CASE-TUTOR™ COURSEWARE FOR STUDENTS

Accompanying this textbook is an optional custom-designed supplement that you can use to help you analyze the cases.

Case-TUTOR™ contains study questions for each of the 35 cases in this book plus custom-designed case preparation exercises for 12 of the cases that walk you through the needed analysis, tutor you in appropriate use of the concepts and tools, and provide number-crunching assistance. The 12 cases for which there's a case preparation exercise on Case-TUTOR are indicated by the Case-TUTOR logo in the Table of Contents.

The study questions for each of the 35 cases serve as a guide for what to think about and what to analyze in preparing the assigned cases for class. You'll find the 12 custom-designed case preparation exercises valuable in learning how to think strategically about a company's situation, applying the tools and concepts covered in the 13 text chapters, and arriving at sound recommendations about what actions management should take to improve the company's performance.

This courseware can be used with any Windows-based PC loaded with Microsoft Excel (either the Office 97 version or the Office 2000 version).

Case-TUTOR™ is **FREE** with the purchase of a new textbook when you use the unique code packaged with the book to download the software.

Strategic | Management
Concepts and Cases

Arthur A. Thompson, Jr.
A. J. Strickland III
Both of the University of Alabama

Thirteenth Edition

McGraw-Hill
Irwin

Boston   Burr Ridge, IL   Dubuque, IA   Madison, WI   New York   San Francisco   St. Louis
Bangkok   Bogotá   Caracas   Kuala Lumpur   Lisbon   London   Madrid   Mexico City
Milan   Montreal   New Delhi   Santiago   Seoul   Singapore   Sydney   Taipei   Toronto

McGraw-Hill Higher Education

A Division of The **McGraw-Hill** *Companies*

STRATEGIC MANAGEMENT: CONCEPTS AND CASES

Published by McGraw-Hill/Irwin, a business unit of The McGraw-Hill Companies, Inc. 1221 Avenue of the Americas, New York, NY, 10020. Copyright © 2003, 2001, 1999, 1998, 1996, 1995, 1993, 1992, 1990, 1987, 1984, 1981, 1978 by The McGraw-Hill Companies, Inc. All rights reserved. No part of this publication may be reproduced or distributed in any form or by any means, or stored in a data base or retrieval system, without the prior written consent of The McGraw-Hill Companies, Inc., including, but not limited to, in any network or other electronic storage or transmission, or broadcast for distance learning. Some ancillaries, including electronic and print components, may not be available to customers outside the United States.

This book is printed on acid-free paper.

domestic   3 4 5 6 7 8 9 0 VNH/VNH 0 9 8 7 6 5 4 3
international 3 4 5 6 7 8 9 0 VNH/VNH 0 9 8 7 6 5 4 3

ISBN 0-07-244371-5

Publisher: *John E. Biernat*
Senior editor: *John Weimeister*
Managing developmental editor: *Laura Hurst Spell*
Senior marketing manager: *Ellen Cleary*
Project manager: *Catherine R. Schultz*
Production supervisor: *Debra R. Sylvester*
Coordinator freelance design: *Mary L. Christianson*
Producer, media technology: *Mark Molsky*
Supplement producer: *Joyce J. Chappetto*
Photo research coordinator: *Jeremy Cheshareck*
Cover and interior freelance designer: *Design Solutions*
Cover image: *SIS/© Guy Crittendon*
Typeface: *10.5/12 Times Roman*
Compositor: *GAC Indianapolis*
Printer: *Von Hoffmann Press, Inc.*

Library of Congress Control Number: 2002103316

INTERNATIONAL EDITION ISBN 0-07-112132-3

Copyright © 2003. Exclusive rights by The McGraw-Hill Companies, Inc. for manufacture and export. This book cannot be re-exported from the country to which it is sold by McGraw-Hill.

The International Edition is not available in North America.

www.mhhe.com

to Hasseline and Kitty

about the | authors

Arthur A. Thompson, Jr., earned his BS and PhD degrees in economics from the University of Tennessee in 1961 and 1965, respectively; spent three years on the economics faculty at Virginia Tech; and served on the faculty of the University of Alabama's College of Commerce and Business Administration for 24 years. In 1974 and again in 1982, Dr. Thompson spent semester-long sabbaticals as a visiting scholar at the Harvard Business School.

His areas of specialization are business strategy, competition and market analysis, and the economics of business enterprises. He has published over 30 articles in some 25 different professional and trade publications and has authored or co-authored five textbooks and four computer-based simulation exercises.

Dr. Thompson is a frequent speaker and consultant on the strategic issues confronting the electric utility industry, particularly as concerns the challenges posed by industry restructuring, re-regulation, competition, and customers' freedom of choice. He spends much of his off-campus time giving presentations to electric utility groups and conducting management development programs for electric utility executives all over the world.

Dr. Thompson and his wife of 41 years have two daughters, two grandchildren, and a Yorkshire terrier.

Dr. A. J. (Lonnie) Strickland, a native of North Georgia, attended the University of Georgia, where he received a bachelor of science degree in math and physics in 1965. Afterward he entered the Georgia Institute of Technology, where he received a master of science in industrial management. He earned a PhD in business administration from Georgia State University in 1969. He currently holds the title of Professor of Strategic Management in the Graduate School of Business at the University of Alabama.

Dr. Strickland's experience in consulting and executive development is in the strategic management area, with a concentration in industry and competitive analysis. He has developed strategic planning systems for such firms as the Southern Company, BellSouth, South Central Bell, American Telephone and Telegraph, Gulf States Paper, Carraway Methodist Medical Center, Delco Remy, Mark IV Industries, Amoco Oil Company, USA Group, General Motors, and Kimberly Clark Corporation (Medical Products). He is a very popular speaker on the subject of implementing strategic change and serves on several corporate boards.

He has served as director of marketing for BellSouth, where he had responsibility for $1 billion in revenues and $300 million in profits.

In the international arena, Dr. Strickland has done extensive work in Europe, the Middle East, Central America, Malaysia, Australia, and Africa. In France he developed a management simulation of corporate decision making that enables management to test various strategic alternatives.

In the area of research, he is the author of 15 books and texts. His management simulations, Tempomatic IV and Micromatic, were pioneering innovations that enjoyed prominent market success for two decades.

Recent awards for Dr. Strickland include the Outstanding Professor Award for the Graduate School of Business and the Outstanding Commitment to Teaching Award for the University of Alabama, in which he takes particular pride. He is a member of various honor leadership societies: Mortar Board, Order of Omega, Beta Gamma Sigma, Omicron Delta Kappa, and Jasons. He is past national president of Pi Kappa Phi social fraternity.

the | preface

The 13th edition of *Strategic Management: Concepts and Cases,* coming on the heels of the 12th edition published in late 2000, features (1) 35 of the freshest and best cases we could find; (2) an extensively revised e-business chapter focused on company use of Internet technology applications to reconfigure value chain activities, why growing Internet usage often acts to intensify competitive forces, and the several strategic options that companies have for using the Internet to position themselves in the marketplace; and (3) updated Illustration Capsules for all 13 chapters. The hallmark of the 13th edition, like that of the 12th edition, is thorough coverage of the landmark changes in business strategy and competitive markets being driven by globalization and Internet technology. You'll find this edition to be "globalized" and "e-commerced" from cover to cover, with on-target chapter content, timely examples, and an unusually interesting and teachable case lineup that includes seven accompanying videos. We have tried our level best to satisfy the market's yearning for a comprehensive teaching/learning package that squarely targets what every student needs to know about crafting, implementing, and executing business strategies in today's market environments.

MEETING THE MARKET DEMAND FOR FRESH CASES

Quite understandably, users of strategy texts have an unrelenting appetite for new and well-researched cases loaded with timely and intriguing issues. With so many business schools offering the strategic management course every term, the case collection in any one edition wears out after a few terms. Sometimes, fast-changing industry and company circumstances cause an otherwise good case to lose its appeal (because outcomes are known or issues are rendered moot by subsequent events). Class discussions always take on an added element of excitement either when a case is hot off the press and poses issues that company managers are still currently trying to resolve or when the jury remains out on the wisdom of actions taken by management. The strong and legitimate interest among adopters in using the very latest and best cases, together with an expanding supply of first-rate cases being written annually, merits this continuing effort on our part to provide an alternate set of the most current and eminently suitable cases for strategic management courses. Only the classic two-page Robin Hood case is carried over from the 12th edition; the remaining 34 cases in this 13th edition are all recently written and contain important, timely teaching points.

THE VASTLY REVISED E-BUSINESS CHAPTER AND UPDATED EXAMPLES

While the pace of new developments in the literature of strategic management generally doesn't warrant revising text chapters every 18 months, we made a partial exception in this edition, electing to radically revise and restructure our chapter on e-business (Chapter 7). The opportunities in e-commerce look much different now than they looked during the euphoric Internet gold rush of the late 1990s. Dot-com business models and strategies have undergone a sobering and thoughtful metamorphosis in the 24 months since we prepared our first chapter on e-business models and strategies for the 12th edition; some important strategic lessons have come to the fore and next-generation dot-com strategies have emerged—there's been more time to assess what works and what doesn't. Furthermore, companies all across the world are actively engaged in incorporating Internet technology into their value chain activities, producing fundamental changes in supply chain management, internal operations, and distribution channel emphasis. Consequently, we determined that the 13th edition ought to include a second-generation Chapter 7 that fully reflects the radically altered e-commerce landscape and the more down-to-earth e-business models and strategies that are now emerging. The newly revised Chapter 7 is organized around key strategy-shaping issues: How is Internet technology altering how companies perform value chain activities? What is the impact of the Internet on competition? Will the Internet prove to be a vehicle for increasing or decreasing industry profitability? Does the Internet enhance or impede company efforts to gain sustainable competitive advantage? The chapter also looks at the strategic mistakes made by some of the early Internet entrepreneurs and the strategic lessons learned from the first wave of the Internet revolution. The chapter concludes with a major section examining the strategic decisions that companies have to make regarding how to utilize the Internet in positioning the company in the marketplace—whether and when to use the Internet as the company's *exclusive* channel for accessing customers, as the company's *primary* distribution channel, as *one of several* important distribution channels, as a *secondary or minor* channel, or as simply *a vehicle* for disseminating product information (with traditional distribution channel partners making all sales to end users). There are general strategy prescriptions for pure dot-com enterprises, companies employing combination brick-and-click strategies, and traditional businesses wishing to leverage use of the Internet.

If you are a user of the 12th edition, shifting to the 13th edition merits consideration (1) as soon as you deem it's time to incorporate a new case collection in your course offering and/or (2) if you see value in incorporating the vastly revised Chapter 7 and the updated Illustration Capsules in your course offering. If you haven't been an adopter of the 12th edition, we hope you'll take a close look at this 13th edition to see if its features (discussed below) meet your needs. There's also a newly published upgraded edition of *The Business Strategy Game* (version 7.20) for use with either the 12th or the 13th edition.

THE CASE COLLECTION IN THE 13TH EDITION

The 35 cases in this edition include 28 new cases not appearing in any of our previous editions, 6 thoroughly updated and revised cases from past editions, and one carryover case from the 12th edition—the now-classic two-page Robin Hood case. As has been our longtime custom, we have grouped the cases under five chapter-related and topical headings to highlight the close links that particular cases have with the strategic management concepts and tools presented in specific chapters. In the Section A grouping are four cases spotlighting the role and tasks of the manager as chief strategy maker and chief strategy implementer; these cases—Andrea Jung's Makeover of Avon Products, The Solar Feeder, World Wrestling Federation (A), and Pi Kappa Phi Fraternity—provide convincing demonstration of why the discussions in Chapters 1 and 2 are relevant to a company's long-term market success. There are follow-on cases for the World Wrestling Federation and Pi Kappa Phi cases that you can pass out in class. Section B contains a 17-case grouping in which the central issues deal with analyzing industry and competitive situations and crafting business-level strategy; these cases drill students in utilizing the concepts and analytical tools presented in Chapters 3 through 8. In Section C are three cases involving strategy assessments and strategy making in diversified or multi-industry companies that give students the opportunity to apply the concepts and tools presented in Chapters 9 and 10. There are nine cases in Section D, all revolving around the managerial challenges of implementing and executing strategy, and all serving as good vehicles for illustrating the relevance of the material covered in Chapters 11, 12, and 13. Section E contains two cases, one on Nike and one on DoubleClick, highlighting the links between strategy, ethics, and social responsibility.

The case lineup in this 13th edition, as in prior editions, reflects our steadfast preference for cases that feature interesting products and companies and that are capable of sparking student interest and lively classroom discussions. At least 24 of the 35 cases involve high-profile companies, products, or people that students will have heard of, know about from personal experience, or can easily identify with. There are four dot-com company cases, plus several others that will provide students with insight into the special demands of competing in industry environments where technological developments are an everyday event, product life cycles are short, and competitive maneuvering among rivals comes fast and furious. At least 20 of the cases involve situations where company resources and competitive capabilities play as large a role in the strategy-making, strategy-implementing scheme of things as industry and competitive conditions do.

Scattered throughout the lineup are eight cases concerning non-U.S. companies, globally competitive industries, and/or cross-cultural situations; these cases, in conjunction with the globalized content of the text chapters, provide ample material for linking the study of strategic management tightly to the ongoing globalization of the world economy—in proper keeping with AACSB standards. You'll also find 10 cases dealing with the strategic problems of family-owned or relatively small entrepreneurial businesses, a nonprofit organization case (Pi Kappa Phi Fraternity), and 19 cases involving public companies about which students can do further research on the Internet or in the library. Seven of the cases (Avon Products, eBay, Southwest Airlines, Dakota Growers Pasta, DoubleClick, Music on the Internet, and Nike) have videotape segments that are available from the publisher, and there is an excellent video for use with World Wrestling Federation (A) that can be ordered from the copyright holder.

The case researchers whose work appears in this edition have done an absolutely first-class job of preparing cases that contain valuable teaching points, illustrate the important kinds of strategic challenges managers face, and allow students to apply the tools of strategic analysis. We believe you will find the 13th edition's collection of 35 cases exceptionally appealing, eminently teachable, and very suitable for drilling students in the use of the concepts and analytical treatments in Chapters 1 through 13. It is an attractive case lineup calculated to capture student interest from beginning to end.

The e-Case Collection and the e-Learning Center

As a way to make it simple and convenient for instructors to supplement the 35 cases included in the text, we've assembled a collection of cases deliverable in downloadable format that includes 33 popular cases from our 11th and 12th editions. Several cases in the e-case collection have companion video segments. The e-cases, coupled with the 35 cases in this volume, give you a total of 68 cases to select from in making case assignments. Moreover, *our plan is to keep the e-case collection updated with fresh cases as fast as we are able to identify newly written cases of suitable quality and content, get them satisfactorily formatted, and secure the rights to post them in the e-Learning Center.* We believe you will find that using cases from our continually replenished and updated e-case collection (which you can preview in the Instructor Center at www.mhhe.com/thompson) will prove a valuable way to supplement the cases in this text and keep your case assignments varied and current.

Our intent is for the e-case collection to consist of 60 to 75 of the latest and best cases that we believe are eminently suitable for use with our text and that you can be confident will work effectively in the classroom. We've tried to organize and present the e-case collection in a manner that makes it easy and convenient for instructors to identify and select the cases best meeting their course needs. Teaching notes for all the e-cases are also available in downloadable or viewable form for instructor perusal and use. If the notion of using e-cases appeals to you, we suggest visiting the Instructor Center at the website for the text (www.mhhe.com/thompson) and browsing through the case listings.

Students can obtain assigned e-cases by going to the redesigned, more user-friendly e-Learning Center at www.mhhe.com/thompson and using a credit card to purchase and then immediately download files of the desired e-cases to their own PC or to a disk. Students can use the e-case file to print a copy for their personal use (or can read the case directly on the monitor). The publisher has completely reworked the first version of the e-Learning Center to eliminate the annoying difficulties that a few users encountered when downloading the e-case files.

The Guide to Case Analysis and Use of the Internet

Following Chapter 13 and prior to Case 1, we have once again included a section called "A Guide to Case Analysis" that gives students positive direction in what case method pedagogy is all about, offers suggestions for approaching case analysis, and provides a useful review of the financial ratios used in evaluating a company's financial strength. The guide features pointers on how to use the Internet to (1) do further research on an industry or company, (2) obtain a company's latest financial results, and (3) get updates on what has happened since the case was written. The industry and company information available on the Internet has mushroomed to the point that the challenge now is for students to learn how to sift through the search engine hits quickly to find what is really pertinent and interesting. While more and more students are adept in locating useful information on the Internet, we think students with weaker Internet search skills will find our list of suggested websites a time-saving and valuable assist in running down the information they are interested in.

CONTENT FEATURES OF THE 13TH EDITION CHAPTERS

Other than a much revamped Chapter 7 and updated Illustration Capsules (some of which are entirely new), the text chapters in this edition are identical to those in the 12th edition. Starting with the 6th edition, our revision cycle has involved new chapters and new cases in even-numbered editions and then carryover chapters and new cases in odd-numbered editions. This being an odd-numbered edition, the chapter content parallels that of the 12th edition, except for the differences noted and explained above. However, the 12th edition chapters represented a radical revision and updating of the 10th/11th edition chapters, so the overall content of the 13th edition chapters remains tolerably close to the cutting edge. We, of course, made the changes in Chapter 7 and the Illustration Capsules to help sustain the timeliness and currency of the text treatments in this edition. Those who are unfamiliar with our 12th edition may find the following brief review of the chapters helpful.

The content of our 12th/13th edition chapters reflects a number of recent developments in the literature of strategic management: use of the term *business model* has become widespread, the strategic importance of entrepreneurship has taken on new meaning, collaborative alliances have grown in scope and in strategic importance, companies have continued to globalize their operations, the effects of global competition have spread, the resource-based view of the firm has become a standard part of strategic analysis, high-velocity change has spread to more industries and company environments, and the Internet has triggered a virtual revolution in both strategy and internal operations. We have made a concerted attempt to incorporate and integrate all these developments. In this edition you'll find much discussion about business models and how they relate to strategy. Considerable attention is paid to the role of collaboration and alliances and how they affect competition—indeed, the collaborative efforts between sellers and their suppliers and between sellers and buyers are now woven into the five-forces model of competition as a way of analyzing the impact of alliances and cooperative agreements on competition. There's solid coverage of the demands of competing in "high-velocity" market environments where the swift pace of change (from whatever source) forces companies to make frequent and sometimes very fundamental changes in their strategies and resource capabilities. The text chapters emphasize that a company's strategy must be matched *both* to its external market circumstances and to its internal resources and competitive capabilities. The chapters on global market environments (Chapter 6) and e-business strategies (Chapter 7) testify to the importance of these topics in contemporary courses in strategic management, but you will find that all 13 chapters have been globalized and e-commerced because the impacts of globalization and Internet technology pervade a company's strategy-making, strategy-implementing actions and ought not to be isolated in a separate chapter. You'll find the resource-based view of the firm prominently integrated into the coverage of crafting business strategy (Chapters 2 through 8) and crafting diversification strategies (Chapters 9 and 10). You'll also find that Chapters 11 and 12 have a strong resource-based perspective as concerns the role of intellectual capital, core competencies, competitive capabilities, and organizational resources in implementing and executing strategy.

We've made extensive use of examples and Illustration Capsules to highlight the close connection between the conceptual presentation and real-world application. There are numerous charts and figures, color photographs, and a four-color design. As in prior editions, there's prominent treatment of ethical and social responsibility issues, plus margin notes in every chapter that highlight basic concepts, strategic management principles, and kernels of wisdom.

Specific Chapter Features and Content

The following rundown summarizes the noteworthy chapter features and topical emphasis in this edition:

- Chapter 1 contains material (starting on page 1) on what is meant by the term *business model* and how a company's business model relates to its strategy. To drive home the point about how the business models of companies sometimes differ quite substantially, we have included a capsule that contrasts Microsoft's business model in operating system software with the business model that Linux uses. The sections on strategic visions and mission statements in Chapters 1 and 2 hammer home the importance of clear direction setting and a motivating strategic vision. Emphasis is placed on why companies have to rapidly adapt strategy to newly unfolding market conditions and why strategy life cycles are often short. We stress how and why a company's strategy emerges from (1) the deliberate and purposeful actions of management and (2) as-needed reactions to unanticipated developments and fresh competitive pressures. There's a section on corporate intrapreneuring to help underscore that a company's strategic plan is a collection of strategies devised by different managers at different levels in the organizational hierarchy. We've taken pains to explain why *all managers are on a company's strategy-making, strategy-implementing team* and why it is imperative for company personnel to be "students of the business" and skilled users of the concepts and tools of strategic management.

- In Chapter 3, Michael E. Porter's traditional "five forces model of competition" has been recast to incorporate the role and importance of alliances and collaborative agreements in the competitive market arena. We argue that on occasion some competitors are able to forge such effective collaborative arrangements with either their suppliers or their customers or both that the whole structure of competition in the industry is affected. Globalization and the Internet are treated as potent driving forces capable of reshaping industry competition—their roles as change agents have become factors that most companies in most industries must reckon with in forging winning strategies. Chapter 3 sets forth the now-familiar analytical tools and concepts of industry and competitive analysis and demonstrates the importance of tailoring strategy to fit the circumstances of a company's industry and competitive environment.

- Chapter 4 establishes the equal importance of doing solid company situation analysis as a basis for matching strategy to organizational resources, competencies, and competitive capabilities. As with the prior edition, Chapter 4 contains a full-blown discussion of all the concepts and analytical tools required to understand why a company's strategy must be well matched to its internal resources and competitive capabilities. The roles of core competencies and organizational resources and capabilities in creating customer value and helping build competitive advantage are *center stage* in the discussions of company resource strengths and weaknesses. SWOT analysis is presented as a valuable tool for assessing a company's resource strengths and resource weaknesses. There are sections on determining the competitive value of specific company resources and assets and on deliberately cultivating and nurturing those competencies and capabilities having the biggest competitive advantage potential. The now-standard tools of value chain analysis, strategic cost analysis, benchmarking, and competitive strength assessments continue to have a prominent role in the methodology of evaluating a company's situation—we believe they are an essential part of understanding a company's relative cost position and competitive standing vis-à-vis rivals. A pedagogically useful feature of this chapter is a section (undergirded with timely examples and an Illustration Capsule) on how the value chains of dot-com companies differ from those of traditional brick-and-mortar companies.

- Together, the material in Chapter 3 and Chapter 4 creates the understanding for why managers must carefully match company strategy both to industry and competitive conditions and to company resources and capabilities. Chapter 3 demonstrates the importance of tailoring strategy to fit the circumstances of a company's industry and competitive environment. Chapter 4 establishes the equal importance of doing solid company situation analysis as a basis for matching strategy to organizational resources, competencies, and competitive capabilities.

- Chapter 5 focuses on how a company can achieve or defend competitive advantage through strategy and through the ways it manages value chain activities. There's continuing coverage of the five generic competitive strategies; extensive treatments on using alliances and cooperative strategies to build competitive advantage; a section on mergers and acquisitions; and material on how astute use of the Internet and e-commerce technologies is allowing companies to reconfigure their value chains to speed the flow of information, enhance efficiency, and reduce costs.

- Chapter 6 examines the issues companies face in crafting strategies suitable for multinational and globally competitive market environments, drawing a careful distinction between competing internationally and competing globally and exploring the reasons why it often makes good strategic sense for a company to expand beyond domestic boundaries. There's a section on cross-country differences in cultural, demographic, and market conditions that lays the foundation for whether multicountry or global competition exists. The chapter is anchored by a major section describing the various strategy options for entering and competing in foreign markets—options ranging from an export strategy to licensing and franchising to multicountry strategies to global strategies to heavy reliance on strategic alliances and joint ventures. This chapter introduces the concepts of profit sanctuaries and cross-market subsidization; explores the special problems associated with entry into the markets of emerging countries; and concludes with a section discussing the strategic options that local companies in such emerging countries as India, China, Brazil, and Mexico can use to defend against the invasion of opportunity-seeking, resource-rich global giants.

- The vastly restructured Chapter 7 features an important section detailing the specific ways that companies are using the Internet and Internet technology applications to streamline supply chain management practices and reconfigure company and industry value chains. There's another important section discussing the impact of the Internet on each of the five competitive forces and why, on average, growing use of the Internet by businesses and consumers acts to intensify competition. The causes of the dot-com crash, the strategic miscalculations of the early Internet entrepreneurs, and the elusiveness of first-mover advantages are explored in another section. The chapter concludes with an in-depth look at the challenges companies face in deciding what role the Internet should play in their strategy and how best to use the Internet in positioning the company in the marketplace. There's consideration of strategy alternatives for pure dot-com enterprises, the competitive advantage potential of combination brick-and-click strategies, and the strategic options of traditional businesses in capitalizing on the Internet and Internet technology.

- Chapter 8 looks at the broad strategy options for companies competing in five different industry environments: (1) emerging industries; (2) turbulent high-velocity markets; (3) mature, slow-growth industries; (4) stagnant and declining industries; and (5) fragmented industries. It also covers the strategy-making challenges that confront companies pursuing rapid growth, companies in industry-leading positions, companies in runner-up positions, and crisis-ridden companies. These nine situations merit special attention in strategy courses because of their widely representative nature and because they reinforce the points made in Chapters 3 and 4 that winning strategies have to be matched both to industry and competitive conditions and to company resources and capabilities.

- The analytical treatment of corporate diversification strategies in Chapters 9 and 10 abandons much of the attention once given to drawing business portfolio matrices and instead puts the analytical spotlight on (1) assessing industry attractiveness, (2) evaluating a multi-industry company's competitive strength in each of its lines of business, and (3) appraising both the *strategic fits* and the *resource fits* among a diversified company's different businesses. You'll find a very strong resource-based view of the firm in the recommended methodology for evaluating the pros and cons of a company's diversification strategy. Chapter 10 incorporates analytical use of the industry attractiveness/business strength portfolio matrix because of its conceptual soundness and practical relevance, but we have abandoned coverage of the flawed growth-share matrix and the little-used life-cycle matrix.

- The three-chapter module on strategy implementation (Chapters 11–13) continues to feature a solid, compelling conceptual framework structured around (1) building the resource strengths and organizational capabilities needed to execute the strategy in competent fashion; (2) developing budgets to steer ample resources into those value chain activities critical to strategic success; (3) establishing strategically appropriate policies and procedures; (4) instituting best practices and mechanisms for continuous improvement; (5) installing information, communication, and operating systems that enable company personnel to carry out their strategic roles successfully day-in and day-out; (6) tying rewards and incentives tightly to the achievement of performance objectives and good strategy execution; (7) creating a strategy-supportive work environment and corporate culture; and (8) exerting the internal leadership needed to drive implementation forward and to keep improving on how the strategy is being executed.

- The eight-task framework for understanding the managerial components of strategy implementation and execution is explained in the first section of Chapter 11. The remainder of Chapter 11 focuses on building an organization with the competencies, capabilities, and resource strengths needed for successful strategy execution. You'll find welcome coverage of what it takes for an organization to build and enhance its competencies and capabilities, develop the dominating depth in competence-related activities needed for competitive advantage, and forge arrangements to achieve the necessary degree of collaboration and cooperation both among internal departments and with outside resource providers. There is extensive treatment of the task of building resource strengths through collaborative alliances and partnerships and considerable emphasis on the importance of intellectual capital and the needs to recruit talented employees and develop a first-rate management team. We no longer spend time discussing functional, geographic, business-unit, and matrix organizational structures, since these are covered in organization behavior and principles of management courses. But there's continuing coverage of the pros and cons of outsourcing noncritical activities, the strategic rationale for downsizing and de-layering hierarchical structures, the merits of employee empowerment, and the use of cross-functional and self-contained work teams. The result is a powerful treatment of building resource capabilities and structuring organizational activities that ties together and makes strategic sense out of all the revolutionary organizational changes sweeping through today's corporations. So far, the efforts of companies across the world to organize the work effort around teams; reengineer core business processes; compete on organizational capabilities (as much as on differentiated product attributes); and install leaner, flatter organization structures are proving to be durable, valuable approaches for improving the caliber of strategy execution.

- Chapter 12 surveys the role of strategy-supportive budgets, policies, reward structures, and internal support systems and explains why the benchmarking of best practices, total quality management, reengineering, and continuous improvement programs are important managerial tools for enhancing organizational competencies in executing strategy.

- Chapter 13 deals with creating a strategy-supportive corporate culture and exercising the internal leadership needed to drive implementation forward. There's coverage of strong versus weak cultures, low performance and unhealthy cultures, adaptive cultures, and the sustained leadership commitment it takes to change a company with a problem culture, plus sections on ethics management and what managers can do to improve the caliber of strategy execution.

- Among the 58 Illustration Capsules, more than 20 have been revised. A substantial number concern global issues and the strategies of non-U.S. companies, each designated by a special "global" logo.

Margin notes that highlight basic concepts, major conclusions, and core truths remain a visible and reader-friendly feature of the 13 text chapters. Their value-added contribution is to distill the subject matter into concise principles, bring the discussion into sharper focus for readers, and give emphasis to what is important.

Our top priority has been to ensure that the content is substantive and covers all the right bases. But, at the same time, we've taken pains to meet reader expectations of clarity and crispness. You won't find much fluff or filler. The conceptual discussions go straight to the point and are laced with enough relevant examples to make them convincing, realistic, and interesting. We aimed squarely at a chapter presentation that is comfortably mainstream, dead center with respect to content, tightly written, and very representative of the best thinking of both academics and practitioners of strategic management.

THE REST OF THE 13TH EDITION PACKAGE

In addition to this book containing 13 text chapters, a guide to case analysis, and 35 cases, the 13th edition package consists of the following companion elements:

- *The previously mentioned e-case collection of 33 popular cases from the 11th and 12th editions, plus appropriate cases from other sources, that instructors can select for case assignments.* Students can visit the newly designed and now more user-friendly e-Learning Center at www.mhhe.com/thompson and use a credit card to purchase and then immediately download to their PC or to a disk the e-cases that instructors have opted to include in their course syllabus. The e-case collection, coupled with the 35 cases in the text, effectively provides instructors with a bank of 68 high-caliber cases to choose from.

- *Concept-TUTOR™ self-tests for each of the 13 chapters that students can utilize to gauge their comprehension of the text material.* The self-tests are available for open student use in the Student Center at www.mhhe.com/thompson. The 25-question tests for each chapter consist of an assortment of true–false, multiple choice, and fill-in-the-blank questions that cover the text presentation rather thoroughly. These tests were deliberately made demanding (given their open-book nature) so as to require careful reading and good comprehension of the material. When the student completes each test, Concept-TUTOR automatically grades the answers, provides a test score, and indicates the questions with right and wrong answers. Students can attempt incorrectly answered questions as many times as they need to arrive at a perfect score of 100.

- *Case-TUTOR™ software containing study questions for all 35 cases and 12 custom-designed case preparation exercises that coach students in doing the appropriate analysis and help them arrive at soundly reasoned action recommendations.* Students can go to the student center at www.mhhe.com/thompson and use the passcode in their text to obtain a onetime download of Case-TUTOR. The study questions for each case provide valuable direction to students in adequately preparing the case prior to coming to class. (The study questions on Case-TUTOR are mostly identical to the suggested assignment questions in the teaching notes for cases.) The 12 case preparation exercises are particularly helpful to students in gaining command of the concepts and tools of analysis. Each exercise is organized around the study questions for the case and coaches students in developing good answers to the questions by using whatever analytical tools are appropriate—whether it be five-forces analysis, strategic group mapping, identification of key success factors, SWOT analysis, value chain analysis, competitive strength assessments, industry attractiveness assessments, or strategic fit matchups. The process of working their way through an analytically structured exercise and developing substantive answers to the study questions pushes students to think about the right things; practice doing the right kind of analysis; and thus arrive at reasoned, supportable action recommendations. The goal of the 12 exercises is to teach students what a good case analysis consists of and how to correctly use and apply the concepts and tools of strategic analysis. The hoped-for outcome is that conscientious completion of the exercise will cause your students to come to class much better prepared, thus greatly enhancing the caliber of the learning and understanding that takes place during class discussion of the case. It is important to recognize that we carefully crafted the case preparation guides to keep the ball squarely in the student's court to do the actual analysis, to decide what story the numbers tell about a company's situation and performance, to figure out their own answers to the study questions, and to think through the options to arrive at recommendations. The Case-Tutor exercises are thus not an "answer give-away" for the cases; rather, they have been designed and structured (we think!!!) as a way of tutoring students in strategic thinking and solid strategic analysis.

- *A website featuring a student center, an instructor center, an information center, and a link to the e-Learning Center, where students obtain e-cases.*
- *An upgraded and slightly revised version of* The Business Strategy Game *(version 7.20).* This global simulation is a companion to the text and functions as an integrative "strategy-in-action" decision-making exercise for capstone courses in strategic management. The simulation is available in both printed and digital formats and has a built-in e-mail feature for distance-learning situations and for eliminating use of disks entirely.
- *Seven video supplements for use with the collection of 35 cases in this edition.*
- *A full array of instructional aids for adopters.*

We think the 13th edition and its companion supplements will help push your course in strategic management to a higher plateau and equip students with what they need to know about crafting, implementing, and executing strategy in today's business environment.

THE BUSINESS STRATEGY GAME OPTION

The Business Strategy Game has five features that make it an uncommonly effective teaching–learning aid for strategic management courses:

1. *The product and the industry.* Producing and marketing athletic footwear is a business that students can readily identify with and understand.
2. *The industry global environment.* Students get up-close exposure to what global competition is like and the kinds of strategic issues that managers in global industries have to address.
3. *The realistic quality of the simulation exercise.* We've designed the simulation to be as faithful as possible to real-world markets, competitive conditions, and revenue–cost–profit relationships.

4. *The wide degree of strategic freedom students have in managing their companies.* We've gone to great lengths to make the game free of bias with regard to the built-in advantages and disadvantages of one strategy versus another.

5. The three-year strategic planning and analysis capabilities it incorporates as an integral part of the exercise of running a company.

These features, wrapped together as a package, provide an exciting and valuable bridge between concept and practice, the classroom and real-life management, and reading textbook wisdom and learning-by-doing. You'll find opportunity after opportunity to use examples and happenings in *The Business Strategy Game* to connect to your lectures on the text chapters.

The Value a Simulation Adds

Our own experiences with simulation games, along with hours of discussions with users, have convinced us that simulation games are *the single best exercise available* for helping students understand how the functional pieces of a business fit together and giving them an integrated, capstone experience. First and foremost, the exercise of running a simulated company over a number of decision periods helps develop students' business judgment and gives them much-needed opportunity to apply what they have learned from all their business courses. Simulation games provide a live case situation where events unfold and circumstances change as the game progresses. Their special hook is an ability to get students personally involved in the subject matter. *The Business Strategy Game* is very typical in this respect. In plotting their competitive strategies each decision period, students learn about risk taking. They have to respond to changing market conditions, react to the moves of competitors, and choose among alternative courses of action. They get valuable practice in reading the signs of industry change, spotting market opportunities, evaluating threats to their company's competitive position, weighing the trade-offs between profits now and profits later, and assessing the long-term consequences of short-term decisions. They are driven to chart a long-term direction for their company, set strategic and financial objectives, and try out different strategies in pursuit of competitive advantage. The simulation environment thrusts them into being active strategic thinkers, industry analysts, and business decision makers. And by having to live with the decisions they make, players experience what it means to be accountable for decisions and responsible for achieving satisfactory results. All this serves to drill students in responsible decision making and to improve their business acumen and managerial judgment.

Second, students learn an enormous amount from working with the numbers; exploring options; and trying to unite production, marketing, finance, and human resource decisions into a coherent strategy. They begin to see ways to apply knowledge from prior courses and figure out what really makes a business tick. The effect is to help students integrate a lot of material, look at decisions from the standpoint of the company as a whole, and see the importance of thinking strategically about a company's competitive position and future prospects. Since a simulation game is, by its very nature, a hands-on exercise, the lessons learned are forcefully planted in students' minds—the impact is far more lasting than what is remembered from lectures. Third, students' entrepreneurial instincts blossom as they get caught up in the competitive spirit of the game. The resulting entertainment value helps maintain an unusually high level of student motivation and emotional involvement in the course throughout the term.

A Bird's-Eye View of the Simulation

We designed *The Business Strategy Game* around athletic footwear because producing and marketing athletic footwear is a business students can readily understand and because the athletic footwear market displays the characteristics of many globally competitive industries—fast growth, worldwide use of the product, competition among companies from several continents, production located in low-wage locations, and a marketplace where a variety of competitive approaches and business strategies can coexist. The simulation allows companies to manufacture and sell their brands in North America, Asia, Europe, and Latin America, plus the option to compete for supplying private-label footwear to North American chain retailers. Branded sales can be pursued through any or all of three distribution channels—independent footwear retailers, company-owned and operated retail stores, and direct sales made online at the company's website.

Competition is head-to-head—each team of students must match their strategic wits against the other company teams. Companies can focus their branded marketing efforts on one geographic market or two or three or all four, and they can compete aggressively or they can de-emphasize branded sales and specialize in private-label production (an attractive strategy for low-cost producers). They can establish a one-country production base or they can manufacture in all four of the geographic markets to avoid tariffs and mitigate the risk of adverse exchange rate fluctuations. Low-cost leadership, differentiation strategies, best-cost producer strategies, and focus strategies are all viable competitive options. Companies can position their products in either the low or high end of the market, or they can stick close to the middle in price, quality, and service; they can have a wide or narrow product line, small or big dealer networks, extensive or limited advertising. Company market shares are based on how each company's product attributes and competitive effort stacks up against the efforts of rivals. Demand conditions, tariffs, and wage rates vary from geographic area to geographic area. Raw materials used in footwear production are purchased in a worldwide commodity market at prices that move up or down in response to supply–demand conditions. If a company's sales volume is unexpectedly low, management has the option to liquidate excess inventories at deep discount prices.

The company that students manage has plants to operate; a workforce to compensate; distribution expenses and inventories to control; capital expenditure decisions to make; marketing and sales campaigns to wage; a website to operate; sales forecasts to consider; and ups and down in exchange rates, interest rates, and the stock market to take into account. Students must weave functional decisions in production, distribution, marketing, finance, and human resources into a cohesive action plan. They have to react to changing market and competitive conditions, initiate moves to try to build competitive advantage, and decide how to defend against aggressive actions by competitors. And they must endeavor to maximize shareholder wealth via increased dividend payments and stock price appreciation. Each team of students is challenged to use their entrepreneurial and strategic skills to become the next Nike or Reebok and ride the wave of growth to the top of the worldwide athletic footwear industry. The whole exercise is representative of a real-world competitive market where companies try to outcompete and outperform rivals—things are every bit as realistic and true to actual business practice as we could make them.

There are built-in planning and analysis features that allow students to (1) craft a three-year strategic plan, (2) evaluate the economics of expanding capacity, (3) draw strategic group maps, (4) quickly prepare and print out an assortment of charts and graphs showing various performance trends, and (5) build different competitive strategy scenarios. Calculations at the bottom of each decision screen provide instantly updated projections of sales revenues, profits, return on equity, cash flow, and other key outcomes as each decision entry is made. The sensitivity of financial and operating outcomes to different decision entries is easily observed on the screen and on detailed printouts of projections. With the speed of today's personal computers, the relevant number-crunching is done in a split second. The game is designed throughout to lead students to decisions based on "My analysis shows . . ." and away from the quicksand of decisions based on "I think," "It sounds good," "Maybe it will work out," and other such seat-of-the-pants approaches.

A separate Instructor's Manual for *The Business Strategy Game* describes how to integrate the simulation exercise into your course, provides pointers on how to administer the game, and contains step-by-step processing instructions. Should you encounter technical difficulties or have questions, technical assistance is directly available from the coauthors.

The Business Strategy Game runs on any PC loaded with Microsoft Excel (preferably the Office 2000 or the Office XP versions), and it is suitable for both senior-level and MBA courses. The software can be installed to run on a network.

The Upgraded 7.20 Version of the Simulation

The recently introduced 7.20 version of *The Business Strategy Game* has a raft of appealing features that propel the simulation to a high plateau of capability:

- *An easy-to-use e-mail feature that makes the simulation ideal for use in distance-learning situations.* This addition is a response to requests from numerous users. The e-mail feature allows company members to click on a built-in e-mail button that will send their decision file to the instructor/game administrator, allows instructors to open e-mailed files and initiate the decision-processing routine with a few clicks, and then lets instructors/game administrators readily e-mail the results back to company members for use in the next round of decision making. We feel that using e-mail to exchange files between students and the game administrator is superior to playing the simulation online because it does not require students to maintain an open Internet connection for several hours and because the simulation runs much faster for players than would be the case with a slow-speed modem connection.

- *An integrated demand forecasting tool.* There's a screen that allows each company to develop fairly accurate sales projections for the number of pairs it is likely to sell in each market segment, given its contemplated marketing effort and given the overall competitive effort it expects to encounter from rival companies. Company members can use these projections as the basis for production and plant operations decisions and for deciding how many pairs need to be shipped to the various distribution centers, and for crafting a marketing strategy that will produce the desired sales and market share. However, the accuracy of the sales projections provided by the demand forecasting tool will be no better than players' ability to anticipate changes in market conditions and the competitive effort they will encounter from rivals.

- *A global market emphasis.* Companies can locate plants and sell their footwear products in any or all of four regions—North America, Asia, Europe, and Latin America. The simulation begins with a tariff of $4 on footwear imported into Europe, a $6 tariff on footwear imported into Latin America, and an $8 tariff on footwear imported into Asia. All companies start the simulation with a 1-million-pair plant in North America and a 2-million-pair plant in Asia. Exchange-rate fluctuations are tied to the U.S. dollar, the euro, the Japanese yen, and the Brazilian real.

- *The Internet marketing and online sales feature.* Companies compete online to sell direct to consumers on the basis of three global factors (comparative selling prices, the number of models and styles offered at the website, and speed of delivery) and three region-specific factors (product quality, image rating, and advertising). As might be expected, there is some channel conflict between online sales and a company's attempt to secure sales through brick-and-mortar retail outlets; company managers have to address the conflict and cannibalization issues if they elect to pursue a "brick-and-clicks" strategy (a situation that many real-world companies have to contend with).

- *The option to open a chain of company retail stores.* Companies have the option of investing in building a chain of company-owned and operated retail megastores in major shopping centers to supplement or substitute for selling at wholesale through independent retail dealers. However, just as is the case with online sales, company-owned stores pose some distribution channel conflict because independent retailers see them as cannibalizing their own sales. Company managers thus have to wrestle with which of three distribution channels to emphasize—independent dealers, company-owned stores, online sales—and they have to try to minimize the impact of channel conflicts.

- *An array of analytical tools.* There are menu options that players can use to assist them in evaluating capacity expansions, drawing strategic group maps, drawing charts and graphs, and preparing a long-range strategic plan. Conscientious use of these analytical tools improves the caliber of players' decisions.

- *The use of Microsoft Excel and PC requirements.* This 7.20 version requires that the simulation be played on PCs loaded with Microsoft Excel—on Office 97, Office 2000, or Office XP. Moreover, the PCs must have a Windows-based operating system (Windows 95, Windows 98, Windows NT, Windows 2000, or Windows XP) and preferably 64 MB of RAM and a 233MHz or faster chip (the program will run on lesser-equipped machines, but at slower-than-desired speeds). If your class does not have access to PCs with a Windows-based operating system and a recent version of Microsoft Excel, then you will need to use the sixth edition version of *The Business Strategy Game.*

- *Extensive onscreen calculations.* Version 7.20 features user-friendly screen layouts and navigation; where feasible, instructions for using the software and "rules of the game" appear directly on the screens (so as to minimize the need for students to look up things in the Player's Manual). There's a particularly rich set of onscreen calculations that give players instantaneous feedback on the revenue–cost–profit consequences of each decision entry. While some screens contain a lot of information and take a while to digest, players will find most all of the information they need to make an informed decision is either directly on the screens or is readily accessible on the menu bar guide at the top of each screen. If students forget some of the information in the Player's Manual, they can quickly access the information online by clicking on the Help button—the Help button takes them directly to screens displaying the related information in the Player's Manual, thus bypassing the need to look up rules and procedures in the manual.

- *A comprehensive Player's Manual.* The Player's Manual is cast around demand forecasting, plant operations, warehousing and shipping, sales and marketing, and the financing of company operations—the very things that are the central focus of the decision screens, the overall strategy-making process, and the company performance reports. A much revised presentation in the Player's Manual, coupled with the information-rich screen layouts, helps students play the simulation in a more sophisticated fashion and, in our experience, reduces the number of questions students have about rules and procedures.

Instructors have numerous ways to stir competition among rival companies and keep things lively as the game progresses—there are options to raise or lower interest rates; alter certain costs up or down; and issue special news flashes announcing new tariff levels, materials cost changes, shipping difficulties, or other new considerations to keep business conditions dynamic and stir the pot a bit as needed. The built-in scoreboard of company performance keeps students constantly informed about where their company stands and how well they are doing.

The effort required for instructors to gear up for this 7th edition is modest, and the overall time it takes to process and administer the game has been significantly reduced. The speed of today's PCs cut the processing time to under 5 minutes—it should take no more than 20 minutes for you or a student assistant to turn the decisions around for an entire industry once you have done it a couple of times.

THE 13TH EDITION INSTRUCTOR'S PACKAGE

A full complement of instructional aids is available to assist adopters in using the 13th edition successfully. A two-volume Instructor's Manual contains suggestions for using the text materials, various approaches to course design and course organization, a sample syllabus, alternative course outlines for both semesters and quarters, a set of over 1,050 multiple-choice and essay questions covering the 13 text chapters, and a comprehensive teaching note for each of the 35 cases.

In addition to the two-volume Instructor's Manual, the instructor support package includes software for generating exams from the 1,050-question test bank, a set of color transparencies depicting the figures and tables in the 13 text chapters, and PowerPoint presentation software containing color slides for classrooms equipped with computer-screen-projection capability. The PowerPoint files can also be used to make black-and-white overheads in the event you use an overhead projector in delivering your lectures on the concepts and tools of strategic management. The PowerPoint package includes over 500 slides that thoroughly cover the material presented in the 13 chapters, thus providing plenty to select from in creating support for your classroom lectures. (We deliberately created an abundance of slides for each chapter to give you an ample number to pick and choose from in putting together a presentation that fits both your preferences and time constraints.)

To help instructors enrich and vary the pace of class discussions of cases, there are companion videos for use with seven cases: Avon Products, eBay, Southwest Airlines, Dakota Growers Pasta, DoubleClick, Music on the Internet, and Nike. Adopters can obtain these on a tape/CD from the publisher. In addition, there is an excellent video you can use as a follow-up to World Wresting Federation (A), but you will have to order it directly from the copyright holder—details are provided in the teaching note for this case.

In concert, the textbook, the three companion supplements, and the comprehensive instructor's package provide a complete, integrated lineup of teaching materials. The package provides exceptional latitude in course design, allows you to capitalize on the latest computer-assisted instructional techniques, arms you with an assortment of visual aids, and offers rich pedagogical options for keeping the nature of student assignments varied and interesting. We've endeavored to equip you with all the text materials and complementary resources you need to create and deliver a course that is very much in keeping with contemporary strategic management issues and that wins enthusiastic student approval.

ACKNOWLEDGMENTS

We have benefited from the help of many people during the evolution of this book. Students, adopters, and reviewers have generously supplied an untold number of insightful comments and helpful suggestions. Our intellectual debt to those academics, writers, and practicing managers who have blazed new trails in the strategy field will be obvious to any reader familiar with the literature of strategic management.

We are particularly indebted to the case researchers whose casewriting efforts appear herein and to the companies whose cooperation made the cases possible. To each one goes a very special thank-you. We cannot overstate the importance of timely, carefully researched cases in contributing to a substantive study of strategic management issues and practices. From a research standpoint, cases in strategic management are invaluable in exposing the generic kinds of strategic issues which companies face, in forming hypotheses about strategic behavior, and in drawing experienced-based generalizations about the practice of strategic management. Pedagogically, cases about strategic management give students essential practice in diagnosing and evaluating strategic situations, in learning to use the tools and concepts of strategy analysis, in sorting through various strategic options, in crafting strategic action plans, and in figuring out successful ways to implement and execute the chosen strategy. Without a continuing stream of fresh, well-researched, and well-conceived cases, the discipline of strategic management would quickly fall into disrepair, losing much of its energy and excitement. There's no question, therefore, that first-class case research constitutes a valuable scholarly contribution.

The following reviewers provided insightful advice regarding ways to improve the 12th and 13th edition packages:

F. William Brown, Montana State University

Anthony F. Chelte, Western New England College

Gregory G. Dess, University of Kentucky

Alan B. Eisner, Pace University

John George, Liberty University

Carle M. Hunt, Regent University

Theresa Marron-Grodsky, University of Maryland

Sarah Marsh, Northern Illinois University

Joshua D. Martin, University of Delaware

William L. Moore, California State University

Donald Neubaum, University of Central Florida

George M. Puia, Indiana State University

Amit Shah, Frostburg State University

Lois M. Shelton, University of Illinois at Chicago

Mark Weber, University of Minnesota

We also express our thanks to Steve Barndt, J. Michael Geringer, Ming-Fang Li, Richard Stackman, Stephen Tallman, Gerardo R. Ungson, James Boulgarides, Betty Diener, Daniel F. Jennings, David Kuhn, Kathryn Martell, Wilbur Mouton, Bobby Vaught, Tuck Bounds, Lee Burk, Ralph Catalanello, William Crittenden, Vince Luchsinger, Stan Mendenhall, John Moore, Will Mulvaney, Sandra Richard, Ralph Roberts, Thomas Turk, Gordon VonStroh, Fred Zimmerman, S. A. Billion, Charles Byles, Gerald L. Geisler, Rose Knotts, Joseph Rosenstein, James B. Thurman, Ivan Able, W. Harvey Hegarty, Roger Evered, Charles B. Saunders, Rhae M. Swisher, Claude I. Shell, R. Thomas Lenz, Michael C. White, Dennis Callahan, R. Duane Ireland, William E. Burr II, C. W. Millard, Richard Mann, Kurt Christensen, Neil W. Jacobs, Louis W. Fry, D. Robley Wood, George J. Gore, and William R. Soukup. These reviewers provided valuable guidance in steering our efforts to improve earlier editions.

As always, we value your recommendations and thoughts about the book. Your comments regarding coverage and contents will be most welcome, as will your calling our attention to specific errors, deficiencies, and oversights. Please e-mail us at athompso@cba.ua.edu or astrickl@cba.ua.edu; fax us at (205) 348-6695; or write us at P. O. Box 870225, Department of Management and Marketing, The University of Alabama, Tuscaloosa, Alabama 35487-0225.

Arthur A. Thompson
A. J. Strickland

brief | contents

part | one   The Concepts and Techniques of Strategic Management   1

1. The Strategic Management Process: An Overview   2
2. Establishing Company Direction: Developing a Strategic Vision, Setting Objectives, and Crafting a Strategy   30
3. Industry and Competitive Analysis   72
4. Evaluating Company Resources and Competitive Capabilities   114
5. Strategy and Competitive Advantage   148
6. Strategies for Competing in Globalizing Markets   198
7. Business Models and Strategies in the Internet Era   224
8. Tailoring Strategy to Fit Specific Industry and Company Situations   248
9. Strategy and Competitive Advantage in Diversified Companies   280
10. Evaluating the Strategies of Diversified Companies   318
11. Building Resource Strengths and Organizational Capabilities   344
12. Managing the Internal Organization to Promote Better Strategy Execution   378
13. Corporate Culture and Leadership—Keys to Effective Strategy Execution   408

part | two   Cases in Strategic Management   C-1

A Guide to Case Analysis   C-2

Section A: The Manager as Chief Strategy Maker and Chief Strategy Implementer

1. Andrea Jung's Makeover of Avon Products, Inc.   C-17
2. The Solar Feeder   C-50
3. World Wrestling Federation (A)   C-61
4. Pi Kappa Phi Fraternity   C-74

Section B: Crafting Strategy in Single-Business Companies

5. ZAP and the Electric Vehicle Industry   C-95
6. Dakota Growers Pasta   C-116
7. Colorado Creative Music   C-138
8. Élan and the Competition Ski Boat Industry   C-153
9. Azalea Seafood Gumbo Shoppe   C-184
10. Kentucky Fried Chicken and the Global Fast Food-Industry   C-203
11. Competition in the Global Wine Industry: A U.S. Perspective   C-225
12. Robert Mondavi Corporation   C-246

13. E. & J. Gallo Winery   C-263

14. Krispy Kreme Doughnuts, Inc.   C-279

15. PFS: Daisytek's Growth Strategy   C-302

16. Music on the Internet: Transformation of the Industry by Sony, Amazon.com, MP3.com, and Napster   C-321

17. The Chicagotribune.com   C-339

18. eBay in 2002: The Challenges of Sustained Growth   C-356

19. Nucor Corporation in 2001: Pursuing Growth in a Troubled Steel Industry   C-392

20. FedEx Corporation: Structural Transformation through e-Business   C-428

21. South African Breweries: Achieving Growth in the Global Beer Market   C-447

Section C: Crafting Strategy in Diversified Companies

22. Unilever's Acquisitions of Slimfast, Ben & Jerry's, and Bestfoods   C-470

23. PepsiCo's Acquisition of Quaker Oats   C-502

24. Avid Technology, Inc.   C-536

Section D: Implementing and Executing Strategy

25. Robin Hood   C-550

26. Moss Adams LLP   C-552

27. Perdue Farms, Inc.: Responding to 21st-Century Challenges   C-565

28. Southwest Airlines, Inc.   C-590

29. Gordon Bethune and the Turnaround of Continental Airlines   C-630

30. Conseco's Implementation Strategy for a Web-Based Cash Management System   C-661

31. West Indies Yacht Club Resort: When Cultures Collide   C-677

32. AES Corporation: Values, Culture, and Operating Practices at a Global Power Company   C-695

33. Optivus Technology   C-732

Section E: Strategy, Ethics, and Social Responsibility

34. Nike's Dispute with the University of Oregon   C-759

35. DoubleClick Inc.: Gathering Customer Intelligence   C-776

indexes

Name   I-1

Organization   I-5

Subject   I-11

table of contents

part | one   The Concepts and Techniques of Strategic
              Management   1

1. The Strategic Management Process: An Overview   2

The Most Trustworthy Signs of Good Management   4
The Five Tasks of Strategic Management: A Bird's-Eye View of This Book   6
Developing a Strategic Vision   6
Setting Objectives   9
Crafting a Strategy   10
Implementing and Executing the Strategy   18
*Evaluating Performance, Monitoring New Developments, and
Initiating Corrective Adjustments   19*
Why Strategic Management Is an Ongoing Process, Not a Start-Stop
Event   20
Characteristics of the Five-Task Process   20
Who Performs the Five Tasks of Strategic Management?   21
*How Strategies Get Crafted—What the Process Is Like and Who
Participates   23*
The Role of the Board of Directors in Crafting and Executing Strategy   27
The Benefits of a Strategic Approach to Managing   28
Suggested Readings   29
illustration capsules
   1. Two Radically Different Business Models: Microsoft and Redhat Linux   5
   2. Examples of Strategic Visions and Company Mission Statements   8
   3. Examples of Strategic and Financial Objectives   11
   4. A Strategy Example: McDonald's   14
   5. Corporate Intrapreneuring Is No Game at Sony   26

2. Establishing Company Direction: Developing a Strategic
       Vision, Setting Objectives, and Crafting a Strategy   30

Developing a Strategic Vision: The First Direction-Setting Task   32
The Three Elements of a Strategic Vision   32
The Mission Statement: A Starting Point for Forming a Strategic Vision   32
From Mission Statement to Strategic Vision   38
Communicating the Strategic Vision   40
Establishing Objectives: The Second Direction-Setting Task   41
What Kinds of Objectives to Set   42
The Concept of Strategic Intent   45

The Need for Long-Range and Short-Range Objectives   46
How Much Stretch Should Objectives Entail?   46
Objectives Are Needed at All Organizational Levels   47

Crafting a Strategy: The Third Direction-Setting Task   48
The Strategy-Making Pyramid   49
Corporate Strategy   50
Business Strategy   54
Functional Strategy   56
Operating Strategy   57
Uniting the Strategy-Making Effort   57

The Factors That Shape a Company's Strategy   58
*Societal, Political, Regulatory, and Citizenship
Considerations   59*
Competitive Conditions and Overall Industry Attractiveness   61
The Company's Market Opportunities and External Threats   62
Company Resource Strengths, Competencies, and Competitive Capabilities   62
*The Personal Ambitions, Business Philosophies, and Ethical Beliefs of
Managers   62*
The Influence of Shared Values and Company Culture on Strategy   63

Linking Strategy with Ethics and Social Responsibility   64

Tests of a Winning Strategy   68

Key Points   70

Suggested Readings   70

illustration capsules

6. Deere and Company's Strategic Vision   33
7. Four Sample Mission Statements: Examples to Critique   37
8. Intel's Two Strategic Inflection Points   40
9. Corporate Objectives at Citigroup, General Electric, McDonald's,
    Anheuser-Busch, Exodus Communications, Motorola, and
    McCormick & Company   44
10. Bank One's New Internet Banking Strategy   50
11. The Enron Debacle: A Bold Vision and Admirable Values Undermined by
    a Flawed Strategy and Unethical Behavior   65
12. The Kroger Company's Commitments to Its Stakeholders   69

3. Industry and Competitive Analysis   72

The Methods of Industry and Competitive Analysis   76
Question 1: What Are the Industry's Dominant Economic
Features?   77
Question 2: What Is Competition Like and How Strong Are
Each of the Competitive Forces?   79
The Five Forces of Competition   79
Strategic Implications of the Five Competitive Forces   92
Question 3: What Is Causing the Industry's Competitive Structure and Business
Environment to Change?   93

The Concept of Driving Forces   93

Environmental Scanning Techniques   99

Question 4: Which Companies Are in the Strongest/Weakest Positions?   100

*Using Strategic Group Maps to Assess the Competitive Positions of
Rival Firms   100*

What Can Be Learned from Strategic Group Maps   101

Question 5: What Strategic Moves Are Rivals Likely to Make Next?   103

Monitoring Competitors' Strategies   103

Evaluating Who the Industry's Major Players Are Going to Be   104

Predicting Competitors' Next Moves   105

Question 6: What Are the Key Factors for Competitive Success?   106

Question 7: Is the Industry Attractive and What Are Its Prospects for Above-
Average Profitability?   108

Actually Doing an Industry and Competitive Analysis   109

Key Points   111

Suggested Readings   113

illustration capsules

13. How the Internet and New Internet-Related Technologies Are Changing the
Business Landscape: Classic Examples of a Driving Force   95

14. Strategic Group Map of Competitors in the Video Game Industry   102

4. Evaluating Company Resources and
Competitive Capabilities   114

Question 1: How Well Is the Present Strategy Working?   116

Question 2: What Are the Company's Resource Strengths and Weaknesses and
Its External Opportunities and Threats?   117

Identifying Company Strengths and Resource Capabilities   117

Identifying Company Weaknesses and Resource Deficiencies   119

Identifying Company Competencies and Capabilities   120

Identifying a Company's Market Opportunities   125

Identifying the Threats to a Company's Future Profitability   127

The Real Value of SWOT Analysis   127

Question 3: Are the Company's Prices and Costs Competitive?   128

Strategic Cost Analysis and Value Chains   129

Benchmarking the Costs of Key Activities   134

Strategic Options for Achieving Cost Competitiveness   137

*From Value Chain Activities to Competitive Capabilities to Competitive
Advantage   139*

Question 4: How Strong Is the Company's Competitive Position?   140

Competitive Strength Assessments   140

Question 5: What Strategic Issues Does the Company Face?   143

Key Points   146

Suggested Readings   147

illustration capsules

15. Motorola Uses Strategy to Identify Threats and Opportunities   126

16. The Value Chain for the Recording and Distributing of Music CDs   135
17. Benchmarking: Ford Takes Advice from Cisco Systems   136
18. Benchmarking and Ethical Conduct   137

5. Strategy and Competitive Advantage   148

The Five Generic Competitive Strategies   150
    Low-Cost Provider Strategies   151
    Differentiation Strategies   163
    Best-Cost Provider Strategies   167
    Focused (or Market Niche) Strategies   168
Cooperative Strategies and Competitive Advantage   172
    The Increasingly Pervasive Use of Alliances   172
    Why and How Strategic Alliances Are Advantageous   174
Merger and Acquisition Strategies   177
Vertical Integration Strategies: A Competitive Plus or a Minus   178
    The Strategic Advantages of Vertical Integration   180
    The Strategic Disadvantages of Vertical Integration   187
    Weighing the Pros and Cons of Vertical Integration   182
Unbundling and Outsourcing Strategies—Narrowing the Boundaries of
the Business   182
    Capability Considerations in Boundary Decisions   184
Using Offensive Strategies to Secure Competitive Advantage   185
    Initiatives to Match or Exceed Competitor Strengths   186
    Initiatives to Capitalize on Competitor Weaknesses   187
    Simultaneous Initiatives on Many Fronts   188
    End-Run Offensives to Move to Less Contested Ground   188
    Guerrilla Offensives   189
    Preemptive Strikes   189
    Choosing Whom to Attack   190
Using Defensive Strategies to Protect Competitive Advantage   191
First-Mover Advantages and Disadvantages   193
Key Points   194
Suggested Readings   197
illustration capsules
19. Nucor Corporation's Low-Cost Provider Strategy   154
20. E-Business Technologies: Powerful Tools for Restructuring Value Chains
    to Create a Low-Cost Advantage   161
21. Differentiating Features That Raise Performance   165
22. Toyota's Best-Cost Producer Strategy for Its Lexus Line   169
23. Focused Strategies in the Lodging Industry: Motel 6 and
    Ritz-Carlton   170
24. Examples of Recent Alliances   176

25. How Clear Channel Communications Used Mergers and Acquisitions to Become a Global Leader in the Media Industry   179

26. Toyota's First-Mover Offensive in Custom-Built Cars   194

6. Strategies for Competing in Globalizing Markets   198

Why Companies Expand into Foreign Markets   200

   The Difference between Competing Internationally and Competing Globally   200

Cross-Country Differences in Cultural, Demographic, and Market Conditions   201
   The Potential for Locational Advantages Stemming from Country-to-Country Cost Variations   202
   Fluctuating Exchange Rates   202
   Host Government Restrictions and Requirements   203

Multicountry Competition or Global Competition?   203

Strategy Options for Entering and Competing in Foreign Markets   204
   Export Strategies   205
   Licensing Strategies   206
   Franchising Strategies   206
   A Multicountry Strategy or a Global Strategy?   206

Pursuing Competitive Advantage by Competing Multinationally   209
   Achieving Locational Advantages   210
   Transferring Competencies and Capabilities across Borders   211
   Coordinating Cross-Border Activities   212

Profit Sanctuaries, Cross-Market Subsidization, and Global Strategic Offensives   213
   Using Cross-Market Subsidization to Wage a Strategic Offensive   213

Strategic Alliances and Joint Ventures with Foreign Partners   213
   The Risks of Strategic Alliances with Foreign Partners   214
   Making the Most of Strategic Alliances with Foreign Partners   215

Competing in Emerging Foreign Markets   217

Strategies for Local Companies in Emerging Markets   219
   Defending against Global Competitors by Using Home-Field Advantages   219
   Transferring the Companies Expertise to Cross-Border Markets   220
   Dodging Global Entrants by Shifting to a New Business Model or Market Niche   220
   Contending on a Global Level   221

Key Points   221

Suggested Readings   223

illustration capsules

27. Multicountry Strategies: Microsoft in PC Software, McDonald's in Fast Food, and Nestlé in Instant Coffee   209

28. Cross-Border Strategic Alliances: The New Shape of Global Business   216

7. Business Models and Strategies in the Internet Era   224

The Internet: Technology and Participants   226
The Demand for Internet Services   226
The Suppliers of Internet Technology and Services   226
The Strategic Challenge of Competing Technologies   228
How Internet Technology Impacts Company and Industry Value Chains   229
How Internet Technology Improves Supply Chain Efficiency   229
How Internet Technology Improves Internal Operating Efficiency   229
How Internet Technology Improves Distribution Channel Efficiency   231
The Pervasive Benefits of Internet Applications   232
How the Internet Reshapes the Competitive Environment   232
The Impact on Competitive Rivalry   232
The Impact on Barriers to Entry   234
The Impact on Buyer Bargaining Power   235
The Impact on Supplier Bargaining Power and Supplier-Seller Collaboration   236
Overall Influence on an Industry's Competitive Structure   237
Other Strategy-Shaping Features of Internet Technology   237
The Difficulty of Relying on Internet Technology to Gain Sustainable Competitive Advantage   240
The First-Mover Advantage Myth   241
Strategic Mistakes Made by Early Internet Entrepreneurs   242
The Mistake of Ignoring Low Barriers to Entry   243
The Mistake of Competing Solely on the Basis of Low Price   243
The Mistake of Selling below Cost and Trying to Make It Up with Revenues from Other Sources   244
E-Commerce Business Models and Strategies for the Future   245
Business Models and Strategies for Pure Dot-Com Enterprises   246
"Brick-and-Click" Strategies: An Appealing Middle Ground   249
Internet Strategies for Traditional Businesses   250
Key Points   253
Suggested Readings   255
illustration capsules
29. How the Internet Can Revamp Manufacturing Economics and Industry Value Chains   233
30. Priceline.com's Unique "Name Your Own Price" Business Model   249
31. Office Depot's Brick-and-Click Strategy   251

8. Tailoring Strategy to Fit Specific Industry and Company Situations   258

Strategies for Competing in Emerging Industries of the Future   290
Strategies for Competing in Turbulent, High-Velocity Markets   262
Strategies for Competing in Maturing Industries   266
Strategic Moves in Maturing Industries   267
Strategic Pitfalls in Maturing Industries   269

Strategies for Firms in Stagnant or Declining Industries   269

Strategies for Competing in Fragmented Industries   271

Strategies for Sustaining Rapid Company Growth   273

Strategies for Industry Leaders   275

Strategies for Runner-Up Firms   277

Strategies for Weak and Crisis-Ridden Businesses   281

   Turnaround Strategies for Businesses in Crisis   281

   Liquidation—the Strategy of Last Resort   283

   End-Game Strategies   283

10 Commandments for Crafting Successful Business Strategies   285

Key Points   287

Suggested Readings   289

illustration capsules

32. Yamaha's Strategy in the Stagnant Piano Industry   271

33. How Microsoft Used Its Muscle to Maintain Market Dominance   278

34. Lucent Technologies' Turnaround Strategy   284

9. Strategy and Competitive Advantage in Diversified Companies   290

When to Diversify   292

   Why Rushing to Diversify Isn't Necessarily a Good Strategy   293

   The Risks of Concentrating on a Single Business   293

   Factors That Signal When It's Time to Diversify   294

Building Shareholder Value: The Ultimate Justification for Diversifying   294

   Three Tests for Judging a Diversification Move   294

Choosing the Diversification Path: Related versus Unrelated Businesses   295

The Case for Related Diversification Strategies   296

   Cross-Business Strategic Fits along the Value Chain   297

   Strategic Fit, Economies of Scope, and Competitive Advantage   301

   Capturing Strategic-Fit Benefits   302

The Case for Unrelated Diversification Strategies   303

   The Pros and Cons of Unrelated Diversification   304

   Unrelated Diversification and Shareholder Value   308

Combination Related-Unrelated Diversification Strategies   309

Strategies for Entering New Businesses   309

   Acquisition of an Existing Business   309

   Internal Start-Up   310

   Joint Ventures and Strategic Partnerships   311

Strategy Options for Companies That Are Already Diversified   312

   Strategies to Broaden a Diversified Company's Business Base   312

   Divestiture Strategies Aimed at Retrenching to a Narrower Diversification Base   314

Corporate Restructuring and Turnaround Strategies   316

Multinational Diversification Strategies   318

What Makes Multinational Diversification So Attractive: The Opportunities for Growth and Added Competitive Advantage   318

Key Points   325

Suggested Readings   327

illustration capsules

35. Tyco International's Diversification Strategy   298
36. Examples of Companies with Related Business Portfolios   301
37. Diversified Companies with Unrelated Business Portfolios   305
38. The Global Scope of Five Prominent Diversified Multinational Corporations   320
39. Honda's Competitive Advantages   324

10. Evaluating the Strategies of Diversified Companies   328

Identifying the Present Corporate Strategy   330

Evaluating Industry Attractiveness: Three Tests   331

Evaluating the Attractiveness of Each Industry the Company Has Diversified Into   332

Each Industry's Attractiveness Relative to the Others   333

The Attractiveness of the Mix of Industries as a Whole   334

Evaluating the Competitive Strength of Each of the Company's Business Units   334

Using a Nine-Cell Matrix to Simultaneously Portray Industry Attractiveness and Competitive Strength   337

Strategic Fit Analysis: Checking for Cross-Business Competitive Advantage Potential   340

Resource Fit Analysis: Determining How Well the Firm's Resources Match Business Unit Requirements   342

Cash Hog and Cash Cow Businesses   343

Competitive and Managerial Resource Fits   344

Ranking the Business Units on the Basis of Past Performance and Future Prospects   346

Deciding on Resource Allocation Priorities and a General Strategic Direction for Each Business Unit   347

Crafting a Corporate Strategy   348

The Performance Test   348

Identifying Additional Diversification Opportunities   350

Managing the Process of Crafting Corporate Strategy   350

Key Points   351

Suggested Readings   353

illustration capsules

40. General Electric's Approach to Managing a Broadly Diversified Business Portfolio   339

11. Building Resource Strengths and Organizational Capabilities   354

A Framework for Executing Strategy   356

The Principal Strategy-Implementing Tasks   357

Leading the Strategy Implementation and Execution Process   358

Building a Capable Organization   359

Staffing the Organization   360

Building Core Competencies and Competitive Capabilities   365

Matching Organization Structure to Strategy   369

Organizational Structures of the Future   382

Key Points   384

Suggested Readings   386

illustration capsules

41. How General Electric Develops a Talented and Deep Management Team   362

42. How Cisco Systems Staffs Its Organization with Talented Employees   364

43. Reengineering Business Processes: How Companies Do It and the Results They Have Gotten   376

44. Cross-Unit Coordination at Three Companies   381

45. Organizational Approaches for International and Global Markets   383

12. Managing the Internal Organization to Promote Better Strategy Execution   388

Linking Budgets to Strategy   390

Creating Strategy-Supportive Policies and Procedures   391

Instituting Best Practices and a Commitment to Continuous Improvement   393

Total Quality Management: A Commitment to Continuous Improvement   395

Capturing the Benefits of Best Practice and Continuous Improvement Programs   398

Installing Support Systems   400

Installing Adequate Information Systems, Performance Tracking, and Controls   403

Designing Strategy-Supportive Reward Systems   405

Strategy-Supportive Motivational Practices   405

Linking the Reward System to Strategically Relevant Performance Outcomes   409

Key Points   414

Suggested Readings   415

illustration capsules

46. Granite Rock's "Short Pay" Policy   393

47. Where Best Practices Come From: The Accomplishments of Three Best Practice Award Winners   394

48. Continuous Improvement Makes Ritz-Carlton Hotels a Two-Time Baldridge Award Winner   399

49. The Rush to Install E-Commerce Support Systems   402
50. Motivation and Reward Techniques of "Best Practice" Companies   408
51. The Folly of the Reward System in the Claims Division of a Large Insurance Company   411

13. Corporate Culture and Leadership—Keys to Effective Strategy Execution   418

Building a Strategy-Supportive Corporate Culture   420
    Where Does Corporate Culture Come From?   420
    Culture: Ally or Obstacle to Strategy Execution?   423
    Strong versus Weak Cultures   424
    Unhealthy Cultures   426
    Adaptive Cultures   427
    Creating a Strong Fit between Strategy and Culture   429
    Building Ethics into the Culture   431
    Building a Spirit of High Performance into the Culture   438
Exerting Strategic Leadership   440
    Staying on Top of How Well Things Are Going   441
    Leading the Effort to Establish a Strategy-Supportive Culture   442
    Keeping the Internal Organization Responsive and Innovative   444
    Exercising Ethics Leadership and Insisting on Good Corporate Citizenship   445
    Leading the Process of Making Corrective Adjustments   447
Key Points   448
Suggested Readings   450
illustration capsules
52. The Culture at Nordstrom   421
53. Adaptive Cultures at Companies That Act and React at Internet Speed   428
54. The Johnson & Johnson Credo   433
55. Corporate Ethics and Values Statements at Lockheed Martin, Pfizer, and J. M. Smucker   434
56. SAS Fosters a Culture of Caring   437
57. A Test of Your Business Ethics   439
58. Lockheed Martin's Corrective Actions after Being Fined for Violating U.S. Antibribery Laws   447

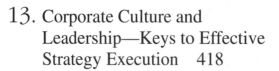

part | two   Cases in Strategic Management   C-1

A Guide to Case Analysis   C-2
Section A: The Manager as Chief Strategy Maker and Chief Strategy Implementer

1. Andrea Jung's Makeover of Avon Products, Inc.   C-17
   John E. Gamble, University of South Alabama

2. The Solar Feeder   C-50
   Lew G. Brown, The University of North Carolina at Greensboro
   Emily Abercrombie, The University of North Carolina at Greensboro

3. World Wrestling Federation (A)   C-61
   Thomas Mannarelli, INSEAD
   Christopher Baty, INSEAD

4. Pi Kappa Phi Fraternity   C-74
   Chris Holoman, The University of Alabama
   Lou Marino, The University of Alabama
   Mark Timmes, CEO, Phi Kappa Phi Fraternity
   A. J. Strickland, The University of Alabama

Section B: Crafting Strategy in Single-Business Companies

5. ZAP and the Electric Vehicle Industry   C-95
   Armand Gilinsky Jr., Sonoma State University
   Robert Ditizio, Sonoma State University

6. Dakota Growers Pasta   C-116
   Michael Boland, Kansas State University
   Christian Freberg, Kansas State University
   David Barton, Kansas State University
   Jeff Katz, Kansas State University

7. Colorado Creative Music   C-138
   Rachel Deane Canetta, University of Denver
   Joan Winn, University of Denver

8. Élan and the Competition Ski Boat Industry   C-153
   Fiona Nairn, The University of Alabama
   A. J. Strickland, The University of Alabama

9. Azalea Seafood Gumbo Shoppe   C-184
   John E. Gamble, University of South Alabama

10. Kentucky Fried Chicken and the Global Fast Food-Industry   C-203
    Jeffrey A. Krug, University of Illinois at Urbana Champaign

11. Competition in the Global Wine Industry: A U.S. Perspective   C-225
    Murray Silverman, San Francisco State University
    Richard M. Castaldi, San Francisco State University
    Sally Baack, San Francisco State University
    Gregg Sorlien, San Francisco State University

12. Robert Mondavi Corporation   C-246
    Murray Silverman, San Francisco State University
    Armand Gilinsky, Sonoma State University
    Michael Guy, San Francisco State University

13. E. & J. Gallo Winery   C-263
    Taylor Green, The University of Alabama
    A. J. Strickland, The University of Alabama

14. Krispy Kreme Doughnuts, Inc.   C-279
Arthur A. Thompson, The University of Alabama

15. PFS: Daisytek's Growth Strategy   C-302
Neil W. Jacobs, Northern Arizona University
Kathryn S. Savage, Northern Arizona University
Mason S. Gerety, Northern Arizona University
Scott Ramsey, Software Architects

16. Music on the Internet: Transformation of the Industry by Sony, Amazon.com, MP3.com, and Napster   C-321
Beatrix Biren, INSEAD

17. The Chicagotribune.com   C-339
Nina Ziv, Polytechnic University

 18. eBay in 2002: The Challenges of Sustained Growth   C-356
Louis Marino, The University of Alabama
Patrick Kreiser, The University of Alabama

 19. Nucor Corporation in 2001: Pursuing Growth in a Troubled Steel Industry   C-392
Frank C. Barnes, University of North Carolina–Charlotte
Beverly B. Tyler, North Carolina State University

20. FedEx Corporation: Structural Transformation through e-Business   C-428
Pauline Ng, The University of Hong Kong

21. South African Breweries: Achieving Growth in the Global Beer Market   C-447
Courtenay Sprague, University of Witwatersrand
Saul Klein, University of Witwatersrand

Section C: Crafting Strategy in Diversified Companies

 22. Unilever's Acquisitions of Slimfast, Ben & Jerry's, and Bestfoods   C-470
Arthur A. Thompson, University of Alabama

 23. PepsiCo's Acquisition of Quaker Oats   C-502
John E. Gamble, University of South Alabama

24. Avid Technology, Inc.   C-536
Philip K. Goulet, University of South Carolina
Alan Bauerschmidt, University of South Carolina

Section D: Implementing and Executing Strategy

 25. Robin Hood   C-550
Joseph Lampel, New York University

26. Moss Adams LLP   C-552
Armand Gilinsky, Jr., Sonoma State University
Sherri Anderson, Sonoma State University

27. Perdue Farms, Inc.: Responding to 21st-Century Challenges   C-565
George C. Rubenson, Salisbury State University
Frank Shipper, Salisbury State University

28. Southwest Airlines, Inc. C-590
Arthur A. Thompson, Jr., The University of Alabama
John E. Gamble, University of South Alabama

29. Gordon Bethune and the Turnaround of Continental Airlines C-630
Arthur A. Thompson, Jr., The University of Alabama
John E. Gamble, University of South Alabama

30. Conseco's Implementation Strategy for a Web-Based Cash Management System C-661
William H. Moates, Indiana State University
Jeffrey S. Harper, Indiana State University
Joseph P. Clarke, Conseco Services, LLC

31. West Indies Yacht Club Resort: When Cultures Collide C-677
Jeffrey P. Shay, University of Montana

32. AES Corporation: Values, Culture, and Operating Practices at a Global Power Company C-695
Arthur A. Thompson, Jr., The University of Alabama

33. Optivus Technology C-732
Lee Hanson, California State University at San Bernardino

Section E: Strategy, Ethics, and Social Responsibility

34. Nike's Dispute with the University of Oregon C-759
Rebecca J. Morris, University of Nebraska at Omaha
Anne T. Lawrence, San Jose State University

35. DoubleClick Inc.: Gathering Customer Intelligence C-776
Ken Mark, University of Western Ontario
Scott Schneberger, University of Western Ontario

indexes
Name I-1
Organization I-5
Subject I-11

Strategic | Management
Concepts and Cases

part one

1

The Concepts and Techniques of Strategic Management

chapter | one

The Strategic Management Process

An Overview

"Cheshire Puss," she [Alice] began . . . "would you tell me, please, which way I ought to go from here?"
"That depends a good deal on where you want to get to," said the Cat.

—Lewis Carroll

Without a strategy the organization is like a ship without a rudder.

—Joel Ross and Michael Kami

Strategic management is not a box of tricks or a bundle of techniques. It is analytical thinking and commitment of resources to action.

—Peter Drucker

The Internet Age implies Internet speed, a different pace and a greater sense of urgency. Clearly we need to invigorate things here.

—Carly Fiorina, CEO, Hewlett-Packard Co.

The tasks of crafting, implementing, and executing company strategies are the heart and soul of managing a business enterprise. A company's **strategy** is the game plan management is using to stake out a market position, conduct its operations, attract and please customers, compete successfully, and achieve organizational objectives. In crafting a strategy, management is saying, in effect, "Among all the paths and actions we could have chosen, we have decided to move in this direction, focus on these markets and customer needs, compete in this fashion, allocate our resources and energies in these ways, and rely on these particular approaches to doing business." A strategy thus entails managerial choices among alternatives and signals organizational commitment to specific markets, competitive approaches, and ways of operating.

Closely related to the concept of strategy is the concept of a company's **business model,** a term now widely applied to management's plan for making money in a particular business. More formally, a company's business model deals with the revenue-cost-profit economics of its strategy—the actual and projected revenue streams generated by the company's product offerings and competitive approaches, the associated cost structure and profit margins, and the resulting earnings stream and return on investment. The fundamental issue surrounding a company's business model is whether a given strategy makes sense from a money-making perspective. A company's business model is, consequently, more narrowly focused than the company's business strategy. Strategy *relates to a company's competitive initiatives and business approaches (irrespective of the financial and competitive outcomes it produces), while the term* business model *deals with whether the revenues and costs flowing from the strategy demonstrate business viability.* Companies that have been in business for a while and are making acceptable profits have a proven business model—there is clear evidence that their strategy is capable of profitability and that they have a viable enterprise. Companies that are

3

Basic Concept
A company's **business model** deals with whether the revenue-cost-profit economics of its strategy demonstrate the viability of the enterprise as a whole.

losing money or are in a start-up mode (like many new dot-com companies) have a questionable business model; their strategies have yet to produce good bottom-line results, putting their viability in doubt. Illustration Capsule 1 contrasts the business models for Microsoft and Redhat Linux in operating system software for personal computers (PCs). Which business model do you think makes the most sense?

Crafting, implementing, and executing a strategy are top-priority managerial tasks for two very big reasons. First, there is a compelling need for managers to *proactively shape* how the company's business will be conducted. It is management's responsibility to exert strategic leadership and commit the enterprise to going about its business in one fashion rather than another. Without a strategy, managers have no prescription for doing business, no road map to competitive advantage, no game plan for pleasing customers or achieving good performance. Lack of a consciously shaped strategy is a surefire ticket for organizational drift, competitive mediocrity, internal wheel-spinning, and lackluster results. Second, there is an equally compelling need to mold the efforts and decisions of different divisions, departments, managers, and groups into a *coordinated, compatible whole*. All the actions being taken in different parts of the business—R&D, design and engineering, production, marketing, customer service, human resources, information technology, and finance—need to be mutually supportive. Absent a purposeful strategy for the entire enterprise, managers have no overarching business rationale for molding the actions and decisions initiated across the organization into a cohesive whole, no underlying business basis for uniting cross-department operations into a team effort, no conscious business model for generating profits.

THE MOST TRUSTWORTHY SIGNS OF GOOD MANAGEMENT

Among all the things managers do, nothing affects a company's ultimate success or failure more fundamentally than how well its management team sets the company's long-term direction, develops competitively effective strategic moves and business approaches, and implements what needs to be done internally to produce good day in, day out strategy execution. Indeed, *good strategy and good strategy execution are the most trustworthy signs of good management.* Managers don't deserve a gold star for designing a potentially brilliant strategy but failing to put the organizational means in place to carry it out in high-caliber fashion—weak implementation undermines the strategy's potential and paves the way for shortfalls in customer satisfaction and company performance. Competent execution of a mediocre strategy scarcely merits enthusiastic applause for management's efforts either. The standards for good management rest to a very great extent on how well-conceived the company's strategy is and how competently it is executed. Any claim of talented management that disregards these standards is likely to be false.

Excellent execution of an excellent strategy is the best test of managerial excellence—and the most reliable recipe for organizational success.

Granted, good strategy combined with good strategy execution doesn't *guarantee* that a company will avoid periods of so-so or even subpar performance. Sometimes organizations with well-conceived strategies, showcase practices, and very capable managers experience performance problems because of unexpected shifts in market conditions or uncontrollable technology delays or unanticipated costs. Sometimes it takes several years for competent strategy-making/strategy-implementing efforts to show good results. But neither the bad luck of unforeseeable events nor the "we need more time" reason excuses mediocre performance year after year. It is the responsibility of a

illustration capsule 1
Two Radically Different Business Models: Microsoft and Redhat Linux

MICROSOFT'S BUSINESS MODEL

Microsoft is one of the world's most successful and profitable companies, partly because of its dominant market position in operating system software for PCs—first DOS, then Windows 95 and Windows NT, and later Windows 98 and Windows 2000. Microsoft's business model for its operating system products is based on the following elements:

- Employ a cadre of highly skilled Microsoft programmers to develop proprietary code; compensate them with premium pay and lucrative stock options. Keep the source code hidden from users.

- Sell the resulting operating system to PC makers and to PC users at relatively attractive prices—around $75 to PC makers and around $100 at retail to consumers. Since most of the costs are fixed (having been incurred in developing the code), each sale generates substantial margins—the variable costs of producing and packaging the CDs provided to users amount to only a couple of dollars per copy.

- Provide technical support to users at no cost.

REDHAT LINUX'S BUSINESS MODEL

Redhat Linux, a start-up company formed to market the Linux operating system in competition with Microsoft's Windows, employs a sharply different business model:

- Give the Linux operating system away free of charge to those who download it (but charge as much as $79 to users who prefer to buy the CD-ROM version—complete with an instruction manual). Redhat is in a position to give Linux away for free because Linux has been created and upgraded through the collaborative efforts of interested programmers from all over the world who volunteer their time and contribute bits and pieces of code to improve and polish the system. The guiding force and visionary of the confederation of volunteer programmers is Linus Torvalds, age 30,

who started development of Linux in 1991 as a sideline hobby while a graduate student at the University of Helsinki and who has shepherded the cobbling together of the code in the intervening years. Torvalds encouraged other programmers to download his software, use it, test it, fix bugs, modify it, add new features as they saw fit, and post their work on the Internet. As the Linux code developed, more and more programmers joined in, contributing their ideas and improvements. The thousands of programmers around the world who work on Linux in their spare time do what they do because they love it, because they are fervent believers that software should be free (as in free speech), and in some cases because they are anti-Microsoft and want to have a part in undoing what they see as a Microsoft monopoly. Their crusade for the cause of free software and competition means that Redhat, unlike Microsoft, essentially has zero product development costs.

- Make the source code open and available to all users, allowing them to make whatever changes they may wish to create a customized version of Linux. Linux users like the ability to modify the source code at will.

- Employ a cadre of technical support personnel who provide technical support to users for a fee. The Linux operating system is a bit quirky and buggy and is said to be hard to install and use in multiserver, multiprocessor applications. Corporate users of Linux thus typically require quite a bit of handholding. Make money on technical support services, not the code.

WHO HAS THE BEST BUSINESS MODEL?

Microsoft's business model—sell proprietary code and give service away free—is a proven moneymaker. But can Redhat make money with a business model that gives software away free and charges users for technical support? What do you think?

Source: Based on information in *Business Week,* February 1, 1999, p. 36; *The New York Times Magazine,* February 21, 1999, pp. 34–37; *PC World,* March 1999, p. 64; and *Smart Money,* October 1999, p. 100.

company's management team to adjust to unexpectedly tough conditions by undertaking strategic defenses and business approaches that can overcome adversity. Indeed, the essence of good strategy making is to build a market position strong enough and an organization capable enough to produce successful performance despite unforeseeable events, potent competition, a rash of delays, or cost surprises. The rationale for using the twin standards of good strategy making and good strategy execution to determine whether a company is well managed is therefore compelling: the better conceived a company's strategy and the more competently it is executed, the more likely it is that the company will be a standout performer and exhibit enviable business practices.

THE FIVE TASKS OF STRATEGIC MANAGEMENT: A BIRD'S-EYE VIEW OF THIS BOOK

The strategy-making/strategy-implementing process consists of five interrelated managerial tasks:

1. *Forming a strategic vision of where the organization is headed*—so as to provide long-term direction, delineate what kind of enterprise the company is trying to become, and infuse the organization with a sense of purposeful action.
2. *Setting objectives*—converting the strategic vision into specific performance outcomes for the company to achieve.
3. *Crafting a strategy to achieve the desired outcomes.*
4. *Implementing and executing the chosen strategy efficiently and effectively.*
5. *Evaluating performance and initiating corrective adjustments in vision, long-term direction, objectives, strategy, or execution in light of actual experience, changing conditions, new ideas, and new opportunities.*

Figure 1.1 displays this process. Together, these five components define what we mean by the term **strategic management.** Let's examine this five-task framework in enough detail to set the stage for the forthcoming chapters.

Developing a Strategic Vision

Very early in the strategy-making process, company managers need to pose a set of questions: "What is our vision for the company—where should the company be headed, what should its future technology-product-customer focus be, what kind of enterprise do we want to become, what industry standing do we want to achieve in five years?" Drawing a carefully reasoned conclusion about what the company's long-term direction should be pushes managers to take a hard look at the company's external and internal environment and form a clearer sense of whether and how its present business needs will change over the next five years and beyond.

Management's views and conclusions about what the organization's long-term direction should be, the technology-product-customer focus it intends to pursue, and its future business scope constitute a **strategic vision** for the company. A strategic vision thus reflects management's aspirations for the organization and its business, providing a panoramic view of "where we are going" and giving specifics about its future business plans. It spells out long-term business purpose and molds organizational identity. A strategic vision points an organization in a particular direction and charts a strategic path for it to follow.

The Difference between a Strategic Vision and a Mission Statement
Whereas the chief concern of a strategic vision is with "where we are going," the term **mission statement,** as it is commonly used, tends to deal with a company's *present* business scope—"who we are and what we do." The mission statements that most companies include in their annual reports or post on their websites almost always stress what the company's present products and services are, what types of customers it serves, and what technological and business capabilities it has. They typically say

---

Basic Concept
The term ***strategic management*** refers to the managerial process of forming a strategic vision, setting objectives, crafting a strategy, implementing and executing the strategy, and then over time initiating whatever corrective adjustments in the vision, objectives, strategy, and execution are deemed appropriate.

Basic Concept
A ***strategic vision*** is a roadmap of a company's future—providing specifics about technology and customer focus, the geographic and product markets to be pursued, the capabilities it plans to develop, and the kind of company that management is trying to create.

figure 1.1 The Five Tasks of Strategic Management

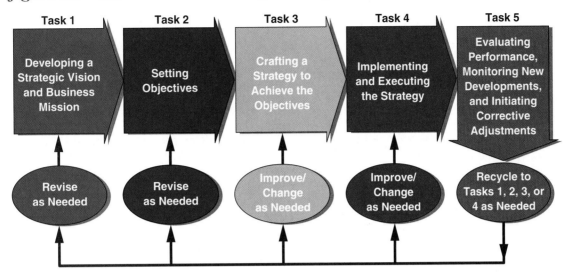

precious little about where the company is headed and its future business scope and business plans. Hence the conceptual distinction between a strategic vision and a mission statement is fairly clear-cut: A strategic vision portrays a company's future business scope ("where we are going"), whereas a company's mission statement describes its present business scope ("who we are and what we do"). Illustration Capsule 2 presents some examples of company mission and vision statements.

If a company's mission statement not only sets forth a clear definition of "who we are and what we do" but also indicates where the company is headed and what its business will become in the years ahead, then it has combined the concepts of company mission (or mission statement) and strategic vision into a single statement describing both where it is now and where it is going. In other words, a strategic vision and a future-oriented mission statement cover essentially the same ground. In practice, however, because the big majority of company mission statements say more about "what our business is now" than "what our business will be later," the distinction between company mission and strategic vision has pragmatic relevance.

Why a Strategic Vision Is Important   While there's a role for a mission statement that speaks to what a company is doing today, a strategic vision generally has much greater direction-setting and strategy-making value. There's an ever-present managerial imperative to look beyond today and think strategically about the impact of new technologies on the horizon, how customer needs and expectations are changing, what it will take to overtake or outrun competitors, which promising market opportunities ought to be aggressively pursued, and all the other external and internal factors that drive what the company needs to be doing to prepare for the future. Managers cannot succeed as organization leaders or strategy makers without first drawing soundly reasoned conclusions about the winds of change and then making some fundamental choices about which of several strategic paths to take. *There's no escaping the need for a strategic vision.* Armed with a clear, well-conceived business course for the organization to follow, managers have a beacon to guide resource allocation and a basis for crafting a strategy to get the company where it needs to go. Companies whose managers neglect the task of thinking strategically about the company's future business path or who are indecisive in committing the company to one direction instead of another are prone to drift aimlessly and lose any claim to being an industry leader.

Basic Concept
A company's *mission statement* is typically focused on its present business scope—"who we are and what we do"; mission statements broadly describe an organization's present capabilities, customer focus, activities, and business makeup.

illustration capsule 2
Examples of Strategic Visions and Company Mission Statements

MICROSOFT CORPORATION

For years, one vision drove what Microsoft did: "A computer on every desk and in every home using great software as an empowering tool." But the emergence of the Internet and non-PC devices like handheld computers and TV-set-top boxes as increasingly integral parts of everyday life prompted Microsoft in 1999 to broaden its vision to "Empower people through great software anytime, anyplace, and on any device." Bill Gates observed: "We see a world where people can use any computing device to do whatever they want to do anytime, anywhere. The PC will continue to have a central role . . . but it will be joined by an incredibly rich variety of digital devices accessing the power of the Internet."

INTEL

"Our vision: Getting to a billion connected computers worldwide, millions of servers, and trillions of dollars of e-commerce. Intel's core mission is being the building-block supplier to the Internet economy and spurring efforts to make the Internet more useful. Being connected is now at the center of people's computing experience. We are helping to expand the capabilities of the PC platform and the Internet."

OTIS ELEVATOR

"Our mission is to provide any customer a means of moving people and things up, down, and sideways over short distances with higher reliability than any similar enterprise in the world."

AVIS RENT-A-CAR

"Our business is renting cars. Our mission is total customer satisfaction."

TRADER JOE'S (a unique grocery store chain)

"The mission of Trader Joe's is to give our customers the best food and beverage values that they can find anywhere and to provide them with the information required for informed buying decisions. We provide these with a dedication to the highest quality of customer satisfaction delivered with a sense of warmth, friendliness, fun, individual pride, and company spirit."

AMERICAN RED CROSS

"The mission of the American Red Cross is to improve the quality of human life; to enhance self-reliance and concern for others; and to help people avoid, prepare for, and cope with emergencies."

3COM

"3Com's mission is to connect more people and organizations to information in more innovative, simple, and reliable ways than any other networking company in the world. Our vision of pervasive networking is of a world where connections are simpler, more powerful, more affordable, more global, and more available to all."

EASTMAN KODAK

"We are in the picture business."

RITZ-CARLTON HOTELS

"The Ritz-Carlton Hotel is a place where the genuine care and comfort of our guests is our highest mission.

"We pledge to provide the finest personal service and facilities for our guests who will always enjoy a warm, relaxed yet refined ambience.

"The Ritz-Carlton experience enlivens the senses, instills well-being, and fulfills even the unexpressed wishes and needs of our guests."

LONG JOHN SILVER'S

"To be America's best quick-service restaurant chain. We will provide each guest great-tasting, healthful, reasonably priced fish, seafood, and chicken in a fast, friendly manner on every visit."

BRISTOL-MYERS SQUIBB

"The mission of Bristol-Myers Squibb is to extend and enhance human life by providing the highest quality health and personal care products. We intend to be the preeminent global diversified health and personal care company."

WIT CAPITAL (an Internet start-up company)

"Our mission is to be the premier Internet investment banking firm focused on the offering and selling of securities to a community of online individual investors."

Source: Company documents and websites.

Setting Objectives

The purpose of setting **objectives** is to convert managerial statements of strategic vision and business mission into specific performance targets—results and outcomes the organization wants to achieve. Setting objectives and then measuring whether they are achieved or not help managers track an organization's progress. Managers of the best-performing companies tend to set objectives that require stretch and disciplined effort. The challenge of trying to achieve bold, aggressive performance targets pushes an organization to be more inventive, to exhibit some urgency in improving both its financial performance and its business position, and to be more intentional and focused in its actions. Setting objectives that require real organizational stretch helps build a firewall against complacent coasting and low-grade improvements in organizational performance. As Mitchell Leibovitz, CEO of automotive parts retailer The Pep Boys—Manny, Moe, & Jack, puts it, "If you want to have ho-hum results, have ho-hum objectives."

Objective setting is required of *all* managers. Every unit in a company needs concrete, measurable performance targets that contribute meaningfully toward achieving company objectives. When companywide objectives are broken down into specific targets for each organizational unit and lower-level managers are held accountable for achieving them, a results-oriented climate builds throughout the enterprise. There's little if any internal confusion over what to accomplish. The ideal situation is a team effort where each organizational unit strives to produce results in its area of responsibility that contribute to the achievement of the company's performance targets and strategic vision.

From a companywide perspective, two very distinct types of performance yardsticks are required: those relating to *financial performance* and those relating to *strategic performance.* Achieving acceptable financial results is crucial. Without adequate profitability, a company's pursuit of its vision, as well as its long-term health and ultimate survival, is jeopardized. Neither shareowners nor lenders will continue to sink additional funds into an enterprise that can't deliver satisfactory financial results. Even so, the achievement of satisfactory financial performance, by itself, is not enough. Managers must also pay attention to the company's strategic well-being—its competitiveness and overall long-term business position. Unless a company's performance reflects improving competitive strength and a stronger long-term market position, its progress is less than inspiring and its ability to continue delivering good financial performance is suspect.

The need for both good financial performance and good strategic performance calls for management to set financial objectives and strategic objectives. **Financial objectives** concern the financial results and outcomes that management wants the organization to achieve. They signal commitment to such outcomes as earnings growth, an acceptable return on investment (or economic value added—EVA),[1] dividend growth, stock price

> **Basic Concept**
> *Objectives* are an organization's performance targets—the results and outcomes it wants to achieve. They function as yardsticks for tracking an organization's performance and progress.

---

[1]*Economic value added (EVA)* is profit over and above the company's cost of debt and equity capital. More specifically, it is defined as operating profit less income taxes less the cost of debt less an allowance for the cost of equity capital. For example, if a company has operating profits of $200 million, pays taxes of $75 million, pays interest expenses of $25 million, has shareholders' equity of $400 million with an estimated equity cost of 15 percent (which translates into an equity cost of capital of $60 million), then the company's EVA is $200 million minus $75 million minus $25 million minus $60 million, or $40 million. The EVA of $40 million can be interpreted to mean that the company's management has generated profits well in excess of the benchmark 15 percent equity cost needed to justify or support the shareholder investment of $400 million—all of which represents wealth created for the owners *above* what they could expect from making an investment of comparable risk elsewhere. Such companies as Coca-Cola, AT&T, and Briggs & Stratton use EVA as a measure of their profit performance.

appreciation (or market value added—MVA),[2] good cash flow, and creditworthiness. In contrast, **strategic objectives** aim at results that reflect increased competitiveness and a stronger business position—outcomes such as winning additional market share, overtaking key competitors on product quality or customer service or product innovation, achieving lower overall costs than rivals, boosting the company's reputation with customers, winning a stronger foothold in international markets, exercising technological leadership, gaining a sustainable competitive advantage, and capturing attractive growth opportunities. Strategic objectives serve notice that management intends not only to deliver good financial performance but also to improve the organization's competitive vitality, business position, and long-range business prospects.

Both financial and strategic objectives ought to involve both near-term and longer-term performance targets. Short-range objectives focus organizational attention on the need for immediate performance improvements and outcomes. Long-range objectives serve the valuable purpose of prompting managers to consider what to do *now* to put the company in position to perform well over the longer term. As a rule, when trade-offs have to be made between achieving long-run objectives and achieving short-run objectives, long-run objectives should take precedence. A company rarely prospers from repeated management actions that put better short-term performance ahead of better long-run performance.

Illustration Capsule 3 shows examples of the kinds of strategic and financial objectives companies set.

Crafting a Strategy

A company's strategy represents management's answers to such fundamental business questions as whether to concentrate on a single business or build a diversified group of businesses, whether to cater to a broad range of customers or focus on a particular market niche, whether to develop a wide or narrow product line, whether to pursue a competitive advantage based on low cost or product superiority or unique organizational capabilities, how to respond to changing buyer preferences, how big a geographic market to try to cover, how to react to newly emerging market and competitive conditions, and how to grow the enterprise over the long term. A strategy thus reflects managerial choices among alternatives and signals organizational commitment to particular products, markets, competitive approaches, and ways of operating the enterprise.

Strategy making brings into play the critical managerial issue of *how* to achieve the targeted results in light of the organization's situation and prospects. Objectives are the "ends," and strategy is the "means" of achieving them. The hows of a company's strategy are typically a blend of (1) deliberate and purposeful actions, (2) as-needed reactions to unanticipated developments and fresh market conditions and competitive pressures,

---

[2]*Market value added (MVA)* is defined as the amount by which the total value of the company has appreciated above the dollar amount actually invested in the company by shareholders. MVA is equal to a company's current stock price times the number of shares outstanding less shareholders' equity investment; it represents the value that management has added to shareholders' wealth in running the business. For example, if a company's stock price is $50, there are 1 million shares outstanding, and shareholders' equity investment is $40 million, then MVA is $10 million ($50 million in market value of existing shares minus $40 million in equity investment); in other words, management has taken the shareholders' investment of $40 million in the company and leveraged it into a current company value of $50 million, creating an additional $10 million in shareholder value. If shareholder value is to be maximized, management must select a strategy and long-term direction that maximizes the market value of the company's common stock. In recent years, MVA and EVA have gained widespread acceptance as valid measures of a company's financial performance.

illustration capsule 3
Examples of Strategic and Financial Objectives

BANC ONE CORPORATION
(Strategic Objective)

"To be one of the top three banking companies in terms of market share in all significant markets we serve."

DOMINO'S PIZZA
(Strategic Objective)

"To safely deliver a hot, quality pizza in 30 minutes or less at a fair price and a reasonable profit."

FORD MOTOR COMPANY
(Strategic Objectives)

"To satisfy our customers by providing quality cars and trucks, developing new products, reducing the time it takes to bring new vehicles to market, improving the efficiency of all our plants and processes, and building on our teamwork with employees, unions, dealers, and suppliers."

ALCAN ALUMINUM
(Strategic and Financial Objectives)

"To be the lowest-cost producer of aluminum and to outperform the average return on equity of the Standard & Poor's industrial stock index."

BRISTOL-MYERS SQUIBB
(Strategic Objective)

"To focus globally on those businesses in health and personal care where we can be number one or number two through delivering superior value to the customer."

ATLAS CORPORATION
(Strategic Objectives)

"To become a low-cost, medium-size gold producer, producing in excess of 125,000 ounces of gold a year and building gold reserves of 1.5 million ounces."

3M CORPORATION
(Financial and Strategic Objectives)

"To achieve annual growth in earnings per share of 10 percent or better, on average; a return on stockholders' equity of 20–25 percent; a return on capital employed of 27 percent or better; and have at least 30 percent of sales come from products introduced in the past four years."

---

and (3) the collective learning of the organization over time—not just the insights gained from its experiences but, more important, the internal activities it has learned to perform quite well and the competitive capabilities it has developed.[3] As illustrated in Figure 1.2, strategy is typically more than what managers carefully plot out in advance and deliberately pursue as part of a visionary strategic plan. It is normal for management's planned strategy to take on a different face as new strategy features are added and others are subtracted in response to shifting market conditions, altered customer needs and preferences, the strategic maneuvering of rival firms, the experience of what is working and what isn't, newly emerging opportunities and threats, unforeseen events, and fresh thinking about how to improve the strategy. Future business conditions are sufficiently uncertain and unpredictable to prevent managers from planning every strategic action in advance without experiencing any learning or seeing any possibilities for improvement. Furthermore, common sense instructs that a company's actions, both planned and reactive, ought to bear close relationship to its competencies and competitive capabilities.

---

[3]See Henry Mintzberg and J. A. Waters, "Of Strategies, Deliberate and Emergent," *Strategic Management Journal* 6 (1985), pp. 257–72; Henry Mintzberg, Bruce Ahlstrand, and Joseph Lampel, *Strategy Safari: A Guided Tour through the Wilds of Strategic Management* (New York: Free Press, 1998), chapters 2, 5, and 7: and C. K. Prahalad and Gary Hamel, "The Core Competence of the Corporation," *Harvard Business Review* 70, no. 3 (May–June 1990), pp. 79–93.

figure 1.2 **A Company's Actual Strategy Is Partly Planned and Partly Reactive**

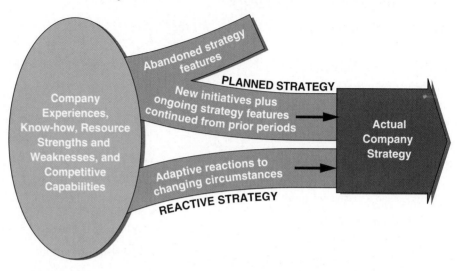

The strategy-making task thus involves developing an *intended strategy;* adapting it as events unfold *(adaptive/reactive strategy);* and linking the firm's business approaches, actions, and competitive initiatives closely to its competencies and capabilities. In short, a company's actual strategy is something managers shape and reshape as events transpire outside the company and as the company's competitive assets and liabilities evolve in ways that enhance or diminish its competitiveness.

> Strategy is both proactive (intended and deliberate) and reactive (adaptive).

What Does a Company's Strategy Consist Of?   Company strategies concern *how:* how to grow the business, how to satisfy customers, how to outcompete rivals, how to respond to changing market conditions, how to manage each functional piece of the business and develop needed organizational capabilities, how to achieve strategic and financial objectives. The hows of strategy tend to be company-specific, customized to a company's own situation and performance objectives. In the business world, companies have a wide degree of strategic freedom. They can diversify broadly or narrowly, into related or unrelated industries, via acquisition, joint venture, strategic alliances, or internal start-up. Insofar as a single business is concerned, prevailing market conditions usually offer enough strategy-making latitude that close competitors can easily avoid carbon-copy strategies—some pursue low-cost leadership, others stress particular differentiating attributes of their product or service, and still others concentrate on serving narrow market segments and developing unique capabilities to meet the special needs and preferences of buyers comprising these segments. Some compete only locally or regionally, others compete nationally, and still others compete globally. Because there are numerous ways for a company to conduct its business internally and position itself in the markets where it elects to compete, descriptions of the content of company strategy necessarily have to be fairly detailed in order to portray the defining characteristics of its strategy.

Figure 1.3 depicts the kinds of actions and approaches that reflect a company's overall strategy. A company's present strategy is typically a blend of holdover approaches and fresh actions and reactions, with perhaps some about-to-be-launched moves and changes that remain under wraps and in the planning stage. Because the holdover approaches and freshly initiated actions are usually visible and have been publicly discussed by company managers or explained in press releases, outside observers can deduce many key

> Company strategies are partly visible and partly hidden to outside view.

figure 1.3   Understanding a Company's Strategy—What to Look For

Actions to diversify the company's revenue base and enter altogether new industries or businesses

Planned actions and initiatives to outcompete rivals

Moves to react and respond to changing external circumstances

Actions to strengthen the company's resource base and competitive capabilities

THE PATTERN OF ACTIONS AND BUSINESS APPROACHES THAT DEFINE A COMPANY'S STRATEGY

Actions to alter geographic coverage

Actions and approaches that define how the company manages R&D, production, sales and marketing, finance, and other key functions

Actions to capitalize on new opportunities or to defend against threats to the company's well-being

Actions to form strategic alliances and collaborative partnerships

Actions to merge with or acquire a rival company to strengthen the company's business position

elements of a company's strategy. Still, there's an unrevealed portion of strategy that outsiders can only speculate about—the-as-yet-unrevealed strategic actions company managers are intending to launch. Managers often, for good reason, choose not to reveal certain elements of their strategy until the company's actions become public.

To get a better understanding of the content of company strategies, see the overview of McDonald's strategy in Illustration Capsule 4.

Strategy and Entrepreneurship   Crafting strategy is partly an exercise in astute entrepreneurship—actively searching for opportunities to do new things or to do existing things in new ways.[4] The faster a company's business environment is changing, the more critical it becomes for its managers to be good entrepreneurs in making both predictions and timely strategic adjustments. Imagine, for instance, the implications for companies that downplay the potential impact of e-commerce or for retailers who ignore the exploding interest of consumers in shopping on the Internet. Managers are always under the gun to pick up on happenings in the external environment that

> Strategy making is fundamentally a market-driven and customer-driven entrepreneurial activity—the essential qualities are a talent for capitalizing on emerging market opportunities and evolving customer needs, a bias for innovation and creativity, an appetite for prudent risk taking, and a strong sense of what needs to be done to grow and strengthen the business.

---

[4]For a fuller discussion of strategy as an entrepreneurial process, see Mintzberg, Ahlstrand, and Lampel, *Strategy Safari,* chapter 5. Also see Bruce Barringer and Allen C. Bluedorn, "The Relationship between Corporate Entrepreneurship and Strategic Management," *Strategic Management Journal* 20 (1999), pp. 421–44; and Jeffrey G. Covin and Morgan P. Miles, "Corporate Entrepreneurship and the Pursuit of Competitive Advantage," *Entrepreneurship: Theory and Practice* 23, no. 3 (Spring 1999), pp. 47–63.

illustration capsule 4
A Strategy Example: McDonald's

In 1999 McDonald's was the leading food-service retailer in the global consumer marketplace, with a strong brand name and systemwide restaurant sales approaching $35 billion. Eighty percent of its 25,000-plus restaurants were franchised to approximately 5,000 owner/operators around the world. Over the past 10 years, the company's systemwide sales had grown an average of 8 percent annually and its stock had provided a 20 percent annual return to investors.

McDonald's food-quality specifications, equipment technology, marketing and training programs, operating systems, site selection techniques, and supply systems were considered industry standards throughout the world. Its vision was to be the world's best quick-service restaurant—*being the best* was defined as consistently satisfying customers better than rivals through outstanding quality, service, cleanliness, and value.

The company's strategic priorities were ensuring continued growth, providing exceptional customer care, remaining an efficient and quality producer, developing people at every level of the organization, sharing best practices among all units worldwide, and reinventing the fast-food concept by fostering innovation in the company's menu, facilities, marketing, operation, and technology.

GROWTH STRATEGY

- Penetrate the market not currently served by adding 1,750 restaurants annually (an average of one every five hours), some company-owned and some franchised, with about 90 percent outside the United States. Establish a leading market position in foreign countries ahead of competitors.

- Promote more frequent customer visits via the addition of attractive menu items, low-price specials, Extra Value Meals, and children's play areas.

- Explore opportunities to exploit the company's global supplier infrastructure and its core competencies in multiunit restaurant management, site location and unit construction, and product marketing.

FRANCHISING STRATEGY

- Grant franchises only to highly motivated, talented entrepreneurs with integrity and business experience, and train them to become active, on-premise owners of McDonald's. (No franchises were granted to corporations, partnerships, or passive investors.)

STORE LOCATION AND CONSTRUCTION STRATEGY

- Locate restaurants on sites offering convenience to customers and profitable growth potential. The company's research indicated that 70 percent of all decisions to eat at McDonald's were made on the spur of the moment, so its goal was to pick locations that were as convenient as possible for customers to visit. In the United States, the company supplemented its traditional suburban and urban locations with satellite outlets in food courts, airports, hospitals, universities, large shopping establishments (Wal-Mart, The Home Depot), and service stations; outside the United States, the strategy was to establish an initial presence in center cities, then open freestanding units with drive-thrus outside center cities.

- Reduce site costs and building costs by using standardized, cost-efficient store designs and by consolidating purchases of equipment and materials via a global sourcing system.

- Make sure restaurants are attractive and pleasing inside and out, and provide drive-thru service and play areas for children, where feasible.

PRODUCT LINE STRATEGY

- Offer a limited menu.

- Improve the taste appeal of the items offered (especially sandwich selections).

- Expand product offerings into new categories of fast food (chicken, Mexican, pizza, adult-oriented sandwiches, and so on) and include more items for health-conscious customers.

(continued)

signal either new opportunities for the enterprise or threats to its present way of doing business. For a company to be successful, its strategy and business model have to be well matched to the company's present and future environment. That won't happen unless managers exhibit first-rate entrepreneurship in steering company activities in whatever new directions are dictated by market conditions and customer preferences. This entails studying market trends, listening to customers and anticipating their changing needs and expectations, scrutinizing the business possibilities that spring

illustration capsule 4

(concluded)

- Roll out new, potentially appealing and exciting items in speedy fashion, but quickly drop those that fail to catch on, learning from whatever mistakes were made and moving promptly on to the next idea. (This strategy element was recently instituted and was a sharp departure from the company's long-standing practice of doing extensive testing to ensure consistent high quality and ample customer appeal before rolling out new menu items systemwide—Chicken McNuggets, for example, took seven years to develop.)

STORE OPERATIONS

- Enforce stringent standards regarding food quality; store and equipment cleanliness; restaurant operating procedures; and friendly, courteous counter service.

- Expand the "Made for You" concept to include a much larger percentage of outlets. The company's Made for You program involved the installation of advanced equipment, sophisticated computer technology, and new preparation methods to allow items to be prepared to customer order.

SALES PROMOTION, MARKETING, AND MERCHANDISING

- Enhance the McDonald's image of quality, service, cleanliness, and value globally via heavy media advertising and in-store merchandise promotions funded with fees tied to a percentage of sales revenues at each restaurant.

- Use Ronald McDonald to create greater brand awareness among children and the *Mc* prefix to reinforce the connection of menu items and McDonald's.

- Project an attitude of happiness and interest in children.

HUMAN RESOURCES AND TRAINING

- Offer wage rates that are equitable and nondiscriminatory in every location; teach job skills; reward both individual and team performance; create career

opportunities; have flexible work hours for student employees.

- Hire restaurant crews with good work habits and courteous attitudes and train them to act in ways that will impress customers; promote promising employees quickly.

- Provide proper training on delivering customer satisfaction and running a fast-food business to franchisees, restaurant managers, and assistant managers. (Instructors at Hamburger University campuses in Illinois, Germany, England, Australia, and Japan annually train over 5,000 students in 22 languages.)

- Promote a global mindset by aggressively transferring best practices and new ideas developed in outlets in one part of the world to outlets in other parts of the world.

SOCIAL RESPONSIBILITY AND COMMUNITY CITIZENSHIP

- Take an active community role—support local charities and community projects; help create a neighborhood spirit; promote educational excellence.

- Sponsor Ronald McDonald Houses. (At year-end 1995, there were 168 houses in 12 countries providing a home away from home for families of seriously ill children receiving treatment at nearby hospitals.)

- . Promote workforce diversity, voluntary affirmative action, and minority-owned franchises. (Over 34 percent of McDonald's franchisees and 70 percent of the franchisee applicants in training were females and minorities.)

- Support education through student scholarships, teacher awards, and free instructional resources.

- Adopt and encourage environmentally friendly practices.

- Provide nutritional information on McDonald's products to customers.

Source: Company annual reports.

from technological developments, building the firm's market position via acquisitions or new-product introductions, and pursuing ways to strengthen the firm's competitive capabilities. Good strategy making is therefore inseparable from good business entrepreneurship. One cannot exist without the other.

How fast company managers adapt to changing market conditions, how boldly they pursue new business opportunities, how much they emphasize out-innovating the competition, and how often they champion actions to improve organizational performance are good barometers of a company's entrepreneurial spirit. Entrepreneurial strategy makers are inclined to be either first-movers or rapid followers, responding quickly and opportunistically to new avenues for building the enterprise and fortifying its market position and capabilities. They are willing to take prudent risks and initiate trailblazing strategies. Today's dot-com companies are examples of entrepreneurship in action. In contrast, entrepreneurially deficient companies are risk-averse, displaying a wariness of deviating very far from the company's tried-and-true business approaches unless absolutely forced to. They either dismiss impending developments as unimportant ("we don't think it will really affect us") or move so slowly that the company is habitually late in responding and adapting to shifting conditions in the marketplace. Entrepreneurially deficient companies often minimize the disadvantages of being late-movers, pointing instead to the cost-saving benefits of avoiding whatever "mistakes" they believe first-movers have made or might make. They prefer gradual strategic change to dramatic or sweeping strategic realignment. Companies still taking a wait-and-see approach to embracing use of the Internet and e-commerce is a classic example of entrepreneurial deficiency.

Why Company Strategies Evolve   Plainly, every company encounters occasions in which it needs to adapt its strategy to shifting industry and competitive conditions, newly emerging buyer preferences and requirements, the initiatives of rival firms to grab increased market share, the appearance of fresh opportunities and threats, advancing technology, and other significant events that affect its business. On occasion, quantum changes in strategy are called for—when an opening appears to shift to a radically new strategy and drive market change, when a competitor makes a revolutionary move that demands a dramatic response, when technological breakthroughs occur, or when crisis strikes and major strategy adjustments are needed very quickly. The America Online–Time Warner merger represented a quantum strategy change for both companies. Just as plainly, ways open up to fine-tune a company's strategy, first in one department or functional area and then in another.

Basic Concept
The march of external and internal developments dictate that a company's strategy change and evolve over time—a condition that makes strategy making an ongoing process, not a one-time event.

Because the march of external and internal events make it commonplace to initiate fresh strategic moves and business approaches of one kind or another in one part of the organization or another, *an organization's strategy re-forms over time as the number of changes and adaptations begin to mount.* It is thus normal, indeed necessary, for a company's strategy to change, sometimes gradually and sometimes rapidly, sometimes reactively (when new developments dictate a response) and sometimes proactively (when attractive new opportunities are spotted or new capabilities are acquired). Consequently, *strategy making is an ongoing process, not a one-time event.* Managers are obliged to reevaluate strategy regularly, refining and recasting it as often and as much as needed to match the organization's changing external and internal circumstances.

Another important facet of strategic change is *the need for actions to improve on how the company is competing today and the need for actions to prepare for tomorrow's markets and competitive conditions.* Whether a company takes a proactive or reactive posture in preparing for future market conditions shapes the character and speed of the adjustments it makes in its strategy over time.

Figure 1.4 illustrates the strategic postures a company can adopt in preparing for future market conditions and coping with the waves of change in the marketplace.[5] In most industries, there are pioneering entrepreneurial companies that seek to be proactive leaders in reshaping their strategies and there are cautious, conservatively managed

---

[5]For a discussion of the need for strategic actions aimed at competing today coupled with strategic actions to prepare for competing tomorrow, see Derek F. Abell, "Competing Today While Preparing for Tomorrow," *Sloan Management Review* 40, no. 3 (Spring 1999), pp. 73–81.

figure 1.4   **Strategic Approaches to Preparing for Future Market Conditions**

COMPANY APPROACHES

	Reactive/Follower	**Proactive/Leader**
Rapid Revolutionary Change	Rushing to catch up to keep from being swamped by the waves	Aggressively altering strategy to make waves and drive change
Gradual Evolutionary Change	Revising strategy (hopefully in time) to catch the waves	Anticipating change and initiating strategic actions to ride the crest of the waves

FUTURE MARKET CONDITIONS

Source: Adapted from Derek F. Abell, "Competing Today While Preparing for Tomorrow," *Sloan Management Review* 40, no. 3 (Spring 1999), p. 75.

companies that end up as reactive followers. Indeed, it is typical for companies to adjust their strategies and prepare for future market conditions at varying speeds and in varying ways—the path each company takes is unique.

However, if managers decide to change strategy so fast and so fundamentally that their business model undergoes major overhaul every year, questions have to be asked. Is rapid strategy change being legitimately driven by rapid-fire technological change, swiftly changing market conditions, volatile buyer behavior, or other hard-to-foresee developments? Or is it the product of poor entrepreneurship, faulty situation analysis, and inept strategizing? As a general rule, frequent and fundamental strategy changes cannot be made repeatedly year after year without creating a zigzag market wake, generating undue confusion among customers and employees, and posing real profitability problems. In most situations, the core elements of well-crafted strategies ought to have a life of several years, even though they may have to undergo modest revision to keep them in tune with changing circumstances.

Strategy and Strategic Plans   Developing a strategic vision and mission, establishing objectives, and deciding on a strategy are basic direction-setting tasks. They map out where the organization is headed, its short-range and long-range performance targets, and the competitive moves and internal action approaches to be used in achieving the targeted business results. Together, they constitute a **strategic plan** for coping with industry and competitive conditions, the expected actions of the industry's key players, and the challenges and issues that stand as obstacles to the company's success.[6]

Basic Concept
A *strategic plan* consists of an organization's mission and future direction, near-term and long-term performance targets, and strategy.

---

[6]For an excellent discussion of why a strategic plan needs to be more than a list of bulleted points and should, in fact, tell an engaging, insightful, stage-setting story that lays out the industry and competitive situation as well as the vision, objectives, and strategy, see Gordon Shaw, Robert Brown, and Philip Bromiley, "Strategic Stories: How 3M Is Rewriting Business Planning," *Harvard Business Review* 76, no. 3 (May–June 1998), pp. 41–50.

In companies committed to regular strategy reviews and the development of explicit strategic plans, the strategic plan may take the form of a written document describing the industry's economics, key success factors, and drivers of change along with the company's strategic plan for dealing with its external and internal environment.

Some companies circulate the strategic plan to most all managers (and perhaps selected employees), although some of the planned strategic initiatives may be expressed in general terms or omitted if they are too sensitive to reveal before they are actually undertaken. In other companies, the strategic plan is not put in writing for widespread distribution but exists only in the form of oral understandings and commitments among managers about where to head, what to accomplish, and how to proceed. Organizational objectives are the part of the strategic plan most often spelled out explicitly and communicated to managers and employees. A number of companies present key elements of their strategic plans in the company's annual report to shareholders or in statements provided to the business media, while others, perhaps for reasons of competitive sensitivity, make only vague general statements about their strategic plans that could apply to most any company.

| The faster a company's external and internal environment changes, the more frequently that its short-run and long-run strategic plans have to be revised and updated—annual changes may not be adequate. In today's world strategy life cycles are growing shorter, not longer.

However, as we noted earlier, formal, written strategic plans seldom anticipate all the strategically relevant events that will transpire in upcoming months and years. Unforeseen events, unexpected opportunities or threats, and the constant bubbling up of new proposals encourage managers to modify planned actions and forge "unplanned" reactions. Postponing the recrafting of strategy until it's time to work on next year's strategic plan is both foolish and unnecessary. Once-a-year strategizing under "have-to" conditions is not a prescription for managerial or business success. *Strategy is something that ought to be modified whenever it is propitious to do so and certainly whenever unfolding events dictate.* In the "Internet economy," developments have been occurring so rapidly that quarterly, monthly, or even weekly reviews of strategy have become essential and common—the notion of annual strategic plans has been abandoned almost entirely. Internet companies have found it essential to revise demand forecasts, update financial projections, and adjust key elements of their strategies at least quarterly and often more frequently.

At Ingram-Micro, a contract manufacturer and distributor of PCs, "rolling forecasts" of financial projections are devised for five quarters out and then updated every 60 days. Bluefly.com, a clothing e-tailer, makes budget revisions weekly to keep up with strategy changes and react to daily sales patterns. To help speed company reactions to fast-changing market conditions, a number of companies have resorted to developing strategic plans for each of several different market and competitive scenarios, enabling them to react more swiftly as one or another of the scenarios turns out to best approximate unfolding events. Because of the speed of change in many of today's industries, *strategy life cycles are increasingly measured in months and single years, not decades or even five-year intervals.*[7]

Implementing and Executing the Strategy

The managerial task of implementing and executing the chosen strategy entails assessing what it will take to develop the needed organizational capabilities and to reach the targeted objectives on schedule. The managerial skill here is figuring out what must be done to put the strategy in place, carry it out proficiently, and produce good results.

---

[7]Gary Hamel, "Bringing Silicon Valley Inside," *Harvard Business Review* 77, no. 5 (September–October 1999), p. 72.

Managing the strategy execution process is primarily a hands-on, close-to-the-scene administrative task that includes the following principal aspects:

Basic Concept
Strategy implementation concerns the managerial exercise of putting a freshly chosen strategy into place. *Strategy execution* deals with the managerial exercise of supervising the ongoing pursuit of strategy, making it work, improving the competence with which it is executed, and showing measurable progress in achieving the targeted results.

- Building an organization capable of carrying out the strategy successfully.

- Allocating company resources so that organizational units charged with performing strategy-critical activities and implementing new strategic initiatives have sufficient people and funds to do their work successfully.

- Establishing strategy-supportive policies and operating procedures.

- Motivating people in ways that induce them to pursue the target objectives energetically and, if need be, modifying their duties and job behavior to better fit the strategy requirements of successful execution.

- Tying the reward structure to the achievement of targeted results.

- Creating a company culture and work climate conducive to successful strategy implementation and execution.

- Installing information, communication, and operating systems that enable company personnel to carry out their strategic roles effectively day in, day out.

- Instituting best practices and programs for continuous improvement.

- Exerting the internal leadership needed to drive implementation forward and to keep improving on how the strategy is being executed.

Good strategy execution involves creating a strong "fit" between the way things are done internally and what it will take for the strategy to succeed. The stronger the methods of implementation fit the strategy's requirements, the better the odds that performance targets will be achieved. The most important fits are between strategy and organizational capabilities, between strategy and the reward structure, between strategy and internal support systems, and between strategy and the organization's culture. Fitting the organization's internal practices to what is needed for strategic success helps unite the organization behind the accomplishment of strategy.

The strategy-implementing/strategy-executing task is easily the most complicated and time-consuming part of strategic management. It cuts across virtually all facets of managing and must be initiated from many points inside the organization. The action agenda for executing strategy emerges from careful assessment of what the organization needs to do differently or better. Each manager has to answer the question "What has to be done in my area to execute my piece of the strategic plan, and how can I best get it done?" How much internal change is needed depends on how much of the strategy is new, how far internal practices and competencies deviate from what the strategy requires, and how well strategy and organizational culture already match. Depending on the amount of internal change involved, full implementation and proficient execution can take several months to several years.

Strategy execution is fundamentally an action-oriented, make-it-happen process—the key tasks are developing competencies and capabilities, budgeting, policy making, motivating, culture-building, and leadership.

Evaluating Performance, Monitoring New Developments, and Initiating Corrective Adjustments

It is always incumbent on management to evaluate the organization's performance and progress. It is management's duty to stay on top of the company's situation, deciding whether things are going well internally, and monitoring outside developments closely. Subpar performance or too little progress, as well as important new external circumstances, will require corrective actions and adjustments in a company's long-term direction, objectives, business model, and/or strategy.

Likewise, one or more aspects of executing the strategy may not be going as well as intended. Revising budgets, changing policies, reorganizing, making personnel changes, building new competencies and capabilities, revamping activities and work processes, making efforts to change the culture, and revising compensation practices are typical managerial actions that may have to be taken to hasten implementation or improve strategy execution. Proficient strategy execution is always the product of much organizational learning. It is achieved unevenly—coming quickly in some areas and proving nettlesome in others. Progress reviews, ongoing searches for ways to continuously improve, and corrective adjustments are thus normal.

WHY STRATEGIC MANAGEMENT IS AN ONGOING PROCESS, NOT A START-STOP EVENT

A company's vision, objectives, strategy, and approach to implementation are never final; evaluating performance, reviewing changes in the surrounding environment, and making adjustments are normal and necessary parts of the strategic management process.

The choice of whether to continue or change the company's vision, objectives, strategy, and implementation approaches always presents itself. Strategic management is an ongoing, neverending process, not a start-stop event that, once done, can be safely put aside for a while. Managers have an ever-present responsibility for detecting when new developments require a strategic response and when they don't. Their job is to track progress, spot problems and issues early, monitor the winds of market and customer change, and initiate adjustments as needed. This is why the task of evaluating performance and initiating corrective adjustments is both the end and the beginning of the strategic management cycle.

Characteristics of the Five-Task Process

Although forming a strategic vision, setting objectives, crafting a strategy, implementing and executing the strategic plan, and evaluating performance portray what strategic management involves, actually performing these five tasks is not so cleanly divided into separate, neatly sequenced compartments. First, there is much interplay and recycling among the five tasks, as was shown in Figure 1.1. For example, deciding on a company mission and vision shades into setting objectives (both involve directional priorities). Objective-setting entails considering current performance, the strategy options available to improve performance, and whether the organization has the resources and capabilities to achieve stretch objectives when pushed and challenged. Clearly, the direction-setting tasks of developing a mission, setting objectives, and crafting strategy need to be integrated and done as a package, not individually. Deciding on a strategy is entangled with whether the organization has what it takes to execute the strategy with sufficient proficiency—it is generally foolhardy to pursue a strategic course ill-suited to the company's competencies, capabilities, and resources.

Strategic management is a tightly-knit process; the boundaries between the five tasks are conceptual, not fences that prevent some or all of them being done together.

Second, the five strategic management tasks have to be done alongside a manager's other duties and responsibilities—administering day-to-day operations, dealing with crises, going to meetings, reviewing information, handling people problems, and taking on special assignments and civic duties. Thus, while the job of managing strategy is the most important managerial function insofar as organizational success or failure is concerned, it certainly isn't all managers must do or be concerned about.

Third, crafting and implementing strategy make erratic demands on a manager's time. Change does not happen in an orderly or predictable way. Events can build quickly or gradually; they can emerge singly or in rapid-fire succession; and their implications for strategic change can be easy or hard to diagnose. Hence the task of reviewing and adjusting the strategic game plan can take up big chunks of management time in some months and little time in other months. As a practical matter, there is as much skill in knowing *when* to institute strategic changes as there is in knowing what to do.

Last, the most time-consuming aspect of strategic management involves a daily effort to get the best strategy-supportive performance out of every individual in the organization and trying to perfect the current strategy by refining its content and execution. Managers usually spend most of their efforts improving bits and pieces of the current strategy rather than developing and instituting radical or sweeping changes. Excessive changes in strategy can be disruptive to employees and confusing to customers, and they are usually unnecessary. Most of the time, there's more to be gained from improving execution of the present strategy. Persistence in making a basically sound strategy work better is often the key to successful strategy management.

WHO PERFORMS THE FIVE TASKS OF STRATEGIC MANAGEMENT?

An organization's chief executive officer, as captain of the ship, is the most visible and important strategy manager. The title of CEO carries with it the mantles of chief direction setter, chief objective setter, chief strategy maker, and chief strategy implementer for the total enterprise. Ultimate responsibility for *leading* the tasks of forming, implementing, and executing a strategic plan for the whole organization rests with the CEO, even though other senior managers normally have significant leadership roles also. What the CEO views as strategically important usually is reflected in the company's strategy, and the CEO customarily puts a personal stamp of approval on big strategic decisions and actions.

Vice presidents for production, marketing, finance, human resources, and other functional departments have important strategy-making and strategy-implementing responsibilities as well. Normally, the production VP has a lead role in developing and executing the company's production strategy, the marketing VP oversees the marketing strategy effort, the financial VP is in charge of devising and implementing an appropriate financial strategy, and so on. Usually, senior executives below the CEO are involved in proposing key elements of the overall company strategy and developing major new strategic initiatives, working closely with the CEO to hammer out a consensus strategy and coordinate various aspects of executing the strategy. Only in comparatively small companies is the strategy-making/strategy-implementing task orchestrated by a single executive.

But managerial positions with strategy-making and strategy-implementing responsibility are by no means restricted to CEOs, other senior executives, and owner-entrepreneurs. Every major organizational unit in a company—business unit, division, staff support group, plant, or district office—normally has a leading or supporting role in the company's strategic game plan. And the manager in charge of that organizational unit, with guidance from superiors, usually ends up doing some or most of the strategy making for the unit and deciding how to execute whatever strategic choices are made. While managers farther down in the managerial hierarchy obviously have a narrower, more specific strategy-making/strategy-implementing role than managers closer to the top, *every manager is a strategy maker and strategy implementer for the area he or she supervises.*

Every company manager has a strategy-making/strategy-implementing role—it is flawed thinking to view strategic management as solely the province of senior executives.

Toshiba is a $45 billion corporation with 300 subsidiaries, thousands of products, and operations extending across the world. The notion that a few senior executives in Toshiba headquarters can orchestrate the crafting, implementing, and executing of all the thousands of pieces of Toshiba's strategy is absurd—it takes Toshiba's whole management team to pull off the strategy-making/strategy-executing process competently.

One of the primary reasons why middle- and lower-echelon managers are part of the strategy-making/strategy-implementing team is that the more geographically scattered and diversified an organization's operations are, the more unwieldy it becomes for headquarters executives to personally craft and lead the implementation of all the necessary initiatives. Managers in the corporate office seldom know enough about the situation in every geographic area and operating unit to direct every strategic move made in the field. It is common practice for top-level managers to delegate strategy-making authority to subordinates who head the organizational subunits where specific strategic results must be achieved. Such delegation fixes accountability for strategic success or failure. When the managers who implement the strategy are also its architects, it is hard for them to shift blame or make excuses if they don't achieve the target results. And, having participated in developing the strategy they are trying to execute, they are likely to support it strongly, an essential condition for effective strategy execution.

In diversified companies where the strategies of several different businesses have to be managed, there are usually four distinct levels of strategy managers:

- The chief executive officer and other senior corporate-level executives who have primary responsibility and personal authority for big strategic decisions affecting the total enterprise and the collection of individual businesses into which the enterprise has diversified.

- Managers who have profit-and-loss responsibility for one specific business unit and who are delegated a major leadership role in crafting and executing a strategy for that business.

- Functional area managers within a given business unit who have direct authority over a major piece of the business (manufacturing, marketing and sales, finance, R&D, personnel) and whose role it is to support the business unit's overall strategy with strategic actions in their own areas.

- Managers of major operating units (plants, sales districts, local offices) who have on-the-scene responsibility for developing the details of strategic efforts in their areas and for executing their piece of the overall strategic plan at the grassroots level.

Single-business enterprises need no more than three of these levels (a business-level strategy manager, functional area strategy managers, and operating-level strategy managers). Proprietorships, partnerships, and owner-managed enterprises typically have only one or two strategy managers since in small-scale enterprises the whole strategy-making/strategy-implementing function can be handled by just a few key people.

Managerial jobs involving crafting and executing strategy abound in not-for-profit organizations as well. In federal and state government, heads of local, district, and regional offices function as strategy managers in the areas they serve (a district manager in Portland may need a slightly different strategy than a district manager in Orlando). In municipal government, the heads of various departments (fire, police, water and sewer, parks and recreation, health, and so on) are strategy managers because they have line authority for the operations of their departments and thus can influence departmental objectives, the formation of a departmental strategy to achieve these objectives, and day-to-day execution of the strategy.

Managerial jobs with strategy-making/strategy-executing roles are thus the norm rather than the exception.[8] The job of crafting and executing strategy touches virtually every managerial job in one way or another, at one time or another. Strategic management is basic to the task of managing; it is not something just top-level managers deal with.

How Strategies Get Crafted—What the Process Is Like and Who Participates

Companies and managers approach the task of crafting a strategy in a variety of ways. At one extreme, strategy emerges as chiefly the product of one person—the CEO, a visionary founder of the business, or an enterprise's current owner. At the other extreme, strategy making is a group or team exercise involving managers and perhaps select other key personnel throughout the whole organization. The process of crafting strategy at most companies tends to take one of the following four forms.[9]

The Chief Architect Approach   In some enterprises, a single person—the owner or CEO—assumes the role of chief strategist and chief entrepreneur, singlehandedly shaping most or all of the major pieces of strategy. This does not mean that one person is the originator of all ideas underlying the resulting strategy or does all the background data gathering and analysis; there may be much brainstorming with subordinates and considerable analysis by specific departments. But it does mean that one person functions as strategic visionary and chief architect of strategy, personally orchestrating the process and putting his or her imprint on what strategy to pursue. The chief architect approach to strategy formation is characteristic of companies that have been founded by the company's present CEO—Michael Dell at Dell Computer, Steve Case at America Online, Bill Gates at Microsoft, and Howard Schultz at Starbucks are prominent examples of corporate CEOs who exert a heavy hand in shaping their company's strategy. The strategies of small entrepreneurial companies, partnerships, and family-owned businesses almost always are primarily the product of the experiences, personal observations and assessments, strategic visions, and business judgments of the owner(s), with perhaps modest contributions from a few key employees or outside advisers.

The Delegation Approach   Here the manager in charge delegates big chunks of the strategy-making task to trusted subordinates, down-the-line managers in charge of key business units and departments, a high-level task force of knowledgeable and talented people from many parts of the company, self-directed work teams with authority over a particular process or function, or, more rarely, a team of consultants brought in specifically to help develop new strategic initiatives. Delegating the brainstorming, analysis, and crafting of major strategy components and certainly most of the detailed pieces of an enterprise's strategy allows for broad participation from many managers and personnel with specialized expertise and on-the-scene knowledge of market and competitive conditions—a big advantage (if not a necessity) in multiproduct, multibusiness enterprises whose operations are far-flung or fast-moving. The more that a

> Broad participation in a company's strategy-creating exercises is usually a strong plus.

---

[8]The strategy-making, strategy-implementing roles of middle managers are thoroughly discussed and documented in Steven W. Floyd and Bill Wooldridge, *The Strategic Middle Manager* (San Francisco: Jossey-Bass, 1996), chapters 2 and 3.

[9]This classification scheme is based on David R. Brodwin and L. J. Bourgeois, "Five Steps to Strategic Action," in *Strategy and Organization: A West Coast Perspective,* ed. Glenn Carroll and David Vogel (Marshfield, MA: Pitman Publishing, 1984), pp. 168–78.

company's operations cut across different products, industries, and geographical areas, the more that headquarters executives are prone to delegate considerable strategy-making authority to personnel who have firsthand knowledge of customer requirements, can better evaluate market opportunities, and are better able to keep the strategy responsive to changing market and competitive conditions. The swifter the pace of market change, the more imperative it is to delegate strategy-making responsibility to down-the-line managers who can act quickly.

While strategy delegators have less of their own imprint on individual elements of strategy, they still typically play an influential role in shaping the major components of the strategy and in turning thumbs up or down on strategy particulars proposed by subordinates. The weakness of the delegation approach is that its success hinges on the business judgments and strategy-making skills of lower-echelon personnel. For instance, the strategizing efforts of subordinates may deal more with how to address today's problems than with positioning the enterprise and adapting its resources to capture tomorrow's opportunities. Subordinates may not have either the clout or the inclination to tackle changing major components of the present strategy.[10] A second weakness is that delegation sends the wrong signal: that strategy development isn't important enough to warrant a big claim on the boss's personal time and attention. Finally, it is a mistake for executives to be too detached from the strategy-making process in case the group's deliberations bog down in disagreement or go in ill-conceived directions.

The Collaborative or Team Approach
This is a middle approach whereby a manager with strategy-making responsibility enlists the assistance and advice of key peers and subordinates in hammering out a consensus strategy. Strategy teams often include line and staff managers from different disciplines and departmental units, a few handpicked junior staffers known for their ability to think creatively, and near-retirement veterans noted for being keen observers, telling it like it is, and giving sage advice.

Electronic Data Systems conducted a year-long strategy review involving 2,500 of its 55,000 employees and coordinated by a core of 150 managers and staffers from all over the world.[11] J. M. Smucker, a maker of jams and jellies, formed a team of 140 employees (7 percent of its 2,000-person workforce) who spent 25 percent of their time over a six-month period looking for ways to rejuvenate the company's growth; the team, which solicited input from all employees, came up with 12 initiatives to double the company's revenues over the next five years. Nokia Group, a Finland-based global leader in wireless telecommunications, involved 250 employees in a strategy review of how different communications technologies were converging, how this would affect the company's business, and what strategic responses were needed. It is increasingly common for strategy teams to involve customers and suppliers in assessing the future market situation and deliberating the various strategy options.

Collaborative efforts are usually led by the manager in charge, but the result is the joint product of all concerned. Such an approach is well suited to situations where strategic issues cut across departments, product lines, and businesses and there's a need to tap the strategic thinking of people with different expertise, experiences, and perspectives. Collaborative strategy making helps win participants' wholehearted commitment to implementation of the strategy that emerges. Involving teams of people to dissect complex situations and find market-driven, customer-driven solutions is becoming increasingly necessary in many businesses. Not only are many strategic issues too far-reaching or too

Collaborative strategy making helps win participants' wholehearted commitment to implementation.

---

[10]For a case in point of where the needed strategy changes were too big for a chartered group of subordinates to address, see Thomas M. Hout and John C. Carter, "Getting It Done: New Roles for Senior Executives," *Harvard Business Review* 73, no. 6 (November–December 1995), pp. 140–44.

[11]"Strategic Planning," *Business Week,* August 26, 1996, pp. 51–52.

involved for a single manager to handle but they often are cross-functional and cross-departmental, thus requiring the contributions of many disciplinary experts and the collaboration of managers from different parts of the organization. Giving people an influential stake in crafting the strategy they must later help implement not only builds motivation and commitment but it also means they can be held accountable for putting the strategy into place and making it work—the excuse "It wasn't my idea to do this" won't fly.

The Corporate Intrapreneur Approach   In the corporate intrapreneur approach, top management encourages individuals and teams to develop and champion proposals for new product lines and new business ventures. The idea is to unleash the talents and energies of promising corporate intrapreneurs, letting them try out business ideas and pursue new strategic initiatives. Executives serve as judges of which proposals merit support, give company intrapreneurs the needed organizational and budgetary support, and let them run with the ball. Thus, important pieces of company strategy originate with those intrapreneuring individuals and teams who succeed in championing a proposal through the approval stage and then end up being charged with the lead role in launching new products, overseeing the company's entry into new geographic markets, or heading up new business ventures.

> Corporate intrapreneuring relies upon middle and lower-level managers and teams to spot new business opportunities, develop strategic plans to pursue them, and create new businesses.

Utilizing the corporate intrapreneur approach successfully requires having an organization populated with ambitious, entrepreneurial people who want the chance to take on strategic and managerial responsibility for a new product or business. With this approach, the total strategy of a company is the collective sum of all the championed initiatives. This approach works well in enterprises where technological advances are coming at a fast and furious pace and/or compelling new opportunities are opening up in a variety of areas.

W. L. Gore & Associates, a privately owned company famous for its Gore-Tex waterproofing film, is an avid and highly successful practitioner of the corporate intrapreneur approach to strategy making. Gore expects all employees to initiate improvements and to display innovativeness. Each employee's intrapreneuring contributions are prime considerations in determining raises, stock option bonuses, and promotions. W. L. Gore's commitment to intrapreneuring has produced a stream of product innovations that has kept the company vibrant and growing for well over a decade. Illustration Capsule 5 describes an example of the corporate intrapreneur approach at Sony.

Comparing the Approaches   These four basic managerial approaches to forming a strategy illuminate several aspects of how strategies come into being. Highly centralized strategy making works fine when the strategy commander-in-chief has a powerful, insightful vision of where to head and how to get there. The primary weakness of the chief architect approach is that the caliber of the strategy depends so heavily on one person's entrepreneurial acumen and strategic judgments. It also breaks down in enterprises with diverse businesses and product lines where there are so many particulars to the strategy that one person cannot orchestrate the strategy-making process.

On the other hand, delegating strategic decisions to others and collaborating to build a consensus strategy have their risks too. The big weakness of delegating much of strategy making to down-the-line-managers is the potential lack of sufficient top-down direction and strategic leadership on the part of senior executives. Down-the-line managers don't always have the breadth of vision or experience to make strategic decisions that later could prove to have far-reaching impact on the enterprise. Furthermore, there may be occasions when lower-level managers elect to play it safe with conservative, middle-of-the-road strategies rather than bold, creative strategies. Delegation also runs the risk that the outcome will be shaped by influential subordinates, by powerful

> Each of the four basic strategy-making approaches has strengths and weaknesses, and each is workable in the "right" situation.

illustration capsule 5
Corporate Intrapreneuring Is No Game at Sony

In today's business environment, technological advances pepper companies so fast that many times managers can barely grasp what's current before it becomes obsolete. That's when intrapreneurship can boost a firm's capacity to innovate and prosper.

At Sony Corporation, intrapreneurship might not have taken hold at all if it weren't for one persistent engineer, Ken Kutaragi. Kutaragi, born in Tokyo and educated at the University of Electro-Communications, joined Sony shortly after graduating in 1975. Fourteen years later, he drafted plans for a new type of computer game that became the PlayStation. At first, he couldn't get top managers interested in the idea of games as serious business. So Kutaragi threatened to quit, and executives eventually allowed him to form a team to fully develop the new idea. This intrapreneurial effort has paid off many times over for Sony.

Today, Kutaragi heads the Sony Computer Entertainment division—the only division at Sony whose products combine both software and hardware. The games division is now a multibillion-dollar enterprise. Less than a decade after its launch, PlayStation (and now PlayStation 2) generates 11 percent of Sony's revenue and 40 percent of the company's profits. About 75 million PlayStation systems have been sold worldwide so far, and the game claims about 47 percent of the market share.

Still, Kutaragi isn't satisfied, and he keeps pushing toward his vision to revolutionize home entertainment. Although PlayStation 2 can play digital video disks (DVDs), Kutaragi is adding broadband Internet connectivity designed to link consumers to a whole new world of interactive entertainment as part of a strategic plan to best competitors Microsoft and Nintendo.

Although Sony supports Kutaragi's intrapreneuerial efforts, he continues to push his new ideas. "We're just going to be forced to educate Sony Corporation a bit," he says. Meanwhile, PlayStation 3 is in its planning stages. Kutaragi remains quiet about the next generation of video gaming, except to hint that it will integrate games, music, and videos over broadband networks—and it will be on store shelves by the year 2005.

Sources: Todd Spangler, "Ken Kutaragi," *Interactive Week* (www.zdnet.com), February 5, 2001; Robert La Franco, "In an Intrapreneur's Shadow," *Red Herring* (www.redherring.com), September 1, 2000; Dean Takahashi, "Reinventing the Intrapreneur," *Red Herring* (www.redherring.com), September 1, 2000.

functional departments, or by majority coalitions that have a common interest in promoting their particular version of what the strategy ought to be. The collaborative approach is conducive to political strategic choices as well, since powerful departments and individuals have ample opportunity to try to build a consensus for their favored strategic approach. Politics and the exercise of power are most likely to come into play in situations where there is no consensus on what strategy to adopt. Collaborative strategy making can also suffer from slower reaction and response times, as group members meet to debate the merits of what to do.

The strength of the corporate intrapreneur approach is also its weakness. The value of corporate intrapreneuring is that it encourages people at lower organizational levels to be alert for profitable market opportunities, to propose innovative strategies to capture them, and to take on responsibility for new business ventures. Individuals with attractive strategic proposals are given the latitude and resources to try them out, thus helping renew an organization's capacity for innovation and growth. However, because they spring from many places in the organization and can fly off in many directions, the various championed actions are not likely to form a coherent pattern or result in a clear strategic direction for the company as a whole without some strong top-down leadership. With intrapreneuring, top-level executives have to work at nurturing proposals that add power to the overall organization strategy; otherwise, strategic initiatives may be launched in directions that have little or no integrating links or fits with the overall business. Another weakness of the corporate intrapreneuring approach is that top executives may be more prone to protect their reputations for prudence and risk avoidance than to support revolutionary strategies, in which case innovative ideas can be doused by corporate orthodoxy.[12] It is not easy for a low-ranking employee to champion an out-of-the-ordinary proposal up the chain of command.

Thus, all four approaches to developing a strategy have strengths and weaknesses. All four can succeed or fail depending on the company's size and business makeup, on how well the approach is managed, and on the business judgments of the individuals involved.

The Role of the Board of Directors in Crafting and Executing Strategy

Since lead responsibility for crafting and executing strategy falls to key managers, the chief strategic role of an organization's board of directors is to exercise oversight and see that the five tasks of strategic management are done in a manner that benefits shareholders (in the case of investor-owned enterprises) or stakeholders (in the case of not-for-profit organizations). The specter of stockholder lawsuits and the escalating costs of liability insurance for directors underscore the responsibility that corporate board members have for overseeing a company's strategic actions. Moreover, holders of large blocks of shares (mutual funds and pension funds), regulatory authorities, and the financial press consistently urge that board members, especially outside directors, be active in their oversight of company strategy and the actions and capabilities of executives.

It is standard procedure for executives to brief board members on important strategic moves and to submit the company's strategic plans to the board for official approval. But directors rarely can or should play a direct, hands-on role in formulating or implementing strategy. Most outside directors lack industry-specific experience; their company-specific knowledge is limited (especially if they are relatively new board members). Boards of directors typically meet once a month (or less) for six to eight hours. Board members can scarcely be expected to have detailed command of all the strategic issues or know the ins and outs of the various strategic options. It is unreasonable to expect them to come up with compelling strategy proposals of their own to debate against those put forward by management. Such a hands-on role is unnecessary for good oversight. The immediate task of directors is to be *supportive critics,* exercising their own independent judgment about whether proposals have been adequately analyzed and whether proposed strategic actions appear to have greater promise than available alternatives.[13] If executive management is bringing well-supported strategy proposals to the board, there's little reason for board members to aggressively challenge everything put before them. Asking perceptive and incisive questions is usually sufficient to test whether the case for the proposals is compelling and to exercise vigilant oversight. However, if the company is experiencing gradual erosion of profits and market share, and certainly when there is a precipitous collapse in profitability, board members have a duty to be proactive, expressing their concerns about the validity of the strategy, initiating debate about the company's strategic path, having one-on-one discussions with key executives and other board members, and perhaps directly intervening as a group to alter both the strategy and the company's executive leadership.

Strategic Management Principle
The central role of the board of directors in the strategic management process is (1) to critically appraise and ultimately approve strategic action plans and (2) to evaluate the strategic leadership skills of the CEO and others in line to succeed the incumbent CEO.

---

[12]See Gary Hamel, "Strategy as Revolution," *Harvard Business Review* 74, no. 4 (July–August 1996), pp. 80–81.

[13]For a good discussion of the role of the board of directors in overseeing the strategy-making, strategy-executing process, see Gordon Donaldson, "A New Tool for Boards: The Strategic Audit," *Harvard Business Review* 77, no. 4 (July–August 1995), pp. 99–107.

The real hands-on role of directors is to evaluate the caliber of senior executives' strategy-making and strategy-implementing skills. The board is always responsible for determining whether the current CEO is doing a good job of strategic management (as a basis for awarding salary increases and bonuses and deciding on retention or removal).[14] Recently, at AT&T, Pacific Corp., Kmart, RiteAid, and Compaq Computer, company directors concluded that top executives were not adapting their company's strategy fast enough and fully enough to the changes sweeping their markets. They pressured the CEOs to resign and installed new leadership to provide the impetus for strategic renewal. Boards must also exercise due diligence in evaluating the strategic leadership skills of other senior executives in line to succeed the CEO. When the incumbent CEO retires, the board must elect a successor, either going with an insider (frequently nominated by the retiring CEO) or deciding that an outsider is needed to perhaps radically change the company's strategic course. Board oversight and vigilance is therefore very much in play in the strategy arena.

THE BENEFITS OF A STRATEGIC APPROACH TO MANAGING

The message of this book is that doing a good job of managing inherently requires good strategic thinking. Today's managers have to think strategically about their company's position and about the impact of changing conditions. They have to monitor the company's external environment and internal capabilities closely enough to know when to institute strategy changes. They have to know the business well enough to determine what kinds of strategic changes to initiate. Simply said, the fundamentals of strategic management need to drive the whole approach to managing organizations. The chief executive officer of one successful company put it well when he said:

> In the main, our competitors are acquainted with the same fundamental concepts and techniques and approaches that we follow, and they are as free to pursue them as we are. More often than not, the difference between their level of success and ours lies in the relative thoroughness and self-discipline with which we and they develop and execute our strategies for the future.

The advantages of first-rate strategic thinking and conscious strategy management (as opposed to freewheeling improvisation, gut feel, and hoping for good luck) include (1) providing better guidance to the entire organization on the crucial point of "what it is we are trying to do," (2) making managers and organizational members more alert to new opportunities and threatening developments, (3) helping to unify the organization, (4) creating a more proactive management posture, (5) promoting the development of a constantly evolving business model that will produce sustained bottom-line success for the enterprise, and (6) providing managers with a rationale for evaluating competing budget requests—a rationale that argues strongly for steering resources into strategy-supportive, results-producing areas.

Trailblazing strategies can be the key to better long-term performance. Business history shows that high-performing enterprises often initiate and lead, not just react and defend. They launch strategic offensives to out-innovate and out-maneuver rivals

---

[14]For an excellent discussion of the board of directors' role in CEO evaluation and succession, see Jay W. Lorsch and Rakesh Khurana, "Changing Leaders: The Board's Role in CEO Succession," *Harvard Business Review* 77, no. 3 (May–June 1999), pp. 96–105.

and secure sustainable competitive advantage, then use their market edge to achieve superior financial performance. Aggressive pursuit of a creative, opportunistic strategy can propel a firm into a leadership position, paving the way for its products and services to become the industry standard. High-achieving enterprises are nearly always the product of astute, proactive management, rather than the result of lucky breaks or a long run of good fortune.

In the chapters to come, we will probe the strategy-related tasks of managers and the methods of strategic analysis much more intensively. When you get to the end of the book, we think you will see that *two factors separate the best-managed organizations from the rest: (1) superior strategy making and entrepreneurship, and (2) competent implementation and execution of the chosen strategy.* There's no escaping the fact that the quality of managerial strategy making and strategy implementing has a significant impact on organization performance. A company that lacks clear-cut direction, has vague or undemanding objectives, has a muddled or flawed strategy, or can't seem to execute its strategy competently is a company whose performance is probably suffering, whose business is at long-term risk, and whose management is lacking. In short, the better conceived a company's strategy and the more proficient its execution, the greater the chances the company will be a leading performer in its markets and truly deserve a reputation for talented management.

suggested | readings

Abell, Derek F. "Competing Today While Preparing for Tomorrow." *Sloan Management Review* 40, no. 3 (Spring 1999), pp. 73–81.

Burgelman, Robert A. *Strategy Is Destiny.* New York: The Free Press, 2000.

Collins, James C., and Jerry I. Porras. "Building Your Company's Vision." *Harvard Business Review* 74, no. 5 (September–October 1996), pp. 65–77.

Farkas, Charles M., and Suzy Wetlaufer. "The Ways Chief Executive Officers Lead." *Harvard Business Review* 74, no. 3 (May–June 1996), pp. 110–122.

Hamel, Gary. "Strategy as Revolution." *Harvard Business Review* 74, no. 4 (July–August 1996), pp. 69–82.

Lipton, Mark. "Demystifying the Development of an Organizational Vision." *Sloan Management Review,* Summer 1996, pp. 83–92.

Markides, Constantinos C. "A Dynamic View of Strategy." *Sloan Management Review* 40, no. 3 (Spring 1999), pp. 55–63.

Mintzberg, Henry. "Crafting Strategy." *Harvard Business Review* 65, no. 4 (July–August 1987), pp. 66–75.

Mintzberg, Henry. Bruce Ahlstrand; and Joseph Lampel. *Strategy Safari: A Guided Tour through the Wilds of Strategic Management.* New York: Free Press, 1998.

Moncrieff, James. "Is Strategy Making a Difference?" *Long Range Planning* 32, no. 2 (April 1999), pp. 273–76.

Porter, Michael E. "What Is Strategy?" *Harvard Business Review* 74, no. 6 (November–December 1996), pp. 61–78.

Shaw, Gordon; Robert Brown; and Philip Bromiley. "Strategic Stories: How 3M Is Rewriting Business Planning." *Harvard Business Review* 76, no. 3 (May–June 1998), pp. 41–50.

chapter  two

Establishing Company Direction

Developing a Strategic Vision, Setting Objectives, and Crafting a Strategy

The last thing IBM needs right now is a vision. (July 1993)
What IBM needs most right now is a vision. (March 1996)
—Louis V. Gerstner Jr., CEO, IBM Corporation

How can you lead if you don't know where you are going?
—George Newman, The Conference Board

Management's job is not to see the company as it is . . . but as it can become.
—John W. Teets, CEO, Greyhound Corporation

A strategy is a commitment to undertake one set of actions rather than another.
—Sharon M. Oster, Professor, Yale University

In this chapter, we present a more in-depth look at the first three of the five strategic management tasks discussed in Chapter 1: developing a strategic vision and business mission, setting performance objectives, and crafting a strategy to produce the desired results. We will also examine which kinds of strategic decisions are made at which levels of management and the major factors that shape a company's strategy. The final two sections of the chapter discuss links between strategy making and ethics, and present some tests for determining whether a proposed strategy is a winner.

DEVELOPING A STRATEGIC VISION: THE FIRST DIRECTION-SETTING TASK

A clear and entrepreneurially astute strategic vision is a prerequisite to effective strategic leadership. Managers cannot function effectively as either leaders or strategy-makers without a future-oriented concept of the business—what customer needs to work toward satisfying, what business activities to pursue, what kind of long-term market position to build vis-à-vis competitors, what kind of company to try to create. Charting a company's course begins with senior management looking at the road ahead and addressing the following questions: "Where do we go from here?" "What changes lie ahead in the business landscape?" and "What difference will these changes make to the company's present business?"

Forming a strategic vision is thus not merely a wordsmithing exercise designed to create a catchy company slogan; rather it is an exercise in thinking carefully about where a company needs to head to be successful. It involves selecting the market arenas in which to participate, putting the company on a strategic path, and making a commitment to follow that path.

See Illustration Capsule 6 for an example of a strategic vision describing what course a company intends to follow.

The Three Elements of a Strategic Vision

Managers have three discernible tasks in forming a strategic vision and making it a useful direction-setting tool:

- Coming up with a *mission statement* that defines what business the company is *presently* in and conveys the essence of "who we are, what we do, and where we are now."

- Using the mission statement as a basis for deciding on a *long-term* course, making choices about "where we are going," and charting a strategic path for the company to pursue.

- Communicating the strategic vision in clear, exciting terms that arouse organization-wide commitment.

The Mission Statement: A Starting Point for Forming a Strategic Vision

Coming up with a mission statement is not as simple as it might seem. Is America Online in the Internet connection business, the online content business, the information business, or the entertainment business? Is Coca-Cola in the soft-drink business (in which case management's strategic attention can be concentrated on outselling and outcompeting Pepsi, 7UP, Dr Pepper, Canada Dry, and Schweppes), or is it in the beverage business (in which case management also needs to think strategically about positioning Coca-Cola products to compete against fruit juices, ready-to-drink teas, bottled water, sports drinks, milk, and coffee)? Whether to take a soft-drink perspective or a beverage perspective is not a trivial question for Coca-Cola management—only partly because Coca-Cola is also the parent of Minute Maid and Hi-C, which make juice products. With a beverage industry vision as opposed to a soft-drink focus, Coca-Cola management can better zero in on, say, how to convince young adults to get their morning caffeine fix by drinking Coca-Cola instead of coffee.

illustration capsule 6
Deere & Company's Strategic Vision

With revenues of more than $14 billion, John Deere has been a truly international company for decades. Use of the company's agricultural equipment in many parts of the world has given the company a respected global brand name. The company has set forth in clear terms who it is, where it is going, and how it plans to get there. The following paragraphs, from Deere's website, spell out the company's strategic vision.

WHO ARE WE?

John Deere has grown and prospered through a long-standing partnership with the world's most productive farmers. Today, John Deere is a global company with several equipment operations and complementary service businesses. These businesses are closely interrelated, providing the company with significant growth opportunities and other synergistic benefits.

WHERE ARE WE GOING?

Deere is committed to providing genuine value to the company's stakeholders, including our customers, dealers, shareholders, employees, and communities. In support of that commitment, Deere aspires to:

- Grow and pursue leadership positions in each of our businesses.
- Extend our preeminent leadership position in the agricultural equipment market worldwide.
- Create new opportunities to leverage the John Deere brand globally.

HOW WILL WE GET THERE?

By pursuing the broader corporate goals of profitable growth and continuous improvement, each of the company's businesses is expected to:

- Achieve world-class performance by attaining a strong competitive position in target markets.
- Exceed customer expectations for quality and value.
- Earn in excess of the cost of capital over a business cycle.

By growing profitably and continuously improving, each of the company's businesses will benefit from and contribute to John Deere's unique intangible assets:

- Our distinguished brand.
- Our heritage of integrity and teamwork.
- Our advanced skills.
- The special relationships that have long existed between the company and our employees, customers, dealers, and other business partners around the world.

HOW WILL WE MEASURE OUR PERFORMANCE?

Each business will make a positive contribution to the corporation's objectives in the pursuit of creating genuine value for our stakeholders. Our "scorecard" includes:

- Human Resources—Employee Satisfaction, Training
- Customer Focus—Loyalty, Market Leadership
- Business Processes—Productivity, Quality, Cost, Environment
- Business Results—Return on Assets, Sales Growth

Source: Deere & Company website (www.deere.com).

The Mission Is Not to Make a Profit Sometimes companies couch their business mission in terms of making a profit. This is misguided—profit is more correctly an *objective* and a *result* of what the company does. The desire to make a profit says nothing about the business arena in which profits are to be sought. Missions based on making a profit do not allow us to distinguish one type of profit-seeking enterprise from another—the business of Amazon.com is plainly different from the business of Toyota, even though both endeavor to earn a profit. A company that says its mission is to make a profit begs the question "What will we do to make a profit?" To understand a company's business purpose, we must know management's real answer to that question.

One of the roles of a mission statement is to give the organization its own special identity, business emphasis, and path for development—one that typically sets it apart from other similarly situated companies.

Incorporating What, Who, and How into the Mission Statement

A strategically revealing mission statement incorporates three elements:[1]

1. Customer needs, or *what* is being satisfied.
2. Customer groups, or *who* is being satisfied.
3. The company's activities, technologies, and competencies, or *how* the enterprise goes about creating and delivering value to customers and satisfying their needs.

> A company's business is defined by what needs it is trying to satisfy, by which customer groups it is targeting, and by the technologies and competencies it uses and the activities it performs.

Defining a business in terms of what to satisfy, whom to satisfy, and how to produce the satisfaction identifies the substance of what a company does to create value for its customers. Defining a business solely in terms of the products or services it provides is incomplete. A product or service becomes a business only when it satisfies a need or want; without demand for the product there is no business. Customer groups are relevant because they pinpoint the market to be served—the geographic domain to be covered and the types of buyers the firm hopes to attract.

> Technology, competencies, and activities are important to defining a company's business because they indicate the boundaries on its operations.

Technology, competencies, and activities are important because they indicate how much of the industry's total production-distribution chain its operations will span. For instance, the business of a *fully integrated firm* extends across the entire range of industry activities that must be performed to get a product or service into the hands of end users. The business of major international oil companies like Exxon, Mobil, BP Amoco, and Royal Dutch/Shell covers all stages of the oil industry's production-distribution chain—these companies lease drilling sites, drill wells, pump oil, transport crude oil in their own ships and pipelines to their own refineries, and sell gasoline and other refined products through their own networks of branded distributors and service station outlets. A *partially integrated firm* participates in some but not all of the industry's stages—raw materials supply, components production, manufacturing and assembly, distribution, or retailing. General Motors is a partially integrated company that makes between 30 and 50 percent of the parts and components used in assembling GM vehicles; the remainder of the needed parts and systems components come from independent suppliers, and GM relies on a network of independent, franchised dealers to handle retail sales and customer service functions. A *specialized firm* concentrates on just one stage of an industry's total production-distribution chain. Wal-Mart, The Home Depot, Toys"R"Us, Lands' End, and The Limited are essentially one-stage firms that focus on the retail end of the production-distribution chain; they don't manufacture the items they sell. Southwest Airlines is a one-stage enterprise that limits its business activities to moving travelers from one location to another via commercial jet aircraft. It doesn't manufacture the airplanes it flies or operate the airports where those planes land.

An example of a company that does a pretty good job of covering the three bases of what, who, and how in its business definition is Cardinal Health, a Fortune 100 company based in Dublin, Ohio:

> Cardinal Health is a leading provider of services supporting health care worldwide. The company offers a broad array of services for health-care providers and manufacturers to help them improve the efficiency and quality of health care. These services include phar-

---

[1]Derek F. Abell, *Defining the Business: The Starting Point of Strategic Planning* (Englewood Cliffs, NJ: Prentice Hall, 1980), p. 169.

maceutical distribution, health-care product manufacturing and distribution, drug delivery systems development, pharmaceutical packaging and repackaging, automated dispensing systems manufacturing, hospital pharmacy management, retail pharmacy franchising, and health-care information systems development.

JDS Uniphase, a Canada-based high-tech telecommunications components company, also has an explicit and comprehensive business definition:

> JDS Uniphase is the leading provider of advanced fiber optic components and modules. These products are sold to the world's leading telecommunications and cable television system providers, which are commonly referred to as OEMs and include Alcatel, Ciena, General Instruments, Lucent, Nortel, Pirelli, Scientific Atlanta, Siemens, and Tyco. Our products perform both optical-only (commonly referred to as "passive") functions and optoelectronic (commonly referred to as "active") functions within fiber optic networks. Our products include semiconductor lasers, high-speed external modulators, transmitters, amplifiers, couplers, multiplexers, circulators, tunable filters, optical switches, and isolators for fiber optic applications. We also supply our OEM customers with test instruments for both system production applications and network installation. In addition, we design, manufacture, and market laser subsystems for a broad range of OEM applications, which include biotechnology, industrial process control and measurement, graphics and printing, and semiconductor equipment.

Russell Corporation, the largest U.S. manufacturer of athletic apparel and uniforms, is another company with a business definition that covers all the bases:

> Russell Corporation is a vertically integrated international designer, manufacturer, and marketer of athletic uniforms, activewear, better knit shirts, leisure apparel, licensed sports apparel, sports and casual socks, and a comprehensive line of lightweight, yarn-dyed woven fabrics. The Company's manufacturing operations include the entire process of converting raw fibers into finished apparel and fabrics. Products are marketed to sporting goods dealers, department and specialty stores, mass merchandisers, golf pro shops, college bookstores, screen printers, distributors, mail-order houses, and other apparel manufacturers.

A Broad or Narrow Business Definition and Mission?

Merck, one of the world's foremost pharmaceutical companies, states that its business mission is "to provide society with superior products and services—innovations and solutions that satisfy customer needs and improve the quality of life." There's nothing specific in this statement that would allow anyone to actually identify Merck's true business; the broad, all-inclusive language Merck uses could just as easily apply to an enterprise engaged in developing innovative computer software, producing and marketing uniquely satisfying snack foods, manufacturing very appealing sports utility vehicles, or providing tax preparation services.

It is perfectly normal for companies in the same industry to have different missions and business definitions. For example, the current mission of a globally active New York bank like Citicorp (a Citigroup subsidiary) has little in common with that of a locally owned hometown bank, even though both are in the banking industry. To truly convey "who we are, what we do, and where we are now," a mission statement must be specific enough to pin down a company's real business arena. Broad-narrow definitions are relative to a company's business focus and intent, however. Consider the following business definitions:

> Good mission statements are highly personalized—unique to the organization for which they are developed.

Broad Definition	Narrow Definition
• Furniture business	• Wrought-iron lawn furniture business
• Telecommunications business	• Long-distance telephone service business
• Beverage business	• Soft-drink business
• Global mail delivery business	• Overnight package delivery business
• Travel and tourism business	• Caribbean cruise ship business

"We're in the furniture business" is probably too broad a definition for a company focused on being the largest manufacturer of wrought-iron lawn furniture in North America. In contrast, "We're a provider of long-distance telephone service" has proved too narrow a definition for AT&T, which, with its desire to capitalize on the convergence of computers and communications, has ventured into cable TV (acquiring TCI and MediaOne) and is launching efforts to become the telecommunications company of the future by bundling long-distance service, local telephone service, cable TV, and Internet access into package offerings to residential and business customers. The U.S. Postal Service successfully operates with a broad definition, providing global mail-delivery services to all types of senders. Federal Express, however, operates with a narrow business definition based on handling overnight package delivery for customers who have emergencies or tight deadlines. The risks of making an overly broad mission statement are lack of business focus and dilution of effort. *Few businesses fail because they are focused on a sharply targeted market opportunity, but many fail or do badly because management's attention is divided and resources are scattered across too many areas.*

Diversified firms, understandably, employ more sweeping business definitions than single-business enterprises. For example, the McGraw-Hill Companies describes itself broadly as a global publishing, financial, information, and media services company (which covers a lot of ground) but then goes on to pin down its business arenas in fairly explicit terms:

> The McGraw-Hill Companies is a global publishing, financial, information and media services company with such renowned brands as Standard & Poor's, Business Week, and McGraw-Hill educational and professional materials. The Company provides information via various media platforms: through books, magazines and newsletters; online over the Internet and electronic networks; via television, satellite and FM sideband broadcast; and through software, videotape, facsimile and CD-ROM products. The McGraw-Hill Companies now creates more than 90 percent of its information on digital platforms and its business units are represented on more than 75 websites.

Federal Express (known formally as FDX Corporation)—also diversified—does a more precise job of laying out its targets of what, who, and how:

> FDX is composed of a powerful family of companies: FedEx®, RPS®, Viking Freight, FDX Global Logistics, and Roberts Express®. These companies offer logistics and distribution solutions on a regional, national and global scale: fast, reliable, time-definite express delivery; expedited surface and air charter delivery of time-critical freight shipments; business-to-business ground small-package delivery; expedited same-day delivery; less-than-truckload (LTL) freight service in the Western U.S.; and integrated information and logistics solutions.
>
> With all of this expertise under one umbrella, the FDX companies can provide businesses with the competitive advantage they need by providing streamlined solutions that are on the cutting edge of technology.

Diversified companies have broader missions and business definitions than single-business enterprises.

illustration capsule 7
Four Sample Mission Statements: Examples to Critique

Incorporating what, who, and how into a brief, revealing sentence or paragraph is not something many companies have done very well. A perusal of company websites, annual reports, and 10-K filings quickly reveals a surprising number of business definitions/mission statements that are deficient. Critique how well each of the following four mission statements cut to the chase in describing what the enterprise is really about and the strategic position it is trying to stake out. Which one is most revealing? Least revealing?

PFIZER INC.

Pfizer is a research-based, global pharmaceutical company. We discover and develop innovative, value-added products that improve the quality of life of people around the world and help them enjoy longer, healthier, and more productive lives.

The company has three business segments: health care, animal health and consumer health care. Our products are available in more than 150 countries.

RITZ-CARLTON HOTELS

The Ritz-Carlton Hotel is a place where the genuine care and comfort of our guests is our highest mission.

We pledge to provide the finest personal service and facilities for our guests, who will always enjoy a warm, relaxed yet refined ambience.

The Ritz-Carlton experience enlivens the senses, instills well-being, and fulfills even the unexpressed wishes and needs of our guests

APPLE COMPUTER

Apple Computer, Inc., ignited the personal computer revolution in the 1970s with the Apple II, and reinvented the personal computer in the 1980s with the Macintosh. Apple is now committed to its original mission—to bring the best personal computing products and support to students, educators, designers, scientists, engineers, business persons and consumers in over 140 countries around the world.

THE GILLETTE COMPANY

The Gillette Company is a globally focused consumer products company that seeks competitive advantage in quality, value-added personal care and personal use products. We compete in four large, worldwide businesses: personal grooming products, consumer portable power products, stationery products and small electrical appliances.

As a Company, we share skills and resources among business units to optimize performance. We are committed to a plan of sustained sales and profit growth that recognizes and balances both short- and long-term objectives.

Mission

Our mission is to achieve or enhance clear leadership, worldwide, in the existing or new core consumer product categories in which we choose to compete.

Current core categories are:

- Male grooming products, including blades and razors, electric shavers, shaving preparations and deodorants and antiperspirants.

- Female grooming products, including wet shaving products, hair removal and hair care appliances and deodorants and antiperspirants.

- Alkaline and specialty batteries and cells.

(continued)

Critically evaluate the caliber of the four mission statements in Illustration Capsule 7.

Mission Statements for Functional Departments   There's also a place for mission statements for key functions and departments within a business—R&D, marketing, finance, human resources, customer service, information systems. Every department can help focus the efforts of its personnel by developing a mission statement that sets forth its principal role and activities, the direction it is headed, and its contribution to the overall company mission. Functional and departmental managers who think through and debate with subordinates and higher-ups what their unit needs to focus on and do have a clearer view of how to lead the unit. Three examples from

illustration capsule 7

(concluded)

- Writing instruments and correction products.
- Certain areas of the oral care market, including tooth-brushes, interdental products and oral care appliances.
- Selected areas of the high-quality small household appliance business, including coffeemakers and food preparation products.

To achieve this mission, we will also compete in supporting product areas that enhance the Company's ability to achieve or hold the leadership position in core categories.

Values

In pursuing our mission, we will live by the following values:

- **People.** We will attract, motivate, and retain high-performing people in all areas of our business. We are committed to competitive, performance-based compensation, benefits, training and personal growth based on equal career opportunity and merit. We expect integrity, civility, openness, support for others and commitment to the highest standards of achievement. We value innovation, employee involvement, change, organizational flexibility and personal mobility. We recognize,

value, and are committed to the benefits in the diversity of people, ideas, and cultures.

- **Customer Focus.** We will invest in and master the key technologies vital to category success. We will offer consumers products of the highest levels of performance for value. We will provide quality service to our customers, both internal and external, by treating them as partners, by listening, understanding their needs, responding fairly and living up to our commitments. We will be a valued customer to our suppliers, treating them fairly and with respect. We will provide these quality values consistent with improving our productivity.

- **Good Citizenship.** We will comply with applicable laws and regulations at all government levels wherever we do business. We will contribute to the communities in which we operate and address social issues responsibly. Our products will be safe to make and to use. We will conserve natural resources, and we will continue to invest in a better environment.

We believe that commitment to this mission and to these values will enable the Company to provide a superior return to our shareholders.

Sources: Company annual reports and websites.

actual companies indicate how a functional mission statement puts the spotlight on a unit's organizational *role* and *scope:*

- The mission of the human resources department is to contribute to organizational success by developing effective leaders, creating high-performance teams, and maximizing the potential of individuals.
- The mission of the corporate claims department is to minimize the overall cost of liability, workers compensation, and property damage claims through competitive cost containment techniques and loss prevention and control programs.
- The mission of corporate security is to provide services for the protection of corporate personnel and assets through preventive measures and investigations.

From Mission Statement to Strategic Vision

A mission statement highlighting the boundaries of the company's current business is a logical vantage point from which to look down the road, decide what the enterprise's business makeup and customer focus need to be, and chart a strategic path for the company to take. As a rule, strategic visions should have a time horizon of five years or more unless the industry is very new or market conditions are so volatile and uncertain that it is difficult to see that far down the road with any degree of confidence. However, choosing a company's path is a daunting task that requires reasoned answers to the following questions:

1. What changes are occurring in the market arenas where we operate, and what implications do these changes have for the direction in which we need to move?
2. What new or different customer needs should we be moving to satisfy?
3. What new or different buyer segments should we be concentrating on?
4. What new geographic or product markets should we be pursuing?
5. What should the company's business makeup look like in five years?
6. What kind of company should we be trying to become?

> The entrepreneurial challenge in developing a strategic vision is to think creatively about how to prepare a company for the future.

The Crucial Role of Entrepreneurship in Forming a Strategic Vision   There's no substitute for good entrepreneurship in addressing the above six questions and making choices about which forks in the road to take.[2] Charting a promising strategic course forces managers to think both creatively and realistically about changing market, competitive, technological, economic, regulatory, and societal conditions and about the company's resources and capabilities. Sometimes, the best clues about where to head come from alertness to users' problems and complaints and listening intently when a customer says, "If only . . ." Such information, if used creatively, points to valuable customer-market-technology opportunities. Moving early and quickly to pursue emerging opportunities can result in competitive advantage.[3] *A well-chosen strategic vision prepares a company for the future.*

> Forming a strategic vision is an exercise in astute entrepreneurship, not a time for pipedreams or fantasies about the company's future.

Recognizing Strategic Inflection Points   Sometimes there's an order of magnitude change in a company's environment that dramatically alters its prospects and mandates radical revision of its strategic course. Intel's chairman Andrew Grove calls such occasions *strategic inflection points*—Illustration Capsule 8 relates Intel's two encounters with strategic inflection points and the resulting alterations in its strategic vision. As the Intel example forcefully demonstrates, when a company reaches a strategic inflection point, management has some tough decisions to make about the company's course. Often, it is a question of what to do to sustain company success, not just how to avoid possible disaster. Responding to the winds of change in timely fashion lessens a company's chances of becoming trapped in a stagnant or declining business or letting attractive new growth opportunities slip away because of inaction.

> Many successful organizations need to change direction not in order to survive but in order to maintain their success.

---

[2]For a discussion of the challenges of developing a well-conceived vision, as well as some in-depth examples, see James C. Collins and Jerry I. Porras, "Building Your Company's Vision," *Harvard Business Review* 74, no. 5 (September–October 1996), pp. 65–77; Robert A. Burgelman and Andrew S. Grove, "Strategic Dissonance," *California Management Review* 38, no. 2 (Winter 1996), pp. 8–25; and Ron McTavish, "One More Time: What Business Are You In?" *Long Range Planning* 28, no. 2 (April 1995), pp. 49–60. For a discussion of some of the alternative ways a company can position itself in the marketplace, see Michael E. Porter, "What Is Strategy?" *Harvard Business Review* 74, no. 6 (November–December 1996), pp. 65–67. Porter argues that the three basic strategic positions are based on (*a*) the range of customer needs to be served, (*b*) the variety of products to be offered (anywhere along the spectrum of one to many), and (*c*) the means by which customers are accessed—the terms Porter uses are *needs-based positioning, variety-based positioning,* and *access-based positioning.* For an empirical study of executive success in formulating and implementing a company vision, and the difficulties encountered, see Laurie Larwood, Cecilia M. Falbe, Mark Kriger, and Paul Miesing, "Structure and Meaning of Organizational Vision," *Academy of Management Journal* 38, no. 3 (June 1995), pp. 740–69.

[3]For a discussion of the role of corporate entrepreneurship in helping build competitive advantage, see Jeffrey G. Colvin and Morgan P. Miles, "Corporate Entrepreneurship and the Pursuit of Competitive Advantage," *Entrepreneurship: Theory and Practice* 23, no. 3 (Spring 1999), pp. 47–63.

illustration capsule 8
Intel's Two Strategic Inflection Points

Intel Corporation has encountered two strategic inflection points within the past 15 years. The first came in the mid-1980s, when memory chips were Intel's principal business and Japanese manufacturers, intent on dominating the memory chip business, began cutting their prices 10 percent below the prices charged by Intel and other U.S. memory chip manufacturers. Each time U.S. companies matched the Japanese price cuts, the Japanese manufacturers responded with another 10 percent price cut. Intel's management explored a number of strategic options to cope with the aggressive pricing of its Japanese rivals—building a giant memory chip factory to overcome the cost advantage of Japanese producers, investing in R&D to come up with a more advanced memory chip, and retreating to niche markets for memory chips that were not of interest to the Japanese.

At the time, Gordon Moore, Intel's chairman and cofounder, and Andrew Grove, Intel's well-known CEO, jointly concluded that none of these options offered much promise and that the best long-term solution was to abandon the memory chip business even though it accounted for 70 percent of Intel's revenue. Grove, with the concurrence of both Moore and the board of directors, then proceeded to commit Intel's full energies to the business of developing ever more powerful microprocessors for personal computers. (Intel had invented microprocessors in the early 1970s but had recently been concentrating on memory chips because of strong competition and excess capacity in the market for microprocessors.)

Grove's bold decision to withdraw from memory chips, absorb a $173 million writeoff in 1986, and go all out in microprocessors produced a new strategic vision for Intel—becoming the preeminent supplier of microprocessors to the personal computing industry, making the PC the central appliance in the workplace and the home, and being the undisputed leader in driving PC technology forward. Grove's new vision for Intel and the strategic course he charted in 1985 produced spectacular results. Going into 2001, over 80 percent of the world's PCs had "Intel inside" and Intel was one of the 10 most profitable U.S. companies in 2000, earning after-tax profits of $7.3 billion on revenues of $29.4 billion.

The company encountered a second inflection point in 1998, opting to refocus on becoming the preeminent building-block supplier to the Internet economy and spurring efforts to make the Internet more useful. Starting in early 1998 and responding to the mushrooming importance of the Internet, Intel's senior management launched major new initiatives to direct attention and resources to expanding the capabilities of the PC platform and the Internet. Management saw Intel as having a major role in getting a billion computers connected to the Internet worldwide, installing millions of servers (containing ever more powerful Intel microprocessors), and building an Internet infrastructure that would support trillions of dollars of e-commerce and serve as a worldwide communications medium.

Communicating the Strategic Vision

Communicating the strategic vision down the line to lower-level managers and employees is almost as important as setting the organization's long-term direction. People need to believe that the company's management knows where it's trying to take the company and what changes lie ahead both externally and internally. Ideally, executives should present their vision for the company in language that reaches out and grabs people, that creates a vivid image in their heads, and that provokes emotion and excitement. Expressing the strategic vision in engaging language has enormous motivational value—"building a cathedral," for example, is more inspiring than "laying stones."

Strategic visions ought to convey a larger sense of purpose—so that employees see themselves as "building a cathedral" rather than "laying stones."

Most organization members will rise to the challenge of pursuing a worthy organizational purpose and trying to be the world's best at something competitively significant and beneficial to customers. Presenting the vision as an endeavor that will please customers and perhaps benefit society is far more motivating than stressing the payoff for shareholders—it goes without saying that the company intends to profit shareholders.[4] When management can paint an inspiring picture of the company's strategic vision it can arouse a committed organizational effort in which people live the business instead of just coming to work. The simple, clear mission statement of the International Red Cross is a good example: "to serve the most vulnerable." Bland language, platitudes, and dull motherhood-and-apple-pie-style verbiage must be scrupulously avoided—they can be a turn-off rather than a turn-on.

> A well-articulated strategic vision creates enthusiasm for the course management has charted and engages members of the organization.

Breaking Down Resistance to a New Strategic Vision   It is particularly important for executives to provide a compelling rationale for a new strategic vision. Failure to understand or accept the need for redirecting organizational efforts often produces resistance to change among employees and makes it harder to move the organization down a newly chosen path. Hence, inducing employee buy-in, lifting spirits, and calming fears are necessary steps in getting an organization ready to move along a new course. Just stating the case for a new direction once is not enough; the vision has to be repeated often and reinforced at every opportunity, until it gains organizationwide acceptance.

Putting the Vision Statement in Writing   Many companies put the strategic visions of senior executives into written vision statements, using them as vehicles to communicate with employees, shareholders, and other constituencies. Usually it is best to keep such vision statements simple and clear, using no more words than it takes to convey unmistakable meaning. A slogan that helps generate enthusiasm for the firm's future course and inspires dedicated effort can be a strong plus. A crisp, clear, often-repeated, inspiring strategic vision has the power to turn heads in the intended direction and create a unified organizational march.

> The best-worded vision statements clearly and crisply illuminate the direction in which an organization is headed.

The Real Payoffs of a Well-Conceived, Well-Worded Vision Statement   A well-conceived, well-stated strategic vision pays off in several respects: (1) it crystallizes senior executives' own views about the firm's long-term direction; (2) it reduces the risk of rudderless decision making; (3) it conveys organizational purpose in ways that motivate organization members to go all out; (4) it provides a beacon that lower-level managers can use to form departmental missions, set departmental objectives, and craft functional and departmental strategies that are in sync with the company's overall strategy; and (5) it helps an organization prepare for the future. When these five benefits have been realized, the first step in organizational direction setting has been successfully completed.

ESTABLISHING OBJECTIVES: THE SECOND DIRECTION-SETTING TASK

Setting objectives converts the strategic vision into specific performance targets. Objectives represent a managerial commitment to achieving specific outcomes and results. Unless an organization's long-term direction is translated into specific performance targets

---

[4]Unless most managers and employees have a significant ownership stake in the enterprise, they will scarcely be motivated and energized by a vision that emphasizes making shareholders richer. Why should they go all out to enhance the pocketbooks of the owners? So, except for companies with employee stock ownership plans that empower and reward employees as owners, there is far more motivational value in a mission/vision that stresses the payoff for customers and/or the general well-being of society, not the payoff for stockholders.

and managers are pressured to show progress in reaching these targets, vision and mission statements are likely to end up as nice words, window dressing, and unrealized dreams. The experiences of countless companies and managers teach that *companies whose managers set objectives for each key result area and then press forward with actions aimed directly at achieving these performance outcomes typically outperform companies whose managers exhibit good intentions, try hard, and hope for the best.*

For objectives to function as yardsticks of organizational performance and progress, they must be stated in *quantifiable,* or measurable, *terms* and they must contain a *deadline for achievement.* They have to spell out *how much* of *what kind* of performance *by when.* This means avoiding generalities like "maximize profits," "reduce costs," "become more efficient," or "increase sales," which specify neither how much or when. As Bill Hewlett, co-founder of Hewlett-Packard, once observed, "You cannot manage what you cannot measure . . . And what gets measured gets done."[5] Spelling out organization objectives in measurable terms and then holding managers accountable for reaching their assigned targets within a specified time frame (1) substitutes purposeful strategic decision making for aimless actions and confusion over what to accomplish and (2) provides a set of benchmarks for judging the organization's performance and progress.

> **Basic Concept**
> **Objectives** represent a managerial commitment to achieving specific performance targets within a specific time frame—they are a call for results that connect directly to the company's strategic vision and core values.

What Kinds of Objectives to Set

Objectives are needed for each key result managers deem important to success.[6] Two types of key result areas stand out: those relating to *financial performance* and those relating to *strategic performance.*[7] Achieving acceptable financial performance is a must; otherwise the organization's financial standing can alarm creditors and shareholders, impair its ability to fund needed initiatives, and perhaps even put its very survival at risk. Achieving acceptable strategic performance is essential to sustaining and improving the company's long-term market position and competitiveness. Representative kinds of financial and strategic performance objectives are listed below:

> **Strategic Management Principle**
> Every company needs both strategic objectives and financial objectives.

---

[5]As quoted in Charles H. House and Raymond L. Price, "The Return Map: Tracking Product Teams," *Harvard Business Review* 60, no. 1 (January–February 1991), p. 93.

[6]The literature of management is filled with references to *goals* and *objectives.* These terms are used in a variety of ways, many of them conflicting. Some writers use the term *goals* to refer to the long-run outcomes an organization seeks to achieve and the term *objectives* to refer to immediate, short-run performance targets. Some writers reverse the usage, referring to *objectives* as the desired long-run results and *goals* as the desired short-run results. Others use the terms interchangeably. And still others use the term *goals* to refer to broad organizationwide performance targets and the term *objectives* to designate specific targets set by operating divisions and functional departments to support achievement of overall company performance targets. In our view, little is gained from semantic distinctions between *goals* and *objectives.* The important thing is to recognize that the results an enterprise seeks to attain vary as to both organizational scope and time frame. Nearly always, organizations need to have companywide performance targets and division/department performance targets for both the near term and the long term. It is inconsequential which targets are called goals and which objectives. To avoid a semantic jungle, we use the single term *objectives* to refer to the performance targets and results an organization seeks to attain. We use the adjectives *long-range* (or *long-run*) and *short-range* (or *short-run*) to identify the relevant time frame, and we try to describe objectives in words that indicate their intended scope and level in the organization.

[7]For another view calling for four different types of performance measures, see Robert S. Kaplan, and David P. Norton, "The Balanced Scorecard—Measures That Drive Performance," *Harvard Business Review* 70, no. 1 (January–February 1992), pp. 71–79.

Financial Objectives	Strategic Objectives
• Growth in revenues	• A bigger market share
• Growth in earnings	• Quicker design-to-market times than rivals (an ability to get newly developed products to market quicker)
• Higher dividends	
• Bigger profit margins	
• Higher returns on invested capital	• Higher product quality than rivals
• Attractive economic value added (EVA) performance*	• Lower costs relative to key competitors
	• Broader or more attractive product line than rivals
• Strong bond and credit ratings	
• Bigger cash flows	• Better e-commerce and Internet sales capabilities than rivals
• A rising stock price	
• Attractive and sustainable increases in market value added (MVA)†	• Superior on-time delivery
	• A stronger brand name than rivals
• Recognition as a "blue-chip" company	• Superior customer service compared to rivals
• A more diversified revenue base	• Stronger global distribution and sales capabilities than rivals
• Stable earnings during periods of recession	
	• Recognition as a leader in technology and/or product innovation
	• Wider geographic coverage than rivals
	• Higher levels of customer satisfaction than rivals

*Economic value added (EVA) is profit over and above the company's weighted average after-tax cost of capital; specifically, it is defined as operating profit less income taxes less the weighted average cost of capital. Such companies as Coca-Cola, AT&T, Briggs & Stratton, and Eli Lilly use EVA as a measure of the profit performance. For more details on EVA, consult footnote 1 in Chapter 1.

†Market value added (MVA) is defined as the amount by which the total value of the company has appreciated above the dollar amount actually invested in the company by shareholders. MVA is equal to a company's current stock price times the number of shares outstanding less shareholders' equity investment; it represents the value that management has added to shareholders' wealth in running the business. If shareholder value is to be maximized, management must select a strategy and long-term direction that maximize the market value of the company's common stock. See footnote 2 in Chapter 1.

Illustration Capsule 9 presents the strategic and financial objectives for seven different companies.

Strategic Objectives versus Financial Objectives: Which Take Precedence?

Even though an enterprise places high priority on achieving both financial and strategic objectives, situations arise where a trade-off has to be made. Should a company under pressure to pay down its debt elect to kill or postpone investments in strategic moves that hold promise for strengthening the enterprise's future business and competitive position? Should a company under pressure to boost near-term profits cut back R&D programs that could help it achieve a competitive advantage over key rivals in the years ahead? The pressures on managers to opt for better near-term financial performance and to sacrifice or cut back on strategic initiatives aimed at building a stronger competitive position become especially pronounced when (1) an enterprise is struggling financially, (2) the resource commitments for strategically beneficial moves will materially detract from the bottom line for several years, and (3) the proposed strategic moves are risky and have an uncertain competitive or bottom-line payoff.

Yet there are dangers in management's succumbing time and again to the lure of immediate gains in profitability when it means forgoing strategic moves that would build a stronger business position. A company that consistently passes up opportunities to

> Strategic objectives need to be competitor-focused, often aiming at unseating a competitor considered to be the industry's best in a particular category.

illustration capsule 9

Corporate Objectives at Citigroup, General Electric, McDonald's, Anheuser-Busch, Exodus Communications, Motorola, and McCormick & Company

CITIGROUP
(*Strategic Objective*)

- To attain 1 billion customers worldwide.

GENERAL ELECTRIC
(*Strategic Objectives*)

- Become the most competitive enterprise in the world.
- Be number one or number two in each business we are in.
- Globalize every activity in the company.
- Embrace the Internet and become a global e-business.

MCDONALD'S
(*Strategic Objective*)

- To achieve 100 percent total customer satisfaction . . . every day . . . in every restaurant . . . for every customer.

ANHEUSER-BUSCH
(*Strategic and Financial Objectives*)

- To make all of our companies leaders in their industries in quality while exceeding customer expectations.
- To achieve a 50 percent share of the U.S. beer market.
- To establish and maintain a dominant leadership position in the international beer market.
- To provide all our employees with challenging and rewarding work, satisfying working conditions, and opportunities for personal development, advancement, and competitive compensation.
- To provide our shareholders with superior returns by achieving double-digit annual earnings per share growth, increasing dividends consistent with earnings growth, repurchasing shares when the opportunity is right, pursuing profitable international beer expansions, and generating quality earnings and cash flow returns.

EXODUS COMMUNICATIONS
(Exodus Communications is a leading provider of network management and Internet hosting solutions for companies with mission-critical Internet operations.)

(*Strategic Objectives*)

- Extend our market leadership and position Exodus as the leading brand name in the category.
- Enhance our systems and network management and Internet technology services.
- Accelerate our domestic and international growth.
- Leverage our technical expertise to address new market opportunities in e-commerce.

MOTOROLA
(*Financial Objectives*)

- Self-funding revenue growth of 15 percent annually.
- An average return on assets of 13 to 15 percent.
- An average return on shareholders' equity investment of 16 to 18 percent.
- A strong balance sheet.

McCORMICK & COMPANY
(*Financial Objectives*)

- To achieve a 20 percent return on equity.
- To achieve a net sales growth rate of 10 percent per year.
- To maintain an average earnings per share growth rate of 15 percent per year.
- To maintain total debt-to-total capital at 40 percent or less.
- To pay out 25 percent to 35 percent of net income in dividends.
- To make selective acquisitions which complement our current businesses and can enhance our overall returns.
- To dispose of those parts of our business which do not or cannot generate adequate returns or do not fit our business strategy.

Source: Company annual reports and websites.

strengthen its long-term competitive position in order to realize better near-term financial gains risks diluting its competitiveness, losing momentum in its markets, and impairing its ability to stave off market challenges from ambitious rivals. The danger of trading off long-term gains in market position for near-term gains in bottom-line performance is greatest when (1) there are lasting first-mover advantages in being a market pioneer (many Internet start-ups, for example, are incurring big short-term losses in their rush to stake out leadership positions in fast-emerging "industries of the future") and (2) a profit-conscious market leader has competitors who invest relentlessly in gaining market share, striving to become big and strong enough to outcompete the leader in a head-to-head market battle. The surest path to sustained future profitability quarter after quarter and year after year is to pursue strategic actions that strengthen a company's *competitiveness* and *business position*. Absent a strong position from which to compete, a company's profitability is at risk.

> **Strategic Management Principle**
> Building a stronger long-term competitive position benefits shareholders more lastingly than improving short-term profitability.

The Concept of Strategic Intent

A company's strategic objectives are important for another reason—they indicate **strategic intent** to stake out a particular business position.[8] Strategic intent can be thought of as a "big, hairy, audacious goal," or BHAG (pronounced *bee-hag*), that generally takes a long time to achieve (maybe even as long as 20 or 30 years).[9] The strategic intent of a large company may be industry leadership on a national or global scale. The strategic intent of a small company may be to dominate a market niche. The strategic intent of an up-and-coming enterprise may be to overtake the market leaders. The strategic intent of a technologically innovative company may be to pioneer a promising discovery and create a whole new array of products that change the way people work and live—as many entrepreneurial companies are now trying to do via the Internet.

> **Basic Concept**
> A company exhibits *strategic intent* when it relentlessly pursues an ambitious strategic objective and concentrates its competitive actions and energies on achieving that objective.

The time horizon underlying a company's strategic intent is *long term*. Ambitious companies almost invariably begin with strategic intents that are out of proportion to their immediate capabilities and market positions. But they set aggressive long-term strategic objectives and pursue them relentlessly, sometimes even obsessively. In the 1960s, Komatsu, Japan's leading earth-moving equipment company, was less than one-third the size of Caterpillar, had little market presence outside Japan, and depended on its small bulldozers for most of its revenue. But Komatsu's strategic intent was to eventually "encircle Caterpillar" with a broader product line and then compete globally against Caterpillar. By the late 1980s, Komatsu was the industry's second-ranking company, with a strong sales presence in North America, Europe, and Asia plus a product line that included industrial robots and semiconductors as well as a broad selection of earth-moving equipment.

The strategic intent of the U.S. government's Apollo space program was to land a person on the moon ahead of the Soviet Union. Throughout the 1980s, Wal-Mart's

---

[8]The concept of strategic intent is described in more detail in Gary Hamel and C. K. Pralahad, "Strategic Intent," *Harvard Business Review* 89, no. 3 (May–June 1989), pp. 63–76; this section draws on their pioneering discussion. See also, Michael A. Hitt, Beverly B. Tyler, Camilla Hardee, and Daewoo Park, "Understanding Strategic Intent in the Global Marketplace," *Academy of Management Executive* 9, no. 2 (May 1995), pp. 12–19. For a discussion of the different ways that companies can position themselves in the marketplace, see Michael E. Porter, "What Is Strategy?" pp. 65–67.

[9]For a discussion of BHAGs, see James C. Collins and Jerry Porras, *Built to Last: Successful Habits of Visionary Companies* (New York: HarperBusiness, 1994); James C. Collins and Jerry I. Porras, "Building Your Company's Vision," *Harvard Business Review* 74, no. 5 (September–October 1996), pp. 65–77; and Jim Collins. "Turning Goals into Results: The Power of Catalytic Mechanisms," *Harvard Business Review* 77, no. 4 (July–August 1999), p. 72.

strategic intent was to "overtake Sears" as the largest U.S. retailer (a feat accomplished in 1991). America Online's strategic intent is to build the strongest, most recognized brand name on the Internet. Internet start-up companies like E-loan, Doubleclick, eBay, etoys, Mortgage.com, and E*Trade are exhibiting strategic intent in rushing to build what they hope will prove to be dominant positions in their target e-commerce niches.

Strategic intent signals a deep-seated commitment to winning—becoming the recognized industry leader, unseating the existing industry leader, remaining the industry leader (and becoming more dominant in the process)—sometimes against long odds. Small, capably managed enterprises determined to achieve ambitious strategic objectives exceeding their present reach and resources often prove to be more formidable competitors than larger, cash-rich companies with modest strategic intents.

Sometimes a company's strategic intent takes on a heroic character, serving as a rallying cry for managers and employees alike to go all out and do their very best. Canon's strategic intent in copying equipment was to "beat Xerox." Nike's strategic intent during the 1960s was to overtake Adidas (which connected nicely with its core purpose "to experience the emotion of competition, winning, and crushing competitors"). Komatsu's motivating battle cry was "Beat Caterpillar." When Yamaha overtook Honda in the motorcycle market, Honda responded with *"Yamaha wo tsubusu"* ("We will crush, squash, slaughter Yamaha"). It is plain that America Online, Amazon.com, and Yahoo! are going all out to build globally dominant market positions in their parts of the mushrooming Internet economy.

The Need for Long-Range and Short-Range Objectives

Organizations need to establish both long-range and short-range objectives. A strong commitment to achieving long-range objectives forces managers to begin taking actions *now* to reach desired performance levels *later.* A company that has an objective of doubling its sales within five years can't wait until the third or fourth year of its five-year strategic plan to begin growing its sales and customer base. By spelling out the near-term results to be achieved, short-range objectives indicate the *speed* at which management wants the organization to progress as well as the *level of performance* being aimed for over the next two or three periods. Short-range objectives can be identical to long-range objectives if an organization is already performing at the targeted long-term level. For instance, if a company has an ongoing objective of 15 percent profit growth every year and is currently achieving this objective, then the company's long-range and short-range objectives for increasing profits coincide. The most important situation where short-range objectives differ from long-range objectives occurs when managers are trying to elevate organizational performance and cannot reach the long-range target in just one year. Short-range objectives then serve as stairsteps or milestones.

How Much Stretch Should Objectives Entail?

Company performance targets should require *organizational stretch*.

As a starter, objectives should be set high enough to produce outcomes at least incrementally better than current performance. But incremental improvements are not necessarily sufficient, especially if current performance levels are subpar. At a minimum, a company's financial objectives must aim high enough to generate the resources to execute the chosen strategy proficiently. But an "enough-to-get-by" mentality is not appropriate in objective setting. Objectives need to be set high enough to generate period-to-period results that will not only please shareholders and Wall Street but also compare favorably with competitors' performance. Ideally, objectives ought to serve as a managerial tool for truly stretching an organization to reach its full potential; this means setting them high enough to be *challenging*—to energize the organization and its strategy.

One school of thought holds that objectives should be set boldly and aggressively high—above levels that many organizational members would consider realistic. The idea here is that more organizational creativity and energy is unleashed when stretch objectives call for achieving performance levels well beyond the reach of the enterprise's immediate resources and capabilities. One of the most avid practitioners of setting stretch objectives and challenging the organization to go all out to achieve them is General Electric, arguably the world's best-managed corporation. Jack Welch, GE's CEO from 1980 to 2001, believed in setting stretch targets that seemed "impossible" and then challenging the organization to go after them. Throughout the 1960s, 1970s, and 1980s, GE's operating margins hovered around 10 percent and its sales-to-inventory ratio averaged about 5 turns per year. In 1991, Welch set stretch targets for 1995 of at least a 16 percent operating margin and 10 inventory turns. Welch's letter to the shareholders in the company's 1995 annual report said:

> 1995 has come and gone, and despite a heroic effort by our 220,000 employees, we fell short on both measures, achieving a 14.4% operating margin and almost seven turns. But in stretching for these "impossible" targets, we learned to do things faster than we would have going after "doable" goals, and we have enough confidence now to set new stretch targets of at least 16% operating margin and more than 10 turns by 1998.

GE's philosophy is that setting very aggressive stretch targets pushes the organization to move beyond being only as good as what is deemed doable to being as good as it possibly can be. GE's management believes challenging the company to achieve the impossible improves the quality of the organization's effort, promotes a can-do spirit, and builds self-confidence. Hence, a case can be made that objectives ought to be set at levels *above* what is doable with a little extra effort; there's merit in setting stretch targets that require something approaching a heroic degree of organizational effort.

Objectives Are Needed at All Organizational Levels

Objective setting does not stop when company performance targets are agreed on. Company objectives must be broken down into performance targets for each of the organization's separate businesses, product lines, functional areas, and departments. Company objectives are unlikely to be reached without each area of the organization doing its part to contribute to the desired companywide outcomes and results. This means setting strategic and financial objectives for each organization unit that support—rather than conflict with—the achievement of companywide strategic and financial objectives. Consistency between company objectives and the objectives of organizational subunits signals that each part of the organization knows its strategic role and is on board in helping the company move down the chosen strategic path and produce the desired results.

The Need for Top-Down Objective Setting. To appreciate why a company's objective-setting process needs to be more top-down than bottom-up, consider the following example. Suppose the senior executives of a diversified corporation establish a corporate profit objective of $500 million for next year. Suppose further that,

Strategic Management Principle

Objective setting needs to be more of a top-down than a bottom-up process in order to guide lower-level managers and organizational units toward outcomes that support the achievement of overall business and company objectives.

after discussion between corporate management and the general managers of the firm's five different businesses, each business is given a stretch profit objective of $100 million by year-end (i.e., if the five business divisions contribute $100 million each in profit, the corporation can reach its $500 million profit objective). A concrete result has thus been agreed on and translated into measurable action commitments at two levels in the managerial hierarchy. Next, suppose the general manager of business unit X, after some analysis and discussion with functional area managers, concludes that reaching the $100 million profit objective will require selling 1 million units at an average price of $500 and producing them at an average cost of $400 (a $100 profit margin times 1 million units equals $100 million profit). Consequently, the general manager and the manufacturing manager settle on a production objective of 1 million units at a unit cost of $400; and the general manager and the marketing manager agree on a sales objective of 1 million units and a target selling price of $500. In turn, the marketing manager breaks the sales objective of 1 million units into unit sales targets for each sales territory, each item in the product line, and each salesperson. It is logical for organizationwide objectives and strategy to be established first so they can guide objective setting and strategy making at lower levels.

A top-down process of setting companywide performance targets first and then insisting that the financial and strategic performance targets established for business units, divisions, functional departments, and operating units be directly connected to the achievement of company objectives has two powerful advantages: One, it helps produce *cohesion* among the objectives and strategies of different parts of the organization. Two, it helps *unify internal efforts* to move the company along the chosen strategic course. If top management, in the interest of involving a broad spectrum of organizational members, allows objective setting to start at the bottom levels of an organization without the benefit of companywide performance targets as a guide, then lower-level organizational units have no basis for connecting their performance targets to the company's. Bottom-up objective setting, with little or no guidance from above, nearly always signals an absence of strategic leadership on the part of senior executives.

CRAFTING A STRATEGY: THE THIRD DIRECTION-SETTING TASK

Strategies represent management's answers to *how* to achieve objectives and *how* to pursue the organization's business mission and strategic vision. Strategy making is all about *how*—how to achieve performance targets, how to outcompete rivals, how to achieve sustainable competitive advantage, how to strengthen the enterprise's long-term business position, how to make management's strategic vision for the company a reality. A strategy is needed for the company as a whole, for each business the company is in, and for each functional piece of each business.

Basic Concept
An organization's strategy deals with *how* to make management's strategic vision for the company a reality—it represents the game plan for moving the company into an attractive business position and building a sustainable competitive advantage.

Strategy making thus entails managerial choices. The hows that comprise the strategy represent organizational commitment to specific competitive approaches and ways of operating—in effect, strategy constitutes management's *business model* for producing good profitability and good business results. Furthermore, strategy is inherently action-oriented; it concerns what to do and when to do it. Unless there is action, unless something happens, unless somebody does something, strategic thinking and planning simply go to waste.

An organization's strategy evolves over time, emerging from the pattern of actions already initiated, the plans managers have for fresh moves, and the ongoing need to react to new or unforeseen developments. The future is too unknowable for management to plan a company's strategy in advance and encounter no reason for changing one piece or another of its intended strategy as time passes. In many of today's industries—especially those where technology is advancing rapidly and those involving the Internet—the pace of industry change is intense and sometimes more than a bit chaotic. Industry environments characterized by high-velocity change require rapid strategy adaption.[10] Illustration Capsule 10 describes Bank One's attempt to adapt to high-velocity change and become a leader in online banking.

Reacting to fresh developments in the surrounding environment is thus a normal and necessary part of the strategy-making process. There is always some new strategic window opening up—whether from advancing technology, new competitive developments, budding trends in buyer needs and expectations, unexpected increases or decreases in costs, mergers and acquisitions among major industry players, new regulations, the raising or lowering of trade barriers, or countless other events that make it desirable to alter first one and then another aspect of the present strategy.[11] This is why the task of crafting strategy is neverending. And it is why a company's actual strategy turns out to be a blend of prior actions, managerial plans and intentions, and as-needed reactions to fresh developments.

While most of the time a company's strategy evolves incrementally, there are occasions when a company can function as an industry revolutionary by creating a *rule-breaking* strategy that redefines the industry or how it operates. A strategy can challenge fundamental conventions by reconceiving a product or service (like creating a single-use, disposable cameras or digital cameras), redefining the marketplace, or redrawing industry boundaries. Internet retailers are trying to become *rule-makers* by marketing their products anywhere at any time rather than being restricted to making their products available at particular locations during normal shopping times. Consumers can now get their credit cards from Shell Oil or General Motors or AOL, or have their checking account at Charles Schwab, or get a home mortgage from Merrill Lynch or Mortgage.com, or shop on the Internet instead of going to the mall.[12]

The Strategy-Making Pyramid

As we emphasized in Chapter 1, strategy making is not just a task for senior executives. In large enterprises, decisions about what business approaches to take and what new moves to initiate involve senior executives in the corporate office, heads of business units and product divisions, the heads of major functional areas within a business or division (manufacturing, marketing and sales, finance, human resources, and the like), plant managers, product managers, district and regional sales managers, and lower-level supervisors. In diversified enterprises, strategies are initiated at four distinct organization levels. There's a strategy for the company and all of its businesses as a whole (*corporate strategy*). There's a strategy for each separate business the company has diversified into (*business strategy*). Then there is a strategy for each specific functional unit within a business (*functional strategy*). Each business usually has a production strategy, a marketing strategy, a finance strategy, and so on. And, finally, there

> A company's *actual strategy* usually turns out to be both more and less than the *planned strategy* as new strategy features are added and others are deleted in response to newly emerging conditions.

---

[10]For an excellent treatment of the strategic challenges posed by high-velocity changes, see Shona L. Brown and Kathleen M. Eisenhardt, *Competing on the Edge: Strategy as Structured Chaos* (Boston, MA: Harvard Business School Press, 1998), chapter 1.

[11]Henry Mintzberg and J. A. Waters, "Of Strategies, Deliberate and Emergent," *Strategic Management Journal* 6 (1985), pp. 257–72.

[12]For an in-depth discussion of revolutionary strategies, see Gary Hamel, "Strategy as Revolution," *Harvard Business Review* 74, no. 4 (July–August 1996), pp. 69–82.

illustration capsule 10
Bank One's New Internet Banking Strategy

In 1999, after having acquired over 100 banks during the past 15 years and built an interstate banking franchise spanning 14 states with 1,900 branch offices, Chicago-based Bank One created an independent Internet bank named WingspanBank.com. The new bank operated entirely separately from Bank One and was accessible only on the Internet.

Whereas a number of other banks, such as Wells Fargo and Bank of America, had already created "Internet branches" that allow customers to pay bills and perform certain other banking functions online, Bank One opted for a strategy of creating an altogether independent Internet bank that could distance itself from Bank One and even compete against Bank One in certain areas.

John McCoy, Bank One's CEO, believed that just having a cyberbranch outpost of Bank One was not the optimal strategy for exploiting the opportunities afforded by the Internet because the financial services market was evolving too fast and because outside software and website developers could build a full-service Internet branch for any bank in about three months for a modest $50,000 fee. McCoy believed that online mutual fund supermarkets, brokerage firms, and mortgage lenders all posed a threat to enter the online banking business and take business away from traditional banking institutions that relied on brick-and-mortar branches, ATMs, and on-site people to deliver

their services. Furthermore, in 1999 Wal-Mart was in the process of seeking approval to acquire a small savings and loan institution that would allow it to offer services ranging from car loans to credit cards in all of its stores.

Bank One's initial strategy for Wingspan included the following elements:

- Creating the capability to approve or reject customer applications for loans in less than a minute.

- Providing credit cards offering a 5 percent discount on purchases from selected Internet retailers, such as Amazon.com.

- Providing free access to Bank One's ATMs and reimbursing customers up to $5 per month for ATM fees incurred at the ATMs of other banks (so that Wingspan customers could get cash out of their accounts). To make deposits, customers had to mail the checks and slips to Wingspan's post office box in Philadelphia.

- Offering a menu of investments, mortgages, and insurance from companies not affiliated with Bank One. Whereas Bank One customers had online access to only 49 mutual funds, Wingspan customers could choose from 7,000 mutual funds. A special search function allowed Wingspan customers to scan the Internet for the lowest available mortgage rate and get an e-mail telling them the location of the best deal.

(continued)

are still narrower strategies for basic operating units—plants, sales districts and regions, and departments within functional areas (*operating strategy*). In single-business enterprises, there are only three levels of strategy making (business strategy, functional strategy, and operating strategy) unless diversification into other businesses becomes an active consideration. Figure 2.1 on page 52 shows the strategy-making pyramids for diversified and single-business companies.

Basic Concept
Corporate strategy concerns how a diversified company intends to establish business positions in different industries and the actions and approaches employed to improve the performance of the group of businesses the company has diversified into.

Corporate Strategy

Corporate strategy is the overall managerial game plan for a diversified company; it extends companywide—an umbrella over all a diversified company's businesses. Corporate strategy consists of the moves made to establish business positions in different industries and the approaches used to manage the company's group of businesses. Figure 2.2 depicts the core elements that identify a diversified company's corporate strategy. Crafting corporate strategy for a diversified company involves four kinds of initiatives:

1. *Making the moves to establish positions in different businesses and achieve diversification*—In a diversified company, a key piece of corporate strategy is how many

illustration capsule 10

(concluded)

Wingspan customers could also shop the Internet for five different kinds of insurance.

- Spending close to $100 million to promote Wingspan coast-to-coast, including pop-up ads on a wide variety of Internet sites, so as to both attract new customers and establish strong brand-name awareness. Bank One executives also believed that quickly establishing dominance in Internet banking would give Wingspan/Bank One an important first-mover advantage that would allow it to out-compete later entrants.

- Creating an advisory board for Wingspan that included a student, a software programmer, and a stay-at-home mother. The iBoard, as it is called, met online as well as in person.

- Using a high-speed transaction-processing system operated by Pennsylvania-based Sanchez Computer Associates to process and account for transactions in real time, as opposed to the catch-up time that Bank One's computers often required. Outsourcing the transaction system also meant that Wingspan did not have to spend months figuring out how to link into Bank One's far-flung and complex data processing system.

- Using the feedback from customers to improve its website and alter its product offerings.

In its first two months of operation, Wingspan attracted 75,000 customers, nearly one-third of all customers then claimed by all the existing independent Internet banks—compared to some 9.5 million customers engaged in online banking at the Internet branches of their traditional bank. But the corporate strategy did not play out the way everyone had hoped. "Pure Internet plays are having a hard time getting off the ground," noted Bank One's executive vice president, Bruce Luecke. "It's harder to make deposits. It's harder to make withdrawals." So in September 2000, Bank One began to decrease its spending to market Wingspan and fold some of Wingspan's systems back into those of Bank One.

Wingspan still existed, but after assigning a group to evaluate and run Bank One's Internet operations, CEO Jamie Dimon announced in June 2001 that the bank's new strategy would be to merge all of Wingspan's 225,000 customers and resources with Bankone.com, the Internet arm of Bank One's overall retail operation. Executives hoped that this move would increase efficiency and profitability for the bank's Internet activities.

Sources: Christopher Bowe, "Wingspan Fails to Take Off," *Financial Times* (http://news.ft.com), June 28, 2001; Maria Twombly, "Bank One Trims Its WingspanBank.com," *Computerworld* (www.computerworld.com), September 21, 2000; and *The Wall Street Journal,* August 25, 1999, pp. A1, A8.

and what kinds of businesses the company should be in—specifically, what industries to enter and whether to enter the industries by starting a new business or acquiring another company (an established leader, an up-and-coming company, or a troubled company with turnaround potential). This piece of corporate strategy establishes whether diversification is based narrowly in a few industries or broadly in many industries and whether the different businesses will be related or unrelated.

2. *Initiating actions to boost the combined performance of the businesses the firm has diversified into*—As positions are created in the chosen industries, corporate strategy making concentrates on ways to strengthen the long-term competitive positions and profitabilities of the businesses the firm has invested in. Corporate parents can help their business subsidiaries be more successful by financing additional capacity and efficiency improvements, by supplying missing skills and managerial know-how, by acquiring another company in the same industry and merging the two operations into a stronger business, or by acquiring new businesses that strongly complement existing businesses. Management's overall strategy for improving companywide performance usually involves pursuing rapid-growth strategies in the most promising businesses, keeping the other core businesses healthy, initiating turnaround efforts in weak-performing businesses with potential, and divesting businesses that are no longer attractive or that don't fit into the organization's long-range plans.

figure 2.1   **The Strategy-Making Pyramid**

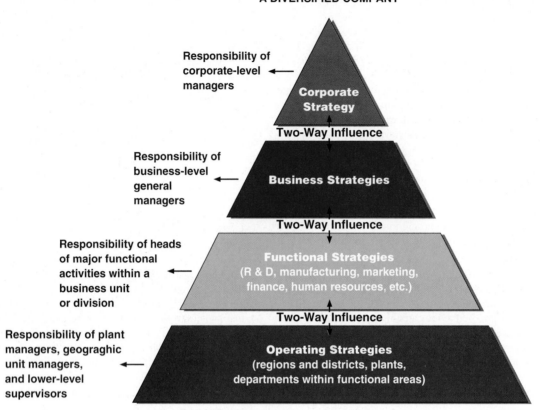

figure 2.2 **Identifying the Overall Corporate Strategy of a Diversified Company**

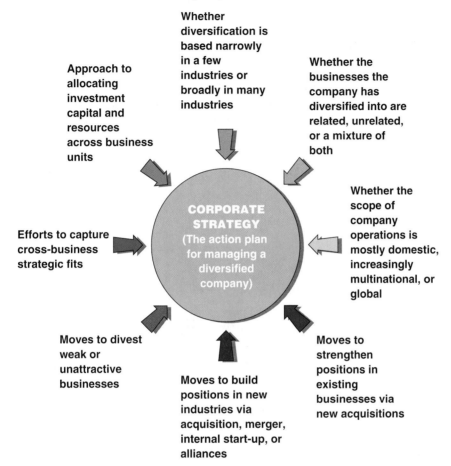

3. *Pursuing ways to capture valuable cross-business strategic fits and turn them into competitive advantage*—When a company diversifies into businesses with related technologies, similar operating characteristics, common distribution channels or customers, or some other synergistic factor, it gains competitive advantage potential not open to a company that diversifies into totally unrelated businesses. When Amazon.com diversified into selling CDs and conducting online auctions, the moves presented opportunities to (*a*) transfer Amazon's skills and expertise in online book sales to online music sales, (*b*) use the same distribution facilities and order fulfillment technology to ship both books and CDs (use of shared facilities and resources meant lower joint costs), (*c*) leverage Amazon's brand name, and (*d*) lay the foundation for Amazon.com to later extend its reach into other product lines and become a one-stop shopping site for online buyers. Such cross-business "strategic fits" strengthen a company's competitiveness and provide a basis for greater profitability.

4. *Establishing investment priorities and steering corporate resources into the most attractive business units*—A diversified company's different businesses are usually not equally attractive from the standpoint of investing additional funds. This facet of corporate strategy making involves channeling resources into areas where earnings potentials

figure 2.3   **Identifying Strategy for a Single Business**

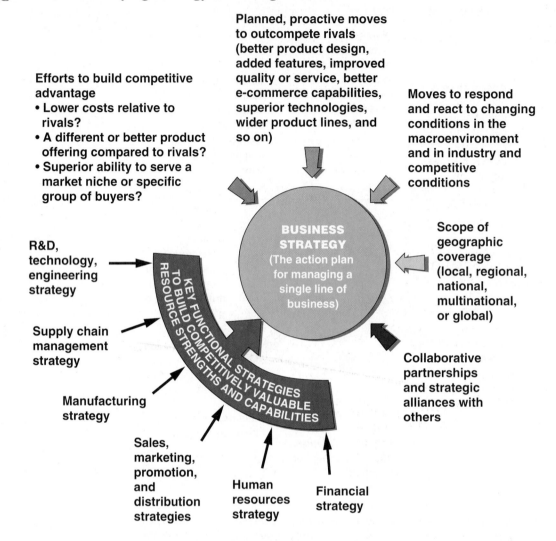

Efforts to build competitive advantage
- **Lower costs relative to rivals?**
- **A different or better product offering compared to rivals?**
- **Superior ability to serve a market niche or specific group of buyers?**

Planned, proactive moves to outcompete rivals (better product design, added features, improved quality or service, better e-commerce capabilities, superior technologies, wider product lines, and so on)

Moves to respond and react to changing conditions in the macroenvironment and in industry and competitive conditions

R&D, technology, engineering strategy

Supply chain management strategy

Manufacturing strategy

Sales, marketing, promotion, and distribution strategies

Human resources strategy

Financial strategy

BUSINESS STRATEGY (The action plan for managing a single line of business)

KEY FUNCTIONAL STRATEGIES TO BUILD COMPETITIVELY VALUABLE RESOURCE STRENGTHS AND CAPABILITIES

Scope of geographic coverage (local, regional, national, multinational, or global)

Collaborative partnerships and strategic alliances with others

---

are higher and away from areas where they are lower. Corporate strategy may include divesting business units that are chronically poor performers or those in an increasingly unattractive industry. Divestiture frees up unproductive investments for redeployment to promising business units or for financing attractive new acquisitions.

Corporate strategy is crafted at the highest levels of management. Senior corporate executives normally have lead responsibility for devising corporate strategy and for choosing among whatever recommended actions bubble up from lower-level managers. Key business-unit heads may also be influential, especially in strategic decisions affecting the businesses they head. Major strategic decisions are usually reviewed and approved by the company's board of directors.

Business Strategy

The term **business strategy** (or business-level strategy) refers to the managerial game plan for a single business. It is mirrored in the pattern of approaches and moves crafted by management to produce successful performance in one specific line of business.

Basic Concept
Business strategy concerns the actions and the approaches crafted by management to produce successful performance in one specific line of business; the central business strategy issue is *how* to build a stronger long-term competitive position.

The core elements of business strategy are illustrated in Figure 2.3. For a single-business company, corporate strategy and business strategy are one and the same.

The central thrust of business strategy is *how* to build and strengthen the company's long-term competitive position in the marketplace. Toward this end, business strategy is concerned principally with (1) forming responses to changes under way in the industry, the economy at large, the regulatory and political arena, and other relevant areas; (2) crafting competitive moves and market approaches that can lead to sustainable competitive advantage; (3) building competitively valuable competencies and capabilities; (4) uniting the strategic initiatives of functional departments; and (5) addressing specific strategic issues facing the company's business.

Clearly, business strategy involves initiating whatever actions and responses managers deem prudent in light of competitive forces, economic trends, technological developments, buyer needs and demographics, new legislation and regulatory requirements, and other such broad external factors. *A good strategy is well-matched to a company's external and internal situation;* as the company's situation changes in significant ways, then adjustments in strategy typically are needed. Whether a company's response to changing conditions is quick or slow tends to be a function of how long events must unfold before managers can assess their implications and how much longer it then takes to form a strategic response. Some changes in a company's external and internal environment, of course, require little or no response, while others call for significant strategy alterations. On occasion, situational factors change in ways that pose a formidable strategic hurdle—for example, cigarette and firearms manufacturers face a tough challenge holding their own against the mounting campaigns against smoking and for stricter gun control. Conventional retailers are rushing to establish their own Internet sales capabilities to defend against competition from thousands of enterprising Internet retailers.

What separates a powerful business strategy from a weak one is the strategist's ability to forge a series of moves, both in the marketplace and internally, that are capable of producing *sustainable competitive advantage.* With a competitive advantage, a company has good prospects for above-average profitability and success in the industry. Without competitive advantage, a company risks being locked into mediocre performance. Crafting a business strategy that yields sustainable competitive advantage has three facets: (1) deciding what product/service attributes (lower costs and prices, a better product, a wider product line, superior customer service, emphasis on a particular market niche) offer the best chance to win a competitive edge; (2) developing expertise, resource strengths, and competitive capabilities that set the company apart from rivals; and (3) trying to insulate the business as much as possible from the actions of rivals and other threatening competitive developments.

> A business strategy is powerful if it produces a sizable and sustainable competitive advantage; it is weak if it results in competitive disadvantage.

A company's strategy for competing is typically both offensive and defensive—some actions are aggressive and amount to direct challenges to competitors' market positions; others aim at countering competitive pressures and the actions of rivals. Three of the most frequently used competitive approaches are (1) striving to be the industry's low-cost provider; (2) pursuing such differentiating features as higher quality, added performance, better service, more attractive styling, technological superiority, or unusually good value; and (3) focusing on a narrow market niche and doing a better job than rivals of serving the special needs and tastes of its buyers.

The most successful business strategies typically aim at building *uniquely strong or distinctive competencies* in one or more areas crucial to strategic success and then using them as a basis for winning a competitive edge over rivals. Distinctive competencies can relate to leading-edge product innovation, better mastery of a technological process, expertise in defect-free manufacturing, specialized marketing and merchandising know-how, potent global sales and distribution capability, superior e-commerce capabilities, better customer service, or anything else that constitutes a competitively valuable

> Having superior internal resource strengths and competitive capabilities is an important way to outcompete rivals.

strength in creating, producing, distributing, or marketing the company's product or service.

On a broader internal front, business strategy must also aim at uniting strategic initiatives in the various functional areas of business. Strategic actions are needed in each functional area to *support* the company's competitive approach and overall business strategy. Strategic unity and coordination across the various functional areas add power to the business strategy.

Business strategy also extends to *action plans* for addressing any special strategy-related issues unique to the company's competitive position and internal situation (such as whether to add new capacity, replace an obsolete plant, increase R&D funding for a promising technology, reduce burdensome interest expenses, form strategic alliances and collaborative partnerships, or build competitively valuable competencies and capabilities via the Internet). Such custom tailoring of strategy to fit a company's specific situation is one of the reasons why companies in the same industry employ different business strategies.

Lead responsibility for business strategy falls in the lap of whoever is in charge of the business. Even if the business head does not personally wield a heavy hand in business strategy making, preferring to delegate many strategy particulars to subordinates, he or she is still accountable for the strategy and the results it produces. The business head, as chief strategist for the business, has at least two other responsibilities. The first is seeing that supporting strategies in each of the major functional areas of the business are well conceived and consistent with each other. The second is getting major strategic moves approved by higher authority (the board of directors and/or corporate-level officers) and keeping them informed of important new developments, deviations from plan, and potential strategy revisions. In diversified companies, business-unit heads may have the additional obligation of making sure business-level objectives and strategy conform to corporate-level objectives and strategy themes.

Functional Strategy

Basic Concept
Functional strategy concerns the managerial game plan for running a major functional activity or process within a business—R&D, production, marketing, customer service, distribution, finance, human resources, and so on; a business needs as many functional strategies as it has major activities.

The term **functional strategy** refers to the managerial game plan for a particular functional activity, business process, or key department within a business. A company's marketing strategy, for example, represents the managerial game plan for running the marketing part of the business. A company's new product development strategy represents the managerial game plan for keeping the company's product lineup fresh and in tune with what buyers are looking for. A company needs a functional strategy for every major business activity and organizational unit. Functional strategy, while narrower in scope than business strategy, adds relevant detail to the overall business game plan. It aims at establishing or strengthening specific competencies calculated to enhance the company's market position. Like business strategy, functional strategy must *support* the company's overall business strategy and competitive approach. A related role is to create a managerial road map for achieving the functional area's objectives and mission. Thus, functional strategy in the production/manufacturing area represents the game plan for how manufacturing activities will be managed to support business strategy and achieve the manufacturing department's objectives and mission. Functional strategy in the finance area consists of how financial activities will be managed in supporting business strategy and achieving the finance department's objectives and mission.

Lead responsibility for conceiving strategies for each of the various important business functions and processes is normally delegated to the respective functional department heads and process managers unless the business-unit head decides to exert a strong influence. In crafting strategy, the manager of a particular business function or process ideally works closely with key subordinates and touches base often with the managers of other functions/processes and the business head. If functional or process managers plot strategy independent of each other or the business head, they open the door for uncoordinated or conflicting strategies. Compatible, collaborative, mutually reinforcing functional strategies are essential for the overall business strategy to have maximum impact. Plainly, a business's marketing strategy, production strategy, finance strategy, customer service strategy, new product development strategy, and human resources strategy should be in sync rather than serving their own narrower purposes. Coordination and consistency among the various functional and process strategies are best accomplished during the deliberation stage. If inconsistent functional strategies are sent up the line for final approval, it is up to the business head to spot the conflicts and get them resolved.

Operating Strategy

Operating strategy concerns the even narrower strategic initiatives and approaches for managing key operating units (plants, sales districts, distribution centers) and for handling daily operating tasks with strategic significance (advertising campaigns, materials purchasing, inventory control, maintenance, shipping). A plant manager needs a strategy for accomplishing the plant's objectives, carrying out the plant's part of the company's overall manufacturing game plan, and dealing with any strategy-related problems that exist at the plant. A district sales manager needs a sales strategy customized to the district's particular situation and sales objectives. A company's advertising manager needs a strategy for getting maximum audience exposure and sales impact from the ad budget.

Operating strategies, while of limited scope, add further detail and completeness to functional strategies and to the overall business plan. Lead responsibility for operating strategies is usually delegated to front-line managers, subject to review and approval by higher-ranking managers.

Even though operating strategy is at the bottom of the strategy-making pyramid, its importance should not be downplayed. Operating-level strategies provide valuable support to higher-level strategies. Consider the case of a distributor of plumbing equipment whose business strategy emphasizes fast delivery and accurate order filling in an effort to deliver better customer service than rivals. In support of this strategy, the firm's warehouse manager (1) develops an inventory stocking strategy that allows 99.9 percent of all orders to be completely filled without back-ordering any item and (2) institutes a warehouse staffing strategy that allows any order to be shipped within 24 hours. Without such operating strategies in place, the plumbing distributor's strategy would fail.

Another instance of the importance of operating strategy occurs in manufacturing companies. A major plant that fails in its strategy to achieve production volume, unit cost, and quality targets can undercut the achievement of company sales and profit objectives and wreak havoc with the whole company's strategic efforts to build a quality image with customers. One cannot reliably judge the strategic importance of a given action by the organizational or managerial level where it is initiated.

Uniting the Strategy-Making Effort

The previous discussion underscores that *a company's strategic plan is a collection of strategies* devised by different managers at different levels in the organizational

---

Basic Concept
Operating strategy concerns how to manage front-line organizational units within a business (plants, sales districts, distribution centers) and how to perform strategically significant operating tasks (materials purchasing, inventory control, maintenance, shipping, advertising campaigns).

Front-line managers are an important part of an organization's strategy-making team because many operating units have strategy-critical performance targets and need to have strategic action plans in place to achieve them.

A company's strategy is at full power only when its many pieces are united.

Objectives and strategies that are unified from top-to-bottom of the organizational hierarchy do not come from an undirected process where managers at each level have objective-setting and strategy-making autonomy. Cross-unit and top-down coordination is essential.

hierarchy. The larger the enterprise, the more points of strategic initiative it has. Management's direction-setting effort is not complete until the separate layers and pieces of strategy are unified into a coherent, supportive pattern. Ideally the pieces and layers of strategy should fit together like a jigsaw puzzle.

To achieve this unity, the strategizing process has to proceed more from the top down than from the bottom up. Direction and guidance have to flow from the corporate level to the business level and from the business level to the functional and operating levels. *Lower-level managers cannot do good strategy making without understanding the company's long-term direction and higher-level strategies.* The strategic disarray that occurs in an organization when senior managers don't exercise strong top-down direction setting and strategic leadership is akin to what would happen to a football team's offensive performance if the quarterback decided not to call a play for the team but instead let each player pick whatever play he thought would work best at his respective position. In business, as in sports, all the strategy makers in a company are on the same team. They are obligated to perform their strategy-making tasks in a manner that benefits the whole company, not in a manner that suits personal or departmental interests. Indeed, functional and operating-level managers have a duty to set performance targets and invent strategic actions that will help achieve *business* objectives and make *business* strategy more effective.

The larger the company and the more geographically scattered its units and subsidiaries, the more tedious and frustrating the task of harmonizing objectives and strategies piece by piece and level by level. Functional managers are sometimes more interested in doing what is best for their own areas, building their own empires, and consolidating their personal power and organizational influence than they are in cooperating with other functional managers to unify behind the overall business strategy. As a result, it's easy for functional area support strategies to conflict, thereby forcing the business-level general manager to spend time and energy refereeing functional strategy conflicts and building support for a more unified approach. Broad consensus is particularly difficult when there is ample room for opposing views and disagreement.

Figure 2.4 portrays the networking of objectives and strategies through the managerial hierarchy. The two-way arrows indicate that there are simultaneous bottom-up and top-down influences on missions, objectives, and strategies at each level. Furthermore, there are two-way influences across related businesses and across related processes, functions, and operating activities within a business. The tighter that coordination is enforced, the tighter the safeguards against organizational units straying from the company's charted strategic course.

THE FACTORS THAT SHAPE A COMPANY'S STRATEGY

Many situational considerations enter into crafting strategy. Figure 2.5 on page 60 depicts the primary factors that shape a company's strategic approaches. The interplay of these factors and the influence that each has on the strategy-making process vary from situation to situation. Very few strategic choices are made in the same context. Even in the same industry, situational factors differ enough from company to company that the strategies of rivals turn out to be quite distinguishable from one another rather than imitative. This is why carefully sizing up all the various situational factors, both external and internal, is the starting point in crafting strategy.

figure 2.4 **The Networking of Strategic Visions, Missions, Objectives, and Strategies in the Strategy-Making Pyramid**

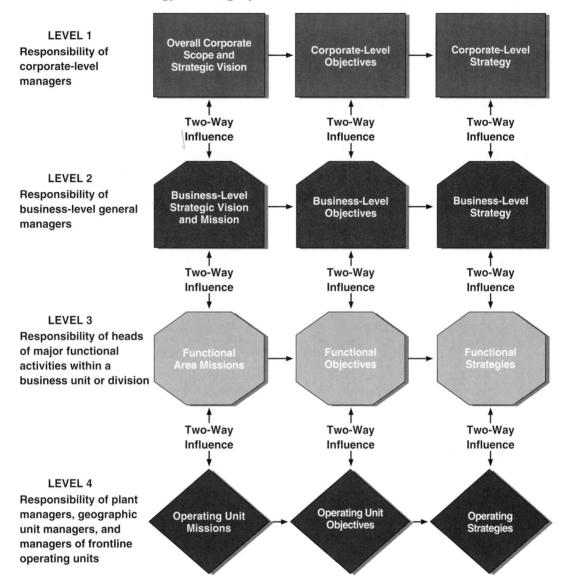

Societal, Political, Regulatory, and Citizenship Considerations

All organizations operate within the broader community of society. What an enterprise can and cannot do strategywise is always constrained by what is legal, by what complies with government policies and regulatory requirements, by what is considered ethical, and by what is in accord with societal expectations and the standards of good community citizenship. Outside pressures also come from other sources—special-interest groups, the glare of investigative reporting, a fear of unwanted political action, and the stigma of

figure 2.5   **Factors Shaping the Choice of Company Strategy**

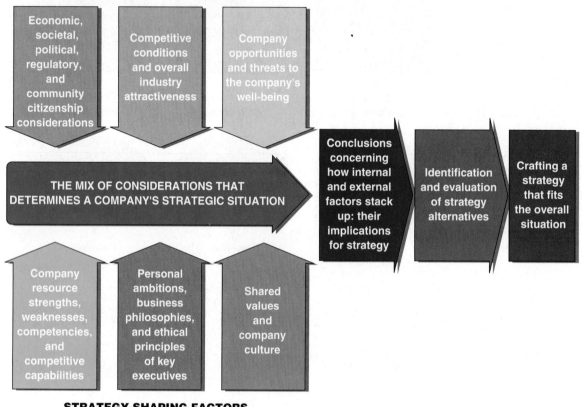

negative opinion. Societal concerns over gun control, health and nutrition, alcohol and drug abuse, smoking, environmental pollution, sexual harassment, and the impact of plant closings on local communities have caused many companies to temper or revise aspects of their strategies. American concerns over jobs lost to foreign manufacturers and political debate over how to cure the chronic U.S. trade deficit are driving forces in the strategic decisions of Japanese and European companies to locate plants in the United States. Heightened consumer awareness about the hazards of saturated fat and cholesterol have driven most food products companies to phase out high-fat ingredients and substitute low-fat ingredients, despite the extra costs.

> Economic, societal, political, regulatory, and citizenship factors limit the strategic actions a company can or should take.

Factoring in societal values and priorities, business ethics, community concerns, and the potential for onerous legislation and regulatory requirements is a regular part of external situation analysis at more and more companies. Intense public pressure and adverse media coverage make such a practice prudent. The task of making an organization's strategy socially responsible means (1) conducting organizational activities within the bounds of what is considered ethical and in the general public interest, (2) responding positively to emerging societal priorities and expectations, (3) demonstrating a willingness to take action ahead of regulatory confrontation, (4) balancing stockholder interests against the larger interests of society as a whole, and (5) being a good citizen in the community.

Corporate social responsibility is showing up in company mission statements. John Hancock, for example, concludes its mission statement with the following sentence:

> In all that we do, we exemplify the highest standards of business ethics and personal integrity, and recognize our corporate obligation to the social and economic well-being of our community.

John Hancock goes on to state its commitment to ethical behavior:

> In order to exemplify the highest standards of business ethics, we conduct the Company's affairs in strict compliance with both the letter and the spirit of the law, and will at all times treat policyholders, customers, suppliers, and all others with whom the Company does business fairly and honorably. Recognizing that our reputation of unquestioned integrity and honesty is our most valued asset, under no circumstances will what we achieve be allowed to take precedence over how we achieve it.[13]

At Sempra Energy, a San Diego–based electricity and natural gas company, management has expressed a strong commitment to enhancing the quality of life in the communities where it does business and stated it is not only good business for the company and its employees to be deeply involved in community activities but also "the right thing to do":

> We have a vested interest in ensuring that businesses thrive, community needs are met, the environment is protected, and our diverse human resources are engaged to their fullest potential.
>
> Our main focus is building and maintaining valuable relationships with communities and community leaders in markets where we do business. We also regularly encourage employee leadership and involvement in civic and community affairs, and make charitable contributions to community and civic organizations through both Sempra Energy and its key affiliates.[14]

Competitive Conditions and Overall Industry Attractiveness

An industry's competitive conditions and overall attractiveness are big strategy-determining factors. A company's strategy has to be tailored to the nature and mix of competitive factors in play—price, product quality, performance features, service, warranties, and so on. When competitive conditions intensify significantly, a company must respond with strategic actions to protect its position. Competitive weakness on the part of one or more rivals presents opportunities for a strategic offensive. Furthermore, fresh moves on the part of rival companies, changes in the industry's price-cost-profit economics, shifting buyer needs and expectations, and new technological developments often alter the requirements for competitive success and mandate reconsideration of strategy. The industry environment, as it exists now and is expected to exist later, thus has a direct bearing on a company's best competitive strategy option and where it should concentrate its efforts. *A company's strategy can't produce real market success unless it fits the industry and competitive situation.* When a firm concludes its industry environment has grown unattractive and it is better off investing company resources elsewhere, it may begin a strategy of disinvestment and eventual abandonment. A strategist, therefore, has to be a student of industry and competitive conditions.

> **Strategic Management Principle**
>
> A company's strategy should be tailored to fit industry and competitive conditions.

---

[13]Information posted on the company's website (www.johnhancock.com) as of September 1999.

[14]Information posted on the company's website (www.sempra.com) as of September 1999.

The Company's Market Opportunities and External Threats

The particular business opportunities open to a company and the threatening external developments that it faces are key influences on strategy. Both point to the need for strategic action. A company's strategy needs to be deliberately aimed at capturing its best growth opportunities, especially the ones that hold the most promise for building sustainable competitive advantage and enhancing profitability. Likewise, strategy should provide a defense against external threats to the company's well-being and future performance. This usually means crafting *offensive* moves to capitalize on the company's most promising market opportunities and crafting *defensive* moves to protect the company's competitive position and long-term profitability. Managers have to scrutinize the kinds of opportunities and threats presented by changes in the marketplace and be prompt and astute in making needed strategic adjustments.

Company Resource Strengths, Competencies, and Competitive Capabilities

One of the most pivotal strategy-shaping internal considerations is whether a company has or can acquire the resources, competencies, and capabilities needed to execute a strategy proficiently. These are the factors that can enable an enterprise to capitalize on a particular opportunity, give the firm a competitive edge in the marketplace, and become a cornerstone of the enterprise's strategy. The best path to competitive advantage is found where a firm has competitively valuable resources and competencies, where rivals do not have matching or offsetting resources and competencies, and where rivals can't develop comparable capabilities except at high cost or over an extended period of time. Intel's long-standing global leadership in microprocessors for PCs, servers, and workstations has much to do with its deep technological expertise, its multibillion-dollar R&D program, its state-of-the-art chip-making plants, and its ability to spend $3–$5 billion annually on new chip-making plants and the latest chip-making equipment. None of its competitors have such depth of resources and capabilities. As a rule, a company's strategy ought to be grounded in its resource strengths and in what it is good at doing (its competencies and competitive capabilities).

   Even if a firm lacks competitively superior competencies and capabilities (as, in fact, many do), its managers still must tailor a strategy that fits the enterprise's particular resource strengths and weaknesses. It is foolish to craft a strategy that cannot be executed with the resources and capabilities a firm is able to assemble. And it is foolish to craft a strategy whose success depends on activities which a company performs poorly or has no experience in performing at all.

The Personal Ambitions, Business Philosophies, and Ethical Beliefs of Managers

Managers do not dispassionately assess what strategic course to steer. Their choices are typically influenced by their own vision of how to compete and how to position the enterprise and by what image and standing they want the company to have. Both casual observation and formal studies indicate that managers' ambitions, values, business philosophies, attitudes toward risk, and ethical beliefs have important influences on strategy.[15] Sometimes the influence of a manager's personal values, experiences, and emotions is conscious and deliberate; at other times it may be unconscious. As one expert noted in explaining the relevance of personal factors to strategy, "People have to have their hearts in it."[16]

Several examples of how business philosophies and personal values enter into strategy-making are particularly noteworthy. Ben Cohen and Jerry Greenfield, cofounders and major stockholders in Ben & Jerry's Homemade, Inc., have consistently insisted that the company's strategy incorporate a strong social mission and be supportive of social causes of their choosing. The strategy crafted by Starbucks' CEO, Howard Schultz, mirrors Schultz's insistence on customers having a very positive experience when patronizing a Starbucks store and his desire to "build a company with soul" and make Starbucks a great place to work. Japanese managers are strong proponents of strategies that take a long-term view and that aim at building market share and competitive position.

Attitudes toward risk also have a big influence on strategy. Risk-avoiders are inclined toward "conservative" strategies that minimize downside risk, have a quick payback, and produce sure short-term profits. Risk-takers lean more toward opportunistic strategies where visionary moves can produce a big payoff over the long term. Risk-takers prefer innovation to imitation and bold strategic offensives to defensive moves aimed at protecting the status quo.

Managerial values also shape the ethical quality of a firm's strategy. Managers with strong ethical convictions take pains to see that their companies observe a strict code of ethics in all aspects of the business. They expressly forbid such practices as accepting or giving kickbacks, badmouthing rivals' products, and buying political influence with political contributions. Instances where a company's strategic actions run afoul of high ethical standards include charging excessive interest rates on credit card balances, employing bait-and-switch sales tactics, continuing to market products suspected of having safety problems, and using ingredients that are known health hazards.

> The personal ambitions, business philosophies, and ethical beliefs of managers are usually stamped on the strategies they craft.

The Influence of Shared Values and Company Culture on Strategy

An organization's policies, practices, traditions, philosophical beliefs, and ways of doing things combine to create a distinctive culture. Typically, the stronger a company's culture, the more that culture is likely to shape the company's strategic actions, sometimes even dominating the choice of strategic moves. This is because culture-related values and beliefs are so embedded in management's strategic thinking and actions that they condition how the enterprise does business and responds to external events. Such firms have a culture-driven bias about how to handle strategic issues and what kinds of strategic moves it will consider or reject. Strong cultural influences partly account for why companies gain reputations for such strategic traits as leadership in technology

> A company's values, policies, practices, and culture can dominate the kinds of strategic moves it considers or rejects.

---

[15]The role of personal values, individual ambitions, and managerial philosophies in strategy-making has long been recognized and documented. The classic sources are William D. Guth and Renato Tagiuri, "Personal Values and Corporate Strategy," *Harvard Business Review* 43, no. 5 (September–October 1965), pp. 123–32; Kenneth R. Andrews, *The Concept of Corporate Strategy,* 3rd ed. (Homewood, IL: Richard D. Irwin, 1987), chapter 4; and Richard F. Vancil, "Strategy Formulation in Complex Organizations," *Sloan Management Review* 17, no. 2 (Winter 1986), pp. 4–5.

[16]Andrews, *The Concept of Corporate Strategy,* p. 63.

and product innovation, dedication to superior craftsmanship, a proclivity for financial wheeling and dealing, a desire to grow rapidly by acquiring other companies, having a strong people orientation and being an especially good company to work for, or unusual emphasis on customer service and total customer satisfaction.

In recent years, many companies have articulated the core beliefs, principles, and values underlying their business approaches. One company expressed its values as follows:

> We are market-driven. We believe that functional excellence, combined with teamwork across functions and profit centers, is essential to achieving superb execution. We believe that people are central to everything we will accomplish. We believe that honesty, integrity, and fairness should be the cornerstone of our relationships with consumers, customers, suppliers, stockholders, and employees.

The commitment of Ritz-Carlton Hotels to providing its guests with the finest personal service and facilities—combined with its principles of trust, respect, honesty, integrity—drive its strategy and operating practices. The company's cultural motto is "We are ladies and gentlemen serving ladies and gentlemen." Wal-Mart's founder, Sam Walton, was a fervent believer in frugality, hard work, constant improvement, dedication to customers, and genuine care for employees. The company's commitment to these values is deeply ingrained in its strategy of low prices, good values, friendly service, productivity through the intelligent use of technology, and hard-nosed bargaining with suppliers.[17] At Hewlett-Packard, the company's basic values, known internally as "the HP Way," include sharing the company's success with employees, showing trust and respect for employees, providing customers with products and services of the greatest value, being genuinely interested in providing customers with effective solutions to their problems, making profit a high stockholder priority, avoiding the use of long-term debt to finance growth, individual initiative and creativity, teamwork, and being a good corporate citizen.[18] At both Wal-Mart and Hewlett-Packard, the value systems are deeply ingrained and widely shared by managers and employees. Whenever this happens, values and beliefs are more than an expression of nice platitudes; they become a way of life within the company.[19] Illustration Capsule 11 provides yet another example of the links between vision, values, and strategy.

LINKING STRATEGY WITH ETHICS AND SOCIAL RESPONSIBILITY

Every strategic action a company takes should be ethical.

Strategy ought to be ethical. It should involve rightful actions, not wrongful ones; otherwise it won't pass the test of moral scrutiny. This means more than conforming to what is legal. Ethical and moral standards go beyond the law and the language of "thou shalt not." They address the issues of *duty* and the language of "should do and should not do." Ethics concern human *duty* and the principles on which this duty rests.[20]

---

[17]Sam Walton with John Huey, *Sam Walton: Made in America* (New York: Doubleday, 1992); and John P. Kotter and James L. Heskett, *Corporate Culture and Performance* (New York: Free Press, 1992), pp. 17, 36.

[18]Kotter and Heskett, *Corporate Culture and Performance*, pp. 60–61.

[19]For another example of the impact of values and beliefs, see Richard T. Pascale, "Perspectives on Strategy: The Real Story behind Honda's Success," in Glenn Carroll and David Vogel, *Strategy and Organization: A West Coast Perspective* (Marshfield, MA: Pitman, 1984), p. 60.

[20]Harry Downs, "Business Ethics: The Stewardship of Power," working paper provided to the authors.

illustration capsule 11

The Enron Debacle: A Bold Vision and Admirable Values Undermined by a Flawed Strategy and Unethical Behavior

Until its crash in the fall of 2001, Enron was one of the world's largest electricity, natural gas, and broadband trading companies, with revenues of over $100 billion. Enron's strategic intent was to become *the* blue-chip energy and communications company of the 21st century through its business efforts in four core areas: Enron Wholesale Services, Enron Broadband Services, Enron Energy Services, and Enron Transportation Services. Enron management claimed that each of these business units supported the company's mission of "offering a wide range of physical, transportation, financial and technical solutions to thousands of customers around the world." Enron had publicly stated its vision and values as follows:

Who We Are

Enron's business is to create value and opportunity for your business. We do this by combining our financial resources, access to physical commodities, and knowledge to create innovative solutions to challenging industrial problems. We are best known for our natural gas and electricity products, but today we also offer retail energy and bandwidth products. These products give customers the flexibility they need to compete today.

What We Believe

We begin with a fundamental belief in the inherent wisdom of **OPEN MARKETS.** Economic activities are better sorted out by markets than they are by governments . . . We are convinced that consumer choice and competition lead to lower prices and innovation.

Enron is a laboratory for **INNOVATION.** That's why we employ the best and the brightest people. And we believe that every employee can make a difference here.

We encourage people to make a difference by creating an environment where everyone is allowed to achieve their full potential and where everyone has a stake in the outcome. We think this entrepreneurial approach stimulates **CREATIVITY** . . .

. . . We value **DIVERSITY.** We are committed to removing all barriers to employment and advancement based on sex, sexual orientation, race, religion, age, ethnic background, national origin, or physical limitation . . .

Our success is measured by the success of our **CUSTOMERS.** We are committed to meeting their energy needs with solutions that offer them a competitive advantage. And we work with them in ways that reinforce the benefits of a long-term partnership with Enron.

In everything we do, we operate safely and with concern for the **ENVIRONMENT** . . . This is a responsibility we take seriously in all the different places around the world where we do business.

. . . We're changing the way energy is delivered, as well as the market for it. We're reinventing the fundamentals of this business by providing energy at lower costs and in more usable forms than it has been provided before . . .

Everything we do is about change . . . **TOGETHER** we're creating the leading energy company in the world. Together, we are defining the energy company of the future.

How We Behave

Respect: We treat others as we would like to be treated ourselves. We do not tolerate abusive or

(continued)

Every business has an ethical duty to each of five constituencies: owners/shareholders, employees, customers, suppliers, and the community at large. Each of these constituencies affects the organization and is affected by it. Each is a stakeholder in the enterprise, with certain expectations as to what the enterprise should do and how it should do it.[21] A company has a *duty to owners/shareholders,* for instance, who rightly expect a return on their investment. Even though investors may individually differ in their preferences for profits now versus profits later, their tolerances for greater risk, and their enthusiasm for exercising social responsibility, business executives have a moral duty to pursue profitable management of the owners' investment.

> A company has ethical duties to owners, employees, customers, suppliers, the communities where it operates, and the public at large.

[21]Ibid.

illustration capsule 11

(concluded)

disrespectful treatment. Ruthlessness, callousness, and arrogance don't belong here.

Integrity: We work with customers and prospects openly, honestly, and sincerely. When we say we will do something, we will do it; when we say we cannot or will not do something, then we won't do it.

Communication: We have an obligation to communicate. Here, we take the time to talk with one another . . . and to listen. We believe that information is meant to move and that information moves people.

Excellence: We are satisfied with nothing less than the very best in everything we do. We will continue to raise the bar for everyone. The great fun here will be for all of us to discover just how good we can really be.

But gaping flaws in Enron's strategy began to emerge in fall 2001, starting with revelations that the company had incurred billions more in debt to grow its energy trading business than was first apparent from its balance sheet. The off-balance-sheet debt was hidden by obscurely worded footnotes to the company's financial statements involving mysterious partnerships in which the company's chief financial officer (CFO) had an interest (and was apparently using to make millions in profits on the side). After Enron's stock price slid from the mid-$80s to the high-$30s despite glowing earnings reports, the company's well-regarded chief executive officer suddenly resigned for "personal reasons" in August 2001. Weeks later, the company's CFO was asked to resign as details of his conflict of interest in the off-balance-sheet partnerships came to light.

Meanwhile, top company executives continued to insist publicly that the company was in sound financial shape and that its business was secure, hoping to keep customers from shifting their business to rivals and to reassure concerned shareholders. But Enron's crown jewel, its energy trading business, which generated about $60 billion in reported revenues, came under increased scrutiny, both for the debt that had been amassed to support such enormous trading volumes and for its very thin profit margins (some of which were suspect due to accounting treatments that had won the stamp of approval of Arthur Andersen, the company's auditor).

Within weeks, Enron filed for bankruptcy, its stock price fell below $1 per share, its stock was delisted from the New York Stock Exchange, and a scandal of unprecedented proportions grew almost daily. Arthur Andersen fired the partner on the Enron account when it appeared that working papers relating to the audit were destroyed in an apparent effort to obstruct a congressional investigation of the details of Enron's collapse. Enron's board fired Arthur Andersen as the company's auditor. Then Enron was caught destroying documents (as late as January 2002) in an apparent attempt to hide the company's actions from investigators. Enron's chairman and CEO resigned; the company's former vice chairman committed suicide after it became public that he had vigorously protested Enron's accounting practices earlier in 2001.

It also came out that senior company officers had sold shares of Enron stock months earlier, when the stock price slide first began. Enron employees—most of whom had their entire 401(K) monies tied up in Enron stock and were precluded from selling their shares, and 4,000 of whom were dismissed in a last-ditch effort to cut costs—watched helplessly as their retirement savings were wiped out by the crash.

The extent of management's unethical behavior is still under investigation. But Enron management clearly did not act in accordance with the principles and values it espoused.

Sources: Company website (www.enron.com); 2000 company annual report; and 1998 company annual report.

A company's *duty to employees* arises out of respect for the worth and dignity of individuals who devote their energies to the business and who depend on the business for their economic well-being. Principled strategy making requires that employee-related decisions be made equitably and compassionately, with concern for due process and for the impact that strategic change has on employees' lives. At best, the chosen strategy should promote employee interests as concerns compensation, career opportunities, job security, and overall working conditions. At worst, the chosen strategy should not disadvantage employees. Even in crisis situations, businesses have an ethical duty to minimize whatever hardships have to be imposed in the form of workforce reductions, plant closings, job transfers, relocations, retraining, and loss of income.

The *duty to the customer* arises out of expectations that attend the purchase of a good or service. Inadequate appreciation of this duty led to product liability laws and a host of regulatory agencies to protect consumers. All kinds of strategy-related ethical issues still abound, however. Should a seller voluntarily inform consumers that its product contains ingredients that, though officially approved for use, are suspected of having potentially harmful effects? Is it ethical for the makers of alcoholic beverages to sponsor college events, given that many college students are under 21? Is it ethical for cigarette manufacturers to advertise at all (even though it is legal)? Is it ethical to short-circuit product testing in order to rush new products to market? Is it ethical for manufacturers to stonewall efforts to recall products they suspect have faulty parts or defective designs? Is it ethical for supermarkets and department store retailers to lure customers with highly advertised "loss-leader" prices on a few select items, but then put high markups on popular or essential items?

Recently, a certain company's chief technology officer helped choose an Internet start-up company's products over that of rivals; the Internet company showed its gratitude by granting the officer rights to purchase 250 shares when the Internet company subsequently went public. The officer bought the shares at the initial offering price of $23; the stock closed at $84 at the end of the first day's trading, kept rising, then split—ultimately giving the officer a profit of about $58,000 when the officer sold the shares several months later. Is it ethical for a company to give gifts to individuals in customer companies when those individuals have had an influential role in selecting the company's products over those of its rivals? Is it ethical for the makers of athletic apparel and equipment to make substantial payments to college coaches in return for having the school's athletic teams wear their apparel or use their equipment?

A company's ethical *duty to suppliers* arises out of the market relationship that exists between them. They are both partners and adversaries. They are partners in the sense that the quality of suppliers' parts affects the quality of a firm's own product and in the sense that their businesses are connected. They are adversaries in the sense that the supplier wants the highest price and profit it can get while the buyer wants a cheaper price, better quality, and speedier service. A company confronts several ethical issues in its supplier relationships. Is it ethical to purchase goods from foreign suppliers who employ child labor, pay substandard wages, or have sweatshop working conditions in their facilities? Is it ethical for supermarket chains to demand "slotting fees" from food suppliers in return for placing their items in favorable shelf locations? Is it ethical to threaten to cease doing business with a supplier unless the supplier agrees not to do business with key competitors? Is it ethical to reveal one supplier's price quote to a rival supplier? Is it ethical to accept an offer to vacation at a supplier's beach house? Is it ethical to pay a supplier in cash? Is it ethical *not* to give present suppliers advance warning of the intent to discontinue using what they have supplied and to switch to components supplied by other enterprises?

A company's ethical *duty to the community at large* stems from its status as a member of the community and as an institution of society. Communities and society are reasonable in expecting businesses to be good citizens—to pay their fair share of taxes for fire and police protection, waste removal, streets and highways, and so on, and to exercise care in the impact their activities have on the environment, on society, and on the communities in which they operate. For example, is it ethical for a brewer of beer to advertise its products on TV at times when these ads are likely to be seen by underage viewers? (Anheuser-Busch responded to such concerns in late 1996, announcing it would no longer run its beer commercials on MTV.) Is it ethical for the manufacturers of firearms to encourage retired policemen and police departments to trade in or return automatic weapons whose manufacture has since been banned by Congress so they can gain access to a supply of resaleable weapons (a loophole in the laws allow them to traffic in such weapons that were manufactured prior to the bans)? Is it ethical for firearms makers to make just enough changes in the designs of their automatic weapons to escape the bans and prohibitions on automatic firearms instituted by Congress? Some years ago, an oil company was found to have spent $2 million on environmental conservation and $4 million advertising its virtue and good deeds—actions that seem deliberately manipulative and calculated to mislead.

A company's community citizenship is ultimately demonstrated by whether it refrains from acting in a manner contrary to the well-being of society and by the degree to which it supports community activities, encourages employees to participate in community activities, handles the health and safety aspects of its operations, accepts responsibility for overcoming environmental pollution, relates to regulatory bodies and employee unions, and exhibits high ethical standards. European consumer goods company Diageo PLC—the maker of Guinness beers and over 50 brands of liquors and wines sold across Europe and the United States—states that it has "a particular responsibility to encourage responsible use of alcohol as part of a healthy lifestyle. [We] are proud of the unique part that alcohol plays in the social lives and celebrations of many cultures. We also recognize that alcohol can be misused, and Diageo will be at the forefront of campaigns to promote moderate and sensible consumption."[22]

Living Up to Ethical Responsibilities   A management that truly cares about business ethics and corporate social responsibility is proactive rather than reactive in linking strategic action and ethics.[23] It steers away from ethically or morally questionable business opportunities and business practices. And it goes to considerable lengths to ensure that its actions reflect integrity and high ethical standards. If any of a company's constituencies conclude that management is not measuring up to ethical standards, they have recourse. Concerned investors can protest at the annual shareholders' meeting, appeal to the board of directors, or sell their stock. Concerned employees can unionize and bargain collectively, or they can seek employment elsewhere. Customers can switch to competitors. Suppliers can find other buyers. The community and society can do anything from staging protest marches and urging boycotts to stimulating political and governmental action.[24]

Illustration Capsule 12 indicates how the Kroger Company intends to satisfy its responsibilities to shareowners, employees, customers, suppliers, and the communities it serves.

TESTS OF A WINNING STRATEGY

What are the criteria for weeding out candidate strategies? How can a manager judge which strategic option is best for the company? What are the standards for determining whether a strategy is successful or not? Three tests can be used to evaluate the merits of one strategy over another:

---

[22]Quoted from information appearing on the company's website (www.diageo.com) as of August 1999.

[23]Joseph L. Badaracco, "The Discipline of Building Character," *Harvard Business Review* 76, no. 2 (March–April 1998), pp. 115–24.

[24]Downs, "Business Ethics: The Stewardship of Power."

illustration capsule 12
The Kroger Company's Commitments to Its Stakeholders

Kroger, one of the leading supermarket chains in the United States, has committed itself to pursuing its mission in a manner that satisfies its responsibilities to shareowners, employees, customers, suppliers, and the communities it serves. Company documents state:

> Our mission is to be a leader in the distribution and merchandising of food, health, personal care, and related consumable products and services. In achieving this objective, we will satisfy our responsibilities to shareowners, employees, customers, suppliers, and the communities we serve.
>
> We will conduct our business to produce financial returns that reward investment by shareowners and allow the Company to grow. Investments in retailing, distribution and food processing will be continually evaluated for their contribution to our corporate return objectives.
>
> We will constantly strive to satisfy consumer needs better than the best of our competitors. Operating procedures will reflect our belief that the organizational levels closest to the consumer are best positioned to respond to changing consumer needs.
>
> We will treat our employees fairly and with respect, openness and honesty. We will solicit and respond to their ideas and reward meaningful contributions to our success.
>
> We value America's diversity and will strive to reflect that diversity in our workforce, the companies with whom we do business, and customers we serve. As a company, we will convey respect and dignity to each individual.
>
> We will encourage our employees to be active, responsible citizens and will allocate researchers for activities that enhance the quality of life for our customers, our employees, and the communities we serve.

Source: Company website (www.kroger.com).

1. *The Goodness of Fit Test*—A good strategy has to be well matched to industry and competitive conditions, market opportunities and threats, and other aspects of the enterprise's external environment. At the same time, it has to be tailored to the company's resource strengths and weaknesses, competencies, and competitive capabilities. Unless a strategy exhibits tight fit with a company's external situation and internal circumstances, it is suspect and likely to produce less than the best possible business results.

2. *The Competitive Advantage Test*—A good strategy leads to sustainable competitive advantage. The bigger the competitive edge that a strategy helps build, the more powerful and effective it is.

3. *The Performance Test*—A good strategy boosts company performance. Two kinds of performance improvements are the most telling of a strategy's caliber: gains in profitability and gains in the company's competitive strength and long-term market position.

Strategic options that clearly come up short on one or more of these tests should be dropped from further consideration. The strategic option that best meets all three tests can be regarded as the best or most attractive strategic alternative. Once a strategic commitment is made and enough time elapses to see results, these same tests can be used to determine whether the chosen strategy qualifies as a winning strategy.

There are, of course, some additional criteria for judging the merits of a particular strategy: completeness and coverage of all the bases, internal consistency among all the pieces of strategy, clarity, the degree of risk involved, and flexibility. These criteria

Strategic Management Principle

The more a strategy fits the enterprise's external and internal situation, builds sustainable competitive advantage, and improves company performance, the more it qualifies as a winner.

are useful supplements and certainly ought to be looked at, but they can in no way re-place the three tests posed above.

key|points

Management's direction-setting tasks involve (1) charting a company's future strategic path, (2) setting objectives, and (3) crafting a strategy. Early on in the direction-setting process, managers need to address the question "What is our business and what will it be?" Management's views and conclusions about the organization's future course, the market position it should try to occupy, and the business activities to be pursued con-stitute a *strategic vision* for the company. A strategic vision indicates management's as-pirations for the organization, providing a panoramic view of "what businesses we want to be in, where we are headed, and the kind of company we are trying to create." It spells out a direction and describes the destination. Effective visions are clear, chal-lenging, and inspiring; they prepare a firm for the future, and they make sense in the marketplace. A well-conceived, well-worded mission/vision statement helps managers manage—serving as a beacon of the enterprise's long-term direction, helping channel organizational efforts and strategic initiatives along the path management has commit-ted to following, building a strong sense of organizational identity and purpose, and creating employee buy-in.

The second direction-setting task is to establish *strategic* and *financial objectives* for the organization to achieve. Objectives convert the mission statement and strategic vision into specific performance targets. The agreed-on objectives need to spell out precisely how much by when, and they need to require a significant amount of organi-zational stretch. Objectives are needed at all organizational levels.

The third direction-setting step entails *crafting a strategy* to achieve the objec-tives set in each area of the organization. A corporate strategy is needed to achieve corporate-level objectives; business strategies are needed to achieve business-unit performance objectives; functional strategies are needed to achieve the performance targets set for each functional department; and operating-level strategies are needed to achieve the objectives set in each operating and geographic unit. In effect, an orga-nization's strategic plan is a collection of unified and interlocking strategies. Typi-cally, the strategy-making task is more top-down than bottom-up. Lower-level strategies should contribute to the achievement of higher-level, companywide objectives.

Strategy is shaped by both external and internal considerations. The major external considerations are societal, political, regulatory, and community factors; competitive conditions and overall industry attractiveness; and the company's market opportunities and threats. The primary internal considerations are company strengths, weaknesses, and competitive capabilities; managers' personal ambitions, philosophies, and ethics; and the company's culture and shared values. A good strategy must be well matched to all these situational considerations. In addition, a good strategy must lead to sustain-able competitive advantage and improved company performance.

suggested|readings

Badaracco, Joseph L. "The Discipline of Building Character," *Harvard Business Review* 76, no. 2 (March–April 1998), pp. 115–24.

Brown, Shona L., and Kathleen M. Eisenhardt. *Competing on the Edge: Strategy as Structured Chaos.* Boston, MA: Harvard Business School Press, 1998.

Campbell, Andrew, and Laura Nash. *A Sense of Mission: Defining Direction for the Large Corporation.* Reading, MA: Addison-Wesley, 1993.

Collins, James C., and Jerry I. Porras. "Building Your Company's Vision." *Harvard Business Review* 74, no. 5 (September–October 1996), pp. 65–77.

Collins, Jim. "Turning Goals into Results: The Power of Catalytic Mechanisms." *Harvard Business Review* 77, no. 4 (July–August 1999), pp. 70–82.

Drucker, Peter. "The Theory of the Business." *Harvard Business Review* 72, no. 5 (September–October 1994), pp. 95–104.

Hamel, Gary. "Strategy as Revolution." *Harvard Business Review* 74 no. 4 (July–August 1996), pp. 69–82.

Hamel, Gary, and C. K. Prahalad. "Strategic Intent." *Harvard Business Review* 67, no. 3 (May–June 1989), pp. 63–76.

———. "Strategy as Stretch and Leverage." *Harvard Business Review* 71, no. 2 (March–April 1993), pp. 75–84.

Hammer, Michael, and James Champy. *Reengineering the Corporation.* New York: Harper Business, 1993, chapter 9.

Ireland, R. Duane, and Michael A. Hitt. "Mission Statements: Importance, Challenge, and Recommendations for Development." *Business Horizons* (May–June 1992), pp. 34–42.

Kahaner, Larry. "What You Can Learn from Your Competitors' Mission Statements." *Competitive Intelligence Review* 6, no. 4 (Winter 1995), pp. 35–40.

Kaplan, Robert S., and David P. Norton. "The Balanced Scorecard—Measures That Drive Performance." *Harvard Business Review* 70, no. 1 (January–February 1992), pp. 71–79.

Lipton, Mark. "Demystifying the Development of an Organizational Vision." *Sloan Management Review,* Summer 1996, pp. 83–92.

McTavish, Ron. "One More Time: What Business Are You In?" *Long Range Planning* 28, no. 2 (April 1995), pp. 49–60.

Mintzberg, Henry. "Crafting Strategy." *Harvard Business Review* 65, no. 4 (July–August 1987), pp. 66–77.

Mintzberg, Henry; Bruce Ahlstrand; and Joseph Lampel. *Strategy Safari: A Guided Tour through the Wilds of Strategic Management.* New York: Free Press, 1998.

Porter, Michael E. "Clusters and the New Economics of Competition," *Harvard Business Review* 76, no. 6 (November–December 1998), pp. 77–90.

———. "What Is Strategy?" *Harvard Business Review* 74, no. 6 (November–December 1996), pp. 65–67.

Shaw, Gordon; Robert Brown; and Philip Bromiley. "Strategic Stories: How 3M Is Rewriting Business Planning." *Harvard Business Review* 76, no. 3 (May–June 1998), pp. 41–50.

Tichy, N. M.; A. R. McGill; and L. St. Clair. *Corporate Global Citizenship.* San Francisco: New Lexington Press, 1997.

Wilson, Ian. "Realizing the Power of Strategic Vision." *Long Range Planning* 25, no. 5 (1992), pp. 18–28.

chapter | three

Industry and Competitive Analysis

Analysis is the critical starting point of strategic thinking.
—Kenichi Ohmae

Things are always different—the art is figuring out which differences matter.
—Laszlo Birinyi

Awareness of the environment is not a special project to be undertaken only when warning of change becomes deafening.
—Kenneth R. Andrews

It is not the strongest of the species that survive, nor the most intelligent, but the one most responsive to change.
—Charles Darwin

C rafting strategy is not a task in which managers can get by with opinions, good instincts, and creative thinking. Judgments about what strategy to pursue need to flow directly from *solid analysis* of a company's external environment and internal situation. The two most important situational considerations are (1) industry and competitive conditions and (2) a company's own competitive capabilities, resources, internal strengths and weaknesses, and market position.

All organizations operate in a *macroenvironment* consisting broadly of the economy at large, population demographics, societal values and lifestyles, governmental legislation and regulation, technological factors, and the company's immediate industry and competitive environment—as depicted in Figure 3.1. The

macroenvironment includes *all relevant forces* outside a company's boundaries—relevant in the sense that they are important enough to have a bearing on the decisions a company ultimately makes about its business model and strategy. While many forces in the macroenvironment are beyond a company's sphere of influence, company managements are nonetheless obliged to monitor them and adapt the company's strategy as may be needed. The forces in a company's macroenvironment having the biggest impact on a company's strategy, however, typically revolve around the company's immediate industry and competitive environment.

Figure 3.2 illustrates what is involved in sizing up a company's overall situation and deciding on a strategy. The analytical sequence is from strategic appraisal of the company's external and internal situation, to evaluation of alternatives, to choice of strategy. Accurate diagnosis of the company's situation is necessary managerial preparation for deciding on a sound long-term direction, setting appropriate objectives, and crafting a winning strategy. Without perceptive understanding of the strategic aspects of a company's external and internal environments, the chances are greatly increased

Managers are not prepared to decide on a long-term direction or a strategy until they have a keen understanding of the company's strategic situation—the exact nature of the industry and competitive conditions it faces and how these conditions match up with its resources and capabilities.

that managers will concoct a strategic game plan that doesn't fit the situation well, that holds little prospect for building competitive advantage, and that is unlikely to boost company performance.

This chapter examines the techniques of *industry and competitive analysis,* the term commonly used to refer to assessing the most strategically relevant aspects of a single-business company's macroenvironment. In Chapter 4, we'll cover the methods of *company situation analysis* and explore how to appraise the strategy-shaping aspects of a firm's internal environment and current market position.

---

figure 3.1   **A Company's Macroenvironment**

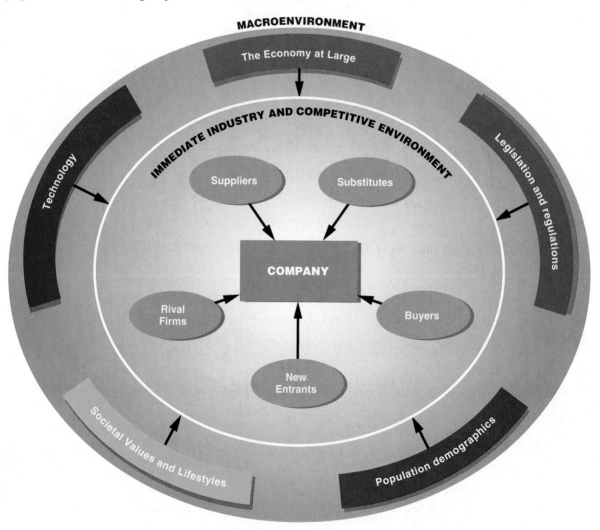

figure 3.2 **How Strategic Thinking and Strategic Analysis Lead to Good Strategic Choices**

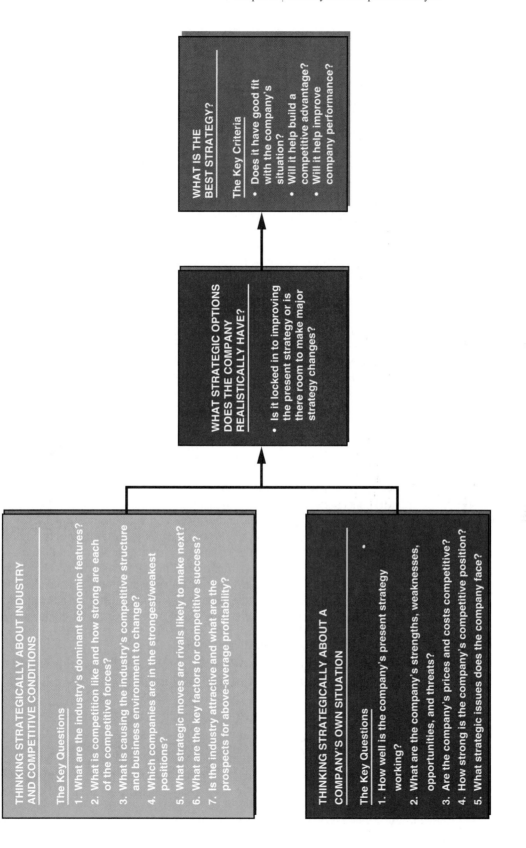

THINKING STRATEGICALLY ABOUT INDUSTRY AND COMPETITIVE CONDITIONS

The Key Questions

1. What are the industry's dominant economic features?
2. What is competition like and how strong are each of the competitive forces?
3. What is causing the industry's competitive structure and business environment to change?
4. Which companies are in the strongest/weakest positions?
5. What strategic moves are rivals likely to make next?
6. What are the key factors for competitive success?
7. Is the industry attractive and what are the prospects for above-average profitability?

THINKING STRATEGICALLY ABOUT A COMPANY'S OWN SITUATION

The Key Questions

1. How well is the company's present strategy working?
2. What are the company's strengths, weaknesses, opportunities, and threats?
3. Are the company's prices and costs competitive?
4. How strong is the company's competitive position?
5. What strategic issues does the company face?

WHAT STRATEGIC OPTIONS DOES THE COMPANY REALISTICALLY HAVE?

• Is it locked in to improving the present strategy or is there room to make major strategy changes?

WHAT IS THE BEST STRATEGY?

The Key Criteria

• Does it have good fit with the company's situation?
• Will it help build a competitive advantage?
• Will it help improve company performance?

THE METHODS OF INDUSTRY AND COMPETITIVE ANALYSIS

Industries differ widely in their economic characteristics, competitive situations, and future profit prospects. The economic and competitive character of the trucking industry bears little resemblance to that of discount retailing. The economic and competitive traits of the fast-food business have little in common with those of Internet service providers. The cable TV business is shaped by industry and competitive considerations radically different from those that dominate the soft-drink business.

The economic character of industries varies according to such factors as overall size and market growth rate, the pace of technological change, the geographic boundaries of the market (which can extend from local to worldwide), the number and size of buyers and sellers, whether sellers' products are virtually identical or highly differentiated, the extent to which costs are affected by economies of scale, and the types of distribution channels used to access buyers. Competitive forces can be moderate in one industry and fierce, even cutthroat, in another. Moreover, in some industries competition focuses on who has the best price, while in others competition is centered on quality and reliability (as in monitors for PCs and laptops) or product features and performance (as in digital cameras) or quick service and convenience (as in online shopping and fast foods) or brand reputation (as in laundry detergents, soft drinks, and beer). In other industries, the challenge is for companies to work cooperatively with suppliers, customers, and maybe even select competitors to create the next round of product innovations and open up whole new vistas of market opportunities (as we are witnessing in wireless telecommunications and personal computers).

An industry's economic traits and competitive conditions, and how they are expected to change, determine whether its profit prospects are poor, average, or excellent. Industry and competitive conditions differ so much that leading companies in unattractive industries can find it hard to earn respectable profits, while even weak companies in attractive industries can turn in good performances.

Industry and competitive analysis uses a tool kit of concepts and techniques to get a clear fix on key industry traits, the intensity of competition, the drivers of industry change, the market positions and strategies of rival companies, the keys to competitive success, and the industry's profit outlook. This tool kit provides a way of thinking strategically about any industry's overall situation and drawing conclusions about whether the industry represents an attractive investment for company funds. The analysis entails examining a company's business in the context of a much wider environment. Industry and competitive analysis aims at developing insightful answers to seven questions:

1. What are the industry's dominant economic features?
2. What is competition like and how strong are each of the competitive forces?
3. What is causing the industry's competitive structure and business environment to change?
4. Which companies are in the strongest/weakest positions?
5. What strategic moves are rivals likely to make next?
6. What are the key factors for competitive success?
7. Is the industry attractive and what are the prospects for above-average profitability?

The answers to these questions build understanding of a firm's surrounding environment and, collectively, form the basis for matching its strategy to changing industry conditions and competitive realities.

QUESTION 1: WHAT ARE THE INDUSTRY'S DOMINANT ECONOMIC FEATURES?

Because industries differ significantly in their basic character and structure, industry and competitive analysis begins with an overview of the industry's dominant economic features. Our working definition of the word *industry* is "a group of firms whose products have so many of the same attributes that they compete for the same buyers." The factors to consider in profiling an industry's economic features are fairly standard:

- Market size.
- Scope of competitive rivalry (local, regional, national, international, or global).
- Market growth rate and position in the business life-cycle (early development, rapid growth and takeoff, early maturity, maturity, saturation and stagnation, decline).
- Number of rivals and their relative sizes—is the industry fragmented into many small companies or concentrated and dominated by a few large companies?
- The number of buyers and their relative sizes.
- Whether and to what extent industry rivals have integrated backward and/or forward.
- The types of distribution channels used to access consumers.
- The pace of technological change in both production process innovation and new product introductions.
- Whether the products and services of rival firms are highly differentiated, weakly differentiated, or essentially identical.
- Whether companies can realize economies of scale in purchasing, manufacturing, transportation, marketing, or advertising.
- Whether key industry participants are clustered in a particular location—the world's best-known cluster locations include Silicon Valley, Hollywood, Italy (for the leather fashion industry), the wine-producing regions of California and France, and New York City (for financial services).[1]
- Whether certain industry activities are characterized by strong learning and experience effects ("learning by doing") such that unit costs decline as *cumulative* output grows.
- Whether high rates of capacity utilization are crucial to achieving low-cost production efficiency.
- Capital requirements and the ease of entry and exit.
- Whether industry profitability is above/below par.

Table 3.1 provides a sample profile of the economic character of the sulfuric acid industry, using the factors (or variations of them) listed above.

An industry's economic features are important because of the implications they have for strategy. For example, in capital-intensive industries where investment in a single plant can run several hundred million dollars, a firm can spread the burden of high fixed costs by pursuing a strategy that promotes high utilization of fixed assets to generate more revenue per dollar of fixed-asset investment. Thus, commercial airlines

> An industry's economic features help frame the window of strategic approaches a company can pursue.

---

[1]For more details on the competitive relevance of clustering, see Michael E. Porter, "Clusters and the New Economics of Competition," *Harvard Business Review* 76, no. 6 (November–December 1998), pp. 77–90.

table 3.1   A Sample Profile of the Dominant Economic Characteristics of the Sulfuric Acid Industry

Market size: $400–$500 million annual revenues; 4 million tons total volume.

Scope of competitive rivalry: Primarily regional; producers rarely sell outside a 250-mile radius of plant due to high cost of shipping long distances.

Market growth rate: 2–3 percent annually.

Stage in life cycle: Mature.

Number of companies in industry: About 30 companies with 110 plant locations and capacity of 4.5 million tons. Market shares of rivals range from a low of 3 percent to a high of 21 percent.

Customers: About 2,000 buyers; most are industrial chemical firms.

Degree of vertical integration: Mixed; 5 of the 10 largest companies are integrated backward into mining operations and also forward in that sister industrial chemical divisions buy over 50 percent of the output of their plants; all other companies are engaged solely in the production of sulfuric acid.

Ease of entry/exit: Moderate entry barriers exist in the form of capital requirements to construct a new plant of minimum efficient size (cost equals $10 million) and ability to build a customer base inside a 250-mile radius of plant.

Technology/innovation: Production technology is standard and changes have been slow; biggest changes are occurring in products using sulfuric acid—1–2 newly formulated specialty chemicals products with sulfuric acid as one of the ingredients are being introduced annually, accounting for nearly all of industry growth.

Product characteristics: Highly standardized; the products of different producers are essentially identical (buyers perceive little real difference from seller to seller except as may relate to time of delivery).

Scale economies: Moderate; all companies have virtually equal manufacturing costs but scale economies exist in shipping in multiple carloads to the same customer and in purchasing large quantities of raw materials.

Learning and experience effects: Not a factor in this industry.

Capacity utilization: Manufacturing efficiency is highest between 90 and 100 percent of rated capacity; below 90 percent utilization, unit costs run significantly higher.

Industry profitability: Subpar to average; the commodity nature of the industry's product results in intense price-cutting when demand slackens, but prices strengthen during periods of strong demand. Profits track the strength of demand for the industry's products.

Basic Concept

When strong economies of learning and experience result in declining unit costs as cumulative production volume builds, a strategy to become the largest-volume manufacturer can yield the competitive advantage of being the industry's lowest-cost producer.

employ strategies to boost the revenue productivity of their multimillion-dollar jets by cutting ground time at airport gates (to get in more flights per day with the same plane) and by using multitiered price discounts to fill up otherwise empty seats on each flight. In industries characterized by one product advance after another, companies must spend enough time and money on R&D to match their technical prowess and innovative capability with that of competitors. A strategy of continuous product innovation becomes a condition of survival.

In industries like semiconductors, strong *learning/experience* effects in manufacturing cause unit costs to decline about 20 percent each time *cumulative* production volume doubles. In other words, if the first 1 million chips costs $100 each to produce, by the time the company reaches a production volume of 2 million the chips would cost $80 each to produce (80 percent of $100), by a production volume of 4 million each chip would cost $64 to produce (80 percent of $80), and so on. When an industry is characterized by sizable economies of experience in its manufacturing operations, a company that initiates production of a new-style product and develops a

figure 3.3 **Comparison of Experience Curve Effects for 10 Percent, 20 Percent, and 30 Percent Cost Reductions for Each Doubling of Cumulative Production Volume**

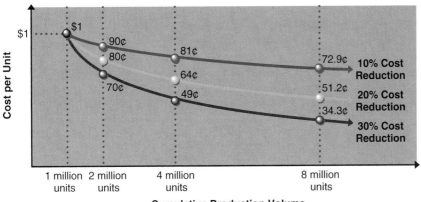

successful strategy to capture the largest market share gains sustainable competitive advantage as the low-cost producer.[2] The bigger the experience curve effect, the bigger the cost advantage of the company with the largest cumulative production volume, as shown in Figure 3.3.

Table 3.2 presents some additional examples of how an industry's economic traits are relevant to managerial strategy making.

QUESTION 2: WHAT IS COMPETITION LIKE AND HOW STRONG ARE EACH OF THE COMPETITIVE FORCES?

One important component of industry and competitive analysis involves delving into the industry's competitive process to discover what the main sources of competitive pressure are and how strong each competitive force is. This analytical step is essential because managers cannot devise a successful strategy without in-depth understanding of the industry's competitive character.

The Five Forces of Competition

Even though competitive pressures in various industries are never precisely the same, the competitive process works similarly enough to use a common analytical framework in gauging the nature and intensity of competitive forces. As Professor Michael

---

[2]There are a large number of studies of the size of the cost reductions associated with experience; the median cost reduction associated with a doubling of cumulative production volume is approximately 15 percent, but there is a wide variation from industry to industry. For a good discussion of the economies of experience and learning, see Pankaj Ghemawat, "Building Strategy on the Experience Curve," *Harvard Business Review* 64, no. 2 (March–April 1985), pp. 143–49.

table 3.2   Examples of the Strategic Importance of an Industry's Key Economic Features

Economic Feature	Strategic Importance
• Market size	• Small markets don't tend to attract big/new competitors; large markets often draw the interest of companies looking to acquire competitors with established positions in attractive industries.
• Market growth rate	• Fast growth breeds new entry; growth slowdowns spawn increased rivalry and a shake-out of weak competitors.
• Capacity surpluses or shortages	• Surpluses push prices and profit margins down; shortages pull them up.
• Industry profitability	• High-profit industries attract new entrants; depressed conditions encourage exit.
• Entry/exit barriers	• High barriers protect positions and profits of existing firms; low barriers make existing firms vulnerable to entry.
• Cost and importance of product	• More buyers will shop for lowest price on big-ticket items than on less important or expensive items.
• Standardized products	• Buyers have more power because it is easier to switch from seller to seller.
• Rapid technological change	• Raises risk factor; equipment and facilities may become obsolete before they wear out.
• Capital requirements	• Big requirements make investment decisions critical and create a barrier to entry and exit; timing becomes important.
• Vertical integration	• Raises capital requirements; often creates competitive differences and cost differences among fully versus partially versus nonintegrated firms.
• Economies of scale	• Increases volume and market share needed to be cost competitive.
• Rapid product innovation	• Shortens product life cycle; increases risk because of opportunities for rivals to bring out next-generation products quicker and leapfrog current market leader.

Porter of the Harvard Business School has convincingly demonstrated, the state of competition in an industry is a composite of *five competitive forces:*[3]

1. The rivalry among competing sellers in the industry.
2. The potential entry of new competitors.
3. The market attempts of companies in other industries to win customers over to their own *substitute* products.
4. The competitive pressures stemming from supplier–seller collaboration and bargaining.
5. The competitive pressures stemming from seller–buyer collaboration and bargaining.

Porter's *five-forces model,* depicted in Figure 3.4, is a powerful tool for systematically diagnosing the principal competitive pressures in a market and assessing how strong and important each one is. Not only is it the most widely used technique of competition analysis, but it is also relatively easy to understand and apply.

---

[3]For a thorough treatment of the five-forces model by its originator, see Michael E. Porter, *Competitive Strategy: Techniques for Analyzing Industries and Competitors* (New York: Free Press, 1980), chapter 1.

figure 3.4   **The Five-Forces Model of Competition: A Key Analytical Tool for Diagnosing the Competitive Environment**

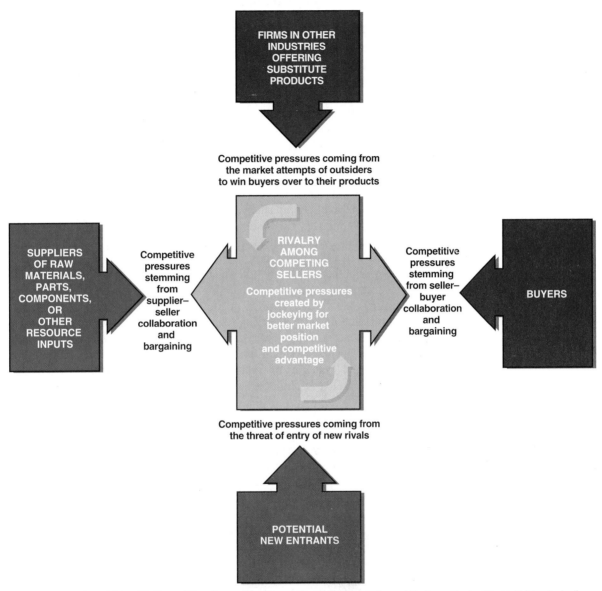

Source: Adapted from Michael E. Porter, "How Competitive Forces Shape Strategy," *Harvard Business Review* 57, no. 2 (March–April 1979), pp. 137–45.

The Rivalry among Competing Sellers   The strongest of the five competitive forces is *usually* the jockeying for position and buyer favor that goes on among rival sellers of a product or service. In some industries, cross-company rivalry is centered on price competition—competing to offer buyers the best (lowest) price is typical among Internet retailers and the sellers of such standard commodities as nails, plywood, sugar, printer paper, and gasoline. Occasionally, price competition can be so lively that market prices temporarily fall below unit costs, forcing losses on some or most rivals. In other industries, price competition is minimal to moderate and rivalry is focused on one or more of the following: offering buyers the most attractive combination of performance features (as occurs in digital cameras), being first to market with innovative products, outcompeting rivals with higher-quality or more durable products, offering buyers longer warranties (as in motor vehicles and replacement tires), providing superior after-the-sale service, or creating a stronger brand image (as in beer, cigarettes, bottled water, electronic brokerage, and quick-service restaurants).

Competitive jockeying among cross-company rivals can heat up when a competitor sees an opportunity to better please customers or is under pressure to improve its market share or profitability. *The intensity of rivalry among competing sellers is a function of how vigorously they employ such tactics as lower prices, snazzier features, expanded customer services, longer warranties, special promotions, and new product introductions.* Rivalry can range from friendly to cutthroat, depending on how frequently and how aggressively companies undertake fresh moves that threaten rivals' profitability. Ordinarily, industry rivals are clever at adding new wrinkles to their product offerings that enhance buyer appeal, and they persist in trying to exploit weaknesses in each other's market approaches.

Irrespective of whether rivalry is lukewarm or heated, every company is challenged to craft a successful strategy for competing—ideally, one that *produces a competitive edge over rivals* and strengthens its position with buyers. The big complication in most industries is that *the success of any one firm's strategy hinges on what strategies its rivals employ and the resources rivals are willing and able to put behind their strategic efforts.* The "best" strategy for one firm depends, in other words, on the competitive capabilities and strategies of rival companies. Such interdependence means that whenever one firm makes a strategic move, its rivals often retaliate with offensive or defensive countermoves.

Principle of Competitive Markets

Competitive jockeying among rival firms is a dynamic, ever-changing process as new offensive and defensive moves are initiated and emphasis swings from one blend of competitive weapons and tactics to another.

This pattern of action and reaction makes competitive rivalry a "war-games" type of contest conducted in a market setting according to the rules of fair competition. Indeed, from a strategy-making perspective, *competitive markets are economic battlefields,* with the intensity of cross-company rivalry ebbing and flowing as competitors initiate fresh offensive and defensive maneuvers and as they endeavor to catch buyers' attention with first one mix of weapons (price, performance features, customer service, and other appealing attributes) and then another. Cross-company rivalry is thus dynamic. The current competitive scene is ever-changing as companies act and react, sometimes in rapid-fire order and sometimes methodically, to outcompete one another and build customer loyalty.

Regardless of the industry, several common factors seem to influence the tempo of cross-company rivalry:[4]

1. *Rivalry intensifies as the number of competitors increases and as competitors become more equal in size and capability.* Competition is not as strong in PC operating systems, where Linux is one of the few challengers to Microsoft, as it is in fast foods and restaurants, where buyers have many choices. Up to a point, the greater the number of competitors, the greater the probability of fresh, creative strategic initiatives. In addition, when rivals are nearly equal in size and capability, they can usually

---

[4]These indicators of what to look for in evaluating the intensity of intercompany rivalry are based on Porter, *Competitive Strategy,* pp. 17–21.

compete on a fairly even footing, making it harder for one or two firms to win the competitive battle and dominate the market.

2. *Rivalry is usually stronger when demand for the product is growing slowly.* In a rapidly expanding market, there tends to be enough business for everybody to grow. Indeed, it may take all of a firm's financial and managerial resources just to keep abreast of the growth in buyer demand, let alone steal rivals' customers. But when growth slows or when market demand drops unexpectedly, expansion-minded firms and/or firms with excess capacity often cut prices and deploy other sales-increasing tactics, thereby igniting a battle for market share that can result in a shake-out of the weak and less efficient firms. The industry then consolidates into a smaller, but individually stronger, number of sellers.

3. *Rivalry is more intense when industry conditions tempt competitors to use price cuts or other competitive weapons to boost unit volume.* When a product is perishable, seasonal, or costly to hold in inventory, or when demand slacks off, competitive pressures build quickly anytime one or more firms decide to cut prices and dump excess supplies on the market. Likewise, whenever fixed costs account for a large fraction of total cost such that unit costs tend to be lowest at or near full capacity, then firms come under significant pressure to cut prices or otherwise try to boost sales. Unused capacity imposes a significant cost-increasing penalty because there are fewer units carrying the fixed-cost burden. In such cases, if market demand weakens or capacity utilization for some reason falls off, the pressure of rising unit costs can push rival firms into secret price concessions, special discounts, rebates, and other sales-increasing tactics, thus heightening competition.

4. *Rivalry is stronger when customers' costs to switch brands are low.* The lower the costs of switching, the easier it is for a rival seller to raid another seller's customers. High buyer switching costs, however, give sellers a more protected customer base and work against the efforts of rivals to promote brand switching among buyers.

5. *Rivalry is stronger when one or more competitors are dissatisfied with their market position and launch moves to bolster their standing at the expense of rivals.* Firms that are losing ground or in financial trouble often react aggressively by acquiring smaller rivals, introducing new products, boosting advertising, discounting prices, and so on. Such actions heighten cross-company rivalry and can trigger a hotly contested battle for market share.

6. *Rivalry increases in proportion to the size of the payoff from a successful strategic move.* The greater the benefits of going after a new opportunity, the more likely that one or more rivals will initiate moves to capture it. Competitive pressures nearly always intensify when several rivals start pursuing the same opportunity. For example, competition in online music sales is heating up with the entry of Amazon.com, barnesandnoble.com, Buy.com. Furthermore, the size of the strategic payoff can vary with the speed of retaliation. When competitors respond slowly (or not at all), the initiator of a fresh competitive strategy can reap benefits in the intervening period and perhaps gain a first-mover advantage that is not easily surmounted. The greater the benefits of moving first, the more likely some competitor will accept the risk and try it.

7. *Rivalry tends to be more vigorous when it costs more to get out of a business than to stay in and compete.* The higher the exit barriers (and thus the more costly it is to abandon a market), the stronger the incentive for existing rivals to remain and compete as best they can, even though they may be earning low profits or even incurring losses.

8. *Rivalry becomes more volatile and unpredictable the more diverse competitors are in terms of their visions, strategic intents, objectives, strategies, resources, and* *countries of origin.* A diverse group of sellers often contains one or more mavericks willing to rock the boat with unconventional moves and "rule-breaking" market approaches, thus generating a livelier and less predictable competitive environment. Globally competitive markets often contain rivals with different views about where the industry is headed and a willingness to employ perhaps radically different competitive approaches. Attempts by cross-border rivals to gain stronger footholds in each other's domestic markets usually boost the intensity of rivalry, especially when the aggressors have lower costs or products with more attractive features. For instance, Motorola has recently faced vigorous competition in cell phones from Europe-based Nokia and Ericcson, largely because these two companies bet on different cell phone technologies than Motorola and because, unlike Motorola, they moved aggressively to make their cell phones work on both analog and digital wireless systems.

9. *Rivalry increases when strong companies outside the industry acquire weak firms in the industry and launch aggressive, well-funded moves to transform their newly acquired competitors into major market contenders.* A concerted effort to turn a weak rival into a market leader nearly always entails launching well-financed strategic initiatives to dramatically improve the competitor's product offering, excite buyer interest, and win a much bigger market share—actions that, if successful, put added pressure on rivals to counter with fresh strategic moves of their own.

Two facets of rivalry need to be underscored. First, a powerful, successful competitive strategy employed by one rival greatly intensifies the competitive pressures on other rivals. Second, the frequency and vigor with which rivals use any and all competitive weapons at their disposal are major determinants of whether the competitive pressures associated with rivalry are cutthroat, fierce, strong, moderate, or weak. Rivalry can be characterized as *cutthroat* or *brutal* when competitors engage in protracted price wars or habitually employ other aggressive tactics that are mutually destructive to profitability. Rivalry can be considered *fierce* to *strong* when competitors are initiating frequent moves and countermoves in a battle for market share so vigorous that profit margins are being squeezed. Rivalry can be characterized as *moderate* when sellers are active in using the various weapons of competition at their command yet are still usually able to earn acceptable profits. Rivalry is *weak* when most companies in the industry are relatively well satisfied with their sales growth and market shares, rarely make concerted attempts to steal customers away from one another, and have comparatively attractive earnings and returns on investment.

The Potential Entry of New Competitors   New entrants to a market bring new production capacity, the desire to establish a secure place in the market, and sometimes substantial resources with which to compete.[5] Just how serious the competitive threat of entry is in a particular market depends on two classes of factors: *barriers to entry* and *the expected reaction of incumbent firms to new entry.* A barrier to entry exists whenever it is hard for a newcomer to break into the market or economic factors put a potential entrant at a disadvantage relative to its competitors. There are several types of entry barriers:[6]

● *Economies of scale*—Scale economies deter entry because they force potential competitors either to enter on a large scale (a costly and perhaps risky move) or to

---

[5]Michael E. Porter, "How Competitive Forces Shape Strategy," *Harvard Business Review* 57, no. 2 (March–April 1979), p. 138.

[6]Porter, *Competitive Strategy,* pp. 7–17.

accept a cost disadvantage and consequently lower profitability. Trying to overcome the disadvantages of small size by entering on a large scale at the outset can result in long-term overcapacity problems for the new entrant (until sales volume builds up), and it can so threaten the market shares of existing firms that they retaliate aggressively (with price cuts, increased advertising and sales promotion, and similar blocking actions) to maintain their positions. Either way, a potential entrant is discouraged by the prospect of lower profits. Entrants may encounter scale-related barriers not just in production but in advertising, marketing and distribution, financing, after-sale customer service, raw materials purchasing, and R&D as well.

- *Cost and resource disadvantages independent of size*—Existing firms may have cost and resource advantages not available to potential entrants. These advantages can include partnerships with the best and cheapest suppliers of raw materials and components, possession of patents and proprietary technology, existing plants built and equipped years earlier at lower costs, favorable locations, and lower borrowing costs.

- *Learning and experience curve effects*—When lower unit costs are partly or mostly a result of experience in producing the product and other learning curve benefits, new entrants face a potentially significant cost disadvantage competing against existing firms with more accumulated know-how.

- *Inability to match the technology and specialized know-how of firms already in the industry*—Successful entry may require technological capability not readily available to a newcomer or skills and know-how not easily learned by a newcomer. Key patents can effectively bar entry, as can lack of technically skilled personnel and an inability to execute complicated manufacturing techniques. Existing firms often carefully guard the know-how that gives them an edge in technology and manufacturing capability. Unless new entrants can gain access to such proprietary knowledge, they cannot compete on a level playing field.

- *Brand preferences and customer loyalty*—Buyers are often attached to established brands. Japanese consumers, for example, are fiercely loyal to Japanese brands of motor vehicles, electronics products, cameras, and film. European consumers have traditionally been loyal to European brands of major household appliances. High brand loyalty means that a potential entrant must commit to building a network of distributors and dealers, and then be prepared to spend enough money on advertising and sales promotion to overcome customer loyalties and build its own clientele. Establishing brand recognition and building customer loyalty can be a slow and costly process. In addition, if it is difficult or costly for a customer to switch to a new brand, a new entrant must persuade buyers that its brand is worth the switching costs. To overcome the switching-cost barrier, new entrants may have to offer buyers a discounted price or an extra margin of quality or service. All this can mean lower expected profit margins for new entrants—something that increases the risk to start-up companies dependent on sizable, early profits to support their new investments.

- *Capital requirements*—The larger the total dollar investment needed to enter the market successfully, the more limited the pool of potential entrants. The most obvious capital requirements are associated with manufacturing plants and equipment, working capital to finance inventories and customer credit, introductory advertising and sales promotion to establish a clientele, and cash reserves to cover start-up losses.

- *Access to distribution channels*—In the case of consumer goods, a potential entrant may face the barrier of gaining adequate access to consumers. Wholesale distributors may be reluctant to take on a product that lacks buyer recognition. A network of retail dealers may have to be set up from scratch. Retailers have to be convinced to give a new brand ample display space and an adequate trial period. The more existing producers tie up present distribution channels, the tougher entry will be. To overcome this barrier, potential entrants may have to "buy" distribution access by offering better margins to dealers and distributors or by giving advertising allowances and other promotional incentives. As a consequence, a potential entrant's profits may be squeezed unless and until its product gains enough acceptance that distributors and retailers want to carry it.

- *Regulatory policies*—Government agencies can limit or even bar entry by requiring licenses and permits. Regulated industries like cable TV, telecommunications, electric and gas utilities, radio and television broadcasting, liquor retailing, and railroads entail government-controlled entry. In international markets, host governments commonly limit foreign entry and must approve all foreign investment applications. Stringent government-mandated safety regulations and environmental pollution standards are entry barriers because they raise entry costs.

- *Tariffs and international trade restrictions*—National governments commonly use tariffs and trade restrictions (antidumping rules, local content requirements, and quotas) to raise entry barriers for foreign firms and protect domestic producers from competition. In 1996, due to tariffs imposed by the South Korean government, a Ford Taurus cost South Korean car buyers over $40,000. The government of India has required that 90 percent of the parts and components used in Indian truck assembly plants be made in India. And to protect European chip makers from low-cost Asian competition, European governments instituted a rigid formula for calculating floor prices for computer memory chips.

Whether an industry's entry barriers ought to be considered high or low depends on the resources and competencies possessed by the pool of potential entrants. Entry barriers can be formidable for start-up enterprises trying to compete against well-established companies. But interested outsiders may, given their resources, competencies, and brand-name recognition, see the industry's entry barriers as relatively easy to hurdle. Likewise, entry barriers may be low for current industry participants that are looking to enter areas of the overall market where they do not yet have a presence. A company already well-established in one market segment or geographic area may possess the resources, competencies, and competitive capabilities to hurdle the barriers of entering a different market segment or new geographic area. In evaluating the potential threat of entry, management must look at (1) how formidable the entry barriers are for each type of potential entrant—start-up enterprises, candidate companies in other industries, and current industry participants looking to expand their market reach—and (2) how attractive the profit prospects are for new entrants. *High profits act as a magnet to firms outside the industry, motivating potential entrants to commit the resources needed to hurdle entry barriers.*[7]

---

[7]When profits are sufficiently attractive, entry barriers are unlikely to be an effective entry deterrent. At most, they limit the pool of candidate entrants to enterprises with the requisite competencies and resources and with the creativity to fashion a strategy for competing with incumbent firms. For a good discussion of this point, see George S. Yip, "Gateways to Entry," *Harvard Business Review* 60, no. 5 (September–October 1982), pp. 85–93.

Even if a potential entrant has or can acquire the needed competencies and resources to attempt entry, it still faces the issue of how existing firms will react.[8] Will incumbent firms offer only passive resistance, or will they aggressively defend their market positions using price cuts, increased advertising, product improvements, and whatever else they can to give a new entrant (as well as other rivals) a hard time? A potential entrant can have second thoughts when financially strong incumbent firms send clear signals that they will stoutly defend their market positions against newcomers. A potential entrant may also turn away when incumbent firms can leverage distributors and customers to retain their business.

The best test of whether potential entry is a strong or weak competitive force in the marketplace is to ask if the industry's growth and profit prospects are attractive enough to induce additional entry. When the answer is no, potential entry is a weak competitive force. When the answer is yes and there are entry candidates with sufficient expertise and resources, then potential entry adds significantly to competitive pressures in the marketplace. The stronger the threat of entry, the more that incumbent firms are driven to fortify their positions against newcomers, endeavoring not only to protect their market shares but also to make entry more costly or difficult.

One additional point: *the threat of entry changes as the industry's prospects grow brighter or dimmer and as entry barriers rise or fall.* For example, the expiration of a key patent can greatly increase the threat of entry. A technological discovery can create an economy-of-scale advantage where none existed before or, alternatively, make it easier for newcomers to gain a market foothold—the Internet, for example, is making it much easier for new e-commerce retailers to compete against some of the strongest and best-known retail chains. New actions by incumbent firms to greatly bolster their e-commerce capabilities, increase advertising, strengthen distributor–dealer relations, step up R&D, or improve product quality can raise the roadblocks to entry. In international markets, entry barriers for foreign-based firms fall as tariffs are lowered, as host governments open up their domestic markets to outsiders, as domestic wholesalers and dealers seek out lower-cost foreign-made goods, and as domestic buyers become more willing to purchase foreign brands.

Principle of Competitive Markets
The threat of entry is stronger when entry barriers are low, when there's a sizable pool of entry candidates, when incumbent firms are unable or unwilling to vigorously contest a newcomer's efforts to gain a market foothold, and when a newcomer can expect to earn attractive profits.

Competitive Pressures from Substitute Products   Firms in one industry are quite often in close competition with firms in another industry because their respective products are good substitutes. The producers of eyeglasses compete with the makers of contact lenses and with eye specialists who perform laser surgery to correct vision problems. The sugar industry competes with companies that produce artificial sweeteners and high-fructose corn syrup. Cotton and wool producers are in head-on competition with the makers of polyester fabrics. Companies providing electric power are in competition with companies providing natural gas for such purposes as cooking, space heating, and water heating. Aspirin manufacturers compete against the makers of acetaminophen, ibuprofen, and other pain relievers. Newspapers are in competition with television in providing late-breaking news and with Internet sources in providing sports results, stock quotes, and job opportunities. E-mail is a substitute for the overnight document delivery services of FedEx, Airborne Express, and the U.S. Postal Service. Just how strong the competitive pressures are from substitute products depends on three factors: (1) whether attractively priced substitutes are available; (2) whether buyers view the substitutes as being satisfactory in terms of quality, performance, and other relevant attributes; and (3) whether buyers can switch to substitutes easily.

---

[8]Porter, "How Competitive Forces Shape Strategy," p. 140, and Porter, *Competitive Strategy,* pp. 14–15.

The presence of readily available and attractively priced substitutes creates competitive pressure by placing a ceiling on the prices an industry can charge for its product without giving customers an incentive to switch to substitutes and risking sales erosion.[9] This price ceiling, at the same time, puts a lid on the profits that industry members can earn unless they find ways to cut costs. When substitutes are cheaper than an industry's product, industry members come under heavy competitive pressure to reduce their prices and find ways to absorb the price cuts with cost reductions.

Principle of Competitive Markets

The competitive threat posed by substitute products is strong when substitutes are readily available and attractively priced, buyers believe substitutes have comparable or better features, and buyers' switching costs are low.

The availability of substitutes inevitably invites customers to compare quality, features, performance, ease of use, and other attributes as well as price. For example, ski boat manufacturers are experiencing strong competition from personal water-ski craft because water sports enthusiasts are finding that personal water-skis have exciting performance features that make them satisfying substitutes. The users of glass bottles and jars constantly weigh the performance trade-offs with plastic containers, paper cartons, and metal cans. Competition from substitute products pushes industry participants to heighten efforts to convince customers their product has attributes that are superior to those of substitutes.

Another determinant of the strength of competition from substitutes is how difficult or costly it is for the industry's customers to switch to a substitute.[10] Typical switching costs include extra price premiums, the costs of additional equipment, the time and cost in testing the quality and reliability of the substitute, the psychic costs of severing old supplier relationships and establishing new ones, payments for technical help in making the changeover, and employee retraining costs. If switching costs are high, sellers of substitutes must offer a major cost or performance benefit in order to entice the industry's customers away. When switching costs are low, it's much easier for sellers of substitutes to convince buyers to change over to their products.

As a rule, then, the lower the price of substitutes, the higher their quality and performance, and the lower the user's switching costs, the more intense the competitive pressures posed by substitute products. Good indicators of the competitive strength of substitute products are the rate at which their sales and profits are growing, the market inroads they are making, and their plans for expanding production capacity.

Competitive Pressures Stemming from Supplier Bargaining Power and Supplier-Seller Collaboration

Whether supplier–seller relationships represent a weak or strong competitive force depends on (1) whether suppliers can exercise sufficient bargaining power to influence the terms and conditions of supply in their favor, and (2) the extent of supplier–seller collaboration in the industry.

How Supplier Bargaining Power Can Create Competitive Pressures
Suppliers have little or no bargaining power or leverage over rivals whenever the items they provide are commodities available on the open market from numerous suppliers with ample capability to fill orders.[11] In such cases, it is relatively simple for rivals to obtain whatever is needed from any of several capable suppliers, perhaps dividing their purchases among two or more suppliers to promote lively competition for orders. Commodity product suppliers have market power only when supplies become quite tight and users are so anxious to secure what they need that they agree to terms more favorable to suppliers.

---

[9]Porter, "How Competitive Forces Shape Strategy," p. 142; and Porter, *Competitive Strategy,* pp. 23–24.
[10]Porter, *Competitive Strategy,* p. 10.
[11]Ibid., pp. 27–28.

Suppliers are likewise relegated to a weak bargaining position whenever there are good substitutes for the item they provide and buyers find it neither costly nor difficult to switch their purchases to the suppliers of alternative items. For example, soft-drink bottlers can counter the bargaining power of aluminum can suppliers on price or delivery by promoting greater use of plastic containers and introducing more attractive plastic container designs.

Suppliers also tend to have less leverage to bargain over price and other terms of sale when the company they are supplying is a *major customer.* In such cases, the well-being of suppliers is closely tied to the well-being of their major customers. Suppliers then have a big incentive to protect and enhance their customers' competitiveness via reasonable prices, exceptional quality, and ongoing advances in the technology of the items supplied.

In contrast, companies may have little bargaining power with *major suppliers.* Consider Intel's position as the world's dominant supplier of microprocessors for PCs. The microprocessor is not only an essential component but also a big part of the cost of a PC, as much as 20 percent in the case of chips for high-performance PCs. It thus matters a great deal to PC makers (and to PC buyers) whether Intel's price for its latest microprocessor chip is $600 or $300 and whether a chip of comparable quality and performance is available from Advanced Micro Devices (AMD), Intel's leading rival. When suppliers provide an item that accounts for a sizable fraction of the costs of an industry's product, is crucial to the industry's production process, or significantly affects the quality of the industry's product, suppliers have considerable influence on the competitive process. This is particularly true when a few large companies control most of the available supplies and have pricing leverage (as in microprocessors for PCs). Likewise, a supplier (or group of suppliers) possesses more bargaining leverage the more difficult or costly it is for users to switch to alternate suppliers. Big suppliers with good reputations and growing demand for their output are harder to wring concessions from than struggling suppliers striving to broaden their customer base or more fully utilize their production capacity.

Suppliers are also more powerful when they can supply a component more cheaply than industry members can make it themselves. For instance, most producers of outdoor power equipment (lawn mowers, rotary tillers, snowblowers, and so on) find it cheaper to source the small engines they need from outside manufacturers rather than make their own because the quantity they need is too little to justify the investment, master the process, and capture scale economies. Specialists in small-engine manufacture, by supplying many kinds of engines to the whole power equipment industry, obtain a big enough sales volume to fully realize scale economies, become proficient in all the manufacturing techniques, and keep costs well below what power equipment firms could realize making the items in-house. Small-engine suppliers, then, are in a position to price the item below what it would cost the user to self-manufacture but far enough above their own costs to generate an attractive profit margin. In such situations, the bargaining position of suppliers is strong *until* the volume of parts a user needs becomes large enough for the user to justify backward integration into self-manufacture of the component. Then the balance of power shifts from suppliers to users. The more credible the threat of such backward integration into the suppliers' business becomes, the more leverage users have in negotiating favorable terms with suppliers.

Another instance in which the relationship between industry members and suppliers is a notable competitive force is when suppliers, for one reason or another, do not have the capability or the incentive to provide items of high or consistent quality. For

Principle of Competitive Markets
The suppliers to a group of rival firms are a strong competitive force whenever they have sufficient bargaining power to put certain rivals at a competitive disadvantage based on the prices they can command, the quality and performance of the items they supply, or the reliability of their deliveries.

example, if a manufacturer's suppliers provide components that have a relatively high defect rate or that fail prematurely, they can so increase the warranty and defective goods costs of the manufacturer that its profits, reputation, and competitive position are seriously impaired.

How Collaborative Partnerships between Sellers and Suppliers Can Create Competitive Pressures   In more and more industries, rival sellers are electing to form long-term strategic partnerships and close working relationships with select suppliers in order to (1) promote just-in-time deliveries and reduced inventory and logistics costs, (2) speed the availability of next-generation components, (3) enhance the quality of the parts and components being supplied and reduce defect rates, and (4) reduce the supplier's costs and pave the way for lower prices on the items supplied. Such benefits can translate into competitive advantage for industry members who do the best job of managing supply chain relationships and form effective collaborative partnerships with suppliers.

Dell Computer has used strategic partnering with key suppliers as a major element in its strategy to be the world's low-cost supplier of branded PCs, servers, and workstations. Because Dell has managed its supply chain relationships in ways that contribute to a low-cost/high-quality competitive edge over rivals in components supply, Dell has put enormous competitive pressure on its PC rivals to try to imitate its supply chain management practices or else run the risk of being at a serious competitive disadvantage. Effective supply chain partnerships on the part of one or more industry rivals can thus become a major source of competitive pressure for other rivals.

Competitive Pressures Stemming from Buyer Bargaining Power and Seller–Buyer Collaboration

Whether seller–buyer relationships represent a weak or strong competitive force depends on (1) whether buyers have sufficient bargaining power to influence the terms and conditions of sale in their favor and (2) the extent and competitive importance of seller–buyer strategic partnerships in the industry.

How Buyer Bargaining Power Can Create Competitive Pressures   Just as with suppliers, the leverage that buyers have in negotiating favorable terms can range from strong to weak. Buyers have substantial bargaining leverage in a number of situations.[12] The most obvious is when buyers are large and purchase a sizable percentage of the industry's output. Typically, purchasing in large quantities gives a buyer enough leverage to obtain price concessions and other favorable terms.

> **Principle of Competitive Markets**
> Buyers are a strong competitive force when they are able to exercise bargaining leverage over price, quality, service, or other terms of sale.

Large retail chains like Wal-Mart, Circuit City, and The Home Depot typically have considerable negotiating leverage in purchasing products from manufacturers because of manufacturers' need for broad retail exposure and favorable shelf space for their products. Retailers may stock one or even several brands but rarely all available brands, so competition among rival manufacturers for the business of popular or high-volume retailers gives such retailers significant bargaining leverage. In the United States and Britain, supermarket chains have sufficient leverage to require food products manufacturers to make lump-sum payments to gain shelf space for new products. Motor vehicle manufacturers have significant bargaining power in negotiating to buy original equipment tires not only because they buy in large quantities but also because tire makers believe they gain an advantage in supplying replacement tires to vehicle owners if their tire brand is original equipment on the vehicle. "Prestige" buyers have

---

[12]Ibid., pp. 24–27.

a degree of clout in negotiating with sellers because a seller's reputation is enhanced by having prestige buyers on its customer list.

Even if buyers do not purchase in large quantities or offer a seller important market exposure or prestige, they may still have some degree of bargaining leverage in the following circumstances:

- *If buyers' costs of switching to competing brands or substitutes are relatively low*—Buyers who have the flexibility to fill their needs by switching brands or sourcing from several sellers often have negotiating room with sellers. When the products of rival sellers are virtually identical, it is relatively easy for buyers to switch from seller to seller at little or no cost and anxious sellers may be willing to make concessions to win a buyer's business. However, if the products of rival sellers are strongly differentiated, buyers may be less able to switch without incurring sizable changeover costs; an alert seller may conclude, often correctly, that the customer is locked in to using its product and therefore may not be inclined to make any substantive concessions.

  > High switching costs create buyer lock-in and weaken a buyer's bargaining power.

- *If the number of buyers is small or if a customer is particularly important to a seller*—The smaller the number of buyers, the less easy it is for sellers to find alternatives when a customer is lost. The prospect of losing a customer not easily replaced often makes a seller more willing to grant concessions of one kind or another.

- *If buyers are well-informed about sellers' products, prices, and costs*—The more information buyers have, the better bargaining position they are in. The mushrooming availability of information on the Internet is giving added bargaining power to individuals. It is relatively easy for buyers to use the Internet to compare prices and features of motor vehicles, obtain mortgages and loans, and purchase big-ticket items such as digital cameras. Bargain-hunting individuals can shop around for the best deal on the Internet and use that information to negotiate with sellers.

- *If buyers pose a credible threat of integrating backward into the business of sellers*—Companies like Anheuser-Busch, Coors, and Heinz have integrated backward into metal can manufacturing to gain bargaining power in obtaining the balance of their can requirements from otherwise powerful metal can manufacturers. Retailers gain bargaining power by stocking and promoting their own private-label brands alongside manufacturers' name brands. Wal-Mart, for example, has elected to compete against Procter & Gamble, its biggest supplier, by introducing its own brand of laundry detergent called Sam's American Choice, which is priced about 25 to 30 percent lower than P&G's Tide.

- *If buyers have discretion in whether and when they purchase the product*—If consumers are unhappy with the sticker prices of new motor vehicles, they can delay purchase or buy a used vehicle instead. If business customers are not happy with the prices or security features of electronic bill payment software systems, they can either delay purchase until next-generation products become available or attempt to develop their own software in-house. If college students believe that the prices of new textbooks are too high, they can purchase used copies.

Buyers typically have weak bargaining power when they buy infrequently or in small quantities and when they face high costs to switch brands. High switching costs can keep a buyer locked in to the present brand. For example, companies that have bought Compaq or Hewlett-Packard engineering and graphics workstations that use

Microsoft's Windows operating systems are not strong candidates to switch to Sun Microsystems' workstation models that run on a UNIX operating system. Switching from Windows to UNIX entails considerable time and relearning on the part of users and can also entail having to abandon all the Windows-based engineering and graphics application software that the user has accumulated over the years and replace it with software applications written for a UNIX-based operating system.

A final point to keep in mind is that *not all buyers of an industry's product have equal degrees of bargaining power with sellers*, and some may be less sensitive than others to price, quality, or service differences among competing sellers. For example, independent tire retailers have less bargaining power in purchasing tires than do Honda, Ford, and DaimlerChrysler (which buy in much larger quantities), and they are also less quality sensitive. Motor vehicle manufacturers are very particular about tire quality and tire performance because of the effects on vehicle performance, and they drive a hard bargain with tire manufacturers on both price and quality. Apparel manufacturers confront significant bargaining power when selling to retail chains like Kmart or Sears or Macy's, but they can command much better prices selling to small owner-managed apparel boutiques.

How Collaborative Partnerships between Sellers and Buyers Can Create Competitive Pressures   Partnerships between sellers and buyers are an increasingly important element of the competitive picture in *business-to-business relationships* as opposed to business-to-consumer relationships. Many sellers that provide items to business customers have found it in their mutual interest to collaborate closely on such matters as just-in-time deliveries, order processing, electronic invoice payments, and online sharing of sales at the cash register. Wal-Mart, for example, provides the manufacturers with whom it does business (like Procter & Gamble) with daily sales data from each of its stores so that they can replenish inventory stocks on time. Dell Computer has partnered with its largest customers to create online systems for over 50,000 corporate customers, providing their employees with information on approved product configurations, global pricing, paperless purchase orders, real-time order tracking, invoicing, purchasing history, and other efficiency tools. Dell also loads a customer's software at the factory and installs asset tags so that customer setup time on the PCs it orders is minimal and helps customers migrate their PC systems to next-generation hardware and software. Dell's partnerships with its customers have put significant competitive pressure on other PC makers to develop packages of offerings to corporate customers that will compare favorably with what Dell offers.

Strategic Implications of the Five Competitive Forces

The special contribution of the five-forces model is the thoroughness with which it exposes what competition is like in a given market—the strength of each of the five competitive forces, the nature of the competitive pressures comprising each force, and the overall structure of competition. *As a rule, the stronger the collective impact of competitive forces, the lower the combined profitability of participant firms.* The most brutally competitive situation occurs when the five forces create market conditions tough enough to impose prolonged subpar profitability or even losses on most or all firms. The competitive structure of an industry is clearly "unattractive" from a profit-making standpoint if rivalry among sellers is very strong, low entry barriers are allowing new rivals to gain a market foothold, competition from substitutes is strong, and both suppliers and customers are able to exercise considerable bargaining leverage. These conditions are approximated in tire manufacturing and apparel, where profit margins have historically been thin.

In contrast, when competitive forces are not collectively strong, the competitive structure of the industry is "favorable" or "attractive" from the standpoint of earning superior profits. The "ideal" competitive environment is one in which both suppliers and customers are in weak bargaining positions, there are no good substitutes, entry barriers are relatively high, and rivalry among present sellers is only moderate. However, even when some of the five competitive forces are strong, an industry can be competitively attractive to those firms whose market position and strategy provide a good enough defense against competitive pressures to preserve their ability to earn above-average profits.

To contend successfully, managers must craft strategies that shield the firm as much as possible from the five competitive forces and that help make the rules, put added pressure on rivals, and perhaps even define the business model for the industry. Managers cannot expect to develop winning competitive strategies without first identifying what competitive pressures exist, gauging the relative strength of each, and gaining a deep understanding of the industry's whole competitive structure. The five-forces model is a powerful tool for giving strategy makers the competitive insights they need to build a successful enterprise—ideally one that enjoys a sustainable competitive advantage.

> A company's competitive strategy is increasingly effective the more it provides good defenses against the five competitive forces, shifts competitive pressures in ways that favor the company, and helps create sustainable competitive advantage.

QUESTION 3: WHAT IS CAUSING THE INDUSTRY'S COMPETITIVE STRUCTURE AND BUSINESS ENVIRONMENT TO CHANGE?

An industry's economic features and competitive structure say a lot about its fundamental character but very little about the ways in which its environment may be changing. All industries are characterized by trends and new developments that gradually or speedily produce changes important enough to require a strategic response from participating firms. The popular hypothesis about industries going through a life cycle helps explain industry change but is still incomplete.[13] The life-cycle stages are strongly keyed to changes in the overall industry growth rate (which is why such terms as *rapid growth, early maturity, saturation,* and *decline* are used to describe the stages). Yet there are more causes of industry change than an industry's position in the life cycle.

The Concept of Driving Forces

While it is important to judge what growth stage an industry is in, there's more analytical value in identifying the specific factors causing fundamental industry and competitive adjustments. Industry and competitive conditions change because forces are in motion that create incentives or pressures for change.[14] The most dominant forces are called **driving forces** because they have the biggest influence on what kinds of changes will take place in the industry's structure and competitive environment. "Driving

> **Basic Concept**
> Industry conditions change because important forces are driving industry participants (competitors, customers, or suppliers) to alter their actions; the *driving forces* in an industry are the *major underlying causes* of changing industry and competitive conditions.

---

[13]For a more extended discussion of the problems with the life-cycle hypothesis, see Porter, *Competitive Strategy,* pp. 157–62.

[14]Porter, *Competitive Strategy,* p. 162.

forces" analysis has two steps: identifying what the driving forces are and assessing the impact they will have on the industry.

The Most Common Driving Forces   Many events can affect an industry powerfully enough to qualify as driving forces. Some are unique and specific to a particular industry situation, but most drivers of change fall into one of the following categories:[15]

- *The Internet and the new e-commerce opportunities and threats it breeds in the industry*—The Internet is unquestionably spawning a sweeping business revolution that alters industry boundaries, opens up all kinds of new business-to-business and business-to-consumer market opportunities and threats, sparks competition from new and entirely different breeds of enterprises, and mandates fundamental changes in business practices. Scarcely any industry or company is unaffected. But the transformation that the Internet is producing varies from industry to industry and company to company, and the industry and competitive implications are continuously evolving as new Internet-related technologies emerge and new Internet-related products hit the market. The challenge here is to assess how growing use of the Internet will alter the industry and competitive landscape. In many industries, the role and impact of the Internet is a critical, if not *the* critical, driver that must be factored into the strategy-making equation. Illustration Capsule 13 explains the power of the Internet and Internet technologies to reshape an industry's environment.

- *Increasing globalization of the industry*—Industries move toward globalization for any of several reasons. One or more nationally prominent firms may launch aggressive long-term strategies to win a globally dominant market position and precipitate a race for world leadership among the industry's major rivals. Demand for the industry's product may start to blossom in more and more countries. Countries may decide to reduce trade barriers or open up once-closed markets to foreign competitors—as is occurring in many parts of Europe, Latin America, and Asia; tariff reductions, deregulation, and privatization of government-owned enterprises bring local competitors eyeball-to-eyeball with ambitious global companies. The spread of technological know-how may pave the way for lesser-known companies in developing countries to enter the industry arena on an international or global scale. Significant differences in labor costs among countries may create a strong reason to locate global-scale plants for labor-intensive products in low-wage countries and use these plants to supply market demand across the whole world. Wages in China, Taiwan, Singapore, Mexico, and Brazil, for example, are about one-fourth those in the United States, Germany, and Japan.

  Significant cost economies may accrue to firms with world-scale volumes as opposed to national-scale volumes. Multinational companies with the ability to transfer their production, marketing, and management know-how from country to country at very low cost can sometimes gain a significant competitive advantage over domestic-only competitors. As a consequence, global competition usually shifts the pattern of competition among an industry's key players, favoring some and disadvantaging others.

  Globalization is most likely to be a driving force in industries (1) where scale economies are so large that rival companies need to market their product in many country markets to gain enough volume to drive unit costs down; (2) where low-cost

---

[15]Much of what follows draws on the discussion in Porter, *Competitive Strategy,* pp. 164–83.

illustration capsule 13

How the Internet and New Internet-Related Technologies Are Changing the Business Landscape: Classic Examples of a Driving Force

Here are three examples of how the Internet is opening up new market opportunities, affecting competition, creating a fundamentally different business environment, and prompting companies to incorporate the capabilities of online technology to transform the way they do business.

TRAVEL BY INTERNET

Traditionally, if you wanted to book a flight or a cruise, you'd call an airline or visit your local travel agent. However, the Internet has changed the strategies used by the travel industry to attract customers.

Consumers who visit the websites for Expedia or Travelocity have a wide range of trip choices at low prices. The companies are profitable because travel "is a virtual product that can be distributed 100 percent electronically, it has complicated pricing, and it's research intensive," says Terrell Jones, Travelocity's CEO.

While online retailers have folded, online travel agencies have survived and begun to diversify into cruises and complete travel packages. USA Networks, which owns the online agency Expedia, is looking to combine several areas of entertainment so that a consumer can book a flight, see a list of events for the destination, and buy tickets for events through Ticketmaster, also owned by USA Networks.

WEYERHAEUSER'S DOORBUILDER

Some years ago, Weyerhaeuser Company's door factory in Wisconsin was besieged with high costs, slack sales, and poor employee morale. The plant—which cuts, glues, drills, and shapes customized doors according to each buyer's order—was plagued with hammering out the details of customer orders over a period of weeks and months since there were over 2 million different door configurations given the options for sizes, styles, veneer color, and hardware. Pricing was a calculation nightmare. Orders, once finalized, were stapled to each door on the production floor, and many order forms would get torn off or lost at various times during production.

Shrewd use of the Internet and creation of a company intranet turned things around. Weyerhaeuser managers installed a state-of-the-art in-house system called DoorBuilder that uses the Internet to compare materials prices and availability from different suppliers, allows customers to design and customize doors online and obtain instant pricing, lets customers submit orders at the plant's website, and checks the order for possible errors (such as whether the desired door hinge conforms with building codes in a particular location). Internally, DoorBuilder has the capability to check plant inventories for all the needed components, determine the cost-price-profit margin on each custom-built door, flag less profitable or unprofitable orders, screen customers' creditworthiness, calculate the volumes a customer has ordered over a period of time to determine how profitable each customer is, track orders as they move through the plant, and completely fill 97 percent of all customer orders on time (up from 40 percent before DoorBuilder).

Since the use of DoorBuilder began, the plant's share of the U.S. commercial door market has gone from 12 to 26 percent and its return on net assets has increased from 2 to 27 percent, which compares very favorably with the companywide objective of 17 percent.

XML FORMAT FOR WEB PAGE CREATION

The Newspaper Association of America is using extensible markup language (XML) for creating Web pages. XML, which is rapidly displacing hypertext markup language (HTML), allows people to find classified jobs or real estate listings from multiple newspapers with a single search. Use of XML enables the exchange of data between otherwise incompatible software systems of different enterprises. Thus, different newspapers can link their classified ads into a single searchable database.

Likewise, XML enables component suppliers, manufacturers, distributors, and end users to exchange data and link their databases, opening up a wealth of new possibilities. A website company could gather a fee schedule and list of routes and timetables from UPS, FedEx, and dozens of other transportation providers and offer business customers point-to-point global delivery services without owning a single truck, airplane, cargo vessel, or railcar. XML enables cyberfirms to offer such services as payment processing in multiple currencies, electronic tax processing for a variety of jurisdictions, and sophisticated searches and analyses of the Securities and Exchange Commission's huge Edgar database of corporate financial filings.

Sources: Greg Dalton, "Airlines Stall While Online Travel Sites Glide," *TheStandard.com,* July 19, 2001; Derek Caney, "USA Networks to Buy Stake in Expedia," Reuters, July 17, 2001; Katherine Hobson, "Bucking the E-Biz Trend," *U.S. News & World Report,* June 4, 2001, pp. 36–38; *Business Week* E.BIZ, July 26, 1999, pp. EB 32–EB 38; and *The Wall Street Journal,* September 16, 1999, pp. B1, B4, and B6.

production is a critical consideration (making it imperative to locate manufacturing facilities in countries where the lowest costs can be achieved); (3) where one or more globally ambitious companies are pushing hard to gain a significant competitive position in as many attractive country markets as they can; (4) where local governments are privatizing government-owned monopolies (e.g., in telecommunications and energy) and opening up their once-closed local markets to competition; and (5) where critical natural resources and raw material supplies (e.g., crude oil, copper, and cotton) are scattered all over the globe.

Globalization has triggered a frantic, fast-paced race for global market leadership in credit cards, PCs, motor vehicles, telecommunications (long-distance telephone service, Internet access, electronic communications), refined petroleum products, and energy.

- *Changes in the long-term industry growth rate*—Shifts in industry growth up or down are a driving force for industry change, affecting the balance between industry supply and buyer demand, entry and exit, and the character and strength of competition. An upsurge in long-term demand triggers a race for growth among established firms and newcomers attracted by the prospects for higher growth. Competition becomes a contest of who can capture the growth opportunities and win a place among the market leaders. A shrinking market heightens competitive pressures, producing an often intense battle for market share and inducing mergers and acquisitions that result in industry consolidation to a smaller number of participants. Some companies may exit the industry and those remaining may be forced to close less efficient plants and retrench to a smaller production base.

- *Changes in who buys the product and how they use it*—Shifts in buyer demographics and new ways of using the product can alter the state of competition by forcing adjustments in customer service offerings (credit, technical assistance, maintenance and repair); opening the way to market the industry's product through a different mix of dealers and retail outlets; and prompting producers to broaden or narrow their product lines, bringing different sales and promotion approaches into play. The mushrooming popularity of the Internet at home and at work is creating new opportunities for electronic shopping, online brokerage services, e-mail services, bulletin board services, data services, and Internet-provider services. The changing demographics generated by longer life expectancies are creating growth markets for residential golf resorts, retirement planning services, mutual funds, and health care.

- *Product innovation*—Product innovation can shake up the structure of competition by broadening an industry's customer base, rejuvenating industry growth, and widening the degree of product differentiation among rival sellers. Successful new product introductions strengthen the market position of the innovating companies, usually at the expense of companies that stick with their old products or are slow to follow with their own versions of the new product. Product innovation has been a key driving force for makers of personal computers, PC software, digital cameras, golf clubs, video games, toys, prescription drugs, frozen foods, and mobile phones.

- *Technological change*—Advances in technology can dramatically alter an industry's landscape, making it possible to produce new and better products at lower cost and opening up whole new industry frontiers. Technological developments can also produce competitively significant changes in capital requirements, minimum efficient plant sizes, distribution channels and distribution logistics, and learning or experience curve effects.

- *Marketing innovation*—When firms are successful in introducing new ways to market their products, they can spark a burst of buyer interest, widen industry demand, increase product differentiation, and lower unit costs—any or all of which can alter the competitive positions of rival firms and force strategy revisions. In today's world, the Internet is the vehicle for all kinds of marketing innovations.

- *Entry or exit of major firms*—The entry of one or more foreign companies into a market once dominated by domestic firms nearly always shakes up competitive conditions. Likewise, when an established domestic firm from another industry attempts entry either by acquisition or by launching its own start-up venture, it usually applies its skills and resources in some innovative fashion that pushes competition in new directions. Entry by a major firm often produces a new ballgame, not only with new key players but also with new rules for competing. Similarly, exit of a major firm changes the competitive structure by reducing the number of market leaders (perhaps increasing the dominance of the leaders who remain) and causing a rush to capture the exiting firm's customers.

- *Diffusion of technical know-how across more companies and more countries*—As knowledge about how to perform a particular activity or execute a particular manufacturing technology spreads, any technically based competitive advantage held by firms originally possessing this know-how erodes. The diffusion of such knowledge can occur through scientific journals, trade publications, on-site plant tours, word-of-mouth among suppliers and customers, and the hiring away of knowledgeable employees. It can also occur when those possessing technological know-how license others to use it for a royalty fee or team up with a company interested in turning the technology into a new business venture. Quite often, technological know-how can be acquired by simply buying a company that has the wanted skills, patents, or manufacturing capabilities.

  In recent years technology transfer across national boundaries has emerged as one of the most important driving forces in globalizing markets and competition. As companies worldwide gain access to technical know-how, they upgrade their manufacturing capabilities in a long-term effort to compete head-on against established companies. Examples of where technology transfer has turned a largely domestic industry into an increasingly global one include automobiles, tires, consumer electronics, telecommunications, and computers.

- *Changes in cost and efficiency*—Widening or shrinking differences in the costs and efficiency among key competitors tends to dramatically alter the state of competition. The low cost of e-mail and fax transmission has put mounting competitive pressure on the relatively inefficient and high-cost operations of the U.S. Postal Service—sending a one-page fax is cheaper and far quicker than sending a first-class letter; sending e-mail is faster and cheaper still. In the electric power industry, sharply lower costs to generate electricity at newly constructed combined-cycle generating plants has put older coal-fired and gas-fired plants under the gun to lower their production costs to remain competitive. E-tailing can have lower-cost economics than brick-and-mortar retailing. In fact, use of wired networks (the Internet and company intranets) is radically transforming the cost structure of doing business in industry after industry.

- *Growing buyer preferences for differentiated products instead of a commodity product (or for a more standardized product instead of strongly differentiated products)*—A shift to differentiated products is signaled when sellers are able to win a bigger and more loyal buyer following by offering made-to-order products, introducing new features, making style changes, offering options and accessories, and creating image differences via advertising and packaging. We have seen growing numbers of buyers decide that a customized "made-to-order" PC suits them better than standardized off-the-shelf models; a similar shift may be happening in car buying where several car manufacturers and online sellers are offering made-to-order vehicles. When a shift from standardized to differentiated products occurs, the driver of change is the contest among rivals to cleverly outdifferentiate one another.

On the other hand, buyers sometimes decide that a budget-priced, mostly look-alike product suits their requirements as well as or better than a premium-priced product with lots of snappy features and personalized services. Online brokers, for example, have used the lure of cheap commissions to attract many investors willing to place their own buy–sell orders via the Internet; growing acceptance of online trading has put significant competitive pressures on full-service brokers whose business model has always revolved around convincing clients of the value of asking for personalized advice from professional brokers and paying their sharply higher high commission fees to make trades. Pronounced shifts toward greater product standardization usually spawn lively price competition and force rival sellers to drive down their costs to maintain profitability. The lesson here is that competition is driven partly by whether the market forces in motion are acting to increase or decrease product differentiation.

- *Regulatory influences and government policy changes*—Government regulatory actions can often force significant changes in industry practices and strategic approaches. Deregulation has proved to be a potent procompetitive force in the airline, banking, natural gas, telecommunications, and electric utility industries. Government efforts to reform Medicare and health insurance have become potent driving forces in the health care industry. In international markets, host governments can drive competitive changes by opening up their domestic markets to foreign participation or closing them off to protect domestic companies.

- *Changing societal concerns, attitudes, and lifestyles*—Emerging social issues and changing attitudes and lifestyles can be powerful instigators of industry change. Growing antismoking sentiment has emerged as the major driver of change in the tobacco industry; initiatives for stricter gun control are having a big impact on gun makers. Consumer concerns about salt, sugar, chemical additives, saturated fat, cholesterol, and nutritional value have forced food producers to revamp food-processing techniques, redirect R&D efforts into the use of healthier ingredients, and compete in coming up with nutritional, good-tasting products. Safety concerns have transformed safety features into a competitive asset in the automobile, toy, and outdoor power equipment industries, to mention a few. Increased interest in physical fitness has spawned whole new industries in exercise equipment, mountain biking, outdoor apparel, sports gyms and recreation centers, vitamin and nutrition supplements, and medically supervised diet programs. Social concerns about air and water pollution have forced industries to incorporate expenditures for controlling environmental pollution into their cost structures. Shifting societal concerns, attitudes, and lifestyles alter the pattern of competition, usually favoring those players that respond quickly and creatively with products targeted to the new trends and conditions.

- *Reductions in uncertainty and business risk*—A young, emerging industry is typically characterized by unproven cost structure, much uncertainty over potential market size, how much time and money will be needed to surmount technological problems, and what distribution channels and buyer segments to emphasize.

Emerging industries tend to attract only risk-taking entrepreneurial companies. Over time, however, if the business model of industry pioneers proves profitable and market demand for the product appears durable, more conservative firms are usually enticed to enter the market. Often, these later entrants are large, financially strong firms looking to invest in attractive growth industries.

Lower business risks and less industry uncertainty also affect competition in international markets. In the early stages of a company's entry into foreign markets, conservatism prevails and firms limit their downside exposure by using less risky strategies like exporting, licensing, joint marketing agreements, and collaborative partnerships and joint ventures with local companies to accomplish entry. Then, as experience accumulates and perceived risk levels decline, companies move more boldly and more independently, making acquisitions, constructing their own plants, putting in their own sales and marketing capabilities to build strong competitive positions in each country market, and beginning to link the strategies in each country to create a more globalized strategy.

The many different *potential driving forces* explain why it is too simplistic to view industry change only in terms of the life-cycle model and why a full understanding of the *causes* underlying the emergence of new competitive conditions is a fundamental part of industry analysis.

However, while many forces of change may be at work in a given industry, no more than three or four are likely to qualify as driving forces in the sense that they will act as *the major determinants* of why and how the industry is changing. Thus, strategic analysts must resist the temptation to label everything they see changing as a driving force; the analytical task is to evaluate the forces of industry and competitive change carefully enough to separate major factors from minor ones.

> The task of driving-forces analysis is to separate the major causes of industry change from the minor ones; usually no more than three or four factors qualify as driving forces.

The Link between Driving Forces and Strategy Sound analysis of an industry's driving forces is a prerequisite to sound strategy making. Without keen awareness of what external factors will produce the biggest potential changes in the company's business over the next one to three years, managers are ill prepared to craft a strategy tightly matched to emerging conditions. Similarly, if managers are uncertain about the implications of each driving force or if their views are incomplete or off-base, it's difficult for them to craft a strategy that is responsive to the driving forces and their consequences for the industry. So driving-forces analysis is not something to take lightly; it has practical strategy-making value and is basic to the task of thinking strategically about where the industry is headed and how to prepare for the changes.

Environmental Scanning Techniques

One way to try to detect future driving forces early on is to systematically scan the environment for new straws in the wind. **Environmental scanning** involves studying and interpreting the sweep of social, political, economic, ecological, and technological events in an effort to spot budding trends and conditions that could become driving forces. Environmental scanning involves time frames well beyond the next one to three years—for example, it could involve judgments about the demand for electric power in the year 2010, what kinds of appliances and computerized electronic controls will be in the "house of the future," how people will be communicating over long distances 10 years from now, or what will happen to the income levels and purchasing habits of retired people in the 21st century if average life expectancies continue to increase. Environmental scanning thus attempts to spot first-of-a-kind happenings and approaches that are catching on, and to extrapolate their possible implications 5 to 20 years into the

> Managers can use *environmental scanning* to spot budding trends and clues of change that could develop into new driving forces.

future. *The purpose of environmental scanning is to raise the consciousness of managers about potential developments that could have an important impact on industry conditions and pose new opportunities or threats.*

Environmental scanning can be accomplished by systematically monitoring and studying current events, constructing scenarios, and employing the Delphi method (a technique for finding consensus among a group of knowledgeable experts). Environmental scanning methods are highly qualitative and subjective. The appeal of environmental scanning, notwithstanding its speculative nature, is that it helps managers lengthen their planning horizon, translate vague inklings of future opportunities or threats into clearer strategic issues (for which they can begin to develop strategic answers), and think strategically about developments in the surrounding environment.[16] Companies that undertake formal environmental scanning on a fairly continuous and comprehensive level include General Electric, AT&T, Coca-Cola, Ford, General Motors, Du Pont, and Shell Oil.

QUESTION 4: WHICH COMPANIES ARE IN THE STRONGEST/WEAKEST POSITIONS?

The next step in examining the industry's competitive structure is to study the market positions of rival companies. One technique for revealing the competitive positions of industry participants is **strategic group mapping**.[17] This analytical tool is useful for comparing the market positions of each firm separately or for grouping them into like positions when an industry has so many competitors that it is not practical to examine each one in depth.

Basic Concept
Strategic group mapping is a technique for displaying the different competitive positions that rival firms occupy in the industry.

Using Strategic Group Maps to Assess the Competitive Positions of Rival Firms

A **strategic group** consists of those rival firms with similar competitive approaches and positions in the market.[18] Companies in the same strategic group can resemble one another in any of several ways: they may have comparable product-line breadth, sell in the same price/quality range, emphasize the same distribution channels, use essentially the same product attributes to appeal to similar types of buyers, depend on identical technological approaches, or offer buyers similar services and technical assistance.[19] An industry contains only one strategic group when all sellers pursue essentially identical strategies and have comparable market positions. At the other extreme, there are as many strategic groups as there are competitors when each rival pursues a distinctively

Dividing industry members into *strategic groups* allows industry analysts to better understand the pattern of competition in complex industries and to pinpoint a firm's closest competitors.

---

[16]For further discussion of the nature and use of environmental scanning, see Roy Amara and Andrew J. Lipinski, *Business Planning for an Uncertain Future: Scenarios and Strategies* (New York: Pergamon Press, 1983); Harold E. Klein and Robert U. Linneman, "Environmental Assessment: An International Study of Corporate Practice," *Journal of Business Strategy* 5, no. 1 (Summer 1984), pp. 55–75; and Arnoldo C. Hax and Nicolas S. Majluf, *The Strategy Concept and Process* (Englewood Cliffs, NJ: Prentice Hall, 1991), chapters 5 and 8.

[17]Porter, *Competitive Strategy,* chapter 7.

[18]Ibid., pp. 129–30.

[19]For an excellent discussion of how to identify the factors that define strategic groups, see Mary Ellen Gordon and George R. Milne, "Selecting the Dimensions that Define Strategic Groups: A Novel Market-Driven Approach," *Journal of Managerial Issues* 11, no. 2 (Summer 1999), pp. 213–33.

different competitive approach and occupies a substantially different competitive position in the marketplace.

The procedure for constructing a *strategic group map* and deciding which firms belong in which strategic group is straightforward:

- Identify the competitive characteristics that differentiate firms in the industry—typical variables are price/quality range (high, medium, low); geographic coverage (local, regional, national, global); degree of vertical integration (none, partial, full); product-line breadth (wide, narrow); use of distribution channels (one, some, all); and degree of service offered (no-frills, limited, full).

- Plot the firms on a two-variable map using pairs of these differentiating characteristics.

- Assign firms that fall in about the same strategy space to the same strategic group.

- Draw circles around each strategic group, making the circles proportional to the size of the group's respective share of total industry sales revenues.

This produces a two-dimensional diagram like the one for the video game industry in Illustration Capsule 14.

Several guidelines need to be observed in mapping the positions of strategic groups in the industry's overall strategy space.[20] First, the two variables selected as axes for the map should *not* be highly correlated; if they are, the circles on the map will fall along a diagonal and strategy makers will learn nothing more about the relative positions of competitors than they would by considering just one of the variables. For instance, if companies with broad product lines use multiple distribution channels while companies with narrow lines use a single distribution channel, then looking at broad versus narrow product lines reveals just as much about who is positioned where as looking at single versus multiple distribution channels; one of the variables is redundant. Second, the variables chosen as axes for the map should expose big differences in how rivals position themselves to compete in the marketplace. This, of course, means analysts must identify the characteristics that differentiate rival firms and use these differences as variables for the axes and as the basis for deciding which firm belongs in which strategic group. Third, the variables used as axes don't have to be either quantitative or continuous; rather, they can be discrete variables or defined in terms of distinct classes and combinations. Fourth, drawing the sizes of the circles on the map proportional to the combined sales of the firms in each strategic group allows the map to reflect the relative sizes of each strategic group. Fifth, if more than two good competitive variables can be used as axes for the map, several maps can be drawn to give different exposures to the competitive positioning relationships present in the industry's structure. Because there is not necessarily one best map for portraying how competing firms are positioned in the market, it is advisable to experiment with different pairs of competitive variables.

What Can Be Learned from Strategic Group Maps

One thing to look for is whether *industry driving forces and competitive pressures favor some strategic groups and hurt others.*[21] Firms in adversely affected strategic groups may try to shift to a more favorably situated group; how hard such a move

---

[20]Ibid., pp. 152–54.

[21]Ibid., pp. 130, 132–38, and 154–55.

illustration capsule 14

Strategic Group Map of Competitors in the Video Game Industry

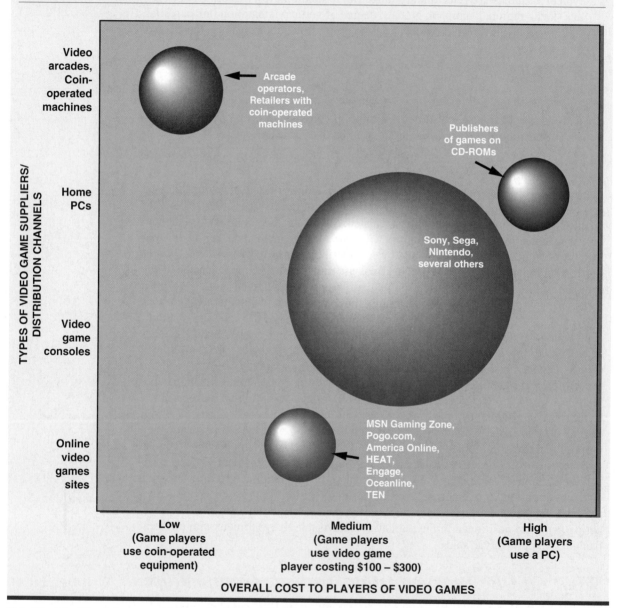

Note: The sizes of the circles are roughly proportional to the market shares of each group of competitors.

proves to be depends on whether entry barriers for the target strategic group are high or low. Attempts by rival firms to enter a new strategic group nearly always increase competitive pressures. If certain firms are known to be trying to change their competitive positions on the map, then attaching arrows to the circles showing the targeted direction helps clarify the picture of competitive jockeying among rivals.

Another consideration is whether *the profit potential of different strategic groups varies due to the strengths and weaknesses in each group's market position.* Differences in profitability can occur because of differing degrees of bargaining leverage or collaboration with suppliers and/or customers, differing degrees of exposure to competition from substitute products outside the industry, differing degrees of competitive rivalry within strategic groups, and differing growth rates for the principal buyer segments served by each group.

Generally speaking, *the closer strategic groups are to each other on the map, the stronger competitive rivalry among member firms tends to be.* Although firms in the same strategic group are the closest rivals, the next closest rivals are in the immediately adjacent groups.[22] Often, firms in strategic groups that are far apart on the map hardly compete at all. For instance, Tiffany & Co. and Wal-Mart both sell gold and silver jewelry, but their clientele and the prices and quality of their products are much too different to justify calling them competitors. For the same reason, Timex is not a meaningful competitive rival of Rolex, and Subaru is not a close competitor of Lincoln or Mercedes-Benz.

> Some strategic groups are usually more favorably positioned than other strategic groups because driving forces and competitive pressures do not affect each group evenly and because profit prospects vary among groups based on the relative attractiveness of their market positions.

QUESTION 5: WHAT STRATEGIC MOVES ARE RIVALS LIKELY TO MAKE NEXT?

Unless a company pays attention to what competitors are doing, it ends up flying blind into competitive battle. A company can't expect to outmaneuver its rivals without monitoring their actions, understanding their strategies, and anticipating what moves they are likely to make next. As in sports, scouting the opposition is essential. **Competitive intelligence** about the strategies rivals are deploying, their latest moves, their resource strengths and weaknesses, and the plans they have announced is essential to anticipating the actions they are likely to take next and what bearing their moves might have on a company's own best strategic moves. Competitive intelligence can help a company determine whether it needs to defend against specific moves taken by rivals or whether those moves provide an opening for a new offensive thrust.

> Successful strategists take great pains in gathering **competitive intelligence** about competitors' strategies, monitoring their actions, sizing up their strengths and weaknesses, and using what they have learned to anticipate what moves rivals are likely to make next.

Monitoring Competitors' Strategies

The best source of information about a competitor's strategy comes from examining what it is doing in the marketplace and from what its management is saying about the company's plans. (Figure 2.3 in Chapter 2 indicates what to look for in identifying a

---

[22]Strategic groups act as good reference points for predicting the evolution of an industry's competitive structure. See Avi Fiegenbaum and Howard Thomas, "Strategic Groups as Reference Groups: Theory, Modeling and Empirical Examination of Industry and Competitive Strategy," *Strategic Management Journal* 16 (1995), pp. 461–76. For a study of how strategic group analysis helps identify the variables that lead to sustainable competitive advantage, see S. Ade Olusoga, Michael P. Mokwa, and Charles H. Noble, "Strategic Groups, Mobility Barriers, and Competitive Advantage," *Journal of Business Research* 33 (1995), pp. 153–64.

company's business strategy.) Additional insights into what a competitor is up to and its future strategy can be gotten by considering the competitor's geographic market arena, strategic intent, market share objective, position on the industry's strategic group map, and willingness to take risks; further, it is important to know whether the competitor's recent moves are mostly offensive or defensive.[23] Good sources for such information include the company's annual report and 10-K filings, recent speeches by its managers, the reports of securities analysts, articles in the business media, company press releases, information on the company's website and other websites, its exhibits at international trade shows, and conversations with a rival's customers, suppliers, and former employees. Many companies have a competitive intelligence unit that regularly gathers information on rivals and makes it available on the company's intranet.

> It is advantageous to know more about your competitors than they know about you.

Gathering competitive intelligence on rivals, however, can sometimes tread the fine line between honest inquiry and unethical or even illegal behavior. For example, calling rivals to get information about prices, the dates of new product introductions, or wage and salary levels is legal, but misrepresenting one's company affiliation during such calls is unethical. Pumping rivals' representatives at trade shows is ethical only if one wears an accurate name tag like everyone else. In 1991, Avon Products secured information about its biggest rival, Mary Kay Cosmetics (MKC), by having its personnel search through the garbage dumpsters outside MKC's headquarters.[24] When MKC officials learned of the action and sued, Avon claimed it did nothing illegal—a 1988 Supreme Court case had ruled that trash left on public property (in this case, a sidewalk) was anyone's for the taking. Avon even produced a videotape of its removal of the trash at the MKC site. Avon won the lawsuit—but the legality of Avon's action does not mean that what the company did was ethical.

Table 3.3 provides an easy-to-apply classification scheme for profiling the objectives and strategies of rival companies. Such profiles, along with a strategic group map, provide a working diagnosis of the strategies and recent moves of rivals and are readily supplemented by whatever additional information is available about each competitor.

Evaluating Who the Industry's Major Players Are Going to Be

It's usually obvious who the *current* major contenders are, but these same firms are not necessarily positioned most strongly for the future. Some may be ill-equipped to compete on the industry's future battleground and may already be losing strength. Smaller companies may be poising for an offensive against larger but vulnerable rivals. Long-standing contenders for market leadership sometimes slide quickly down the industry's ranks; others end up being acquired. Today's market leaders don't automatically become tomorrow's.

> The company that consistently has more and better information about its competitors is better positioned to prevail, other things being equal.

In deciding which competitors are favorably or unfavorably positioned to gain market ground, company strategists need to focus on why there is potential for some rivals to do better or worse than other rivals. Usually, how securely a company holds its present market share is a function of its vulnerability to driving forces and competitive pressures, whether it has a competitive advantage or disadvantage, and whether it is the

---

[23]For a discussion of legal ways of gathering competitive intelligence on rival companies, see Larry Kahaner, *Competitive Intelligence* (New York: Simon & Schuster, 1996).

[24]Kahaner, *Competitive Intelligence*, pp. 84–85.

table 3.3   Profiling the Objectives and Strategies of Competitors

Competitive Scope	Strategic Intent	Market Share Objective	Competitive Position/ Situation	Strategic Posture	Competitive Strategy

• Local
• Regional
• National
• Multicountry
• Global
	• Be the dominant leader
	• Overtake the present industry leader
	• Be among the top 5 industry leaders
	• Move into the top 10
	• Move up a notch or two in the industry rankings
	• Overtake a particular rival (not necessarily the leader)
	• Maintain position
	• Just survive
		• Aggressive expansion via both acquisition and internal growth
		• Expansion via internal growth (boost market share at the expense of rival firms)
		• Expansion via acquisition
		• Hold on to present share (by growing at a rate equal to the industry average)
		• Give up share if necessary to achieve short-term profit objectives (stress profitability, not volume)
			• Getting stronger; on the move
			• Well-entrenched; able to maintain its present position
			• Stuck in the middle of the pack
			• Going after a different market position (trying to move from a weaker to a stronger position)
			• Struggling; losing ground
			• Retrenching to a position that can be defended
				• Mostly offensive
				• Mostly defensive
				• A combination of offense and defense
				• Aggressive risk-taker
				• Conservative follower
					• Striving for low-cost leadership
					• Mostly focusing on a market niche:
					  —High end
					  —Low end
					  —Geographic
					  —Buyers with special needs
					  —Other
					• Pursuing differentiation based on:
					  —Quality
					  —Service
					  —Technological superiority
					  —Breadth of product line
					  —Image and reputation
					  —More value for the money
					  —Other attributes

Note: Since a focus strategy can be aimed at any of several market niches and a differentiation strategy can be keyed to any of several attributes, it is best to be explicit about what kind of focus strategy or differentiation strategy a given firm is pursuing. All focusers do not pursue the same market niche, and all differentiators do not pursue the same differentiating attributes.

likely target of offensive attack from other industry participants. Pinpointing which rivals are poised to gain market position and which rivals seem destined to lose market share helps a strategist anticipate what kinds of moves they are likely to make next.

Predicting Competitors' Next Moves

Predicting competitors' next moves is the hardest yet most useful part of competitor analysis. Good clues about what moves a specific company may make next come from studying its strategic intent, monitoring how well it is faring in the marketplace, and determining how much pressure it is under to improve its financial performance. Whether a company will continue its present strategy usually depends on how well it is doing and how satisfied it is with its current performance. Content rivals are likely to continue their present strategy with only minor fine-tuning. Ailing rivals can be performing so poorly that fresh strategic moves, either offensive or defensive, are virtually certain. Aggressive rivals with ambitious strategic intent are strong candidates for pursuing emerging market opportunities and exploiting the vulnerabilities of weaker rivals.

Since managers generally operate from assumptions about the industry's future and beliefs about their own firm's situation, insights into the strategic thinking of rival managements can be gleaned from their public pronouncements about where the industry is headed and what it will take to be successful, what they are saying about their firm's situation, information from the grapevine about what they are doing, and their past actions and leadership styles. Another thing to consider is whether a rival has the flexibility to make major strategic changes or whether it is locked in to pursuing its same basic strategy with minor adjustments.

> Managers who fail to study competitors closely risk being blindsided by surprise actions on the part of rivals.

To succeed in predicting a competitor's next moves, company strategists need to have a good feel for the rival's situation, how its managers think, and what its options are. Doing the necessary detective work can be tedious and time-consuming since the information comes in bits and pieces from many sources. But scouting competitors well enough to anticipate their next moves allows managers to prepare effective countermoves (perhaps even beat a rival to the punch) and to take rivals' probable actions into account in designing the best course of action.

QUESTION 6: WHAT ARE THE KEY FACTORS FOR COMPETITIVE SUCCESS?

An industry's **key success factors (KSFs)** are those things that most affect industry members' ability to prosper in the marketplace—the particular strategy elements, product attributes, resources, competencies, competitive capabilities, and business outcomes that spell the difference between profit and loss and, ultimately, between competitive success or failure. KSFs by their very nature are so important that *all firms* in the industry must pay close attention to them—they are the prerequisites for industry success or, to put it another way, KSFs are the rules that shape whether a company will be financially and competitively successful. The answers to three questions help identify an industry's key success factors:

> **Basic Concept**
> *Key success factors* concern the product attributes, competencies, competitive capabilities, and market achievements with the greatest direct bearing on company profitability.

- On what basis do customers choose between the competing brands of sellers? What product attributes are crucial?
- What resources and competitive capabilities does a seller need to have to be competitively successful?
- What does it take for sellers to achieve a sustainable competitive advantage?

In the beer industry, the KSFs are full utilization of brewing capacity (to keep manufacturing costs low), a strong network of wholesale distributors (to gain access to as many retail outlets as possible), and clever advertising (to induce beer drinkers to buy a particular brand and thereby pull beer sales through the established wholesale/retail channels). In apparel manufacturing, the KSFs are appealing designs and color combinations (to create buyer interest) and low-cost manufacturing efficiency (to permit attractive retail pricing and ample profit margins). In tin and aluminum cans, because the cost of shipping empty cans is substantial, one of the keys is having plants located close to end-use customers so that the plant's output can be marketed within economical shipping distances (regional market share is far more crucial than national share). Table 3.4 provides a shopping list of the most common types of key success factors.

Determining the industry's key success factors, given prevailing and anticipated industry and competitive conditions, is a top-priority analytical consideration. At the

table 3.4 Common Types of Key Success Factors

Technology-related KSFs
- Scientific research expertise (important in such fields as pharmaceuticals, high-speed Internet access, mobile communications, space exploration, and other high-tech industries)
- Technical capability to make innovative improvements in production processes
- Product innovation capability
- Expertise in a given technology
- Capability to use the Internet for all kinds of e-commerce activities

Manufacturing-related KSFs
- Low-cost production efficiency (achieve scale economies, capture experience curve effects)
- Quality of manufacture (fewer defects, less need for repairs)
- High utilization of fixed assets (important in capital-intensive/high-fixed-cost industries)
- Low-cost plant locations
- Access to adequate supplies of skilled labor
- High labor productivity (important for items with high labor content)
- Low-cost product design and engineering (reduces manufacturing costs)
- Ability to manufacture or assemble products that are customized to buyer specifications

Distribution-related KSFs
- A strong network of wholesale distributors/dealers (or electronic distribution capability via the Internet)
- Gaining ample space on retailer shelves
- Having company-owned retail outlets
- Low distribution costs
- Accurate filling of customer orders
- Short delivery times

Marketing-related KSFs
- Fast, accurate technical assistance
- Courteous customer service
- Accurate filling of buyer orders (few back orders or mistakes)
- Breadth of product line and product selection
- Merchandising skills
- Attractive styling or packaging
- Customer guarantees and warranties (important in mail-order and online retailing, big-ticket purchases, new product introductions)
- Clever advertising

Skills-related KSFs
- Superior workforce talent (important in professional services like accounting and investment banking)
- Quality control know-how
- Design expertise (important in fashion and apparel industries and often one of the keys to low-cost manufacture)
- Expertise in a particular technology
- An ability to develop innovative products and product improvements
- An ability to get newly conceived products past the R&D phase and out into the market very quickly

Organizational capability
- Superior information systems (important in airline travel, car rental, credit card, and lodging industries)
- Ability to respond quickly to shifting market conditions (streamlined decision making, short lead times to bring new products to market)
- Superior ability to employ the Internet and other aspects of electronic commerce to conduct business
- Managerial experience

Other types of KSFs
- Favorable image or reputation with buyers
- Overall low cost (not just in manufacturing)
- Convenient locations (important in many retailing businesses)
- Pleasant, courteous employees in all customer contact positions
- Access to financial capital (important in newly emerging industries with high degrees of business risk and in capital-intensive industries)
- Patent protection

very least, managers need to understand the industry situation well enough to know what is more important to competitive success and what is less important. They need to know what kinds of resources are competitively valuable. Misdiagnosing the industry factors critical to long-term competitive success greatly raises the risk of a misdirected strategy. In contrast, a company with perceptive understanding of industry KSFs can gain sustainable competitive advantage by training its strategy on industry KSFs and devoting its energies to being *distinctively better* than rivals on one or more of these factors. Indeed, companies that stand out on a particular KSF enjoy a stronger market position for their efforts—*being distinctively better than rivals on one or more key success factors presents a golden opportunity for gaining competitive advantage.* Hence, using the industry's KSFs as *cornerstones* for the company's strategy and trying to gain sustainable competitive advantage by excelling at one particular KSF is a fruitful competitive strategy approach.[25]

> **Strategic Management Principle**
>
> A sound strategy incorporates efforts to be competent on all industry key success factors and to excel on at least one factor.

Key success factors vary from industry to industry and even from time to time within the same industry as driving forces and competitive conditions change. Only rarely does an industry have more than three or four key success factors at any one time. And even among these three or four, one or two usually outrank the others in importance. Managers, therefore, have to resist the temptation to include factors that have only minor importance on their list of key success factors—the purpose of identifying KSFs is to make judgments about what things are more important to competitive success and what things are less important. To compile a list of every factor that matters even a little bit defeats the purpose of concentrating management attention on the factors truly critical to long-term competitive success.

QUESTION 7: IS THE INDUSTRY ATTRACTIVE AND WHAT ARE ITS PROSPECTS FOR ABOVE-AVERAGE PROFITABILITY?

The final step of industry and competitive analysis is to use the answers to the previous six questions to draw conclusions about the relative attractiveness or unattractiveness of the industry, both near-term and long-term. Company strategists are obligated to assess the industry outlook carefully, deciding whether industry and competitive conditions present an attractive business opportunity for the company or whether the company's growth and profit prospects are gloomy. The important factors on which to base such conclusions include:

- The industry's growth potential.
- Whether competition currently permits adequate profitability and whether competitive forces will become stronger or weaker.
- Whether industry profitability will be favorably or unfavorably affected by the prevailing driving forces.
- The company's competitive position in the industry and whether its position is likely to grow stronger or weaker. (Being a well-entrenched leader or strongly positioned contender in an otherwise lackluster industry can still produce good profitability;

---

[25]Some experts dispute the strategy-making value of key success factors. Professor Ghemawat claims that the "whole idea of identifying a success factor and then chasing it seems to have something in common with the ill-considered medieval hunt for the *philosopher's stone*, a substance which would transmute everything it touched into gold." Pankaj Ghemawat, *Commitment: The Dynamic of Strategy* (New York: Free Press, 1991), p. 11.

however, having to fight an uphill battle against much stronger rivals can make an otherwise attractive industry unattractive.)

- The company's potential to capitalize on the vulnerabilities of weaker rivals (perhaps converting an unattractive *industry* situation into a potentially rewarding *company* opportunity).
- Whether the company is able to defend against or counteract the factors that make the industry unattractive.
- The degrees of risk and uncertainty in the industry's future.
- The severity of problems confronting the industry as a whole.
- Whether continued participation in this industry adds importantly to the firm's ability to be successful in other industries in which it may have business interests.

As a general proposition, *if an industry's overall profit prospects are above average, the industry can be considered attractive; if its profit prospects are below average, it is unattractive.* However, it is a mistake to think of industries as being attractive or unattractive to all industry participants and all potential entrants. Attractiveness is relative, not absolute, and conclusions one way or the other are in the eye of the beholder— industry attractiveness always has to be appraised from the standpoint of a particular company. Industry environments unattractive to weak competitors may be attractive to strong competitors. Despite the obvious problems of the cigarette industry, for example, Philip Morris has managed to grow market share and maintain reasonable profitability. Industries attractive to insiders, like soft drinks, may be unattractive to outsiders (because of high entry barriers and the global competitive capabilities of Coca-Cola and PepsiCo). Companies on the outside may look at an industry's environment and conclude that it is an unattractive business for them to get into, given the prevailing entry barriers, their particular resources and competencies, the difficulty of challenging current market leaders, and the more profitable opportunities they seem to have elsewhere. But a favorably positioned company already in the industry may survey the very same business environment and conclude that the industry is attractive because it has the resources and competitive capabilities to take sales and market share away from weaker rivals, build a strong leadership position, and earn good profits.

> A company that is uniquely well-situated in an otherwise unattractive industry can, under certain circumstances, still earn unusually good profits.

An assessment that the industry is fundamentally attractive typically suggests that current industry participants employ strategies calculated to strengthen their long-term competitive positions in the business, expanding sales efforts and investing in additional facilities and equipment as needed. If the industry and competitive situation is judged relatively unattractive, more successful industry participants may choose to invest cautiously, look for ways to protect their long-term competitiveness and profitability, and perhaps acquire smaller firms if the price is right; over the longer term, strong companies may consider diversification into more attractive businesses. Weak companies in unattractive industries may consider merging with a rival to bolster market share and profitability or, alternatively, begin looking outside the industry for attractive diversification opportunities.

ACTUALLY DOING AN INDUSTRY AND COMPETITIVE ANALYSIS

Table 3.5 provides a format for presenting the pertinent findings and conclusions of industry and competitive analysis. It embraces all seven questions discussed above and leads would-be analysts to do the strategic thinking and evaluation needed to draw perceptive conclusions about the state of the industry and competitive environment.

table 3.5　Sample Form for an Industry and Competitive Analysis Summary

1. Dominant Economic Characteristics of the Industry Environment (market size and growth rate, geographic scope, number and sizes of buyers and sellers, pace of technological change and innovation, scale economies, experience curve effects, capital requirements, and so on)	**4. Competitive Position of Major Companies/Strategic Groups** ● Those that are favorably positioned, and why ● Those that are unfavorably positioned, and why
2. Competition Analysis ● Rivalry among competing sellers (a strong, moderate, or weak force; weapons that rivals are relying upon in their efforts to outcompete one another) ● Threat of potential entry (a strong, moderate, or weak force; assessment of entry barriers) ● Competition from substitutes (a strong, moderate, or weak force, and why) ● Power of suppliers (a strong, moderate, or weak force, and why) ● Power of customers (a strong, moderate, or weak force, and why)	**5. Competitor Analysis** ● Strategic approaches/predicted moves of key competitors ● Whom to watch, and why **6. Industry Key Success Factors** **7. Industry Prospects and Overall Attractiveness** ● Factors making the industry attractive ● Factors making the industry unattractive ● Special industry issues/problems
3. Driving Forces	● Profit outlook (favorable/unfavorable)

　　Two things should be kept in mind in doing industry and competitive analysis. First, the task of analyzing a company's external situation cannot be reduced to a mechanical exercise in which facts and data are plugged in and definitive conclusions come pouring out. Strategic analysis always leaves room for differences of opinion about how all the factors add up and what future industry and competitive conditions will be. There can be several appealing scenarios about how an industry will evolve, whether it will be an attractive or unattractive business to be in, and how good the profit outlook is. However, while no strategy analysis methodology can guarantee a single conclusive diagnosis, it doesn't make sense to shortcut strategic analysis and rely on opinion and casual observation. Managers become better strategists when they know what analytical questions to pose, have the skills to read clues about industry and competitive changes, and can use situation analysis techniques to find answers and identify strategic issues. This is why we concentrated on suggesting the right questions to ask, explaining concepts and analytical approaches, and indicating the kinds of things to look for.

Second, sweeping industry and competitive analyses need to be done every one to three years; in the interim, managers are obliged to continually update and reexamine their thinking as events unfold. There's no substitute for being a good student of industry and competitive conditions and staying on the cutting edge of what's happening in the industry. Anything else leaves a manager unprepared to initiate shrewd and timely strategic adjustments.

key|points

Thinking strategically about a company's external situation involves probing for answers to the following seven questions:

1. *What are the industry's dominant economic features?* Industries differ significantly on such factors as market size and growth rate, the geographic scope of competitive rivalry, the number and relative sizes of both buyers and sellers, ease of entry and exit, whether sellers are vertically integrated, how fast basic technology is changing, the extent of scale economies and experience curve effects, whether the products of rival sellers are standardized or differentiated, and overall profitability. An industry's economic characteristics are important because of the implications they have for crafting strategy.

2. *What is competition like and how strong are each of the five competitive forces?* The strength of competition is a composite of five forces: the rivalry among competing sellers, the presence of attractive substitutes, the potential for new entry, the competitive pressures stemming from supplier–seller collaboration and bargaining, and the competitive pressures stemming from seller–buyer collaboration and bargaining. The task of competition analysis is to understand the competitive pressures associated with each force; determine whether these pressures add up to a strong or weak competitive force in the marketplace, and then think strategically about what sort of competitive strategy, given the rules of competition in the industry, the company will need to employ to (*a*) insulate the firm as much as possible from the five competitive forces, (*b*) influence the industry's competitive rules in the company's favor, and (*c*) gain a competitive edge.

3. *What is causing the industry's competitive structure and business environment to change?* Industry and competitive conditions change because forces are in motion that create incentives or pressures for change. The most common driving forces are the industry changes being wrought by the Internet and mushrooming e-commerce transactions, globalization of competition in the industry, changes in the long-term industry growth rate, changes in buyer composition, product innovation, entry or exit of major firms, changes in cost and efficiency, changing buyer preferences for standardized versus differentiated products or services, regulatory influences and

government policy changes, changing societal and lifestyle factors, and reductions in uncertainty and business risk. Sound analysis of driving forces and their implications for the industry is a prerequisite to sound strategy making.

4. *Which companies are in the strongest/weakest positions?* Strategic group mapping is a valuable, if not necessary, tool for understanding the similarities, differences, strengths, and weaknesses inherent in the market positions of rival companies. Rivals in the same or nearby strategic groups are close competitors, whereas companies in distant strategic groups usually pose little or no immediate threat.

5. *What strategic moves are rivals likely to make next?* This analytical step involves identifying competitors' strategies, deciding which rivals are likely to be strong contenders and which weak contenders, evaluating their competitive options, and predicting what moves they are likely to make next. Scouting competitors well enough to anticipate their actions can help a company prepare effective countermoves (perhaps even beat a rival to the punch) and allows managers to take rivals' probable actions into account in designing their own company's best course of action. Managers who fail to study competitors closely risk being blindsided by surprise actions on the part of rivals. A company can't expect to outmaneuver its rivals without monitoring their actions and anticipating their next moves.

6. *What are the key factors for competitive success?* An industry's key success factors (KSFs) are the particular strategy elements, product attributes, competitive capabilities, and business outcomes that spell the difference between profit and loss and, ultimately, between competitive success or failure. KSFs by their very nature are so important that *all firms* in the industry must pay close attention to them— they are the *prerequisites* for industry success or, to put it another way, KSFs are *the rules* that shape whether a company will be financially and competitively successful. Frequently, a company can gain sustainable competitive advantage by training its strategy on industry KSFs and devoting its energies to being distinctively better than rivals at succeeding on these factors. Companies that only dimly or incompletely perceive what factors are truly crucial to long-term competitive success are less likely to have winning strategies.

7. *Is the industry attractive and what are its prospects for above-average profitability?* The answer to this question is a major driver of company strategy. An assessment that the industry and competitive environment is fundamentally attractive typically suggests employing a strategy calculated to build a stronger competitive position in the business, expanding sales efforts and investing in additional facilities and equipment as needed. If the industry is relatively unattractive, outsiders considering entry may decide against it and look elsewhere for opportunities, weak companies in the industry may merge with or be acquired by a rival, and strong companies may restrict further investments and employ cost-reduction strategies or product innovation strategies to boost long-term competitiveness and protect their profitability. On occasion, an industry that is unattractive overall is still very attractive to a favorably situated company with the skills and resources to take business away from weaker rivals.

Good industry and competitive analysis is a prerequisite to good strategy making. A competently done industry and competitive analysis tells a clear, easily understood story about the company's external environment. It provides the understanding of a company's macroenvironment needed for shrewdly matching strategy to the company's external situation.

suggested | readings

D'Aveni, Richard A. *Hypercompetition.* New York: Free Press, 1994, chapters 5 and 6.

Ghemawat, Pankaj. "Building Strategy on the Experience Curve." *Harvard Business Review* 64, no. 2 (March–April 1985), pp. 143–49.

Kahaner, Larry. "What You Can Learn from Your Competitors' Mission Statements." *Competitive Intelligence Review* 6 no. 4 (Winter 1995), pp. 35–40.

Langley, Ann. "Between 'Paralysis by Analysis' and 'Extinction by Instinct.'" *Sloan Management Review* (Spring 1995), pp. 63–75.

Linneman, Robert E., and Harold E. Klein. "Using Scenarios in Strategic Decision Making." *Business Horizons* 28, no. 1 (January–February 1985), pp. 64–74.

Porter, Michael E. *Competitive Strategy: Techniques for Analyzing Industries and Competitors.* New York: Free Press, 1980, chapter 1.

———. *Competitive Advantage.* New York: Free Press, 1985, Chapter 2.

———. "Clusters and the New Economics of Competition." *Harvard Business Review* 76, no. 6 (November–December 1998), pp. 77–90.

Thomas, Howard; Timothy Pollock; and Philip Gorman. "Global Strategic Analyses: Frameworks and Approaches." *Academy of Management Executive* 13, no.1 (February 1999), pp. 70–82.

Zahra, Shaker A., and Sherry S. Chaples. "Blind Spots in Competitive Analysis." *Academy of Management Executive* 7, no. 2 (May 1993), pp. 7–28.

chapter | four

Evaluating Company Resources and Competitive Capabilities

The real question isn't how well you're doing today against your own history, but how you're doing against your competitors.

—Donald Kress

Organizations succeed in a competitive marketplace over the long run because they can do certain things their customers value better than can their competitors.

—Robert Hayes, Gary Pisano, and David Upton

The greatest mistake managers make when evaluating their resources is failing to assess them relative to competitors'.

—David J. Collis and Cynthia A. Montgomery

If a company is not "best in world" at a critical activity, it is sacrificing competitive advantage by performing that activity with its existing technique.

—James Brian Quinn

Only firms who are able to continually build new strategic assets faster and cheaper than their competitors will earn superior returns over the long term.

—C. C. Markides and P. J. Williamson

In Chapter 3 we described how to use the tools of industry and competitive analysis to strategically assess a company's external environment. In this chapter we discuss the techniques of evaluating a company's resource capabilities, relative cost position, and competitive strength versus rivals. Company situation analysis prepares the groundwork for matching the company's strategy both to its external market circumstances and to its internal resources and competitive capabilities. The spotlight of company situation analysis is trained on five questions:

1. How well is the company's present strategy working?
2. What are the company's resource strengths and weaknesses and its external opportunities and threats?
3. Are the company's prices and costs competitive?
4. How strong is the company's competitive position relative to its rivals?
5. What strategic issues does the company face?

To explore these questions, we'll be using four analytical techniques: SWOT analysis, value chain analysis, strategic cost analysis, and competitive strength assessment. These techniques are basic strategic management tools that serve to illuminate a company's resource strengths and deficiencies, its best market opportunities, the outside threats to its future profitability, and its competitive standing relative to rivals. Insightful company situation analysis is a precondition for identifying the strategic issues that management needs to address and for tailoring strategy to company resources and competitive capabilities as well as to industry and competitive conditions.

QUESTION 1: HOW WELL IS THE PRESENT STRATEGY WORKING?

In evaluating how well a company's present strategy is working, a manager has to start with what the strategy is. (See Figure 2.3 in Chapter 2 to review the key components of business strategy.) The first thing to pin down is the company's competitive approach. Is the company striving to be a low-cost leader *or* stressing ways to differentiate its product offering from rivals? Is it concentrating its efforts on serving a broad spectrum of customers *or* a narrow market niche? Another strategy-defining consideration is the firm's competitive scope within the industry—how many stages of the industry's production-distribution chain it operates in (one, several, or all), what its geographic market coverage is, and the size and makeup of its customer base. The company's functional strategies in production, marketing, finance, human resources, information technology, new product innovation, and so on further characterize company strategy. In addition, the company may have initiated some recent strategic moves (for instance, price cuts, design improvements, stepped-up advertising, entry into a new geographic area, or merger with a competitor) that are integral to its strategy and that aim at securing an improved competitive position and, optimally, a competitive advantage. The strategy being pursued can be further nailed down by probing the logic behind each competitive move and functional approach.

While there's merit in evaluating the strategy from a *qualitative* standpoint (its completeness, internal consistency, rationale, and suitability to the situation), the best *quantitative* evidence of how well a company's strategy is working comes from studying the company's recent strategic and financial performance and seeing what story the numbers tell about the results the strategy is producing. The two best empirical indicators are (1) whether the company is achieving its stated financial and strategic objectives, and (2) whether the company is an above-average industry performer.[1] Persistent shortfalls in meeting company performance targets and weak performance relative to rivals are reliable warning signs that the company suffers from poor strategy making, less-than-competent strategy execution, or both. Sometimes company objectives are not explicit enough (especially to company outsiders) to benchmark actual performance against, but it is nearly always feasible to evaluate the performance of a company's strategy by looking at:

- Whether the firm's sales are growing faster, slower, or about the same pace as the market as a whole, thus resulting in a rising, eroding, or stable market share.
- Whether the company is acquiring new customers at an attractive rate as well as retaining existing customers.
- Whether the firm's profit margins are increasing or decreasing and how well its margins compare to rival firms' margins.
- Trends in the firm's net profits, return on investment, and economic value added, and how these compare to the same trends for other companies in the industry.
- Whether the company's overall financial strength and credit rating are improving or on the decline.

---

[1]For an excellent discussion of performance measures that reveal how well a company's strategy is working, see Robert S. Kaplan and David P. Norton, "The Balanced Scorecard—Measures That Drive Performance," *Harvard Business Review* 70, no. 1 (January–February 1992), pp. 71–79.

- Whether the company can demonstrate continuous improvement in such internal performance measures as unit cost, defect rate, scrap rate, employee motivation and morale, number of stockouts and customer back orders, fewer days of inventory, and so on.
- How shareholders view the company based on trends in the company's stock price and shareholder value (relative to the market value added of other companies in the industry).
- The firm's image and reputation with its customers.
- Whether the company is regarded as a leader in technology, product innovation, e-commerce, product quality, short times from order to delivery, having the best prices, getting newly developed products to market quickly, or other relevant factors on which buyers base their choice of brands.

> The stronger a company's financial performance and market position, the more likely it has a well-conceived, well-executed strategy.

The stronger a company's current overall performance, the less likely the need for radical changes in strategy. The weaker a company's financial performance and market standing, the more its current strategy must be questioned. Weak performance is almost always a sign of weak strategy, weak execution, or both.

QUESTION 2: WHAT ARE THE COMPANY'S RESOURCE STRENGTHS AND WEAKNESSES AND ITS EXTERNAL OPPORTUNITIES AND THREATS?

Sizing up a firm's resource strengths and weaknesses and its external opportunities and threats, commonly known as *SWOT analysis*, provides a good overview of whether a firm's business position is fundamentally healthy or unhealthy. SWOT analysis is grounded in the basic principle that *strategy-making efforts must aim at producing a good fit between a company's resource capability* (as reflected by its balance of resource strengths and weaknesses) *and its external situation* (as reflected by industry and competitive conditions, the company's own market opportunities, and specific external threats to the company's profitability and market standing). Perceptive understanding of a company's resource capabilities and deficiencies, its market opportunities, and the external threats to its future well-being is essential to good strategy-making. Otherwise, the task of conceiving a strategy that capitalizes on the company's resources, aims squarely at capturing the company's best opportunities, and neutralizes the threats to its well-being becomes a chancy proposition indeed.

Identifying Company Strengths and Resource Capabilities

A *strength* is something a company is good at doing or a characteristic that gives it enhanced competitiveness. A strength can take any of several forms:

- *A skill or important expertise*—low-cost manufacturing capabilities, strong e-commerce expertise, technological know-how, a proven track record in defect-free manufacture, expertise in providing consistently good customer service, excellent mass merchandising skills, or unique advertising and promotional talents.
- *Valuable physical assets*—state-of-the-art plants and equipment, attractive real estate locations, worldwide distribution facilities, ownership of valuable natural

resource deposits, cutting-edge computer networks and information systems, or sizable amounts of cash and marketable securities.

- *Valuable human assets*—an experienced and capable workforce, talented employees in key areas, motivated and energetic employees, cutting-edge knowledge and intellectual capital, astute entrepreneurship and managerial know-how, or the collective learning embedded in the organization and built up over time.[2]

- *Valuable organizational assets*—proven quality control systems, proprietary technology, key patents, mineral rights, a base of loyal customers, a strong balance sheet and credit rating, cutting-edge supply chain management systems, a well-functioning company intranet, and e-commerce systems for accessing and exchanging information with suppliers and key customers, computer-assisted design and manufacturing systems, systems for conducting business on the Internet, or a comprehensive list of customers' e-mail addresses.

- *Valuable intangible assets*—brand-name image, company reputation, buyer goodwill, or a motivated and energized workforce.

- *Competitive capabilities*—short development times in bringing new products to market, a strong dealer network, strong partnerships with key suppliers, an R&D organization with the ability to keep the company's pipeline full of innovative new products, a high degree of organizational agility in responding to shifting market conditions and emerging opportunities, a cadre of highly trained customer service representatives, or state-of-the-art systems for doing business via the Internet.

- *An achievement or attribute that puts the company in a position of market advantage*—low overall costs, market share leadership, a superior product, a wide product selection, strong name recognition, state-of-the-art e-commerce technologies and practices, or exceptional customer service.

- *Alliances or cooperative ventures*—fruitful collaborative partnerships with suppliers and marketing allies that enhance the company's own competitiveness.

Company strengths thus have diverse origins. Sometimes they relate to fairly specific skills and expertise (like know-how in researching consumer tastes and buying habits or training customer contact employees to be cordial and helpful) and sometimes they flow from different resources teaming together to create a competitive capability (like continuous product innovation—which tends to result from a combination of knowledge of consumer needs, technological know-how, R&D, product design and engineering, cost-effective manufacturing, market testing, and other types of intellectual capital).[3] The regularity with which employees from different parts of the organization pool their knowledge and expertise, their skills in exploiting and building on the organization's physical and intangible assets, and the effectiveness with which they collaborate can

---

[2]Many business organizations are coming to view cutting-edge knowledge and intellectual resources as a valuable competitive asset and have concluded that explicitly managing these assets is an essential part of their strategy. See Michael H. Zack, "Developing a Knowledge Strategy," *California Management Review* 41, no. 3 (Spring 1999), pp. 125–45 and Shaker A. Zahra, Anders P. Nielsen, and William C. Bogner, "Corporate Entrepreneurship, Knowledge, and Competence Development," *Entrepreneurship Theory and Practice,* Spring 1999, pp. 169–89.

[3]For a discussion of how to measure the competitive power of a company's resource base, see Nick Bontis, Nicola C. Dragonetti, Kristine Jacobsen, and Goran Roos, "The Knowledge Toolbox: A Review of the Tools Available to Measure and Manage Intangible Resources," *European Management Journal* 17, no. 4 (August 1999), pp. 391–401.

figure 4.1 **Mobilizing Company Resources to Produce Competitive Advantage**

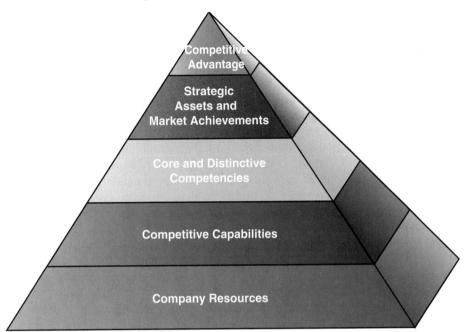

create competitive capabilities not otherwise achievable by a single department or organizational unit within the enterprise.

Taken together, a company's skills and expertise, its intellectual capital, its competitive capabilities, its uniquely strong competencies, its collection of strategically valuable assets, and its market achievements determine the complement of *resources* with which it competes. The caliber of its resources and its ability to mobilize them in a manner calculated to result in competitive advantage are the biggest determinants of how well the company will be able to perform in light of the prevailing industry and competitive conditions—see Figure 4.1.[4]

Basic Concept
A company is positioned to succeed if it has a competitively valuable complement of resources at its command.

Identifying Company Weaknesses and Resource Deficiencies

A *weakness* is something a company lacks or does poorly (in comparison to others) or a condition that puts it at a disadvantage. A company's internal weaknesses can relate to (1) deficiencies in competitively important skills or expertise or intellectual capital

---

[4]In the past decade, there's been considerable research into the role a company's resources and competitive capabilities play in crafting strategy and in determining company profitability. The findings and conclusions have coalesced into what is called the resource-based view of the firm. Among the most insightful articles are Birger Wernerfelt, "A Resource-Based View of the Firm," *Strategic Management Journal,* September–October 1984, pp. 171–80; Jay Barney, "Firm Resources and Sustained Competitive Advantage," *Journal of Management* 17, no. 1 (1991), pp. 99–120; Margaret A. Peteraf, "The Cornerstones of Competitive Advantage: A Resource-Based View," *Strategic Management Journal,* March 1993, pp. 179–91; Birger Wernerfelt, "The Resource-Based View of the Firm: Ten Years After," *Strategic Management Journal* 16 (1995), pp. 171–74; and Jay B. Barney, "Looking Inside for Competitive Advantage," *Academy of Management Executive* 9, no. 4 (November 1995), pp. 49–61.

of one kind or another; (2) a lack of competitively important physical, organizational, or intangible assets; or (3) missing or weak competitive capabilities in key areas. *Internal weaknesses are thus shortcomings in a company's complement of resources.* A weakness may or may not make a company competitively vulnerable, depending on how much the weakness matters in the marketplace and whether it can be overcome by the resources and strengths in the company's possession.

Table 4.1 indicates the kinds of factors to be considered in determining a company's resource strengths and weaknesses. Sizing up a company's complement of resource capabilities and deficiencies is akin to constructing a *strategic balance sheet* where resource strengths represent *competitive assets* and resource weaknesses represent *competitive liabilities.* Obviously, the ideal condition is for the company's strengths/competitive assets to outweigh its weaknesses/competitive liabilities by an ample margin—a 50-50 balance is definitely not the desired condition!

> **Basic Concept**
>
> A company's resource strengths represent competitive assets; its resource weaknesses represent competitive liabilities.

Once managers identify a company's resource strengths and weaknesses, the two compilations need to be carefully evaluated for their competitive value and strategy-making implications. Some resource strengths and competencies are *competitively* more important than others because they add greater power to the company's strategy or are bigger factors in contributing to a strong market position and higher profitability. Likewise, some weaknesses can prove fatal if not remedied, while others are inconsequential, easily corrected, or offset by company strengths. A company's resource weaknesses suggest a need to review its resource base: What existing resource deficiencies need to be remedied? Does the company have important resource gaps that need to be filled? What needs to be done to augment the company's future resource base?

Identifying Company Competencies and Capabilities

The Related Concepts of Company Competence and Competitive Capability   Identifying and evaluating what a company is really good at doing and what capabilities it has for competing is a critical component of assessing a company's situation. A **company competence** is nearly always the product of experience, representing an accumulation of learning over time and the buildup over time of *real proficiency.* Competencies have to be consciously built and developed—they don't just happen. A company competence originates with deliberate efforts to develop the organizational ability to do something, however imperfectly or inefficiently. Such efforts entail selecting people with the requisite knowledge and skills, upgrading or expanding individual abilities as needed, and then molding the efforts and work products of individuals into a cooperative group effort to create organizational ability. Then as experience builds, such that the company reaches a level of ability to perform the activity consistently well and at an acceptable cost, the ability begins to translate into a true competence.

> **Basic Concept**
>
> A *company competence* is the product of learning and experience and represents real proficiency in performing an internal activity.

Examples of competencies include skills in merchandising and product display, the ability to create attractive and easy-to-use websites, expertise in a specific technology, proven ability to select good locations for retail outlets, skills in working with customers on new applications and uses of the product, and expertise in just-in-time inventory management practices. Company competencies are normally bundles of skills, know-how, resources, and technologies—as opposed to a single discrete skill or resource or technology.

table 4.1   SWOT Analysis—What to Look For in Sizing Up a Company's Strengths, Weaknesses, Opportunities, and Threats

Potential Resource Strengths and Competitive Capabilities	Potential Resource Weaknesses and Competitive Deficiencies
• A powerful strategy supported by competitively valuable skills and expertise in key areas • A strong financial condition; ample financial resources to grow the business • Strong brand name image/company reputation • A widely recognized market leader and an attractive customer base • Ability to take advantage of economies of scale and/or learning and experience curve effects • Proprietary technology/superior technological skills/important patents • Superior intellectual capital relative to key rivals • Cost advantages • Strong advertising and promotion • Product innovation skills • Proven skills in improving production processes • Sophisticated use of e-commerce technologies and processes • Superior skills in supply chain management • A reputation for good customer service • Better product quality relative to rivals • Wide geographic coverage and/or strong global distribution capability • Alliances/joint ventures with other firms that provide access to valuable technology, competencies, and/or attractive geographic markets	• No clear strategic direction • Obsolete facilities • A weak balance sheet; burdened with too much debt • Higher overall unit costs relative to key competitors • Missing some key skills or competencies/lack of management depth/a deficiency of intellectual capital relative to leading rivals • Subpar profitability because . . . • Plagued with internal operating problems • Falling behind rivals in putting e-commerce capabilities and strategies in place • Too narrow a product line relative to rivals • Weak brand image or reputation • Weaker dealer network than key rivals and/or lack of adequate global distribution capability • Subpar e-commerce systems and capabilities relative to rivals • Short on financial resources to fund promising strategic initiatives • Lots of underutilized plant capacity • Behind on product quality and/or R&D and/or technological know-how • Not attracting new customers as rapidly as rivals due to ho-hum product attributes
Potential Company Opportunities	**Potential External Threats to Company's Well-Being**
• Serving additional customer groups or expanding into new geographic markets or product segments • Expanding the company's product line to meet a broader range of customer needs • Utilizing existing company skills or technological know-how to enter new product lines or new businesses • Using the Internet and e-commerce technologies to dramatically cut costs and/or to pursue new sales growth opportunities • Integrating forward or backward • Falling trade barriers in attractive foreign markets • Openings to take market share away from rivals • Ability to grow rapidly because of sharply rising demand in one or more market segments • Acquisition of rival firms or companies with attractive technological expertise • Alliances or joint ventures that expand the firm's market coverage or boost its competitive capability • Openings to exploit emerging new technologies • Market openings to extend the company's brand name or reputation to new geographic areas	• Likely entry of potent new competitors • Loss of sales to substitute products • Mounting competition from new Internet start-up companies pursuing e-commerce strategies • Increasing intensity of competition among industry rivals—may cause squeeze on profit margins • Technological changes or product innovations that undermine demand for the firm's product • Slowdowns in market growth • Adverse shifts in foreign exchange rates and trade policies of foreign governments • Costly new regulatory requirements • Growing bargaining power of customers or suppliers • A shift in buyer needs and tastes away from the industry's product • Adverse demographic changes that threaten to curtail demand for the firm's product • Vulnerability to industry driving forces

Companies consist of a collection of competencies and competitive capabilities.

A company competence becomes a meaningful **competitive capability** when customers deem the competence valuable and beneficial, when it helps differentiate a company from its competitors, and when it enhances its competitiveness. However, it is important to understand that competitive capabilities are not all equal—*some merely enable survival* because they are common to most all rivals while *others hold potential for changing the basis of competition* because they are unique, proprietary, and deliver considerable customer value. But *it is useful to think of a company as consisting of a collection of capabilities,* some difficult to disentangle from one another and some stronger and more competitively valuable than others.

Core Competencies: A Valuable Company Resource   One of the most valuable resources a company has is the ability to perform a competitively relevant activity very well. A competitively important internal activity that a company performs better than other competitively important internal activities is termed a **core competence.** While a core competence is something a company does well internally, what makes it a *core* competence as opposed to just a competence is that it is central to a company's competitiveness and profitability rather than peripheral. A company's core competence can relate to any of several aspects of its business: expertise in building networks and systems that enable e-commerce, speeding new or next-generation products to market, good after-sale service, skills in manufacturing a high-quality product, innovativeness in developing popular product features, speed and agility in responding to new market trends and changing competitive conditions, know-how in creating and operating a system for filling customer orders accurately and swiftly, and expertise in integrating multiple technologies to create families of new products.

Basic Concept
A *core competence* is something that a company does well relative to other internal activities; a *distinctive competence* is something a company does well relative to competitors.

A company may have more than one core competence in its resource portfolio but rare is the company that can legitimately claim more than two or three core competencies. Plainly, *a core competence gives a company competitive capability* and thus qualifies as a genuine company strength and resource.[5]

Most often, *a company's core competence resides in its people and in its intellectual capital, not in its assets on the balance sheet.* Core competencies tend to be grounded in cross-department and cross-functional combinations of skills, resources, and technologies. Knowledge and intellectual capital, more than physical assets and tangible organizational resources, are the key ingredients of a core competence and a firm's competitive capability.

Distinctive Competencies: A Competitively Superior Company Resource   Whether a company's core competence represents a **distinctive competence** depends on how good the competence is relative to what competitors are capable of—is it a competitively superior competence or just a standout internal company competence? A distinctive competence is something a company does well in comparison to its competitors.[6] Most every company does one competitively important activity enough better than the other things it does internally that it can claim that activity as a core competence. But what a company does best internally doesn't translate into a

---

[5]For a more extensive discussion of how to identify and evaluate the competitive power of a company's capabilities, see David W. Birchall and George Tovstiga, "The Strategic Potential of a Firm's Knowledge Portfolio," *Journal of General Management* 25, no. 1 (Autumn 1999), pp. 1–16; also see David Teece, "Capturing Value from Knowledge Assets: The New Economy, Markets for Know-How, and Intangible Assets," *California Management Review* 40, no. 3 (Spring 1998), pp. 55–79.

[6]For a fuller discussion of the core competence concept, see C. K. Prahalad and Gary Hamel, "The Core Competence of the Corporation," *Harvard Business Review* 68, no. 3 (May–June 1990), pp. 79–93.

distinctive competence unless the company performs that activity better than rivals and thus enjoys *competitive superiority*. For instance, most all retailers believe they have core competencies in product selection and in-store merchandising, but many retailers who build strategies on these competencies run into trouble in the marketplace because they encounter rivals whose competencies in these areas are better than theirs. Consequently, *a core competence becomes a basis for competitive advantage only when it is a distinctive competence.*

> **Strategic Management Principle**
> A distinctive competence empowers a company to build competitive advantage.

Sharp Corporation's distinctive competence in flat-panel display technology has enabled it to dominate the worldwide market for liquid crystal displays (LCDs). The distinctive competencies of Toyota and Honda in low-cost, high-quality manufacturing and in short design-to-market cycles for new models have proved to be considerable competitive advantages in the global market for motor vehicles. Intel's distinctive competence in rapidly developing new generations of ever more powerful semiconductor chips for personal computers has helped give the company a dominating presence in the personal computer industry. Starbucks' distinctive competence in store ambience and innovative coffee drinks has propelled it to the forefront among coffee retailers. Motorola's distinctive competence in virtually defect-free manufacture (six-sigma quality—an error rate of about 3.4 per million) has contributed significantly to the company's world leadership in cellular telephone equipment. Rubbermaid's distinctive competence in developing innovative rubber and plastics products for household and commercial use has made it the clear leader in its industry.

The importance of a distinctive competence to strategy-making rests with (1) the competitively valuable capability it gives a company, (2) its potential for being a cornerstone of strategy, and (3) the competitive edge it can produce in the marketplace. It is always easier to build competitive advantage when a firm has a distinctive competence in performing activities important to market success, when rival companies do not have offsetting competencies, and when it is costly and time-consuming for rivals to imitate the competence. A distinctive competence is thus potentially the mainspring of a company's success—unless it is trumped by more powerful resources of rivals.

Determining the Competitive Value of a Company Resource No two companies are alike in their resources. They don't have the same skill sets; assets (physical, human, organizational, and intangible); competitive capabilities; or market achievements—a condition that results in different companies having different strengths and weaknesses. *Differences in company resources account for why some companies are more profitable and more competitively successful than others.* A company's success is more certain when it has appropriate and ample resources with which to compete, and especially when it has a valuable strength, asset, capability, or achievement with the potential to produce competitive advantage.

For a particular company resource to qualify as the basis for sustainable competitive advantage, it must pass four tests of competitive value:[7]

- *Is the resource hard to copy?* The more difficult and more expensive it is to imitate a resource, the greater its potential competitive value. Hard-to-copy resources limit competition, making any profit stream they are able to generate more sustainable. Resources can be difficult to copy because of their uniqueness (a fantastic real estate location, patent protection), because they must be built over time in ways

---

[7]See David J. Collis and Cynthia A. Montgomery, "Competing on Resources: Strategy in the 1990s," *Harvard Business Review* 73, no. 4 (July–August 1995), pp. 120–23.

that are difficult to imitate (a brand name, mastery of a technology), and because they carry big capital requirements (a new cost-effective plant to manufacture semiconductor chips can cost $1 to $2 billion).

- *How long does the resource last?* The longer a resource lasts, the greater its value. Some resources lose their value quickly because of the rapid speeds with which technologies or industry conditions are moving. The value of Eastman Kodak's resources in film and film processing is rapidly being undercut by the growing popularity of digital cameras. The value of 3Com's expertise in PC modem technology is fast being eroded by the onslaught of cable modems and by the efforts of chip manufacturers to incorporate modem functions directly into the microprocessor instruction set. The investments that commercial banks have made in branch offices is a rapidly depreciating asset because of growing use of direct deposits, ATMs, and telephone and Internet banking options.

- *Is the resource really competitively superior?* Companies have to guard against pridefully believing that their core competences are distinctive competences or that their brand name is more powerful than the brand names of rivals. Who can really say whether Coca-Cola's consumer marketing skills are better than Pepsi-Cola's or whether Mercedes-Benz's brand name is more powerful than BMW's or Lexus's?

- *Can the resource be trumped by the different resources/capabilities of rivals?* Many commercial airlines (American Airlines, Delta Airlines, United Airlines, Singapore Airlines) have succeeded because of their resources and capabilities in offering safe, convenient, reliable air transportation services and in providing an array of amenities to passengers. However, Southwest Airlines has been a more consistently profitable air carrier by building the capabilities to provide safe, reliable, basic services at radically lower fares. The prestigious brand names of Cadillac and Lincoln have faded as dominating factors in choosing what luxury cars to buy—Mercedes, BMW, and Lexus have introduced the most appealing luxury vehicles in recent years. Amazon.com is putting a big dent in the business prospects of brick-and-mortar bookstore chains like Barnes & Noble and Borders; likewise, online retailers of toys and Wal-Mart (with its lower prices) are putting major competitive pressure on Toys "R" Us, at one time the leading toy retailer.

The vast majority of companies are not well endowed with competitively valuable resources, much less with competitively superior resources capable of passing the above four tests with flying colors. Most businesses have a mixed bag of resources—one or two quite valuable, some good, many satisfactory to mediocre. Only a few companies, usually the strongest industry leaders or up-and-coming challengers, possess a competitively superior resource. Furthermore, nearly all companies have competitive liabilities, whether they be labeled internal weaknesses, a lack of assets, missing expertise or capabilities, or resource deficiencies.

Strategic Management Principle
Successful strategists seek to capitalize on what a company does best—its expertise, resource strengths, and strongest competitive capabilities.

Even if a company doesn't possess a competitively superior resource, the potential for competitive advantage is not lost. Sometimes a company derives significant competitive vitality, even competitive advantage, from a collection of good to adequate resources which, in combination, have competitive power in the marketplace. Toshiba's laptop computers were the market share leader throughout most of the 1990s—an indicator that Toshiba was good at something. Yet Toshiba's laptops were not demonstrably faster than rivals' laptops, nor did they have superior performance features (bigger screens, more memory, longer battery power, a better pointing device, and so on), nor did Toshiba provide clearly superior technical support services to buyers of its laptops. And Toshiba laptops were definitely not cheaper, model for model, than the comparable models of its rivals. Toshiba laptops seldom ranked first in the overall performance ratings done by various organizations. Rather, Toshiba's market share leadership stemmed from a *combination* of good resource strengths and capabilities—its strategic partnerships with suppliers of laptop components, its efficient assembly capability, its design expertise, its skills in choosing quality components, its creation of a wide selection of models, the attractive mix of built-in performance features found in each model when balanced against price, the much-better-than-average reliability of its laptops (based on buyer ratings), and its very good technical support services (based on buyer ratings). The verdict from the marketplace was that PC buyers considered Toshiba laptops as better, all things considered, than competing brands.

Matching Strategy to the Company's Resource Strengths and Weaknesses   From a strategy-making perspective, a company's resource strengths are significant because they can form the cornerstones of strategy and the basis for creating competitive advantage. If a company doesn't have the resources and competitive capabilities around which to craft an attractive strategy, managers need to take decisive remedial action to upgrade existing organizational resources and capabilities and add others as needed. At the same time, managers have to look toward correcting competitive weaknesses that make the company vulnerable, hold down profitability, or disqualify it from pursuing an attractive opportunity. The strategy-making principle here is simple: *a company's strategy should be tailored to fit its resources—taking both strengths and weaknesses into account.* As a rule, managers should build their strategies around exploiting and leveraging company capabilities—its most valuable resources—and avoid strategies that place heavy demands on areas where the company is weakest or has unproven ability. Companies fortunate enough to have a distinctive competence or other competitively superior resource must be wise in realizing that its value will be eroded by time and competition.[8] So attention to building a strong resource base for the future and to maintaining the competitive superiority of an existing distinctive competence are ever-present needs.

Selecting the Competencies and Capabilities to Concentrate On   Enterprises succeed in a competitive marketplace over time because they can do certain things that their customers value better than their rivals. The essence of astute strategy making is selecting the competencies and capabilities to concentrate on and use to underpin the strategy. Sometimes the company already has competitively valuable competencies and capabilities in place and sometimes it has be proactive in developing and building new competencies and capabilities to complement and strengthen its existing resource base. Sometimes the desired competencies and capabilities need to be developed internally and sometimes it is best to acquire them through partnerships or strategic alliances with firms possessing the needed expertise.

Identifying a Company's Market Opportunities

Market opportunity is a big factor in shaping a company's strategy. Indeed, managers can't properly tailor strategy to the company's situation without first identifying each company opportunity and appraising the growth and profit potential each one holds. Depending on the prevailing circumstances, a company's opportunities can be plentiful or

---

[8]Collis and Montgomery, "Competing on Resources: Strategy in the 1990s," p. 124.

illustration capsule 15
Motorola Adjusts Strategy to New Threats and Opportunities

A vital part of any executive's job is to identify threats to a company's survival in the marketplace and devise ideas for capitalizing on opportunities to help keep the company a step ahead of the competition. When it became evident that cell phones were actually becoming commodities—products differentiated more by marketing techniques and pricing than by innovative new features—Motorola, the inventor of the cell phone, began to take a beating in an industry that it had previously dominated. Threats included an industrywide slump in sales, Motorola's failure to shift from analog to digital technology, and its late entry into the replacement cell phone market. In addition, Motorola's semiconductor unit experienced a low profit margin in an already changeable chip industry.

Company officials of the Chicago-area firm realized they had to formulate a new strategy. In July 2001, Motorola announced that it would begin selling all of its technology necessary to build mobile phones to other manufacturers, including competitors. As unusual as the strategy might sound, executives saw the move as an opportunity for Motorola, whose greatest strength had always been its technology. "Motorola intends to accelerate the evolution of the handset industry . . . by removing technological barriers to entry and allowing handset manufacturers to focus on brand loyalty, marketing, features, and style," explained Fred Shlapak, president of Motorola's semiconductor unit. The company said that it would begin to offer the technology based on the next-generation Global Packet Radio Service (GPRS) technology for digital phones. Company

officials explained that they expected the mobile communications chip business to constitute a $35 billion market by 2004. At the time of the announcement, Motorola's semiconductor unit had revenues of $7.9 billion. "I'd like to double that," said Ray Burgess, corporate vice president of Motorola's semiconductor unit.

In addition to selling technology to existing manufacturers, Motorola recognized another opportunity—the company signed an agreement with the Chinese government to provide the technology for a whole new approach to cell phone manufacturing and operation in that country. Finally, during the same time period, Motorola announced a new alliance with Palm, a company with which it had partnered in the past. "Motorola has been a long-time Palm partner, and we are very pleased to be working with that team in new ways," said Alan Kessler, vice president and general manager of Platform Solutions Group at Palm, Inc. "We expect this new program to be a win for all constituencies involved."

Although some industry experts questioned how these strategies would fit the company's overall corporate vision and whether they would succeed, it was clear that Motorola needed to target new opportunities and make new moves. Despite the questions and doubts about its strategies raised by outsiders, Motorola executives felt compelled to bank on the company's greatest strength—technology—and find ways to convert the company's technological know-how into new sources of revenue.

Sources: "Motorola Breathes Fire into Portable Handheld Market, Announces Alliance with Palm, Inc.," company press release, July 24, 2001; Yukari Iwatani, "Motorola to Wholesale Mobile Phone Technology," Reuters, July 23, 2001; Barnaby J. Feder, "Motorola to Sell Inner Workings of Cell Phones to Rivals," *New York Times* (www.nytimes.com), July 23, 2001.

Strategic Management Principle

A company is well-advised to pass on a particular market opportunity unless it has or can build the resource capabilities to capture it.

scarce and can range from wildly attractive (an absolute "must" to pursue) to marginally interesting (low on the company's list of strategic priorities). Table 4.1 presents a checklist of things to be alert for in identifying a company's market opportunities.

In evaluating a company's market opportunities and ranking their attractiveness, managers have to guard against viewing every *industry* opportunity as a *company* opportunity. Not every company in an industry is equipped with the resources to successfully pursue each opportunity that exists in the industry. Some companies are more capable of going after particular opportunities than others, and a few companies may be hopelessly outclassed in trying to contend for a piece of the action. Deliberately adapting a company's resource base to put it in position to contend for attractive growth opportunities is something strategists must pay keen attention to. *The market opportunities most relevant to a company are those that offer important avenues for profitable growth, those where a company has the most potential for competitive advantage, and those that match up well with the company's financial and organizational resource capabilities.*

Identifying the Threats to a Company's Future Profitability

Often, certain factors in a company's external environment pose *threats* to its profitability and competitive well-being. Threats can stem from the emergence of cheaper or better technologies, rivals' introduction of new or improved products, the entry of lower-cost foreign competitors into a company's market stronghold, new regulations that are more burdensome to a company than to its competitors, vulnerability to a rise in interest rates, the potential of a hostile takeover, unfavorable demographic shifts, adverse changes in foreign exchange rates, political upheaval in a foreign country where the company has facilities, and the like. External threats may pose no more than a moderate degree of adversity (all companies confront some threatening elements in the course of doing business) or they may be so imposing as to make a company's situation and outlook quite tenuous. It is management's job to identify the threats to the company's future well-being and to evaluate what strategic actions can be taken to neutralize or lessen their impact.

> **Strategic Management Principle**
> Successful strategists aim at capturing a company's best growth opportunities and creating defenses against external threats to its competitive position and future performance.

Table 4.1 presents a list of potential threats to a company's future profitability and market position. Opportunities and threats not only affect the attractiveness of a company's situation but, more important, they point to the need for strategic action. Tailoring strategy to a company's situation entails (1) pursuing market opportunities well suited to the company's resource capabilities and (2) taking actions to defend against external threats to the company's business.

The Real Value of SWOT Analysis

SWOT analysis is more than an exercise in making four lists. The really valuable part of SWOT analysis is determining what story the four lists tell about the company's situation and thinking about what actions are needed. Understanding the story involves evaluating the strengths, weaknesses, opportunities, and threats and drawing conclusions about (1) how the company's strategy can be matched to both its resource capabilities and its market opportunities, and (2) how urgent it is for the company to correct which particular resource weaknesses and guard against which particular external threats.[9] To have managerial and strategy-making value, SWOT analysis must be a basis for action. It also needs to provoke thinking and answers to several questions about what *future* resource strengths and capabilities the company will need to respond to emerging industry and competitive conditions and to produce successful bottom-line results. Will the current strengths matter as much in the future? Are there resource gaps that need to be filled? Do new types of competitive capabilities need to be put in place? Which resources and capabilities need to be given greater emphasis and which merit lesser emphasis? SWOT analysis has not served its purpose until the lessons about the company's situation have been distilled from the four lists.

> Simply listing a company's strengths, weaknesses, opportunities, and threats is not enough; the payoff of SWOT analysis comes from the evaluations and conclusions that flow from the four lists.

---

[9]See Jack W. Duncan, Peter Ginter, and Linda E. Swayne, "Competitive Advantage and Internal Organizational Assessment," *Academy of Management Executive* 12, no. 3 (August 1998), pp. 6–16.

QUESTION 3: ARE THE COMPANY'S PRICES AND COSTS COMPETITIVE?

Assessing whether a company's costs are competitive with those of its close rivals is a necessary part of company situation analysis.

Company managers are often stunned when a competitor cuts price to "unbelievably low" levels or when a new market entrant comes on strong with a very low price. The competitor may not, however, be "dumping" (an economic term for selling large amounts of goods below market price), buying market share, or waging a desperate move to gain sales; it may simply have substantially lower costs. One of the most telling signs of whether a company's business position is strong or precarious is whether its prices and costs are competitive with industry rivals. Price-cost comparisons are especially critical in a commodity-product industry where the value provided to buyers is the same from seller to seller, price competition is typically the ruling market force, and lower-cost companies have the upper hand. But even in industries where products are differentiated and competition centers on the different attributes of competing brands as much as on price, rival companies have to keep their costs *in line* and make sure that any added costs they incur and price premiums they charge create ample buyer value.

Competitors usually don't incur the same costs in supplying their products to end users. The cost disparities can range from tiny to competitively significant and can stem from any of several factors:

- Differences in the prices paid for raw materials, components parts, energy, and other items purchased from suppliers.
- Differences in basic technology and the age of plants and equipment. Because rival companies usually invest in plants and key pieces of equipment at different times, their facilities have somewhat different technological efficiencies and different fixed costs (depreciation, maintenance, property taxes, and insurance). Older facilities are typically less efficient, but if they were less expensive to construct or were acquired at bargain prices, they *may* still be reasonably cost-competitive with modern facilities.
- Differences in production costs from rival to rival due to different plant efficiencies, different learning and experience curve effects, different wage rates, different productivity levels, and the like.
- Differences in marketing costs, sales and promotion expenditures, advertising expenses, warehouse distribution costs, and administrative costs.
- Differences in inbound transportation costs on purchased items and outbound shipping costs on goods sold.
- Differences in forward channel distribution costs (the costs and markups of distributors, wholesalers, and retailers associated with getting the product from the point of manufacture into the hands of end users).

Principle of Competitive Markets

The higher a company's costs are above those of close rivals, the more competitively vulnerable it becomes.

- Differences in rival firms' exposure to the effects of inflation, changes in foreign exchange rates, and tax rates (a frequent occurrence in global industries where competitors have operations in different nations with different economic conditions and governmental taxation policies).

For a company to be competitively successful, its costs must be in line with those of close rivals. While some cost disparity is justified so long as the products or services of closely competing companies are sufficiently differentiated, a high-cost firm's market position becomes increasingly vulnerable the more its costs exceed those of close rivals.

Strategic Cost Analysis and Value Chains

Competitors must be ever alert to how their costs compare with rivals'. While every firm engages in internal cost analysis to stay on top of what its own costs are and how they might be changing, **strategic cost analysis** goes a step further to explore how costs compare against rivals. Strategic cost analysis focuses on a firm's cost position relative to its rivals'.

Every company's business consists of a collection of activities undertaken in the course of designing, producing, marketing, delivering, and supporting its product or service. Each of these activities give rise to costs. The combined costs of all these various activities define the company's internal cost structure. Further, the cost of each activity contributes to whether the company's overall cost position relative to rivals is favorable or unfavorable. The task of strategic cost analysis is to compare a company's costs activity by activity against the costs of key rivals and to learn which internal activities are a source of cost advantage or disadvantage. A company's relative cost position is a function of how the overall costs of the activities it performs in conducting business compare to the overall costs of the activities performed by rivals.

The Concept of a Company Value Chain   The primary analytical tool of strategic cost analysis is a **value chain** identifying the separate activities, functions, and business processes that are performed in designing, producing, marketing, delivering, and supporting a product or service.[10] The chain of value-creating activities it takes to provide a product or service starts with raw materials supply and continues on through parts and components production, manufacturing and assembly, wholesale distribution, and retailing to the end user of the product or service.

A company's value chain shows the linked set of activities and functions it performs internally (see Figure 4.2). The value chain includes a profit margin because a markup over the cost of performing the firm's value-creating activities is customarily part of the price (or total cost) borne by buyers—creating value that exceeds the cost of doing so is a fundamental objective of business. Disaggregating a company's operations into strategically relevant activities and business processes exposes the major elements of the company's cost structure. Each activity in the value chain incurs costs and ties up assets; assigning the company's operating costs and assets to each individual activity in the chain provides cost estimates for each activity. Quite often, there are links between activities such that the manner in which one activity is done can affect the costs of performing other activities. For instance, Japanese producers of videocassette recorders were able to reduce VCR prices from around $1,300 in 1977 to under $300 in 1984 by spotting the impact of an early step in the value chain (product design) on a later step (production) and deciding to change the product design to drastically reduce the number of parts.[11]

Why the Value Chains of Rival Companies Often Differ   A company's value chain and the manner in which it performs each activity reflect the evolution of its own particular business and internal operations, its strategy, the approaches it is

Basic Concept
Strategic cost analysis involves comparing how a company's unit costs stack up against the unit costs of key competitors *activity by activity*, thereby pinpointing which internal activities are a source of cost advantage or disadvantage.

Basic Concept
A company's *value chain* identifies the primary activities that create value for customers and the related support activities.

---

[10]Value chains and strategic cost analysis are described at greater length in Michael E. Porter, *Competitive Advantage* (New York: Free Press, 1985), chapters 2 and 3; Robin Cooper and Robert S. Kaplan, "Measure Costs Right: Make the Right Decisions," *Harvard Business Review* 66, no. 5 (September–October, 1988), pp. 96–103; and John K. Shank and Vijay Govindarajan, *Strategic Cost Management* (New York: Free Press, 1993), especially chapters 2–6 and 10.

[11]M. Hegert and D. Morris, "Accounting Data for Value Chain Analysis," *Strategic Management Journal* 10 (1989), p. 183.

figure 4.2   **Representative Company Value Chain**

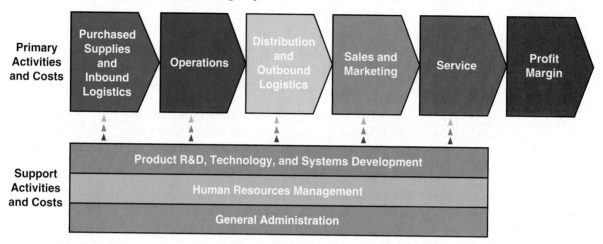

Primary Activities

- **Purchased Supplies and Inbound Logistics**—Activities, costs, and assets associated with purchasing fuel, energy, raw materials, parts components, merchandise, and consumable items from vendors; receiving, storing, and disseminating inputs from suppliers; inspection; and inventory management.
- **Operations**—Activities, costs, and assets associated with converting inputs into final product form (production, assembly, packaging, equipment maintenance, facilities, operations, quality assurance, environmental protection).
- **Distribution and Outbound Logistics**—Activities, costs, and assets dealing with physically distributing the product to buyers (finished goods warehousing, order processing, order picking and packing, shipping, delivery vehicle operations, establishing and maintaining a network of dealers and distributors).
- **Sales and Marketing**—Activities, costs, and assets related to sales force efforts, advertising and promotion, market research and planning, and dealer/distributor support.
- **Service**—Activities, costs, and assets associated with providing assistance to buyers, such as installation, spare parts delivery, maintenance and repair, technical assistance, buyer inquiries, and complaints.

Support Activities

- **Research, Technology, and Systems Development**—Activities, costs, and assets relating to product R&D, process R&D, process design improvement, equipment design, computer software development, telecommunications systems, computer-assisted design and engineering, new database capabilities, and development of computerized support systems.
- **Human Resources Management**—Activities,costs, and assets associated with the recruitment, hiring, training, development, and compensation of all types of personnel; labor relations activities; development of knowledge-based skills and core competencies.
- **General Administration**—Activities, costs, and assets relating to general management, accounting and finance, legal and regulatory affairs, safety and security, management information systems, forming strategic alliances and collaborating with strategic partners, and other "overhead" functions.

Source: Adapted from Michael E. Porter, *Competitive Advantage* (New York: The Free Press, 1985), pp. 37–43.

using to execute its strategy, and the underlying economics of the activities themselves.[12] Because these factors differ from company to company, the value chains of rival companies sometimes differ substantially—a condition that complicates the task of assessing rivals' relative cost positions. For instance, competing companies may differ in their degrees of vertical integration. Comparing the value chain for a fully integrated rival against a partially integrated rival requires adjusting for differences in scope of

---

[12]Porter, *Competitive Advantage*, p. 36.

activities performed. Clearly the internal costs for a manufacturer that *makes* all of its own parts and components will be greater than the internal costs of a producer that *buys* the needed parts and components from outside suppliers and only performs assembly operations.

Likewise, there is legitimate reason to expect value chain and cost differences between a company that is pursuing a low-cost/low-price strategy and a rival that is positioned on the high end of the market with a product that has prestige quality and a wealth of features. In the case of the low-cost firm, the costs of certain activities along the company's value chain should indeed be relatively low, whereas the high-end firm may understandably be spending relatively more to perform those activities that create the added quality and extra features.

Moreover, cost and price differences among rival companies can have their origins in activities performed by suppliers or by forward channel allies involved in getting the product to end users. Suppliers or forward channel allies may have excessively high cost structures or profit margins that jeopardize a company's cost competitiveness even though its costs for internally performed activities are competitive. For example, when determining Michelin's cost competitiveness vis-à-vis Goodyear and Bridgestone in supplying replacement tires to vehicle owners, we have to look at more than whether Michelin's tire manufacturing costs are above or below Goodyear's and Bridgestone's. Let's say that a buyer has to pay $400 for a set of Michelin tires and only $350 for a comparable set of Goodyear or Bridgestone tires; Michelin's $50 price disadvantage in the replacement tire marketplace can stem not only from higher manufacturing costs (reflecting, perhaps, the added costs of Michelin's strategic efforts to build a better-quality tire with more performance features) but also from (1) differences in what the three tire makers pay their suppliers for materials and tire-making components and (2) differences in the operating efficiencies, costs, and markups of Michelin's wholesale–retail dealer outlets versus those of Goodyear and Bridgestone. Thus, determining whether a company's prices and costs are competitive from an end user's standpoint requires looking at the activities and costs of competitively relevant suppliers and forward allies, as well as the costs of internally performed activities.

The Value Chain System for an Entire Industry   As the tire industry example makes clear, a company's value chain is embedded in a larger system of activities that includes the value chains of its upstream suppliers and downstream customers or allies engaged in getting its product or service to end users.[13] *Accurately assessing a company's competitiveness in end-use markets requires that company managers understand the entire value chain system for delivering a product or service to end users, not just the company's own value chain.* At the very least, this means considering the value chains of suppliers and forward channel allies (if any)— as shown in Figure 4.3.

Suppliers' value chains are relevant because suppliers perform activities and incur costs in creating and delivering the purchased inputs used in a company's own value chain; the cost and quality of these inputs influence a company's own cost and/or differentiation capabilities. Anything a company can do to reduce its suppliers' costs or improve suppliers' effectiveness can enhance its own competitiveness—a powerful reason for working collaboratively with suppliers.

Forward channel value chains are relevant because (1) the costs and margins of downstream companies are part of the price the end user pays and (2) the activities

> A company's cost competitiveness depends not only on the costs of internally performed activities (its own value chain) but also on costs in the value chains of suppliers and forward channel allies.

---

[13]Porter, *Competitive Advantage*, p. 34.

figure 4.3   **Representative Value Chain for an Entire Industry**

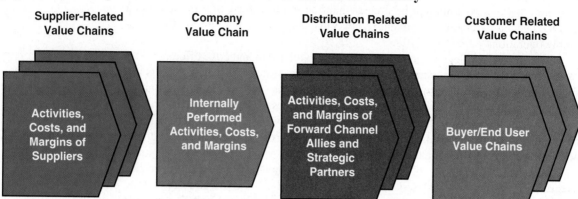

Source: Adapted from Michael E. Porter, *Competitive Advantage* (New York: Free Press, 1985), p. 35.

forward channel allies perform affect the end user's satisfaction. Thus, a company should work closely with its forward channel allies to revise or reinvent their value chains in ways that enhance their mutual competitiveness. Furthermore, a company may be able to improve its competitiveness by undertaking activities that beneficially impact both its own value chain and its customers' value chains.

For instance, some aluminum can producers constructed plants next to beer breweries and delivered cans on overhead conveyors directly to brewers' can-filling lines. This resulted in significant savings in production scheduling, shipping, and inventory costs for both container producers and breweries.[14] Many automotive parts suppliers have built plants near the auto assembly plants they supply to facilitate just-in-time deliveries, reduce warehousing and shipping costs, and promote close collaboration on parts design and production scheduling. In the California wine country, grape growers, irrigation equipment companies, suppliers of grape-harvesting and wine-making equipment, and firms making barrels, wine bottles, caps and corks, and labels are clustered together to be close to the nearly 700 wine makers they supply.[15] The lesson here is that a company's relative cost position and overall competitiveness are linked to the entire industry value chain and to customers' value chains as well.

Although the value chains in Figures 4.2 and 4.3 are representative, actual value chains vary by industry and by company. Value chains for products differ from value chains for services. The major value chain elements for the pulp and paper industry (timber farming, logging, pulp mills, papermaking, printing, and publishing) differ from the major chain elements for the home appliance industry (parts and components manufacture, assembly, wholesale distribution, retail sales). The value chain for the soft-drink industry (processing of basic ingredients, syrup manufacture, bottling and can filling, wholesale distribution, retailing) differs from that for the computer software industry (programming, disk loading, marketing, distribution). A producer of bathroom and kitchen faucets depends heavily on the activities of wholesale distributors and building supply retailers in winning sales to homebuilders and do-it-yourselfers; a producer of

---

[14]Hegert and Morris, "Accounting Data for Value Chain Analysis," p. 180.

[15]For more on how and why the clustering of suppliers and other support organizations matter to a company's costs and competitiveness, see Michael E. Porter, "Clusters and the New Economics of Competition," *Harvard Business Review* 76, no. 6 (November–December 1998), pp. 77–90.

small gasoline engines controls its own market share destiny by selling directly to the makers of lawn and garden equipment. A wholesaler's most important activities and costs deal with purchased goods, inbound logistics, and outbound logistics. A hotel's most important activities and costs are in operations—check-in and check-out, maintenance and housekeeping, dining and room service, conventions and meetings, and accounting. A global public accounting firm's most important activities and costs revolve around customer service and human resources management (recruiting and training a highly competent professional staff). Outbound logistics is a crucial activity at Domino's Pizza but comparatively insignificant at Blockbuster. Sales and marketing are dominant activities at Coca-Cola but only minor activities at interstate gas pipeline companies. Consequently, generic value chains like those in Figures 4.2 and 4.3 are illustrative, not absolute, and may require adaptation to fit a particular company's circumstances.

Developing the Data for Strategic Cost Analysis   Once the major elements of the value chain are identified, the next step in strategic cost analysis involves breaking down a firm's departmental cost accounting data into the costs of performing specific activities.[16] The appropriate degree of disaggregation depends on the economics of the activities and how valuable it is to develop cross-company cost comparisons for narrowly defined activities as opposed to broadly defined activities. A good guideline is to develop separate cost estimates for activities having different economics and for activities representing a significant or growing proportion of cost.[17]

Traditional accounting identifies costs according to broad categories of expenses—wages and salaries, employee benefits, supplies, travel, depreciation, R&D, and other fixed charges. *Activity-based costing* entails defining expense categories based on the specific activities being performed and then assigning costs to the appropriate activity responsible for creating the cost. An illustrative example is shown in Table 4.2.[18] Perhaps 25 percent of the companies that have explored the feasibility of activity-based costing have adopted this accounting approach. To fully understand the costs of activities all along the industry value chain, cost estimates for activities performed in the competitively relevant portions of suppliers' and customers' value chains also have to be developed.

To benchmark the firm's cost position against rivals, costs for the same activities for each rival must be estimated—an advanced art in competitive intelligence. But despite the tediousness of developing cost estimates activity by activity and the imprecision of some of the estimates for rivals, the payoff in exposing the costs of particular internal tasks and functions and the cost competitiveness of a company's position vis-à-vis rivals makes activity-based costing a valuable strategic analysis tool.[19] Illustration Capsule 16 shows a representative value chain for the music CD industry.

The most important application of value chain analysis is to expose how a particular firm's cost position compares with the cost positions of its rivals. What is needed

[16]For discussions of the accounting challenges in calculating the costs of value chain activities, see Shank and Govindarajan, *Strategic Cost Management*, pp. 62–72 and Chapter 5; and Hegert and Morris, "Accounting Data for Value Chain Analysis," pp. 175–88.

[17]Porter, *Competitive Advantage*, p. 45.

[18]For a discussion of activity-based cost accounting, see Cooper and Kaplan, "Measure Costs Right: Make the Right Decisions," pp. 96–103; Shank and Govindarajan, *Strategic Cost Management*, chapter 11; and Joseph A. Ness and Thomas G. Cucuzza, "Tapping the Full Potential of ABC," *Harvard Business Review* 73 no. 4 (July–August 1995), pp. 130–38.

[19]Shank and Govindarajan, *Strategic Cost Management*, p. 62.

table 4.2   The Difference between Traditional Cost Accounting and Activity-Based Cost Accounting: The Case of Purchasing

Traditional Cost Accounting Categories in Purchasing Department Budget		Cost of Performing Specific Purchasing Department Activities Using Activity-Based Cost Accounting	
Wages and salaries	$340,000	Evaluate supplier capabilities	$100,300
Employee benefits	95,000	Process purchase orders	82,100
Supplies	21,500	Collaboration with suppliers on just-in-time deliveries	140,200
Travel	12,400	Data-sharing activities with suppliers	59,550
Depreciation	19,000	Check quality of items purchased	94,100
Other fixed charges (office space, utilities)	112,000	Check incoming deliveries against purchase orders	48,450
Miscellaneous operating expenses	40,250	Dispute resolution	15,250
		Internal administration	100,200
	$640,150		$640,150

Source: Adapted from information in Terence P. Paré, "A New Tool for Managing Costs," *Fortune*, June 14, 1993, pp. 124–29.

are competitor-versus-competitor cost estimates for supplying a product or service to a well-defined customer group or market segment. The size of a company's cost advantage or disadvantage can vary from item to item in the product line, from customer group to customer group (if different distribution channels are used), and from geographic market to geographic market (if cost factors vary across geographic regions).

Benchmarking the Costs of Key Activities

Many companies today are *benchmarking* their costs of performing a given activity against competitors' costs (and/or against the costs of a noncompetitor in another industry that efficiently and effectively performs much the same activity or business process). Benchmarking is a tool that allows a company to determine whether the manner in which it performs particular functions and activities represents industry "best practices" when both cost and effectiveness are taken into account.

> Benchmarking the costs of company activities against rivals provides hard evidence of a company's cost competitiveness.

Benchmarking entails doing cross-company comparisons of how basic functions and processes in the value chain are performed—how materials are purchased, how suppliers are paid, how inventories are managed, how products are assembled, how fast the company can get new products to market, how the quality control function is performed, how customer orders are filled and shipped, how employees are trained, how payrolls are processed, and how maintenance is performed—and comparing the costs of these activities.[20] The objectives of benchmarking are to identify the best practices in

[20]For more details, see Gregory H. Watson, *Strategic Benchmarking: How to Rate Your Company's Performance Against the World's Best* (New York: John Wiley, 1993); and Robert C. Camp, *Benchmarking: The Search for Industry Best Practices That Lead to Superior Performance* (Milwaukee: ASQC Quality Press, 1989). See also Alexandra Biesada, "Strategic Benchmarking," *Financial World*, September 29, 1992, pp. 30–38.

illustration capsule 16
The Value Chain for the Recording and Distributing of Music CDs

The table below presents the representative costs and markups associated with producing and distributing a music CD that retails for $15.

1. Record company direct production costs:		$ 2.40
Artists and repertoire	$0.75	
Pressing of CD and packaging	1.65	
2. Royalties		0.99
3. Record company marketing expenses		1.50
4. Record company overhead		1.50
5. Total record company costs		6.39
6. Record company's operating profit		1.86
7. Record company's selling price to distributor/wholesaler		8.25
8. Average wholesale distributor markup to cover distribution activities and profit margins		1.50
9. Average wholesale price charged to retailer		9.75
10. Average retail markup over wholesale cost		5.25
11. Average price to consumer at retail		$15.00

Source: Developed from information in "Fight the Power," a case study prepared by Adrian Aleyne, Babson College, 1999.

performing an activity, to learn how other companies have actually achieved lower costs or better results in performing benchmarked activities, and to take action to improve a company's competitiveness whenever benchmarking reveals that its costs and results of performing an activity do not match those of other companies (either competitors or noncompetitors).

In 1979, Xerox became an early pioneer in the use of benchmarking when Japanese manufacturers began selling midsize copiers in the United States for $9,600 each—less than Xerox's production costs.[21] Although Xerox management suspected its Japanese competitors were dumping, it sent a team of line managers to Japan, including the head of manufacturing, to study competitors' business processes and costs. Fortunately, Xerox's joint venture partner in Japan, Fuji-Xerox, knew the competitors well. The team found that Xerox's costs were excessive due to gross inefficiencies in its manufacturing processes and business practices; the study proved instrumental in Xerox's efforts to become cost-competitive and prompted Xerox to embark on a long-term program to benchmark 67 of its key work processes against companies identified as having the "best practices" in performing these processes. Xerox quickly decided not to restrict its benchmarking efforts to its office equipment rivals but to extend them to any company regarded as "world class" in performing *any activity* relevant to Xerox's business.

---

[21]Jeremy Main, "How to Steal the Best Ideas Around," *Fortune*, October 19, 1992, pp. 102–3.

illustration capsule 17
Benchmarking: Ford Borrows from Cisco Systems

For some time, top executives at Ford Motor Company have believed that the company's technology strategy is the key to Ford's future. They also recognized that to achieve competence with information technologies, Ford could benefit from the experiences of companies that were acknowledged technological leaders.

Recently, senior Ford executives went to Cisco Systems to get advice and to benchmark Ford's design and manufacturing systems against Cisco's, which are built around Internet technology. Cisco executives recommended that Ford place Internet-savvy executives at the top. During a two-day visit with Cisco CEO John Chambers and other managers at Cisco's headquarters in California, Ford executives learned strategies for revamping their processes. "It was so fundamentally different than our business," recalls one Ford executive. "I got it."

The results of meetings with Cisco have included Ford's new FordDirect.com website, which links buyers with dealers; its new Customer Knowledge System, which creates a profile of each customer; and revamping of its internal design and production processes around the Net. Ford executives regularly benchmark the company's e-commerce activities against those of companies like Cisco, Amazon.com, Dell Computer, and others recognized as having "model" websites and being particularly astute in using Internet technology to good advantage.

Sources: Edward Robinson and William Hoffman, "The Re-Education of Jaques Nasser," *Business 2.0,* May 29, 2001; Stan Gibson, "Say It Again: Channel Transparency," *eWeek* (www.zdnet.com), September 4, 2000; and Bob Wallace, "FordDirect.com Could Be Win–Win for Ford, Dealers, Customers," *InformationWeek* (www.internetwk.com), August 25, 2000.

Basic Concept
Benchmarking
has proven to be a potent tool for learning which companies are best at performing particular activities and then utilizing their techniques (or "best practices") to improve the cost and effectiveness of a company's own internal activities.

Thus, benchmarking has quickly come to be a tool not only for comparing a company against rivals on cost but also for comparing itself to others on most any relevant activity or competitively important measure. Toyota managers got their idea for just-in-time inventory deliveries by studying how U.S. supermarkets replenished their shelves. Southwest Airlines reduced the turnaround time of its aircraft at each scheduled stop by studying pit crews on the auto racing circuit. Illustration Capsule 17 describes one of Ford Motor Company's benchmarking experiences in accounts payable. Over 80 percent of *Fortune 500* companies reportedly engage in some form of benchmarking.

The tough part of benchmarking is not whether or how to do it but rather gaining access to information about other companies' practices and costs. Sometimes benchmarking can be accomplished by collecting information from published reports, trade groups, and industry research firms and by talking to knowledgeable industry analysts, customers, and suppliers. On occasion, customers, suppliers, and joint-venture partners often make willing benchmarking allies. Usually, though, benchmarking requires field trips to the facilities of competing or noncompeting companies to observe how things are done, ask questions, compare practices and processes, and perhaps exchange data on productivity, staffing levels, time requirements, and other cost components. The problem is that benchmarking involves competitively sensitive cost information and close rivals can't be expected to be completely open, even if they agree to host facilities tours and answer questions. Making reliable cost comparisons is complicated by the fact that participants often use different cost accounting systems.

However, the explosive interest of companies in benchmarking costs and identifying best practices has prompted consulting organizations (e.g., Andersen Consulting, A. T. Kearney, Best Practices Benchmarking & Consulting, and Towers Perrin) and several newly formed councils and associations (the International Benchmarking Clearinghouse and the Strategic Planning Institute's Council on Benchmarking) to gather benchmarking data, do benchmarking studies, and distribute information about best practices and the costs of performing activities to clients or members without

illustration capsule 18
Benchmarking and Ethical Conduct

Because discussions between benchmarking partners can involve competitively sensitive data, conceivably raising questions about possible restraint of trade or improper business conduct, the Strategic Planning Institute's Council on Benchmarking and the International Benchmarking Clearinghouse urge all individuals and organizations involved in benchmarking to abide by a code of conduct grounded in ethical business behavior. The code is based on the following principles and guidelines:

- In benchmarking with competitors, establish specific ground rules up front, such as, "We don't want to talk about those things that will give either of us a competitive advantage; rather, we want to see where we both can mutually improve or gain benefit." Do not discuss costs with competitors if costs are an element of pricing.

- Do not ask competitors for sensitive data or cause the benchmarking partner to feel that sensitive data must be provided to keep the process going. Be prepared to provide the same level of information that you request. Do not share proprietary information without prior approval from the proper authorities of both parties.

- Use an ethical third party to assemble and blind competitive data, with inputs from legal counsel, for direct competitor comparisons.

- Consult with legal counsel if any information gathering procedure is in doubt (e.g., before contacting a direct competitor).

- Treat any information obtained from a benchmarking partner as internal, privileged information. Any external use must have the partner's permission.

- Do not:
  —Disparage a competitor's business or operations to a third party.
  —Attempt to limit competition or gain business through the benchmarking relationship.
  —Misrepresent yourself as working for another employer.

- Demonstrate commitment to the efficiency and effectiveness of the process by being adequately prepared at each step, particularly at initial contact. Be professional, honest, and courteous. Adhere to the agenda and maintain focus on benchmarking issues.

Sources: The Strategic Planning Institute's Council on Benchmarking; the International Benchmarking Clearinghouse; and conference presentation of AT&T Benchmarking Group, Des Moines, Iowa, October 1993.

identifying the sources. Having an independent group gather the information and report it in a manner that disguises the names of individual companies permits companies to avoid having to disclose competitively sensitive data to rivals and reduces the risk of ethical problems. The ethical dimension of benchmarking is discussed in Illustration Capsule 18.

Strategic Options for Achieving Cost Competitiveness

Value chain analysis and benchmarking can reveal a great deal about a firm's cost competitiveness. One of the fundamental insights of strategic cost analysis is that a company's competitiveness depends on how well it manages its value chain relative to how well competitors manage theirs.[22] Examining the makeup of a company's own value chain and comparing it to rivals' indicates who has how much of a cost advantage or disadvantage and which cost components are responsible. Such information is vital in crafting strategies to eliminate a cost disadvantage or create a cost advantage.

> Strategic actions to eliminate a cost disadvantage need to be linked to the location in the value chain where the cost differences originate.

Looking again at Figure 4.2, observe that there are three main areas in a company's overall value chain where important differences in the costs of competing firms

---

[22]Shank and Govindarajan, *Strategic Cost Management*, p. 50.

can occur: in the suppliers' part of the industry value chain, in a company's own activity segments, or in the forward channel portion of the industry chain. If a firm's lack of cost competitiveness lies either in the backward (upstream) or forward (downstream) sections of the value chain, then reestablishing cost competitiveness may have to extend beyond the firm's own in-house operations.

Attacking the High Costs of Items Purchased from Suppliers   When a firm's cost disadvantage is principally associated with the costs of items purchased from suppliers (the upstream end of the industry chain), company managers can pursue any of several strategic actions to correct the problem:[23]

- Negotiate more favorable prices with suppliers.
- Work with suppliers on the design and specifications for what is being supplied to identify cost savings that will allow them to lower their prices.
- Switch to lower-priced substitute inputs.
- Collaborate closely with suppliers to identify mutual cost-saving opportunities. For example, finding ways to expedite just-in-time deliveries can lower a company's inventory and internal logistics costs and may also allow its suppliers to economize on their warehousing, shipping, and production scheduling costs—a win–win outcome for both (instead of a zero-sum game where the company's gains match supplier concessions).[24]
- Integrate backward to gain control over the costs of purchased items—seldom an attractive option.
- Try to make up the difference by cutting costs elsewhere in the chain—usually a last resort.

Attacking Cost Disadvantages in the Forward Portion of the Industry Value Chain   A company's strategic options for eliminating cost disadvantages in the forward end of the value chain system include:[25]

- Pushing distributors and other forward channel allies to reduce their markups.
- Working closely with forward channel allies to identify win–win opportunities to reduce costs. A chocolate manufacturer learned that by shipping its bulk chocolate in liquid form in tank cars instead of 10-pound molded bars, it could not only save its candy-bar manufacturing customers the costs associated with unpacking and melting but also eliminate its own costs of molding bars and packing them.
- Changing to a more economical distribution strategy, including switching to cheaper distribution channels (perhaps direct sales via the Internet) or perhaps integrating forward into downstream businesses.
- Trying to make up the difference by cutting costs earlier in the cost chain—usually a last resort.

---

[23]Porter, *Competitive Advantage*, chapter 3.

[24]In recent years, most companies have moved aggressively to collaborate with key suppliers to implement better supply chain management, often achieving cost savings of 5 to 25 percent. For a discussion of how to develop a cost-saving supply chain strategy, see Shashank Kulkarni, "Purchasing: A Supply-Side Strategy," *Journal of Business Strategy* 17, no. 5 (September–October 1996), pp. 17–20.

[25]Porter, *Competitive Advantage*, chapter 3.

Attacking the High Costs of Internally Performed Activities   When the source of a firm's cost disadvantage is internal, managers can use any of the following eight strategic approaches to restore cost parity:[26]

1. Implement the use of best practices throughout the company, particularly for high-cost activities.

2. Try to eliminate some cost-producing activities altogether by revamping the value chain. Examples include cutting out low-value-added activities, shifting to a different business model, bypassing the value chains and associated costs of distribution allies and marketing directly to end users (the approach used by Gateway and Dell in PCs), or using e-commerce retailing. A brokerage firm, for example, could switch to online stock trading systems rather than maintaining an elaborate network of local offices staffed by professional brokers; when investors must call or visit brokers in person to handle their trades, the commissions are sharply higher than for online trading. In retailing, Amazon.com, eMusic, mortgage.com, and others have sliced brick-and-mortar activities out of the value chain.

3. Relocate high-cost activities (such as R&D or manufacturing) to geographic areas where they can be performed more cheaply.

4. Search out activities that can be outsourced from vendors or performed by contractors more cheaply than they can be done internally.

5. Invest in productivity-enhancing, cost-saving technological improvements (robotics, flexible manufacturing techniques, and state-of-the-art electronic networking).

6. Innovate around the troublesome cost components—computer chip makers regularly design around the patents held by others to avoid paying royalties; automakers have substituted lower-cost plastic and rubber for metal at many exterior body locations.

7. Simplify the product design so that it can be manufactured or assembled quickly and more economically.

8. Try to make up the internal cost disadvantage by achieving savings in the backward and forward portions of the value chain system—usually a last resort.

From Value Chain Activities to Competitive Capabilities to Competitive Advantage

How well a company manages its value chain activities relative to competitors can allow it to build valuable competencies and capabilities and leverage them into sustainable competitive advantage. With rare exceptions, a firm's products or services are not a dependable basis for sustained competitive advantage; it is too easy for resourceful competitors to clone, improve on, or find an effective substitute for them.[27] Rather, sustaining a company's competitive edge is best grounded in competencies and capabilities critical to market success and to pleasing customers—competencies and capabilities that rivals don't have or can't quite match.

Merck and Glaxo, two of the world's most competitively capable pharmaceutical companies, built their business positions around expert performance of a few competitively crucial activities: extensive R&D to achieve first discovery of new drugs, a

> **Strategic Management Principle**
>
> Performing value chain activities in ways that give a company the capabilities to outmatch rivals is a source of competitive advantage.

---

[26]Ibid.

[27]James Brian Quinn, *Intelligent Enterprise* (New York: Free Press, 1993), p. 54.

carefully constructed approach to patenting, skill in gaining rapid and thorough clinical clearance through regulatory bodies, and unusually strong distribution and sales force capabilities.[28] FedEx has linked and integrated the performance of its aircraft fleet, truck fleet, support systems, and personnel so tightly and smoothly across the company's different value chain activities that it has created the capability to provide customers with guaranteed overnight delivery services. McDonald's can turn out identical-quality fast-food items at some 25,000-plus outlets around the world—an impressive demonstration of its capability to replicate its operating systems at many locations via an omnibus manual of detailed rules and procedures for each activity and intensive training of franchise operators and outlet managers.

QUESTION 4: HOW STRONG IS THE COMPANY'S COMPETITIVE POSITION?

Systematic assessment of whether a company's overall competitive position is strong or weak relative to close rivals is an essential step in company situation analysis.

Using the tools of value chains, strategic cost analysis, and benchmarking to determine a company's cost competitiveness is necessary but not sufficient. A more broadranging assessment needs to be made of a company's competitive position and competitive strength. Particular issues that merit examination include (1) whether the firm's market position can be expected to improve or deteriorate if the present strategy is continued (allowing for fine-tuning); (2) how the firm ranks relative to rivals on each key success factor and each relevant measure of competitive strength and resource capability; (3) whether the firm enjoys a competitive advantage over rivals or is currently at a disadvantage; and (4) the firm's ability to protect and improve its market position in light of industry driving forces, competitive pressures, and the anticipated moves of rivals.

Table 4.3 lists some indicators of whether a firm's competitive position is strong or weak compared to rivals. But company managers need to do more than just identify the areas of competitive strength and weakness. They have to *judge how all the signs of strength and weakness add up*. The answers to two questions are of particular interest: Does the company have a net competitive advantage or disadvantage vis-à-vis major competitors? Can the company's market position and performance be expected to improve or deteriorate under the current strategy?

Competitive Strength Assessments

The most telling way to determine how strongly a company holds its competitive position is to *quantitatively* assess whether the company is stronger or weaker than close rivals on each industry key success factor and each competitively essential resource and capability. Much of the information for competitive position assessment comes from previous analyses. Industry and competitive analysis reveals the key success factors and competitive capabilities that separate industry winners from losers. Competitor analysis and benchmarking data provide a basis for judging the strengths and capabilities of rivals on such competitively important factors as cost, product quality, customer service, image and reputation, financial strength, technological skills, speed to market, distribution capability, and the possession of competitively important resources and capabilities.

---

[28]Quinn, *Intelligent Enterprise*, p. 34.

table 4.3   The Signs of Strength and Weakness in a Company's Competitive Position

Signs of Competitive Strength	Signs of Competitive Weakness
• Important resource strengths, core competencies, and competitive capabilities	• Confronted with competitive disadvantages
• A distinctive competence in a competitively important value chain activity	• Losing ground to rival firms with stronger positions in global and/or e-commerce markets
• Strong market share (or a leading market share)	• Eroding market share and below-average growth in revenues
• A pacesetting or distinctive strategy that is hard for rivals to copy or match	• Short on financial resources to pursue new opportunities
• Ahead of rivals in expanding into global markets and/or in building an e-commerce presence	• Weaker brand-name recognition than rivals and/or a slipping reputation with customers
• A better-known brand-name and reputation than rivals	• Trailing in product development and product innovation capability
• Growing customer base and customer loyalty	• In a strategic group destined to lose ground
• In a favorably situated strategic group	• Weak in areas where there is the most market potential—foreign markets, e-commerce
• Well-positioned in attractive market segments	• A higher-cost producer
• Strongly differentiated products	• Too small to be a major factor in the marketplace
• Cost advantages	• Not in good position to deal with emerging threats
• Above-average profit margins	• Subpar product quality
• Above-average technological and innovational capability	• Lacking skills, resources, and competitive capabilities in key areas
• A creative, entrepreneurially alert management	• Weaker distribution capability than rivals
• Ample financial resources	

Step 1 is to make a list of the industry's key success factors and most telling measures of competitive strength or weakness (6 to 10 measures usually suffice). Step 2 is to rate the firm and its rivals on each factor. Numerical rating scales (e.g., from 1 to 10) are best to use, although ratings of stronger ($+$), weaker ($-$), and about equal ($=$) may be appropriate when information is scanty and assigning numerical scores conveys false precision. Step 3 is to sum the individual strength ratings to get an overall measure of competitive strength for each competitor. Step 4 is to draw conclusions about the size and extent of the company's net competitive advantage or disadvantage based on the strength assessments and to take specific note of areas where the company's competitive position is strongest and weakest.

> High competitive strength ratings signal a strong competitive position and possession of competitive advantage; low ratings signal a weak position and competitive disadvantage.

Table 4.4 provides two examples of competitive strength assessment. The first one employs an *unweighted rating scale*. With unweighted ratings each key success factor/competitive strength measure is assumed to be equally important (a rather dubious assumption). Whichever company has the highest strength rating on a given measure has an implied competitive edge on that factor; the size of its edge is mirrored in the margin of difference between its rating and the ratings assigned to rivals. Summing a company's ratings on all the measures produces an overall strength rating. The higher a company's overall strength rating, the stronger its competitive position. The bigger the difference between a company's overall rating and the scores of lower-rated rivals, the greater its implied net competitive advantage. Thus, ABC's total score of 61 (see the top half of Table 4.4) signals a greater net competitive advantage over Rival 4 (with a score of 32) than over Rival 1 (with a score of 58).

However, it is better methodology to use a weighted rating system because the different measures of competitive strength are unlikely to be equally important. In a

table 4.4   Illustrations of Unweighted and Weighted Competitive Strength Assessments

A. Sample of an Unweighted Competitive Strength Assessment
Rating scale: 1 = Very weak; 10 = Very strong

Key Success Factor/Strength Measure	ABC Co.	Rival 1	Rival 2	Rival 3	Rival 4
Quality/product performance	8	5	10	1	6
Reputation/image	8	7	10	1	6
Manufacturing capability	2	10	4	5	1
Technological skills	10	1	7	3	8
Dealer network/distribution capability	9	4	10	5	1
New product innovation capability	9	4	10	5	1
Financial resources	5	10	7	3	1
Relative cost position	5	10	3	1	4
Customer service capabilities	5	7	10	1	4
Unweighted overall strength rating	61	58	71	25	32

B. Sample of a Weighted Competitive Strength Assessment
Rating scale: 1 = Very weak; 10 = Very strong

Key Success Factor/Strength Measure	Weight	ABC Co.	Rival 1	Rival 2	Rival 3	Rival 4
Quality/product performance	0.10	8/0.80	5/0.50	10/1.00	1/0.10	6/0.60
Reputation/image	0.10	8/0.80	7/0.70	10/1.00	1/0.10	6/0.60
Manufacturing capability	0.10	2/0.20	10/1.00	4/0.40	5/0.50	1/0.10
Technological skills	0.05	10/0.50	1/0.05	7/0.35	3/0.15	8/0.40
Dealer network/distribution capability	0.05	9/0.45	4/0.20	10/0.50	5/0.25	1/0.05
New product innovation capability	0.05	9/0.45	4/0.20	10/0.50	5/0.25	1/0.05
Financial resources	0.10	5/0.50	10/1.00	7/0.70	3/0.30	1/0.10
Relative cost position	0.30	5/1.50	10/3.00	3/0.95	1/0.30	4/1.20
Customer service capabilities	0.15	5/0.75	7/1.05	10/1.50	1/0.15	4/0.60
Sum of weights	1.00					
Weighted overall strength rating		5.95	7.70	6.85	2.10	3.70

commodity-product industry, for instance, having low unit costs relative to rivals is nearly always the most important determinant of competitive strength. In an industry with strong product differentiation the most significant measures of competitive strength may be brand awareness, amount of advertising, reputation for quality, and distribution capability. In a *weighted rating system* each measure of competitive strength is assigned a weight based on its perceived importance in shaping competitive success. The largest weight could be as high as 0.75 (maybe even higher) in situations where one particular competitive variable is overwhelmingly decisive or as low as 0.20 when two or three strength measures are more important than the rest. Lesser competitive strength indicators can carry weights of 0.05 or 0.10. No matter whether the differences between the weights are big or little, *the sum of the weights must add up to 1.0.*

Weighted strength ratings are calculated by deciding how a company stacks up on each strength measure (using the 1 to 10 rating scale) and multiplying the assigned

> A weighted competitive strength analysis is conceptually stronger than an unweighted analysis because of the inherent weakness in assuming that all the strength measures are equally important.

rating by the assigned weight (a rating score of 4 times a weight of 0.20 gives a weighted rating of 0.80). Again, the company with the highest rating on a given measure has an implied competitive edge on that measure, with the size of its edge reflected in the difference between its rating and rivals' ratings. The weight attached to the measure indicates how important the edge is. Summing a company's weighted strength ratings for all the measures yields an overall strength rating. Comparisons of the weighted overall strength scores indicate which competitors are in the strongest and weakest competitive positions and who has how big a net competitive advantage over whom.

The bottom half of Table 4.4 shows a sample competitive strength assessment for ABC Company using a weighted rating system. Note that the unweighted and weighted rating schemes produce a different ordering of the companies. In the weighted system, ABC Company dropped from second to third in strength, and Rival 1 jumped from third into first because of its high strength ratings on the two most important factors. Weighting the importance of the strength measures can thus make a significant difference in the outcome of the assessment.

Competitive strength assessments provide useful conclusions about a company's competitive situation. The ratings show how a company compares against rivals, factor by factor or capability by capability, thus revealing where it is strongest and weakest, and against whom. Moreover, the overall competitive strength scores indicate how all the different factors add up—whether the company is at a net competitive advantage or disadvantage against each rival. The firm with the largest overall competitive strength rating enjoys the strongest competitive position, with the size of its net competitive advantage reflected by how much its score exceeds the scores of rivals.

Knowing where a company is competitively strong and where it is weak in comparison to specific rivals is valuable in deciding on specific actions to strengthen its long-term competitive position. As a general rule, a company should try to leverage its competitive strengths (areas where it scores higher than rivals) into sustainable competitive advantage and take strategic actions to protect against its competitive weaknesses (areas where it scores are below those of rivals). At the same time, the competitive strength ratings point to which rival companies may be vulnerable to competitive attack and the areas where they are weakest. When a company has important competitive strengths in areas where one or more rivals are weak, it makes sense to consider offensive moves to exploit rivals' competitive weaknesses.

> High competitive strength ratings vis-à-vis competitors signal opportunity for a company to improve its long-term market position.

> Good strategy entails looking for opportunities to leverage company strengths into competitive advantage, often by using company strengths to attack the competitive weaknesses of rivals.

QUESTION 5: WHAT STRATEGIC ISSUES DOES THE COMPANY FACE?

The final analytical task is to zero in on the strategic challenges that stand as obstacles to the company's future success. This involves using the results of both company situation analysis and industry and competitive analysis to identify as sharply and as clearly as possible the strategic issues and problems confronting the company. Pinpointing the things that management needs to worry about most sets the agenda for putting together an effective strategic action plan. The "worry list" of obstacles and issues that have to be wrestled with can include such things as *how* to meet the challenges posed by global competition, *how* to combat the product innovations of rivals, *how* to reduce the company's high costs, *how* to sustain the company's present rate of growth or grow the business at a faster rate, *how* to gain better market visibility for the company's products, or *how* to capture the e-commerce opportunities. Other issues

Identifying the strategic issues a company faces is a prerequisite to effective strategy making. It involves developing a "worry list" of strategic challenges concerning "how to . . .", whether to . . .", and "what to do about . . ."

might be *whether* to expand the company's product offerings, put more emphasis on new product R&D, add more production capacity, cut prices in response to the actions of competitors, add new features that will boost the performance of the company's products, or go forward with investments in foreign markets. Finally, managers may ask *what to do about* proposed new regulations that will significantly raise costs, lagging buyer interest in the company's latest new products, or the aging demographics of the company's customer base.

In determining the issues that merit strategic attention, managers need to draw on all the prior analysis, put the company's overall situation into perspective, and lock in on what challenges have to be overcome and what issues have to be resolved in order for the company to be financially and competitively successful in the years ahead. This step should not be taken lightly. Without a precise fix on the challenges and issues, managers are not prepared to start crafting a strategy. Questions that can help pinpoint the right strategic issues to address include the following:

- Is the present strategy adequate for protecting and improving the company's market position in light of the five competitive forces—particularly those that are expected to intensify in strength?
- Is the company vulnerable to the competitive efforts of one or more rivals?
- Should the present strategy be adjusted to better respond to the *driving forces* at work in the industry?
- Is the present strategy closely matched to the industry's *future* key success factors?
- Does the present strategy adequately capitalize on the company's resource strengths and capabilities?
- Which of the company's opportunities merit top priority? Which should be given low priority? Which are best suited to the company's resource strengths and capabilities?
- How important is it for the company need to correct its resource weaknesses? Are there things the company can do to lessen the impact of external threats?
- Does the company have competitive advantage, or must it work to offset competitive disadvantage?
- Where are the strong spots and weak spots in the present strategy?

Strategic Management Principle
A good strategy must contain ways to deal with all the strategic issues that stand in the way of the company's financial and competitive success in the years ahead.

The answers to these questions and the worries management has about "how to . . . ," "whether to . . . ," and "what to do about . . ." signal whether the company can continue the same basic strategy with minor adjustments or whether major overhaul is called for. If a company's current strategy is well matched to its external environment and to its resource strengths and capabilities, there is little need to contemplate big shifts in strategy. If, however, the present strategy is not well suited for the road ahead, the task of crafting a better strategy has got to go to the top of management's action agenda.

Table 4.5 provides a format for doing company situation analysis. It incorporates the concepts and analytical techniques discussed in this chapter and provides a way of reporting the results of company situation analysis in a systematic, concise manner.

table 4.5   Company Situation Analysis

1. Strategic performance indicators

	1997	1998	1999	2000	2001
Market share	___	___	___	___	___
Sales growth	___	___	___	___	___
Net profit margin	___	___	___	___	___
Return on equity investment	___	___	___	___	___
Other (specify): _____	___	___	___	___	___

2. Internal resource strengths and competitive capabilities:

Internal weaknesses and resource deficiencies:

External opportunities:

External threats to the company's well-being:

3. Competitive strength assessment

  Rating scale: 1 = Very weak; 10 = Very strong.

Key Success Factor/ Competitive Strength Measure	Weight	Firm A	Firm B	Firm C	Firm D	Firm E
Quality/product performance	___	___	___	___	___	___
Reputation/image	___	___	___	___	___	___
Manufacturing capability	___	___	___	___	___	___
Technological skills	___	___	___	___	___	___
Dealer network/ distribution capability	___	___	___	___	___	___
New product innovation capability	___	___	___	___	___	___
Financial resources	___	___	___	___	___	___
Relative cost position	___	___	___	___	___	___
Customer service capability	___	___	___	___	___	___
Sum of weights	1.0					
Overall strength rating		___	___	___	___	___

4. Conclusions concerning competitive position:

  (Improving/slipping? Competitive advantages/disadvantages?)

5. Major strategic issues the company must address:

key|points

There are five key questions to consider in performing company situation analysis:

1. *How well is the present strategy working?* This involves evaluating the strategy from a qualitative standpoint (completeness, internal consistency, rationale, and suitability to the situation) and also from a quantitative standpoint (the strategic and financial results the strategy is producing). The stronger a company's current overall performance, the less likely the need for radical strategy changes. The weaker a company's performance and/or the faster the changes in its external situation (which can be gleaned from industry and competitive analysis), the more its current strategy must be questioned.

2. *What are the company's resource strengths and weaknesses and its external opportunities and threats?* A SWOT analysis provides an overview of a firm's situation and is an essential component of crafting a strategy tightly matched to the company's situation. A company's resource strengths, competencies, and competitive capabilities are important because they are the most logical and appealing building blocks for strategy; resource weaknesses are important because they may represent vulnerabilities that need correction. External opportunities and threats come into play because a good strategy necessarily aims at capturing a company's most attractive opportunities and at defending against threats to its well-being.

3. *Are the company's prices and costs competitive?* One telling sign of whether a company's situation is strong or precarious is whether its prices and costs are competitive with industry rivals. Strategic cost analysis and value chain analysis are essential tools in benchmarking a company's prices and costs against rivals, determining whether the company is performing particular functions and activities cost effectively, learning whether its costs are in line with competitors, and deciding which internal activities and business processes need to be scrutinized for improvement. Value chain analysis teaches that how competently a company manages its value chain activities relative to rivals is a key to building valuable competencies and competitive capabilities and then leveraging them into sustainable competitive advantage.

4. *How strong is the company's competitive position?* The key appraisals here involve whether the company's position is likely to improve or deteriorate if the present strategy is continued, how the company matches up against key rivals on industry key success factors and other chief determinants of competitive success, and whether and why the company has a competitive advantage or disadvantage. Quantitative competitive strength assessments, using the methodology presented in Table 4.4, indicate where a company is competitively strong and weak and provide insight into the company's ability to defend or enhance its market position. As a rule a company's competitive strategy should be built around its competitive strengths and should aim at shoring up areas where it is competitively vulnerable. Also, the areas where company strengths match up against competitor weaknesses represent the best potential for new offensive initiatives.

5. *What strategic issues does the company face?* The purpose of this analytical step is to zero in on the strategic challenges that stand as obstacles to the company's future success. It involves using the results of both company situation analysis and industry and competitive analysis to identify the issues and problems that management needs to address. The objective is to pinpoint the things that management needs to worry about most. Identifying what challenges have to be overcome and

what issues have to be resolved in order for the company to be financially and competitively successful in the years ahead frames the strategic agenda that management needs to act on.

Good company situation analysis, like good industry and competitive analysis, is a crucial prerequisite to good strategy-making. A competently done evaluation of a company's resources and competencies exposes strong and weak points in the present strategy, company capabilities and vulnerabilities, and the company's ability to protect or improve its competitive position in light of driving forces, competitive pressures, and the competitive strength of rivals. Managers need such understanding to craft a strategy that fits the company's situation well.

suggested | readings

Birchall, David W., and George Tovstiga. "The Strategic Potential of a Firm's Knowledge Portfolio." *Journal of General Management* 25, no. 1 (Autumn 1999), pp. 1–16.

Bontis, Nick; Nicola C. Dragonetti; Kristine Jacobsen; and Goran Roos. "The Knowledge Toolbox: A Review of the Tools Available to Measure and Manage Intangible Resources." *European Management Journal* 17, no. 4 (August 1999), pp. 391–401.

Collis, David J., and Cynthia A. Montgomery. "Competing on Resources: Strategy in the 1990s." *Harvard Business Review* 73 no. 4 (July–August 1995), pp. 118–28.

Duncan, W. Jack; Peter M. Ginter; and Linda E. Swayne. "Competitive Advantage and Internal Organizational Assessment." *Academy of Management Executive* 12, no. 3 (August 1998), pp. 6–16.

Fahey, Liam, and H. Kurt Christensen. "Building Distinctive Competencies into Competitive Advantages." In *The Strategic Planning Management Reader*, ed. Liam Fahey. Englewood Cliffs, NJ: Prentice Hall, 1989, pp. 113–18.

Fisher, Marshall L. "What Is the Right Supply Chain for Your Product?" *Harvard Business Review* 75, no. 3 (March–April 1997), pp. 105–16.

Gadiesh, Orit, and James L. Gilbert. "Profit Pools: A Fresh Look at Strategy." *Harvard Business Review* 76, no. 3 (May–June 1998), pp. 139–47.

Kaplan, Robert S., and David P. Norton. "The Balanced Scorecard—Measures That Drive Performance." *Harvard Business Review* 70, no. 1 (January–February 1992), pp. 71–79.

Prahalad, C. K., and Gary Hamel. "The Core Competence of the Corporation." *Harvard Business Review* 70, no. 3 (May–June 1990), pp. 79–93.

Shank, John K., and Vijay Govindarajan. *Strategic Cost Management: The New Tool for Competitive Advantage.* New York: Free Press, 1993.

Stalk, George; Philip Evans; and Lawrence E. Shulman. "Competing on Capabilities: The New Rules of Corporate Strategy." *Harvard Business Review* 70, no. 2 (March–April 1992), pp. 57–69.

Teece, David. "Capturing Value from Knowledge Assets: The New Economy, Markets for Know-How, and Intangible Assets." *California Management Review* 40, no. 3 (Spring 1998), pp. 55–79.

Watson, Gregory H. *Strategic Benchmarking: How to Rate Your Company's Performance Against the World's Best.* New York: John Wiley & Sons, 1993.

Zack, Michael H. "Developing a Knowledge Strategy." *California Management Review* 41, no. 3 (Spring 1999), pp. 125–45.

chapter | five

Strategy and Competitive Advantage

Successful business strategy is about actively shaping the game you play, not just playing the game you find.
—Adam M. Brandenburger and Barry J. Nalebuff

The essence of strategy lies in creating tomorrow's competitive advantages faster than competitors mimic the ones you possess today.
—Gary Hamel and C. K. Prahalad

Competitive strategy is about being different. It means deliberately choosing to perform activities differently or to perform different activities than rivals to deliver a unique mix of value.
—Michael E. Porter

Strategies for taking the hill won't necessarily hold it.
—Amar Bhide

Nothing focuses the mind better than the constant sight of a competitor who wants to wipe you off the map.
—Wayne Calloway, Former CEO, PepsiCo

[S]trategic partnerships have become central to competitive success in fast changing global markets.
—Yves L. Doz and Gary Hamel

Winning business strategies are grounded in sustainable competitive advantage. A company has *competitive advantage* whenever it has an edge over rivals in attracting customers and defending against competitive forces. There are many routes to competitive advantage, but the most basic is to provide buyers with what they perceive as superior value—a good product at a low price,

a superior product that is worth paying more for, or a best-value offering that represents an attractive combination of price, features, quality, service, and other attributes buyers find attractive. Delivering superior value—whatever form it takes—nearly always requires performing value chain activities differently than rivals and building competencies and resource capabilities that are not readily matched.

This chapter focuses on how a company can achieve or defend competitive advantage through the strategy it employs and its management of the value chain.[1] We begin by describing the basic types of competitive strategies in some depth. Next are sections examining the merits of cooperative strategies (strategic alliances and collaborative partnerships), merger and acquisition strategies, and vertical integration versus outsourcing. There are also sections surveying the use of offensive moves to build competitive advantage and the use of defensive moves to protect competitive advantage. In the concluding section we look at the competitive importance of timing strategic moves—when it is advantageous to be a first-mover and when it is better to be a fast-follower or late-mover.

Investing aggressively in creating sustainable competitive advantage is a company's single most dependable contributor to above-average profitability.

----

[1]The definitive work on building and defending competitive advantage is Michael E. Porter, *Competitive Advantage* (New York: Free Press, 1985). A substantial portion of this chapter draws on Porter's pioneering contribution.

THE FIVE GENERIC COMPETITIVE STRATEGIES

A company's competitive strategy consists of the business approaches and initiatives it undertakes to attract customers and fulfill their expectations, to withstand competitive pressures, and to strengthen its market position. *Competitive strategy* has a narrower scope than *business strategy*. Competitive strategy deals exclusively with management's action plan for competing successfully and providing superior value to customers. Business strategy concerns not only how to compete but also how management intends to address all of the other strategic issues confronting the business.

> The objective of competitive strategy is to knock the socks off rival companies by doing a significantly better job of providing what buyers are looking for.

The competitive aim, quite simply, is to do a significantly better job of providing what buyers are looking for, thereby enabling the company to earn a competitive advantage and outcompete rivals in the marketplace. The core of a company's competitive strategy consists of its internal initiatives to deliver superior value to customers. But it also includes offensive and defensive moves to counter the maneuvering of rivals, actions to shift resources around to improve the firm's long-term competitive capabilities and market position, and tactical efforts to respond to whatever market conditions prevail at the moment.

Companies the world over are imaginative in conceiving strategies to win customer favor, outcompete rivals, and secure a market edge. Because a company's strategic initiatives and market maneuvers are usually tailor-made to fit its specific situation and industry environment, there are countless variations in the competitive strategies that companies employ—strictly speaking, there are as many competitive strategies as there are competitors. However, when one strips away the details to get at the real substance, the biggest and most important differences among competitive strategies boil down to (1) whether a company's market target is broad or narrow and (2) whether it is pursuing a competitive advantage linked to low costs or product differentiation. Five distinct competitive strategy approaches stand out:[2]

1. *A low-cost provider strategy*—appealing to a broad spectrum of customers based on being the overall low-cost provider of a product or service.

2. *A broad differentiation strategy*—seeking to differentiate the company's product offering from rivals' in ways that will appeal to a broad spectrum of buyers.

3. *A best-cost provider strategy*—giving customers more value for the money by incorporating good-to-excellent product attributes at a lower cost than rivals; the target is to have the lowest (best) costs and prices compared to rivals offering products with comparable upscale attributes.

4. *A focused (or market niche) strategy based on lower cost*—concentrating on a narrow buyer segment and outcompeting rivals by serving niche members at a lower cost than rivals.

5. *A focused (or market niche) strategy based on differentiation*—concentrating on a narrow buyer segment and outcompeting rivals by offering niche members customized attributes that meet their tastes and requirements better than rivals' products.

Each of these five generic competitive approaches stakes out a different market position—as shown in Figure 5.1. Each involves distinctively different approaches to

---

[2]The classification scheme is an adaptation of one presented in Michael E. Porter, *Competitive Strategy: Techniques for Analyzing Industries and Competitors* (New York: Free Press, 1980), chapter 2, especially pp. 35–39 and 44–46.

figure 5.1 **The Five Generic Competitive Strategies**

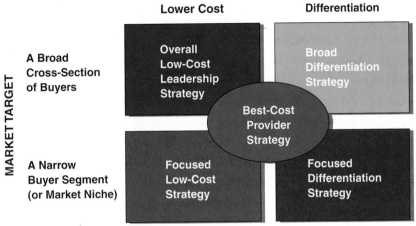

Source: Adapted from Michael E. Porter, *Competitive Strategy* (New York: Free Press, 1980), pp. 35–40.

competing and operating the business. The listing in Table 5.1 highlights the contrasting features of these five competitive strategies; for simplicity, the two strains of focused strategies are combined under one heading since they differ fundamentally on only one feature—the basis of competitive advantage.

Low-Cost Provider Strategies

Striving to be the industry's overall low-cost provider is a powerful competitive approach in markets with many price-sensitive buyers. The aim is to operate the business in a highly cost-effective manner and open up a sustainable cost advantage over competitors. A low-cost provider's strategic target is low cost relative to competitors, not the absolutely lowest possible cost—a company achieves low-cost leadership when it becomes the industry's lowest-cost provider rather than just being one of perhaps several competitors with comparatively low costs.

In trying to keep costs below those of rivals, managers must take care to include features and services that buyers consider essential—a product offering that is too spartan weakens rather than strengthens a firm's competitiveness. *Pursuing cost reduction in a manner that sabotages the attractiveness of the company's product offering turns buyers off.* Furthermore, it matters greatly whether the company achieves its cost advantage in ways difficult for rivals to copy or match. The value of a cost advantage depends on its sustainability. If rivals find it relatively easy or inexpensive to imitate the leader's low-cost methods, then the leader's advantage will be too short-lived to yield a valuable edge in the marketplace.

A low-cost provider has two options for achieving superior profit performance. Option 1 is to use the lower-cost edge to underprice competitors and attract price-sensitive buyers in great enough numbers to increase total profits. The trick to profitably underpricing rivals is either to keep the size of the price cut smaller than the size of the firm's cost advantage (thus reaping the benefits of both a bigger profit margin per unit sold and the added profits on incremental sales) or to generate enough added volume

> A low-cost leader's basis for competitive advantage is lower overall costs than competitors. Successful low-cost leaders are exceptionally good at finding ways to drive costs out of their businesses.

table 5.1   Distinctive Features of the Generic Competitive Strategies

Type of Feature	Low-Cost Provider	Broad Differentiation	Best-Cost Provider	Focused Low-Cost and Focused Differentiation
• Strategic target	• A broad cross-section of the market	• A broad cross-section of the market	• Value-conscious buyers	• A narrow market niche where buyer needs and preferences are distinctively different from the rest of the market
• Basis of competitive advantage	• Lower costs than competitors	• An ability to offer buyers something different from competitors	• More value for the money	• Lower cost in serving the niche (focused low cost) or special attributes that appeal to the tastes or requirements of niche members (focused differentiation)
• Product line	• A good basic product with few frills (acceptable quality and limited selection)	• Many product variations, wide selection, strong emphasis on differentiating features	• Good-to-excellent attributes, several-to-many upscale features	• Features and attributes that appeal to the tastes and/or special needs of the target segment
• Production emphasis	• A continuous search for cost reduction without sacrificing acceptable quality and essential features	• Creation of value for buyers; strive for product superiority	• Incorporation of upscale features and attributes at low cost	• Tailor-made for the tastes and requirements of niche members
• Marketing emphasis	• Try to make a virtue out of product features that lead to low cost	• Build in whatever features buyers are willing to pay for • Charge a premium price to cover the extra costs of differentiating features	• Either underprice rival brands with comparable features or match the price of rivals and provide better features—to build a reputation for delivering the best value	• Communicate how the focuser's product attributes and capabilities aim at catering to niche member tastes and/or specialized requirements
• Sustaining the strategy	• Offer economical prices/good value • Aim at contributing to a sustainable cost advantage—the key is to manage costs down, year after year, in every area of the business	• Communicate the points of difference in credible ways • Stress constant improvement and use innovation to stay ahead of imitative competitors • Concentrate on a few key differentiating features; tout them to create a reputation and brand image	• Develop unique expertise in simultaneously managing costs down and upscaling features and attributes	• Remain totally dedicated to serving the niche better than other competitors; don't blunt the firm's image and efforts by entering other segments or adding other product categories to widen market appeal

to increase total profits despite thinner profit margins (larger volume can make up for smaller margins provided the price reductions bring in enough extra sales). Option 2 is to refrain from price cutting altogether, be content with the present market share, and use the lower-cost edge to earn a higher profit margin on each unit sold, thereby raising the firm's total profits and overall return on investment.

Illustration Capsule 19 describes Nucor Corporation's strategy for gaining low-cost leadership in manufacturing a variety of steel products.

Ways to Achieve a Cost Advantage   To achieve a cost advantage, a firm's cumulative costs across its value chain must be lower than competitors' cumulative costs. There are two ways to accomplish this:[3]

- Do a better job than rivals of performing internal value chain activities efficiently and of managing the factors that can drive down the costs of value chain activities.
- Revamp the firm's value chain to bypass some cost-producing activities altogether.

Let's look at each of the two avenues for gaining a cost advantage.

Controlling the Cost Drivers   There are nine major cost drivers that come into play in determining a company's costs in each activity segment of the chain:[4]

1. *Economies or diseconomies of scale*—The costs of a particular value chain activity are often subject to economies or diseconomies of scale. Economies of scale arise whenever activities can be performed more cheaply at larger volumes than smaller volumes and from the ability to spread out certain costs like R&D and advertising over a greater sales volume. Astute management of activities subject to scale economies or diseconomies can be a major source of cost savings. For example, manufacturing economies can usually be achieved by simplifying the product line, scheduling longer production runs for fewer models, and using common parts and components in different models. In global industries, making separate products for each country market instead of selling a mostly standard product worldwide tends to boost unit costs because of lost time in model changeover, shorter production runs, and inability to reach the most economic scale of production for each country model. Scale economies or diseconomies also arise in how a company manages its sales and marketing activities. A geographically organized sales force can realize economies as regional sales volume grows because a salesperson can write larger orders at each sales call or reduce travel time between calls; in contrast, a sales force organized by product line can encounter travel-related diseconomies if salespersons have to spend disproportionately more travel time calling on distantly spaced customers. Boosting local or regional market share can lower sales and marketing costs per unit, whereas opting for a bigger national share by entering new regions can create scale diseconomies unless and until market penetration in the newly entered regions reaches efficient proportions.

2. *Learning and experience curve effects*—The cost of performing an activity can decline over time due to economies of experience and learning. Experience-based cost savings can come from much more than just personnel learning how to perform their tasks more efficiently and the debugging of new technologies. Other valuable sources of learning/experience economies include seeing ways to improve plant layout and

---

[3] Porter, *Competitive Advantage,* p. 97.

[4] The list and explanations are condensed from Porter, *Competitive Advantage,* pp. 70–107.

illustration capsule 19
Nucor Corporation's Low-Cost Provider Strategy

Nucor Corporation is the leading minimill producer of such steel products as rolled steel, finished steel, steel joists, joist girders, steel decks, and grinding balls. It has over $4 billion in sales annually and produces over 10 million tons of steel annually. The company has pursued a strategy that has made it among the lowest-cost producers of steel in the world and has allowed the company to consistently outperform its rivals in terms of financial and market performance.

Nucor's low-cost strategy aims to give it a cost and pricing advantage in the commodity like steel industry and leaves no part of the company's value chain neglected. The key elements of the strategy include:

- Using electric arc furnaces where scrap steel and directly reduced iron ore are melted and then sent to a continuous caster and rolling mill to be shaped into steel products, thereby eliminating an assortment of production processes from the value chain used by traditional integrated steel mills. Nucor's "minimill" value chain makes the use of coal, coke, and iron ore unnecessary; cuts investment in facilities and equipment (eliminating coke ovens, blast furnaces, basic oxygen furnaces, and ingot casters); and requires fewer employees than integrated mills.

- Nucor strives hard for continuous improvement in the efficiency of its plants, frequently investing in state-of-the-art equipment to reduce unit costs. Nucor is known for its technological leadership and its aggressive pursuit of innovation.

- The company selects its plant sites carefully to minimize inbound and outbound shipping costs and to take advantage of low rates for electricity (electric arc furnaces are heavy users of electricity). It also avoids geographic areas where labor unions are a strong influence.

- Nucor prefers a nonunion work force because it uses team-based incentive compensation systems (often opposed by unions). Operating and maintenance employees and supervisors are paid weekly bonuses based on the productivity of their work group. The size of the

bonus is based on the capabilities of the equipment employed and ranges from 80 to 150 percent of an employee's base pay; no bonus is paid if the equipment is not operating. Nucor's compensation program has boosted the company's labor productivity to levels nearly double the industry average while rewarding productive employees with annual compensation packages that exceed what their union counterparts earn by as much as 20 percent. Nucor has been able to attract and retain highly talented, productive, and dedicated employees. In addition, the company's healthy culture and results-oriented self-managed work teams allow the company to employ fewer supervisors than what would be needed with an hourly union workforce. Nucor is proud of the more than 7,000 employees that make up the total Nucor team.

- Nucor puts heavy emphasis on consistent product quality and has rigorous quality systems.

- Nucor minimizes general and administrative expenses by maintaining a lean staff at its corporate headquarters (fewer than 125 employees) and allowing only four levels of management between the CEO and production workers. Headquarters offices are modestly furnished and located in an inexpensive building. The company minimizes reports, paperwork, and meetings to keep managers focused on value-adding activities. Nucor is noted not only for its streamlined organizational structure but also its frugality in travel and entertainment expenses—the company's top managers set the example by flying coach class, avoiding pricey hotels, and refraining from taking customers out for expensive dinners.

Nucor management's outstanding execution of its low-cost strategy and its commitment to drive out non-value-adding costs throughout its value chain has allowed it to grow at a considerably faster rate than its integrated steel mill rivals and maintain high industry-relative profit margins while aggressively competing on price.

Source: Company annual reports, news releases, and website.

work flows, to make product design modifications that enhance manufacturing efficiency, to redesign machinery and equipment to gain increased operating speed, and to tailor parts and components in ways that streamline the assembly process. Learning can also reduce the cost of constructing and operating websites, new retail outlets, new plants, or new distribution facilities. There are also learning benefits associated with getting samples of a rival's products and having design engineers study how they are made, benchmarking company activities against the performance of similar activities in other companies, and interviewing suppliers, consultants, and ex-employees of rival firms to tap into their wisdom. Learning tends to vary with the amount of management attention devoted to capturing the benefits of experience of both the firm and outsiders. Astute managers make a conscious effort not only to capture learning benefits but also to keep the benefits proprietary by building or modifying production equipment in-house, endeavoring to retain knowledgeable employees (to reduce the risk of them going to work for rivals firms), limiting the dissemination of cost-saving information through employee publications that can fall into rivals' hands, and enforcing strict nondisclosure provisions in employment contracts.

3. *The cost of key resource inputs*—The cost of performing value chain activities depends in part on what a firm has to pay for key resource inputs. Competitors do not all incur the same costs for items purchased from suppliers or for resources used in performing value chain activities. How well a company manages the costs of acquiring key resource inputs is often a big driver of costs. Input costs are a function of three factors:

- *Union versus nonunion labor*—Avoiding the use of union labor is often a key to low-cost manufacturing, not just to escape paying high wages but rather to escape union work rules that stifle productivity. Such prominent low-cost manufacturers as Nucor and Cooper Tire are noted for their incentive compensation systems that allow nonunion workers to earn more than their unionized counterparts at rival companies.
- *Bargaining power vis-à-vis suppliers*—Many large enterprises (Wal-Mart, The Home Depot, the world's major motor vehicle producers) have used their bargaining clout in purchasing large volumes to wrangle good prices on their purchases from suppliers. Differences in buying power among industry rivals can be an important source of cost advantage or disadvantage.
- *Locational variables*—Locations differ in their prevailing wage levels, tax rates, energy costs, inbound and outbound shipping and freight costs, and so on. Opportunities may exist for reducing costs by relocating plants, field offices, warehousing, or headquarters operations.

4. *Link with other activities in the company or industry value chain*—When the cost of one activity is affected by how other activities are performed, costs can be managed downward by making sure that linked activities are performed in cooperative and coordinated fashion. For example, when a company's quality control costs or materials inventory costs are linked to the activities of suppliers, cost savings can be achieved by working cooperatively with key suppliers on the design of parts and components, quality-assurance procedures, just-in-time delivery, integrated materials supply, and online order processing. The costs of new product development can often be managed downward by having cross-functional task forces (perhaps including representatives of suppliers and key customers) jointly work on R&D, product design, manufacturing plans, and market launch. Links with forward channels tend to center on location of warehouses, materials handling, outbound shipping, and packaging. Nail manufacturers, for example, learned that nails delivered in prepackaged 1-lb., 5-lb., and 10-lb. assortments instead of 100-lb. bulk cartons could reduce a hardware dealer's labor costs in filling individual customer orders. The lesson here is that effective coordination of linked activities anywhere in the value chain system holds potential for cost reduction.

5. *Sharing opportunities with other organizational or business units within the enterprise*—Different product lines or business units within an enterprise can often share the same order processing and customer billing systems, utilize a common sales force to call on customers, share the same warehouse and distribution facilities, or rely on a common customer service and technical support team. Such combining of like activities and the sharing of resources across sister units can create significant cost savings. Cost sharing can help achieve scale economies, shorten the learning curve in mastering a new technology, and/or promote fuller capacity utilization. Furthermore, there are times when the know-how gained in one division or geographic unit can be used to help lower costs in another; sharing know-how across organizational lines has significant cost-saving potential when the activities are similar and know-how is readily transferred from one unit to another.

6.   *The benefits of vertical integration versus outsourcing*—Partially or fully integrating into the activities of either suppliers or forward channel allies can allow an enterprise to detour suppliers or buyers with considerable bargaining power. Vertical integration forward or backward also has potential if there are significant cost-savings from having a single firm perform adjacent activities in the industry value chain. But, more often, it is cheaper to outsource certain functions and activities to outside specialists, who by virtue of their expertise and volume can perform the activity/function more cheaply.

7.   *Timing considerations associated with first-mover advantages and disadvantages*—Sometimes the first major brand in the market is able to establish and maintain its brand name at a lower cost than later brand arrivals. This is proving true in new Internet businesses where being first and biggest creates potent brand-name recognition. Cases in point include eBay, Yahoo!, and Amazon.com. On other occasions, such as when technology is developing fast, late-purchasers can benefit from waiting to install second- or third-generation equipment that is both cheaper and more efficient; first-generation users often incur added costs associated with debugging and learning how to use an immature and unperfected technology. Likewise, companies that follow rather than lead new product development efforts sometimes avoid many of the costs that pioneers incur in performing pathbreaking R&D and opening up new markets.

8.   *The percentage of capacity utilization*—Capacity utilization is a big cost driver for those value chain activities that have substantial fixed costs associated with them. Higher rates of capacity utilization allow depreciation and other fixed costs to be spread over a larger unit volume, thereby lowering fixed costs per unit. The more capital-intensive the business, or the higher the percentage of fixed costs as a percentage of total costs, the more important this cost driver becomes because there's such a stiff unit-cost penalty for underutilizing existing capacity. In such cases, finding ways to operate close to full capacity year-round can be an important source of cost advantage.

A firm can improve its capacity utilization by (*a*) serving a mix of accounts with peak volumes spread throughout the year, (*b*) finding off-season uses for its products, (*c*) serving private-label customers that can intermittently use the excess capacity, (*d*) selecting buyers with stable demands or demands that are counter to the normal peak/valley cycle, (*e*) letting competitors serve the buyer segments whose demands fluctuate the most, and (*f*) sharing capacity with sister units having a different seasonal production pattern (e.g., producing snowmobiles for the winter season and personal water-ski craft for summer water sports).

9.   *Strategic choices and operating decisions*—A company's costs can be driven up or down by a fairly wide assortment of managerial decisions:

- Adding/cutting the services provided to buyers.
- Incorporating more/fewer performance and quality features into the product.

- Paying higher/lower wages and fringes to employees relative to rivals and firms in other industries.
- Increasing/decreasing the number of different channels utilized in distributing the firm's product.
- Lengthening/shortening delivery times to customers.
- Putting more/less emphasis than rivals on the use of incentive compensation to motivate employees and boost worker productivity.
- Raising/lowering the specifications for purchased materials.

Managers intent on achieving low-cost leader status have to possess a sophisticated understanding of how the above nine factors drive the costs of each activity in the value chain. Then they have to not only use their knowledge about the cost drivers to reduce costs for every activity where cost savings can be identified but do so with enough ingenuity and unswerving commitment that the company ends up with a sustainable cost advantage over rivals.

> Outperforming rivals in controlling the factors that drive costs is a very demanding managerial exercise.

Revamping the Value Chain   Dramatic cost advantages can emerge from finding innovative ways to restructure processes and tasks, cut out low-value activities, eliminate frills, and provide the basics more economically. The primary ways companies can achieve a cost advantage by reconfiguring their value chains include:

- *Shifting to e-business technologies*—Use of the Internet can enable online shopping and purchases (thus reducing or eliminating the need for human order takers and brick-and-mortar stores), online order processing and bill payment, online data sharing with suppliers, fast e-mail communication and teleconferencing, and other such techniques can streamline the value chain and greatly reduce the costs of doing business. Ford Motor Company has aggressively adopted videoconferencing and computer-assisted design and manufacturing technologies—its new cars and trucks are being developed by teams of designers stationed at Ford locations around the world who use an online computer network to share ideas, create the actual designs, integrate the designs for the various parts and components (the chassis, engine, transmission, body, and instrumentation), and build and test prototypes via computer simulations.
- *Using direct-to-end-user sales and marketing approaches*—Costs in the wholesale-retail portions of the value chain frequently represent 35–50 percent of the price final consumers pay. Software developers are increasingly using the Internet to market and deliver their products directly to buyers; downloading software direct from the Internet eliminates the costs of producing and packaging CDs and cuts out the host of activities, costs, and markups associated with shipping and distributing their products through wholesale and retail channels—see Figure 5.2. By cutting all these costs and activities out of the value chain, software developers have the pricing room to boost their profit margins and still sell their products below levels that retailers would have to charge.
- *Simplifying product design*—Utilizing computer-assisted design techniques, reducing the number of parts, standardizing parts and components across models and styles, shifting to an easy-to-manufacture product design all can simplify the value chain.
- *Stripping away the extras*—Offering only basics products or services can help a company cut costs associated with multiple features and options—a favorite technique of the no-frills airlines like Southwest Airlines.

figure 5.2 **Reconfiguring Value Chain Systems to Lower Costs: The Case of the Software Industry**

A. Value Chain System of Software Developers Using Traditional Wholesale-Retail Channels

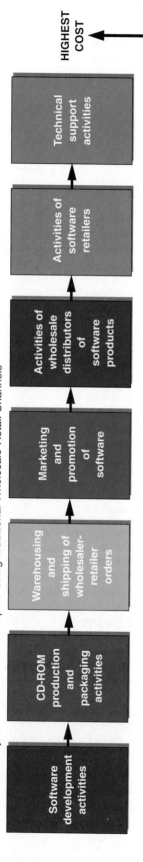

B. Value Chain System of Software Developers Using Direct Sales and Physical Delivery of CDs

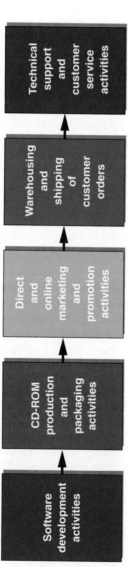

C. Value Chain System of Software Developers Using Online Sales and Internet Delivery

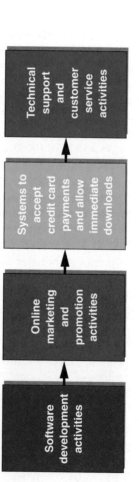

- *Shifting to a simpler, less capital-intensive, or more streamlined or flexible technological process*—Computer-assisted design and manufacture, or other flexible manufacturing systems, can accommodate both low-cost efficiency and product customization.

- *Bypassing the use of high-cost raw materials or component parts*—High-cost raw materials and parts can be designed out of the product.

- *Relocating facilities*—Moving plants closer to suppliers, customers, or both can help curtail inbound and outbound logistics costs.

- *Dropping the "something for everyone" approach*—Focusing on a limited product or service to meet a special, but important, need of the target buyer can eliminate activities and costs associated with numerous product versions.

- *Reengineering core business processes to consolidate work steps and cut out low-value-added activities*—Some companies have been able to reduce the costs of reengineered activities by 30 to 70 percent, compared to the 5 to 10 percent possible with creative tinkering and adjusting.

An example of significant cost advantages from creating altogether new value chain systems can be found in the beef-packing industry. The traditional cost chain involved raising cattle on scattered farms and ranches, shipping them live to labor-intensive, unionized slaughtering plants, and then transporting whole sides of beef to grocery retailers whose butcher departments cut them into smaller pieces and packaged them for sale to grocery shoppers. Iowa Beef Packers revamped the traditional chain with a radically different strategy—large automated plants employing nonunion workers were built near economically transportable supplies of cattle, and the meat was partially butchered at the processing plant into small, high-yield cuts (sometimes sealed in plastic casing ready for purchase) before being boxed and shipped to retailers. Iowa Beef's inbound cattle transportation expenses, traditionally a major cost item, were cut significantly by avoiding the weight losses that occurred when live animals were shipped long distances; major outbound shipping cost savings were achieved by not having to ship whole sides of beef with their high waste factor. Iowa Beef's strategy was so successful that it became the largest U.S. meatpacker, surpassing the former industry leaders, Swift, Wilson, and Armour.[5]

Federal Express innovatively redefined the value chain for rapid delivery of small parcels. Traditional firms like Emery Worldwide and Airborne Express operated by collecting freight packages of varying sizes, shipping them to their destination points via air freight and commercial airlines, and then delivering them via truck to the addressee. FedEx opted to focus only on the market for overnight delivery of small packages and documents. These were collected at local drop points during the late-afternoon hours and flown on company-owned planes during early-evening hours to a central hub in Memphis. From 11 PM to 3 AM each night all parcels were sorted, then reloaded on company planes, and flown during the early-morning hours to their destination points, where they were delivered the next morning by company personnel using company trucks.[6] FedEx's hub-and-spoke system produced a cost structure low enough to guarantee next-day delivery of a small parcel anywhere in the United States for as little as $13.

Southwest Airlines has reconfigured the traditional value chain of commercial airlines to lower costs and thereby offer dramatically lower fares to passengers. It has

---

[5]Porter, *Competitive Advantage,* p. 109.
[6]Ibid., p. 109.

mastered fast turnarounds at the gates (about 15 minutes versus 45 minutes for rivals); because the short turnarounds allow the planes to fly more hours per day, Southwest can schedule more flights per day with fewer aircraft. Southwest does not offer in-flight meals, assigned seating, baggage transfer to connecting airlines, or first-class seating and service, thereby eliminating all the cost-producing activities associated with these features. The company's online system for making reservations and purchasing an electronic ticket along with automated ticketing at its airport check-in counters encourages customers to bypass travel agents (thereby escaping payment of commissions and the costs associated with helping maintain the centralized computerized reservation systems accessed by travel agents) and also reduces the need for so many agents at check-in counters. Southwest's full-service rivals have higher costs because they must perform all the activities associated with providing meal service, assigned seating, premium classes of service, interline baggage checking, and computerized reservation systems.

Dell Computer has proved a pioneer in revamping the value chain in assembling and marketing PCs. Whereas Compaq Computer, Toshiba, Hewlett-Packard, Sony, and several other PC makers produce their models in volume and sell them through independent resellers and retailers, Dell has elected to market directly to customers, building its PCs as customers order them and shipping them to customers within a few days of receiving the order. Dell's value chain approach has proved cost-effective in coping with the PC industry's blink-of-an-eye product life cycle (new models equipped with faster chips and new features appear every few months)—the build-to-order strategy enables the company to avoid misjudging buyer demand for its various models and being saddled with fast-obsoleting excess components and finished goods inventories. Also, its sell-direct strategy slices reseller/retailer costs and margins out of the value chain (although some of these savings are offset by the cost of Dell's direct marketing and customer support activities—functions that would otherwise be performed by resellers and retailers). Partnerships with suppliers that facilitate just-in-time deliveries of components and minimize Dell's inventory costs, coupled with Dell's extensive use of e-commerce technologies (online sales of PCs exceed $30 million per day), further reduce Dell's costs. Dell's value chain approach is widely considered to have made it the global low-cost leader in the PC industry.

See Illustration Capsule 20 for how e-business technologies are fast becoming pervasive in value chain restructuring and creation of a low-cost advantage.

The Keys to Success in Achieving Low-Cost Leadership

To succeed with a low-cost-provider strategy, company managers have to scrutinize each cost-creating activity and determine what drives its cost. Then they have to use this knowledge about the cost drivers to manage the costs of each activity downward, exhaustively pursuing cost savings throughout the value chain. They have to be proactive in restructuring the value chain to eliminate nonessential work steps. Normally, low-cost producers work diligently to create cost-conscious corporate cultures that feature broad employee participation in continuous cost improvement efforts and limited perks and frills for executives. They strive to operate with exceptionally small corporate staffs to keep administrative costs to a minimum. Many successful low-cost leaders also benchmark costs against best-in-class performers of an activity to keep close tabs on how well they are doing at cost control.

But while low-cost providers are champions of frugality, they are usually aggressive in investing in resources and capabilities that promise to drive costs out of the business. Wal-Mart, for example, employs state-of-the-art technology throughout its operations—its distribution facilities are an automated showcase, it uses online systems

Success in achieving cost advantages over rivals comes from exploring all avenues for reducing costs and pressing for continuous cost reductions across all aspects of the company's operations year after year after year.

illustration capsule 20

E-Business Technologies: Powerful Tools for Restructuring Value Chains to Create a Low-Cost Advantage

The creation of low-cost "electronic value chains" is fast becoming the norm in industry after industry. Electronic brokerages, for example, using e-business technologies and the Internet to offer online trading and deliver a growing assortment of investment information and research, are revolutionizing the business model of the stock brokerage industry. The sharply lower costs of the electronic value chains employed by online brokerages allow them to profitably execute trades for a small fraction of what traditional brokerages charge.

A number of enterprising firms have created electronic value chains that enable them to function as "Internet middlemen" and use the instant communications capability of the Internet to match buyers and sellers. Chemdex provides one-stop shopping for scientists and researchers at its website containing the catalogs of scores of pharmaceutical and biotech suppliers from around the world. Chemdex makes money by charging vendors a transactions fee below the percentage markup of traditional distributors; it then passes the savings on to buyers. Similarly, Wells Fargo and Chase Manhattan both operate websites where corporate purchasing agents can pool their purchases to get better deals or special treatment from suppliers; they too make money by charging a fee for transactions. Singapore-based Advanced Manufacturing Online provides an Internet-based system that enables Asian suppliers and customers to send orders and solicit price quotations—users include Motorola,

Matsushita, and Taiwan Semiconductor Manufacturing. These new e-markets where buyers and sellers gather electronically not only allow buyers to conveniently shop for better terms but also give sellers quick access to buyers, allowing them to save on selling and marketing costs. The whole market process becomes more efficient, compared to the traditional methods where salespeople contact customers in person or where buyers survey the offerings of various suppliers via telephone or fax.

Company websites can easily function as retail showrooms, thereby creating an alternative distribution channel that allows many kinds of business-to-consumer transactions in cyberspace to be handled faster, more conveniently, and less expensively than in the physical world of the marketplace—an outcome that is forcing traditional wholesalers and retailers to revamp their value chain structures to protect their sales and market shares. Internet companies (such as Carorder.com) have developed software capability that allows prospective motor vehicle buyers to place orders online for custom-equipped cars and trucks and pick up their vehicles at designated delivery points, thus bypassing the car dealership part of the automotive value chain. Other innovative Internet companies are creating electronic value chain systems to provide buyers with mortgages, loans, insurance, new and used textbooks, groceries, flowers—the list goes on and on.

---

to order goods from suppliers and manage inventories, it equips its stores with cutting-edge sales-tracking and check-out systems, and it operates a private satellite communications system that daily sends point-of-sale data to 4,000 vendors. Its information and communications systems and capabilities are more sophisticated than those of virtually any other retail chain in the world.

Companies that employ low-cost provider strategies include Lincoln Electric in arc welding equipment, Briggs & Stratton in small gasoline engines, Bic in ballpoint pens, Black & Decker in power tools, Stride Rite in footwear, Beaird-Poulan in chain saws, Nucor in steelmaking, General Electric and Whirlpool in major home appliances, and Ameritrade in electronic brokerage.

When a Low-Cost Provider Strategy Works Best   A competitive strategy predicated on low-cost leadership is particularly powerful when:

> In markets where rivals compete mainly on price, low cost relative to competitors is the only competitive advantage that matters.

1. *Price competition among rival sellers is especially vigorous*—Low-cost providers are in the best position to compete offensively on the basis of price, to use the appeal of lower price to grab sales (and market share) from rivals, to remain profitable in the face of strong price competition, and to survive price wars.

2. *The industry's product is essentially standardized or a commodity readily available from a host of sellers*—Commoditylike conditions set the stage for lively price competition; in such markets, it is less efficient, higher-cost rivals whose profits get squeezed the most.

3. *There are few ways to achieve product differentiation that have value to buyers*— When the differences between brands do not matter much to buyers, buyers are nearly always very sensitive to price differences and shop the market for the best price.

4. *Most buyers utilize the product in the same ways*—with common user requirements, a standardized product can satisfy the needs of buyers, in which case low selling price, not features or quality, becomes the dominant factor in causing buyers to choose one seller's product over another's.

5. *Buyers incur low switching costs in changing from one seller to another*—Low switching costs give buyers the flexibility to shift purchases to lower-priced sellers having equally good products or to attractively priced substitute products. A low-cost leader is better positioned to use low price to induce its customers not to switch to rival brands or substitutes.

6. *Buyers are large and have significant power to bargain down prices*—Low-cost providers have partial profit-margin protection in bargaining with high-volume buyers, since powerful buyers are rarely able to bargain price down past the survival level of the next most cost-efficient seller.

7. *Industry newcomers use introductory low prices to attract buyers and build a customer base*—The low-cost leader can use price cuts of its own to make it harder for a new rival to win customers; the pricing power of the low-cost provider acts as a barrier for new entrants.

> A low-cost leader is in the strongest position to win the business of price-sensitive buyers, set the floor on market price, and still earn a profit.

As a rule, the more price-sensitive buyers are and the more inclined they are to base their purchasing decisions on which seller offers the best price, the more appealing a low-cost strategy becomes. A low-cost company's ability to set the industry's price floor and still earn a profit erects protective barriers around its market position.

The Pitfalls of a Low-Cost Provider Strategy   Perhaps the biggest pitfall of a low-cost provider strategy is getting carried away with overly aggressively price cutting and ending up with lower, rather than higher, profitability. A low-cost/low-price advantage results in superior profitability only if (1) prices are cut by less than the size of the cost advantage or (2) the added gains in unit sales are large enough to bring in a bigger total profit despite lower margins per unit sold. A company with a 5 percent cost advantage cannot cut prices 20 percent, end up with a volume gain of only 10 percent, and still expect to earn higher profits!

A second big pitfall is not emphasizing avenues of cost advantage that can be kept proprietary or that relegate rivals to playing catch-up. The value of a cost advantage depends on its sustainability. Sustainability, in turn, hinges on whether the company achieves its cost advantage in ways difficult for rivals to copy or match.

> A low-cost provider's product offering must always contain enough attributes to be attractive to prospective buyers—low price, by itself, is not always appealing to buyers.

A third pitfall is becoming too fixated on cost reduction. Low cost cannot be pursued so zealously that a firm's offering ends up being too features-poor to generate buyer appeal. Furthermore, a company driving zealously to push its costs down has to guard against misreading or ignoring subtle but significant market swings—like growing buyer interest in added features or service, declining buyer sensitivity to price, or new developments that start to alter how buyers use the product. A low-cost zealot risks getting left behind if buyers begin to opt for enhanced quality, innovative performance features, faster service, and other differentiating features.

Even if these mistakes are avoided, a low-cost competitive approach still carries risk. Cost-saving technological breakthroughs or the emergence of still-lower-cost value chain models can nullify a low-cost leader's hard-won position. The current leader may have difficulty in shifting quickly to the new technologies or value chain approaches because heavy investments lock it in (at least temporarily) to its present value chain approach.

Differentiation Strategies

Differentiation strategies are an attractive competitive approach whenever buyers' needs and preferences are too diverse to be fully satisfied by a standardized product or by sellers with identical capabilities. To be successful with a differentiation strategy, a company has to study buyers' needs and behavior carefully to learn what buyers consider important, what they think has value, and what they are willing to pay for. Then the company has to incorporate buyer-desired attributes into its product or service offering that will set it visibly and distinctively apart from rivals. Competitive advantage results once a sufficient number of buyers become strongly attached to the differentiated attributes. The more that a company's differentiated offering appeals to buyers, the more customers *bond* with the company and the stronger the resulting competitive advantage.

> The essence of a differentiation strategy is to be unique in ways that are valuable to customers and that can be sustained.

Successful differentiation allows a firm to

- Command a premium price for its product, and/or
- Increase unit sales (because additional buyers are won over by the differentiating features), and/or
- Gain buyer loyalty to its brand (because some buyers are strongly attracted to the differentiating features and bond with the company and its products).

Differentiation enhances profitability whenever the extra price the product commands outweighs the added costs of achieving the differentiation. Company differentiation strategies fail when buyers don't value the brand's uniqueness enough to buy it instead of rivals' brands and/or when a company's approach to differentiation is easily copied or matched by its rivals, thus eliminating the basis of differentiation.

Types of Differentiation Themes   Companies can pursue differentiation from many angles: a unique taste (Dr Pepper, Listerine); multiple features (Microsoft Windows, Microsoft Office); wide selection and one-stop shopping (The Home Depot, Amazon.com), superior service (FedEx in next-day delivery); spare parts availability (Caterpillar guarantees 48-hour spare parts delivery to any customer anywhere in the world or else the part is furnished free); more for the money (McDonald's, Wal-Mart); engineering design and performance (Mercedes, BMW); prestige and distinctiveness (Rolex in watches); product reliability (Johnson & Johnson in baby products); quality manufacture (Karastan in carpets, Michelin in tires, Honda in automobiles); technological leadership (3M Corporation in bonding and coating products); a full range of services (Charles Schwab in stock brokerage); a complete line of products (Campbell's soups); and top-of-the-line image and reputation (Ralph Lauren in menswear, Chanel in women's fashions and accessories, Ritz-Carlton in hotels, Cross in writing instruments).

> Easy-to-copy differentiating features cannot produce sustainable competitive advantage.

The most appealing approaches to differentiation are those that are hard or expensive for rivals to duplicate. Indeed, resourceful competitors can, in time, clone almost any product or feature or attribute. If American Airlines creates a program for frequent fliers, so can Delta; if Ford offers a 50,000-mile bumper-to-bumper warranty on its new vehicles, so can Volkswagen and Nissan. This is why *sustainable* differentiation usually has to be linked to core competencies, unique competitive capabilities, and superior management of value chain activities. When a company has competencies and capabilities that competitors cannot readily match and/or manages its value chain activities in ways that promote unique differentiation, then its basis for differentiation is more sustainable. As a rule, differentiation yields a longer-lasting and more profitable competitive edge when it is based on new product innovation, technical superiority, product quality and reliability, comprehensive customer service, and unique competitive capabilities. Buyers widely perceive such differentiating attributes as having value, and they tend to be tougher for rivals to copy or offset profitably.

Where along the Value Chain to Create the Differentiating Attributes

Differentiation is not something hatched in marketing and advertising departments, nor is it limited to the catchalls of quality and service. Differentiation opportunities can exist in activities all along an industry's value chain; possibilities include:

1. *Purchasing and procurement activities* that ultimately spill over to affect the performance or quality of the company's end product. McDonald's gets high ratings on its french fries partly because it has very strict specifications on the potatoes purchased from suppliers.

2. *Product R&D activities* that aim at improved product designs and performance features, expanded end uses and applications, more frequent first-on-the-market victories, wider product variety and selection, added user safety, greater recycling capability, or enhanced environmental protection.

3. *Production R&D and technology-related activities* that permit custom-order manufacture at an efficient cost; make production methods safer for the environment; or improve product quality, reliability, and appearance. Many manufacturers have developed flexible manufacturing systems that allow different models to be made or different options to be added on the same assembly line. Being able to provide buyers with made-to-order products can be a potent differentiating capability.

4. *Manufacturing activities* that reduce product defects, prevent premature product failure, extend product life, allow better warranty coverages, improve economy of use, result in more end-user convenience, or enhance product appearance. The quality edge enjoyed by Japanese automakers stems partly from their distinctive competence in performing assembly-line activities.

5. *Outbound logistics and distribution activities* that allow for faster delivery, more accurate order filling, and fewer warehouse and on-the-shelf stockouts.

6. *Marketing, sales, and customer service activities* that result in superior technical assistance to buyers, faster maintenance and repair services, more and better product information provided to customers, more and better training materials for end users, better credit terms, quicker order processing, or greater customer convenience.

Managers need keen understanding of the sources of differentiation and the activities that drive uniqueness to devise a sound differentiation strategy and evaluate various differentiation approaches.[7]

---

[7]Ibid., p. 124.

illustration capsule 21
Differentiating Features That Raise Performance

To enhance the performance a buyer gets from using its product or service, a company can incorporate features and attributes that:

- Provide buyers greater reliability, durability, convenience, or ease of use.

- Make the company's product or service cleaner, safer, quieter, or more maintenance-free than rival brands.

- Exceed environmental or regulatory standards.

- Meet the buyer's needs and requirements more completely, compared to competitors' offerings.

- Give buyers the option to add on or to upgrade later as new product versions come on the market.

- Give buyers more flexibility to tailor their own products to the needs of their customers.

- Do a better job of meeting the buyer's future growth and expansion requirements.

Source: Adapted from Michael E. Porter, *Competitive Advantage* (New York: Free Press, 1985), pp. 135–38.

Achieving a Differentiation-Based Competitive Advantage

While it is easy enough to grasp that a successful differentiation strategy must entail creating buyer value in ways unmatched by rivals, the hard thing is to figure out *how* to create unique attributes that buyers will consider valuable. Any of four basic approaches can be used. First is to *incorporate product attributes and user features that lower the buyer's overall costs of using the company's product.* Making a company's product more economical for a buyer to use can be done by reducing the buyer's raw materials waste (providing cut-to-size components), reducing a buyer's inventory requirements (providing just-in-time deliveries), increasing maintenance intervals and product reliability so as to lower a buyer's repair and maintenance costs, using online systems to reduce a buyer's procurement and order processing costs, and providing free technical support and assistance.

> A differentiator's basis for competitive advantage is either a product/service offering whose attributes differ significantly from the offerings of rivals or a set of capabilities for delivering customer value that rivals don't have or can't quite match.

A second approach is to *incorporate features that raise the performance a buyer gets out of the product.* Illustration Capsule 21 contains differentiation avenues that enhance product performance and buyer value. A third approach is to *incorporate features that enhance buyer satisfaction in noneconomic or intangible ways.* Goodyear's new Aquatread tire design appeals to safety-conscious motorists wary of slick roads in rainy weather. Rolls-Royce, Tiffany, and Gucci have differentiation-based competitive advantages linked to buyer desires for status, image, prestige, upscale fashion, superior craftsmanship, and the finer things in life. L. L. Bean makes its mail-order customers feel secure in their purchases by providing an unconditional guarantee with no time limit: "All of our products are guaranteed to give 100 percent satisfaction in every way. Return anything purchased from us at any time if it proves otherwise. We will replace it, refund your purchase price, or credit your credit card, as you wish."

A fourth approach is to compete on the basis of capabilities—*to deliver value to customers via competitive capabilities that rivals don't have or can't afford to match.*[8] A capability has differentiating competitive value when it allows a firm to perform an activity that delivers value to customers in ways rivals cannot. The strategy-making challenge is selecting which differentiating capabilities to develop. Successful capabilities-driven

---

[8]For a more detailed discussion, see George Stalk, Philip Evans, and Lawrence E. Schulman, "Competing on Capabilities: The New Rules of Corporate Strategy," *Harvard Business Review* 70, no. 2 (March–April 1992), pp. 57–69.

differentiation begins with a deep understanding of what customers need and ends with building organizational capabilities to satisfy these needs better than rivals. The Japanese auto manufacturers have the capability to bring new models to market faster than American and European automakers, thereby allowing them to satisfy changing consumer preferences for one vehicle style versus another. CNN has the capability to cover breaking news stories faster and more completely than the major networks. Microsoft, with its Windows operating systems and assorted application software, its ability to assemble large project teams composed of highly talented and antibureaucratic programmers who thrive on developing complex products and systems, and its marketing savvy and know-how, has stronger capabilities to design, create, distribute, advertise, and sell an array of software products for PC applications than any of its rivals.

The Importance of Perceived Value and Signaling Value
Buyers seldom pay for value they don't perceive, no matter how real the unique extras may be.[9] Thus, the price premium commanded by a differentiation strategy reflects *the value actually delivered* to the buyer and *the value perceived* by the buyer (even if not actually delivered). Actual and perceived value can differ whenever buyers have trouble assessing what their experience with the product will be. Incomplete knowledge on the part of buyers often causes them to judge value based on such signals as price (where price connotes quality), attractive packaging, extensive ad campaigns (i.e., how well-known the product is), ad content and image, the quality of brochures and sales presentations, the seller's facilities, the seller's list of customers, the firm's market share, the length of time the firm has been in business, and the professionalism, appearance, and personality of the seller's employees. Such signals of value may be as important as actual value (1) when the nature of differentiation is subjective or hard to quantify, (2) when buyers are making a first-time purchase, (3) when repurchase is infrequent, and (4) when buyers are unsophisticated.

> A firm whose differentiation strategy delivers only modest extra value but clearly signals that extra value may command a higher price than a firm that actually delivers higher value but signals it poorly.

Keeping the Cost of Differentiation in Line
Company efforts to achieve differentiation usually raise costs. The trick to profitable differentiation is either to keep the costs of achieving differentiation below the price premium the differentiating attributes can command in the marketplace (thus increasing the profit margin per unit sold) or to offset thinner profit margins with enough added volume to increase total profits. It usually makes sense to incorporate extra differentiating features that are not costly but add to buyer satisfaction. Federal Express installed systems that allowed customers to track packages in transit by connecting to FedEx's website and entering the airbill number; some hotels and motels provide in-room coffee-making amenities or free continental breakfasts in their lobbies; many McDonald's outlets have play areas for small children.

When a Differentiation Strategy Works Best
Differentiation strategies tend to work best in market circumstances where:

- *There are many ways to differentiate the product or service and many buyers perceive these differences as having value*—Without this condition, profitable differentiation opportunities are very restricted.

- *Buyer needs and uses are diverse*—Some buyers prefer one combination of features and other buyers another. The more diverse buyer preferences are, the more

---

[9]This discussion draws from Porter, *Competitive Advantage,* pp. 138–42. Porter's insights here are particularly important to formulating differentiating strategies because they highlight the relevance of "intangibles" and "signals."

room firms have to pursue different approaches to differentiation and thereby avoid trying to outdifferentiate one another on much the same attributes.

- *Few rival firms are following a similar differentiation approach*—There is less head-to-head rivalry when differentiating rivals go separate ways in pursuing uniqueness and try to appeal to buyers on different combinations of attributes.

- *Technological change and product innovation are fast-paced and competition revolves around rapidly evolving product features*—Rapid product innovation and frequent introductions of next-version products help maintain buyer interest in the product and provide space for companies to pursue separate differentiating paths.

The Pitfalls of a Differentiation Strategy   There are, of course, no guarantees that differentiation will produce a meaningful competitive advantage. If buyers see little value in the unique attributes or capabilities a company stresses, then its differentiation strategy will get a ho-hum market reception. In addition, attempts at differentiation are doomed to fail if competitors can quickly copy most or all of the appealing product attributes a company comes up with. Rapid imitation means that no rival achieves differentiation, since whenever one firm introduces some aspect of uniqueness that strikes the fancy of buyers, fast-following copycats quickly reestablish similarity. Thus, to build competitive advantage through differentiation a firm must search out sources of uniqueness that are time-consuming or burdensome for rivals to match. Other common pitfalls and mistakes in pursuing differentiation include:[10]

> Any differentiating element that works well tends to draw imitators.

- Trying to differentiate on the basis of something that does not lower a buyer's cost or enhance a buyer's well-being, as perceived by the buyer.
- Overdifferentiating so that price is too high relative to competitors or that product quality or service levels exceed buyers' needs.
- Trying to charge too high a price premium (the bigger the price differential the harder it is to keep buyers from switching to lower-priced competitors).
- Ignoring the need to signal value and depending only on intrinsic product attributes to achieve differentiation.
- Not understanding or identifying what buyers consider as value.

A low-cost provider strategy can defeat a differentiation strategy when buyers are satisfied with a basic product and don't think "extra" attributes are worth a higher price.

Best-Cost Provider Strategies

Best-cost provider strategies aim at giving customers *more value for the money.* The objective is to deliver superior value to buyers by satisfying their expectations on key quality-service-features-performance attributes and beating their expectations on price (given what rivals are charging for much the same attributes). A company achieves best-cost status from an ability to incorporate attractive attributes at a lower cost than rivals. To become a best-cost provider, a company must have the resources and capabilities to achieve good-to-excellent quality at a lower cost than rivals, incorporate appealing features at a lower cost than rivals, match product performance at a lower cost than rivals, provide good-to-excellent customer service at a lower cost than rivals, and so on. The term *best-cost provider* is used because this strategy entails striving to have the best (*lowest*) cost relative to rivals offering products/services with comparable attributes.

> The most successful best-cost producers have competencies and capabilities to simultaneously manage unit costs down and product caliber up.

---

[10]Porter, *Competitive Advantage*, pp. 160–62.

As Figure 5.1 indicates, best-cost provider strategies stake out a middle ground between pursuing a low-cost advantage and a differentiation advantage and between appealing to the broad market as a whole and a narrow market niche. From a competitive positioning standpoint, best-cost strategies are a *hybrid,* balancing a strategic emphasis on low cost against a strategic emphasis on differentiation (superior value). *The market target is value-conscious buyers,* perhaps a very sizable part of the market. *The competitive advantage of a best-cost provider is lower costs than rivals* in incorporating good-to-excellent attributes, putting it in a position to underprice rival brands with similar appealing attributes.

A best-cost provider strategy is very appealing in certain market situations. In markets where buyer diversity makes product differentiation the norm *and* where many buyers are also sensitive to price and value, a best-cost producer strategy can be more advantageous than either a pure low-cost producer strategy or a pure differentiation strategy keyed to product superiority. This is because a best-cost provider can position itself near the middle of the market with either a medium-quality product at a below-average price or with a very good product at a medium price. Often, substantial numbers of buyers prefer midrange products rather than the cheap, basic products of low-cost producers or the expensive products of top-of-the-line differentiators. But unless a company has the resources, know-how, and capabilities to incorporate upscale product or service attributes at a lower cost than rivals, this strategy is ill-advised.

Illustration Capsule 22 describes how Toyota has used a best-cost approach with its Lexus models.

The Big Risk of a Best-Cost Provider Strategy   The danger of a best-cost provider strategy is that a user will get squeezed between the strategies of firms using low-cost and differentiation strategies. Low-cost cost leaders may be able to siphon customers away with the appeal of a lower price. High-end differentiators may be able to steal customers away with the appeal of better product attributes. Thus, to be successful, a best-cost provider must offer buyers *significantly* better product attributes in order to justify a price above what low-cost leaders are charging. Likewise it has to achieve significantly lower costs than a high-end differentiator in providing upscale features so that it can outcompete high-end differentiators on the basis of a significantly lower price.

Focused (or Market Niche) Strategies

What sets focused strategies apart from low-cost or differentiation strategies is concentrated attention on a narrow piece of the total market. The target segment or niche can be defined by geographic uniqueness, by specialized requirements in using the product, or by special product attributes that appeal only to niche members. The aim of a focused strategy is to do a better job of serving buyers in the target market niche than rival competitors. *A focuser's basis for competitive advantage is either (1) lower costs than competitors in serving the market niche or (2) an ability to offer niche members something they perceive is better suited to their own unique tastes and preferences.* A focused strategy based on low cost depends on there being a buyer segment whose requirements are less costly to satisfy compared to the rest of the market. A focused strategy based on differentiation depends on there being a buyer segment that is looking for special product attributes or seller capabilities.

Examples of firms employing some version of a focused strategy include eBay (in online auctions); Porsche (in sports cars); Cannondale (in top-of-the-line mountain

---

The most powerful competitive strategy of all is relentlessly striving to become a lower-and-lower-cost provider of a higher-and-higher-caliber product. The closer a firm can get to the ultimate of being the industry's absolute lowest-cost provider and, simultaneously, the provider of the industry's overall best product, the less vulnerable it becomes to rivals' actions.

illustration capsule 22
Toyota's Best-Cost Producer Strategy for Its Lexus Line

Toyota Motor Co. is widely regarded as a low-cost producer among the world's motor vehicle manufacturers. Despite its emphasis on product quality, Toyota has achieved absolute low-cost leadership because of its considerable skills in efficient manufacturing techniques and because its models are positioned in the low-to-medium end of the price spectrum, where high production volumes are conducive to low unit costs. But when Toyota decided to introduce its new Lexus models to compete in the luxury-car market, it employed a classic best-cost provider strategy. Toyota's Lexus strategy had three features:

- Transferring its expertise in making high-quality Toyota models at low cost to making premium-quality luxury cars at costs below other luxury-car makers, especially Mercedes and BMW. Toyota executives reasoned that Toyota's manufacturing skills should allow it to incorporate high-tech performance features and upscale quality into Lexus models at less cost than other luxury-car manufacturers.

- Using its relatively lower manufacturing costs to underprice Mercedes and BMW, both of which had models selling in the $40,000 to $75,000 range (and some even higher). Toyota believed that with its cost advantage it could price attractively equipped Lexus cars low enough to draw price-conscious buyers away

from Mercedes and BMW and perhaps induce dissatisfied Lincoln and Cadillac owners to switch to a Lexus.

- Establishing a new network of Lexus dealers, separate from Toyota dealers, dedicated to providing a level of personalized, attentive customer service unmatched in the industry.

The Lexus 400 series models, priced in the $48,000 to $55,000 range, compete against Mercedes's 300/400E series, BMW's 540/740 series, Nissan's Infiniti Q45, Cadillac Seville, Jaguar, and Lincoln Continental. The lower-priced Lexus 300 series, priced in the $30,000 to $40,000 range, competes against Cadillac deVille, Acura Legend, Infiniti J30, Buick Park Avenue, Mercedes's C-Class series, BMW's 315 series, and Oldsmobile's Aurora line. More recently, Lexus has introduced sport-utility vehicles to compete against those from Mercedes, Lincoln, Cadillac, BMW, Infiniti, and Jeep.

Lexus's best-cost producer strategy was so successful that Mercedes introduced a new, lower-priced C-Class series, to become more competitive. The Lexus LS 400 models and the Lexus SC 300/400 models have consistently ranked among the top 10 models in the widely watched J. D. Power & Associates quality survey. In the 1999 model year, Lexus was the second best-selling luxury brand in the United States.

bikes); commuter airlines like Horizon, Comair, and Atlantic Southeast (specializing in low-traffic, short-haul flights linking major airports with small cities 100 to 250 miles away); Jiffy Lube International (a specialist in quick oil changes, lubrication, and simple maintenance for motor vehicles); Enterprise Rent-a-Car (specializing in providing rental cars to repair garage customers); and Bandag (a specialist in truck tire recapping that promotes its recaps aggressively at over 1,000 truck stops). Microbreweries, local bakeries, bed-and-breakfast inns, and local owner-managed retail boutiques are all good examples of enterprises that have scaled their operations to serve narrow or local customer segments. Illustration Capsule 23 describes Motel 6's focused low-cost strategy and Ritz-Carlton's focused differentiation strategy.

Focused low-cost strategies are fairly common. Producers of private-label goods are able to achieve low product development, marketing, distribution, and advertising costs by concentrating on making generic items imitative of name-brand merchandise and selling directly to retail chains wanting a basic house brand to sell at a discount to price-sensitive shoppers. Discount stock brokerage houses have lowered costs by focusing on customers who are willing to forgo the investment research, advice, and financial services offered by full-service firms like Merrill Lynch in return for 30 percent or more commission savings on their buy-sell transactions. Pursuing a cost advantage

illustration capsule 23

Focused Strategies in the Lodging Industry: Motel 6 and Ritz-Carlton

Motel 6 and Ritz-Carlton compete at opposite ends of the lodging industry. Motel 6 employs a focused strategy keyed to low cost; Ritz-Carlton employs a focused strategy based on differentiation.

Motel 6 caters to price-conscious travelers who want a clean, no-frills place to spend the night. To be a low-cost provider of overnight lodging, Motel 6 (1) selects relatively inexpensive sites on which to construct its units (usually near interstate exits and high traffic locations but far enough away to avoid paying prime site prices); (2) builds only basic facilities (no restaurant or bar and only rarely a swimming pool); (3) relies on standard architectural designs that incorporate inexpensive materials and low-cost construction techniques; and (4) has simple room furnishings and decorations. These approaches lower both investment costs and operating costs. Without restaurants, bars, and all kinds of guest services, a Motel 6 unit can be operated with just front desk personnel, room cleanup crews, and skeleton building-and-grounds maintenance. To promote the Motel 6 concept with travelers who have simple overnight requirements, the chain uses unique, recognizable radio ads done by nationally syndicated radio personality Tom Bodett; the ads describe Motel 6's clean rooms, no-frills facilities, friendly atmosphere, and dependably low rates (usually under $40 per night).

In contrast, Ritz-Carlton caters to discriminating travelers and vacationers willing and able to pay for top-of-the-line accommodations and world-class personal service. Ritz-Carlton hotels feature (1) prime locations and scenic views from many rooms; (2) custom architectural designs; (3) fine restaurants with gourmet menus prepared by accomplished chefs; (4) elegantly appointed lobbies and bar lounges; (5) swimming pools, exercise facilities, and leisure-time options; (6) upscale room accommodations; (7) an array of guest services and recreation opportunities appropriate to the location; and (8) large, well-trained professional staffs who do their utmost to make each guest's stay an enjoyable experience.

Both companies concentrate their attention on a narrow piece of the total market. Motel 6's basis for competitive advantage is lower costs than competitors in providing basic, economical overnight accommodations to price-constrained travelers. Ritz-Carlton's advantage is its capability to provide superior accommodations and unmatched personal service for a well-to-do clientele. Each is able to succeed, despite polar opposite strategies, because the market for lodging consists of diverse buyer segments with diverse preferences and abilities to pay.

via focusing works well when a firm can lower costs significantly by limiting its customer base to a well-defined buyer segment.

At the other end of the market spectrum, focusers like Godiva Chocolates, Chanel, Rolls-Royce, Häagen-Dazs, and W. L. Gore (the maker of Gore-Tex) employ successful differentiation-based focused strategies targeted at upscale buyers wanting products and services with world-class attributes. Indeed, most markets contain a buyer segment willing to pay a big price premium for the very finest items available, thus opening the strategic window for some competitors to pursue differentiation-based focused strategies aimed at the very top of the market pyramid. Another successful focused differentiator is a "fashion food retailer" called Trader Joe's, a 150-store East and West Coast chain that is a combination gourmet deli and food warehouse.[11] Customers shop Trader Joe's as much for entertainment as for conventional grocery items—the store stocks all

---

[11]Gary Hamel, "Strategy as Revolution," *Harvard Business Review* 74, no. 4 (July–August 1996), p. 72. For an interesting and entertaining presentation of Trader Joe's mission, strategy, and operating practices, see the information the company has posted at www.traderjoes.com.

kinds of out-of-the-ordinary culinary treats like raspberry salsa, salmon burgers, and jasmine fried rice, as well as the standard goods normally found in supermarkets. What sets Trader Joe's apart is not just its unique combination of food novelties and competitively priced grocery items but the opportunity it provides to turn an otherwise mundane shopping excursion to the grocery into a whimsical treasure hunt that is just plain fun. Blue Mountain Arts, a focused differentiator in greeting cards, stands apart from Hallmark and American Greetings not only regarding the distinctive look, feel, and content of its cards but also with respect to its focus on electronic greeting cards.

When Focusing Is Attractive   A focused strategy based either on low cost or differentiation becomes increasingly attractive as more of the following conditions are met:

- The target market niche is big enough to be profitable and offers good growth potential.
- Industry leaders do not see that having a presence in the niche is crucial to their own success—a condition that reduces rivalry from major competitors.
- It is costly or difficult for multisegment competitors to put capabilities in place to meet the specialized needs of the target market niche and, at the same time, satisfy the expectations of their mainstream customers.
- The industry has many different niches and segments, thereby allowing a focuser to pick a competitively attractive niche suited to its resource strengths and capabilities.
- Few, if any, other rivals are attempting to specialize in the same target segment— a condition that reduces the risk of segment overcrowding.
- The focuser can compete effectively against challengers based on the capabilities and resources it has to serve the targeted niche and the customer goodwill it may have built up.

When an industry has many different niches and segments, the strength of competition varies across and within segments, a condition that makes it important for a focuser to pick a niche that is both competitively attractive and well suited to its resource strengths and capabilities. A focuser's specialized competencies and capabilities in serving the target market niche provide the strongest and most dependable basis for contending successfully with competitive forces. Rivalry in the target niche is weaker when there are comparatively few players in the niche and when multisegment rivals have trouble truly meeting the expectations of the focused firm's target clientele along with the expectations of the other types of customers they cater to. A focuser's unique capabilities in serving the market niche also act as an entry barrier—difficulties in matching a focuser's capabilities can dissuade potential newcomers from attempting entry. They also present a hurdle that makers of substitute products must overcome. Even if some niche buyers have substantial bargaining leverage, their power is blunted somewhat by the downside of shifting their business to rival companies less capable of meeting their expectations.

> Even though a focuser may be small, it still may have substantial competitive strength because of the attractiveness of its product offering and its strong expertise and capabilities in meeting the needs and expectations of niche members.

The Risks of a Focused Strategy   Focusing carries several risks. One is the chance that competitors will find effective ways to match the focused firm in serving the target niche—perhaps by coming up with more appealing product offerings or by developing expertise and capabilities that offset the focuser's strengths. A second is the potential for the preferences and needs of niche members to shift over time toward the product attributes desired by the majority of buyers. An erosion of the differences across buyer segments lowers entry barriers into a focuser's market niche and provides an open invitation for rivals in adjacent segments to begin competing for the focuser's customers. A third risk is that the segment becomes so attractive it is soon inundated with competitors, intensifying rivalry and splintering segment profits.

COOPERATIVE STRATEGIES AND COMPETITIVE ADVANTAGE

In the past 10 years, companies in all types of industries and in all parts of the world have formed strategic alliances and partnerships to complement their own strategic initiatives and strengthen their competitiveness in domestic and international markets. This is an about-face from times past, when the vast majority of companies were content to go it alone, confident that they already had or could independently develop whatever resources and know-how were needed to be successful in their markets. But globalization of the world economy, revolutionary advances in technology across a broad front, and untapped opportunities in national markets in Asia, Latin America, and Europe that are opening up, deregulation, and/or undergoing privatization have made strategic partnerships of one kind or another integral to a firm's competitiveness.

Alliances and partnerships are a necessity in racing against rivals to build a strong global presence and/or to stake out a position in the industries of the future.

Many companies now find themselves thrust in the midst of two very demanding competitive races: (1) *the global race to build a market presence in many different national markets* and to establish an attractive position among the global market leaders and (2) *the technology race to capitalize on today's technological and information age revolution* and build the resource strengths and business capabilities to compete successfully in the industries and product markets of the future.[12] Even the largest and most financially strong companies have concluded that simultaneously running the races for global market leadership and for a stake in the industries of the future requires more diverse and expansive skills, resources, technological expertise, and competitive capabilities than they can assemble and manage alone.

Indeed, the gaps in resources and competitive capabilities between industry rivals have become painfully apparent to disadvantaged enterprises. Allowing such gaps to go unaddressed can put a company in a precarious competitive position or even prove fatal. When rivals can develop new products faster or achieve better quality at lower cost or have more resources and know-how to exploit opportunities in attractive new market arenas, a company has little option but to try to close the resource and competency gaps quickly; the fastest way to do this is often with the capabilities and strengths of new strategic allies. In today's rapidly changing world, a company that cannot position itself quickly misses important opportunities, whether they be in cyberspace or foreign countries. More and more enterprises are concluding that well-chosen alliances can allow them to bypass the comparatively slower and more costly process of building one's own capabilities internally to access new opportunities.

The Increasingly Pervasive Use of Alliances

Strategic alliances and collaborative partnerships have thus emerged as an attractive and timely means of breaching the technology and resource gaps that firms now commonly encounter. *Alliances have, in fact, become so essential to the competitiveness of*

---

[12]Yves L. Doz and Gary Hamel, *Alliance Advantage: The Art of Creating Value through Partnering* (Boston: Harvard Business School Press, 1998), pp. xiii and xiv.

companies in many industries that they are a core element of today's business strategies. They are especially prevalent in industries where change is rapid. General Electric has formed over 100 cooperative partnerships in a wide range of areas; IBM has joined in over 400 strategic alliances.[13] Oracle is said to have over 15,000 alliances. Alliances are so central to Corning's strategy that the company describes itself as a "network of organizations." Toyota has forged a network of long-term strategic partnerships with its suppliers of automotive parts and components. Microsoft collaborates very closely with independent software developers that create new programs to run on the next-generation versions of Windows. A recent study indicates that the average large corporation is involved in around 30 alliances today, versus fewer than 3 a decade ago.

In the PC industry cooperative alliances are pervasive because the different components of PCs and the software to run them are supplied by so many different companies—one set of companies provides the microprocessors, another group makes the motherboards, another the monitors, another the disk drives, another the memory chips, and so on. Moreover, their facilities are scattered across the United States, Japan, Taiwan, Singapore, Malaysia, and parts of Europe. Close collaboration is required on product development, logistics, production, and the timing of new product releases. Consequently, Intel has formed collaborative partnerships with numerous makers of PC components and software developers to jointly pursue new technologies and to bring new products to market in parallel so that consumers can get the maximum benefits from new PCs running on Intel's next-generation microprocessors. Without extensive cooperation and collaboration between Intel, the makers of other key PC components, PC makers, and software developers in both new technology and new product development, there would be all kinds of bottlenecks, delays, and incompatibility problems in bringing new computer hardware and software products into the marketplace—obstacles that would dramatically slow the pace of advance in PC capabilities and applications.

The convergence of cable TV, telecommunications, and computer technologies is spawning entirely new kinds of services and new means of content delivery and creating a need for all kinds of alliances. Companies such as AT&T, MCI WorldCom, America Online, the regional Bell companies, Qwest Communications, Deutsche Telekom, Motorola, Nokia, Ericcson, and many others have put together webs of different alliances and partnerships, some collaborative and some competing, to pursue the races for global market leadership and for a major participating role in the telecommunication industry of the future. America Online, which from the outset formed partnerships with a host of companies to deliver content to its subscribers, has entered into alliances with Hughes Satellite, several of the regional Bell companies, and others to develop high-speed Internet access alternatives; AOL's objective is to assemble competitive alternatives to what AT&T (which has acquired two large cable companies that now make it the largest provider of cable TV service in the United States) is endeavoring to deliver via its cable TV connections. Moreover, there are assorted alliances among enterprises promoting wireless telecommunications systems going head-to-head against assorted alliances of telecommunications companies promoting fiber-optic, digital signal line (DSL), and cable types of connections. Collaborative alliances are essential in creating the capabilities for digital banking and credit card transactions on the Internet because "seamless" networks have to be built and made compatible across the operations of many different enterprises using different brands and types of hardware and software.

> Alliances and cooperative arrangements, whether they bring together companies from different parts of the industry value chain or different parts of the world, are a fact of life in business today.

> Growing use of alliances is shifting the basis of competition to groups of companies against groups of companies.

---

[13]Michael A. Hitt, Beverly B. Tyler, Camilla Hardee, and Daewoo Park, "Understanding Strategic Intent in the Global Marketplace," *Academy of Management Executive* 9, no. 2 (May 1995), p. 13.

Why and How Strategic Alliances Are Advantageous

Strategic alliances are cooperative agreements between firms that go beyond normal company-to-company dealings but fall short of merger or full joint venture partnership with formal ownership ties. (Some strategic alliances do involve arrangements whereby one or more allies have minority ownership in certain of the other alliance members, however.) But the value of an alliance stems not from the agreement or deal itself but rather from the capacity of the partners to defuse organizational frictions, collaborate effectively over time, and work their way through the maze of changes that lie in front of them—technological and competitive surprises, new market developments (that may come at a rapid-fire pace), and changes in their own priorities and competitive circumstances. Collaborative alliances nearly always entail an *evolving* relationship, with the benefits and competitive value ultimately depending on mutual learning, effective cooperation over time, and successfully adapting to change. Competitive advantage emerges when a company acquires valuable resources and capabilities through alliances that it could not otherwise obtain on its own and that give it an edge over rivals—this requires real in-the-trenches collaboration between the partners to create new value together, not merely an arm's-length exchange of ideas and information. Unless partners value the skills, resources, and contributions each brings to the alliance and the cooperative arrangement results in win-win outcomes, it will amount to little or fail.

> The competitive attraction of alliances is to bundle competences and resources that are more valuable in a joint effort than when kept separate.

The most common reasons why companies enter into strategic alliances are to collaborate on technology or the development of promising new products, to overcome deficits in their technical and manufacturing expertise, to acquire altogether new competencies, to improve supply chain efficiency, to gain economies of scale in production and/or marketing, and to acquire or improve market access through joint marketing agreements.[14] A company that is racing for global market leadership needs alliances to help it do what it cannot easily do alone:

> Alliances are highly beneficial in racing against rivals for global market leadership.

- Get into critical country markets quickly and accelerate the process of building a potent global market presence.
- Gain inside knowledge about unfamiliar markets and cultures through alliances with local partners.
- Access valuable skills and competencies that are concentrated in particular geographic locations (such as software design competencies in the United States, fashion design skills in Italy, and efficient manufacturing skills in Japan).

A company that is racing to stake out a strong position in an industry of the future needs alliances to:

> Alliances are also highly beneficial in racing against rivals to build the expertise and market position needed to win a strong position in the industries of the future.

- Establish a beachhead for participating in the target industry.
- Master new technologies and build new expertise and competencies faster than would be possible through internal efforts.
- Open up expanded opportunities in the target industry by melding the firm's own capabilities with the expertise and resources of partners.

Allies can learn much from one another in performing joint research, sharing technological know-how, and collaborating on complementary new technologies and products—sometimes enough to enable them to pursue other new opportunities on their own.

---

[14]Porter, *The Competitive Advantage of Nations* (New York: Free Press, 1990), p. 66.

Manufacturers typically pursue alliances with parts and components suppliers to gain the efficiencies of better supply chain management and to speed new products to market. By joining forces in components production and/or final assembly, companies may be able to realize cost savings not achievable with their own small volumes—Volvo, Renault, and Peugeot formed an alliance to make engines together for their large car models precisely because no one of them needed enough such engines to operate their own engine plant economically. Manufacturing allies can also learn much about how to improve their quality control and production procedures by studying one another's manufacturing methods. Often alliances are formed to utilize common dealer networks or for joint promotion of complementary products, thereby mutually strengthening their access to buyers and economizing on forward channel distribution costs. Diageo (parent of Häagen-Dazs, Burger King, Pillsbury, and other name-brand foods and beverages) and Swiss-based Nestlé (the world's largest consumer foods company) recently allied in a joint venture to distribute Häagen-Dazs ice cream and Nestlé frozen dessert treats through the same U.S. distribution pipeline and to use common display cases; the allies expected to both expand the market access for their products and economize on distribution costs.

Not only can alliances offset competitive disadvantages or create competitive advantages but they also can result in the allied companies' directing their competitive energies more toward mutual rivals and less toward one another. Potential rivals can sometimes be effectively neutralized by engaging them in a collaborative alliance. Who partners with whom affects the pattern of industry rivalry. Many runner-up companies, wanting to preserve their independence, resort to alliances rather than mergers to try to close the competitive gap on leading companies—*they rely on collaboration with others to enhance their organizational capabilities, develop valuable new strategic resources, and compete effectively.* Industry leaders pursue cooperative alliances in order to better fend off ambitious rivals as well as to open up new opportunities.

Strategic cooperation is a much-favored, indeed necessary, approach in industries where new technological developments are occurring at a furious pace along many different paths and where advances in one technology spill over to affect others (often blurring industry boundaries). Whenever industries are experiencing high-velocity technological change in many areas simultaneously, firms find it virtually essential to have cooperative relationships with other enterprises to stay on the leading edge of technology and product performance even in their own area of specialization. They cooperate in technology development, in sharing R&D information, in developing new products that complement each other in the marketplace, and in building networks of dealers and distributors to handle their respective products.

Illustration Capsule 24 contains examples of recent high-profile alliances.

> While a few firms can pursue their strategies alone, it is becoming increasingly common for companies to pursue their strategies in collaboration with suppliers, distributors, makers of complementary products, and sometimes even select competitors.

Alliances and Partnerships with Foreign Companies   Cooperative strategies and alliances to penetrate international markets are also common between domestic and foreign firms. Such partnerships are useful in putting together the resources and capabilities to do business over a wider number of country markets. For example, U.S., European, and Japanese companies wanting to build market footholds in the fast-growing Chinese market have all pursued partnership arrangements with Chinese companies to help in dealing with government regulations, to supply knowledge of local markets, to provide guidance on adapting their products to better match the buying preferences of Chinese consumers, to set up local manufacturing capabilities, and to assist in distribution, marketing, and promotional activities. The policy of the Chinese government has long been one of giving privileged market access to a few select outsiders while excluding others and requiring the favored outsiders to partner in one way or another with local enterprises.

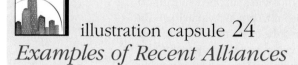

illustration capsule 24
Examples of Recent Alliances

- *Pfizer and Warner-Lambert*—formed an alliance to market cholesterol-reducing drug Lipitor. Warner-Lambert contributed the product; Pfizer's contribution was the skills of its sales force in marketing the product to physicians.

- *America Online with Gateway, Motorola, Palm, Direct TV, and Hughes Electronics*—AOL has partnered with Gateway to develop and co-market Internet appliances and home networking devices; it has partnered with Motorola to make its Instant Messenger service available on Motorola wireless phones and pagers; it has teamed with Palm to put AOL's e-mail service on Palm's handheld PCs; and it has allied with satellite broadcaster Direct TV and Hughes Electronics to bring AOL to TV screens via set-top boxes.

- *Hewlett-Packard and Qwest Communications*—entered into an alliance to create a business called CyberCenters that offers end-to-end Internet solutions, with customer service available 24 hours a day, seven days a week. Hewlett-Packard contributed server hardware, software, and services; Qwest provided Internet access, a base of customers, and a lead role in delivering services to customers.

- *IBM and Dell Computer*—formed an alliance whereby Dell agreed to purchase $16 billion in parts and components from IBM for use in Dell's PCs, servers, and workstations over a three-year period. Dell determined that IBM's growing expertise and capabilities in PC components justified using IBM as a major supplier even though Dell and IBM competed vigorously in supplying laptop computers to corporate customers.

- *Johnson & Johnson and Merck*—entered into an alliance to market Pepcid AC. Merck developed the stomach distress remedy and J&J has functioned as marketer. The alliance has made Pepcid AC the best-selling such remedy.

- *General Electric's Aircraft Engines Division and Pratt & Whitney*—formed an alliance to develop and sell a new engine for Airbus Industries' super jumbo airplane, the A3XX. Both GE Aircraft and Pratt & Whitney make aircraft engines and are fierce competitors in the market for jet engines for commercial aircraft. The partnership was formed to compete with Rolls-Royce for the Airbus contract.

- *United Parcel Service, AT&T, and Microsoft*—UPS joined with its suppliers AT&T and Microsoft to provide free Internet access for UPS's 1.7 million customers using its online shipping and digital document delivery services.

- *United, American, Continental, Delta,* and *Northwest Airlines*—created an alliance to form Orbitz, an Internet travel site designed to compete with Expedia and Travelocity to provide consumers with low-cost airfares, rental cars, lodging, cruises, and vacation packages. About a month after the site's launch, Orbitz announced another alliance—this time with Internet travel discounter Hotwire. Under this agreement, Hotwire and Orbitz promote each other's services and provide links to each other's sites. Hotwire and Orbitz complement each other because Orbitz targets time-sensitive business travelers and those who prefer certain airlines, while Hotwire offers discounts for flights that aren't expected to fill to capacity.

Source: "Orbitz, Hotwire Form Alliance," Associated Press, July 19, 2001; Erich Luening, "Web Users Gravitate to Orbitz," *CNET News.com* (http://news.cnet.com), June 15, 2001; company press releases; and *Business Week,* October 25, 1999, pp. 112–30.

Why Many Alliances Are Unstable or Break Apart Whether an alliance will stand the test of time or break apart hinges on how well the partners work together, their success in responding and adapting to changing internal and external conditions, and their willingness to renegotiate the bargain if circumstances so warrant. Unless partners value the skills, resources, and contributions each brings to the alliance and the cooperative arrangement results in win–win outcomes, it is doomed. A recent study by Andersen Consulting revealed that 61 percent of alliances were either outright failures or "limping along."[15]

---

[15]Cited in *Business Week,* October 25, 1999, p. 110.

More alliances come apart than stay together. Many reasons account for the high "divorce rate," diverging objectives and priorities, an inability to work well together, the emergence of more attractive technological paths, and marketplace rivalry between one or more allies.[16] An example of the complications caused by the unpredictability of emerging technologies comes from the efforts of Merck in the early 1990s to assemble a large group of research institutes, universities, entrepreneurial biotech companies, and other organizations to pursue the development of AIDS cures and vaccines; the market need was clear and urgent, but the uncertainties of the evolving AIDS virus and the often unsystematic manner in which miracle drugs are discovered and wind their way to market meant there was no way for Merck and its allies to judge which, if any, of the R&D alliances might prove fruitful.[17] Ongoing commitment, mutual learning, and continued close collaboration are essential to keeping alliances like Merck's functioning productively.

> Many alliances fail and break apart, never reaching their intended potential, because of frictions and conflicts among the allies.

The Strategic Dangers of Relying Heavily on Alliances and Cooperative Partnerships   The Achilles heel of alliances and cooperative strategies is the danger of becoming dependent on other companies for *essential* expertise and capabilities over the long term. To be a market leader (and perhaps even a serious market contender), a company must ultimately develop its own capabilities in areas where internal strategic control is pivotal to protecting its competitiveness and building competitive advantage. Moreover, some alliances hold only limited potential because the partner guards its most valuable skills and expertise; in such instances, acquiring or merging with a company possessing the desired resources is a better solution.

MERGER AND ACQUISITION STRATEGIES

Mergers and acquisitions are a much-used strategic option.[18] They are especially suited for situations where alliances and partnerships do not go far enough in providing a company with access to the needed resources and capabilities. Ownership ties are more permanent than partnership ties, allowing the operations of the merger/acquisition participants to be tightly integrated and creating more in-house control and autonomy.

Merging with or acquiring another company, often a competitor, can dramatically strengthen a company's market position and open new opportunities for competitive advantage. Combining operations with a rival can fill resource gaps, allowing the new company to do things which the prior companies could not do alone. Together, the companies may have stronger technological skills, more or better competitive capabilities, a more attractive lineup of products and services, wider geographic coverage, and/or greater financial resources with which to invest in R&D, add capacity, or expand into new areas. Moreover, combining operations may offer considerable cost-saving opportunities, transforming otherwise high-cost companies into a competitor with average or below-average costs.

> No company can afford to ignore the strategic and competitive benefits of acquiring or merging with another company to strengthen its market position and open up avenues of new opportunity.

---

[16]Doz and Hamel, *Alliance Advantage,* pp. 16–18.

[17]Ibid., p. 17.

[18]A *merger* is a combination and pooling of equals, with the newly created company often taking on a new name. An *acquisition* is when one company, the acquirer, purchases and absorbs the operations of another, the acquired. The difference between a merger and an acquisition relates more to the details of ownership, management control, and financial arrangements than to strategy and competitive advantage. The resources, competencies, and competitive capabilities of the newly created enterprise end up much the same whether the combination is the result of acquisition or merger.

The race for global market leadership is prompting numerous companies to make acquisitions to build a market presence in countries where they currently do not compete. Similarly, the race to establish attractive positions in the industries of the future is prompting companies to merge or make acquisitions to fill in resource or technological gaps, build important technological capabilities, and move into position to launch next-wave products and services. These benefits can be quite substantial and explain why companies resort to mergers and acquisitions.

WorldCom's bold acquisitions of MCI and Sprint has created a powerhouse company capable of challenging AT&T head-on, competing strongly in the European market, and establishing itself as a leader in the Internet-driven telecommunications industry of the future (as opposed to simply being a provider of long-distance telephone service in the United States). Nestlé, Kraft (a subsidiary of Philip Morris Companies), Unilever, Procter & Gamble, and several other prominent food and consumer products companies have all made numerous acquisitions in racing to establish a stronger global presence. Daimler-Benz merged with Chrysler to create a broader product line and a stronger global presence in the world's motor vehicle industry, enhancing the combined companies' ability to compete with Toyota, Ford, and General Motors. America Online acquired CompuServe to give it stronger appeal to customers wanting Internet access. Intel has made over 300 acquisitions in the past five or so years to broaden its technological base and put it in a stronger position to be a major supplier of Internet technology and less dependent on supplying microprocessors for PCs. Likewise, Cisco Systems has been an active acquirer, purchasing over 40 technology companies to buttress its standing as the world's biggest supplier of systems for building the infrastructure of the Internet. Illustration Capsule 25 describes how Clear Channel Communications has used mergers and acquisitions to build a leading global position in outdoor advertising and radio and TV broadcasting.

However, mergers and acquisitions do not always produce the hoped-for outcomes, sometimes because of exaggerated expectations and sometimes because capturing the benefits proves much harder than anticipated. Combining the operations of two companies, especially large and complex ones, often entails formidable resistance from rank-and-file organization members, hard-to-resolve conflicts in management styles and corporate cultures, and tough problems of integration. The expected cost savings, expertise sharing, and enhanced competitive capabilities may take substantially longer than expected to realize or, worse, may never materialize at all. A number of previously applauded acquisitions have yet to live up to expectations—AT&T's acquisition of AtHome/Excite, Ford's acquisition of Jaguar, Walt Disney's acquisition of Capital Cities/ABC, and Deutsche Bank's acquisition of Banker's Trust are prime examples. Ford paid a handsome price to acquire Jaguar but has yet to make the Jaguar brand a major factor in the luxury car segment in competition against Mercedes, BMW, and Lexus. Novell acquired WordPerfect for $1.7 billion in stock in 1994, but the combination never generated enough punch to compete against Microsoft Word and Microsoft Office; Novell sold WordPerfect to Corel for $124 million in cash and stock less than two years later. Other deals that proved disastrous are Viacom's acquisition of Blockbuster and USA Waste's acquisition of Waste Management.

VERTICAL INTEGRATION STRATEGIES: A COMPETITIVE PLUS OR A MINUS

Vertical integration extends a firm's competitive scope within the same industry. It involves expanding the firm's range of activities backward into sources of supply and/ or forward toward end users of the final product. Thus, if a manufacturer invests in

illustration capsule 25

How Clear Channel Communications Used Mergers and Acquisitions to Become a Global Leader in the Media Industry

In 2000, Clear Channel Communications was the fourth largest media company in the world behind Disney, Time Warner, and Viacom/CBS. The company, founded in 1972 by Lowry Mays and Billy Joe McCombs, got its start by acquiring an unprofitable country-music radio station in San Antonio, Texas. Over the next 10 years, Mays learned the radio business and slowly bought other radio stations in a variety of states. The company went public in 1984, helping it raise the equity capital needed to fuel its strategy of expanding by acquiring radio stations in additional geographic markets.

In the late 1980s, following the decision of the Federal Communications Commission to loosen the rules regarding the ability of one company to own both radio and TV stations, Clear Channel broadened its strategy and began acquiring small, struggling TV stations. Soon thereafter, Clear Channel became affiliated with the Fox network, which was starting to build a national presence and challenge ABC, CBS, and NBC. Meanwhile, the company began selling programming services to other stations, and in some markets where it already had stations it took on the function of selling advertising for cross-town stations it did not own.

By 1998, Clear Channel had used acquisitions to build a leading position in radio and television stations. It owned, programmed, or sold airtime for 69 AM radio stations, 135 FM stations, and 18 TV stations in 48 local markets in 24 states. The TV stations included affiliates with FOX, UPN, ABC, NBC, and CBS. It had purchased a 29 percent ownership interest in Heftel Broadcasting Co., a domestic Spanish-language radio broadcaster. Clear Channel also owned two radio stations and a cable audio channel in Denmark and had acquired ownership interests in radio stations in Australia, Mexico, New Zealand, and the Czech Republic.

In 1997, Clear Channel acquired Phoenix-based Eller Media Company, an outdoor advertising company with over 100,000 billboard facings. Additional acquisitions of outdoor advertising companies quickly followed, the most important of which were:

- ABC Outdoor in Milwaukee, Wisconsin.
- Paxton Communications, with operations in Tampa and Orlando, Florida.
- Universal Outdoor.
- The More Group, with outdoor operations and 90,000 displays in 24 countries.

Then in October 1999, Clear Channel made another major strategic move, merging with AMFM, Inc., to form the world's largest out-of-home media enterprise. After divesting some 125 properties needed to gain the anticipated regulatory approval, Clear Channel Communications (the name adopted by the merged companies) had operations in 32 countries and included 830 radio stations, 19 TV stations, more than 425,000 outdoor displays, and significant ownership interests in other leading radio broadcasting and outdoor advertising properties.

The company's strategy was to buy radio, TV, and outdoor advertising properties with operations in many of the same local markets, share facilities and staffs to cut costs, improve programming, and sell advertising to customers in packages for all three media simultaneously. Packaging ads for two or three media allowed the company to combine its sales activities and have a common sales force for all three media, achieving significant cost savings and boosting profit margins.

Sources: Company documents and *Business Week,* October 19, 1999, p. 56.

facilities to produce certain component parts that it formerly purchased from outside suppliers, it remains in essentially the same industry as before. The only change is that it has business units in two production stages in the industry's value chain. Similarly, if a paint manufacturer, Sherwin-Williams for example, elects to integrate forward by opening 100 retail stores to market its paint products directly to consumers, it remains in the paint business even though its competitive scope extends further forward in the industry chain.

Vertical integration strategies can aim at *full integration* (participating in all stages of the industry value chain) or *partial integration* (building positions in selected stages of the industry's total value chain). A firm can accomplish vertical integration by starting its own operations in other stages in the industry's activity chain or by acquiring a company already performing the activities it wants to bring in-house.

The Strategic Advantages of Vertical Integration

The only good reason for investing company resources in vertical integration is to strengthen the firm's competitive position.[19] Unless vertical integration produces sufficient cost savings to justify the extra investment or adds materially to a company's technological and competitive strengths or truly helps differentiate its product offering, it has no real payoff profitwise or strategywise.

> A vertical integration strategy has appeal *only* if it significantly strengthens a firm's competitive position.

Integrating Backward to Achieve Greater Competitiveness   Integrating backward generates cost savings only when the volume needed is big enough to capture the same scale economies suppliers have and when suppliers' production efficiency can be matched or exceeded with no dropoff in quality. The best potential for being able to reduce costs via backward integration exists in situations where suppliers have sizable profit margins, where the item being supplied is a major cost component, and where the needed technological skills are easily mastered or can be gained by acquiring a supplier with the desired technological know-how. Integrating backward can sometimes significantly enhance a company's technological capabilities and give it expertise needed to stake out positions in the industries and products of the future. Intel, Cisco, and many other Silicon Valley companies have been active in acquiring companies that will help them speed the advance of Internet technology and pave the way for next-generation families of products and services.

Backward vertical integration can produce a differentiation-based competitive advantage when a company, by performing in-house activities that were previously outsourced, ends up with a better-quality product/service offering, improves the caliber of its customer service, or in other ways enhances the performance of its final product. On occasion, integrating into more stages along the industry value chain can add to a company's differentiation capabilities by allowing it to build or strengthen its core competencies, better master key skills or strategy-critical technologies, or add features that deliver greater customer value.

Backward integration can also spare a company the uncertainty of being dependent on suppliers of crucial components or support services, and it can lessen a company's vulnerability to powerful suppliers that raise prices at every opportunity. Stockpiling, fixed-price contracts, multiple-sourcing, long-term cooperative partnerships, or the use of substitute inputs are not always attractive ways for dealing with uncertain supply conditions or with economically powerful suppliers. Companies that are low on a key supplier's customer priority list can find themselves waiting on shipments every time supplies get tight. If this occurs often and wreaks havoc in a company's own production and customer relations activities, backward integration can be an advantageous strategic solution.

Integrating Forward to Enhance Competitiveness   The strategic impetus for forward integration is much the same as that for backward integration. In many industries, independent sales agents, wholesalers, and retailers handle competing

---

[19]See Kathryn R. Harrigan, "Matching Vertical Integration Strategies to Competitive Conditions," *Strategic Management Journal* 7, no. 6 (November–December 1986), pp. 535–56; for a discussion of the advantages and disadvantages of vertical integration, see John Stuckey and David White, "When and When *Not* to Vertically Integrate," *Sloan Management Review* (Spring 1993), pp. 71–83.

brands of the same product; they have no allegiance to any one company's brand and tend to push "what sells" and earns them the biggest profits. Halfhearted commitments by distributors and retailers can frustrate a company's attempt to boost sales and market share, give rise to costly inventory pileups and frequent underutilization of capacity, and disrupt the economies of steady, near-capacity production. In such cases, it can be advantageous for a manufacturer to integrate forward into wholesaling or retailing via company-owned distributorships, franchised dealer networks, or a chain of retail stores. But often a company's product line is not broad enough to justify stand-alone distributorships or retail outlets. This leaves the option of integrating forward into the activity of selling directly to end users—perhaps via the Internet. Bypassing regular wholesale-retail channels in favor of direct sales and Internet retailing may lower distribution costs, produce a relative cost advantage over certain rivals, and result in lower selling prices to end users.

The Strategic Disadvantages of Vertical Integration

Vertical integration has some substantial drawbacks, however. It boosts a firm's capital investment in the industry, increasing business risk (what if industry growth and profitability goes sour?) and perhaps denying financial resources to more worthwhile pursuits. A vertically integrated firm has vested interests in protecting its present investments in technology and production facilities. Because of the high costs of abandoning such investments before they are worn out, fully integrated firms tend to adopt new technologies slower than partially integrated or nonintegrated firms. Second, integrating forward or backward locks a firm into relying on its own in-house activities and sources of supply (that later may prove more costly than outsourcing) and potentially results in less flexibility in accommodating buyer demand for greater product variety.

Third, vertical integration can pose problems of balancing capacity at each stage in the value chain. In motor vehicle manufacturing, for example, the most efficient scale of operation for making axles is different from the most economic volume for radiators and different yet again for both engines and transmissions. Producing just the right number of axles, radiators, engines, and transmissions—and doing so at the lowest unit costs for each—is the exception, not the rule. If internal capacity for making transmissions is deficient, the difference has to be bought externally. Where internal capacity for radiators proves excessive, customers need to be found for the surplus. And if by-products are generated—as occurs in the processing of many chemical products—they require arrangements for disposal.

Fourth, integration forward or backward often calls for radically different skills and business capabilities. Parts and components manufacturing, assembly operations, wholesale distribution and retailing, and direct sales via the Internet are different businesses with different key success factors. Managers of a manufacturing company should consider carefully whether it makes good business sense to invest time and money in developing the expertise and merchandising skills to integrate forward into wholesaling and retailing. Many manufacturers learn the hard way that company-owned wholesale-retail networks present many headaches, fit poorly with what they do best, and don't always add the kind of value to their core business they thought they would. Selling to customers via the Internet poses still another set of problems—it is usually easier to put systems in place to use the Internet to sell to business customers than to consumers.

Integrating backward into parts and components manufacture isn't as simple or profitable as it sometimes sounds either. Personal computer makers, for example, frequently

The big disadvantage of vertical integration is that it locks a firm deeper into the industry; unless operating across more stages in the industry's value chain builds competitive advantage, it is a questionable strategic move.

have trouble getting timely deliveries of the latest semiconductor chips at favorable prices, but most don't come close to having the resources or capabilities to integrate backward into chip manufacture; the semiconductor business is technologically sophisticated and entails heavy capital requirements and ongoing R&D effort, and mastering the manufacturing process takes a long time.

Fifth, backward vertical integration into the production of parts and components can reduce a company's manufacturing flexibility, lengthening the time it takes to make design and model changes and to bring new products to market. Companies that alter designs and models frequently in response to shifting buyer preferences often find vertical integration into parts and components burdensome because of constant retooling and redesign costs and the time it takes to implement coordinated changes throughout the value chain. Outsourcing parts and components is often cheaper and less complicated than making them in-house, allowing a company to be more flexible and more nimble in adapting its product offering to fast-changing buyer preferences. Most of the world's automakers, despite their expertise in automotive technology and manufacturing, have concluded that purchasing many of their key parts and components from manufacturing specialists results in higher quality, lower costs, and greater design flexibility as compared to the vertical integration option of supplying their own needs via in-house manufacture.

Weighing the Pros and Cons of Vertical Integration

All in all, therefore, a strategy of vertical integration can have both important strengths and weaknesses. Which direction the scales tip on vertical integration depends on (1) whether it can enhance the performance of strategy-critical activities in ways that lower cost, build expertise, or increase differentiation, (2) its impact on investment costs, flexibility and response times, and administrative overhead associated with coordinating operations across more stages, and (3) whether it creates competitive advantage. The merits of vertical integration strategies hinge on which capabilities and value-chain activities truly need to be performed in-house and which can be better performed by outsiders. Absent solid benefits, integrating forward or backward is not likely to be an attractive competitive strategy option. In a growing number of instances, companies are proving that deintegrating and focusing on a narrower portion of the industry value chain is a cheaper and more flexible competitive strategy.

UNBUNDLING AND OUTSOURCING STRATEGIES— NARROWING THE BOUNDARIES OF THE BUSINESS

Over the past decade, some companies have found vertical integration to be so competitively burdensome that they have adopted *vertical deintegration,* or *unbundling, strategies.* Moreover, a number of single-business enterprises have found it useful to focus more narrowly on certain value chain activities and rely on outsiders to perform the remaining value chain activities; they have begun *outsourcing* activities formerly performed in-house and concentrating their energies on a narrower portion of the value chain. Thus, executives at many companies are asking, "Which value chain activities should be brought within the boundary of the firm and which value chain activities should be outsourced?"

Deintegration and outsourcing involves withdrawing from certain stages/activities in the value chain system and relying on outside vendors to supply the needed products, support services, or functional activities. Outsourcing pieces of the value chain formerly performed in-house to narrow the boundaries of a firm's business makes strategic sense whenever:

- An activity can be performed better or more cheaply by outside specialists. Many PC makers, for example, have shifted from in-house assembly to utilizing contract assemblers to make their PCs because of sizable scale economies in purchasing PC components in larges volumes and in the assembly process itself. Cisco outsources most all production and assembly of its routers and switching equipment to contract manufacturers that operate 37 factories, all linked via the Internet.

- The activity is not crucial to the firm's ability to achieve sustainable competitive advantage and won't hollow out its core competencies, capabilities, or technical know-how. Outsourcing of maintenance services, data processing, accounting, and other administrative support activities to companies specializing in these services has become commonplace.

- It reduces the company's risk exposure to changing technology and/or changing buyer preferences.

- It streamlines company operations in ways that improve organizational flexibility, cut cycle time, speed decision-making, and reduce coordination costs.

- It allows a company to concentrate on its core business and do what it does best.

> Outsourcing makes good strategic sense in a number of instances.

Often, many of the advantages of bringing or keeping value chain activities in-house can be captured and many of the disadvantages avoided by forging close, long-term cooperative partnerships with key suppliers and tapping into the important competitive capabilities that able suppliers have painstakingly developed. In years past, many companies maintained arm's-length relationships with suppliers, granting them short-term contracts to supply items to precise specifications.[20] Although a company might engage the same supplier repeatedly, there was no expectation that this would be the case; price was usually the determining factor for which a supplier got a contract, and companies maneuvered for leverage over suppliers to get the lowest possible prices. The threat of switching suppliers was the company's primary weapon. To make this threat credible, short-term contracts with multiple suppliers were preferred to long-term ones with single suppliers in order to promote lively competition among suppliers. Today, most companies are abandoning such approaches in favor of alliances and strategic partnerships with fewer, highly capable suppliers. Cooperative relationships are replacing contractual, purely price-oriented relationships.

Dell Computer's partnerships with the suppliers of PC components have allowed it to operate with fewer than seven days of inventory, to realize substantial savings in inventory costs, and to get PCs equipped with next-generation components into the marketplace in less than a week after the newly upgraded components start shipping. Cisco's contract suppliers work so closely with Cisco that they can ship Cisco products to Cisco customers without a Cisco employee ever touching the gear, generating savings to Cisco of $500 to $800 million annually compared to what it would cost Cisco to own and operate the plants itself.[21] Hewlett-Packard, IBM, Silicon Graphics (now SGI), and others have sold plants to suppliers and then contracted to purchase the output. Starbucks finds purchasing coffee beans from independent growers far more advantageous than trying to integrate backward into the business.

---

[20]Robert H. Hayes, Gary P. Pisano, and David M. Upton, *Strategic Operations: Competing Through Capabilities* (New York: Free Press, 1996), pp. 419–22.

[21]"The Internet Age," *Business Week,* October 4, 1999, p. 104.

Capability Considerations in Boundary Decisions

There are numerous reasons why it is burdensome or costly for a company to create and maintain certain capabilities in-house as opposed to outsourcing them from firms that specialize in the capabilities it needs.[22] Sometimes creating or sustaining a capability involves a long, difficult learning process that is impossible to short-circuit at an acceptable cost. Sometimes it is unclear what actions a company needs to take to create or sustain a needed capability—there may be multiple competing hypotheses about how to create the capabilities and no easy way to test which hypothesis is best. Occasionally, there are hidden assets or socially complex organizational considerations involved in creating the needed capabilities, such as having the right culture, having a committed and energetic workforce, enjoying the trust of customers and suppliers—these are generally beyond the ability of managers to change in the short-term and must be put in place gradually.

While acquiring a company with the needed capabilities is an obvious option for acquiring missing capabilities, such an acquisition may pose legal problems, come with unwanted baggage, or be costly to reverse if it does not work as well as anticipated. Rarely are the desired capabilities of an acquired firm conveniently located within a single division or group; most usually they are spread across the enterprise and entangled with other of its resources and capabilities. An alliance or collaborative partnership may therefore be a much more attractive option than an acquisition. In an uncertain, fast-changing market environment, acquiring another firm to gain access to its capabilities is often a less flexible strategic option than a strategic alliance which can be terminated if conditions unexpectedly change.

The Advantages of Outsourcing

Relying on outside specialists to perform certain value chain activities offers a number of strategic advantages:[23]

- Obtaining higher quality and/or cheaper components or services than internal sources can provide.

- Improving the company's ability to innovate by interacting and allying with "best-in-world" suppliers who have considerable intellectual depth and innovative capabilities of their own.

- Enhancing the firm's strategic flexibility should customer needs and market conditions suddenly shift—seeking out new suppliers with the needed capabilities already in place is frequently quicker, easier, less risky, and cheaper than hurriedly retooling internal operations to disband obsolete capabilities and put new ones in place.

- Increasing the firm's ability to assemble diverse kinds of expertise speedily and efficiently.

- Allowing the firm to concentrate its resources on performing those activities internally that it can perform better than outsiders and/or that it needs to have directly under its own strategic control.

Using outsourcing to narrow a company's business boundaries offers significant advantages.

---

[22]Jay B. Barney, "How a Firm's Capabilities Affect Boundary Decisions," *Sloan Management Review* 40, no. 3 (Spring 1999), pp. 140–42.

[23]For more details, see James Brian Quinn, "Strategic Outsourcing: Leveraging Knowledge Capabilities," *Sloan Management Review* 40, no. 4 (Summer 1999), pp. 9–21.

The Pitfalls of Outsourcing

The biggest danger of outsourcing is that a company will farm out too many or the wrong types of activities and hollow out its own capabilities. In such cases, a company loses touch with the very activities and expertise that over the long run contribute to and determine its success. Cisco guards against loss of control and protects its manufacturing expertise by designing the production methods that its contract manufacturers must use. Cisco is thus the source of all improvements and innovations and keeps the source code for its design proprietary. Further, Cisco uses the Internet to monitor the factory operations of contract manufacturers around the clock, enabling it to know of problems immediately and to get involved when needed.

USING OFFENSIVE STRATEGIES TO SECURE COMPETITIVE ADVANTAGE

Competitive advantage is nearly always achieved by successful *offensive* strategic moves—initiatives calculated to yield a cost advantage, a differentiation advantage, or a resource advantage. Defensive strategies, in contrast, can protect competitive advantage but rarely are the basis for creating the advantage. How long it takes for a successful offensive to create an edge varies with the competitive circumstances.[24] The *buildup period,* shown in Figure 5.3, can be short, if the requisite resources and capabilities are already in place awaiting deployment or if the offensive produces immediate buyer response (as can occur with a dramatic price cut, an imaginative ad campaign, or a new product that proves to be a smash hit). Or the buildup can take much longer, if winning consumer acceptance of an innovative product will take some time or if the firm may need several years to debug a new technology or put new network systems or production capacity in place. Ideally, an offensive move builds competitive advantage quickly; the longer it takes, the more likely rivals will spot the move, see its potential, and begin a counterresponse. The size of the advantage, indicated on the vertical scale in Figure 5.3, can be large (as in pharmaceuticals, where patents on an important new drug produce a substantial advantage) or small (as in apparel, where popular new designs can be imitated quickly).

> Competitive advantage is usually acquired by employing a creative offensive strategy that isn't easily thwarted by rivals.

Following a successful competitive offensive is a *benefit period* during which the fruits of competitive advantage can be enjoyed. The length of the benefit period depends on how much time it takes rivals to launch counteroffensives and begin closing the competitive gap. A lengthy benefit period gives a firm valuable time to earn above-average profits and recoup the investment made in creating the advantage. The best strategic offensives produce big competitive advantages and long benefit periods.

As rivals respond with counteroffensives to close the competitive gap, the *erosion period* begins. Competent, resourceful competitors can be counted on to counterattack with initiatives to overcome any market disadvantage they face—they are not going to stand idly by and passively accept being outcompeted without a fight.[25] Thus, to sustain

> Competent, resourceful rivals will exert strong efforts to overcome any competitive disadvantage they face— they won't be outcompeted without a fight.

---

[24]Ian C. MacMillan, "How Long Can You Sustain a Competitive Advantage?" *The Strategic Planning Management Reader,* ed. Liam Fahey (Englewood Cliffs, NJ: Prentice Hall, 1989), pp. 23–24.

[25]Ian C. MacMillan, "Controlling Competitive Dynamics by Taking Strategic Initiative," *The Academy of Management Executive* 2, no. 2 (May 1988), p. 111.

figure 5.3   **The Building and Eroding of Competitive Advantage**

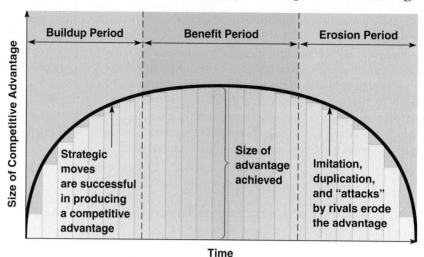

an initially won competitive advantage, a firm must come up with follow-on offensive and defensive moves. Unless the firm stays a step ahead of rivals by initiating one series of offensive and defensive moves after another to protect its market position and retain customer favor, its market advantage will erode.

There are six basic types of strategic offensives:[26]

- Initiatives to match or exceed competitor strengths.
- Initiatives to capitalize on competitor weaknesses.
- Simultaneous initiatives on many fronts.
- End-run offensives to move to less contested ground.
- Guerrilla offensives.
- Preemptive strikes.

Initiatives to Match or Exceed Competitor Strengths

> One of the most powerful offensive strategies is to challenge rivals with an equally good or better product at a lower price.

There are two instances in which it makes sense to mount offensives aimed at neutralizing or overcoming the strengths and capabilities of rival companies. The first is when a company has no choice but to try to whittle away at a strong rival's competitive advantage. The second is when it is possible to gain profitable market share at the expense of rivals despite whatever resource strengths and capabilities they have. Attacking a powerful rival's strengths may be necessary when the rival has either a *superior* product offering or *superior* organizational resources and capabilities. Advanced Micro Devices (AMD), wanting to grow its sales of microprocessors for PCs, recently elected to attack Intel head-on, offering a faster alternative to Intel's Pentium chips at a lower

[26]Philip Kotler and Ravi Singh, "Marketing Warfare in the 1980s," *The Journal of Business Strategy* 1, no. 3 (Winter 1981), pp. 30–41; Philip Kotler, *Marketing Management,* 5th ed. (Englewood Cliffs, NJ: Prentice Hall, 1984), pp. 401–6; and Ian MacMillan, "Preemptive Strategies," *Journal of Business Strategy* 14, no. 2 (Fall 1983), pp. 16–26.

price. AMD recognized that its survival depended on eliminating the performance gap and was willing to risk that its offensive might prompt Intel to counter with lower prices of its own and accelerated development of faster Pentium chips.

The classic avenue for attacking a strong rival is to offer an equally good product at a lower price.[27] This can produce market share gains if the targeted competitor has strong reasons for not resorting to price cuts of its own and if the challenger convinces buyers that its product is just as good. However, such a strategy increases total profits only if the gains in additional unit sales are enough to offset the impact of lower prices and thinner margins per unit sold. A more potent and sustainable basis for mounting a price-aggressive challenge is to *first achieve a cost advantage* and then hit competitors with a lower price.[28] Price cutting supported by a cost advantage can be continued indefinitely. Without a cost advantage, price cutting works only if the aggressor has more financial resources and can outlast its rivals in a war of attrition.

> Challenging larger, entrenched competitors with aggressive price cutting is foolhardy unless the aggressor has either a cost advantage or greater financial strength.

Other strategic options for attacking a competitor's strengths include leapfrogging into next-generation technologies to make the rival's products obsolete, adding new features that appeal to the rival's customers, running comparison ads, constructing major new plant capacity in the rival's backyard, expanding the product line to match the rival model for model, and developing customer service capabilities that the targeted rival doesn't have.

As a rule, challenging a rival on competitive grounds where it is strong is an uphill struggle. Success can be long in coming and usually hinges on developing a cost advantage, a service advantage, a product with attractive differentiating features, or unique competitive capabilities (fast design-to-market times, greater technical know-how, or agility in responding to shifting customer requirements). Absent good prospects for added profitability and a more solid competitive position, such an offensive is ill-advised.

Initiatives to Capitalize on Competitor Weaknesses

A company can take the initiative to gain market inroads by directing its competitive attention to the *weaknesses* of rivals. There are a number of ways to achieve competitive gains at the expense of rivals' weaknesses:

- Go after the customers of those rivals whose products lag on quality, features, or product performance; in such cases, a challenger with a better product can often convince the most performance-conscious customers to switch to its brand.

- Make special sales pitches to the customers of those rivals who provide subpar customer service. It may be relatively easy for a service-oriented challenger to win a rival's disenchanted customers.

- Try to move in on rivals that have weak brand recognition. A challenger with strong marketing skills and a recognized brand name can often win customers away from lesser-known rivals.

- Concentrate on geographic regions where a rival has a weak market share or is exerting less competitive effort.

- Pay special attention to buyer segments that a rival is neglecting or is weakly equipped to serve.

---

[27]Kotler, *Marketing Management*, p. 402.
[28]Ibid., p. 403.

As a rule, initiatives that exploit competitor weaknesses stand a better chance of succeeding than do those that challenge competitor strengths, especially if the weaknesses represent important vulnerabilities and the rival is caught by surprise with no ready defense.[29]

Simultaneous Initiatives on Many Fronts

On occasion a company may see merit in launching a grand competitive offensive involving multiple initiatives (price cuts, increased advertising, new product introductions, free samples, coupons, in-store promotions, rebates) across a wide geographic front. Such all-out campaigns can throw a rival off balance, diverting its attention in many directions and forcing it to protect many pieces of its customer base simultaneously. Microsoft employed a grand offensive to establish a prominent Internet presence that goes well beyond just being a developer for PC software. It rapidly introduced upgraded versions of Internet Explorer (to try to overtake Netscape's Navigator Web browser), incorporated Explorer in its Windows operating system, allowed Internet users to download Explorer free, negotiated deals with Internet service providers to feature Internet Explorer, put several thousand programmers to work on a variety of Internet-related projects and to reprogram Microsoft products to incorporate a host of features for creating Web pages and better interfacing with the evolving capabilities of the Internet, created a new cable channel called MSNBC in a joint venture with NBC, formed alliances with a host of companies to provide content for Microsoft Network and MSNBC, and developed software for use in cable modems and portable wireless devices that can connect to the Internet.

Multifaceted offensives have their best chance of success when a challenger not only comes up with an especially attractive product or service but also has a brand name and reputation to secure broad distribution and retail exposure. Then it can blitz the market with innovative new products and advertising, perhaps enticing large numbers of buyers to switch their brand allegiance.

End-Run Offensives to Move to Less Contested Ground

End-run offensives seek to avoid head-on challenges tied to aggressive price cutting, escalated advertising, or costly efforts to outdifferentiate rivals. Instead the idea is to maneuver *around* competitors, capture unoccupied or less contested market territory, and change the rules of the competitive game in the aggressor's favor. Examples of end-run offensives include:[30]

> A successful end-run offensive allows a company to gain a significant first-mover advantage in a new arena and force competitors to play catch-up.

- *Introducing new products that redefine the market and the terms of competition*— Netscape's Navigator, first marketed in 1994, catapulted the company to the top in Web browsers (heretofore an ignored market) and thrust Microsoft and others into a catch-up mode.

- *Launching initiatives to build strong positions in geographic areas where close rivals have little or no market presence*—The race for global market leadership in

---

[29]For a discussion of the use of surprise, see William E. Rothschild, "Surprise and the Competitive Advantage," *Journal of Business Strategy* 4, no. 3 (Winter 1984), pp. 10–18.

[30]For an interesting discussion of the Netscape-Microsoft battle and the use of end-run offensive strategy, see David B. Yoffie and Michael A. Cusumano, "Judo Strategy: The Competitive Dynamics of Internet Time," *Harvard Business Review* 77, no. 1 (January–February 1999), pp. 70–81.

PCs, servers, and Internet infrastructure products is prompting some contenders to launch early end-run offensives to build positions in less contested markets in Latin America and Asia.

- *Trying to create new segments by introducing products with different attributes and performance features to better meet the needs of selected buyers*—Witness the success that Lexus and BMW have had with carlike sport-utility vehicles. The introduction of PCs below $1,000 proved a smash hit. This initiative works well when new product versions satisfy certain buyer needs that heretofore have been ignored or neglected.
- *Leapfrogging into next-generation technologies to supplant existing technologies, products and/or services*—A number of telecommunications firms are trying to use new-style cable modems to displace the role of local telephone firms in providing Internet access. The makers of thin, trim flat-panel monitors are moving aggressively to improve the cost effectiveness of their technology and production processes to leapfrog the technology of heavier, more bulky CRT monitors.

Guerrilla Offensives

Guerrilla offensives are particularly well suited to small challengers who have neither the resources nor the market visibility to mount a full-fledged attack on industry leaders.[31] A guerrilla offensive uses the hit-and-run principle, selectively trying to grab sales and market share wherever and whenever an underdog catches rivals napping or spots an opening through which to lure their customers away. Guerrilla offensives can involve making scattered, random raids on the leaders' customers with such tactics as occasional lowballing on price (to win a big order or steal a key account); surprising key rivals with sporadic but intense bursts of promotional activity (offering a 20 percent discount for one week to draw customers away from rival brands); or undertaking special campaigns to attract buyers away from rivals plagued with a strike or problems in meeting delivery schedules.[32] Guerrillas can promote the quality of their products when rivals have quality control problems or announce guaranteed delivery times when competitors' deliveries are running behind or significantly boost their commitment to prompt technical support when buyers are frustrated by the caliber of the support offered by industry leaders. If rivals employ unfair or unethical competitive tactics and the situation merits it, a guerrilla can file legal actions charging antitrust violations, patent infringement, or unfair advertising.

> Guerrillas are a thorn in the side of larger competitors, quick to take advantage of whatever opportunities come their way yet careful not to provoke concerted competitive retaliation.

Preemptive Strikes

Preemptive strategies involve moving first to secure an advantageous position that rivals are foreclosed or discouraged from duplicating. What makes a move "preemptive" is its one-of-a-kind nature—whoever strikes first stands to acquire competitive assets

---

[31]For an interesting study of how small firms can successfully employ guerrilla-style tactics, see Ming-Jer Chen and Donald C. Hambrick, "Speed, Stealth, and Selective Attack: How Small Firms Differ from Large Firms in Competitive Behavior," *Academy of Management Journal* 38, no. 2 (April 1995), pp. 453-82.

[32]For more details, see Ian MacMillan, "How Business Strategists Can Use Guerrilla Warfare Tactics," *Journal of Business Strategy* 1, no. 2 (Fall 1980), pp. 63–65; Kathryn R. Harrigan, *Strategic Flexibility* (Lexington, MA: Lexington Books, 1985), pp. 30–45; and Liam Fahey, "Guerrilla Strategy: The Hit-and-Run Attack," in *The Strategic Management Planning Reader*, ed. Liam Fahey (Englewood Cliffs, NJ: Prentice Hall, 1989), pp. 194–97.

that rivals can't readily match. There are several ways a firm can bolster its competitive capabilities with preemptive moves:[33]

- Acquire a company that has exclusive control of or commanding expertise in a valuable technology, thereby giving the firm a hard-to-match technological advantage.

- Secure exclusive or dominant access to the best distributors in a particular geographic region or country.

- Tie up the best (or the most) raw material sources or the most reliable, high-quality suppliers via exclusive partnership, long-term contracts, or acquisition. DeBeers became the dominant world distributor of diamonds by buying up the production of most of the important diamond mines.

- Secure the best geographic locations. An attractive first-mover advantage can often be locked up by moving to obtain the most favorable site along a heavily traveled thoroughfare, at a new interchange or intersection, in a new shopping mall, in a natural beauty spot, close to cheap transportation or raw material supplies or market outlets, and so on.

- Obtain the business of prestigious customers, thereby boosting the company's reputation and winning the confidence of otherwise hesitant buyers.

- Expand capacity well ahead of market demand in hopes of discouraging rivals from following with expansions of their own. When rivals are "bluffed" out of adding capacity for fear of creating long-term excess supply and having to struggle with the bad profit economics of underutilized assets, the preemptor stands to win a bigger market share as market demand grows and it has the production capacity to take on new orders.

- Build an image that is unique, hard to copy, and establishes a compelling psychological appeal. Examples include Nike's "Just do it" tag line and its endorsement contract with Tiger Woods, Avis's well-known "We try harder" theme, Yahoo's image as an Internet portal, and Prudential's "piece of the rock" image of safety and permanence.

> **Successful preemptive strikes relegate rivals to competing for second-best positions.**

To be successful, a preemptive move doesn't have to totally block rivals from following or copying; it merely needs to give a firm a prime position that is not easily circumvented. Fox's stunning four-year, $6.2 billion contract to televise NFL football in the mid-1990s represented a bold and (successful) strategic move to transform Fox into a major TV network alongside ABC, CBS, and NBC. Du Pont's aggressive capacity expansions in titanium dioxide, while not blocking all competitors from expanding, did discourage enough to give it a leadership position in the titanium dioxide industry.

Choosing Whom to Attack

Aggressor firms need to analyze which of their rivals to challenge as well as how to outcompete them. Any of four types of firms can make good targets:[34]

1. *Market leaders*—Offensive attacks on a market leader make the best sense when the leader in terms of size and market share is not a "true leader" in terms of serving the

---

[33]The use of preemptive moves is treated comprehensively in Ian MacMillan, "Preemptive Strategies," pp. 16–26. What follows in this section is based on MacMillan's article.

[34]Kotler, *Marketing Management,* p. 400.

market well. Signs of leader vulnerability include unhappy buyers, an inferior product line, a weak competitive strategy in terms of low-cost leadership or differentiation, strong emotional commitment to an aging technology the leader has pioneered, outdated plants and equipment, a preoccupation with diversification into other industries, and mediocre or declining profitability. Offensives to erode the positions of market leaders have real promise when the challenger is able to revamp its value chain or innovate to gain a fresh cost-based or differentiation-based competitive advantage.[35] Attacks on leaders don't have to result in making the aggressor the new leader to be judged successful; a challenger may "win" by simply wresting enough sales from the leader to make the aggressor a stronger runner-up. Caution is well advised in challenging strong market leaders—there's a significant risk of squandering valuable resources in a futile effort or precipitating a fierce and profitless industrywide battle for market share.

2. *Runner-up firms*—Runner-up firms are an especially attractive target when a challenger's resource strengths and competitive capabilities are well suited to exploiting their weaknesses.

3. *Struggling enterprises that are on the verge of going under*—Challenging a hard-pressed rival in ways that further sap its financial strength and competitive position can weaken its resolve and hasten its exit from the market.

4. *Small local and regional firms*—Because these firms typically have limited expertise and resources, a challenger with broader capabilities is well-positioned to raid their biggest and best customers—particularly those who are growing rapidly, have increasingly sophisticated requirements, and may already be thinking about switching to a supplier with more full-service capability.

Choosing the Basis for Attack   A firm's strategic offensive should, at a minimum, be tied to what it does best—its core competencies, resource strengths, and competitive capabilities. Otherwise the prospects for success are indeed dim. The centerpiece of the offensive can be an important core competence, a unique competitive capability, an innovative new product, technological superiority, a cost advantage in manufacturing or distribution, or some kind of differentiation advantage. If the challenger's resources and competitive strengths amount to a competitive advantage over the targeted rivals, so much the better.

> At the very least, an offensive must be tied to a firm's resource strengths; more optimally, it is grounded in competitive advantage.

USING DEFENSIVE STRATEGIES TO PROTECT COMPETITIVE ADVANTAGE

In a competitive market, all firms are subject to challenges from rivals. Market offensives can come both from new entrants in the industry and from established firms seeking to improve their market positions. The purpose of defensive strategy is to lower the risk of being attacked, weaken the impact of any attack that occurs, and influence challengers to aim their efforts at other rivals. While defensive strategy usually doesn't enhance a firm's competitive advantage, it helps fortify a firm's competitive position, protect its most valuable resources and capabilities from imitation, and sustain whatever competitive advantage it does have. There are two basic approaches to defensive strategy: moving to block challengers and signaling the likelihood of strong retaliation.

> The foremost purpose of defensive strategy is to protect competitive advantage and fortify the firm's competitive position.

---

[35]Porter, *Competitive Advantage*, p. 518.

Blocking the Avenues Open to Challengers

The most frequently employed approach to defending a company's present position involves actions that foreclose a challenger's options for initiating competitive attack. There are any number of obstacles that can be put in the path of would-be challengers.[36] A defender can participate in alternative technologies to reduce the threat that rivals will attack with a better technology. A defender can introduce new features, add new models, or broaden its product line to close off gaps and vacant niches to would-be challengers. It can thwart the efforts of rivals to attack with a lower price by maintaining economy-priced options of its own. Shortly after America Online acquired CompuServe, it cut the price of CompuServe's service and positioned it as a lower-priced alternative to AOL, thereby countering the efforts of rivals to draw AOL users away on the basis of a cheaper price. A defender also can hire talented employees to broaden or deepen the company's base of core competencies or capabilities in key areas (so as to be able to overpower rivals that attempt to imitate its skills and resources). It can try to discourage buyers from trying competitors' brands by lengthening warranty coverages, offering free training and support services, developing the capability to deliver spare parts to users faster than rivals can, providing coupons and sample giveaways to buyers most prone to experiment, and making early announcements about impending new products or price changes to induce potential buyers to postpone switching, It can challenge the quality or safety of rivals' products in regulatory proceedings—a favorite tactic of the pharmaceutical firms in trying to delay the introduction of generic prescription drugs. It can grant dealers and distributors volume discounts or better financing terms to discourage them from experimenting with other suppliers, or it can convince them to handle its product line *exclusively* and force competitors to use other distribution outlets.

Moves such as these not only buttress a firm's present position but also present competitors with a moving target. Protecting the status quo isn't enough. A good defense entails adjusting quickly to changing industry conditions and, on occasion, being a first-mover to block or preempt moves by would-be aggressors. A mobile defense is preferable to a stationary defense.

> There are many ways to throw obstacles in the path of would-be challengers.

Signaling Challengers That Retaliation Is Likely

A second approach to defensive strategy entails signaling challengers that strong retaliation is likely in the event of an attack. The goal is either to dissuade challengers from attacking at all by raising their expectations that the resulting battle will be more costly than it is worth or at least to divert them to less threatening options. Would-be challengers can be signaled by:[37]

- Publicly announcing management's commitment to maintain the firm's present market share.

- Publicly announcing plans to put adequate capacity in place to meet and possibly surpass the forecasted growth in industry volume.

- Giving out advance information about a new product, technology breakthrough, or the planned introduction of important new brands or models in hopes that challengers will be induced to delay moves of their own until they see if the announced actions actually are forthcoming.

---

[36]Ibid., pp. 489–94.

[37]Ibid., pp. 495–97. The list here is selective; Porter offers a greater number of options.

- Publicly committing the company to a policy of matching competitors' terms or prices.
- Maintaining a war chest of cash and marketable securities.
- Making an occasional strong counterresponse to the moves of weak competitors to enhance the firm's image as a tough defender.

Another way to dissuade rivals is to try to lower the profit inducement for challengers to launch an offensive. When a firm's or industry's profitability is enticingly high, challengers are more willing to tackle high defensive barriers and combat strong retaliation. A defender can deflect attacks, especially from new entrants, by deliberately forgoing some short-run profits and using accounting methods that obscure profitability.

FIRST-MOVER ADVANTAGES AND DISADVANTAGES

When to make a strategic move is often as crucial as *what* move to make. Timing is especially important when *first-mover advantages* or *disadvantages* exist.[38] Being first to initiate a strategic move can have a high payoff when (1) pioneering helps build a firm's image and reputation with buyers; (2) early commitments to new technologies, new-style components, distribution channels, and so on can produce an absolute cost advantage over rivals; (3) first-time customers remain strongly loyal to pioneering firms in making repeat purchases; and (4) moving first constitutes a preemptive strike, making imitation extra hard or unlikely. The bigger the first-mover advantages, the more attractive that making the first move becomes.[39] In e-commerce, for example, whoever is first with a new technology or a new network solution often enjoys lasting first-mover advantages in gaining the visibility and reputation needed to emerge as the dominant market leader. America Online, Amazon.com, Yahoo!, eBay, Broadcast.com, DoubleClick, Priceline.com, Inktomi, and several others have demonstrated the power of moving first and forcing rivals into a desperate race to catch up. Illustration Capsule 26 discusses Toyota's first-mover offensive in custom-built cars.

> Because of first-mover advantages and disadvantages, competitive advantage is often attached to *when* a move is made as well as to *what* move is made.

However, being a rapid follower or even a wait-and-see late-mover doesn't always carry a significant or lasting competitive penalty. There are times when a first-mover's skills, know-how, and actions are easily copied or even surpassed by late-movers, allowing them to catch or overtake the first-mover in a relatively short period. And there are times when there are actually advantages to being an adept follower rather than a first-mover. Late-mover advantages (or first-mover disadvantages) arise when (1) pioneering leadership is more costly than imitating followership and only negligible experience curve benefits accrue to the leader—a condition that allows a follower to end up with lower costs than the first-mover; (2) the products of an innovator are somewhat primitive and do not live up to buyer expectations, thus allowing a clever follower to win disenchanted buyers away from the leader with better performing products; and (3) technology is advancing rapidly, giving fast followers the opening to leapfrog a first-mover's products with more attractive and full-featured second- and third-generation products.

---

[38]Porter, *Competitive Strategy*, pp. 232–33.

[39]For research evidence on the effects of pioneering versus following, see Jeffrey G. Covin, Dennis P. Slevin, and Michael B. Heeley, "Pioneers and Followers: Competitive Tactics, Environment, and Growth," *Journal of Business Venturing* 15, no. 2 (March 1999), pp.175–210.

illustration capsule 26
Toyota's First-Mover Offensive in Custom-Built Cars

In fall 1999 Toyota Motor Company announced that it would begin a program to allow U.S. car shoppers to order custom-equipped vehicles for delivery within five days. The move was seen as an attempt to shift from a "build-for-dealer-inventory" business model in North America to a "build-to-order" business model, which was already relatively common in Japan and Europe. But the move was further interpreted as a shrewd strategic initiative by Toyota to gain competitive advantage by being the first North American manufacturer to make this transition.

Surveys of car buyers indicated that close to 50 percent were unable to find the model, color, or equipment configuration they preferred when shopping dealer lots. Traditionally, dealers made educated guesses as to what model, color, and equipment options buyers would prefer, placed their orders with manufacturers, and hoped that car buyers would find what they wanted from the array of vehicles they had in stock. To induce customers to compromise if what they wanted was not in stock, manufacturers offered rebates and dealers would make price concessions. Custom-ordered vehicles could be obtained, but delivery times often ranged from 30 to 60 days.

Toyota's competitive move to five-day delivery on custom orders was intended not only to better satisfy car buyers and encourage brand loyalty but also to gain the benefits of tighter supply chain management and reduce reliance on costly promotions to push sales of slow-selling models. A build-to-order business model (similar to that used by Dell, Gateway, and other PC makers) permitted tighter just-in-time delivery of parts and components to Toyota assembly plants, plus a reduced need for profit-eroding rebates and discounts on unpopular models and configurations. It also paved the way for dealers to drastically cut the number of vehicles kept in stock (thus driving down their inventory-financing costs). If the build-to-order approach caught on with car buyers, a dealer would only have to stock a minimal number of showroom models for inspection and test drives, a limited number of vehicles for immediate delivery, and function mainly as a pickup point for custom orders. Investing in acres of real estate at visible, high-traffic locations would be less necessary.

A build-to-order model would also work to the advantage of Internet car-buying services, since it would be easy for car shoppers to do their research online, make price comparisons, and place their orders.

From Toyota's perspective, the issue was whether its first-mover offensive would provide a lasting competitive advantage. Would buyers respond in attractive numbers? Would Toyota realize significant cost-savings and gain a valuable cost advantage over rivals? How long would it take for rival manufacturers to develop the capability to match Toyota's five-day delivery, build-to-order option?

Source: Jeffrey Bodenstab, "An Automaker Tries the Dell Way," *The Wall Street Journal,* August 30, 1999, p. 26.

While being an adept fast follower has its advantages, rarely does a company gain from being a slow follower and concentrating on avoiding the "mistakes" of early movers. Habitual late-movers, while able to survive, are usually fighting to retain their customers and struggling to keep pace with more progressive and innovative rivals.

key|points

The challenge of competitive strategy—whether it be overall low-cost, broad differentiation, best-cost, focused low-cost, or focused differentiation—is to create a competitive advantage for the firm. Competitive advantage comes from positioning a firm in the marketplace so it has an edge in coping with competitive forces and in attracting buyers.

A strategy of trying to be the low-cost provider works well in situations where:

● The industry's product is essentially the same from seller to seller (brand differences are minor).

● Many buyers are price-sensitive and shop for the lowest price.

- There are only a few ways to achieve product differentiation that have much value to buyers.
- Most buyers use the product in the same ways and thus have common user requirements.
- Buyers' costs in switching from one seller or brand to another are low or even zero.
- Buyers are large and have significant power to negotiate pricing terms.

To achieve a low-cost advantage, a company must become more skilled than rivals in controlling structural and executional cost drivers and/or it must find innovative cost-saving ways to revamp its value chain. Successful low-cost providers usually achieve their cost advantages by imaginatively and persistently ferreting out cost savings throughout the value chain. They are good at finding ways to drive costs out of their businesses.

Differentiation strategies seek to produce a competitive edge by incorporating attributes and features into a company's product/service offering that rivals don't have. Anything a firm can do to create buyer value represents a potential basis for differentiation. Successful differentiation is usually keyed to lowering the buyer's cost of using the item, raising the performance the buyer gets, or boosting a buyer's psychological satisfaction. To be sustainable, differentiation usually has to be linked to unique internal expertise, core competencies, and resources that give a company capabilities its rivals can't easily match. Differentiation tied just to unique physical features seldom is lasting because resourceful competitors are adept at cloning, improving on, or finding substitutes for almost any feature that appeals to buyers.

Best-cost provider strategies combine a strategic emphasis on low cost with a strategic emphasis on more than minimal quality, service, features, or performance. The aim is to create competitive advantage by giving buyers more value for the money; this is done by matching close rivals on key quality-service-features-performance attributes and beating them on the costs of incorporating such attributes into the product or service. To be successful with a best-cost provider strategy, a company must have unique expertise in incorporating upscale product or service attributes at a lower cost than rivals; it must have the capability to manage unit costs down and product/service caliber up simultaneously.

The competitive advantage of focusing is earned either by achieving lower costs in serving the target market niche or by developing an ability to offer niche buyers something different from rival competitors—in other words, it is either cost-based or differentiation-based. A focused strategy based either on low cost or differentiation becomes increasingly attractive as more of the following conditions are met:

- The target market niche is big enough to be profitable and offers good growth potential.
- Industry leaders do not see that having a presence in the niche is crucial to their own success—a condition that reduces rivalry from major competitors.
- It is costly or difficult for multisegment competitors to put capabilities in place to meet the specialized needs of the target market niche and, at the same time, satisfy the expectations of their mainstream customers.
- The industry has many different niches and segments, thereby allowing a focuser to pick a competitively attractive niche suited to its resource strengths and capabilities.

- Few, if any, other rivals are attempting to specialize in the same target segment—a condition that reduces the risk of segment overcrowding.
- The focuser can compete effectively against challengers based on the capabilities and resources it has to serve the targeted niche and the customer goodwill it may have built up.

Many companies are turning to strategic alliances and collaborative partnerships as ways to help them in the global race to build a market presence in many different national markets and in the technology race to capitalize on today's technological and information age revolution. Even large and financially strong companies have concluded that simultaneously running both races requires more diverse and expansive skills, resources, technological expertise, and competitive capabilities than they can assemble and manage alone. Strategic alliances are an attractive, flexible, and often cost-effective means for companies to gain access to missing technology, expertise, and business capabilities. The competitive attraction of alliances is to bundle competences and resources that are more valuable in a joint effort than when kept separate. Competitive advantage emerges when a company acquires valuable resources and capabilities through alliances that it could not otherwise obtain on its own and that give it an edge over rivals.

Mergers and acquisitions are another attractive strategy for strengthening a firm's competitiveness. Companies racing for global market leadership frequently make acquisitions to build a market presence in countries where they currently do not compete. Similarly, companies racing to establish attractive positions in the industries of the future merge or make acquisitions to fill in resource or technological gaps, build important technological capabilities, and move into position to launch next-wave products and services. Mergers and acquisitions allow a company to fill resource gaps or correct competitive deficiencies; combining operations can result in lower costs, stronger technological skills, more or better competitive capabilities, a more attractive lineup of products and services, wider geographic coverage, and/or greater financial resources with which to invest in R&D, add capacity, or expand into new areas.

Vertically integrating forward or backward makes strategic sense only if it strengthens a company's position via either cost reduction or creation of a differentiation-based advantage. Otherwise, the drawbacks of vertical integration (increased investment, greater business risk, increased vulnerability to technological changes, and less flexibility in making product changes) outweigh the advantages (better coordination of production flows and technological know-how from stage to stage, more specialized use of technology, greater internal control over operations, greater scale economies, and matching production with sales and marketing). There are ways to achieve the advantages of vertical integration without encountering the drawbacks.

Outsourcing pieces of the value chain formerly performed in-house makes strategic sense whenever (1) an activity can be performed better or more cheaply by outside specialists; (2) the activity is not crucial to the firm's ability to achieve sustainable competitive advantage and won't hollow out its core competencies, capabilities, or technical know-how; (3) it reduces the company's risk exposure to changing technology and/or changing buyer preferences; (4) it streamlines company operations in ways that improve organizational flexibility, cut cycle time, speed decision-making, and reduce coordination costs; and/or (5) it allows a company to concentrate on its core business and do what it does best. In many situations outsourcing is a superior strategic alternative to vertical integration.

A variety of offensive strategic moves can be used to secure a competitive advantage. Strategic offensives can be aimed either at competitors' strengths or at their weaknesses; they can involve end runs or grand offensives on many fronts; they can be designed as guerrilla actions or as preemptive strikes; and the target of the offensive can be a market leader, a runner-up firm, or the smallest and/or weakest firms in the industry.

Defensive strategies to protect a company's position usually take the form of making moves that put obstacles in the path of would-be challengers and fortify the company's present position while undertaking actions to dissuade rivals from even trying to attack (by signaling that the resulting battle will be more costly to the challenger than it is worth).

The timing of strategic moves is important. First-movers sometimes gain strategic advantage; at other times, it can be cheaper and easier to be a fast follower than a pioneering leader.

suggested | readings

Barney, Jay B. *Gaining and Sustaining Competitive Advantage.* Reading, MA: Addison-Wesley, 1997, especially chapters 6, 7, 9, 10, and 14.

D'Aveni, Richard A. *Hypercompetition: The Dynamics of Strategic Maneuvering* (New York: Free Press, 1994), chapters 1, 2, 3, and 4.

Dess, Gregory G., and Joseph C. Picken. "Creating Competitive (Dis)advantage: Learning from Food Lion's Freefall." *Academy of Management Executive* 13, no. 3 (August 1999), pp. 97–111.

Hamel, Gary. "Strategy as Revolution." *Harvard Business Review* 74, no. 4 (July–August 1996), pp. 69–82.

Hayes, Robert H.; Gary P. Pisano; and David M. Upton. *Strategic Operations: Competing Through Capabilities* (New York: Free Press, 1996).

Porter, Michael E. *Competitive Advantage* (New York: Free Press, 1985), chapters 3, 4, 5, 7, 14, and 15.

———. "What Is Strategy?" *Harvard Business Review* 74, no. 6 (November–December 1996), pp. 61–78.

Schnarrs, Steven P. *Managing Imitation Strategies: How Later Entrants Seize Markets from Pioneers.* New York: Free Press, 1994.

Stuckey, John, and David White. "When and When *Not* to Vertically Integrate." *Sloan Management Review* (Spring 1993), pp. 71–83.

Venkatesan, Ravi. "Strategic Outsourcing: To Make or Not to Make." *Harvard Business Review* 70, no. 6 (November–December 1992), pp. 98–107.

Yoffie, David B., and Michael A. Cusumano. "Judo Strategy: The Competitive Dynamics of Internet Time." *Harvard Business Review* 77, no. 1 (January–February 1999), pp. 71–81.

chapter | six

Strategies for Competing in Globalizing Markets

You have no choice but to operate in a world shaped by globalization and the information revolution. There are two options: Adapt or die.

—Andrew S. Grove, Chairman, Intel Corporation

You do not choose to become global. The market chooses for you; it forces your hand.

—Alain Gomez, CEO, Thomson, S.A.

[T]here's no purely domestic industry anymore.

—Robert Pelosky and Morgan Stanley

[I]ndustries actually vary a great deal in the pressures they put on a company to sell internationally.

—Niraj Dawar and Tony Frost, Professors, Richard Ivey School of Business

ny company that aspires to industry leadership in the 21st century must think in terms of global market leadership, not domestic market leadership. The world economy is globalizing at an accelerating pace as countries heretofore closed to foreign companies open up their markets, as the Internet shrinks the importance of geographic distance, and as ambitious, growth-minded companies race to stake out competitive positions in the markets of more and more countries. Globalization of the world economy is a market condition that demands bold offensive strategies to carve out new market positions and potent defensive strategies to protect positions previously won.

This chapter examines the issues companies face in crafting strategies suitable for multinational and globally competitive industry environments. We will be introducing a number of new concepts, such as profit sanctuaries, cross-market subsidization, and the distinction between multicountry competition and global competition. There are sections on the special features of doing business in foreign markets, the different strategies for entering and competing in the foreign arena, the growing role of alliances with foreign partners, the importance of locating operations in the most advantageous countries, and the special circumstances of competing in such emerging country markets as China, India, and Brazil.

WHY COMPANIES EXPAND INTO FOREIGN MARKETS

Companies opt to expand outside their domestic market for any of four major reasons:

- *To gain access to new customers*—Expanding into the markets of foreign countries offers potential for increased revenues, profits, and long-term growth and becomes an especially attractive option when a company's home markets are mature. Firms like Cisco Systems, Intel, Sony, Nokia, and Toyota, which are racing for global leadership in their respective industries, must move rapidly and aggressively to extend their market reach into all corners of the world.

- *To achieve lower costs and enhance the firm's competitiveness*—Many companies are driven to sell in more than one country because the sales volume achieved in their own domestic markets is not large enough to fully capture manufacturing economies of scale and experience curve effects and thereby substantially improve a firm's cost competitiveness. The relatively small size of country markets in Europe explains why companies like Michelin and Nestlé long ago began selling their products all across Europe and then moved into markets in North America and Latin America.

- *To capitalize on its core competencies*—A company with competitively valuable competencies and capabilities may be able to leverage them into a position of competitive advantage in foreign markets as well as just domestic markets. Nokia's competencies and capabilities in mobile phones have propelled it to global market leadership in the wireless telecommunications business.

- *To spread its business risk across a wider market base*—A company spreads business risk by operating in a number of different foreign countries rather than depending entirely on operations in its own domestic market. Thus, if the economies of certain Asian countries turn down for a period of time, the company may be sustained by buoyant sales in Latin America or Europe.

In a few cases, companies in natural resource–based industries (like oil and gas, minerals, rubber, and lumber) often find it necessary to operate in the international arena because attractive raw material supplies are located in foreign countries.

Basic Concept
A company is an *international* (or *multinational*) *competitor* when it competes in a select few foreign markets. It is a *global competitor* when it has or is pursuing a market presence on most continents and in virtually all of the world's major countries.

The Difference between Competing Internationally and Competing Globally

Typically, a company will *start* to compete internationally by entering just one or maybe a select few foreign markets. Competing on a truly global scale comes later, after the company has established operations on several continents and is racing against rivals for global market leadership. Thus, there is a meaningful distinction between the competitive scope of a company that operates in a select few foreign countries (with perhaps modest ambitions to expand further) and a company that markets its products in 50 to 100 countries and is expanding its operations into additional country markets annually. The former is most accurately termed an **international** (or **multinational**) **competitor,** while the latter qualifies as a **global competitor.** In the discussion that follows, we'll continue to make a distinction between strategies for competing internationally and strategies for competing globally.

CROSS-COUNTRY DIFFERENCES IN CULTURAL, DEMOGRAPHIC, AND MARKET CONDITIONS

Regardless of a company's motivation for expanding outside its domestic markets, the strategies it uses to compete in foreign markets have to be *situation-driven*; cultural, demographic, and market conditions vary significantly among the countries of the world. Cultures and lifestyles are the most obvious country-to-country differences. Market demographics are close behind. Consumers in Spain do not have the same tastes, preferences, and buying habits as consumers in Norway; buyers differ yet again in Greece, in Chile, in New Zealand, and in Taiwan. Less than 10 percent of the populations of Brazil, India, and China have annual purchasing power equivalent to $20,000. Middle-class consumers represent a much smaller portion of the population in these and other emerging countries than in North America, Japan, and much of Europe.[1] Sometimes, product designs suitable for one country are inappropriate in another—for example, in the United States electrical devices run on 110-volt electrical systems, but in some European countries the standard is a 240-volt electric system, necessitating the use of different electrical designs and components. In France consumers prefer top-loading washing machines, while in most other European countries consumers prefer front-loading machines. Northern Europeans want large refrigerators because they tend to shop once a week in supermarkets; southern Europeans can get by on small refrigerators because they shop daily. In parts of Asia refrigerators are a status symbol and may be placed in the living room, leading to preferences for stylish designs and colors—in India bright blue and red are popular colors. In other Asian countries, household space is constrained and many refrigerators are only four feet high so the top can be used for something else. In Hong Kong the preference is for compact, European-style appliances, but in Taiwan large American-style appliances are more popular.

The potential for rapid market growth varies significantly from country to country. In emerging markets like India, China, Brazil, and Malaysia, market growth potential is far higher than in the more mature economies of Britain, France, Canada, and Japan. In India there are efficient, well-developed national channels for distributing trucks, scooters, farm equipment, groceries, personal care items, and other packaged products to the country's 3 million retailers, whereas in China distribution is primarily local and provincial and there is no national network for distributing most products. The marketplace is intensely competitive in some countries and only moderately contested in others. Industry driving forces may be one thing in Italy and quite another in Canada or Israel or Argentina or South Korea.

One of the biggest concerns of companies competing in foreign markets is whether to customize their offerings in each different country market to match the tastes and preferences of local buyers or whether to offer a mostly standardized product worldwide. While being responsive to local tastes makes a company's products more appealing to local buyers, customizing a company's products country by country *may* have the effect of raising production and distribution costs due to the greater variety of designs and components, shorter production runs, and the complications of

> Competing in foreign markets where there are significant cross-country variations in cultural, demographic, and market conditions poses a much bigger strategy-making challenge than just competing at home.

> Being responsive to cross-country differences in cultural, demographic, and market conditions complicates the task of competing in the world market arena. The challenge is to balance pressures to be responsive to local situations in each country against pressures for lower costs and prices.

---

[1]For an insightful discussion of how much significance these kinds of demographic and market differences have, see C. K. Prahalad and Kenneth Lieberthal, "The End of Corporate Imperialism," *Harvard Business Review* 76, no. 4 (July–August 1999), pp. 68–79.

added inventory handling and distribution logistics. Greater standardization of the company's product offering, on the other hand, can lead to scale economies and experience curve effects, thus contributing to the achievement of a low-cost advantage. The tension between the market pressures to customize and the competitive pressures to lower costs is one of the big strategic issues that participants in foreign markets have to resolve.

Aside from the basic cultural and market differences from country to country, a company also has to pay special attention to locational advantages that stem from country-to-country variations in manufacturing and distribution costs, the problems of fluctuating exchange rates, and the economic and political demands of host governments.

The Potential for Locational Advantages Stemming from Country-to-Country Cost Variations

Differences in wage rates, worker productivity, inflation rates, energy costs, tax rates, government regulations, and the like create sizable variations in manufacturing costs from country to country. Plants in some countries have major manufacturing cost advantages because of lower input costs (especially labor), relaxed government regulations, or unique natural resources. In such cases, the low-cost countries become principal production sites, with most of the output being exported to markets in other parts of the world. Companies with production facilities in low-cost countries (or that source their products from contract manufacturers in these countries) have a competitive advantage over rivals with plants in countries where costs are higher. The competitive role of low manufacturing costs is most evident in low-wage countries like Taiwan, South Korea, China, Singapore, Malaysia, Vietnam, Mexico, and Brazil, which have become production havens for goods with high labor content. Likewise, concerns about short delivery times and low shipping costs make some countries better locations than others for establishing distribution center facilities.

The quality of a country's business environment also offers locational advantages—the governments of some countries are anxious to attract foreign investments and go all out to create a business climate that outsiders will view as favorable. A good example is Ireland, which has one of the world's most pro-business environments, offering very low corporate tax rates, a government that is responsive to the needs of industry, and a policy of aggressively recruiting high-tech manufacturing facilities and multinational companies. The single biggest foreign investment in Ireland's history is Intel's largest non-U.S. chip manufacturing plant, a $2.5 billion facility employing over 4,000 people. Ireland's pro-industry policies were a significant force in making it the most dynamic, fastest-growing nation in Europe during the 1990s. Another locational advantage is the clustering of suppliers of components and capital equipment, infrastructure suppliers (universities, vocational training providers, research enterprises), trade associations, and makers of complementary products in a geographic area (the benefits of which were discussed in Chapter 4).

A company's potential for gaining competitive advantage based on where it locates its foreign activities or being at a disadvantage because rivals have lower-cost locations is a matter of considerable strategic concern.

Fluctuating Exchange Rates

The volatility of exchange rates greatly complicates the issue of geographic cost advantages. Currency exchange rates often fluctuate as much as 20 to 40 percent annually. Changes of this magnitude can totally wipe out a country's low-cost advantage or transform a former high-cost location into a competitive-cost location. A strong U.S.

dollar makes it more attractive for U.S. companies to manufacture in foreign countries. Declines in the value of the dollar against foreign currencies can eliminate much of the cost advantage that foreign manufacturers have over U.S. manufacturers and can even prompt foreign companies to establish production plants in the United States.

Host Government Restrictions and Requirements

National governments enact all kinds of measures affecting business conditions and the operation of foreign companies in their markets. Host governments may set local content requirements on goods made inside their borders by foreign-based companies, impose tariffs or quotas on imports, put restrictions on exports to ensure adequate local supplies, and regulate the prices of imported and locally produced goods. In addition, outsiders may face a web of regulations regarding technical standards, product certification, prior approval of capital spending projects, withdrawal of funds from the country, and minority (sometimes majority) ownership by local citizens. Some governments also provide subsidies and low-interest loans to domestic companies to help them compete against foreign-based companies. Other governments, anxious to obtain new plants and jobs, offer foreign companies a helping hand in the form of subsidies, privileged market access, and technical assistance. In China, the government is hostile to the Internet and imposes severe restrictions; as a consequence fewer than 3 million Chinese were estimated to have Internet access in 1999 in a country of 1.2 billion people, and the total was not expected to reach 25 million until 2004. In contrast, it has been predicted that the percentage of the population with Internet access in 2004 would exceed 50 percent of the households in the United States, Japan, and several Western European countries.

MULTICOUNTRY COMPETITION OR GLOBAL COMPETITION?

There are important differences in the patterns of international competition from industry to industry.[2] At one extreme is **multicountry** or **multidomestic competition,** where each country market is self-contained—buyers have different expectations and like different styling and features, competition in each national market is essentially independent of competition in other national markets, and the set of rivals comprising the selling side of the market differ from country to country. For example, there is a banking industry in France, one in Brazil, and one in Japan, but market conditions and buyer expectations in banking differ markedly among the three countries, the lead banking competitors in France differ from those in Brazil or in Japan, and the competitive battle going on among the leading banks in France is unrelated to the rivalry taking place in Brazil or Japan. Because each country market is separate in multicountry competition, a company's reputation, customer base, and competitive position in one nation have little or no bearing on its ability to compete successfully in another. As a consequence, the power of a company's strategy in any one nation and any competitive advantage it yields are largely confined to that nation and do not spill over to other countries where it operates. *With multicountry competition there is no international or global market, just a collection of self-contained country markets.* Industries characterized by

> **Basic Concept**
> ***Multicountry*** (or ***multidomestic***) ***competition*** exists when competition in one national market is independent of competition in another national market—there is no "international market," just a collection of self-contained country markets.

---

[2]Michael E. Porter, *The Competitive Advantage of Nations* (New York: Free Press, 1990), pp. 53–54.

multicountry competition include beer, life insurance, apparel, metals fabrication, many types of food products (coffee, cereals, canned goods, frozen foods), and many types of retailing.

Basic Concept
Global competition exists when competitive conditions across national markets are linked strongly enough to form a true international market and when leading competitors compete head to head in many different countries.

At the other extreme is **global competition,** where prices and competitive conditions across country markets are strongly linked together and the term international or *global market* has true meaning. In a globally competitive industry, a company's competitive position in one country both affects and is affected by its position in other countries. Rival companies compete against each other in many different countries, but especially so in countries where sales volumes are large and where having a competitive presence is strategically important to building a strong global position in the industry. In global competition, a firm's overall competitive advantage grows out of its entire worldwide operations; the competitive advantage it creates at its home base is supplemented by advantages growing out of its operations in other countries (having plants in low-wage countries, being able to transfer expertise from country to country, having the capability to serve customers who also have multinational operations, and maintaining a brand reputation that is transferable from country to country). *A global competitor's market strength is directly proportional to its portfolio of country-based competitive advantages.* Global competition exists in automobiles, television sets, tires, telecommunications equipment, copiers, watches, and commercial aircraft.

In multicountry competition, rival firms vie for national market leadership. In globally competitive industries, rival firms vie for worldwide leadership.

An industry can have segments that are globally competitive and segments where competition is country by country.[3] In the hotel-motel industry, for example, the low- and medium-priced segments are characterized by multicountry competition because competitors mainly serve travelers within the same country. In the business and luxury segments, however, competition is more globalized. Companies like Nikki, Marriott, Sheraton, and Hilton have hotels at many international locations and use worldwide reservation systems and common quality and service standards to gain marketing advantages in serving businesspeople and other travelers who make frequent international trips.

For a company to be successful in foreign markets, its strategy must take varying country-to-country business and competitive environments into account.

In lubricants, the marine engine segment is globally competitive because ships move from port to port and require the same oil everywhere they stop. Brand reputations in marine lubricants have a global scope, and successful marine engine lubricant producers (Exxon Mobil, BP Amoco, and Shell) operate globally. In automotive motor oil, however, multicountry competition dominates. Countries have different weather conditions and driving patterns, production is subject to limited scale economies and shipping costs are high, and retail distribution channels differ markedly from country to country. Thus, domestic firms—like Quaker State and Pennzoil in the United States and Castrol in Great Britain—can be leaders in their home markets without competing globally.

All these situational considerations affecting the business and competitive environment, along with the obvious cultural and political differences between countries, shape a company's strategic approach to competing in foreign markets.

STRATEGY OPTIONS FOR ENTERING AND COMPETING IN FOREIGN MARKETS

There are a host of generic strategic options for a company that decides to expand outside its domestic market and compete internationally or globally.

---

[3]Ibid., p. 61.

1. *Maintain a national (one-country) production base and export goods to foreign markets* utilizing either company-owned or foreign-controlled forward distribution channels.

2. *License foreign firms to use the company's technology or produce and distribute the company's products.*

3. *Employ a franchising strategy.*

4. *Follow a multicountry strategy,* varying the company's strategic approach (perhaps a little, perhaps a lot) from country to country in accordance with local conditions and differing buyer tastes and preferences. The company's hoped-for competitive edge over local rivals might be lower cost in some countries, differentiated product attributes in other countries, or better value for the money in still others. The target customer base may vary from *broad* in some countries to *narrowly focused* in others. Furthermore, strategic moves in one country are made independent of initiatives taken in another country; cross-country strategy coordination is a lower priority than matching company strategy to host-country market and competitive conditions.

5. *Follow a global strategy,* using essentially the same competitive strategy approach in all country markets where the company has a presence. Any of the generic strategy options can be used. A company can employ *a global low-cost strategy* and strive for low-cost leadership over both global rivals and local rivals. Alternatively, it can opt for a *global differentiation strategy,* endeavoring to set itself apart from rivals on the same products attributes in all countries to create a globally consistent image and a consistent market position. It can follow *a global best-cost strategy* and strive to provide buyers with the overall best value in most or all of the world's major markets. Or, it can adopt *a global focus strategy,* serving the same identifiable niche in each of many strategically important country markets and striving for competitive advantage based on either low-cost or differentiation. Whichever generic theme is chosen, a global strategy entails only minimal country-to-country variation to accommodate local tastes and local market conditions. Furthermore, strategic actions are coordinated globally to achieve consistency worldwide.

6. *Use strategic alliances or joint ventures with foreign companies as the primary vehicle for entering foreign markets* and perhaps also using them as an ongoing strategic arrangement aimed at maintaining or strengthening its competitiveness.

Export Strategies

Using domestic plants as a production base for exporting goods to foreign markets is an excellent *initial strategy* for pursuing international sales. It minimizes both risk and capital requirements, and it is a conservative way to test the international waters. With an export strategy, a manufacturer can limit its involvement in foreign markets by contracting with foreign wholesalers experienced in importing to handle the entire distribution and marketing function in their countries or regions of the world. If it is more advantageous to maintain control over these functions, a manufacturer can establish its own distribution and sales organizations in some or all of the target foreign markets. Either way, a firm minimizes its direct investments in foreign countries because of its home-based production and export strategy. Such strategies are commonly favored by Chinese, Korean, and Italian companies—products are designed and manufactured at home and then distributed through local channels; the primary functions performed abroad relate chiefly to establishing a network of distributors and dealers and perhaps selected sales promotion and brand awareness activities.

Whether an export strategy can be pursued successfully over the long run hinges on the relative cost competitiveness of a home-country production base. In some industries, firms gain additional scale economies and experience curve benefits from centralizing production in one or several giant plants whose output capability exceeds demand in any one country market; obviously, to capture such economies a company must export to markets in other countries. However, an export strategy is vulnerable when manufacturing costs in the home country are substantially higher than in foreign countries where rivals have plants or when it has relatively high shipping costs. Unless an exporter can keep its production and shipping costs competitive with rivals having low-cost plants in locations close to end-user markets, its success will be limited.

Licensing Strategies

Licensing makes sense when a firm with valuable technical know-how or a unique patented product has neither the internal organizational capability nor the resources to enter foreign markets. Licensing also has the advantage of avoiding the risks of committing resources to country markets that are unfamiliar, present considerable economic uncertainty, or are politically volatile. By licensing the technology or the production rights to foreign-based firms, the firm does not have to bear the costs and risks of entering foreign markets on its own, yet it is able to generate income from royalties. The big disadvantage of licensing is the risk of providing valuable technological know-how to foreign companies and thereby losing some degree of control over its use; monitoring licensees and safeguarding the company's proprietary know-how can prove quite difficult in some circumstances.

Franchising Strategies

While licensing works well for manufacturers, franchising is often better suited to the global expansion efforts of service and retailing enterprises. McDonald's, Tricon Global Restaurants (the parent of Pizza Hut, Kentucky Fried Chicken, and Taco Bell), and Hilton Hotels have all used franchising to build a presence in foreign markets. Franchising has much the same advantages as licensing. The franchisee bears most of the costs and risks of establishing foreign locations; a franchiser has to expend only the resources to recruit, train, and support franchisees. The big problem a franchiser faces is maintaining quality control; foreign franchisees do not always exhibit strong commitment to consistency and standardization, perhaps because the local culture does not stress or put much value on the same kinds of quality concerns.

A Multicountry Strategy or a Global Strategy?

The need for a multicountry strategy derives from the sometimes vast differences in cultural, economic, political, and competitive conditions in different countries. The more diverse national market conditions are, the stronger the case for a *multicountry strategy* where the company tailors its strategic approach to fit each host country's market situation. Usually, but not always, companies employing a multicountry strategy use the same basic competitive theme (low-cost, differentiation, or best-cost) in each country, making whatever country-specific variations are needed to best satisfy customers and to position themselves against local rivals. They may aim at broad market targets in some countries and focus more narrowly on a particular niche in others.

The bigger the country-to-country variations, the more a company's overall international strategy becomes a collection of its individual country strategies. But country to country variations still allow room to connect the strategies in different countries by making an effort to transfer ideas, technologies, competencies, and capabilities that work successfully in one country market to other country markets. Toward this end, it is useful to view operations in each country as "experiments" that result in learning and in capabilities that merit transfer to other country markets.[4]

While multicountry strategies are best suited for industries where multicountry competition dominates and a fairly high degree of local responsiveness is competitively imperative, global strategies are best suited for globally competitive industries. A *global strategy* is one where the company's approach is *mostly the same* in all countries. Although *minor* country-to-country differences in strategy do exist to accommodate specific competitive conditions in host countries, the company's fundamental competitive theme (low-cost, differentiation, best-cost, or focused) remains the same worldwide. Moreover, a global strategy involves (1) integrating and coordinating the company's strategic moves worldwide and (2) selling in many if not all nations where there is significant buyer demand. Table 6.1 provides a point-by-point comparison of multicountry versus global strategies. The question of which of these two strategies to pursue is the foremost strategic issue firms face when they compete in international markets.

The strength of a multicountry strategy is that it matches the company's competitive approach to host-country circumstances. A multicountry strategy is essential when there are significant country-to-country differences in customers' needs and buying habits (see Illustration Capsule 27), when buyers in a country insist on special-order or highly customized products, when host governments enact regulations requiring that products sold locally meet strict manufacturing specifications or performance standards, and when the trade restrictions of host governments are so diverse and complicated they preclude a uniform, coordinated worldwide market approach. However, a multicountry strategy has two big drawbacks: it is very difficult to transfer a company's competencies and resources across country boundaries, and it does not promote building a single, unified competitive advantage—especially one based on low cost. The primary orientation of a multicountry strategy is responsiveness to local country conditions, not building well-defined cross-country competencies and competitive capabilities that can ultimately produce a competitive advantage over other international or global competitors and the domestic companies of host countries. Companies employing a multicountry strategy face big hurdles in achieving low-cost leadership unless they find ways to customize their products and still be in position to capture scale economies and experience curve effects—the capability to implement mass customization assembly at relatively low cost (as Dell, Gateway, and Toyota have demonstrated) greatly facilitates effective use of a multicountry approach.

A global strategy, because it is more uniform from country to country, can concentrate on building the resource strengths to secure a sustainable low-cost or differentiation-based competitive advantage over both domestic rivals and global rivals racing for world market leadership. Whenever country-to-country differences are small enough to be accommodated within the framework of a global strategy, a global strategy is preferable to a multicountry strategy because of the value of uniting a company's efforts worldwide to create strong, competitively valuable competencies and capabilities not readily matched by rivals.

> A multicountry strategy is appropriate for industries where multicountry competition dominates and local responsiveness is essential. A global strategy works best in markets that are globally competitive or beginning to globalize.

---

[4]For more details on the usefulness of such "transnational" strategy opportunities, see C. A. Bartlett and S. Ghoshal, *Managing Across Borders: The Transnational Solution*, 2nd ed. (Boston: Harvard Business School Press, 1998), pp. 79–80 and chapter 9.

table 6.1   Differences between Multicountry and Global Strategies

	Multicountry Strategy	Global Strategy
Strategic arena	• Selected target countries and trading areas	• Most countries where there is high demand for the product; most global companies will have operations in North America, the Asian Pacific, and Latin America
Business strategy	• Custom strategies to fit the circumstances of each host country situation; little or no strategy coordination across countries	• Same basic strategy worldwide; minor country-to-country variations where essential
Product-line strategy	• Adapted to local culture and the particular needs and expectations of local buyers	• Mostly standardized products sold worldwide; moderate customization where and when necessary
Production strategy	• Plants scattered across many host countries, each producing versions suitable for the surrounding locale	• Plants located on the basis of maximum competitive advantage (in low-cost countries, close to major markets, geographically scattered to minimize shipping costs, or use of a few world-scale plants to maximize economies of scale and experience curve effects—as most appropriate)
Source of supply for raw materials and components	• Suppliers in host country preferred (local facilities meeting local buyer needs; some local sourcing may be required by host government)	• Attractive suppliers from anywhere in the world
Marketing and distribution	• Adapted to practices and culture of each host country	• Much more worldwide coordination; minor adaptation to host-country situations if required
Cross-country strategy connections	• Efforts made to transfer ideas, technologies, competencies, and capabilities that work successfully in one country to another country whenever such a transfer appears advantageous	• Efforts made to use much the same technologies, competencies, and capabilities in all country markets (to promote use of a mostly standard strategy), but new strategic initiatives and competitive capabilities that prove successful in one country are transferred to other country markets
Company organization	• Form subsidiary companies to handle operations in each host country; each subsidiary operates more or less autonomously to fit host country conditions	• All major strategic decisions closely coordinated at global headquarters; a global organizational structure is used to unify the operations in each country

illustration capsule 27

Multicountry Strategies: Microsoft in PC Software, McDonald's in Fast Food, and Nestlé in Instant Coffee

MICROSOFT

In order to best serve the needs of users in foreign countries, Microsoft localizes many of its software products to reflect local languages. In France, for example, all user messages and documentation are in French and all monetary references are in French francs. In the United Kingdom, monetary references are in British pounds and user messages and documentation reflect certain British conventions. Various Microsoft products have been localized into more than 30 languages.

MCDONALD'S

McDonald's has been highly successful in markets outside the United States, partly because it has been adept in altering its menu offerings to cater to local tastes. In Taiwan and Singapore, McDonald's outlets offer a bone-in fried chicken dish called Chicken McCrispy. In Great Britain, there's McChicken Tikka Naan to appeal to British cravings for Indian food. In India, McDonald's features the Maharajah Mac sandwich (an Indian version of the Big Mac); in Japan, there's the Chicken Tatsuta sandwich and a Teriyaki Burger sandwich; in Australia, there's a McOz Burger. However, the infrastructure and operating systems that are employed in the outlets are largely the same, enabling McDonald's to achieve low-cost leadership status once it builds volume up at its outlets (sometimes a 5-year process) and once it has enough outlets operating in a country to achieve full economies of scale (sometimes a 5- to 10-year process in the largest foreign markets).

NESTLÉ

Swiss-based Nestlé, the largest food company in the world, is also the largest producer of coffee. With a total workforce of 22,541 people operating in nearly 480 factories in 100 countries, Nestlé's presence is clearly multinational. Chief executive Peter Brabeck-Letmathe advocates understanding the distinctions between the cultures where Nestlé markets its products. "[If] you are open to new languages, you are also open to new cultures," he explains. Thus, instant coffee names like Nescafé, Taster's Choice, Ricore, and Ricoffy line grocery shelves in various countries. If customers prefer roast or ground coffee, they can purchase Nespresso, Bonka, Zoegas, or Loumidis, depending on where they live.

Nestlé produces 200 types of instant coffee, from lighter blends for the U.S. market to dark espressos for Latin America. To keep its instant coffees matched to consumer tastes in different countries (and areas within some countries), Nestlé operates four coffee research labs, to experiment with new blends in aroma, flavor, and color. The strategy is to match the blends marketed in each country to the tastes and preferences of coffee drinkers in that country, introducing new blends to develop new segments when opportunities appear and altering blends as needed to respond to changing tastes and buyer habits. In Britain, Nescafé was promoted extensively to build a wider base of instant coffee drinkers. In Japan, where Nescafé was considered a luxury item, the company made its Japanese blends available in fancy containers suitable for gift-giving.

Sources: Nestlé website (www.nestle.com), accessed August 15, 2001; "Nestlé S.A.," Hoover's Online (www.hoovers.com), accessed August 15, 2001; Tom Mudd, "Nestlé Plays to Global Audience," *Industry Week* (www.industryweek.com), August 13, 2001; company annual reports; Shawn Tully, "Nestlé Shows How to Gobble Markets," *Fortune,* January 16, 1989, pp. 74–78; and "Nestlé: A Giant in a Hurry," *Business Week,* March 22, 1993, pp. 50–54.

PURSUING COMPETITIVE ADVANTAGE BY COMPETING MULTINATIONALLY

There are three ways in which a firm can gain competitive advantage (or offset domestic disadvantages) by expanding outside its domestic market.[5] One way exploits a multinational or global competitor's ability to deploy R&D, parts manufacture, assembly, distribution centers, sales and marketing, customer service centers and other activities among various countries in a manner that lowers costs or achieves greater product differentiation. A second way involves efficient and effective transfer of competitively

---

[5]Porter, *The Competitive Advantage of Nations*, p. 54.

valuable competencies and capabilities from its domestic markets to foreign markets. A third way draws on a multinational or global competitor's ability to deepen or broaden its resource strengths and capabilities and to coordinate its dispersed activities in ways that a domestic-only competitor cannot.

Achieving Locational Advantages

To use location to build competitive advantage, a company must consider two issues: (1) whether to concentrate each activity it performs in a few select countries or to disperse performance of the activity to many nations, and (2) in which countries to locate particular activities. Companies tend to concentrate their activities in a limited number of locations:

- *When the costs of manufacturing or other activities are significantly lower in particular geographic locations than in others*—For example, much of the world's athletic footwear is manufactured in Asia (China and Korea) because of low labor costs; much of the production of motherboards for PCs is located in Taiwan because of both low costs and the high-caliber technical skills of the Taiwanese labor force.

> Companies can pursue competitive advantage in world markets by locating activities in the most advantageous nations; a domestic-only competitor has no such opportunities.

- *When there are significant scale economies in performing the activity*—The presence of significant economies of scale in components production or final assembly means that a company can gain major cost savings from operating a few superefficient plants as opposed to a host of small plants scattered across the world. Important marketing and distribution economies associated with multinational operations can also yield low-cost leadership. In situations where some competitors are intent on global dominance, being the worldwide low-cost provider is a powerful competitive advantage. Achieving low-cost producer status often requires a company to have the largest worldwide *manufacturing share,* with production centralized in one or a few world-scale plants in low-cost locations. Manufacturing share (as distinct from brand share or market share) is significant because it provides more certain access to production-related scale economies. Several Japanese companies have used their large manufacturing share to establish a low-cost advantage over rivals. For example, although less than 40 percent of all the videocassette recorders sold in the United States carry a Japanese brand name, Japanese companies do 100 percent of the manufacturing—all sellers source their videocassette recorders from Japanese manufacturers.[6] In microwave ovens, Japanese brands have less than a 50 percent share of the U.S. market, but the manufacturing share of Japanese companies is over 85 percent.

- *When there is a steep learning or experience curve associated with performing an activity in a single location*—In some industries experience curve effects in parts manufacture or assembly are so great that a company establishes one or two large plants from which it serves the world market. The key to riding down the experience curve and achieving lower costs is to concentrate production in a few locations to increase the accumulated volume at a plant (and thus the experience of the plant's workforce) as rapidly as possible.

- *When certain locations have superior resources, allow better coordination of related activities, or offer other valuable advantages*—A research unit or a sophisticated production facility may be situated in a particular nation because of its pool

---

[6]C. K. Prahalad and Yves L. Doz, *The Multinational Mission* (New York: Free Press, 1987), p. 60.

of technically trained personnel. Samsung became a leader in memory chip technology by establishing a major R&D facility in Silicon Valley and transferring the know-how gained back to headquarters and its plants in South Korea. Where just-in-time inventory practices yield big cost savings and/or where the assembly firm has long-term partnering arrangements with its key suppliers, parts manufacturing plants may be clustered around final assembly plants. An assembly plant may be located in a country in return for the host government's allowing freer import of components from large-scale, centralized parts plants located elsewhere. A customer service center or sales office may be opened in a particular country to help develop strong relationships with pivotal customers.

However, in several instances, *dispersing activities is more advantageous than concentrating them.* Buyer-related activities—such as distribution to dealers, sales and advertising, and after-sale service—usually must take place close to buyers. This means physically locating the capability to perform such activities in every country market where a global firm has major customers (unless buyers in several adjoining countries can be served quickly from a nearby central location). For example, firms that make mining and oil-drilling equipment maintain operations in many international locations to support customers' needs for speedy equipment repair and technical assistance. Large public accounting firms have numerous international offices to service the foreign operations of their multinational corporate clients. A global competitor that effectively disperses its buyer-related activities can gain a service-based competitive edge in world markets over rivals whose buyer-related activities are more concentrated—this is one reason the Big Five public accounting firms have been so successful relative to second-tier firms. Dispersing activities to many locations is also competitively advantageous when high transportation costs, diseconomies of large size, and trade barriers make it too expensive to operate from a central location. Many companies distribute their products from multiple locations to shorten delivery times to customers. In addition, it is strategically advantageous to disperse activities to hedge against the risks of fluctuating exchange rates, supply interruptions (due to strikes, mechanical failures, and transportation delays), and adverse political developments. Such risks are greater when activities are concentrated in a single location.

The classic reason for locating an activity in a particular country is low cost.[7] Even though multinational and global firms have strong reason to disperse buyer-related activities to many international locations, such activities as materials procurement, parts manufacture, finished goods assembly, technology research, and new product development can frequently be decoupled from buyer locations and performed wherever advantage lies. Components can be made in Mexico, technology research done in Frankfurt, new products developed and tested in Phoenix, and assembly plants located in Spain, Brazil, Taiwan, or South Carolina. Capital can be raised in whatever country it is available on the best terms.

Transferring Competencies and Capabilities across Borders

Expanding outside the domestic market is a way for companies to leverage their core competencies and resource strengths, using them as a basis for competing successfully in additional country markets and growing sales and profits in the process.

---

[7]Porter, *The Competitive Advantage of Nations*, p. 57.

Transferring competencies, capabilities, and resource strengths from country to country contributes to the development of broader or deeper competencies and capabilities—ideally helping a company achieve *dominating depth* in some competitively valuable area. Dominating depth in a competitively valuable capability or resource or value chain activity is a strong basis for sustainable competitive advantage over other multinational or global competitors and especially so over small domestic competitors in host countries. Domestic companies are usually not able to achieve dominating depth because a one-country customer base is too small to support such a resource buildup or because their market is just emerging and sophisticated resources have not been required.

Wal-Mart is rapidly expanding its operations into other parts of the world with a strategy that involves transferring its considerable domestic expertise in distribution and discount retailing to other countries. Its status as the largest, most resource-deep, and most sophisticated user of distribution-retailing know-how has served it well in rapidly building its foreign sales and profitability.

Coordinating Cross-Border Activities

Aligning and coordinating company activities located in different countries contributes to sustainable competitive advantage in several different ways. Companies that compete in multiple locations across the world can choose where and how to challenge rivals. A multinational or global competitor may decide to retaliate against an aggressive rival in the country market where the rival has its biggest sales volume or its best profit margins in order to reduce the rival's financial resources for competing in other country markets. It may decide to wage a price-cutting offensive against weak rivals in their home markets, capturing greater market share and subsidizing any short-term losses with profits earned in other country markets.

If a firm learns how to assemble its product more efficiently at its Brazilian plant, the accumulated expertise can be easily transferred via the Internet to assembly plants in other world locations. Knowledge gained in marketing a company's product in Great Britain can readily be exchanged with company personnel in New Zealand or Australia. A company can shift production from one country to another to take advantage of exchange rate fluctuations, to enhance its leverage with host country governments, and to respond to changing wage rates, components shortages, energy costs, or changes in tariffs and quotas. Production schedules can be coordinated worldwide; shipments can be diverted from one distribution center to another if sales rise unexpectedly in one place and fall in another.

Using the Internet, companies can collect ideas for new and improved products from customers and sales and marketing personnel from all over the world, permitting informed decisions about what can be standardized and what should be customized. Likewise, the Internet can be used to involve the company's best design and engineering personnel (wherever they are located) in coming up with next-generation products. If workloads are heavy in one location, they can be shifted to locations where personnel are underutilized.

A company can enhance its brand reputation by consistently incorporating the same differentiating attributes in its products in the various worldwide markets where it competes. The reputation for quality that Honda established worldwide first in motorcycles and then in automobiles gave it competitive advantage in positioning Honda lawn mowers at the upper end of the U.S. outdoor power equipment market—the Honda name gave the company instant credibility with U.S. buyers.

PROFIT SANCTUARIES, CROSS-MARKET SUBSIDIZATION, AND GLOBAL STRATEGIC OFFENSIVES

Profit sanctuaries *are country markets in which a company derives substantial profits because of its strong or protected market position.* Japan, for example, is a profit sanctuary for most Japanese companies because trade barriers erected around Japanese industries by the Japanese government effectively block foreign companies from competing for a large share of Japanese sales. Protected from the threat of foreign competition in their home market, Japanese companies can safely charge somewhat higher prices to their Japanese customers and thus earn attractively large profits on sales made in Japan. In most cases, a company's biggest and most strategically crucial profit sanctuary is its home market, but multicountry and global companies may also enjoy profit sanctuary status in other nations where they have a strong competitive position, big sales volume, and attractive profit margins.

> **Basic Concept**
> Companies with large, protected *profit sanctuaries* have competitive advantage over companies that don't have a protected sanctuary. Companies with multiple profit sanctuaries have a competitive advantage over companies with a single sanctuary.

Using Cross-Market Subsidization to Wage a Strategic Offensive

Profit sanctuaries are valuable competitive assets, providing the financial strength to support strategic offensives in selected country markets and aid a company's race for global market leadership. The added financial capability afforded by multiple profit sanctuaries gives a global or multicountry competitor the financial strength to wage a market offensive against a domestic competitor whose only profit sanctuary is its home market. Consider the case of a purely domestic company in competition with a company that has multiple profit sanctuaries and that is racing for global market leadership. The global company has the flexibility of lowballing its prices in the domestic company's home market and grabbing market share at the domestic company's expense, subsidizing razor-thin margins or losses with the healthy profits earned in its sanctuaries—a practice called **cross-market subsidization.** The global company can adjust the depth of its price-cutting to move in and capture market share quickly, or it can shave prices slightly to make gradual market inroads over a decade or more, so as not to threaten domestic firms precipitously and perhaps trigger protectionist government actions. If the domestic company retaliates with matching price cuts, it exposes its entire revenue and profit base to erosion; its profits can be squeezed substantially and its competitive strength sapped, even if it is the domestic market leader.

> **Basic Concept**
> *Cross-market subsidization*—supporting competitive offensives in one market with resources and profits diverted from operations in other markets—is a powerful competitive weapon.

    There are numerous instances across the world where domestic companies, rightly or wrongly, have accused foreign competitors of "dumping" goods at unreasonably low prices and deliberately attempting to put them in dire financial straits and perhaps drive them out of business. Many governments have antidumping laws aimed at protecting domestic firms from "unfair" pricing by foreign rivals. In the United States in 1999, for example, the federal government imposed antidumping sanctions against Japanese steel companies for selling steel products at ultralow prices.

STRATEGIC ALLIANCES AND JOINT VENTURES WITH FOREIGN PARTNERS

Strategic alliances and cooperative agreements of one kind or another with foreign companies are a favorite and potentially fruitful means for entering a foreign market or

Strategic alliances can help companies in globally competitive industries strengthen their competitive positions while still preserving their independence.

strengthening a firm's competitiveness in world markets. Historically, export-minded firms in industrialized nations sought alliances with firms in less-developed countries to import and market their products locally—such arrangements were often necessary to win approval from the host country's government to enter its market. More recently, companies from different parts of the world have formed strategic alliances and partnership arrangements to strengthen their mutual ability to serve whole continents and move toward more global market participation. Both Japanese and American companies are actively forming alliances with European companies to strengthen their ability to compete in the 15-nation European Union and to capitalize on the opening up of Eastern European markets. Many U.S. and European companies are allying with Asian companies in their efforts to enter markets in China, India, and other Asian countries.

Of late, the number of alliances, joint ventures, and other collaborative efforts has exploded, involving joint research efforts, technology sharing, joint use of production facilities, marketing one another's products, and joining forces to manufacture components or assemble finished products. Cooperative arrangements between domestic and foreign companies have strategic appeal for reasons besides gaining wider access to attractive country markets.[8] One is to capture economies of scale in production and/or marketing—the cost-reductions can be the difference that allows a company to be cost competitive. By joining forces in producing components, assembling models, and marketing their products, companies can realize cost savings not achievable with their own small volumes. A second reason is to fill gaps in technical expertise and/or knowledge of local markets (buying habits and product preferences of consumers, local customs, and so on). Allies learn much from one another in performing joint research, sharing technological know-how, studying one another's manufacturing methods, and understanding how to tailor sales and marketing approaches to fit local cultures and traditions. A third reason is to share distribution facilities and dealer networks, thus mutually strengthening their access to buyers. Fourth, allied companies can direct their competitive energies more toward mutual rivals and less toward one another; teaming up may help them close the gap on leading companies. And finally, alliances can be a particularly useful way to gain agreement on important technical standards—they have been used to arrive at standards for VCRs, assorted PC devices, Internet-related technologies, and mobile phones and other wireless communications devices.

The Risks of Strategic Alliances with Foreign Partners

Alliances and joint ventures have their pitfalls, however. Achieving effective collaboration between independent companies, each with different motives and perhaps conflicting objectives, is not easy.[9] It requires many meetings of many people working in good faith over a period of time to iron out what is to be shared, what is to remain proprietary, and how the cooperative arrangements will work. Cross-border allies typically have to overcome language and cultural barriers; the communication, trust-building, and coordination costs are high in terms of management time. Often, once the bloom is off the

---

[8]Porter, *The Competitive Advantage of Nations,* p. 66; see also Yves L. Doz and Gary Hamel, *Alliance Advantage* (Boston, MA: Harvard Business School Press, 1998), especially chapters 2–4.

[9]For an excellent discussion of company experiences with alliances and partnerships, see Doz and Hamel, *Alliance Advantage,* chapters 2–7 and Rosabeth Moss Kanter, "Collaborative Advantage: The Art of the Alliance," *Harvard Business Review* 72, no. 4 (July–August 1994), pp. 96–108.

rose, partners discover they have deep differences of opinion about how to proceed and conflicting objectives and strategies. Tensions build up, working relationships cool, and the hoped-for benefits never materialize.[10]

Another major problem is getting alliance partners to make decisions fast enough to respond to rapidly advancing technological developments. The large telecommunications companies' strategy to achieve "global connectivity" has involved extensive use of alliances and joint ventures with foreign counterparts, but they are encountering serious difficulty in reaching agreements on which of several technological approaches to employ and how to adapt to the swift pace at which all of the alternatives are advancing. AT&T and British Telecom, who formed a $10 billion joint venture to build an Internet-based global network linking 100 major cities, took eight months to find a CEO to head the project and even longer to come up with a name.

Many times allies find it difficult to collaborate effectively in competitively sensitive areas, thus raising questions about mutual trust and forthright exchanges of information and expertise. There can also be clashes of egos and company cultures. The key people on whom success or failure depends may have little personal chemistry, be unable to work closely together or form a partnership, or be unable to come to consensus. For example, an alliance between Northwest Airlines and KLM Royal Dutch Airlines linking their hubs in Detroit and Amsterdam resulted in a bitter feud among the top officials of both companies (who, according to some reports, refused to speak to each other) and precipitated a battle for control of Northwest Airlines engineered by KLM. The dispute was rooted in a clash of business philosophies (the American way versus the European way), basic cultural differences, and an executive power struggle.[11]

Another danger of collaborative partnerships is that of becoming overly dependent on another company for essential expertise and capabilities over the long term. To be a serious market contender, a company must ultimately develop internal capabilities in all areas important to strengthening its competitive position and building a sustainable competitive advantage. When learning from allies holds only limited potential (because those allies guard their most valuable skills and expertise), acquiring or merging with a company possessing the desired know-how and resources is a better solution. If a company is aiming for global market leadership, then cross-border merger or acquisition may be a better alternative than cross-border alliances or joint ventures. Illustration Capsule 28 relates the experiences of various companies with cross-border strategic alliances.

> Strategic alliances are more effective in helping establish a beachhead of new opportunity in world markets than in achieving and sustaining global leadership.

Making the Most of Strategic Alliances with Foreign Partners

Whether a company realizes the potential of alliances and collaborative partnerships with foreign enterprises seems to be a function of six factors:[12]

1. *Picking a good partner*—A good partner shares the company's vision about the purpose of the alliance and has the desired expertise and capabilities. Experience indicates that it is generally wise to avoid partnering with foreign companies

---

[10]Jeremy Main, "Making Global Alliances Work," p. 125.

[11]Details of the disagreements are reported in Shawn Tully, "The Alliance from Hell," *Fortune,* June 24, 1996, pp. 64–72.

[12]Doz and Hamel, *Alliance Advantage,* chapters 4–8.

illustration capsule 28

Cross-Border Strategic Alliances: The New Shape of Global Business

As the chairman of British Aerospace recently observed, a strategic alliance with a foreign company is "one of the quickest and cheapest ways to develop a global strategy." Cross-border strategic alliances are fast reshaping competition in world markets, pitting one group of allied global companies against other groups of allied global companies. High-profile global alliances include the following:

- Airbus Industrie, one of the world's two leading makers of commercial aircraft, was formed by an alliance of aerospace companies from Britain, Spain, Germany, and France that included British Aerospace, Daimler-Benz Aerospace, and Aerospatiale. Airbus and Boeing vie for world leadership in large commercial aircraft (over 100 passengers).

- General Electric and SNECMA, a French maker of jet engines, have had a longstanding 50-50 partnership to make jet engines to power aircraft made by Boeing and Airbus Industrie. Their partnership company is called CFM International. The GE/SNECMA alliance is regarded as a model because it has enjoyed great success since the 1970s, winning market shares for aircraft with 100+ passengers of about 35 percent through the 1980s and market shares approaching 50 percent since 1995. CFM International had over 200 customers worldwide using its engines as of 2000.

- Renault of France has recently entered into an alliance with struggling Nissan of Japan to create a global partnership capable of being more competitive with DaimlerChrysler, General Motors, Ford, and Toyota,

all of which were engaged in numerous alliances of their own. During the past decade, hundreds of strategic alliances have been formed in the motor vehicle industry as car and truck manufacturers and automotive parts suppliers moved aggressively to compete globally. Not only have there been joint marketing alliances between automakers strong in one region of the world and automakers strong in another region but there have also been strategic alliances between vehicle makers and parts suppliers.

- Vodaphone AirTouch PLC and Bell Atlantic Corporation in 1999 agreed to a collaborative partnership to create a wireless business with a single brand and common digital technology covering the entire U.S. market and to work together on global business synergies in handset and equipment purchases, global corporate account programs, global roaming agreements, and the development of new products and technologies. At the time, Vodaphone AirTouch, based in Great Britain, was the world's largest mobile communications company, and Bell Atlantic was completing a merger with GTE to make it one of the premier telecommunications service providers in the United States and a participant in the global telecommunications market, with operations and investments in 25 countries.

- American Express entered into an alliance with Tata Finance of India to provide money-changing and foreign exchange services in India.

Source: Company websites and press releases; Yves L. Doz and Gary Hamel, *Alliance Advantage: The Art of Creating Value through Partnering* (Boston, MA: Harvard Business School Press, 1998).

where there is strong potential of direct competition because of overlapping product lines or other conflicting interests—agreements to jointly market each other's products hold much potential for conflict unless the products are complements rather than substitutes.

2. *Being sensitive to cultural differences*—Unless the outsider exhibits respect for the local culture and local business practices and unless there is good chemistry among key personnel, productive working relationships are unlikely to emerge.

3. *Recognizing that the alliance must benefit both sides*—Information must be shared as well as gained, and the relationship must remain forthright and trustful. Many alliances fail because one or both partners grow unhappy with what they are learning. Also, if either partner plays games with information or tries to take advantage of the other, the resulting friction can quickly erode the value of further collaboration.

4. *Ensuring that both parties live up to their commitments*—Both parties have to deliver on their commitments for the alliance to produce the intended benefits. The division of work has to be perceived as fairly apportioned and the caliber of the benefits received on both sides has to be perceived as adequate.

5. *Structuring the decision-making process so that actions can be taken swiftly when needed*—In many instances, technology and competitive changes occur at such a fast pace that decisions need to be made fast. If the parties get bogged down in discussions among themselves or in gaining internal approval from higher-ups, the alliance can turn into an anchor of delay and inaction.

6. *Managing the learning process and then adjusting the alliance agreement over time to fit new circumstances*—In today's fast-moving markets, few alliances can succeed by holding only to initial plans. One of the keys to longevity and success is learning to adapt to change and adjusting the terms and objectives of the alliance as may be needed.

Most alliances with foreign companies that aim at technology-sharing or providing market access turn out to be temporary, serving their purpose after a few years because the benefits of mutual learning have occurred and because the businesses of both partners have developed to the point where they are ready to go their own ways. In such cases, it is important for the company to learn thoroughly and rapidly about a partner's technology, business practices, and organizational capabilities and then transfer valuable ideas and practices into its own operations promptly. Although long-term alliances sometimes prove mutually beneficial, most partners don't hesitate to terminate the alliance and go it alone when the payoffs run out.

Alliances are more likely to be long-lasting when (1) they involve collaboration with suppliers or distribution allies and each party's contribution involves activities in different portions of the industry value chain or (2) both parties conclude that continued collaboration is in their mutual interest, perhaps because new opportunities for learning are emerging or perhaps because further collaboration will allow each partner to extend its market reach beyond what it could accomplish on its own.

COMPETING IN EMERGING FOREIGN MARKETS

Companies racing for global leadership have to consider competing in big and *emerging-country markets* like China, India, Brazil, Indonesia, and Mexico—countries where the business risks are considerable but where the opportunities for growth are huge as their economies develop and living standards increase toward levels in the modern world.[13] With the world now comprising more than 6 billion people—fully one-third of whom are in India and China, and hundreds of millions more in other emerging countries of Asia and Latin America—a company that aspires to world market leadership (or to sustained rapid growth) cannot ignore the market opportunities or the base of technical and managerial talent such countries offer. This is especially true given that once-high protectionist barriers in most of these countries are in the process of crumbling. Coca-Cola, for example, has predicted that its $2 billion investment in China, India, and Indonesia— which together hold 40 percent of the world's population—can produce sales in those

[13]Much of this section is based on Prahalad and Lieberthal, "The End of Corporate Imperialism," pp. 68–79; and David J. Arnold and John A. Quelch, "New Strategies in Emerging Markets," *Sloan Management Review* 40, no. 1 (Fall 1998), pp. 7–20.

countries that double every three years for the foreseeable future (compared to a modest 4 percent growth rate that Coca-Cola averaged in the United States during the 1990s).[14]

Tailoring products for these big emerging markets often involves more than making minor product changes and becoming more familiar with their local cultures.[15] Ford's attempt to sell a Ford Escort in India at a price of $21,000—a luxury car price, given that India's best-selling Maruti-Suzuki model sold at the time for $10,000 or less, and that fewer than 10 percent of Indian households have annual purchasing power greater than $20,000—met with less than enthusiastic market response. McDonald's has had to offer vegetable burgers in parts of Asia and to rethink its prices, which are often high by local standards and affordable only by the well-to-do. Kellogg has struggled to introduce its cereals successfully because consumers in many emerging countries do not eat cereal for breakfast—changing habits is difficult and expensive. Coca-Cola has found that advertising its world image does not strike a chord with the local populace in several emerging countries. Single-serving packages of detergents, shampoos, pickles, cough syrup, and cooking oils are very popular in India because they allow buyers to conserve cash by purchasing only what they need immediately. Because telephones are not widely available in China, people use pagers to send entire messages, which prompted Motorola to redesign its pagers to display more lines and then to expand capacity to keep up with climbing demand for its product.

Strategy Implications   Consumers are highly focused on price in emerging markets, in many cases giving local low-cost competitors the edge. Companies wishing to succeed in these markets have to attract buyers with bargain prices as well as better products—an approach that can entail a radical departure from the strategy used in other parts of the world. If building a market for the company's products is likely to be a long-term process and involve reeducation of consumers, a company must not only be patient with regard to sizable revenues and profits but also prepared in the interim to invest sizable sums to alter buying habits and tastes. Also, specially designed or packaged products may be needed to accommodate local market circumstances. For example, when Unilever entered the market for laundry detergents in India, it realized that 80 percent of the population could not afford the brands it was selling to affluent consumers in India (as well as in wealthier countries). To compete against a very low-priced detergent made by a local company, Unilever came up with a low-cost formula that was not harsh to the skin, constructed new low-cost production facilities, packaged the detergent (named Wheel) in single-use amounts so that it could be sold very cheaply, utilized distribution by hand carts to local merchants, and crafted an economical marketing campaign that included painted signs on buildings and demonstrations near stores—the new brand captured $100 million in sales in a relatively short period of time. Unilever later replicated the strategy in South America with a brand named Ala.

Because managing a new venture in an emerging market requires a blend of global knowledge and local sensitivity to the culture and business practices, the management team must usually consist of a mix of expatriate and local managers. Expatriate managers are needed to transfer technology, business practices, and the corporate culture and serve as conduits for the flow of information between the corporate office and local operations; local managers bring needed understanding of the area's nuances and deep commitment to its market.

> Profitability in emerging country markets rarely comes quickly or easily—new entrants have to be very sensitive to local conditions, be willing to invest in developing the market for their products over the long term, and be patient in earning a profit.

---

[14]Arnold and Quelch, "New Strategies in Emerging Markets," p. 7.
[15]Prahalad and Lieberthal, "The End of Corporate Imperialism," pp. 72–73.

figure 6.1 **Strategy Options for Local Companies in Competing against Global Challengers**

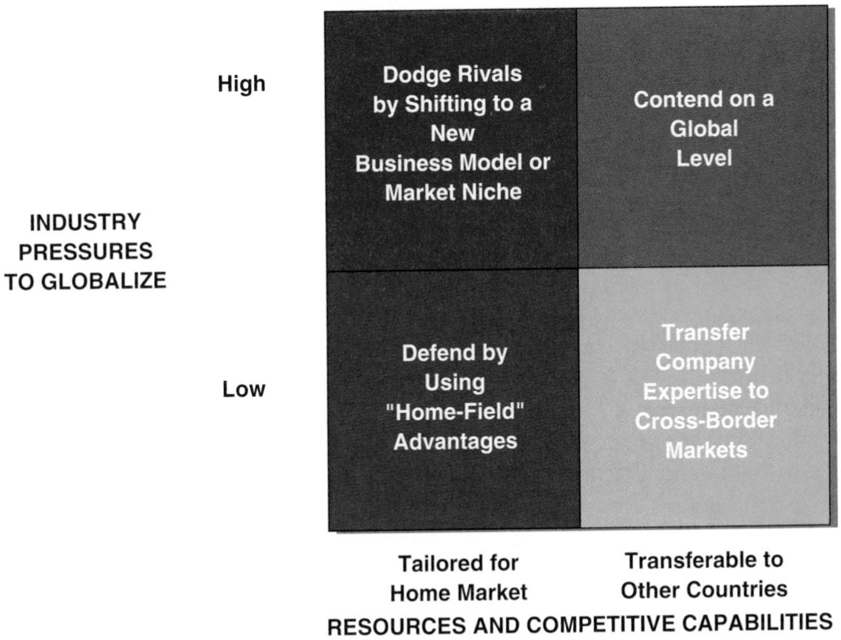

INDUSTRY PRESSURES TO GLOBALIZE

High
- Dodge Rivals by Shifting to a New Business Model or Market Niche
- Contend on a Global Level

Low
- Defend by Using "Home-Field" Advantages
- Transfer Company Expertise to Cross-Border Markets

Tailored for Home Market   Transferable to Other Countries

RESOURCES AND COMPETITIVE CAPABILITIES

Source: Adapted from Niraj Dawar and Tony Frost, "Competing with Giants: Survival Strategies for Local Companies in Emerging Markets," *Harvard Business Review* 77, no. 1 (March–April, 1999), p. 122.

STRATEGIES FOR LOCAL COMPANIES IN EMERGING MARKETS

If large, opportunity-seeking, resource-rich companies are looking to enter the markets of emerging countries, what are the strategy options for local companies in these same markets wishing to survive against the entry of global giants? As it turns out, the prospects for local companies are by no means grim. Their optimal strategic approach hinges on (1) whether a firm's competitive assets are suitable only for the home market or can be transferred abroad and (2) whether industry pressures to move toward global competition are strong or weak. The four generic options are shown in Figure 6.1.

Defending against Global Competitors by Using Home-Field Advantages

When the pressures for global competition are weak and a local firm has competitive strengths well suited to the local market, a good strategy option is to concentrate on the advantages enjoyed in the home market, cater to customers who prefer a local touch, and accept the loss of customers attracted to global brands.[16] A local company may be

[16]Niraj Dawar and Tony Frost, "Competing with Giants: Survival Strategies for Local Companies in Emerging Markets," *Harvard Business Review* 77 no. 2 (March–April, 1999), pp. 122–23. See also Guliz Ger, "Localizing in the Global Village: Local Firms Competing in Global Markets," *California Management Review* 41, no. 4 (Summer 1999), pp. 64–84.

able to astutely exploit its local orientation—its familiarity with local preferences, its expertise in traditional products, its long-standing customer relationships. A local company, in many cases, enjoys a significant cost advantage over global rivals (perhaps because of simpler product design, lower operating and overhead costs), allowing it to compete on the basis of a lower price. Its global competitors often aim their products at upper- and middle-income urban buyers, who tend to be more fashion-conscious, willing to experiment with new products, and view global brands as attractive. Bajaj Auto, India's largest producer of scooters, has defended its turf against Honda (which entered the Indian market with a local joint venture partner to sell scooters, motorcycles, and other vehicles on the basis of its superior technology, quality, and brand appeal) by focusing on buyers who wanted low-cost, durable scooters and easy access to maintenance in the countryside. Bajaj designed a rugged, cheap-to-build scooter for India's rough roads, invested more in R&D to improve reliability and quality, and created an extensive network of distributors and roadside-mechanic stalls, a strategic approach that served it well—while Honda captured about an 11 percent market share, Bajaj maintained a share above 70 percent, close to its 77 percent share prior to Honda's entry. In fall 1998, Honda announced it was pulling out of its scooter manufacturing joint venture with its Indian partner.

Transferring the Company's Expertise to Cross-Border Markets

When a company has resource strengths and capabilities suitable for competing in other country markets, launching initiatives to transfer its expertise to cross-border markets becomes a viable strategic option.[17] Televisa, Mexico's largest media company, used its expertise in Spanish culture and linguistics to become the world's most prolific producer of Spanish-language soap operas. Jollibee Foods, a family-owned company with 56 percent of the fast-food business in the Philippines, combated McDonald's entry by upgrading service and delivery standards, then used its expertise in seasoning hamburgers with garlic and soy sauce and in noodle and rice meals made with fish to open outlets catering to Asian residents in Hong Kong, the Middle East, and California.

Dodging Global Entrants by Shifting to a New Business Model or Market Niche

When industry pressures to globalize are strong, any of three options make the most sense: (1) shift the business to a piece of the industry value chain where the firm's expertise and resources provide competitive advantage, (2) enter into a joint venture with a globally competitive partner, or (3) sell out to (be acquired by) a global entrant into the home market who concludes the company would be a good entry vehicle.[18] When Microsoft entered China, local software developers shifted from cloning Windows products to developing Windows application software customized to the Chinese market. When the Russian PC market opened to IBM, Compaq, and Hewlett-Packard, local Russian PC maker Vist focused on assembling very low-cost models, marketing

---

[17]Dawar and Frost, "Competing with Giants," p. 124.
[18]Ibid., p. 125.

them through exclusive distribution agreements with selected local retailers, and opening company-owned full-service centers in dozens of Russian cities. Vist focused on providing low-cost PCs, giving lengthy warranties, and catering to buyers who felt the need for local service and support. Vist's strategy allowed it to remain the market leader, with a 20 percent share.

Contending on a Global Level

If a local company in an emerging market has transferable resources and capabilities, it can sometimes launch successful initiatives to meet the pressures for globalization head-on and start to compete on a global level itself.[19] When General Motors decided to outsource the production of radiator caps for all of its North American vehicles, Sundaram Fasteners of India pursued the opportunity; it purchased one of GM's radiator cap production lines, moved it to India, and became GM's sole supplier of radiator caps in North America—at 5 million units a year. As a participant in GM's supplier network, it learned about emerging technical standards, built its capabilities, and became one of the first Indian companies to achieve QS 9000 certification, a quality standard that GM now requires for all suppliers. Sundaram's acquired expertise in quality standards enabled it then to pursue opportunities to supply automotive parts in Japan and Europe.

key|points

Companies opt to expand outside their domestic market for any of four major reasons: to gain access to new customers for their products or services, to achieve lower costs and become more competitive on price, to leverage its core competencies, and to spread its business risk across a wider market base. A company is an *international* or *multinational competitor* when it competes in several foreign markets; it is a *global competitor* when it has or is pursuing a market presence in virtually all of the world's major countries.

The strategies a company uses to compete in foreign markets have to be *situation-driven*—cultural, demographic, and market conditions vary significantly among the countries of the world. One of the biggest concerns of competing in foreign markets is whether to customize the company's offerings to cater to the tastes and preferences of local buyers in each different country market or whether to offer a mostly standardized product worldwide. While being responsive to local tastes makes a company's products more appealing to local buyers, customizing a company's products country-by-country may have the effect of raising production and distribution costs due to the greater variety of designs and components, shorter production runs, and the complications of added inventory handling and distribution logistics. Greater standardization of the company's product offering, on the other hand, enhances the capture of scale economies and experience curve effects, contributing to the achievement of a low-cost advantage. The tension between the market pressures to customize and the competitive pressures to lower costs is one of the big strategic issues that participants in foreign markets have to resolve.

Multicountry (or *multidomestic*) *competition* exists when competition in one national market is independent of competition in another national market—there is no

---

[19]Ibid., p. 126.

"international market," just a collection of self-contained country markets. *Global competition* exists when competitive conditions across national markets are linked strongly enough to form a true international market and when leading competitors compete head-to-head in many different countries. A multicountry strategy is appropriate for industries where multicountry competition dominates, but a global strategy works best in markets that are globally competitive or beginning to globalize. Other strategy options for competing in world markets include maintaining a national (one-country) production base and exporting goods to foreign markets, licensing foreign firms to use the company's technology or produce and distribute the company's products, employing a franchising strategy, and using strategic alliances and collaborative partnerships to enter a foreign market or strengthen a firm's competitiveness in world markets.

The number of global strategic alliances, joint ventures, and collaborative arrangements has exploded in recent years. Cooperative arrangements with foreign partners have strategic appeal from several angles: gaining wider access to attractive country markets, allowing capture of economies of scale in production and/or marketing, filling gaps in technical expertise and/or knowledge of local markets, saving on costs by sharing distribution facilities and dealer networks, helping gain agreement on important technical standards, and helping combat the impact of alliances that rivals have formed. Cross-border strategic alliances are fast reshaping competition in world markets, pitting one group of allied global companies against other groups of allied global companies.

There are three ways in which a firm can gain competitive advantage (or offset domestic disadvantages) in global markets. One way involves locating various value chain activities among nations in a manner that lowers costs or achieves greater product differentiation. A second way involves efficient and effective transfer of competitively valuable competencies and capabilities from its domestic markets to foreign markets. A third way draws on a multinational or global competitor's ability to deepen or broaden its resource strengths and capabilities and to coordinate its dispersed activities in ways that a domestic-only competitor cannot.

Profit sanctuaries are country markets in which a company derives substantial profits because of its strong or protected market position. They are valuable competitive assets, providing the financial strength to support competitive offensives in one market with resources and profits diverted from operations in other markets, and aid a company's race for global market leadership. The cross-subsidization capabilities provided by multiple profit sanctuaries gives a global or multinational competitor a powerful offensive weapon. Companies with large, protected profit sanctuaries have competitive advantage over companies that don't have a protected sanctuary. Companies with multiple profit sanctuaries have a competitive advantage over companies with a single sanctuary.

Companies racing for global leadership have to consider competing in *emerging-country markets* like China, India, Brazil, Indonesia, and Mexico—countries where the business risks are considerable but the opportunities for growth are huge. To succeed in these markets, it is usually necessary to attract buyers with bargain prices as well as better products—an approach that can entail a radical departure from the strategy used in other parts of the world. Moreover, building a market for the company's products in these markets is likely to be a long-term process, involving the investment of sizable sums to alter buying habits and tastes and reeducate consumers. Profitability is unlikely to come quickly or easily.

The outlook for local companies in emerging-country markets wishing to survive against the entry of global giants is by no means grim. The optimal strategic approach hinges on whether a firm's competitive assets are suitable only for the home market or can be transferred abroad and whether industry pressures to move toward global competition are strong or weak. Local companies can compete against global newcomers by (1) defending on the basis of home-field advantages, (2) transferring their expertise to cross-border markets, (3) dodging large rivals by shifting to a new business model or market niche, or (4) launching initiatives to compete on a global level themselves.

suggested | readings

Arnold, David J., and John A. Quelch. "New Strategies in Emerging Markets." *Sloan Management Review* 40, no. 1 (Fall 1998), pp. 7–20.

Bolt, James F. "Global Competitors: Some Criteria for Success." *Business Horizons* 31, no. 1 (January–February 1988), pp. 34–41.

Das, T. K., and Bing-Sheng Teng. "Managing Risks in Strategic Alliances." *Academy of Management Executive* 13, no. 4 (November 1999), pp. 50–62.

Dawar, Niraj, and Tony Frost. "Competing with Giants: Survival Strategies for Local Companies in Emerging Markets." *Harvard Business Review* 77, no. 2 (March–April 1999), pp. 119–29.

Doz, Yves L., and Gary Hamel. *Alliance Advantage: The Art of Creating Value through Partnering.* Boston, MA: Harvard Business School Press, 1998.

Ger, Guliz. "Localizing in the Global Village: Local Firms Competing in Global Markets." *California Management Review* 41, no. 4 (Summer 1999), pp. 64–84.

Inkpen, Andrew C. "Learning and Knowledge Acquisition through International Strategic Alliances." *Academy of Management Executive* 12, no. 4 (November 1998), pp. 69–81.

Kanter, Rosabeth Moss, and Thomas D. Dretler. " 'Global Strategy' and Its Impact on Local Operations: Lessons from Gillette Singapore." *Academy of Management Executive* 12, no. 4 (November 1998), pp. 60–68.

Lei, David. "Strategies for Global Competition." *Long Range Planning* 22, no. 1 (February 1989), pp. 102–9.

Ohmae, Kenichi. "The Global Logic of Strategic Alliances." *Harvard Business Review* 67, no. 2 (March–April 1989), pp. 143–54.

Parkhe, Arvind. "Building Trust in International Alliances." *Journal of World Business* 33, no. 4 (Winter 1998), pp. 417–37.

Rackham, Neil; Lawrence Friedman; and Richard Ruff. *Getting Partnering Right: How Market Leaders Are Creating Long-Term Competitive Advantage.* New York: McGraw-Hill, 1996.

Sugiura, Hideo. "How Honda Localizes Its Global Strategy." *Sloan Management Review* 33 (Fall 1990), pp. 77–82.

Thomas, Howard; Timothy Pollock; and Philip Gorman. "Global Strategic Analyses: Frameworks and Approaches." *Academy of Management Executive* 13, no. 1 (February 1999), pp. 70–82.

Zahra, Shaker A., and Hugh M. O'Neill. "Charting the Landscape of Global Competition." *Academy of Management Executive* 12, no. 4 (November 1998), pp. 36–42.

chapter | seven

Business Models and Strategies in the Internet Era

It's easy to understand why investors fled dot-coms like a house on fire. Lots of Net companies constructed dwellings out of highly flammable cards. But not everything they built burned to the ground. Collectively, they left a rich legacy: a huge leap in information technology.

—Robert D. Hof, *Business Week*

The key question is not whether to deploy Internet technology—companies have no choice if they want to stay competitive—but how to deploy it.

—Michael Porter, Professor, Harvard Business School

If we want to stay competitive, we need to be in e-commerce.

—Jessica Chu, Marketing Manager, Aaeon Technology, Taiwan

Our strategy is to integrate the Internet into all of our core businesses.

—Thomas Middelhoff, CEO, Bertelsmann AG, Germany

There can be no doubt that the Internet and Internet technology represent a driving force of historical and revolutionary proportions, fundamentally affecting how business is conducted and how markets function. Everyday use of the Internet by businesses and consumers adds an important distribution channel, gives businesses an important technological tool for improving some value chain activities and bypassing others, and alters the five competitive forces. The Internet has spawned entirely new industries—online auctions; website hosting; online brokerage; Internet service provision; and online commodity markets that match buyers and sellers for such products as steel, chemicals, and natural gas. Leading-edge e-commerce capabilities can give a company competitively valuable resource strengths; conversely, failure to make Internet technology an integral part of a company's strategy and business operations can prove to be a competitive weakness. The Internet is a powerful enabling technology that can be used, wisely or unwisely, in almost every industry and as part of almost every company's strategy.[1] The strategic skill with which a company deploys Internet technology and makes the Internet a central part of its strategy holds enormous potential for affecting its competitiveness vis-à-vis rivals.

This chapter first examines an assortment of strategic issues surrounding the Internet and e-commerce: How is Internet technology altering the ways in which companies perform value chain activities? What is the impact of the Internet on competition? Will the Internet prove to be a vehicle for increasing or decreasing industry profitability? Does the Internet enhance or impede company efforts to gain sustainable competitive advantage? Next, we look at the strategic mistakes made by some of the early Internet entrepreneurs and the strategic lessons learned from the first wave of the Internet revolution. The chapter concludes with an examination of business models and strategies for pure dot-com enterprises, combination brick-and-click strategies, and Internet strategies for traditional businesses.

---

[1]Michael E. Porter, "Strategy and the Internet," *Harvard Business Review* 79, no. 3 (March 2001), p. 64.

THE INTERNET:
TECHNOLOGY AND PARTICIPANTS

The Internet is an integrated network of users' connected computers, banks of servers and high-speed computers, digital switches and routers, and telecommunications equipment and lines. The backbone of the Internet consists of telecommunications lines (fiber-optic lines and high-capacity copper wires) criss-crossing countries and continents. These lines allow computers to transfer data in digital form at very high speeds. The bandwidth of the line determines the capacity or speed of the data transfer. Computerlike digital switches move traffic along the backbone lines; many of these switches act as routers, deciding which way to direct the traffic and how to handle the requests of users' computers to send or obtain data, given the destinations and degree of line congestion. Users gain access to the network via a local-area network server or an Internet service provider's computerized switch that has the capability to route traffic to and from end users directly connected to it. Companies need specialized software to design multifunctional websites and to take advantage of the growing number of Internet technology applications.

The Demand for Internet Services

There were an estimated 400 million people worldwide using the Internet in 2001—about 167 million in North America, 105 million in Europe, 122 million in the Asia-Pacific region, 21 million in Latin America, and 7 million in the rest of the world.[2] Projections called for 600 to 700 million Internet users globally by 2003. A growing majority of businesses across the world were connected to the Internet. Uses of the Internet varied widely among individuals and businesses—from e-mail communications to information gathering to shopping to entertainment to a growing number of business applications.

The Suppliers of Internet Technology and Services

The gold rush atmosphere surrounding the Internet and rapidly advancing Internet technology has given rise to a diverse collection of firms and industries on the supply side of the "Internet economy":

- *The makers of specialized Internet-related communications components and equipment*—Cisco Systems is the world's leading provider of switches and routers; other prominent companies in this group include JuniperNetworks, Lucent Technologies, Corning, F5 Networks, Nortel, Foundry Networks, Broadcom, PMC Sierra, 3Com, and JDS Uniphase.

| The supply side of the Internet economy consists of diverse kinds of enterprises. |

- *The providers of Internet communications services*—Internet communication companies develop and install the communications networks that enable connectivity and traffic flow. They include backbone providers, "last-mile" providers, and Internet service providers. Last-mile companies, which install and maintain the *physical assets* needed to connect users to the Internet, include local telephone companies, cable companies, and wireless communications providers. Leading backbone providers include WorldCom, AT&T, Qwest Communications, Deutsche Telekom, British Telecom, Verizon, and SBC Communications.

---

[2]Based on estimates made by Nua (www.nua.com), a leading source of Internet trends and statistics, and estimates in *Business2.0*, February 2001.

- *The suppliers of computer components, computer hardware, and wireless handheld devices*—There are hundreds of companies engaged in components manufacture, assembly, and marketing of PCs, servers, data storage devices, and related peripheral equipment. Examples of companies in this category include Intel, Sun Microsystems, Seagate Technology, IBM, Taiwan Semiconductor, Fujitsu, NEC, Matsushita/Panasonic, Dell Computer, KLA-Tencor, EMC Corp., Philips Electronics, Toshiba, Network Appliance, and Hewlett-Packard. Still others, like Nokia, Ericsson, Motorola, and PalmPilot, are making an assortment of wireless handheld devices with Internet access capability.

- *The developers of specialized software*—Software developers write the programs that enable commercial transactions on the Internet. These programs involve numerous functions and features: encryption; order/payment processing; shopping-cart purchase tracking; browser image; banner ads; Web page design; the functioning of cable modems and wireless devices; and the functioning of PCs, workstations, and local-area networks. Important developers of software and e-commerce systems include Microsoft, IBM, SAP, Seibel Systems, Oracle, Inktomi, Sun Microsystems, DoubleClick, VeriSign, Check Point Software Technologies, Macromedia, and Novell.

- *E-commerce enterprises*—This category of businesses includes (1) business-to-business merchants like Cisco, Intel, and Dell Computer, which conduct most of their business with corporate customers online, and Exodus Communications, which provides Web hosting services; (2) business-to-consumer merchants like eBay, Amazon.com, FTD.com, Priceline.com, Buy.com, and Charles Schwab; (3) media companies such as Disney, Nintendo, Electronic Arts, and Sony that provide online entertainment; and (4) content providers like America Online, Yahoo!, The Motley Fool, TheStreet.com, Edmunds.com, and iVillage.

The volume of business done online is forecast to exceed $6 trillion by the end of 2005. In 2001, three companies—Dell Computer, Intel, and Cisco Systems—were doing over $120 million of business daily on the Internet and General Electric transacted all of its business with its suppliers online.

Throughout most of the last decade, the suppliers of Internet equipment and Internet technology have enjoyed booming demand. The many different efforts to establish a globally connected Internet infrastructure—building out the telecommunications system, installing millions of servers, providing Internet connections to hundreds of millions of businesses and households, and developing the necessary software—presented Internet-related suppliers with sometimes exploding market opportunities. In addition to Internet buildout opportunities, there were market opportunities associated with the rush of companies setting up websites, opening e-businesses of all types, and putting Internet applications in place. In the process, several altogether new industries have been created—Internet service provision, website design and maintenance, Web hosting, specialized Internet application software, the manufacture of various parts and components needed to make the Internet work, website content provision, e-retailing in a variety of product categories, and online gaming, to mention a few.

Of course, once the building of a globally interconnected infrastructure approaches completion, Internet technology suppliers will confront a much more mature marketplace, with demand for their products stemming chiefly from (1) ongoing advances in Internet technology that open up opportunities to further upgrade performance for Internet users looking for new applications and capabilities and (2) supplying the needs of new and expanding e-businesses. Thus, the rapid growth of many Internet technology suppliers will not go on indefinitely—some are already experiencing slowdowns and are shifting from strategies designed for a rapid growth mode to those more suitable for a maturing market environment.

The Strategic Challenge of Competing Technologies

One of the toughest strategic issues many Internet technology providers face is vigorous competition among alternative technologies for building various components of the Internet infrastructure and creating a globally wired economy. For example, in wireless communications, several digital cellular standards are competing on the world market:

Area of World/Country	Major Wireless Platforms in Use
North America	CDMA, WAP, GSM
Western Europe	GSM/GPRS, WAP
Central and South America	TDMA, CDMA
Africa	WAP
Asia-Pacific	GSM, CDMA, i-mode, 3G, WAP
China	GSM/GPRS, CDMA, WAP
Japan	i-mode, 3G
South Korea	CDMA, GSM, 3G

Key: WAP = wireless application protocol; CDMA = code division multiple access; TDMA = time division multiple access; GSM = global system for mobile communications; GPRS = general packet radio service; i-mode is an Internet-based system utilizing a simplified version of hypertext markup language (HTML) that is designed for use in Japan; 3G stands for 3rd generation and is a combination of technologies and standards said to have global allocation potential.

The hodgepodge of mobile communication systems poses formidable technological and competitive challenges for all the various market participants in establishing mobile systems capable of connecting all users irrespective of location and wireless platform.

Other things being equal, the low-cost technological solution typically wins out. But other things are seldom equal. Often, competing technologies have materially different performance pluses and minuses, with the trade-offs unclear enough that industry participants disagree about which of the competing technologies represent the best options. In other cases, the competing technologies are incompatible, preventing users of one from interfacing with users of the other. If the economics of installing and maintaining parallel technological systems is prohibitive, progress is slowed (and business risks are increased) until consensus emerges around one as the industry standard. There's a natural tendency for those with vested interests in a particular technological approach to maneuver to make their favored technological solution the industry standard. Technology rivals typically employ any of several strategic initiatives in waging the battle for technological supremacy:

- *Investing aggressively in R&D to win the technological race against rivals;* spending tends to be aimed at improving performance features, curing performance weaknesses, and reducing the costs of installing and maintaining the company's technological approach.

- *Forming strategic alliances* with suppliers, potential customers, and those with complementary technologies to build consensus for favored technological approaches and industry standards.

- *Acquiring other companies with complementary technological expertise* so as to broaden and deepen the company's technological base and thereby drive advances in its technology faster than rivals are able to advance theirs.

- *Hedging the company's bets* by investing sufficient resources in mastering one or more of the competing technologies so that the company has the capability to shift to another technological approach should that approach win out.

HOW INTERNET TECHNOLOGY IMPACTS COMPANY AND INDUSTRY VALUE CHAINS

Internet technology applications open up a host of opportunities for reconfiguring company and industry value chains. Table 7.1 lists ways in which companies can utilize the Internet to improve the efficiency and effectiveness of particular value chain activities. While many of these applications are self-explanatory, some uses of Internet technology are producing such fundamental changes in operating practices and how value chain activities are managed that further discussion is merited.

How Internet Technology Improves Supply Chain Efficiency

Internet technology is a powerful tool for facilitating supply chain management: procuring items from suppliers, reducing inventory requirements, expediting the design and production of new components, and otherwise engaging in mutually beneficial collaboration with suppliers. With software from Commerce One, Oracle, SAP, Ariba, and others, company procurement personnel can—with only a few mouse clicks within one seamless system—check materials inventories against incoming customer orders, check suppliers' stocks, check the latest prices for parts and components at auction and e-sourcing websites, and check FedEx delivery schedules. Electronic data interchange software permits the relevant details of incoming customer orders to be instantly shared with the suppliers of needed parts and components. All this lays the foundation for just-in-time deliveries of parts and components and for the production of parts and components to be matched closely to assembly plant requirements and production schedules— and such coordination produces savings for both suppliers and manufacturers. Via the Internet, manufacturers can collaborate closely with parts and components suppliers in designing new products and reducing the time it takes to get new products into production. Warranty claims and product performance problems involving supplier components can be made available instantly to the relevant suppliers so that corrective fixes can be expedited. Various e-procurement software packages streamline the purchasing process by eliminating much of the manual handling of data and by substituting electronic communication for paper documents such as requests for quotations, purchase orders, order acceptances, and shipping notices.

   All told, the many e-procurement applications now available permit comprehensive revision of purchasing and inbound logistics activities, with incentives for both companies and their suppliers to collaborate closely and achieve mutual cost savings and operating improvements.

> Opportunities to apply Internet technology exist all along company and industry value chain systems, offering considerable potential for improving operating efficiency, reconfiguring value chains, and lowering costs.

How Internet Technology Improves Internal Operating Efficiency

Using the Internet, manufacturers can link the orders of customers to production at their plants and to deliveries of components from suppliers. Real-time sharing of customer orders with suppliers helps suppliers both hold down the costs of making

Table 7.1   Ways to Integrate the Internet into Value Chain Activities

Primary Activities and Costs				
Purchased Supplies and Inbound Logistics	**Operations**	**Distribution and Outbound Logistics**	**Sales and Marketing**	**Service**
• Data sharing with suppliers to coordinate production schedules and just-in-time deliveries • Coordination of parts and components design • Real-time diagnosis of customer experiences with parts failures and defective performance • Use of Internet auctions and e-markets to procure selected parts and components • Online systems for ordering, order processing, and payment of suppliers	• Build-to-order capabilities • Interplant coordination of production • Real-time production and inventory data provided to sales force and distribution channel allies • Production coordination with contract manufacturers	• Online dealer ordering and order processing • Customer and dealer access to delivery schedules and order status • Collaborative data sharing of real-time sales • Collaborative sales forecasting with distribution channel partners • Real-time coordination of shipping needs with shipping partners	• Customer ordering capabilities at website • Online product catalogs containing extensive product information and product specs • Real-time access to customer account data • Online software that permits customers to specify build-to-order configurations • Online price quotes • Online marketing tailored to customer profiles and buying habits • Online announcements of special sales and promotions	• Extensive online product information • Online support for customers via online customer service reps, e-mail, chat rooms, PC voice communications, and streaming video • Real-time order status reports • Online customer ordering at company website • Online order processing, invoicing, and electronic payment for purchases • Online processing of warranty claims

Support Activities and Costs		
Technology and New Product Development	**Human Resource Management**	**General Administration**
• Collaborative product design across all company locations and with other value chain partners • R&D access to online sales and service data for use in correcting performance problems and designing new products and models	• Online training programs • Online posting of job openings, résumé submission • Self-service benefits administration • Online personnel files	• Web-based dissemination of company information across all locations • Online investor information (financial reports, press releases, and business information) • Real-time monitoring of sales at various company locations and real-time calculations of revenues, costs, profits, and cash flows • E-mail communication systems

just-in-time deliveries to manufacturers and slice parts inventory costs. It also allows both manufacturers and their suppliers to gear production to match demand for both components and finished goods. Online systems that monitor actual sales permit more accurate demand forecasting, thereby helping both manufacturers and their suppliers adjust their production schedules as swings in buyer demand are detected.

Data sharing, starting with customer orders and going all the way back to components production, coupled with the use of enterprise resource planning (ERP) and manufacturing execution system (MES) software, can make custom manufacturing just as cheap as mass production—and sometimes cheaper. It can also greatly reduce production times and labor costs. J. D. Edwards, a specialist in ERP software, teamed with Camstar Systems, a specialist in MES software, to cut Lexmark's production time for computer printers from four hours to 24 minutes. General Motors, Ford Motor Company, and DaimlerChrysler have programs under way to incorporate e-procurement technologies into their supply chain systems as part of their plans to give buyers the option of having their new vehicles built to order and custom equipped.

The instant communications features of the Internet, combined with all the real-time data sharing and information availability, have the further effect of breaking down corporate bureaucracies and reducing overhead costs. The whole "back-office" data management process (order processing, invoicing, customer accounting, and other kinds of transaction costs) can be handled fast, accurately, and with less paperwork and fewer personnel. The time savings and transaction cost reductions associated with doing business online can be quite significant across both company and industry value chains.

How Internet Technology Improves Distribution Channel Efficiency

Internet technology alters the distribution portion of industry value chains in two basic ways: (1) it allows manufacturers to bypass wholesale/retailer dealers and sell directly to end users, and (2) it permits tighter collaboration between manufacturers and distribution channel partners to wring out distribution cost savings. Figure 5.2 in Chapter 5 depicted how software developers can use the Internet to create a low-cost value chain system for marketing and delivering their software directly to end users, thereby eliminating the markups imposed by traditional software distributors and retailers.

In addition to offering opportunities to cut out intermediaries, online retailers sometimes have asset-based advantages over traditional brick-and-mortar retailers. For instance, as of 1999 Amazon.com had invested about $56 million in fixed assets to achieve sales of $1.2 billion (equal to the sales of about 235 Barnes & Noble bookstores), whereas Barnes & Noble had invested about $462 million in 1,000-plus stores and was paying additional sums in rent and leasing fees.[3]

Internet-based collaboration between manufacturers and their distribution channel partners entails real-time data exchange; the use of online systems to lower manufacturer–distributor transactions costs (via online ordering and invoicing, online customer service, and electronic funds transfer to pay for shipments); and mutual efforts to speed deliveries and reduce inventories. Online data sharing allows manufacturers to monitor retail sales and inventories on a real-time basis, and it allows retailers to monitor manufacturer–wholesaler inventories and delivery times. Build-to-order manufacturing capabilities reduce the need for wholesalers and retailers to stock so many models and styles for immediate purchase. To the extent that manufacturers can quickly adjust the production and shipment of particular models and styles up or down in response to daily sales, distributors and dealers are less likely to be plagued with

> The Internet is the most powerful and broad-ranging tool currently available for improving the efficiency of company and industry value chains.

---

[3]As reported in *Business Week*, October 4, 1999, p. 90.

stockouts of fast-selling items or the need to have markdown sales to clear out over-stocked items. Tying shippers into online data-sharing systems can shorten delivery times, facilitate shipping in more economical volumes, and keep out-of-stock conditions to a minimum.

Utz Quality Foods, the number three maker of salty snacks in the United States, with sales of $200 million, has put in place an Internet-based sales-tracking system called UtzFocus that monitors sales of the company's chips and pretzel products at each supermarket and convenience store that carries the brand. The 500 drivers/sales-people who deliver Utz snacks directly to retail stores from Massachusetts to North Carolina use handheld computers to upload daily sales data (product by product and store by store) to headquarters. Managers carefully monitor the results to spot missed deliveries, pinpoint stores with lagging sales, and measure the effectiveness of special promotions. The UtzFocus system also keeps delivery personnel up-to-date on which stores are running specials on Utz products so that drivers can make sure they have ample supplies of the right products on their trucks—and since drivers get a 10 percent commission on sales, they have a stake in making UtzFocus work. The company has been installing machines with monitoring capabilities in all of its plants, and efforts are under way to hook them up to the company's intranet to generate real-time data on the usage of ingredients, measure how close chip-slicing machines are coming to the ideal thickness of .057 of an inch, track how many bags of chips the main factory's seven lines are turning out, and keep inventories of ingredients and plastic bags matched to production and sales requirements. Management has found these systems valuable in improving Utz's production and distribution operation and in boosting sales.

The Pervasive Benefits of Internet Applications

All told, the efficiency-enhancing potential of Internet technology on company and industry value chains is so pervasive that it is driving fundamental changes in how business is conducted internally and with suppliers, wholesalers, retailers, and end users. Today, companies across the world are pursuing the operational benefits of Internet technology and making the use of online systems and applications a normal part of everyday operations. An example of how the use of Internet technology alters manufacturing and industry value chains to increase efficiency, reduce costs, and streamline the production process is provided in Illustration Capsule 29.

HOW THE INTERNET RESHAPES THE COMPETITIVE ENVIRONMENT

One of the most important impacts of the Internet is how it alters the strength and balance of competitive forces, frequently intensifying the competitive pressures that companies face.

The Impact on Competitive Rivalry

The Internet widens the geographic market, increasing the number of rivals a company faces and escalating rivalry among sellers in adjacent geographic areas to unprecedented levels. In the brick-and-mortar world of retailing, a consumer electronics store in Tuscaloosa, Alabama, does not compete intensively with similar stores in Birmingham, 60 miles away. In the virtual world of the Internet, however, it competes with

illustration capsule 29
How the Internet Can Revamp
Manufacturing Economics and Industry Value Chains

In years past, PC companies like Compaq Computer and Hewlett-Packard made PCs for their corporate and business customers by "guesstimating" which models and options would be preferred, making variously equipped models in quantity, and then shipping them to resellers. Resellers not only maintained inventories of a wide selection of PC models, as well as parts to reconfigure those models to buyer specifications, but also handled marketing and servicing. However, pressured by the lower-cost economics of Dell Computer's build-to-order and sell-direct business model, many PC makers have been forced to revamp their value chain approach.

Recently, Compaq Computer and Hewlett-Packard (HP) entered into arrangements with Ingram Micro, the largest global PC distributor and reseller and also an assembler of PCs, and Solectron Corporation, a contract manufacturer of PCs, to supply custom PCs to their corporate customers. The new value chain model the partners worked out is depicted below. This new value chain model was expected to cut production costs substantially and reduce the amount of time a PC sat in inventory from as much as several months to a matter of hours.

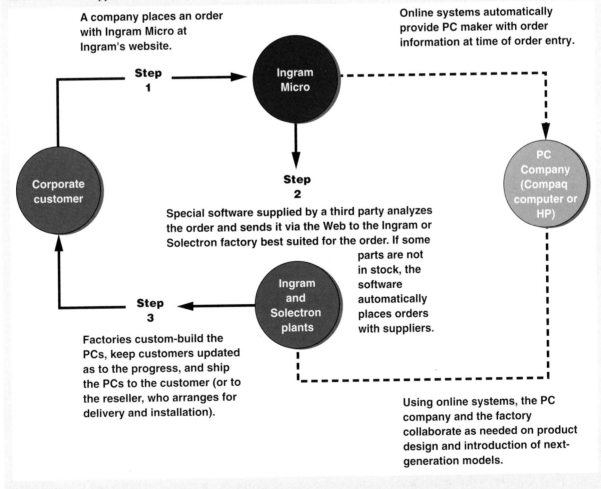

Source: Business Week, March 22, 1999, pp. EB 15 and EB 18, and information supplied by Ingram Micro, Inc., and Solectron Corp.

Growing use of the Internet by businesses and consumers widens the geographic market and intensifies rivalry among competing sellers.

online electronics retailers like Buy.com (whose actual locations are unknown and irrelevant) and the Web stores of electronics retailers in Birmingham become competitively relevant. In effect, the Internet eliminates the geographic protection of distance that has traditionally given small-town businesses an advantage of being the only source within reasonable driving distance—using the Internet, an individual can buy a digital camera from Buy.com rather than a local camera retailer, readily negotiate purchase of a vehicle with an auto dealer a hundred miles away, get auto financing and insurance from online providers, download recordings of music artists at EMusic.com, order toys instead of going to the local Wal-Mart or Toys "R" Us, and shop for any number of items at Amazon.com. Online shopping is not for everyone, of course, and local retailers will continue to enjoy geographic advantages, particularly for items that buyers prefer to inspect and shop for in person.

Rivalry among industry participants is often intensified by freshly launched e-commerce strategies of existing rivals and by the entry of enterprising dot-com rivals. A number of online sellers, believing their sell-direct approach gives them a lower-cost value chain than that of traditional brick-and-mortar retailers, have used the Internet to promote their lower prices, thus heightening price competition and shifting the competitive focus away from performance features, service, quality, and other attributes.

Rivalry is also increased when an industry's competitive structure pits pure online sellers against combination brick-and-click sellers against pure brick-and-mortar sellers. The varying emphasis that such rivals place on the Internet as a distribution channel for accessing buyers raises the stakes for which of the several channels for accessing customers will gain or diminish in importance. Effective use of the Internet adds a valuable weapon to the competitive arsenal of rival sellers, giving them yet another way to jockey for market position and competitive advantage.

The Impact on Barriers to Entry

Entry barriers into the e-commerce world are relatively low. It is relatively easy for dot-com start-ups to gain entry into some industries, and it is even easier for existing enterprises to expand into new geographic markets via online selling at their websites. Many of the value chain activities requisite for doing business on the Internet can be *outsourced* from suppliers offering specialized services and know-how. The software necessary for establishing an e-commerce website is readily available from any of several software providers, and the costs are relatively modest—for example, a bank can obtain the software needed to operate its own Internet banking site for under $50,000. There are companies that specialize in designing and maintaining Web pages, answering e-mail inquiries, and providing warehousing and shipping services. Dozens of companies operate "server farms" for the purpose of hosting the websites of client companies, thus relieving companies of the costs and hassle of purchasing their own servers and hiring personnel capable of providing customers with reliable, around-the-clock website access. Indeed, for a relatively modest $200 monthly fee and up-front costs of less than $5,000, Web hosting companies can design, operate, and maintain an online store on behalf of any small enterprise that wants to sell its products over the Internet. If need be, manufacturing and assembly can be contracted out to others as well.

The relative ease with which dot-com start-ups and expansion-minded existing enterprises can enter new geographic markets via online selling signals a strong likelihood that companies in many industries will experience a net increase in both the number of rivals and the intensity of the rivalry.

Perhaps the biggest entry barrier facing dot-com start-ups is the sometimes significant outlays required to create brand awareness and draw traffic to a new website. Even so, there are a number of online businesses that entrepreneurs can start and operate out of their home. *Relatively low entry barriers for dot-com start-ups explain why there are already hundreds of thousands of newly formed e-commerce firms and perhaps hundreds of thousands more to spring up around the world in years to come.*[4] And the number of existing companies that are selling their products online and extending their reach into new geographic markets is growing daily.

Thus, companies in many industries are likely to experience a net increase in the number of rivals and the intensity of rivalry in their geographic markets.

The Impact on Buyer Bargaining Power

The Internet makes it easy and convenient for buyers to gather extensive information about competing products and brands. The websites of rival sellers are only a few clicks apart and are "open for business" 24 hours a day every day of the year, giving buyers unprecedented ability to research the product offerings of rival sellers and shop the market for the best value. Wholesalers and retailers can use the information gleaned about the prices and features of rival manufacturers to decide which brands to stock and to pressure manufacturers to meet or beat the deals offered by rivals. Individual consumers, relying on their Internet research about the features, quality, and specifications of competing brands and the prices of different retailers, are at the very least in a position to make wiser, more informed choices of which brand to buy and which retailer to patronize. In some instances, consumers can haggle with retailers over price; some online retailers permit individuals to put up bids for how much they are willing to pay for an item. Informed buyers, knowledgeable about competing products and brands and alert to price differences among rival sellers, are thus in an enhanced bargaining position. Buyers can readily avoid sellers with high prices or unattractive product attributes. Such *widespread efforts among buyers to seek out the best deal foster active competition among rivals*—an outcome that tilts the competitive scales toward buyers and away from sellers.

> Extensive product and price knowledge on the part of buyers tends to reduce their switching costs—there's little reason for buyers to remain loyal to their present brand unless they are getting the best overall value.

Buyer bargaining power is enhanced in other ways as well. The Internet has created opportunities for manufacturers, wholesalers, retailers, and sometimes individuals to join online buying groups to pool their purchasing power and approach vendors for better terms than could be gotten individually. A multinational manufacturer's geographically scattered purchasing groups can use Internet technology to pool their orders with parts and components suppliers and bargain for volume discounts. Purchasing agents at some companies are banding together at third-party websites to pool corporate purchases to get better deals or special treatment—at PurchasingCenter.com, for example, companies can participate in a buying pool for industrial goods such as bits and motors.

> Extensive buyer use of the Internet often translates into greater buyer bargaining power.

On the other hand, the information that buyers can glean from the Internet does not always give them the upper hand in bargaining with sellers. There are instances where manufacturers can counter the bargaining power of influential wholesalers and retailers by using the Internet to begin selling directly to end users. Sellers are not entirely disadvantaged by buying pools, for example, because they gain ready access to large, well-defined groups of buyers, allowing them to save on selling and transactions costs. Many commercial airlines are encouraging air travelers to go directly to airline websites to check flight schedules, make reservations, and buy tickets, thus cutting deeply into the business of travel agents and lowering agent commissions. Manufacturers of

---

[4]For a discussion of how the Internet and e-commerce are attracting entrepreneurs and capital, see Gary Hamel, "Bringing Silicon Valley Inside," *Harvard Business Review* 77, no. 5 (September–October 1999), pp. 70–84.

consumer goods have also begun selling directly to consumers via the Internet. Sony has begun selling its electronics products directly to consumers in Japan (to the consternation of Japanese retailers); several automakers are testing Web-direct sales in Canada; and Mattel has begun selling its Barbie and Fisher-Price products online, a move that could counter the significant bargaining power of two of the biggest toy retailers—Wal-Mart and Toys "R" Us. At Nike.com, consumers can design their own shoes, choose colors, and even have custom phrases such as "Air Ryan" put on the back of the shoe. So whether the Internet tilts bargaining power more to buyers or more to sellers can vary with the situation.

The Impact on Supplier Bargaining Power and Supplier-Seller Collaboration

> Because the Internet allows companies to cast a wider geographic net for the best suppliers, shop the market for the best prices and values, and use e-markets to source certain items, it gives companies some measure of added bargaining power vis-à-vis suppliers.

All the various e-procurement options now available to companies through the Internet tend to give them added bargaining power vis-à-vis suppliers as compared with the pre-Internet period. There are several reasons why this is so. *The Internet makes it feasible for companies to reach beyond their borders to find the best suppliers and, further, to collaborate closely with them to achieve efficiency gains and cost savings.* While a number of companies have relied on foreign suppliers for low-cost components and assembly for some years, in a globally-connected world, the Internet allows many more companies to identify and then integrate foreign suppliers into their supply chain. Similarly, local and regional companies can extend their geographic search for suppliers via the Internet, shopping the market for candidates with better quality, prices, and/or capabilities than present suppliers.

In addition, companies can now use the services of online marketplaces, or "e-markets," to efficiently sort through all the various supplier choices. The roughly 1,500 e-markets now in operation can range from a website that simply aggregates the electronic catalogs of alternative suppliers to online auctions to online communities that use the instant communications capability of the Internet to match buyers and sellers. For example, FreeMarkets operates global e-sourcing of over 185 categories of goods and services from 150,000 different qualified suppliers in 70 countries. Global sourcing via e-markets benefits all participants. Buyers can conveniently locate qualified suppliers and get ready access to product information and competitive pricing. Suppliers are inclined to participate in e-markets because they gain wide access to buyers at low expense. For both buyers and sellers, e-markets entail low transactions costs, eliminating the sometimes tedious process of contacting one another via fax, e-mail, or telephone regarding pricing and availability. But, on balance, e-markets work in favor of buyers rather than suppliers. Via e-markets, a buyer with an urgent need for supplies can shop anonymously with thousands of potential suppliers, comparing prices and avoiding the potential of price gouging when they urgently need a particular item. E-markets lower buyer switching costs, thus fostering price competition among suppliers. Buyers can use the information about prices and alternative suppliers provided at various e-market sites to bargain more aggressively with present suppliers.

The Impact on Seller–Supplier Collaboration   As discussed earlier, e-procurement techniques foster greater seller–supplier collaboration across a wide front. Companies and their suppliers have strong incentive to leverage use of the Internet to streamline purchasing and inbound logistics activities—with both parties likely to realize substantial cost savings and operating improvements. Such collaboration promotes long-term partnerships with suppliers. However, most companies make it clear that they are willing to partner with a supplier only so long as that supplier continues to offer the best value. And to the extent that a company uses e-sourcing techniques to do a first-rate job of supply chain management, it may be able to put added competitive pressure on its rivals.

Overall Influence on an Industry's Competitive Structure

The preceding discussion should leave no doubt that Internet technology is driving important shifts in competitive forces—in the majority of industries, the results include intensified rivalry, greater entry threats, somewhat greater bargaining power over suppliers, a better bargaining positioning on the part of buyers, and incentives for all kinds of seller–supplier and seller–distributor collaboration. On balance, Internet technology tends to increase the strength of competitive pressures that companies face, thus tending to weaken industry attractiveness from a profit perspective. Internet technology allows a company to enhance its profitability and gain a competitive edge only to the extent that it can clearly do a better job of capitalizing on that technology than its rivals can.

> Internet technology applications are driving important shifts in an industry's competitive forces—shifts that, on balance, act to intensify competitive pressures and reduce profitability.

OTHER STRATEGY-SHAPING FEATURES OF INTERNET TECHNOLOGY

Aside from the impacts on company/industry value chains and on competitive forces, Internet technology has several other features that are strategically relevant:

- *The Internet is a force for globalizing competition and expanding the geographic arena in which firms have a market presence.* A company's Web store is open to buyers all over the world. Language barriers can be accommodated by giving site visitors the option to browse in any of several languages. A company whose products have globally appropriate attributes and can be shipped economically can pursue sales opportunities beyond its domestic borders at relatively low incremental costs. National boundaries mean little in an e-commerce world—for example, someone putting an item up for bid on eBay's auction site can connect with a buyer in Europe or Latin America, and eBay provides detailed instructions for shipping auctioned goods internationally. Growing numbers of transportation providers can handle shipments to any part of the world. Companies can use Internet technology to reach beyond their borders to find the best suppliers, and suppliers can participate in e-markets to broaden their geographic customer base.

> Distance and location matter less in a connected world; indeed, the Internet is a globalizing force that promotes the formation of a world community and fosters cross-country commerce in many categories of goods and services.

- *Internet and PC technologies are advancing at uncertain speeds and in unexpected directions.* A few years ago, both Intel and Microsoft were focusing all their energies on boosting the performance and capabilities of PCs and expanding the role of PCs as a multifunctional appliance in both businesses and households. Both companies misjudged the technological and business significance of the Internet and had to initiate crash programs to redirect their efforts. Also a few years ago, investors considered Iomega one of hottest growth stocks because of the potential for Iomega's Zip drives and high-capacity Zip disks to displace the standard 3.5-inch floppy disk. Iomega signed up numerous PC makers to include its Zip drive as an option on PCs. Its business model called for keeping prices attractively low on Zip drives to gain greater market penetration and then making money on the sale of the disks, which retailed for about $10 each. Just as the Zip drive was gaining a solid foothold in the market, the makers of computer hard drives unexpectedly hit upon ways to greatly increase hard drive capacity (to unheard of levels—20 to 80 gigabytes) and at the same time to lower hard drive production costs dramatically. PC makers and PC users quickly shifted to PCs with bigger hard drives and bypassed significant use of Iomega's Zip drives and disks. Iomega's stock price declined steadily and the company fell upon hard times, despite concerted efforts to come up with innovative new products.

Deployment of broadband technology to permit high-speed Internet access has turned out to be more complicated and has therefore proceeded more slowly than originally envisioned. The many companies involved in developing various facets of broadband technology have had problems deciding which of several technological approaches to employ. Lack of common standards and compatible technological approaches has obstructed mass adoption by businesses and households. Meanwhile, using digital subscriber line (DSL) technology to provide high-speed Internet access in homes and businesses has proved to involve higher-than-anticipated investments on the part of local telephone companies; moreover, installing DSL service takes technicians a fair amount of time, and users have reported annoying difficulties in getting DSL to interface smoothly with their PCs. Likewise, cable companies have encountered higher-than-expected investment and installation costs for cable modems. The so-far higher prices for DSL and cable modem Internet connections, together with the tedious process of working out all the bugs, have slowed the deployment of broadband technology and made it difficult for many PC and Internet features that require broadband (like high-quality streaming video and voice communications via PCs) to gain wide market penetration. The lagging deployment of broadband technology contributed to the burst of the dot-com bubble in 2000 and has slowed build-out of the global Internet infrastructure.

- *Internet technologies tend to reduce variable costs and tilt the cost structure more toward fixed costs.*[5] Putting Internet technology and applications in place is largely a fixed-cost exercise determined by the nature of the application and the scale of company operations (how many PCs, sets of software, servers, and related equipment are required and what the associated costs of IT support personnel are). Once the application is in place, there are very few variable costs associated with using it and, more important, the cost reductions flowing from the application are likely to take the form of labor savings, lower transactions costs, and other operating economies—all of which are usually classified as variable costs because they relate directly to unit sales volume. The high fixed cost/low variable cost structure of many e-commerce businesses accounts for why dot-com start-ups typically incur significant losses for the first few years as they invest in the internal infrastructure needed to support operations; profitability is achieved if and when sales volume climbs to levels sufficient to cover modest variable costs and the sizable built-in fixed costs of website operations. The high fixed-cost structure of e-commerce enterprises is exacerbated by fast-paced advances in website technology that mandate ongoing fixed-cost outlays to maintain, freshen, and upgrade the website. Obligatory outlays for next-generation Internet technologies drive up the break-even volume needed to achieve profitability; ever-higher break-even volumes often strain a company's ability to raise the necessary capital to fund operations until revenues grow sufficiently to turn the corner on profitability.

Many Internet applications entail high fixed costs and relatively low variable costs; many dot-com start-ups therefore incur losses until unit volume builds enough to cover the sizable built-in fixed costs of website operations.

---

[5]Porter, "Strategy and the Internet," p. 66.

- *The Internet results in much faster diffusion of new technology and new ideas across the world.* Companies in all countries now use Internet communications to monitor the latest technological and market developments. Breaking news takes only a matter of hours to spread across world markets. Details about new technologies or particular company and market developments can be gleaned quickly from a growing number and variety of websites. The exploding amount of information available on the Internet and the speed with which news travels make it unlikely that a company can conceal from competitors and other interested parties any market testing, facilities expansion, or efforts to launch new strategic initiatives. Innovative products or business concepts that gain acceptance in one part of the world market can be copied or adapted by opportunistic companies in other parts of the world. Some first-mover advantages may thus prove short lived.

  > The Internet speeds the diffusion of new technologies and business approaches, making first-mover advantages short lived.

- *Widespread adoption of Internet technology puts companies under the gun to move swiftly—"in Internet time" or "at Internet speed."* Just a few years ago, companies that were nimble and operated with short response times could expect to have a competitive advantage over slower-moving rivals. With companies everywhere now putting Internet technology in place and alert to the faster pace of events, speed is a condition of survival. New developments of one kind or another occur daily. Fast-moving market and competitive conditions sometimes put the businesses of late-movers at risk.

  > High-velocity change is the norm in the Internet era.

- *The Internet can be an economical means of delivering customer service.* The Internet provides innovative opportunities for handling customer service activities, supplementing or even replacing on-site personnel. By handling customer service issues over the Internet, companies need fewer people to send out to customers' locations, staff telephone lines at call centers, or respond to other customer communications. For example, using specially designed software, Dell Computer can take a digital reading of a customer's troubled computer system, pinpoint the problem, and send repairs over the Internet—all without human intervention.[6] Direct online customer support systems may well prove inexpensive and highly effective in a number of industries.

- *The capital for funding e-commerce businesses is readily available for ventures with solidly attractive business models and strategies and has dried up for ventures with dubious prospects.* Investor excitement about the business opportunities spawned by the Internet and Internet technology initially created a climate where venture capitalists were quite willing to fund start-up enterprises with most any plausible idea and business plan. Up until early 2000, when the investor euphoria over the Internet fell back to earth, dot-com start-ups found it unusually easy to raise hundreds of millions, even billions, of dollars to fund their proposed ventures.[7] More capital was raised through initial public offerings of stock in the 1990s than in all previous decades combined.[8] Internet initial public offerings (IPOs) became commonplace, and rapid bidding up of their stock prices put dot-com companies in a strong position to make acquisitions and to raise additional equity capital to fund start-up losses. But, in 2000, investors in start-up enterprises, concerned about sizable and sometimes mounting losses as revenues rose, began pressuring dot-com executives for better bottom-line performance. When it became

---

[6]As reported in *Business Week,* March 22, 1999, p. EB 31.
[7]See Hamel, "Bringing Silicon Valley Inside," pp. 77–83.
[8]According to a study cited on CNBC, January 6, 2000.

Although the gold rush investment mentality has come to a sudden and dramatic halt, dot-com ventures with real bottom-line promise can still attract start-up capital.

evident that the business models and strategies of many dot-com companies were flawed and held little prospect of generating near-term profitability, the stock prices of most all dot-com companies plummeted. Companies with sizable losses, negative cash flows, and a need for capital infusions to continue operations fell upon hard times; some went bankrupt, others slashed their operating budgets and laid off a big percentage of their work forces to conserve cash and gain time to reformulate their business and strategies. The result was a return to business fundamentals, with traditional bottom-line requirements dominating performance expectations. Notwithstanding the earlier excesses and fallout, venture capital and equity capital continues to be available to Internet-related companies that have a promising technology or idea, an attractive business model, and a well-thought-out strategic plan. But the investment climate is decidedly more skeptical, and the gold rush mentality appears to have come to a sudden halt. Capital requirements may well prove more of an entry barrier in the years ahead than they did in the immediate past.

THE DIFFICULTY OF RELYING ON INTERNET TECHNOLOGY TO GAIN SUSTAINABLE COMPETITIVE ADVANTAGE

Companies the world over are rapidly gaining experience in using Internet technology and learning how to capture the benefits it affords. Most all companies in most all industries are putting Internet applications into place. Scarcely any part of company and industry value chains is going untouched by online applications that ease and speed the exchange of real-time information. As might be expected with any significant new technological tool, experimentation is much in evidence and refinements are ongoing.

Most companies in most industries are deploying Internet applications, often utilizing off-the-shelf packages marketed by software developers.

But much Internet technology that has been put in place so far involves the use of generic, off-the-shelf software packages marketed by such vendors as Oracle, Commerce One, and Ariba and readily available to all companies. The Internet's "open platform" (that is, its standard architecture and navigation procedures), coupled with widespread reliance on generic software packages, makes it very difficult for a company to gain sustainable competitive advantage via aggressive, cutting-edge adoption of Internet technology. There's little to prevent rivals from obtaining comparable software and instituting similar online applications within a matter of months. For instance, a leading drugstore chain, CVS, implemented a sophisticated e-procurement system in 60 days.[9]

There's little chance that a company can gain competitive advantage implementing Internet applications with generic software packages when rivals are implementing much the same applications with much the same software.

Indeed, there's reason to believe that the vast majority of competitors in an industry are gravitating to many of the same operating-related Internet applications (e-procurement systems, extensive data sharing with value chain partners, e-communications, product information displays at company websites, online customer ordering systems) and achieving comparable operating benefits. Most companies today are scouring the market for best-of-breed Internet applications and are "e-commerce-ing" internal value chain activities to squeeze out cost savings and improve operating effectiveness. Given the broad, intensive efforts of companies in all industries to incorporate Internet technology, rare will be the company that can gain durable operating advantages by doing a world-class job of incorporating Internet technology across its value chain system. One company that has defied the odds of using the Internet to gain sustainable competitive

---

[9]Porter, "Strategy and the Internet," p. 71.

advantage is Dell Computer. Dell's deployment of Internet technology has contributed significantly to its emergence as the global low-cost provider of PC hardware and, so far, no rival has been able to match the sophistication and efficiency of Dell's e-commerce systems; however, a substantial portion of the Internet technology Dell employs is *proprietary* rather than based on generic applications—the Dell lesson is that proprietary Internet applications are harder for rivals to duplicate and therefore offer more durable competitive advantages.

The First-Mover Advantage Myth

During the Internet gold rush atmosphere of the 1990s, when the focus was on all the things the Internet could do and the dramatic speed with which Internet use was growing, conventional wisdom held that competitive advantage and above-average profitability would accrue to aggressive first-movers that developed snazzy and useful websites, generated high and growing traffic volumes from both repeat and first-time users, built widespread name recognition and a strong new-economy brand name, and cultivated website loyalty with fresh features and product offerings. First-movers, it was argued, could compound early successes by accumulating knowledge of site users' preferences and buying behavior and using that knowledge to provide tailored offerings, service, and convenience. Over time, then, they could solidify user loyalty by expanding into additional product categories that complemented their initial offerings or matched site-user profiles and buying preferences.

Furthermore, the advantages accruing to successful first-movers were allegedly durable because of (1) high switching costs on the part of site users and (2) "network effects," where a site's features became more valuable as more people used them.[10] Companies expected that site users, having invested time in becoming familiar with a particular site and being used to its conveniences, would not be inclined to incur the trouble and annoyance of finding, registering with, and learning to use a rival's site. Network effects are present for such applications as e-mail, auctions, message boards, instant messaging, and chat rooms—the more people using them, the more useful and effective they become. The greater the network effect associated with using a particular site, so the argument went, the more that competitive rivalry would become a winner-take-all contest in which one or maybe two sites would end up dominating the market.

But such thinking about the power and durability of so-called first-mover advantages, while appealing on the surface, proved flawed. In most cases switching costs are relatively low for Internet users. Rival sites not only are easy to locate and sometimes interesting to explore but also involve minimal registration time. Furthermore, site switching and multiple site use is getting easier. New Web technologies now enable customers to register their personal information and credit card numbers at a central location and then shop at different sites without entering the same data again and again. Content consolidation software allows users to build customized Web pages that draw and record information from many different Internet sites, eliminating the need to go back to sites over and over to retrieve the desired information. Growing use of extensible markup language (XML) standards frees companies from much of the burden of revising their online ordering systems when switching suppliers.

Meanwhile, companies found it harder than expected to establish dominating brand names that created high competitive barriers for rivals. While some dot-coms got

> Lower-than-expected switching costs, weaker-than-expected network effects, and weaker-than-expected brand-name power have resulted in low site-user loyalty, causing first-mover advantages, once thought powerful and durable, to evaporate quickly or never materialize at all.

---

[10]Ibid., p. 68.

something of a head start with big advertising campaigns, equally ambitious rivals wasted little time in countering with heavy advertising expenditures of their own. Advertising wars in several industries—online brokerage is a prime example—produced something of a standoff in brand-name recognition and brand-name power, with a number of rivals able to claim some success in attracting sales and winning market share. But very few dot-com companies that were first to enter a particular market have been able to overwhelm other online rivals with the power of their brand name and the attraction of their website. This is partly because many Internet users like to explore alternative sites, curious to see what they can find and what other sites have to offer.

At the same time, network effects have turned out to be fairly weak, further failing to block competition from rivals and making market dominance hard to achieve. For network effects to pose strong entry barriers to rivals and allow dominance, they need to be based on a company's own proprietary systems and features that prove hard for competitors to duplicate. But since the software needed to establish e-mail, chat rooms, message boards, and auctions is widely available, rival companies can easily incorporate such features as part of their websites with modest effort and cost. Moreover, Internet users are widely familiar with how e-mail, chat rooms, message boards, and auction software works, thus posing little or no switching costs to users in moving from site to site. America Online and eBay are perhaps the best examples of companies with proprietary systems that have exploited network effects successfully—but they are the exception rather than the rule.

On balance, it has proved hard for first-movers to achieve durable competitive advantage. Innovative fast-followers have found that they can compete effectively. Only a few Internet companies have converted their first-mover status into durable competitive advantages and powerful brand names—America Online, Amazon.com, Yahoo!, eBay, and Priceline.com are among the most prominent examples. And, of these, only America Online and eBay have demonstrated attractive profitability; Amazon has lost billions of dollars trying to establish itself as an online retailer and just recently is showing signs of becoming marginally profitable.

What the dot-com debacle has taught us is that being a first-mover in some absolute sense is not nearly as important to strategic success as being a smart-mover—it matters greatly whether or not a company's actions are based on sound revenue-cost-profit economics. *The proper goal of a first-mover is to be first to put together a combination of features, customer value, and revenue-cost-profit economics that unlocks an attractive market opportunity.*[11] Sometimes the company that unlocks a profitable market opportunity is the first one to try to do so, and sometimes it is not—but the company that comes up with the key is surely the smart-mover. One more point warrants mention: *Just because some dot-coms failed as first-movers does not render the concept of first-mover advantages invalid.* Such failures merely underscore the importance of (1) making smart, well-timed first moves and (2) capturing durable first-mover advantages as opposed to chasing fleeting or, worse, illusory advantages. Counting on all first-movers to stumble, fall, and come up empty-handed is a bad bet.

> Remarkably few first-movers have emerged as dominant market leaders in the Internet arena; even fewer have demonstrated attractive profitability.

> Because some dot-coms foolishly rushed to capture first-mover advantages that later proved fleeting or illusory does not mean that moving first is always a strategically perilous path or one lacking in potential competitive advantage.

STRATEGIC MISTAKES MADE BY EARLY INTERNET ENTREPRENEURS

While revolutionary new technologies often give entrepreneurs room to experiment with fresh strategies and business models, the rise of the Internet to center stage in the

---

[11]Gary Hamel, "Smart Mover, Dumb Mover," *Fortune*, September 3, 2001, p. 195.

economy during the 1990s resulted in an unusually large number of new business models and strategies, some of which violated fundamental business principles. The following sections look at a few of the strategic mistakes made by the early Internet entrepreneurs.

The Mistake of Ignoring Low Barriers to Entry

Dot-coms multiplied rapidly during the 1990s in part because venture capitalists and investors, enamored with the wide-ranging business opportunities afforded by the Internet and motivated by potentially huge capital gains if a new business hit it big, provided unprecedented amounts of capital to start-up enterprises. In many cases, venture capitalists and investors gave the business plans and proposed strategies of entrepreneurial start-ups little critical scrutiny. Believing that time was of the essence (because of assumed first-mover advantages), many investors committed huge sums of capital to start-up ventures without first requiring the start-ups to do the spadework and market testing necessary to demonstrate that their business models were viable. They often gave their go-ahead based solely on entrepreneurs' arguments that their innovative products would make the Internet work better or that their idea for an online business could cannibalize the business of traditional brick-and-mortar enterprises.

With ample capital available to hurdle whatever entry barriers might exist, start-up enterprises multiplied faster than was justified by the opportunities. Some pursued questionable "opportunities" and then fell by the wayside when buyer interest proved minimal to nonexistent. But where legitimate market opportunity existed, the artificially low entry barriers created by eager capital providers paved the way for market overcrowding and fierce rivalry—conditions conducive to lower-than-expected profitability or even losses, especially if revenues grew more slowly than anticipated. Although they had capital sufficient to see them through two or three years of operations, many start-ups began to burn through their cash reserves in 1999–2001 when competition stiffened, revenues fell short of projections, and investor skepticism about the viability of their business models and strategies dried up access to additional capital. Strategy overhauls, deep budget cutbacks, downsizing, and bankruptcies swept through much of the so-called Internet economy, exposing the flawed business models and strategic mistakes of the first wave of Internet entrepreneurs.

> Low entry barriers signal a strong threat of potential entry and nearly always produce a net gain in the number of competitors.

The ensuing shakeout has been basically healthy, producing sounder analysis of industry and competitive conditions and legitimate market opportunities and the use of better business models and strategies. The second wave of Internet investment and entrepreneurship, now under way, will likely produce a much bigger percentage of businesses and companies with staying power and acceptable profitability.

The Mistake of Competing Solely on the Basis of Low Price

A number of online retailers, believing that online sales entail inherently lower costs than brick-and-mortar retailing, cut their prices below those of traditional retailers and promoted the savings of buying online. Price became the predominant, attention-getting competitive variable, with e-tailers making little effort to tout the advantages of convenience, in-depth product information and product reviews, online service, specialized offerings for particular buyer needs and uses, customized or built-to-order products, and other value-added features that would justify charging prices more in line with those of traditional retailers. Competition in many product categories turned into a battle for market share and revenue growth, with sellers resorting to heavy advertising, discount specials, giveaway promotions, and incentives for distribution partners in order to build unit volume. The quest for near-term profits quickly deteriorated into a hope for profits later, if and when unit volume built up and the margins over variable costs generated enough dollars to more than cover fixed operating costs.

Meanwhile, bargain-hunting shoppers drawn by the prospect of saving money by buying online and coming to expect low online prices, became adept at searching the Internet for the lowest prices on items they wanted. This further fostered fierce price competition among Internet retailers and drove prices to rock-bottom levels that at best allowed meager profits and at worst inflicted losses on most sellers.

Such vigorous price competition and indiscriminate price discounting among e-tailers eroded industry attractiveness (just as it would in any industry) by undermining the market and competitive conditions requisite for good profitability. The price war atmosphere proved very difficult to reverse, especially once buyers grew accustomed to the discount-price strategies of many online retailers. Equally important, the excessive reliance on price cutting to attract buyers and win market share violated three tried-and-true strategic principles:

> Successful price discounting strategies are linked to a low-cost advantage over rivals and require low enough costs to make the discounted price profitable.

- Avoid competing on the basis of low price without first having a low-cost advantage over rivals.
- Do not cut prices so deep as to preclude an attractive profit margin at the low price.
- Incorporate and promote such value chain activities as superior service, build-to-order products, convenience, superior product information, and other attributes that deliver buyer value so as to command an attractively profitable price.

The Mistake of Selling below Cost and Trying to Make It Up with Revenues from Other Sources

Some online companies, like Buy.com, have sought to build a large and loyal clientele by selling products at deeply discounted prices—sometimes below cost (and occasionally at or below what it cost to purchase the items from manufacturers). Their business model called for attracting so many site visitors that they could sell sufficient advertising at their sites not only to cover the losses on items sold but also to eke out an acceptable profit. In addition to selling website advertising, e-tailers also pursued such other revenue supplements such as charging Internet partners for click-throughs to their websites and selling the data they collected from monitoring buyer browsing patterns and shopping preferences to manufacturers and others interested in learning about buyer use of the Internet.

> Dot-com business models that are highly dependent on advertising revenues to cover costs and earn a profit are highly risky at best and highly suspect at worst (witness the number that are losing money and have gone bankrupt).

There are three problems with this business model and strategy. One is the tendency (discussed in the preceding section) to employ price discounting strategies without a commensurate cost advantage and to ignore other differentiating value-added features to command higher prices. A second is becoming totally reliant upon ever-rising advertising revenues. Selling below cost means bigger and bigger dollar losses as unit volume grows; to cover these losses and also grow profits over time requires a bigger and bigger stream of revenues from advertising (or from other sources). To generate ever-growing ad revenues, a website must not only grow site traffic but also deliver value to advertisers—that is, advertisers must see a concrete payoff from their expenditures on the website.

The third problem is the strong bargaining power of Internet advertisers. Internet advertisers, initially enthusiastic about running ads on high-traffic websites to maximize "eyeball exposure" and willing to ad pay rates linked to the number of page views or unique site visitors, soon began questioning the value of what they were getting for their Internet advertising dollars. Research has indicated that banner ads are not especially effective—most Internet users pay them little or no attention. Recognizing their strong bargaining position (due to low switching costs and the online sellers' dependence on ad revenues), advertisers began demanding better results from the ad dollars they were spending. As starters, they insisted on a different set of metrics for determining advertising rates, refusing to pay ad rates based on eyeballs and instead bargaining for ad rates based on the number of click-throughs to their own website or on the even tougher standard of how many dollars of sales were generated from click-throughs to their website. Some advertisers began reallocating their Internet advertising budgets to those sites frequented by members of their target market rather than simply buying ads where they could maximize eyeballs or ad views.

As it became harder for ad-dependent websites to generate the sizable increases in advertising revenues they so desperately needed to operate profitably, the misguided nature of their strategy and business model became evident. Most users of this strategy have now scrambled to revise their business model. The revisions have involved raising the prices of their products to reflect smaller discounts off regular retail prices; seeking other revenue sources; coming up with more creative ways to display ads on their sites (using streaming video, audio, and different page positions); using targeted e-mail promotions to generate more buyer interest in their product offerings; and experimenting with expanded product offerings.

Not all dot-coms fell prey to the mistake of selling below cost, however. America Online and Microsoft Network have been able to generate heavy site traffic with multifunctional websites that offer news, weather, stock quotes, stock portfolio tracking, search engine capabilities, e-mail, online calendars and address books, chat rooms, personalized Web pages, and shopping opportunities. By creating content and features that attract millions of users daily, they are able to charge monthly subscription fees and sell advertising to companies wanting to get a message to site users—the same business model used by newspapers. Yahoo!, because it also attracts millions of site users daily, has covered the costs of site operations and earned profits by selling sufficient advertising—essentially the same business model used by the major TV networks. But these examples really are the exceptions that prove the rule—building a dot-com enterprise that is heavily dependent on advertising revenues for success is risky, and only a handful have done it successfully.

E-COMMERCE BUSINESS MODELS AND STRATEGIES FOR THE FUTURE

As use of the Internet continues to weave its way into the fabric of everyday business and personal life, and as the second wave of Internet entrepreneurship takes root, companies of all types are being forced to address how best to make the Internet a fundamental part of their business and their competitive strategies. It is thus worthwhile to take a hard look at what kinds of business models and strategies are attractive in the maturing Internet economy. What strategic principles need to be observed? What strategies and business models make sense for companies that operate exclusively online (i.e., "pure dot-com enterprises")? Is the combination brick-and-click model likely to be a good strategic positioning option? Are there any guidelines that can be prescribed for traditional businesses threatened in one way or another by e-commerce business approaches?

Business Models and Strategies for Pure Dot-Com Enterprises

As the second wave of the Internet revolution unfolds, the strategies of successful dot-com enterprises will exhibit several common features.

One of the lessons of the dot-com crash of 2000–2001 is that while the Internet does indeed change a lot of things about how business is conducted, it doesn't change everything. The Internet does not make the rules of competition obsolete, nor does it allow companies to ignore sound business fundamentals and strategy-making principles. Just like traditional companies, online companies must carefully analyze industry and competitive conditions and craft strategies well matched to these conditions—ill-conceived business models and strategies are just as perilous for online as for brick-and-mortar businesses.

That said, what guidelines can be given to pure dot-com enterprises on the road ahead? The evidence thus far indicates that successful dot-com strategies will incorporate the following features:

- *A distinctive strategy that delivers unique value to buyers and makes buying on-line very appealing*—Winning strategies almost always stand apart from the strategies of rivals and succeed in drawing buyers because of the value being delivered. This means competing on far more than just low price—indeed, many dot-coms are already working to tilt the basis for competing away from low price and more toward build-to-order products, convenience, superior product information, attentive online service, and other ways of making online buying an experience that buyers will find very appealing (as compared with buying from offline sellers). Distinctiveness also requires shrewd matching of strategy to the particulars of the company's immediate industry and competitive situation. It is unwise to think in terms of "e-business" or "e-commerce" strategies—winning strategies are almost never generic, off-the-shelf approaches broadly used by companies confronting different sorts of competitive pressures and market circumstances and having different resource strengths and weaknesses.

- *Deliberate efforts to engineer a value chain that enables differentiation or lower costs or better value for the money*—Striving for sustainable competitive advantage is just as essential for online businesses as for traditional brick-and-mortar businesses. This means employing strategies and value chain approaches that hold potential for low-cost leadership, competitively valuable differentiating attributes, or a best-cost provider advantage. If a firm is positioning itself to sell at below-market prices, then it must possess cost advantages in those activities it performs, and it must outsource the remaining activities to low-cost specialists. If an online firm is going to differentiate itself on the basis of a superior buying experience and top-notch customer service, then it needs to concentrate on having an easy-to-navigate website, an array of functions and conveniences for customers, "Web reps" who can answer questions online, and logistical capabilities to deliver products quickly. If it is going to deliver more value for the money, then it must manage value chain activities in a manner calculated to deliver upscale products and services at lower costs than rivals.

- *Clear focus on a limited number of competencies and a relatively specialized number of value chain activities in which proprietary Internet applications and capabilities can be developed*—low-value-added activities can be delegated to outside specialists. Durable competitive advantage is far more likely to emerge from efforts to develop proprietary Internet applications than from using the software packages of third-party developers. Outsourcing value chain activities where there is little potential for proprietary advantage or little opportunity for differentiation from rivals allows an enterprise to concentrate on what it can do best and the particular value chain activities where advantage can be gained.

- *Strong capabilities in cutting-edge Internet technology*—Ongoing advances in Internet technology are inevitable since, compared with other technologies throughout history, Internet technology is still in the early stages of development. The capability to employ state-of-the-art Internet technology is a definite key success factor.

- *Innovative marketing techniques that are efficient in reaching the targeted audience and effective in stimulating purchases (or boosting ancillary revenue sources like advertising)*—Marketing campaigns that just result in heavy site traffic and lots of page views are seldom sufficient; the best test of effective marketing is the ratio at which page views are converted into revenues and profits (the "look-to-buy" ratio). For example, in 2001 the traffic at brokerage firm Charles Schwab's website averaged 40 million page views per day and resulted in an average of $5 million daily in online commission revenues; in contrast, Yahoo!'s site traffic averaged 1.2 *billion* page views daily but generated only about $2 million in daily revenues.

- *Minimal reliance on ancillary revenues*—Online businesses have to charge fully for the value delivered to customers rather than subsidizing artificially low prices and collecting revenues from advertising and other ancillary sources. Companies should view revenue extras as a way to *boost* the profitability of an already profitable core businesses, not as a means of covering core business losses.

- *An innovative, fresh, and entertaining* website—Just as successful brick-and-mortar retailers employ merchandising strategies to keep their stores fresh and interesting to shoppers, online retailers must be good Web merchandisers, exerting ongoing efforts to add innovative site features and capabilities, enhance the look and feel of their sites, heighten viewer interest with audio and live video, and have fresh product offerings and special promotions. Web pages need to be easy to read and interesting, with lots of eye appeal. Website features that are distinctive, engaging, and entertaining add value to the experience of spending time at the site and are thus strong competitive assets. The online auction house eBay, for example, has gone to great lengths to foster a strong sense of community among users and visitors as part of its strategy to set itself apart from rival auction sites. Moreover, websites have to be cleverly marketed. Unless Web surfers hear about the site, like what they see on their first visit, and are intrigued enough to return again and again, a pure dot-com company will not generate the traffic and revenues necessary to its survival.

The Issue of Broad versus Narrow Product Offerings   Given that shelf space on the Internet is unlimited, online sellers have to make shrewd decisions about how to position themselves on the spectrum of broad versus narrow product offerings. A one-stop shopping strategy like that employed by Amazon.com has the appealing economics of helping spread fixed operating costs over a wide number of items and a large customer base. Amazon has diversified its product offerings beyond books to include music, online auctions, electronics, toys, video games, camera and photo products, health and beauty aids, software, kitchen and houseware items, tools and hardware, cars, and outdoor living products; it has also allowed small specialty-item e-tailers to market their products on the Amazon website. The company's tag line "Earth's Biggest Selection" seems accurate: In 2001, Amazon had some 34 million customers at websites in the United States, Britain, France, Germany, and Japan. Other e-tailers, such as eToys, have adopted classic focus strategies—building a website aimed at a sharply defined target audience shopping for a particular product or product category. Focusers seek to build customer loyalty based on attractively low prices or better value or wide selection of models and styles or convenient service or nifty options or some other differentiating attribute. They pay special attention to the details that will please their narrow target audience.

The Order Fulfillment Issue   Another big strategic issue for dot-com retailers is whether to perform order fulfillment activities internally or to outsource them. Building central warehouses, stocking them with adequate inventories, and developing systems to pick, pack, and ship individual orders requires substantial start-up capital but may result in lower overall unit costs than would paying the fees of order fulfillment specialists who make a business of providing warehouse space, stocking inventories, and shipping orders for e-tailers. Outsourcing is likely to be economical unless an e-tailer has high unit volume and the capital to invest in its own order fulfillment capabilities. Buy.com, an online superstore consisting of some 30,000 items, obtains products from name-brand manufacturers and uses outsiders to stock and ship those products; thus, its focus is not on manufacturing or order fulfillment but rather on selling.

Opportunities for Unconventional Business Models and Strategies
There are times when the Internet presents opportunities for using unconventional or truly innovative business models and strategies. Aside from ventures like Yahoo!, America Online, and Microsoft Network that depend on advertising for profitability, Web entrepreneurs have hit upon several other revenue-building techniques for trying to profit from website operations:

- *Subscription fees*—Some information providers, like the online edition of *The Wall Street Journal,* charge subscription fees. A number of Internet users are willing to pay Consumer Reports Online $3.95 a month or $24 per year because the information provided on the website is valuable in making wise purchases. But subscription fees generate considerable resistance from Internet users, most of whom are unwilling to pay for content and are adept at scouring the Web to find the information they want for free.

- *Transaction* fees—Rather than selling their software outright at a set price per copy, some Internet software developers have adopted a business model whereby they collect a small fee for every transaction their software performs. Inktomi sells its search engine software to companies and Web portals, collecting a fraction-of-a-cent fee per Web page retrieved from each query. The fee-per-transaction model provides a continuing revenue stream and is particularly appealing to software makers when (1) there's a potential for the software to perform millions of transactions and (2) the number of websites requiring such software is relatively small (thus limiting the potential number of copies that can be sold). Customers for such software may readily accept a fee-per-transaction arrangement because it lowers their front-end costs for the software and they end up paying only for actual services rendered.

- *Pay-per-use*—Developers of online video games and educational programs are pursuing a pay-per-use business model. For about $3, entertainment seekers can log on to PlayNow.com and run a program as much as they like during a 48-hour

illustration capsule 30
Priceline.com's Unique "Name Your Own Price" Business Model

Priceline.com's business involves operating an "e-market" for the buyers and sellers of airline tickets, hotel rooms, rental cars, new cars, home financing, and long-distance calling. The company's business model is simple but innovative. Take the case of airline tickets: Buyers submit a "guaranteed offer" (typically the lowest price they think they can get away with) to Priceline and secure the offer with a credit card. Priceline compares the bids with confidential discounted fares on unsold seats supplied to it by participating airline partners. If Priceline can buy a ticket from an airline partner's unsold seat inventory at a low enough cost, add a margin to cover its own costs along with a margin for profit, and resell the ticket to the buyer at the buyer's bid price, it executes the transaction. Bidders learn within 15 minutes whether their bid is accepted. Once accepted, a bid cannot be canceled, and bidders must agree to whatever flight schedule is submitted (layovers of two to five hours may be involved at connecting airports if flights with shorter connection times are filled to capacity).

"Name your own price" bids for hotel rooms, rental cars, new cars, and long-distance calling work in essentially the same fashion. In the case of home mortgages and home equity loans, bidders specify the amount to be financed and the interest rate they are willing to pay.

Priceline.com's patented "virtual business model" has allowed for rapid scaling using the Internet. The company is able to electronically communicate consumer bids directly to the appropriate sellers, who in turn electronically match the bids against their unsold inventory. Sellers can opt to fill as many of the guaranteed bids as they wish. By requiring consumers to be flexible with respect to brands, sellers, and/or product features, Priceline's e-market enables sellers to generate incremental revenue without disrupting their existing distribution channels or retail pricing structures.

In 2001, Priceline was able to accept about half of the bids it received for airline tickets, hotel rooms, and rental cars. Overall, it was booking purchases for about 1 million of the 2 million bids it received monthly. Approximately 11 million customers had made purchases from Priceline, and over 60 percent of its purchase offers came from repeat customers. The company reported revenues of $365 million in the second quarter of 2001 and earnings of $2.8 million—its first quarterly profit since its founding.

Source: Information posted at Priceline.com (www.priceline.com) as of August 9, 2001.

period. The business models of fee-based online education programs are basically no different from those used by universities and the marketers of professional seminars and training programs.

Priceline.com's business model, described in Illustration Capsule 30, embraces an unconventional and innovative business approach that is demonstrating profitability.

"Brick-and-Click" Strategies: An Appealing Middle Ground

Many traditional retailers, threatened by the potential of consumers using the Internet as a substitute for shopping at local stores, have opened their own online shopping sites. Toys "R" Us, for example, has launched a website to combat eToys (now bankrupt) and other online toy merchants. Merrill Lynch now offers customers the option of trading online to discourage commission-sensitive customers from moving their accounts to cheaper online brokerages such as Charles Schwab, E*Trade, and TD Waterhouse. Wal-Mart, too, has launched a website.

Combination brick-and-click strategies that give customers the option of shopping either online or in stores can be an effective way of combating competition from pure

In many industries and product categories, brick-and-click strategies are competitively superior to pure dot-com strategies.

online retailers, especially when customers sometimes want to see and touch a product before making a purchase or prefer to transact some aspects of their business in person. In banking, a brick-and-click strategy can easily defeat a pure dot-com strategy because banking customers like the convenience of local branches and ATMs for depositing checks and getting cash while using online systems to pay bills, check account balances, and transfer funds. Wells Fargo, Bank One, Citibank, Bank America, and other established banks have far more customers going online to do banking transactions than do the Internet banks (most of which are struggling because they do not have a local presence).

Brick-and-mortar businesses can enter online retailing at relatively low cost—all they need is a Web store and systems for filling and delivering individual customer orders. Brick-and-click strategies have two big appeals: they are an economic means of expanding a company's geographic reach, and they give both existing and potential customers another choice of how to communicate with the company, shop for product information, make purchases, or resolve customer service problems. In a number of instances, brick-and-mortar businesses can shift to brick-and-click strategies by using their current distribution centers and/or retail stores for picking orders from on-hand inventories and making deliveries. A number of supermarket chains, taking note of the $800 million market for online grocery sales, have begun giving shoppers the option of ordering groceries online. A chain's website may forward the order to the supermarket nearest the customer's home; store personnel then gather the order in shopping carts and deliver the groceries to the customer's home—usually the same day the order is placed. At Walgreen's, a leading drugstore chain, customers can order a precription online and then pick it up personally at the location they patronize (the drive-through window, in some cases). Many industrial distributors are finding it efficient for customers to place their orders over the Web rather than phoning them in or waiting for salespeople to call in person.

In the years to come, traditional brick-and-mortar companies will make use of Internet technology and e-commerce capabilities such a core part of their operations that the distinction between dot-com and traditional businesses will be reduced to whether a company uses the Internet as its exclusive distribution channel or as one of several channels.

Web ordering from distributors/retailers can thus actually increase the value of local brick-and-mortar facilities, which serve as local stocking and delivery/pick-up points for nearby buyers and thus eliminate the need for central warehousing and the expense of shipping orders via FedEx, United Parcel Service, or other carrier. In a number of businesses, it is cheaper to make bulk deliveries to local warehouses or retail stores than it is to pick, pack, and ship individual customer orders from a central warehouse, thus giving brick-and-click retailers a cost advantage over e-tailers. Illustration Capsule 31 describes how Office Depot has successfully made the Internet a core part of its business and migrated from a traditional brick-and-mortar strategy to a competitively attractive brick-and-click strategy.

Internet Strategies for Traditional Businesses

Because the Internet has forever altered how companies and customers learn about each other, communicate, and transact business, few if any businesses can escape making some effort to integrate the Internet into their operations and to use Internet applications to squeeze out cost savings from the performance of value chain activities. This much is a given—anything less will put a company at a competitive disadvantage. Thus, the real strategic issues for a traditional business boil down to two things: (1) what specific Internet applications to implement and (2) how to make the Internet a fundamental part of its strategy—in particular, how much emphasis to place on the Internet as a distribution channel for accessing buyers.

Most companies are well along in the process of implementing Internet applications to improve operational effectiveness and value chain efficiency. Which Internet

illustration capsule 31
Office Depot's Brick-and-Click Strategy

Office Depot was in the first wave of retailers to adopt an e-commerce strategy. In 1996, it began allowing business customers to use the Internet to place orders. These customers could thus avoid having to make a call, generate a purchase order, and pay an invoice—while still getting same-day or next-day delivery.

Office Depot built its Internet business around its existing network of 750 retail stores; 30 warehouses; 2,000 delivery trucks; $1.3 billion in inventories; and phone-order sales department, which handled large business customers. It already had a solid brand name and enough purchasing power with its suppliers to counter discount-minded e-commerce rivals trying to attract buyers on the basis of super-low prices. Office Depot's incremental investment to enter the e-commerce arena was extremely low since all it needed to add was a website where customers could see pictures and descriptions of the items it carried, their prices, and in-stock availability; marketing costs have been less than $10 million.

In setting up customized Web pages for 37,000 corporate and educational customers, Office Depot designed sites that allowed the customer's employees varying degrees of freedom to buy supplies. A clerk might be able to order only copying paper, toner cartridges, computer disks, and paper clips up to a preset dollar limit per order, while a vice president might have carte blanche to order any item Office Depot sold. Office Depot's online prices were the same as its store prices; the company's strategy was to promote Web sales on the basis of service, convenience, and lower customer costs for order processing and inventories.

In 2001, 40 percent of Office Depot's major customers were ordering most of their supplies online because of the convenience and the savings in transactions costs. Bank of America, for example, was ordering 85 percent of its office supplies online from Office Depot.

Customers reported that using the website cut their costs of issuing purchase orders and paying invoices by up to 80 percent; plus, Office Depot's same-day or next-day delivery capability gave them the ability to reduce the amount of office supplies they kept in inventory.

Website sales cost Office Depot less than $1 per $100 of goods ordered, compared with about $2 for phone and fax orders. And since Web sales eliminated the need to key in transactions, order-entry errors have been virtually eliminated and product returns cut by 50 percent. Billing is handled electronically.

Office Depot's online unit accounted for $982 million in sales in 2000, nearly double that of Staples, its largest competitor. Office Depot expected its online sales in 2001 to increase by 50 percent, to $1.5 billion, contributing 14 percent to the company's overall sales and making the company the second-largest online retailer behind Amazon. Unlike those of Amazon, however, Office Depot's online operations have been profitable from the start. Online rivals like AtYourOffice.com (with 30,000 items available online) and TotalOfficeSupply.com had captured less than 5 percent of the online market as of early 2001.

Industry experts believe that Office Depot's success is based on the company's philosophy of maintaining a strong link between the Internet and its stores. "Office Depot gets it," noted one industry analyst. "It used the Net to build deeper relationships with customers."

Source: "Office Depot's e-Diva," *BusinessWeek Online* (www.businessweek.com), August 6, 2001; Laura Lorek, "Office Depot Site Picks Up Speed," *Interactive Week* (www.zdnet.com/intweek), June 25, 2001; "Why Office Depot Loves the Net," *Business Week*, September 27, 1999, pp. EB 66, EB 68; and *Fortune*, November 8, 1999, p. 17.

applications make the most sense for a traditional business vary from industry to industry and company to company—generic prescriptions are suspect. But the compilation in Table 7.1(p. 230) provides a good menu of possibilities.

Although many companies have websites, more than a website is needed if the Internet is to be an integral part of a company's strategy for competing. *Decisions have to be made about how to use the Internet in positioning the company in the marketplace*—whether to use the Internet as the company's *exclusive* channel for accessing customers, as the company's *primary* distribution channel, as *one of several* important distribution channels, as a *secondary or minor* channel, or as simply a vehicle for disseminating product information (with traditional distribution channel partners making

Companies today must wrestle with the issue of how to use the Internet in positioning themselves in the marketplace—whether to use the Internet as the company's only distribution channel, as the primary distribution channel, as one of several distribution channels, as a minor channel, or just as a vehicle for disseminating product information (with traditional distribution partners making all sales to end users).

all sales to end users). While it is hard to be definitive about how brick-and-mortar businesses can make strategic use of the Internet (since the answers vary according to specific industry and company circumstances), the following Internet-related strategy initiatives merit consideration:

- *Operating a website that provides existing and potential customers with extensive product information but that relies on click-throughs to distribution channel partners to handle orders and transactions (or, in the case of retailers, that informs site visitors where nearby retail stores are located)*—This is an attractive market positioning option for manufacturers and/or wholesalers that have established retail dealer networks and face nettlesome channel conflict issues if they try to sell online in direct competition with their dealers. A manufacturer or wholesaler that aggressively pursues online sales to end users is signaling both a weak strategic commitment to its dealers and a willingness to cannibalize dealers' sales and growth potential. To the extent that strong partnerships with wholesale and/or retail dealers are critical to accessing end users, initiating online sales with a brick-and-click strategy is a very tricky road to negotiate. A manufacturer's efforts to try to use its website to sell around its dealers is certain to anger distribution channel allies, many of whom may stock the brands of several manufacturers. If these dealers respond by putting more effort into marketing the brands of rival manufacturers who don't sell online, a manufacturer may stand to lose more sales through its dealers than it gains from its own online sales effort. Moreover, dealers may be in better position to employ a brick-and-click strategy than a manufacturer is because dealers have a local presence to complement their online sales approach (which consumers may find more appealing). Consequently, in industries where the strong support and goodwill of dealer networks is essential, manufacturers may conclude that their website should be designed to partner with dealers rather than compete with them—just as the auto manufacturers are doing with their franchised dealers.

- *Using online sales as a relatively minor distribution channel for achieving incremental sales, gaining online sales experience, and doing marketing research*—If channel conflict poses a big obstacle to online sales, or if only a small fraction of buyers can be attracted to make online purchases, then companies are well advised to pursue online sales with the strategic intent of gaining experience, learning more about buyer tastes and preferences, testing reaction to new products, creating added market buzz about their products, and boosting overall sales volume a few percentage points. Nike, for example, has begun selling some of its footwear online, giving buyers the option of specifying certain colors and features. Such a strategy is unlikely to provoke much resistance from dealers and could even prove beneficial to dealers if footwear buyers become enamored with custom-made shoes that can be ordered through and/or picked up at Nike retailers. A manufacturer may be able to glean valuable marketing research data from tracking the browsing patterns of website visitors and incorporating what generates the most interest and appeal into its mainstream product offerings. The behavior and actions of Web surfers are a veritable gold mine of information for companies seeking to respond more precisely to buyer preferences.

- *Employing a brick-and-click strategy to sell directly to consumers and to compete directly with traditional wholesalers and retailers*—Software developers have used the Internet as a highly effective distribution channel to complement sales through wholesalers and retailers. Selling online directly to end users has the advantage of cutting out the costs and margins of software wholesalers and retailers (often 35 to 50 percent of the retail price). In addition, allowing customers to download their software purchases immediately via the Internet eliminates the costs of producing and packaging CDs. However, software developers are still strongly motivated to continue to distribute their products through wholesalers and retailers (to maintain broad access to existing and potential users who, for whatever reason, may be reluctant to buy online). Despite the channel conflict, there are two major reasons why manufacturers might want to aggressively pursue online sales and establish the Internet as an important new distribution channel alongside traditional channels: (1) they make a far bigger profit margin from online sales and (2) it helps educate buyers to the ease and convenience of purchasing online, thus encouraging more and more buyers to migrate to buying online (where company profit margins are greater). This sell-direct positioning strategy is well suited for companies in industries where there are good long-term prospects for the Internet to *evolve* into a company's primary distribution channel. In such instances, incurring the channel conflict in the short term and competing against traditional distribution allies makes good strategic sense.

- *Making greater use of build-to-order manufacturing and assembly as a basis for bypassing traditional distribution channels entirely*—This positioning strategy is well suited for manufacturers that can also use the Internet to shift to build-to-order manufacturing and assembly and then economically ship custom orders directly to buyers. Companies in the PC industry have already used the Internet to make cost-effective build-to-order options a reality. Similarly, several motor vehicle companies have initiated actions to streamline build-to-order manufacturing capbilities and reduce delivery times from 30 to 60 days on custom orders to as few as 5 to 10 days; most all vehicle manufacturers already have software on their Internet sites that permits motor vehicle shoppers to select the models, colors, and optional equipment they would like to have. Online music retailers already have options that allow shoppers to create custom CDs from a library of artists' recordings; however, using the Internet, recording studios can market recordings directly, allowing music lovers to download digital files of the particular artist recordings they want and bypassing distributors and music retailers to capture the full retail price for themselves. In industries where build-to-order options can result in substantial cost savings along the industry value chain and permit sizable price reductions, companies have to consider making build-to-order and sell-direct an integral part of their market positioning strategy. Over time, such a strategy could minimize (or eventually cannibalize entirely) sales through distribution allies.
- *Building systems to pick and pack products that are shipped individually or else contracting with order fulfillment specialists to handle this function*—Order fulfillment is important for companies that opt for brick-and-click strategies.

key|points

The Internet is an integrated network of users' connected computers, banks of servers and high-speed computers, digital switches and routers, and telecommunications equipment and lines. The Internet represents an important new technological tool for companies to improve operating efficiency and operating effectiveness, and it is an important new distribution channel that greatly extends a company's geographic market reach. The strategic skill with which a company deploys Internet technology and makes the Internet a central part of its strategy holds enormous potential for affecting its competitiveness vis-à-vis rivals.

Internet technology applications open up a host of opportunities for reconfiguring company and industry value chains in ways that yield big gains in supply chain efficiency, internal operating efficiency, and distribution channel efficiency. As Table 7.1 illustrates, there are opportunities for Internet technology applications throughout company value chains. Today, the vast majority of companies are pursuing the operational benefits of Internet technology and making the use of online systems and applications a normal part of everyday operations. Hence, the once-critical distinction between old-economy and new-economy companies is fast becoming meaningless.

Growing use of the Internet and Internet technology produces important shifts in an industry's competitive forces—intensifying rivalry, posing greater entry threats, enhancing the bargaining position of customers, improving the bargaining position of companies vis-à-vis suppliers, and possibly improving the bargaining position of companies vis-à-vis powerful distributors and retailers. On balance, Internet technology tends to increase the strength of competitive pressures that companies face, thus tending to weaken industry attractiveness from the standpoint of earning above-average profits.

In addition, the Internet and Internet technology applications have several other effects:

- Globalizing competition and expanding the geographic arena in which firms have a market presence.
- Producing much faster diffusion of new technology and new ideas across the world.
- Reducing variable costs and tilting the cost structure toward fixed costs.
- Being an economical means of delivering customer service.
- Putting companies under the gun to move swiftly—"at Internet speed."

The Internet is still in its early stages, and next-generation advances are likely to be somewhat unpredictable with regard to the speed at which they will occur and the direction they will take.

During the rise of the Internet to center stage in the economy during the 1990s, a number of dot-com start-ups deployed business models and strategies that were either flawed or ill conceived. Three of the most common mistakes were (1) ignoring low barriers to entry, (2) relying too heavily on price discounting without having a commensurate cost advantage, and (3) selling below cost and trying to cover the losses with ancillary revenue sources.

Moreover, many dot-coms erroneously believed that high switching costs on the part of site users and "network effects" (increases in the value of a site's features as more people use them) would give them durable first-mover advantage protection against competition from rivals. In fact, switching costs have proved relatively low for Internet users, and network effects have proved weak, producing greater competitive rivalry than expected. At the same time, very few dot-com companies that were first to enter a particular market have been able to overwhelm other online rivals with the power of their brand name, despite having spent heavily (and sometimes extravagantly) on advertising.

On the road ahead, dot-com success is likely to come from (1) having a distinctive strategy that delivers unique value to buyers and makes buying online very appealing; (2) engineering a value chain that enables differentiation, lower costs, or better value;

(3) focusing on a limited number of competencies and performing a relatively special- ized number of value chain activities where proprietary Internet applications and ca- pabilities can be developed; (4) using innovative marketing techniques that are efficient in reaching the targeted audience and effective in stimulating purchases (or boosting ancillary revenue sources like advertising); (5) having strong capabilities in cutting-edge Internet technology; (6) relying minimally on ancillary revenues; and (7) keeping websites fresh, entertaining, and exciting. Dot-coms also have to figure out economical solutions to order fulfillment and choose wisely between broad or narrow product offerings.

Combination brick-and-click strategies, which give customers the option of shop- ping either online or in stores, can be an effective way of combating competition from pure online retailers, especially when customers sometimes want to see and touch a product before making a purchase or prefer to transact some aspects of their business in person. Brick-and-click strategies have two big appeals: they are an economical means of expanding a company's geographic reach and they give both existing and po- tential customers *another choice* of how to communicate with the company, shop for product information, make purchases, or resolve customer service problems. In a num- ber of products and businesses, it is cheaper to make bulk deliveries to local ware- houses or retail stores than it is to pick, pack, and ship individual customer orders from a central warehouse, thus giving brick-and-click retailers a cost advantage over e-tailers. In a number of product markets, brick-and-click strategies are likely to prove more competitively powerful than pure dot-com strategies.

Whether to make the Internet an integral feature of strategy is an issue that many traditional companies are struggling with. Decisions have to be made about whether to use the Internet as the company's *exclusive* channel for accessing customers, as the company's *primary* distribution channel, as *one of several* important distribution chan- nels, as a *secondary or minor* channel, or as simply a vehicle for disseminating product information (with traditional distribution channel partners making all sales to end users). The choice often hinges on how best to resolve channel conflict. Manufacturers and/or wholesalers that depend heavily on established retail dealer networks trigger complicated channel conflict issues if they try to sell online in direct competition with their dealers. Where channel conflict is a big obstacle to deploying a brick-and-click strategy, traditional companies may be well advised to enter online sales only with the intent of gaining experience with online sales, researching the preferences of site visi- tors, testing reaction to new products, creating added market buzz about their products, and perhaps boosting overall sales volume a few percentage points—as well as avoid- ing any appearance of moving to cannibalize the sales of distribution partners. Other manufacturers may pursue online sales more aggressively, endeavoring to establish the Internet as an important new distribution channel alongside traditional channels (be- cause they make a far bigger profit margin from online sales). Still others may find it strategically advantageous to use the Internet to shift to build-to-order manufacturing and assembly and then economically ship custom orders directly to buyers, perhaps sig- naling a long-term competitive effort to bypass traditional distribution channels entirely.

suggested |readings

Batua, Anitish; Prabhudev Konana; Andrew B. Whinston; and Fang Yin. "Managing E- Business Transformation: Opportunities and Value Assessment." *Sloan Management Review*, forthcoming.

Evans, Philip, and Thomas S. Wurster. "Getting Real about Virtual Commerce." *Harvard Business Review* 77, no. 6 (November–December 1999), pp. 84–94.

Griffith, David A., and Jonathan W. Palmer. "Leveraging the Web for Corporate Success." *Business Horizons* 42, no. 1 (January–February 1999), pp. 3–10.

Hamel, Gary. "Bringing Silicon Valley Inside." *Harvard Business Review* 77, no. 5 (September–October 1999), pp. 70–84.

Porter, Michael E. "Strategy and the Internet." *Harvard Business Review* 79, no. 3 (March 2001), pp. 63–78.

Rosenoer, Johnathan; Douglas Armstrong; and J. Russell Gates. *The Clickable Corporation: Successful Strategies for Capturing the Internet Advantage.* New York: Free Press, 1999.

Tapscott, Don; David Ticoll; and Alex Lowy. *Digital Capital: Harnessing the Power of Business Webs.* Boston, MA: Harvard Business School Press, 2000.

chapter | eight

Tailoring Strategy to Fit Specific Industry and Company Situations

The best strategy for a given firm is ultimately a unique construction reflecting its particular circumstances.

—Michael E. Porter

Competing in the marketplace is like war. You have injuries and casualties, and the best strategy wins.

—John Collins

It is much better to make your own products obsolete than allow a competitor to do it.

—Michael A. Cusamano and Richard W. Selby

In Chapters 6 and 7 we examined strategies for competing in global and e-commerce environments. This chapter looks at the strategy-making task in nine other commonly encountered situations:

1. Companies competing in emerging industries of the future.
2. Companies competing in turbulent, high-velocity markets.
3. Companies competing in mature, slow-growth industries.
4. Companies competing in stagnant or declining industries.
5. Companies competing in fragmented industries.
6. Companies pursuing rapid growth.
7. Companies in industry leadership positions.
8. Companies in runner-up positions.
9. Companies in competitively weak positions or plagued by crisis conditions.

We selected these situations to shed still more light on the whys and hows of matching strategy (1) to industry and competitive conditions and (2) to a company's own resource strengths and weaknesses, competitive capabilities, opportunities and threats, and market position. When you finish this chapter, you will have a strong appreciation for why it is so important for managers to customize a company's strategy and you'll have a better idea of how to weigh the various external and internal considerations and balance the pros and cons of the various strategic options that are open to a company.

STRATEGIES FOR COMPETING IN EMERGING INDUSTRIES OF THE FUTURE

An *emerging industry* is one in the early, formative stage. Examples include wireless Internet communications, high-definition TV, assisted living for the elderly, online education, and electronic banking. Most companies racing against rivals to establish a strong foothold in an emerging industry of the future are in a start-up mode; they are perfecting technology, adding people, acquiring or constructing facilities, gearing up operations, and trying to broaden distribution and gain buyer acceptance. The business models and strategies of companies in an emerging industry are unproven—what appears to be a promising business concept and strategy may stall out, never passing the test of generating attractive bottom-line profitability. Often, there are important product design problems and technological problems that remain to be worked out.

Competing in emerging industries thus presents managers with some unique strategy-making challenges:[1]

- Because the market is new and unproven, there may be much speculation and many opinions about how it will function, how fast it will grow, and how big it will get. The little historical data available is virtually useless in making sales and profit projections. There's lots of guesswork about how rapidly buyers will be attracted to use the product and how much they will be willing to pay for it. For example, digital video disc (DVD) players were much slower to catch on than expected. Currently, there is great uncertainty about how quickly the demand for high-definition TV sets will grow once the law requiring all U.S. TV stations to broadcast digital programs goes into effect in 2003.

- In many cases, much of the technological know-how underlying the products of emerging industries is proprietary and closely guarded, having been developed in-house by pioneering firms; patents and unique technical expertise are key factors in securing competitive advantage. In other cases, the technology is multifaceted, entailing parallel or collaborative efforts on the part of several enterprises and perhaps competing technological approaches.

- Often, there is no consensus regarding which of several competing technologies will win out or which product attributes will prove decisive in winning buyer favor. Until market forces sort these things out, wide differences in product quality and performance are typical. Rivalry therefore centers on each firm's efforts to get the market to ratify its own strategic approach to technology, product design, marketing, and distribution.

- Entry barriers tend to be relatively low, even for entrepreneurial start-up companies. Large, well-known, opportunity-seeking companies with ample resources and competitive capabilities are likely to enter if the industry has promise for explosive growth or if its emergence threatens their present business. For instance, many traditional local telephone companies, seeing the potent threat of wireless communications technology, have opted to enter the mobile communications business in one way or another.

- Strong experience curve effects may be present, allowing significant cost and price reductions as volume builds.

- Since in an emerging industry all buyers are first-time users, the marketing task is to induce initial purchase and to overcome customer concerns about product features, performance reliability, and conflicting claims of rival firms.

---

[1]Michael E. Porter, *Competitive Strategy* (New York: Free Press, 1980), pp. 216–23.

- Many potential buyers expect first-generation products to be rapidly improved, so they delay purchase until technology and product design mature.
- Sometimes, firms have trouble securing ample supplies of raw materials and components (until suppliers gear up to meet the industry's needs).
- Undercapitalized companies, finding themselves short of funds to support needed R&D and get through several lean years until the product catches on, end up merging with competitors or being acquired by financially strong outsiders looking to invest in a growth market.

The two critical strategic issues confronting firms in an emerging industry are (1) how to finance initial operations until sales and revenues take off, and (2) what market segments and competitive advantages to go after in trying to secure a front-runner position.[2] Competitive strategies keyed either to low cost or differentiation are usually viable. Focusing makes good sense when resources and capabilities are limited and the industry has too many technological frontiers or too many buyer segments to pursue at once. The lack of established "rules of the game" gives industry participants considerable freedom to experiment with a variety of different strategic approaches. Nonetheless, a firm with solid resource capabilities, an appealing business model, and a good strategy has a golden opportunity to shape the rules and establish itself as the recognized industry front-runner.

Dealing with all the risks and opportunities of an emerging industry is one of the most challenging business strategy problems. To be successful in an emerging industry, companies usually have to pursue one or more of the following strategic avenues:[3]

1. Try to win the early race for industry leadership with risk-taking entrepreneurship and a bold, creative strategy. Broad or focused differentiation strategies keyed to technological or product superiority typically offer the best chance for early competitive advantage.

2. Push to perfect the technology, to improve product quality, and to develop additional attractive performance features.

3. As technological uncertainty clears and a dominant technology emerges, adopt it quickly. (However, while there's merit in trying to be the industry standard bearer on technology and to pioneer the dominant product design, firms have to beware of betting too heavily on their own preferred technological approach or product design—especially when there are many competing technologies, R&D is costly, and technological developments can quickly move in surprising new directions.)

4. Form strategic alliances with key suppliers to gain access to specialized skills, technological capabilities, and critical materials or components.

5. Acquire or form alliances with companies that have related or complementary technological expertise so as to outcompete rivals on the basis of technological superiority.

6. Try to capture any first-mover advantages associated with early commitments to promising technologies, allying with the most capable suppliers, expanding product selection, improving styling, capturing experience curve effects, and getting well positioned in new distribution channels.

> Strategic success in an emerging industry calls for bold entrepreneurship, a willingness to pioneer and take risks, an intuitive feel for what buyers will like, quick response to new developments, and opportunistic strategy making.

---

[2]Charles W. Hofer and Dan Schendel, *Strategy Formulation: Analytical Concepts* (St. Paul, MN: West Publishing, 1978), pp. 164–65.

[3]Phillip Kotler, *Marketing Management,* 5th ed. (Englewood Cliffs, NJ: Prentice Hall, 1984), p. 366, and Porter, *Competitive Strategy,* chapter 10.

7. Pursue new customer groups, new user applications, and entry into new geographical areas (perhaps utilizing strategic partnerships or joint ventures if financial resources are constrained).

8. Make it easy and cheap for first-time buyers to try the industry's first-generation product. Then as the product becomes familiar to a wide portion of the market, begin to shift the advertising emphasis from creating product awareness to increasing frequency of use and building brand loyalty.

9. Use price cuts to attract the next layer of price-sensitive buyers into the market.

The short-term value of winning the early race for growth and market share leadership has to be balanced against the longer-range need to build a durable competitive edge and a defendable market position.[4] Well-financed outsiders are certain to move in with aggressive strategies as industry sales start to take off and the perceived risk of investing in the industry lessens. A rush of new entrants, attracted by the growth and profit potential, may crowd the market and force industry consolidation to a smaller number of players. Resource-rich latecomers, aspiring to industry leadership, may be able to become major players by acquiring and merging the operations of weaker competitors and then launching strategic offensives to build market share and gain quick brand-name recognition. Strategies must be aimed at competing for the long haul; often, this means sacrificing some degree of short-term profitability in order to invest in the resources, capabilities, and market recognition needed to sustain early successes.

Young companies in fast-growing markets face three strategic hurdles: (1) managing their own rapid expansion, (2) defending against competitors trying to horn in on their success, and (3) building a competitive position extending beyond their initial product or market. Up-and-coming companies can help their cause by selecting knowledgeable members for their boards of directors, by hiring entrepreneurial managers with experience in guiding young businesses through the start-up and takeoff stages, by concentrating on out-innovating the competition, and perhaps by merging with or acquiring another firm to gain added expertise and a stronger resource base.

> The early leaders in an emerging industry cannot afford to relax and rest on their laurels; they must drive forward to strengthen their resource capabilities and build a position strong enough to ward off newcomers and compete successfully for the long haul.

STRATEGIES FOR COMPETING IN TURBULENT, HIGH-VELOCITY MARKETS

More and more companies are finding themselves in industry situations characterized by rapid-fire technological change, short product life cycles (because of the pace with which next-generation products are being introduced), entry of important new rivals into the marketplace, frequent launches of new competitive moves by rivals (including mergers and acquisitions to build a stronger, if not dominant, market position), and rapidly evolving customer requirements and expectations—all occurring at once. Since news of this or that important competitive development is a daily happening, it is an imposing task just to monitor and assess developing events. High-velocity change is plainly the prevailing condition in personal computer hardware and software, video games, networking, wireless telecommunications, medical equipment, biotechnology, prescription drugs, and in the growing number of industries being swept along by the torrential changes in the whole arena of cyberspace.

> High-velocity change is the striking feature of contemporary business.

---

[4]Hofer and Schendel, *Strategy Formulation,* pp. 164–65.

The central strategy-making challenge in a turbulent market environment is managing change.[5] As illustrated in Figure 8.1, a company can assume any of three strategic postures in dealing with high-velocity change:[6]

- *It can react to change.* For instance, it can respond to a rival's new product with a better product. It can counter an unexpected shift in buyer tastes and buyer demand by redesigning or repackaging its product, or shifting its advertising emphasis to different product attributes. Reacting is a defensive strategy and is therefore unlikely to create fresh opportunity, but it is nonetheless a necessary component in a company's arsenal of options.

- *It can anticipate change.* Anticipation entails looking ahead to analyze what is likely to occur and then preparing and positioning for that future. It entails studying buyer behavior, buyer needs, and buyer expectations to get insight into how the market will evolve, then lining up ahead of time the necessary production and distribution capabilities. Like reacting to change, anticipating change is still fundamentally defensive in that forces outside the enterprise are in the driver's seat. Anticipation, however, can open up new opportunities and thus is a better way to manage change than just pure reaction.

- *It can lead change.* Leading change entails initiating the market and competitive forces that others must react and respond to—*it is an offensive strategy aimed at putting a company in the driver's seat.* Leading change means being first to market with an important new product or service. It means being the technological leader, rushing next generation products to market ahead of rivals, and having products whose features and attributes shape customer preferences and expectations. It means proactively seeking to shape the rules of the game.

> Reacting to change and anticipating change are basically defensive postures; leading change is an offensive posture.

As a practical matter, a company's approach to managing change should, ideally, incorporate all three postures (though not in the same proportion). The best-performing companies in high-velocity markets consistently seek to lead change with proactive strategies. Even so, an environment of relentless change makes it incumbent on any company to anticipate and prepare for the future and react in timely manner to unpredictable or uncontrollable new developments.

> Industry leaders are proactive agents of change, not reactive followers and analyzers. Moreover, they improvise, experiment, and adapt rapidly.

Competitive success in fast-changing markets tends to hinge on a company's ability to improvise, experiment, adapt, reinvent, and regenerate as market and competitive conditions shift rapidly and sometimes unpredictably.[7] It has to constantly reshape its strategy and its basis for competitive advantage. While the process of altering offensive and defensive moves every few months or weeks to keep the overall strategy closely matched to changing conditions is inefficient, the alternative—a fast-obsolescing strategy—is worse. The following strategic moves seem to offer the best payoffs:

[5]The strategic issues companies must address in fast-changing market environments are thoroughly explored in Richard A. D'Aveni, *Hyper-Competition: Managing the Dynamics of Strategic Maneuvering* (New York: Free Press, 1994). See also Richard A. D'Aveni, "Coping with Hypercompetition: Utilizing the New 7S's Framework," *Academy of Management Executive* 9, no. 3 (August 1995), pp. 45–56; and Bala Chakravarthy, "A New Strategy Framework for Coping with Turbulence," *Sloan Management Review* (Winter 1997), pp. 69–82.

[6]Shona L. Brown and Kathleen M. Eisenhardt, *Competing on the Edge: Strategy as Structured Chaos* (Boston: Harvard Business School Press, 1998), pp. 4–5.

[7]Ibid., p. 4.

figure 8.1   **Meeting the Challenge of High-Velocity Change**

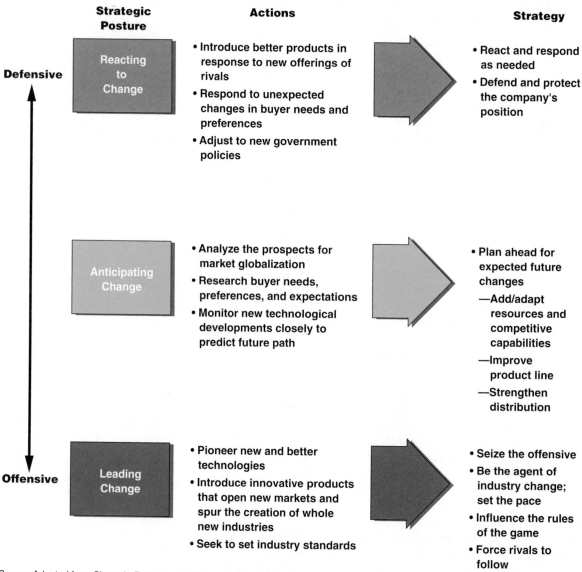

Source: Adapted from Shona L. Brown and Kathleen M. Eisenhardt, *Competing on the Edge: Strategy as Structured Chaos* (Boston: Harvard Business School Press, 1998) p. 5.

   1. *Invest aggressively in R&D to stay on the leading edge of technological know-how.* Translating technological advances into innovative new products (and remaining close on the heels of whatever advances and features are pioneered by rivals) is a necessity in industries where technology is the primary driver of change. But it is often desirable to focus the R&D effort in a few critical areas not only to avoid stretching the company's resources too thin but also to deepen the firm's expertise, master the technology, fully capture learning-curve effects, and become the dominant leader in a particular technology or product category.[8] When a fast-evolving market environment

---

[8]For insight into building competitive advantage through R&D and technological innovation, see Shaker A. Zahra, Sarah Nash, and Deborah J. Bickford, "Transforming Technological Pioneering into Competitive Advantage," *Academy of Management Executive* 9, no. 1 (February 1995), pp. 32–41.

entails many technological areas and product categories, competitors have little choice but to employ some type of focus strategy and concentrate on being the leader in a particular product/technology category.

2. *Develop and maintain the organizational capability to respond quickly to the moves of rivals and surprising new developments.* Because no company can predict or foresee all of the changes that will occur, it is crucial to have the organizational capability to react, respond, and improvise quickly. This means shifting resources internally, adapting existing competencies and capabilities, creating new competencies and capabilities, and not falling far behind rivals. Companies that are habitual late-movers are destined to be industry also-rans.

3. *Rely on strategic partnerships with outside suppliers and with companies making tie-in products.* In many high-velocity industries, technology is branching off to create so many new technological paths and product categories that no company has the resources and competencies to pursue them all. Specialization (to promote the necessary technical depth) and focus strategies (to preserve organizational agility and leverage the firm's expertise) are desirable strategies. Companies build their competitive position not just by strengthening their own internal resource base but also by partnering with those suppliers making state-of-the-art parts and components and by collaborating closely with both the developers of related technologies and the makers of tie-in products. For example, personal computer companies like Gateway, Dell, Compaq, and Acer rely heavily on the makers of faster chips, the makers of monitors and screens, the makers of built-in faxes and modems, and software developers for innovative advances in PCs. None of the PC makers have done much in the way of integrating backward into parts and components because they have learned that the most effective way to provide PC users with a state-of-the-art product is to outsource the latest, most advanced components from technologically sophisticated suppliers who make it their business to stay on the cutting edge of their specialization and who can achieve economies of scale by mass-producing components for many PC assemblers. An outsourcing strategy also allows a company the flexibility to replace suppliers that fall behind on technology or product features or that cease to be competitive on price. The managerial challenge here is to strike a good balance between building a rich internal resource base that, on the one hand, keeps the firm from being at the mercy of its suppliers and allies and, on the other hand, maintains organizational agility by relying on the resources and expertise of capable (and perhaps "best-in-world") outsiders.

4. *Initiate fresh actions every few months, not just when a competitive response is needed.* In some sense, change is partly triggered by the passage of time rather than solely by the occurrence of events. A company can be proactive by making *time-paced moves*—introducing a new or improved product every four months, rather than when the market tapers off or a rival introduces a next-generation model.[9] Similarly, a company can expand into a new geographic market every six months rather than waiting for a new market opportunity to present itself; it can also refresh existing brands every two years rather than waiting until their popularity wanes. The keys to successfully using time-pacing as a strategic weapon are choosing intervals that make sense internally and externally, establishing an internal organizational rhythm for change, and choreographing the transitions. 3M Corporation has long pursued an objective of having 25 percent of its revenues come from products less than four years old, a force that established the rhythm of change and created a relentless push for new products. Recently, the firm's

---

[9]Brown and Eisenhardt, *Competing on the Edge,* pp. 14–15. See, also, Kathleen M. Eisenhardt and Shona L. Brown, "Time Pacing: Competing in Markets That Won't Stand Still," *Harvard Business Review* 76, no. 2 (March–April 1998), pp. 59–69.

CEO upped the tempo of change at 3M by increasing the percentage from 25 percent to 30 percent.

5. *Keep the company's products and services fresh and exciting enough to stand out in the midst of all the change that is taking place.* One of the risks of rapid change is that products and even companies can get lost in the shuffle of events. The marketing challenge here is to keep the firm's products and services in the limelight and, further, to keep them innovative and well matched to the changes that are occurring in the marketplace.

In fast-paced markets, in-depth expertise, speed, agility, innovativeness, opportunism, and resource flexibility are critical organizational capabilities.

Cutting-edge know-how and first-to-market capabilities are very valuable competitive assets in fast-evolving markets. Moreover, the action-packed competition demands that a company have quick reaction times and flexible, adaptable resources—organizational agility is a huge competitive asset. Even so, companies will make mistakes and some things a company does are going to work better than others. When a company's strategy doesn't seem to be working well, it has to quickly regroup—probing, experimenting, improvising, and trying again and again until it finds something that strikes the right chord with buyers and that puts it in sync with market and competitive realities.

STRATEGIES FOR COMPETING IN MATURING INDUSTRIES

A maturing industry is one that is moving from rapid growth to significantly slower growth. An industry is said to be mature when nearly all potential buyers are already users of the industry's products; market demand thus consists mainly of replacement sales to existing users, with growth hinging on the industry's ability to attract new buyers and convince existing buyers to up their usage. Consumer goods industries that are mature typically have a growth rate under 5 percent—roughly equal to the growth of the customer base or economy as a whole.

An industry's transition to maturity does not begin on an easily predicted schedule. Industry maturity can be forestalled by the emergence of new technological advances, product innovations, or other driving forces that keep rejuvenating market demand. Nonetheless, when growth rates do slacken, the onset of market maturity usually produces fundamental changes in the industry's competitive environment:[10]

1. *Slowing growth in buyer demand generates more head-to-head competition for market share.* Firms that want to continue on a rapid-growth track start looking for ways to take customers away from competitors. Outbreaks of price cutting, increased advertising, and other aggressive tactics to gain market share are common.

2. *Buyers become more sophisticated, often driving a harder bargain on repeat purchases.* Since buyers have experience with the product and are familiar with competing brands, they are better able to evaluate different brands and can use their knowledge to negotiate a better deal with sellers.

3. *Competition often produces a greater emphasis on cost and service.* As sellers all begin to offer the product attributes buyers prefer, buyer choices increasingly depend on which seller offers the best combination of price and service.

---

[10]Porter, *Competitive Strategy,* pp. 238–40.

4. *Firms have a "topping-out" problem in adding new facilities.* Reduced rates of industry growth mean slowdowns in capacity expansion for manufacturers and slowdowns in new store growth for retail chains. With slower industry growth, adding too much capacity too soon can create oversupply conditions that adversely affect company profits well into the future.

5. *Product innovation and new end-use applications are harder to come by.* Producers find it increasingly difficult to create new product features, find further uses for the product, and sustain buyer excitement.

6. *International competition increases.* Growth-minded domestic firms start to seek out sales opportunities in foreign markets. Some companies, looking for ways to cut costs, relocate plants to countries with lower wage rates. Greater product standardization and diffusion of technological know-how reduce entry barriers and make it possible for enterprising foreign companies to become serious market contenders in more countries. Industry leadership passes to companies that succeed in building strong competitive positions in most of the world's major geographic markets and in winning the biggest global market shares.

7. *Industry profitability falls temporarily or permanently.* Slower growth, increased competition, more sophisticated buyers, and occasional periods of overcapacity put pressure on industry profit margins. Weaker, less-efficient firms are usually the hardest hit.

8. *Stiffening competition induces a number of mergers and acquisitions among former competitors, drives the weakest firms out of the industry, and produces industry consolidation in general.* Inefficient firms and firms with weak competitive strategies can achieve respectable results in a fast-growing industry with booming sales. But the intensifying competition that accompanies industry maturity exposes competitive weakness and throws second- and third-tier competitors into a survival-of-the-fittest contest.

Strategic Moves in Maturing Industries

As the new competitive character of industry maturity begins to hit full force, any of several strategic moves can strengthen a firm's competitive position: pruning the product line, improving value chain efficiency, trimming costs, accelerating sales promotion efforts, expanding internationally, and acquiring struggling competitors.[11]

Pruning Marginal Products and Models   A wide selection of models, features, and product options sometimes has competitive value during the growth stage, when buyers' needs are still evolving. But such variety can become too costly as price competition stiffens and profit margins are squeezed. Maintaining many product versions works against achieving design, parts inventory, and production economies at the manufacturing levels and can increase inventory stocking costs for distributors and retailers. In addition, the prices of slow-selling versions may not cover their true costs. Pruning marginal products from the line opens the door for cost savings and permits more concentration on items whose margins are highest and/or where a firm has a competitive advantage.

More Emphasis on Value Chain Innovation   Efforts to "reinvent" the industry value chain can have a fourfold payoff: lower costs, better product or service

---

[11]The following discussion draws on Porter, *Competitive Strategy,* pp. 241–46.

quality, greater capability to turn out multiple or customized product versions, and shorter design-to-market cycles. Manufacturers can mechanize high-cost activities, re-design production lines to improve labor efficiency, build flexibility into the assembly process so that customized product versions can be easily produced, and increase use of advanced technology (robotics, computerized controls, and automatic guided vehicles). Suppliers of parts and components, manufacturers, and distributors can collaborate on the use of Internet technology and e-commerce techniques to streamline various value chain activities and implement cost-saving innovations.

A Stronger Focus on Cost Reduction   Stiffening price competition gives firms extra incentive to drive down unit costs. Company cost-reduction initiatives can cover a broad front. Some of the most frequently pursued options are pushing suppliers for better prices, implementing tighter supply chain management practices, cutting low-value activities out of the value chain, developing more economical product designs, reengineering internal processes using e-commerce technology, and shifting to more economical distribution arrangements.

Increasing Sales to Present Customers   In a mature market, growing by taking customers away from rivals may not be as appealing as expanding sales to existing customers. Strategies to increase purchases by existing customers can involve providing complementary items and ancillary services, and finding more ways for customers to use the product. Convenience stores, for example, have boosted average sales per customer by adding video rentals, automated teller machines, gasoline pumps, and deli counters.

Purchasing Rival Firms at Bargain Prices   Sometimes a firm can acquire the facilities and assets of struggling rivals quite cheaply. Bargain-priced acquisitions can help create a low-cost position if they also present opportunities for greater operating efficiency. In addition, an acquired firm's customer base can provide expanded market coverage and opportunities for greater scale economies. The most desirable acquisitions are those that will significantly enhance the acquiring firm's competitive strength.

Expanding Internationally   As its domestic market matures, a firm may seek to enter foreign markets where attractive growth potential still exists and competitive pressures are not so strong. Many multinational companies are expanding into such emerging-country markets as China, India, Brazil, Argentina, and Malaysia, where the long-term growth prospects are quite attractive. Strategies to expand internationally also make sense when a domestic firm's skills, reputation, and product are readily transferable to foreign markets. For example, even though the U.S. market for soft drinks is mature, Coca-Cola has remained a growth company by upping its efforts to penetrate foreign markets where soft-drink sales are expanding rapidly.

Building New or More Flexible Capabilities   The stiffening pressures of competition in a maturing or already mature market can often be combated by strengthening the company's resource base and competitive capabilities. This can mean adding new competencies or capabilities, deepening existing competencies to make them harder to imitate, or striving to make core competencies more adaptable to changing customer requirements and expectations. Microsoft has responded to competitors' challenges by expanding its already large cadre of talented programmers. Chevron has developed a best-practices discovery team and a best-practices resource map to enhance the speed and effectiveness with which it is able to transfer efficiency improvements from one oil refinery to another.

Strategic Pitfalls in Maturing Industries

Perhaps the biggest strategic mistake a company can make as an industry matures is steering a middle course between low cost, differentiation, and focusing—blending efforts to achieve low cost with efforts to incorporate differentiating features and efforts to focus on a limited target market. Such strategic compromises typically result in a firm ending up stuck in the middle, with a fuzzy strategy, too little commitment to winning a competitive advantage, an average image with buyers, and little chance of springing into the ranks of the industry leaders.

Other strategic pitfalls include being slow to adapt existing competencies and capabilities to defend against stiffening competitive pressures, concentrating more on protecting short-term profitability than on building or maintaining long-term competitive position, waiting too long to respond to price cutting by rivals, overexpanding in the face of slowing growth, overspending on advertising and sales promotion efforts in a losing effort to combat the growth slowdown, and failing to pursue cost reduction soon enough or aggressively enough.

> One of the greatest strategic mistakes a firm can make in a maturing industry is pursuing a compromise between low-cost, differentiation, and focusing such that it ends up "stuck in the middle," with a fuzzy strategy, an average image, an ill-defined market identity, no competitive advantage, and little prospect of becoming an industry leader.

STRATEGIES FOR FIRMS IN STAGNANT OR DECLINING INDUSTRIES

Many firms operate in industries where demand is growing more slowly than the economywide average or is even declining. Although harvesting the business to obtain the greatest cash flow, selling out, or preparing for closedown are obvious end-game strategies for uncommitted competitors with dim long-term prospects, strong competitors may be able to achieve good performance in a stagnant market environment.[12] Stagnant demand by itself is not enough to make an industry unattractive. Selling out may or may not be practical, and closing operations is always a last resort.

Businesses competing in stagnant or declining industries must resign themselves to performance targets consistent with available market opportunities. Cash flow and return-on-investment criteria are more appropriate than growth-oriented performance measures, but sales and market-share growth are by no means ruled out. Strong competitors may be able to take sales from weaker rivals, and the acquisition or exit of weaker firms creates opportunities for the remaining companies to capture greater market share.

> Achieving competitive advantage in stagnant or declining industries usually requires pursuing one of three competitive approaches: focusing on growing market segments within the industry, differentiating on the basis of better quality and frequent product innovation, or becoming a lower cost producer.

In general, companies that succeed in stagnant industries employ one of three strategic themes:[13]

1. *Pursue a focused strategy aimed at the fastest-growing market segments within the industry.* Stagnant or declining markets, like other markets, are composed of numerous segments or niches. Frequently, one or more of these segments is growing rapidly, despite stagnation in the industry as a whole. An astute competitor who

---

[12]R. G. Hamermesh and S. B. Silk, "How to Compete in Stagnant Industries," *Harvard Business Review* 57, no. 5 (September–October 1979), p. 161.

[13]Ibid., p. 162.

zeroes in on fast-growing segments and does a first-rate job of meeting the needs of buyers comprising these segments can often escape stagnating sales and profits and even gain decided competitive advantage. For instance, both Ben & Jerry's and Häagen-Dazs have been successful focusing on the growing luxury or super-premium segment of the otherwise stagnant market for ice cream; revenue growth and profit margins are substantially higher for high-end ice creams sold in supermarkets and in scoop shops than is the case in the other market segments.

2. *Stress differentiation based on quality improvement and product innovation.* Either enhanced quality or innovation can rejuvenate demand by creating important new growth segments or inducing buyers to trade up. Successful product innovation opens up an avenue for competing besides meeting or beating rivals' prices. Differentiation based on successful innovation has the additional advantage of being difficult and expensive for rival firms to imitate. Sony has built a solid business selling high-quality TVs, an industry where market demand has been relatively flat in the world's industrialized nations for some years.

3. *Strive to drive costs down and become the industry's low-cost leader.* Companies in stagnant industries can improve profit margins and return on investment by pursuing innovative cost reduction year after year. Potential cost-saving actions include (*a*) cutting marginally beneficial activities out of the value chain, (*b*) outsourcing functions and activities that can be performed more cheaply by outsiders, (*c*) redesigning internal business processes to exploit cost-reducing e-commerce technologies, (*d*) consolidating underutilized production facilities, (*e*) adding more distribution channels to ensure the unit volume needed for low-cost production, (*f*) closing low-volume, high-cost retail outlets, and (*g*) pruning marginal products from the firm's offerings. Nucor Steel has been one of the most successful steel producers in the United States for the past decade because of its innovative production methods and low-cost operating culture; Nucor is widely considered to be one of the most efficient producers of steel products in the world and the low-cost leader in the North American market.

These three strategic themes are not mutually exclusive.[14] Introducing innovative versions of a product can *create* a fast-growing market segment. Similarly, relentless pursuit of greater operating efficiencies permits price reductions that create price-conscious growth segments. Note that all three themes are spinoffs of the generic competitive strategies, adjusted to fit the circumstances of a tough industry environment. The most attractive declining industries are those in which sales are eroding only slowly, there is large built-in demand, and some profitable niches remain.

The most common strategic mistakes companies make in stagnating or declining markets are (1) getting trapped in a profitless war of attrition, (2) diverting too much cash out of the business too quickly (thus further eroding performance), and (3) being overly optimistic about the industry's future and spending too much on improvements in anticipation that things will get better.

Illustration Capsule 32 describes the creative approach taken by Yamaha to reverse the declining market demand for pianos.

---

[14]Ibid., p. 165.

illustration capsule 32
Yamaha's Strategy in the Stagnant Piano Industry

For some years now, worldwide demand for pianos has been declining—in the mid-1980s the decline was 10 percent annually. Modern-day parents have not put the same stress on music lessons for their children as prior generations of parents did. In an effort to see if it could revitalize its piano business, Yamaha conducted a market research survey to learn what use was being made of pianos in households that owned one. The survey revealed that the overwhelming majority of the 40 million pianos in American, European, and Japanese households were seldom used. In most cases, the reasons the piano had been purchased no longer applied. Children had either stopped taking piano lessons or were grown and had left the household; adult household members played their pianos sparingly, if at all—only a small percentage were accomplished piano players. Most pianos were serving as a piece of fine furniture and were in good condition despite not being tuned regularly. The survey also confirmed that the income levels of piano owners were well above average.

Beginning in the late 1980s, Yamaha's piano strategists saw the idle pianos in these upscale households as a potential market opportunity. The strategy that emerged entailed marketing an attachment that would convert the piano into an old-fashioned automatic player piano capable of playing a wide number of selections recorded on disks. Concurrently, Yamaha introduced Disklavier, an upright acoustic player piano model that could record and play back performances up to 90 minutes long, making it simple to monitor student progress.

Over the past 15 years, Yamaha has introduced a host of Disklavier pianos—grand pianos, minigrand, upright, and console designs in a variety of styles and finishes. It has partnered with recording artists and music studios to make thousands of digital disks available for Yamaha piano owners, allowing them to enjoy concert-caliber performances in their home. And it has created a global music education program for both teachers and students. Together, these efforts have helped rejuvenate and sustain Yamaha's piano business.

STRATEGIES FOR COMPETING IN FRAGMENTED INDUSTRIES

A number of industries are populated by hundreds, even thousands, of small and medium-sized companies, many privately held and none with a substantial share of total industry sales.[15] The standout competitive feature of a fragmented industry is the absence of market leaders with king-sized market shares or widespread buyer recognition. Examples of fragmented industries include book publishing, landscaping and plant nurseries, real estate development, convenience stores, banking, health and medical care, mail order catalog sales, computer software development, custom printing, kitchen cabinets, trucking, auto repair, restaurants and fast food, public accounting, apparel manufacture and apparel retailing, paperboard boxes, hotels and motels, and furniture.

Any of several reasons can account for why the supply side of an industry is fragmented:

● Market demand is so extensive and so diverse that very large numbers of firms can easily coexist trying to accommodate the range and variety of buyer preferences and requirements and to cover all the needed geographic locations. This is true in

---

[15]This section is summarized from Porter, *Competitive Strategy,* Chapter 9.

the hotel and restaurant industry in New York City, London, or Tokyo, and the market for apparel. Likewise, there is ample room in the marketplace for numerous auto repair outlets, gasoline and convenience store retailers, and real estate firms.

- Low entry barriers allow small firms to enter quickly and cheaply.
- An absence of scale economies permits small companies to compete on an equal cost footing with larger firms.
- Buyers require relatively small quantities of customized products (as in business forms, interior design, kitchen cabinets, and advertising). Because demand for any particular product version is small, sales volumes are not adequate to support producing, distributing, or marketing on a scale that yields advantages to a large firm.
- The market for the industry's product or service is becoming more global, putting companies in more and more countries in the same competitive market arena (as in apparel manufacture).
- The technologies embodied in the industry's value chain are exploding into so many new areas and along so many different paths that specialization is essential just to keep abreast in any one area of expertise.
- The industry is young and crowded with aspiring contenders, with no firm having yet developed the resource base, competitive capabilities, and market recognition to command a significant market share (as in online business-to-consumer retailing via the Internet).

Some fragmented industries consolidate over time as growth slows and the market matures. The stiffer competition that accompanies slower growth produces a shake-out of weak, inefficient firms and a greater concentration of larger, more visible sellers. Others remain atomistic because it is inherent in the nature of their businesses. And still others remain stuck in a fragmented state because existing firms lack the resources or ingenuity to employ a strategy powerful enough to drive industry consolidation.

Competitive rivalry in fragmented industries can vary from moderately strong to fierce. Low barriers tend to make entry of new competitors an ongoing threat. Competition from substitutes may or may not be a major factor. The relatively small size of companies in fragmented industries puts them in a relatively weak position to bargain with powerful suppliers and buyers, although sometimes they can become members of a cooperative formed for the purpose of using their combined leverage to negotiate better sales and purchase terms. In such an environment, the best a firm can expect is to cultivate a loyal customer base and grow a bit faster than the industry average. Competitive strategies based either on low cost or product differentiation are viable unless the industry's product is highly standardized or a commodity (like sand, concrete blocks, paperboard boxes). Focusing on a well-defined market niche or buyer segment usually offers more competitive advantage potential than striving for broad market appeal. Suitable competitive strategy options in a fragmented industry include

> In fragmented industries competitors usually have wide enough strategic latitude (1) to either compete broadly or focus and (2) to pursue a low-cost, differentiation-based, or best-cost competitive advantage.

- *Constructing and operating "formula" facilities*—This strategic approach is frequently employed in restaurant and retailing businesses operating at multiple locations. It involves constructing standardized outlets in favorable locations at minimum cost and then operating them superefficiently. Tricon Global Restaurants (with its Pizza Hut, Taco Bell, and Kentucky Fried Chicken restaurants), The Home Depot, and 7-Eleven pursue this strategy.
- *Becoming a low-cost operator*—When price competition is intense and profit margins are under constant pressure, companies can stress no-frills operations featur-

ing low overhead, high-productivity/low-cost labor, lean capital budgets, and dedicated pursuit of total operating efficiency. Successful low-cost producers in a fragmented industry can play the price-discounting game and still earn profits above the industry average. Many e-retailers compete on the basis of superlow prices; so do local tire retailers and supermarkets and gasoline stations.

- *Specializing by product type*—When a fragmented industry's products include a range of styles or services, a strategy to focus on one product or service category can be very effective. Some firms in the furniture industry specialize in only one furniture type such as brass beds, rattan and wicker, lawn and garden, or early American. In auto repair, companies specialize in transmission repair, body work, or speedy oil changes.

- *Specialization by customer type*—A firm can stake out a market niche in a fragmented industry by catering to those customers who are interested in low prices, unique product attributes, customized features, carefree service, or other extras. A number of restaurants cater to take-out customers; others specialize in fine dining experiences, and still others cater to the sports bar crowd.

- *Focusing on a limited geographic area*—Even though a firm in a fragmented industry can't win a big share of total industrywide sales, it can still try to dominate a local or regional geographic area. Concentrating company efforts on a limited territory can produce greater operating efficiency, speed delivery and customer services, promote strong brand awareness, and permit saturation advertising, while avoiding the diseconomies of stretching operations out over a much wider area. Supermarkets, banks, convenience stores, and sporting goods retailers successfully operate multiple locations within a limited geographic area.

In fragmented industries, firms generally have the strategic freedom to pursue broad or narrow market targets and low-cost or differentiation-based competitive advantages. Many different strategic approaches can exist side by side.

STRATEGIES FOR SUSTAINING RAPID COMPANY GROWTH

Companies that are focused on growing their revenues and earnings at a rapid or above-average pace year after year generally have to craft a portfolio of strategic initiatives covering three horizons:[16]

Horizon 1: Strategic initiatives to fortify and extend their position in existing businesses—Horizon 1 initiatives typically include adding new items to the company's present product line, expanding into new geographic areas where the company does not yet have a market presence, and launching offensives to take market share away from rivals. The objective is capitalize fully on whatever growth potential exists in the company's present business arenas.

Horizon 2: Strategic initiatives to leverage existing resources and capabilities by entering new businesses with promising growth potential—Growth companies have to be alert for opportunities to jump into new businesses where there is promise of rapid growth and where their experience, intellectual capital, technological

---

[16]Eric D. Beinhocker, "Robust Adaptive Strategies," *Sloan Management Review* 40, no. 3 (Spring 1999), p. 101.

know-how, and capabilities will prove valuable in gaining rapid market penetration. While Horizon 2 initiatives may take a back seat to Horizon 1 initiatives as long as there is plenty of untapped growth in the company's present businesses, they move to the front as the onset of market maturity dims the company's growth prospects in its present business(es).

Horizon 3: Strategic initiatives to plant the seeds for ventures in businesses that do not yet exist—Such initiatives can entail pumping funds into long-range R&D projects, setting up an internal venture capital fund to invest in promising start-up companies attempting to create the industries of the future, or acquiring a number of small start-up companies experimenting with technologies and product ideas that complement the company's present businesses. Intel, for example, has set up a multibillion-dollar fund to invest in over 100 different projects and start-up companies, the intent being to plant seeds for Intel's future, broadening its base as a global leader in supplying building blocks for PCs and the worldwide Internet economy. Royal Dutch/Shell, with over $140 billion in revenues and over 100,000 employees, put over $20 million into rule-breaking, game-changing ideas put forth by free-thinking employees; the objective was to inject a new spirit of entrepreneurship into the company and sow the seeds of faster growth.[17]

The three strategy horizons are illustrated in Figure 8.2. Managing such a portfolio of strategic initiatives is not easy, however. The tendency of most companies is to focus on Horizon 1 strategies and devote only sporadic and uneven attention to Horizon 2 and 3 strategies. But a recent McKinsey & Company study of 30 of the world's leading growth companies revealed a relatively balanced portfolio of strategic initiatives covering all three horizons. The lesson of successful growth companies is that keeping a company's record of rapid growth intact over the long term entails crafting a diverse population of strategies, ranging from short-jump incremental strategies to grow present businesses to long-jump initiatives with a 5- to 10-year growth payoff horizon.[18] Having a mixture of short-jump, medium-jump, and long-jump initiatives not only increases the odds of hitting a few home runs but also provides some protection against unexpected adversity in present or newly entered businesses.

The Risks of Pursuing Multiple Strategy Horizons   There are, of course, risks to pursuing a diverse strategy portfolio aimed at sustained growth. A company cannot, of course, place bets on every opportunity that appears on its radar screen, lest it stretch itself too thin. And medium-jump and long-jump initiatives can cause a company to stray far from its core competencies and end up trying to compete in businesses for which it is ill suited. Moreover, it can be difficult to achieve competitive advantage in medium- and long-jump product families and businesses that prove not to mesh well with a company's present businesses and resource strengths. The payoffs of long-jump initiatives often prove elusive; not all of the seeds a company sows will bear fruit, and only a few may evolve into truly significant contributors to the company's revenue and profit growth. The losses from those long-jump ventures that do not take root may

---

[17]Gary Hamel, "Bringing Silicon Valley Inside," *Harvard Business Review* 77, no. 5 (September–October 1999), p. 73.

[18]Beinhocker, "Robust Adaptive Strategies," p. 101.

figure 8.2 **The Three Strategy Horizons for Sustaining Rapid Growth**

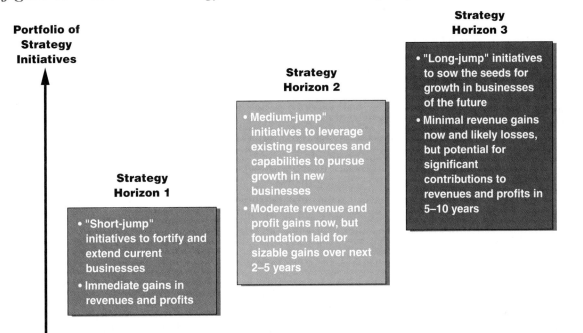

Source: Adapted from Eric D. Beinhocker, "Robust Adaptive Strategies," *Sloan Management Review* 40, no. 3 (Spring 1999), p. 101.

erode significantly the gains from those that do, resulting in disappointingly modest gains in overall profits.

STRATEGIES FOR INDUSTRY LEADERS

The competitive positions of industry leaders normally range from "stronger than average" to "powerful." Leaders typically are well known, and strongly entrenched leaders have proven strategies (keyed either to low-cost leadership or to differentiation). Some of the best-known industry leaders are Anheuser-Busch (beer), Starbucks (coffee drinks), Microsoft (computer software), McDonald's (fast food), Gillette (razor blades), Campbell's Soup (canned soups), Gerber (baby food), AT&T (long-distance telephone service), Eastman Kodak (camera film), Wal-Mart (discount retailing), Amazon.com (online shopping), eBay (online auctions), and Levi Strauss (jeans).

The main strategic concern for a leader revolves around how to defend and strengthen its leadership position, perhaps becoming the *dominant* leader as opposed to just *a* leader. However, the pursuit of industry leadership and large market share per se is primarily important because of the competitive advantage and profitability that accrue to being the industry's biggest company. Three contrasting strategic postures are open to industry leaders and dominant firms:[19]

---

[19]Kotler, *Marketing Management,* chapter 23; Michael E. Porter, *Competitive Advantage* (New York: Free Press, 1985), chapter 14; and Ian C. MacMillan, "Seizing Competitive Initiative," *Journal of Business Strategy* 2, no. 4 (Spring 1982), pp. 43–57.

1. *Stay-on-the-offensive strategy*—The central goal of a stay-on-the-offensive strategy is to be a first-mover.[20] It rests on the principle that staying a step ahead and forcing rivals into a reactive, catch-up mode is the surest path to industry prominence and potential market dominance—as the saying goes, the best defense is a good offense. Being the industry standard setter entails relentless pursuit of continuous improvement and innovation—being out front with technological improvements, new or better products, more attractive performance features, quality enhancements, improved customer service, ways to cut operating costs, and ways to make it easier and less costly for potential customers to switch their purchases from runner-up firms to its own products. A low-cost leader must set the pace for cost reduction, and a differentiator must constantly initiate new ways to keep its product set apart from the brands of imitative rivals in order to be the standard against which rivals' products are judged. The array of options for a potent stay-on-the-offensive strategy can also include initiatives to expand overall industry demand—spurring the creation of new families of products, making the product more suitable for consumers in emerging-country markets, discovering new uses for the product, attracting new users of the product, and promoting more frequent use.

Furthermore, unless a leader's market share is already so dominant that it presents a threat of antitrust action (a market share under 60 percent is usually safe), a potent stay-on-the-offensive strategy entails actions aimed at growing faster than the industry as a whole and wresting market share from rivals. A leader whose growth does not equal or outpace the industry average is losing ground to competitors.

2. *Fortify-and-defend strategy*—The essence of "fortify and defend" is to make it harder for challengers to gain ground and for new firms to enter. The goals of a strong defense are to hold on to the present market share, strengthen current market position, and protect whatever competitive advantage the firm has. Specific defensive actions can include:

- Attempting to raise the competitive ante for challengers and new entrants via increased spending for advertising, higher levels of customer service, and bigger R&D outlays.
- Introducing more product versions or brands to match the product attributes that challenger brands have or to fill vacant niches that competitors could slip into.
- Adding personalized services and other "extras" that boost customer loyalty and make it harder or more costly for customers to switch to rival products.
- Keeping prices reasonable and quality attractive.
- Building new capacity ahead of market demand to discourage smaller competitors from adding capacity of their own.
- Investing enough to remain cost-competitive and technologically progressive.
- Patenting the feasible alternative technologies.
- Signing exclusive contracts with the best suppliers and dealer distributors.

A fortify-and-defend strategy best suits firms that have already achieved industry dominance and don't wish to risk antitrust action. It is also well suited to situations where a firm wishes to milk its present position for profits and cash flow because the indus-

> The two best tests of success of a stay-on-the-offensive strategy are (1) the extent to which it keeps rivals in a reactive mode, scrambling to keep up, and (2) whether the leader is growing faster than the industry as a whole and wresting market share from rivals

---

[20]The value of being a frequent first-mover and leading change is documented in Walter J. Ferrier, Ken G. Smith, and Curtis M. Grimm, "The Role of Competitive Action in Market Share Erosion and Industry Dethronement: A Study of Industry Leaders and Challengers," *Academy of Management Journal* 42, no. 4 (August 1999), pp. 372–88.

try's prospects for growth are low or because further gains in market share do not appear profitable enough to go after. But a fortify-and-defend strategy always entails trying to grow as fast as the market as a whole (to stave off market-share slippage) and requires reinvesting enough capital in the business to protect the leader's ability to compete.

3. *Muscle-flexing strategy*—Here a dominant leader plays competitive hardball (presumably in an ethical and competitively legal manner) when smaller rivals rock the boat with price cuts or mount new market offensives that directly threaten its position. Specific responses can include quickly matching and perhaps exceeding challengers' price cuts, using large promotional campaigns to counter challengers' moves to gain market share, and offering better deals to their major customers. Dominant leaders may also court distributors assiduously to dissuade them from carrying rivals' products, provide salespersons with documented information about the weaknesses of competing products, or try to fill any vacant positions in their own firms by making attractive offers to the better executives of rivals that get out of line.

> Industry leaders can strengthen their long-term competitive positions with strategies keyed to aggressive offense, aggressive defense, or muscling smaller rivals and customers into behaviors that bolster its own market standing.

The leader may also use various arm-twisting tactics to pressure present customers not to use the products of rivals. This can range from simply forcefully communicating its displeasure should customers opt to use the products of rivals to pushing them to agree to exclusive arrangements in return for better prices to charging them a higher price if they use any competitors' products. As a final resort, a leader may grant certain customers special discounts or preferred treatment if they do not use any products of rivals.

The obvious risks of a muscle-flexing strategy are running afoul of the antitrust laws (as did Microsoft—see Illustration Capsule 33), alienating customers with bullying tactics, and arousing adverse public opinion. A company that tries to throw its weight around to protect and enhance its market dominance has got to be judicious, lest it cross the line from allowable tactics to what buyers, rivals, and antitrust officials consider unfair and unethical competitive practices.

STRATEGIES FOR RUNNER-UP FIRMS

Runner-up or "second-tier" firms have smaller market shares than "first-tier" industry leaders. Some runner-up firms are up-and-coming *market challengers,* employing offensive strategies to gain market share and build a stronger market position. Other runner-up competitors are *focusers*, seeking to improve their lot by concentrating their attention on serving a limited portion of the market. There are, of course, always a number of firms in any industry that are destined to be *perennial runners-up,* lacking the resources and competitive strengths to do more than continue in trailing positions and/or content to follow the trendsetting moves of the market leaders.

In industries where big size is definitely a key success factor, firms with small market shares have some obstacles to overcome: (1) less access to economies of scale in manufacturing, distribution, or marketing and sales promotion; (2) difficulty in gaining customer recognition; (3) weaker ability to use mass media advertising; and (4) difficulty in funding capital requirements.[21] When significant scale economies give large-volume competitors a *dominating* cost advantage, small-share firms have only two viable strategic options: initiate offensive moves to gain sales and market share (so as to build the volume of business needed to approach the scale economies enjoyed by

---

[21]Hamermesh, Anderson, and Harris, "Strategies for Low Market Share Businesses," p. 102.

illustration capsule 33
How Microsoft Used Its Muscle to Maintain Market Dominance

In 1999 in *U.S.* v. *Microsoft*, U.S. District Judge Thomas Penfield Jackson concluded that Microsoft repeatedly had used heavy-handed tactics to routinely pressure customers, crush competitors, and throttle competition. Judge Jackson painted Microsoft as a domineering company that rewarded its friends and punished its enemies, pointing to the following examples:

- Gateway and IBM, both of which resisted Microsoft's efforts to dissuade them from using or promoting competitors' products on their PCs, were forced to pay higher prices for installing Microsoft's Windows operating system on their PCs than Dell Computer, Hewlett-Packard, and Compaq Computer, which had less contentious relationships with Microsoft. Microsoft's beef with IBM stemmed from IBM's efforts to market PCs loaded with IBM's own internally developed OS/2 operating system rather than Windows and, also, its own Lotus SmartSuite rather than Microsoft Office.

- Microsoft tried to persuade Netscape to halt its development of platform-level technologies for Windows 95, arguing that Netscape's Navigator browser should be designed to run on Windows 95 only rather than be designed in a way that could serve as an alternative operating system platform and substitute for use of Windows. Microsoft wanted Netscape to agree to a special alliance with Microsoft that would allow Microsoft to incorporate Navigator's functionality into Windows. When Netscape refused, Microsoft withheld information about its Windows 95 code until after it released Windows 95 and its own new version of Internet Explorer. Microsoft also refused to give Netscape a license to one of its scripting tools, thereby preventing Netscape from doing business with certain Internet service providers for a time. Simultaneously, Microsoft

pressured PC makers to install its Internet Explorer browser as the preferred alternative to Netscape Navigator. When Compaq removed the Internet Explorer icon from the opening screen of its computers and preinstalled the Navigator icon, Microsoft threatened to revoke Compaq's license to install Windows 95.

- Microsoft tried to convince Intel not to ship its newly developed Native Signal Processing (NSP) software (intended to help spark demand for Intel's most advanced microprocessors) because Microsoft felt that the NSP software represented an incursion into Microsoft's operating system platform territory. It also asked Intel to reduce the number of people working on software at Intel. Microsoft assured Intel that if it would stop promoting NSP that Microsoft would accelerate its own work to incorporate the functions of NSP into Windows. At the same time, Microsoft pressured PC makers not to install Intel's NSP software on their PCs.

- When Compaq Computer entered into an agreement with America Online to promote AOL above all online services and began to ship its computers with the Microsoft Network (MSN) icon removed and the AOL icon installed, Microsoft wrote Compaq a letter stating its intention to terminate Compaq's license for Windows 95 if it did not restore the MSN icon to its original position on the opening screen.

Since the 1999 decision, Microsoft has continued to face challenges to its muscle-flexing strategies. In 2001, the company reduced its support for Java in its release of the new Windows XP operating system. Microsoft also increased its pressure on PC makers to display three of its own icons—for MSN online, Windows Media player, and Internet Explorer—on the Windows XP desktop.

Source: Don Clark, "Microsoft Raises Requirements on Icon Use by Computer Makers," *The Wall Street Journal* (www.wsj.com), August 9, 2001; D. Ian Hopper, "Microsoft Appeals to Supreme Court," Associated Press, August 8, 2001; John R. Wilke and Don Clark, "Senate Judiciary Committee Plans Microsoft Hearings," *The Wall Street Journal* (http://public.wsj.com), July 24, 2001; John R. Wilke and Don Clark, "Microsoft Pulls Back Support for Java," *The Wall Street Journal* (www.wsj.com), July 19, 2001; and transcript of Judge Jackson's findings of fact in *U.S.* v. *Microsoft,* November 5, 1999.

larger rivals) or withdraw from the business (gradually or quickly). The competitive strategies most underdogs use to build market share and achieve critical scale economies are based on (1) using lower prices to win customers from weak, higher-cost rivals; (2) merging with or acquiring rival firms to achieve the size needed to capture greater scale economies; (3) investing in new cost-saving facilities and equipment, perhaps relocating operations to countries where costs are significantly lower; and

(4) pursuing technological innovations or radical value chain revamping to achieve dramatic cost savings.

But *it is erroneous to view runner-up firms as inherently less profitable or unable to hold their own against the biggest firms.* Many small and medium-sized firms earn healthy profits and enjoy good reputations with customers. Assuming that scale economies or experience curve effects are relatively small and result in no important cost advantage for big-share firms, runner-up companies have considerable strategic flexibility and can consider any of the following six approaches.

Offensive Strategies to Build Market Share   A challenger firm interested in improving its market standing needs a strategy aimed at building a competitive advantage of its own. Rarely can a runner-up firm improve its competitive position by imitating the strategies of leading firms. A cardinal rule in offensive strategy is to avoid attacking a leader head-on with an imitative strategy, regardless of the resources and staying power an underdog may have.[22] Moreover, if a challenger has a 5 percent market share and needs a 20 percent share to earn attractive returns, it needs a more creative approach to competing than just "Try harder."

> Rarely can a runner-up firm successfully challenge an industry leader with a copycat strategy.

Ambitious runner-up companies desirous of joining the ranks of first-tier industry leaders have to make some waves in the marketplace if they want to make big market share gains. The best "mover-and-shaker" offensives usually involve one of the following approaches:

- Pioneering a leapfrog technological breakthrough.
- Getting new or better products into the market consistently ahead of rivals and building a reputation for product leadership.
- Being more agile and innovative in adapting to evolving market conditions and customer expectations than slower-to-change market leaders.
- Forging attractive strategic alliances with key distributors, dealers, or marketers of complementary products.
- Finding innovative ways to dramatically drive down costs and then using the attraction of lower prices to win customers from higher-cost, higher-priced rivals. A challenger firm can pursue aggressive cost reduction by eliminating marginal activities from its value chain, streamlining supply chain relationships, improving internal operating efficiency, using various e-commerce techniques, and merging with or acquiring rival firms to achieve the size needed to capture greater scale economies.
- Crafting an attractive differentiation strategy based on premium quality, technological superiority, outstanding customer service, rapid product innovation, or convenient online shopping options.

Without a potent offensive strategy to capture added market share, runner-up companies have to patiently nibble away at the lead of first-tier firms and build sales at a more moderate pace over time.

Growth-via-Acquisition Strategy   One of the most frequently used strategies employed by ambitious runner-up companies is merging with or acquiring rivals to form an enterprise that has greater competitive strength and a larger share of the overall market. For an enterprise to succeed with this strategic approach, senior management must have the skills to assimilate the operations of the acquired companies,

---

[22]Porter, *Competitive Advantage*, p. 514.

eliminating duplication and overlap, generating efficiencies and cost savings, and structuring the combined resources in ways that create substantially stronger competitive capabilities. Many banks owe their growth during the past decade to acquisition of smaller regional and local banks. Likewise, a number of book publishers have grown by acquiring small publishers. HealthSouth, an operator of outpatient surgery centers and rehabilitation and diagnostics clinics, has grown into a $4 billion health care provider by acquiring hundreds of clinics and facilities across the United States and in several foreign countries.

Vacant-Niche Strategy   This version of a focused strategy involves concentrating on customer or end-use applications that market leaders have bypassed or neglected. An ideal vacant niche is of sufficient size and scope to be profitable, has some growth potential, is well suited to a firm's own capabilities and skills, and for one reason or another is hard for leading firms to serve. Two examples where vacant-niche strategies have worked successfully are (1) regional commuter airlines serving cities with too few passengers to fill the large jets flown by major airlines and (2) health-food producers (like Health Valley, Hain, and Tree of Life) that cater to local health-food stores—a market segment traditionally given little attention by Pillsbury, Kraft General Foods, Heinz, Nabisco, Campbell Soup, and other leading food products firms.

Specialist Strategy   A specialist firm trains its competitive effort on one technology, product or product family, end use, or market segment (often one in which buyers have special needs). The aim is to train the company's resource strengths and capabilities on building competitive advantage through leadership in a specific area. Smaller companies that successfully use a specialist focused strategy include Formby's (a specialist in stains and finishes for wood furniture, especially refinishing); Blue Diamond (a California-based grower and marketer of almonds); Canada Dry (known for its ginger ale, tonic water, and carbonated soda water); and American Tobacco (a leader in chewing tobacco and snuff). Many companies in high-tech industries concentrate their energies on being the clear leader in a particular technological area; their competitive advantage is superior technological depth, technical expertise that is highly valued by customers, and the capability to consistently beat out rivals in pioneering technological advances.

Superior Product Strategy   The approach here is to use a differentiation-based focused strategy keyed to superior product quality or unique attributes. Sales and marketing efforts are aimed directly at quality-conscious and performance-oriented buyers. Fine craftsmanship, prestige quality, frequent product innovations, and/or close contact with customers to solicit their input in developing a better product usually undergird this superior product approach. Some examples include Bombay and Tanqueray in gin, Tiffany in diamonds and jewelry, Chicago Cutlery in premium-quality kitchen knives, Baccarat in fine crystal, Cannondale in mountain bikes, Bally in shoes, and Patagonia in apparel for outdoor recreation enthusiasts.

Distinctive Image Strategy   Some runner-up companies build their strategies around ways to make themselves stand out from competitors. A variety of strategic approaches can be used: creating a reputation for charging the lowest prices, providing prestige quality at a good price, going all out to give superior customer service, designing unique product attributes, being a leader in new product introduction, or devising unusually creative advertising. Examples include Dr Pepper's strategy in calling attention to its distinctive taste, Apple Computer's making it easier and more interesting for people to use its Macintosh PCs, and Mary Kay Cosmetics' distinctive use of the color pink.

Content Follower Strategy   Content followers deliberately refrain from initiating trendsetting strategic moves and from aggressive attempts to steal customers away from the leaders. Followers prefer approaches that will not provoke competitive retaliation, often opting for focus and differentiation strategies that keep them out of the leaders' paths. They react and respond rather than initiate and challenge. They prefer defense to offense. And they rarely get out of line with the leaders on price. They are content to simply maintain their market position, albeit sometimes struggling to do so. Followers have no urgent strategic questions to confront beyond "What strategic changes are the leaders initiating and what do we need to do to follow along and maintain our present position?" The marketers of private-label products tend to be followers, imitating many of the features of name-brand products and content to sell to price-conscious buyers at prices modestly below those of well-known brands.

STRATEGIES FOR WEAK AND CRISIS-RIDDEN BUSINESSES

A firm in an also-ran or declining competitive position has four basic strategic options. If it can come up with the financial resources, it can launch an *offensive turnaround strategy* keyed either to low-cost or "new" differentiation themes, pouring enough money and talent into the effort to move up a notch or two in the industry rankings and become a respectable market contender within five years or so. It can employ a *fortify-and-defend* strategy, using variations of its present strategy and fighting hard to keep sales, market share, profitability, and competitive position at current levels. It can opt for an *immediate abandonment strategy* and get out of the business, either by selling out to another firm or by closing down operations if a buyer cannot be found. Or it can employ an *end-game strategy*, keeping reinvestment to a bare-bones minimum and taking actions to maximize short-term cash flows in preparation for an orderly market exit.

> The strategic options for a competitively weak company include waging a modest offensive to improve its position, defending its present position, being acquired by another company, or employing an end-game strategy.

Turnaround Strategies for Businesses in Crisis

Turnaround strategies are needed when a business worth rescuing goes into crisis; the objective is to arrest and reverse the sources of competitive and financial weakness as quickly as possible. Management's first task in formulating a suitable turnaround strategy is to diagnose what lies at the root of poor performance. Is it an unexpected downturn in sales brought on by a weak economy? An ill-chosen competitive strategy? Poor execution of an otherwise workable strategy? High operating costs? Important resource deficiencies? An overload of debt? Can the business be saved, or is the situation hopeless? Understanding what is wrong with the business and how serious its strategic problems are is essential because different diagnoses lead to different turnaround strategies.

Some of the most common causes of business trouble are taking on too much debt, overestimating the potential for sales growth, ignoring the profit-depressing effects of an overly aggressive effort to "buy" market share with deep price cuts, being burdened with heavy fixed costs because of an inability to use plant capacity, betting on R&D efforts to boost competitive position and profitability and failing to come up with effective innovations, betting on technological long shots, being too optimistic about the ability to penetrate new markets, making frequent changes in strategy (because the previous strategy didn't work out), and being overpowered by more successful rivals.

Curing these kinds of problems and achieving a successful business turnaround can involve any of the following actions:

- Selling off assets to raise cash to save the remaining part of the business.
- Revising the existing strategy.
- Launching efforts to boost revenues.
- Pursuing cost reduction.
- Using a combination of these efforts.

Selling Off Assets   Asset-reduction strategies are essential when cash flow is a critical consideration and when the most practical ways to generate cash are (1) through sale of some of the firm's assets (plant and equipment, land, patents, inventories, or profitable subsidiaries) and (2) through retrenchment (pruning of marginal products from the product line, closing or selling older plants, reducing the workforce, withdrawing from outlying markets, cutting back customer service). Sometimes crisis-ridden companies sell off assets not so much to unload losing operations and to stem cash drains as to raise funds to save and strengthen the remaining business activities. In such cases, the choice is usually to dispose of noncore business assets to support strategy renewal in the firm's core businesses.

Strategy Revision   When weak performance is caused by bad strategy, the task of strategy overhaul can proceed along any of several paths: (1) shifting to a new competitive approach to rebuild the firm's market position; (2) overhauling internal operations and functional area strategies to better support the same overall business strategy; (3) merging with another firm in the industry and forging a new strategy keyed to the newly merged firm's strengths; and (4) retrenching into a reduced core of products and customers more closely matched to the firm's strengths. The most appealing path depends on prevailing industry conditions, the firm's particular strengths and weaknesses, its competitive capabilities vis-à-vis rival firms, and the severity of the crisis. A situation analysis of the industry, major competitors, and the firm's own competitive position and its skills and resources is a prerequisite for action. As a rule, successful strategy revision must be tied to the ailing firm's strengths and near-term competitive capabilities and directed at its best market opportunities.

Boosting Revenues   Revenue-increasing turnaround efforts aim at generating increased sales volume. There are a number of revenue-building options: price cuts, increased promotion, a bigger sales force, added customer services, and quickly achieved product improvements. Attempts to increase revenues and sales volumes are necessary (1) when there is little or no room in the operating budget to cut expenses and still break even, and (2) when the key to restoring profitability is increased utilization of existing capacity. If buyer demand is not especially price sensitive because of differentiating features, the quickest way to boost short-term revenues may be to raise prices rather than opt for volume-building price cuts.

Cutting Costs   Cost-reducing turnaround strategies work best when an ailing firm's value chain and cost structure are flexible enough to permit radical surgery, when operating inefficiencies are identifiable and readily correctable, when the firm's costs are obviously bloated and there are many places where savings can be quickly achieved, and when the firm is relatively close to its break-even point. Accompanying a general belt-tightening can be an increased emphasis on paring administrative overheads, elimination of nonessential and low-value-added activities in the firm's value chain, modernization of existing plant and equipment to gain greater productivity, delay of nonessential capital expenditures, and debt restructuring to reduce interest costs and stretch out repayments.

Combination Efforts   Combination turnaround strategies are usually essential in grim situations that require fast action on a broad front. Likewise, combination actions frequently come into play when new managers are brought in and given a free hand to make whatever changes they see fit. The tougher the problems, the more likely the solutions will involve multiple strategic initiatives—see the story of the turnaround at Continental Airlines in Illustration Capsule 34.

Turnaround efforts tend to be high-risk undertakings, and they often fail. A landmark study of 64 companies found no successful turnarounds among the most troubled companies in eight basic industries.[23] Many of the troubled businesses waited too long to begin a turnaround. Others found themselves short of both the cash and entrepreneurial talent needed to compete in a slow-growth industry characterized by a fierce battle for market share. Better-positioned rivals simply proved too strong to defeat in a long, head-to-head contest. Even when successful, turnaround may involve numerous attempts and management changes before long-term competitive viability and profitability are finally restored.

Liquidation—the Strategy of Last Resort

Sometimes a business in crisis is too far gone to be salvaged or is not worth salvaging given the resources it will take and its profit prospects. Closing a crisis-ridden business down and liquidating its assets is sometimes the best and wisest strategy. Of all the strategic alternatives, liquidation is the most unpleasant and painful because of the hardships of job eliminations and the effects of business closings on local communities. Nonetheless, in hopeless situations, an early liquidation effort usually serves owner-stockholder interests better than an inevitable bankruptcy. Prolonging the pursuit of a lost cause merely exhausts an organization's resources further and leaves less to salvage, not to mention the added stress and potential career impairment for all the people involved. The problem, of course, is differentiating between when a turnaround is achievable and when it isn't. It is easy for owners or managers to let their emotions and pride overcome sound judgment when a business gets in such deep trouble that a successful turnaround is remote.

End-Game Strategies

An *end-game strategy* steers a middle course between preserving the status quo and exiting as soon as possible. *Harvesting* is a phasing-down strategy that involves sacrificing market position in return for bigger near-term cash flows or current profitability. The overriding financial objective is to reap the greatest possible harvest of cash to deploy to other business endeavors. The operating budget is chopped to a rock-bottom level; reinvestment in the business is held to a bare minimum. Capital expenditures for

---

[23]William K. Hall, "Survival Strategies in a Hostile Environment," *Harvard Business Review* 58, no. 5 (September–October 1980), pp. 75–85. See also Frederick M. Zimmerman, *The Turnaround Experience: Real-World Lessons in Revitalizing Corporations* (New York: McGraw-Hill, 1991), and Gary J. Castrogiovanni, B. R. Baliga, and Roland E. Kidwell, "Curing Sick Businesses: Changing CEOs in Turnaround Efforts," *Academy of Management Executive* 6, no. 3 (August 1992), pp. 26–41.

illustration capsule 34
Lucent Technologies' Turnaround Strategy

By the summer of 2001, the situation was desperate. Lucent Technologies, the famous AT&T spinoff that had once been the superstar of the telecommunications industry, was floundering. The combination of lost sales to competitors and a general downturn in the economy had thrown the company into a nosedive out of which many industry watchers believed it could not pull itself. In one year alone, Lucent had lost more than $6 billion and 80 percent of its market value. Furthermore, experts forecast a slow recovery of sales of voice and data-switching equipment and Internet routers because of a capacity glut that had made growth of the market in general sluggish.

But Lucent was not to be defeated. Revising its previous strategies, which were effective when the economy was strong and the telecommunications market growing, Lucent was forced to devise instead a combination of turnaround strategies to ensure its survival.

First came cost cutting. Lucent announced that it would eliminate 15,000 to 20,000 jobs worldwide as part of a plan to turn itself into a leaner, more efficient maker of telecommunications equipment. Eventually, company managers said, the workforce would be cut by more than half, from 150,000 to 60,000. In addition, Lucent announced that some of its plants would be consolidated. But officials hastened to say that these job and plant cuts would not decrease the company's ability to provide service to its top customers, who represented nearly 75 percent of the company's sales and on whom Lucent now focused most of its attention in a fortify-and-defend strategy. "We've left more than enough human and financial capital to execute this plan," noted CEO Henry Schacht, who was called out of retirement to lead the company's turnaround plan. Lucent then dedicated special customer teams to serve approximately 30 top customers in 20 countries.

Next, Lucent had to find ways to raise cash and reassure investors. So the company sold both stock and assets: convertible preferred stock worth $1.82 billion and its fiber optic operations. The sale of both raised about $6 billion in cash. When outsiders questioned the motivation for the sale of Chromatis Networks, Lucent's fiber-optics firm, company spokesperson Frank Briamonte countered, "This is purely a strategic restructuring. It's not a product failure at all." Then the company reached an agreement with its group of banks to realign the terms of $4 billion in loans. "We want to take this [cash] issue off the table," stated CEO Schacht. "We believe we have the liquidity to fund this plan to fruition."

Finally, although engaged in deep cost cuts, including dropping some product lines, Lucent announced plans to launch a major new group of optical products as well as a spinoff of Agere Systems, a microelectronics company, in an effort to eventually boost revenues.

It is too early to predict whether the company's turnaround efforts will produce the intended results. An analyst with Forrester Research noted that Lucent's combination strategies "focus on the right products and customers" but that the general slowdown in spending on telecommunications equipment would probably last several more years. So Lucent might have to increase its efforts to lure business away from such competitors as Nortel Networks and Cisco Systems. But Schacht, in defense of his company's strategy, commented, "The plan is conservatively based and does not require a market recovery." In fact, company officials insisted that their plan took into account a slow recovery of the economy and the telecommunications market. "We're optimistic about our ability to get where we're going," said Schacht.

Sources: Yuki Noguchi, "Lucent Closes Herndon's Chromatis," *Washington Post* (www.washingtonpost.com), August 29, 2001; Simon Romero, "Lucent Maps Out Route to Profit by the End of Next Year," *New York Times* (www.nytimes.com), August 24, 2001; Peter J. Howe, "Lucent Fires 290 More at Massachusetts Sites," *Boston Globe* (www.boston.com), August 24, 2001; and Sara Silver, "Lucent Cuts 2,200 Jobs," Associated Press, August 23, 2001.

new equipment are put on hold or given low financial priority (unless replacement needs are unusually urgent); instead, efforts are made to stretch the life of existing equipment and make do with present facilities as long as possible. Promotional expenses may be cut gradually, quality reduced in not-so-visible ways, nonessential customer services curtailed, and the like. Although such actions may result in shrinking sales and market share, if cash expenses can be cut even faster, then after-tax profits and cash flows are bigger (at least temporarily). The business gradually declines, but not before sizable amounts of cash have been harvested.

An end-game strategy is a reasonable strategic option for a weak business in the following circumstances:[24]

1. When the industry's long-term prospects are unattractive—as seems to be the case for the cigarette industry, for the manufacture and sale of VCRs and videocassettes (which are now being replaced by DVD players and both CDs and DVDs), and for the 3.5-inch floppy disk business.

2. When rejuvenating the business would be too costly or at best marginally profitable—as could be the case at Iomega, which is struggling to maintain sales of its Zip drives in the face of rapidly expanding hard disk drives on PCs, or at Polaroid, which has experienced stagnant sales for its instant-developing cameras and film.

3. When the firm's market share is becoming increasingly costly to maintain or defend—as could be the case with the makers of film for traditional cameras.

4. When reduced levels of competitive effort will not trigger an immediate or rapid falloff in sales—the makers of dot-matrix printers will not likely experience much of a decline in sales of either dot-matrix printers or ribbons if they spend all of their ad budgets on laser printers.

5. When the enterprise can redeploy the freed resources in higher-opportunity areas—the makers of dot-matrix printers are better off devoting their resources to the production and sale of low-cost, good-quality laser printers.

6. When the business is not a crucial or core component of a diversified company's overall lineup of businesses—gradually letting a sideline business decay is strategically preferable to deliberately letting a mainline or core business decline.

7. When the business does not contribute other desired features (sales stability, prestige, a well-rounded product line) to a company's overall business portfolio.

The more of these seven conditions that are present, the more ideal the business is for harvesting.

End-game strategies make the most sense for diversified companies that have sideline or noncore business units in weak competitive positions or in unattractive industries. Such companies can withdraw the cash flows from unattractive, noncore business units and reallocate them to business units with greater profit potential or spend them on the acquisition of new businesses.

10 COMMANDMENTS FOR CRAFTING SUCCESSFUL BUSINESS STRATEGIES

Business experiences over the years prove again and again that disastrous strategies can be avoided by adhering to good strategy-making principles. We've distilled the lessons learned from the strategic mistakes companies most often make into 10 commandments that serve as useful guides for developing sound strategies:

---

[24]Phillip Kotler, "Harvesting Strategies for Weak Products," *Business Horizons* 21, no. 5 (August 1978), pp. 17–18.

1. *Place top priority on crafting and executing strategic moves that enhance the company's competitive position for the long term.* An ever-stronger competitive position pays off year after year, but the glory of meeting one quarter's or one year's financial performance targets quickly fades. Shareholders are never well served by managers who let short-term financial performance considerations rule out strategic initiatives that will meaningfully bolster the company's longer-term competitive position and competitive strength. The best way to protect a company's long-term profitability is with a strategy that strengthens the company's long-term competitiveness.

2. *Be prompt in adapting to changing market conditions, unmet customer needs, buyer wishes for something better, emerging technological alternatives, and new initiatives of competitors.* Responding late or with too little often puts a company in the precarious position of having to play catch-up. While pursuit of a consistent strategy has its virtues, adapting strategy to changing circumstances is normal and necessary. Moreover, long-term strategic commitments to achieve top quality or lowest cost should be interpreted relative to competitors' products as well as customers' needs and expectations; the company should avoid singlemindedly striving to make the absolute highest quality or lowest cost product possible no matter what.

3. *Invest in creating a sustainable competitive advantage.* Having a competitive edge over rivals is the single most dependable contributor to above-average profitability. As a general rule, a company must play aggressive offense to build competitive advantage and aggressive defense to protect it.

4. *Avoid strategies capable of succeeding only in the most optimistic circumstances.* Expect competitors to employ countermeasures and expect times of unfavorable market conditions. A good strategy works reasonably well and produces tolerable results even in the worst of times.

5. *Don't underestimate the reactions and the commitment of rival firms.* Rivals are most dangerous when they are pushed into a corner and their well-being is threatened.

6. *Consider that attacking competitive weakness is usually more profitable and less risky than attacking competitive strength.* Attacking capable, resourceful rivals is likely to fail unless the attacker has deep financial pockets and a solid basis for competitive advantage.

7. *Be judicious in cutting prices without an established cost advantage.* Only a low-cost producer can win at price cutting over the long term.

8. *Strive to open up very meaningful gaps in quality or service or performance features when pursuing a differentiation strategy.* Tiny differences between rivals' product offerings may not be visible or important to buyers.

9. *Avoid "stuck in the middle" strategies that represent compromises between lower costs and greater differentiation and between broad and narrow market appeal.* Compromise strategies rarely produce sustainable competitive advantage or a distinctive competitive position—well-executed best-cost producer strategies are the only exception where a compromise between low cost and differentiation succeeds. Usually, companies with compromise strategies end up with average costs, average differentiation, an average image and reputation, a middle-of-the-pack industry ranking, and little prospect of industry leadership.

10. *Be aware that aggressive moves to wrest market share away from rivals often provoke retaliation in the form of a marketing "arms race" or price war—to the*

detriment of everyone's profits. Aggressive moves to capture a bigger market share invite cutthroat competition, particularly when the market is plagued with high inventories and excess production capacity.

key|points

It is not enough to understand a company's basic competitive strategy options, overall low-cost leadership, broad differentiation, best cost, focused low cost, and focused differentiation, and that there are a variety of offensive, defensive, first-mover, and late-mover initiatives and actions to choose from. The lessons of this chapter are that some strategic options are better suited to certain specific industry and competitive environments than others and that some strategic options are better suited to certain specific company situations than others. This chapter portrays the multifaceted task of matching strategy to a firm's external and internal circumstances in nine types of situations.

Rather than try to summarize the main points we made about choosing strategies for these nine sets of circumstances (the relevant principles are not readily capsuled in three or four sentences each), we think it more useful to conclude by outlining a broader framework for matching strategy to *any* industry and company situation. Aligning a company's strategy with its overall situation starts with a quick diagnosis of the industry environment and the firm's competitive standing in the industry:

1. What basic type of industry environment does the company operate in (emerging, rapid-growth, high-velocity, mature, global, commodity-product)? What strategic options and strategic postures are usually best suited to this generic type of environment?

2. What position does the firm have in the industry (leader, runner-up, or also-ran; strong, weak, or crisis-ridden)? How does the firm's market standing influence its strategic options given the industry and competitive environment—in particular, which courses of action have to be ruled out?

Next, strategists need to factor in the primary external and internal situational considerations (as discussed in Chapters 3 and 4—see again Figure 3.2 for a convenient overview) and decide how all the factors add up. Nearly always, weighing the various considerations makes it clear that some strategic options can be ruled out. Listing the pros and cons of the remaining options can help reach a decision as to the best overall strategy.

The final step is to custom-tailor the chosen generic strategic approach (low-cost, differentiation, best-cost, focused low-cost, focused differentiation) to fit *both* the industry environment and the firm's standing vis-à-vis competitors. Here, it is important to be sure that (1) the customized aspects of the proposed strategy are well matched to the firm's competencies and competitive capabilities and (2) the strategy addresses all issues and problems the firm confronts.

In weeding out less attractive strategic alternatives and weighing the pros and cons of the most attractive ones, the answers to the following questions often help point to the best course of action, all things considered:

- What kind of competitive edge can the company *realistically* achieve? Can the company execute the strategic moves necessary to secure this edge?

- Does the company have the organizational capabilities and financial resources to succeed in these moves and approaches? If not, can they be acquired?

table 8.1   Sample Format for a Strategic Action Plan

1. Strategic Vision and Mission	**5. Supporting Functional Strategies** • Production
2. Strategic Objectives • Short-term • Long-term	• Marketing/sales • Finance • Personnel/human resources
3. Financial Objectives • Short-term • Long-term	• Other
	6. Recommended Actions to Improve Company Performance • Immediate
4. Overall Business Strategy	• Longer-range

- Once built, how can the competitive advantage be protected? Is the company in a position to lead industry change and set the rules by which rivals must compete? What defensive strategies need to be employed? Will rivals counterattack? What will it take to blunt their efforts?

- Are any rivals particularly vulnerable? Should the firm mount an offensive to capitalize on these vulnerabilities? What offensive moves need to be employed?

- What additional strategic moves are needed to deal with driving forces in the industry, specific threats and weaknesses, and any other issues/problems unique to the firm?

As the choice of strategic initiatives is developed, there are several pitfalls to avoid:

- Designing an overly ambitious strategic plan—one that overtaxes the company's resources and capabilities.

- Selecting a strategy that represents a radical departure from or abandonment of the cornerstones of the company's prior success—a radical strategy change need not be rejected automatically, but it should be pursued only after careful risk assessment.

- Choosing a strategy that goes against the grain of the organization's culture or that conflicts with the values and philosophies of the most senior executives.

- Being unwilling to *commit wholeheartedly* to one of the five competitive strategies—picking and choosing features of the different strategies usually produces so many compromises between low cost, best cost, differentiation, and focusing that the company fails to achieve any kind of advantage and ends up stuck in the middle.

Table 8.1 provides a generic format for outlining a strategic action plan for a single-business enterprise. It contains all of the pieces of a comprehensive strategic action plan that we discussed at various places in the previous seven chapters.

suggested | readings

Afuah, Allan. "Strategies to Turn Adversity into Profits." *Sloan Management Review* 40, no. 2 (Winter 1999), pp. 99–109.

Beinhocker, Eric D. "Robust Adaptive Strategies." *Sloan Management Review* 40, no. 3 (Spring 1999), pp. 95–106.

Bleeke, Joel A. "Strategic Choices for Newly Opened Markets." *Harvard Business Review* 68, no. 5 (September–October 1990), pp. 158–65.

Brenneman, Greg. "Right Away and All at Once: How We Saved Continental." *Harvard Business Review* 76, no. 5 (September–October 1998), pp. 162–79.

Cooper, Arnold C., and Clayton G. Smith. "How Established Firms Respond to Threatening Technologies." *Academy of Management Executive* 6, no. 2 (May 1992), pp. 55–57.

D'Aveni, Richard A. *Hypercompetition: Managing the Dynamics of Strategic Maneuvering.* New York: Free Press, 1994, chapters 3 and 4.

Day, George S. "Strategies for Surviving a Shakeout." *Harvard Business Review* 75, no. 2 (March–April 1997), pp. 92–102.

Feldman, Lawrence P., and Albert L. Page. "Harvesting: The Misunderstood Market Exit Strategy." *Journal of Business Strategy* 5, no. 4 (Spring 1985), pp. 79–85.

Finkin, Eugene F. "Company Turnaround." *Journal of Business Strategy* 5, no. 4 (Spring 1985), pp. 14–25.

Gordon, Geoffrey L.; Roger J. Calantrone; and C. Anthony di Benedetto. "Mature Markets and Revitalization Strategies: An American Fable." *Business Horizons* (May–June 1991), pp. 39–50.

Mayer, Robert J. "Winning Strategies for Manufacturers in Mature Industries." *Journal of Business Strategy* 8, no. 2 (Fall 1987), pp. 23–31.

Rackham, Neil; Lawrence Friedman; and Richard Ruff. *Getting Partnering Right: How Market Leaders Are Creating Long-Term Competitive Advantage.* New York: McGraw-Hill, 1996.

Zimmerman, Frederick M. *The Turnaround Experience: Real-World Lessons in Revitalizing Corporations.* New York: McGraw-Hill, 1991.

chapter | nine

Strategy and Competitive Advantage in Diversified Companies

...to acquire or not to acquire: that is the question.
—Robert J. Terry

Strategy is a deliberate search for a plan of action that will develop a business's competitive advantage and compound it.
—Bruce D. Henderson

Fit between a parent and its businesses is a two-edged sword: a good fit can create value: a bad one can destroy it.
—Andrew Campbell, Michael Goold, and Marcus Alexander

In this chapter and the next, we move up one level in the strategy-making hierarchy, from strategy making in a single-business enterprise to strategy making in a diversified enterprise. Because a diversified company is a collection of individual businesses, corporate strategy making is a bigger-picture exercise than line-of-business strategy making. In a single-business enterprise, management has to contend with only

one industry environment and the question of how to compete successfully in it. But in a diversified company corporate managers must strategize for several different business divisions competing in diverse industry environments and craft a multi-industry, multi-business strategy.

The task of crafting corporate strategy for a diversified company encompasses four areas:

1. *Picking the new industries to enter and deciding on the means of entry*—The first concern in diversifying is what new industries to get into and whether to enter by starting a new business from the ground up, acquiring a company already in the target industry, or forming a joint venture or strategic alliance with another company. A company can diversify narrowly into a few industries or broadly into many industries. The choice of whether to enter an industry via a new start-up operation or a collaborative joint venture or by acquisition of an established leader, an up-and-coming company, or a troubled company with turnaround potential shapes what position the company will initially stake out for itself.

2. *Initiating actions to boost the combined performance of the businesses the firm has entered*—As positions are created in the chosen industries, corporate strategists typically focus on ways to strengthen the long-term competitive positions and profitabilities of the businesses the firm has invested in. Corporate parents can help their business subsidiaries be more successful by providing financial resources, by supplying missing skills or technological know-how or managerial expertise to better perform key value chain activities, or by providing new avenues for cost reduction. They can also acquire another company in the same industry and merge the two operations into a stronger business, or acquire new businesses that strongly complement existing businesses. Typically, a company will pursue rapid-growth strategies in its most promising businesses, initiate turnaround efforts in weak-performing businesses with potential, and divest businesses that are no longer attractive or that don't fit into management's long-range plans.

3. *Pursuing opportunities to leverage cross-business value chain relationships and strategic fits into competitive advantage*—A company that diversifies into

businesses with related value chain activities (pertaining to technology, supply chain logistics, production, overlapping distribution channels, common customers), gains competitive advantage potential not open to a company that diversifies into businesses whose value chains are totally unrelated. Related diversification presents opportunities to transfer skills, share expertise, or share facilities, thereby reducing overall costs, strengthening the competitiveness of some of the company's products, or enhancing the capabilities of particular business units.

4.   *Establishing investment priorities and steering corporate resources into the most attractive business units*—A diversified company's different businesses are usually not equally attractive from the standpoint of investing additional funds. It is incumbent on corporate management to (*a*) decide on the priorities for investing capital in the company's different businesses, (*b*) channel resources into areas where earnings potentials are higher and away from areas where they are lower, and (*c*) divest business units that are chronically poor performers or are in an increasingly unattractive industry. Divesting poor performers and businesses in unattractive industries frees up unproductive investments for redeployment to promising business units or for financing attractive new acquisitions.

These four tasks are sufficiently demanding and time-consuming that corporate-level decision makers generally refrain from becoming immersed in the details of crafting and implementing business-level strategies, preferring instead to delegate lead responsibility for business strategy to the heads of each business unit.

In this chapter we describe the various paths through which a company can become diversified, explain how a company can use diversification to create or compound competitive advantage for its business units, and survey the strategic options an already-diversified company has to improve its overall performance. In Chapter 10 we will examine the techniques and procedures for assessing the strategic attractiveness of a diversified company's business portfolio.

WHEN TO DIVERSIFY

So long as a company has its hands full trying to capitalize on profitable growth opportunities in its present industry, there is no urgency to pursue diversification. But when growth opportunities in the company's mainstay business begin to peter out, diversification is usually the most viable option for reviving the firm's prospects. Diversification also has to be considered when a firm possesses technological expertise, core competencies, and resource strengths that are uniquely well suited for competing successfully in other industries.

> When to diversify depends partly on a company's growth opportunities in its present industry and partly on the opportunities to utilize its resources, expertise, and capabilities in other market arenas.

As part of the decision to diversify into new businesses, the company must ask itself, "What kind and how much diversification?" The strategic possibilities are wide open. A company can diversify into closely related businesses or into totally unrelated businesses. It can expand into industries whose technologies and products complement and enhance its present business. It can leverage existing competencies and capabilities by expanding into businesses where these same resource strengths are key success factors and valuable competitive assets. It can pursue opportunities to get into other product markets where its present technological know-how can be applied and possibly yield competitive advantage. It can diversify to a small extent (less than 10 percent of total revenues and profits) or to a large extent (up to 50 percent of revenues and profits). It can move into one or two large new businesses or a greater number of small ones. Joint ventures in new fields of endeavor are another possibility.

Why Rushing to Diversify Isn't Necessarily a Good Strategy

Companies that continue to concentrate on a single business can achieve enviable success over many decades without relying on diversification to sustain their growth. Mc-Donald's, Southwest Airlines, Coca-Cola, Domino's Pizza, Apple Computer, Wal-Mart, Federal Express, Timex, Campbell Soup, Anheuser-Busch, Xerox, Gerber, and Ford Motor Company all won their reputations in a single business. In the nonprofit sector, continued emphasis on a single activity has proved successful for the Red Cross, Salvation Army, Christian Children's Fund, Girl Scouts, Phi Beta Kappa, and American Civil Liberties Union. Coca-Cola, wanting to escape market maturity for soft drinks in the United States, abandoned most of its early efforts to diversify (into wine and into entertainment) when management concluded that the opportunities to sell Coca-Cola products in foreign markets (especially in China, India, and other parts of Asia) could produce attractive sales and profit growth well into the 21st century.

> Diversification doesn't need to become a strategic priority until a company begins to run out of attractive growth opportunities in its main business.

Concentrating on a single line of business (totally or with a small dose of diversification) has important advantages. It entails less ambiguity about "who we are and what we do." The energies of the total organization are directed down one business path, creating less chance that senior management's time will be diluted or organizational resources will be stretched thin by the demands of several different businesses. The company can devote the full force of its organizational resources to expanding into geographic markets it doesn't serve and to becoming better at what it does. Important competencies and competitive skills are more likely to emerge. Entrepreneurial efforts can be trained exclusively on keeping the firm's business strategy and competitive approach responsive to industry change and evolving customer preferences and buying patterns. With management's attention focused exclusively on one business, the probability is higher that good ideas will emerge on how to improve production technology, better meet customer needs with innovative new product features, and enhance efficiencies or differentiation capabilities along the value chain. All the firm's managers, especially top executives, can have hands-on contact with the core business and in-depth knowledge of operations. Most senior officers will usually have risen through the ranks and possess firsthand experience in field operations. (In broadly diversified enterprises, corporate managers seldom have had the opportunity to work in more than one or two of the company's businesses.) The more successful a single-business enterprise is, the more able it is to parlay its accumulated experience, distinctive competence, and reputation into a sustainable position as one of the leading firms in its industry.

> There are important organizational, managerial, and strategic advantages to concentrating on just one business.

The Risks of Concentrating on a Single Business

The big risk of remaining concentrated on a single business, of course, is putting all of a firm's eggs in one industry basket. If the market becomes saturated, competitively unattractive, or is eroded by the appearance of new technologies or new products or fast-shifting buyer preferences, then a company's prospects can quickly dim. It is not unusual for changing customer needs, technological innovation, or new substitute products to undermine or wipe out a single-business firm. Consider, for example, what digital cameras are doing to the market for film and film processing, what compact disc technology is doing to the market for cassette tapes and 3.5-inch disks, and what good-tasting, low-fat food products are doing to the sales of high-fat food products.

Factors That Signal When It's Time to Diversify

There's no formula for determining when a company ought to diversify. Judgments about when to diversify have to be made on the basis of a company's own situation. Generally speaking, a company is a prime candidate for diversifying when it has: (1) diminishing growth prospects in its present business, (2) opportunities to add value for its customers or gain competitive advantage by broadening its present business to include complementary products or technologies, (3) attractive opportunities to transfer its existing competencies and capabilities to new business arenas, (4) cost-saving opportunities that can be exploited by diversifying into closely related businesses and (5) the financial and organizational resources to support a diversification effort. Indeed, because companies in the same industry occupy different market positions and have different resource strengths and weaknesses, it is entirely rational for them to choose different diversification approaches and launch them at different times.

BUILDING SHAREHOLDER VALUE: THE ULTIMATE JUSTIFICATION FOR DIVERSIFYING

To create share-holder value, a diversifying company must get into businesses that can perform better under common management than they could perform as stand-alone enterprises.

Diversification is justifiable only if it builds shareholder value. To enhance shareholder value, the company must accomplish more than simply spreading its business risk across various industries. Shareholders can easily diversify risk on their own by purchasing stock in companies in different industries or investing in mutual funds. Strictly speaking, *diversification does not create shareholder value unless the chosen businesses perform better under a single corporate umbrella than they would perform operating as independent, stand-alone businesses.* For example, let's say that company A diversifies by purchasing company B. If A and B's consolidated profits in the years to come prove no greater than what each could have earned on its own, then A's diversification won't provide its shareholders with added value. Company A's shareholders could have achieved the same 1 + 1 = 2 result by merely purchasing stock in company B. Shareholder value is not created by diversification unless it produces a 1 + 1 = 3 effect where sister businesses perform better together as part of the same firm than they could have performed as independent companies.

Three Tests for Judging a Diversification Move

The problem with such a strict rule for whether diversification is justified is that it requires speculative judgments about how well a diversified company's businesses would have performed on their own. Comparisons of actual and hypothetical performances are never very satisfactory, and besides they represent after-the-fact assessments. Strategists have to base diversification decisions on *expectations*. Attempts to gauge the impact of particular diversification moves on shareholder value do not have to be abandoned, however. Corporate strategists can make before-the-fact assessments of whether a particular diversification move is capable of increasing shareholder value by using three tests:[1]

1. *The industry attractiveness test:* The industry chosen for diversification must be attractive enough to yield consistently good returns on investment. Whether an industry is attractive depends chiefly on the presence of favorable competitive conditions and a market environment conducive to long-term profitability. Such factors as rapid growth or a currently hot-selling product are unreliable as indicators of attractiveness.

2. *The cost-of-entry test:* The cost to enter the target industry must not be so high as to erode the potential for good profitability. A catch-22 can prevail here, however. The more attractive the industry, the more expensive it can be to get into. Entry barriers for start-up companies are nearly always high; were barriers low, a rush of new entrants would soon erode the potential for high profitability. And buying a company already in an industry with strong appeal often entails a high acquisition cost. Costly entry undermines the prospects of above-average profitability and enhanced shareholder value.

3. *The better-off test:* Diversifying into a new business must offer potential for the company's existing businesses and the new business to perform better together than apart. The best chance of a $1 + 1 = 3$ outcome occurs when a company diversifies into businesses that have competitively important value chain matchups with its existing businesses—matchups that offer opportunities to reduce costs, to transfer skills or technology from one business to another, to create valuable new competencies and capabilities, or to leverage existing resources (such as brand name reputation). Absent such strategic fits, a firm ought to be skeptical about the potential for the businesses to perform better together than apart.

Diversification moves that satisfy all three tests have the greatest potential to build shareholder value over the long term. Diversification moves that can pass only one or two tests are suspect.

CHOOSING THE DIVERSIFICATION PATH: RELATED VERSUS UNRELATED BUSINESSES

Once the decision is made to pursue diversification, the firm must choose whether to diversify into *related* businesses, *unrelated* businesses, or some mix of both—see Figure 9.1. *Businesses are said to be related when there are competitively valuable relationships among the activities comprising their respective value chains.* The appeal of related diversification is exploiting these value chain matchups to realize a $1 + 1 = 3$ performance outcome and build shareholder value. *Businesses are said to be unrelated when the activities comprising their respective value chains are so dissimilar that no real potential exists to transfer skills or technology from one business to another or to combine similar activities and reduce costs or to otherwise produce competitively valuable benefits from operating under a common corporate umbrella.*

Most companies favor related diversification strategies, attracted by the performance-enhancing potential of cross-business synergies. However, some companies

---

[1]Michael E. Porter, "From Competitive Advantage to Corporate Strategy," *Harvard Business Review* 45, no. 3 (May–June 1987), pp. 46–49.

figure 9.1   **Strategy Alternatives for a Company Looking to Diversify**

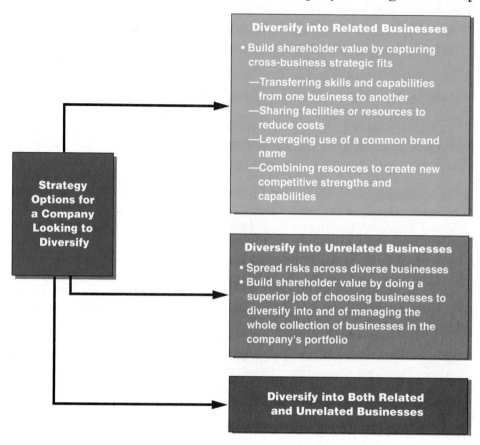

have, for one reason or another, pursued unrelated diversification. And a few have diversified into both related and unrelated businesses. The next two sections explore the ins and out of related and unrelated diversification.

THE CASE FOR RELATED DIVERSIFICATION STRATEGIES

A related diversification strategy involves adding businesses whose value chains possess competitively valuable "strategic fits" with the value chain of the company's present business, as shown in Figure 9.2. *Strategic fit* exists whenever one or more activities comprising the value chains of different businesses are sufficiently similar as to present opportunities for:[2]

---

[2]Michael E. Porter, *Competitive Advantage* (New York: Free Press, 1985), pp. 318–19 and pp. 337–53; Kenichi Ohmae, *The Mind of the Strategist* (New York: Penguin Books, 1983), pp. 121–24; and Porter, "From Competitive Advantage to Corporate Strategy," pp. 53–57. For an empirical study confirming that strategic fits are capable of enhancing performance (provided the resulting resource strengths are competitively valuable and difficult to duplicate by rivals), see Constantinos C. Markides and Peter J. Williamson, "Corporate Diversification and Organization Structure: A Resource-Based View," *Academy of Management Journal* 39, no. 2 (April 1996), pp. 340–67.

figure 9.2 **Value Chains for Related Businesses**

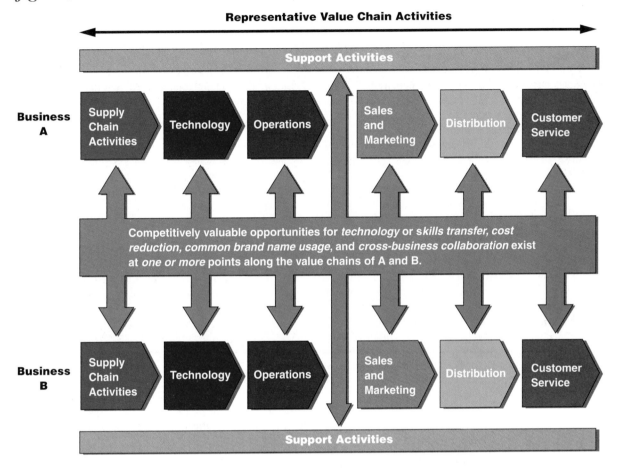

- Transferring competitively valuable expertise or technological know-how or capabilities from one business to another.
- Combining the related activities of separate businesses into a single operation to achieve lower costs.
- Exploiting common use of a well-known brand name.
- Cross-business collaboration to create competitively valuable resource strengths and capabilities (see Illustration Capsule 35).

Related diversification thus has strategic appeal from several angles. It allows a firm to reap the competitive advantage benefits of skills transfer, lower costs, common brand names, and/or stronger competitive capabilities and still spread investor risks over a broad business base. Furthermore, the relatedness among the different businesses provides sharper focus for managing diversification and a useful degree of strategic unity across the company's various business activities.

Cross-Business Strategic Fits along the Value Chain

Cross-business strategic fits can exist anywhere along the value chain—in R&D and technology activities, in supply chain activities and relationships with suppliers, in

Strategic fits among related businesses offer the competitive advantage potential of *(a)* efficient transfer of key skills, technological expertise, or managerial know-how from one business to another, *(b)* lower costs, *(c)* ability to share a common brand name, or *(d)* creation of competitively valuable resource strengths and capabilities.

illustration capsule 35
Tyco International's Diversification Strategy

They call Dennis Kozlowski, Tyco International's CEO, the "deal a day man." That's because part of Tyco's overall strategy is to grow by acquiring companies in a variety of different manufacturing businesses.

Tyco, which has 240,000 employees in more than 100 countries, currently controls more than 200 businesses operating in six industry segments worldwide. It had 2001 revenues of approximately $36 billion. The company's largest unit specializes in electronics. Then there are the health care and specialty products division, which churns out bandages and crutches; the fire and security services unit, a world leader; the flow control group, which makes pipe and tubing; and the telecommunications division, which produces undersea fiber-optic cable. Further, Tyco entered the financial services segment by buying the commercial loan firm CIT.

Tyco's experience in assimilating the operations of the companies it acquired had resulted in the company developing a "formula" for making sure that the operations of acquired companies produced satisfactory profits. In recent years, Tyco had made between 6 and 15 significant acquisitions and dozens of small acquisitions annually. Most of the new acquisitions complemented or were extensions of the businesses in Tyco's six industry segments.

When Wall Street analysts began to question Tyco's ability to continue to acquire and successfully manage so many new and existing businesses, Tyco announced in January 2002 that it would "unlock tens of billions of dollars of shareholder value by separating Tyco into four independent, publicly traded companies. Weeks later, Tyco came under scrutiny for its accounting practices and failure to report all its acquisitions, precipitating a 40 percent drop in its stock price. Kozlowski defended the company's strategy and actions.

Sources: "Tyco International Ltd.," Hoovers Online (www.hoovers.com), accessed August 30, 2001; Peter Marsh, "Tyco Searches for Directors in Europe and Asia," *Financial Times* (http://news.ft.com), July 15, 2001; William C. Symonds, "The Most Aggressive CEO," *BusinessWeek Online* (www.businessweek.com), May 28, 2001; and Tyco press release, January 22, 2002.

manufacturing, in sales and marketing, in distribution activities, or in administrative support activities.[3]

R&D and Technology Activities Diversifying into businesses where there is potential for sharing common technology, exploiting the full range of business opportunities associated with a particular technology and its derivatives, or transferring technological know-how from one business to another has considerable appeal. Businesses with technology-sharing benefits can perform better together than apart because of potential cost savings in R&D, because of potentially shorter times in getting new products to market, and/or because technological advances in one leads to increased sales of both. Technological innovations were the driver behind AT&T's diversification into cable TV (via the acquisition of TCI and MediaOne). Now that there are ways to provide local and long-distance telephone service, cable TV service, and Internet access to residential and commercial customers in a single "pipe," AT&T can offer its customers all of these services in a single package.

Supply Chain Activities Businesses that have supply chain strategic fits can perform better together because of the potential for skills transfer in procuring materials, greater bargaining power in negotiating with common suppliers, the benefits of added collaboration with common supply chain partners, and/or added leverage with shippers in securing volume discounts on incoming parts and components. Dell

---

[3]For a discussion of the strategic significance of cross-business coordination and insight into how it works, see Jeanne M. Liedtka, "Collaboration across Lines of Business for Competitive Advantage," *Academy of Management Executive* 10, no. 2 (May 1996), pp. 20–34.

Computer's strategic partnerships with leading suppliers of microprocessors, motherboards, disk drives, memory chips, monitors, modems, flat-panel displays, long-life batteries, and other desktop and laptop components have been an important component of its strategy to diversify into servers and workstations—products that include many components common to PCs and that can be sourced from the same strategic partners that provide Dell with PC components.

Manufacturing Activities   Cross-business strategic fits in production-related activities can represent an important source of competitive advantage in situations where a diversifier's expertise in quality manufacture, in cost-efficient production methods, in just-in-time inventory practices, or in training and motivating workers can be transferred to another business. When Emerson Electric diversified into the chain-saw business, it transferred its expertise in low-cost manufacture to its newly acquired Beaird-Poulan business division; the transfer drove Beaird-Poulan's new strategy to be the low-cost provider of chain-saw products and fundamentally changed the way Beaird-Poulan chain saws were designed and manufactured. Another benefit of value chain matchups in production may involve cost-saving opportunities stemming from the ability to perform manufacturing or assembly activities jointly in the same facility rather than independently, thus making it feasible to consolidate production into a smaller number of plants and significantly reduce overall production costs. When snowmobile maker Bombardier diversified into motorcycles, it was able to set up assembly lines for its motorcycles in the same manufacturing facility where it was assembling its snowmobiles.

Distribution Activities   Businesses with closely related distribution activities can perform better together than apart because of potential cost savings in sharing the same distribution facilities or using many of the same wholesale distributors and retail dealers to access customers. When Sunbeam acquired Mr. Coffee, it was able to consolidate the distribution centers for its own line of small household appliances and the distribution centers for Mr. Coffee's lineup of coffeemakers; cutting back on the number of distribution centers the company had to operate generated considerable cost savings. Likewise, since Sunbeam products were sold to many of the same retailers as Mr. Coffee products (Wal-Mart, Kmart, department stores, home centers, hardware chains, supermarket chains, and drugstore chains), Sunbeam was able to convince many of the retailers carrying Sunbeam appliances to also take on the Mr. Coffee line and to convince retailers that stocked Mr. Coffee products to also begin carrying Sunbeam products.

Sales and Marketing Activities   A variety of cost-saving opportunities spring from diversifying into businesses with closely related sales and marketing activities. Sales costs can often be reduced by using a single sales force for the products of both businesses rather than having separate sales forces for each business. When the products are distributed through many of the same wholesale and retail dealers or are sold directly to the same customers, it is usually feasible to give one salesperson the responsibility for handling the sales of both products (rather than have two different salespeople call on the same customer). The products of related businesses can be promoted at the same website, and included in the same media ads and sales brochures. After-sale service and repair organizations for the products of closely related businesses can often be consolidated into a single operation. There may be opportunities to reduce costs by coordinating delivery and shipping, coordinating order processing and billing, and using common promotional tie-ins (cents-off couponing, free samples and trial offers, seasonal specials, and the like). When global power-tool maker Black & Decker acquired General Electric's domestic small household appliance business, it was able to use its own global sales force and global distribution facilities in power tools to sell and distribute small appliances (toasters, irons, mixers, and coffeemakers) because the types of customers that carried its power tools (discounters like Wal-Mart and Kmart, home centers, and hardware stores) also stocked small appliances. The economies of combining and then downsizing the sales forces and distribution centers for power tools and small appliances were substantial.

A second category of benefits arises when different businesses use similar sales and marketing approaches; in such cases, there may be competitively valuable opportunities to transfer selling, merchandising, advertising, and product differentiation skills from one business to another. Philip Morris, a leading cigarette manufacturer, pursued a related diversification strategy by purchasing Miller Brewing, General Foods, and Kraft Foods and transferring its competencies and capabilities in advertising, promoting, and marketing cigarettes to the marketing of beer and food products. Procter & Gamble's lineup of products includes Jif peanut butter, Duncan Hines cake mixes, Folger's coffee, Tide laundry detergent, Crisco vegetable oil, Crest toothpaste, Ivory soap, Charmin toilet tissue, and Head and Shoulders shampoo. All of these have different competitors and different supply chain and production requirements, but they all move through the same wholesale distribution systems, are sold in common retail settings to the same shoppers, are advertised and promoted in the same ways, and require the same marketing and merchandising skills.

A third set of benefits arises from related sales and marketing activities when a company's brand name and reputation in one business is transferable to other businesses. Black & Decker's strong brand name in power tools and cordless items like the Dustbuster vacuum greatly facilitated a successful transfer of the B&D brand name to the products in GE's household appliance line. Honda's name in motorcycles and automobiles gave it instant credibility and recognition in entering the lawn-mower business, allowing it to achieve a significant market share without spending large sums on advertising to establish a brand identity for its lawn mowers. Canon's reputation in photographic equipment was a competitive asset that facilitated the company's diversification into copying equipment. Panasonic's name in consumer electronics (radios, TVs) was readily transferred to microwave ovens, making it easier and cheaper for Panasonic to diversify into the microwave oven market.

Managerial and Administrative Support Activities Often, different businesses require comparable types of skills, competencies, and managerial know-how, thereby allowing know-how in one line of business to be transferred to another. Ford transferred its automobile financing and credit management know-how to the savings and loan industry when it acquired some failing savings and loan associations during the 1989 bailout of the crisis-ridden S&L industry. At General Electric, managers who were involved in GE's geographic expansion into Russia were able to expedite entry because of information gained from GE managers involved in expansions into other emerging-country markets. The lessons GE managers learned in China were passed along to GE managers in Russia, allowing them to anticipate that the Russian government would demand that GE build production capacity in the country rather than enter the market through exporting or licensing and that GE would be required to aid in the country's national economic development efforts. In addition, GE's managers in Russia were better able to develop realistic performance expectations and make tough up-front decisions since experience in China and elsewhere warned them (1) that there would likely be increased short-term costs during the early years of start-up and (2) that if GE committed to the Russian market for the long term and aided the country's economic development it could eventually expect to be given the freedom to pursue profitable penetration of the Russian market.[4]

---

[4]"Beyond Knowledge Management: How Companies Mobilize Experience," *The Financial Times*, February 8, 1999, p. 5.

illustration capsule 36
Examples of Companies with Related Business Portfolios

Presented below are the business portfolios of four companies that have pursued related diversification. See if you can identify the strategic fits and value chain relationships that exist among their businesses.

GILLETTE

- Blades and razors
- Toiletries (Right Guard, Foamy, Dry Idea, Soft & Dry, White Rain)
- Oral-B toothbrushes
- Writing instruments and stationery products (Paper Mate pens, Parker pens, Waterman pens, Liquid Paper correction fluids)
- Braun shavers, coffeemakers, alarm clocks, mixers, hair dryers, and electric toothbrushes
- Duracell batteries

DARDEN RESTAURANTS

- Olive Garden restaurant chain (Italian-themed)
- Red Lobster restaurant chain (seafood-themed)
- Bahama Breeze restaurant chain (Caribbean-themed)

JOHNSON & JOHNSON

- Baby products (powder, shampoo, oil, lotion)
- Band-Aids and other first-aid products
- Women's health and personal care products (Stayfree, Carefree, Sure & Natural)
- Neutrogena and Aveeno skin care products
- Nonprescription drugs (Tylenol, Motrin, Pepcid AC, Mylanta, Monistat)
- Prescription drugs
- Prosthetic and other medical devices
- Surgical and hospital products
- Accuvue contact lenses

PEPSICO, INC.

- Soft drinks (Pepsi, Diet Pepsi, Pepsi ONE, Mountain Dew, Mug, Slice, Storm)
- Fruit juices (Tropicana and Dole)
- New Age and other beverages (Aquafina bottled water, Lipton ready-to-drink tea, Starbucks ready-to-drink coffee, All Sport isotonic beverages)
- Snack foods (Fritos, Lays, Ruffles, Doritos, Tostitos, Santitas, Smart Food, Rold Gold pretzels, Chee-tos, Grandma's cookies, Sun Chips, Cracker Jack, salsas, sandwich crackers)

Source: Company annual reports.

Likewise, different businesses sometimes entail the same types of administrative support facilities. For instance, an electric utility that diversifies into natural gas, water, cable TV, appliance sales and repair services, and home security services can use the same customer data network, the same customer call centers and local offices, the same billing and customer accounting systems, and the same customer service infrastructure to support all of its products and services.

Illustration Capsule 36 shows the business portfolios of four companies that have pursued a strategy of related diversification.

Strategic Fit, Economies of Scope, and Competitive Advantage

As the preceding discussion illustrates, related diversification can lead to cost savings whenever there are opportunities to consolidate one or more of the value chain activities being performed in different businesses. Such savings are termed **economies of scope**—a concept distinct from *economies of scale*. Economies of *scale* are cost savings that accrue from increases in size or number; for example, unit costs are lower in

> **Basic Concept**
> *Economies of scope* arise from the ability to eliminate costs by operating two or more businesses under the same corporate umbrella; the cost-saving opportunities can stem from strategic fit relationships anywhere along the businesses' value chains.

a large plant than in a small plant, lower in a large distribution center than in a small one, lower for large-volume purchases of components than for small-volume purchases. Economies of *scope* are cross-business cost-saving opportunities.

Economies of scope are pretty much a phenomenon of related diversification, arising whenever it is less costly to perform certain value chain activities for two or more businesses operated under centralized management than it is for these activities to be performed independently. Sharing technology, performing R&D together, sharing manufacturing or distribution facilities, using a common sales force or distributor/dealer network, sharing an established brand name, and sharing administrative support functions can all help a diversified company save money. *The greater the economies of scope associated with cross-business cost-saving opportunities, the greater the potential for creating a competitive advantage based on lower costs.*

What makes related diversification an attractive strategy is the opportunity to convert the strategic fit relationships between the value chains of different businesses into competitive advantage over business rivals that have not diversified or that have diversified in ways that don't give them access to such strategic-fit benefits. The greater the relatedness among the businesses of a diversified company, the greater the opportunities for skills transfer and/or combining value chain activities to achieve lower costs and/or collaborating to create new resource strengths and capabilities and the bigger the window for creating competitive advantage.

Moreover, *a diversified firm that exploits cross-business value-chain matchups and captures the benefits of strategic fit can achieve a consolidated performance greater than the sum of what the businesses can earn pursuing independent strategies.* The competitive edge flowing from strategic fits along the value chains of related businesses provides a dependable basis for them performing better together than as stand-alone enterprises where no such competitive edge exists. The bigger the strategic-fit benefits, the more that related diversification is capable of $1 + 1 = 3$ performance—thereby satisfying the better-off test for building shareholder value.

> What makes related diversification attractive is the opportunity to turn cross-business strategic fits into competitive advantage.

> Competitive advantage achieved through cross-business strategic fits adds to the performance potential of the firm's individual businesses; this extra source of competitive advantage allows related diversification to have a $1 + 1 = 3$ effect on shareholder value.

Capturing Strategic-Fit Benefits

It is one thing to diversify into industries with strategic fit and another to actually capture the benefits associated with having interrelated value chains.[5] To capture the cost-saving benefits of cross-business strategic fits, the related value chain activities must usually be merged into a single functional unit and coordinated; then the cost savings must be squeezed out. Because merging functions can entail reorganization costs, management must decide whether the benefit of some centralized strategic control is great enough to warrant sacrifice of business-unit autonomy. Likewise, where skills or technology transfer is the cornerstone of strategic fit, managers must find a way to make the transfer effective without stripping too many skilled personnel from the business that has the expertise. The more a company's diversification strategy is tied to skills or technology transfer, the more it has to develop a big enough and talented enough pool of specialized personnel not only to supply new businesses with the skill or technology but also to master the skill or technology sufficiently to create competitive advantage.

There is one additional benefit that flows from becoming adept at capturing cross-business strategic fits: the competitive advantage potential for the firm to expand its pool of resources and strategic assets and to create new ones *faster and more cheaply* than

> A company that can expand its stock of strategic assets faster and at lower cost than rivals obtains sustainable competitive advantage.

[5]For one view of how to capture strategic fit benefits, see Kathleen M. Eisenhardt and D. Charles Galunic, "Coevolving: At Last, a Way to Make Synergies Work," *Harvard Business Review* 78, no. 1 (January–February 2000), pp. 91–101.

rivals who are not diversified across related businesses.[6] One reason some diversified firms perform better over the long term than others is that they are more accomplished in exploiting the links between their related businesses; such know-how translates into an ability to *accelerate* the creation of valuable new core competencies and competitive capabilities. Given the rapid pace of change in many industries in today's world, having the ability to build new resource strengths and capabilities faster than rivals is a potent and dependable way for a diversified company to earn superior returns over the long term.

THE CASE FOR UNRELATED DIVERSIFICATION STRATEGIES

Despite the strategic-fit benefits associated with related diversification, a number of companies opt for unrelated diversification strategies. These companies exhibit a willingness to diversify into *any industry* with a good profit opportunity. *In unrelated diversification there is no deliberate effort to seek out businesses having strategic fit with the firm's other businesses*—see Figure 9.3. While companies pursuing unrelated diversification may try to make certain their diversification targets meet the industry-attractiveness and cost-of-entry tests, the conditions needed for the better-off test are either disregarded or relegated to secondary status. Decisions to diversify into one industry versus another are the product of an opportunistic search for "good" companies to acquire—*the basic premise of unrelated diversification is that any company that can be acquired on good financial terms and that has satisfactory profit prospects represents a good business to diversify into.* Much time and effort goes into finding and screening acquisition candidates, using such criteria as:

- Whether the business can meet corporate targets for profitability and return on investment.
- Whether the new business will require substantial infusions of capital to replace out-of-date plants and equipment, fund expansion, and provide working capital.
- Whether the business is in an industry with significant growth potential.
- Whether the business is big enough to contribute significantly to the parent firm's bottom line.
- Whether there is a potential for union difficulties or adverse government regulations concerning product safety or the environment.
- Whether there is industry vulnerability to recession, inflation, high interest rates, or shifts in government policy.

> A strategy of unrelated diversification involves diversifying into whatever industries and businesses hold promise for attractive financial gain; exploiting strategic-fit relationships is secondary.

Sometimes, companies with unrelated diversification strategies concentrate on identifying acquisition candidates that offer quick opportunities for financial gain because of their "special situation." Two types of businesses may hold such attraction:

- *Companies whose assets are undervalued*—Opportunities may exist to acquire such companies for less than full market value and make substantial capital gains by reselling their assets and businesses for more than their acquired costs.
- *Companies that are financially distressed*—Such businesses can often be purchased at a bargain price, their operations turned around with the aid of the parent company's financial resources and managerial know-how, and then either held as long-term investments in the acquirer's business portfolio (because of their strong earnings or cash flow potential) or sold at a profit, whichever is more attractive.

---

[6]Constantinos C. Markides and Peter J. Williamson, "Related Diversification, Core Competences and Corporate Performance," *Strategic Management Journal* 15 (Summer 1994), pp. 149–65.

figure 9.3   **Value Chains for Unrelated Businesses**

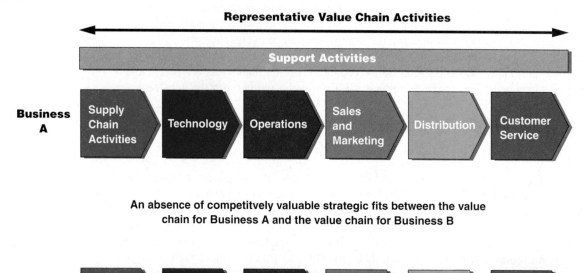

Companies that pursue unrelated diversification nearly always enter new businesses by acquiring an established company rather than by forming a start-up subsidiary within their own corporate structures. Their premise is that growth by acquisition translates into enhanced shareholder value. Suspending application of the better-off test is seen as justifiable so long as unrelated diversification results in sustained growth in corporate revenues and earnings and so long as none of the acquired businesses end up performing badly.

Illustration Capsule 37 shows the business portfolios of several companies that have pursued unrelated diversification. Such companies are frequently labeled *conglomerates* because their business interests range broadly across diverse industries.

The Pros and Cons of Unrelated Diversification

Unrelated diversification has appeal from several financial angles:

1.   Business risk is scattered over a set of *diverse* industries—a superior way to diversify financial risk as compared to related diversification because the company's investments can be spread over businesses with totally different technologies, competitive forces, market features, and customer bases.[7]

---

[7]While such arguments have logical appeal, there is research showing that related diversification is less risky from a financial perspective than is unrelated diversification; see Michael Lubatkin and Sayan Chatterjee, "Extending Modern Portfolio Theory into the Domain of Corporate Diversification: Does It Apply?" *Academy of Management Journal* 37, no. 1 (February 1994), pp. 109–36.

illustration capsule 37
Diversified Companies with Unrelated Business Portfolios

DIAGEO PLC

- Burger King fast-food restaurants
- Guinness—a leading beer brewer and maker of stout
- Häagen-Dazs ice cream products
- Pillsbury and Martha White flours and baking products
- Old El Paso Mexican food products
- Progresso soups
- Totino's pizza
- Frescarina fresh pasta
- B&M baked beans
- Green Giant, Giant Vert, and Gigante brands of canned and frozen vegetables
- Spirits and wines—Smirnoff, Popov vodka, Johnny Walker, Gordon's, Tanqueray, George Dickel, J&B, Moët, Henessey, Gilbey's, Bailey's, Cinzano, Jose Cuervo, Beaulieu Vineyards, Glen Ellen Wines, Rutherford Estates wines, Dom Perignon, and some 50 other brands of liquors, cordials, wines, and brandies

UNITED TECHNOLOGIES, INC.

- Pratt & Whitney aircraft engines
- Carrier heating and air-conditioning equipment
- Otis elevators
- Sikorsky helicopters
- Hamilton Substrand aerospace subsystems and components

THE WALT DISNEY COMPANY

- Theme parks
- Disney Cruise Line
- Resort properties
- Movie production (for both children and adults)
- Video production
- Television broadcasting (ABC, Disney Channel, Toon Disney, Classic Sports Network, ESPN, E!, Lifetime, and A&E networks)
- Radio broadcasting (Disney Radio)
- Theatrical productions
- Musical recordings
- Animation art sales
- Anaheim Mighty Ducks NHL franchise
- Anaheim Angels Major League Baseball franchise (25 percent ownership)
- Book and magazine publishing
- Interactive software and Internet sites
- The Disney Store retail shops

COOPER INDUSTRIES

- Crescent wrenches, pliers, and screwdrivers
- Nicholson files and saws
- Diamond horseshoes and farrier tools
- Lufkin measuring and layout products
- Gardner-Denver electric power tools
- Electrical construction materials
- Lighting fixtures, fuses, and circuit protection devices
- Electric utility products (transformers, relays, capacitor controls, switches)
- Emergency lighting, fire detection, and security systems

TEXTRON, INC.

- Bell helicopters
- Cessna Aircraft
- E-Z-Go golf carts
- Textron Automotive (instrument panels, plastic fuel tanks, plastic interior and exterior trim)
- Textron Fastening Systems (the global leader)
- Fluid and power systems
- Textron Financial Services
- Jacobsen turf care equipment
- Ransomes turf care and utility vehicles
- Tools and testing equipment for the wire and cable industry

(continued)

illustration capsule 37

(concluded)

AMERICAN STANDARD

- Trane and American Standard furnaces, heat pumps, and air conditioners
- Plumbing products (American Standard, Ideal Standard, Standard, Porcher lavatories, toilets, bathtubs, faucets, whirlpool baths, and shower basins)
- Automotive products (commercial and utility vehicle braking and control systems)
- Medical systems (DiaSorin disease assessment and management products)

VEBA GROUP

VEBA is a German-based company with revenues of $43 billion and a ranking of 46 on the Fortune Global 500.

- PreussenElektra—Germany's second largest generator of electricity

- Degussa-Huls—one of the world's largest specialty chemicals companies whose products include feed additives, hydrogen peroxide, industrial carbon black, silicic acids, and phenol
- VEBA Oel—a crude oil producer and a refiner of petroleum and petrochemical products
- MEMC Electronic Materials—a Missouri-based manufacturer of silicon wafers, with production facilities in the United States, Asia, and Europe
- VEBA Telecom—a seller of wireless service to private and business customers and a participant in the telecommunications markets in Switzerland and France
- Viterra—Germany's market leader in real estate and real estate services
- VEBA Electronics and Stinnes—business interests in distribution/logistics

Source: Company annual reports.

2. The company's financial resources can be employed to maximum advantage by investing in *whatever industries* offer the best profit prospects (as opposed to considering only opportunities in related industries). Specifically, cash flows from company businesses with lower growth and profit prospects can be diverted to acquiring and expanding businesses with higher growth and profit potentials.

3. Company profitability may prove somewhat more stable because hard times in one industry may be partially offset by good times in another—ideally, cyclical downswings in some of the company's businesses are counterbalanced by cyclical upswings in other businesses the company has diversified into.

4. To the extent that corporate managers are exceptionally astute at spotting bargain-priced companies with big upside profit potential, shareholder wealth can be enhanced.

> The two biggest drawbacks to unrelated diversification are the difficulties of competently managing many different businesses and being without the added source of competitive advantage that cross-business strategic fit provides.

While entry into an unrelated business can often pass the industry attractiveness and cost-of-entry tests (but rarely the better-off test), a strategy of unrelated diversification has drawbacks. One Achilles' heel of conglomerate diversification is the big demand it places on corporate-level management to make sound decisions regarding fundamentally different businesses operating in fundamentally different industry and competitive environments. The greater the number of businesses a company is in and the more diverse they are, the harder it is for corporate managers to oversee each subsidiary and spot problems early, to have real expertise in evaluating the attractiveness of each business's industry and competitive environment, and to judge the caliber of strategic actions and plans proposed by business-level managers. As one president of a diversified firm expressed it:

We've got to make sure that our core businesses are properly managed for solid, long-term earnings. We can't just sit back and watch the numbers. We've got to know what the real issues are out there in the profit centers. Otherwise, we're not even in a position to check out our managers on the big decisions.[8]

With broad diversification, corporate managers have to be shrewd and talented enough to (1) discern a good acquisition from a bad acquisition, (2) select capable managers to run each of many different businesses, (3) discern when the major strategic proposals of business-unit managers are sound, and (4) know what to do if a business unit stumbles.[9] Because every business tends to encounter rough sledding, a good way to gauge the risk of diversifying into new unrelated areas is to ask, "If the new business got into trouble, would we know how to bail it out?" When the answer is no, unrelated diversification can pose significant financial risk and the business's profit prospects are more chancy.[10] As the former chairman of a Fortune 500 company advised, "Never acquire a business you don't know how to run." It takes only one or two big strategic mistakes (misjudging industry attractiveness, encountering unexpected problems in a newly acquired business, or being too optimistic about how hard it will be to turn a struggling subsidiary around) to cause a precipitous drop in corporate earnings and crash the parent company's stock price.

Second, without the competitive advantage potential of strategic fit, consolidated performance of an unrelated multibusiness portfolio tends to be no better than the sum of what the individual business units could achieve if they were independent, and it may be worse to the extent that corporate managers meddle unwisely in business-unit operations or hamstring them with corporate policies. Except, perhaps, for the added financial backing that a cash-rich corporate parent can provide, a strategy of unrelated diversification does nothing for the competitive strength of the individual business units. Each business is on its own in trying to build a competitive edge. Unrelated diversification offers no basis for cost reduction, skills transfer, or technology sharing. In a widely diversified firm, the value added by corporate managers depends primarily on how good they are at deciding what new businesses to add, which ones to get rid of, how best to deploy available financial resources to build a higher-performing collection of businesses, and the quality of the decision-making guidance they give to the general managers of their business subsidiaries.

Third, although in theory unrelated diversification offers the potential for greater sales-profit stability over the course of the business cycle, *in practice, attempts at countercyclical diversification fall short of the mark*. Few attractive businesses have opposite up-and-down cycles; the great majority of businesses are similarly affected by economic good times and hard times. There's no convincing evidence that the consolidated profits of broadly diversified firms are more stable or less subject to reversal in periods of recession and economic stress than the profits of less diversified firms.

---

[8]Carter F. Bales, "Strategic Control: The President's Paradox," *Business Horizons* 20, no. 4 (August 1977), p. 17.

[9]For a review of the experiences of companies that have pursued unrelated diversification successfully, see Patricia L. Anslinger and Thomas E. Copeland, "Growth through Acquisitions: A Fresh Look," *Harvard Business Review* 74, no. 1 (January–February 1996), pp. 126–35.

[10]Of course, management may be willing to assume the risk that trouble will not strike before it has had time to learn the business well enough to bail it out of almost any difficulty. But there is research that shows this is very risky from a financial perspective; see, for example, Lubatkin and Chatterjee, "Extending Modern Portfolio Theory," pp. 132–33.

Despite these drawbacks, unrelated diversification can sometimes be a desirable corporate strategy. It certainly merits consideration when a firm needs to diversify away from an endangered or unattractive industry and has no distinctive competencies or capabilities it can transfer to an adjacent industry. There's also a rationale for pure diversification to the extent that owners have a strong preference for investing in several unrelated businesses instead of a family of related ones. Otherwise, the argument for unrelated diversification hinges on the case-by-case prospects for financial gain.

A key issue in unrelated diversification is how wide a net to cast in building the business portfolio. In other words, should the corporate portfolio contain few or many unrelated businesses? How much business diversity can corporate executives successfully manage? A reasonable way to resolve the issue of how much diversification comes from answering two questions: "What is the least diversification it will take to achieve acceptable growth and profitability?" and "What is the most diversification that can be managed given the complexity it adds?"[11] The optimal amount of diversification usually lies between these two extremes.

Unrelated Diversification and Shareholder Value

Unrelated diversification is fundamentally a *financial* approach to creating shareholder value, whereas related diversification is fundamentally *strategic*. Related diversification represents a strategic approach to building shareholder value because it is predicated on exploiting the links between the value chains of different businesses to lower costs, transfer skills and technological expertise across businesses, and gain other strategic-fit benefits. As we stressed earlier, the objective is to convert cross-business strategic fits into an extra measure of competitive advantage that goes beyond what business subsidiaries are able to achieve on their own. The added competitive advantage a firm achieves through related diversification is the driver for building greater shareholder value.

In contrast, unrelated diversification is predicated on astute deployment of corporate financial resources and executive skill in spotting financially attractive business opportunities. Since unrelated diversification entails no cross-business strategic-fit opportunities of consequence, corporate strategists can't build shareholder value by acquiring companies that exploit value chain matchups to perform better together than as stand-alone entities—in a conglomerate of unrelated businesses, competitive advantage doesn't go beyond what each business subsidiary can achieve independently through its own competitive strategy. Consequently, for unrelated diversification to result in enhanced shareholder value (above the $1 + 1 = 2$ effect that shareholders could obtain by purchasing ownership interests in a variety of businesses to spread investment risk on their own behalf), corporate strategists must exhibit superior skills in creating and managing a portfolio of diversified business interests. This specifically means:

- Doing a superior job of diversifying into new businesses that can produce consistently good returns on investment (satisfying the attractiveness test).
- Doing an excellent job of negotiating favorable acquisition prices (satisfying the cost-of-entry test).
- Making astute moves to sell previously acquired business subsidiaries at their peak and getting premium prices. (This requires skills in discerning when a business subsidiary is on the verge of confronting adverse industry and competitive conditions and probable declines in long-term profitability.)

> Unrelated diversification is a *financial* approach to creating shareholder value; related diversification, in contrast, represents a *strategic* approach.

> For corporate strategists to build shareholder value in some way other than through strategic fits and competitive advantage, they must be smart enough to produce financial results from a group of businesses that exceed what business-level managers can produce.

---

[11]Peter Drucker, *Management: Tasks, Responsibilities, Practices* (New York: Harper & Row, 1974), pp. 692–93.

- Being shrewd in shifting corporate financial resources out of businesses where profit opportunities are dim and into businesses where rapid earnings growth and high returns on investment are occurring.

- Doing such a good job overseeing the firm's business subsidiaries and contributing to how they are managed (by providing expert problem-solving skills, creative strategy suggestions, and decision-making guidance to business-level managers) that the businesses perform at a higher level than they would otherwise be able to do (a possible way to satisfy the better-off test).

To the extent that corporate executives are able to craft and execute a strategy of unrelated diversification that produces enough of the above outcomes for an enterprise to consistently outperform other firms in generating dividends and capital gains for stockholders, a case can be made that shareholder value has truly been enhanced. Achieving such results consistently requires supertalented corporate executives, however. Without them, unrelated diversification is a very dubious and unreliable way to try to build shareholder value. There are far more who have tried it and failed than who have tried it and succeeded.

COMBINATION RELATED-UNRELATED DIVERSIFICATION STRATEGIES

There's nothing to preclude a company from diversifying into both related and unrelated businesses. Indeed, in actual practice the business makeup of diversified companies varies considerably. Some diversified companies are really *dominant-business enterprises*—one major "core" business accounts for 50 to 80 percent of total revenues and a collection of small related or unrelated businesses accounts for the remainder. Some diversified companies are *narrowly diversified* around a few (two to five) related or unrelated businesses. Some diversified companies are *broadly diversified* and have a wide-ranging collection of either related businesses or unrelated businesses or a mixture of both. And a few multibusiness enterprises have diversified into unrelated areas but have a collection of related businesses within each area—thus giving them a business portfolio consisting of *several unrelated groups of related businesses.* There's ample room for companies to customize their diversification strategies to incorporate elements of both related and unrelated diversification, as may suit their own risk preferences and strategic vision.

STRATEGIES FOR ENTERING NEW BUSINESSES

Entry into new related or unrelated businesses can take any of three forms: acquisition, internal start-up, and joint ventures/strategic partnerships.

Acquisition of an Existing Business

Acquisition is the most popular means of diversifying into another industry. Not only is it a quicker way to enter the target market than trying to launch a brand-new operation from the ground up but it offers an effective way to hurdle such entry barriers as acquiring technological experience, establishing supplier relationships, becoming big enough to match rivals' efficiency and unit costs, having to spend large sums on introductory advertising and promotions to gain market visibility and brand recognition, and securing adequate distribution.[12] In many industries, going the internal start-up route and trying to develop the knowledge, resources, scale of operation, and market reputation necessary to become an effective competitor can take years. Acquiring an already established concern allows the entrant to move directly to the task of building a strong market position in the target industry.

However, finding the right kind of company to acquire sometimes presents a challenge.[13] The big dilemma an acquisition-minded firm faces is whether to pay a premium price for a successful company or to buy a struggling company at a bargain price. If the buying firm has little knowledge of the industry but ample capital, it is often better off purchasing a capable, strongly positioned firm—unless the price of such an acquisition is prohibitive and flunks the cost-of-entry test. However, when the acquirer sees promising ways to transform a weak firm into a strong one and has the resources, the know-how, and the patience to do it, a struggling company can be the better long-term investment.

The cost-of-entry test requires that the expected profit stream of an acquired business provide an attractive return on the total acquisition cost and on any new capital investment needed to sustain or expand its operations. A high acquisition price can make meeting that test improbable or difficult. For instance, suppose that the price to purchase a company is $3 million and that the business is earning after-tax profits of $200,000 on an equity investment of $1 million (a 20 percent annual return). Simple arithmetic requires that the acquired business's profits be tripled for the purchaser to earn the same 20 percent return on the $3 million acquisition price that the previous owners were getting on their $1 million equity investment. Building the acquired firm's earnings from $200,000 to $600,000 annually could take several years—and require additional investment on which the purchaser would also have to earn a 20 percent return. Since the owners of a successful and growing company usually demand a price that reflects their business's future profit prospects, it's easy for such an acquisition to fail the cost-of-entry test. A would-be diversifier can't count on being able to acquire a desirable company in an appealing industry at a price that still permits attractive returns on investment.

> One stumbling block to entering attractive industries by acquisition is the difficulty of finding a suitable company at a price that satisfies the cost-of-entry test.

Internal Start-Up

Achieving diversification through *internal start-up* involves creating a new company under the corporate umbrella to compete in the desired industry. A newly formed organization not only has to overcome entry barriers but also has to invest in new production capacity, develop sources of supply, hire and train employees, build channels of distribution, grow a customer base, and so on. Generally, forming a start-up company is more attractive when (1) there is ample time to launch the business from the ground up, (2) incumbent firms are likely to be slow or ineffective in responding to a new entrant's efforts to crack the market, (3) internal entry has lower costs than entry via acquisition, (4) the company already has in-house most or all of the skills it needs to compete effectively, (5) adding new production capacity will not adversely impact the supply-demand balance in the industry, and (6) the targeted industry is populated

> The biggest drawbacks to entering an industry by forming a start-up company internally are the costs of overcoming entry barriers and the extra time it takes to build a strong and profitable competitive position.

---

[12]In recent years, hostile takeovers have become a hotly debated and sometimes abused approach to acquisition. The term *takeover* refers to the attempt (often sprung as a surprise) of one firm to acquire ownership or control over another firm against the wishes of the latter's management (and perhaps some of its stockholders).

[13]Michael E. Porter, *Competitive Strategy: Techniques for Analyzing Industries and Competitors* (New York: Free Press, 1980), pp. 354–55.

with many relatively small firms so the new start-up does not have to compete head-to-head against larger, more powerful rivals.[14]

Joint Ventures and Strategic Partnerships

Joint ventures typically entail forming a new corporate entity owned by the partners, whereas strategic partnerships represent a collaborative arrangement that usually can be terminated whenever any one of the partners so chooses. Most joint ventures have involved two partners and, historically, were normally formed to pursue opportunities that were somewhat peripheral to the strategic interests of the partners; very few companies have used joint ventures to diversify into new industries central to their corporate strategy. In recent years, strategic partnerships/alliances have replaced joint ventures as the favored mechanism for joining forces to pursue strategically important diversification opportunities because they can readily accommodate multiple partners and are more flexible and adaptable to rapidly changing technogological and market conditions than a formal joint venture.

A strategic partnership or joint venture can be a useful way to gain access to a new business in at least three types of situations.[15] First, a strategic alliance/joint venture is a good way to pursue an opportunity that is too complex, uneconomical, or risky for a single organization to pursue alone. Second, strategic alliances/joint ventures make sense when the opportunities in a new industry require a broader range of competencies and know-how than any one organization can marshal. Many of the opportunities in satellite-based telecommunications, biotechnology, and network-based systems that blend hardware, software, and services call for the coordinated development of complementary innovations and integrating a host of financial, technical, political, and regulatory factors. In such cases, pooling the resources and competencies of two or more independent organizations is essential to generate the capabilities needed for success.

Third, joint ventures are sometimes the only way to gain entry into a desirable foreign market when market entry is restricted by government and companies must secure a local partner to gain entry; for example, the Chinese government closed entry in the automotive industry to all but a few select automakers and in the elevator industry it originally permitted only Otis, Schindler, and Mitsubishi to establish joint ventures with local partners. (Although this number was later expanded, the three early entrants were able to retain a market advantage over later entrants.)[16] Joint ventures with local partners can also be a useful way to surmount tariff barriers and import quotas. Alliances with local partners have become a favorite mechanism for global companies to establish footholds in desirable foreign country markets. Local partners offer outside companies the benefits of local knowledge about market conditions, local customs and cultural factors, and customer buying habits; they can also be a source of managerial and marketing personnel and provide access to distribution outlets. The foreign partner's role is usually to provide specialized skills, technological know-how, and other resources needed to crack the local market and serve it efficiently.

However, such partnerships are not without their difficulties, often posing complicated questions about how to divide efforts among the partners and about who has effective control.[17] Conflicts between foreign and domestic partners can arise over

---

[14]Ibid., pp. 344–45.

[15]Yves L. Doz and Gary Hamel, *Alliance Advantage: The Art of Creating Value through Partnering* (Boston: Harvard Business School Press, 1998), chapters 1 and 2. See also Drucker, *Management: Tasks, Responsibilities, Practices,* pp. 720–24.

[16]Doz and Hamel, *Alliance Advantage,* p. 46.

[17]Porter, *Competitive Strategy,* p. 340.

whether to use local sourcing of components, how much production to export, whether operating procedures should conform to the local partner's or the foreign company's standards, and the extent to which the local partner is entitled to make use of the foreign partner's technology and intellectual property. As the foreign partner acquires experience and confidence in the local market, its need for the local partner typically diminishes, posing the strategic issue of whether the alliance/joint venture should be dissolved. This happens frequently in alliances between global manufacturers and local distributors.[18] Japanese car makers have abandoned their European distribution partners and set up their own dealer networks; BMW did the same thing in Japan. On the other hand, several ambitious local partners have used their alliances with global companies to master technologies and build key competitive skills, then capitalized on the acquired know-how to launch their own entry into the international arena. Taiwan's Acer Computer Group used its alliance with Texas Instruments as a stepping stone for entering the world market for desktop and laptop computers.

STRATEGY OPTIONS FOR COMPANIES THAT ARE ALREADY DIVERSIFIED

We can better understand the strategic issues corporate managers face in managing a diversified group of businesses by looking at four post-diversification strategy alternatives:

1. Broadening the firm's business base by diversifying into additional businesses.
2. Retrenching to a narrower diversification base by divesting some of its present businesses.
3. Corporate restructuring and turnaround strategies.
4. Multinational diversification strategies.

Figure 9.4 summarizes the central thrust of each of these diversification options.

Strategies to Broaden a Diversified Company's Business Base

Diversified companies sometimes find it desirable to build positions in new related or unrelated industries, perhaps because the company's growth is sluggish and it needs the revenue and profit boost of a newly acquired business, because it has resources and capabilities that are eminently transferable to other related or complementary businesses, or because the opportunity to acquire an attractive company unexpectedly lands at its doorstep. Making new acquisitions to broaden a company's diversification base can become close to imperative when rapidly changing conditions in one of a company's core industries are blurring the boundaries with adjoining industries. For instance, the recent passage of legislation in the United States allowing banks, insurance companies, and stock brokerages to enter each other's businesses is likely to propel a blurring between these historically distinct industries and result in the creation of enterprises that offer banking, insurance, and brokerage services to their customers. Already companies with business interests in one of the three industries are acquiring companies in the others and merging their operations so as to reposition themselves as financial services firms of the future.

---

[18]Doz and Hamel, *Alliance Advantage*, p. 48.

figure 9.4   **Strategy Options for a Company That Is Already Diversified**

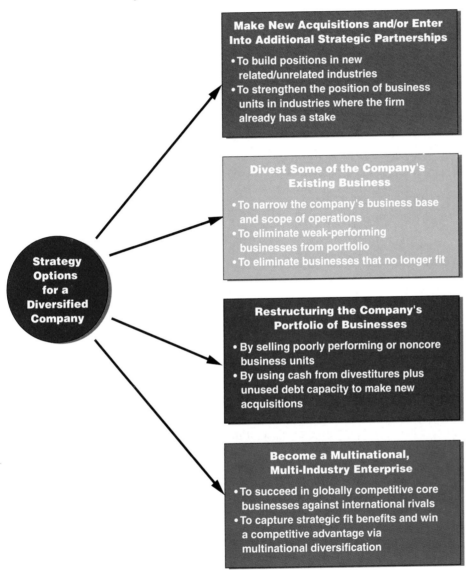

Alternatively, a diversified company may find it highly desirable to make new acquisitions to complement and strengthen the market position and competitive capabilities of one or more of its present businesses. Viacom's acquisition of CBS strengthened and extended its reach into various media businesses (shown at top of page 304).

Numerous pharmaceutical and high-tech companies have been active in acquiring new businesses to broaden their competitive reach and extend their technological expertise into new areas. The latest diversification rage has been for companies to diversify broadly into numerous types of Internet-related businesses. Companies like CMGI, Internet Capital Group, and Softbank Corporation have invested in Internet technology and hardware providers, e-commerce software developers, Web publishers, e-retailers, online brokerages, Web portals, assorted e-commerce service providers, and media and content providers to create diversified enterprises broadly positioned

Viacom's Businesses	CBS's Businesses
• Paramount Pictures and Paramount Home Video	• CBS Television Network
• Paramount Television (production); 50% ownership of UPN TV broadcasting network	• King World Productions (programs include *The Oprah Winfrey Show* and *Wheel of Fortune*); Infinity Broadcasting (radio)
• 19 local TV stations	• 15 local TV stations
• Cable TV networks (MTV, MTV2, Nickelodeon, VH1, Showtime, The Movie Channel, Comedy Central, and several others)	• CBS Cable (Country Music Television, The Nashville Network, Home Team Sports)
• Simon & Schuster (book publishing)	• TDI Outdoor Advertising
• Internet businesses (Red Rocket online educational toy retailer, SonicNet.com, vh1.com, mtv.com, nick.com)	• Internet businesses (Sportsline USA, CBS Marketwatch.com, Medscape, Rx.com, office.com, Hollywood.com)
• Blockbuster video and music	
• Famous Players and United Cinemas International movie theaters	

across many aspects of the Internet economy. A number of Internet-focused venture capital companies are building broadly diversified portfolios of Internet start-up companies, some investing in several new companies each month.

Divestiture Strategies Aimed at Retrenching to a Narrower Diversification Base

Focusing corporate resources on a few core businesses is usually a superior strategy to diversifying broadly and potentially stretching resources and management attention too thin.

A number of highly diversified firms have had difficulty managing broad diversification and have elected to divest certain of their businesses to focus their total attention and resources on a lesser number of core businesses. Retrenching to a narrower diversification base is usually undertaken when corporate management concludes that the firm's diversification efforts have ranged too far afield and that the key to improved long-term performance lies in concentrating on building strong positions in a smaller number of businesses. Retrenchment is usually accomplished by divesting businesses (1) that have little or no strategic fit with the businesses that management wants to concentrate on, or (2) that are too small to make a sizable contribution to earnings. Divesting such businesses frees resources that can be used to reduce debt, to support expansion of the remaining businesses, or to make acquisitions that materially strengthen the company's competitive position in one or more of the remaining core businesses. Hewlett-Packard recently spun off its testing and measurement businesses into a new company called Aligent Technologies so that it could better concentrate on its PC, workstation, server, printer and peripherals, and electronics businesses. PepsiCo divested its entire restaurant group of businesses, consisting of KFC, Pizza Hut, Taco Bell, and California Pizza Kitchens, so that it could better focus its attention and resources on its soft-drink business (which had recently been losing market share to Coca-Cola) and its faster-growing and more profitable Frito-Lay snack foods business. Kmart divested itself of its OfficeMax, Sports Authority, and Borders Bookstores businesses in order to refocus its efforts on discount retailing.

These and other similarly-motivated divestitures confirm the difficulties that companies encounter when trying to manage broad diversification. So few companies have demonstrated the capability to profitably manage broad diversification that investors question the wisdom of broad diversification and place a lower valuation on companies that pursue such strategies. Indeed, because conglomerates often have lower price-earnings ratios than companies with narrow diversification, some broadly diversified companies have divested a number of their businesses and retrenched to a narrower business base. Recent research indicates that pruning businesses and narrowing a firm's diversification base improves corporate performance.[19]

But there are other important reasons for divesting a portion of a company's present businesses. Sometimes diversified firms retrench because they can't make certain businesses profitable after several frustrating years of trying or because they lack funds or other resources to support the operating and investment requirements of all of their business subsidiaries. Even a shrewd corporate diversification strategy can result in the acquisition of business units that, down the road, just do not work out. Mistakes cannot be completely avoided because it is difficult to foresee how getting into a new line of business will actually work out. In addition, long-term industry attractiveness changes with the times; what was once a good diversification move into an attractive industry may later turn sour because of deteriorating market and competitive conditions. Subpar performance by some business units is bound to occur, thereby raising questions of whether to divest them or keep them and attempt a turnaround. Other business units, despite adequate financial performance, may not mesh as well with the rest of the firm as was originally thought.

Sometimes, a diversification move that seems sensible from a strategic-fit standpoint turns out to be a poor *cultural fit*.[20] Several pharmaceutical companies had just this experience. When they diversified into cosmetics and perfume, they discovered their personnel had little respect for the "frivolous" nature of such products compared to the far nobler task of developing miracle drugs to cure the ill. The absence of shared values and cultural compatibility between the medical research and chemical-compounding expertise of the pharmaceutical companies and the fashion-marketing orientation of the cosmetics business was the undoing of what otherwise was diversification into businesses with technology-sharing potential, product-development fit, and some overlap in distribution channels.

When a particular line of business loses its appeal, the most attractive solution usually is to sell it. Normally such businesses should be divested as fast as is practical. To drag things out serves no purpose unless time is needed to get it into better shape to sell. The more business units in a diversified firm's portfolio, the more likely that it will have occasion to divest poor performers and misfits. A useful guide to determine if and when to divest a business subsidiary is to ask, "If we were not in this business today, would we want to get into it now?"[21] When the answer is no or probably not, divestiture should be considered. Another useful signal that a business should become a divestiture candidate is whether it is worth more to another company than to the present parent.[22]

> A business needs to be considered for divestiture when corporate strategists conclude it no longer fits or is an attractive investment.

Options for Accomplishing Divestiture

Divestiture can take either of two forms—spinning the business off as a financially and managerially independent company or selling it outright. When a corporate parent decides to spin off one of its businesses as a separate company, there's the issue of whether to retain partial ownership

> Divestiture usually takes one of two forms—spinning a business off as an independent company or selling it to another company.

---

[19]See, for example, Constantinos C. Markides, "Diversification, Restructuring and Economic Performance," *Strategic Management Journal* 16 (February 1995), pp. 101–18.

[20]Drucker, *Management: Tasks, Responsibilities, Practices*, p. 709.

[21]Ibid., p. 94.

[22]See David J. Collis and Cynthia A. Montgomery, "Creating Corporate Advantage," *Harvard Business Review* 76, no. 3 (May–June 1998), pp. 72–80.

or forgo any ownership interest whatsoever in the new company. Retaining partial ownership makes sense when the business to be divested has good profit prospects. When 3Com elected to divest its Palm Pilot business, which investors saw as having very promising profit potential, it elected to retain a substantial ownership interest in the newly formed company.

When the parent decides to sell a business outright, the problem becomes finding a buyer. This can prove hard or easy, depending on the business. As a rule, a company selling a business should not ask, "Whom can we pawn this business off on, and what is the most we can get for it?"[23] Instead, it is wiser to ask, "For what sort of company would this business be a good fit, and under what conditions would it be viewed as a good deal?" Enterprises for which the business is a good fit are likely to pay the highest price. Sometimes a parent, anxious to divest itself of a particular business and not finding a buyer with ready cash, will agree to a *leveraged buyout.* A leveraged buyout typically involves selling the business to the managers who have been running it (and perhaps other outside investors brought in as partners) for a minimal equity down payment and loaning the balance of the purchase price to the new owners. Of course, if a buyer willing to pay an acceptable price cannot be found, then the decision must be made whether to keep the business until a buyer appears, whether to spin it off as a separate company, or whether, in the case of a crisis-ridden business that is losing substantial sums, to simply close it down and liquidate the remaining assets. Liquidation is obviously a last resort.

Corporate Restructuring and Turnaround Strategies

Corporate restructuring and turnaround strategies come into play when a diversified company's management has to restore an ailing business portfolio to good health. Diversified companies may find themselves struggling because of large losses in one or more business units that pull the corporation's overall financial performance down, a disproportionate number of businesses in unattractive industries, a bad economy adversely affecting many of the firm's business units, an excessive debt burden with interest costs that eat deeply into profitability, ill-chosen acquisitions that haven't lived up to expectations, or the appearance of new technologies that threaten the survival of one or more of the company's important core businesses. *Restructuring strategies* involve divesting some businesses and acquiring new businesses so as to put a whole new face on the company's business makeup; *corporate turnaround strategies,* in contrast, concentrate exclusively on restoring a diversified company's money-losing businesses to profitability.

Strategies to Restructure a Diversified Company's Business Mix

Corporate restructuring efforts attack poor overall performance by performing radical surgery on the nature and mix of businesses in the portfolio. For instance, one struggling diversified company over a two-year period divested 4 business units, closed down the operations of 4 others, and added 25 new lines of business to its portfolio, 16 through acquisition and 9 through internal start-up. Other diversified companies have approached restructuring from the standpoint of splitting their businesses up into two or more independent companies. AT&T, for instance, in the mid-1990s divided into three companies—one for long-distance and other telecommunications services that retained the AT&T name, one for manufacturing telecommunications equipment (called Lucent Technologies), and one for computer systems (called NCR) that essentially represented the divestiture of AT&T's earlier acquisition of NCR. A few years after the split-up, AT&T acquired TCI Communications and MediaOne, both cable companies, and

> Corporate restructuring involves making radical changes in the composition of the businesses in the company's portfolio.

---

[23]Ibid., p. 719.

restructured itself into a "new-age" telecommunications company offering bundled local and long-distance service, cable TV, and high-speed Internet access to its customers.

Restructuring can be prompted by any of several conditions: (1) when a strategy review reveals that the firm's long-term performance prospects have become unattractive because the portfolio contains too many slow-growth, declining, or competitively weak business units; (2) when one or more of the firm's principal businesses fall prey to hard times; (3) when a new CEO takes over and decides to redirect the company; (4) when "wave-of-the-future" technologies or products emerge and a major shake-up of the portfolio is needed to build a position in a potentially big new industry; (5) when the firm has a unique opportunity to make an acquisition so big that it has to sell several existing business units to finance the new acquisition; (6) when major businesses in the portfolio have become more and more unattractive, forcing a shake-up in the portfolio in order to produce satisfactory long-term corporate performance; or (7) when changes in markets and technologies of certain businesses proceed in such different directions that it is better to split the company into separate pieces rather than remain together under the same corporate umbrella.

Candidates for divestiture typically include not only weak or up-and-down performers or those in unattractive industries, but also those that no longer fit a company's revised diversification strategy (even though they may be profitable or in an attractive industry). Business units incompatible with the new related diversification criteria are divested, the remaining units regrouped and aligned to capture more strategic-fit benefits, and new acquisitions made to strengthen the parent company's business position in the industries it has chosen to emphasize.[24] Recently, a few broadly diversified companies have pursued restructuring by splitting into several independent companies. Notable examples include ITT, Westinghouse, and Britain's Imperial Chemical and Hanson, PLC. Before beginning to divest in 1995, Hanson owned companies with more than $20 billion in revenues in industries as diverse as beer, exercise equipment, tools, construction cranes, tobacco, cement, chemicals, coal mining, electricity, hot tubs and whirlpools, cookware, rock and gravel, bricks, and asphalt; understandably, investors and analysts had a hard time making sense of the company and its strategies. By early 1997, Hanson had restructured itself into a $3.8 billion enterprise focused more narrowly on gravel, crushed rock, cement, asphalt, bricks, and construction cranes; the remaining businesses were divided into four groups and divested.

Strategies to Turn Ailing Businesses Around Corporate turnaround strategies focus on efforts to restore a diversified company's money-losing businesses to profitability instead of divesting them. The intent is to get the whole company back in the black by curing the problems of those businesses in the portfolio that are most responsible for pulling overall performance down. Turnaround strategies are most appropriate in situations where the reasons for poor performance are short term, the ailing businesses are in attractive industries, and divesting the money-losers does not make long-term strategic sense.

The specifics of the turnaround efforts in each poorly performing business necessarily need to vary according to the causes underlying each business's weak performance and flow from a diagnosis of prevailing industry and competitive conditions and the business's particular resource strengths, weaknesses, opportunities, and threats. The strategic options for turning a poorly performing business around in a diversified company are the same as discussed in Chapter 8 for a single-business company:

---

[24]Evidence that corporate restructuring produces improved corporate performance is contained in Markides, "Diversification, Restructuring and Economic Performance."

- Selling or closing down a portion of its operations (usually those where losses are greatest and/or future prospects are poorest).
- Shifting to a different, and hopefully better, business-level strategy.
- Launching new initiatives to boost the business's revenues.
- Pursuing cost reduction.
- Using a combination of these efforts.

However, turnaround efforts in a diversified company as compared to a single-business company have the advantage of being able to draw on the corporate parent for needed financial resources and managerial know-how and perhaps on related businesses for an infusion of competitively valuable skills and expertise.

Multinational Diversification Strategies

The distinguishing characteristics of a multinational diversification strategy are a *diversity of businesses* and a *diversity of national markets.*[25] Such diversity makes multinational diversification a particularly challenging and complex strategy to conceive and execute. Managers have to develop business strategies for each industry (with as many multinational variations as conditions in each country market dictate). Then, opportunities for cross-business and cross-country collaboration and strategic coordination have to be pursued and managed in ways calculated to result in competitive advantage and enhanced profitability.

Moreover, the geographic operating scope of individual businesses within a diversified multinational company (DMNC) can range from one country only to several countries to many countries to global. Thus, each business unit within a DMNC often competes in a somewhat different combination of geographic markets than its sister businesses—adding another element of strategic complexity—and perhaps an element of opportunity to try to grow certain lines of business by entering country markets where sister businesses already have a market presence.

What Makes Multinational Diversification So Attractive: The Opportunities for Growth and Added Competitive Advantage

Despite their complexity, multinational diversification strategies have considerable appeal. They offer two avenues for long-term growth in revenues and profitability. One is to grow by entering additional businesses and the other is to grow by extending the operations of existing businesses into additional country markets. Moreover, multinational diversification offers six ways to build competitive advantage:

1. Full capture of economies of scale and experience curve effects.
2. Opportunities to capitalize on cross-business economies of scope.
3. Opportunities to transfer competitively valuable resources from one business to another and from one country to another.
4. Ability to leverage use of a well-known and competitively powerful brand name.
5. Ability to capitalize on opportunities for cross-business and cross-country collaboration and strategic coordination.[26]

---

[25]C. K. Prahalad and Yves L. Doz, *The Multinational Mission* (New York: Free Press, 1987), p. 2.
[26]Ibid., p. 15.

6. Opportunities to use cross-business or cross country subsidization to outcompete rivals.

Each of these will be discussed in turn below.

Illustration Capsule 38 shows the scope of five prominent diversified multinational corporations.

Opportunities to Capture Full Economies of Scale and Experience Curve Effects

In some businesses, the volume of sales needed to realize full economies of scale and/or benefit from experience curve effects is rather sizable, perhaps exceeding the volume that can be achieved operating within the boundaries of a single country market, especially a small one. *The chance to drive down unit costs through expanding sales to additional country markets is one reason why a diversified multinational may seek to acquire a business and then expand its operations into additional foreign markets as fast as possible.* Expanding into additional country markets to capture scale economies makes good strategic sense when cross-country buyer preferences are homogeneous; it is then feasible to market common product versions across different country markets. Expansion also makes sense if a company has the capability to pursue customized mass production and economically produce different versions of a product for different country markets. With the greater sales volumes provided from selling to buyers in a greater number of country markets, companies can drive harder bargains with components suppliers. Plants can gain the economies of longer production runs in world-scale plants, make efficient use of high-speed equipment, and/or accelerate capture of learning-curve effects. Distribution facilities can be scaled to a size that justifies use of state-of-the-art technology and automated processes. Both plants and distribution facilities can be located in whatever country locations prove most cost effective. In short, expanding into additional country markets is advantageous whenever it helps a company achieve an efficient scale of operation in production, distribution, or marketing and spread fixed overhead costs over a greater volume of unit sales.

> Expanding into additional country markets helps a company capture full economies of scale and experience curve effects.

Opportunities to Capitalize on Cross-Business Economies of Scope

Diversifying into related businesses can help a multinational firm benefit from cost-reducing economies of scope. For example, a diversified multinational company that utilizes much the same distributors and retail dealers worldwide can diversify into new businesses using these same worldwide distribution channels at relatively little incremental expense by piggybacking distribution for the newly entered businesses on the dealer network already in place. Likewise, diversifying into new distribution-related businesses may present opportunities to draw on existing distribution capabilities in many or all of the same country markets where it already has operations and a solid base of customers. A third source of distribution-related economies of scope comes from gaining added bargaining leverage with retailers in securing attractive display space for any new products and businesses as its family of businesses grows in number and sales importance to the retailer.

> Multinational diversification can open up opportunities to achieve economies of scope, reduce costs, and build a low-cost advantage over less diversified rivals.

Sony, for example, has enjoyed competitive advantage in diversifying into the video game industry to take on giants like Nintendo and Sega because (1) it has well-established distribution capabilities in consumer electronics worldwide that can be used for video game products; (2) it has in-place capability to go after video game sales in all country markets where it presently does business in other product categories (TVs, computers, DVD players, VCRs, radios, CD players, and digital and video cameras); and (3) it has the marketing clout to persuade retailers and e-tailers to give Sony video game products prominent visibility in their merchandising efforts. The cost-savings that flow from economies of scope open up opportunities to build a low-cost advantage over less diversified rivals.

illustration capsule 38
The Global Scope of Five Prominent Diversified Multinational Corporations

Sony, Philip Morris, Nestlé, Siemens, and Samsung are among the world's most prominent diversified multinational companies. The table below provides a glimpse of their reach into different lines of business and the geographic scope of their operations across the various countries of the world.

Company	Global Scope	Businesses into Which the Company Has Diversified
Sony	Operations in more than 100 countries and sales offices in more than 200 countries	• Televisions, VCRs, DVD players, radios, CD players and home stereos, digital cameras and video equipment, PCs and Trinitron computer monitors • PlayStation game consoles and video game software • Columbia, Epic, and Sony Classical pre-recorded music • Columbia TriStar motion pictures, syndicated television programs • Insurance • Other businesses (financing, entertainment complexes, Internet-related businesses)
Philip Morris Companies	Operations in 92 countries and sales offices in more than 150 countries	• Cigarettes (Marlboro, Virginia Slims, Benson & Hedges, and numerous other brands) • Miller Brewing Company (Miller Genuine Draft, Miller Lite, Icehouse, Red Dog, Molson, Foster's, and numerous other brands) • Kraft Foods (Maxwell House, Sanka, Oscar Mayer, Kool-Aid, Jell-O, Post cereals, Miracle Whip, Bullseye barbecue sauce, Kraft cheeses, Crystal Light, Tombstone pizza)
Nestlé	Operations in 70 countries and sales offices in more than 200 countries	• Beverages (Nescafe and Taster's Choice coffees, Nestea, Perrier, Arrowhead, & Calistoga mineral and bottled waters) • Milk products (Carnation, Gloria, Neslac, Coffee Mate, Nestlé ice cream and yogurt) • Pet foods (Friskies, Alpo, Fancy Feast, Mighty Dog) • Contadina, Libby's, and Stouffer's food products and prepared dishes • Chocolate and confectionery products (Nestlé Crunch, Smarties, Baby Ruth, Butterfinger, KitKat) • Pharmaceuticals (Alcon opthalmic products, Galderma dermatological products)
Siemens	Operations in 160 countries and sales offices in more than 190 countries	• Electrical power generation, transmission, and distribution equipment and products • Manufacturing automation systems, industrial motors, industrial computers, industrial machinery, industrial tools, plant construction and maintenance • Information and communications (solutions and services needed for corporate communication networks, telephones, PCs, mainframes, computer network products, consulting services)

illustration capsule 38

(concluded)

Company	Global Scope	Businesses into Which the Company Has Diversified
Samsung	Operations in more than 60 countries and sales in more than 200 countries	• Mass transit and light rail systems, rail cars, locomotives • Medical equipment, health care management services • Semiconductors, memory components, microcontrollers, capacitors, resistors • Lighting (bulbs, lamps, theater and television lighting systems) • Home electronics, large home appliances, vacuum cleaners • Financial services (commercial lending, pension administration, venture capital) • Procurement and logistics services, business consulting services • Electronics (computers, peripherals, displays, televisions, telecommunications equipment, semiconductors, memory chips, circuit boards, capacitors, information technology services, systems integration) • Machinery and heavy industry (shipbuilding, oil and gas storage tank construction, marine engines, aircraft and aircraft parts, gas turbines, military hardware, industrial robots, factory automation systems) • Automotive (passenger cars, commercial trucks) • Chemicals (general chemicals, petrochemicals, fertilizers) • Financial services (insurance, credit card services, securities trading, consumer credit services, trust management) • Other affiliated companies (theme parks, hotels, medical centers, apparel, professional sports teams, film, music, and television production)

Source: Company annual reports and websites.

Opportunities to Transfer Competitively Valuable Resources from One Business to Another and from One Country to Another

Diversification into new businesses with resource-related strategic fits at various points along the value chain offers significant competitive advantage potential. Technological expertise and know-how in one business can be transferred to other existing or newly entered businesses with opportunities to make competitively advantageous use of such expertise. Manufacturing skills, sales and marketing skills, e-commerce capabilities, and managerial expertise can likewise be transferred across businesses, allowing the receiving businesses to perform better as part of the diversified multinational company than as a stand-alone enterprise.

> Multinational diversification offers a firm the opportunity to build competitive advantage through cross-business and cross-country resource transfer.

Furthermore, competing multinationally allows a company to transfer the experience and expertise it has gained in operating in particular country markets to sister businesses that are in the process of entering these same country markets. It can also transfer its multicountry operating experiences and know-how to newly entered country markets. The understanding of local markets and buyer behavior and customs gained in one country often provides valuable clues and faster learning about markets and buyer behavior in new country markets that a multinational company is presently entering or planning to enter.

Opportunities to Leverage Use of a Competitively Powerful Brand Name

A number of diversified multinational companies have gone to great lengths to establish brand names that are well known and respected in many parts of the world. Such companies can deliberately exploit the value of that name by transferring it to newly entered businesses and benefiting from the added sales and market share they can gain simply on the strength of the trust that buyers have in their brand name. For example, Sony's well-established, global brand-name recognition gives it an important marketing and advertising advantage over rivals with lesser-known brands. When Sony diversifies into new businesses or product families and goes into the marketplace with the stamp of the Sony brand on them, it can command prominent display space with retailers. It can expect to win sales and market share simply on the confidence that buyers place in products carrying the Sony name. While it may spend money to make consumers aware of the availability of its new products, it does not have to spend as heavily to gain brand recognition and market acceptance as would a lesser known competitor looking at the marketing and advertising costs of entering the same new product/business/country markets and trying to go head-to-head against Sony. Further, if Sony moves into a new country market for the first time and does well selling Sony PlayStations and video games, it faces lower market barriers in proceeding to introduce the products of its other businesses (say, consumer electronics products) in that same country. Once it has established the Sony brand strongly in the minds of buyers in one product family or line of business, it can leverage its investment in establishing its brand name by marketing its other product families and business lines under the same brand. In short, a diversified multinational company's global brand name is more than a valuable competitive or strategic asset; it is a source of potential competitive advantage.

> Diversified multinational companies with well-known and respected brand names have lower barriers to entering new businesses in those country markets where they already have a presence.

Ability to Coordinate Strategic Activities and Strategic Initiatives across Businesses and Countries

Multinational diversification presents a host of opportunities for cross-business and cross-country coordination of a company's strategic activities and initiatives. For instance, by channeling corporate resources directly into a combined R&D/technology effort for all related businesses, as opposed to letting each business unit fund and direct its own R&D effort however it sees fit, a diversified multinational company can merge its expertise and efforts *worldwide* to advance the core technology, pursue promising technological avenues to create altogether new businesses, generate technology-based manufacturing economies within and across product/business lines, expedite across-the-board product improvements in existing businesses, and develop new products that complement and enhance the sales of existing products—all significant contributors to competitive advantage and better corporate performance.

> A diversified multinational company with expertise in a core technology and a family of businesses using this technology can capture competitive advantage through a collaborative and strategically coordinated R&D effort on behalf of all the related businesses as a group.

If, on the other hand, R&D activities are decentralized and put totally under the direction of each existing business unit, R&D/technology investments are more prone to end up narrowly aimed at each business's own product-market opportunities. A splintered R&D effort is unlikely to produce the range and depth of strategic fit benefits as a broad, coordinated companywide effort to advance and exploit the company's full technological expertise.[27] Illustration Capsule 39 describes how Honda has exploited gasoline engine technology and its well-known name by diversifying into a variety of products powered by gasoline engines.

Aside from cross-business technological coordination, a company can gain cost savings by cross-business and cross-country coordination of purchasing and procurement from suppliers, from collaborative introduction and shared use of e-commerce technologies and online sales efforts, and from coordinated product introductions and promotional campaigns. Firms that are less diversified and less global in scope have less such cross-business and cross-country collaborative opportunities.

Opportunities to Use Cross-Business or Cross-Country Subsidization to Outcompete Rivals   A diversified multinational company can use the financial and organizational resources it has from operations in other countries or other lines of business to cross-subsidize a competitive assault on the market position of rivals. Both a one-country competitor and a one-business competitor are at a disadvantage defending their market positions against a DMNC determined to establish a solid long-term competitive position in their market and willing to accept lower short-term profits in order to do so. A one-business domestic company has only one profit sanctuary—its home market. A diversified one-country competitor may have profit sanctuaries in several businesses but all are in the same country market. A one-business multinational company may have profit sanctuaries in several country markets, though all are in the same business. All three are vulnerable to an aggressive DMNC that launches a major strategic offensive in their profit sanctuaries and lowballs its prices and/or spends extravagantly on advertising to win market share at their expense. A DMNC's ability to keep hammering away at competitors with lowball prices year after year may reflect either a cost advantage growing out of its related diversification strategy or a willingness to cross-subsidize low profits or even losses with earnings from its profit sanctuaries in other country markets and/or its earnings from other businesses. Sony, for example, by pursuing related diversification keyed to product-distribution-technology strategic fit and managing its product families on a global scale, has the ability to put strong competitive pressure on its two main video game rivals, Nintendo and Sega, neither of which are diversified. If need be, Sony can lowball its prices on its PlayStations or fund extravagant promotions for its latest video game products, using earnings from its other business lines to help wrest market share away from Nintendo and Sega in video games. At the same time, Sony can draw on its considerable resources in R&D, its ability to transfer electronics technology from one electronics product family to another, and its expertise in product innovation to introduce better video game players, perhaps players that are multifunctional and do more than just play video games. Such competitive actions not only enhance Sony's own brand image but also make it very tough for Nintendo and Sega to match its prices, advertising, and product development efforts and still earn acceptable profits. Sony can turn its attention to making its video game business more attractively profitable once the battle for market share and competitive position against Nintendo and Sega is won.[28]

> A well-diversified family of businesses and a multinational market base give a DMNC the power and resource strength to subsidize a long-term market offensive against one-market or one-business competitors with earnings from profit sanctuaries in other countries or businesses.

The Combined Effects of These Advantages Is Potent   Companies with a strategy of (1) diversifying into *related* industries and (2) competing *globally* in each of these industries thus can draw on any of several competitive advantage opportunities to overcome a domestic-only rival or a single-business rival. There's evidence that

> Although cross-subsidization is a potent competitive weapon, it can only be used sparingly because of its adverse impact on overall corporate profitability.

---

[27]Prahalad and Doz, *The Multinational Mission,* pp. 62–63.

[28]Ibid.

illustration capsule 39
Honda's Competitive Advantages

At first blush anyone looking at Honda's lineup of products—cars, motorcycles, lawn mowers, power generators, outboard motors, snowmobiles, snowblowers, and garden tillers—might conclude that Honda has pursued unrelated diversification. But underlying the obvious product diversity is a common core: Honda's expertise in the technology of gasoline engines.

Honda's strategy involves transferring the company's expertise in gasoline engine technology to additional products, exploiting its capabilities in low-cost/high-quality manufacturing, using the widely known and respected Honda brand name on all the products, and promoting several products in the same ad. One Honda ad teased consumers with the question "How do you put six Hondas in a two-car garage?" and then showed a garage containing a Honda car, a Honda motorcycle, a Honda snowmobile, a Honda lawn mower, a Honda power generator, and a Honda outboard motor.

The relatedness in the value chains for the products in Honda's business lineup produces competitive advantage for Honda in the form of economies of scope, beneficial opportunities to transfer technology and capabilities from one business to another, and economical use of a common brand name.

Honda's Competitive Advantage

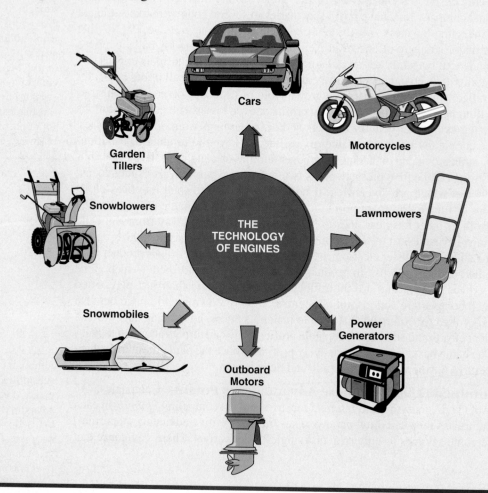

Source: Adapted from C. K. Prahalad and Yves L. Doz, *The Multinational Mission* (New York: Free Press, 1987), p. 62.

these advantages are significant enough to help a DMNC achieve above-average returns and have lower overall business risk.[29] A DMNC's biggest competitive advantage potential comes from concentrating its diversification efforts in those industries where there are resource-sharing and resource-transfer opportunities and where there are important economies of scope and brand-name benefits. The more a company's diversification strategy yields these kinds of strategic-fit benefits, the more powerful a competitor it becomes and the better its profit and growth performance is likely to be. Relying on cross-business strategic fit advantages to outcompete rivals is inherently more attractive than resorting to the profit-eroding tactics of cross-subsidization.

While a DMNC can employ cross-subsidization tactics to help muscle its way into attractive new markets or outcompete a particular rival, its ability to use cross-subsidization is limited by the need to maintain respectable levels of overall company profitability. It is one thing to occasionally use a portion of the profits and cash flows from existing businesses to cover reasonable short-term losses to gain entry to a new business or a new country market or wage a competitive offensive against certain rivals. It is quite another thing to regularly use cross-subsidization tactics to fund competitive inroads in new areas and weaken overall company performance on an ongoing basis. A DMNC is under the same pressures as any other company to demonstrate consistently acceptable profitability across its whole business portfolio. At some juncture, every business and every market entered needs to make a profit contribution or become a candidate for abandonment. So using cross-subsidization as a competitive tactic is constrained by the need to preserve acceptable levels of corporate profitability. As a general rule, *cross-subsidization is justified only if there is a good prospect that the short-term impairment to corporate profitability will be offset by stronger competitiveness and better overall profitability over the long term.*

key|points

Most companies have their business roots in a single industry. Even though they may have since diversified into other industries, a substantial part of their revenues and profits still usually comes from the original or "core" business. Diversification becomes an attractive strategy when a company runs out of profitable growth opportunities in its core business. The purpose of diversification is to build shareholder value. Diversification builds shareholder value when a diversified group of businesses can perform better under the auspices of a single corporate parent than they would as independent, stand-alone businesses and thereby realize important $1 + 1 = 3$ performance benefits. Whether a particular diversification move is capable of increasing shareholder value hinges on the attractiveness test, the cost-of-entry test, and the better-off test.

There are two fundamental approaches to diversification—into related businesses and into unrelated businesses. The rationale for *related* diversification is *strategic:* diversify into businesses with strategic fits along their respective value chains, capitalize on strategic-fit relationships to gain competitive advantage, and then use competitive advantage to achieve the desired $1 + 1 = 3$ impact on shareholder value. Businesses have strategic fit when their value chains offer potential (1) for realizing economies of scope or cost-saving efficiencies associated with sharing technology, facilities, functional activities, distribution outlets, or brand names; (2) for competitively valuable cross-business transfers of technology, skills, know-how, or other resource capabilities;

---

[29]See, for example, W. Chan Kim, Peter Hwang, and Willem P. Burgers, "Multinationals' Diversification and the Risk-Return Trade-off," *Strategic Management Journal* 14 (May 1993) pp. 275–86.

(3) for leveraging use of a well-known and trusted brand name, and (4) for competitively valuable cross-business collaboration.

The basic premise of unrelated diversification is that any business that has good profit prospects and can be acquired on good financial terms is a good business to diversify into. *Unrelated* diversification is basically a *financial* approach; strategic fit is a secondary consideration compared to the expectation of financial gain. Unrelated diversification surrenders the competitive advantage potential of strategic fit in return for such advantages as (1) spreading business risk over a variety of industries and (2) providing opportunities for quick financial gain (if candidate acquisitions have undervalued assets, are bargain-priced and have good upside potential given the right management, or need the backing of a financially strong parent to capitalize on attractive opportunities). In theory, unrelated diversification also offers greater earnings stability over the business cycle, a third advantage. However, achieving these three outcomes consistently requires corporate executives who are smart enough to avoid the considerable disadvantages of unrelated diversification. The greater the number of businesses a conglomerate is in and the more diverse these businesses are, the harder it is for corporate executives to know enough about each business to distinguish a good acquisition from a risky one, select capable managers to run each business, know when the major strategic proposals of business units are sound, or wisely decide what to do when a business unit stumbles. Unless corporate managers are exceptionally shrewd and talented, unrelated diversification is a dubious and unreliable approach to building shareholder value when compared to related diversification.

Entry into new related or unrelated businesses can take any of three forms: acquisition, internal start-up, and joint ventures/strategic partnerships. Each has its pros and cons, but acquisition is the most frequently used.

Once diversification is accomplished, corporate management's task is to manage the collection of businesses for maximum long-term performance. There are four different strategic paths for improving a diversified company's performance: (1) broadening the firm's business base by diversifying into additional businesses, (2) retrenching to a narrower diversification base by divesting some of its present businesses, (3) corporate restructuring and turnaround strategies, and (4) multinational diversification.

Broadening the diversification base is attractive when growth is sluggish and the company needs the revenue and profit boost of a newly acquired business, when it has resources and capabilities that are eminently transferable to related or complementary businesses, or when the opportunity to acquire an attractive company unexpectedly lands on its doorstep. Furthermore, there are occasions when a diversified company makes new acquisitions to complement and strengthen the market position and competitive capabilities of one or more of its present businesses.

Retrenching to a narrower diversification base is usually undertaken when corporate management concludes that the firm's diversification efforts have ranged too far afield and that the best avenue for improving long-term performance is to concentrate on building strong positions in a smaller number of businesses. Retrenchment is usually accomplished by divesting businesses (1) that have little or no strategic fit with the businesses that management wants to concentrate on and/or (2) that are too small to make a sizable contribution to earnings. Divesting such businesses frees resources that can be used to reduce debt, to support expansion of the remaining businesses, or to make acquisitions that materially strengthen the company's competitive position in one or more of the remaining core businesses. Most of the time, companies divest businesses by selling them to another company, but sometimes they spin them off as financially and managerially independent enterprises in which the parent company may or may not retain an ownership interest.

Corporate restructuring and turnaround strategies come into play when corporate management has to restore an ailing business portfolio to good health. Poor performance can be caused by large losses in one or more businesses that pull overall corporate performance down, by too many business units in unattractive industries, by an excessive debt burden, or by ill-chosen acquisitions that haven't lived up to expectations. Corporate turnaround strategies aim at restoring money-losing businesses to profitability instead of divesting them. Restructuring strategies involve radical portfolio shake-ups, divestiture of some businesses and acquisition of others to create what is perceived as a more attractive group of businesses with better long-term performance potential.

Multinational diversification strategies feature a diversity of businesses and a diversity of national markets. Despite the complexity of having to devise and manage so many strategies (at least one for each industry, with as many variations for country markets as may be needed), multinational diversification strategies have considerable appeal. They offer two avenues for long-term growth in revenues and profitability—one is to grow by entering additional businesses and the other is to grow by extending the operations of existing businesses into additional country markets. Moreover, multinational diversification offers six ways to build competitive advantage: (1) full capture of economies of scale and experience curve effects, (2) opportunities to capitalize on cross-business economies of scope, (3) opportunity to transfer competitively valuable resources from one business to another and from one country to another, (4) ability to leverage use of a well-known and competitively powerful brand name, (5) ability to capitalize on opportunities for cross-business and cross-country collaboration and strategic coordination, and (6) opportunities to use cross-business or cross-country subsidization to wrest sales and market share from rivals.

suggested | readings

Barney, Jay B. *Gaining and Sustaining Competitive Advantage*. Reading, MA: Addison-Wesley, 1997, chapters 11 and 13.

Campbell, Andrew; Michael Goold; and Marcus Alexander. "Corporate Strategy: The Quest for Parenting Advantage." *Harvard Business Review* 73, no. 2 (March–April 1995), pp. 120–32.

———. "The Value of the Parent Company." *California Management Review*, 38, no. 1 (Fall 1995), pp. 79–97.

Collis, David J., and Cynthia A. Montgomery. "Creating Corporate Advantage." *Harvard Business Review* 76, no. 3 (May–June 1998), pp. 70–83.

Doz, Yves L., and Gary Hamel. *Alliance Advantage: The Art of Creating Value through Partnering*. Boston: Harvard Business School Press, 1998.

Eisenhardt, Kathleen M., and D. Charles Galunic. "Coevolving: At Last, a Way to Make Synergies Work." *Harvard Business Review* 78, no. 1 (January–February 2000), pp. 91–101.

Goold, Michael, and Andrew Campbell. "Desperately Seeking Synergy." *Harvard Business Review* 76, no. 5 (September–October 1998), pp. 130–43.

Goold, Michael, and Kathleen Luchs. "Why Diversify? Four Decades of Management Thinking." *Academy of Management Executive* 7, no. 3 (August 1993), pp. 7–25.

Hax, Arnoldo, and Nicolas S. Majluf. *The Strategy Concept and Process*. Englewood Cliffs, NJ: Prentice Hall, 1991, chapters 9, 11, and 15.

Hoffman, Richard C. "Strategies for Corporate Turnarounds: What Do We Know about Them?" *Journal of General Management* 14, no. 3 (Spring 1989), pp. 46–66.

Liedtka, Jeanne M. "Collaboration across Lines of Business for Competitive Advantage." *Academy of Management Executive* 10, no. 2 (May 1996), pp. 20–34.

chapter ten

Evaluating the Strategies of Diversified Companies

If we can know where we are and something about how we got there, we might see where we are trending—and if the outcomes which lie naturally in our course are unacceptable, to make timely change.

—Abraham Lincoln

The corporate strategies of most companies have dissipated instead of created shareholder value.

—Michael Porter

Achieving superior performance through diversification is largely based on relatedness.

—Philippe Very

The acid test for any corporate strategy is that the company's businesses must not be worth more to another owner.

—David G. Collis and Cynthia A. Montgomery

Make winners out of every business in your company. Don't carry losers.

—Jack Welch, CEO, General Electric

O nce a company diversifies and has operations in a number of different industries, three issues dominate the agenda of the company's top strategy makers:

1. How attractive is the group of businesses the company is in?
2. Assuming the company sticks with its present lineup of businesses, how good is its performance outlook in the years ahead?
3. If the answers to the previous two questions are not satisfactory:
   a. Should the company divest itself of low-performing or unattractive businesses?
   b. What actions should the company take to strengthen the growth and profit potential of the businesses it intends to remain in?
   c. Is further diversification into additional businesses warranted to boost the company's long-term performance prospects?

Crafting and implementing action plans to improve the overall attractiveness and competitive strength of a company's business lineup is the central strategic task of corporate-level managers.

Strategic analysis of diversified companies builds on the concepts and methods used for single-business companies. But there are also new aspects to consider and additional analytical approaches to master. The evaluation procedure involves the following steps:

1. *Identifying the present corporate strategy*—whether the company is pursuing related or unrelated diversification (or a mixture of both), the nature and purpose of any recent acquisitions and divestitures, and the kind of diversified company that corporate management is trying to create.
2. *Applying the industry attractiveness test*—evaluating the long-term attractiveness of each industry the company is in and the attractiveness of all the industries as a group.
3. *Applying the competitive strength test*—evaluating the competitive strength of the company's business units to see which ones are strong contenders in their respective industries.
4. *Applying the strategic-fit test*—determining the competitive advantage potential of cross-business value chain relationships and strategic fits among the company's various business units.

5. *Applying the resource-fit test*—determining whether the firm's resource strengths match the resource requirements of its present business lineup.

6. *Ranking the businesses*—analyzing both historical performance and future prospects.

7. *Ranking the business units in terms of priority for resource allocation*—deciding whether the strategic posture for each business unit should be aggressive expansion, fortify and defend, overhaul and reposition, or harvest/divest. (The task of initiating specific business-unit strategies to improve the business unit's competitive position is usually delegated to business-level managers, with corporate-level managers offering suggestions and having authority for final approval.)

8. *Crafting new strategic moves to improve overall corporate performance*—changing the makeup of the portfolio via acquisitions and divestitures, improving coordination among the activities of related business units to achieve greater cost-sharing and skills-transfer benefits, and steering corporate resources into the areas of greatest opportunity.

The rest of the chapter describes this eight-step process and introduces analytical techniques managers need in order to arrive at sound corporate strategy appraisals.

IDENTIFYING THE PRESENT CORPORATE STRATEGY

Analysis of a diversified company's situation and prospects needs to begin with an understanding of its present strategy and business makeup. As shown in Figure 10.1, we can get a good handle on a diversified company's corporate strategy by looking at

> Evaluating a diversified firm's business portfolio needs to begin with a clear identification of the firm's diversification strategy.

- The extent to which the firm is diversified (as measured by the proportion of total sales and operating profits contributed by each business unit and by whether the diversification base is broad or narrow).
- Whether the firm is pursuing related or unrelated diversification, or a mixture of both.
- Whether the scope of company operations is mostly domestic, increasingly multinational, or global.
- Any moves to add new businesses to the portfolio and build positions in new industries.
- Any moves to divest weak or unattractive business units.
- Recent moves to boost performance of key business units or strengthen existing business positions.
- Management efforts to capture cross-business strategic-fit benefits and leverage cross-business value chain relationships into competitive advantage.
- The percentage of total capital expenditures allocated to each business unit in prior years (a strong indicator of the company's resource allocation priorities).

Getting a clear fix on the current corporate strategy and its rationale sets the stage for probing the strengths and weaknesses in its business portfolio and, subsequently, for drawing conclusions about whatever refinements or major alterations in strategy are appropriate.

figure 10.1   **Identifying a Diversified Company's Strategy—
What to Look For**

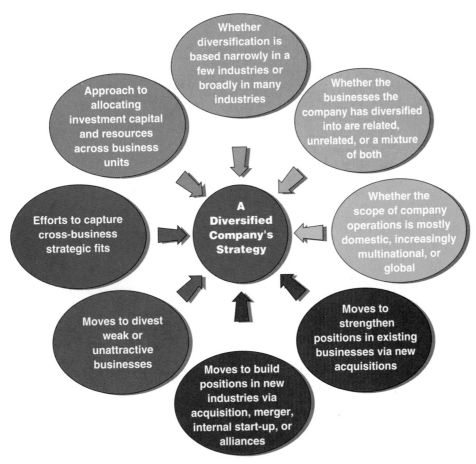

EVALUATING INDUSTRY ATTRACTIVENESS: THREE TESTS

A principal consideration in evaluating a diversified company's business makeup and the caliber of its strategy is the attractiveness of the industries into which it has diversified. The more attractive these industries, the better the company's long-term profit prospects. Industry attractiveness needs to be evaluated from three angles:

1. *The attractiveness of each industry represented in the business portfolio*—Each industry must be scrutinized from the standpoint of whether it represents a good business for the company to be in. What are the industry's prospects for long-term growth? Are competitive conditions and the overall market environment conducive to long-term profitability? Ideally, each industry in which the firm operates will pass the attractiveness test.

2. *Each industry's attractiveness relative to the others*—The question here is "Which industries in the portfolio are the most attractive and which are the least attractive?" Comparing the attractiveness of the industries and ranking them from most

> The more attractive the industries that a company has diversified into, the better its performance prospects.

attractive to least attractive is a prerequisite to drawing conclusions about the attractiveness of the industries as a group and deciding how to allocate corporate resources across the various businesses.

3. *The attractiveness of all the industries as a group*—The question here is "How appealing is the whole group of industries in which the company has invested?" The answer points to whether the company may be in too many relatively unattractive businesses, whether the portfolio of industries holds promise for attractive growth and profitability, or whether some form of portfolio restructuring needs to be considered. A company whose revenues and profits come chiefly from businesses in unattractive industries probably needs to look at building positions in additional industries that qualify as highly attractive.

Evaluating the Attractiveness of Each Industry the Company Has Diversified Into

All the industry attractiveness considerations discussed in Chapter 3 come into play here:

- *Market size and projected growth rate*—Big industries are more attractive than small industries, and fast-growing industries tend to be more attractive than slow-growing industries or industries with uncertain prospects, other things being equal.

- *The intensity of competition*—Industries where competitive pressures are relatively weak are more attractive than industries where competitive pressures are strong.

- *Emerging opportunities and threats*—Industries with promising opportunities and minimal threats on the near horizon are more attractive than industries with modest opportunities and imposing threats.

- *Seasonal and cyclical factors*—Industries where buyer demand is relatively steady year-round and not unduly vulnerable to economic ups and downs are more attractive than industries where there are wide swings in buyer demand within or across years.

- *Resource requirements*—Industries having resource requirements within the company's reach are more attractive than industries where capital and other resource requirements could strain corporate financial resources and organizational capabilities.

- *The presence of cross-industry strategic fits and resource fits*—An industry is more attractive to a particular firm if its value chain and resource requirements match up well with the value chain activities of other industries the company has diversified into and with the company's resource capabilities.

- *Industry profitability*—Industries with healthy profit margins and high rates of return on investment are generally more attractive than industries where profits have historically been low or where the business risks are high.

- *Social, political, regulatory, and environmental factors*—Industries with significant problems in such areas as consumer health, safety, or environmental pollution or that are subject to intense regulation are less attractive than industries where such problems are not burning issues.

- *Industry uncertainty and business risk*—Industries with less uncertainty on the horizon and lower overall business risk are more attractive than industries whose future prospects for one reason or another are quite uncertain, especially when the industry has formidable resource requirements.

How well each industry stacks up on these factors determines how many are able to satisfy the attractiveness test. The ideal situation is for all of the industries represented in the company's portfolio to be attractive.

Each Industry's Attractiveness Relative to the Others

It is not enough, however, that an industry be attractive. There is strong reason for corporate managements to steer resources into those industries of *greatest* long-term opportunity. Shrewd resource allocation is aided by ranking the industries in the company's business portfolio from most attractive to least attractive—an analytical procedure that calls for quantitative measures of industry attractiveness.

The first step in arriving at a formal, quantitative measure of long-term industry attractiveness is to select a set of industry attractiveness measures (such as those listed above). Next, weights are assigned to each attractiveness measure—it is weak methodology to assume that the various measures are equally important. While judgment is obviously involved in deciding how much weight to put on each attractiveness measure, it makes sense to place the most weight on those measures that are important to achieving corporate objectives and that fit the company's circumstances. The weights must add up to 1.0. Each industry is then rated on each of the chosen industry attractiveness measures, using a rating scale of 1 to 5 or 1 to 10 (where a *high* rating signifies *high* attractiveness and a *low* rating signifies *low* attractiveness or unattractiveness). Weighted attractiveness ratings are calculated by multiplying the industry's rating on each factor by the factor's weight. For example, a rating score of 8 times a weight of 0.25 gives a weighted rating of 2.00. The sum of weighted ratings for all the attractiveness factors provides a quantitative measure of the industry's long-term attractiveness. The procedure is shown below:

Industry Attractiveness Factor	Weight	Attractiveness Rating	Weighted Industry Rating
Market size and projected growth	0.10	5	0.50
Intensity of competition in the industry	0.25	8	2.00
Strategic fits and resource fits with other industries represented in the company's business portfolio	0.15	5	0.75
Resource requirements	0.15	7	1.05
Emerging industry opportunities and threats	0.05	6	0.30
Seasonal and cyclical influences	0.05	4	0.20
Social, political, regulatory, and environmental factors	0.05	2	0.10
Industry profitability	0.10	4	0.40
Industry uncertainty and business risk	0.10	5	0.50
Sum of the assigned weights	1.00		
Industry attractiveness rating			**5.80**

Rating scale: (1 = Very unattractive; 10 = Very attractive)

Once industry attractiveness ratings are calculated for each industry in the corporate portfolio, it a simple task to rank the industries from most to least attractive.

There are two difficulties with calculating industry attractiveness scores. One is deciding on appropriate weights for the industry attractiveness measures. The other is getting reliable data on which to assign accurate and objective ratings. Without good information, the ratings necessarily become subjective, and their validity hinges on whether management has probed industry conditions sufficiently to make dependable judgments. Generally, a company can come up with the statistical data needed to compare its industries on such factors as market size, growth rate, seasonal and cyclical influences, and industry profitability. The presence of important cross-industry value chain relationships and strategic fits with other industries or businesses represented in the company's business portfolio typically greatly enhances an industry's attractiveness because of the competitive advantage potential such relationships can yield. The attractiveness measure where judgment weighs most heavily is in comparing the industries on intensity of competition. It is not always easy to conclude whether competition in one industry is stronger or weaker than in another industry because of the different types of competitive influences that prevail and the differences in their relative importance. Nonetheless, industry attractiveness ratings are a reasonably reliable method for ranking a diversified company's industries from most attractive to least attractive—they tell a valuable story about just how and why some of the industries a company has diversified into are more attractive than others.

The Attractiveness of the Mix of Industries as a Whole

For a diversified company to be a strong performer, a substantial portion of its revenues and profits must come from business units judged to be in attractive industries—those with relatively high attractiveness scores. It is particularly important that the company's principal businesses be in industries with a good outlook for growth and above-average profitability. Having a big fraction of the company's revenues and profits come from industries that are growing slowly or have low returns on investment tends to drag overall company performance down. Business units in the least attractive industries are potential candidates for divestiture, unless they are positioned strongly enough to overcome the unattractive aspects of their industry environments or they are a strategically important component of the portfolio.

EVALUATING THE COMPETITIVE STRENGTH OF EACH OF THE COMPANY'S BUSINESS UNITS

The task here is to evaluate whether each business unit in the corporate portfolio is well positioned in its industry and the extent to which it already is or can become a strong market contender. Doing an appraisal of each business unit's strength and competitive position in its industry not only reveals its chances for industry success but also provides a basis for comparing the relative competitive strength of the different business units to determine which ones are strongest and which are weakest. Quantitative measures of each business unit's competitive strength and market position can be calculated using a procedure similar to that for measuring industry attractiveness.[1] Assessing the competitive strength of a diversified company's business subsidiaries should be based on such factors as:

---

[1]The procedure also parallels the method for doing competitive strength assessments presented in Chapter 4 (see Table 4.4).

- *Relative market share*—Business units with higher relative market shares normally have greater competitive strength than those with lower shares. A business unit's *relative market share* is defined as the ratio of its market share to the market share held by the largest rival firm in the industry, with market share measured in unit volume, not dollars. For instance, if business A has a 15 percent share of its industry's total volume and A's largest rival has 30 percent, A's relative market share is 0.5. If business B has a market-leading share of 40 percent and its largest rival has 30 percent, B's relative market share is 1.33.[2] Using relative market share is analytically superior to using actual or absolute market share to measure competitive strength. A 10 percent market share, for example, is not very strong if the leader's share is 50 percent, but a 10 percent share is actually quite strong if the leader's share is 12 percent.[3]

- *Costs relative to competitors*—Business units that are very cost competitive tend to be more strongly positioned in their industries than business units struggling to maintain cost parity with major rivals.

- *Ability to match or beat rivals on key product attributes*—A company's competitiveness depends in part on being able to satisfy buyer expectations with regard to features, product performance, reliability, service, and other important attributes.

- *Ability to exercise bargaining leverage with key suppliers or customers*—Having bargaining leverage signals competitive strength and can be a source of competitive advantage.

- *Caliber of alliances and collaborative partnerships with suppliers and/or buyers*— Well-functioning alliances and partnerships may signal a potential competitive advantage vis-à-vis rivals and thus add to a business's competitive strength.

- *Ability to benefit from strategic-fit relationships with sister businesses*— Strategic-fit relationships with sister businesses are a source of added competitive advantage.

- *Technology and innovation capabilities*—Business units recognized for their technological leadership and track record in product innovation are usually strong competitors in their industry.

- *How well the business unit's competitive assets and competencies match industry key success factors*—The more a business unit's resource strengths and competitive capabilities match the industry's key success factors, the stronger its competitive position tends to be.

---

[2]Given this definition, only business units that are market share leaders in their respective industries will have relative market shares greater than 1.0. Business units that trail rivals in market share will have ratios below 1.0. The further below 1.0 a business unit's relative market share, the weaker is its competitive strength and market position relative to the industry's market share leader.

[3]Equally important, relative market share is likely to reflect relative cost based on experience in producing the product and economies of large-scale production. Businesses with large relative market shares may be able to operate at lower unit costs than low-share firms because of technological and efficiency gains that attach to larger production and sales volume. As was discussed in Chapter 3, the phenomenon of lower unit costs can go beyond just the effects of scale economies; as the cumulative volume of production increases, the knowledge gained from the firm's growing production experience can lead to the discovery of additional efficiencies and ways to reduce costs even further. For more details on how the relationship between experience and cumulative production volume results in lower unit costs, see Figure 3.1 in Chapter 3. A sizable experience curve effect in an industry's value chain places a strategic premium on market share: the competitor that gains the largest market share tends to realize important cost advantages that, in turn, can be used to lower prices and gain still additional customers, sales, market share, and profit. Such conditions are an important contributor to the competitive strength that a company has in that business.

- *Brand-name recognition and reputation*—A strong brand name is a valuable competitive asset in most industries.
- *Profitability relative to competitors*—Business units that consistently earn above-average returns on investment and have bigger profit margins than their rivals usually have stronger competitive positions than business units with below-average profitability for their industry. Moreover, above-average profitability signals competitive advantage, while below-average profitability usually denotes competitive disadvantage.

Other competitive strength indicators include uniquely strong knowledge of customers and markets, unique production capabilities, skills in supply chain management, marketing skills, ample financial resources, and the caliber of management (particularly whether management has experience, knowledge, and depth in making the kinds of major business changes that may be needed).

Analysts have a choice between rating each business unit on the same generic factors or rating each business unit on those strength measures most pertinent to its industry. Either approach can be defended, although using strength measures specific to each industry is conceptually stronger because the relevant measures of competitive strength, along with their relative importance, vary from industry to industry. Where adequate information is available, it is desirable to do a SWOT analysis (see Chapter 4) of each business unit and use the results in doing the competitive strength assessments.

As was done in evaluating industry attractiveness, weights need to be assigned to each of the strength measures to indicate their relative importance. Using different weights for different business units is conceptually stronger when the importance of the strength measures differs significantly from business to business. As before, the weights must add up to 1.0. Each business unit is then rated on each of the chosen strength measures, using a rating scale of 1 to 5 or 1 to 10 (where a *high* rating signifies *high* competitive strength and a *low* rating signifies *low* strength). Weighted strength ratings are calculated by multiplying the business unit's rating on each strength measure by the assigned weight. For example, a strength score of 8 times a weight of 0.20 gives a weighted strength rating of 1.60. The sum of weighted ratings across all the strength measures provides a quantitative measure of a business unit's overall market strength and competitive standing. The procedure is shown below:

Competitive Strength Measure	Weight	Strength Rating	Weighted Strength Rating
Relative market share	0.15	5	0.75
Costs relative to competitors	0.20	8	1.60
Ability to match rivals on key product attributes	0.05	7	0.35
Bargaining leverage with suppliers/buyers; caliber of alliances	0.10	6	0.60
Strategic-fit relationships with sister businesses	0.15	7	1.05
Technology and innovation capabilities	0.05	4	0.20
How well resources are matched to industry key success factors	0.10	7	0.70
Brand-name reputation/image	0.10	4	0.40
Degree of profitability relative to competitors	0.10	5	0.50
Sum of the assigned weights	1.00		
Competitive strength rating			**6.15**

Rating scale: (1 = Low strength; 10 = High strength)

Business units with relatively high overall competitive strength ratings (above 6.7 on a rating scale of 1 to 10) are strong market contenders in their industries. Businesses with relatively low overall ratings (below 3.3 on a rating scale of 1 to 10) are in competitively weak market positions.[4] Managerial evaluations of which businesses in the portfolio are strong and weak market contenders are a valuable consideration in deciding where to steer resources.

Shareholder interests are generally best served by concentrating corporate resources on businesses that can contend for market leadership in their industries.

Using a Nine-Cell Matrix to Simultaneously Portray Industry Attractiveness and Competitive Strength

The industry attractiveness and business strength scores can be used to portray the strategic positions of each business in a diversified company. Long-term industry attractiveness is plotted on the vertical axis and competitive strength on the horizontal axis. A nine-cell grid emerges from dividing the vertical axis into three regions (high, medium, and low attractiveness) and the horizontal axis into three regions (strong, average, and weak competitive strength). High attractiveness is associated with scores of 6.7 or greater on a rating scale of 1 to 10, medium attractiveness is assigned to scores of 3.3 to 6.7, and so on; likewise, strong competitive strength is defined as a score greater than 6.7, average strength entails scores of 3.3 to 6.7, and so on—as shown in Figure 10.2. Each business unit in the corporate portfolio is plotted on the nine-cell matrix according to its overall attractiveness score and strength score, and then shown as a "bubble." The size of each bubble is scaled to what percentage of revenues the business generates relative to total corporate revenues.

In the attractiveness-strength matrix, each business's location is plotted using quantitative measures of long-term industry attractiveness and business strength/competitive position.

The attractiveness-strength matrix helps in assigning investment priorities to each of the company's business units. Top investment priority is normally given to businesses in the three cells at the upper left, where long-term industry attractiveness and competitive strength/competitive position are both favorable. The general strategic prescription for businesses falling in these three cells is "grow and build," with businesses in the high-strong cell having the highest claim on investment funds. Next in priority come businesses positioned in the three diagonal cells stretching from the lower left to the upper right. These businesses are usually given medium or intermediate priority. They merit *selective* reinvestment, depending on their specific circumstances—size, profitability, strategic and resource fits, role in the company's overall strategy, and so on.

Some businesses in the medium-priority diagonal cells are likely to be more attractive than others. For example, a small business in the upper right cell of the matrix, despite being in a highly attractive industry, may occupy too weak a competitive position in its industry relative to stronger rivals to justify the investment and resources needed to turn it into a strong market contender and shift its position leftward in the matrix over time. If, however, a business in the upper right cell has an unusually attractive strategic opening to win a stronger market position, it may merit a higher investment priority and be given the resources to pursue a "grow-and-build" strategy.

A company may earn larger profits over the long term by investing in a business with a competitively strong position in a moderately attractive industry than by investing in a weak business in a glamour industry.

---

[4]If analysts lack sufficient data to do detailed strength ratings, they can rely on their knowledge of each business unit's competitive situation to classify it as being in a "strong," "average," or "weak" competitive position. If trustworthy, such subjective assessments of business-unit strength can substitute for quantitative measures.

figure 10.2 **A Representative Nine-Cell Industry Attractiveness–Competitive Strength Matrix**

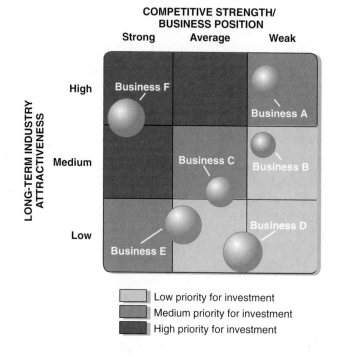

The strategy prescription for businesses in the three cells in the lower right corner of the matrix is typically "harvest or divest." In exceptional cases where good turnaround potential exists, it can be "overhaul and reposition" using some type of turnaround approach.[5]

The nine-cell attractiveness-strength grid provides strong logic for concentrating resources in those businesses that enjoy a higher degree of attractiveness and competitive strength, being very selective in making investments in businesses with intermediate positions, and withdrawing resources from businesses that are lower in attractiveness and strength unless they offer exceptional turnaround potential. This is why a diversified company needs to consider both industry attractiveness and business strength in allocating resources and investment capital to its different businesses.

More and more diversified companies are concentrating their resources on industries where they can be strong market contenders and divesting businesses that are not good candidates for becoming market leaders. At General Electric, the whole thrust of corporate strategy and corporate resource allocation over the past two decades has been to put GE's businesses into a number one or two position in both the United States and globally—see Illustration Capsule 40.

---

[5]At General Electric, each business actually ended up in one of five types of categories: (1) *high-growth-potential businesses* deserving top investment priority, (2) *stable base businesses* deserving steady reinvestment to maintain position, (3) *support businesses* deserving periodic investment funding, (4) *selective pruning or rejuvenation businesses* deserving reduced investment funding, and (5) *venture businesses* deserving heavy R&D investment.

illustration capsule 40

General Electric's Approach to Managing a Broadly Diversified Business Portfolio

Most knowledgeable observers believe General Electric has done a superlative job of profitably operating a broadly diversified portfolio of most unrelated businesses, anointing it as the world's most successful conglomerate.

GE's climb to global prominence began when Jack Welch became CEO of General Electric in 1981 and launched a series of corporate revitalization initiatives to reshape the company's diversified business portfolio. Early on, Welch issued a challenge to GE's business-unit managers to become number one or number two in their industry. Failing that, the business units either had to capture a decided technological advantage translatable into a competitive edge or face possible divestiture. By 1990, GE was a different company, having divested operations worth $9 billion, made additional acquisitions totaling $24 billion, and cut its workforce by 100,000. Twelve of GE's 14 primary business groups had attained a leading market position in the United States and/or globally. (The company's financial services and TV broadcasting businesses served markets too fragmented to rank.)

Under Welch's leadership, acquisitions, divestitures, and portfolio reshuffling continued at a fast and furious pace during the 1990s. GE acquired hundreds of new companies during the 1990s, including 108 in 1998 and 64 during a 90-day period in 1999. Most of the acquisitions were in Europe, Asia, and Latin America and aimed at transforming GE into a truly global enterprise. Weak-performing businesses were either divested or merged with stronger GE businesses.

GE'S BUSINESS PORTFOLIO IN 2001

Going into 2001, General Electric's business portfolio consisted of over 250 business divisions grouped into 10 business categories:

- *Aircraft Engines*—the world's largest producer of large and small jet engines for commercial and military aircraft. Throughout the 1990s, more than 50 percent of the world's large commercial jet engine orders were awarded to GE businesses.

- *Appliances*—one of the largest manufacturers of major appliances in the world, producing Monogram, Profile Performance, Profile, GE, and Hotpoint refrigerators and freezers, ovens, ranges and cooktops, microwave ovens, washers and dryers, dishwashers, disposals and compactors, room air conditioners, and water purification systems.

- *GE Equity*—a subsidiary of GE Capital that offers flexible and innovative deal structures to clients. GE Equity employs 120 investment professionals throughout five business units and has a portfolio of 150 companies worldwide.

- *Industrial Systems*—a leading supplier of products used to distribute, protect, operate and control electrical power and equipment, as well as services for commercial and industrial applications. Major products and services include circuit breakers, switches, transformers, switchboards, switchgear, meters, relays, adjustable-speed drives, control and process automation systems, a full range of AC and DC electric motors, and comprehensive technical engineering and power management solutions.

- *Lighting*—a leading supplier of lighting products for global consumer, commercial, and industrial markets. Products include incandescent, fluorescent, high-intensity discharge, halogen and holiday lamps, along with portable lighting fixtures, lamp components, and quartz products. GE also manufactures outdoor lighting fixtures, residential wiring devices, and commercial lighting controls.

- *Medical Systems*—a world leader in medical diagnostic imaging technology, services, and health care productivity. Products include computed tomography (CT) scanners, X-ray equipment, magnetic resonance imaging (MRI) systems, nuclear medicine cameras, ultrasound systems, patient monitoring devices, and mammography systems.

- *NBC*—the nation's first broadcast network and now an international media company. In addition to the NBC Television Network and its 13 stations, NBC owns CNBC; operates MSNBC in partnership with Microsoft; and maintains equity interests in Arts & Entertainment, the History Channel, and Rainbow Media Holdings. The NBC division also includes NBCi, ShopNBC, CNBC Europe, CNBC Asia, and an equity interest in National Geographic Channels International.

(continued)

illustration capsule 40

- *Plastics*—a world leader in versatile, high-performance engineered plastics used in the computer, electronics, data storage, office equipment, automotive, building, and construction industries.

- *Power Systems*—a global leader in the design, manufacture, and service of gas, steam, and hydroelectric turbines and generators for power production, pipeline and industrial applications. Power Systems also provides nuclear fuels, services, and related equipment.

- *Real Estate*—offers financing for commercial estate, including office buildings, rental apartments, and shopping centers. Loans might range from $2 million to several hundred million dollars, made on a variety of terms, from fixed to floating rate and, in some cases, equity on a joint venture basis. GE Real Estate also provides loan servicing and asset management to other real estate investors. GE Capital Investment Advisors work in conjunction with GE Real Estate for some services.

GE'S INTERNAL INITIATIVES TO PROFITABLY MANAGE BROAD DIVERSIFICATION

During the 1990s, Jack Welch orchestrated a series of internal initiatives to dramatically boost productivity in all of the company's businesses, reduce the size of the corporation's bureaucracy, and create a "boundaryless" organization where new ideas, technology, experience, and other forms of intellectual capital could be readily transferred from one GE business to another. Company programs to profitably manage a broadly diversified and global portfolio of businesses included:

- Emphasis on being a learning organization with no boundaries. Stress was placed on finding better ways to do things—borrowing ideas from other companies and relentlessly transferring ideas and best practices from one GE business to another. The operative assumption at GE was that someone, somewhere has a better idea; and the operative compulsion was to find who has that better idea, learn it, and put it into action as quickly as possible. Cross-business idea sharing was promoted by job rotations and transfers of people across businesses and geographic areas and by sending individuals or teams to visit facilities inside or outside the company that had put an innovative idea in place and achieved outstanding results. For example, when the company transferred a manager from its aircraft engine business to a GE appliance plant, that manager was expected to learn firsthand the success of the appliance division's Quick Response Plan that reduced the division's inventory by $200 million and increased its return on investment by 8.5 percent; on returning, the individual was under the gun to use that learning to help implement inventory savings in the aircraft engine business. Transfers and regular job rotations also built personal relationships between individuals across business units that aided in continued knowledge transfer after the rotation and helped block out insular thinking within each business unit.

- Instituting a six sigma quality program (led and taught by highly trained GE employees) all across GE that introduced rigorous thinking and analysis into the management process—a six sigma quality program

(continued)

STRATEGIC FIT ANALYSIS: CHECKING FOR CROSS-BUSINESS COMPETITIVE ADVANTAGE POTENTIAL

One essential part of evaluating a diversified company's strategy is to check its business portfolio for the extent to which there are competitively valuable matchups (i.e., strategic fit) among the company's existing businesses:

- Which business units have value chain matchups that offer opportunities to combine the performance of certain activities and thereby reduce costs? Potential value chain matchups typically include purchasing (where combining materials purchases could lead to greater bargaining leverage with suppliers), common use of e-commerce systems, manufacturing (where it may be possible to share manufacturing facilities), or distribution (where it may be possible to share warehousing, sales forces, distributors, dealers, or online sales channels).

illustration capsule 40

(concluded)

generates fewer than 3.4 defects per million operations in a manufacturing or service process. GE's six sigma initiative was introduced in late 1995 (when it was running at a sigma level between 3 and 4) in a concerted effort to reduce costs, improve efficiency, and boost customer satisfaction. The gap between GE's sigma level of 3 to 4 and the target level of 6 was estimated to cost GE between $8 billion and $14 billion in inefficiencies and lost productivity. By year-end 1998, GE reported that its six sigma initiative had improved the company's operating margins to 16.7 percent (from 13.6 percent in 1995) and helped increase GE's working capital turns to 9.2 (from 5.8 in 1995).

- Strong reliance on "workout sessions" where GE managers and employees gathered in a room for as many hours or days as it took to focus on a problem or an opportunity, confront issues, share and debate their views, and develop a decisive plan of action for taking swift corrective action and moving the business or company forward. Workout, like the concept of a boundaryless company, was an integral component of GE's global culture.

- Encouraging managers and employees to fight bureaucracy and to go all out to kill bureaucratic practices and behavior at GE.

- Becoming an Internet company—the company's newest initiative. The goal was to fully incorporate use of the Internet and e-commerce practices in all of GE's 250 business divisions within 18 months and transform GE into a global e-business.

- Consciously molding a deep, talent-rich team of managers with strong leadership skills, the ability to make tough decision, and the ability to produce good business results. In a *Business Week* interview, Jack Welch said, "This place runs by its great people. The biggest accomplishment I've had is to find great people. An army of them . . . They are big hitters . . . We're in the cat-and-dog insurance business in England. I don't really want to be in that business, but the guy who brought me that idea wanted to be in it, and I trust him. He'll take it and make it work."

GE's commitment to cross-business learning and its determination to create a boundaryless organization are just two of the reasons that the company grew throughout the 1990s to become a global force. As chairman Jack Welch prepared to retire in 2001, he noted ironically, "I came in a bad economy and I'm leaving in a bad economy." But he placed confidence in his successor, Jeff Immelt. "He is going to take this thing to whole new heights," predicted Welch. "I'm excited that the future looks better than the past." Meanwhile, the deal making continues. The same month that Welch was slated to retire, GE Americom signed a long-term agreement with Viacom for enhanced satellite communications worldwide.

Source: GE website (www.ge.com), accessed September 4, 2001; "Viacom Signs with GE Americom for Next-Generation Satellites," press release (www.ge.com), September 4, 2001; Richard Waters, "Welch Will Step Down Earlier as GE Revenues Fall," *Financial Times* (http://news.ft.com), July 12, 2001; Drew Ross Sorkin, "Rare Miscalculation for Jack Welch," *New York Times* (www.nytimes.com), July 3, 2001; company documents; John A. Byrne, "How Jack Welch Runs GE," *Business Week,* June 8, 1998, pp. 88–95; and assorted other articles in the business press.

- Which business units have value chain matchups that offer opportunities to transfer skills or technology or intellectual capital from one business to another?

- Which business units offer opportunities to use a common and well-respected brand name to command prominent display space with retailers and gain credibility with buyers?

- Which business units have value chain matchups that offer opportunities to create valuable new competitive capabilities or to leverage existing resources?

Figure 10.3 illustrates the process of searching for competitively valuable cross-business strategic fits and value chain matchups. Absent significant strategic fits, one has to be skeptical about the potential for a diversified company's businesses to perform better together than apart.

figure 10.3   **Comparing Value Chains to Identify Strategic Fits among a Diversified Company's Business Units**

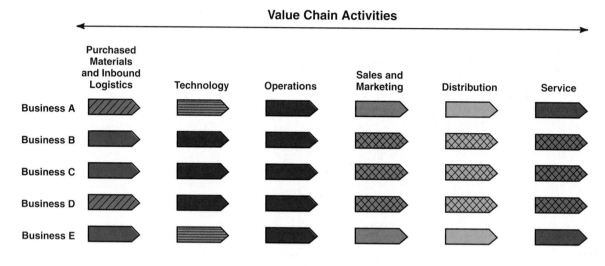

Opportunities to combine purchasing activities and gain greater leverage with suppliers

Opportunities to share technology, transfer technical skills, combine R&D

Opportunities to combine/share sales and marketing activities, utilize common distribution channels, leverage use of a common brand name, and/or combine after-sale service activities.

No strategic fit opportunities

A second aspect of strategic fit that bears checking out is whether there are any businesses in the portfolio that do not fit in well with the company's overall long-term direction and strategic vision. Sometimes a business, despite possessing certain value chain matchups, doesn't mesh well with the strategic markets or customer groups or product categories that corporate management is concentrating on—in other words, it doesn't fit strategically into the company's future plans and performance objectives. A business may also lack long-term strategic appeal if it lacks growth potential or is marginally profitable or requires sizable annual capital investments to replace outdated plants and equipment. Such businesses probably need to be considered for divestiture despite having value chain fits with sister businesses. Businesses with little long-term strategic value often end up being treated like an unwanted stepchild and are a distraction to top management.

RESOURCE FIT ANALYSIS: DETERMINING HOW WELL THE FIRM'S RESOURCES MATCH BUSINESS UNIT REQUIREMENTS

The businesses in a diversified company's lineup need to exhibit good *resource fit* as well as good strategic fit. Resource fit exists when (1) businesses add to a company's resource strengths, either financially or strategically, and (2) a company has the resources to adequately support its businesses as a group without spreading itself too thin. One important dimension of resource fit concerns whether the company's business lineup is well matched to its financial resources.

Cash Hog and Cash Cow Businesses

Different businesses have different cash flow and investment characteristics. For example, business units in rapidly growing industries are often *cash hogs*—so labeled because the annual cash flows they are able to generate from internal operations aren't big enough to cover their annual capital requirements. To keep pace with rising demand, rapid-growth businesses frequently are looking at sizable annual capital investments for some years to come—for new facilities and equipment, for new product development or technology improvements, and for additional working capital to support inventory expansion and a larger base of operations. A business in a fast-growing industry becomes an even bigger cash hog when it has a relatively low market share and is pursuing a strategy to outgrow the market and gain enough market share to become an industry leader. When a rapid-growth business cannot generate a big enough cash flow from operations to finance its capital requirements internally, the needed financial resources must be provided by the corporate parent. Corporate management has to decide whether it is strategically and financially worthwhile to fund the perhaps considerable investment requirements of a cash hog.

Business units with leadership positions in mature industries may, however, be *cash cows*—or businesses that generate substantial cash surpluses over what is needed for capital reinvestment and competitive maneuvers to sustain their present market position. Market leaders in slow-growth industries often generate sizable positive cash flows *over and above what is needed for reinvestment in operations* because their industry-leading position tends to give them the sales volumes and reputation to earn attractive profits and because the slow-growth nature of their industry often entails relatively modest annual investment requirements. Cash cows, though not always attractive from a growth standpoint, are valuable businesses from a financial resource perspective. The surplus cash flows they generate can be used to pay corporate dividends, finance acquisitions, and provide funds for investing in the company's promising cash hogs. It makes good financial and strategic sense for diversified companies to keep cash cows in healthy condition, fortifying and defending their market position so as to preserve their cash-generating capability over the long term and thereby have an ongoing source of financial resources to deploy elsewhere.

Viewing a diversified group of businesses as a collection of cash flows and cash requirements (present and future) is a major step forward in understanding the financial aspects of corporate strategy. Determining which businesses in a diversified company's portfolio are cash hogs and which are cash cows highlights opportunities for shifting financial resources between business subsidiaries to optimize the performance of the whole corporate portfolio, explains why priorities for corporate resource allocation can differ from business to business, and provides good rationalizations for both invest-and-expand strategies and divestiture. For instance, a diversified company can use the excess cash generated by cash cows to fund the investment requirements of promising cash hogs, eventually growing the hogs into self-supporting "stars" having strong competitive positions in attractive, high-growth markets.[6] *Star businesses* are the cash cows of the future—when the markets of star businesses begin to mature and their growth

> A *cash hog* business is one whose internal cash flows are inadequate to fully fund its needs for working capital and new capital investment.

> A *cash cow* business is a valuable part of a diversified company's business portfolio because it generates cash for financing new acquisitions, funding the capital requirements of cash hogs, and paying dividends.

---

[6]A star business, as the name implies, is one with a leading market share, a widely respected reputation, a solid track record of profitability, and excellent future growth and profit opportunities. Star businesses vary as to their cash hog status. Some can cover their investment needs with self-generated cash flows; others require capital infusions from their corporate parents to stay abreast of rapid industry growth. Normally, strongly positioned star businesses in industries where growth is beginning to slow tend to be self-sustaining in terms of cash flow and make little claim on the corporate parent's treasury. Young stars, however, may require substantial investment capital *beyond what they can generate on their own* and still be cash hogs.

slows, their competitive strength should produce self-generated cash flows more than sufficient to cover their investment needs. The "success sequence" is thus cash hog to young star (but perhaps still a cash hog) to self-supporting star to cash cow.

If, however, a cash hog has questionable promise (either because of low industry attractiveness or a weak competitive position), then it becomes a logical candidate for divestiture. Pursuing an aggressive invest-and-expand strategy for a competitively weak cash hog seldom makes sense because it requires the corporate parent to keep pumping more capital into the business to keep abreast of fast-paced market growth *and* to build an attractively strong competitive position. Such businesses are a financial drain and lack good financial resource fit. Divesting a less attractive cash hog business is usually the best alternative unless (1) it has valuable strategic fits with other business units or (2) the capital infusions needed from the corporate parent are modest relative to the funds available and there's a decent chance of growing the business into a solid bottom-line contributor yielding a good return on invested capital.

Aside from cash flow considerations, a business has good financial fit when it contributes to the achievement of corporate performance objectives (profit growth, above-average return on investment, recognition as an industry leader, and so on) and when it materially enhances shareholder value. A business exhibits poor financial fit if it soaks up a disproportionate share of the company's financial resources, if it is a subpar or inconsistent bottom-line contributor, if it is unduly risky and failure would jeopardize the entire enterprise, or if it is too small to make a material earnings contribution even though it performs well. In addition, a diversified company's business portfolio lacks financial fit if its financial resources are stretched across too many businesses. Severe financial strain can occur if a company borrows so heavily to finance new acquisitions that it has to trim way back on new capital expenditures for existing businesses and use the big majority of its financial resources to meet interest obligations and to pay down debt. Some diversified companies have found themselves so financially overextended or overleveraged that they have had to sell off some businesses to raise the money to meet existing debt obligations and fund essential capital expenditures for the remaining businesses.

Competitive and Managerial Resource Fits

A diversified company's strategy must aim at producing a good fit between its resource capability and the competitive and managerial requirements of its businesses.[7] Diversification is more likely to enhance shareholder value when the company has or can develop the competitive and managerial capabilities to be successful in the businesses/industries it has diversified into. Businesses where resource fit is lacking is a serious enough problem to make such businesses prime divestiture candidates. Likewise, when a company's resources and capabilities match the key success factors of industries it is not presently in, it makes sense to take a hard look at acquiring companies in these industries and expanding the company's business lineup.

> Business subsidiaries that don't exhibit good strategic fit and good resource fit should be considered for divestiture unless their financial performance is outstanding.

Checking a diversified company's business portfolio for competitive and managerial resource fits involves the following:

- *Determining whether the company's resource strengths are well matched to the key success factors of the businesses it has diversified into*—A close match between

---

[7]For an excellent discussion of how to assess these fits, see Andrew Campbell, Michael Goold, and Marcus Alexander, "Corporate Strategy: The Quest for Parenting Advantage," *Harvard Business Review* 73, no. 2 (March–April 1995), pp. 120–32.

industry key success factors and company resources and capabilities is a solid sign of good resource fit.

- *Determining whether the company has ample resource depth to support all its businesses*—A diversified company has to guard against stretching its resource base too thin and trying to do too many things. The broader the diversification, the greater the concern about whether the company has sufficient managerial depth and expertise to cope with the diverse range of managerial and operating problems its wide business lineup presents (plus those it may be contemplating getting into).

- *Determining whether one or more businesses can benefit from the transfer of resources and/or competitive capabilities from sister businesses*—Capabilities that are often good candidates for transfer include short development times in bringing new products to market, strong partnerships with key suppliers, an R&D organization capable of generating technological and product opportunities in several different industry arenas simultaneously, a high degree of organizational agility in responding to shifting market conditions and emerging opportunities, or state-of-the-art systems for doing business via the Internet. The ability to transfer competitively valuable resources or capabilities from one business to another is a strong signal of resource fit.

- *Determining whether the company needs to invest in upgrading its resources or capabilities in order to stay ahead of (or at least abreast of) the efforts of rivals*—In a world of fast-paced change and competition, managers have to be alert to the need to continually invest in and upgrade the company's resources, however potent its current resources are. All resources depreciate in value as competitors mimic them or retaliate with a different (and perhaps more attractive) resource combination.[8] Upgrading resources and competencies often means going beyond just strengthening what the company already is capable of doing. It may involve adding new capabilities (like the ability to manage a group of diverse international manufacturing plants, technological expertise in related or complementary disciplines, a state-of-the-art-company intranet, or an innovative website that draws many visits and gives all business units greater market exposure); building competencies that allow the company to enter another attractive industry; or widening the company's range of capabilities to match certain competitively valuable capabilities of rivals.

The complement of resources and capabilities at a firm's command determines its competitive strengths. The more a company's diversification strategy is tied to leveraging its resources and capabilities in new businesses, the more it has to develop a big enough and deep enough resource pool to supply these businesses with sufficient capability to create competitive advantage. Otherwise its strengths end up being stretched too thin across too many businesses and the opportunity for competitive advantage is lost.

Some Notes of Caution Many diversification strategies built around cross-business transfer of resource capabilities never live up to their promise because the transfer process proves problematic. Developing a resource capability in one business nearly always involves much trial and error and much organizational learning, the product of close collaboration among many people over a period of time. The first step in transferring knowledge from one business to another involves moving people with the requisite know-how to the new business. These people not only have to learn the

> Diversifying into businesses with seemingly good resource fit is, by itself, not sufficient to produce success.

---

[8]David J. Collis and Cynthia A. Montgomery, "Competing on Resources: Strategy in the 90s," *Harvard Business Review* 73, no. 4 (July–August 1995), p. 124.

ins and outs of the new business well enough to see how best to integrate the capability into the operations of the receiving business but they also have to be adept in implanting all the appropriate organizational learning from the donor business. As a practical matter, resource transfers require the receiving business to undergo significant organizational learning and team building on its own to get up to speed in executing the transferred capability. It takes time, money, and patience for the transferred capability to become operational. Sometimes unforeseen problems result in debilitating delays or prohibitive expenses or inability on the part of the receiving business to execute the capability proficiently. As a consequence, the business receiving the resource transfer may never perform up to expectations.

A second reason for the failure of a diversification move into a new business with seemingly good resource fit is that the causes of a firm's success in one business are sometimes quite entangled and hard to replicate.[9] It is easy to be overly optimistic about the ease with which a company that has hit a home run in one business can enter a new business with similar resource requirements and hit a second home run. Noted British retailer Marks & Spencer, despite possessing a range of impressive resource capabilities (ability to choose excellent store locations, having a supplier chain that gives it both low costs and high merchandise quality, loyal employees, an excellent reputation with consumers, and strong management expertise) that have made it one of Britain's premier retailers for 100 years, has failed repeatedly in its efforts to diversify into department store retailing in the United States.

A third reason for diversification failure, despite apparent resource fit, is misjudging the resource strengths of rivals. For example, even though Philip Morris had built powerful consumer marketing capabilities in its cigarette and beer businesses, it floundered in soft drinks and ended up divesting its acquisition of 7UP after several frustrating years because of difficulties in competing against strongly entrenched and resource-capable rivals like Coca-Cola and PepsiCo.

RANKING THE BUSINESS UNITS ON THE BASIS OF PAST PERFORMANCE AND FUTURE PROSPECTS

Once a diversified company's businesses have been rated on the basis of industry attractiveness, competitive strength, strategic fit, and resource fit, the next step is to evaluate which businesses have the best performance prospects and which ones the worst. The most important considerations in judging business-unit performance are sales growth, profit growth, contribution to company earnings, and the return on capital invested in the business. (As we noted in Chapter 1, more and more companies are evaluating business performance on the basis of economic value added—the return on invested capital over and above the firm's cost of capital.) Sometimes, cash flow generation is a big consideration, especially for cash cows and businesses with potential for harvesting.

Information on each business's past performance can be gleaned from a company's financial records.[10] While past performance is not necessarily a good predictor of future performance, it does signal which businesses have been strong performers

---

[9]Ibid., pp. 121–22.

[10]Financial performance by line of business is typically contained in a company's annual report, usually in the notes to corporate financial statements. Line-of-business performance can also be found in a publicly owned firm's 10-K report filed annually with the Securities and Exchange Commission.

and which have been weak performers. The industry attractiveness–business strength evaluations should provide a solid basis for judging future prospects. Normally, strong business units in attractive industries have significantly better prospects than weak businesses in unattractive industries.

The growth and profit outlooks for a diversified company's principal or core businesses generally determine whether its portfolio as a whole is capable of strong, mediocre, or weak performance. Noncore businesses with subpar track records and hazy or uncertain long-term prospects are logical candidates for divestiture. Business subsidiaries with the brightest profit and growth prospects and solid strategic and resource fits generally should head the list for corporate resource support.

DECIDING ON RESOURCE ALLOCATION PRIORITIES AND A GENERAL STRATEGIC DIRECTION FOR EACH BUSINESS UNIT

Using the information and results of the preceding evaluation steps, corporate strategists can allocate resources to the various business units and settle on a general strategic direction for each business unit. The task here is to draw some conclusions about which business units should have top priority for corporate resource support and new capital investment and which business units should carry the lowest priority. In doing the ranking, managers need to give special attention to whether and how corporate resources and capabilities can be used to enhance the competitiveness of particular business units.[11] Opportunities for resource transfer, activity combining, or infusions of new financial capital become especially important when improvement in some key success area could make a big difference to a particular business unit's performance.

Ranking a diversified company's businesses from highest to lowest priority should also reveal the most appropriate strategic approach for each business unit—*invest-and-grow* (aggressive expansion), *fortify-and-defend* (protect current position by strengthening and adding resource capabilities in needed areas), *overhaul-and-reposition* (make major competitive strategy changes to move the business into a different and ultimately stronger industry position), or *harvest-divest*. In deciding whether to divest a business unit, corporate managers should rely on a number of evaluating criteria: industry attractiveness, competitive strength, strategic fit with sister businesses, resource fit, performance potential (profit, return on capital employed, economic value added, contribution to cash flow), compatibility with the company's strategic vision and long-term direction, and ability to contribute to enhanced shareholder value.

To get ever-higher levels of performance out of a diversified company's business portfolio, corporate managers have to do an effective job of steering resources out of low-opportunity areas into high-opportunity areas. Divesting marginal businesses is one of the best ways of freeing unproductive assets for redeployment. Surplus funds from cash cows and businesses being harvested also add to the corporate treasury. Options for allocating a diversified company's financial resources include (1) investing in ways to strengthen or expand existing businesses, (2) making acquisitions to establish positions in new industries, (3) funding long-range R&D ventures, (4) paying off

> Improving a diversified company's long-term financial performance entails concentrating company resources on businesses with the best prospects and most solid strategic and resource fits.

---

[11]Collis and Montgomery, "Competing on Resources: Strategy in the 90s," pp. 126–28; Hofer and Schendel, *Strategy Formulation: Analytical Concepts,* p. 80; and Michael E. Porter, *Competitive Advantage* (New York: Free Press, 1985), chapter 9.

existing long-term debt, (5) increasing dividends, and (6) repurchasing the company's stock. The first three are *strategic* actions to add shareholder value; the last three are *financial* moves to enhance shareholder value. Ideally, a company will have enough funds to do what is needed, both strategically and financially. If not, strategic uses of corporate resources should usually take precedence unless there is a compelling reason to strengthen the firm's balance sheet or divert financial resources to pacify shareholders.

CRAFTING A CORPORATE STRATEGY

The preceding analytical steps set the stage for crafting strategic moves to improve a diversified company's overall performance. The basic issue of "what to do" hinges on the conclusions drawn about the strategic and financial attractiveness of the group of businesses the company has diversified into.[12] Key questions here are: Does the company have enough businesses in very attractive industries? Will the proportion of mature or declining businesses cause corporate growth to be sluggish? Are the company's businesses overly vulnerable to seasonal or recessionary influences or to threats from emerging new technologies? Are the prospects hazy or uncertain for too many of the industries or businesses the company is in? Is the firm burdened with too many businesses in average-to-weak competitive positions? Is there ample strategic fit among the company's different businesses? Does the portfolio contain businesses that the company really doesn't need to be in? Is there ample resource fit among the company's business units? Does the firm have enough cash cows to finance the cash hogs with potential to be star performers? Can the company's principal or core businesses be counted on to generate dependable profits and/or cash flow? Does the makeup of the business portfolio put the company in good position for the future? Answers to these questions indicate whether corporate strategists should consider divesting certain businesses, making new acquisitions, restructuring the makeup of the portfolio, significantly altering the pattern of corporate resource allocation, or sticking closely with the existing business lineup and pursuing the opportunities they present.

The Performance Test

A good test of the strategic and financial attractiveness of a diversified firm's business portfolio is whether the company can attain its performance objectives with its current lineup of businesses and resource capabilities. If so, no major corporate strategy changes are indicated. However, if a performance shortfall is probable, corporate strategists can take any of several actions to close the gap:[13]

1. *Alter the strategic plans for some or all of the businesses in the portfolio.* This option involves renewed corporate efforts to get better performance out of its present business units. Corporate managers can push business-level managers for strategy changes that yield better business-unit performance and perhaps provide higher-than-planned corporate resource support for these efforts. However, pursuing better short-term performance by zealously trimming resource initiatives aimed at

---

[12]Barry Hedley, "Strategy and the Business Portfolio," *Long Range Planning* 10, no. 1 (February 1977), p. 13; and Hofer and Schendel, *Strategy Formulation*, pp. 82–86.

[13]Hofer and Schendel, *Strategy Formulation*, pp. 93–100.

bolstering a business's long-term competitive position has dubious value—it merely trades off better long-term performance for better short-term financial performance. In any case there are limits on how much extra near-term performance can be squeezed out to reach established targets.

2. *Add new business units to the corporate portfolio.* Boosting overall performance by making new acquisitions or starting new businesses internally raises some new strategy issues. Expanding the corporate portfolio means taking a close look at (*a*) whether to acquire related or unrelated businesses, (*b*) what size acquisitions to make, (*c*) how the new units will fit into the present corporate structure, (*d*) what specific features to look for in an acquisition candidate, and (*e*) whether acquisitions can be financed without shortchanging present business units on their new investment requirements. Nonetheless, adding new businesses is a major strategic option, one frequently used by diversified companies to escape sluggish earnings performance.

3. *Divest weak-performing or money-losing businesses.* The most likely candidates for divestiture are businesses in a weak competitive position, in a relatively unattractive industry, or in an industry with minimal strategic fit with sister business and/or a lack of resource fit. Funds from divestitures can, of course, be used to finance new acquisitions, pay down corporate debt, or fund new strategic thrusts in the remaining businesses.

4. *Form cooperative alliances to try to alter conditions responsible for subpar performance potentials.* In some situations, cooperative alliances with domestic or foreign firms, suppliers, customers, or special interest groups may help ameliorate adverse performance prospects.[14] Instituting resource sharing agreements with suppliers, select competitors, or firms with complementary products and collaborating closely on mutually advantageous initiatives are often fruitful avenues for improving the competitiveness and performance potential of a company's businesses. Forming or supporting a political action group may be an effective way of lobbying for solutions to import-export problems, tax disincentives, and onerous regulatory requirements.

5. *Upgrade the company's resource base.* Achieving better performance may well hinge on corporate efforts to develop new resource strengths that will help select business units match the competitively valuable capabilities of their rivals or, better still, allow them to secure competitive advantage. One of the biggest ways that corporate-level managers of diversified companies can contribute to added shareholder value is to lead the development of cutting-edge capabilities and to marshal new kinds of corporate resources for deployment in a number of the company's businesses.

6. *Lower corporate performance objectives.* Adverse market circumstances or declining fortunes in one or more core business units can render companywide performance targets unreachable. So can setting overly ambitious objectives. Closing the gap between actual and desired performance may then require downward revision of corporate objectives to bring them more in line with reality. Lowering performance objectives is usually a last resort, used only after other options come up short.

---

[14]For an excellent discussion of the benefits of alliances among competitors in global industries, see Kenichi Ohmae, "The Global Logic of Strategic Alliances," *Harvard Business Review* 67, no. 2 (March–April 1989), pp. 143–54.

Identifying Additional Diversification Opportunities

One of the major corporate strategy-making concerns in a diversified company is whether to pursue further diversification and, if so, how to identify the "right" kinds of industries and businesses to get into. For firms pursuing unrelated diversification, the issue of where to diversify next is relatively wide open—the search for acquisition candidates is based more on spotting a good financial opportunity and having the financial resources to pursue it than on industry or strategic criteria. Decisions to diversify into additional unrelated businesses are usually based on such considerations as whether the firm has the financial ability to make another acquisition, whether new acquisitions are badly needed to boost overall corporate performance, whether one or more acquisition opportunities have to be acted on before they are purchased by other firms, whether the timing is right for another acquisition (corporate management may have its hands full dealing with the current portfolio of businesses), and whether corporate management believes it possesses the range and depth of expertise to take on the supervision of an additional business.

> Firms with unrelated diversification strategies hunt for businesses that offer attractive financial returns—regardless of what industry they're in.

With a related diversification strategy, however, the search for new industries to diversify into is aimed at identifying other businesses (1) whose value chains have fits with the value chains of one or more businesses represented in the company's business portfolio and (2) whose resource requirements are well matched to the firm's corporate resource capabilities.[15] Once corporate strategists identify strategic-fit and resource-fit opportunities in attractive new industries, they must determine which ones have important competitive advantage potential. The size of the competitive advantage potential depends on whether the fits are competitively significant or marginal and on the costs and difficulties of merging or coordinating the business unit interrelationships to capture the fits.[16] Often, careful analysis reveals that while there are many actual and potential business unit interrelationships, only a few have enough strategic importance to generate meaningful competitive advantage.

> Further diversification in firms with related diversification strategies involves identifying attractive industries having good strategic or resource fit with one or more existing businesses.

Managing the Process of Crafting Corporate Strategy

Although formal analysis and entrepreneurial brainstorming normally undergird the corporate strategy-making process, there is more to where corporate strategy comes from and how it evolves. Rarely is there an all-inclusive grand formulation of the total corporate strategy. Instead, corporate strategy in major enterprises emerges incrementally as many different internal and external events unfold; it is the result of probing the future, experimenting, gathering more information, sensing problems, building awareness of the various options, spotting new opportunities, developing ad hoc responses to unexpected crises, communicating consensus as it emerges, and acquiring a feel for all the strategically relevant factors, their importance, and their interrelationships.[17]

Strategic analysis is not something that the executives of diversified companies do all at once in comprehensive fashion. Such big reviews are sometimes scheduled, but research indicates that major strategic decisions emerge gradually rather than from

---

[15]Porter, *Competitive Advantage,* pp. 370–71.

[16]Ibid., pp. 371–72.

[17]Ibid., pp. 58, 196.

periodic, full-scale analysis followed by prompt decision. Typically, top executives approach major strategic decisions a step at a time, often starting from broad, intuitive conceptions and then embellishing, fine-tuning, and modifying their original thinking as more information is gathered, as formal analysis confirms or modifies their judgments about the situation, and as confidence and consensus build for what strategic moves need to be made. Often attention and resources are concentrated on a few critical strategic thrusts that illuminate and integrate corporate direction, objectives, and strategies.

key|points

Strategic analysis in diversified companies is an eight-step process:

Step 1: *Get a clear fix on the present strategy.* Determine whether the company's strategic emphasis is on related or unrelated diversification; whether the scope of company operations is mostly domestic or increasingly multinational, what moves have been made recently to add new businesses and build positions in new industries, the rationale underlying recent divestitures, the nature of any efforts to capture strategic fits and create competitive advantage based on economies of scope and/or resource transfer, and the pattern of resource allocation to the various business units. This step sets the stage for thorough evaluation of the need for strategy changes.

Step 2: *Evaluate the long-term attractiveness of the industries into which the firm has diversified.* Industry attractiveness needs to be evaluated from three angles: the attractiveness of each industry on its own, the attractiveness of each industry relative to the others, and the attractiveness of all the industries as a group. Quantitative measures of industry attractiveness tell a valuable story about just how and why some of the industries a company has diversified into are more attractive than others. The two hardest parts of calculating industry attractiveness scores are deciding on appropriate weights for the industry attractiveness measures and knowing enough about each industry to assign accurate and objective ratings.

Step 3: *Evaluate the relative competitive strength of each of the company's business units.* Again, quantitative ratings of competitive strength are preferable to subjective judgments. The purpose of rating the competitive strength of each business is to gain clear understanding of which businesses are strong contenders in their industries, which are weak contenders, and the underlying reasons for their strength or weakness. Join the conclusions about industry attractiveness with the conclusions about competitive strength by drawing an industry attractiveness/competitive strength matrix displaying the positions of each business on a nine-cell grid; use the attractiveness/strength matrix to help determine the prospects of each business and what priority they should have in allocating corporate resources and investment capital.

Step 4: *Check for cross-business value chain relationships and strategic fit.* A business is more attractive strategically when it has value chain relationships with sister business units that present opportunities to transfer skills or technology, reduce overall costs, share facilities, or share a common brand name—any of which can represent a significant avenue for producing competitive advantage beyond what any one business can achieve on its own. The more businesses with competitively valuable strategic fits, the greater a diversified company's potential for achieving economies of scope, enhancing the competitive capabilities of particular business units, and/or strengthening the competitiveness of its product and business lineup, thereby realizing a combined performance greater than the units could achieve operating independently.

Step 5: *Determine whether the firm's resource strengths fit the resource requirements of its present business lineup.* The businesses in a diversified company's lineup need to exhibit good *resource fit* as well as good strategic fit. Resource fit exists when (1) businesses add to a company's resource strengths, either financially or strategically, (2) a company has the resources to adequately support the resource requirements of its businesses as a group without spreading itself too thin, and (3) there are close matches between a company's resources and industry key success factors. One important dimension of resource fit concerns whether the company's business lineup is well matched to its financial resources. Assessing the cash requirements of different businesses in a diversified company's portfolio and determining which are cash hogs and which are cash cows highlights opportunities for shifting corporate financial resources between business subsidiaries to optimize the performance of the whole corporate portfolio, explains why priorities for corporate resource allocation can differ from business to business, and provides good rationalizations for both invest-and-expand strategies and divestiture.

Step 6: *Rank the different business units on past performance and future prospects.* The most important considerations in judging business-unit performance are sales growth, profit growth, contribution to company earnings, and the return on capital invested in the business. Sometimes, cash flow generation is a big consideration. Normally, strong business units in attractive industries have significantly better performance prospects than weak businesses or businesses in unattractive industries.

Step 7: *Decide on priorities for resource allocation and whether the general strategic direction for each business unit should be aggressive expansion, fortify and defend, overhaul and reposition, or harvest/divest.* In doing the ranking, special attention needs to be given to whether and how corporate resources and capabilities can be used to enhance the competitiveness of particular business units. Options for allocating a diversified company's financial resources include (1) investing in ways to strengthen or expand existing businesses, (2) making acquisitions to establish positions in new industries, (3) funding long-range R&D ventures, (4) paying off existing long-term debt, (5) increasing dividends, and (6) repurchasing the company's stock. Ideally, a company will have the financial strength to accomplish what is needed strategically and financially; if not, strategic uses of corporate resources should usually take precedence.

Step 8: *Use the preceding analysis to craft a series of moves to improve overall corporate performance.* Typical actions include (1) making acquisitions, starting new businesses from within, entering into new strategic alliances, and divesting marginal businesses or businesses that no longer match the company's long-term direction and strategy; (2) devising moves to strengthen the long-term competitive positions of the company's businesses; (3) capitalizing on strategic-fit and resource-fit opportunities and turning them into long-term competitive advantage; and (4) steering corporate resources out of low-opportunity areas and into high-opportunity areas.

suggested | readings

Campbell, Andrew; Michael Goold; and Marcus Alexander. "Corporate Strategy: The Quest for Parenting Advantage." *Harvard Business Review* 73, no. 2 (March–April 1995), pp. 120–32.

Collis, David J., and Cynthia A. Montgomery. "Creating Corporate Advantage." *Harvard Business Review* 76, no. 3 (May–June 1998), pp. 70–83.

Eisenhardt, Kathleen M., and Shona L. Brown. "Patching: Restitching Business Portfolios in Dynamic Markets." *Harvard Business Review* 77, no. 3 (May–June 1999), pp. 72–82.

Haspeslagh, Phillippe C., and David B. Jamison. *Managing Acquisitions: Creating Value through Corporate Renewal.* New York: Free Press, 1991.

Porter, Michael E. "From Competitive Advantage to Corporate Strategy." *Harvard Business Review* 65, no. 3 (May–June 1987), pp. 43–59.

chapter | eleven Building Resource Strengths and Organizational Capabilities

The best game plan in the world never blocked or tackled anybody.

—Vince Lombardi

Strategies are intellectually simple; their execution is not.

—Lawrence A. Bossidy, Former CEO, Allied-Signal

We would be in some form of denial if we didn't see that execution is the true measure of success.

—C. Michael Armstrong, CEO, AT&T

Organizing is what you do before you do something, so that when you do it, it is not all mixed up.

—A. A. Milne

Flat organizations of empowered people are critical to gaining quick decisions in a global marketplace that moves at Net speed.

—John Byrne

Managers can't assume that strategy and capability will come together automatically.

—Thomas M. Hout and John C. Carter

O nce managers have decided on a strategy, the emphasis turns to converting it into actions and good results. Putting a strategy into place and getting the organization to execute it well call for different sets of managerial skills. Whereas crafting strategy is largely a market-driven activity, implementing strategy is primarily an operations-driven activity revolving around the management of people and business processes. Whereas successful strategy making depends on business vision, shrewd industry and competitive analysis, and good resource fit, successful strategy implementation depends on doing a good job of leading, working with and through others, allocating resources, building and strengthening competitive capabilities, installing strategy-supportive policies, and shaping

how the organization performs its core business activities. Executing strategy is an action-oriented, make-things-happen task that tests a manager's ability to direct organizational change, motivate people, develop core competencies, build valuable organizational capabilities, achieve continuous improvement in business processes, create a strategy-supportive corporate culture, and meet or beat performance targets.

Experienced managers, savvy in strategy making and strategy implementing, are emphatic in declaring that it is a whole lot easier to develop a sound strategic plan than it is to execute the plan and achieve the planned outcomes. According to one executive, "It's been rather easy for us to decide where we wanted to go. The hard part is to get the organization to act on the new priorities."[1] What makes executing strategy a tougher, more time-consuming management challenge than crafting strategy is the wide array of managerial activities that have to be attended to, the many ways managers can proceed, the demanding people-management skills required, the perseverance necessary to get a variety of initiatives launched and moving, the number of bedeviling issues that must be

> The manager's task is to convert the strategic plan into action and get on with what needs to be done to achieve the vision and targeted objectives.

---

[1]As quoted in Steven W. Floyd and Bill Wooldridge, "Managing Strategic Consensus: The Foundation of Effective Implementation," *Academy of Management Executive* 6, no. 4 (November 1992), p. 27.

worked out, the resistance to change that must be overcome, and the difficulties of integrating the efforts of many different work groups into a smoothly functioning whole.

Just because managers announce a new strategy doesn't mean that subordinates will agree with it or cooperate in implementing it. Senior executives cannot will things to happen when they launch new strategic initiatives, nor can they simply communicate with a few hundred people at the top of the organization and expect change to occur. Some managers and employees may be skeptical about the merits of the strategy, seeing it as contrary to the organization's best interests, unlikely to succeed, or threatening to their own careers. Moreover, different employees may interpret the new strategy differently, be uncertain about how their departments will fare, and have different ideas about what internal changes are needed to execute the new strategy. Long-standing attitudes, vested interests, inertia, and ingrained organizational practices don't melt away when managers decide on a new strategy and start to implement it—especially when only a handful of people have been involved in crafting the strategy and when the rationale for strategic change has to be sold to enough organizational members to root out the status quo. It takes adept managerial leadership to convincingly communicate the new strategy and the reasons for it, overcome pockets of doubt and disagreement, build consensus and enthusiasm for how to proceed, secure the commitment and energetic cooperation of concerned parties, and move forward to get all the implementation pieces into place and integrated. Depending on how much consensus building, motivating, and organizational change is involved, the implementation process can take several months to several years.

> Companies don't implement and execute strategies, people do.

A FRAMEWORK FOR EXECUTING STRATEGY

Implementing and executing strategy entails converting the organization's strategic plan into action and then into results. Like crafting strategy, it's a job for the whole management team, not just a few senior managers. While an organization's chief executive officer and the heads of major units (business divisions, functional departments, and key operating units) are ultimately responsible for seeing that strategy is implemented successfully, the implementation process typically affects every part of the firm, from the biggest operating unit to the smallest frontline work group. Every manager has to think through the answer to "What has to be done in my area to implement our part of the strategic plan, and what should I do to get these things accomplished?" In this sense, *all managers become strategy-implementers in their areas of authority and responsibility, and all employees are participants.*

> Every manager has an active role in the process of executing the firm's strategic plan and all employees are participants.

One of the keys to successful implementation is for management to communicate the case for organizational change so clearly and persuasively to organizational members that there is determined commitment throughout the ranks to carry out the strategy and meet performance targets. The ideal condition is for managers to arouse enough enthusiasm for the strategy to turn the implementation process into a companywide crusade. *Management's handling of the strategy implementation process can be considered successful if and when the company achieves the targeted strategic and financial performance and shows good progress in realizing its long-range strategic vision.*

Unfortunately, there are no 10-step checklists, no proven paths, and few concrete guidelines for tackling the job. Strategy implementation is the least charted, most open-ended part of strategic management. The best dos and don'ts come from the reported experiences and "lessons learned" of managers and companies—and the wisdom they yield is inconsistent. What's worked well for some managers has been tried by others and found lacking. The reasons are understandable. Not only are some managers more effective than others in employing this or that recommended approach to organizational change but each instance of strategy implementation takes place in a different organizational context. Different business practices, competitive circumstances, work environments, cultures, policies, compensation incentives, mixes of personalities, and organizational histories all require a customized approach to strategy implementation—one based on individual company situations and circumstances, the strategy-implementer's best judgment, and the implementer's ability to use particular change techniques adeptly.

Managing strategy implementation is more art than science.

THE PRINCIPAL STRATEGY-IMPLEMENTING TASKS

While managers should tailor their approaches to the situation, certain bases have to be covered no matter what the organization's circumstances; these include:

1. Building an organization with the competencies, capabilities, and resource strengths to carry out the strategy successfully.
2. Developing budgets to steer ample resources into those value chain activities critical to strategic success.
3. Establishing strategy-supportive policies and procedures.
4. Instituting best practices and pushing for continuous improvement in how value chain activities are performed.
5. Installing information, communication, e-commerce, and operating systems that enable company personnel to carry out their strategic roles successfully day in and day out.
6. Tying rewards and incentives to the achievement of performance objectives and good strategy execution.
7. Creating a strategy-supportive work environment and corporate culture.
8. Exerting the internal leadership needed to drive implementation forward and keep improving on how the strategy is being executed.

These managerial tasks crop up repeatedly in the strategy implementation process, no matter what the specifics of the situation, and drive the priorities on the strategy implementer's agenda—as depicted in Figure 11.1. One or two of these tasks usually end up being more crucial or time-consuming than others, depending on whether there are important resource weaknesses to correct or new competencies to develop, the strength of ingrained behavior patterns that have to be changed, any pressures for quick results and near-term financial improvements, and other such factors particular to the company's circumstances.

In devising an action agenda, *strategy implementers should begin with a probing assessment of what the organization must do differently and better to carry out the strategy successfully.* They should then consider how to make the necessary internal changes as rapidly as possible. Successful strategy implementers have a knack for diagnosing what their organizations need to do to execute the chosen strategy well, and they are creative in finding ways to perform key value chain activities effectively and efficiently.

figure 11.1   **The Eight Big Managerial Components of Implementing Strategy**

LEADING THE STRATEGY IMPLEMENTATION AND EXECUTION PROCESS

One make-or-break determinant of successful strategy implementation and execution is how well management leads the process. Managers can employ any of several leadership styles in pushing the implementation process along. They can play an active, visible, take-charge role or a quiet, low-key, behind-the-scenes one. They can make decisions authoritatively or on the basis of consensus; delegate much or little; be personally involved in the details of implementation or stand on the sidelines and coach others; proceed swiftly (launching implementation initiatives on many fronts) or deliberately (remaining content with gradual progress over a long time frame). How managers lead the strategy execution process tends to be a function of (1) their experience and knowledge of the business; (2) whether they are new to the job or veterans; (3) their network of personal relationships in the organization; (4) their own diagnostic, administrative, interpersonal, and problem-solving skills; (5) the authority they've been given; (6) the leadership style they're comfortable with; and (7) their view of the role they need to play to get things done.

Although major initiatives to implement corporate and business strategies usually have to be led by the CEO and other senior officers, top-level managers still have to rely on the active support and cooperation of middle and lower managers to push strategy changes into functional areas and operating units and to carry out the strategy effectively on a daily basis. Middle and lower-level managers not only are responsible for initiating and supervising the execution process in their areas of authority but also are instrumental in getting subordinates to continuously improve on how strategy-critical value chain activities are performed and in producing the front-line results that allow company performance targets to be met. How successful middle and lower managers are in using the resources at their command to strengthen organizational capabilities determines how proficiently the company executes its strategy on a daily basis—their role on the company's strategy execution team is by no means minimal.

> It is the job of middle and lower-level managers to push needed implementation actions on the front lines and to see that the strategy is well executed on a daily basis.

In big organizations with geographically scattered operating units, the action agenda of senior-level strategy implementers mostly involves communicating the case for change to others, building consensus for how to proceed, installing strong allies in positions where they can push implementation along in key organizational units, urging and empowering subordinates to get the process moving, establishing measures of progress and deadlines, recognizing and rewarding those who achieve implementation milestones, reallocating resources, and personally presiding over the strategic change process. Thus, the bigger the organization, the more the success of the chief strategy implementer depends on the cooperation and implementing skills of operating managers who can push needed changes at the lowest organizational levels. In small organizations, the chief strategy implementer doesn't have to work through middle managers and can deal directly with frontline managers and employees, personally orchestrating the action steps and implementation sequence, observing firsthand how implementation is progressing, and deciding how hard and how fast to push the process along. Regardless of the organization's size and whether implementation involves sweeping or minor changes, the most important leadership trait is a strong, confident sense of "what to do" to achieve the desired results. Knowing what to do comes from understanding the circumstances of both the organization and the industry as a whole.

> The real strategy-implementing skill is being good at figuring out what it will take to execute the strategy proficiently.

In the remainder of this chapter and the next two chapters, we survey the manager's role as chief strategy implementer. The discussion is framed around the eight managerial components of the strategy implementation process shown in Figure 11.1 and the most often-encountered issues associated with each. This chapter explores the management tasks of building a capable organization. Chapter 12 looks at budget allocations, policies, best practices, internal support systems, and strategically appropriate reward structures. Chapter 13 deals with creating a strategy-supportive corporate culture and exercising strategic leadership.

BUILDING A CAPABLE ORGANIZATION

Proficient strategy execution depends heavily on competent personnel, better-than-adequate competitive capabilities, and effective internal organization. Building a capable organization is thus always a top priority in strategy execution. As shown in Figure 11.2, three types of organization-building actions are paramount:

figure 11.2   **The Components of Building a Capable Organization**

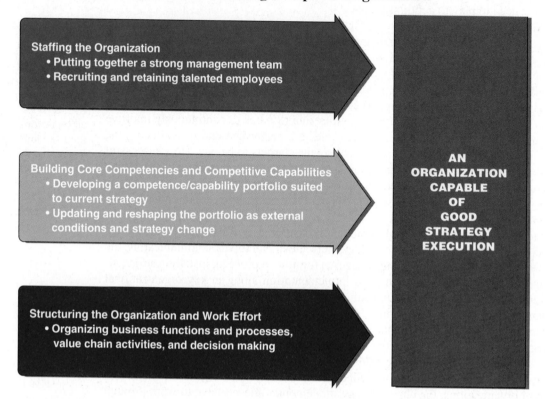

- *Staffing the organization*—includes putting together a strong management team, and recruiting and retaining employees with the needed experience, technical skills, and intellectual capital.
- *Building core competencies and competitive capabilities* that will enable good strategy execution and then keeping the competence/capability portfolio updated as strategy and external conditions change.
- *Structuring the organization and work effort*—organizing business functions and processes, value chain activities, and decision making in a manner conducive to successful strategy execution.

Staffing the Organization

No company can hope to perform the activities required for successful strategy execution without attracting capable managers and without employees that give it a suitable knowledge base and portfolio of intellectual capital.

Putting Together a Strong Management Team   Assembling a capable management team is one of the first cornerstones of the organization-building task. Strategy implementers must determine the kind of core management team they need and then find the right people to fill each slot on the team. Sometimes the existing management team is suitable; sometimes it needs to be strengthened or expanded by promoting qualified people from within or by bringing in outsiders whose experience, skills, and leadership styles suit the situation. In turnaround and rapid-growth situations, and in instances when a company doesn't have insiders with the requisite experience and management know-how, filling key management slots from the outside is a fairly standard organization-building approach. In 1998 Gateway founder Ted Waitt determined that the company, whose sales had rocketed to over $6 billion but whose profits were sagging, needed a fundamental shaking up in the top executive ranks.[2] He brought in consultants Smart & Associates to evaluate Gateway's top 100 managers, many of whom he had hired and who had good credentials. The company decided to replace 10 of the top 14 executives with outsiders and to recruit a new CEO. Following the consultants' recommendations, Waitt decided to recruit only "A players," coach the company's B and C players to become A players or move them into positions where they could become A players, or, failing that, move them out. Two years later, in early 2000, all of the major new hires were still in their jobs and the company's earnings and profit margins were much improved.

The important skill in assembling a core executive group is discerning what mix of backgrounds, experiences, know-how, values, beliefs, management styles, and personalities will contribute to successful strategy execution. The personal chemistry needs to be right, and the talent base needs to be appropriate for the chosen strategy. Picking a solid management team is an essential organization-building function—often the first strategy implementation step to take.[3] Until key managerial slots are filled with able people, it is hard for strategy implementation to proceed at full speed.

Illustration Capsule 41 describes General Electric's approach to assembling an "A" caliber management team to execute its strategy of broad diversification.

> Putting together a strong management team with the right personal chemistry and mix of skills is one of the first strategy-implementing steps.

Recruiting and Retaining Talented Employees

A good management team is not enough. Staffing the organization with talented people must go much deeper than managerial jobs in order to assemble the human resources and knowledge base needed for effective strategy execution. Companies like General Electric, Procter & Gamble, PepsiCo, Hewlett-Packard, Nike, Electronic Data Systems (EDS), Cisco, Microsoft, and McKinsey & Company (one of the world's premier management consulting companies) make a concerted effort to recruit the best and brightest talent they can find and then retain them with excellent compensation packages, opportunities for rapid advancement and professional growth, and challenging and interesting assignments. Having a cadre of people with strong skill sets and budding management potential is essential to their business. EDS requires college graduates to have at least a 3.5 grade point average (on a 4.0 scale) just to qualify for an interview. Microsoft makes a point of hiring the very brightest and most talented programmers it can find and motivating them with both good monetary incentives and the challenge of working on cutting-edge software design projects. McKinsey recruits MBAs only at the top 10 business schools. The Big Five accounting firms endeavor to screen candidates not only on the basis of their accounting expertise but also on whether they possess the people skills needed to relate well with clients and colleagues. Southwest Airlines goes to considerable lengths to hire people who can have fun and be fun on the job; it uses specially developed methods, including interviews with customers, to determine whether applicants for customer-contact jobs have outgoing personality traits that match its strategy of creating a high-spirited, fun-loving, in-flight atmosphere for passengers. The company is so selective that only about 3 percent of the candidates interviewed are offered jobs.

> Talented people in possession of superior intellectual capital are not only a resource that enables proficient strategy execution but also a prime source of competitive advantage.

For dot-com companies trying to carve out a future in the Internet economy, the resource in shortest supply is intellectual capital. Their biggest challenge is to staff their organizations with gifted, imaginative, and energetic people who can bring life to new

---

[2]Geoffrey Colvin, "The Truth Can Hurt—Get Used to It," *Fortune,* February 7, 2000, p. 52.

[3]For an analytical framework in top-management team analysis, see Donald C. Hambrick, "The Top Management Team: Key to Strategic Success," *California Management Review* 30, no. 1 (Fall 1987), pp. 88–108.

illustration capsule 41
How General Electric Develops a Talented and Deep Management Team

General Electric is widely considered to be one of the best-managed companies in the world, with capabilities that go deep into the management ranks and one of the world's best programs for developing managers into people with outstanding leadership, business, and decision-making skills. The company focuses on attracting talented people with high potential for executive leadership and then goes to great lengths to develop their leadership, business, and decision-making skills. There are several key elements of GE's strategy for assembling a talent-rich stable of managers and executives:

- GE makes a practice of transferring managers across divisional, business, or functional lines for sustained periods of time. Such transfers allow managers to develop relationships with colleagues in other parts of the company, help break down insular thinking in business "silos," and promote cross-business idea sharing and best practice sharing. There is an enormous emphasis at GE on transferring ideas and best practices from business to business and making GE a "boundaryless" company despite its strategy of broad, mostly unrelated diversification (see Illustration Capsule 40 in Chapter 10).

- In selecting executives for key positions, GE is strongly disposed to candidates who exhibit what are called the four E's—enormous personal *energy,* the ability to motivate and *energize* others, *edge* (a GE code word for instinctive competitiveness and the ability to make tough decisions in a timely fashion, saying yes or no, and not maybe), and *execution* (the ability to carry things through to fruition).

- All managers are expected to be proficient at what GE calls "workout"—a process where managers and employees come together to confront issues as soon as they come up, pinpoint the root cause of the issue, and bring about quick resolutions to the issue so the business can move forward. In 1999 and early 2000, managers and employees in all of GE's businesses were engaged in workout sessions on how to make proficient use of the Internet, "e-commerce" the whole company, and transform GE into a global e-business.

- GE operates a Leadership Development Center in Croton-on-Hudson, New York (referred to as Crotonville by GE managers), that is regarded as one of the best corporate training centers in the world. Each

---

In the Internet economy and many other industries, there is a seismic shift under way from the importance of capital investment to the importance of investing in intellectual capital.

ideas quickly and inject into the organization what one Dell Computer executive calls "hum."[4] In a very real way, their most important investment is in intellectual capital, not in tangible assets such as facilities and equipment. The saying "People are our most important asset" may seem hollow elsewhere, but it fits Internet and high-technology companies dead on. This is why such companies as Amazon.com, DoubleClick, America Online, Cisco Systems, and Dell are breaking new ground in recruiting, hiring, cultivating, developing, and retaining talented employees—most all of whom are in their 20s and 30s. Compensation packages include not only attractive pay and benefits but also lucrative stock options. Much attention is devoted to creating exciting work environments where people work hard but have fun and are passionate about being on the cutting edge and doing incredible new things that will affect the future of the world. DoubleClick puts all new employees through a week-long orientation program called ClickerCamp, where all senior executives discuss what the company is doing and a concerted effort is made to explain the company's vision, introduce new hires to DoubleClick's culture, and begin making them a part of the DoubleClick team.[5] All Dou-

[4]John Byrne, "The Search for the Young and Gifted," *Business Week*, October 4, 1999, p. 108.
[5]Ibid., p. 112.

illustration capsule 41

(concluded)

year GE sends about 10,000 newly hired and long-time managers to Crotonville for a three-week course on the company's six sigma quality initiative. More than 5,000 "Master Black Belt" and "Black Belt" six sigma experts have graduated from Crotonville to drive forward thousands of quality initiatives throughout the corporation. Almost every GE professional manager holds at least a "Green Belt" in six sigma education. CEO Jack Welch's inspirational lectures on quality and performance are seen on video by nearly all of GE's employees. Six sigma training is an ironclad requirement for promotion to any professional and managerial position and any stock option award.

Welch has visited the company's training facility more than 250 times over the past 17 years to lecture, cajole, and engage 15,000-plus GE managers in discussions. Welch encourages managers attending the three-week development course to speak their minds, challenge, argue and disagree with his positions, and offer up their own thoughts.

GE's Crotonville development center also offers advanced courses for senior managers that may focus on a single management topic for a month. All classes at Crotonville involve managers from different GE businesses and different parts of the world. Some of the most valuable learning at Crotonville comes in between formal class sessions when GE managers from different businesses trade ideas about how to improve processes and better serve the customer. This knowledge sharing not only spreads best practices throughout the organization but also improves each GE manager's knowledge.

- Each of GE's 85,000 managers and professionals is graded in an annual process that divides them into five groups: the top 10 percent, the next 15 percent, the middle 50 percent, the next 15 percent, and the bottom 10 percent. Everyone in the top tier gets stock options, nobody in the fourth tier gets options, and most of those in the fifth tier become candidates for being weeded out. Business heads are pressured to wean out "C" players. Jack Welch personally reviews the performance of GE's top 3,000 managers. Senior executive compensation is heavily weighted toward six sigma commitment and producing successful business results.

According to Jack Welch, "The reality is, we simply cannot afford to field anything but teams of 'A' players."

Sources: 1998 Annual Report; www.ge.com; John A. Byrne, "How Jack Welch Runs GE," *Business Week,* June 8, 1998, p. 90; Miriam Leuchter, "Management Farm Teams," *Journal of Business Strategy,* May 1998, pp. 29–32; and "The House That Jack Built, *The Economist,* September 18, 1999.

bleClick employees rate their manager annually on 25 criteria, intended to reveal whether managers hired good people and whether employees liked working for them. Besides checking closely for functional and technical skills, Dell Computer tests applicants for their tolerance of ambiguity and change, their capacity to work in teams, and their ability to learn on the fly. Illustration Capsule 42 discusses Cisco Systems' approach to recruiting talented employees.

The best companies use a variety of practices to develop their knowledge base and build intellectual capital:

1. Spend considerable effort in screening and evaluating job applicants, selecting only those with suitable skill sets, energy, initiative, judgment, and aptitudes for learning and adaptability to the company's work environment and culture. Many companies take extraordinary pains to seek out the right people to fill job openings—in 1997, Southwest Airlines got 150,000 resumés but hired only 5,000 people.

2. Put employees through training programs that continue not just through their early years but usually throughout their careers.

3. Give them challenging, interesting, and skills-stretching assignments.

illustration capsule 42

How Cisco Systems Staffs Its Organization with Talented Employees

Cisco Systems is the world's leading producer of switches, routers, and other network components used to access the Internet. The company's revenues and earnings increased about 50 percent each year from 1995 to 2000. During this period, Cisco's rapid growth required workforce additions of as many as 1,000 new employees per quarter. In early 2002, Cisco had close to 38,000 employees worldwide, with more than 430 sales and support offices in 60 countries. Cisco CEO John Chambers believes in hiring only the highest-caliber people. One way he finds them is by acquiring other companies; between 1993 and 2001, Cisco bought 71 companies. While Chambers and other executives hammered out a deal, human resource managers like Mimi Gigoux visited the prospect's headquarters to inform potential new employees about Cisco and persuade them of the merits of staying on should Cisco take over the company. But this is only one of Cisco's recruiting methods.

Finding so many star engineers, programmers, managers, salespeople, and support personnel has been a challenge for Cisco, given the superheated job market and the competition for top talent. Because Cisco operates with few levels of management, it requires employees who not only have strong skill sets but also work well without direct supervision and can make quick, sound decisions. The innovative tactics Cisco uses to staff its organization with talented high performers include the following:

- Cisco does not advertise specific jobs in newspapers, but runs ads featuring its Web address and an invitation to apply at Cisco. The employment opportunities section of Cisco's website contains job listings for all Cisco locations around the world and provides a great deal of information about each job. To attract applicants, Cisco also runs ads in movie theaters and on billboards along commuter routes and sends recruiters to art fairs, microbrewery festivals, and home and garden shows in Silicon Valley and other locations where it has facilities to collect business cards and speak informally with potential prospects.

- Since many prospects visit Cisco's website from their jobs (peak usage of the employment Web pages occurs between 10 AM and 3 PM), it can tell where they work (with software that automatically checks the Internet address of those who visit its site) and, at times, has greeted visitors from highly regarded firms with a screen that says "Welcome to Cisco. Would you like a job?" Cisco's employment Web pages contain an escape button featuring a grimacing face with the caption "Oh no: My boss is coming." When job seekers click on the face, they are immediately taken to a page that lists "Seven habits of a successful employee," "Lists of gift ideas for my boss and workmates," and "Things to do today."

- Job prospecting visitors to Cisco's website can fill out an application online. Part of the online application process involves use of a tool Cisco calls Profiler that asks a series of questions tailored to the applicant's experience. The profile gives Cisco recruiters more detailed information about an applicant than what might be included in a résumé.

4. Rotate them through jobs that not only have great content but that span functional and geographic boundaries. Providing people with opportunities to gain experience in a variety of international settings is increasingly considered an essential part of career development in multinational or global companies.

5. Encourage employees to be creative and innovative, to challenge existing ways of doing things and offer better ways, and to submit ideas for new products or businesses. Progressive companies work hard at creating a work environment where ideas and suggestions bubble up from below rather than proceed from the top down. Employees are made to feel their opinions count.

6. Foster a stimulating and engaging work environment, such that employees will consider the company "a great place to work."

7. Exert efforts to retain high-potential, high performing employees with salary increases, performance bonuses, stock options and equity ownership, and other

illustration capsule 42

(concluded)

- Cisco recruiters target passive job seekers—people who are happy and successful where they are. According to Cisco's human resources vice president, "The top 10% are not typically found in the first round of layoffs from other companies, and they usually aren't cruising through the want ads." To learn how to find and entice talented people to move to Cisco, the company held focus groups with such recruiting targets as marketing professionals and senior engineers at other companies to discover how happily employed people could be persuaded to interview for a job. These sessions revealed that people were most likely to consider a job change if a friend told them about a job opportunity that was better than their current job. So the company launched an initiative to get Cisco personnel actively involved in making friends with prospects, telling them what it was like to work at Cisco, mentioning attractive job openings, and putting them in touch with Cisco employees in the same job or with similar interests who could give them a realistic preview of the job and attempt to remove the fear and uncertainty from a job move. At one point, a thousand Cisco employees participated in the "friends initiative," enticed by a referral fee (starting at $500) and a lottery ticket for a free trip to Hawaii for each prospect they befriended who was ultimately hired. The program was so successful that a Friends@Cisco section was added to the company's website, giving prospects a way to communicate directly with Cisco employees in job functions or departments of interest and get their views on Cisco's work environment, culture, and career opportunities.

- The company has a staff of 100 in-house professional headhunters to review applicant profiles and résumés and submit a short list of qualified applicants to line managers for interviews. Cisco management believes that it is best to hire people when they are "hot" and that any compensation premium for "hot" prospects (as well as the costs of headhunters and recruiting) is more than offset by the benefits of quickly hiring top-tier people to support Cisco's own rapid growth.

- In May 2001, Cisco Systems announced a relationship with Monster.com, the Internet job search website. Under the new agreement, students enrolled in the Cisco Networking Academy program will have instant access to Monster.com's global jobs database, as well as résumé-building assistance and other tips. The Cisco Networking Academy program is a 560-hour, eight-semester program that teaches students and in-transition workers to design, build, and maintain computer networks. More than 6,800 of these "academies" are located in high schools, technical schools, and colleges.

With the economic downturn of the early 2000s, Cisco has made some structural changes as the communications market consolidates, but it continues to emphasize high quality staff. "You are still dealing with one of the strongest companies in the world," notes Rand Blazer, CEO of KPMG Consulting.

Sources: "Cisco Systems Announces New Organizational Structure," press release (http://newsroom.cisco.com), August 23, 2001; "Cisco and Monster.com Announce Career Search Relationship," press release (http://newsroom.cisco.com), May 15, 2001; Stephanie N. Mehta, "Cisco Fractures Its Own Fairy Tale," *Fortune,* (www.fortune.com), May 14, 2001; Kim Girard, "Cisco or Crisco?" *Business 2.0* (www.business2.com), May 2001; Cisco's website (www.cisco.com); and Patricia Nakache, "Cisco's Recruiting Edge," *Fortune,* September 29, 1997, pp. 275–76.

long-term incentives. Average performers are coached to do better, while underperformers and benchwarmers are weeded out.

Building Core Competencies and Competitive Capabilities

High among the organization-building concerns in the strategy implementing/executing process is the need to build competitively valuable core competencies and organizational capabilities that give the firm a competitive edge over rivals in performing one or more critical value chain activities. When it is relatively easy for rivals to copy smart strategies, making it difficult or impossible to outstrategize rivals and beat them on the

Strategic Management Principle

Building core competencies, resource strengths, and organizational capabilities that rivals can't match is a sound foundation for sustainable competitive advantage.

basis of a superior strategy, the other main avenue to lasting competitive advantage is to outexecute them (beat them with superior strategy execution). Superior strategy execution is essential in situations where rival firms can readily duplicate one another's successful strategic maneuvers. Building core competencies, resource strengths, and organizational capabilities that rivals can't match is one of the best ways to outexecute them. This is why one of management's most important strategy-implementing tasks is to guide the building of core competencies and organizational capabilities in competitively advantageous ways.

Developing and Strengthening Core Competencies   Core competencies can relate to any strategically relevant factor. Honda's core competence is its depth of expertise in gasoline engine technology and small engine design (see Illustration Capsule 39 in Chapter 9). Intel's is in the design of complex chips for personal computers. Procter & Gamble's core competencies reside in its superb marketing-distribution skills and its R&D capabilities in five core technologies—fats, oils, skin chemistry, surfactants, and emulsifiers.[6] Sony's core competencies are its expertise in electronic technology and its ability to translate that expertise into innovative products (cutting-edge video game hardware, miniaturized radios and video cameras, TVs and DVDs with unique features, attractively designed PCs). Most often, a company's core competencies emerge incrementally as it moves either to bolster skills that contributed to earlier successes or to respond to customer problems, new technological and market opportunities, and the competitive maneuverings of rivals.[7] Wise company managers try to foresee changes in customer-market requirements and proactively build new competencies and capabilities that offer a competitive edge over rivals.

Four traits concerning core competencies and competitive capabilities are important to organization building:[8]

- Core competencies rarely consist of narrow skills or the work efforts of a single department. More often, they are bundles of skills and know-how growing out of the combined efforts of cross-functional work groups and departments performing complementary activities at different locations in the firm's value chain.

- Because core competencies typically reside in the combined efforts of different work groups and departments, individual supervisors and department heads can't be expected to see building the overall corporation's core competencies as their responsibility. Rather, the building and nurturing of core competencies is a senior management responsibility.

- The key to leveraging a company's core competencies into competitively valuable capabilities with potential for long-term competitive advantage is concentrating more effort and more talent than rivals on deepening and strengthening these competencies.

- Because customers' needs and market conditions change in often unpredictable ways, it is difficult to fully anticipate the specific know-how and intellectual capital needed for future competitive success. A company's selected bases of competence thus need to be broad enough and flexible enough to respond to an unknown future.

---

[6]James Brian Quinn, *Intelligent Enterprise* (New York: Free Press, 1992), p. 76.
[7]Ibid.
[8]Ibid., pp. 52–53, 55, 73, and 76.

Thus, building and strengthening core competencies is an exercise in (1) managing human skills, knowledge bases, and intellect, and (2) coordinating and networking the efforts of different work groups and departments at every related place in the value chain. It's an exercise best orchestrated by senior managers who appreciate the strategy-executing significance of creating valuable competencies/capabilities and who have the clout to enforce the necessary networking and cooperation among individuals, groups, departments, and external allies. Moreover, organization builders have to concentrate enough resources and management attention on core competence–related activities to achieve the *dominating depth* needed for competitive advantage.[9] This does not necessarily mean spending more money on such activities than present or potential competitors, but it does mean consciously focusing more talent on them and making appropriate internal and external benchmarking comparisons to move toward best-in-industry, if not best-in-world, status.

> Core competencies don't come into being or reach strategic fruition without conscious management attention.

To achieve dominance on lean financial resources, companies like Cray in large computers, Lotus in software, and Honda in small engines leveraged the expertise of their talent pool by frequently re-forming high-intensity teams and reusing key people on special projects.[10] The experiences of these and other companies indicate that the usual keys to successfully building core competencies are superior employee selection, thorough training and retraining, powerful cultural influences, cooperative networking, motivation, empowerment, attractive incentives, organizational flexibility, short deadlines, and good databases—not big operating budgets.[11]

Developing and Strengthening Organizational Capabilities   Whereas the essence of astute strategy making is selecting the competencies and capabilities to underpin the strategy, the essence of good strategy execution is *building and strengthening* the company's competencies and capabilities. Sometimes the company already has the needed competencies and capabilities in place, in which case managers can concentrate on nurturing them to promote better strategy execution. More usually, however, management has to be proactive in upgrading existing capabilites to promote more proficient strategy execution and developing new competencies and capabilities to execute new strategic initiatives.

Capability-building is a time-consuming, hard-to-replicate exercise. Capabilities are difficult to purchase (except through outsiders who already have them and will agree to supply them) and difficult to acquire just by watching others. Just as one cannot become a good golfer by watching Tiger Woods play golf, a company cannot put a new capability in place by creating a new department and assigning it the task of emulating a capability rivals have. Building capability requires a series of organizational steps:

> Building capabilities takes time, conscious effort, and considerable organizing skill.

- First, the organization must develop the *ability* to do something, however imperfectly or inefficiently. This entails selecting people with the requisite skills and experience, upgrading or expanding individual abilities as needed, and then molding the efforts and work products of individuals into a cooperative group effort to create organizational ability.

---

[9]Ibid., p. 73.
[10]Ibid.
[11]Ibid., pp. 73–74.

- Then as experience builds, and the organization reaches a level of ability to accomplish the activity consistently well and at an acceptable cost, the ability begins to translate into a *competence* or a *capability*.
- Should the organization get so good (by continuing to polish and refine and deepen its skills and know-how) that it is better than rivals at the activity, the capability becomes a *distinctive competence* and carries the potential for competitive advantage.

One organization-building question is whether to develop the desired competencies and capabilities internally or to outsource them by partnering with key suppliers or forming strategic alliances. The answer depends on what can be safely delegated to outside suppliers or allies versus what internal capabilities are key to the company's long-term success. Either way, though, calls for action. Outsourcing means launching initiatives to identify the most attractive providers and to establish collaborative relationships. Developing the capabilities in-house means hiring new personnel with relevant skills and experience, linking the individual skills to form organizational capability, building the desired levels of proficiency through repetition (practice makes perfect), and establishing links with related value chain activities.[12] Strong links with related activities are important. Complex activities (like designing and manufacturing a sports utility vehicle or creating software that allows secure credit card transactions over the Internet) usually involve a number of component skills, technological disciplines, competencies, and capabilities—some performed in-house and some provided by suppliers/allies. An important part of the organization-building function is to think about which competencies and capabilities need to be linked and made mutually reinforcing and then to forge the necessary collaboration both internally and with outside resource providers.

| Organizational competencies and capabilities can emerge from collaborative efforts with allies and from acquiring a company having the desired capabilities. |

Sometimes these steps can be short-circuited by acquiring the desired capability through collaborative efforts with external allies or by buying a company that has the requisite capability and integrating its competencies into the firm's value chain. Indeed, a pressing need to acquire certain capabilities quickly is one reason to acquire another company—an acquisition aimed at building greater capability can be every bit as competitively valuable as an acquisition aimed at adding new products or services to the company's business lineup. Capabilities-motivated acquisitions are essential (1) when an opportunity can disappear faster than a needed capability can be created internally, and (2) when industry conditions, technology, or competitors are moving at such a rapid clip that time is of the essence.

Updating and Reshaping Competencies and Capabilities as External Conditions and Company Strategy Change   Even after core competencies and competitive capabilities are in place and functioning, company managers can't relax. Competencies and capabilities that grow stale can impair competitiveness unless they are refreshed and modified, with some even being phased out and replaced with altogether new ones, in response to ongoing customer-market changes and to shifts in company strategy. Indeed, the buildup of knowledge and experience over time, coupled with the imperatives of keeping capabilities in step with ongoing

---

[12]Robert H. Hayes, Gary P. Pisano, and David M. Upton, *Strategic Operations: Competing through Capabilities* (New York: Free Press, 1996), pp. 503–7.

strategy and market changes, makes it appropriate to view a company as *a bundle of evolving competencies and capabilities.* Management's organization-building challenge is one of continuously adapting and adjusting the company's portfolio of competencies and capabilities, deciding when and how to tune and recalibrate existing competencies and capabilities, and when and how to develop new ones. Although the task is formidable, ideally it produces a dynamic organization with "hum" and momentum. But dedicated and ongoing management efforts to keep core competencies finely honed and in step with shifting external and internal circumstances provide a big executional advantage. Moreover, cutting-edge core competencies and organizational capabilities are not easily duplicated by rival firms; thus any competitive edge they produce is likely to be sustainable, paving the way for above-average organizational performance.

> Continuously tuning and recalibrating a company's competencies and capabilities to match new strategic requirements, evolving market conditions, and customer expectations is a solid basis for sustaining both effective strategy execution and competitive advantage.

The Strategic Role of Employee Training   Training and retraining are important when a company shifts to a strategy requiring different skills, competitive capabilities, managerial approaches, and operating methods. Training is also strategically important in organizational efforts to build skills-based competencies. And it is a key activity in businesses where technical know-how is changing so rapidly that a company loses its ability to compete unless its skilled people have cutting-edge knowledge and expertise. Successful strategy implementers see to it that the training function is both adequately funded and effective. If the chosen strategy calls for new skills, deeper technological capability, or building and using new capabilities, training should be placed near the top of the action agenda.

The strategic importance of training has not gone unnoticed. Over 600 companies have established internal "universities" to manage the task of keeping employee and managerial skills and expertise up-to-date, facilitate continuous organizational learning, and aid in the task of upgrading company competencies and capabilities. Many companies conduct orientation sessions for new employees, fund an assortment of competence-building training programs, and reimburse employees for tuition and other expenses associated with obtaining additional college education, attending professional development courses, and earning professional certification of one kind or another. A number of companies offer online, just-in-time training courses to employees around the clock. Increasingly, employees at all levels are expected to take an active role in their own professional development, assuming responsibility for continuous learning.

Matching Organization Structure to Strategy

There are few hard-and-fast rules for organizing the work effort to support strategy. Every firm's organization chart is idiosyncratic, reflecting prior organizational patterns, varying internal circumstances, executive judgments about reporting relationships, and the politics of who gets which assignments. Moreover, every strategy is grounded in its own set of key success factors and value chain activities. So a customized organization structure is appropriate. But despite the need for situation-specific organization structures, some considerations are common to all companies. These are summarized in Figure 11.3 and discussed in turn below.

Identifying Strategy-Critical Activities   In any business, some activities in the value chain are always more critical to strategic success and competitive advantage than others. From a strategy perspective, a certain portion of an organization's work

figure 11.3   **Structuring the Organization to Promote Successful Strategy Execution**

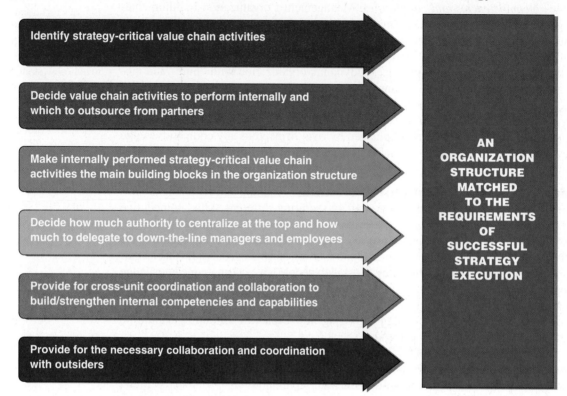

Strategy-critical activities and capabilities vary according to the particulars of a firm's strategy, value chain make-up, competitive requirements, and external market conditions.

involves routine administrative housekeeping (doing the payroll, administering employee benefit programs, managing cash flows, handling grievances and the usual assortment of people problems, providing corporate security, managing stockholder relations, maintaining fleet vehicles, and complying with regulations). Other activities are support functions (information technology and data processing, accounting, training, public relations, market research, legal and legislative affairs, and purchasing). Among the primary value chain activities are certain crucial business processes that have to be performed either exceedingly well or in closely coordinated fashion for the organization to deliver on the capabilities needed for strategic success. For instance, hotel/motel enterprises have to be good at fast check-in/check-out, room maintenance, food service, and creating a pleasant ambience. A manufacturer of chocolate bars must be skilled in purchasing, production, merchandising, and promotional activities; buying quality cocoa beans at low prices is vital, and reducing production costs by a fraction of a cent per bar can mean a seven-figure improvement in the bottom line. In discount stock brokerage, the strategy-critical activities are fast access to information, accurate order execution, efficient record keeping and transactions processing, and good customer service. In specialty chemicals, the critical activities are R&D, product innovation, getting new products onto the market quickly, effective marketing, and expertise in assisting customers. In consumer electronics, where advancing technology drives new product innovation, rapidly getting cutting-edge, next-generation products to market is a critical organizational capability.

Two questions help pinpoint an organization's strategy-critical activities: "What functions or business processes have to be performed extra well or in timely fashion to achieve sustainable competitive advantage?" and "In what value chain activities would poor execution seriously impair strategic success?"[13] The answers generally point to the crucial activities where attentive, strategy-supportive organization is required.

Reasons to Consider Outsourcing "Noncritical" Value Chain Activities Managers too often spend inordinate amounts of time, psychic energy, and resources wrestling with functional support groups and other internal bureaucracies, which diverts their attention from the company's strategy-critical activities. One way to reduce such distractions is to cut the number of internal staff support activities and, instead, source more support functions and noncritical value chain activities from outside vendors.

Each supporting activity in a firm's value chain and within its traditional staff groups can be considered a "service."[14] Indeed, most of a company's overhead consists of services the company chooses to produce internally. However, many such services can be purchased from outside vendors. What makes outsourcing attractive is that an outsider, by concentrating specialists and technology in its area of expertise, can frequently perform certain services as well or better, and usually more cheaply, than a company that performs these services only for itself.

But there are strong reasons to consider outsourcing besides lower costs and less internal hassle. Approached from a strategic point of view, outsourcing noncrucial support activities can decrease internal bureaucracies, flatten the organization structure, speed decision making, heighten the company's strategic focus, improve its innovative capacity (through interaction with "best in world" suppliers), and increase competitive responsiveness.[15] The experiences of companies that obtain many support services from outside vendors indicate that such outsourcing allows a company to concentrate its own energies and resources on those value chain activities where it can create unique value, where it can be best in the industry (or, better still, best in the world), and where it needs strategic control to build core competencies, achieve competitive advantage, and manage key customer-supplier-distributor relationships.[16]

Critics contend that the danger of outsourcing is that a company can go overboard and hollow out its knowledge base and capabilities, leaving itself at the mercy of outside suppliers and short of the resource strengths to be master of its own destiny.[17] However, a number of companies have found ways to successfully rely on outside components suppliers, product designers, distribution channels, advertising agencies,

> Outsourcing non-critical value chain activities can produce many advantages—lower costs, less internal bureaucracy, speedier decision making, more flexibility, and heightened strategic focus.

---

[13]Peter F. Drucker, *Management: Tasks, Responsibilities, Practices* (New York: Harper & Row, 1974), pp. 530, 535.

[14]Quinn, *Intelligent Enterprise,* p. 32.

[15]Quinn, *Intelligent Enterprise,* pp. 33 and 89; and James Brian Quinn, "Strategic Outsourcing: Leveraging Knowledge Capabilities," *Sloan Management Review* 40, no. 3 (Summer 1999), p. 9. See also James Brian Quinn and Frederick G. Hilmer, "Strategic Outsourcing," *Sloan Management Review* (Summer 1994), pp. 43–55.

[16]Quinn, *Intelligent Enterprise,* p. 47; and Quinn, "Strategic Outsourcing: Leveraging Knowledge Capabilities," p. 9.

[17]Quinn, *Intelligent Enterprise,* pp. 39–40.

and financial services firms to perform significant value chain activities.[18] For years
Polaroid Corporation bought its film from Eastman Kodak, its electronics from Texas
Instruments, and its cameras from Timex and others, while it concentrated on producing its unique self-developing film packets and designing its next generation of cameras and films. Nike concentrates on design, marketing, and distribution to retailers,
while outsourcing virtually all production of its shoes and sporting apparel. Likewise,
a number of PC manufacturers outsource the assembly of the PCs, concentrating their
energies on product design, sales and marketing, and distribution. Many mining companies outsource geological work, assaying, and drilling. Ernest and Julio Gallo Winery outsources 95 percent of its grape production, letting farmers take on the weather
and other grape-growing risks while it concentrates on wine production and the mar-
keting-sales function.[19] The major airlines outsource their in-flight meals even though
food quality is important to travelers' perception of overall service quality. Eastman
Kodak, Ford, Exxon, Merrill Lynch, and Chevron have outsourced their data processing activities to computer service firms, believing that outside specialists can perform
the needed services at lower costs and equal or better quality. Prior to merging with
Germany's Daimler-Benz, Chrysler tranformed itself from a high-cost producer into a
low-cost producer by abandoning internal production of many parts and components
and instead outsourcing them from more efficient parts/components suppliers; greater
reliance on outsourcing enabled Chrysler to shorten its design-to-market cycle for new
models. Companies like Ford, Boeing, Aerospatiale, AT&T, BMW, and Dell Computer
have learned that their central R&D groups cannot begin to match the innovative
capabilities of a well-managed network of suppliers.[20] Consequently, deciding what activities to perform internally and what activities to outsource is indeed of considerable
strategic significance.

**Reasons to Consider Partnering with Others to Gain Added Com-
petitive Capabilities**   There is another, equally important reason to look outside
for resources to compete effectively aside from just the cost savings and agility that outsourcing can permit. *Partnerships can add to a company's arsenal of capabilities and
contribute to better strategy execution.* By building, continually improving, and then
leveraging collaborative partnerships, a company enhances its overall organizational
capabilities and builds resource strengths—strengths that deliver value to customers,
that rivals can't quite match, and that consequently pave the way for competitive
success.

Automobile manufacturers work closely with their suppliers to advance the design
and functioning of parts and components, to incorporate new technology, to better integrate individual parts and components to form engine cooling systems, transmission

---

[18]The growing tendency of companies to outsource important activities and the many reasons for building
cooperative, collaborative alliances and partnerships with other companies is detailed in James F. Moore,
The Death of Competition (New York: HarperBusiness, 1996); see especially chapter 3.

[19]Quinn, *Intelligent Enterprise,* p. 43.

[20]Quinn, "Strategic Outsourcing: Leveraging Knowledge Capabilities," p. 17.

systems, electrical systems, and so on—all of which helps shorten the cycle time for new models, improve the quality and performance of those models, and boost overall production efficiency. Soft-drink producers (Coca-Cola and PepsiCo) and beer producers (Anheuser-Busch and Miller Brewing) all cultivate their relationships with their bottlers and distributors to strengthen access to local markets and build the loyalty, support, and commitment for corporate marketing programs, without which their own sales and growth are weakened. Similarly, fast-food enterprises like McDonald's and Taco Bell find it essential to work hand-in-hand with franchisees on outlet cleanliness, consistency of product quality, in-store ambience, courtesy and friendliness of store personnel, and other aspects of store operations. Unless franchisees continuously deliver sufficient customer satisfaction to attract repeat business, a fast-food chain's sales and competitive standing will suffer quickly. *Strategic partnerships, alliances, and close collaboration with suppliers, distributors, the makers of complementary products, and even competitors all make good strategic sense whenever the result is to enhance organizational resources and capabilities.*

Making Strategy-Critical Activities the Main Building Blocks The rationale for making strategy-critical activities the main building blocks in structuring a business is compelling: if activities crucial to strategic success are to have the resources, decision-making influence, and organizational impact they need, they have to be centerpieces in the organizational scheme. Plainly, implementing a new or changed strategy is likely to entail new or different key activities, competencies, or capabilities and, therefore, require new or different organizational arrangements. If workable organizational adjustments are not forthcoming, the resulting mismatch between strategy and structure can open the door to execution and performance problems.[21] Hence, attempting to carry out a new strategy with an old organizational structure is usually unwise. Just as a company's strategy evolves to stay in tune with changing external circumstances, so must an organization's structure evolve to fit shifting requirements for proficient strategy execution.

> **Strategic Management Principle**
>
> Matching structure to strategy requires making strategy-critical activities and strategy-critical organizational units the main building blocks in the organization structure.

---

[21]The importance of matching organization design and structure to the particular needs of strategy was first brought to the forefront in a landmark study of 70 large corporations conducted by Professor Alfred Chandler of Harvard University. Chandler's research revealed that changes in an organization's strategy bring about new administrative problems that, in turn, require a new or refashioned structure for the new strategy to be successfully implemented. He found that structure tends to follow the growth strategy of the firm—but often not until inefficiency and internal operating problems provoke a structural adjustment. The experiences of these firms followed a consistent sequential pattern: new strategy creation, emergence of new administrative problems, a decline in profitability and performance, a shift to a more appropriate organizational structure, and then recovery to more profitable levels and improved strategy execution. That managers should reassess their company's internal organization whenever strategy changes is pretty much common sense. A new or different strategy is likely to entail new or different key activities, competencies, or capabilities, and therefore to require new or different internal organizational arrangements. For more details, see Alfred Chandler, *Strategy and Structure* (Cambridge, MA: MIT Press, 1962).

An evolving organization structure is needed to stay in step with the new strategy-executing requirements of an evolving strategy.

Although the stress here is on designing the organization structure around the needs of effective strategy execution, it is worth noting that structure can and does influence the choice of strategy. A good strategy must be doable. When an organization's present structure is so far out of line with the requirements of a particular strategy that the organization would have to be turned upside down to implement it, the strategy may not be doable and should not be given further consideration. In such cases, structure shapes the choice of strategy. The point here, however, is that once strategy is chosen, structure must be modified to fit the strategy if, in fact, an approximate fit does not already exist. Any influences of structure on strategy should, logically, come before the point of strategy selection rather than after it.

The primary organizational building blocks within a business are usually a combination of traditional functional departments (R&D, engineering and design, production and operations, sales and marketing, information technology, finance and accounting, and human resources) and process-complete departments (supply chain management, filling customer orders, customer service, speeding new products to market, quality control, e-commerce).[22] In enterprises with operations in various countries around the world, the basic building blocks may also include geographic organizational units, each of which has profit-loss responsibility for its assigned geographic area. In vertically integrated firms, the major building blocks are divisional units performing one (or more) of the major processing steps along the value chain (raw materials production, components manufacture, assembly, wholesale distribution, retail store operations); each division in the value chain may operate as a profit center for performance measurement purposes. The typical building blocks of a diversified company are its individual businesses, with each business unit usually operating as an independent profit center and with corporate headquarters performing assorted support functions for all the businesses.

Functional specialization can result in the pieces of strategically relevant activities and capabilities being scattered across many different departments.

Managers need to be particularly alert to the fact that in traditional functionally organized structures, pieces of strategically relevant activities and capabilities often end up scattered across many departments. Consider, for example, how a functional structure ends up with pieces of the following strategy-critical activities and organizational capabilities being performed in different departments:

1. *Filling customer orders accurately and promptly*—a process that cuts across sales (which wins the order); finance (which may have to check credit terms or approve special financing); production (which must produce the goods and replenish warehouse inventories as needed); warehousing (which has to verify whether the items are in stock, pick the order from the warehouse, and package it for shipping); shipping (which has to choose a carrier to deliver the goods and release the goods to the carrier).[23]

2. *Speeding new products to market*—a process that is fragmented among R&D, engineering, purchasing, manufacturing, and marketing.

[22]There are many ways a company can organize around functions other than those just cited. A technical instruments manufacturer may be organized around research and development, engineering, production, technical services, quality control, marketing, personnel, and finance and accounting. A hotel may have a functional organization based on front-desk operations, housekeeping, building maintenance, food service, convention services and special events, guest services, personnel and training, and accounting. A discount retailer may organize around such functional units as purchasing, warehousing and distribution, store operations, advertising, merchandising and promotion, customer service, and corporate administrative services. Likewise, process organization assumes a form that matches a company's processes.

[23]Michael Hammer and James Champy, *Reengineering the Corporation* (New York: HarperBusiness, 1993), pp. 26–27.

3. *Improving product quality*—a process that often involves the collaboration of personnel in R&D, engineering and design, components purchasing from suppliers, in-house components production, manufacturing, and assembly.

4. *Supply chain management*—a collaborative process that cuts across such functional areas as purchasing, engineering and design, components purchasing, inventory management, manufacturing and assembly, and warehousing and shipping.

5. *Building the capability to conduct business via the Internet*—a process that involves personnel in information technology, supply chain management, production, sales and marketing, warehousing and shipping, customer service, finance, and accounting.

6. *Obtaining feedback from customers and making product modifications to meet their needs*—a process that involves personnel in customer service and after-sale support, R&D, engineering and design, components purchasing, manufacturing and assembly, and marketing research.

So many handoffs lengthen completion time and frequently drive up administrative costs, since coordinating the fragmented pieces can soak up hours of effort on the parts of many people.[24] This is not a fatal condemnation of functional organization—organizing around specific functions has worked to good advantage in support activities like finance and accounting, human resource management, and engineering, and in such primary activities as R&D, manufacturing, and marketing, despite the fragmentation of strategy-critical activities which accompanies such organization structures. But fragmentation is an important weakness of functional organization, accounting for why we indicated that a company's competencies and capabilities are a composite of activities and do not reside in the activities of a single functional department.

Increasingly during the last decade, companies have found that rather than continuing to scatter related pieces of a business process across several functional departments and scrambling to integrate their efforts, it is better to reengineer the work effort and create *process departments*. This is done by pulling the people who performed the pieces in functional departments into a group that works together to perform the whole process. Pulling the pieces of strategy-critical processes out of the functional silos and creating process departments or cross-functional work groups charged with performing all the steps needed to produce a strategy-critical result has been termed *business process reengineering*. Bell Atlantic used business process reengineering to streamline its bureaucratic procedures for connecting a telephone customer to its long-distance carrier.[25] In Bell Atlantic's functional structure, when a business customer requested a connection between its telephone system and a long-distance carrier for data services, the request traveled from department to department; the internal processing required two to four weeks. In reengineering that process, Bell Atlantic pulled workers from the many functional departments and put them on teams that could handle most customer requests in a matter of days or even hours. Because the work was recurring—similar customer requests had to be processed daily—the teams were permanently grouped into a process department. In the electronics industry, where product life cycles run

[24]Although functional organization incorporates Adam Smith's division-of-labor principle (every person/department involved has specific responsibility for performing a clearly defined task) and allows for tight management control (everyone in the process is accountable to a functional department head for efficiency and adherence to procedures), *no one oversees the whole process and its result.* Hammer and Champy, *Reengineering the Corporation,* pp. 26–27.

[25]Hammer and Champy, *Reengineering the Corporation,* pp. 66–68.

illustration capsule 43

Reengineering Business Processes: How Companies Do It and the Results They Have Gotten

Reengineering strategy-critical business processes to reduce fragmentation across traditional departmental lines and cut bureaucratic overhead has proved to be a legitimate organization design tool. It's not a passing fad or another management program-of-the-month. Process organization is every bit as valid an organizing principle as functional specialization. Strategy execution is improved when the pieces of strategy-critical activities and core business processes performed by different departments are properly integrated and coordinated.

Companies that have reengineered some of their business processes have ended up compressing formerly separate steps and tasks into jobs performed by a single person and integrating jobs into team activities. Reorganization then follows as a natural consequence of task synthesis and job redesign. Successes in this area suggest attacking process fragmentation and overhead reduction in the following fashion:

- Develop a flow chart of the total business process, including its interfaces with other value chain activities.

- Try to simplify the process first, eliminating tasks and steps where possible and streamlining the performance of what remains.

- Determine which parts of the process can be automated (usually those that are repetitive, time-consuming, and automatic); consider introducing advanced technologies that can be upgraded to achieve next-generation capability and provide a basis for further productivity gains down the road.

- Reengineer, then reorganize.

- Evaluate each activity in the process to determine whether it is critical or not. Strategy-critical activities are candidates for benchmarking to achieve best-in-industry or best-in-world performance status.

- Weigh the pros and cons of outsourcing activities that are noncritical or that contribute little to organizational capabilities and core competencies.

- Design a structure for performing the activities that remain; reorganize the personnel and groups who perform these activities into the new structure.

When done properly, reengineering can produce dramatic gains in productivity and organizational capability. In the order-processing section of General Electric's circuit breaker division, elapsed time from order receipt to delivery was cut from three weeks to three days by consolidating six production units into one, reducing a variety of former inventory and handling steps, automating the design system to replace a human custom-design process, and cutting the organizational layers between managers and workers from three to one. Productivity rose 20 percent in one year, and unit manufacturing costs dropped 30 percent.

(continued)

three to six months due to the speed of advancing technology, companies have formed process departments charged with cutting the time it takes to bring new technologies and products to commercial fruition. Illustration Capsule 43 discusses the procedures for reengineering fragmented processes and the results that several organizations have gotten from their reengineering efforts. [26]

Determining the Degree of Authority and Independence to Give Each Unit and Each Employee Companies must decide how much authority to give managers of each organization unit (especially the heads of business subsidiaries, functional departments, and process departments) and how much decision-making latitude to give individual employees in performing their jobs. *In a highly centralized organization structure, top executives retain authority for most strategic and operating decisions and keep a tight rein on business-unit heads and department heads; compara-*

[26]For a detailed review of one company's experiences with reengineering, see Donna B. Stoddard, Sirkka L. Jarvenpaa, and Michael Littlejohn, "The Reality of Business Reengineering: Pacific Bell's Centrex Provisioning Process," *California Management Review* 38, no. 3 (Spring 1996), pp. 57–76.

illustration capsule 43

(concluded)

Northwest Water, a British utility, used reengineering to eliminate 45 work depots that served as home base to crews who installed and repaired water and sewage lines and equipment. Now crews work directly from their vehicles, receiving assignments and reporting work completion from computer terminals in their trucks. Crew members are no longer employees but contractors to Northwest Water. These reengineering efforts not only eliminated the need for the work depots but also allowed Northwest Water to eliminate a big percentage of the bureaucratic personnel and supervisory organization that managed the crews.

At acute care hospitals such as Lee Memorial in Fort Myers, Florida, and St. Vincent's in Melbourne, Australia, medical care has been reengineered so that it is delivered by interdisciplinary teams of health care professionals organized around the needs of the patients and their families rather than around functional departments within the hospital. Both hospitals created focused care or treatment-specific wards within the hospital to treat most of a patient's needs, from admission to discharge. Patients are no longer wheeled from department to department for procedures and

tests; instead, teams have the equipment and resources within each focused care unit to provide total care for the patient. While the hospitals had some concern about functional inefficiency in the use of some facilities, process organization has resulted in substantially lower operating cost, faster patient recovery, and greater satisfaction on the part of patients and caregivers.

In the late 1990s, executives at Dell Computer decided that instead of building more factories to keep up with demand, it would be more efficient to reengineer the way it assembled computers. Dell's goal was to reduce the number of worker touches per machine and thus cut assembly time and costs. Dell came up with a plan called Metric 12, which reorganized the factory space and gave assembly workers more responsibilities. Prior to Metric 12, Dell used a standard assembly line process, where one person after another installed a component until the PC was complete. In this progressive build system, it took up to 25 people to assemble one machine. With the Metric 12 reengineering, small teams of workers have their own compact cell and assemble a complete machine using components in racks in front of them.

Sources: Based on information in Stewart Deck, "Fine Line," *CIO Magazine* (www.cio.com), February 1, 2000. James Brian Quinn, *Intelligent Enterprise* (New York: Free Press, 1992), p. 162; T. Stuart, "GE Keeps Those Ideas Coming," *Fortune,* August 12, 1991; Gene Hall, Jim Rosenthal, and Judy Wade, "How to Make Reengineering Really Work," *Harvard Business Review* 71, no. 6 (November–December 1993), pp. 119–31; Ann Majchrzak and Qianwei Wang, "Breaking the Functional Mind-Set in Process Organizations," *Harvard Business Review* 74, no. 5 (September–October 1996), pp. 93–99; and Iain Somerville and John Edward Mroz, "New Competencies for a New World," in *The Organization of the Future,* ed. Frances Hesselbein, Marshall Goldsmith, and Richard Beckard (San Francisco: Jossey-Bass, 1997), p. 71.

tively little discretionary authority is granted to subordinate managers and individual employees. The command-and-control paradigm of centralized structures is based on the underlying assumption that the people actually performing work have neither the time nor the inclination to monitor and control it, and that they lack the knowledge to make informed decisions about how best to do it—hence the need for prescribed procedures, close supervision, and tight managerial control. A serious shortcoming of hierarchical command-and-control is that it makes an organization sluggish because of the time it takes for the review-approval process to run up all the layers of the management bureaucracy. Furthermore, to work well, centralized decision making requires top-level managers to gather and process whatever knowledge is relevant to the decision. When the relevant knowledge resides at lower organizational levels or is technical, detailed, or hard to express in words, it is difficult and time-consuming to get all of the facts and nuances in front of a high-level executive located far from the scene of the action—knowledge cannot be readily copied from one mind to another. Very often, it is better (and certainly faster) to put decision-making authority in the hands of the people closest to and most familiar with the situation and train them to exercise good judgment.

There are serious disadvantages to having a small number of top-level managers micro-manage the business by personally making decisions or by requiring they approve the recommendations of lower-level subordinates before actions can be taken.

In a highly decentralized organization, managers (and, increasingly, many non-managerial employees) are empowered to act on their own in their areas of responsibility. Plant managers are empowered to order new equipment as needed and make arrangements with suppliers for parts and components; work teams are empowered to manage and improve their assigned process; and employees with customer contact are empowered to do what it takes to please customers. At Starbucks, for example, employees are empowered to exercise initiative in promoting customer satisfaction—there's the story of a store employee who, when the computerized cash register system went offline, enthusiatically offered free coffee to waiting customers.[27] In a diversified company operating on the principle of decentralized decision making, business-unit heads have broad authority to run the subsidiary with comparatively little interference from corporate headquarters; moreover, the business head gives functional and process department heads considerable decision-making latitude.

> The purpose of decentralization is not to push decisions down to lower levels but to lodge decision-making authority in those persons or teams closest to and most knowledgeable about the situation.

Delegating greater authority to subordinate managers and employees creates a more horizontal organization structure with fewer management layers. Whereas in a centralized vertical structure managers and workers have to go up the ladder of authority for an answer, in a decentralized horizontal structure they develop their own answers and action plans—making decisions and being accountable for results is part of their job. Decentralized decision making usually shortens organizational response times, plus it spurs new ideas, creative thinking, innovation, and greater involvement on the part of subordinate managers and employees.

During the past decade, there's been a growing shift from authoritarian, multilayered hierarchical structures to flatter, more decentralized structures that stress employee empowerment. The new preference for leaner management structures and empowered employees is grounded in three tenets:

1. *With the world economy moving swiftly into the Internet Age, traditional hierarchical structures built around functional specialization have to undergo radical surgery to capitalize on both the external market and internal operating potentials of e-commerce technologies.* Companies the world over are having to reinvent their organization structures and internal business approaches in order to (*a*) incorporate productivity-enhancing, cost-reducing benefits of Internet technologies; (*b*) enhance their capabilities to act and react quickly; and (*c*) create, package, and rapidly move information to the point of need.

2. *Decision-making authority should be pushed down to the lowest organizational level capable of making timely, informed, competent decisions.* In practice this means giving meaningful decision-making authority to those people (managers or nonmanagers) nearest the scene who are knowledgeable about the issues and trained to weigh all the factors. Insofar as the five tasks of strategic management are concerned, decentralization means that the managers of each organizational unit should not only lead the crafting of their unit's strategy but also lead the decision making on how to execute it. Decentralization thus requires selecting strong managers to head each organizational unit and holding them accountable for crafting and executing appropriate strategies for their units. Managers who consistently produce unsatisfactory results have to be weeded out.

3. *Employees below the management ranks should be empowered to exercise judgment on matters pertaining to their jobs.* The case for empowering employees to make decisions and holding them accountable for their performance is based on the belief that a

---

[27]Iain Somerville and John Edward Mroz, "New Competencies for a New World," in *The Organization of the Future,* ed. Frances Hesselbein, Marshall Goldsmith, and Richard Beckard (San Francisco: Jossey-Bass, 1997), p. 70.

company that draws on the combined intellectual capital of all its employees can outperform a command-and-control company. The thesis is that employee empowerment shortens organizational response times and spurs new ideas, creative thinking, innovation, and greater involvement on the part of subordinate managers and employees. With employee empowerment, jobs can be defined more broadly, several tasks can be integrated into a single job, and people can direct their own work. Fewer managers are needed because deciding how to do things becomes part of each person's or team's job. Further, given today's electronic communication systems, it is easy and relatively inexpensive for people at all organizational levels to have direct electronic access to data, other employees, managers, suppliers, and customers. They can access information quickly (via the Internet or company intranet), readily check with superiors or whomever else as needed, and take responsible action. Typically, there are genuine morale and productivity gains when well-informed people are allowed to operate in a self-directed way.

Increasing numbers of organizations all across the world are acknowledging the wisdom of these three tenets. There's strong and growing consensus that authoritarian, hierarchical organizations are not as well suited to implementing and executing strategies in an era where they use electronic technologies to operate at Internet speed and where a big fraction of the organization's most valuable assets is intellectual capital and resides in the knowledge and capabilities of its employees. Many companies have therefore begun empowering lower-level managers and employees throughout their organizations, giving them greater discretionary authority to make strategic adjustments in their areas of responsibility and decide what needs to be done to put new strategic initiatives into place and execute them proficiently. But empowerment presents its own organizing challenge: how to exercise adequate control over the actions of empowered employees so that the business is not put at risk at the same time that the benefits of empowerment are realized.[28]

> Decentralization of authority is an appropriate response to today's seismic shifts toward an Internet economy and toward the dominating role of intellectual capital.

Further, decentralizing strategy-related decisions and giving business heads full operating rein poses a problem in diversified companies with related businesses. Cross-business strategic fits are often best captured by either centralizing strategic-fit-related decision-making authority at the corporate level or else by enforcing close cooperation and shared decision making.[29] For example, if businesses with overlapping process and product technologies have their own independent R&D departments, each pursuing their own priorities, projects, and strategic agendas, it's hard for the corporate parent to prevent duplication of effort, capture either economies of scale or economies of scope, or broaden the company's R&D efforts to embrace new technological paths, product families, end-use applications, and customer groups. Likewise, centralizing control over the related activities of separate businesses makes sense when there are opportunities to share a common sales force, use common distribution channels, rely on a common field service organization to handle customer requests for technical assistance or provide maintenance and repair services, use common e-commerce systems and approaches, and so on. And for reasons previously discussed, limits also have to

> In diversified companies, there's merit in retaining some strategy-implementing authority at the corporate level to enforce cross-business collaboration and achieve tight coordination of related value chain activities.

---

[28]Exercising adequate control in businesses that demand short response times, innovation, and creativity is a serious requirement. For example, a prominent Wall Street securities firm lost $350 million when a trader allegedly booked fictitious profits; Sears took a $60 million write-off after admitting that employees in its automobile service departments recommended unnecessary repairs to customers. For a discussion of the problems and possible solutions, see Robert Simons, "Control in an Age of Empowerment," *Harvard Business Review* 73 (March–April 1995), pp. 80–88.

[29]For a discussion of the importance of cross-business coordination, see Jeanne M. Liedtka, "Collaboration across Lines of Business for Competitive Advantage," *Academy of Management Executive* 10, no. 2 (May 1996), pp. 20–34.

be placed on the independence of functional managers when pieces of strategy-critical processes are located in different organizational units and require close coordination for maximum effectiveness.

Providing for Cross-Unit Coordination   The classic way to coordinate the activities of organizational units is to position them in the hierarchy so that those most closely related report to a single person (a functional department head, a process manager, a geographic area head). Managers higher up in the pecking order generally have authority over more organizational units and thus the clout to coordinate, integrate, and arrange for the cooperation of units under their supervision. In such structures, the chief executive officer, chief operating officer, and business-level managers end up as central points of coordination because of their positions of authority over the whole unit. When a firm is pursuing a related diversification strategy, coordinating the related activities of independent business units often requires the centralizing authority of a single corporate-level officer. Also, diversified companies commonly centralize such staff support functions as public relations, finance and accounting, employee benefits, and information technology at the corporate level.

But, as explained earlier, the functional organization structures employed in most businesses often result in pieces of certain strategy-critical activities being fragmented across several departments rather than being unified under the coordinating authority of a single executive. To combat fragmentation, most companies supplement their functional organization structures with coordinating teams, cross-functional task forces, dual reporting relationships, informal organizational networking, voluntary cooperation, incentive compensation tied to group performance measures, and strong executive-level insistence on teamwork and cross-department cooperation (including removal of recalcitrant managers who stonewall collaborative efforts). At ABB, a $30 billion European-based company that makes power generation and electrical equipment and offers a wide range of engineering services, a top executive promptly replaced the managers of several plants who were not fully committed to collaborating closely on eliminating duplication in product development and production efforts among plants in several different countries. Earlier, the executive, noting that negotiations among the managers had stalled on which labs and plants to close, had met with all the managers, asked them to cooperate to find a solution, discussed with them which options were unacceptable, and given them a deadline to find a solution. When the asked-for teamwork wasn't forthcoming, several managers were replaced.

See Illustration Capsule 44 for how 3M Corporation puts the necessary organizational arrangements into place to create worldwide coordination on technology matters.

The key in weaving support activities into the organization design is to establish reporting and coordinating arrangements that

- Maximize how support activities contribute to enhanced performance of the primary functional and strategy-critical capabilities in the firm's value chain.
- Contain the costs of support activities and minimize the time and energy internal units have to spend on doing business with each other.

Without such arrangements, the cost of transacting business internally becomes excessive, and the managers of individual organizational units, forever diligent in guarding their turf and protecting their prerogatives to run their areas as they see fit, can weaken the strategy execution effort and become part of the strategy-implementing problem rather than part of the solution.

Assigning Responsibility for Collaboration with Outsiders   Someone or some group must be authorized to collaborate as needed with each major outside

illustration capsule 44
Cross-Unit Coordination at Three Companies

Many companies have embraced the benefits of cross-unit coordination. At 3M, management formed a Technical Council, composed of the heads of the major labs, which meets regularly to discuss ways to improve cross-unit transfer of technology and other issues of common interest. It also created a Technical Forum, composed of scientists and technical experts chosen to facilitate grassroots communication among employees in all the labs. These collaborative efforts have resulted in a portfolio of more than 100 technologies and the capability to use them routinely in production applications.

At Whole Foods Market, the largest U.S. natural foods grocer, employees are called team members, and job titles reflect functions rather than hierarchy. Each of the Whole Foods 40-plus markets is an autonomous profit unit comprising about 10 self-managed teams—for produce, grocery, prepared foods, and the like—all with designated leaders. Those leaders form a store team, and store leaders form regional teams. Whole Foods' teamwork has boosted revenues to over $500 million—roughly double the industry average.

The Container Store managers encourage employees to "think outside the box" in their daily work. The company, a Dallas-based chain of retail stores that sells gadgets for organizing consumers' homes and lives, integrates many work functions. Human resource managers have responsibilities ranging from payroll to store operations. "We know this helps in so many ways, from reduced turnover to clearer lines of communication," notes Barbara Anderson, director of community services and staff development.

Sources: Cindy Royal, "Finding Fame in Fortune," *Austin Business Journal* (http://austinbcentral.com), August 11, 2000; Karen M. Kroll, "Container Store a Hit with Customers, Employees," *Shopping Centers Today* (www.icsc.org), May 1, 2000; Jennifer Koch Laabs, "Thinking Outside the Box at the Container Store," *Workforce* (www.workforce.com), March 2001, pp. 34–38; Charles Fishman, "Whole Foods Is All Teams," *Fast Company* (www.fastcompany.com), April 1996; Sumantra Ghoshal and Christopher A. Bartlett, "Changing the Role of Top Management: Beyond Structure to Process," *Harvard Business Review* 73, no. 1 (January–February 1995), pp. 93–94.

constituency involved in strategy execution. Forming alliances and cooperative relationships presents immediate opportunities and opens the door to future possibilities, but nothing valuable is realized until the relationship grows, develops, and blossoms. Unless top management sees that constructive organizational bridge-building with strategic partners occurs and that productive working relationships emerge, the value of alliances is lost and the company's power to execute its strategy is weakened. If close working relationships with suppliers are crucial, then supply chain management must be given formal status on the company's organization chart and a significant position in the pecking order. If distributor/dealer/franchisee relationships are important, someone must be assigned the task of nurturing the relationships with foward channel allies. If working in parallel with providers of complementary products and services contributes to enhanced organizational capability, then cooperative organizational arrangements have to be put in place and managed to good effect.

> The key to cooperative alliances and partnerships is effectively managing the relationship and capturing the potential gain in resource capability, not in doing the deal.

Building organizational bridges with external allies can be accomplished by appointing "relationship" managers with responsibility for making particular strategic partnerships or alliances generate the intended benefits. Relationship managers have many roles and functions: getting the right people together, promoting good rapport, seeing that plans for specific activities are developed and carried out, helping adjust internal organizational procedures and communication systems to link the partners better and iron out operating dissimilarities, and nurturing interpersonal ties. Multiple cross-organization ties have to be established and kept open to ensure proper communication and coordination.[30] There has to be enough information sharing to make the relationship work and periodic frank discussions of conflicts, trouble spots, and changing situations.[31]

---

[30]Rosabeth Moss Kanter, "Collaborative Advantage: The Art of the Alliance," *Harvard Business Review* 72, no. 4 (July–August 1994), pp. 105–6.

[31]For an excellent review of ways to effectively manage the relationship between alliance partners, see Kanter, "Collaborative Advantage," pp. 96–108.

Perspectives on Organizing the Work Effort and Building Capabilities   All organization designs have their strategy-related strengths and weaknesses. To do a good job of matching structure to strategy, strategy implementers first have to pick a basic design and modify it as needed to fit the company's particular business makeup. They must then (*a*) supplement the design with appropriate coordinating mechanisms (cross-functional task forces, special project teams, self-contained work teams, and so on), and (*b*) institute whatever networking and communication arrangements it takes to support effective execution of the firm's strategy. While companies may not set up "ideal" organizational arrangements to avoid disturbing certain existing reporting relationships or to accommodate the personalities of certain individuals involved, internal politics, and other situational idiosyncrasies, they must work toward the goal of building a competitively capable organization.

> There's no perfect or ideal organization structure.

The ways and means of developing stronger core competencies and organizational capabilities (or creating altogether new ones) tend to be idiosyncratic to each company, its culture, and its circumstances. Not only do different companies and executives tackle the capabilities-building challenge in different ways but different capabilities require different organizing techniques. Thus, generalizing about how to build capabilities has to be done cautiously. What can be said unequivocally is that building an organization with the competencies and capabilities to execute strategy proficiently entails a process of consciously knitting the efforts of individuals and groups together. Competencies and capabilities emerge from establishing and nurturing cooperative working relationships among people and groups to perform activities in a more customer-satisfying fashion, not from rearranging boxes on an organization chart. Furthermore, organization building is a task senior management must lead and be deeply involved in. Indeed, effectively managing both internal organization processes and external collaboration to create and develop competitively valuable competencies and capabilities ranks very high on the "to-do" list of senior executives in today's companies.

> Organizational capabilities emerge from a process of consciously knitting together the efforts of different work groups, departments, and external allies, not from how the boxes on the organization chart are arranged.

ORGANIZATIONAL STRUCTURES OF THE FUTURE

Many of today's companies are winding up the task of remodeling their traditional hierarchical structures once built around functional specialization and centralized authority. Much of the corporate downsizing movement in the late 1980s and early 1990s was aimed at recasting authoritarian, pyramidal organizational structures into flatter, decentralized structures. The change was driven by growing realization that command-and-control hierarchies were proving a liability in businesses where customer preferences were shifting from standardized products to custom orders and special features, product life cycles were growing shorter, custom mass production methods were replacing standardized mass production techniques, customers wanted to be treated as individuals, the pace of technological change was accelerating, and market conditions were fluid. Layered management hierarchies with lots of checks and controls that required people to look upward in the organizational structure for answers and approval were bogging down, failing to deliver responsive customer service and adapt fast enough to changing conditions. Likewise, functional silos, task-oriented work, and fragmentation of strategy-critical activities further contributed to an erosion of competitiveness in fluid or volatile business environments.

> During the past decade, new strategic priorities and rapidly shifting competitive conditions have triggered revolutionary changes in how companies are organizing the work effort.

illustration capsule 45

Organizational Approaches for International and Global Markets

A study of 43 large U.S.-based consumer products companies conducted by McKinsey & Co., a leading management consulting firm, identified internal organizational actions with the strongest and weakest links to rapidly growing sales and profits in international and global markets.

ORGANIZATIONAL ACTIONS STRONGLY LINKED TO INTERNATIONAL SUCCESS

- Centralizing international decision making in every area except new product development.

- Having a worldwide management development program and more foreigners in senior management posts.

- Requiring international experience for advancement into top management.

- Linking global managers with video conferencing and electronic mail.

- Having product managers of foreign subsidiaries report to a country general manager.

- Using local executives to head operations in foreign countries. (However, this is rapidly ceasing to distinguish successful companies because nearly everyone has implemented such a practice.)

ORGANIZATIONAL ACTIONS WEAKLY LINKED TO INTERNATIONAL SUCCESS

- Creating global divisions.

- Forming international strategic business units.

- Establishing centers of excellence where a single company facility takes global responsibility for a key product or emerging technology (too new to evaluate pro or con).

- Using cross-border task forces to resolve problems and issues.

- Creating globally integrated management information systems.

However, the lists of organizational dos and don'ts are far from decisive. In general, the study found that internal organizational structure doesn't matter as much as having products with attractive prices and features. It is wrong to expect good results just because of good organization. Moreover, certain organizational arrangements, such as centers of excellence, are too new to determine whether they positively affect sales and profit growth.

Source: Based on information reported by Joann S. Lublin, "Study Sees U.S. Businesses Stumbling on the Road to Globalization," *The Wall Street Journal,* March 22, 1993, p. B4B.

In today's fast-changing markets where many companies are racing for global leadership in their industries and/or racing to build strong positions in the industries of the future, the necessary organizational themes are lean, flat, agile, responsive, and innovative. The necessary tools of organizational design are managers and workers empowered to act on their own judgments, reengineered work processes, self-directed work teams, rapid incorporation of Internet technologies and a cutting-edge e-commerce infrastructure, and networking with outsiders to improve existing organization capabilities and create new ones. The necessary organizational imperative is building a company capable of outcompeting rivals on the basis of superior resource strengths and competitive capabilities—capabilities that are increasingly based on intellectual capital. In a growing number of companies and industries, there is no alternative but to restructure the internal organization so it can operate at Internet speed and to ingrain e-commerce business practices in day-to-day operations throughout the company.

Illustration Capsule 45 reports the results of a study of trends in organizational arrangements in multinational and global companies.

The organizations of the future will have several new characteristics:

- Fewer barriers between different vertical ranks, between functions and disciplines, between units in different geographic locations, and between the company and its suppliers, distributors/dealers, strategic allies, and customers.
- A capacity for change and rapid learning.
- Collaborative efforts among people in different functional specialities and geographic locations—essential to create organization competencies and capabilities.
- Extensive use of e-commerce technology and e-commerce business practices—real-time data and information systems, heavy reliance on e-commerce systems for transacting business with suppliers and customers, and Internet-based communication and collaboration with suppliers, customers, and strategic partners.

key|points

The job of strategy execution is to convert strategic plans into actions and good results. The test of successful strategy execution is whether actual organization performance matches or exceeds the targets spelled out in the strategic plan. Shortfalls in performance signal weak strategy, weak execution, or both.

In deciding how to implement a new or revised strategy, managers have to determine what internal conditions are needed to execute the strategic plan successfully. Then they must create these conditions as rapidly as practical. The process of implementing and executing strategy involves:

- Building an organization with the competencies, capabilities, and resource strengths to carry out the strategy successfully.
- Developing budgets to steer ample resources into those value chain activities critical to strategic success.
- Establishing strategy-supportive policies and procedures.
- Instituting best practices and pushing for continuous improvement in how value chain activities are performed.
- Installing support systems that enable company personnel to carry out their strategic roles successfully day in and day out.
- Tying rewards and incentives to the achievement of performance objectives and good strategy execution.
- Creating a strategy-supportive work environment and corporate culture.
- Exerting the internal leadership needed to drive implementation forward and to keep improving on how the strategy is being executed.

The challenge is to create a series of tight fits (1) between strategy and the organization's competencies, capabilities, and structure; (2) between strategy and budgetary allocations; (3) between strategy and policy; (4) between strategy and internal support systems; (5) between strategy and the reward structure; and (6) between strategy and the corporate culture. The tighter the fits, the more powerful strategy execution becomes and the more likely targeted performance can actually be achieved.

Implementing strategy is not just a top-management function; it is a job for the whole management team. *All managers function as strategy implementers* in their respective areas of authority and responsibility. All managers have to consider what actions to take in their areas to achieve the intended results—they each need an action agenda.

The three major organization-building actions are (1) filling key positions with able people, (2) building the core competencies and organizational capabilities needed to perform value chain activities proficiently, and (3) structuring the internal work effort and melding it with the collaborative efforts of strategic allies. Selecting able people for key positions tends to be one of the earliest strategy implementation steps because it takes a full complement of capable managers and employees to get changes in place and functioning smoothly.

Building strategy-critical core competencies and competitive capabilities not easily imitated by rivals is one of the best ways to gain a competitive advantage. Core competencies emerge from skills and activities performed at different points in the value chain that, when linked, create unique organizational capability. The key to leveraging a company's core competencies into long-term competitive advantage is to concentrate more effort and more talent than rivals do on strengthening and deepening organizational competencies and capabilities. The multiskill, multiactivity character of core competencies and capabilities makes achieving dominating depth an exercise in (1) managing human skills, knowledge bases, and intellect, and (2) coordinating and networking the efforts of different work groups, departments, and collaborative allies. It is a task that senior mangement must lead and be deeply involved in chiefly because it is senior managers who are in the best position to guide and enforce the necessary networking and cooperation among individuals, groups, departments, and external allies.

Building organizational capabilities means more than just strengthening what a company already does. There are times when management has to be proactive in developing new competencies and capabilities to complement the company's existing resource base and promote more proficient strategy execution. It is useful here to think of companies as a bundle of evolving competencies and capabilities, with the organization-building challenge being one of developing new capabilities and strengthening existing ones in a fashion calculated to achieve competitive advantage through superior strategy execution.

One capability-building issue is whether to develop the desired competencies and capabilities internally or whether it makes more sense to outsource them by partnering with key suppliers or forming strategic alliances. Decisions about whether to outsource or develop in-house capability often turn on the issues of (1) what can be safely delegated to outside suppliers versus what internal capabilities are key to the company's long-term success and (2) whether noncritical activities can be outsourced more effectively or efficiently than they can be performed internally. Either way, though, calls for action. Outsourcing means launching initiatives to identify the most attractive providers and to establish collaborative relationships. Developing the capabilities in-house means hiring new personnel withs skills and experience relevant to the deired organizational competence/capability, then linking the individual skills/know-how to form organizational capability.

Matching structure to strategy centers around making strategy-critical activities the main organizational building blocks, finding effective ways to bridge organizational lines of authority and coordinate the related efforts of separate internal units and individuals, and effectively networking the efforts of internal units and external collaborative partners. Other big considerations include what decisions to centralize and what decisions to decentralize.

All organization structures have strategic advantages and disadvantages; *there is no one best way to organize.* Functionally specialized organization structures have traditionally been the most popular way to organize single-business companies. Functional organization works well where strategy-critical activities closely match discipline-specific activities and minimal interdepartmental cooperation is needed. But it has significant drawbacks: functional myopia, empire building, interdepartmental rivalries, excessive process fragmentation, and vertically layered management hierarchies. In recent years, *business process reengineering* has been used to circumvent many of the disadvantages of functional organization.

Whatever basic structure is chosen, it usually has to be supplemented with interdisciplinary task forces, incentive compensation schemes tied to measures of joint performance, empowerment of cross-functional and/or self-directed work teams to perform and unify fragmented processes and strategy-critical activities, special project teams, relationship managers, and special top management efforts to knit the work of different individuals and groups into valuable competitive capabilities. Building core competencies and competitive capabilities emerges from establishing and nurturing collaborative working relationships between individuals and groups in different departments and between a company and its external allies, not from how the boxes are arranged on an organization chart.

New strategic priorities like short design-to-market cycles, multiversion production, personalized customer service, aggressive pursuit of e-commerce opportunities, and winning the race for positions of leadership in global markets and/or industries of the future have prompted increasing numbers of companies to create lean, flat, horizontal structures that are responsive and innovative. Such designs for matching structure to strategy involve fewer layers of management authority, managers and workers empowered to act on their own judgment, reengineered work processes to reduce cross-department fragmentation, collaborative partnerships with outsiders (suppliers, distributors/dealers, companies with complementary products/services, and even select competitors), increased outsourcing of selected value chain activities, leaner staffing of internal support functions, and rapidly growing use of e-commerce technologies and business practices.

suggested | readings

Argyris, Chris. "Empowerment: The Emperor's New Clothes." *Harvard Business Review* 76, no. 3 (May–June 1998), pp. 98–105.

Hall, Gene; Jim Rosenthal; and Judy Wade. "How to Make Reengineering Really Work." *Harvard Business Review* 71, no. 6 (November–December 1993), pp. 119–31.

Hambrick, Donald C. "The Top Management Team: Key to Strategic Success." *California Management Review* 30, no. 1 (Fall 1987), pp. 88–108.

Hammer, Michael, and James Champy. *Reengineering the Corporation.* New York: Harper-Business, 1993, chapters 2 and 3.

Kanter, Rosabeth Moss. "Collaborative Advantage: The Art of the Alliance." *Harvard Business Review* 72, no. 4 (July–August 1994), pp. 96–108.

Katzenbach, Jon R., and Douglas K. Smith. "The Discipline of Teams." *Harvard Business Review* 71, no. 2 (March–April 1993), pp. 111–24.

Majchrzak, Ann, and Qianwei Wang. "Breaking the Functional Mind-Set in Process Organizations." *Harvard Business Review* 74, no. 5 (September–October 1996), pp. 93–99.

Markides, Constantinos C., and Peter J. Williamson. "Corporate Diversification and Organizational Structure: A Resource-Based View." *Academy of Management Journal* 39, no. 2 (April 1996), pp. 340–67.

Pfeffer, Jeffrey. *The Human Equation: Building Profits by Putting People First.* Boston, MA: Harvard Business School Press, 1999.

————. "Producing Sustainable Competitive Advantage through the Effective Management of People." *Academy of Management Executive* 9, no. 1 (February 1995), pp. 55–69.

Pfeffer, Jeffrey, and John F. Veiga. "Putting People First for Organizational Success." *Academy of Management Executive* 13, no. 2 (May 1999), pp. 37–48.

Prahalad, C. K., and Gary Hamel. "The Core Competence of the Corporation." *Harvard Business Review* 68 (May–June 1990), pp. 79–93.

Rackham, Neil; Lawrence Friedman; and Richard Ruff. *Getting Partnering Right: How Market Leaders Are Creating Long-Term Competitive Advantage.* New York: McGraw-Hill, 1996.

Stalk, George; Philip Evans; and Lawrence E. Shulman. "Competing on Capabilities: The New Rules of Corporate Strategy." *Harvard Business Review* 70, no. 2 (March–April 1992), pp. 57–69.

Wetlaufer, Suzy. "Organizing for Empowerment: An Interview with AES's Roger Sant and Dennis Bakke." *Harvard Business Review* 77, no. 1 (January–February 1999), pp. 110–23.

chapter | twelve

12

Managing the Internal Organization to Promote Better Strategy Execution

Winning companies know how to do their work better.
—Michael Hammer and James Champy

If you talk about change but don't change the reward and recognition system, nothing changes.
—Paul Allaire, former CEO, Xerox Corporation

If you want people motivated to do a good job, give them a good job to do.
—Frederick Herzberg

You ought to pay big bonuses for premier performance . . . be a top payer, not in the middle or low end of the pack.
—Lawrence Bossidy, former CEO, AlliedSignal

In Chapter 11 we emphasized the importance of building organization capabilities and structuring the work effort so as to perform strategy-critical activities in a coordinated and highly competent manner. In this chapter we discuss five additional managerial tasks common to the strategy-implementing/strategy-executing process:

1. Reallocating resources to ensure that strategy-critical units have sufficient budgets to do their work successfully.
2. Establishing strategy-supportive policies.
3. Instituting best practices and mechanisms for continuous improvement.
4. Installing support systems that enable company personnel to carry out their strategic roles proficiently day in, day out.
5. Motivating and compensating employees in ways that enhance organizationwide commitment to good strategy execution.

LINKING BUDGETS TO STRATEGY

Implementing and executing strategy forces managers to consider how the firm's resources are being allocated. Organizational units need sufficient budgets and resources to carry out their parts of the strategic plan effectively and efficiently. There has to be ample funding of efforts to strengthen existing competencies and capabilities and/or to develop new ones. Managers with budgetary responsibility must screen subordinates' requests for more people, bigger operating budgets, and more or better facilities and equipment, distinguishing between requests that would be nice and requests that hold promise for making a cost-justified contribution to strategy execution and enhanced competitive capabilities. Moreover, strategy implementers have to make a persuasive, documented case to superiors to acquire the resources they need to execute their assigned pieces of company strategy.

How well budget allocations are linked to the needs of strategy can either promote or impede the implementation process. Too little funding slows progress and impedes the ability of organizational units to execute their pieces of the strategic plan proficiently. Too much funding wastes organizational resources and reduces financial performance. Both outcomes argue for managers charged with implementing and executing strategy to be deeply involved in the budgeting process, closely reviewing programs and budget proposals and endeavoring to ensure adequate resources are allocated to strategy-critical organization units.

A change in strategy nearly always calls for budget reallocations. Units important in the prior strategy may now be oversized and overfunded. Units that now have a bigger and more critical strategic role may need more people, new equipment, additional facilities, and above-average increases in their operating budgets. Strategy implementers need to be active and forceful in shifting resources, downsizing some areas and upsizing others, to not only amply fund activities with a critical role in the new strategy but also avoid inefficiency and achieve profit projections. They have to exercise their power to put enough resources behind new strategic initiatives to make things happen and make the tough decisions to kill projects and activities that are no longer justified. The essential condition is that the funding requirements of the new strategy must drive how capital allocations are made and the size of each unit's operating budgets. Underfunding organizational units and activities pivotal to strategic success can defeat the whole implementation process.

Forceful actions to reallocate operating funds and move people into new organizational units signal a determined commitment to strategic change and are frequently needed to catalyze the implementation process and give it credibility. Microsoft has made a practice of regularly shifting hundreds of programmers to new high-priority programming initiatives within a matter of weeks or even days. At Harris Corporation, where the strategy was to diffuse research ideas into areas that were commercially viable, top management regularly shifted groups of engineers out of government projects and moved them as a group into new commercial venture divisions. But fast-moving developments in many markets are prompting companies to move at Internet speed in reallocating resources and updating budgets. Companies are finding it desirable, if not necessary, to abandon traditional annual or semiannual budgeting and resource allocation cycles in favor of cycles that match the strategy changes a company makes in response to newly developing events. Annual or semiannual budget and resource reallocation reviews do not work when companies make strategic shifts weekly. Bluefly.com, a discount Internet apparel retailer, revises its

Strategic-Management Principle

Depriving strategy-critical groups of the resources needed to execute their pieces of the strategy can undermine the implementation process.

New strategies usually call for significant budget reallocations.

budgets and shifts resources weekly. Bluefly.com's CEO observed, "For us, 11 months is long-term planning."[1]

Fine-tuning the implementation of a company's existing strategy seldom requires big movements of people and money from one area to another. The desired improvements can usually be accomplished through above-average budget increases to organizational units where new initiatives are contemplated and below-average increases (or even small cuts) for the remaining organizational units. The chief exception occurs where a prime ingredient of strategy is to create altogether new capabilities or to generate fresh products and business opportunities within the existing budget. Then, as proposals and business plans worth pursuing bubble up from below, managers have to make decisions regarding where the needed capital expenditures, operating budgets, and personnel will come from. Companies like 3M, GE, and Boeing shift resources and people from area to area as needed to support the launch of new products and new business ventures. They empower "product champions" and small bands of would-be entrepreneurs by giving them financial and technical support and by setting up organizational units and programs to help new ventures blossom more quickly.

CREATING STRATEGY-SUPPORTIVE POLICIES AND PROCEDURES

Changes in strategy generally call for some changes in work practices and internal operations. Asking people to alter established procedures always upsets the internal order of things. It is normal for pockets of resistance to develop and for people to exhibit some degree of stress and anxiety about how the changes will affect them, especially when the changes may eliminate jobs. Questions are also likely to arise over what activities need to be done in rigidly prescribed fashion and where there ought to be leeway for independent action.

Prescribing policies and operating procedures aids the task of implementing strategy in several ways:

1. New or revised policies and procedures provide top-down guidance to operating managers, supervisory personnel, and employees regarding how certain things now need to be done and what behavior is expected, thus establishing some degree of regularity, stability, and dependability in how management has decided to try to execute the strategy and operate the business.

2. Policies and procedures help align actions and behavior with strategy throughout the organization, placing limits on independent action and channeling individual and group efforts along the intended path. Policies and procedures counteract tendencies for some people to resist or reject common approaches. Most people refrain from violating company policy or ignoring established practices without first gaining clearance or having strong justification.

3. Policies and standardized operating procedures help enforce needed consistency in how particular strategy-critical activities are performed in geographically scattered operating units (different plants, sales regions, customer service centers, or the individual outlets in a chain operation). Eliminating significant differences in the

---

[1]Marcia Stepanek, "How Fast Is Net Fast?" *Business Week*, November 1, 1999, pp. EB-52–EB-54.

operating practices and procedures of organizational units performing common functions is frequently desirable to avoid sending mixed messages to internal personnel and to customers who do business with the company at multiple locations.

4. Because dismantling old policies and procedures and instituting new ones invariably alter the internal work climate, strategy implementers can use the policy-changing process as a powerful lever for changing the corporate culture in ways that produce a stronger fit with the new strategy.

Company managers therefore need to be inventive in devising policies and practices that can provide vital support to effective strategy implementation and execution.

McDonald's policy manual, in an attempt to steer "crew members" into stronger quality and service behavior patterns, spells out procedures in detail; for example, "Cooks must turn, never flip, hamburgers. If they haven't been purchased, Big Macs must be discarded in 10 minutes after being cooked and french fries in 7 minutes. Cashiers must make eye contact with and smile at every customer." Caterpillar Tractor has a policy of guaranteeing its customers 24-hour parts delivery anywhere in the world; if it fails to fulfill the promise, it supplies the part for free. Hewlett-Packard requires R&D people to make regular visits to customers to learn about their problems, talk about new product applications, and in general keep the company's R&D programs customer-oriented. Mrs. Fields Cookies has a policy of establishing hourly sales quotas for each store outlet; furthermore, it is company policy that cookies not sold within two hours after being baked have to be removed from the case and given to charitable organizations. Illustration Capsule 46 describes Granite Rock's "short pay" policy for promoting high levels of customer service and customer satisfaction.

Thus, there is a definite role for new and revised policies and procedures in the strategy implementation process. Wisely constructed policies and procedures help channel actions, behavior, decisions, and practices in directions that promote good strategy execution. When policies and practices aren't strategy-supportive, they become a barrier to the kinds of attitudinal and behavioral changes strategy-implementers are trying to promote. Often, people opposed to certain elements of the strategy or certain implementation approaches will hide behind or vigorously defend long-standing policies and operating procedures in an effort to stall implementation or divert the approaches to implementation along a different route. Anytime a company alters its strategy, managers should review existing policies and operating procedures, proactively revise or discard those that are out of sync, and formulate new ones to facilitate execution of new strategic initiatives.

None of this implies that companies need thick policy manuals to guide strategy execution and daily operations. Too much policy can be as stifling as wrong policy or as chaotic as no policy. There is wisdom in a middle approach: prescribe enough policies to give organization members clear direction in implementing strategy and to place desirable boundaries on their actions, then empower them to act within these boundaries however they think makes sense. Allowing company personnel to decide and act anywhere between the "white lines" is especially appropriate when individual creativity and initiative are more essential to good strategy execution than standardization and strict conformity. Creating a strong supportive fit between strategy and policy can therefore mean more policies, fewer policies, or different policies. It can mean policies that require things to be done a certain way or policies that give employees leeway to do activities the way they think best.

> Well-conceived policies and procedures aid implementation; out-of-sync policies are barriers.

illustration capsule 46

Granite Rock's "Short Pay" Policy

The owners of Granite Rock, a 100-plus-year-old supplier of crushed gravel, sand, concrete, and asphalt in Watsonville, California, set two big, hairy, audacious goals (BHAGs) for the company: to achieve total customer satisfaction and a reputation for service that met or exceeded that of Nordstrom, the upscale department store famous for pleasing its customers. To drive the implementation effort, the owners decided to forgo all the various hoopla events it could have used to fire up its 725-plus employees. Instead it instituted a radical new policy called "short pay," to signal to both employees and customers that Granite Rock was deadly serious about its two strategic commitments. At the bottom of every Granite Rock invoice was the following statement:

> If you are not satisfied for any reason, don't pay us for it. Simply scratch out the line item, write a brief note about the problem, and return a copy of this invoice along with your check for the balance.

Customers did not have to call and complain and were not expected to return the product. They were given complete discretionary power to decide whether and how much to pay based on their satisfaction level.

The policy has worked exceptionally well, providing unmistakable feedback and spurring company managers to correct any problems quickly in order to avoid repeated short payments. Granite Rock has enjoyed market share increases, while charging a 6 percent price premium for its commodity products in competition against larger rivals. Its profit margins and overall financial performance have improved. Granite Rock won the prestigious Malcolm Baldrige National Quality Award in 1992, about five years after instituting the policy. *Fortune* rated it as one of the 100 best companies to work for in America in 1997 (ranked 23rd), 1998 (ranked 33rd), and 1999 (ranked 19th). Company employees receive an average of 43 hours of training annually. Entry-level employees, called job owners, start at $16 per hour and progress to such positions as "accomplished job owner" and "improvement champion" (base pay of $26 per hour). The company has a no-layoff policy.

Source: Based on information in Jim Collins, "Turning Goals into Results: The Power of Catalytic Mechanisms," *Harvard Business Review* 77, no. 4 (July–August 1999), pp. 72–73; and Robert Levering and Milton Moskowitz, "The 100 Best Companies to Work For," *Fortune*, January 10, 2000, p. 88.

INSTITUTING BEST PRACTICES AND A COMMITMENT TO CONTINUOUS IMPROVEMENT

If value chain activities are to be performed as effectively and efficiently as possible, each organizational unit needs to benchmark how it performs specific activities against best-in-industry or best-in-world performers. A strong commitment to searching out and adopting best practices is integral to implementing strategy and then continuously improving on how well it is executed—especially for strategy-critical and big-dollar activities where better quality or lower costs significantly impact bottom-line performance.[2]

As we noted in Chapter 4, benchmarking how well a company performs particular activities and processes against "best in industry" and "best in world" performers provides valuable yardsticks for gauging how well a company is executing pieces of its strategy and represents a solid methodology for identifying areas in which to improve. It can also be useful to look at "best in company" performers of an activity if a company has a number of different organizational units performing much the same function at different

Identifying and implementing best practices is a journey, not a destination.

[2]For a discussion of the value of benchmarking in implementing strategy, see Yoshinobu Ohinata, "Benchmarking: The Japanese Experience," *Long-Range Planning* 27, no. 4 (August 1994), pp. 48–53.

illustration capsule 47

Where Best Practices Come From: The Accomplishments of Three Best Practice Award Winners

Arthur Andersen sponsors a Best Practices Awards program to help businesses learn the innovative practices of small and mid-sized companies from different parts of the world. Three of the award winners in 1998 were Cloud 9 Shuttle, the Amalgamated Sugar Company, and Great Plains Software (which has been selected four times as one of the top 100 companies to work for in America).

CLOUD 9 SHUTTLE

Cloud 9 Shuttle, San Diego's largest "share ride" airport ground transportation company, was created in 1994 out of the ashes of a predecessor company whose dispatchers used magnets on a map to track the location of company vehicles. The predecessor stored customer service information in rarely used file folders and put customers through a lengthy procedure when they called to make reservations.

The new owners had a good vision of where they wanted to take the company, recognizing that service standards had to be increased and costs lowered. But resources were limited. They opted to use technology in very pragmatic ways. One innovation was to use a cellular telephone technology called cellular triangularization that allows reservationists and dispatchers to see the location of any Cloud 9 vehicle in San Diego County on a computer screen around the clock; the system identifies each vehicle's speed and direction as well as the street and nearest cross street.

New information systems were installed that permitted the integration of reservations, dispatch, and cashiering functions, both to provide better customer service and to provide key operating data to management—passengers per hour, revenue per hour per driver, passengers per gallon of fuel, and so on. This information is used to control costs and schedule drivers—driver hours were reduced by 11 percent while their income rose 7 percent.

The new systems and practices—coupled with employee empowerment, training, and a progressive company culture—have allowed Cloud 9 to deploy a fleet of more than 100 vehicles (the precedessor company could only handle 60 vehicles with its operating practices), triple revenues, and operate profitably.

THE AMALGAMATED SUGAR COMPANY

Amalgamated's business is converting sugar beets into sugar. A key success factor is how much sugar can be extracted from the beets before it is lost to molasses. Since sugar sells for $550 per ton versus $75 per ton for molasses, the incentive to improve sugar yield is high.

Amalgamated engineers developed and patented a computer-optimized separator system based on "simulated

locations. The innovative manner in which activities or processes are performed by companies considered "best in industry" or "best in world" (or internal units considered "best in company")—commonly termed *best practices*—provides useful performance targets for organization units to achieve or compare themselves against. But it is not enough just to identify the best practices of other companies, especially companies in other industries, because copying them exactly is usually neither feasible nor desirable owing to differences from one situation and application to another. More usually, the best practices of other companies need to be modified and adapted to a company's own specific situation—and then later improved on as time passes. Hence, benchmarking nearly always involves creativity and innovative application of the best practices of outsiders.

A substantial number of companies engage in benchmarking. A recent survey of over 4,000 managers in 15 countries indicated that over 85 percent were using benchmarking to measure the efficiency and effectiveness of their internal activities. During the past decade, growing numbers of companies have instituted best practice programs as an integral part of their efforts to fine-tune strategy execution. Such programs, creatively pursued, tend to result in company personnel being innovative in developing best practices out of their own efforts as well as searching out and adapting the best

illustration capsule 47

(concluded)

moving bed chromatography" that has enabled the company to recover more than 80 percent of the sugar ordinarily lost to the molasses by-product.

Amalgamated also developed a computer technology to perform 1,500 individual analytic tests daily at each of its four plants to maximize plant performance. Company representatives also developed software that helped the company's sugar beet growers to set standards and use sophisticated agronomic practices in producing sugar beets.

Amalgamated's management believes the company's constant innovation and use of advanced technology has enabled it to become the most efficient sugar beet processor in the world.

GREAT PLAINS

Great Plains, based in Fargo, South Dakota, is a leading provider of enterprise business management software for mid-sized companies. The company has annual revenues of about $135 million and nearly 1,000 employees; it was rated 15th on the 1999 list of the 100 best companies to work for in America. It won awards for best practices in exceeding customer expectations and in motivating and retaining employees.

Great Plains' management believes superior customer service is a key success factor in the enterprise software business. In 1987, in an effort to provide immediate solutions to customers' problems, Great Plains established "guaranteed response times" to set customer expectations for prompt service and technical support. Although Great Plains' customer support teams handle more than 20,000 cases each month (most of them involving "how-to" questions and productivity issues), they have met the company's guaranteed response times more than 99 percent of the time. In 1998, the company broke its own record by serving more than 250,000 consecutive customer support calls without missing a single guarantee.

Among the key employee-oriented practices are an automated performance management process, company-wide and team-based recognition events, stock ownership opportunities for all employees, on-site services for employees such as dry cleaning, discounts for health clubs and retail stores, flexible work hours, and paid sabbaticals. There's also a no-layoff policy. Employees have strong feelings of belonging to a family; according to one employee, "Work feels a whole lot more like hanging out with your friends than going to work."

Source: Arthur Andersen and articles in *Fortune* reporting the 100 best companies to work for: January 12, 1998, and January 10, 2000.

practices of others. Illustration Capsule 47 provides examples of three small and mid-sized companies that have won best practice awards because of their own innovations.

Total Quality Management: A Commitment to Continuous Improvement

The benchmarking movement to search out, study, implement, and improve on best practices has stimulated greater management awareness of the importance of business process reengineering, *total quality management* (TQM), and other continuous improvement techniques. *TQM is a philosophy of managing a set of business practices that emphasizes continuous improvement in all phases of operations, 100 percent accuracy in performing activities, involvement and empowerment of employees at all levels, team-based work design, benchmarking, and fully satisfying customer expectations.* Management interest in quality improvement programs has historically originated in such activities as fabrication and assembly in manufacturing enterprises, teller transactions in banks, order picking and shipping at catalog firms, and customer-contact interfaces at websites and in service organizations. Occasionally, interest begins with executives who hear TQM presentations, read about TQM, or talk to people in other companies that have benefited from total quality programs. Usually, interested managers either have quality

table 12.1   Components of Popular TQM Approaches and 1992 Baldrige Award Criteria

DEMING'S 14 POINTS	THE JURAN TRILOGY	CROSBY'S 14 QUALITY STEPS
1. Constancy of purpose	1. *Quality planning*	1. Management commitment
2. Adopt the philosophy	• Set goals	2. Quality improvement teams
3. Don't rely on mass inspection	• Identify customers and their needs	3. Quality measurement
4. Don't award business on price	• Develop products and processes	4. Cost of quality evaluation
5. Constant improvement		5. Quality awareness
6. Training	2. *Quality control*	6. Corrective action
7. Leadership	• Evaluate performance	7. Zero-defects committee
8. Drive out fear	• Compare to goals and adapt	8. Supervisor training
9. Break down barriers	3. *Quality improvement*	9. Zero-defects day
10. Eliminate slogans and exhortations	• Establish infrastructure	10. Goal-setting
11. Eliminate quotas	• Identify projects and teams	11. Error cause removal
12. Pride of workmanship	• Provide resources and training	12. Recognition
13. Education and retraining	• Establish controls	13. Quality councils
14. Plan of action		14. Do it over again

THE 1992 BALDRIGE AWARD CRITERIA (1,000 points total)

1. *Leadership* (90 points)
   • Senior executive
   • Management for quality
   • Public responsibility
2. *Information and analysis* (80 points)
   • Scope and management of quality and performance data
   • Competitive comparisons and benchmarks
3. *Strategic quality planning* (60 points)
   • Strategic quality and planning process
   • Quality and performance plans
4. *Human resource development and management* (150 points)
   • Human resource management
   • Employee involvement
   • Employee education and training
   • Employee performance and recognition
   • Employee well-being and morale

5. *Management of process quality* (140 points)
   • Design and introduction of products and services
   • Process management—production and delivery
   • Process management—business and support
   • Supplier quality
   • Quality assessment
6. *Quality and operational results* (180 points)
   • Product and service quality
   • Company operations
   • Business process and support services
   • Supplier quality
7. *Customer focus and satisfaction* (300 points)
   • Customer relationships
   • Commitment to customers
   • Customer satisfaction determination
   • Customer satisfaction results
   • Customer satisfaction comparisons
   • Future requirements and expectations

Source: As presented in Thomas C. Powell, "Total Quality Management as Competitive Advantage," *Strategic Management Journal* 16, no. 1 (January 1995), p. 18, and based on M. Walton, *The Deming Management Method* (New York: Pedigree, 1986); J. Juran, *Juran on Quality by Design* (New York: Free Press, 1992); Philip Crosby, *Quality Is Free: The Act of Making Quality Certain* (New York: McGraw-Hill, 1979); and S. George, *The Baldrige Quality System* (New York: Wiley, 1992).

and customer-satisfaction problems they are struggling to solve or are under the gun of competition and customer expectations to dramatically improve certain quality attributes. Surveys indicate that over 95 percent of manufacturing companies and 70 percent of service companies have used some form of quality improvement program.[3] Another survey found that 55 percent of American executives and 70 percent of Japanese executives used quality improvement information at least monthly as part of their assessment of overall

---

[3]Judy D. Olian and Sara L. Rynes, "Making Total Quality Work: Aligning Organizational Processes, Performance Measures, and Stakeholders," *Human Resource Management* 30, no. 3 (Fall 1991), p. 303; and Darrell K. Rigby, "What's Today's Special at the Consultant's Café?" *Fortune,* September 7, 1998, p. 163.

table 12.2   12 Aspects Common to TQM and Continuous
Improvement Programs

1. **Committed leadership:** a near-evangelical, unwavering, long-term commitment by top managers to the philosophy, usually under a name something like Total Quality Management, Continuous Improvement (CI), or Quality Improvement (QI).

2. **Adoption and communication of TQM:** using tools like the mission statement, and themes or slogans.

3. **Closer customer relationships:** determining customers' (both inside and outside the firm) requirements, then meeting those requirements no matter what it takes.

4. **Closer supplier relationships:** working closely and cooperatively with suppliers (often sole-sourcing key components), ensuring they provide inputs that conform to customers' end-use requirements.

5. **Benchmarking:** researching and observing operating competitive practices.

6. **Increased training:** usually includes TQM principles, team skills, and problem-solving.

7. **Open organization:** lean staff, empowered work teams, open horizontal communications, and a relaxation of traditional hierarchy.

8. **Employee empowerment:** increased employee involvement in design and planning, and greater autonomy in decision-making.

9. **Zero-defects mentality:** a system in place to spot defects as they occur, rather than through inspection and rework.

10. **Flexible manufacturing:** (applicable only to manufacturers) can include just-in-time inventory, cellular manufacturing, design for manufacturability (DFM), statistical process control (SPC), and design of experiments (DOE).

11. **Process improvement:** reduced waste and cycle times in all areas through cross-departmental process analysis.

12. **Measurement:** goal-orientation and zeal for data, with constant performance measurement, often using statistical methods.

Source: Thomas C. Powell, "Total Quality Management as Competitive Advantage," *Strategic Management Journal* 16, no. 1 (January 1995), p. 19.

business performance.[4] An Arthur D. Little study reported that 93 percent of the 500 largest U.S. firms had adopted TQM in some form as of 1992, and a 1998 *Fortune* survey of over 4,000 managers in 15 countries showed that TQM usage was just under 60 percent in 1997. Analysts have credited TQM with helping propel Japanese companies to global prominence in manufacturing quality products. Table 12.1 displays the different kinds of features emphasized by the leading proponents of TQM and the criteria employed in selecting winners of the Malcolm Baldrige Award for Quality.

While TQM concentrates on the production of quality goods and the delivery of excellent customer service, it is more successful when it is extended to employee efforts in all departments—HR, billing, R&D, engineering, accounting and records, and information systems—that may lack less-pressing customer-driven incentives to improve. This is because the institution of best practices and continuous improvement programs involves re-forming the corporate culture and shifting to a total quality/continuous improvement business philosophy that permeates every facet of the organization—see Table 12.2 for the features common to most TQM programs.[5] TQM aims at instilling enthusiasm and commitment to doing things right from top to bottom of the

> Quality improvement processes have now become a globally pervasive part of the fabric of implementing strategies keyed to defect-free manufacture, superior product quality, superior customer service, and total customer satisfaction.

> TQM entails creating a total quality culture bent on continuously improving the performance of every task and value chain activity.

---

[4]Olian and Rynes, "Making Total Quality Work," p. 303.

[5]For a discussion of the shift in work environment and culture that TQM entails, see Robert T. Amsden, Thomas W. Ferratt, and Davida M. Amsden, "TQM: Core Paradigm Changes," *Business Horizons* 39, no. 6 (November–December 1996), pp. 6–14.

organization. It entails a restless search for continuing improvement, the little steps forward each day that the Japanese call *kaizen*. TQM is thus a race without a finish. The managerial objective is to kindle an innate, burning desire in people to use their ingenuity and initiative to progressively improve on how tasks and value chain activities are performed. TQM preaches that there's no such thing as "good enough" and that everyone has a responsibility to participate in continuous improvement. See Illustration Capsule 48, which describes Ritz-Carlton's success in pursuing its version of TQM and continuous improvement.

> The ability to generate continuous improvements in important value chain activities is a valuable competitive asset and resource strength.

Effective use of TQM/continuous improvement techniques is a valuable asset in a company's resource portfolio—one that can produce important competitive capabilities (in product design, cycle time, cost, product quality and reliability, service, and customer satisfaction) and be a source of competitive advantage.[6] Not only do ongoing incremental improvements add up over time and strengthen organizational capabilities but TQM/continuous improvement programs have hard-to-imitate aspects. While it is relatively easy for rivals to undertake benchmarking, process improvement, and quality training, it is much more difficult for them to implant a total quality culture, do an effective job of empowering employees, and generate deep and genuine management commitment to TQM philosophy and practices throughout their organizations. Successful implementation of TQM initiatives requires a substantial investment of management time and effort; some managers and employees resist TQM, viewing it as ideological or faddish. It is expensive (in terms of training and meetings), and it seldom produces short-term results. The long-term payoff depends heavily on management's success in instilling a culture within which TQM philosophies and practices can thrive.

The Difference between TQM and Process Reengineering   Best practices, business process reengineering, and continuous improvement efforts like TQM all aim at improved efficiency and reduced costs, better product quality, and greater customer satisfaction. The essential difference between business process reengineering and TQM is that reengineering aims at quantum gains on the order of 30 to 50 percent or more whereas total quality programs stress incremental progress, striving for inch-by-inch gains again and again in a never-ending stream. The two approaches to improved performance of value chain activities are not mutually exclusive; it makes sense to use them in tandem. Reengineering can be used first to produce a good basic design that yields dramatic improvements in performing a business process. Total quality programs can then be used as a follow-on to gradually make improvements in the efficiency and effectiveness of the process over time. Such a two-pronged approach to implementing organizational change is like a marathon race where you run the first four laps as fast as you can, then gradually pick up speed the remainder of the way.

> Reengineering seeks one-time quantum improvement; TQM seeks ongoing incremental improvement.

Capturing the Benefits of Best Practice and Continuous Improvement Programs

Research indicates that some companies benefit from reengineering and TQM and some do not.[7] Usually, the biggest beneficiaries are companies that view such programs not

---

[6]Thomas C. Powell, "Total Quality Management as Competitive Advantage," *Strategic Management Journal* 16 (1995), pp. 15–37. See also, Richard M. Hodgetts, "Quality Lessons from America's Baldrige Winners," *Business Horizons* 37, no. 4 (July–August 1994), pp. 74–79; and Richard Reed, David J. Lemak, and Joseph C. Montgomery, "Beyond Process: TQM Content and Firm Performance," *Academy of Management Review* 21, no. 1 (January 1996), pp. 173–202.

[7]See, for example, Gene Hall, Jim Rosenthal, and Judy Wade, "How to Make Reengineering Really Work," *Harvard Business Review* 71, no. 6 (November–December 1993), pp. 119–31.

illustration capsule 48
Continuous Improvement Makes Ritz-Carlton Hotels a Two-Time Baldrige Award Winner

The best companies know that quality isn't a destination; rather, it's an ongoing journey. No one knows this better than the 22,000 men and women who work at the 36 luxury Ritz-Carlton Hotels located in North America, Europe, Asia, Australia, the Middle East, Africa, and the Caribbean. In fact, Ritz-Carlton employees are referred to as "The Ladies and Gentlemen of the Ritz-Carlton," a label that reflects the company's expectations of high-quality performance. All of the Ritz-Carlton hotels have received four- or five-star ratings from the *Mobil Travel Guide* and diamond ratings from the American Automobile Association. In addition, the company itself has been the recipient of the coveted Malcolm Baldrige National Quality Award twice, in 1992 and 1999.

The Ritz-Carlton Hotel Company is based on a set of core values collectively called The Gold Standards: The Credo, The Three Steps of Service, The Motto, and The Twenty Basics. Every employee is expected to embrace these quality guidelines, find new ways to interpret them, and put them into practice during every moment of their working shift. If they forget any of the standards, they can refer to a condensed version on a pocket-sized laminated card.

All new employees receive orientation to The Gold Standards, and each day they are reinforced in staff meetings. In addition, workers receive ongoing quality training geared toward the standards. "Although much-imitated, The Gold Standards as embodied in The Credo Card remain an industry first and are a blueprint for our success," notes Simon Cooper, president and chief operating officer of Ritz-Carlton.

Even after winning the Baldrige award in 1992, Ritz-Carlton looked for new ways to improve. Goals for customer satisfaction were raised to top priority. Efforts were made to reduce employee turnover and energize morale. Top management revamped its strategic planning process to make it more systematic. The company instituted a new approach of "customer customization," which gathers extensive data on guests to anticipate their needs and take steps to ensure the best, most comfortable stay at any of the Ritz-Carlton hotels. In fact, it may be the company's attention to detail at every level that makes it such a winner in the eyes of its guests, 99 percent of whom report satisfaction with their stays—perhaps more significant than any quality award the company could win.

Sources: Malcolm Baldrige National Quality Award website; "The Ritz-Carlton Hotel Company, L.L.C." (www.nist.gov), accessed October 5, 2001; company website (www.ritzcarlton.com), accessed October 2, 2001; Ken Ryan, "At Ritz-Carlton, Quality Is Job One," Hotel Interactive (www.hotelinteractive.com), May 25, 2000.

as ends in themselves but as tools for implementing and executing company strategy more effectively. The skimpiest payoffs from best practices, TQM, and reengineering occur when company managers seize them as something worth trying—novel ideas that could improve things. In most such instances, they result in strategy-blind efforts to simply manage better. There's an important lesson here. Best practices, TQM, and reengineering all need to be seen and used as part of a bigger-picture effort to execute strategy proficiently. Only strategy can point to which value chain activities matter and what performance targets make the most sense. Absent a strategic framework, managers lack the context in which to fix things that really matter to business-unit performance and competitive success.

To get the most from benchmarking, best practices, reengineering, TQM, and related tools for enhancing organizational competence in executing strategy, managers have to start with a clear fix on the indicators of successful strategy execution. Examples of such performance indicators include minimal manufacturing defects, on-time delivery percentages, low overall costs relative to rivals, few customer complaints and survey data indicating high percentages of pleased customers, shorter cycle times, and a higher percentage of revenues coming from recently introduced

> When best practices, reengineering, and TQM are not part of a wider-scale effort to improve strategy execution and business performance, they deteriorate into strategy-blind efforts to manage better.

products. Benchmarking best-in-industry and best-in-world performance of most or all value chain activities provides a realistic basis for setting internal performance milestones and longer-range targets.

Then comes the managerial task of building a total quality culture and instilling the necessary commitment to achieving the targets and performance measures that the strategy requires. The action steps managers can take include:[8]

- Visible, unequivocal, and unyielding commitment to total quality and continuous improvement, including a quality vision and specific, measurable objectives for boosting quality and making continuous improvement.
- Nudging people toward TQ-supportive behaviors by initiating such organizational programs as
  —Screening job applicants rigorously and hiring only those with attitudes and aptitudes right for quality-based performance.
  —Quality training for most employees.
  —Using teams and team-building exercises to reinforce and nurture individual effort (expansion of a TQ culture is facilitated when teams become more cross-functional, multitask, and increasingly self-managed).
  —Recognizing and rewarding individual and team efforts regularly and systematically.
  —Stressing prevention (doing it right the first time), not inspection (instituting ways to correct mistakes).
- Empowering employees so that authority for delivering great service or improving products is in the hands of the doers rather than the overseers.
- Using online systems to provide all relevant parties with the latest best practices and actual experiences with them, thereby speeding the diffusion and adoption of best practices throughout the organization and also allowing them to exchange data and opinions about how to upgrade the prevailing best practices.
- Preaching that performance can, and must, be improved because competitors are not resting on past laurels and customers are always looking for something better.

If the targeted performance measures are appropriate to the strategy and if all organizational members (top executives, middle managers, professional staff, and line employees) buy into the process of continuous improvement, then the work climate will be conducive to proficient strategy execution and good bottom-line business performance.

Strategic Management Principle

Innovative, state-of-the-art support systems can be a basis for competitive advantage if they give a firm capabilities that rivals can't match.

INSTALLING SUPPORT SYSTEMS

Company strategies can't be implemented or executed well without a number of support systems for business operations. Southwest, American, United, Delta, and other major airlines cannot hope to provide world-class passenger service without a computerized reservation system, an accurate and expeditious baggage handling system, and a strong

---

[8]Olian and Rynes, "Making Total Quality Work," pp. 305–6 and 310–11; and Paul S. Goodman and Eric D. Darr, "Exchanging Best Practices Information through Computer-Aided Systems," *Academy of Management Executive* 10, no. 2 (May 1996), p. 7.

aircraft maintenance program. FedEx has internal communication systems that allow it to coordinate its 44,500 vans nationwide to handle an average of 3.2 million packages per day. Its leading-edge flight operations systems allow a single controller to direct as many as 200 FedEx aircraft simultaneously, overriding their flight plans should weather or special emergencies arise. In addition, FedEx has created a series of e-business tools for customers that allow them to ship and track packages online (either at FedEx's website or on their own company intranets or websites), create address books, review shipping history, generate custom reports, simplify customer billing, reduce internal warehousing and inventory management costs, purchase goods and services from suppliers, and respond faster to changing customer demands. All of FedEx's systems support the company's strategy of next-day package delivery when "it absolutely, positively has to be there" and boost its competitiveness against UPS, Airborne Express, and the U.S. Postal Service.

Otis Elevator has a sophisticated support system called OtisLine to coordinate its maintenance efforts nationwide.[9] Trained operators take all trouble calls, input critical information on a computer screen, and dispatch people directly via a beeper system to the local trouble spot. From the trouble-call inputs, problem patterns can be identified nationally and the information communicated to design and manufacturing personnel, allowing them to quickly alter design specifications or manufacturing procedures when needed to correct recurring problems. Also, much of the information needed for repairs is provided directly from faulty elevators through internally installed microcomputer monitors, further lowering outage time.

Arthur Andersen uses the Internet and digital technology to link more than 70,000 people in 382 offices in 81 countries. Its Knowledge Xchange system has data, voice, and video capabilities and includes an electronic bulletin board for posting customer problems, allowing personnel from all over the world to organize around a customer's problem. The system also has the capability to collect, index, and distribute files containing information on particular subjects, customers, solutions, and company resources.[10] Knowledge Xchange thus helps Andersen personnel capture the lessons learned in the company's daily work and research and makes those lessons available to all other Andersen personnel 24 hours a day. Wal-Mart's computers transmit daily sales data to Wrangler, a supplier of blue jeans; Wrangler then uses a model that interprets the data, and software applications that act on these interpretations, in order to ship specific quantities of specific sizes and colors to specific stores from specific warehouses—the system lowers logistics and inventory costs and leads to fewer stockouts.[11] Domino's Pizza has computerized systems at each outlet to facilitate ordering, inventory, payroll, cash flow, and work control functions, thereby freeing managers to spend more time on supervision, customer service, and business development activities.[12] Most telephone companies, electric utilities, and TV broadcasting systems have online monitoring systems to spot transmission problems within seconds and increase the reliability of their services. At

---

[9]James Brian Quinn, *Intelligent Enterprise* (New York: Free Press, 1992), p. 186.

[10]James Brian Quinn, Philip Anderson, and Sydney Finkelstein, "Leveraging Intellect," *Academy of Management Executive* 10, no. 3 (November 1996), p. 9.

[11]Stephan H. Haeckel and Richard L. Nolan, "Managing by Wire," *Harvard Business Review* 75, no. 5 (September–October 1993), p. 129.

[12]Quinn, *Intelligent Enterprise,* p. 181.

illustration capsule 49
The Rush to Install E-Commerce Support Systems

Companies everywhere are rushing to install the support systems they need to participate in one or more segments of the rapidly expanding Internet economy and enable better execution of their business strategies. Investment in Internet-related support systems is occurring in a host of different arenas:

- Building attractive, user-friendly websites and installing adequate and reliable server capacity.

- Creating electronic data interchange capabilities, starting with the details of sales to customers and flowing real-time information all the way back through company supply chains to the relevant suppliers.

- Developing software and systems to gather and analyze data from online sales, thus enabling "real-time market research" and rapid response to shifting customer demand.

- Installing software and systems to handle buyer credit card payments (in the case of business-to-consumer transactions) and electronic payment of invoices (in the case of business-to-business transactions).

- Installing the hardware systems and software to handle and tie together such "back-office" functions as automated order processing and invoicing for both customers and suppliers, accounts receivable and other customer/supplier-related accounting functions, management of both materials and finished goods inventories, and distribution logistics. Companies such as Computer Associates, Oracle, Ariba, Siebel Systems, i2 Technologies, and Germany's SAP (the world's largest) supply complex software allowing companies to weave together such basic internal

operations as procurement, accounting, manufacturing, shipping, order processing, and all interactions with customers.

- Putting warehousing and shipping facilities and systems in place to follow through on delivering customers' online orders in a timely and economical manner.

- Installing software and systems to enable customers to track their orders online and to get online technical support and customer service.

- Connecting more employees to the Internet and company intranets so that (1) e-mail can be used as the prime means of internal and external communication, (2) employees can readily access needed databases, (3) company personnel can engage in online collaboration with external allies and partners, (4) communications with target customer groups can be optimized, and (5) internal activities can be tied together with software and coordinated easily and more quickly.

Rapidly advancing Internet and e-commerce technologies are revolutionizing the manner in which company operations are conducted internally, as well as the manner in which business is conducted externally—with suppliers and customers and alliance partners. Because this revolution is only in its early stages, it is difficult to forecast the outcome, except to say that it is generating major gains in productivity, lowering costs, and spawning an overhaul of daily operating practices that no business can afford to ignore. There can be no doubt that cutting-edge e-commerce support systems can greatly enrich a company's long-term competitiveness and strategy execution capabilities.

Mrs. Fields Cookies, computer systems monitor hourly sales and suggest product mix changes, promotional tactics, or operating adjustments to improve customer response. Many companies have installed software systems on their company intranets to catalog best practices information and promote faster best practices transfer and implementation organizationwide.[13]

Well-conceived, state-of-the-art support systems not only facilitate better strategy execution but also can strengthen organizational capabilities enough to provide a

---

[13]Such systems speed organizational learning by providing fast, efficient communication, creating an organizational memory for collecting and retaining best practice information, and permitting people all across the organization to exchange information and updated solutions. See Goodman and Darr, "Exchanging Best Practices Information through Computer-Aided Systems," pp. 7–17.

competitive edge over rivals. For example, a company with a differentiation strategy based on superior quality has added capability if it has systems for training personnel in quality techniques, tracking product quality at each production step, and ensuring that all goods shipped meet quality standards. A company striving to be a low-cost provider is competitively stronger if it has a benchmarking system that identifies opportunities to implement cost-saving best practices and drive costs out of the business. Fast-growing companies get an important assist from having the internal capabilities in place to recruit and train new employees in large numbers and from investing in high-capacity systems and infrastructure that give them the capability to handle rapid growth as it occurs. It is nearly always better to put infrastructure and support systems in place ahead of the time they are actually needed than to be caught short and have to scramble to catch up to customer demand. In businesses such as public accounting and management consulting where large numbers of professional staff need cutting-edge technical know-how, companies need well-functioning systems for training and retraining employees regularly and keeping them supplied with up-to-date information. Companies that rely on empowered customer service employees to act promptly and creatively in pleasing customers have to have state-of-the-art information systems that put essential data at employees' fingertips and give them instantaneous communications capabilities.

> In today's business environment, competitive advantage goes to those firms most able to mobilize information and create systems to use knowledge effectively.

Installing Adequate Information Systems, Performance Tracking, and Controls

Accurate information is an essential guide to action. Every organization needs systems for gathering and storing data, tracking key performance indicators, identifying and diagnosing problems, and reporting strategy-critical information. Telephone companies have elaborate information systems to measure signal quality, connection times, interrupts, wrong connections, billing errors, and other measures of reliability. To track and manage the quality of passenger service, airlines have information systems to monitor gate delays, on-time departures and arrivals, baggage handling times, lost baggage complaints, stockouts on meals and drinks, overbookings, and maintenance delays and failures. Virtually all companies now provide customer-contact personnel with instant electronic access to customer databases so that they can respond effectively to customer inquiries and personalize customer services. Companies that rely on empowered employees need measurement and feedback systems to monitor the performance of empowered workers and guide them to act within specified limits so that unwelcome surprises are avoided.[14]

> Accurate, timely information allows organizational members to monitor progress and take corrective action promptly.

The age of real-time information spawned by the Internet allows company managers to monitor implementation initiatives and daily operations, steering them to a successful conclusion in case early steps don't produce the expected progress or things seem to be drifting off course. Information systems need to cover five broad areas: (1) customer data, (2) operations data, (3) employee data, (4) supplier/partner/collaborative ally data, and (5) financial performance data. All key strategic performance indicators have to be measured as often as practical. Many retail companies generate daily sales reports for each store and maintain up-to-the-minute inventory and sales records on each

---

[14]For a discussion of the need for putting appropriate boundaries on the actions of empowered employees and possible control and monitoring systems that can be used, see Robert Simons, "Control in an Age of Empowerment," *Harvard Business Review* 73 (March–April 1995), pp. 80–88.

Effective companies gather, analyze, and communicate data and information at Internet speed.

item. Manufacturing plants typically generate daily production reports and track labor productivity on every shift. Many retailers and manufacturers have online data systems connecting them with their suppliers that monitor the status of inventories, process orders and invoices, and track shipments. Monthly profit-and-loss statements and monthly statistical summaries, long the norm, are fast being replaced by daily statistical updates and even up-to-the-minute performance monitoring that electronic technology makes possible. Such diagnostic control systems allow managers to detect problems early, intervene as appropriate, and adjust either the strategy or how it is being implemented. Early experiences are sometimes difficult to assess, but they yield the first hard data and should be closely scrutinized as a basis for corrective action. Ideally, data analysis procedures should flag big or unusual variances from preset performance standards.

Statistical information gives the strategy implementer a feel for the numbers; reports and meetings provide a feel for new developments and problems; and personal contacts add a feel for the people dimension. All are good barometers of overall performance and good indicators of which things are on and off track. Managers have to identify problem areas and deviations from plan before they can take actions either to improve implementation or fine-tune strategy.

Exercising Adequate Controls over Empowered Employees   A major problem facing today's managers is how to ensure that the actions of empowered subordinates stay within acceptable bounds and don't expose the organization to excessive risk.[15] There are dangers to leaving employees to their own devices in meeting performance standards. Media stories abound with reports of employees whose decisions or behavior went awry, sometimes costing a company huge sums or producing lawsuits aside from just generating embarrassing publicity. Managers can't spend all their time making sure that everyone's decisions and behavior are between the white lines, yet they have a clear responsibility to institute adequate checks and balances and protect against unwelcome surprises. One of the main purposes of diagnostic control systems to track performance is to relieve managers of the burden of constant monitoring and give them time for other issues. But diagnostic controls are only part of the answer. Another valuable lever of control is establishing clear boundaries on behavior without telling employees what to do. Strictly prescribed rules and procedures that leave no room for discretion can discourage employee creativity and turn work into pure drudgery. It is better to set forth what not to do, allowing freedom of action within specified limits. Another control device is face-to-face meetings to review information, assess progress and performance, reiterate expectations, and discuss the next action steps.

When a company relies on team-based organizations and self-managed work groups, one of the biggest payoffs is that teams substitute peer-based control for hierarchical control of work.[16] This is because team members feel accountable and responsible for the success and performance of the whole team and tend to be relatively intolerant of a team member's behavior or actions that weaken team performance or put team accomplishments at risk. Because peer evaluation is so powerful a control device, companies organized on the basis of teams find that they can remove some layers of the management hierarchy, avoiding the costs of having people whose job it is to

---

[15]Ibid. See also, David C. Band and Gerald Scanlan, "Strategic Control through Core Competencies," *Long Range Planning* 28, no. 2 (April 1995), pp. 102–14.

[16]Jeffrey Pfeffer and John F. Veiga, "Putting People First for Organizational Success," *Academy of Management Executive* 13, no. 2 (May 1999), pp. 41–42.

watch other people do the work. This is especially true when a company has the information systems capability to closely monitor team performance.

DESIGNING STRATEGY-SUPPORTIVE REWARD SYSTEMS

It is important for both organization subunits and individuals to be enthusiastically committed to executing strategy and achieving performance targets. Company managers typically try to enlist organizationwide commitment to carrying out the strategic plan by motivating people and rewarding them for good performance. A manager has to do more than just talk to everyone about how important new strategic practices and performance targets are to the organization's future well-being. No matter how inspiring, talk seldom commands people's best efforts for long. *To get employees' sustained, energetic commitment, management has to be resourceful in designing and using motivational incentives—both monetary and nonmonetary.* The more a manager understands what motivates subordinates and the more he or she relies on motivational incentives as a tool for implementing strategy, the greater will be employees' commitment to good day in, day out execution of the company's strategic plan.

> The role of the reward system is to align the well-being of organization members with realizing the company's vision, so that organization members benefit by helping the company execute its strategy competently and fully satisfy customers.

While financial incentives (salary increases, performance bonuses, stock options, and retirement packages) are the core component of most companies' reward systems, managers normally make extensive use of such nonmonetary carrot-and-stick incentives as frequent words of praise (or constructive criticism), special recognition at company gatherings or in the company newsletter, more (or less) job security, stimulating assignments, opportunities to transfer to attractive locations, increased (or decreased) job control and decision-making autonomy, and rapid promotion (or the risk of being "sidelined" in a routine or dead-end job). Effective managers are further alert to the motivating power of giving people a chance to be part of something exciting, giving them an opportunity for greater personal satisfaction, challenging them with ambitious performance targets, creating a stimulating and engaging work environment, and the intangible bonds of group acceptance and a "family" work environment. But the motivation and reward structure has to be used *creatively* and tied directly to achieving the performance outcomes necessary for good strategy execution.

Strategy-Supportive Motivational Practices

Successful strategy implementers inspire and challenge employees to do their best. They get employees to buy into the strategy and commit to making it work. They structure individual efforts into teams and work groups in order to facilitate an exchange of ideas and foster a climate of support. They allow employees to participate in making decisions about how to perform their jobs, and they try to make jobs interesting and satisfying and the company's whole work climate engaging and fun. They devise strategy-supportive motivational approaches and use them effectively. Consider some actual examples:

> One of the biggest strategy implementing challenges is to employ motivational techniques that build wholehearted commitment and winning attitudes among employees.

- Several Japanese automobile producers, believing that providing employment security is a valuable contributor to worker productivity and company loyalty, elect not to lay off factory workers but instead put them out in the field to sell vehicles when business slacks off for a period. Mazda, for example, during a sales downturn in Japan in the 1980s, shifted factory workers to selling its models door-to-door, a common practice in Japan. At the end of the year, when awards were given out to the best salespeople, Mazda found that its top 10 salespeople were all factory workers, partly because they were able to explain the product effectively. When business picked up and the factory workers returned to the plant, their experiences in talking to customers yielded useful ideas in improving the features and styling of Mazda's product line.[17] Southwest Airlines, FedEx, Lands' End, and Harley-Davidson (all companies that have been listed among the 100 best companies to work for in America), along with over a dozen other companies on the same list, have also instituted no-layoff policies and use employment security as both a positive motivator and a means of reinforcing good strategy execution.[18] At Southwest Airlines (ranked second on the 1999 list), for example, the company's partnership with employees is a critical component of its strategy to make flying a fun experience for passengers and to have a more productive workforce that helps it contain costs and keep its fares lower than competitors. Southwest management believes that its no-layoff policy keeps workers from fearing that by boosting their productivity they will work themselves out of their jobs.[19]

- More than 35 of the 58 publicly held companies on *Fortune*'s 1999 list of the 100 best companies to work for in America (including Cisco Systems, Procter & Gamble, Merck, Charles Schwab, General Mills, Amgen, and Tellabs) provide stock options to all employees. Tellabs gives every employee options on 200 shares every year. Having employee-owners who share in a company's success is widely viewed as a positive motivator, most especially when a company's stock is rising sharply and making employees wealthy—as has been the case at numerous dotcom companies that have gone public in the last several years. A big majority of Internet companies have found it necessary to use lucrative stock options to attract the kinds of talented, innovative, energetic, committed employees needed to run and win the race for leadership in some niche of the Internet economy.

- Nordstrom typically pays its retail salespeople an hourly wage higher than the prevailing rates paid by other department store chains, plus it pays them a commission on each sale. Spurred by a culture that encourages salespeople to go all out to satisfy customers, to exercise their own best judgment, and to seek out and promote new fashion ideas, Nordstrom salespeople often earn twice the average incomes of sales employees at competing stores.[20] Nordstrom's rules for employees are simple: "Rule #1: Use your good judgment in all situations. There will be no additional rules."

- Cisco Systems offers on-the-spot bonuses of up to $2,000 for exceptional performance.

- Microsoft, realizing that software creation is a highly individual effort, interviews hundreds of prospective programmers to find the few most suited to write code for its programs. It places new recruits onto teams of three to seven people under experienced mentors to work on the next generation of software programs. While project team members can expect to put in 60- to 80-hour workweeks to meet

---

[17]Ibid., p. 62.

[18]*Fortune*'s 1997 and 1999 lists of the 100 best companies to work for in America—see the January 12, 1998, and January 10, 2000, issues.

[19]Pfeffer and Veiga, "Putting People First for Organizational Success," p. 40.

[20]Jeffrey Pfeffer, "Producing Sustainable Competitive Advantage through the Effective Management of People," *Academy of Management Executive* 9, no. 1 (February 1995), pp. 59–60.

deadlines for getting new programs to market, the best programmers seek out and stay with Microsoft largely because they believe that Microsoft will determine where the industry moves in the future and that working for Microsoft will allow them to share in the excitement, challenge, and rewards of working on this frontier (and only partly because of Microsoft's very attractive pay scales and lucrative stock option program).[21]

- Lincoln Electric, a company deservedly famous for its piecework pay scheme and incentive bonus plan, rewards individual productivity by paying workers for each good piece produced. Workers have to correct quality problems on their own time— defects can be traced to the worker who caused them. The piecework plan motivates workers to pay attention to both quality and volume produced. In addition, the company sets aside a substantial portion of its profits above a specified base for worker bonuses. To determine bonus size, Lincoln Electric rates each worker on four equally important performance measures: dependability, quality, output, and ideas and cooperation. The higher a worker's merit rating, the higher the incentive bonus earned; the highest rated workers in good profit years receive bonuses of as much as 110 percent of their piecework compensation.[22]

- At a California automobile assembly plant run by Toyota, there's a big emphasis on symbolic egalitarianism. All employees (managers and workers alike) wear blue smocks, there are no reserved spaces in the employee parking lot, there's no executive dining room—everyone eats in the same plant cafeteria, and there are only two job classifications for skilled trades and only one job classification for all other workers.[23] Many companies are discovering that reducing the status distinctions that separate individuals and groups makes organization members feel important and raises their commitment.

- Monsanto, FedEx, AT&T, Whole Foods Markets, Advanced Micro Devices, W.L. Gore & Associates, and many other companies have tapped into the motivational power of self-managed teams and achieved very good results. Team performance is enhanced because team members put considerable peer pressure on co-workers to pull their weight and help achieve team goals and expectations. At W.L. Gore (a regular member on annual listings of the 100 best companies to work for), each team member's compensation is based on other team members' rankings of his or her contribution to the enterprise.

- GE Medical Systems uses a program called Quick Thanks! in which an employee can nominate any colleague to receive a $25 gift certificate redeemable at certain stores and restaurants in appreciation of a job well done. Employees often hand out the award personally to deserving co-workers (in a recent 12-month period over 10,000 Quick Thanks! awards were presented). Peers prove to be tougher than executives in praising colleagues; for the recipient, the approving acknowledgment of co-workers matters more than the $25.[24]

The above approaches to motivation, compensation, and people management (and those presented in Illustration Capsule 50) accentuate the positive; others blend positive

---

[21]Quinn, Anderson, and Finkelstein, "Leveraging Intellect," p. 8.

[22]Pfeffer, "Producing Sustainable Competitive Advantage through the Effective Management of People," p. 59.

[23]Ibid., p. 63.

[24]Steven Kerr, "Risky Business: The New Pay Game," *Fortune*, July 22, 1996, p. 95.

illustration capsule 50
Motivation and Reward Techniques of "Best Practice" Companies

Companies have been innovative in coming up with all kinds of novel motivational and reward practices to help create a work environment that supports strategy execution. Here's a glimpse of what some companies believe are best practices:

- *Providing attractive perks and benefits*—The various options here include on-site child care, on-site gym facilities and massage therapists, vacation and getaway opportunities at company-owned recreational facilities (beach houses, ranches, resort condos), personal concierge services, subsidized cafeterias and free lunches, casual dress every day, personal travel services, paid sabbaticals, profit-sharing plans, maternity leaves, paid leaves to care for ill family members, telecommuting, compressed workweeks (four 10-hour days, instead of five 8-hour days), reduced summer hours, college scholarships for children, on-the-spot bonuses for exceptional performance, and relocation services.

- *Making sure that the ideas and suggestions of employees are valued and respected*—Research indicates that the moves of many companies to push decision making down and empower employees increases employee motivation and satisfaction, as well as boosting their productivity. The use of self-managed teams has much the same effect.

- *Creating a work atmosphere where there is genuine sincerity, caring, and mutual respect among workers and between management and employees*—Companies where people are on a first-name basis and there is strong camaraderie are increasingly the rule because of the beneficial impact on the work climate.

- *Providing inspiring leadership and making employees feel they are a part of doing something very worthwhile in a larger social sense*—Jobs with noble purpose tend to turn employees on. At Medtronic, Merck,

and most other pharmaceutical companies, it is the notion of helping sick people get well and restoring patients to full life; at Whole Foods Market (a natural-foods grocery chain), it is improving human health and nutrition; at many Internet companies, it is creating a global village and revolutionizing the world landscape.

- *Sharing information with employees about financial performance, strategy, operational measures, market conditions, and competitors' actions*—This conveys to people that they are trusted and that there are no secrets. Keeping employees in the dark denies them information useful to performing their job, prevents them from being "students of the business," and usually turns employees off.

- *Having "knockout facilities"*—An impressive corporate compound for employees to work in usually has decidedly positive effects on morale and productivity.

- *Relying on promotion from within whenever possible*—This practice helps bind workers to their employer and employers to their workers, plus it is an incentive for good performance. Promotion from within also helps ensure that people in positions of responsibility actually know something about the business, technology, and operations they are managing.

- *Being flexible in how the company approaches people management (motivation, compensation, recognition, recruitment) in multinational, multicultural environments*—Managers and employees in countries whose customs, habits, values, and business practices vary from those at the "home office" often become frustrated with insistence on consistent people management practices worldwide. But the one area where consistency is essential is conveying the message that the organization values people of all races and cultural backgrounds and that discrimination on the basis of race, gender, or culture will not be tolerated.

Sources: Articles in *Fortune* on the 100 best companies to work for (1998, 1999, and 2000); Jeffrey Pfeffer and John F. Veiga, "Putting People First for Organizational Success," *Academy of Management Executive* 13, no. 2 (May 1999), pp. 37–45; and Linda K. Stroh and Paula M. Caligiuri, "Increasing Global Competitiveness through Effective People Management," *Journal of World Business* 33, no. 1 (Spring 1998), pp. 1–16.

and negative features. At companies such as McKinsey & Company and other management consulting firms, General Electric, the leading public accounting firms, and other companies that put a premium on high performance, there's an "up-or-out" policy—managers and professionals whose performance is considered marginal or not good enough to warrant promotion are denied bonuses and stock options and systematically weeded out. Some companies, despite having attractive pay packages, expect employees to put in long hours (nights and weekends), put them under the pressure of heavy workloads and tight deadlines, and push them hard to achieve ambitious stretch objectives. Business heads and other senior managers in underperforming organization units are usually under the gun to boost performance to acceptable levels or risk being replaced.

Balancing Positive and Negative Motivational Considerations   If an organization's motivational approach and reward structure induces too much stress, internal competitiveness, and job insecurity, the impact on work force morale and strategy execution can be counterproductive. Evidence shows that a manager's push for improving strategy execution should incorporate more positive than negative motivational elements because when cooperation is positively enlisted and rewarded, rather than strong-armed by orders and threats (implicit or explicit) of retribution, people tend to respond with more enthusiasm, effort, creativity, and initiative. Yet it is unwise to completely eliminate pressure for good individual and group performance and the stress and anxiety it evokes. There is no evidence that a no-pressure work environment leads to superior strategy execution or sustained high performance. As the CEO of a major bank put it, "There's a deliberate policy here to create a level of anxiety. Winners usually play like they're one touchdown behind."[25] *High-performing organizations need a cadre of ambitious people who relish the opportunity to climb the ladder of success, love a challenge, thrive in a performance-oriented environment, and find some competition and pressure useful to satisfy their own drives for personal recognition, accomplishment, and self-satisfaction.* Unless meaningful compensation, career, and job satisfaction consequences are associated with successfully implementing strategic initiatives and hitting strategic performance targets, few people will respond to top management urgings for dedicated effort to execute strategic initiatives and achieve the company's vision and objectives.

> Positive motivational approaches generally work better than negative ones, but completely eliminating pressure for good performance lacks merit.

Linking the Reward System to Strategically Relevant Performance Outcomes

The most dependable way to keep people focused on organizational objectives and to make achieving these performance targets a way of life up and down the organization is to *generously* reward and recognize individuals and groups who achieve their assigned performance targets and deny rewards and recognition to those who don't. *The use of incentives and rewards is the single most powerful tool management has to win strong employee commitment to diligent, competent strategy execution.* Failure to use these tools wisely and powerfully weakens the entire strategy implementation/execution process. Decisions on salary increases, incentive compensation, promotions, key assignments, and the ways and means of awarding praise and recognition are potent attention-getting, commitment-generating devices. Such decisions seldom escape the closest employee scrutiny, saying more about what is expected and who is considered to be doing a good job than any other factor. A company's system of incentives and rewards thus ends up being the vehicle by which its strategy is emotionally ratified in the form of real workforce commitment. Performance-based incentives make it in employees' self-interest to exert

> **Strategic Management Principle**
> A properly designed reward structure is management's most powerful tool for mobilizing organizational commitment to successful strategy execution.

---

[25] As quoted in John P. Kotter and James L. Heskett, *Corporate Culture and Performance* (New York: Free Press, 1992), p. 91.

their best efforts to achieve strategy-critical performance targets and to execute the strategy competently.[26]

The key to creating a reward system that promotes good strategy execution is to
make strategically relevant measures of performance *the dominating basis* for designing incentives, evaluating individual and group efforts, and handing out rewards. Strat-
egy-driven performance targets have to be established for every organization unit, every
manager, every team or work group, and perhaps every employee—targets that measure
whether strategy execution is progressing satisfactorily. If the company's strategy is to
be a low-cost provider, the incentive system must reward actions and achievements that
result in lower costs. If the company has a differentiation strategy predicated on superior quality and service, the incentive system must reward such outcomes as zero defects, infrequent need for product repair, low numbers of customer complaints, and
speedy order processing and delivery. If a company's growth is predicated on a strategy
of new product innovation, incentives should be tied to factors such as the percentages
of revenues and profits coming from newly introduced products.

A number of prominent companies—Southwest Airlines, W. L. Gore & Associates, Bank One, Nucor Steel, Lincoln Electric, Wal-Mart, Remington Products, and
Mary Kay Cosmetics—owe much of their success to a set of incentives and rewards
that induce people to do the things critical to good strategy execution and competing
effectively in the marketplace. At Bank One (one of the 10 largest U.S. banks and also
one of the most profitable based on return on assets), operating in a manner that produces consistently high levels of customer satisfaction makes a big competitive difference in how well the company fares against rivals; customer satisfaction ranks high on
Bank One's list of strategic priorities. To enhance employee commitment to the task of
pleasing customers, Bank One ties the pay scales in each branch office to that branch's
customer satisfaction rating—the higher the branch's ratings, the higher that branch's
pay scales. By shifting from a theme of equal pay for equal work to one of equal pay
for equal performance, Bank One has focused the attention of branch employees on the
task of pleasing, even delighting, their customers.

Nucor's strategy is to be *the* low-cost producer of steel products. Because labor
costs are a significant fraction of total cost in the steel business, successful implementation of Nucor's low-cost leadership strategy entails achieving lower labor costs per
ton of steel than competitors'. Nucor management designed an incentive system to
promote high worker productivity and drive labor costs per ton below rivals'. Management organized each plant's workforce into production teams (each assigned to perform particular functions) and, working with the teams, has established weekly
production targets for each team. Base pay scales are set at levels comparable to wages
for similar manufacturing jobs in the local areas where Nucor has plants, but workers
can earn a 1 percent bonus for each 1 percent that their output exceeds target levels. If
a production team exceeds its weekly production target by 10 percent, team members
receive a 10 percent bonus in their next paycheck; if a team exceeds its quota by 20
percent, team members earn a 20 percent bonus. Bonuses are paid every two weeks
based on the prior two weeks' actual production levels measured against the targets.
Nucor's piece-rate incentive plan has resulted in labor productivity levels 10 to 20 percent above the average of the unionized workforces of large, integrated steel producers like U.S. Steel and Bethlehem Steel, given Nucor a cost advantage over most rivals,
and made Nucor workers among the best-paid in the U.S. steel industry.

---

[26]For a countervailing view on the merits of incentives, see Alfie Kohn, "Why Incentive Plans Cannot
Work," *Harvard Business Review* 71, no. 6 (September–October 1993), pp. 54–63.

illustration capsule 51
The Folly of the Reward System in the Claims Division of a Large Insurance Company

The past reward practices of the health care claims division of a large insurance company demonstrate the folly of hoping for one behavior but rewarding another behavior. Seeking to encourage employees to be accurate in paying surgical claims, the company tracked the number of returned checks and letters of complaint filed by policyholders. However, employees in the claims department frequently found it hard to tell from physician filings which of two surgical procedures, with different allowable benefits, was performed. Since writing to the physicians for clarification greatly reduced the number of claims paid within two days of receipt (a performance standard the company stressed), the workers' norm quickly became "When in doubt, pay it out." Thus, while it appeared that employee accuracy increased (since fewer policyholders complained about nonpayment), the company lost money to overpayment of claims.

This practice was made worse by the firm's reward system, which called for merit increases of 5 percent for "outstanding" employees, 4 percent for "above-average" employees (most employees not rated as outstanding were designated as above average), and 3 percent for all other employees. Many employees were indifferent to the potential of an extra 1 percent reward for avoiding overpayment errors and working hard enough to be rated as outstanding.

However, employees were not indifferent to a rule that stated that employees forfeited their entire merit raise at the next six-month merit review if they were absent or late for work three or more times in any six-month period. The company, while hoping for performance, was rewarding attendance. But the absent-late rule was not as stringent as it might seem because the company counted the number of "times" rather than the number of "days"—a one-week absence counted the same as a one-day absence. A worker in danger of getting a third absence within a six-month period could sometimes stay away from work during the second absence until the first absence was over six months old; the limiting factor was that after a certain number of days the worker was paid sickness benefits instead of his or her regular pay. For workers with 20 or more years of service, the company provided tax-free sickness benefits of 90 percent of normal salary.

Source: Steven Kerr, "On the Folly of Rewarding A While Hoping for B," *Academy of Management Executive* 9, no. 1 February 1995), p.11.

As the example in Illustration Capsule 51 so vividly demonstrates, compensating and rewarding organization members on criteria not directly related to successful strategy execution undermines organization performance and condones the diversion of time and energy in less strategically relevant directions.

The Importance of Basing Incentives on Achieving Results, Not on Performing Assigned Functions   To create a strategy-supportive system of rewards and incentives, a company must emphasize rewarding people for accomplishing results, not for just dutifully performing assigned functions. Focusing jobholders' attention and energy on what to *achieve* as opposed to what to *do* makes the work environment results-oriented. It is flawed management to tie incentives and rewards to satisfactory performance of duties and activities in hopes that the by-products will be the desired business outcomes and company achievements.[27] In any job, performing assigned tasks is not equivalent to achieving intended outcomes. Working hard, staying busy, and diligently attending to assigned duties do not guarantee results. (As any student knows, just because an instructor teaches and students are going to class

> It is folly to reward one outcome in hopes of getting another outcome.

---

[27]See Steven Kerr, "On the Folly of Rewarding A While Hoping for B," *Academy of Management Executive* 9, no. 1 (February 1995), pp. 7–14; Kerr, "Risky Business: The New Pay Game," pp. 93–96; and Doran Twer, "Linking Pay to Business Objectives," *Journal of Business Strategy* 15, no. 4 (July–August 1994), pp. 15–18.

doesn't mean students are learning. Teaching and going to class are activities, and learning is a result. The enterprise of education would no doubt take on a different character if teachers were rewarded for the result of what is learned instead of the activity of teaching.)

Incentive compensation for top executives is typically tied to company profitability (earnings growth, return on equity investment, return on total assets, economic value added), the company's stock price performance, and perhaps such measures as market share, product quality, or customer satisfaction that indicate the company's market position, overall competitiveness, and future prospects have improved. However, incentives for department heads, teams, and individual workers may be tied to performance outcomes more closely related to their strategic area of responsibility. In manufacturing, incentive compensation may be tied to unit manufacturing costs, on-time production and shipping, defect rates, the number and extent of work stoppages due to labor disagreements and equipment breakdowns, and so on. In sales and marketing, there may be incentives for achieving dollar sales or unit volume targets, market share, sales penetration of each target customer group, the fate of newly introduced products, the frequency of customer complaints, the number of new accounts acquired, and customer satisfaction. Which performance measures to base incentive compensation on depends on the situation—the priority placed on various financial and strategic objectives, the requirements for strategic and competitive success, and what specific results are needed in different facets of the business to keep strategy execution on track.

> The whats to accomplish—the performance measures on which rewards and incentives are based—must be tightly connected to the requirements of successful strategy execution and good company performance.

Guidelines for Designing Incentive Compensation Systems   The concepts and company experiences discussed above yield the following prescriptive guidelines for creating an incentive compensation system to help drive successful strategy execution:

1. *The performance payoff must be a major, not minor, piece of the total compensation package.* Payoffs must be at least 10 to 12 percent of base salary to have much impact. Incentives that amount to 20 percent or more of total compensation are big attention-getters, likely to really drive individual or team effort; incentives amounting to less than 5 percent of total compensation have comparatively weak motivational impact. Moreover, the payoff for high-performing individuals and teams must be substantially greater than the payoff for average performers, and the payoff for average performers substantially bigger than for below-average performers.

2. *The incentive plan should extend to all managers and all workers, not just top management.* It is a gross miscalculation to expect that lower-level managers and employees will work their hardest to hit performance targets just so a few senior executives can get lucrative rewards.

3. *The reward system must be administered with scrupulous care and fairness.* If performance standards are set unrealistically high or if individual/group performance evaluations are not accurate and well documented, dissatisfaction with the system will overcome any positive benefits.

4. *The incentives must be tightly linked to achieving only those performance targets spelled out in the strategic plan.* Incentives should not include factors that get thrown in because they are thought to be nice occurrences. Performance evaluation based on factors not tightly related to the strategy signal that either the strategic

plan is incomplete (because important performance targets were left out) or management's real agenda is something other than what was stated in the strategic plan.

5. *The performance targets each individual is expected to achieve should involve outcomes that the individual can personally affect.* The role of incentives is to enhance individual commitment and channel behavior in beneficial directions. This role is not well served when the performance measures an individual is judged by are outside his or her arena of influence.

6. *Keep the time between the performance review and payment of the reward short.* A lengthy interval between review and payment breeds discontent and works against reinforcing cause and effect.

7. *Make liberal use of nonmonetary rewards; don't rely solely on monetary rewards.* When used properly, money is a great motivator, but there are potent advantages to be gained from praise, special recognition, handing out plum assignments, and so on.

8. *Absolutely avoid skirting the system to find ways to reward nonperformers.* It is debatable whether exceptions should be made for people who've tried hard, gone the extra mile, yet still come up short because of circumstances beyond their control—arguments can be made either way. The problem with making exceptions for unknowable, uncontrollable, or unforeseeable circumstances is that once good excuses start to creep into justifying rewards for nonperformers, the door is open for all kinds of reasons why actual performance failed to match targeted performance. In short, people at all levels have to be held accountable for carrying out their assigned parts of the strategic plan, and they have to know their rewards are based on the caliber of their strategic accomplishments.

Once the incentives are designed, they have to be communicated and explained. Everybody needs to understand how their incentive compensation is calculated and how individual/group performance targets contribute to organizational performance targets. Moreover, the reasons for anyone's failure or deviations from targets have to be explored fully to determine whether the causes are attributable to poor individual/group performance or to circumstances beyond the control of those responsible. The pressure to achieve the targeted strategic and financial performance and continuously improve on strategy execution should be unrelenting. A "no excuses" standard has to prevail.[28] But with the pressure to perform must come deserving and meaningful rewards. Without an ample payoff, the system breaks down, and the strategy implementer is left with the unworkable option of barking orders and pleading for compliance.

Performance-Based Incentives and Rewards in Multinational Enterprises

In some foreign countries, incentive pay runs counter to local customs and cultural norms. Professor Steven Kerr cites the time he lectured an executive education class on the need for more performance-based pay and a Japanese manager protested, "You shouldn't bribe your children to do their homework, you shouldn't bribe your wife to prepare dinner, and you shouldn't bribe your employees to work for the company."[29] Singling out individuals and commending them for unusually good

---

[28]Tom Peters and Nancy Austin, *A Passion for Excellence* (New York: Random House, 1985), p. xix.

[29]Kerr, "Risky Business: The New Pay Game," p. 96. For a more general criticism of why performance incentives are a bad idea, see Kohn, "Why Incentive Plans Cannot Work," pp. 54–63.

effort can also be a problem; Japanese culture considers public praise of an individual an affront to the harmony of the group. In some countries, employees have a preference for nonmonetary rewards—more leisure time, important titles, access to vacation villages, and nontaxable perks. Thus, multinational companies have to build some degree of flexibility into the design of incentives and rewards in order to accommodate cross-cultural traditions and preferences.

key|points

A change in strategy nearly always calls for budget reallocations. Reworking the budget to make it more strategy-supportive is a crucial part of the implementation process because every organization unit needs to have the people, equipment, facilities, and other resources to carry out its part of the strategic plan (but no more than what it really needs). Implementing a new strategy often entails shifting resources from one area to another—downsizing units that are overstaffed and overfunded, upsizing those more critical to strategic success, and killing projects and activities that are no longer justified.

Anytime a company alters its strategy, managers are well advised to review existing policies and operating procedures, deleting or revising those that are out of sync and deciding if additional ones are needed. Prescribing new or freshly revised policies and operating procedures aids the task of implementation (1) by providing top-down guidance to operating managers, supervisory personnel, and employees regarding how certain things need to be done; (2) by putting boundaries on independent actions and decisions; (3) by promoting consistency in how particular strategy-critical activities are performed in geographically scattered operating units; and (4) by helping to create a strategy-supportive work climate and corporate culture. Thick policy manuals are usually unnecessary. Indeed, when individual creativity and initiative are more essential to good execution than standardization and conformity, it is better to give people the freedom to do things however they see fit and hold them accountable for good results rather than try to control their behavior with policies and guidelines for every situation. Hence, creating a supportive fit between strategy and policy can mean many policies, few policies, or different policies.

Competent strategy execution entails visible, unyielding managerial commitment to best practices and continuous improvement. Benchmarking, the discovery and adoption of best practices, reengineering core business processes, and total quality management programs all aim at improved efficiency, lower costs, better product quality, and greater customer satisfaction. *All these techniques are important tools for learning how to execute a strategy more proficiently.* Benchmarking provides a realistic basis for setting performance targets. Instituting "best-in-industry" or "best-in-world" operating practices in most or all value chain activities provide a means for taking strategy execution to a higher plateau of competence and nurturing a high-performance work environment. Reengineering is a way to make quantum progress toward becoming a world-class organization, while TQM instills a commitment to continuous improvement. Effective use of TQM and continuous improvement techniques is a valuable competitive asset in a company's resource portfolio—one that can produce important competitive capabilities (in reducing costs, speeding new products to market, or improving product quality, service, or customer satisfaction) and be a source of competitive advantage.

Company strategies can't be implemented or executed well without a number of support systems to carry on business operations. Well-conceived, state-of-the-art support systems not only facilitate better strategy execution but can also strengthen organizational capabilities enough to provide a competitive edge over rivals. In the age of the Internet, real-time information and control systems, growing use of e-commerce technologies and business practices, company intranets, and wireless communications capabilities, companies can't hope to outexecute their competitors without cutting-edge information systems and technologically sophisticated operating capabilities that enable fast, efficient, and effective organization action.

Strategy-supportive motivational practices and reward systems are powerful management tools for gaining employee buy-in and commitment. The key to creating a reward system that promotes good strategy execution is to make strategically relevant measures of performance *the dominating basis* for designing incentives, evaluating individual and group efforts, and handing out rewards. Positive motivational practices generally work better than negative ones, but there is a place for both. There's also a place for both monetary and nonmonetary incentives.

For an incentive compensation system to work well (1) the monetary payoff should be a major percentage of the compensation package, (2) the use of incentives should extend to all managers and workers, (3) the system should be administered with care and fairness, (4) the incentives should be linked to performance targets spelled out in the strategic plan, (5) each individual's performance targets should involve outcomes the person can personally affect, (6) rewards should promptly follow the determination of good performance, (7) monetary rewards should be supplemented with liberal use of nonmonetary rewards, and (8) skirting the system to reward nonperformers should be scrupulously avoided.

suggested | readings

Denton, Keith D. "Creating a System for Continuous Improvement." *Business Horizons* 38, no. 1 (January–February 1995), pp. 16–21.

Grant, Robert M.; Rami Shani; and R. Krishnan. "TQM's Challenge to Management Theory and Practice." *Sloan Management Review* (Winter 1994), pp. 25–35.

Herzberg, Frederick. "One More Time: How Do You Motivate Employees?" *Harvard Business Review* 65, no. 4 (September–October 1987), pp. 109–20.

Katzenbach, Jon R., and Jason A Santamaria. "Firing Up the Front Line." *Harvard Business Review* 77, no. 3 (May–June 1999), pp. 107–17.

Kerr, Steven. "On the Folly of Rewarding A While Hoping for B." *Academy of Management Executive* 9, no. 1 (February 1995), pp. 7–14.

Kohn, Alfie. "Why Incentive Plans Cannot Work." *Harvard Business Review* 71, no. 5 (September–October 1993), pp. 54–63.

Luthans, Fred, and Alexander D. Stajkovic. "Reinforce for Performance: The Need to Go beyond Pay and Even Rewards." *Academy of Management Executive* 13, no. 2 (May 1999), pp. 49–57.

Ohinata, Yoshinobu. "Benchmarking: The Japanese Experience." *Long Range Planning* 27, no. 4 (August 1994), pp. 48–53.

Olian, Judy D., and Sara L. Rynes. "Making Total Quality Work: Aligning Organizational Processes, Performance Measures, and Stakeholders." *Human Resource Management* 30, no. 3 (Fall 1991), pp. 303–33.

Pfeffer, Jeffrey. "Producing Sustainable Competitive Advantage through the Effective Management of People." *Academy of Management Executive* 9, no. 1 (February 1995), pp. 55–69.

———. "Six Dangerous Myths about Pay." *Harvard Business Review* 76, no. 3 (May–June 1998), pp. 108–19.

Pfeffer, Jeffrey, and John F. Veiga. "Putting People First for Organizational Success." *Academy of Management Executive* 13, no. 2 (May 1999), pp. 37–48.

Simons, Robert. "Control in an Age of Empowerment." *Harvard Business Review* 73 (March–April 1995), pp. 80–88.

chapter | thirteen 13

Corporate Culture and Leadership— Keys to Effective Strategy Execution

Weak leadership can wreck the soundest strategy; forceful execution of even a poor plan can often bring victory.

—Sun Zi

Leadership is accomplishing something through other people that wouldn't have happened if you weren't there . . . Leadership is being able to mobilize ideas and values that energize other people . . . Leaders develop a story line that engages other people.

—Noel Tichy

[A] leader lives in the field with his troops.

—H. Ross Perot

An organization's capacity to execute its strategy depends on its "hard" infrastructure—its organizational structure and systems—and on its "soft" infrastructure—its culture and norms.

—Amar Bhide

Ethics is the moral courage to do what we know is right, and not to do what we know is wrong.

—C. J. Silas

The biggest levers you've got to change a company are strategy, structure, and culture. If I could pick two, I'd pick strategy and culture.

—Wayne Leonard, CEO, Entergy

In the previous two chapters we examined six of the strategy-implementer's tasks—building a capable organization, steering ample resources into strategy-critical activities and operating units, establishing strategy-supportive policies, instituting best practices and programs for continuous improvement, creating internal support systems to enable better execution, and employing appropriate motivational practices and compensation incentives. In this chapter we explore the two remaining implementation tasks: creating a strategy-supportive corporate culture and exerting the internal leadership needed to drive implementation forward.

BUILDING A STRATEGY-SUPPORTIVE CORPORATE CULTURE

Every company has a unique organizational culture. Each has its own business philosophy and principles, its own ways of approaching problems and making decisions, its own work climate, its own embedded patterns of "how we do things around here," its own lore (stories told over and over to illustrate company values and what they mean to stakeholders), its own taboos and political don'ts—in other words, its own ingrained beliefs, behavior and thought patterns, business practices, and personality that define its **corporate culture.** The bedrock of Wal-Mart's culture is dedication to customer satisfaction, zealous pursuit of low costs, a strong work ethic, Sam Walton's legendary frugality, the ritualistic Saturday-morning headquarters meetings to exchange ideas and review problems, and company executives' commitment to visiting stores, talking to customers, and soliciting suggestions from employees. At McDonald's the constant message from management is the overriding importance of quality, service, cleanliness, and value; employees are drilled over and over on the need for attention to detail and perfection in every fundamental of the business. At General Electric, the culture is founded on a hard-driving, results-oriented atmosphere (where all of GE's businesses are held to a standard of being number one or two in their industries as well as achieving good business results); the concept of a boundaryless organization (where ideas, best practices, and learning flow freely from business to business); the reliance on "workout sessions" to identify, debate, and resolve burning issues; a commitment to six sigma quality; and globalization of the company. At Microsoft, there are stories of the long hours programmers put in, the emotional peaks and valleys in encountering and overcoming coding problems, the exhilaration of completing a complex program on schedule, the satisfaction of working on cutting-edge projects, the rewards of being part of a team responsible for a popular new software program, and the tradition of competing aggressively. Illustration Capsule 52 describes the culture at Nordstrom.

> **Basic Concept**
> *Corporate culture* refers to a company's values, beliefs, business principles, traditions, ways of operating, and internal work environment.

Where Does Corporate Culture Come From?

The taproot of corporate culture is the organization's beliefs and philosophy about how its affairs ought to be conducted—the reasons why it does things the way it does. A company's culture is manifested in the values and business principles that management preaches and practices, in its ethical standards and official policies, in its stakeholder relationships (especially its dealings with employees, unions, stockholders, vendors, and the communities in which it operates), in the traditions the organization maintains, in its supervisory practices, in employees' attitudes and behavior, in the legends people repeat about happenings in the organization, in the peer pressures that exist, in the organization's politics, and in the "chemistry" and the "vibrations" that permeate the work environment. All these sociological forces, some of which operate quite subtly, combine to define an organization's culture.

> An organization's culture is bred from a complex combination of sociological forces operating within its boundaries.

Beliefs and practices that become embedded in a company's culture can originate anywhere: from one influential individual, work group, department, or division, from the bottom of the organizational hierarchy or the top.[1] Very often, many components of the culture originate with a founder or certain strong leaders who articulated them as a company philosophy or as a set of principles to which the organization should rigidly

---

[1] John P. Kotter and James L. Heskett, *Corporate Culture and Performance* (New York: Free Press, 1992), p. 7.

illustration capsule 52
The Culture at Nordstrom

The culture at Nordstrom, a department store retailer noted for exceptional commitment to its customers, revolves around the company's motto: "Respond to unreasonable customer requests." Living up to the company's motto is so strongly ingrained in behavior that employees learn to relish the challenges that some customer requests pose. For example, the phone is always answered within three rings. Salespeople walk customers to fitting rooms rather than pointing the way. Customers receive thank-you notes for purchases and phone calls when back-ordered items arrive. In return, a favorite salesclerk might receive a Valentine or a souvenir from a customer's trip overseas.

At Nordstrom, each out-of-the-ordinary customer request is seen as an opportunity for a "heroic" act by an employee and a way to build the company's reputation for great service. Nordstrom encourages these acts by promoting employees noted for outstanding service, keeping scrapbooks of heroic acts, and basing the compensation of salespeople mainly on commission. It is not unusual for good salespeople at Nordstrom to earn double what they would at other department stores.

Nordstrom starts new employees, even those with advanced degrees, out on the sales floor. Promotion is strictly from within, and when a new store is opened, its key people are recruited from other stores around the country to help perpetuate Nordstrom's culture and values and to make sure the new store is run the Nordstrom way.

Nordstrom strives to provide superior customer service at its website, as well. Alissa Kozuh's job is to make sure that her customers can easily find the items they want. "That's the difference between bringing a human element into this process and leaving it to technology," she says.

Source: Based on information in Kathy Mulady, "Nordstrom Way Is Legendary in Shopping," *Seattle Post-Intelligencer* (http://seattlep-i.nwsource.com), June 26, 2001; Ron Lieber, "She Reads Customer's Minds," *Fast Company* (www.fastcompany.com), February 2001; Tracy Goss, Richard Pascale, and Anthony Athos, "Risking the Present for a Powerful Future," *Harvard Business Review* 71, no. 6 (November–December 1993), pp. 101–2; and Jeffrey Pfeffer, "Producing Sustainable Competitive Advantage through the Effective Management of People," *Academy of Management Executive* 9, no. 1 (February 1995), pp. 59–60, 65.

adhere or as company policies. Over time, these cultural underpinnings take root, become embedded in how the company conducts its business, come to be shared by company managers and employees, and then persist as new employees are encouraged to adopt and follow the professed values and practices. Fast-growing companies risk creating a culture by chance rather than by design if they rush to hire employees mainly for their technical skills and credentials and neglect to screen out candidates whose values, philosophies, and personalities aren't compatible with the organizational character, vision, and strategy being articulated by the company's founder and top managers.

The Role of Stories   Frequently, a significant part of a company's culture emerges from the stories that get told over and over again to illustrate to newcomers the importance of certain values and beliefs and ways of operating. FedEx, of course, is world renowned for the reliability of its next-day package delivery guarantee. One of the folktales at FedEx is about a deliveryman who had been given the wrong key to a FedEx drop box. Rather than leave the packages in the drop box until the next day when the right key was available, the deliveryman unbolted the drop box from its base, loaded it into the truck, and took it back to the station. There, the box was pried open and the contents removed and sped on their way to their destination the next day. The story vividly communicates the kind of commitment the company wants every employee to exhibit in helping the company live up its reputation of reliable delivery.

Perpetuating the Culture   Once established, company cultures can be perpetuated by screening and selecting new group members according to how well their values and personalities fit in (as well as on the basis of talents and credentials), by systematic indoctrination of new members in the culture's fundamentals, by the efforts of senior group members to reiterate core values in daily conversations and pronouncements, by the telling and retelling of company legends, by regular ceremonies honoring members who display cultural ideals, and by visibly rewarding those who follow cultural norms and penalizing those who don't.[2] The staffing of an organization with new employees is one of the most important ways in which a company's culture is perpetuated. Company managers tend to hire people they feel comfortable with and think will fit in—which tends to mean hiring people with values and beliefs and personalities that will embrace the prevailing culture. Job seekers tend to accept jobs at companies where they expect to be comfortable and happy. Employees who don't hit it off at a company tend to leave quickly, while employees who thrive and are pleased with the work environment move into senior roles and positions of greater responsibility. The longer people stay at an organization, the more their values and beliefs tend to be molded by mentors, fellow workers, company training programs, and the reward structure and the more that they come to embrace and mirror the corporate culture. Sometimes gradually and sometimes more rapidly, the culture takes root, the agglomeration and product of all the social forces at work.

Forces That Can Cause Culture to Evolve   However, even stable cultures aren't static—just like strategy and organization structure, they evolve, if only slightly. Internal crises, revolutionary technologies (like the Internet), and new challenges breed new ways of doing things and cultural evolution. Arrival of new leaders and turnover of key members often spawn new or different values and practices that alter the culture. Diversification into new businesses, expansion into different geographical areas (especially foreign countries), rapid growth that adds new employees, and merger with or acquisition of another company can all precipitate cultural changes. Indeed, globalization and the Internet are today driving significant changes in the culture of companies all over the world.

Company Subcultures: The Problems Posed by New Acquisitions and Multinational Operations   Although it is common to speak about corporate culture in the singular, companies typically have multiple cultures (or subcultures).[3] Values, beliefs, and practices can vary significantly by department, geographic location, division, or business unit. A company's subcultures can clash, or at least not mesh well, if they have conflicting managerial styles, business philosophies, and operating approaches or if important differences between a company's culture and those of recently acquired companies have not yet been ironed out. *Global and multinational companies tend to be at least partly multicultural* because cross-country organization units have different operating histories and traditions, as well as members who have different values and beliefs and who speak different languages. The human resources manager of a global pharmaceutical company who took on an assignment in the Far East discovered, to his surprise, that one of his biggest challenges was to persuade his company's managers in China, Korea, Malaysia, and Taiwan to accept promotions—their cultural values were such that they did not believe in competing with their peers for career rewards or personal gain, nor did they relish breaking ties to their local communities to assume cross-national responsibilities.[4] Many companies that have merged with or acquired foreign companies have to deal with language- and custom-based cultural differences.

---

[2]Ibid., pp. 7–8.

[3]Ibid., p. 5.

[4]John Alexander and Meena S. Wilson, "Leading across Cultures: Five Vital Capabilities," in *The Organization of the Future,* ed. Frances Hesselbein, Marshall Goldsmith, and Richard Beckard (San Francisco: Jossey-Bass, 1997), pp. 291–92.

Nonetheless, the different subcultures that may exist within a global or multinational company's culture do not preclude there being important areas of commonality and compatibility. For example, General Electric's cultural traits of boundarylessness, workout, and six sigma quality can be implanted and practiced successfully in different countries. Multinational companies are learning how to make strategy-critical cultural traits travel across country boundaries and create a workably uniform culture worldwide. Likewise, company managements have learned to consider the importance of cultural compatibility in making acquisitions and the importance of addressing how to merge and integrate the cultures of newly acquired companies.

Culture: Ally or Obstacle to Strategy Execution?

The beliefs, vision, objectives, and business approaches and practices underpinning a company's strategy may be compatible with its culture or they may not. When they are, the culture becomes a valuable ally in strategy implementation and execution. When the culture is in conflict with some aspect of the company's direction, performance targets, or strategy, the culture becomes a stumbling block that impedes successful strategy implementation and execution.[5]

> An organization's culture is either an important contributor or an obstacle to successful strategy execution.

How Culture Can Promote Better Strategy Execution A culture grounded in values, practices, and behavioral norms that match what is needed for good strategy execution helps energize people throughout the company to do their jobs in a strategy-supportive manner, adding significantly to the power and effectiveness of strategy execution. For example, a culture where frugality and thrift are values strongly shared by organizational members is very conducive to successful execution of a low-cost leadership strategy. A culture where creativity, embracing change, and challenging the status quo are pervasive themes is very conducive to successful execution of a product innovation and technological leadership strategy. A culture built around such business principles as listening to customers, encouraging employees to take pride in their work, and giving employees a high degree of decision-making responsibility is very conducive to successful execution of a strategy of delivering superior customer service.

> Strong cultures promote good strategy execution when there's fit and hurt execution when there's little fit.

A tight culture–strategy alignment acts in two ways to channel behavior and influence employees to do their jobs in a strategy-supportive fashion:[6]

- *A work environment where the culture matches the conditions for good strategy execution provides a system of informal rules and peer pressure regarding how to conduct business internally and how to go about doing one's job.* Strategy-supportive cultures shape the mood, temperament, and motivation of the workforce, positively affecting organizational energy, work habits and operating practices, the degree to which organizational units cooperate, and how customers are treated. Culturally approved behavior thrives, while culturally disapproved behavior gets squashed and often penalized. In a company where strategy and culture are misaligned, ingrained values and operating philosophies don't cultivate strategy-supportive ways of operating; often, the very kinds of behavior needed to execute strategy successfully run afoul of the culture and attract negative recognition rather than praise and reward.

> A deeply rooted culture well matched to strategy is a powerful lever for successful strategy execution.

- *A strong strategy-supportive culture nurtures and motivates people to do their jobs in ways conducive to effective strategy execution; it provides structure, standards,*

---

[5]Kotter and Heskett, *Corporate Culture and Performance,* p. 5.

[6]Ibid., pp. 15–16.

and a value system in which to operate; and it promotes strong employee identification with the company's vision, performance targets, and strategy. All this makes employees feel genuinely better about their jobs and work environment and the merits of what the company is trying to accomplish. Employees are stimulated to take on the challenge of realizing the company's vision, do their jobs competently and with enthusiasm, and collaborate with others as needed to bring the strategy to fruition.

This says something important about the task of leading strategy implementation: *anything so fundamental as implementing a strategic plan involves moving the organization's culture into close alignment with the requirements for proficient strategy execution.* The optimal condition is a work environment that mobilizes organizational energy in strategy-supportive fashion, promoting "can-do" attitudes and acceptance of change where needed, enlisting and encouraging people to perform strategy-critical activities in superior fashion, and breeding needed organizational competencies and capabilities.

The Perils of Strategy–Culture Conflict   Conflict between culture and strategy sends mixed signals to organization members and forces an undesirable choice. Should organization members be loyal to the culture and company traditions (as well as their own personal values and beliefs, which are likely to be compatible with the culture) and resist actions to pursue the strategy? Or should they go along with announced strategic priorities and engage in actions that will erode certain valued aspects of the culture and go against their own ingrained values and beliefs? Such conflict weakens commitment to culture or strategy or both.

When a company's culture is out of sync with what is needed for strategic success, the culture has to be changed as rapidly as can be managed—this, of course, presumes that it is one or more aspects of the culture that are out of whack rather than the strategy. While correcting a strategy–culture conflict can occasionally mean revamping strategy to produce cultural fit, more usually it means revamping the mismatched cultural features to produce strategy fit. The more entrenched the mismatched aspects of the culture, the greater the difficulty of implementing new or different strategies until better strategy–culture alignment emerges. A sizable and prolonged strategy–culture conflict weakens and may even defeat managerial efforts to make the strategy work.

Strong versus Weak Cultures

Company cultures vary widely in the degree to which they are embedded in company practices and behavioral norms. Some are strong and go directly to a company's heart and soul; others are weak, with shallow roots that support little in the way of a definable corporate character.

In a strong-culture company, values and behavioral norms are like crabgrass: deeply rooted and difficult to weed out.

Strong-Culture Companies   A company's culture can be strong and cohesive in the sense that the company conducts its business according to a clear and explicit set of principles and values, that management devotes considerable time to communicating these principles and values to organization members and explaining how they relate to its business environment, and that the values are shared widely across the company—by senior executives and rank-and-file employees alike.[7] Strong-culture

---

[7]Terrence E. Deal and Allen A. Kennedy, *Corporate Cultures* (Reading, MA: Addison-Wesley, 1982), p. 22.

companies typically have creeds or values statements, and executives regularly stress the importance of using these values and principles as the basis for decisions and actions taken throughout the organization. In strong-culture companies, values and behavioral norms are so deeply rooted that they don't change much when a new CEO takes over—although they can erode over time if the CEO ceases to nurture them. And they may not change much as strategy evolves and the organization acts to make strategy adjustments, either because the new strategy is compatible with the present culture or because the dominant traits of the culture are strategy neutral and can be used to support any number of plausible strategies.

Three factors contribute to the development of strong cultures: (1) a founder or strong leader who establishes values, principles, and practices that are consistent and sensible in light of customer needs, competitive conditions, and strategic requirements; (2) a sincere, long-standing company commitment to operating the business according to these established traditions, thereby creating an internal environment that supports decision making and strategies based on cultural norms; and (3) a genuine concern for the well-being of the organization's three biggest constituencies—customers, employees, and shareholders. Continuity of leadership, small group size, stable group membership, geographic concentration, and considerable organizational success all contribute to the emergence and sustainability of a strong culture.[8]

During the time a strong culture is being implanted, there's nearly always a good strategy–culture fit (which partially accounts for the organization's success). Mismatches between strategy and culture in a strong-culture company tend to occur when a company's business environment undergoes significant rapid-fire change, prompting a drastic strategy revision that clashes with the entrenched culture. In such cases, a major culture-changing effort has to be launched. IBM went through wrenching culture changes to adapt to the new computer industry environment now driven by the so-called Wintel standard—Microsoft (with its Windows operating systems for PCs and its Windows-based PC software programs) and Intel (with its successive generations of faster microprocessors for PCs). IBM's bureaucracy and mainframe culture clashed with the shift to a PC-dominated world and the emergence of the Internet economy. Many electric utilities, long used to operating as slow-moving regulated monopolies with captive customers, are in the midst of a massive cultural shift, as they try to cope with the transition to a competitive marketplace and freedom of customer choice. The new circumstances of electric utilities are prompting a shift away from cultures predicated on risk avoidance, centralized control of decision making, and the politics of regulatory relationships to cultures where the new values and beliefs revolve around entrepreneurial risk taking, innovation, competitive thinking, superior customer service, and growing the business.

> A strong culture is a valuable asset when it matches strategy and a dreaded liability when it doesn't.

Weak-Culture Companies In direct contrast to strong-culture companies, a company's culture can be weak and fragmented in the sense that many subcultures exist, few values and behavioral norms are widely shared, and there are few sacred traditions. In weak-culture companies, there's little cohesion and glue across organization units—top executives don't repeatedly espouse any business philosophy or exhibit commitment to particular values or extol use of particular operating practices. Because of a dearth of common values and ingrained business approaches, organization members typically have no deeply felt sense of corporate identity. While they may have some bonds of identification with and loyalty toward their department, their colleagues, their

---

[8]Vijay Sathe, *Culture and Related Corporate Realities* (Homewood, IL: Richard D. Irwin, 1985).

union, or their boss, the weak company culture breeds no strong employee allegiance to what the company stands for. The lack of a definable corporate character tends to result in many employees viewing the company as a place to work and their job as a way to make a living. As a consequence, *weak cultures provide little or no strategy implementing assistance* because there are no traditions, beliefs, values, common bonds, or behavioral norms that management can use as levers to mobilize commitment to executing the chosen strategy. While a weak culture does not usually pose a strong barrier to strategy execution, it provides no assist either.

Unhealthy Cultures

There are a number of unhealthy cultural characteristics that can undermine a company's business performance.[9] One unhealthy trait is a politicized internal environment that allows influential managers to operate autonomous "fiefdoms" and resist needed change. In politically dominated cultures, many issues get resolved on the basis of turf, vocal support or opposition by powerful executives, personal lobbying by a key executive, and coalitions among individuals or departments with vested interests in a particular outcome. What's best for the company plays second fiddle to personal aggrandizement.

A second unhealthy cultural trait, one that can plague companies suddenly confronted with fast-changing business conditions, is hostility to change and to people who champion new ways of doing things. Executives who don't value managers or employees with initiative often put a damper on experimentation and on efforts to improve. Avoiding risks, not fouling up, not rocking the boat, and accepting the status quo become more important to a person's career advancement than entrepreneurial successes, innovative accomplishments, and championing better ways to do things. Hostility to change is most often found in companies with multilayered management bureaucracies that have enjoyed considerable market success in years past but whose business environments have been hit with accelerating change. General Motors, IBM, Sears, and Eastman Kodak are classic examples—all four gradually became burdened by a stifling bureaucracy that rejected innovation and are now struggling to reinvent the cultural approaches that caused them to succeed in the first place.

A third unhealthy characteristic is promoting managers who are good at staying within their budgets, exerting close supervisory control over their units, and handling administrative detail as opposed to managers who understand vision, strategies, and culture building and who are good leaders, motivators, and decision makers. While the former are adept at internal organizational maneuvering, they may lack the entrepreneurial skills a company needs among its senior executives to introduce new strategies, reallocate resources, build new competitive capabilities, and fashion a new culture— and such a lack will ultimately erode long-term performance.

A fourth characteristic of unhealthy cultures is an aversion to looking outside the company for superior practices and approaches. Sometimes a company enjoys such great market success and reigns as an industry leader for so long that its management becomes inbred and arrogant. It believes it has all the answers or can develop them on its own. Insular thinking, inward-looking solutions, and a must-be-invented-here syndrome often precede a decline in company performance. Kotter and Heskett cite Avon, BankAmerica, Citicorp, Coors, Ford, General Motors, Kmart, Kroger, Sears, Texaco,

---

[9]Kotter and Heskett, *Corporate Culture and Performance*, chapter 6.

and Xerox as examples of companies that had unhealthy cultures during the late 1970s and early 1980s.[10] Several—most notably General Motors, Kmart, and Sears—still exhibit many unhealthy culture traits.

Adaptive Cultures

In fast-changing business environments, the capacity to introduce new strategies and organizational practices is a necessity if a company is to achieve superior performance over long periods of time.[11] Strategic agility requires a culture that quickly accepts and supports company efforts to adapt to environmental change rather than a culture that has to be coaxed and cajoled to change.

> Adaptive cultures are a valuable competitive asset—sometimes a necessity—in fast-changing environments.

In adaptive cultures, members share a feeling of confidence that the organization can deal with whatever threats and opportunities come down the pike; they are receptive to risk taking, experimentation, innovation, and changing strategies and practices whenever necessary to satisfy the legitimate interests of stakeholders—customers, employees, shareowners, suppliers, and the communities where the company operates. Hence, members willingly embrace a proactive approach to identifying issues, evaluating the implications and options, and implementing workable solutions. There's a spirit of doing what's necessary to ensure long-term organizational success *provided core values and business principles are upheld in the process.*[12] Entrepreneurship is encouraged and rewarded. Managers habitually fund product development initiatives, evaluate new ideas openly, and take prudent risks to create new business positions. Strategies and traditional operating practices are modified as needed to adjust to or take advantage of changes in the business environment. The leaders of adaptive cultures are adept at changing the right things in the right ways, not changing for the sake of change and not compromising core values or business principles. Adaptive cultures are very supportive of managers and employees at all ranks who propose or help initiate useful change; indeed, executives consciously seek, train, and promote individuals who display these leadership traits.

> Today's dot-com companies are classic examples of adaptive cultures.

Today's dot-com companies are perfect illustrations of adaptive cultures. Internet-related companies thrive on change—driving it, leading it, and capitalizing on it (but sometimes also succumbing to change when they make the wrong move or are swamped by better technologies or the superior business models of rivals). From the outset, Internet companies established cultures with the capability to act and react rapidly. They are avid practitioners of entrepreneurship and innovation, with a demonstrated willingness to take bold risks to create altogether new products, new businesses, and new industries. They have carefully and deliberately staffed their organizations with people who are proactive, who rise to the challenge of change, and who have an aptitude for adapting. Because of the revolution in business strategies, business organization, and business practices spawned largely by companies comprising the Internet economy, traditional companies are overhauling their cultures to become more adaptive and are learning to move at

---

[10]Ibid., p. 68.

[11]This section draws heavily from Kotter and Heskett, *Corporate Culture and Performance,* chapter 4.

[12]There's no inherent reason why new strategic initiatives should conflict with core values and business principles. While conflict is always possible, most strategy makers lean toward choosing strategic initiatives that are compatible with the company's character and culture and that don't go against ingrained values and beliefs. After all, the company's culture is usually something that strategy makers have had a hand in building and perpetuating, so they are not often anxious to undermine core values and business principles without serious soul-searching and compelling business reasons.

illustration capsule 53
Adaptive Cultures at Companies That Act and React at Internet Speed

Fast-changing industry and competitive conditions, driven partly by the e-commerce revolution and mushrooming use of the Internet, have made it more desirable than ever for companies to establish adaptive cultures. Acting and responding at Internet speed is rapidly becoming a cultural and business necessity. Internet retailers typically monitor consumer buying preferences every few days and make changes to their product lineup whenever it appears that buying preferences have changed. Companies like software and e-services firm Portera Systems hold weekly meetings to analyze sales reports and customer requests and decide whether to institute changes in their software products or shifts in strategy. New entrants can become viable competitors before they are even noticed by most industry incumbents—for example, within 10 weeks, home furnishings start-up GoodHome.com went from an idea to a business plan to venture capital funding to a merger.

The ability to act and react at Internet speed hinges largely on having an adaptive culture. Corporate cultures that are resistant to change impede actions to quickly plot and pursue a new strategic course when customer preferences or other circumstances so dictate. Companies with adaptive organizational cultures typically create flat organizational structures that push decision making to the front lines. They staff the organization with people who thrive on change and ambiguity. And they foster a "sensing-and-responding mind-set" that comes from ongoing

communications with customers, attentive monitoring of rivals' actions, and awareness of technological developments. The CEO of Accompany, an online buying club, reports that his company is "not interested in people who can only deal in black and white—they'd slow us down."

Building an adaptive culture that moves at Internet speed also entails providing employees with timely information about strategic changes. According to an IBM executive, "You can't keep people in the dark when you're moving really fast or they start thinking that change is something sinister." Accompany uses e-mail and group meetings to communicate strategy shifts to its employees within hours of management's decisions.

Solutia, a Monsanto spin-off, speeds its ability to respond to market changes by building scenarios in its strategic planning sessions. For every new strategic initiative, the company's managers plan four different short-term outcomes and establish "signposts" to indicate when it's time to change strategic direction. When signpost events begin to appear, management relies on its scenarios and discussions to alter strategy, sometimes within hours.

Sun Microsystems has weekly "whack-o-meter" sessions where the company's president and key decision makers meet to assess the company's vulnerabilities or ways that competitors might "whack" Sun. Sun's managers then try to identify responses that can be implemented at the first sign of a rival's offensive move.

Source: Based on Marcia Stepanek, "How Fast Is Net Fast?" *Business Week*, November 1, 1999, pp. EB 52–EB 54.

Internet speed. Illustration Capsule 53 describes what dot-com companies are doing to build adaptive cultures that can act and react at Internet speed.

One outstanding trait of adaptive cultures is that top management, while orchestrating responses to changing conditions, proceeds in a manner that demonstrates genuine care for the well-being of all key constituencies—customers, employees, stockholders, major suppliers, and the communities where the company operates—and tries to satisfy all their legitimate interests simultaneously. No group is ignored, and fairness to all constituencies is a decision-making principle—a commitment often described as "doing the right thing."[13] Pleasing customers and protecting, if not enhancing, the company's long-term well-being is seen as the best way of looking out for the interests of employees, stockholders, suppliers, and communities where the company operates. Management concern for the well-being of employees is a big factor in gaining employee support for

---

[13]Kotter and Heskett, *Corporate Culture and Performance,* p. 52.

change—employees understand that changes in their job assignments are part of the process of adapting to new conditions and that their employment security will not be threatened in the process of adapting to change unless the company's business unexpectedly reverses direction. In cases where workforce downsizing becomes necessary, management concern for employees dictates that separation be handled humanely, making employee departure as pleasant as possible. Management efforts to make the process of adapting to change fair for customers, employees, stockholders, suppliers, and communities where the company operates, keeping adverse impacts to a minimum insofar as possible, breeds acceptance of and support for change among all organization stakeholders.

In less-adaptive cultures where skepticism about the importance of new developments and resistance to change are the norm, managers avoid risk taking and prefer waiting until the fog of uncertainty clears before steering a new course or making fundamental adjustments to their product line or embracing a major new technology.[14] They believe in moving cautiously and conservatively, preferring to follow others rather than take decisive action to be in the forefront of change. In change-resistant cultures, there's a premium placed on not making mistakes, prompting managers to lean toward safe, "don't-rock-the-boat" options that will have only a ripple effect on the status quo, protect or advance their own careers, and guard the interests of their immediate work groups.

Creating a Strong Fit between Strategy and Culture

It is the *strategy maker's* responsibility to select a strategy compatible with the "sacred" or unchangeable parts of prevailing corporate culture. It is the *strategy implementer's* task, once strategy is chosen, to change whatever facets of the corporate culture hinder effective execution.

Changing a Problem Culture   Changing a company's culture to align it with strategy is among the toughest management tasks—easier to talk about than do. Changing problem cultures is very difficult because of the heavy anchor of deeply held values and habits—people cling emotionally to the old and familiar. It takes concerted management action over a period of time to replace an unhealthy culture with a healthy culture or to root out certain unwanted cultural obstacles and instill ones that are more strategy-supportive.

> Once a culture is established, it is difficult to change.

The first step is to diagnose which facets of the present culture are strategy-supportive and which are not. Then, managers have to talk openly and forthrightly to all concerned about those aspects of the culture that have to be changed. The talk has to be followed swiftly by visible, aggressive actions to modify the culture—actions that everyone will understand are intended to establish a new culture more in tune with the strategy. The menu of culture-changing actions includes revising policies and procedures in ways that will help drive cultural change, altering incentive compensation (to reward the desired cultural behavior), visibly praising and recognizing people who display the new cultural traits, recruiting and hiring new managers and employees who have the desired cultural values and can serve as role models for the desired cultural behavior, replacing key executives who are strongly associated with the old culture, and taking every opportunity to communicate to employees the basis for cultural change and its benefits to all concerned.

---

[14]Ibid., p. 50.

Sometimes executives succeed in changing the values and behaviors of small groups of managers and even whole departments or divisions, only to find the changes eroded over time by the actions of the rest of the organization. What is communicated, praised, supported, and penalized by an entrenched majority undermines the new emergent culture and halts its progress. Executives, despite revamping the formal organization, bringing in managers from the outside, introducing new technologies, and opening new facilities, can still fail at altering embedded cultural traits and behaviors because of skepticism about the new directions and covert resistance to altering traditional methods.

Symbolic Culture-Changing Actions   Managerial actions to tighten the culture–strategy fit need to be both symbolic and substantive. Symbolic actions are valuable for the signals they send about the kinds of behavior and performance strategy-implementers wish to encourage. The most important symbolic actions are those that top executives take to serve as role models—leading cost reduction efforts by curtailing executive perks; emphasizing the importance of responding to customers' needs by requiring all officers and executives to spend a significant portion of each week talking with customers and understanding their requirements; and initiating efforts to alter policies and practices identified as hindrances in executing the new strategy. Another category of symbolic actions includes the events organizations hold to designate and honor people whose actions and performance exemplify what is called for in the new culture. Many universities give outstanding teacher awards each year to symbolize their commitment to and esteem for instructors who display exceptional classroom talents. Numerous businesses have employee-of-the-month awards. The military has a long-standing custom of awarding ribbons and medals for exemplary actions. Mary Kay Cosmetics awards an array of prizes—from ribbons to pink automobiles—to its beauty consultants for reaching various sales plateaus.

> Awards ceremonies, role models, and symbols are a fundamental part of culture-shaping and reshaping efforts.

The best companies and the best executives expertly use symbols, role models, ceremonial occasions, and group gatherings to tighten the strategy–culture fit. Low-cost leaders like Wal-Mart and Nucor are renowned for their spartan facilities, executive frugality, intolerance of waste, and zealous control of costs. Executives sensitive to their role in promoting strategy–culture fits make a habit of appearing at ceremonial functions to praise individuals and groups that "get with the program." They honor individuals who exhibit cultural norms and reward those who achieve strategic milestones. They participate in employee training programs to stress strategic priorities, values, ethical principles, and cultural norms. Every group gathering is seen as an opportunity to repeat and ingrain values, praise good deeds, reinforce cultural norms, and promote changes that assist strategy execution. Sensitive executives make sure that current decisions and policy changes will be construed by organizational members as consistent with cultural values and supportive of the company's new strategic direction.[15]

Substantive Culture-Changing Actions   While being out front personally and symbolically leading the push for new behaviors and communicating the reasons for new approaches is crucial, strategy implementers have to convince all those concerned that the culture-changing effort is more than cosmetic. Talk and symbolism have to be complemented by substantive actions and real movement. The actions taken have to be credible, highly visible, and unmistakably indicative of the seriousness of

---

[15]Judy D. Olian and Sara L. Rynes, "Making Total Quality Work: Aligning Organizational Processes, Performance Measures, and Stakeholders," *Human Resource Management* 30, no. 3 (Fall 1991), p. 324.

management's commitment to new strategic initiatives and the associated cultural changes. There are several ways to accomplish this. One is to engineer some quick successes that highlight the benefits of strategy–culture changes, thus making enthusiasm for the changes contagious. However, instant results are usually not as important as having the will and patience to create a solid, competent team psychologically committed to pursuing the strategy in a superior fashion. The strongest signs that management is truly committed to creating a new culture include replacing old-culture traditionalist managers with "new-breed" managers, changing long-standing policies and operating practices that are dysfunctional or that impede new initiatives, undertaking major reorganizational moves that bring structure into better alignment with strategy, tying compensation incentives directly to the new measures of strategic performance, and making major budgetary reallocations that shift substantial resources from old-strategy projects and programs to new-strategy projects and programs.

Implanting the needed culture-building values and behavior depends on a sincere, sustained commitment by the chief executive coupled with extraordinary persistence in reinforcing the culture at every opportunity through both word and deed. Neither charisma nor personal magnetism is essential. However, personally talking to many departmental groups about the reasons for change *is* essential; organizational changes are seldom accomplished successfully from an office. Moreover, creating and sustaining a strategy-supportive culture is a job for the whole management team. Major cultural change requires many initiatives from many people. Senior officers, department heads, and middle managers have to reiterate values, "walk the talk," and translate the organization's philosophy into everyday practice. In addition, for the culture-building effort to be successful, strategy implementers must enlist the support of firstline supervisors and employee opinion leaders, convincing them of the merits of practicing and enforcing cultural norms at the lowest levels in the organization. Until a big majority of employees join the new culture and share an emotional commitment to its basic values and behavioral norms, there's considerably more work to be done in both instilling the culture and tightening the culture–strategy fit.

The task of making culture supportive of strategy is not a short-term exercise. It takes time for a new culture to emerge and prevail; it's unrealistic to expect an overnight transformation. The bigger the organization and the greater the cultural shift needed to produce a culture–strategy fit, the longer it takes. In large companies, changing the corporate culture in significant ways can take two to five years. In fact, it is usually tougher to reshape a deeply ingrained culture that is not strategy-supportive than it is to instill a strategy-supportive culture from scratch in a brand-new organization.

Building Ethics into the Culture

A strong corporate culture founded on ethical business principles and moral values is a vital driving force behind continued strategic success. Many executives are convinced that *a company must care about how it does business*; otherwise a company's reputation, and ultimately its performance, is put at risk. Corporate ethics and values programs are not window dressing; they are typically undertaken to create an environment of strongly held values and convictions and to make ethical conduct a way of life. Moral values and high ethical standards nurture the corporate culture in a very positive way—they connote integrity, "doing the right thing," and genuine concern for stakeholders. *Value statements serve as a cornerstone for culture building; a code of ethics*

An ethical corporate culture has a positive impact on a company's long-term strategic success; an unethical culture can undermine it.

table 13.1   Topics Frequently Covered in Value Statements and Codes of Ethics

Topics Covered in Values Statements	Topics Covered in Codes of Ethics
• Importance of customers and customer service • Commitment to quality • Commitment to innovation • Respect for the individual employee and the duty the company has to employees • Importance of honesty, integrity, and ethical standards • Duty to stockholders • Duty to suppliers • Corporate citizenship • Importance of protecting the environment	• Honesty and observance of the law • Conflicts of interest • Fairness in selling and marketing practices • Using inside information and securities trading • Supplier relationships and procurement practices • Payments to obtain business/Foreign Corrupt Practices Act • Acquiring and using information about others • Political activities • Use of company assets, resources, and property • Protection of proprietary information • Pricing, contracting, and billing

serves as a cornerstone for developing a corporate conscience.[16] Table 13.1 indicates the kinds of topics such statements cover.

Companies establish values and ethical standards in a number of different ways.[17] Tradition-steeped companies with a rich folklore rely heavily on word-of-mouth indoctrination and the power of tradition to instill values and enforce ethical conduct. But many companies today convey their values and codes of ethics to stakeholders and interested parties in their annual reports, on their websites, and in documents provided to all employees. They are hammered in at orientation courses for new employees and in refresher courses for managers and employees. The trend of making stakeholders aware of a company's commitment to ethical business conduct is partly attributable to greater management understanding of the role these statements play in culture building and partly attributable to a growing trend by consumers to search out "ethical" products, a greater emphasis on corporate social responsibility by large investors, and increasing political and legal pressures on companies to behave ethically.

However, there is a considerable difference between saying the right things (having a well-articulated corporate values statement or code of ethics) and truly managing a company in an ethical and socially responsible way. Companies that are truly committed to ethical conduct make ethical behavior *a fundamental component of their corporate culture.* They put a stake in the ground, explicitly stating what the company intends and expects. Values statements and codes of ethical conduct are used as benchmarks for judging both company policies and individual conduct. Illustration Capsule 54 presents the Johnson & Johnson Credo, one of the most publicized and celebrated codes of ethics among U.S. companies; J&J's CEO has called the credo "the unifying

---

[16]For a discussion of the strategic benefits of formal statements of corporate values, see John Humble, David Jackson, and Alan Thomson, "The Strategic Power of Corporate Values," *Long Range Planning* 27, no. 6 (December 1994), pp. 28–42. For a study of the status of formal codes of ethics in large U.S. corporations, see Patrick E. Murphy, "Corporate Ethics Statements: Current Status and Future Prospects," *Journal of Business Ethics* 14 (1995), pp. 727–40.

[17]The Business Roundtable, *Corporate Ethics: A Prime Asset,* February 1988, pp. 4–10.

illustration capsule 54
The Johnson & Johnson Credo

- We believe our first responsibility is to the doctors, nurses, and patients, to mothers and all others who use our products and services.
- In meeting their needs everything we do must be of high quality.
- We must constantly strive to reduce our costs in order to maintain reasonable prices.
- Customers' orders must be serviced promptly and accurately.
- Our suppliers and distributors must have an opportunity to make a fair profit.
- We are responsible to our employees, the men and women who work with us throughout the world.
- Everyone must be considered as an individual.
- We must respect their dignity and recognize their merit.
- They must have a sense of security in their jobs.
- Compensation must be fair and adequate, and working conditions clean, orderly, and safe.
- Employees must feel free to make suggestions and complaints.
- There must be equal opportunity for employment, development, and advancement for those qualified.

- We must provide competent management, and their actions must be just and ethical.
- We are responsible to the communities in which we live and work and to the world community as well.
- We must be good citizens—support good works and charities and bear our fair share of taxes.
- We must encourage civic improvements and better health and education.
- We must maintain in good order the property we are privileged to use, protecting the environment and natural resources.
- Our final responsibility is to our stockholders.
- Business must make a sound profit.
- We must experiment with new ideas.
- Research must be carried on, innovative programs developed, and mistakes paid for.
- New equipment must be purchased, new facilities provided, and new products launched.
- Reserves must be created to provide for adverse times.
- When we operate according to these principles, the stockholders should realize a fair return.

Source: 1982 Annual Report and company website.

force for our corporation." Illustration Capsule 55 presents the ethics and values statements for Lockheed Martin, Pfizer, and J. M. Smucker.

Once values and ethical standards have been formally set forth, they must be institutionalized and ingrained in the company's policies, practices, and actual conduct. Implementing the values and code of ethics entails several actions:

> Values and ethical standards must not only be explicitly stated but must also be ingrained into the corporate culture.

- Incorporation of the statement of values and the code of ethics into employee training and educational programs.
- Explicit attention to values and ethics in recruiting and hiring to screen out applicants who do not exhibit compatible character traits.
- Communication of the values and ethics code to all employees and explaining compliance procedures.
- Management involvement and oversight, from the CEO down to firstline supervisors.
- Strong endorsements by the CEO.
- Word-of-mouth indoctrination.

illustration capsule 55
Corporate Ethics and Values Statements at Lockheed Martin, Pfizer, and J. M. Smucker

LOCKHEED MARTIN
Our Value Statements

- *Ethics*—We will be well informed in the regulations, rules, and compliance issues that apply to our businesses around the world. We will apply this knowledge to our conduct as responsible employees of Lockheed Martin, and will adhere to the highest standards of ethical conduct in all that we do.

- *Excellence*—The pursuit of superior performance infuses every Lockheed Martin activity. We excel at meeting challenging commitments even as we achieve total customer satisfaction. We demonstrate leadership by advancing new technologies, innovative manufacturing techniques, enhanced customer service, inspired management, and the application of best practices throughout our organization. Each of us leads through our individual contributions to Lockheed Martin's core purpose.

- *"Can-Do"*—We demonstrate individual leadership through a positive approach to every task, a "can-do" spirit, and a restless determination to continually improve upon our personal bests. We aggressively pursue new business, determined to add value for our customers with ingenuity, determination and a positive attitude. We utilize our ability to combine strength with speed in responding enthusiastically to every new opportunity and every new challenge.

- *Integrity*—Each of us brings to the workplace personal values which guide us to meet our commitments to customers, suppliers, colleagues, and others with whom we interact. We embrace truthfulness and trust, and we treat everyone with dignity and respect—as we wish to be treated ourselves.

- *People*—Outstanding people make Lockheed Martin unique. Success in rapidly changing markets requires that we continuously learn and grow as individuals and as an organization. We embrace lifelong learning through individual initiative, combined with company-sponsored education and development programs, as well as challenging work and growth opportunities.

- *Teamwork*—We multiply the creativity, talents, and contributions of both individuals and businesses by focusing on team goals. Our teams assume collective accountability for their actions, share trust and leadership, embrace diversity, and accept responsibility for prudent risk-taking. Each of us succeeds individually . . . when we as a team achieve success.

Our Ethical Principles

- *Honesty*—To be truthful in all our endeavors; to be honest and forthright with one another and with our customers, communities, suppliers, and shareholders.

- *Integrity*—To say what we mean, to deliver what we promise, and to stand for what is right.

- *Respect*—To treat one another with dignity and fairness, appreciating the diversity of our workforce and the uniqueness of each employee.

- *Trust*—To build confidence through teamwork and open, candid communication.

- *Responsibility*—To speak up—without fear of retribution—and report concerns in the workplace, including violations of laws, regulations and company policies, and seek clarification and guidance whenever there is doubt.

- *Citizenship*—To obey all the laws of the United States and the other countries in which we do business and to do our part to make the communities in which we live better.

PFIZER, INC.

To fulfill our purpose and achieve our mission, we abide by the enduring values that are the foundation of our business:

- *Integrity*—We demand of ourselves and others the highest ethical standards, and our products and processes will be of the highest quality. Our conduct as a company, and as individuals within it, will always reflect the highest standards of integrity. We will demonstrate open, honest, and ethical behavior in all dealings with customers, clients, colleagues, suppliers, partners, the public, and governments. The Pfizer name is a source of pride to us and should inspire trust in all with whom we come in contact. We must do more than simply do things right—we must also do the right thing.

- *Respect for People*—We recognize that people are the cornerstone of Pfizer's success. We come from many

illustration capsule 55

(continued)

different countries and cultures, and we speak many languages. We value our diversity as a source of strength. We are proud of Pfizer's history of treating employees with respect and dignity and are committed to building upon this tradition.

We listen to the ideas of our colleagues and respond appropriately. We seek a business environment that fosters personal and professional growth and achievement. We recognize that communication must be frequent and candid and that we must support others with the tools, training, and authority they need to succeed in achieving their responsibilities, goals, and objectives.

- *Teamwork*—We know that to be a successful company we must work together, frequently transcending organizational and geographic boundaries to meet the changing needs of our customers.

We want all of our colleagues to contribute to the best of their ability, individually and in teams. Teamwork improves the quality of decisions and increases the likelihood that good decisions will be acted upon. Teamwork sustains a spirit of excitement, fulfillment, pride, and passion for our business, enabling us to succeed in all of our endeavors and continually learn as individuals and as a corporation.

- *Performance*—We strive for continuous improvement in our performance. When we commit to doing something, we will do it in the best, most complete, most efficient, and most timely way possible. Then we will try to think of ways to do it better the next time. We will measure our performance carefully, ensuring that integrity and respect for people are never compromised. We will compete aggressively, establishing challenging but achievable targets and rewarding performance against those targets. We wish to attract the highest caliber employees, providing them with opportunities to develop to their full potential and to share in the success that comes from winning in the marketplace.

- *Innovation*—Innovation is the key to improving health and sustaining Pfizer growth and profitability. The quest for innovative solutions should invigorate all of our core businesses and pervade the Pfizer community worldwide.

In our drive to innovate, we support well-conceived risk-taking and understand that it will not always lead to success. We embrace creativity and consistently pursue new opportunities. We look for ways to make our research and development capabilities, our products and services more useful to our customers, and our business practices, processes, and systems more efficient and effective. We listen to and collaborate with our customers to identify and make widely available potential new products.

- *Customer Focus*—We are deeply committed to meeting the needs of our customers and constantly focus on customer satisfaction. We take genuine interest in the welfare of our customers, whether internal or external. We recognize that we can prosper only if we anticipate and meet customer needs, respond quickly to changing conditions, and fulfill customer expectations better than our competitors. We seek long-term relationships based on our comprehensive understanding of all our customers' needs and on the value we provide through superior products and services.

- *Leadership*—Leaders advance teamwork by imparting a clarity of purpose, a shared sense of goals, and a joint commitment to excellence. Leaders empower those around them by sharing knowledge and authority and by recognizing and rewarding outstanding individual effort. We are dedicated to providing opportunities for leadership at all levels in our organization.

Leaders are those who step forward to achieve difficult goals, envisioning what needs to happen and motivating others. They utilize the particular talents of every individual and resolve conflict by helping others to focus on common goals. Leaders build relationships with others throughout the company to share ideas, provide support, and help assure that the best practices prevail throughout Pfizer.

- *Community*—We play an active role in making every country and community in which we operate a better place to live and work. We know that the ongoing vitality of our host nations and localities has a direct impact on the long-term health of our business. As a company and as individuals, we give of ourselves to serve the needs of communities and people in need throughout the world.

THE J. M. SMUCKER COMPANY

Our Basic Beliefs are an expression of the values and principles that guide corporate and individual behavior at the

(continued)

illustration capsule 55

(concluded)

Company. These Basic Beliefs are deeply rooted in the philosophy and heritage of the Company's founder, J. M. Smucker. Present policies are based on these time-honored principles:

- *Quality*—Quality applies to our products, our manufacturing methods, our marketing efforts, our people, and our relationships with each other. We will only produce and sell products that enhance the quality of life and well-being. These will be the highest quality products offered in our respective markets because the Company's growth and business success have been built on quality. We will continuously look for ways to achieve daily improvements which will, over time, result in consistently superior products and performance.

    At The J. M. Smucker Company, quality comes first. Sales growth and earnings will follow.

- *People*—We will be fair with our employees and maintain an environment that encourages personal responsibility within the Company and the community. In return, we expect our employees to be responsible for not only their individual jobs but for the Company as a whole.

    We will seek employees who are committed to preserving and enhancing the values and principles inherent in our Basic Beliefs through their own actions. We firmly believe that the highest quality people produce the highest quality products and services; that the highest business ethics require the highest personal ethics; and that responsible people produce exceptional results.

- *Ethics*—The same strong, ethical values on which our Company was founded provide the standards by which we conduct our business as well as ourselves. We accept nothing less regardless of the circumstances. Therefore, we will maintain the highest standards of business ethics with our customers, suppliers, employees, and shareholders and with the communities in which we work.

- *Growth*—Along with day-to-day operations, we are also concerned with the potential of our Company. Growing is reaching for that potential whether it be in the development of new products and new markets, the discovery of new manufacturing or management techniques, or the personal growth and development of our people and their ideas.

    We are committed to strong balanced growth that will protect or enhance our consumer franchise within prudent financial parameters. We want to provide a fair return for our stockholders on their investment in us.

- *Independence*—We have a strong commitment to stewardship of the Smucker name and heritage. We will remain an independent company because of our desire and motivation to control our own direction and succeed on our own. We strive to be an example of a company which is successful by operating under these Basic Beliefs within the free enterprise system.

These Basic Beliefs regarding quality, people, ethics, growth and independence have served as a strong foundation throughout our history, and will continue to be the basis for future strategy, plans, and achievements.

Sources: Company websites and annual reports.

Illustration Capsule 56 describes the innovative ways that SAS Institute, one of the world's leading software providers, embedded its values into its culture and operating practices.

In the case of codes of ethics, special attention must be given to sections of the company that are particularly vulnerable—procurement, sales, and political lobbying. Employees who deal with external parties are in ethically sensitive positions and often are drawn into compromising situations. Company personnel assigned to subsidiaries in foreign countries can find themselves trapped in ethical dilemmas if bribery and corruption of public officials are common practices or if suppliers or customers are accustomed to kickbacks of one kind or another.

illustration capsule 56
SAS Fosters a Culture of Caring

In today's frenzied high-tech business world when it seems routine to work 18 hours a day (and to expect your employees to do so), to decline vacations, and to hire more and more child care for your kids, SAS Institute cofounders Jim Goodnight and John Sall are decidedly unfashionable. They believe that their employees should have lives outside their jobs. They also believe that employees should be motivated to work because they love what they do. So they've fostered a corporate culture that supports family values, quality of life, and genuine company loyalty. And they've profited by it.

SAS Institute is the world's largest privately held software specialist, and it isn't even located in Silicon Valley. Instead, the company makes its home in Cary, North Carolina. SAS writes software that enables users to gather and understand data—to cull oceans of data for patterns and meaning. Originally, Jim Goodnight developed the software to analyze agricultural research data in North Carolina. But the software is so flexible and easy to use that today a wide range of businesses rely on it. Marriott Hotels uses it to manage its frequent-visitor program; Merck & Co. uses it to develop new drugs; and the U.S. government uses it to calculate the consumer price index. "At SAS, our mission is to deliver superior software and services that give people the power to make the right decisions," notes the company's mission statement. "We want to be the most valued competitive weapon in business decision making."

The mission statement might appear to be setting up employees for a life of complete dedication to their computer terminals, but in fact, the opposite is true. Employees frequently describe the atmosphere at SAS as "relaxed."

Company headquarters has 36,000 square feet of gym space, outdoor soccer and softball fields, and massage rooms. Weekly classes in golf, African dance, tennis, and tai chi are offered to employees who like to exercise during downtime. SAS also offers child care, as well as a host of other work–life benefits, including a health clinic and a laundry service.

If all of this sounds more like summer camp than work, David Russo, head of human resources, insists that it's not. Instead, incorporating quality-of-life values into the corporate culture is part of a well-thought-out strategy—the point of which is to remove distractions that impede employees from focusing on work. "Jim [Goodnight]'s idea is that if you hire adults and treat them like adults, then they'll behave like adults," explains Russo.

SAS values accountability on the part of its workers—in other words, in giving employees the freedom to manage their lives and their jobs, the company expects them to do exactly that, and to be able to document their performance. "If you're out sick for six months," says Russo, "you'll get cards and flowers, and people will come to cook dinner for you. If you're out sick for six Mondays in a row, you'll get fired. We expect adult behavior."

SAS also values the efforts of individuals, meaning that each employee is responsible for his or her actions. "You're given the freedom, the flexibility, and the resources to do your job," says Kathy Passarella, who trains new R&D employees in computer skills. Because you're treated well, you treat the company well." She notes that, contrary to what one might expect when reading the list of work–life benefits the company provides, "when you walk

(*continued*)

Structuring the Ethics Enforcement Process   Procedures for enforcing ethical standards and handling potential violations have to be developed. The compliance effort must permeate the company, extending into every organizational unit. The attitudes, character, and work history of prospective employees must be scrutinized. Every employee must receive adequate training. Line managers at all levels must give serious and continuous attention to the task of explaining how the values and ethical code apply in their areas. In addition, they must insist that company values and ethical standards become a way of life. In general, instilling values and insisting on ethical conduct must be looked on as a continuous culture-building, culture-nurturing exercise. Whether the effort succeeds or fails depends largely on how well corporate values and ethical standards are visibly integrated into company policies, managerial practices, and actions at all levels.

As a test of your ethics, take the quiz in Illustration Capsule 57 on page 439.

illustration capsule 56

(concluded)

through the halls here, it's rare that you hear people talking about anything but work." That's because SAS has deftly removed the other topics of small talk that might travel along the employee grapevine—worry about reaching a child care center on time, trying to get to and from a gym during lunch, deciding whether to leave work to see a doctor for a cold or a prescription. Without those distractions, employees have no reason not to focus on work—and no excuse for failing to devote 100 percent of their focus and efforts on their jobs during the workday. With freedom comes responsibility at SAS.

The strategy of developing a positive atmosphere in which to work has paid off for SAS. "I believe that a person's surroundings have a lot to do with how a person feels," says Jim Goodnight. "We try to have nice surroundings here." If he sounds like a talk-show psychologist, he doesn't seem to mind. SAS has enjoyed nearly a quarter of a century of double-digit growth; it serves more than 37,000 customers in 111 countries; and 98 percent of the top Fortune 500 companies are SAS customers. The company that has been called *The Good Ship Lollipop* is the envy of many of its competitors. Somehow, its founders have managed to make success fun.

Sources: Company website (www.sas.com), accessed September 6, 2001; Melanie Austria Farmer, "Software Giant Hires First COO in 24 Years," CNET News.com (http://news.cnet.com), September 15, 2000; Chris Fishman, "Sanity Inc.," *Fast Company* (www.fastcompany.com), January 1999.

Building a Spirit of High Performance into the Culture

An ability to instill strong individual commitment to strategic success and to create an atmosphere in which there is constructive pressure to perform is one of the most valuable strategy-implementing/strategy-executing skills. When an organization performs consistently at or near peak capability, the outcome is not only improved strategic success but also an organizational culture permeated with a spirit of high performance. Such a spirit should not be confused with whether employees are happy or satisfied or whether they get along well together, although the latter are certainly desirable conditions. *An organization with a spirit of high performance emphasizes achievement and excellence. Its culture is results-oriented, and it uses people-management practices that inspire workers to do their best.*[18]

> A results-oriented culture that inspires people to do their best is conducive to superior strategy execution.

Companies with a spirit of high performance typically are intensely people-oriented, and they reinforce their concern for individual employees on every conceivable occasion in every conceivable way. They treat employees with dignity and respect, train each employee thoroughly, encourage employees to use their own initiative and creativity in performing their work, set reasonable and clear performance expectations, use the full range of rewards and punishment to enforce high-performance standards, hold managers at every level responsible for developing the people who report to them, and grant employees enough autonomy to stand out, excel, and contribute. Creating a results-oriented organizational culture generally entails making champions out of the people who turn in

---

[18] For a more in-depth discussion of what it takes to create a climate and culture that nurture success, see Benjamin Schneider, Sarah K. Gunnarson, and Kathryn Niles-Jolly, "Creating the Climate and Culture of Success," *Organizational Dynamics,* Summer 1994, pp. 17–29.

illustration capsule 57
A Test of Your Business Ethics

As a gauge of your own ethical and moral standards, take the following quiz and see how you stack up against other members of your class. How do you think your future employer would want you to answer each of these questions—in which instances would an employer be indifferent as to your answers?

---

1. Is it unethical to make up data to justify the introduction of a new product if, when you start to object, your boss tells you to "just do it"?
    _____ Yes _____ No _____ Need more information

2. Do you think that it is acceptable to give your boss a $100 gift to celebrate a birthday or holiday?
    _____ Yes _____ No _____ Need more information

3. Would it be wrong to accept a $100 gift from your boss (who is of the opposite sex) to celebrate your birthday?
    _____ Yes _____ No _____ Need more information

4. Is it unethical to accept an invitation from a supplier to spend a holiday weekend skiing at the supplier company's resort home in Colorado? (Would your answer be different if you were presently considering a proposal from that supplier to purchase $1 million worth of components?)
    _____ Yes _____ No _____ Need more information

5. Is it unethical to give a customer company's purchasing manager free tickets to the Super Bowl if he or she is looking for tickets and is likely to make a large purchase from your company?
    _____ Yes _____ No _____ Need more information

6. Is it unethical to use sick days provided in your company benefits plan as personal days so that you can go shopping or leave early for a weekend vacation?
    _____ Yes _____ No _____ Need more information

7. Would it be wrong to keep quiet if you, as a junior financial analyst, had just calculated that the projected return on a possible project was 18 percent and your boss (a) informed you that no project could be approved without the prospect of a 25 percent return and (b) told you to go back and redo the numbers and "get them right"?
    _____ Yes _____ No _____ Need more information

8. Would it be unethical to allow your supervisor to believe that you were chiefly responsible for the success of a new company initiative if it actually resulted from a team effort or major contributions by a co-worker?
    _____ Yes _____ No _____ Need more information

9. Is it unethical to fail to come forward to support an employee wrongfully accused of misconduct if that person is a source of aggravation for you at work?
    _____ Yes _____ No _____ Need more information

10. Is it wrong to use your employer's staff to prepare invitations for a party that you will give provided clients or customers are among those invited?
    _____ Yes _____ No _____ Need more information

11. Is it wrong to browse the Internet while at work if all your work is done and there is otherwise nothing you ought to be doing? (Would your answer be the same if the websites you visited were pornographic?)
    _____ Yes _____ No _____ Need more information

12. Is it unethical to keep quiet if you are aware that a co-worker is being sexually harassed by his or her boss?
    _____ Yes _____ No _____ Need more information

13. Is there an ethical problem with using your employer's copier to make a small number of copies for personal use (for example, your tax returns, your child's school project, or personal correspondence)?
    _____ Yes _____ No _____ Need more information

14. Is it unethical to install company-owned software on your home computer without the permission of your supervisor and the software vendor?
    _____ Yes _____ No _____ Need more information

15. Is it unethical to okay the shipment of products to a customer that do not meet the customer's specifications without first checking with the customer?
    _____ Yes _____ No _____ Need more information

ANSWERS:

We think a strong case can be made that the answers to questions 1, 3, 4, 5, 6, 7, 8, 9, 10, 11, 12, 13, 14, and 15 are yes and that the answer to question 2 is no. Most employers would consider the answers to questions 10 and 13 to be yes unless company policy allows personal use of company resources under certain specified conditions.

winning performances. Some companies symbolize the value and importance of individual employees by referring to them as Cast Members (Disney), crew members (McDonald's), co-workers (Kinko's and CDW Computer Centers), job-owners (Granite Rock), partners (Starbucks), or associates (Wal-Mart, Lenscrafters, W. L. Gore, Edward Jones, Publix Supermarkets, and Marriott International). Companies like Mary Kay Cosmetics, Tupperware, and McDonald's actively seek out reasons and opportunities to give pins, buttons, badges, and medals for good showings by average performers—the idea being to express appreciation and give a motivational boost to people who stand out in doing "ordinary" jobs. General Electric and 3M Corporation make a point of ceremoniously honoring individuals who believe so strongly in their ideas that they take it on themselves to hurdle the bureaucracy, maneuver their projects through the system, and turn them into improved services, new products, or even new businesses.

What makes a spirit of high performance come alive is a complex network of people-management practices, words, symbols, styles, values, and policies pulling together that produces extraordinary results with ordinary people. The drivers of a spirit of high performance are a belief in the worth of the individual, strong company commitment to job security and promotion from within, managerial practices that encourage employees to exercise individual initiative and creativity in doing their jobs, and pride in doing the "itty-bitty, teeny-tiny things" right.[19] A company that treats its employees well generally benefits from increased teamwork, higher morale, greater loyalty, and increased employee commitment to making a contribution.

While promoting and nurturing a spirit of high performance nearly always accentuates the positive, there are negative reinforcers too. Managers whose units consistently perform poorly have to be replaced. Low-performing workers and people who reject the cultural emphasis on dedication and high performance have to be weeded out or at least moved to out-of-the-way positions. Average performers have to be candidly counseled that they have limited career potential unless they put forth more effort and acquire better skills and work habits.

EXERTING STRATEGIC LEADERSHIP

The litany of good strategic management is simple enough: craft a sound strategic plan, implement it, execute it to the fullest, adjust as needed, win! But it's easier said than done. Exerting take-charge leadership, being a "spark plug," ramrodding things through, and getting things done by coaching others to do them are difficult tasks.[20] Moreover, a strategy manager has many different leadership roles to play: visionary, chief entrepreneur and strategist, chief administrator and strategy implementer, culture builder, resource acquirer and allocator, capabilities builder, process integrator, coach, crisis solver, taskmaster, spokesperson, negotiator, motivator, arbitrator, consensus builder, policy maker, policy enforcer, mentor, and head cheerleader.[21] Sometimes it is

---

[19]Jeffrey Pfeffer, "Producing Sustainable Competitive Advantage through the Effective Management of People," *Academy of Management Executive* 9, no.1 (February 1995), pp. 55–69.

[20]For an excellent survey of the problems and pitfalls in making the transition to a new strategy and to fundamentally new ways of doing business, see John P. Kotter, "Leading Change: Why Transformation Efforts Fail," *Harvard Business Review* 73, no. 2 (March–April 1995), pp. 59–67. See also, Thomas M. Hout and John C. Carter, "Getting It Done: New Roles for Senior Executives," *Harvard Business Review* 73, no. 6 (November–December 1995), pp. 133–45 and Sumantra Ghoshal and Christopher A. Bartlett, "Changing the Role of Top Management: Beyond Structure to Processes," *Harvard Business Review* 73, no. 1 (January–February 1995), pp. 86–96.

[21]For a very insightful and revealing report on how one CEO leads the organizational change process, see Noel Tichy and Ram Charan, "The CEO as Coach: An Interview with Allied Signal's Lawrence A. Bossidy," *Harvard Business Review* 73, no. 2 (March–April 1995), pp. 68–78.

useful to be authoritarian and hardnosed; sometimes it is best to be a perceptive listener and a compromising decision maker; sometimes a strongly participative, collegial approach works best; and sometimes being a coach and adviser is the proper role. Many occasions call for a highly visible role and extensive time commitments, while others entail a brief ceremonial performance with the details delegated to subordinates.

For the most part, major change efforts have to be top-down and vision-driven. Leading change has to start with diagnosing the situation and then deciding which of several ways to handle it. Managers have five leadership roles to play in pushing for good strategy execution:

1. Staying on top of what is happening, closely monitoring progress, ferreting out issues, and learning what obstacles lie in the path of good execution.

2. Promoting a culture and esprit de corps that mobilizes and energizes organizational members to execute strategy in a competent fashion and perform at a high level.

3. Keeping the organization responsive to changing conditions, alert for new opportunities, bubbling with innovative ideas, and ahead of rivals in developing competitively valuable competencies and capabilities.

4. Exercising ethics leadership and insisting that the company conduct its affairs like a model corporate citizen.

5. Pushing corrective actions to improve strategy execution and overall strategic performance.

Staying on Top of How Well Things Are Going

To stay on top of how well the strategy execution process is going, a manager needs to develop a broad network of contacts and sources of information, both formal and informal. The regular channels include talking with key subordinates, attending presentations and meetings, reading reviews of the latest operating results, talking to customers, watching the competitive reactions of rival firms, exchanging e-mail and holding telephone conversations with people in outlying locations, and gathering information firsthand through on-site visits and listening to rank-and-file employees. However, some information is more trustworthy than the rest, and the views and perspectives offered by different people can vary widely. Presentations and briefings by subordinates may represent the truth but not the whole truth. Bad news or problems may be minimized or in some cases not reported at all as subordinates delay conveying failures and problems in hopes that more time will give them room to turn things around. Hence, strategy managers have to make sure that they have accurate information and a feel for the existing situation. They have to confirm whether things are on track, identify problems, learn what obstacles lie in the path of good strategy execution, and develop a basis for determining what, if anything, they can personally do to move the process along.

One way strategy leaders stay on top of things is by making regular visits to the field and talking with many different people at many different levels. The technique of *managing by walking around (MBWA)* is practiced in a variety of styles. Wal-Mart executives have had a long-standing practice of spending two to three days every week visiting Wal-Mart's stores and talking with store managers and employees. Sam Walton, Wal-Mart's founder, insisted, "The key is to get out into the store and listen to what the associates have to say." Jack Welch, CEO of General Electric, not only spends several days each month personally visiting GE operations and talking with major customers but also arranges his schedule so that he can spend time talking with and listening to GE managers from all over the world who are attending classes at the

MBWA is one of the techniques effective leaders use to stay informed on how well strategy implementation and execution are proceeding.

company's leadership development center near GE's headquarters. Some companies have weekly get-togethers in each division (often on Friday afternoons), attended by both executives and employees, to create a regular opportunity for tidbits of information to flow freely between down-the-line employees and executives. In a number of offices, executives operate out of open cubicles in big spaces populated with open cubicles for other office personnel so that they can interact easily and frequently with co-workers. Some manufacturing executives make a point of strolling the factory floor talking with workers and meeting regularly with union officials.

Most managers rightly attach great importance to spending time with people at various company facilities and gathering information and opinions firsthand from diverse sources about how well various aspects of the strategy execution process are going. Such contacts give managers a feel for the progress being made, the problems being encountered, and whether additional resources or different approaches may be needed. Just as important, on-site visits and MBWA provide opportunity to talk informally to many different people at different organizational levels, speak with encouragement, lift spirits, shift attention from the old to the new priorities, and create some excitement—all of which generate positive energy and help mobilize organizational efforts behind strategy execution.

Leading the Effort to Establish a Strategy-Supportive Culture

Managers with responsibility for crafting and executing strategy have to be out front in establishing a strategy-supportive organizational climate and culture. When major strategic changes are being implemented, a manager's time is best spent personally leading the changes for whatever cultural adjustments are needed. Showing gradual incremental progress is often not enough. Conservative incrementalism seldom leads to major cultural adaptations; more usually, gradualism is defeated by the resilience of entrenched cultures and the ability of vested interests to thwart or minimize the impact of piecemeal change. Only with bold leadership and concerted action on many fronts can a company succeed in tackling so large and difficult a task as major cultural change. When only strategic fine-tuning is being implemented, it takes less time and effort to bring values and culture into alignment with strategy, but there is still a lead role for the manager to play in pushing ahead and prodding for continuous improvements.

The single most visible factor that distinguishes successful culture-change efforts from failed attempts is competent leadership at the top. Effective culture-changing leadership has several attributes:[22]

- A "stakeholders-are-king" philosophy that links the need for culture change to the need to serve the long-term best interests of all key constituencies.

- Challenging the status quo with very basic questions: Are we giving customers what they really need and want? Why aren't we taking more business away from rivals? Why do our rivals have lower costs than we do? How can we drive costs out of the business and be more competitive on price? Why can't design-to-market cycle time be halved? Why aren't we moving faster to make better use of the Internet and e-commerce technologies and practices? How can we grow company revenues at 15 percent instead of 10 percent? What can we do to speed up our decision making and shorten response times?

> Successful culture changes have to be personally led by top mangement; it's a task that can't be delegated to others.

---

[22]Kotter and Heskett, *Corporate Culture and Performance,* pp. 84, 144, and 148.

- Creating events where everyone in management is forced to listen to angry customers, dissatisfied strategic allies, alienated employees, or maybe disenchanted stockholders—a tactic that raises awareness levels and helps lay the basis for realistically assessing which traits of the culture support strategy and which do not.

- Making a compelling case for why the company's new direction and a different cultural atmosphere are in the organization's best interests and why individuals and groups should commit themselves to making it happen despite the obstacles. Skeptics have to be convinced that all is not well with the status quo. And the messages of strategic and cultural change have to be repeated at every opportunity to continue to drive the points home.

- Initiating substantive and forceful actions to flush out the undesirable cultural traits and replace them with the desired new ones.

- Recognizing and generously rewarding those who exhibit new cultural norms and who lead successful change efforts—this helps cultivate expansion of the coalition for change.

What organizational leaders say and do plants the seeds of cultural change.

Great power is needed to force major cultural change—to overcome the spring-back resistance of entrenched cultures—and great power normally resides only at the top. But senior executives must not only use the power and influence that come with their position, they must also *lead by example.* For instance, if the organization's strategy involves a drive to become the industry's low-cost producer, senior managers must display frugality in their own actions and decisions: inexpensive decorations in the executive suite, conservative expense accounts and entertainment allowances, a lean staff in the corporate office, scrutiny of budget requests, and so on. The CEO of SAS Airlines, Jan Carlzon, symbolically reinforced the primacy of quality service for business customers by flying coach instead of first class and by giving up his seat to wait-listed travelers.[23] In addition, effective culture-change leaders frequently rely on stories to convey new values, create new role models, and connect the case for change to organization members.

Only top management has the power and organizational influence to bring about major change in a company's culture.

Leading Culture Change Efforts in Multinational and Global Companies In multinational and global companies, where some cross-border diversity in the corporate culture is normal, the leadership requirements of culture-changing efforts are even more complex. Company personnel in different countries sometimes fervently insist on being treated as distinctive individuals or groups, making a one-size-fits-all rationale for cultural change and a common leadership approach potentially inappropriate. Leading cross-border culture-change initiatives requires sensitivity to prevailing cross-border cultural differences, discerning how to adapt the case for cultural change to each situation and discerning when diversity has to be accommodated and when cross-border differences can be and should be narrowed.[24] Many multinational and global companies are finding, however, that most of their core cultural values and beliefs travel well across country borders and strike a chord with managers and workers in many different areas of the world, despite the diversity of local cultures and behavioral norms. AES Corporation, which operates power plants in a growing number of culturally diverse companies across the world, has managed to institute a reasonably uniform corporate culture by relying on a set of corporate values

[23]Olian and Rynes, "Making Total Quality Work," p. 324.
[24]For a discussion of this dimension of leadership, see Alexander and Wilson, "Leading across Cultures: Five Vital Capabilities," pp. 287–94.

and beliefs that are well received in virtually all of the countries where it has plants.[25] At AES, the culture is built around respect for the worth and dignity of individuals, a strong sense of social responsibility and corporate citizenship, respect for the environment, decentralization of authority and decision making to local country managers (most of whom are natives to the country), and heavy reliance on employee empowerment at each of its power plants.

Keeping the Internal Organization Responsive and Innovative

Generating fresh ideas, identifying new opportunities, and developing innovative products and services are not solely managerial tasks. They are organizationwide tasks, particularly in large corporations. One of the toughest parts of exerting strategic leadership is generating a dependable supply of fresh ideas and suggestions for improvement from the rank and file, along with promoting an entrepreneurial spirit among managers and employees. A flexible, responsive, innovative internal environment is critical in fast-moving high-technology industries, in businesses where products have short life cycles and growth depends on new product innovation, in companies with widely diversified business portfolios (where opportunities are varied and scattered), in markets where successful product differentiation depends on out-innovating the competition, and in situations where low-cost leadership hinges on continuous improvement and new ways to drive costs out of the business. Managers cannot mandate such an environment by simply exhorting people to "be creative."

> The faster a company's business environment changes, the more attention managers must pay to keeping the organization innovative and responsive.

Empowering Champions   One useful leadership approach is to take special pains to foster, nourish, and support people who are willing to champion new technologies, new operating practices, better services, new products, and new product applications and are eager for a chance to try turning their ideas into better ways of operating, new product families, new businesses, and even new industries. One year after taking charge at Siemens-Nixdorf Information Systems, Gerhard Schulmeyer produced the first profit in the merged company, which had been losing hundreds of millions of dollars annually since 1991; he credited the turnaround to the creation of 5,000 "change agents," almost 15 percent of the workforce, who volunteered for active roles in the company's change agenda while continuing to perform their regular jobs. As a rule, the best champions are persistent, competitive, tenacious, committed, and fanatic about their idea and seeing it through to success.

> Identifying and empowering champions helps promote an environment of innovation and experimentation.

To promote an organizational climate where champion innovators can blossom and thrive, strategy managers need to do several things:

- Individuals and groups have to be encouraged to be creative, hold informal brainstorming sessions, let their imaginations fly in all directions, and come up with proposals. The culture has to nurture, even celebrate, experimentation and innovation. Everybody must be expected to contribute ideas, exercise initiative, and pursue continuous improvement. The trick is to keep a sense of urgency alive in the business so that people see change and innovation as necessities.

- People with maverick ideas or out-of-the-ordinary proposals have to be tolerated and given room to operate. Above all, would-be champions who advocate radical or different ideas must not be looked on as disruptive or troublesome.

---

[25]Suzy Wetlaufer, "Organizing for Empowerment: An Interview with AES's Roger Sant and Dennis Bakke," *Harvard Business Review* 77, no. 1 (January–February 1999), pp. 110–23.

- Managers have to induce and promote lots of "tries" and be willing to tolerate mistakes and failures. Most ideas don't pan out, but the organization learns from a good attempt even when it fails.

- Strategy managers should be willing to use all kinds of ad hoc organizational forms to support ideas and experimentation—venture teams, task forces, "performance shootouts" among different groups working on competing approaches, informal "bootlegged" projects composed of volunteers, and so on.

- Strategy managers have to see that the rewards for successful champions are large and visible and that people who champion an unsuccessful idea are not punished or sidelined but rather encouraged to try again.

In effect, the leadership task is to create an adaptive, innovative culture that embraces organizational responses to changing conditions rather than fearing the new conditions or seeking to minimize them. Companies with conspicuously innovative cultures include Sony, 3M, Nokia, Amazon.com, W. L. Gore, Dell Computer, and Enron.

Leading the Process of Developing New Capabilities   Often, effectively responding to changing customer preferences and competitive conditions requires top management intervention. Senior management usually has to lead the effort because core competencies and competitive capabilities typically reside in the combined efforts of different work groups, departments, and collaborative allies. The tasks of managing human skills, knowledge bases, and intellect and then integrating them to forge competitively advantageous competencies and capabilities is an exercise best orchestrated by senior managers who appreciate their strategy-implementing significance and who have the clout to enforce the necessary networking and cooperation among individuals, groups, departments, and external allies.

Effective company managers try to anticipate changes in customer-market requirements and proactively build new competencies and capabilities that offer a competitive edge over rivals. Senior managers are in the best position to see the need and potential of new capabilities and then to play a lead role in the capability-building, resource-strengthening process. Proactively building new competencies and capabilities ahead of rivals to gain a competitive edge is strategic leadership of the best kind, but strengthening the company's resource base in reaction to newly developed capabilities of pioneering rivals occurs more frequently.

Exercising Ethics Leadership and Insisting on Good Corporate Citizenship

For an organization to display consistently high ethical standards, the CEO and those around the CEO must be openly and unequivocally committed to ethical and moral conduct. It is never enough for senior executives to assume activities are being conducted ethically, nor can it be assumed that employees understand they are expected to act with integrity. Leading the enforcement of ethical behavior means iterating and reiterating to employees that it is their duty not only to observe the company's ethical codes but also to report ethical violations. While ethically conscious companies have provisions for disciplining violators, *the main purpose of enforcement is to encourage compliance rather than administer punishment.*

There are several concrete things managers can do to exercise ethics leadership. First and foremost, they must set an excellent ethical example in their own behavior and establish a tradition of integrity. Company decisions have to be seen as ethical—actions speak louder than words. Second, managers and employees have to be educated about what is ethical and what is not; ethics training programs may have to be established and

It's a constant organization-building challenge to broaden, deepen, or modify organization capabilities and resource strengths in response to ongoing customer-market changes.

High ethical standards cannot be enforced without the open and unequivocal commitment of the chief executive.

Managers are an organization's ethics teachers—what they do and say sends signals and what they don't do and don't say sends signals.

gray areas pointed out and discussed. Everyone must be encouraged to raise issues with ethical dimensions, and such discussions should be treated as a legitimate topic. Third, top management should regularly reiterate its unequivocal support of the company's ethical code and take a strong stand on ethical issues. Fourth, top management must be prepared to act as the final arbiter on hard calls; this means removing people from key positions or terminating them when they are guilty of a violation. It also means reprimanding those who have been lax in monitoring and enforcing ethical compliance. Failure to act swiftly and decisively in punishing ethical misconduct is interpreted as a lack of real commitment.

If a company is really serious about enforcing ethical behavior, it probably needs to do two things:

- Conduct an annual audit of each manager's efforts to uphold ethical standards and formal reports on the actions taken by managers to remedy deficient conduct.
- Require all employees to sign a statement annually certifying that they have complied with the company's code of ethics.

See Illustration Capsule 58 for a discussion of the actions Lockheed Martin took when it was fined nearly $25 million for an ethics violation and its status as a major U.S. defense contractor was put in jeopardy.

Corporate Citizenship and Social Responsibility: Another Dimension of Model Ethical Behavior   Strong enforcement of a corporate code of ethics by itself is not sufficient to make a company a good corporate citizen. Business leaders who want their companies to be regarded as exemplary corporate citizens not only must see that their companies operate ethically but also must display a social conscience in decisions that affect stakeholders, especially employees, the communities in which they operate, and society at large. Corporate citizenship and socially responsible decision making are demonstrated in a number of ways: having family-friendly employment practices, operating a safe workplace, taking special pains to protect the environment (beyond what is required by law), taking an active role in community affairs, interacting with community officials to minimize the impact of layoffs or hiring large numbers of new employees (which could put a strain on local schools and utility services), and being a generous supporter of charitable causes and projects that benefit society. For example, Chick-fil-A, an Atlanta-based fast-food chain with 700 outlets, has a charitable foundation, supports 10 foster homes and a summer camp, funds two scholarship programs, and participates in a number of one-on-one programs with children.[26] Toys "R" Us supports initiatives addressing the issue of child labor and fair labor practices around the world. Community Pride Food Stores is assisting in revitalizing the inner city of Richmond, Virginia, where the company is based. The owner of Malden Mills Industries in Malden, Massachusetts, kept employees on the company's payroll for months while a fire-razed plant was rebuilt and re-equipped.

What separates companies that make a sincere effort to carry their weight in being good corporate citizens from companies that are content to do only what is legally required of them are strategy leaders who believe strongly in good corporate citizenship. Companies with socially conscious strategy leaders and with cultures where corporate social responsibility is a core value are the most likely to conduct their affairs in a manner befitting a good corporate citizen.

---

[26]Archie B. Carroll, "The Four Faces of Corporate Citizenship," *Business and Society Review* 100/101 (1998), p. 6.

illustration capsule 58

Lockheed Martin's Corrective Actions after Being Fined for Violating U.S. Antibribery Laws

Lockheed Martin Corporation is among the world's leading producers of aeronautics and space systems with 1999 sales of over $25 billion. Since 1914, when the company first delivered aircraft to the U.S. Army Signal Corps, Lockheed has designed and built military aircraft and spacecraft for the U.S. military and its allies, including the P-38 fighter, B-29 bomber, U-2 and SR-71 reconnaissance aircraft, C-130 cargo planes, F-104 Starfighter, F-16 Fighting Falcon, F-22 Raptor, and Titan and Trident missiles. It has been a major contractor on the Mercury, Gemini, Apollo, Skylab, and Shuttle space programs. In 1999 the company's sales to the U.S. government accounted for more than 70 percent of its annual revenues.

Lockheed Martin's status as a U.S. government contractor was jeopardized in 1995 when company officials admitted that the company had conspired to violate U.S. antibribery laws. The infraction occurred in 1990 when Lockheed Martin paid an Egyptian lawmaker $1 million to help the company secure a contract to supply Egypt with C-130 cargo planes. The U.S. government fined Lockheed Martin $24.8 million and placed it on a three-year probationary period during which further ethics violations could bar the company from bidding on government contracts.

After the conviction, Lockheed Martin's CEO and other senior executives engineered the development of a comprehensive ethics compliance program that used the company's computer systems and Internet capabilities to guard against subsequent violations. Software programs like Qwizard and Merlin allow employees to go online to complete mandatory ethics training related to the Lockheed Martin's Code of Ethics and Business Conduct. The system records when employees complete online sessions on such topics as sexual harassment, security, software-license compliance, labor charging, insider trading, and gratuities. The Internet-based training program also allows the company to conduct up-to-the-minute ethics audits to determine how many hours of training have been completed by each of Lockheed Martin's 170,000 employees.

Lockheed Martin's ethics software programs also provide company managers with a variety of statistics related to ethics violations that do occur at the company. The system compiles data and prepares reports concerning detected violations like misuse of company resources, conflicts of interest, and security breaches. In addition, the system gives an accounting of the number of Lockheed Martin employees discharged, suspended, and reprimanded for ethics violations. The information maintained by Lockheed Martin's systems has aided both managers and the U.S. government in assessing the state of business ethics at the company.

Lockheed Martin's renewed commitment to honesty, integrity, respect, trust, responsibility, and citizenship and its method for monitoring ethics compliance not only reduced the likelihood of being barred from the defense contracting business but also paved the way for the company to receive the 1998 American Business Ethics Award. Upon receiving the award, the company's chairman and CEO Vance Coffman said, "At Lockheed Martin, we have stressed that the first and most important unifying principle guiding us is ethical conduct, every day and everywhere we do business. Receiving the American Business Ethics Award is a strong signal that we are achieving our goal of putting our Corporation on a firm ethical foundation for the challenges of the 21st Century."

Sources: Lockheed Martin website; and *The Wall Street Journal*, October 21, 1999, p. B1.

Leading the Process of Making Corrective Adjustments

The leadership challenge here is twofold: deciding when to make adjustments and deciding what adjustments to make. Both decisions are a normal and necessary part of a strategy manager's job since no strategic plan and no scheme for implementing and executing strategy can foresee all the events and problems that will arise. There comes a time at every company when managers have to alter the company's direction, revise objectives, modify strategy, or fine-tune the approaches to strategy execution.

The *process* of making corrective adjustments varies according to the situation. In a crisis, the typical leadership approach is to have key subordinates gather information,

> Corrective adjustments in the company's approach to executing strategy are normal and have to be made as needed.

identify and evaluate options (crunching whatever numbers may be appropriate), and perhaps prepare a preliminary set of recommended actions for consideration. The strategy leader then usually meets with key subordinates and personally presides over extended discussions of the proposed responses, trying to build a quick consensus among members of the executive inner circle. If no consensus emerges and action is required immediately, the burden falls on the strategy manager to choose the response and urge its support.

When the situation allows managers to proceed more deliberately in deciding when to make changes and what changes to make, strategy managers seem to prefer a process of incrementally solidifying commitment to a particular course of action.[27] The process that managers go through in deciding on corrective adjustments is essentially the same for both proactive and reactive changes: they sense needs, gather information, broaden and deepen their understanding of the situation, develop options and explore their pros and cons, put forth action proposals, generate partial (comfort-level) solutions, build a managerial consensus, and finally formally adopt an agreed-on course of action.[28] The time frame for deciding what corrective changes in vision, objectives, strategies, capabilities, implementation/execution approaches to initiate can take a few hours, a few days, a few weeks, or even a few months if the situation is particularly complicated. Success usually hinges on thorough analysis of the situation and the exercise of good business judgment.

All this, once again, highlights the fundamental nature of strategic management: the job of crafting, implementing, and executing strategy is a five-task process with much looping and recycling to fine-tune and adjust strategic visions, objectives, strategies, capabilities, implementation approaches, and cultures to fit one another and to fit changing circumstances. The process is continuous, and the conceptually separate acts of crafting and executing strategy blur and join together in real-world situations. The best tests of good strategic leadership are whether the company has a good strategy and whether that strategy is being competently executed. If these two conditions exist, the chances are excellent that the company is improving its financial and strategic performance, is capable of adapting to multiple changes, and is a good place to work.

key|points

Building a strategy-supportive corporate culture is important to successful strategy execution because it produces a work climate and organizational esprit de corps that thrive on meeting performance targets and being part of a winning effort. An organization's culture emerges from why and how it does things the way it does, the values and beliefs that senior managers espouse, the ethical standards expected of organization members, the tone and philosophy underlying key policies, and the traditions the organization maintains. Culture thus concerns the atmosphere and feeling a company has and the style in which it gets things done.

Very often, the elements of company culture originate with a founder or other early influential leaders who articulate the values, beliefs, and principles to which the company should adhere, and that then get incorporated into company policies, a creed or values statement, strategies, and operating practices. Over time, these values and practices become shared by company employees and managers. Cultures are perpetuated as new leaders act to reinforce them, as new employees are encouraged to adopt

---

[27]James Brian Quinn, *Strategies for Change: Logical Incrementalism,* Homewood, IL: Richard D. Irwin, 1980, pp. 20–22.
[28]Ibid., p. 146.

and follow them, as stories of people and events illustrating core values and practices are told and retold, and as organization members are honored and rewarded for displaying cultural norms.

Company cultures vary widely in strength and in makeup. Some cultures are strongly embedded, while others are weak and fragmented. Some cultures are unhealthy; these are often dominated by self-serving politics, resistance to change, and inward focus. Such cultural traits are often precursors to declining company performance. In fast-changing business environments, adaptive cultures are best because people tend to accept and support company efforts to adapt to environmental change; the work climate in adaptive-culture companies is receptive to new ideas, experimentation, innovation, new strategies, and new operating practices provided such changes are compatible with core values and beliefs. One significant defining trait of adaptive cultures is that top management genuinely cares about the well-being of all key constituencies—customers, employees, stockholders, major suppliers, and the communities where it operates—and tries to satisfy all their legitimate interests simultaneously.

The philosophy, goals, and practices implicit or explicit in a new strategy may or may not be compatible with a firm's culture. A close strategy–culture alignment promotes implementation and good execution; a mismatch poses real obstacles. Changing a company's culture, especially a strong one with traits that don't fit a new strategy's requirements, is one of the toughest management challenges. Changing a culture requires competent leadership at the top. It requires symbolic actions and substantive actions that unmistakably indicate serious commitment on the part of top management. The stronger the fit between culture and strategy, the less managers have to depend on policies, rules, procedures, and supervision to enforce what people should and should not do; rather, cultural norms are so well observed that they automatically guide behavior.

Healthy corporate cultures are also grounded in ethical business principles, moral values, and socially responsible decision making. Such standards connote integrity, "doing the right thing," and genuine concern for stakeholders and for how the company does business. To be effective, corporate ethics and values programs have to become a way of life through training, strict compliance and enforcement procedures, and reiterated management endorsements. Moreover, top managers must practice what they preach, serving as role models for ethical behavior, values-driven decision making, and a social conscience.

Successful managers do a number of things to exercise strategy-executing leadership. They keep a finger on the organization's pulse by spending considerable time outside their offices, listening and talking to organization members, coaching, cheerleading, and picking up important information. They take pains to reinforce the corporate culture through the things they say and do. They encourage people to be creative and innovative in order to keep the organization responsive to changing conditions, alert to new opportunities, and anxious to pursue fresh initiatives. They support champions of new approaches or ideas who are willing to stick their necks out and try something innovative. They work hard at building consensus on how to proceed, what to change, and what not to change. They enforce high ethical standards and insist on socially responsible corporate decision making. And they actively push corrective actions to improve strategy execution and overall strategic performance.

Because each instance of executing strategy occurs under different organizational circumstances, a strategy implementer's action agenda always needs to be situation-specific—there's no neat generic procedure to follow. And, as we said at the beginning, executing strategy is an action-oriented, make-the-right-things-happen task that challenges a manager's ability to lead and direct organizational change, create or reinvent business processes, manage and motivate people, and achieve performance targets. If you now better understand the nature of the challenge, the range of available approaches, the issues that need to be considered, and why the action agenda for implementing and executing strategy sweeps across so many aspects of administrative and managerial work, then we will look on our discussion in these last three chapter as a success.

suggested | readings

Badaracco, Joseph L. *Defining Moments: When Managers Must Choose between Right and Wrong.* Boston: Harvard Business School Press, 1997.

Badaracco, Joe, and Allen P. Webb. "Business Ethics: A View from the Trenches." *California Management Review* 37, no. 2 (Winter 1995), pp. 8–28.

Carroll, Archie B. "The Four Faces of Corporate Citizenship." *Business and Society Review* 100/101 (1998), pp. 1–7.

Clement, Ronald W. "Culture, Leadership, and Power: The Keys to Organizational Change." *Business Horizons* 37, no. 1 (January–February 1994), pp. 33–39.

Driscoll, Dawn-Marie, and W. Michael Hoffman. "Gaining the Ethical Edge: Procedures for Delivering Values-Driven Management." *Long Range Planning* 32, no. 2 (April 1999), pp. 179–89.

Farkas, Charles M., and Suzy Wetlaufer. "The Ways Chief Executive Officers Lead." *Harvard Business Review* 74, no. 3 (May–June 1996), pp. 110–22.

Floyd, Steven W., and Bill Wooldridge. "Managing Strategic Consensus: The Foundation of Effective Implementation." *Academy of Management Executive* 6, no. 4 (November 1992), pp. 27–39.

Ghoshal, Sumantra, and Christopher A. Bartlett. "Changing the Role of Top Management: Beyond Structure to Processes." *Harvard Business Review* 73, no. 1 (January–February 1995), pp. 86–96.

Goffee, Robert, and Gareth Jones. *The Character of a Corporation.* New York: HarperCollins, 1998.

Goleman, Daniel. "What Makes a Leader." *Harvard Business Review* 76, no. 6 (November–December 1998), pp. 92–102.

Hamel, Gary. "Reinvent Your Company." *Fortune* 141, no. 12 (June 12, 2000), pp. 98–118.

Heifetz, Ronald A., and Donald L. Laurie. "The Work of Leadership." *Harvard Business Review* 75, no. 1 (January–February 1997), pp. 124–34.

Kirkpatrick, Shelley A., and Edwin A. Locke. "Leadership: Do Traits Matter?" *Academy of Management Executive* 5, no. 2 (May 1991), pp. 48–60.

Kotter, John P. "What Leaders Really Do." *Harvard Business Review* 68, no. 3 (May–June 1990), pp. 103–11.

———."Leading Change: Why Transformation Efforts Fail." *Harvard Business Review* 73, no. 2 (March–April 1995), pp. 59–67.

Kotter, John P., and James L. Heskett. *Corporate Culture and Performance.* New York: Free Press, 1992.

Miles, Robert H. *Corporate Comeback: The Story of Renewal and Transformation at National Semiconductor.* San Francisco: Jossey-Bass, 1997.

Murphy, Patrick E. "Corporate Ethics Statements: Current Status and Future Prospects." *Journal of Business Ethics* 14 (1995), pp. 727–40.

Paine, Lynn Sharp. "Managing for Organizational Integrity." *Harvard Business Review* 72, no. 2 (March–April 1994), pp. 106–17.

Schneider, Benjamin; Sarah K. Gunnarson; and Kathryn Niles-Jolly. "Creating the Climate and Culture of Success." *Organizational Dynamics* (Summer 1994), pp. 17–29.

Scholz, Christian. "Corporate Culture and Strategy—The Problem of Strategic Fit." *Long Range Planning* 20 (August 1987), pp. 78–87.

part | two

2

Cases in Strategic Management

A Guide to Case Analysis

I keep six honest serving men
(They taught me all I knew);
Their names are What and Why and When;
And How and Where and Who.
—Rudyard Kipling

In most courses in strategic management, students use cases about actual companies to practice strategic analysis and to gain some experience in the tasks of crafting and implementing strategy. A case sets forth, in a factual manner, the events and organizational circumstances surrounding a particular managerial situation. It puts readers at the scene of the action and familiarizes them with all the relevant circumstances. A case on strategic management can concern a whole industry, a single organization, or some part of an organization; the organization involved can be either profit-seeking or not-for-profit. The essence of the student's role in case analysis is to diagnose and size up the situation described in the case and then to recommend appropriate action steps.

WHY USE CASES TO PRACTICE STRATEGIC MANAGEMENT?

A student of business with tact
Absorbed many answers he lacked.
But acquiring a job,
He said with a sob,
"How does one fit answer to fact?"

The above limerick was used some years ago by Professor Charles Gragg to characterize the plight of business students who had no exposure to cases.[1] The truth is that the mere act of listening to lectures and sound advice about managing does little for anyone's management skills. Accumulated managerial wisdom cannot effectively be passed on by lectures and assigned readings alone. If anything had been learned about the practice of management, it is that a storehouse of readymade textbook answers does not exist. Each managerial situation has unique aspects, requiring its own diagnosis, judgment, and tailor-made actions. Cases provide would-be managers with a valuable way to practice wrestling with the actual problems of actual managers in actual companies.

The case approach to strategic analysis is, first and foremost, an exercise in learning by doing. Because cases provide detailed information about conditions and problems of different industries and companies, your task of analyzing company after company and situation after situation has the twin benefit of boosting your analytical skills and exposing you to the ways companies and managers actually do things. Most college students have limited managerial backgrounds and only fragmented knowledge

---

[1]Charles I. Gragg, "Because Wisdom Can't Be Told," in *The Case Method at the Harvard Business School,* ed. M. P. McNair (New York: McGraw-Hill, 1954), p. 11.

about companies and real-life strategic situations. Cases help substitute for on-the-job experience by (1) giving you broader exposure to a variety of industries, organizations, and strategic problems; (2) forcing you to assume a managerial role (as opposed to that of just an onlooker); (3) providing a test of how to apply the tools and techniques of strategic management; and (4) asking you to come up with pragmatic managerial action plans to deal with the issues at hand.

OBJECTIVES OF CASE ANALYSIS

Using cases to learn about the practice of strategic management is a powerful way for you to accomplish five things:[2]

1. Increase your understanding of what managers should and should not do in guiding a business to success.
2. Build your skills in sizing up company resource strengths and weaknesses and in conducting strategic analysis in a variety of industries and competitive situations.
3. Get valuable practice in identifying strategic issues that need to be addressed, evaluating strategic alternatives, and formulating workable plans of action.
4. Enhance your sense of business judgment, as opposed to uncritically accepting the authoritative crutch of the professor or "back-of-the-book" answers.
5. Gaining in-depth exposure to different industries and companies, thereby acquiring something close to actual business experience.

If you understand that these are the objectives of case analysis, you are less likely to be consumed with curiosity about "the answer to the case." Students who have grown comfortable with and accustomed to textbook statements of fact and definitive lecture notes are often frustrated when discussions about a case do not produce concrete answers. Usually, case discussions produce good arguments for more than one course of action. Differences of opinion nearly always exist. Thus, should a class discussion conclude without a strong, unambiguous consensus on what do to, don't grumble too much when you are *not* told what the answer is or what the company actually did. Just remember that in the business world answers don't come in conclusive black-and-white terms. There are nearly always several feasible courses of action and approaches, each of which may work out satisfactorily. Moreover, in the business world, when one elects a particular course of action, there is no peeking at the back of a book to see if you have chosen the best thing to do and no one to turn to for a provably correct answer. The only valid test of management action is *results*. If the results of an action turn out to be good, the decision to take it may be presumed right. If not, then the action chosen was wrong in the sense that it didn't work out.

Hence, the important thing for a student to understand in case analysis is that the managerial exercise of identifying, diagnosing, and recommending builds your skills; discovering the right answer or finding out what actually happened is no more than frosting on the cake. Even if you learn what the company did, you can't conclude that it was necessarily right or best. All that can be said is "Here is what they did . . . "

---

[2]Ibid., pp. 12–14; and D. R. Schoen and Philip A. Sprague, "What Is the Case Method?" in *The Case Method at the Harvard Business School,* ed. M. P. McNair, pp. 78–79.

The point is this: *The purpose of giving you a case assignment is not to cause you to run to the library or surf the Internet to discover what the company actually did but, rather, to enhance your skills in sizing up situations and developing your managerial judgment about what needs to be done and how to do it.* The aim of case analysis is for *you* to become actively engaged in diagnosing the business issues and managerial problems posed in the case, to propose workable solutions, and to explain and defend your assessments—this is how cases provide you with meaningful practice at being a manager.

PREPARING A CASE FOR CLASS DISCUSSION

If this is your first experience with the case method, you may have to reorient your study habits. Unlike lecture courses in which you can get by without preparing intensively for each class and have latitude to work assigned readings and reviews of lecture notes into your schedule, a case assignment requires conscientious preparation before class. You will not get much out of hearing the class discuss a case you haven't read, and you certainly won't be able to contribute anything yourself to the discussion.

To get ready for class discussion of a case, you must study the case, reflect carefully on the situation presented, and develop some reasoned thoughts. Your goal should be to end up with a sound, well-supported analysis of the situation and a sound, defensible set of recommendations. The Case-TUTOR software package that accompanies this edition will assist you in preparing the cases—it contains a set of study questions for each case and step-by-step tutorials to walk you through the process of analyzing and developing reasonable recommendations.

To prepare a case for class discussion, we suggest the following approach:

1. *Skim the case rather quickly to get an overview of the situation it presents.* This quick overview should give you the general flavor of the situation and indicate the kinds of issues and problems you will need to wrestle with. If your instructor has provided you with study questions for the case, now is the time to read them carefully.

2. *Read the case thoroughly to digest the facts and circumstances.* On this reading, try to gain full command of the situation presented in the case. Begin to develop some tentative answers to the study questions from your instructor or in the Case-TUTOR software package, which you can download at the Web site for the text. If your instructor has elected not to give you assignment questions or has not recommended regular use of the Case-TUTOR, then start forming your own picture of the overall situation being described.

3. *Carefully review all the information presented in the exhibits.* Often, there is an important story in the numbers contained in the exhibits. Expect the information in the case exhibits to be crucial enough to materially affect your diagnosis of the situation.

4. *Decide what the strategic issues are.* Until you have identified the strategic issues and problems in the case, you don't know what to analyze, which tools and analytical techniques are called for, or otherwise how to proceed. At times the strategic issues are clear—they are either stated directly in the case or easily inferred from it. At other times you will have to dig out the issues from all the information

given; if so, the study questions and the case preparation exercises provided in the Case-TUTOR software will guide you.

5. *Start your analysis of the issues with some number crunching.* A big majority of strategy cases call for some kind of number crunching—calculating assorted financial ratios to check out the company's financial condition and recent performance, calculating growth rates of sales or profits or unit volume, checking out profit margins and the makeup of the cost structure, and understanding whatever revenue-cost-profit relationships are present. See Table 1 on the next page for a summary of key financial ratios, how they are calculated, and what they show. If you are using Case-TUTOR, some of the number crunching has been computerized and you'll spend most of your time interpreting the growth rates, financial ratios, and other calculations provided.

6. *Apply the concepts and techniques of strategic analysis you have been studying.* Strategic analysis is not just a collection of opinions; rather, it entails applying the concepts and analytical tools described in Chapters 1 through 13 to cut beneath the surface and produce sharp insight and understanding. Every case assigned is strategy related and presents you with an opportunity to usefully apply what you have learned. Your instructor is looking for you to demonstrate that you know *how* and *when* to use the material presented in the text chapters. The case preparation guides on Case-TUTOR will point you toward the proper analytical tools needed to analyze the case situation.

7. *Check out conflicting opinions and make some judgments about the validity of all the data and information provided.* Many times cases report views and contradictory opinions (after all, people don't always agree on things, and different people see the same things in different ways). Forcing you to evaluate the data and information presented in the case helps you develop your powers of inference and judgment. Resolving conflicting information comes with the territory because a great many managerial situations entail opposing points of view, conflicting trends, and sketchy information.

8. *Support your diagnosis and opinions with reasons and evidence.* Most important is to prepare your answers to the question "Why?" For instance, if after studying the case you are of the opinion that the company's managers are doing a poor job, then it is your answer to "Why do you think so?" that establishes just how good your analysis of the situation is. If your instructor has provided you with specific study questions for the case or if you are using the case preparation guides on Case-TUTOR, by all means prepare answers that include all the reasons and number-crunching evidence you can muster to support your diagnosis. Work through the case preparation exercises on Case-TUTOR *conscientiously,* or, if you are using study questions provided by the instructor, *generate at least two pages of notes!*

9. *Develop an appropriate action plan and set of recommendations.* Diagnosis divorced from corrective action is sterile. The test of a manager is always to convert sound analysis into sound actions—actions that will produce the desired results. Hence, the final and most telling step in preparing a case is to develop an action agenda for management that lays out a set of specific recommendations. Bear in mind that proposing realistic, workable solutions is far preferable to casually tossing out top-of-the-head suggestions. Be prepared to explain why your recommendations

table 1   Key Financial Ratios, How They Are Calculated, and What They Show

Ratio	How Calculated	What It Shows
Profitability ratios		
1. Gross profit margin	$$\frac{\text{Sales} - \text{Cost of goods sold}}{\text{Sales}}$$	An indication of the total margin available to cover operating expenses and yield a profit.
2. Operating profit margin (or return on sales)	$$\frac{\text{Profits before taxes and before interest}}{\text{Sales}}$$	An indication of the firm's profitability from current operations without regard to the interest charges accruing from the capital structure.
3. Net profit margin (or net return on sales)	$$\frac{\text{Profits after taxes}}{\text{Sales}}$$	Shows after-tax profits per dollar of sales. Subpar profit margins indicate that the firm's sales prices are relatively low or that costs are relatively high, or both.
4. Return on total assets	$$\frac{\text{Profits after taxes}}{\text{Total assets}}$$ or $$\frac{\text{Profit after taxes} + \text{interest}}{\text{Total assets}}$$	A measure of the return on total investment in the enterprise. It is sometimes desirable to add interest to the after-tax profits to form the numerator of the ratio since total assets are financed by creditors as well as by stockholders; hence, it is accurate to measure the productivity of assets by the returns provided to both classes of investors.
5. Return on stockholders' equity (or return on net worth)	$$\frac{\text{Profits after taxes}}{\text{Total stockholders' equity}}$$	A measure of the rate of return on stockholders' investment in the enterprise.
6. Return on capital employed	$$\frac{\text{Profits after taxes} - \text{Preferred stock dividends}}{\text{Total stockholders' equity} + \text{total debt} - \text{Par value of preferred stock}}$$	A measure of the rate of return on the total capital investment in the enterprise.
7. Earnings per share	$$\frac{\text{Profits after taxes and after preferred stock dividends}}{\text{Number of shares of common stock outstanding}}$$	Shows the earnings available to the owners of each share of common stock.
Liquidity ratios		
1. Current ratio	$$\frac{\text{Current assets}}{\text{Current liabilities}}$$	Indicates the extent to which the claims of short-term creditors are covered by assets that are expected to be converted to cash in a period roughly corresponding to the maturity of the liabilities.
2. Quick ratio (or acid-test ratio)	$$\frac{\text{Current assets} - \text{Inventory}}{\text{Current liabilities}}$$	A measure of the firm's ability to pay off short-term obligations without relying on the sale of its inventories.
3. Inventory to net working capital	$$\frac{\text{Inventory}}{\text{Current assets} - \text{Current liabilities}}$$	A measure of the extent to which the firm's working capital is tied up in inventory.
Leverage ratios		
1. Debt-to-assets ratio	$$\frac{\text{Total debt}}{\text{Total assets}}$$	Measures the extent to which borrowed funds have been used to finance the firm's operations. Debt includes both long-term debt and short-term debt.
2. Debt-to-equity ratio	$$\frac{\text{Total debt}}{\text{Total stockholders' equity}}$$	Provides another measure of the funds provided by creditors versus the funds provided by owners.

table 1   (*concluded*)

Ratio	How Calculated	What It Shows
Leverage ratios (*cont.*)		
3. Long-term debt-to-equity ratio	$\dfrac{\text{Long-term debt}}{\text{Total stockholders' equity}}$	A widely used measure of the balance between debt and equity in the firm's long-term capital structure.
4. Times-interest-earned (or coverage) ratio	$\dfrac{\text{Profits before interest and taxes}}{\text{Total interest charges}}$	Measures the extent to which earnings can decline without the firm becoming unable to meet its annual interest costs.
5. Fixed-charge coverage	$\dfrac{\text{Profits before taxes and interest} + \text{Lease obligations}}{\text{Total interest charges} + \text{Lease obligations}}$	A more inclusive indication of the firm's ability to meet all of its fixed-charge obligations.
Activity ratios		
1. Inventory turnover	$\dfrac{\text{Sales}}{\text{Inventory of finished goods}}$	When compared to industry averages, it provides an indication of whether a company has excessive or perhaps inadequate finished goods inventory.
2. Fixed assets turnover	$\dfrac{\text{Sales}}{\text{Fixed assets}}$	A measure of the sales productivity and utilization of plant and equipment.
3. Total assets turnover	$\dfrac{\text{Sales}}{\text{Total assets}}$	A measure of the utilization of all the firm's assets; a ratio below the industry average indicates the company is not generating a sufficient volume of business, given the size of its asset investment.
4. Accounts receivable turnover	$\dfrac{\text{Annual credit sales}}{\text{Accounts receivable}}$	A measure of the average length of time it takes the firm to collect the sales made on credit.
5. Average collection period	$\dfrac{\text{Accounts receivable}}{\text{Total sales} \div 365}$ or $\dfrac{\text{Accounts receivable}}{\text{Average daily sales}}$	Indicates the average length of time the firm must wait after making a sale before it receives payment.
Other ratios		
1. Dividend yield on common stock	$\dfrac{\text{Annual dividends per share}}{\text{Current market price per share}}$	A measure of the return to owners received in the form of dividends.
2. Price-earnings ratio	$\dfrac{\text{Current market price per share}}{\text{After-tax earnings per share}}$	Faster-growing or less-risky firms tend to have higher price-earnings ratios than slower-growing or more-risky firms.
3. Dividend payout ratio	$\dfrac{\text{Annual dividends per share}}{\text{After-tax earnings per share}}$	Indicates the percentage of profits paid out as dividends.
4. Cash flow per share	$\dfrac{\text{After-tax profits} + \text{Depreciation}}{\text{Number of common shares outstanding}}$	A measure of the discretionary funds over and above expenses that are available for use by the firm.

Note: Industry-average ratios against which a particular company's ratios may be judged are available in *Modern Industry and Dun's Reviews* published by Dun & Bradstreet (14 ratios for 125 lines of business activities), Robert Morris Associates' *Annual Statement Studies* (11 ratios for 156 lines of business), and the FTC-SEC's *Quarterly Financial Report* for manufacturing corporations.

are more attractive than other courses of action that are open. You'll find Case-Tutor's case preparation guides helpful in performing this step, too.

As long as you are conscientious in preparing your analysis and recommendations,
and have ample reasons, evidence, and arguments to support your views, you shouldn't
fret unduly about whether what you've prepared is "the right answer" to the case. In
case analysis there is rarely just one right approach or set of recommendations. Managing a company and crafting and executing strategies are not such exact sciences that
there exists a single provably correct analysis and action plan for each strategic situation. Of course, some analyses and action plans are better than others; but, in truth,
there's nearly always more than one good way to analyze a situation and more than one
good plan of action. So, if you have carefully prepared the case using either the Case-
Tutor case preparation guides or your instructor's assignment questions, don't lose
confidence in the correctness of your work and judgment.

PARTICIPATING IN CLASS DISCUSSION OF A CASE

Classroom discussions of cases are sharply different from lecture classes. In a case
class students do most of the talking. The instructor's role is to solicit student participation, keep the discussion on track, ask "Why?" often, offer alternative views, play
the devil's advocate (if no students jump in to offer opposing views), and otherwise
lead the discussion. The students in the class carry the burden of analyzing the situation and of being prepared to present and defend their diagnoses and recommendations. Expect a classroom environment, therefore, that calls for *your* size-up of the
situation, *your* analysis, what actions *you* would take, and why *you* would take them.
Do not be dismayed if, as the class discussion unfolds, some insightful things are said
by your fellow classmates that you did not think of. It is normal for views and analyses to differ and for the comments of others in the class to expand your own thinking
about the case. As the old adage goes, "Two heads are better than one." So it is to be
expected that the class as a whole will do a more penetrating and searching job of case
analysis than will any one person working alone. This is the power of group effort, and
its virtues are that it will help you see more analytical applications, let you test your
analyses and judgments against those of your peers, and force you to wrestle with differences of opinion and approaches.

To orient you to the classroom environment on the days a case discussion is scheduled, we compiled the following list of things to expect:

1.   Expect the instructor to assume the role of extensive questioner and listener.

2.   Expect students to do most of the talking. The case method enlists a maximum of
     individual participation in class discussion. It is not enough to be present as a
     silent observer; if every student took this approach, there would be no discussion.
     (Thus, expect a portion of your grade to be based on your participation in case
     discussions.)

3.   Be prepared for the instructor to probe for reasons and supporting analysis.

4.   Expect and tolerate challenges to the views expressed. All students have to be will-
     ing to submit their conclusions for scrutiny and rebuttal. Each student needs to
     learn to state his or her views without fear of disapproval and to overcome the hes-
     itation of speaking out. Learning respect for the views and approaches of others is
     an integral part of case analysis exercises. But there are times when it is OK to

swim against the tide of majority opinion. In the practice of management, there is always room for originality and unorthodox approaches. So while discussion of a case is a group process, there is no compulsion for you or anyone else to cave in and conform to group opinions and group consensus.

5. Don't be surprised if you change your mind about some things as the discussion unfolds. Be alert to how these changes affect your analysis and recommendations (in the event you get called on).

6. Expect to learn a lot in class as the discussion of a case progresses; furthermore, you will find that the cases build on one another—what you learn in one case helps prepare you for the next case discussion.

There are several things you can do on your own to be good and look good as a participant in class discussions:

- Although you should do your own independent work and independent thinking, don't hesitate before (and after) class to discuss the case with other students. In real life, managers often discuss the company's problems and situation with other people to refine their own thinking.

- In participating in the discussion, make a conscious effort to contribute, rather than just talk. There is a big difference between saying something that builds the discussion and offering a long-winded off-the-cuff remark that leaves the class wondering what the point was.

- Avoid the use of "I think," "I believe," and "I feel"; instead, say, "My analysis shows—" and "The company should do . . . because—" Always give supporting reasons and evidence for your views; then your instructor won't have to ask you "Why?" every time you make a comment.

- In making your points, assume that everyone has read the case and knows what it says; avoid reciting and rehashing information in the case—instead, use the data and information to explain your assessment of the situation and to support your position.

- Bring the printouts of the work you've done on Case-TUTOR or the notes you've prepared (usually two or three pages' worth) to class and rely on them extensively when you speak. There's no way you can remember everything—especially the results of your number crunching. To reel off the numbers or to present all five reasons why, instead of one, you will need good notes. When you have prepared thoughtful answers to the study questions and use them as the basis for your comments, *everybody* in the room will know you are well prepared, and your contribution to the case discussion will stand out.

PREPARING A WRITTEN CASE ANALYSIS

Preparing a written case analysis is much like preparing a case for class discussion, except that your analysis must be more complete and put in report form. Unfortunately, though, there is no ironclad procedure for doing a written case analysis. All we can offer are some general guidelines and words of wisdom—this is because company situations and management problems are so diverse that no one mechanical way to approach a written case assignment always works.

Your instructor may assign you a specific topic around which to prepare your written report. Or, alternatively, you may be asked to do a comprehensive written case analysis, where the expectation is that you will (1) *identify* all the pertinent issues that management needs to address, (2) perform whatever *analysis* or *evaluation* is appropriate, and (3) propose an *action plan* and *set of recommendations* addressing the issues you have identified. In going through the exercise of identify, evaluate, and recommend, keep the following pointers in mind.[3]

Identification

It is essential early on in your paper that you provide a sharply focused diagnosis of strategic issues and key problems and that you demonstrate a good grasp of the company's present situation. Make sure that you can identify the firm's strategy (use the concepts and tools in Chapters 1–10 as diagnostic aids) and that you can pinpoint whatever strategy implementation issues may exist (consult the material in Chapters 11–13 for diagnostic help). Consult the key points we have provided at the end of each chapter for further diagnostic suggestions. Review the study questions for the case on Case-TUTOR. Consider beginning your paper with an overview of the company's situation, its strategy, and the significant problems and issues that confront management. State problems/issues as clearly and precisely as you can. Unless it is necessary to do so for emphasis, avoid recounting facts and history about the company (assume your professor has read the case and is familiar with the organization).

Analysis and Evaluation

This is usually the hardest part of the report. Analysis is hard work! Check out the firm's financial ratios, its profit margins and rates of return, and its capital structure, and decide how strong the firm is financially. Refer back to Table 1, which contains a summary of various financial ratios and how they are calculated. Use it to assist in your financial diagnosis. Similarly, look at marketing, production, managerial competence, and other factors underlying the organization's strategic successes and failures. Decide whether the firm has valuable resource strengths and competencies and, if so, whether it is capitalizing on them.

Check to see if the firm's strategy is producing satisfactory results and determine the reasons why or why not. Probe the nature and strength of the competitive forces confronting the company. Decide whether and why the firm's competitive position is getting stronger or weaker. Use the tools and concepts you have learned about to perform whatever analysis or evaluation is appropriate. Work through the case preparation exercise on Case-TUTOR if one is available for the case you've been assigned.

In writing your analysis and evaluation, bear in mind four things:

1.   You are obliged to offer analysis and evidence to back up your conclusions. Do not rely on unsupported opinions, overgeneralizations, and platitudes as a substitute for tight, logical argument backed up with facts and figures.

---

[3]For some additional ideas and viewpoints, you may wish to consult Thomas J. Raymond, "Written Analysis of Cases," in *The Case Method at the Harvard Business School,* ed. M. P. McNair, pp. 139–63. Raymond's article includes an actual case, a sample analysis of the case, and a sample of a student's written report on the case.

2. If your analysis involves some important quantitative calculations, use tables and charts to present the calculations clearly and efficiently. Don't just tack the exhibits on at the end of your report and let the reader figure out what they mean and why they were included. Instead, in the body of your report cite some of the key numbers, highlight the conclusions to be drawn from the exhibits, and refer the reader to your charts and exhibits for more details.

3. Demonstrate that you have command of the strategic concepts and analytical tools to which you have been exposed. Use them in your report.

4. Your interpretation of the evidence should be reasonable and objective. Be wary of preparing a one-sided argument that omits all aspects not favorable to your conclusions. Likewise, try not to exaggerate or overdramatize. Endeavor to inject balance into your analysis and to avoid emotional rhetoric. Strike phrases such as "I think," "I feel," and "I believe" when you edit your first draft, and write in "My analysis shows," instead.

Recommendations

The final section of the written case analysis should consist of a set of definite recommendations and a plan of action. Your set of recommendations should address all of the problems/issues you identified and analyzed. If the recommendations come as a surprise or do not follow logically from the analysis, the effect is to weaken greatly your suggestions of what to do. Obviously, your recommendations for actions should offer a reasonable prospect of success. High-risk, bet-the-company recommendations should be made with caution. State how your recommendations will solve the problems you identified. Be sure the company is financially able to carry out what you recommend; also check to see if your recommendations are workable in terms of acceptance by the persons involved, the organization's competence to implement them, and prevailing market and environmental constraints. Try not to hedge or weasel on the actions you believe should be taken.

By all means state your recommendations in sufficient detail to be meaningful— get down to some definite nitty-gritty specifics. Avoid such unhelpful statements as "The organization should do more planning" or "The company should be more aggressive in marketing its product." For instance, do not simply say, "The firm should improve its market position" but state exactly how you think this should be done. Offer a definite agenda for action, stipulating a timetable and sequence for initiating actions, indicating priorities, and suggesting who should be responsible for doing what.

In proposing an action plan, remember there is a great deal of difference between, on the one hand, being responsible for a decision that may be costly if it proves in error and, on the other hand, casually suggesting courses of action that might be taken when you do not have to bear the responsibility for any of the consequences. A good rule to follow in making your recommendations is: *Avoid recommending anything you would not yourself be willing to do if you were in management's shoes.* The importance of learning to develop good managerial judgment is indicated by the fact that, even though the same information and operating data may be available to every manager or executive in an organization, the quality of the judgments about what the information means and which actions need to be taken does vary from person to person.[4]

---

[4]Gragg, "Because Wisdom Can't Be Told," p. 10.

It goes without saying that your report should be well organized and well written. Great ideas amount to little unless others can be convinced of their merit—this takes tight logic, the presentation of convincing evidence, and persuasively written arguments.

PREPARING AN ORAL PRESENTATION

During the course of your business career it is very likely that you will be called on to prepare and give a number of oral presentations. For this reason, it is common in courses of this nature to assign cases for oral presentation to the whole class. Such assignments give you an opportunity to hone your presentation skills.

The preparation of an oral presentation has much in common with that of a written case analysis. Both require identification of the strategic issues and problems confronting the company, analysis of industry conditions and the company's situation, and the development of a thorough, well-thought-out action plan. The substance of your analysis and quality of your recommendations in an oral presentation should be no different than in a written report. As with a written assignment, you'll need to demonstrate command of the relevant strategic concepts and tools of analysis, and your recommendations should contain sufficient detail to provide clear direction for management. The main difference between an oral presentation and a written case is in the delivery format. Oral presentations rely principally on verbalizing your diagnosis, analysis, and recommendations and visually enhancing and supporting your oral discussion with colorful, snappy slides (usually created with Microsoft's PowerPoint software).

Typically, oral presentations involve group assignments. Your instructor will provide the details of the assignment—how work should be delegated among the group members and how the presentation should be conducted. Some instructors prefer that presentations begin with issue identification, followed by analysis of the industry and company situation analysis, and conclude with a recommended action plan to improve company performance. Other instructors prefer that the presenters assume that the class has a good understanding of the external industry environment and the company's competitive position and expect the presentation to be strongly focused on the group's recommended action plan and supporting analysis and arguments. The latter approach requires cutting straight to the heart of the case and supporting each recommendation with detailed analysis and persuasive reasoning. Still other instructors may give you the latitude to structure your presentation however you and your group members see fit.

Regardless of the style preferred by your instructor, you should take great care in preparing for the presentation. A good set of slides with good content and good visual appeal is essential to a first-rate presentation. Take some care to choose a nice slide design, font size and style, and color scheme. We suggest including slides covering each of the following areas:

- An opening slide covering the "title" of the presentation and names of the presenters.
- A slide showing an outline of the presentation (perhaps with presenters' names by each topic).
- One or more slides showing the key problems and strategic issues that management needs to address.
- A series of slides covering your analysis of the company's situation.

- A series of slides containing your recommendations and the supporting arguments and reasoning for each recommendation—one slide for each recommendation and the associated reasoning has a lot of merit.

You and your team members should carefully plan and rehearse your slide show to maximize impact and minimize distractions. The slide show should include all of the pizzazz necessary to garner the attention of the audience, but not so much that it distracts from the content of what group members are saying to the class. You should remember that the role of slides is to help you communicate your points to the audience. Too many graphics, images, colors, and transitions may divert the audience's attention from what is being said or disrupt the flow of the presentation. Keep in mind that visually dazzling slides rarely hide a shallow or superficial or otherwise flawed case analysis from a perceptive audience. Most instructors will tell you that first-rate slides will definitely enhance a well-delivered presentation but that impressive visual aids accompanied by weak analysis and poor oral delivery still add up to a substandard presentation.

RESEARCHING COMPANIES AND INDUSTRIES VIA THE INTERNET AND ONLINE DATA SERVICES

Very likely, there will be occasions when you need to get additional information about some of the assigned cases, perhaps because your instructor has asked you to do further research on the industry or company or because you are simply curious about what has happened to the company since the case was written. These days it is relatively easy to run down recent industry developments and to find out whether a company's strategic and financial situation has improved, deteriorated, or changed little since the conclusion of the case. The amount of information about companies and industries available on the Internet and through online data services is formidable and expanding rapidly.

It is a fairly simple matter to go to company Web sites, click on the investor information offerings and press release files, and get quickly to useful information. Most company Web sites are linked to databases containing the company's quarterly and annual reports and 10K and 10Q filings with the Securities and Exchange Commission. Frequently, you will find mission and vision statements, values statements, codes of ethics, and strategy information, as well as charts of the company's stock price. The company's recent press releases typically contain reliable information about what of interest has been going on—new product introductions, recent alliances and partnership agreements, recent acquisitions, and other late-breaking company developments. Some company Web pages also include links to the home pages of industry trade associations where you can find information about industry size, growth, recent industry news, statistical trends, and future outlook. Thus, an early step in researching a company on the Internet is always to go to its Web site and see what's available.

Online Data Services

Lexis-Nexis, Bloomberg Financial News Services, and other online subscription services available in many university libraries provide access to a wide array of business reference material. For example, the Web-based Lexis-Nexis Academic Universe contains business news articles from general news sources, business publications, and industry trade publications. Broadcast transcripts from financial news programs are also available through Lexis-Nexis, as are full-text 10-Ks, 10-Qs, annual reports, and company profiles for more than 11,000 U.S. and international companies. Your business librarian should be able to direct you to the resources available through your library that will aid you in your research.

Public and Subscription Web sites with Good Information

In addition to company Web pages and online services provided by your university library, almost every major business publication has a subscription site available on the Internet. *The Wall Street Journal Interactive Edition* not only contains the same information that is available daily in its print version of the paper but also maintains a searchable database of all *Wall Street Journal* articles published during the past few years. The newspaper's online subscription site also has a Briefings Books section that allows you to conduct research on a specific company and track its financial and market performance in near–real time. *Fortune* and *Business Week* also make the content of the most current issue available online to subscribers as well as provide archives sections that allow you to search for articles related to a particular keyword that were published during the past few years.

The following Web sites are particularly good locations for company and industry information:

Securities and Exchange Commission EDGAR database (contains company 10-Ks, 10-Qs etc.)	www.sec.gov/cgi-bin/srch-edgar
NASDAQ	www.nasdaq.com
CNNfn: The Financial Network	www.cnnfn.com
Hoover's Online	www.hoovers.com
The Wall Street Journal Interactive Edition	www.wsj.com
Business Week	www.businessweek.com
Fortune	www.fortune.com
MSN Money Central	www.moneycentral.msn.com
Yahoo! Finance	www.quote.yahoo.com
Individual News Page	www.individual.com

Some of these Internet sources require subscriptions in order to access their entire databases.

Using a Search Engine

Alternatively, or in addition, you can quickly locate and retrieve information on companies, industries, products, individuals, or other subjects of interest using such Internet search engines as Lycos, Go, Excite, Snap, and Google. Search engines find articles and other information sources that relate to a particular industry, company name, topic, phrase, or keyword of interest. Search engine technology is becoming highly intuitive in retrieving Web pages related to your query and will likely direct you to the company Web site and other sites that contain timely and accurate information about the company. However, keep in mind that the information retrieved by a search engine is unfiltered

table 2   The 10 Commandments of Case Analysis

To be observed in written reports and oral presentations, and while participating in class discussions.

1. Go through the case twice, once for a quick overview and once to gain full command of the facts; then take care to explore the information in every one of the case exhibits.

2. Make a complete list of the problems and issues that the company's management needs to address.

3. Be thorough in your analysis of the company's situation. Either work through the case preparation exercises and/or study questions on Case-Tutor or make a minimum of one to two pages of notes detailing your diagnosis.

4. Use every opportunity to apply the concepts and analytical tools in the text chapters— all of the cases in the book have very definite ties to the concepts/tools in one or more of the text chapters and you are expected to apply them in analyzing the cases.

5. Do enough number crunching to discover the story told by the data presented in the case. (To help you comply with this commandment, consult Table 1 in this section to guide your probing of a company's financial condition and financial performance.)

6. Support any and all opinions with well-reasoned arguments and numerical evidence; don't stop until you can purge "I think" and "I feel" from your assessment and instead are able to rely completely on "My analysis shows."

7. Prioritize your recommendations and make sure they can be carried out in an acceptable time frame with the available resources.

8. Support each recommendation with persuasive argument and reasons as to why it makes sense and should result in improved company performance.

9. Review your recommended action plan to see if it addresses all of the problems and issues you identified—any set of recommendations that does not address all of the issues and problems you identified is incomplete and insufficient.

10. Avoid recommending any course of action that could have disastrous consequences if it doesn't work out as planned; therefore, be as alert to the downside risks of your recommendations as you are to their upside potential and appeal.

and may include sources that are not reliable or that contain inaccurate or misleading information. Be wary of information that is provided by authors who are unaffiliated with reputable organizations or publications or that doesn't come from the company or a credible trade association—be especially careful in relying on the accuracy of information you find posted on various bulletin boards. Articles covering a company or issue should be copyrighted or published by a reputable source. If you are turning in a paper containing information gathered from the Internet, you should cite your sources (providing the Internet address and date visited); it is also wise to print Web pages for your research file (some Web pages are updated frequently).

The Learning Curve Is Steep

With a modest investment of time, you will learn how to use Internet sources and search engines to run down information on companies and industries quickly and efficiently. And it is a skill that will serve you well into the future. Once you become familiar with the data available on the different Web sites mentioned above and with one or more search engines, you will know where to go to look for the particular information that you want. Search engines nearly always turn up too many information sources that match your request rather than too few; the trick is to learn to zero in on those most relevant to what you are looking for. As with most things, once you get a little experience under your belt on how to do company and industry research on the Internet, you will find that you can readily find the information you need.

THE 10 COMMANDMENTS OF CASE ANALYSIS

As a way of summarizing our suggestions about how to approach the task of case analysis, we have compiled what we like to call "The 10 Commandments of Case Analysis." They are shown in Table 2 on the previous page. If you observe all or even most of these commandments faithfully as you prepare a case either for class discussion or for a written report, your chances of doing a good job on the assigned cases will be much improved. Hang in there, give it your best shot, and have some fun exploring what the real world of strategic management is all about.

case 1 Andrea Jung's Makeover of Avon Products, Inc.

John E. Gamble
University of South Alabama

As 2001 came to a close, Avon Products, Inc., was the world's largest direct seller of beauty and beauty-related products—a position it had held for over a century. However, there were many ways beyond direct selling for women to purchase color cosmetics, hair care products, fragrances, bath products, skin care products, or jewelry. Supermarkets, drugstores, discount stores, specialty retailers, and department stores accounted for approximately 93 percent of the industry's $140 billion global sales. With retailing becoming increasingly sophisticated and saturated with a worldwide proliferation of malls and supercenter-style discount stores, stand-alone specialty retailers, and Internet sales, one Avon board member asked, "Is the day of the Avon rep over?"[1]

When former CEO Charles Perrin stepped down and Andrea Jung was promoted from president to CEO of Avon in November 1999, the company was in serious trouble, with annual sales growth of less than 1.5 percent and a crashing stock price during the greatest economic boom in history. Jung took on the role of an "Avon lady" during her first month as CEO to better understand what customers thought about the company's products and to find out what it was like to be a member of Avon's direct sales force. Jung heard customer complaints about Avon's image, poor-quality products, lack of interesting new lines, and unattractive catalogs. She also learned that Avon's sales representatives at times could not reorder popular items and very often did not receive the correct items ordered. After one month as CEO, Andrea Jung outlined a bold new vision and strategic plan for Avon that called for it to introduce highly innovative new products; build new lines of business; transform its value chain and business processes; make the Internet a critical link in its direct selling business model; rebuild its image; enter the retail sector; and most important, update its direct sales model (developed in the late 1800s) to better fit the 21st century.

At the second anniversary of Jung's appointment as Avon's CEO, all indicators suggested that the new vision, strategy, and implementation efforts were working to near perfection. Even though the U.S. economy had officially entered a recession in mid-2001 and had slowed further following the September 11 terrorist attacks on the World Trade Center and the Pentagon, the company's 2001 revenues were expected to

[1]"It Took a Lady to Save Avon," *Fortune*, October 15, 2001, p. 203.

increase by 6 percent, its sales force was expected to expand by 15 percent, operating profits were expected to grow by 7 percent, and operating margins were expected to reach the highest level in over a decade at 14 percent. Jung's push into new products, business models, business lines, and promotional campaigns all contributed to sales increases, while value chain realignment and business process reengineering created additional resources to support such activities, and simultaneously improved margins. In addition, during Jung's first 24 months as CEO, Avon's common shares had increased by approximately 90 percent, whereas indexes such as the S&P 500 had fallen by nearly 25 percent. Just prior to the completion of Andrea Jung's second year as the company's chief executive, Avon's board of directors endorsed her performance by announcing to investors that Jung would become chairman of the board in addition to CEO. Avon's financial performance for 1991–2000 and market performance for 1991–2001 are presented in Exhibits 1 and 2.

ANDREA JUNG: CHAIRMAN AND CEO OF AVON PRODUCTS, INC.

Andrea Jung was born in Toronto, Canada, but raised in Wellesley, Massachusetts, as a member of a demanding family with high expectations for achievement. Andrea's father was born in Hong Kong and received a master's degree in architecture from the Massachusetts Institute of Technology after moving to the United States. Her mother was born in Shanghai and was a chemical engineer before becoming an accomplished pianist. Jung's parents expected commitment and determination from Andrea and her younger brother from early ages. In an October 2001 interview with a *Fortune* journalist, Jung suggested that her parents' expectations for excellence contributed greatly to her successful career. She recalled that when she was in the fourth grade, she desperately wanted a box of 120 colored pencils. Her parents indicated that if she were to make straight A's for the school year, she could have the pencils. By Jung's own admission to the reporter, she was not a natural student and had to miss birthday parties and other activities to make the grades necessary to receive the pencils. At the end of year, Jung delivered all A's to her parents and, in return, they took her to purchase the pencils. Jung found meaning in the life example given by her parents: "I'll never forget that. My parents ingrained in me early on that the perfect score is always something to strive for. I want to win and I want to succeed no matter what."[2]

Jung attended Princeton University and in 1979 graduated magna cum laude with a degree in English literature. Joining Bloomingdale's as a management trainee, Jung achieved early success before moving to I. Magnin, where she rose to second in command before age 30. At age 32, she was in charge of women's apparel for Neiman Marcus. Two years later, in 1994, she left to marry Bloomingdale's CEO and move to Manhattan. Once in Manhattan, Jung joined Avon as president of U.S. product marketing and quickly impressed then-CEO James Preston, making a name for herself with her decisiveness and no-nonsense style. When asked to assess whether the company should move into retail sales, Jung shocked some at Avon by forcefully recommending that the company avoid retail sales, arguing that neither the products nor the sales agents were ready for such a move. Among her most widely recognized successes as president of marketing was her decision to replace the company's assortment of regional brands

---

[2]Ibid., p. 208.

with global brands. Andrea's ability to unhesitatingly make bold decisions—even those likely to be second-guessed, like cutting 40 percent of the company's catalog items and dismissing the company's advertising agency—made her a standout and landed her the position of president and a spot on Avon's board before Preston's retirement. At age 40, Jung became CEO, and in 2001, at age 42, she was listed fourth on *Fortune*'s ranking of the 50 Most Powerful Women in American Business.

COMPANY HISTORY

Avon, originally known as the California Perfume Company, was founded in 1886 by a New York book salesman named David H. McConnell. McConnell entered the fragrances and cosmetics business after noting that many of the housewives who purchased books during his door-to-door sales calls weren't really interested in the books but rather in the free bottles of perfume he provided as a gift with each purchase. Upon opening an office in New York, McConnell immediately began to build a door-to-door sales force for his new company and hired Mrs. P. F. E. Albee as its first sales agent. Albee not only proved to be a stellar sales agent but also helped McConnell pioneer the company's direct sales approach. By the turn of the 20th century, the company employed more than 10,000 representatives and supported their efforts with a growing line of cosmetics, fragrances, and other beauty products developed and produced at its newly constructed Suffern, New York, research laboratory and production facility. By the early 1900s, the California Perfume Company had expanded its sales offices beyond New York to San Francisco, California; Luzerne, Pennsylvania; and Davenport, Iowa.

In 1914, the company began selling its products in Canada and reached a sales milestone of 5 million units. Sales had grown to $2 million by 1928, when the company first launched a line of beauty products under the Avon brand. McConnell branded the new line Avon as a tribute to the beauty of Stratford-upon-Avon in England—a city he had visited during his travels. The Avon products were top sellers, and California Perfume Company's name was changed to Avon Products, Inc., in 1939 by David McConnell Jr., who became president of the company after his father's death in 1937. Avon Products, Inc., went public in 1946, and its sales grew at annual rates of 25 percent or more during the 1950s as the company rapidly expanded its product line; entered nearly a dozen international markets; launched its well-known "Avon Calling" advertising campaign; and, most important, expanded its network of sales representatives. Avon's direct sales model was almost tailor-made to the economic conditions and societal norms of the 1950s and 1960s, a time in which only a small percentage of women held professional careers. Avon offered many middle-class U.S. homemakers an opportunity to earn extra income—an "Avon lady" could sell cosmetics to her friends and neighbors and still maintain her family obligations. By 1960, Avon's sales force had helped increase the company's U.S. sales to $250 million and make it the world's largest cosmetics company overall (not just the largest direct seller).

Even though Avon held on to its lead in the global cosmetics industry until the mid-1980s—when its annual sales averaged more than $3 billion—signs of trouble began to appear during the recession of the mid-1970s as middle-class homemakers began to enter the workforce. By 1980, Avon's sales had begun to decline as fewer middle-class women were satisfied with part-time sales jobs and, accordingly, fewer women purchased products sold door-to-door. In addition, Avon's products had little appeal with teens, and many lower-income women found Avon's products too expensive. With

exhibit 1 Selected Financial and Operating Highlights, Avon Products, Inc., 1991–2000 (in millions, except per share and employee data)

	2000	1999	1998	1997	1996	1995	1994	1993	1992	1991
Net sales	$5,673.7	$5,289.1	$5,212.7	$5,079.4	$4,814.2	$4,492.1	$4,266.5	$3,844.1	$3,660.5	$3,441.0
Other revenue	40.9	38.8	35.0	—	—	—	—	—	—	—
Total revenue	5,714.6	5,327.9	5,247.7	5,079.4	4,814.2	4,492.1	4,266.5	3,844.1	3,660.5	3,441.0
Operating profit	788.7	549.4	473.2	537.8	538.0	500.8	489.5	427.4	339.9	430.9
Interest expense	84.7	43.2	34.7	35.5	33.2	34.6	44.7	39.4	38.4	71.6
Income from continuing operations before taxes, minority interest, and cumulative effect of accounting changes	691.0	506.6	455.9	534.9	510.4	465.0	433.8	394.6	290.0	352.9
Income from continuing operations before minority interest and cumulative effect of accounting changes	489.3	302.4	265.1	337.0	319.0	288.6	270.3	243.8	169.4	209.3
Income from continuing operations before cumulative effect of accounting changes	485.1	302.4	270.0	338.8	317.9	286.1	264.8	236.9	164.2	204.8
Income (loss) from discontinued operations, net	—	—	—	—	—	(29.6)	(23.8)	2.7	10.8	(69.1)
Cumulative effect of accounting changes, net	(6.7)	—	—	—	—	—	(45.2)	(107.5)	—	—
Net income	$478.4	$302.4	$270.0	$338.8	$317.9	$256.5	$195.8	$132.1	$175.0	$135.7
Earnings (loss) per share, basic										
Continuing operations	$2.04	$1.18	$1.03	$1.28	$1.19	$1.05	$0.94	$0.82	$0.57	$0.65
Discontinued operations	—	—	—	—	—	(0.11)	(0.09)	0.01	0.04	(0.24)
Cumulative effect of accounting changes	(0.03)	—	—	—	—	—	(0.16)	(0.37)	—	—
Net income	2.01	1.18	1.03	1.28	1.19	0.94	0.69	0.46	.61	.41

exhibit 1 (*continued*)

	2000	1999	1998	1997	1996	1995	1994	1993	1992	1991
Earnings (loss) per share, diluted										
Continuing operations	$ 2.02	$ 1.17	$ 1.02	$1.27	$1.18	$1.05	$0.93	$0.82	$0.57	$0.71
Discontinued operations	—	—	—	—	—	(0.11)	(0.08)	0.01	0.04	(0.24)
Cumulative effect of accounting changes	(0.03)	—	—	—	—	—	(0.16)	(0.37)	—	—
Net income	1.99	1.17	1.02	1.27	1.18	0.94	0.69	0.46	0.61	0.47
Cash dividends per share										
Common	$0.74	$0.72	$0.68	$0.63	$0.58	$0.53	$0.48	$0.43	$0.38	$1.10
Preferred	—	—	—	—	—	—	—	—	—	0.253
Balance sheet data										
Total assets	$2,826.4	$2,528.6	$2,433.5	$2,272.9	$2,222.4	$2,052.8	$1,978.3	$1,918.7	$1,692.6	$1,693.3
Long-term debt	1,108.2	701.4	201	102.2	104.5	114.2	116.5	123.7	177.7	208.1
Total debt	1,213.6	1,007.4	256.3	234.3	201.6	161.5	177.7	194.1	215	351.9
Shareholders' (deficit) equity	(215.8)	(406.1)	285.1	285	241.7	192.7	185.6	314	310.5	251.6
Number of employees	43,000	40,500	33,900	35,000	33,700	31,800	30,400	29,500	29,400	30,100

Source: Avon Products, Inc., 2000 10-K.

exhibit 2   Monthly Performance on Avon Products, Inc.'s Stock Price, 1991 to December 2001

Trend in Avon Product, Inc.'s Common Stock Price

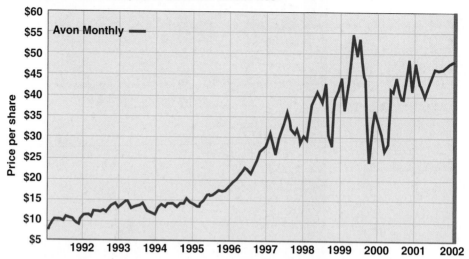

Performance of Avon Product, Inc.'s Stock Price versus the S&P 500 Index

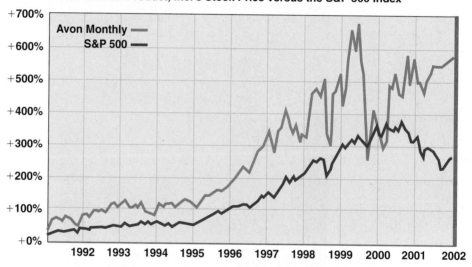

stalled sales growth in its core cosmetics business, Avon pursued business diversification to boost its revenues. It acquired the prestigious jeweler Tiffany & Company in 1979; fragrance retailers Giorgio Beverly Hills and Parfums Stern in 1987; and a variety of unrelated businesses such as magazines, retirement properties, health care products, children's toys, and menswear. The company's foray into diversification failed to produce the hoped-for level of performance, and the multitude of acquisitions were all eventually divested. Avon sold Tiffany's to a management buyout team in 1983, Parfums Stern was sold in 1990, and Giorgio Beverly Hills' retail stores were divested in

1994. All of the company's businesses unrelated to cosmetics were either abandoned or divested by 1999.

INITIAL STEPS IN REVITALIZING AVON

With Avon's cosmetics business achieving only modest revenue and earnings growth throughout the early and mid-1990s, the board of directors took steps toward revitalizing the company upon the retirement of CEO James Preston in 1997. The board's succession plan called for outsider Charles Perrin to lead Avon with the aid of two chief lieutenants, Andrea Jung and Susan Kropf. Perrin had been head of Duracell International from 1994 until its acquisition by Gillette in 1996 and had been a member of Avon's board since 1996. Jung and Kropf had both held executive positions with Avon under Preston, who was noted for fast-tracking women. By the end of Preston's tenure in mid-1998, women at Avon held more than one-third of officer positions, more than two-thirds of management positions, and one-half of the seats on Avon's board. Jung became the company's president and chief operating officer, while Kropf became executive vice president and president of North American operations. Both Jung and Kropf were also elected to the board, and Jung was identified as Perrin's eventual successor. Avon's board of directors was criticized by women's organizations and the news media for bypassing Jung, Kropf, and other proven women at Avon in favor of Perrin, but the board justified its selection by pointing to Perrin's previous experience as a chief executive and his success in building Duracell into a global brand.

Among Charles Perrin's first tasks as Avon CEO was to direct a $400 million restructuring program drafted by outgoing CEO Preston and intended to fuel more rapid growth. During Perrin's first year as Avon's chief executive, the company's business process reengineering efforts freed up more than $120 million; this money was used to develop new products, increase advertising, increase dividends, and buy back outstanding shares. In addition, Avon's business process redesign improved gross margins by 1.7 points and operating margins by 1.5 points by year-end 1998. Perrin's strategy also called for Avon to improve its image with consumers around the world, shorten product development times, develop new brands and products that could be marketed worldwide, and use technology to aid sales representatives in placing and tracking orders. Perrin believed that Avon needed to rejuvenate its dated direct sales model and create more lucrative income opportunities for sales representatives.

As Avon's president and chief operating officer, Andrea Jung collaborated with Perrin in the development and execution of strategies directed at improving Avon's competitive strength in the global cosmetics, fragrances, and toiletries (CFT) industry. Specific undertakings begun in 1998 by Perrin and Jung included the establishment of Avon's Global Development Center, which replaced duplicative local product development efforts with a coordinated global approach to develop brands that would have worldwide appeal. Avon's simultaneous launch of its Women of Earth fragrance in 54 countries in late 1998 exceeded the initial sales of Far Away (Avon's previous sales launch leader) by 31 percent. Two other early Global Development Center successes were lines targeted toward younger consumers and Techniques, a premium hair care line. Avon management believed that hair care was a particularly attractive product category since personal care products accounted for 50 percent of the $140 billion retail value of the global CFT market.

The improvement of Avon's image was another strategic initiative advanced by Jung and Perrin during 1998. Market research had found that many consumers considered Avon's products to be almost commodity-like with regard to quality and innovativeness—and not in the least glamorous. Avon attacked this image with new global products, a new global advertising campaign, and the opening of its 20,000-square-foot Avon Centre in New York's Trump Tower. Intended to illustrate the luxuriousness of Avon's products, the Avon Centre included an elegantly appointed spa and salon; 5,000 square feet of meeting rooms; and select beauty products like the Avon Spa collection, created for exclusive use at the Avon Centre.

Avon improved its website under Perrin by making it easier for customers to purchase products online, and it began testing a Web-based ordering system for the company's sales representatives in Japan. In 1998, Avon held its first-ever Representative National Convention, during which 6,000 representatives learned about new products, received sales training, and discussed areas of improvement for the company. The convention revealed a number of barriers to representatives' success. In response, Avon launched a pilot program in Japan that allowed representatives to order more than once during a sales campaign; in addition, it set up telephone, fax, and interactive computer voice ordering and speeded up deliveries to improve sales representative satisfaction.

At the direction of Perrin and Jung, Avon also began experimenting with new ways to make the company's products available to consumers who found it inconvenient to purchase from an Avon sales representative. In 1998, the company tested Avon Beauty Centers in 40 malls across the United States. Avon Beauty Centers were freestanding kiosks where passersby could purchase the latest Avon products. The Beauty Centers were modeled after the company's 200 Avon Beauty Boutiques in Malaysia, which accounted for 68 percent of the company's sales in that country. Another major shift in strategy initiated by Perrin was the development of Avon's Leadership Opportunity Program. The network marketing plan allowed representatives not only to receive commissions on their own sales but also to receive bonuses based on the sales of their recruits and trainees. Previously, Avon used a sales force structure that included sales zone managers who recruited new sales representatives but did not receive commissions on the recruits' sales. The strategies and implementation efforts of Perrin's management team led to a 3 percent sales increase and a 17 percent earnings increase before one-time charges for 1998.

OVERVIEW OF THE GLOBAL COSMETICS, FRAGRANCE, AND TOILETRY INDUSTRY

In 2001, the global cosmetics, fragrance, and toiletry (CFT) industry was highly fragmented, with distribution channels beyond direct selling and multiple subcategories existing within each product category. For example, within the color cosmetics category, products like eyeliner, mascara, foundation, concealer, nail polish, and lipstick could be purchased from direct sellers like Avon or from supermarkets, drugstores, discounters, specialty retailers, and department stores. Products in the hair care category, available through the same channels, included such subcategories as home permanents, shampoo, wave-setting lotions, cream rinses and conditioners, hair coloring, and hair spray. The percentage of sales accounted for by channel tended to vary widely by product category with, for example, drugstores being the largest U.S. retail sellers of cosmetics and hair care products and discounters the greatest sellers of fragrances. In addition, the sales growth rates for the subcategories of beauty products could also

exhibit 3   U.S. Sales of Cosmetics, Fragrances, and Toiletries
by Retail Channel, 1996 and 2000

Channel	1996		2000		Compound Average Growth Rate (1996–2000)
	Dollar Value (in billions)	Percent of Total	Dollar Value (in billions)	Percent of Total	
Supermarkets	$4.6	17.9%	$5.3	16.3%	+3.6%
Drugstores	4.8	18.7	5.4	16.6	+3.0
Mass merchandisers	5.6	21.8	8.0	24.6	+9.3
Department stores	5.5	21.4	6.8	20.9	+5.4
Specialty stores	2.3	8.9	3.3	10.2	+9.4

Source: Investor update meeting, Avon Products, Inc., May 8, 2001.

exhibit 4   U.S. Cosmetics, Fragrances, and Toiletries Market Sizes by Product Category,
1996, 2000, and 2005 (projected)

Product Category	1996		2000		2005		Compound Average Growth Rate (1996–2000)
	Dollar Value (in billions)	Percent of Total	Dollar Value (in billions)	Percent of Total	Dollar Value (in billions)	Percent of Total	
Hair care	$6.6	25.9%	$8.2	25.2%	$8.6	21.6%	5.3%
Fragrance	4.7	18.4	5.1	15.6	6.0	15.0	1.7
Cosmetics	4.6	17.8	6.4	19.7	8.4	21.1	8.7
Skin care	4.3	16.7	6.3	19.5	9.4	23.7	10.3
Bath and other personal care products	5.4	21.2	6.5	20.1	7.4	18.6	4.6
Total	$25.7	100.0%	$32.5	100.1%	$39.8	100.0%	6.1%

Source: Investor update meeting, Avon Products, Inc., May 8, 2001.

vary greatly. For example, between 2000 and 2001, the U.S. sales of eye shadow increased by nearly 14 percent, while the sales of foundation declined by 2 percent. Exhibit 3 presents U.S. CFT sales by retail channel for 1996 and 2000. The U.S. CFT market by product category for 1996, 2000, and 2005 (projected) is shown in Exhibit 4.

The market for beauty products was also segmented by consumer demographics and by geography. The product characteristics sought by teen consumers, for example, differed greatly from those sought by baby boomers. Country-specific differences in consumer preferences and complexions further fragmented the global CFT industry, while market penetration rates created varying growth opportunities across the world. The $6 billion U.S. cosmetics market offered the least growth potential worldwide but was twice as large as the next largest country market for cosmetics. The combined $8 billion sales of cosmetics in Japan and Western Europe approximately matched cosmetics sales in the rest of the world. China and Mexico were among the world's fastest-growing markets, with annual growth rates of 16 percent and 8 percent, respectively. As with cosmetics sales, the market growth rates for hair care products, skin care products, fragrances, and bath products varied greatly between countries.

Product Innovation in the Cosmetics Industry

As the global CFT industry entered the 21st century, sales increases were being driven primarily by product innovation. Beginning in the mid-1990s, skin care became the fastest-growing product category in the global CFT industry, growing at annual rates approaching 15 percent. The category's growth was fueled by new product introductions that responded to a worldwide consumer focus on wellness and youthfulness. Manufacturers formulated skin care products with natural active ingredients like vitamins and plant extracts. The goal was to move product benefits beyond cleansing and moisturizing and into such areas as antiaging, antipollution, firming, and sebum regulation. Skin care product formulations including vitamins C, E, and A had the greatest popularity because consumers were familiar with the benefits of these vitamins when taken as supplements. The use of retinol, a form of vitamin A, as a skin care additive spurred the most growth in sales to women over 30 since the pharmaceutical industry had demonstrated the efficacy of retinol in visibly reducing the signs of aging. By the late 1990s, almost all skin care producers offered products with retinol as an additive. Because retinol is prone to oxidation, many companies developed innovative airtight packaging and scientific delivery systems (such as liposomes, nanoparticles, and microencapsulation) that improved the effects of retinol and other unstable additives. Others offered SPF 15 sunscreens that allowed retinol to be used during the day.

Scientific research had also shown vitamin C to improve skin elasticity and to even out skin pigmentation, and vitamin E had become accepted as an antioxidant. Medical researchers had found that antioxidant intervention slowed basal skeletal muscle oxidation, which caused the body to age. Studies conducted by Alberto-Culver showed that St. Ives's Multivitamin Retinol Anti-Wrinkle Cream, which included vitamins A, E, and C, reduced the appearance of wrinkles by 34 percent in two weeks. Manufacturers also introduced products containing plant extracts that had been shown to be antioxidants. Both Lancôme and L'Oréal had introduced lines of creams and lotions that included grape polyphenols, which had been found to be powerful antioxidants that could protect the skin against free radicals. Free radicals are created when molecules break down and leave previously paired atoms with an unpaired electron to search out bonds with other atoms. The presence of free radicals is damaging to skin and other body tissues since free radicals break down other bonded atoms in the repairing process, which creates new free radicals. Antioxidants are known by scientists as free-radical scavengers since they contain a free electron that can bond with and neutralize free radicals. Skin care research was expected to focus on improving skin hydration since dehydration is a major contributor to premature aging of the skin. Another future research area was improving skin sensitivity, since people tend to lose sensitivity as they age.

Since the scientific formulations could be confusing to most consumers, manufacturers of skin care products attempted to promote the benefits of their products' additives without a lengthy discussion of scientific theory. Many products, like cleansing wipes, were frequently merely marketed as hypoallergenic rather than promoted for their inclusion of specific additives. However, some manufacturers had found that younger consumers were less likely to be confused by scientific claims, opening an opportunity for brands like Clinique to target the niche of 15- to 19-year-olds with products containing additives such as salicylic acid and tricolsan (to combat blemishes) and extracts such as sea whip, yeast, and green tea (to reduce skin discoloration).

Innovation also drove sales in cosmetics and hair care. Estée Lauder's Lightsource line of cosmetics contained not only active ingredients like amino acids and micronutrients found in skin care products but also microcrystals to deflect light and thus mask wrinkles. Innovative lipstick products that were popular in 2001 included Helena Rubinstein's Lip Sculptor (said to firm and plump lips) and long-wear products that reduced the need to frequently reapply lipstick. Cover Girl and Max Factor both introduced highly popular products (Outlast and Lipfinity, respectively) that contained Permatone, a semipermanent color base that kept lipstick in place for up to eight hours. New hair care products also benefited from innovations. Products that touted aromatherapy, herbal, or other natural benefits; protected colored or highlighted hair; and enhanced volume and body achieved the greatest sales growth. Gels, waxes, and creams were also gaining in popularity as hair treatment products intended to match the tousled or ultrasmooth styles seen in fashion magazines and on runways. Other products like L'Oréal's Elvive Citrus shampoos and conditioners contained active ingredients intended to clean the hair and rebalance its surface to prevent the accumulation of impurities. Products with a natural image, like Clairol's Herbal Essence, seemed to have an enduring appeal worldwide.

Although their beneficial effects were anecdotal rather than scientific, aromatherapy and herbal products had also led sales growth in the bath products and fragrance categories of the CFT industry. The Fragrance Foundation reported in its *Fall 2001/ Winter 2002 Trends Report*: "Wellness is the growth area for all fragrance items—the association of feelings, emotions, and fragrances and how they interact with one another."[3] Category leader Coty improved its strength in the bath market by extending its Healing Garden and Calgon bath lines to include aromatherapy products beginning in 1997. Similarly, Bath & Body Works increased its product offerings by adding high levels of fruit and floral fragrances that provided a therapeutic and mood-enhancing environment. In addition, fruit-based fragrances were popular sellers in the perfume and cologne categories of the CFT industry.

Consumer Demographics and Cosmetics

Many of the product innovations in skin care, cosmetics, and hair care were developed specifically to address the concerns of baby boomers who wished to fight the aging process. Antiaging products accounted for most of the 2 percent annual growth in the overall CFT industry during the late 1990s and 2000–2001, and for much of the growth in such categories as hair care, cosmetics, and skin care. However, the teen and preteen market rivaled that of the baby boomers, since the average weekly disposable income of the 23 million U.S. teens was $85. The U.S. teen and preteen market was so attractive that specialty retailers like Hotfox, Limited Too, Charlotte Russe, and Hot Topic carried only items appealing to preteens. With the help of his daughter, designer Ralph Lauren developed his Ralph fragrance line, targeted toward young women and color-coded to suit the personality of the purchaser. Givenchy, Donna Karan, and FUBU also introduced fragrances in 2000 and 2001 specifically targeted toward teens and preteens. Skin care was a particularly attractive product category in the teen market since nearly 80 percent of teen girls used complexion care products on a daily basis. Cleansing

---

[3]"Market Undergoes Sea Change," *MMR*, June 25, 2001, p. 103.

cloths from Nivea, Biore, and Johnson & Johnson were targeted to young women tired of the traditional routine of using a separate cleanser and toner. Annual sales growth for these cloths reached rates as high as 40 percent during 2000 and 2001.

Product innovations also focused on the needs of women in their 20s and 30s who were concerned with the oncoming effects of aging. Nivea's Visage Time Defying Fluid was targeted toward women aged 20 to 35 who were not yet ready for an anti-wrinkle product but wished to take a proactive approach to delaying the first signs of aging. The product's active ingredient, Alpha Flavon, was said to activate the skin's own age protection system and slow the formation of wrinkles and skin discoloration. The men's market had remained elusive, with few men adopting a daily skin care routine, but some manufacturers had achieved modest success with cleaning and mois-turizing products. The most successful men's daily skin care products focused on avoiding technical claims and making skin care simple, quick, and fuss-free.

African Americans and other consumers with dark complexions had skin care and cosmetics needs that differed substantially from those of women with European heritage. Much of the product innovation directed toward reducing the effects of aging was less important to women with darker complexions since the higher melanin and oil content found in dark-colored skin naturally discouraged wrinkles. A marketing executive for Color Me Beautiful, Inc., whose cosmetics brands include Iman, Flori Roberts, Interface Cosmetics, and Patti La Belle, suggested that the skin care needs of African American women had gone largely unmet. Their concerns focused mainly on the availability of cosmetics pigments suitable for darker skin, skin oiliness, and hyperpigmentation caused by abrasions, blemishes, or excessive exposure to the sun. The skin care concerns of Asian women, too, differed from those of women of Euro-pean ancestry, with emphasis placed on maintaining natural or pale skin tones.

Key Rivals in the Global Cosmetics, Fragrance, and Toiletry Industry

Even though Avon was the world's largest direct seller of cosmetics, fragrances, and toiletries in 2001, it was only about half the size of industry leader L'Oréal, whose 2000 sales exceeded $12 billion. Rivals in the CFT industry ranged from companies like L'Oréal and Avon (whose business focus was limited to a single line of business) to highly diversified companies such as Procter & Gamble and LVMH (whose busi-ness diversification included a wide variety of consumer products). Distribution strate-gies also varied in the industry, with many of the largest sellers like L'Oréal, Procter & Gamble, and Estée Lauder choosing to sell their products through department store, drugstore, and discounter channels, while others chose to vertically integrate into di-rect selling or the operation of cosmetics retail stores. The specialty retail store chan-nel was the fastest-growing channel in the industry, with Sephora, Bath & Body Works, and Victoria's Secret Beauty accounting for the greatest share of industry re-tail sales growth. Specialty retailers' broad lines of cosmetics were available both in their stores dedicated to the sale of CFT products and through their catalogs and web-sites. Exhibit 5 presents the corporate and personal care revenues for 2000, and lists well-known personal care brands. The following subsections describe Avon's key rivals in detail.

L'Oréal   L'Oréal's history dates to 1907, when French chemist Eugene Schueller developed a safe hair dye that he sold to Parisian hairdressers. The product's ability to make a lasting color change without damaging the hair or irritating the scalp was a

exhibit 5 Corporate Revenues, Global Personal Care Sales, and Personal Care Brands of Leading Cosmetics, Fragrances, and Toiletry Producers

Rank	Company	2000 Corporate Revenues (in billions)	2000 Personal Care Sales (in billions)	Personal Care Brands
1	L'Oréal	$10.6	$10.3	L'Oréal, Lancôme, Giorgio Armani, Vichy, La Roche-Posay, Matrix, Redken, Maybelline, Ralph Lauren, Helena Rubinstein, Carson, Biotherm
2	Procter & Gamble	$40.1	$7.3	Cover Girl, Max Factor, Hugo Boss, Giorgio Beverly Hills, Head & Shoulders, Pantene Pro-V, Pert Plus, Vidal Sassoon, Olay, Clairol, Nice 'n Easy, Herbal Essences, Aussie, Infusium, Zest, Safeguard
3	Estée Lauder	$4.4	$4.4	Estée Lauder, Clinique, Donna Karan, Kate Spade, Tommy Hilfiger, Aramis, Bobbi Brown, Aveda, Prescriptives, Origins, M•A•C, Bumble and bumble, jane
4	Avon Products	$5.7	$3.5	Avon, Skin-So-Soft, Anew, Far Away, BeComing
5	Intimate Brands	$5.1	$2.4	Victoria's Secret Beauty, Bath & Body Works, Dream Angels, PINK, Rapture, Victoria
6	Alberto-Culver	$2.3	$2.2	Sally Beauty, Alberto VO5, St. Ives, TCB, TREsemmé, Consort, Motions
7	Coty	$1.8	$1.8	Coty, Davidoff, Lancaster, Joop!, Chopard, Jil Sander, Isabella Rossellini/Manifesto, Vivienne Westwood, Stetson, Adidas, Aspen, Jovan, Calgon, Rimmel, Yue-Sai Kan
8	LVMH	$9.7	$1.7	Christian Dior, Givenchy, Bliss, Hard Candy, BeneFit, Urban Decay, Fresh, Make Up For Ever
10 (tie)	Johnson & Johnson	$29.1	$1.5	Neutrogena, Aveeno, Clean & Clear, Shower to Shower, Johnson's, Sundown
10 (tie)	Revlon	$1.5	$1.5	Revlon, Almay, Ultima II, African Pride, Flex, Charlie
11	Mary Kay	$1.2	$1.2	Mary Kay, Journey, Elige, Belara

Source: HAPPI (Household and Personal Products Industry), July 2001, p. 73; company websites.

welcome product innovation—and one that allowed Schueller to almost immediately develop export market opportunities in Holland, Austria, Italy, Russia, the Far East, and the United States. As a chemist, Schueller sought to make his company known for quality and innovation. By 1936, he had diversified the company's product line beyond hair care products to high-quality fragrances, skin care products, and cosmetics. In 2001, L'Oréal remained known for its quality products, processes, and business practices. In a review of global corporations' strategies and operations conducted by INSEAD in 2001, L'Oréal was rated the Best of the Best across such themes as mission and vision, client orientation, and innovation. In addition, the company took pride in its 383 million euro ($321 million) R&D budget, its 2,500+ researchers, and its 420 patents registered in 2000 alone.

In 2001, L'Oréal was the leader in developing products designed to neutralize free radicals and was steering its research toward the development of products to rehydrate the skin, improve skin sensitivity, and change color characteristics with lighting. A L'Oréal laboratory executive explained how the company's new makeup lines would change tone with available light:

> When light strikes the surface of the new generation pigments, it modifies their molecular structure and brings about changes in color. That explains how different colored effects could be obtained under different light exposure. Other pigments change color according to the angle at which they are observed: this is the goniometric effect. Their multi-lamellar structure absorbs and re-emits the light at several levels in shades that vary depending on the observer's position. This means that tomorrow, we can use a single product to reproduce a sophisticated star-class makeup instead of using many different products to achieve this result, as is the case today. The technology also produces effects on the contours of the face. By associating powders of variable shapes (flat or spherical), of different chemical composition (mineral or synthetic), we can influence the path of the light ray and modulate the light. This is the principle behind Lancôme's Photogenic foundation, which guarantees optimal luminosity for the face, whatever the type of lighting. At the other end, there is absolute transparency where certain formulas integrate soft-focus agents to create a luminous halo for hiding contours that are too sharp.[4]

In 2001, L'Oréal manufactured and marketed more than 500 brands and 2,000 products in more than 150 countries. The company's products were sold in the department stores around the world and, in some cases, to hair care professionals and pharmacies. The company's mass-market products represented nearly 55 percent of its 2000 sales of 12.671 billion euros ($10.6 billion) and experienced a 15 percent sales increase from 1999. The company's luxury brands accounted for 27 percent of its 2000 corporate sales and increased by 20 percent from the prior year. Products sold to hair care professionals increased by nearly 28 percent during 2000 and accounted for 12 percent of the company's sales. L'Oréal also developed and sold dermo-cosmetic health care brands that could be prescribed by dermatologists and purchased from pharmacies. These brands made up about 5 percent of the company's 2000 sales and grew by 15 percent during the year. Approximately 50 percent of L'Oréal's sales were generated in Western Europe, with 30 percent originating in North America and the remaining 20 percent coming from other parts of the world.

L'Oréal had aggressively expanded its global reach during the 1990s by offering a wider selection of brands in countries outside Western Europe and making strategic acquisitions of brands popular outside of Europe. In 2000 L'Oréal acquired Carson, the number one brand in the U.S. ethnic cosmetics market; Kiehl's, an exclusive luxury brand that relied only on its worldwide reputation and personalized relationships as marketing tactics; and Matrix, the number three brand worldwide in professional hair care products. The company also made acquisitions in 2000 to strengthen its position in Argentina and Scandinavia.

Procter & Gamble   The Procter & Gamble Company (P&G) was begun when immigrants William Procter and James Gamble settled in Cincinnati, Ohio, in 1837 and soon thereafter married sisters. At the urging of their father-in-law, the two men, one a candle maker and the other a soap maker, created a partnership to manufacture and market their products in the Cincinnati area. The company's sales reached $1 million by 1859, but the company had yet to produce and market a national brand. Then, in

---

[4]"What Will Tomorrow's Makeup Look Like?" http://www.loreal.com/us/index.asp.

1879, James Norris Gamble, son of the founder and a trained chemist, developed Ivory soap. Ivory quickly transformed Procter & Gamble into a national consumer products company; by 1890, P&G had 30 brands and production facilities across the United States and Canada. The company added a food products division in 1911, when it introduced Crisco, and began a chemicals division in 1917 to formalize its research procedures and develop new products. P&G entered the hair care business in 1934 when it developed the first detergent-based shampoo. P&G's commitment to research allowed it to continue to introduce popular-selling brands like Camay, Tide, Crest, Pampers, and Downy throughout the 1940s, 1950s, and 1960s.

P&G's presence in the CFT industry strengthened when the company acquired Richardson-Vicks in 1985 and Noxell in 1989. Richardson-Vicks was the producer of Oil of Olay and Pantene products, and Noxell manufactured and marketed Cover Girl, Noxema, and Clarion branded products. The company's research efforts resulted in the development of Pert Plus, the first combination shampoo/conditioner, while its marketing expertise transformed Pantene from a little-known brand into the world's fastest-growing shampoo brand. Procter & Gamble acquired Max Factor in 1991 and Giorgio Beverly Hills fragrances in 1994. In 2000, P&G recorded revenues of $40.1 billion through the manufacturing and marketing of more than 250 brands sold in 130 countries. The company budgeted over $1.7 billion for research and development in 2000 and collaborated with nearly 100 universities worldwide in the development and refinement of its consumer products and more than 40 prescription pharmaceutical products. The company's worldwide sales of cosmetics, hair care products, and fragrances exceeded $7 billion in 2000. The acquisition of Clairol, approved by the U.S. government in November 2001, was expected to add $1.6 billion annually to the company's beauty product sales. Like P&G's other brands Clairol products were found primarily in discount stores, supermarkets, and drugstores.

Estée Lauder   The Estée Lauder Company was founded in 1946 when Estée Lauder and her husband, Joseph, began to market four skin care products in New York City. The company quickly developed a reputation for quality and innovation, and in 1948 prestigious retailer Saks Fifth Avenue began carrying the Lauders' products in its New York store. In 1953, Estée Lauder extended its product line into fragrances with the introduction of Youth Dew—the first bath oil that doubled as a perfume. The company expanded internationally in 1960 when its products became available at Harrod's in London. Within the next six years, Estée Lauder's sales operations were expanded to Canada, Puerto Rico, Central America, Denmark, Italy, Spain, Switzerland, Australia, Netherlands, Belgium, France, Finland, Greece, Germany, Norway, Austria, Singapore, Thailand, and Japan.

Estée Lauder extended its product line to men's fragrances with the introduction of Aramis in 1964. It then launched Clinique, the first dermatologist-guided, allergy-tested, fragrance-free cosmetics brand, in 1968. Its Prescriptives line of cosmetics was introduced in 1979, while Origins, a line of skin care, makeup, and bath products, was launched in 1990. In the 1990s, the company acquired two makeup artist brands (M·A·C and Bobbi Brown); Sassaby (the owner of the color cosmetics brand jane); and Aveda Corporation (a leader in the U.S. luxury hair care industry). Also during the 1990s, Estée Lauder acquired Stila Cosmetics (a prestige cosmetics brand) and Jo Malone (the London–based marketer of prestige skin care and fragrance products). In 2000, the company acquired a majority equity interest in New York–based Bumble and bumble (a premier hair salon) and Bumble and bumble Products (a developer, marketer, and distributor of quality hair care products). The Estée Lauder Companies also held the global licensee for fragrances and cosmetics for the Tommy Hilfiger, Donna Karan New York, DKNY, and Kate Spade brands.

In 2000, the company recorded sales of $4.4 billion and its products could be found in more than 120 countries. In addition, the company's Clinique and Estée Lauder brands were the top two brands of cosmetics sold in the United States. Estée Lauder brands were usually found in department stores but could also be purchased in specialty retail stores and via the Internet. Estée Lauder launched an aggressive Internet strategy in 2001 that made its products available for sale at www.esteelauder.com and www.gloss.com. Estée Lauder also operated 320 freestanding specialty stores located in prominent shopping districts where its M·A·C, Origins, and Estée Lauder branded products were showcased. Ms. Lauder, who was in her 90s in 2001, had not made public appearances for the company for many years, but the majority of the company's stock was controlled by the Lauder family and several key positions within the company—including the positions of chairman, president, and various vice presidencies—were held by Lauder family members.

Intimate Brands   Intimate Brands was created through a spinoff from The Limited in 1995 and, in 2001, was among the world's largest specialty retailers of intimate apparel and beauty and personal care products. The company's sales in 2000 were $5.1 billion. One of its brands, Victoria's Secret, was the largest retailer of intimate apparel in the United States, with nearly 1,000 stores and sales of $2.3 billion in 2000. Intimate Brands' Bath & Body Works carried bath, skin care, and hair care products; with more than 1,400 stores and 2000 sales of $1.8 billion, it was the largest specialty retailer in the United States. The company's White Barn Candle Company, launched in 1999, specialized in the retail sales of home fragrance and home decor business. More than 130 White Barn Candle stores had been opened by 2001.

Intimate Brands also operated Victoria's Secret Beauty (VSB) stores that sold its own VSB-branded lines of cosmetics, fragrances, and skin care products. Proprietary brands sold in VSB stores included PINK, Heavenly, Halo, and Divine fragrances; Body by Victoria skin care products; and PINK, Rapture, Victoria, and Garden Collection cosmetics. Victoria's Secret Beauty was among the fastest-growing specialty retailers of cosmetics, with 2000 sales of $377 million and 480 stores located side-by-side with Victoria's Secret stores, 450 niche locations within Victoria's Secret stores, and 80 freestanding stores. Victoria's Secret Beauty cosmetics, fragrances, skin care products, and beauty accessories could also be purchased online at www.victoriassecret.com/beauty. Intimate Brands expected VSB to achieve $1 billion in sales by 2005 through the aggressive addition of stores, growing Internet sales, and the development of new beauty products.

Alberto-Culver   In 2001 Alberto-Culver was a leading manufacturer and marketer of hair care products, with over $2.3 billion sales in the previous year. The company was established in 1955 and gained its initial success selling its VO5 conditioning hairdressing to Hollywood hair stylists. The company moved its operations from California to Chicago in 1960 and gradually introduced new products, including VO5 shampoo and VO5 hairspray. In 1969, the company acquired Sally Beauty Supply, a New Orleans–based discount beauty supply business that catered to beauticians and stylists. Alberto-Culver diversified into the manufacture and sale of spices and laundry products in 1983 with its acquisition of Mrs. Dash, Molly McButter, and Static Guard. In 1996, the company acquired St. Ives Laboratories and its global line of hair care and skin care products. In 2000 Alberto-Culver expanded its line of products developed for the African American market with its acquisition of Pro-Line Corporation—the second-largest hair care products company focusing on the niche. Alberto-Culver's hair care products were sold through drugstore, supermarket, and discount store channels in more than 120 countries. Its Sally Beauty Supply chain, with 2,350 stores, was the largest marketer of professional beauty care products in the world.

Coty   In 2001, Coty was the world's leading manufacturer and marketer of fragrances and was among the largest producers of cosmetics and skin care products. Its 2000 revenues were nearly $1.8 billion. Founded in 1904 by François Coty in Paris, the company was based in Germany for many years until its headquarters was moved to New York City in 1996. The privately held company distributed its products through both mass-market and prestige retail channels around the world and maintained production and sales operations in 29 countries. Coty's mass-market brands included Adidas, The Healing Garden, Calgon, Stetson, and Jovan, while its prestige fragrance and cosmetics brands (distributed by its Paris-based Lancaster Group) included Lancaster, Davidoff, JOOP!, Isabella Rossellini's Manifesto, Vivienne Westwood, and Yue-Sai Kan.

Coty's strategy had not only yielded a number one global ranking in fragrances with its brands appealing mainly to price-sensitive consumers, but the company's upscale brands of cosmetics had allowed it to become the market leader in several international markets. For example, the company's RIMMEL London line of cosmetics was the top-selling brand of cosmetics in the United Kingdom and was expected to quickly build share in the United States after being introduced to the market in March 2000. Coty was also China's leading cosmetics brand in the department store channel. The company's cosmetics and skin care products sold in China were developed through an alliance with Yue-Sai Kan, one of China's most beloved and respected personalities. *People* magazine called Yue-Sai Kan "the most famous woman in China," and market research indicated that more than 95 percent of China's 1.3 billion citizens were aware of the Yue-Sai brand of cosmetics.[5] Coty management believed that the Yue-Sai brand had global appeal because, according to Yue-Sai Kan, it reflected the "sensibilities of an empowered, intelligent, feminine and modern Asian woman."[6]

LVMH   Moët Hennessy Louis Vuitton (LVMH) was the world's leading luxury products group, with annual sales of 11.6 billion euros ($9.7 billion) in 2000. The company's brands, some of which dated to 18th-century France, were among the most prestigious names in wine and spirits, fashion, perfumes and cosmetics, watches and jewelry, and specialty retailing. Some of LVMH's best-known brands included Dom Pérignon, Louis Vuitton, Givenchy, Parfums Christian Dior, Christian Lacroix, TAG Heuer, Ebel, and Solstice. LVMH added to its impressive lineup of brands in November 2001 when it acquired not only Donna Karan International but also controlling interests in Fendi and Prada.

The company's perfumes and cosmetics business grew by 22 percent in 2000 to reach $2.1 billion euros ($1.7 billion) and grew by another 15 percent during the first six months of 2001. The company's growth was attributed to its strong brands; new product introductions (which included J'Adore by Christian Dior, Hot Couture by Givenchy, and Michael by Michael Kors); and the success of its Sephora retail cosmetics operations. Sephora was the leading retail beauty chain in France and the

---

[5]"China's Top Selling Color Cosmetics Introduces New Look; Coty Inc.'s Yue Sai Kan Relaunches Color Cosmetics Line," Coty, Inc., press release, April 18, 2000.

[6]Ibid.

United States and the second-largest beauty chain in Europe. In 2001, Sephora operated more than 225 stores in Europe, more than 80 stores in the United States, and 7 stores in Japan. Sephora stores carried LVMH's products and other prestigious brands of cosmetics, fragrances, and skin care products including Chanel, Dolce and Gabbana, Elizabeth Arden, Hugo Boss, Naomi Campbell, Gianni Versace, and Burberry. In 2001, Sephora.com offered the largest and most diverse selection of beauty products on the Internet, with over 11,000 products and more than 230 brands. LVMH cosmetics, fragrance, and skin care brands were also sold by prestigious retailers around the world.

Johnson & Johnson Johnson & Johnson (J&J) was founded in 1886 by Robert Wood Johnson to provide surgeons with sterile surgical dressings that were wrapped and sealed in individual packages and ready for use. Johnson's new product was a major development in the fight against postsurgery infection, which at the time contributed to postoperative mortality rates as high as 90 percent in some hospitals. Johnson was driven to develop his antiseptic dressings and write *Modern Methods of Antiseptic Wound Treatment* after learning of Sir Joseph Lister's discovery that airborne germs were the source of most infections in the operating room. Johnson joined with his two brothers in developing a growing line of surgical products; by the time of his death in 1910, J&J was firmly established as the leader in health care products. In 2001, Johnson & Johnson remained a leader in the pharmaceutical industry, with sales of $29 billion and R&D expenditures of nearly $3 billion in the prior year.

Johnson & Johnson first introduced a baby powder in 1893 and baby lotions and oils in the 1920s, but its presence in the skin care and cosmetics industry was bolstered with the acquisitions of RoC, S.A., of France in 1993 and Neutrogena in 1994. J&J purchased the Aveeno line of colloidal oatmeal and other skin care products from S. C. Johnson & Son in 1999. The company also produced Ortho prescription dermatological products, which were proved in clinical trials to reduce fine wrinkles. Johnson & Johnson's competencies in the pharmaceutical industry aided its product development efforts in consumer skin and hair care and cosmetics, which were well regarded in terms of quality and innovativeness. In fact, Neutrogena's full line of color cosmetics, hair care products, and skin care products were commonly recommended by dermatologists to patients with sensitive skin. J&J skin and hair care products and cosmetics were distributed primarily through drugstores, supermarkets, and discount stores. Johnson & Johnson's 2000 sales of Aveeno, RoC, and Neutrogena skin and hair care products and Neutrogena cosmetics accounted for approximately $1.5 billion.

Revlon Revlon was established in 1932 by Charles and Joseph Revson, along with a chemist, Charles Lachman, who contributed the L to the Revlon name. Lachman had developed a unique nail polish that used pigments instead of dyes and was able to create a rich-looking, opaque nail enamel in shades never before available. Revlon sold the new nail polish first in beauty salons and then through department stores and drugstores. Within six years of the company's founding, annual sales exceeded $1 million. Revlon expanded beyond nail polish to cosmetics in the 1950s and entered the fragrance market in 1973 when it introduced Charlie, which became the top-selling fragrance in the world by 1975. Revlon's annual sales surpassed the $1 billion mark in 1977 and in the mid-1990s Revlon became the number one brand of color cosmetics in mass-market channels. In 2000, Revlon's annual revenues were approximately $1.5 billion and the company's cosmetics, skin care products, hair care products, and fragrances were sold in approximately 175 countries.

In 2001, Revlon's products were marketed globally under such well-known brands as Revlon, ColorStay, Revlon Age Defying, Almay, and Ultima in cosmetics; Moon

Drops, Eterna 27, Ultima and Jeanne Gatineau in skin care; Charlie and Fire & Ice in fragrances; and Flex, Outrageous, Mitchum, ColorStay, Colorsilk, Jean Naté, Bozzano, and Colorama in personal care products. Also that year, Revlon remained the world's number one brand of cosmetics sold in mass market channels and held the number one positions in lipstick and nail polish. Revlon had held the worldwide number one position in nail polish for 25 consecutive years. Revlon's products could be purchased at drugstores, supermarkets, and discount stores and over the Internet through marketing agreements with www.drugstore.com, www.ulta.com, and www.walgreens.com. The agreements allowed consumers viewing products at www.revlon.com to be directed to an appropriate page on one of the three retailers' sites where they could immediately select and purchase the product. As of 2001, Revlon had not vertically integrated into the retail sales of cosmetics.

Mary Kay   Of all cosmetics manufacturers and marketers, Mary Kay Cosmetics was the one whose business model most closely resembled that of Avon. In 2001, Mary Kay was the second-largest direct seller of cosmetics, fragrances, skin care products, and dietary supplements, with more than 200 products. Its 2000 revenues of $1.2 billion at the wholesale level equated to more than $2.5 billion at retail.

Mary Kay was founded by Mary Kay Ash in 1963 with $5,000 and the help of her 20-year-old son, Richard Rogers. Ash had recently retired from a career in direct sales and, after making a list of both winning and poor management practices she had observed during her career, was moved to create a principled company for women wanting unlimited opportunity for personal and financial success. One of Mary Kay Ash's central goals for the company was creating opportunity for women, and she used the Golden Rule as her guiding philosophy. She believed that her independent sales force should prioritize their lives with God first, family second, and career third. Her vision and principles allowed the company to build a sales force of more than 800,000 "independent beauty consultants" in 37 countries and become recognized by *Fortune* as one of the "100 Best Companies to Work for in America" and one of the "10 Best Companies for Women" in 1984, 1993, and 1998. *Fortune* also listed Mary Kay among its "Most Admired Corporations" in America in 1995. Ash was an inspiration to many women around the world; she died in November 2001, but her legacy was expected to live on for decades. During her lifetime Mary Kay Ash published three best-selling books, received awards for aiding the financial needs of women, and was the only woman profiled in *Forbes Greatest Business Stories of All Time.*

In 2001 Mary Kay offered a full line of color cosmetics, skin care products, fragrances, and bath products. Mary Kay also offered a men's line of skin care products and fragrances. The company maintained a staff of experts in cosmetics, dermatology, biochemistry, process technology, package engineering; and quality engineering to develop, test, and produce its products in its plants located in Dallas, Texas; China; and Switzerland. The company's products were available only through one of its 850,000 independent beauty consultants. Consumers could order from a beauty consultant during a sales call, over the phone, or by visiting www.marykay.com and entering their consultant's name and then selecting items to purchase. Visitors to the site who did not have a beauty consultant could enter their zip code and either immediately make purchases that were then credited to a nearby consultant or have the consultant contact them for a beauty consultation. A unique characteristic of Mary Kay was the bond of sisterhood shared by many independent consultants. Mary Kay Ash's deep concern for the welfare of her consultants cultivated a culture of unity at Mary Kay, which was evident during Seminar—an annual gathering of tens of thousands of independent consultants, and in the following testimonials posted on Mary Kay's website after her death in November 2001:[7]

> Laura Bush, First Lady: "Mary Kay is someone I have always admired. I believe that America's greatness is due in large part to courageous people like Mary Kay who have never been afraid to stand up for what is right."

> Doretha Dingler, Mary Kay Executive National Sales Director: "Mary Kay blazed the trail in the area of economic liberation for women! She has empowered women and enabled them to build a better life for themselves and their families. Mary Kay will go down in history as one of the greatest female humanitarians and visionaries of our time."

> Fannie Flagg, author of *Fried Green Tomatoes*: "Mary Kay is my heroine. She cares so much for women, and she meant so much to my mother and so much to my mother's friends who changed their lives in Alabama."

> Nancy Tiejten, Mary Kay Executive National Sales Director: "Mary Kay . . . had a vision to change the world for women. She had a dream, and she worked her whole life to make our dreams a reality. She wanted to build a company for women who wanted to be the best they could be, to be financially independent, and to help them fulfill their dreams."

> Rev. Dr. Robert Schuller, Crystal Cathedral, Garden Grove, California: "Mary Kay Ash has set an example of how our free enterprise system works that is thrilling indeed. Her life is a glowing testimony of a person who sets goals, follows them through with determination, uses innovative methods in a creative manner, but at the same time is motivated by a genuine desire to help people achieve unusual success."

ANDREA JUNG AND AVON'S NEW STRATEGIC DIRECTION

When Andrea Jung became Avon's new CEO in November 1999, the company's annual sales growth had slowed to less than 1.5 percent and its stock price had fallen from a high of $55 to a three-year low of $25. The strategies initiated by Charles Perrin had resulted in some initial improvement in operating ratios and yielded some modest sales growth during 1998, but in late 1999 it was clear that Avon was in need of a bold new direction. After 16 months as Avon CEO, Perrin resigned, concluding that his lack of experience in direct sales limited his effectiveness with the company. Avon's board took little time in turning to Andrea Jung to rejuvenate the 113-year-old beauty products company. Jung's first task as CEO was to hit the streets of her neighborhood, ringing doorbells, to better understand the desires of customers and needs of sales agents. Jung heard customer gripes over discontinued colors, mishandled orders, out-of-date catalogs, unattractive packaging, lack of innovative products, and confusing promotions. The new CEO also discovered firsthand the structural obstacles to achieving success as an Avon lady. Policies that required sales agents to place orders only during the beginning of a campaign with no opportunity to reorder hot-selling items, procedures that required 40-page order forms to be filled out by hand and either mailed or faxed to Avon, and orders that, according to Avon's own estimates, were improperly filled more than 30 percent of the time all made it difficult for sales agents to increase their sales volumes and commissions.

---

[7]Presented at www.marykay.com.

In Andrea Jung's fourth week on the job, she asked Avon executives and market analysts to convene for the presentation of her turnaround plan. She called for the launch of an entirely new line of business, the development of innovative products, new packaging, new channels of distribution, a new approach to supply chain management, new sales models, and new approaches to image building. Jung promised to pay for the increased expenditures for everything from R&D to Internet-based sales support. She proposed that additional process reengineering would cut hundreds of millions in non-value-adding costs from the company's value chain. At the close of Jung's conference, few believed that she could successfully implement the ambitious plan. A Paine Webber analyst's comment that the plan had "a high probability of disappointment" was not a unique view.[8]

Jung's Vision for Avon

Andrea Jung envisioned an Avon that would be the "ultimate relationship marketer of products and services for women."[9] Jung's view of a new Avon was that of a company going far beyond selling cosmetics to becoming a trusted source for almost any type of good or service that women need. Andrea Jung's Avon would allow women to purchase not only beauty products but ultimately such goods and services as financial services, in whatever manner the customer found most convenient—through an Avon representative, in a store, or online. Under Jung, Avon's vision statement read, "Our vision is to be the company that best understands and satisfies the product, service and self-fulfillment needs of women globally. Our dedication to supporting women touches not only beauty—but health, fitness, self-empowerment and financial independence."

In late 1999, however, the company was far from what Jung envisioned. In an era when 75 percent of American women worked and direct selling accounted for less than 7 percent of cosmetics and toiletries sold in the United States, the sales model perfected by David McConnell and Mrs. P. F. E. Albee in the late 1800s seemed dated by two generations. However, with approximately 98 percent of Avon's annual sales generated by its 3.5 million sales agents, Avon could ill afford to alienate its sales force with moves that might reduce direct selling revenues. Avon's representatives were vigilant in protecting their customers and sales, and they were aggressive in reversing strategies that might increase sales for Avon but limit sales growth opportunities for sales representatives. In 1997, Avon launched a basic website where a small number of products could be purchased online, but when it placed its Web address on the back of Avon catalogs, sales representatives revolted, covering the Web address with their own stickers until they were successful in forcing the company to remove the website.

Avon sales representatives were similarly displeased with any recommendation to make Avon products available for sale in department stores or malls. The company was also limited by its dowdy brand image; market research found that most women viewed Avon as "my grandmother's brand" or "not for me."[10] In addition, Avon had no products in some of the fastest-growing CFT categories, and it had not introduced a hit product in decades. Other problems at Avon included distribution inefficiencies, limited income opportunity for the average sales representative, and the difficulty of selling the company's products to busy women. One Avon board member helped

[8]"It Took a Lady to Save Avon," p. 204.

[9]As quoted in "Avon: The New Calling," *Business Week*, September 18, 2000, p. 136.

[10]"Avon Calling," *Ad Age Global*, October 1, 2001, p. 26

explain the dilemma of Avon's direct selling model: "Do you have an Avon rep? I don't . . . people like us should be able to buy the product."[11]

Jung identified the following strategic priorities to help correct Avon's competitive liabilities and set the company on a new course:

- Grow global beauty category sales through continued investment in new product development, advertising, and sampling.
- Provide representatives with greater career opportunities through sales leadership, enhanced Internet capabilities, and training.
- Reduce inventory levels while at the same time improving service to representatives.
- Improve operating margins 50–100 basis points through business process redesign.
- Successfully launch Avon Wellness line of nutritional supplements and vitamins.
- Begin to build a profitable retail business to fuel future growth.
- Develop e-commerce opportunities for Avon and its sales representatives.
- Pursue market opportunities in China and Eastern Europe.

Exhibit 6 presents a list of specific objectives under Avon's major strategic priorities.

New Strategies to Increase Sales

Andrea Jung's strategies for Avon were intended to grow revenues and market share by correcting many of the company's competitive liabilities, but not at the expense of its proven direct sales force: "If we don't include them in everything we do, then we're just another retail brand, just another Internet site, and I don't see the world needing more of those."[12] Jung believed that the Internet could be among Avon's best hopes for future growth and that an e-commerce business model at Avon would benefit the company's representatives. Jung initiated the eRepresentative sales concept, which allowed representatives to direct customers to www.avon.com to purchase products 24 hours a day, seven days a week. However, before the company's e-commerce plans were finalized, Avon was careful to gain input from its independent sales reps through multiple surveys and focus groups. Once the plan was implemented, Avon's eRepresentatives received commissions of 20 to 25 percent on Web orders shipped direct from Avon and commissions of 30 to 50 percent on Internet orders that they personally delivered to customers' homes. Visitors to www.avon.com who did not have an Avon representative were asked whether or not they'd like an eRepresentative before they completed the checkout process. Within the first nine months of the program, almost 12,000 of Avon's 500,000 sales representatives in the United States each paid $15 per month to become an eRepresentative. Jung also believed that use of the Internet could speed order processing and reduce paperwork for both sales representatives and corporate personnel. Even though 54 percent of Avon's sales representatives did not own a computer, the company hoped to get all representatives online by offering Gateway PCs plus an Internet connection for $19.95 per month.

Another opportunity for sales representatives to increase their income was a concept called Sales Leadership—an idea that had been talked of for years and was

---

[11]"The New Calling," *Business Week*, September 18, 2000, p. 136.
[12]Ibid.

exhibit 6 Avon's Strategic and Financial Objectives, 1997–2004

Marketing Transformations	2000	2004
Active beauty product SKUs	5,000	4,000
Breakthrough innovation frequency	3 years	2 years
Product development (average)	88 weeks	50 weeks
Campaign development	52 weeks	26 weeks
Supply Chain Improvement	**2000**	**2004**
Days of inventory	119	8–10
Forecasting accuracy	Baseline	+30%
Order fill rate	68%	90%
Sales Leadership	**2000**	**2004**
Leadership downlines per U.S. district	110	214
Representatives per U.S. district	322	440
Growth in active representatives	2–3%	2–3%
Growth in average rep earnings	—	25–30%
E-commerce and Internet	**2000**	**2002**
eRepresentative participation	13%	50%
Representative support cost savings	$3 million	+$20 million
Geographic market penetration	U.S., Japan, Taiwan	20 markets
International	**2000**	**2004**
Local currency sales growth	50%	20–30%
Representative growth	25%	20–30%
Sales outlets (China)	3,463	6,000
Financial	**1997–2000**	**2001–2004**
Sales growth	9%	10%+
Beauty growth	10%	12%+
Operating margin improvement	+3.2 points	50+ basis points/year
Cash flow from operations	$350 million	$700 million
Capital expenditures	$200 million (2000)	$225 million average/year

Source: Avon investor presentation, Susan Kropf, president and COO, 2000.

partially developed under Charles Perrin. Avon's direct sales model provided Avon representatives with no training and with commissions only on their own sales. Individuals who came to Avon with developed sales skills or a natural ability to sell the company's products prospered—approximately 20 percent of Avon's reps accounted for 80 percent of the company's revenues. In 1999, the annual earnings for a typical Avon sales representative in the United States was $2,400 and earnings of $7,500 or more allowed agents to gain admittance into the company's President's Club. Turnover was high among representatives who had difficulty reaching adequate sales levels, and Avon was having trouble adding new reps to replace those who dropped out. However, Sales Leadership allowed Avon's seasoned sales representatives to recruit new sales agents who they believed might have a knack for sales and to share in their successes. It also included a Beauty Advisors program that allowed sales reps to receive training in sales tactics and beauty and cosmetics tips.

Jung recognized that Avon's sales force, regardless of how well organized and trained, relied on appealing products to increase sales. As CEO, she aggressively pushed the company's plan to develop global brands, repackage existing products, and launch blockbuster products. The company's market research showed that Avon's largely working- and middle-class customers couldn't afford prestige brands like Lancôme or Estée Lauder but craved the elegance of those brands. To improve the company's image, Jung called for a redesign of the packaging of Avon's products to better match the look of upscale department store brands, launched a "Let's Talk" advertising campaign, and signed tennis stars Venus and Serena Williams to endorsement contracts.

Recognizing that her earlier efforts to transform Avon's many regional brands into single global brands had produced considerable success (global brands grew from 11 percent of Avon's sales in 1993 to 70 percent of sales in 2000), Jung stressed to the company's product development teams that new lines should be marketable globally whenever possible. Most of all, Jung understood the importance of innovation to the success of new lines. She added nearly 50 percent to Avon's R&D budget during her first fiscal year as CEO and demanded that the company's researchers develop innovative new lines within two years instead of the company's usual product development time of three-plus years.

To make products available to women who either were too busy to shop with a sales agent or preferred to shop for beauty products in retail stores, Jung pushed forward Perrin's plans to make the company's products available in malls. Even though retail sales accounted for 93 percent of the global CFT market, Avon had largely avoiding retail channels in fear of competing against its representatives. However, Jung was able to gain the support of Avon's sales reps by offering the kiosks as franchises after the test marketing had been completed. Avon opened 50 franchised mall kiosks in Jung's first year as CEO and, in 2001, entered agreements with Sears and JCPenney to operate Avon Center store-within-a-store concepts that would dedicate 400 to 1,000 square feet to an entirely new product line: Avon beComing. The beComing line of products could not be purchased from independent representatives and was priced higher than Avon's other lines, but it was less expensive than department store brands like Clinique, Lancôme, or Estée Lauder.

Avon had achieved success internationally before Andrea Jung became CEO, but she wanted more aggressive growth in emerging international markets like China, Eastern Europe, the Middle East, and Africa. China had been identified by Avon management as an attractive market because it had 20 percent of the world's population, its population was relatively young, and it represented a large and growing market for beauty products. Avon was the first and largest international direct seller in China from 1990 until April 1998, when direct selling was banned by the Chinese government. Avon quickly found retail stores to process sales of Avon products while its sales reps, now banned, became sales promoters who steered customers to retail stores to maintain their sales commissions. Jung's strategy for China continued the development of sales promoters but also expanded the products into class A department stores and hypermarts in major cities and introduced Avon products to Dealer Beauty counters in boutiques and class B and C department stores in smaller towns.

Jung found the emerging markets in Eastern Europe, the Middle East, and Africa (EEMEA) attractive because of the more than 200 million women age 15 and older living in the regions, the young average age of consumers, and the $7.5 billion market size. The company's direct selling model was well suited to these markets since there were no governmental restrictions to limit independent sales representatives. Jung's strategies for the EEMEA markets focused on representative recruitment, the development of local leaders, ongoing market research, and significant spending for advertising and promotions. Avon also intended to maintain a focused product line in EEMEA markets, with limited stock keeping units (SKUs) and 95 percent of sales coming from the sales of cosmetics, fragrances, and toiletries.

Strategy Execution and Business Results under Andrea Jung and COO Susan Kropf

Business Process Reengineering   The heart of Avon's strategy implementation efforts was its ability to eliminate the costs of low-value-added activities from its value chain. Jung wanted to spend $100 million annually to support product development, e-commerce initiatives, better commission opportunities for independent reps, and global image building, but funding for these activities hinged on Avon's president and COO Susan Kropf being able to squeeze out $100 million in cost savings elsewhere. Kropf's business process reengineering (BPR) efforts achieved great success in 2000, delivering cost savings of more than $150 million. The company's BPR efforts had begun under Charles Perrin in 1997 and had saved more than $400 million between 1998 and 2000. Kropf's efforts also improved Avon's operating margins by 3.2 points in 2000, as she left no component of the company's value chain untouched. Although Avon's BPR efforts were expected to result in a 2001 $80–$90 million pretax charge related to costs to accelerate business transformation initiatives, they were also expected to improve operating margins by 50 basis points during the year.

Much of Kropf's reengineering had to do with improving the company's manufacturing and distribution systems. The company saved $56 million annually after cutting its number of suppliers from 300 to 75, and it used information systems to automate order processing and logistics to reduce transportation costs by $22 million, shipping segmentation costs by $17 million, and order entry costs by $8 million. Other BPR implementation efforts focused on continued efficiency improvement, improved demand forecasting, and an overall end-to-end supply chain reconfiguration. Exhibit 7 provides examples of specific operating strategies and implementation efforts undertaken to accomplish Avon's strategic and financial objectives.

Sales Representatives   The recruitment and retention of sales reps was a strategic objective that led to the implementation of Jung's Sales Leadership program. "If Avon stopped adding numbers of active representatives, you know, the fuel and the lifeblood of the business slows down," explained Jung when asked about the importance of growth in the number of sales representatives.[13] Jung said Avon needed "double digit growth [in the number of Avon reps] every year. . . . We had 15 percent last year and to date 11 to 12 percent [in 2001]. Probably one of the biggest indicators to us of the health of the direct sales operation is how many people we are attracting."[14] With Sales Leadership, Avon reps could earn commissions on the sales of their recruits. In 2001, Leadership Executive Unit Leaders earned (on average) $46,500 and Senior Executive Unit Leaders earned $185,000.

---

[13]"It Took a Lady to Save Avon," p. 208.
[14]"Avon Calling," p. 26.

***exhibit* 7**   Avon's Operating Strategies and Implementation Initiatives, 2000–2001

Marketing transformations
- Higher-quality, timely market intelligence
- Category-, brand-, and concept-focused marketing strategy
- Flexible product development cycles
- Comprehensive product screening
- Fewer, more highly innovative new products
- Integrated category, brand, and campaign planning
- Significantly shortened campaign planning and brochure creation
- Use of high-style, glamorous catalogs

Supply chain improvement
- Supplier management/sourcing savings
- Leverage supply chain planning tools to reduce cost and inventory levels
- Consensus-based forecasting
- Strong linkages and focus between marketing and supply chain operations
- ABC planning and product segmentation
- Centralized inventory distribution hubs

Sales Leadership
- Faster growth through expanded coverage
- Improved representative earnings opportunities
- Full implementation of eRepresentative concept to Poland, Taiwan, Japan
- Expand pilot eRepresentative program in Brazil, Chile, Argentina, and the United Kingdom
- Continue existing pilot eRepresentative program in Italy and Venezuela
- Redesign pilot eRepresentative program for Canada and Germany

International
- Sales Leadership and training
- Geographic expansion
- New market entries
- Expansion of outlets in China
- Establish a customer club in China
- Triple advertising to 7% of sales in China

E-commerce and Internet
- Utilization of Internet in manufacturing/sourcing (job bidding, e-auctions, international transfers)
- Internet-based customer service functions including electronic ordering, contract processing, product information, and order status
- Utilization of Internet to provide representatives with ordering information, account status, online appointments, sales training, and field reporting
- Create global website style guide
- Maximize and leverage existing sites in the United States, Japan, and Taiwan

Source: Avon investor presentation, Susan Kropf, president and COO, 2000.

Even though all representatives enrolled in the Sales Leadership program were required to sell products totaling at least $500 per month, some spent more time recruiting and training new members than selling products. A New York rep who said she spent "Saturdays outside the supermarket trying to talk people into becoming an Avon Lady" recruited 350 new reps in 18 months and grossed more than $1.3 million in sales—half of which came from her recruits.[15] By late 2001, more than one-third of Avon's representatives were participating in the Sales Leadership program and the company was progressing with implementation in international markets.

A by-product of Sales Leadership was Avon's ability to recruit younger sales representatives. Before Sales Leadership, the company had trouble recruiting younger reps; its greatest success was with women over 40. The introduction of youth to Avon's sales force was important since the younger women's network of customers might be less brand loyal and more likely to try new products. The changing face of Avon's sales force is shown below:

Age	New Reps	Total Reps	All U.S. Women
Under 35	52%	17%	34%
35+	48%	83%	66%
Average age	35	48	46

Source: Avon Products, Inc.

E-commerce and the Internet   Jung and Kropf saw the Internet as the driver of transformation in the relationships between representatives, customers, and the company's marketing and supply chain operations. The company could use the Internet to accept bids from sourcing contractors and vendors; create global sales aids and online literature; and provide representatives with electronic ordering, contract processing, product information, and order status. Avon's Web-based ordering process eliminated paperwork for eRepresentatives and reduced Avon's internal cost of order processing from 90 cents to 30 cents per order. In 2001, Avon had added most items to its website for online purchasing but also hoped to expand www.avon.com to include virtual makeovers, online appointments, sales training for its representatives in the United States, Japan, Taiwan, and eventually 17 other country markets.

The company's Internet sales strategy achieved early success in 2000 when Avon management found that 4 to 6 percent of site visitors made purchases versus a typical purchase rate of 1 to 2 percent for most business-to-consumer sites. Avon management also found that eRepresentatives increased sales by 30 percent on average after linking to www.avon.com. Andrea Jung suggested that the sales increases were attributable to the Web's ability to keep representatives constantly connected to customers. She also suggested that eReps experienced "higher average order productivity as the geographic borders and time differences disappear."[16] Avon hoped to have 250,000 U.S. reps enrolled as eRepresentatives by 2002.

Image Enhancement   The transformation of Avon's image called for new products, new packaging, celebrity endorsements, stylish new catalogs, and new advertising campaigns. Avon increased the company's expenditures for advertising by 50 percent (to $90 million) in 2000, and Jung wanted Avon's advertising budget to grow from 2 percent to approximately 4 percent of total beauty sales by 2004. The company's advertising focused on its global "Let's Talk" campaign, which attempted to

---

[15]"It Took a Lady to Save Avon," p. 208.

[16]"Avon Calling," p. 26.

portray Avon as a lively, energetic, fashionable brand. Management saw the company's endorsement by Venus and Serena Williams as an embodiment of Avon's values of empowerment and self-fulfillment. The company also completely redesigned its catalog to better reflect the glamour associated with the cosmetics industry. Prior to the redesign, Avon's catalog had the look of an industrial products catalog, with beauty products usually depicted in photos on a plain background with some limited graphics. The new catalog, first tested in the United Kingdom in 2000, had the slick look of fashion and cosmetics ads seen in magazines like *Glamour* or *Cosmopolitan*—copy was printed in stylish fonts, and products were displayed by fashion models. During the U.K. test, the catalog helped Avon not only improve sales, average order sizes, and market share but also move from number four in the U.K. market to number three. Avon's redesigned catalog for the U.S. market was scheduled for launch in late 2001.

Changing Avon's image and developing of global campaigns involved new approaches to market intelligence, marketing strategy, new product development, and marketing planning. Kropf called for better and more timely market intelligence on various consumer groups, channels, and competitors, as well as the development of a consumer-needs-based marketing strategy. In addition, Kropf required Avon's marketers to integrate their decisions with others in the organization, including product developers. The cross-functional product development effort called for shorter development cycles, more highly innovative products, and more frequent development of breakthrough products. Once new products were developed, Avon's marketers were to create integrated category and brand campaigns in shorter time frames so that products could go to market earlier. Market research conducted by Avon indicated that the company's efforts to enhance the Avon brand image had achieved some modest success by mid 2001. The U.S. brand image indexes of Avon and selected competitors in June 1999 and March 2001 are shown below:

Brand	June 1999	March 2001
Cover Girl	150	146
Clinique	150	138
Revlon	138	131
Maybelline	107	107
Avon	89	96
Mary Kay	96	96
L'Oréal	104	96
Oil of Olay	86	93

Source: Avon Products, Inc.

Product Development   In 2000, Avon's R&D team responded to Andrea Jung's challenge to develop a blockbuster product within two years by introducing Anew Retroactive—an antiaging skin cream. Retroactive, developed in just under one year, recorded sales of $100 million in its first year on the market—twice the first year's sales of any other previous new Avon product. Jung's emphasis on product innovation also aided Avon's move into the development of new lines of business. Avon's R&D personnel collaborated with pharmaceuticals manufacturer Roche Holding, Ltd., in the development of vitamins and supplements designed to promote general health or address

exhibit 8   Avon Products, Inc.'s Net Sales by Major Product Line Categories, 1998–2000 (in millions)

	2000	1999	1998
Cosmetics, fragrances, and toiletries	$3,501.3	$3,220.8	$3,181.1
Beauty Plus			
Fashion jewelry	323.4	313.4	294.5
Accessories	275.8	223.9	222.4
Apparel	476.3	474.5	469.1
Watches	68.6	49.8	42.1
	$1,144.1	$1,061.6	$1,028.1
Beyond Beauty and Other*	1,028.3	1,006.7	1,003.5
Total net sales	$5,673.7	$5,289.1	$5,212.7

*Beyond Beauty and Other primarily includes home products, gift and decorative, health and nutrition, and candles.

Source: Avon Products, Inc., 2000 10-K.

specific health problems such as lack of energy, poor memory, stress, cardiovascular disease, arthritis, loss of bone density, and hormone imbalance. In addition, Avon and Roche developed the VitaTonics line of bath and skin care products, which offered therapeutic benefits provided by vitamins A, B, and C. Other Avon Wellness products included aromatherapy products, books, videos, music, and teas. Avon's Wellness line accounted for an estimated $75 million in sales during 2001. Exhibit 8 presents Avon's sales contribution by product line.

In addition to Anew Retroactive and the VitaTonics bath products, new Avon products introduced in 2000 included Color IV cosmetics; 22 shampoos, conditioners, and hair treatments; and VitAdvance vitamins and nutritional supplements. Avon also developed two new fragrance brands, Incandessence (a floral scent inspired by the warmth of the sun) and Little Black Dress (a scent that was said to be timeless and perfect for almost any occasion). Avon's new products aided in market share gains of 0.8 percent in color cosmetics, 2.2 percent in antiaging, and 0.3 percent overall among mass market brands. Avon's Wellness line exceeded sales estimates by 300 percent and achieved a 46 percent penetration rate during its first year on the market.

International   Avon pushed its innovative new products like Anew Retroactive into emerging markets like China, Poland, Russia, Hungary, and Slovakia; redesigned catalogs to illustrate the glamour of the Avon brand; and allocated up to 7 percent of sales to advertising in each country market. In China, Avon brand awareness improved from 41 to 53 percent, annual usage rates increased from 26 to 31 percent, and sales improved by 47 percent during 2000. In the EEMEA region Avon entered into new markets, implemented Sales Leadership and sales rep training, and aggressively increased spending on advertising and promotions. Avon's efforts in EEMEA improved its share of the makeup subcategory from 8.7 percent in 1999 to 11.5 percent in 2001, increased its share of fragrance sales from 6.5 percent in 1999 to 9.3 percent in 2001, and increased its market share in the skin care category from 7.7 percent in 1999 to 10.6 percent in 2001. Also, Avon had the highest beauty brand image index among global CFT

exhibit 9   Avon Products, Inc.'s Net Sales and Operating Profit by Geographic Region, 1998–2000 (in millions)

	2000		1999		1998	
	Net Sales	Operating Profit	Net Sales	Operating Profit	Net Sales	Operating Profit
North America						
United States	$1,894.9	$ 343.5	$1,809.3	$329.3	$1,774.0	$302.8
Other*	253.0	24.7	241.0	31.8	259.7	29.3
Total	$2,147.9	$ 368.2	$2,050.3	$361.1	$2,033.7	$332.1
International						
Latin America North**	848.8	215.2	731.7	181.6	636.0	156.4
Latin America South**	992.0	200.3	909.0	184.9	1,057.0	198.9
Latin America	1,840.8	415.5	1,640.7	366.5	1,693.0	355.3
Europe	885.6	129.5	878.0	126.2	862.7	102.2
Pacific	799.4	117.8	720.1	102.1	623.3	62.5
Total	3,525.8	662.8	3,238.8	594.8	3,179.0	520.0
Total from operations	$5,673.7	$1,031.0	$5,289.1	$955.9	$5,212.7	$852.1
Global expenses		(242.3)		(255.3)		(224.5)
Special and nonrecurring charges		—		(151.2)		(154.4)
Operating profit		$ 788.7		$549.4		$473.2

*Includes operating information for Canada and Puerto Rico.

**Latin America North includes the major markets of Mexico, Venezuela, and Central America. Latin America South includes the major markets of Brazil, Argentina, Chile, and Peru.

Source: Avon Products, Inc., 2000 10-K.

brands in Hungary, Poland, Russia, and Ukraine, and the second-highest index in Slovakia and the Czech Republic. Avon's net sales and operating profit by geographic region for 1998–2000 are presented in Exhibit 9.

Retail Channels   The company's Avon Centers planned for JCPenney and Sears stores represented a substantial growth opportunity since, in 2000, Sears and JCPenney combined had nearly 2,000 stores with total cosmetics sales of $700 million. Also, estimates indicated that 58 to 60 percent of all women shopped in Sears or JCPenney and preferred premium mass-market, specialty, or entry-level prestige CFT lines. This group of customers matched Avon management's target market for a new retail line of cosmetics, but one standout characteristic of Sears and JCPenney shoppers was that they tended to reject direct selling. Avon's initial agreements with Sears and JCPenney called for 195 Avon Centers in 2001, with an additional 650 store-within-a-store openings in 2002. However, Sears abandoned the plan in July 2001, just weeks before the first Avon Center opening was scheduled. Still, Avon pushed forward with the opening of its Avon Centers in 75 JCPenney stores and the launch of its beComing CFT line with 400 SKUs, upscale prestige packaging, and value pricing. Avon Centers provided shoppers with free samples and were staffed by uniformed sales employees who had undergone thorough training to recommend beComing products best suited to customers' complexions. Following are Avon's pricing points for its beComing product line in comparison with core Avon, mass-market, and prestige brands:

Product	Core Avon	Mass-Market Brands	beComing	Prestige Brands
Lipstick	$3–$7	$6–$9	$9.50	$12–$16
Nail polish	$2–$4	$3–$5	$6.50	$8–$12
Antiaging treatment	$16–$24	$13–$22	$20–$40	$30–$60
Fragrance	$20	$20	$30	$45+

Source: Avon Products, Inc., investor update meeting, May 8, 2001.

AVON'S PERFORMANCE AT ANDREA JUNG'S SECOND ANNIVERSARY AS CEO

As Andrea Jung completed her second year as CEO of Avon Products, Inc., she was able to celebrate a number of strategic successes. Avon's sales growth had increased from 1.5 percent in 1999 to an expected 6 percent in 2001; the company's sales force was expected to expand by 15 percent; operating profits were expected to grow by 7 percent; and operating margins were expected to reach the highest level in more than 10 years, at 14 percent. The company's business process reengineering efforts had saved more that $400 million in costs during its first three years and had improved operating margins by more than 350 basis points. In a conference call with investors in December 2001, Jung noted: "We are moving rapidly into the implementation phase of business transformation initiatives . . . Cost savings should accelerate as we transform our operating processes, reengineer our global supply chain, and streamline our organizational structure." She continued by saying, "Business transformation also gives us further confidence that we will achieve at least a 50 basis point improvement in operating margin in 2002, with significantly higher margin expansion beyond next year as we ramp up additional transformation initiatives. Moreover, the savings we expect to generate will enable us to invest further in consumer growth strategies in 2002, on top of the $130 million incremental investment over the past two years."[17]

By December 2001, Avon's strategic investments were recording successes: Little Black Dress had become the company's number two fragrance SKU since its launch in October 2001, beComing sales were meeting expectations, and overall sales in the United States were above projections despite increasingly global recessionary economic effects. In addition, Avon's international sales grew at double-digit rates, with the strongest performance coming in Eastern Europe and Asia. Avon sales growth was expected to remain strong into 2003 due in part to the highly anticipated early-2003 launch of a line of cosmetics and skin care products developed exclusively for teens. Even though Jung had said in December 2001 that the current strategic plan included all necessary elements to accomplish Avon's objectives and meet shareholder's expectations, she had emphasized that there was more to be done: "This turnaround is far from complete. I'm probably thinking that we need to be even bolder and faster."[18]

The company's financial statements for 1998–2000 are shown in Exhibits 10 and 11.

---

[17]Avon Products, Inc., press release, December 7, 2001.

[18]"It Took a Lady to Save Avon," p. 208.

exhibit 10   Avon Products, Inc.'s Consolidated Statements of Income, 1998–2000 (in millions, except per share amounts)

	2000	1999	1998
Net sales	$5,673.7	$5,289.1	$5,212.7
Other revenue	40.9	38.8	35.0
Total revenue	$5,714.6	$5,327.9	$5,247.7
Costs, expenses, and other			
Cost of sales˙	$2,122.7	$2,031.5	$2,053.0
Marketing, distribution, and administrative expenses	2,803.2	2,641.8	2,605.0
Special charges	—	105.2	116.5
Operating profit	788.7	549.4	473.2
Interest expense	84.7	43.2	34.7
Interest income	−8.5	−11.1	−15.9
Other expense (income), net	21.5	10.7	−1.5
Total other expenses	$97.7	$42.8	$17.3
Income from continuing operations before taxes, minority interest, and cumulative effect of accounting change	$691.0	$506.6	$455.9
Income taxes	201.7	204.2	190.8
Income before minority interest and cumulative effect of accounting change	489.3	302.4	265.1
Minority interest	−4.2	0.0	4.9
Income from continuing operations before cumulative effect of accounting change	485.1	302.4	270.0
Cumulative effect of accounting change, net of tax	−6.7	—	—
Net income	$478.4	$302.4	$270.0
Basic earnings per share			
Continuing operations	$2.04	$1.18	$1.03
Cumulative effect of accounting change	−0.03	—	—
	$2.01	$1.18	$1.03
Diluted earnings per share			
Continuing operations	$2.02	$1.17	$1.02
Cumulative effect of accounting change	−0.03	—	—
	$1.99	$1.17	$1.02

˙1999 and 1998 include special and nonrecurring charges of $46.0 and $37.9, respectively, for inventory write-downs.

Source: Avon Products, Inc., 2000 10-K.

exhibit 11   Avon Products, Inc.'s Consolidated Balance Sheets,
1999–2000 (in millions)

	Year Ended December 31	
	2000	1999
Assets		
Current assets		
Cash, including cash equivalents of $23.9 and $49.6	$ 122.7	$ 117.4
Accounts receivable (less allowance for doubtful accounts of $39.2 and $40.0)	499.0	495.6
Income tax receivable	95.2	—
Inventories	610.6	523.5
Prepaid expenses and other	218.2	201.3
Total current assets	1,545.7	1,337.8
Property, plant, and equipment (at cost)		
Land	53.0	55.1
Buildings and improvements	659.5	653.4
Equipment	810.6	763.5
	1,523.1	1,472.0
Less accumulated depreciation	754.7	737.2
	768.4	734.8
Other assets	512.3	456.0
Total assets	$2,826.4	$2,528.6
Liabilities and shareholders' (deficit) equity		
Current liabilities		
Debt maturing within one year	$ 105.4	$ 306.0
Accounts payable	391.3	435.9
Accrued compensation	138.2	165.8
Other accrued liabilities	251.7	411.6
Sales and taxes other than income	101.1	107.5
Income taxes	371.6	286.0
Total current liabilities	$1,359.3	$1,712.8
Long-term debt	$1,108.2	$ 701.4
Employee benefit plans	397.2	398.1
Deferred income taxes	31.3	36.7
Other liabilities (including minority interest of $40.7 and $32.7)	95.2	85.7
Commitments and contingencies		
Share repurchase commitments	51.0	—
Shareholders' (deficit) equity		
Common stock, par value $.25—authorized: 800,000,000 shares; issued 354,535,840 and 352,575,924 shares	88.6	88.1
Additional paid-in capital	824.1	819.4
Retained earnings	1,139.8	837.2
Accumulated other comprehensive loss	(399.1)	(349.7)
Treasury stock, at cost—116,373,394 and 114,680,525 shares	(1,869.2)	(1,801.1)
Total shareholders' (deficit) equity	(215.8)	(406.1)
Total liabilities and shareholders' (deficit) equity	$2,826.4	$2,528.6

Source: Avon Products, Inc., 2000 10-K.

case 2 The Solar Feeder

Lew G. Brown
The University of North Carolina at Greensboro

Emily Abercrombie
The University of North Carolina at Greensboro

"I guess the first thing everyone wants to know is how we came up with the idea for a solar-powered bird feeder," Bo Haeberle remarked, smiling, as he stood in the noisy assembly area. In the background, Glen Thomas continued assembling feeders, undisturbed by Bo and his two guests. In the center of the large room, lines of bird feeders, in various stages of assembly, stretched across large tables. Along one wall, three shelves were filled with beta versions of the feeder—many showing the signs of weather and squirrel attacks.

Bo related that Ed Welsh, one of Bo's friends, actually had the idea for the solar-powered feeder. Six years earlier, Ed had been watching basketball with his brother, Richard, who was an avid basketball fan. While watching one particularly difficult game, Richard, who was already upset, glanced out his window to see a squirrel assaulting the bird feeder on his recently constructed deck. Besides eating the seed, scattering it all over, and loading up their cheeks with seed to take back to their nests, the squirrels also kept the birds away and often destroyed the feeders. Seeing his brother's frustration at both the basketball team and the squirrel, Ed vowed to do something about the age-old problem of squirrels attacking bird feeders.

Bo continued,

Ed placed a car battery near the bird feeder and hooked it up to the feeder. He then ran a line inside the house to a switch that he installed near Richard's chair. When Richard threw the switch, a charge would build up in the feeder, and if a squirrel was on the feeder or got on it, the squirrel got a pretty good jolt. The shock did not hurt the squirrels, but they sure got off the feeder quickly.

This sounds pretty neat, but squirrels are smart animals. It seems that when Richard threw the switch, there was a brief time lapse before the feeder was charged. The squirrels quickly figured out if Richard was in his chair (they could see him through the window) and if they saw him move to throw the switch, they would simply jump off the feeder. This led to hilarious episodes of Richard trying to hide or to throw the switch without the squirrels seeing him.

This hide-and-seek process was too much for Richard, so he just started leaving the switch on. However, the squirrels seemed to know the switch was on and would stay away until the feeder lost its charge. Then, they were back.

Then, I think it was in 1996, we came up with the idea of the solar cell. The solar cell would eliminate the need for the battery, at least that's what we thought. The squirrels,

The authors wish to thank SDI, Inc., for its cooperation in development of this case and the anonymous reviewers for their constructive suggestions to improve the case. The case is for classroom discussion purposes only.

however, figured out that they were okay if they ate in the early morning before the sun charged the cell or in the early evening after the sun had gone down. So, we put a battery in the unit to keep it charged on cloudy or rainy days and in the mornings and evenings. That electronics arrangement is pretty much what we have in the solar feeder today.

"This reminds me of the old saying about the better mousetrap," one of Bo's guests observed. "Perhaps the invention of the squirrel-proof bird feeder has become man's ultimate struggle over the rodent, replacing the search for the better mousetrap!"

"That's an interesting observation," Bo replied. "I seem to remember the quotation mentioned the world beating a path to your door. I hope that happens, but I've got to come up with a good marketing plan for our feeder that builds on what we've learned over these past few years. We are also going to need some help from investors, like yourselves, if we are going to be successful."

BO'S INVOLVEMENT GROWS

Ed Welsh had developed the idea for the feeder while he was working for Bo at Visual Design, Inc., a Greensboro, North Carolina, firm Bo founded to design retail store interiors. Bo had become interested in the bird feeder project as he heard Ed describe Richard's saga. Bo realized how much time and effort his friend spent fighting squirrels and feeding birds. When Ed added the solar device, Bo took a more active interest in the feeder.

"At first, I saw the solar feeder as a challenge—a fun problem," Bo observed. "As you get more into it, however, you realize how clever and gifted squirrels are." Prior to the solar feeder project, Bo and Ed had often gotten together on Wednesday nights for a beer and a game of pool. As they got deeper and deeper into the challenge, they paid less and less attention to the game and talked more and more about the feeder. Bo and Ed also did a little market research by visiting some local stores that sold bird feeders and talking to the stores' owners. However, they really did very little market research.

By fall 1997, things were really getting charged up. Ed took the feeder to a Habitat for Humanity auction. The feeder generated more interest than any other product at the charity auction and earned the highest price bid for any item! In early 1998, Ed took the feeder to the Bird Watch America trade show, the national birding convention. To everyone's surprise, the solar feeder won the award for the best new product.

On the basis of the product's success, Bo decided in October 1998 to begin to cut back on his other business and move towards devoting full time to the solar feeder. He joined forces with Ed, formed Squirrel Defense, Inc. (SDI) as an S corporation, and opened a small shop in Greensboro to begin production of the solar feeder so they could take orders for the product. Little did Bo know about the complexity of building bird feeders!

THE SOLAR FEEDER—HOW IT WORKS

"We developed the product without an engineer," Bo noted as he showed his guests around the shop. "We've done it the way, you know, you make the thing and see if it works. And, you have to learn. If you are an engineer, you can skip a lot of steps because you know something won't work. So we've had to spend a lot of money on product development so we could move from a 'craft' manufactured item to a manufactured product that we can produce in high volume at low cost. This meant reducing our labor costs anywhere we could."

exhibit 1   Solar Feeder Models

And you thought all squirrel-proof bird feeders were ugly?
"Amazing solar technology allows you to train your squirrels to stay away."

Solar FEEDER™

Red Cedar Country Style   **Town Style**

The solar feeder was a unique twist on the typical bird feeder. It resembled a typical birdhouse, but it housed feed instead. Bo and Ed developed design possibilities for their product. With the help of a third partner, Scott Wilson, they decided to produce the solar feeder in two styles, "Town" and "Country" (Exhibit 1). The Country style was a western red cedar house with a copper roof. The Town style offered a contemporary appearance with its white finish and copper roof. They designed the Town style as a higher-end model for construction with Sintra, a material similar to PVC, which provided durability against the elements. The partners estimated that it cost them $90 to $100 to produce one Town solar feeder and $100 to $110 to produce one Country solar feeder. They projected that, at higher production levels, they could produce the Town feeder for as low as $50. However, the lowest production cost for the Country feeder could not be less than $85 at any production level because of the cost of the red cedar and the difficulty of working with that material.

To prevent squirrels from taking the birdseed, the solar feeder produced an electric shock. The feeder had two small copper tubes on either side that served as perches for the birds. A squirrel trying to get the birdseed would touch both of the tubes and/or one of the tubes and the copper roof. Once the squirrel completed the circuit, it received a mild electric shock and jumped from the feeder. The shock did not affect birds because their legs were made of cartilage, and they did not have sweat glands.

The copper roof had an area cut out of it that provided a place for the solar panel. Powered by the solar cell during the day and by a D-cell battery at night, the solar feeder's seed supply was protected around the clock. The unit also featured an on-off switch, so the owner could turn it off if he or she chose to do so.

"The biggest problem with the feeder," Bo noted, "is explaining how it works. We made a video that showed the feeder in action. But people don't understand that it doesn't hurt squirrels. It's friendly. Many people see the cooper tubes and the solar panel and think there must be hot water in the tubes; therefore, the squirrels jump off because the tubes are hot."

Along with the two feeder styles, SDI produced three possible mounting options: the deck mount, patio kit, and yard kit. The deck mount allowed the owner to attach the feeder directly to the deck railing with a short post and mounting plate. The patio kit provided a longer post attached to a moveable base. The yard kit utilized a ground socket (like a very large screw attached to a post) to install the post and feeder in one's yard. This kit eliminated the hassle of digging holes to set up the feeder. The Country feeder offered one other mounting option, the planter box. It attached in the same way as the patio kit, but the base doubled as a planter box for flowers or other greenery. The mountings were available in two finishes: white, to match the Town feeder, and cedar, to match the Country feeder.

Commenting on the feeder's design, Bo pointed out,

> Sometimes people ask me why our feeders are mounted in some way versus the feeders that they have seen that hang from wires that run between two posts or two trees. We found that "squirrel-proof" feeders that are hung or suspended fail because of the squirrels' acrobatics. The squirrels jump onto those kinds of feeders, causing them to swing and send seed everywhere. We have actually seen squirrels swing these feeders until they dump all the seed on the ground.

The solar feeder came with a 30-day, money-back satisfaction guarantee and a one-year warranty on parts. Consumers had to send in a warranty card, however, to validate the warranty.

According to Scott, SDI had been "horribly back-ordered" for the last six months, to the point where the company intentionally slowed sales so production could catch up with demand. Scott commissioned a local manufacturer to perform some production tasks to reduce some of the pressure, but SDI still performed primary assembly. Even though the bird feeder was a relatively simple product, tolerances for cut or machined parts were very tight, and final assembly often involved having to make time-consuming adjustments to parts that were not in tolerance.

In addition to the difficulty of manufacturing the product, Bo learned that starting business in October caused other problems. The retailers to whom the company wanted to sell the bird feeders typically placed their orders for the year during the January through March period, using the money they had earned during the Christmas season. However, with an October start, SDI was not ready to fill large orders by the first quarter of 1999 and missed the ordering window for 1999. Therefore, the company limped along during most of 1999, filling small orders it generated here and there.

By November 1999, production had reached almost 115 feeders per month, and Scott hoped to push it higher to 200 or 300 feeders per week in the coming months. SDI sold the feeders at wholesale prices shown in Exhibit 2. Retailers set a retail price of $280 to $300 for the feeders. "Originally, I priced the feeders based on how much I wanted to make per unit—forget about what the market would pay," Bo observed. "I didn't care. If they buy it—they buy it. If they don't buy it, OK. But, if the interest and demand were there, I'd pursue the project. That was my attitude then.

"Now, my attitude is directed to what the market wants. Our Town feeder needs to sell retail at or below $150 to $160. This price is based on our competitors' prices, and how much we believe our customers will pay for a superior product. Stores want a 100 percent markup on their cost, our wholesale price. So, for a retail price of $160, I need to be able to sell the feeder to stores at $75 to $80 a unit to allow them to make a profit."

exhibit 2   SDI Price List and Terms

Product	Recommended Retail	Wholesale Price	Drop-Ship Price
Original Solar Feeder	$229	$138	$117.30
White Solar Feeder	269	161	136.85
Cedar Yard Install Kit	47	28	23.80
White Yard Install Kit	47	28	23.80
Cedar Deck Install Kit	35	23	19.55
White Deck Install Kit	35	23	19.55
Cedar Patio Kit	58	35	29.75
White Patio w/4×4	58	35	29.75
Cedar Planter w/4×4	75	45	38.25
White Planter w/4×4	75	45	38.25
Cedar Mount	13.50	8	6.80
White Mount	13.50	8	6.80
Cedar 4×4×48	26.50	16	13.60
White 4×4×48	20	12	10.20
Cedar 4×4×72	43	26	22.10
White 4×4×72	26.50	16	13.60

Terms and Conditions

Minimum opening order $350. No minimums on reorders.

New orders should be prepaid, COD, MasterCard, or Visa.

Our standard terms are net 30, with 1% discount if payment is made within 10 days. Terms are available after first order, with verification of references. Service charge of 1.5% per month on late invoices.

We ship UPS, FedEx, and commercial carrier. Shipping paid by buyer. Shipping charges are nonrefundable.

Damage claims must be made within 5 days of receipt of shipment.

25% restocking fee on all canceled orders.

Bo's primary responsibility was to generate interest in the product and find sales outlets for the solar feeder. The feeder won two more "best new product" awards in 1999. These awards contributed to the product's exposure and sales. For 1999, Bo reported that SDI sold 112 Town-style and 334 Country-style feeders. Bo estimated he sold about one mounting kit for each three feeders.

The partners promoted the solar feeder through trade shows to traditional and high-end birding stores, and through the company's website. They chose to promote the product to lawn and garden stores, as well as nurseries and birding stores, such as Wild Bird Center and Wild Birds Unlimited. They thought that other outlets, such as Lowe's and Home Depot, would eventually be interested if SDI could develop a cheaper model.

To distribute the feeder, SDI decided to work with several large companies that distributed garden supplies to retailers. Small retailers used these distributors' catalogs to place orders for everything from rakes to seeds. The distributors consolidated orders from one area and made deliveries, which allowed them to have delivery costs that were lower than UPS costs. The distributors had salespeople who called on the retailers to take orders and provide service.

Because SDI could not yet produce large quantities of the solar feeder, it took orders from the distributors and shipped the feeders directly to the retailers by using UPS. SDI charged about 10 to 12 percent for shipping. After SDI had shipped a feeder to a store, it billed the distributor. SDI had good relationships with the distributors and found that they paid SDI promptly.

Advertising consisted of a retro theme, with images of 1950s "mom-and-pop" people (Exhibits 3 and 4). SDI produced flyers and materials in loud oranges and greens, as well as psychedelic greens and yellows. Also, the partners created a video showing the effectiveness of the product; consumers could watch the video on the website.

"However," Bo noted, "the video doesn't download well and our website is not easy to use. We designed it for us, but we find that the typical person who buys the feeder is a 35- to 75-year-old affluent woman and typically on the higher end of that range. This person may not be handy with a computer. Thus, although our website has had good response, it's produced limited sales.

Bo believed some customers were purchasers of high-end products and were buying based on novelty and appearance. "We figured that our product would attract the bird enthusiast, preferably an older crowd of retired men and women. However, we also find that the product is attracting younger consumers who are homeowners, 30 years or older, and are typically housewives."

Bo noted that a student group from a local university had recently done some research for him. The group found a 1996 survey by the U.S. Fish and Wildlife Service and an American Birding Association (ABA) study that estimated that there were 50.4 million bird watchers in the United States. The most popular activity among residential wildlife watchers was feeding wild birds. A 1993 U.S. Department of Interior study estimated that consumers spent $843 million per year on feeders, baths, and nesting boxes.

Further, the students found that the average member of the American Birding Association was between 40 and 60 years old with an annual average income of $60,000. Sixty-five percent of the members were male, with women comprising 35 percent, up from just 25 percent in 1989. More than 80 percent of ABA members had a college degree. The five states with the most members were California, Florida, Pennsylvania, Texas, and Illinois, in that order. ABA membership had tripled in the 1990s, reaching 20,456 by 1998.

COMPETITION

Even though SDI priced the solar feeder above some competitive products, in the partners' eyes there did not appear to be much competition. The only competition they had seen was a product called "WildBills." It was also electric-shock-based and had been dubbed the "squirrel-stinger." The feeder was dome shaped and came in two sizes, 8- and 12-port feeders. According to the

exhibit 3   Sample Solar Feeder Advertisement

Source: SDI, Inc.

exhibit 4   Sample Solar Feeder Advertisement

Source: SDI, Inc.

exhibit 5   Competition

squirrel-free bird feeder

As seen on TV! If you are tired of squirrels stealing bird seed, destroying your bird feeders and costing you money, a hi-tech WildBills Squirrel-Free Bird Feeder may be just the feeder for you. They electronically teach squirrels to go away and stay away. Power source—9 volt battery. We have two models available.

Source: Company website.

partners, it served functionality only, whereas the solar feeder offered appearance as well. WildBills was significantly cheaper, with a retail price of $89.95 to $99.95 (Exhibit 5).

Vari-Crafts manufactured a squirrel-proof bird feeder that fended off squirrels by utilizing a wire cage that permitted only small birds to enter and feed. It sold for approximately $75 (Exhibit 6).

The BIG TOP, created by Droll Yankee, had a dome top that prevented squirrels and other animals from stealing seed as well. It offered a lifetime guarantee and had a price of just $57.95 (Exhibit 7).

To the partners, these competitors did not appear to be viable opponents because the feeders were unappealing and did not offer the solar feeder's technology.

The student group had also done some research on competition. Students had visited a local specialty nursery, a large independent hardware/garden supply store, and a branch of a national home-improvement retailer. Exhibit 8 presents results of the group's research.

LATER THAT DAY

After the guests left, Bo returned to his office. Sitting at his desk, he began to examine his financial statements (Exhibits 9 and 10), wondering how a little company like his could have all these best new product awards and orders, but no cash.

Bo heard a noise and looked up to see Ed Welsh walking into the office. Ed looked worried also. "Ed, we have a problem. Our cash flow is not where it needs to be. I don't understand it. We've more orders than we can fill, and we are still not breaking even. I need more feeders, and I need them to be cheaper."

exhibit 6   Competition

Squirrel-Proof Bird Feeder, Vari-Crafts

Stops pesky gray squirrels from eating seed. Wire cage also allows only small songbirds access to feeding ports while excluding larger starlings, grackles, and jays. 18 lb. mixed-seed chamber requires only weekly filling for convenience. Features easy-filling screw-off top, vented seed chamber to eliminate condensation, and easy disassembly for cleaning. Small songbirds enter the wire mesh to feed at six ports. Interior tube is PVC. Hang or post mount. 60″ poll and ground socket included.

Source: Company website.

exhibit 7   Competition

BIG TOP by Droll Yankee

The best squirrel-proof bird feeder. It is made of UV-stabilized polycarbonate, brass hardware, and die-cast metal hooks. A quality gift. A long-time favorite, the BIG TOP gives both weather and squirrel protection. The adjustable seed valve lets you offer any type of seed. By lowering the 15″ diameter dome, large birds are kept out. Hang a suet bag from the hook below. Rated #1 bird feeder by the Cornell Lab of Ornithology, "My favorite feeder is the BIG TOP by Droll Yankee." Scott Shalaway, columnist and radio show host of Birds & Nature. Lifetime guarantee.

Source: Company website.

"I've been looking at this feeder for six years now and have become pretty jaded," Ed responded. "At this point, I'm just putting them in boxes and shipping them. What else can I do?"

Scott Wilson walked in from the workshop just in time to catch the end of Ed's statement. "Let me guess. You are discussing our cash flow problems? Maybe we should consider the way we are taking this to the consumer. I have been working on

exhibit 8   Competition Survey

Store	Manufacturer	Type	Squirrel Resistant	Lawn Appeal	Price
New Garden Nursery	Vari-Crafts	Cylinder	No	5	$44.99
		Caged	Yes	4	$79.99
	Droll Yankee	Domed	Yes	6	$39.99
	Duncraft	Caged	Yes	4	$74.99
	K feeder	Dome guard	Yes	4	$22.49
	Wildlife Wood Products	Classic wood	No	6	$42.99
	ERVA	Post guard	Yes	2	$19.99
	Heritage Farms	Classic	Yes	5	$91.99
Fleet Plumber	Heritage Farms	Classic	Yes	5	$69.99
	Wildlife Wood Products	Classic wood	No	6	$42.99
	Hyde	Caged	Yes	4	$34.99
	RubberMaid	Dome Guard	Yes	2	$14.99
	Lazy Hill Farms	Custom	No	8	$299.99
		Custom	No	9	$549.99
	Princess Jamica	Custom	No	8	$169.99
		Custom	No	8	$359.99
	Other custom	Custom	No	6	$79.99
		Custom	No	7	$109.99
		Custom	No	8	$129.99
Lowe's	Homestead	Classic	Yes	4	$29.96
	Country Home	Classic cedar	No	5	$34.99
	National Garden	Cylinder	No	5	$49.96
	ArtLine	Classic plastic	No	2	$12.99
	Others	Cylinder	No	2	$12.99
		Classic	No	3	$24.99
		Gazebo	No	4	$29.99
Other competitive products mentioned in a *Wall Street Journal* survey published October 17, 1999:					
	L.L. Bean Absolute II	House	Yes		$74.00
	Smith & Hawken	Cylinder with cage	Yes		$79.00
	Good Catalog				
	Infinite Feeder	Cylinder	Yes		$139.00
	Duncraft WildBill's 12 Port	Cylinder/ electronic	Yes		$119.95

Survey as of April 2000.

Lawn appeal on scale of 1–10, with 10 being high. Represent surveyor's opinion.

Source: Student survey and *Wall Street Journal* article cited.

some ideas such as new brochures and advertising materials, but honestly, things just are not working in production. The feeders are expensive and time consuming to make."

"Who were those people I saw you with earlier, Bo?" Ed asked.

"A couple of potential investors I've been talking to. They're impressed with the product; but, like everyone else, they want to see a marketing plan. I told them I'm working on one.

"You remember those SCORE people (Service Corps of Retired Executives) I was working with last year?" Bo continued. "They also wanted me to write a business plan, but I really didn't know what to write. It's a little like the chicken and the egg: How can you have a plan before you have a business? A year and a half ago, I would not have been able to write a plan because I didn't know where all the problems were. Now, I know, and I think we are ready. It's time to implement our plan to increase our sales and production and to reduce our costs. These financials tell me that we don't have much time."

exhibit 9   SDI's Balance Sheet, 1998–1999

	December 31, 1999	December 31, 1998
Assets		
Current assets		
Checking/savings	$ (7,308)	$ (701)
Loan receivable—Ed Welsh	7,180	4,830
Total current assets[a]	(128)	4,129
Fixed assets	1,416	715
Total assets	$ 1,288	$ 4,844
Liabilities and equity		
Current liabilities		
Credit card debt	$ 0	$ (2,140)
Payroll expense	2,418	0
Total current liabilities	2,418	(2,140)
Long-term debt		
Loan payable—Wayne Garrison	2,500	0
Loan payable—Scott Wilson	10,000	0
Loan payable—VID	14,493	9,500
Total long-term debt	26,993	9,500
Total liabilities	29,411	7,360
Equity		
Capital stock	10,473	9,473
Retained earnings	(11,989)	0
Net income	(26,607)	(11,989)
Total equity	(28,123)	(2,516)
Total liabilities and equity	$ 1,288	$ 4,844

[a]The balance sheet contained no entry for inventory.

exhibit 10   SDI's Income Statement, 1998–1999

	December 31, 1999	December 31, 1998
Net Sales	$ 56,071	$ 18,001
Cost of goods sold:		
Contract labor	1,545	2,950
Purchases	21,170	8,128
Total cost of goods sold	22,715	11,078
Gross profit	33,356	6,923
Expenses		
Advertising	5,334	1,353
Automobile expense	859	0
Bank service charge*	1,496	885
Depreciation expense	0	85
Education	149	0
Equipment rental	53	0
Filing fees	75	0
Freight & shipping	1,425	1,057
Gross wages**	19,285	0
Payroll taxes	1,574	0
License & permits	0	757
Miscellaneous†	2,925	0
Payroll taxes	1,574	0
Postage & delivery	408	0
Professional fees	1,654	3,425
Rent	7,274	5,230
Supplies	9,386	2,773
Taxes	548	0
Telephone	2,679	1,045
Trade show expense	2,788	2,015
Travel & entertainment	1,053	0
Utilities	979	287
Total expenses	59,963	18,912
Net income	$(26,607)	$(11,989)

*Bank service charges include credit card charges and interest charges.

**Gross wage includes wages for production workers.

†Miscellaneous charges include charges for miscellaneous materials and expenses.

case 3 World Wrestling Federation (A)

Thomas Mannarelli
INSEAD

Christopher Baty
INSEAD

PREFACE

It would come to be called the match of the century. Canadian hero Bret "The Hitman" Hart versus American bad boy "The Heartbreak Kid" Shawn Michaels. The World Wrestling Federation's top two contenders, squaring off on November 9, 1997, in Montreal.

It is Remembrance Day weekend in Canada, and it will also turn out to be the final night of world champion Hart's 14-year career with the World Wrestling Federation. Despite efforts to keep it quiet, speculation is running high that Hart signed that week with Ted Turner's rival wrestling league, World Championship Wrestling. More than 20,000 fans have come down to the Molson Center to see him off, many carrying signs with words of encouragement. "Don't Go, Bret," reads one; "Where Bret Goes, We Go," reads another.

As with all professional wrestling matches, the outcome of the Montreal showdown has been decided beforehand. Hart's looming defection to the World Championship Wrestling league, however, introduces a worrisome note of uncertainty into the proceedings. Thanks to a story leaked on the Internet, some of the audience knows that off-camera differences between Hart and Michaels came to a violent head in June, with simmering resentments boiling over into unscripted slurs and a real locker-room fight. The match, should Hart decide to use it as such, would provide him a golden opportunity to settle old scores in front of a hometown crowd.

It is one of the rare times in the history of professional wresting when no one, from WWF scriptwriters on down, can be completely sure of the outcome.

At 8:00 PM, backed by pyrotechnic explosions and thundering rock music, the show begins.

INTRODUCTION

In 2000, oversaturation became the watchword of the wrestling industry. The reasons were obvious: with over 15 hours of wrestling programming on U.S. television every week, industry analysts feared the business might become a victim of its own success.

Much to the delight of the two major wrestling companies, the World Wrestling Federation (WWF) and World Championship Wrestling (WCW), though, professional wrestling's growth showed no signs of slowing.

The industry produced revenues of over $1 billion a year in the United States, with over 35 million viewers tuning in every week for a dose of the body-slamming, pile-driving, high-flying action. Pay-per-view broadcasts enticed as many as 7 million subscribers each year to pay $30 per event to watch the action from home. The sports-entertainment hybrid had also found eager audiences all over the world: American wrestling programs were televised in 120 countries and translated into 11 languages.

Wrestling had not always been such big business. Many of the secrets of the industry's rise in popularity resided in innovations implemented over the past two decades. This case will examine those changes with a view toward understanding an ethical and managerial dilemma faced by Vince McMahon, owner of the WWF. After a primer on wrestling's past, the case will focus on the challenge cable mogul Ted Turner posed to McMahon's wrestling empire, and explain the way Turner's entry into the wrestling world brought McMahon into conflict with one of his top employees, Bret "The Hitman" Hart.

LEARNING THE ROPES: WRESTLING HISTORY

The First 50 Years: Ups, Downs, and the Arrival of Television

Born in the circus sideshows of the 1890s, professional wrestling had long been an industry of soaring boom times followed by unceremonious busts. At the dawn of the 20th century, wrestling was America's favorite spectacle. Frank Gotch, the era's top contender, visited the White House twice as a guest of President Teddy Roosevelt. With the advent of radio, however, wrestling took a back seat to boxing, baseball, comedy, and other entertainment forms that translated better to the medium. That, combined with fiscal woes brought on by the Depression, sidelined the industry through the 1930s and 1940s.

However, the pseudosport proved to be a resilient entertainment form. Midcentury, professional wrestling was on the rise again, as the nascent television networks scrambled to find low-cost, easy-to-film programming. Wrestling fit the bill perfectly, and its top talent soon became national celebrities. Wrestlers such as "Nature Boy" Buddy Rogers and Gorgeous George, with their embellished histories and cartoonish personas, were loved and reviled coast-to-coast.

Times and tastes changed, however, and by the end of the 1950s wrestling's popularity had begun to wane. Networks had a limited number of broadcast slots available, and television viewers were demanding more sophisticated programs. In a time of dramatic leaps in production quality, ringside bouts with their static wide-angle shots, quickly became outdated. By 1960, wrestling had disappeared from the networks entirely.

Regional Markets, Amicable Neighbors

Professional wrestling's departure from the networks did not signal the industry's demise. The demand for wrestling on a local level was still strong, and a new crop of promoters arose to fill the need. By the 1970s, the wrestling world had fragmented into

30 or so local markets, each operated by a regional promoter. These promoters produced weekly wrestling bouts for local television and gave out free tickets to draw small audiences to their tapings, usually held in cramped television studios. These televised matches were used primarily as a vehicle to build up fan interest in the feuds, which would be settled in the industry's bread and butter: live matches in larger arenas.

The scale was limited, but there was no money to be made. With all promoters getting a piece of the pie, relations between markets remained cordial. Wrestlers typically worked on short-term contracts, usually being paid on a per-appearance basis. With the exception of a handful of national stars, their incomes were meager. There was plenty of work, however, and when a wrestler had saturated one market, he could start fresh in another. Then, after an absence of, say, six months, he could make a triumphant return to the previous market with renewed fan interest.

To add both credibility and celebrity luster, most territories were affiliated with a larger alliance. Each alliance recognized its own world champion, and the reigning champion would travel to different territories within his alliance, challenging the local hero. These match-ups routinely packed small auditoriums across North American cities. Despite the ease with which wrestlers could travel to different regions, borders between territories were clearly drawn. Unless an agreement was first struck between promoters, attempts at expansion were viewed harshly. "Muscling in" on a territory was a serious breach of the gentlemen's agreement that had governed wrestling for two decades.

By the end of the 1970s, the circuits were well worn, and the territories firmly established. Wrestling had carved a comfortable niche for itself as a lucrative, but no-growth, business.

No one was in a better place to reap the benefits of the system than Vince McMahon Sr. Compared to other promoters', his territory was vast, encompassing most of the major cities on the eastern seaboard. Through his World Wrestling Federation, McMahon Sr. controlled live and televised wrestling events in major markets such as Philadelphia, Washington, D.C., Boston, and New York City.

By the beginning of the 1980s, though, the territory McMahon Sr. had built was imperiled by his failing health. With his cancer spreading, McMahon Sr. sold his business to his son, Vince McMahon Jr., in 1982. Professional wrestling in the United States, and eventually the world, would never be the same.

A NEW KIND OF WRESTLING: THE WWF

Disruptive and Violent: Vince McMahon Jr.'s Early Years

Before he came to work for his father, the future looked grim for Vince McMahon. Raised by his mother and a succession of physically abusive stepfathers in Havelock, North Carolina, McMahon spent most of his childhood in trouble. His home life was a constant battle. According to McMahon, his stepfathers would sometimes hit him with tools or baseball bats when he stuck up for his mother. Suffering from both dyslexia and attention deficit disorder, his disruptive antics in the classroom eventually got him shipped off to Fishburne Military School in Waynesboro, Virginia. His rebelliousness continued unabated, and, although he graduated, he was the first student in the school's history to be court-martialed.

It took him five years, with summer school every year, to get his degree. McMahon was eager to join his father in the WWF, but McMahon Sr. discouraged those aspirations. His son's future, he thought, would be more secure in a traditional career as a lawyer. Out of school with little direction, McMahon drifted from job to job, selling everything from paper cups to adding machines. He got his big break when one of the ringside announcers from his father's television program failed to show up for a taping. The young McMahon was hastily added as a replacement. McMahon Jr. displayed an immediate talent for ring announcing, and his father reluctantly allowed his son to join the company.

Sr. and Jr. Together

On joining the WWF in 1971, McMahon discovered something that inspired and challenged him. Ambition, deadened from years of poor scholastic performance and unrewarding sales jobs, returned. The wrestling world was a new start for McMahon, and his academic trials and childhood of physical abuse had taken the sting away from potential failure. As he explained in 1985.

> Even when I was a kid, my philosophy was basically, if I wanted something and somebody else didn't want me to have it, the worst that could happen was I might get the hell kicked out of me.

Armed with this brash confidence, a 24-year-old McMahon dove into the role of apprentice promoter. From his father, he learned how to deal with large metropolitan venues (such as New York City's Madison Square Garden) and also had a chance to study the television side of the operation. By taking up the post of full-time ring announcer, McMahon was able to hone his performing skills and see close up what worked in the ring and what did not.

Still working for his father but looking to try something on his own, McMahon put some of his newly learned promotional skills to the test, buying a 5,000-seat arena in Yarmouth, Massachusetts. The concerts he staged there encouraged his hopes of someday becoming an entertainment promoter in his own right. They also gave him his first insight into the potential of marrying wrestling with the pyrotechnics and elaborate sets of rock concerts.

First Steps

With his father dying of cancer, McMahon seemed the obvious choice to take over control of the WWF. McMahon Sr., though, refused to just hand over the company he had built. Because the young McMahon lacked the capital to buy the WWF outright, father and son arranged a payment plan whereby McMahon Jr. paid for the company in several lump sums, due throughout the year. If he missed any of the payments, the company would revert to McMahon Sr. and the other stockholders.

The first year was predictable touch-and-go, as the new owner struggled to make payment on the business. The resourceful McMahon managed to meet every payment obligation, however, and despite the capital drain incurred by the purchase, he quickly moved to expand the WWF. One of his first major moves as the "new kid in town" was to assert his position as one who would not abide by the artificial territorial borders that had been drawn by his predecessors. As McMahon explains, the days of the gentlemen's agreement were over:

In the old days, there were wrestling fiefdoms all over the country, each with its own little lord in charge. Each little lord respected the rights of his neighboring little lord. No takeovers or raids were allowed . . . I, of course, had no allegiance to those little lords.

Empire Building

The first signs that the old order was crumbling came when news leaked out that McMahon had convinced a station in Los Angeles, the second-largest TV market in the United States, to air WWF wrestling. St. Louis, long a bastion of professional wrestling, soon followed. He then used his presence in those markets to leverage spots in others. Soon, the WWF could be seen in local markets across half the country. Predictably, the move did not go over well with other promoters, including McMahon's father. McMahon recalls:

> My dad would have never sold me the business had he known what I was going to do with it . . . He would receive phone calls every single day from his cronies in the wrestling business that I was invading. He'd say, "Vinny, what the hell are you doing now? My God, you know you're going to wind up at the bottom of a river." These were pretty tough guys that we were competing with.

The WWF was now wholly McMahon's, but it was not making the kind of money that could support simultaneous battles on 30 territorial fronts. McMahon gambled that many of his competitors would take note of the WWF's enormous television presence and overestimate McMahon's capital reserves, selling out to him or quitting outright. McMahon explains:

> Most of the promoters we were competing with were former wrestlers, most middle aged, none of whom had a very strong work ethic. Their typical day in the office may have been several hours if, in fact, they went into the office at all . . . I was counting upon the fact, based on their egos, that they wouldn't even be able to go to lunch together, much less cooperate with one another.

McMahon's gamble paid off. As local television stations fell into WWF hands across the country, so did most of the rival territories. Those that tried to compete were undermined, as their top talent signed lucrative contracts with the WWF. Fans watched, shocked, as alliance champions disappeared from local broadcasts overnight and reappeared as WWF contenders. On several occasions, McMahon was able to orchestrate embarrassing hiring coups where a big-name wrestler appeared simultaneously on a competitor's (taped) program and the WWF's more recent one.

McMahon's work had a snowball effect. Increased exposure meant increased revenues, which further raised production values. With the new camera equipment and sets, WWF wrestling could be filmed in front of 10,000 screaming fans—a much more exciting backdrop than a cramped, dim studio. The show's slicker look created more programming openings, which in turn added still more cash to the WWF coffers.

Cable television was on the rise in the United States at this time, and McMahon was one of the first promoters to have the resources (and the vision) to take advantage of it. McMahon recognized cable's potential for helping the WWF strengthen its hold on a national audience. McMahon quickly signed a deal with the recently founded USA Network, and for the first time in three decades professional wrestling was beamed coast-to-coast.

As with cable, McMahon also took advantage of another new medium, the pay-per-view broadcast. McMahon envisioned pay-per-view as the vehicle for an annual event where the feuds of all his top stars would be settled. Previously used primarily for boxing matches, pay-per-view became an important source of revenue, beginning in 1985 with the first big Wrestlemania extravaganza. Fans who couldn't make the live event could, for a one-time fee, watch it from home. Over time, McMahon added four more annual pay-per-view events, eventually ratcheting the number up to 12 per year.

Changes and Innovations

On top, with the resources to stay there, McMahon was not content to just sit and reap the bounty. Instead, he embarked on a tireless campaign to redefine and expand what he termed "sports entertainment."

Perhaps the most important of these innovations was the attention paid to character development. All WWF wrestlers were given a persona, along with costumes and props to support it. Even established wrestlers coming in from other leagues were given a gimmick and often a complete change of identity. The Million Dollar Man used his money to humiliate others. Mr. Perfect was infallible. The Common Man looked out for the little people. The Big Boss Man, a former correctional officer, used his nightstick to enforce his evil justice.

The availability of inexpensive videotape helped move the action away from the ring and into the wrestlers' lives. Copious interviews helped fans keep track of the byzantine feuds and alliances. Skits and other segments allowed fans to go to the golf course with Mr. Perfect and watch him sink impossible putts, or follow the Common Man as he helped garbage men collect the trash on his block. Viewers despised the Million Dollar Man before he had wrestled a single match in a WWF ring, having been subjected to a series of vignettes in which he humiliated ordinary citizens, including children, by paying them $100 to make fools of themselves (he would always take the money back from them in the end, adding to his villainous persona). Nonwrestling parts of the show, previously an occasional occurrence, became a major part of every broadcast.

For every wrestler, McMahon created a total package. And he was able to use these packages to implement the second of his major innovations: turning wrestling into mainstream family entertainment. McMahon cleansed the ring of blood. By publicly admitting that the outcome of matches was predetermined, he made the violence seem closer to *The Three Stooges* than to *Rambo*. Elements of humor were stressed, lightening the mood of the show. Under his control, WWF "good guy" wrestlers always triumphed in the end and became role models that parents could feel comfortable allowing their children to emulate. Hulk Hogan, one of the WWF's biggest stars in the 1980s, was known for enjoining children to say their prayers and take their vitamins. McMahon even added a Saturday-morning wrestling-oriented cartoon show, hosted by Hogan, to his lineup.

Catering to a younger audience proved incredibly successful. Merchandise and licensing revenues soared as the WWF introduced action figures, ice cream bars, breakfast cereals, foam fingers, and countless other toys to capitalize on wrestling's popularity with children. Through another innovation—that of trademarking and copyrighting the characters' names and personas—McMahon was able to keep the lion's share of the wealth generated by his creations. His ownership of their identities also prevented wrestlers from using their WWF names, costumes, and catchphrases outside of WWF-sanctioned activities.

With his audience and revenues increasing, McMahon was able to implement another important innovation: bringing celebrities into the wrestling fold. One of the most successful cases was Cyndi Lauper, a top-of-the-charts pop singer who had a high-profile role in WWF story lines. Vince McMahon touted the new alliance between the wrestling and musical entertainment worlds as "the rock and wrestling connection." It was a bridge he had dreamed of building since his days staging concerts in Massachusetts. The wrestling set came to resemble a rock concert stage, with explosions, elevated platforms, and cameramen running throughout, capturing all the action for the millions watching at home.

McMahon increased the visibility of WWF Wrestlers by pushing them to record albums, to appear in movies, and go on talk shows. The glitziness of the performers and the WWF programming alienated many traditionalists, who felt that the actual in-ring wrestling now took a back seat to showmanship. But for every viewer lost, the WWF gained five new ones. The mix of music, myth, and athleticism attracted larger audiences with each spectacle-filled broadcast. McMahon explained the draw:

> Our shows are extremely unique . . . There's no place you can go where you can see a soap opera, action-adventure, rock show, talk show, comedy, all that stuff rolled into one. Every format that is successful in television, we dabble in that.

This borrowing of elements far removed from the traditional in-ring drama transformed the WWF from a wrestling company into a brand name. When McMahon discussed his product, he consciously avoided the word *wrestling*, choosing instead to speak of "WWF matches." His employees were not "wrestlers," but "WWF Superstars." Much as *Kleenex* became synonymous with *tissues* and *Band-Aid* came to replace *bandage*, *WWF* was gradually replacing the term *professional wrestling*.

Despite tremendous growth and a ballooning cast of characters, Vince McMahon kept a tight rein over his domain. Publicly, his only role in the WWF was as a ring announcer, giving blow-by-blow commentary on the matches alongside the "bad guy" ring announcers who would routinely insult their boss. Insiders knew, however, that McMahon made the daily decisions on which wrestlers would get a "push" (promotion signaled by increased involvement in story lines and high-level bouts). It was also up to him to pick the moment's "babyface" (good guy) and chief "heel" (bad guy). If the WWF was, as McMahon often stated, in the business of storytelling, McMahon was the company's chief raconteur.

It was a golden age for the WWF. Merchandise revenues were soaring, live event business was booming, pay-per-view broadcasts were bringing in millions, and the annual Wrestlemania events set indoor attendance records. With the decade heading for a close, though, a portentous development was shaping up on wrestling's periphery. Atlanta businessman and billionaire Ted Turner had noticed how lucrative wrestling had become, and he wanted in on the action.

McMahon was about to have some very unwelcome company.

ENTER TED TURNER AND THE WCW

A Deal Sours and a League Is Born

Ted Turner, who owned several sports franchises, built a cable television empire around his entertainment and news networks. One of his stations, TBS, was a home to WWF programming in Atlanta until 1985. That year, Turner invited McMahon to be his guest at an Atlanta Braves baseball game. According to McMahon, Turner used the opportunity to raise objections to what he saw as an overly generous arrangement between TBS and the WWF. Turner also expressed interest in buying stock in the WWF. As McMahon explained:

> We gave Turner the best numbers he ever had back in the early eighties. Then Turner began to notice what we were doing. He invited me to a Braves game down in Atlanta and said: "Vince, you are too damned successful; you have to sell me some of your stock." I told him the WWF was a private company, a family-owned company, and that he couldn't have any.

Disagreements over the TBS/WWF deal eventually led McMahon to decide to pull WWF programming from the station. Looking to get out of the Atlanta area, McMahon sold the Georgia territory to promoter Jim Crockett and considered his dealings with Turner over.

In 1988, however, McMahon received a call from Turner. McMahon recalls the conversation:

> Ted picks up the phone and announces "Guess what?" Of course you can never guess with Ted. "What, Ted?" He says, "I'm in the wrasslin' business."

Turner Broadcasting Systems had just bought the same Georgia territory that McMahon had abandoned three years earlier. Press releases announcing the $5 million purchase also laid out plans for the expansion of the existing wrestling programming, using Turner's cable network as a conduit. It was the first rumblings of a war that McMahon would come to see as the fight of his life. McMahon, never one to be intimidated, reacted to Turner's call with his trademarked cockiness:

> I said, "Well, congratulations Ted, I'm glad to know that. I'm in the entertainment business. Big difference."

Turner's World Championship Wrestling

The Turner-funded wrestling league, called World Championship Wrestling, got off to a shaky start. Its affiliation with TBS gave the WCW national exposure, but television ratings and ticket sales were disappointing. Turner was at a loss to come up with anything to match the enthusiasm generated by the WWF. This made the WCW vulnerable to pillaging by McMahon, who would entice wrestlers away from the WCW as soon as they achieved a degree of notoriety. Turner's WCW was viewed by most as a farm system for the major leagues: the WWF.

To make matters worse for the WCW, the WWF debuted a weekly prime-time cable show, *Monday Night RAW*. The popularity of the program, which mixed previously taped bouts with a healthy dose of live broadcasts (unheard of until then), further widened the gap between the competing leagues. Despite Ted Turner's financial and television backing, the WCW continued to lose money.

Eric Bischoff and Nitro

The WCW's turnaround began in 1993 when Ted Turner brought in Eric Bischoff to run the league. Young, handsome, and arrogant, Bischoff had cut his teeth as a ring announcer for an ailing Minnesota-based wrestling alliance in the 1980s. Bischoff knew that the WWF was in a vulnerable state, having waged several costly legal battles, the most significant of which involved the U.S. government's investigation of a steroid drug distribution scandal. With Turner's blessings, Bischoff went on a spending spree, offering unprecedented amounts of money and a 50 percent reduction in work days to entice dozens of big-name wrestlers to join the WCW. Bischoff's offer was especially appealing to older WWF stars, such as Hulk Hogan and Randy "Macho Man" Savage, who were no longer as high-profile as they once were in the WWF. Following the signing of Hogan and Savage, a dozen other former WWF Superstars who had made their name during the golden days of the 1980s joined the WCW.

With the "name" talent secured, Bischoff got the green light to begin production on a live, prime-time WCW wrestling program, scheduled to air Monday nights directly opposite *RAW*. Insiders and fans alike saw it as a recipe for disaster: the WCW's brand recognition was far below that of the WWF, and it would have to compete for viewers in a market McMahon had essentially created.

But Bischoff was confident in his strategy: mimic and outspend the WWF. The result, called *Monday Nitro*, was a sports entertainment program built on the McMahon model and brought to life with stars hired directly from the WWF. Critics (McMahon the loudest of them) claimed that the WCW was an untenably expensive WWF knock-off, one that would fold in an instant if it were not for Ted Turner's willingness to absorb huge financial losses.

The War for Monday Night

The first shots of the battle between the two leagues were fired on September 4, 1995, when *Monday Nitro* debuted. Taking advantage of *RAW*'s preemption by the U.S. Open tennis tournament, *Nitro* pulled out all the stops to present itself as serious competition to the WWF. Bischoff accomplished this goal with aplomb, and showed that he had studied McMahon's playbook closely. Wrestling fans watched, shocked, as WWF mainstay wrestler Lex Luger appeared on the live *Nitro* broadcast to ridicule McMahon and the WWF. Luger was under intense contract negotiation with the WWF at the time, and was in the midst of a high-profile "push" within the league. When Luger appeared on *Monday Nitro*, the WWF (who had no idea Luger was even considering a jump) had to scramble to cut him from several weeks' worth of already taped shows and commercials.

The signing of Luger was important, signaling a new strategy by Bischoff to go after the current, younger WWF talent. Critics could soon no longer claim that the WCW was merely the WWF's retirement home.

The following Monday was the first head-to-head competition between *Nitro* and *RAW*. On the strength of their powerful opening the previous week, *Nitro* carried the night, garnering 2.5 Nielsen ratings points to *RAW*'s 2.2.[1] Those who had predicted immediate annihilation for the WCW were wrong, and talk began circulating around the wrestling world of an upset in the making.

The shows swapped ratings wins for the next couple of months, but Bischoff again humiliated the WWF with a high-profile defection in December. The WWF's reigning women's champion appeared on *Nitro*, signifying her new allegiance by throwing the WWF championship belt in a garbage can. It was another embarrassment for *RAW* and a nightmare for the WWF's storywriters, who now had to account for the disappearance of both their top women's star and the championship belt.

The high-profile defections—more followed that spring—were troubling enough for the WWF, but Bischoff compounded these problems with some innovations of his own. With the program doing well, Bischoff convinced Turner's network to grant him an additional hour on Monday nights. *Nitro* began running from 8:00 to 10:00 PM, giving it an hour's jump on *RAW*. Because Ted Tuner owned the broadcast medium, the

---

[1]Nielsen is the official ratings system in U.S. television. Each point translates to 1 percent of the total American viewing audience (with millions of dollars in advertising revenues at stake).

two hours of *Nitro* could be carefully orchestrated, with key matches beginning just as *RAW* cut away to commercials. With *Nitro* live every week, Bischoff made the controversial decision to begin announcing the results of taped *RAW* shows before they were broadcast, taking the impact out of WWF story lines.

Bischoff also worked to attract the traditionalist fans disgruntled by the declining emphasis on wrestling action in the WWF. Bischoff filled out his roster of superstars with an undercard of young lightweight wrestlers from leagues in Japan and Mexico. These athletic unknowns willingly performed the dangerous stunts and high-flying maneuvers considered too risky by the more established wrestlers.

Beginning in June, *Nitro* picked up steam and pulled away from *RAW*, winning the ratings war every Monday night for the rest of the year. By *Nitro*'s birthday in September 1996, the show had reason to celebrate. The costs had been high, but they were winning a ratings battle many had considered unwinnable.

The second year of the head-to-head competition opened with McMahon facing another crisis: the contract of his top wrestler, Bret "The Hitman" Hart, was about to expire.

BRET "THE HITMAN" HART

Bret Hart was the most famous son of Canada's first family of professional wrestling. His father had been a well-known wrestler and promoter in Calgary, and the Hart patriarch had high hopes that his eight sons would follow his footsteps into the ring. All the boys did eventually find careers as wrestlers, referees, or trainers. (The four daughters did their part by marrying wrestlers.)

Hart began wrestling for the WWF in 1983, one year after Vince McMahon took over the company. The Hitman character developed over time as a good-hearted Canadian patriot. Decked out in pink-and-black spandex, he began his fights against the forces of evil by removing his wraparound sunglasses and carefully giving them to a young fan in the audience.

Hart took his job deadly seriously. For 14 years, he kept up with the grueling touring schedule, wrestled while sick and injured, and took pride in having never accidentally hurt another wrestler in the ring. For Hart, wrestling was about much more than money or a bigger vacation package. Wrestling was about honoring the sport and the WWF fans that loved him. His dedication showed, and Bret Hart was recognized within the industry as someone with immense integrity.

Different from most of the cartoonish wrestlers around him, Hart was neither flamboyant nor particularly charismatic. He was in top shape physically, and he put on dynamic matches. But apart from his flair for in-ring drama, it was sometimes hard to understand why he became such a fan favorite. Perhaps it was Hart's "regular guy" image that made him stand out in an industry so based on outlandishness. For its part, the WWF recognized the fans' fondness for the atypical wrestler and allowed Hart the stage to become a superstar, giving him all of the major belts, including the WWF World Heavyweight title.

The Bidding War for Bret

In October 1996, Bret Hart was given the golden opportunity offered to so many of his wrestling colleagues. His contract with the WWF expired at the end of the month, freeing him to pursue a deal with the WCW for much more money and a lighter work schedule. Hart's loyalty was to McMahon and the WWF, but the deal the WCW offered gave him pause for thought. Hart, almost 40 years old at that point, felt he could continue to wrestle for three more years. With retirement looming, Hart's friends encouraged him to get as much as he could for his last years in the ring. Eric Bischoff offered Hart a three-year contract worth $9 million, a salary far beyond anything McMahon could match. In addition, Hart would only be required to work half as many dates as he had been for the WWF.

The battle for Bret Hart, though, was one McMahon was determined to win. WWF executives had been warning McMahon that losing Hart would have a devastating impact on the WWF's sagging ratings and that it would be financial suicide to let Hart go. McMahon felt that he could not allow Ted Turner to humiliate him one more time. Unable to match the money the WCW was offering, McMahon drew on Hart's desire to stay with the company that had created him. With the negotiations down to the wire, McMahon offered Hart a 20-year contract with the WWF. The contract stipulated three years of wrestling, followed by 17 years' guaranteed work in the front office.

It was the sign of approval from McMahon that Hart had been looking for. The bidding war had been a very public one, and McMahon and Hart agreed to announce its conclusion the next Monday night on *RAW*. Striding out into the ring to the cheers of his fans, Bret took the microphone:

> When you get offered a great offer you have to decide which one you're going to take. Nobody has any idea how much soul-searching I've done over this. But when it comes right down to it everything I've ever done, and everything I ever plan on ever doing, I owe to my WWF fans. I'll be with the WWF forever.

Backstage, Bret explained that the fans were not the only consideration in his decision. His concern for McMahon had also weighed heavy on his mind:

> You know my relationship with Vince McMahon was always sort of like a father. If I left it would have been a little bit like leaving my dad, especially when the chips were down. The WCW is breathing down his neck, they've overtaken him in the ratings. It's easy to jump and switch sides and say "Thanks for everything." Loyalty's important.

A final deal-making point had been McMahon's assurances that the Hitman would remain a fan favorite for years to come. According to Hart, McMahon also told him that the WWF would base many of the coming years' story lines around him. "I know one thing," Hart said after signing his 20-year contract, " in the WWF I'll always be able to go out the hero."

The Fans Pick a New Kind of Hero

Vince McMahon had won the battle for Bret Hart, but the war with Ted Turner's WCW waged on. The second year of head-to-head competition saw McMahon matching the WCW by adding another hour to *Monday Night RAW*. He also renamed the show *RAW Is WAR*, a nod to the contest with Turner's league that had turned into a struggle for survival. *RAW Is WAR* went live every week for the second half of the year, stymieing the WCW's ability to give away its match results. Regardless, the year again belonged to Bischoff and the WCW. Going for the jugular, the WCW added a third hour of programming to *Nitro,* and won all 44 of the head-to-head ratings battles. Vince McMahon, the undisputed king of the ring since his transformation of the sport in the early 1980s, was in freefall.

One of McMahon's few glimmers of hope for the future of the WWF was a wrestler from Texas, "Stone Cold" Steve Austin. Dressed in plain back trunks, with a shaved head and goatee, Austin was cast as a perpetually angry, remorseless villain. He guzzled beer before matches, made obscene gestures at the cameras and fans, and was merciless in the ring. Initially, fans hated him (as they were supposed to), but then something went wrong: Austin began getting cheers.

As the year wore on, Austin's misbehaving antics continued, but nothing could stem the growing tide of fan enthusiasm. "Stone Cold" merchandise was flying off the shelves, and audiences erupted when Austin entered arenas. McMahon knew he had to reposition Austin to take advantage of his popularity, and there was only one spot that was big enough for him: the top "good guy" spot, then occupied by Bret Hart.

Hart Goes Bad

On March 10, 1996, McMahon approached Hart to ask him to "turn heel" and become a bad guy. Initially opposed to the idea, Hart eventually relented and agreed. Together they concocted an anti-American angle whereby Hart could be a villain in the United States and remain a hero in Canada and the rest of the world. Coached by McMahon, Hart began opening matches by insulting America and American fans.[2]

The heel turn may have been unappetizing to Hart, but the alternative—being the second banana fan favorite to Austin—was even worse. Besides, haranguing American fans was something Hart could do and still remain true to himself. The Americans' love of the villainous "Stone Cold" character was unsettling to Hart, who saw Austin's ascendancy as a sign that Americans had lost their moral bearings.

Hart was also uncomfortable with the negative direction the WWF was taking on several fronts. In an attempt to boost ratings, McMahon had begun pushing the envelope on the Monday night shows. Knowing that Turner and Bischoff, hemmed in by the family orientation of their network, would be reluctant to follow his lead, McMahon added racial angles, sexually suggestive story lines, adult language, and obscene gestures as increasingly regular aspects of *RAW Is WAR*. A merger between Turner and Time Warner further constrained Bischoff's freedom to match the WWF's adult themes. Hart began complaining (both privately to McMahon and publicly in interviews) that the WWF was heading into dangerous territory. As Hart explained:

> It's gotten a lot more raunchier. A lot more sexual. The show's very sexual . . . in a bad way. I don't think you watch wrestling for sex. I don't think it's something presentable to your children . . . It's just become something I don't want to associate myself with.

Hart also began speaking publicly about his dissatisfaction with the Hitman's lowered visibility in the WWF, as he did in this 1997 interview for Canadian television:

> I don't mind taking a backseat once in a while. But I think it would be fair to say that it kind of ruffled my feathers to be on four pay-per-views and play a secondary role, if that. Maybe a third-rate role. Which I don't think is fair to me, and I don't think is fair to my fans.

To add to his worries about the rise of "Stone Cold" Steve Austin, Hart had lately been eclipsed by "The Heartbreak Kid" Shawn Michaels. Looking every part the bronzed Californian, Michaels was known as an exceptionally talented athlete who brought a new level of acrobatics and stunts to the ring. He also had a reputation for being exasperatingly temperamental, impetuously quitting when things did not go his way. Michaels had just returned to the WWF after leaving over an altercation with Hart caused by Michaels's insinuations that Hart was having an affair with a female WWF

---

[2]In one graphic illustration of the change in the Hitman character, Hart found himself in Pittsburgh, Pennsylvania, announcing to the entire booing arena that if he were to give the United States an enema, the first place he'd stick the hose was Pittsburgh. ("I didn't want to say that," confided Hart afterwards. "That's not me.")

employee. A physical confrontation over the matter had resulted in Michaels's departure, claiming an unsafe work environment.

At McMahon's urging, Michaels and Hart made peace and Michaels began wrestling again. For Michaels's return, McMahon created a new slant on the Heartbreak Kid persona. Michaels was to become a villain. With "Stone Cold" Steve Austin out temporarily injured,[3] McMahon made a rivalry between Michaels and Hart the biggest story in the WWF.[4] As part of this feud, the two were encouraged to take verbal shots at one another in interview segments. According to Hart, Michaels took this too far, delving into the off-limits topic of Hart's family. The choreographed rivalry was scheduled to culminate in the November 9 *Survivor Series*, but it looked like the two might come to blows well before that.

Apart from a personal dislike for Michaels, Hart felt threatened by the Heartbreak Kid's rise in popularity. Michaels had no reservations about pushing the envelope or going along with McMahon's tabloid-style story lines. The Heartbreak Kid was comfortable playing the nasty villain and was well on his way toward occupying the coveted position of most-hated superstar in the WWF. Hart feared his character would be forgotten. As he explained:

> I came from being the number one good guy in the world. And I gave that job up to become the number one bad guy. And now you've given my bad guy job to Shawn Michaels, how can I become a good guy again? I've bashed the American people. That's where I perform 95 percent of the time. I'm stuck in limbo. I'm in purgatory. I can't be a great good guy anymore and I can't be a great bad guy. I'm stuck with nothing.

Poor Returns on a 20-Year Investment

Ten months after convincing Bret Hart to sign the 20-year contract, Vince McMahon began to have second thoughts. Signing Hart had been an expensive gamble for McMahon, and, with essentially no dent made in the WCW's ratings dominance, it looked like it had not paid off. Previously invincible, Hart was also coming up injured more often. And Hart's issues with Shawn Michaels and criticisms of the show had become trying to McMahon.

On September 8, 1997, McMahon called Hart in for a meeting. The company, McMahon explained to Hart, was in fiscal peril.[5] McMahon asked for permission to cut Hart's weekly salary in half, with the money to be paid to him once the WWF was back on its feet financially. Hart, afraid that he might not ever see the money if he consented, declined.

At a *RAW Is WAR* taping in New York City two weeks later, McMahon was more blunt. Again citing the WWF's poor financial health, McMahon informed Hart that he could not afford to keep him around. McMahon told a stunned Hart that Hart would be doing him a favor if he went back to the WCW and asked for another shot at signing with them. Hart was reluctant, but he agreed to contact the WCW.

The WCW still wanted Hart and made him roughly the same offer as it had a year earlier. On November 1, 1997, Hart was on the verge of signing with the WCW. Before accepting the $9 million offer from Eric Bischoff, though, Hart gave McMahon a final chance to convince him to stay in the WWF.

---

[3]Ironcially, Steve Austin had been hurt in a match against Bret Hart's brother Owen.

[4]Only WWF employees and in-the-know fans that routinely surfed the Internet's "insider" wrestling Web pages were aware how close to reality the feud really was.

[5]The actual extent of the WWF's financial difficulties at this point is unknown.

case 4 Pi Kappa Phi Fraternity

Chris Holoman
University of Alabama

Lou Marino
University of Alabama

Mark Timmes, CEO
Pi Kappa Phi Fraternity

A. J. Strickland
University of Alabama

Jason McKenna, a senior majoring in management, was sitting in his fraternity house at the University of Alabama (UA). President of the Omicron chapter of Pi Kappa Phi, McKenna was trying to decide what to say at the chapter meeting that was starting in a few minutes. The Omicron chapter, with a long legacy of rich traditions on the UA campus, was facing mounting pressure from the National Council of Pi Kappa Phi to agree to become a "leadership chapter" and take on the challenge of revamping its chapter operations in ways that would put far more emphasis on the positive aspects of fraternal societies. The national officers of Pi Kappa Phi were trying to coax most of its local chapters to help lead the arduous and slippery task of reshaping the troubled and oft-criticized Greek culture at both the local and national levels—in recent years, fraternity chapters on many campuses across the United States had come under increased scrutiny from university administrators for their wild parties, binge drinking, drug use, occasional hazing incidents, and weak emphasis on academics. In supporting initiatives for basic reforms at its local chapters, personnel at Pi Kappa Phi's national headquarters had invested substantial resources in creating unique programs, such as The Journey, that were intended to enrich fraternity membership and rejuvenate dwindling chapter rosters.

While McKenna clearly saw the benefits of The Journey and other initiatives that National was promoting, he was not sure they were a good fit with what his brothers in the Omicron chapter wanted to get out of their fraternity experience. Omicron's activities and the concerns and priorities of its members were not substantively different from those at the other 25 fraternities on the UA campus. The truth of the matter was that, while making decent grades was important to many of McKenna's fraternity brothers, winning the All Sports Trophy and having parties with the best sororities were even more important. In fact, on the UA campus, a fraternity's reputation hinged chiefly on how well its intramural sports teams performed and grapevine comments about how good its parties were. McKenna was, of course, very aware that the university's administration had long-standing concerns about what went on in UA's fraternity houses—over the years, a number of chapters had been put on probation (some several times) or had their houses shut down for a time for one violation or another. For well over a decade, UA officials had been urging and pressuring campus fraternity officers to purge all hazing, strictly enforce an antidrug policy, monitor alcohol consumption closely, conduct their parties in a responsible fashion, and promote better academic standards among their membership.

McKenna, along with many other fraternity officers at UA, thought that university administrators had exaggerated the extent of so-called abuses and negatives of fraternity life at UA, but there was no doubt that university officials wanted to crack down on fraternities and either reform the fraternity system or engineer its demise on the UA campus. While the Omicron chapter was currently in good standing with the University of Alabama, McKenna realized that recent racially embarrassing incidents involving two fraternities at nearby Auburn University, coupled with the growing anti-Greek sentiment among the university's administration, heightened the risk of potentially serious trouble for Omicron down the road. McKenna didn't see that simply coasting along with the status quo was a wise option. His conversations with Omicron's academic adviser, a professor in UA's College of Business Administration, and with a couple of the people at National had persuaded him that for the good of the house he needed to convince his brothers to adopt and implement National's Journey program and become a Leadership Chapter. But his immediate problem was figuring out what he could do and say at the upcoming meeting to win a majority vote for such an action—especially given that the main item on the agenda for the meeting was planning the chapter's annual "Animal House" party.

Six hundred miles away in Charlotte, North Carolina, Mark Timmes, the CEO of Pi Kappa Phi, was sitting in his office preparing for an upcoming meeting of the National Council (the fraternity's board of directors) and wrestling with ways that National could alter the direction and culture of the local chapters and accentuate the many positives of membership in a Greek organization such as Pi Kappa Phi. Like many university officials, Pi Kappa Phi's national officers saw that the fraternity system as presently constituted was slowly sinking and in danger of losing its raison d'être; they were even more worried about deteriorations in the overall strength of the fraternity's local chapters. Pi Kappa Phi had made a "bet your company" decision on implementing The Journey throughout its 140 chapters across the United States as a way to try to turn things around. Pi Kappa Phi had spent a small fortune developing materials for implementing the program at its local chapters. There were videos, interactive websites, and leadership training programs specially developed for Pi Kappa Phi members by Steven Covey's Covey Leadership Center. The fraternity had made funds available to pay a modest stipend to local professors to become academic advisers to assist the local chapters. With these support systems in place and broad authority at the national level, Timmes was confident that he had the means to drive significant cultural changes and reforms at the chapter level throughout Pi Kappa Phi. However, Timmes realized that the future of the fraternity was in the hands of the local chapter officers, current members, and interested alumni. Like Jason McKenna, Mark Timmes faced the challenge of convincing these brothers that the fraternity's future rested with successful adoption and execution of The Journey by local chapters.

As McKenna and Timmes finished preparing for their meetings, both realized that implementing and executing a bold new vision and strategy for their organizations was a challenging assignment. While both knew it was a Herculean task, Timmes recognized that it was one needed for survival and McKenna was less certain. Both understood, however, that first step was to convince their brothers of the necessity for change.

HISTORY OF FRATERNITIES

In 1776, America became free to determine its destiny when 13 colonies declared their independence from England. In that same year, the first college fraternity was formed. From this first small group, America's fraternity system had grown and expanded to involve millions of citizens, 20 U.S. presidents, a majority of all congressmen, and most modern business leaders.

It all started with a group of students at the College of William and Mary. With politics in such a volatile state in 1776, college professors wanted the minds of their students focused on books, not on social activities. Discipline and rules about dress and behavior were extremely strict. Just as students today seek some escape from the daily grind of schoolwork, the students at William and Mary found theirs. On certain evenings, a group of young men calling themselves the Flat Hat Club would gather in an upstairs room at a local tavern to talk, joke, and socialize over a bowl of punch. While membership in the Flat Hat Club was unofficial by today's standards, the club reportedly included some prestigious names—many believe that Thomas Jefferson founded the club.

Other groups at William and Mary followed the Flat Hat Club's lead but soon caught the notice of disapproving faculty members. To win faculty acceptance, these groups incorporated educational elements of "literary societies" into their meetings: oratorical contests and debate and critiques of various literary works. When John Heath, a student at William and Mary, was denied membership in one of these groups in 1776, he gathered four of his friends and formed Phi Beta Kappa. By giving his organization a Greek name and instituting certain secrets for the society, Heath made Phi Beta Kappa even more exclusive. Phi Beta Kappa created many of the features that characterize modern fraternities—use of Greek letters, a secret grip, a motto, a ritual of initiation, a distinctive membership badge, and a constitution of fraternal laws. As Phi Beta Kappa thrived, its members believed that students at other colleges would enjoy secret fraternal societies; they formed a second chapter at Yale University in 1780 and then a third at Harvard in 1781.

When an anti–secret society movement caught momentum in the United States in the 1830s, the members of Phi Beta Kappa were forced to divulge the society's secrets, including the meaning of their Greek letters ("Philosophy, the Guide of Life"). By the second half of the 20th century, Phi Beta Kappa fraternity had become the highest recognized honor fraternity for collegiate men and women of superior academic achievement. But before it relinquished its secret aspects, Phi Beta Kappa had sparked a movement among college students to form a variety of Greek-letter organizations; the Greek movement flourished, and chapters sprang up on a growing number of new campuses.

At Union College in Schenectady, New York, in 1825, students formed the Kappa Alpha (KA) Society, a relatively small national fraternity that still exists. This was America's first true social fraternity, and it precipitated the first conflict between a college's administration and a Greek organization. Some faculty at Union College feared the KA Society's secrecy and thus did not welcome the formation of this group, but the society's members defiantly continued to meet. KA Society's success spurred the formation of two other fraternities in 1827: Sigma Phi and Delta Phi. Students at Union College went on to found three other national fraternities, earning the college the nickname "The Mother of Fraternities."

In 1847, the first recorded expulsion of a Greek organization from an institution of higher learning took place at Miami University of Oxford, Ohio; all the members of two fraternities, Alpha Delta Phi and Beta Theta Pi, were expelled after leading a so-called snow rebellion in protest against an unpopular administration. The two fraternities had teamed up and piled snow in front of Miami University's administration building, blocking the entrance of the faculty and university officials and causing the university to close down for two days. The expulsions of the Alpha Delta Phi and Beta Theta Pi members left a void, and two more fraternities, Phi Delta Theta and Sigma Chi, were formed.

In the early days, fraternities typically met in rented rooms or private homes. However, as time went on, fraternities began to follow the example of Chi Psi, which built the first fraternity house in 1854 at the University of Michigan. The mushrooming popularity of fraternity houses forever changed the Greek world. The introduction of fraternity houses made fraternity management more complex and increased the need for alumni involvement to help manage and fund the properties. As college student enrollment rose and as more women entered college, the demand for university housing grew and the construction of fraternity and sorority houses was generally encouraged by college administrations. Independently financed Greek housing not only helped solve the housing shortage on America's campuses but also provided a place where fraternity brothers could live together, thus strengthening the unity and bonds among the members.

Women's fraternities (sororities) had their beginnings in Macon, Georgia, in the 1850s when the Adelphian Society (later Alpha Delta Pi) and the Philomathean Society (later Phi Mu) were formed at Wesleyan Female College. The first recognized women's Greek-letter fraternity was Kappa Alpha Theta, founded in 1870 at DePauw University in Greencastle, Indiana. The word *sorority* was created in 1874 when Gamma Phi Beta was founded.

By 1860, the year in which the Civil War began, 22 of the 61 national fraternities that existed in 2001 had been founded. But the advent of the war tested the survival of the American fraternity system, particularly in the South, where it was common to find whole fraternity chapters leaving together to join the Confederate cause. In some cases, members tried to keep their fraternal organizations active on the war front. When the Civil War ended, fraternities offered one viable avenue for mending the divisiveness that existed and restoring bonds between men. In post–Civil War Virginia, five more fraternities were founded (Alpha Tau Omega, Kappa Alpha Order, Pi Kappa Alpha, Sigma Nu, and Kappa Sigma).

In the first half of the 20th century, fraternities continued to grow and prosper, interrupted only by the two world wars, during which college enrollment drop-offs due to military service forced many chapters to close temporarily. At the end of World War II, the convergence of several factors led to the golden age of fraternities. First, there was a large influx of returning soldiers and too few job opportunities to absorb them all. To aid the transition of servicemen back into American society, Congress passed the GI Bill to make it easier for war veterans seeking to continue their education to finance the costs of going to college. The GI Bill allowed thousands of returning military personnel, from a wide range of backgrounds, to attend colleges all across the United States. Familiarity with military-style training regimens (where men formed a strong esprit de corps and worked together in harsh and violent circumstances) was conducive to joining a fraternity. More important, the potential benefits of a military-style training experience were evident to the student/soldiers who were joining fraternities, and fraternity chapters across the country rapidly adopted the practice of putting pledges through a sometimes rigorous training program prior to initiation. It quickly became commonplace for fraternity pledgeships to involve some form of hazing. Although pledges faced semester-long periods with hazing that might range from paddling (if they could not correctly answer questions about fraternity history or the hometowns of actives) to being required to perform whatever physically demanding or lewd acts that actives might think up, fraternities flourished during the 1950s.

The 1960s and 1970s were an adjustment period for fraternities, as the young people of those eras questioned and rebelled against the establishment. Fraternities and their regimens were seen as part of this establishment, and membership suffered accordingly. Indeed, a popular movie of that time, *Animal House,* portrayed an unconventional group of antiestablishment fraternity brothers triumphing over hyperconformist fraternities as well as a college administration that persecuted them and eventually threw the group off campus.

However, fraternity membership rebounded, growing rather briskly at most U.S. college campuses during the 1980s. Undergraduates were interested in the social life fraternities offered; as one member said, "All fraternities are about social life. You make friendships and, as far as careers go, connections. Being in a fraternity is all about having a house to have parties and the social funds to do it right." As membership reached roughly 450,000 undergraduates in the early 1990s, the outlook for the fraternity system seemed rosy. But underneath the healthy membership gains and popularity of the fraternity system, there were some distressing signs. Problems regarding alcohol abuse, drug use, overemphasis on partying, and low academic performance were mounting at many chapters on many campuses. Numerous observers, including the national officers of fraternities, felt that local chapters on many campuses were straying from their national fraternity's original roots and purposes, fostering a culture that was out of step and misdirected.

THE DARK SIDE OF FRATERNITIES

During the 1990s, there was a steady stream of negative and embarrassing headlines in the media implicating fraternities in irresponsible and dangerous acts—hazing, excessive drinking, illegal drug use (including overdosing), on-premise drug dealing, and out-of-control partying—that resulted in arrests, injuries, and occasional deaths, as well as university probation for the guilty chapters. Reporters claimed that Greek organizations had not changed much since the stereotypical 1980s, when rowdy keg parties and sophomoric pranks aided in recruiting fun-loving freshmen. Fraternity values and culture were said to clash with those of non-Greek students and with the behavioral expectations of university administrators and society at large.

Despite diligent efforts on the part of national fraternity officers and university officials, hazing proved difficult to flush out of the fraternity culture. Incidents of hazing continued to surface on many campuses. On campuses where hazing frequently took place, it was common for students to gossip about the kinds of hazing that fraternity pledges were subjected to; stories and rumors circulated through the campus grapevine on a fairly regular basis.

During the 1990s, interest in fraternity activities steadily eroded among incoming freshmen, resulting in membership declines of as much as 30 percent by 2001. Undergraduate membership in Alpha Tau Omega nationwide had declined from 9,100 in 1989 to 6,300 in 2000; membership in Theta Chi fraternity was off 27 percent, and membership in Phi Delta Theta was down nearly 30 percent. At Michigan State, Greek membership dropped from 6,000 in 1989 to 3,100 in fall 1999. At Bowling Green State University, the percentage of undergraduates belonging to fraternities was down from 19 percent in 1990 to 12 percent in 2000. An officer of the National Interfraternity Conference estimated that 350,000 undergraduates belonged to fraternities in 2000, down from about 400,000 members in 1990. By 1998, the average size of the fraternity chapters on college campuses had fallen to 38 men, down from an average of 54 men in 1990 and not far from the lows of the Vietnam War era, when the average chapter size was 34 members. However, the average chapter size of the 26 sororities belonging to the National Panhellenic Conference had risen from 46 in 1980 to 54 in 2000. Exhibit 1 provides data on Greek membership for the years 1982–2000.

The nationwide falloff in Greek membership had numerous causes. Fewer students seemed inclined to shell out hundreds of dollars in monthly dues and fees to be part of a system that had a reputation for excessive partying, engaged in sometimes offensive behavior, and, in some cases, endangered members' lives. Some fraternities experienced high dropout rates among existing members, generally for financial reasons, low grades, or eroding interest in what the fraternity had to offer. The Beta Theta Pi chapter at Michigan State, which had 130 members and was known for throwing the wildest beer bashes on the campus in the 1980s, was down to 25 members in 1995; according to a former chapter president, "They partied themselves into an oblivion." The somewhat precipitous decline in membership and eroding financial conditions at uneconomically small chapters led to the shutdown of many chapters.

However, falling membership was not wholly due to faulty chapter recruitment practices and eroding retention rates. The national officers at the various fraternities recognized that excessive partying and alcohol had become a far too prominent part of Greek life and, further, that growing numbers of students saw fraternities as conflicting with their academic and career pursuits. According to Ron Foster, executive director of Tau Kappa Epsilon, "Today's college students are more serious about their studies and career goals than they were in the 1980s. Many students say they simply don't see any reason to join a fraternity." Tom Strong, dean of students at the University of Alabama (which had more than 300 student organizations), observed, "At one point, being Greek was very traditional and it was the thing to do. But now there are so many more organizations on campus that the lure of the Greek system is not what it used to be." Other reasons for declining interest in joining a fraternity were (1) the high numbers of students who were working part-time to help defray their college expenses and who thus had little time to devote to fraternity life and little inclination to spend what discretionary funds they had on fraternity dues, and (2) the increasing ethnic and multicultural diversity of student populations—many nonwhite students had almost no prior exposure to the legacy of fraternities and were not disposed to even consider joining such groups, even if they were extended bids.

Traditional Greek-letter organizations were mostly white as of 2001, despite a rising number of minority students on campus. At campuses like the University of Alabama, where several thousand black students were enrolled, the Greek population

exhibit 1   Greek Organization Membership Trends, 1982–2000

Year	Number of Institutions Reporting	Fraternity Actives	Fraternity Pledges	Sorority Actives	Sorority Pledges
1982	285	122,711	35,948	114,867	29,116
1984	371	165,698	49,025	131,574	42,304
1986	429	196,884	67,400	155,620	54,657
1988	392	194,260	62,406	157,498	58,346
1990	398	197,974	59,417	169,953	59,675
1992	292	162,820	48,998	144,521	47,454
1997	346	133,210	59,166	134,248	68,508
2000	324	115,222	40,935	127,110	45,515

Note: These data require careful use and intrepretation because of the year-to-year variations in the number and composition of the reporting institutions.

Source: www.indiana.edu/~cscf/faqs.htm, December 20, 2001.

included a number of predominantly black fraternities and sororities. In 2001, on a number of campuses across the United States, ethnic and multicultural fraternities were booming—Latino, Asian American, and other multicultural fraternities were springing up alongside black fraternities as alternatives to the traditional Anglo-American Greek organizations.[1] A student at Michigan State University who had joined Sigma Lambda Beta, a Latino fraternity, said, "As one Latino with new ideas going into a room of 30 to 40 Anglo-Americans, I don't see my voice being heard."[2] Since 1995, black, Latino, Asian American, and multicultural fraternities and sororities had formed 9 chapters on the Michigan State campus; 10 such chapters had sprung up at Penn State University; and 6 Latino and Asian American groups had formed chapters at Purdue University.

From time to time, the Greek system had been plagued by complaints from people offended by certain Greek activities with racist and politically incorrect undertones. At George Mason University in 1991, a member of Sigma Chi fraternity appeared in blackface at an "ugly woman" skit at a campus fund-raiser; the university suspended the Sigma Chi chapter for two years, but the U.S. Court of Appeals ruled in 1993 that the skit was protected by the First Amendment and nullified the suspension. In 1992, Texas A&M University fined the Sigma Alpha Epsilon chapter on its campus $1,000 for holding a jungle party in which students painted their faces black and wore grass skirts. In 1997, the Zeta Beta Tau fraternity at Indiana University–Bloomington was suspended for sending its pledges on a scavenger hunt to find, among other things, pictures of "any funny-lookin' Mexican." In 2001, members of the Tau Kappa Epsilon fraternity at the University of Louisville attended a Halloween party in blackface, accompanied by one of their African American brothers dressed in a Ku Klux Klan outfit that he burned during the party. The chapter was suspended (which in this instance meant the chapter could hold no parties) pending completion of an investigation by university officials. Also in 2001, two fraternities at Auburn University—Delta Sigma Phi and Beta Theta Pi—held Halloween parties that some members attended wearing blackface; more than 20 pictures of members in blackface inadvertently appeared on

---

[1]Leo Reisberg, "Ethnic and Multicultural Fraternities Are Booming on Many Campuses," *Chronicle of Higher Education* (http://chronicle.com), January 7, 2000.

[2]As quoted in ibid.

the Internet at www.partypics.com shortly thereafter.[3] The pictures showed members in blackface, Afro wigs, gold jewelry, and T-shirts with the Greek letters of Omega Psi Phi, a historically black fraternity; one of the pictures from the Delta Sigma Phi party had a Confederate battle flag in the background and showed one student posing in a Ku Klux Klan outfit brandishing a rifle and holding a rope noosed around the neck of another student in blackface. The media in Alabama had a field day describing the pictures and the resulting fallout. Both chapters were shut down by their national organizations, and Auburn University withdrew its official recognition of the two fraternities (meaning, in this case, that members had to vacate their on-campus houses).[4] These incidents and others like them put university officials in the tricky position of denouncing offensive behavior while not running afoul of constitutional protection of free expression.

The 2001 incidents at Auburn and Louisville were variously described as being in "bad taste," reflecting "poor judgment," and being "isolated"; however, Lloyd Jordan, national president of Omega Psi Phi, called the blackface costumes at the two Auburn fraternity parties "acts of racial terrorism" because, in his view, they were intended to threaten and provoke black students—he stated that the offending Auburn students should be expelled.[5] A black member of Auburn University's board of trustees echoed Jordan's outrage and called for "appropriate action." Feeling heat from all the adverse publicity, Auburn University's president, supported by the board of trustees, decided to expel 10 members of the Beta Theta Pi Fraternity and 5 members of the Delta Sigma Phi Fraternity for wearing blackface and racially offensive costumes at the two Halloween parties; Auburn's black trustee said the expelled students should not be readmitted before 2005. Shortly thereafter, the 10 expelled members of Beta Theta Pi sued the president of Auburn University, the board of trustees, the dean of students, and their national fraternity for $300 million in compensatory and punitive damages, alleging that the university and the national office of Beta Theta Pi violated their constitutional and civil rights, including freedom of speech, freedom of association, and privacy as guaranteed by the First and Fourteenth Amendments. The suit also claimed that Auburn University officials defamed the students by publicly deploring their conduct and portraying them in a false light and by characterizing them and their conduct as racist. A circuit judge in Lee County (where Auburn University is located) subsequently ordered the 10 suspended Auburn students reinstated pending further hearings in their case.

NATIONAL FRATERNITY EFFORTS TO ADDRESS LOCAL CHAPTER PROBLEMS

In an effort to improve the reputation of the Greek movement and to protect their organizations from an increasingly litigious society, national fraternity executives had made some tough choices in the last decade. For example, from 1993 to 1995, Alpha Tau Omega shut down 40 chapters because of low membership or incidents relating

---

[3]Thomas Bartlett, "An Ugly Tradition Persists at Southern Fraternity Parties," *Chronicle of Higher Education*, November 30, 2001.

[4]The Beta Theta Pi chapter at Auburn had about 140 members, a 3.2 overall grade-point average, and a $2.5 million house; a number of its members were officers of prominent campus organizations. The chapter was regarded by the national organization as one of its most outstanding chapters in all of North America.

[5]Bartlett, "An Ugly Tradition Persists."

to alcohol, drugs, and/or hazing. These tough measures were the result of "zero tolerance" attitudes and policies that were adopted by national fraternity and university officials. Under these policies, evidence of improper conduct by a fraternity led to strict sanctions or outright closing of the chapter. A second action involved the efforts of some national fraternity organizations to reduce risk at chapter events by having alcohol-free chapter houses. The rise in the number of dry fraternities began in 1997 when the national leadership of Sigma Nu and Phi Delta Theta made the decision to become alcohol-free by 2000. Others fraternities were following suit. By the end of 2000, over 30 national fraternities were pursuing the implementation of alcohol-free chapter houses. Dry rush (recruiting without alcohol) had become the norm on U.S. campuses as a way of helping reduce alcohol abuse in fraternity chapters.

In 1992, to attack the problem cultures of many of its chapter houses, the national office of Sigma Phi Epsilon (SPE) had initiated a project called Balanced Man, which tracked the personal development of members throughout their college careers; each member had to go through three steps—the Sigma, the Phi, and the Epsilon Challenges. The project eliminated the concept of pledgeship periods; according to one member, "From Day 1, you're a brother. I see no point in breaking someone down just to build them back up." New groups were required to adopt the Balanced Man approach in order to colonize; 149 of SPE's 249 chapters had signed on to the Balanced Man project during the 1992–2000 period. But the SPE chapters that had not become part of the project—and even a few that had—were reluctant to give up the tradition of pledging, and the hazing that sometimes went with it. Some chapters were still struggling with membership numbers, behavior, and grades. According to one SPE national officer, "Until we get a lot of other fraternities on our campuses to institute similar models of development, our chapters will continue to fight the battle of being different."[6] From 1992 to 1999, SPE closed 58 chapters, including nine Balanced Man chapters, for low membership, alcohol abuse, hazing, or other violations involving what SPE's national officers considered risky behaviors. Although emphasis on academics was a key part of SPE's Balanced Man project, seven years after the start of the program, only 49 percent of the Balanced Man chapters had grade-point averages above their respective campus averages—26 percent of the non–Balanced Man chapters were above their campus averages. A few SPE chapters were going all-out to combat undesirable behavior on the part of members; for example, the newly colonized SPE chapter at the University of Georgia required a minimum 3.0 grade-point average and community service of all members, and the chapter took a strong stand against underage drinking—when two members under 21 were caught drinking in 1999, each had to write a five-page paper on how alcohol abuse could destroy a fraternity.

Despite increased self-policing, on-campus fraternity chapters as a group had faced mounting pressure and regulation from college administrations around the country for at least the past five years. More and more colleges and universities were enacting strict rules governing fraternities that were often distinct and more rigorous than the rules for other on-campus student organizations. These new rules governing fraternities sometimes included accreditation requirements that had to be met on an ongoing basis to remain in good standing; typical of these rules were the deferring of freshmen rush to the second semester, having to maintain a specified-minimum grade-point average, and reducing or completely eliminating pledgeship periods. Even with these

---

[6]Reisberg, "Ethnic and Multicultural Fraternities Are Booming."

restrictions and requirements, some college administrators saw the fraternities on their campus as troublesome nuisances with more negatives than positives. Anti-Greek administrators at some universities had cut back on institutional support for Greek-life staff members and programs and, in a few extreme instances, had banned fraternities from campus all together.

Other universities were initiating efforts to restore the luster of fraternities. Emory University in Atlanta had introduced its Phoenix Plan in 1997 to "raise the fraternity system out of the ashes." The plan involved the university purchasing the rundown and often unsafe fraternity houses from alumni corporations, remodeling them into sparkling residences with state-of-the-art kitchens and top-of-the-line furnishings, and providing housekeeping and maintenance. Emory also put live-in house directors on its payroll to serve as role models and keep an eye on what needed fixing—from a leaky roof to an out-of-control party. Nine of Emory's 11 fraternities had elected to participate in the plan in 2000, but the two holdouts symbolized the resistance to change that university administrators and national fraternities often encountered from local fraternity chapters. An officer of the Kappa Sigma fraternity, one of the two holdouts, said of Emory's Phoenix Plan:

> We hate it. The Phoenix Plan equals no fun and sucky fraternity life. It severely hurts what being in a fraternity is all about, which is having a good time and having parties.[7]

At the time the officer made this statement, his Kappa Sigma chapter house was rundown, with crumbling columns, broken windows, a leaky roof that had stained the ceiling, and a side yard littered with beer bottles and a broken couch. In contrast, the houses of the nine fraternities that had opted to participate in the Phoenix Plan were filled almost to capacity. Emory University officials believed the Phoenix Plan had been a success, pointing out that, by 2000, fraternity membership at Emory had climbed above 1997 levels when the Phoenix Plan was launched and that the new chapter house arrangements had produced positive cultural changes within the nine participating fraternities.

GREEK ORGANIZATIONS AT THE UNIVERSITY OF ALABAMA

Although historically the Greek system at the University of Alabama had been very strong, it was not immune from the same challenges facing Greek organizations around the country. In 2001, the university had a total enrollment of around 22,000 students on its main Tuscaloosa campus; roughly 20 percent belonged to Greek fraternities and sororities. The Greek system consisted of 26 fraternities and 19 sororities, with the sororities having about twice as many total members as the fraternities. Traditionally, Greeks permeated all levels of campus leadership and involvement, effectively dominating student government and campus elections. The political activities of Greek organizations had recently extended into community political circles when a 25-year-old former Greek UA student was elected to the Tuscaloosa city council in 1997 (with many of his votes coming from UA students who had registered to vote in Tuscaloosa—some for the purpose of voting in this particular election).

---

[7]Reisberg, "Ethnic and Multicultural Fraternities Are Booming."

In addition to political interests, Greeks had visible and often leading roles in community service, scholarship development, social activities, and intramural sports. While some traditions of UA's Greek system had proved to be great assets to the fraternities, others had put the current system under great strain. Over the last decade, the Greek system and the university administration had been in a virtual state of war. Fraternities had been more or less constantly in trouble for violations involving hazing, drinking, fighting, and pulling pranks, and university administrators were always pressing for one or another changes in the Greek system or student government (controlled by the Greeks), further heightening the friction between the groups. Issues at the forefront of the debate were delayed rush, a push on the part of the university faculty and others for greater diversity (there had been very limited racial and cultural integration of fraternities and sororities), and the requirements and standards for a Greek organization to remain in good standing.

Frequent stories in the local and state media in 2001 concerning one or another aspects of Greek life (especially regarding the admission of blacks to the mostly all-white fraternities and sororities) had exacerbated an already tense situation. Most stories spotlighted what reporters saw as "problems" and the negative aspects of fraternal life; little mention was ever made in the media when something positive occurred in the Greek segment of the campus. The negative reporting had fostered unfavorable public sentiment against the Greek system and, rightly or wrongly, had helped toughen the stance that university administrators were taking in their dealing with fraternities and sororities.

THE PI KAPPA PHI FRATERNITY

Three lifelong friends who had grown up together in Charleston, South Carolina, founded Pi Kappa Phi fraternity at the College of Charleston on December 10, 1904. The fraternity was formed so that its members could compete effectively with existing fraternities for influence over campus life. The three cofounders were already heavily involved in activities across the campus. From football, basketball, and baseball to elite academic and honor societies, these men strived for excellence in everything they did. In accordance with their high ideals and personal goals, they based the foundation of their new fraternity on the principles of scholarship, leadership, service, and brotherhood.

Pi Kappa Phi grew quickly and became very popular and influential at Charleston. In 1906, the chapter was offered a charter by another national fraternity. Although this might have been the easiest way to achieve permanence and would have provided an excellent vehicle for growth, the men instead chose to expand and create more chapters of Pi Kappa Phi. Shortly thereafter, the fraternity chartered a second chapter at Presbyterian College. At that time, there was a state law banning fraternities at state-supported schools. Presbyterian and the College of Charleston did not receive state funds and thus were the only colleges in South Carolina where fraternities openly existed. In order to protect the fraternity's name, the members moved to secure articles of incorporation, which legally registered Pi Kappa Phi in the state of South Carolina in 1907.

Later that year, one of the original members of Pi Kappa Phi, Theodore B. Kelley, moved from Charleston to attend college at the University of California. There he founded the third chapter of Pi Kappa Phi and thus began the process of establishing the fraternity on a national level. Over the next 30 years, 49 new chapters were established across the United States. Pi Kappa Phi grew at a rate of almost two new chapters per year. In 1970, the fraternity became the fastest growing in America in terms of members.

In 2001, Pi Kappa Phi had 140 chapters across the United States, was continuing to expand at a rapid rate, and ranked in the top 25 percent in the number of chapters, pledges, and active members. The fraternity was governed by a seven-member National Council that consisted of a president, vice president, treasurer, secretary, historian, chaplain, and chancellor. The staff at the national headquarters served as the chapters' "chamber of commerce," promoting the expansion of Pi Kappa Phi to college campuses across the country.

While Pi Kappa Phi looked very solid in 2001 when benchmarked against other fraternities, the reality was that many of the chapters had substandard academic performance, mediocre leaders, alcohol issues, limited alumni involvement, and minimal outreach to the community. To address these problems, Pi Kappa Phi had developed and was currently instituting a new broad-based, value-building strategic plan called The Journey.

Evolution of The Journey Project at Pi Kappa Phi

In 1995, the National Council of Pi Kappa Phi realized that after two centuries of growth and successful operation, America's fraternity system was facing some tough and unprecedented challenges. In response, it created The Journey to meet these challenges head-on. The goal of The Journey was to refocus the national fraternity and local chapters on the fraternity's founding values, beliefs, and principles. Seven guiding principles, or beacons, formed the core of the metaphoric journey on which the National Council envisioned local chapter members would embark:

- *Balance*—"Individuals who are balanced in their mental, physical and spiritual development are happier than those whose lives are out of balance."
- *Excellence*—"Excellence is more than a state of being; it is a process."
- *Accountability*—"Actions have consequences and we must individually be held responsible for our actions."
- *Commitment*—"Commitment is the desire to get the job done, be it by hard work, allocation of resources or whatever means possible."
- *Opportunity*—"Always seek out new opportunities."
- *No Limits*—"Eliminating self-imposed limits that impair the pursuit of excellence."
- *Stewardship*—"Practice service beyond self."

The concept and purpose of The Journey project were well received by external constituencies. The fraternity received numerous national awards for introduction of the initiative, and one prestigious businessman went so far as to describe The Journey as "a true renaissance of the fraternal movement."

Recognizing the truth in John F. Kennedy's statement that only 50 percent of a college education comes through what you learn in a classroom, The Journey aimed at providing a goodly portion of the other 50 percent and was specifically aimed at building better men, not simply building better chapters. Through the value-building programs and educational efforts built into The Journey, every Pi Kappa Phi chapter was offered the opportunity to meet higher standards and provide its members with a valuable way to enhance their personal development and leadership potential. While all chapters could profit from taking on the challenge of meeting the higher standards built into Level I of The Journey (see Exhibit 2), chapters aspiring to Level II status had to commit to higher performance standards and a new set of operating practices, including

exhibit 2   The Three Levels of Pi Kappa Phi's Journey Project

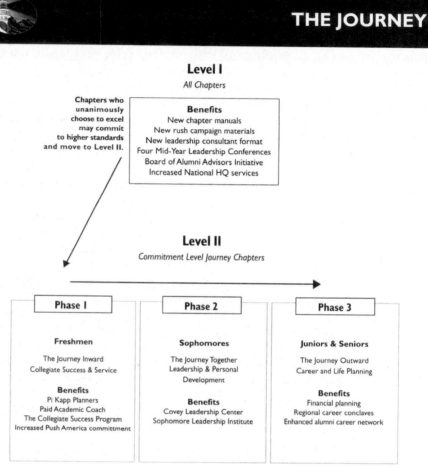

Source: "Built to Last," Pi Kappa Phi's strategic plan for 2000–2004.

- *Higher academic requirements*: The chapter had to have a grade-point average of no lower than a 2.50 on a 4.0 scale.
- *Chapter size requirements*: The chapter had to have an above-average number of members (relative to all Pi Kappa Phi chapters) or else be in the top half in chapter size among all the fraternities on its campus and have no less than 35 initiated members.
- *Governance and oversight*: The chapter had to establish an actively functioning advisory board consisting of a minimum of a chapter advisor, a financial advisor, and an academic advisor and work to include two to four more advisors made up of alumni, parents, faculty and staff, and community leaders, none of whom could be members of Pi Kappa Phi.
- *Standards*: The chapter had to establish a standards board charged with holding members individually accountable to the standards expected of Pi Kappa Phis.
- *Annual retreat*: The chapter had to hold an annual alcohol-free, off-campus retreat attended by 100 percent of the chapter.
- *Member conduct*: The chapter had to devise and implement a code of conduct for members.

In addition, a Level II chapter was expected to implement a three-phase program intended to "build better men." Member participation in the three phases was based on a member's class (freshman, sophomore, junior, senior) and time in the fraternity. Phase 1, called The Journey Inward: Collegiate Success & Service, was for first-year pledges/members, typically freshmen. Participants in this phase received a free Pi Kappa Phi planner and were given access to a paid academic coach responsible for overseeing the Collegiate Success Program (a series of lessons designed to help first-year pledges/members strive for balance in their lives and to help them maintain high academic standards); the academic coach tracked each member's progress in absorbing The Journey Inward lessons and could insist that a member redo all or parts of Phase 1 to achieve the intended learning and developmental objectives. First-year members were also expected to devote significant time and energy to Pi Kappa Phi's chapterwide annual community service event, Push America (a transcontinental bike ride that used service and education to promote greater understanding of persons with disabilities and that had raised over $3 million for this cause).

In Phase 2, called The Journey Together: Leadership & Personal Development, second-year members (typically sophomores) were trained in leadership through the Sophomore Leadership Institute, an arm of the Covey Leadership Center, using programs specifically developed for Pi Kappa Phi members and grounded around Stephen Covey's best-selling book, *Seven Habits of Highly Effective People*. Leadership consultants affiliated with the Pi Kappa Phi's national office helped chapter leaders apply these concepts in daily chapter operations. In Phase 3, The Journey Outward: Career & Life Planning, Pi Kappa Phi alumni volunteered as mentors to help juniors and seniors choose appropriate careers and master the skills necessary to secure a job; completion of this phase involved résumé workshops and mock interviews. In turn, juniors and seniors were expected to mentor first- and second-year members going through the Phase 1 and 2 programs.

So far, The Journey had been very successful, with over 75 chapters voting to become Level II chapters by 2001. Building on this success, the National Council decided to do an in-depth strategic analysis of the whole Pi Kappa Phi fraternity organization and use the findings as a basis for (1) creating a new vision for the fraternity (to be in place by Pi Kappa Phi's centennial year, 2004), and (2) identifying a set of specific action steps to get the organization and its chapters well along the road to achieving the vision. While the National Council recognized that The Journey was an integral part of the fraternity's future, it was evident that the program was not sufficient. Pi Kappa Phi patterned its new initiative after James C. Collins and Jerry I. Porras's best-selling book *Built to Last,* which dealt with what some of the world's most successful companies had done to achieve sustained success. The task force charged with developing the strategic plan for 2000–2004 was asked to consider three questions:

1. What does Pi Kappa Phi want to be in the year 2004 and beyond?
2. What will it take to get there?
3. How will we know if we are successful?

The National Council's intent was to transform the fraternity into a visionary organization, not simply an organization led by visionary men. The task force identified 11 critical issues that the fraternity needed to address (see Exhibit 3). The strategic plan that emerged (titled "Built to Last") contained the following:

- *Mission*: Building leading men for life's journey through leading chapters.
- *Vision*: Pi Kappa Phi will be America's Leading Fraternity with leading men in leading chapters. Pi Kappa Phi members will be citizens, leaders, gentlemen,

exhibit 3   Critical Issues Faced by Pi Kappa Phi's Local Chapters and National Organization

1. **Recruitment.** Fraternities are perceived negatively by incoming students and parents. Recruitment numbers are down. Student members are unable to articulate the benefit of the fraternity experience other than alcohol and women. Chapters recruit binge drinkers.

2. **Retention.** Significant number of members have de-pledged or gone inactive after initiation. Many of them "window shop" and either do not "buy" or have "buyer's remorse."

3. **Member education.** There has been a breakdown in the assimilation of new members with emphasis on rote memorization or menial tasks for the brothers as compared to teaching them how to become a fully functioning member of the chapter.

4. **Quality of student leadership.** Many student officers are "caretakers" and take no ownership in their respective office, nor plan for the future which leads to a rapid breakdown in the chapter infrastructure. They are improperly trained and are in critical need of guidance and oversight. The developmental stage of male college students and the level of intelligence issue are factors here. Complete turnover in executive officer ranks contributes to the officers' lack of preparation since the elected member typically will not have served in another capacity.

5. **Standards enforcement.** Today's college students find it difficult to hold each other accountable and have a misplaced sense of brotherhood. Due to rapid turnover in the chapter, it is necessary to constantly reeducate and reaffirm. It takes only two years to establish tradition—both good and bad.

6. **Financial management.** Local chapters carry significant accounts receivable balances from its members and rely on inexperienced students to serve as the local bookkeeper for this small business. Members begrudgingly pay their local obligation and resent any national fees. Finances are mismanaged without adequate budgeting and internal controls.

7. **Quality of housing.** Most chapter houses are in significant need of remodeling, and need health and fire code upgrades. Typically the chapter houses are trashed and smell like a bar.

8. **National staff.** Although Pi Kappa Phi is a volunteer based organization, staff provides significant support. Staff are typically entry level who need significant training and oversight in their respective jobs. Once trained they tend to leave and the cycle is repeated.

9. **Alumni volunteers.** Significant oversight is needed for the students. There has been a significant breakdown in the identification and recruitment, training, communication with and supervision of our volunteers.

10. **Alcohol abuse.** Alcohol abuse and binge drinking is the number one problem on college campuses, as with the fraternity system.

11. **Lack of "Esprit de Corps."** Too many members think that the fraternity is only a club and are unable to articulate what its true meaning is. At best, members participate in only a few chapter activities and never develop a sense of lifelong brotherhood and fellowship.

Source: "Built to Last," Pi Kappa Phi's strategic plan for 2000–2004.

scholars, servants, lifelong brothers. (See Exhibit 4 for the complete vision statement.)

- *Vision outcome*: Men of CLASS (*C*itizenship, *L*eadership Development, *A*ccountability, *S*cholastic Achievement, and Commitment to *S*ervice). (See Exhibit 5 for the standards expected for achieving CLASS status.)

- *Long-range objective*: Pi Kappa Phi will become and remain the leading fraternal organization in the world.

exhibit 4   Pi Kappa Phi Vision Statement, 2000

Pi Kappa Phi will become *America's Leading Fraternity*
Augmenting the Education of America's finest men
at campuses across the nation
through its uncompromising passion
To maintain the lofty **Standards**
which teach all members
the true meaning of **Brotherhood.**

As our students and alumni begin
this **Lifelong Journey of Brotherhood,**
Pi Kappa Phi will foster the development of
Scholarship,
Service and Values,
as well as
Leadership and Personal Development,
while providing a network of opportunity for
Career and Life Planning.

Pi Kappa Phi will kindle
Alumni Involvement
by providing avenues for direct
Interaction with collegians as the alumni assist
them in their **Personal Development.**
This interaction will give both students and alumni
a better understanding of the Journey of **Pi Kappa Phi** Fraternity.

Source: "Built to Last," Pi Kappa Phi's strategic plan for 2000–2004.

- *General goal*: Augment the education of America's finest men at campuses across the nation by promoting lifelong member development.
- *Core strategy*: Lifelong member development program based upon CLASS.
- *Substrategies*: Promote character and accountability
    Provide leadership development opportunities
    Encourage academic achievement
    Promote commitment to service
    Promote a spirit of team work and selfless contribution
- *Target behavior*: Members utilize opportunities for lifelong enrichment
- *Measurable outcomes*: Attendance at local, regional, and national events
    Percent of members involved in other student organizations
    Number utilizing alumni/career network mentors
    Percent of members remaining active for four years
    Chapter accounts receivable status
    Percent meeting initiation grade requirement
    Percent graduating versus campus average
    Number of honors graduates and number in honor societies
    Number of conduct violations

exhibit 5   Pi Kappa Phi's Journey Standards for Men of CLASS

THE JOURNEY STANDARD

Citizen

Participates in self governance of chapter (recruitment, ritual, committees, chapter).

Participates in chapter and alumni events.

Upholds faithfully the traditions and activities of their college by participating in Greek, campus and community events.

Diligently prepares himself and serves as a responsible citizen upon graduation.

Leader

Serves as a leader in the chapter.

Joins another student organization and becomes a campus leader.

Attends local, regional and national leadership events.

Accountable

Takes personal responsibility and is accountable for his actions.

Serves as a role model by living the ritual everyday.

Expects others to live the ritual and holds them accountable.

Safeguards the reputation of his chapter by keeping careful watch over his personal conduct.

Whose loyalty transcends any personal selfishness.

Bears his share of the financial burden of the chapter and the national organization.

Scholar

Strives to attain the highest possible standard of scholarship and performs above the all-men's grade point average.

Member in good standing academically.

Graduates with honors and is recognized for his scholastic achievement.

Servant

Serves as a lifelong volunteer in both community and Push America activities.

Is a lifelong brother who stays active throughout his college career and stays in touch with the brotherhood and participates in alumni activities.

Is a senior mentor in the chapter.

Gives back to the Fraternity as both a volunteer and donor.

Source: "Built to Last," Pi Kappa Phi's strategic plan for 2000–2004.

The plan identified four core objectives delivered through two initiatives:

- *Building Leading Men* by making The Journey of Pi Kappa Phi (formerly The Journey Project) available to all chapters with no distinction between levels, no application process, no separate standards, and no Journey Retreat. Leading men were able to quickly and succinctly articulate what Pi Kappa Phi stands for and were challenged to be men of CLASS (*C*itizenship, *L*eadership Development, *A*ccountability, *S*cholastic Achievement, and Commitment to *S*ervice. The fraternity also offered the Star Assignment Alcohol Education Program to help support the initiative of building better men.

- *Building Leading Chapters* through the America's Leading Fraternity initiative. This initiative encompassed the Seven Objectives of Chapter Excellence (Recruitment Success, Superior Associate Member Education, Scholastic Achievement, Sound Chapter Operations, Living the Ritual, Commitment to Service, Effective Alumni Relations), defining chapter achievement at three levels, with a leading chapter meeting the highest one. Leading chapters would focus chapter support through a customized strategic plan.

- *Promoting Lifelong Brotherhood* by shifting resources to make Pi Kappa Phi a lifelong experience. To meet this goal, the fraternity intended to employ systematic communication in the form of chapter alumni newsletters and e-mails, developing member benefit packages, and sponsoring annual chapter- and city-based alumni events.

- *Becoming the Leading National Headquarters* by allowing the national headquarters to serve as a chamber of commerce and the staff to act as volunteer coordinators to help members and chapters be successful and to maintain the standards of the fraternity.

The plan set forth two detailed action initiatives for achieving these four objectives and also identified the resources that would be made available to chapter members in pursuing Journey standards and producing men of CLASS. The plan included over 20 measures for tracking the progress being made in implementing the plan and achieving the target outcomes.

As Mark Timmes got ready to head to the National Council meeting, he worried whether all the money and energy that the national fraternity had spent on The Journey and on "Built to Last" was going to produce the desired results and allow Pi Kappa Phi to lay legitimate claim to its tag line of "America's Best Fraternity." The plan seemed to look pretty good on paper, but Timmes realized the real test was yet to come—local chapters, most especially the ones that were struggling, had to be convinced to buy into The Journey concept and then National had to deliver on making The Journey experience something that the big majority of chapter members would find truly worthwhile and meaningful. Otherwise, the plan would produce little of tangible value and National would be back at square one.

THE OMICRON CHAPTER OF PI KAPPA PHI

One day in 1917, a group of young men at the University of Alabama applied for a charter to the Pi Kappa Phi National Fraternity. One month later, on April 25, 1917, a charter was issued establishing the Omicron chapter of Pi Kappa Phi. Omicron was the 15th chapter to be chartered by the young national organization, and the first in the state of Alabama. The chapter soon became a leader in both Pi Kappa Phi and on the university campus.

The first permanent chapter house, acquired in 1921, was occupied by Omicron until the present chapter house on University Boulevard was built in 1963. The brothers who occupied the original chapter house won the first Alabama All Sports Championship, beginning a tradition of excellence in athletics for the Omicron chapter.

In keeping with Pi Kappa Phi's spirit of growing through the relentless pursuit of excellence, the brothers of the Omicron chapter overcame many obstacles over the years. In 1960, the university notified the chapter that the property on which its original chapter house stood would be needed for expansion of the law school. When it appeared that funds could not be raised in time to build a new fraternity house and meet the deadline for vacating the existing house, Omicron's president, along with several other chapter members, went to a local bank and pledged their cars as collateral for a loan to start construction of the present chapter house.

While some years produced more honors, awards, and championships than others, Omicron thrived. It was regarded as one of Pi Kappa Phi's strongest chapters, and it was among the most highly regarded fraternities on the UA campus. On the national level, the Omicron chapter generated more national presidents of Pi Kappa Phi and more Mr. Pi Kappa Phis (the fraternity's highest honor) than any other chapter. However, in 1996, in what proved to be a traumatic event for the chapter, the University of Alabama cited Omicron for hazing. According to grapevine rumor, a number of UA fraternities still surreptitiously engaged in the hazing of pledges in the mid-1990s, despite long-standing university efforts to halt the practice and despite assurances from fraternity officers that it had ended in their chapters. University officials imposed swift and harsh penalties on the Pi Kappa Phi chapter (as they had done with other fraternities when hazing had been discovered). The punishment handed down was so severe that it was whispered among other Greek organizations that the Pi Kappa Phi chapter had received a "death sentence." Omicron's fraternity house was closed, the prominent Pi Kappa Phi letters removed from the facade, and all on-campus operations and activities of the fraternity were suspended for three years. As might be expected, the three-year suspension for hazing hit the chapter hard, severely disappointing their national officers and marring Omicron's reputation on campus.

The suspension presented chapter officers and members with a dilemma—they could simply disband the chapter and try to resurrect operations after the three-year suspension ended, or they could move to an off-campus location and fight to hold the chapter together until they were allowed to return to their on-campus house and resume normal fraternity activities. Not surprisingly, in keeping with the tradition of the chapter, the members chose to find a suitable location off campus where they could at least maintain some semblance of a chapter house and gather enough strength to return to the campus after the three-year suspension ended. To find a facility large enough for the weekly chapter meetings, Omicron turned to a local drinking establishment and rented the facility on Sunday nights when it was closed (local county ordinances banned serving alcohol on Sunday). Following a series of gut-wrenching meetings in which there was hot debate about how Omicron came to find itself in such dire straits and what now needed to be done, members vowed to clean up their act. The chapter worked hard on boosting members' academic performance during the suspension period and made giant strides, raising the chapter's grade-point average from the lowest among 26 fraternities on the UA campus (at the time the suspension was handed down) to the highest of all 26 chapters by 1999 (when the suspension ended).

Though times were rocky during the three-year suspension, Omicron's brothers were able to keep the chapter functional, albeit in a weakened state except for the dramatic improvement in the chapter's academic performance. When the chapter returned to campus in 1999, Omicron's members were anxious to resume a leading position in the Greek hierarchy on the UA campus and indicated to university officials that they were committed to instituting a hazing-free pledge program. Both goals proved challenging. Campus administrators were not sure whether chapter members were truly ready to purge all hazing; they discounted what Omicron's officers said and preferred to let the chapter's future actions tell the story one way or the other. Omicron had to work especially hard to rebuild its membership roster to former levels, finding that the chapter's suspension-tarnished reputation caused a number of the "best" rushees to shy away. Nonetheless, the size of the chapter increased from just over 30 members when the suspension was lifted in 1999 to just over 70 members in 2001.

Chapter members were heartened, too, by the strong alumni support they received in resuming on-campus chapter operations and rebuilding the chapter. To welcome and thank the returning alumni offering assistance and moral support, the chapter held scholarship dinners (that highlighted the chapter's academic achievements) and provided pregame lunches at home football games. The chapter alumni who volunteered to help restore the chapter's strength were quick to impart their experiences and advice based on the "glory days" of how things were done when they were members. A few of the alumni brothers were openly skeptical of hazing-free pledge programs, arguing that a strong brotherhood was built on the experiences of pledges who had to overcome the adversity of a tough pledgeship regimen; these alumni brothers told Omicron's current members a raft of stories about the camaraderie fostered by the antics they shared as pledges and as brothers training new pledges. While the current members realized that some of the alumni's stories involved clear examples of hazing, other stories seemed to involve harmless fun and were enticing. All the alumni folklore, coupled with hearsay about what transpired at several other fraternity houses on the UA campus, began to spread sentiments among Omicron's members to maintain some semblance of the chapter's pledge-training traditions rather than to make a clean break with the past.

Omicron Chapter in 2001

In the fall of 2001, the short-term and long-term consequences of Omicron's 1996–99 suspension lingered in the minds of some members of the Omicron chapter; there was a contingent of members who didn't want any part of another suspension and were willing to break with past traditions—at least as far as haze-free pledging was concerned. Other members, enamored with the chapter's long-standing traditions and "glory days" culture, were willing to push the envelope with regard to a tough pledge-training regimen. Most the chapter's 74 members were generally antagonistic toward what they saw as an anti-Greek attitude on the part of the university administration; there was considerable sentiment for hanging tough and taking a hard-line stance against most of the so-called reforms being proposed by university officials.

Thus, Jason McKenna felt himself being pulled in several opposing directions as he contemplated the chapter's future. He was acutely aware of the chapter's need to avoid another serious run-in with the university and to institute whatever chapter reforms might be necessary to remain in good standing. He was also aware that 75 other Pi Kappa Phi chapters had already chosen to join The Journey and that, from National's perspective, it would not reflect well on Omicron to delay its participation much longer. Yet McKenna knew that convincing the membership to vote to become a leadership chapter and implement The Journey program would be a hard sell—the old-style way of running the chapter, with all its attendant problems (toleration of alcohol abuse, a lingering tradition of hazing pledges, preoccupation with winning the All Sports Trophy, and a full-fledged party atmosphere), was the clear preference of a majority of the brothers. He was not seeing any genuine enthusiasm among the membership for making fundamental changes; on the contrary, there was much comfort with the status quo and with stonewalling on most of the changes in the Greek system the university administration proposed. McKenna sensed that his brothers' interest in National's Journey initiative was lukewarm at best.

As he headed for the chapter meeting, Jason McKenna continued to mull over several questions. Should he stick his neck out for The Journey and, if so, what could he say that would carry the day? If he did not bring it up tonight, how much longer could he wait to put the issue squarely before the chapter? What was his responsibility as chapter president—to carry out the wishes of the majority of the members, or to exercise leadership and make a persuasive case for changing the long-term direction of the chapter? The choices were not easy ones, but the time to make some decisions was close at hand.

(For additional data on trends in fraternity membership, you can browse the information at http://chronicle.com/free/v46/i18/18a06101/htm.)

case | 5

ZAP and the Electric Vehicle Industry

Armand Gilinsky Jr.
Sonoma State University

Robert Ditizio
Sonoma State University

Soon after winning the 2000 Oscar for best actor, Kevin Spacey made his appearance on *The Late Show with David Letterman* by riding a Zappy electric scooter. It was at that moment that Gary Starr, the CEO and cofounder of ZAP Corporation, felt his efforts at creating electric vehicles (EVs) for the masses had reached a milestone. ZAP designed, manufactured, and marketed electric bicycles, scooters, motorcycles, and other short-range electric transportation products. Following a recent return in popularity of nonpowered "kick" scooters, ZAP had experienced a rise in sales of its electric-powered Zappy scooter. As sales figures approached record levels, ZAP was poised to take a leadership position in the emerging alternative short-range transportation industry, an industry that Starr predicted could grow to $5 billion by 2005.

The appearance of the Zappy on the Letterman show was a high point in a marketing campaign that had included associated tie-ins with Old Navy, Sprite, and the 2000 Olympics in Sydney. Yet the unplanned appearance of ZAP's flagship product also left Starr with several unanswered questions: Should his company ramp up production to meet a sudden spike in demand, or should it follow a more carefully controlled growth path? Would demand be sustained, or was the resurgence of scooters a fad? What position could ZAP's electrically powered bicycles and scooters occupy in an evolving market for alternative transportation?

By 2001, Starr and his management team were considering ways to match ZAP's internal resources and capabilities with external market demand. An internal debate raged over how to allocate ZAP's resources between its flagship scooter products and the remaining product line in order to put the company on a path to profitability. In the company's early years, Starr had often relied on gut feelings to forecast demand. As ZAP had matured as a business, however, Starr felt that proper demand forecasting by his team was necessary to assemble the needed capital, manufacturing facilities, marketing, and staff to take the company to the next level. An onslaught of new, lower-cost competitors had recently entered the EV market. Starr knew that he needed to act quickly to assemble a critical mass of resources in order to protect ZAP's early market leadership.

This case was originally presented at the 2001 meeting of the North American Case Research Association in Memphis, TN. Copyright © 2001 by the case authors. Used with permission.

COMPANY HISTORY

In 1994, James McGreen and Gary Starr founded ZAP Power Systems in Sebastopol, California, a town of 7,750 located 56 miles north of San Francisco in the heart of the Sonoma County wine grape and apple-growing region. ZAP, an acronym for Zero Air Pollution, arose out of McGreen and Starr's residual interests in U.S. Electricar, a now-defunct organization that made a run at producing electric automobiles. Having spent their careers designing electric vehicles, McGreen and Starr had been encouraged by the growing public attention on curbing fossil fuel emissions.

In 1996, ZAP began to sell its electrically powered bikes through auto dealerships and started offering products through catalogs. The company's business began to improve in 1997, when ZAP and electric scooter maker Motivity formed ZAP Europa to cross-distribute products. The company also signed manufacturing and distribution agreements that year with Dantroh Japan, XtraMOBIL of Switzerland, and Forever Bicycle Company in Shanghai, China.

ZAP began selling its stock directly to the public via the Internet in 1997, the first Internet initial public offering in history. It then opened an outlet store in San Francisco. A year later it introduced the Zappy scooter, which boosted sales. The company changed its name to Zapworld.com just prior to the Internet frenzy that was to follow shortly thereafter. Although the Internet represented a significant marketing tool and sales outlet, the company name was changed back to ZAP in April 2001 following an industrywide shake-out in which hundreds of dot-com companies went out of business.

In November 1999, an agreement was reached with ZEV Technologies of Syracuse, New York, for the exclusive right to distribute its electric Pedicab, a three-wheeled vehicle capable of carrying a driver and one or two passengers. In December 1999, an agreement was reached to purchase EV maker emPower, a developer of advanced electric scooters founded by Massachusetts Institute of Technology engineers. ZAP then acquired emPower in exchange for 525,000 shares of common stock. In that same month, a second company-owned EV store was opened, in Key West, Florida.

In February 2000, ZAP bought EV Systems, an EV company based in Los Altos, California. EV Systems produced a two-wheeled vehicle designed to tow skaters and skateboarders. EV Systems was obtained for 25,000 shares of common stock. Looking to further broaden ZAP's product lines, in May 2000 Starr introduced a new generation of nonpowered scooter (called the Kick™) that used inline skate technology. This compact scooter could be folded to fit into a backpack. In the same month ZAP also acquired Aquatic Propulsion Technology, Inc., a company that developed a product called a sea scooter, which pulled scuba divers, snorkelers, and other swimmers through water. This deal was secured in exchange for 120,000 shares of common stock.

In August 2000, ZAP formed a joint venture agreement with Nongbo Topp Industrial Company Ltd. of China to manufacture and distribute EVs in China. This joint venture purchased key components from ZAP, assembled and distributed the Zappy scooter in China, and paid royalties on each electric scooter sold in China. ZAP also received a share of the profits from the joint venture.

In September 2000, *Automotive News* recognized Starr as one of the 10 most influential EV authorities. The following month, at the 17th International EV Symposium in Montreal, Quebec, Starr spoke to a plenary session:

> Light EVs don't require the development of sophisticated hybrid or fuel cell technologies to bring them to market. With nearly 20 different models of EVs now available, ZAP is already delivering thousands of EVs to consumers. This industry [segment] has already surpassed the market for all other electric transportation.

Later that month, ZAP purchased Electric Motorbike Inc., a firm that developed electric scooters, motorbikes, and motorcycles. As with most of the other acquisitions, under the terms of this purchase agreement, ZAP acquired all assets, customer contacts, engineering capabilities, and technology, including the components and designs for the Lectra motorcycle and its proprietary VR24 drive system. The Lectra motorcycle was capable of reaching speeds of over 50 mph and, at the time, was the world's only electric motorcycle in production.

An exclusive distribution contract with Oxygen SpA of Italy was signed in October 2000 to sell the Zappy folding electric scooter and other ZAP EVs in Italy and three other European countries. In February 2001, this agreement was expanded to allow ZAP to distribute the Lepton in North America. The Lepton was a moped-class sit-on scooter built by Oxygen SpA.

Internal product development efforts also aided Starr's efforts to expand his product base. In 2001, five new personal electric transportation products were unveiled at the industry Super Show in Las Vegas, Nevada. These products included the Zappy Jr., a smaller version of the Zappy targeted at younger riders, and the Zappy Turbo, an improved version of the popular Zappy electric scooter. The Zappy and Kick lines of products accounted for approximately 85 percent of total sales in 2000, and product expansions and improvements were necessary to secure ZAP's market position in the face of increasing competition. Other products under development included an electrically powered tricycle called the Golfcycle™, specifically designed for golf courses. This single-passenger golf vehicle was equipped with a hybrid human-electric propulsion system and room to carry a set of golf clubs, and was offered as an alternative to the ubiquitous golf cart. Also scheduled for release in 2001 was a new electric motor device called ZapAdapt™, which attached to manual wheelchairs. This device provided an affordable, convenient means of power assistance without the need to purchase a fully powered wheelchair.

The string of acquisitions and marketing agreements, along with ongoing internal product development efforts, resulted in a product line of personal EVs consisting of offerings in over 10 different product categories. (See Exhibit 1 for a list of ZAP's most popular products.) Accessories for these products also contributed to increasing sales. The promotional publicity garnered by ZAP's products created a source of momentum for the entire product line and contributed to a doubling of revenues for the small company for the year 2000 versus 1999. Recent financial statements for the company are provided in Exhibits 2 and 3.

ZAP'S MARKETING EFFORTS AND OVERALL STRATEGY

After the most recent acquisitions and product development efforts, ZAP's electrically powered product offerings included scooters, bicycles, power skis, patrol bikes, tricycles, sit-down scooters (similar to a moped), motorbikes, pedicabs, underwater propulsion devices, and neighborhood cars. ZAP also offered the ZAP Power System™ to address the market of the do-it-yourselfer who preferred to transform his or her own bicycle into an electric bike.

Through internal development and acquisition, ZAP had procured 14 patents associated with EV design implementation. This strong patent portfolio was secured as a means to protect the company's interests in light of increasing competition. Although the patent position represented a significant investment for ZAP, Starr conceded in a recent interview that patents simply gave companies the right to sue and that in a competitive environment, litigation could become burdensome and costly. Nonetheless, he was forced to hire legal counsel in early 2001 in an attempt to stop patent infringers from stealing ZAP's technology.

exhibit 1   Most Popular Items in ZAP's Product Line in 2001

Zappy™

The Zappy folding electric scooter is what the Company calls a "destination vehicle." Folded, the Zappy is just over three feet long and stores easily almost anywhere. Lightweight at only 36 pounds, the Zappy can be carried or rolled like luggage, and an optional tote bag makes transporting the Zappy even easier. Due to its small size when folded, the Zappy can be transported via a number of means including car, train, bus, and commercial airlines. When they're ready to roll, users simply pop up the Zappy's handlebar, stand up, and push off. The powerful electric drive system propels the Zappy at speeds up to 13 mph for a fast, safe, and fun trip, without poisoning the environment. Line extensions include the Zappy Turbo (higher performance model capable of 19 mph), Zappy Stap fighter (a Star Wars promotional model), the Zappy Mobility (a model with an added seat), the Skootr-X (a less expensive alternative to the Zappy capable of 12 mph), and the Zappy Junior (classified as a toy with maximum speed of 8 mph).

Kick™

The Kick weighs only nine pounds and folds to the size of a tennis racquet. No assembly is required. With its lightweight design, the Kick is easier to ride than a skateboard. Inline-style wheels provide a smooth ride. This foot-powered scooter, built with high-tensile steel, can handle bumps, jumps, and other obstacles and includes a convenient rear compression foot brake. It has an adjustable handlebar and folds small enough to fit in a locker or backpack. The heavy-duty steel construction and rigid braced frame design provide riders with an extremely quiet and effortless ride, while competitive models have been found to produce annoying buzzes and rattles.

PowerBike®

Introduced in 1995, the PowerBike is one of the original electric bikes in America. The PowerBike combines a rugged mountain-bike-style frame with the world-record-breaking ZAP Power System. The PowerBike is designed for long rides out on the open road, with an easy "ZAP" boost for passing, assistance on hills, or short rests on the fly. With the electric "power-assist" benefits of the PowerBike, riders are able to enjoy the outdoor environment without polluting it. The PowerBike unit includes a tough, high-tensile steel mountain bike frame, 18-speed index shifting, and the revolutionary ZAP Power System. PowerBike also features front suspension, V-style brakes, a spring saddle, and a choice of power systems tailored to the budget and power preferences of the consumer.

ElectriCruizer

The ElectriCruizer brings back the "retro" look of older bicycle styles with a futuristic ZAP power system. The new ElectriCruizer is the ultimate way to cruise any neighborhood. Designed for trips around town, commuting, errands, and just plain old fun, this bike features an eye-catching frame made of rugged, high-tensile steel; high-quality, six-speed grip shifting; and front and rear cantilever brakes. Wide, semislick whitewall road tires and a springy contour saddle help smooth out even the bumpiest roads, and the curved handlebars make for an even more comfortable upright riding position. Equipped with the ZAP Power System, the ElectriCruizer has the power to climb virtually any hill. Accessories for this ElectriCruizer include front and rear fenders, baskets, rear racks, lights, and horns. The ZAP ElectriCruizer SX (for "Single Speed") is equipped with a single-motor system, and although the top speed is less than the DX ("Dual Speed") standard, its range is greater. After being pedaled to start, the ElectriCruizer SX reaches approximately 14 mph and has a range of up to 20 miles. The DX offers a more powerful motor with a higher top speed.

ZAP Patrol Bike™

ZAP's police bike looks and pedals like a normal bicycle. But, with the flip of a switch, the bike leaps forward with a silent burst of speed, working in conjunction with leg power to help peace officers arrive on the scene faster and in better physical condition to handle the situation. The ZAP Patrol Bike is designed to maneuver through busy city traffic with an available zap of acceleration for sticky situations. Silent electric power gives officers stealth when approaching areas of suspected criminal activity, and the Quick Release Battery system allows for around-the-clock operation. The ZAP Patrol law enforcement bicycle is identifiable with decals (police, sheriff, EMT, etc.), front suspension, 24-speed index shifting, front and rear V-brakes, heavy-duty Continental Goliath tires, rear rack, and the NiteRider Pursuit Kit. The kit includes dual red-and-white or blue-and-white headlamps with night and flashing pursuit settings, a 115-decibel siren, a rear rack with taillight, and the ZAP Power System.

exhibit 1 (*continued*)

ZAP Trike™

The ZapTrike was designed for those who have trouble pedaling heavy three-wheelers. The burden of pedaling is taken away with the on-board ZAP Power System. This vehicle is popular among seniors and can be an inexpensive alternative for commercial use. The unit includes a sturdy high-tensile steel frame, wide semislick road tires, front side-pull and coaster brakes, a comfortable extra-wide contour saddle, and a large rear basket. The ZAP Trike Power System includes a two-speed dual motor with a long-range (33 ah) battery.

ZAP Kits

ZAP provides everything needed to turn virtually any bicycle into a quiet, nonpolluting, fun electric vehicle. A complete conversion kit includes a motor, a maintenance-free battery, a heavy-duty battery bag, controller, automatic portable charger (either 110 or 220 volts), on/off switch, wiring and mounting hardware. At 22 pounds, the system is so light that it is barely noticeable, yet it is powerful enough to provide extra bursts for passing or climbing hills. The patented Auto Engagement Feature allows the bike to be pedaled normally with the system off. The typical range of bicycles utilizing a ZAP kit varies from 5 to 20 miles per charge, depending on model, user input, and riding conditions.

ZAP kits come in four varieties: DX, SX, Step Thru, and Trike. The DX motor is a dual motor assembly designed for higher speeds. People who want the most power to supplement their pedaling for short bursts of turbo power for hills, like the police, find the DX most appropriate. The DX also features a Regenerative ("Regen") Mode, which recharges the battery by coasting the bike down a big hill. It turns the system's motors into generators, helping to recharge some of the lost electricity. (ZAP-powered bikes are the only electric bikes with regenerative braking.) The SX is a single motor designed for greater range. The Step-Thru systems are designed for a woman's-style bike frame and have the battery mounted on a rear rack rather than in the frame. The Trike kit is great for seniors or people with disabilities.

ElectriCycle™

The ElectriCycle is powered by two 12-volt batteries and a 24-volt DC motor. This vehicle is very similar in performance to a standard 50-cubic-centimeter gas scooter without the fumes and noise. It has a range of up to 20 miles and can top out at up to 25 mph, going from 0 to 18 mph in six seconds. The ElectriCycle features front and rear drum brakes, a power indicator, a speedometer, and an on-board charger that charges the battery in two to eight hours.

Lectra™ Motorbike

Lectra developed one of the world's only electric motorcycles, which represents a world-class application of the most advanced technologies available in electric energy storage, display, and delivery. The Lectra offers superior acceleration, braking, and handling, and the advanced electric drive system is accurately controlled from the fingertips. The antilock, electrically assisted, regenerating rear brake and floating caliper front disk brake provide smooth, powerful braking. Also featured are the convenience of on-board, fully automatic charging and a maintenance-free energy storage system.

Electric Pedicab

Developed with the support of the New York State Energy Research and Development Authority, the ZAP Pedicab is an all-new three-wheeled electric bicycle capable of carrying a driver and two passengers. Operating at 24 volts DC, the Pedicab has a top speed of 15 mph and a 20-mile range. Each ZAP Pedicab is equipped with an onboard 120-volt charging system that will completely recharge the vehicle in less than three hours from any standard power outlet. A convenient state-of-charge meter provides the operator with current information about the vehicle's remaining range and the amount of energy it consumes. The ZAP Pedicab is capable of navigating through spaces that are inaccessible to cars and buses. As a result, for-hire pedicabs can be found in many cities around the world, including several in the United States.

PowerSki®

The PowerSki is a radical new form of personal transportation that creates a downhill skating or skiing environment on flat ground. Much like a water-skier, an inline or roller skater holds onto poles as the PowerSki tows them along at speeds of up to 15 mph. The PowerSkier has complete control of the trigger switch and speed. A single battery charge lasts up to seven miles, and the PowerSki has enough torque to pull an average man up just about any hill, taking PowerSkiers practically anywhere their feet can take them, including on the street, over rough terrain, and up and down hills. This powerful design gives skaters a new form of transportation, exercise, and pure skating fun.

(*continued*)

exhibit 1 (*concluded*)

Swimmy/Sea Scooter

The Swimmy is a fun new water-sport device for the whole family. Whether you're snorkeling in a tropical paradise or swimming in your backyard pool, the Swimmy offers a totally new underwater experience. This "sea scooter" pulls the swimmer through the water, providing more enjoyment in swimming pools and less exertion in reaching coral reefs and other underwater sights.

Neighborhood Cars

Neighborhood EVs (NEVs) are engineered like an automobile for dependable performance on both street and turf. Standard features include a rear brake light and backup alarm, anchored seatbelts, windshield wipers and a safety-glass windshield, auto-style headlights, a rearview mirror, and turn signals.

exhibit 2   ZAP's Consolidated Statement of Operations, 1995–2000 (in thousands, except per share amounts)

	Year Ended December 31					
	2000	**1999**	**1998**	**1997**	**1996**	**1995**
Net sales	$12,443	$ 6,437	$ 3,519	$ 1,640	$1,171	$ 651
Cost of goods sold	7,860	4,446	2,391	1,275	863	465
Gross profit	4,583	1,991	1,127	366	308	215
Operating expenses						
Selling	2,204	1,187	968	633	477	90
General and administrative	3,824	1,945	979	820	555	282
Research and development	699	365	203	246	100	75
Total operating expenses	6,727	3,497	2,150	1,700	1,132	447
Loss from operations	(2,144)	(1,506)	(1,022)	(1,334)	(824)	(232)
Other income (expense)						
Interest expense	(21)	(267)	(100)	(85)	(11)	(3)
Interest income						
Miscellaneous	269	81	14	11	20	222*
Total other income	248	186	(86)	(74)	8	219
	(1,896)	(1,693)	(1,109)	(1,408)	(817)	(13)
Provision for income taxes	1	1	1	2	2	4
Net loss	$ (1,897)	$(1,694)	$(1,109)	$(1,409)	$ (817)	$ (16)
Net loss attributable to shares						
Net loss	(1,897)	(1,694)	(1,109)	(1,409)	(817)	(16)
Preferred dividend	(2,649)	—	—	—	—	—
Total	$ (4,546)	$(1,694)	$(1,109)	$(1,409)	$ (817)	$ (16)
Net income/(loss) per common share, basic and diluted	$(0.85)	$(0.43)	$(0.42)	$(0.62)	$(0.45)	$(0.01)
Weighted average of common shares outstanding	5,361,905	3,927,633	2,614,563	2,289,165	1,805,317	1,582,656

*Includes $210,000 in royalty income and $20,000 in grant income.

exhibit 3 ZAP's Consolidated Balance Sheets, 1995–2000 (in thousands, except per share amounts)

	Years Ending December 31					
	2000	1999	1998	1997	1996	1995
Assets						
Cash	$3,543	$ 3,184	$ 475	$ 691	$ 162	$ 22
Accounts receivable	1,613	353	284	122	61	31
Inventories	2,898	1,725	634	267	247	58
Prepaid expenses and other assets	696	323	98	66	116	—
Total current assets	8,750	5,585	1,491	1,145	585	111
Property and equipment, net	510	350	177	163	100	66
Patents and trademarks, less accumulated amortization	1,432	1,176	—	—	—	—
Goodwill, less accumulated amortization	2,023	112	—	—	—	—
Advance to retail stores and technology companies		479	—	—	—	—
Intangibles, net of accumulated amortization			80	20	7	8
Deposits and other	112	25	12	14	78	6
Total assets	$12,827	$ 7,727	$ 1,760	$ 1,342	$ 770	$191
Liabilities and stockholders' equity						
Current liabilities						
Accounts payable	$ 398	$742	$ 334	$ 162	$ 301	$ 94
Accrued liabilities and customer deposits	1,167	368	151	189	67	13
Notes payable, current maturities of long-term debt	99	15	867	52	249	22
Current maturities of obligations under capital leases	32	9	10	16	13	—
Income taxes payable						3
Total current liabilities	1,696	1,134	1,362	418	629	131
Long-term debt, less current maturities	95	24	11	60	5	—
Obligations under current leases, less current	31	14	1	11	24	—
Total liabilities	1,822	1,172	1,374	489	657	131
Stockholders' equity						
Preferred stock*	1,812					
Paid in common stock†	19,117	12,053	3,732	3,169	1,019	150
Accumulated deficit	(9,664)	(5,118)	(3,346)	(2,316)	(907)	(90)
Unearned compensation	(42)	(96)	—	—	—	—
Less notes receivable from shareholders	(218)	(285)	—	—	—	—
Total stockholder's equity	11,005	6,555	386	853	112	60
Total liabilities and stockholder's equity	$12,827	$ 7,727	$ 1,760	$ 1,342	$ 770	$191

*Shares of preferred stock issued and outstanding (10 million shares authorized): 4

†Shares of common stock issued and outstanding (20 million shares authorized): 5,816 | 5,109 | 2,665 | 2,543 | 2,077 | 1,644

The increasing popularity of electrically powered vehicles, coupled with increasing political and social activity favoring environmentally friendly transportation, resulted in other unplanned exposure for ZAP. Twelve electric bikes were used at the

2000 Olympics in Sydney for regular patrols of the Olympic Village. Other unsolicited product exposure included Zappy appearances on popular television sitcoms such as the *Drew Carey Show* and *Just Shoot Me* and in television commercials with the popular Blue Man Group for Intel Corporation. The Swimmy sea scooter was selected as a finalist for the NASDAQ Sports Product of the Year. The PowerSki product was featured in a segment of the popular morning talk program *The Today Show*, as Matt Lauer demonstrated his prowess with the device on the streets of New York City. Other ZAP products were also slated to appear in four big-screen movie productions to be released in the summer of 2001.

Increasing demand coupled with increasing competition prompted Starr to shift production of high-volume products to Taiwan to trim costs and to allow the company to focus its efforts on improving distribution. Although Starr strongly believed that ZAP must continue its efforts at product development, competitive pressures required that ZAP begin to shift more of its resources to finding ways to reach the customer. In early 2001, a new Zapworld retail store and test track for customers was opened in a shopping mall in Santa Rosa, California. Planning was under way to open similarly configured retail outlets around the country to improve distribution and to build name recognition. The number of independent retail outlets that carried ZAP products in the United States also continued to grow and had exceeded 100 by this time.

Although Starr and his team had expended much effort in creating a broad range of offerings, he also knew that he needed to find new ways to reach consumers. By midyear 2001, after shifting much of ZAP's manufacturing operations overseas, Starr announced that he and his management team were "undertaking a significant repositioning of ZAP from an electric scooter–only company to an overall provider of premier EV products."

Under the plan, ZAP would be positioned as a distributor of high-margin foreign-manufactured products, with a primary focus on aggressive sales activity. ZAP would continue to place an emphasis on the research and development of new EV products, although acquisition plans remained a significant part of the new plan, allowing the company to diversify its product line more rapidly.

With regard to ZAP's developments and repositioning plans, Starr commented:

> ZAP took a bold step to introduce electric bicycles and scooters during the '90s when electric cars seemed to be the center stage. Today, we have proven to the world there is a market for low-speed EVs, but we need to continue to be a pioneer and a leader in this industry, introducing new products and opening up new markets. We must draw on all of our talents to design superior vehicles, manufacture those products at competitive prices, and market them with utmost creativity. We believe we have the entrepreneurial team to accomplish all of the above, backing our mission to make ZAP the name in clean transportation.

ZAP MANAGEMENT

Starr assembled a board of directors that included ZAP's former president, John Dabels. Dabels had come to ZAP after having served as CFO and member of the board of EV Global Motors, an electric bicycle company founded and chaired by Lee Iacocca, the former CEO of Chrysler. Starr felt that the Dabels's experience provided a necessary element for managing the growth of ZAP. In early 2001, however, Dabels left ZAP to spend more time with his family. Dabels's departure left a considerable vacancy on the board for Starr to fill and put added pressure on the other board members to guide the organization. Biographies of the current board members and management team for ZAP are provided in Exhibit 4.

exhibit 4   Biographies of ZAP's Board of Directors and Management Team, 2001

Gary Starr, 45, CEO of ZAP, has been a director and executive officer since 1994, and chief executive officer since September 1999. Starr founded U.S. Electricar's EV operation in 1983 and has been building, designing, and driving electric cars for more than 25 years. He has overseen the marketing of more than 50,000 electric bicycles and other EVs and has invented several solar electric products and conservation devices. Starr was named one of the 10 most influential electric car authorities by *Automotive News* and has appeared on numerous radio, television talk, and television news shows, and is a published author of articles and books on energy efficiency and electric vehicles. He has received several recognition awards for his contributions to clean air, including awards from the American Lung Association of San Francisco, Calstart, and U.S. senator Barbara Boxer. He holds a bachelor of science degree in environmental consulting and advocacy from the University of California–Davis.

Robert E. Swanson, 53, chairman of the board of ZAP since 1999, is chairman of the board, sole director, and sole stockholder of Ridgewood Capital Corporation. Swanson is also chairman of the board of the fund, president, and registered principal and sole stockholder of Ridgewood Securities Corporation. In addition, Swanson is president and sole shareholder of Ridgewood Energy, Ridgewood Power, and Ridgewood Power Management Corporation. Ridgewood Power is a managing shareholder of each of the prior programs, and Swanson is the president of each prior program. Since 1982, Swanson, through a number of entities, has sponsored and been a principal of more than 47 investment programs involved in oil and gas exploration and development; these programs have raised approximately $200 million from the sale of investment units. Swanson was also a tax partner at the former New York and Los Angeles law firm of Fulop & Hardee and an officer in the Investment Division of Morgan Guaranty Trust Company. His specialty was in personal tax and financial planning, including income, estate, and gift taxes. Swanson is a member of the New York State and New Jersey bars. He is a graduate of Amherst College and Fordham University Law School. Swanson and his wife, Barbara Mardinly Swanson, are the authors of *Tax Shelters: A Guide for Investors and Their Advisors,* published by Dow Jones–Irwin in 1982 and published in revised editions in 1984 and 1985.

Douglas R. Wilson, 40, director of ZAP, is vice president of acquisitions at RCC and the Ridgewood Fund. He was a principal of Monhegan Partners, Inc., which provided acquisition and financial advisory for Ridgewood Power and the Prior Programs, from October 1996 until September 1998, when he joined Ridgewood Power and RCC. He has over 14 years of capital markets experience, including specialization in complex lease and project financings and in energy-related businesses. He has a bachelor of business administration from the University of Texas and a master's degree in business administration from the Wharton School of the University of Pennsylvania.

Lee Sannella, M.D., 84, director of ZAP, has been an active researcher in the fields of alternative transportation, energy, and medicine for more than 25 years. Dr. Sannella has been a founding shareholder in many start-up high-tech companies and is a best-selling author. He has served on advisory boards of the City of Petaluma, California, on the board of directors of the San Andreas Health Council of Palo Alto, the Veritas Foundation of San Francisco, and the AESOP Institute. He is a graduate of Yale Medical School.

William D. Evers, 73, director of ZAP, is one of the leading SEC attorneys in California with extensive experience in start-up and emerging companies, specializing for a number of years in private placements, Section 25102(n) offerings, small corporate offering registration, Regulation A exemptions, and small business registrations. He has handled numerous mergers and acquisitions. Evers heads the Evers and Hendrickson Internet Law Group, with its emphasis on Internet relationships. Evers has also had extensive experience in franchising and has been the CEO or president of various business ventures. He holds a bachelor of arts degree from Yale University and doctor of jurisprudence degree from University of California–Berkeley.

Harry Kraatz, 51, became a director of ZAP on December 7, 2000. Since investing in ZAP in 1998, he has provided franchise consulting and certain financial services. Beginning in June 1986, Kraatz has been the sole officer and director of the Embarcadero Group II, and T.E.G. Inc., a franchise management and financial consulting company located in San Francisco, California. Working with those companies, he has provided consulting services to numerous finance and franchising companies, including Montgomery Medical Ventures, Commonwealth Associates, Westminster Capital, and World Wide Wireless Communications, Inc. He received a degree from Southwest Missouri State University in 1971.

Andrew Hutchins, 40, was appointed vice president for operations of ZAP in October 1999. He joined the company in December 1996 and since June 1997 has been the general manager. Successful as an entrepreneur, Hutchins started, developed, and managed a retail bicycle business for 11 years prior to selling it for several times his initial investment. In 1982, Hutchins received a bachelor of arts degree with a double major in business economics and communication studies from the University of California–Santa Barbara.

Scott Cronk, 35, was the founder of Electric MotorBike, Inc. and served as its president from 1995 to 1999. Previously, as director of business development and international programs, he led strategic venturing activities for U.S. Electricar, Inc. Cronk was appointed vice president of business development of ZAP in December 1999 shortly after ZAP acquired Electric Motorbike, Inc. Cronk has a bachelor of science degree in electrical engineering from GMI Engineering & Management Institute (now Kettering University) and a master of business administration degree from the City University of London, England.

exhibit 5   ZAP's Organization in 2001

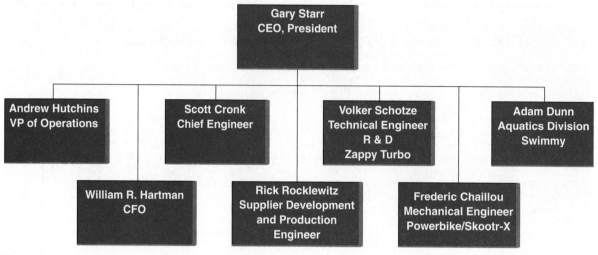

Source: Company records.

Starr oversaw day-to-day operations at ZAP—see the organization chart in Exhibit 5. Andrew Hutchins, vice president of operations, oversaw production of the various products that ZAP manufactured, such as the Zappy line of scooters. One of Hutchins's primary responsibilities in early 2001 was to ensure a smooth transition of the Zappy manufacturing operation to Taiwan. Rick Rocklewitz filled in as supplier development and production engineer in Taiwan to assist in the transition. Product development at ZAP was split into specific product categories. Volker Schotze handled development of extensions of the Zappy scooter line. Frederic Chaillou oversaw the PowerBike line. Adam Dunn was in charge of the Aquatics Division. Starr was looking to each of these individuals to identify and fill market niches with extensions of existing products or development of new products. Their charge was to build on the technology base that had been developed internally at ZAP and via acquisition.

THE ELECTRIC VEHICLE INDUSTRY

The overall electric vehicle industry was very broad in scope. Vehicles in production ranged in size and sophistication—from military tanks and large transport vehicles used in airports at the high end, to plastic toys for toddlers at the low end. Included within this wide range of cost and complexity were golf carts, personal transport vehicles for disabled persons, and electric automobiles.

In 2000, Peter Harrop, a consultant to the EV industry, estimated that industry sales would exceed $6 billion in 2000 and $26 billion by 2010. Harrop's 10-year estimates of unit sales volumes and value by individual market segments for the EV industry are provided in Exhibits 6 and 7. Harrop described the market forces driving growth in the EV industry:

> Contrary to popular opinion, pollution control is not often the primary reason why EVs are bought today or will be bought in future. Even those solely concerned with pollution would do well to make their vehicles more acceptable by featuring other, more compelling attributes. Blockbuster EVs usually capture the imagination, make something new possible,

exhibit 6 Forecasted Worldwide Sales Volume of EVs, by Market Segment, 2000–2010 (in thousands of units)

	2000	2001	2002	2003	2005	2010
Heavy industrial	230	240	250	255	260	350
Light industrial/commercial	64	100	120	150	250	400
Disabled	420	470	530	590	740	1,300
Two-wheel	500	700	1,000	1,300	3,000	6,000
Golf carts and caddies	256	265	280	300	320	330
Cars	60	100	150	200	500	1,250
Military	2	2	2	3	6	10
Mining	2	2	3	3	4	6
Mobile robots	10	30	300	400	1,000	2,800
Others	15	14	17	20	25	30
Total	1,559	1,923	2,652	3,221	6,105	12,476

Source: Peter Harrop, "Electric Vehicle Markets, Players, and Forecasts," www.footnoteanalysis.com.

exhibit 7 Forecasted Dollar Value of Worldwide EV Sales, by Market Segment, 2000–2010 (in billions of dollars)

	2000	2001	2002	2003	2005	2010
Heavy industrial	$2.80	$2.90	$3.07	$ 3.26	$ 3.35	$ 3.35
Light industrial/commercial	0.55	0.65	0.80	1.00	1.60	2.50
Disabled	0.42	0.47	0.53	0.59	0.74	1.30
Two-wheel	0.40	0.54	0.71	0.94	1.50	3.00
Golf carts and caddies	0.51	0.53	0.55	0.56	0.60	0.60
Cars	0.60	1.01	2.00	3.00	4.50	10.00
Military	0.18	0.21	0.24	0.30	0.60	1.00
Mobile robots (except toys)	0.08	0.10	0.90	1.12	2.50	2.80
Mining	0.44	0.46	0.50	0.67	1.00	1.50
Other (mainly marine)	0.23	0.28	0.25	0.40	0.50	0.60
Total	$6.21	$6.68	$9.55	$11.84	$16.89	$26.65
Annual growth rate	15%	11%	43%	24%	19%	11%

Source: Peter Harrop, "Electric Vehicle Markets, Players, and Forecasts," www.footnoteanalysis.com.

replace human effort, and/or save cost over the life of the product. Even where they save cost over life, it is not necessarily against a vehicle powered by an internal combustion engine (ICE). For example, an EV access platform replaces scaffolding and ladders and the attendant high labor costs. EVs usually create new markets with EV bicycles and three- or four-wheel, single-seat vehicles for the slightly infirm being recent examples. Home robots are likely to emerge in this category next.

Harrop also described the growth factors driving several EV market segments:

Heavy industrial vehicles
Heavy industrial vehicles, such as the archetypal forklift, are increasingly used to replace human effort in enclosed factories and warehouses, and laws increasingly call for them to

be used in orchards. Most growth in heavy industrial EV sales derives from the demands of the fast-moving consumer goods (FMCG) logistic chain and from the industrialization of third-world countries.

It is increasingly accepted that there is about 30 percent reduction in cost-over-life versus ICE anyway, so penetration will also rise steadily, encouraged by increased use of hybrids and later fuel cell EVs for the high-energy, long-range applications.

Two-wheel vehicles (bikes, scooters, etc.)

Projected growth is very substantial for this sector because there are many strong influences. This is the only sector where prices have halved in three years, and where fashion and draconian new pollution laws are brought to bear together.

This is, and will remain, most true in East Asia, where most of the world's conventional bicycles and scooters reside anyway. China's ban on further purchases of ICE two-wheelers in several major cities will continue to provide a large boost to output of two-wheel EVs, as will the promotion of the EV industry in China as a whole. However, most usually EVs replace human effort and not ICE vehicles.

Increasing success of two-wheel scooters and later motorcycles increases the average selling price of the two-wheel sector, but volume production and severe competition causing price erosion with bicycles is more than an offset.

The market drivers are likely to be performance and pollution issues. Motorcycle EVs and their derivatives are barely selling at all in 2001, but they will become popular within five years. Improved batteries and hybrids, rather than fuel cells, are key to the larger two-wheel EVs selling strongly in the next few years. There is a real possibility that tens of millions of two-wheel EVs will be sold in 2010.

Golf carts and caddies

Market growth for golf carts and motorized golf caddies has slowed because golf course construction in the United States has slowed and the rest of the world is not compensating. There is some growth from the expansion of leisure activities globally and from changes in local bylaws that increasingly permit golf carts on public roads in Europe and North America.

There is also some growth from the cost saving over the life of the product being accepted as an argument by most golf clubs worldwide. The current 60–70 percent penetration of electric vehicles may slowly rise to 90 percent or so, but most are leased to golf clubs, keeping prices down despite the small number of suppliers.

Vehicles for the disabled

The EV market segment for the disabled can be divided into wheelchairs for supervised severely disabled people, where increased concern and funding are creating market growth, and the larger market for mobility aids for unsupervised, less-disadvantaged people such as those who are pregnant, temporarily injured, or old rather than registered disabled. These same products may start to appear in locations such as airports for those with a lot to carry.

Such people have increasing disposable income and will purchase on impulse from the expanding variety of single-rider EVs being made available to them, such as ones for the home, for country paths, for the obese, or for folding into a car trunk. More countries are enjoying these products, and an increasing number are on free loan in large buildings, supermarkets, town centers, and leisure parks, having been bought by local government or large companies. A fairly strong growth rate is anticipated in this market segment.

Special EV applications

Emerging types of EVs include special models for mining, marine, police, military, research, and leisure beyond golf carts and two-wheelers. That covers everything from silent airships to disposable handheld $1,000 military surveillance aircraft, "pigs" in pipelines, and leisure boats for silent surface trolling or wildlife study. Pure EV leisure submarines, power assistance for scuba divers, and remote-controlled undersea search robots are also in this category.

Noise, air, and water pollution are all relevant in some of the new EV markets. This sector is rife with innovation and includes thousands of mobile robots sold for the first time in Japan in 1999 and in the West in 2000. These robots variously perform multiple tasks such as vacuum cleaning, fetching and carrying, and monitoring the elderly. They are not toys, however, in the sense of small remote-controlled or preprogrammed boats, cars, dogs, and cats. Mobile robots save human effort and make new things possible. These products have little or nothing to do with reduction in pollution.

Most of the serious new products make possible something new, creating markets from thin air. To look at the preparation of yet other new EV products in universities and elsewhere, explosive growth will occur. Initially this growth will occur through the adoption of military EVs, home robots, and marine EVs.

A remarkable variety of new concepts is being proved every year, giving great optimism about the future. Robots searching for earthquake survivors or doing the gardening will come, as will seagoing hybrid electric ships and much more. Trials are being carried out today. This is not science fiction.

Like Harrop, some industry observers predicted that the short-range EV industry was poised to experience record global growth in the foreseeable future. The industry was offering various alternatives for urban commuters and a direct means for lessening pollution. Between bicycles and automobiles lay a broad range of short-range vehicles that fell into the category of individual transportation vehicles. Unlike the maturing bicycle market, which had achieved a high level of market penetration, with over 1.4 billion bicycles in service worldwide by 2000, the individual electric transportation market was considered to have greater opportunity for growth.

The unexpected boom in popularity of nonpowered scooters in recent years provided an indication of the strength of demand for alternatives in this market and the potential for growth. Although kick scooters had been introduced over 50 years ago, their resurgence in 2000 suggested that there was unmet demand for alternatives to the bicycle and other recreational short-range modes of transportation such as inline skates and skateboards. With almost no demand for scooters in 1999, sales of nonpowered scooters were estimated at between 2 and 5 million units in 2000 for models priced in the range of $50 to $120—see Exhibit 8. The preliminary expectations for the nonpowered kick scooter market, based on sluggish sales since the 2000 Christmas buying season, were that sales for 2001 would be significantly lower than for the previous year. It was not yet clear whether the forecast decline in sales was due to rapid market saturation or an indication that the nonpowered scooter was a short-lived fad.

The largest segment of the individual transportation industry belonged to the bicycle industry, which had experienced a resurgence of its own since the introduction of the mountain bike in 1981. Year 2000 sales volumes in the U.S. bicycle market reached levels in excess of 16 million units, with revenues of over $5 billion. The worldwide bicycle market exceeded 60 million units in 2000—see Exhibits 9 and 10. In the 1990s, bicycle manufacturing in the United States was, for the most part, left to manufacturers of high-end specialty bikes. By the end of the decade, most bicycles targeted for the mass market in the United States were made in Taiwan. Exhibit 10 shows the reduction in U.S. domestic production of bicycles and the associated increase in bicycle imports for the years 1991 to 1998. In 1998, U.S. domestic production of bicycles had fallen to 2.3 million units from its 1993 peak of 9.9 million units. The corresponding retail sales values for each year are also provided in Exhibit 10. Bicycles were sold as a means of transportation and for recreational purposes. Only about 5 percent of bicycles sold in the United States were used by commuters, the primary market for alternatives such as electric vehicles. A breakdown of U.S. retail sales in 1999 and 2000

exhibit 8   Estimated Unit Shipments and Dollar Sales Volume of
Nonpowered Scooters, 1999–2001

Year	Units Shipped	Industry Sales Volume
1999	—	$5–$10 million
2000	2–5 million	$100–$600 million
2001	1–2.5 million	$50–$300 million

Source: Rita Haberman, "Wheels of Fortune or Passing Fad?"
www.redchip.com, August 25, 2000.

exhibit 9   Bicycles Sold in the U.S. Market, by Wheel Size, 1973–2000

Year	Wheel Sizes 20 Inches and Up (millions)	All Wheel Sizes (millions)
2000	11.9*	18.1*
1999	11.6*	17.5*
1998	11.1*	15.8*
1997	11.0*	15.2*
1996	10.9	15.4
1995	12.0	16.1
1994	12.5	16.7
1993	13.0	16.8
1992	11.6	15.3
1991	11.6	
1990	10.8	
1989	10.7	
1988	9.9	
1987	12.6	
1986	12.3	
1985	11.4	
1984	10.1	
1983	9.0	
1982	6.8	
1981	8.9	
1973	15.2 (record high)	

Source: Bicycle Manufacturers Association. Asterisks indicate projections
from the Bicycle Council based on a compilation from numerous sources.
Available at www.nbda.com/statpak.htm. (Note: The Bicycle Manufacturers
Association no longer exists.)

by market segment for nonpowered bicycles is shown in Exhibit 11, along with the average selling price for each segment.

Electric power-assist add-ons to enable conversion of almost any nonpowered bicycle were developed and introduced by a number of manufacturers and were targeted for the 1.4 billion nonpowered bikes that had already been sold. These add-ons ranged in price and complexity of installation.

exhibit 10   Selected Statistics for U.S. Bike Market, 1991–1998

Year	Total Unit Sales (millions)	Imports (millions of units)	Domestic (millions of units)	Market Value (in billions)
1990	—	—	—	$3.6
1991	15.1	6.5	8.6	4.0
1992	15.4	6.3	9.0	4.5
1993	17.0	7.1	9.9	4.3
1994	16.7	7.0	9.7	5.0
1995	16.0	7.2	8.8	5.2
1996	15.5	7.5	8.0	5.2
1997	15.8	9.8	6.0	5.4
1998	16.1	13.9	2.3	5.6

Source: Bicycle Retailer and Industry News website (www.nbda.com/statpak.htm).

exhibit 11   Average Prices and Unit Sales Percentages of Top 13 Brands of Bicycles Sold in the United States, by Type of Bicycle, 1999–2000

Bicycle Type	2000	1999	Average Retail Price
Mountain	43.10%	46.40%	$ 449
Youth	25.10	27.50	206
Comfort	13.50	8.70	338
Hybrid	11.50	11.80	368
Road	3.85	2.60	1,109
Cruiser	2.60	2.60	297
Tandem	0.13	0.12	1,069

Source: National Bicycle Dealers Association, Retail Data Capture Program (www.nbda.com/stat-pak.htm).

Sales of EVs were expected to grow not just because of their appeal to recreational riders but also because they cut across many other market segments. Aging baby boomers were finding it increasingly difficult to get outdoors and exercise, and the lack of short-range vehicle alternatives put their independent lifestyles in jeopardy. Seniors were turning to electrically powered vehicles as a way to extend their present habits and preferences. Electric bicycles were thoroughly practical, both for personal transit and transporting moderate loads. Improved battery technology, worsening traffic congestion, and new community infrastructure (bike lanes, bike racks, secure parking, etc.) were also thought to be major attractions to prospective consumers of electric bikes.

Police and law enforcement agencies were also discovering the benefits of EVs. Officers on local patrols could respond more quickly than their bicycle-pedaling colleagues and were not as susceptible to the traffic snarls experienced by patrol cars. These officers also required less training to handle an electrically powered bike or scooter than those trained to ride a motorcycle or horse. In Florida, electrically powered bike sales began to experience significant growth due to law enforcement agencies' purchases of those vehicles for use in resort areas.

Short-range EVs were also becoming popular in a range of industrial applications, on golf courses, in parks, at airports, and in other environments in which the traditional automobile proved inconvenient. Commuters, frustrated with traffic congestion and parking limitations, also found EVs to be a practical transportation choice.

COMPETITIVE FORCES IN THE EV MARKETPLACE

By 2000, competition in manufacturing, developing, and marketing EVs had increased in expectation of sustained industry growth rates. Major manufacturers mainly sold products to Japan and Europe. Smaller manufacturers sold products in U.S., European, and Asian markets. Prices for e-bikes typically fell within the range of $500 to $1,000 for a typical bicycle with an electric power-assist, add-on package. High-end electric bikes with integrated drive trains, such as those offered by EV Global, ranged from $1,000 for the base model to $2,000 for the high-end model. A list of the top 23 electric bike manufacturers is provided in Exhibit 12. Most EV manufacturers had their roots entirely in the electric bicycle industry. As shown in Exhibit 12, Taiwanese manufacturers dominated offshore production of EVs.

Many short-range EVs were marketed as alternatives to existing gasoline-powered vehicles. Stand-up scooters with small gas-powered engines, although relative newcomers to the marketplace, offered consumers the ability to refuel in a matter of minutes as opposed to the time it took to recharge a battery. A relatively noisy two-stroke engine, however, accompanied this convenience.

The potential for two-wheeled EVs induced large established automakers and manufacturers of nonpowered bicycles to introduce models under new brand names. Th!nk Mobility was an enterprise of Ford Motor Company that designed and marketed electric bicycles. Mercedes-Benz introduced its own version of the electric bicycle. Trek, Schwinn, and Murray, three of the largest nonpowered bicycle sellers in the United States, also introduced electrically powered bicycles, as did a number of large foreign bicycle companies, such as Giant, a China-based manufacturer.

Estimated unit sales volumes and dollar sales volumes of powered bicycles for the four largest geographic markets are provided in Exhibits 13 and 14. Data for the adoption rate of electric bicycles worldwide since 1993 are shown in Exhibit 15, along with projected sales volumes to 2003. Several key players in the electric-powered scooter industry are listed in Exhibit 16. Estimated sales volumes for electric scooters in 2000 and projected sales volumes for 2001 in the United States, the primary market for these vehicles, are provided in Exhibit 17.

Differentiation in the electric scooter market began to emerge as manufacturers raced to identify new niche markets. Some manufacturers focused on stand-up scooters (rider stands while driving); others produced scooters with attachable seats, scooters with built-in seats, and moped-like scooters. Higher-performance (i.e., faster than 15 mph) stand-up scooters were also under development, ahead of legislation that would permit their usage on public roadways. Top speed and expected mileage between charges were considered performance benchmarks for these high-end models.

Advances in battery technology were also driving the rise in interest and investment in the short-range EV market. Batteries were now much safer, more compact, and more affordable than ever before and could be charged more quickly and easily. Significant short-term innovations in battery technology were expected to arrive in the marketplace with increasing global utilization of electric-powered vehicles. Future advances in battery technology were also expected to continue to invigorate the EV

exhibit 12   Estimated Sales of Major Electric Bicycle Manufacturers, 2000

Brand or Manufacturer	Place of Final Assembly	Estimated Quantity Sold*
EV Rider	Taiwan	62,000
Currie Technologies	Taiwan/Thailand	39,000
ZAP	USA/Taiwan	33,000
Giant Bicycle Company	Taiwan	20,000
EV Global	Taiwan	17,000
Master Shine	China	15,000
ETC	Taiwan	10,000
JD Components	Taiwan	6,000
Sunpex	Taiwan	3,500
Merida	Taiwan	3,000
Bikit	China	2,500
HCF	Taiwan	2,500
Schwinn	Taiwan	800
Badsey	USA	500
Trek	USA	500
Heinzmann	Germany	400
SRAM	Germany	300
Th!nk Mobility	Taiwan	250
Denali	USA	200
Diamond Firefly	China	200
Mercedes	Germany	165
Moterrad	Germany	100
Electricbike factory	USA	100

Note: Sales volumes include totals of electric bikes and electric scooters where applicable.
Source: Casewriter communication with Ed Benjamin.

exhibit 13   Estimated Unit Sales Volumes of Electric Bicycles in Four Largest Markets, 1998–2000

	Japan	China	Europe	United States	Total
1998	270,000	40,000	35,000	25,000	370,000
1999	200,000	200,000	40,000	25,000	465,000
2000	200,000	250,000	55,000	30,000	535,000

Source: Casewriter communication with Ed Benjamin.

exhibit 14   Estimated Dollar Sales of Electric Bicycles in Four Largest Markets, 1998–2000 (in millions)

	Japan	China	Europe	United States	Total
1998	$175.5	$12.0	$26.3	$17.5	$231.3
1999	130.0	60.0	30.0	17.5	237.5
2000	130.0	75.0	41.3	21.0	267.3

Source: Casewriter communication with Ed Benjamin.

exhibit 15   Estimated Worldwide Unit Sales of Electric Bicycles and Electric Scooters, 1993–2003

	Estimated Actual Sales	
Year	Annual	Cumulative
1993	36,000	36,000
1994	60,000	96,000
1995	116,000	212,000
1996	133,000	345,000
1997	285,000	630,000
1998	400,000	1,030,000
1999	470,000	1,500,000
	Projected Unit Sales	
	Annual	Cumulative
2000	800,000	2,300,000
2001	1,000,000	3,300,000
2002	1,200,000	4,500,000
2003	1,500,000	6,000,000

Source: Casewriter communication with Ed Benjamin.

exhibit 16   Top Electric Scooter Manufacturers in the U.S. Market, 2001

Electric Scooter Manufacturer	Products	Estimated Price Range
ZAP	SkootrX, Zappy	$200–$700
Currie Technologies	Phat Phantom, Phat Flyer	$570–$700
Badsey	Hot Scoot, Cruiser, Racer	$1,000–$3,000
Go-Ped	Hoverboard	$800
BatteryBikes	CityBug, Citibug e^2	$500–$600
Nova Cruz Products	Xootr, eX3	$269–$1,100

Sources: Prices and product offerings compiled by the case researchers from a survey of numerous retail websites.

exhibit 17   Estimated U.S. Sales Volume for Electric Scooters in 2000, with Projections for 2001

Year	Sales Volume
2000 (estimated)	80,000
2001 (projected)	500,000

Source: Casewriter communication with Ed Benjamin.

industry, as creative individuals discovered new and exciting ways to attach the latest batteries to new and existing modes of transportation.

Rapidly rising gasoline prices and an electric power crisis in California during 2000 and early 2001 contributed to the level of uncertainty in the external environment for EVs. Global environmental pressures, higher oil prices, population pressures, and urban traffic congestion were expected to contribute to rising demand for short-range transportation solutions. Increasing energy costs translated into higher operating costs and a potential backlash from consumers. Electricity had historically been an inexpensive source of power with a typical charge on an electric bicycle costing a few cents. Higher electric energy costs had the potential of altering this perception in the minds of consumers.

The legal environment for short-range EVs was also changing. The failure of the automobile industry to provide nonpolluting alternatives to the internal combustion engine resulted in a series of extensions for automobile manufacturers to meet a mandate initiated by the State of California, the largest U.S. market for automobiles and the market with the highest antipollution standards. Initiated by the California Air Resources Board in the early 1990s, the mandate required that 4 percent of all vehicles sold in the state by 2003 fall into the category of zero emission vehicles. Other states, including New York, Vermont, and Massachusetts, had adopted similar legislation. In California and elsewhere, extensions had been necessary to provide automobile manufacturers with more time to develop automobiles that could compete in price and reliability against vehicles based on internal combustion engines. Industry analysts suggested that gas/electric hybrids such as the Toyota Prius and the Honda Insight were an interim alternative until further improvements in battery technology made electric automobiles more practical to produce. Missed deadlines nevertheless stirred concern among hard-core environmentalists, who increased their pressure on lawmakers to pass legislation expediting development of nonpolluting alternatives.

As of early 2001, light EVs in most states and countries did not generally require an operating license, insurance, or registration. New legislation was on the docket in many states to provide reclassification of EVs to broaden their acceptance in the marketplace and to remove potential legal barriers to widespread acceptance. Pressure on lawmakers in California, for example, resulted in the adoption of legislation in 2000 legalizing roadway usage of electric scooters that traveled at top speeds of 15 mph. Prior to January 1, 2000, these vehicles had not been permitted on California roads.

A 2000 study by the National Renewable Energy Laboratory noted that 45 million automobiles in the United States drove less than 20 miles per day, within the range of many EVs then on the market. Investments in new short-range transportation infrastructure at federal, state, and local levels began emerging as a means to provide equal access for alternatives to the automobile and to provide open space for recreational purposes. Programs such as Rails-to-Trails were initiated to convert unused railway rights-of-way to bicycle trails. As of September 2000, over 11,000 miles of old railways in the United States had been converted for bicycle usage. Similar projects to improve access and safety for short-range transportation vehicles included bike lanes and limited access areas for gas-powered vehicles in urban centers. Continued investment in these programs was expected to play a major role in the market acceptance for EVs.

ZAP'S CHALLENGES

At the same time that ZAP was transferring its manufacturing overseas, it was attempting to reposition itself as "an overall provider of premier EV products with a primary focus on aggressive sales activity." In the United States, ZAP's primary market for electric bicycle and electric scooter sales, a combined estimated total of 120,000 units had been sold in 2000, with scooter sales leading bicycle sales by a ratio of approximately 7:1. This breakdown implied that electric scooter sales had reached approximately 105,000 units and electric bicycle sales approximately 15,000 units for the year. In the future, more sizable markets for EV products were expected to emerge abroad.

In early 2001, widespread advertising by competitors for a new electric scooter priced at under $200 had resulted in increased sales in mass-market channels. These channels included Target, Toys "R" Us, and other "big box" chain stores. Competitors had created a new price point that ZAP was then forced to meet by developing a low-end version of the Zappy, called the Skootr-X.

In light of these trends, Starr called a meeting of his product launch team in May 2001 to develop a long-range product strategy. Starr led the product-launch team, which included Hutchins, Cronk, Rocklewitz, Schotze, and Chaillou. The team was charged with creating a forecast of the expected demand for scooters and electric bicycles, ZAP's two best-selling product lines. Starr argued that sales forecasts of the Zappy electric scooter and ZAP PowerBike had to be made within the context of similar recreational products, such as the bicycle. Other team members felt strongly that sales forecasts could be obtained only after careful study of market demographics and environmental variables to arrive at a projected adoption rate that could be used to project future sales.

The team also debated ZAP's generic strategy to stake out a position in an industry that was still in its infancy. Starr made the case for the benefits of a "market penetration strategy," meaning higher volume sales at lower prices. Lower pricing had the potential of increasing demand and limiting future opportunity for lower-priced competitors that were already driving down the average selling price for electrically powered scooters and bicycles. Other team members argued for a "skimming strategy," that is, restricting demand by maintaining a high price. Higher pricing might provide for enhanced profit margins and allow ZAP's products, which had become benchmarks of quality and performance, to maintain a position of superiority in the industry. Regardless of which approach the ZAP team ultimately chose, the probable reactions of competitors were expected to have a major impact on the success or failure of ZAP's long-range strategy.

Bibliography

Analyst Report on Zapworld.com. Donner Corporation International website (www.donner.corp.com), June 12 and September 5, 2000.

Benjamin, Ed. *Electric Bicycle Market Information Report.*

———. *Is There an Electric Bike in Your Future?* Prepared for Earth Options Institute.

———. Personal communication with casewriters.

Bicycle Retailer and Industry News website (www.bicycleretailer.com/public_pages/pubstats.html).

"Electric Bikes: Practical Transportation for Errands and Short Commutes." ZAP Electric Bikes and Scooters website (www.electric-bikes.com).

Haberman, Rita. "Wheels of Fortune or Passing Fad?" www.redchip.com, August 25, 2000.

Harrop, Peter. "Electric Vehicle Markets, Players, and Forecasts." www.footnoteanalysis.com.

———. Personal communication with casewriters.

International Bicycle Fund website (www.ibike.org/statistics.htm).

"2000 NBDA Statpak." National Bike Dealers Association website (www.nbda.com/statpak.htm).

Union Atlantic Corporation, LC. *Research Report on Zapworld.com.* February 16, 2001.

"ZAP CEO Gary Starr Predicts $5 Billion Industry for Light Electric Transportation by 2005." Zapworld.com press release (www.zapworld.com), October 18, 2000.

"ZAP Previews Italian Electric Scooter to Motorcycle Industry at Indianapolis Dealer Expo." Zapworld.com press release (www.zapworld.com), February 16, 2001.

Zapworld.com website (www.zapworld.com).

Zapworld.com. 10-KSB filings, 1996–2000.

case 6 Dakota Growers Pasta

Michael Boland
Kansas State University

Christian Freberg
Kansas State University

David Barton
Kansas State University

Jeff Katz
Kansas State University

Borden Foods announced that it would close 5 of its 10 plants in North America, including the two we are seeking to acquire in Minneapolis, Minnesota. We believe that there's a big opportunity with Borden shrinking its store brand business. If consumption continues to increase, it is going to give us a chance to grow our business. We've been very successful in aligning ourselves with major supermarkets and food-service companies that have a very aggressive sales strategy. Of course, as they're growing, we grow because when we have a supply agreement with them, we can take advantage of their increased sales. Actually, this year (1998), we are anticipating as much as a 10 percent growth just within our core customer base.

Tim Dodd was general manager of Dakota Growers Pasta (DGP), an integrated pasta company headquartered in Carrington, North Dakota. Tim and the board of directors reviewed a proposal in July 1998 to purchase two pasta plants formerly owned by Borden that would add another 200 million pounds of pasta capacity to DGP's existing 240 million pounds. Tim was putting together his remarks on the subject for the board. He needed to present both points of view concerning the acquisition decision.

Tim Dodd was well known in the durum milling and pasta industry. He had been involved in virtually every integrated durum milling and pasta operation during his career. In addition, durum wheat producers found him very trustworthy, which was valuable during the formation of DGP. Both he and Gary Mackintosh, DGP's national sales manager who had helped get DGP started, felt strongly that locating DGP in Carrington, North Dakota, made sense economically, and its rural location would help to attract the right kind of labor needed to run an integrated durum milling and pasta plant. Tim appeared to be a risk taker to many who had followed his career, but those who knew him well discovered that he had established strong and credible relationships with his customers and other key players in this industry. His ability to access information through these relationships had played a key role in his success.

I started with International Multifoods in 1977 after graduating with a degree in grain science from Kansas State University and was responsible for the first integrated durum milling and pasta production plant in North America, the Noodles by Leonardo start-up at Cando, North Dakota. Then, I supervised the construction of a "state-of-the-art" flour mill in Texas before coming over to American Italian Pasta Company in 1988, where I ran the manufacturing operations at Excelsior Springs. Finally, my family and I went back to North Dakota and started DPG.

PASTA CONSUMPTION AND MARKETS

Pasta consumption in the United States was relatively stable between 1967 and 1984 at approximately six to seven pounds of durum wheat–based food products (pasta) per capita.[1] Since then, U.S. pasta consumption had risen about one pound per year, reaching a maximum of 14 pounds per capita in 1994, and then decreasing slightly (see Exhibit 1).

The U.S. Department of Agriculture noted that there were four primary reasons for the per capita increase in demand for pasta: changing lifestyles, increased availability of pasta sauces, increased attention to healthy eating, and increased numbers of Italian restaurants.[2] In addition, the number of American households with two working parents

exhibit 1   Consumption of Semolina and Durum Flour Products, 1965 to 1998[*]

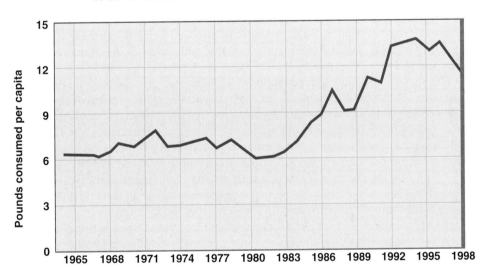

*Consumption is equal to wholesale disappearance of pasta product.

Source: Putnam and Allshouse.

---

[1]Judith Jones Putnam and Jane E. Allshouse, *Food Consumption, Prices, and Expenditures,* 1970–97, Food and Rural Economics Division, Economic Research Service, U.S. Department of Agriculture. Statistical Bulletin No. 965, 1999. Available online at www.ers.usda.gov/epubs/pdf/sb965/.

[2]James N. Barnes and Dennis A. Shields, "The Growth in U.S. Wheat Food Demand," in *USDA Wheat Yearbook,* Market and Trade Economics Division, Economic Research Service, U.S. Department of Agriculture, WHS-1998. Available online at usda.mannlib.cornell.edu/reports/erssor/field/whs_bby/wheat_yearbook_03.30.98.

exhibit 2   Favorite Shapes of Pasta Purchased by U.S. Consumers in 1998

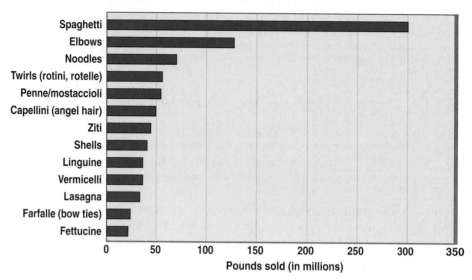

Source: National Pasta Association.

increased, leading to changes in where and how meals were prepared and eaten. Meals that were healthful, easy, and relatively quick to prepare had become commonplace, and pasta fit that description. The abundance of prepared sauces had served as a "complementary catalyst" and had improved the quality and variety of the choices available for consumption.

The increase of Italian-style restaurants fueled the growth in the food-service sector of the pasta industry. Italian food had become a mainstream food, evident by the growth of the number of Italian restaurants. Reasons for this trend were that consumers were eating outside of the home more often; they were eating more healthful foods; and per capita incomes were increasing. Americans spent 46 percent of their food expenditures on away-from-home meals in 1998, up from 34 percent in 1970 and 39 percent in 1980.

A study by the National Pasta Association found that consumers typically had three to five packages of dry pasta products on their shelves at any one time. Spaghetti was by far the most favorite pasta dish (40 percent) cited by consumers, followed by lasagna (12 percent), and macaroni and cheese (6 percent).[3] Spaghetti was the most widely sold pasta shape, followed by elbow macaroni, noodles, and other different shapes of pasta (see Exhibit 2).

The plateau and slight decline in consumption were attributable to several things. First, it was suspected that the USDA was having measurement problems. The use of older conversion factors for new processes for developing pasta may have overestimated pasta consumption in the mid-1990s. Another reason was that although pasta consumption had increased because it was regarded as a "healthful" food that could be prepared quickly and easily, the food industry had developed other such foods, and consumers might have substituted away from pasta. Finally, the denominator in the consumption figure was population. Pasta was consumed primarily by single households or

---

[3]National Pasta Association, *American Pasta Report,* 2000. Available online at www.ilovepasta.org/industrystatistics.html.

exhibit 3 Dry Pasta Market Segments in 1999

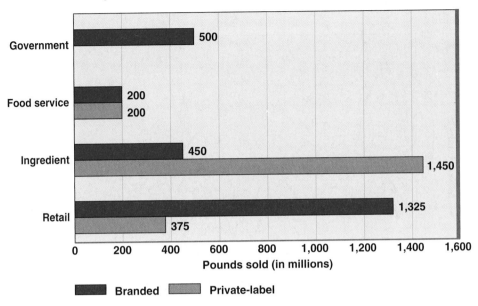

Pounds sold (in millions)

Branded   Private-label

families. As the U.S. population increased and aged, the proportion of those eating pasta may have declined as a proportion of the total population.

Pasta Market Segments

Five billion pounds of pasta (4.5 billion in dry pasta and 0.5 billion in frozen and fresh pasta) were consumed in 1998 compared with about 4 billion pounds in 1992. The 1998 total value was $2.6 billion. There were four principal dry pasta market segments: ingredient (43 percent), private- and brand-label retail (37 percent of the market), food service (10 percent), and government bids (10 percent).

Within each segment, there were both private-label and brand-label products (see Exhibit 3). Private-label products were products manufactured by a firm that had another firm's label on them. For example, a company such as Mueller's that had brand assets but no manufacturing assets would contract its brand production with a company that had manufacturing assets such as American Italian Pasta Company. Within the retail market segment, private-label pasta had been growing at a faster rate than brand-label pasta: Private-label sales had increased from 19 percent to almost 24 percent of total pasta sales during the 1994 to 1998 time period. In the ingredient market segment, 75 percent was manufactured by firms for their own internal needs, with the remainder being sold to food producers with no pasta-making capacity. About half the food-service market segment was private-label, and the government market segment was considered brand-label.

Pasta manufacture had undergone change as large pasta firms, which had produced both private labels and brand labels, had exited private-label production to focus strictly on their core brands. Some retailers preferred private labels because of higher margins and greater control of merchandising. Although there was no direct evidence, retailers and pasta manufacturers believed that consumers preferred "Italian" brand names and regarded imported Italian pasta as higher quality. Thus, some firms were beginning to develop domestic pasta with an Italian brand name. The perceived quality of a brand was related to its image as well as product characteristics such as shorter

exhibit 4   U.S. Durum Wheat Production, Consumption, and Exports, 1980 to 1998

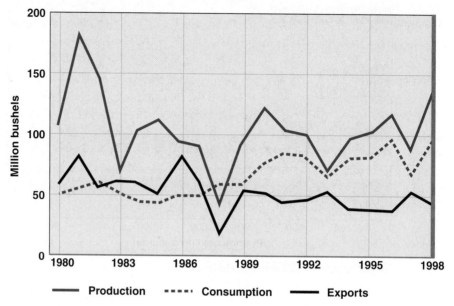

Source: USDA Wheat Outlook Situation and Yearbook.

cooking time, ease of cleaning (e.g., less stickiness inside a pan), and innovative products that were easy to prepare and convenient to use by consumers. Using lower-cost technology, new entrants in the pasta industry had launched innovative pasta products, sometimes manufacturing them for sale under the name brands of rival firms. Thus, private-label producers were gaining sales and market share because their product offerings had attractive attributes and were priced competitively.

The Durum Milling and Pasta Industries

The pasta production chain was divided into three different stages: durum wheat, semolina flour, and pasta product. Production had increased as consumption increased; exports remained fairly constant over time (see Exhibit 4). Approximately 67 million bushels of durum wheat were milled into more than 3 billion pounds of semolina (a granular product used to make pasta) and durum wheat flour in 1998 (see Exhibit 5).[4] The majority of value was added through further processing. Exports and shrinkage accounted for the difference.

Durum Wheat Production

Durum wheat was particularly well-suited for making pasta due to its high protein percentage, which is higher than any other type of wheat. Poor-quality durum resulted in pasta noodles that broke easily and caused problems in packaging. North Dakota,

---

[4]*USDA Wheat Outlook Situation and Yearbook.* Market and Trade Economics Division, Economic Research Service, U.S. Department of Agriculture, WHS-2000. Available online at usda.mannlib.cornell.edu/reports/erssor/field/whs_bby/whs2000.pdf.

exhibit 5   The Pasta Value Chain

Durum product	Semolina product	Pasta production	Distribution	Retail sales
Durum Product	**Semolina Product**	**Pasta Production**	**Distribution**	**Retail Sales**
Producers supply durum wheat. The 1997 average price was $4.65 per bushel.	Durum wheat was milled into semolina flour. The average price of semolina was $12.60 per 100 pounds in 1997.	Semolina flour was manufactured into pasta for retail, food service, or ingredient use. The Bureau of Census reported that the value of durum wheat purchased by pasta plants was $1,045,198,000 and *Milling and Baking News* estimated that 64,663,000 bushels of durum wheat were milled in 1997.	The Bureau of Census reported that the value of pasta shipments was $1,766,358 in 1997.	Pasta was sold at retail for about $1.25 per pound.

eastern Montana, northwest Minnesota, southern Alberta, and southern Saskatchewan were the primary production regions due to cool nights and warm but not hot summers, which were ideal for durum wheat. Although durum wheat was also grown in Arizona and California, the northern Great Plains states were expected to remain production leaders in the future.

Durum Milling Leads to Semolina Flour and Pasta Manufacturing

Producers delivered their durum wheat to a durum milling plant. There it was sampled, weighed, precleaned, and loaded into grain silos. Within these silos, the wheat was preblended and fed into the mill, where it was cleaned and dampened to the appropriate moisture level needed for milling. The wheat was then ground, sifted, and purified into high-quality semolina flour. In addition to semolina, other products were created, including granulars, first clear (higher grade) flour, second clear (lower grade) flour, semolina/durum flour blends, and mill feed. Mill feed and second clear flour were sold as livestock feed to neighboring livestock producers. A 60-pound bushel of wheat was milled into approximately 36 pounds of semolina product, 6 pounds of flour, and 18 pounds of mill feed product.

The semolina was blended with first clear flour and used to make pasta, which was basically a mixing, extrusion, and drying process. Pasta "dough" was extruded through dies that created individual shapes. The entire process was computerized for maximum efficiency and control.

Durum Milling Industry

There were 13 major companies that milled durum wheat in the United States. There had been significant change over the 1991 to 1998 time period. Well-known firms had

exhibit 6   Original Durum Milling Capacity in 1991 and 1998, by Firm

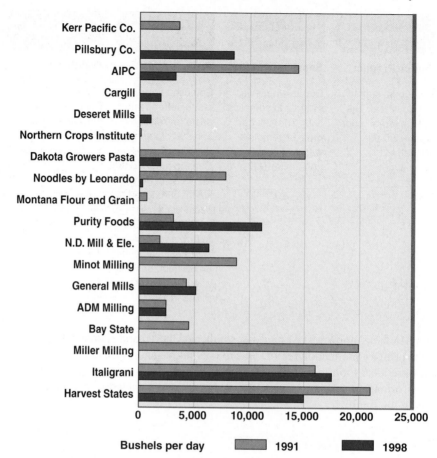

Source: Industry annual report, *Milling and Baking News.*

exited durum milling (for example, Pillsbury, Cargill) and new firms had entered (for example, American Italian Pasta Company, Dakota Growers Pasta), with shifting capacity shares as shown in Exhibit 6. By the late 1990s, Italigrani USA, Harvest States Cooperatives, and Miller Milling Company operated about 60 percent of total U.S. durum milling capacity. Durum milling plants had traditionally been located near durum wheat production or in regions with favorable rail transportation access to North Dakota. Milling capacity increases had kept pace with consumption in the early 1990s but outgrew consumption by 1995. Then capacity began to decline as older and higher-cost plants began to be shut down (see Exhibit 7). By the late 1990s, capacity was concentrated in Minnesota, North Dakota, and midwestern states such as Missouri that were on a direct line to eastern North Dakota (see Exhibit 8).[5]

[5]"Industry News Report," *Milling and Baking News,* various issues, 1990 to 2000. Available online at www.sosland.com.

exhibit 7 Durum Milling Industry Capacity and Number of Mills, 1990–1998

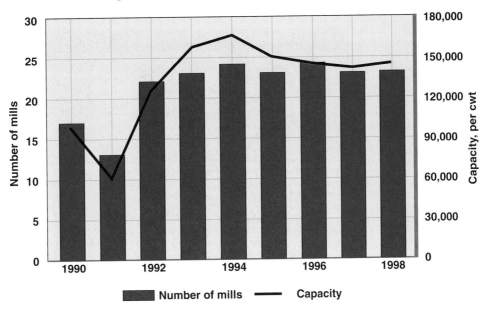

Source: Industry annual report, *Milling and Baking News.*

exhibit 8 Durum Milling Capacity by U.S. Geographic Region,
1990–1998

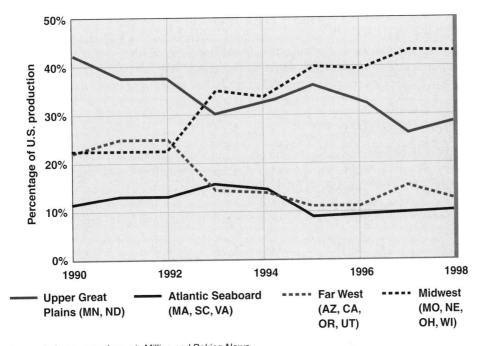

Source: Industry annual report, *Milling and Baking News.*

exhibit 9   Annual Pasta Production Capacity in
the United States, 1998*

Firm	Capacity, Million Pounds
American Italian Pasta Company	800
Hershey Pasta Group	688
Borden Food Holdings	350
Dakota Growers Pasta	270
Primo Piatto	200
Barilla	200

*Assuming all announced plant expansions occurred.

Dry Pasta Industry

There were 141 pasta plants that manufactured dry pasta in the United States, but 67 accounted for the majority of sales in 1998.[6] Vertically integrated firms such as American Italian Pasta Company (AIPC), which was a new entrant with little market share in 1991, had the largest capacity in 1998 (see Exhibit 9). Hershey Foods, AIPC, Borden Food Holdings Company, DGP, Philadelphia Macaroni Company, A. Zerega Sons, Inc., and Gooch Foods (owned by Archer Daniels Midland) were the main U.S. pasta manufacturers, with a combined market share of about 55 percent.

Another 25 percent of market share was owned by Kraft Foods, General Foods, Inc., American Home Foods Products, Con Agra, Inc., Pillsbury, Campbell Soup Company, and Stouffers Corporation; these companies produced pasta for their own brands of pasta products. An Italian pasta manufacturer, Barilla, had recently built a plant in Iowa.[7] Pasta imports had increased in the 1990s and then decreased when a trade ruling asserted that several Italian pasta companies were importing U.S. durum wheat and then exporting pasta to the United States at prices below their variable costs (i.e., dumping pasta). Imports represented 10 percent of sales in 1998 (see Exhibit 10).[8] Total domestic capacity was estimated at 3.8 billion pounds per year.

Price Volatility

Shifts in durum milling capacity and geographic location, coupled with imports, had increased durum wheat and semolina flour price volatility in the late 1990s (see Exhibit 11).[9] The Minneapolis Grain Exchange had established a durum futures contract in February 1998, but it was not widely used due to lack of liquidity. Durum wheat prices rose because of increased demand for pasta and lower production yields

---

[6]U.S. Department of Commerce, *Dry Pasta Manufacturing,* 1997 Economic Census Manufacturing Series, Economics and Statistics Administration, U.S. Census Bureau, EC97M-3118F, 1999. Available online at www.census.gov/prod/ec97/97m3118f.pdf.

[7]M. I. Sosland, "Barilla Sees U.S. as Major Step in Global Presence," *Milling and Baking News,* December 9, 1997. Available online at www.sosland.com/content/mbn/1997/120997.htm.

[8]Foreign Agricultural Trade of the United States, *U.S. Agricultural Trade Update,* various issues, 2000. Available online at www.ers.usda.gov/briefing/AgTrade/htm/Public.htm.

[9]"Ingredient Prices," *Milling and Baking News,* various issues, 1985 to 2000.

exhibit 10   Volume of Imported Pasta and Noodle Products,
1990 to 1998

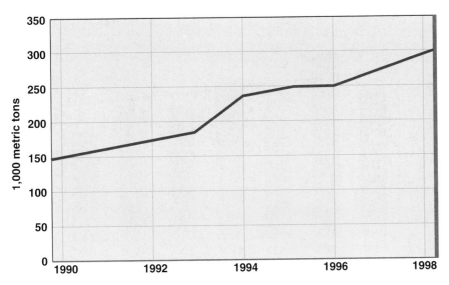

Source: Foreign Agricultural Trade of the United States.

exhibit 11   Minneapolis Semolina Flour and Durum Wheat Prices,
1980 to 1998

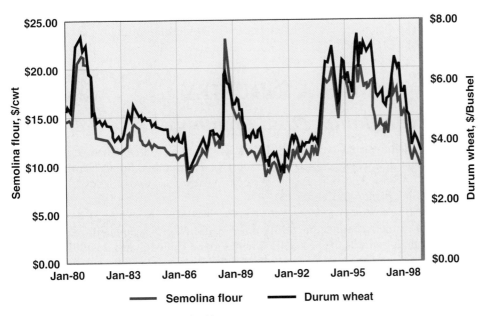

Source: Ingredient prices, *Milling and Baking News.*

in North Dakota due to disease problems (see Exhibit 12). In addition, the increase in milling capacity in the late 1990s had helped increase demand for durum wheat, which increased durum prices. As durum and semolina flour prices rose and pasta demand

exhibit 12   North Dakota Durum Wheat Yields, 1991 to 1998

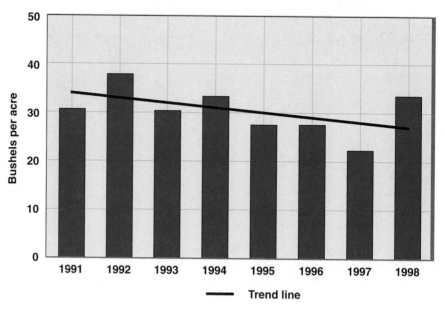

Source: USDA Wheat Situation Outlook and Yearbook.

began to plateau, pasta manufacturers found it more difficult to pass along higher input costs, and their margins began to decline, driving down profitability. With all the projected expansion, it was believed that by 1999, durum milling capacity would be greater than pasta demand.

COMPETITION IN THE PASTA INDUSTRY

American Italian Pasta Company

American Italian Pasta Company (AIPC) was formed in 1988 and had vertically integrated plants in Excelsior Springs, Missouri, and Columbia, South Carolina. A new pasta plant was located in Kenosha, Wisconsin, next to Harvest States Cooperatives durum milling plant (see Exhibit 13).

One AIPC customer (25 percent of sales) was Mueller's (owned by Bestfoods, which had exited pasta manufacturing in 1998). Mueller's accounted for almost 200 million pounds and was the best-selling brand in the United States. In 1995, AIPC began marketing an all-natural flavored pasta under the brand name Pasta LaBella, which was sold to retailers and through SYSCO Corporation (27 percent of sales), the largest marketer and distributor of food-service products. Other customers included Wal-Mart's Sam's Club stores (20 percent of sales) and 15 of the 16 largest grocery retailers, all of whom had their own private-label pasta brands. AIPC's brands included American Italian, AIPC, and Pasta LaBella.

Its relationship with Wal-Mart enabled AIPC to sell its pasta on a cost-plus basis (production cost plus specified profit per pound). It had a strong reputation in category management of its brands and used Nielsen's supermarket data to help provide expertise to its customers regarding new products. It had also developed electronic data

exhibit 13   Selected Financial Data for American Italian Pasta Growers Company, 1993–1998 (in thousands)

	1993	1994	1995	1996	1997	1998
Net revenue	47,872	69,465	92,903	21,149	29,143	189,390
Net income	6,699	2,182	476	(3,490)	5,057	15,314
Dividends/share	.64	.21	.05	(.33)	.42	1.03
Total assets	66,337	93,629	135,424	141,688	158,175	259,381
Long-term debt	40,024	62,375	97,452	93,284	100,137	48,519
Members' equity	16,973	19,401	20,067	15,688	42,984	176,784

Source: AIPC 10-K reports.

exhibit 14   Selected Financial Data for Hershey's Pasta Division, 1994–1998 (in thousands)

	1994	1995	1996	1997	1998
Net revenue	$397,770	$419,090	$407,370	$386,218	$373,096
Net income*	17,126	18,437	18,693	25,157	25,914
Total assets	293,678	259,731	246,563	231,920	225,017
Equity Investment	234,450	194,155	183,698	162,777	166,944

*Net income did not include interest expense as a division of Hershey Foods Corporation, and Hershey's corporate long-term debt was not parcelled out to its product divisions. No 1993 data were available.

Source: Hershey 10-K reports.

interchange (EDI) systems with its customers to better forecast demand and inventory. There was considerable speculation that AIPC was contemplating building a plant In Italy and importing Italian pasta into the United States for its customers who wanted Italian pasta.

Hershey Pasta Group

Hershey's brands had approximately a 27 percent share of the branded segment of the retail pasta market, with three of the top six brands in the United States in 1998 (see Exhibit 14). Hershey Foods had entered the pasta industry in 1966 with the purchase of San Giorgio brand. Skinner Macaroni was acquired in 1979, American Beauty was acquired from Pillsbury in 1984, and Ronzoni was purchased from Kraft (General Foods) in 1990. Hershey Pasta Group's brands held the highest retail market share in 22 of the top 64 markets (12 of the top 20), second-highest market share in another 25 markets, and third-highest market share in an additional 18 markets. However, Hershey Pasta Group was not a core part of Hershey Foods' business, and in 1996 it had combined its pasta sales force with its general foods force and significantly reduced its marketing and promotional expenses.

Almost 70 percent of its semolina needs was purchased from Miller Milling Company, which had total capacity of 688 million pounds with locations in Winchester, Virginia; Lebanon, Pennsylvania; Omaha, Nebraska; Fresno, California; Louisville, Kentucky; and Kansas City, Missouri. Miller Milling Company had established mills alongside the Virginia and Lebanon pasta plants, enabling these two plants to be vertically integrated. However, approximately 30 percent of its total capacity was not being used at the current time.

Borden Food Holdings Corporation

Borden Food Holdings Corporation was a privately held chemical and food company. It had recently sold 6 of its 10 pasta plants but had signed short-term supply agreements with the buyers. Its major brands were Prince, Creamette, Catelli, Merlino's, and Anthony. It was the largest pasta sauce manufacturer in the United States. No financial information was released on its pasta foods.

Other Pasta Companies

There were several privately held companies (for example, Philadelphia Macaroni Company, A. Zerega Sons, Inc.) that did not publicly release information, and little was known about their markets. Durum millers and pasta plant competitors in North Dakota included Philadelphia Macaroni's Conte Luna plant in Grand Forks (specialty pasta) and their Minot Milling plant (durum milling) in Minot; Noodles by Leonardo in Cando and Devil's Lake (integrated durum milling and pasta); and Farmers Choice Pasta at Leeds (specialty pasta). A new entrant, Prairie Pasta Producers at Minot, was expected to be an integrated milling and pasta plant, and D&B Specialty Foods in Grand Forks, Minnesota, was building a specialty pasta plant.[10]

Competitive Rivalry

Firms competed in this industry through five principal methods: (1) degree of capacity utilization (achieve lowest average cost production); (2) product distribution capabilities; (3) service capability; (4) ability to provide consistent quality to customer specifications; and (5) access to durum wheat.

AIPC and DGP had almost 100 percent capacity utilization due to their supply management agreements with their customers. Access to favorable rail transportation had helped new entrants (AIPC, DGP) achieve low distribution costs. The use of EDI had also helped AIPC, DGP, and Hershey's Pasta Group to provide marketing services to their customers. In addition, high durum wheat prices in recent years resulted in semolina flour accounting for 30 to 40 percent of total pasta cost of goods sold. Dakota Growers Pasta and AIPC had been able to achieve success through access to high-quality durum wheat despite low yields and poor quality; this allowed them to provide consistent quality at low average cost.

DAKOTA GROWERS PASTA

The 1,084 members of DGP were durum wheat producers who operated in the states of North Dakota, Minnesota, and Montana. DGP's mission was to help its members become more profitable:

> Dakota Growers Pasta was founded on the dream to provide farmers with the means to secure a future for themselves and their families.

---

[10]M. A. Boland, "Cooperative Entrants in the Durum Milling and Pasta Industries in North Dakota," Unpublished report, Department of Agricultural Economics, Kansas State University, Manhattan, Kansas, 2000.

To succeed in this endeavor, our owners and employees pledge to always apply the "Quality Assured" idea in everything we do.

We believe that the customer is our single most important asset and that we must constantly strive to improve and to do it better than the day before.

We take great pride and care in everything we do, because it is our past as well as our future.

Dakota Growers Pasta was organized as a cooperative.[11] Cooperatives were a unique organization form compared to C corporations, limited liability companies, partnerships, and proprietorships. Most of DGP's competitors were C corporations. Cooperatives were common in agriculture-related industries but much less common in other industries. Nonagricultural cooperatives included credit unions, mutual insurance companies, rural electric utilities, and telephone cooperatives. Essentially, cooperatives were business organizations whose members were also the users of the cooperative's business or services.

In DGP's case, durum wheat producers were the users. The users were the voting members who controlled the co-op, the owners who provided the equity capital, and the patrons who received the benefits of use, including (1) a market or buyer for their durum wheat and (2) a share of the profits based on use or patronage. Profits or net income was usually distributed as patronage refunds per bushel.

Many farmers had provided equity to organize and finance cooperatives, because in many cases, private investor equity or competitive markets for farm products were not available (commonly called market failure) during the early 1900s. Then, in the early 1990s, another wave of cooperative formation started in North Dakota and Minnesota and moved south into South Dakota, Nebraska, and Kansas. Producers invested over $2 billion in processing beyond grain handling, including corn wet milling, pasta, and soybean processing plants in North Dakota, South Dakota, Minnesota, Nebraska, and Kansas. Tim had recited the story of DGP's formation at countless meetings:

> The farmers had been talking about it for years and years. Farmers wanted to see more of a profit from the durum they grew. In 1991, a group of them decided to see if their ideas could be put into action. A feasibility study was quickly undertaken, and an interim board of directors was elected. Then, the real sales pitch began as that core group of farmers began selling stock to their peers. Producers paid $125 to join the cooperative as a member and paid $3.85 (par value) per share, which represents an obligation to deliver one bushel of durum wheat. The $3.85 just happens to be the historical per bushel average for North Dakota durum wheat.

Dakota Growers Pasta was organized in late 1991 as a closed membership cooperative. Producer-users or members were required to purchase one share of stock for each bushel of durum wheat they wanted to sell annually to DGP. The total number of shares sold matched the capacity of the mill. Shares in the first stock offering were priced at $3.85 each, and they conveyed a right and an obligation to deliver durum wheat as specified in the "Growers Agreement."

The DGP members' "Growers Agreement" obligated each member to deliver a set amount of durum wheat to the company from their own production, based on the number of shares they had purchased. If the member could not supply the wheat with the desired quality, DGP would purchase the wheat on behalf of the member and charge

[11]David Coltrain, David Barton, and Michael Boland. "Differences between New Generation Cooperatives and Traditional Cooperatives." Arthur Capper Cooperative Center, Department of Agricultural Economics, Cooperative Extension Service, Kansas State University. Available online at www.agecon.ksu.edu/accc/kcdc/PDF%20Files/differences.pdf.

them the current market price. The member was exposed to price risk, as they must purchase durum wheat to be delivered to the company on behalf of the member. A growers agreement gave Dakota Growers a competitive advantage because it allowed them to source high-quality durum wheat. The stock was an asset that could be traded or exchanged between members at a privately negotiated price. This meant the stock price could appreciate or depreciate in value from the initial issue price or subsequent exchange price. However, DGP always carried the stock on its books at its nominal issue or book price.

Plant Description

Tim was one of the first in the industry to recognize that vertical integration meant opportunity:

> The beauty of it is that we are integrated all the way through. We are a highly efficient pasta plant because we work directly with growers, keeping them informed about what we need and integrating them in the milling and manufacturing. They have a real stake in the end product.

Dakota Growers Pasta owned and operated a state-of-the-art durum wheat mill and pasta production facility in Carrington, North Dakota; the facility was completed in 1994. The cooperative had gone through many changes since its inception (see Exhibit 15). The company used its semolina in its own pasta production process. The vertically integrated facility consisted of a grain elevator; a mill; four pasta production lines, two of which manufactured short goods (such as macaroni) and two of which produced long goods (such as spaghetti); and a warehouse to store the finished goods.

The elevator had a storage capacity of 370,000 bushels (two weeks' storage); the mill had capacity to grind 3.2 million bushels each year; and the pasta production complex had the ability to manufacture 240 million pounds of pasta annually. The company's flexible packaging operation could pack the pasta into boxes or film that ranged in size from 7¼ ounces to 2,000 pounds. The facility was constructed to accommodate a future expansion of double the current milling capacity and the addition of one pasta production line without any further plant construction other than the purchase and installation of the necessary equipment.

The cost savings from integration provided a competitive advantage relative to other firms. Dakota Growers Pasta had become successful in a very short period of time (see Exhibits 16 and 17). Members had received patronage refunds (sometimes called patronage dividends) in 1996, 1997, and 1998. For example, in 1996 patronage refunds were $.30 per bushel (see Exhibit 18). In addition, a three-for-two equity stock split had been declared in July 1997. The company had been profitable over its brief history by increasing the value that members received for their durum wheat relative to nonmembers in North Dakota who had not invested in DGP. Because the plant had lower costs relative to others in the industry, it had increased market share and, therefore, net income. The total increase in value can be seen in Exhibit 18, where the sum of purchase price, patronage refund, and stock appreciation is greater than the average cash price for the durum wheat.

Market Segments

In the beginning, Tim focused mainly on the private-label business because that was the quickest way to enter this industry:

exhibit 15 Dakota Growers Pasta Timeline of Activities, 1990–1998

Year	Transaction
1990	North Dakota durum wheat farmers contributed cash for a feasibility study of an integrated durum milling/pasta manufacturing plant.
1991	Results came back positive (15% return on investment over and above the 10-year durum wheat average price per bushel of $3.85). Tim Dodd was hired as general manager and Gary Mackintosh as national sales manager in December.
January–February 1992	1,200 durum wheat farmers from western Minnesota, North Dakota, and northeastern Montana pledged $12.5 million in equity toward a $40 million durum mill and pasta plant in Carrington, North Dakota.
July 1995	Completion of its first year of operation with 3.2 million bushels of durum milling capacity and 120 million pounds of pasta (almost perfectly aligned because 36 pounds of semolina in a bushel of durum wheat yields 115.2 bushels of semolina flour for pasta).
October 1995	Board of directors decided to double durum wheat capacity.
February 1996	1,085 producers contributed over $9.7 million in equity toward the expansion.
Summer 1996	Durum mill expansion (6 million bushels of durum per year).
Summer 1997	Pasta plant expansion was completed (240 million pounds).
Fall 1998	Analyzed possible acquisition of Primo Piatto (200 million pounds of pasta) and to expand Carrington facility to 12 million bushels of durum milling per year and add an additional 30 million pounds of pasta capacity.

Source: DGP 10-K reports.

exhibit 16 Selected Financial Data for Dakota Growers Pasta,
1993–1998* (in thousands)

	1993	1994	1995	1996	1997	1998[†]
Net revenue	$0	$19,706	$40,441	$49,558	$69,339	$124,869
Net income	(423)	(206)	1,436	2,618	6,926	4,559
Dividends/share	0	0	0	30	485	51
Total assets	24,818	45,215	47,842	49,894	68,739	124,534
Long-term debt	1,557	28,477	29,097	19,752	30,218	66,056
Members' equity	12,183	12,107	13,497	24,866	29,956	36,875

*Dakota Growers Pasta was formed December 16, 1991, and was in development stage through July 31, 1993. Full operations began January 1, 1994.

[†]Assumed acquisition occurred.

Source: DGP 10-K reports.

We had no plans to market our own label, but our members and employees began asking to purchase the product they had a part in producing. So we put our brand, Pasta Growers, on the market, but most of our sales increase has been in the private-label business. We market in three different segments. The retail segment consists primarily of brand and store-brand pasta. We've introduced three labels since we entered the brand arena. Again, that takes a lot of capital and so we are just slowly starting to pursue that. We also market pasta

exhibit 17   Condensed Balance Sheets for Dakota Growers Pasta, 1996–1998 (in thousands)*

	1998	1997	1996
Assets			
Cash and cash equivalents	$ 182	$ 5	$ 1,448
Receivables	13,146	8,287	5,917
Inventories	21,935	8,700	6,737
Prepaid expenses	3,915	536	150
Total current assets	39,178	17,528	13,532
Property and equipment (net)	81,137	48,472	33,584
Investment in St. Paul Bank for Cooperatives	2,086	1,804	1,710
Other assets	2,136	883	1,068
Total assets	$124,537	$68,739	$49,894
Liabilities and members' investment			
Notes payable and			
Current portion of long-term debt	$ 4,033	$ 2,634	$ 72
Accounts payable	5,748	3,432	2,889
Excess outstanding checks over cash on deposit	2,336	2,457	0
Accrued grower payments	1,354	1,116	1,845
Accrued liabilities	2,894	1,560	542
Total current liabilities	16,365	11,199	5,348
Long-term debt, net of current portion	66,056	27,131	18,860
Deferred income taxes	4,900		
Other liabilities	88		
Total liabilities	87,409	38,330	24,208
Redeemable preferred stock	253	453	820
Members' investment			
Convertible preferred stock	2,304		
Membership stock	137	135	135
Equity stock	18,390	18,881	18,881
Additional paid-in capital	4,101	3,610	3,610
Accumulated allocated earnings	2,914	413	0
Accumulated unallocated earning	9,029	6,917	2,240
Total members' investment	36,875	29,956	24,866
Total liabilities and members' investment	$124,537	$68,739	$49,894

*Figures for 1998 are projected assuming the acquisition occurred.
Source: Dakota Growers Pasta 10-K reports.

in the food-service sector to the large food-service companies. Most of them are the major, private-label food-service distributors that create a lot of high volume for us. They're interested in very high-quality pasta at very reasonable prices, of course. Our third market for pasta is the ingredient sector, which consists of food processors that use our product as an ingredient in their process. These would be similar to value-added products such as Hamburger Helper™ or Healthy Choice™.

During the plant's first two years, it produced, among other things, pasta for other companies that were short on inventory due to unexpected demand or shortage of

exhibit 18   Durum Wheat Prices: Dakota Growers Pasta Member vs. Average North Dakota Price, 1994 to 1998[*]

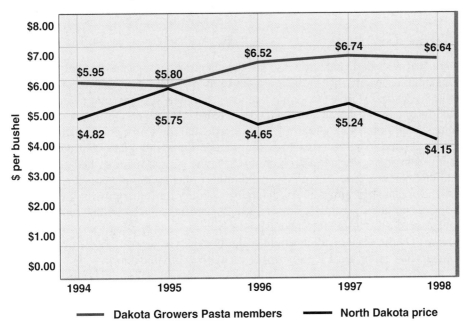

    ——— **Dakota Growers Pasta members**   ——— **North Dakota price**

[*]The DPG price represents the purchase price, patronage refund, and stock appreciation on a per bushel basis.
Source: Dakota Growers Pasta annual report.

durum wheat (this was called co-packing). However, DGP's sales increased to where co-packing was less than 1 percent of sales. The retail private-label and ingredient market segments made up the bulk of DGP's sales. Branded pasta products represented an important market segment for the company. Approximately 50 percent of its business in 1997 was retail (primarily private-label), followed by 25 percent in food-service and 25 percent in ingredient market segments. The majority of DGP sales were under private labels, although it had its own label, Dakota Growers, as well as Pasta Sanita and Zia Briosa.

CRITICAL ISSUES FOR 1999

In the fall of 1997, Borden Food Holdings abruptly announced that the firm intended to close 6 of its 10 North America pasta plants. The company wanted to focus on its core food businesses, one of which was pasta sauce. A partnership, consisting of Borden's employees, purchased two of the plants located in New Hope, Minnesota, and Minneapolis, Minnesota, and formed Primo Piatto ("First Course" in Italian) in August 1997. The plants produced 200 million pounds of pasta per year and had a three-year contract with Borden. However, it was soon apparent that Primo Piatto might require a partner or sale to DGP. Dakota Growers Pasta was supplying Primo Piatto semolina until DGP's own pasta line expansion was completed, and then it would use the semolina internally. The expansion was set for completion in the fall of 1998.

Primo Piatto contacted Tim Dodd about a possible partnership. Tim and the board of directors were considering several issues, including future growth, branding, and shareholder profitability.

Future Growth

Dakota Growers Pasta had grown so fast that the Carrington plant was already running at maximum capacity. The firm would not be able to sustain any new growth without additional capacity. The marketing and sales staff felt strongly that additional sales could be obtained if production could be increased. However, these new sales opportunities were in the southeastern United States, and the Carrington location was not ideally situated to serve this expanding market. Obtaining additional durum wheat from its members was not a problem because the typical member had only enough shares to market an average of 10 percent of his or her total production.

The organic pasta market was another possibility for future growth. Consumption of organic products was increasing at about 20 percent annually in the late 1990s. Several customers had asked for organic products in the past, but there was never enough volume. The new acquisition would make Dakota Growers more flexible. Several members had expressed a willingness to try to grow organic durum.

Private Label versus Brand Label Retail Markets

Prior to the 1960s, the pasta industry was dominated by regional brands, usually family-owned and located in regional population centers. During the 1960s and 1970s, large national firms such as Pillsbury, Hershey, General Foods, Borden, and Coca-Cola purchased these smaller regional firms. In the late 1980s and early 1990s, some of these companies sold off their pasta interests, leading to further consolidation. Throughout this period of consolidation, regional brand names remained the retail leaders, although they were owned by these national firms. Price competition among retail brands had lowered the average price of retail brand pasta within the past two years. Thus, the price differential between private-label pasta and brand-label pasta declined, slowing private-label pasta growth. Tim expected that if the acquisition occurred, DGP's distribution of sales would increase to 60 percent retail, 20 percent ingredient, and 20 percent food service. Most, but not all, of this market share would still be private label.

Tim Dodd wondered about competing in the brand-label pasta market versus continuing to grow in the private-label market. If DGP moved to the brand-label market, it would have to upgrade its image and perhaps even change its brand identity. It would be important to judge its market share prospects after the acquisition occurred and what actions competitors would take in response. Its members had long wanted to see DGP's own brand in retail stores outside North Dakota. However, Tim had warned the board that DGP's initial entry into the pasta industry had to be private label because of the entrenched competition. Tim believed that the acquisition would provide enough capacity that it might be conceivable to further penetrate the brand-label market. Finally, he and the board had discussed the possibility of investigating a joint venture or similar alliance with an Italian pasta manufacturer as a way to present an Italian image.

Shareholder Profitability

Additional capital would be needed to support any capacity expansion or brand product development. Yield losses caused by the wheat scab disease had pushed durum production further away from the plant. This was increasing the members' durum procurement costs. Over the past decade, wet summers had led to mold forming in the wheat, which had reduced yields. Dakota Growers Pasta procured over 6 million bushels of durum per year. Lower yields and increased costs had also reduced member profits, which might dampen members' willingness to provide additional equity capital for the acquisition and for increased marketing expenses associated with branding. Although DGP had returned profits to its members, the durum wheat sold through DGP was typically a small percentage of their total farm output. Low profits in agriculture in general meant that future equity capital might be hard to find. New capacity in the industry also meant that firms had to be very competitive on price.

Dakota Growers Pasta was contemplating hiring a plant breeder to begin developing durum wheat varieties that were not only resistant to scab disease but also had quality attributes desired by their customers. This would increase costs. Tim believed that the equity was there for an expansion. Tim knew all of his members. Many were good managers who had used risk management tools including crop insurance, crop diversification, and contracting to shield them from much of the low profitability seen in the rest of the industry.

However, it was a concern. Durum wheat was grown in a crop rotation with other crops such as sugar beets, malt barley, potatoes, corn, and spring wheat. Some DGP members who participated in the success of DGP were also investors in other closed cooperatives to process sugar beets (American Crystal Sugar), high fructose corn syrup (ProGold), and frozen bread dough (United Spring Bakers). American Crystal Sugar was under financial stress, ProGold was suffering major losses in producer equity, and United Spring Bakers was still searching for a plant location.

DETAILS ABOUT THE ACQUISITION

Tim had told the board the advantages of Primo Piatto:

> Primo Piatto has its own market that it is satisfying. These two plants have continued to produce private-label brands, including some for our customers. It is an attractive acquisition in that sense, but we will need to be more proactive in the research and development of new meal solutions, creative pasta shapes, and more packaging ideas. Primo Piatto brings some of that experience. This should give us about 470 million pounds of pasta per year (240 of existing capacity, 200 through the acquisition, and 30 of additional expansion). We will be perfectly matched if we add the capacity at Carrington. We will be able to mill enough semolina to produce pasta without having to source from anyone else. In addition, we will be on a direct rail-link from Carrington to Minneapolis. Total integration has been the key to our success. This will quadruple our original capacity, and we can still add 10 percent more capacity at both pasta manufacturing plants, if need be, in the future.

Tim looked down at the figures from his accountants. The Primo Piatto acquisition would cost $13.3 million, $11 million of it in cash, with the remainder consisting of preferred stock in DGP. DGP's accountants had projected sales with the acquisition (see Exhibits 19 and 20). Another $1.5 million would be needed to update the software and link the two Minneapolis plants with the Carrington plant. Because DGP was perfectly integrated, any increase in pasta capacity would require an increase in durum milling capacity in order to remain internally self-sufficient across all production stages. The economies of scale were such that DGP would have to add another 6 million bushels of durum milling capacity (i.e., DGP would have to double its existing durum milling capacity). However, it would also leave DGP with excess semolina

exhibit 19   Primo Piatto Balance Sheet, May 29 (date of inception) to September 30, 1997 (in thousands)

Assets	
Current assets	
Cash	$ 1,697
Accounts receivable	4,785
Inventories	2,388
Prepaid expenses	122
Deferred tax asset	28
Total current assets	9,021
Property, plant, and equipment (net)	10,964
Deferred financing cost (net)	54
Total assets	**$20,040**
Liabilities and stockholder's equity	
Current liabilities	
Current portion of long-term debt	$ 3,877
Accounts payable	3,445
Accrued expenses	665
Total current liabilities	7,987
Long-term debt	1,595
Deferred tax liability	48
Total liabilities	9,630
Stockholders' equity	
Common stock	224
Retained earnings	186
Total stockholders' equity	410
Total liabilities and stockholders' equity	**$20,040**

Source: DGP 10-K reports.

flour. To keep capacity matched from stage to stage, DGP would have to add pasta capacity at Carrington because the two Primo Piatto plants had no room for expansion. The scale economies for pasta production were lower, but there was room for a 30-million-pound expansion at Carrington. They would also need more storage capacity at Carrington (620,000 bushels compared with the existing 370,000). Storage costs were estimated at $3.09 per bushel. The milling and pasta expansion would be an $11 million investment, and the total cost of the acquisition investments would be $25.8 million (plus storage costs).

Thus, if the acquisition went forward, DGP would acquire 200 million pounds of pasta production capacity and add another 30 million pounds at Carrington for an overall total of 470 million pounds. In addition, DGP would add another 6 million bushels of durum milling capacity at Carrington. Such moves would enable DGP to keep capacity in balance at each stage.

By using the delivery right stock sale and growers agreement, DGP would ensure mat enough durum wheat could be procured to supply all three plants' needs. Primo Piatto enabled DGP to increase its research base for packaging and new products that would help develop differentiated products. In addition, me acquisition would give DGP a larger sales and marketing staff.

exhibit 20 Primo Piatto Income Statement, May 29 (date of inception) to September 30, 1997 (in thousands)

Net sales	$5,915
Cost of sales	4,915
Gross profit	1,000
Selling and administrative	555
Operating income	44
Other expense	—
Interest expense	133
Other	2
Total other expense	135
Income before taxes	309
Income taxes (includes deferrable)	123
Net income	$ 186

Source: DGP.

CONCLUSION

Tim summed up what the acquisition would mean for DGP:

> Our strategy is to increase our brands. We've got three brands on the market now. We're marketing Zia Briosa with the Costco stores. A second label that is the Pasta Grower label in the upper Midwest is targeted more toward Minnesota, North Dakota, and South Dakota. In the discount stores, we have a label that's called Pasta Sanita. It's our strategy to increase our brand presence. That takes a lot of capital if you're going to go out and actually buy those markets. You have to be able to have deep pockets to compete.

Tim Dodd and the DGP board of directors planned to discuss the acquisition in light of all the changes going on in the pasta industry. Tim felt that the acquisition made perfect sense and was in keeping with DGP's vertical integration strategy. He believed that the board's main questions would be related to the future profitability of DGP with respect to where the industry was going, overall effect on market share, and what competitive rivalry might look like in the future.

case 7 Colorado Creative Music

Rachel Deane Canetta
University of Denver

Joan Winn
University of Denver

I was a good musician, so I thought, what better thing to start than a music company?
—Darren Skanson

Darren Skanson, lead artist and CEO of Colorado Creative Music (CCM), settled into his flight on Friday, March 9, 2001. He was heading to New Smyrna Beach, Florida, where he would perform at the Images arts festival. As lead artist, Darren had been traveling all over the country performing light classical guitar and selling his line of CDs. As CCM's biggest money machine, Darren was performing 40 two- or three-day weekends a year. As CEO, Darren was increasingly concerned. He was being pulled in too many directions. He realized that he couldn't continue to travel and perform as much as he had been and still manage the growth of his record label. While he waited for the plane to take off, he thought about how to turn the nightmare that his company had become into the dream that he believed it could be.

DARREN CURTIS SKANSON

I've always been a performer; music was in our household from very early on. When I first saw what a musical group, a band, can do to an audience—just the excitement and the adulation that they received—that moment changed my life. I said, "I want to do that."

Darren Curtis Skanson was born and raised on a farm seven miles outside of Fertile, a small town of about 800 people in the northwest part of Minnesota. Darren's father was an elementary school teacher, and his mother was a piano teacher and a teacher's aide. Darren was the oldest of four boys.

Darren's passion for music began at an early age. Some of his earliest memories were of singing with his brother Brant in church at the age of four. Darren traced his dream of being a rock star to watching the crowd respond to a high school band performance:

Partial funding for preparation of this case was provided by the John E. and Jeanne T. Hughes Charitable Foundation Entrepreneurship Education and Awareness Grant. All events and individuals in this case are real, but some names may have been disguised. Copyright © 2001 by Rachel Deane Canetta and Joan Winn. Used with permission.

I was in 7th or 8th grade and one of my best friends, a 10th-grader, was playing with a bunch of seniors. They played a pep rally for a sporting event, and the school all comes down and gets together. Everyone came out of the bleachers and went up to the stage and, you know, it was a pretty strong experience . . . The first night that I ever played live with a band on stage and got a similar response just reinforced it.

With the encouragement of his parents, Darren went to Moorhead State University, graduating with a BA in music in 1989. This education helped him discover the intellectual and emotional aspects of music. Darren had originally intended to get a music industry degree, which required a minor in business. But during his senior year, the music took over, and he ended up without enough business courses to fulfill the minor. Darren regretted that now, but, he said, "you know when you are 22 years old you don't really foresee the future very well. You see the ideals and not the practicalities."

Just out of college, Darren began performing as lead guitarist in a heavy metal band called Mata Hari. The band toured the United States playing in small venues and opening for bigger bands in larger venues. After four years Darren was frustrated. The band had produced only one CD, and the band members did not want to move to a place that was more conducive to making a break in heavy metal. They had been living and performing out of Fargo, North Dakota, which was not a hotbed for performing artists. When Jack, the lead singer, left the band to get married, Darren was ready to call it quits and break up the band.

In March 1993, Mata Hari's last stretch of a tour put the group in Denver. Darren liked Denver and looked for an excuse to stay. He found an ad in the newspaper soliciting a guitarist for a classical/New Age duo called Watson and Company. Darren's classical training gave him the courage he needed to call and set up an audition. He got the job, which turned out to be a major turning point in his musical career.

Malcolm Watson was a classical violinist who was making his living by performing at art festivals around Colorado and selling his CDs. Darren and Malcolm produced Watson and Company's third CD. Darren's college friend Jennifer was hired to serve as Watson and Company's booking agent. She began booking the duo nationwide, and within a year Watson and Company's annual sales increased from $100,000 to $250,000.

Darren believed that there were ways to capitalize on the knowledge the team had about the art festivals. He saw art festivals as a strong distribution venue that could be tapped. Darren's vision was to sign on other artists in a way that kept them tied in so that they could not just absorb the knowledge and leave. Discouraged that Malcolm wanted to move more slowly, Darren and Jennifer decided to end their relationship with Watson and Company.

Jennifer began booking other artists, taking a percentage of their sales. Darren wanted to move beyond booking artists to forming a company that would manage and promote artists. His vision was to record, produce, and sell his own music as well as the music of a cohesive group of artists that would make up a unique record label and distribution company. Jennifer was helpful as a booking agent, but Darren's vision of a viable business venture differed from hers. Jennifer was not the person Darren was looking for in a business partner.

COLORADO CREATIVE MUSIC

I've always been a very driven person, and I got tired of waiting or depending on other people to get things done. I was always the spearhead in getting stuff done in every other organization or business relationship I was in.

Darren started Colorado Creative Music in January 1995. Working solo, Darren produced two CDs and sold them at the art festivals that Jennifer booked for him. He did this on his own for two and a half years, and as sales grew and doing business got more complicated he began seeing a need for bringing others on board.

In June 1997, Darren's cousin Ted, a business school student at St. Cloud State University in Minnesota, contacted him about doing a business internship. Darren and Ted began writing down everything about how the business was run. "We started transferring the knowledge to my cousin, and then into processes," Darren said. At the end of Ted's internship, Darren tried to find someone who could continue the work Ted had begun, with hopes of fine-tuning the processes into a workable set of operational systems. In early 1998, Darren hired Ryan, a young musician who was familiar with the music industry, to continue documenting processes and also to help with equipment repairs and recordings. By summer, CCM was so busy that Darren started to look for someone to take over some of the day-to-day operations, like filling and mailing orders and handling the bookkeeping. In late fall he hired Andy Harling, a classical guitarist, to help with the office work and the maintenance of instruments and equipment. When Ryan left CCM to go back to school to finish his music degree, Andy inherited the task of examining the business processes to make CCM operate more efficiently.

Soon after Andy was hired, Jennifer, who had continued to act as Darren's booking agent, had openings for two shows that had been left vacant by a musician who had canceled at the last minute. Darren was already booked for other gigs, but felt it was important to find another artist to do the shows. Darren quickly recorded a CD of Andy's repertoire, duplicated it in-house, and sent Andy out to do the two gigs. To Darren's excitement, Andy was successful. But now that Andy had actually gone out and done an art festival under Darren's direction, Andy had valuable knowledge of how to capitalize on art festivals. Darren felt there was a risk that Andy could leave and become his competitor. Recognizing this as an opportunity, Darren signed Andy to a recording contract. Andy's first full CD with CCM was launched under the title *Andrew Thomas Harling*.

As Andy's responsibilities expanded into more and more performing, CCM needed someone else to help answer telephones and fill orders. Amy was hired in August 2000 as Andy's assistant.

Darren's growing company required more space, so Darren moved CCM from his one-bedroom office and recording studio to a large rental house. A spacious laundry room in the basement was transformed into a well-organized mailroom; a spare bedroom served as an office. Darren built a workbench for repairing equipment and turned another room in the basement into a nearly soundproof recording studio. The garage served as a warehouse, with all inventory and equipment neatly organized on labeled shelves and workbenches.

THE PERFORMANCE MUSIC RECORDING INDUSTRY AND THE DIGITAL REVOLUTION

> What used to be a quarter-of-a-million-dollar piece of gear 10 years ago, say in the late 80s, you can get now for $5,000, and the quality is just as good, maybe even better.

Traditionally, the record industry was the exclusive domain of five or six major record labels. These major labels had large staffs, big budgets, and huge distribution. The cost of recording and pressing vinyl was very high. In the early 1980s, a professional recording studio could cost several million dollars. Although most performances were recorded on tape, editing was virtually nonexistent. Music was typically recorded onto a multimaster track. This was then mixed down to a half-inch tape called the master. The master was then transferred to vinyl. In order to cut anything, the half-inch tape had to be physically spliced with a razor. Because of the high cost of recording and of pressing in vinyl, a company had to produce a minimum of about 5,000 copies of any given album just to cover fixed expenses. The costs and difficulty of building a major record label kept industry competition in the hands of a few established companies.

With the digital revolution came the compact disc. The cost of digitally recording and burning a CD was significantly less expensive than creating copies from a vinyl or tape master. In 2000, a professional recording studio could be assembled for about $5,000. In addition, the hardware and computers used to edit music were affordable, even for the spare-room hobbyist. The ability to edit music and manipulate it via computer became far more comprehensive than in the past. Not only were digital recording and editing cheap, CDs were cheap to duplicate, even in small quantities. Producer and writer Kashif estimated that 500 CDs cost between $1.90 and $3.63 per CD to duplicate. A production run of 2,000 CDs would bring the cost down to under $1 per unit.[1]

Unlike vinyl or tape masters, digital recordings could be duplicated without deterioration of the master disc. A musician could create a master CD on his own home computer, design and print attractive labels, and duplicate 500 to 1,000 without investing in expensive equipment or contracting with a professional studio. The size and weight of compact discs made storage and shipping cheap and convenient, thus opening the music recording and distribution industry to an uncountable number of players in even remote locations.

Production costs represented only part of the total cost picture to launch a recording. Major recording labels invested heavily in marketing, promotion, distribution, royalties, and image building, often exceeding $1 million. On the other end of the spectrum, "anyone with talent and a business perspective can start their own virtual reality or vanity label."[2]

With the availability of cheap production equipment and easy access to Internet marketing and distribution, the industry became fragmented and distinct segments appeared. Music production companies, or labels, generally fell into four categories, or levels. Exhibit 1 gives some examples of the labels within these categories.

The "first tier companies" consisted of the major labels such as Columbia, BMG, EMI, and Sony Music. These labels had national or even international distribution. Typically, they had more than 100 artists under contract, representing a broad array of musical styles. They tended not to focus on just one genre. CCM did not really compete with major labels, and Darren Curtis Skanson didn't want to position himself to compete directly with classical guitarists such as Christopher Parkening and John Williams, whose music was produced by Sony's Classical Division.

Independent labels were the next-largest segment of the industry. Many of these companies were managed by a musician/artist, but larger independents were run by professional managers. Independent labels had anywhere from 10 to 100 artists under contract. Some of these labels may have been comparable in size to some of the major labels, but independents tended to focus on one or two genres of music. Narada, whose focus was New Age music, was a typical example of a successful independent label. Another producer of New Age music was Higher Octave. Metal Blade Records was an

---

[1]Kasif, *Everything You'd Better Know about the Record Industry* (Venice, CA: Brooklyn Boy Books, 1996).

[2]L. E. Wacholtz, "The New Music Business: Internet Entrepreneurial Opportunities in the Performing Arts," *Proceedings of the 2001 USASBE/SBIDA National Conference,* Orlando, Florida, August 2001.

exhibit 1   Record Label Company Categories

Major Labels Over 100 artists	Independent Labels 10–100 artists	Microlabels 2–10 artists	Vanity Labels 1 artist
Sony Columbia BMG EMI Giant Records Warner Brothers Elektra Records Atlantic Records	Soundings of the Planet (inspirational/ healing) Narada (New Age) Higher Octave Metal (New Age) Metal Blade Records (heavy metal) Rhino Records (compilations) W.A.R. (punk, rock, reggae) Windham Hill (light classical, easy listening)	Etherian (meditative) Evol Egg Nart (rock/pop) Cuneiform Records (progressive jazz) CCM (light acoustic)	Bob Culbertson Lisa Lynn Franco Watson and Company Lao Tizer Esteban Ramirez

Note: Gary Hustwit, in *Releasing an Independent Record* (San Diego: Rockpress, 1998), lists over 1,000 major and independent labels. This table illustrates CCM's perceived competitor and/or partner labels.

independent label that focused on heavy metal. Rhino Records focused on re-releasing compilations. Soundings of the Planet produced several easy-listening and classical offerings that directly competed with CCM. Some of the larger independent labels had national distribution, but most were regional or specialty distributors.

The next tier of recording companies were known as the microlabels. These labels typically had fewer than 10 artists under contract and tended to be more tightly focused than the independent labels. The microlabels had small staffs, and the owner/manager was often the lead artist. Microlabels seldom had formal distribution systems, relying on direct sales to fans and wholesale to clubs and specialty retailers. Because of the size of these labels and the small distribution networks they commanded, they existed only because of the low costs involved in digital recording. Etherian was an established microlabel that competed directly with Colorado Creative Music.

The most specialized segment of the music industry consisted of the vanity labels. These labels were created by independent artists who wanted to record and sell their own music. They were usually one-person operations with no formal distribution. These artists relied on direct sales to concertgoers and loyal fans. Musicians such as Bob Culbertson, Lisa Franco, Watson and Company, Peruvian Bands, and Lao Tizer had been successful at direct selling at art festivals.

While it was fairly common for a vanity label to move up to microlabel status, it was quite uncommon for a microlabel to move up to the independent label level. Soundings of the Planet was one example of a record label that was able to do this. It was virtually unheard of for an independent to compete at the major label level, although some independent labels had been acquired by major label companies.

Marketing and Promotion

A key element in recorded-music sales was getting music heard. In general, people didn't want to buy music they had not heard. The major labels used their established

exhibit 2 The Recording Industry Distribution Chain

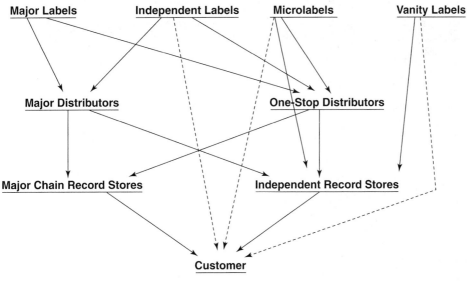

——— **Traditional Distribution Channel**
- - - - - **Direct Sales to Customers**

relationships with prominent radio stations for tremendous leverage in getting new music played on prime-time programs. Command of distributors and capital to produce in large quantities allowed major record labels to offer new recordings for sale at the same time that radio stations gave the music airplay. Music was a fashionable business, and sales were heavily correlated to good timing.

The radio stations' primary relationship was with the major labels, so independents, microlabels, and vanity labels had to rely on other means of getting their music heard. Many bands on these smaller labels relied on touring and performing. Big Head Todd and the Monsters (Giant Records), Phish (Warner Brothers), and Widespread Panic (Capricorn Records) found their fame through the college circuit, performing and selling their music all over the country. Musicians who recorded their music on vanity labels often played small local venues, such as bars, coffee houses, and bookstores.

Because getting music heard was so essential, there were promotional companies that specialized in getting music airplay. These companies called stations to negotiate airplay, promotional giveaways, and interviews. While many independent labels might have had the funding for this, smaller labels could rarely afford such extensive promotional campaigns.

Distribution

Most recorded music was distributed through major distributors and "one-stops" (see Exhibit 2). Major distributors contracted with large chain stores like Tower Records, Sam Goody, Barnes & Noble, and Borders Books and Music. It was very difficult for small record labels to use a major distributor because of the large order requirements and risky payment policies that had become standard for the industry. These distributors generally operated on a 60–90-day turnaround with full return. This meant that if a CD sold, the producer would typically be paid two or three months later. In addition,

exhibit 3   CCM's Income Statements, 1997–2000

	Year Ending			
	2000	1999	1998	1997
Income				
GIG sales	$181,451.92	$148,839.76	$145,721.78	$129,445.25
Wholesale	12,238.83	19,556.04	17,587.02	10,887.02
Mail and phone orders	11,442.24	2,928.72	3,148.00	—˙
Website sales	6,419.35	760.50	0.00	0.00
Other	1,758.79	1,417.89	3,714.98	1,259.59
Total sales	213,311.13	173,502.91	170,171.78	141,591.86
Other income	3,302.92	2,750.09	4,329.00	1,527.28
Total Income	216,614.05	176,253.00	174,500.78	143,119.14
Cost of goods sold	22,034.33	23,311.38	36,468.62	36,226.52
Gross profit	$194,579.72	$152,941.62	$138,032.16	$106,892.62
Expenses				
Advertising expense	$10,422.83	$4,388.71	$11,432.35	$ 4,110.43
Automobile expense	0.00	2,279.01	1,644.83	4,016.88
Bad check expense	156.00	583.14	416.99	1,072.50
Bank service charges	5,320.39	4,790.75	3,070.60	2,509.47
Commissions	32,861.14	31,333.92	30,283.59	27,828.66
Dues and subscriptions	10.00	0.00	0.00	397.45
Depreciation expense	0.00	5,820.00	0.00	0.00
Equipment rental	491.14	0.00	0.00	0.00
Furniture and fixtures	0.00	0.00	329.95	656.84
Insurance	2,344.79	2,655.51	2,109.19	1,173.00
Interest expense	631.96	0.00	0.00	0.00

all those CDs that didn't sell were returned to the label or producer. Major distributors also wanted large quantities of inventory. A label might have to front the money for 40,000 CDs, which required a large amount of working capital, with no guarantee that the CDs would sell.

One-stops started out mainly to service independent music stores like Joe's Records on the corner. These one-stops allowed stores to buy in smaller quantities than from a major distributor. One-stops would sometimes carry music from major labels, but were similar to an independent label in that they tended to specialize in one type of music.

FROM MUSICIAN TO ENTREPRENEUR

I started this business because I was a good guitar player, so I thought a music company is perfect. But what you need to start a business—to be an entrepreneur—is different than being a guitar player. So I had to learn not to concentrate so much on the musical end of things, and instead to concentrate on the entrepreneurial things. That was a huge shift that started with Acoustitherapy. That is really where that whole process began, when I said I don't need to make guitar music, I can make any kind of music, I just have to look at it as a businessman not a musician.

Darren Skanson soon realized that the physical work involved in setting up a studio was much easier than building and managing a business. His music degree did not

exhibit 3   *(continued)*

	Year Ending			
	2000	**1999**	**1998**	**1997**
Licenses and permits	0.00	0.00	218.00	327.09
Miscellaneous	580.37	1,077.27	1,462.62	2,282.64
Parking expense	308.75	661.00	348.00	258.00
Payroll	15,515.76	6,660.29	5,150.64	0.00
Payroll expenses/taxes	3,143.38	11,671.74	0.00	0.00
Postage and delivery	6,432.22	2,321.22	1,626.06	2,150.97
Printing and reproduction	4,691.82	1,818.19	4,414.28	7,409.34
Professional fees†	29,719.26	2,242.50	217.10	1,145.00
Rent and storage fees	14,080.45	13,368.07	9,973.29	2,174.75
Repairs and maintenance	2,531.25	1,863.00	3,217.77	2,229.01
Royalties	17,283.39	8,848.99	1,776.91	746.57
Shipping	3,776.97	3,257.89	2,804.05	2,345.05
Subscriptions	80.95	443.18	472.76	0.00
Supplies	13,142.81	7,343.05	5,343.78	8,247.67
Taxes	4,744.94	4,678.58	7,961.01	6,796.28
Telephone	4,399.22	5,269.83	4,860.00	4,754.38
Travel and entertainment	16,156.64	23,889.21	17,759.91	19,092.13
Utilities	1,461.29	1,262.04	511.78	244.92
Total expense	$190,287.72	$148,527.09	$117,405.46	$101,969.03
Net income	$ 4,292.00	$ 4,414.53	$ 20,626.70	$ 4,923.59

*Included with wholesale.

†This includes payments to backup musicians at live performances and an independent music consultant to direct the production of the "Classica" and "A Christmas Story" CDs.

prepare him for the tasks of marketing and promoting his music, nor did it provide a framework for creating a workable system of operations and control.

When Darren began Colorado Creative Music out of his bedroom in 1995, he did everything himself. He was his own accountant, desktop publisher, database manager, newsletter editor, website designer, and copywriter. Early on, he started transferring his stack of art festival contacts from three-by-five-inch notecards to a computerized database. By 1997, he switched to a computerized accounting system.

Using only his own savings to finance the company, Darren was concerned about keeping overhead low and expenses down. (See Exhibit 3 for summaries of CCM's income statements.) To save time, Darren would purchase rolls of stamps and apply postage to packages according to their weight. This sometimes resulted in overpostaging some packages. Stamps and address labels were affixed by hand, since CCM didn't have enough mail orders to warrant purchasing an automated postage system. As mail order demand grew, the wastefulness of the system became significant.

Promotion was most effective at art festivals, but Darren understood the need for retail distribution to increase sales. He approached some retailers himself, but found that it was an onerous and time-consuming task:

> I tried to take care of it myself, going out there trying to get CDs into stores, but it's too big a job for me. I have too many things pulling me into too many other directions. I actually hired a sales guy in the summer of '98, and he turned out to be worthless. He basically

didn't do anything; he took the money and didn't do anything—the employer's nightmare. Then I tried friends who wanted to do it part-time, but that didn't work out either.

Then we hooked up with one of the one-stops here in Colorado. Basically, a one-stop has a huge catalog of stuff. If the demand is there, the stores will ask the one-stop, "Do you have any Darren Curtis Skanson CDs?" The thing we ran into with that is we had some Barnes & Noble stores calling the one-stop to get our stuff, but the one-stop put such a markup on the CDs that B&N didn't want to buy from them. He's got to make money too, that I understand, but B&N would call us wanting to get more CDs and we'd tell them, "That's great, but we're doing business with John over there at USA One-Stop. Just give him a call and he'll set you up." Then they call us back, and tell us that John is charging them a ridiculous amount for the CDs wholesale, and they say, "We don't want to deal with John, we want to deal with you." And you're back to where you started from.

In 1999, feeling overwhelmed with the tasks of running a business, Darren outsourced the accounting function and made a list of tasks and systems that needed to be codified (Exhibit 4). He also began reading books on entrepreneurship, searching for a way to organize Colorado Creative Music and to make it more profitable.

CREATING A SUSTAINABLE ENTERPRISE

Darren wanted *Colorado Creative Music* and *Darren Curtis Skanson* to become identifiable names, with enough demand to make distribution through large book and record stores feasible. He envisioned a promotional spot on the evening news, with thousands of people watching and then heading out to buy his CD in a store. He wanted someone browsing the shelves to see a Darren Curtis Skanson CD, recognize him from the newscast, and buy it.

> I think you always start with a vision, and of course that vision was to record, produce, and sell my own music. And that of course still is a major part of CCM. Your vision always changes. I'm amazed at how much your vision changes as you learn and grow as a business person.

Darren's early success in selling his and Andy's recordings led him to realize the potential for profitability and growth that the digital revolution had opened up. He knew enough about the music industry to be wary of labeling himself New Age or classical or folk, competing with established artists. He decided to call his own music light classical, and position CCM as a company that handled a portfolio of artists, each with a distinctive light acoustic style.

The first step in "branding" CCM was a promotional catalog that could be handed out to people who approached his sales table at art festivals and shopping malls. He enclosed the catalog with every sale and offered it for free on CCM's website.

CCM's first catalog was a small brochure. With the addition of new CCM offerings, Darren felt the need for an upgrade that would portray a high-quality image. He was able to reproduce an attractive catalog for about 12 cents apiece. He was pleased with the appearance of catalogs, but he wasn't sure how to manage them as inventory or how to decide how many to produce at one time. He didn't want a box of 1,000 old catalogs on hand when he needed to add a new product to the order form. The company was adding two new titles a year, which made sales and inventory increasingly difficult to manage.

By December of 2000, CCM had four product lines and 11 different records. The four product lines (or brand names) were Darren Curtis Skanson, Acoustitherapy, Andrew Thomas Harling, and Music for Candles.

exhibit 4   Colorado Creative Music Task List

Research and Development	Operations	Brand Marketing	Sales
Musical	**Accounting**	**Live Performance**	**Direct**
1. Song Writing	**Fulfillment**	1. Malls	1. Live performance
2. Arranging	**Maintenance**	2. Art festivals	2. 800 #
3. Pre-production	1. Instruments and gear	3. Concerts	3. Website
4. Recording, producing, Engineering	2. Office equipment	**Website**	4. Mail order catalog
5. Mastering	Gear preparation for shows	Essential elements	5. After sale:
Books to read	Duplication	Books to read	Thank-you letter
Pirsig, *Zen and the Art of Motorcycle Maintenance*	Inventory management	*Front-Page 2000 for Dummies*	Direct letters from database
	Database management	Software to know	Direct response
Market	Design	Front-Page 2000	Books to read
1. CCM R+D Worksheet	Books to read		Levinson, *Guerilla Marketing*
2. Artwork	Gerber, *The E-Myth*	**Publicity**	**Indirect**
Books to read	Software to know	1. Airplay: Radio, TV, Internet Radio	Traditional
Reis/Trout, *Positioning: The Battle for Your Mind*	Quickbooks 2000 Pro	2. Live Interviews: Radio, TV	1. Chain music stores
Reis, *22 Immutable Laws of Branding*	Microsoft Access	3. Print Press: Reviews, Features, Events listings	2. Chain book stores
Trout, *The New Positioning*	Microsoft Works		3. Independent music stores
Levinson, *Guerilla Marketing*	Microsoft Word 2000	**Promotions**	Nontraditional
Kottler, *Kottler on Marketing*		1. In store	1. Retail chains
		2. Contests	2. Catalogs
		3. Sponsoring	3. Gift stores
		4. Giveaway	4. Independent bookstores
		E-mail	5. Health, massage, yoga, t'ai chi, day care
		Monthly Newsletter	6. Christian: chains and independents
		Books to read	
		Levinson, *Guerilla Marketing*	
		Software to know	
		Aureate Group Mail	

(handwritten annotation: "Strength")

Darren Curtis Skanson

Darren described this line of music as "light classical guitar." The Darren Curtis Skanson line was marketed as a gentle and intimate approach to classical music, positioned against more purist classical guitarists such as John Williams and Christopher Parkening. Darren had released five titles under this brand name. *Peace, Earth, and Guitars* was released in September 1995. Due to the success of this title, CCM released *Peace, Earth, and Guitars, Volume II* in January 1997. Darren's next title was a Christmas album, *Angels, Guitars, and Joy*, released in October 1996. *Classica* was released in May 2000; *A Christmas Story* was released in November 2000. These last two releases featured a cello backup to Darren's solo guitar, in an effort to broaden Darren's audience appeal.

Acoustitherapy

The Acoustitherapy line of records was Darren's response to what many customers wanted from instrumental music. Customers specifically wanted acoustic instrumental music that was slow, soft, and soothing. Darren collected music from various artists who wrote original music and performed on a variety of acoustic instruments. *Relaxation* and *Regeneration* were released in September 1997. *Gentle Passion* was released in October 1998, and in July 2000 *World Meditations* was released. Acoustitherapy was marketed as soft and soothing music for the mind, body, heart, and soul.

Andrew Thomas Harling

Andy's debut CD, *The Road to the Soul,* was a combination of traditional melodies and new compositions written by modern classical guitarists. A second CD was in the making, to be released by August 2001.

Music for Candles

CCM engineered and produced a CD called *Starry Night* for the vanity label Music for Candles. In 2001, CCM carried this product in its catalog under a distribution contract with the Music for Candles artists. Darren hoped to produce and distribute CDs for other labels to expand CCM's catalog offerings and promote CCM's name recognition.

PUSHING THE PRODUCTS

Darren knew that he needed to understand his customers and cater to their tastes. He had noticed that the people who approached him at the art festivals and shopping malls where he sold his CDs were generally white, middle-class adults, mostly women in the mid-40s to 60 age range, whose children were grown. These people expressed their delight in meeting Darren personally, and often asked for his autograph. Phone orders appeared to be coming from a similar demographic, with callers enthusiastic about talking with Darren personally when they placed an order for one of his recordings. Darren was careful to keep this personal touch and sent regular e-mails to his growing list of fans.

Darren understood quickly that these people were not classical music enthusiasts but rather were drawn to his music for its blend of soft acoustic sounds and familiar classical tunes. He chose his music offerings carefully, trying to maintain a distinction between himself and other artists. He knew that his company would need to offer a variety of titles to gain the sales volume he needed to compete for retail space.

Darren had an easy time selling his CDs in local music and book stores, but he had not been able to set up distribution beyond his home state. Out of town, Darren relied

exhibit 5   CCM Pricing Structure for Recorded Compact Discs

At Live Shows		Mail, E-Mail, and 800 Number Orders
1 CD	$17.00	$16.00 per CD
2 CDs	28.00	$ 1.75 shipping and handling per CD
3 CDs	38.00	$17.75 total per CD*
4 CDs	47.00	
5 CDs	55.00	
6 CDs	62.00	
7 CDs	68.00	

*No mail-order discount for multiples.

on live performances to sell his recordings. For these shows (art festivals, shopping malls, and concerts), he set up a pricing structure that he hoped would encourage the purchase of more than one CD (see Exhibit 5). Darren wanted to encourage an impulse buy with customers that were harder to reach on a regular basis.

With regular appearances at two local upscale malls, Darren's pricing structure appeared to create some saturation. Many customers were returning fans who already had all his CDs. For this reason he changed the price at local mall performances to $17 per CD. Darren's rationale was clear: "If we are going to be playing at these places over and over again, we can't be shooting ourselves in the foot by selling five CDs at a great price, then when the customer comes back, he or she has everything. We might even be too late on that. We may have shot ourselves in the foot already."

Darren was also concerned that Jennifer was not finding many new venues for him, preferring to book him at the regular shows and festivals where he already had a strong presence. Traveling around the country gave him exposure to a wider customer base, but he was afraid that bookings at the same shows year after year limited his ability to reach a broader market. As he brought more musicians on board, Darren believed that he could produce music that would appeal to a broader audience. By rotating artists, he could allow each performer to do different festivals each year, minimizing the saturation problem.

In addition to festival and shopping mall distribution, Darren wanted to be able to offer his CDs in retail outlets nationwide. He knew he couldn't compete with the major labels, but he did not know how to break into the traditional industry distribution networks. From some of his reading on entrepreneurship, Darren concluded that it was important to think in terms of company "saleability" as a measure of business success, even though selling CCM to a major label was not his ultimate goal. He felt he could build a stronger, more focused business if he thought of CCM in terms of its attractiveness as a potential acquisition or investment. That meant that he needed to build enough volume for CCM products to be sold nationally through traditional distribution channels. Major labels expected sales of 15,000 copies of a recording in one year before they would consider offering a contract. This was the benchmark that Darren set for himself.

DARREN'S DILEMMA

The major dilemma is that we have built the backbone of our company on direct sales, whether it is at the gig, in the mall, or in the back end (800 number, website, mail order). That has been a very profitable thing for us, but as I discovered this last Christmas, I only have so many hours of performance in me to be out there direct selling—which is the engine that drives all of the other back-end sales.

Darren realized that he had a long way to go in getting national distribution. By the end of 2000, Colorado Creative Music had sold over 30,000 *Darren Curtis Skanson* CDs, but that number included all five Darren Curtis Skanson titles over six years. Over a seven-month period, CCM sold 4,100 units of his CD *Classica,* which was released in May 2000. Most of these were from direct sales, stemming from Darren's tireless efforts as performer, publicity agent, promoter, and salesman.

Darren started to list his goals and think about his options:

1. To create a profitable record label with a complementary range of artists.
2. To position Darren Curtis Skanson to compete with artists on a recording label on par with Sony Classical. This required selling records in stores through traditional distribution methods.
3. To create a product line, such as Acoustitherapy, that was saleable, and use the funds to work towards accomplishing goals 1 and 2.

Feeling strongly that something was missing in his efforts to make CCM and his music more successful, Darren began researching and reading books about marketing and positioning. He was searching for a way to position Acoustitherapy and Darren Curtis Skanson against the competition:

> One of the better books I found was *The E-Myth* by Michael Gerber. He talks about thinking about a business as a franchise. You can be successful if you can define everything in your business, like a franchise does, like McDonald's does. They say, cook these fries for three minutes at *x* number of degrees and plop them out there and leave them in the drainer for 30 seconds. It's the same thing with me. The thing I need to concentrate on now is my promotion and publicity processes. How do you promote a record? It should be a fairly simple process, but I should have a process for it.

When Darren began thinking of CCM as a franchise, he thought in terms of having a system into which he could plug other artists. He felt that by putting Andy into the systems that he had tried and tested, he was franchising the company. As he fine-tuned these processes, Darren started seeking out other artists who he felt would fit well into the system. Darren wanted to train each artist to sell in a way that would allow them to focus their energies on performing without having to worry about the business end of things. Darren had already compiled a procedures manual that included checklists for equipment necessary to take to a show, settings for the soundboard and speakers, and even a script for making sales. Darren saw his main weakness in the area of marketing:

> I had always thought that the better-quality product always wins. So I had to be a better guitar player, I had to be faster and all those things. When I read those books I realized that quality matters, but it is not nearly as important as the position that you own in the mind of whomever. If you say classical guitar to someone, most people would say "Andre Segovia," and then they'd say "John Williams" or "Christopher Parkening." There's an implicit ranking, a product ladder in people's minds. There is no way that I will compete—EVER compete—with those people. It doesn't really matter if I'm a better musician. The reality or the truth makes no difference. In people's minds, truth and perception become melded. So I need to work on the image, the perception in people's minds, of the CCM label and the artists it employs.

Having been bitten by this marketing mind-set, Darren became driven in his pursuit of product positioning and image creation. He began formulating a worksheet for positioning CCM products and documenting a process for publicity. He created a system for writing press releases that included information on the timing and frequency of sending press releases. Darren purchased a nationwide publicity database to help prepare in advance for every trip.

Even with all of these new ideas being put into action, Darren was still traveling about 40 weekends a year to perform at art festivals and shopping malls, where the largest portion of direct sales could be made. Most phone, mail, and e-mail orders were still directly related to Darren's art festival appearances. Although website (Internet) sales increased threefold in 2000, this was still a small portion of overall direct sales.

In December 2000, when Darren was playing a 10-day stint at a shopping mall in Denver, the reality of Darren's limitations began to set in. He began feeling the pains of tendonitis in his left elbow, and soon after Christmas he realized he had a significant problem. His plan to put out two new Darren Curtis Skanson CDs in order to ride a wave of recent publicity would have to be put on hold.

With the harsh realization that he could not continue to perform at his previous level, Darren knew he needed to find other musicians to drive sales. In January 2001, he began to formulate some ideas for growing the label that would take some of the pressure for performance off him.

First he decided to produce only one new Darren Curtis Skanson CD, and instead produce a second Andrew Thomas Harling CD. Darren felt that if Andy had another CD he would be in a better position to take over some of the bigger art festivals that Darren had been doing himself.

To compensate for the fact that CCM would produce only one Darren Curtis Skanson CD (which might not be released until November), Darren knew he had to do something different to attract a bigger crowd of listeners. He decided to look for violists or violinists to play with him when he played larger Colorado festivals, capitalizing on the success of the cello-enhanced *Classica*. He transcribed the cello harmonies from *Classica* into a score for viola and violin and auditioned musicians who would make a commitment to do a certain number of shows. He found musicians, set up rehearsals, and sold more CDs at their first show together than he had sold alone the previous year with the initial release of *Classica*.

Darren also began actively searching for other artists who would fit well with the CCM label. He began negotiations with a pianist and a violinist, but both sets of talks eventually broke down. The pianist wanted 50 percent ownership of CCM, which made Darren nervous.

THE NEXT STEP

In order for us to get legitimate, and our product lines to be legitimate in the "standard music industry," we have to have distribution through retail stores. It's just how the music business machine works. That's the distribution dilemma. Of course personally, I would like Darren Curtis Skanson the brand name to be courted by Sony Classical because we've sold 15,000 of my next CD through established chains. And they'd be calling and asking who Darren Curtis Skanson is, saying that they want to sign him. And we could say, "Well, CCM has his contract and we would let him go for *x* number of dollars," or whatever deal you negotiate.

I guess in a nutshell the dilemma is this, in order to (a) grow the company or (b) sell the product lines to an entity larger than CCM, those entities want to see your sales in traditional outlets. But in order to get it into those outlets, you have to either commit to a huge product run or be satisfied with pounding away at it or just incrementally working your sales up. I would love to get bigger distribution because bigger distribution means bigger sales, but I can't handle huge distribution without a bigger base of performers and a bigger push for publicity. In the short term, making direct sales is good for cash flow, it's good for the bottom line, it's good for the business; but in the long term, in order to turn any one of our product lines into something bigger than just making direct sales, you have to make a significant amount of sales through the established music business machine, which is record stores.

I think ultimately one-stops and distributors is the way you have to go, that's the way the whole industry works, but I don't believe that I can do that myself. That is going to have to be someone's job. If it means hiring a guy part-time to start, it's just going to have to be his responsibility—that is, all he does is chase that down.

Darren was caught in a chicken-and-egg dilemma. He knew that CCM needed more sales to be attractive to the retail distributors, and he needed retail distribution to increase sales. Unless he could produce more CDs, Darren's festival performances would not yield the sales volume he needed to keep CCM profitable. Even if he produced another Darren Curtis Skanson CD, he was not sure that it would sell if he could not actively promote it himself. Until his elbow healed, his performance schedule would have to be curtailed.

As CCM's lead performer, Darren had hoped to turn over the sales and managerial functions to others. Now he was forced to rethink his role. Darren knew that he still wanted to perform, but it was clear that he could not keep up his current performance schedule. Should he work harder to get other musicians on board to tour and publicize the CCM name while he acted as master manager and coach? Should he hire a sales manager or focus his energies on getting CCM's products into retail outlets himself? Should he concentrate on recording-studio activities to increase CCM's product offerings and try to push the catalogue sales, which had higher profit margins? Would hiring an experienced marketing manager help Darren uncover new arenas for growth? Could a new salesperson free Darren up to explore alternative performance venues? Or were his talents best directed at refining the CCM "system" and managing the recording studio?

Darren felt that his company was at a crossroads. His first love was music, and he loved to perform, but he knew that his personal satisfaction hinged on building a profitable company. He understood that growth and profitability were directly tied to maintaining and building CCM's customer base. As the plane started its descent into the Orlando airport, Darren tried to ready himself for the performance weekend ahead. But visions of CCM as a sought-after label were not far from his mind. He wished he could build a business as easily as he could serenade a crowd.

case 8 Élan and the Competition Ski Boat Industry

Fiona Nairn
The University of Alabama

A. J. Strickland
The University of Alabama

Ben Favret, professional water-skier, World Champion, U.S. Champion, and Pro-Tour champion, was resting on the dock after a slalom training run one afternoon when a call came through on his cell phone. Jay Blossman, his high school tennis partner and now politician, was on the other end. Out of the blue, Jay announced to Ben that he was buying American Skier, the competition ski boat company owned by financially troubled American Performance Marine. Ben instantly knew that Jay had found himself a great boat and suspected that he was getting a great deal in buying the company, but he also realized that while Jay was an excellent tennis player, Jay lacked the necessary insider knowledge about building, marketing, and selling ski boats. Excited and eager to be involved in this rare opportunity, Ben was on the next flight to New Orleans to meet Jay and look into the situation.

As Ben took the tour of the American Performance Marine plant in Kentwood, Louisiana, he learned that the company had recently filed for bankruptcy. Ben concluded that with his firsthand knowledge of the waterskiing industry and the boat-building capabilities that lay before him in the Kentwood plant, he and Jay ought to be able to resurrect the ailing company. With all the enthusiasm and high hopes of an entrepreneur entering the industry of a sport he loves, Ben Favret dove headfirst into building ski boats. In keeping with this excitement and attitude, Ben renamed the company Élan Boats. (The word élan means "vigorous spirit and enthusiasm.")

HISTORY OF THE COMPETITION SKI BOAT INDUSTRY

Waterskiing began in 1922 when Ralph Samuelson became the first American to invent and ride a pair of water skis. The skis were simply crude wooden boards with rubber

Aimee Hagedorn, author of an earlier case on the competition ski boat industry and graduate of The University of Alabama, was most helpful in helping edit this case. Fiona Nairn, the lead case writer, was the 1998, 1999, and 2001 NCWSA National Collegiate Overall Women's Champion in waterskiing. Aimee Hagedorn was the 1997 and 2001 AWSA Women 2 Slalom National Champion. Information about both of these world-class water skiers can be found on the Internet by putting their names into any of the search engines.

foot straps and were roughly twice the length and width of today's skis. Throughout the 1920s and 1930s, enthusiasm for waterskiing spread; in 1939, the American Water Ski Association (AWSA) was formed as a nonprofit organization to promote the sport. That same year, the first National Water Ski Championships were held. The towboat for the first competition was an open wooden boat built of overlapping boards or strakes (similar to a wood johnboat) and powered by a four-cylinder outboard engine. The national championships were not held during World War II, and recreational boat manufacture was minimal during this time; after the war, however, interest and activity in the recreational boating industry increased as the economy boomed.

During the late 1940s and early 1950s, wooden inboard boats made by Chris-Craft and Century Resorters, along with the Atom Skier by Correct Craft, were favored by most skiers. These boats were the most powerful ski boats of the time, yet skier performance suffered due to the large wakes these boats produced. Boats with outboard motors had a smaller wake but did not have enough power until the advent of the twin-rig concept in the early 1950s. Twin-rig outboards quickly gained popularity among competition skiers and dominated the scene for the rest of the decade and into the 1960s. Companies such as Mercury Marine, Evinrude, and Johnson recognized the potential market in waterskiing and invented the concept of promotional boats, whereby manufacturers provided specially equipped boats for use in waterskiing tournaments. Twin rigs, however, were difficult to set up and had high fuel consumption.

In search of the perfect ski boat, Leo Bentz, who operated a ski school in Florida, designed and built an inboard boat specifically for waterskiing. In the spring of 1960, the first Ski Nautique was displayed at the Southern Regional Championships in Birmingham, Alabama. It was the first inboard made of fiberglass and had a hull design that produced a smaller wake than its predecessors. Originally marketed and sold by Glass Craft Boat Company, the Ski Nautique concept was bought by Correct Craft the following year when Bentz approached the company's owners to sell them his mold. Correct Craft refined the Ski Nautique's design, and the performance of the Ski Nautique brand became a standard for rivals to emulate. The Ski Nautique was highly successful, prompting a resurgence in ski boats with inboard motors.

In 1968, Rob Shirley, a competitive skier, noticed the growing market and absence of much competition among ski boat makers, so he designed and built his own ski boat, known as MasterCraft. Throughout the 1970s and early 1980s, Correct Craft and MasterCraft dominated the market and led the industry in innovations and technology. By the 1980s, inboards came to be used almost exclusively in AWSA-sanctioned tournaments, and many start-up companies tried to compete with the two leaders. Yet there still existed an opportunity for outboards as other water ski disciplines—such as barefooting, kneeboarding, and show skiing—emerged.

RECENT TRENDS IN THE SKI BOAT INDUSTRY

Traditionally, ski boat companies focused their R&D efforts on creating the best pull for the die-hard slalom skiers training on private, sport-specific, man-made lakes. Their top-of-the-line flagship models were endorsed by popular professional skiers and competed against one another to be named as the "official towboats" of prestigious waterski tournaments around the world.

Competition ski boats typically had closed bows with direct drive inboard engines mounted in the center of the boat for optimal balance and performance. This configuration, however, took up a lot of space inside the boat, leaving little room for passengers and cargo. The ski pole was also mounted in the center of the boat to minimize the impact of the skiers' pull on the boat path. Passengers could not sit behind the pole (in the back of the boat) when a skier was being towed because the rope swung back and forth above the rear seats at head height. These boats had sports-car-like handling to navigate the tight dimensions of the man-made lakes and were flat bottomed to produce the desired low and soft wake for slalom skiers to cut through. Because of their flat bottoms, the boats were awful performers in the rough, jarring waters of large public lakes.

In the economic boom of the 1990s, recreational boat sales shot upward, driven partly by the development of easy-to-ride shaped skis and by growing popularity of wakeboards and riding on inner tubes. People who had never seen a slalom course or even knew man-made ski lakes existed were buying recreational boats powered for waterskiing and other water-related activities. More and more "weekend warriors" were hitting public waters and finding that on these large lakes competition ski boats were less than satisfactory for recreational waterskiing and wakeboarding. Wakeboarding—the waterborne equivalent of snowboarding that debuted in the early 1990s—had lower course and equipment requirements and a far easier learning curve than tournament slalom skiing. It was also more social and was generating a cult following among the younger generation. In the second half of the 1990s, there was a massive surge of wakeboarding participants; one of the leading manufacturers in traditional water skis, HO, derived half of its 2000 sales revenues from the sale of wakeboards. Industry leaders MasterCraft and Correct Craft scrambled to cater to this new market niche by producing specialty wakeboard boats. These boats were typically much larger, with an open bow and a V-drive engine mounted in the rear of the boat. The resulting spaciousness allowed for wraparound seating and accommodation of up to 11 people. The boats had built-in ballast systems that filled with water to weight the boat down and create a bigger wake for the riders to launch off, a slalomer's worst nightmare. The boats were additionally equipped with flight towers, which raised the rope up to 86 inches above the water and improved the height wakeboarders got on their aerial maneuvers (see Exhibit 1).

MARKET SIZE AND GROWTH

In 2000, the National Marine Manufacturers Association (NMMA) estimated retail sales of all new and used boats and related products (including motors, engines, accessories, safety equipment, docking, and storage) to be $25.6 billion, a 15 percent increase over sales in 1999. These results reflected a steady growth trend in spending after a sharp dip in the early 1990s (see Exhibit 2). According to industry estimates, there were over 16.9 million recreational boats in use in 2000 and 72.2 million people participating in recreational boating activities (see Exhibit 3). The growth in the number of recreational boats in use had stalled over the past 10 years, and the estimated number of participants had recently declined.

According to the National Sporting Goods Association (NSGA), the number of people participating in waterskiing also dipped in 2000, dropping to 5.9 million, down 18 percent from the 1998 level of 7.2 million (see Exhibit 4). The NSGA study ranked motor boating and waterskiing 13th and 40th, respectively, in terms of participation in the United States. It also noted that 66 percent of power boaters also waterskied. By state, Michigan had the largest number of registered boats, with California and Florida 2nd and 3rd, respectively; the District of Columbia, Hawaii, and Alaska had the least number of registered boats. The United States was the largest boating/water skiing nation in the world, followed by Australia and Canada.

exhibit 1   A Traditional Competition Ski Boat and a Wakeboard Boat

A Traditional Competition Ski Boat

A Wakeboard Boat

Sources: www.correctcraft.com/ski_index.cfm and www.mastercraft.com/showroom/2002/xseries/x_star/index.htm

DEMOGRAPHIC AND MARKET CONDITIONS

Exhibit 5 shows the demographic characteristic of recent boat buyers based on data compiled by National Marine Manufacturers Association (NMMA). Because boats were luxury items, the boating industry suffered during periods of economic decline. In 2001, the U.S. economic doldrums spelled bad news for the industry. Since 1998, NMMA statistics indicated the number of recreational boaters had been declining at a steady 1–2 percent rate, and many industry analysts feared the economic downturn in 2000–2001 would accelerate the decline. Analysts speculated that any spare money consumers had would be reserved for home improvements, education, or maybe even potential unemployment expenses rather than being used for boating-related purchases. The largest segment to be affected was expected to be the newcomers purchasing entry-level boats; a sales decline in this segment would cause ripple effects through the market over the

exhibit 2   Estimated Retail Expenditures on Boating, 1984–2000
               (in billions of dollars)

Year	Retail Expenditures on Boating
1984	$12.34
1985	13.28
1986	14.48
1987	16.50
1988	17.93
1989	17.14
1990	13.73
1991	10.56
1992	10.32
1993	11.25
1994	14.07
1995	17.23
1996	17.75
1997	19.34
1998	19.00
1999	22.21
2000	25.63

exhibit 3   Selected Waterskiing and Boating Statistics, 1998–2000

	2000	1999	1998
People participating in recreational boating	72,269,000	73,208,000	74,847,000
Water-skiers	10,446,000	11,376,000	10,314,000
All boats in use	16,965,200	16,772,600	16,657,200
Outboard boats owned	8,282,300	8,211,200	8,193,500
Inboard boats owned	1,634,900	1,616,800	1,601,000
Stern-drive boats owned	1,708,100	1,665,300	1,620,700
Personal water craft	1,078,400	1,096,000	1,100,000
Sailboats owned	1,642,800	1,647,300	1,669,000
Miscellaneous water craft (canoes, etc.)	997,800	973,000	949,000
Other unregistered boats and water craft	1,620,900	1,563,000	1,524,000
Outboard motors owned	8,696,400	8,621,800	8,603,200
Inboard engines owned (includes gasoline, diesel, and jet-drive marine engines)	2,157,100	2,133,200	2,112,400
Boat trailers owned	7,455,600	7,313,700	7,170,900
Marina, boatyards, yacht clubs, dockominiums, parks, and other	12,000	11,500	10,320

Note: $25,629,734,000 was spent at retail during 2000 for new and used boats, motors and engines, trailers, accessories, and other associated costs. There were 12,746,301 boat registrations as of December 31, 1999, for the United States and territories.

exhibit 4   Number of Participants* Seven Years of Age and Older in
Selected Sports, 1990–2000 (in millions)

Sport	2000	1998	1996	1994	1992	1990
Exercise walking	86.3	77.6	73.3	70.8	67.8	71.4
Swimming	60.7	58.2	60.2	60.3	63.1	67.5
Camping	49.9	46.5	44.7	42.9	47.3	46.2
Fishing	49.3	43.6	45.6	45.7	47.6	46.9
Bicycle riding	43.1	43.5	53.3	49.8	54.6	55.3
Golf	26.4	27.5	23.1	24.6	24.0	23.0
Hiking	24.3	27.2	26.5	25.3	21.6	22.0
Boating, motor/power	24.2	25.7	28.8	26.4	22.3	28.6
Running/jogging	22.8	22.5	22.2	20.6	21.9	23.8
Skiing (alpine)	7.4	7.7	10.5	10.6	10.8	11.4
Snorkeling	5.5	7.3	7.1	5.9	4.8	n.a.
Waterskiing	**5.9**	**7.2**	**7.4**	**7.4**	**7.9**	**10.5**
Canoeing	6.2	7.1	8.4	8.5	7.2	8.9
Snowboarding	4.3	3.6	3.1	2.1	1.2	1.5
Sailing	2.5	3.6	4.0	4.1	3.5	4.9
Kayaking/rafting	3.1	3.2	3.6	n.a.	n.a.	n.a.
Skiing (cross-country)	2.3	2.6	3.4	3.6	3.5	5.1
Scuba diving (open water)	1.6	2.6	2.4	2.2	2.2	2.6
Surfboarding	1.2	1.3	n.a.	n.a.	n.a.	1.5
Windsurfing	0.5	0.6	0.7	0.7	0.8	0.9

n.a. = not available
*Must have participated more than once to qualify as a participant.
Source: National Sporting Goods Association, Mount Prospect, Illinois.

exhibit 5   Demographic Characteristics of Boat Buyers in 2000

	Total	Cruiser	Runabout	Fishing Fiberglass	Fishing Aluminum	PWC Owners
Median age	48	50	44	46	46	37
Median income (000)	$71	$134	$67	$64	$53	$68
Owners with children 18 years old and younger	37%	33%	42%	41%	41%	53%
Married	86%	86%	84%	89%	85%	73%
Managerial, professional, executive	48%	70%	49%	44%	35%	53%
Retired	14%	11%	13%	9%	14%	2%
Other	38%	19%	38%	47%	51%	45%

Source: National Marine Manufacturers Association, 2000.

2002–2005 period, as a dearth of first-time buyers in 2001 would mean fewer people moving on to purchase more upscale second and third boats in 2003–2005. Furthermore, to the extent that income-constrained households opted out of recreational boating, a surge of used boats would flood the market, putting downward pressure on new and used boat prices and the volume of new boat sales. Unsold 2001 boats would sit in inventory until the 2002 boating season, adversely impacting prices on both the 2001 and new

2002 models. However, an upside to economic downturns was that technology and innovation always seemed to accelerate in troubled times, as the leading companies strove to carve out every competitive edge possible in a dwindling market.

It was estimated that interest in waterskiing would double if competition skiing became an Olympic event. Over the past 10 years, the International Water Ski Federation (IWSF) and its 92 member federations worldwide (over 30 million skiers) had worked hard at lobbying the International Olympic Committee (IOC). But inclusion of waterskiing as an Olympic sport had been delayed over concerns about variations among towboat brands and the influence of the boat driver. A skier's performance could be affected by a boat driver's error and/or bias. However, the introduction of cruise control systems such as Perfect Pass and Accu-ski had eliminated driver error (driving slower than or faster than actual speed), and videotaping the driver's boat path was implemented to control bias (moving the boat to either help or hurt the skier). Waterskiing came very close to being included in the 2004 games in Athens. The Athens committee had unanimously accepted waterskiing as their sole choice of new sports to be added, and the IWSF was confident that it had cleared the last hurdle. However, in December 2000 the IOC announced that the number of athletes at the games was to be kept under 10,000 and no new sports were to be added. IWSF was now focusing its sights on the 2008 games in Beijing, where waterskiing was highly supported.

Despite being excluded from the Olympics, waterskiing and wakeboarding were included in many other high-profile multisport events, such as the World Games, X-games, and Gravity Games. The 2001 World Games hosted in Akita, Japan, included sports not yet part of the Olympic program, namely powerlifting, karate, and rugby. Wakeboarding also enjoyed exposure in both the ESPN X-games and the Gravity Games. These extreme sports events were centered on action, music, and lifestyle. In 2000, the Gravity Games drew 370,000 spectators to Providence, Rhode Island, and their NBC telecast drew a Nielsen rating of 1.6, making it the highest-rated action sports event of the year. The Gravity Games included 250 athletes from 17 countries competing in 16 sports. MasterCraft had agreed to a three-year contract to be the exclusive provider of the towboat for the Gravity Games.

BOAT SHOWS

Boat shows were a key boat-selling tool and very influential in the boat-buying process. The boating industry held approximately 200 boat shows annually across the nation. Research confirmed that almost all recent buyers had attended at least one boat show and that two-thirds attended one or more boat shows during the six months prior to purchase. More than 40 percent of recent new boat buyers either ordered their boat at a show or bought it from a dealer they spoke with at a show. For both boat manufacturers and retail dealers, boat shows were an occasion to compare competitive products and test buyer response. Guided by the amount of consumer interest generated at national and regional shows, manufacturers would decide how many of each model boat to manufacture for the upcoming year, how best to market each product, and where to focus advertising efforts. Dealers would also base their orders on the consumer interest indicated at regional and local shows. Interest level was gauged by the percentage of people coming through a dealer's or manufacturer's booth at a show and expressing an interest to buy as well as by the number of boats sold at the show.

Of specific interest to competition ski boat manufacturers was the Wakeboard and Waterski Expo, a trade show for the industry held in September each year in Orlando, Florida. While the ski boat industry and the water-ski industry in general tended to get overlooked at the large marine trade shows such as the International Marine Trades

exhibit 6   Information Sources Used to Shop for Boats

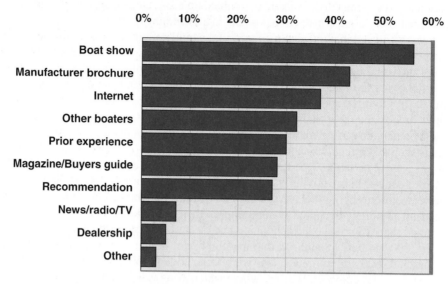

Source: J. D. Power and Associates, 2001 Marine Sales and Service Study, p. 17.

Exhibit and Convention, the Wakeboard and Waterski Expo focused on these two watersport segments. Manufacturers were able to network and introduce their new products to dealers and retailers without getting lost in the crowd.

As a follow-up selling method, manufacturers like Correct Craft encouraged their dealers to host Demo Days on weekends after the boat shows. These were generally invitation-only affairs for serious buyers whom salespeople had met at the show. At these events prospective buyers were able to test-drive and inspect the product. A recent study by J. D. Power and Associates showed that the 32 percent of buyers who took test drives before deciding on which boat to purchase reported much higher levels of satisfaction than those who did not test-drive.

LEADING FACTORS IN CHOOSING A SKI BOAT

For the majority of consumers, the quality of a ski boat was judged according to several factors: reliability and durability, wake and spray characteristics, and performance (tracking and turning ability, speed control, and engine power). A market tracking study conducted by the Water Sports Industry Association (WSIA) revealed that price and quality were the most important factors in the brand selection of boats and water-ski products for the general population of water-skiers; quality and brand reputation were more important for experienced skiers. The main concern of 77 percent of potential new boat buyers was the cost of purchasing and maintaining a boat. This was also a main concern for 65 percent of former owners and 46 percent of recent buyers.

For the average buyer, the time taken between deciding to purchase a boat and actually signing on the dotted line was six months. This lapse was attributed to two main causes: (1) a desire to select the right type of boat from the vast array available and (2) the difficulty of obtaining reliable information. To combat the lack of readily available and reliable information, potential buyers visited boat shows, consulted manufacturer's brochures, researched on the Internet, and talked with friends and other boaters (see Exhibit 6).

A recent survey by J. D. Power and Associates revealed that the main source of consumer dissatisfaction was the level of after-sale service from their dealership's service department. "Plugging the service gap" was a major concern of the industry. The J. D. Power report said, "The biggest issue is the time a customer has to give up a boat to have it serviced. Given the relatively short boating season in certain portions of the country, the ability of a dealer's service department to diagnose and fix problems quickly is paramount." The study also strongly indicated that the manufacturers whose dealerships had efficient service departments were "much more likely to retain that customer next time they are in the market for a new boat."

The sport expanded rapidly up until the mid-1990s, becoming the fastest-growing segment in the marine industry. Personal water craft (PWC) sales peaked in 1995, with 200,000 units sold at an average cost of $6,300, equal to $1.2 billion in sales. Ever since then, unit sales had spiraled dramatically downward. In 2000, only 92,000 PWC were sold. On average, each unit cost $7,800, generating sales of nearly $720 million (see Exhibit 7). There were approximately 1.1 million PWCs in use in the year 2000 (see Exhibit 3). The decline in PWC use was partly attributable to the rowdy manner in which some were operated, earning PWCs a bad reputation among boaters and law enforcers alike. Also, because of numerous accidents (mostly from lack of product use education), many regulations had been imposed on the vehicles. In 1997, there were 83 fatalities associated with PWCs. According to the U.S. Coast Guard, 506 people had been killed and more than 11,000 injured during the last 10 years of PWC use. The Coast Guard claimed that a PWC user was six times as likely to be injured on a PWC as in a motorboat. One alarming statistic about PWC safety was that the leading cause of death was not drowning in a PWC accident but rather blunt trauma from crashing into stationary objects or other boats.

A new concept that expanded the PWC market was the Solo. Founder Robin Sells designed the Solo for people who loved to ski on smooth, quiet early-morning waters but had trouble rounding up the family or friends required for the legal trio of driver, observer, and skier. The Solo, which retailed for around $7,000, resembled a riderless PWC and was maneuvered by the water-skier using controls in the towrope—Nintendo style. The Solo towrope was 40 feet long, shorter than the standard 75-foot line used for skiing. The Solo could reach speeds of up to 40 mph and was powered by a two-stroke, 95 horsepower Polaris engine. When the skier fell, either the two kill-switches on the handle or the one attached as a lanyard to the skier's life jacket shut down the engine. The Solo was legal in 40 states, but there were many concerns over its safety. Opponents were concerned about the visibility of the small Solo craft to other boats and the ability of a water skier to control both the skis and the boat at the same time. Issues about injured fallen skiers who were unable to swim back to the craft had also been raised.

Another way to enjoy waterskiing without owning a boat was to patronize a cable park, where an overhead cable towed a water-skier around a lake. This concept was extremely popular in Europe and was beginning to take hold in the United States thanks to the rising numbers of young wakeboarders who wanted to ride but couldn't afford a boat or were too young to drive. The world's largest cable park was a 14-hectare lake in a high-profile location along the Bee Line Highway in Orlando Florida. This unique park had two cables, one specifically for slalom and one for wakeboarding; according to estimates, 70 percent of the park's users were wakeboarders. The complex had capacity for 600 skiers a day, with each cable carrying up to 9 skiers at a time. Local boat company Correct Craft did not see the cable park as a threat but rather as a way to introduce newcomers who would eventually become boat buyers. Other cable parks in

exhibit 7   Selected Statistics for the Pleasure and Ski Boat Market, 1998–2000

	1998*	1999*	2000
Outboard boats			
Total units sold	213,700	230,200	241,600
Retail value	$1,547,188,000	$1,988,928,000	$2,256,544,000
Average unit cost	$7,240	$8,640	$9,340
Outboard motors			
Total units sold	314,000	331,900	348,700
Retail value	$2,155,610,000	$2,602,096,000	$2,901,881,400
Average unit cost	$6,865	$7,840	$8,322
Boat trailers			
Total units sold	174,000	168,000	167,000
Retail value	$189,660,000	$190,008,000	$195,390,000
Average unit cost	$1,090	$1,131	$1,170
Inboard boats—runabouts			
Total units sold	10,900	12,100	13,200
Retail value	$253,348,700	$308,429,000	$340,494,000
Average unit cost	$23,243	$25,490	$25,795
Inboard boats—cruisers			
Total units sold	6,700	7,000	8,000
Retail value	$1,704,245,500	$1,799,420,000	$2,349,920,000
Average unit cost	$254,365	$257,060	$293,740
Stern-drive boats			
Total units sold	77,700	79,600	77,800
Retail value	$1,746,696,000	$2,054,476,000	$2,228,192,000
Average unit cost	$22,480	$25,810	$28,640
Canoes			
Total units sold	107,800	121,000	111,800
Retail value	$64,033,200	$67,034,000	$64,844,000
Average unit cost	$594	$554	$580
Personal water craft			
Total units sold	130,000	106,000	92,000
Retail value	$868,530,000	$771,044,000	$720,176,000
Average unit cost	$6,681	$7,274	$7,828
Jet boats			
Total units sold	10,100	7,800	6,500
Retail value	$124,644,100	$132,678,000	$118,820,000
Average unit cost	$12,341	$17,010	$18,280
Sailboats*			
Total units sold	18,200	21,200	27,800
Retail value	N/A	$589,360,000	N/A
Average unit cost	N/A	$27,800	N/A

*1998 and 1999 market estimates revised in 2000.
N/A = not available.
Source: 2000 Annual Sailing Business Review.

the United States were in North Carolina and southern Florida, where day passes ran around $35 and hourly slots could be bought for $15.

SUPPLIERS TO THE INBOARD BOAT MANUFACTURERS

The major suppliers to the inboard boat industry were engine manufacturers Indmar, PCM, and MerCruiser. Of the 17 inboard manufacturers whose boats were reviewed in *WaterSki* magazine's 2001 Boat Buyer's Guide, four powered their products with PCM engines, four with Indmar, and six with MerCruiser. As the world's largest privately held manufacturer of gasoline-powered inboard marine engines, Indmar supplied the lion's share of inboard engines to the makers of ski/wakeboard boats, including industry leaders MasterCraft and Malibu. Almost 85 percent of Indmar's business came from the sale of private-label engines, with MasterCraft being its largest private-label customer. Indmar offered these customers an exclusive customization and calibrations program called Power Partners, in which engines were dialed in specifically for the performance and application needs specific to the boatmaker's products. This program covered initial engine development, prototype installation, and extensive field testing.

Under its private-label agreement with MasterCraft, Indmar was the first engine manufacturer to bring electronic fuel injection (EFI) to the inboard market. To counter the harsh marine environment, the company worked closely with American automobile manufacturers to develop an EFI system robust enough to withstand the rugged, wet conditions. The resulting engines were highly efficient because of a three-dimensional computerized management system that controlled all aspects of combustion. The optimum mix of fuel, air, and spark was delivered to compensate for changing load demands, weather conditions, gasoline quality, and altitude changes. The main payoff from owning an EFI engine was turnkey starting (prior generations of inboard motors were notoriously difficult to start), smoother and faster acceleration, increased fuel economy, and reduced emissions. Indmar manufactured its own subcomponents for its engines, choosing not to expose itself to what it considered the hit-and-miss quality standards of outside suppliers.

Over the years, Indmar had achieved considerable name recognition and brand awareness within the waterskiing industry. This was due mainly to its sponsorship and support of numerous professional tournaments as well as to being visible at grassroots waterskiing competitions around the nation.

THE PLEASURE AND SKI BOAT MARKET

The $4.3 billion pleasure and ski boat market had three main segments: inboards, outboards, and stern drives (inboard/outboards). Inboards were further classified as either runabouts or cruisers, and runabouts could have an open or closed bow. Outboards, stern drives, and inboard runabouts were generally 16 to 25 feet long, while cruisers were anywhere from 30 to 50 feet long. Traditionally, outboards were the biggest sellers, followed by stern drives and inboards, although outboard and stern-drive manufacturers had always outnumbered inboard manufacturers. Over the past 20 years, sales for each segment had fluctuated, with each segment experiencing intermittent periods of increasing and decreasing sales (see Exhibit 7). An estimated 8.2 million boaters owned outboards, 1.7 million owned stern drives, and 1.6 million owned inboards. There were approximately 17 million pleasure and ski boats in use in 2000.

In 2000, 13,200 inboard boats were sold at an average price of $25,795, generating industry revenues of $340 million (up 10 percent from 1999). The outboard and

exhibit 8   An Outboard Boat

stern-drive segments also displayed strong growth in 2000, while the personal water craft sector declined sharply—see Exhibit 7.

Outboards

Perhaps the greatest advantage of outboard ski boats (see Exhibit 8) was that they had excellent maneuverability, especially at low speeds. Also, with the trim function, they had the ability to cruise through shallow waters with little difficulty. Outboards generally had good power at top speeds and relatively low noise levels. Power steering was offered on some models, with power trimming usually a standard feature. Engines could be easily upgraded. Outboards were roomy as well, with plenty of walk-around and storage room. However, outboards did not make very good ski boats for several reasons. First, they had turbulent wakes and a rough table (the flat part in between the crests of the wake); second, they had marginal handling ability in ski sites with tight dimensions; and, third, their controls lacked the smoothness and precision needed for serious competition skiing. They were not as naturally balanced as inboards, and they had no platform on the back of the boat for the convenience and ease of putting on skis.

Another disadvantage of outboards was that they required a specially trained mechanic for tune-ups, adjustments, and repairs. Typically, outboards did not come "packaged" from the manufacturer; that is, the controls for steering, throttle, shift, and trim had to be set by a mechanic, although some manufacturers had begun prepackaging their products.

Competition Inboards

Competition inboards had a closed bow and a direct-drive tournament inboard motor. These 19- to 20-foot-long boats were excellent performers, designed with the serious skier's needs and demands in mind. For riders, their most noticeable aspects were their sports-car feel and fingertip control. Competition inboards had quick and easy handling in tight dimensions, excellent tracking ability, and low steering effort and play, resulting in easy operator effort. Standard features on inboards included a precise speedometer, some form of cruise control, a tachometer, a large dash-mounted mirror, a platform, and a ski pylon (an upright steel bar mounted in front of the engine to which ski ropes can be attached). Engine installation for inboards was simpler than for outboards and stern drives, and was easily built into the overall design of the boat.

Inboard engines were mounted in the center of the boat and were therefore easily serviceable. Since the propeller was fixed, there was no trimming function. Wakes were defined at lower speeds and small at higher speeds, making them suitable (and desirable) for slaloming, tricking, and jumping, while spray coming from the back of the boat was minimal.

The greatest drawbacks of inboards included less-than-adequate slow-speed handling (because only the rudder was being turned), high interior and drive-by noise level, less interior and storage space due to the centrally mounted engine, and high retail prices. Yet the resale value of inboards, whether open or closed bow, was generally the highest of all the ski boat types. This was attributed to the high quality, durability, and long life of inboards, as well as to the fact that the inboard market was the smallest of the four segments.

Open-Bow/Family Pleasure Boats

Open-bow boats began appearing in the early 1980s in response to demand from both recreational and serious skiers who had growing families but also wanted a quality water ski boat with more room and luxury features. Open-bow inboards were nearly comparable to their closed-bow counterparts in performance and standard features, yet they were longer (20 to 24 feet) and wider than the closed-bow boats, thus offering increased roominess and comfort. Because of differing demands, the family inboards usually came in a variety of models and styles. Perhaps the only complaint of the open bow was that the ride in the front of the boat was not as smooth as in the back of the boat, sometimes resulting in a "wet ride" as water splashed up over the nose of the boat. Many new buyers of family inboards included those who, after skiing behind an inboard, decided to convert from a stern-drive boat.

Stern Drives/(Inboard/Outboards)

Stern drives combined attributes of both inboards and outboards. The actual engine was housed inside the boat with the propeller extending out the back, much like an outboard. There was the runabout-sized boat, ranging in length from 17 to 20 feet, and the family-sized boat, at lengths of 20 to 23 feet. These boats had historically been aimed at recreational boaters and skiers by not providing such "serious" skier necessities as a rearview mirror, a ski pylon, a platform, and precise speedometers and steering/tracking ability. However, many stern-drive manufacturers were making serious inroads toward "skier-izing" their products.

Like the outboard, stern-drive boats had excellent maneuverability and low-speed control as well as power steering and the trimming function to aid in speed, tracking and acceleration, and shallow-water operations. They were also relatively quiet and roomy, with plenty of walk-about room and storage capacity. Like inboards, stern drives had marinized automotive engines, allowing for easy serviceability. The bow usually stayed dry, yet it had a high planing attitude, thereby impairing drivers' visibility at the start of the ride. Such planing attitude resulted in a well-defined wake for tricking but turbulent wakes for slaloming.

V-Drives

As the demand for "watersports towboats" grew, a new niche for boating manufacturers was created. The V-drive evolved to fill the gap and gained prominence in the early to mid-1990s. The V-drive offered the in-boat roominess of a stern drive combined with more comparable performance to its direct-drive inboard counterparts. Due to the rear positioning of the V-drive, a ski boat no longer had to be cramped by a center-mounted engine; ski boats thus suddenly became acceptable to mom and the kids. Wakewise, the V-drives were adequate for slaloming and excellent for wakeboarding, tubing, and family boating.

The advantages over a stern drive were the increase in power due to the lack of a complex gear train. Also, as the propeller was fixed under the boat's hull rather than extending off the stern (as both stern drives and outboards do), it was much safer and allowed for a ski platform to be attached, as in a competition inboard for skier convenience. The V-drive was the basis for the specialty wakeboard boat. Having the engine in the rear meant a bigger, peakier wake for boarders to launch off, and the increased room inside the boat was ideal for the bring-all-your-friends wakeboard culture.

INNOVATIONS IN COMPETITION INBOARDS

In the sport of competition waterskiing, the boat driver had always been an extremely influential factor. A biased boat driver had the ability to make or break a skier's performance by playing with the throttle to make the boat go faster or slower than regulation. Since the push to make the sport an Olympic event required the boat driver's influence to be eliminated, a market for cruise control systems for ski boats was created. The two main cruise control system players in 2001 were Perfect Pass and Accuski, with Perfect Pass gaining overwhelming market share and consumer acceptance. The Perfect Pass system required the driver to enter the weight of the skier and the desired speed. The cruise control then set and monitored the engine revolutions to produce incredibly accurate and even boat performance, which relegated the driver's role to that of steering the boat in a straight, true path for the skier. The Perfect Pass system came with a circular in-dash display that replaced one of the boat's speedometers. By 2001, the Perfect Pass system had become so standard that in most cases it was being preinstalled at boat factories before shipping. Although the system was originally designed for competition skiers, a cheaper scaled-down version included on recreational model boats improved the skiing and driving experience at all levels.

Another recent industry advance was an increase in engine horsepower and torque, precipitated largely by boat manufacturers' efforts to partner with engine makers in making private-label engines especially for their boat models. Engines with 310 horsepower became the standard, with some monster engines over 400 horsepower also available. MasterCraft boats produced The Beast, a competition inboard boat with a 450 horsepower engine designed specifically to tow the spectacular new Ski Flying event. Ski Flying, in which skiers set the boat speed at 45 mph to launch themselves over 300 feet in the air off a six-foot-high ski ramp, required enormous engine power.

To cater to the new breed of boater who wanted the versatility of a boat that combined slalom, wakeboarding, tubing, and family boating in one, manufacturers had begun to offer a wider range of models and styles. The demand for "watersports towboats" was created when the general boating public became dissatisfied with the inability of competition ski boats to perform all the different functions they were looking for. The family pleasure boating segment was many times larger than the competition towboats preferred by competition skiers practicing their routines on private lakes. Consequently, a flood of boat models sporting such family-oriented features as more room, wraparound seating, and greater versatility were introduced in the 1990s. MasterCraft led the charge with its Maristar Sport-V concept in 1993. The Maristar's all-around characteristics had wide mass appeal, and MasterCraft aggressively marketed this model to a variety of boat users. To take the versatility concept even further, manufacturers began to implement systems that changed the characteristics of a boat's wake and the way it performed, depending on the type of watersport being undertaken. The manufacturer of the Tige brand came up with the Tige Adjustable Performance System, a skid plate that sat behind the propeller and adjusted the wake's characteristics; with the flick of a switch, Tige boats could change from producing low, soft-slalom wakes to big, peaky wakeboard wakes. Along the same lines, Malibu Boats came up with the Malibu Wedge, a similar performance-altering device.

As the sport of wakeboarding evolved, riders came to prefer the biggest wake possible. They piled as many friends and family members into the boat as possible and began loading down their inboards and V-drives with water-filled bladders called fat-sacs. This added weight caused the boat to displace more water, which consequently formed a larger wake when the extra displaced water came back together again behind the boat. The increased number of passengers also meshed nicely with the exhibitionist nature of wakeboarding. A second wakeboarding innovation was to extend the height of the tow pylon by attaching telescopic "high poles." These poles allowed the wakeboarders to get more "lift" off the wake as the higher rope pulled them upward toward the sky. Both the fat-sacs and the high poles became the vogue for waveboarders, but the inconvenience factor of both boat features was significant. Fat-sacs covered the entire floor space and took up to half an hour to fill with a pump-and-tube device pulling water from the lake. The high pole had guy wires attached to the nose of the boat; these were inconvenient and difficult to set up, and the elevated single point of contact made the boat rock unsteadily when a wakeboarder made a hard cut out to the side of the wake. However, boat manufacturers soon introduced specialty wakeboard boats with innovations that solved these problems (see Exhibit 9). A tower was added to eliminate the need for a high pole and also increase steadiness. Clip systems were attached to the tower to hold boards and create more passenger room inside the boat. An inbuilt ballast system made fat-sacs unnecessary, and the tanks could be filled in a matter of minutes with the flick of a switch. High-quality sound systems and inbuilt coolers were also added to enhance the party image of the boat.

USA WATER SKI

USA Water Ski, headquartered in Polk County, Florida, was the national governing body for organized waterskiing in the United States. Affiliated sport divisions included the following:

- American Water Ski Association.
- American Barefoot Club.
- American Kneeboard Association.
- National Collegiate Water Ski Association.
- National Show Ski Association.
- National Water Ski Racing Association.
- American Wakeboard Association.
- Water Skiers with Disabilities Association.

As a nonprofit organization, USA Water Ski's mission was "to promote the growth and development of recreational water skiing, and organizing and governing the sport of competitive water skiing." It was the largest water-ski federation in the world. In 2001,

exhibit 9   Wakeboard Boat Showing Inbuilt Ballast System and Tower

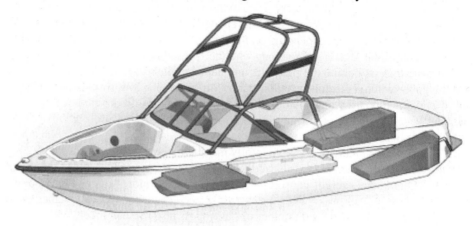

Source: www.correctcraft.com/ballast.cfm

USA Water Ski had a salaried staff of 20 who served 37,500 members in five regions across the country; 60 percent of the organization's members were competitive skiers, and 40 percent were recreational skiers. Three-fourths of USA Water Ski members were college graduates, and many were professionals such as physicians, attorneys, psychologists, business owners, and administrators. Roughly 70 percent of the association's members had yearly household incomes of more than $50,000, and 53 percent had annual incomes of more than $65,000.

The backbone of USA Water Ski was the 630 affiliated active water-ski clubs that existed across the United States in 2001. It was mainly through these clubs that USA Water Ski was able to grow its membership base. Clubs provided volunteers and workers for any local USA Water Ski programs, put on ski shows, hosted tournaments, and held clinics for water-ski instruction, as well as instruction for tournament officials. Yet another supporting branch of AWSA was the American Water Ski Educational Foundation (AWSEF). This entity maintained the Water Ski Museum/Hall of Fame, supervised college scholarship programs, and helped support U.S. water-ski teams in recognized international competitions. Additionally, USA Water Ski was a member of the International Water Ski Federation, the world governing body of waterskiing, and was an Affiliated Sports Organization member of the U.S. Olympic Committee.

In 2001, USA Water Ski sanctioned some 800 tournaments. These tournaments ranged from small, fun competitions for beginners to World Championship tournaments and cash-prize professional events. To compete in USA Water Ski–sanctioned tournaments, one had to be an active member, which cost $50 per year. Membership provided $10,000 medical and liability insurance, a subscription to *The Water Skier* magazine (published nine times a year), and eligibility for special offers and programs (including legislative/regulatory assistance concerning the use of local waterways, water-ski instructor certification, and towboat insurance).

For traditional three-event waterskiing competitions held under the auspices of the American Water Ski Association, the largest of USA Water Ski's sport divisions, skiers competed in one of five regions based on where they lived or skied: the West, Midwest, South, South Central, or East. On the basis of the number of members, the Midwest was the largest AWSA region.

REGULATORY DEVELOPMENTS

As the number of boating and waterskiing participants grew, the nation's waterways became increasingly crowded. Safety, courtesy, and environmental issues became more prevalent, sometimes drawing debate and controversy. Speed limit, noise limits, and environmental laws to regulate boat wakes and protect against bank erosion had been imposed on boaters/skiers by virtually every state. In 1991, Florida's Department of Natural Resources proposed legislation to establish a statewide boating speed limit of 30 mph for all waters. The boating industry feared that if such a bill was passed, other states might follow suit.

In response to such actions, USA Water Ski created a Waterways Education Committee that focused on educating skiers about legislation and teaching them how to organize to fight adverse legislation and burdensome regulations. The committee compiled a database of each state's laws and regulations concerning use of the waterways, produced a manual on how to lobby legislatures, and explored the development of a lawyer/lobby referral service made up of USA Water Ski members.

BOAT TESTS

In 1983, AWSA began testing ski boats to encourage manufacturers to strive for continuous improvement in their products and to certify towboats for use in USA Water Ski–sanctioned tournaments, including traditional three-event, kneeboard, barefoot, show ski, collegiate, and disabled tournaments. USA Water Ski's Towboat and Speed Control committees, technical experts, and elite water-ski athletes conducted the annual evaluations. Each boat had to pass a series of 11 tests and subtests to qualify as an approved towboat; boats were evaluated on

- Power and acceleration.
- Handling and maneuverability.
- Engineering.
- Drivability.
- Sound level.
- Slalom course center-line drivability.
- Slalom spray.
- Jumping center-line deviation.
- Jumping wake.
- Slalom wake.
- Tricks wake.

Each approved towboat met or exceeded a set of predefined standards on each of the above tests to ensure optimum conditions in tournaments. Once a boat was approved, manufacturers were encouraged to participate in sanctioned tournaments. If the manufacturer was involved in a predetermined number of tournaments, its towboats were eligible to pull the Regional Championships. If a manufacturer's towboat met the tournament quota and pulled Regionals, its towboats could pull skiers in the U.S. National Championships, the largest water-ski competition in the world, where more than 800 contestants competed in 24 divisions over five days. At the 2001 National Championships, the only manufacturers qualified were Malibu, Correct Craft, MasterCraft, and Infinity.

In 1982, only four towboats were in use at competitions. Since the inception of the boat tests in 1983, the number of manufacturers participating and the number of boats tested had steadily increased. For 2001, 12 boats passed the rigorous tests. These included Correct Craft's Ski Nautique, the Infinity ZX-1 closed bow and open bow, the Malibu Response LX, MasterCraft's ProStar 190 and 197, and the American Skier Pro (Élan).

ENTRY BARRIERS AND MANUFACTURING COSTS

Capital expenditures to start a boat company were the industry's largest barrier to entry. The R&D, shaping, and design of a new boat mold cost in excess of $400,000 per model. A less expensive route was to buy or modify an existing mold at a cost of around $100,000. To produce 100 boats per year, at least a 20,000-square-foot facility was required; minimum-scale plants cost a minimum of $350,000. Tools, vehicles, employee training, office equipment, and staffing could run $100,000 or more. Construction time for one boat was approximately 10 to 13 days, depending on the model and the features.

A second barrier to entry was customer loyalty to the well-established names of MasterCraft, Malibu, and Correct Craft. These three industry leaders had established large dealer networks and were able to achieve greater economies of scale in manufacturing by getting orders early and planning production. Additionally, because of their size, they had the advantage of greater bargaining power over suppliers and received lower pricing, better terms, and reduced shipping costs.

Because of the capital requirements and manufacturing and design know-how, actual and potential participants in the competition ski boat market consisted mainly of existing boat manufacturers that viewed the ski boat segment as an attractive opportunity.

COMPETITIVE RIVALRY

Competition in inboard ski boats was centered mainly on differentiation, innovation, and quality. Some companies also relied on their visibility and long-standing brand-name recognition in the industry; a few manufacturers competed on the basis of lower prices, although there had been no price wars in the industry as yet. Manufacturers sold their products to retail dealers, who in turn sold to the general public.

Most companies did the majority of their advertising in boating and waterskiing magazines, and promoted their products at boat shows, major pro tournaments, and amateur tournaments. Many also had a promotional boat program in which the company chose certain interested individuals with some degree of influence in their skiing community to use its product as a "promo boat." These promo boats were taken to local and regional tournaments for use and exposure. A promo person received a new boat each year at a discounted price under an agreement to use it in a specified number of tournaments within his or her region. The owner was reimbursed for charges incurred to transport the boat and also received a stipend for each tournament in which the boat participated. The owner was usually responsible for the sale of the boat at the end of the competition season.

The latest study by Statistical Surveys revealed a closely fought battle between MasterCraft and Malibu Boats for the number one position in the ski boat market—see Exhibit 10.

MASTERCRAFT

MasterCraft was the world's largest manufacturer of inboard towboats and luxury performance inboards. According to data compiled by Statistical Surveys, the company

exhibit 10   Estimated Sales of Competition Ski Boats, First Six
Months of 2001

Ski Boat Brand	Second Quarter, 2001	First Six Months, 2001	First Six Months, 2000
MasterCraft	1,091	1,434	1,530
Malibu Boats	1,056	1,392	1,518
Correct Craft	589	764	951
Skier's Choice	467	605	573
Tige Boats	362	473	487
Centurion	241	323	289
M. B. Sports	77	120	125
Sanger Boats	75	102	127
Calabria Boats	64	85	84
Ski Supreme	35	52	33
Gekko	35	44	43
Toyota	29	36	99
American Skier (Élan)	6	10	7
Infinity Ski Boats	5	9	7

Source: Statistical Surveys Inc. study, November 2001, p. 33.

ranked number one in retail sales in 2000, with a 30 percent market share in the competitive inboard category; Mastercraft led all manufacturers in both retail sales and market share in the United States in 1999. However, Statistical Surveys' data did not include international sales or unregistered sales on private lakes, which, according to MasterCraft president John Dorton, had increased considerably in 2000–2001.

In 2000, when other ski boat companies were struggling due to a less-than-favorable economic situation, MasterCraft reported a production sellout. In fact, 2000 was the best year in MasterCraft's 33-year history. Also, in what was predicted to be a slow winter selling season, MasterCraft's orders for its 2001 product line were up another 10 percent from this all-time high. Scott Crutchfield, Mastercraft's vice president of worldwide sales, attributed the company's strong performance to "having the right product, well-informed dealers and an excellent array of marketing and sales materials that inform, entertain and ultimately, create a reason to buy." MasterCraft's diverse product line included 15 models across its tournament ProStar series, X-series, and Maristar series. This diverse lineup reflected management's vision for MasterCraft—to "create an atmosphere of industry leadership, by offering more choices in models than any other inboard boat company" and "build the best product in every significant inboard category." The MasterCraft ProStar 209/X9 was recently awarded *Powerboat* magazine's Tow Boat of the Year Award, considered by many as the industry's most prestigious award. A sample MasterCraft ProStar model is shown in Exhibit 11.

MasterCraft was founded in 1968, when skier Rob Shirley, unhappy with the quality of boats available for towing ski schools, decided to do something about it. His boat company originated in Florida, then later on was transplanted to Tennessee. MasterCraft had a recently upgraded 172,000-square-foot facility in Vonore, where 485 employees manufactured 16 to 18 boats per day. The company was recently sold in 2000 and bought up by members of the senior management team and their equity partners Poushine Capital Partners LP. Mastercraft's president, John Dorton, believed it was important for managers to be enthusiasts to fully understand the inboard niche.

exhibit 11   Sample MasterCraft Model Displayed in Company's Web
Showroom, 2002

Even though it's a twenty-one footer and weighs in at over 2,700 lbs., the ProStar 209 can dance fancifully and furtively
through the water.

This gentle giant is USA Water Ski's most capable record-producer and a big reason why this MasterCraft was named
2001 Tow Boat of the Year by a leading industry magazine. Our engineers flared out the hull sides to 96 inches, to
keep the running surface nimble, while creating **spacious interior lounging** and **cavernous storage areas**. The
roominess of the 209's open bow is the largest in its class and ideal for housing your family and friends.

Don't be deceived by this behemoth. The ProStar 209 has a **310** hp fuel-injected MasterCraft Power by Indmar engine
with such incredible low-end torque, smooth acceleration and solid pull that you will think it's on steroids. Throttle up!
See how the water transforms from clean-shaven ramps to deep, sexy curls for footers and offers the perfect boost for a
behind-the-rope experience like no other.

In '02, we improved on the Towboat of the Year. How about a new **polished aluminum steering wheel, chrome
throttle knob, thicker windshield extrusion,** new **drip-molded decals** and **MasterView driver's seat?**

**In any package, the 209 delivers wake size and shape for every discipline, proving that this gentle giant
rightfully owns its place in the towboat hierarchy.**

SAMMY DUVALL SPECIAL EDITION: This unique
package offers additional amenities for skiers
demanding distinction. The spacious interior is
wrapped with monochromatic lambskin vinyl and is
accented with Sammy Duvall's embroidered
autograph. Both the trailer and boat have special
edition graphics. Even the standard 330 hp LTR has
Sammy's signature style.

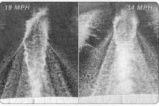

19- AND 34-MPH WAKES: With wakes like these
it's no wonder ski schools are making the ProStar
209 their top choice for transporting and training
elite athletes.

Source: www.mastercraft.com, February 22, 2002.

exhibit 12 Mastercraft X-Trek Concept Boat

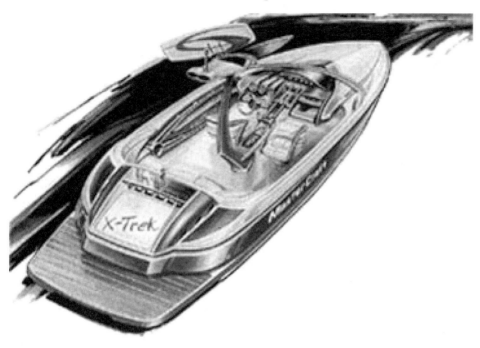

Source: www.mastercraft.com

Consequently, his new management team was made up of watersports and boating aficionados.

Shortly after its inception in 1972, MasterCraft pulled its first nationals and a year later towed its first world record. The now-indispensable swim platform on competition ski boats originated on the back of a MasterCraft, and the company also pioneered the use of triple fins on the underside of the hull for better tracking and handling. In 1984, President Rob Shirley and MasterCraft founded the Water Ski Pro tour, increasing exposure for the company as well as making waterskiing a viable career choice for the sports elite.

In the 1990s, MasterCraft was first-to-market with EFI engines, forcing all other manufacturers to hurriedly play catchup. In 1993, the company rocked the lagging market with its introduction of the V-drive Maristar series, the first of the all-around watersports towboats. MasterCraft aggressively marketed this boat to both water-skiers and industry outsiders, drawing a new type of consumer into the ski-specific market. In 1997 MasterCraft unveiled the X-star, the first true high-performance wakeboard boat. It was a V-drive with standard water ballast system to increase the size of the wakes and had a premium stereo system and an extended pylon to raise the height of the tow rope. The X-Star caused enough of a stir that wake boarders were lined up at dealerships before the boat even arrived. This initial X-Star has since evolved into the 2001 X-Star, a leader in wakeboard boats and the official towboat of the ESPN X-games and the Gravity games.

Enhancing its image of being a revolutionary market leader, MasterCraft recently teamed up with Marine Design Resource Alliance (MDRA) to design, build, and promote the first ever MasterCraft concept boat, The X-Trek (see Exhibit 12). MasterCraft saw the X-Trek concept boat as a way to get consumer feedback without the heavy expense associated with immediately going into production. Concept boats designed in partnership with MDRA were said to have generated over $640,000 in free press coverage.

Despite the company's recent product-line expansion into wakeboard and family boats, the MasterCraft ProStar 190 Evo had remained one of the front runners in competition inboards. The 2001 Evo featured a new and exciting look, with MasterCraft departing from its traditional lines and designing "creases" into the sides of the hull. The hull and deck shape were also completely new.

CORRECT CRAFT

In its fourth generation of family ownership, Correct Craft had a "77-year history on the waters of the world." The company's flagship model, the Ski Nautique, introduced in 1961 was the first tournament inboard boat and had been a major player ever since, claiming more world records than any other towboat on the market.

The Ski Nautique received a massive overhaul in 1997, resulting in the Total Surface Control (TSC) hull, which, according to Correct Craft, produced the flattest, smoothest wakes of any boat on the market. It was deemed to have the perfect "footprint" for a competition inboard and its length of 19 feet, 6 inches and width of 7 feet, 6 inches was widely copied throughout the industry. The TSC owned both the men's and women's world slalom records in 2000. In 2001, Correct Craft did stern-to-stern redesign of the hull, only the fifth in Ski Nautique's 42-year history. The TSC2 featured four major changes that worked together to further enhance the boat's performance. These included keel relief pockets that reduced the rooster tail (a hard plume of water in the center of the wake that adversely affects skier performance), strakes in the hull to give lift while the boat was on plane, a change in the shaft angle to minimize the wake, and a four-blade prop made on a milling machine to ensure that every Nautique performed the same. Additionally, any steering problem of pulling to the left or right could be easily fixed by adjusting the Ski Nautique's turnable rudder. The interior roominess of this redesigned boat increased by 11 percent, a response to users' comments about the need for more space.

The Correct Craft lineup featured eight models in addition to the Ski Nautique. This included two open-bow family direct drives and one open-bow V-drive aimed at skiers and five Air Nautiques, the company's specialty wakeboard boat line. The Air series was made up of three direct-drive boats, for those wanting "do-it-all" versatility, and two V-drive versions, for the really serious wakeboarders.

The Pro Air was the first wakeboard boat to house a totally integrated ballast system. It also sported the industry's first tower (the Flight Control Tower), which replaced the awkward high poles. The Flight Control Tower raised the rope 84 inches above the floor of the boat and was far more stable than a high pole. An added bonus to this innovation was that boards could be strapped to the side of the tower with the Nautique "Flight Clips" board-rack system to reduce equipment clutter in the boat. The flight control towers on the Air Nautique models were a success, and Correct Craft was contesting other companies' towers, which it said infringed on its flight tower patents.

Every boat that came out of the Correct Craft factory was water-tested on a lake before shipment, where, among other things, steering, speed, and noise level were checked. Few other companies could boast such quality-control measures. As an industry first, Correct Craft also offered a "Bumper-to-Bumper Five Year Warranty," which covered everything from stern to stern. The company had paid full retail shop rates for all warranty-covered repairs and services for over 10 years.

exhibit 13   Sample Correct Craft Ad for Ski Nautique

Correct Craft had a comprehensive set of endorsements, sponsoring a large number of tournaments, world champions, record holders and masters champions. Correct Craft and the Ski Nautique had exclusive towboat rights to the World Championships, the Masters Championships, and the Melbourne Masters in Australia, three of the largest and most prestigious water-ski tournaments in the world. Perhaps its most famous sponsored skier was Andy Mapple, the Michael Jordan of slalom. Mapple had been associated with Nautique since 1983, an unprecedented 18 years, and was brought on as product manager to lead the R&D team in the TSC2 hull redesign. Exhibit 13 shows a sample ad for Correct Craft's Ski Nautique.

MALIBU BOATS

Known for innovation and quality, Malibu Boats had won *Powerboat* magazine's TowBoat of the Year award eight times, more than any other boat company. Founded in 1982 by Robert Alkema, an ex–plant manager of the Ski Centurion boat company, Malibu went from being a small upstart to the "most popular inboard boat in the world" (according to *Boating News* magazine). Alkema had a quest for continuous innovation and was often quoted as saying, "Nothing is ever as good as it could be." This constant striving and company-defining out-of-the-box thinking had helped Malibu garner an unparalleled 17 Product Excellence Awards from industry experts.

Headquartered in Merced, California, Malibu was the only player in the industry to have multiple manufacturing sites—its three plants were in California, Tennessee, and Albury, Australia. Malibu had purchased the Australian ski boat company Flight-craft in 1989, and since then had gone on to capture 22 percent of the Australian market. Malibu's sales in Australia had grown 75 percent in the past three years, forcing a plant expansion to twice current capacity. This expansion was expected to push Malibu's Australian market share to 28 percent. According to Xavier West, Malibu Boats of Australia's CEO, "Increased production in the Southern Hemisphere will allow Malibu to supply boats to international sales channels at a much lower freight cost than the Malibu factories stateside."

Malibu's expansions were not just limited to Australia; despite tough U.S. economic conditions in 2000–2001, Malibu experienced rising demand for its models, especially east of the Mississippi. In 2001, Malibu's production increased 12 percent, resulting in a doubling of the Tennessee plant's capacity. Expansion of the Tennessee facility to 89,500 square feet had resulted in lower freight costs and improved customer service to Malibu dealers and owners all over the United States.

One characteristic that distinguished Malibu from its competitors was its employee stock ownership program; in 1989 employees were awarded stock equal to 10 percent of their annual salary. In 2001, Malibu was the only company in the industry with employee stock owners. Malibu operated with a worker-oriented environment in order to promote quality workmanship, reduce defects and warranty costs, and instill greater pride and job satisfaction. Malibu workers were the first in the industry to use computer-aided design in the development of new hulls and decks and the first to use CNC machinery in everyday production.

For 2002, Malibu expanded its product line to 15 models, including the addition of three new wakeboarding boats and a "true cross-training" model. Malibu's wakeboard boats featured the innovative Malibu Wedge concept, a hydrofoil attached to the underside of the boat. Lowering the wedge provided the equivalent of over 1,000 pounds of down force, enhancing the size of the wake without adding weight to the boat.

Malibu sponsored the U.S. Open waterski tournament each year, and in 2001 the company had 23 professional skiers, wakeboarders, and barefooters endorsing its product.

INFINITY BOATS

Rob Shirley, the driving force behind Infinity boats, was also the founding father of industry leader MasterCraft. Shirley sold MasterCraft in 1984 when the company was number one in sales. Rob had decided he wanted to spend more time with his family and moved to the Cayman Islands. But in 1998, Rob's passion for waterskiing and boats reignited and he decided to enter the ski boat industry again. In his opinion, the leaders of the ski boat industry had "lost sight of the competitive skier." According to Shirley, the scramble of manufacturers to satisfy the needs of wakeboarders and the general boating public had left an unfulfilled niche where the "real ski boats" had once been. Shirley believed that the die-hard skiers were being neglected, and to rectify this situation, he set about to make Infinity the best competition ski boat ever.

To make his vision a reality, Shirley had formed a "dream team" that included his son, Mike Shirley, and friends Kris La Point and Gary Mahler. Kris La Point was an incredible slalom champion who had dominated the sport for decades. Kris was the world record holder five times, masters champion eight times, and a prolific winner on the pro circuit. Gary Mahler was a well-respected tournament boat driver who served as the national director of the AWSA and was a representative on the boat drivers committee. Mike Shirley was also an accomplished skier, and his skills were augmented by a

exhibit 14   Sample Infinity Ad

degree in mechanical engineering. The resulting collaboration became known as Infinity Ski Boats.

According to Rob Shirley, "The mission of Infinity Ski Boats is to build the finest boats available. But that's not all. Our commitment is to total innovation, constant testing and continuing improvement, which means new and exciting boats for serious water skiers." Reflecting this mission, Infinity's marketing approach focused on performance, and not just that of the boat, but the improved performance of the skier behind the boat. A slogan in an Infinity print advertisement read, "The ZX-1 is a hard core competition ski boat made for one reason: to help skiers ski better" (see Exhibit 14). The strategy of catering entirely to the avid skier was also reflected in Infinity's very narrow product line, which consisted of only three boats: the ZX-1 closed bow, the almost identical ZX-1 open bow, and a wakeboard offering.

The ZX-1 featured many radical innovations. The center-mounted inboard motor sat farther back than in most boats, while the prop and rudder were positioned farther forward. This meant the ZX-1 felt much smaller than it really was; its 20 feet in length handled more like 16 or 17 feet, making it more nimble than its competitors. The Infinity's gas tank was situated in the middle of the boat (as opposed to the normal position in the back). The end result was a boat that planed quickly, accelerated faster, and had lower wakes than any other competition ski boat. The angle of Infinity's drive shaft was set at 12 degrees in order to reduce prop slippage and increase efficiency; most boats ran at 16 degrees. Because of this, the ZX-1 planed at a lower speed and had no bow rise, running at 3 degrees bow up versus an industry average of 5 degrees. A lower bow rise meant the driver had greater visibility of the water in front of the boat. In an effort to please the competitive skier, Infinity designed a built-in spray trap system to eliminate spray off the side of the boat. This was a crucial feature for short-line slalom skiers who were distracted by spray hitting their face when crossing the wake. The ZX-1, with its novel engine setup, combined with other space-saving initiatives, was the most spacious competition ski boat on the market.

In recognition of Infinity's commitment to producing a focused competition ski boat, Infinity qualified to pull the National Championships in its very first year of production. This was an industry first, as all other boats usually took many years to reach this pinnacle of achievement.

Infinity was comparatively a very small company. In 2000, Infinity's 45 employees produced approximately 10 units per week and had dealer orders through the entire model year. The company had established 20 dealerships in key boating markets. Infinity boats were manufactured outside of Orlando, Florida, where Shirley's second company, Specialty Marine Group, produced custom dive boats. Because of the company's small size, personal touches were made to each of its products; Kris La Point took every boat to the lake to personally set up the Perfect Pass cruise control system.

While the competitive skier niche was small, Infinity's marketing manager, Terry Temple, claimed it to be lucrative. Also, the size of the company matched the size of the market; Infinity's management didn't want to expand too rapidly. According to Temple, "Time will tell if the market forces dictate that Infinity must enter the run-about family market." According to a report by Statistical Surveys, Infinity sold only seven registered boats in the year 2000 (see Exhibit 10).

ÉLAN BOATS

American Performance Marine had been building its American Skier models "to the highest possible standards" since 1975, earning a reputation for high quality, exceptional product performance, and cutting-edge innovation. But during the 1990s, the company had become unfocused, poorly managed, and undercapitalized. The American Skier plant closed its doors in January 2001 and filed for bankruptcy.

As Ben Favret took his first tour of American Performance Marine's 24,000-square-foot production facility, he wondered just why the company had gone bankrupt. Four reasons soon became apparent: excessive debt, high manufacturing costs, little or no marketing, and poor management (lack of staffing, cash flow, inventory control, and ordering). As he continued the plant tour, Ben also reflected on the industry situation. As a World Champion water-skier, he was aware of "excessive customer dissatisfaction in the market" fostered by overpriced boats that underperformed. Ben weighed the pros of purchasing the business at a bargain-basement price, thus giving the aspiring owners low overhead cost, a debt-free company, and, because of his own connections in the industry, the ability to recruit top talent in manufacturing, sales, and marketing. Favret believed all the signs pointed to go, paving the way for him to make history as the first professional skier ever to purchase a ski boat manufacturing company. Favret and his partner, Jay Blossman, came up with the following mission for the new company:

> The mission of Élan boats is to be hyperefficient in the manufacturing and marketing of Inboard Runabout Boats for recreational and competitive water sports enthusiasts. Élan boats is dedicated to building long-term relationships with customers through superior training and customer support. We will do business consistent with the definition of the company's name. Élan—vigorous spirit or enthusiasm. Synonyms: Style, Confidence, Flair, Elegance, Flamboyance.

Using the same drive and determination that had propelled him to the top of the waterskiing world, Ben wanted Élan to be the "true market leader in profitability, quality, manufacturing cost efficiency and eventually sales"; as he saw it, Élan was "gunning for, and will take down MasterCraft, Correct Craft, and Malibu." Favret believed an offensive attack on the major competitors was the best option, given prevailing industry conditions. Ben viewed the leaders as vulnerable due to unhappy buyers, sliding profits, excess capacity, and heavy debt. He assessed the situations of the two industry leaders as follows:

- *MasterCraft:* Very high overhead due to its large production facility, extensive marketing programs, and unnecessary employees. In order to rope in expenditures, MasterCraft's new management team will "let go" of some of its sponsored Pro Skiers, giving Élan an opportunity to pick up some prime athletes.

- *Correct Craft:* Sales declined 17.2 percent in 2000 due to poor marketing focus and being outflanked by "dare-to-be-different" competitors. This is an old company that is stodgy and slow to change.

Because none of the industry leaders were particularly cost-efficient, Élan aimed to attack its rivals first by revamping and streamlining its activity cost chain to achieve a cost advantage and then by pursuing first an "ours-is-better-than-theirs" approach—the idea was to offer a better boat at a lower price. Additionally, Favret and Blossman wanted to aim their competitive offensive at rivals who had done a poor job of servicing customers. Their objective was to win over the leaders' disenchanted customers by being a service-oriented company.

Élan also sought to dominate its own backyard, the Gulf Coast region. Targeted states were Texas, Louisiana, Mississippi, Alabama, Georgia, and Florida. By concentrating facilities and marketing activities in a limited territory, Élan hoped to produce greater sales force efficiency, expedite delivery and customer service, and achieve saturation advertising while avoiding the diseconomies of trying to employ the strategy on a national scale. To accomplish this, Élan planned to bypass boat retailers and sell directly to the end user.

Élan's saturation advertising strategy centered on creating a distinctive image via a corporate identity and logo that stood out from its competitors and ads targeted at the undermarketed competition ski boat segment. The goal was to make Élan boats attractive to competition skiers and wakeboard enthusiasts by offering a "free week of ski school" for new boat owners or a "free lesson and boat demo" for prospective buyers. Élan also negotiated cross-marketing ventures with numerous water-ski and wakeboard manufacturers and retailers to give boat owners a onetime discount on all skis and equipment. The target demographic for Élan's marketing campaign was white males between the ages of 25 and 55 with a college education and income greater than $50,000.

Élan's strategy was to cater to the skiing and wakeboarding enthusiast with eight models comprising three series (see Exhibit 15). The American Skier models were aimed at filling the "neglected" tournament skier niche and meeting the needs and expectations of the "hard-core enthusiast who demanded performance." The American Skier brand name was retained to capitalize on tradition, brand recognition, and goodwill toward the 26-year-old company. The Volante range was the company's luxury model, for affluent boaters who viewed their boat as more of a definition of who they were rather than a functional tool. Élan's wakeboard models were the Eagle Air series. Both the Eagle 7.3 and Volante 7.3 were V-drives. Each model was available in a variety of colors and a multitude of standard features, with Élan boats being noted for

exhibit 15   Élan's Product Line

American Skier Series	Volante Series	Eagle Air Series
American Skier Pro	Volante 6.2	Eagle 5.8
American Skier Comp	Volante 7.3	Eagle 6.2
American Skier Classic		Eagle 7.3

having more standard features than those of the competition. As of 2000, Élan Boats had 30 clients. Ben projected growth to at least 50 clients in 2001, 60 in 2002, and 72 in 2003. Élan's facility in Kentwood had capacity of 150 units a year. Ben anticipated investing in a new manufacturing facility in Covington Industrial Park in 2004.

Exhibits 16–18 show Élan's actual and projected financial statements. Exhibit 19 shows projected financial ratios.

exhibit 16   Elan's Actual and Projected Statements of Income, Start-up through 2004

	Actual		Projected		
Formation	Start-up thru August 31, 2001	10 Months	1st Year 2002	2nd Year 2003	3rd Year 2004
Revenues					
Boats	$ 32,240	$1,594,320	$1,626,560	$1,951,820	$2,342,210
Trailers		165,750	165,750	198,900	238,680
Parts		24,700	24,700	29,640	35,620
Net revenue	32,240	1,784,770	1,817,010	2,180,360	2,616,510
Cost of goods sold					
Direct materials - boats	17,160	861,900	879,060	1,054,820	1,265,810
Direct materials - trailers		72,930	72,930	87,490	105,040
Direct labor - boats	5,590	179,010	184,600	221,520	265,850
Direct labor - trailers		39,780	39,780	47,710	57,200
Freight		16,250	16,250	19,500	23,400
Parts and supplies		12,090	12,090	14,560	17,420
Plant supplies		3,380	3,380	4,030	4,810
Sales commissions		52,650	52,650	65,390	78,520
Warranty work		17,550	17,550	21,060	25,220
Total cost of goods sold	22,750	1,255,540	1,278,290	1,536,060	1,843,270
Gross profit	9,490	529,230	538,720	644,280	773,240
Gross margin	29.4%	29.7%	29.6%	29.5%	29.6%
Operating expenses					
Advertising and marketing	3,250	52,910	56,160	60,710	65,520
Insurance - worker's comp		16,250	16,250	17,550	18,980
Insurance - P & C	1,950	32,760	34,710	37,440	40,430
Insurance - health	650	14,430	15,080	16,250	17,550
Payroll - office and mgmt	14,300	119,600	133,900	144,560	156,130
Payroll - taxes		39,000	39,000	42,120	45,500
Sales consulting		42,900	42,900	46,280	49,920
Rent		23,400	23,400	25,220	27,300
R & D tooling		13,650	13,650	14,690	15,860
Utilities	1,040	35,100	36,140	39,000	42,120
Telephone	390	7,800	8,190	8,840	9,490
Permits and licenses	1,040	1,950	2,990	3,250	3,510
Travel		7,800	7,800	8,450	9,100
Meals and entertainment		3,120	3,120	3,380	3,640
Fuel		4,290	4,290	4,680	5,070
Auto - maintenance	260	1,560	1,820	1,950	2,080
Office supplies/postage		4,680	4,680	5,070	5,460
Professional fees	5,200	3,900	9,100	9,880	10,660
Repairs and maintenance		1,560	1,560	1,690	1,820
Miscellaneous	780	16,900	17,680	19,110	20,670
Total operating expenses	28,860	443,560	472,420	510,120	550,810
Operating income - EBITDA	(19,370)	85,670	66,300	134,160	222,430
Depreciation	1,170	17,810	18,980	19,370	19,370
Interest expense	260	15,990	16,250	13,520	13,260
Earnings before taxes	(20,800)	51,870	31,070	101,270	189,800
Tax required distributions	0	10,530	10,530	29,900	60,060
Net income	$(21,060)	$ 41,340	$ 20,540	$ 71,370	$ 129,740

Source: Company records.

exhibit 17   Elan's Actual and Projected Balance Sheet, Start-up through 2004

Formation	Actual	Projected		
	Start-up thru August 31, 2001	Year-End 2002	Year-End 2003	Year-End 2004
Assets				
Current assets				
Cash on hand and in bank	$ (3,510)	$ 1,170	$ 24,700	$ 25,610	$ 19,240
Accounts receivable		—	34,970	89,570	179,270
Work-in-process		23,270	46,540	46,540	69,810
Inventory—boats and trailers	92,950	92,950	139,490	232,440	278,850
Prepaid expenses		9,750	9,750	9,750	9,750
Total current assets	89,440	127,140	255,450	403,910	556,920
Equipment and leasehold improvements					
Equipment, furniture, and fixtures—LA					
Truck and trailer		32,500	62,920	62,920	62,920
Equipment, furniture, and fixtures	34,060	34,060	34,060	34,060	34,060
Less: accumulated depreciation			(18,980)	(38,350)	(57,720)
Net property and equipment	34,060	66,560	78,000	58,630	39,260
Other assets					
Patents, trademarks, and intangibles			0	0	0
Utility and other deposits		1,300	1,300	1,300	1,300
Total other assets	0	1,300	1,300	1,300	1,300
Total assets	$123,500	$195,000	$334,750	$463,840	$597,480
Liabilities and shareholders' equity					
Current liabilities					
Accounts payable—trade		$ 0	$ 0	$ 82,290	$ 98,800
All other accruals		0	0	0	0
Operating loan		32,500	162,500	149,500	149,500
Current portion—long-term debt		0	10,790	11,570	12,610
Total current liabilities	0	32,500	173,290	243,360	260,910
Long-term debt					
Note payable—new trucks, vehicles		26,000	17,420	8,190	(1,820)
Note payable new equipment		13,000	10,790	8,450	5,850
Less: current portion long-term debt above	0	0	(10,790)	(11,570)	(12,610)
Net long-term debt	0	39,000	17,420	5,070	(8,580)
Stockholders' equity					
Treasury stock	123,500	123,500	123,500	123,500	123,500
Retained earnings (deficit)			0	20,540	91,910
Operating income—YTD		0	20,540	71,370	129,740
Total equity	123,500	123,500	144,040	215,410	345,150
Total liabilities and equity	$123,500	$195,000	$334,750	$463,840	$597,480

Source: Company records.

exhibit 18   Elan's Projected Statements of Cash Flows, 2002–2004

	2002	2003	2004
Operating activities			
Net income (loss) from operations	$ 20,540	$ 71,370	$129,740
Adjustments needed to reconcile income to cash:			
Depreciation and amortization	18,980	19,370	19,370
Increases and decreases in the operating assets and liabilities			
Accounts receivable	(34,970)	(54,600)	(89,700)
Work-in-process	(46,540)	—	(23,270)
Inventory—boats and trailers	(46,540)	(92,950)	(46,410)
Prepaid expenses			
Accounts payable—trade	—	82,290	16,510
All other accruals	—	—	—
Operating loan	162,500	(13,000)	—
Net cash provided or (used) from operating activities	$ 64,220	$ 12,480	$ 6,240
Investing activities			
Truck and trailer	(62,920)	—	—
Equipment, furniture and fixtures	—	—	—
Patents, trademarks, and intangibles	—	—	—
Utility and other deposits	(1,300)	—	—
Net cash provided or (used) from investing activities	$(64,220)	—	—
Financing activities			
Note payable—new trucks, vehicles	17,420	(9,230)	(10,010)
Note payable new equipment	10,790	(2,340)	(2,600)
Net cash provided or (used) from financing activities	28,210	(11,570)	(12,610)
Net increase (decrease) in cash	28,210	910	(6,370)
Cash—beginning of period	(3,510)	24,700	25,610
Net cash balance at period's end	$ 24,700	$ 25,610	$ 19,240

Source: Company records.

exhibit 19   Elan's Projected Operating Ratios, 2002–2004

	2002	2003	2004
Return on assets	6.1%	15.4%	21.7%
(Net income/Total assets)			
Return on equity	14.3%	33.1%	37.6%
(Net income/Equity)			
Current ratio	1.5	1.7	2.1
(Current assets/Current liabilities)			
Working capital efficiency	22.1	13.6	8.8
(Total sales/[Current assets − Current liabilities])			
Inventory turnover	6.9	5.5	5.3
(Cost of goods sold/WIP and inventory Boats & trailers)			
Return on investment	10.3%	40.7%	51.1%
(Earnings before taxes/Equity)			
Return on capital employed	9.3%	26.5%	38.1%
(Earnings before taxes/[Equity + LT debt + ST debt])			
Debt to equity	1.3	0.8	0.4
([Operating loan + LT debt]/Equity)			
Interest coverage	0.3	0.8	1.3
(EBITDA/Interest payment)			
Debt to EBITDA	2.88	1.24	0.69
(Operating loan + Long-term debt + CP LT debt/EBITDA)			

Note: EBITDA = Earnings before interest, taxes, depreciation, and amortization.
Source: Company records.

case 9 Azalea Seafood Gumbo Shoppe

John E. Gamble
University of South Alabama

The aroma of boiling crawfish and shrimp and the sound of "A Pirate Looks at Forty" filled the air on Monterey Street on the temperate May 2001 evening as block party guests mingled and sampled the libations provided by their hosts. Jimmy Buffett songs were frequently heard during such events in Mobile, Alabama, since the famous musician lived there until his graduation from McGill-Toolen High School in the late 1960s. The Monterey Street Spring Fling block party was one of Mobile's great traditions. Mardi Gras balls had concluded more than two months earlier, and weekend trips to the cottages and antebellum homes along Mobile Bay's Eastern Shore were still a few weeks off. For many, the third Saturday evening in May was best spent socializing with old friends and new acquaintances amid the residential street's 100-year-old live oaks and mix of Craftsman, Victorian, and Georgian homes that dated to the early 1900s.

Mike Rathle and John Addison had tended the boiling 25-gallon pots of crawfish and shrimp since late afternoon. As they cooked pot after pot of shellfish, they had chances to catch up with old friends—some of whom asked about their business. Azalea Seafood Gumbo Shoppe catered special events like the Monterey Street block party, but, more important, it was among the largest producers of ready-to-eat gumbo, with annual revenues in 2000 of more than $1 million. In 2001 Azalea's products could be found in approximately 1,000 supermarkets and were served in about 300 restaurants in the southeastern United States. Mike Rathle commented on why he and his partner dabbled in catering:

> Our catering activities provide very little revenue for the company, but John and I enjoy it and it's great for public relations. In a way, I feel kind of obligated to do these events since we used crawfish to prevent robberies when we first began running our business, which at the time was just a small retail seafood shop. During our first few years of selling fresh fish and gumbo, we always had a pot of crawfish cooking. We had not been out of college too long and it seemed that there were always about 5 to 10 guys at our store just hanging around eating crawfish—especially on Friday and Saturday nights. One spring there was a rash of robberies at the intersection where our business was located. Every business at that intersection was robbed—some more than once. On any given weekend we probably had $1,000 to $2,000 cash in the building, but we were never robbed. I guess the prospects of holding up a business where the parking lot was almost full didn't seem too appealing to whoever was responsible for the robberies.

The case author is grateful for the assistance and cooperation of Mike Rathle and John Addison in preparing this case. Copyright © 2001 by the case author.

The event also gave Rathle and Addison an opportunity to discuss the future of their business while they prepared more than 1,200 pounds of shrimp and crawfish that filled and refilled a five-foot replica of a wooden fishing boat where partyers could serve themselves throughout the evening. As the two men were about to begin their second decade as partners, Addison reflected briefly on the company's success and brought up some points for consideration:

> Our growth has been phenomenal since we bought the seafood shop in 1991. We have successfully transitioned from a small retail seafood shop to one of the largest producers of gumbo in the United States. We've gained distribution to supermarkets, Wal-Mart Supercenters, Sam's Clubs, and probably half the seafood restaurants within 100 miles of here. However, I think that we need to consider what our sales and profit expectations for the business are. Are we satisfied with $1 million a year in sales or do we want annual sales of $1.5 million? Do we want sales of $5 million? $10 million? If we want greater sales, how will we achieve our growth? Should more of our sales come from supermarkets or food service? Do we need a new location? Can we improve our packaging? Are our prices too low? Also, should we extend our product line to different sized packages or other items?

Rathle agreed that Addison's questions would have to be answered soon and suggested that the 10th anniversary of the partnership underscored the importance of evaluating the company's strategy and its opportunities for further growth.

COMPANY HISTORY AND BACKGROUND

Azalea Seafood Gumbo Shoppe was established in Mobile, Alabama, in 1971 by Pat Lodds. Mobile was an attractive market for seafood sales because the city's location on the northern coast of the Gulf of Mexico made fresh seafood readily available and because seafood dishes were staples in most Mobilians' diets. Many established families in Mobile took pride in some recipe for a seafood dish that had been handed down for generations. A cookbook, first published in 1964, that contained seafood recipes from some of Mobile's oldest families had been reprinted a number of times and remained a popular seller over the next decades and into the new century. Azalea Seafood Gumbo Shoppe, like other seafood shops in Mobile, offered customers fresh snapper, grouper, flounder, and shrimp caught in Mobile Bay and the Gulf of Mexico, but Azalea differed from its rivals by also selling prepared seafood gumbo that could be taken home for dinner.

The shop was located near the busy McGregor Avenue and Airport Boulevard intersection in a concrete-block building that had been a fried chicken restaurant in the mid-1960s. Azalea's sales of seafood were brisk from almost the day the store opened, and its gumbo (made using Lodds's 100-year-old family recipe) became popular within months as the word spread. Many Mobilians possessed their own treasured gumbo recipes, but since gumbo was very difficult and time-consuming to prepare, it was much more convenient to drop by Azalea Seafood Gumbo Shoppe to pick up high-quality gumbo for that evening's dinner. The most trying aspect of preparing gumbo was making its roux base—a mixture of flour and oil that was cooked at a very high temperature. The skill, which involved cooking the flour-and-oil mixture until it reached a deep brown color without being scorched, took some time for most cooks to master.

Pat Lodds owned and operated Azalea Seafood Gumbo Shoppe until 1981, when it was sold to Jim Hartman. Hartman continued to sell fresh fish and freshly prepared gumbo to the walk-in customers, and he began to freeze large gallon containers for sale to local seafood restaurants that might not be able to cook a good gumbo. Hartman also began to prepare and sell shrimp creole to walk-in customers and area restaurants because the product required ingredients similar to those found in gumbo and used a similar preparation process. However, gumbo was by far the more popular seller of the two prepared food products. By 1991, Azalea's seafood gumbo was distributed by three food-service suppliers to about 30 restaurants along the Gulf Coast and its sales remained relatively stable at about $10,000 to $15,000 per month. Even though the store was doing well, Jim Hartman began to grow tired of the daily routine and mentioned to a few business contacts and friends that he would entertain offers on the business. Three of Hartman's previous employees heard that the business was for sale and began to think about the possibility of purchasing Azalea Seafood Gumbo Shoppe.

Mike Rathle, John Addison, and Bill Sibley had been friends since attending McGill-Toolen High School together, and all worked at the seafood shop after school during their senior year. Upon high school graduation, Rathle and Addison attended the University of South Alabama, where Rathle obtained a marketing degree and Addison graduated with a degree in international business. Sibley began a career with International Paper and was employed at the company's Mobile mill as a safety coordinator when he heard that Jim Hartman was interested in selling his seafood business. Immediately intrigued, Sibley contacted his two longtime friends to discuss forming a partnership to purchase the business. Rathle and Addison were both busy operating a small construction company at the time but were interested in the opportunity. After hearing the details, Rathle believed that he could leverage the knowledge he had gained while employed by Brach's Candy as an area sales manager to expand Azalea's gumbo into supermarkets. Addison, believing that Azalea could be an attractive investment opportunity if the company's gumbo sales could be expanded into supermarkets and additional restaurants, agreed to join his two friends in the new venture.

The three friends approached Jim Hartman with an offer, and by August 1991 they owned and operated the seafood gumbo shop where they had once worked after school. Sibley oversaw the company's gumbo production, while Rathle immediately began to call on area supermarkets and restaurants to gain access to new customers for the company's prepared gumbo. Addison was still involved with a number of construction projects but joined Rathle in Azalea's marketing efforts within a few months.

Shortly before the company's first anniversary of new ownership, the three partners were notified that their building lease would not be renewed because a shopping center would be built on the property where Azalea Seafood Gumbo Shoppe had operated since 1971. Relocating would be a problem since it would be difficult to move the kitchen equipment and freezers without disrupting the company's production. The three partners spent several days following the eviction notice dreading the prospects of moving, but before they had an opportunity to look at other properties, they were approached by a competing gumbo producer who was retiring. The competitor offered Azalea his kitchen equipment and freezers for $5,000; in addition, Azalea could assume his building lease. Mike Rathle stated that the timing of the offer was a godsend: "We were able to pick up our ingredients and move to a turnkey operation without losing a beat."

Azalea's new 2,200-square-foot production facility, much larger than its previous building, was located on a one-acre parcel of land that also included a frame house built in the 1930s. The house was located only about 100 feet from the concrete-block plant and could be used as an office. The only drawback to the new building was that its location on a quiet street outside the city limits was too far from high-traffic areas to support retail sales of fresh seafood and prepared gumbo. Before they knew of their pending lease termination, however, the partners had considered giving up retail sales and focusing on commercial accounts—the move was the deciding factor. With a clear vision of Azalea's future business and the new facility's eight-ton-per-day production capacity, Rathle and Addison began to aggressively pursue new supermarket and food-service accounts. They were able to land account after account over the next 10 years, and in 2001 Azalea Seafood Gumbo Shoppe produced more than 45 tons of gumbo and other seafood products each month. Bill Sibley sold his interest in the business to Rathle and Addison in early 2001 so that he could pursue other business opportunities.

OVERVIEW OF THE VALUE-ADDED SEAFOOD INDUSTRY

Value-added seafood products included any type of packaged food item with seafood as an ingredient. Value-added seafood producers purchased fresh, frozen, or cooked seafood to use in creating products for sale to restaurants, supermarkets, or other types of food retailers. Food companies that sold seafood products either used their own marketing staffs to sell and distribute products to retailers and restaurants or contracted with food brokers to provide the marketing and logistical support needed to distribute their products. Packaged seafood products were also distributed by jobbers, independent sellers who purchased packaged food products directly from manufacturers and sold them to restaurants and grocers after a 15–20 percent markup.

Suppliers

Value-added seafood producers could readily obtain ingredients from seafood processors, fruit and vegetable producers, canned and dry goods producers, or large food wholesalers that specialized in such ingredients. Large processed food companies had considerable latitude in their choice of suppliers since most ingredients were commoditylike and readily available from multiple sources. In some instances, large food companies were able to further improve their ability to negotiate with suppliers by their own production of some key ingredients. Many times, smaller value-added producers did not have adequate volume to negotiate directly with the producer of ingredients but were able to select from a variety of wholesalers to obtain the best mix of quality and price for purchased ingredients.

Production

Packaged food production in the United States was regulated and monitored by the U.S. Food and Drug Administration (FDA), the U.S. Department of Agriculture (USDA), and state departments of public health. State departments of public health usually monitored only the cleanliness of food producers' cooking areas and other facilities with monthly inspections, whereas the FDA required food producers to develop and implement a Hazard Analysis Critical Control Point (HACCP) system for their operations and comply with the provisions of the Food and Nutritional Labeling Act. The Nutritional Labeling and Education Act of 1990 required all packaged foods to bear nutrition labels that listed ingredients and nutritional facts about the product. The act also established standardized definitions for such terms as *low fat* or *light*. The USDA enforced the Federal Meat Inspection Act, which established sanitation standards for producers of meat and poultry products.

All seafood processors were required to develop an HACCP plan using guidelines provided by the FDA to ensure that packaged foods were free from such health hazards as pathogens and toxins. HACCP plans were required to provide general information about the company's product and processes, describe the food, describe the method of distribution and storage, identify the intended use and consumer, and develop a flow diagram of the company's value chain. Food companies were also required to identify potential species-related and process-related health hazards and identify critical hazard control points. Once a food producer had set critical limits for health hazards, a monitoring procedure was developed and followed. Food companies were required to establish record-keeping and verification procedures that could be evaluated by the FDA during inspections.

Distribution

Processed food items were distributed either by the producer or by food brokers who represented a large number of companies producing many types of products. Sometimes a food broker might represent companies producing products in nearly every category found in supermarkets. Food brokers had become larger and their product offerings broader during the 1990s. A wave of acquisitions and mergers reduced the number of food brokers in the United States from about 2,500 in 1990 to about 200 in 2001. Consolidation among food brokers was driven primarily by consolidation among food producers and food retailers. However, there remained a large number of small food brokers that focused on representing food companies for the sale of their products to restaurants.

Consolidation of Packaged Food Companies   Throughout the 1990s, large global food companies like Unilever, Nestlé, and Kraft Foods had acquired smaller companies to fill gaps in their product lines and expand their global presence. Food brokers were forced to alter their business practices as the food industry consolidated since larger food companies had greater service demands than small, independent food producers. Smaller companies were typically pleased with a broker that could deliver products to supermarkets within a limited geographic region and assure that items were in stock and located in appropriate locations within stores. Large food companies that chose to outsource distribution considered contracts with brokers competitive resources that could be used to provide broader geographic coverage for their brands and that could contribute to efficient inventory management and replenishment systems. Global food manufacturers had also begun to demand in-store marketing services from brokers in return for distributing their multiple brands. Brokers could be required to report stockouts, make price checks, and deliver up-to-the-minute inventory data to manufacturers' distribution centers. Brokers might also be asked to set up in-store displays, discuss new products with store managers, and conduct in-store product sampling. Small food manufacturers had much less ability to demand such services from food brokers. In fact, some small food producers found it difficult to secure the services of a national food broker and, if a large broker did agree to distribute their product, would likely receive only minimal attention to their brand.

Consolidation of Supermarkets and Other Grocers   Consolidation among grocery retailers also supported the trend toward fewer, larger food brokerages. In 2000, 38.2 percent of the $494 billion supermarket industry was accounted for by Kroger, Wal-Mart, Albertson's, Safeway, and Royal Ahold. In 1995, the top five supermarket companies had accounted for only 26.5 percent of industry sales. There were 60 mergers and acquisitions in the supermarket industry between 1997 and 2000, and industry analysts expected between 15 and 20 mergers and acquisitions in 2001.

exhibit 1   Estimated Sales and Number of Supermarket Locations for the Top 20 U.S. Grocers, Year-End 2000

Rank	Company	Estimated Sales (in millions)	Number of Supermarket Locations (store sales of $2 million or greater)
1	The Kroger Co.*	$43,120	2,366
2	Albertson's	31,461	1,715
3	Safeway	28,829	1,482
4	Wal-Mart*	22,947	908
5	Royal Ahold	20,022	974
6	Food Lion	15,042	1,435
7	Winn-Dixie	13,731	1,081
8	Publix	13,021	645
9	A&P	8,075	553
10	SUPERVALU	7,197	539
11	H-E-B Grocery Co.	6,704	270
12	Shaw's	4,001	165
13	Pathmark	3,807	138
14	Military	3,607	190
15	Meijer*	3,545	144
16	Hy-Vee	3,383	184
17	Fleming	3,120	200
18	Raley's	2,982	149
19	Giant Eagle	2,856	120
20	Aldi	2,522	697

*Supercenter statistics reduced to include only traditional supermarket items.
Source: Progressive Grocer annual report, April 2001.

Much of the industry's merger activity had occurred as a result of traditional supermarket companies' attempts to better compete with Wal-Mart. Although Wal-Mart did not enter the grocery industry until 1988, when it opened its first Supercenter, it was crowned the U.S. supermarket leader in 2001, with annual grocery sales of $57.2 billion. Competition in the industry was expected to intensify further with Wal-Mart's annual addition of 150–175 new Supercenters and 15–20 smaller Neighborhood Markets to expand its chain of more than 1,500 stores. The industry's other leading grocery companies believed that mergers between the larger companies and acquisitions of smaller chains would provide greater purchasing power to meet Wal-Mart's discount pricing. Exhibit 1 presents estimated sales and number of stores with annual sales exceeding $2 million for the top 20 U.S. grocers.

The grocery industry experienced more than $15 billion in grocery bankruptcies between 1997 and 2001, and analysts believed bankruptcies totaling another $15 billion would occur in the retail grocery industry between 2002 and 2005. One such bankruptcy involved Delchamps, Inc., a former Mobile, Alabama–based grocery chain that was acquired by Jackson, Mississippi's Jitney-Jungle in 1997 in an attempt by both companies' management to gain greater purchasing power. In 1999, the Jitney-Jungle/Delchamps chain included 198 stores with annual sales of approximately $2 billion, but the company was forced to file for bankruptcy protection that same year and was dissolved in late 2000. The new company had been able to achieve some cost savings in purchasing, but any cost savings from lower prices on packaged goods were more than offset by the interest expense and debt service that accompanied the buyout. Jitney-Jungle's stores and fixtures were purchased by Winn-Dixie, a chain with more than 1,000 stores in 14 states, and by Bruno's, a 153-store chain operating in Alabama, Florida, Georgia, and Mississippi. Bruno's had emerged from its own Chapter 11 bankruptcy protection just months before it purchased 17 of Jitney-Jungle's stores.

Like the large global food companies, large national grocers expected food brokers to provide national coverage and take a large role in inventory management and replenishment efforts. The grocery industry's razor-thin margins required that supermarkets have access to cutting-edge information systems to reduce spoilage of perishable items and keep popular items on the shelf while keeping store inventory levels at a minimum. SUPERVALU, the largest distributor of food products to U.S. grocers, offered comprehensive procurement, distribution, and replenishment services to more than 5,500 supermarkets, mass merchandisers, and e-tailers in the United States. The company's logistics services featured activity-based costing, cross-docked warehouses, on-time delivery, 24/7 service, and Web-based ordering and invoicing. In addition to inventory management benefits, both large and small grocery chains profited from SUPERVALU's $40 billion purchasing power. Like many other large food brokers, SUPERVALU had made a number of acquisitions in recent years to boost its ability to provide better service and broader geographic coverage to food companies and grocers. The company's 1999 acquisition of Richfield Holdings for approximately $1.5 billion was completed to boost SUPERVALU's distribution capabilities in the mid-Atlantic region of the United States. In 2001, SUPERVALU was also the nation's 10th-largest supermarket chain, with 1,200 stores and retail sales of $9.3 billion.

Distribution in the Food Service Industry

Distribution in the Food Service Industry   Even though the $175 billion U.S. food-service industry was highly fragmented, with more than 3,500 broadline food-service distributors and 15,000 specialty product suppliers that provided various food items to restaurants and other locations where prepared food was served, many industry participants believed that the industry would soon consolidate. Large food-service companies like SYSCO Corporation and U.S. Foodservice had begun to acquire food-service distributors of all types and in all geographic locations in the United States. SYSCO, the largest food-service company in the United States, with 2000 sales of $19.3 billion, provided more than 275,000 products to 356,000 different customers in all 50 states and in portions of Canada.

SYSCO had completed more than 20 acquisitions between 1991 and 2000 to expand its line of fresh and frozen meats, seafood, poultry, fruits and vegetables, canned and dry foods, equipment and supplies, beverages, bakery items, dairy products, disposables, medical and surgical products, and chemical and sanitation items sold to restaurants, hotels, schools, hospitals, and other locations where food was prepared. In early 2001, SYSCO acquired a distributor of hotel housekeeping supplies and guest personal care items; a Houston, Texas, specialty meat supplier; and a Canadian distributor of prepared food and cleaning and paper supplies. SYSCO management intended for its acquisitions of distributors serving food-service niches to improve its 11 percent market share and gain more of the industry's 850,000 customers.

U.S. Foodservice, the second-largest food-service company in the United States, held about a 7 percent share of the food-service market, with 2000 sales of $12 billion. U.S. Foodservice had stepped up its acquisition efforts after it was acquired by Dutch supermarket giant Royal Ahold in April 2000. Royal Ahold was the fifth-largest supermarket chain in the United States, with approximately 1,300 supermarkets and 2000 sales of $27.5 billion. Royal Ahold's stores in Europe, Latin America, and Asia brought the company's worldwide sales to more than $50 billion in 2000. U.S. Foodservice's acquisitions in 2000 and 2001 included the $1.5 billion acquisition of PYA/Monarch, a leading food-service distributor in the southeastern United States; the purchase of Parkway Food Service, a broadline distributor in western Florida with more than 1,000 accounts; and Mutual Wholesale Company, a Florida food-service company with more than 4,200 accounts. The rapid growth through acquisition by SYSCO and U.S. Foodservice had encouraged other food-service distributors to rapidly advance their own acquisition plans.

The growing size and strength of food-service distributors had little effect on jobbers since jobbers had traditionally been forced to call on small accounts or distribute items needed by restaurants only on an infrequent basis. A jobber was usually a one-person operation with company assets limited to a single refrigerated truck. Jobbers lacked any formal relationship with food producers and usually operated on a cash-and-carry basis. Jobbers typically purchased only a few cases of an item at any given time for their daily calls to small restaurants that might need a case or two of some food item. Although few had annual sales of over $400,000, jobbers were an important distributor for small restaurants that lacked the sales volume to establish an account with a large food-service company.

Food brokers also played a role in the food-service industry. Many small- and medium-sized food companies would contract with food brokers to promote their products to restaurants served by food-service distributors that purchased their products. For example, once a food-service distributor agreed to purchase a food company's product, food brokers could be hired to create pull for that product by marketing the product directly to the food distributor's restaurant customers. In return, food brokers typically received a 5 percent commission on a food company's sales increases to food distributors.

Growth in Sales of Meals Eaten Away from Home   Consolidation of the U.S. food-service industry was also likely because of opportunities presented by the rapid growth in meals eaten away from home. In 2000, more than 54 billion meals were eaten in nearly 850,000 restaurants, schools, work cafeterias, hospitals, nursing homes, and other places where meals were served. Restaurants' share of the food dollar had grown from 33 percent in 1980 to 46 percent in 2001. Americans were projected to spend 53 percent of their food dollars in restaurants by 2010. In addition, the restaurant industry's sales were projected to grow from $399 billion in 2001 to $577 billion in 2010. Companies like SYSCO and Royal Ahold were willing to make further investments in the food-service industry to capture a greater share of the rapidly growing industry. Also, food service offered Royal Ahold the chance to diversify beyond sales of food items in supermarkets while not straying too far from its core competencies developed in the grocery business.

AZALEA SEAFOOD GUMBO SHOPPE IN 2001

In 2001, Azalea Seafood Gumbo Shoppe's seafood gumbo, crawfish etouffee, shrimp creole, and shrimp-and-crabmeat bisque were distributed to more than 1,000 supermarkets, 20 Sam's Clubs, and approximately 300 restaurants in the southeastern United States. The company's sales had grown at a compounded rate of 33 percent between

exhibit 2   Azalea Seafood Gumbo Shoppe, Income Statements, 1996–2000*

	2000	1999	1998	1997	1996
Revenues					
Wholesale sales	$1,036,570	$1,222,452	$1,327,346	$944,522	$880,914
Catering	18,937	16,146	10,613	20,575	5,980
Allowances/damages	−11,936	−5,800	−4,453	−1,855	−1,669
Sales discounts	−2,004	−3,627	−13,683	−8,291	−9,742
Total revenues	$1,041,567	$1,229,171	$1,319,823	$954,951	$875,484
Cost of goods sold					
Cost of ingredients	440,673	501,554	555,873	449,086	401,812
Cost of containers	82,813	94,368	97,520	67,120	57,519
Freight and shipping	24,249	26,384	35,925	8,039	10,494
Payroll–officers	84,186	123,260	138,363	108,480	107,873
Payroll–other	97,248	107,016	123,446	50,206	46,101
Commission/brokerage	480	463	4,708	0	2,206
Cost of goods sold	729,650	853,046	955,833	682,931	626,005
Gross profit	$311,917	$376,125	$363,990	$272,020	$249,479
Expenses					
Advertising	$ 3,973	$16,633	$14,626	$ 9,217	$ 2,421
Bad debt expense	0	5,634	0	0	0
Bank charges	1,316	5,682	4,367	9,437	1,260
Contract labor	2,071	687	976	1,103	254
Contributions	607	1,646	816	1,081	1,294
Depreciation expense	31,202	39,738	41,000	20,388	19,496
Dues and subscriptions	909	83	286	183	264
Equipment rental	1,265	296	1,658	943	326
Entertainment and meals	1,909	2,414	1,592	342	2,442

1992 and 1999. However, its 2000 sales fell by 15 percent after Jitney-Jungle filed for Chapter 11 bankruptcy protection and later ceased operations. As an unsecured supplier, Azalea had no ability to recover the outstanding account of more than $100,000. The company's 2000 sales were also adversely affected by a kitchen worker's decision to stamp gumbo containers with a date stamp after a stamp showing a lot number broke. The company eventually had to recall more than $100,000 worth of gumbo when consumers and retailers believed that the stamp showed an expiration date that had passed. Revenues were decreased further when Publix supermarkets stopped placing orders with Azalea because of the recall. Azalea Seafood Gumbo Shoppe's income statements for 1996 through 2000 are presented in Exhibit 2. The company's balance sheets for 1996 through 2000 are presented in Exhibit 3.

Azalea's Product Line

Azalea sold fully cooked seafood gumbo, crawfish etouffee, shrimp creole, and shrimp-and-crabmeat bisque in pint, quart, half-gallon, and gallon containers. The company's seafood products were sold frozen and were ready to serve after thawing and heating.

exhibit 2 *(continued)*

	2000	1999	1998	1997	1996
Insurance	43,442	28,275	31,741	21,681	21,522
Interest expense	12,133	11,188	12,623	5,298	6,268
Janitorial and pest control	3,177	4,473	4,394	7,102	2,026
Miscellaneous	179	190	0	817	0
Postage	169	356	961	410	334
Office expense	2,510	3,141	4,635	2,884	3,662
Payroll tax expense	16,249	19,911	21,988	12,627	12,341
Penalties	1,134	5,800	847	529	0
Product demo costs	10,368	45,344	105,683	30,520	46,951
Product sampling	250	670	1,785	2,512	0
Professional fees	6,085	5,813	6,457	6,177	7,554
Rent	14,560	14,560	15,718	11,030	14,339
Repairs and maintenance	26,258	19,553	7,799	3,462	11,368
Service charges	3,863	3,662	2,108	1,660	4
Security	283	1,692	1,180	728	1,037
Supplies	3,219	9,775	6,360	1,667	1,554
Taxes and licenses	1,222	2,782	1,488	2,103	2,899
Telephone	13,015	16,405	16,899	11,595	12,613
Travel	2,927	4,343	5,333	3,317	864
Truck lease	16,891	15,820	18,894	13,721	13,984
Truck expenses	15,375	10,526	5,543	5,553	8,067
Uniforms and laundry	1,999	3,913	3,664	2,113	1,796
Utilities	21,816	21,527	19,767	17,526	19,445
Total expenses	$260,376	$322,530	$361,186	$207,726	$216,384
Net income	$51,541	$53,595	$2,804	$64,294	$33,094

˙Azalea Seafood Gumbo Shoppe's financial statements have been disguised. However, the relationships remain intact.

Azalea's pint- and quart-sized containers were sold in supermarkets and wholesale clubs, and its half-gallon and gallon containers were sold to restaurants and other food-service customers. The company's gumbo was its best-selling item, accounting for approximately 90 percent of annual sales. Azalea's seafood gumbo, like other gumbos, was a stewlike soup containing okra, crabmeat, shrimp, and spices in a roux base; it traced its roots to the Acadians who were forced from Canada in the late 1700s and settled in the New Orleans area. In perfecting many of today's Cajun recipes, the Acadians borrowed heavily from the Native Americans and the French and Spanish settlers who lived near the Mississippi Delta. Azalea Seafood Gumbo Shoppe's authentic Louisiana-style seafood gumbo had been featured in the Taste of America sponsored by the National Press Club in Washington, D.C., and had been served in the White House during the Reagan presidency.

Azalea Seafood Gumbo Shoppe added a white cream sauce–based shrimp-and-crabmeat bisque in 1997 and introduced a crawfish etouffee in 1998. Etouffee was another Cajun-style dish that was usually served over rice but could also be served in a bread bowl, in a pie shell, or alone. Azalea's crawfish etouffee received the San Francisco Seafood Show's Silver Award for Best New Product in 1998. Exhibit 4 provides technical data for Azalea's products. Nutritional label information for all four products

exhibit 3   Azalea Seafood Gumbo Shoppe, Balance Sheets, 1999–2000*

	2000	1999	1998	1997	1996
Assets					
Current assets					
Cash	$ (12,249)	$ (22,689)	$ 6,467	$ (23,542)	$ (18,345)
Accounts receivable	98,347	130,043	93,444	99,777	62,143
Other current assets					
Inventory—finished goods	6,337	11,189	11,145	9,134	6,580
Inventory—raw materials	21,503	34,686	33,990	34,223	29,913
Prepaid insurance	10,554	7,771	5,940	6,325	5,316
Total other current assets	38,393	53,646	51,074	49,681	41,810
Total current assets	124,491	160,999	150,985	125,916	85,608
Fixed assets					
Equipment and machinery	293,064	206,477	198,423	150,484	106,616
Office equipment and furniture	9,966	9,966	9,966	7,406	7,406
Leasehold improvements	12,147	12,147	12,147	1,663	1,663
Vehicles	31,055	31,055	17,819	16,134	16,134
Accumulated depreciation	(196,989)	(165,788)	(126,050)	(80,902)	(60,514)
Total fixed assets	149,243	93,858	112,305	94,785	71,305
Other assets					
Stockholders' loans	27,624	22,850	28,932	29,055	33,083
Total other assets	27,624	22,850	28,932	29,055	33,083
Total assets	$301,357	$277,707	$292,222	$249,757	$189,996
Liabilities and equity					
Current liabilities					
Accounts payable	$126,635	$126,100	$119,345	$ 99,874	$ 51,831
Other current liabilities					
Notes payable	$ 13,805	$ 5,261	$ 5,185	$ 46,305	$ 6,297
Payroll taxes payable	4,411	5,528	8,642	6,728	4,625
Current portion of long-term debt	46,136	64,606	44,692	29,253	19,561
Total other current liabilities	$ 64,352	$ 75,396	$ 58,520	$ 82,286	$ 30,483
Long-term liabilities					
Notes payable	$131,222	$ 93,132	$112,834	$ 47,848	$ 60,379
Less current portion	(46,136)	(64,606)	(44,692)	(29,253)	(19,561)
Total long-term liabilities	$ 85,086	$ 28,526	$ 68,141	$ 18,595	$ 40,818
Equity					
Common stock	$ 300	$ 300	$ 300	$ 300	$ 300
Paid in capital	19,698	19,692	19,692	19,692	19,692
Retained earnings	5,286	27,693	26,225	29,009	46,872
Total equity	$ 25,284	$ 47,685	$ 46,217	$ 49,001	$ 66,864
Total liabilities and equity	$301,357	$277,707	$292,222	$249,757	$189,996

*Azalea Seafood Gumbo Shoppe's financial statements have been disguised. However, the relationships remain intact.

exhibit 4   Technical Information for Azalea Seafood Gumbo Shoppe's
Prepared Seafood Dishes*

Available Size†	Count per Case	Case Dimensions (inches)	Pallet Configuration
Pint (16 oz.)	12	14⅜ × 9⅝ × 6⅞	N/A
Quart (30 oz.)	12	18½ × 12⅛ × 7	Tie 7 × 6 = 42
Half-gallon (64 oz.)	8	15 × 15 × 10½‡	Tie 6 × 7 = 42
Gallon (117 oz.)	4	16½ × 16½ × 6¾	Tie 6 × 6 = 36

*Seafood gumbo, shrimp-and-crabmeat bisque, shrimp creole, crawfish etouffee.

†All items packed in reusable plastic containers.

‡11 inches for shrimp bisque.

Note: Shelf life: frozen, one year; refrigerated, four to five days. Cooking instructions: Microwave, open skillet, slow cooker, or crock pot; serve over cooked rice; add hot sauce to taste.

is presented in Exhibit 5. The company's wholesale prices and a retail pricing survey from April 2001 are shown in Exhibit 6.

Azalea's Production Process

Azalea operated on a just-in-time production schedule with relatively short production runs that were initiated as needed to fill orders from distributors and retailers. Rathle and Addison shared responsibility for planning and organizing the company's overall production process, but the company's kitchen manager was responsible for day-to-day kitchen operations and coordinating the efforts of Azalea's three full-time and two part-time kitchen workers. Rathle's responsibility for planning and organizing the kitchen operations included scheduling the batch-cooking activities and purchasing ingredients. The company purchased fresh vegetables, fresh cooked crabmeat, cooked frozen shrimp, and packaging directly from manufacturers. It purchased other ingredients and supplies from one primary and two secondary food distributors. Most of the company's supply of crabmeat and crawfish was landed and processed by Gulf Coast fisheries, but Rathle and Addison had found that shrimp landed, cooked, and flash-frozen in California could be purchased at better prices than that from the nearby Gulf.

Azalea attempted to eliminate as much preparation as possible and concentrate only on the production of its gumbo, bisque, etouffee, and creole items. The company purchased diced vegetables and cooked shrimp, crabmeat, and crawfish to eliminate labor-intensive preparation activities. In addition, the purchase of processed vegetables and seafood reduced food waste and allowed for shorter cleanup periods.

Gumbo was cooked to order each day in the company's 150-gallon insulated steam kettle. Shrimp-and-crabmeat bisque, shrimp creole, and crawfish etouffee were not cooked every day since orders for those products were less frequent than for the company's gumbo. The gumbo and other products were cooked for approximately one and a half hours in the steam kettle before being transferred to pint or quart plastic tubs that would be stocked in supermarket freezers. Azalea's quart container is shown in Exhibit 7. The food prepared in the 150-gallon kettle was moved to a vertical agitator where the ingredients were evenly distributed. Shrimp, however, could not be added to the agitator because the machine's vertical structure, combined with the weight of the shrimp, allowed the shrimp to settle to the bottom rather than being distributed evenly.

exhibit 5   Nutritional Facts For Azalea Seafood Gumbo Shoppe's Seafood Dishes

Seafood Gumbo
Nutrition Facts

Serving Size 1 cup (228g)

Amount Per Serving

Calories 60   Calories from Fat 15

		% Daily Value*
Total Fat	2g	3%
Saturated Fat	0g	0%
Cholesterol	30mg	11%
Sodium	410mg	17%
Total Carbohydrate	6g	2%
Dietary Fiber	0g	0%
Sugars	5g	
Protein	5g	

Vitamin A 4%	•	Vitamin C 8%
Calcium 2%	•	Iron 4%

*Percent Daily Values are based on a 2,000-calorie diet.

Shrimp-and-Crabmeat Bisque
Nutrition Facts

Serving Size 2/3 cup (140g)

Servings Per Container approx. 14

Amount Per Serving

Calories 120   Calories from Fat 50

		% Daily Value*
Total Fat	26g	9%
Saturated Fat	1.5g	9%
Cholesterol	50mg	16%
Sodium	580mg	24%
Total Carbohydrate	9g	3%
Dietary Fiber	0g	0%
Sugars less than	1g	
Protein	7g	

Vitamin A 2%	•	Vitamin C 4%
Calcium 2%	•	Iron 4%

*Percent Daily Values are based on a 2,000-calorie diet.

Shrimp Creole
Nutrition Facts

Serving Size 2/3 cup (139g)

Amount Per Serving

Calories 40   Calories from Fat 10

		% Daily Value*
Total Fat	1g	2%
Saturated Fat	0g	0%
Cholesterol	20mg	6%
Sodium	300mg	13%
Total Carbohydrate	5g	2%
Dietary Fiber	0g	0%
Sugars	3g	
Protein	3g	

Vitamin A 6%	•	Vitamin C 10%
Calcium 2%	•	Iron 4%

*Percent Daily Values are based on a 2,000-calorie diet.

Crawfish Etouffee
Nutrition Facts

Serving Size 2/3 cup (140g)

Amount Per Serving

Calories 100   Calories from Fat 40

		% Daily Value*
Total Fat	4.5g	7%
Saturated Fat	1g	4%
Cholesterol	40mg	13%
Sodium	710mg	30%
Total Carbohydrate	9g	3%
Dietary Fiber less than	1g	2%
Sugars	7g	
Protein	7g	

Vitamin A 4%	•	Vitamin C 8%
Calcium 2%	•	Iron 6%

*Percent Daily Values are based on a 2,000-calorie diet.

To ensure consistent protein content, shrimp were weighed on a scale and placed by hand into each container. Once the frozen cooked shrimp were added to the containers, kitchen workers drew gumbo or other seafood mixtures from the 150-gallon kettle into four-gallon containers and then manually filled each tub. As soon as the workers filled batches of containers, they placed lids on each container and applied a safety seal around the rim of the lid. The filling process usually involved slight spills or overfills that would require cleaning the tubs before applying the safety seal. Filled and sealed

exhibit 6   Retail Pricing Survey and Wholesale Prices of Azalea
             Seafood Gumbo Shoppe's Seafood Dishes

Retail Pricing Survey		
Grocery Chain	**Item**	**Retail Price**
Winn-Dixie	1-quart seafood gumbo	$5.99
	1-quart crawfish etouffee	6.99
Wal-Mart Supercenters	1-quart seafood gumbo	5.47
	1-quart shrimp creole	5.47
Bruno's	1-quart seafood gumbo	5.98
	1-quart shrimp creole	5.98
	1-quart shrimp-and-crabmeat bisque	5.98
Greer's	1-quart seafood gumbo	5.98
	1-quart shrimp creole	5.98
Randall's	1-quart seafood gumbo	5.99
	1-quart shrimp creole	5.99
	1-quart shrimp-and-crabmeat bisque	5.99

Wholesale Prices		
Product	**Container Size**	**Wholesale Price**
Seafood gumbo	Gallon	$15.50
	Half gallon	8.00
	Quart	3.60
	Pint	2.00
Shrimp creole	Gallon	15.50
	Half gallon	8.00
	Quart	3.60
	Pint	2.00
Crawfish etouffee	Gallon	18.00
	Half gallon	9.25
	Quart	4.00
	Pint	2.25
Shrimp-and-crabmeat bisque	Gallon	16.50
	Half gallon	8.25
	Quart	3.60
	Pint	2.00

containers were then moved to a freezer where the temperature was brought down from about 150 degrees Fahrenheit to −10 degrees Fahrenheit within four hours.

The company had begun to use a new packaging process for its half-gallon and gallon food-service packages that added automation to replace many of the labor-intensive activities called for in its current packaging process. After gumbo or other products were cooked in the steam kettle, the cooked product was transferred by a piston pump through a three-inch-diameter stainless-steel pipe to a horizontal paddle wheel agitator where shrimp and other ingredients were evenly distributed. The seafood products were then conveyed by stainless-steel piping from the agitator to a vertical form/fill/seal machine that accurately metered the product into plastic boil-in

exhibit 7   Azalea Seafood Gumbo Shoppe's Quart Packaging
for Gumbo

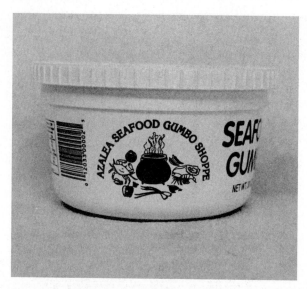

bags. The form/fill/seal machine had the capability to fill and seal 15 gallon-sized plastic bags per minute or 30 half-gallon pouches per minute. In production testing, the form/fill/seal machine filled quart and pint bags at the rate of about 40 per minute. The form/fill/seal machine left no residue on the filled and sealed boil-in bags. Each sealed bag of gumbo, etouffee, bisque, or creole was then moved to a 1,000-gallon chill tank that was able to lower the products' temperature from approximately 150 degrees Fahrenheit to about 35 degrees Fahrenheit within 15 minutes. The cooled packages were then moved to the company's freezer, where temperatures were lowered to −10 degrees Fahrenheit. The frozen seafood products were then placed in individual boxes and prepared for shipping. Once frozen, the prepared seafood products had a shelf life of one year.

Sales and Marketing

John Addison and Mike Rathle were both responsible for the company's sales and marketing efforts. When either partner identified a potential new customer, typically he would give price quotes over the phone and ship samples of the product to the company to evaluate. If the grocer or food-service distributor was interested in the new product, meetings would be set up to finalize the details. The partners' approach to developing new accounts had been successful with grocery accounts established with Wal-Mart, Bruno's, Winn-Dixie, Publix, Greer's, and Randall's. (See Exhibit 8 for a listing of Azalea's supermarket accounts.) The company used the same approach to develop food-service accounts and had been able to gain access to more than 300 restaurants through distribution agreements with PYA/Monarch and Wood Fruitticher. Usually establishing an account with a regional office of a national grocer took time, hard work, and some good fortune. Rathle explained how personal contacts, persistence, and salesmanship played a role in Azalea's gaining access to distribution in about 300 Wal-Mart Supercenters and 20 Sam's Clubs in the southeastern United States:

exhibit 8 Estimated Sales and Number of Locations for Azalea
Seafood Gumbo Shoppe's Supermarket Customers, 2000

Company	Estimated 2000 Sales (in millions)	Number of Stores (store sales of 2 million or greater)
Wal-Mart*	$22,947	908
Winn-Dixie	13,731	1,081
Randall's†	2,600	117
Bruno's	2,139	172
Jitney-Jungle/Delchamps	1,985	119
Greer's	90	38

*Supercenter statistics reduced to include only traditional supermarket items.
†Randall's is a subsidiary of Safeway.
Source: Progressive Grocer annual report, April 2001; company websites.

We got into Wal-Mart because a local Supercenter manager liked our product and asked that we sell to him on a direct delivery basis. Our product was selling well in that one store and I found out that a person I knew while working for Brach's was a grocery manager for Wal-Mart. I called him up and said, "You guys need to get me in the warehouse. Look at the volume I'm selling down here in this one store." Two weeks later we were in the warehouse selling to 300 Wal-Marts and 20 Sam's stores.

We were also lucky in the way that Wood Fruitticher became a distributor for our gumbo. John just called them up one day and they told them what volume we could supply and they said, "Ship it." Other accounts are very difficult to land. We've been in Winn-Dixie regionally for a long time, but we've made no progress working with their corporate people to get our gumbo distributed on a national basis.

Addison and Rathle's marketing efforts to grocers also included trying to keep a favorable product placement in its distribution network of 1,000 supermarkets. This was a challenging task since it was impossible for the two partners to call on all 1,000 store managers or seafood managers. Many times, store managers might decide to move items around in the store and Azalea's gumbo might be moved to an unfavorable freezer location without Addison or Rathle's knowledge. The company had hired a number of food brokers in the past to ensure a favorable placement but had only recently found a broker willing to devote sufficient attention to the company's products. The company had achieved some success in guaranteeing good in-store placement by purchasing nine-cubic-foot display-box freezers to place in some stores where its products were found. The bin-style display-box freezers contained only Azalea products and were usually placed in the center of the seafood department. The company's in-store placement in Wal-Mart and Sam's Clubs was not a concern since Wal-Mart maintained a Plan-O-Gram that standardized product placement in all stores. Rathle explained how the product's placement in the store had such a large bearing on its sales:

One of our biggest problems in supermarkets is having our product moved down to the end of a freezer aisle by the bait shrimp or getting stuck at the top-right corner of stand-up freezer. The best placement is center face—right at eye level. We usually have good placement in Wal-Mart or Sam's because we've proven our product sells and we've worked with them to get a good Plan-O-Gram placement. The Plan-O-Gram goes out to every Supercenter and Sam's so that every store has the exact same store schematic. As long as we've got a good spot on the Plan-O-Gram, the biggest part of the battle is won.

It's also very hard for us to get a good broker to distribute our products. We just aren't large enough to get the interest of a SUPERVALU. So we've been forced to work with corporate buyers to work on our placement. We have found a broker that is small enough to be interested in us, but yet he has a very good relationship with Winn-Dixie. He's done a great job getting us a good Plan-O-Gram placement with Winn-Dixies in Alabama and Mississippi, but we really need more brokers with relationships like his.

In some ways, Azalea's competition in supermarkets was limited since there were few companies that specialized in gumbo. However, when discussing competition, Addison explained how in other ways everything in the store competed with his gumbo:

Our competitor is every other product in the store or on the menu. A customer can purchase gumbo or they can buy fish. They can buy gumbo or they can buy steak or chicken. But as far as other gumbo producers, there are only about four or five out there. Usually they appear whenever we land a new supermarket account. When we were only in Bruno's, we had no real competition. Then we got into Delchamps and here came everyone out of the woodwork trying to take away the account. The same thing happened when we showed up in Wal-Mart. However, we've never really permanently lost business to a competitor. Sometimes a newcomer or existing competitor will pay a big slotting fee to get on the shelf, but if their product doesn't taste as good as ours or is overpriced, they'll be gone in three or four months. There are a couple of other companies that sell gumbo to food-service distributors, but we haven't really experienced any strong price competition in that segment.

Azalea's food-service accounts with food distributors were highly attractive because they required virtually no continued sales and promotion support after the account was established. Once the food distributor began to carry a prepared food item, it promoted the products it carried and placed regular orders with its manufacturers. About 10 percent of Azalea's production volume was dedicated to its food-service accounts. Most of the company's gumbo and other products were sold to large food-service accounts like U.S. Foodservice, but about 20 percent of Azalea's food-service sales were made to jobbers. Addison and Rathle believed that the company's just-in-time production process helped keep its costs low and improved cash flow, but since the company had very little inventory on hand, it frequently did not have any cases to sell to jobbers who stopped by.

Addison and Rathle had also gained some food-service accounts by calling directly on the corporate offices of various restaurant chains. The partners had been able to gain accounts with a few small regional chains, but had been unable to land accounts with larger chains even though many chain buyers liked the gumbo samples and were comfortable with Azalea's pricing. Rathle discussed how the company's austere facilities had been a problem for some corporate buyers:

I made a presentation to Applebee's a year or so ago to try to get them to serve our gumbo. The meeting was going very well with the buyer saying how great our gumbo was, but then she started talking about how the manufacturers of their food items had these state-of-the-art facilities. It seemed that she went on forever about the automation that she sees in the plants and manufacturers' use of statistical quality control techniques. I knew that the meeting was a waste of time when she asked when she could come down and inspect our plant.

We later had a similar opportunity with Cracker Barrel. We had sent a sample and they called to say that they liked the product and were coming down to work out the details of a contract. We knew from our meeting with Applebee's that we needed to impress these people with our facility. Well, we did the best we could do. We painted everything, did a lot of yard maintenance, and generally cleaned everything up. They never showed up. Actually, I think that they did show up, but didn't come in. On the day of the meeting, I was sitting in the office when I saw a rental Suburban full of suits pull into our driveway, sit for a while, and then turn around and pull off. Now I don't know if those were the guys from Cracker Barrel, but I never did receive a phone call about why they never showed for the meeting. But I can't really blame them. They probably pulled in here and said, "This is it? These guys can't do anything for us."

OPPORTUNITIES FOR FURTHER GROWTH

As Addison and Rathle began to break down the cooking equipment used at the Monterey Street block party, Rathle addressed some of the questions Addison had raised earlier in the evening. Rathle was so pleased with the new boil-in bags used for the company's half-gallon and gallon food-service packages that he was convinced the company should move to boil-in bags for its pint and quart packages sold in supermarkets:

> You know, I am really happy with the new boil-in bags we're using for the food-service packages. I've been thinking that we might want to get rid of our pint and quart tubs. First, we'll have less wear and tear on the freezer and lower utility expenses. Right now we're running at a high load factor because we're bringing 150-degree gumbo down to −10 degrees. We've got to set the freezer at −25 degrees to do that. By using the chill tank for all of our gumbo, we'll take gumbo at 35 degrees down to −10 degrees—so we'll only need to set the freezer at −10 degrees. I've run some numbers and I think that the lower load factor will save about 30 percent per month in utility expense and about $2,000 per year in freezer maintenance. We'll have some labor cost savings because we won't have to weigh shrimp, safety-seal the tubs, or wipe spilled gumbo from the tubs, but that will probably be offset by the cost of boxes needed for the boil-in bags.
>
> Another advantage of the boil-in bags is our products' appearance and the flexibility it gives us for new product introductions. John, you know as neat of a pourer as I am, I can't keep those containers from sloshing around as they are racked and wheeled into the freezer. When they come out of the freezer we've either got gumbo down the side of the tub or under the safety seal.
>
> Also, the boxes will look more like what people are used to seeing from national brands. We can have a full-color photo-quality image of our product right on the front of the box. Initially, the boxes are going to cost about 50 percent more per container than what we pay for the tubs, but I think we'll get better placement in the stores with a box that is attractive and can be stood on end in a freezer near other seafood items. I believe that our sales will increase by at least 20 percent because of the more attractive packaging. Right now, I'm not sure that anyone knows what's in our tubs unless they're already familiar with the product. Also, we haven't raised our prices in two years. Maybe a price increase could accompany a packaging change. Also, the additional cost of the box will eventually fall below what we currently pay for tubs once our order size increases.

Addison agreed with Rathle's observations but pointed out that gumbo could be wiped off the tub before shipping and that they had rarely heard a complaint from a retailer about gumbo under the safety seal. Rathle replied,

> Well, it bugs me because I know it doesn't look good. I wouldn't buy a product that's coming out of the container. Plus, I think that we could sell true ready-to-serve meals if we put a bag of rice and a gumbo boil-in bag in the same box where both could be dropped in a pot of boiling water and served within 10 minutes. The individual servings might also be a hit with restaurants since instead of cooking a gallon of gumbo that might not be completely used, they could take out a six-ounce pack that could be boiled or microwaved whenever someone ordered a cup of gumbo.

Rathle mentioned that his only reservation with changing to boil-in bags for retail sales was the potential for the bags to contain varying amounts of shrimp:

I've tested and tested the paddle wheel agitator and it seems that the number of shrimp in the bags is always consistent, but I know and you know that someone out there is going to buy a pint of gumbo that doesn't contain as many shrimp as what they are used to. I'd just hate for someone to say, "Gosh, it had more shrimp in it last time."

Addison didn't comment on the consistency issue and shifted the conversation to the need for a new production facility:

You know I really think that we're going to have to move to a new facility before we can land many more accounts—especially in food service. It just seems that large customers are worried about our sanitation, which has never been a problem, and our ability to meet their production needs. They see this 2,200-square-foot building and think we can't do as much volume as we can. We'll need about $120,000 in new equipment if we move. Also, our rent will probably go up by about $1,000–$1,500 per month, but we have about $5,000 in monthly payments on equipment loans that will pay out within the next six months. Plus, if the people in Bentonville wanted our product in 100 Sam's locations, I'm not sure we could do it with our current facility.

Also, if we had a larger building specifically designed for food processing, we could become USDA certified. USDA certification would allow us to add new products like chicken gumbo that would sell at a lower price point than seafood gumbo. We could also add new products like Red Beans and Sausage or Cajun Stuffed Chicken Breasts. We could also do custom entrées for our food-service customers. None of that will happen in our current building since we don't have 12-foot ceilings, two bathrooms, an office for the USDA inspector to park, or isolation freezers for raw food.

With the last of the cooking equipment loaded, Addison and Rathle got in the truck to return to the plant. Addison mentioned to Rathle that Azalea's current production capacity would allow the company to increase annual sales to about $1.5 million without any further investment. He believed that both partners could live very well if the company could grow sales by another 50 percent without the addition of debt or increased rental expenses. However, Addison went on to comment that the highest return on their investment of time and money hinged on their ability to grow revenues and earnings by an additional five- to tenfold to become an acquisition candidate for a large food company or food distributor.

case 10 Kentucky Fried Chicken and the Global Fast-Food Industry

Jeffrey A. Krug

University of Illinois at Urbana-Champaign

Kentucky Fried Chicken Corporation (KFC) was the world's largest chicken restaurant chain and third largest fast-food chain in 2000. KFC had a 55 percent share of the U.S. chicken restaurant market in terms of sales and operated more than 10,800 restaurants in 85 countries. KFC was one of the first fast-food chains to go international in the late 1950s and was one of the world's most recognizable brands. KFC's early international strategy was to grow its company and franchise restaurant base throughout the world. By early 2000, however, KFC had refocused its international strategy on several high-growth markets, including Canada, Australia, the United Kingdom, China, Korea, Thailand, Puerto Rico, and Mexico. KFC planned to base much of its growth in these markets on company-owned restaurants, which gave KFC greater control over product quality, service, and restaurant cleanliness. In other international markets, KFC planned to grow primarily through franchises, which were operated by local business-people who understood the local market better than KFC. Franchises enabled KFC to more rapidly expand into smaller countries that could only support a small number of restaurants. KFC planned to aggressively expand its company-owned restaurants into other major international markets in Europe and Latin America in the future. Latin America was an appealing area for investment because of the size of its markets, its common language and culture, and its geographical proximity to the United States. Mexico was of particular interest because of the North American Free Trade Agreement (NAFTA), which went into effect in 1994 and created a free-trade zone between Canada, the United States, and Mexico. However, other fast-food chains such as McDonald's, Burger King, and Wendy's were rapidly expanding into other countries in Latin America such as Venezuela, Brazil, Argentina, and Chile. KFC's tasks in Latin America were to select the proper countries for future investment and to devise an appropriate strategy for penetrating the Latin American market.

COMPANY HISTORY

In 1952, fast-food franchising was still in its infancy when Harland Sanders began his travels across the United States to speak with prospective franchisees about his "Colonel Sanders Recipe Kentucky Fried Chicken." By 1960, "Colonel" Sanders had granted KFC franchises to more than 200 take-home retail outlets and restaurants across the United States. He had also established a number of franchises in Canada. By 1963, the number of KFC franchises had risen to more than 300 and revenues topped $500 million. The Colonel celebrated his 74th birthday the following year and was eager to lessen the load of running the day-to-day operations of his business. Thus, he looked for potential buyers and sold his business to two Louisville businessmen—Jack Massey and John Young Brown Jr.—for $2 million. The Colonel stayed on as a public relations man and goodwill ambassador for the company. During the next five years, Massey and Brown concentrated on growing KFC's franchise system across the United States. In 1966, they took KFC public and the company was listed on the New York Stock Exchange. By the late 1960s, KFC had established a strong foothold in the United States, and Massey and Brown turned their attention to international markets. In 1969, KFC entered into a joint venture with Mitsuoishi Shoji Kaisha, Ltd. that involved the rights to operate franchises in Japan and England. KFC subsidiaries were later established in Hong Kong, South Africa, Australia, New Zealand, and Mexico. By 1971, KFC had established 2,450 franchised restaurants and 600 company-owned restaurants in 48 countries.

Heublein, Inc.

In 1971, KFC entered into negotiations with Heublein, Inc. to discuss a possible merger. The decision to consider a merger was partially driven by Brown's desire to pursue other interests including a political career (Brown was elected governor of Kentucky in 1977). Several months later, Heublein acquired KFC. Heublein was in the business of producing vodka, mixed cocktails, dry gin, cordials, beer, and other alcoholic beverages; however, it had little experience in the restaurant business. Conflicts quickly erupted between Colonel Sanders and Heublein management. In particular, Colonel Sanders became increasingly distraught over quality-control issues and restaurant cleanliness. By 1977, new restaurant openings had slowed to only 20 a year, few restaurants were being remodeled, and service quality had declined. To combat these problems, Heublein sent in a new management team to redirect KFC's strategy. A "back-to-the-basics" strategy was implemented and new restaurant construction was halted until existing restaurants could be upgraded and operating problems eliminated. A program for remodeling existing restaurants was implemented, an emphasis was placed on cleanliness and service, marginal products were eliminated, and product consistency was reestablished. This strategy enabled KFC to gain better control of its operations and it was soon again aggressively building new restaurants.

R. J. Reynolds Industries, Inc.

In 1982, R. J. Reynolds Industries, Inc. (RJR), acquired Heublein and merged it into a wholly owned subsidiary. The acquisition of Heublein was part of RJR's corporate strategy of diversifying into unrelated businesses such as energy, transportation, food, and restaurants to reduce its dependence on tobacco. Tobacco had driven RJR's sales since its founding in North Carolina in 1875; however, sales of cigarettes and tobacco products, while profitable, were declining because of reduced consumption in the

United States. Reduced consumption was primarily the result of an increased awareness among Americans of the negative health consequences of smoking.

RJR, however, had little more experience in the restaurant business than Heublein when it acquired KFC 11 years earlier. In contrast to Heublein, which tried to actively manage KFC using its own managers, RJR allowed KFC to operate autonomously with little interference. RJR believed that KFC's executives were better qualified to operate the business than their own managers were. By leaving KFC's top management team largely intact, RJR avoided many of the operating problems that plagued Heublein during its ownership of KFC.

In 1985, RJR acquired Nabisco Corporation for $4.9 billion. The acquisition of Nabisco was an attempt to redefine RJR as a world leader in the consumer foods industry. Nabisco sold a variety of well-known cookies, crackers, and other grocery products, including Oreo cookies, Ritz crackers, Planters peanuts, LifeSavers candies, and Milk-Bone dog biscuits. RJR subsequently divested many of its non-consumer-food businesses. It sold KFC to PepsiCo, Inc. one year later.

PepsiCo, Inc.

Corporate Strategy   PepsiCo, Inc. was formed in 1965 with the merger of the Pepsi-Cola Co. and Frito-Lay Inc. The merger created one of the largest consumer-products companies in the United States. Pepsi-Cola's traditional business was the sale of soft-drink concentrates to licensed independent and company-owned bottlers that manufactured, sold, and distributed Pepsi-Cola soft drinks. Pepsi-Cola's best-known trademarks were Pepsi-Cola, Diet Pepsi, and Mountain Dew. Frito-Lay manufactured and sold a variety of leading snack foods that included Lay's potato chips, Doritos tortilla chips, Tostitos tortilla chips, and Ruffles potato chips. Soon after the merger, PepsiCo initiated an aggressive acquisition program, buying a number of companies in areas unrelated to its major businesses such as North American Van Lines, Wilson Sporting Goods, and Lee Way Motor Freight. However, PepsiCo lacked the management skills required to operate these businesses, and performance failed to live up to expectations. In 1984, chairman and chief executive officer Don Kendall restructured PepsiCo's operations. Businesses that did not support PepsiCo's consumer-product orientation (including North American Van Lines, Wilson Sporting Goods, and Lee Way Motor Freight) were divested. PepsiCo's foreign bottling operations were then sold to local business-people who better understood their country's culture and business practices. Last, PepsiCo was organized into three divisions: soft drinks, snack foods, and restaurants.

Restaurant Business and Acquisition of KFC   PepsiCo believed that the restaurant business complemented its consumer product orientation. The marketing of fast food followed many of the same patterns as the marketing of soft drinks and snack foods. Pepsi-Cola soft drinks and fast-food products could be marketed together in the same television and radio segments, thereby providing higher returns for each advertising dollar. Restaurant chains also provided an additional outlet for the sale of Pepsi soft drinks. Thus, PepsiCo believed it could take advantage of numerous synergies by operating the three businesses under the same corporate umbrella. PepsiCo also believed that its management skills could be transferred among the three businesses. This practice was compatible with PepsiCo's policy of frequently moving managers among its business units as a means of developing future executives. PepsiCo first entered the restaurant business in 1977 when it acquired Pizza Hut. Taco Bell was acquired one year later. To complete its diversification into the restaurant industry, PepsiCo acquired

KFC in 1986. The acquisition of KFC gave PepsiCo the leading market share in the chicken (KFC), pizza (Pizza Hut), and Mexican-food (Taco Bell) segments of the fast-food industry.

Management Following its acquisition of KFC, PepsiCo initiated sweeping changes. It announced that the franchise contract would be changed to give PepsiCo greater control over KFC franchisees and to make it easier to close poorly performing restaurants. Staff at KFC was reduced in order to cut costs and many KFC managers were replaced with PepsiCo managers. Soon after the acquisition, KFC's new personnel manager, who had just relocated from PepsiCo's New York headquarters, was overheard in the KFC cafeteria saying, "There will be no more homegrown tomatoes in this organization."

Rumors spread quickly among KFC employees about their opportunities for advancement within KFC and PepsiCo. Harsh comments by PepsiCo managers about KFC, its people, and its traditions; several restructurings that led to layoffs throughout KFC; the replacement of KFC managers with PepsiCo managers; and conflicts between KFC and PepsiCo's corporate cultures created a morale problem within KFC. KFC's culture was built largely on Colonel Sanders's laid-back approach to management. Employees enjoyed good job security and stability. A strong loyalty had been created among KFC employees over the years as a result of the Colonel's efforts to provide for his employees' benefits, pension, and other non-income needs. In addition, the southern environment in Louisville resulted in a friendly, relaxed atmosphere at KFC's corporate offices. This corporate culture was left essentially unchanged during the Heublein and RJR years.

In contrast to KFC, PepsiCo's culture was characterized by a much stronger emphasis on performance. Top performers expected to move up through the ranks quickly. PepsiCo used its KFC, Pizza Hut, Taco Bell, Frito-Lay, and Pepsi-Cola divisions as training grounds for its executives, rotating its best managers through the five divisions on average every two years. This practice created immense pressure on managers to demonstrate their management skills within short periods in order to maximize their potential for promotion. This practice also reinforced the feelings of KFC managers that they had few opportunities for promotion within the new company. One PepsiCo manager commented, "You may have performed well last year, but if you don't perform well this year, you're gone, and there are 100 ambitious guys with Ivy League MBAs at PepsiCo's headquarters in New York who would love to have your job." Unwanted effects of this performance-driven culture were: employee loyalty was often lost and turnover was higher than in other companies.

Kyle Craig, president of KFC's U.S. operations, commented on KFC's relationship with its corporate parent:

> The KFC culture is an interesting one because it was dominated by a lot of KFC folks, many of whom have been around since the days of the Colonel. Many of those people were very intimidated by the PepsiCo culture, which is a very high performance, high accountability, highly driven culture. People were concerned about whether they would succeed in the new culture. Like many companies, we have had a couple of downsizings which further made people nervous. Today, there are fewer old KFC people around and I think to some degree people have seen that the PepsiCo culture can drive some pretty positive results. I also think the PepsiCo people who have worked with KFC have modified their cultural values somewhat and they can see that there were a lot of benefits in the old KFC culture.
>
> PepsiCo pushes their companies to perform strongly, but whenever there is a slip in performance, it increases the culture gap between PepsiCo and KFC. I have been involved in two downsizings over which I have been the chief architect. They have been probably the two most gut-wrenching experiences of my career. Because you know you're dealing with peoples' lives and their families, these changes can be emotional if you care about the

people in your organization. However, I do fundamentally believe that your first obligation is to the entire organization.

A second problem for PepsiCo was its poor relationship with KFC franchisees. A month after becoming KFC's president and chief executive officer in 1989, John Cranor addressed KFC's franchisees in Louisville in order to explain the details of the new franchise contract. This was the first contract change in 13 years. It gave PepsiCo greater power to take over weak franchises, relocate restaurants, and make changes in existing restaurants. In addition, restaurants would no longer be protected from competition from new KFC units and PepsiCo would have the right to raise royalty fees on existing restaurants as contracts came up for renewal. After Cranor finished his address, there was an uproar among the attending franchisees, who jumped to their feet to protest the changes. KFC's franchise association later sued PepsiCo over the new contract. The contract remained unresolved until 1996, when the most objectionable parts of the contract were removed by KFC's new president and CEO, David Novak. A new contract was ratified by KFC's franchisees in 1997.

PepsiCo's Divestiture of KFC, Pizza Hut, and Taco Bell   PepsiCo's strategy of diversifying into three distinct but related markets—soft drinks, snack foods, and fast-food restaurants—created one of the world's largest consumer product companies and a portfolio of some of the world's most recognizable brands. Between 1990 and 1996, PepsiCo's sales grew at an annual rate of more than 10 percent, surpassing $31 billion in 1996. PepsiCo's growth, however, masked troubles in its fast-food businesses. Operating margins (operating profit as a percent of sales) at Pepsi-Cola and Frito Lay averaged 12 and 17 percent, respectively, between 1990 and 1996. During the same period, margins at KFC, Pizza Hut, and Taco Bell fell from an average of more than 8 percent in 1990 to a little more than 4 percent in 1996. Declining margins in the fast-food chains reflected increasing maturity in the U.S. fast-food industry, more intense competition, and the aging of KFC and Pizza Hut's restaurant bases. As a result, PepsiCo's restaurant chains absorbed nearly one-half of PepsiCo's annual capital spending during the 1990s, but they generated less than one-third of PepsiCo's cash flows. This meant that cash had to be diverted from PepsiCo's soft drink and snack food businesses to its restaurant businesses. This reduced PepsiCo's corporate return on assets, made it more difficult to compete effectively with Coca-Cola, and hurt its stock price. In 1997, PepsiCo decided to spin off its restaurant businesses into a new company called Tricon Global Restaurants, Inc. The new company was based at KFC's headquarters in Louisville, Kentucky (see Exhibit 1).

PepsiCo's objective was to reposition itself as a beverage and snack food company, strengthen its balance sheet, and create more consistent earnings growth. PepsiCo received a one-time distribution from Tricon of $4.7 billion, $3.7 billion of which was used to pay off short-term debt. The balance was earmarked for stock repurchases. In 1998, PepsiCo acquired Tropicana Products, which controlled more than 40 percent of the U.S. chilled orange juice market. Because of the divestiture of KFC, Pizza Hut, and Taco Bell, PepsiCo's sales fell by $11.3 billion and its assets fell by $7.0 billion between 1997 and 1999. Profitability, however, soared. Operating margins rose from 11 percent in 1997 to 14 percent in 1999, and return on assets rose from 11 percent in 1997 to 16 percent in 1999. By focusing on high-cash-flow market leaders, PepsiCo raised profitability while decreasing its asset base.

FAST-FOOD INDUSTRY

According to the National Restaurant Association, food-service sales increased by 5.4 percent, to $358 billion, in 1999. More than 800,000 restaurants and food outlets made

exhibit 1   Tricon Global Restaurants, Inc., Organization Chart, 2000

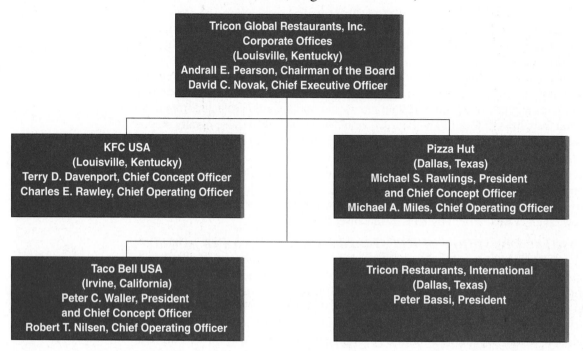

up the U.S. restaurant industry, which employed 11 million people. Sales were highest in the full-service, sit-down sector, which grew by 7 percent, to $121 billion. Fast-food sales grew at a slower rate, rising by about 5 percent, to $110 billion. Fast-food sales surpassed the full-service sector during the mid-1990s; however, maturation of the fast-food sector and rising incomes among many Americans helped full-service restaurants again overtake fast-food outlets as the largest sector in the restaurant industry. The full-service and fast-food segments were expected to make up about 65 percent of total food-service industry sales in 2000.

Major Fast-Food Segments

Eight major segments made up the fast-food sector of the restaurant industry: sandwich chains, pizza chains, family restaurants, grill buffet chains, dinner houses, chicken chains, nondinner concepts, and other chains. Sales data for the leading restaurant chains in each segment are shown in Exhibit 2. McDonald's, with sales of more than $19 billion in 1999, accounted for 15 percent of the sales of the nation's top 100 restaurant chains. The second-largest chain—Burger King—had less than a 7 percent share of the market.

Sandwich chains made up the largest segment of the fast-food market. McDonald's accounted for 35 percent of the sandwich segment, while Burger King ran a distant second, with a 16 percent market share. Despite continued success by some chains like McDonald's, Carl's Jr., Jack in the Box, Wendy's, and White Castle, other chains like Hardee's, Burger King, Taco Bell, and Checkers were struggling. McDonald's generated the greatest per store sales—about $1.5 million per year. The average U.S.

exhibit 2 1999 Sales and Market Shares of Top 50 U.S. Fast-Food Restaurants, Grouped by Segment ($ in millions)

Rank	Sandwich Chains	Sales	Share	Rank	Dinner Houses	Sales	Share
1	McDonald's	$19,006	35.0%	9	Applebee's	$ 2,305	14.9%
2	Burger King	8,659	16.0	15	Red Lobster	2,005	13.0
3	Wendy's	5,250	9.7	16	Outback Steakhouse	1,729	11.2
4	Taco Bell	5,200	9.6	17	Olive Garden	1,610	10.4
7	Subway	3,200	5.9	19	Chili's Grill & Bar	1,555	10.1
10	Arby's	2,260	4.2	22	T.G.I. Friday's	1,364	8.8
11	Dairy Queen	2,145	4.0	30	Ruby Tuesday	920	5.9
12	Hardee's	2,139	3.9	49	Lone Star Steakhouse	468	3.0
18	Sonic Drive-In	1,589	2.9		Other chains	3,520	22.7
20	Jack in the Box	1,510	2.8		Total segment	$15,476	100.0%
32	Carl's Jr.	887	1.6				
46	Whataburger	503	0.9				
	Other chains	1,890	3.5				
	Total segment	$54,238	100.0%				

Rank	Pizza Chains	Sales	Share	Rank	Chicken Chains	Sales	Share
5	Pizza Hut	$ 5,000	44.0%	6	KFC	$4,378	55.2%
8	Domino's	2,560	22.5	28	Popeyes	986	12.7
21	Papa John's	1,426	12.6	29	Chick-fil-A	946	12.1
23	Little Caesars	1,200	10.6	34	Boston Market	855	11.0
50	Sbarro	466	4.1	38	Church's	705	9.0
	Other chains	703	6.2		Total segment	$7,870	100.0%
	Total segment	$11,355	100.0%				

Rank	Family Restaurants	Sales	Share	Rank	Other Dinner Chains	Sales	Share
13	Denny's	$2,079	22.7%	37	Long John Silver's	$ 716	15.7%
24	Cracker Barrel	1,163	12.7	41	Walt Disney Co.	666	14.7
26	IHOP	1,077	11.8	43	Old Country Buffet	589	13.0
33	Shoney's	869	9.5	47	Luby's Cafeteria	502	11.0
35	Perkins	790	8.6	48	Captain D's Seafood	499	11.0
36	Bob Evans	727	8.0		Other chains	1,574	34.6
40	Friendly's	671	7.3		Total segment	$4,546	100.0%
42	Waffle House	620	6.8				
	Other chains	1,144	12.6				
	Total segment	$9,140	100.0%				

Rank	Grill Buffet Chains	Sales	Share	Rank	Nondinner Concepts	Sales	Share
31	Golden Corral	$ 899	32.3%	14	Dunkin' Donuts	$2,007	42.9%
39	Ryan's	704	25.3	25	7-Eleven	1,117	23.8
45	Ponderosa	560	20.1	27	Starbucks	987	21.1
	Other Chains	621	22.3	44	Baskin-Robbins	573	12.2
	Total segment	$2,784	100.0%		Total segment	$4,684	100.0%

Source: *Nation's Restaurant News.*

chain generated $800,000 in sales per store in 1999. Per store sales at Burger King remained flat, and Hardee's per store sales declined by 10 percent. Franchisees at Burger King complained of leadership problems within the corporate parent (London-based Diageo PLC), an impending increase in royalties and franchise fees, and poor advertising. Hardee's corporate parent (CKE Enterprises), which also owned Carl's Jr. and Taco Bueno, planned to franchise many of its company-owned Hardee's restaurants and to allow the system to shrink as low-performing units were closed. It also planned to refocus Hardee's strategy in the southeastern part of the United States, where brand loyalty remained strong.

Dinner houses made up the second largest and fastest-growing fast-food segment in 1999. Sales of dinner houses increased by more than 13 percent during the year, surpassing the average increase of 6 percent among all fast-food chains. Much of the growth in dinner houses came from new unit construction, a marked contrast with other fast-food chains, which had already slowed U.S. construction because of market saturation. Much of the new unit construction took place in new suburban markets and small towns. Applebee's and Red Lobster dominated the dinner-house segment. Each chain generated more than $2 billion in sales in 1999. The fastest-growing dinner houses, however, were chains generating less than $500 million in sales such as On The Border, The Cheesecake Factory, O'Charley's, Romano's Macaroni Grill, and Hooters. Each of these chains increased sales by more than 20 percent in 1999.

Increased growth among dinner houses came at the expense of slower growth among sandwich chains, pizza chains, grilled buffet chains, and family restaurants. Too many restaurants chasing the same customers was responsible for much of the slower growth in these other fast-food categories. However, sales growth within each segment differed from one chain to another. In the family segment, for example, Friendly's and Shoney's were forced to shut down restaurants because of declining profits, but Steak n Shake and Cracker Barrel each expanded its restaurant base by more than 10 percent. Within the pizza segment, Pizza Hut and Little Caesars closed underperforming restaurants, but Papa John's and Chuck E. Cheese's continued to aggressively grow their U.S. restaurant bases. The hardest-hit segment was grilled buffet chains, which generated the lowest increase in sales (less than 4 percent). Dinner houses, because of their more upscale atmosphere and higher-ticket items, were better positioned to take advantage of the aging and wealthier U.S. population, which increasingly demanded higher-quality food in more attractive settings. Even dinner houses, however, faced the prospect of market saturation and increased competition in the near future.

Chicken Segment

KFC continued to dominate the chicken segment, with sales of $4.4 billion in 1999 (see Exhibit 3). Its nearest competitor, Popeyes, ran a distant second, with sales of $1.0 billion. KFC's leadership in the U.S. market was so extensive that it had fewer opportunities to expand its U.S. restaurant base, which was only growing at about 1 percent per year. Despite its dominance, KFC was losing market share as other chicken chains increased sales at a faster rate. KFC's share of chicken segment sales fell from 71 percent in 1989 to less than 56 percent in 1999, a 10-year drop of 15 percent. During the same period, Chick-fil-A and Boston Market increased their combined market share by 17 percent (see Exhibit 4). In the early 1990s, many industry analysts predicted that Boston Market would challenge KFC for market leadership. Boston Market was a new restaurant chain that emphasized roasted rather than fried chicken. It successfully created the image of an upscale deli offering healthy, "home-style" alternatives to fried

exhibit 3 Comparative Statistics for Top U.S. Chicken Chains, 1994–99

	1994	1995	1996	1997	1998	1999	Growth Rate
Sales (in millions)							
KFC	$3,587	$3,740	$3,935	$4,002	$4,171	$4,378	4%
Popeyes	614	660	677	720	843	986	10
Chick-fil-A	451	502	570	643	767	946	16
Boston Market	371	754	1,100	1,197	929	855	18
Church's	465	501	526	574	620	705	9
Total	$5,488	$6,157	$6,808	$7,136	$7,330	$7,870	7
Number of U.S. restaurants							
KFC	5,081	5,103	5,078	5,092	5,105	5,231	1%
Popeyes	853	889	894	945	1,066	1,165	6
Chick-fil-A	534	825	717	749	812	897	11
Boston Market	534	829	1,087	1,166	889	858	10
Church's	937	953	989	1,070	1,105	1,178	5
Total	7,939	8,599	8,765	9,022	8,977	9,329	3
Sales per unit ($000s)							
KFC	706	733	775	786	817	837	3%
Popeyes	720	742	757	762	790	847	3
Chick-fil-A	845	608	795	859	945	1,055	5
Boston Market	695	910	1,012	1,027	1,045	997	7
Church's	496	526	532	536	561	598	4
Average	691	716	777	791	816	844	4

Source: Tricon Global Restaurants, Inc., 1999 annual report; Chick-fil-A, corporate headquarters, Atlanta; Boston Chicken, Inc., 1999 annual report; *Nation's Restaurant News*, 2000.

exhibit 4 Market Shares of Top U.S. Chicken Chains
Based on Annual Sales, 1989–99

	KFC	Popeyes	Chick-fil-A	Boston Market	Church's	Total
1989	70.8%	12.0%	6.2%	0.0%	11.0%	100.0%
1990	71.3	12.3	6.6	0.0	9.8	100.0
1991	72.7	11.4	7.0	0.0	8.9	100.0
1992	71.5	11.4	7.5	0.9	8.7	100.0
1993	68.7	11.4	8.0	3.0	8.9	100.0
1994	65.4	11.2	8.2	6.7	8.5	100.0
1995	60.7	10.7	8.2	12.3	8.1	100.0
1996	57.8	9.9	8.4	16.2	7.7	100.0
1997	56.1	10.1	9.0	16.8	8.0	100.0
1998	56.9	11.5	10.5	12.7	8.4	100.0
1999	55.6	12.5	12.0	10.9	9.0	100.0
1994–99 change	−9.8%	1.3%	3.8%	4.2%	0.5%	
1989–99 change	−15.2%	0.5%	5.8%	10.9%	−2.0%	

chicken and other fast food. In order to distinguish itself from more traditional fast-food concepts, it refused to construct drive-throughs and it established most of its units outside of shopping malls rather than at major city intersections.

On the surface, it appeared that Boston Market and Chick-fil-A's market-share gains were achieved primarily by taking customers away from KFC. Another look at the data, however, reveals that KFC's sales grew at a stable rate in the 1990s. Boston Market, rather than drawing customers away from KFC, appealed primarily to consumers who did not regularly frequent KFC and wanted healthy, nonfried chicken alternatives. Boston Market was able to expand the chicken segment beyond its traditional emphasis on fried chicken by offering nonfried chicken products that appealed to this new consumer group. After aggressively growing its restaurant base through 1997, however, Boston Market was unable to handle mounting debt problems. It soon entered bankruptcy proceedings. McDonald's acquired Boston Market in 2000, following acquisition of Denver, Colorado-based Chipotle Mexican Grill in 1998 and Columbus, Ohio-based Donatos Pizza in 1999. McDonald's hoped the acquisitions would help it expand its U.S. restaurant base, since the U.S. was approaching saturation with McDonald's locations. Chick-fil-A's growth came primarily from its aggressive shopping-mall strategy where it was capitalizing on the trend to establish large food courts in shopping malls. Despite gains by Boston Market and Chick-fil-A, KFC's customer base remained loyal to the KFC brand because of its unique taste. KFC has also continued to dominate the dinner and take-out segments of the industry.

Popeyes replaced Boston Market as the second-largest chicken chain in 1999. Popeyes and Church's had traditionally followed similar strategies—to compete head-on with other "fried chicken" chains. Popeyes, however, was in the process of shifting its focus to Cajun fast food, after it successfully launched its Louisiana Legends One-Pot Cajun Meals of jambalaya, gumbo, shrimp, and crawfish etoufee. Church's was determined to distinguish itself by placing a heavier emphasis on its "made-from-scratch" southern image. In 1999, it broadened its menu to include buffalo chicken wings, macaroni and cheese, beans and rice, and collard greens. Chick-fil-A focused on pressure-cooked and char-grilled skinless chicken breast sandwiches, which it had traditionally sold to customers in sit-down restaurants in shopping malls. As more malls added food courts, however, malls became less enthusiastic about allocating separate store space to restaurants. Therefore, Chick-fil-A began to open smaller units in shopping mall food courts, hospitals, and colleges as a way of complementing its existing sit-down restaurants in shopping malls. It also began to open freestanding units in selected locations.

Demographic Trends

A number of demographic and societal trends influenced the demand for food eaten outside of the home. During the last two decades, rising incomes, greater affluence among a greater percentage of American households, higher divorce rates, and the fact that people married later in life contributed to the rising number of single households and the demand for fast food. More than 50 percent of women worked outside of the home, a dramatic increase since 1970. This number was expected to rise to 65 percent by 2010. Double-income households contributed to rising household incomes and increased the number of times families ate out. Less time to prepare meals inside the home added to this trend. Countering these trends, however, was a slower growth in the U.S. population and an oversupply of fast-food chains that increased consumer alternatives and intensified competition.

Baby boomers aged 35 to 50 constituted the largest consumer group for fast-food restaurants. Generation Xers (ages 25 to 34) and the "mature" category (ages 51 to 64) made up the second and third largest groups. As consumers aged, they became less enamored with fast food and were more likely to patronize dinner houses and full-service restaurants. Sales of many Mexican-food restaurants, which were extremely popular during the 1980s, began to slow as Japanese, Indian, and Vietnamese restaurants became more fashionable. Ethnic foods in general were rising in popularity as U.S. immigrants, which constituted 10 percent of the U.S. population in 2000, looked for establishments that sold their native foods.

The greatest concern for fast-food operators was the shortage of employees in the 16-to-24 age category. Most Americans in this age category had never experienced a recession or an economic downturn. During the 1970s, Americans experienced double-digit inflation, high interest rates, and high unemployment, as well as two major oil crises that resulted in gas shortages. The U.S. economy began to expand again during the early 1980s and continued to expand almost unabated through 2000. Unemployment was at its lowest point in more than two decades, and many high school and college graduates, especially those in business and engineering, enjoyed a robust job market that made it more difficult for fast-food operators to find capable employees.

Labor costs made up about 30 percent of a fast-food chain's total costs, second only to food and beverage costs. Intense competition, however, made it difficult for restaurants to increase prices sufficiently to cover the increased cost of labor. Consumers made decisions about where to eat partially based on price. Therefore, profit margins were squeezed. In order to reduce costs, restaurants eliminated low-margin food items, increased portion sizes, and improved product value to offset price increases. Restaurants also attempted to increase consumer traffic through discounting, by accepting coupons from competitors, by offering two-for-one specials, and by making limited-time offerings.

Costs could also be lowered and operations made more efficient by increasing the use of technology. According to the National Restaurant Association, most restaurant operators viewed computers as their number one tool for improving efficiency. Computers could be used to improve labor scheduling, accounting, payroll, sales analysis, and inventory control. Most restaurant chains were also using point-of-sale systems that recorded the selected menu items and gave the cashier a breakdown of food items and the ticket price. These systems decreased serving times and increased cashier accuracy. Chains like McDonald's and Carl's Jr. converted to new food preparation systems that allowed them to prepare food more accurately and to prepare a great variety of sandwiches using the same process.

Higher costs and poor availability of prime real estate was another trend that negatively affected profitability. A plot of land suitable for a normal-sized freestanding restaurant cost between $1.5 and $2.5 million. Leasing was a less costly alternative to buying. Nevertheless, market saturation decreased per store sales as newer units cannibalized sales from existing units. As a result, most food chains began to expand their U.S. restaurant bases into alternative distribution channels in hospitals, airports, colleges, highway rest areas, gas stations, shopping mall food courts, and large retail stores or by dual branding with other fast-food concepts.

While the news media touted the benefits of low-fat diets during the 1970s and 1980s, consumer demand for beef began to increase again during the 1990s. The U.S. Department of Agriculture estimated that Americans ate an average of 64 pounds of red meat each year. The growing demand for steak and prime rib helped fuel the growth in dinner houses that continued into 2000. According to the National

Restaurant Association, other food items that were growing in popularity included chicken, hot and spicy foods, smoothies, wraps and pitas, salads, and espresso and specialty coffees. Starbucks, the Seattle-based coffee retailer, capitalized on the popularity of specialty coffees by aggressively expanding its coffee-shop concept into shopping malls, commercial buildings, and bookstores such as Barnes & Noble. Starbucks increased its store base by 28 percent in 1999, the greatest increase of any major restaurant chain.

International Fast-Food Market

As the U.S. market matured, many restaurants expanded into international markets as a strategy for growing sales. Foreign markets were attractive because of their large customer bases and comparatively little competition. McDonald's, for example, operated 46 restaurants for every 1 million U.S. residents; outside the United States, it operated only 1 restaurant for every 3 million residents. McDonald's, KFC, Burger King, and Pizza Hut were the earliest and most aggressive chains to expand abroad beginning in the late 1950s. By 2000, at least 35 chains had expanded into at least one foreign country. McDonald's operated the largest number of restaurants (more than 12,000 U.S. units and 14,000 foreign units) in the most countries (119). In comparison, Tricon Global Restaurants operated more than 20,000 U.S. and close to 30,000 non-U.S. KFC, Pizza Hut, and Taco Bell restaurants in 85 countries. Because of their early expansion abroad, McDonald's, KFC, Burger King, and Pizza Hut had all developed strong brand names and managerial expertise in international markets. This made them formidable competitors for fast-food chains investing abroad for the first time.

Exhibit 5 lists the world's 35 largest restaurant chains in 2000. The global fast-food industry had a distinctly American flavor. Twenty-eight chains (80 percent of the total) were headquartered in the United States. U.S. chains had the advantage of a large domestic market and ready acceptance by the American consumer. European firms had less success developing the fast-food concept, because Europeans were more inclined to frequent more midscale restaurants, where they spent several hours enjoying multi-course meals in a formal setting. KFC had trouble breaking into the German market during the 1970s and 1980s because Germans were not accustomed to buying take-out or ordering food over the counter. McDonald's had greater success penetrating the German market, because it made a number of changes to its menu and operating procedures to appeal to German tastes. German beer, for example, was served in all of McDonald's restaurants in Germany. In France, McDonald's used a different sauce on its Big Mac sandwich that appealed to the French palate. KFC had more success in Asia and Latin America, where chicken was a traditional dish.

Aside from cultural factors, international operations carried risks not present in domestic-only operations. Long distances between headquarters and foreign franchises made it more difficult to control the quality of individual restaurants. Large distances also caused servicing and support problems. Transportation and other resource costs were sometimes higher than encountered domestically. In addition, time, culture, and language differences increased communication and operational problems. As a result, most restaurant chains limited expansion to their domestic market as long as they were able to achieve corporate profit and growth objectives. As companies gained greater expertise abroad, they turned to profitable international markets as a means of expanding restaurant bases and increasing sales, profits, and market share. Worldwide demand for fast food was expected to grow rapidly during the next two decades, because rising per capita incomes worldwide made eating out more affordable for greater

exhibit 5   Global Coverage of the World's 35 Largest Fast-Food Chains in 2000

Chain	Headquarters Location	Parent Country	No. of Countries with Restaurants
1. McDonald's	Oakbrook, Illinois	United States	119
2. Pizza Hut	Dallas, Texas	United States	88
3. KFC	Louisville, Kentucky	United States	85
4. Subway Sandwiches	Milford, Connecticut	United States	73
5. TCBY	Little Rock, Arkansas	United States	68
6. Domino's Pizza	Ann Arbor, Michigan	United States	64
7. Burger King	Miami, Florida	United Kingdom	58
8. T.G.I. Friday's	Dallas, Texas	United States	53
9. Baskin-Robbins	Glendale, California	United States	52
10. Dunkin' Donuts	Randolph, Massachusetts	United States	41
11. Wendy's	Dublin, Ohio	United States	29
12. Sizzler	Los Angeles, California	United States	22
13. A&W Restaurants	Livonia, Michigan	United States	21
14. Popeyes	Atlanta, Georgia	United States	21
15. Chili's Grill & Bar	Dallas, Texas	United States	20
16. Little Caesars	Detroit, Michigan	United States	19
17. Dairy Queen	Edina, Minnesota	United States	18
18. Taco Bell	Irvine, California	United States	15
19. Carl's Jr.	Anaheim, California	United States	15
20. Outback Steakhouse	Tampa, Florida	United States	13
21. Hardee's	Rocky Mt., North Carolina	United States	11
22. Applebee's	Overland Park, Kansas	United States	10
23. Arby's	Ft. Lauderdale, Florida	United States	10
24. Church's Chicken	Atlanta, Georgia	United States	9
25. PizzaExpress	London, England	United Kingdom	9
26. Denny's	Spartansburg, South Carolina	United States	6
27. Mos Burger	Tokyo	Japan	5
28. Taco Time	Eugene, Oregon	United States	5
29. Yoshinoya	Tokyo	Japan	5
30. Loterria	Tokyo	Japan	4
31. Orange Julius	Edina, Minnesota	United States	4
32. Quick Restaurants	Brussels	Belgium	4
33. Skylark	Tokyo	Japan	4
34. IHOP	Glendale, California	United States	3
35. Red Lobster	Orlando, Florida	United States	3

Source: Case writer research.

numbers of consumers. In addition, the development of the Internet was quickly breaking down communication and language barriers. Greater numbers of children were growing up with computers in their homes and schools. As a result, teenagers in Germany, Brazil, Japan, and the United States were equally likely to be able to converse about the Internet. The Internet also exposed more teenagers to the same companies and products, which enabled firms to more quickly develop global brands and a worldwide consumer base.

KENTUCKY FRIED CHICKEN CORPORATION

Marketing Strategy

Many of KFC's problems during the 1980s and 1990s surrounded its limited menu and inability to quickly bring new products to market. The popularity of its Original Recipe Chicken allowed KFC to expand through the 1980s without significant competition from other chicken chains. As a result, new product introductions were not a critical part of KFC's overall business strategy. KFC suffered one of its most serious setbacks in 1989 as it prepared to introduce a chicken sandwich to its menu. KFC still experimented with the chicken sandwich concept when McDonald's test-marketed its Mc-Chicken sandwich in the Louisville market. Shortly after, McDonald's rolled out the McChicken sandwich nationally. By beating KFC to the market, McDonald's developed strong consumer awareness for its sandwich. This significantly increased KFC's cost of developing awareness for its own sandwich, which KFC introduced several months later. KFC eventually withdrew the sandwich because of low sales. Today, about 95 percent of chicken sandwiches are sold through traditional hamburger chains.

By the late 1990s, KFC had refocused its strategy. The cornerstone of its new strategy was to increase sales in individual KFC restaurants by introducing a variety of new products and menu items that appealed to a greater number of customers. After extensive testing, KFC settled on three types of chicken: Original Recipe (pressure cooked), Extra Crispy (fried), and Tender Roast (roasted). It also rolled out a buffet that included some 30 dinner, salad, and dessert items. The buffet was particularly successful in rural locations and suburbs. It was less successful in urban locations because of space considerations. KFC then introduced its Colonel's Crispy Strips and five new chicken sandwiches to appeal to customers who preferred boneless chicken products. KFC estimated that its Crispy Strips and chicken sandwiches accounted for $250,000 (30 percent) of the $837,000 in sales that KFC restaurants averaged. One of the problems with these items, however, was that they cannibalized sales of its fried-chicken items; they were less expensive and easier for customers to handle. The latter was especially appealing to drive-through customers.

Overcapacity in the U.S. market made it more difficult to justify the construction of new freestanding restaurants. Fewer sites were available for new construction and those sites, because of their increased cost, drove profit margins down. KFC initiated a three-pronged distribution strategy that helped beef up sales. First, it focused on building smaller restaurants in nontraditional outlets such as airports, shopping malls, universities, and hospitals. It also experimented with units that offered drive-through and carry-out service only, snack shops in cafeterias, scaled-down outlets for supermarkets, and mobile units that could be transported to outdoor concerts and fairs. Second, KFC continued to experiment with home delivery, which was already firmly established in the Louisville, Las Vegas, and Los Angeles markets. Third, KFC established "2-in-1" units that sold both KFC and Taco Bell (KFC/Taco Bell Express) or KFC and Pizza Hut (KFC/Pizza Hut Express) products. By early 2000, Tricon Global Restaurants was operating 700 multibranded restaurants that simultaneously sold products from two of the three chains. It was also testing "3-in-1" units that sold all three brands.

Refranchising Strategy

When Colonel Sanders began to expand the Kentucky Fried Chicken system in the late 1950s, he established KFC as a system of independent franchisees. This strategy helped the Colonel minimize his involvement in the operations of individual restaurants and to concentrate on the things he enjoyed the most—cooking, product development, and public relations. The franchise system resulted in a fiercely loyal and independent group of KFC franchises. When PepsiCo acquired KFC in 1986, a primary objective was to integrate KFC's operations into the PepsiCo system to take advantage of operational, financial, and marketing synergies. This strategy, however, led to greater interference by PepsiCo management in franchise menu offerings, financing, marketing, and operations. This interference was met by resistance from KFC franchisees. PepsiCo attempted to decrease these problems by expanding KFC's restaurant base through company-owned restaurants rather than through franchising. It also used its strong cash flows to buy back unprofitable franchises. Many of these restaurants were converted into company-owned restaurants. By 1993, company-owned restaurants accounted for 40 percent of KFC's worldwide system. When PepsiCo spun off its restaurants into Tricon Global Restaurants in 1994, Tricon's new top management team began to sell company-owned restaurants back to franchisees they believed knew the business better than they did. By 2000, company-owned restaurants had fallen to about 27 percent of the total KFC system.

International Operations

KFC's early experiences operating abroad put it in a strong position to take advantage of the growing trend toward international expansion. By 2000, more than 50 percent of KFC's restaurants were located outside the United States. Historically, franchises made up a large portion of KFC's international restaurant base, because franchises were owned and operated by local entrepreneurs who had grassroots understanding of local language, culture, customs, law, financial markets, and marketing characteristics. Franchising was also a good strategy for establishing a presence in small countries like Grenada, Bermuda, and Suriname, which could only support a single restaurant. The costs of operating company-owned restaurants were prohibitively high in these small markets. Of the 5,595 KFC restaurants located outside the United States in 1999, 69 percent were franchised, while 21 percent were company-owned and 10 percent were licensed restaurants or joint ventures. In larger markets such as Mexico, China, Canada, Australia, Puerto Rico, Korea, Thailand, and the United Kingdom, there was a stronger emphasis on building company-owned restaurants. By coordinating purchasing, recruiting and training, financing, and advertising, fixed costs could be spread over a larger number of restaurants. Increased bargaining power also enabled KFC to negotiate lower prices from suppliers. KFC was also better able to control product and service quality.

Latin American Strategy

KFC operated 438 restaurants in Latin America in 2000 (see Exhibit 6). Its primary presence was in Mexico, Puerto Rico, and the Caribbean. KFC established subsidiaries in Mexico and Puerto Rico beginning in the late 1960s and expanded through company-owned restaurants. Franchises were used to penetrate other countries in the Caribbean whose market size prevented KFC from profitably operating company-owned restaurants. Subsidiaries were later established in the Virgin Islands, Venezuela, and Brazil. KFC had planned to expand into these regions using company-owned restaurants. The Venezuelan subsidiary, however, was later closed because of the high costs of operating the small subsidiary. KFC had opened eight restaurants in Brazil but

exhibit 6   Latin America Restaurant Count—McDonald's, Burger King, KFC, and Wendy's, 2000

	McDonald's	Burger King	KFC	Wendy's
Mexico	170	108	157	7
Puerto Rico	121	148	67	30
Caribbean Islands	59	57	91	23
Central America	80	85	26	26
Regional subtotal	430	398	341	86
% of total	24%	80%	78%	60%
Colombia	21	0	19	3
Ecuador	7	12	18	0
Peru	10	10	17	0
Venezuela	83	13	6	33
Other Andean	6	7	0	0
Andean region subtotal	127	42	60	36
% of total	7%	9%	14%	25%
Argentina	205	25	0	21
Brazil	921	0	8	0
Chile	61	25	29	0
Paraguay and Uruguay	32	5	0	0
Southern cone subtotal	1,219	55	37	21
% of total	69%	11%	8%	15%
Latin America total	1,776	495	438	143
Total %	100%	100%	100%	100%

Source: Restaurant data obtained from corporate offices at McDonald's Corp. (as of December 1999), Burger King Corp. (as of June 30, 2000), Tricon Global Restaurants, Inc. (as of June 30, 2000), and Wendy's International (as of May 15, 2000).

decided to close them in 1999 because it lacked the cash flow needed to support an expansion program in that market. Franchises were opened in other markets that had good growth potential such as Chile, Ecuador, Peru, and Colombia.

KFC's early entry into Latin America gave it a leadership position over McDonald's in Mexico and the Caribbean. It also had an edge in Ecuador and Peru. KFC's Latin America strategy represented a classic internationalization strategy. It first expanded into Mexico and Puerto Rico because of their geographic proximity, as well as political and economic ties, to the United States. From these regions, KFC expanded its franchise system throughout the Caribbean, gradually moving away from its U.S. base as its experience in Latin America grew. Only after it had established a leadership position in Mexico and the Caribbean did it venture into South America. McDonald's pursued a different strategy. It was late to expand into the region. Despite a rapid restaurant construction program in Mexico during the 1990s, McDonald's still lagged behind KFC. But McDonald's had initiated a first-mover strategy in Brazil and Argentina, large markets where KFC had no presence. By early 2000, more than 63 percent of McDonald's restaurants in Latin America were located in these two countries. Wendy's pursued a slightly different strategy. It first expanded into Puerto Rico, the

Caribbean Islands, and Central America because of their geographical proximity to the United States. The shorter distance to the United States made these restaurants easier to manage. Wendy's late entry into Latin America, however, made it more difficult to penetrate the Mexican market, where KFC, McDonald's, and Burger King had already established a strong presence. Wendy's announced plans to build 100 Wendy's restaurants in Mexico by 2010; however, its primary objective was to establish strong positions in Venezuela and Argentina, where most U.S. fast-food chains had not yet been established.

COUNTRY RISK ASSESSMENT IN LATIN AMERICA

Latin America comprised some 50 countries, island nations, and principalities that were settled primarily by the Spanish, Portuguese, French, Dutch, and British during the 1500s and 1600s. Spanish was spoken in most countries, the most notable exception being Brazil, whose official language was Portuguese. Catholicism was the predominant religion, though Methodist missionaries successfully exported Protestantism into many regions of Latin America in the 1800s, most notably on the coast of Brazil. Despite commonalities in language, religion, and history, however, political and economic policies often differed significantly from one country to another. Historically, frequent changes in governments and economic instability increased the uncertainty of doing business in the region.

Most U.S. and Canadian companies were beginning to realize, however, that they could not overlook the region. Geographic proximity made communications and travel easier and quicker between countries, and the North American Free Trade Agreement (NAFTA) had eliminated tariffs on goods shipped between Canada, Mexico, and the United States. Mercosur—a customs union agreement signed in 1991 between Argentina, Paraguay, Uruguay, and Brazil—eliminated tariffs on trade among those four countries. Many countries such as Chile and Argentina had also established free-trade policies that were beginning to stimulate growth. These factors made Latin America an attractive location for investment. The primary task for companies investing in the region was to accurately assess the different risks of doing business in Latin America and to select the proper countries for investment.

In 1992, researcher Kent D. Miller developed a framework for analyzing country risk that was a useful tool for analyzing the attractiveness of a country for future investment. He argued that firms must examine country, industry, and firm factors in order to fully assess country risk. Country factors addressed the risks associated with changes in the country's political and economic environment that potentially affected the firm's ability to conduct business. They included the following:

1. Political risk (e.g., war, revolution, changes in government, price controls, tariffs and other trade restrictions, appropriation of assets, government regulations, and restrictions on the repatriation of profits).

2. Economic risk (e.g., inflation, high interest rates, foreign exchange rate volatility, balance-of-trade movements, social unrest, riots, and terrorism).

3. Natural risk (e.g., rainfall, hurricanes, earthquakes, and volcanic activity).

Industry factors addressed changes in the structure of the industry that inhibited the firm's ability to successfully compete in its industry. They included the following:

1. Supplier risk (e.g., changes in quality, shifts in supply, and changes in supplier power).

2. Product market risk (e.g., changes in consumer tastes and availability of substitute products).
3. Competitive risk (e.g., rivalry among competitors, new market entrants, and new product innovations).

Firm factors examined the firm's ability to control its internal operations. They included the following:

1. Labor risk (e.g., labor unrest, absenteeism, employee turnover, and labor strikes).
2. Supplier risk (e.g., raw material shortages and unpredictable price changes).
3. Trade-secret risk (e.g., protection of trade secrets and intangible assets).
4. Credit risk (e.g., problems collecting receivables).
5. Behavioral risk (e.g., control over franchise operations, product quality and consistency, service quality, and restaurant cleanliness).

Many U.S. companies believed that Mexico was an attractive country for investment. Its population of 103 million was more than one-third as large as the U.S. population and represented a large market for U.S. goods and services. In comparison, Canada's population of 31 million was only one-third as large as Mexico's. Mexico's proximity to the United States meant that transportation costs between the United States and Mexico were significantly lower than to Europe or Asia. This increased the competitiveness of U.S. goods in comparison with European and Asian goods, which had to be transported to Mexico across the Atlantic or Pacific Ocean at significantly greater cost. The United States was in fact Mexico's largest trading partner. More than 80 percent of Mexico's total trade was with the United States. Many U.S. firms also invested in Mexico to take advantage of lower wage rates. By producing goods in Mexico, U.S. goods could be shipped back to the United States or to third markets at a low cost.

Despite the advantages of doing business in Mexico, Mexico only accounted for about 20 percent of the United States' total trade. Beginning in the early 1900s, the percentage of total U.S. exports going to Latin America declined as exports to other regions of the world such as Canada and Asia increased. The growth in economic wealth and consumer demand in Canada and Asia has generally outpaced Mexico for most of the last century. However, the volume of trade between the United States and Mexico has increased significantly since the North American Free Trade Agreement went into effect in 1994.

A commonly held perception among many Americans was that Japan was the United States' largest trading partner. In reality, Canada was the United States' largest trading partner by a wide margin. Canada bought more than 22 percent ($154 million) of all U.S. exports in 1998; Japan bought less than 9 percent ($58 billion). Canada accounted for about 19 percent of all goods imported into the United States ($178 billion); Japan accounted for 13 percent ($125 billion). The perception that Japan was the largest U.S. trading partner resulted primarily from extensive media coverage of the long-running U.S. trade deficit with Japan. Less known to many Americans was the fact that the United States was running a balance-of-trade deficit with China that almost equaled the deficit with Japan. China was positioned to become the United States' largest trading partner in Asia within the next few years.

The lack of U.S. investment in and trade with Mexico during the 20th century was mainly the result of Mexico's long history of restricting foreign trade and investment. The Institutional Revolutionary Party (PRI), which came to power in Mexico during the 1920s, had a history of promoting protectionist economic policies to shield Mexico's economy from foreign competition. The government owned or controlled many industries and many Mexican companies focused on producing goods for the domestic market without much attention to building exports. High tariffs and other trade barriers restricted imports into Mexico, and foreign ownership of assets in Mexico was largely prohibited or heavily restricted.

Mexico's dictatorial and entrenched government bureaucracy, corrupt labor unions, and a long tradition of anti-Americanism among government officials and intellectuals also reduced the motivation of U.S. firms to invest in Mexico. The nationalization of Mexico's banks in 1982 led to higher real interest rates and lower investor confidence. This forced the Mexican government to battle high inflation, high interest rates, labor unrest, and lower consumer purchasing power during the early to mid-1980s. Investor confidence in Mexico, however, improved after 1988, when Carlos Salinas de Gortari was elected president. Salinas embarked on an ambitious restructuring of the Mexican economy. He initiated policies to strengthen the free-market components of the economy, lowered top marginal tax rates, and eliminated many restrictions on foreign investment.

The privatization of government-owned companies came to symbolize the restructuring of Mexico's economy. In 1990, legislation was passed to privatize all government-run banks. By the end of 1992, more than 800 of 1,200 government-owned companies had been sold, including Mexicana and AeroMexico, the two largest airline companies in Mexico, and Mexico's 18 major banks. More than 350 companies, however, remained under government ownership. These represented a significant portion of the assets owned by the state at the start of 1988. Therefore, the sale of government-owned companies in terms of asset value was still modest. A large percentage of the remaining government-owned assets was controlled by government-run companies in certain strategic industries such as steel, electricity, and petroleum. These industries had long been protected by government ownership. However, President Salinas opened up the electricity sector to independent power producers in 1993 and Petroleos Mexicanos (Pemex), the state-run petrochemical monopoly, initiated a program to sell off many of its nonstrategic assets to private and foreign buyers.

North American Free Trade Agreement (NAFTA)

Prior to 1989, Mexico levied high tariffs on most imported goods. In addition, many other goods were subjected to quotas, licensing requirements, and other nontariff trade barriers. In 1986, Mexico joined the General Agreement on Tariffs and Trade (GATT), a world trade organization designed to eliminate barriers to trade among member nations. As a member of GATT, Mexico was required to apply its system of tariffs to all member nations equally. Mexico subsequently dropped tariff rates on a variety of imported goods. In addition, import license requirements were dropped for all but 300 imported items. During President Salinas's administration, tariffs were reduced from an average of 100 percent on most items to an average of 11 percent.

On January 1, 1994, the North American Free Trade Agreement (NAFTA) went into effect. The passage of NAFTA created a trading bloc with a larger population and a larger gross domestic product than the European Union. All tariffs on goods traded between the United States, Canada, and Mexico were eventually phased out. NAFTA was expected to benefit Mexican exporters, since reduced tariffs made their goods more competitive compared to goods exported to the United States from other countries. In 1995, one year after NAFTA went into effect, Mexico posted its first balance-of-trade surplus in six years. A large part of this surplus was attributed to greater exports to the United States.

Despite its supporters, NAFTA was strongly opposed by farmers and unskilled workers. The day after NAFTA went into effect, rebels rioted in the southern Mexican province of Chiapas on the Guatemalan border. After four days of fighting, Mexican troops drove the rebels out of several towns the rebels had earlier seized. Around 150 people—mostly rebels—were killed. Later in the year, 30 to 40 masked men attacked a McDonald's restaurant in the tourist section of Mexico City. The men threw cash registers to the floor, smashed windows, overturned tables, and spray-painted "No to Fascism" and "Yankee Go Home" on the walls. Such protests continued through 2000, when Mexican farmers dumped gallons of spoiled milk in the streets to protest low tariffs on imported farm products. Farmers also protested the Mexican government's practice of allowing imports of milk powder, corn, and wheat from the United States and Canada above the quotas established as part of NAFTA. The continued opposition of Mexican farmers, unskilled workers, and nationalists posed a constant threat to the stability of NAFTA.

Another problem was Mexico's failure to reduce restrictions on U.S. and Canadian investment in a timely fashion. Many U.S. firms experienced problems getting required approvals for new ventures from the Mexican government. A good example was United Parcel Service (UPS), which sought government approval to use large trucks for deliveries in Mexico. Approvals were delayed, forcing UPS to use smaller trucks. This put UPS at a competitive disadvantage vis-à-vis Mexican companies. In many cases, UPS was forced to subcontract delivery work to Mexican companies that were allowed to use larger, more cost-efficient trucks. Other U.S. companies such as Bell Atlantic and TRW faced similar problems. TRW, which signed a joint venture agreement with a Mexican partner, had to wait 15 months longer than expected before the Mexican government released rules on how it could receive credit data from banks. TRW claimed that the Mexican government had slowed the approval process to placate several large Mexican banks.

Foreign Exchange and the Mexican Peso Crisis of 1995

Between 1982 and 1991, a two-tiered exchange rate system was in force in Mexico. The system consisted of a controlled rate and a free-market rate. A controlled rate was used for imports, foreign debt payments, and conversion of export proceeds. An estimated 70 percent of all foreign transactions were covered by the controlled rate. A free-market rate was used for other transactions. In 1989, President Salinas instituted a policy of allowing the peso to depreciate by 1 peso per day against the dollar. In 1991, the controlled rate was abolished and replaced with an official free rate. The peso was thereafter allowed to depreciate by 0.20 pesos per day against the dollar. When Ernesto Zedillo became Mexico's president in December 1994, one of his objectives was to continue the stability of prices, wages, and exchange rates achieved by Carlos Salinas during his tenure as president. This stability, however, was achieved primarily on the basis of price, wage, and foreign exchange controls. While giving the appearance of stability, an overvalued peso continued to encourage imports that exacerbated Mexico's balance-of-trade deficit. At the same time, Mexican exports became less competitive on world markets.

Anticipating a devaluation of the peso, investors began to move capital into U.S. dollar investments. On December 19, 1994, Zedillo announced that the peso would be

exhibit 7   Selected Economic Data for Mexico, 1994–99

	1994	1995	1996	1997	1998	1999	Average Annual Growth Rate
Population (millions)	93	91	97	96	100	102	2%
Gross domestic product	13%	29%	36%	27%	19%	21%	24%
Money supply (M1)	4%	5%	43%	33%	19%	26%	22%
Inflation (CPI)	7%	35%	34%	21%	16%	17%	
Money market rate	17%	61%	34%	22%	27%	24%	
Peso devaluation against U.S. dollar	71%	44%	3%	3%	22%	−4%	
Unemployment rate	3.6%	4.7%	3.7%	2.6%	2.3%	n/a	

Source: International Monetary Fund, *International Financial Statistics*, 2000.

allowed to depreciate by an additional 15 percent per year against the dollar. The maximum allowable depreciation at the time was 4 percent per year. Within two days, continued pressure on the peso forced Zedillo to allow the peso to float freely against the dollar. By mid-January 1995, the peso had lost 35 percent of its value against the dollar and the Mexican stock market plunged by 20 percent. By the end of the year, the peso had depreciated from 3.1 pesos per dollar to 7.6 pesos per dollar. In order to thwart a possible default by Mexico, the U.S. government, the International Monetary Fund, and the World Bank pledged $25 billion in emergency loans. Shortly thereafter, Zedillo announced an emergency economic package, called the "pacto," which reduced government spending, increased sales of government-run businesses, and placed a freeze on wage increases.

By 2000, there were signs that Mexico's economy had stabilized. Gross domestic product was increasing at an average annual rate of 24 percent, and unemployment had decreased to slightly more than 2 percent (see Exhibit 7). Interest rates and inflation were also low by historical standards (24 and 17 percent in 1999), far below their highs of 61 and 35 percent in 1995. Interest rates and inflation in Mexico were, however, still considerably higher than in the United States. Higher relative interest rates and inflation put continued pressure on the peso to depreciate against the dollar. This led to higher import prices and contributed to inflation.

A number of social concerns also plagued President Zedillo's government. These included a lack of success in controlling organized crime surrounding the drug trade; high-profile political murders (e.g., the murder of a Roman Catholic cardinal at the Guadalajara airport in 1993); and a high poverty rate, particularly in southern Mexico. These social problems, and voters' disenchantment over allegations of continued political corruption, led to strong opposition to the ruling PRI. In 2000, the PRI lost its first presidential election in five decades when Vicente Fox, leader of the opposition National Action Party, was elected president. Fox took office on December 1, 2000.

RISKS AND OPPORTUNITIES

KFC faced a variety of risks and opportunities in Mexico. It had eliminated all of its franchises in Mexico and operated only company-owned restaurants that enabled it to better control quality, service, and restaurant cleanliness. Company-owned restaurants, however, required more capital than franchises did. This meant that KFC would not be able to expand as quickly as it could using a franchised restaurant base. KFC still had the largest number of restaurants in Mexico of any fast-food chain. However, McDonald's was growing its restaurant base rapidly and was beating KFC in terms of sales. KFC's other major competitors included Burger King and El Pollo Loco (The Crazy Chicken). Wendy's had also announced plans to open 100 restaurants in Mexico by 2010, though Wendy's emphasis in Latin America continued to be in Venezuela and Argentina. Another threat came from Habib's, Brazil's second largest fast-food chain, which opened its first restaurant in Mexico in 2000. Habib's served traditional Middle Eastern dishes such as falafel, hummus, kafka, and tabbouleh at prices below KFC or McDonald's. It planned to open 400 units in Mexico between 2000 and 2005.

Another concern was the long-term value of the peso, which had depreciated at an average annual rate of 23 percent against the U.S. dollar since NAFTA went into effect. This translation risk lowered Tricon Global's reported profits when peso profits were translated into dollars. It also damaged Tricon Global's stock price. From an operational point of view, however, KFC's Mexico operations were largely insulated from currency fluctuations, because it supplied most of its needs using Mexican sources. KFC purchased chicken primarily from Tyson Foods, which operated two chicken-processing plants in Mexico. Tyson was also the primary supplier of chicken to McDonald's, Burger King, Applebee's, and Wal-Mart in Mexico.

KFC faced difficult decisions surrounding the design and implementation of an effective Latin American strategy over the next 20 years. It wanted to sustain its leadership position in Mexico and the Caribbean, but it also hoped to strengthen its position in other regions in South America. Limited resources and cash flow, however, constricted KFC's ability to aggressively expand in all countries simultaneously. What should KFC's Latin American strategy be? KFC's strategy in 2000 focused on sustaining its position in Mexico and the Caribbean, but postponed plans to expand into other large markets like Venezuela, Brazil, and Argentina. This strategy carried significant risk, since McDonald's and Wendy's were already building first-mover advantages there. A second strategy was to invest more capital in these large markets to challenge existing competitors, but such a strategy might risk KFC's leadership position in Mexico and the Caribbean. Another strategy was to focus on building a franchise base throughout Latin America, in order to build KFC's brand image and prevent competitors from establishing first-mover advantages. This strategy, however, was less effective in building a significant market share in individual countries, since market leadership often required a country subsidiary that actively managed both franchised and company owned restaurants and took advantage of synergies in purchasing, operations, and advertising. A country subsidiary could only be justified if KFC had a large restaurant base in the targeted country.

references

Direction of Trade Statistics. Washington, DC: International Monetary Fund.

International Financial Statistics. Washington, DC: International Monetary Fund.

Miller, Kent D. "A Framework for Integrated Risk Management in International Business." *Journal of International Business Studies* 23, no. 2 (1992), pp. 311–31.

Quickservice Restaurant Trends. Washington, DC: National Restaurant Association.

case 11 Competition in the Global Wine Industry: A U.S. Perspective

Murray Silverman
San Francisco State University

Richard M. Castaldi
San Francisco State University

Sally Baack
San Francisco State University

Gregg Sorlien
San Francisco State University

The global wine market in 1998 was an estimated 6.8 billion gallons, down from 6.9 billion gallons in 1997 and 7.1 billion gallons in 1996. About 25 percent of the total volume of wine produced was being purchased outside the country in which the wine was produced; this represented an increase over the 17 percent volume for which exports accounted during the 1991–95 period. The increasing percentage of wines being exported was due primarily to the higher strategic priority that wineries were placing on exporting as a growth strategy. Historically, wines were locally produced and locally consumed, but that paradigm had changed in the last few decades as per capita consumption in many wine-producing countries had stagnated. At the same time that older wine-producing countries had begun to put more emphasis on pursuing export opportunities, the wine industry was seeing the emergence of wine production in a number of new countries—Australia, Chile, Argentina. The result was increased competition in the global wine market. Exhibits 1, 2, and 3 provide an overview of wine production and the global wine industry.

In 2000, the United States was the fourth-largest producer of wine in the world (see Exhibit 1), yet it accounted for only approximately 4.2 percent of the total wine export market based on volume (see Exhibit 2). This was mainly due to the low level

The authors gratefully acknowledge a Business and International Education (BIE) grant from the U.S. Department of Education and a matching grant from the College of Business at San Francisco State University in support of this research. Copyright © 2001 by the case authors. Used with permission.

exhibit 1   World Wine Production, 1996–98 (in millions of gallons)

Country	1996	1997	1998
Italy	1,551	1,343	1,430
France	1,506	1,414	1,390
Spain	818	876	800
United States	498	580	539
Argentina	334	356	334
Germany	228	224	286
South Africa	230	232	215
Australia	177	162	195
Chile	100	120	144
Romania	202	176	132
Hungary	110	118	110
Yugoslavia	92	106	106
Rest of world	1,296	1,195	1,150
World total	7,142	6,902	6,831

Source: IV International, based on data from Office International de la Vigne et du Vin (OIV).

exhibit 2   Percentage Shares of the World Wine Production, Consumption, World Wine Market, and Export Market, Based on Volume, 1998

Country*	% Share of Production	% Share of Consumption	% Share of World Market	% Share of Export Market	World Export Market Rank
Italy	21.0%	14.3%	20.8%	25.3%	1
France	20.4	15.9	20.3	25.1	2
Spain	11.7	6.7	10.6	15.6	3
United States	7.9	9.3	8.4	4.2	4
Argentina	4.9	6.1	6.4	1.7	10
Germany	4.2	8.5	4.1	3.6	5
Australia	2.9	1.6	2.3	3.0	8
Chile	2.1	1.0	2.0	3.5	6
Portugal	1.4	2.2	2.5	3.4	7
Others	23.5	34.4	22.6	14.6	
Total	100.0%	100.0%	100.0%	100.0%	

*Sorted by % share of production.
Source: Office International de la Vigne et du Vin (OIV), 1999.

of strategic importance most U.S. wineries placed on exporting. Traditionally, most U.S. wineries resorted to exporting only when they had excess supplies that could not be sold domestically—the relatively attractive growth opportunities in the U.S. wine industry prompted most U.S. wineries to see little gain from establishing a strategic presence in the wine markets of other countries. More recently, however, their interest in exports had increased because the U.S. market was maturing, domestic competition was strong, the industry was consolidating to a smaller number of big players, and

exhibit 3   Per Capita Consumption of Wine in Selected Countries, 1995–99 (in liters)

Rank	Country	Population*	1996	1997	1998
1	Luxembourg	388,000	62.89	69.07	70.36
2	France	58,109,160	59.88	61.09	61.09
3	Italy	58,261,971	59.55	52.96	54.92
4	Slovenia	2,051,522	54.79	51.74	48.74
5	Croatia	4,547,000	37.61	47.26	47.66
6	Portugal	10,562,388	54.91	49.45	47.34
7	Switzerland	7,084,984	41.36	40.93	40.93
8	Argentina	34,292,742	38.97	39.05	39.52
9	Spain	39,404,348	36.69	37.02	38.07
10	Uruguay	3,222,716	29.88	33.57	35.13
33	United States	267,636,000	7.82	7.69	7.88

Source: Office International de la Vigne et du Vin (OIV), 1999.

more U.S. wineries were switching from family management to professional management. As a case in point, in February 2000, Lew Platt, the former chairman and CEO of Hewlett-Packard, was named CEO of Kendall-Jackson winery in Napa Valley. With signs that the world wine industry was globalizing and with the mounting competition in the United States among both import and domestic brands, many wine industry analysts believed that the leading U.S. wineries needed to develop or sharpen their export skills to compete successfully in what the analysts saw as a more globally competitive industry environment.

WINE INDUSTRY OVERVIEW

Wine has been a part of Western history since the Neolithic period (8,500–4,000 B.C.), when humans first started to develop permanent communities and stopped being nomadic hunter-gatherers (one of the earliest written records of the consumption of wine is in the Bible). The impact of wine on Mediterranean cultures became pronounced over the years as the geopolitical situation stabilized in the region under the Roman Empire. Roman imperialism helped spread the production of wine across most of the countries in the empire, which included most of northern Africa and southern Europe. During that same era, wine became ingrained in the Christian faith and is still used in Catholic mass today. The close tie between wine and the Christian faith aided the spread of wine production and wine consumption across Europe in the ages after the fall of the Roman Empire and eventually throughout the world with the European imperialism of the 15th–19th centuries. The wine-producing and wine-consuming countries consisted primarily of western European countries and their ex-colonies, with most of them being historically Catholic (see Exhibits 1 and 2).

There has never been a universally accepted system for naming styles of wine. Currently, there are two prominent systems for naming wine, varietal and appellation. *Appellation* is a French term that, in the context of the wine industry, means the name of the region or specific area in which a wine is produced. In France, when the appellation convention was created, it was accepted that certain geographic locations, due to *terroir* (the land where the grapes are grown), were better prepared to produce a specific type of grape and therefore a specific style of wine. For example, that is why champagne (wine with a degree of carbonation) comes from the Champagne region in France, east of Paris. Some appellations that have been created around the world are Bordeaux (France), Burgundy (France), Chablis (France), Tuscany (Italy), Maipo (Chile), Mendoza (Argentina), New South Wales (Australia), Napa Valley (California) and Sonoma County (California). The word *varietal* refers to a descriptive naming convention based on the type of grape used to produce a wine. Varietals are predominantly used in the U.S. industry to segment the market; common wine varietals include Zinfandel, White Zinfandel, Riesling, Chardonnay, Burgundy, Shiraz, Petite Shiraz, Merlot, Pinot Noir, and Cabernet Sauvignon.

Terroir was considered a determining factor in the quality of the wine. The idea was that the quality of a wine was influenced not so much by who made the wine or what methods they used as it was by the quality of the grape. Environmental factors—the temperature in the region, the amount of light to which the grapevines were exposed, the annual amount of rain that the area received, and the characteristics of the soil—largely determined the flavors and sugar content in the grape. A vineyard that had all of the desirable environmental qualities, of course, still required considerable agricultural work to remain healthy and free of insects and/or molds that damaged the vines' ability to produce quality grapes. The combinations of attributes needed to grow a high-quality grape for winemaking were not very common throughout the world. The amount of good *terroir* was limited, and therefore so was the ability to produce fine wines.

The complexity of the winemaking process created many opportunities to either enhance or damage the quality of the product. The process started in late fall, when the grapes were cut from the vine and laid on the ground to dry for a short time in the sun. Sun drying increased the ratio of sugar to water in the grape, thus creating the opportunity to make a sweeter wine. Next, the grapes were put into a vat and crushed to remove the juice. The longer the skin of the grape remained with the juice, the darker the wine would be. For white wines, the skins of the grapes were removed soon after the crush; for red wines, the skins of the grapes were left in with the juice for an extended period. The juice was then placed in a wooden cask or stainless-steel vat and aged for, on average, a year. The aging process not only allowed the natural yeast from the sugar in the grape to ferment and produce alcohol but also allowed the wine to absorb flavors from the container. After being aged, the wine was bottled, labeled, and shipped to the market.

WINE-PRODUCING COUNTRIES

Wine-producing countries were classified into two broad categories: Old World and New World. The largest of the Old World producers were France and Italy. The larger New World producers included Australia, Chile, and Argentina. The United States, also a New World producer, will be discussed later in this case.

New World Producers

Australia Grapevines were first introduced to Australia in 1788 by English immigrants. The wine industry was born in the 1860s when European immigrants added the skilled workforce necessary to develop the commercial infrastructure. Despite its long history, the winemaking industry in Australia was stagnant until the 1960s when several key factors transformed it. Among these factors were innovative techniques that improved the quality of Australian wine while keeping costs down. Soon after the wineries were in a position to produce quality wine at many price points, domestic and international demand began to rise. Since Australia (with a population of only 17 million) has a very limited domestic market, its wineries realized that if the industry was to continue to grow, it would have to do so in the international market.[1] In the late 1990s, Australia was the eighth-largest producer of wine in the world (see Exhibit 1), with output of 177 million gallons in 1996 and 195 million gallons in 1998. In the export market, Australia had 3 percent of the total and was ranked eighth in the world for 1998 (see Exhibit 2).

At the same time that the Australian wine industry was starting to show strong growth, the government was considering legislation that would severely tax wine sales. To protect the industry, the local wineries joined together with government officials to develop a plan that would keep the government from levying taxes, and the result was the formulation of a business strategy labeled "Strategy 2025."[2] The consensus between the wineries and the government was that growing the industry would better serve the government and national economy than would instigating high taxes. Strategy 2025 outlined how Australian wines would expand domestically and internationally. The vision was that by the year 2025 the Australian wine industry would achieve $4.5 billion in annual sales by being the world's most influential and profitable supplier of branded wines and by pioneering wine as a universal first-choice lifestyle beverage. The wineries were even bold enough to name the specific markets that they would target: the United Kingdom, the United States, Germany, and Japan. Australia's top five markets in 1999 were the United Kingdom, the United States, New Zealand, Canada, and Germany. With $343 million in sales, the United Kingdom accounted for over half of the revenue gained by Australia in the export market, while the United States came in second, with $160 million. The next three countries—New Zealand, Canada, and Germany—accounted for sales of only $97 million, or 16.1 percent of total export sales. Despite being a target market in Strategy 2025, Japan was not on the list of Australia's top five export markets. Australia had targeted select Asian countries due to the large forecasted growth of their populations and economies.

Chile   The first vines were introduced to Chile in the 16th century by a Spanish priest. Over the years the amount of land under cultivation grew slowly until the late 19th century, when wine began to be produced on a large scale. Due to political and economic instability, the wine industry was not able to develop and take on a global perspective until 1979, when Chile began to focus on exporting natural resources to strengthen its economy.

The Andean climate is very good for the production of high-quality red wines. Chilean wines were of higher quality than those of neighboring Argentina. In 1996, the Chilean government took an active role in maintaining the quality of wine for export by implementing the Denomination of Origin (DO), a set of laws that regulated the origin and variety of grapes used in wine as well as restricting varietal labeling to develop a consistent system. Chile had four wine-producing regions that had appellations of origin and were monitored by the ministry of agriculture: Aconcagua, Maipo, Maule, and Rapel. In 1999, the top five export markets for Chilean wines were the United Kingdom, United States, Canada, Denmark, and Japan. The United Kingdom

---

[1]Australian Wine Foundation, *Strategy 2025: The Australian Wine Industry,* June 1996.

[2]Paul Franson, "U.S. Wineries Consider Long-Term Strategy to Maintain Competitiveness," *Vineyard & Winery Management,* May/June 1999.

accounted for the most revenue, with $116 million, and the United States accounted for $107 million. Canada, Denmark, and Japan accounted, respectively, for $35, $25, and $24 million in export sales, 27 percent of the top five countries' total.[3] Chile was the ninth-largest producer of wine in the world (see Exhibit 1), with output of 100 million gallons in 1996 and 144 million gallons in 1998. Despite being only the ninth-largest producer, Chile had 3.5 percent of the total export market and was ranked sixth in the world in exports for 1998 (see Exhibit 2).

Argentina   Like Chile, Argentina had a long history of making wine. However, the overall quality of Argentine wines was relatively low due to the country's small area of land capable of producing high-quality grapes. The production of wine in Argentina had increased over the years, but the wine produced tended to be for local consumption, not for export, due to low quality and strict government regulations. In recent years Argentina had developed several organizations to help boost the quality of its wines so that it could increase its presence in the export market. These organizations included the Original Denomination (OD), Controlled Original Denomination (COD), and Guaranteed Controlled Original Denomination (GCOD), all of which had the task of regulating the production and labeling of Argentine wine to create a higher-quality image in the global wine market. Many foreign companies looked to Chile to create joint ventures, but this was not the case in Argentina. The four main areas of wine production in Argentina were La Rioja, Mendoza, Rio Negro, and San Juan. In 1999, the total volume of the top eight markets for Argentine wine was 58 million liters, with volume shipments being 12 million liters for Paraguay, 11 million for the United Kingdom, 10 million for the United States, 7 million for Japan, 5 million for Bolivia, 5 million for Uruguay, 4 million for Chile, and 4 million for Germany. A significant portion of the export volume, 45 percent, went to other South American countries where low prices were a major factor. Argentina was the world's fifth-largest wine producer (see Exhibit 1), with output of 334 million gallons in both 1996 and 1998, and in 1998 it ranked ninth in total exports (see Exhibit 2).

The Old World Producers

France   France had been a longtime world leader in the production of wine due to historical and cultural factors. In terms of volume, France was the world's number two producer of wine (see Exhibit 1), with output of 1,506 million gallons in 1996 and 1,390 million gallons in 1998. The French developed the Vins d'appellation d'origine contrôlée (AOC) system centuries ago to help ensure that the quality of French wine stayed high. The AOC regulated the areas of production, wine production and storage methods, and minimum alcohol content. There were many regions in which quality grapes could be grown in France, and the dominant position that France had in the export segment reflected its extensive grape-producing capabilities. Some of the better-known appellations in France were Bordeaux, Burgundy, Champagne, and Rhône.

Italy   Italy, like France, also had a very old and established wine industry that relied on the appellation method to control the quality of its wines. Italy was the world's largest producer of wine (see Exhibit 1), with output of 1,551 million gallons in 1996 and 1,430 million gallons in 1998. The two main organizations responsible for the

---

[3]Robert M. Nicholson, "New World Wine Exporters Continued Growth in '99," *Wines & Vines,* July 2000.

control of the quality in Italian wine were the Denominazione di Origine Controllata and the Denominazione di Origine Controllata e Garantita. The second appellation control system was developed in recent years to help raise the quality of Italian wines.

New World versus Old World Producers

While wineries in the New World countries generally used more modern methods of production and innovative approaches, those in France and Italy were more likely to use older methods of production that had become a part of these countries' "wine culture." Wineries in all of the countries profiled in this case, with the exception of Argentina, were capable of shipping brands that could compete at a wide range of price points. Argentine wines usually had a hard time competing in the premium market, although one region in Argentina was capable of producing grapes suitable for better-quality wines. A number of French wineries turned out premium-quality wines that were positioned in the high end of the wine market, and it was not uncommon for top-of-the-line French wines to retail for over $100 a bottle—many brands of premium French wines retailed in the range of $20 to $50 per bottle. Italian wines, which had the reputation of being good to have with meals, seldom commanded the price premiums of French wines; Italian wines competed chiefly in the middle and lower price categories.

MAJOR WORLD MARKETS FOR WINE

While several of the major wine-producing countries were also major wine-consuming countries, a number of countries and regions had little wine-producing capability and relied on imports to satisfy consumer demand.

The Market in Major Wine-Producing Countries

Australia   In Australia rising per capita consumption of wine was being driven by a shift toward a Mediterranean-style diet, growing awareness of the health benefits of wine, and increased participation in recreational activities and general entertainment. In 1998, Australia ranked 18th in the world with regard to per capita consumption; Australians drank 19.89 liters of wine per capita (Exhibit 3), up from 17.94 liters per capita in 1996. In 1998, Australia imported 7.5 million gallons of wine (see Exhibit 4), which translated into about a 5 percent market share for imported wines based on volume. The low share for imports was attributable to the high quality and low price of domestic brands. In 1996, 6 percent of the brands sold in Australia accounted for more than 75 percent of sales.

Argentina   In 1998, Argentina had the eighth-highest per capita consumption of wine in the world, with 39.52 liters in 1998, up from 38.97 liters in 1996 (see Exhibit 3). Imported wines totaled 1.3 million gallons (see Exhibit 4), equal to a 0.4 percent market share based on volume. It was difficult for imported wines to compete against the low-priced domestic brands. Most wine consumers in Argentina were more price-conscious than quality-conscious.

France and Italy   France and Italy were second and third, respectively, in per capita wine consumption in 1998 (see Exhibit 3). Both countries had a long history of wine production and consumption, but their consumption levels were flat to declining.

exhibit 4   Wine Imports by Country, 1996–98 (in thousands of gallons)

Country	1996	1997	1998
Germany	306.7	318.2	318.6
United Kingdom	197.0	211.8	233.9
France	140.0	153.8	148.0
United States	96.3	122.2	111.1
Japan	28.4	38.3	84.8
Russia	62.0	106.8	76.9
Netherlands	57.2	73.4	76.3
Canada	44.8	47.1	53.6
Switzerland	48.9	48.9	49.8
Denmark	40.3	44.3	46.1
Portugal	13.5	11.0	39.0
Sweden	30.2	28.0	29.6
Italy	4.5	30.4	28.3
Spain	30.2	3.9	23.6
Australia	3.7	5.5	7.5
Argentina	1.1	1.3	1.3
Chile	0.1	0.1	0.1
Rest of world	280.0	265.0	268.3
Total	1,384.9	1,510.0	1,596.8

Source: Office International de la Vigne et du Vin (OIV), 1999.

Italian wine consumers preferred Italian wines, with imported brands accounting for only 2.8 percent of volume in 1998; imported wines were much more popular in France where imported brands had a 1998 market share of 13.4 percent.

Major Importing Countries

Imported wines accounted for a majority of consumption in the United Kingdom, Canada, Japan, and most Asian countries. The United Kingdom had a very small domestic wine industry, and its wine market was said to be open and competitive. Only Germany imported more wine in 1998 than Britain did, and German and French wines made up most of the United Kingdom's imports. The United Kingdom ranked 23rd in per capita wine consumption in the late 1990s, and consumption levels were rising slightly. The situation was very similar in Canada, except that the government there placed more restraints on competition in the wine industry. In 1998, Canada ranked 30th in per capita wine consumption among the countries of the world.

Although wine imports were rising in Japan, the Japanese were not big wine consumers and Japan did not rank among the top 33 countries in per capita consumption. Japanese wine consumers were, however, very quality-conscious and were willing to pay for premium-quality wines. While no Asian country had a high per capita consumption of wine in comparison with Western countries, Asia was seen as presenting a great opportunity for wine producers around the world because it was a very large market that had yet to be tapped. China alone had 1.27 billion people (out of a world population of 6 billion people).

exhibit 5   Percentage Market Shares of U.S. Table Wine Market, 1994–98 (based on volume)

Company	1994	1996	1998
E. & J. Gallo Winery	34.3%	27.7%	27.5%
Canandaigua Wine	17.7	15.5	14.8
The Wine Group	9.7	11.4	14.6
Beringer Wine Estates*	3.2	2.5	4.0
Robert Mondavi Winery	3.2	3.6	3.8
Next three competitors	13.7	11.9	12.9
All others (1,600+)	19.2	27.4	22.4
Total	100.0%	100.0%	100.0%

*Named "Wine World Estates" in 1994.

Source: Adams Wine Handbook, 1999.

THE U.S. WINE INDUSTRY

The wine industry in the United States in 1999 was an $18.1 billion market; dollar volume had been growing at an annual average rate of 8.5 percent since 1994. There were over 1,600 U.S. wineries in operation, most of which were low-volume, family-managed enterprises. Fewer than a dozen large-volume producers dominated the market—see Exhibit 5.

Even though in its early decades much of the United States had a large European immigrant population, Americans had not been as culturally disposed to drink wine as were people in France, Germany, and Italy. In the 19th century, when the United States was developing, vineyards were few and the U.S. wine production infrastructure was quite small—production and consumption were relegated to niche areas comprised of ethnic enclaves or well-to-do individuals who saw wine as a good accompaniment to food. The first alcoholic beverages to be mass-produced nationwide were beer and whiskey. With beer and whiskey being more affordable as well as readily available in the United States, wine was viewed as more of an elite drink and was not embraced by a substantial part of the general public until the second half of the 20th century.

Demographic analysis of U.S. wine consumers revealed several distinct wine-consuming segments. According to the 1998 *Adams Wine Handbook,* women were slightly more likely to consume wine than men, with the majority of drinkers being in the baby boom generation. Wine drinkers also tended to be professionals or managers who were college graduates and made over $60,000 annually. According to one estimate, about 15.7 million U.S. adults made up the core of wine drinkers. The members of this segment had wine at least once a week and consumed approximately 88 percent of the wine by volume.

Internationally, the image of the U.S. wine industry until the mid-1970s was that of a low-quality jug wine producer. This image stemmed from the efforts of large U.S. wineries like E. & J. Gallo to make low-priced wines for the mass market. The U.S. wineries that produced high-quality wines did so in low volumes, so it was easy for their reputation to be overshadowed by that of the Old World producers who had proven track records. This changed in 1976 during a blind wine-tasting contest in Paris, France, in which California wines from Napa Valley beat out several well-established

exhibit 6   Share of Bottled California Table Wine, Shipments by Color, 1990–98 (based on volume)

Color	1990	1992	1994	1996	1998
Red	14.7%	19.6%	23.6%	27.2%	31.9%
Rose	15.6	13.1	9.2	9.5	6.2
White	52.9	48.7	50.3	46.8	40.5
Blush	16.8	18.6	16.9	16.5	21.4
Total	100.0%	100.0%	100.0%	100.0%	100.0%

Source: Adams Wine Handbook, 1999.

European wines for the top honors. From that time forward, U.S. wines have been held in growing esteem and many wineries in the Napa Valley and Sonoma County regions of California have focused on developing high-quality wines worthy of competing with the brands of Old World producers.

The United States had one of the world's most open markets for imported wines, with few restrictions placed on wine imports and with import brands free to capture whatever market share they could get in competition against domestic brands. Despite this, California wines had traditionally dominated the domestic market due to the state's ideal growing conditions and to aggressive marketing and branding on the part of some of California's large wineries. The U.S. market share of imported wines had fluctuated over time, but had changed little in recent years (rising slightly from 16 percent in 1992 to 17 percent in 1998). Both New and Old World producers had begun implementing strategies targeted closely to specific groups of consumers and market niches. California wines were also experiencing increased competition from wines produced in Washington and New York—the market shares of wineries in these states had risen from 6.2 percent in 1992 to 14 percent in 1998.

The eight largest U.S. wine companies accounted for 77.6 percent of the wine sold in the U.S. in 1998 (based on volume), while an estimated 1,600-plus other wineries produced the remaining 22.4 percent (see Exhibit 5). A small number of wine companies had dominated the majority of production for many years; however, the companies in the top eight had changed from time to time as some initiated moves to build better brand portfolios and as brand popularity shifted. The consolidation trend in the market took on a new twist in 2000—instead of U.S. wineries acquiring or merging with each other, foreign companies were shopping to acquire U.S. wineries. Foreign producers saw acquisition as the quickest and best way to gain access to the U.S. market; by purchasing a U.S. winery, a foreign producer could tap the acquired firm's distribution channels, existing suppliers, and market knowledge.

Exhibit 6 shows how customer preferences for the colors, or varietals, of wine shifted from white to red during the 1990–98 period. White wines accounted for 52.9 percent of the volume shipped in 1990 but only 40.5 percent of volume by 1998. The demand for red and blush wines rose from 14.7 percent and 16.8 percent in 1990 to 31.9 percent and 21.4 percent in 1998, respectively. Exhibit 7 shows the U.S. balance of trade for wine for the years 1992–98. The deficit grew in absolute numbers but shrank proportionally over the six-year period. Also, with the value per gallon for imports rising from $15.36 in 1992 to $17.14 in 1998, it seemed that foreign wineries were targeting the premium wine segment of the U.S. market.

exhibit 7   United States Balance of Trade for Wine, 1992–98

By Volume (in millions of gallons)				
	1992	1994	1996	1998
Imports	71,081	72,611	94,928	109,730
Exports	37,107	31,134	46,473	71,106
Trade deficit	33,974	41,477	48,455	38,624
Ratio: imports to exports	1.9:1	2.3:1	2.0:1	1.5:1
By Value				
	1992	1994	1996	1998
Total value of imports ($ millions)	$1,091.8	$1,050.0	$1,434.6	$1,880.8
Value per gallon ($)	$15.36	$14.46	$15.11	$17.14
Total value of exports ($ millions)	$174.7	$192.1	$320.0	$531.9
Value per gallon ($)	$4.71	$6.17	$6.89	$7.48
Trade deficit ($ millions)	$917.1	$857.9	$1,114.6	$1,348.9
Ratio: imports to exports	6.2:1	5.5:1	4.5:1	3.5:1

Source: *Adams Wine Handbook,* 1999; U.S. Department of Commerce.

Wine industry suppliers included grape producers, makers of wine-producing equipment, bottle manufacturers, suppliers of label-printing services, and ad agencies. The amount of capital required to start a winery depended on the scale of production. Very small wineries could be started with a capital investment of roughly $1 million and could source grapes from outside growers. However, it was not uncommon for wineries to compete aggressively for the high-quality grapes of certain reputable suppliers and thus bid up prices. Hence, most wineries opted either to purchase vineyards and assume the higher capital investment and agricultural maintenance costs or to enter into long-term contracts with dependable grape suppliers.

THE WINE DISTRIBUTION SYSTEM

In the United States, a law enacted after the repeal of Prohibition in 1933 mandated use of a three-tier distribution system. To access wine drinkers, wine producers had to sell to a wholesaler, who then sold to an established customer base of grocery stores, liquor stores, hotels, and/or restaurants. A winery could sell directly to consumers only if it had a gift shop located on its premises. Mailing lists and direct sales via the Internet could be used in only a limited number of states because most states had made direct shipments illegal. Direct sales volumes were very low compared with sales through wholesale distributors. Since wholesale distributors had a vested interest in keeping wineries from being able to sell directly to consumers, there was an industrywide push by distributors to keep wine sales over the Internet from being legal. Distributors and concerned citizens' groups argued that legalizing Internet sales would allow minors to purchase wine with just a few mouse clicks. The role of wholesale distribution channels was taking on greater strategic importance as the industry consolidated and as wineries proceeded to expand their geographic market reach. The challenge for wine producers was gaining access to more domestic and international markets without

exhibit 8   Estimated 1999 California Table Wine Shipments by Price Class

Retail Price per Bottle	Price Segment	Percent of Total Volume	Percent of Total Revenue
Over $14	Ultra-Premium	7%	25%
$7 to $14	Super-Premium	16	27
$3 to $7	Popular Premium	33	31
Below $3	Jug Wine and Others	44	17
Total		100%	100%

Source: Estimated by Gomberg, Fredrikson, and Associates. Excludes exports.

adding significantly to their marketing budgets and capital requirements. Moreover, mergers and acquisitions among wholesale wine distributors were making it increasingly difficult for smaller wineries to find distributors willing to take on the job of marketing low-volume wines.

As with all branded products, image was a very important dimension in marketing wine to consumers. With the target market for wine being educated professionals in the upper-income brackets, having the image of a premium-quality, low-volume "boutique" winery could be a significant advantage. The so-called garage wines being produced in France were a case in point: Their low volumes made their products hard to acquire, and if a garage winery could convey a convincing image of superpremium quality, it could command $20 to $500 a bottle. A significant fraction of the consumers of high-end wines were not only very knowledgeable about different brands and vintages but also particular about the wines they drank. The keys to success for a small winery were finding a market niche and then exploiting its image and the taste of its wines. To set themselves apart, some small wineries had built strong associations with a specific cuisine, lifestyle trait, or local distribution channels. The competitive environment was harsh; according to one industry analyst, small wineries had to "stay small or perish" due to the tremendous costs and other obstacles of scaling up to large-volume production. Exhibit 8 gives a breakdown of California table wine shipments based on the retail price per bottle.

The mix of channels and distribution strategies that wineries used to reach their target market varied greatly depending on the winery's marketing approach and the price/taste/vintage/quality segments in which its brands were positioned. For instance, premium brands were marketed primarily through upscale restaurants, resorts, bars, and liquor stores; wines with low or moderate prices were sold primarily through supermarkets, megastores like Sam's or Costco, popular restaurant chains, and liquor stores located in low- and middle-income neighborhoods.

U.S. WINE INDUSTRY EXPORTING

The dollar value of U.S. wine exports increased from $137 million in 1990 to $548 million in 1999 (see Exhibit 9). Exhibits 10 and 11 provide a breakdown of the dollar value of U.S. wine exports by country and area of the world. A majority of the 1,600-plus U.S. wineries had little experience in wine exporting. Small wineries lacked the resources to pursue expansion into the international arena, and the poor image of U.S.

exhibit 9   U.S. Wine Exports, 1986–99

Year	Volume (millions of gallons)	Value (millions of dollars)
1999	75.4	$548
1998	71.9	537
1997	60.0	425
1996	47.5	326
1995	38.8	241
1994	35.2	196
1993	34.9	182
1992	38.9	181
1991	33.1	153
1990	29.0	137
1989	21.9	98
1988	16.9	85
1987	11.9	61
1986	7.3	35

Source: U.S. Department of Commerce, National Trade Data Bank; The Wine Institute.

wines prior to the 1976 Paris wine-tasting competition resulted in meager foreign demand. With domestic demand for wine growing fairly briskly, most wineries elected to focus their scarce marketing resources on growing their sales in the U.S. market. But while interest in exporting became strategically more important to the more ambitious and well-financed U.S. wineries in the 1990s, the difficulties of exporting remained formidable—trade barriers as well as local business practices and customs prevented entry. To boost their export sales, wineries were relying on agents and brokers and seeking out wholesale distributors and wine importers in foreign countries to take on the distribution of their brands. Some wineries had also entered into joint ventures.

Export Barriers

Many countries around the world subsidized their local industries by giving them money for research, brand building, and exporting—in the European Union countries, subsidies totaled $1 billion in 1997. Governments in some European countries did not recognize the production methods and branding practices of U.S. wineries; to gain entry into these country markets, U.S. wineries had to seek temporary import approval. Government-owned monopoly liquor stores and quotas on wine imports to help protect local producers were common in several countries around the world. Some countries imposed high tariffs on wine imports, sometimes to protect local producers and sometimes to discourage consumption of foreign products. In 1997, Japan had a 21 percent tariff on U.S. wine imports and Hong Kong had a 30 percent tariff on U.S. wines, while Taiwan's government monopoly instigated a flat $3.62 tax per liter; these barriers meant that U.S. wines tended to retail for "premium prices" in these countries even if the quality of the wine did not warrant such a price. Canada had one of the most regulated markets for wine in the world, and trade issues included state-owned monopoly liquor stores, subsidies for the limited local production of wine, and a distribution

exhibit 10 U.S. Bottled Table Wine Exports to Selected Countries and World Totals, Based on Dollar Value, 1997–99

Country	1997	1998	% Change 1997–98	1999	% Change 1998–99
United Kingdom	$ 98,373	$134,509	37%	$122,187	−9%
Canada	58,877	68,909	17	68,950	0
Japan	20,702	55,226	167	46,235	−16
Netherlands	7,782	43,273	456	68,249	58
Switzerland	14,331	18,797	31	21,026	12
Germany	22,082	15,663	−29	12,947	−17
Denmark	6,968	9,156	31	11,052	21
Ireland	6,599	10,191	54	10,678	5
Belgium	5,205	7,107	37	5,937	−16
Sweden	10,011	12,130	21	9,196	−24
France	4,632	7,059	52	5,758	−18
Mexico	1,944	1,384	−29	2,820	104
Taiwan	13,334	5,247	−61	4,197	−20
Hong Kong	8,676	5,005	−42	3,331	−33
Singapore	2,515	1,799	−28	2,964	65
Finland	2,746	2,131	−22	2,395	12
Norway	1,844	2,452	33	2,458	0
South Korea	2,123	79	−63	1,480	87
Netherlands Antilles	1,126	1,304	16	989	−24
China	927	39	−58	1,040	166
Thailand	2,261	17	−92	501	190
Country total	293,058	402,696	37%	404,390	0%
All other countries	14,910	17,961	20	21,399	19
World total	$307,968	$420,657	37%	$425,789	1%

Source: U.S. Department of Commerce, National Trade Data Bank; The Wine Institute.

system that curtailed the ability of foreign companies to market their products. In Mexico, wine export sales had dropped due to a trade dispute over brooms; as a result, tariffs on U.S. wines had gone up and Mexico had a zero-tariff trade agreement with Chile (which had boosted the sales of Chilean wines in Mexico). The World Trade Organization (WTO) was helping alleviate some of these trade issues and helping foster a more open market system on a global scale, but its success had been limited with regard to the wine industry.

Agents and Brokers

An agent was a person or firm that took ownership of a product and then resold it in established channels. It could be very advantageous for a winery to partner with an agent that had a distribution network and set of retail contacts suited to promoting and selling that winery's brand. However, a winery had no control over agent's channels or marketing plans, and little access to data about the foreign consumers who purchased its wines. Agents tended to represent a number of different brands, some of which competed against each other, and seldom hesitated to drop one brand in favor of a

exhibit 11   U.S. Wine Exports by Region, Based on Dollar Value,
                1993–97 (in thousands)

Region	1993	1994	1995	1996	1997
European Union	$ 72,485	$ 68,447	$ 96,841	$151,160	$205,629
Canada	47,271	52,424	53,784	72,440	79,124
Asia	31,535	37,270	49,114	57,078	89,503
Other Europe	5,084	8,545	14,646	16,566	20,677
Mexico	5,456	7,151	2,816	3,961	3,550
Latin America	5,162	5,972	6,948	7,791	8,142
Caribbean	10,440	10,477	11,620	13,393	13,314
Eastern Europe and Russian Federation	1,989	3,091	1,739	1,831	1,768
Africa	855	687	533	709	1,028
Middle East	319	151	154	307	687
All other areas	1,350	1,640	2,918	914	1,705
Total	$182,287	$196,271	$241,640	$326,589	$425,127

Source: The Wine Institute, *International Trade Barriers Report,* 1998.

better-selling brand or an opportunity to take on the brand of a more reputable winery. In other words, agents tended to do what was most profitable for themselves and were not always strongly committed to gaining market penetration of all the wine brands they currently carried.

Brokers functioned in the same manner as agents except that brokers did not take ownership of the product. Thus, the advantages and disadvantages of using a broker were the same as those of using an agent except that with a broker, revenue for the product was not forthcoming until the broker actually consummated the sale of the product to a wholesale distributor or retail establishment.

Distributors/Importers

The role of wholesale distributors (some of whom specialized in imported wines) was to handle the marketing of a winery's products to local wine retailers in the geographic area served by the distributor. For a winery looking to expand its geographic reach, it was important to select distributors with the capabilities to access the targeted wine consumers in the targeted geographic areas. An example of how a particular distributor/importer's capabilities mattered was in Europe, where wine consumers were shifting away from specialty wine stores and toward larger "hyperstores" and grocery stores. By the late 1990s, 47.9 percent of European consumers were buying their wines from hyperstores or supermarkets and 60–70 percent of the wine sold in Europe was being retailed through this channel.

Joint Ventures

Some U.S. wineries had entered into joint ventures with foreign wineries to gain local knowledge of foreign markets and, in return, to share their knowledge of the U.S. market with their foreign partner. Many such ventures had resulted in joint marketing agreements in which each partner shared its access to local distribution channels with its foreign partner. In addition, joint ventures were a particularly useful device for facilitating the export of U.S. bulk wines, which were blended with host-country wines to satisfy local import regulations. Joint ventures could also be useful from the standpoint of technology sharing.

PROFILES OF SELECTED U.S. EXPORTERS

This section profiles four U.S. wineries that have long histories in the industry. Each profile describes the winery's strategies for going after specific market segments and its means of expansion in the international marketplace.

E. & J. Gallo Winery

E. & J. Gallo was the largest winemaker in the world. In July 2000, industry magazine *Wines & Vines* reported that Gallo's production capacity was 330 million gallons (see Exhibit 12)—roughly equivalent to that of all of Argentina (see Exhibit 1). Gallo produced approximately a third of all the bottled wine consumed in the United States. Founded in 1933 in Modesto, California, by two brothers, Ernest and Julio Gallo, the company early on adopted the strategy of having its sales force "push" for very visible shelf space in liquor stores and grocery stores to help drive sales. The emphasis on favorable shelf space and active promotion of the Gallo brand name worked very well, and Gallo's sales grew at a fast rate.

In order to get more control over costs and to help position Gallo products in retail outlets, the company integrated forward into wholesale distribution and backward into vineyards, bottling, and foil production. Ernest and Julio Gallo were also pioneers in developing new wine production techniques and growing high-quality grapes. The company's innovations in those two areas made it a low-cost producer of low- and moderate-quality wines, paving the way for Gallo brands to capture a very large portion of the low-end table wine market in the United States. After establishing a dominant position in this market segment, the Gallo brothers began gradual expansion into medium-quality, medium-priced wines by purchasing land in the Napa Valley region of California (north of its Sonoma County operations) and creating several new brands. By 1998, Gallo had 17 of the top 75 best-selling brands—see Exhibit 13.

Ernest and Julio Gallo were regarded as very aggressive competitors in an industry that liked to consider itself a gentleman's industry. Gallo was sued by Kendall-Jackson for creating a label very similar to one of Kendall-Jackson's best-selling products; the case was eventually settled out of court. Financial data on Gallo's performance were not publicly available because the company was family-owned. The third generation of the Gallo family was currently taking over the operations of the winery and planned to continue the strategies crafted largely by Ernest and Julio in making Gallo the largest wine producer in the world. In September 2000, Gallo announced that a brand called Alcott Ridge Vineyards would be sold in all Wal-Mart stores worldwide.

E. & J. Gallo exported to an estimated 86 country markets, but its international focus was for the most part on such major markets as Great Britain, Japan, Canada, and Germany. Gallo exported about 13 percent of its production overseas in 1997, and its total volume of exports was more than those of all other California wineries combined (see Exhibit 14). Gallo's forward and backward integration strategy in the U.S. wine market was also an integral part of its export strategy. Gallo brands were featured in a front-aisle display at Harrods' new wine shop in London. Approximately three of every

exhibit 12   Winery Production Capabilities (in thousands of gallons)

Company	Capacity
E. & J. Gallo	330,000
Beringer	17,800
Robert Mondavi	17,387
Wente	5,100

Source: Wines & Vines, July 2000.

exhibit 13   Number of Brands in the Top 75 in the United States, 1996 and 1998 (based on volume)

Company	Number in top 75, 1996	Highest Rank, 1996	Number in top 75, 1998	Highest Rank, 1998
E. & J. Gallo Winery	11	1	17	2
Robert Mondavi	1	8*	2	8
Beringer	3	10	2	9
Wente	0	N/A	0	N/A

*Includes volumes for all domestically produced Mondavi wines.
Source: Adams Wine Handbook, 1997 and 1999.

exhibit 14   Top California Wine Exporters, 1997 (based on volume)

1997 Rank	Company	Selected Brands	Exports (in thousands of gallons)	Percent of Total Sales
1	E. & J. Gallo	Gallo, Turning Leaf	17,555	13%
4	Robert Mondavi	Woodbridge, Mondavi	1,302	8
11	Wente	Wente, Concannon	485	61
12	Beringer	Beringer, Meridian	345	3

Source: San Francisco Chronicle Research.

five bottles of California wine on the shelves of U.K. retailers were Gallo brands. In 1998, Gallo launched a brand named Garnet Point tailored to appeal to British tastes.

Robert Mondavi Corporation

Something of a niche player in the wine market, Robert Mondavi Corporation focused exclusively on premium and superpremium wines. Mondavi's production capacity was substantial, but the company was very small compared with E. & J. Gallo (see Exhibit 12). Robert Mondavi founded the company in 1966 after he was asked to leave his previous position as sales manager at a winery owned by his family. Mondavi was reportedly such an excellent salesman that his family's winery could not increase production to keep up with his sales. While part of the family wine business, Mondavi

exhibit 15   Robert Mondavi Winery, Financial Summary, 1995–99
                    (in millions)

	1995	1996	1997	1998	1999
Net revenue	$199.5	$240.8	$300.8	$325.2	$370.6
Gross profit	$ 93.0	$117.9	$151.0	$151.3	$169.7
Operating income	$ 28.9	$ 47.2	$ 71.2	$ 61.3	$ 6.6
Net income	$ 12.3	$ 24.1	$ 38.1	$ 30.2	$ 34.5
Volume (9-liter case equivalent)	4.5	5.4	6.5	6.8	7.6

Source: Company records.

helped create and bring to market several innovations. One of these was cold fermentation, which created a lighter and fruitier taste that differentiated Mondavi's wines
from European and other California wines. Another innovation was the use of French
oak barrels for aging wine. These barrels gave wine a distinctive flavor that rivaled the
French wines dominating the international market at the time. Mondavi was also responsible for combining the French appellation and California varietal naming conventions, thereby elevating the brand image of his wines due to the associations with
both French wines and the Napa Valley region.

When Robert Mondavi left the family winery, he utilized all of his prior innovations to begin creating a new winery that would produce fine wines. Mondavi believed
that love of wine came from a way of life and that that way of life involved fine dining, travel, and love of the arts. The company never spent money on advertising, relying instead on trade shows, awards, salesmanship, and showmanship. Its brands were
sold in restaurants, hotels, supermarkets, liquor stores, and specialty wine shops; prices
for the various Mondavi brands ranged from as little as $6 per bottle to over $100 per
bottle. An example of Robert Mondavi's dedication to fine wines was the company's
joint venture with Baron Philippe de Rothschild of France to produce the Opus One label; Opus One was considered one of the finest wines in the world and retailed for over
$100 per bottle. The Robert Mondavi Corporation went public in 1993, but the family
still owned 92 percent of the stock. The company's recent financial performance is
shown in Exhibit 15.

In 1999, Mondavi wines were marketed in an estimated 77 countries. Exporting
and growing the company's presence in the global premium wine market was a priority for Mondavi. The company expected to export a minimum of 20 percent of its production in the future.

Beringer Wine Estates, Inc.

The Beringer winery was founded by Jacob and Frederick Beringer, brothers who emigrated from the Rhine Valley in Germany. Beringer was the oldest continuously operating winery in Napa Valley, its first crush having occurred in 1877. Beringer wines
were well regarded by the turn of the century because of their high quality. In 1971, the
Beringer winery was sold by the family to Nestlé USA, Inc. At the time, the company
was underperforming, chiefly because the family had not reinvested in the vineyards
or in the production process, thus impairing the quality of its wines. Nestlé renamed
the company Wine World Estates and launched a long-term effort to refurbish production facilities and improve the vineyards, but it sold the winery in 1996 for $350 mil-
lion and Beringer Wine Estates Inc. was formed. Soon thereafter, the new Beringer did

exhibit 16   Beringer Financial Summary, 1995–99 (in millions)

	1995	1996	1997	1998	1999
Net revenue	$202.0	$231.7	$269.5	$318.4	$376.2
Adjusted gross profit	$100.7	$116.1	$134.9	$163.7	$194.6
Adjusted operating income	$34.8	$43.9	$56.3	$70.5	$83.0
Adjusted net income	$16.8	$15.6	$15.1	$29.5	$39.3
Volume (9-liter case equivalent)	4.6	5	5.4	6.1	6.8
Total assets	$289.9	$438.7	$467.2	$543.6	$644.3
Total debt	N/A	$289.2	$319.1	$277.2	$328.0

Source: Beringer Wine Estates, 1999 annual report.

several more acquisitions, focused its brands on the moderate and upscale segments, and then went public in 1997. The company's recent financial performance is presented in Exhibit 16.

In the fall of 2000, Beringer Wine Estates was purchased for $1.2 billion by Foster's Brewing Group Limited, the Australian parent company of Foster's Lager. Foster's planned to combine Beringer's portfolio of wines with its own wine subsidiary, Mildara Blass Limited, to create the largest premium wine company in the world, with combined revenues of $886 million in fiscal year 2000. Mildara Blass currently had a 25 percent share of the premium wine market in Australia, and its main export markets were the United States, the United Kingdom, and Europe. Foster's saw the Beringer acquisition as giving it access to a broader distribution system and planned to leverage Beringer's U.S. distribution network to grow sales of Mildara Blass wines. It also planned to use its Australian distribution capabilities to grow the sales of Beringer brands in Australia.

Wente Bros.

Wente was a family-owned winery founded in California's Livermore Valley in 1885. Unlike most other U.S. wineries, Wente's strategy focused more on the export market than on the domestic market. Wente sold its wines in an estimated 160 country markets and exported about 61 percent of its total production capacity in 1997 (see Exhibit 14). Wente's marketing strategies were country-specific, varying in a manner calculated to appeal to local tastes and preferences. In contrast to other U.S. wineries, which tended to focus their export efforts on a few larger country markets with limited service to smaller country markets, Wente was willing to patiently develop a country market when it saw future opportunities.

To draw attention to its wines, Wente had opened wine bars in airports from Africa to the Pacific Rim. It was the number one wine retailer in the world through duty-free shops in airports; to help drive sales, it had created special gift boxes that contained French wines specifically for duty-free shops. Wente also claimed that it sold more wine to more airlines than any other winery in the world, with a focus on airlines serving Asia and the Pacific Rim—Thai Airways, All Nippon Airways, Singapore Air, Philippine Airlines, Cathay Pacific Airlines, Malaysian Air, Vietnam Airlines, and Garuda—plus Delta and United flights in the region. In the 1980s, Wente invested heavily in building its relationships with distributors in Japan; this move later paid off when a Japanese news program ran a segment on the health benefits of wine—Wente soon sold out its entire stock on hand and gained an advantage in securing distribution of its wines in Japan. In China, Wente's brands were sold in restaurants, liquor stores, and hotels.

Wente had formed many joint ventures throughout the world. Some involved producing premium wines in conjunction with established foreign wineries; others were aimed at partnering simply to help gain access to the markets of a particular country. Wente's joint venture with Indage Group in India allowed Wente to become the first foreign winery to import into the Indian market; the agreement stipulated that Wente had to export Indage wine to other markets and that all Wente wine sold in India had to be bottled locally. (These terms were required by the Indian government as a condition of approving the joint venture and granting import access to Wente—the terms allowed the government to offset the import and export credits between the participating countries.) Indage was also planning to enter into similar joint venture arrangements with French and German wineries. A joint venture between Wente and Luigi Cecchi & Sons of Italy was formed to produce an ultrapremium wine to be sold in the U.S. domestic market by 2003. Wente had entered into a joint venture with an Israeli firm named Segal Winery to produce a kosher wine. Another Wente joint venture was formed with Bodegas de Santo Tomas, a Mexican winery, to sell a brand named Duetto in the United States and Mexico; the motivation for this venture was to get around high import tariffs established by Mexico in retaliation for the American government's penalizing Mexican companies for dumping cheap brooms in the U.S. market. The high import tariffs made shipping bottled wine to Mexican markets too expensive for Wente to compete in Mexico. To detour the tariff barrier, Wente started shipping bulk wine to Bodegas de Santo Tomas; this wine was then blended, bottled, and marketed locally by Wente's Mexican partner.

Over the years, Wente had encountered a number of problems in executing its export strategy. It had been forced to exit the wine market in Myanmar due to political pressure, and it pulled out of Russia when the ruble collapsed. Wente had proved its commitment to responding to local market conditions by developing and marketing varietal wines in Africa to accompany such nontraditional foods as zebra and antelope.

FUTURE CHALLENGES AND OPPORTUNITIES

In 2000–2001, U.S. wineries were confronting increased competitive pressures. In 1999 and early 2000, import brands upped their share of the U.S. market to 20 percent (up from 17 percent in 1998), owing to inroads made by Australian, Argentine, and Chilean wines. And while U.S. wine exports had grown impressively from $137 million in 1990 to $548 million in 1999, domestic competition was making exporting more strategically important. The U.S. wine industry exported only 13 percent of its production, while Old World wineries in France, Italy, and Spain exported, on average, more than 25 percent of the wine they produced. New World producer Australia exported over 40 percent of its production, and Chile exported over 80 percent.

bibliography

Adam Wine Handbook. New York: Adam Business Media, 1999.

"American Wine in the 21st Century." *Wine Vision,* July 6, 2000.

Australian Wine Foundation, *Strategy 2025: The Australian Wine Industry,* June 1996.

Beringer Wine Estates press release, August 28, 2000.

Britannica.com search on wine, October 2000.

Brown-Forman Corporation annual report, 2000.

"Brown-Forman Taps Wines from Down Under." *Beverage Industry,* December 1999.

"California Vintners Try to Quench China's Thirst for Wine." *Contra Costa Times,* October 10, 1997.

"California's Wente Vineyards Halts Shipments to Myanmar." *Contra Costa Times,* November 8, 1996.

Cartiere, Richard. "New World Global Wine Boom Shows No Sign of Faltering." *Wine Market Report,* May 16, 2000.

Clawson, James B.; Jeannie Boone; and Alan Atkinson. *International Trade Barriers Report 1998.* Washington, DC: JBC International, May 1998.

Courtney, Kevin, and Carson, L. Pierce. "What He Did Right—and Wrong—in the Creation of His World Wine Empire." *Napa Valley Register,* October 21, 1998.

Durkan, Andrew, and John Cousins. *Wine Appreciation,* Chicago: NTC Publishing Group, 1995.

Elliott-Fisk, Deborah. *The Geography of Soils.* University of California.

Franson, Paul. "U.S. Wineries Consider Long-Term Strategy to Maintain Competitiveness." *Vineyard & Winery Management,* May/June 1999.

"Globalization, Who's Leading the Way?" *Wines & Vines,* April 2000.

Ivie International, California Wine Export Program. "United States Wine Exports, Imports and Balance of U.S. Wine Trade 1999." July 24, 2000.

Johnson, Hugh. " All about Wine." www.reedbooks.co.uk/docs/mitchell/wine/allabout.htm.

Koerber, Kristine. "Fueling Increased." *Wine Business Monthly* 7, no. 5 (May 2000).

Marketing Intelligence Services Ltd. "Gallo Garnet Point Wine." September 21, 1998.

"Monterey County, Calif., Wine Exports Increase." *Monterey County Herald,* November 14, 1998.

"Multicultural Wine Trade: A New Red Is Being Made with Grapes from Northern California and Baja. The Blend Skirts Mexican Tariffs." *Orange County (CA) Register,* September 19, 1998.

Nicholson, Robert M. "New World Wine Exporters Continued Growth in '99." *Wines & Vines,* July 2000.

"On Your Mark—Get Set—Consolidate." *Wine Business Insider* 10, no 35 (September 2, 2000).

Prial, Frank. "Controversy Swirls around $1,000 Garage Wines." *New York Times,* October 25, 2000.

Sawyer, Abby, and Jim Hammett. "American Appellations Earn Distinction as a Marketing Tool." *Wine Business Monthly,* June 2000.

Sinton, Peter. "California Wines Quenching in the World: Exports from the States Have Doubled in the Past Five Years. *San Francisco Chronicle,* January 23, 1999.

University of Pennsylvania, Museum of Archaeology and Anthropology website (www.upenn.edu/museum), October, 2000.

"Vintners Uncork Indian Market." *South China Morning Post,* March 21, 1999.

Wal-Mart press release, September 29, 2000.

"Wente and Bichot Forge New Partnership." *Duty-Free News International,* December 15, 1999.

"Wente Bros." *Impact,* December 15, 1995.

case 12 Robert Mondavi Corporation

Murray Silverman
San Francisco State University

Armand Gilinsky
Sonoma State University

Michael Guy
San Francisco State University

In January 1999, Michael Mondavi, the 55-year-old CEO of the Robert Mondavi Corporation (RMC) and son of its founder, Robert Mondavi, announced the reorganization of the company and the layoff of 4 percent of the workforce. RMC had experienced a shortfall in supplying its Woodbridge Chardonnay brand. Disgruntled distributors had begun substituting competing Chardonnay brands on retailers' shelves. Once Woodbridge production levels returned to normal, some distributors remained reluctant to carry the brand, putting a more lasting dent in company sales. Subsequently, RMC's stock was downgraded by Wall Street analysts, and its stock price fell nearly 60 percent. Recent company financial data are shown in Exhibits 1 through 5.

At the same time that Michael Mondavi announced the layoffs in January 1999, senior management was completing the process of reconfiguring RMC's future strategies. One camp argued for a return to the original vision, complaining that RMC had been so busy focusing on launching new brands and pursuing international ventures that it had neglected its core domestic brands, which made up 90 percent of revenues. Another group of managers argued for continued diversification. After all, RMC had introduced three new brands in the previous year: two through global partnerships in Chile and Italy and one domestic brand. Many of the managers in this camp had been involved in orchestrating the development and launch of new brands in the domestic and global markets. Michael Mondavi was caught between the two camps.

COMPANY BACKGROUND

Robert Mondavi, the son of a poor Italian immigrant, founded the Robert Mondavi Winery in 1966 at the age of 54, after a bitter departure stemming from a dispute over

The authors gratefully acknowledge a Business and International Education (BIE) grant from the U.S. Department of Education and a matching grant from the College of Business at San Francisco State University in support of this research.

exhibit 1   Robert Mondavi Corporation, Statements of Income, Fiscal
Years 1997–99 (dollar amounts in millions, except per share
amounts)

	Fiscal Years Ending		
	June 1999	June 1998	June 1997
Revenue	$370.6	$325.2	$300.8
Cost of goods sold	205.4	175.7	166.0
Gross profit	165.2	149.5	134.8
Gross profit margin	44.6%	46.0%	44.8%
Selling, general, and administrative expenses	104.6	90.0	79.8
Operating income	60.6	59.5	55.0
Operating margin	16.4%	18.3%	18.3%
Nonoperating income	3.0	0.4	1.0
Nonoperating expenses	14.2	12.3	10.6
Income before taxes	50.1	47.6	46.2
Income taxes	19.3	18.6	18.0
Net income after taxes	30.8	29.0	28.2
Net profit margin	8.3%	8.9%	9.4%
Diluted EPS	$1.94	$1.83	$1.80
Dividends per share ($)	—	—	—

control of the family-owned Krug Winery. Using personal savings and loans from
friends, Mondavi founded his Napa Valley winery with a simple vision: "To do whatever it took to make great wines and to put Napa Valley on the map, right alongside the
great winemaking centers of Europe."

Wine in the United States was classified into the following categories: table wine
(7 to 14 percent in alcohol by volume), sparkling wine/champagne, dessert wine, and
other wine products (e.g., wine coolers, sherry). Table wine represented approximately
66 percent of U.S. volume and was further divided into varietal and nonvarietal wine.
In order to classify a wine as varietal, the law stated that 75 percent of the juice that
went into it had to be from a single grape variety. The current most popular white varietal was Chardonnay. Cabernet Sauvignon and Merlot were the standards in red
wines, and White Zinfandel in blush wines. Table wine also was categorized into price
brackets: jug wine (under $3 per 750-milliliter bottle) and premium wine (over $3 per
750-milliliter bottle). The premium wine segment was further subdivided into popular
premium, superpremium, and ultrapremium categories. While the jug wine category
accounted for 44 percent of the table-wine market by volume, it accounted for only 17
percent of the revenue by 1999—see Exhibit 6. Wines also were classified by their appellation, the name of the geographic area in which the grapes were grown. This was
because the climate and soil conditions imparted different characteristics and tastes to
the wine. The winemaking process provided many opportunities to affect a wine's
characteristics, increasing the potential for differentiating wine brands.

Robert Mondavi set out to be the first in California to produce premium wines that
were intended to compete with the premium European brands. At the time, many wine
industry observers considered Mondavi's venture to be financial suicide. In his 1998

exhibit 2   Robert Mondavi Corporation, Balance Sheets, Fiscal Years
1997–99 (dollar amounts in millions)

	Fiscal Years Ending		
	June 1999	June 1998	June 1997
Assets			
Cash	$ 4.0	$ 2.7	$ 0.2
Net receivables	82.0	68.7	59.2
Inventories	262.4	226.1	167.7
Other current assets	4.0	10.3	7.3
Total current assets	353.9	307.8	234.3
Net fixed assets	249.6	215.3	187.0
Other noncurrent assets	25.8	24.8	23.6
Total assets	$629.3	$548.0	$444.9
Liabilities and shareholders' equity			
Accounts payable	$ 19.4	$ 18.9	$ 14.8
Short-term debt	10.3	11.0	15.5
Other current liabilities	26.4	20.3	18.1
Total current liabilities	56.1	50.2	48.4
Long-term debt	243.8	222.6	158.1
Other noncurrent liabilities	7.0	7.0	6.4
Total liabilities	$325.0	$294.0	$223.7
Common stock equity	$304.4	$254.0	$221.2
Total equity	304.4	254.0	221.2
Total liabilities and equity	$629.3	$548.0	$444.9
Shares outstanding (mil.)	15.5	15.4	15.2

Note: Some figures may not add up due to rounding.

exhibit 3   Robert Mondavi Corporation, Statements of Cash Flow,
Fiscal Years 1997–99 (dollar amounts in millions)

	Fiscal Years Ending		
	June 1999	June 1998	June 1997
Net operating cash flow	$27.9	$(18.5)	$(3.4)
Net investing cash flow	$(47.6)	$(39.9)	$(41.3)
Net financing cash flow	$21.5	$60.9	$44.8
Net change in cash	$1.9	$2.5	$0.2
Depreciation and amortization	$15.8	$13.7	$12.6
Capital expenditures	$(50.8)	$(49.5)	$(42.6)
Cash dividends paid	$0	$0	$0

exhibit 4   Robert Mondavi Corporation, 10-Year Highlights, 1990–99

Fiscal Year	Revenue ($ millions)	Net Income ($ millions)	Net Profit Margin (%)	Employees
1999	$370.6	$30.8	8.3%	750
1998	325.2	29.0	8.9	1,098
1997	300.8	28.2	9.4	890
1996	240.8	24.4	10.1	989
1995	210.4	17.8	8.5	906
1994	167.0	9.5	5.7	—
1993	177.7	8.7	4.9	—
1992	154.3	7.1	4.6	—
1991	125.1	4.3	3.4	—
1990	115.7	8.1	7.0	—

Source: Hoover's Company Capsules, 2000.

exhibit 5   Robert Mondavi Corporation, Stock Price History, 1993–98

Year	Fiscal Year Stock Price			Price-Earnings Ratio		Per Share ($)		
	High	Low	Close	High	Low	Earnings	Dividend	Book Value
1998	$56.75	$27.63	$28.38	31	15	$1.83	0	$16.54
1997	47.38	26.25	47.25	26	15	1.80	0	14.58
1996	34.75	17.38	31.50	22	11	1.61	0	12.59
1995	17.75	6.25	17.50	13	4	1.39	0	9.75
1994	11.25	7.75	7.88	15	10	0.75	0	8.35
1993	14.25	10.50	11.25	17	13	0.83	0	7.61

Source: Hoover's Company Capsules, 2000.

exhibit 6   Estimated 1999 California Table Wine Shipments by Price Class

Retail Price per Bottle	Price Segment	% of Total Volume	% of Total Revenue
Over $14	Ultrapremium	7.0%	25.0%
$7 to $14	Superpremium	16.0	27.0
$3 to $7	Popular premium	33.0	31.0
Below $3	Jug wine and other	44.0	17.0
Total		100.0%	100.0%

Source: 1999 estimates by Gomberg, Fredrikson, and Associates (excludes exports).

book on the history of the company, *Harvests of Joy: How the Good Life Became a Great Business,* Mondavi recalled:

> We in California had enormous potential; I knew we could become one of the great wine-producing regions of the world. But the American wine industry was still in its infancy, and no one seemed to have the knowledge, the vision, or the guts to reach for the gold, to make wines that could stand proudly next to the very best from France and Italy, Germany, and Spain.

Robert Mondavi's initial business plan called for building RMC's reputation by producing a limited quantity of super- to ultrapremium wines using the most prestigious noble varietal grapes: Cabernet Sauvignon, Pinot Noir, Chardonnay, and Johannesburg Riesling. At the time, these four varietals commanded the highest prices in the marketplace and had the highest profit margin per bottle. In order to generate cash flow to expand the business, RMC planned to produce less-expensive wines in high volumes to be sold in the premium market. Mondavi felt that the path to success in producing super- to ultrapremium wines began with high-quality grapes, so he set out to find the best vineyard in Napa Valley to locate the new RMC. He eventually purchased a 12-acre portion of the famous To-Kalon vineyard in Oakville for the winery location. This vineyard was able to supply RMC with high-quality estate-grown Cabernet Sauvignon grapes in its first year of operation. The To-Kalon vineyard has provided Cabernet Sauvignon grapes ever since, enabling RMC to create a prestige label.

To meet initial production targets, Mondavi began purchasing grapes from other growers around the Napa Valley and convinced many of Krug's top grape suppliers during these early years to sign long-term contracts with RMC. Mondavi then worked closely with growers to improve grape quality and structured their contracts so that their compensation was tied to the grape quality and crop yields. Mondavi also was able to convince Krug's top two suppliers to take a financial stake in his new winery.

Next, Mondavi set out to build a state-of-the-art winemaking facility that was both functional for making premium wines and distinctive enough to make a statement. Mondavi enlisted Cliff May, a highly respected architect, to design an eye-catching Spanish mission–style landmark. May's design for the winery became the backdrop of every wine label RMC has since produced. In his 1998 book, Mondavi wrote about his design requirements for the new winery:

> The winery I envisioned was to be a showcase for the most advanced winemaking techniques and equipment in America, if not the world. Aesthetics would be key. In France, the great chateaux were temples of style, tradition, and refinement. This was the lead I wanted to follow. I wanted my winery to have elegance and style, to be a place that would properly highlight our talents and the work going on inside. I also wanted it to be a place that would attract streams of visitors.

The winery became a laboratory for developing what were to become some of the California wine industry's best practices in the production of world-class premium wines. Among these practices were (1) assembling a team of experts in the areas of viticulture and winemaking, from industry professionals to university professors; (2) developing new technology to permit gentle handling of wine grapes and cold fermentation of white wines; and (3) introducing process innovations, such as steel fermentation tanks, vacuum corking of bottles, and aging of wines in new French oak barrels. These innovative practices have since become standards in the California wine industry. In his book, Mondavi described his pursuit of excellence:

> From the outset, I wanted my winery to draw inspiration and methods from the traditional Old World chateaux of France and Italy, but I also wanted to become a model of state-of-

the-art technology, a pioneer in research and a gathering place for the finest minds in our industry. I wanted our winery to be a haven of creativity, innovation, excitement, and that unbelievable energy you find in a start-up venture when everyone is committed, heart and soul, to a common cause and a common quest.

Although Mondavi had managed to slowly improve the quality of RMC's wines throughout the 1970s, he struggled to get his super- to ultrapremium RMC wines into reputable five-star restaurants and top wine shops across the country. Mondavi spent lavishly on entertaining influential people within the industry and invited the top wine writers to the RMC facility for free meals. He then would conduct blind tastings of the RMC wines against reputable French and Italian wines so that the wine writers could taste for themselves what RMC was producing. For over a decade, Mondavi traveled extensively throughout the country and abroad as the company's chief salesperson, promoting his vision for RMC and Napa Valley. Often, while dining alone on business trips, Mondavi invited the chefs, sommeliers, wait staff, and restaurateurs to blind-taste RMC wines against the restaurant's best European wines. One restaurant at a time, Mondavi managed to get his wines on the wine lists of the best five-star restaurants in the United States. By the close of the 1970s, Mondavi's persistence began to pay off. Restaurant owners, famous wine connoisseurs, and the press were now very interested in RMC's products. With increasing recognition of and demand for his wine, Mondavi began slowly raising the prices of his products until they were selling for as much as comparable French wines.

Michael Mondavi, one of Robert Mondavi's sons, became a winemaker for RMC in 1966. He worked his way up through several management positions, and in 1994 he was appointed president and CEO. Robert Mondavi became chairman of the board.

RMC ultimately reached the capacity to produce approximately 500,000 cases annually of premium to ultrapremium wines. These wines were composed of reserves and district-designated and varietal wines, such as Cabernet Sauvignon, Pinot Noir, Chardonnay, and Fumé Blanc. Approximately 40 percent of the wines produced at RMC were made from estate-grown grapes in the Stag's Leap, Carneros, and Oakville districts of the Napa Valley. The winery progressively expanded the breadth of its wines by releasing ultrapremium reserves and district-designated varietal wines in more limited quantities. In the works was a vineyard-designated wine program to produce limited releases of popular varietals, such as a Cabernet Sauvignon from Marjorie's Block of the To-Kalon Vineyard. These ultrapremium wines were available in limited quantities and at higher prices than the regular RMC wines.

In the 1998 fiscal year, RMC sold 6.8 million cases of wine throughout the United States and in some 90 countries worldwide, grossing $341.1 million in sales. RMC's workforce had grown to more than 1,000 people. All of RMC's domestic sales came through its top 16 distributors, which represented approximately 96 percent of 1998 gross revenues. Brokers and agents handled product sales into export markets, and worldwide wine sales in 1998 accounted for 8 percent of the company's gross revenues.

DOMESTIC BRAND DIVERSIFICATION

Starting in the late 1970s and continuing throughout the 1980s, RMC set out to build a portfolio of premium wine brands to fill various price points and niches in the domestic wine market. Robert Mondavi became very interested in exploring opportunities to develop new brands from the new wine appellations that had begun springing up in the California wine country. RMC expanded its brand portfolio by acquiring and

exhibit 7   Robert Mondavi's Brands

Brands	Popular Premium ($3 to $7)	Super-premium ($7 to $14)	Ultra-premium* ($14 to $25)	Super Ultra-premium (over $25)
Domestic Brands				
Robert Mondavi Winery		X	X	X
Opus One				X
Woodbridge	X	X		
RM Coastal		X		
Io			X	
Byron		X	X	
La Famiglia		X	X	
Import Brands				
Dazante (Italy)		X		
Luce & Lucente (Italy)			X	X
Seña (Chile)				X
Caliterra (Chile)	X	X		
Vichon Med. (France)†	X	X		
Percentage of fiscal year 1999 revenues	55%	26%	11%	8%

*RMC further divided the ultrapremium category into two categories, which has not been adopted by the industry to date.

†Bulk wine from France was imported for the Vichon brand, but the wine was finished and bottled at the RMC facility.

Source: Robert Mondavi Bank of America Securities Conference, February 16, 2000.

developing the Woodbridge, Byron, and Coastal brands, and along the way also acquiring new vineyard properties in California. RMC used long-term debt to finance its move into additional brands and wine varieties. By 1999, RMC owned five winemaking facilities and associated vineyards across California, and was marketing its wines under seven domestic brands and six international brands—see Exhibits 7 and 8.

The Woodbridge Brand

In 1979, RMC purchased Cherokee Vineyard Winery to expand the production of table wines under the RMC label. RMC remodeled the Cherokee Vineyard Winery and renamed it Woodbridge, after the small town in which the winery was located. Woodbridge began producing high-volume premium wines using the same quality-driven winemaking techniques employed by RMC. Over the course of the 1980s, the Robert Mondavi Table Wine brand, previously made at RMC, was migrated into the Woodbridge brand. Wines sold under the Woodbridge label represented approximately 55 percent of company revenue by 1998. The brand had become the second-largest premium wine in U.S. food stores, as measured by ACNielsen/Adams Business Research. Woodbridge produced six moderately priced varietal wines—Cabernet Sauvignon, Zinfandel, Chardonnay, Sauvignon Blanc, Merlot, and White Zinfandel—all of which were positioned in the popular premium and low-end superpremium wine market segments. RMC projected that Woodbridge sales would continue to grow at 10 to 15 percent a year indefinitely. Management believed that more vineyards would be needed to enable the Woodbridge brand to meet future production goals and keep costs under control.

exhibit 8   Acres of RMC-Owned Vineyards

County	Planted	Fallow	Total
Napa Valley	694	302	996
Carneros, Napa Valley	452	—	452
Mendocino	260	170	430
Monterey	549	618	1,167
San Joaquin	93	—	93
San Luis Obispo	434	—	434
Santa Barbara	1,295	300	1,595
Total	3,777	1,390	5,167

The Byron Brand

To supply the Woodbridge brand, RMC started searching for additional sources of grapes in the central California coastal regions in the mid-1980s. In the late 1970s, winemaker Byron "Ken" Brown, owner of the Byron Winery, had recognized the tremendous promise of the region's cool, ocean-influenced climate to grow high-quality Pinot Noir and Chardonnay grapes, and he was one of the first to introduce these Rhône-style grape varietals to the appellation. Robert Mondavi was so impressed by the wines Brown was creating that in 1989 he purchased the Byron Winery and 55 acres of vineyards in Santa Barbara and Santa Maria counties. After the purchase, Brown was left in charge of Byron while RMC injected needed capital and expertise into the winery and vineyard operations. Tim Mondavi, RMC's head winemaker, was sent to work closely with Brown to incorporate the winemaking and viticulture techniques developed at RMC into Byron's operations. A new 80,000-case Byron Winery was completed in August 1996. RMC also expanded the vineyard holdings at Byron by replanting the estate vineyards with high-density plantings, bringing the total amount of land in production up to 1,420 acres in 1998. In addition to the Byron brand, RMC planned to release a new brand produced out of the Byron acreage under the label Io. Io was to be a limited-production Rhône-style wine, consisting of a unique blend of Syrah, Mourvedre, and Grenache grapes. It was to be priced at $40 a bottle and sold exclusively to RMC's top accounts.

The Coastal Brand

The Robert Mondavi Coastal wines were developed in May 1994 to fill a price niche in the premium to superpremium market below Byron's wines. Wines under the Coastal label retailed from $8 to $12 a bottle and featured Cabernet Sauvignon, Merlot, Pinot Noir, Zinfandel, Chardonnay, and Sauvignon Blanc varietal wines. Despite opposition from other California winemakers, RMC sought to differentiate the California coastal regions by creating a new Central Coast appellation that emphasized the Coastal origin of source grapes used in the wines and that featured a sea-meets-land motif as a backdrop to the brand's labels. RMC did not maintain an exclusive winery for the production of the Coastal brand but instead contracted with Golden State Vintners of Soledad to crush the grapes and then used facilities at the RMC and Woodbridge wineries to make and bottle the Central Coast wine varieties. Several larger competitors in the premium market were also known to be developing vineyards and wineries in the coastal regions, and RMC management foresaw stiff competition ahead for its Coastal brand.

In order to maintain retail shelf space, RMC sought to lower its production costs and to increase the volume of wine produced as the brand entered nationwide distribution. A major constraint to the brand's growth was grape supply, as most grapes for the Coastal brand were sourced from 25 growers, accounting for approximately 2,500 acres of vineyard production. RMC owned an additional 1,200 acres of land in the Salinas Valley, of which only 35 percent were planted. RMC sought additional vineyard acquisitions in the region so that 80 percent of grape sourcing for the brand in the future would come from company-owned vineyards. Sales for this brand were expected to surpass 1 million cases by 1999, a full year ahead of projections.

The La Famiglia di Robert Mondavi Brand

The La Famiglia di Robert Mondavi brand was introduced in 1995 and was devoted to producing Italian-style varietal wines in California for the ultrapremium market. After decades of growing traditional French varietal grapes in California, RMC decided to experiment by growing Italian varietals in California. Management felt that the Napa Valley might be suited for cultivating these Italian varietals and was especially interested in making wines from Sangiovese grapes, one of the most popular varietal wines in Italy. RMC produced small quantities of seven wines under the La Famiglia di Robert Mondavi brand. This brand featured Barbera, Sangiovese, and Pinot Grigio varietals. Wines under the La Famiglia label were produced at the former Oakville Vichon Winery, which RMC renamed the La Famiglia di Robert Mondavi Winery.

GLOBAL PARTNERSHIPS

In the 1980s, RMC began pursuing global ventures and looking for suitable partners in France, Italy, and Chile. By the mid-1990s, the company had entered into three multinational partnerships, one in Napa with the Rothschild family, one in Chile with the Chadwick family, and the other in Italy with the Marchesi de' Frescobaldi family. These partnerships yielded several new global brands, including Opus One, Caliterra, and Lucente.

Opus One

RMC took the initial steps to expand its brand portfolio beyond California when it entered into a joint partnership with Baron Philippe de Rothschild, owner of the famed Château Mouton-Rothschild in Bordeaux, France, to form Opus One. The Opus One partnership began one morning in 1979, when Mondavi and Rothschild were dining in the baron's bedroom in Bordeaux. In his 1998 book, Mondavi outlined the basis for their partnership:

> We agreed to form a fifty-fifty partnership with one guiding ambition: to make a great wine, a wine that would stand alone in spirit and quality. The idea was to take our different cultures and traditions, along with the best materials and know-how from Bordeaux and California, merge them, fuse them, and see if we could find that touch of magic that produces a wine great enough to be referred to as "bottled poetry." We'd draw our inspiration from Mouton's Premier Grand Cru Classe and the Mondavi Cabernet Reserve, but our aim was to create a wine like no other, a great wine with its own style, character, and breeding.
>
> No one in the past fifty years had done more for French wine than the Baron and everyone knew it. The fact that he wanted to have a joint venture with our winery immediately elevated us into a unique position in the California wine industry. The Baron wanted

to do business in America, with a Napa Valley winery as a partner, and we were chosen. He said: "I want a fifty-fifty partnership. Because I don't know the local culture. I don't know the local history. I don't know the local people. And those three will make the difference between producing wine and producing great wine."

The prestige value was enormous—and so was the publicity. When we announced the creation of the joint venture, I'd say we got over a million dollars' worth of free advertising. At the same time, this partnership gave us real international standing, and it set the stage for a series of other foreign ventures that we developed in the years ahead.

Work to create the first vintages of Opus One wine commenced immediately with RMC selling 35 acres of the company's best vineyards from the To-Kalon block. The partnership then purchased two more vineyards across Highway 29 from RMC, where the Opus One Winery would eventually be built. Château Mouton-Rothschild's winemaker Lucien Sionnea and Timothy Mondavi began working together at RMC to make the first vintage of Opus One. Over the next five years, the two winemakers worked closely to blend the two different cultural styles and techniques of winemaking. Ten years in the making, the Opus One Winery was completed in 1991. The winery featured a state-of-the-art barrel room where temperature and humidity were kept at precise specifications using an electronic climate control system. Opus One, a Bordeaux-style Cabernet Sauvignon, consisted of a blend of 80 percent Cabernet Sauvignon mixed with Cabernet Franc and Merlot. Production was limited to 30,000 cases per year, and bottles of the wine sold for between $90 and $100 in more than 65 world markets. Due to its limited production, demand for Opus One exceeded supply. Distributors and individual customers had to order well in advance of the wine's release. Opus One thus became America's first ultrapremium wine. By the mid-1980s, it had made the transition into the French, English, German, and Swiss markets. This was not only a first for American wines but also an opportunity for RMC to showcase its other wines in those markets.

The Chadwick Family Partnership

RMC recognized that Chile possessed wine regions with the same favorable climatic and soil characteristics as those found in the Napa Valley. In 1996, RMC entered into a 50/50 joint partnership with Eduardo Chadwick and his family to form the Viña Caliterra S.A. joint venture, which would now be responsible for producing the Caliterra brand of premium Chilean wines. Under the terms of the partnership, the Caliterra wines would be produced at the Viña Errazuriz Winery until a new winemaking facility could be built. Caliterra wine intended for the United States market would be shipped in bulk to be finished at the Woodbridge facility, whereas wine intended for the global markets would be produced and finished in the Viña Errazuriz Winery. The terms of the Viña Caliterra partnership also provided RMC with exclusive rights to distribute the Viña Errazuriz brand of wines in the United States. Michael Mondavi commented on the Caliterra partnership:

> We saw the same potential in Chile that we saw in Napa Valley 30 years ago. But most importantly, with Caliterra we saw people who are dedicated to producing wines that belong in the company of the greatest wines in the world.

After forming Viña Caliterra, each partner provided sufficient capital to expand the Caliterra operations and to purchase La Arboleda, a 1,000-hectare estate in Chile's Colchagua Valley. Viña Caliterra planned to source additional grape supplies from independent growers located throughout the Colchagua Valley's various appellations.

RMC anticipated that the new Caliterra Winery would be completed and in full production by 1999 harvest. The Viña Caliterra partnership produced four varietal wines under the Caliterra label—Cabernet Sauvignon, Merlot, Sauvignon Blanc, Chardonnay—and two reserve varietals. These wines were priced between $7 and $10 a bottle. Despite a slowdown of imported wines to the U.S. market in the late 1990s, the Caliterra brand was one of the fastest-growing import brands. Worldwide sales of Caliterra in 1997 reached an estimated 300,000 cases.

Partnering with Italy's Marchesi de' Frescobaldi Family

In 1996, RMC formed a partnership with the Marchesi de' Frescobaldi family, a highly respected Italian viticulture family with three generations of winemaking experience, to produce Italian-style wines in Tuscany, using traditional Italian varietals. The partnership purchased the 11-hectare Solaria Estate Vineyard in the Montalcino region of Tuscany. The partnership produced approximately 20,000 cases a year of ultrapremium wines under the Luce and Lucente labels in Italy. Luce was first introduced to the international wine markets in June 1997, and this Tuscany-style blend of Merlot and Sangiovese varietals recently was listed as one of the world's top 40 red wines by *Wine Spectator* magazine. Lucente was later released in 1998. Both wines were priced in the range of $55 to $60 and were available in select U.S. and European markets.

GOING PUBLIC

By the early 1990s, RMC began to develop severe financial constraints brought on by the combination of expansion, increased competition, and a phylloxera infestation.[1] Several of the company's Napa County vineyards were dying from phylloxera, forcing the company to replant many of its vineyards at a time when its debt was already high from the acquisitions of the 1980s. Further compounding the competitive and operating problems for the company were some 200 new wineries in the Napa Valley, many of which were now producing premium to ultrapremium wines that directly competed with RMC brands. A growing number of these wineries in the premium market were owned by multinational corporations that could afford to replant phylloxera-infested vineyards and to pay higher prices for grape supplies until the replanted vineyards returned to production. Small, family-owned wine operations were at a financial disadvantage against large, fully integrated, and in many cases conglomerate-owned firms, and were faced with either selling off assets or borrowing heavily to finance existing operations. Due to dwindling capital resources, Robert Mondavi felt that RMC would not be in the position to take advantage of future opportunities and that it risked being forced aside in the premium market by larger competitors—unless additional capital could be obtained.

After five years of careful study of other family-controlled public companies, Robert Mondavi, with the help of the investment banking firm Goldman Sachs, devised a deal to raise enough money for RMC to continue expansion while maintaining

---

[1]Phylloxera, an aphidlike insect that attacks the roots of grapevines, began appearing in Napa Valley vineyards in 1983. By 1989, a University of California–Davis phylloxera task force determined that widespread vineyard decline had been due to phylloxera. The root louse sucks the nutrients from the roots and slowly starves the vine, creating dramatic decreases in fruit production.

family control. An initial public offering (IPO) for the company was structured with two classes of stock: a Class A common stock to be issued to Mondavi family members, and a Class B common stock to be offered to the public. Class A shares carried 10 votes per share, and Class B 1 vote per share. Providing that Mondavi family members retained their shares, the family could retain control over RMC's destiny.

On June 10, 1993, RMC issued 3.7 million Class B shares at $13.50 a share and began trading on the NASDAQ exchange under the symbol MOND. The IPO raised approximately $49.95 million, giving the company a market capitalization of $213.3 million. Within days, the stock was trading at around $8 a share and six months later at $6.50 a share, wiping away over half of the company's value and half of the Mondavi family's fortune. Investors and analysts alike had difficulty valuing RMC, due to a lack of information on the company and the wine industry as a whole. At the time, only two other publicly traded wine companies existed, both of which were in the low-end jug wine market segment and not in the premium wine segments. In addition, the California industry was facing large expenditures and uncertainty related to the phylloxera infestation. In his 1998 book, Robert Mondavi approached the stock valuation problem much as he approached marketing wine:

> The wine industry was not highly regarded by the investment community. So I knew we had to educate them, show them we had the knowledge and know-how to build a strong, enduring business, based on a product line of the highest-quality wines, plus quality table wines we could sell in very high volumes. And we had to explain to them what we were doing globally. Opus One was a huge success; it had cemented our international prestige. We had to make investors understand that Opus was only the beginning. We had to explain that we were going to establish other joint ventures of similar quality, in many parts of the world—something no other winery had ever done. I also realized that to get our message across we had to put on major presentations for the top stock analysts around America. We had to send a team to New York, Boston, and Chicago to put on first-class presentations, receptions, and tastings—all to show them, in the most visceral, penetrating way possible, what we were doing....Well, we had to mount an effective campaign and take it right to them, and not just explain our approach but put our wines right in their hands! Let them taste, in their own mouths, our expertise and commitment to excellence.

INDUSTRY AND COMPETITION

The U.S. wine industry was composed of approximately 1,500 wineries. The industry, however, was highly concentrated, with the top 10 wineries accounting for 70 percent (by volume) of U.S. production, according to the 1999 *Adams Wine Handbook*. Market shares for some of the larger wineries are shown in Exhibit 9. Wine was produced in every state except Alaska. California dominated the U.S. wine industry in that it had over 800 wineries and accounted for more than 90 percent of the wine produced in and exported by the United States. Northwest wineries (Washington, Oregon, and Idaho) were composed of approximately 200 wineries and were developing an export presence as well as an excellent reputation for quality wines.

Wine was sold through a three-tier distribution system. Wineries (the first tier) or importers sold wine to wholesalers (the second tier), who provided legal fulfillment of wine products to local retail businesses (the third tier) within a certain state. Wine was a controlled substance, and laws in each state differed regarding how it could be sold. Typically, wine passed through each tier of the distribution system, making direct shipping to retailers or selling wine through the Internet difficult or impossible in most states.

exhibit 9   Percentage Market Shares of Selected Competitors, United
States Table Wine Market, 1994–98 (based on volume)

Company	Market Share, 1994	Market Share, 1996	Market Share, 1998
E. & J. Gallo Winery	34.3%	27.7%	27.5%
Canandaigua Wine	17.7	15.5	14.8
The Wine Group	9.7	11.4	14.6
Beringer Wine Estates	3.2	2.5	4.0
Robert Mondavi Winery	3.2	3.6	3.8
Next three competitors	13.7	11.9	12.9
All other competitors	18.2	27.4	22.4
Total	100.0%	100.0%	100.0%

Source: *Adams Wine Handbook*, 1999.

The third tier of the distribution system consisted of retail and nonretail outlets. Supermarkets, convenience stores, club stores, mail order and Internet retailers, specialty stores, and wine clubs accounted for 78 percent of total sales volume. Supermarkets alone accounted for 52 percent of retail wine sales and were very influential in wine distribution. They were dominant in food-and-drink retailing and made one-stop shopping an appealing concept for consumers. Furthermore, supermarkets had considerable bargaining leverage with wholesalers. The role of specialty stores in wine distribution diminished due to the increasing power of supermarkets. Specialty stores' share of retail wine sales was about 30 percent in 1998. Nevertheless, specialty stores were not likely to disappear soon; they provided superior customer service and their sales staffs had extensive knowledge of wines. They also carried specialty brands and limited production labels, attracting wine connoisseurs and enthusiasts. Nonretail outlets accounted for the remaining 22 percent of wine volume in the United States, according to the *Adams Wine Handbook.*

The Wine Institute estimated that 1999 U.S. wine market retail sales were $18 billion, up from $11.7 billion in 1990. The U.S. wine market ranked third in the world behind those of France and Italy. However, the United States ranked 30th in the world in per capita consumption of wine in 1999. The greatest concentration of table wine consumers was in the 35-to-55 age bracket. About the same proportion of men and women consumed wine. While all income levels consumed wine, higher income was associated with greater wine consumption. In 1998, adults in families earning over $75,000 annually represented 18.7 percent of the population and 31.4 percent of the domestic table wine consumption.

Export Markets

Wine was produced commercially in over 60 countries, and 23 percent (by volume) of world production was exported to international markets, according to *Wines & Vines* magazine. Leading wine producers included the Old World wineries in France, Italy, and Spain, which were also the leading exporters. New World producers—such as the United States, Australia, Chile, Argentina, and South Africa—had been making both production and export inroads globally over the past few decades. For example,

France, Italy, and Spain all exported more than 25 percent of the wine they produced; Australia exported over 40 percent; and Chile exported over 80 percent. Many observers attributed these export numbers to the small size of the home markets.

Until the mid-1990s, the U.S. wine market remained largely a domestic industry, with some imports from France, Italy, and Spain competing with U.S. wineries. By 1999, however, imports had risen to 20 percent of the U.S. market share, which was seven percentage points above where it was in 1995, according to *Wine Business Monthly*. Tremendous inroads had been made by Australian and Chilean wines, in particular, into the U.S. market. For example, from 1995 to 1999, Argentina increased the value of its exports to the United States by 243 percent, and Chile by 152 percent. Since 1995, the unfavorable balance of trade for wine in the United States had increased by 78 percent, according to the 2000 *World Vineyard, Grape, and Wine Report*.

U.S. wine exports also grew consistently, from a base of $137 million in 1990 to $548 million in 1999, according to the U.S. Department of Commerce. Also, the U.S. industry enjoyed the highest rate of increased wine exports (19.3 percent) in 1998 among the major wine-producing countries, according to the 2000 *World Vineyard, Grape, and Wine Report*. While this export growth was impressive, U.S. wineries also face increasing threats to their domestic market share due to increased competition from foreign wineries exporting to the United States.

Wines & Vines reported in 1999 that the United States had only 4.2 percent (by volume) of the world export wine market, while producing 8 percent (by volume) of the wine produced in the world. The U.S. wine industry exported only 13 percent of the wine it produced, while other countries had more intensely developed their export markets. Tariffs and trade barriers played a pivotal role in obstructing U.S. wineries' access to various country markets. Ten U.S. wineries accounted for more than 89 percent of exports. Nearly 50 percent of U.S. wineries exported their products, although most exported only a small percentage. The leading U.S. exporter by volume was E. & J. Gallo, accounting for about half of U.S. exports and more than four times the volume of its nearest export competitor. Gallo exported approximately 13 percent of its total production. Wente Vineyards was a notable exception among U.S. wineries. Wente made exports a cornerstone of its long-term strategy: 60 percent of its annual case sales were from 147 country markets.

Competition   The nature of competition within the U.S. wine market varied by wine category. While the basis of competition in the lower segments of the wine market (jug to premium) was primarily driven by price, retail shelf space, and brand imaging, competition at the higher segments (superpremium and above) was driven more by quality and brand image. Wine producers in the jug to premium market segments relied heavily on the retail chains for most of their sales. Retail chains demanded that these wine producers be able to produce an adequate supply of the most popular varietal wines within specified price ranges (price points) because consumers of these wines tended to be price-sensitive. In addition, wines targeted to the lower segments required sufficient consumer demand (depletion rates) for retail chains. Although many retail chains carried superpremium to ultrapremium wines, obtaining shelf space was of lesser concern for producers of these brands.

Typically, high-end wines were made in smaller quantities, and demand often exceeded supply for acclaimed wines. Wholesalers could increase their markups on top-selling superpremium to ultrapremium wines by moving these wines through alternate distribution channels, such as restaurants, hotels, and specialty wine shops. For the top superpremium to ultrapremium brands, wholesalers were often willing to enter into future contracts with producers to buy the most popular wines before they were released, thereby generating advance revenue for the producers. Producers also were able to sell their best superpremium to ultrapremium wines through direct sales at the winery or through mail order wine clubs that were allowed by law in selected states.

Building brand awareness to drive sales for wines in the lower market segments was typically done through traditional advertising campaigns and retail promotions, whereas brand awareness for wines in the higher market segments was built more through "pull" marketing strategies. Rarely did producers resort to television or mass print advertising to promote their superpremium or ultrapremium brands. Instead, these producers built awareness through wine competitions, public relations campaigns, direct marketing, and wine tourism. Most superpremium to ultrapremium wine producers entered their best wines into local, state, national, and international wine competitions, with some going so far as holding back portions of their best inventory to be released later at prestigious competitions. Medal winners often were featured in magazine articles, newspapers, and wine enthusiast newsletters. These write-ups helped to build the public's awareness for the best superpremium to ultrapremium wines each year.

Historically, Gallo, a family-owned wine business since 1933, had almost completely dominated the jug wine segment both in the U.S. and global markets. However, during the 1980s, large alcoholic beverage companies—such as Canandaigua, The Wine Group, and Brown Forman—were able to compete with Gallo in the jug wine market segment. Although it was still the single largest wine producer in the world, making up approximately 45 percent of California wine sales, Gallo had failed to capitalize on changes in consumer demand toward a preference for premium wines. In recent years Gallo, like many of the other jug wine producers, had sought to enter the premium wine market, choosing to develop and launch new Gallo brands from 2,300 acres of prime vineyards in Sonoma County acquired to supply the new brands.

Besides the alcoholic beverage companies, several large food and beverage conglomerates—Nestlé, Pillsbury, Suntory, PepsiCo, Coca-Cola—entered the premium market by acquiring premium to ultrapremium wineries in the 1970s. However, during the 1980s, many of these food and beverage companies divested their wine holdings, choosing instead to focus on their core businesses. The beneficiaries of these divestitures were the wine and alcoholic beverage companies that continued to build their portfolios of wine brands. Wine industry analysts expected further consolidation in the wine industry as large wine and alcoholic beverage companies continued to acquire smaller winery operations to gain access to premium and ultrapremium brands.

The superpremium-to-ultrapremium market was highly fragmented, composed of hundreds of individual, small to large operations that were all competing to produce the most acclaimed wines each year. Although larger producers held advantages in scale and capital, the smaller wineries were able to compete by consistently producing high-quality wines in limited quantities that gained critical acclaim from wine enthusiasts. Smaller wine producers, however, were at a disadvantage when trying to compete for grape sources against larger, better-financed competitors such as Beringer, RMC, Kendall-Jackson, Sebastian Vineyards, UDV NA Wines, Gallo, and Canandaigua. Many of these rival firms owned portfolios of brands, invested in winemaking facilities and vineyards across California and abroad, and produced wines across the price spectrum of the premium, superpremium, and ultrapremium market segments.

SEEKING CONSENSUS

Michael Mondavi remained confident that future releases of small-lot ultrapremium wines from RMC could help to build the company's overall image of prestige and quality. RMC had spent $50 million during the early 1990s replanting the RMC estate vineyards with high-density plantings in the traditional French planting style. RMC hoped to showcase these high-quality grapes with special small-lot, vineyard-designated wines once those vineyards came into production after 1999.

Throughout the mid-1990s, RMC struggled to secure an adequate supply of grapes to meet domestic production targets. RMC had been unable to purchase sufficient quantities of Chardonnay grapes for its Woodbridge brand during the 1996 harvest, and management foresaw a revenue shortfall in fiscal year 1998 (the year in which its 1996 vintage Chardonnay was scheduled for release). Due to poor growing conditions and phylloxera infestation in 1996, many other Chardonnay wine producers suffered the same grape supply problems. RMC had been especially hard hit, as only 12 percent of its grape sources came from company-owned vineyards. RMC purchased the remaining supply from some 300 independent growers across California, increasing the company's susceptibility to fluctuations in the price, quantity, and quality of grapes on the open market.

However, RMC was currently at capacity and required an estimated $27 million remodeling job to add capacity for small-lot, ultrapremium vineyard and district-designated wines. With additional production capacity, RMC could produce more high-end reserve and vineyard-designated wines at higher price points.

At the same time, Michael Mondavi had spent considerable time in 1998 traveling to Chile and Europe promoting RMC's new brands. He said at the time:

> Our globalization started, I believe, from my father's quest to learn how to make wines better. All the time we were growing up, he was always tasting wines. Not just the wines of Charles Krug, the Napa Valley, or of California, but from around the world. And he wasn't tasting them to say which was better. He would taste these wines to study them, to say "What in this wine was soil? What was the climate? What was the grape variety, or the clone of that grape variety? What was the pruning technique? What was the art of the winemaker." In essence, be was asking "What do we have to learn from the way this wine was made? And how can we improve on it?"

Michael Mondavi believed the formation of global joint ventures would become an integral part of RMC's future business and a way for the company to continue to innovate and develop world-class wines. He wanted RMC to become a truly global company by growing, producing, and selling wines in all the best wine-growing regions in the world.

bibliography

Adams Wine Handbook. New York: Adams Business Media, 1999.

"And Now the Numbers." *Wine & Vines*, July 1999.

Appel, T. "Deal Closed for Tip Wineries Sale, Include Beringer, a Record." *Santa Rosa Press Democrat*, November 22, 1995.

"Big Firms, Less Brands Seen Wine Industry's Future," Reuters, September 17, 1999.

Evans, Mark. "Investment Group to Buy Largest Winery in Sonoma." *Orange County Register*, May 26, 1996.

Love, John M. "United States Wine Producers Face Increasing Competition." *Wine Business Monthly*, June, 2000.

Mondavi, Robert. *Harvests of Joy: How the Good Life Became a Great Business.* San Diego: Harcourt, 1998.

———. Bank of America Securities Conference, February 16, 2000.

"Mondavi Overhaul: 36 Jobs to Be Cut." *Santa Rosa Press Democrat,* January 14, 1999.

1999 Annual Wine Industry Review. San Francisco: Gomberg, Fredrikson & Associates, 1999.

Robert Mondavi Corporation. Annual Report, 1999, and 405k report, June 1999.

———. Fourth-quarter conference call (www.corporate-ir.net/ireye/ir_site.zhtml?ticker= MOND&script=1100&layout=7), 1999.

"History of Caliterra." Caliterra website (www.caliterra.com/history.html), 2000.

Sinton, Peter. "California Wines Quenching in the World." *San Francisco Chronicle,* January 23, 1999.

U.S. Department of Commerce. National Trade Data Bank, 2000.

Wine Institute website (www.wineinstitute.org), 2000.

"Wine World Completes Chateau St. Jean Buyout." *Santa Rosa Press Democrat,* April 9, 1996.

Wines & Vines Directory and Buyer's Guide, vol. 79. San Rafael, CA: The Hearing Company, December 1999.

World Vineyard, Grape, and Wine Report, San Francisco: California Wine Export Program, July 2000.

E. & J. Gallo Winery

Taylor Green
The University of Alabama

J. Strickland
The University of Alabama

In 2001, dessert wines represented a 32-million-gallon, $500 million business. Included within the dessert wine category was a group of cheap, low-grade, and highly controversial "high-proof" or "fortified" wines that contained added alcohol to increase their potency and additional sugar or sweetener to enhance their taste—see Exhibit 1. Most natural wine products had about 8 to 12 percent alcohol by volume, since the yeasts that were used in the fermentation process were killed by higher alcohol concentrations. Many of the cheap fortified wine products were deliberately made and sold at the highest potency because they were the low-cost alcoholic beverage favored by skid-row alcoholics, teenagers and college students, and other people with low incomes.[1] Canandaigua's Wild Irish Rose was the leading seller in this category, followed by Gallo's Thunderbird brand and Mogen David MD 20/20. Canandaigua's Cisco wine cooler, known as "liquid cocaine" on the streets, had the fourth-leading market share in the dessert wine segment. For several decades, low-end dessert and fortified wines had been a profitable, high-volume market segment that winemakers had targeted. *The Wall Street Journal* reported in 1988 that of all the wine brands sold in America, Richard's Wild Irish Rose (named after the founder's son, Richard Sands, who had been Canandaigua's president until 1999) was the number 6 best-seller, Thunderbird was 10th, and MD 20/20 was 16th.

Originally, fortified wines were made by adding brandy (distilled wine) to ordinary wine in order to raise the alcohol content so as to help prevent spoilage during shipping and to extend the shelf life—the higher alcohol content killed off bacteria and other organisms. Port and sherry wines were good examples of high-quality fortified wines. However, the makers of low-grade fortified wines often used cheaper grain alcohol (far cheaper than brandy) to raise the alcohol content to 14 to 20 percent. Low-grade fortified wines like Richard's Wild Irish Rose, Thunderbird, Night Train (another Gallo product), and Boone's Farm generally sold for less than $3 per 750 milliliter bottle and for between $1 and $2 per 375 milliliter bottle (about 12.5 ounces). They produced more intoxication for less money than just about any other type of alcoholic beverage. The dose of alcohol in a typical 12.5-ounce Cisco wine cooler or a pint of

---

[1]William J. Bailey, "Factline on High Potency Alcoholic Beverages," Indiana Prevention Resource Center, Indiana University (www.drugs.indiana.edu/publications/iprc/factline/high_potency.html), September 7, 1998.

exhibit 1   Examples of Low-End Fortified Wines That Had Attracted
Criticism

Thunderbird was five times the dose of alcohol in a 12-ounce can of beer, a 4- to 5-
ounce serving of wine, or a 1.25-ounce shot of bourbon—see Exhibit 2.

A typical critic of fortified wines was Mark Dalton, a social worker for the State
of Washington Division of Alcohol and Substance Abuse, who believed that "fortified
wines and cheap strong beer are packaged and marketed to alcoholics, and that corner
stores who sell them are making profits while contributing to a cycle of addiction as
well as a public nuisance."[2] Addiction professionals had dubbed cheap, fortified wine
"the most seriously abused drug in this country."[3] It was common for people who were
charged with trying to help the chronic alcoholics who drank cheap fortified wines to
express the view that manufacturing and selling these and other, similar alcoholic beverages was unethical, even bordering on being criminal; they often charged that the
providers (wineries and retail stores selling such products) had no conscience and that
their actions were repulsive. A drug and alcohol counselor from Mountain View Hospital in Gadsden, Alabama, told of crack addicts' stories about buying Mad Dog (the
street name for MD 20/20) to help to them come off their crack high; according to the
counselor, addicts said they chose Mad Dog because it was "cheap and strong." The
president of one winery said, "Fortified wines lack any socially redeeming values." In
a 1988 *Wall Street Journal* article, Paul Gillette, publisher of *Wine Investor*, said,
"Makers of skid-row wines are the dope-pushers of the wine industry. And these companies are the largest producers and appear the most successful wineries."[4]

---

[2]Kelly Payne, "Drying Up the Square"
(www.realchangenews.org/pastarticles/features/articles/new_dec_Boozeban.html).

[3]"Banning the Saturday-Night Special of Booze," *Newsweek*, March 10, 1986.

[4]Alix Freedman, "Market Misery—Winos and Thunderbird Are a Subject Gallo Doesn't Like to Discuss," *The Wall Street Journal*, February 25, 1988, pp. 1, 18.

exhibit 2   Alcohol Content of Selected Alcoholic Beverages

Alcoholic Beverage	Alcohol Content (ounces)
12 ounces of 4 percent beer	0.48
5 ounces of 10 percent wine	0.50
1.25 ounces of 40 percent vodka (80 proof)	0.50
1.25 ounces of 43 percent whiskey (86 proof)	0.52
40-ounce bottle of 8 percent malt liquor	3.20
1.25-ounce shot of 151 proof rum	0.94
12.5-ounce bottle of 6 percent wine cooler	0.75
12.5-ounce bottle of 20 percent fortified wine cooler	2.50

Examples of high-potency alcoholic beverages:

- Fortified wines (most low-cost brands are sold at or near 20 percent alcohol by volume).
- Wine coolers (most are about 6 percent alcohol by volume, 1.5 times more potent than typical beer).
- Specialty wine coolers, such as Cisco (up to 20 percent alcohol by volume).
- Malt liquors (up to 8 percent alcohol by volume, nearly twice the potency of typical American beer).
- Neutral grain spirits, such as Everclear (95 percent alcohol by volume).
- High-proof liquors, such as 151 Rum (75.5 percent alcohol by volume, about twice the potency of other rums).

Source: William J. Bailey, "Factline on High-Potency Alcoholic Beverages," Indiana Prevention Resource Center, Indiana University (www.drugs.indiana.edu/publications/iprc/factline/high_potency.html).

In many states, fortified wines were effectively limited to a maximum of 20 percent alcohol content by tax and licensing laws. For example, Indiana law defined "wine" as a beverage "that does not contain 21 percent or more alcohol." This meant that a wine with a higher alcohol content could not be sold in grocery and convenience stores (which were typically licensed to sell only beer and wine); wines with more than the legal alcohol content limit were taxed at the much higher rates set for distilled spirits. Federal taxes also jumped up for wines with an alcohol content above 20 percent.

The major producers and marketers of such low-end dessert and fortified wines defended their products and disputed the critics' characterization of the buyers of fortified wines. Sid Abrams of the Wine Institute, which represented California vintners, said, "There are a lot of people who just like the flavor. And some older people buy inexpensive sherry because they can't afford the more expensive product."[5] The problem of street alcoholics presents a dilemma, Abrams said, "but I don't think you can blame the manufacturers." Another defense was that since it was legal to produce and market cheap fortified wines, there was nothing wrong with winemakers and store retailers pursuing the market opportunities that existed. However, the producers of low-end fortified wines typically distanced themselves from their fortified-wine product offerings by leaving their corporate names off the labels—an omission critics interpreted as being deliberately intended to obscure the producer's link to these brands.

[5]As quoted in Warren King, "Ethics of Manufacturing Profits from Drunks," *Seattle Times*, January 20, 1998.

THE E. & J. GALLO WINERY

The Early Years

The E. & J. Gallo Winery, the largest wine producer in the world, was founded by Ernest and Julio Gallo in 1933. The Gallo brothers got their start in the wine business working during their spare time in their father's vineyard near Modesto, California. Their father, Joseph Gallo, had immigrated from the Piedmont region in northwestern Italy and was a small-time grape grower and shipper of California wine. He survived Prohibition because the government permitted the personal production of no more than 100 gallons of wine per year (an amount many Californians produced if they could get the grapes). This loophole allowed Joseph Gallo to sell grapes in bulk shipments to private brewers. But the Depression was tough, and his company almost went under. During the spring of 1933, the family was scarred by a tragedy when the boys' parents were found dead in an apparent murder/suicide in which Joseph Gallo shot his wife and then himself.

Following his parents' deaths, Ernest became head of the family and the business. The Gallo brothers, both in their early 20s, decided it would be a good idea to integrate forward into making wine even though neither knew anything about the process. Ernest and Julio found two thin pamphlets on winemaking in the Modesto Public Library and, with $5,900 to their names, began to invest in winemaking capability. Julio oversaw the vineyards and the winemaking operation, while Ernest handled marketing and distribution; their youngest brother, Joe, was an employee. Ernest pushed to build the company, aiming at a broad national market and envisioning E. & J. Gallo as becoming the "Campbell Soup Company of the wine industry." He drove himself and his employees hard, sometimes working 16-hour days and taking long trips around the country by car to make sales calls and learn about consumers' wine-drinking preferences and habits. It was his practice to study the company's markets and customers very carefully and to base the winery's marketing strategy on detailed market research concerning buyer behavior and preferences.

With the end of Prohibition, the Gallo brothers set out to become market leaders in what was then a relatively small and mostly downscale American wine market. Ernest effectively marketed cheap fortified (20 percent alcohol content) wines like White Port and lemon-flavored Thunderbird in inner-city markets. Thunderbird, introduced in the late 1950s and named after the ritzy Thunderbird Hotel in Las Vegas, Nevada, became Gallo's first phenomenal success. A catchy radio jingle helped send Thunderbird to the top of the sales charts in many inner-city and low-income neighborhoods across the United States: "What's the word? / Thunderbird / How's it sold? / Good and cold / What's the jive? / Bird's alive / What's the price? / Thirty twice." There were stories, which Gallo denied, that the winery got the idea for citrus-flavored Thunderbird from reports that liquor stores in Oakland, California, were catering to the tastes of certain customers by attaching packages of lemon Kool-Aid to bottles of white wine to be mixed at home. According to author Ellen Hawkes, who wrote an unauthorized history of the Gallo family called *Blood and Wine*, Ernest later delighted in telling the story of driving through a tough inner-city neighborhood; upon seeing a man walking down the sidewalk, Gallo pulled up alongside, rolled down his window, and called out, "What's the word?" The man's immediate answer was "Thunderbird."

The Gallos began researching varietal grapes in 1946, planting more than 400 varieties in experimental vineyards during the 1950s and 1960s and testing each variety in the different grape-growing regions of California for its ability to produce fine table wines. Their greatest difficulty was to persuade growers to convert from common grape varieties to the delicate, thin-skinned varietals because it took at least four years for a vine to begin bearing and perhaps two more years to develop typical varietal characteristics. As an incentive, in 1967, Gallo offered long-term contracts to growers, guaranteeing the prices for their grapes every year, provided the fruit met Gallo quality standards. With a guaranteed long-term buyer for their crops, growers were able to borrow the needed capital to finance the costly replanting, and the winery's staff of skilled viticulturists provided technical assistance to aid contract growers.

While most California wineries concentrated on production and sold their wines through wholesale distributors, Gallo pursued a vertical integration strategy and participated in every aspect from growing grapes, to making wine, to marketing the product, to owning and operating its wine distributorships. E. & J. Gallo Winery owned the wholesale distributors of Gallo wines in about 10 geographic markets and probably would have bought many of the more than 300 independent distributors handling its wines if laws in most states had not prohibited it. The entrepreneurial freedom that came with private ownership, the wise stewardship of Ernest and Julio Gallo, low-cost mass production, and strong distribution were the major competitive advantages contributing to Gallo's success. Because they owned the business, the Gallo brothers could use low prices and paper-thin margins to win market share from higher-cost rivals and could absorb occasional losses in introducing new brands and widening the company's geographic reach, whereas wineries that were publicly held had to appease earnings-minded stockholders. While Gallo bought about 95 percent of its grapes, it virtually controlled its 1,500 growers through long-term contracts. Gallo's trucking company, Fairbanks, hauled wine out of Modesto and brought raw materials in. Gallo was the only winery that manufactured its own bottles (2 million a day) and screw-top caps.

Gallo's Gradual Shift to More Upscale Wines

Gallo's major competitive weakness over the years had always been its reputation as a maker of low-end wines in screw-top bottles—an image that flowed partly from its Thunderbird and Night Train brands. This was not so much a liability in the early days, when wine sales in the United States were heavily concentrated in the low end of the market, but Gallo's low-end image became an increasing liability in the 1980s as wine consumers began to purchase better-quality table wines in increasing numbers and as wine became a favored beverage at cocktail parties. As the company grew over the years, first becoming the largest winemaker in the United States and then the largest in the world, the Gallo brothers initiated a series of moves to shed the winery's image as a maker of low-end wines sold in screw-top bottles and jugs. Gallo's new strategy was to distance itself from the Thunderbird and Night Train brands and begin the long-range task of repositioning itself as a maker of better-quality, moderately priced table wines and then later as a maker of truly fine wines.

From 1985 to 2000, the company spent hundreds of millions of dollars on advertising aimed at boosting consumer perceptions of Gallo wines and cultivating a clientele for its new, more upscale wines.[6] At the same time, the company invested in production facilities to make more upscale table wines under a variety of labels, some of which were created internally and some of which were acquired. Ernest Gallo continued to study the markets the company targeted and the tastes and wine-drinking

---

[6]*Standard Directory of Advertisers*, 2000.

habits of consumers very carefully—from the high end to the low end of the price/quality scale. By the mid-1990s the company had been reasonably successful in attracting more upscale wine-drinkers to try its newly introduced brands. In 1998, one of the company's estate-bottled premium Chardonnay wines was rated 94 points on *Wine Spectator*'s 100-point scale.[7] In 1998 and again in 2001, Gallo won the Premio Gran Vinitaly at the International Wine and Distilled Fair in Verona, Italy, making Gallo the only foreign winery to win twice in the history of the award. As of 2001, the company had more than 75 brands in its product lineup and was exporting wines to countries all over the world.

Ernest and Julio Gallo were active contributors to political campaigns, with Ernest contributing largely to Democrats and Julio giving to Republicans. Over the years, the Gallos reportedly contributed $381,000 to Senator Robert Dole and about $900,000 to foundations with which Dole was connected.[8] In 1998, Ernest help bring in $100,000 for a Clinton fund-raising lunch in San Francisco only weeks after the *Los Angeles Times* reported that he had met privately with President Clinton to discuss Chilean wine imports (which had recently been gaining market share in the low-priced end of the U.S. wine market). Shortly after Ernest's meeting with the president, Congress delayed any action to authorize increases in Chilean wine imports and also passed increased funding for a wine promotion program that funneled millions of dollars to Gallo to promote its wines overseas. A bipartisan group of senators included this program in a 1998 listing of a "dirty dozen" examples of corporate welfare.

E. & J. Gallo Winery in 2001

In 2001, the Gallo Winery was continuing to operate as a privately owned and family-operated corporation. Second-generation family members Joseph and Robert Gallo were co-presidents of the company in 2001, but Ernest Gallo, who was in his 90s, still exercised supervision and made his views known. (Julio had died in a 1993 car accident.) Julio's grandson Matt was a winegrower in the family's vineyards, and Julio's granddaughter Gina was a member of the company's winemaking team. Gina's views on winemaking were featured at the company's website:

> For me, wine is a pleasure. It has to be beautiful to look at and smell and astonishing to taste.
>
> But I don't want to make obvious wines. I want depth and a little mystery, and I want some "wow" in there too. Along with the rest of my family, I was very proud when Gallo of Sonoma was named Winery of the Year in 1996, 1998, and again in 2001. As a winemaker, however, I've never forgotten a secret that my grandpa once told me. The true test of a wine, he said, happens in the face of someone when they drink it for the first time. If they smile before their eyes meet yours, then the wine is a success. They have already told you so, without ever saying a word.[9]

Matt Gallo commented on the company's grape-growing practices and technological advances in how Gallo's vineyards in California's Sonoma wine region were now being managed:

---

[7]Jeff Morgan, "Gallo of Sonoma," *Wine Spectator Online,* June 30, 1999.

[8]"So You Want to Buy a President," *Frontline,* Public Broadcasting System (www.pbs.org/wgbh/pages/frontline/president/players/gallo.html).

[9]Posted at www.gallo.com as of December 11, 2001.

Many of the vineyards I look after today were planted by my grandfather, Julio. He was an early pioneer of sustainable agriculture in this county. At a time when farmers took what they could get from the land, Julio was conserving—the soil, the water, and the natural environment. Only half of the property we own in Sonoma is actually cultivated, thanks to the 50/50 Give Back Program he created. Julio didn't just believe in the land—he showed people that redwoods and vineyards could thrive together.

From my father, Bob Gallo, I learned how to focus my efforts on the fruit. He was forever experimenting with new rootstock, trellising techniques, and better ways of harvesting the grapes. As a result, every vine at Gallo of Sonoma is "touched" at least six times prior to harvest to ensure the growing conditions are optimal.

Fortunately, I have access to new technologies—tools Dad and Grandpa didn't have—that can help. For instance, I can pinpoint weather conditions in a certain section of a vineyard using the latest technology. The accuracy is unbelievable, especially when you cross-reference it with soil and crop data. Does that mean less time in the vine rows, tasting grapes and touching the soil? Not by a long shot. Computers have memory, but farmers have a feeling for the land—a feeling that someday I hope to hand down to my kids.

In April 2001, Ernest Gallo received the Lifetime Achievement Award from the prestigious James Beard Foundation; in presenting the award, Charles Osgood spoke about "the power and persistence of the Gallo mission to make not just the most, but the best wines possible."[10] John Deluca, chairman of the Wine Institute, further elaborated on Ernest Gallo and the Gallo legacy: "He has really created the modern wine industry in America. . . . The Gallo brothers have been the most important force in the positive transformation of the California wine industry this last century." Marvin Shanken, publisher of *Wine Spectator*, said, "All Americans who drink wine at their dinner table today are in his debt." But what always seemed to go unsaid was that, despite the company's industry prominence and the growing market success and quality of Gallo table wines, the cheap bottles of Thunderbird and Night Train still continued to be among the best-selling and most notorious wines that E. & J. Gallo Winery produced and marketed. In 2001, Gallo's website featured many of its award-winning wines and highlighted the care and attention paid by the company's winemakers to making quality wines, but there was no mention of Thunderbird or any of the company's other low-end fortified and jug wines.

Exhibit 3 shows the 10 largest U.S. wineries. Information on Gallo's finances was not publicly available, since the company was family-owned and the Gallo family maintained a tight lid on financial details. However, industry analysts estimated that Gallo's sales in 2000 were $1.35 billion.[11] By comparison, Canandaigua, the second leading winery based on volume and producer of Richard's Wild Irish Rose, had approximately $2.5 billion in 2000 sales revenues.[12] Canandaigua's founder and majority stockholder, Marvin Sands, had named the company's best-selling dessert wine after his son, Richard.

Gallo's 75 different wine brands were visible in many segments of the wine industry, both domestic and foreign. According to *Wine Spectator*, Gallo's E. & J. Wine Cellars was the "largest-selling global brand." Gallo produced the top-selling red and white table wines in the United States based on unit volume. Its Blush Chablis became the best-selling blush-style wine within the first year of its national introduction. Gallo's award-winning varietal wines were among the top sellers in their classification. During 1999 and 2000, Gallo's Carlo Rossi and Livingston Cellars brands outsold all

---

[10]www.gallo.com/UK/html/ernestaward.htm.

[11]*Hoover's Handbook of Private Companies,* 2001.

[12]*Standard Directory of Advertisers.*

exhibit 3   The 10 Largest U.S. Wineries Based on Volume, 2000

Winery	Brands	Number of Winemaking Facilities	Gallons Produced
1. E. & J. Gallo Winery	Gallo, Turning Leaf, Carlo Rossi, Thunderbird, Night Train, Sonoma County, Barelli Creek, Stefani, Laguna, Frei, New Russian River, over 60 others	4	330,000,000
2. Canandaigua Wine Company	Wild Irish Rose, Cisco, Taylor California Cellars, Paul Masson, Almaden, Inglenook, Columbia, Cook's champagne, and others, plus a variety of beers and liquors	15	182,800,000
3. The Wine Group	Franzia, Mogen David	4	87,000,000
4. Golden State Vintners	Edgewood Estate, Monthaven, Summerfield, bulk wines	6	68,000,000
5. JFJ Bronco		1	62,945,000
6. Vie-Del Company		2	50,000,000
7. Korbel & Bros.	Korbel champagne and brandy, Kenwood	5	45,399,000
8. Delicato Vineyards	Delicato, Monterra, Delicato Family Vineyards	2	43,422,000
9. Trinchero Family Estates	Sutter Home, Trinity Oaks, M. Trinchero, Montevina	4	37,150,000
10. UDV North America, Inc.	Glen Ellen, Beaulieu	3	19,800,000

Sources: Gale Group, Hiaring Company, and compilations by the case researchers from various Internet sites.

other popular-priced wines except Franzia. Gallo's Andre Champagne brand was by far the best-selling champagne in the United States, and E. & J. Brandy outsold the number two and three brands combined. Gallo's Bartles and Jaymes brand had been a leader in the wine cooler segment since its introduction in the 1980s, and it was the top-ranking seller in 2000. The company's Gallo of Sonoma winery was named Winery of the Year in 1996, 1998, and 2001.

So why does Gallo, after winning so many awards and apparently having done so well in other parts of the wine market, still produce skid-row wines?

THE U.S. WINE INDUSTRY

Wine sales in the United States grew from about 72 million gallons in 1940 to a peak of nearly 600 million gallons in 1986; since then, both volume and per capita consumption had stagnated—see Exhibits 4 and 5. In 2000, U.S. wine sales at retail were approximately $19 billion, representing a volume of 565 million gallons.

Per capita consumption of wine in the United States was relatively low prior to the 1970s because wine was perceived as a drink either for the very wealthy or for down-

exhibit 4 Consumption of Wine in the United States, 1935–2000

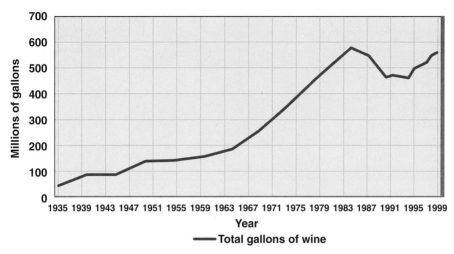

Source: The Wine Institute, and Gomberg, Fredrikson & Associates.

exhibit 5 Per Capita Wine Consumption in the United States, 1935–2000

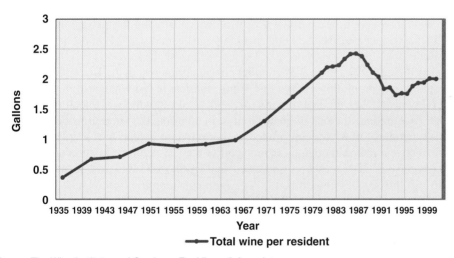

Source: The Wine Institute, and Gomberg, Fredrikson & Associates.

and-out winos. Fortified dessert wines were the top-selling wines of the 1935–1970 period. The first surge in consumption in the late 1960s was the result of the introduction of "pop" wines, such as Boone's Farm, Cold Duck, and Sangria. These wines were bought by baby boomers, who were then college-aged young adults; sweet pop wines with a kick were better suited to the high-energy party atmosphere in which they were consumed than were the more pricey table wines. By the mid-1970s, pop wine drinkers began moving up to Lambruscos and trendy wine spritzers. The introduction of wine coolers helped drive several years of rising consumption in the 1984–88 period; by

exhibit 6   U.S. Wine Sales by Category, 1991–2000

	Millions of Gallons				
Year	Table Wine*	Dessert Wine†	Champagne/ Sparkling Wine	Total Wine	Total Retail Value (billions)
2000	505	32	28	565	$19.0
1999	483	31	37	551	$18.1
1998	466	30	30	526	$17.0
1997	461	30	29	520	$16.1
1996	439	31	29	500	$14.3
1995	404	30	30	464	$12.2
1994	394	33	31	458	$11.5
1993	381	35	33	449	$11.0
1992	405	37	33	476	$11.4
1991	394	39	33	466	$10.9

*Includes all still wines not over 14 percent alcohol. Excludes unshipped foreign bulk wines.
†Includes all still wines over 14 percent alcohol.
Sources: The Wine Institute; U.S. Department of Commerce; and Gomberg, Fredrikson & Associates.

1987 sales of wine coolers totaled 72.6 million nine-liter cases, with Gallo's Bartles and Jaymes brand rising quickly to a market-leading position. Some of the slowdown in wine consumption in the 1985–95 period was attributed to the national obsession with fitness, increases in the legal drinking age from 18 to 21, and crackdowns on drunk driving.

During the 1990s, there was growing consumer interest in the United States in better-quality and premium-quality table wines; interest in red wines had increased considerably because of medical reports that a glass of red wine was "healthy" owing to its ability to reduce the risk of heart disease. In addition, the booming stock market of the 90s and busy lifestyles contributed to more dining out and thus increased sales of wine in restaurants. Although more than half of the U.S. adult population enjoyed wine occasionally in 2001, research indicated that by global standards, most Americans were still infrequent wine drinkers. Per capita consumption in the United States was less than 2 gallons per year in 2000, compared with about 18 gallons in France and Italy, where drinking wine with meals was part of the local culture.

The Dessert and Fortified Wine Segment

During the 1980s, dessert wine sales totaled about 55 million gallons annually (about 10 percent of total wine sales based on volume); sales of low-end brands accounted for 43 million gallons (nearly 80 percent of all dessert wines). Approximately 50 percent of the low-end fortified dessert wines were sold in half-pints; buyers of high-proof dessert wines were said to like pint bottles because they fit well in the back pocket of a pair of pants and gave skid-row drinkers a more secure feeling. However, dessert wine volume had trended down in the 1990s, to around 32 million gallons in 2000 (Exhibit 6), the majority of which continued to be low-end fortified wines. Whereas dessert wines accounted for almost 10 percent of total wine sales (based on volume) in the late 1980s, by 2000 the category accounted for just 5.7 percent of total volume—the percentage drop was chiefly attributable to a decline in the popularity of wine coolers. The approximately $500 million in fortified wine sales in 2000 represented about 2.6 percent of the estimated $19 billion in U.S. wine sales at retail.

The most popular distribution outlet for fortified wine sales was food and convenience stores with a low-income clientele. Wines selling for less than $3 a bottle accounted for almost 40 percent of the total wine sales in food stores—see Exhibit 7.

The dessert wine category was typically a profitable market segment for low-end wine producers to pursue because many of the wines in this category were made with less expensive ingredients, packaged in less expensive containers, and could be sold with little or no marketing and promotion. Canandaigua estimated that profit margins in this category were as much as 10 percent higher than those of ordinary table wines. Gallo said that this was not true for its products, but the company did not reveal its figures.

According to wine industry analysts, local wine distributors were eager to handle the low-end dessert and fortified wines because the margins were relatively large and it was generally easy to convince food retailers in low-income neighborhoods to stock them. As one distributor said, "All you have to do is to put it on the shelf in the right zip codes and it sells itself." Little or no advertising or sales promotion was needed—although in 1988, one magazine reported that Gallo sales representatives, in attempting to gain customers in newly entered markets, had on occasion gone so far as to trash the streets with empty bottles of Thunderbird and Night Train as a way to advertise to winos. Since distributors owned by Gallo were restricted by law from handling spirits (bourbon, vodka, scotch, gin, etc.), they were eager to stock and distribute low-end wines because the sizable volumes and good profit margins were a major contributor to covering fixed costs and ensuring decent profitability.

A sales representative for an Alabama distributor of Gallo wines indicated that his company distributed Thunderbird and other high-proof wines to retail outlets in ethnic and low-income neighborhoods, with bottle sizes varying according to the time of the month. The representative indicated that it was the distributor's practice at the first of the month, when many people in poorer ethnic neighborhoods were cashing their government checks, to stock area retailers' shelves with larger containers of wines (jugs and 1.5-liter bottles). Then toward the middle and end of the month, when customers were likely to have less cash in their pockets, the wine distributor made sure that retailer shelves were amply stocked with pint bottles that retailed anywhere from $.99 to $1.49 per bottle.

exhibit 7   Consumer Wine Purchases in Food Stores, 2000

Price Category	Volume Share	Percent Change in Volume from 1999	Percent Change in Revenue from 1999
Up to $3	39%	−4%	−4%
$3 to $7	41	3	3
$7 up to $10	13	22	24
$10 up to $14	5	23	25
$14 and over	2	18	24

Source: Gomberg, Fredrikson & Associates, from ACNielsen/Adams data.

Low-End Fortified Wines and Pop Culture

Cheap fortified wines had, over the years, found their way into the pop culture in the United States, often coming to symbolize the plight of the poor and less fortunate. They were seen as what people drank when they were sad or miserable, or when they just wanted to get drunk. Gallo's Night Train Express, an apple-flavored wine that was known as "the pocket rocket" and was popular with both street alcoholics and teenagers, was alluded to in Guns N' Roses' debut album, *Appetite for Destruction,* on which Axl Rose sang "Nightrain":

> Loaded like a freight train / flying like an aeroplane
> Speeding like a space brain / one more time tonight
> I'm on a Nightrain / bottoms up
> I'm on a Nightrain / fill my cup
> I'm on the Nightrain / I love that stuff
> I'm on the Nightrain / I can never get enough.

Wild Irish Rose was the inspiration for a song written and sung by Neil Diamond. In 1970, on a Canadian Indian reservation where there were many more men than women, Diamond observed that men left without a date on Saturday night made wine their "woman for the night." He decided to compose "Cracklin' Rosie" to characterize the relationship of a lonely wine-drinker and his bottle of Richard's Wild Irish Rose:

> Cracklin' Rosie, make me a smile
> God if it lasts for an hour, that's alright
> We got all night
> To set the world right
> Find us a dream that don't ask no questions, yeah
>
> Oh, I love my Rosie child
> You got the way to make me happy
> You and me, we go in style
> Cracklin' Rosie, you're a store-bought woman
> You make me sing like a guitar hummin'
> So hang on to me, girl
> Our song keeps runnin' on . . .

PRODUCT REVIEWS OF LOW-END FORTIFIED WINES

By and large, low-end fortified wines did not fare well in product reviews, even when the reviewers were members of the target clientele and experienced drinkers. Adam Martin, a college-age writer for a California-based website called West Oakland Wine Tasting, offered his take on the appeal of low-end wines to the college crowd and presented colorful ratings of five brands:

> We live in one of the great wine producing regions of the world and it's a crying shame that nobody around here gives a #@&%. I know I don't. We could be in France, taking all kinds of wine baths and I would still be craving Pabst Blue Ribbon and Milwaukee's Best. As a young, unrefined student on a budget, I simply can't afford to be a wine aficionado. I couldn't, that is, until last Friday, when, along with a panel of experts (namely Wrath and the Reverend, my good-for-nothing-except-drinking-cheap-wine-when-I-buy-it roommates), I ventured out into my neighborhood to see what good old Grand Foods had to offer for the sacred palate. The following review focuses on five wines popular in West Oakland and the surrounding areas (North Oakland and East Oakland). Wines are rated on packaging, taste, alcohol content, and some other stuff.

Night Train Express—17.5% apv, $3.49 for 750 ml.

This bottle looks foreboding at first because of the spooky-ass train on the front. It's all dark, done in deep maroons and yellows. There's a heavy fog and the train is probably loaded with all kinds of dangerous cargo and people. Wrath points out, however, that although it's scary at first, if you look close you can see how the windows on the front of the engine make bright little eyes, the single headlight a perfect button nose, and the rim of the tank right above the cow-catcher a wide, welcoming grin. "I'm not nearly as afraid to drink it any more," he proclaimed, and fell to it. We also liked the ornate cursive writing at the bottom of the label explaining how it's a product of Modesto, and the instruction to "serve very cold."

Night Train is thick, heavy, syrupy stuff, but for some reason it still tastes pretty bad. It's sort of like sucking on a rotten lollipop or something. We decided that, while Brussels sprouts taste good, and chocolate tastes good, you wouldn't want a chocolate Brussels sprout, and that's what this is. It's strong, though, and one bottle will get you very drunk. Night Train is the classic hobo wine, celebrated in story and song, so get a bottle if for no other reason than to celebrate our American heritage.

Thunderbird—17.5% apv, $3.49 for 750 ml.

Thunderbird is by far the burliest wine we tasted, and we are still afraid to say anything bad about it for fear it will come hunt us down and kill us in our sleep. I dare you to drink a whole bottle. Seriously, I dare you. Even looking at it makes me shiver. The word "Thunderbird" is written in a boldly slanted, straight lined typeface in white on a red background with a gold border. Directly under that word is the instruction to "Serve Cold," and under that is written "The American Classic." Then there is this . . . logo of an eagle wearing a crown. It looks like a state seal or something—the state of being all drunk and mean.

Wrath thought this was the most likely to give you whiskey face, and once we finished it I agreed with all three of him. Drink this wine if you want to get in a fight. But make sure the other person has also drunk a bottle of T-bird, too, or you'll get beat up. Thunderbird doesn't help you once you're in the fight. It just helps you get started. Even though it has the same amount of alcohol as Night Train and slightly less than Wild Irish Rose, it will still kick both of their asses and then yours. Watch it, punk.

Carlo Rossi California Sangria—10% apv, $4.00 per 1.5 liter bottle

While Burgundy is generally the favorite in Carlo Rossi's circles, the California Sangria definitely wins, as far as we were concerned. For starters, it has that classic "moonshine jug" shape that can't be beat, with the round bottle, and little finger loop on the neck. The proper way to take a slug of Carlo Rossi is to hook your finger through the loop and rest the bottle on the outside of your elbow while you drink it over your shoulder . . .

The flavor of Carlo Rossi is better than the others because it's spicy as well as sweet. It has a nice light flavor with a little kick to it, and you can definitely nurse it for a while. Sure, you could nurse a bottle of the burgundy for a while too, but the Sangria won't turn your mouth all purple and make you throw up. Compared to the other wines we tasted, this is the easiest to drink. It also has the most pretensions toward serious winehood, although this may be a strike against its image.

Wild Irish Rose—18% apv, $3.49 for 750 ml.

Wild Irish Rose has a simple, understated bottle with a picture of a rose above its name, and the accurate (if vague) description "100 percent pure grape wine." What's nice about this bottle is that it kind of knows it's being treated more like a liquor than a wine. The bottle is flat on the sides and kind of rectangular which makes it look more like a bottle of gin. This may be why it needs to say the word "wine" at least three times on the bottle. For a fun party game, see who can find all three the fastest. If you're drinking alone, see how fast you can find them and then try to break that record.

Tastewise, Wild Irish Rose is surprisingly agreeable. . . . We thought it was the best value for the money because it was the strongest and still really cheap. Also, even though it still had the same "death" aftertaste as Night Train and Thunderbird, it wasn't as prominent. We licked our lips and howled at the moon after Wild Irish Rose. Try it. It's a winner.

Boone's Farm Kiwi-Strawberry—8% apv, $2.90 for 750 ml.
This crap needs to stay on the store shelf. It's weak, bubbly and sweet in just the wrong ways. Both bottle and drink are bland as hell. The label just has this boring old picture of some farm-house (presumably Boone's) and nothing else really eye-catching. It tastes like weak strawberry soda, but . . . you could drink Vintage soda for about a third of the price and still get just as loaded. Unless you're a sixteen-year-old girl, don't bother with the stuff.[13]

Brian Gnatt, a college reviewer writing for *The Michigan Daily Online* at the University of Michigan, had the following to say about low-end fortified wines and their appeal to younger consumers of alcoholic beverages:

For those who don't care for the taste of beer or hard alcohol, those who can't afford to buy quality alcohol, or for those who simply like the taste and effects of drinking cheap wine, usually out of a bottle with a screw-off cap, there's a line of alcoholic beverages just for you that adds a splash of color to liquor store shelves everywhere. Best of all, the bottles come in various shapes, sizes and colors; the wine comes in different flavors and most important, various strengths so everyone can find one to their liking.

From the bright rainbow colors of MD 20/20 (a.k.a. Mad Dog) to the lighter pastels of Boone's, ghetto wines look quite similar to wine coolers or even Kool-Aid. But don't be deceived—their punch is stronger than Bartles and Jaymes or the Kool-Aid Man. Ranging from about 5 percent alcohol (similar to beer) to 18 percent (about half of hard alcohol), cheap wines offer easy, economical and colorful ways to get drunk.

The fact that the wines are cheap, easy and appealing are some of the reasons many young people enjoy drinking the less-than-tasty beverages. When I first started drinking, Mad Dog was my drink of choice. And I thought it was great; memories of skipping high school and watching reruns of *Alf* with friends and a bottle of Wild Berry 20/20—life didn't get much better. But as I got older, and my taste buds refined a bit, I realized Mad Dog and Thunderbird weren't the best drinks in the world, but that they're not all that bad either.

Years later, the occasional bottle of wine still hits the spot. Now, however, it usually includes ridicule by friends and other onlookers who respond with the customary "Mad Dog? Yuck!" Nevertheless, cheap wine will always have a place in my heart, even though I have moved on to some finer forms of fermented fruit drinks, like Franzia, a.k.a. "wine in a box."

While all wino-wines may get a bad rap for being a little pungent, there still are better cheap wines. The *Michigan Daily* taste-tested a number of the area's top-selling rot-gut wines to find which ones are the best bargains in the cheap wine market.

The Test
Finding cheap wine isn't a problem in Ann Arbor. Just about every beer, wine and liquor store sells some variation of the drink, most for less than $4. While all of our selections aren't available at every store, they are all available within walking distance of campus . . .

For the taste test, we gathered 11 different bottles of wine: five of Mad Dog (Hawaiian Blue, Lightning Creek, Pink Grapefruit, Red Grape Wine and Wild Berry), two Boone's (Snow Creek Berry and Strawberry Hill), two Wild Irish Rose varieties (regular and White Label), a bottle of Thunderbird and a bottle of Night Train. Then we tasted. Here's the findings:

Out of the 11 samples, Boone's Snow Creek Berry was the best tasting of all the samples, but to no surprise. The lightly carbonated drink is only about 5 percent alcohol, while many of the other samples had more than three times that amount. It was sweet, fruity and fresh, and the taste of alcohol was almost non-existent.

Boone's Strawberry Hill variety ranked No. 2 on the list, weighing in at 7.5 percent alcohol. The alcohol was a bit more prevalent and the wine had a bit of a sharp taste—drinkable, yet not as enjoyable as the Snow Creek Berry. Again though, the relatively small

---

[13]Adam Martin, "What to Do When You've Only got $5.22 and a Serious Liquor Monkey on Your Back," West Oakland Wine Tasting (www.readsatellite.com/culture/2.4/wine.martin.2.4.1.htm).

amount of alcohol almost nullifies Boone's from the contest, and forces it to stand alone in its own lightweight wine category.

The Mad Dog flavors were the next most successful in the taste test, with the Pink Grapefruit flavor ranking No. 3, after the weaker Boone's. At 13.5 percent alcohol, Pink Grapefruit was fairly smooth and had less of a church-wine taste than the rest of the MD 20/20 flavors. It was tangy and not too sweet, for a somewhat refreshing flavor.

Wild Berry Mad Dog (13.5 percent alcohol) was the next-best, but was quite sweet and sharp and had a lasting aftertaste. Mad Dog's Red Grape Wine (18 percent alcohol) followed at No. 5, the first drink to ever make me hurl. The wine was quite sweet, a bit dry and very grapey, but still drinkable. At No. 6 was Lightning Creek (17 percent alcohol), the clear variety of Mad Dog for all of you who don't like artificial colors in your food. The smell of rubbing alcohol and a taste of watered-down alcohol made this selection the turning point in the tasting, and the wines went downhill from here.

Next in line was the potent Thunderbird (18 percent alcohol)—with "An American Classic" as the slogan on the bottle. With its strong alcohol flavor, Thunderbird is strong at first taste, but it doesn't linger on the palate as much as some of the other selections, mainly the Wild Irish Rose and the Hawaiian Blue Mad Dog, which followed Thunderbird for a No. 8 ranking. With its 2,000 Flushes aqua blue color, alcohol flavor and a hint of coconut, Hawaiian Blue coats your system like a good bathtub scum, with its only redeeming quality being it's a pretty color.

Wild Irish Rose Wine (18 percent) ranked in at No. 9, with its red color, hint of grape flavor and plain taste. Not very tasty, to say the least. The infamous Night Train (18 percent) pulled into the station at No. 10, pushing a train wreck for anyone who could top of the entire bottle of wine. It had a rather nasty, pungent and incarcerating taste and side effects to back up its poor reputation.

Coming in last was Wild Irish Rose's White Label (18 percent alcohol), a harsh, sharp and brutal wine without any flavor whatsoever. The White Label produced breath of fire, and left nothing to be desired.

For all it's worth, cheap wine still has its virtues, even if it doesn't have a very desirable taste. All but the Boone's could probably get you drunk for less than the price of the average beer at the average bar. So if drunk's what you want, and $3 is all you've got, a not-so-good bottle of wine is all you need to cure those sobriety blues.[14]

ATTEMPTS TO CONTROL EXCESSIVE CONSUMPTION OF HIGH-PROOF WINES

Public drunkenness in inner cities and low-income neighborhoods, alcoholism, and binge drinking on college campuses had provoked concerns among various citizens groups, community organizations, churches, government agencies, the makers of alcoholic beverages, and some wine companies. In June 1989, Gallo conducted an experiment whereby it stopped distributing Thunderbird and Night Train wines in the Tenderloin District of San Francisco for six months. Canandaigua Wine Company indicated it would cooperate in the experiment by pulling Wild Irish Rose from the shelves, but it failed to follow through during the trial period because it said the ultimate decision to halt sales was up to its local distributors. But there was reportedly little beneficial impact because, as local winos said, "you can't get it in one store, you get it in another . . . or you just drink something else." The minimal impact of pulling Gallo's Thunderbird and Night Train wines off retailer shelves in San Francisco was

---

[14]Brian A. Gnatt, "A Touch of Underclass: Cheap Wine, an Alternative, Proletariat Potable," *Michigan Daily Online* (www.pub.umich.edu/daily/1997/apr/04-10-97/arts/art3.html).

taken as validation of the oft-stated views within the wine industry (and elsewhere as well) that alcoholics, if deprived of one source, would simply seek out alternatives to satisfy their desire for alcohol.

In addition to Gallo's mostly independent effort in San Francisco, several cities had experimented with ways to remove cheap fortified wines from inner-city stores, as a means of defeating the efforts of people looking for a cheap way to get drunk. Salt Lake City and Portland tried imposing bans on the sales of such wines, with somewhat conflicting results. Both cities reported substitute alcohol sales up. However, while Salt Lake City reported a decline in public drunkenness, in Portland the conclusion was that winos just drank something else.

Banning Cisco, one of the most potent fortified wine coolers, became a cause célèbre during the early 1990s, because it was packaged deceptively similar to normal wine coolers and was shelved in the same beverage cases in convenience stores and supermarkets. Cisco's very sweet flavorings made it a favorite target of young adolescent shoplifters. Former U.S. Surgeon General Antonio Novello referred to heavily fortified wine coolers as "wine foolers"—innocent-looking bottles of wine and sugared fruit juices that looked like a regular wine cooler but packed more than three times the punch (Exhibit 2).

One defense of winemakers who were profiting from producing and marketing cheap fortified wines to skid-row alcoholics was offered by Professor Edward Freeman, a nationally prominent ethicist at the University of Virginia's Darden Graduate School of Business Administration. Freeman stated, "There is a long tradition of freedom of contract in our country. People are free to make their own mistakes."[15] Freeman emphasized that the problem of street alcoholics was far more complex than just the sale of the products. The root issue, he claimed, was the underlying social conditions that helped push alcoholics into their disease: "Not selling this stuff is like moving the deck chairs on the Titanic. The question is, do you really want to be a company associated with these products that are so abused? In our system, we let the companies decide."

---

[15]As quoted in Warren King, "Ethics of Manufacturing Profits from Drunks," *Seattle Times,* January 20, 1998.

case | 14 Krispy Kreme Doughnuts, Inc.

Arthur A. Thompson
The University of Alabama

"We think we're the Stradivarius of doughnuts."
—Scott Livengood, President and CEO, Krispy Kreme Doughnuts, Inc.

With 181 Krispy Kreme stores in 28 states, Krispy Kreme Doughnuts in 2001 was rapidly building something of a cult following for its light, warm, melt-in-your-mouth doughnuts. Sales were on an impressive climb, exceeding 3.5 million doughnuts a day. The company's business model called for 20 percent annual revenue growth, mid-single-digit comparable store sales growth, and 25 percent annual growth in earnings per share.

But a number of securities analysts doubted whether Krispy Kreme's strategy and growth potential merited a stock price nearly 70 times projected 2002 earnings per share of $0.69 and 85 times actual 2001 earnings of $0.55 per share. The company's stock, which was trading in the $46–$50 range and had been as high as $54, had been a favorite of short sellers for several months—the 2.5 million shorted shares in May 2001 represented nearly 10 percent of the company's outstanding shares. According to one analyst, "It [the stock] has had a good run, but the numbers just don't work"; another analyst commented, "The odds are against this stock for long-term success." A third said, "Single-product concepts only have so many years to run." Indeed, restaurants with quick-service products presently had the slowest revenue growth of any restaurant type.

COMPANY BACKGROUND

In 1933, Vernon Rudolph bought a doughnut shop in Paducah, Kentucky, from Joe LeBeau. His purchase included the company's assets, goodwill, the Krispy Kreme name, and rights to a secret yeast-raised doughnut recipe that LeBeau had created in New Orleans years earlier. Several years thereafter, Rudolph and his partner, looking for a larger market, moved their operations to Nashville, Tennessee; other members of the Rudolph family joined the enterprise, opening doughnut shops in Charleston, West Virginia, and Atlanta, Georgia. The business consisted of producing, marketing, and delivering fresh-made doughnuts to local grocery stores. Then, during the summer of 1937, Rudolph quit the family business and left Nashville, taking with him a 1936 Pontiac, $200 in cash, some doughnut-making equipment, and the secret recipe. After some disappointing efforts to find another location, he settled on opening the first Krispy Kreme doughnut shop in Winston-Salem, North Carolina. Rudolph was drawn to Winston-Salem because the city was developing into a tobacco and textiles hub in the Southeast, and he thought a doughnut shop would make a good addition to the thriving local economy. Rudolph and his two partners, who accompanied him from Nashville, used their last $25 to rent a building across from Salem College and Academy. With no money left to buy ingredients, Rudolph convinced a local grocer to lend them what they needed, promising payment once the first doughnuts were sold. To deliver the doughnuts, he took the backseat out of the 1936 Pontiac and installed a delivery rack. On July 13, 1937, the first Krispy Kreme doughnuts were made at Rudolph's new Winston-Salem shop and delivered to grocery retailers.

Soon afterward, people began stopping by the shop to ask if they could buy hot doughnuts. There were so many requests that Rudolph decided to cut a hole in the shop's wall so he could sell doughnuts at retail to passersby. Krispy Kreme doughnuts proved highly popular in Winston-Salem, and Rudolph's shop prospered.

In the early 1950s, Vernon Rudolph met Mike Harding, who was then selling powdered milk to bakeries. Rudolph was looking for someone to help grow the business, and Harding joined the company as a partner in 1954. Starting with six employees, the two began building an equipment department and a plant for blending doughnut mixes. They believed the key to Krispy Kreme's expansion was to have control over each step of the doughnut-making process and to be able to deliver hot doughnuts to customers as soon as they emerged from the frying and sugar-glazing process. By the late 1950s, Krispy Kreme had 29 shops in 12 states, with each shop having the capacity to produce 500 dozen doughnuts per hour. In 1960, they decided to standardize all Krispy Kreme shops with a green roof, red-glazed brick exterior, viewing window inside, overhead conveyor for doughnut production, and bar stools, creating a look that became the Krispy Kreme trademark during that era.

Harding focused on operations, while Rudolph concentrated on finding promising locations for new stores and getting bank financing to support expansion into other southeastern cities and towns. Harding became Krispy Kreme's president in 1958 and, when Rudolph died in 1973, chief executive officer. Under Harding and Rudolph, Krispy Kreme's revenues grew from less than $1 million in 1954 to $58 million when Harding retired in 1974. Corporate headquarters remained in Winston-Salem.

In 1976, Beatrice Foods bought Krispy Kreme and proceeded to make a series of changes. The recipe was changed and the company's script-lettered signs were altered to produce a more modern look. Customers reacted negatively to Beatrice's changes, and business declined. A group of franchisees, led by Joseph McAleer, bought the company from Beatrice in 1982 in a $22 million leveraged buyout (LBO). The new owners quickly reinstated the original recipe and the original script-lettered signs. Sales rebounded, but with double-digit interest rates in the early 1980s, it took years to pay off the LBO debt, leaving little for expansion.

To grow revenues, the company relied mainly on franchising "associate" stores, opening a few new company-owned stores—all in the southeastern United States, and boosting store volume through off-premise sales. Associate stores operated under a 15-year licensing agreement that permitted them to use the Krispy Kreme system within a specific geographic territory. They paid royalties of 3 percent of on-premise sales and 1 percent of all other branded sales (to supermarkets, convenience stores, charitable organizations selling doughnuts for fund-raising projects, and other wholesale buyers); no royalties were paid on sales of unbranded or private-label doughnuts. The primary emphasis of the associate stores and many of the company stores was on wholesaling both Krispy Kreme doughnuts and private-label doughnuts to local groceries and supermarkets. Corporate revenues rose gradually to $117 million in 1989 and then flattened for the next six years.

New Leadership and a New Strategy

In the early 1990s, with interest rates falling and much of the debt paid down, the company began experimenting cautiously with expanding under Scott Livengood, the company's newly appointed president and chief operating officer. Livengood, 48, joined Krispy Kreme's human relations department in 1978 three years after graduating from the University of North Carolina at Chapel Hill with a degree in industrial relations and a minor in psychology. Believing strongly in the company's product and long-term growth potential, he rose through the management ranks, becoming president and chief operating officer in 1992, a member of the board of directors in 1994, president and CEO in 1998, and president, CEO, and chairman of the board in 1999.

Shortly after becoming president in 1992, Livengood became increasingly concerned about stagnant sales and shortcomings in the company's strategy: "The model wasn't working for us. It was more about selling in wholesale channels and less about the brand." He and other Krispy Kreme executives, mindful of the thousands of "Krispy Kreme stories" told by passionate customers over the years, concluded that the emphasis on off-premise sales did not adequately capitalize on the enthusiasm and loyalty of customers for Krispy Kreme's doughnuts. A second shortcoming was that the company's exclusive focus on southeastern U.S. markets unnecessarily handcuffed efforts to leverage the company's brand equity and product quality in the rest of the United States. The available data also indicated that the standard-size stores (7,000+ square feet) were uneconomic to operate in all but very-high-volume locations.

By the mid-1990s, with fewer than 100 franchised and company-owned stores and corporate sales stuck in the $110–$120 million range for six years, company executives determined that it was time for a new strategy and aggressive expansion outside the Southeast. Beginning in 1996, Krispy Kreme began implementing a new strategy to reposition the company, shifting the focus from a wholesale bakery strategy to a specialty retail strategy that promoted sales at the company's own retail outlets and emphasized the "hot doughnut experience" so often stressed in customers' Krispy Kreme stories. Doughnut sizes were also increased. The second major part of the new strategy was to expand the number of stores nationally using both area franchisees and company-owned stores. In preparing to launch the strategy, the company tested several different store sizes, eventually concluding that stores in the range of 2,400 to 4,200 square feet were better suited for the company's market repositioning and expansion plans.

The franchising part of the strategy called for the company to license territories, usually defined by metropolitan statistical areas, to select franchisees with proven experience in multi-unit food operations. Franchisees were expected to be thoroughly familiar with the local area market they were to develop and also to have the capital and organizational capability to open a prescribed number of stores in their territory within a specified time period. The minimum net worth requirement for franchised area developers was $5 million total or $750,000 per store, whichever was greater. Area developers paid Krispy Kreme a franchise fee of $20,000 to $40,000 for each store they opened. They also were required to pay a 4.5 percent royalty fee on all sales and to contribute 1 percent of revenues to a company-administered advertising and public relations fund. Franchisees were expected to strictly adhere to high standards of quality and service.

By early 2000, the company had signed on 13 area developers operating 33 Krispy Kreme stores and committed to open another 130 stores in their territories within five years or less. In addition, the company was operating 61 stores under its own management. Sales had zoomed to $220 million, and profits were a record $6 million.

After a decision was made to take the company public, the company spent much of late 1999 and early 2000 preparing for an initial public offering (IPO) of the company's stock in April 2000. The old corporate structure (Krispy Kreme Doughnut Corporation) was merged into a new company (Krispy Kreme Doughnuts, Inc.). The new company planned to use the proceeds from its IPO to remodel or relocate older company-owned stores, to repay debt, to make joint venture investments in franchised stores, and to expand its capacity to make doughnut mix.

The IPO of 3.45 million shares was oversubscribed at $21.00 per share, and when the stock began trading in April under the ticker symbol KREM, the price quickly rose. Over the next 12 months, the company's stock price more than quadrupled; after a 2-for-1 split in March 2001, the company's stock was trading in the high 40s in May 2001—up from the low 30s in early April 2001 and down slightly from its all-time high of $54.25 in November 2000. Krispy Kreme was the second-best-performing stock among all IPO offerings in the United States in 2000. In fiscal year 2001, Krispy Kreme reported sales of $301 million and profits of $14.7 million. The company's stock began trading on the New York Stock Exchange in May 2001 under the symbol KKD.

Exhibit 1 presents a summary of Krispy Kreme's financial performance and operations for fiscal years 1995–2001.

KRISPY KREME'S BUSINESS MODEL AND STRATEGY

Krispy Kreme's business model involved generating revenues and profits from three sources:

- Sales at company-owned stores.
- Royalties from franchised stores and franchise fees from new store openings.
- Sales of doughnut mixes and customized doughnut-making equipment to franchised stores.

Exhibit 2 shows revenues, operating expenses, and operating income by business segment.

The company was drawn to franchising because it minimized capital requirements, provided an attractive royalty stream, and put responsibility for local store operations in the hands of successful franchisees who knew the ins and outs of operating multi-unit chains efficiently.

Krispy Kreme had developed a vertically integrated supply chain whereby it manufactured the mixes for its doughnuts at company plants in North Carolina and Illinois and also manufactured proprietary doughnut-making equipment for use in both company-owned and franchised stores. The sale of mixes and equipment, referred to as "KK manufacturing & distribution" by the company, generated a substantial fraction of both revenues and earnings (see Exhibit 2).

Many of the stores built prior to 1997 were designed primarily as wholesale bakeries, and their formats and site locations differed considerably from the newer stores being located in high-density areas where there were lots of people and high traffic counts. In order to improve on-premise sales at these older stores, the company was implementing a program to either remodel them or relocate them to sites that could better attract on-premise sales. In new markets, the company's strategy was to focus initial efforts on on-premise sales and then leverage the interest generated in Krispy Kreme products to secure supermarket and convenience store accounts.

exhibit 1 Summary of Krispy Kreme's Financial and Operating Performance, Fiscal Years 1995–2001
(dollar amounts in thousands, except per share)

				Fiscal Years Ending			
	Jan. 29, 1995	Jan. 28, 1996	Feb. 2, 1997	Feb. 1, 1998	Jan. 31, 1999	Jan. 30, 2000	Jan. 28, 2001
Statement of operations data							
Total revenues	$114,986	$118,550	$132,614	$158,743	$180,880	$220,243	$300,715
Operating expenses	98,587	104,717	116,658	104,207	159,941	190,003	250,690
General and administrative expenses	7,578	6,804	7,630	9,530	10,897	14,856	20,061
Depreciation and amortization expenses	2,764	2,799	3,189	3,586	4,278	4,546	6,457
Provision for restructuring	—	3,000	—	—	9,466	—	—
Income (loss) from operations	6,057	1,230	5,137	5,420	(3,702)	10,838	23,507
Interest expense, net, and other	(1,291)	930	1,091	895	1,577	1,232	276
Income (loss) before income taxes	7,348	300	4,046	4,525	(5,279)	9,606	23,783
Provision (benefit) for income taxes	2,731	120	1,169	1,811	(2,112)	3,650	9,058
Net income (loss)	$ 4,617	$ 180	$ 2,427	$ 2,714	$ (3,167)	$ 5,956	$ 14,725
Net income (loss) per share:							
Basic	$0.32	$0.01	$0.17	$0.19	$(0.19)	$0.32	$0.60
Diluted	$0.32	$0.01	$0.17	$0.19	$(0.19)	$0.30	0.55
Shares used in calculation of net income (loss) per share:							
Basic	14,568	14,568	14,568	14,568	16,498	18,680	24,592
Diluted	14,568	14,568	14,568	14,568	16,498	19,640	26,828
Cash dividends declared per common share	$0.08	$0.08	$0.08	$0.08	$0.08	—	—
Operating data							
Systemwide sales	$146,715	$151,693	$167,592	$203,439	$240,316	$318,854	$448,129
Number of stores at end of period:							
Company-owned	48	53	61	58	61	58	63
Franchised	40	42	55	62	70	86	111
Systemwide total	88	95	116	120	131	144	174

(*continued*)

C-283

exhibit 1 (concluded)

	Fiscal Years Ending						
	Jan. 29, 1995	Jan. 28, 1996	Feb. 2, 1997	Feb. 1, 1998	Jan. 31, 1999	Jan. 30, 2000	Jan. 28, 2001
Increase in comparable store sales:							
Company-owned	n.a.	n.a.	n.a.	11.5%	11.1%	12.0%	22.9%
Franchised	n.a.	n.a.	n.a.	12.7%	9.7%	14.1%	17.1%
Average weekly sales per store:							
Company-owned	$45	$39	$39	$42	$47	$54	$69
Franchised	22	23	22	23	28	38	43
Balance sheet data							
Current assets				$ 25,792	$ 33,780	$ 41,038	$ 67,611
Current liabilities				16,641	25,672	29,586	38,168
Working capital	$ 7,730	$ 5,742	$ 10,148	9,151	8,108	11,452	29,443
Total assets	67,257	72,888	78,005	81,463	93,312	104,958	171,493
Long-term debt, including current maturities	12,533	18,311	20,187	20,870	21,020	22,902	—
Total shareholders' equity	35,817	35,033	36,516	38,265	42,247	47,755	125,679
Cash flow data							
Net cash provided by operating activities			$ 2,652	$ 7,126	$ 11,682	$ 8,890	$ 30,576
Purchase of property and equipment			(9,592)	(6,708)	(12,376)	(11,335)	(25,655)
Proceeds from disposal of property and equipment			5,430	1,740	—	—	1,419
Net cash used for investing activities			(3,426)	(5,896)	(11,827)	(11,826)	(67,288)
Net proceeds from long-term borrowings			1,876	683	150	1,682	(19,375)
Proceeds from stock offering					4,619	—	65,637
Cash dividends paid			(1,159)	(1,173)	(1,180)	(1,518)	(7,005)
Net cash provided by (used for) financing activities			759	(456)	1,525	(84)	40,555
Cash and cash equivalents at end of year			2,158	2,933	4,313	3,183	7,026

Source: Company SEC filings and annual reports.

exhibit 2 Krispy Kreme's Performance by Business Segment, Fiscal Years 1997–2001 (in millions of $)

	Fiscal Years Ending				
	Feb. 2, 1997	Feb. 1, 1998	Jan. 31, 1999	Jan. 30, 2000	Jan. 20, 2001
Revenues by business segment					
Company store operations	$113,940	$132,826	$145,251	$164,230	$213,677
Franchise operations	1,709	2,285	3,236	5,529	9,445
KK manufacturing & distribution	16,965	23,632	32,393	50,484	77,593
Total	$132,614	$158,743	$180,880	$220,243	$300,715
Operating expenses by business segment (excluding depreciation and amortization)					
Company store operations	$100,655	$117,252	$126,961	$142,925	$181,470
Franchise operations	1,575	2,368	2,731	4,012	3,642
KK manufacturing & distribution	14,428	20,587	27,913	43,066	65,578
Total	$116,658	$140,207	$157,605	$190,003	$250,690
Operating income by business segment (before depreciation and amortization)					
Company store operations	$ 13,285	$ 15,574	$ 18,290	$ 21,305	$ 32,207
Franchise operations	134	(83)	505	1,517	5,803
KK manufacturing & distribution	2,537	3,045	4,480	7,418	12,015
Total	$ 15,956	$ 18,536	$ 23,275	$ 30,240	$ 50,025
Unallocated general and administrative expenses	$ (7,630)	$ (10,476)	$(12,020)	$(16,035)	$ (21,305)
Depreciation and amortization expenses					
Company store operations	n.a.	$ 2,339	$ 2,873	$ 3,059	$ 4,838
Franchise operations	n.a.	100	57	72	72
KK manufacturing & distribution	n.a.	201	225	236	303
Corporate administration	n.a.	946	1,123	1,179	1,244
Total	$ 3,189	$ 3,586	$ 4,278	$ 4,546	$ 6,457

Source: Company SEC filings and annual reports.

So far, the company had spent very little on advertising to introduce its product to new markets, relying instead on local media publicity, product giveaways, and word of mouth. In almost every instance, local newspapers had run big features headlining the opening of the first Krispy Kreme stores in their area; in some cases, local radio and TV stations had sent news crews to cover the opening and conduct on-the-scene interviews. The grand opening in Austin, Texas, was covered live by five TV crews and four radio station crews (there were 50 people in line at 11:30 P.M. the night before the 5:30 A.M. store opening). At the first San Diego store opening, there were five remote TV trucks on the scene; radio reporters were out interviewing customers camped out in their pickup trucks in the parking lot; and a nationally syndicated radio show broadcast "live" at the site. It was common for customers to form lines at the door and at the drive-through well before the initial day's 5:30 A.M. grand opening when the "Hot Doughnuts Now" sign was first turned on. In a number of instances, there were traffic jams at the turn-in to the store—a Buffalo, New York, traffic cop said, "I've never seen anything like this . . . and I mean it." As part of the grassroots marketing effort surrounding new-store openings, Krispy Kremes were typically given away at public events as a treat for participants—then, as one franchisee said, "the Krispy Kremes seem to work their own magic and people start to talk about them."

Krispy Kreme had originally financed its expansion strategy with the aid of long-term debt. However, the April 2000 IPO raised enough equity capital to completely pay off all long-term debt (see Exhibit 1). When the company went public, it ceased paying dividends to shareholders; currently all earnings were being used to help grow the business.

COMPANY OPERATIONS

Products and Product Quality

Krispy Kreme produced about 20 varieties of doughnuts, the biggest seller of which was the company's signature "hot original glazed" doughnut made from Joe LeBeau's original yeast-based recipe. Exhibit 3 shows the company's doughnut varieties as of May 2001. Exhibit 4 indicates the nutritional content for a representative selection of Krispy Kreme doughnuts.

Company research indicated that Krispy Kreme's appeal extended across all major demographic groups, including age and income. Many customers purchased doughnuts by the dozen for their office, clubs, and family. According to one enthusiastic franchisee:

> We happen to think this is a very, very unique product which has what I can only describe as a one-of-a-kind taste. They are extremely light in weight and texture. They have this incredible glaze. When you have one of the hot original doughnuts as they come off the line, there's just nothing like it.

The company received an average of 3,500 e-mails and letters monthly from customers. By all accounts, most were from customers who were passionate about Krispy Kreme products, and there were always some from people pleading for stores to be opened in their area. Exhibit 5 presents sample comments from customers and franchisees. According to Scott Livengood:

> You have to possess nothing less than a passion for your product and your business because that's where you draw your energy. We have a great product . . . We have loyal customers, and we have great brand equity. When we meet people with a Krispy Kreme story, they always do it with a smile on their faces.

exhibit 3   Varieties of Krispy Kreme Doughnuts

• Original Glazed	• Chocolate Iced Custard Filled	• Glazed Cruller
• Chocolate Iced	• Raspberry Filled	• Powdered Cake
• Chocolate Iced with Sprinkles	• Lemon Filled	• Glazed Devil's Food
• Maple Iced	• Cinnamon Apple Filled	• Chocolate Iced Cruller
• Chocolate Iced Creme Filled	• Powdered Blueberry Filled	• Cinnamon Bun
• Glazed Creme Filled	• Chocolate Iced Cake	• Glazed Blueberry
• Traditional Cake		• Glazed Sour Cream

Source: www.krispykreme.com, May 3, 2001.

exhibit 4 Nutritional Content of Selected Varieties of Krispy Kreme Doughnuts

| Product | Calories | Calories from Fat | Total Fat | | Saturated Fat | | Cholesterol | Sodium | Carbohydrates | | Sugars |
			Grams	% Daily Value*	Grams	% Daily Value*			Grams	% Daily Value*	
Original Glazed	210	110	12g	19%	4g	19%	<5mg	65mg	22g	7%	13g
Fudge Iced Glazed	280	130	14g	22%	4g	22%	<5mg	75mg	36g	12%	22g
Maple Iced Glazed	200	80	9g	14%	2.5g	13%	0mg	100mg	28g	9%	18g
Powdered Blueberry Filled	270	110	13g	20%	4g	20%	<5mg	170mg	33g	11%	40g
Fudge Iced Creme Filled	340	160	18g	28%	5g	25%	<5mg	160mg	39g	13%	22g
Glazed Creme Filled	350	120	20g	31%	5g	25%	<5mg	135mg	39g	13%	24g
Traditional cake	200	100	11g	17%	3g	14%	15mg	280mg	22g	7%	7g
Glazed Cruller	250	140	16g	25%	4g	20%	5mg	190mg	24g	8%	15g
Cinnamon Bun	220	100	11g	17%	3g	15%	0mg	160mg	26g	9%	7g
Glazed Devil's Food	390	220	24g	37%	5g	25%	<5mg	250mg	41g	14%	30g

*Based on a 2,000-calorie diet.

Source: www.krispykreme.com, May 3, 2001.

exhibit 5　Sample Comments from Krispy Kreme Customers and Franchisees

Customer comments

"I ate one and literally it brought a tear to my eye. I kid you not."

"Oh my gosh, this is awesome. I wasn't even hungry, but now I'm going to get two dozen."

"We got up at 3 o'clock this morning. I told them I would be late for work. I was going to the grand opening."

"They melt in your mouth. They really do."

"Krispy Kreme rocks."

"It's hot, good and hot. The way a doughnut should be."

"The doughnut's magnificent. A touch of genius."

"I love doughnuts, but these are different. It's terrible for your weight because when you eat just one, you feel like you've barely tasted it. You want more. It's like popcorn."*

"When you bite into one it's like biting into a sugary cloud. It's really fun to give one to someone who hasn't had one before. They bite into one and just exclaim."†

Franchisee comments

"Krispy Kreme is a 'feel good' business as much as it is a doughnut business. Customers come in for an experience which makes them feel good—they enjoy our doughnuts and they enjoy the time they spend in our stores watching the doughnuts being made."

"We're not selling doughnuts as much as we are creating an experience. The viewing window into the production room is a theater our customers can never get enough of. It's fun to watch doughnuts being made and even more fun to eat them when they're hot off the line."

"Southern California customers have responded enthusiastically to Krispy Kreme. Many of our fans first came to Krispy Kreme not because of a previous taste experience but rather because of the 'buzz' around the brand. It was more word of mouth and publicity that brought them in to sample our doughnuts. Once they tried them, they became loyal fans who spread the word that Krispy Kreme is something special . . . We witness the excitement every day, especially when we're away from the store and wearing a hat or shirt with the Krispy Kreme logo. When people see the logo, we get the big smile and are always asked, 'When will we get one in our neighborhood?' . . . The tremendous local publicity coupled with the amazing brand awareness nationwide has helped us make the community aware of our commitment to support local charities. Our fund-raising program, along with product donations to schools, churches, and other charitable organizations have demonstrated our real desire to give back. This commitment also impacts our employees who understand firsthand the value of supporting the needy as well as the worthy causes in our neighborhoods."

"In all my many years of owning and operating multiple food franchise businesses, we have never been able to please—until Krispy Kreme—such a wide range of customers in the community. Its like an old friend has come to town when we open our doors: we're welcomed with open arms . . . Quite frankly, in my experience, publicity for Krispy Kreme is like nothing I have ever seen. It is truly unprecedented."

"We happen to think this is a very, very unique product which has what I can only describe as a one-of-a-kind taste. They are extremely light in weight and texture. They have this incredible glaze. When you have one of the hot original doughnuts as they come off the line, there's just nothing like it."

*Quoted in "Winchell's Scrambles to Meet Krispy Kreme Challenge," *Los Angeles Times*, September 30, 1999, p. C1.

†Quoted in Greg Sukiennik, "Will Dunkin' Donuts Territory Take to Krispy Kreme?" The Associated Press State & Local Wire, April 8, 2001.

Source: Krispy Kreme's 2000 and 2001 annual reports, except for the two quotes noted above.

Coffee   Krispy Kreme was making a concerted effort to improve the caliber and appeal of its on-premise coffee and beverage offerings, aligning them more closely with the hot doughnut experience in its stores. In early 2001, Krispy Kreme acquired Digital Java, Inc., a small Chicago-based coffee company that sourced and roasted premium quality coffees and that marketed a broad line of coffee-based and non-coffee beverages. Scott Livengood explained the reasons for the acquisition:

> We believe the Krispy Kreme brand naturally extends to a coffee and beverage offering that is more closely aligned with the hot doughnut experience in our stores. Vertical integration of our coffee business provides the capability to control the sourcing and roasting of our coffee. Increasing control of our supply chain will help ensure quality standards, recipe formulation and roast consistency. With this capability, one of our first priorities will be the research and benchmarking necessary to develop premier blends and roasts of coffee which will help make Krispy Kreme a coffee destination for a broader audience. Beyond coffee, we intend to offer a full line of beverages including expresso-based drinks and frozen beverages. We believe we can substantially increase the proportion of our business devoted to coffee specifically and beverages generally by upgrading and broadening our beverage offering.

In 2000, beverage sales accounted for about 10 percent of store sales, with coffee accounting for about half of the beverage total and the other half divided among milk, juices, soft drinks, and bottled water.

Store Operations

Each store was designed as a "doughnut theater" where customers could watch the doughnuts being made through a 40-foot glass window. New stores ranged in size between 2,400 and 4,200 square feet (see Exhibit 6 for representative stores and store scenes). Stores had a drive-through window and a dining area that would seat 50 or more people—a few of the newer and larger stores had special rooms for hosting Krispy Kreme parties. Store decor was a vintage 1950s look with mint green walls and smooth metal chairs; some of the newest stores had booths. A typical store employed about 125 people, including about 65 full-time positions. Approximately half of on-premise sales occurred in the morning hours and half in the afternoon and evening. Many stores were open 24 hours a day, with much of the doughnut making for off-premise sales being done between 6 P.M. and 6 A.M. Production was nearly always under way during peak in-store traffic times. In several large metropolitan areas, however, the doughnut making for off-premise sales was done in a central commissary specially equipped for large-volume production, packaging, and local area distribution.

Each batch of doughnuts took about one hour to make. After the ingredients were mixed into dough, the dough was rolled and cut. The pieces went into a 12-foot-tall machine where each piece rotated on a wire rack for 33 minutes under high humidity and low heat (126 degrees Fahrenheit) to allow the dough to rise. When the rising process was complete, the doughnuts moved along a conveyor to be fried on one side, flipped, fried on the other side, drained, and inspected. Doughnuts destined to be glazed were directed through a waterfall of warm, sugary topping; the others were directed to another part of the baking section to be filled and/or frosted. Exhibit 7 depicts the mixing, rising, frying, draining, and glazing parts of the process. Depending on store size and location, a typical day's production ranged between 2,400 and 6,000 dozen doughnuts.

Each producing store featured a prominent Hot Doughnuts Now® neon sign (see Exhibit 6) signaling customers that freshly made "original glazed doughnuts" were

exhibit 6   Representative Krispy Kreme Stores and Store Scenes

exhibit 7   Making the Doughnuts

Mixing Ingredients

Rising

Frying and Flipping

Inspection and Draining

Drying and Entering Glazing

Exiting Glazing

Packaging

coming off the bakery conveyor belt and were available for immediate purchase. Generally, the signs glowed from around 6 A.M. until 11 A.M. and then came on again during the late afternoon and stayed on into the late-night hours.

At one California franchise, Krispy Kreme's original glazed doughnuts sold for $0.70 each or $4.99 per dozen; a mixed dozen sold for $5.49. They were packaged in white boxes with small green polka dots and the Krispy Kreme logo. At a franchise in Alabama, original glazed doughnuts were $0.60 each or $4.29 per dozen; other varieties were $0.65 each or $4.79 a dozen—customers got a $1.00 per dozen discount on purchases of two or more dozen.

Stores generated revenues in several ways:

- On-premise sales of doughnuts.
- Sales of coffee and other beverages.
- Off-premise sales of branded and private-label doughnuts to local supermarkets, convenience stores, and fund-raising groups.

The company had developed a highly effective system for delivering fresh doughnuts, both packaged and unpackaged, to area retail stores. Route drivers had the capability to take customer orders and deliver products directly to retail accounts where they were typically merchandised either from Krispy Kreme branded displays or from bakery cases (as unbranded doughnuts). Krispy Kreme stores actively promoted sales to schools, churches, and civic groups for fund-raising drives.

The franchisee for Krispy Kreme stores in San Francisco had arranged to sell a four-pack of Krispy Kremes for $5 at San Francisco Giant baseball games at Pacific Bell Park—Krispy Kreme ran out of 2,100 packs by the third inning of the first game and, despite increasing supplies, sold out after the fourth and sixth innings of the next two games; stadium vendors were supplied with 3,450 four-packs for the fourth game. The franchisee of the Las Vegas stores had a website where on-the-job customers could place orders online before 2 P.M. and have them delivered to their place of work by a courier service.

A Texas franchisee was building a new 18,000-square-foot production and distribution center to supply Metroplex supermarkets, convenience stores, and other area retailers with Krispy Kreme 12-packs because newly opened local stores did not have the baking capacity to keep up with both on-premise and off-premise demand; there were similar franchiser-operated wholesale baking and distribution centers in Nashville, Cincinnati, Atlanta, Chicago, and Philadelphia. Several of these centers had established delivery capability to supply Krispy Kremes to retailers in outlying areas deemed too small to justify a stand-alone Krispy Kreme store. Target Corporation, which had already entered into an agreement with Starbucks to put Starbucks kiosks in all of its SuperTarget stores, was experimenting with adding a Krispy Kreme doughnuts section to its SuperTarget format.

The cost of opening a new store ranged from $1.0 to $2.5 million, depending on land costs and store size. Site selection was based on household density, proximity to both daytime employment and residential centers, and proximity to other retail traffic generators. The company planned to open 36 stores in fiscal year 2002, and agreements were in place for franchisees to open more than 250 new stores by 2006. Exhibit 8 shows data on store opening activity. Exhibit 9 shows the economics of unit operations.

exhibit 8 Krispy Kreme Store Openings, Closings, and Transfers, Fiscal Years 1997–2001

	Company-Owned	Franchised	Total
Year ended February 2, 1997			
Beginning count	53	42	95
Opened	7	15	22
Closed	0	(1)	(1)
Transferred*	1	(1)	0
Ending count	61	55	116
Year ended February 1, 1998			
Beginning count	61	55	116
Opened	0	7	7
Closed	(2)	(1)	(3)
Transferred*	(1)	1	0
Ending count	58	62	120
Year ended January 31, 1999			
Beginning count	58	62	120
Opened	0	14	14
Closed	0	(3)	(3)
Transferred*	3	(3)	0
Ending count	61	70	131
Year ended January 30, 2000			
Beginning count	61	70	131
Opened	2	19	21
Closed	(5)	(3)	(8)
Transferred*	0	0	0
Ending count	58	86	144
Year ended January 28, 2001			
Beginning count	58	86	144
Opened	8	28	36
Closed	(3)	(3)	(6)
Transferred*	0	0	0
Ending count	63	111	174

New Stores in New Markets, 2001	New Stores in Existing Markets, 2001
Denver	Baton Rouge
Oklahoma City	Charleston
Syracuse	Greensboro
Albuquerque	Alexandria
Wichita	Davenport
Minneapolis	New Orleans
Pittsburgh	Orlando
Seattle	Dallas
Reno	Richmond
Little Rock	New York City
West Palm Beach	

*Transferred stores represent stores sold between the company and franchisees.

Source: Company SEC filings and annual reports; Deutsche Banc Alex. Brown estimates.

exhibit 9   Estimated Krispy Kreme Store Economics

Store revenues	$3,600,000
Cash flow (after operating expenses)	960,000
Cash flow margin	27%
Owner's equity investment to construct store	$1,050,000
Cash flow return on equity investment	91%

Source: As estimated by Deutsche Banc Alex. Brown.

Performance of New Krispy Kreme Stores

In 2000, Krispy Kreme's first stores in 10 new geographic markets averaged $234,000 in sales the first week, attracting an average of more than 50,000 visitors, and producing an average of 23,500 transactions. Sales in succeeding weeks averaged $93,400. First-week sales in new stores opened in existing marketplaces in 2000 averaged $150,000, with about 30,000 visitors—this compared favorably with average opening-week sales of $123,000 in fiscal year 1999 and $85,600 in fiscal year 1998. Weekly sales at newly opened stores tended to moderate after several months of operation, but the company expected its newer stores to have annual sales averaging more than $3 million in their first year of operation.

The record opening-week revenue for a new Krispy Kreme store in a new market was $369,000. The store, located in Denver, grossed $1 million in revenues in its first 22 days of operation, commonly had waiting lines running out the door with a one-hour wait for doughnuts, and, according to local newspaper reports, one night had 150 cars in line for the drive-through window at 1:30 A.M. The store was said to have paid off-duty sheriff's deputies $12,000 to help direct traffic from Tuesday through Sunday between 5 A.M. and 11 P.M. on opening week.[1] The prior sales record for a first-week new-store opening was $365,000, when the first Krispy Kreme opened in San Diego.

Average weekly sales of Krispy Kreme stores opened in 1997 and 1998 were about $40,000 per week in 2000. Average weekly sales at Class of 1999 stores were $69,000, and sales at Class of 2000 stores averaged $79,000. Krispy Kreme management had advised franchisees that on-premise sales should not exceed $50,000 per week in order to provide good service and ample seating.

KK Manufacturing and Distribution

All the doughnut mix and equipment used in the stores was manufactured and supplied by the company, partly as a means of ensuring consistent recipe quality and doughnut making throughout the chain and partly as a means of generating sales and profits from franchise operations. Sales of the KKM&D unit were up 357 percent since the end of fiscal year 1997, and operating income was up 374 percent; KKM&D was the second largest contributor to Krispy Kreme's overall operating income and had attractive profit margins (see Exhibit 2). The company's line of custom stainless-steel doughnut-making machines ranged in capacity from 230 to 600 dozen doughnuts per hour.

---

[1] *Rocky Mountain News,* March 30, 2001.

Krispy Kreme had recently put plans in place to construct a state-of-the-art 187,000-square-foot manufacturing and distribution facility in Illinois, dedicated to the blending and packaging of prepared doughnut mixes and to distributing mixes, equipment, and other supplies to stores in the Midwest and the western half of North America. This facility was expected to lower Krispy Kreme's unit costs. A new doughnut-making equipment manufacturing facility was under construction in Winston-Salem, where the current ingredient-mixing facility was also located. Krispy Kreme had a state-of-the-art laboratory that tested all key ingredients and each batch of mix produced.

Training

Since mid-1999, Krispy Kreme had invested resources in its training program, creating a multimedia management training curriculum. The program included classroom instruction, computer-based and video training modules, and in-store training experiences. The online part of the training program made full use of graphics, video, and animation, as well as seven different types of test questions. Every Krispy Kreme store had access to the training over the company's intranet and the Internet; employees who registered for the course could access the modules from home using their Internet connection. Learners' test results were transferred directly to a Krispy Kreme human resources database; learners were automatically redirected to lessons where test scores indicated that the material was not well absorbed on the first attempt. The online course was designed to achieve 90 percent mastery from 90 percent of the participants and could be updated as needed. The company expected that some 250 managers would have completed the course by early 2002.

The course for managers had been recast into a program suitable for hourly employees. The course could also be divided into small pieces and customized to fit individual needs.

Growth Potential

With only 181 stores in May 2001, Krispy Kreme management believed the company was in the infancy of its growth. The company's highest priority was on expanding into markets with over 100,000 households; management believed these markets were attractive because the dense population characteristics offered opportunities for multiple store locations, gave greater exposure to brand-building efforts, and afforded multi-unit operating economies. However, the company believed that secondary markets with fewer than 100,000 households held significant sales and profit potential—it was exploring smaller-sized store designs suitable for secondary markets. Krispy Kreme's management further believed the food-service and institutional channel of sales offered significant opportunity to extend the brand into colleges and universities, business and industry facilities, and sports and entertainment complexes. Management had stated that the company's strong brand name, highly differentiated product, high-volume production capability, and multichannel market penetration strategy put the company in a position to become the recognized leader in every market it entered.

As of May 2001, the company had stopped accepting franchise applications for U.S. locations, indicating that there were no open territories. However, it was accepting applications from interested developers interested in franchised stores in international markets. According to Scott Livengood, "Krispy Kreme is a natural to become a global brand. Looking at our demographics, we appeal to a very broad customer base.

We receive lots of interest on a weekly basis to expand into international locations and we are confident our brand will be received extremely well outside the U.S."

In December 2000, the company hired Donald Henshall, 38, to fill the newly created position of president of international development; Henshall was formerly managing director of new business development with London-based Overland Group, a maker and marketer of branded footwear and apparel. Henshall's job was to refine the company's global strategy, develop the capabilities and infrastructure to support expansion outside the U.S., and consider inquiries from qualified parties wanting to open Krispy Kreme stores in foreign markets.

INDUSTRY ENVIRONMENT

By some estimates, the doughnut industry in the United States was a $4.7 billion market in both 1998 and 1999. Americans consumed an estimated 10 billion doughnuts annually—just over three dozen per capita. There was little indication that the health-consciousness craze that had swept the United States in recent years had cut much into sales; industry observers and company officials attributed this in part to doughnuts being an affordable indulgence and the tendency of many people to treat themselves occasionally.

The dominant and longtime industry leader was Dunkin' Donuts, with worldwide 2000 sales of $2.32 billion, 5,200 outlets, and close to a 45 percent U.S. market share based on dollar sales volume. According to data compiled by Technomic, a marketing research specialist in foods, doughnut chains in the United States had combined sales of $2.73 billion in 1999, of which $2.1 billion was accounted for by Dunkin' Donuts—a 77 percent market share based on sales revenues of all doughnut chains. No other doughnut chain had as much as a 10 percent market share in 1999, and the big majority of fresh-doughnut makers were local mom-and-pop bakeries and supermarket bakeries whose products were mostly undifferentiated with regard to product quality. Overall growth in doughnut sales had been quite small the past five years.

In recent years, a proliferation of bakery departments in supermarkets had squeezed out many locally owned doughnut shops and, to some extent, had constrained the growth of doughnut chains. Doughnuts were a popular item in supermarket bakeries, with many customers finding it more convenient to buy them when doing their regular supermarket shopping than to make a special trip to a local bakery. Doughnut aficionados, however, tended to pass up doughnuts in the grocery store, preferring the freshness, quality, and variety offered by doughnut specialty shops. Most patrons of doughnut shops frequented those in their neighborhoods or normal shopping area; it was unusual for them to make a special trip of more than a mile or two for doughnuts.

Small independent doughnut shops usually had a devoted clientele, drawn from neighborhood residents and regular commuters passing by on their way to and from work. A longtime employee at a family-owned shop in Denver said, "Our customers are very loyal to us. Probably 80 percent are regulars."[2] Owners of independent shops seemed to believe that new entry by popular chains like Krispy Kreme posed little competitive threat, arguing that the market was big enough to support both independents and franchisers, that the Krispy Kreme novelty was likely to wear off, and that unless a doughnut franchiser located a store close to their present location the impact

---

[2]Quoted in "Dough-Down at the Mile High Corral," *Rocky Mountain News*, March 25, 2001, p. 1G.

would be minimal at worst. A store owner in Omaha said, "Our doughnut sales increased when Krispy Kreme came to town. We benefit every time they advertise because doughnuts are as popular as ever."[3]

KRISPY KREME'S CHIEF COMPETITORS

Dunkin' Donuts

Dunkin' Donuts was the largest coffee-and-baked-goods chain in the world, selling 6.4 million donuts and 1.8 million cups of coffee daily. The chain was owned by British-based Allied Domecq PLC, a diversified enterprise whose other businesses included the Baskin-Robbins ice cream chain, ToGo's Eateries (sandwiches), and an assortment of alcoholic beverage brands (Kahlúa, Beefeater's, Maker's Mark, Courvoisier, Tia Maria, and many others). In 2000 the Dunkin' Donuts chain had annual sales of $2.32 billion, 5,200 stores worldwide, 3,600 U.S. outlets, and comparable store sales growth of 7 percent. In New England alone, Dunkin' Donuts operated 1,200 stores, including 600 in the Greater Boston area, where the chain was founded in 1950 and where a Krispy Kreme franchisee was in the process of opening 16 stores.

Compared to Krispy Kreme, Dunkin' Donuts put more emphasis on coffee and convenience. According to one Dunkin' Donuts executive, "People talk about our coffee first. We're food you eat on the go. We're part of your day. We're not necessarily a destination store." Roughly half of all purchases at Dunkin' Donuts included coffee without a doughnut.[4] The Dunkin' Donuts menu included doughnuts (50 varieties), muffins, bagels, cinnamon buns, cookies, brownies, Munchkins doughnut holes, cream cheese sandwiches, nine flavors of fresh coffee, and iced coffees. In areas where there were clusters of Dunkin' Donuts outlets, most baked items were supplied from centrally located kitchens rather than being done on-site.

The nutritional content of the chain's 50 doughnut varieties ranged between 200 and 340 calories, between 8 and 19 grams of fat, between 1.5 and 6 grams of saturated fat, and between 9 and 31 grams of sugar; its cinnamon buns had 540 calories, 15 grams of fat, 4 grams of saturated fat, and 42 grams of sugar. Whereas Krispy Kreme's best-selling original glazed doughnuts had 210 calories, 12 grams of fat, 4 grams of saturated fat, and 13 grams of sugar, the comparable item at Dunkin' Donuts had 180 calories, 8 grams of fat, 1.5 grams of saturated fat, and 6 grams of sugar. Several Dunkin' Donuts customers in the Boston area who had recently tried Krispy Kreme doughnuts reported that Krispy Kremes had more flavor and were lighter.[5]

Dunkin' Donuts had successfully fended off competition from national bagel chains and Starbucks. When national bagel chains, promoting bagels as a healthful alternative to doughnuts, opened new stores in areas where Dunkin' Donuts had stores, the company responded by adding bagels and cream cheese sandwiches to its menu offerings. Dunkin' Donuts had countered threats from Starbucks by adding a wider variety of hot-and-cold coffee beverages—and whereas coffee drinkers had to wait for a

---

[3]Quoted in "Hole-ly War: Omaha to Be Battleground for Duel of Titans," *Omaha World Herald*, September 7, 1999, p.14.

[4]According to information in Hermoine Malone, "Krispy Kreme to Offer Better Coffee as It Tackles New England," *Charlotte Observer*, March 16, 2001.

[5]"Time to Rate the Doughnuts: Krispy Kreme Readies to Roll into N.E. to Challenge Dunkin' Donuts," *The Boston Globe*, February 21, 2001, p. D1.

Starbucks barista to properly craft a $3 latte, they could get coffee and a doughnut on the fly at Dunkin' Donuts for less money. Quick and consistent service was a Dunkin' Donuts forte. Management further believed that the broader awareness of coffee created by the market presence of Starbucks stores had actually helped boost coffee sales at Dunkin' Donuts. In markets such as New York City and Chicago where there were both Dunkin' Donuts and Krispy Kreme stores, sales at Dunkin' Donuts had continued to rise. In commenting on the competitive threat from Krispy Kreme, a Dunkin' Donuts vice president said:

> We have a tremendous number of varieties, a tremendous level of convenience, tremendous coffee and other baked goods. I think the differentiation that Dunkin' enjoys is clear. We're not pretentious and don't take ourselves too seriously, but we know how important a cup of coffee and a donut or bagel in the morning is. Being able to deliver a great cup of coffee when someone is on their way to something else is a great advantage.[6]

In 2000, Dunkin' Donuts began opening tri-brand stores in partnership with sister businesses Baskin-Robbins (for ice cream) and ToGo (for sandwiches).

Winchell's Donut House

Winchell's, founded by Verne Winchell in 1948, was owned by Shato Holdings Ltd. of Vancouver, Canada. There were approximately 600 Winchell's units located in 10 states west of the Mississippi River, along with international franchises in Guam, Saipan, Korea, Egypt, Saudi Arabia, and New Zealand. Winchell's had 110 restaurants in Southern California, a market that had about 1,600 doughnut shops and a market that Krispy Kreme had recently entered. To combat Krispy Kreme's entry into Southern California, Winchell's launched a Warm 'n Fresh program as a pilot in seven California stores. The pilot program called for fresh, glazed doughnuts in display cases to be replaced every 15 to 20 minutes between 6 A.M. and 9 A.M. daily; a flashing red light on display cases signaled that a fresh batch of glazed doughnuts was available. Starting in June 1999, Winchell's rolled out a modified Warm 'n Fresh concept to all outlets, offering customers a Warm 'n Fresh doughnut between 6 A.M. and 11 A.M. daily. Consideration was being given to expanding the hours of the Warm 'n Fresh program.

As of May 2001, a "Winchell's dozen" of 14 doughnuts sold for $5.99 and a double dozen (28) sold for $9.99. Winchell's bakery offerings included 20 varieties of doughnuts, 14 flavors of muffins, croissants, bagels (breakfast bagel sandwiches were available at select locations), éclairs, tarts, apple fritters, and bear claws. It served three varieties of its "legendary" coffees: Dark Roast Supreme, Legendary Blend and Legendary Decaf, all using only 100 percent arabica beans (considered by many as the finest coffee beans in the world). Other beverages included cappuccino, frozen cappuccino, soft drinks, milk, and juices.

In 2000 Winchell's began an expansion program in six U.S. cities where company sales were strong to recruit fast-food franchises to add Winchell's kiosks to their stores. Winchell's had already succeeded in getting kiosks into Subway sandwich shop franchises in Las Vegas and several Blimpie's Subs and Salads in Southern California. In Los Angeles, Winchell's had opened kiosks inside 11 Lucy's LaundryMat locations. Winchell's also offered co-branding partners the option to add a full-blown Winchell's World Donut Factory, as opposed to a Winchell's Express. One of the cities chosen for

---

[6]As quoted in Hermoine Malone, "Krispy Kreme to Offer Better Coffee As It Tackles New England," *The Charlotte Observer*, March 16, 2001.

Winchell's co-branding effort was Omaha, Nebraska, where two Krispy Kreme locations had recently opened. The Omaha Krispy Kreme franchisee was not planning additional Omaha stores but was adding convenience store customers, supplying them with nightly deliveries from the two existing Omaha locations.

A second co-branding initiative involved featuring Hershey's chocolate in some of Winchell's doughnuts and muffins. A third initiative Winchell's had in the works was introducing a Winchell's Lighter Side line of low-fat doughnuts, muffins, and bagels. It was also considering bringing back its traditional glazed and jelly doughnuts, which were 40 percent smaller than the sizes presently offered.

Winchell's corporate goal for the next five years was to triple its sales.

Tim Hortons

Tim Hortons, a subsidiary of Wendy's International, was one of North America's largest coffee-and-fresh-baked-goods chains, with more than 1,900 stores across Canada and a steadily growing base of more than 120 locations in key markets within the United States. In Canada, Tim Hortons was regarded as something of an icon. The chain was named for a popular Canadian-born professional hockey player who played for the Toronto Maple Leafs, Pittsburgh Penguins, and Buffalo Sabres; Horton was born in 1930, started playing hockey when he was five years old, and died in an auto accident in 1974.

Most of the stores were franchised operations. The chain specialized in coffee and fresh baked goods (doughnuts, bagels, muffins, coffee cakes, cakes, and cookies) but had recently added specialty coffee drinks, soups, stews, chili, and deli-style sandwiches to its menu lineup to increase lunchtime traffic and broaden customer appeal. Plans were in place to introduce fresh-baked baguettes in 2002. One of the chain's biggest drawing cards was its special blend of fresh-brewed coffee, which was also sold in cans for customers' use at home. About half of the purchases at Tim Hortons included coffee without a doughnut.

Tim Hortons locations ranged from full standard stores with in-store baking facilities, to combo units with Wendy's and Tim Hortons under one roof, to carts and kiosks in shopping malls, highway outlets, universities, airports, and hospitals. Most Tim Hortons full standard locations offered 24-hour drive-through service. Tim Hortons promoted its full standard stores as neighborhood meeting places and was active in promoting its products for group fund-raisers and community events. The chain opened its 1,000th store in 1995 and its 2,000th store in December 2000. Tim Hortons was named "Company of the Year" for 2000 at *Foodservice & Hospitality* magazine's Pinnacle Awards.

Executives at Tim Hortons did not feel threatened by Krispy Kreme's expansion into Canada and those parts of the United States where it had stores (Michigan, New York, Ohio, Kentucky, Maine, and West Virginia). According to David House, Tim Hortons president, "We really welcome them. Anyone who draws attention to doughnuts can only help us. It is a big market and a big marketplace. I would put our doughnut up against theirs any day."[7] The Tim Hortons outlets in the United States had reportedly been quite successful, and House believed that the real war for doughnut supremacy was already being waged on U.S. soil. A Canadian retailing consultant familiar with Tim Hortons and Krispy Kreme said, "This is the Canadian elephant and the

---

[7]Quoted in "Can Krispy Kreme Cut It in Canada?" *The Ottawa Citizen*, December 30, 2000, p. H1.

U.S. mouse. Listen, if there's anything where Canadians can kick American butt, it is in doughnuts."[8] Another Canadian retailing consultant said, "It [Krispy Kreme] is an American phenomenon. These things are sickeningly sweet."[9] Hortons planned to add 33 outlets in the United States during 2001, upping its total to 155.

Canada was reputed to have more doughnut shops per capita than any other country in the world. Aside from Tim Hortons, other chains in Canada featuring doughnuts included Dunkin' Donuts, Robin's Donuts, Country Style, and Coffee Time.

LaMar's Donuts

Headquartered in Kansas City, Missouri, LaMar's was a small, privately held chain that had doughnut shops in Missouri, Kansas, Nebraska, Colorado, Nevada, New Jersey, and Alabama. Ray LaMar opened the original LaMar's Donuts shop in 1960 on Linwood Avenue in Kansas City and quickly turned it into a local institution. On a typical day, lines started forming before 6:00 A.M. and, by closing time, about 11,000 doughnuts would be sold. Based on the doughnut shop's success and reputation, Ray and his wife Shannon decided in the early 1990s to franchise LaMar's.

Hundreds of LaMar's devotees applied for the limited number of franchises made available in the Kansas City area; 15 were granted over a few months. Given the success of Kansas City franchising effort, the LaMars concluded their concept could expand beyond the confines of Kansas and Missouri and made plans to take LaMar's Donuts to the next level. In 1997, Franchise Consortium International, headed by Joseph J. Field, purchased majority interest in LaMar's Franchising, renamed the company LaMar's Donuts International, and began laying the groundwork for a national expansion program scheduled to reach its peak in about 2008. LaMar's planned 35 stores for the Denver area alone by 2006, versus 5 that were on the drawing board for Krispy Kreme. In mid-2001, Lamar's had 29 store locations in 22 cities and plans for nearly 500 stores by late 2004. Its stores were typically located along neighborhood traffic routes.

LaMar's utilized a secret recipe and its doughnuts were "artisan quality," being handmade daily with all-natural ingredients and no preservatives. Day-old doughnuts were never sold at the shops but were donated at day's end to the needy. In addition to 20 varieties of doughnuts, LaMar's menu included coffee and cappuccino. LaMar's had recently partnered with Dazbog Coffee Company in Denver, Colorado, and created over a dozen customized specialty coffee blends under the "LaMar's Old World Roast" label. Beans were handpicked from Costa Rica and then slow-roasted in an authentic Italian brick fire oven. Coffee products at LaMar's shops included cappuccinos, espressos, lattes, iced coffee drinks, and chai teas. Exhibit 10 shows Lamar's lineup of baked goods and nutritional information for each product.

The company used the tag line "Simply a better doughnut." Joe Fields said, "People come in and try the product and they are surprised. They are wowed, in a very different way than Krispy Kreme. They say, 'Oh my god, this is the best doughnut I've had in my life.'" The *Zagat Survey*, a well-known rater of premier dining spots nationwide, described LaMar's Donuts as "extraordinary; fit for kings." *Gourmet* magazine, in search of the country's favorite doughnut, conducted a nationwide poll; the winner was a LaMar's doughnut.

---

[8] Quoted in ibid.
[9] Quoted in ibid.

exhibit 10 Nutritional Content of Selected LaMar's Doughnut Products, 2001

Product	Calories	Calories From Fat	Total Fat	Saturated Fat	Cholesterol	Sodium	Carbohydrates	Sugars
Ray's Original Glazed Donut	220	90	10g	2.5g	0mg	260mg	31g	13g
Chocolate Iced LaMar's Bar (Unfilled)	540	200	22g	6g	0mg	440mg	81g	49g
Cinnamon Twist	770	240	26g	7g	0mg	1190mg	120g	32g
Old Fashioned Sour Cream Donut	420	160	18g	4.5g	15mg	380mg	60g	40g
Cherry Filled Bizmark	550	170	19g	5g	0mg	560mg	88g	45g
Apple Fritter	650	230	26g	7g	0mg	1020mg	91g	13g
Cinnamon Roll	690	220	25g	6g	0mg	1020mg	106g	30g
Raisin Nut Cinnamon Roll	850	240	27g	6g	0mg	1020mg	137g	62g
Chocolate Iced LaMar's Bar (White Fluff Filled)	810	320	35g	9g	0mg	460mg	120g	85g
Ray's Chocolate Glazed Donut	290	100	11g	3g	0mg	260mg	44g	25g
White Iced Cake Donut	320	160	17g	4.5g	0mg	320mg	38g	23g

Source: LaMar's Donuts International, Inc., 2001.

case 15 PFS: Daisytek's Growth Strategy

Neil W. Jacobs
Northern Arizona University

Kathryn S. Savage
Northern Arizona University

Mason S. Gerety
Northern Arizona University

Scott Ramsey
Software Architects

> Our view of PFS in the early days was that you pour something in the top of the Daisytek fulfillment engine and dollars spit out the botttom. Well, what we found as we built PFS is that every deal has its unique aspects.
> —Chris Yates, Senior VP–Business Development

> When we present PFS to a potential client, we have to be aggressive, stretch our capabilities to the limit, and sell our capabilities. Then, when people begin to nod their heads in agreement that—by golly—what you do is really good and you have a deal, then, reality checks in and you start to talk about how to get it done. Some things may not be easy to do, but then you do it. We view the impossible as something to get done.
> —Steve Graham, Senior VP and Chief Information Officer

On November 6, 1996, Daisytek president and CEO Mark Layton; senior vice president and chief information officer (CIO) Steve Graham; and senior vice president for business development Chris Yates met to discuss Daisytek's largest-ever proposal to provide distribution services for a client. Only a month earlier, they had begun working on the proposal. Now, it was time to finalize key decisions because their bid was due November 7. The decision to bid was significant: If successful, this contract would dramatically increase the size of Daisytek's outsourcing subsidiary and could be the springboard for Daisytek's growth strategy. Their discussion revolved around four questions. Given the limited information they had on the customer's operations, how aggressive should they be? How much risk could they afford to take? How much cushion should they build into the proposal? Could their organization respond to the unforeseen surprises and problems that were likely to occur?

---

exhibit 1   Daisytek Quarterly High and Low Stock Prices

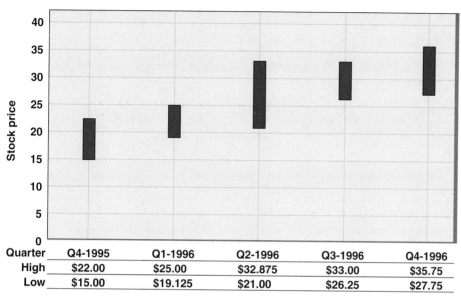

Quarter	Q4-1995	Q1-1996	Q2-1996	Q3-1996	Q4-1996
High	$22.00	$25.00	$32.875	$33.00	$35.75
Low	$15.00	$19.125	$21.00	$26.25	$27.75

Fiscal year quarter
(Fiscal year-end March 31)

DAISYTEK INTERNATIONAL

Founded in 1977 as a manufacturer of paper-handling products for Daisywheel print-ers, Daisytek subsequently became a major reseller of computer supplies. In 1982, ISA, a European distributor of computer supplies, acquired Daisytek but split it off three years later when ISA's founder, David Heap, purchased Daisytek's stock. Subse-quently, Heap shifted the firm's business to the sales and distribution of office con-sumables. By 1996, Daisytek served more than 24,000 customer locations in more than 50 countries. The company went public in January 1995 and completed a second stock offering in 1996. (Quarterly stock prices from January 1995 through March 1996 are shown in Exhibit 1.) In recent years, Daisytek had experienced dramatic growth, with sales escalating from $4.3 million in 1981 to over $464 million in 1996 (see Exhibit 2). Net income in 1996 was $10.8 million—an amount more than one and one-half times the 1995 net income of $6.5 million. Total assets were $128.6 million in 1996 com-pared with $94.4 million in 1995.

In 1996, Daisytek expanded its lines of business with a subsidiary, Priority Ful-fillment Services (PFS), in order to provide services to firms who wanted to outsource part, or all, of their sales and distribution functions. Cliff Defee, vice president of op-erations for PFS, explained the value-added provided by PFS to its outsourcing clients:

> We will take the telephone calls, interface with the customers, do the selling on an inbound basis, administer the product, warehouse it, pick, pack and ship everything in the cus-tomer's name. We even answer the phone in the customer's name. We are a virtual infra-structure.

Mark Layton described the environment at Daisytek as one that "encourages strategic and creative thinking, risk-taking, teamwork, and a commitment to quality."

exhibit 2   Daisytek Revenue

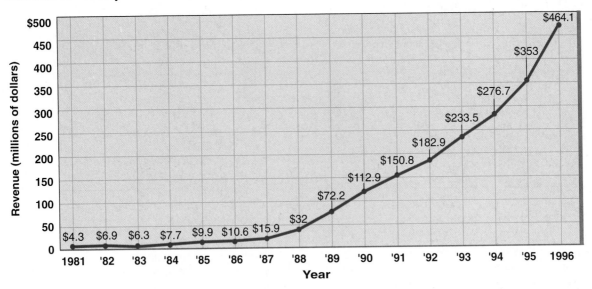

Daisytek considered itself the world's leading distributor of computer and office automation supplies and accessories, such as ink-jet and toner cartridges, diskettes and
other data storage media, copier supplies, and printer ribbons.

THE INDUSTRY

Daisytek's primary business—the distribution of computer and office-automation consumables—was part of a generally healthy and growing industry with reported sales of
$14 billion in 1995 and projected sales of $25 billion by the year 2000.[1] Growth in the
industry had been fueled by the increasing amount of automation in the workplace and
by changes in the technology of printing—most notably by the shift from dot matrix to
color ink-jet printers. Ninety percent of the lifetime cost of ownership and use for dot
matrix printers was equipment cost; consumable supplies accounted for only 10 percent of total cost. In contrast, only 32 percent of the lifetime cost of a color ink-jet
printer was equipment, and 68 percent of total cost was spent on consumables. Industry projections predicted that by the year 1998, worldwide sales volume from printer
consumables would exceed worldwide sales volume from printer hardware.

In spite of the fact that market growth was expected to continue, competition in the
industry was fierce, margins were low, and the industry had undergone significant restructuring. According to Mark Layton, the customer base for Daisytek and its competitors changed dramatically as chain stores such as Office Depot, Office Max, and
Staples replaced independent mom-and-pop office products dealers. Another major
customer group, contract stationers, had also consolidated, significantly reducing the

---

[1]Business Products Industry Association and BIS strategic decisions.

number of independent entities that delivered office products on demand to local customers. Mark Layton summarized the industry changes:

> Every market in the U. S. had a contract stationer, and over the last couple of years there has been a big play to roll up all the contract stationers in big towns. So, the top 300 of our large customers, these contract stationers, have been bought by five companies within the last five years.

The restructuring caused serious difficulties for distributors who were bypassed, as the "big players" were able to buy directly from manufacturers. Layton continued:

> Office Depot got direct contracts with HP, Canon, Lexmark, Epson from day one, primarily because the manufacturers wanted their hardware in those stores, and supplies were part of the package. So the superstores grew and crushed many of our bread-and-butter customers and converted business that was going through wholesale distribution back to manufacturer direct distribution.

Although more than 250 distributors competed with Daisytek in the U.S. market, the company's chief rivals were divisions of three larger corporations—Micro United, Ingram Micro, and Abitibi-Price.

Micro United, Computer Supplies Division of United Stationers

Micro United was a U.S. wholesaler of computer products and services, whose stock was traded on the NASDAQ. The firm sold a variety of business products, including furniture, facilities management supplies, and computer supplies with their own proprietary brands of key products. Corporate net sales for 1996 totaled $2.3 billion. The firm operated 41 computer-driven distribution centers in 31 states and used a fleet of 350 trucks as well as UPS for deliveries.

Ingram Micro, Computer Products

Ingram Micro was a worldwide distributor of microcomputer products—the largest in the world—whose corporate net sales for 1995 totaled $8.7 billion. Its stock had been traded on the New York Stock Exchange since the firm's initial public offering in 1996. The firm operated in 19 countries, but resellers in 120 countries handled its products. Distribution centers were located in the United States, Mexico, Canada, Singapore, Malaysia, and across Europe.

Azerty Division, Abitibi-Price Inc.

Abitibi-Price was a Canadian company whose major line of business was forest products, including newsprint. The firm's Azerty Division distributed office products in North America and western Europe. Corporate sales for 1996 totaled $2.6 billion (Canadian), of which $647 million (Canadian) were from the Azerty Division.

Daisytek estimated that it had the largest share of the wholesale distribution market for nonpaper consumables and imaging supplies, with most of the balance split among its three major competitors. Both the competing units of United Stationers and Ingram Micro sold broader product lines than Daisytek, offering "one-stop shopping" for all office needs; the Azerty Division of Abitibi-Price offered a range of products slightly broader than Daisytek's, distributing computer peripherals as well as consumables. All

exhibit 3   Dupont Analysis of Daisytek and Its Three Main Competitors

Competitor	ROE (net income/ equity)	Leverage (assets/ equity)	Return on Assets (net income/ assets)	Asset Turnover (sales/assets)	Profit Margin (net income/sales)
United Stationers	39.90%	14.64	2.73%	2.07	1.32%
Abitibi-Price	9.30	2.24	4.16	1.04	4.02
Ingram Micro	13.41	4.08	3.29	3.57	.92
Daisytek	20.84	2.49	8.37	3.61	2.32

Source: Annual reports of companies shown.

three competitors followed the pattern of conventional distributors: Products were bought from original equipment manufacturers (OEMs) and supplies manufacturers and resold to office product dealers, computer resellers, office product superstores, mail order companies, and mass merchandisers.

Profit margins in the industry were low. Exhibit 3 provides financial ratios for Daisytek and the three primary competitors of Daisytek. One significant motivation for becoming an outsourcing provider was a possible increase in margin. Daisytek's management believed that they could leverage their cost advantages in distribution through PFS and significantly increase margin, even in the short run. Although they were only able to guess at prospective profit margins for PFS, they hoped for an increase in Daisytek's 2.3 percent existing margin to near 6 percent for PFS.

DAISYTEK'S BUSINESS STRATEGY

Although the major players in the markets in which Daisytek competed had chosen different product mixes, all faced fierce competitive pressures because of the changing nature of the industry. As a strategic response to the competition, Daisytek focused on distributing "trailing edge" products with "leading edge" technology. The firm's 1996 annual report explained:

> We define "trailing edge" products as consumables that are less dependent on new technology introductions and more dependent on the existing installed base of office automation machines. Just as the razor uses many blades, these machines use numerous consumables for many years. As a result, these products are less likely to "go out of style" or become obsolete.

The company's mission statement reinforced management's commitment to maintaining Daisytek's competitive edge and market position:

> Daisytek International will be a low-cost, high-growth distributor and outsourcing services provider. We will dominate our chosen markets by embracing change, maximizing profitability and efficiency for our customers and ourselves, and constantly pursuing quality solutions . . . and we'll have fun doing it.

Overall, the company measured its operating performance in terms of service, productivity, and error-free operations. Two critical performance measures were service level, measured by cycle time per order, and order accuracy (lack of errors). Accuracy and productivity were expected to increase while exceptional service continued to be a company hallmark.

Part of Daisytek's ability to compete on a cost basis came from a strategic alliance with Federal Express (FedEx). In 1992, management negotiated a very favorable FedEx rate for the firm—an action that was coupled with the opening of a Memphis superhub to centralize the firm's distribution activities near FedEx's terminal. (FedEx employees actually worked in the Daisytek distribution center, weighing outgoing packages.) The proximity of FedEx, the favorable rate, and technologically sophisticated call center and distribution systems allowed Daisytek to provide low-cost, fast service.

Daisytek's top management team was committed to using technology to lower cost and improve service quality. Still, in the long run, the overall effect of these efforts on profitability was problematic. The future profitability of the firm was constrained by the increasingly competitive battle for market share in the office consumables industry and the decreasing marginal return that could be realized from efficiency efforts. Mark Layton was not content to "ride the industry out as it matured." His long-run strategy was to alter the basic Daisytek business model with PFS to leverage the infrastructure already present in Daisytek, and to branch out of the office consumables industry by providing outsourcing services to firms in a variety of industries.

DAISYTEK'S GROWTH STRATEGY— PRIORITY FULFILLMENT SERVICES (PFS)

The PFS outsourcing services initiative was triggered by financial goals and a perceived opportunity to build on Daisytek's capabilities. In the long run, Mark Layton believed that the computer consumables distribution industry would continue to experience substantial margin pressures. Daisytek had been able to maintain margins (see Exhibit 4; complete financial statements are included in Exhibit 5) by effective use of technology and a focus on high-margin product lines; however, as Layton explained:

> We knew we were coming to the end of what we could gain from operational improvements based on technology. One of the primary motives behind PFS was to find a business that would give us higher margin capabilities, a better way to take the infrastructure that we had in place to the market, and keep our gross margins up. We wanted to stay at that premium margin. PFS was developed because we are continually striving to find margin opportunities. (See box below.)

Initial PFS Deals: Telescoping Golf Clubs and Nursing Bras

For the first year and a half, Daisytek did what Mark Layton describes as Donkey Kong deals, in which an inventor lacked the money to mass-market a new product. The inventors ran ads in magazines or on late-night TV, and Daisytek handled the 800-number response calls. The initial deals were for small, undercapitalized companies. Mark Layton recalled two of the more humorous undertakings:

- The telescoping golf club was collapsible and had a removable club head that you could carry in a little yellow pouch. The inventor was marketing these clubs in magazines to golfers who wanted to practice while they were on the road. It fit our weight characteristics perfectly. He made about 3,000 of them. We shipped about two and ended up giving the others away.

- After that, we were into nursing bras and breast-milking kits and mats for Lamaze classes. It was the first time the Lamaze organization had ever allowed its name to be used in a product-licensing arrangement, and this inventor approached us for help in distributing these items. I think we sold four.

exhibit 4 Overview of Daisytek Operations

Daisytek Revenue and Profit (thousands)				
	1995	1996	Q1 1997	Q2 1997
Sales	$352,963	$464,169	$138,148	$136,894
Gross profit	36,971	47,970	13,589	13,670
Net income	6,496	10,767	2,955	3,041

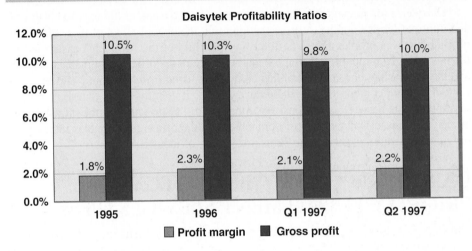

Profit margin effects of the traditional Daisytek distribution business and the PFS outsourcing business could differ dramatically. With the traditional distribution business, the company had to fight other distributors for market share. Increasing sales in the distribution market provided Daisytek a gross margin of somewhere between 8 and 10 percent, and ultimately a profit margin before taxes of about 4 percent. In contrast, Layton described the PFS model:

> In the PFS model we end up with 100 percent of the business, but we don't own the inventory or receivables. We physically possess the inventory, but we don't own it. Therefore, our accountants allow us to recognize revenue equal to our fees (instead of the sales value of the product). In the PFS model, we bid our outsourcing services as a percent of revenue. This "transaction" fee thus becomes our revenue. Our costs are typically about 50 percent of that fee. The beauty of this model is that we make a bit more money and see the impact this has on our financial statements. The returns generated by this type of business are infinite. I can go to Wall Street showing return on capital numbers in the 50 percent to 60 percent range, whereas in the computer supply business, we are at 18 percent to 19 percent. So, in addition to having a model that is financially attractive to investors, we don't have the risk of ownership. We are just being paid for our intellectual value.

Layton viewed the future of PFS from a supply chain perspective.

> The superstores, such as Sam's Club, exist today because they believed wholesale distribution was a redundant step that was not required. PFS is value-added; so manufacturers find that it is considerably cheaper for us to use our existing technology and small package distribution capabilities to service thousands of phone calls than it is for them to handle calls themselves.

In some cases, the attractiveness of PFS was heightened by the fact that, in addition to the direct costs of starting its own distribution centers, many manufacturing

exhibit 5   Daisytek International's Consolidated Statements of
Operations and Balance Sheets, 1995–96
(dollar amounts in thousands, except per share data)

	March 31	
	1996	1995
Income Statement Data		
Net sales	$464,169	$352,953
Cost of sales	416,199	316,982
Gross profit	47,970	36,971
Selling, general, and administrative expenses	29,024	23,260
Income from operations	18,946	12,711
Interest expense	1,482	2,050
Income before income taxes	17,464	10,661
Provision for income taxes		
Current	6,460	4,470
Deferred	237	(305)
Net income	$ 10,767	$ 6,496
Net income per common share	$1.59	$1.17
Weighted-average common share outstanding (000)	7,757	5,542
Assets		
Current assests		
Cash	$ 204	$ 408
Accounts receivable, net	69,169	51,099
Employee receivables, net	571	599
Inventories, net		
Inventories, excluding PFS	44,358	32,249
Inventories, PFS	0	0
Prepaid expenses	2,120	343
Deferred taxes	762	999
Total current assets	117,184	85,697
Property and equipment	15,631	10,686
Less—accumulated depreciation	(6,136)	(3,906)
Net property and equipment	9,495	6,780
Employee receivables	395	367
Excess of cost over assets acquired, net	1,527	1,577
Total assets	$128,601	$ 94,421
Liabilities and shareholders' Equity		
Current Liabilities		
Current portion of long-term debt	$ 650	$ 571
Trade accounts payable	44,726	28,187
Accrued expenses	4,230	3,052
Income tax payable	419	908
Other current liabilities	10,486	9,552
Total current liabilities	60,521	42,270
Long-term debt (less current portion)	16,419	11,334
Shareholders' equity		
Preferred stock, $1.00 par	—	
Common stock, $.01 par	63	62
Additional paid-in capital	30,874	30,796
Retained earnings	21,736	10,969
Cumulative foreign currency translation adjustment	(1,012)	(1,010)
Total liabilities and shareholders' equity	$128,601	$ 94,421

divisions were burdened with corporate investment-related overhead. Often, large manufacturers did not have any idea what it cost them to do things because their information systems did not provide detailed information on distribution costs. Experience indicated that the performance of managers of product fulfillment units in large firms was often evaluated on their direct costs plus a corporate overhead charge of 4 or 5 percent; cost as a percentage of revenue for handling product fulfillment internally might be as much as 15 percent. As an alternative, they could outsource to PFS for substantially less, never get burdened with the overhead, and end up looking very good.

Top management was convinced there was major growth potential in outsourcing. Further, they were convinced higher margins were available by providing outsourcing services. Beyond continuing to use technology to improve cost and service competitiveness in its core business, Daisytek's long-term strategy was focused on the PFS initiative.

IMPORTANCE OF B2B AND B2C E-COMMERCE

Both business-to-business (B2B) and business-to-consumer (B2C) e-commerce were important to Daisytek. As a reseller that operated between product manufacturers and wholesalers and retailers, Daisytek was an intermediary in B2B business. To remain competitive as a distributor to resellers and retailers, Daisytek's costs and the services provided had to yield advantages over those offered by competitors. PFS was subject to the same competitive pressures as Daisytek. To the extent that PFS added clients who were resellers like Daisytek, the effects of B2B developments would be increased.

PFS was also in the B2C business. Clients such as IBM and HP used PFS's service to supply consumers in the name of IBM or HP. To these consumers, the fact that PFS was providing the service was not evident. For this reason, PFS in particular stood to benefit from the growth of B2C e-commerce through clients seeking to do B2C e-commerce without adding the logistics capabilities that PFS could provide. The emerging B2C market fueled by the Internet was an important development supporting PFS's strategy.

COMPETITION FOR PFS

As Daisytek pursued the PFS initiative, there was little direct competition for the full range of services that PFS offered. Potential entrants into the business of fulfilling orders and handling customer service functions for e-commerce enterprises included

- Daisytek's primary competitors, namely Micro United, Ingram Micro, and Azerty.
- Other traditional wholesalers, both inside and outside the computer supplies product industry.
- Direct marketers (e.g., Fingerhut).

The relative strengths of all these firms were (1) their experience providing fulfillment services for their own businesses and (2) their size advantage over Daisytek. The smallest was five times the size of Daisytek. Also, if PFS's profitability projections were valid, new firms might be formed to compete with PFS.

OVERVIEW OF DAISYTEK AND PFS OPERATIONS

One of the things that PFS has helped Daisytek understand is that PFS not only sells surplus Daisytek capacity, it crafts solutions. Now we know that the solutions must contain a reasonable component of the core engine; otherwise, we have to start over with each new client, and we can't afford to do that.
—Chris Yates

exhibit 6   Overview of Daisytek Operations

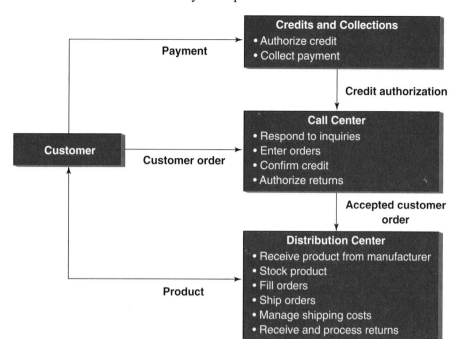

Daisytek operations included closely coordinated systems and processes that handled all transactions from the taking of a customer's order by phone to collecting payment. Specifically, the tightly integrated processes allowed PFS employees to perform the following activities for its clients:

1. Accept customer orders by phone, simultaneously process credit authorization, and enter the order into Daisytek's information system.
2. Generate picking tickets, packaging, and freight instructions at Daisytek's semi-automated Memphis Distribution Center.
3. Route packaged orders so orders placed by 8:30 PM would be assured delivery via Federal Express the next day.
4. Handle any follow-up queries from customers.
5. Bill customers and collect accounts receivable.
6. Provide performance reports to clients.

The operational units that performed these activities included call center operations, credit and collections, and the distribution center. Exhibit 6 highlights the activities performed by each unit and illustrates the relationship of the operational units to customers. In addition, sales worked with prospective clients, provided consultation, developed proposals, negotiated business agreements, and managed client relationships; information technology provided information systems and communications support.

PFS piggybacked on Daisytek's operations by doing much of its work in a shared environment. For example, a call center operator might answer the telephone as Daisytek one time and IBM the next. Daisytek's information systems allowed operators to keep each transaction tied to the appropriate business (e.g., Daisytek or IBM) while gaining the necessary efficiencies and economies of scale by combining Daisytek's own business with all of the business handled through PFS. The relationship between the client, the client's customer, and PFS is diagrammed in Exhibit 7. A comparison of the differences

exhibit 7   Priority Fulfillment Services, Inc. (PFS) Outsourcing Relationship*

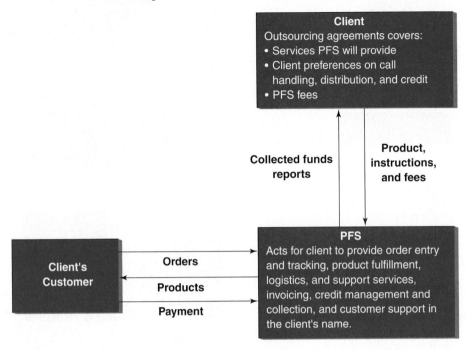

*PFS is a wholly-owned subsidiary of Daisytek International Corporation.

between in-house and outsourcing operations for the client and the client's customers is shown in Exhibit 8.

Top management at Daisytek believed they could use the PFS fulfillment engine as a springboard into a major position in the outsourcing services market. They also hoped to capitalize on a deal with IBM, which Daisytek had landed in 1996. CEO Mark Layton recalled:

> Once IBM decided to outsource the manufacturing and distribution for printing supplies, they came to us as a potential distribution partner. Although it didn't turn out to be the size of deal that we expected, it is a nice contract for us, and we make good money out of it. More importantly, however, is that having IBM as a customer put PFS on the map.

A MAJOR OPPORTUNITY FOR PFS—BASF

> In outsourcing, timing means everything. My personal view on outsourcing is that people are a lot more likely to consider the possibility of outsourcing if they are financially forced to do it. People typically don't go to their organization and reengineer the whole thing un-less they have to. In a lot of cases, this seems to come either early or late in the lift cycle of the business. Early in the life cycle, the incentive is to avoid investment in infrastructure, and late, the incentive is near desperation, that is, unless we do something we are on the road to nowhere right now.
> —Chris Yates

In late 1996, Mark Layton was approached by representatives of the U.S. division of BASF, a German company that manufactured and marketed data and video recording media. In the United States, BASF had built a large sales, marketing, support, admin-

exhibit 8   Operational Differences When a PFS Client Uses PFS

Activity	Before Using PFS	When Using PFS
Contacts with client's customers, including order placement, inquiries, and so forth	Client does internally	PFS call center performs these activities with no difference perceivable by the client's customer.
Order processing, including response to inquiries, order entry, confirmation of credit, and authorization of returns	Client does internally	PFS call center and distribution center perform these duties in the client's name according to the outsourcing agreement.
Distribution center operations, including product receipt, stocking, order filling and processing, packing and shipping, management of shipping costs, and returned items processing	Client does internally	PFS distribution center performs these operations.
Credit and collections, including authorization of credit, collection of payments, follow-up on overdue accounts, and management of bad debt allowance	Client does internally	PFS credit and collection department performs these operations according to client's instructions with no perceivable difference by the client's customer.
Management information system (MIS)	Client provides and maintains own information systems infrastructure and systems for product fulfillment operations	Client interfaces with PFS systems on desired performance measures, but infrastructure is provided by PFS and transactions are processed using PFS customized systems.

istration, and distribution organization, which included its own information systems department.

Unfortunately, the American divisions were losing millions of dollars annually, and the parent company planned to close down this operation. In an attempt to cut costs and save the U.S. operations, two of BASF's U.S. vice presidents came up with the idea of outsourcing to eliminate the U.S. infrastructure. Ultimately, two former sales divisions were spun out to the two vice presidents as independent firms with exclusive U.S. sales agent rights for BASF media products. As part of their restructuring, the two new owners brought in PFS and a competitor to bid on outsourcing.

Although sales projections for the divisions were not provided, the bidders knew that sales for the previous year were about $110 million. To Daisytek, the chance to increase revenue by the amount of PFS's outsourcing fee on $110 million of product shipments, and contribute 50 percent of that fee to gross profit, was exciting. Mark and his top management team began a crash project to develop a bid proposal.

Developing an Outsourcing Proposal: The Role of Organizational Units

Finding the information on which to base a bid is extremely difficult because those who are in charge of a business that is being outsourced probably won't go out of their way to tell you what their real costs are or to tell you how you can improve on what they are already doing.
—Chris Yates

Developing the outsourcing proposal for BASF involved considerable uncertainty, as Daisytek knew from prior experience. Like many prospective clients, BASF had scant or spotty information on the activities being outsourced. As Chris Yates remembered, this presented a challenge:

> They [BASF] asked us to guarantee freight at a set percentage of revenue, a number that only they knew or claimed to know. Other data were suspect, to say the least. The one thing that we knew was that they had sales of about $110 million the year before.
>
> We thought of the deal in two phases. First, capital investment to cover starting up the services, e.g., racks for the warehouse or computer terminals at their end. Second, processing transactions that represented an ongoing cost. Because of other difficulties in understanding the exact nature of these transactions, we decided to bid this project on a percentage of revenue basis.

The short time frame for the bid made a quick response imperative and limited the opportunities for information gathering. Yates continued:

> They [BASF] had to scramble to shift fulfillment services to an outsourcing firm. This discussion was taking place in November 1996; and the go date was January 1, 1997. After that, support from the parent company in Germany would cease, and the U.S. support people would be jobless.

Chris Yates and the bid team from PFS had to compile relevant cost data before they could create a bid. A number of the organizational units—call center, credit and collections, the distribution center, and IT—had to provide input, though everyone understood that these cost estimates were inexact. Information regarding the role and cost structure of each major unit needed to be analyzed before Chris could formulate a complete bid. He began with call center operations.

CALL CENTER OPERATIONS

Call center operations processed customer orders, handled order status inquiries, and provided technical assistance, depending on the agreement with the client. The call center had evolved over the prior four years. It began as an order-taking or message center desk. In its second year, automatic call direction call-handling technology was introduced to create an inbound call center with increased operational speed. Employees were trained on call-handling processes, urged to answer the phone in less than 12 seconds, and encouraged to handle 18 calls per hour. In year three, skill-based routing of incoming calls (where calls were routed to specialists who dealt with specific customer transactions) was added to establish what Daisytek called a customer-care center. Finally, a customer service center was added to help clinch the sale.

Developing an Outsourcing Proposal for Call Center Operations

Martin Anderson, vice president for call center operations, explained the process for developing a bid proposal at PFS:

> First, we start with estimates of projected revenue and numbers of transactions over time, and we determine how many transactions will fall out of the projected revenue. Then, we identify specific types of transactions or services that we have to provide.

We have a standard template of basic assumptions that we refer to as our call-handle model. From the assumptions and the client's data, we formulate call-handling scenarios. We establish the call-handling characteristics, e.g., the different types of calls and the length of each one by type. This tell us, for example, whether we need a 7 × 24 (7-day, 24-hour) operation for this customer, or a 5 × 8. It depends on the client's needs and determines how many call handlers we will need.

One cost driver is the services we must provide, such as order-taking, product advice, and technical support. Another is how quickly we must answer a call. Our goal is to answer 90 percent of our calls in 30 seconds. How quickly we answer the phone, the nature of the calls we handle, and the number of phone or Internet orders all affect cost.

Donna Barnes, manager for call center inbound operations, elaborated:

We'll actually go through a role-play for each type of call to find out how much time it takes to take an order, handle a return, or whatever. Then, we have Wizmo calls, our name for calls asking, "Where's my order?" We go through each type of call and estimate the time each takes. We also determine how many calls of each type we can anticipate.

Martin Anderson continued:

The call-handling matrix is the basis for call center production costs. The components are labor, long distance, and special initiatives the client wants. Long-distance cost is a cost per minute for servicing an account. Then, we factor in all the special initiatives the client selects, such as how many calls that client wants us to monitor for quality purposes. We do a random sampling of 30 to 40 percent, depending on what the client chooses.

Martin Anderson's cost estimate for the BASF bid was detailed by the month and by the call or order. Martin assumed 4,000 calls per month to support 2,000 orders. Of these 2,000 orders, he assumed 300 would be placed by phone, using significant operator time, and 1,700 would be placed by fax, following one or more phone calls from the customer. From these assumptions, Martin estimated BASF phone costs and included incremental fixed overhead costs.[2] Martin used these activity levels and costs to provide Chris Yates the estimated call center costs shown in Exhibit 9. Costs shown in Exhibit 9 did not include the labor component, assumed to be 60 percent of the costs of the phone system.

CREDIT AND COLLECTIONS

Chris Yates also needed cost data from the credit and collections department. This department authorized credit, set up new accounts, invoiced clients' customers, processed payment receipts, called delinquent accounts, and managed collection of accounts receivable. John Lagerman, credit manager, supervised a staff of five.

Developing an Outsourcing Proposal for Credit and Collections

For a bid like BASF, even though PFS would not own the receivables, a major collection cost would be time and effort expended on collection of bad accounts. Because PFS would inherit most accounts from BASF, solid information on BASF's receivables

---

[2]Incremental fixed overhead costs refer to those costs that are incremental for the BASF bid but fixed with respect to volume; that is, they are independent of the number of calls handled or orders processed.

exhibit 9   BASF Bid—Estimated Monthly Costs for Call Center

Activity	Monthly Assumptions	Average Monthly Cost	Cost per Call	Cost per Order (1,700 fax, 300 voice)
Phone system				
"800" setup	Monthly service fee	$ 98	$0.0245	$0.049
"800" calls	4,000 @ 4 min. @ .19	3,040	0.76	—
Dedicated fax	1,700 inbound calls	140	0.082	0.082
Call center				
Incremental fixed costs		12,852	3.21	6.43

and delinquent debt would significantly improve the quality of the bid; however, this information was not available from BASF. In addition, PFS would need to evaluate potential new customers. As John Lagerman explained:

> When I make credit decisions, I want to base them on the financial welfare of the company. I focus more on things like cash flow and less on things like references. They may have 10 great references but if their business is not producing positive cash flow, if they don't have any banking arrangement that provides for cash flow, we will not be paid on time. We look at their business trends. If we have the last three years' financial data, we can analyze it and examine some of their key ratios.
>
> We go through the credit approval process for all new customers and then review accounts as they approach their credit limit. Periodically, we may have a customer whose balance is $180,000 on a credit limit of $200,000, and they have an order for $70,000. At this point, we check to see if they are financially able to handle it. We look at financial information and cash flow and call their bank to see if they have a revolving line of credit. If we have their credit limit at $200,000 and they have a $2 million open line of credit with the bank, then they are using only $1.8 million of their total line of credit. From a cash flow perspective, I'm reassured.

John assessed whether the existing staff would be able to handle the increased workload. A few costs were relatively fixed, such as reporting to the client, but most costs were variable and depended on the number of the client's customers. John tracked the productivity of his department and used this information to estimate the impact of a new client and whether additional staff would be required. Productivity could vary from one account to another because each outsourcing client provided guidelines for credit and collections to use with their customers. John continued:

> If we don't have better data from a prospective client, we use our averages as a basis. We know how many customers they have, and we decide whether we need an additional person to manage the increased workload.

John estimated costs for the BASF bid to include one new employee at $3,250 per month, plus miscellaneous incremental overhead costs of $1,700 per month that would be incurred to support the BASF contract.

DISTRIBUTION CENTER (DC)

Scott Talley, Daisytek's director of distribution, came to Memphis in 1992 after 18 months at headquarters working with Mark Layton on the issue of multiple versus single distribution centers. Dave Reese, PFS director of distribution, had worked at distribution facilities handling steel and then consumer products before he was hired at Daisytek in 1995.

Scott and Dave enjoyed trying to anticipate and resolve problems related to business growth and direction. Service, productivity, and errors were important watchwords in discussions of DC performance. Measurement reports addressed overall distribution center performance for each PFS customer and for each Daisytek customer group, as well as productivity and accuracy down to the individual level. Scott described the DC's mode of operation:

> We do 100 percent every day, in every department. If we get 80 (product) returns in—we do 80 returns today. If we get 1,000 receipts in—we do 1,000 receipts. To accomplish this, we must be sophisticated in how we schedule; our activity fluctuates widely, and it isn't unusual for us to have 100 percent volume fluctuations in some areas.

The distribution center was expected to ship, in a given day, 100 percent of all orders received before that day's evening cutoff. If the service commitments for a day were not met, then Talley had to call (usually after midnight) Mark Layton to inform him. Fortunately, this did not happen very often. As a result of the emphasis placed on service level, 99.5 percent of orders were shipped the same day they were received, which was an execution rate Daisytek believed was faster than many other distributors in the industry. Accuracy was vital, too. Routinely implemented in receiving, stocking, replenishment, and shipping, additional accuracy checks were built into the fill-and-packing line. In addition, an internal audit staff in the DC periodically checked 100 percent of a given customer's orders for accuracy to be sure that the shipment was correct.

Developing an Outsourcing Proposal for the Distribution Center

Operating costs were easily determined for the DC because most costs were driven by volume. The DC maintained inventories, filled and shipped orders, managed transportation arrangements and cost, and processed returns. Located in Memphis, Tennessee, the DC was established in 1992 to consolidate the multiple distribution centers that existed previously. Operating characteristics of the various departments were as follows:

Receiving   Although the DC operated 24 hours per day, 5 days per week, incoming deliveries occurred from midnight until 6 AM, with an average of 50 trucks arriving during the delivery period. Deliveries were sorted according to supplier in the receiving area. Then, each delivery was scanned by purchase order number, and receiving reports were produced to facilitate checking of deliveries before the items included were stocked. Workers confirmed they received only the items ordered, checked item counts, and recorded any discrepancies. Each palletted shipment received a locator sticker, and the bar code of items was scanned into the system. Pallets cost $7.90 each, and the shipping skids cost $7.60 each. Normally, items were stored at the most convenient open location. Receiving expected to hire some additional labor if PFS received the contract from BASF.

Order Filling   Semiautomated fill lines used Computer Identics' systems to read box bar codes and direct boxes to one of 17 filling zones. Stock attendants scanned the orders on the boxes and were directed by the "pick to light" system first to the proper row and then to the proper bin for filling. By pushing a button on the bin, the attendant told the system that the item was in the shipment. Passing the box bar code past the zone

exhibit 10   Estimate of Distribution Center Costs for BASF Bid

Item	Per Order
Receiving pallets	$ 7.90
Shipping truck skid	7.60
Returns processing	0.75
Replenishment	0.08
Supervision	2.25
Supplies (shrinkwrap, etc.)	3.35
Storage	5.00
Routine handling, clerical	3.75
Capital equipment	1.50
Subtotal	$32.18
Overhead (15%)	4.83
Total	$37.01

Note: Cost per order is based on an average order.

scanner, the attendant told the system that he was finished. Then the attendant pushed the box back onto the main flow conveyor. The box passed another scanner, which recognized the order by the box bar code, checked Daisytek's information system to see if the order was complete, and then routed the box to either additional stock zones or to packaging. If it was complete, box weight was recorded and checked against an expected standard for the contents of the order; if the weight was not within prescribed limits, the box was sent onto a special conveyor for problem resolution. To do all this for BASF, the DC expected it would need additional workers and supervision.

Packing   As each open box entered the packing area, an overhead camera photographed it to create a digital record. Next, a sensor that determined which packing line the box should take, popcorn or paper dunnage, depending on customer specification, recognized the box. Packing used supplies such as shrinkwrap, labels, and outer packaging. After packing, the order was weighed again, this time by FedEx employees working in the DC. Any shipment under 200 pounds was sent to one of the waiting FedEx trailers; anything heavier was routed to waiting freight carrier trucks.

All cost estimates from the DC had to include labor for returns processing, inventory storage, routine handling, clerical support, and a monthly capital equipment replacement charge. In addition, PFS customarily allocated an additional 15 percent of the costs of the distribution center as overhead. For the upcoming bid for the BASF contract, Scott Talley and Dave Reese estimated DC costs as detailed in Exhibit 10.

INFORMATION TECHNOLOGY (IT)

One particularly critical part of a successful outsourcing bid was the support provided by information technology (IT). The IT organization, headed by Steve Graham, Daisytek's chief information officer (CIO), created and provided information systems for the integration of clients' product distribution.

Daisytek utilized an IBM AS/400 platform and had five AS/400s worldwide. Three were located in Plano, Texas (including a Web server and data warehouse system), one was in Australia, and another was in Memphis, Tennessee. The distribution engine in

Plano mirrored its data to the Memphis system in real time. In Plano, one major AS/400 ran the distribution application for the entire globe; a second supported a powerful data warehouse that was used by Canada, the United States, and Miami for queries; and a third was a website server, which supported all international affiliates. The data-warehousing system allowed users to track their own accounts. As Steve Graham put it: "Thanks to the Internet, all websites and e-commerce can be run from one server."

Daisytek prided itself on its globally networked system, which allowed the company to sell products in Australia from Plano or to sell to India from Mexico City. Steve Graham described this:

> We can do this because we run the same system everywhere in the world. It allows us to service all clients uniformly. So I could do the same for BASF; all they have to do is get going. Our system easily accommodates growth and change. I'm on the right version of an excellent IT platform that I can adjust to expand several times over what it is now.

Developing an Outsourcing Proposal for Information Technology

Steve commented on the challenges IT faced with learning enough about prospective clients' operations and information systems to confidently develop a proposal.

> Ideally, there are hundreds of questions we should ask to be sure we fully understand the IT integration task when we take on a new outsourcing client. What kind of business is it? Who is going to take over; who is going to hold the product, ship it? How are we going to ship the product, and how are receivables to be handled? But this takes time, and you run the risk of scaring off the customer. The BASF proposal illustrates this struggle. From an I/S standpoint, I would be very comfortable with a very detailed statement of work. The customer isn't comfortable with buying off on that. BASF, for example, wants a very, very short, vague deal. They don't understand the mechanics of a true outsourcing deal, and putting them through a detailed statement of work is not feasible. Deliverables and milestones are lost on them. They just want to know what percentage of sales we require.

What will IT costs add to the BASF operation? On a monthly basis, over a 24-month window, Steve projected $3,500 per month for setup, conversion, test, and maintenance of required system support, but it all depended on the exact details of tasks to be performed, which were still unknown.

DECIDING WHAT TO BID

With the bid due the next day, Mark Layton, Chris Yates, and Steve Graham met to decide whether to offer a proposal for the BASF contract and, if so, how to price it. They had learned that at least one other firm, which they suspected was Azerty, was bidding on the BASF business.

Chris Yates was cautiously excited about the opportunity. He did feel some trepidation about the "softness" of the bidding process. Because BASF was eliminating the jobs associated with their North American operations, information about the actual scale of the operations, especially the costs of their in-house distribution system and freight expenses, had been sparse and incomplete. However, in spite of the fluid numbers, he knew the BASF project could provide an important boost to PFS, support its growth goals, and add to its credibility in the marketplace, if successful.

Steve Graham was wary about unforeseen surprises that would impair his IT organization's ability to support needed changes to information systems. Establishing

exhibit 11　Proposed Format for Structuring BASF Bid

Area	Estimated Cost for Handling $110 Million of Product Consisting of 2,000 Orders per Month	Percent of $110 Million
Call Center		
IT		
Distribution Center		
Credit and Collections		
Contingency		
Profit		
Total		

smooth-working information systems with a new firm was always a challenge from an operations and IT standpoint.

Because of the size of the BASF business opportunity and significance of PFS to Daisytek's growth strategy, Mark Layton wanted to present a bid, but he was uneasy about the information on which the bidding process was based and the possible impact on targeted profit margins. Meeting the PFS 50 percent profit margin target for this bid was important for Daisytek's strategy; however, given that PFS was operating at a significant information disadvantage, Mark felt a bid should include compensation for the inherent risk.

One thing was certain: The bid had to be submitted tomorrow. If a bid was offered, cost numbers had to be translated into a finished bid proposal, one that would assure a successful, profitable project for Daisytek.

Chris proposed the format for structuring the decision on the bid, shown in Exhibit 11.

Turning to Chris and Steve, Mark said, "Let's see the numbers."

case 16

Music on the Internet: Transformation of the Industry by Sony, Amazon.com, MP3.com, and Napster

Beatrix Biren
INSEAD

INTRODUCTION

Meet Joyce King a teenager and a sophomore in a liberal arts college. She is a smart young woman involved in many activities, including music and musicals in her college. Like any other teenager, she spends a great amount of time on the Internet. Lately Joyce indulges in a new hobby: She makes her own music CDs. She connects to various sites including MP3, downloads the music, writes them to a CD, and then plays them. Of course she would like to have an MP3 player for her next birthday so that she can play those music CDs on the MP3 player directly. Joyce cannot get all she wants free from MP3 sites, so she goes to the Sony Corporation's site and downloads music for which she has to pay. Although it "sucks" to pay, there is no other way to get these "cool" new songs!

Joyce's dad, Alex, a professor in a business school, is a conservative man. He surfs the Net a lot but stays mostly on the news and financial pages. He uses Amazon.com to buy books, and he occasionally uses Amazon.com for DVDs and music CDs. Alex likes buying from Amazon.com, because the price is right and there is no local sales tax—which is quite hefty. Also, he does not want to fight the mall parking.

Prepared under the supervision of Professor Soumitra Dutta and Luk Van Wassenhove, both of INSEAD. The support of Professor Alek Chakrabarti of the New Jersey Institute of Technology is gratefully acknowledged. Copyright © 2001, INSEAD, Fontainebleau, France.

exhibit 1   Deconstructing Musical Copyrights

Type of Right	Right
Performance rights	This right entitles the holder of a musical copyright to receive payment for almost any broadcast and public performance of that composition.
Mechanical rights	The right to reproduce musical works on sound recordings.
Synchronization or sync rights	The right to record music that is timed to the display of visual images in films or videotape soundtracks.

Alex and Joyce represent a growing number of people who are using the Internet to get their music. Not only has the Internet changed the distribution systems for music, but also it raises many different legal and ethical issues. Joyce and Alex have changed the business model for the music industry in many ways.

MUSIC INDUSTRY IN TRANSITION

Many industries could not exist without the protection of intellectual property laws such as patent and trademark. The piracy of copyrighted works can destroy industries. The music industry was challenged by the prospect of music distribution online; new formats such as MP3 allowed consumers to download music relatively swiftly and easily, and websites sprang up to service this content.[1]

The Internet could not change who owned the copyright of songs, films, or books, but it could radically alter how these works were distributed. While the legal control of music copying was straightforward, any attempt to control distribution raised more complex legal questions. Although courts and legislatures were quick to prevent and punish copyright theft, the protection of intellectual property had to be balanced with the needs of consumers and unsigned artists (see Exhibit 1 on deconstructing musical copyrights).

Hilary Rosen, president and CEO of the Recording Industry Association of America (RIAA), commented:

> Perhaps no other decade in history has contributed as much to the growth of the music industry as the 90s, the digital decade. Consumers are going digital; they are also going online. Compression breakthroughs have made it easy to quickly download and distribute music files. This distribution can allow customers to discover and follow new bands and to meet other fans with shared interests. The opportunities offered by the new technologies seem limitless for the music industry: fans, artists, and record companies. The challenge is that artists who produce the music are not taken advantage of.[2]

The $38 billion music industry had long been wary of threats from the Internet, especially the emergence of the popular MP3 format, in which files could be downloaded onto a personal computer and used on commercially available portable hi-fi. The International Federation of the Phonographic Industry (IFPI) saw this as a significant problem with enormous consequences for the development of a legitimate business model.

---

[1]Denis Kelleher, "Computimes: The Bandwagon Plays On—Litigation Shows Online Music Providers Won't Be Replacing the Record Companies Just Yet," *Financial Times*, July 17, 2000.
[2]www.riaa.com.

Columnist Darren O'Neill wrote in ZDNET News online:

> I love the MP3 format and in the long run it can be a good thing for the record labels, if they harness the technology correctly. We all heard how the cassette tape was going to kill tapes. We heard how recordable CDs were going to kill sales. We heard how VCRs were going to kill movie sales. Guess what? None of those happened! Neither will MP3 kill the music industry.

THE TRADITIONAL BUSINESS MODEL

The music industry was the quintessential illustration of the middleman. For artists to get their music into the local record shop, they had to pass through many layers—each layer taking a slice of the revenue (see Exhibits 2 and 3 for a description of the value chain). This is why less than $1, on average, of a $16 CD made it back to the artist.

Andrew Artherton said in the report "Music's Online Future,"[3]

> The "real-world" music stores and the current giants of the music industry will find themselves in the line of fire as the Internet squeezes out the middleman. Major labels will concentrate on volume marketing and promotion of an artist—their core competency. The role of the Internet will be discovering the artist.[4]

It is no secret that the music industry had been diligently fighting music piracy in the United States and around the world, but its slow pace in embracing new technologies and streamlining its own industry was the reason why the problem became so prevalent. Further compounding the problem was the fact that just a handful of companies dominated the music industry, largely controlling distribution and marketing channels. There were six major players: Bertelsmann, EMI-Capitol, Universal, Polygram, Sony Music, and Warner Music. These companies controlled distribution and marketing channels, making it an uneven playing field for smaller labels. Until music piracy began to substantially eat into that profit, there was little motivation to change the way the industry worked. In the absence of alternatives to buying what many consider overpriced music and limited sources, customers were creating their own alternatives. But so far, the financial impact seemed to be minimal. Indeed, according to the IFPI, the global music market was worth $38.5 billion—up by 1 percent in 1999 (see Exhibit 4).

It seemed that the music giants were aware of the possibilities and technologies, but were hesitant to embrace a digital system that would endanger the current retail model. Established music companies were avoiding the pain of adopting new commercial models that might displace some of their existing business. However, the Internet demonstrated its power to force change on even the most entrenched industries. Digital distribution became inevitable due to the Internet. Embracing it would open the doors sooner to new types of products delivered much more cost-efficiently and provide music lovers with true alternatives where previously there were none. The *Financial Times* stated:

> Ask record executives to describe their worst fear, and it would probably be the threat of artists breaking away from record labels to distribute their own music.[5]

---

[3]Study sponsored by Lucent Technologies, 1999.

[4]www.zdnet.com/eweek/news/.

[5]"Music Company Internet Fears Start to Come True: Online Distribution Rap Rebel Bypasses Record Labels," *Financial Times*, January 16, 1999.

exhibit 2   The Value Chain

The value chain is comprised of the following links in sequence: artists and repertoire development, recording, manufacturing, marketing, distribution, and retail. Recording, manufacture, and retail are frequently outsourced, even by the Big Five (EMI Recorded Music, Warner Music Group, BMG Entertainment, Universal, and Sony Music Group).

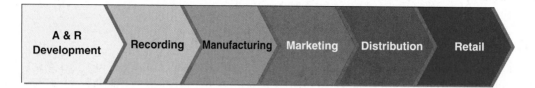

Artists and Repertoire (A&R) Development: Record labels advance all money necessary to develop bands and their music, to develop the musical repertoire, to promote and arrange concerts and tours, and to prepare all merchandising.

Recording: Major labels own and operate their own recording studios, although they may still outsource this link of the value chain. Costs derive from equipment and mixing.

Manufacturing: The physical manufacturing of a CD typically constitutes 10% of the total production cost. There are few CD manufacturers in the world, however, due to overcapacity, and costs remain reasonably contained in light of the limited number of competitors and the high barriers to entry. There is high seasonal variability in CD manufacturing, as pre-Christmas is typically a boom period.

Marketing: Marketing activities typically constitute 30% of the total production cost of a CD. Marketing costs are comprised of television and print advertising assaults upon the release of a new music or of new tour information and promotional events. Marketing costs may also include the preparation of music videos and public relations tours.

Distribution: This constitutes approximately 40% of the production cost of a CD. Distribution involves the packaging and physical transport of CDs from their place of manufacture to the distributor or directly to the retailer. One of the primary reasons that distribution costs are this high is that, because there are few manufacturing facilities in the world, delivery distances may be far. Additionally, as delivery is typically needed on short notice, costs are further elevated.

Retailing: The major labels and also the Internet superstores like Amazon.com and CDnow carry out these operations.

Source: BT Alex.Brown report on EMI Group, November 26, 1998.

THE NEW BUSINESS MODEL

The Internet had made it easier to acquire free or cheaper music by expanding the netizens' connectivity to a worldwide population. Beyond creating an alternative to the traditional dissemination of music, the Internet offered artists increased ease of exposure to the music-buying public. The low cost of entry and the possibility to communicate with an enormous market of potential consumers meant that there was increasingly little need for record labels, as artists themselves could produce and market their own music. For consumers the motivation to turn to the Internet was to hear artists they could not listen to on the radio (see Exhibit 5). A survey commissioned by the digital music distribution industry found that nearly 80 percent of respondents would buy more music if they had immediate information about the artist and title of the song; more than 60 percent would purchase more music if they could buy a song as soon as they hear it; more than 80 percent wanted to buy songs individually; and of

exhibit 3   Schematic Diagram for Music Distribution

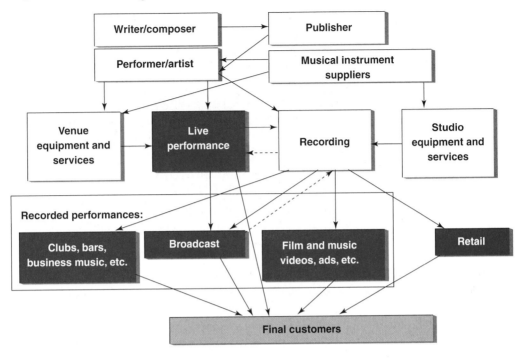

exhibit 4   Proportion of Value of World Recorded Music Sales by Geographic Area, 1999

Total = $38.5 billion

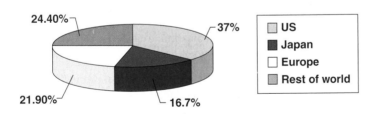

Source: Recording Industry Association of America website (www.riaa.com).

those who regularly listened to music on the Internet, one-third were more likely to purchase CDs in stores after hearing the music online.[6]

Music distribution on the Internet had taken two forms: (1) ordering via the Internet with delivery via mail and (2) direct digital downloading. In 1998, according to Music Business International's compilation of Market Tracking International data,[7] $143 million of music was sold through the Internet. While the proportion of this

[6]Dick Kelsey, "Online Music Leads to Offline Purchases," *Newsbytes*, June 15, 2000.

[7]Music Business International, "Digital Music Market Will Be Worth Dollars 4 bn," *Financial Times*, March 11, 1999, p. 5.

exhibit 5   Costs Involved in the Digital Distribution

Upload: Using Liquid Audio's programs designed for independent musicians to upload their music onto the Internet, we can identify the following costs. For between $60 and $250 per track (depending on the prominence of the resellers through which the artist wishes to sell his or her material), artists can upload individual tracks to the Liquid Audio network. For $495 plus a $39 monthly storage fee, artists can upload 100 megabytes of music (15 tracks, 65 minutes) to the Liquid Audio site, where this music will be sold directly to consumers. A larger version of the same program is available at $995 plus $69 per month. A popular San Francisco band named JoJo is currently selling its music in this fashion.

Direct Digital Download: These sites typically charge $1.00 per track downloaded ($8.99 per CD), approximately 50% less than the price of a CD at a conventional retailer. This new "transparency" is expected to drive down retail prices in the short term. However, mere MP3.com-type free download sites may not have a profitable future. The BBC quoted a British Phonographic Industry spokesman saying that free downloads were not expected by the BPI to be a profitable business.* Nor are 99-cent individual tracks.

---

*BBC, as quoted in the *Financial Times*, April 22, 1999.
Source: www.liquidaudio.com.

figure that was sold via direct download was not specified, it was anticipated that the overwhelming majority was merely through Internet retailing with mail delivery. The total Internet music sales figure was expected to increase to $4 billion in 2004. Internet CD sales for 1999 were expected to be 2 percent of all CD sales.[8] Indicative of a trend toward music download, portals revealed that approximately one of every five search requests of their portal were for MP3 tracks. Next to "sex," "MP3" was the most widely entered term in Internet searches.

The case will focus on Sony, a traditional record label; Amazon.com, one of the fastest-growing Internet superstores; MP3.com, a new entrant to the digital music industry; and Napster and Gnutella, both file-sharing networks, to understand the rapidly changing dynamics of the music industry.

SONY CORPORATION

Sony Corporation, founded in 1946 in Japan and headquartered in Tokyo, was a leading manufacturer of audio, video, communication, and information technology products for the consumer and professional markets. Its music, motion pictures, television production, computer entertainment operations, and online businesses made Sony one of the most comprehensive entertainment companies in the world. Sony was among the leading music companies in the United States and worldwide as well as among the leading audiovisual electronics and technology companies. Sony was engaged in the development, production, manufacturing, and distribution of recorded music, in all commercial formats and musical genres worldwide, through Sony Music Entertainment Inc. (SMEI) and, in Japan, though Sony Music Entertainment (Japan) Inc. (SMEJ).

Success in the music entertainment business was dependent to a large extent on the artistic and creative abilities of employees and outside talent, and was subject to the

---

[8]"Seagram Unveils Alliance with Bertelsmann Entertainment: Canadian Group Shares Soar on News of Internet Sales Venture with German Company," *Financial Times*, April 8, 1999, p. 13.

vagaries of public taste. Although SMEI was one of the largest recorded music companies in the world, its competitive position depended on its continuing ability to attract and develop talent that could achieve a high degree of public acceptance.

Sony had been one of the forerunners in musical equipment manufacturing. Twenty years ago, music listening was revolutionized by a pocket-sized 14-ounce dynamo—the Sony Walkman® personal stereo. Since its introduction, the Walkman portable stereo had been a huge product and marketing success. In fact, led by the Walkman, Sony created a new industry of personal entertainment. Millions of portable stereos have been sold. In fact, Sony Walkman personal stereos (cassette, compact disc, and Minidisk) sales approached 100 million in 1999.[9]

The MP3 Threat

MP3 was the popular (but unofficial) current standard for digital music transmission, but had not been accepted by record labels because MP3 offered no antiprivacy protection.[10] Invented in 1997, it compressed digital audio information to a size that made it relatively practical to send over the Internet, and hundreds, perhaps thousands, of websites offered free MP3 music files ready for downloading. Software that played MP3 files, with names like WinAmp and FreeAmp, was available on the Internet, and the Netshow software in Windows 98 included an MP3 player. MP3 offered near CD-quality sound and compressed music tracks to 1 megabyte per minute of music. A three-minute song could be downloaded via a 56kbps modem in approximately eight minutes. Many websites were offering free MP3 copies of music released by the major recording companies. Ordinary music CDs were digital master copies that could be easily copied or turned into computer-sound files. Performers, songwriters, publishers, and recording companies received no income when computer users downloaded those files. On college campuses in particular, where many students had fast Internet access, music in the MP3 format was extremely popular. To students, the MP3 movement was an innocuous exciting fad that promoted musicians and their music to audiences that might otherwise never be exposed to them.

Other digital distribution technologies existed (see Exhibit 6) that either did not allow free downloading or could place a security feature in the offering. These all conformed on some level with the traditional model of music that was run by the record labels.

Sony's Reactions to MP3

A few years ago, it would have raised eyebrows for a manufacturer of any product to compete with its dealers by opening an online retail store. However, with the rising percentage of the CDs sold over the Internet in the United States, the leading music companies and record labels were promoting joint ventures and creating a series of Internet sites to promote and sell music. Sony had started to distribute music through the Internet. Single songs were available at prices from $1.73 to $2.60. This was significantly cheaper than CD singles distributed through the stores at an average price of $9.

---

[9]www.sony.com.

[10]MPEG Layer 3, known as MP3, is a digital audio format for quick-downloading files that sound almost as good as CDs. With an MP3 player, you can listen to free or very cheap music downloaded from the Web. With a ripper and an encoder, you can create your own MP3 files from CDs that you own. Then you can transfer the MP3 files into a portable player and take the music with you anywhere you go.

exhibit 6   Digital Distribution Technologies Available

MP3: MP3 is an abbreviation for MPEG1, audio layer 3. It is a music compression standard meeting the audio quality requirements set by the Motion Picture Experts Group. Thomson Multimedia and Fraunhofer Institute own the patents to the digital compression technology utilized by the MP3 format. While MP3 is the popular (but unofficial) current standard for digital music transmission, it has not been accepted by record labels because MP3 offers no antiprivacy protection. MP3 offers near CD-quality sound and compresses music tracks to one megabyte per minute of music. A three-minute song can be downloaded via a 56k modem in approximately eight minutes.

MS Audio 4.0: Microsoft is one of various software manufacturers that have created an alternative to MP3. Microsoft claims that the recently released MS Audio 4.0 offers higher quality sound than does MP3 and compresses files more effectively (allowing faster download). This format is yet unproven. In addition, Microsoft is building a sophisticated back-end system into Windows 2000 that will be able to encrypt, manage, and track digital files as they are passed from one user to the next over the Net.

Liquid Audio: This is another alternative to MP3, offering protection and acoustic quality. This format is significantly slower to download than MP3, taking approximately 15 minutes to download a three-minute song via a 56k modem. Liquid Audio recently announced an initiative to develop hardware with Texas Instruments for handheld devices that play downloaded music files.

A2B: This is an alternative format recently introduced by AT&T's Bell Labs. It is not yet widely utilized as a compression and transmission standard.

VQF: This compression technology creates files that are approximately 30% smaller than the benchmark MP3 format, and its proponents claim the sound is noticeably better, especially in the treble range. VQF files are compressed at a 1/18 ratio, while MP3 is at 1/11. Nippon Telegraph and Telephone developed the VQF format, officially named Twin VQ, several years ago. NTT licenses the technology to Yamaha for the SoundVQ player and the Solid Audio portable player. VQF's proprietary status could be its biggest drawback, as software developers have to comply with one company's licensing terms if they want to build products for it.

Madison Project: IBM is working with five major record labels to test its Madison Project platform, the details of which are yet to be disclosed.

In an attempt to counter the MP3 threat, Sony Corporation announced the development of new copyright management technologies that could revolutionize the way in which digital music content was delivered, used, and enjoyed. The company planned to promote the solutions to the music and technology industries and propose them to the Secure Digital Music Initiative (SDMI) to study various copyright protection technologies. Sony engaged in a number of technologies to counter the piracy issues (see Exhibit 7).

"As a company which has strong commitments to both electronics and entertainment, Sony enthusiastically supports the mission of the Secure Digital Music Initiative. We respect the rights of artists and other copyright holders and look forward to providing a comprehensive copyrights management solution that will expand the entire audio market and offer our customers new ways to enjoy digital music content,"[11] stated Ted Masaki, deputy president of Sony Corporation of America.

Sony's efforts were welcomed by the Recording Industry Association of America (RIAA). In a press conference,[12] leaders of the RIAA and chief executives of the five major recording companies said they would work with major technology companies to

---

[11] Sony press release, Tokyo, February 25, 1999.

[12] www.riaa.com.

exhibit 7   Copyright Protection Technologies Used by Sony

Super MagicGate employs network servers that handle content distribution, secured payments, and other functions as well as compliant products, such as PCs, portable player/recorders, and IC recording media. Features include:

Authentication and Content Encryption: Before music content is transmitted between products, authentication is conducted to ensure that both devices are compliant. If authentication is successfully completed, protected content can then be transferred and recorded in an encrypted format. This provides robust protection against the unauthorized accessing, copying, and distributing of digital music content.

Flexible Usage Settings: Super MagicGate accommodates flexible usage settings that give content providers more choice in setting conditions under which digital music content can be provided and enjoyed. For example, promotional tracks could be limited to a single playback whereas other content could be played back freely, a certain number of times, or over a limited playback period.

Active Rights Management: Usage and billing settings can be changed even after content has been delivered. For example, users could choose to purchase a music track after sampling it once for free or users could receive a limited playback version of a song for upgrade to unlimited playback at a later date.

Offline Usage Management: Super MagicGate provides for offline tracking of usage and payment information. This allows flexible content usage and active rights management features to be applied to content enjoyed on portable audio player/recorders and products that are not directly connected to a network.

Other Copyright Protection: The development of MagicGate, OpenMG, and Super MagicGate is just one part of Sony's efforts to develop and implement appropriate copyright protection technologies for various types of digital AV content.

Sony is also promoting the 5C DTCP (Digital Transmission Content Protection) method, a bus encryption technology for use across the i.LINK (IEEE1394) digital interface that supports existing copy protection and serves as an important link in a secure digital content delivery chain that can be used for a broad range of applications, including network, broadcast, and package media. In addition, Sony supports the video watermarking technology for digital content developed and promoted by the Galaxy Group. Video watermarks are capable of surviving digital-to-analog and analog-to-digital conversions as well as various types of video processing, including compression. This versatile technology offers potential applications both as a playback control mechanism and a means of identifying the origin of digital AV content.

Each of these technologies offers a different layer of protection that is best suited to certain types of digital content and/or certain applications. Sony intends to promote the adoption of various different copyright protection measures to be used either separately or in combination.

Source: Press releases at www.sony.com.

develop the SDMI (see Exhibit 8), which sought to get the recording, electronics, and computer industries to adopt a unified standard for the delivery of music over the Internet. This standard would let copyright owners control the distribution of their music while making it available for sale. The initiative intended to create technological specifications for music distribution that would be encouraged to suggest approaches to digital music security and to work together to establish and document an open architecture and specification and for protection music.

As Hilary Rosen, the CEO of RIAA, said:

Those companies have been reluctant to sell music directly through the Internet for fear of piracy. We need copyright protection but we must not stifle technology to get it. They would be likely to include copy protection (limiting the number of copies that can be made), encryption (a way of making sure that only an authorized consumer can play back

exhibit 8   Secure Digital Music Initiative Mission Statement

The mission of SDMI is to enable consumers to conveniently access music in all forms, artists and recording companies to protect their intellectual property, and technology and music companies to build successful businesses in their chosen areas.

To accomplish this goal, SDMI will actively help develop an open and interoperable means for providing security for copyrighted music in all existing and emerging digital formats and their respective delivery channels.

Led by members of the worldwide recording industry, SDMI will create the SDMI Forum, which is an open body of companies involved in digital music. Forum members will be invited to bring their individual approaches to the task of developing an open music security architecture and specification. The companies will work together to make their varying products and solutions interoperable. The final specifications will be available to all interested parties.

Initiative rationale

The worldwide recording industry recognizes that many companies are developing approaches and solutions to provide security for music that is digitally distributed via CD, high-density disc, the Internet and other means.

For example, some companies are currently working to develop standards for high-density discs, which may become the medium for the next generation of music. Others are launching marketplace trials for the digital distribution of music, which may open a new marketplace for the consumption of recorded music.

The technologies and standards involved in these initiatives provide an opportunity to positively impact the security of copyrighted music. However, there is also a risk that the marketplace will develop with incompatible products and services, which would be detrimental to consumers, artists and recording companies. SDMI will build upon and harmonize these ongoing efforts, as well as deal with other issues not currently being addressed.

The goal is to encourage a marketplace of interoperable products that will benefit consumers and spur innovation.

Source: www.riaa.com/tech/sdmimis.htm.

the music) and watermarking, which would show the source of the music, a way to trace back pirated music to its source. Whether consumers would be buying individual songs, full albums or other formats would be up to recording companies and musicians once the standard has been accepted.[13]

As a leading entertainment company, Sony also tried to take advantage of opportunities in consumer electronic devices. In 2000, it introduced a digital music player, Music Clip, that could be a PC peripheral. Consumers could download music files from the PC to the Music Clip and play it later. This device used software that converted MP3 files into a different format that could be protected from copying. The secure music download was ensured by Sony's Open MG copyright protection technology, which was compliant with the SDMI guidelines.

AMAZON.COM[14]

Amazon.com, online since 1995, is a name that had become synonymous with Internet bookselling. More than just a place to find and buy a book, Amazon.com was the place to find a seemingly endless number of reviews and interviews claiming to cover more

---

[13]www.riaa.com.

[14]The description of Amazon.com is taken partially from the company website (www.amazon.com) and partly from 10-K documents filed with the SEC (www.sec.gov/edgar).

than 4.7 million books, music CDs, videos, DVDs, computer games, and other titles at discounts of up to 40 percent. A proven technology leader, it offered its customers a superior shopping experience by providing value and a high level of customer service. The Web could offer attractive benefits to customers, including greater selection, convenience, ease of use, competitive pricing, and personalization. Customers entering Amazon.com websites could, in addition to ordering books and other products, purchase gift certificates, conduct targeted searches, browse highlighted selections, view best-seller lists and other features, read and post reviews, register for personalized services, participate in promotions, and check order status. The key components of Amazon.com's offering included browsing, searching, reviews and content, recommendations and personalization, 1-Click technology, secure credit card payment, and availability and fulfillment (see Exhibit 9). Amazon.com's websites promoted brand loyalty and repeat purchases by providing an inviting experience that encouraged customers to return frequently and to interact with other customers.

Amazon.com expanded its product offering beyond books with the June 1998 launch of its music store. In the third quarter of 1998, its first full quarter of online music sales, Amazon.com became the number one online music seller. Amazon.com reported sales of $1.3 billion in 1999. In DVD and video products, sales reached $250 million.[15] The online distribution of music was expected to rise to $3 billion in 2001 from $200 million in 1998. Amazon.com was the market leader, with 40 percent market share, while its closest rival, CDnow, held only a 20 percent market share.

Competition

The online commerce market was rapidly evolving. In addition, the retail book, music, and video industries were intensely competitive. Amazon's current or potential competitors included online booksellers and vendors of other products such as CDs, videotapes, and DVDs. There were also a number of indirect competitors, including Web portals and Web search engines, such as Yahoo! and AOL, that were involved in online commerce either directly or in collaboration with other retailers, publishers, distributors, and retail vendors of books, music, videos, and other products—including Barnes & Noble, Inc., Bertelsmann AG, and other large specialty booksellers and media corporations, many of which possessed significant brand awareness, sales volume and customer bases—and traditional retailers who sold, or who might sell, products or services through the Internet. In addition, there had been a series of consolidations and alliances in this industry that involved players in various segments of the value chain (see Exhibit 10).

As an early-stage online commerce company, Amazon.com had an evolving and unpredictable business model, whereas many of its current and potential competitors had longer operating histories, larger customer bases, greater brand recognition and significantly greater financial, marketing, and other resources. Customer functionality requirements, preferences, and technology in the online commerce industry were changing rapidly. Competitors often introduced new products and services with new technologies. With the emergence of new industry standards and practices, Amazon.com had to continuously respond to these changing technologies on a cost-effective and timely basis.

The Amazon Advantage Program

The Advantage Program was designed to increase the visibility and sales of titles from artists and labels. It offered artists a compelling solution to the problem of securing widespread distribution of their work. It allowed them to sell their music at

---

[15]www.amazon.com.

exhibit 9 Key Components of Amazon.com's Service Offerings

Browsing: The Amazon.com sites offer visitors a variety of highlighted subject areas, styles, and special features arranged in a simple, easy-to-use fashion, intended to enhance product search and selection. In addition, the website presents a variety of products and services and topical information. To enhance the customers' shopping experience and increase sales, the company features a variety of products and services on a rotating basis throughout the stores.

Searching: A primary feature of Amazon.com websites is their interactive, searchable catalogs of more than 4.7 million books, music CDs, videos, computer games, and other titles. The company provides a selection of search tools to find books, music, videos, and other products based on keyword, title, subject, author, artist, musical instrument, label, actor, director, publication date, or ISBN. Customers can also use more complex and precise search tools such as Boolean search queries. The company licenses some of its catalog and other information from third parties.

Reviews and Content: The Amazon.com stores offer numerous forms of content to enhance the customer's shopping experience and encourage purchases. Various types of content are available for particular titles, including cover art, synopses, annotations, reviews by editorial staff and other customers, and interviews by authors and artists.

Recommendations and Personalization: Amazon.com personalizes its products and service offerings. These features include greeting customers by name, instant and personalized recommendations, best-seller and chart-topper listings, personal notification services, purchase pattern filtering, and a number of other related features. The company believes that personalization of a customer's shopping experience at the company's websites is an important element of the value proposition it offers to customers and intends to continue to enhance its personalized services.

1-Click Technology: Amazon.com provides customers with a streamlined ordering process using 1-Click technology. If a customer has previously activated 1-Click functionality, he or she can place an order by clicking one button without having to fill out an order form. The customer's shipping and billing information is automatically referenced on the company's secure server.

Secure Credit Card Payment: Amazon.com utilizes secure server software for secure commerce transactions. It encrypts all of the customer's personal information, including credit card number, name and address, so that it cannot be read as the information travels over the Internet.

Availability and Fulfillment: Many of the company's products are available for shipment within 24 hours, others are available within two to three days, and the remainder are generally available within four to six weeks, although some products may not be available at all. Out-of-print books generally are available in one to three months, although some books may not be available at all. Customers can select from a variety of delivery options, including overnight and various international shipping options, as well as gift-wrapping services. The company uses e-mail to notify customers of order status under various conditions and provides links to shipping carriers so that the customers can track their shipments.

Return Policy: Within 30 days following the customer's receipt of an order, Amazon.com will provide a full refund for any book in its original condition; any Amazon.com recommended book in any condition; any unopened music CD, DVD, VHS tape, or software; or any other merchandise item in new condition, with its original packaging and accessories.

Source: www.amazon.com.

the Amazon.com store and to enjoy the same level of exposure as major artists and labels.

Commenting on the relevance of the program, Dara Quinn of Seattle's Rockin' Teenage Combo, Amazon.com's Advantage charter band, said:

exhibit 10   Alliances in the Music Industry

The industry shake-up resulting from the arrival of the Internet and the industry's failure to foresee the Internet's effect has forced existing players to ally with one another in self-defense. These alliances also offer a unique opportunity for new players to attain a substantial foothold in the "new" industry landscape. The Association of Independent Music (AIM) announced that it is seeking the alliance of software developers, media groups, and Internet service providers to create a digital music sales service. The *Financial Times* suggests that such an alliance is intended to help independent music labels (e.g., Beggar's Banquet) remain competitive against the major labels and to remain competitive against online retail giants such as Amazon.com.[*] Other such alliances are indicated below:[†]

1. IBM and Lycos set up an MP3 download site that was shut down by an injunction resulting from legal action initiated by the RIAA.

2. Lycos recently announced an alliance with Fast.no, one of the most complete FTPs specializing in downloadable music (claiming directions to over 100,000 music tracks).

3. Madison project is a multilabel (including the Big Five—see Exhibit 2) digital download initiative to be commenced and run by IBM beginning summer 1999.

4. BMG and Universal Music Group have created a joint venture to promote and sell music online. According the *Financial Times*,[††] the new entity (Getmusic.com) is intended to promote only the music of BMG and Universal artists, but will sell music from other labels as well. While music will initially be delivered by mail, Getmusic has indicated that it intends to direct download in the future as standards of encryption and download are established.

5. Sony Music and Time Warner have also announced the creation of a joint venture online music store called "Total E." Sony Music has also indicated that it is pursuing an online joint venture with the EMI Group.

6. The musician Alanis Morissette announced that she has transferred a partial interest in her Maverick Records to Musicmaker.com in exchange for an ownership interest there. This represents an artist/new intermediary alliance.

---

[*]"Microsoft Plans Internet Music," *Financial Times*, April 13, 1999, p. 10.

[†]Due to the speed at which the issues discussed in this report are developing, mergers, acquisitions, and other news occur on a daily basis. The alliances listed here are merely a sampling of current trends.

[††]"Microsoft Plans Internet Music," p. 10.

No matter how slammin' your band is, it is really hard to get distribution without being signed to a major label. Even if we could get our CDs stocked in stores in every city we play when we're on tour, who has the time and money to print and distribute all those CDs?

Finding the right customer for a CD was a challenge. In most music stores, shelf space was limited, with a focus only on the best-sellers. Not so at Amazon.com! With 16 music category areas and hundreds of best-seller lists, the CD had a better chance of finding its audience. Features like "If You Like This Artist" and "MoodMatcher" in the recommendation center also matched CDs to customers by their areas of interest. And by making it easy for customers to conduct searches by artist, CD title, song title, and label, Amazon.com made it easy for the artist to sell his or her CD.

Within one week of approval of the CDs, Amazon.com ordered copies from the artists and stocked them in their distribution center. It could scan the cover, prepare sound clip files, and put up the artists' information. It monitored inventory and, on the basis of the previous sales and the recent sales performance of the title, automatically reordered via e-mail when it got low. The artists did not even have to bother with invoicing or collecting. Amazon.com automatically paid for copies the month after they were sold. The artists also had the option of choosing the retail selling price of their album and the methods of payment.

The Amazon.com website explained its offering to the artists as follows:

> With Amazon.com, you can reach millions of customers, find the audience for your CD, and personally hand-sell your CD directly to customers. Join for free, and sell more music. Get the Amazon.com Advantage, and make it easy for millions of music fans worldwide to discover and buy your music. You'll never hear fans say "I couldn't find your CD anywhere" again! Now everyone everywhere who hears the buzz about your CD can get it with just a few clicks at Amazon.com.

MP3.COM

MP3.com was pioneering a revolutionary approach to the promotion and distribution of music. It used the Internet and file formats that make music files smaller to enable a growing number of artists to distribute and promote their music worldwide and to enable consumers to conveniently access an expanding music catalog. Consumers could search for, listen to, and download music. As the premier online Music Service Provider (MSP), the company was dedicated to growing the digital music space. It allowed users to access, manage, and listen to their personal music collection anytime and anywhere in the world, using any Web-enabled device or application.[16] The site claimed 300,000 daily visitors.

MP3.com CEO Mike Robertson described the growth of the new company:

> In a short span of less than a week, MP3.com is signing up about a hundred bands a day. Just the fact that it's adding almost two gigabytes of songs every day is a very big engineering challenge and a lot of the money is being spent on the engineering infrastructure to support this growth.[17]

At the New York Music and Internet Expo, Robertson said:

> When you look at record labels, they were dropping artists that were selling 200,000 CDs or less. That same artist can move to the Internet, sell 25,000 CDs in a year, make US$5 a CD, and make 125 grand. The record label model today only works with the multi-platinum and the platinum sellers and I think that's the beauty of the Internet—it has that potential to work for artists who sell fewer CDs.[18]

In January 1998, when Sequoia Capital, Idealab capital partners, and a few others invested $11 million in the startup MP3.com, the rush was on to find the player that would matter in the new world of downloadable music. The goal of the investors behind MP3.com was to make it the Yahoo! of music on the Web. Indeed, MP3.com had more than 10 million downloads; a chart-ranking system and artist sign-up areas served as guides. CEO Robertson gave this description of MP3.com's growth since the beginning of 1998:

> We started off with news, but fairly early on it became apparent that the content area was really where the opportunity was. And although 15 months ago the majority of the MP3 activity was the unauthorized, illegal songs, we thought that there would be a large number of artists and record labels that would really want to aggressively use MP3 to market and sell their music. We created a content area where artists and record labels could sign up to

---

[16]"MP3.com Nominated for Best Overall Music Site at Yahoo," *Financial Times*, July 21, 2000.

[17]www.mp3.com press release, July 24, 2000.

[18]www.mp3.com press release, July 10, 2000.

gain marketing and exposure and build their fan bases. And from there we moved on to CD manufacturing and distribution. We learned that a lot of artists wanted to sell CDs, but couldn't get over the start-up of having to order 500 CDs and getting them mastered. So we decided to offer a service where any artist in the world could manufacture and distribute CDs. There are no start-up fees or monthly fees to the artist; it's a non-exclusive arrangement and we don't take ownership of their master recording—unlike a traditional record label. We give them half of the money of the sale price of the CD right off the top for every CD they sell. It's a dramatically different program than artists would encounter if they signed with a traditional record label.[19]

In January 2000, the major recording companies sued MP3.com for violation of copyrights. However, in September 2000, the company had settled its copyright infringement lawsuit with four of the Big Five record companies: EMI Recorded Music, Warner Music Group, BMG Entertainment, and Sony Music Group. Included in the settlements were nonexclusive licensing deals that allowed MP3.com's service to stream songs from recently purchased CDs. Although financial details were not disclosed, the settlements and licensing fees would total millions of dollars in payments. The stock price traded as high as $64.63 and as low as $6.50 between September 1999 and September 2000. Labels profited from streaming their songs since they were not losing control of the products. Streaming songs to consumers also eliminated downloads and the sharing of files.[20]

Nevertheless, MP3.com strengthened its leadership position in the online digital music space by continuing to anticipate and deliver the music products and services that music fans looked for on the Internet. For its second quarter, ended June 30, 2000, the company had reached record levels in attracting artists and content to its site: Approved artists increased to over 81,000, and content reached 515,000 songs and audio files. The number of listens (songs delivered online, played, or saved) grew to more than 100 million during the second quarter. This made MP3.com clearly the destination for people to find music.[21]

NAPSTER

Napster was the world's leading file-sharing community. Napster's software application enabled users to locate and share media files from one convenient, easy-to-use interface. Although it stored files on users' PCs anywhere on the network, it held a central directory on its own servers. Users could log on to a central directory and identify the song they wanted, and the directory connected them with someone who had it. Files were then passed in a form of "peer-to-peer" sharing. Under this model, the Web no longer served as a network where information was deposited and withdrawn from websites. Rather, it allowed anyone to reach out to any other computer and get files from it. The Web transformed itself from an information bank to an electronic octopus. Napster also provided media fans with a vehicle to identify new artists and a forum to communicate their interests and tastes with one another via instant messaging, chat rooms, and hot list user bookmarks. The service had put its finger on precisely what online music consumers wanted: fast access to a comprehensive library of songs to download. The shortcomings of Napster were guaranteed file quality and virus protection.

---

[19]Interview with CNET news.com, June 13, 2000.

[20]CNET New.com, August 2, 2000.

[21]Press release, www.mp3.com, July 2000.

Napster founder Shawn Fanning said:

I believe the Naptser technology can help everyone involved in music—including artists, consumers, and the industry. New technologies can be a win-win situation if we work together on building new models, and we at Napster are eager to do so.[22]

The RIAA reached violently to Napster. It claimed that such software was a tool to pirate digital music. The RIAA sued Napster, claiming the music-sharing network encouraged copyright infringement by allowing people to swap songs for free. The RIAA also claimed that Napster harmed the industry by slowing CD sales.

A study issued by research firm Jupiter Communications Inc. revealed that, on the contrary, users of Napster software were more likely to buy more records than non-Napster users. Jupiter surveyed more than 2,200 online music fans about their purchasing habits. The only group that wasn't likely to increase its music spending was that of the 18- to 24-year-old cashstrapped, computer-savvy user. Jupiter analyst Aram Sinnreich said:

Because Napster users are music enthusiasts, it's logical to believe that they are more likely to increase their music spending in the future. When we conducted our consumer survey, we found that Napster usage is one of the strongest determinants of increased music buying.[23]

Many people believed that file-sharing services were here to stay and that the record labels were making a mistake by not embracing the technology and finding ways to profit from and pay royalties to the artists and songwriters. Stephen Bradley, a senior analyst at Gartner Group, a leading U.S. e-business management consultancy company, described the attempts to close down Napster's website as shortsighted, because they could severely damage the record industry. He warned:

The record companies should be careful about what they ask for. The closure of Napster's website would spur millions of its users to adopt existing "anarchistic" Internet music sharing technologies that cannot be controlled.[24]

New music sites were pitching themselves as "legitimate" Napster clones, differing only in that they would pay record companies to carry their music. Everyone seemed to be moving to capitalize on the huge demand for cheap, easy-to-download music—the grassroots groundswell that catapulted Napster into dot-com legend.[25]

GNUTELLA

Gnutella was a network that was not owned by anyone and had no central server. The difference between Gnutella and the Napster model was that in Gnutella there was no central directory. It was only a program that could link a PC user with as many other PC users as it could find. For example, if a PC user wanted to download the "xyz" song, he could run the Gnutella program and it could link him with a guy in Lima, Peru, who was online and had it in his files. The other side of Gnutella was giving back. Every client on the GnutellaNet was also a server, so that one could not only find stuff but also make things available for the benefit of others.[26]

---

[22]News release at www.napster.com, July 28, 2000.

[23]Derek Caney, "Napster Increases Music Sales," Reuters, July 21, 2000.

[24]Tom Foremski, "Napster Dispute Raises Piracy Level," *Financial Times*, July 31, 2000.

[25]Brad Stone, "The Day the Music (Almost) Died," *Newsweek,* July 20, 2000.

[26]www.gnutella.wego.com.

While Napster fought for its life against the gigantic record labels and brands (e.g., Metallica), Gnutella and others continued to swap songs and other property without paying royalties. The music industry could sue a company like Napster, but it could not sue a program. Gnutella could not be attacked legally because it was not owned by anyone, made no money, and had no assets to seize. Gnutella was no more than a label for a process or what amounted to a virtual library. Only this library was as large, or as small, as the number of individuals who linked to one another through it.

"Napster would never have existed if the labels had fulfilled the demand for individual songs, in MP3 format, from major artists," noted Marty Fries, coauthor of *The MP3 and Internet Audio Handbook*. "People are fed up with spending money for CDs with only one good song and a lot of filler. The industry needs to transition back to offering singles and eventually offer subscription services, similar to Napster."

LOOKING AHEAD

The five major record labels all had their own music-downloading services in the trial or planning stage, but the scope of available tunes was only a fraction of what Napster's 20 million users collectively served up. The labels did not have the ability to aggregate an offering in the way a third party could. They could not achieve a complete product offering for consumers. Napster could still survive if a record company bought it, or if it convinced the labels to let it sell the music to its users. For record companies the challenge was to compete online instead of litigating, or else they would have to watch a lawsuit-proof pirating technology emerge on the Net:

> While Universal Music, Sony Music, Warner Music Group and Bertelsmann were involved in a lawsuit against Napster, Bertelsmann suddenly broke ranks with the other labels. In October 2000, they signed a deal with Napster to install a membership-based service with royalty payments. Bertelsmann believed that most of Napster's 40 million users would be prepared to pay for music downloads from the web.[27]

While the peer-to-peer network quickly became a powerful Internet platform, one critical success factor for the continued growth of this technology was contingent on how easily e-commerce capabilities could be integrated into them. So far, there was no way to transfer files and collect payment simultaneously. New technologies addressed this issue.[28]

The ability to protect intellectual property seemed to be fraught with difficulties, but Internet companies attempted to create systems that would thwart piracy using high-tech codes similar to those that protect a customer's credit card details. Experts in the field claimed that this was not the death of copyright, only a copyright gap as the technology for protecting intellectual property was catching up with the systems available.[29]

The *Financial Post* described another scenario of how the music business would work in the future:

> Instead of signing a contract with a big record company, and its legal department, to make a CD, an artist will go to an Internet Service Provider and stage his or her own pay-per-

---

[27]Jean Chua and Lydia Zajc, "Sound Policies Marry Tradition and Technology," *South China Morning Post*, December 5, 2000.

[28]"Dynamic Transactions Announces Next Generation Technology for Developers of Peer-to-Peer Networks," *Financial Times*, August 1, 2000.

[29]"E-World: In the Age of Napster, Protecting Copyright Is a Digital Arms Race," *The Wall Street Journal*, July 24, 2000.

view concert. The artist will also get money by taking their new and old music on the road in the form of live concerts and by endorsing products and selling merchandise. Corporate music empires will no longer be able to control, or demand payment from everyone who listens to or borrows or copies a CD. This is a cultural disintermediation and not the death of artistry. Performers will find other middlemen to help them gain an audience and make money. Or they won't, and will go directly to consumers.[30]

Forrester Research senior analyst Mark Hardie pointed out:

We are seeing a lot of rhetoric about MP3 vs. the music business, but the rhetoric is confusing because no one's comparing apples to apples. Web music companies are comparing apples to oranges and saying the oranges are a better fruit. Ask any garage band right now, "Would you trade a contract with Sony for 50% of all downloads with MP3.com?" They'd pick Sony, noting that Internet companies still can't match the recording industry's ability to market, promote, and distribute an artist's work to a widespread mainstream audience by putting a lot of funds up front. This still remains its key advantage over companies like MP3.com.[31]

Jupiter Communciations analyst Mark Mooradian added:

Can MP3 help you as a distribution tool? Yes. Is it a great marketing device? Yes, but the format in itself is not going to make a star. The quality has to be there. There's a plethora of bad MP3 bands.[32]

CONCLUSION

The Internet had transformed the rules of the music industry. New entrants were changing the rules of the game and forcing traditional players to reevaluate their strategic options.

There are several open questions:

- Which are the business models that will be successful?
- To which customer segments will they appeal?
- What pricing strategies will emerge?
- Is there a need for international laws and authorities to enforce the laws on copyright globally?

---

[30]"Gnutella Torching the Music Business," *Financial Post*, August 3, 2000.

[31]News release at www.zdnet.com.

[32]News release at www.zdnet.com.

case 17 The Chicagotribune.com

Nina Ziv

Polytechnic University

As he sat in his office in the Tribune Tower in downtown Chicago on a sunny morning in August 1999, Owen Youngman, director of interactive media for the *Chicago Tribune,* reflected on what it was like to manage the Chicagotribune.com:

> The big deal is that you get up in the morning and come to work and you are on the bus and you know you'll make a mistake today. You don't know what it is and you may not know for a long time. Whereas in the newspaper business, there's a lot more certainty regardless of what part of the business you are talking about. And adjusting to that reality is different. And so you manage differently as a result. Some things you hedge; others you don't.[1]

Youngman, a seasoned veteran of the *Chicago Tribune* for over 28 years, was used to a culture that valued innovation but was steeped in 150 years of tradition. He now found himself managing in an environment characterized by constant change, instantaneous feedback from readers, a volatile marketplace, and competitors who had never been on his radar screen. True, in its foray into the online world, the *Tribune* had been very successful. As a leader and innovator in developing an online newspaper, the *Tribune* had not only developed a distinctive persona for its online paper but also been innovative at integrating the digital and physical aspects of the paper and providing unique online offerings for its readers. It had been recognized for its efforts by such prestigious organizations as the Newspaper Association of America (NAA) as well as the bible of the newspaper business, *Editor & Publisher* magazine. In the summer of 1997, the Chicagotribune.com was named Best Newspaper Site (in the largest circulation category) by the NAA. In 1998, *Editor & Publisher* honored the Chicagotribune.com as 1998's Best Online Newspaper among publications with print circulations of more than 100,000. The online newspaper also won awards for the best business section and the best design.

But clearly, the Chicagotribune.com faced significant challenges in its fourth year of operation. Perhaps the most important challenge was creating a digital brand that would build on the reputation of the print newspaper but offer its readers features they could not get in print. Most online news sites obtained up to 70 percent of their online content simply by reusing and reformatting print stories for the online market, a prac-

---

This case was made possible by the cooperation of the Tribune Company.

[1]The remarks by Owen Youngman throughout this case study were taken from a taped interview with the casewriter in Chicago on August 10, 1999.

exhibit 1   Tribune Company Structure, 2000

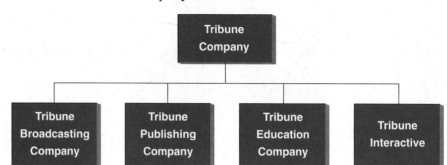

tice known in the industry as "shoveling."[2] Rather than just providing its readers with an electronic version of the print edition, Youngman and his staff were committed to exploiting the strength of each medium and constantly fine-tuning the interaction between them. In order to do this, the organization currently in place would need to be restructured to accommodate the new medium and the right kind of talent would need to be recruited that could adapt to this hybrid environment.

Closely linked to the development of the brand was the challenge of defining what business the newspaper should be in as it positioned itself in the new media industry. Should the Chicagotribune.com be in the business of providing news to its readership, or should it become an e-commerce business with news as just one of its many products? Unlike many new media companies that operated independently, the Chicagotribune.com was part of the Tribune Company, a media conglomerate, and thus its development as an online entity was linked to the overall strategy of the parent company. In May 1999, the Tribune Company consolidated its national and local online businesses into one business unit, a move that could have a significant impact on the development of the Chicagotribune.com. Tribune Interactive, which joined publishing, broadcasting, and education as the Tribune Company's fourth line of business (Exhibit 1), brought together the interactive functions of the *Tribune*'s four newspapers and 17 television stations. In addition, other Internet products and services—such as Black-Voices, Go2Orlando, and Digital City—were placed under the umbrella of the business unit (see Exhibit 2).

The purpose of the consolidation was to enable the *Tribune* to develop new products for the online environment more rapidly and achieve economies of scale. Yet Jeff Scherb, the chief technology officer of the *Tribune* and president of Tribune Interactive (TI), stated on numerous occasions that the "goal is for TI to be an e-commerce company enabled by great content."[3] Scherb understood that the mission of the newspaper was to focus on coverage of events and breaking news, but his vision also entailed building Internet businesses that would provide consumers with the utility and convenience of one-stop shopping on the Web.

Whether or not the e-commerce mission of the online edition delineated by Scherb was realized, executives at the *Tribune* saw the Chicagotribune.com as one part of their plan to leverage the rich content of old media newspapers and evolve the Tribune

[2]Martha Stone, "Print to Web: It Takes Teamwork," *Editor & Publisher Online,* July 10, 1999.

[3]"PaineWebber Media Conference," press release, (www.tribune.com/about/news/1999/pw.htm), December 8, 1999.

exhibit 2 Tribune Company Holdings by Business Unit, 2000

Tribune Broadcasting Company

Television

WPIX (WB)	WLIV (WB)	KHWB (WB)
New York	Boston	Houston
KWGN (WB)	WTIC (FOX)	WPMT (FOX)
Denver	Hartford	Harrisburg
KTLA (WB)	KDAF (WB)	KCPQ (FOX)
Los Angeles	Dallas	Seattle
KTXL (FOX)	WXMI (FOX)	WEWB (WB)
Sacramento	Grand Rapids	Albany
WGN (WB)	WBDC (WB)	KTWB
Chicago	Washington	Seattle
KSWB (WB)	WGNO (ABC)	WPHL (WB)
San Diego	New Orleans	Philadelphia
WATL (WB)	WBZL (WB)	WXIN (FOX)
Atlanta	Miami	Indianapolis
WNOL (WB)		
New Orleans		

Radio

WGN-AM	KEZW-AM	KOSI-FM
Chicago	Denver	Denver
KKHK-FM		
Denver		

TV programming

Tribune Entertainment Company, Los Angeles develops and distributes first-run television programming for the Tribune station group and national syndication

Baseball

Chicago National League Ball Club Inc. (Chicago Cubs)

Investments

The WB Television Network (25% stake), TV Food Network (29% stake)

Tribune Publishing Company

Daily newspapers

Chicago Tribune	*Sun-Sentinel*	*Orlando Sentinel*	*Daily Press*
Chicago	South Florida	Orlando	Hampton Roads, Virginia

Weekly newspapers

Sun-Sentinel Community News Group; Exito

Entertainment listings and syndications

Tribune Media Services, Chicago—TV, cable, and movie listings; comics, features, and opinion columns; online and wire services; advertising networks

Cable Programming

CLTV News Chicago; Central Florida News 13, Orlando, a 50% partnership with Time Warner Communications

Other products and services

Chicago, Illinois: Auto Finder, Job Finder, Mature Adult, New Homes Guide, Silicon Prairie, RELCON Apartment Guide, Tribune Direct Marketing

exhibit 2   *(continued)*

Orlando, Florida: Auto Finder, Black Family Today Central, Florida Family, Hot Properties, O Arts, The Orlando City Book, RELCON Apt. Renter's Book, Sentinel Direct

South Florida: Florida New Homes & Condominium Guides, Gold Coast Shopper South, Florida Parenting, Vital Signs

Newport News, Virginia: Hampton Roads Gardening and Home

Investments

BrassRing Inc. (36% owned); CareerPath.com (16%); Classified Ventures (17%); Knight Ridder/Tribune Information Services (50%)

Tribune Education Company

Educational products for schools

The Wright Group

Everyday Learning/Creative Publications Group

NTC/Contemporary Publishing Group

Instructional Fair Group

Educational Products for Consumers

NTC/Contemporary Publishing Group

Instructional Fair Group

Landoll

Investments

Discourse Technologies (19% owned); ImageBuilder Software (22%)

Tribune Interactive

National businesses

BlackVoices.com

Cubs.com

Go2Orlando.com

Local businesses

Chicagotribune.com

Dailypress.com

Orlandosentinel.com

Sun-sentinel.com

Metromix.com

Showtimeinteractive.com

HRticket.com

ChicagoSports.com

Websites for all Tribune television and radio stations

Classified businesses

Automotive—cars.com

Real estate—apartments.com, newhomenetwork.com

Recruitment—BlackVoices.com, BrassRing.com, CareerPath.com, Siliconprairie.com, thepavement.com

General merchandise—Auctions.com

Source: Tribune Company annual report, 1999.

Company into a cross-media company with multiple outlets serving a wide-ranging audience. Indeed, with the acquisition of the Times Mirror Company, which owned several newspapers in major cities such as Los Angeles and New York City, the Tribune Company was in a strong position to develop what John Madigan, chairman and president of the company, called a "national platform rich in content and the ability to develop e-commerce."[4, 5]

As the Tribune Company redefined its role in the media industry on a national level, another challenge for the Chicagotribune.com was how best to serve its Chicago-based readership in a complex environment where competitors were emerging from nontraditional sectors of the community and where making the right partnerships and alliances was essential. For example, new media companies such as Yahoo! had emerged over the past few years that were providing news services and thus making inroads on the audiences that had traditionally been considered in the *Tribune*'s domain. With the proliferation of cellular phones and personal digital assistants, technology companies could also play a major role in shaping the way information was distributed and formatted for the "small screen." During the past nine years, the Tribune Company had made numerous investments in online companies and formed alliances and partnerships with these companies. The Chicagotribune.com now had the task of cultivating these relationships and integrating the offerings of these companies in a way that would enhance the online edition and differentiate it from its competitors.

How the online newspaper would deal with the challenges outlined above remained to be seen. Would the Chicagotribune.com remain a strong, forward-looking pioneer in the new media industry, or would it struggle to survive in the vast media network of the Tribune Company?

THE TRIBUNE AS INNOVATOR

The *Chicago Tribune* was founded in 1847 and during its 150-year history had been an innovative pioneer in the media industry. Very early in its history, Colonel Robert McCormick, who took over the *Tribune* in 1911, expanded the reach of the newspaper to include the *Washington Times-Herald* and the *Daily News* of New York. In 1924, when radio was a new medium, McCormick bought WDAP, one of the first radio stations in Chicago, because he viewed it as another way to reach his audience. Later the *Tribune* invested in television stations even though most major newspapers saw television as a threat (see Exhibit 3).

With its history of innovation, "it was really no big leap for the Tribune Company to view interactive media as another way to do what it had done successfully so many times before." said Owen Youngman. Moreover, key members of senior management were very much in favor of moving in this direction. Jack Fuller, president of the Tribune Company, recognized early on that the Internet would be a positive force for the newspaper industry and promoted this idea in his 1996 book, *New Values*. Fuller's vision of the convergence between this new medium and the traditional newspaper business proved to be a driving force in enabling the culturally conservative *Tribune* to develop its online offering. Charles Brumback, the chairman of the Tribune Company from the late 1970s until 1995, also believed that computer services would be crucial

---

[4]Mark Fitzgerald, "The Team Riding the Tiger," *Editor & Publisher Online,* March 27, 2000.

[5]For further discussion of the merger with Times Mirror, see the *Chicagotribune.com: Creating a Newspaper for the New Economy (B),* Institute for Technology and Enterprise, November 2000.

exhibit 3   History of the Chicago Tribune

1847	The *Chicago Tribune* is founded by two newspapermen (John E. Wheeler and Joseph K. C. Forrest) and a leather merchant (James Kelly). The first edition was a four-page newspaper, the *Chicago Daily Tribune,* of which 400 copies were printed.
1848	The *Tribune* becomes the first paper in the West to receive regular news by wire. By the end of 1849, circulation was near 1,000.
1852	The subscription price for the *Tribune* is raised to 15 cents.
July 1, 1858	The *Chicago Daily Tribune* and the *Democratic Press* merge to become the *Chicago Daily Press and Tribune.*
1861	The *Tribune* takes over Chicago's oldest paper, the *Daily Democrat.*
1871	The Great Chicago Fire. The buildings housing the paper are totally destroyed by the fire.
1897	The newspaper prints its first halftone image.
1903	The first daily spot color begins running.
1912	The *Tribune* builds its first paper mill in Ontario.
1924	The paper expands into local radio.
1925	The Tribune Tower is dedicated.
1931	The "Dick Tracy" comic strip begins publishing.
1939	The *Tribune* prints the first-ever full-color spot news photo.
1948	The *Tribune*'s television station, WGN, begins broadcasting.
1981	The Tribune Company purchases the Chicago Cubs baseball team.
1983	The Tribune Company goes public.
1991	The Tribune Company makes a $5 million investment in America Online.
1992	The *Tribune* goes digital with Chicago Online, available via America Online.
October 1995	CareerPath is formed as an employment information service in conjunction with the *Boston Globe, Los Angeles Times, New York Times, San Jose Mercury News,* and *Washington Post.*
March 1996	The *Tribune* launches its website, Chicagotribune.com.
September 1996	Digital City Arlington Heights is unveiled—Chicago's first virtual community.
June 10, 1997	The *Tribune* marks its 150th anniversary with a free public celebration. The *Tribune* is older than the *New York Times* (146 years old), *Washington Post* (120), *Los Angeles Times* (116), and *The Wall Street Journal* (108).
July 1997	Community websites are expanded to 20.
February 1998	Chicagotribune.com is redesigned so that news and advertising are divided into seven categories.
December 1998	The Chicago Tribune's Media Services launch FanStand. This site provides online shopping for film and television-related merchandise.
March 1999	The Tribune Company announces that it will digitize its entire archive of news clippings (1985 to date is already online). The completed database will house 15 million images and include content from as early as 1920. Images and full text of every front page since 1849 will also be available, as will obituaries and death notices.
April 1999	Tribune Ventures makes an investment in SuperMarkets Online.
May 1999	Tribune Interactive is created.
November 1999	The *Tribune* announces it will no longer produce a special edition for AOL.

Source: Tribune Company annual report, 1999.

exhibit 4 Tribune Ventures as of April 2000

Public investments	
America Online	America's largest online service, with more than 14 million subscribers
Exactis	Customizable, scalable e-mail marketing solutions for business
Excite@Home	Leading provider of broadband Web services and open access to the Internet via cable
iVillage	A leading online network targeted to women, with top brands Parent Soup and Better Health
Lightspan	Developer of electronic education curriculum products; products used in more than 500 school districts
Peapod	Online grocery shopping service, with more than 75,000 customers and operations in eight U.S. cities
VarsityBooks.com	Nation's premier online college bookstore
Private investments	
BlackVoices.com	The leading online African American community
Food.com	The Internet's largest takeout and delivery service
iExplore	One-stop resource for adventure and experiential travel
iOwn.com	Online mortgage broker and real estate service
Legacy.com	Publisher of online memorials and related information
PseudoPrograms	Online entertainment network; produces more than 40 Internet-television programs
ReplayNetworks	Creators of next-generation television products using advanced digital technologies
SocialNet.com	Destination site to meet people for work, leisure, housing, and romance
Teach.com	Premier provider of training solutions focused on improving knowledge worker productivity
ValuPage	A website service through which consumers receive coupon savings on leading national brands at local supermarkets

Source: Tribune Company annual report, 1999.

to the development of newspapers, and it was he who initiated the Tribune Company's investments in various online ventures.[6]

The Tribune Company began to amass its portfolio of online companies in 1991 when it bought a 10 percent share in America Online (AOL), then known as Quantum. Over time, the newspaper sold off its shares and invested the money into other new media opportunities. As of August 1999, the *Tribune*'s portfolio, which included stakes in public companies like AOL, Excite@Home, iVillage, and Peapod, and private companies such as WB Network, Lightspan Partnership, and Digital City, was valued at more than $812 million (see Exhibit 4).[7]

In addition to the potential financial gains from making such investments, John Madigan, the Tribune Company's chairman, president, and chief executive officer, said

[6]Mark Fitzgerald, "The Team Riding the Tiger," *Editor & Publisher Online,* March 27, 2000.

[7]Jeff Borden, "Trib Co. Buys Low, Flies High with Shrewd Internet Buys," *Crain's Chicago Business* (www.pcreprints.com/eprint/tribune/buvlow.htm). August 30, 1999.

the investments were "our form of R&D."[8] Owen Youngman elaborated on Madigan's idea:

> Being an early investor in AOL gave the company an up-close view of the mind-set that it takes to be successful in this space. AOL, first and foremost, is a great marketer. And so, seeing their marketing techniques up close, and the speed with which they'd move and with which they would change, helped us to make decisions about what we should be doing. No, we're not spending the same percentage of revenues on promotion that AOL did, but it's a good leading indicator that spending promotional money early on can help to build a powerful brand down the line.

Thus, the newspaper viewed its investments in new media companies as an avenue for learning about how to operate effectively in the new media environment and understand how some of these companies could affect the long-term development of the newspaper. Indeed, some of these companies were threatening one of the newspaper's most important sources of revenue—advertising. In an August 1999 report, Forrester Research, predicted that by 2003, newspapers would lose over 23 percent of their total ad revenues.[9] Yet the Tribune Company's strategy was to incorporate these online opportunities and use them to enhance its own media offerings.

For example, in mid-2000, the newspaper invested in Supermarkets Online. The company, which is based in Greenwich, Connecticut, provides electronic coupons that are accepted at over 9,000 brick-and-mortar grocery stores nationwide. In making this investment, Andy Oleszczuk, Tribune Venture president, said:

> With Supermarkets Online, we see a company that represents the future of consumer packaged goods promotion and helps our traditional media properties serve the needs of our consumers and advertisers.[10]

For the *Tribune,* a company such as Supermarkets Online, which offered digital coupons, could potentially threaten the supermarket advertising business that had been so lucrative for the newspaper in the past. However, rather than view this as a threat, newspaper executives saw it as an opportunity to integrate the content offerings of the newspaper with advertising and create a richer online experience, especially for the local consumer.

The Tribune Company's investments and innovative strategies appeared to have paid off. The company's 1999 annual report indicated that the Tribune had continued to be profitable (see Exhibit 5). In a press release detailing the full-year results of the Tribune Company's operations in 1999, John W. Madigan reported:

> This is our eighth consecutive year of earnings growth. In our media businesses, we increased our operating cash flow margins once again in 1999. Our daily newspapers' operating cash flow margins of 35 percent are among the best in the industry. And operating cash flow margins from our television stations expanded to more than 41 percent. Our television group—the largest station group not owned by a network—has been the most significant driver of earnings growth. The fundamentals of all of our businesses are strong, and we're looking forward to continued growth in 2000.[11]

---

[8]James P. Miller, "How Tribune Grabbed a Media Prize," *The Wall Street Journal,* March 14, 2000.

[9]Chalene Li, "Internet Advertising Skyrockets," *Forrester Research Report,* August 1999.

[10]"Chicago Media Company Increases Internet Investments," *Editor & Publisher Online,* April 9, 1999.

[11]"Tribune Reports Record 4Q and Full Year Earnings," press release (www.tribune.com/about/news/2000/4q99.htm), January 21, 2000.

exhibit 5 Tribune Company Financial Highlights, 1998–99
(in thousands, except per share date)

	For the Year		
	1999	1998	Change
Operating revenues	$3,221,890	$2,980,889	+ 8%
Operating profit	$770,440	$702,289	+ 10%
Net income			
Before nonoperating items	$415,446	$350,809	+18%
Including nonoperating items	1,483,050	414,272	—
Cumulative effect of accounting change, net	(3,060)	—	—
Total	$1,479,990	$414,272	—
Diluted earnings per share			
Before nonoperating items	$1.54	$1.27	+ 21%
Including nonoperating items	5.62	1.50	—
Cumulative effect of accounting change, net	(.01)	—	—
Total	$5.61	$1.50	—
Common dividends per share:	$.36	$.34	+ 6%
Common stock price per share:			
High	$60.88	$37.53	
Low	$30.16	$22.38	
Close	$52.56	$33.32	

	At Year-End		
	December 26, 1999	December 27, 1998	Change
Total assets	$8,797,691	$5,935,570	+ 48%
Total debt	$2,724,881	$1,646,161	+ 66%
Shareholders' equity	$3,469,898	$2,356,617	+ 47%
Common shares outstanding	237,792	238,004	—

**Common stock
11-year price history**
(Dollars based on closing
price each quarter)

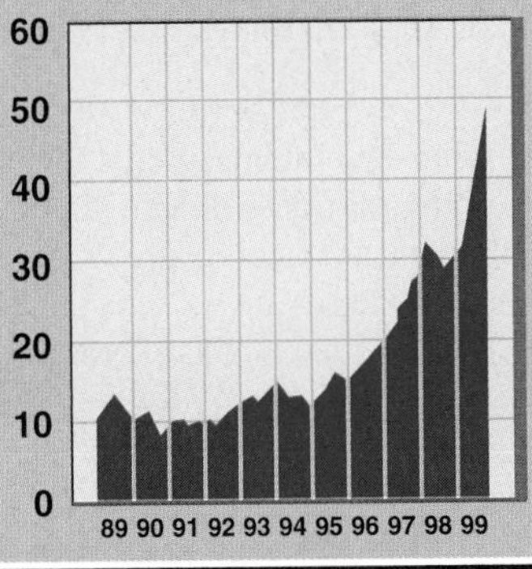

**Operating
revenues**
(Dollars in billions)

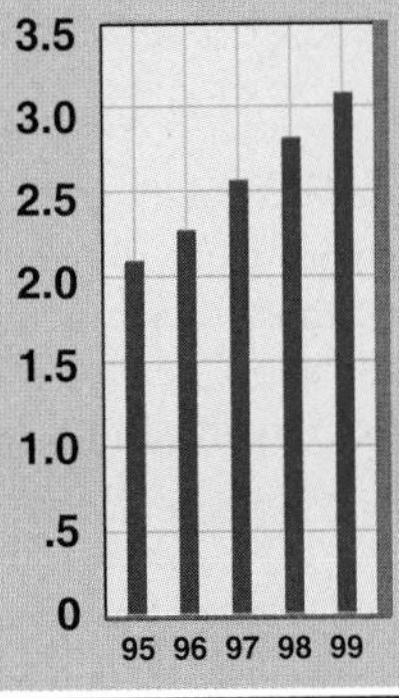

**Operating
profit**
(Dollars in millions)

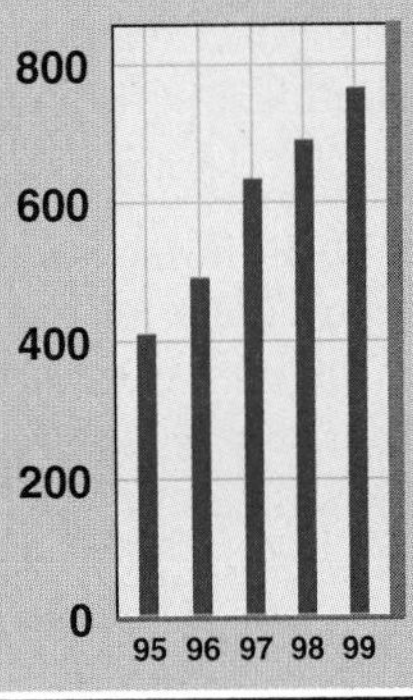

Source: Tribune Company annual report, 1999.

ORGANIZATIONAL CHALLENGES FOR THE CHICAGOTRIBUNE.COM

The first online edition of the *Tribune* was launched in 1992 and could be accessed only through America Online. As the World Wide Web became more pervasive, the *Tribune* launched its own website in March 1996, the Chicagotribune.com, which featured stories from the daily paper as well as original content such as election news.

Even with Jack Fuller and the rest of the senior management behind the effort, Youngman, who was charged with developing the new online edition, described his role as a mediator between two cultures:

> There is a culture of innovation that suffuses the newspapers. That is helpful. There is a willingness to take measured risks. That's helpful. On the other hand, there are elements of the culture that are very hidebound and traditional. It's a balancing act, and one of my key roles is sort of mediating and juggling all that stuff and deciding when to push and when not to push.

As he juggled these two disparate cultures, one of Youngman's immediate tasks was to develop an organization that could successfully produce an online edition of the newspaper. While the standard departments such as marketing, finance, advertising, and customer services would all continue to exist in the new online organization, the old ways of gathering, validating, and presenting the news were no longer suitable, and the organization, as well as the people in it, would have to reflect this.

Many newspapers faced with developing news in two media simply used their print reporters to staff their online editions and 'integrated' their print and online operations.[12] In contrast, the *Tribune* was the first newspaper to build a team of reporters whose primary responsibility was to produce online content. By mid-1997, the newspaper had hired 130 "digital journalists," the largest staff of any online newspaper.[13] While these online reporters worked in a separate unit, they were just as adept at posting a breaking story on the newspaper's website as writing a longer article about the same issue for the print edition. Indeed, the expansion of the online staff was initially intended not only to help the Chicagotribune.com but also to enhance the market share for the print edition of the paper, especially in the area of local news. This hybrid organizational model continued to evolve because the management at the *Tribune* ensured that the two organizations interact at various levels. Thus, the top online editors attended news meetings with the print editors and reporters, and worked with their print counterparts to post early versions of print stories on the website.[14]

Youngman soon discovered that aside from the ability to be conversant in both print and online media, the most successful new hires had other attributes that enabled them to thrive in this environment:

> We started off early—because there was not much of an established Internet model for employees in 1995—hiring people with skills that were going to translate into the new medium. But over time what we've learned is that flexibility and adaptability are more important than almost any other skills and when we hire people we say now, "This is what we're hiring you for today, but three months, three days from now we might ask you to do

---

[12]Rob Runett, "Study: Joint Newsrooms Still Dominate," *The Digital Edge* (www.digitaledge.org/monthly/2000_04/mediaincyberspace.html), April 2000.

[13]Scott Kirsner, "Explosive Expansion at Tribune Website, *Editor & Publisher Online,* July 7, 1997.

[14]Martha Stone, "Print to Web: It Takes Teamwork," *Editor & Publisher Online,* July 10, 1999.

something different." The business is changing rapidly. We're trying to learn from our mistakes, leverage our success and there are really very few people in the whole organization, two to three at most, that are doing the same thing today that they were originally hired to do. And you have to be comfortable with that amount of change and to some degree comfortable with the ambiguity in order to thrive.

Along with finding the right people who could work in an environment that was constantly undergoing change, Youngman suggested that a significant challenge for a traditional media company like the *Tribune* was trying to understand the nature of the new media workforce. Not only were new media employees more mobile and less likely to stay at the *Tribune* for the length of their career, but the competition for top-notch human talent was coming from unexpected quarters. Instead of the *Chicago Sun-Times,* technology companies such as Sun Microsystems, AOL, and Microsoft were luring away the *Tribune*'s people:

> For old media companies that are in the new media space, the biggest differences are workforce issues. The *Chicago Tribune,* the *New York Times,* the *Washington Post,* the *LA Times* are destination newspapers. People will generally go there and that is where they stay. In the Internet space, it's a different competitive set. We are not competing with the *Sun-Times* for people. We're competing with Sun or AOL or Excite. And we've lost people to those companies and more. We're adjusting to the sort of rent-a-player mentality, where you know when you hire somebody they are not likely to be a career employee but you want to help them. You want to keep them as long as you can, help them build their skills knowing they are ultimately going to leave but wanting to get as much value out of them as you can.

Indeed, John Madigan was concerned about the constant turnover and whether there would be enough of the right kind of people to manage the newspaper in the future:

> I worry about whether we have the right people in the right places to deal with the issues that will be most significant in the future. Are you growing the right people, hiring at entry and middle management level, the kind of people who will develop into the positions of the future? Are you recruiting enough from the outside to immediately provide the management talent for tomorrow's needs? It's something I think about every day.[15]

BUILDING A BRAND

While the Chicagotribune.com was able to capitalize on the brand name of its print counterpart, the *Chicago Tribune,* it was important that the online organization build a brand that went beyond this legacy. Instead of being merely an electronic version of the newspaper, the online edition would have to offer stories and information not readily available in the print edition.

In order to differentiate itself, the Chicagotribune.com began to experiment with producing various content unique to the Web. One of the most successful features it implemented was "Metro Daywatch," a breaking news feature that was launched in January 1999. This feature exploited the unique capabilities of the online edition. Unlike the print edition, which had one production cycle, the online version had a constant deadline cycle that enabled online reporters to deliver the news in a timely fashion even after the print newspaper edition has been finalized. For example, when an Amtrak train crashed in a Chicago suburb, online reporters were able to go to the

---

[15]Jeff Borden, "A Collision of Media," *Crain's Chicago Business* (www.pcreprints.com/eprint/tribune), June 7, 1999.

scene immediately and post stories throughout the night. The crash occurred after midnight, long after the print edition had been "put to bed." In the morning, the website had fresh information about the crash while the print edition had none.

Ben Estes, editor of the Chicagotribune.com, believed that features like breaking news were important for developing a readership for the online newspaper: "We have a lot to offer the reader who wants to know the latest. That's where our future is."[16] In fact, the ability of the Chicagotribune.com to provide in-depth coverage on breaking news stories enabled the online newspaper to significantly increase its user base. When Walter Payton died in November 1999, the Chicagotribune.com had extensive coverage on Payton within hours of his death. In just three days, there were over 600,000 page views on that story line alone.

One of the keys to development of the unique online features that characterized the Chicagotribune.com's brand was the incorporation of various technologies into the newspaper's infrastructure. Early in the development of the Chicagotribune.com, a major investment was made in a technology called Story Server, a content management system for the Web. CNET had originally developed the technology called Presentation of Real-Time Interactive Service Material (PRISM) to maintain high-volume websites. CNET sold this technology to Vignette, an Austin, Texas–based company, in mid-1996. After becoming a beta test site for the new technology, the Chicagotribune.com implemented Story Server in the spring of 1997. Mike Guilino, the *Tribune*'s manager of interactive technology, viewed the acquisition of Story Server as a way to improve the handling of the vast amount of information that existed online. "There's now a way to support our efforts statically," he said. "Discrete, independent files live in the directory structures and the larger they get, the more difficult it decomes."[17]

The first *Tribune* operation to use Story Server was Silicon Prairie (www.chicagotribune.com/tech), a feature that focuses on delivering the latest technology news and job listings to Chicago's high-tech professionals. With the help of Story Server, the majority of the stories on the Silicon Prairie site were original, with only two columns coming from the print *Tribune*. Writers sent the editor stories by e-mail; the stories were then edited before being posted on the website. In addition to holding the stories on the site, Story Server created relationships between articles. Thus, in several Silicon Prairie columns, headlines and links for the previous ten stories were available at the end.[18]

Owen Youngman saw that in addition to providing technical improvements for managing the online content, technologies such as Story Server were a way of harnessing the productivity of his employees and making some sections of the print newspaper more efficient:

> One of my goals in building Metromix was to move the newspaper away from its inefficient way of putting listings in the paper, which is: Rudy gets a press release, opens up a file, and types in the information. Next week, he gets another press release, opens it up, deletes last week's, and types in another one. Awful. So we built a database for Metromix of events so that Rudy can now get the press release, type in a whole year's worth of events, and it's fielded. So every week we just do a dump from the database to create the nine-zone listing for the newspaper, which is localized. We've decreased the error rate in them from 12 per page to 3 per page—typos and so on. Because it's all databased, it's only typed once. Huge deal. Huge deal.

---

[16]Stone, "Print to Web."

[17]"Web Databasics," *NAA Presstime* (www.naa.org/presstime/9707/wb2.html) July/August 1997.

[18]"Web Databasics," *NAA Presstime* (www.naa.org/presstime/9707/wb2.html) July/August 1997.

Technology was also used to enhance the online edition by providing readers with access to vast amounts of information in easy-to-use formats. For example, the online newspaper offered data on Illinois school districts that included statistics on standardized tests in math and reading. In addition to articles on the results, an interface to the database was designed so that the readers were able not only to access their own district statistics but also to do comparisons with the statistics of other school districts in Chicago.

Another example of the use of technology was the online paper's ability to provide in-depth coverage of elections. Along with the standard information usually provided about candidates, the Chicagotribune.com provided all the contribution records and the paper's endorsements of the candidates. In addition, the online edition provided copies of the questionnaires that the candidates filled out in seeking the paper's endorsement so that voters could understand the paper's rationale in endorsing a particular candidate. Youngman said that this type of information could not be offered in the print edition because "there's no room in the newspaper to do that. Print is expensive and there is just not space for it. But here [at the Chicagotribune.com] we can do that and do it powerfully."

The technology also enabled reporters to tell their stories in nontraditional, innovative ways that invariably enhanced what they could have done in the print edition. Using a process called nonlinear storytelling, reporters could provide a variety of ways for viewing and reading a story. Since the Web was structured so that links from one computer page location could lead to another, a story could be told in components or from several points of view, and could encompass different media such as video, audio, and text.

Thus, during the 1996 Democratic convention, *Tribune* reporter Darnell Little developed a historical tour of some of the previous 25 political conventions in the city. Little, who holds degrees in both engineering and journalism, used a variety of media and devised three parallel tours, which included tours of some of the conventions, a behind-the-scenes look at what was happening in Chicago at the time of the conventions, and archives and cartoons of the various periods. Little also used a technique called layering, which guided the reader from one section of the story to the next. Unlike a print newspaper page, which usually had ample space for a story, a computer screen might only contain the first "layer" of a digital story in the form of a headline, photograph, or text. The reader was given the option to click on the first layer and proceed in a logical order to other aspects of the story.[19]

While the use of technology had a significant impact on the type of information offered to its readers, the Chicagotribune.com's competitive edge lay in part in its ability to provide solid reporting and compelling writing just as its print counterpart had done for 150 years. In a well-publicized thrust into the new media business, Microsoft developed a group of Web entries called Sidewalk. Aimed at providing an entertainment guide for cities around the country, including Chicago, Sidewalk was poised to be a significant threat to online ventures like the Chicagotribune.com. Microsoft even tried to recruit away editorial people from the *Tribune* to work on Sidewalk.

The *Tribune* responded by developing Metromix (http://metromix.com), which Youngman said was far superior to Sidewalk in terms of content and focus on the Chicago market. Though Microsoft's technological capabilities far outweighed that of

---

[19]Christopher Harper, "Journalism in a Digital Age," lecture given at the Democracy and Digital Media Conference held at MIT, May 8–9, 1998. For a discussion about content innovation at the Chicagotribune.com, see George Szarka, "Chicago Tribune Internet Edition," unpublished paper, Institute for Technology and Enterprise, Polytechnic University, Spring 1999.

an online newspaper like the Chicagotribune.com, according to Jack Fuller the newspaper could respond to this threat because of the news values that were part of the newspaper's culture and define its brand. Fuller believed that though people could get information from anywhere, they still needed filters for selecting and creating meaning out of the vast amount of information that they were given, and the newspaper could act as such a filter. In a discussion of the role of the newspaper in the new media environment, Fuller wrote:

> Whether delivered on paper or electronically, the newspaper must have human editors. It must continue to embody the complexities of human personality, to demonstrate judgment and character, to have a distinctive voice that relates well to the community it serves. All these elements come together in what the marketers like to call brand identity, which in a fragmented, targeted environment, will be vital to differentiating one source of information from another . . . Out of the welter of products on a supermarket shelf, a few stand out because of their comfortable familiarity. Organizations with the most brand loyalty—earned by staying close to their communities and by adhering strictly to proper new values—will be the ones that thrive.[20]

It was open to question whether Fuller's vision of a brand that garnered loyalty by espousing particular values and catering to its constituent communities was viable in a future characterized by a proliferation of content and a variety of news media that provide coverage on the Web. It remained to be seen whether the vast audience of users would be interested in a comprehensive newspaper like the Chicagotribune.com or prefer more Yahoo!-type short takes on newsworthy events.

CONTENT, COMMUNITY AND COMMERCE

As the Chicagotribune.com developed, it became apparent that if the newspaper was going to succeed, it would need to rethink its strategy vis-à-vis the various stakeholders, both traditional and nontraditional, who were becoming an influential part of the community in which the *Tribune* operated. Indeed, the management of the *Tribune* realized that the nature of the interactive medium had changed the way the newspaper related to its partners, its competitors and its readers. Owen Youngman pointed out that the competitive landscape had changed dramatically: "The nature of this business is changing so much that our best customers are turning into competitors, and our competitors are turning into potential collaborators."[21] For example, some of the local media and publishing organizations that used to be competitors of the *Tribune* were forming alliances with the Chicagotribune.com. *Crain's Chicago Business* now had a relationship with the online newspaper, as did several radio stations that had online presences. Conversely, real estate agencies, which used to be a traditional source of classified ad revenues for the newspaper, were now setting up websites that bypassed the newspaper and offered property directly to the consumer.

Because of this dramatic shift in alliances, Youngman spent much of his time seeking out a variety of strategic partners with whom the newspaper could form mutually beneficial alliances. When he realized that cultivating relationships was an intrinsic part of the new online business, Youngman created a position in his organization, the strate-

---

[20]Jack Fuller, *News Values: Ideas for an Information Age* (Chicago: University of Chicago Press, 1996), pp. 229–30.

[21]"Meeting the Online Competition," *Editor & Publisher Online,* January 8, 1997.

gic relationship manager, which would focus on managing such strategic partnerships. Youngman considered this to be one of the most important jobs in his organization:

> Going it alone did not make any sense. Six months into this, it became clear to me that we needed to have a focus in the digital arena on this. If you are going to make these relationships, someone is going to have to manage them and make sure they work for everybody. Sorting it out is a full-time thing, and making sure that those relationships accrue to the benefit of our organization and our partners' organization requires a full-time focus.[22]

In addition, Jack Fuller appointed a vice president for acquisitions and alliances at the newspaper itself. In another iteration of the hybrid organization that evolved at the *Tribune,* the two relationship managers worked closely together and met regularly with Youngman.

The thrust of the newspaper toward reaching out to the larger community of partners echoed Jeff Scherb's tripartite strategy of "content, community and commerce." Scherb, who recently became president of Tribune Interactive, believed that while the first goal of the newspaper was to be the premier provider of local news and information, this was only one aspect of a newspaper's mission. Providing up-to-the-minute news through such features as Metrowatch also drove traffic to local e-commerce sites, thus serving the local community in a multidimensional way. An example of this blend of content, community, and commerce was the news coverage and related advertising that appeared before and during Hurricane Floyd in September 1999. Along with weather updates and breaking news stories, the Chicagotribune.com teamed up with Lowe's, a home products retailer, which provided information on the availability of supplies that would be useful during the storm.[23]

The importance of the community of readers for the *Tribune* was also reflected in several features of the Chicagotribune.com website. There was Metromix, a site devoted to providing up-to-the-minute information on movies, restaurants, art exhibits, and other entertainment events; a network of community websites devoted to local events and groups; and, most recently, the addition of Chicagosports.com (www.chicagosports.com), a website devoted exclusively to in-depth coverage of Chicago sports teams and events and linked to the Chicagotribune.com home page.

Because of the nature of the interactive medium, readers were not only passive receivers of information; they were active participants in content creation on several levels. For example, a decision was made in early 1998 to change the newspaper page metaphor that was the *Tribune*'s home page and redesign it so that it looked like a television screen with content in different channels. Because of the overwhelming negative response to the redesign from the user community, the newspaper switched back so that it would look like the other newspaper sites, such as those of the *New York Times* and *The Wall Street Journal.* In addition, readers had become active participants within their own online communities. Using a self-publishing software tool, local community groups could post news and events on their particular community websites.

EMERGING ISSUES

On March 14, 2000, the Tribune Company and the Times Mirror Company announced that they would merge. The combined company, which would own 11 daily newspapers, 22 television stations, and 4 radio stations, would have a combined circulation of

---

[22]Ibid.

[23]Paine Webber Media Conference, December 8, 1999.

3.6 million copies ranking the new company third among newspaper companies after Gannett and Knight Ridder.[24] Along with a more powerful presence on the print side, the addition of the Times Mirror websites would give Tribune Interactive an audience of 34 million unique visitors, more than the websites of the *New York Times* (www.nytimes.com) and USA.com (www.usa.com) combined.[25]

While the creation of a nationwide website was something *Tribune* executives envisioned, the company had no immediate plans to combine content on any of the websites. Instead, the company would create a national network of locally targeted sites and focus on how it can leverage the advertising, promotional, and technological possibilities that the merger would bring. For example, the company expected to explore how to manage the technology of its entire group of websites more efficiently and see if common content management platforms and search engines could be developed.[26]

For the Chicagotribune.com, the proposed merger was expected to affect its development as a strong local online newspaper. Clearly, there would be more opportunities for online advertisers both locally and nationally, and the emphasis on advertising at the expense of good content could threaten the brand that Owen Youngman and his staff had been building over the last four years. Even before the merger, there were organizational changes that were seen by many as a step in the wrong direction. Indeed, after the creation of Tribune Interactive in March 1999, more than 15 percent of the Chicagotribune.com's staff left, including Howard Witt, associate managing editor of the paper. Staffers said they left because the company was de-emphasizing writing and journalism and focusing more on promotion and profit.[27]

Yet in an interview in December 1999 with the *Digital Edge,* Digby Solomon, who had just been appointed as the new general manger of Tribune Interactive's Chicago division, defended the focus on e-commerce and suggested that the content needed to be changed in order to compete with pure Internet companies such as AOL and Yahoo!: "Let's face it—we created many products that audiences didn't want to read and that advertisers wouldn't pay for, because they were legacies of our traditional newspaper businesses. We needed to focus on content that drove ratings."[28] Solomon also insisted that the editorial quality of the online newspaper would not suffer and that "our properties will still follow the journalistic values of our newspaper and television newsrooms."[29]

While the conflict between profitability and good journalism continued, online newspapers such as the Chicagotribune.com had to search for additional sources of revenue to sustain their operations. One such potential revenue source was subscriptions. With the exception of *The Wall Street Journal Interactive,* which had a subscription fee since its inception, other online newspapers did not charge for access to their sites. Moreover, in a recent survey released by ScreamingMedia.com, 89 percent of the 1,232 respondents said they had never paid for news or information on the Web and 83

---

[24]Felicity Barringer and Laura M. Holson, "Tribune Company Agrees to Buy Times Mirror," *New York Times,* March 14, 2000, p A1.

[25]Jason Williams, "The New Spider in the Web," *Editor & Publisher Online,* March 20, 2000.

[26]Jim Benning, "Mergers—Times Mirror and Tribune: A Powerhouse Is Born?" *Online Journalism Review* (www.ojr.usc.edu/content/print.cfm?print=346), March 14, 2000.

[27]Martha L. Stone, "Defections Hit Tribune Co.'s Interactive Unit," *Editor & Publisher Online,* September 8, 1999.

[28]Rob Runett, "Solomon Grabs Point Position as Tribune Restructures Sites, *Digital Edge* (www.digitaledge.org/monthly/1999_12/digbyprofile.html), December 1999.

[29]Ibid.

percent said that they were not willing to pay.[30] Nevertheless, Owen Youngman thought that this should change and was investigating what users would pay for: "We're conducting research on what people will pay for and what they won't and how much they'll pay for it. We're looking at what [content] is highly commoditized."[31] Another potential source of revenue was subscriptions to mobile services. The *New York Times* already had a free service that provided daily updated coverage of top stories downloadable to handheld devices. However, users might be willing to pay for subscriptions to such features as breaking news and stock reports.

After four years of operation, the Chicagotribune.com remained one of the premier online newspapers. Yet its leadership knew that in the rapidly changing business environment, flexibility, adaptability, and constantly reassessing the competitive landscape were key if the newspaper was going to continue to be recognized for its high-quality reporting and features. Owen Youngman knew this very well:

> It's literally true that every day I question whether what we're doing is going to continue next week, next month, next year, or in five years. If you let a week go by without evaluating what you're doing, you can be left behind.[32]

---

[30]Felicity Barringer, "Web Surfers Want the News Fast and Free," *New York Times,* May 1, 2000, p. C12.

[31]Martha L. Stone, "Chicago Tribune Web Site Moving to Registration," *Editor & Publisher Online,* March 3, 1999.

[32]Jeff Borden, "A Collision of Media," *Crain's Chicago Business* (www.pcreprints.com/eprint/tribune), June 7, 1999.

case 18 eBay in 2002: The Challenges of Sustained Growth

Louis Marino
The University of Alabama

Patrick Kreiser
The University of Alabama

The online auction industry had experienced substantial growth and rapid evolution since eBay had invented it in the mid-1990s. The complexion of the industry changed almost daily with the entry of new competitors, the exit of existing firms, and the introduction of strategic initiatives by firms of all sizes. While its fortunes had risen with those of other e-commerce industries during the Internet euphoria of the 1990s, the on-line auction industry was blazing its own trail in 2002. Many e-commerce firms were adversely affected by an economic slowdown in the United States in 2001, but sales at online auction sites in May 2001 were up 149 percent from the preceding year.[1] Despite swiftly evolving industry conditions, two factors that had not varied were eBay's dominance of the market and its unspotted record of positive net income. See Exhibit 1 for eBay's growth performance during the 1996–2001 period.

Founder Pierre Omidyar (pronounced oh-*mid*-ee-ar) initially conceived eBay as a democratized, efficient online marketplace that would facilitate a person-to-person trading community in which everyone could have equal access through the same medium, the Internet. Capitalizing on its unique business model and the growing popularity of the Internet, eBay grew to include over 29.7 million registered users from numerous countries and, as of early 2002, conducted over 2.1 million auctions daily. The base of registered eBay users in 2002 was far more diverse than it had been in the company's early years. Whereas the buyers and sellers who used eBay originally consisted of bargain hunters and individuals looking to generate cash from the sale of unwanted items, by 2002 eBay's clientele was quite diverse, ranging from high school and college students looking to make a few extra dollars, to individuals auctioning a used car, to Fortune 500 companies such as IBM selling excess inventory, to large government agencies like the U.S. Post Office selling undeliverable parcels. Moreover, eBay auctions were increasingly involving participants from outside the United States, with eBay auction sites functioning in a number of foreign countries and projections of more to come.

[1]Troy Wolverton, "eBay riding Net auction industry's wave," www.cnet.com, June 28, 2001.

exhibit 1   Selected Indicators of eBay's Growth, 1996–2001

	1996	1997	1998	1999	2000*	2001*
Number of registered users	41,000	341,000	2,181,000	10,006,000	22,500,000	42,400,000
Gross merchandise sales	$7 million	$95 million	$745 million	$2.8 billion	$5.4 billion	$9.3 billion
Number of auctions listed	289,000	4,394,000	33,668,000	129,560,000	264,700,000	423,000,000

*2000 and 2001 figures include combined numbers from eBay and Half.com.
Source: Company records.

While most bidders applauded the widening selection of items available on eBay, there was a growing and somewhat vocal segment of small sellers who felt that eBay had "sold out" to large companies. These small sellers claimed that the spreading influence of eBay auctions involving the sale of merchandise by "name" companies was prompting eBay to neglect the needs and interests of the individuals and collectors who had been so instrumental in spreading the popularity of online auctions.

This perception of neglect held by some longtime eBay community members was exacerbated by eBay's continuous efforts to increase its product offerings through acquiring other companies, adding new product categories, and entering new geographic markets. Even though eBay had, so far, successfully fought off challenges from other auction sites looking to siphon off its dominant market share, Pierre Omidyar and Margaret (Meg) Whitman (eBay's president and CEO) were intent on improving and refining eBay's business model and strategy; they had insisted on building eBay's cash reserves and financial strength to support future initiatives to sustain the company's rapid growth. In September 2001, eBay registered with the Securities and Exchange Commission to raise up to $1 billion through new stock issues over an unspecified period of time. Initial reaction to the filing was predictable—eBay's shares fell 10 percent because of investor fears of diluted earnings. But investor confidence in the company's growth and earnings potential boosted the stock price back to its former level within four days.

With access to a substantial war chest and with the company's position as the dominant player in the online auction industry largely uncontested, eBay's top management team began to plan its next moves in more detail. There were indications that eBay was considering further expansion in the international market, targeting either China or Taiwan, as well as intending to fully integrate Half.com with eBay's website. In the midst of these expansion plans, however, Omidyar and Whitman had to explore the possibility that eBay's phenomenal growth had led to erosion of one of the company's key competencies, the sense of community that helped establish eBay's position in the market.

THE GROWTH OF E-COMMERCE AND ONLINE AUCTIONS

The Internet was first conceived in the 1960s, but it wasn't until the 1990s that it garnered widespread use and became a part of everyday life. The *Computer Industry Almanac* estimated that by the end of 2000 there were approximately 550 million Internet users in over 150 countries and that the number would grow to over 625 million worldwide by the end of 2001 and to over 1 billion by 2005.[2] While the top 15 countries ac-

---

[2]www.c-i-a.com, press releases, April 2001 and July 2001.

counted for more than 70 percent of the computers in use, slightly more than one-third of Internet users (168.8 million) resided in the United States. The areas where Internet usage was expected to grow fastest were Asia, Latin America, and Eastern Europe, with much of this growth coming from increased access through such new technologies as Web-enabled cell phones.

The Gartner Group estimated that business-to-business (B2B) e-commerce would grow from $919 billion in 2001 to over $8.5 trillion by 2005. Similarly Gartner predicted that business-to-consumer revenues from online sales would climb from $31.2 billion in 1999 to over $380 billion in 2003. Forrester Research expected about 28 percent of worldwide business-to-business transactions to occur in the Asia/Pacific region. Within the business-to-consumer segment, where eBay operated, U.S. e-commerce accounted for over 65 percent of all Internet transactions in 1999 but was expected to account for only about 38 percent in 2003 as Internet usage expanded rapidly in other parts of the world, especially Asia (where usage was expected to be spurred by the 2001 decision to admit China into the World Trade Organization). Business-to-consumer e-commerce in Europe was projected to grow from $5.4 billion in 1999 (17.3 percent of the world total) to over $115 billion (more than 30 percent of the world total) by 2003. According to one estimate, online auction sales of collectibles and personal merchandise were expected to represent an $18.7 billion market in 2002—see Exhibit 2.

Key Success Factors in Online Retailing

While it was relatively easy to create a website that functioned like a retail store, the more significant challenge for an online retailer was to generate traffic to the site in the form of both new and returning customers. To reach new customers, some online retailers partnered with shopping search engines (such as www.mysimon.com or www.streetprices.com) that allowed customers to compare prices for a given product from many retailers. Other tactics employed to build traffic included direct e-mail, online advertising at portals and content-related sites, and some traditional advertising such as print ads and television commercials. For customers who found their way to a site, most online retailers endeavored to provide extensive product information, include pictures of the merchandise, make the site easily navigable, and have enough new things happening at the site to keep customers coming back. (A site's ability to generate repeat visitors was known as *stickiness.*) Retailers also had to help new users overcome their nervousness about using the Internet itself to shop for items they generally bought at stores. Both new and experienced Internet shoppers were concerned about credit card security and the possible sale of personal information to marketing firms. Online retailing had severe limitations in the case of those goods and services people wanted to see in person. From the retailer's perspective, there was the issue of collecting payment from buyers who wanted to use checks or money orders instead of credit cards.

HISTORY OF AUCTIONS

The first known auctions were held in Babylon around 500 BC. In these auctions, women were sold for marriage to the highest bidder. In ancient Rome, soldiers would auction the spoils of their victories and wealthy citizens would auction their expensive belongings and prized possessions. In 193 AD, the entire Roman Empire was put up for

exhibit 2 Estimated Growth in Global E-Commerce and Online Auction Sales, 1995–2005

	1999	2000	2001	2002	2003	2004	2005
Estimated worldwide B2B sales (in billions)	$150	$433	$919	$1,900	$3,600	$6,000	$8,500

Source: GartnerGroup.

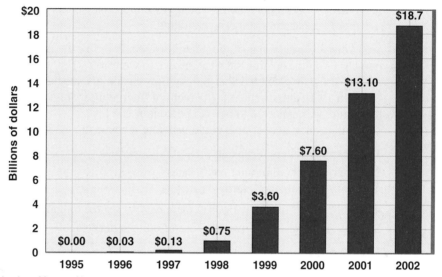

Online Auction Sales of Collectibles
and Personal Merchandise
(in billions of dollars)

Source: Keenan Vision Inc., Mercury News.

auction after the emperor Pertinax was executed. Didius Julianus bid 6,250 drachmas per royal guard and was immediately named emperor of Rome. However, Julianus was executed only two months later, and thus may have been the first-ever victim of the winner's curse (bidding more than the good would cost in a non-auction setting).

In the late 16th century, auctions began to be held in taverns and alehouses in Great Britain. Sotheby's was founded in 1744, and Christie's was established in 1766; both have now become world-renowned auction houses for rare and valuable items. Auctions for tobacco, horses, and other domestic animals were commonplace in colonial America.

Auctions have endured throughout history for several reasons. First, they give sellers a convenient way to find a buyer for something they would like to dispose of. Second, auctions are an excellent way for people to collect difficult-to-find items, such as certain Beanie Babies or historical memorabilia, that have a high value to them personally. Finally, auctions are one of the "purest" markets that exist for goods, in that they bring buyers and sellers into contact to arrive at a mutually agreeable price. Experts estimated that the national market for auctions, garage sales, flea markets, and classified ad listings was greater than $130 billion in 2001.

ONLINE AUCTIONS

Online auctions worked in essentially the same way as traditional auctions, the difference being that buyers and sellers were not physically present at a specific geographic location. In 2002, there were three basic categories of online auctions:

1. Business-to-business auctions involving such items as computers, used equipment, and surplus merchandise. Such auctions accounted for $2.5 billion in sales in 1998. Forrester Research predicted that B2B auctions would grow to $52.6 billion in 2002.
2. Business-to-consumer auctions, in which businesses sold goods and services to consumers via the Internet. Many such auctions involved companies interested in selling used or discontinued goods, or liquidating unwanted inventory.
3. Person-to-person auctions, which gave interested sellers and buyers the opportunity to engage in competitive bidding.

Since eBay's pioneering of the person-to-person online auction process in 1995, the number of online auction sites had grown to well over 2,750 by the end of 2001. Forrester Research predicted that 6.5 million customers would use online auctions in 2002. In 1999, an estimated 8.2 percent of Internet users registered at an auction site; that figure was expected to be 14.5 percent in 2002.

Online auction operators could generate revenue in any of five principal ways:

1. Charging sellers for listing their good or service.
2. Charging a commission on all sales.
3. Selling advertising on their websites.
4. Selling their own new or used merchandise via the online auction format.
5. Selling goods (their own or those of other sellers) in a fixed-price format.

Most sites charged sellers either a fee or a commission and sold advertising to companies interested in promoting their goods or services to users of the auction site. The fifth revenue generation option—selling goods at fixed prices—was a more recent development.

Auction Software Packages

In 1996, OpenSite Technologies began to offer packaged software applications to firms interested in creating their own auction websites. Moai Technologies and Ariba, Inc., were other sources for auction software. The ready availability of commercial software packages made it easy for firms to create and operate online auction sites. OpenSite had marketed over 600 auction packages to such companies as The Sharper Image, CNET, and John Deere. OpenSite claimed that its purpose was to bring together "buyers and sellers, helping businesses dynamically manage inventory, create sales channels, attract customers, and test market new products, to create efficient markets for goods and services."

Providers of Site Hosting and Online Auction Services

Auction firms could, if they wished, outsource all the hosting functions associated with online auctions to independent site-hosting enterprises and could even turn the entire auction process over to an independent online auction specialist. FairMarket, the leader in auction outsourcing in 1999, provided companies such as ZDNet, MicroWarehouse, and CollegeBytes.com with a means of selling their goods at online auction at Fair-Market's website. The use of site hosts and independent online auction services was a particularly appealing option for companies that wanted to use online auctions as a distribution channel but preferred to devote only minimal time and energy to site construction and upkeep. By paying FairMarket an annual hosting fee between $2,000 and $10,000, as well as a percentage fee on all transactions, firms were able to have an auction site without having to worry about the hassle of site upkeep.

In 2000, as another option for sites wishing to cash in on the online auction boom without investing significant resources, eBay created the Application Program Interface, which allowed new sites to "use the eBay commerce engine to power [their] business, eliminating time and expense from the start-up process."[3] According to eBay's Meg Whitman, an entrepreneur running a content site for motorcycles could import all the eBay motorcycle auctions onto the entrepreneur's own site, with eBay functioning as the commerce engine for the site.[4]

Online Auction Users

Participants in online auctions could be grouped into six categories: (1) bargain hunters, (2) hobbyist/collector buyers, (3) professional buyers, (4) casual sellers, (5) hobbyist/collector sellers, and (6) corporate and power sellers.

Bargain Hunters Bargain hunters viewed online auctions primarily as a form of entertainment; their objective usually was to find a great deal. One bargain hunter described the eBay experience as follows:

> A friend and I would spend one day a week going flea marketing and auctioning. Since school has started again, time has become a hot commodity. We've found that we can use eBay to fill that flea marketing, auctioning need. We'll call each other, then get on eBay and hunt and find things together even though we can't be together. EBay has definitely been a great way to spend quality time together!

Bargain hunters were thought to make up only 8 percent of active online users but 52 percent of eBay visitors. To attract repeat visits from bargain hunters, industry observers said, sites must appeal to them on both rational and emotional levels, satisfying their needs for competitive pricing, the excitement of the search, and the desire for community.

Hobbyist/Collector Buyers Hobbyists and collectors used auctions to search for specific goods that had a high value to them personally. They were very concerned with both price and quality. Collectors prized eBay for its wide variety of product offerings. One user commented:

> My sister collects Princess House hand-blown ornaments. She needed the first three to complete her series. I posted to the Wanted Board several times, and also put a note on my About Me page. Well, we have now successfully completed her series. We could never have done this without eBay because the first one is so hard to find. Thanks eBay!

Professional Buyers As the legitimacy of online auctions grew, a new type of buyer began to emerge: the professional buyer. Professional buyers covered a broad range of purchasers, from purchasing managers acquiring office supplies to antique and gun dealers purchasing inventory. Like bargain hunters, professional buyers were

---

[3]eBay 10-K report, March 28, 2001.

[4]Rex Moore, "Microsoft and eBay Team," Fool.com, March 13, 2001.

looking for a way to help contain costs; and, like hobbyists and collectors, some professional buyers were seeking unique items to supplement their inventory. The primary difference between professional buyers and other types, however, was their affiliation with commercial enterprises. With the growth of online auction sites dedicated to business-to-business auctions, professional buyers were becoming an increasingly important element of the online auction landscape.

Casual Sellers   Casual sellers included individuals who used eBay as a substitute for a classified ad listing or a garage sale to dispose of items they no longer wanted. While many casual sellers listed only a few items, some used eBay to raise money for one new project or another. One such seller stated:

> Thank you! After just starting to use your site less than a month ago, I have increased my earnings by over $1,000. I have not yet received all the cash, but so far the response has been fantastic. This all started with a Kool-Aid container and four cups I had that were collecting dust in a box in the attic. I was "browsing for bargains" and saw someone else had made $29.00 from those plastic things! I was AMAZED! Needless to say, I listed them. I only made $8.00, but I received my first positive feedback. Since then I am listing daily.
>
> My wife and I are scrimping to save for an adoption of a baby. The fees are much more than our modest income can afford, and this extra cash will come in handy. My wife and I sincerely thank you and your company for the opportunity to be a part of eBay.

Hobbyist/Collector Sellers   Sellers who were hobbyists or collectors typically dealt in a limited category of goods and looked to eBay as a way to sell selected items in their collections to others who might want them. Items ranged from classic television collectibles, to hand-sewn dolls, to coins and stamps. The hobbyists and collectors used a range of traditional and online outlets to reach their target markets. A number of the sellers used auctions to supplement their retail operations, while others sold exclusively through online auctions and in fixed-price formats such as Half.com.

Power and Corporate Sellers   Power sellers were typically small to medium-sized businesses that favored eBay as a primary distribution channel for their goods and often sold tens of thousands of dollars' worth of goods every month on the site. One estimate suggested that while these power sellers accounted for only 4 percent of eBay's population, they were responsible for 80 percent of eBay's total business.[5] Individuals who were power sellers could often make a full-time job of the endeavor; for example, according to information posted on eBay's website:

> Brian and Rossio (UserID: digitalmaster) went from out-of-work Web developers to successful PowerSellers in just one year! In 1998, the couple's Web development business went under; in 1999 they found eBay—and profitability. "To our surprise, selling records and CDs on eBay was a bigger success than we thought it would be," Brian says. By year 2000, they were generating $3,000 to $10,000 per month. "With the money made on eBay, we bought a 2-story, 4-bedroom house with a pool after just one year of selling!"[6]

Commercial enterprises were becoming an increasingly important part of the online auction industry and some achieved power seller status relatively rapidly. Some of the new power sellers on eBay were IBM, Compaq, and the U.S. Post Office (which sold undeliverable items under the user name "usps-mrc").

PIERRE OMIDYAR AND THE FOUNDING OF eBAY

Pierre Omidyar was born in Paris, France, to parents who had left Iran decades earlier. The family emigrated to the United States when Pierre's father began a residency at

---

[5]Claire Tristram, "'Amazoning' Amazon," www.contextmag.com, November 1999.

[6]www.pages.ebay.com/services/buyandsell/powersellers.html.

Johns Hopkins University Medical Center. Pierre grew up in modest circumstances; his parents divorced when he was two but remained near each other so he could be with both of them. Pierre's passion for computers began at an early age; he would sneak out of gym class in high school to play with computers. While still in high school, he took his first computer-related job in the school's library, where he was hired for $6.00 an hour to write a program to print catalog cards. After high school Pierre attended Tufts University, where he met his future wife, Pamela Wesley, who came to Tufts from Hawaii to get a degree in biology. Upon graduating in 1988, the couple moved to California, where Pierre, who had earned a BS in computer science, joined Claris, an Apple Computer subsidiary in Silicon Valley, and wrote a widely used graphics application, MacDraw. In 1991, Omidyar left Claris and cofounded Ink Development (later renamed eShop), which became a pioneer in online shopping and was eventually sold to Microsoft in 1996. In 1994, Omidyar joined General Magic as a developer services engineer and remained there until mid-1996, when he left to pursue full-time development of eBay.

Internet folklore has it that eBay was founded solely to allow Pamela to trade Pez dispensers with other collectors. While Pamela was certainly a driving force in launching the initial website, Pierre had long been interested in how one could establish a marketplace to bring together a fragmented market. Pierre saw eBay as a way to create a person-to-person trading community based on a democratized, efficient market where everyone could have equal access through the same medium, the Internet. Pierre set out to develop his marketplace and to meet both his and Pamela's goals. In 1995, he launched the first online auction under the name of Auctionwatch at the domain name of www.eBay.com. The name *eBay* stood for "electronic Bay area," coined because Pierre's initial concept was to attract neighbors and other San Francisco Bay area residents to the site to buy and sell items of mutual interest. The first auctions charged no fees to either buyers or sellers and contained mostly computer equipment (and no Pez dispensers). Pierre's fledgling venture generated $1,000 in revenue the first month and an additional $2,000 the second. Traffic grew rapidly, however, as word about the site spread in the Bay area; a community of collectors emerged, using the site to trade and chat—some marriages resulted from exchanges in eBay chat rooms.[7]

By February 1996, the traffic at Pierre Omidyar's site had grown so much that his Internet service provider informed him that he would have to upgrade his service. When Pierre compensated for this by charging a listing fee for the auction, and saw no decrease in the number of items listed, he knew he was on to something. Although he was still working out of his home, Pierre began looking for a partner and in May asked his friend Jeffrey Skoll to join him in the venture. While Jeff had never cared much about money, his Stanford MBA degree provided the firm with the business background that Pierre lacked. With Pierre as the visionary and Jeff as the strategist, the company embarked on a mission to "help people trade practically anything on earth."

Their concept for eBay was to "create a place where people could do business just like in the old days—when everyone got to know each other personally, and we all felt we were dealing on a one-to-one basis with individuals we could trust."

In eBay's early days, Pierre and Jeff ran the operation alone, using a single computer to serve all of the pages. Pierre served as CEO, chief financial officer, and president, while Jeff functioned as co-president and director. It was not long until Pierre and Jeff grew the company to a size that forced them to move out of Pierre's living room, due to the objections of Pamela, and into Jeff's living room. Shortly thereafter, the operations moved into the facilities of a Silicon Valley business incubator for a time

---

[7]Quentin Hardy, "The Radical Philanthropist," *Forbes*, May 1, 2000, p. 118.

exhibit 3   eBay's Income Statements, 1996–2001 (in thousands of $, except per share figures)

	1996	1997	1998	1999	2000	2001
Net revenues	$32,051	$41,370	$86,129	$224,724	$431,424	$748,821
Cost of net revenues	6,803	8,404	16,094	57,588	95,453	134,816
Gross profit	25,248	32,966	70,035	167,136	335,971	614,005
Operating expenses:						
Sales and marketing	13,139	15,618	35,976	95,956	166,767	253,474
Product development	28	831	4,640	23,785	55,863	75,288
General and administrative	5,661	6,534	15,849	43,055	74,577	105,784
Payroll expense (stock options)					2,337	2,442
Amortization of acquired intangibles		—	805	1,145	1,443	36,591
Merger related costs		0	—	4,359	1,550	—
Total operating expenses	18,828	22,983	57,270	168,300	300,977	473,549
Income (loss) from operations	6,420	9,983	12,765	−1,164	34,994	140,426
Interest and other income (expense), net	(2,607)	(1,951)	(703)	21,377	42,963	38,762
Income before income taxes	3,813	8,032	12,062	20,213	77,957	162,943
Minority interests in consolidated companies	—	—	—	—	3,062	7,514
Provision for income taxes	(475)	(971)	(4,789)	(9,385)	(32,725)	(80,009)
Net income	$ 3,338	$ 7,061	$ 7,273	$ 10,828	$ 48,294	$ 90,448
Net income per share:						
Basic	$0.39	$0.29	$0.07	$0.04	$0.19	$0.34
Diluted	.07	0.08	0.03	0.04	0.17	0.32
Weighted average shares:						
Basic	8,490	24,428	52,064	108,235	251,776	268,971
Diluted	45,060	84,775	116,759	135,910	280,346	280,595

Source: Company financial documents.

until the company settled in its current facilities in San Jose, California. Exhibits 3 and 4 present eBay's recent financial statements.

eBAY'S TRANSITION TO PROFESSIONAL MANAGEMENT

From the beginning, Pierre Omidyar intended to hire a professional manager to serve as the president of eBay: "[I would] let him or her run the company so . . . [I could] go play."[8] In 1997 both Omidyar and Skoll agreed that it was time to locate an experienced professional to function as CEO and president. In late 1997, eBay's headhunters came up with a candidate for the job: Margaret Whitman, then general manager for Hasbro Inc.'s preschool division. Whitman had received her BA in economics from Princeton and her MBA from the Harvard Business School; her first job was in brand management at Procter & Gamble. Her experience also included serving as the president and CEO of FTD, the president of Stride Rite Corporation's Stride Rite Division,

---

[8]Susan Moran, "The Candyman," *Business 2.0,* June 1999.

exhibit 4   eBay's Consolidated Balance Sheets, 1997-2001 (in thousands of $)

	Fiscal Year Ending December 31				
	1997	**1998**	**1999**	**2000**	**2001**
Assets					
Current assets:					
Cash and cash equivalents	$3,723	$ 37,285	$219,679	$ 201,873	$ 523,969
Short-term investments	—	40,401	181,086	354,166	199,450
Accounts receivable, net	1,024	12,425	36,538	67,163	101,703
Other current assets	220	7,479	22,531	52,262	58,683
Total current assets	4,967	97,590	459,834	675,464	883,805
Property and equipment, net	652	44,062	111,806	125,161	142,349
Investments	—	—	373,988	344,587	416,612
Deferred tax asset	—	—	5,639	13,892	21,540
Intangible and other assets, net	—	7,884	12,675	23,299	214,223
Total assets	$5,619	$149,536	$963,942	$1,182,403	$1,678,529
Liabilities and Stockholders' Equity					
Current liabilities:					
Accounts payable	$ 252	$ 9,997	$ 31,538	$ 31,725	$ 33,235
Accrued expenses and other current liabilities	—	6,577	32,550	60,882	94,593
Deferred revenue and customer advances	128	973	5,997	12,656	15,583
Debt and leases, current portion	258	4,047	12,285	15,272	16,111
Income taxes payable	169	1,380	6,455	11,092	20,617
Deferred tax liabilities	—	1,682	—	—	—
Other current liabilities	128	5,981	7,632	5,815	—
Total current liabilities	1,124	24,656	88,825	137,442	180,139
Debt and leases, long-term portion	305	18,361	15,018	11,404	12,008
Other liabilities	157	—	—	6,549	19,493
Minority interests	—	—	—	13,248	37,751
Total liabilities	1,586	48,998	111,475	168,643	249,391
Series B mandatorily redeemable convertible preferred stock and Series B warrants	3,018	—	—	—	—
Total stockholders' equity	1,015	100,538	852,467	1,013,760	1,429,138
Total liabilities and stockholders' equity	$5,619	$149,536	$963,942	$1,182,403	1,678,529

Source: Company financial documents.

and as the senior vice president of marketing for the Walt Disney Company's consumer products division.

     When first approached by eBay, Whitman was not especially interested in joining a company that had fewer than 40 employees and less than $6 million in revenues the previous year. It was only after repeated pleas that Whitman agreed to meet with Omidyar in Silicon Valley. After a second meeting, Whitman understood the company's enormous growth potential and agreed to give eBay a try. According to Omidyar, Meg Whitman's experience in global marketing with Hasbro's Teletubbies, Playskool, and Mr. Potato Head brands made her "the ideal choice to build upon eBay's leadership position in the one-to-one online trading market without sacrificing the quality and personal touch our users have grown to expect."[9] In addition to convincing Whitman to head eBay's operations, Omidyar had been instrumental in helping bring in other talented senior executives and in assembling a capable board of directors. Notable members of eBay's board of directors included Scott Cook, the founder of Intuit, a highly successful financial software company, and Howard Schultz, the founder and CEO of Starbucks. (For a profile of eBay's senior management team, check out the Company Overview section at www.pages.ebay.com/community/aboutebay/overview/management.html.)

Whitman ran the operation from the time she came on board. Omidyar, who as of April 17, 2001, owned 25.7 percent of eBay's stock (worth approximately $4.7 billion as of December 2001), spent considerable time in Paris. He and Pamela, still in their mid-30s and concerned about the vast wealth they had accumulated in such a short period of time, were devoting a substantial amount of their energy to exploring philanthropic causes.[10] They had decided to give most of their fortune to charity and were scrutinizing alternative ways to maximize the impact of their philanthropic contributions on the overall well-being of society. Jeffrey Skoll owned 14.8 percent of eBay's shares (worth about $2.7 billion), and Margaret Whitman owned 4.2 percent (worth about $750 million).

HOW AN eBAY AUCTION WORKED

EBay endeavored to make it very simple to buy and sell goods (see Exhibits 5 and 6). In order to sell or bid on goods, users first had to register at the site. Once they registered, users selected both a user name and a password. Unregistered users were able to browse the website but were not permitted to bid on any goods or list any items for auction.

On the website, search engines helped customers determine what goods were currently available. When registered users found an item they desired, they could choose to enter a single bid or to use automatic bidding (called proxy bidding). In automatic bidding the customer entered an initial bid sufficient to make him or her the high bidder. Then the bid would be automatically increased as others bid for the same object until the auction ended and either the bidder won or another bidder surpassed the original customer's maximum specified bid. Regardless of which bidding method they chose, users could check bids at any time and either bid again, if they had been outbid, or increase their maximum amount in the automatic bid. Users could choose to receive e-mail notification if they were outbid.

Once the auction had ended, the buyer and seller were notified of the winning bid and were given each other's e-mail address. The parties to the auction would then privately arrange for payment and delivery of the good.

Fees and Procedures for Sellers

Buyers were not charged a fee for bidding on items on eBay, but sellers were charged an insertion fee and a "final value" fee; they could also elect to pay additional fees to

---

[9]eBay press release, May 7, 1998.
[10]Quentin Hardy, "The Radical Philanthropist," *Forbes,* May 1, 2000.

exhibit 5   eBay's Instructions for Becoming a New Bidder

promote their listing. Listing, or insertion, fees ranged from 30 cents for auctions with opening bids, minimum values, or reserve prices under $10 to $3.30 for auctions with opening bids, minimum values, or reserve prices of $200.00 and up. Final value fees ranged from 1.25 to 5 percent of the final sale price and were computed according to a graduated fee schedule in which the percentage fell as the final sales price rose. As an example, in a basic auction with no promotion, if the item had brought an opening bid of $200 and eventually sold for $1,500, the total fee paid by the seller would be $35.18—the $3.30 insertion fee plus 5 percent of the first $25.00 (or $1.25), 2.5 percent of the additional amount between $25.01 and $1,000.00 (or $24.38), and 1.25 percent of the additional amount between $1,000.01 and $1,500.00 (or $6.25).

A seller who wished to promote an item could choose a variety of options ranging from adding a bold heading (for a fee of $2.00) to highlighting the item with a yellow band (for $5.00). A seller with a favorable feedback rating (discussed below) could have his or her auction listed as either a "Featured Plus Auction" (for $19.95), which featured the seller's item in a specific category, or a "Home Page Feature" (for $99.95), which allowed the seller's item to be rotated on the eBay home page.

In addition, a seller could post a photograph on a website and provide eBay with the appropriate Web address, which would then be included in the item's description. Items could be showcased in the Gallery section with a catalog of pictures rather than text. A seller who used a photograph in his or her listing could have this photograph

exhibit 6 eBay's Instructions for Becoming a New Seller

home | my eBay | site map | sign in

Browse | Sell | Services | Search | Help | Community

basics | buyer guide | seller guide | my info | billing | rules & safety

▸ Billpoint, the best way to send and receive payment on eBay!
▸ Business Exchange—eBay's small business marketplace.
▸ Local Trading--buy or sell in a region near you!

Search

☐ Search titles **and** descriptions

Smart Search

New to Selling?

It's so easy—you'll love it! Here's what to do . . .

1. First, you'll need to register, if you haven't done so already.
2. **Set up your selling account.** Place your credit card on file with eBay and you're ready to sell! If you'd like to accept credit card payments from winning bidders, sign up for Billpoint online payments.
3. **Gather the info** you'll need before you prepare your listing:
   - your item description
   - the URL (web site address) for any photos (see the photo tutorial)
   - the category you'll list under
4. Go to the Sell Your Item form, **fill in the info,** and review your listing. Be sure to check the information carefully, then click on Submit My Listing.
5. You'll see a confirmation page; **jot down the info,** such as your item number. This will be helpful if you want to update your listing, and to keep track of your item's status as your very own auction progresses!
6. When your auction closes, **contact your winning bidder** or bidders within three business days. You'll want to confirm the final cost, including any shipping charges, and tell them where to send payment. When the bidder meets your payment terms, you fulfill your end of the agreement by sending them your item. Your auction forms a binding contract between you and the winning bidder or bidders.

And then that's it—your item is sold!

Source: www.pages.eBay.com/help/basics/n-selling.html.

included in the Gallery section for 25 cents or featured there for $19.95. A Gallery section was available in all categories of eBay. Certain categories of items—such as real estate ($50.00 insertion fee), automobiles ($25.00 insertion fee, $25.00 final value fee), and "Great Collections"—had special promotion rates.

To attract sellers, eBay introduced several features, such as minimum opening bids and reserve prices. If the bidding did not top the reserve price, the seller was under no obligation to sell the item to the highest bidder and could relist the item for free. Sellers could also set a "buy it now" price that allowed bidders to pay a set amount for a listed item and thus end the auction immediately.

As of June 11, 2001, eBay sellers were required to provide both a credit card number and bank account information. While eBay admits that these requirements are extreme, it argues that they help protect everyone in the community against fraudulent sellers. They ensure that sellers are of legal age and are serious about listing the item on eBay.

How Transactions Were Completed

Under the terms of eBay's user agreement, if a seller received one or more bids above the stated minimum, or reserve, price, the seller was obligated to complete the transaction, although eBay had no enforcement power beyond suspending a noncompliant buyer or seller from using eBay's service. In the event the buyer and seller were unable to complete the transaction, the seller notified eBay, which then credited the seller the amount of the final value fee.

When an auction ended, the eBay system verified that the bid fell within the acceptable price range. If the sale was successful, eBay automatically notified the buyer and seller via e-mail; the buyer and seller could then work out the transaction details independent of eBay, or they could use eBay's checkout and payments services to complete the transaction. In its original business model, eBay did not take possession of either the item being sold or the buyer's payment at any point during the process. However, in an effort to increase revenues, eBay began to accept credit card payments and electronic funds transfers on behalf of the seller. Also, through an alliance with the U.S. Postal Service, it began allowing sellers to purchase and print postage online for a monthly fee of $14.95 (the service was named Simply Postage). However, the buyer and seller still had to independently arrange shipping terms (with buyers typically paying for shipping), and the items were sent directly from the seller to the buyer unless an independent escrow service was arranged to help ensure security.

To encourage sellers to use eBay's ancillary services, the company offered an automated checkout service designed to help expedite communication, payment, and delivery between buyers and sellers.

Feedback Forum

In early 1996, eBay pioneered a feature called Feedback Forum to build trust among buyers and sellers and to facilitate the establishment of reputations within its community. Feedback Forum encouraged individuals to record comments about their trading partners. At the completion of each auction, both buyer and seller were allowed to leave positive, negative, or neutral comments about each other. Individuals could dispute feedback left about them by annotating comments in question.

By assigning values of $+1$ for a positive comment, 0 for a neutral comment, and -1 for a negative comment, traders earned a ranking that was attached to their user name. Color-coded star symbols displayed next to a user's name indicated the amount of positive feedback. Well-respected high-volume traders could have rankings well into the thousands. The highest ranking a trader could receive was "over 100,000," indicated by a red shooting star.

Users who received a sufficiently negative net feedback rating (typically a -4) had their registrations suspended and were thus unable to bid on or list items for sale. Buyers could review a person's feedback profile before deciding to bid on an item listed by that person or before choosing payment and delivery methods. A sample user profile is shown in Exhibit 7.

The terms of eBay's user agreement prohibited actions that would undermine the integrity of the Feedback Forum, such as leaving positive feedback about oneself

***exhibit* 7** A Sample Feedback Forum Profile

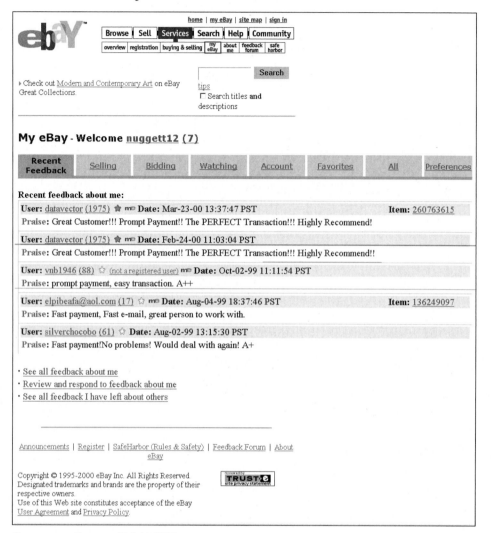

Source: www.eBay.com, April 14, 2000.

through other accounts or leaving multiple negative comments about someone else through other accounts. The Feedback Forum had several automated features designed to detect and prevent different forms of abuse. For example, feedback posted from the same account, positive or negative, could not affect a user's net feedback rating by more than one point, no matter how many comments an individual made. Furthermore, a user could make comments about his or her trading partners in completed transactions only.

The company believed its Feedback Forum was extremely useful in overcoming users' initial hesitancy about trading over the Internet, since it reduced the uncertainty of dealing with an unknown trading partner. However, there was growing concern among sellers and bidders that feedback might be positively skewed, as many eBayers chose not to leave negative feedback for fear of unfounded retribution that could damage their carefully built reputations.

eBAY'S STRATEGY TO SUSTAIN ITS MARKET DOMINANCE

Meg Whitman assumed the helm of eBay in February 1998 and began acting as the public face of the company. In an effort to stay in touch with eBay customers, Whitman hosted an auction on eBay herself. She found the experience so enlightening that she required all of eBay's managers to sell on eBay. When Whitman took over as CEO, Pierre Omidyar stepped back to function as chairman of eBay's board of directors, focusing his time and energy on overseeing eBay's strategic direction and growth, business model and site development, and community advocacy. Jeff Skoll, who became the vice president of strategic planning and analysis, concentrated on competitive analysis, new business planning and incubation, the development of the organization's overall strategic direction, and supervision of customer support operations.

Becoming a Public Company

Within months of assuming the presidency of eBay, Whitman took on the challenge of preparing the company to raise capital for expansion through an initial public offering (IPO) of common stock. Through a series of road shows designed to convince investors of the potential of eBay's business model, Whitman and her team generated significant interest in eBay's IPO. When the shares opened for trading on September 24, 1998, eBay's executives had high hopes for the offering, but none of them dreamed that it would close the day at $47, up more than 160 percent over the initial offering price of $18 per share. The IPO generated $66 million in new capital for the company and was so successful that *Bloomberg Personal* magazine designated eBay as the "Hot IPO of 1998"; *Euromoney* magazine named eBay as the "Best IPO in the U.S. Market" in January 1999. The success of the September 1998 offering led eBay to issue a follow-up offering in April 1999 that raised an additional $600 million. As a qualification to the IPOs, eBay's board of directors retained the right to issue as many as 5 million additional shares of preferred stock with no further input from the current shareholders in case of a hostile takeover attempt.

With the funds received from the IPOs, eBay launched strategic initiatives aimed at six specific objectives:[11]

1. Growing the eBay community and strengthening the eBay brand, both to attract new members and to maintain the vitality of the eBay community.

2. Broadening the company's trading platform by growing existing product categories, promoting new product categories, and offering services for specific regions.

3. Fostering eBay community affinity and increasing community trust and safety through services such as user verification and insurance.

4. Enhancing website features and functionality through the introduction of personalization features such as About Me, which permits users to create their own home page free of charge, and the Gallery, an opportunity for sellers to showcase their items as pictures in a photo catalog.

5. Expanding pre- and post-trade value-added services, such as assistance with scanning and uploading photographs of listed items, third-party escrow services, and arrangements to make shipping of purchased items easier.

---

[11]eBay S-1 report, filed March 25, 1999, p. 4.

6. Developing international markets by actively marketing and promoting the eBay website in selected countries.

To pursue these objectives, eBay employed three main competitive tactics. First, it sought to build strategic partnerships in all stages of its value chain, creating an impressive portfolio of over 250 strategic alliances with companies such as America Online (AOL), Yahoo!, Lycos, Compaq, and Warner Brothers. Second, it actively sought customer feedback and made improvements based on this information. Third, it actively monitored the external environment for developing opportunities.

Establishing a Business Model

The business model eBay established was based on creating and maintaining a person-to-person (or company-to-individual) trading community where buyers and sellers could readily and conveniently exchange information and goods. EBay's role was to function as a value-added facilitator of online buyer–seller transactions by providing a supportive infrastructure that enabled buyers and sellers to come together in an efficient and effective manner. Success depended not only on the quality of eBay's infrastructure but also on the quality and quantity of buyers and sellers attracted to the site; in management's view, this entailed maintaining a compelling trading environment, a number of trust and safety programs, a cost-effective and convenient trading experience, and strong community affinity. By developing the eBay brand name and increasing the customer base, eBay endeavored to attract a sufficient number of high-quality buyers and sellers necessary to meet the organization's goals. The online auction format meant that eBay carried zero inventory and could operate a marketplace without the need for a traditional sales force.

Management believed that eBay's business model had six specific elements that were key to the company's success:[12]

1. A position as the largest online trading forum with a critical mass of buyers, sellers, and items listed for sale. (At the end of 2000, eBay had more than 6 million items listed for sale in the auction format and an additional 8 million listed on Half.com in a fixed-price format.)

2. A compelling and entertaining trading environment that featured strong values and established rules and procedures to facilitate communication and trade between buyers and sellers.

3. Established trust and safety programs such as Safeharbor™. This program provided guidelines for trading, aided in resolving disputes, and warned and suspended (both temporarily and permanently) users who violated eBay's rules.

4. A cost-effective convenient trading system.

5. A strong community affinity.

6. A user interface that was easy to navigate, arranged by topics, and fully automated.

eBay's Strategy in 2002

Heading into 2002, eBay's strategy revolved around on five key action initiatives:[13]

---

[12]eBay 10-K report, filed March 3, 2001, pp. 4–6.
[13]eBay 10-K report, filed March 28, 2001.

1. *Broadening the existing trading platform* within existing product categories, across new product categories, through geographic expansion (both local and international), and through introduction of additional pricing formats such as fixed-price sales.

2. *Fostering eBay community affinity* by instilling a vibrant, loyal eBay community experience and maintaining a critical mass of frequent buyers and sellers with a vested interest in the eBay community.

3. *Enhancing features and functionality* by continually updating the eBay and Half.com websites to ensure continuous improvement in the trading experience.

4. *Expanding value-added services* to provide a comprehensive end-to-end personal trading service through offering a variety of pre- and post-trade services that enhanced the user's experience and made trading easier.

5. *Developing U.S. and international markets* via the deployment of efficient, opportunity-specific trading platforms that would gradually evolve into a seamless, truly global trading platform.

Broadening the Existing Trading Platform

Efforts to broaden the eBay trading platform concentrated on growing the content within current categories, broadening the range of products offered according to user preferences, and developing regionally targeted offerings. Growth in existing product categories was facilitated by deepening the content within the categories through the use of content-specific chat rooms and bulletin boards as well as targeted advertising at trade shows and in industry-specific publications.

To broaden the range of products offered, eBay developed new product categories, introduced specialty sites, and developed eBay stores. Over 2,000 new categories were added in 1998 and 1999, with an additional 5,000 launched in 2000, bringing the total to 8,000 categories (greatly expanded from the original 10 categories in 1995). Since its early days, eBay had developed a number of significant new product categories and specialty sites:

- *Great Collections* began as a category that showcased rare collectibles such as coins, stamps, jewelry, and timepieces as well as fine art and antiques from leading auction houses. Its success led eBay to expand Great Collections into a specialty site by tapping dealers, collectors, auction houses, and galleries and offering a database covering works of art, sales schedules, and art-related content through an alliance with ArtNet.com. EBay also offered a guarantee worth up to $50,000 for items sold through its site if issues regarding authenticity arose and could not be resolved.

- *EBay Motors* also began as a category and was developed when eBay noticed that an increasing number of automobile transactions were taking place on its site. According to Whitman, "One month, we saw the miscellaneous category had a very rapid growth rate, and someone said we have to find out what's going on. It was the buying and selling of used cars. So we said, maybe what we should do is give these guys a separate category and see what happens. It worked so well that we created eBay Motors."[14] In partnership with AutoTrader.com, this category was later expanded to a specialty site.

---

[14]"Q&A with eBay's Meg Whitman," *Business Week e.biz,* December 3, 2001.

- *LiveAuctions* allowed live bidding via the Internet for auctions occurring in brick-and-mortar auction houses around the world. Through an alliance with Icollector.com, eBay users had access to more than 300 auction houses worldwide. Auction houses that participated in this agreement were well rewarded, as more than 20 percent of their sales went to online bidders. An auction broadcast on the LiveAuctions site in February 2001 featured items from a rare Marilyn Monroe collection, including a handwritten note from Monroe that listed her reasons for divorcing her first husband.

- *Professional Services* offered professionals and freelancers a wide variety of products and services, ranging from business plan writing, to website and software development, to translation services and data entry. On this site prospective customers could post a project and allow professionals to bid on it.

- *The fixed-price format* established via the acquisition of Half.com allowed eBay to compete more directly with competitors such as Amazon.com. Half.com employed a fixed-price, person-to-person format that enabled buyers and sellers to trade books, CDs, movies, and video games at prices starting at generally half of the retail price. Similar to eBay, Half.com offered a feedback system that helped buyers and sellers build a solid reputation. EBay intended to eventually fully integrate both Half.com's listings and the feedback system into eBay's current site.

- *A business-to-business exchange category,* launched in March 2000, targeted businesses with fewer than 100 employees.

- *A real estate category* fostered eBay's emerging real estate marketplace. The offerings within this category were significantly enhanced by eBay's August 2001 acquisition of Homesdirect; which specialized in the sale of foreclosed properties owned by government agencies such as Housing and Urban Development and the Veterans Administration.

- *A partnership with Boats.com* offered buyers and dealers of boats a unique Internet site for the sale of boats and other marine products.

In June 2001, eBay introduced "eBay stores" to complement new offerings, to make it easier for sellers to build loyalty and for buyers to locate goods from specific sellers, and to prevent sellers from driving bidders to the seller's own website. In an eBay store, the entirety of a seller's auctions would be listed in one convenient location. These stores could also offer a fixed-price option from a seller and the integration of a seller's Half.com listings with its eBay auction listings. While numerous sellers of all sizes moved to take advantage of eBay stores, the concept was especially appealing to the larger retailers—such as IBM, Hard Rock Café, Sears, and Handspring—that were auctioning a growing array of items on eBay to take advantage of eBay's reach and distribution power.

Between 1999 and 2001, eBay launched over 60 regional sites to offer a more local flavor to its offerings. These regional sites focused on the 50 largest metropolitan areas in the United States. Regional auction sites were intended to encourage the sale of items that were prohibitively expensive to ship, items that tended to have only a local appeal, and items that people preferred to view before purchasing. To supplement the regional sites, in mid-2001 eBay began offering sellers the option of having their items listed in a special eBay seller's area in the classified sections of local newspapers. In these classifieds, sellers could highlight a specific item, their eBay store, or their user ID.

Other notable moves to broaden the platform included:

- Developing "eBay Anywhere" to allow eBayers to use mobile technology (personal digital assistants, cell phones, etc.) to access eBay.
- Launching the "Application Program Interface (API) and Developers Program" to allow other companies to use eBay's commerce engine and technology to build new sites.

Fostering eBay Community Affinity From its founding, eBay considered developing a loyal, vivacious trading community to be a cornerstone of its business model. This community was nurtured through open and honest communication and was built on five basic values that eBay expected its members to honor:

- We believe people are basically good.
- We believe everyone has something to contribute.
- We believe that an honest, open environment can bring out the best in people.
- We recognize and respect everyone as a unique individual.
- We encourage you to treat others the way that you want to be treated.[15]

EBay recognized that these values could not be imposed by fiat. According to Omidyar,

> As much as we at eBay talk about the values and encourage people to live by those values, that's not going to work unless people actually adopt those values. The values are communicated not because somebody reads the Web site and says, "Hey, this is how we want to treat each other, so I'll just starting treating people that way." The values are communicated because that's how they're treated when they first arrive. Each member is passing those values on to the next member. It's little things, like you receive a note that says, "Thanks for your business."[16]

Consistent with its desire to stay in touch with its customers and be responsive to their needs, eBay flew in 10 new sellers every few months to hold group meetings known as Voice of the Customer. These sellers suggested 75 to 80 percent of the company's new features.

An example of eBay values in action took place when eBay introduced a feature that referred losing bidders to similar auctions from other eBay sellers. The new policy elicited a strong outcry from some sellers, who demanded to know why eBay was stealing their sales by referring bidders to other auctions. One longtime seller went so far as to auction a rare eBay jacket so he could use the auction as a forum to complain about "eBay's new policy of screwing the folks who built them."[17] This caught the attention of Omidyar and Whitman, who met with the seller in his home for 45 minutes. After the meeting, eBay abandoned the practice of referring losing bidders to similar auctions by other eBay sellers.

Recognizing that many new users were perhaps not getting the most out of their eBay experience, and hoping to introduce new entrepreneurs to the community, the company created eBay University in August 2000. EBay University personnel traveled across the country, holding two-day seminars in various cities. These seminars attracted between 400 and 500 people, who each paid $25 for the experience. Courses ranged from "freshmen-level" classes that offered an introduction to buying and

---

[15]www.pages.ebay.com/help/community/values.html, January 1, 2002.

[16]"Q&A with eBay's Meg Whitman."

[17]Ibid.

selling to "graduate" classes that taught the intricacies of bulk listing and competitive tactics. EBay University was so successful that the company partnered with Evoke Communications to offer an online version of the classes. While community members gained knowledge from these classes, so did eBay. The company kept careful track of questions and concerns and used them to uncover areas that needed improvement.

A second important initiative to make the eBay community more inclusive was aimed at the fastest-growing segment of the U.S. population: adults aged 50 and over. In an effort to bridge the digital divide, eBay launched the Digital Opportunity Program for Seniors and set a goal of training and bringing online 1 million seniors by 2005. Specific elements of this plan included partnering with SeniorNet, the leading nonprofit computer technology trainer of seniors, and donating $1 million to this organization for establishing 10 new training facilities by 2005, developing a volunteer program for training seniors, and creating a specific area on eBay for Senior Citizens (www.ebay.com/seniors).

To foster a sense of community among eBay users, the company employed tools and tactics designed to promote both business and personal interactions between consumers, to create trust between bidders and sellers, and to instill a sense of security among traders. Interactions between community members were facilitated through the creation of chat rooms based on personal interests. These chat rooms allowed individuals to learn about their chosen collectibles and to exchange information about items they collected.

So that the company could manage the flow of information in the chat rooms, eBay employees went to trade shows and conventions to seek out individuals who had both knowledge about and a passion for either a specific collectible or a category of goods. These enthusiasts would act as community leaders or ambassadors; they were never referred to as employees, but they were compensated $1,000 a month to host online discussions with experts.

Although personal communication between members fostered a sense of community, as eBay's community grew from "the size of a small village to a large city" additional measures were necessary to ensure a continued sense of trust and honesty among users.[18] One of eBay's earliest trust-building efforts was the 1996 creation of the Feedback Forum, described earlier. Unfortunately, the Feedback Forum was not always sufficient to ensure honesty and integrity among traders. Although eBay estimated that far less than 1 percent of the millions of auctions completed on the site involved some sort of fraud or illegal activity, some users, like Clay Monroe, disagreed. Monroe, a Seattle-area trader of computer equipment, estimated that "ninety percent of the time everybody is on the up and up . . . [but] ten percent of the time you get some jerk who wants to cheat you." Fraudulent or illegal acts perpetrated by sellers included misrepresenting goods; trading in counterfeit goods or pirated goods that infringed on others' intellectual property rights; failing to deliver goods paid for by buyers; and using a false bidder to artificially drive up the price of a good (a practice known as *shill bidding*). Buyers could manipulate bids by placing an unrealistically high bid on a good to discourage other bidders and then withdraw their bid at the last moment to allow an ally to win the auction at a bargain price. Buyers could also fail to deliver payment on a completed auction.

Recognizing that fraudulent activities represented a significant danger to eBay's future, management took the Feedback Forum a step further in 1998 by launching the

---

[18]Claire Tristram, "'Amazoning' Amazon," www.contextmag.com, November 1999.

SafeHarbor program to provide guidelines for trade, provide information to help re-solve user disputes, and respond to reports of misuse of the eBay service. The Safe-Harbor initiative was expanded in 1999 to provide additional safeguards and to actively work with law enforcement agencies and members of the trading community to make eBay more secure. New elements of SafeHarbor included:

- Free insurance, with a $25 deductible, through Lloyd's of London for transactions under $200.
- Enhancements to the Feedback Forum such as listing whether the user was a buyer or a seller in a transaction.
- A new class of verified eBay users with an accompanying icon.
- Easy access to escrow services.
- Tougher policies relating to nonpaying bidders and shill bidders.
- Clarification of which items were not permissible to list for sale (such as items as-sociated with Nazi Germany or with organizations such as the Ku Klux Klan that glorify hate, racial intolerance, or violence).
- A strengthened antipiracy and anti-infringement program known as the Verified Rights Owner (VeRO) program, and the introduction of dispute resolution services.

The use of verified buyer and seller accounts was viewed as especially significant because it allowed eBay to ensure that suspended users did not open new eBay ac-counts under different names. User information was verified through Atlanta-based Equifax, Inc. To further ensure that suspended users didn't register new accounts with different identities, eBay partnered with Infoglide, whose similarity search technology allowed the company to examine new registrant information.

Implementing these new initiatives meant increasing the number of positions (full-time or contract) in eBay's SafeHarbor department from 24 to 182. The company also organized the department around the functions of investigations, community watch, and fraud prevention. The investigations group was responsible for examining reported trading violations and possible misuses of eBay. The fraud prevention group mediated customer disputes over such things as the quality of the goods sold. If a written com-plaint of fraud was filed against a user, eBay generally suspended the alleged of-fender's account, pending an investigation.

The community watch group worked with over 100 industry-leading companies—ranging from software publishers to toy manufactures to apparel makers—to protect intellectual property rights. To ensure that illegal items were not being sold and that sale items listed did not violate intellectual property rights, this SafeHarbor group au-tomated daily keyword searches on auction content. Offending auctions were closed, and the seller was notified of the violation. Repeated violations resulted in suspension of the seller's account.

As eBay expanded its categories, new safeguards were introduced to meet the unique needs of the Great Collections and automobile categories. In the eBay Great Collections category, the company partnered with Collector's Universe to offer au-thentication and grading services for specific products such as trading cards, coins, and autographs. In the automobile area, eBay partnered with Saturn to provide users with access to Saturn models nationwide.

Enhancing Features and Functionality   In designing its website, eBay went to great lengths to make it intuitive, easy to use by both buyers and sellers, and reliable. Efforts to ensure ease of use ranged from narrowly defining categories (to allow users to quickly locate desired products) to introducing services designed to personalize a user's eBay experience. One such service, developed by eBay and launched in 1998, was My eBay, which gave users centralized access to confidential, current information regarding their trading activities. From his or her My eBay page, a user could view information pertaining to his or her current account balances with eBay; feedback rating; the status of any auctions in which he or she was participating, as either a buyer or a seller; and auctions in favorite categories. In October of the same year, eBay introduced the About Me service, which allowed users to create customized home pages that could be viewed by all other eBay members and could include elements from the My eBay page such as user ratings or items the user had listed for auction, as well as personal information and pictures. This service not only increased customer ease of use but also contributed to the sense of community among the traders; one seller stated, "[The About Me service] made it easier and more rewarding for me to do business with others."[19] New features and services added in 2000 included Highlight and Feature Plus (new listing functions that could make an auction stand out), a cross-listing feature that allowed sellers to list their products in two categories, a tool to set prequalification guidelines for bidders, a new imaging and photo hosting service that made it easier for sellers to include pictures of their goods, and Buy It Now (a tool that sped up the buying process).

When eBay first initiated service, the only computer resource it had was a single Sun Microsystems setup with no backup capabilities. By 1999, eBay's explosive growth required 200 Windows NT servers and a Sun Microsystems server to manage the flow of users on the site, process new members, accept bids, and manage the huge database containing the list of all items sold on the site. On June 10, 1999, the strain of managing these processes while attempting to integrate new product and service offerings proved too much for the system—the eBay site crashed and stayed down for 22 hours. The outage shook user confidence in eBay's reliability and cost the company some $4 million in fees. The company's stock price reacted to the outage by falling from $180 to $136.20.

Unfortunately, the June 10 site crash proved to be the first in a string of outages. While none were as significant as the first (most lasted only one to four hours), confidence in eBay continued to decline in both the online community and on Wall Street—pushing eBay's stock price down to $88 in August 1999. To counter its outage problems, eBay sought out Maynard Webb, a premier software engineer and troubleshooter who was working at Gateway Computer. Webb put a moratorium on new features until system stability was restored. He believed that it was virtually impossible to completely eliminate outages, so he set a goal of reducing system downtime and limiting outages to one hour.[20] To achieve this goal, Webb believed, he would need a backup for the 200 Windows NT servers, another for the Sun Microsystems unit, and a better system for managing communications between the Windows NT and Sun systems. In attacking these challenges, eBay acquired seven new Sun servers, each valued at $1 million, and outsourced its technology and website operations to Exodus Communications and Abovenet. These outsourcing agreements were intended to allow Exodus and Abovenet to "manage network capacity and provide a more robust backbone" while eBay focused on its core business.[21] While eBay still experienced minor outages

---

[19]Ann Pearson, in an eBay press release dated October 15, 1998.

[20]Julie Pita, "Webb Master," *Forbes*, December 13, 1999.

[21]eBay press release, October 8, 1999.

when it changed or expanded services (for example, a system crash coincided with the introduction of the original 22 regional websites), system downtime decreased. However, the stability of the system under eBay's explosive growth and continuous introduction of new features and services was a major and continuing management concern. In 2001, eBay formed an alliance with IBM to upgrade eBay's technological infrastructure in a project referred to as V3.

The V3 project used WebSphere, IBM's "e-frastructure" software, to provide the technological foundation for eBay's next-generation trading platform. This platform was designed to improve the overall user experience by allowing eBay to easily add new features, user tools, and businesses while improving site dependability. According to Webb, "WebSphere, with its Java-based J2EE technology framework, gives us tremendous business advantages. EBay will be able to grow reliably and cost effectively, and we will be able to do so while providing our users with the new services they want to transact more business."[22]

Expanding Value-Added Services   Since its earliest days, eBay realized that in order to be successful, its service had to be both easy to use and convenient to access. The company continuously sought to add services to fill these needs by offering a variety of pre- and post-trade services to enhance the user experience and provide an end-to-end trading experience.

Early efforts in this direction included alliances with

- A leading shipping service (Parcel Plus).
- Two companies that helped guarantee that buyers would get what they paid for (Tradesafe and I-Escrow).
- The world's largest franchiser of retail business, communications, and postal service centers (Mailboxes, Etc.).
- The leader in multicarrier Web-based shipping services for e-commerce (iShip.com).

To facilitate person-to-person credit card payments, eBay acquired Billpoint, a company that specialized in transferring money from one cardholder to another. Using the newly acquired capabilities of Billpoint, eBay was able to offer sellers the option of accepting credit card payments from other eBay users; for this service, eBay charged sellers a small percentage of the transaction. EBay's objective was to make credit card payment a "seamless and integrated part of the trading experience."[23] In March 2000, eBay and Wells Fargo, the owner-operator of the largest Internet bank, entered into an arrangement whereby Wells Fargo would purchase a minority stake in Billpoint and, in turn, Billpoint would use Wells Fargo's extensive customer care and payment processing infrastructure to process credit card payments from eBay buyers to eBay sellers.

Developing U.S. and International Markets   As competition increased in the online auction industry, eBay began to seek growth opportunities in international markets. While international buyers and sellers had been trading on eBay for some time, there were no facilities designed especially for the needs of these community members. In entering international markets, eBay considered three options. It could

---

[22]eBay press release, September 6, 2001.
[23]eBay press release, May 18, 1999.

build a new user community from the ground up, acquire a local organization, or form a partnership with a strong local company. In an effort to create a global trading community, eBay employed all three strategies.

In late 1998, eBay's initial efforts at international expansion into Canada and the United Kingdom relied on building new user communities. The first step in establishing these communities was creating customized home pages for users in those countries.

These home pages were designed to provide content and categories locally customized to the needs of users in specific countries, while providing them with access to a global trading community. Local customization in the United Kingdom was facilitated through the use of local management, grassroots and online marketing, and participation in local events.[24] In February 1999, eBay partnered with PBL Online, a leading Internet company in Australia, to offer a customized Australian and New Zealand eBay home page. When the site went live in October of that year, transactions were denominated in Australian dollars. While buyers could bid on auctions anywhere in the world, they could also search for items located exclusively in Australia. Further, eBay designed local chat boards to facilitate interaction between Australian users and offered country-specific categories, such as Australian coins and stamps as well as cricket and rugby memorabilia.

Seeking to further expand its global reach, eBay acquired Germany's largest online person-to-person trading site, Alando.de AG, in June 1999. EBay's management handled the transition of service in a manner calculated to be smooth and painless for Alando.de AG's users. While users would have to comply with eBay rules and regulations, the only significant change for Alando.de AG's 50,000 registered users was that they would have to go to a new URL to transact their business.

To establish an Asian presence, eBay formed a joint venture with NEC in February 2000 to launch eBay Japan. According to the new CEO of eBay Japan, Merle Okawara, an internationally renowned executive, NEC was pleased to help eBay in leveraging the tried-and-trusted eBay business model to provide Japanese consumers with access to a global community of active online buyers and sellers. In customizing the site to the needs of Japanese users, eBay wrote the content exclusively in Japanese and allowed users to bid in yen. The site had over 800 categories, ranging from those that were internationally popular (such as computers, electronics, and Asian antiques) to those with a local flavor (such as Hello Kitty, Pokémon, and pottery). The eBay Japan site also debuted a new merchant-to-person concept known as Supershops, which allowed consumers to bid on items listed by companies.

In 2001, eBay expanded into South Korea through an acquisition of a majority ownership position in the country's largest online trading service, Internet Auction Co. Ltd., and into Belgium, Brazil, Italy, France, the Netherlands, Portugal, Spain, and Sweden through the acquisition of Europe's largest online trading platform, iBazar. Further expansion in 2001 included the development of a local site in Singapore, and an equity-based alliance with the leading online auction site for the Spanish- and Portuguese-speaking communities in Latin America, MercadoLibre.com, that would give eBay access to Argentina, Chile, Colombia, Ecuador, Mexico, Uruguay, and Venezuela.

EBay perceived this rapid international expansion as one of the keys to attaining its goal of having $3 billion in annual revenues by 2005. Growth opportunities were

---

[24]eBay 10-K report, filed March 30, 2000.

exhibit 8   Comparative Ratings of Site Characteristics of Selected Leading Online Auction Sites, December 2001

Rating scale: Excellent = 4, Good = 3, Average = 2, Below average = 1)

| | Site Characteristics | | | | | |
Auction Site	Inventory	Bidding	Services/Fees	Support	Functionality	Community
eBay	4	3	3	2	3	4
Amazon.com Auctions	4	2	4	3	4	2
Dell Auctions	2	2	3	3	3	1
eHammer	3	4	3	3	2	1
Excite Auctions	2	2	4	3	2	1
uBid	3	3	3	4	3	N/A
Yahoo Auctions	4	3	3	1	4	2

Source: www.auctionwatch.com, December 5, 2001.

especially appealing in Asia (due to rapid increases in Internet access) and Europe. According to a spokesperson for eBay, the company was particularly interested in expanding to large markets that had significant levels of Internet usage such as China and Taiwan. While eBay recognized the challenges represented by linguistic, cultural, and legal issues, it expected its international operations to achieve profitability in 2002.[25]

HOW eBAY'S AUCTION SITE COMPARED WITH THAT OF RIVALS

Auction sites varied in a number of respects: their inventory, the bidding process, extra services and fees, technical support, functionality, and sense of community. AuctionWatch, a company that helped Internet users select which online auction companies to do business with, ranked the leading online auction sites based on these characteristics. Exhibit 8 shows the AuctionWatch ratings of several online auction competitors as of December 5, 2001.

eBAY'S PRINCIPAL COMPETITORS

In the broadest sense, eBay competed with classified advertisements in newspapers, garage sales, flea markets, collectibles shows, and other venues such as local auction houses and liquidators. As eBay's product mix had broadened beyond collectibles to include practical household items, office equipment, toys, and so on, the company's competitors had broadened to include brick-and-mortar retailers, import/export companies, and catalog and mail order companies. EBay considered itself to be competing in a broad sense with a number of other online retailers, such as Wal-Mart, Kmart, Target, Sears, JCPenney, and Office Depot. The company also felt that it was competing

---
[25]Stephen Lawson, "eBay Outlines International Expansion Plans," www.thestandard.com, November 14, 2001.

exhibit 9   Number of Unique Monthly Visitors at Leading Online
Auction Sites, November 1999 through November 2000

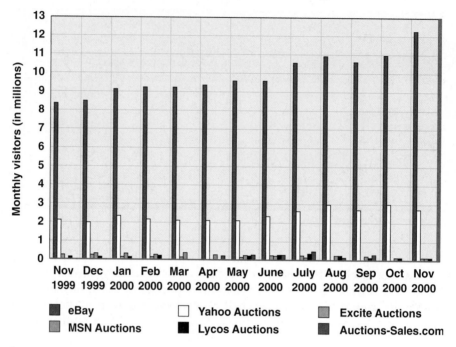

Source: www.auctionwatch.com/awdaily/reviews/metrics/index.html\.

with a number of specialty retailers, such as Christie's (antiques), KB Toys (toys), Blockbuster (movies), Dell (computers), Footlocker (sporting goods), Ticketmaster (tickets), and Home Depot (tools).[26]

While eBay controlled 64.3 percent of the online auction revenue share in May 2001, uBid.com had emerged as eBay's main competitor during this time (with 14.7 percent of online auction revenue). The three next-largest competitors, Egghead.com (4.0 percent), Yahoo! Auctions (2.4 percent), and Amazon Auctions (2.0 percent), represented less than 10 percent of the revenue share in the online auction market in mid-2001. EBay considered several factors—such as the ability to attract buyers, the volume of transactions and selection of goods, customer service, and brand recognition—as being the most important competitive factors in the online auction industry. In addition to these principal factors, eBay was also attempting to compete along several other dimensions: sense of community, system reliability, reliability of delivery and payment, website convenience and accessibility, level of service fees, and quality of search tools.[27] Exhibit 9 displays the number of unique monthly visitors to several of the main online auction sites in 1999–2000.

EBay management saw traditional competitors as inefficient because their fragmented local and regional nature made it expensive and time-consuming for buyers and sellers to meet, exchange information, and complete transactions. Moreover, traditional auction houses suffered from three other deficiencies: (1) they tended to offer

---

[26]eBay 10-Q annual report, November 14, 2001.
[27]Ibid.

limited variety and breadth of selection as compared to the millions of items available on eBay, (2) they often had high transactions costs, and (3) they were "information inefficient" in the sense that buyers and sellers lacked a reliable and convenient means of setting prices for sales or purchases. EBay's management saw its online auction format as competitively superior to these rivals because it (1) facilitated buyers and sellers meeting, exchanging information, and conducting transactions; (2) allowed buyers and sellers to bypass traditional intermediaries and trade directly, thus lowering costs; (3) provided global reach to greater selection and a broader base of participants; (4) permitted trading at all hours and provided continuously updated information; and (5) fostered a sense of community among individuals with mutual interests.

uBid.com

UBid's mission was to "become the most recognized and trusted e-commerce auction site that consistently delivers exceptional value and service to its customers and supplier partners."[28] The company's business model centered on offering brand-name merchandise in 16 categories. In early 2002, its product categories ranged from computers and their peripherals, to travel and events, to linen and apparel at up to 70 percent off retail prices. Users had three options for buying and selling products on uBid's site. First, the company offered Internet auctions consisting of its own products. Second, the company offered uBid Preferred Partner Auctions, which consisted of products listed by uBid-approved businesses. Third, uBid conducted auctions through the uBid Consumer Exchange, where consumers listed items for auction with no listing fees.

UBid had experienced rapid growth due in part to the warranties it offered on almost all of its products. The company's website had 6 million visitors during December 2000, an 80 percent increase from December 1999. The company's revenues also increased by 60 percent during this same period. The website sold 350,000 items in December 2000 (a 60 percent increase over 1999) and experienced 66 million page views (a 50 percent increase). While other online auction sites were experiencing a stagnant period due to the mediocre performance of e-commerce in 2000, uBid had continued to prosper. Many industry analysts saw the company emerging as eBay's most significant competitor down the road. Alan Cohen, senior vice president of marketing at uBid, credited his company's success and growth to their ability to "convert niche focus into consumer loyalty . . . [with the] incredible value we provide consumers through a niche business-to-consumer/small business marketplace."[29]

UBid was founded in April 1997 and became a public company with an initial public offering of common stock in December 1998; the company's stock traded on the NASDAQ. UBid generated revenues of $204.9 million in 1999. In April 2000, uBid entered into an agreement with CMGI (a public venture-capital firm that invested in dot-com start-ups) and since that time had formed alliances with such CMGI affiliates as AltaVista and AuctionWatch. In May 2001, the uBid website offered 12,000 products daily in 16 different product categories. The company had approximately 3 million registered users and was second only to eBay in the online auction market with a 14.7% share of market revenues.

---

[28]www.ubid.com/about/companyinfo.asp.

[29]uBid press release, July 7, 2001.

exhibit 10   A Sample uBid Auction

UBid had been the recipient of several honors and awards. The company was ranked one of the top 30 online merchants in 2001, received the first annual e.Millenium Award in 2000, was mentioned by Ernst & Young as one of the favorite sites of 2000, and was reported by Nielsen as one of the top 15 e-tailers of the 2000 Christmas season. An example of an auction from uBid is shown in Exhibit 10.

Yahoo! Auctions

Yahoo!, the first online navigational guide to the Web, launched Yahoo! Auctions in 1998. Yahoo! offered services to nearly 200 million users every month, and the Yahoo! Network operated in North America, Europe, Asia, and Latin America. The website was available in 24 different countries and 12 different languages. Yahoo! reported net revenues of $1.11 billion in 2000 (up 88 percent from 1999) and net income of $290 million. The company's user base grew from 120 million to over 180 million during 2000. In December 2000, Yahoo! averaged 900 million page views per day (up 94 percent from 1999). Yahoo! had entered into numerous alliances and marketing agreements to generate additional traffic and was investing in new technology to improve the performance and attractiveness of its site.

Its auction services were provided to users free of charge in the early days, and the number of auctions listed on Yahoo! increased from 670,000 to 1.3 million during the second half of 1999. However, when Yahoo! decided to start charging users a listing fee in January 2001, listings fell from over 2 million to about 200,000.[30] Yahoo! Auctions also offered many extra services to its users. For example, the Premium Sellers Program was designed to reward the sellers that were consistently at the top of their category. These premium sellers were allowed enhanced promotions, premium placement, and direct access to customer support. In recognition of the fall in listings due to the listing fee, Yahoo! Auctions announced a revamped performance-based pricing model for its U.S. auctions in November 2001. In this system, which was relatively similar to eBay's, listing fees were reduced and sellers were charged according to the value of an item sold. In response to this change, the number of listings rose to more than 500,000 by December 7, 2001.

Yahoo! Auctions expanded its geographic coverage to include auctions in Hong Kong, Taiwan, Korea, Mexico, Brazil, and Denmark by year-end 1999 and to include auctions in France, Germany, Italy, Spain, Ireland, Australia, New Zealand, Japan, Singapore, and Canada by early 2001. Localized Yahoo! auctions outside the United States were being conducted in 16 countries in 11 different languages going into 2002. Yahoo! Japan Auctions was the largest localized online auction service in Japan. An example of an auction from Yahoo! Auctions is shown in Exhibit 11.

Amazon.com Auctions

Amazon.com's strategic objective was to "be the world's most customer-centric company where customers can find and discover anything they may want to buy online."[31] The company was created in July 1995 as an online bookseller and had rapidly transitioned into a full-line, one-stop-shopping retailer with a product offering that included books, music, toys, electronics, tools and hardware, lawn and patio products, video games, and software. Its mall of boutiques was called zShops. Amazon.com was the Internet's number one music, video, and book retailer. The company's 2000 revenues of $2.76 billion were up 68 percent over 1999. Despite the company's rapid revenue growth, it had incurred huge losses since its inception (see Exhibit 12).

While Amazon's management was under mounting pressure to control expenses and to prove to investors that its business model and strategy were capable of generating good bottom-line profitability, it was clear that management's decisions and strategy were focused on the long term and on solidifying Amazon's current position as a market leader. The company's customer base rose from 14 million to 20 million during 2000. The company invested more than $300 million in infrastructure in 1999 and opened two international sites, Amazon.co.uk and Amazon.de. These two sites, along with Amazon.com, were the three most popular online retail domains in Europe. International sales grew to $381 million in 2000, up from $168 million in 1999. Amazon

---

[30]Wolverton, "eBay Seeks to Sail into New Territory."

[31]Amazon annual report, 2000.

exhibit 11 A Sample Yahoo! Auction

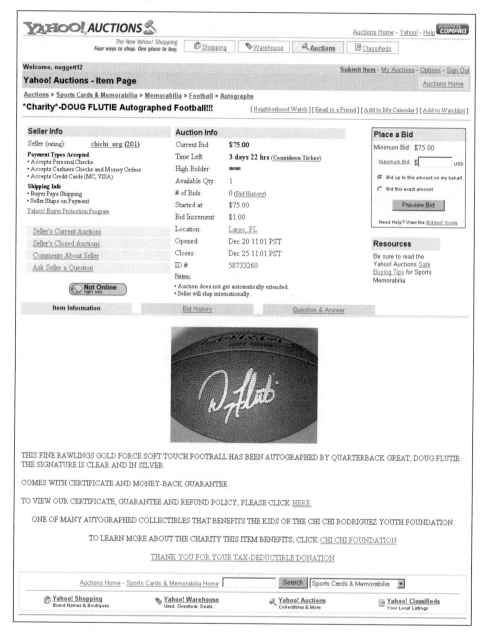

also entered into a number of strategic alliances. During September 2000, the company announced a co-branded toy and video game store with Toysrus.com. It already had e-commerce partnerships with Ashford.com, Drugstore.com, CarsDirect.com, and Sotheby's (a leading auction house for art, antiques, and collectibles), among others.

With its customer base of 20 million users in over 150 countries and a very well known brand name, Amazon.com was considered an imposing competitive threat to eBay. Amazon.com launched its online auction site in March 1999. The site charged sellers for listing their products and also a commission on sales. Although Amazon's selection of auctions did not match that of eBay, the company reported that online auc-

exhibit 12   Amazon's Net Revenue (Loss) 1996–2000

Year	Net Loss
1996	$ 6.2 million
1997	31.0 million
1998	124.5 million
1999	720.0 million
2000	1.41 billion

tions were the fastest-growing part of its business in 1999. Amazon.com offered three major marketplaces for its users: Auctions, zShops, and Sothebys.amazon.com. Its auction site formed partnerships with DreamWorks to promote the movies *Stuart Little* and *American Beauty* (72 auctions, averaging 27 bids per auction, total gross merchandise sales of over $25,000, yielding an average of over $400 per item) and with Oprah Winfrey (25 auctions, averaging 38 bids per auction, total gross merchandise sales of over $130,000, yielding an average of over $6,000 per item). An example of an auction from the Amazon.com website is shown in Exhibit 13.

Amazon's Acquisition of Egghead.com Assets.   In December 2001, Amazon.com paid $6.1 million in cash to acquire Egghead.com's website name; selected intellectual property; and almost all of the company's product information, business documents, and website data. Prior to filing for bankruptcy in mid-2001, Egghead.com had 3 million customers, had expected total revenues of $350 million, and was third in market revenues in the online auction industry.

Egghead was founded in Seattle in 1984 and specialized in the sale of electronics, computers, and related merchandise. In 1998, the company closed its physical stores and decided to operate entirely online. Egghead.com merged with Onsale.com in 1999, forming a company to compete in online auctions against eBay. In commenting on the usefulness of the assets acquired from Egghead, Amazon management said, "The Egghead brand is very well-known and well-respected. This will be a good opportunity for those customers who previously shopped with Egghead to continue to do so and also enjoy the added benefits and convenience of shopping with Amazon."[32]

eBAY'S NEW CHALLENGES

To successfully grow from a niche player to the world's largest online auction site, eBay had to overcome a number of challenges. The company faced each new challenge with an eye on its founding values and an ear for community members. According to Omidyar,

> What we do have to be cautious of, as we grow, is that our core is the personal trade, because the values are communicated person-to-person. It can be easy for a big company to start to believe that it's responsible for its success. Our success is really based on our members' success. They're the ones who have created this, and they're the ones who will create it in the future. If we lose sight of that, then we're in big trouble.[33]

---

[32]http://money.excite.com/jsp/nw/nwdt_rt.jsp?news_id=reu-n0446919-u1&feed=reu&date=20011204.

[33]"Q&A with eBay's Pierre Omidyar," *Business Week e.biz,* December 3, 2001.

exhibit 13   An Example Auction from Amazon.com

Going into 2002, industry analysts believed eBay faced two fundamental challenges:

1. Could eBay retain its traditional values and community culture, given its rapid growth and the changing size and composition of its user base?
2. How far could the company expand before its core business model began to erode or expansion into new auction categories put it in direct competition with large, well-known, well-funded, and resourceful rivals?

Growth, Values, and the Disgruntlement of Some Small Sellers

By 2002, the main core of buyers on eBay had changed from collectors seeking unique items to bargain hunters looking for values. The shifting buyer composition had affected final bid prices. Prices for consumer collectibles in 2001 were about 25 percent below 2000 levels, whereas the final bid price of some electronics items up for auction was comparable to the prices charged by online electronics retailers. As the number of value-conscious shoppers grew, eBay auctions became increasingly attractive to large retail stores and liquidators looking to unload overstocked inventories and/or second-quality merchandise. Some sellers welcomed the entry of larger companies, citing their ability to draw more bidders who would then pursue eBay's other offerings. Other sellers were indifferent to the new entrants; according to one regular eBay seller, "I'm not worried much about competing with larger businesses. I'm a micro-business, and I can run circles around the big guys. They're paying overhead on things that I don't—rent, payroll, utilities, and other things."[34] There was, however, a growing number of small sellers who felt that eBay's attempt to attract large companies was a clear sign that eBay was abandoning its traditional customer base and values. In response to a 2001 announcement that over half of eBay's revenues were coming from sales of practical items such as clothes and electronics, with larger retailers and wholesalers entering the eBay marketplace, one small seller stated, "It just continues the trend of ignoring/stepping on the non-corporate sellers who built eBay . . . EBay isn't fun anymore."[35] Comments left by two small sellers, one of whom had been on eBay since 1998, summed up the frustration of many of the disgruntled small merchants:

> The reason eBay will no longer be a place for the small vendor is the same reason the small vendor is absent wherever big vendors show up. Whether the challenge is price competition or site real estate competition, large vendors coming to eBay bodes ill for small sellers of collectables or anything else . . . eBay cannot have two masters. Whatever type of seller at eBay brings in the most revenue at the least cost will dictate who eBay caters to . . . Even if large vendors bring in more buyers, what will it cost a small vendor to even have a chance to be seen by these buyers? Do you think a large vendor or eBay will permit your item to be listed for 50 cents in the same vicinity as their merchandise? You don't need an MBA to figure this out.[36]

> I feel like many of the sellers at eBay feel! Many of us feel that eBay has betrayed us in many ways and it's really sad because I liked it here. If there was a better online auction site I would have gone long ago. The fact of the matter is, that eBay is still by far the best online auction site out there, so I will continue to sell on eBay until a better site comes along![37]

Omidyar and Whitman recognized the importance of eBay's culture and were aware of the potential impact rapid growth and the evolution of the product line could have on this valued asset. When asked about the importance of the culture, Omidyar said, "If we lose that, we've pretty much lost everything."[38] Whitman agreed on the importance of eBay's culture, but she did not see the influx of larger retailers and liquidators as a significant problem:

> Today, the big companies probably represent less than 1% of our gross merchandise revenues. So I think we have a long way to go before a small number of big companies accounts for a large percentage of our business. But we're going to keep our eye on that.[39]

Expansion into New Product Categories

Coupled with efforts to reach out to new types of sellers and bidders, eBay's additional expansion initiatives were designed to transform the business model from an online garage sale to the preeminent online marketplace where individuals and businesses

---

[34]"The eBay Outlook," www.auctionwatch.com message center, January 3, 2002.
[35]Ibid.
[36]Ibid.
[37]Ibid.
[38]"The People's Company," *Business Week e.biz,* December 3, 2001.
[39]"Q&A with eBay's Meg Whitman," December 3, 2001.

from nations all over the globe would come to buy and sell. Both the eBay community and Wall Street welcomed inclusion of new categories and international expansion that brought new eyes to sellers' listings and new revenues to eBay's pockets. This was true even though the international expansion brought with it increasing legal and economic complexities due to the new legal systems and exchange rate issues eBay encountered. As eBay expanded further from its original model to include the fixed-price options in eBay stores and Half.com (as well as entering the online software market through the API initiative), concerns arose among some industry analysts regarding whether eBay's top management had the knowledge and experience to grow these new businesses and whether the new competition eBay would face in these markets would hurt profitability.

Few were concerned that any of eBay's rivals would seriously threaten eBay in its core auction business in the near future; but with eBay stores and Half.com, eBay came into more direct retailing competition with Amazon.com and with such marketers of e-commerce solutions as Microsoft, Oracle, and IBM. Whitman dismissed these concerns, saying:

> EBay has a different brand proposition than an Amazon.com. The two companies do two quite different things very well. We're not going to be the retailer. And unlike an Amazon, the items are going to be unique and hard to find or value items. This is our only business. A lot of our competitors' businesses are primarily something else. We know more about managing a marketplace than anyone else in the world. Brands are like quick-drying cement. It's very hard to expand a brand beyond what the true core of the company is.[40]

Even with Whitman's assurances, concerns still existed regarding eBay's ability to simultaneously battle several large competitors on multiple fronts while dealing with the complexities of expanding into international markets. For example, eBay's operations in the European Union allowed Rolex to file a suit against eBay for facilitating the sale of counterfeit merchandise, even though eBay made no direct claims regarding the authenticity of goods auctioned on its site.

THE FUTURE

With approval from the U.S. Securities and Exchange Commission to raise up to $1 billion in equity capital (via the issue of new shares of stock), a hefty share price in the mid-60s, and a high price–earnings ratio that reflected strong investor confidence, eBay appeared able to fund new strategic initiatives and grow the company (see Exhibit 14). But it was not clear which opportunities eBay ought to pursue. Should it continue its aggressive expansion strategy or focus its efforts on maintaining the character of the eBay community (which was of great interest to some of eBay's long-standing small sellers who felt overwhelmed and ignored by all the strategic changes eBay was instituting)? If the decision was to continue rapid expansion, which opportunities should be accorded the highest priority? Should additional expansion in the international markets be the highest priority? If so, where? Alternately or in addition, should eBay concentrate on further broadening its offerings to include more categories, an increased number of specialty sites and sellers, and new fixed-price options? If management chose to continue expanding, should it do so by growing eBay's current businesses or through acquisitions? Would slower expansion open the door for significant competition from ambitious, well-funded rivals seeking to steal market share

---

[40]"Q&A with eBay's Meg Whitman," December 3, 2001.

exhibit 14   eBay's Stock Price Performance, September 1998–January 2002

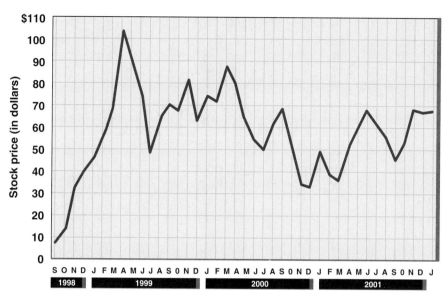

Source: www.bigcharts.com.

away from eBay or from smaller specialty sites catering to selected auction market niches?

In choosing among these opportunities, analysts and eBayers alike were forced to wonder just how much eBay could put on its plate to sustain its rapid growth, especially given Meg Whitman's philosophy about the danger of trying to do too much at once:

> You really need to do things 100 percent. Better to do 5 things at 100 percent than 10 things at 80 percent. Because the devil in so much of this is in the detail and while we have to move very, very fast, I think you are not well served by moving incredibly rapidly and not doing things that well.[41]

---

[41]"What's Behind the Boom at eBay?" *Business Week Online,* May 21, 1999.

19 Nucor Corporation in 2001: Pursuing Growth in a Troubled Steel Industry

Frank C. Barnes
University of North Carolina–Charlotte

Beverly B. Tyler
North Carolina State University

Nucor Corporation emerged from relative obscurity and near bankruptcy in 1966 to become one of the fastest-growing steel companies in America and one of the world's lowest-cost producers of steel products in 1990. Revenues had increased from $21 million in 1966 to nearly $1.5 billion in 1990, and earnings were $75 million, up from $1.3 million in 1966. Despite an economic recession in 1991, it appeared that Nucor had a virtually unstoppable strategy to grow into one of the biggest and best-known global producers of steel. Customers liked Nucor's expanding product line and low prices; investors were pleased with the company's relatively strong earnings and stock price performance; and Nucor, with Ken Iverson as a "model company president," had become a media darling and one of the most admired U.S. companies.

But by fall 2001, a little more than 10 years later, so much had changed. The steel industry worldwide had far more production capacity than was needed to meet market demand, forcing many companies to operate in the red. An unprecedented number of steel producers were flirting with bankruptcy. The economic recession that hit Asia and Europe in the late 1990s reached the United States in 2000–2001 and then orders for steel eroded further after the September 11, 2001, terrorist attacks. The slowing economy affected such major steel-consuming industries as construction, automobiles, and farm equipment. Hamstrung by overcapacity, foreign steel producers with few market opportunities abroad were dumping steel in the U.S. market at cut-rate prices. Although many domestic steel producers had imitated Nucor's innovative production processes and cut their costs to help them be more price-competitive, 30 U.S. steel companies had been forced to file for bankruptcy protection since late

1997. As Nucor entered the 21st century still pursuing a strategy of long-term growth, achieving expansion profitably was not as simple as it had been in preceding decades and opportunities in steel were harder to come by. Nucor still expected to improve its position as the second-biggest U.S. steelmaker and overtake U.S. Steel as the industry leader, but the challenges ahead were as great as in any period in the company's history.

COMPANY HISTORY AND BACKGROUND

Nucor's roots went back to auto manufacturer Ransom E. Olds, who founded Oldsmobile and then Reo Motor Cars. Through a series of transactions associated with Reo's decline toward bankruptcy, Reo Motor Cars eventually became the Nuclear Corporation of America (NCA) in 1955. NCA proceeded to diversify, acquiring various high-tech businesses making radiation sensors, semiconductors, air-conditioning equipment, and other products. However, from 1955 through 1965, NCA had eight money-losing years. A fourth reorganization of the company in 1965 led to the installation of F. Kenneth Iverson as president and Samuel Siegel as vice president of finance in 1966. This change in management resulted in a total restructuring of NCA and a decision to divest the money-losing businesses and rebuild the company around its only profitable operation—the steel joist businesses in Florence, South Carolina, and Norfolk, Nebraska, called Vulcraft. NCA moved its headquarters from Phoenix, Arizona, to Charlotte, North Carolina, in 1966, and expanded the joist business with new operations in Texas and Alabama. Management then decided to integrate backward into steelmaking by building its first steel bar mill in Darlington, South Carolina, in 1968. In 1972, the company formally adopted the name Nucor Corporation and began its journey to join the ranks of the world's leading steel companies.

Ken Iverson

Ken Iverson had joined the navy after high school in 1943 and had been transferred from officer training school to Cornell University's Aeronautical Engineering Program. On graduation, he selected mechanical engineering/metallurgy for a master's degree to avoid the long drafting apprenticeship in aeronautical engineering. His college work with an electron microscope earned him a job with International Harvester. After five years in that company's lab, his boss, and mentor, prodded him to expand his vision by going with a smaller company.

Over the next 10 years, Iverson worked for four small metals companies, gaining technical knowledge and increasing his exposure to other business functions. He enjoyed working with the presidents of these small companies and admired their ability to achieve outstanding results. NCA, after failing to buy the company Iverson worked for, hired him as a consultant to find another metals business for it to buy. In 1962, Iverson came upon a small joist plant in South Carolina named Vulcraft; NCA acquired the company and put Iverson in charge of running the new joist business.

Over the next four years, Iverson built the Vulcraft division into a profitable operation, even as the rest of NCA's businesses lost money. NCA's president, David Thomas, was described as a great promoter and salesman but a weak manager. In 1966, when NCA was on the edge of bankruptcy, Ken Iverson was named president. Iverson wasted little time in moving company headquarters to Charlotte, proceeding to divest NCA's unprofitable businesses, and then focusing the company's resources first on growing its profitable steel joist business and second on integrating backward into steel production. By 1984, the renamed company, Nucor, had six joist plants and four state-of-the-art steel minimills that used electric arc furnaces to recycle scrap steel into new steel products; the company's 1984 revenues were $660 million and its pretax earnings were $78.5 million.

From the beginning, Iverson required the people running the various plants, called divisions, to make all the major decisions about how to build and run Nucor. Nucor's board of directors and key decision makers consisted of Iverson, Sam Siegel (Nucor's chief financial officer), and Dave Aycock, who had been with the South Carolina joist company before NCA acquired it. Siegel had joined NCA as an accountant in 1961; he had quit earlier but agreed to return if Iverson was named president. Aycock and Siegel were named vice presidents at the time Iverson was named president.

Dave Aycock

Dave Aycock was the last of eight children raised on a small farm in the poor community of Wadesboro, North Carolina. He attended the University of North Carolina at Chapel Hill for one month, before financial considerations convinced him to join the navy as an enlisted man. For the next three years and eight months, he specialized as a metalsmith. On leaving the service in 1954, he got a job at Vulcraft as a welder. Over the next six years, he worked his way up to production supervisor and assistant plant manager, and then to sales manager. Aycock was very impressed with the owner of Vulcraft, Sanborn Chase. He described Chase as "the best person I've ever known" and as "a scientific genius." Specifically, Aycock viewed Chase as a man of great compassion who understood the atmosphere necessary for people to self-motivate. Chase devised the incentive system for production workers that later formed the core of Nucor's compensation programs in both its joist plants and its steel mills.

Aycock met Ken Iverson when NCA purchased Vulcraft in 1962, and they worked together closely for the next year and a half. At the corporate headquarters in Phoenix, Aycock reported directly to Iverson and had authority over all the joist operations, along with the task of planning and building a new joist plant in Texas. In late 1963, Aycock moved to Norfolk, Nebraska, to run the joist plant there and also to help oversee the operations of the company's other joist plants. Then, in 1977, he was named the manager of Nucor's new Darlington, South Carolina, steel plant.

Aycock had this to say about Iverson: "Ken was a very good leader, with an entrepreneurial spirit. He is easy to work with and has the courage to do things, to take lots of risks. Many things didn't work, but some worked very well." Nucor was very innovative in steel and joists. Its plants in Norfolk were years ahead in wire rod welding. In the late 1960s, the Norfolk operations not only had one of the first computer inventory management systems and design/engineering programs but also were very sophisticated in purchasing, sales, and managing and often beat out rivals because of their speedy design capabilities.

In 1984, Aycock became Nucor's president and chief operating officer, with Iverson functioning as chairman and CEO. While Iverson was an enthusiastic spokesman for Nucor's story, Aycock's role was more internal and low key. On one occasion, Aycock commented, "I was never as consumed by the excitement of making hot metal. To me, Nucor is a company with lots of employees and investors." Aycock saw Nucor's purpose as one of creating value for stockholders and employees; the fact that it did so by making steel was secondary.

The Nucor Success Story

By 1985, Nucor had become the seventh-largest steel company in the United States. It had two basic lines of business, the first being six steel joist plants that made the steel frames seen in many buildings and the second consisting of its four steel mills that utilized innovative minimill technology to supply both its joist plants and outside customers. It was a fairytale story. Management expert Tom Peters cited Nucor as an example of an excellently managed company. *The New Yorker* serialized a book about how Nucor, a relatively small American steel company, built an enterprise that led the whole world into a new era of steelmaking. NBC featured Nucor's success on one of its documentaries, "If Japan Can, Why Can't We?" The company's nonunion hourly workers had never seen a layoff and earned not only more than the unionized workers of old-line steel companies (U.S. Steel and Bethlehem) but also more than 85 percent of the people in the states where they worked. Many Nucor employees were financially secure.

Building on the Initial Base of Success, 1986–2000

Over the next 15 years, Nucor continued to be the prime mover in the U.S. steel industry. In a seemingly risky move in 1986, the company began construction of a $25 million plant in Indiana to manufacture steel fasteners. Imports had grown to 90 percent of this market as U.S. companies failed to do the things necessary to be competitive on cost and price. Iverson said, "We're going to bring that business back; we can make bolts as cheaply as foreign producers." A second fastener plant built in 1995 gave Nucor 20 percent of the U.S. market for steel fasteners. Nucor also acquired a steel bearings manufacturer in 1986, which Iverson called "a good fit with our business, our policies, and our people."

The Crawfordsville Plant and Nucor's Entry into Flat-Rolled Sheet Steel
In early 1986, Iverson announced plans for a revolutionary $250 million plant at Crawfordsville, Indiana, the first minimill in the world to attempt to manufacture flat-rolled sheet steel, a product segment heretofore the exclusive province of fully integrated steel manufacturers. The market for flat-rolled sheet steel was twice the size of the existing markets for minimill products; buyers included automakers, appliance manufacturers, and other durable goods manufacturers. The plant was expected to have half the labor costs of the integrated manufacturers' plants and to produce flat-rolled sheet at costs $50 to $75 per ton below the costs of integrated manufacturers, a highly significant cost advantage given the going market price of $400 per ton. Nucor's projections indicated that if the new plant's technology worked as planned, Nucor's profit from this one plant would almost equal the profit the company was earning in all the rest of its operations. A *Forbes* article said, "If any mini-mill can meet the challenge, it's Nucor. But expect the going to be tougher this time around." Nucor had the licensing rights to the world's next two plants built with this technology.

Nucor had spent millions trying to develop the process for manufacturing flat-rolled sheet when it heard of some promising developments at a German company. In the spring of 1986, Dave Aycock flew to Germany to see the pilot machine at SMS Schloemann-Siemag AG. In December, the Germans came to Charlotte for the first of what they thought would be many meetings to hammer out a deal with Nucor. Iverson shocked them when he announced that Nucor was ready to proceed to build the first plant of its kind.

Keith Busse was given the job of heading up the construction of the Crawfordsville, Indiana, sheet steel plant. Though an accountant by training, Busse had designed and built Nucor's state-of-the-art bolt factory. A midwesterner of German extraction, Busse ran a gun supermarket in Fort Wayne, Indiana, as a sideline and was the biggest machine gun dealer in the northern part of the state. Author Robert Preston, who wrote a book chronicling the pioneering effort at the Crawfordsville plant, told of a dinner conversation between Iverson and Busse during the construction phase: Thinking about the future, Busse was worried that Nucor might someday become a bureaucratic hierarchy like Big Steel, with vice presidents stacked on vice presidents, research departments, assistants to assistants, and so on. Concerned that the span of control was getting wider and wider for Iverson and the corporate staff as new plants and new divisions were added, Busse wondered, "How do we allow Nucor to grow without expanding the bureaucracy?" Iverson agreed that avoiding bureaucracy was essential. Busse suggested to Iverson, "Maybe we're going to need group vice presidents." Iverson's heated response was "Do you want to ruin the company? That's the old Harvard Business School thinking. They would only get in the way, slow us down." Iverson said the company could at least double in size to revenues of $2 billion before it added a new level of management. He then said, "I hope that by the time we have group vice presidents I'll be collecting Social Security."

Nucor's gamble on the new plant paid off and Busse, named the general manager of the Crawfordsville plant, played a key role within Nucor. The new mill began operations in August 1989 and reached 15 percent of capacity by year-end. In June 1990, the plant had its first profitable month, and Nucor announced the construction of a second flat-rolled sheet steel plant in Arkansas.

Leveraging the Success at Crawfordsville

In December 1992, Nucor signed a letter of intent with Oregon Steel Mills to build a sheet mill on the West Coast to begin production in 1994, but the project was later canceled partly because Iverson was becoming increasingly concerned about the adequacy of scrap steel supplies and the potential for higher scrap steel prices. In early 1993, Nucor announced the construction of a plant on the island of Trinidad to supply its mills with iron carbide pellets, which could be used as a partial substitute for scrap steel. The innovative plant would cost $60 million and take 18 months to complete. In 1994, Nucor moved forward, expanding its two existing flat-rolled sheet mills and announcing a new $500 million, 1.8-million-ton sheet mill in South Carolina, to begin operation in early 1997.

John Correnti Comes on Board

In 1987, Nucor began a joint venture with Yamato Kogyo, Ltd., to make structural steel products in an Arkansas mill near the Mississippi River; Nucor's entry into structural steel put it into another product segment dominated by the Big Three integrated steel companies (U.S. Steel, Bethlehem, and LTV). Ken Iverson put John Correnti in charge of the operation. Correnti, born in the Finger Lakes region of western New York, received a degree in civil engineering from Clarkson University in 1969. Correnti recalled, "I was a C/F student my first two years and an A/B student my last two years." With 17 offers, he accepted a job in U.S. Steel's construction department. He was energetic and ambitious, and became one of the youngest people to ever become a construction superintendent at U.S. Steel. The members of U.S. Steel's construction group were considered mavericks in the rest of the company and specialized in overcoming the company's bureaucracy and paperwork requirements. While employed by U.S. Steel, Correnti conducted projects in a wide range of steel operations across the country.

Working on a project in Texas in 1980, Correnti married a Texan and decided to leave U.S. Steel rather than move his wife out of Texas. A headhunter showed him a construction manager job with Nucor, a company he had never heard of. Ken Iverson convinced Correnti to join the company and move to Salt Lake City to build a bar plant. Correnti, who was used to operating independently, recalled, "I just started doing things, and I figured that when they didn't want me do something, I'd hear from somebody. I never heard from anybody." His second project was to build a Vulcraft plant in Utah, which Iverson then asked him to run.

In 1984, Correnti moved up to the more challenging job of vice president and general manager of the Utah bar mill, which was not performing well. He wasted no time getting everyone focused on cost-cutting, pointing out examples of wasted pens in one man's desk and the possibility of washing and reusing gloves. The plant office, dubbed the Taj Mahal by people in the plant, was too far from the main operations, so Correnti had it torn down and moved the staff into an engineering building nearer to the plant. He wouldn't let the salespeople have carpeting until their sales reached the desired level. By the time he left in 1986, to head construction of the Nucor-Yamato plant in Arkansas, the division was profitable.

Correnti became the general manager of Nucor-Yamato when it began production in 1988. In 1991, he surprised many people by deciding to double Nucor-Yamato's capacity by 1994. Nucor-Yamato became Nucor's largest division and the largest producer of wide-flange structural steel in the United States. By 1995, Bethlehem Steel was the only other wide-flange producer of structural steel products left—and it had plans to leave the business. In 1993, when Ken Iverson developed heart problems and had to have surgery, John Correnti was elevated to CEO of Nucor, with Iverson retaining the position of chairman of the board of directors.

Expansion into Other Products and Market Segments   Nucor started up its first facility to produce metal buildings in 1987. A second metal-buildings facility began operations in late 1996 in South Carolina, and a new steel-deck facility, in Alabama, was announced for 1997. At the end of 1997, the Arkansas sheet mill was undergoing a $120 million expansion to include a galvanizing facility.

In 1995, Nucor became involved in its first international venture, an ambitious project with Brazil's Companhia Siderurgica National to build a $700 million steel mill in the state of Ceara. While other minimills were cutting deals to buy plants and sell abroad, Nucor was planning to ship iron from Brazil and process it in Trinidad.

Nucor set records for sales and net earnings in 1997. In the spring of 1998, as Iverson approached his 73rd birthday, he was commenting, "People ask me when I'm going to retire. I tell them our mandatory retirement age is 95, but I may change that when I get there." Thus, it came as a surprise when, in October 1998, Nucor announced that Ken Iverson was retiring as Nucor's chairman at the end of the year and giving up his position on Nucor's board of directors. As the Iverson era came to a close, Nucor's management made a number of moves to strengthen the company in light of declining 1998 revenues and profits. Start-up began at the new South Carolina mill and at the Arkansas sheet mill expansion. The plans for a 1-million-tons-per-year steel plate mill in Hertford County, North Carolina, were announced, a move that would push Nucor's total steel production capacity to over 12 million tons per year when the plant came on line in 2000. The plant in Trinidad, which had proved much more expensive than expected, was deemed unsuccessful and closed. And Nucor's board approved the repurchase of up to 5 million shares of Nucor stock.

Despite revenue declines of 3 percent and earnings declines of 7 percent in 1999, Nucor continued to press forward with new investments. Expansions were under way in the steel mills, and a third building systems facility was under construction in Texas. Nucor was actively searching for a site for a joist plant in the Northeast. A letter of intent was signed with Australian and Japanese companies to form a joint venture to commercialize the strip casting technology. The Hertford steel plate mill began production in October 2000; the start-up was successful, and the steel plate was of high quality.

Nucor had 2000 revenues of $4.6 billion, 2001 production capacity of close to 13 million tons (up from 120,000 tons in 1970), production in 2000 of 11.3 million tons, and a product line that included carbon and alloy steel in bars, beams, sheet, and plate; steel joists and joist girders; steel deck; cold-finished steel; steel fasteners; and metal building systems. The company had production operations in nine states and was known for its strong emphasis on employee relations, quality, productivity, and aggressive pursuit of innovation and technical excellence. The company had a very streamlined organizational structure, incentive-based compensation systems, rigorous quality systems, and mills that were among the most modern and efficient in the United States. It had more than 8,000 employees and recycled more than 10 million tons of scrap steel annually.

Exhibit 1 presents a summary of tons produced by product category, average revenue per ton, and average profit per ton for the period 1970–2001. Exhibit 2 presents a financial summary for Nucor for the period 1990–2000. Nucor had operated profitably every year and every quarter since 1966. Nucor's directors had approved the purchase of up to 15 million shares of Nucor common stock; during 1998, 1999, and 2000, Nucor repurchased approximately 10.8 million shares at a cost of approximately $445 million.

NUCOR'S ORGANIZATION

By the early 1990s, Nucor had 22 divisions (one for every plant); each division/plant had a general manager who was also a vice president of the corporation. The divisions were of three basic types: joist plants, steel mills, and miscellaneous plants. The division general managers/vice presidents reported directly to the CEO. The corporate staff consisted of fewer than 25 people because Iverson wanted headquarters to consist of a small cadre of executives who would guide a decentralized operation where liberal authority was delegated to managers in the field. Iverson described how the decentralized structure functioned:

> Each division is a profit center, and the division manager has control over the day-to-day decisions that make that particular division profitable or not profitable. We expect the division to provide contribution, which is earnings before corporate expenses. We do not allocate our corporate expenses, because we do not think there is any way to do this reasonably and fairly. We do focus on earnings. And we expect a division to earn a 25 percent return on total assets employed, before corporate expenses, taxes, interest, or profit sharing. And we have a saying in the company—if a manager doesn't provide that for a number of years, we are either going to get rid of the division or get rid of the general manager, and it's generally the division manager.

A joist division manager saw Nucor's organization structure (which had only four levels of management) as an advantage:

exhibit 1 Nucor's Sales Volumes, Revenues, Average Prices per Ton, and Pretax Earnings, 1970–2001

| Year | Sales Tons (thousands) | | | | | | | | | | Net Sales | Composite Sales Price per Ton | Earnings before Federal Income Taxes | |
| | Steel | | | | | Steel Joists | Steel Deck | Cold-Finished Steel | Other | Total Tons | | | Amount | Per Ton |
	Sheet	Bars	Structural	Plate	Total Steel									
2001 (9 mo.)	3,891	2,054	2,043	359	8,347	404	260	161	101	9,273	$3,159,681,000	$341	$132,995,000	$16
2000	4,456	2,209	3,094	20	9,779	613	353	250	194	11,189	4,586,146,000	410	478,308,000	48
1999	4,293	1,988	2,453	—	8,734	616	375	243	208	10,176	4,009,346,000	394	379,189,000	42
1998	3,939	1,970	2,253	—	8,162	600	342	261	247	9,612	4,151,232,000	432	415,309,000	49
1997	4,118	2,082	2,235	—	8,435	568	287	256	240	9,786	4,184,498,000	428	460,182,000	53
1996	3,232	1,858	2,162	—	7,252	543	256	221	187	8,459	3,647,030,000	431	387,769,000	52
1995	2,994	1,799	1,952	—	6,745	552	234	234	178	7,943	3,462,046,000	436	432,335,000	62
1994	2,580	1,792	1,608	—	5,980	487	207	239	168	7,081	2,975,596,000	420	356,933,000	57
1993	2,038	1,669	1,230	—	4,937	417	170	213	154	5,891	2,253,738,000	383	187,110,000	35
1992	965	1,462	1,072	—	3,499	414	132	187	146	4,378	1,619,235,000	370	117,326,000	30
1991	707	1,335	1,075	—	3,117	378	124	163	123	3,905	1,465,457,000	375	95,816,000	28
1990	420	1,382	1,002	—	2,804	443	134	163	104	3,648	1,481,630,000	406	111,215,000	35
1989	6	1,344	630	—	1,980	446	140	157	105	2,828	1,269,007,000	449	85,636,000	34
1988	—	1,367	70	—	1,437	444	147	155	81	2,264	1,061,364,000	469	107,581,000	48
1987	—	1,313	—	—	1,313	444	154	133	54	2,098	851,022,000	406	83,234,000	40
1986	—	1,140	—	—	1,140	453	176	108	33	1,910	755,229,000	395	84,239,000	44
1985	—	1,152	—	—	1,152	471	169	87	23	1,902	758,495,000	399	106,178,000	56
1984	—	990	—	—	990	424	118	90	22	1,644	660,260,000	402	78,548,000	48
1983	—	1,030	—	—	1,030	331	95	62	17	1,535	542,531,000	353	47,564,000	31
1982	—	812	—	—	812	319	83	43	7	1,264	486,018,000	385	37,792,000	30
1981	—	919	—	—	919	342	89	33	—	1,383	544,821,000	394	44,829,000	32
1980	—	677	—	—	677	373	96	13	—	1,159	482,420,000	416	76,060,000	66
1975	—	144	—	—	144	243	—	—	—	387	121,467,000	314	11,682,000	30
1970	—	4	—	—	4	203	—	—	—	205	50,751,000	245	2,156,000	10

Source: Information posted at www.nucor.com, November 30, 2001.

exhibit 2 Financial Summary, Nucor Corp., 1990–2000

	2000	1999	1998	1997	1996	1995	1990
For the year							
Net sales	$4,586,145,981	$4,009,346,082	$4,151,232,283	$4,184,497,854	$3,647,030,387	$3,462,045,648	$1,481,630,011
Costs and expenses:							
Cost of products sold	3,925,478,540	3,480,478,687	3,591,782,838	3,578,941,039	3,139,157,919	2,900,168,171	1,293,082,950
Marketing, administrative and other expenses	183,175,557	154,773,600	147,973,101	145,409,693	120,387,357	130,677,162	70,461,830
Interest expense (income)	(816,104)	(5,095,299)	(3,832,252)	(35,318)	(283,837)	(1,134,190)	6,869,970
	4,107,837,993	3,630,156,988	3,735,923,687	3,724,315,414	3,259,261,439	3,029,711,143	1,370,414,750
Earnings before federal income taxes	478,307,988	379,189,094	415,308,596	460,182,440	387,768,948	432,334,505	111,215,261
Federal income taxes	167,400,000	134,600,000	151,600,000	165,700,000	139,600,000	157,800,000	36,150,000
Net earnings	$ 310,907,988	$ 244,589,094	$ 263,708,596	$ 294,482,440	$ 248,168,948	$ 274,534,505	$ 75,065,261
Net earnings per share	$3.80	$2.80	$3.00	$3.35	$2.83	$3.14	$0.88
Dividends declared per share	.60	.52	.48	.40	.32	.28	.12
Percentage of earnings to sales	6.8%	6.1%	6.4%	7.0%	6.8%	7.9%	5.1%
Return on average equity	14.2%	11.3%	13.4%	16.9%	16.6%	21.9%	12.1%
Capital expenditures	$ 415,404,602	$ 374,717,759	$ 502,910,263	$ 306,749,422	$ 537,438,406	$ 263,421,786	$ 85,764,316
Depreciation	259,365,173	256,637,460	253,118,608	218,764,101	182,232,851	173,887,657	51,133,482
Sales per employee	597,193	547,762	591,596	622,554	572,038	570,353	271,859
At year-end							
Current assets	$1,381,446,907	$1,538,508,511	$1,129,467,383	$1,125,508,464	$ 828,380,585	$ 830,741,318	$ 312,637,487
Current liabilities	558,068,452	531,030,898	486,897,157	524,453,610	465,652,755	447,136,311	202,789,294
Working capital	823,378,455	1,007,477,613	642,570,226	601,054,854	362,727,830	383,605,007	109,848,192
Current ratio	2.5	2.9	2.3	2.1	1.8	1.9	1.5
Property, plant and equipment	2,340,340,812	2,191,339,477	2,097,078,473	1,858,874,894	1,791,152,821	1,465,400,015	723,248,574
Total assets	3,721,787,719	3,729,847,988	3,226,545,856	2,984,383,358	2,619,533,406	2,296,141,333	1,035,886,060
Long-term debt	460,450,000	390,450,000	215,450,000	167,950,000	152,600,000	106,850,000	28,777,000
Percentage of debt to capital	15.9%	13.3%	8.4%	7.2%	7.5%	6.2%	3.8%
Stockholders' equity	2,130,951,640	2,262,247,906	2,072,551,781	1,876,425,866	1,609,290,193	1,382,112,159	652,757,216
Per share	$27.47	$25.96	$23.73	$21.32	$18.33	$15.78	$7.59
Shares outstanding	77,582,948	87,133,737	87,352,906	87,996,583	87,795,947	87,598,517	85,950,696
Stockholders	51,000	55,000	62,000	50,000	39,000	39,000	27,000
Employees	7,900	7,500	7,200	6,900	6,600	6,200	5,500

Source: Company records.

> I've been a division manager four years now and at times I'm still awed by it: the opportunity I was given to be a Fortune 500 vice president . . . I think we are successful because it is our style to pay more attention to our business than our competitors . . . We are kind of a "no-nonsense" company.

Hamilton Lott, a plant manager in Nucor's Vulcraft steel joist division (and group executive vice president in 2001), commented in 1997, "We're truly autonomous; we can duplicate efforts made in other parts of Nucor. We might develop the same computer program six times. But the advantages of local autonomy make it worth it." Joe Rutkowski, manager at Nucor's Darlington plant, agreed: "We're not constrained; headquarters doesn't restrict what I spend. I just have to make my profit contribution at the end of year."

Nucor's divisions operated as decentralized profit centers, with engineering, manufacturing, selling, accounting, and personnel management all being performed at the division level. A steel division manager, when questioned about Florida Steel, which had a large plant 90 miles away, commented, "I expect they do have more of a corporate hierarchy. I think they have central purchasing, centralized sales, centralized credit collections, centralized engineering, and most of the major functions."

Nucor spent some monies from time to time to research new ways to improve the efficiency of its production processes, but the main thrust of the company's R&D strategy was to be very diligent in monitoring R&D activities in steel production processes worldwide—it quickly reviewed newly emerging technical applications for possible adoption. Though Nucor was known for constructing state-of-the-art facilities at the lowest possible costs and for investing aggressively in plant modernization and efficiency improvements, its corporate-level engineering and construction team consisted of only three individuals. Nucor pursued strong alliances with outside suppliers. The company had developed working relationships with several construction companies whose managers knew the kind of work Nucor expected. Nucor did not specify exact equipment parameters on new purchases but instead asked its equipment suppliers to provide recommendations and accept responsibility for proper functioning of what was installed. It bought 95 percent of its scrap steel from an independent broker who followed the market and made recommendations regarding scrap purchases. Nucor did not have a corporate advertising department, corporate public relations department, or a corporate legal or environmental department—it preferred to outsource what needed to be done in these areas.

South magazine observed that Iverson had established a "stripped down, no nonsense" organization at Nucor. "Jack Benny would like this company," observed Roland Underhill, an analyst with Crowell, Weedon and Co. of Los Angeles. Underhill pointed out that Nucor's thriftiness didn't end with its lean corporate staff and spartan corporate facilities: "There are no corporate perquisites. No company planes. No country club memberships. No company cars." Ken Iverson was noted for flying coach class and taking the subway when he was in New York City. Nucor managers reflected a simple, businesslike style in operating their divisions; the offices of division general managers and vice presidents were like plant offices typically found in manufacturing facilities.

DIVISION MANAGERS

Nucor's corporate personnel manager described management relations at Nucor as informal, trusting, and not bureaucratic. He indicated there was a minimum of paperwork, that a phone call was more common than memos, and that no confirming memo was thought to be necessary. A Vulcraft manager commented:

> We have what I would call a very friendly spirit of competition from one plant to the next. And of course all of the vice presidents and general managers share the same bonus systems, so we are in this together as a team even though we operate our divisions individually. When I came to this plant four years ago, I saw we had too many people, too much overhead. We had 410 people at the plant and I could see, from my experience at the Nebraska plant, we had many more than we needed. Now with 55 fewer men, we are still capable of producing the same number of tons as four years ago.

The divisions managed their activities with a minimum of contact with Nucor's corporate staff. Each day, disbursements were reported to corporate office. Payments flowed into regional lockboxes. On a weekly basis, joist divisions reported total quotes, sales cancellations, backlogs, and production numbers. Steel mills reported tons rolled, outside shipments, orders, cancellations, and backlogs. Each month, each division prepared a two-page "operations analysis" distributed to all Nucor general managers and to the corporate office.

Nucor's general managers met three times a year. In late October they presented preliminary budgets and capital requests. In late February they met to finalize budgets and treat miscellaneous matters. Then, at a meeting in May, they handled personnel matters, such as wage increases and changes of policies or benefits. The general managers as a group considered the raises for the department heads, the next lower level of management for all the plants.

VULCRAFT: THE JOIST DIVISIONS

One of Nucor's major businesses was the manufacture and sale of open-web steel joists, joist girders, and steel deck at six Vulcraft divisions, located in Florence, South Carolina; Norfolk, Nebraska; Fort Payne, Alabama; Grapeland, Texas; Saint Joe, Indiana; and Brigham City, Utah. A new $50 million joist plant was under construction in Chemung, New York; start-up was scheduled for the third quarter of 2001.

Open-web joists, in contrast to solid joists, were made of steel angle iron separated by round bars or smaller angle iron (see Exhibit 3). Compared with solid joists, the open-web joists cost less and were of greater strength for many applications. They were used primarily as the roof support systems in large buildings such as warehouses and shopping malls.

The joist segment of the steel industry was characterized by intense competition among many manufacturers for many small customers. With an estimated 40 percent of the joist market, Nucor was the largest joist supplier in the United States, and it had a 30 percent share of the domestic market for steel deck. In 2000, Vulcraft produced 613,000 tons of steel joists and joist girders, a decrease from the record 616,000 tons produced in 1999; Vulcraft's steel deck sales were 353,000 tons in 2000, down 6 percent from the 375,000 tons sold in 1999. It utilized national advertising campaigns and prepared competitive bids on 80 to 90 percent of the buildings using joists. Competition was based on price and delivery. Nucor had developed computer programs to prepare designs for customers and to compute bids based on current prices and labor standards. In addition, each Vulcraft plant maintained its own engineering department to help customers with design problems or specifications. The Florence plant manager commented,

exhibit 3   Sample Vulcraft Products

Steel Joists Made by Vulcraft

Examples of Steel Decking Made by Vulcraft

Here on the East Coast we have six or seven major competitors; of course, none of them are as large as we are. The competition for any order will be heavy, and we will see six or seven different prices. I think we have a strong selling force in the marketplace. It has been said to us by some of our competitors that in this particular industry we have the finest selling organization in the country.

Nucor aggressively sought to be the lowest-cost producer in the industry. Materials and freight were two important elements of cost. Nucor maintained its own fleet of almost 150 trucks to ensure on-time delivery to customers in all states, although most business was regional due to transportation costs. Plants were located in rural areas near the markets they served. Nucor's move into steel production was a move to lower the cost of steel used by the joist and steel deck businesses.

Joist Production

On the joist divisions' basic assembly line, three or four of which might make up any one plant, about six tons of joists would be assembled per hour. In the first stage, eight people cut the angles to the right lengths or bent the round bars to the desired form. These bars and angles were then moved on a roller conveyer to six-man assembly stations, where the component parts would be tacked together for the next stage, welding. Drilling and miscellaneous work were done by three people between the lines. The nine-man welding station completed the welds before passing the joists on roller conveyers to two-man inspection teams. The last step before shipment was the painting.

Plant workers had control over, and responsibility for, quality. An independent quality control inspector had the authority to reject the run of joists and cause them to be reworked. The quality control people were not under the incentive system and reported to the engineering department.

Daily production might vary widely, since joists were custom made to match the requirements of each construction project. The wide range of joists being produced made efficient scheduling of the tasks at each workstation in the plant difficult; bottlenecks might arise anywhere along the line. Each workstation was responsible for identifying delays so that the foreman could reassign people promptly to maintain productivity. Since workers knew most of the jobs along the production line, including those requiring good welding skills, they could be shifted as needed. Work on the line was described by one general manager as "not machine type but mostly physical labor." He said the important thing was to avoid bottlenecks that slowed overall joist production.

There were four lines of about 28 people each on two shifts at the Florence joist plant. The jobs on the line were rated according to their degree of responsibility and were assigned a base wage, from $11 to $13 per hour. In addition to the base wage, workers were paid a weekly production bonus based on the total output of each line or shift. Each worker on a production line/shift received the same percent bonus. At the Vulcraft joist plant in Texas (which was representative), worker bonuses for production above the standard volume averaged 125 percent of base pay, pushing total compensation up to around $27 an hour in 1999.

The "standard" amount of time to make a joist (for purpose of determining worker bonuses) was established on the basis of experience (typically at the time plant operation began); one general manager indicated he had seen no time studies to recalculate the standard in his 15 years with the company. The Florence general manager stated, "In the last 9 or 10 years we have not changed a standard." Standards were, however, usually reset if a plant underwent significant modernization or important new pieces of equipment were installed that greatly affected labor productivity. As a job was bid, the cost of each joist was estimated using company-developed software. The estimated time depended on the length, number of panels, depth of the joist, the prevailing labor standard, and other relevant factors.

Vulcraft's Grapeland plant utilized a time chart to estimate the labor standard appropriate for on a particular job and type of joist. Plant team productivity was then measured against the designated standard time for bonus purposes. The chart of various standards was based on the historical time required on different types of joist jobs. Every few years, the time chart at Grapeland was updated and a new labor standard set.

exhibit 4   Productivity at Nucor's Florence Joist Plant, 1977–2000
           (in tons per man-hour)

Year	Tons per Man-Hour
1977	0.163
1978	0.179
1979	0.192
1980	0.195
1981	0.194
1982	0.208
1983	0.215
1984	0.214
1985	0.228
1986	0.225
1987	0.218
1998	0.249
1999	0.251
2000	0.241

Because some of the changes in the productivity performance of the production teams were due to equipment changes, generally the Grapeland chart for labor standards would be increased by half the total time change and employees would benefit in bonus pay from the other half. The most recent change in standards at Grapeland resulted in worker bonus increases in some departments of as much as 10 percent. The production manager at Grapeland had started in an entry position and risen through the ranks to his present position over a workforce of 200 people.

Exhibit 4 shows the productivity of Nucor's Florence, South Carolina, joist plant. The plant set a productivity record for overall tonnage in 1999. The manager explained that the small drop in 2000 was due to managerial changes; he was new to the division and had brought two new managers with him.

NUCOR'S STEEL DIVISIONS

Nucor expanded into the steelmaking business in 1969 to provide low-cost steel to its Vulcraft plants. Iverson said, "We got into the steel business because we wanted to build a mill that could make steel as cheaply as we were buying it from foreign importers or from offshore mills." To determine what type mill the company should construct, a task force of four Nucor people toured the world to investigate new technological advancements. This group decided that Nucor should adopt the latest and best minimill technology that used electric arc furnaces to recycle scrap steel into new steel products. A Harvard Business School casewriter described the early development of Nucor's steel divisions:

> By 1967 about 60 percent of each Vulcraft sales dollar was spent on materials, primarily steel. Thus, the goal of keeping costs low made it imperative to obtain steel economically. In addition, in 1967 Vulcraft bought about 60 percent of its steel from foreign sources. As the Vulcraft Division grew, Nucor became concerned about its ability to obtain an adequate economical supply of steel and in 1968 began construction of its first steel mill in

Darlington, South Carolina. By 1972 the Florence, South Carolina, joist plant was purchasing over 90 percent of its steel from this mill. The Fort Payne, Alabama, joist plant bought about 50 percent of its steel from Darlington. The other joist plants in Nebraska, Indiana, and Texas found transportation costs from the Darlington plant prohibitive and continued to buy their steel from other steel companies, both foreign and domestic. Since the Darlington mill had excess capacity, Nucor began to market its steel products to outside customers. In 1972, 75 percent of the shipments of Nucor steel was to Vulcraft and 25 percent was to other customers.

Between 1973 and 1981, Nucor constructed three more bar mills with accompanying rolling mills to convert the steel billets into bars, flats, rounds, channels, and other steel products. Iverson explained in 1984:

> In constructing these mills we have experimented with new processes and new manufacturing techniques. We serve as our own general contractor and design and build much of our own equipment. In one or more of our mills we have built our own continuous casting unit, reheat furnaces, cooling beds, and in Utah even our own mill stands. All of these to date have cost under $125 per ton of annual capacity—compared with projected costs for large integrated mills of $1,200–$1,500 per ton of annual capacity, 10 times our cost. Our mills have high productivity. We currently use less than four man-hours to produce a ton of steel. This includes everyone in the operation: maintenance, clerical, accounting, sales, and management. On the basis of our production workers alone, it is less than three man-hours per ton. Our total employment costs are less than $60 per ton compared with the average employment costs of the seven largest U. S. steel companies of close to $130 per ton. Our total labor costs are less than 20 percent of our sales price.

Nucor's 1989 entry into the flat-rolled sheet steel segment opened up another 50 percent of the total steel market to Nucor. Nucor's first sheet steel plant in Crawfordsville, Indiana, proved profitable, and three additional sheet mills were constructed between 1989 and 1990. Through the years, these flat-rolled sheet steel plants were significantly modernized and expanded to a total capacity of 3 million tons per year by 1999, at a capital cost of less than $170 per ton of capacity. In 2000, Nucor's production capacity at its three sheet steel mills was 5.9 million tons per year, with capital costs averaging $305 per ton of annual capacity.

Each of Nucor's four steel bar mills consisted of two mills operating side by side—one concentrating on making large-diameter bar products (which had distinct product specifications and customer requirements) and the other concentrating on smaller-diameter bar stock. In 2000, the total capital cost of all four Nucor bar mills averaged about $170 per ton of current annual capacity; total capacity of the four bar mills exceeded 3 million tons per year.

About 87 percent of Nucor's 10 steel mills' production in 2000 was sold to outside customers, and the balance was used internally by the Vulcraft Group, Cold Finish Group, Building Systems Group, and Fastener Division. Steel sales to outside customers in 2000 were a record 9,779,000 tons, 12 percent higher than the 8,734,000 tons in 1999. Throughout Nucor, each operation was housed in its own separate building with its own staff. Nucor designed its processes to limit work-in-process inventory, minimize space requirements, use a pull approach to material usage, and have operating flexibility.

Nucor's Approach to Pricing

Starting in 1984, Nucor broke with the industry pattern of basing the price of an order of steel on the quantity ordered and abandoned offering quantity discounts; Iverson explained why: "Some time ago we began to realize that with computer order entry and billing, the extra charge for smaller orders was not cost justified." Nucor also broke away from traditional steel industry practice on pricing. The steel industry had established a pattern of absorbing shipping costs, so all users paid the same delivered price regardless of their distance from the mill. Nucor stopped the practice of including freight charges in its prices and began pricing its products at the mill. Nucor's strategy was to quote the same price and sales terms to all customers, with the customer paying all shipping charges. Its prices were customarily the lowest or close to the lowest in the industry.

In order to gain the advantage of low shipping costs, two tube manufacturers, two steel service centers, and a cold-rolling facility had located adjacent to Nucor's Arkansas plant—these customers accounted for 60 percent of the shipments from the mill. Nucor plants were linked electronically to each other's production schedules and thus could function in a just-in-time inventory mode. All new mills were built on large enough tracts of land to accommodate expansion and collaborating businesses.

THE STEELMAKING PROCESS AT NUCOR

Nucor minimills had an annual capacity of 200,000–1,200,000 tons, small compared with the 7-million-ton capacity of Bethlehem Steel's fully integrated Sparrow's Point, Maryland, plant, which made steel from scratch using iron ore. Mini-mill operations involved two phases: preparation of steel of the proper "chemistry," and the forming of the steel into the desired shapes and products.

A charging bucket fed loads of scrap steel into electric arc furnaces. The melted load, called a *heat,* was poured into a ladle to be carried by overhead crane to the casting machine. In the casting machine the liquid steel was extruded as a continuous red-hot solid bar of steel and cut into "billets"—lengths measuring four inches by 20 feet and weighing some 900 pounds. In a typical plant, a billet was held temporarily in a pit where it cooled to normal temperatures. Periodically, cooled billets were moved to the rolling mill and placed in a reheat oven to bring them up to 2,000 degrees Fahrenheit, at which temperature they would be malleable. In the rolling mill, presses and dies progressively converted the billet into the desired round bars, angles, channels, flats, and other products. After being cut to standard lengths, the finished products were moved to the warehouse for shipping.

Plant Economics

Nucor's first steel mill, in Darlington, South Carolina, employed more than 500 people. The mill, with its three electric arc furnaces, operated 24 hours per day, 5½ days per week. Nucor had made a number of improvements in the melting and casting operations. The general manager of the Darlington plant developed a system that involved preheating the ladles, allowing for the faster flow of steel into the caster and resulting in better control of the steel characteristics. Thus, less time and lower capital investment were required at Darlington than at other minimills at the time of its construction. In contrast to older machines that used a batch method, the casting machines were "continuous casters." The objective in the front of the mill was to keep the casters working. At the time, the Darlington plant was also perhaps the only mill in the country that moved hot billets directly to the rolling mill, thus avoiding the cost of reheating the billets; this continuous-processing approach saved $10–$12 per ton in fuel usage and losses due to oxidation of the steel. The cost of developing this process had been $12 million. Not all of Nucor's efforts at process innovation were successful, however. The company had spent approximately $2 million in an unsuccessful effort to utilize resistance heating and had lost even more on a failed effort at induction melting. As Iverson told *Metal Producing*, "That costs us a lot of money. Timewise it was very expensive. But you have got to make mistakes and we've had lots of failures."

The Darlington design became the basis for Nucor plants in Nebraska, Texas, and Utah. The capital costs to build the Texas plant were under $80 per ton of annual capacity. Whereas the construction costs for a typical minimill at the time were approximately $250 per ton, the average capital cost of Nucor's first four mills was under $135 per ton of capacity. Capital costs for a traditional integrated mill (like those used by such Nucor competitors as U.S. Steel and Bethlehem Steel) that converted iron ore into steel generally ran between $1,200 and $1,500 per ton.

Scrap steel and scrap substitutes were the most significant element in the total cost of steel products at Nucor. Nucor's average cost for scrap steel increased to about $120 per gross ton used in 2000, up from $111 per gross ton in 1999.

Nucor's Use of Production Incentives at Its Steel Mills

The Darlington plant was organized into 12 groups of workers for the purpose of incentive pay. The two mill facilities at Darlington each operated two production shifts with three groups or teams of workers—one each for melting and casting, the rolling mill operation, and finishing. In melting and casting there were three or four different production standards, depending on the material, each established by the department manager years ago based on historical performance. The general manager stated, "We don't change the standards." The caster, key to the amount produced, was operated at 92 percent of rated capacity—one percentage point greater than the claims of the manufacturer. For every good ton of billet above the standard hourly rate for the week, workers in the group received a 4 percent bonus. For example, for a standard of 10 tons per run hour and an actual rate for the week of 28 tons per run hour, workers would receive a bonus of 72 percent of their base rate in the week's paycheck.

In the rolling mill there were more than 100 products, each with a different historical standard. Workers received a 4 to 6 percent bonus for every good ton sheared per hour for the week over the computed standard. The Darlington general manager said the standard would be changed only if there was a major machinery change and that a standard had not been changed since the initial development period for the plant. He observed that worker efforts to exceed the standard and get a bonus did not involve working harder so much as they involved good teamwork to avoid problems and to quickly collaborate in solving problems that did develop: "If there is a way to improve output, they will tell us." Another manager added: "Meltshop employees don't ask me how much it costs Chaparral or LTV to make a billet. They want to know what it costs Darlington, Norfolk, or Jewitt to put a billet on the ground—scrap costs, alloy costs, electrical costs, refractory, gas, etc. Everybody from Charlotte to Plymouth watches the nickels and dimes."

In 2000, Nucor's employment costs averaged about 10 percent of corporate revenues, a very low number compared to labor costs at the mills of rival companies.

MANAGEMENT PHILOSOPHY

Aycock, when he was the Darlington plant manager, stated:

The key to making a profit when selling a product with no aesthetic value, or a product that you really can't differentiate from your competitors, is cost. I don't look at us as a fantastic marketing organization, even though I think we are pretty good; but we don't try to overcome unreasonable costs by mass marketing. We maintain low costs by keeping the employee force at the level it should be, not doing things that aren't necessary to achieve our goals, and allowing people to function on their own and by judging them on their results.

To keep a cooperative and productive workforce you need, number one, to be completely honest about everything; number two, to allow each employee as much as possible to make decisions about that employee's work, to find easier and more productive ways to perform duties; and number three, to be as fair as possible to all employees. Most of the changes we make in work procedures and in equipment come from the employees. They really know the problems of their jobs better than anyone else. We don't have any industrial engineers, nor do we ever intend to, because that's a type of specialist who tends to take responsibility off the top division management and give them a crutch.

To communicate with my employees, I try to spend time in the plant and at intervals have meetings with the employees. Usually if they have a question they just visit me. Recently a small group visited me in my office to discuss our vacation policy. They had some suggestions and, after listening to them, I had to agree that the ideas were good.

Nucor's manager at the Florence plant described his philosophy for dealing with the workforce:

I believe very strongly in the incentive system we have. We are a nonunion shop and we all feel that the way to stay so is to take care of our people and show them we care. I think that's easily done because of our fewer layers of management . . . I spend a good part of my time in the plant, maybe an hour or so a day. If a man wants to know anything, for example, an insurance question, I'm there and they walk right up to me and ask me questions, which I'll answer the best I know how.

We don't lay our people off and we make a point of telling our people this. In the slowdown of 1994, we scheduled our line for four days, but the men were allowed to come in the fifth day for maintenance work at base pay. The men in the plant on an average running bonus might make $17 to $19 an hour. If their base pay is half that, on Friday they would only get $8 to $9 an hour. Surprisingly, many of the men did not want to come in on Friday. They felt comfortable with just working four days a week. They are happy to have that extra day off." About 20 percent of the people took the fifth day at base rate, but still no one had been laid off, in an industry with a strong business cycle.

In an earlier downcycle, Nucor's executive committee decided that economic conditions made a pay freeze necessary. Nucor employees normally received an increase in base pay the first of June. When the decision was made to freeze wages, company officers, as a show of good faith, took a 5 percent pay cut. In addition to announcing the freeze via a stuffer in workers' pay envelopes, each production group met in the plant conference room with all the plant foremen, the plant production manager, and the division manager. The production manager explained the economic crisis facing the company and answered workers' questions.

NUCOR'S HUMAN RESOURCE PRACTICES AND INCENTIVE COMPENSATION SYSTEM

Nucor had set forth four principles to guide the company's approach to employee relations:

1. Management is obligated to manage Nucor in such a way that employees will have the opportunity to earn according to their productivity.

2. Employees should be able to feel confident that if they do their jobs properly, they will have a job tomorrow.

3. Employees have the right to be treated fairly and must believe that they will be.

4. Employees must have an avenue of appeal when they believe they are being treated unfairly.

The hallmark of Nucor's human resources strategy was its incentive pay plan for production exceeding the standard. Another major personnel policy was providing job security. All Nucor employees received the same fringe benefits. There was only one group insurance plan. Holidays and vacations did not differ by job. Every child of every Nucor employee received up to $1,200 a year for four years if they chose to go to college or technical school. The company had no executive dining rooms or restrooms, no fishing lodges, no company cars, and no reserved parking places.

Jim Coblin, Nucor's vice president of human resources, described Nucor's systems for *HR Magazine* in a 1994 article entitled "No-Frills HR at Nucor: A Lean, Bottom-Line Approach at This Steel Company Empowers Employees." Coblin, as benefits administrator, received part-time help from one of the secretaries in the corporate office. The plants typically assigned someone from their finance department to handle compensation issues, although two plants had personnel generalists. Nucor plants did not utilize job descriptions, believing they caused more problems than they solved, given the teamwork atmosphere and the close collaboration among work group members. Coblin also believed performance appraisal was a waste of time and added paperwork. If a Nucor employee was not performing well, the problem was dealt with directly by supervisory personnel and the peer pressure of work group members (whose bonuses were adversely affected). Coblin further noted that when promotional opportunities became available, performance appraisals were seldom much help in filling open positions. Coblin believed the best approach to workforce management was to pay employees directly for productivity and not to put a maximum on what they could earn. Ken Iverson had insisted that bonuses be paid weekly rather than quarterly, semiannually, or annually so that employees would be rewarded immediately for their efforts and, further, that bonus calculations involve no discretion on the part of a manager.

Employees were kept informed about company and division performance. Charts showing the division's results in return on assets and bonus payoff were posted in prominent places in the plant. Nucor's personnel manager noted that as he traveled around to all the plants, he found everyone in the company could tell him the level of profits in their division. The general managers held dinner meetings at least once (but usually twice) a year with division employees. Attendance at any one dinner was restricted to 50 or 60 employees at a time (resulting in as many as 20 dinners per year) to allow time for more interaction with employees. After introductory remarks at each dinner, the floor was opened for questions and discussion of any work-related problems. Nucor had a new employee orientation program and an employee handbook that contained personnel policies and rules. Nucor had a formal grievance procedure, although the Darlington manager couldn't recall the last grievance he had processed. The corporate office sent all news releases to each division, where they were posted on bulletin boards. Each employee in the company also received a copy of Nucor's annual report. For the last several years, the cover of the annual report had contained the names of all Nucor employees.

Neither absenteeism nor tardiness was a problem at Nucor. Each employee had four days of absences per year before pay was reduced. In addition to these, missing work was allowed for jury duty, military leave, or the death of close relatives. After this, a day's absence cost a worker the entire bonus pay for that week. Being more than a half hour late to work on a given day resulted in no bonus payment for the day. Safety was a concern of Nucor's critics. With 10 fatalities in the 1980s, Nucor was committed to doing better. Safety administrators had been appointed in each plant, and safety at Nucor plants had improved in the 1990s.

Nucor had conducted attitude surveys every three years for over two decades. These provided management insight into employee attitudes on 20 issues and allowed comparisons across plants and divisions. There were some concerns and differences, but most employees appeared very satisfied with Nucor as an employer, especially with regard to total compensation.

The average hourly worker's pay at Nucor was over twice the average earnings paid by other manufacturing companies in the states where Nucor's plants were located. In many rural communities where Nucor had located, the company provided better worker compensation than most other area manufacturers. At Nucor's new $450 million plant in Hertford County, North Carolina, an area in which jobs were scarce and poverty was common, Nucor employees were expected to earn $60,000 or more a year, three times the local average manufacturing wage. Nucor had recently begun developing its plant sites with the expectation of other companies co-locating nearby to save shipping costs. Four companies had announced plans to locate close to Nucor's new North Carolina plant, adding another 100 to 200 jobs. The average compensation for jobs at Nucor's Darlington plant was $70,000. While Nucor didn't try to set pay "a buck over Wal-Mart," it made a practice of trying to hire the best workers in the area. Nucor considered high pay appropriate because steel mills were hot and dangerous and the work was hard.

Incentive Compensation at Nucor

There were four incentive programs at Nucor, one each for (1) production workers, (2) department heads, (3) professional and clerical personnel, and (4) senior officers, which included the division managers. Payments under all these incentive programs were based on group performance.

Production Worker Incentives   For production, incentive payments were tied to the productivity of groups ranging in size from 25 to 30 people. The company believed that an incentive program should be simple and that any bonuses should be paid with the regular pay the following week. According to Ken Iverson, "We don't have any discretionary bonuses—zero. It is all based on performance. We don't want anyone to sit in judgment, because it never is fair." A bonus was not paid when equipment was not operating; Nucor's philosophy was that when equipment was not operating, everybody suffered and the bonus for downtime ought to be zero. Production foremen were also part of a group and received the same bonus as the employees they supervised.

Department Head Incentives   The incentive program for department heads in the various divisions was based on division contribution, defined as the division earnings before corporate expenses and profit sharing are determined. Bonuses ranged between 0 and 90 percent of a person's base salary, with the average being 35–50 percent. The base salaries for department heads were pegged at 75 percent of the steel industry norm.

Incentives for Professional and Clerical Employees   The bonus plan for people who were not production workers, department managers, or senior managers was linked to either the employee's division return on assets or the corporate return on assets depending on the unit the person was a part of. Bonuses for people in these positions were typically 30 percent or more of a person's base salary.

Senior Officer Incentives   Nucor's senior officers had no employment contracts, pension or retirement plans, or other perquisites. Their base salaries were set at about 75 percent of what an individual doing similar work in other companies would receive. Once Nucor's corporate return on equity reached 9 percent (slightly below the norm for manufacturing firms), then 5 percent of Nucor's earnings before taxes went into a pool, which was divided among the officers on the basis of their salaries. In addition to profit-sharing bonuses, senior officers were entitled to stock bonuses. Ken Iverson explained, "If return on equity for the company reaches, say 20 percent, which it has, then we can wind up with as much as 190 percent of our base salaries and 115 percent on top of that in stock. We get both." Half the profit-sharing bonus was paid in cash, and half was deferred compensation. Depending on Nucor's performance, individual bonuses could range from zero to several hundred percent of an officer's base salary; over recent years bonuses had run in the 75 to 150 percent range. But when industry conditions were bad and Nucor's performance was subpar, Nucor officers could find their compensation swinging widely. In 1982, Nucor's return on equity was only 8 percent and executives received no bonus. Iverson's compensation in 1981 was approximately $300,000, but the amount dropped to $110,000 in 1982, causing him to say, "I think that, ranked by total compensation, I was the lowest-paid CEO in the Fortune 500. I was kind of proud of that, too." In his 1997 book, *Plain Talk: Lessons from a Business Maverick*, Iverson wrote, "Can management expect employees to be loyal if we lay them all off at every dip of the economy, while we go on padding our own pockets?"

Other Compensation

In lieu of a retirement plan for employees, Nucor had a profit-sharing plan with a deferred trust. Each year, 10 percent of pretax earnings was put into profit sharing for all employees below officer level. Twenty percent of the contributed amount was set aside to be paid to employees in the following March as a cash bonus, and the remaining 80 percent was put into a trust for each employee, with each employee's share being equal proportional to his or her earnings as a percent of total earnings by all workers covered by the plan. An employee's share of the profits became vested after one full year of employment. Employees received a quarterly statement of their balance in profit sharing.

The company had a monthly stock investment plan for employees whereby Nucor added 10 percent to the amount an employee contributed toward the purchase of Nucor shares; Nucor paid the commission on all share purchases. After each five years of service with the company, Nucor employees received a service award consisting of five shares of Nucor stock. Moreover, extraordinary bonus payments were made to employees in years when Nucor's profits were very good—in December 1998, each employee received a special $800 bonus.

Ken Iverson explained the company's policy regarding charitable contributions:

> I think the first obligation of the company is to the stockholder and to its employees. I find in this country too many cases where employees are underpaid and corporate management is making huge social donations for self-fulfillment. We regularly give donations, but we have a very interesting corporate policy. First, we give donations where our employees are. Second, we give donations that will benefit our employees, such as to the YMCA. It is a

difficult area and it requires a lot of thought. There is certainly a strong social responsibility for a company, but it cannot be at the expense of the employees or the stockholders.

THE U.S. STEEL INDUSTRY IN THE 1980s

The early 1980s were the worst years in decades for the steel industry. Data from the American Iron and Steel Institute showed shipments falling from 100 million tons in 1979 to the mid-80 levels in 1980 and 1981. A slowing economy, particularly in auto sales, led the decline. In 1986, when industry capacity was at 130 million tons, the outlook was for a continued decline in per capita consumption and movement toward capacity in the range of 90–100 million tons. The chairman of Armco saw "millions of tons chasing a market that's not there: excess capacity that must be eliminated."

The large, integrated steel firms, such as U.S. Steel and Armco, which made up the major part of the industry, were the hardest hit. *The Wall Street Journal* stated, "The decline has resulted from such problems as high labor and energy costs in mining and processing iron ore, a lack of profits and capital to modernize plants, and conservative management that has hesitated to take risks."

The integrated companies produced a wide range of steels using a process that started with iron ore processed in blast furnaces. Because of high costs, they had difficulty competing with imported steel, usually from Japan, and had lost market share to foreign imports. They sought the protection of import quotas. Imported steel accounted for 20 percent of the U.S. steel consumption, up from 12 percent in the early 1970s. The U.S. share of world production of raw steel declined from 19 percent to 14 percent over the period. Imports of light bar products accounted for less than 9 percent of the U.S. consumption of those products in 1981, according to the U.S. Commerce Department, while imports of wire rod totaled 23 percent of U.S. consumption.

Iron Age stated that exports, as a percent of shipments in 1985, were 34 percent for Nippon, 26 percent for British Steel, 30 percent for Krupp, 49 percent for USINOR of France, and less than 1 percent for every American producer on the list. The consensus of steel experts was that imports would average 23 percent of the market in the last half of the 1980s.

Iverson was one of the very few in the steel industry to oppose import restrictions. He saw an outdated U.S. steel industry that had to change:

> We Americans have been conditioned to believe in our technical superiority. For many generations a continuing stream of new inventions and manufacturing techniques allowed us to far outpace the rest of the world in both volume and efficiency of production. In many areas this is no longer true and particularly in the steel industry. In the last three decades, almost all the major developments in steelmaking were made outside the United States. There were 18 continuous casting units in the world before there was one in this country. I would be negligent if I did not recognize the significant contribution that the government has made toward the technological deterioration of the steel industry. Unrealistic depreciation schedules, high corporate taxes, excessive regulation and jaw-boning for lower steel prices have make it difficult for the U.S. steel industry to borrow or generate the huge quantities of capital required for modernization.

By the mid-1980s the integrated mills were moving fast to get back into the game: They were restructuring, cutting capacity, dropping unprofitable lines, focusing on fewer products, and trying to become responsive to the market. The industry made a pronounced move toward segmentation. Integrated producers focused on mostly flat-rolled and structural grades, reorganized steel companies retrenched to product categories where they were most cost-competitive, minimills dominated the bar and light structural product areas, and specialty steel firms sought niches. The industry saw an accelerated shutdown of older plants, elimination of products by some firms, and the installation of new product lines with new technologies by others. High-tonnage mills restructured to handle sheets, plates, structural beams, high-quality bars, and large pipe and tubular products; such moves allowed resurgence of specialized mills: cold-finished bar manufacturers, independent strip mills, and minimills.

For the integrated mills, the road was not easy. Tax laws and accounting rules inhibited the closing of inefficient plants. Shutting down a big plant could require a firm to establish a cash reserve of $100 million to fund health, pension, and insurance liabilities for former plant employees. One steel industry executive noted, "Liabilities associated with a planned shutdown are so large that they can quickly devastate a company's balance sheet."

Joint ventures among competing steel companies were formed to produce steel for a specific market or region. The chairman of USX (the parent of U.S. Steel) called the joint ventures "an important new wrinkle in steel's fight for survival" and stated, "If there had been more joint ventures like these two decades ago, the U.S. steel industry might have built only half of the dozen or so hot-strip mills it put up in that time and avoided today's overcapacity."

The American Iron and Steel Institute reported steel production in 1988 of 99.3 million tons, up from 89.2 million tons in 1987, and the highest total in seven years. As a result of plant modernization programs, 60.9 percent of production involved the use of continuous casting equipment. U.S. exports of steel increased and the volume of foreign imports fell. Some steel industry analysts believed U.S. steel companies were now cost-competitive with the Japanese steel producers. In 1989, steel production in the United States was hampered by the onset of an economic recession, the expiration of the voluntary import restraints, and labor negotiations at several companies. Declines in motor vehicle production and consumer durable goods hit the producers of flat-rolled sheet steel hard. According to the forecast of one knowledgeable industry expert, "The U.S. steel market has peaked. Steel consumption is trending down. By 1990, we expect total domestic demand to dip under 90 million tons."

THE U.S. STEEL INDUSTRY IN THE 1990s

The economic slowdown of the early 1990s did lead to a decline in the demand for steel through early 1993, but by 1995 conditions in the U.S. steel industry were the best in 20 years, and, 6 years after Nucor pioneered the low-cost German technology in Crawfordsville, Indiana, a number of rival steelmakers were building new minimills to make flat-rolled sheet steel—what a *Business Week* article described as "the race of the Nucor look-alikes." Ten new flat-rolled steel mills with 20 million tons of capacity were under construction, pushing U.S. production capabilities up as much as 40 percent by 1998. Most of these mills opened in 1997 just as the steel industry in the United States was predicted to move into a cyclical slump. The newly added capacity intensified worldwide competition, as domestic companies rushed to find export opportunities to keep the new plants operating as close to capacity as possible. The push into foreign markets was a new phenomenon for U.S. firms, most all of whom had been preoccupied with defending their home markets against foreign imports for decades. U.S. minimills focused their exporting efforts primarily on markets in Asia and South America.

Meanwhile in 1994, U.S. Steel, North America's largest integrated steel producer, began a major business process reengineering project to improve order fulfillment performance and customer satisfaction on the heels of a decade of internal restructuring to improve its competitiveness. According to an article in *Steel Times International*, "U.S. Steel had to completely change the way it did business. Cutting labor costs, and increasing reliability and productivity took the company a long way towards improving profitability and competitiveness. However, it became clear that this leaner organization still had to implement new technologies and business processes if it was to maintain a competitive advantage." The goals of U.S. Steel's business process reengineering effort included a sharp reduction in cycle time, greatly decreased levels of inventory, shorter order lead times, and the ability to offer real-time promised delivery dates to customers. In 1995, the company successfully installed integrated planning/production/order fulfillment software, and results were very positive. Executives at U.S. Steel believed that the reengineering project favorably positioned the company for a future of increased competition, tighter markets, and raised customer expectations.

In late 1997 and again in 1998, declining demand for steel prompted Nucor and other U.S. companies to reduce prices to better compete against an unprecedented surge of imported steel. Steel companies in the United States filed unfair trade complaints with U.S. trade regulators, claiming that foreign steel companies were dumping steel in the United States at below-market prices, causing steel prices in the spot market to drop sharply in August and September 1998 before they stabilized. The U.S. secretary of commerce, William Daley, stated, "I will not stand by and allow U.S. workers, communities and companies to bear the brunt of other nations' problematic policies and practices. We are the most open economy of the world. But we are not the world's dumpster." In early 1999, officials at the American Iron and Steel Institute commented on market conditions. One said, "With many of the world's economies in recession, and no signs of recovery on the horizon, it should come as no surprise that the United States is now seen as the only reliable market for manufactured goods. This can be seen in the dramatic surge of imports." Another observed, "While there are different ways to gauge the impact of the Asian crisis, believe me, it has already hit. Just ask the 163,000 employees of the U. S. steel industry."

The Commerce Department concluded in March 1999 that steel companies in six countries had illegally dumped stainless steel in the United States at prices below production costs or home market prices. The Commerce Department study found that companies in Canada, South Korea, and Taiwan were guilty only of dumping, while the governments of Belgium, Italy, and South Africa also gave their steel producers unfair subsidies that effectively lowered prices. However, in June 1999, *The Wall Street Journal* reported that the U.S. Senate decisively shut off an attempt to restrict imports of foreign steel despite the complaints of U.S. steel companies that a flood of cheap imports was driving them out of business. Advisers to President Clinton were reported to have said the president would likely veto the bill if it passed. Administration officials said they opposed the Senate bill because it would violate international trade law and leave the United States open to retaliation.

The American Iron and Steel Institute reported that U.S. steel mills shipped 8,330,000 net tons in May 1999, a decrease of 6.7 percent from the 8,927,000 net tons shipped in May 1998. The institute also stated that shipments were 41,205,000 net tons for the first five months of 1999, down 10 percent from the same period in 1998. AISI president and CEO Andrew Sharkey III said, "Once again, the May data show clearly that America's steel trade crisis continues. U.S. steel companies and employees continue to be injured by high levels of dumping and subsidized imports . . . In addition,

exhibit 5   Average Import Value per Net Ton for Selected Steel
Products, May 1999 versus First Quarter 1998

Product	Import Value per Net Ton		% Change
	May 1999	1st Quarter 1998	
Wire rods	$275	$350	−21.50%
Structural shapes	267	379	−29.60
Plates cut lengths	456	490	−6.90
Plates in colis	257	377	−31.70
Reinforcing bars	198	300	−33.90
Line pipe	429	524	−18.20
Black plate	551	627	−12.20
Sheet hot rolled	242	304	−20.40
Sheets cold rolled	400	549	−27.10
Sheet and strip galvanized electrolytic	483	609	−20.70%
Total—All steel mill products	332	455	−27.00%

Source: American Iron and Steel, press release, June 24, 1999

steel inventory levels remain excessive, and steel operating rates continue to be very low." Exhibit 5 compares the average import customer's value per net ton of steel for May 1999 with the first quarter of 1998, and Exhibit 6 compares U.S. imports of steel mill products by country of origin for the first five months in 1999 compared with the same periods in 1997 and 1998.

Going into 2000, Nucor was the second-largest steel producer in the United States, trailing only U.S. Steel. The company's market capitalization was about two times that of the next-smaller competitor.

STEEL TECHNOLOGY AND THE MINIMILL

Electric arc furnace minimills that used scrap steel as their basic raw material emerged in the United States during the 1970s as a low-cost alternative to making steel in traditional fashion from iron ore and coke at so-called integrated steel mills, where all of the steelmaking functions were performed at a single large-scale plant. Initially, minimill technology was too unsophisticated to manufacture any more than a narrow range of low-value steel products—reinforcing rods (or rebar), structural bolts (used by coal mines), angle irons, and fasteners. The leading U.S. minimill companies in the 1980s were Nucor, Florida Steel, Georgetown Steel, North Star Steel, and Chaparral Steel. Between the late 1970s and the late 1980s, the integrated mills' share of total domestic shipments fell from about 90 percent to about 60 percent, with the integrated steel companies averaging a 7 percent return on equity, the minimills averaging 14 percent, and some minimill firms, such as Nucor, achieving returns on equity investment in the 25 percent range. The market share gains of minimills reflected growing technological capabilities that allowed minimills to expand into a growing range of steel products (namely, flat-rolled sheet steel and structural steel) that previously could be manufactured only at integrated mills. In the 1990s minimills tripled their output, driving the market share of integrated mills down to around 40 percent.

exhibit 6   U.S. Imports of Steel Mill Products by Country of Origin, Selected Periods of 1997–99

	Imports (in thousands of net tons)			5 Months 1999 vs. 5 Months 1998 % Change	5 Months 1999 vs. 5 Months 1997 % Change
	5 Months 1999 (Prelim.)	5 Months 1998	5 Months 1997		
European Union	2,569	2,634	3,048	−2.5	−15.7
Canada	2,157	2,146	2,035	0.5	6.0
Japan	1,452	2,099	1,015	−30.8	43.1
Mexico	1,444	1,263	1,432	14.3	0.8
Brazil	1,428	987	1,565	44.7	−8.8
Korea	1,330	1,064	643	25.0	106.8
Russia	343	1,583	1,680	−78.3	−79.6
Australia	316	366	121	−13.7	161.2
South Africa	252	214	120	17.8	110.0
China	243	177	274	37.3	−11.3
India	170	118	90	70.3	123.3
Indonesia	187	116	33	61.2	466.7
Turkey	148	232	209	−36.2	−29.2
Ukraine	105	392	290	−73.2	−63.8
Others	1,546	1,188	1,038	27.5	46.0
Total	13,690	14,578	13,593	−6.1	0.7

Source: American Iron and Steel, press release, June 24, 1999.

Some steel industry experts believed that a relatively new technology, the twin shell electric arc furnace, would help minimills increase production and lower costs and take additional market share. According to the *Pittsburgh Business Times*, "With a twin shell furnace, one shell—the chamber holding the scrap to be melted—is filled and heated. During the heating of the first shell, the second shell is filled. When the heating is finished on the first shell, the electrodes move to the second. The first shell is emptied and refilled before the second gets hot." Twin shell furnace technology increased production capacity by 60 percent and had been widely adopted in the last few years. Nucor began running a twin shell furnace in November 1996 in Berkeley, South Carolina, and installed another in Norfolk, Nebraska, which began operations in 1997. "Everyone accepts twin shells as a good concept because there's a lot of flexibility of operation," said Rodney Mott, vice president and general manager of Nucor-Berkeley. However, the accelerating move toward twin shell furnaces was expected to greatly tighten the supply of scrap steel, possibly creating shortages and causing scrap steel prices to rise.

According to a September 1997 *Industry Week* article, steelmakers around the world were closely monitoring the development of continuous "strip casting" technology, which was said to hold potential to be the next technological leap forward for the industry: "The objective of strip casting was to produce thin strips of steel (in the 1-mm to 4-mm range) as liquid steel flowed from a tundish—the stationary vessel which received molten steel from the ladle. This would eliminate the slab-casting stage and all of the rolling that now takes place in a hot mill." Strip casting was reported to have some difficult technological challenges, but companies in Germany, France,

Japan, Australia, Italy and Canada had strip-casting projects under way. In fact, all of the significant development work in strip casting was taking place outside the United States.

Larry Kavanaph, American Iron and Steel Institute vice president for manufacturing and technology, said, "Steel is a very high-tech industry, but nobody knows it." In 2001, the most productive steelmaking facilities incorporated advanced metallurgical practices, sophisticated process-control sensors, state-of-the art computer controls, and the latest refinements in continuous casting and rolling mill technology. Another industry expert said, "You don't survive in this industry unless you have the technology to make the best products in the world in the most efficient manner."

ENVIRONMENTAL AND POLITICAL ISSUES

Not all stakeholders were happy with Nucor's environmental practices. In June 1998, *Waste News* reported that Nucor's mill in Crawfordsville, Indiana, had been cited by the Environmental Protection Agency for alleged violations of federal and state clean-air rules. The Pamlico-Tar River Foundation, the North Carolina Coastal Federation, and the Environmental Defense Fund had concerns about North Carolina's decision to allow Nucor to start building its new Hertford County plant before all environmental reviews were completed. According to the *Charlotte News & Observer*, "The environmental groups charge that the mill will discharge 6,720 tons of pollutants into the air each year."

Moreover, there were other concerns about the fast-track approval of the Hertford County facility. The plant was located on the banks of one of the most important and sensitive stretches of the Chowan River, a principal tributary to the national treasure Albemarle Sound and the last bastion of North Carolina's once-vibrant river-herring fishery. North Carolina passed a law in 1997 that required the restoration of this fishery through a combination of measures designed to prevent overfishing, restore spawning and nursery habitats, and improve water quality in the Chowan River. "New federal law requires extra care in protecting essential habitat for the herring, which spawn upstream," according to an article in the *Business Journal*. Another concern was whether the promise of 300 well-paying jobs in Hertford County were worth $155 million in tax breaks the state of North Carolina was giving Nucor to locate its plant in the state.

NUCOR'S NEW MANAGEMENT TEAM, 1998–2001

As Nucor opened new plants, each was made a division and given a general manager with complete responsibility for all aspects of the business. The corporate office did not involve itself in the routine functioning of the divisions. There was no centralized purchasing, hiring and firing, or division accounting. Despite the company's revenue growth and plant additions over the years, at the start of 1999 the total corporate staff still numbered fewer than 25 people, about the same number as in 1985.

When Dave Aycock moved into Nucor's corporate office as president in 1984 and Ken Iverson assumed the titles of CEO and chairman, three people functioned as an executive committee to provide overall direction to the company—Iverson, Aycock, and Sam Siegel, the company's chief financial officer. By 1990, Dave Aycock, who had invested his money wisely, owned over 600,000 shares of Nucor stock and five hotels and farms in three states. He was 60, five years younger than Iverson, and was concerned that if he waited to retire, he and Iverson might be leaving the company at the same time. Two people stood out as candidates for the presidency, Keith Busse and John Correnti. In November, Iverson called Correnti to the Charlotte airport and offered him the job. Aycock commented, "Keith Busse was my choice, but I got outvoted." In June 1991, Aycock retired and Keith Busse left Nucor to build an independent sheet mill in Indiana for a group of investors. Aycock, however, remained a member of Nucor's board of directors.

For the next two years, Iverson, Correnti, and Siegel led the company. In 1993, Iverson developed heart problems and had major surgery. Correnti took over the CEO role in 1996, in addition to functioning as president and COO. Nucor's board of directors had always been small, consisting of the three-person executive team and one or two past Nucor vice presidents. Several institutional owners of large blocks of Nucor stock began pressing Nucor's leadership to diversify its board membership and add outside directors. In 1996, Jim Hlavacek, head of a small consulting firm and friend of Ken Iverson, was added to the board.

Only five, not six, members were in attendance during the board of directors meeting in October 1998, due to the recent death of Jim Cunningham. Near the end of the meeting, Dave Aycock read a motion, drafted by Sam Siegel, that Ken Iverson be removed as Nucor's chairman. It was seconded by Hlavacek and passed. Later in October 1998, it was announced that Iverson would stay on as chairman emeritus and a director but, after continuing disagreements between Iverson and other board members, Iverson decided to leave the company completely. It was agreed Iverson would receive $500,000 a year for five years. Dave Aycock agreed to come out of retirement and temporarily serve as chairman of Nucor's board of directors until a suitable replacement could be found.

The basic disagreements over the company's management and direction (that precipitated Iverson's leaving) did not become publicly known until June 1999 when John Correnti also resigned following disagreements with the board. Dave Aycock then took on the added role of CEO. The developments came as a complete surprise to investors and drove Nucor's stock price down 10 percent. Siegel stated that "the board felt Correnti was not the right person to lead Nucor into the 21st century." Aycock assured everyone he would be happy to move back into retirement as soon as replacements could be found. In December 1999, Correnti was named chairman and CEO of rival Birmingham Steel, a struggling company with a corporate staff of 156 people. Commenting on Nucor's organizational changes, Correnti said, "Nucor's trying to centralize and do more mentoring. That's not what grew the company to what it is today."

In the second half of 1999, Dave Aycock moved expeditiously to add outside directors to Nucor's board. New members included Harvey Gantt, a principal in his own architectural firm and former mayor of Charlotte, North Carolina; Victoria Haynes, formerly BF Goodrich's chief technology officer and currently the president of the Research Triangle Institute; and Peter Browning, chief executive officer of Sonoco Products Company. Then Aycock added a new layer of corporate management, appointing four executive vice presidents to head each of Nucor's four business areas. The corporate staff was further expanded by adding two specialist jobs in strategic planning and steel technology. When Siegel retired, Aycock promoted Terry Lisenby to CFO and treasurer, and a director of information technology was hired who reported to Lisenby. Exhibit 7 presents Nucor's organization chart as of 2001. Exhibit 8 shows the composition of Nucor's senior management and board of directors during the 1990–2000 period.

exhibit 7 Nucor Organization Chart, 2001

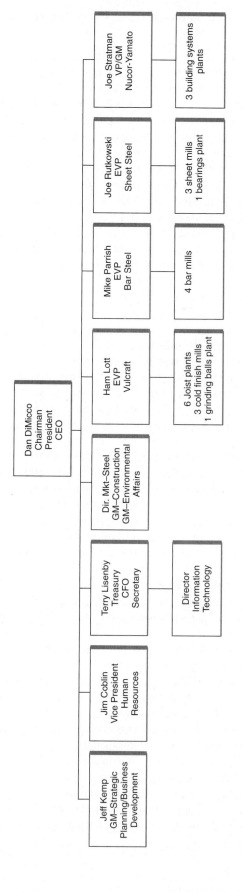

exhibit 8   Nucor's Board of Directors and Executive Management
                  1990–2000

To 1990
Board: Iverson, Aycock, Siegel, Vandekieft
Executive office: Iverson, Aycock, Siegel

In 1990
Board: Iverson, Aycock, Cunningham, Siegel, Vandekieft
Executive office: Iverson, Aycock, Siegel

1991 to 1994
Board: Aycock, Correnti, Cunningham, Iverson, Siegel
Executive office: Iverson, Siegel, Correnti, Lisenby, Prichard

1995 to 1996
Board: Aycock, Correnti, Cunningham, Hlavacek, Iverson, Siegel
Executive office: Iverson, Correnti, Siegel, Doherty, Prichard

In 1997
Board: Aycock, Correnti, Cunningham, Hlavacek, Iverson, Siegel
Executive office: Iverson, Correnti, Siegel, Lisenby, Prichard

At the end of 1998
Board: Aycock, Browning, Correnti, Gantt, Haynes, Hlavacek, Siegel (Iverson "resigned" in October)
Executive office: Aycock, Correnti, Siegel, Parrish, Rutowski, Lisenby, Prichard

1999 to 2000
Board: Aycock, Browning, Gantt, Haynes, Hlavacek, Siegel
Executive office: Aycock, Lisenby, DiMicco, Lott, Parrish, Rutowski, Coblin, Prichard

Source: Company records.

A New Strategic Vision and Operating Scheme Begins to Evolve

Jim Coblin, Nucor's vice president of human resources, believed the time had come to expand the size of Nucor's executive management team and add a new layer of group executive vice presidents to the organization structure. He noted that the 24 Nucor plants/divisions had different business cards and plant signs (some did not even want a Nucor sign at their plant) and that sometimes as many as six different Nucor sales representatives would call on the same customer, each promoting and selling just the products of one plant/division. Coblin indicated, "There is no manager of human resources in the plants, so at least we needed to give additional training to the person who does most of that work at the plant." Along with the new management additions, there were two important new corporate-level committees appointed, one for environmental issues and a second for auditing.

Coblin believed the old span of control of 24 division managers/vice presidents reporting to a single CEO worked well when there was less competition, but Aycock considered it ridiculous, saying, "It was not possible to properly manage, to know what was going on. The top managers have totally lost contact with the company." Coblin was optimistic that the new executive vice presidents would infuse more strategic thinking from a companywide and/or business group point of view rather than from the perspective of what was best for an individual Nucor plant. The three meetings of the general managers each year had slowly increased in length from about 1½ days to about 2½ days and become more immersed in the operating details of particular plants/divisions. With the advent of the new group EVP positions, Coblin believed the meetings would take on more of a strategic focus. Instead of 15 detailed presentations about different aspects of company operations given by various general managers, each general manager within a Nucor business group would now give a five-minute briefing and then there would be an in-depth presentation on the operation of the group as a whole by the group's executive vice president, with participation from all general managers within the group. After some training by Lisenby, the divisions had recently done a pretty good job with an analysis of strengths, weaknesses, opportunities, and threats (a SWOT analysis). Coblin thought these changes would make Nucor a stronger global player.

To Jeff Kemp, the new general manager of strategic planning and business development, the big issue was how to sustain Nucor's earnings growth in an industry where there were too many marginal competitors and too much production capacity. The U.S. government had recently given almost $1 billion in subsidies to nine mills, allowing them to remain in operation. Kemp was looking for opportunities for Nucor within the steel industry. He questioned why Nucor had bought a steel bearings company. Kemp's experience in the chemical industry suggested a need for Nucor to establish a position of superiority and grow globally, driving industry competition rather than reacting. He argued that a company should protect its overall market position, which could mean sacrifices for individual plants. Aycock liked Kemp's background in law and accounting, and had specifically sought someone from outside the steel industry to head up Nucor's strategic planning. By June 2000, Kemp had conducted studies of other steel companies in the U.S. market and developed a working document that identified opportunities worthy of further analysis.

According to Dave Aycock, "Every company hits a plateau. You can't just go out and build plants to grow. How do you step up to the next level? I wouldn't say it's a turning point but we have to get our strategic vision and strategic plans. We are beginning Nucor's first ever strategic planning sessions; it was not necessary before." Nucor had recently received the results of a study done by an outside consulting firm of how the company's top 10 to 15 managers and selected outsiders viewed the company—see Exhibit 9.

Aycock believed Nucor needed to be quick to recognize developing technology in all production areas. He made special note of Nucor's new joint venture to develop a new "strip caster" that could cast flat-rolled sheet in a more finished form. He believed the impact could be explosive, allowing Nucor to build smaller plants close to end-use customers, an outcome that would be particularly helpful on the West Coast. Nucor would own the U.S. and Brazilian rights, and its partners would own the rights for the rest of the world. Aycock was looking forward to the next generation of steel mills and believed this time Nucor should own the rights to new technologies; he praised Ken Iverson's skill at seeing the potential of new technology and committing early to it.

Aycock had expressed an interest in acquisitions provided they fit strategically. He indicated a bar mill in the upper-central Midwest and a flat-rolled plant in the Northeast would be good for Nucor. He also believed there was a significant opportunity for Nucor in preengineered buildings. Looking ahead, Aycock saw Nucor concentrating on steel for the next five to six years, achieving an average growth rate of 15 percent per year. Aycock thought that Nucor needed to be ready in about seven years to move into other areas, indicating that Nucor had already "picked the low-hanging grapes" and would need to be careful in its next moves.

exhibit 9 Nucor's 2000 Image Survey

In early 2000, Nucor had an outside consulting firm conduct a survey of the company's image as seen by the top 10 to 15 managers, including corporate office. The consulting firm also gathered the views of a few analysts and media personnel. The survey produced several major findings:

- Nucor managers still agreed that the company valued risk taking, innovation, and a lean management structure with aggressive, hardworking employees who accepted the responsibility of failure along with the opportunity for success.
- Nucor managers seemed to see the company as a way of doing business—not just a way of making steel. They placed a high value on Nucor's operating practices and ways of doing business.
- When Nucor managers were asked to associate Nucor's persona with a public figure, John Wayne was the clear choice.
- Nucor managers in the field seemed to believe the new layer of management was needed and were not concerned about a loss of decentralization. They liked the new management team and the changes so far, particularly the improved communications with corporate office.
- Corporate-level managers thought the company was changing much faster than did division managers. They also held a more positive view of the company on such things as how good the company was in their community or with the environment.
- The business media people surveyed had positive views of Nucor, characterizing it as hardworking and committed to its employees and as an innovative, risk-taking economic powerhouse.
- Outsiders most familiar with the company believed Nucor management needed to do a better job of communicating its vision during a period of transition.

Source: Nucor records.

STEEL AND NUCOR IN 2000–2001

In September 2000, David Aycock stepped aside as Nucor's president and CEO as he had planned when the board elected Daniel R. DiMicco, one of the four new group executive vice presidents, as Nucor's new president and CEO. At the time of his appointment, Dan DiMicco had responsibility over Nucor-Yamato Steel, Nucor Steel Hertford (plate division), and Nucor Building Systems (three plants). He had graduated from Brown University in 1972 with a bachelor of science in engineering, metallurgy and materials science. He received a master's degree in metallurgy from the University of Pennsylvania in 1975. He was with Republic Steel in Cleveland as a research metallurgy and project leader until he joined Nucor in 1982 as plant metallurgist and manager of quality control for Nucor Steel in Utah. In 1988, he became melting and castings manager. In 1991 he was promoted to general manager of Nucor-Yamato and was appointed a vice president in 1992. In addition to DiMicco's appointment, at the same September 2000 meeting, Peter Browning, a recent addition to Nucor's board of directors, was elected chairman of Nucor's board. Aycock retired from the Nucor's board in 2001.

In 2000, Nucor's sales revenues and earnings were at record levels (Exhibits 1 and 2). While 2000 had begun on a strong footing for Nucor, the domestic steel market had turned weak by year-end. Nucor remained profitable, but other steel companies were in deep financial trouble. A new Vulcraft plant was under construction in New York, the company's first venture into the Northeast. Nucor was also attempting a break-through technological step in strip casting at Crawfordsville with its new Castrip process. Nucor sold its grinding-ball facilities and bearing products operation, indicating these operations no longer fit into its core business.

In early 2001, *The Wall Street Journal* predicted that all but two of the biggest steelmakers in the United States would post fourth-quarter 2000 losses. AK Steel Holding Corporation and Nucor Corporation were expected to have profits for the last quarter of 2000, while U.S. Steel Group, a unit of USX Corporation (the largest U.S. steel manufacturer) was expected to post a profit for all of 2000 but not the fourth quarter.

In Nucor's 2000 annual report (issued in March 2001), Dan DiMicco laid out Nucor's plans for 2001 and beyond:

> Our targets are to deliver an average annual earnings growth of 10–15 percent over the next 10 years, to deliver a return well in excess of our cost of capital, to maintain a minimum average return on equity of 14 percent, and to deliver to return on sales a 8–10 percent. Our strategy will focus on Nucor becoming a "Market Leader" in every product group and business in which we compete. This calls for significant increases in market share for many of our core products and the maintenance of market share where we currently enjoy a leadership position.
>
> . . . In the past Nucor grew almost exclusively through "Greenfield" expansion. It would be impossible in today's market to rely on this mechanism for all of our future projected growth. While Nucor will continue to expand through Greenfield construction, there will now be a heavy focus on growth through acquisitions. We will also continue growing through the commercialization of new disruptive and leapfrog technologies.
>
> We believe that there are several unique opportunities today to grow through acquisition and industry consolidation. These opportunities exist because of the historically low valuations for steel-making assets . . . Nucor has always approached every cloud on the economic landscape as an opportunity to grow. Our job is to find the opportunities that best fit our culture, our core businesses, and our strategic plan for profitable growth.
>
> . . . The year 2001 will see us implement a company-wide benchmarking and best practices program that will involve every employee.

Between October 2000 and October 2001, 29 steel companies in the United States, including Bethlehem Steel Corporation and LTV Corporation, the nation's third- and fourth-largest steel producers, respectively, filed for bankruptcy protection. Bankrupt steel mills accounted for about 25 percent of U.S. steelmaking capacity. Later in October 2001, *The Economist* noted that of the 14 steel companies tracked by Standard & Poor, only Nucor was indisputably healthy. Some experts believed that close to half of the U.S. steel industry's production capacity might be forced to close; since 1997, nearly 47,000 jobs in the U.S. steel industry have vanished. In November 2001, LTV announced that its cash reserves were depleted and that it no longer had the funds to operate all of its facilities; management indicated the company was petitioning the bankruptcy judge to permit the company to shut down operations and put some of its steelmaking facilities up for sale. Nucor's stock price rose $4 per share on the day of the LTV announcement.

Worldwide, the steel industry was in the midst of one of its most unprofitable and volatile periods ever, in part due to a glut of steel that had sent prices tumbling 32 percent (since 1997) to 20-year lows. While many U.S. steel producers were mired in red ink, many foreign steelmakers desperately needed to continue to sell in the relatively open U.S. market to stay profitable (or survive). The industry was hovering around 75 percent capacity utilization, a level too low to be profitable for many companies. Three European companies—France's Usinor SA, Luxembourg's Arbed SA, and Spain's Aceralia Corporation—were in the process of merging to form the world's largest steel company. Two Japanese companies—NKK Corporation and Kawasaki Steel Corporation—were in merger talks that would create the world's second-biggest steelmaker.

exhibit 10   Summary of Nucor's Performance for the First Nine Months of 2001

Quarter	Total Tons Sold	Percent Change vs. Prior Year	Revenues (in billions)	Percent Change vs. Prior Year	Average Sales Price per Ton	Pretax Earnings (in millions)	Percent Change vs. Prior Year	Average Pretax Profit per Ton
1	2,980,000	3.5%	$1.028	(14.3)%	$345	$50.3	(60.2)%	$19
2	3,237,000	11.4	1.079	(11.2)	333	51.3	(59.5)	17
3	3,066,000	7.9	1.053	(9.5)	345	31.4	(70.3)	11
Year-to-date	9,283,000	7.6	$3.160	(11.7)	341	$133.0	(62.9)	16

Some analysts believed these new megasteelmakers could outmuscle U.S. competitors, which were generally less efficient, smaller, and financially weaker than competitors in Asia and Europe. The largest U.S. steelmaker, USX–U.S. Steel Group, was currently only the 11th-largest producer in the world, and consolidation in the industry could push it further down the list. In spite of these worsening conditions, global steel production increased 7 percent in 2000, to a record 747 million tons, and efforts were under way to negotiate a worldwide reduction in steel production. According to the Organization for Economic Cooperation and Development, total global steel capacity was 1 billion tons annually. The OECD expected 2001 production to reach 835 million tons, but consumption was seen at 721 million tons. Estimated overcapacity worldwide was 200 million tons.

In addition to cheap imports, U.S. steel producers were facing higher energy prices, weakening demand by customer industries, increasingly tough environmental rules, and a changing cost structure among producers. While a recession might push energy prices down and lower operating costs, a recession would adversely affect such steel-using industries as construction, motor vehicles, and farm equipment. Tougher environmental rules could lead to costly modifications and closings of old plants, which produced coke along with vast clouds of ash and acrid green smoke. In 1990, minimills accounted for 36 percent of the domestic steel market, but by 2000 the more efficient minimill had seized 50 percent of the market and the resulting competition had driven prices lower. The Bush administration was under mounting pressure to impose 40 percent import tariffs and quotas that would provide relief for the beleaguered integrated mills in the U.S.

Nucor's Performance and Strategy Adjustments in 2001.   The first nine months of 2001 were tough for Nucor. Despite record production and shipments, revenues and earnings were down as compared with the first nine months of 2000—see Exhibit 10. DiMicco attributed the drop-offs in revenues and earnings directly due to global overcapacity and price cutting, stating that "all the U.S. mills could close and there would still be excess capacity [worldwide]." Exhibit 11 shows Nucor's average sales prices and cost for scrap steel by quarter for 2000 and the first nine months of 2001.

In March 2001, Nucor made its first acquisition in 10 years, purchasing a 400,000-ton steel bar minimill in Auburn, New York, from Japanese-based Sumitomo Metal Industries for $115 million. Nucor had hired about five people to help plan for future acquisitions. DiMicco commented, "It's taken us three years before our team has felt this is the right thing to do and get started making acquisitions." In the present over-

exhibit 11   Nucor's Average Sales Prices per Ton and Scrap Steel Costs, 2000–2001

	Average Sales Prices per Ton								Average Scrap and Scrap Substitute Cost per Ton Used
	Sheet Steel	Steel Bars	Structural Steel	Steel Plate	Total Steel	Steel Joists	Steel Deck	Cold-Finished Steel	
2001									
1st Quarter	$267	$288	$380	$269	$301	$810	$672	$561	$103
2nd Quarter	273	282	340	261	290	785	640	552	102
First Half	270	285	361	264	295	796	654	556	102
3rd Quarter	279	286	356	267	300	729	598	550	101
Nine Months	273	285	359	265	297	771	634	554	102
2000									
1st Quarter	$348	$341	$404		$363	$845	$723	$568	$126
2nd Quarter	353	335	401		365	830	712	576	126
First Half	351	338	402		364	837	718	572	126
3rd Quarter	329	310	407		349	823	699	575	118
Nine Months	344	328	404		359	832	711	573	123
4th Quarter	288	302	403		326	827	688	577	109
Full Year	$332	$322	$404		$352	$831	$705	$574	$120

Source: Posted at www.nucor.com as of November 30, 2001.

supplied market, analysts believed it would be cheaper for growth-minded companies to purchase existing plant capacity rather than to build new plants (but this conclusion hinged on existing plants being able to operate with costs reasonably comparable to state-of-the-art plants). Until this acquisition, Nucor's strategy had been to invest in its own newly constructed state-of-the-art plants to get the production capacity to take sales and market share away from competitively weaker, higher-cost competitors. Nucor planned to use the steel mill in Auburn to supply 90 percent of the raw materials for its newly constructed Vulcraft joist plant in New York, 80 miles away. Then in November 2001, Nucor announced the acquisition of Trico Steel for $120 million; Trico was in Chapter 11 bankruptcy proceedings and its primary asset, a 2.2-million-ton sheet steel mill in Decatur, Alabama, built in 1997 at a cost of $465 million, was presently shut down. Trico was a joint venture of LTV (which owned a 50 percent interest) and two of the world's leading international steel companies—Sumitomo Metal Industries and British Steel, each of which had a 25 percent interest. Nucor indicated that the timing of the start-up of the newly acquired sheet mill in Alabama would depend on market conditions and that the mill, which had the capability to make thin sheet steel with a superior surface quality, would be a strong complement to Nucor's flat-rolled sheet strategy.

case 20 FedEx Corporation: Structural Transformation through e-Business

Pauline Ng,
The University of Hong Kong

> [FedEx] has built superior physical, virtual and people networks not just to prepare for change, but to shape a change on a global scale; to change the way we all connect with each other in the new Network Economy[1]

> [FedEx] is not only reorganizing its internal operations around a more flexible network computing architecture, but it's also pulling-in and in many cases locking-in customers with an unprecedented level of technological integration.[2]

Since its inception in 1973, Federal Express Corporation (FedEx)[3] had transformed itself from an express delivery company to a global logistics and supply chain management company. Over the years, the company had invested heavily in information technology systems, and with the launch of the Internet in 1994, the potential for further integration of systems to provide services throughout its customers' supply chains became enormous. With all the investment in the systems infrastructure over the years and the $88 million acquisition of Caliber Systems, Inc., in 1998, the company had built a powerful technical architecture that had the potential to pioneer in Internet commerce. However, despite having all the ingredients for the makings of a successful e-

The case is part of a project funded by a teaching development grant from the University Grants Committee (UGC) of Hong Kong SAR. This case was an award-winner in the 2000 Paper Awards Competition hosted by the Society of Information Management. Copyright © 2000 The University of Hong Kong. This case was prepared under the supervision of Dr. Ali F. Farhoomand and is not intended to show effective or ineffective handling of decision or business processes.

[1]Federal Express, annual report, 1999.

[2]M. Janah and C. Wilder, "Special Delivery," *Information Week* (www.FedExcorp.com/media/infowktop100thml), 1997.

[3]The company was incorporated as Federal Express Corporation in 1971. In 1994, the company was renamed FedEx Corporation and subsequently renamed FDX Corporation in 1998 and then FedEx Corporation in 2000. However, throughout the case the company is referred to as FedEx to avoid confusion.

business, the company's logistics and supply chain operations were struggling to shine through the historical image of the company as simply an express delivery business. Furthermore, competition in the transportation/express delivery industry was intense, and there were reports that FedEx's transportation volume growth was slowing down, even though the company was poised to take advantage of the surge in traffic that e-tailing and electronic commerce (EC) were supposed to generate. Hence, on January 19, 2000, FedEx announced major reorganizations in the group's operations in the hope of making it easier to do business with the entire FedEx family. The mode of operation for the five subsidiary companies was to function independently but to compete collectively. In addition to streamlining many functions, the group announced that it would pool its sales, marketing, and customer services functions such that customers would have a single point of access to the whole group. The reorganization was expected to cost $100 million over three years. Was this simply a new branding strategy or did FedEx have the right solution to leverage its cross-company synergies and its information and logistics infrastructure to create e-business solutions for its customers?

THE EXPRESS TRANSPORTATION AND LOGISTICS INDUSTRY

FedEx invented the air/ground express industry in 1973. Although United Parcel Service (UPS) was founded in 1907 and became America's largest transportation company, it did not compete with FedEx directly in the overnight delivery market until 1982. Competition began with a focus on customer segmentation, pricing, and quality of service. For most businesses, physical distribution costs often accounted for 10–30 percent of sales or more. As competition put pressure on pricing, businesses began to look at ways to cut costs yet improve customer service. The solution was to have a well-managed logistics operation to reduce the length of the order cycle and thus generate a positive effect on cash flow.

The growth of the express transportation and logistics industry was brought about by three main trends: the globalization of businesses, advances in information technology (IT), and the application of new technology to generate process efficiencies, and the changing market demand for more value-added services. As businesses expanded beyond national boundaries and extended their global reach to take advantage of new markets and cheaper resources, so the movement of goods created new demands for the transportation and logistics industry. With this, the competitiveness of transportation companies depended upon their global network of distribution centers and their ability to deliver to wherever their customers conducted business. Speed became of significance to achieve competitiveness, not only for the transportation companies but also for their customers. The ability to deliver goods quickly shortened the order-to-payment cycle, improved cash flow, and created customer satisfaction.

Advances in IT promoted the globalization of commerce. The ability to share information between operations/departments within a company and between organizations to generate operational efficiencies, reduce costs, and improve customer service was a major breakthrough for the express transportation industry. However, of even greater significance was the way in which new technology redefined logistics. At a time when competition within the transportation industry was tough and transportation companies were seeking to achieve competitive advantages through value-added services, many of these companies expanded into logistics management services. Up until the 1980s, logistics was merely the handling, warehousing, and transportation of goods. By combining the functions of materials management and physical distribution, logistics took on a new and broader meaning. It was concerned with inbound as well as outbound material flow, within companies as well as the movement of finished goods from dock to dock. With this, the transportation industry responded by placing emphasis not only on the physical transportation but also on the coordination and control of storage and movement of parts and finished goods. Logistics came to include value-added activities such as order processing, distribution center operations, inventory control, purchasing, production, and customer and sales services. Interconnectivity through the Internet and intranets and the integration of systems enabled businesses to redefine themselves and to reengineer their selling and supply chains. Information came to replace inventory. Just-in-time inventory management helped to reduce costs and improve efficiency. With the advent of IT, express transportation became an aggregation of two main functions: the physical delivery of parcels, and the management and utilization of the flow of information pertaining to the physical delivery (i.e., control over the movements of goods).

FEDEX CORPORATION

FedEx was the pioneer of the express transportation and logistics industry. Throughout the 27 years of its operation, FedEx's investment in IT had earned the company a myriad of accolades. Since 1973, FedEx had won over 194 awards for operational excellence. Fundamental to the success of the FedEx business was the vision of its founder.

The Visionary behind the Business

> If we're all operating in a day-to-day environment, we're thinking one to two years out. Fred's thinking five, ten, fifteen years out.
> —William Conley, VP, FedEx Logistics, Managing Director Europe

Fred Smith, chairman, president, and chief executive officer of FedEx Corporation, invented the express distribution industry in March 1973. By capitalizing on the needs of businesses for speed and reliability of deliveries, FedEx shortened lead times for companies. Its next-day delivery service revolutionized the distribution industry. The success of FedEx's distribution business in those early days rested on Smith's commitment to his belief that the opportunities were excellent for a company able to provide reliable overnight delivery of time-sensitive documents and packages. Despite losses in the first three years of operation due to high capital investments in the physical transportation infrastructure of the business, FedEx began to see profits from 1976 onward. To compete on a global basis, the key components of the physical infrastructure had to be in place to connect the world's gross domestic product (GDP). The underlying philosophy was that wherever business was conducted, there was going to have to be the movement of physical goods.

Under Smith's leadership, the company had set a few records with breakthrough technology. In the 1980s, FedEx gave away more than 100,000 sets of personal computers loaded with FedEx software, designed to link and log customers into FedEx's ordering and tracking systems. FedEx was also the first to issue its drivers handheld scanners that alerted customers of when packages were picked up or delivered. Then, in 1994, FedEx became the first big transportation company to launch a website that included tracking and tracing capabilities. Very early on, Smith could foresee that the Internet was going to change the way businesses would operate and the way people would interact. By applying IT to the business, FedEx leapfrogged the rest of the industry. Smith was the visionary who forced his company and other companies to think outside of the proverbial box. The core of FedEx's corporate strategy was to "use IT to help customers take advantage of international markets."[4] By 1998, FedEx was a $10 billion company spending $1 billion annually on IT development plus millions more on capital expenditure. It had an IT workforce of 5,000 people.

Building the Transportation and Logistics Infrastructure

In the early years of the FedEx transportation business, Smith insisted that the company should acquire its own transportation fleet, while competitors were buying space on commercial airlines and subcontracting their shipment to third parties. The strategy of expanding through acquiring more trucks and planes continued. By the 10th year of operation, FedEx earned the accolade of being the first U.S. company to achieve the $1 billion revenue mark within a decade without corporate acquisitions and mergers.

FedEx was cited as being the inventor of customer logistics management.[5] As early as 1974, FedEx started logistics operations with the Parts Bank. In those days, a few small parts distributors approached FedEx with their warehousing problems and decided on the idea of overnight distribution of parts. With those propositions, FedEx built a small warehouse on the end of its sorting facilities at Memphis. This was FedEx's first attempt at multiple-client warehousing. Customers would call up and order the dispatch of parts, and the order would be picked up on the same day. That was also FedEx's first value-added service beyond basic transportation. From there, the logistics side of the business snowballed.

Throughout the next three decades, FedEx's transportation business growth was attributable to a number of external factors that FedEx was quick to capitalize on. These included:

- Government deregulation of the airline industry, which permitted the landing of larger freight planes, thus reducing operating costs for FedEx.
- Deregulation of the trucking industry, which allowed FedEx to establish a regional trucking system to lower costs further on short-haul trips.
- Trade deregulation in Asia Pacific, which opened new markets for FedEx. Expanding globally became a priority for FedEx.
- Technological breakthroughs and applications innovations, which promoted significant advances for customer ordering, package tracking, and process monitoring.
- Rising inflation and global competition, which gave rise to greater pressures on businesses to minimize the costs of operation, including implementation of just-in-time inventory management systems and so forth. This also created demands for speed and accuracy in all aspects of business.

As of January 2000, FedEx served 210 countries (making up more than 90 percent of the world's GDP), operated 34,000 drop-off locations, and managed over 10 million square feet of warehouse space worldwide. It had a fleet of 648 aircraft and more than

---

[4]Garten, 1998.

[5]R. F. Bruner and D. Bulkley, "The Battle for Value: Federal Express Corporation versus United Parcel Service of America, Inc. (Abridged)," University of Virginia Darden School Foundation, 1995.

exhibit 1   FedEx's Record of Systems Innovations, 1979–99

1979	Customer Operations Service Master On-line System (COSMOS), a global shipment tracking network based on a centralized computer system to manage vehicles, people, packages, routes, and weather scenarios on a real-time basis. COSMOS integrated two essential information systems: information about goods being shipped and information about the mode of transportation.
1980	Digitally Assisted Dispatch System (DADS), a system that coordinated on-call pickups for customers. It allowed couriers to manage their time and routes through communication via a computer in their vans.
1984	The first PC-based automated shipping system, later named FedEx PowerShip, a stand-alone DOS-based system for customers with five or more packages per day. The customer base was immediately transformed into a network that allowed customers to interact with the FedEx system and download software and shipping information.
1984	PowerShip Plus, a DOS-based shipping system that integrated with customers' order-entry, inventory-control, and accounting systems, for customers who shipped more than 100 packages per day.
1985	Bar-code labeling. FedEx was the first to introduce such labeling to the ground transportation industry.
1986	The SuperTracker, a handheld bar-code scanner system that captured detailed package information.
1989	An on-board communications system that used satellite tracking to pinpoint vehicle location.
1991	Rite Routing, which demonstrated the value of a nationwide, centralized transportation management service.
1991	PowerShip PassPort, a Pentium-class PC system that combined best of PowerShip and PowerShip Plus for customers who shipped more than 100 packages a day (1,500 users).
1993	MultiShip, the first carrier-supplied customer automation system to process packages shipped by other transportation providers.
1993	FedEx ExpressClear Electronic Customs Clearance System, which expedited regulatory clearance while cargo was en route.
1993	PowerShip 3, a client-server shipping system for customers who shipped three or more packages per day.
1994	The FedEx website (www.fedex.com), the first to offer online package status tracking so that customers could actually conduct business via the Internet.
1994	DirectLink, software that let customers receive, manage, and remit payments of FedEx invoices electronically.

60,000 vehicles, with a staff of nearly 200,000. It was the world's largest overnight package carrier, with a market share of about 30 percent.

Building the Virtual Information Infrastructure

We are really becoming a technology company enabled by transportation.
—David Edmonds, VP, Worldwide Services Group, FedEx[6]

Even as early as 1979, a centralized computer system—Customer Operations Service Master On-line System (COSMOS)—kept track of all packages handled by the com-

---

[6]K. Krause, "Not UPS with a Purple Tint," *Traffic World* (www.trafficworld.com/reg/news/special/s101899.html), October 1999.

exhibit 1   FedEx's Record of Systems Innovations 1979–99 (*cont.*)

1995	FedEx Ship, a Windows-based shipping and tracking software program that allowed customers to process and manage shipping from their desktop (650,000 users). It extended the benefits of PowerShip to all FedEx's customers, providing software and toll-free dial-up to the FedEx network.
1995	The AsiaOne network, a transportation routing system.
1996	FedEx interNetShip, available through www.fedex.com, which made FedEx the first company to allow customers to process shipments on the Internet (65,000 users). This allowed customers to create shipping labels, request courier pickups, and send e-mail notifications to recipients of the shipments, all from the FedEx website.
1996	FedEx VirtualOrder, a software program that linked Internet ordering with FedEx delivery and online tracking. It also put customers' catalogs on their websites for them.
1997	E-Business Tools, which allowed easier connection with FedEx shipping and tracking applications.
1998	FedEx Ship for Workgroups, a Windows-based software program housed on a server that let users share information, such as address-book information, and gave them access to shipping logs and a tracking database. The server could be connected to FedEx via either modem or the Internet.
1998	PowerShip mc, a multicarrier electronic shipping system.
1999	The FedEx Marketplace, at www.fedex.com, which provided easy access to online merchants that offered fast, reliable FedEx express shipping. Through this new portal, shoppers had one-click access to several top online merchants that utilized FedEx's delivery services, including Value America, L. L. Bean, and HP Shopping Village (Hewlett-Packard's consumer EC website).
1999	The EuroOne network, which linked 16 cities to FedEx's Paris hub by air and another 21 cities by road-air. Like AsiaOne, this was a transportation routing system.
1999	A deal with Netscape that allowed FedEx to offer a suite of delivery services at its Netcenter portal. This entailed automatically integrating Netscape with the FedEx site. Although customers of Netscape could choose not to use FedEx, the use of an alternative shipper meant that they would not benefit from the efficiencies of the integrated systems. Considering that the Netscape Netcenter had more than 13 million members, the deal was a winner for FedEx.

Note: PowerShip had 850,000 online customers worldwide; PowerShip, PowerShip 3, and PowerShip Pass-Port were hardware-based products.

pany. This computer network relayed data on package movement, pickup, invoicing, and delivery to a central database at Memphis headquarters. This was made possible by placing a bar code on each parcel at the point of pickup and scanning the bar code at each stage of the delivery cycle.

In 1984, FedEx started to launch a series of technological systems, the PowerShip program, aimed at improving efficiency and control, which provided the most active customers (over 100,000) with proprietary online services. (See Exhibit 1 for a chronological list of FedEx systems.) In summary, these PowerShip systems provided additional services to the customer, including storing of frequently used addresses, label printing, online package pickup request, package tracking, and much more.

The emergence of electronic data interchange (EDI) and the Internet allowed companies to build one-to-one relationships with their customers. This was the perfect scenario for many manufacturers: the ability to match supply to demand without waste. FedEx took advantage of such new technologies and started to track back along the supply chain to the point of raw materials. As it did so, it identified points along the supply chain where it could provide management services. Often, these services included transportation, order processing and related distribution center operations, fulfillment inventory control, purchasing, production, and customer and sales services. The ability to interconnect and distribute information to all the players in a supply chain became the focus of FedEx's attention. For many of its customers, logistics was viewed as a key means for differentiating their products or services from those of their competitors (see Exhibit 2 for examples of some customer solutions). In other words, logistics became a key part of strategy formulation. As businesses were placing more emphasis on the order cycle as the basis for evaluating customer services levels, FedEx's role in providing integrated logistics systems formed the basis of many partnership arrangements. By helping them to redefine sources and procurement strategies so as to link in with other parties in the supply chain, such as raw materials suppliers, customers were outsourcing their supply chain management functions to FedEx, functions that were seen as peripheral to the core of their business (see Exhibit 3 and 4 for FedEx's coverage of the supply chain through integrated systems). Improving, tightening, and synchronizing the various parts to the supply chain showed customers the benefits of squeezing time and inventory out of the system. Tighter supply chain management was no longer viewed as a competitive advantage but a competitive imperative.

Businesses sought ways to improve their return on investment and became interested in any business process that could be integrated and automatically triggered (e.g., proof of delivery and payment) as proposed to being separately invoked. So not only was FedEx pushing its customers for integration, but its innovative customers were also demanding greater integration. Some customers had even jumped ahead of FedEx. Cisco Systems, for example, had developed an extranet that allowed its customers to order FedEx services without leaving the Cisco website. By integrating its services within the supply chain of its customers, and thus generating increases in customer loyalty and in customers' switching costs, FedEx managed to effectively raise the barriers to entry for competitors.

The Internet refined the COSMOS system. Wherever new information was entered into the system by FedEx or by customers through the Internet, all related files and databases were automatically updated. For example, when a FedEx customer placed an order through Fedex.com, the information would find its way to COSMOS, FedEx's global package-tracking system. The courier's Route Planner—an electronic mapping toll—would facilitate the pickup and delivery of the order from the customer. A product movement planner would schedule the order through the company's global air and courier operations. The customer would be able to track the status of the shipment through PowerShip or FedEx Ship. The COSMOS system handled 54 million transactions per day in 1999.

In 1998, FedEx decided to overhaul its internal IT infrastructure under Project GRID (Global Resources for Information Distribution). The project involved replacing 60,000 terminals and some PCs with over 75,000 network systems. The decision to go with network computers was made to avoid the "desktop churn" found with PCs.[7] The network computers linked over a global Internet Protocol network aimed to enhance the quality and quantity of services FedEx could deliver to it customers. For example, FedEx employees at any location at any time could track a package through the vari-

---

[7]"Desktop churn" refers to the rapid obsolescence of PCs as new applications eat up processing power.

exhibit 2   Examples of FedEx Solutions for Customers

Dell Computers pioneered the direct selling model in the computer industry and succeeded because it was able to keep inventory very low. FedEx provided the system to track and monitor the assembly of each PC on order. Because the assembly line could be in any one of five manufacturing locations around the world, however, FedEx described itself as the conveyor belt for that manufacturing line. FedEx was a key partner for Dell, allowing customized, built-to-order products to be delivered within days of a customer placing an order, a huge advantage in an industry whose components become obsolete at the rate of 2 percent per month.

In 1995, **National Semiconductor Corporation (NatSemi)** decided to outsource its warehousing and distribution to FedEx. By 1999, virtually all of NatSemi's products, manufactured by six factories (three being subcontractors), were shipped directly to FedEx's distribution warehouse in Singapore. Hence, FedEx had control over the goods, the warehouse, and the dispatch of orders (via FedEx transportation, of course). Having complete visibility of NatSemi's order systems allowed FedEx to reduce the average customer delivery cycle from four weeks to two days, and distribution costs from 2.9 percent of sales to 1.2 percent. FedEx could pack and fulfill orders without NatSemi having to notify the company. In effect, it became the logistics department of NatSemi. Furthermore, this arrangement enabled NatSemi to dispense with seven regional warehouses in the United States, Asia, and Europe. NatSemi reported savings in the region of $8 million over the five-year period (see Exhibit 4).

For **Omaha Steaks,** when orders were received, they would be relayed from Omaha Steaks' IBM AS/400 to its warehouse and simultaneously to FedEx by dedicated line. FedEx would generate the tracking and shipping labels, and the orders would be delivered to one of FedEx's regional hubs for onward delivery.

Cisco Systems was a Silicon Valley Internet hardware maker that transacted 80 percent of its business over the Web. At the end of 1999, FedEx signed an agreement with Cisco to coordinate all of Cisco's shipping over the next two years, and to gradually eliminate Cisco's warehousing over the following three years. Cisco had factories in the United States, Mexico, Scotland, Taiwan, and Malaysia. The finished parts were stored in warehouses near the factories awaiting completion of the whole order before it was dispatched to the customer. But Cisco did not want to build more warehouses, pay for reshipping, and hold massive volumes of inventory in transit. So the solution was to merge the orders in transit. As soon as parts were manufactured, they would be shipped to customers. Once all the parts had arrived at the customer's site, assembly would take place, thus doing away with warehousing. (This was known as the "merge-in-transit" program offered to companies such as Micron Computers.) FedEx created a unique system for Cisco that would automatically select routes and pick the most effective and economical mode of transportation, which included carriers other than FedEx's fleet of trucks and planes. Just as critical, however, was that the real-time information status of the synchronization operation was constantly available on the Internet.

ous steps in the FedEx chain. Other applications planned to be launched included COSMOS Squared, which allowed Non-Event Tracking, a feature that triggered alerts when scheduled events, such as the arrival of a package, did not occur. Through a 24-hour, seven-day operation called the Global Operations Command Center, the central nervous system of FedEx's worldwide system in Memphis, FedEx was able to provide efficient gathering and dissemination of real-time data. The operation housed huge screens covering the walls that tracked world events, weather patterns, and the real-time movement of FedEx trucks and aircraft. New systems were also introduced to predict with greater accuracy the amount of inbound traffic. This system allowed FedEx to prioritize the hundreds of variables involved in the successful pickup,

exhibit 3   FedEx Solutions for the Entire Supply Chain

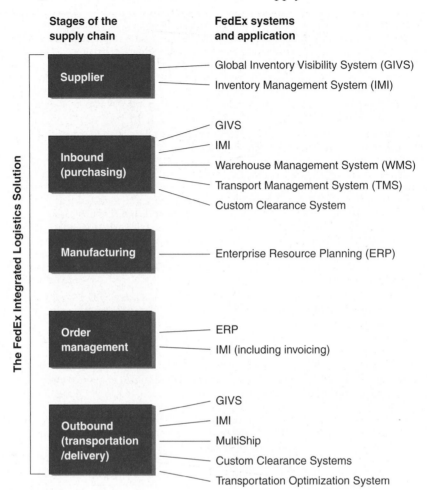

processing, and delivery of a parcel. Senior managers at FedEx believed that having current and accurate information helped them reduce failure in the business.

As well as the data center in Memphis, FedEx operated other centers in Colorado Springs, Miami, Orlando, Dallas–Fort Worth, Singapore, and Brussels.

Also in 1999, FedEx signed an agreement with Netscape to adopt Netscape software as the primary technology for accessing its corporate intranet sites. FedEx's intranet included more than 60 websites, created for its end users and in some cases by its end users. Customers could build integrated websites using FedEx Applications Programming Interfaces (API) or FedEx intraNetShip (free downloads from Fedex.com) and incorporate a link that would allow them to track packages directly from their own site. Over 5,000 websites fed hundreds of thousands of tracking requests through to the Fedex.com site.

> Our API solutions are designed to give global visibility and access across the supply chain, from manufacturing to customer service to invoicing. We've managed to wipe out those ir-

exhibit 4   Example of Integrated Customer Order Process Management: National Semiconductor

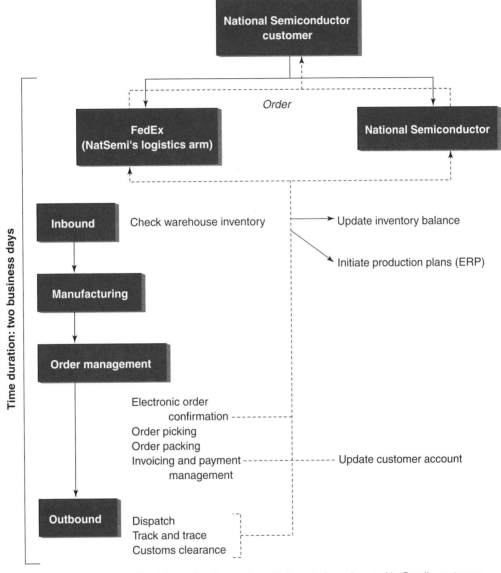

------------------ The information flow value of integrated services to NatSemi's customer

ritating WISMO (Where Is My Order) calls because we've seamlessly linked our customers to their customers.

—Mike Janes, former VP, Electronic Commerce & Logistics Marketing, FedEx[8]

At the beginning of 1999, FedEx launched an enhancement to its package-tracking service. Customers could query and receive package status information for up to 25 shipments simultaneously, and forward this information on to up to three e-mail recipients.

---

[8]C. Gentry, "FedEx API's Create Cinderella Success Stories" (www.fedex.com/us/about/api.html), October 1998.

Furthermore, users in France, Japan, Italy, Germany, the Netherlands, and Portuguese- and Spanish-speaking countries could access this information online in their native languages through Fedex.com.

FedEx claimed to have the largest online client server network in the world that operated in real time. Information became an extremely critical part of its business.

> We're in the express transportation business, but we've discovered how to lock up a lot of value in the information that we have.
> —Mark Dickens, VP, Electronic Commerce & Customer Services[9]

> Even when on the physical side of the business, we outsource, for instance, the pickup or the delivery or the warehousing activity for a customer, we have never outsourced the information. Protecting the brand has always been very, very critical for us.
> —William Conley

The benefits of these services were not limited to FedEx's customers. For FedEx, its online services, which in 1999 handled 60 million transactions per day, saved FedEx the cost of 200,000 customer service employees. In turn, the company reported spending 10 percent of its $17 billion annual revenue on IT in 1999. Information had allowed FedEx to lower its costs such that the cost to customers of using FedEx in 1999 was lower than it was 25 years ago.

Going beyond delivery services, FedEx aimed to fully integrate its corporate partners every step of the way along the supply chain. Fundamental to FedEx's strategy for establishing its e-business and logistics operations was how well it could forge technology links with customers.

> It's all about integration, whether it's inside FedEx, with our technology partners, or with our customers.
> —Laurie Tucker, Senior VP, Logistics Electronic Commerce & Catalog[10]

> Integration of Internet services with our transportation offerings is not an addition to our core business; it is our core business.
> —Dennis Jones, CIO[11]

> When it comes to managing synergies across businesses, we've found that seamless information integration is a critical component.[12]

MANAGEMENT AND OPERATIONS ISSUES

Branding and Business Structure up until January 19, 2000

In the first 21 years of business, FedEx operated under the corporate name of Federal Express Corporation. Its customers came to recognize it as FedEx for short, and the brand took off as the company grew and expanded its service offerings under the purple-and-orange flag. Hence, in 1994, it seemed natural that the company should change its brand name to FedEx.

---

[9]Janah and Wilder, "Special Delivery."

[10]Ibid.

[11]E. Cone and M. Duvall, "UPS Keeps Truckin'; FedEx: A Documented Success," *Inter@ctive Week,* November 16, 1999.

[12]Federal Express, annual report, 1999.

The Parts Bank was given official recognition when it became a division of FedEx Corporation in 1988 and became known as Business Logistics Services (BLS). It operated as a separate and independent company. In line with the express transportation side of the business, BLS developed expertise in the high-value, high-tech industries. It was involved in the express inbound, outbound, and redistribution of goods. However, it focused mainly on the small parcel business. FedEx based its solutions on just-in-time logistics. As the business grew, concern was raised that the logistics business was not generating revenue for the express transportation business but rather feeding this through to other carriers. Hence, in 1994, BLS was renamed FedEx Logistics, and it became mandatory for the logistics business to include FedEx transportation as part of its solution to customers. In 1996, the division changed its name yet again, to FedEx Logistics and Electronic Commerce (FLEC). The company started to focus its resources on doing business on the Internet, and the name change was to reflect the changes in the marketplace.

Following the acquisition of Caliber Systems, Inc., in 1998, five separate subsidiary companies were formed: Federal Express, RPS, Roberts Express, Viking Freight, and FDX Logistics. The latter four were Caliber businesses. Each subsidiary was managed independently and was responsible for its own accounts (see Exhibit 5). However, Caliber and FedEx's logistics operations were fundamentally different in that they had completely distinct customer bases and service offerings. Caliber developed expertise in moving raw materials, plates of steel, and steel bars and in managing work-in-progress. It would manage the manufacturing of cars and forklift trucks. Caliber provided an elaborate logistics operation concentrating mainly on high-priced goods industries, and it provided a fuller supply chain solution than FLEC did, whereas FLEC was primarily focused on finished goods, transportation logistics, and reverse logistics (i.e., handling returns). One was concentrating its business at the front end of the supply chain (e.g., receiving, work-in-progress) while the other was more involved in the back-end operations of the supply chain (i.e., warehousing, transportation). Hence, the two operations continued to operate independently of each other. Logistics systems and applications were also developed independently. Caliber Logistics became a subsidiary company under FDX Logistics, while FLEC continued as a division within Federal Express, the express transportation arm.

The acquisition served to reinforce FedEx's commitment to becoming more than just an express delivery company. Yet commentators and customers continued to associate the FedEx brand with transportation, and FedEx fought to transform the image of the company outside of this mold. One solution was to rename the company. With the acquisition, the company created a holding company, FDX Corporation. However, FedEx did very little to promote its new FDX corporate brand. Furthermore, its transportation subsidiary continued to operate under the Federal Express name with the purple-and-orange FedEx brand on its trucks and vans. The FedEx brand lived on, but with no advertising or aggressive promotion of FDX, the name did not resonate in the marketplace. While the likes of UPS had the advantage of promoting just one brand—UPS—to sell the entire company and its many service offerings, FedEx was trying to promote five different subsidiary companies with completely unrelated names and business logos under the FDX banner through distinctly separate sales and customer service teams. Furthermore, with two separate logistics businesses within the group, separate sales forces selling services offered by different parts of the company, separate customer services staff to deal with different queries, and IT resources spread across the group, customers were confused and resources were duplicated.

Despite the confusion, by 1999 FedEx purported to offer companies "total one-stop shopping" for solutions at all levels of the supply chain. Each subsidiary continued to

exhibit 5   Subsidiary Companies of FedEx Following the Acquisition of Caliber Systems Inc. in 1998

- **Federal Express** was the world leader in global express distribution, offering 24–48-hour delivery to 211 countries that composed 90 percent of the world's GDP. In 1998, FedEx was the undisputed leader in the overnight package delivery business. It had a fleet of 44,500 ground vehicles and 648 planes that gave support to the $14-plus billion business. It had 34,000 drop-off locations, and 67 percent of its U.S. domestic shipping transactions were generated electronically. Goods shipped ranged from flowers to lobsters to computer components. This company was constantly running in crisis mode, seeking to move packages through all weather and conditions to fulfill shipments overnight. The underlying philosophy that ensured high service levels was that every package handled could make a difference to someone's life. The company handled nearly 3 million shipments per day in 1998.

- **RPS** was North America's second-largest provider of business-to-business ground small-package delivery. It was a low-cost, nonunion, technology-savvy company acquired with the Caliber purchase. The company specialized in business-to-business shipments in one to three days, a service that FedEx could not match because it was unable to offer prices low enough to attract enough volume. Being a 15-year-old company, RPS prized itself on having one of the lowest-cost models in the transportation industry. It employed only owner-operators to deliver its packages. In terms of volume and revenue growth, RPS outperformed FedEx. For the future, plans were to grow RPS's business-to-consumer delivery service to take advantage of the growth of electronic commerce, thus carving a niche in the burgeoning residential delivery market. In 2000, the company owned 8,600 vehicles, achieved annual revenues of $1.9 billon and employed 35,000 people, including independent contractors. It handled 1.5 million packages per day.

- **Viking Freight** was the first less-than-truckload freight carrier in the western United States. The company employed 5,000 people, managed a fleet of 7,660 vehicles and 64 service centers, and shipped 13,000 packages per day.

- **Roberts Express** was the world's leading surface-expedited carrier for nonstop, time-critical, and special-handling shipments. The service offered by Roberts Express has been likened to a limousine service for freight. In 1999, the company handled more than 1,000 shipments per day. It was the smallest company within the FedEx Group. Urgent shipments could be loaded onto trucks within 90 minutes of a call, and shipments would arrive within 15 minutes of the promised time 96 percent of the time. Once loaded, shipments could be tracked by satellite every step of the way. Goods such as works of art or critical manufacturing components often required exclusive-use truck services. Exclusivity allowed customers greater control but at a price. This service was an infrequent necessity for most customers. Roberts had exclusive use of a handful of FedEx aircrafts, but the company still had to pay for use and for crew time.

- **Caliber Logistics** was a pioneer in providing customized, integrated logistics and warehousing solutions worldwide. The acquisition of Caliber in January 1998 brought with it over-the-road transportation and warehousing capabilities. Since the acquisition, FedEx tried to move away from traditional logistics offerings to providing total supply chain management solutions, and Caliber Logistics was renamed FDX Logistics. To the customer, this meant that FedEx could provide warehousing services, but only if this was part of a bigger deal. In September 1999, FedEx bought its first freight forwarder, Caribbean Transport Services (formerly GeoLogistics Air Services). Caribbean had a strong overseas network. FDX Logistics was the parent company of FedEx Supply-chain Services and Caribbean Transportation Services.

operate independently, with separate accounting systems and customer service staff, while competing collectively. However, while maintaining the autonomy of each subsidiary company, the challenge for FedEx was how to bring the companies closer together to create those synergies. Providing customers with a single point of access to the whole group was the ultimate goal. In practical terms, the task was to decide how each of the subsidiary companies should leverage its skills and services to a broader audience.

EVENTS LEADING UP TO THE JANUARY 2000 REORGANIZATION

FedEx needed to address a number of factors that would affect the prospects of the company.

FedEx's Performance

In the year ending May 31, 1999, FDX Corp. had outperformed analyst expectations, posting record earnings of 73 percent, an increase of 28 percent over the previous year.[13] Net income had risen 30 percent, to $221 million. However, results took a downturn in the following financial year. For the first quarter ended August 31, 1999, FDX announced that rising fuel prices had severely impacted the company's net income, causing it to miss its first-quarter target. With no sign of improvements in fuel prices and with the U.S. domestic market growth slowing down, FedEx warned that earnings for the second quarter and the full fiscal year might fall below analyst expectations. If one bears in mind that the express transportation business (mainly FedEx and RPS) accounted for over 80 percent of the group's revenue, and that the U.S. market accounted for approximately $10 billion of the group's revenue, both trends had a significant negative impact on net income.

Sure enough, FDX reported that for the quarter ended November 30, 1999, operating income was down by 10 percent from the previous year and net income was down by 6 percent. The company was not achieving the level of U.S. domestic growth it expected. Rising fuel prices continued to erode operating income. However, operations other than express transportation (i.e., Viking Freight, Roberts Express, FDX Logistics, and Caribbean Transportation Services) achieved revenue and operating income increases of 27 percent and 12 percent, respectively, in the second quarter. With the adverse fuel prices alone, the company anticipated that operating income could be down by more than $150 million for the year ending May 31, 2000. This called for some immediate remedial action.

Other trends within the express transportation and logistics market were also putting pressure on the company to rethink its business strategy.

The Internet Market and e-Tailing

The Internet changed the basis for competition for most business. Its low cost and diversity of applications make it appealing and accessible. The Internet leveled the playing field such that once a company was online, as long as it fulfilled its orders to the expectations of its customers, the size of the company was of no significance. The impact of the Internet on FedEx was twofold. First, it opened up opportunities in logistics management for FedEx as businesses were using the Internet to reengineer

---

[13]S. Gelsi, "FDX Posts Stronger-than-Expected Profit," CBS MarketWatch June 30, 1999 (http://cbs.marketwatch.com/archive . . . /current/fdx.htm?source=&dist=srch), February 2000.

their supply chains. So long as customers were satisfied, it really did not matter whether the goods were warehoused or not, whether the goods came directly from a factory in some distant location, or whether the goods had been made to order. Integration with customer supply chains was the key.

Second, the express transportation needs associated with the growth in e-tailing (expected to reach $7 billion in 2000) and business-to-business EC (expected to reach $327 billion by 2002) presented enormous opportunities for companies such as FedEx.[14, 15]

FedEx was sure that it had the right business model to take advantage of these opportunities.

> We're right at the center of the new economy . . . Businesses are utilizing the Internet to reengineer the supply chain. In the new economy, the Internet is the neural system. We're the skeleton—we make the body move.
> —Fred Smith[16]

But so were its competitors.

The Competition

In January 2000, *CBS MarketWatch Live* reported that FedEx's express delivery business was maturing and was not growing as fast as it used to.[17] Furthermore, the industry was loaded with companies, local and global, that provided a myriad of transportation services to a wide range of businesses. Competition was fierce. All major transportation and delivery companies were betting big on technology. Although FedEx pioneered the Web-based package-tracking system, such systems became the industry norm rather than a competitive advantage.

The four leading companies in the international courier business were DHL, FedEx, UPS, and TNT. Between them they held more than 90 percent of the worldwide market.[18]

UPS   Since 1986, UPS had spent $9 billion on IT; it had formed five alliances in 1997 to disseminate its logistics software to EC users. However, while FedEx developed all its IT software in-house, UPS made a point in stating that it was not a software developer and that companies taking that route were "trying to go a bridge too far."[19]

In early 1998, UPS formed a strategic alliance with Open Market, Inc., a U.S.-based provider of Internet software, to deliver a complete Internet commerce solution providing integrated logistics and fulfillment. It was also working with IBM and Lotus to standardize formats on its website.

---

[14]T. Lappin, "The Airline of the Internet," *Wired* 4, no. 12
(www.wired.com/wired/4.12/features/ffedex.html), December 1996.

[15]B. Erwin; M. A. Modahl; and J. Johnson, "Sizing Intercompany Commerce," *Business Trade & Technology Strategies* 1, no.1 (Forrester Research, Cambridge, MA 1997).

[16]H. Collingwood, 1999.

[17]D. Adamson, "FDX Corp. Changes Name to FedEx, "*CBS MarketWatch Live,* January 19, 2000.

[18]D. Murphy and K. Hernly, "Air Couriers Soar despite Mainland Gloom," *South China Morning Post,* May 30, 1999.

[19]D. A. Blackmon, "Ante Up! Big Gambles in the New Economy: Overnight Everything Changed for FedEx," *The Wall Street Journal Interactive Edition*
(www.djreprints.com/jitarticles/trx0001272701445.html), November 4, 1999.

In 1999, UPS raised $5.47 billion through its initial public offering (IPO), the largest in U.S. IPO history. The company shipped more than 55 percent of goods ordered over the Internet and offered a full range of logistics solutions to its customers.

DHL   In 1993, DHL announced a four-year, $1.25-billion worldwide capital spending program aimed at investing in handling systems, automation, facilities, and computer technology. The company launched its website in 1995. It was 25 percent owned by Deutsche Post and 25 percent owned by Lufthansa Airlines. Plans were under way for an initial public offering in the first half of 2001. Though the company dominated the U.K. market, it projected an increase in worldwide revenues of 18 percent, to $5.26 billion.[20]

TNT   In 1998, TNT launched a Web Collection facility on the Internet. Later the same year, TNT launched the world's first global Price Checker service on its website that allowed customers to calculate the price of sending a consignment from one place to another anywhere in the world. Other applications were under development that would allow customers to integrate with TNT's online services. Then in 1999, TNT launched QuickShipper, a one-stop online access to TNT's entire range of distribution services, from pricing to delivery. This new service was to be integrated with existing online tools such as Web Collection and Price Checker.

Also in March 1999, TNT launched the express industry's first dedicated customer extranet, Customized Services environment. This offered regular customers easy access to detailed and personalized shipment information through the use of user IDs and passwords. With this came a host of service offerings.

While FedEx had pioneered many logistics solutions that had helped it to achieve economies of scale faster than its competitors, the advantages were quickly eroding as newer technologies became even more powerful and less expensive.

THE JANUARY 2000 ANNOUNCEMENT

> All of your transportation and logistics needs can now be met by one organization—FedEx Corporation.[21]

On January 19, 2000, FedEx announced three major strategic initiatives:

- A new branding strategy that involved changing the company's name to FedEx Corporation and extending the FedEx brand to four of its five subsidiary companies. The subsidiary companies became:
  - FedEx Express (formerly Federal Express).
  - FedEx Ground (formerly RPS).
  - FedEx Custom Critical (formerly Roberts Express).
  - FedEx Logistics (formerly Caliber Logistics).
  - Viking Freight (no change).

  Exhibit 6 describes some of the internal changes flowing from the reorganization announcement.

---

[20]J. Exelby, "Interview—DHL UK Foresees Tough Market" (http://biz.yahoo.com/rf/000117/mq.html), January 17, 2000.

[21]FedEx Corporation Corporate Overview (www.fedexcorp.com/aboutfdx/corporateoverview.html) January 20, 2000.

exhibit 6   Before and After the FDX Reorganization

Before	After
Multiple brands under FDX umbrella	A single branding system leveraging the power of the FedEx brand so more customers can use FedEx reliability as a strategic competitive advantage
Separate sales force with directed cooperation	A single, expanded sales force especially targeting small and medium-sized businesses, cross-selling a wide portfolio of services and pricing schemes
Multiple invoices and account numbers	A single invoice and single account number from FedEx
Multiple automation platforms offering all FDX services	Streamlined customer automation systems to handle electronic transactions and database management needs for small and large businesses
Separate customer service, claims trace functions	Single customer service, claims, and trace functions by calling 1-800-G0-FedEx® (800-463-3339) or visiting its website at www.fedex.com

● Major internal reorganization aimed at creating one point of access to sales, customer service, billing, and automation systems. With these consolidations, the company announced intentions to form a sixth subsidiary, called FedEx Corporate Services Corporation, in June 2000 (see Exhibit 7 for new group structure). The new subsidiary would pool together the marketing, sales, customer services, information technology, and electronic commerce resources across all of FDX. The invoicing functions would also be combined for all the companies.

● Introduction of a new low-cost residential delivery service, FedEx Home Delivery, to be launched in the United States.

Of significance was the merging of the two logistics operations (Caliber Logistics and FLEC) into FedEx Logistics. The two companies seemed to complement each other in terms of their service offerings and customer base. Both had a few of the same customers but many different ones. Furthermore, Caliber's presence was mainly in North America and Europe, while FLEC had expanded into other continents. FedEx Logistics brought together all the splintered operations of logistics in all the subsidiary companies, streamlining costs, presenting one menu of logistics service offerings to customers, and aligning R&D of systems upon common, agreed platforms. This reorganization also brought about another major change in operations. It was no longer mandatory for the logistics business to use FedEx transportation as part of its solutions to customers. Being "carrier-agnostic" meant that FedEx Logistics would use FedEx transportation where it fit, both in terms of cost and in terms of geographic coverage. The decision would also rest on customer preference and the kind of goods being transported. For example, Caliber was transporting forklift trucks, cars, and steel plates that FedEx did not have the physical capacity to handle.

Combining the two operations brought together the IT expertise and the know-how of the logistics business. Under one CIO, standards were set for the development of systems on a worldwide basis, including vendor selection. In the past, regions de-

exhibit 7   FDX Corporation's Group Structure

A. Structure at the end of 1999

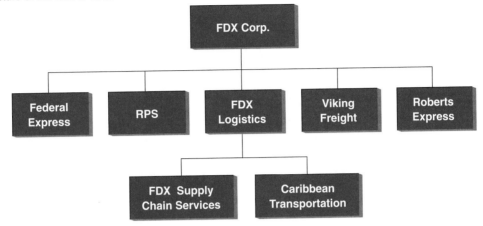

B. Structure following the January 2000 reorganization

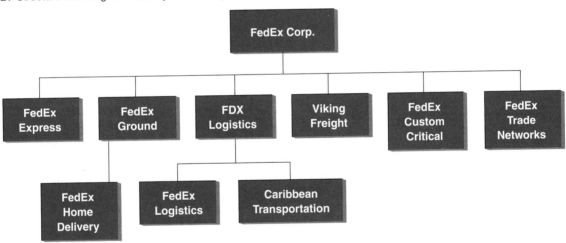

veloped their own solutions and operated in isolation. However, the Internet forced the company to consolidate its systems and solutions as customers demanded global solutions. Through the IT groups located in Memphis, Leiden (Holland), and Singapore, the company resolved to develop global systems for worldwide implementation, with functions such as multiple currencies and multiple languages. FedEx Logistics forecast a 70 percent growth rate in the year ending May 31, 2000. However, the business so far failed to generate any profit. The company aimed to build on its expertise in the five market segments: health care, industrial, high-tech, automotive, and consumer.

The company anticipated having to spend $100 million on these changes over three years. The intention was to take advantage of one of its greatest assets, the FedEx brand name—the name that customers could count on for "absolutely, positively" reliable service and cutting-edge innovation. The value of the brand had been ignored, particularly when the company decided to change its corporate name to FDX in 1998. Realizing its mistake, the renaming of the company as FedEx Corporation, and the extension of the brand to its subsidiaries fell in line with its intention to provide customers with an integrated set of business solutions. Customers wanted to deal with one company to meet their transportation and logistics needs.

Each subsidiary company was to continue operating independently, but collectively the group would provide a wide range of business solutions. It was this collective synergy of solutions that FedEx believed would form the competitive advantage of the company in the future. For customers, the benefits included easier means of doing business with FedEx. There was to be one toll-free telephone number, one website, one invoice and account number, one sales team, one customer service team, and a streamlined customer automation platform to handle electronic transactions for small and large businesses. The new organization was aimed at helping businesses of all sizes to achieve their shipping, logistics, supply chain, and e-business objectives. However, analysts questioned whether the new group structure would work, given that there would still be different teams of delivery and pickup staff for the different operations. Hence, one person could pick up one package sent by ground and another person could pick up another package sent by express from the same company. Companies such as UPS, on the other hand, would have one person pick up both types of packages.

In addition to these changes, FedEx anticipated growth in consumer e-commerce and planned to start a new service called FedEx Home Delivery (within the FedEx Ground subsidiary company) to meet the needs of businesses specializing in business-to-consumer e-tailing. FedEx had been successful in providing services to the business-to-business e-commerce market. Now it aimed to achieve the same leadership status in the business-to-consumer e-commerce market. However, expanding the residential delivery business was one segment that FedEx consciously made a decision not to pursue throughout the 1990s. This gave UPS the opportunity to lead in residential delivery services.

In late 1997, Smith was quoted as saying,

> We've made huge investments in our networks, and now that bow wave has passed. We think we have a good chance of harvesting a lot of that investment.[22]

In the two years that followed, the results of the company showed little signs of a harvest. Was the January 2000 restructuring going to bring in the harvest? The announcement certainly served to tell investors that FedEx was making some major changes to address competitive issues. However, analysts took a pragmatic view of the announcement, saying that "the proof is in the pudding."[23]

> Our biggest challenge is to correctly manage everything that's on our plate.
> —Fred Smith[24]

Was the reorganization going to leverage the power of the networks and the information and logistics infrastructures that FedEx had built? Did it provide the right ingredients to achieve the objectives of creating value for FedEx customers while at the same time improving profitability for FedEx? Given the speed at which technology and the marketplace were changing, would the new organization structure be adaptable to the changing business environment? Were there better alternative solutions that the company could have considered?

---

[22]L. Grant, "Why FedEx Is Flying High" (http:/pathfinder.com/fortune/1997/971110/fed.html), November 10, 1997.

[23]C. Bazdarich, "What's in a Name? Traders Swayed by Nominal Changes," *CBS MarketWatch,* January 21, 2000 (http://cbs.marketwatch.com/archive . . . st.htx?source=htx/http2_mw&dist=na), February 2000.

[24]Collingwood, 1999.

case 21 South African Breweries: Achieving Growth in the Global Beer Market

Courtenay Sprague
University of the Witwatersrand

Saul Klein
University of the Witwatersrand

In May 2000, Graham Mackay, group chief executive of South African Breweries (SAB), faced a difficult decision regarding the company's global strategy. Under Mackay's leadership, SAB had moved from a diversified South African conglomerate that shed its noncore businesses to become a fairly focused, global beer company. By the end of 1999, SAB had become the fourth-largest brewer in the world by volume. It had long been the dominant player in Africa and was growing rapidly in other emerging markets. SAB held a 98 percent share of the beer market in South Africa alone. Growth had been achieved across the African continent, and SAB had initiated brewing operations in Europe and Asia.

In early 2000, devastating floods ravaged the southern African region (especially Mozambique). A civil war continued in Angola, and political instability wracked Zimbabwe. With wars in the Democratic Republic of Congo, Ethiopia/Eritrea, and Sierra Leone, Africa was once again being portrayed in the international media as "the lost continent." The South African rand and other regional currencies plunged against the U.S. dollar. High political risk and volatility were attached to these emerging market economies, and SAB's ratings on the international financial markets were inevitably affected. As a result, SAB was challenged to reach the same growth in hard currency earnings as was obtained by its global competitors. Aiming to increase its globalization efforts, make acquisitions, and compete in developed markets, SAB had shifted its headquarters to London and listed its stock on the London Stock Exchange in March 1999.

While the global brewing industry remained highly fragmented, a race for consolidation had begun. Brewers were under pressure to move quickly to acquire, or else they might be acquired themselves. Despite SAB's movement overseas, the company was primarily an emerging market brewer, and closely associated with South Africa—an economy out of favor at the time. Mackay was considering several options for SAB. The company could try to merge with a major developed-country brewer, one that would complement SAB's competencies and geographical strengths. This tactic could be used to firmly entrench SAB in the top tier of premier international brewers. Alternatively, SAB could find a large emerging market brewer to acquire. Third, SAB could continue to focus on emerging market growth opportunities by building critical mass and rounding out its portfolio of beer brands, possibly staging small acquisitions when opportunities arose. SAB would then wait for the cycle of poor political risk to turn, and for emerging markets to return to favor before considering growth options in developed countries. In the interim, the focus would remain on improving organizational effectiveness, rendering operations even more cost-effective in order to increase efficiency and profits.

COMPANY BACKGROUND

Johannesburg, nicknamed the "city of gold" or E-Goli, was established as a mining town in 1886. South African Breweries followed in 1895, with £650 000 in combined capital and debentures. At the time, the local drink of choice was raw potato spirit mixed with tobacco juice and pepper. Beer created powerful competition. In 1896, SAB established a bar on company land in central Johannesburg, and in 1898 Castle Lager was launched. A London headline at the time read: "Castle Lager beer a phenomenal success. Taste its brilliancy, taste its flavour, 6 pence per glass."[1] In spite of the dire economic and social effects of the second Anglo-Boer War (raging from 1899 to 1902), SAB's annual profits rose to £100 000, while assets surpassed £1 million— making SAB the fastest-growing nonmining firm locally, by the early 1900s.

In the 1940s, SAB began to expand its brewing portfolio to include small hotels. In the 1950s taxes on beer resulted in reduced demand for beer, and South Africa's three largest brewers consolidated: Ohlsson's, United Breweries, and SAB. Although SAB was the smallest of the three, it managed to retain its name. The newly formed company emerged with 90 percent of the lager beer market. In order to expand its range of products in the 1960s, SAB acquired control of Stellenbosch Farmers' Winery. On August 15, 1962, the restriction on the drinking of alcohol by black South Africans was lifted, and a phenomenal market opportunity for SAB was created.

Between 1978 and 1990, SAB experienced extremely high organic growth rates in South Africa. From the mid-1960s to the early 1990s, SAB also followed a strategy of growth through diversification. In 1966, a hotel division was launched. SAB then added the furniture, footwear, and discount retailer OK Bazaars. In 1974, SAB acquired the Pepsi bottling division in South Africa (which converted to Coca-Cola in 1977) and the beer interests of the Rembrandt Group. In 1979, SAB obtained a 49 percent share in Appletiser,[2] obtaining control in 1982. In 1981 and 1982, SAB entered the apparel retail sector with the purchase of the Scotts Stores Group and Edgars. South African Breweries went on to invest in the Lion Match Company, Da Gama Textiles,

---

[1] From SAB history archives (www.sabcentenary.co/za/sabhistory).

[2] Early on, Appletiser was the most international of SAB's interests. By the mid-80s the brand was sold in the United States, Europe, and the United Kingdom.

exhibit 1   SAB's Involvement in Africa

Swaziland	Swaziland Brewers and Bottling, which originated in 1976, is the only brewer and soft-drink bottler in the country.
Botswana	SAB began operations with its neighbor in 1977. The company is the sole domestic producer of clear and sorghum beer, as well as Coca-Cola products.
Lesotho	Lesotho Brewing, established in 1980, is the only producer of beer, spirits, and soft drinks with a dominant market share.
Angola	SAB manages a brewery in Lubango on behalf of the Angolan government, under a three-year contract to rehabilitate the brewery.
Mozambique	SAB invested in Cervejas de Moçambique in 1995, which has an 84 percent market share. A sorghum plant was opened in Maputo in 1999.
Zimbabwe	SAB holds a 23 percent interest in Delta, one of the largest industrial companies listed on the Harare Stock exchange, and owner of Zimbabwe Breweries.
Zambia	In 1998, SAB acquired Zambian Breweries. From an initial market share of 28 percent, the market share increased to 90 percent in 1998.
Tanzania	SAB became a privatization partner with the Tanzanian government in 1993, becoming a shareholder in Tanzania Breweries—which owns the country's most popular beer brands, and has a licence to distribute Castle Lager.
Kenya	In April 1997, construction of a brewery began in Thika near Nairobi, with a planned capacity of 500,000 hectolitres. Brewing commenced in October 1998.
Uganda	Also in 1997, the company acquired a 40 percent stake in Nile Breweries, assuming management responsibility. Two of the Nile Breweries brands are the leading brands in Uganda.
Ghana	Entering the West African market in 1997, SAB acquired an initial 50.5 percent of Accra Brewery, a leading brewery in Ghana. This shareholding later increased to 69 percent.

Source: "SAB: Making Beer Making Friends," SAB brochure, 1999, pp. 50–56.

and Plate Glass in 1987, 1989, and 1992, respectively. The diversification strategy was a consequence of the political isolation of South Africa and the fact that SAB already had a 98 percent share of the South African lager beer market.[3]

SAB extended its operations in sub-Saharan Africa in the 1970s, beginning with a brewery in each of the neighboring countries, Swaziland, Botswana, and Lesotho. By the late 1990s, SAB held brewing interests in Zimbabwe, Tanzania, Mozambique, Angola, Ghana, Uganda, Kenya, and Zambia, and was the largest brewer in Africa, producing over half of all beer consumed on the continent (see Exhibit 1).[4]

By the early 1980s, SAB was also negotiating small acquisitions overseas. SAB bought a company in the United States called Sundoor, which it sold in 1987 to Procter & Gamble, one of the largest manufacturers of soap and household goods. In the mid-

---

[3]All company history based on the following sources: South African Breweries PLC; Hoover Online Company Profile (www.Hoovers.com/premium/profile); SAB's website (www.sab.com.za), including the archives footnoted previously; "SAB: Making Beer Making Friends," SAB brochure, 1999; and interview with Mike Simms, MD Europe, September 22, 2000.

[4]"SAB: Making Beer Making Friends."

exhibit 2   SAB's Involvement in Europe and Asia

Poland	With Euro Agro Centrum, SAB has control of two Polish breweries: one in Poznan (western Poland) and one in Silesia (southern Poland). Poland is one of SAB's fastest-growing markets in Europe. The brewery also distributes Beck's beer.
Romania	The company has a 93 percent interest in the Ursus brewing business, which has three breweries. Ursus has become the biggest brand in Romania, with a 16 percent market share.
Hungary	SAB acquired a 98.3 percent interest in Dreher, the owner and operator of two Hungarian breweries. Dreher has a well-positioned portfolio of beers, including Dreher, Arany Aszok, while Hofbrau and Tuborg are brewed under license.
Slovakia	In 1997, SAB acquired a 97.6 percent interest in an Eastern Slovakian brewery, Saris, the second-largest brewing company in the country.
Russia	In 1998, SAB acquired a brewery 180 kilometers southwest of Moscow. Sales commenced in May 1999.
Czech Republic	SAB acquired a 51 percent interest in a joint venture with Nomura in two breweries: Pilsner Urquell and Radegast. The deal enables SAB to increase its stake by 100 percent in the year 2001.
Canary Islands	SAB has a 51 percent stake in CCC, the sole established brewery in the Canary Islands. There are two modern, efficient breweries on the two major islands. The dominant local brands are Dorada and Tropical.
China	SAB owns 49 percent of CREB in China, with China Resources Enterprises Limited owning the remaining 51 percent. CREB has six breweries in China, in Shenyang, Dalian, Mianyang, Jilin, and Tianjin. China is the second-largest beer market in the world, and it is growing by 10 percent per annum.
India	In December of 1998, SAB entered into a joint venture to operate a brewery in India. This is presently under way.

Source: "SAB: Making Beer Making Friends," SAB brochure, 1999, pp. 50–56.

1980s, SAB acquired Rolling Rock[5], a small U.S. brewer, but was forced to sell it several years later, owing to anti-apartheid legislation and the accompanying negative sentiment toward South Africa. At the time, SAB realized it was limited to growing the domestic market, with anti-apartheid sanctions threatening any movement overseas.[6]

When sanctions were lifted in the early 1990s, SAB began to advance operations overseas once again—acquiring stakes in Hungary in 1993, China in 1994, and Poland and Romania in 1996. Graham Mackay became managing director in 1996, and CEO in 1999. During these years, the company refocused on core brewing activities. Non-core interests were sold, such as textiles, furniture, matches, and retail. In 1999, SAB gained control of the Czech brewers Radegast and Pilsner Urquell,[7] to become the

---

[5]Following SAB's disinvestments, Rolling Rock went on to become one of the most popular college beers in the United States.

[6]Based on interview with Mike Simms, MD Europe, September 22, 2000.

[7]A pils or pilsner is a pale lager beer that is highly hopped. It takes its name from the town of Pilsen, in the former Czechoslovakia, where the bottom fermentation process used to produce a pale beer was invented in 1842. Lager is often used as a synonym for pils. From www.beer.com. See "beer glossary."

exhibit 3   SAB Earnings and Volume Splits

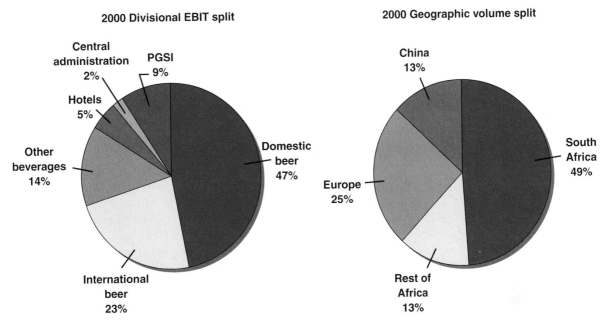

Source: Adapted from Deutsche Bank, "Emerging Markets Brewing," December 1999.

largest brewer in eastern Europe.[8] South African Breweries acquired a 97 percent share in a Slovakian beer company and purchased a brewery in Moscow. In Asia, SAB became active in China and India (see Exhibits 2 and 3).

The capstone of SAB's recent international movement occurred in March 1999, when SAB shifted its primary stockmarket listing to London to facilitate the raising of hard currency for acquisitions. The rationale for the listing included membership in the Financial Times Stock Exchange Index (FTSE 100), which would ensure an international rating, in turn enhancing global competitiveness in raising capital. Toward that end, SAB targeted South African, British, and U.S. investors.[9] In fact, several months after the listing, the investor base had altered significantly. Prior to the listing, 15 percent of SAB's investor base was international. Following the listing, the figure doubled to 30 percent.[10] Added benefits to the company that were associated with the London listing included access to equity and debt for growth and a rerating of its shares.

DOMESTIC CONTEXT: SOUTH AFRICA

Of every 50 beers that South Africans quaff, spill or slosh over steaks on the braai, 49 are brewed by SAB. Its brands . . . are tasty enough, but that does not explain the firm's

---

[8]Geographically, eastern Europe is presently comprised of the following countries: Poland, Lithuania, Latvia, Belarus, Czech Republic, Slovakia, Hungary, the former Yugoslavian countries, Albania, Bulgaria, Romania, Moldova, Russia, and Ukraine. In the geographic (as opposed to ideological) sense, western Europe is comprised of the central European countries, as well as Belgium, the Netherlands, Spain, Italy, Greece, France, and the United Kingdom.

[9]From internal document, SAB, 1999

[10]Ibid.

dominance. SAB's strength derives from its abnormal skill at coping with the demands of a highly abnormal market.[11]

The larger socioeconomic and legislative environment in South Africa greatly affected SAB's operations. Legislative changes introduced in the 1990s included competition and labor legislation, affirmative action, black economic empowerment, and liquor market reregulation, as well as granting licensing to a small number of shebeens (pubs in the informal sector). The ensuing reregulation of the liquor market could increase the number of legal liquor establishments, adding import to the informal sector. Such changes created an opportunity for innovation in sales and distribution practices in order for SAB to meet the "service requirements of a diverse customer base, while at the same time optimizing the cost-effectiveness of these services."[12]

In the late 1990s, per capita beer consumption in South Africa was in decline, and SAB was working hard to sustain revenue growth. The fall in consumption was attributed to a number of factors, including the sluggish South African economy, legalization of gambling and the establishment of casinos, the creation of a national lottery, a burgeoning cellular telephone market, and the impact of HIV-AIDS.

The company's vision was to be rated one of the top five brewing companies in the world, by any measure. SAB's mission was to be a world-class brewer and marketer of fine-quality beers, while behaving in a socially responsible and progressive manner. Indeed, SAB believed the company served the public interest in many ways. The company donated 1.75 percent of post-tax profits to corporate social investment programs. SAB also developed initiatives with communities, including the development of AIDS education programs in several townships and donating vehicles to the Alexandra Crime Prevention Unit. SAB also maintained that it served the public interest by providing service excellence, monitoring environmental impacts, and ensuring the health and safety of employees and the safety of company products.[13] The company aimed to build on the values it had developed over time (See Exhibit 4).

Increased Competition

South Africa's recent re-admission to the international community will result in increased globalization, necessitating an increased focus on, and benchmarking against, world class standards in order to ensure competitiveness.[14]

With the transition to a multiparty democracy, the globalization of South Africa's markets and its economic performance as a leader on the African continent, SAB observed that South Africa's emerging market economy would become an increasingly attractive destination for international brewers, particularly as the country's political and economic profile improved. SAB management had long argued that its 98 percent share of the South African beer market could be a temporary phenomenon. However, as *The Economist* noted: "Since the end of apartheid, foreign brewers have considered trying to break SAB's near monopoly, but decided that it would be too difficult. For one thing, its prices are off-puttingly low"[15] (see Exhibit 5). In addition, its distribution skills were regarded as second to none in South Africa.

---

[11]*The Economist,* August 12, 2000.

[12]SAB Three Year Business Plan, F97–F99.

[13]From SAB Corporate Citizenship Review 1999.

[14]SAB Three Year Business Plan, F97–F99.

[15]August 12, 2000.

exhibit 4   SAB's Company Values

VALUES	SAB and its employees share a commitment to and responsibility for:
	CUSTOMER SERVICE—Providing quality and value to satisfy the requirements of all our internal and external customers.
	PRODUCT QUALITY—Providing products of uncompromising quality to meet the needs of our customers and consumers.
	CONTINUOUS IMPROVEMENT—Being creative and innovative in all we do, to ensure continuous learning and improvement.
	RESPECT, DIGNITY AND EQUAL OPPORTUNITY—Treating each other with trust and respect, upholding human dignity and ensuring treatment and equal opportunity.
	PARTICIPATION AND EMPOWERMENT—Employee participation in problem-solving and decision-making processes through effective individual and team empowerment.
	WEALTH CREATION, REWARD AND RECOGNITION—Optimizing the creation of wealth to provide security, fair reward and recognition for the contributors of all our stakeholders.
	COMMUNICATION—Open, honest, respectful communication and freedom of expression.
	EMPLOYEE DEVELOPMENT—Creating the environment for all individuals and teams to develop to their potential for the benefit of themselves and the company.
	SAFE AND HEALTHY WORK ENVIRONMENT—Ensuring a safe and healthy work environment for all employees.
	COMMUNITY AND ENVIRONMENTAL COMMITMENT—Active involvement in the improvement of the environment and quality of life in the communities within which we operate.

Source: Adapted from "SAB: Making Beer, Making Friends," SAB brochure, 1999, p.4.

To lessen SAB's stranglehold on the market, new entrants would have to match SAB's prices, building large enough breweries and lean enough distribution channels to be a force. However, building growth in the market would be a long process and SAB could easily cut prices to defend market share. Nonetheless, access to South Africa's beer market could be achieved through alliances and joint ventures, as well as through direct imports. SAB's established brands could also face increasing competition from microbrewers and premium brands. In addition, wine and spirits could gain market share, particularly with less expensive brands, as could locally produced sorghum beer. SAB outlined the company's position: "Notwithstanding our marketing and sales and distribution responses to these challenges, our long term defense will be critically dependent on our ability to simultaneously improve our product quality, brand portfolio, service excellence and cost leadership."[16]

GLOBAL BREWING INDUSTRY

Beer is surprisingly local . . . The beer industry is a collection of tiny players.[17]

---

[16]SAB Three Year Business Plan, F97–F99.

[17]*The McKinsey Quarterly,* no. 1, 1999.

exhibit 5   Financial Highlights, South African Breweries, 1995–2000
(in millions of rand)

	95/96	96/97	97/98	98/99	99/00E
Cash Flow					
EBIT	3,511	3,742	3,929	4,012	4,177
Depreciation	1,086	1,169	1,379	1,439	1,700
Increase, decrease (−) in provisions	50	54	1	(322)	64
Operating cash flow	4,290	4,305	4,881	4,860	7,576
Interest paid (−) and received	(603)	(425)	(343)	(464)	(531)
Tax paid	(889)	(942)	(1,002)	(1,042)	(1,043)
Dividend paid	(29)	(263)	(375)	0	(272)
Capital expenditures	(1,956)	(1,824)	(2,562)	(3,451)	(2,936)
Net other investments	(245)	(625)	(1,614)	(1,309)	(927)
Other cash flow related items	(44)	(116)	(389)	1,184	(2,489)
Change in net debt (−) cash (+)	551	1,918	(1,380)	1,412	(621)
Balance sheet					
Net working capital	1,282	1,317	(229)	(3,154)	(1,591)
Net financial debt (−) cash (+)	(3,218)	(1,301)	(2,681)	(1,269)	(1,890)
Gross tangible fixed assets	12,876	14,676	16,486	18,358	22,221
Net tangible fixed assets	8,480	9,284	10,329	11,711	13,407
Goodwill	1,094	1,454	3,040	2,971	2,080
Other long term assets	227	401	413	2,025	0
Other long-term provisions	405	459	460	138	2,550
Other LT liabilities	0	0	0	0	0
Stated shareholder's equity	6,364	8,654	9,613	13,389	10,936
Minorities	2,510	3,010	2,159	1,001	1,641
Total net worth	8,874	11,664	11,772	14,390	12,577
Shareholder's equity after goodwill write-off	5,270	7,200	6,573	10,418	8,856

Source: Deutsche Bank, "Emerging Markets Brewing," 1999, p. 79; SAB annual reports, 1999, 2000.

By early 2000, the globalization trend had spread to most industries. Information technology was perhaps the most visible example. This trend was forecast to increase due to improved telecommunications, transport, and infrastructure.

When a few companies in a single industry succeeded in gaining world-class capability in one piece of the value chain, they left the others behind. These few superior companies gained advantages of scale through the declining costs of transactions, increased access to market, and deregulation. The value that was created by the few was so pronounced that the rest of the industry players reaggregated along the same model.[18] McKinsey claimed that this had already happened in the area of computers. For electric utilities and telecommunications, globalization had just begun. The big question facing international brewers was whether or not the beer industry would follow this trend.

---

[18]Ibid., p.4

exhibit 6   Ranking of Top 10 Global Brewers by 1999 Volume (million hl)

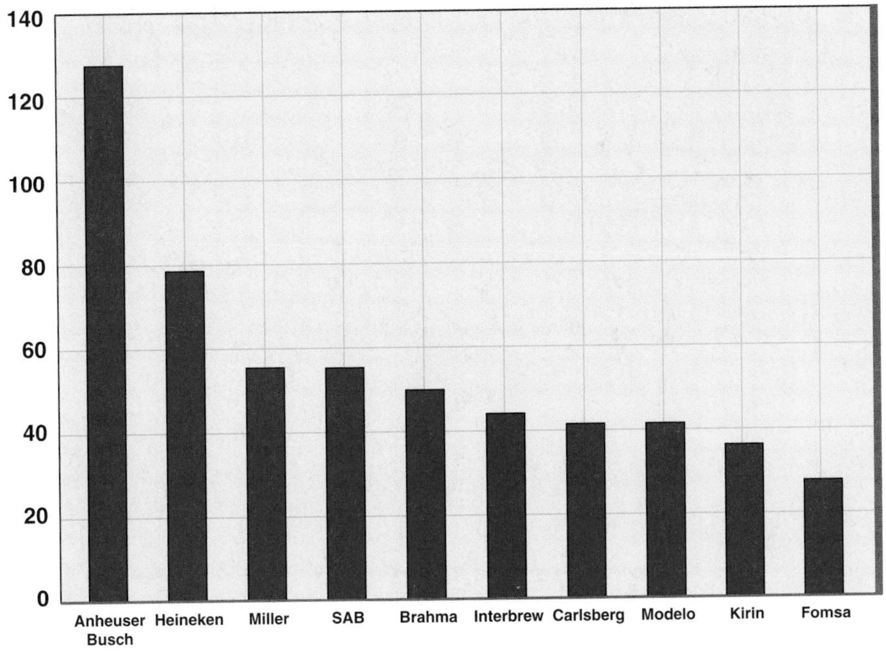

Source: Deutsche Bank Estimates.

By early 2000, there was no dominant player commanding the global beer market. Instead, there were a number of top brewers (see Exhibit 6), most of whom dominated their home country markets. For instance, the top two or three brewers in a country often held more than an 80 percent market share of the national market (see Exhibit 7).

Traditionally, the difficulty of storing and transporting beer resulted in most beer being bought, sold, and drunk locally. Local brands tended to be dominant, and most consumers across countries tended to prefer their local brands, perhaps due to their greater availability. National brewers traditionally dominated the wholesale distribution network, and new entrants to market had to obtain licenses from local authorities, which could be extremely bureaucratic and time consuming. In addition, the capital outlays and investment involved in setting up operations could be quite extensive, both for foreign investors and new local competitors. McKinsey analysts noted that "in South Africa, such major players as Heineken and Guinness have chosen to license their local production, distribution, and marketing to South African Breweries, the dominant local player, rather than try to do business on their own."[19]

In the late 1990s, Meyer Kahn, chairman of SAB, argued: "Because of the passion the mass beer drinker has for his brand, and the nationalism that goes with it, there will never be a world beer brand like Coca-Cola. What we have chosen to do is give each emerging market consumer their own local, emotional, passionate brand."[20] In keeping with the globalization of the industry, however, Graham Mackay called for a feasibility

---

[19]Ibid., p. 5.
[20]Meyer Kahn, group chairman of SAB, March 28, 1997. SAB documents, 1997.

exhibit 7 National Beer Markets, Percentage Share of Top Brewers, 1999

	Number of Brewers	Percentage Share
Argentina	1	76%
Australia	2	96
Brazil	2*	74
Chile	1	89
China	3	8
Czech Republic	2	60
Germany	3	23
Mexico	2	100
Namibia	1	90
New Zealand	1	55
Philippines	1	83
Poland	2	61
Russia	2	39
South Africa	1	98
Turkey	1	79
United States	2	77

*The two Brazilian brewers were merging.

Source: Adapted from Deutsche Bank, "Emerging Markets Brewing," December 1999.

study, "to see whether there was an international opportunity for the Castle brand."[21] It had already been acknowledged within SAB that investment in brand building was needed.

Industry analysts identified four indicators that marked the increasing pace of globalization:[22]

1. *Convergence in consumer choice.* Gradually, consumer preferences for beer around the world had begun to converge. By the 1990s consumer tastes were shifting from bottles to cans, and consumers were choosing lager instead of ale.[23] Taste, packaging, and delivery channels were all determinants in the overall "success package" of a beer, and these were beginning to standardize across national borders.

---

[21]Based on interview with Miles Saxby, head of exports, August 31, 2000. SAB's brand portfolio currently consists of 16 brands. The key brand is Castle Lager, which accounted for over 50 percent of the South African Beer Division's sales in recent years. Other major brands include Carling Black Label, Hansa Pilsener, and Lion Lager. Both Castle Lager and Lion Lager have been established brands in South Africa since the beginning of the 20th century. From www.sab.co.za; see "beer interests."

[22]*The McKinsey Quarterly,* no. 1, 1999, pp. 5–8.

[23]The two major categories of beer are ales and lagers, and the yeast used in fermentation determines the differences between the two. Ales are fermented at warm temperatures for short periods of time, typically a week. This yeast ferments in warmer temperatures to produce a fruity flavor that characterizes ale. Ales are aged, or conditioned, for one to three weeks. Ales should be served at room or cellar temperature— about 13° C (about 55° F.) Lagers are usually drier, crisper, and less fruity in taste than ales. Source: Encarta Encyclopedia (www.encarta.com).

exhibit 8   Country Groups, Growth Opportunities

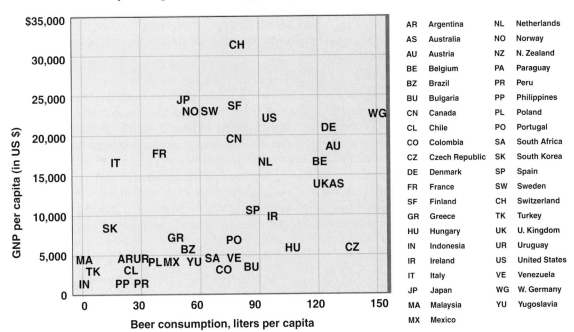

Note: Sample consists of 41 countries that consume 75 percent of the world's beer production.
Source: World Drink Trends 1991; Brewers' Society 1991; press releases; World Bank; ERC. In most cases, 1989 data are used.

2. *Easier access to consumers.* Lower tariffs and partnerships between local brewers and foreign brands allowed consumers and multinationals to access the same markets. Corona beer, for example, was available in 140 countries. Beer companies were able to raise the capital to fund their overseas expansion. VereinsBank in Germany, for example, established a mutual fund to support the growth of small companies in emerging markets, including many local brewers that had listed publicly. Additionally, a growing number of consumers in developing countries could now afford beer, as their incomes had risen. A 93 percent correlation was seen to exist between GDP growth per capita and beer consumption (see Exhibit 8). Brewers with plans for global expansion targeted new and growing consumer populations that exhibited similar patterns in terms of flavor, packaging, and preference for location of beverage consumption (in a pub, in a restaurant, or at home).

3. *Specialization in high-value areas of industries that were previously vertically integrated.* As global contenders acquired extensive knowledge and expertise of a single part of the business, they developed a specific advantage—in technology or process. Specialization allowed a company to gain a greater market share, and perhaps become the dominant player, nationally as well as overseas. One example of specialization was that of the Boston Beer Company in the United States. Boston Beer focused on developing recipes and marketing the Samuel Adams brand. The company outsourced the remainder of the value chain (brewing, packaging, and distribution) to a number of low-cost suppliers.

4. *Benefits of intangible scale.* In the past, local brewers sought dominance by attaining cost advantages through physical scale. However, physical scale alone was

no longer a recipe for competitive advantage. Relatively small brewers could achieve economies of scale by producing in excess of 500,000 hectoliters per year. As physical scale ceased to be a distinguishing feature, intangible assets became more important. These assets provided the ability to leverage brands, people, skills, and relationships.

ABN-AMRO analysts outlined five basic drivers of industry consolidation. The desire to achieve growth in sales was the most significant factor. As markets grew stagnant, brewers logically sought new markets and premium brands to catalyze growth. Second, the "U-curve theory" demonstrated that it was highly profitable to operate as a niche brewer or a major mainstream brewer, securing a dominant market share, but mainstream medium-sized brewers in fragmented markets often suffered from low profitability. Research indicated that consolidating a market could double profitability. Third, to a large degree, domestic consolidation had reached a holding pattern. This caused brewers to look overseas for opportunities to enhance margins. Fourth, adding premium brands to an existing portfolio significantly increased the margin over time. Lastly, international brewers found they could add value to the distribution strategies of local operations by introducing cost control and relationship marketing.[24]

Competitive Success

If the beer industry were to consolidate on a global scale, as it had on the national level, there could be a small number of global players dominating worldwide markets. Global economies of scale would then be the determining factor. Those brewers that eventually gained global dominance and captured the most profits would be on a par with companies such as Nike or Coca-Cola. If consolidation did not occur, due to forces of nationalism and localism, the determinants of success were much less clear.

Graham Mackay observed, "My own view is that the number of beer brands in the world will decline dramatically, [and] there will be a move towards premium branding throughout. But at the end of that, you will have several dozen well known brands, if not more." Deutsche Bank analysts agreed: "We do not envisage a Coca-Cola scenario, we expect a handful of global brewers and brands to continue to widen the gap between themselves and the rest of the pack."[25] The debate led to very different behaviors and strategic directions.

Several criteria could determine the success of a beer company on a global scale. Market capitalization was one indicator of a company's financial resources, which could fuel growth and expansion. In contrast, a lack of resources could indicate vulnerability to takeovers. Raising market capitalization required achieving economies of scale, with respect to marketing in particular. For instance, becoming a global brewer would require innovation, brand development (i.e., a brand that was globally recognizable), or a global presence (i.e., creating successful local brands on a global scale). Another key to success was finding ways to access new markets without putting up vast amounts of capital up front. This could involve strategic partnerships.

Deutsche Bank analysts identified a number of winning characteristics that a top global brewer would need to demonstrate:[26]

---

[24]ABN-AMRO, "Global Beer Industry Consolidation Takes Off," May 2000.
[25]Deutsche Bank, "Emerging Markets Brewing," December 1999.
[26]Ibid.

exhibit 9 SAB's Volume Sales, International and South Africa, 1994–99

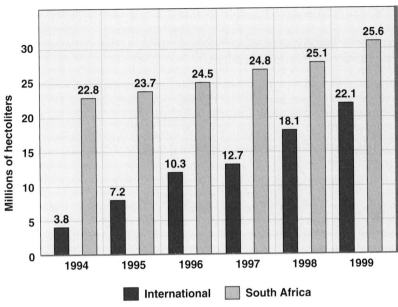

Source: Adapted from Deutsche Bank, "Emerging Markets Brewing," December 1999.

- A brand that could become a global mainstream brand, with a portfolio of strong local mainstream brands.
- Strong management, with a will to relocate to emerging markets, and significant emerging market exposure.
- Access to capital.
- Strong acquisition strategy driving global expansion.
- Strong local partners to facilitate transitions from national to global brands.

Developed versus Emerging Markets

> We believe that most of the excitement in future global beer volume growth will come from emerging markets. Per capita consumption is low in most emerging markets and is trending upwards.[27]

With demand for beer increasing in the developing countries, and best practices being adopted globally, the international profit pool[28] from beer was forecast to increase to an estimated $28 billion by 2010, from $18 billion in 1999. Future growth was expected to come primarily from Latin America, Asia, and eastern Europe—with western Europe also providing some opportunity. For SAB, international sales volume was rapidly catching up to domestic sales (see Exhibit 9). If China continued its current growth path of 10 percent per annum, the country would become the largest beer market in the world, by virtue of sheer size. There were two key assumptions made in the international profit pool forecast:

[27]Ibid.

[28]Measured by EBITDA, or earnings before interest, taxes, depreciation, and amortization. From *The McKinsey Quarterly,* no.1, 1999.

- Labor costs and margins in developing countries would improve. Brewing technology could be expensive, but developing economies generally had low labor costs.

- Beer prices would rise in the developing world; in the more mature developed markets, they would remain constant.

The major differentials between developed and emerging markets were price and volume. Volume growth was easier to achieve in emerging markets, but pricing power was low. As a result, emerging market strategies often balanced volume growth against price in order to ensure profitable growth in volume. In developed markets, flat or declining volume was counteracted by a product mix featuring more expensively priced premium brands.[29]

SAB INTERNATIONAL STRATEGIC OPTIONS

South African Breweries identified two core challenges for the company. The first was in continuing to make incremental operational improvements in the short term, while making the fundamental changes required of SAB, in order to be successful in the longer term. The second was in balancing the demand to become international, and the need to be perceived as a leader by South African society.

The company conducted a major strategic review in 1989–90. In 1990, the Berlin Wall was demolished. At the same time the world's gaze was fixed on South Africa, where Nelson Mandela was being released from his prison cell on Robben Island. Malcolm Wyman, group corporate finance and development director, stated:

> Things were changing, not only internationally but we could see the impact on SA . . . We decided two things: first of all we didn't think it was appropriate at that time for us to enter the first world market . . . the principle that we looked at was the fact that in the first world market there was little growth and a lot of competition from large well-established brewers. We had to start from scratch with a very low financial base and that meant we were limited as to what we could acquire. Secondly . . . we felt those skills we learnt in southern Africa would serve us best in emerging markets . . . Essentially Africa was something that we had experience of, but over many years our operations in some African countries had been nationalized. We could see the privatization coming in Africa, which would allow us to re-establish our presence. Our experience, particularly around southern Africa, meant that we were more familiar with these markets than our competitors, and our lines of communication were shorter and our ability to provide resources quicker.[30]

Wyman outlined SAB's thinking toward other emerging market regions:

> We believed that over time eastern Europe would become part of Europe as a whole. Whilst western European beer markets were mature and highly competitive, eastern European beer markets provided us with opportunities to buy positions, use our skills in production and sales and distribution, and to build a sensible operation in Europe over time. We saw China as another leg. The fourth emerging market was Latin America, which we decided against entering, as the opportunities there did not appear as attractive.[31]

---

[29]Deutsche Bank, "Emerging Markets Brewing."

[30]Events outlined and subsequent quotations based on interview, September 19, 2000.

[31]Based on interview with Malcolm Wyman, September 19, 2000.

exhibit 10 SAB Executive Directors—Strategic Management Team

Ernest Arthur Graham Mackay (50)	Norman Joseph Adami (45)
BSc (Eng) Bcom	BbusSc MBA
Chief Executive	Managing Director, Beer South Africa
Mr. Mackay joined SAB in 1978.	Mr. Adami Joined SAB Limited in 1979.
Nigel Geoffrey Cox (52)	Richard Llewellyn Lloyd (56)
CA (SA) CA	MA (Cantab) MBA
Financial Director	Director
Mr. Cox joined the group in 1973.	Mr. Lloyd joined SAB in 1971.
Michael Hugh Simms (51)	Malcolm Ian Wyman (53)
BSc MBA	CA (SA) CA
Managing Director, Europe	Corporate Finance and Development Director
Mr. Simms joined SAB in 1978.	Mr. Wyman joined SAB in 1986.

Source: Adapted from www.SAB.co.za.

SAB's Resource Strengths

SAB identified its competitive advantage in the company's ability to sustain and improve in two areas: value-adding capability and cost leadership. In accordance with this aim, the group targeted specific areas on which to focus:

- Maintain and enhance product quality and brand equity.
- Strengthen new product development capabilities.
- Pursue differentiated customer service and trade marketing.

SAB's core competencies were geared toward emerging market economies: understanding developing world conditions, understanding how to utilize assets, cost management, and the delivery of a product that was both high quality and low cost. Norman Adami, managing director of Beer South Africa, emphasized that in terms of competencies such as brand building, low-cost operations, people management and development, and managing reputation, "SAB is as strong in these areas as first world competitors."[32] Some consultants noted that SAB remained "close to customers and its own performance." The company was in tune with the South African environment, and was responsive to local issues. SAB's depth of experience also provided the company with an excellent base on which to draw (see Exhibit 10).[33]

Mike Simms observed: "That ability to actually improve the quality and drinkability of the beer is something that we have evolved and believe in very deeply. We have done that everywhere . . . in China, in Africa . . . even in the Czech Republic." Simms continued: "We don't realize that our technical abilities are extraordinary by any standards in the world." Simms highlighted the company's unique capability: "One strength has certainly been the ability to make things work. You know the Afrikaans expression ' 'n boer maak 'n plan'—[literally] 'a farmer makes a plan.' Whether he is using chewing gum or string, it's the 'can do' attitude. I think of some of the guys that went out, literally armed with a pair of pliers and a hammer, and they got breweries running that hadn't worked for four or five years."[34]

---

[32]Based on interview, June 27, 2000.

[33]Analyst reports and presentations, PricewaterhouseCoopers and *McKinsey & Company,* 1998-1999.

[34]Based on interview with Mike Simms, September 22, 2000.

SAB's Resource Weaknesses/Threats

Critics noted that despite SAB's success in emerging markets, it had yet to establish itself in developed countries or to create international brands. The firm remained vulnerable to takeovers and other market forces, earning the lion's share of its profits in soft currencies. There was the ever-present challenge to raise sufficient capital. A further loss of confidence in emerging markets could quickly affect the company, and spontaneously lead to another dip in the share price. *Business Day* highlighted the challenge for South African (SA) companies "to distance themselves from their SA roots by diversifying geographically their earnings streams as quickly as possible. But to varying degrees, they still rely on Africa for their bread and butter . . . [A]ny SA company wishing to make it in the big wide world has to move quite quickly to internationalize its earnings. In some cases, this requires the assumption of a fair amount of risk."[35] It was also noted by consultants that SAB was slow to transfer best practices, and slow to master global business issues, while the company had exhibited an inconsistent approach to performance improvement.[36]

SAB acknowledged that it could not replicate the success factors underlying its achievements in Africa in other markets, particularly in Europe. In Africa, SAB was associated with an African heritage (while European beers were generally even older), and in Europe, SAB could not replicate the association with quality, as items coming from Africa were generally not recognized as being of high quality. SAB sought to expand its position in other countries, while pursuing growth at home and identifying the synergies with others that would, ideally, add value. SAB needed to maintain its rating, growth, and the accompanying growth proposition. Mackay noted: "[T]here are a number of . . . developments that put things into sharper focus. One of those is clearly the rand's ongoing . . . seemingly never ending decline . . . It has a huge bearing because it sources our cash, shaping both current results, but also perceptions for future growth."[37]

In early 2000 the southern African region was beset with political instability in Zimbabwe. The South African rand and other regional currencies plunged against the dollar. High political risk and volatility were attached to these emerging market economies, and SAB's ratings on the international financial markets were inevitably affected. SAB's share price was trading at what Mackay believed to be a significant discount below its true value, and raising capital was therefore an expensive proposition. Malcolm Wyman stated: "We see ourselves as having positioned ourselves fairly well. We do have a depressed share price right at the moment, but we also feel that some of the other first world brewers also have depressed prices."[38] Norman Adami observed that the political risk attached to emerging market economies in turn attached risk to SAB's profile, essentially making SAB "a victim of its own success."[39]

Strategic Positions among Brewers

Determining the future of the brewing industry was a guessing game, as the pace of consolidation fluctuated. Among the events in 1999 alone, Scottish & Newcastle, in moves which illustrated the company's evolution from a parochial UK brewer to an in-

---

[35]August 14, 2000.

[36]McKinsey analyst report, 1999.

[37]Based on interview with Graham Mackay, September 20, 2000.

[38]Based on interview with Malcolm Wyman, September 19, 2000.

[39] Based on interview with Graham Mackay, September 20, 2000.

exhibit 11   Rand, Effective Exchange Rates, 1995-2000

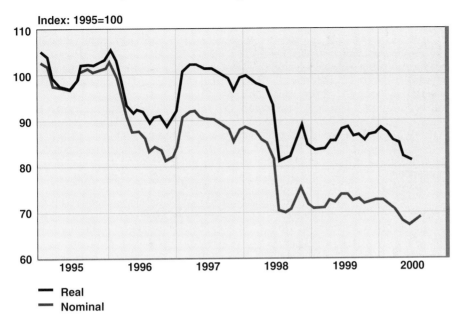

Index: 1995=100

■ **Real**
■ **Nominal**

Source: South African Reserve Bank quarterly bulletin, September 2000.

ternational brewer, acquired Danone's beer businesses in France and Kronenbourg in the United Kingdom, while declaring its intent to purchase Centralcer, a large brewer in Portugal. Interbrew acquired Whitbread, while Carlsberg was negotiating a deal with Albani Brewery, a domestic competitor. Woverhampton & Dudley, a British regional brewer, considered a takeover offer from Botts, a London-based equity firm.[40]

South African Breweries acquired Pilsner-Urquell, a premium brand in the Czech Republic, indicating that SAB might seek to exploit selected brands on a global basis. Graham Mackay pointed to a lack of immediate activity most recently. Mackay suggested: "I think there is a hiatus at the moment . . . because possible sellers have one or two expectations, either of being consolidators . . . or selling at an unrealistically high price." He continued: The "flurry of activity that happened in Europe early this year . . . dispelled a general impression of a horizon containing many many possibilities," also highlighting the problem of the high selling prices that brewers were demanding (see Exhibit 12).

Deutsche Bank analysts observed: "We believe that the future winners will need strong brands, sound management and significant emerging market exposure. Our estimate of the ranking of the winning brewers in ten years' time is Anheuser Busch, Heineken and SAB."[41] McKinsey analysts made their selection: "Heineken now has the single best prospect of ranking among the global giants of the future. It has a global brand; a widespread presence, both in its own right and through alliances; and strong skills in such areas as marketing and production. As the company expands, these skills will help it create value . . . by improving the operations it acquires."

---

[40]*The Economist,* August 26, 2000.

[41]ABN-AMRO, Deutsche Bank, "Emerging Markets Brewing."

exhibit 12   Profiles of SAB Major Competitors/Potential Partners

Anheuser-Busch

Anheuser-Busch (A-B) was the largest brewer in the world. It controlled 46% of the U.S. beer industry compared with less than 20% for Miller and about 10% for Coors. Economies of scale included advertising; A-B could spend more but pay less than its competitors on a per hectoliter basis. Thus, A-B had some of the best beer advertising campaigns in the United States, which it had been able to use prominently. This, combined with savvy pricing, efficient production, and excellent distribution, drove A-B's market share gains and volume growth. Although the U.S. beer market was growing only 2% annually, A-B expected to gain market share and grow at a 3% or faster pace.

A-B traded at premium multiples because of its dominant position in the huge U.S. beer industry and growing presence throughout the world. It dwarfed its competitors, and this created economies of scale advantages in production, administration, and marketing. These advantages contributed to its growth worldwide.

A-B was building Budweiser into a global brand. A-B's objectives were to participate in rapidly growing markets worldwide in conjunction with leading brewers. Outside of the U.S., Canada (in association with Labatt Brewing Co.) was the largest market for A-B in terms of volume. The UK and Ireland (in association with Guinness Ireland) were generating strong results. Budweiser had been growing in Italy, Spain, France, and Greece through partnerships with local brewers. In Latin America, A-B owned 50% of Modelo, Mexico's leading brewer, and 10.7% of CCU Argentina. In Brazil, A-B recently ended its joint venture with Antarctica. In Asia, Budweiser was gaining share and establishing a strong position. Budweiser was the leading premium foreign brand in both China and the Philippines. A-B's increasing presence around the world positioned it for growth over the medium to long term.

AmBev/Brahma

Brahma was the largest brewer in Brazil with approximately a 50% market share. Antarctica had a 22% market share. Competition, however, remained intense because of the soft drink business, which was integrally linked to the beer industry in Brazil due to shared distribution. Small local soft drink competitors were aggressive, often taking advantage of their skill in evading taxes. Coca-Cola was also a major player in Brazil's soft drink market, and the Coke bottlers, in conjunction with Heineken and the Coca-Cola Company, owned Kaiser, now Brazil's second-largest brewer with a 17% market share.

In March, Brahma received regulatory approval to merge with its primary beer competitor, Antarctica. The new enterprise, the American Beverage Company (AmBev) was expected to dominate the Brazilian beer industry with over 70% market share, and become the third-largest brewer in the world. The company estimated efficiencies from the merger to be at least $200 million.

Brahma's current owners acquired the company in 1988. At that time, Brahma was losing market share, operating inefficiently, and generating minimal profit, similar to Antarctica's performance prior to the merger agreement. The new management was aggressive, market-driven, and cost conscious and turned Brahma into a market leader with rising sales and profits. The strength of management was demonstrated following the devaluation of Brazil's currency in early 1999, when Brahma turned in surprisingly strong results that could be attributed only to management strength and cost control. Management was focusing on consolidation of the two brewers and reducing its excess production capacity.

Carlsberg

Carlsberg's main activity was the production and distribution of beer. More than 88% of beer sales were generated outside Denmark. Production took place in fully owned facilities, associated companies, or through license agreements. Carlsberg's beer sales in Denmark were 4 million hectoliters and outside Denmark amounted to 33 million hectoliters in 1998–99. Sales of soft drinks were managed through a Coca-Cola joint venture in Scandinavia. Sales of soft drinks in Denmark were 3.2 million hectoliters and outside Denmark sales amounted to 10.6 million hectoliters in 1998–99.

(continued)

exhibit 12   Profiles of SAB Major Competitors/Potential Partners *(cont.)*

Focus and expansion mainly drove Carlsberg's strategy plan. Its future focus was expected to be on beer and soft drinks. Carlsberg was number seven in the world in terms of beer sales and its objective was to become one of the top five. Acquisitions were at the top of its agenda. In April 2000, the principal shareholder of Carlsberg—the Carlsberg Foundation—adjusted its status so that it no longer needed to hold 51% of Carlsberg's shares. This meant Carlsberg would be able to issue new shares to fund major acquisitions. It also meant that Carlsberg could participate in an agreed merger to expand in the soft drink area with Coca-Cola. So far, Carlsberg had been limited to the Scandinavian region, but an expansion into the Baltic countries was likely. Carlsberg was also working on selling its majority holding in Royal Scandinavia and its minority in Tivoli.

Adolph Coors Co.

Coors's management was aggressive and performance-oriented, leading the company in an impressive turnaround. Coors was gaining market share and increasing profitability. During this process, management improved expense discipline, capital planning, and cash management, enabling the company to use the increasing cash flow to repay debt and buy back stock. Coors's balance sheet could now support additional expansion. In 1992, Pete Coors took control of the family business and began a major restructuring. He split off Coors's nonbeer businesses, installed professional, marketing-oriented management, and cut administration. Coors had two important strengths on which to build: a quality product and strong brand equity. A new selling team was built and, since 1996, advertising, promotions, packaging improvements, and innovations became additional strengths on which Coors could compete. The sales team began to work closely with Coors's 600 distributors, an area of past weakness. Management then shifted its focus to growing volume, increasing product quality, and further raising operational efficiency.

Improving profitability was key to Coors's ability to compete. Headcount was cut from nearly 7,000 to 5,800, but productivity was still below that at Miller and Anheuser-Busch. To cut distribution expenses, Coors increased shipments of beer directly to distributors, reducing handling time and inventories while increasing working capital and improving product freshness. Coors's products still traveled more than 1,000 miles, compared with 150 miles for Miller or Anheuser-Busch, a distance Coors planned to reduce to 500–600 miles in the next few years. Labor, productivity, and transportation were three areas that Coors had targeted for continued improvement.

Femsa

Femsa was an integrated beverage company with operations in beer, soft drinks, packaging, and retail convenience stores. Labatt of Canada (majority owned by Interbrew) owned 30% of the beer subsidiary. Femsa was the second player in Mexico's beer duopoly with a 45% market share (Modelo had 55%). After having lost market share consistently following a difficult merger in the late 1980s, Femsa's position had stabilized in the last four years. The Mexican beer industry was highly competitive in terms of marketing and purchase of exclusive contracts, but had not involved aggressive price discounting. Femsa was strongest in northern Mexico, the more industrial part of the country closest to the United States.

Foster's Brewing Group

Foster's was surprisingly large on the international beer stage. From a base of market leadership in Australia (55.9% market share), Foster's continued its expansion on the world stage via its flagship Foster's brand, now available in more than 140 countries worldwide. Foster's was the eighth-most-consumed beer in Europe, primarily on its number one ranking in London and number two in the United Kingdom. Foster's exited the Molson joint venture in 1998 to concentrate on Asia. This included the sale of two Chinese breweries and acquiring breweries in India and Vietnam.

In the last three years Foster's had transformed itself from a beer company into a total provider of alcoholic beverages. While beer sales still accounted for some 56% of revenue (down from 76% in 1997), the strong growth opportunities were in nonbeer areas: pubs and hospitality (including local gaming) and wine. Foster's was one of the few

(continued)

exhibit 12   Profiles of SAB Major Competitors/Potential Partners *(cont.)*

beer companies with the potential to compete on the world stage and was well positioned to benefit from expected Asian consumption growth (both beer and wine). Considered a "safe haven" growth company, Foster's had underperformed the Australian market over the past year.

Foster's had successfully grown the flagship brand at greater than 10% annually by promoting its "Australianness." With the Australian beer market static in terms of volume, Foster's strategy was to expand across Asia by buying ownership interests in local breweries. Internationally, expansion was primarily through licensing agreements, such as that with Molson in North America and Scottish & Newcastle in UK/Europe.

Grupo Modelo

Modelo was the leader in the Mexican beer market with a 55% share. Modelo exported beer worldwide to more than 140 countries. Corona, Modelo's flagship brand, was recognized as a global brand and the leader in the U.S. imported beer sector. Modelo's other brands were also growing rapidly in the U.S. market.

Modelo stock traded at valuation multiples in line with global brewers, yet its base market (Mexico) was growing more rapidly, and it was expanding sales in the United States faster than any major importer. Modelo had no debt and was 50% owned by Anheuser-Busch (Anheuser-Busch did not have operating control).

Modelo invested heavily in markets to build equity of its premium-priced brands and then penetrated the market through distribution. Production was efficient because of large-scale, modern plants which it operated at high utilization levels. Low labor costs in Mexico further reduced its low cost levels. Operating margins were in the mid-20s and generally rose 60–80 basis points per year. Modelo intended to be one of the top five brewers in the world (it was number eight currently). Modelo was expanding capacity to achieve its growth objectives.

Guinness Anchor

Guinness Anchor was the dominant stout producer, controlling over 90% of the Malaysian stout market. Its arsenal included three key blonde beers—Anchor, Heineken, and Tiger. Tiger was one of the fastest-growing beers in the country, with growth averaging 22.5% over the last three years.

GAB had been reborn, with "economic profit," "portfolio management," and "channeling" the new mantras for the company. Instead of distributors being brand-specific, they managed GAB's entire portfolio of brands, with dedicated teams to deal with the categories such as "Hypermarkets" and "Sundry Shops." Direct draught sales increased to 70% of total sales to ensure product "freshness" and better stock/credit controls. GAB had been investing heavily in its brands, most notably Tiger Beer. Tiger was the fastest-growing beer in Malaysia and, according to management, grew by 17% year on year. The company was also investing in new efficient equipment. With new production lines coming on stream, the company provided RM16 million in the year to June 2000 for retrenchment and asset write-offs.

Heineken

Heineken was the world's second-largest brewing group and the largest outside of the United States. Total volume was 68 million hectoliters in 1999. Its most important countries were the United States (number two import brand), the Netherlands (54% market share), France (33% share), Italy (36% share), and Greece (76% share). Beer sales in these countries made up almost 70% of profits. Following recent acquisitions, Poland and Spain were expected to increase in prominence. Outside the Netherlands and the United Kingdom, the Heineken brand carried a strong premium image. Heineken sold 20 million hectoliters under the Heineken brand and 8 million under the Amstel label. Significant ownerships included 50% in Asia Pacific Breweries, 15% in Quilmes, and 15% in Kaiser. A quarter of the company was in the founding family's hands, which had effective control of the company.

Heineken was the world's largest measured by nondomestic shipments, and it was the premier beer industry consolidator. It had been at the vanguard of consolidating local

(continued)

exhibit 12   Profiles of SAB Major Competitors/Potential Partners *(cont.)*

beer markets to improve their profitability, and its major market shares had also enabled the highly profitable Heineken brand to grow into the world's most international beer brand.

Heineken's strategy was twofold. In the mass market, it actively participated in consolidation. Heineken had shown that if the top two players in a market had more than 65% and it was one of them, profits could be dramatically increased through cost reductions, price stabilization, and improving the mix toward premium brands such as Heineken. This strategy was successfully executed in France and Italy (acquisitions in 1995 and 1996) and was being deployed in Poland (acquisitions 1998) and Spain (Cruzcampo acquired in 2000). The company was actively pursuing acquisition opportunities, providing shareholder value could be created. Otherwise, the company focused on the Heineken premium brand in the United States (Heineken had 20% of the import market) and China.

Interbrew

Thirty acquisitions in the 1990s had propelled Interbrew from a parochial European brewer to sixth place worldwide and second place in terms of international volumes. Volumes had grown almost fourfold since the Labatt acquisition in 1995, and Interbrew's 45 breweries had a consolidated volume of 49 million hectoliters in 1999, selling 120 brands in over 80 countries. The Belgium-domiciled multinational brewer was currently a private company but recently had announced its intention to seek a stock market listing in 2000. Currently the world's sixth-largest brewer, it was second-largest in terms of nondomestic shipments, and offered a combination of strong market shares in developed, hard currency markets (Belgium, Canada, the Netherlands, France), with exposure to growth markets (Mexico, South Korea, Russia, Ukraine, Bosnia, China, and U.S. imports).

Interbrew had a 56% market share in Belgium (Stella Artois, Jupiter, Leffe) and a 45% share in Canada (Labatt). Other developed-country market positions included the Netherlands (16% share, Dommelsch, Hertog Jan, Hoegaarden, Oranjeboom); France (8% share); and the United Kingdom, where Stella Artois, brewed by Whitbread under license, was the best-selling premium beer (5% market share). Interbrew had made significant acquisitions in growth markets. It had a 49% market share in Korea (Cass, OB Lager), and in eastern Europe it was the market leader in Bulgaria (42% share, Pleven). It had a 26% market share in Hungary and a 9% share in Romania. The SUN Interbrew joint venture (50% controlled by Interbrew) had the second-largest market share in Russia (17%, Klinskoe), and third-largest in Ukraine (23%). Interbrew owned 80% of two breweries in Nanjing, China.

Interbrew saw itself as the "World's Local Brewer," which meant a focus on local brands and a partnership approach to expansion. The premium brand of worldwide expansion was clearly Stella Artois, which had recently been pushed into the U.S. market (riding the wave for Belgian cuisine). The company was actively seeking synergies in the form of global purchasing and the exchange of best practices between its many operations.

Scottish & Newcastle

Scottish Courage, S&N's UK brewing subsidiary, was the UK's largest brewer with a 29% market share. Its major brands were Foster's, Kronenbourg, Miller, Beck's, and John Smith's, all of which, with the exception of John Smith's, were brewed under license. S&N's acquisition of Kronenbourg from Danone was expected to close in June 2000 and would take S&N into France (with a 44% market share), Belgium (16% share), and Italy (a 24% stake in Peroni which had a 29% share of the market).

S&N had been slow to address its strategic weakness. Because of government regulations, S&N was unable to acquire more UK beer market share. It had operated under these constraints since 1998. The acquisition of Kronenbourg demonstrated the company's intention to expand its brewing interests rather than to find another leg to its business. Because of the constraints on acquisitions in UK brewing, S&N's growth was reliant on exploiting those areas of the UK beer market that were growing in a market which was in overall volume decline. This meant lager, which was growing at the expense of ale, and premium brands in both ale and lager (although S&N has little interest in ale).

(continued)

exhibit 12   Profiles of SAB Major Competitors/Potential Partners *(concl.)*

It owned the UK and continental European rights to the Foster's brand in perpetuity, and paid a royalty to the Australian brewer that owned the brand. It also licensed Kronenbourg in the UK and had invested heavily in marketing the brand in competition with the category leader, Stella Artois.

Whitbread

Whitbread was the third-largest UK brewer with a 15% market share. Its major brands were Stella Artois and Heineken (which it brewed under license from Interbrew and Heineken, respectively) and Boddington's ale. It was the most diversified of the major UK brewers.

As with Bass, Whitbread was likely to dispose of its brewing division in the near future. In 1999, Whitbread tried to buy Allied Domecqu's UK retail business and said it would dispose of its brewing division in order to avoid contravening UK brewing regulations. That acquisition failed when it was referred to the Competition Commission. The episode highlighted how Whitbread's growth in leisure was constrained by its ownership of a brewing business that contributed only 10% of profits. Whitbread had been very successful over the last five years in growing Stella Artois into a highly profitable premium-quality brand. By contrast, it had allowed Heineken, which was positioned as a standard brand in the United Kingdom, to decline.

Source: Adapted in part from ABN-AMRO, "Global Beer Industry Consolidation Takes Off," May 2000.

From ABN-AMRO analysis: "We believe that the 1999 acquisition of Pilsner Urquell was the first of many large deals involving SAB. The company lacks exposure to stable currency cash flows, and partnership with a more balanced developed/emerging player would make sense."[42] Anheuser-Busch appeared bent on globalizing the Budweiser brand, but the company could also change tactics and launch a bid for local brewers, perhaps those with whom the company had an existing relationship. Some analysts noted that Anheuser-Busch had an enormous amount of untapped brand equity.[43] Its associate company, Modelo, declared its intent to become a global brewer ranking in the top five.

It was likely that AmBev could launch some international movement. Foster's had changed its focus, becoming a provider of a "full portfolio of alcoholic drinks"; the brewer's interests in Canada ended, but acquisitions were made in Asia. Kirin began its international acquisitions with Lion Nathan (of New Zealand) and developed a partnership with Anheuser-Busch. Heineken, the most international of brewers, sold its beer in over 170 countries. The company had some emerging market exposure.

LOOKING AHEAD

By early 2000 SAB was under pressure to move into developed-country markets. This push had increased following SAB's move to London. Financial analysts observed the realities of an emerging-market company plagued by a devaluing rand and associated risk, and a more diverse and demanding shareholder base.

Responding to the pressure to enter developed markets, Wyman noted: "We have a very solid emerging market business . . . We proved that we can extract growth in

---

[42]ABN-AMRO, "Global Beer Industry Consolidation Takes Off."

[43]Deutsche Bank, "Emerging Markets Brewing."

many areas, e.g., China. However, we believe that, in addition to the emerging market business, which we will continue to build, we may acquire a first world position where such investments will be synergistic with our existing international operations, whether geographically, in production or sales and distribution, or through enhancement of our brand portfolio." Graham Mackay seconded this notion: "SAB is seeking expansion into first world markets . . . Our long-term strategy is basically to participate in consolidation and growth opportunities . . . in the first world, as well as in emerging markets."[44]

Mackay considered several options for SAB's international growth strategy. The first option was that SAB would merge with a major developed-country brewer as a means for ensuring global success. In short, the merger option. The chief challenge would be finding a partner that would supplement SAB's existing competencies and strengths. A second option was one of acquisitions in emerging markets. Third, SAB could continue to focus on organic growth in emerging markets, growing a presence and rounding out its portfolio. SAB would then focus on improving organizational effectiveness, rendering operations even more cost-effective, to increase both efficiency and profits. SAB could wait for the cycle of poor political risk to shift, and for emerging markets to return to favor, revisiting the growth options at a later date.

---

[44]March 29, 2000.

case 22 Unilever's Acquisitions of SlimFast, Ben & Jerry's, and Bestfoods

Arthur A. Thompson
The University of Alabama

Following several years of sluggish performance, Unilever's top management announced a new five-year Path to Growth strategy in February 2000 to rejuvenate the company and restructure its wide-ranging portfolio of food, home, and personal care businesses. The new strategy initiative fashioned by Unilever co-chairmen Niall FitzGerald and Antony Burgmans came on the heels of a decline in Unilever PLC's stock price from a peak of 690 pence in June 1998 to 341 pence just prior to the announcement.

Unilever's Path to Growth initiative involved greatly reducing the size of the company's brand portfolio, concentrating R&D and advertising on the company's leading brands, divesting a number of underperforming brands and businesses, boosting product innovation, making new acquisitions, and achieving faster growth in sales and earnings. Focusing on key brands was expected to allow Unilever to concentrate its advertising and marketing efforts on higher-margin businesses and build brand value, thus gaining increased pricing power with supermarket retailers. The five-year initiative was expected to cost a total some 5 billion euros (€); entail closing or selling 100 factories and laying off some 25,000 employees (10 percent of Unilever's workforce) so as to consolidate production at fewer plants; and ultimately produce annual savings of €1.5 billion through better strategic fits, a streamlined supply chain, and greater operating efficiencies. By 2004, Unilever management predicted, the company would be expanding its sales 5 to 6 percent annually and have boosted its operating profit margins from 11 to over 16 percent, sufficient to produce double-digit growth in earnings per share.

Following the announcement of its Path to Growth strategy, which was met with considerable skepticism on the part of industry analysts, Unilever management undertook a series of actions over the next 12 months to deliver on its commitments to boost the company's sales and profits. By March 2001, the company had

- Made 20 new acquisitions worldwide, including SlimFast diet foods; Ben & Jerry's ice cream; Bestfoods (whose 1999 sales totaled $8.6 billion across 110 countries and whose major brands included Hellmann's mayonnaise, Skippy peanut butter, Mazola corn oil and margarines, and Knorr packaged soup mixes); Corporacion Jaboneria Nacional (an Ecuadorian company, with sales of approximately €114 million, that had strong market positions in detergents, toilet soaps, skin creams, dental care, margarine and edible oils); Grupo Cressida (a leading consumer products company in Central America); and Amora-Maille (a French maker of mustards, mayonnaises, ketchups, pickles, vinegars, spices, and cooking sauces with 1999 sales of about $365 million).

- Cut the company's brand portfolio from 1,600 brands to 970. (To reach the 2004 corporate goal of focusing on about 400 core brands, Unilever's brand reduction strategy called for letting certain brands wither and decline without active promotion and support, selling those brands that no longer fit in with Unilever's future strategy, and discontinuing the rest.)

- Launched 20 internal initiatives to deliver additional sales of €1.5 billion on an annualized basis.

- Divested 27 businesses, including the company's Elizabeth Arden cosmetics business, the Elizabeth Taylor and White Shoulders fragrances, the company's European bakery business, the Bestfoods Baking Company (a U.S. bakery business inherited from the acquisition of Bestfoods), most of its European dry soups and sauces businesses, and an assortment of small businesses that produced and marketed lesser-known European grocery brands.

- Reorganized the company into two roughly equal-sized global divisions, one including all of the company's food products and the other including all of its household and personal care products.

- Started two new businesses—Cha, a chain of tea houses, and Myhome, a laundry and home cleaning service test-marketed in Britain in 2000 and being tested in the United States and India in 2001.

Unilever's operating results after the first year of the Path to Growth initiative were somewhat encouraging. In February 2001, the company announced that sales growth in the company's major brands had accelerated to 4.9 percent in the fourth quarter of 2000. Revenues in 2000, including acquisitions, were up 16 percent, to €47.6 billion. Net profits, however, were down from €2.97 billion in 1999 to €1.1 billion in 2000, largely due to €1.3 billion in restructuring charges associated with the Path to Growth initiative. Management said it was ahead of schedule in its restructuring efforts.

COMPANY BACKGROUND

Unilever was created in 1930 through the merger of Margarine Unie, a Dutch margarine company, and British-based Lever Brothers, a soap and detergent company. Margarine Unie had grown through mergers with other margarine companies in the 1920s. Lever Brothers was founded in 1885 by William Hesketh Lever, who originally built the business by establishing soap factories around the world. In 1917, Lever Brothers began to diversify into foods, acquiring fish, ice cream, and canned foods businesses. At the time of their merger, the two companies were purchasing raw materials from many of the same suppliers, both were involved in large-scale marketing of household products, and both used similar distribution channels. Between them, they had operations in over 40 countries.

Searching for Focus and Identity

Over the next decades, Unilever continued acquiring companies and brands, gradually moving into more food and household products categories in more and more countries. Still, as late as the mid-1970s, more than half of Unilever's profits came from its West African plantations that produced bulk vegetable oils for margarine and washing powders. In the 1970s and early 1980s, Unilever diversified beyond food and household products into specialty chemicals, advertising, packaging, market research, and a U.K.-based franchise for Caterpillar heavy equipment. The specialty chemicals business transformed products from some of the company's plantations into ingredients for food and household products; Unilever also had shipping lines that transported Unilever products. However, during the late 1980s and 1990s, the specialty chemicals, advertising, packaging, shipping, and market research businesses were divested in an attempt to shed the company's image as a conglomerate and focus resources on the company's core businesses.

Unilever's broad-based product and geographic diversification in foods, personal care products, and household products spawned a complex management structure that gave considerable decision-making power to country managers to set their own priorities and to tailor products to local tastes. From time to time, Unilever's top executives had launched new initiatives and reorganization plans aimed at giving the company more focus as a multinational marketer of food, personal care, and household products. Still, in 2000, the company had 1,600 brands of food, personal care, and household products, with sales exceeding $43 billion and operations in 88 countries. Unilever was one of the world's 5 largest food and household products companies and had been ranked among the top 60 of *Fortune*'s Global 500 largest corporations since 1995. According to Irish co-chairman Niall FitzGerald, "We're not a manufacturing company any more. We're a brand marketing group that happens to make some of its products."[1]

In early 2000, at the time the Path to Growth initiative was announced, the top 400 of Unilever's 1,600 brands—some global brands like Lipton's and Dove and some local jewels like Persil (the leading brand of detergent in Great Britain)—accounted for over 85 percent of the company's annual revenues. A number of Unilever brands had either the highest or second highest share in their respective markets. Exhibit 1 shows Unilever's product and brand portfolio in February 2000.

Organization and Management

To preserve the company's Dutch and British heritage, Unilever maintained two headquarters—one in Rotterdam and one in London—and operated under two co-chairmen. The company's headquarters group in Rotterdam, headed by Antony Burgmans, was in charge of food products, while the London headquarters group, under Niall FitzGerald, was in charge of personal care and household products. FitzGerald had been chairman of the London-based portion of Unilever since 1996 and was said to have been instrumental in reorganizing Unilever's 1,600-brand portfolio around 14 groups as opposed to the former 57 groups. Company observers regarded FitzGerald as one of the most able and innovative Unilever chairmen in decades. Officially, the two co-chairmen had equal status and responsibilities. Each had offices in both Rotterdam and London, shuttling between the two headquarters' locations every couple of weeks. They kept in contact via phone daily. To complement its unique dual headquarters/dual co-chair approach, the company had a dual holding company structure whereby Unilever's own-

---

[1]Quoted in *The Financial Times*, February 23, 2000, p. 27.

exhibit 1   Unilever's Business and Product Line Portfolio in Early 2000

Unilever Foods Group		
Product Category	**Brands**	**Comments**
Margarines, spreads, and cooking oils	I Can't Believe It's Not Butter, Country Crock, Imperial, Take Control, and Promise spreads, Brummel & Brown spreads and sprays, Bertolli and Puget olive oils, Flora/Becel spreads and cooking products	The world leader in margarine and related spreads and olive oil, with sales in more than 50 countries, Unilever had significant oil plantations in the Democratic Republic of Congo, Côte d'Ivoire, Ghana, and Malaysia.
Frozen foods	Birds Eye frozen foods (sold in U.K.), Iglo frozen foods (sold in most other European countries), Gorton's frozen seafood products, Findus pan-prepared meals, and Quattro Stelle meal solutions	
Ice cream and frozen novelties	Breyers, Magnum, Solero, Walt's, Langnese, Ola, Algida, Cornetto, Viennetta, Pinguino, Carte d'Or, Klondike, Popsicle, and Good Humor ice cream products	Unilever had ice cream sales in more than 90 countries worldwide.
Tea-based beverages	Lipton, Lipton Ice Tea and Lipton Brisk (ready-to-drink teas), Brooke Bond and Beseda teas	Lipton was the world's most popular tea brand—Unilever had extensive tea plantations in India, Tanzania, and Kenya that supplied tea for its own brands and the tea market in general
Culinary products	Ragú and Five Brothers pasta and pizza sauces, Colmans mustard and sauces, Amora and Maille mustards, ketchup, and dressings, Lawry's seasonings, Upron Spices and seasonings, Wishbone and Calvé salad dressings; Calvé peanut butter; Slotts and Klocken mustards, ketchup and seasonings, Sizzle & Stir sauces, Wishbone salad dressings, Oxo stock cubes, Batchelor's dry soup mixes (a U.K. brand), Royco dry soup mixes (sold in France and Belgium), Heisse Tasse dry soup mixes (sold in Germany), and instant Cup-A-Soup, Recipe, McDonnell's, Bla Band, and Lipton soups	Ragú was Unilever's biggest selling culinary brand; Calvé was Unilever's most widely used culinary brand with sales in Greece, Russia, Romania, and much of Europe. Amora mustard was the best-selling mustard brand in France. A number of the dry soups and sauces businesses were sold to Campbell Soup in January 2001 for approximately €1 billion.
Desserts	Carte d'Or	
Bakery products	Bread and confectionery mixes, baking ingredients, frozen bakery products such as Danish pastries, muffins, and croissants	Had operations across 13 European countries, with sales of €860 million, operating profits of €60 million, and a workforce of approximately 3,900 people

(continued)

ership was divided into two classes—some shareholders owned Unilever NV stock (based largely on food products) that traded on the Dutch stock exchange, and some shareholders owned Unilever PLC stock (based largely on personal care and household products) that traded on the London FTSE and was included as part of the FTSE 100 Index. Since Unilever stock was also traded on the New York Stock Exchange, the company reported its financial results in euros, British pounds, and U.S. dollars. The two companies, Unilever NV and Unilever PLC, operated as nearly as practicable as a single entity; a series of intercompany agreements ensured that the position of shareholders in both companies was virtually the same as having shares in a single company.

exhibit 1   (*concluded*)

Unilever Home & Personal Care Group (operations in 60-plus countries)		
Product Category	**Brands**	**Comments**
Prestige fragrances	Calvin Klein, Chloé, Cerruti, Valentino, Lagerfeld, Nautica, Elizabeth Taylor, White Shoulders, Vera Wang	Unilever's fragrance brands represented one of the largest fragrance businesses in the world.
Deodorants and toiletry products	Rexona/Sure, Axe/Lynx, Dove, Degree, Brut, Suave, Impulse	Rexona/Sure was the world's number one deodorant brand.
Hair care	ThermaSilk, Sunsilk, Mod's Hair (Japan), Finesse, Suave, Caress, Dove, Salon Selectives, Timotei, and Organics shampoos; AquaNet and Rave hair care products	
Oral care and oral products	Aim, Pepsodent, Mentadent, and Close-up (Asia-Pacific, United States), Signal (Europe), Zhongua (China) toothpastes; Signal and Mentadent chewing gums	
Soaps, lotions, and skin care products	Dove, Lux, Degree, Caress, Lever 2000, Lifebuoy, and Shield soap bars; Pond's, Vaseline, and Fair & Lovely skin care products; Hazeline shampoos and skin care products (sold in China); Q-tips cotton swabs and balls	Dove was the world's number one brand of soap.
Laundry detergents and fabric conditioners	Wisk, Oxo, Omo, Surf, Ala, Persil, All, and Skip detergents; Snuggle, Cajoline, and Comfort fabric conditioners.	Snuggle was the number two brand of fabric softener in the United States with annual sales of about $350 million.
Household care and cleaning products	Domestos surface cleaners, Cif household cleaners, Sunlight dish detergents, and Solvol (a heavy-duty hand cleaner marketed in Australia and New Zealand)	Domestos was marketed in 43 countries, and Cif was marketed in 53 countries.
Diagnostics	Unipath pregnancy tests	
Professional cleaning	Diversey/Lever commercial cleaning products	These products were sold to institutional, laundry, and food and beverage customers.

Source: Compiled by the case researcher from a variety of company sources.

Longtime company analysts regarded Unilever management as a slow-moving, unwieldy, and inherently conservative Anglo-Dutch bureaucracy—one that operated in a staid manner resembling the civil service approach of government agencies. As one analyst put it, "Historically, Unilever has been a very inbred business. People used to join the company from college and leave it when they were carried out in a box. It was a cradle-to-grave company."[2] In 2001, about 90 percent of the company's managers were locally recruited and trained.

Company critics, moreover, saw Unilever as burdened by lack of a coherent corporate strategy and an array of lesser-known, low-volume brands; very few of Unilever's brands had global standing or qualified as "power" brands. In emerging-country markets, where there was the greatest potential to grow sales of food and household products, Unilever's performance was said to be lackluster.

Unilever's food businesses had traditionally been organized around countries, with each country having its own factories engaged in making products for mostly national and sometimes regional geographic markets. Some countries had multiple brands of

[2]Quote attributed to David Lang, consumer industry analyst at brokerage firm Investec Henderson Crosthwaite, in an article by John Thornhill in the *Financial Times,* London edition, August 5, 2000, p. 12.

exhibit 2   Summary of Unilever's Performance, 1995–2000 (dollars and euros in millions, unadjusted for cross-year exchange rate fluctuations)

Year	Revenues Dollars	Revenues Euros	Net Income	Fixed Assets (Including Goodwill and Intangibles)	Employees
2000	$43,809	€47,582	$1,017	$34,852	295,000
1999	43,680	40,977	2,953	27,940	255,000
1998	44,908	40,437	3,270	35,807	267,000
1997	48,761	41,105	5,463	31,671	287,000
1996	52,067	39,785	2,500	30,993	306,000
1995	49,738	36,234	2,325	30,077	308,000

Source: Unilever annual report for 2000 data; *Fortune Global 500* statistics for 1995–99 data; and Wright Investors Service for revenues in euros.

the same product—for example, American shoppers could choose from seven Unilever brands of margarine (Promise, Imperial, Country Crock, Brummel & Brown, Mazola, Take Control, and I Can't Believe It's Not Butter!); in the United Kingdom there were nine Unilever margarine brands, although only three were supported by advertising. The strategy in margarine was to cater to a wide range of tastes—from a German preference for lighter-colored spreads to British preferences for spreads with a higher fat content to American tastes for flavorful and healthier spreads. There were cases where the same Unilever products—Magnum ice cream bars, for instance—did not utilize uniform names, logos, or packaging from country to country.

Performance Issues

Unilever shareholders had not been particularly happy with the company's performance in recent years (see Exhibit 2). During the 1990s, Unilever's sales grew at an average annual rate of 2 percent, well under management's target rate of 5–6 percent and below the 3.1 percent achieved by Nestlé (the world's largest food products company) and the 4.9 percent achieved by Procter & Gamble. The share price of Unilever's London-based operation, Unilever PLC, had lagged the FTSE 100 Index by almost 40 percent since 1995. Unilever had sales per employee of around $160,000 in 2000, compared with $360,000 for Procter & Gamble, $205,000 for Nestlé, $458,000 for Kellogg's, and $605,000 for General Mills.

Unilever executives believed the Path to Growth initiative would rectify the company's mediocre performance. Concentrating the lion's share of R&D, advertising and promotion, and management time on the top 400 brands, they believed, would deliver 5–6 percent annual growth in revenues. Faster revenue growth, coupled with cost-saving efficiencies from better strategic and resource fits among the top 400 brands, was expected to push operating profit margins up from 11 to 16 percent and permit double-digit earnings growth by 2004. Much of the margin improvement was expected to come from pruning the low-volume, local brands and thereby simplifying and streamlining the company's supply chain.

To stimulate more innovation and entrepreneurial thinking, Unilever had begun stepping up efforts to attract talented managers from outside the company. In addition, Unilever had revised its incentive compensation system. In the old system, the top 300–400 managers could earn an annual bonus worth up to 40 percent of their salaries, with the average bonus rate being 15 to 25 percent. Under the recently introduced system, outstanding managers who hit exacting growth and earnings targets could earn up to 100 percent bonuses. A further move was to alter the award of stock options from giving equal amounts to all managers at a particular level (based on the company's overall performance) to making awards of shares based on individual performance.

INDUSTRY ENVIRONMENT

The food and household products industry was composed of many subsectors, each with differing growth expectations, profit margins, competitive intensity, and business risks. Industry participants were constantly challenged to respond to changing consumer preferences and to fend off maneuvers from rival firms to gain market share. Competitive success started with creating a portfolio of attractive products and brands; from there success depended largely on product-line growth through acquisitions (it was generally considered cheaper to buy a successful brand than to build and grow a new one from scratch) and on the ability to continually grow sales of existing brands and improve profit margins. Advertising was considered a key to increasing unit volume and helping drive consumers toward higher margin products; sustained volume growth also usually entailed gaining increased international exposure for a company's brands. Improving a company's profit margins included not only shifting sales to products with higher margins but also boosting efficiency and driving down unit costs.

In 2000, there was a wave of megamergers involving high-profile food and household products companies (see Exhibit 3). Three factors were driving consolidation pressures in the food industry—slower growth rates in the food sector, rapid consolidation in retail grocery chains (which enhanced the buying power of supermarket chains and enhanced their ability to demand and receive "slotting fees" for allocating manufacturers favorable shelf space on their grocery aisles), and fierce competition between branded food manufacturers and private-label manufacturers.

The earnings growth picture for many food companies had been bleak for several years, and the trend was expected to continue. In the United States, for example, sales of food and household products were, on average, growing 1–2 percent, slightly higher than the 1 percent population growth. More women working outside the home, decreasing household sizes, and greater numbers of single-person and one-parent households were causing a shift of food and beverage dollars from at-home outlays to away-from-home outlays. The growth rate for food and household products across the industrialized countries of Europe was in the 2 percent range, with many of the same growth-slowing factors at work as in the United States. Food industry growth rates in emerging or less-developed countries were more attractive—in the 3–4 percent range, prompting most growth-minded food companies to focus their efforts on markets in Latin America, Asia, Eastern Europe, and Africa.

Since 1985, the share of private-label food and beverages sold in the United States had risen steadily, accounting for roughly 25 percent of total grocery sales in 2000, up from 19 percent in 1992. Growing shopper confidence in the leading supermarket chains and other food retailers like Wal-Mart (which had begun selling a full line of grocery and household items at its Supercenters) had opened the way for retail chains to effectively market their own house-brand versions of name-brand products, provided the house brand was priced attractively below the competing name brands. Indeed, with the aid of checkout scanners and computerized inventory systems, retailers knew as well or better (and more quickly) than manufacturers what customers were buying and what price differential it took to induce shoppers to switch from name brands to private-label brands. These developments tilted the balance of power firmly

exbibit 3 Mergers and Acquisitions among Food and Household Products Companies in 2000

Companies Involved	Value of Deal	Brand Portfolio of Acquiring Company	Brand Portfolio of Company Being Acquired
General Mills acquired the Pillsbury unit of Diageo (a U.K.-based company with a wide-ranging portfolio of alcoholic beverage brands and the parent of Burger King and Pillsbury)	$10.5 billion in cash	*General Mills brands:* Big G cereals (Wheaties, Cheerios, Total, Lucky Charms, Trix, Chex, Golden Grahams); Betty Crocker desserts and side dishes; Gold Medal flours; Bisquick; Hamburger Helper; Lloyd's; Yoplait and Colombo yogurts; Pop Secret; Chex Mix snacks; Nature Valley, Bugles	*Pillsbury brands:* Pillsbury and Martha White flours, baking mixes, and baking products; Häagen-Dazs ice cream and frozen yogurt; Green Giant frozen and canned vegetables; Old El Paso Mexican foods; Totino's and Jeno's pizzas; Progresso; Hungry Jack
Philip Morris (the parent of Kraft Foods) acquired Nabisco	$19 billion in cash, stock, and debt	*Kraft Foods brands:* Kraft cheeses, mayonnaise, salad dressings, barbeque sauces, and dinners; Post cereals; Jell-O; Velveeta; Cheez Whiz; Cracker Barrel, Di Giorgo and Hoffman's cheeses; Claussen pickles; Maxwell House, Yuban, and Sanka coffees; Minute rice; Tobler and Toblerone chocolates; Louis Rich and Oscar Mayer meats; Miracle Whip; Shake 'N Bake; Breakstone; Cool Whip; Planters; Kool-Aid; Stove Top; Altoids	*Nabisco brands:* Nabisco cookies, crackers, and snacks; Grey Poupon French mustards
Kellogg's acquired Keebler	$4.4 billion	*Kellogg's brands:* Kellogg's cereals, Eggo, Nutri-Grain, Pop-Tarts, Kashi cereal and breakfast bars, Rice Crispies Treats, Snack'Ums	*Keebler brands:* Keebler cookies; Murray cookies; Keebler snack foods (Cheez-It, Wheatables, Toasteds, Munch'ems, Harvest Bakery, Snax Stix); Krispy and Zesta saltine crackers; Club crackers; Hi-Ho crackers; Golden Vanilla Wafers; Ready Crust pie shells
ConAgra acquired International Home Foods	$2.9 billion	*ConAgra brands:* Armour, Banquet, Butterball, Blue Bonnet and Parkay margarines, Chun King, La Choy, Orville Redenbacher's and Act II popcorns, Peter Pan peanut butter, County Line cheeses, Morton prepared foods, Eckrich meats, Fleischmann's, Egg Beaters, Healthy Choice, Hunt's	*International Home Foods brands:* Chef Boyardee, Pam cooking spray, Louis Kemp/Bumblebee seafood products, Libbey's canned meats, Gulden's mustard
PepsiCo acquired Quaker Oats	$12.4 billion in cash and stock	*PepsiCo brands:* Pepsi soft drinks, Mountain Dew, Frito-Lay snack foods, Tropicana juices	*Quaker brands:* Gatorade, Quaker Oats cereals, Rice-A-Roni, Aunt Jemima, Near East, Golden Grain–Mission pastas
Cadbury Schweppes acquired the Snapple Beverage Group from Triarc, Inc.	$1.45 billion	*Cadbury Schweppes brands:* Schweppes and Canada Dry tonics, sodas, and ginger ales; 7UP; Dr Pepper; A&W; Mott's apple juices; Clamato juices; Cadbury chocolates and confectionery items; Trebor, Pascall, Cadbury Éclair, and Bassett candies	*Snapple brands:* Snapple ready-to-drink teas and beverages

toward retailers. Thus, competition between private-label goods and name-brand goods in supermarkets was escalating rapidly, since retailers' margins on private-label goods often exceeded those on name-brand goods. The battle for market share between private-label and name-brand goods was expected to continue as private-label manufacturers improved their capabilities to match the quality of name-brand products, while also gaining the scale economies afforded by a growing market share.

Brand-name manufacturers were trying to counteract the bargaining power of large supermarket chains and the growth of private-label sales by building a wide-ranging portfolio of strong brands—the thesis being that retailers, fearful of irritating shoppers by not carrying well-known brands, would be forced to stock all of the manufacturer's name-brand products and, in many cases, award them favorable shelf space. At the same time, because they faced pressures on profit margins in negotiating with retailers and combating the competition from rival brands (both name-brand rivals and private-label rivals), manufacturers were trying to squeeze out costs, weed out weak brands, focus their efforts on those items they believed they could develop into global brands, and reduce the number of versions of a product they manufactured wherever local market conditions allowed (to help gain scale economies in production).

Exhibit 4 provides a brief profile of selected competitors of Unilever. Other competitors included Sara Lee, H. J. Heinz, Kellogg's, and well over 100 regional and local food products companies around the world. Many of the leading food products companies had a "food-service" division that marketed company products to restaurants, cafeterias, and institutions (such as schools, hospitals, college student centers, private country clubs, corporate facilities) to gain access to the growing food-away-from-home market.

UNILEVER'S BUSINESSES AND BRAND PORTFOLIO

Analysts familiar with the household products business and with Unilever were skeptical that there were meaningful strategic and resource fits between food products and household/personal care products. Some saw Unilever's reorganization into a foods group and a home and personal care group as a possible precursor to the breakup of Unilever, an outcome denied by Unilever executives.

The Foods division, known as Unilever Bestfoods following the 2000 acquisition and integration of Bestfoods, was organized around the six product categories: spreads and dressings; tea and tea-based beverages; culinary products; frozen foods; ice cream; and the global food-service business. The Foods division generated slightly more than half of Unilever's sales. The Home and Personal Care (HPC) division consisted of eight categories: deodorants, hair care, household care, laundry, mass skin care, oral care, personal wash, and fragrances and cosmetics. The Foods Division and the Home and Personal Care Division were each headed by a director who had global profit responsibility and executive authority for aligning brand strategy with operations worldwide.[3] Underneath the division heads were directors for each product category and regional presidents who were responsible for profitability in their respective regions. Both divisions had an executive committee—composed of the division director (acting as chairperson), the directors for each product category, and the regional presidents—that was responsible for the overall results and performance of Unilever. Most research and new product development activities were integrated into the divisional structure, but the company had formed a small number of "global innovation centers" to interlink

---

[3]Company press release describing the realignment of the senior management structure at Unilever, August 3, 2000.

exhibit 4   Profile of Selected Unilever Competitors

Company (Headquarters)	Product Categories/Brands	Sales	Profits	Key Facts
Nestlè (Swiss)	• Chocolates and candies (Nestlé, Crunch, KitKat, Smarties, Butterfinger, Cailler, Frigor, Chokito, Galak/Milkybar, Yes, Quality Street, Baci, After Eight, Baby Ruth, Lion, Nuts, Rolo, Aero, Polo) • Dairy (Carnation, Milkmaid, Nespray, Nido, Neslac, Gloria, Bärenmarke) • Coffee (Nescafé, Taster's Choice, Bonka, Zoegas, Ricoffy, Loumidis, Coffee-mate) • Beverages (Nesquik, Nestea, Carnation, Libby's, Perrier, San Pellegrino, Poland Spring, Calistoga, Vittel, Valvert, Arrowhead, Buxton, Vera) • Frozen Foods (Stouffer's, Maggi, Buitoni) • Culinary products (Maggi, Libby's, Crosse & Blackwell, Buitoni) • Ice Cream (Nestlé, Frisco, Dairy Farm) • Pet care (Friskies, Fancy Feast, Alpo, Mighty Dog, Gourmet, Ralston Purina) • Cosmetics (L'Oréal) • Others (PowerBar, Nestlé cereal, Alcon eye care products) • Food services	2000: Fr 81.4b* 1999: Fr 74.7b 1998: Fr 71.7b 1997: Fr 70.0b 1996: Fr 60.5b	2000: Fr 5.76b* 1999: Fr 4.72b 1998: Fr 4.20b 1997: Fr 4.18b 1996: Fr 3.59b	World's largest food company with sales in almost every country of the world; 509 factories; 231,000 employees.
Procter & Gamble (U.S.)	• Baby care (Pampers, Luvs) • Laundry products (Tide, Cheer, Downy, Bounce, Bold, Dreft, Era, Gain, Ivory Snow, Ariel) • Household cleaners (Joy, Cascade, Dawn, Comet, Mr. Clean/Top Job) • Food/Beverage (Folgers, Jif, Crisco, Pringles, Sunny Delight, Millstone) • Health and oral care (Crest, Pepto-Bismol, Metamucil, Vicks, Nyquil) • Feminine care (Always, Tampax) • Paper products (Bounty, Charmin, Puffs) • Personal care (Ivory, Camay, Safeguard, Zest, Secret, Old Spice, Cover Girl, Max Factor, Head & Shoulders, Olay, Pert, Vidal Sassoon, Pantene, Physique, Noxema, Hugo Boss) • Pet care (Iams)	2000: $40.0b 1999: $38.1b 1998: $37.2b 1997: $35.8b 1996: $35.3b	2000: $3.54b 1999: $3.76b 1998: $3.78b 1997: $3.42b 1996: $3.05b	Sales in over 140 countries; on-the-ground operations in more than 70 countries, 110,000 employees; and 300 brands. Tide's market share was over 4 times larger than its nearest competitor; Ariel laundry detergent was sold in 115 countries (with the highest or second highest share in 25 countries). Tide and Ariel had combined sales greater than any other P&G brand.
Colgate-Palmolive (U.S.)	• Oral care (Colgate toothpaste, toothbrushes, dental floss; Kolynos—Latin America) • Personal care (Irish Spring, Softsoap, Protex, Palmolive, Speed Stick, Afta, Mennen) • Household care (Palmolive, Ajax, Murphy's Oil, Javex) • Fabric care (Fab, Dynamo, Fleecy, Suavitel, Ajax) • Pet foods (Hill's Science Diet and Prescription Diet)	2000: $9.36b 1999: $9.12b 1998: $8.97b 1997: $9.06b 1996: $8.75b	2000: $1.06b 1999: $0.94b 1998: $0.85b 1997: $0.74b 1996: $0.64b	Sales in over 200 countries and territories; 70% of sales outside the United States; 38% of 2000 sales came from new products introduced in past five years.

(continued)

*Swiss francs.

exhibit 4   (*continued*)

Company (Headquarters)	Product Categories/Brands	Sales	Profits	Key Facts
Kraft Foods (U.S.) —a subsidiary of Philip Morris Companies	• Chocolates and candies (Life Savers, Creme Savers, Altoids and Gummi Savers; Cote d'Or, Terry's, Gallito, Milka, and Toblerone chocolate and confectionery products; Jell-O ready-to-eat refrigerated desserts) • Snacks and crackers (Nabisco, Oreo, Chips Ahoy!, SnackWell's cookies; Ritz, Premium, Triscuit, Wheat Thins, Cheese Nips; Planters nuts; Balance Bar nutrition and energy snacks; Lyux salty snacks; Terrabusi, Canale, Club Social, Cerealitas, Trakinas, Lucky biscuits) • Meats (Oscar Mayer and Louis Rich cold cuts, hot dogs and bacon; Boca Burger soy-based meat alternatives; Simmenthal meats in Italy) • Cereals (Post Raisin Bran, Grape-Nuts and other ready-to-eat cereals; Cream of Wheat and Cream of Rice) • Culinary products (Jell-O, Cool Whip frozen whipped topping; Miracle Whip; Kraft and Good Seasons salad dressings; A-1 steak sauce; Kraft and Bull's-Eye barbecue sauces; Grey Poupon premium mustards; Claussen pickles; Royal dry packaged desserts and baking powder; Kraft and ETA peanut butter; Vegemite yeast spread, Miracoli pasta dinners and sauces, Shake 'N Bake coatings) • Convenient meals (DiGiorno, Tombstone, Jack's, and Delissio frozen pizzas; Kraft macaroni & cheese dinners; Minute rice, Stove Top meal kits; Lunchables) • Beverages (Maxwell House, General Foods International Coffees, Yuban, Jacobs, Gevalia, Carte Noire, Jacques Vabre, Kaffe, HAG, Grand' Mere, Kenco, Saimaza, and Dadak coffees; Capri Sun, Tang, Crystal Light, Country Time, Royal, Verao, Fresh, Frisco, Q-Refres-Ko, and Ki-Suco powdered soft drinks; Suchard Express, O'Boy, Milka and Kaba chocolate drinks) • Cheeses (Kraft, Velveeta, Cracker Barrel, Eden, and Dairylea cheeses; Philadelphia cream cheese, Cheez Whiz process cheese sauce; Knudsen and Breakstone's cottage cheese and sour cream)	2000: $26.5b 1999: $26.8b 1998: $27.3b 1997: $27.7b 1996: $27.9b	2000: $4.62b† 1999: $4.25b 1998: $4.18b 1997: $4.20b 1996: $3.36b	International sales accounted for about 35% of the total; Kraft had 228 manufacturing plants (147 outside the United States) and 550 distribution centers and depots (176 outside the United States); in the United States, Kraft brands had number one market share ranking based on dollar volume in 23 grocery and food categories; in international markets, Kraft brands were number one based on unit volume in one or more countries in 10 product categories.

(*continued*)

†Operating earnings—Philip Morris does not report net income separately for its business divisions.

exhibit 4   (*continued*)

Company (Headquarters)	Product Categories/Brands	Sales	Profits	Key Facts
Groupe Danone (France)	• Dairy (Danone and Dannon yogurts, cream cheese, yogurt-style cheeses, and fresh dairy desserts, Actimel, Galbani, La Serenisima) • Bottled water (Evian, Volvic, Aqua, Boario, Crystal Springs, Ferrarelle) • Biscuits and crackers (LU, Bagley, Danone, Opavia, Bolshevik, Jacobs, Saiwa, Britannia, Griffin's, several others) • Culinary (Lea & Perrins, HP steak sauce, Amoy Asian products) • Baby foods (Blédini—France) • Cheese (Galbani—Italy)	2000: €14.3b 1999: €12.9b 1998: €13.5b 1997: €12.8b 1996: €12.1b	2000: €721m 1999: €598m 1998: €559m 1997: €506m 1996: €325m	World leader in fresh dairy products (15.1% share worldwide); bottled waters have a number one market share in several countries and a 10.8% share worldwide; LU crackers was the number one brand in several countries in Asia-Pacific region; had a 9% market share in biscuits/crackers worldwide. Sales in 120 countries (38% outside the European Union); 148 production plants, 86,000 employees.
Campbell's Soup (U.S.)	• Soups (Campbell's, Healthy Request, Simply Home, Swanson's broth, Liebeg, Erasco, Homepride, Stock Pot) • Bakery (Pepperidge Farm, Arnott's) • Culinary (Pace, V8, Prego, Swanson's, Franco-American, Homepride Pasta Bake, Kimball sauces) • Chocolates (Godiva)	2000: $6.27b 1999: $6.42b 1998: $6.70b 1997: $7.96b 1996: $7.68b	2000: $714m 1999: $724m 1998: $660m 1997: $713m 1996: $802m	Campbell's was the number one wet soup brand in the world; Arnott's was the market leader in biscuits and crackers in Australia and was the number two brand in New Zealand; Pace, Liebeg, V8, Pepperidge Farm. Erasco, and Homepride were also the market leaders in their segments.

(*continued*)

with R&D at the division level and the company's worldwide brand innovation organization. Unilever's local companies were the key interface with customers and consumers, responding to local market needs. Unilever executives saw the formation of two global divisions as having three benefits:

- Improving the company's focus on foods and HPC activities regionally and globally.
- Accelerating decision making and execution through tighter alignment of brand strategy with operations.
- Strengthening innovation capability through more effective integration of R&D into the divisional structure and the creation of global innovation centers.

As part of the company's organizational restructuring, Unilever was closing 100 plants in Europe and North America, and trimming 25,000 jobs to concentrate production

exhibit 4   *(concluded)*

Company (Headquarters)	Product Categories/Brands	Sales	Profits	Key Facts
General Mills/ Pillsbury (U.S.)	• Flours and baking mixes (Pillsbury, Martha White, Gold Medal, Bisquick, Robin Hood) • Snacks and Beverages • Ice cream and dairy (Häagen-Dazs, Yoplait and Trix yogurts) • Desserts (Betty Crocker) • Cereals (Cheerios, Wheaties, Total, Lucky Charms, Trix, Cocoa Puffs, many others) • Frozen and refrigerated foods (Green Giant, Totino's, Pillsbury, Jeno's) • Dinner mixes (Betty Crocker, Hamburger Helper, Farmhouse) • Culinary (Progresso soups, Old El Paso Mexican foods, Green Giant) • Snacks (Chex Mix, Nature Valley, Pop Secret) • Food service	2000: $6.70b 1999: $6.25b 1998: $6.03b 1997: $5.61b 1996: $5.42b	2000: $614m 1999: $535m 1998: $422m 1997: $445m 1996: $476m	The acquisition of Pillsbury in 2001 made General Mills a $13 billion company with a wider and stronger product/brand portfolio; still, about 95% of sales were in the United States.

Source: Compiled by the case researcher from company websites and company documents.

at 150 key sites and 130 ancillary sites. Efficiencies and cost savings associated with consolidating manufacturing were a key part of the company's Path to Growth plan to realize annual savings of €1.5 billion (after restructuring charges of €5.0 billion). In 2000, Unilever spent about €1.2 billion for R&D and €6.5 billion on advertising and brands promotions. Unilever's ice cream and beverage categories had a bad year in 2000, with losses increasing from €22 million in the third quarter to €60 million in the fourth quarter, following a poor summer in Europe. Unilever said it "had a cracking year" in Asia, while in Latin America management characterized the performance as "a good recovery." Interest charges in 2000 rose sharply to €632 million, up from €14 million in 1999, owing to the debt-financed acquisitions.

The company had reduced its brand portfolio from 1,600 to 970 as of February 2001, with the top 400 accounting for 78 percent of total revenues in 2000. An additional 250–300 brands had been targeted for pruning by 2002. Another 200 had been designated as suitable for "merger and migration" into the product families of the top 400 brands. According to Niall FitzGerald, "This [migration] is a complex process. No one else has [done it] on this scale. It is easy to change a name—the marketing challenge is to bring the consumer with you."[4] Also, by year-end 2000, 20 of the planned 100 factories had been closed, with related workforce reductions of 5,300 people.

Some analysts had criticized Unilever for paying too much for several of its acquisitions. For example, Unilever paid a purchase price of €715 million to acquire Amora Maille (equal to 16.6 times Amora Maille's 1999 operating earnings of €43 million)—a price well above the earnings multiples commanded by other food businesses and an amount said to be double what the present owners paid to acquire Amora Maille from Group Danone in 1997. Unilever paid 14.1 times EBITDA (earnings

---

[4]Quoted in "Unilever Unveils 'Big Hit' Innovations, Brand Cull Progress," *Euromarketing via E-mail* 4, no. 3 (February 9, 2001).

exhibit 5   Selected Financial Performance Statistics for SlimFast,
1997 through the First Quarter of 2000 (dollars in millions)

	1997	1998	1999	Q1 2000
Sales revenues	$390	$505	$611	$194*
Advertising and promotional expenditures	87	102	142	n.a.
Earnings before interest, taxes, depreciation, and amortization (EBITDA)	78	117	133	n.a.
Earnings before interest and taxes (EBIT)—operating profits	76	112	125	39†
EBIT % (operating profit margin)	19.4%	22.2%	20.5%	20.1%

*Up 21% over Q1 1999.

†Up 28% over Q1 1999.

Source: www.unilever.com, April 17, 2001.

before interest, taxes, depreciation, and amortization) for Bestfoods—a record high for a foods company and above the 12.8 times EBITDA that Philip Morris/Kraft paid for Nabisco and the 12.1 times EBITDA that PepsiCo paid for Tropicana in 1999. Unilever defended its price for Amora Maille, saying it was justified based on the superior growth prospects the business would deliver relative to other grocery products and on the 19.3 times EBIT (earnings before interest and taxes) that PepsiCo paid for Tropicana in 1999 and the 16.5 times EBIT that Frito-Lay paid for Australia-based Smith's Snackfoods Company in 1997.

THE SLIMFAST ACQUISITION

Two months after announcing the new Path to Growth strategy in February 2000, Unilever negotiated an agreement to acquire SlimFast diet foods for $2.3 billion cash. SlimFast, a privately held company headquartered in Miami, Florida, was the U.S. market leader, with a 45 percent market share, in the $1.3 billion North American weight management and nutritional supplement industry. The company's nearest competitor had a market share of just over 25 percent. SlimFast had sales of $611 million in 1999, up 20 percent over 1998 (see Exhibit 5); the company's net assets totaled $160 million at the time of acquisition. SlimFast's ready-to-drink selections (72 percent of total sales), powders (16 percent), and bars (12 percent) all had the leading positions in their category segments. An estimated 2 million U.S. consumers used SlimFast products daily, and an additional 5 million used SlimFast products occasionally. About 94 percent of SlimFast's sales were in North America. Studies showed the SlimFast brand name had an unaided 89 percent recognition rate among U.S. consumers. SlimFast produced a portion of its products at a company-owned manufacturing facility in Tennessee and sourced the remainder from contract suppliers. It had a strong sales and distribution network, having been successful in gaining shelf space in most supermarkets and drugstores, and had spent over $400 million on advertising and promotion during the past four years.

The company's products were made from "natural ingredients" supplemented with added vitamins and minerals to provide a strong nutritional profile—no appetite suppressants were used. Promotional efforts centered on the themes of good health, balanced nutrition, great taste, and convenient product formats (ready-to-drink products, powders, and bars). SlimFast had conducted extensive clinical trials to validate the performance of its products. The company had a strong physician education program and enjoyed good relationships with the U.S. Food and Drug Administration (FDA) and other regulatory agencies.

Unilever was attracted to SlimFast because the company was growing about 20 percent annually and because people all across the world were increasingly interested in living a longer, healthier, and more vital life. Market research indicated that in the United States, Germany, and the United Kingdom nutrition was the number one dietary concern and that weight was number three. In the United States, Western Europe, Australia, and the largest cities in the rest of the world, between 40 and 55 percent of the population were overweight and 15 to 25 percent were obese. According to the World Health Organization, the number of people who were either overweight or obese was increasing at an alarming rate.

Unilever management saw opportunities to use the company's global distribution capabilities to introduce SlimFast in Europe, Australia, and cities in developing countries, perhaps doubling SlimFast's sales within two to three years. According to independent market research, the world market for diet products and nutritional foods was about $31.7 billion annually and was growing annually at 11.3 percent. Unilever executives believed SlimFast products would appeal to weight-conscious Europeans; according to co-chairman Antony Burgmans, "Europe at the moment is underdeveloped. We are in a perfect position to boost the presence of this brand."[5] Company projections indicated that SlimFast would begin to contribute positively to Unilever's cash flows in 2002 and to earnings in 2003. Unilever believed that SlimFast had a strong management team.

THE BEN & JERRY'S ACQUISITION

After considering offers from Unilever, Diageo (at the time, the parent company of arch-rival Häagen-Dazs), Nestlé, Roncadin (an Italian company), and Dreyer's (a rival maker of super premium ice cream products and a long-time distributor of Ben & Jerry's products), the board of directors of Ben & Jerry's Homemade, Inc., in April 2000 agreed to accept Unilever's offer of $43.60 for all of the company's 7.48 million shares, resulting in an acquisition price of $326 million. The $43.60 price represented a premium of 23 percent over the closing price the day prior to the announcement of the agreement and was well above the $15.80 to $20.00 range the stock traded in prior to the five buyout offers becoming public knowledge in December 1999. Exhibit 6 shows Ben & Jerry's recent financial highlights. The Ben & Jerry's acquisition put Unilever in the high-end superpremium segment of the ice cream market for this first time and made Unilever the world's large marketer of ice cream products.

Company Background

Ben & Jerry's began active operations in 1978 when Ben Cohen and Jerry Greenfield, two former hippies with counterculture lifestyles and very liberal political beliefs, opened a scoop shop in a renovated gas station in Burlington, Vermont. Soon thereafter, the cofounders decided to package their ice cream in pint cartons and wholesale them to area groceries and mom-and-pop stores—their logo became "Vermont's Finest All Natural Ice Cream" and the carton design featured a picture of the cofounders on the lid and unique handstyle lettering to project a homemade impression. The cartons were inscribed with a sales pitch by Ben and Jerry:

> This carton contains some of the finest ice cream available anywhere. We know because we're the guys who made it. We start with lots of fresh Vermont cream and the finest

---

[5]Quoted in an article by Mark Bendeich, "Unilever Buys U.S. Health Foods Firm for $2.3 billion," and posted at www.economictimes.com, April 12, 2000.

exhibit 6   Financial Performance Summary, Ben & Jerry's Homemade, Inc., 1994–99
(in thousands except per share data)

	1999	1998	1997	1996	1995	1994
Income statement data						
Net sales	$237,043	$209,203	$174,206	$167,155	$155,333	$148,802
Cost of sales	145,291	136,225	114,284	115,212	109,125	109,760
Gross profit	91,752	72,978	59,922	51,943	46,208	39,042
Selling, general & administrative expenses	78,623	63,895	53,520	45,531	36,362	36,253
Special charges*	8,602					6,779
Other income (expense)—net	681	693	(118)	(77)	(441)	228
Income (loss) before income taxes	5,208	9,776	6,284	6,335	9,405	(3,762)
Income taxes	1,823	3,534	2,388	2,409	3,457	(1,869)
Net income (loss)	3,385	6,242	3,896	3,926	5,948	(1,869)
Net income (loss) per share—diluted	$ 0.46	$ 0.84	$ 0.53	$ 0.54	$ 0.82	$ (0.26)
Shares outstanding—diluted	7,405	7,463	7,334	7,230	7,222	7,148
Balance sheet data						
Working capital	$ 42,805	$ 48,381	$ 51,412	$ 50,055	$ 51,023	$ 37,456
Total assets	150,602	149,501	146,471	136,665	131,074	120,296
Long-term debt and capital lease obligations	16,669	20,491	25,676	31,087	31,977	32,419
Stockholders' equity†	89,391	90,908	86,919	82,685	78,531	72,502

*The special charge in 2000 concerned a writedown of Springfield, Vermont, plant assets and employee severance costs associated with outsourced novelty ice cream products. The 1994 charge stemmed from early replacement of certain software and equipment installed at the plant in St. Albans, Vermont, and included a portion of the previously capitalized interest and project management costs.

†No cash dividends have been declared or paid by the company on its capital stock since the company's organization in 1978. Earnings were used to provide needed working capital and to finance future growth.

Source: Company annual reports.

flavorings available. We never use any fillers or artificial ingredients of any kind. With our specially modified equipment, we stir less air into the ice cream, creating a denser, richer, creamier product of uncompromising high quality. It costs more and it's worth it.

A *Time* magazine article on the superpremium ice cream craze appeared in August 1981 with the opening sentence, "What you must understand is that Ben & Jerry's in Burlington, Vermont, makes the best ice cream in the world." Sales at Ben & Jerry's took off, rising to $10 million in 1985 and to $78 million in 1990. By 1994, Ben & Jerry's products were distributed in all 50 states, the company had 100 scoop shops, and it was marketing 29 flavors in pint cartons and 45 flavors in bulk cartons.

Products and Operations in 2000

Headquartered in Burlington, Vermont, Ben & Jerry's in 2000 produced and marketed over 50 superpremium ice cream flavors, ice cream novelties, low-fat ice cream flavors, low-fat frozen yogurts, and sorbets, using Vermont dairy products and high-quality, all-natural ingredients. Like other superpremium ice creams, Ben & Jerry's products were high in calories (about 300 per serving), had a fat content equal to 40 to 55 percent of the recommended daily allowance for saturated fat per serving, and were high in cholesterol content (20 to 25 percent of the recommended daily allowance). About 35 of the flavors were packaged in pint cartons for sale in supermarkets, grocery stores, and convenience stores; the rest were packaged in bulk tubs for sale in about 200 franchised and company-owned Ben & Jerry's scoop shops, restaurants, and food-service accounts. To stimulate buyer interest, the company came up with attention-getting names for its flavors: Chunky Monkey, Chocolate Chip Cookie Dough, Bovinity Divinity, Coconut Cream Pie, Chubby Hubby, Double Trouble, Totally Nuts, and Coffee Olé. Many of the flavors contained sizable chunks of cookies or candies, a standout attribute of the company's products. Retail prices for a pint of Ben & Jerry's were around $3.25 in May 2001.

At year-end 1999, Ben & Jerry's had 164 franchised scoop shops; 8 PartnerShop franchises (not-for-profit organizations that operated scoop shops); 19 Featuring Franchises (scoop shops within airports, stadiums, college campus facilities, and similar venues); 12 Scoop Station franchises (prefabricated units that operated within other large retail establishments); and 9 company-owned scoop shops (4 in Vermont, 2 in Las Vegas, and 3 in Paris, France). Internationally, there were nine franchised Ben & Jerry's scoop shops in Israel, four in Canada, three in the Netherlands, one in Lebanon, and one in Peru. The company began exporting from its Vermont plants to Japan in 1997, selling single-serve containers through an exclusive arrangement with 7-Eleven Japan. In 1999, it established a wholly owned subsidiary in Japan for the purpose of importing, marketing, and distributing its products through Japanese retail grocery stores. Beginning in January 2000, Ben & Jerry's imported all products into Japan through an agreement with a Japanese trading company.

Distribution   The company's products were distributed throughout the United States and in several foreign countries. Company trucks, along with several local distributors, handled deliveries to retailers in Vermont and upstate New York. In the rest of the United States, Ben & Jerry's relied on distribution services provided by other ice cream manufacturers and marketers. It was the distributors' job to sell retailers on stocking a brand, deliver supplies to each retail location, and stock the freezer cases with the agreed-on flavors and number of facings. Up until 1998, Ben & Jerry's utilized two primary distributors, Sut's Premium Ice Cream for much of New England and Dreyer's Grand Ice Cream for states in the Midwest and West. To round out its national coverage, the company had a number of other distributors that serviced limited market areas. In 1994, Dreyer's accounted for 52 percent of Ben & Jerry's net sales. The arrangement with Dreyer's was somewhat rocky, and in 1998 Ben & Jerry's began redesigning its distribution network to gain more company control. Under the redesign, Ben & Jerry's increased direct sales calls by its own sales force to all grocery and convenience store chains and set up a network where no distributor had a majority percentage of the company's sales. Starting in 1999, much of the distribution responsibility in certain territories was assigned to Ice Cream Partners (a joint venture of Nestlé and Pillsbury, the parent of Häagen-Dazs); the balance of U.S. deliveries was assigned to Dreyer's and several other regional distributors, but Dreyer's territory was smaller than before and entailed Ben & Jerry's receiving a higher price than formerly for products distributed through Dreyer's.

Manufacturing   Ben & Jerry's operated three manufacturing plants, two shifts a day, five to seven days per week, depending on demand requirements. Superpremium ice cream and frozen yogurt products packed in pint cartons were manufactured at the company's Waterbury, Vermont, plant. The company's Springfield, Vermont, plant was used for the production of ice cream novelties and ice cream, frozen yogurt, low-fat ice cream, and sorbets packaged in bulk, pints, quarts, and half gallons. The St. Albans, Vermont, plant manufactured superpremium ice cream, frozen yogurt, frozen smoothies, and sorbet in pints, 12-ounce, and single-serve containers. Beginning in October

1999, in order to reduce costs and improve its profit margins, the company ceased production of ice cream novelties at its Springfield plant and began outsourcing its requirements from third-party co-packers.

Competitors

Ben & Jerry's two principal competitors were Dreyer's/Edy's (which had introduced its Dreamery and Godiva superpremium brands in 1999) and Häagen-Dazs (part of Pillsbury—which was formerly a subsidiary of Diageo but which was acquired by General Mills in 2000—see Exhibit 3). Other significant frozen dessert competitors were Colombo frozen yogurts (a General Mills brand), Healthy Choice ice creams (a ConAgra brand), Breyer's ice creams and frozen yogurts (Unilever), Kemps ice cream and frozen yogurts (a brand of Marigold Foods), and Starbucks (whose coffee ice cream flavors were distributed by Dreyer's). In the ice cream novelty segment, Ben & Jerry's products (S'Mores, Phish Sticks, Vanilla Heath Bar Crunch pops, Cookie Dough pops, Cherry Garcia frozen yogurt pops, and several others) competed with Häagen-Dazs bars, Dove bars (made by a division of Mars, Inc.), Good Humor bars (a Unilever brand), an assortment of Nestlé products, and many private-label brands.

Häagen-Dazs was considered the global market leader in the superpremium segment, followed by Ben & Jerry's. Ben & Jerry's had only a negligible market share in ice cream novelties and a low single-digit share of the frozen yogurt segment. Whereas close to 90 percent of Ben & Jerry's sales were in the United States, Häagen-Dazs was represented in substantially more foreign markets, including markets in Europe, Japan, and other Pacific Rim countries. Like Ben & Jerry's, Häagen-Dazs marketed several ice cream flavors using pieces of cookies and candies as ingredients.

Management and Culture

Since 1988 Ben & Jerry's had formalized its business philosophy by adopting and pursuing a three-part mission statement:

- *Product mission*: To make, distribute, and sell the finest quality all-natural ice cream and related products in a wide variety of innovative flavors made from Vermont dairy products.

- *Economic mission*: To operate the company on a sound financial basis of profitable growth, increasing value for our shareholders, and creating career opportunities and financial rewards for our employees.

- *Social mission*: To operate the company in a way that actively recognizes the central role that business plays in the structure of society by initiating innovative ways to improve the quality of life of a broad community—local, national, and international.

Pursuing the Company Mission   The three parts of the mission were deemed equally important, and management strived to integrate their pursuit in its day-to-day business decision making. Starting in 1988, the company's annual report had contained a "social report" on the company's performance during the year, with emphasis on workplace policies and practices, concern for the environment, and the social mission accomplishments. To support its social mission activities, Ben & Jerry's had a policy of allocating 7.5 percent of pretax income (equal to $1.1 million in 1999) to support various social causes through the Ben & Jerry's Foundation, corporate grants made by the company's director of social mission development, and employee community action teams. In addition, the company made a practice of sourcing some of its ingredients from companies that gave jobs to disadvantaged individuals who would otherwise be unemployed, strived to operate in an environmentally friendly manner, and partnered with environmentally and socially conscious organizations working to make the world a healthier and more humane place. Over the years, the company had been actively involved with hundreds of grassroots organizations working for progressive social change, including Greenpeace, the Children's Defense Fund, the National Association of Child Advocates, the Coalition for Environmentally Responsible Economies, the Environmental Working Group, and the Institute for Sustainable Communities. It had contributed to efforts to save the rain forests in Brazil. One day each year, the company hosted a "free cone day" at its scoop shops as a way of thanking customers for their patronage.

Ben & Jerry's had selected Vermont communities with high unemployment rates for all three of its plants. It had created a blueberry ice cream so it could buy blueberries exclusively from a tribe of Maine Indians and help support their economy. In 1991, Ben & Jerry's had entered into an agreement with St. Albans Cooperative Creamery (a group of Vermont dairy farmers) to pay not less than a specified minimum price for its dairy products in order to bring prices up to levels the company deemed fair and equitable. In 1994, this agreement was amended to include, as a condition of paying the premium price, assurance that the milk and cream purchased by the company would not come from cows that had been treated with recombinant bovine growth hormone (rBGH), a synthetic growth hormone approved by the FDA. The company quit selling a handmade brownie-and-ice-cream sandwich upon discovering that workers' hands were developing repetitive strain injuries. In 1999, Ben & Jerry's became the first U.S. ice cream company to convert a significant portion of its pint containers to a more environmentally friendly unbleached paperboard. (Bleaching paper with chlorine to make it whiter was said to be one of the largest causes of toxic water pollution in the United States.)

Company Culture   The work environment at Ben & Jerry's was characterized by informality, casual dress, attempts to make the atmosphere fun and pleasurable, and frequent communications between employees and management. Ben Cohen was noted for not owning a suit. Efforts were made to treat employees with fairness and respect; employee opinions were sought out and given serious consideration. Rank and hierarchy were viewed with distaste, and until the late 1990s executive salaries were capped at no more than seven times the pay for entry-level jobs. Compensation levels were above average, compared to pay scales in the Vermont communities where Ben & Jerry's operated. Ben & Jerry's had instituted a very liberal benefits package for its nearly 850 employees that included health benefits for the gay or lesbian partners of employees, maternity leave for fathers as well as mothers, leave for the parents of newly adopted children, $1,500 contributions toward adoption costs, on-site cholesterol and blood pressure screening, smoking cessation classes, tuition reimbursement for three classes per year, a profit-sharing plan, a 401(k) plan, an employee stock purchase plan that allowed employees to buy shares 15 percent below the current market price, a housing loan program, a sabbatical leave program, free health club access, and free ice cream. Nonetheless, the company had experienced occasions where employees expressed dissatisfaction with one or another aspects of their jobs; the periodic meetings management held to discuss issues and concerns with employees had often provoked hot debates.

Ben & Jerry's had long prided itself on treating workers so fairly that they did not need and would not want to be represented by a union. But in late 1998 the company became embroiled in a union controversy at its St. Albans plant, where the International Brotherhood of Electrical Workers (IBEW) was trying to organize a group of 19 maintenance workers. Management refused the IBEW's request to recognize the union voluntarily. Company lawyers, appearing before the National Labor Relations Board (NLRB), opposed the IBEW organizing attempt, arguing that the vote should be held among all workers at the plant, not just among the 19 maintenance workers. Production workers, who made up the majority of the plant's workforce, did not support the union's organizing effort as strongly. In early 1999, following an NLRB ruling that the maintenance workers at the St. Albans plant were an appropriate bargaining unit, the 19 maintenance workers voted narrowly for representation by the IBEW. Even though the 19 workers constituted less than 3 percent of the company's full-time workforce, top management at Ben & Jerry's was concerned that the voting outcome raised questions about the quality of employer-employee relations at Ben & Jerry's.

Management Changes   When Ben Cohen, the creative driving force in the company from the beginning, decided to step down as CEO in 1994, the search for a replacement included an essay contest in which anyone wishing to be considered for the CEO position was asked to state in 100 words or less "why I want to be a great CEO for Ben & Jerry's." Robert Holland, a former consultant at McKinsey & Co., was selected to become the company's CEO in February 1995; he helped transition the company from a founder-led to a professional management structure and helped begin the company's ventures into international markets. Holland resigned in October 1996, partly because of growing disagreements with the founders over how the company was being operated; he was replaced by Perry Odak, who had held senior management positions at Armour-Dial, Atari, Jovan, Dellwood Foods (a dairy products company), and, most recently, at U.S. Repeating Arms Co. (the maker of Winchester firearms) and Browning, a manufacturer of firearms and other sporting goods.

Company Image and Events Leading Up to the Acquisition   Ben & Jerry's counterculture values, unconventional policies, and passionate commitment to social causes were widely known and, in many respects, had emerged as the company's biggest brand asset. Frequent and usually favorable stories in the New England and national press describing Ben & Jerry's proactive approach to "caring capitalism" had fostered public awareness of the company and helped mold a very positive image of the company and its business philosophy. Indeed, substantial numbers of the company's customers patronized Ben & Jerry's ice cream products because they were suspicious of giant corporations, shared many of the same values and beliefs about how a company ought to conduct its business, and wanted to support the company's efforts and good deeds. So strong was the anti-big-business feeling of some customers, employees, and shareholders that, when the press reported Ben & Jerry's was considering various acquisition offers, there were protest rallies at company facilities in Vermont and a Save Ben & Jerry's website (www.savebenandjerrys.com) sprang up for followers to express their displeasure and to help mount a public relations campaign to block a sale. Hundreds of messages were posted at the site—one message said, "My friend and I will not buy Ben & Jerry's again if you sell out. It would not taste the same." Most messages conveyed concerns that Ben & Jerry's would lose its character and social values, ceasing to be a model for other businesses to emulate. Vermont's governor told Reuters, "This company has really come to symbolize Vermont to the country and the world. It would be a shame if it were sucked into the corporate homogenization that's taking over the planet."[6]

Reportedly, neither Ben Cohen nor Jerry Greenfield was enthusiastic about selling the company; both had publicly expressed their desires for the company to remain in-

---

[6]Quoted in an article by Mike Mills in *The Vermont Post*, December 9, 1999.

dependent. But the company's languishing stock price and the attractive offers of interested buyers forced the board of directors to consider being acquired. To counter an offer of $38 per share from Dreyer's, Ben Cohen had entered into negotiations with Meadowbrook Lane Capital (one of the company's large shareholders) and others to take the company private. This fell through when Unilever made its offer of $43.60 per share. In agreeing to accept Unilever's price, Cohen netted over $39 million for his controlling interest in the company, while Odak received over $16 million and Greenfield got $9.6 million. A substantial fraction of Ben & Jerry's 11,000 shareholders were Vermont (or former Vermont) residents.

Developments Following the Acquisition

To win approval for the acquisition from the cofounders and the board, Unilever agreed to keep Ben & Jerry's headquarters in Vermont, to operate the company separately from Unilever for a period of time, to maintain employment at current levels for at least two years, to hold employee benefits at current levels for at least five years, and to contribute 7.5 percent of pretax income annually to the Ben & Jerry's Foundation (historically, the foundation had been managed by a nine-member employee board of directors that considered proposals relating to children and families, disadvantaged groups, and the environment). Unilever further agreed to form an independent 11-member board of directors for Ben & Jerry's to monitor how well these conditions were being met, with 8 of the board members to be named by Ben & Jerry's management, 1 by Unilever, and 2 by Meadowbrook Lane Capital. Ben Cohen and Jerry Greenfield were also to continue to have active roles in management.

In a joint statement announcing the acquisition, Unilever's co-chairmen said, "Ben & Jerry's is an incredibly strong brand name with a unique consumer message. We are determined to nurture its commitment to community values." Ben Cohen said, "The best and highest use for Ben & Jerry's is to try to influence what goes on at Unilever. It's a gargantuan task. Who knows how far we'll get? Who knows how successful we'll be?"

In November 2000, Unilever announced that Yves Couette had been appointed CEO of Ben & Jerry's, to succeed existing CEO Perry Odak. Couette, a native of France, was one of the top executives in Unilever's ice cream group and had worked in the United States, Mexico, Indonesia, and the United Kingdom. Couette had recently been managing director of Unilever's ice cream business in Mexico, where he had turned Unilever's Helados Holanda business into a solid success with distinctive local brands and scoop shops. In commenting on his appointment, Couette said,

> Ben & Jerry's is a unique company, with highly professional and committed people from whom I look forward to learning and connecting to Unilever's world-class knowledge of ice cream. In addition, I am determined to deliver on Ben & Jerry's social mission commitment.

Perry Odak remained with the company until January 2001 to assist Yves Couette in the transition.

THE BESTFOODS ACQUISITION

Bestfoods was a global company engaged in manufacturing and marketing consumer foods. The company had offices and manufacturing operations in 60 countries and marketed its products in 110 countries. About 60 percent of the company's $8.6 billion in sales in 1999 came from outside the United States. Bestfoods employed approximately

44,000 people, of which about 28,000 were at non-U.S. locations. Food industry analysts considered Bestfoods to be one of the best-managed American food companies, and it was one of the 10 largest U.S.-based food products companies at the time it was acquired by Unilever. Once known as CPC International, the company renamed itself Bestfoods after spinning off its cyclical $1.5 billion corn refining business in late 1997.

Exhibit 7 shows Bestfoods' product portfolio in mid-2000 when Unilever first offered to acquire the company. During the decade of the 1990s, Bestfoods had grown revenues at a 7.8 percent annual rate, operating earnings at a 10.5 percent annual rate, and earnings per share at a 12.1 percent annual rate; the company had increased its dividends for 14 consecutive years. Growth had slowed during the 1997–99 period, however. In 1999, Bestfoods' sales were up 2.7 percent over 1998, unit volumes were up 4.1 percent, and operating income was up 9.0 percent (see Exhibit 8). Bestfoods' corporate strategy had four core elements:

- *Globalization of the company's core consumer businesses*—the Knorr product line, salad dressings, and food-service operations.
- *Continual improvement in cost-effectiveness.*
- *Seeking out and exploiting new market opportunities* (via both new product introductions and extending sales of existing products to additional country markets).
- *Using free cash flow to make strategic acquisitions.* Since the 1980s, Bestfoods had made over 60 acquisitions to expand its lineup of products and brands and to position the company in new geographic markets.

Exhibits 9 and 10 show Bestfoods' recent performance and market positions in various country markets.

After several weeks of back-and-forth negotiations and increases in Unilever's offer price from the $61–$64 per share range to $66 per share to $72 per share and finally to $73 per share, Bestfoods in June 2000 agreed to be acquired by Unilever for what amounted to $20.3 billion in cash (equivalent to €23.6 billion), plus assumption of Bestfoods net debt (which amounted to $3.1 billion as of June 30, 2000). The $73 per share buyout agreement represented a price 44 percent higher than the nearly $51 price at which Bestfoods' shares were trading before Unilever's overtures became public and represented about a 20 percent premium over the $59–$62 range where Bestfoods shares were trading in late 1999. Bestfoods was, by far, the largest acquisition ever undertaken by Unilever and the largest combination of food companies in 12 years.

Unilever management believed that combining and integrating the operations of Bestfoods and Unilever would "result in pre-tax cost savings of approximately $750 million annually through combined purchase savings, greater efficiencies in operations and business processes, synergy in distribution and marketing, streamlining of general and administrative functions, and increased economies of scale." In addition, management said that the complementary nature of Unilever's and Bestfoods' product portfolios and geographic market coverage better positioned the combined company for faster revenue growth through:

- Creating a "more robust" combined business in the U.S. market.
- Maximizing the complementary strengths of Unilever and Bestfoods in Europe.
- Building on the strength of Bestfoods in Latin America to accelerate the growth of Unilever's brands.
- Using Unilever's distribution network strengths in the Asia-Pacific area to grow the sales of Bestfoods' brands.
- Utilizing Bestfoods' food-service channel to gain increased sales for Unilever's portfolio of spreads, teas, and culinary products.

exhibit 7   Bestfoods Product Portfolio, June 2000

Products/Brands	Comments
Hellmann's mayonnaise and salad dressings; Bestfoods, Lady's Choice, and Lesieur mayonnaise and salad dressings; Dijonnaise creamy mustard; Henri's and Western salad dressings	Worldwide sales of about $2 billion, with the leading market share in mayonnaise in North America, Latin America, and many countries of Asia and Europe. In parts of the United States, Hellmann's products were marketed under the Bestfoods brand; Lesieur mayonnaise products were marketed in France and had the second highest market share in that country.
Knorr dry soups, sauces, bouillons, and related products	Worldwide sales of about $3 billion. Knorr products were sold in virtually all of the 110 countries where Bestfoods had a market presence. It was the number two soup brand, behind Campbell's.
Mazola corn and canola oils and Mazola margarine; Mazola No-Stick and Pro Chef cooking sprays; RightBlend oils	Marketed in 35 countries.
Skippy peanut butter	One of the leading brands in the United States and also strong in parts of Asia
Karo and Golden Griddle syrups	
Argo, Kingsford's, Canada, Benson's, and Maziena corn starches	The Maziena brand of corn starch and other basic nutritional foods was marketed primarily in Latin America.
Mueller's pastas	
Rit dyes and laundry products	
Entemann's bakery goods; Thomas' English muffins; Arnold, Brownberry, Oroweat, and Freihofer's breads; Boboli pizza crusts	The Bestfoods Baking division was the largest baker of fresh premium products in the United States; Entemann's was the number one brand of fresh bakery-style cakes and pastries in the United States; Boboli had a 57 percent share of the market for fresh pizza crusts; Bestfoods total sweet baked goods share was 19.2 percent in 1998.
Glaxose-D energy drinks	A newly-acquired business in Pakistan.
Globus dressings, condiments, and liquid sauces	A newly-acquired brand in Hungary.
Alsa and Ambrosia ready-to-eat desserts, dessert mixes, and baking aids	Marketed primarily in Europe; sales of about $280 million in 1999.
AdeS soy beverages	Marketed throughout Latin America.
Captain Cook salt	A packaged salt business in India.
Bestfoods (in the United States) and Caterplan (outside the United States) food services	Provided food-service packs of company products, specially formulated products, and menu-planning and other unique services to support restaurants, cafeterias, and institutions in the growing global market for food prepared and consumed away from home—geographic coverage in virtually all of the countries where Bestfoods operated. The food-service division had worldwide sales of $1.4 billion in 1999.
Others: Pfanni potato products (Germany), Pot Noodle instant hot snacks (United Kingdom), Telma soups and instant foods products (Israel), Bovril bouillons, Marmite spread, Santa Rosa jams, Sahara pita breads, Goracy Kubek instant soups (Poland), Delikat seasonings (Central Europe), Molinos de la Plata mayonnaise, ketchup, and mustard (Argentina)	

exhibit 8   Selected Financial Statistics for Bestfoods, 1997–99
               (in millions of dollars, except for per share amounts)

	1999	1998	1997
Selected income statement data			
Net sales	$8,637	$8,413	$8,438
Cost of sales	4,546	4,562	4,693
Gross profit	4,091	3,851	3,745
Marketing expenses	996	976	978
Selling, general, and administrative expenses	1,765	1,655	1,659
Operating income	1,330	1,187	866
Financing costs	183	166	162
Income from continuing operations before income taxes	1,147	1,021	704
Provision for income taxes	384	352	250
Net income	$ 717	$640	$ 429
Earnings per share of common stock (diluted)	$ 2.48	$ 2.09	$ 1.15
Selected balance sheet data			
Inventories	$ 792	$ 827	$ 818
Current assets	2,204	2,405	2,188
Plant, property, and equipment	1,964	1,965	1,941
Intangible assets, including goodwill associated with acquiring businesses at costs exceeding net assets	1,811	1,854	1,742
Total assets	6,232	6,435	6,100
Current liabilities	2,368	2,312	2,347
Long-term debt	1,842	2,053	1,818
Total stockholders' equity	938	981	1,042
Selected cash flow data			
Net cash flows from operating activities	$1,110	$ 819	$ 915
Capital expenditures	278	304	321
Payments for acquired businesses	225	121	298
Net cash flows used for investing activities	477	264	732
Repayment of long-term debt	153	94	99
Dividends paid on common and preferred stock	295	277	256
Net cash flows used for financing activities	697	440	267

Source: Company annual reports, 1998 and 1999.

According to a statement issued by Antony Burgmans and Niall FitzGerald, the Bestfoods acquisition would give Unilever "a portfolio of powerful worldwide and regional brands with strong growth prospects." Knorr, with $3 billion in annual sales, would become Unilever's biggest food brand.

To finance the $21.4 billion Bestfoods acquisition, Unilever arranged for a $20 billion line of credit from several banks, with annual interest costs that analysts expected to exceed $1 billion. It was anticipated that Unilever would ultimately finance the transaction with longer-term debt securities having a currency profile paralleling the geographic composition of the business.

In February 2001, Unilever announced the sale of the Bestfoods Baking Company to George Weston, a Canadian food and supermarkets group, for $1.76 billion in cash.

exhibit 9   Summary of Bestfoods Worldwide Business Results, 1997–99

1999 Sales and Operations, by Geographic Region							
Geographic Region	**Sales Revenues (in millions)**		**Fixed Assets (in millions)**		**Areas of Operation, 1999**		**Number of Plants, 1999**
Europe, Africa/ Middle East	1999 $3,598 1998 3,490 1997 3,539		1999 $1,568 1998 1,809 1997 1,637		Operations in 33 countries of Europe, Africa, and Middle East		59
North America	1999 $3,594 1998 3,452 1997 3,412		1999 $1,682 1998 1,507 1997 1,547		Operations in the U.S. Canada, and the Caribbean		36
Latin America	1999 $1,071 1998 1,149 1997 1,105		1999 $ 277 1998 284 1997 291		Operations in 16 countries		19
Asia	1999 $ 374 1998 322 1997 382		1999 $ 124 1998 120 1997 101		Operations in 12 countries, including joint ventures in 7 countries		18

1999 Sales by Product Group				
Product Group	**Region**	**Sales (in millions)**	**% Change**	**Volumes**
Knorr soups, sauces, bouillons and related products	Europe	$2,091	+4.2%	+9.8%
	North America	470	+10.3	10.3
	Latin America	342	−9.0	−7.6
	Asia	185	+17.0	+25.0
	Total/average	$3,088	+4.1%	6.8%
Dressings	Europe	$464	+2.7%	+7.9%
	North America	1,001	+4.8	5.4
	Latin America	443	−5.7	+1.7
	Asia	96	+14.0	+10.2
	Total/average	$2,004	+2.2%	5.4%
Baking	United States	$1,697		
Starches	Worldwide	$569		
Bread Spreads	Worldwide	$406		
Desserts	Worldwide	$280		
All other sales	Worldwide	$593		
Bestfoods and Caterplan food services	Worldwide	$1,400 (distributed across several of the product groups above)	+8.4%	Included in the appropriate product groups above

Unilever had announced its intention to divest Bestfoods Baking Company two weeks after closing its merger with Bestfoods on October 4, 2000, noting that the characteristics of the baking business did not fit other Unilever products and that "bakery products" was a category no longer in existence at Unilever. Bestfoods Baking was entirely U.S.-based, with 19 plants across the country, a strong management team, 12,000 employees, and one of the best distribution systems for delivering fresh-baked products directly to retail stores. In 1999, Bestfoods Baking had sales of $1.7 billion (up 2.3 percent over 1998) and an operating profit margin of 8 percent (good for the baking business).

exhibit 10 Market Positions of Selected Bestfoods Products, by Country, 1999

1 Leader in Market Share / 2 Second in Market Share / • Present in the Market	Soups*	Sauces*	Bouillons	Meal Kits*	Potato Products	Pasta/Pasta Dishes	Mayonnaise	Pourable Dressings	Corn Oil	Foodservice†	Peanut Butter	Starches	Desserts (Ambient)	Premium Baking
North America, Caribbean														
Canada	2	2	1				1		1	•	2	1		
Dominican Republic	2		2				•		•	•		1		
United States	•	•	2	•	•	•	1	•	1	•	2	1	•	1
Europe														
Austria	1	1	1	1	1				1	•		1		
Belgium	1	1	1	1						•		1		
Bulgaria	•	•	•		•					•				
Czech Republic	2	2	2	2	•		1	1		•				
Denmark	1	1	1	1	2			2	1	•		1	•	
Finland	1	1	1	2					1	•		2		
France	1	2	2				2	2				1	1	
Germany	2	2	2	2	1		•		1	•		1	•	
Greece	1	1	1		2	1	1	1		•		2	2	
Hungary	1	1	1	2	1		2			•			•	
Ireland	1	1	1	1	1	•	1	2	•	•		2	1	
Italy	1	•	2		1		•		•	•		1		
Netherlands	2	1	2	2	•				•	•		2		
Norway	•	2	•						•	•		1		
Poland	1	1	1	1	1		2			•			•	
Portugal	1	•	1		2		1	2		•		1	2	
Romania	1		1							•			•	
Russia	2	1	2		1		•		•	•	•			
Slovak Republic	2	•	•	•	•		1			•				
Slovenia														
Spain	2	•	2	•		•	•	•		•		1	2	
Sweden	1	2	1	1				•	1	•	1	1		
Switzerland	1	1	1	1	1		•		•	•		1	•	
United Kingdom	•	•	2	•		•	1	2	1	•		1	1	
Africa/Middle East														
Egypt														
Israel	1	2	2	1	•	•	1		1	•	1		2	
Jordan	2	2								•				
Kenya	1	2							•	•	2	1		
Morocco	1	•	1							•		1	1	
Saudi Arabia							2		2	•	•	•		
South Africa	1	2	1	1			•	1	•	•	•	1	•	
Tunisia	1	•	1				•			•		2	•	
Turkey	1	2	•							•		1	•	

(continued)

exhibit 10   (*concluded*)

1 Leader in Market Share 2 Second in Market Share • Present in the Market	Soups*	Sauces*	Bouillons	Meal Kits*	Potato Products	Pasta/Pasta Dishes	Mayonnaise	Pourable Dressings	Corn Oil	Foodservice†	Peanut Butter	Starches	Desserts (Ambient)	Premium Baking
Latin America														
Argentina	1		1		1	1	1	1	2	•		1		
Bolivia	•		•				2			•		1		
Brazil	2		1			2	1	1	1	•		1		
Chile	•		•		2		1	1	1	•		1	•	
Colombia	•	2	2	2	•		1	•	•	•		1	1	
Costa Rica	2	1			•		1	1	1	•	•	1		
Ecuador	2	•	•	2			•		1			•		
El Salvador	•	•	•				•	•	1		•	1		
Guatemala	•	•	•		•		•	1	1	•	•	1		
Honduras		•					•		1			2		
Mexico	1	•	1	1		1	2	•	2	•		1	•	
Panama	•	•	•				•	•	•	•		1		
Paraguay	2		2	2	•		1		2	•		1		
Peru	2	•	2		2	2	1	2	1	•		1		
Uruguay	1		1		1	•	1		2	•		1		
Venezuela	2	•	2	1			•	•		•		1		
Asia														
China	•	•	•				•			•	•	•	•	•
Hong Kong	•	•	1		•		2			•	•	1	1	1
India	1			1								1	1	
Indonesia	1	•	•				2	2	1	•	1			
Japan	1	•	1	•			2	2	1	•	•			
Malaysia	1	•	2				1	1	1	•		1	1	2
Pakistan	1	•	1	•			2		1	•		1		1
Philippines	1	•	1			1	1	•	•	•	1	•	1	
Singapore	1		1				2	2	•	•		1	1	1
Sri Lanka	2	1	2						2	•				
Taiwan	1		1				2	•	•	•		1		
Thailand	1	1	1	2		1	1		1	•		1	•	•
Vietnam	2		1				•			•				

*Dehydrated products only.

†Bestfoods foodservice (catering) products hold leading share positions in many of the categories in which they compete.

Source: Company annual report, 1999.

UNILEVER IN 2001

The company's 2000 annual report characterized Unilever as a "truly multi-local, multinational company dedicated to meeting the everyday needs of people everywhere." Unilever management was generally pleased with first-year results of the company's five-year Path to Growth initiative. Management believed its recent acquisitions had greatly strengthened the company's competitive position, giving it a "world-beating brand portfolio and unrivaled geographic coverage" (see Exhibit 11). Management also believed the company had built a solid platform for rapid growth in the food-service segment.

In 2000 Unilever divested its positions in baked goods, selling its European baking business to a Dutch food products company in July 2000 for €700 million in cash and then, as noted earlier, finding a buyer for the Bestfoods Baking Company several months after completing the Bestfoods acquisition.

In January 2001, Unilever sold its European dry soups and sauces businesses (including the Batchelors, Oxo, Royco, McDonnell's, Bla Band, and Heisse Tasse brands) to Campbell Soup for €1 billion; also included in the sale was the Lesieur brand of the mayonnaise products sold in France. The brands sold to Campbell's had combined sales of €435 million in 2000; EBITDA of €87 million, EBIT of €78 million, assets of €100 million, and about 1,300 employees; overall sales of the products had grown at 1 percent annually over the last three years. Unilever's divestiture of these brands was undertaken to alleviate market power concerns expressed by the European Commission and gain the commission's approval of Unilever's acquisition of Bestfoods.

Exhibits 12 and 13 present Unilever's most recent financial statements. By year-end 2000, Unilever had refinanced much of the short-term debt used to finance the Bestfoods acquisition through various bond issues. Interest costs on the company's debt were said to average less than 7 percent and were expected to decline through 2001. Exhibits 14 and 15 present comparisons of Unilever's performance in 2000 versus 1999, by business group and by geographic region of the world.

In the first quarter of 2001, Unilever reported revenue gains of 20 percent over the first quarter of 2000 (partly due to the contributions of acquisitions made in 2000), total operating profit gains of 38 percent, and an operating profit margin of 12.4 percent. Global sales growth of the company's leading brands was 4.3 percent on an annualized basis, excluding acquisitions. Unlever's sales growth performance by geographic region was said to be in line with the Path to Growth strategy:

Region	1st Quarter 2001 versus 1st Quarter 2000	Growth due to Acquisitions Made in 2000	Sales Growth of Leading Unilever Brands
Western Europe	12%	9%	3%
North America	31	"Strong"	2
Africa, Middle East, Turkey	13	8%	8
Asia and Pacific	8	Not reported	9
Latin America	7	Not reported	10

exhibit 11   Market Standing of Core Products and Brands in Unilever's Portfolio, Year-end 2000

Product Category	Market Standing at Year-End 2000				
	North America	Europe	Latin America	Rest of World	Global
Mayonnaise/salad dressings	#1	#1	#1	#1	#1
Bouillons and hot sauces	#1	#1	#1	#2	#1
Dry soups	#1	#1	#2	#2	#1
Ice cream	#1	#1	#1	#1	#1
Margarines and spreads (excluding butter)	#1	#1	#1	#1	#1
Tea (black)	#1	#1	#1	#1	#1

Source: Unilever slide presentation posted at <www.unilever.com>, April 2001.

exhibit 12   Unilever's Consolidated Statement of Profit and Loss, 2000 versus 1999

2000 (€ million)	1999 (€ million)		2000 ($ million)	1999 ($ million)
47,582	40,977	**Group revenues**	**43,809**	43,650
44,637	40,977	Continuing operations	**41,098**	43,650
2,945		Acquisitions	**2,711**	
(44,280)	(36,674)	Operating costs	**(40,769)**	(39,066)
5,729	4,595	Group operating profit before exceptional items and amortization of goodwill and intangibles	**5,274**	4,895
(1,992)	(269)	Exceptional items	**(1,834)**	(287)
(435)	(23)	Amortization of goodwill and intangibles	**(400)**	(24)
3,302	4,303	**Group operating profit**	**3,040**	4,584
3,363	4,303	Continuing operations	**3,096**	4,584
(61)		Acquisitions	**(56)**	
57	42	Add: Share of operating profit of joint ventures	**52**	45
3,359	4,345	**Total operating profit**	**3,092**	4,629
3,408	4,345	Continuing operations	**3,137**	4,629
(49)		Acquisitions	**(45)**	
(4)	10	Other income from fixed investments	**(3)**	10
(632)	(14)	Interest	**(582)**	(15)
2,723	4,341	**Profit on ordinary activities before taxation**	**2,507**	4,624
(1,403)	(1,369)	Taxation on profit on ordinary activities	**(1,292)**	(1,458)
1,320	2,972	**Profit on ordinary activities after taxation**	**1,215**	3,166
(215)	(201)	Minority interests	**(198)**	(214)
1,105	2,771	**Net profit**	**1,017**	2,952
675	1,761	Attributable to: **NV**	**621**	1,876
430	1,010	**PLC**	**396**	1,076
(1,458)	(1,265)	Dividends	**(1,343)**	(1,348)
(44)	(20)	Preference dividends	**(41)**	(22)
(1,414)	(1,245)	Dividends on ordinary capital	**(1,302)**	(1,326)
(353)	1,506	**Result for the year retained**	**(326)**	1,604

Source: Unilever's annual review, 2000.

exhibit 13   Unilever's Consolidated Balance Sheet and Cash Flow Statement, 1999–2000 (at December 31)

Balance Sheet at 31 December					
2000 (€ million)	1999 (€ million)			2000 ($ million)	1999 ($ million)
37,463	9,606	**Fixed assets**		34,852	9,650
26,467	643	Goodwill and intangible assets		24,622	646
10,996	8,963	Other fixed assets		10,230	9,004
		Current assets			
5,421	5,124	Stocks		5,043	5,147
7,254	5,742	Debtors due within one year		6,749	5,768
2,563	1,943	Debtors due after more than one year		2,384	1,952
1,666		Acquired business held for resale		1,550	
3,273	5,473	Cash and current investments		3,045	5,498
20,177	18,282			18,771	18,365
		Creditors due within one year			
(16,675)	(2,936)	Borrowings		(15,513)	(2,949)
(11,689)	(9,198)	Trade and other creditors		(10,874)	(9,241)
(8,187)	6,148	**Net current assets**		(7,616)	6,175
29,276	15,754	**Total assets less current liabilities**		27,236	15,825
		Creditors due after more than one year			
13,066	1,853	Borrowings		12,155	1,862
1,019	979	Trade and other creditors		948	982
6,404	4,582	**Provisions for liabilities and charges**		5,958	4,603
618	579	**Minority interests**		575	581
8,169	7,761	**Capital and reserves**		7,600	7,797
6,300	6,122	Attributable to: **NV**		5,861	6,150
1,869	1,639	**PLC**		1,739	1,647
29,276	15,754	**Total capital employed**		27,236	15,825

Cash Flow Statement for the Year Ended 31 December					
2000 (€ million)	1999 (€ million)			2000 ($ million)	1999 ($ million)
6,738*	5,654	**Cash flow from operating activities**		6,203	6,023
38	28	Dividends from joint ventures		35	29
(798)	(156)	Returns on investments and servicing of finance		(735)	(167)
(1,734)	(1,443)	Taxation		(1,596)	(1,538)
(1,061)	(1,501)	Capital expenditure and financial investment		(977)	(1,599)
(27,373)	(362)	Acquisitions and disposals		(24,142)	(388)
(1,365)	(1,266)	Dividends paid on ordinary share capital		(1,257)	(1,348)
	(6,093)	Special dividend			(6,491)
(25,555)	(5,139)	**Cash flow before management of liquid resources and financing**		(22,469)	(5,479)
2,464	5,675	Management of liquid resources		2,268	6,047
22,902	(146)	Financing		21,085	(156)
(189)	390	**Increase/(decrease) in cash in the period**		884	412
(27,152)	(5,094)	**(Decrease)/increase in net funds in the period**		(25,310)	(6,101)

*Includes payments of €550 million to settle share options and similar obligations in Bestfoods consequent to the change of control.

Source: Unilever's annual review, 2000.

exhibit 14 Summary of Unilever's Performance, 2000 versus 1999, by Group (in billions of Euros and Dollars)

| | Euros | | | | U.S. Dollars | |
	2000 (at constant 1999 exchange rates)	2000 (at current 2000 exchange rates)	1999 (at current 1999 exchange rates)	Percent change† (at constant 1999 exchange rates)	2000 (at current 2000 exchange rates)	1999 (at current 1999 exchange rates)
Revenues						
Food Group	22.3	23.9	20.3	9%	22.0	21.7
Home and Personal Care Group	20.8	22.8	19.8	5%	21.0	21.1
Operating profit						
Food Group	1.6	1.7	1.8	(8)%	1.6	1.9
Home and Personal Care Group	1.5	1.5	2.4	(38)%	1.4	2.5
Operating profit BEIA*						
Food Group	2.6	2.7	2.0	26%	2.5	2.2
Home and Personal Care Group	2.7	3.0	2.4	11%	2.7	2.6

*BEIA = Before exceptional items and amortization of goodwill and intangibles.
†Calculated using unrounded numbers for revenues and operating profits.
Source: Unilever annual review, 2000.

exhibit 15 Summary of Unilever's Performance, 2000 versus 1999, by Geographic Area (in billions of Euros and Dollars)

| | Euros | | | | U.S. Dollars | |
	2000 (at constant 1999 exchange rates)	2000 (at current 2000 exchange rates)	1999 (at current 1999 exchange rates)	Percent change† (at constant 1999 exchange rates)	2000 (at current 2000 exchange rates)	1999 (at current 1999 exchange rates)
Revenues						
Europe	19.2	19.8	18.8	2%	18.2	20.0
North America	10.0	11.6	8.8	13%	10.7	9.4
Africa & Middle East	2.4	2.4	2.3	3%	2.3	2.4
Asia & Pacific	7.2	8.0	6.7	7%	7.4	7.2
Latin America	5.0	5.7	4.3	14%	5.2	4.6
Operating profit						
Europe	1.7	1.8	2.2	(20)%	1.6	2.3
North America	0.1	0.2	0.8	(83)%	0.2	0.9
Africa & Middle East	0.2	0.2	0.3	(10)%	0.2	0.3
Asia & Pacific	0.7	0.8	0.6	11%	0.7	0.7
Latin America	0.3	0.3	0.4	(21)%	0.3	0.4
Operating profit BEIA*						
Europe	2.4	2.5	2.3	6%	2.3	2.4
North America	1.3	1.5	1.0	30%	1.4	1.0
Africa & Middle East	0.3	0.3	0.3	9%	0.3	0.3
Asia & Pacific	0.8	0.9	0.7	23%	0.8	0.7
Latin America	0.5	0.6	0.4	24%	0.6	0.5

*BEIA = Before exceptional items and amortization of goodwill and intangibles.

†Calculated using unrounded numbers for revenues and operating profits.

Source: Unilever annual review, 2000.

case 23
PepsiCo's Acquisition of Quaker Oats

John E. Gamble
University of South Alabama

In 2001, PepsiCo was the world's fifth-largest food and beverage company, with such brands as Lay's, Tostitos, Mountain Dew, Pepsi, Doritos, Aquafina, and Lipton contributing to revenues of approximately $26 billion. PepsiCo's revenues had reached $31 billion in 1996, but a new corporate strategy embarked upon in 1997 slimmed the company's portfolio from a collection of fast-food restaurants, snack foods, and beverages to a sharply focused lineup of convenience foods and beverages. Between 1997 and 1999, CEO Roger Enrico spun off Kentucky Fried Chicken (KFC), Taco Bell, and Pizza Hut as one independent, publicly traded company; created a stand-alone soft-drink bottling business through an initial public offering; and entered additional snack and beverage categories with the acquisitions of Cracker Jack and Tropicana. Enrico's focus on convenience foods and beverages placed PepsiCo in food and beverage categories that grew at twice the 2 percent industry growth rate and gave it a 2-to-1 market share lead over its nearest competitor in the convenience food and beverage industry.

Roger Enrico and Quaker Oats Company's CEO, Robert Morrison, jointly announced on December 4, 2000, that PepsiCo would acquire Quaker Oats. The move would combine PepsiCo's 13 brands (with retail sales of more than $1 billion each) with Quaker's market-leading Gatorade sports drinks and Quaker granola bars and hot breakfast products. The merger was approved by the U.S. Federal Trade Commission in August 2001 and gave PepsiCo a platform to continue to lead the food and beverage industry not only in revenue growth but also in operating profit and earnings growth. PepsiCo's chairman and CEO Steve Reinemund, who succeeded Roger Enrico in May 2001, commented that the acquisition of Quaker Oats would insert the leading sports drink into PepsiCo's portfolio and provide ample opportunities for revenue growth and cost sharing through synergies existing between PepsiCo's and Quaker's brands:

> Quaker brings to PepsiCo a very wide range of benefits that touch virtually every one of our businesses. With Gatorade, we'll add the leading isotonic brand to our beverage portfolio. Quaker's high-efficient broker-warehouse system will help Tropicana accelerate national distribution and growth of its shelf stable products. The Quaker brand and the company's line of wholesome snacks gives us an ideal way to expand beyond salty snacks. And bringing our companies together will create literally hundreds of millions of dollars in purchasing, manufacturing and distribution synergies.[1]

[1] "PepsiCo and Quaker Complete Their Merger, Forming the Fifth Largest Food and Beverage Company," *PR Newswire,* August 2, 2001.

PepsiCo's chief managers anticipated that, by 2004, the inclusion of Quaker Oats brands in PepsiCo's portfolio would also increase annual operating cash flow by $4 billion and improve return on invested capital by 100 basis points per year, to reach 30 percent by 2005. With the exception of volatility in the months following the Quaker acquisition announcement, the market had reacted favorably to the transformation of PepsiCo, with the value of its common shares improving from about $30 in 1997 to over $45 in late 2001. Summaries of PepsiCo's and Quaker Oats' financial performance are shown in Exhibits 1 and 2, respectively. Exhibit 3 tracks PepsiCo's market performance between 1991 and 2001.

COMPANY HISTORY

PepsiCo was founded in 1965 when Pepsi-Cola's CEO and president at the time, Donald M. Kendall, approached Herman Lay, Frito-Lay's chairman and CEO, with a proposition: "You make them thirsty, and I'll give them Pepsi."[2] Kendall envisioned a food and beverage company with complementary products that would provide ample opportunities for cost sharing, joint merchandising, and knowledge and skills transfer. The new company was founded with annual revenues of $510 million and such well-known brands as Pepsi-Cola, Mountain Dew, Fritos, Lay's, Chee-tos, Ruffles, and Rold Gold. PepsiCo's roots can be traced to 1898, when Caleb Bradham, a pharmacist in New Bern, North Carolina, created the formula for a carbonated beverage he named Pepsi-Cola. The history of the company's salty snacks began in 1932 when Elmer Doolin of San Antonio, Texas, purchased the recipe for an unknown product called a corn chip and began manufacturing and marketing the chips he branded Fritos. Another event that occurred in 1932 that marked the beginning of Frito-Lay was the decision of Nashville, Tennessee, businessman Herman W. Lay to start a potato chip distribution business. Sales increased such that, in 1938, Lay bought the company that supplied him with chips and renamed it H. W. Lay Company. Doolin and Lay agreed to merge Fritos and the H. W. Lay Company in 1961.

Kendall, who retained the role of CEO of the newly merged company, pushed PepsiCo's growth forward with new product introductions, expansion into international markets, and clever advertising campaigns. Under Kendall, PepsiCo introduced Doritos and Funyuns; entered markets in Japan and eastern Europe; and launched Mountain Dew's first advertising campaign, which proclaimed, "Yahoo Mountain Dew." Kendall also oversaw not only rapid capacity expansion that averaged one new snack food plant per year but also the development of Pepsi-Cola's "Pepsi Generation" advertising campaign, intended to appeal to the youthful baby boomers of the late 1960s. By the time Kendall turned over the reins to Andrall Pearson in 1971, PepsiCo had more than doubled its revenues, to $1 billion.

Pearson, like Kendall, pursued growth through new product development, international expansion, and aggressive marketing. One of Pearson's first moves was to change the hillbilly theme of Mountain Dew's advertising and packaging graphics to action-oriented scenes. The advertising and packaging changes, along with the new slogan "Put a little yahoo in your life," made Mountain Dew one of the 10 best-selling soft drinks in the United States within a year. PepsiCo became the first foreign product sold in the Soviet Union in 1972, expanded into China in 1982, and by 1984 sold products in nearly 150 countries and territories. New brands launched under Pearson's

---

[2]"The Sweet Spot of Convenient Food and Beverages," *Business Week Online*, April 10, 2000.

exhibit 1 Financial Summary for PepsiCo, Inc., 1991–2000 (in millions, except per share amounts)

	2000	1999	1998	1997	1996	1995	1994	1993	1992	1991
Net sales	$20,438	$20,367	$22,348	$20,917	$31,645	$30,421	$28,472	$25,021	$21,970	$19,292
Operating profit	3,225	2,818	2,584	2,662	2,546	2,987	3,201	2,907	2,371	2,112
Interest expense, net	145	245	321	353	474	555	555	484	472	452
Gain on bottling transactions	—	1,000	—	—	—	—	—	—	—	—
Income from continuing operations before income taxes and cumulative effect of accounting changes	3,210	3,656	2,263	2,309	2,047	2,432	2,664	2,423	1,899	1,660
Income taxes—current and deferred	1,027	1,606	270	818	898	826	880	835	597	580
Income from continuing operations before cumulative effect of accounting changes	2,183	2,050	1,993	1,491	1,149	1,606	1,784	1,588	1,302	1,080
Cumulative effect of accounting changes	—	—	—	—	—	—	(34)	—	(928)	—
Net income	$ 2,183	$ 2,050	$ 1,993	$ 1,491	$ 1,149	$ 1,606	$ 1,752	$ 1,588	$ 374	$ 1,080
Net income per share	$ 1.51	$ 1.40	$ 1.35	$ 0.98	$ 0.70	$ 1.00	$ 1.09	$ 0.98	$ 0.23	$ 0.68
Cash dividends declared per share	$ 0.56	$ 0.54	$ 0.52	$ 0.49	$ 0.45	$ 0.39	$ 0.35	$ 0.30	$ 0.26	$ 0.23
Total assets	$18,339	$17,551	$22,660	$20,101	$24,512	$25,432	$24,792	$23,706	$20,951	$18,775
Long-term debt	$ 2,346	$ 2,812	$ 4,028	$ 4,946	$ 8,174	$ 8,439	$ 8,509	$ 8,841	$ 7,443	$ 7,965
Capital spending	$ 1,067	$ 1,118	$ 1,405	$ 1,506	$ 2,287	$ 2,104	$ 2,253	$ 1,982	$ 1,550	$ 1,458

Source: PepsiCo, Inc., 2000 10-K.

exhibit 2 Financial Summary for Quaker Oats Company, 1995–2000 (in millions, except per share amounts)

	2000	1999	1998	1997	1996	1995
Net sales	$5,041.0	$4,725.2	$4,842.5	$5,015.7	$5,199.0	$5,954.0
Gross profit	2,752.7	2,588.4	2,468.1	2,450.8	2,391.5	2,659.6
Income (loss) before income taxes	551.1	618.3	396.6	−1,064.3	415.6	1,220.5
Provision (benefit) for income taxes	190.5	163.3	112.1	−133.4	167.7	496.5
Net income (loss)	$ 360.6	$ 455.0	$ 284.5	($930.9)	$ 247.9	$ 724.0
Per common share:						
Net income (loss)	$ 2.71	$ 3.36	$ 2.04	($6.80)	$ 1.80	$ 5.39
Net income (loss)—diluted	$ 2.61	$ 3.23	$ 1.97	($6.80)	$ 1.78	$ 5.23
Dividends declared:						
Common stock	$ 149.3	$ 151.8	$ 155.2	$ 155.9	$ 153.3	$ 150.8
Per common share	$ 1.14	$ 1.14	$ 1.14	$ 1.14	$ 1.14	$ 1.14
Average number of common shares outstanding (in thousands)	131,689	134,027	137,185	137,460	135,466	134,149
Financial statistics						
Working capital	$ 153.3	$ 58.4	$ 105.9	$ 187.3	($465.0)	($621.6)
Property, plant, and equipment—net	$1,120.0	$1,106.7	$1,070.2	$1,164.7	$1,200.7	$1,167.8
Depreciation expense	$ 123.5	$ 114.0	$ 116.3	$ 122.0	$ 119.1	$ 115.3
Total assets	$2,418.8	$2,396.2	$2,510.3	$2,697.0	$4,394.4	$4,620.4
Long-term debt	$ 664.1	$ 715.0	$ 795.1	$ 887.6	$ 993.5	$1,051.8
Common shareholders' equity	$ 354.7	$ 197.3	$ 151.0	$ 228.0	$1,229.9	$1,079.3
Market price range of common stock:						
High	$98 15/16	$71	$65 9/16	$55 1/8	$39 1/2	$37 1/2
Low	45 13/16	50 7/8	48 1/2	34 3/8	30 7/8	30 1/4

Source: Quaker Oats Company 2000 10-K.

exhibit 3   Monthly Performance of PepsiCo, Inc.'s Stock Price,
1991 to December 2001

(a) Trend in PepsiCo, Inc.'s Common Stock Price

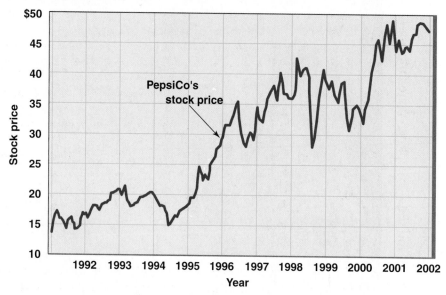

(b) Performance of PepsiCo, Inc.'s Stock Price versus the S&P 500 Index

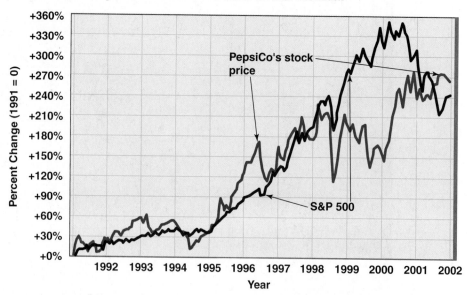

tenure as president and CEO included Pepsi Light in 1975, Grandma's cookies in
1980, Tostitos in 1981, Pepsi Free in 1982, and Slice in 1984.

In addition, Pearson crafted a corporate strategy that called for PepsiCo's diversification into quick-service restaurants. PepsiCo had diversified beyond snack foods
and soft drinks with the acquisitions of North American Van Lines in 1968 and Wilson
Sporting Goods in 1970, but the company's acquisition of Pizza Hut in 1977 signifi-

cantly shaped the strategic direction of PepsiCo for the next 20 years. The acquisitions of Taco Bell in 1978 and Kentucky Fried Chicken in 1986 created a business portfolio described by Wayne Calloway, PepsiCo's CEO between 1986 and 1996, as a balanced three-legged stool. Pearson and Calloway believed that, whereas soft drinks and snack foods were complementary businesses offering skills transfer and cost sharing benefits, quick-service restaurants offered a captive market for Pepsi-Cola's fountain drinks and positioned the company in an additional high-growth industry. Furthermore, PepsiCo's considerable marketing expertise could be leveraged in the marketing of fried chicken, pizza, and Mexican fast foods. North American Van Lines and Wilson Sporting Goods were divested from PepsiCo's three-legged stool portfolio in 1984 and 1985, respectively.

PepsiCo strengthened its portfolio during the 1980s and early to mid-1990s with such snack food and beverage acquisitions as Mug root beer and 7UP International in 1986, and the UK's Walker's Crisps and Smith's Crisps and U.S. ready-to-eat popcorn brand Smartfood in 1989. Mexican cookie company Gamesa was added in 1990, and SunChips was acquired in 1991. Calloway added Hot 'N Now (a drive-through-only hamburger chain) in 1990; California Pizza Kitchen in 1992; and East Side Mario's, D'Angelo's Sandwich Shop, and Chevys Mexican Restaurants in 1993.

The company expanded beyond carbonated beverages with a 1992 agreement with Ocean Spray to distribute single-serving juices; the 1993 introduction of Lipton ready-to-drink teas; and the 1994 introduction of Aquafina bottled water, All Sport isotonic sports drinks, and Frappucino ready-to-drink coffees. The company became a leader in the use of celebrities to endorse its soft drinks and snack foods during the 1980s and 1990s with memorable ads featuring Michael Jackson, Michael J. Fox, Ray Charles, Billy Crystal, George Foreman, Shaquille O'Neal, and André Agassi. PepsiCo's business portfolio was refocused on soft drinks and snack foods in 1997 when CEO Roger Enrico spun off all of the company's restaurants as an independent, publicly traded company. PepsiCo shareholders received one share of the new company, Tricon Global Restaurants, for every 10 shares they held in PepsiCo.

During the late 1990s, PepsiCo acquired Cracker Jack from Borden Foods, Tropicana from Seagram Company Ltd., and Smith's Snackfood Company in Australia from United Biscuits Holdings. The company also introduced Doritos 3D's tortilla chips and Pepsi One during the 1990s. In 2000, PepsiCo launched its FruitWorks line of fruit drinks and Sierra Mist lemon-lime soda, and Aquafina became the number one brand of bottled water sold in the United States. South Beach Beverage Company, the maker of SoBe teas and alternative beverages; Tasali Snack Foods, the leader in the Saudi Arabian salty snack market; and the Quaker Oats Company were acquired by PepsiCo in 2001. Also in 2001, PepsiCo continued its tradition of utilizing high-profile celebrities with a multiyear endorsement agreement with Britney Spears. Exhibit 4 presents PepsiCo's portfolio of brands and products in 2001.

PEPSICO'S BUSINESS PORTFOLIO AND PERFORMANCE UNDER WAYNE CALLOWAY

Wayne Calloway, PepsiCo's chairman of the board and chief executive officer from 1986 to 1996, believed that a portfolio of beverages, snack foods, and fast-food restaurants offered valuable synergy and strategic fit opportunities because of the similarity of each industry's value chain and key success factors. Competitive success in all three industries was, in large part, a function of a company's ability to create a distinctive

exhibit 4   PepsiCo's Brand and Product Portfolio, 2001

Frito-Lay Brands	Pepsi-Cola brands	Gatorade brands
Lay's potato chips	Pepsi-Cola	Gatorade thirst quencher
Baked Lay's potato crisps	Diet Pepsi	Gatorade Frost
Ruffles potato chips	Pepsi One	Gatorade Fierce
Baked Ruffles potato chips	Wild Cherry Pepsi	Gatorade energy bar
Doritos tortilla chips	Mountain Dew	Propel fitness water
3D's snacks	Mountain Dew Code Red	**Quaker brands**
Tostitos tortilla chips	Slice	Quaker Oats
Baked Tostitos tortilla chips	Mug	Quaker instant oatmeal
Santitas tortilla chips	Sierra Mist	Cap'n Crunch cereal
Fritos corn chips	FruitWorks	Life cereal
Chee-tos cheese flavored snacks	Lipton Brisk (Partnership)	Quaker Toasted Oatmeal cereal
Rold Gold pretzels	Lipton's Iced Tea (Partnership)	Quaker 100% Natural cereal
Funyons onion flavored rings	Aquafina	Quaker Toasted Oatmeal
SunChips multigrain snacks	Frappuccino (Partnership)	Squares cereal
Cracker Jack candy-coated popcorn	SoBe	Quisp cereal
Chester's popcorn	**Pepsi-Cola outside the United States**	King Vitaman cereal
Grandma's cookies		Quaker Bagged cereals
Munchos potato crisps	Mirinda	Quaker Ohs! cereal
Smartfood popcorn	7UP	Mother's cereal
Baken-ets fried pork skins	Pepsi Max	Quaker rice cakes
Oberto meat snacks	**Tropicana brands**	Quaker Crispy Mini's rice snacks
Frito-Lay dips and salsa	Tropicana Pure Premium	Quaker Chewy granola bars
Frito-Lay outside the United States	Tropicana Season's Best	Quaker Fruit & Oatmeal bars
Bocabits wheat snacks	Tropicana Twister	Rice-A-Roni
Crujitos corn snacks	Dole (Under license)	Pasta Roni
Fandangos corn snacks	Tropicana Pure Tropics	Near East couscous/pilafs
Hamkas snacks	**Tropicana outside the United States**	Aunt Jemima mixes & syrups
Niknaks cheese sticks		Quaker grits
Quavers potato snacks	Loóza	**Quaker outside the United States**
Sabritas potato chips	Copella	FrescAvena beverage powder
Twisties cheese snacks	Frui'Vita	Toddy chocolate powder
Walker's potato crisps	Tropicana 100	ToddYnho chocolate drink
Jack's snacks		Coqueiro canned fish
Simba snacks		Sugar Puffs cereal
		Harvest Crunch cereal
		Cruesli cereal
		Quaker Oatso Simple hot cereal
		Scott's Porage Oats
		Quaker Snack-a-Jacks rice cakes
		Quaker Dipps granola bars

Source: PepsiCo website.

image and to develop innovative and tasty new products. Under Calloway, PepsiCo made it a regular practice to move its best managers from positions in one business unit to assignments in the other two business segments to promote the transfer of skills, practices, know-how, and innovative ideas from one business to another. Calloway believed that such shifting of key personnel helped PepsiCo capture strategic fit relationships among its different businesses, build stronger competitive capabilities, and keep managers' thinking fresh and innovative.

Experience in the company's soft-drink business was essential for managers wishing to rise through the ranks since it was PepsiCo's oldest and largest business. In 1996, the Pepsi-Cola business unit was the world's second-largest manufacturer and marketer of soft drinks. Frito-Lay was also an essential stop for advancing managers since it was PepsiCo's most profitable division—accounting for 28 percent of company sales and 48 percent of its profits in 1995. Frito-Lay had captured over one-half of the $12.1 billion U.S. salty snack food market, and its pound volume grew 10 times faster than the industry in 1995. A Frito-Lay executive assessed the company's competitive position in the industry: "Basically, we are the category."[3]

The inclusion of quick-service restaurants was the most distinctive characteristic of PepsiCo's business portfolio under Wayne Calloway. In 1996, PepsiCo's restaurant segment was comprised of three worldwide fast-food franchise systems (Pizza Hut, Taco Bell, and KFC) and a group of five lesser restaurant chains (California Pizza Kitchen, Chevys Mexican Restaurants, Hot 'N Now, East Side Mario's, and D'Angelo's Sandwich Shops); together, these formed the largest restaurant conglomerate in the world. KFC, Pizza Hut, and Taco Bell, collectively had over 28,500 units and worldwide sales of $11.3 billion in 1995. All three were ranked among the top five U.S. chains. The company and its franchisees operated over 8,000 international units located in 94 countries and had international systemwide sales of $6.5 billion in 1995.

Pizza Hut, the leading pizza chain in the world in 1995, had a 51 percent market share of the $15.6 billion U.S. franchised pizza market. Taco Bell was the leading Mexican fast-food chain, with only a few regional competitors; its 1995 systemwide domestic sales of $4.9 billion represented 68 percent of the $7.2 billion Mexican fast-food industry segment. KFC had domestic system sales of about $7.3 billion in 1995 and accounted for 70 percent of the U.S. chicken market. With over 5,000 units, it had more than four times as many U.S. restaurants as the next-largest chicken chain.

Whereas PepsiCo's early restaurant acquisition strategy was to acquire established market leaders, the company later acquired small, relatively unknown companies that might be entering a rapid period of growth. Hot 'N Now was acquired in 1990 and California Pizza Kitchen, a joint venture formed in 1992, was a full-service restaurant that featured pizzas cooked in wood-fired ovens. East Side Mario's, and D'Angelo's Sandwich shops, and Chevys Mexican Restaurants were all acquired in 1993. East Side Mario's and D'Angelo's were operated by Pizza Hut management. All D'Angelo's were integrated within Pizza Hut units. Chevys and Hot 'N Now were part of the Taco Bell organization.

Pearson and Calloway found the quick-service restaurant industry appealing because, beginning in the late 1960s, Americans had spent a rising portion of their food dollars at restaurants. Demographic factors, such as more two-income families and an increase in the number of households made up of singles, along with a growing desire for better-quality leisure time, had combined to make eating out an attractive alternative to preparing meals at home. In 1995, consumers worldwide spent over $150 billion dollars at fast-food restaurants. U.S. fast-food sales grew at a compounded annual rate of 6 percent between 1990 and 1996 to reach $100 billion as Americans increased

[3]*Brandweek,* March 18, 1996, p. 33.

the percentage of food dollars spent in restaurants from 33 percent in 1980 to 50 percent in 1996.

Even though consumers were eating a greater number of meals away from home, the fast-food segment of the restaurant industry became challenged by market saturation and increasing price competition during the 1990s. Fast-food companies not only expanded the number of freestanding locations convenient to motorists but also expanded to such nontraditional locations as sports stadiums, airports, large-scale discount warehouses, shopping malls, university dining halls, and gasoline stations. In 1995, the 191,000 fast-food restaurants in the United States represented a 74 percent increase since 1980. The growing numbers of fast-food outlets and value-conscious consumers produced strong price competition among the leading fast-food chains, with an increasing reliance on discounted value meals to increase volume at the expense of margins.

As the U.S. market became more saturated and competitive, the leading franchised restaurants focused greater attention on international markets as a source of growth. While the international fast-food market was approximately half the size of the U.S. market, many countries offered faster near-term growth rates and even greater long-term potential as their markets for fast food developed. Even though international markets were attractive to U.S.-based fast-food companies, there were many risks associated with entering international markets. In addition to the challenge of satisfying international taste preferences, fast-food companies experienced difficulties in repatriating profits because of local government restrictions and international currency fluctuations. Also, site development costs abroad were frequently higher than in the United States, and qualified suppliers were not readily available.

In 1996, as the attractiveness of the global fast-food industry continued to decline, a number of investors and Wall Street analysts expressed the opinion that PepsiCo should divest or spin off its restaurant businesses. Hot 'N Now and Chevys had both experienced operating losses in 1995, and, while KFC units had steady same store sales in 1996, the same store sales of Taco Bell and Pizza Hut had been in decline since 1994. A summary of operating results for PepsiCo's three business units during 1993–96 is provided in Exhibit 5. Annual revenues and the number of units for the leading U.S. quick-service chicken, Mexican, and pizza chains in 1995 are given in Exhibit 6.

ROGER ENRICO AND THE RESTRUCTURING OF PEPSICO'S PORTFOLIO

Early in 1996, Wayne Calloway announced that he would resign as CEO of PepsiCo because of his ongoing battle with cancer. PepsiCo shareholders had fared well during Calloway's 10-year reign, with the company's stock price increasing from $4⅜ in 1986 to its year-end 1995 price of $27¹⁵⁄₁₆. PepsiCo's shares appreciated 54 percent in 1995 alone. Roger Enrico, a 25-year veteran of the company with experience in all three of the company's business segments, became PepsiCo's new chief executive officer on April 1, 1996. Enrico joined PepsiCo in Frito-Lay's marketing department in 1971, where he remained until becoming president and CEO of PepsiCo's beverage segment in 1983. Roger Enrico left the Pepsi-Cola beverages unit in 1991 to become CEO of Frito-Lay. In 1994, Enrico moved from Frito-Lay to head up the company's restaurant businesses.

exhibit 5   Selected Financial Results for PepsiCo's Three Major Lines
of Business, 1993–96 (in millions)

	Beverages	Restaurants	Snack Foods	Corporate
North American sales				
1996	$ 7,725	$9,110	$6,618	
1995	7,400	9,202	5,863	
1994	6,541	8,694	5,356	
1993	5,918	8,026	4,674	
International sales				
1996	$ 2,799	$2,331	$3,062	
1995	2,982	2,126	2,682	
1994	2,535	1,827	2,908	
1993	2,148	1,330	2,353	
North American operating profits				
1996	$ 1,428	$ 370	$1,286	
1995	1,249	726	1,149	
1994	1,115	637	1,043	
1993	804	685	901	
International operating profits				
1996	$ (846)	$ 153	$ 346	
1995	117	112	301	
1994	136	86	354	
1993	97	109	285	
Assets				
1996	$ 9,816	$6,435	$6,279	$ 607
1995	10,032	6,759	5,451	1,555
1994	9,566	7,203	5,044	1,684
1993	9,105	6,412	4,995	2,103
Depreciation				
1996	$ 440	$ 546	$ 346	$7
1995	445	579	304	7
1994	385	539	297	7
1993	359	457	279	7
Capital expenditures				
1996	$ 648	$ 657	$ 973	$ 9
1995	566	750	769	34
1994	677	1,072	532	7
1993	491	1,005	491	21

Source: 1996 PepsiCo, Inc. 10-K.

Each of the three PepsiCo business segments had prospered under Enrico's leadership. In the 1980s, Enrico initiated and launched a new advertising campaign for Pepsi-Cola that included the combination of new slogans, taste testing, and endorsements from celebrities like Michael Jackson and Madonna and quickly revitalized

exhibit 6 Sales and Units of Leading U.S. Restaurants in the Chicken, Pizza, and Mexican Segments, 1995

	Sales (in millions)	Units
Chicken segment		
KFC	$7,275	5,142
Church's Chicken	737	1,165
Popeye's Famous Fried Chicken & Biscuits	710	907
Chick-fil-A	502	592
Kenny Rogers Roasters	285	250
El Pollo Loco	200	250
Boston Market	159	1,023
Grandy's	156	184
Lee's Famous Recipe Chicken	152	274
Bojangle's Famous Chicken & Biscuits	101	206
Pizza segment		
Pizza Hut	$7,900	10,648
Domino's Pizza	2,650	5,079
Little Caesars	2,000	4,700
Papa John's	458	632
Round Table Pizza	376	562
Chuck E. Cheese's	263	332
Shakey's	250	450
Godfather's	250	522
Pizza Inn	233	475
California Pizza Kitchen	171	70
Mexican segment		
Taco Bell	$4,925	5,950
Chi-Chi's	341	1,375
El-Torito	237	105
Del Taco	216	266
Taco John's	166	420
Taco Cabana	158	127
Chevys Fresh Mex	150	54
El Chico	144	94
Taco Time	115	306
Don Pablo's	89	76

Source: *Restaurants & Institutions,* July 1, 1996.

Pepsi-Cola's stodgy image. Enrico's marketing strategy was so successful that it was credited with enticing Coca-Cola into the disastrous introduction of New Coke in 1985. Roger Enrico detailed the rivalry between the two soft-drink companies and the failure of New Coke in his 1986 book, *The Other Guy Blinked: How Pepsi Won the Cola Wars.*

While at Frito-Lay, Enrico improved the snack food division's performance by dramatically cutting costs and improving the quality of Frito-Lay's products. During his tenure as head of PepsiCo Worldwide Restaurants, Enrico pushed successfully for new product introductions that helped bolster same-store sales. He also instituted a restaurant refranchising plan intended to lessen the restaurant group's dependency on capital and cash infusions from PepsiCo's other business segments to finance the construction of new restaurants.

Within months of taking over, however, Roger Enrico found himself having to deal with a number of fairly serious problems at PepsiCo. The company's beverage business began to fall behind Coca-Cola by a growing margin in both domestic and international markets. Also, PepsiCo's restaurant businesses were plagued with declining same-store sales and narrowing profit margins. Enrico's solutions to strategic issues confronting PepsiCo gradually unfolded between 1996 and 2001 and involved restructuring PepsiCo's business portfolio.

Enrico's Spinoff of KFC, Pizza Hut, and Taco Bell

In late 1996, Roger Enrico proposed to PepsiCo's board that the company's restaurants should be eliminated from the company's portfolio of businesses with its three major restaurant chains spun off as an independent publicly traded company and its lesser-known chains being divested prior to the spinoff. The board approved the plan in January 1997, and in October that year the divestitures of KFC, Taco Bell, and Pizza Hut had been completed with the creation of Tricon Global Restaurants. Analysts and investors applauded the spinoff since there was a pervasive belief that PepsiCo's restaurants limited investment in the company's snack food and beverage businesses and severely impaired the corporation's overall operating and profit margins. When asked to discuss the initial acquisitions of KFC, Taco Bell, and Pizza Hut and the 1997 spinoff, Enrico commented:

> Clearly, you can't say it was a total failure for PepsiCo to be in the restaurant business. That would be completely wrong. The things that were important to those businesses when PepsiCo got in, PepsiCo had an ability to contribute: cash . . . we had lots of cash. [Also] we could provide the same people standard and process [as what was found at Frito-Lay and Pepsi-Cola]. And the third was marketing, because you had to build these brands. When we bought Pizza Hut, it wasn't a very big business. When we bought Taco Bell, it was this tiny business. Shakey's was bigger than Pizza Hut when we bought it.
>
> But now we were faced with a different strategic situation. The [restaurant] business was built out for the most part. What was going to be important going forward was the operating side of the business—the customer service, the quality of the product, the value equation. Those things really needed a restaurant culture and processes. They had nothing to do with Pepsi-Cola or Frito-Lay. You can't have two different cultures in a corporation. One culture has to be dominant. The Frito-Pepsi culture is very similar. Our culture was not conducive to what you needed to win in restaurants. It was a good business for us right up until the late '80s, when the industry was faced with overcapacity, with too many units and demand slowing down. And we got into casual dining [Chevys Mexican Restaurants and California Pizza Kitchen] just as demand almost collapsed.[4]

The Acquisition of Cracker Jack

PepsiCo acquired Borden Foods' 104-year-old snack mix of candy-coated popcorn and peanuts—Cracker Jack— in late 1997. In the year prior to its acquisition by PepsiCo, Cracker Jack recorded sales of $40 million and had failed to break even for its fifth

---

[4]"The Sweet Spot of Convenient Food and Beverages."

consecutive year. Borden Foods had neglected the brand, with little advertising since the late 1970s and no innovations to the product formulation or packaging. Enrico saw the product as a natural fit with Frito-Lay's product line and believed that the brand could quickly grow sales through Frito-Lay's direct-store delivery system that could put Cracker Jack in 470,000 retail outlets within weeks of the acquisition. A Frito-Lay executive who championed the acquisition discussed the additional appeal of Cracker Jack: "We were missing out on 50 percent of the snacking opportunity because when people snack, they first decide whether to go for a salty treat or a sweet one." The executive also commented that the product met Frito-Lay's "mindlessly nibbling test" since "once you open the bag, you just keep eating them until they're gone."[5]

PepsiCo retained Cracker Jack's iconic box, but also made the sweet snack available in new four- and eight-ounce bags and added 10 percent more peanuts and better prizes. New prizes in Cracker Jack packages included, for the first time since the early 1960s, plastic whistles and miniature baseball gloves, balls, and caps. Cracker Jack turned a profit during its first year under Frito-Lay management and increased its sales to more than $100 million within two years of the acquisition.

The Tropicana Acquisition

PepsiCo acquired Tropicana Products from Seagram Company Ltd. in August 1998 for $3.3 billion. The acquisition was the largest ever undertaken by PepsiCo and gave the company the world's largest producer and marketer of branded juices, with such well-known brands as Tropicana Pure Premium, Tropicana Season's Best, and Dole. Some analysts questioned Tropicana's $3.3 billion price given its 1997 sales of approximately $2 billion, but its 71 percent market share in the not-from-concentrate category of the orange juice market gave PepsiCo an almost four-to-one advantage over Coca-Cola's Minute Maid. In addition, PepsiCo's vast distribution system was expected to increase Tropicana's availability, and some believed that the orange juice market was far from mature. Tropicana's top executive argued that the brand could achieve rapid growth since fewer than 20 percent of breakfasts in North America included orange juice and since ample opportunity for international growth existed through PepsiCo's global distribution network.

The Spinoff and Initial Public Offering of PepsiCo's Bottling Operations

Throughout most of PepsiCo's history, management held the belief that corporate ownership of local bottling and distribution operations was critical to the overall success of the Pepsi-Cola Company. The company's management believed that control over local production and distribution would give it an advantage over Coca-Cola, which relied on independent bottlers to produce and distribute soft drinks to retailers. Small, local Coca-Cola bottlers began to disappear in the 1980s and 1990s, but the acquisitions were made by independent publicly traded companies such as Coca-Cola Enterprises and Coca-Cola Consolidated rather than by Coca-Cola. Coca-Cola Enterprises was the largest bottler and distributor of Coca-Cola products, with operations in 46 U.S. states; all 10 provinces in Canada; and portions of Europe including Belgium, France, Great Britain, Luxembourg, Monaco; and the Netherlands. Coca-Cola Enterprises' distribu-

---

[5]"PepsiCo's New Formula," *Business Week Online,* April 10, 2000.

tion of Coca-Cola products made it the world's largest bottler of nonalcoholic beverages. After more than a dozen acquisitions throughout the southeastern United States, Coca-Cola Consolidated became the second-largest Coca-Cola bottler, with selling territories in 11 states and a consumer base of more than 18 million people. Coca-Cola's strategy allowed it to keep low-margin, capital-intensive bottling operations (which required plants, trucks, and thousands of employees) off of its financial statements and focus on global marketing and high-margin sales of concentrate to bottlers.

In 1999, PepsiCo spun off more than 50 percent of its bottling operations around the world in four transactions that created four independent anchor bottlers. PepsiCo recorded a $1 million gain on the initial public offering (IPO) of the Pepsi Bottling Group (PBG) in March 1999. As an independent entity, PepsiCo believed that PBG would benefit from a sharper definition of its role and would be better able to execute its business strategy on a local market level. The spinoff would also allow PepsiCo to focus on the development of new products and marketing programs to support them. At the conclusion of the IPO, PBG became Pepsi-Cola's largest bottler, accounting for approximately 50 percent of the company's unit sales in the United States and 30 percent of unit sales worldwide. PepsiCo retained an equity interest in PBG of approximately 36 percent. Also in 1999, PepsiCo combined other bottling operations with those of three independent bottlers—Whitman Corporation; PepCom Industries, Inc.; and PepsiAmericas, Inc. PepsiCo maintained an equity interest in each of the expanded independent bottlers. In December 2000, Whitman Corporation merged with Pepsi-Americas.

Assessment of PepsiCo's Portfolio in 2000

PepsiCo's stock had traded erratically since Roger Enrico became the company's CEO, with the market seemingly unimpressed with the spinoff of the company's fast-food businesses, the IPO of its bottling operations, and the acquisition of Tropicana. Some analysts commented that Enrico lacked a corporate vision and overarching corporate strategy, but had repositioned the company through a series of isolated opportunistic moves. In a 2000 interview with *Business Week* reporters, Enrico explained the unfolding of his strategy for PepsiCo and took some blame for the company's poor market performance. He also suggested that PepsiCo's poor market performance was partly attributable to the popularity of technology sector stocks.

> Probably because we didn't articulate a strategy that [explained our decisions], we did confuse [investors]. To some degree that was my fault. If I had to do it over again, I would have come to these conclusions more quickly. Spin off the restaurants. IPO the bottling. Buy Tropicana—that was opportunistic. It had to be for sale. And I would have articulated these strategies we were going to embark on.
>
> Instead, so as not to be disruptive, we pooh-poohed the notion that we would do these things. But we had not decided to do them at the time. It would have been better had I decided these things more quickly and started with a very quick agenda rather than let it play out the way it did. I also felt it was important to have some success behind us. It probably caused me to procrastinate. If I went out and said, this was the strategy and here's why, I could have generated just as much support. But it would have been a lot to digest. The problem was, that if you articulated the strategy and then took a year to do it, you could have a disaster on your hands. As it was, we were very nervous. It took us nine months to do the spinoff of the restaurants because of IRS rules. It was hard enough then to keep it together.
>
> What I worry the most about is, "When will the financial market recognize that we are there?" Right now, I worry more about the stock price than I should. And [I worry more

exhibit 7   PepsiCo, Inc.'s Consolidated Statements of Income, 1998–2000 (in millions, except per share amounts)

	2000	1999	1998
Net sales			
New PepsiCo	$20,438	$18,244	$14,686
Bottling operations	—	2,123	7,662
Total net sales	20,438	20,367	22,348
Costs and expenses			
Cost of sales	7,943	8,198	9,330
Selling, general, and administrative expenses	9,132	9,103	9,924
Amortization of intangible assets	138	183	222
Impairment and restructuring charges	—	65	288
Total costs and expenses	17,213	17,549	19,764
Operating profit			
New PepsiCo	3,225	2,765	2,460
Bottling operations and equity investments	—	53	124
Total operating profit	3,225	2,818	2,584
Bottling equity income, net	130	83	—
Gain on bottling transactions	—	1,000	—
Interest expense	(221)	(363)	(395)
Interest income	76	118	74
Income before income taxes	3,210	3,656	2,263
Provision for income taxes	1,027	1,606	270
Net income	$ 2,183	$ 2,050	$ 1,993
Net income per share—basic	$1.51	$1.40	$1.35
Average shares outstanding—basic	1,446	1,466	1,480
Net income per share—assuming dilution	$1.48	$1.37	$1.31
Average shares outstanding—assuming dilution	1,475	1,496	1,519

Source: PepsiCo, Inc., 2000 10-K.

about] investor perceptions of this company more than I should. Some of that is the whole sector issue: The average consumer product company lost a quarter of its market value last year. That doesn't make me feel too good.

I absolutely think the stock in this company is undervalued. And I want to make sure that people are making their valuation judgments on the facts and on the new Pepsi and not on suppositions from the old Pepsi. I'm not sure I can convince people to change their sector allocations from the Internet to companies like ours. I think a lot of people are going to get burned big time on these ridiculously valued companies. And when that happens, I hope they don't get scared and rush their money out of the stock market but that they put it in more substantive investments like Pepsi.[6]

PepsiCo's consolidated statements of income from 1998 to 2000 are presented in Exhibit 7. The company's balance sheets for 1999 and 2000 are shown in Exhibit 8.

---

[6]"The Sweet Spot of Convenient Food and Beverages."

exhibit 8   PepsiCo, Inc.'s Consolidated Balance Sheets, 1999–2000 (in millions, except per share amounts)

	2000	1999
Assets		
Current assets		
Cash and cash equivalents	$ 864	$ 964
Short-term investments, at cost	466	92
Accounts and notes receivable, net	1,799	1,704
Inventories	905	899
Prepaid expenses and other current assets	570	514
Total current assets	4,604	4,173
Property, plant, and equipment—net	5,438	5,266
Intangible assets—net	4,485	4,735
Investments in unconsolidated affiliates	2,978	2,846
Other assets	834	531
Total assets	$18,339	$17,551
Liabilities and shareholders' equity		
Current liabilities		
Short-term borrowings	$ 72	$ 233
Accounts payable and other current liabilities	3,815	3,399
Income taxes payable	48	156
Total current liabilities	3,935	3,788
Long-term debt	2,346	2,812
Other liabilities	3,448	2,861
Deferred income taxes	1,361	1,209
Shareholders' equity		
Capital stock, par value 1⅔ cents per share: authorized 3,600 shares, issued 1,726 shares	29	29
Capital in excess of par value	955	1,081
Retained earnings	15,448	14,066
Accumulated other comprehensive loss	(1,263)	(989)
	15,169	14,187
Less: repurchased shares, at cost: 280 million shares and 271 million shares, respectively	(7,920)	(7,306)
Total shareholders' equity	7,249	6,881
Total liabilities and shareholders' equity	$18,339	$17,551

Source: PepsiCo, Inc., 2000 10-K.

The Quaker Oats Acquisition

Roger Enrico's worries about PepsiCo's share price came to an end not long after his interview with *Business Week,* as his analysis of Internet stocks proved correct, with such stocks as Amazon.com falling from nearly $100 per share in early 2000 to less than $20 per share in late 2000. Online auction company eBay's share price fell from over $120 to approximately $30 over the same period of time. PepsiCo's stock price appreciated by 40 percent within one year of Enrico's *Business Week* interview, and many investment analysts continued to rate PepsiCo as a buy when, in December 2000, Enrico and Quaker Oats CEO Robert Morrison jointly announced PepsiCo's proposed $14.15 billion acquisition of Quaker Oats Company. A Putnam portfolio manager told *Fortune* magazine in early 2001, "If Pepsi handles Quaker well, there could be a lot more upside here."[7]

At year-end 2000, Quaker Oats was a 99-year-old company that had achieved annual sales growth that, at 7 percent, outpaced the food and beverage industry; a 14 percent operating income growth rate; and, for the third consecutive year, an earnings growth rate in excess of 20 percent. The company also boasted some of the best-known brands in grain products: Quaker Oatmeal was the number one brand of hot cereals in the United States with a 60+ percent category share; Cap'n Crunch and Rice-A-Roni were brands many Americans had grown up with; and the company's Quaker rice cakes and Quaker Chewy Granola and Fruit & Oatmeal bars made it the leader in the U.S. rice/popcorn cake and cereal bar categories. However, Quaker's most valuable asset in its arsenal of brands was Gatorade.

Gatorade was developed by University of Florida researchers in 1965 but was not marketed commercially until the formula was sold to Stokely–Van Camp in 1967. When Quaker Oats acquired the brand from Stokely–Van Camp in 1983, Gatorade gradually made a transformation from a regionally distributed product with annual sales of $90 million to a $2 billion international powerhouse. At the time of Gatorade's acquisition by Quaker Oats, the beverage was available only in two flavors—lemon-lime and orange—and packaged only in one-quart glass bottles. Quaker Oats grew Gatorade into one of the largest beverage brands in the United States with the addition of 17 new flavors, various sized packaging, celebrity endorsements, and annual advertising expenditures of more than $75 million. In 1999, Gatorade's advertising budget of $81 million was five times greater than what Coca-Cola spent to support Powerade and 500 times as much as PepsiCo allocated to All Sport. Many of Gatorade's ads featured Michael Jordan, who signed a 10-year endorsement contract to promote the sports beverage in 1991. Quaker also signed athletes like soccer star Mia Hamm and New York Yankees shortstop Derek Jeter to broaden Gatorade's appeal. In 2000, Gatorade was the official drink of every major sports league except the National Hockey League, which adopted Powerade as its official isotonic beverage. Gatorade was also popular with college and high school sports programs and weekend athletes, who usually purchased Gatorade in grocery stores or convenience stores. Quaker Oats management had also begun to increase Gatorade's availability in vending machines and kiosks near golf courses, parks, and schools in 1999 and 2000.

Gatorade was able to grow by more than 10 percent annually during the 1990s, with no new entrant to the isotonic beverage category posing a serious threat to the brand's dominance. Its market share had held near 85 percent throughout the 1990s and in 2000, while over 100 new entrants to the category came and went. Neither Coke nor Pepsi was able to exploit its vast distribution systems to become a key challenger to Gatorade. A Quaker executive assessed the relative competitive strengths of Gatorade, Powerade, and All Sport by suggesting, "Coke and Pepsi had distribution,

---

[7]"Guess Who's Winning the Cola Wars," *Fortune* (Internet edition), April 2, 2001.

but we had brand equity."[8] The editor of *Beverage Digest* was impressed that Coke could win as much as an 11 percent market share in 1999 and commented on Coca-Cola's and Pepsi's difficulty in upending Gatorade: "Even for marketing powerhouses like Coke and Pepsi, competing against a brand which is well-established, strong, and continuously well-marketed is very difficult."[9]

PepsiCo, Coca-Cola, France's Danone Group, and Swiss food giant Nestlé all were attracted to Gatorade because of its commanding market share and because of the expected growth in the isotonic beverage category. In a trend that began in the 1980s, consumers were increasingly drawn to healthy food choices. Beginning in the late 1990s, beverages and food products with nutraceutical qualities—ingredients such as vitamins, herbs, and other dietary supplements—were growing at rapid rates. Gatorade, which was a borderline nutraceutical that included sodium, potassium, and chloride, appeared to have begun benefiting from the trend in 1999 when its sales grew by 18 percent. Gatorade's sales were up 15 percent during the first nine months of 2000, and many analysts projected that Gatorade's sales could grow by as much as 20 percent annually between 2000 and 2010. In 2000, Quaker Oats began marketing Gatorade Energy Bars and Propel fitness water—a bottled water including four B vitamins and two antioxidants (vitamins A and C)—to further capture growth in the demand for nutraceutical food and beverage products and exploit the Gatorade brand.

PepsiCo became the successful bidder for Quaker Oats and Gatorade with an agreement struck in December 2000; but this agreement would not receive U.S. Federal Trade Commission (FTC) approval until August 2001. The FTC's primary concern over the merger was that Gatorade's inclusion in PepsiCo's portfolio of snacks and beverages might give the company too much leverage in negotiations with convenience stores and ultimately force smaller snack food and beverage companies out of convenience store channels. The FTC was also concerned that PepsiCo's proposed sale of its All Sport isotonic brand to Monarch Company—a small, privately held beverage company that sold Dad's root beer and Moxie soft drinks—would allow All Sport to wither and eventually fail as an industry participant. All Sport was already a weak rival to Gatorade and Powerade, with total advertising expenditures from 1999 to mid-2001 of less than $380,000 and a 4 percent market share. The four-member panel of FTC commissioners was divided on blocking the merger but announced that the deal could proceed in August 2001 after voting 2–2 to prevent the merger. A 3–1 vote was required to block the merger. However, PepsiCo was required to make concessions that included agreeing to distribute All Sport for Monarch for a 10-year period and delaying the joint distribution of Gatorade with PepsiCo's soft drinks for 10 years. Under the terms of the merger, Quaker Oats shareholders received 2.3 shares of PepsiCo in exchange for each share of Quaker's common stock.

Quaker Oats' income statements for 1998–2000 and balance sheets for 1999–2000 are presented in Exhibits 9 and 10. The company's sales by product category and geography between 1998 and 2000 are shown in Exhibit 11. Exhibit 12 presents selected operating segment data for Quaker Oats from 1998 to 2000. PepsiCo also acquired a majority stake in South Beach Beverage Company—maker of SoBe noncarbonated beverages—and Tasali Snack Foods, the leader in the Saudi Arabian salty snack market, in 2001.

---

[8]"Gotta Get That Gatorade," *Business Week Online,* November 27, 2000.
[9]Ibid.

exhibit 9   Quaker Oats Company's Income Statements, 1998–2000
            (in millions, except per share amounts)

	2000	1999	1998
Net sales	$5,041.0	$4,725.2	$4,842.5
Cost of goods sold	2,288.3	2,136.8	2,374.4
Gross profit	2,752.7	2,588.4	2,468.1
Selling, general, and administrative expenses	1,968.8	1,904.1	1,872.5
Restructuring charges, asset impairments, and (gains) losses on divestitures—net	182.5	−2.3	128.5
Interest expense	54.0	61.9	69.6
Interest income	−9.0	−11.7	−10.7
Foreign exchange loss—net	5.3	18.1	11.6
Income before income taxes	551.1	618.3	396.6
Provision for income taxes	190.5	163.3	112.1
Net income	360.6	455.0	284.5
Preferred dividends—net of tax	4.2	4.4	4.5
Net income available for common	$ 356.4	$ 450.6	$ 280.0
Per common share			
Net income	$2.71	$3.36	$2.04
Net income—diluted	$2.61	$3.23	$1.97
Dividends declared	$1.14	$1.14	$1.14
Average number of common shares outstanding (in thousands)	131,689	134,027	137,185

Source: Quaker Oats Company, 2000 10-K.

BUILDING SHAREHOLDER VALUE IN 2001

In 2001, PepsiCo was the second-largest food products company in the United States (behind Kraft Foods) and was diversified into salty and sweet snacks, soft drinks, orange juice, bottled water, ready-to-drink teas and coffees, nutraceutical and isotonic beverages, hot and ready-to-eat breakfast cereals, grain-based products, and breakfast condiments. Many PepsiCo brands held number one or number two positions in their respective food and beverage categories.

PepsiCo's New Senior Management Team

The task of integrating Quaker Oats Company's brands and products into PepsiCo's organization fell on a new top management team since 56-year-old Roger Enrico stepped down as CEO in May 2001. Enrico announced a succession plan in October 2000 that called for his transition from the position of CEO by year-end 2001. His retirement was not a complete surprise since he had reluctantly accepted the positions of head of PepsiCo's restaurant division in 1994 and that of CEO in 1996. During the succession announcement, Enrico commented:

exhibit 10   Quaker Oats Company's Consolidated Balance Sheets, 1998–2000 (in millions, except per share amounts)

	2000	1999
Assets		
Current assets		
Cash and cash equivalents	$ 174.3	$ 282.9
Marketable securities	0.3	0.3
Trade accounts receivable—net of allowances	298.0	254.3
Inventories:		
Finished goods	213.9	186.6
Raw materials	39.0	50.0
Packaging materials and supplies	34.5	29.6
Total inventories	287.4	266.2
Other current assets	253.7	193.0
Total current assets	1,013.7	996.7
Property, plant, and equipment		
Land	27.1	28.2
Buildings and improvements	430.6	407.6
Machinery and equipment	1,469.9	1,416.1
Property, plant, and equipment	1,927.6	1,851.9
Less accumulated depreciation	807.6	745.2
Property—net	1,120.0	1,106.7
Intangible assets—net of amortization	229.2	236.9
Other assets	55.9	55.9
Total assets	$2,418.8	$2,396.2
Liabilities and shareholders' equity		
Current liabilities		
Short-term debt	$ 81.6	$ 73.3
Current portion of long-term debt	48.0	81.2
Trade accounts payable	212.3	213.6
Accrued payroll, benefits, and bonus	135.9	139.1
Accrued advertising and merchandising	126.7	138.7
Income taxes payable	15.6	40.1
Other accrued liabilities	240.3	252.3
Total current liabilities	860.4	938.3
Long-term debt	664.1	715.0
Other liabilities	518.0	523.1
Preferred stock, series B, no par value, authorized 1,750,000 shares; issued 1,282,051 of $5.46 cumulative convertible shares (liquidating preference of $78 per share.)	100.0	100.0
Deferred compensation	(27.2)	(38.5)
Treasury preferred stock, at cost, 441,469 and 366,069 shares, respectively	(51.2)	(39.0)
Common shareholders' equity		
Common stock, $5 par value, authorized 400 million shares	840.0	840.0
Additional paid-in capital	136.4	100.7
Reinvested earnings	1,061.7	854.6
Accumulated other comprehensive income	(111.3)	(95.1)
Deferred compensation	(21.2)	(45.5)
Treasury common stock, at cost	(1,550.9)	(1,457.4)
Total common shareholders' equity	354.7	197.3
Total liabilities and shareholders' equity	$2,418.8	$2,396.2

Source: Quaker Oats Company, 2000 10-K.

exhibit 11   Quaker Oats Company's Sales by Product Category
and Geography, 1998–2000 (in millions, except
per share amounts)

	2000	1999	1998
Enterprise net sales			
U.S. hot cereals	$ 514.6	$ 485.5	$ 430.8
U.S. ready-to-eat cereals	689.7	724.5	711.9
U.S. grain-based snacks	341.3	304.6	290.8
U.S. flavored rice and pasta	334.9	344.3	340.5
U.S. other foods	298.2	306.0	318.3
Total U.S. foods	$2,178.7	$2,164.9	$2,092.3
Canadian foods	$ 202.5	$ 194.6	$ 181.8
Latin American foods	345.9	308.4	372.9
European and Asia/Pacific foods	210.0	215.4	202.9
Total foods	$2,937.1	$2,883.3	$2,849.9
U.S. beverages	$1,693.0	$1,469.0	$1,306.8
Canadian beverages	35.4	33.3	31.4
Latin American beverages	273.9	229.1	267.7
European and Asia/Pacific beverages	101.6	103.8	103.1
Total beverages	$2,103.9	$1,835.2	$1,709.0
Total ongoing businesses	$5,041.0	$4,718.5	$4,558.9
U.S. divested	—	—	206.7
Foreign divested	—	6.7	76.9
Total divested businesses	—	6.7	283.6
Total consolidated	$5,041.0	$4,725.2	$4,842.5
Geographic net sales			
Total U.S.	$3,871.7	$3,633.9	$3,605.8
Total foreign	1,169.3	1,091.3	1,236.7
Total consolidated	$5,041.0	$4,725.2	$4,842.5

Source: Quaker Oats Company 2000 10-K.

When I was elected CEO I said I hoped to have the perseverance to stay long enough to get the job done and the wisdom not to remain too long. By the end of 2001, I will have been a part of the PepsiCo team for 30 terrific years. I'm sure it will be surprising to very few people that I now feel it is time to move on to creating a new chapter in my life.

In my mind, getting the job done meant re-focusing our company on the vibrant convenient food and beverage market. The performance our PepsiCo team has delivered over the last six quarters since the completion of our restructuring clearly demonstrates they have successfully built the capability to consistently deliver healthy mid-to-upper-single-digit revenue growth, double-digit earnings growth, and higher returns on invested capital.[10]

Steve Reinemund, PepsiCo's president and chief operating officer was selected as Enrico's successor. Reinemund joined PepsiCo in 1984 in its Pizza Hut business before

[10]PepsiCo, Inc., press release, October 4, 2000.

exhibit 12 Selected Operating Segment Data, Quaker Oats Company, 1998–2000 (in millions, except per share amounts)

	2000	1999	1998
Net sales			
Foods			
U.S. and Canadian	$2,381.2	$2,359.5	$2,274.1
Latin American	345.9	308.4	372.9
Other	210.0	215.4	202.9
Total foods	$2,937.1	$2,883.3	$2,849.9
Beverages			
U.S. and Canadian	$1,728.4	$1,502.3	$1,338.2
Latin American	273.9	229.1	267.7
Other	101.6	103.8	103.1
Total beverages	$2,103.9	$1,835.2	$1,709.0
Total ongoing businesses	$5,041.0	$4,718.5	$4,558.9
Total divested businesses	—	6.7	283.6
Total sales	$5,041.0	$4,725.2	$4,842.5
Operating income (loss)			
Foods			
U.S. and Canadian	$ 458.5	$ 399.8	$ 369.8
Latin American	26.8	26.2	28.2
Other	25.2	21.1	(1.2)
Total foods	$ 510.5	$ 447.1	$ 396.8
Beverages			
U.S. and Canadian	$ 273.7	$ 253.9	$ 214.9
Latin American	30.9	16.5	25.6
Other	(6.8)	(7.3)	(7.4)
Total beverages	$ 297.8	$ 263.1	$ 233.1
Total ongoing businesses	808.3	710.2	629.9
Total divested businesses	—	—	−2.4
Total operating income	$ 808.3	$ 710.2	$ 627.5
Identifiable assets			
Foods			
U.S. and Canadian	$1,120.8	$1,124.6	$1,187.0
Latin American	187.4	174.0	167.7
Other	110.2	110.1	92.1
Total foods	$1,418.4	$1,408.7	$1,446.8
Beverages			
U.S. and Canadian	$ 684.5	$ 522.7	$ 464.2
Latin American	105.0	105.4	94.6
Other	77.4	79.6	109.5
Total beverages	$ 866.9	$ 707.7	$ 668.3
Total ongoing businesses	$2,285.3	$2,116.4	$2,115.1
Total divested businesses	—	—	37.5
Total operating segments	$2,285.3	$2,116.4	$2,152.6
Corporate	133.5	279.8	357.7
Total consolidated	$2,418.8	$2,396.2	$2,510.3

(Continued)

exhibit 12   *(cont.)*

	2000	1999	1998
Capital expenditures			
Foods			
U.S. and Canadian	$117.6	$ 70.6	$102.7
Latin American	10.3	9.6	13.2
Other	3.9	3.7	5.7
Total foods	$131.8	$ 83.9	$121.6
Beverages			
U.S. and Canadian	$140.2	$106.0	$ 57.6
Latin American	11.5	25.4	12.1
Other	2.1	7.1	5.5
Total Beverages	$153.8	$138.5	$ 75.2
Total ongoing businesses	285.6	222.4	196.8
Total divested businesses	—	—	7.9
Total consolidated	$285.6	$222.4	$204.7
Depreciation and amortization			
Foods			
U.S. and Canadian	$ 67.0	$ 66.9	$ 65.2
Latin American	6.0	5.9	6.7
Other	4.3	3.5	6.3
Total foods	$ 77.3	$ 76.3	$ 78.2
Beverages			
U.S. and Canadian	$ 45.0	$ 36.2	$ 31.5
Latin American	6.3	5.0	5.8
Other	4.4	5.4	4.7
Total beverages	$ 55.7	$ 46.6	$ 42.0
Total ongoing businesses	133.0	122.9	120.2
Total divested businesses	—	—	11.4
Total operating segments	$133.0	$122.9	$131.6
Corporate	—	0.9	0.9
Total consolidated	$133.0	$123.8	$132.5

Source: Quaker Oats Company 2000 10-K.

becoming the chief executive of Frito-Lay in 1992. Reinemund, a U.S. Naval Academy graduate, ex-marine, and marathon runner, was known as reserved, serious, and detail oriented. He was also known for his enthusiasm for rolling up his sleeves and attacking the problem at hand. A story recounted many times at Frito-Lay involves Reinemund's stopping by a convenience store on a Christmas Eve and, finding a Frito-Lay delivery man still at work, jumping in to stock shelves.

Reinemund's first selection to his management team was that of Indra Nooyi as the company's president and chief financial officer. Nooyi emigrated to the United States in 1978 to attend Yale's Graduate School of Business and worked with Boston Consulting Group, Motorola, and Asea Brown Boveri before arriving at PepsiCo in 1994. Reinemund was impressed with Nooyi as a tough negotiator who engineered the 1997 spin-off of Pepsi's restaurants, spearheaded the 1998 acquisition of Tropicana, played a crit-

exhibit 13   PepsiCo, Inc.'s U.S. and International Sales and
Long-Lived Assets, 1998–2000 (in millions, except
per share amounts)

	2000	1999	1998
Net sales			
United States	$13,179	$11,772	$ 8,782
International	7,259	6,472	5,904
Combined segments	20,438	18,244	14,686
Bottling operations/investments	—	2,123	7,662
Total	$20,438	$20,367	$22,348
Long-lived assets			
United States	$ 8,179	$ 7,980	$ 6,732
International	4,722	4,867	4,276
Combined segments	12,901	12,847	11,008
Bottling operations/investments	—	—	6,702
Total	$12,901	$12,847	$17,710

Source: PepsiCo, Inc., 2000 10-K.

ical role in the 1999 IPO of Pepsi's bottling operations, and closed the 2001 acquisition
of Quaker Oats. PepsiCo's new top management team also included promotions at
Frito-Lay North America, Pepsi-Cola North America, Tropicana, and Frito-Lay's international operations. Quaker Oats CEO Robert Morrison became vice chairman of PepsiCo and president of Gatorade/Tropicana upon completion of the acquisition.

PepsiCo's Organizational Structure

Prior to the Quaker Oats acquisition, PepsiCo's businesses were organized by product
line and geography into Frito-Lay North America, Frito-Lay Europe/Africa/Middle
East, Frito-Lay Latin America/Asia Pacific/Australia, Pepsi-Cola North America,
Pepsi-Cola International, and Tropicana. In 2000, the company's U.S. sales were more
than 80 percent greater than its international sales and the global sales of Frito-Lay
products accounted for more than 60 percent of the company's total revenues.
PepsiCo's U.S. and international sales and long-lived assets for 1998–2000 are shown
in Exhibit 13. Selected financial data for each of PepsiCo's business segments from
1998 through 2000 are presented in Exhibit 14.

The Quaker acquisition brought changes to the company's organizational structure
with all snack food operations consolidated within Frito-Lay North America and Frito-
Lay International units and all beverage operations except North American Tropicana
and Gatorade operations organized geographically within Pepsi-Cola North America
and PepsiCo Beverages International. The North American operations of Gatorade and
Tropicana beverages were included in its Gatorade/Tropicana North American business unit and the company's grain-based snacks, dinner items, and breakfast cereals
and Aunt Jemima syrups were consolidated under the company's Quaker Oats North
American division.

exhibit 14   Selected Financial Data for PepsiCo, Inc.'s Business Segments, 1998–2000 (in millions, except per share amounts)

	2000	1999	1998
Net sales			
Frito-Lay			
North America	$ 8,562	$ 7,865	$ 7,474
International	4,319	3,750	3,501
Pepsi-Cola			
North America	3,289	2,605	1,389
International	1,842	1,771	1,600
Tropicana	2,426	2,253	722
New PepsiCo	20,438	18,244	14,686
Bottling operations/investments	—	2,123	7,662
	$20,438	$20,367	$22,348
Operating profit			
Frito-Lay			
North America	$ 1,851	$ 1,580	$ 1,424
International	493	406	367
Pepsi-Cola			
North America	833	751	732
International	148	108	99
Tropicana	225	170	40
Combined segments	3,550	3,015	2,662
Corporate	−325	−250	−202
New PepsiCo	3,225	2,765	2,460
Bottling operations/investments	—	53	124
	$ 3,225	$ 2,818	$ 2,584
Total assets			
Frito-Lay			
North America	$ 4,119	$ 4,013	$ 3,915
International	4,085	4,170	4,039
Pepsi-Cola			
North America	836	729	547
International	1,432	1,454	1,177
Tropicana	3,743	3,708	3,661
Combined segments	14,215	14,074	13,339
Corporate	1,592	1,008	215
Bottling operations/investments	2,532	2,469	9,106
	$18,339	$17,551	$22,660

The new organizational structure called for a new unit to be formed within Frito-Lay North America that would be dedicated exclusively to convenience food snacks

exhibit 14 *(cont.)*

	2000	1999	1998
Amortization of intangible assets			
Frito-Lay			
North America	$ 7	$ 8	$ 7
International	46	46	43
Pepsi-Cola			
North America	2	2	3
International	14	13	8
Tropicana	69	70	22
Combined segments	138	139	83
Bottling operations/investments	—	44	139
	$ 138	$ 183	$ 222
Depreciation and other amortization expense			
Frito-Lay			
North America	$ 366	$ 338	$ 326
International	172	149	142
Pepsi-Cola			
North America	94	72	30
International	91	85	64
Tropicana	83	81	27
Combined segments	806	725	589
Corporate	16	10	8
Bottling operations/investments	—	114	415
	$ 822	$ 849	$1,012
Other noncash items			
Frito-Lay North America		$37	$54
Pepsi-Cola International		—	6
Combined segments		37	60
Bottling operations/investments		—	194
		$37	$254
Capital spending			
Frito-Lay			
North America	$ 502	$ 472	$ 402
International	264	282	314
Pepsi-Cola			
North America	59	22	21
International	72	82	46
Tropicana	134	123	50
Combined segments	1,031	981	833
Corporate	36	42	29
Bottling operations/investments	—	95	543
	$1,067	$1,118	$1,405

such as Quaker granola and cereal bars, Quaker rice cakes, Cracker Jack, Gatorade energy bars, and Oberto's meat snacks. The new unit focused on convenience foods was developed to allow the company to focus on opportunities outside its core salty snack business, achieve purchasing, manufacturing, and distribution synergies, and promote knowledge sharing within the snack foods unit. The new Frito-Lay International division combined the company's operations outside of North America with Quaker's snack businesses outside North America. The new international division was intended to improve the distribution of Quaker snack products outside North America and develop cost-sharing opportunities internationally for all PepsiCo snack businesses. The company's new Gatorade/Tropicana North America business unit would allow the company to combine the production of Gatorade, Tropicana Twister, Dole, Season's Best, SoBe, and other hot fill products to gain production efficiencies and cost savings. In addition, the new division would allow Tropicana to exploit Gatorade's broker/warehouse system and distribution network. The new organizational structure also allowed PepsiCo to coordinate and consolidate materials purchasing across divisions for items such as bottles and paperboard that were needed for food and beverage products packaging.

Frito-Lay North America

In 2000 Frito-Lay brands accounted for 58 percent of the sales of snack chips in the $20.6 billion U.S. salty snack industry. Frito-Lay North America's volume growth of 4 percent and revenue growth of 7 percent during 2000 outpaced the 6.4 percent growth rate of the U.S. snack food industry. In 2000 Frito-Lay owned the top-selling chip brand in each U.S. salty snack category and claimed 9 of the top 10 best selling snack chip brands sold in U.S. supermarkets. The sales and market shares of PepsiCo's major brands and products are presented in Exhibit 15.

Almost one-third of Frito-Lay North America's revenue growth in 2000 was attributable to the success of its new Snack Kit and Snack Mix products and Oberto's natural beef jerky snacks. Meat snacks were a rapidly growing snack food category; they were popular with preteen and teen boys because of their bold flavor, and with dieting adults since they were low in fat and carbohydrates. Frito-Lay North America's fastest-growing products in terms of volume were its core products such as Lay's and Ruffles potato chips, Chee-tos cheese puffs, and Tostitos tortilla chips. Frito-Lay's new Scoops! Fritos and Scoops! Tostitos were other rapidly growing products that appealed to snackers who ate chips with dips. Among the few failures at Frito-Lay North America were the company's low-fat WOW!, Baked Lay's, and Baked Tostitos brands of chips—sales of these products were declining.

Frito-Lay International

Frito-Lay was the largest snack chip company in the world, with sales of more than $5.9 billion outside the United States and a 28 percent share of the international snack chip industry in 2000. Frito-Lay's international operations were among its fastest-growing and most profitable, with 13 percent volume growth, 14 percent revenue growth, and 19 percent growth in operating profits in 2000. Frito-Lay not only marketed its own brands of chips in international markets but also entered into international joint ventures and acquired established chip companies outside the United States to further increase sales and market shares within various country markets. For example, in 2000 Frito-Lay International was able to boost market share in Colombia from

Exhibit 15 U.S. Food and Beverage Category Size and Sales, Market Share, and Category Rank of PepsiCo's Major Products, 2000 (dollar amounts in millions)

Product Category/Product	2000 Sales	Category Size	Market Share	Category Rank
Potato chips				
Lay's	$ 908.8		36.3%	1
Ruffles	363.4		14.5	2
Wavy Lay's	201.3		8.0	3
Ruffles Flavor Rush	79.1		3.2	5
Ruffles WOW!	61.9		2.5	8
Lay's WOW!	54.5		2.2	9
Ruffles The Works	17.4		0.7	15
Category	$1,686.4	$2,506.3	67.3%	
Tortilla chips				
Doritos	$ 784.6		38.8%	1
Tostitos	690.9		34.2	2
Santitas	69.4		3.4	4
Baked Tostitos	57.5		2.8	5
Tostitos WOW!	29.9		1.5	7
Doritos WOW!	25.2		1.2	8
Category	$1,657.5	$2,023.0	81.9%	
Corn chips				
Fritos	$ 234.9		42.0%	1
Fritos Scoops	139.4		24.9	2
Doritos 3D's	67.4		12.1	3
Fritos Chili and Scoops	17.4		3.1	5
Fritos Sloppy Joe and Scoops	9.7		1.7	7
Fritos Fiesta Cheese and Scoops	2.4		0.4	9
Category	$ 471.2	$ 558.9	84.3%	
Cheese snacks				
Chee-tos	$ 348.2	$ 542.5	64.2%	1
Pretzels				
Rold Gold	$ 168.6	$ 561.4	30.0%	1
Dips				
Frito-Lay Fritos dip	$ 99.6		49.0%	1
Frito-Lay dip	34.1		16.8	2
Category	$ 133.7	$ 203.1	65.8%	
Salsas				
Tostitos salsa	$ 264.0	$ 943.4	28.0%	1
Snack bars				
Quaker Chewy Snack Bars	$ 149.6	$1,358.1	11.0%	1
Quaker Fruit & Oatmeal Bars	59.5		4.4	8
Category	$ 209.1	$1,358.1	15.4%	

exhibit 15   *(cont.)*

Product Category/Product	2000 Sales	Category Size	Market Share	Category Rank
Rice/popcorn cakes				
Quaker rice cakes	$69.5		43.1%	1
Quaker Crispy Minis rice cakes	41.9		26.0	2
Category	$111.4	$161.2	69.1%	
Soft drinks				
Pepsi-Cola	$1,422.5		13.9%	2
Mountain Dew	730		7.1	4
Diet Pepsi	500.3		4.9	7
Caffeine-Free Diet Pepsi	96		0.9	13
Diet Mountain Dew	90.2		0.9	14
Mug	80.7		0.8	16
Caffeine-Free Pepsi	70		0.7	19
Pepsi One	66.7		0.7	21
Slice	49.5		0.5	27
Wild Cherry Pepsi	28.7		0.3	30
Diet Slice	6.7		0.1	42
Others (includes Sierra Mist)	16.1		0.2	
Category	$3,157.4	$10,218.7	30.9%	
Bottled water				
Aquafina	$203.2	$2,170.0	9.4%	1
Ready-to-drink tea				
Lipton	$670		41.1%	1
SoBe	35		2.1	5
Category	$705	$1,630	43.3%	
Chilled juices				
Tropicana Pure Premium, Tropicana Twister, Dole, Season's Best	$2,400	$6,850	35.0%	1
Isotonic beverages				
Gatorade	$1,700	$2,000	85.0%	1
Hot cereals				
Quaker oatmeal, Quaker instant oatmeal	$515	$850	60.6%	1
Ready-to-eat cereals				
Cap'n Crunch, Life, Quaker Toasted Oatmeal	$690	$7,500	9.2%	4
Flavored grains				
Golden Grain Rice-A-Roni, Pasta Roni, Near East	$334	$1,005	33.2%	1
Other breakfast				
Quaker grits	$76	$100	76.0%	1
Aunt Jemima syrup	$95	$560	17.0	1
Aunt Jemima pancake mix	$70	$310	22.6%	1

Sources: Snack Food Association; June 2001 issue of *Snack Food & Wholesale Bakery* magazine; "Top 10 Soft Drink Review," *Beverage World,* March 15, 2001; "Beverages Represent Big-Time Opportunity," *MMR,* September 3, 2001; "The U.S. Ready-to-Drink Tea Market," *Beverage Aisle,* April 2001; Quaker Oats and PepsiCo annual reports.

21 percent to nearly 50 percent with the acquisition of Margarita snacks and became the snack chip leader in India with the purchase of Uncle Chipps. Also in 2000, the company's acquisition of Symba Ltd. gave it 58 percent of the growing market for salty snacks in South Africa. In early 2001, Frito-Lay International was able to increase its market share to 60 percent in Egypt and over 45 percent in Saudi Arabia with joint ventures and mergers in those countries. Also in 2001, Frito-Lay International announced that it would invest $40 million to build a state-of-the-art manufacturing facility in Russia to support its $20 million distribution system that reached over 70 percent of the country. Frito-Lay agricultural experts began working with Russian farmers, using the company's proprietary agrotechnology, to ensure a supply of consistent and high-quality potatoes. The company's acquisitions and joint ventures made it the number one snack company in over 30 countries, including 9 of the 15 largest snack chip markets. Mexico and Chile were two of Frito-Lay's strongest markets globally, with 80 percent and 90 percent shares of the markets, respectively.

Pepsi-Cola North America

Pepsi-Cola had comfortably held the position of runner-up to soft-drink leader Coca-Cola for most of the two companies' 100-plus-year histories, but during the mid-1990s Pepsi-Cola fell further behind its chief rival in the industry at a disturbing rate. Almost every Pepsi-Cola brand except Mountain Dew was losing market share to Coca-Cola's brands. Coca-Cola's CEO at the time, Roberto Goizueta, had stated that the company's strategic intent was to control 50 percent of the U.S. cola market by 2000. Market share was essential in the $30 billion U.S. soft-drink market since, even though approximately 50 percent of all beverages consumed were soft drinks, industry growth approximated only about 0.5 percent annually. Pepsi-Cola's competitive strength was eroding so quickly that Goizueta summed up his worries about Pepsi as a key rival in an October 28, 1996, *Fortune* article entitled "How Coke Is Kicking Pepsi's Can" by saying, "As they've become less relevant, I don't need to look at them very much anymore." Enrico commented on Coca-Cola's aggressiveness and Pepsi-Cola's ability to respond to the challenge in a 2000 *Business Week* article:

> Coca-Cola was flat out trying to put us out of business. They had an objective to achieve a 50% share by the year 2000. And they had gained a fair amount of share in the early 1990s, but obviously they didn't come even close to a 50% share.
>
> People have been questioning Pepsi's ability to compete against the larger competitor ever since I can remember, and our ability isn't going to end any time soon. I look at these things over a longer perspective and say soft drinks is a great business. It is tremendously profitable, and it can generate good growth. The demographics and lifestyles are still in our favor, and they are likely to continue to be so for a long time.[11]

Pepsi-Cola management engineered a dramatic comeback by taking advantage of a tumultuous management transition after Goizueta became terminally ill with cancer, stressed the rapid implementation of new ideas rather than spending years developing and testing new products, and focused on strategies to improve local distribution. Among Pepsi's most successful strategies to build volume and share in soft drinks was its Power of One strategy, which attempted to achieve the synergistic benefits of a combined Pepsi-Cola and Frito-Lay envisioned by Donald Kendall in 1965. PepsiCo had found that, as Kendall and Lay had believed, chips and soft drinks were consumed together much of the time, but the idea that Frito-Lay chips and Pepsi would be

---

[11]"The Sweet Spot of Convenient Food and Beverages."

purchased together was rarely the case. Pepsi's market research indicated that even though Frito-Lay and Pepsi-Cola products were consumed together 58 percent of the time, they were purchased together only 22 percent of the time. The Power of One strategy called for supermarkets to place Pepsi and Frito-Lay products side-by-side on shelves. Roger Enrico visited the CEOs of the 25 largest supermarket chains to encourage their companies to participate in the plan, citing research findings that Frito-Lay and Pepsi-Cola products were the number one drivers of retailer sales growth and retailer profit growth. Enrico also cited market research that found supermarket profit margins on PepsiCo's products were typically 9 percent, compared with an average profit margin of 2 percent on other items sold by supermarkets. In addition, Enrico stressed that PepsiCo products accounted for only 3 percent of supermarket sales, but 20 percent of retailers' cash flows. PepsiCo's Power of One strategy allowed top-ranking grocery chains to increase sales of soft drinks and salty snacks by as much as 10 percent. In 2001 Power of One and other PepsiCo strategies allowed Pepsi-Cola to draw within two percentage points of market leader Coca-Cola.

Although carbonated beverages made up more than 90 percent of Pepsi-Cola North America's total beverage volume, much of the division's growth was attributable to the success of its noncarbonated beverages. Aquafina, the number one brand in the $2.17 billion U.S. bottled water market, grew by 32 percent in 2000. Bottled water was a particularly attractive segment for PepsiCo since U.S. bottled water consumption had increased from 2.2 billion gallons in 1990 to 4.6 billion gallons in 1999. The category was the fastest-growing beverage category in 2000, with 8.3 percent growth during the year, and consumption was projected to reach 6.8 billion gallons by 2004. Coca-Cola's Dasani was a rapidly growing bottled water brand, but it trailed Aquafina by five places in the industry's ranking of top-selling brands. PepsiCo had also beat Coca-Cola into new beverage categories with products like Frappucino and Lipton teas that had quickly become category leaders. The ready-to-drink tea category was relatively mature, with 4.5 percent growth in 2000, but Lipton's 16-point lead over Coca-Cola's Nestea added to the category's importance in PepsiCo's brand portfolio. Coca-Cola's Minute Maid was the leading brand of single-serve juices, but Pepsi management expected to improve the company's standing with the recent launches of FruitWorks and Dole single-serving products. PepsiCo's $370 million acquisition of South Beach Beverage Company was among its more significant achievements in 2001 since sales of the company's SoBe line of herbal juices and teas had grown by 40 percent in 2000. Pepsi management hoped to exploit SoBe's expertise in developing innovative beverage formulations in developing new products in all beverage categories.

PepsiCo Beverages International

PepsiCo found that it could grow international sales through its Power of One strategy. A Pepsi-Cola executive explained how the company's soft-drink business could gain shelf space through the strength of Frito-Lay's brands: "You go to Chile, where Frito-Lay has over 90% of the market, but Pepsi is in lousy shape. Frito-Lay can help Pepsi change that."[12] Pepsi-Cola's sales in Mexico increased by more than 26 percent in 2000 as 8,000 retailers in that country adopted the company's Power of One strategy. PepsiCo management expected to have 40,000 retailers in Mexico signed on to Power of One by 2002. Enrico also believed that Pepsi-Cola needed to abandon its longtime

---

[12]"PepsiCo's New Formula."

strategy of battling Coca-Cola head-to-head in international markets. In 2000, more than 60 percent of Coca-Cola's sales were from international markets and Coke enjoyed 80-plus percent market share in many markets. Enrico shifted the international beverage division's growth strategy from a broad global span to picking emerging markets where there was yet to be a decided leader. Enrico suggested that Pepsi-Cola had adopted a self-defeating strategy in many international markets by "beating our heads in markets that Coke won 20 years ago."[13] "The key thing is not to merely plant flags," echoed Pepsi-Cola's chief manager, "It's to make sure you build a business, customer by customer, block by block, day by day."[14]

In 2000, Pepsi-Cola's greatest international growth was in Russia, China, India, Thailand, and Mexico (where it recorded double-digit growth). Pepsi benefited from its 1999 reorganization of its international bottling operations and its 10-year agreement to supply Tricon's restaurants with fountain drinks, but Pepsi also made impressive gains in developing markets by making successful local business owners franchisees to distribute soft drinks in sometimes nontraditional manners. For example, most of Pepsi's products in India were distributed by three-wheeled bicycles rather than by trucks that were used in more developed markets. In 2000, PepsiCo's international beverage business increased market share in most of its top-25 markets and was able to increase operating income by 37 percent through increased soft-drink concentrate pricing and volume gains. Also by year-end 2000, Pepsi's international beverage business had grown faster than Coca-Cola in international markets for 9 of the 10 most recent quarters.

PepsiCo Beverages International was also responsible for production and distribution of Tropicana and Gatorade in markets outside North America. PepsiCo managers believed that a single international beverage company would provide greater economies of scale in production and distribution and would allow for coordinated product development and better information sharing between brands. In addition, a single international beverage distributor was expected to allow Gatorade to achieve greater success internationally than what was possible with Quaker Oats, which had lacked a strong international distribution system. However, there was some disagreement within the company concerning the integration of distribution networks for soft drinks and juices since markets for such products varied considerably in some countries.

Gatorade/Tropicana

Not only was Tropicana the number one brand of not-from-concentrate orange juice, but its flagship Tropicana Pure Premium brand was the fastest-growing major brand of orange juice in 2000. Tropicana achieved double-digit volume growth during 2000 to become the third-largest brand among all products sold in U.S. supermarkets. Even though the orange juice category grew by only 1.4 percent in 2000, Tropicana had grown its volume and revenues with the introduction of new products featuring, for example, no-pulp, low-acid, and calcium-fortified formulations. A shift to glass bottles in single-serve products helped Season's Best, Dole, and Tropicana Twister juices grow by as much as 13 percent in 2000. In addition to new product formulations, PepsiCo management brought greater profitability to Tropicana as it more than doubled its operating income from 1998 to 2000. The 2001 launch of single-serve Smoothies (which combined fruit juices and nonfat yogurt) was intended to capture a share of the $1 bil-

---

[13]Ibid.

[14]Ibid.

lion smoothie market, which had grown by as much as 50 percent annually during the late 1990s.

Gatorade surpassed the $2 billion global sales mark in 2000 when its sales grew by 15 percent. The brand had grown by more than $500 million since 1998 and had recorded 16 consecutive years of growth with the introduction of new flavors, new container sizes and designs, new multipacks, and world-class advertising and added points of distribution. Gatorade's sales outside the United States reached $375 million in 2000 as the company's worldwide sales averaged an annual growth rate of 9 percent between 1996 and 2000 and its operating income grew by an annual rate of 29 percent over the same five-year period. Gatorade's operating income increased by 13 percent in 2000, despite its investment in the development of Propel fitness water. Gatorade's $1.7 billion sales in the U.S. and Canadian markets gave it an 85 percent share in the U.S./Canadian isotonic sports beverage market, which grew by 7.5 percent in 2000.

PepsiCo management expected Gatorade's broker-distribution system to expand Tropicana's availability into new retail locations, and analysts believed that Gatorade could experience a 10 percent volume increase merely from becoming available in Pepsi vending machines. PepsiCo's expertise in new product development and production efficiency was also expected to improve Gatorade's sales and profits. Some analysts were skeptical that Gatorade's inclusion in PepsiCo's portfolio would bring the expected growth in revenues and profits since the operations of Gatorade differed substantially from those of Pepsi's soft-drink business. Whereas Pepsi produced concentrate and sold it to bottlers for distribution to retail outlets, Gatorade's operations spanned the entire beverage value chain—from making some ingredients to beverage production and container filling to distribution. Soft-drink sales were particularly profitable for PepsiCo since the operating profit margins on the sales of concentrate to bottlers approximated 24 percent. Gatorade's scope of operations provided it with an operating profit margin that was about half that of Pepsi-Cola North America. The FTC's prohibition on bundled beverage contracts with retailers and joint Gatorade–soft-drink distribution also led some analysts to believe that the full benefits of the acquisition might not be achieved for 10 years.

Quaker Foods North America

Quaker Oats was the leading producer of hot and ready-to-eat cereals, grain-based snacks, and rice and pasta side dishes in the United States and Canada, with 2000 sales of $2.9 billion. Quaker dominated the oatmeal category of the breakfast food industry with new product innovations that included new flavors, microwavable cups, and vitamin-fortified formulations. The combined sales of Quaker's ready-to-eat cereals like Cap'n Crunch, Life, and Toasted Oatmeal made it a distant number four to General Mills, Kellogg's, and Post. Quaker held a 10 percent share of the $7.5 billion U.S. cereal market and relied heavily on price promotions to increase sales. Quaker was not alone in its reliance on price promotions to increase its share of the cereal category; the industry had failed to grow since 1995, and the three main cereal producers saw sales and profits fall almost every year during the late 1990s. Rice-A-Roni, Pasta Roni, and Near East side dishes held leading positions in the flavored rice and pasta categories, but experienced 3 percent sales declines in 2000. Competing in relatively mature categories, Quaker grits, Masa Harina tortilla flour and corn meal, and Aunt Jemima pancake mix and syrup all enjoyed market leading positions. Even though Quaker nonsnack products competed in mature food categories, the businesses required little capital investment and generated free cash flow in excess of $100 million annually.

Value Chain Alignment between PepsiCo Brands and Products

PepsiCo's new management team estimated that the company could achieve annual cost savings of $140 to $175 million by the end of 2002 and could achieve savings of $400 million annually by 2005 through the reorganization of activities in the value chains of the company's snack and beverage businesses. Value chain alignment between PepsiCo brands and products was also expected to contribute to a four percentage point improvement in operating margins by year-end 2001, a $1.5 to $4 billion increase in operating cash flow by 2005, and a 30 percent improvement in return on invested capital by 2005.

The combined corporatewide procurement for product ingredients and packaging materials was expected to produce an estimated $160 million in cost savings by 2005, while the combination of Gatorade and Tropicana hot fill operations was expected to save $120 million annually by 2005. The joint distribution of Quaker snacks and Frito-Lay products was expected to reduce distribution expenses by $40 million by 2005, and PepsiCo management believed that synergies between Frito-Lay International and PepsiCo Beverages International could produce $50 million annually in combined cost savings and revenue increases by 2005. PepsiCo management also believed that the company could reduce corporate costs by $30 million annually by combining administrative activities.

PepsiCo had developed a sophisticated value chain alignment tracking process that utilized online scorecards. These cards were updated monthly to track over 130 individual projects designed to capture synergistic benefits. In addition, return on capital was individually reviewed for each project and baseline performance was tracked separately from performance resulting from synergies. PepsiCo also gave its chief manager direct communication lines to corporate and division presidents and CFOs, and made 2002 bonuses dependent on achieving synergies.

By November 2001, PepsiCo had successfully consolidated its corporate activities, combined the Tropicana and Gatorade sales forces, made Quaker snacks available in Frito-Lay vending machines, and combined all international beverages in its PepsiCo Beverages International division. The company had also created a North American hot fill manufacturing unit and formed a worldwide procurement unit.

PEPSICO'S PERFORMANCE GOING INTO 2002

PepsiCo's portfolio restructuring continued to show positive results for shareholders in late 2001 as the company delivered double-digit earnings growth for its eighth consecutive quarter. Every division reported volume, revenue, and operating profit gains during the company's third quarter of 2001. Also during the quarter, the company's worldwide snack sales increased by 6 percent and its North American sales of soft drinks, bottled water, and teas grew by 20 percent. Gatorade/Tropicana sales increased 8 percent during the quarter, while international sales of beverages increased 2 percent and Quaker nonsnack food products increased by 3 percent. The effects of the company's efforts to align the value chain activities of its food and beverage businesses had yet to have an effect on the company's performance, since the acquisition was not approved by the FTC until the seventh week of PepsiCo's third quarter in 2001.

case 24 Avid Technology, Inc.

Philip K. Goulet
University of South Carolina

Alan Bauerschmidt
University of South Carolina

"I think that any company that is very successful can be a victim of its own success," proclaimed David Krall in the fall of 2000 as he pondered Avid Technology's past performance. He was Avid's third CEO in almost as many years. Poor financial performance had led the board to replace a company founder in 1996 with a successful outside executive from a large high-tech company to turn Avid around. Results were slow in coming, however, causing the board to replace the executive three years later with Krall, one of the company's divisional chief operating officers.

The burden of a second attempt at a turnaround was placed squarely on the shoulders of the 39-year-old Krall. Though a relatively young man with only four years' experience in one of the company's divisions, Krall had a history as an innovator. He had won Harvard Business School's Entrepreneur of the Year Award for an invention he had patented (a backup battery for laptop computers), and he had guided Digidesign, the Avid division he headed, to strong performance even as the overall company suffered poor results. Avid's board was counting on the entrepreneurial Krall to orchestrate the strategic renewal the company desperately needed.

Avid Technology, Inc., was the quintessential high-tech success story. Sales grew rapidly following the company's first product shipment in late 1989. Avid achieved high growth rates and accolades from customers and industry analysts by applying digital technology to processes used to manipulate pictures, graphics, and sound in the creation of movies, television programs, and news broadcasts. In effect, Avid built "a better mouse trap" in the way moving pictures, graphics, and sound were captured, edited, and then reproduced for an audience's viewing and listening pleasure.

However, by 1995, sales growth had begun to slow. Bringing in new management at the end of 1996, Avid hoped to turn its fortunes around and place the company once again on a profitable growth path. The turnaround attempt, though, was a tumultuous one. The new management team made several strategic decisions but failed to achieve sustainable results and soon lost the confidence of the company's board. That team's departure was indicative of Avid's failure to find the strategic prescription to solve the problems that plagued the company.

By decisively replacing top management for a second time, the board sent a strong signal to the company's newest management team that nothing short of Avid's immediate turnaround was expected. Understanding what had happened to Avid over the past few years was the urgent task now facing Krall. The new CEO had to determine what the prior two CEOs had done, or not done, that had turned Avid's fortunes so quickly. And, more important, Krall had to decide on a new direction and strategy to rejuvenate Avid's growth and profitability.

COMPANY OVERVIEW AND HISTORY

Traditional analog technology required various people to capture moving pictures, graphics, and sound on magnetic tape; cut and splice this tape to edit picture sequences; and then duplicate this tape for distribution. Digital technology captured moving pictures, graphics, and sound in the form of binary codes recognizable by computers. Editing the digitized pictures, graphics, and sound sequences was similar to editing a word processing file (which consists of digitized text)—the editor used a mouse to cut and paste the pictures, graphics, and sound into the desired sequence on the computer. The resulting movie, for example, was a computer file of digitized pictures, graphics, and sound. Digital editing not only was faster and less costly than traditional analog editing but also provided editors with greater capabilities for creating special effects. Moreover, while analog film showed wear and tear after 15 to 25 showings, digital films did not lose quality.

Located within the high-tech metropolitan area of Boston, Massachusetts, Avid Technology was an industry leader in several digital technology markets. Avid developed computer systems for digital editing in newsrooms that helped create content for television news programs. Additionally, the company developed digital audio systems for professional use. Avid's products were used worldwide in film studios; network, affiliate, independent, and cable television stations; recording studios; advertising agencies; government and educational institutions; and corporate video departments. The special effects in the new *Star Wars* series were created and edited with Avid products. Similarly, producers employed Avid systems to make actor Gary Sinise (Lieutenant Dan Taylor) appear to be a double amputee in the movie *Forrest Gump*. Corporate uses included video applications by real estate firms to display property listings and by professional sports teams, such as the Green Bay Packers, to analyze game plays.

Avid was founded in 1987 by William Warner, who left his position at Apollo Computer, Inc., a manufacturer of computer systems, to pursue his revolutionary idea of digitizing moving pictures and sound so that they could be edited by computer. Joining Warner in 1988 were Curt Rawley, former president of Racal Design Services, a designer of printed circuit boards, and Eric Peters, former engineer at Apollo Computer and Digital Equipment Corporation (now Compaq Computer).

The three entrepreneurs developed Media Composer, the product upon which the new company was launched. Product shipments began in the fourth quarter of 1989. Sales grew rapidly, rising from $1 million in 1989 to $7 million, $20 million, and $52 million in 1990, 1991 and 1992, respectively.

To finance the company's growth, Avid went public in 1993 (NASDAQ: AVID), generating additional capital of $53 million. In the same year, sales more than doubled, to $113 million. The company rose to the fifth position in *Inc.* magazine's list of "100 Fastest Growing Small Public U.S. Companies" and ranked ninth on *Fortune*'s list of "100 Fastest Growing American Companies." Rapid growth continued, with Avid recording revenues of $204 million in 1994 and $407 million in 1995, an 81 percent and 100 percent increase over the prior year, respectively. Through 1995, Avid was achieving its objectives to quickly gain market share and develop a leadership position in its markets. However, sales growth following 1995 slowed, with revenues increasing by only 5 percent, to $429 million, in 1996; 10 percent, to $471 million, in 1997; and 2 percent, to $482 million, in 1998. In 1999, revenues decreased for the first time in the company's history, dropping 6 percent, to $453 million. Exhibit 1 provides a consolidated statement of operations, and Exhibit 2 shows a consolidated balance sheet for the company. Avid had about 1,700 employees by the end of 1999.

A key factor in Avid's rapid sales growth was its ability to establish a channel for international sales during its earliest days. Avid established sales offices in 7 different countries by 1993, and by 1999 it had offices in 20 different countries. Sales outside North America quickly grew from 11 percent of revenues in 1990, to 42 percent in 1992, and to 51 percent in 1999, with Avid selling to over 75 foreign markets. European sales showed the most promise, representing approximately 87 percent of total international sales. Sales from the Asian region were disappointing but were expected to generally improve as the economy of the region, especially that in Japan, came out of recession.

AVID'S MARKETS

Avid served three markets. Avid's primary revenue source was the film, television, and related industries. The film and television industries came to recognize digital technology as state of the art, and Avid as the leader in this technology. Exhibit 3 provides a sample listing of films and television programs that were created using Avid products.

The estimated $1 billion film industry was a rapid adopter of new technology and thus quickly migrated from analog to digital products, giving Avid more than an 80 percent share of the market segments it served in this industry. However, the $2 billion television industry was still predominantly tape-based, as was the $900 million audio industry. These industries represented a significant growth opportunity for the company. The $985 million corporate and institutional video industry was also predominantly tape-based, with Avid holding the leadership position in the digital segment (Avid's total industry share was 13 percent, versus all other digital-based competitors, which together made up 27 percent.) Thus, the company saw an opportunity for significant growth in this industry as well.

Avid's second most important revenue source was the $350 million news broadcast industry. Although the company had focused on this market since 1993, its efforts to gain a strong foothold were less successful than its efforts in the film and television industries. A key factor was the cost of the large integrated systems these customers required, which ran into the millions of dollars. Additionally, Avid did not offer products that could perform all the functions required in the highly complex process of news broadcast creation. To satisfy the diverse needs of news broadcast customers, the company's products required bundling with digital or analog products made by other vendors.

Further, the news broadcast industry was still predominantly analog based. Its migration from an analog to a digital format was significantly delayed by the high switching costs involving capital outlays and personnel training, as well as the perceived risks associated with systems that could have an unwieldy mix of both analog and digital devices. However, news broadcast firms were expected to make the transition to digital technology more readily as their expensive analog equipment reached replacement age.

exhibit 1 Avid Technology's Consolidated Statement of Operations, 1989-2000 (in millions, except per share data)

	1989	1990	1991	1992	1993	1994	1995	1996	1997	1998	1999	2000
Net revenues	$ 0.9	$ 7.4	$ 20.1	$51.9	$112.9	$203.7	$406.6	$429.0	$471.3	$482.4	$ 452.6	$476.0
Cost of sales	0.5	3.4	9.6	23.7	54.1	99.9	198.8	238.8	221.5	190.2	205.9	234.4
Gross profit	0.4	4	10.5	28.2	58.8	103.8	207.8	190.2	249.8	292.2	246.7	241.6
Operating expenses	2.1	6.3	10.5	24.7	55.7	87	185.2	220.5	219.7	242.6	246.9	229.8
Nonrecurring costs	0	0.6	1	0.9	0	0	5.5	29	0	28.4	14.5	0
Amortization of acquired assets	0	0	0	0	0	0	0	0	0	34.2	79.9	66.9
Other income (expenses)	0	0.1	0.1	0	1.5	1	1.4	3.4	8.1	8.6	3.5	3.7
Income taxes	0	0	0	1.2	0.9	4.8	8.6	(17.9)	11.8	(0.8)	46.4	5
Net income (loss)	$ (1.7)	$ (2.8)	$ (0.9)	$ 1.4	$ 5.5	$ 13	$ 15.4	$ (38)	$ 26.4	$ (3.6)	$(137.5)	$(56.4)
Net income (loss) per common share	$(0.57)	$(0.84)	$(0.27)	$0.29	$ 0.38	$ 1.10	$ 0.77	$ (1.80)	$ 1.08	$ (0.15)	$ (5.75)	$ (2.28)
Common stock value												
High	n/a	n/a	n/a	n/a	$27.16	$43.50	$48.75	$25.88	$38.00	$47.75	$ 34.25	$24.50
Low	n/a	n/a	n/a	n/a	16.00	20.50	16.75	10.13	9.00	11.06	10.00	9.38

Note: Nonrecurring costs primarily relate to write-offs resulting from restructurings and/or acquisitions.

Amortization of acquired assets relates to the Softimage acquisition.

Source: Avid annual reports and 10Ks, 1993–2000.

exhibit 2   Avid Technology's Consolidated Balance Sheet, 1998–2000 (in millions)

	1998	1999	2000
Assets			
Cash and marketable securities	$111.8	$72.8	$83.2
Accounts receivable, net	89.8	76.2	90.0
Inventories	11.1	15.0	21.1
Other current assets	29.0	12.6	11.7
Total current assets	241.7	176.4	206.1
Property, plant, and equipment, net	35.4	32.7	26.1
Other assets	209.6	102.9	34.2
Total assets	$486.7	$312.0	$266.4
Liabilities and Stockholders' Equity			
Accounts payable	$24.3	$24.0	$28.8
Other accrued charges	75.4	61.8	56.2
Deferred revenues	22.9	20.3	24.5
Total current liabilities	122.6	106.1	109.5
Long-term debt	13.3	14.2	13.4
Other	60.5	23.8	5.7
Stockholders' equity			
Common stock	0.3	0.3	0.3
Additional paid-in-capital	349.3	366.6	359.1
Retained earnings	14.3	(128.1)	(197.8)
Treasury stock	(68.0)	(66.5)	(15.6)
Deferred compensation	(3.8)	(1.9)	(4.8)
Cumulative translation adjustment	(1.8)	(2.5)	(3.4)
Total stockholders' equity	290.3	167.9	137.8
Total liabilities and stockholders' equity	$486.7	$312.0	$266.4

Source: Avid annual reports and 10Ks, 1998–2000.

Other factors limiting Avid's performance in this industry were the company's relative size and experience compared to competitors such as Sony. When making investments of $1 million or more in highly critical areas of their operations, news broadcast firms relied heavily on longtime suppliers with financial stability and established performance records. Avid, a small high-tech company (i.e., one with less than $500 million in sales) and a relative newcomer, realized that establishing a strong presence in this market would take time.

Avid's third source of company revenues was the retail consumer market. The company entered this market in 1994. Buyers of Avid products included individuals who, for example, edited home videos or photos on their personal computers. Several firms were producing products to serve the home market, yet no one firm had yet emerged as the market leader. Avid competed in this market with its Avid Cinema product. Avid Cinema was created by the company as an easy-to-use video software package for the retail consumer. Individuals with videotapes of school plays, sporting events, weddings, birthdays, and family get-togethers, for example, could use Avid

exhibit 3   Films and Television Programs Created Using Avid Products
(sample listing only)

Films	Television Programs
Lethal Weapon 4	Ally McBeal
Lost in Space	Frasier
The Perfect Storm	Friends
Star Trek: Insurrection	Just Shoot Me
Titanic	Survivor II
The X-Files: Fight the Future	Veronica's Closet

Note: 85 percent of films made in the United States in 2000 were edited on Avid systems, and 95 percent of prime time television programs in 2000 were edited on Avid systems.

Source: Avid Technology, Inc., public documents; *The Boston Globe*, April 30, 2001.

Cinema to add special effects, songs from favorite CDs, and professional-looking titles to turn their tapes into entertaining movies. Avid Cinema had received positive industry reviews. It was named finalist in 1999 for best digital video product by the editors of *Popular Photography* magazine and DigitalFocus, the leading digital imaging newsletter publisher. The previous year, it had been named "Best New Product" at Retail Xchange n8 and had been nominated for a best-of-show list at Comdex (both industry trade shows).

Because the retail consumer market was still in its infancy, sales were expected to remain modest over the next few years. However, Avid realized that the market held great sales potential as individuals gained an understanding of and appreciation for digital editing technology as a standard home-computer application. Excitement was being generated in this market as the cost of high-quality digital cameras (products that enhanced the utility of Avid Cinema) fell under $500, and as computer retailers such as Best Buy and CompUSA began reporting that digital cameras were one of their fastest-moving electronic/computer accessories.

PRODUCT DEVELOPMENT

Avid's first product, Media Composer, was designed specifically for the film and television industries. Indeed, the company's rapid growth was largely attributed to the market's acceptance of this initial product. Although Avid offered other products to the film and television industry, Media Composer contributed the most to both revenues and company profits.

Avid was dedicated to new product development. The company maintained a consistent level of R&D activity approximating 17 percent of sales, which mirrored the industry average. In addition, Avid engaged in several acquisitions to gain leading technology that the company believed complemented its existing in-house technology (see Exhibit 4). As a result of these acquisitions, Avid was able to develop a presence in the news broadcast industry (with systems installations at CBS, NBC, CNN, CNBC, and the BBC, for example) as well as in the audio and special effects markets. Avid also formed alliances with other firms to help develop new technologies (these alliances are discussed later in this case).

exhibit 4   Significant Avid Acquisitions, 1993–2000

Year	Company	Revenues (in millions)	Cost (in millions)	Description
1993	Digital Video Applications Corporation	n/a	$4.6	Developed video editing and presentation software products targeted for sale to nonprofessional video editors
1994	Basys Automation Systems (newsroom division)			Developed newsroom automation systems
	Softech Systems	$26*	$5*	Developed newsroom automation software
1995	Digidesign, Inc	$39	$205	Leading provider of computer-based, digital audio production systems for the professional music, film, broadcast, multimedia, and home recording markets
	Elastic Reality			Developed digital image manipulation software
	Parallax Software	$12†	$45†	Developed paint and compositing software
1998	Softimage	$37	$248	Leading developer of 3D animation, video production, 2D cel animation, and compositing software
2000	The Motion Factory			Developed 3D media for games and the Web
	Pluto Technologies International	n/a	$2.3‡	Developed newsroom storage and networking products

*Combined totals for Basys Automation Systems and Softech Systems acquisitions.

†Combined totals for Elastic Reality and Parallax Software acquisitions.

‡Combined totals for The Motion Factory and Pluto Technologies International acquisitions.

Note:

1. Digital Video Applications Corporation was acquired to give Avid a presence in the nonprofessional video market as well as enhance its existing market capabilities.

2. Basys Automation Systems (newsroom division) and Softech Systems were acquired to provide Avid access to the news broadcast industry.

3. Digidesign, Inc. was acquired to give Avid a leadership position in the digital audio market.

4. Elastic Reality and Parallax Software were acquired to form Avid's graphics and effects group; the companies developed a range of image manipulation products that allow users in the video and film post-production and broadcast markets to create graphics and special effects for use in feature films, television programs and advertising, and news programs. The Softimage acquisition significantly strengthened Avid's capabilities and market presence in these areas.

5. The Motion Picture Factory was acquired to enhance Avid's gaming and Web capabilities.

6. Pluto Technologies International was acquired to diversify Avid's product offerings for the news broadcast industry.

Source: Avid annual reports, public documents, and on-site interview with company representative; Computer Reseller News, October 31, 1994; Newsbytes News Network), March 31, 1995; *Boston Herald,* October 22, 1998, and June 30, 2000; and CCN Disclosure, September 10, 2000.

Avid's products could be classified into six general categories: video and film editing products, audio products, digital news gathering systems, newsroom computer systems, graphics and special effects products, and storage systems. The company offered numerous products that ranged widely in cost and target market. For example, Avid Symphony, a sophisticated film editing system, cost $150,000 and was designed for professional editors. In contrast, Avid Cinema cost $139 and was marketed to retail consumers using personal computers.

ESTABLISHING INDUSTRY STANDARDS

As a pioneer in digital technology, Avid took the lead in developing and promoting open industry standards. The company released into the public domain the platform of basic digital technology it developed and applied to specific product creations. This platform, or basic standards observed in the creation of digital media products, became known as Open Media Framework (OMF). OMF grew into a cooperative effort involving more than 150 leading manufacturers of digital products. Products based on OMF standards were compatible with other OMF-based media products (whether graphics, video, audio, animation, or text), allowing different products from different vendors to be used simultaneously during the production process.

Avid understood the advantages of releasing its basic digital technology to firms providing competing as well as complementary products. Open standards resulted in increased development of innovative digital media technology and products, with more firms producing complementary as well as competing products. This increased the speed at which industries migrated from analog to digital technology. Additionally, by establishing industry standards, Avid ensured that its products would be compatible with complementary products of other firms—such capability increased the utility of Avid products. However, by making its basic digital technology available to other firms, Avid lost the ability to distinguish itself in this respect from competitors.

STRATEGIC ALLIANCES

To enhance its competitiveness, Avid engaged in several horizontal and vertical alliances with other technology firms. Avid products were originally designed to operate solely on Apple computers; however, during the 1990s personal computer (PC) manufacturers began to erode product performance differences between Apple and IBM-compatible computers. As a result, Apple's market share dropped, causing some industry experts to question the company's continued viability. Avid realized the risk of being dependent on Apple technology to run its software and thus entered into a vertical alliance with Intel to develop the technology necessary to migrate the company's software to Microsoft Windows/Intel–based PCs (commonly referred to as Wintel). This pact also included Intel's taking a subsequent 6.75 percent ownership stake in Avid in 1997, providing the company with $14.7 million in cash to help fund the process. By 1994, Avid began shipping comparable products on both Apple and Wintel platforms and continued to migrate and develop additional products to and for Wintel systems. Consequently, Avid reduced the uncertainty connected with being dependent on Apple's PCs while at the same time making its products available to a wider market of both Apple and Wintel PC users.

Another partnership formed by Avid was the 1993 vertical alliance with filmmaker George Lucas and his Lucas Film and Lucas Digital groups. This agreement allowed for cooperation on the development of an extended line of special-effects products for the film industry. Avid provided software and hardware, and Lucas provided design specifications. Avid also entered into a partnership with Ikegami Tsushinki Company, Ltd., in 1994 to develop the world's first full-motion digital camera.

More recent arrangements included Avid's 1998 acquisition of Softimage, a Canadian company located in Montreal. Although criticized by some industry analysts for missing product development deadlines and not maintaining product quality, Softimage was recognized as a leader in 3D software designed to generate special effects in movies and advertisements using Microsoft operating systems. Softimage was formerly a division of Microsoft and was considered a fringe competitor of Avid. As part of the $248 million acquisition that included $128 million in goodwill, Microsoft took a 9.1 percent ownership stake in Avid. Microsoft's changed status from that of competitor to that of part owner effectively aligned Avid with one of the most powerful firms in the technology industry.

In 1998, Avid also entered into a horizontal strategic alliance with Tektronix. This agreement resulted in a joint venture between the two competitors. Avid and Tektronix were able to identify mutual needs in responding to competition in the news broadcast market. Tektronix, a diversified organization with revenues of $2 billion, had advantages in the areas of digital storage technology as well as in its network of customers in the news broadcast industry. Although Avid produced digital storage devices, it conceded that those produced by Tektronix were more widely accepted by the industry. In addition, being relatively new to the news broadcast industry, Avid had yet to develop a customer network on a par with that of Tektronix. Further, the market would perceive Avid to have greater financial stability if it partnered its operations with those of a larger firm. At the same time, Tektronix conceded that Avid's digital editing products were superior to its own.

The joint venture was called Avstar. Each partner took a 50 percent ownership position in the venture and, in 1999, each contributed an initial $2 million in cash and assets. Through Avstar, Avid and Tektronix planned to combine their competencies in both digital editing and storage technology, while further enhancing innovation and product development in the news broadcast market. Together, they expected to grow market share in this industry more quickly, while reducing the risk each would face if it sought to develop the market on its own.

AVID MANAGEMENT

From its founding in 1989 through 1995, Avid's cofounders sequentially held the position of CEO. William Warner was first, and kept the title until 1991, when he left to start another, noncompeting company. Subsequently, Curt Rawley held the position until 1995. They both answered to a board of directors chaired by the general partner of Greylock Management Corporation, a venture capital firm that played a significant role in the company's initial equity funding.

While the cofounders led Avid through a period of remarkable growth and success, Avid's initial objectives to gain market share and develop a position of industry leadership eventually took their toll on company profitability. Lack of strong controls to monitor growth resulted in large write-downs in 1996 of various assets, including obsolete inventories and uncollectable receivables. At the same time, sales growth slowed, thus exacerbating the impact of insufficient controls on the company's bottom line.

Slowing sales and decreasing profits during this period led Avid's board of directors to recognize the need for a new management team that could institute the functional competencies necessary to halt the company's deteriorating financial performance. As a consequence, Avid shifted its emphasis from being driven by market share to seeking balanced growth with increased profitability. The board decided that to make it through these trying times, the company needed an "outside" individual with proven experience running a large technology firm in a highly competitive environment.

In 1996, Bill Miller, 53, a seasoned executive in the technology industry, was hired to turn the fortunes of Avid around. As former chair and CEO of Quantum Computers, Miller had proved his leadership ability in the computer hard-drive industry. Under Miller, Quantum had grown from $1.1 billion in revenues to $3.4 billion in five years.

Miller's responsibilities as Avid's new CEO included implementing the controls necessary to reduce the company's cost structure and reestablishing Avid as a profitable growth company. Understanding the need for Avid's quick turnaround, the board provided Miller with a high level of authority. He was appointed to the positions of both CEO and chairman of Avid's board of directors. The remaining eight board members were all nonexecutive directors.

AVID ATTEMPTS A TURNAROUND

Bill Miller was excited about Avid's prospects and its competitive staying power, saying that "in a world in which media can be used for virtually any message and delivered across the airwaves, a cable, or a computer network, we intend to continue to provide the tools that people use to tell their story." To Miller, the proliferation of television channels alone signaled Avid's potential: "The average cable household will soon have 90 channels, and with the fast spread of digital signals, that number may increase very quickly. More channels mean more programming to edit with software like Avid's."

However, Miller also recognized that Avid had outgrown the capabilities of its management, and that market leadership had to be paired with superior profitability. As a result, he began his tenure by building a new management team. This included hiring a new chief financial officer (CFO) to establish necessary financial control systems to decrease costs. Inventories and accounts receivables were significantly reduced, from $63.4 million and $107.9 million, respectively, in 1995, to $9.8 million and $79.8 million, respectively, in 1997. These efforts improved the company's cash flow while reducing risks associated with inventory obsolescence and the collectibility of receivables. The turnaround entailed streamlining the organization, eliminating approximately 70 staff positions, and discontinuing the development and sale of certain products. The total one-time cost to the company was $15.8 million.

In an effort to boost company growth and profitability, Miller began to make significant changes in operations. One such change involved the company's product distribution channels. During Miller's tenure, Avid developed stronger relationships with firms that could distribute its products to a broad base of commercial and retail customers. As this channel grew, Avid was able to reduce its direct sales (in-house) activities to only key accounts that required a significant amount of time during and after the sales process. Avid was thus able to take advantage of the well-developed networks of its indirect channel members (independent distributors, value-added resellers, and dealers) while reducing overall operating expenses relating to in-house sales and marketing activities. Sales through indirect channel members (as opposed to the direct, in-house sales function) grew from 50 percent of total annual sales in 1996 to 85 percent in 1999.

The company also focused on its customer support function, by expanding resources and restructuring the function to increase customer satisfaction. For example, according to a 1998 *Forbes* article, after Miller increased training for his support staff, Avid's ability to fix a problem on the first service call improved from under 50 percent to over 90 percent, and the period of time customers had to wait for technical help decreased to about two minutes.

Under Miller's leadership, Avid worked toward realizing its mission statement of becoming the leading provider of powerful digital content creation tools used to "entertain and inform the world." The company not only sought to expand its presence in its existing digital media markets but also targeted new markets and continued to drive and support open industry standards.

However, the benefits of Miller's restructuring were short lived. The Softimage acquisition—Miller's most significant strategic action while running Avid, and perhaps the most important single transaction in the company's history—was more difficult for the company to digest than originally expected. Additionally, three years into Miller's tenure as Avid's chief executive, sales growth and profits remained elusive. In 1999, Avid recorded revenues of $452.6 million (a 6 percent decrease from 1998) and a net loss of $137.5 million—the company's worst performance in its 10-year history. Further, from 1998 to 1999, cash and marketable securities decreased from $111.8 million to $72.8 million; the current ratio decreased from 2:1 to 1.7:1, and long-term debt as a percentage of equity increased from 4.6 percent to 8.5 percent (see Exhibits 1 and 2).

This resulted in the board of directors once again taking action by replacing top management. In late 1999, Bill Miller, CEO and chair of the board, and Clifford Jenks, president, both resigned. A few months later in early 2000, William Flaherty, CFO under Miller, resigned. The company stated that its business plan was no longer achievable given rapid changes in the market. As a result, the board determined that another thorough restructuring was necessary to position the company for future growth and profitability.

Krall, who was chief operating officer (COO) of Avid's Digidesign division, was appointed to the position of CEO in April 2000. The Digidesign division had been a bright spot for Avid; it had achieved record sales and operating income while the company as a whole was performing below expectations. In making the latest round of top management changes, the board decided not to appoint David Krall as chairman. The board chair position (also held by Miller during his reign) was filled by Robert Halperin, a nonexecutive board member. Krall was the only executive on the now six-member board. The restructuring also entailed an 11 percent reduction in staff. About 200 jobs were terminated, at a $10 million cost to the company. Avid expected the restructuring to reduce forward costs by $20 million annually. The company also announced that it would discontinue the development and sale of a limited number of existing products. The recently acquired Softimage was, for the most part, spared any significant restructuring and allowed to continue operating as a relatively autonomous division of the company.

THE COMPETITIVE LANDSCAPE

Avid benefited from introducing digital technology to the film and television industries. The company's success was achieved by providing superior digital products as a substitute for traditional analog products. The new digital technology was originally developed and marketed by small, innovative firms, many of which had since failed or been acquired by Avid or other firms in an attempt to establish industry leadership.

However, competition was intensifying. As digital technology became more firmly established, competition was expected from some of the big, well-entrenched analog firms that were beginning (or expected to begin) to produce their own digital products. These firms, such as Sony and Panasonic, were much larger than Avid and had significantly greater financial, technical, distribution, support, and marketing resources. Avid also expected to face competition in one or more of its markets from computer manufacturers such as IBM, Compaq, and Hewlett-Packard, and software vendors such as Oracle and Sybase. All of these firms had announced their intentions to enter some or all of the company's target markets, specifically the broadcast news and special effects markets. Exhibit 5 provides further information on key competitors.

exhibit 5   Avid's Key Competitors* (excluding music production markets)

Company Name	Sales Fiscal Year 2000 (in millions)
Digital (direct competition)	
Adobe	$ 1,266
Alias/Wavefront (subsidiary of Silicon Graphics)	2,331[†]
BTS (subsidiary of Philips Electronics)	35,253[†]
Discreet Logic (subsidiary of Autodesk)	936[†]
Kinetix (subsidiary of Autodesk)	936[†]
Lightworks USA (subsidiary of Tektronix)	1,103[†]
Media 100	73
Panasonic (subsidiary of Matsushita)	63,470[†]
The Grass Valley Group (subsidiary of Tektronix)	1,103[†]
Analog (indirect competition)	
Sony	63,607
Matsushita	63,470
Tektronix	1,103[‡]

*Includes video and film production and postproduction markets, broadcast news market, and graphics and special effects market; does not include the music production and postproduction markets.

[†]Annual sales represent that of the parent company's total operations; most subsidiaries represent acquisitions by larger firms as a means to enter Avid's markets.

[‡]Tektronix annual sales at the time of the 1998 joint venture with Avid were $2.1 billion. The decrease from 1998 to 2000 is due to divestitures of certain businesses in 1999 and 2000.

Source: Avid annual reports, public documents, and on-site interview with company representative; individual company 10K/10Q filings.

KRALL'S DILEMMA

"We revolutionized the digital content industry," said Krall. "We build the best content creation tools in video, film, 3D, and audio; 85 percent of films made in the U.S. actually utilize Avid tools." Additionally, Avid equipment was used to edit 95 percent of prime-time television programs. The company had established a leadership position in several markets by applying new technology in a timely fashion to meet emerging customer needs. However, for Avid to remain a leader, it had to maintain an accurate understanding of customer needs, technological advancements, and competitive dynamics in the markets it served.

Krall and the new management team he needed to build faced many challenges. Concern existed over the slowed rate of growth in company revenues and the staggering losses. Some industry analysts viewed the purchase of Softimage as a signal for investors to wait and see, wondering whether the sheer magnitude of Avid's first cross-border acquisition was too much for the company to manage. Krall acknowledged that "it's easy for expenses to get ahead of revenues," and indicated that "the company's first goal was to bring expenses back in line [with company revenues]." He also noted that the company's "second goal was to lay the foundation for growth in the future." Meanwhile, Avid risked competition from major international firms, such as

Sony and Panasonic, that were attracted to opportunities offered by the digital technologies the company had pioneered. Avid's ability to compete effectively against these well-established firms would be severely tested.

Krall's four years' experience at Avid included stints as Digidesign's director of program management, vice president of engineering, and COO. His strong technical background, with BS and MS degrees from MIT and an MBA from Harvard, as well as his company and industry knowledge, would come to bear on the strategic decisions he would have to make to turn Avid around. During his first year as CEO, the proactive Krall announced a new focus on Internet-related editing products and once again set Avid on an acquisition track. In 2000, Avid purchased Pluto Technologies International and The Motion Factory for an aggregate $2.3 million. Pluto Technologies specialized in storage and networking products for the news broadcast industry, and The Motion Factory specialized in interactive games for the Web. These were Avid's first acquisitions since its 1998 acquisition of Softimage. Krall also oversaw an alliance with Intel and Microsoft to develop products for creating interactive digital television.

Krall finished his first year with Avid on a modestly successful note. Avid's 2000 revenues were up 5 percent from 1999, and, although the company incurred a net loss of $56 million, it was significantly less than the $137 million loss incurred in 1999.

As Avid entered 2001, Krall had to reevaluate his first-year decisions and determine what new strategic actions, if any, he should take to ensure Avid's successful turnaround. With competition intensifying, Krall knew he had to act fast. His strategic decisions to further diversify the company into the Internet, gaming, and digital television markets as well as to further commit to the news broadcast market would have to be weighed against the company's performance in 2000. Krall had to assess whether he had addressed the causes of the company's past performance problems. Another downturn in Avid's financial performance would not only result in further turmoil within the company and investment community but also jeopardize the company's ability to survive as an independent entity. With his keen sense of humor, the youthful Krall stated, "If you look at Avid's history, it has roughly had a new CEO every three years. One could guess that perhaps I've got two years left on my clock."

bibliography

"Advancing the Film: For Those Who Want to Beam Photos over the Internet, Digital Cameras May Be the Way to Go." *The Wall Street Journal,* March 22, 1999, p. R6.

Ankeny, Jan. :A Summertime Trip to Avid." *TV Technology,* June 27, 1998.

"Avid Acquires Pluto, Expanding Its Broadcast and Post-Production Product Line-up." *CNN Disclosure,* September 10, 2000.

"Avid Acquires The Motion Picture Factory." *Boston Herald,* June 30, 2000, p. 30.

"Avid Agrees to Buy Softimage Unit from Microsoft." *The Wall Street Journal,* June 16, 1998, p. B7.

"Avid's Acquisition Posted Losses." *Boston Herald,* October 22, 1998.

"Avid, Microsoft, Intel Alliance." *DTV Business* 14, no. 8 (April 17, 2000).

Avid Technololgy. 10-K reports, 1998–2000; 10-Q reports, March 31, 1998, June 30, 1998, September 30, 1998, and March 31, 2001; annual reports, 1993–2000; Business Overview, Prudential Securities Technology Conference, fall 1998; "Leadership and Vision," 1998; "NAB '98 Avid Teaser"; prospectuses, March 1, 1993, and September 21, 1995; "Corporate Overview," August 14, 1998; various press releases, 1998–2001; website (www.avid.com); and on-site interview with company official.

"Avid Technology Acquired Two Software Companies, Elastic Reality and The Parallax Software Group, for $45 Million." *Newsbytes News Network,* March 31, 1995.

"Avid Technology Inc Staff to Be Trimmed 11% under Restructuring Plan." *The Wall Street Journal,* November 11, 1999, p. B23.

"Avid Technology to Acquire Digidesign in a Stock-Swap Merger Worth about $205 Million." *Computer Reseller News* 602 (October 31, 1994), p. 231.

"Best Buy Co.: December Sales Rose 21% on Strong DVD Purchasing." *The Wall Street Journal,* January 7, 1999.

"CEO Interviews." *Wall Street Transcript* 47, no. 12 (December 29, 1997).

"Cheaper PCs Start to Attract New Customers." *The Wall Street Journal,* January 26, 1998, p. B1.

"CompUSA Net Rises 44% as Revenue Jumps 22% to $1.46 Billion." *The Wall Street Journal,* January 29, 1998, p. A10.

Dickson, Glen. "Avid Makes New Friend in Las Vegas; Forms Alliances with Hewlett-Packard and Panasonic." *Broadcasting & Cable* 126, no. 17 (April 17, 1996), p. 12.

———. "Avid's Turnaround Man." *Broadcasting & Cable,* October 9, 2000, p. 81.

Film & Television 2, no. 1 (first quarter, 1998).

Griffith, Bill. CNBC on-air interview, October 20, 2000.

Linsmayer, Anne. "The Customer Knows Best." *Forbes,* August 24, 1998, pp. 92–93.

Shadid, Anthony. "Fast Forward: There's No Firm More Avid for Digital Film Technology." *Boston Globe,* April 30, 2001, p. C2.

"Softimage Enters Agreement with Microsoft to Develop Tools and Middleware for Xbox." *Business Wire,* May 15, 2001.

"Who's News: Avid Technology Inc." *The Wall Street Journal,* April 27, 2000.

case 25 | Robin Hood

Joseph Lampel
New York University

It was in the spring of the second year of his insurrection against the High Sheriff of Nottingham that Robin Hood took a walk in Sherwood Forest. As he walked he pondered the progress of the campaign, the disposition of his forces, the Sheriff's recent moves, and the options that confronted him.

The revolt against the Sheriff had begun as a personal crusade. It erupted out of Robin's conflict with the Sheriff and his administration. However, alone Robin Hood could do little. He therefore sought allies, men with grievances and a deep sense of justice. Later he welcomed all who came, asking few questions and demanding only a willingness to serve. Strength, he believed, lay in numbers.

He spent the first year forging the group into a disciplined band, united in enmity against the Sheriff and willing to live outside the law. The band's organization was simple. Robin ruled supreme, making all important decisions. He delegated specific tasks to his lieutenants. Will Scarlett was in charge of intelligence and scouting. His main job was to shadow the Sheriff and his men, always alert to their next move. He also collected information on the travel plans of rich merchants and tax collectors. Little John kept discipline among the men and saw to it that their archery was at the high peak that their profession demanded. Scarlock took care of the finances, converting loot to cash, paying shares of the take, and finding suitable hiding places for the surplus. Finally, Much the Miller's son had the difficult task of provisioning the ever-increasing band of Merrymen.

The increasing size of the band was a source of satisfaction for Robin, but also a source of concern. The fame of his Merrymen was spreading, and new recruits were pouring in from every corner of England. As the band grew larger, their small bivouac became a major encampment. Between raids the men milled about, talking and playing games. Vigilance was in decline, and discipline was becoming harder to enforce. "Why," Robin reflected, "I don't know half the men I run into these days."

The growing band was also beginning to exceed the food capacity of the forest. Game was becoming scarce, and supplies had to be obtained from outlying villages. The cost of buying food was beginning to drain the band's financial reserves at the very moment when revenues were in decline. Travelers, especially those with the most to lose, were now giving the forest a wide berth. This was costly and inconvenient to them, but it was preferable to having all their goods confiscated.

Robin believed that the time had come for the Merrymen to change their policy of outright confiscation of goods to one of a fixed transit tax. His lieutenants strongly resisted this idea. They were proud of the Merrymen's famous motto: "Rob the rich and give to the poor." "The farmers and the townspeople," they argued, "are our most important allies. How can we tax them, and still hope for their help in our fight against the Sheriff?"

Robin wondered how long the Merrymen could keep to the ways and methods of their early days. The Sheriff was growing stronger and becoming better organized. He now had the money and the men and was beginning to harass the band, probing for its weaknesses. The tide of events was beginning to turn against the Merrymen. Robin felt that the campaign must be decisively concluded before the Sheriff had a chance to deliver a mortal blow. "But how," he wondered, "could this be done?"

Robin had often entertained the possibility of killing the Sheriff, but the chances for this seemed increasingly remote. Besides, killing the Sheriff might satisfy his personal thirst for revenge, but it would not improve the situation. Robin had hoped that the perpetual state of unrest, and the Sheriff's failure to collect taxes, would lead to his removal from office. Instead, the Sheriff used his political connections to obtain reinforcement. He had powerful friends at court and was well regarded by the regent, Prince John.

Prince John was vicious and volatile. He was consumed by his unpopularity among the people, who wanted the imprisoned King Richard back. He also lived in constant fear of the barons, who had first given him the regency but were now beginning to dispute his claim to the throne. Several of these barons had set out to collect the ransom that would release King Richard the Lionheart from his jail in Austria. Robin was invited to join the conspiracy in return for future amnesty. It was a dangerous proposition. Provincial banditry was one thing, court intrigue another. Prince John had spies everywhere, and he was known for his vindictiveness. If the conspirators' plan failed, the pursuit would be relentless, and retributions swift.

The sound of the supper horn startled Robin from his thoughts. There was the smell of roasting venison in the air. Nothing was resolved or settled. Robin headed for camp promising himself that he would give these problems his utmost attention after tomorrow's raid.

Armand Gilinsky Jr.
Sonoma State University

Sherri Anderson
Sonoma State University

In early January 2001, Jeff Gutsch, senior manager at the Santa Rosa, California, office of Moss Adams LLP, a West Coast accounting firm, met with his team to discuss the progress of a new initiative for developing the firm's accounting practice to serve clients in the northern California wine industry. At the meeting, Gutsch and his wine niche team reviewed the strategic plan for the coming year (see Exhibit 1).

The meeting took place just before the height of the busy tax and audit season. Gutsch, 39, had been concentrating on the firm's clients in its construction industry niche. He had not made as much headway as he had hoped developing new business with wine industry clients. He opened the meeting by saying:

> I think the issue we are all struggling with is how to break into a well-established mature niche. Do we discount fees? If so, is that our desired position in servicing the wine industry? Do we advertise? Seems like a big commitment for something that we can't be sure will produce results. Do we just get on every panel we can and shake as many hands as we can? I'm still trying to find the right formula.

Chris Pritchard, an accounting manager who had worked with Gutsch for two years to develop the wine niche, said:

> Sorry, Jeff, but I've been too busy working in health care. Health care is taking off, so my time is limited on the wine side. There's something missing, sort of a spark in this niche. There's not as much of a hunger to close, to go out and actually close a deal, or at least go out and meet with somebody. I think that's what's lacking for our success right now. I think we have all of the tools we need. But we don't have an aggressive nature to go out and start shaking hands and asking for business. We're doing everything else except asking for the business. We don't follow up.

Neysa Sloan, a senior accountant, nodded in assent:

> I personally do not see us making our objectives of gathering 20 percent of the market share in the regional wine industry over the next three to five years. Our marketing tactics are not up to the challenge. We need to seriously look at what we have done in the last year or two, what we are currently doing, and what we are proposing to do in regard to marketing. If we looked at this objectively, we would see that we have not gained much ground in the past using our current tactics—why would it work now? If you allowed more individuals to market and be involved, we might get somewhere.

This case was originally presented at the 2001 meeting of the North American Case Research Association in Memphis, Tennessee. The authors gratefully acknowledge the support of Moss Adams LLP and the Wine Business Program at Sonoma State University for assistance in preparation of this case.

exhibit 1   Moss Adams's Wine Niche Strategic Plan, 2001

Moss Adams LLP
Santa Rosa Office
2001 Strategic Plan to Serve Wine Industry Clients

Mission Statement

Our goal is to become the dominant accounting and business consulting firm serving the wine industry by providing superior, value-added services tailored to the needs of Northern California vineyards and wineries, as well as becoming experts in the industry.

● We expect to achieve this goal by December 31, 2004.

Five-Year Vision

We are recognized as the premier wine industry accounting and business consulting firm in Sonoma, Mendocino, and Napa Counties. We are leaders in the Moss Adams firmwide wine industry group, helping to establish Moss Adams as the dominant firm in the Washington and Oregon wine regions. We have trained and developed recognized industry experts in tax accounting and business consulting. Our staff is enthusiastic and devoted to the niche.

The Market

● A firmwide objective is to increase the average size of our business client. We expect to manage the wine niche with that objective in mind. However, during the first two to three years, we intend to pursue vineyards and wineries smaller than the firm's more mature niches would. When this niche is more mature we will increase our minimum prospect size. This strategy will help us gain experience and build confidence in Moss Adams in the industry, as it is an industry that tends to seek firms that are well established in the wine industry.

● There are approximately 122 wineries in Sonoma County, 168 in Napa County, and 25 in Mendocino County. Of these, approximately 55% have sales over $1 million, and up to one-third have sales in excess of $10 million. In addition to these, there are over 450 vineyards within the same three counties.

● The wine industry appears to be extremely provincial. That combined with the fact that most of our stronger competitors (see "Competition" below) are in Napa County, we consider Sonoma County to be our primary geographic market. However, Mendocino County has a growing wine industry, and we certainly will not pass up opportunities in Napa and other nearby counties in 2001.

Our Strengths

The strengths Moss Adams has in competing in this industry are:

● We are large enough to provide the specific services demanded by this industry.

● Our firm's emphasis is on serving middle-market businesses, while the "Big 5" firms are continually increasing their minimum client size. The majority of the wine industry is made up of middle-market companies. This "Big 5" trend increases our market each year.

● We do not try to be all things to all people. We focus our efforts in specialized industries/niches, with the goal of ultimately becoming dominant in those industries.

● We emphasize value-added services, which create more client satisfaction, loyalty, and name recognition.

● We have offices located throughout the West Coast wine regions.

● We have individuals within the firm with significant wine industry experience, including tax accounting and consulting. We also have experts in closely related industries such as orchards and beverage and food manufacturing.

● Within California, we have some high-profile wine industry clients.

● The majority of our niche members have roots in Sonoma County, which is important to Sonoma County wineries and grape growers.

exhibit 1   (continued)

- Our group is committed to being successful in and ultimately dominating the industry in Sonoma, Napa, and Mendocino Counties.

Challenges

- Our experience and credibility in the wine industry are low compared to those of other firms.
- There has been a perception in the Sonoma County area that we are not local to the area. As we continue to grow and become better known, this should be less of an issue.

If we can minimize our weaknesses by emphasizing our strengths, we will be successful in marketing to the wine industry, allowing us to achieve our ultimate goal of being dominant in the industry.

Competition

There are several CPA firms in Northern California that service vineyards and wineries. The "Big 5" firms are generally considered our biggest competitors in many of the industries we serve, and some have several winery clients. But as noted earlier, their focus seems to be on larger clients, which has decreased their ability to compete in this industry. Of the firms with significant wine industry practices, the following firms appear to be our most significant competitors:

- *Motto Kryla & Fisher*—This firm is a well-established wine industry leader, with the majority of its client base located in Napa County, although it has many Sonoma County clients. It is moving away from the traditional accounting and tax compliance services, concentrating its efforts on consulting and research projects. We can take advantage of this—along with the perception of many in the industry that Motto Kryla & Fisher is becoming too much of an insider—and gain additional market share.
- *Dal Pagetto & Company*—This firm was a split off from Deloitte & Touche several years ago. It is located in Santa Rosa, and has several vineyard and winery clients. At this time, it is probably our biggest Sonoma County competitor; however, it may be too small to compete once our momentum builds.
- Other firms that have significant wine industry practices that we will compete against include G & J Seiberlich & Co., Brotemarkle Davis & Co., Zainer Reinhart & Clarke, Pisenti & Brinker, Deloitte & Touche, and PriceWaterhouseCoopers. The first two are wine industry specialists headquartered in Napa County, and although very competitive there, they each do not appear to have a large Sonoma County client base. The next two are general practice firms with several wine industry clients. However, each of these firms has struggled to hold itself together in recent years, and none appear to have well-coordinated wine industry practices. The last two firms listed above are "Big 5" firms that, as noted earlier, focus mostly on the largest wineries.

Annual Marketing Plan

Our marketing strategy will build on the foundation we laid during the prior two years. We have established the following as our marketing plan:

- Increase and develop industry knowledge and expertise:
  - Work with other Moss Adams offices, particularly Stockton, to gain knowledge and experience from their experienced staff. Additionally, work with Stockton to have Santa Rosa Wine Niche staff assigned to two of their winery audits.
  - Continue to attend industry CPE, including the Vineyard Symposium, the Wine Industry Symposium, the California State Society of CPAs sponsored wine industry conferences in Napa and San Louis Obispo, and selected Sonoma State University and UC Davis courses. We would like 8 hours of wine industry–specific CPE for each Senior Level and above committed member of the Wine Niche. Jeff will have final approval on who will attend which classes.

exhibit 1   (continued)

- Continue to build our relationship with Sonoma State University (SSU). Our wine niche has agreed to be the subject of an SSU case study on the development of a CPA firm wine industry practice. We feel this case study will help us gain additional insight into what it will take to be competitive, as well as give us increased exposure both at SSU and in the industry. We will also seek to become more involved in SSU's wine industry educational program by providing classroom guest speakers twice a year.
  - Attract and hire staff with wine industry experience. We should strongly consider candidates who have attained a degree through the SSU Wine Business Program. We should also work to recruit staff within the office that have an interest in the industry.

- Continue to form alliances with industry experts both inside and outside the firm. We are building relationships with Ray Blatt, of the Moss Adams Los Angeles office, who has expertise in wine industry excise and property tax issues. Cheryl Mead, of the Santa Rosa office, has developed as a cost segregation specialist with significant winery experience.

- Develop and use relationships with industry referral sources:
  - Work with bankers and attorneys who specialize in the wine industry. From these bankers and attorneys, we would like to see three new leads per year.
  - Partner with other CPA firms in the industry. Smaller firms may need to enlist the services of a larger firm with a broader range of services, while the "Big 5" firms may want to use a smaller firm to assist with projects that are below their minimum billing size for the project type. We will obtain at least two projects per year using this approach.
  - Leverage the relationships we have to obtain five referrals and introductions to other wine industry prospects per year.
  - Maintain a matrix of Sonoma, Mendocino, and Napa County wineries and vineyards, including addresses, controller or top financial officer, current CPA, and banking relationship. This matrix will be updated as new information becomes available. From this matrix, we will send at least one mailing per quarter.

- Increase our involvement in the following industry trade associations by attending regular meetings and getting to know association members. In one of the following associations, each committed niche member will seek to obtain an office or board position:
  - Sonoma County Wineries Association
  - Sonoma County Grape Growers Association
  - Sonoma State University Wine Business Program
  - Zinfandel Advocates and Producers
  - Women for Winesense
  - California Association of Winegrape Growers
  - Wine Institute

- Establish an environment within the niche that promotes and practices the PILLAR concept. Encourage staff in the niche to be creative and strive to be the best. Provide interesting projects and events for the niche to make participation more interesting.

- Use the existing services that Moss Adams offers to market the firm. These include:
- BOSS
- Business Valuations
- Cost Segregation
- SCORE
- SALT
- Business Assurance Services
- Income Tax Compliance Services

exhibit 1   *(concluded)*

- Make use of firm resources
  - Use Moss Adams's InfoEdge (document management system) to share and refer to industry-related proposals and marketing materials.
    - All wine niche proposals will be entered into and updated in InfoEdge as completed.
    - All wine niche marketing letters will be entered into InfoEdge as created.
- Continue to have monthly wine industry niche meetings. We will review the progress on this plan at our March, April, and September niche meetings. Within our niche, we should focus our marketing efforts on Sonoma County, concentrating on smaller prospects that we can grow with, which will enable us to increase our prospect size over time. We would like to be in position to attract the largest wineries in the industry by 2004.
- Establish a Quarterly CFO/Controller roundtable group, with the Moss Adams Wine Industry Group working as facilitator. We will have the group established and have our first meeting in the summer.
- Quarterly, at our niche meetings, monitor progress on the quantifiable goals in this strategic plan.

Summary

In 2001, one of our goals is to add a minimum of three winery clients to our client base. We feel this is a reasonable goal as long as we continue to implement our plan as written.

We believe we can make the wine industry niche a strong niche in the Santa Rosa office. The firm defines niche dominance as having a minimum of $500,000 in billings, and a 20 percent market share, and having 40 percent of the services provided be in value-added service codes. We expect to become the dominant industry force in Sonoma, Mendocino, and Napa Counties by 2004.

We are also willing to assist other offices within the firm establish wine industry niches, eventually leading to a mature niche within the firm. We believe with the proper effort we can accomplish each of these goals.

Cheryl Mead, a senior manager whose specialty was conducting cost segregation[1] studies, commented:

> Growing wineries are looking for help. We need to focus on wineries that are expanding their facilities, and then grow with their growing businesses. Value-added services like cost segregation could represent as much as 40 percent of our wine industry practice. If we want to get in, we've got to do much more networking, marketing, and presentations. The challenge for us here in Santa Rosa is how to manage our resources. Career choices are changing; you can't be a generalist anymore. We need both people-related and technical skills, but those don't usually go hand-in-hand. We need someone who is famous in the field, a "who's who" in the wine accounting industry.

Claire Calderon, also a senior tax manager, said to the team:

> This is a hard niche to break into, Jeff. It takes a long time to develop relationships in specific industries. It could take a couple of years. First you find forums to meet people, get to know people, get people to trust you, and then you get an opportunity to work on a project and you do a good job. It takes a while. Our goal is to become a trusted adviser and that doesn't happen overnight.

---

[1]Cost segregation is a process of breaking a large asset into its smaller components so that depreciation may be taken on an accelerated basis.

Gutsch replied:

> While consolidation is happening in the wine industry, many of the wineries we are targeting are still privately owned. When you're dealing with privately owned businesses it's much more personal than with public companies.

Calderon added:

> That might explain part of it, Jeff, but the reality is that there are two other fledgling niches that are doing well and going like gangbusters. This niche is off to a slow start!

Barbara Korte, a senior accountant, reassured him:

> Jeff, you have been very focused, very enthusiastic about this project. You've put a lot of time into it. As a leader, I think you are a real good manager.

At stake was the opportunity to generate significant incremental client fee revenues. More than 600 wine producers and vineyards (grape growers) were in business in the premium northern California wine-growing region encompassing Napa, Sonoma, and Mendocino Counties. According to the Summer 2000 issue of *Marketplace*, there were 168 wine producers and 228 vineyards in Napa; 122 wine producers and 196 vineyards in Sonoma; and 25 wine producers and 61 vineyards in Mendocino. Few of these operations were large, according to *Marketplace*. Napa and Sonoma each had 14 wine producers reporting over $10 million in sales, and Mendocino only one.

COMPANY BACKGROUND

Moss Adams was a regional accounting firm. It had four regional hubs within the firm: southern California, northern California, Washington, and Oregon. By late 2000, Moss Adams had become one of the 15 largest accounting firms in the United States, with 150 partners, 740 CPAs, and 1,200 employees. Founded in 1913 and headquartered in Seattle, the full-service firm specialized in middle-market companies, those with annual revenues of $10 to $200 million.

Each office had a managing partner. Art King was the managing partner of the Santa Rosa office—see Exhibit 2 for the Santa Rosa office organization chart. The firm was considered midsize and its client base tended to mirror that size. King reflected on Moss Adams's advantages of size and location:

> It is an advantage to be a regional firm with a strong local presence. For one thing, there just aren't that many regional firms, especially out here on the West Coast. In fact, I think we're the only true West Coast regional firm. That gives us access to a tremendous number of resources that the larger firms have. We have the added advantage of being a big part of Sonoma County. Sonoma County companies want the same kind of services they can get from the Big Five operating out of places like San Francisco, but they also like to deal with local firms that are active in the community. Our staff is active in Rotary, 20-30, the local chambers of commerce, and so on, and that means a lot to the businesspeople in the area. Sonoma County companies will go to San Francisco for professional services, but only if they have to, so we offer the best of both worlds.

Each office within the firm was differentiated. An office like Santa Rosa had the ability to be strong in more niches because it was one of the dominant firms in the area. Moss Adams did not have to directly compete with the Big Five accounting firms (Andersen Worldwide, PriceWaterhouseCoopers, Ernst & Young, Deloitte & Touche, and KPMG) as they did not focus on providing services to small businesses. Since it was a

exhibit 2   Moss Adams's Organizational Chart for Santa Rosa Office

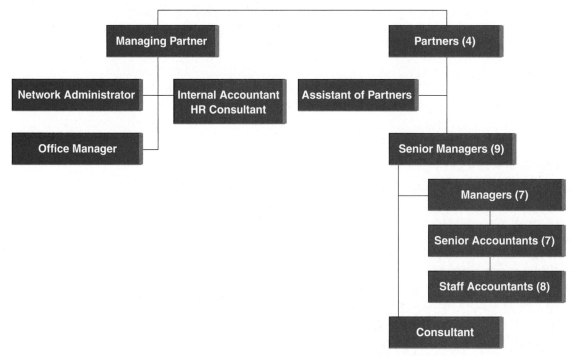

regional firm, Moss Adams was able to offer a depth of services that most local firms were not able to match. This gave Moss Adams a competitive advantage when selling services to the middle-market company segment.

Moss Adams provided services in four main areas of expertise: business assurance (auditing), tax, international, and consulting. Auditing constituted approximately 35 to 40 percent of Moss Adams's practice, the remainder being divided among tax work in corporate, partnerships, trusts and estates, and individual taxation. In its Santa Rosa office, Moss Adams serviced corporate clients and very wealthy individuals.

On the international side, Moss Adams was a member of Moores Rowland International, a worldwide association of accounting firms. Moss Adams primarily worked with local companies that did business overseas or that wanted to set up a foreign location. It also did a lot of work with local companies that had parent firms located overseas.

On the consulting side, Moss Adams had about 80 full-time consultants, and this line of business represented probably 15 to 20 percent of the total practice. A large part of the consulting work performed by Moss Adams was in mergers and acquisitions. Its M&A division helped middle-market companies, which formed the bulk of its clientele, develop a coherent, consistent strategy, whether they were planning on selling the business and needed to find an appropriate buyer or were looking for a good acquisition target.

The Big Six (now Big Five) accounting firms had developed industry-specific strategies in the 1980s, and Moss Adams had been one of the first midlevel accounting firms in the nation to use a focus strategy and build its practice around specific industry niches. Adopting a niche strategy had allowed Moss Adams to provide specialized services to a particular industry of regional importance. As niche clients were attracted,

Moss Adams made sure that it had "famous people" (or true industry experts) in that niche. These in-house people became the "go-to persons," the leaders of Moss Adams's practice in that niche.

The high-technology sector represented one of the fastest-growing parts of Moss Adams's business. According to King:

> It's big in the Seattle area [where Moss Adams has its headquarters], and with the development of Telecom Valley, it's certainly becoming big in Sonoma County. We're finding that a great deal of our work is coming from companies that are offshoots of other large high-tech companies in the area. Financial institutions represent another client group that's growing rapidly, as is health care. With all of the changes in the health care and medical fields, there's been a good deal of turmoil. We have a lot of expertise in the health care and medical areas, so that's a big market for us. Have I seen a drop-off? No, not really. The interesting thing about the accounting industry is that even when the economy slows down, there's still a lot of work for a CPA firm. There might not be as many large, special projects as when the economy is really rolling, but the work doesn't slow down.

THE INDUSTRY AND THE MARKET

Accounting was a large and relatively stable service industry, according to the *Journal of Accountancy*, the industry's most widely read trade publication. The Big Five accounting firms dominated the global market in 1998 with combined global revenue exceeding $58 billion, well over half the industry's total revenue. All of the Big Five firms reported double-digit growth rates in 1998. However, some of the most spectacular growth was achieved by firms outside the top 10, some of which registered increases of nearly 60 percent over 1997 revenues. Ninety of the top 100 firms had revenue increases, and 58 of them had achieved double-digit gains.

In 1999, accounting industry receipts in the United States exceeded $65 billion. The industry employed more than 632,000 people. However, the industry was expected to post more modest growth in revenues and employment into the 21st century. Finding niche markets, diversifying services, and catering to global markets were key growth strategies for companies in the industry. Large international firms, including the Big Five, had branched out into management consulting services in the late 1980s and early 1990s.

Accounting firms and certified public accountants (CPAs) nationwide began offering a wide array of services in addition to traditional accounting, auditing, and bookkeeping services. This trend was partially a response to clients' demand for "one-stop shopping" for all their professional services needs. Another cause was the relatively flat growth in demand for traditional accounting and auditing services over the past 10 years, as well as the desire of CPAs to develop more value-added services. The addition of management consulting, legal, and other professional services to the practice mix of large national accounting networks was transforming the industry.

Many firms began offering information technology consulting because of growing client demand for Internet and electronic commerce services. *Accounting Today*'s 1999 survey of CPA clients indicated that keeping up with technology was *the* strategic issue of greatest concern, followed by recruiting and retaining staff, competing with larger companies, planning for executive succession, and maximizing productivity.

However, according to the *CPA Journal,* the attractive consulting fees may have led many firms to ignore potential conflicts of interest in serving as an auditor and as a management consultant to the same client. The profession's standards could be jeopardized by the entrance of non-CPA partners and owners in influential accounting firms. Many companies facing these problems had split their accounting and management consulting operations. In January 2001, Arthur Andersen had spun off its consulting division into an independent company named Accenture, partly to avoid conflict of interests.

Still, CPA firms could be expected to continue to develop their capabilities and/or strategic alliances to meet clients' demands. Areas of expansion among accounting firms included administrative services, financial and investment planning services, general management services, government administration, human resources, international operations, information technology and computer systems consulting, litigation support, manufacturing administration, marketing, and research and development. Many small and medium-size independent firms were merging or forming alliances with large service companies such as American Express, H&R Block, and Century Business Services.

By the late 1990s, a trend toward consolidation got under way in the accounting industry. Several factors were fueling the drive toward consolidation. Large increases in revenue among the top 100 accounting firms between 1997 and 1998 were partially attributable to this trend toward consolidation. Consolidators wanted access to the large volume of business currently being done by independent CPAs. The trust that small businesses and individuals had in their CPAs was considered very valuable, and consolidators wanted to leverage the potential of an individual firm's integrity to expand their own businesses. Consolidation caused a decline in the number of independent accounting firms that offered only tax and accounting services. The New York State Society of CPAs estimated that up to 50 of the largest accounting firms in the United States could merge with other entities by the end of 2000. In the San Francisco Bay Area, the Big Five dominated the industry—see Exhibit 3.

THE WINE INDUSTRY NICHE

The wine industry was a newly targeted niche not only for the Santa Rosa office, but also for Moss Adams. Moss Adams allowed any employee to propose a niche. All accounting firms bill at fairly standard rates—so the more billable hours generated, the better. Moss Adams felt it was in the firm's long-term best interest to allow employees to focus on areas in which they were interested. The firm would benefit from revenues generated, but, more important, employees would likely stay with a firm that allowed a degree of personal freedom and promoted professional growth.

Gutsch and Pritchard had begun pursuing wine industry clients in mid-1998 for several reasons. First, both had an interest in the industry. Second, Sonoma and Napa Counties had over 200 wineries and numerous vineyard operations. Third, Moss Adams had expertise in related or similar business lines such as orchards, as well as significant related experience in providing services to the manufacturing sector. Finally, the wine industry had been historically serviced either by large firms that considered the typical winery a small client or by smaller firms that were not able to offer the range of services that Moss Adams could provide.

Sara Rogers, a senior accountant and member of the wine niche team, recalled:

> It first started with Jeff Gutsch and Chris Pritchard and another senior manager, who was in our office until November, 1999. Anyway, I think it was their motivation that really started the group. The three of them were doing everything in building the niche. When the senior manager left, it sort of fell flat on its face for a little while. I think it got stagnant. Pretty much nobody said anything about it until last summer, when Jeff started the organization

exhibit 3 Top 20 Accounting Firms in San Francisco Bay Area, Ranked by Number of Bay Area CPAs, June 2000

Rank	1999 Rank	Company	No. of Bay Area CPAs	No. of Company CPAs	No. of Bay Area Employees	1999 Billings, Bay Area	No. of Partners in Bay Area	No. of Company Partners	Fiscal Year Ending	U.S. Net Revenue ($ mil.)	% Change vs. Prior Year
1	2	Deloitte & Touche LLP	439	8,380	1,437	NR	172	2,066	May-99	$5,336	24.2
2	1	PricewaterhouseCoopers LLP	430	430	2,000	NR	138	9,000	Sep-99	6,956	18.7
3	3	KPMG Peat Marwick LLP	316	NR	1,778	NR	157	6,800	Jun-99	4,112	21.5
4	4	Arthur Andersen	312	6,161	821	NR	63	3,059	Aug-99	3,300	17.9
5	5	Ernst & Young LLP	300	NR	850	NR	77	2,465	Sep-99	6,100	10.0
6	6	BDO Seidman LLP	72	1,650	122	NR	15	360	Jun-00	408	36.9
7	14	Seiler & Co. LLP	44	44	110	NR	12	12	NR	NR	NR
8	7	Frank, Rimerman & Co. LLP	43	51	76	NR	12	13	May-99	17	9.2
9	9	Hood & Strong LLP	42	42	89	NR	12	12	NR	NR	NR
10*	10	Harb, Levy & Weiland LLP	38	38	80	NR	13	13	NR	NR	NR
10*	13	Ireland San Filippo LLP	38	38	81	12.7M	13	17	Apr-00	13	15.8
12	15	Burr, Pilger & Mayer	35	35	110	NR	10	10	NR	NR	NR
13	11	Armanino McKenna LLP	34	34	87	NR	13	13	NR	NR	NR
14	14	Novogradac & Co. LLP	31	36	80	NR	6	8	NR	NR	NR
15	12	RINA Accountancy Corp.	26	29	59	7.3M	13	14	NR	NR	NR
16*	16	Grant Thornton LLP	25	1,300	90	NR	10	300	Jul-00	416	10.9
16*	18	Shea Labagh Dobberstein	25	25	35	NR	3	3	NR	NR	NR
18	18	Moss Adams LLP	24	800	39	NR	7	144	Dec-99	109	31.3
19	16	Lindquist, von Husen & Joyce	23	23	47	NR	5	5	NR	NR	NR
20	21	Lautze & Lautze	21	28	39	NR	9	11	NR	NR	NR

NR = Not Reported

*Tie in ranking.

Sources: Viva Chan, *San Francisco Business Times* 14, no. 46 (June 16, 2000), p. 28; Strafford Publications, *Public Accounting Reports*, vol. 24, June 2000.

of it again and brought in more people, and then he approached people that he wanted to work with.

Gutsch felt that Moss Adams was in a position to move forward to make the wine industry niche a strong one both in the Santa Rosa office and eventually in the firm as a whole. He was committed to that goal and expected to achieve it within five years. Gutsch saw this niche as his door to future partnership. Moss Adams's marketing strategy included the following:

1. Develop industry marketing materials that communicate Moss Adams's strengths and commitment.
2. Develop a distinctive logo for use in the industry.
3. Create an industry brochure similar to that of the firm's construction industry group.
4. Develop industry service information flyers such as the business life cycle, Research & Exploration (R&E) credit, excise tax compliance, and Business Ownership Succession Services (BOSS).
5. Develop relationships with industry referral sources (e.g., bankers and attorneys that specialized in the wine industry or current clients who served or had contacts in the industry).
6. Join and become active in industry trade associations.
7. Use existing relationships with industry contacts to obtain leads into prospective wineries and vineyards.
8. Use the existing services that Moss Adams offered to market the firm, particularly in cost segregation.
9. Focus efforts on Sonoma County, as well as adjacent wine-growing regions, which would enable Moss Adams to increase its prospect size over time.

Pritchard reflected on those early days:

The first thing we did was to develop a database of regional wineries and send out an introduction letter. The other thing we did was to develop marketing materials. Jeff developed a logo. We used a top-down approach pyramid for an introduction letter, starting out general and then with an action step at the end to call us. So we used that at first. Usually with that we'd get about 2 percent response, which is good out of 300 letters or whatever we sent out.

According to King, however, the major issue in growing the wine industry practice was selling:

The thing about selling in public accounting is that you have to have a lot of confidence in what you do and what you can do for the client. You have to have confidence that you know something about the industry. If you go into a marketing meeting or a proposal meeting and you're saying, "Well, we do a couple of wineries but we really want to do more and get better at it," you're not going to get the work. You gain confidence by knowing how to talk the language, knowing the buzzwords, knowing some of the players in the industry. You go into a meeting, all of a sudden you're on an equal footing with them. From a confidence standpoint, that's huge. You can't sell public accounting services unless you're confident about you and your firm and the people that are going to do the work. Over the last two years, Jeff has gone to the classes, gone to the meetings and his confidence level is much higher than it was a year ago. When he goes into these meetings he's going to be at a level where he doesn't have to make excuses for not having a lot of winery clients, because we have a lot of activity in the wine and the beverage processing industries. So, I think that's going to help a lot. That's where he's going to have more success because we're getting the at bats, we just need to get some hits.

One of the roles of the managing partner was to mentor potential partners and help them attain the role of partner. The training process included marketing and helping them build a practice, according to King:

> When we're talking with senior managers, I explain to them what they need to do to get to that next level. I had this conversation with Jeff because his primary focus when he came was "I need to build a big practice, nothing else matters." He trusts the system now. He's transferred some clients to others and received some clients. You have to work well with people, you have to train people, you have to have some responsibilities, and you have to get along with your peers.

The firm's philosophy was to encourage people to really enjoy what they did. Anyone was allowed to propose a niche, *even* a senior manager. Pritchard explained:

> Well, part of the way our firm works is, there is a "four-bucket" tier to make partner. One of the buckets is to become a famous person, and the fastest way of doing that is through the niche base; within a niche you get the experience and the reputation faster than you would as a generalist. Jeff is a senior manager, so now he's trying to figure out a way to become partner. I work on Bonny Doon Winery. I have a grower client in Kenwood, so I do have some experience with that. I also like wine because I make wine. It's an untapped market in Sonoma County for our firm. So we both got together—I had the entrepreneurial spirit to start and Jeff had the need.

King described in detail the "four-bucket" evaluation system at Moss Adams:

> We have four criteria that get evaluated by the partner and the compensation committee on a scale of 1 to 10. All of these are weighted equally, 25 percent, with a possibility of 40 points. The first is financial. We take a look at the potential partner's financial responsibilities, what their billings are, what their fee adjustments are, what their charge hours are. I've transferred many clients to people in the office. That's one way I help others grow their practices. I'm still responsible for some of those clients, because I'm the one who brought them in and I'm still the primary contact. My billing numbers may be this, but my overall financial responsibility may be bigger. That's an objective measure because we look at the numbers, we look at the trends.
>
> The second is responsibility. The managing partner of a big office gets more points than the managing partner of a smaller office does, who in turn gets more points than a person in charge of a niche, who in turn gets more points than a line partner. Somebody who is a partner and is responsible for the tax department, let's say, might get an extra point or half a point, whereas someone in charge of a niche might get an extra point. If they're in charge of an office they get more points.
>
> The third is personnel. Personnel is a very big initiative within Moss Adams. Upstream and downstream evaluations are conducted by our HR person for each office and measures staff retention and the quality of our mentoring program. Each partner is also evaluated up or down from an overall office rating score. For example, our office may get a 7, but I may get an 8 because I'm really good with people. Somebody who's really hard on people would get a lower rating.
>
> The fourth and final "bucket" is peer evaluation. We have three other partners evaluate each partner. They evaluate the partner for training, mentoring, marketing, and involvement in their community. Then, evaluations are used by the Compensation Committee to review individual partner compensation. They are also used for partner counseling sessions.

King also assured a "soft landing" to the participants of the niche teams. This meant that if a niche didn't work out, the firm would find the individual another one. This, it was hoped, fostered entrepreneurial behaviors that had their potential upsides and downsides. According to King:

> A high level of practice responsibility for a partner would be $1 million in this office. The range is anywhere from $600,000 to $1 million in billings a year. We try to get people involved in at least two niches in the office, until a niche becomes large enough that you can spend full-time in it. The upside, potentially, of the wine niche would be a practice of from $500,000 to $1 million based on Sonoma and maybe some Napa County wineries. So the upside is a very mature, profitable niche that fits right into our model of our other niches of middle market companies that have the need for not only client services but also our value-added services.
>
> If for some reason the wine niche didn't take off, Jeff would become more involved in the manufacturing niche—well, wine is manufacturing anyway, but it's just a subset of manufacturing. It might slow his rate to partner. It could also turn out that—all of a sudden—Jeff gets four great referrals in the manufacturing niche this year, he builds this great big practice in manufacturing, and as a result he has less time for the wine niche. The downside is we've spent some money on marketing, and Jeff has spent some time on marketing when he could have been doing something else. Then, we abandon the project. If that happens, then Jeff's time becomes available and the money becomes available to go after some other initiative or something we're already doing or some new initiative. Nobody is going to lose his or her job over it. We haven't lost a lot of money over it.

THE AFTERMATH

After the January 2001 meeting, Gutsch pondered how he should proceed to overcome some major roadblocks to building his team. King took Gutsch aside for counseling:

> Target the $10 million to under $20 million winery, for which we can provide a full range of services. There's nobody else with our range of services that's really doing a good job in that area. There's an underserved market for those middle market companies. When you started, I knew it would take two or three years to really get the ball rolling. This is really going to be your year, Jeff. If it isn't, well, we'll reevaluate at the end of the year. Our overall marketing budget is probably in the area of 1.5 to 2 percent of total client billings. In 1999, the first year for the wineries, we probably spent somewhere in the neighborhood of $5,000 to $8,000, which wasn't a lot but you joined some organizations and you did some training. Last year we probably spent $10,000 to $12,000. Now, Jeff, I know that some of our other offices spend a lot more on marketing than we do. We'll have to decide: Is this the best use of your time? Is this the best use of our resources to try to go after an industry where we just tried for three years and haven't made any inroads?

The decision to develop a niche had been based on a gut feeling. Moss Adams did not use any litmus test or hurdle rate of return to screen possible niches. This was because, with the exception of nonprofits, most clients had similar fee realization rates. Moss Adams looked at the potential volume of business and determined whether it could handle that volume. Yet Moss Adams remained unknown in the wine industry. Time was running out.

case 27 Perdue Farms, Inc.: Responding to 21st-Century Challenges

George C. Rubenson
Salisbury State University

Frank Shipper
Salisbury State University

I have a theory that you can tell the difference between those who have inherited a fortune and those who have made a fortune. Those who have made their own fortune forget not where they came from and are less likely to lose touch with the common man.
—Bill Sterling, *Eastern Shore News,* March 2,1988

In 1917, Arthur W. Perdue, a Railway Express agent and descendant of a French Huguenot family named Perdeaux, bought 50 leghorn chickens for a total of $5 and began selling table eggs near the small town of Salisbury, Maryland, a region alternately known as the Eastern Shore or Delmarva Peninsula. Initially, the business amounted to little more than a sideline, but in 1920 when Railway Express asked Arthur Perdue to move to a station away from the Eastern Shore, he quit his job and entered the egg business full-time. Arthur Perdue's only child, Franklin Parsons Perdue, was also born in 1920.

In 1924, Mr. Arthur, as he was called, bought some leghorn roosters (for $25) from Texas to improve the quality of his flock. He soon expanded his egg market and began shipments to New York. Practicing small economies such as mixing his own chicken feed and using leather from his old shoes to make hinges for his chicken coops, he stayed out of debt and prospered. He tried to add a new chicken coop every year. By the time young Frank was 10, he had 50 chickens or so of his own to look after, earning money from their eggs. He worked along with his parents (not always enthusiastically) to feed the chickens, clean the coops, dig the cesspools, and gather and grade the

The authors are indebted to Frank Perdue, Jim Perdue, and the numerous associates at Perdue Farms, Inc., who generously shared their time and information about the company. In addition, the authors would like to thank the anonymous librarians at Blackwell Library, Salisbury State University, who routinely review area newspapers and file articles about the poultry industry—the most important industry on the Delmarva Peninsula. Without their assistance, this case would not have been possible. Copyright 2001 by the authors. Used with permission.

eggs. A shy, introverted country boy, Frank went for five years to a one-room school near his home, went on to graduate from Wicomico High School, and attended State Teachers College in Salisbury for two years before returning to the farm in 1939 to work full-time with his father.

By 1940, Perdue Farms was already known for quality products and fair dealing in a tough, highly competitive market. The company began offering chickens for sale when both Mr. Arthur and Frank realized that the future lay in selling chickens, not eggs. In 1944, Mr. Arthur made Frank a full partner in A. W. Perdue and Son, Inc. In 1950, Frank took over leadership of the company, which employed 40 people. By 1952, company revenues had reached $6 million from the sale of 2.6 million broilers. During this period, the company began to vertically integrate, operating its own hatchery, starting to mix its own feed formulations, and operating its own feed mill. Also in the 1950s, Perdue Farms began to contract with others to grow chickens for them. By furnishing the growers with peeps (baby chickens) and feed, the company was better able to control quality.

In the 1960s, Perdue Farms continued to vertically integrate by building its first grain receiving and storage facilities and Maryland's first soybean processing plant. By 1967, annual sales had increased to about $35 million. However, it became clear to Frank that profits lay in processing chickens. Frank recalled in a September 15, 1972, interview for *Business Week,* "Processors were paying us 10 cents a live pound for what cost us 14 cents to produce. Suddenly, processors were making as much as 7 cents a pound."

A cautious, conservative planner, Arthur Perdue had not been eager for expansion and Frank Perdue himself was reluctant to enter poultry processing. But economics forced his hand and, in 1968, the company bought its first processing plant, a Swift and Company operation in Salisbury, and became a vertically integrated operation that hatched eggs, delivered baby chicks to growers, bought grain and mixed feed, supplied feed and litter to growers, and processed broilers and shipped them to market. The newly acquired Salisbury plant was renovated and equipped with machines capable of processing 14,000 broilers per hour. Nutritionists were brought on board to devise feeding formulas that enabled birds to reach their growth potential sooner, and veterinarians were put on staff to keep the flocks healthy.

Frank Perdue's drive for quality became legendary both inside and outside the poultry industry. (In 1985, Frank Perdue and Perdue Farms were featured in the book *A Passion for Excellence,* by Tom Peters and Nancy Austin.) From the first batch of chickens that it processed, Perdue Farms' standards were higher than what the federal government required for Grade A chickens. The state grader on the first batch of chickens processed at the Salisbury plant was fond of telling how, as he finished his inspections for that first day of processing, he was worried that he had rejected too many of the plant's chickens as not meeting Grade A standards. He then saw Frank Perdue headed his way, clearly unhappy. Frank started inspecting the birds himself but never argued over one that was rejected. Next, Frank went through the ones that the grader had passed and began to toss some of them over with the rejected birds. Finally, realizing that few of the birds met his own standards, Frank put all of them in the reject pile.

From the beginning, Frank Perdue refused to permit his broilers to be frozen for shipping, arguing that it resulted in unappetizing black bones and loss of flavor and moistness when cooked. Instead, Perdue chickens were (and some still are) shipped fresh to market (though packed in ice), justifying the company's advertisements at that time that it sold only "fresh, young broilers." However, this policy also limited the company's market to those locations that could be serviced overnight from the Eastern

Shore of Maryland—chiefly the densely populated towns and cities of the East Coast (Baltimore, Philadelphia, and particularly New York City, which consumed more Perdue chicken than all other brands combined). During the 1970s, Perdue Farms also expanded geographically to areas north of New York City—Boston, Providence, Hartford, and other portions of Massachusetts, Rhode Island, and Connecticut. Facilities were expanded rapidly to include a new broiler processing plant and protein conversion plant in Virginia, a processing plant and a hatchery in North Carolina, a processing plant in Delaware, and feed mills in Delaware and North Carolina.

In 1970, Perdue Farms established breeding and genetic research programs. Through selective breeding, Perdue developed a chicken with more white breast meat than the typical chicken. Selective breeding had been so successful that Perdue chickens were in demand by other processors. There were rumors to the effect that Perdue-breed chickens had been stolen from growers on occasion in an attempt by competitors to improve their flocks.

In 1971, Perdue Farms began an extensive marketing campaign featuring Frank Perdue. In the company's early advertisements, Frank Perdue became well known in eastern U.S. households for saying things like "If you want to eat as good as my chickens, you'll just have to eat my chickens." The Perdue Farms ad campaign was one of the first to succeed in branding what was generally considered a commodity product.

In 1977, Mr. Arthur died at the age of 91, leaving behind a company with annual sales of nearly $200 million, an average annual growth rate of 17 percent (compared with an industry average of 1 percent), the potential for processing 78,000 broilers per hour, and annual production of nearly 350 million pounds of poultry per year. Frank Perdue said of his father, "I learned everything from him." Of himself, Frank Perdue said, "I am a B-minus student. I know how smart I am. I know a B-minus is not as good as an A."

In April 1981, Frank Perdue was in Boston at the invitation of the Babson College Academy of Distinguished Entrepreneurs, established in 1978 to recognize the spirit of free enterprise and business leadership. The College's president, Ralph Z. Sorenson, inducted Perdue into the academy, whose membership at the time numbered 18 men and women from four continents. Perdue had the following to say to the college students in accepting the award:

> There are none, nor will there ever be, easy steps for the entrepreneur. Nothing, absolutely nothing, replaces the willingness to work earnestly, intelligently towards a goal. You have to be willing to pay the price. You have to have an insatiable appetite for detail, have to be willing to accept constructive criticism, to ask questions, to be fiscally responsible, to surround yourself with good people and, most of all, to listen.

During the early 1980s, Perdue Farms expanded its market reach southward into Virginia, North Carolina, and Georgia. It also bought out such producers as Carroll's Foods, Purvis Farms, Shenandoah Valley Poultry Company, and Shenandoah Farms. The latter two acquisitions broadened the company's product line to include turkey. The company also introduced a line of fully cooked fresh chicken products featuring chicken breast nuggets, cutlets, and tenders under the brand Perdue Done It! James A. (Jim) Perdue, Frank's only son, joined the company as a management trainee in 1983 and soon became a plant manager.

But the latter 1980s tested the mettle of Perdue Farms. The company's considerable geographic and product-line expansion led a consulting firm to conclude that top management's span of control was too broad and to recommend that the company form several decentralized strategic business units, each responsible for running its own operations. Soon after, the chicken market leveled off and then declined for a period. In 1988, Perdue Farms experienced its first year in the red, losing as much as $1 million per week for a time, partly because the shift to independent business unit operations led to duplication of effort and sharply higher administrative costs. The costs for management information systems, for example, tripled. The firm's expansion into turkey products and prepared chicken products, where it had little experience, contributed to the losses. Frank Perdue decided to refocus the company, concentrating on efficiency of operations, improving communications throughout all segments, and paying close attention to detail.

On June 2, 1989, Frank celebrated 50 years with Perdue Farms, Inc. At a morning reception in downtown Salisbury, the governor of Maryland proclaimed it "Frank Perdue Day." The governors of Delaware and Virginia did the same. In 1991, Frank gave up direct control of the company and stepped back to the position of chairman of the executive committee; Jim Perdue became the company's CEO and chairman of the board. Quieter, gentler, and more formally educated, Jim Perdue focused attention on operations, pushing for even stronger devotion to quality control and a bigger commitment to strategic planning. Frank Perdue continued to have a role in Perdue Farms' advertising campaigns and public relations efforts. Gradually, as Jim Perdue matured in his role of company leader, he became the company spokesperson and began to appear in the company's advertisements.

Under Jim Perdue's leadership, Perdue Farms' strategic initiatives in the 1990s were dominated by market expansion southward into Florida and westward to Michigan and Missouri. In 1992, the company formalized its international business segment, serving customers in Puerto Rico, South America, Europe, Japan, and China. By fiscal year 1998, international sales were $180 million per year. International sales were seen as very beneficial because U.S. customers preferred white meat while customers in most other countries preferred dark meat.

Food-service sales to commercial consumers also became a major market. New retail product lines focused on what management considered value-added items—individual quick-frozen items, home meal replacement items, and products for store delicatessens. The company's Fit 'n Easy label—applied to skinless, boneless chicken and turkey products—was featured as part of an appeal to nutrition-conscious consumers.

The 1990s also saw the increased use of technology and the building of distribution centers to better serve the customer. For example, all of Perdue's over-the-road trucks were equipped with satellite two-way communications and geographic positioning, allowing real-time tracking and rerouting if needed, and providing store retailers accurate information about exactly when to expect product arrival. In 2000, Perdue Farms had revenues of more than $2.5 billion and nearly 20,000 associates.

MISSION, VALUES, AND VISION

Starting in the company's early days, Mr. Arthur's philosophy was to "create a quality product, be aware of your customers, deal fairly with people, and work, work hard, work hard." In 1991, Frank Perdue, in reflecting on the firm's success, said,

> If you were to ask me what was the biggest factor in whatever success we have enjoyed, I would answer that it was not technology, or economic resources, or organizational structure. It . . . has been our conscious decision that, in order to be successful, we must have a sound set of beliefs on which we premise all our policies and actions . . . Central to these beliefs is our emphasis on quality . . . Quality is no accident. It is the one absolutely necessary ingredient of all the most successful companies in the world.

Jim, Frank, and Mr. Arthur Perdue . . . three generations of Perdue Farms leadership.

The quality theme was prominent in the company's statement of its mission, values, and vision (see Exhibit 1).

MANAGEMENT AND ORGANIZATION

From 1950 until 1991, Frank Perdue was the primary force behind Perdue Farms' strategy and growth. During Frank's years as CEO, the chicken industry enjoyed comparatively strong growth in volume. Many industry executives had come up through the ranks during the industry's infancy. A big fraction had little formal education and started their careers in the barnyard, building chicken coops and cleaning them out. They often spent their entire careers with one company, progressing from supervisor of grow-out facilities to management of processing plants to corporate executive positions. Perdue Farms was not unusual in that respect. An entrepreneur through and through, Frank Perdue epitomized his marketing slogan "It takes a tough man to make a tender chicken." The company's organization structure was highly centralized, with decision-making authority being retained by Frank Perdue or delegated to a few trusted, senior executives whom he had known for a lifetime (see Exhibit 2). Workers were expected to do their jobs.

exhibit 1   Perdue Farms' Quality Policy: Mission, Values, and Vision, 2000

Stand on Tradition

Perdue was built upon a foundation of quality, a tradition described in our Quality Policy . . .

Our Quality Policy

We shall produce products and provide services
at all times which meet or exceed the expectations of our customers.

We shall not be content to be of
equal quality to our competitors.

Our commitment is to be increasingly superior.

Contribution to quality is a responsibility
shared by everyone in the Perdue organization.

Focus on Today

Our mission reminds us of the purpose we serve . . .

Our Mission

"Enhance the quality of life with great food and agricultural products."

While striving to fulfill our mission, we use our values to guide our decisions . . .

Our Values

- **Quality:** We value the needs of our customers. Our high standards require us to work safely, make safe food and uphold the Perdue name.

- **Integrity:** We do the right thing and live up to our commitments. We do not cut corners or make false promises.

- **Trust:** We trust each other and treat each other with mutual respect. Each individual's skill and talent are appreciated.

- **Teamwork:** We value a strong work ethic and ability to make each other successful. We care what others think and encourage their involvement, creating a sense of pride, loyalty, ownership and family.

Look to the Future

Our vision describes what we will become and the qualities that will enable us to succeed . . .

Our Vision

To be the leading quality food company with $20 billion in sales in 2020.

Perdue in the Year 2020

- **To our customers:** We will provide food solutions and indispensable services to meet anticipated customer needs.

- **To our consumers:** A portfolio of trusted food and agricultural products will be supported by multiple brands throughout the world.

- **To our associates:** Worldwide, our people and our workplace will reflect our quality reputation, placing Perdue among the best places to work.

- **To our communities:** We will be known in the community as a strong corporate citizen, trusted business partner and favorite employer.

- **To our shareholders:** Driven by innovation, our market leadership and our creative spirit will yield industry-leading profits.

exhibit 2 Perdue Farms Organization Chart as of 2000

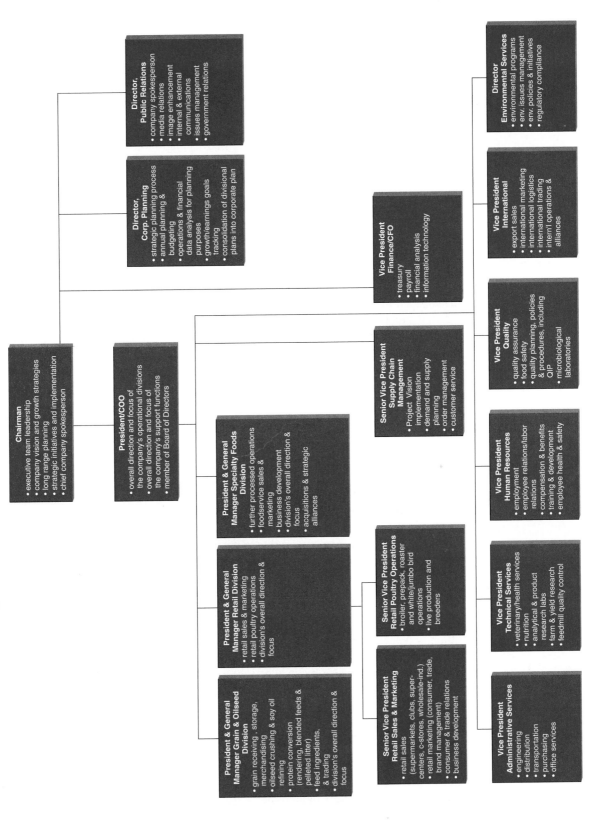

Chairman
- executive team leadership
- company vision and growth strategies
- long range planning
- strategic initiatives and implementation
- chief company spokesperson

President/COO
- overall direction and focus of the company's operational divisions
- overall direction and focus of the company's support functions
- member of Board of Directors

Director, Corp. Planning
- strategic planning process
- annual planning & budgeting
- operations & financial data analysis for planning purposes
- growth/earnings goals tracking
- consolidation of divisional plans into corporate plan

Director, Public Relations
- company spokesperson
- media relations
- image enhancement
- internal & external communications
- issues management
- government relations

President & General Manager Grain & Oilseed Division
- grain receiving, storage, merchandising
- oilseed crushing & soy oil refining
- protein conversion (rendering, blended feeds & pelleted litter)
- feed ingredients, & trading
- division's overall direction & focus

President & General Manager Retail Division
- retail sales & marketing
- retail poultry operations
- division's overall direction & focus

President & General Manager Specialty Foods Division
- further processed operations
- foodservice sales & marketing
- business development
- division's overall direction & focus
- acquisitions & strategic alliances

Vice President Finance/CFO
- treasury
- payroll
- financial analysis
- information technology

Senior Vice President Supply Chain Management
- Project Vision implementation
- demand and supply planning
- order management
- customer service

Vice President Administrative Services
- engineering
- distribution
- transportation
- purchasing
- office services

Senior Vice President Retail Sales & Marketing
- retail sales (supermarkets, clubs, super-centers, c-stores, wholesale-ind.)
- retail marketing (consumer, trade, brand management)
- consumer & trade relations
- business development

Senior Vice President Retail Poultry Operations
- broiler, prepack, roaster and white/jumbo bird operations
- live production and breeders

Vice President Technical Services
- veterinary/health services
- nutrition
- analytical & product research labs
- farm & yield research
- feedmill quality control

Vice President Human Resources
- employment
- employee relations/labor relations
- compensation & benefits
- training & development
- employee health & safety

Vice President Quality
- quality assurance
- food safety
- quality planning, policies & procedures, including QIP
- microbiological laboratories

Vice President International
- export sales
- international marketing
- international logistics
- international trading
- intern'l operations & alliances

Director Environmental Services
- environmental programs
- env. issues management
- env. policies & initiatives
- regulatory compliance

As time went on, however, Frank Perdue loosened the reins, increasingly emphasizing employee involvement in quality issues and operational decisions; employees came to be known as "associates." Outside analysts of the company saw the mounting shift to more employee participation in decision making as one of the factors that helped make the transfer of power in 1991 to Jim Perdue unusually smooth and uneventful. Although Jim grew up in the family business, he spent almost 15 years earning an undergraduate degree in biology from Wake Forest University, a master's degree in marine biology from the University of Massachusetts at Dartmouth, and a doctorate in fisheries from the University of Washington in Seattle. Returning to Perdue Farms in 1983, he earned an executive master of business administration degree from Salisbury State University and held positions as plant manager, divisional quality control manager, and vice president of quality improvement process (QIP) prior to becoming chairman and CEO.

Jim Perdue had a people-first management style. Company goals centered on what Jim Perdue termed the three P's: people, products, and profitability. He believed that business success rested on satisfying customer needs with quality products but also that both of these factors depended on associates: "If [associates] come first, they will strive to assure superior product quality—and satisfied customers." This philosophy had shaped the company's culture, reflecting one of management guru Tom Peters's views: "Nobody knows a person's 20 square feet better than the person who works there." Jim Perdue's approach was to gather ideas and information from everyone in the organization and maximize productivity by transmitting these ideas throughout the organization.

A key part of the "employees first" policy was an effort to build and maintain a stable, productive workforce, a difficult task in an industry where many jobs were physically demanding and had to be performed under sometimes stressful and unpleasant conditions. A significant number of Perdue associates were Hispanic immigrants who had a poor command of the English language, were often undereducated, and lacked basic health care. In order to increase the opportunity for advancement among Hispanic associates, Perdue Farms had instituted a series of programs—there were English-language classes to help non-English-speaking employees assimilate and support for helping less-educated associates earn the equivalent of a high school diploma.

To deal with physical stress, the company had an ergonomics committee in each plant that studied job requirements and sought to redesign jobs that were inherently stressful, unattractive, or risky. Perdue Farms also had an impressive wellness program that included clinics at 10 plants, staffed by professional medical people working for medical practice groups under contract to Perdue Farms. Associates had universal access to all Perdue-operated clinics and could visit a doctor for anything from a muscle strain to prenatal care to screening tests for a variety of diseases. Dependent care was available as well. Management saw such programs as benefiting the company through reductions in lost time for medical office visits; lower turnover; and a happier, healthier, more productive, and more stable workforce.

MARKETING

In the early days of the chicken industry, chicken was sold to butcher shops and neighborhood groceries as a commodity—that is, producers sold it in bulk, butchers cut and wrapped it, and shoppers had no idea what firm grew or processed the chicken they were buying. Frank Perdue was convinced that higher profits could be made if his company's products could be marketed as premium quality and sold at a premium price. But the only way the premium-quality concept would work was if customers could be convinced that all chicken was not alike—and that meant Perdue's chicken products had to be differentiated and people "taught" what premium qualities to look for. Frank Perdue's innovative marketing strategy was to promote Perdue Farms' chickens as superior-quality, broader breasted chickens with a healthy golden color (which could be achieved by putting marigold petals in the feed to enhance the natural yellow color that corn provided).

In 1968, Perdue Farms spent $50,000 on radio advertising. In 1969, Frank Perdue added $80,000 in TV advertising to the company's radio budget—against the advice of his advertising agency. Although the early TV ads increased sales, Frank Perdue decided the agency he was dealing with didn't match one of the basic Perdue tenets: "The people you deal with should be as good at what they do as you are at what you do." That decision set off a storm of activity on Frank's part. In order to select an ad agency that met his standards, Frank began a 10-week immersion on the theory and practice of advertising. He read books and papers on advertising. He talked to sales managers of every newspaper, radio, and television station in the New York area, consulted experts, and interviewed 48 ad agencies. In April 1971, he selected Scali, McCabe, Sloves as Perdue Farms' new advertising agency. As agency executives tried to figure out how to successfully "brand" a chicken—something that had never been done—they realized that Frank Perdue was their greatest ally; as one of the ad agency executives noted, "He looked a little like a chicken himself, and he sounded a little like one, and he squawked a lot!"

McCabe decided that Perdue should be the firm's spokesman. Initially Frank resisted, but in the end he accepted the role and the campaign based on "It takes a tough man to make a tender chicken" was born. The firm's very first television commercial showed Frank on a picnic in the Salisbury City Park saying:

> A chicken is what it eats . . . And my chickens eat better than people do . . . I store my own grain and mix my own feed . . . And give my Perdue chickens nothing but pure well water to drink . . . That's why my chickens always have that healthy golden yellow color . . . If you want to eat as good as my chickens, you'll just have to eat my chickens.

Additional ads, touting high quality and the broader breasted chicken read as follows:

> Government standards would allow me to call this a grade A chicken . . . but my standards wouldn't. This chicken is skinny . . . It has scrapes and hairs . . . The fact is, my graders reject 30% of the chickens government inspectors accept as grade A . . . That's why it pays to insist on a chicken with my name on it . . . If you're not completely satisfied, write me and I'll give you your money back . . . Who do you write in Washington? . . . What do they know about chickens?

> The Perdue Roaster is the master race of chickens.

> Never go into a store and just ask for a pound of chicken breasts . . . Because you could be cheating yourself out of some meat . . . Here's an ordinary one-pound chicken breast, and here's a one-pound breast of mine . . . They weigh the same. But as you can see, mine has more meat, and theirs has more bone. I breed the broadest breasted, meatiest chicken you can buy . . . So don't buy a chicken breast by the pound . . . Buy them by the name . . . and get an extra bite in every breast.

The ads paid off. In 1968, Perdue Farms accounted for about 3 percent of the New York market for broilers. By 1972, one out of every six chickens eaten in New York

SCALI, McCABE, SLOVES INC.

CLIENT: PERDUE FOODS INC.

PRODUCT: PERDUE CHICKENS

TITLE: "MY CHICKENS EAT BETTER THAN PEOPLE"

LENGTH: 30 SECONDS

COMMERCIAL NO.: TV-PD-30-2C

1. FRANK PERDUE: A chicken is what it eats. And my chickens eat better than . . .

2. people do. I store my own grain and mix my own feed.

3. And give my Perdue chickens nothing but pure well water to drink.

4. That's why my chickens always have that healthy golden-yellow color.

5. If you want to eat as good as my chickens, you'll just have to eat my chickens.

6. That's really good.

Frank Perdue's first TV commercial.

was a Perdue chicken and 51 percent of New Yorkers recognized the Perdue Farms brand. Scali, McCabe, Sloves credited Frank Perdue's "believability" for the success of the advertising campaign; according to one of its executives, "This was advertising in which Perdue had a personality that lent credibility to the product. If Frank Perdue didn't look and sound like a chicken, he wouldn't be in the commercials." Frank had a different view. As he told a Rotary Club audience in Charlotte, North Carolina, in March 1989, "The product met the promise of the advertising and was far superior to the competition. Two great sayings tell it all: 'Nothing will destroy a poor product as quickly as good advertising,' and 'A gifted product is mightier than a gifted pen!'"

By the 1990s, branded chicken was ubiquitous. However, chicken industry analysts in 2000 believed that the market for fresh poultry had peaked whereas sales of prepared and frozen chicken products were expected to continue to grow at a healthy rate. Although domestic retail sales accounted for about 60 percent of Perdue Farms revenues in fiscal year 2000, food-service sales accounted for another 20 percent, international sales accounted for 5 percent, and grain and oilseed contributed the remaining 15 percent. Perdue management expected food-service, international, and grain and oilseed sales to continue to grow as a percentage of the company's total revenues.

The Domestic Retail Market Segment

In 2000, retail grocery customers were increasingly looking for items that were easy and quick to prepare (commonly termed *value-added products*). The move toward value-added products had significantly changed the composition and look of meat departments in modern supermarkets. There were now five distinct store locations for poultry:

1. The fresh meat counter—for whole chickens and parts.

2. The delicatessen—for turkey and rotisserie chicken.

3. The frozen food case—for individually quick frozen items such as chicken tenders, wings, and breasts; breaded and cooked items such as tenders and buffalo wings; and whole chickens, turkeys, and Cornish hens.

4. Home meal replacement—for fully prepared entrées such as Perdue brand "Short Cuts" and Deluca brand entrees (the Deluca brand was acquired and products are marketed under its own name) that are sold along with salads and desserts so that you can assemble your own dinner.

5. Canned meats—for canned chicken products.

Because Perdue Farms had always used the phrase "fresh young chicken" as the centerpiece of its marketing strategy, growing consumer interest in value-added products and frozen chicken products posed a possible conflict with past marketing themes. To answer the questions of whether frozen and prepared products were compatible with the company's marketing image and how the company should convey the notion of quality in this broader product environment, Perdue Farms was studying what the term "fresh young chicken" meant to customers, especially those who preferred quick, easy meal preparation and/or who put many of their fresh meat purchases in the freezer once they got home. One view was that the appeal of the term "fresh young chicken" came from customer perceptions that "quality" and "freshness" were closely associated. Another view was that "brand trust" was the real issue, in which case the marketing challenge was to get customers to believe that Perdue products, whether fresh or frozen, were dependable and of the best quality available.

The Food-Service Market Segment

The food-service segment consisted of a wide variety of public and private customers, including restaurants, cafeterias, hospitals, schools, prisons, airports, and institutions that served meals and thus were regular buyers of food products. Historically, the vast majority of food-service customers had not been brand-conscious, preferring to do business with food suppliers that met their strict specifications at the lowest prices; their willingness to trade premium quality for lower price made food-service enterprises a less-than-ideal fit for Perdue Farms. However, with American consumers eating an ever larger percentage of their meals away from home and traditional supermarket sales flattening, Perdue Farms felt compelled to put greater emphasis on pursuing the faster growing food-service segment. The food-service segment accounted for approximately 50 percent of total poultry sales in the United States, while approximately 20 percent of Perdue Farms' revenues came from this category.

Because Perdue Farms had neither strength nor expertise in the food-service segment, management's strategy for gaining better penetration of this segment was to acquire companies that already had food-service expertise. In September 1998, Perdue completed the acquisition of Tennessee-based Gol-Pak Corporation, a company with about 1,600 employees and revenues of about $200 million per year.

The International Segment of the Poultry Industry

In the early 1990s, Perdue Farms began exporting specialty products such as chicken feet (known as "paws") to customers in China. Although not approved for sale for human consumption in the United States, paws were considered a delicacy in China. By

exhibit 3   International Volume of Broiler Sales, Perdue Farms, 1992–98

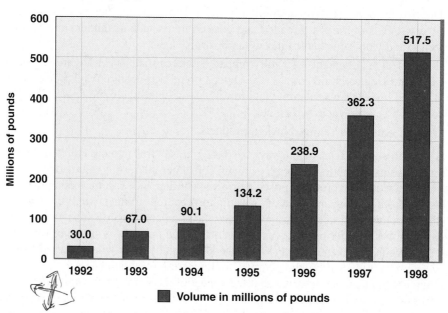

Volume in millions of pounds

1992, international sales, consisting principally of paws, had become a small but profitable business of about 30 million pounds per year. Building on this initial success, Perdue Farms was, by 1998, generating more than $140 million in revenues and exporting more than 500 million pounds of poultry products annually to China, Japan, Russia, and Ukraine (see Exhibit 3).

Management considered Japan an excellent fit for Perdue Farms' products because Japanese consumers were very quality-conscious and willing to pay a premium price for quality chicken products. Moreover, Asian consumers preferred dark meat, a serendipitous complement to the U.S. preference for white breast meat that provided a ready market channel for disposing of whatever supplies of dark meat could not be sold in the United States. However, Asian consumers had not embraced the concept of branded chicken, making it difficult for Perdue to capitalize on the premium quality of its products.

To better serve export markets, Perdue Farms had developed a portside freezing facility in Newport News, Virginia. This permitted freshly processed poultry to be shipped directly to the docks, reducing processing costs and helping offset the added costs of shipping to Asia (which were in the range of two-thirds cents per pound for a shipload—a shipload was equal to 300–500 truckloads). Exporting poultry to Asian markets was not without problems, though. For example, delivery trucks in China were seldom refrigerated, which limited warehouse-to-store transit times since the thawing process began as soon as the frozen poultry products were loaded. One shipload of Perdue Farms chicken bound for Russia "vanished"—it had been inappropriately impounded using forged documents, but Perdue Farms eventually recovered most of the dollar value of the shipment.

Initial demand for Perdue products in Russia, Poland, and Eastern Europe was quite strong. By fiscal year 1998, a significant portion of Perdue's international volume was being exported to Russia. Unfortunately, the crumbling of Russia's economy had a devastating effect, and Perdue Farms' exports to Russia in 2000 were off significantly from earlier levels. Such instability of demand, coupled with rampant corruption in Russia, had made Perdue management reluctant to commit significant capital investment to building its Russian export business.

Import duties and taxes were also a barrier to increasing exports. In China, according to the U.S. Department of Agriculture (USDA), import duty rates for poultry were 45 percent for favored countries and 70 percent for unfavored countries; plus, China imposed a 17 percent value-added tax on imports from all countries. High import duties and taxes in Russia had proved a significant hurdle to earning good profit margins as well.

Perdue Farms had created a joint partnership with Jiang Nan Feng (JNF) in order to develop a small processing plant in Shanghai—Perdue management wanted a local partner to help with the development of local markets due to major cultural differences between the U.S. and Chinese poultry markets. Brand recognition was being built through the use of normal marketing tools. The products used the first "tray pack" wrapping available in Shanghai supermarkets. Perdue management felt the JNF partnership showed promise because in China it was a significant competitive advantage to be able to sell homegrown, fresh dark meat. Additionally, while USDA regulations did not currently permit foreign-grown poultry to be imported, the future possibility of importing excess white meat from Shanghai to the United States was attractive—Perdue management believed that the Shanghai facility would have difficulty finding attractive markets for all of the white breast meat that was available from locally grown poultry.

OPERATIONS

Two words summed up the Perdue approach to operations—*quality* and *efficiency,* with more emphasis given to the first than to the second. Perdue Farms was strongly committed to the use of total quality management (TQM) principles and did everything it could to live up to the slogan "Quality, a journey without end." Milestones in the quality improvement process at Perdue Farms are presented in Exhibit 4.

Both quality and efficiency were improved through close attention to detail. Exhibit 5 depicts the structure and product flow of a generic, vertically integrated broiler company. Broiler companies had some discretion in choosing which steps in the process they wanted to perform internally and which they preferred to outsource. Perdue Farms had consciously opted for maximum vertical integration in order to control every detail of the process and better ensure product quality. It bred and hatched its own eggs (19 hatcheries); selected its contract growers; built Perdue-engineered chicken houses; formulated and manufactured its own feed (12 poultry feedmills, one specialty feedmill, two ingredient blending operations); oversaw the care and feeding of the chicks; operated its own processing plants (21 processing/further processing plants); shipped via its own trucking fleet; and marketed the products—see Exhibit 5. Total process control formed the basis for Frank Perdue's claims that Perdue Farms poultry was, indeed, premium quality. The claims Frank Perdue had made in the company's early ads—"I store my own grain and mix my own feed . . . And give my Perdue chickens nothing but well water to drink"—could be backed up, given the internal control afforded by the company's vertical integration strategy. Full vertical integration also enabled Perdue Farms to minimize waste and maintain tight control over operating efficiency. Eight measurable items—hatchability, turnover, feed conversion, livability, yield, birds per man-hour, utilization, and grade—were tracked routinely.

exhibit 4   Milestones in the Quality Improvement Process at Perdue Farms

1924	Arthur Perdue buys leghorn roosters for $25
1950	Perdue Farms adopts the company logo of a chick under a magnifying glass
1984	Frank Perdue attends Philip Crosby's Quality College
1985	Perdue recognized for its pursuit of quality in *A Passion for Excellence*
	200 Perdue managers attend Quality College
	Quality Improvement Process (QIP) adopted
1986	Corrective Action Teams (CATs) established
1987	Quality Training for all associates established
	Error Cause Removal (ECR) process implemented
1988	Steering Committee formed
1989	First annual Quality Conference held
	Team Management implemented
1990	Second annual Quality Conference held
	Values and corporate mission codified
1991	Third annual Quality Conference held
	Customer satisfaction defined
1992	Fourth annual Quality Conference held
	How to implement customer satisfaction explained to team leaders and Quality Improvement Teams (QITs)
	Quality Index created
	Customer Satisfaction Index (CSI) created
	"Farm to Fork" quality program created
1999	Raw Material Quality Index launched
2000	High Performance Team Process initiated

Perdue Farms had a strictly enforced policy that nothing artificial could be fed to or injected into the birds. A chemical-free and steroid-free diet was fed to the chickens. Young chickens were vaccinated against disease. Selective breeding was used to improve the quality of the chicken stock and yield more white breast meat. To benchmark the quality of its poultry products and to track quality in the industry, the company bought and analyzed competitors' products regularly. Inspection associates graded the products of rival processors and reported the results to senior executives. In addition, the company's Quality Policy (Exhibit 6) was displayed at all company locations and taught to all associates in quality training.

RESEARCH AND DEVELOPMENT

Perdue Farms was an acknowledged industry leader in the use of research and technology to provide quality products and service to its customers. The company spent more on research as a percent of revenues than any other poultry processor. This practice went back to Frank Perdue's focus on finding ways to differentiate the company's poultry products on the basis of quality and value. The company's most significant R&D achievement was the selective breeding program to increase the breast size and white meat yield of its flocks. While other processors had made strides in improving the quality of their stocks, Perdue Farms executives believed that Perdue was still the industry leader. A list of some of Perdue Farms' technological accomplishments is presented in Exhibit 7.

exhibit 5   Perdue Farms' Vertically Integrated Operations

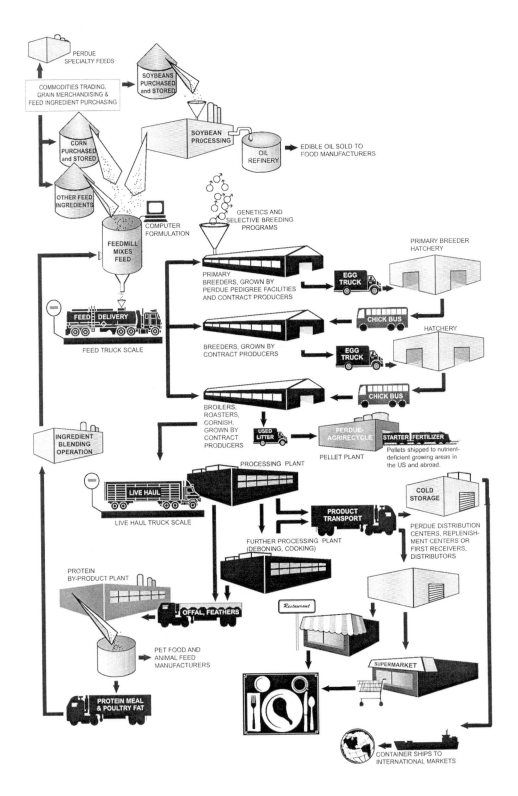

exhibit 6   Perdue Farms' Quality Policy

- WE SHALL produce products and provide services at all times that meet or exceed the expectations of our customers.
- WE SHALL not be content to be of equal quality to our competitors.
- OUR COMMITMENT is to be increasingly superior.
- CONTRIBUTION TO QUALITY is a responsibility shared by everyone in the Perdue organization.

exhibit 7   Perdue Farms' Technological Accomplishments

- Conducts more research than all competitors combined
- Breeds chickens with consistently more breast meat than any other birds in the industry
- First to use digital scales to guarantee weights to customers
- First to package fully cooked chicken products in microwavable trays
- First to have a box lab to define quality of boxes from different suppliers
- First to test both its chickens and competitors' chickens on 52 quality factors every week
- Improved on time deliveries 20% between 1987 and 1993
- Built state-of-the-art analytical and microbiological laboratories for feed and end-product analysis
- First to develop best management practices for food safety across all areas of the company
- First to develop commercially viable pelletized poultry litter.

The company employed specialists in avian science, microbiology, genetics, nutrition, and veterinary science. Because of its research and development capabilities, Perdue Farms was often involved in USDA field tests with pharmaceutical suppliers. Perdue had the most extensive and expensive vaccination program in the industry. In 2000, the company was doing collaborative studies of the practices of several European producers that used completely different methods. The company's research in designing feed mixes had been a contributing factor in reducing the time it took to grow chickens. In the 1950s, it took 14 weeks to grow a three-pound chicken. In 2000, it took only seven weeks to grow a five-pound chicken. This gain in efficiency was due principally to improvements in the conversion rate of feed to chicken. At current conversion rates, it took about two pounds of feed to produce one pound of chicken. Feed represented about 65 percent of the cost of growing a chicken. Studies indicated that if Perdue Farms could improve the conversion rate of feed to chicken by just 1 percent, it would represent estimated additional income of $2.5–$3 million per week or $130–$156 million per year.

FINANCE

Perdue Farms, Inc., was a privately held company and considered its financial information to be proprietary. Publicly available financial and operating data were limited. Most of the stock was held by the family, with a limited number of shares owned by

exhibit 8   Compound Growth Rates, Perdue Farms, 1980–2000

	Revenue	Associates	Sales/Associate
Past 20 years	10.60%	6.48%	3.87%
Past 15 years	8.45	4.48	4.48
Past 10 years	7.39	4.75	2.52
Past 5 years	8.39	0.99	7.33

senior executives. The media and the poultry industry analysts pegged Perdue Farms' revenues for fiscal year 2000 at about $2.5 billion and the number of associates at nearly 20,000. *Forbes* magazine had estimated the company's fiscal year 2000 operating profits at about $160 million and net profits at about $22 million.

The firm's compound growth rate in revenues had been slowly decreasing during the past 20 years, mirroring the general slowdown in the poultry industry's overall growth. However, the company annual growth rates varied significantly by market segment:

- Retail chicken segment—5 percent.
- Sales of chicken and turkey products to the food service segment—12 percent.
- International sales—64 percent.
- Sales of grain and oilseed—10 percent.

Perdue had compensated for slowing growth rates internally by automating its processes and boosting labor productivity. Whereas during the period 1980–2000 each 1.6 percent increase in revenues required a 1 percent increase in workforce size, in the 1995–2000 period the company was able to grow revenues about 8.4 percent for each 1 percent increase in workforce size (see Exhibit 8).

Since its founding, Perdue Farms had been profitable every year, with the exceptions of 1988 and 1996. Company officials believed the loss in 1988 was caused by industrywide overproduction and by higher administrative costs stemming from the abortive shift to decentralized business unit organization. Management attributed the loss in 1996 to the impact of high corn prices.

Perdue Farms employed conservative financial management practices, using retained earnings and internal cash flows to finance the replacement of existing assets and normal growth. Long-term debt was used to finance major expansion projects and acquisitions; creditors for such financing included domestic and foreign banks and insurance companies. The target debt limit was 55 percent of equity. The debt strategy was to match asset lives with liability maturities and to have a mix of fixed-rate and variable-rate debt. Management indicated that it currently took about $1 in new investment capital to generate each $2 increase in revenues.

ENVIRONMENTAL ISSUES

Environmental issues presented a constant challenge to all poultry processors. Industry detractors claimed that growing, slaughtering, and processing poultry was dangerous to workers, inhumane to the poultry, and hard on the environment. Others noted that processed chicken was sometimes unsafe for consumers. Media headlines such as "Human Cost of Poultry Business Bared," "Animal Rights Advocates Protest Chicken

Coop Conditions," "Processing Plants Leave a Toxic Trail," or "EPA Mandates Poultry Regulations" were routine.

Perdue Farms tried to be proactive in managing environmental issues. In April 1993, the company created an Environmental Steering Committee whose mission was "to provide all Perdue Farms work sites with vision, direction, and leadership so that they can be good corporate citizens from an environmental perspective today and in the future." The committee was responsible for overseeing how the company was doing in such environmentally sensitive areas as waste water, storm water, hazardous waste, solid waste, recycling, biosolids, and human health and safety.

Disposing of dead birds had long been an industry problem. Perdue Farms developed small composters for use on each farm. Using this approach, carcasses were reduced to an end product that resembled soil in a matter of a few days. The disposal of hatchery waste was another environmental challenge. Historically, manure and unhatched eggs had been shipped to a landfill. More recently, Perdue Farms had instituted procedures that reduced the waste by 50 percent and was selling the liquid fraction to a pet-food processor that cooked it for protein; the remaining 50 percent was recycled through a rendering process. In 1990, Perdue Farms spent $4.2 million to upgrade the existing treatment facilities at its plants in Accomac, Virginia, and Showell, Maryland; the new state-of-the-art systems used forced hot air (heated to 120 degrees) to cause the microbes to digest all traces of ammonia, even during the cold winter months.

In the late 1980s, North Carolina's Occupational Safety and Health Administration cited Perdue Farms for an unacceptable level of repetitive stress injuries at its processing plants in Lewiston and Robersonville, North Carolina. This citation sparked a major research program in which Perdue Farms worked with Health and Hygiene Inc. of Greensboro, North Carolina, to learn more about the repetitive movements required to accomplish specific jobs. The result was a new program, launched in 1991, that videotaped employees at all of Perdue Farms' plants as they worked in order first to identify and measure and then to mitigate the amount of stress associated with various tasks. Although the cost of the program was substantial, it had been instrumental in reducing workers compensation claims by 44 percent, cutting lost-time reports to just 7.7 percent of the industry average, decreasing the incidence of serious repetitive stress cases by 80 percent, and reducing certain types of injuries by 50 percent.[1]

In 1997, the organism *Pfiesteria piscicida,* a toxic microbe, burst into Eastern Shore media headlines when massive numbers of dead fish with lesions turned up along the Chesapeake Bay in Maryland. Initial indications pointed to manure runoff from area poultry facilities as a probable cause. Political constituencies quickly called for increased regulation to ensure proper manure storage and fertilizer use. Perdue Farms readily admitted that "the poultry process is a closed system. There is lots of nitrogen and phosphorus in the grain, it passes through the chicken and is returned to the environment as manure. Obviously, if you bring additional grain into a closed area such as the Delmarva Peninsula, you increase the amount of nitrogen and phosphorus in the soil unless you find a way to get rid of it." Scientists speculated that soil erosion was producing phosphorus runoff that threatened nearby streams, rivers, and larger bodies of water such as the Chesapeake Bay.

Although it was still not clear what role poultry-related nitrogen and phosphorus runoff played in the *Pfiesteria* outbreak on the Eastern Shore, regulators believed the

---

[1]Shelley Reese, "Helping Employees Get a Grip," *Business and Health,* August 1998.

microorganism feasted on the algae that grew when too much nitrogen and phosphorus were present in the water. The Environmental Protection Agency and various states were considering new regulations. Currently, contract growers were responsible for either using or disposing of the manure from their chicken houses. But some regulators and environmentalists believed that (1) it was too complicated to police the utilization and disposal practices of thousands of individual farmers, and (2) only the big poultry companies had the financial resources to properly dispose of the waste. Thus, they wanted to make poultry companies responsible for all waste disposal, a move that the poultry industry strongly opposed. Some experts had called for measures limiting the density of chicken houses in a given area or even requiring a percentage of existing chicken houses to be taken out of production periodically. Following the negative publicity and extensive investigation by both poultry processors and state regulatory agencies into the *Pfiesteria* outbreak on the Eastern Shore, the State of Maryland passed the Water Quality Act of 1998, requiring nutrient management plans.

Working with AgriRecycle Inc. of Springfield, Missouri, Perdue Farms was pursuing a solution whereby poultry companies would process excess manure into pellets for use as fertilizer outside poultry growing regions. Advocates of this approach estimated that as much as 120,000 tons—nearly one-third of the surplus nutrient from manure produced each year on the Delmarva Peninsula—could be sold to corn growers in other parts of the country. Prices of $25–$30 per ton for the pelletized fertilizer would enable a small profit.

Perdue Farms' executives and poultry industry officials believed that solving environmental problems presented at least five major challenges to poultry processors:

- Maintaining the trust of the poultry consumer.
- Ensuring that the poultry remained healthy.
- Protecting the safety of employees and the integrity of poultry processing.
- Satisfying legislators who needed to show their constituents that they were taking firm action when environmental problems occurred.
- Keeping environmental costs at an acceptable level.

Jim Perdue summed up Perdue Farms' position as follows: "We must not only comply with environmental laws as they exist today, but look to the future to make sure we don't have any surprises. We must make sure our environmental policy statement is real, that there's something behind it and that we do what we say we're going to do." Exhibit 9 presents Perdue Farms' environmental policy.

LOGISTICS AND INFORMATION SYSTEMS

The explosion of poultry products and increasing number of customers during recent years placed a severe strain on the capabilities of Perdue Farms' existing logistics system, which had been developed at a time when there were far fewer products, fewer delivery points, and lower volume. These strains were limiting the company's ability to improve service levels, support further growth, and introduce innovative services that might provide a competitive edge over rival poultry brands.

In general, poultry processing companies were faced with two significant logistics problems: short shelf life for fresh chicken products and uncertainty regarding the volume that consumers would buy during the upcoming days. The shelf life of fresh poultry products was measured in days, making it important for processors to keep

exhibit 9 Perdue Farms' Environmental Policy Statement

Perdue Farms is committed to environmental stewardship and shares that commitment with its farm family partners. We're proud of the leadership we're providing our industry in addressing the full range of environmental challenges related to animal agriculture and food processing. We've invested—and continue to invest—millions of dollars in research, new technology, equipment upgrades, and awareness and education as part of our ongoing commitment to protecting the environment.

- Perdue Farms was among the first poultry companies with a dedicated Environmental Services department. Our team of environmental managers is responsible for ensuring that every Perdue facility operates within *100 percent compliance of all applicable environmental regulations and permits.*

- Through our joint venture, Perdue AgriRecycle, Perdue Farms is investing $12 million to build in Delaware a first-of-its-kind pellet plant that will convert surplus poultry litter into a starter fertilizer that will be marketed internationally to nutrient deficient regions. The facility, which will serve the entire Delmarva region, is scheduled to begin operation in April 2001.

- We continue to explore new technologies that will reduce water usage in our processing plants without compromising food safety or quality.

- We invested thousands of man-hours in producer education to assist our family farm partners in managing their independent poultry operations in the most environmentally responsible manner possible. In addition, all our poultry producers are required to have nutrient management plans and dead-bird composters.

- Perdue Farms was one of four poultry companies operating in Delaware to sign an agreement with Delaware officials outlining our companies' voluntary commitment to help independent poultry producers dispose of surplus chicken litter.

- Our Technical Services department is conducting ongoing research into feed technology as a means of reducing the nutrients in poultry manure. We've already achieved phosphorous reductions that far exceed the industry average.

- We recognize that the environmental impact of animal agriculture is more pronounced in areas where development is decreasing the amount of farmland available to produce grain for feed and to accept nutrients. That is why we view independent grain *and* poultry producers as vital business partners and strive to preserve the economic viability of the family farm.

At Perdue Farms, we believe that it is possible to preserve the family farm; provide a safe, abundant and affordable food supply; and protect the environment. However, we believe that can best happen when there is cooperation and trust between the poultry industry, agriculture, environmental groups and state officials. We hope Delaware's effort will become a model for other states to follow.

production levels closely matched to customer demand and make sure that deliveries of the needed volume arrived in stores in a timely fashion. On the one hand, estimating requirements too conservatively could produce unwanted stockouts in supermarkets—megacustomers like Wal-Mart took a dim view of product shortages that led to empty shelves and lost sales. On the other hand, overly generous estimates could lead to outdated products that could not be sold and losses for Perdue Farms. A common expression in the poultry industry is "You either sell it or smell it."

Forecasting has always been extremely difficult in the poultry industry because processors need to know approximately 18 months in advance how many broilers will be needed in order to properly size hatchery supply flocks and contract with growers to provide the requisite number of live broilers. Most customers (grocers, food-service buyers) have a far shorter planning and ordering window. Further, there was no way for

Perdue Farms to know when rival poultry processors would put a particular product on special, cutting into Perdue Farms' near-term sales, or when bad weather and other uncontrollable events might unexpectedly cause swings in sales. Historically, poultry companies used past demand trends and assorted industry contacts to estimate sales and production requirements. Although product-line proliferation had complicated the forecasting task, the steady movement away from fresh product to frozen product provided welcome flexibility.

Perdue Farms was making use of new information technology to stay in close touch with customers and market conditions. In 1987, customer service associates were provided with PCs to enable them to enter customer orders directly. In the 1990s, systems were developed that tracked inventories of every product and that put dispatchers in direct contact with every truck in the fleet, providing real-time information product inventory and truck location at all times. In 2000, the company's information technology group was moving to establish online communications with each of the company's customers with the objective of shortening the time from order to delivery.

The company's logistics operations were further complicated by different requirements for different distribution channels:

1. *Bulk fresh deliveries*—Here, timeliness and frequency of delivery were critical to ensure product freshness and maximize shelf life. To achieve the lowest distribution costs, deliveries needed to be in large quantities.

2. *Domestic frozen and further processed products*—Temperature integrity was critical; this channel lent itself to dual temperature trailer systems and load consolidation. Customers expected frequent, timely deliveries.

3. *Exports*—Temperature integrity, high volume, and low shipping costs were essential; this channel lent itself to consolidation of orders from customers from each country/port of entry and custom loading of vessels.

4. *Consumer packaged goods (fresh, prepared, and deli products)*—Products in this channel tended to be differentiated from rivals with respect to either product attributes or the nature and variety of services offered. Customers frequently wanted short order-to-delivery times while the company strived for holding down delivery costs.

As a consequence, managing the distribution of Perdue's products in a cost-effective and customer-aware fashion increasingly entailed use of a sophisticated supply chain management system. In order to better operate the entire supply chain management process, Perdue Farms had recently purchased a multimillion-dollar information technology system that represented the biggest nontangible asset expense in the company's history. This integrated, state-of-the-art information system required completely reengineering Perdue Farms' data system, materials handling, and product distribution functions, a project that took 18 months and required training 1,200 associates.

Major goals of the new system were to (1) make it easier and more desirable for the customer to do business with Perdue Farms, (2) make it easier for Perdue Farms associates to get the job done, and (3) take as much cost out of the process as possible. Perdue's system strived to efficiently integrate all facets of the company's operations, including grain and oilseed activities; hatcheries and growing facilities; processing plants (which produced more than 400 products at more than 20 locations); distribution facilities; and deliveries to distributors, supermarkets, food-service customers, and export markets. To underscore the growing importance of supply chain management,

exhibit 10   U.S. Consumption per Capita of Chicken, Beef, and Pork
               in the 1990s and Projected Consumption for 2000, 2001

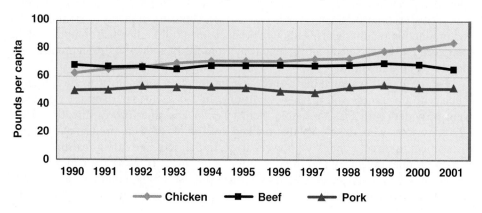

Perdue Farms had recently created a new executive position, senior vice president for supply chain management.

A recently undertaken initiative to strengthen the company's distribution infrastructure was the building of "replenishment centers" to serve as inventory buffers between the processing plants and customers. In addition, the portside facility in Norfolk, Virginia, from which all products for export were shipped, was being expanded and a new freezer facility installed.

Demand forecasts for each of the company's products were converted into an optimized production schedule. As products came off the production line, they were directed from company processing plants to the replenishment and freezer centers nearest the customer locations where orders had been received or were expected to be received. Perdue Farms trucks delivered these products in bulk to the centers in finished or semifinished form. At the centers, further finishing and packaging were undertaken as needed. Specific customer orders were custom palletized and loaded on trucks (either Perdue owned or contracted) for delivery to individual customers. All shipments to customers were made up from replenishment center inventory.

INDUSTRY TRENDS

In 2000, chicken was the number one meat consumed in the United States, with a 40 percent market share (see Exhibits 10 and 11). According to USDA data, annual consumption of meat per capita equaled about 81 pounds of chicken, 69 pounds of beef, and 52 pounds of pork. Chicken was becoming the most popular meat in the world. In 1997, U.S. exports of poultry were a record $2.5 billion. Although U.S. exports fell by 6 percent in 1998, the decrease was attributed to temporary conditions in the Russian economy and the economies of certain Asian countries.

The growing popularity of poultry products was attributed to both nutritional and economic issues. Poultry products contained significantly less fat and cholesterol than other meat products. In the United States, the demand for boneless, skinless breast meat, the leanest meat on poultry, was so great that dark meat often was sold at a discount or else shipped overseas.

exhibit 11   Chicken as a Percentage of Worldwide Meat Consumption, 1960–2000

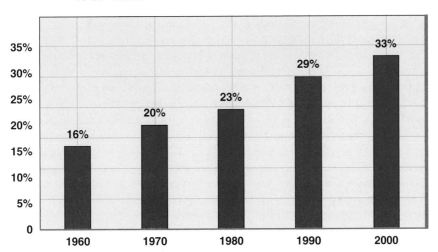

Another industry trend was falling demand for whole birds used as the base dish for home meals and rising demand for poultry products that had been further processed for either home or restaurant consumption. Turkey or chicken hot dogs, fully cooked sliced chicken or turkey, and turkey pastrami (which neither looks nor tastes like turkey) could be found in most deli cases. Many supermarkets sold hot rotisserie chicken (whole or parts). Almost all fast-food restaurants had at least one sandwich based on poultry products. Many upscale restaurants featured poultry products that were shipped to them frozen and partially prepared in order to expedite restaurant meal preparation.

The poultry industry was consolidating as larger companies in the industry bought out smaller local and regional processors. In 2000, there were about 35 major poultry firms in the United States, but this number was expected to drop to 20–25 by 2010 or sooner. There were several reasons for industry consolidation. Slowing U.S. demand and excess processing capacity had created downward price pressures that made it difficult for smaller firms to operate profitably. In addition, efficiency improvements often required sizable capital outlays. Finally, megaretailers such as Sam's Club and Royal Ahold (the Dutch owner of several U.S. supermarket chains) preferred to deal with a few large processing firms rather than contracting with numerous smaller processors to meet their requirements.

The poultry industry was regulated on several fronts. The U.S. Food and Drug Administration (FDA) monitored product safety. The USDA inspected poultry as it arrived at processing plants. After killing, each bird was again inspected by a USDA inspector for avian diseases, contamination of feces, or other foreign material. All birds that did not meet regulations were destroyed under USDA supervision. USDA inspectors also examined the plant, equipment, operating procedures, and personnel for compliance with sanitary regulations. Congress had mandated that the USDA make this information available online. Additional intensive inspections of statistically selected samples of poultry products had been recommended by the National Academy of Sciences, and additional FDA regulations for product quality were anticipated.

All meat industries were experiencing increased scrutiny by the Environmental Protection Agency (EPA) regarding the disposal of waste. In general, waste generated at processing plants was subject to regulation and monitoring by several different agencies that had the power to impose stiff fines for noncompliance.

Still, the most difficult environmental problems that the poultry industry had to deal with were those stemming from numerous poultry processors operating in a relatively limited area. As previously discussed, high levels of poultry production in a limited geographic area intensified poultry manure disposal problems. In manmade fertilizer, phosphorous and nitrogen existed in a ratio of approximately 1:8, whereas in poultry manure the ratio could be as high as 1:1. As a consequence, high concentrations of poultry manure could result in excessive phosphorous runoff into streams and rivers, potentially resulting in aquatic disease and degradation of water quality—as occurred in the 1997 outbreak of *Pfiesteria* in the tributaries of the Chesapeake Bay. Although the poultry industry insisted that there were many possible reasons for high phosphorus concentrations, the media and most regulatory spokespersons attributed them primarily to phosphorous runoff from chicken manure. Environmental advocates wanted the EPA to impose additional, stricter federal environmental regulations on the disposal of poultry manure. Recent regulatory activity had continued to spotlight the Eastern Shore area, where Perdue had extensive operations. However, new studies from the U.S. Geological Survey suggested that the vast majority of nutrients affecting the Chesapeake Bay came from rivers that did not flow through the poultry-producing regions of the Eastern Shore. These studies also found that improved agricultural management practices had reduced nutrient runoff from farmlands. Jim Perdue stated, "While the poultry industry must accept responsibility for its share of nutrients, public policy should view the watershed as a whole and address all the factors that influence water quality."

Other government agencies whose regulations impacted the industry included the Occupational Safety and Health Administration (OSHA) for employee safety and the Immigration and Naturalization Service (INS) for undocumented workers. OSHA enforced its regulations via periodic inspections, and levied fines when work safety violations were found—a Hudson Foods poultry plant was fined more than a $1 million for allegedly willful violations causing ergonomic injury to workers. The INS made periodic inspections to spot use of undocumented workers; it estimated that undocumented aliens working in the poultry industry ranged from 3 to 78 percent of the workforce at individual plants. Plants employing undocumented workers could be heavily fined, especially if they were repeat offenders.

THE FUTURE

Perdue Farms planned to use customer service to further differentiate itself from rivals. The strategic objective was to become indispensable to the customer by taking cost out of the product and delivering it exactly the way the customer wanted it, where and when the customer wanted it. According to Jim Perdue, "Perdue Farms wants to become so easy to do business with that the customer will have no reason to do business with anyone else."

In the poultry business, customer purchase decisions, as well as company profitability, often hinged on 1–2 cents per pound or less. One of the cost drivers was the location of processing facilities. Historically, Perdue Farms had been an Eastern Shore company, but in 2000, it cost Perdue Farms about 1½ cents more per pound to grow poultry on the Eastern Shore versus what poultry could be grown for in Arkansas. This was attributable to differences in the costs of labor, the costs of complying with federal and state environmental laws, certain resource costs (e.g., feed grain), and several lesser factors.

Supermarket chains were consolidating in order not only to better compete with Wal-Mart (which had recently emerged as the biggest supermarket retailer with its new Supercenter store format) and Royal Ahold but also to gain greater buying power in dealing with the suppliers of food and grocery products. Wal-Mart and Royal Ahold gained efficiency by concentrating their purchases among a few selected suppliers and then using their buying muscle to wrangle low prices and get suppliers to take on more functions. Perdue Farms was in the process of developing the capability to employ sophisticated distribution and information systems to manage the entire meat department requirements for several of its supermarket chain customers. Management saw such capability as supportive of its strategic objective of becoming indispensable to its mainstream grocery customers.

To respond to the growing demand for preprepared and easy-to-cook poultry products, Perdue Farms planned to open several additional cooking plants. These plants would put the company in better position to serve the needs of food-service customers and to supply supermarkets with prepared and ready-to-eat poultry products for the delicatessen, frozen, home meal replacement, and canned goods/shelf stable segments. One challenge facing Perdue Farms was designing a distribution system that could efficiently organize hundreds of customer orders for more than 400 different products that were processed and further prepared at more than 20 facilities throughout the Southeast for delivery on a single truck.

Perdue executives viewed international markets as something of a conundrum. On the one hand, Perdue Farms' international revenue had grown from an insignificant side business in 1994 to about $140 million in 1999—approximately 5 percent of total revenues and a significant profit contributor. Poultry was popular in many countries, and demand was growing. On the other hand, different cultures valued different parts of the chicken and preferred different meat color, preparation, and seasoning. Parts not in demand in a particular country had to be sold at severely reduced prices, used as feed, or shipped frozen to a different market where demand existed. Demand in some country markets was sometimes volatile.

Executives at Perdue Farms saw the future as holding many opportunities for the company. But none of them were without risk, and choices had to be made about where to direct the company's resources.

case 28 Southwest Airlines, Inc.

Arthur A. Thompson Jr.
The University of Alabama

John E. Gamble
University of South Alabama

In June 2001, Southwest Airlines, responding to anxious investor concerns about the company's leadership succession plans, began an orderly transfer of power and responsibilities from its longtime CEO and cofounder, Herb Kelleher, age 70, to two of his most trusted protégés. James F. Parker, 54, Southwest's general counsel, was elevated to CEO, and Colleen Barrett, 56, Southwest's executive vice president–customers and self-described keeper of Southwest's pep-rally corporate culture, became president and chief operating officer. Kelleher was, however, scheduled to stay on as chairman of Southwest's board of directors and the head of the board's executive committee and continue to be in charge of strategy, expansion to new cities and aircraft scheduling, and governmental and industry affairs through December 2003; his contract called for an annual salary of $450,000, plus bonuses and stock options. Many observers and longtime employees did not expect Kelleher to ever fully remove himself from management of the company—as long as his health held up (Kelleher had undergone treatment for prostate cancer in 1999).

Southwest's board of directors passed over three higher-ranking executives in selecting Parker as the company's new CEO. Parker's name had not come up in speculation about a potential successor to Kelleher, a hard-driving, whiskey-drinking chain-smoker whose witty and unconventional management style had made him a legend in the airline business and won him the admiration and respect of the vast majority of Southwest's 30,000 employees. Parker, also known for his wit within Southwest, joked at a conference announcing the new management lineup that he and Barrett had already divided up some of Kelleher's key responsibilities: "Colleen will handle the smoking and I'll take the extra drinking."[1] As for his new role, Kelleher said, "I'll try to cut back the hours I put in each week a little, but I'll still be full-time. I'll try to keep it under 100 hours per week."

COMPANY BACKGROUND

In late 1966, Rollin King, a San Antonio, Texas, entrepreneur who owned a small commuter air service, marched into Herb Kelleher's law office with a plan to start a

---

[1]As quoted in the *Fort Worth Star-Telegram*, March 20, 2001, p. 1.

low-cost/low-fare airline that would shuttle passengers between San Antonio, Dallas, and Houston.[2] Kelleher thought King's idea was off the wall but agreed to discuss it with him over cocktails in a nearby San Antonio club. King told Kelleher about the success of Pacific Southwest Airlines, a low-fare intrastate carrier in California, where the economy was booming and major cities were far enough apart to make air travel an attractive alternative to driving. King argued that the situation in Texas paralleled that in California and scrawled out on a cocktail napkin how a local airline could fly between Houston, San Antonio, and Dallas (the "Golden Triangle") conveniently and economically. King was convinced that local air travel needs in Texas were not being met—fares were too high, flight schedules were inconvenient, ticketing was too complicated, and the time required to drive to airports, park, and take off was too lengthy. In many instances, it was simpler and less annoying to drive rather than fly. Over the years, King had heard many Texas businesspeople complain about how long it took to drive between the three cities and the expense of flying the airlines currently serving these cities. Rollin King's business concept for the airline was simple: Attract passengers by flying convenient schedules, getting passengers to their destination on time at the lowest possible fares, and making sure they had a good experience. King's intent was to create an intra-Texas airline that would (1) meet the needs of travelers going between Dallas, San Antonio, and Houston and (2) make fares competitive with travel by automobile. Kelleher, despite lingering skepticism, dug further into the possibilities during the next few weeks and concluded that a new airline was feasible; he agreed to handle the necessary legal work and also to invest $10,000 of his own funds in King's proposed venture.

In early 1967, Kelleher filed papers to incorporate the new airline. Later the same year, he filed an application with the Texas Aeronautics Commission (TAC) for the new company to begin serving Dallas, Houston, and San Antonio.[3] The TAC unanimously approved the application, but the day after the approval three airlines—Braniff, Continental, and Trans Texas (soon to become Texas International)—obtained a temporary court order that prohibited the TAC from issuing Southwest a certificate to fly. The case went to trial in the summer of 1968 with the plaintiffs presenting testimony that the markets Southwest wanted to serve did not have enough traffic to support another carrier. Kelleher, representing Southwest, countered with witnesses who claimed that the markets were growing and that passenger traffic would increase significantly given the low fares that Southwest planned to charge. The trial was bitterly contested, with heated exchanges and emotional outbursts on both sides. The district court ruled that the cities Southwest proposed to serve were already adequately served by the existing carriers and could not support another carrier. Southwest appealed the decision to the state court of civil appeals; seven months later, the appellate court upheld the district court in a 2–1 decision.

Even though legal expenses had depleted the $543,000 in capital contributed by the initial investors, Kelleher's fighting spirit prevailed. He said to the board, "Gentlemen, let's go one more round with them."[4] The board agreed to an appeal to the Texas Supreme Court, with Kelleher committing to pay the court costs out of his own pocket and delay billing on any further legal fees. Kelleher argued the case before the Texas

[2]Kevin Freiberg and Jackie Freiberg, *NUTS!: Southwest Airlines' Crazy Recipe for Business and Personal Success* (New York: Broadway Books, 1998), p 15.

[3]Ibid., pp. 16–18.

[4]Ibid., p. 17.

Supreme Court and won over a majority, but Braniff, Continental, and Trans Texas then decided to appeal to the U.S. Supreme Court. In late 1970, however, the Court refused to hear the appeal, clearing the way for Southwest to proceed with its plans to initiate service. Southwest set June 17, 1971, as the date.

In January 1971, Lamar Muse was brought in as Southwest's CEO to get operations under way. Muse was an aggressive and self-confident airline veteran who knew the business well and who had the entrepreneurial skills necessary to tackle the challenges of building the airline from scratch and then competing head-on with the major carriers. Herb Kelleher recalled, "He was exactly what we needed. He was tough and he was iconoclastic in his thinking."[5] With the company strapped for cash, Muse started raising new capital to purchase planes and equipment and get through the first year of operations. Through private investors and an initial public offering of stock in June 1971, Muse was able to raise $7 million in capital to finance the start-up. He proceeded to negotiate a deal with Boeing to purchase three new 737-200s that the aircraft maker had in inventory and had been unable to sell; Boeing agreed to discount its price from $5 million to $4 million per plane and to finance 90 percent of the $12 million deal.

Because the airline industry was in a slump in the early 1970s, Muse was able to recruit a talented senior staff that included a number of veteran executives from other carriers. He particularly sought out people who were innovative, wouldn't shirk from doing things differently or unconventionally, and were motivated by the challenge of building an airline from scratch. Muse wanted his executive team to be willing to think like mavericks and not be lulled into instituting practices at Southwest that were merely imitative. According to Rollin King, "It was our one opportunity to do it right . . . We all understood that this was our opportunity to decide how to do it our way. Our philosophy was, and still is, we do whatever we have to do to get the job done."[6]

Meanwhile, Braniff and (the newly renamed) Texas International (TI) filed complaints with the Civil Aeronautics Board (CAB) protesting Southwest's start-up. Two days before Southwest was to make its inaugural flights, the CAB rejected the Braniff-TI complaint, but lawyers from Braniff and TI convinced a district court judge in Austin, Texas, to issue an injunction to keep Southwest from beginning airline service. Kelleher was angry: "The constant proceedings had gradually come to enrage me. There was no merit to our competitors' legal assertions. They were simply trying to use their superior economic power to squeeze us dry so we would collapse before we ever got into business. I was bound and determined to show that Southwest Airlines was going to survive and was going into operation."[7] He immediately headed to the Texas Supreme Court building in Austin, met with the justice who had written the 1970 decision, told him what was happening, and got him to schedule a hearing the next day. The ruling came in Southwest's favor, and on June 17, 1971, the lower court judge was ordered not to enforce the injunction. Southwest began service the next day.

The Early Days: Getting Airborne

On June 18, 1971, four years after being incorporated, Southwest made its first flights. The schedule soon included 6 round-trips between Dallas and San Antonio and 12 round-trips between Houston and Dallas. Initially, Southwest instituted $20 one-way

---

[5]Ibid., p. 18.
[6]Ibid., p. 41.
[7]Katrina Brooker, "The Chairman of the Board Looks Back," *Fortune,* May 28, 2001, p. 66.

fares to fly the Golden Triangle, well below the $27 and $28 fares charged by rivals. But passenger loads were disappointingly meager on a number of the flights—some days the total number of passengers on all 18 flights would be fewer than 250.

To try to gain attention for its service and drum up more passengers, Southwest decided that it would have to do more than just run ads in the media—the company had budgeted $700,000 for advertising in its first year of operation, and half of that had been spent in the first month to publicize Southwest's market entry. Word-of-mouth advertising became the obvious alternative. Company officials decided that, aside from hoping satisfied passengers told other people about the pleasurable experience they had flying Southwest, they could generate talk by making their company outrageously different from its rivals. One of the first outrageous things Southwest decided to try was to dress its flight hostesses in colorful hot pants and white knee-high boots with high heels. Recruiting ads for Southwest's first group of hostesses were headlined "Attention, Raquel Welch: You can have a job if you measure up." Two thousand applicants responded, and those selected for interviews were asked to come dressed in hot pants to show off their legs. Over 30 of Southwest's first graduating class of 40 flight attendants consisted of young women who had been cheerleaders and majorettes in high school and thus had experience performing in front of people while skimpily dressed.

A second attention-getting action was to give passengers free alcoholic beverages during daytime flights. Most passengers on these flights were business travelers. Southwest management's thinking was that since most flights lasted less than one hour and since many passengers did not drink during the day, it would be cheaper simply to give drinks away rather than to collect the money from the few passengers who did order drinks.

Another promotional ploy took a cue from the airline's being based at Dallas's Love Field. Southwest began using the tag line "Now there's somebody else up there who loves you." The routes between Houston, Dallas, and San Antonio became known as the Love Triangle. Southwest's planes were referred to as Love Birds, drinks became Love Potions, peanuts were called Love Bites, drink coupons were Love Stamps, and tickets were printed on Love Machines. The "love" campaign set the tone for Southwest's approach to its customers and for its efforts to make flying Southwest an enjoyable, fun, and differentiating experience.

In September 1971, Lamar Muse decided to purchase a fourth Boeing 737 to provide out-of-state charter service and to add more flights in the Love Triangle. But competitors protested and a federal court ruling prohibited Southwest from flying charters out of state. Southwest did not have sufficient passenger traffic on its in-state routes to justify keeping the fourth plane, so Muse generated much-needed cash by selling the plane to Frontier Airlines for a $500,000 profit. The lack of a fourth plane, however, put Southwest in a bind. Muse did not want to cut back on flights that had been instituted when the new plane was acquired. Bill Franklin, the head of Southwest's ground operations, figured out that Southwest could avoid cutting back its schedule if ground crews for each of the three remaining planes could off-load passengers and baggage, refuel the plane, clean the cabin and restock the galley, on-load passengers and baggage, do the necessary preflight checks and paperwork, and push away from the gate—all within 10 minutes. Franklin knew from his experience at Trans Texas that such rapid turns were feasible. Like Muse, Franklin was an action-oriented, make-it-happen kind of guy and—with Southwest still unprofitable and struggling for survival—he directed the station managers to figure out how to do 10-minute turns. Station employees, many of whom did not have previous work experience at an airline and thus did not know the difficulty, took on the challenge of off-loading and then on-loading passengers and baggage and doing the necessary plane checks and paperwork within 10 minutes—realizing that the company's survival was on the line. Jack Vidal, former vice president of maintenance and engineering, recalled:

> The tough part was getting the fellows who had come from other major airlines to see that changing a tire, checking the oil, and getting the plane turned could happen in 10 minutes. We'd get our fastest guys and show them. Ten minutes later the tires have been changed, oil checked, and off it goes—everything in order. And the guys say, "Oh, it can be done."[8]

The 10-minute turn became one of Southwest's signatures. (In later years, as passenger volume grew and many flights were filled to capacity, the turnaround time expanded to 15 minutes and then 20 minutes—because it took more time to unload and load 125 passengers than just 60–65. Even so, turnaround times at Southwest were still shorter than the 40–60 minutes typical at other major airlines.)

Lamar Muse, Rollin King, and several other executives regularly mingled with employees, drinking beer with them after work hours and monitoring how well things were going.[9] Muse made a point of querying flight attendants about what customers were saying to better learn what Southwest could do to improve service and customer satisfaction. He also spent 25 to 30 hours per month riding various Southwest flights to give himself a chance to see employees in action, talk personally with passengers, and check out what was happening in the terminals and at Southwest's gates. Muse and King made a point of encouraging flight and station personnel to be creative and inventive and to go out of their way to be nice to passengers.

Throughout 1971, the small number of passengers flying Southwest stretched the company's financial resources to the limit.[10] At one point, Lamar Muse bought fuel for several months using his personal credit card. The company was short of ground equipment, and most of what it had was used and worn. Plane maintenance had to be done at night when the planes were not flying, and money for parts and tools was tight—on occasion, company personnel got on the phone with acquaintances at rival airlines operating at the terminal and arranged to borrow needed parts and tools. Nonetheless, morale and enthusiasm remained high; company personnel displayed can-do attitudes and adeptness at getting by on whatever resources were available. Rollin King said, "We had absolute honest communications with employees. We told them from the very outset that we were going to be in a fight for survival and that we really had to be better than everybody else, and they accepted it."[11]

In late November 1971, Southwest needed to send one of its planes in Houston to Dallas for routine maintenance over the weekend. Rather than have a crew fly the plane empty to Dallas, Lamar Muse came up with the idea of offering a $10 fare to passengers on the Friday-night Houston–Dallas flight, believing that some revenue was better than nothing. Even with no advertising, the 112-seat flight sold out. This led Muse to realize that Southwest was serving two quite distinct types of travelers in the Golden Triangle market: (1) time-sensitive business travelers who wanted weekday flights at times suitable for conducting business and (2) price-sensitive leisure travelers who wanted low fares and had more flexibility about when to fly.[12] He came up with a two-tier on-peak/off-peak pricing structure in which all seats on weekday flights

---

[8]Freiberg and Freiberg, *NUTS!*, p. 34.

[9]Ibid., p. 41.

[10]Ibid., p. 42.

[11]Ibid., p. 42.

[12]Ibid., p. 31.

departing before 7 PM were priced at $26 and all seats on other flights were priced at $13. Passenger traffic increased significantly—and systemwide on-peak/off-peak pricing soon became standard across the whole airline industry.

Things Start to Look Up a Bit

Southwest's first big breakthrough came when the company decided in 1972 to move its flights in Houston from the newly opened Houston Intercontinental Airport (where it was losing money and where it took 45 minutes to get to downtown) to the abandoned Houston Hobby Airport (located much closer to downtown Houston). Despite being the only carrier to fly into Houston Hobby, the results were spectacular—business travelers who flew to Houston frequently from Dallas and San Antonio found the Houston Hobby location far more convenient, and passenger traffic doubled almost immediately. Braniff and Texas International then transferred some of their intrastate flights to Hobby to take back the market share being lost to Southwest, and Braniff launched an aggressive ad campaign matching Southwest's low fares. Southwest initiated ads of its own reminding passengers that the other two carriers would never have reduced their fares if Southwest had not come to Hobby with low fares first. The company also gained a reputation among passengers for its on-time flights and lack of lines at the ticket counter. Southwest won the market share battle at Houston Hobby, and in 1975 Braniff and Texas International discontinued their flights into that airport.

Fare Wars

On January 22, 1973, in an attempt to fill empty seats on its San Antonio–Dallas flights, Southwest cut its regular $26 fare to $13 for all seats, all days, and all times. On February 1, 1973, Braniff retaliated by cutting its $26 Houston–Dallas fares in half and running full-page ads in Dallas announcing the $13 fares so that Dallas–Houston passengers could "get acquainted" with Braniff (even though the airline had been in business for 40 years). The Dallas–Houston route was only a small part of Braniff's operations, but it was Southwest's only profitable route at the time. With low cash reserves, Muse knew that Southwest had to respond; Kelleher flew in from San Antonio and, along with the Bloom Agency (Southwest's advertising firm), helped Muse write the ad that finally emerged. Headlined "Nobody Is Going to Shoot Southwest Airlines Out of the Sky for a Lousy $13," the ad contained copy saying that Braniff was trying to run Southwest out of business. The ad announced that Southwest would not only match Braniff's $13 fare but also give passengers the choice of buying a regular-priced ticket for $26 and receiving a complimentary fifth of Chivas Regal scotch, Crown Royal Canadian whiskey, or Smirnoff vodka (or, for nondrinkers, a leather ice bucket). Initially, over 75 percent of Southwest's Dallas–Houston passengers opted for the $26 fare (charging the ticket to their expense accounts and keeping the free bottle of liquor for themselves), but the percentage dropped to 20 percent as the two-month promotion wore on and corporate controllers began insisting that company employees use the $13 fare. As the local and national media picked up the story of Southwest's offer, proclaiming the battle as a David-versus-Goliath struggle in which the upstart Southwest did not stand much of a chance against the much larger and well-established Braniff, grassroots sentiment in Texas swung to Southwest's side.

The fare war with Braniff spread to other areas of operations. Kelleher recalled:

> One time some Braniff people went up to the roof of the terminal in Houston and hung a sign over the edge to advertise their service to Dallas. Our station manager went up there

and tried to cut it down with a knife. He ended up getting into a tussle with their people right there on top of the terminal. Another time Braniff didn't have enough room to move one of its planes away from the terminal and they asked us to move our airplane. We said no. So they tried to power it out using all their engines and blew out two of them. That was a great day. Finally the FAA told us, "Guys, unless you two quit this, we're going to throw you both out of here."[13]

Despite the bitter rivalry with Braniff, Southwest reported its first-ever annual profit in 1973. It has been profitable every year since—in an industry noted for its vulnerability to economic cycles and big swings in bottom-line performance. (For instance, the airline industry as a whole lost $3.5 billion in 1992 when events surrounding the Gulf War produced a slowdown in air traffic, and the industry was expected to lose as much as $4 billion in 2001 due to a slowing economy.)

More Legal and Regulatory Battles

Another round of legal battles began when Southwest refused to move its flights from Dallas's Love Field, located 10 minutes from downtown, out to the newly opened Dallas–Fort Worth (DFW) Regional Airport, which was 30 minutes from downtown Dallas. Local officials were furious with Southwest over its refusal to shift its flights to DFW because they were counting on fees from Southwest's flights in and out of DFW to help service the debt on the bonds issued to finance the construction of the new airport. But Southwest stood firm; it had not been ordered to move by the Texas Aeronautics Commission—moreover, the company's headquarters were located at Love Field. Initial hearings began in federal district court in March 1973. The judge ruled that Southwest's operations could remain at Love Field; the decision was appealed to the U.S. Fifth Circuit Court of Appeals in New Orleans, which upheld the district court's decision in mid-1974. Southwest's opponents decided to take the case on to the U.S. Supreme Court, but they were denied a hearing.

In 1973, Lamar Muse began exploring ways to expand by serving some of the smaller cities in Texas. He settled on the Rio Grande Valley and filed an application with the Texas Aeronautics Commission to fly into Harlingen Airport, a market served primarily by Texas International. A year-long battle ensued, with TI arguing vigorously that the market was already well served and could not support another carrier. The TAC ruled in Southwest's favor, prompting TI to seek an interim restraining order in the courts. But while proceedings dragged on for two years, the order never materialized, partly because TI became embroiled in a labor strike that grounded its service in the Rio Grande Valley and partly because Southwest's arguments that its service would greatly expand the market proved accurate. In the year before Southwest initiated service, 123,000 passengers flew from Harlingen Airport to Houston, Dallas, or San Antonio; in the 11 months following Southwest's initial flights, 325,000 passengers flew to the same three cities—chiefly because Southwest's low fares enabled more people to fly.

Unfair Competitive Practices   Believing that Braniff and Texas International were deliberately engaging in tactics to harass Southwest's operations, Southwest convinced the U.S. government to investigate what it considered predatory tactics by its chief rivals. In February 1975, Braniff and Texas International were indicted by a federal grand jury for conspiring to put Southwest out of business; such conspiracy was a violation of the Sherman Antitrust Act. Among other things, the

---

[13]Brooker, "The Chairman of the Board Looks Back," p. 66.

indictment alleged that Braniff and Texas International had conspired to pressure Southwest's investment bankers to withdraw from underwriting Southwest's initial public offering of stock, to boycott vendors doing business with Southwest, to keep Southwest from using the fuel hydrant system at Houston's Intercontinental Airport, and to blackball Southwest from membership in the airline credit card system. The two airlines pleaded no contest to the charges, signed cease-and-desist agreements, and were fined a modest $100,000 each.

Countering Opposition to Out-of-State Flights   When Congress passed the Airline Deregulation Act in 1978, Southwest was still an intrastate carrier serving parts of Texas. It decided to take advantage of the new interstate route opportunities afforded by deregulation and applied to the Civil Aeronautics Board (now the Federal Aviation Agency) to fly between Houston and New Orleans. The application was vehemently opposed by local government officials and airlines operating out of DFW because of the potential for passenger traffic to be siphoned away from DFW. The opponents solicited the aid of Fort Worth congressman Jim Wright, the powerful majority leader of the U.S. House of Representatives. Wright testified against Southwest's application, but the CAB approved it, and Southwest initiated service between Dallas and New Orleans in September 1979. Undeterred by the CAB ruling, Jim Wright took the matter to the floor of the House of Representatives and won approval of a bill to ban all interstate air service into and out of Love Field. Herb Kelleher and Colleen Barrett, with the aid of Washington lobbyists, then sought the aid of influential senators to defeat Wright's bill in the Senate. They ultimately won enough support in the Senate to gain what was known as the Love Field Compromise—under terms of the Wright Amendment of 1979, airlines operating out of Love Field may provide nonstop or through-plane service only to locations within Texas or within states bordering Texas (Louisiana, Oklahoma, Arkansas, and New Mexico). The amendment, which continues in effect as of 2001, means that Southwest cannot advertise, publish schedules or fares, or check baggage for travel from Dallas Love Field to any city it serves outside Texas, Louisiana, Arkansas, Oklahoma, and New Mexico.

The legal and regulatory battles that Southwest fought in its early years created an esprit de corps and a survival mentality. With newspaper and TV stories reporting Southwest's difficulties regularly, employees came to understand that the airline was fighting for its very existence. Had the company been forced to move from Love Field, it would most likely have gone under, an outcome that Southwest's employees, its rivals, and local government officials understood well. According to Colleen Barrett, the obstacles thrown in Southwest's path by competitors and local officials were instrumental in building Herb Kelleher's passion for Southwest Airlines and the corporate culture:

> They would put twelve to fifteen lawyers on a case and on our side there was Herb. They almost wore him to the ground. But the more arrogant they were, the more determined Herb got that this airline was going to go into the air—and stay there.
>
> The warrior mentality, the very fight to survive, is truly what created our culture.[14]

New Leadership

In March 1978, following a long series of run-ins and disagreements with Rollin King, Lamar Muse resigned as Southwest's president and CEO. Herb Kelleher was appointed interim president, CEO, and chairman of the board. In July 1978, Southwest's

---

[14]Freiberg and Freiberg, *NUTS!*, pp. 26–27.

board voted unanimously to appoint Howard Putnam, a group vice president of marketing services at United Airlines, as Southwest's president and CEO. Kelleher was named permanent chairman of the board. With the advent of airline deregulation in 1978 and opportunities for Southwest to fly interstate routes opening up, Putnam and several of the company's senior officers went on a two-day retreat to revisit Southwest's purpose and mission. Putnam told the group, "We aren't going to leave this room until we can write up on the wall, in a hundred words or less, what we are going to be when we grow up." The group decided that Southwest should continue with the same low-fare, short-haul, point-to-point strategy that it had been pursuing from the beginning, but with one major addition— it would gradually expand service to more cities outside Texas.

In September 1981, Putnam announced his resignation at Southwest, accepting an offer to become president and chief operating officer at Braniff International. Southwest's board asked Kelleher to assume Putnam's duties as president and CEO on an interim basis. In February 1982, Kelleher agreed to become Southwest's permanent president, CEO, and chairman. When Kelleher took over, Southwest had $270 million in revenues, 2,100 employees, and 27 planes flying to 14 cities.

In the years following Kelleher's move from being the company's courtroom warrior to being its CEO, Southwest Airlines prospered, racking up many industry firsts and expanding into more geographical areas. Some of the milestones during the Kelleher era are shown in Exhibit 1.

In 2001, Southwest was operating 353 jets to 58 airports in 57 cities in the continental U.S. (see Exhibit 2). It was the dominant carrier at four airports: Baltimore/Washington, Las Vegas, Kansas City, and Chicago Midway. Southwest was also the leading carrier in intrastate air travel in California, Texas, and Florida. During its 30 years of operations, Southwest had discontinued service to three cities—Beaumont/Port Arthur, Texas (1980); Denver (1986); and San Francisco (2001). In all three cases, Southwest was unable to generate sufficient traffic to operate profitably.

Exhibit 3 provides a 10-year summary of Southwest's financial and operating performance. Exhibit 4 provides industrywide data on airline travel for the 1995–2000 period.

HERB KELLEHER

Herb Kelleher majored in philosophy at Wesleyan University in Middletown, Connecticut, graduating with honors. He earned his law degree at New York University, again graduating with honors and also serving as a member of the law review. After graduation, he clerked for a New Jersey Supreme Court justice for two years and then joined a law firm in Newark. Upon marrying a woman from Texas and becoming enamored with the state, he moved to San Antonio, where he became a successful lawyer and came to represent Rollin King's small aviation company.

When Lamar Muse resigned, Southwest's board wanted Herb Kelleher to take over as chairman and CEO. But Kelleher enjoyed practicing law, and he asked the board to bring someone else in as CEO. However, when Howard Putnam came in as CEO, he asked Kelleher to become more involved in Southwest's day-to-day operations. Over the next three years, Kelleher got to know many of the company's personnel and observe them in action. He made a point of visiting with maintenance personnel to check on how well the planes were running and talking with the flight attendants. Kelleher did not do much managing from his office, preferring instead to be out among the troops as

exhibit 1   Milestones in Southwest Airlines Growth during the
               Kelleher Era, 1983–2001

1983	Three additional Boeing 737s are purchased; Southwest flies over 9.5 million passengers.
1984	Southwest is ranked first in customer satisfaction among U.S. airlines for the fourth straight year.
1985	Service begins to St. Louis and Chicago Midway airports. Southwest names the Ronald McDonald House as its primary charity—the tie-in was the result of an effort by a Southwest pilot who lost a daughter to leukemia and who believed that Ronald McDonald Houses were a worthy way to demonstrate Southwest's community spirit.
1986	Southwest flies over 13 million passengers.
1988	Southwest becomes the first U.S. airline to win the Triple Crown (best on-time record, fewest reports of mishandled baggage, and fewest complaints per 100,000 passengers) for a single month.
1990	Revenues reach $1 billion; Southwest was the only major U.S. airline to record both an operating profit and a net profit.
1992	Southwest wins its first annual Triple Crown for best on-time record, best baggage handling, and fewest customer complaints; for the second year running, Southwest was the only major U.S. airline to record both an operating profit and a net profit.
1993	Southwest begins operations on the East Coast and wins its second annual Triple Crown; revenues exceed $2 billion and profits exceed $100 million. For the third consecutive year, Southwest was the only major U.S. airline to record both an operating profit and a net profit.
1994	Southwest leads the industry by introducing ticketless travel in four cities; Southwest wins its third Triple Crown and acquires Morris Air, based in Salt Lake City.
1995	Ticketless travel becomes available systemwide; Southwest wins fourth consecutive Triple Crown.
1996	Service to Florida begins; Southwest wins fifth consecutive Triple Crown. Southwest and its employees contributed almost $740,000 to help support Ronald McDonald Houses, including $34,000 in cash donations from the company and $302,500 in free air travel for families staying at Ronald McDonald Houses in cities served by Southwest.
1997	Service begins to Southwest's 50th city; over 50 million people fly Southwest.
1998	Southwest is named by *Fortune* as the best company to work for in America.
1999	Service is added to three more cities.
2000	The number of passengers on Southwest flights exceeds 60 million and revenues surpass the $5 billion mark; the company records its 28th consecutive year of profitability and 9th consecutive year of increased profits. Southwest becomes the fourth-largest U.S. airline in terms of passengers carried.
2001	Southwest's market capitalization of $14 billion (May 2001) exceeded the combined market capitalization of United Airlines, American Airlines, and Continental Airlines. In the first quarter of 2001, Southwest reported net profits of $121 million—Delta, United, American, and U.S. Airways reported losses.

often as he could. His style was to listen and observe and to offer encouragement. When the flight attendant leadership told Kelleher it was time to get rid of the out-of-fashion hot pants, he was receptive. Then, when he got a petition from customer service agents arguing to keep the hot pants, Kelleher helped engineer a compromise—those who wanted could tie a wraparound skirt over their hot pants. Kelleher attended most graduation ceremonies of flight attendants from "Southwest University," and he

exhibit 2   Airports and Cities Served by Southwest Airlines, 2001

Southwest's Top 10 Airports			
	Daily Departures	Number of Gates	Nonstop Cities Served
Phoenix	181	23	35
Las Vegas	169	16	42
Houston (Hobby)	151	14	25
Dallas (Love Field)	139	15	14
Baltimore/Washington	127	13	31
Oakland	123	11	16
Chicago (Midway)	123	17	25
Los Angeles	117	13	16
Nashville	89	9	28
St. Louis	85	12	21
Other Airports Served by Southwest Airlines			
Albany	El Paso	Midland/Odessa	Rio Grande Valley
Albuquerque	Fort Lauderdale	New Orleans	Sacramento
Amarillo	Hartford/Springfield	Norfolk	Salt Lake City
Austin	Houston (Bush Intercontinental)	Oklahoma City	San Antonio
Birmingham	Indianapolis	Omaha	San Jose
Boise	Long Island/Islip	Ontario, CA	Seattle
Buffalo	Jackson, MS	Orange County, CA	Spokane
Burbank	Jacksonville	Orlando	Tampa
Cleveland	Little Rock	Portland, OR	Tucson
Columbus, OH	Louisville	Providence	Tulsa
Corpus Christi	Lubbock	Raleigh-Durham	West Palm Beach
Detroit (Metro)	Manchester, NH	Reno/Tahoe	

Source: Southwest Airlines.

often appeared to help load bags on "Black Wednesday," the busy travel day before Thanksgiving.

Kelleher had an affinity for bold-print Hawaiian shirts, owned a tricked-out motorcycle, and made no secret of his love for cigarettes and Wild Turkey whiskey. He loved to make jokes and engage in pranks and corporate antics, prompting some people to refer to him as the "clown prince" of the airline industry. He once appeared at a company gathering dressed in an Elvis costume. On another occasion, accompanied by bandoleers holding airline-size bottles of Wild Turkey, Kelleher arm-wrestled a South Carolina aviation company executive in an old Dallas wrestling arena before an audience of employees and the media for rights to an advertising slogan.[15] The South Carolina company had begun using the slogan "Plane Smart" a year before Southwest began using its version, "Just Plane Smart." Rather than pay lawyers to hash things out, the chairman of the South Carolina company proposed holding a friendly three-round arm-wresting contest to settle the dispute. Kelleher accepted the offer and insisted on representing Southwest in the event, which came to be billed as "Malice in Dallas." The loser of each round had to donate $5,000 to a charity of the winner's choice. Kelleher lost, but the event quickly became a favorite story told by Southwest employees—

---

[15]Ibid., pp. 246–47.

despite its victory the South Carolina company decided to let Southwest keep using the slogan "Just Plane Smart."

Kelleher was well known inside and outside the company for his combativeness, particularly when it came to beating back competitors. On one occasion, he reportedly told a group of veteran employees, "If someone says they're going to smack us in the face—knock them out, stomp them out, boot them in the ditch, cover them over, and move on to the next thing. That's the Southwest spirit at work."[16] On another occasion, he said, "I love battles. I think it's part of the Irish in me. It's like what Patton said, 'War is hell and I love it so.' That's how I feel. I've never gotten tired of fighting."[17]

While Southwest was deliberately combative and flamboyant in some aspects of its operations, when it came to the financial side of the business Kelleher insisted on fiscal conservatism, a strong balance sheet, comparatively low levels of debt, and zealous attention to bottom-line profitability. Kelleher was a strong believer in being prepared for adversity, the competitive maneuvers of rivals, and economic downturns—his philosophy was "Manage in good times so that you're ready for bad times." But he had an aversion to having groups of Southwest managers and employees spending time drawing up all kinds of formal strategic plans, saying, "Reality is chaotic; planning is ordered and logical. The meticulous nit-picking that goes on in most strategic planning processes creates a mental straitjacket that becomes disabling in an industry where things change radically from one day to the next." Instead, Kelleher preferred that Southwest managers look down the road, think ahead, have contingency plans, and be ready to act when it appeared that the future held significant risks or when new conditions suddenly appeared and demanded prompt responses.

In 1999, Kelleher became concerned that jet-fuel prices of 45 to 55 cents per gallon would not last (the going price for crude oil at the time was around $12 per barrel) and that the company was getting a bit lax about controlling costs—an internal cost study initiated by Kelleher showed that Southwest's nonfuel costs had risen 22 percent faster than those of rival airlines for the past several years. To guard against the potential for rising jet-fuel costs, Southwest hedged 80 percent of its anticipated 2000–2001 fuel requirements at prices equivalent to $22 per barrel of crude oil—a move that paid off handsomely when jet-fuel prices spiked to the range of 70 to 90 cents in 2000–2001(crude oil prices were in the $25–$35 range from early 2000 to fall 2001). To attack the upward creep in costs, Kelleher wrote a letter to all employees asking each one to institute actions that would save the company $5 per day in nonfuel costs; his letter generated the hoped-for response—Southwest's nonfuel costs in 2000 dropped 5.6 percent below 1999 levels.

Kelleher was a strong believer in the principle that employees—not customers—come first:

> You have to treat your employees like your customers. When you treat them right, then they will treat your outside customers right. That has been a very powerful competitive weapon for us. You've got to take the time to listen to people's ideas. If you just tell somebody no, that's an act of power and, in my opinion, an abuse of power. You don't want to constrain people in their thinking.[18]

Another indication of the importance that Kelleher placed on employees was the message he had penned in 1990 that was prominently displayed in the lobby of Southwest's headquarters in Dallas:

---

[16]As quoted in the *Dallas Morning News,* March 20, 2001.

[17]Brooker, "The Chairman of the Board Looks Back," p. 64.

[18]As quoted in ibid., p. 72.

exhibit 3 Summary of Southwest Airlines' Financial and Operating Performance, 1991–2000

	2000	1999	1998	1997
Operating revenues:				
Passenger[9]	$ 5,467,965	$ 4,562,616	$ 4,010,029	$ 3,669,821
Freight	110,742	102,990	98,500	94,758
Other[9]	70,853	69,981	55,451	52,242
Total operating revenues	5,649,560	4,735,587	4,163,980	3,816,821
Operating expenses	4,628,415	3,954,011	3,480,369	3,292,585
Operating income	1,021,145	781,576	683,611	524,236
Other expenses (income), net	3,781	7,965	(21,501)	7,280
Income before income taxes	1,017,364	773,611	705,112	516,956
Provision for income taxes[3]	392,140	299,233	271,681	199,184
Net income[3]	$ 625,224[10]	$ 474,378	$ 433,431	$ 317,772
Net income per share, basic[3]	$1.25[10]	$.94	$.87	$.64
Net income per share, diluted[3]	$1.18[10]	$.89	$.82	$.62
Cash dividends per common share	$.02200	$.02150	$.01889	$.01471
Total assets	$ 6,669,572	$ 5,653,703	$ 4,715,996	$ 4,246,160
Long-term debt	$760,992	$ 871,717	$ 623,309	$628,106
Stockholders' equity	$ 3,451,320	$ 2,835,788	$ 2,397,918	$ 2,009,018
Consolidated financial ratios[1]				
Return on average total assets	10.1%[10]	9.2%	9.7%	8.0%
Return on average stockholders' equity	19.9%[10]	18.1%	19.7%	17.4%
Consolidated operating statistics[2]				
Revenue passengers carried	63,678,261	57,500,213	52,586,400	50,399,960
RPMs (000s)	42,215,162	36,479,322	31,419,110	28,355,169
ASMs (000s)	59,909,965	52,855,467	47,543,515	44,487,496
Passenger load factor	70.5%	69.0%	66.1%	63.7%
Average length of passenger haul	663	634	597	563
Trips flown	903,754	846,823	806,822	786,288
Average passenger fare[9]	$85.87	$79.35	$76.26	$72.81
Passenger revenue yield per RPM[9]	12.95¢	12.51¢	12.76¢	12.94¢
Operating revenue yield per ASM	9.43¢	8.96¢	8.76¢	8.58¢
Operating expenses per ASM	7.73¢	7.48¢	7.32¢	7.40¢
Fuel cost per gallon (average)	78.69¢	52.71¢	45.67¢	62.46¢
Number of employees at year-end	29,274	27,653	25,844	23,974
Size of fleet at year-end[8]	344	312	280	261

[1]The Selected Consolidated Financial Data and Consolidated Financial Ratios for 1992 and 1991 have been restated to include the financial results of Morris Air Corporation (Morris).

[2]Prior to 1993, Morris operated as a charter carrier; therefore, no Morris statistics are included for these years.

[3]Pro forma for 1992 and 1991 assuming Morris, an S corporation prior to 1993, was taxed at statutory rates.

[4]Excludes cumulative effect of accounting changes of $15.3 million ($.03 per share).

[5]Excludes cumulative effect of accounting change of $12.5 million ($.03 per share).

The people of Southwest Airlines are "the creators" of what we have become—and of what we will be.

Our people transformed an idea into a legend. That legend will continue to grow only so long as it is nourished—by our people's indomitable spirit, boundless energy, immense goodwill, and burning desire to excel.

1996	1995	1994	1993	1992[1]	1991[1]
$ 3,285,178	$ 2,767,835	$ 2,497,765	$ 2,216,342	$ 1,623,828	$ 1,267,897
80,005	65,825	54,419	42,897	33,088	26,428
40,987	39,091	39,749	37,434	146,063	84,961
3,406,170	2,872,751	2,591,933	2,296,673	1,802,979	1,379,286
3,055,335	2,559,220	2,275,224	2,004,700	1,609,175	1,306,675
350,835	313,531	316,709	291,973	193,804	72,611
9,473	8,391	17,186	32,336	36,361	18,725
341,362	305,140	299,523	259,637	157,443	53,886
134,025	122,514	120,192	105,353	60,058	20,738
$ 207,337	$ 182,626	$ 179,331	$ 154,284[4]	$97,385[5]	$33,148
$.42	$.38	$.37	$.32[4]	$.21[5]	$.08
$.41	$.37	$.36	$.31[4]	$.20[5]	$.07
$ .01303	$ .01185	$.01185	$.01146	$.01047	$.00987
$ 3,723,479	$ 3,256,122	$ 2,283,071	$ 2,576,037	$ 2,368,856	$ 1,854,331
$ 650,226	$ 661,010	$ 583,071	$639,136	$ 735,754	$ 617,434
$ 1,648,312	$ 1,427,318	$ 1,238,706	$ 1,054,019	$ 879,536	$ 635,793
5.9%	6.0%	6.6%	6.2%[4]	4.6%[5]	2.0%
13.5%	13.7%	15.6%	16.0%[4]	12.9%[5]	5.3%
49,621,504	44,785,573	42,742,602[6]	36,955,221[6]	27,839,284	22,669,942
27,083,483	23,327,804	21,611,266	18,827,288	13,787,005	11,296,183
40,727,495	36,180,001	32,123,974	27,511,000	21,366,642	18,491,003
66.5%	64.5%	67.3%	68.4%	64.5%	61.1%
546	521	506	509	495	498
748,634	685,524	624,476	546,297	438,184	382,752
$66.20	$61.80	$58.44	$59.97	$58.33	$55.93
12.13¢	11.86¢	11.56¢	11.77¢	11.78¢	11.22¢
8.36¢	7.94¢	8.07¢	8.35¢	7.89¢	7.10¢
7.50¢	7.07¢	7.08¢	7.25¢[7]	7.03¢	6.76¢
65.47¢	55.22¢	53.92¢	59.15¢	60.82¢	65.69¢
22,944	19,933	16,818	15,175	11,397	9,778
243	224	199	178	141	124

[6]Includes certain estimates for Morris.

[7]Excludes merger expenses of $10.8 million.

[8]Includes leased aircraft.

[9]Includes effect of reclassification of revenue reported in 1999 through 1995 related to the sale of flight segment credits from Other to Passenger due to the accounting change implementation in 2000.

[10]Excludes cumulative effect of accounting change of $22.1 million ($.04 per share).

Our thanks—and our love—to the people of Southwest Airlines for creating a marvelous family and a wondrous airline.

Over the years, Kelleher had been highly visible in the organization. He knew the names of thousands of Southwest employees and was held in the highest regard by

exhibit 4   Commercial Airline Revenues, Scheduled Revenue Passenger Miles, and Overall Load Factor for Major U.S. Airline Carriers, 1995–2000

Year	Total Revenues (in billions)	Scheduled Revenue Passenger Miles* (in billions)	Operating Profit (in billions)	Load Factor†
1995	$73.5	509.6	$4.92	67.3%
1996	78.5	534.7	5.27	69.8
1997	83.5	570.0	7.52	70.8
1998	84.6	583.0	7.47	71.3
1999	89.6	616.8	6.00	71.4
2000	98.1	651.8	5.50	72.8

*Scheduled revenue passenger miles is the total number of miles flown by all passengers on all scheduled flights.

†Load factor is the total number of passengers boarded as a percentage of total seats available.

Source: Department of Transportation, Office of Aviation Analysis, *Airline Quarterly Financial Review, Majors,* fourth quarters, 1995–2000.

Southwest employees. When he attended a Southwest employee function, he was swarmed like a celebrity.

SOUTHWEST AIRLINES' STRATEGY

In 2001, Southwest was the only major short-hop, low-fare, point-to-point carrier in the U.S. airline industry. Its fares were among the lowest in the industry, accounting for 90 percent of the low-fare competition to rival U.S. carriers. From its inception, Southwest had pursued a low-cost/low-price/no-frills strategy that featured offering passengers a single class of service at the lowest possible fares and making air travel affordable to a wide segment of the U.S. population—hence its use of the tag line "The freedom to fly." Southwest's management was a strong believer in the concept of price elasticity, maintaining that cut-rate fares would grow passenger traffic so significantly that the revenue erosion from reduced fares would be more than compensated for by the revenue gains from increased ticket sales and the volume of passenger traffic. For instance, when Southwest entered the Florida market, it offered an introductory $17 fare from Tampa to Fort Lauderdale; in the first year, the number of annual passengers flying the Tampa–Fort Lauderdale route jumped 50 percent, to more than 330,000. In 2000, the Tampa–Fort Lauderdale fare averaged $56 and annual traffic was approaching 500,000; Southwest had 11 flights daily each way between Tampa and Fort Lauderdale. In Manchester, New Hampshire, passenger counts went from 1.1 million in 1997, the year prior to Southwest's entry, to 3.5 million in 2000 and average one-way fares dropped from just over $300 to $129. The company's strategy was to add flights as passenger traffic at a particular airport grew, thus offering customers more flight times to particular locations and, usually, an expanded number of destination options as well. Southwest's success in stimulating higher passenger traffic at airports across the United States via low fares and frequent flights had been coined the "Southwest Effect" by personnel at the U.S. Department of Transportation.

Southwest's market focus was flying between pairs of cities from 150 to 700 miles apart where there was high traffic potential and the company could offer a sizable number of flights. As a general rule, Southwest did not initiate service to an airport unless it envisioned the potential for originating at least eight flights a day there. Throughout the past 10 years, Southwest consistently had ranked first in market share in 80 to 90 percent of its top 100 city-pair routes and had an overall 65 percent share of the passenger traffic on its biggest 100 city-pair routes. Southwest carried the most passengers in the top 100 U.S. markets, despite serving only 40 of them.

Cost-Reduction Efforts

Southwest management fully understood that its low fares necessitated zealous pursuit of low operating costs so as to keep Southwest's operating costs per passenger mile attractively below the revenue generated per passenger mile. Southwest had, over the years, perfected a number of operating strategies for keeping its costs below those of rival carriers:

- The company's aircraft fleet consisted entirely of Boeing 737s. Having one type of aircraft minimized the need for spare parts inventories, made it easier to train maintenance and repair personnel, improved the proficiency and speed with which maintenance routines could be done, and simplified the task of scheduling planes for particular flights. Furthermore, as the launch customer for Boeing's 737-300, 737-500, and 737-700 models, Southwest acquired its new aircraft at favorable prices. See Exhibit 5 for statistics on Southwest's aircraft fleet.

- Southwest encouraged customers to make reservations and purchase tickets at the company's website, thus bypassing the costs paid to travel agents for handling the ticketing process and reducing the number of personnel needed to staff Southwest's own reservation centers. Selling a ticket on its website cost Southwest one-tenth as much as delivering a ticket through a travel agent and about half of the cost of processing a paper ticket through its own internal reservation system. In January 2001, Southwest cut the commissions paid to travel agents to 8 percent of the price of an electronic ticket and 5 percent of the price of a paper ticket (down from 10 percent paid on both), with a commission cap of $60 for a round-trip ticket (either electronic or paper)—management estimated the move would save the company $40 million in 2001. In 2000, about 30 percent of Southwest's revenue came from ticket sales through travel agents (versus 40 percent in 1998); and in the first quarter of 2001, close to 35 percent of ticket sales were occurring at the company's website. Ticketless travel accounted for over 80 percent of all sales, which significantly reduced paperwork and back-office processing.

- The company tried to steer clear of congested airports, stressing instead serving airports relatively near major metropolitan areas and in medium-sized cities. This helped produce better-than-average on-time performance and helped reduce the fuel costs associated with planes sitting in line on crowded taxiways or circling airports waiting for clearance to land. It also allowed the company to avoid paying the higher landing fees and terminal gate costs at high-traffic airports, where landing slots were controlled and rationed to those airlines willing to pay the high fees. In several cases, Southwest was able to compete on the perimeters of several big metropolitan areas by flying into nearby airports with less-congested air space. For example, Southwest drew some Boston-area passengers away from Boston's Logan International by initiating service into nearby Providence, Rhode Island, and Manchester, New Hampshire. Similarly, it initiated flights into Islip, Long Island, which siphoned some passengers away from New York's LaGuardia and Kennedy International airports. Emphasis on using less-congested airports furthered Southwest's objective of trying to minimize total travel time for passengers—driving to the airport, parking, ticketing, boarding, and flight time.

- Southwest's point-to-point system of scheduling flights was more cost-efficient than the hub-and-spoke systems used by rival airlines. Hub-and-spoke systems involved

exhibit 5   Southwest's Aircraft Fleet as of June 2001

Type of Aircraft	Number	Seats	Comments
Boeing 737-200	33	122	
Boeing 737-300	194	137	Southwest was Boeing's launch customer for this model
Boeing 737-500	25	122	Southwest was Boeing's launch customer for this model
Boeing 737-700	101	137	Southwest was Boeing's launch customer for this model

Other Statistical Facts

Average age of aircraft fleet—8.4 years.

Average aircraft trip length—509 miles.

Average aircraft utilization in 2000—8 flights per day; 11 hours, 18 minutes per day flight time.

Fleet size—1990: 106, 1995: 224, 1996: 243, 1997: 261, 1998: 280, 1999: 312, 2000: 344.

Firm orders for new aircraft—2001: 25, 2002: 27, 2003: 13, 2004: 29, 2005: 5, 2006: 22, 2007: 25.

passengers on many different flights coming in from spoke locations (or perhaps another hub) to a central hub within a short span of time and then connecting to an outgoing flight to their destination—a spoke location or another hub. Most flights arrived and departed a hub across a two-hour window, creating big peak–valley swings in airport personnel workloads and gate utilization—airport personnel and gate areas were very busy when hub operations were in full swing and then were underutilized in the interval awaiting the next round of inbound/outbound flights. In contrast, Southwest's point-to-point routes helped minimize the time that planes had to be parked at the gate (there was no need to wait for passengers from several different incoming flights to land, unload, walk to the gates for their connecting flight, and board) and also minimized the number of gates that Southwest needed for its operations (since incoming/outgoing flights were spaced somewhat evenly across the day). Compared to hub-and-spoke systems, Southwest's point-to-point route system resulted in higher utilization of aircraft and terminal facilities, reducing both the number of aircraft and terminal gates needed to support flight operations. Furthermore, with a relatively even flow of incoming/outgoing flights and gate traffic, Southwest could staff its terminal operations to handle a fairly steady workload across a day. Southwest management believed its point-to-point system resulted in higher labor productivity and was one of several reasons why its labor costs were lower than those of rival airlines—see Exhibit 6.

- To economize on the amount of time it took terminal personnel to check passengers in and to simplify the whole task of making reservations, Southwest dispensed with the practice of assigning each passenger a reserved seat. Instead, passengers were given color-coded plastic cards with numbers on them when they checked in at the boarding gate. Passengers then boarded in groups of 30, according to the color and number on their card, sitting in whatever seat was open when they got on the plane—a procedure described by some as a "cattle call." Passengers who were particular about where they sat had to arrive at the gate early to get a low number on their boarding cards and then had to be up front when it was their group's turn to board.

- Southwest flight attendants were responsible for cleaning up trash left by deplaning passengers and otherwise getting the plane presentable for passengers to board

exhibit 6 Comparative Operating Cost Statistics, Major U.S. Airlines, 1995–2000 (in cents per average seat mile)

Carrier	Year	Food	Salaries and Benefits	Aircraft Fuel and Oil	Commissions	Landing Fees	Advertising	Other Operating and Maintenance Expenses	Total Operating Expenses	Rent and Leasing Fees	Interest
American	1995	0.41¢	3.70¢	1.01¢	0.80¢	0.15¢	0.15¢	3.23¢	9.45¢	0.73¢	0.36¢
	1996	0.41	3.38	1.23	0.77	0.16	0.13	2.97	9.05	0.71	0.24
	1997	0.41	3.51	1.21	0.79	0.16	0.11	3.18	9.37	0.69	0.11
	1998	0.40	3.72	1.00	0.75	0.15	0.12	3.24	9.38	0.68	0.00
	1999	0.43	3.81	1.01	0.68	0.16	0.12	3.33	9.54	0.71	(0.02)
	2000	0.44	4.18	1.48	0.60	0.17	0.13	3.49	10.49	0.74	(0.00)
Alaska	1995	0.31¢	2.60¢	1.07¢	0.55¢	0.15¢	0.12¢	3.10¢	7.89¢	1.17¢	0.29¢
	1996	0.30	2.74	1.31	0.60	0.15	0.12	3.03	8.26	1.17	0.20
	1997	0.30	2.99	1.25	0.65	0.16	0.11	3.13	8.60	1.15	0.14
	1998	0.29	3.06	0.94	0.56	0.15	0.13	3.13	8.27	1.15	0.08
	1999	0.28	3.22	1.14	0.53	0.16	0.15	3.29	8.77	1.13	0.06
	2000	0.29	3.53	1.76	0.38	0.18	0.38	3.72	10.25	1.08	0.14
Continental	1995	0.22¢	2.45¢	1.11¢	0.74¢	0.18¢	0.16¢	3.82¢	8.67¢	1.20¢	0.33¢
	1996	0.23	2.65	1.29	0.76	0.20	0.13	4.05	9.31	1.18	0.23
	1997	0.25	2.80	1.34	0.76	0.20	0.15	3.77	9.27	1.12	0.18
	1998	0.26	3.05	1.02	0.69	0.18	0.14	4.08	9.41	1.16	0.16
	1999	0.28	3.10	0.97	0.63	0.18	0.14	4.21	9.51	1.22	0.23
	2000	0.28	3.30	1.62	0.54	0.18	0.07	4.21	10.20	1.23	0.23
Delta	1995	0.26¢	3.25¢	1.11¢	0.85¢	0.20¢	0.13¢	3.06¢	8.86¢	0.81¢	0.19¢
	1996	0.25	3.43	1.35	0.78	0.19	0.09	3.45	9.54	0.69	0.15
	1997	0.26	3.35	1.31	0.73	0.18	0.10	3.15	9.07	0.68	0.12
	1998	0.31	3.36	1.08	0.66	0.16	0.09	3.37	9.04	0.71	0.10
	1999	0.30	3.44	1.07	0.53	0.16	0.10	3.50	9.11	0.73	0.15
	2000	0.27	3.73	1.27	0.42	0.16	0.08	3.51	9.43	0.72	0.28
America West	1995	0.19¢	2.08¢	0.96¢	0.64¢	0.16¢	0.19¢	3.07¢	7.29¢	1.30¢	0.32¢
	1996	0.11	1.91	1.20	0.62	0.16	0.15	3.69	7.84	1.31	0.22
	1997	0.10	1.90	1.13	0.64	0.15	0.13	3.29	7.35	1.32	0.17
	1998	0.10	1.99	0.85	0.48	0.14	0.08	3.72	7.36	1.37	0.14
	1999	0.11	2.07	1.00	0.44	0.13	0.05	3.80	7.60	1.41	0.11
	2000	0.12	2.21	1.54	0.32	0.13	0.09	4.17	8.57	1.58	0.08

(continued)

Carrier	Year	Food	Salaries and Benefits	Aircraft Fuel and Oil	Commissions	Landing Fees	Advertising	Other Operating and Maintenance Expenses	Total Operating Expenses	Rent and Leasing Fees	Interest
Northwest	1995	0.28¢	3.47¢	1.24¢	0.93¢	0.27¢	0.16¢	2.80¢	9.15¢	0.70¢	0.27¢
	1996	0.26	3.30	1.49	0.90	0.24	0.17	2.84	9.21	0.64	0.21
	1997	0.26	3.25	1.43	0.86	0.23	0.14	2.89	9.06	0.62	0.21
	1998	0.26	3.72	1.19	0.73	0.23	0.20	3.34	9.68	0.64	0.32
	1999	0.27	3.57	1.19	0.71	0.24	0.14	3.03	9.15	0.61	0.35
	2000	0.29	3.65	1.80	0.61	0.24	0.13	3.24	9.96	0.67	0.31
TWA*	1995	0.27¢	3.16¢	1.20¢	0.69¢	0.19¢	0.16¢	2.88¢	8.56¢	0.71¢	0.40¢
	1996	0.27	3.19	1.44	0.66	0.18	0.17	3.34	9.25	0.74	0.31
	1997	0.23	3.45	1.32	0.66	0.18	0.14	3.21	9.20	1.02	0.31
	1998	0.26	3.71	1.00	0.57	0.19	0.17	3.74	9.65	1.33	0.34
	1999	0.25	3.80	1.11	0.51	0.21	0.15	4.23	10.26	1.54	0.27
	2000	0.23	3.72	1.65	0.34	0.20	0.11	3.89	10.14	1.79	0.24
United	1995	0.37¢	3.34¢	1.06¢	0.93¢	0.21¢	0.13¢	2.84¢	8.89¢	0.94¢	0.21¢
	1996	0.37	3.50	1.28	0.90	0.21	0.13	2.95	9.34	0.90	0.13
	1997	0.37	3.74	1.22	0.89	0.21	0.14	2.97	9.53	0.87	0.11
	1998	0.36	3.75	1.03	0.76	0.20	0.15	2.99	9.25	0.83	0.15
	1999	0.37	3.86	1.01	0.65	0.21	0.16	3.15	9.41	0.84	0.17
	2000	0.38	4.16	1.43	0.59	0.20	0.20	3.64	10.60	0.88	0.19
US Airways	1995	0.25¢	4.93¢	1.04¢	0.90¢	0.19¢	0.11¢	4.18¢	11.61¢	1.16¢	0.51¢
	1996	0.24	5.53	1.25	0.93	0.22	0.09	4.64	12.90	1.16	0.49
	1997	0.27	5.39	1.19	0.90	0.20	0.08	5.56	13.58	1.20	0.43
	1998	0.29	5.34	0.90	0.84	0.19	0.06	5.72	13.34	1.15	0.42
	1999	0.29	5.57	1.01	0.74	0.20	0.07	6.09	13.97	1.15	0.30
	2000	0.28	5.35	1.72	0.51	0.20	0.08	5.73	13.88	1.11	0.36
Southwest	1995	0.02¢	2.56¢	1.01¢	0.39¢	0.23¢	0.27¢	2.61¢	7.09¢	0.71¢	0.16¢
	1996	0.03	2.63	1.19	0.40	0.24	0.29	2.73	7.51	0.70	0.09
	1997	0.03	2.72	1.11	0.40	0.25	0.27	2.63	7.40	0.67	0.10
	1998	0.02	2.89	0.82	0.37	0.24	0.27	2.72	7.32	0.64	0.06
	1999	0.03	2.94	0.93	0.33	0.23	0.28	2.73	7.47	0.60	0.04
	2000	0.03	2.99	1.38	0.30	0.22	0.26	2.55	7.72	0.55	0.07

*Acquired by American Airlines in late 2000.

Source: U.S. Department of Transportation, Bureau of Transportation Statistics, Office of Airline Information, Form 41B, Form 41P, Form T100.

for the next flight (other carriers had cleaning crews come on board to perform this function). Attendants usually had planes ready for boarding within minutes of the last passenger's exit from the plane. On occasion, pilots pitched in to help with facilitating turnarounds.

- Southwest did not have a first-class section in any of its planes and had no fancy clubs for its frequent flyers to relax in at terminals. It served no meals on its flights—passengers were offered beverages, peanuts, and, more recently, raisins. (In 2000, Southwest provided passengers with 90.9 million packages of peanuts and 7.3 million packages of raisins.) Serving no meals on flights made reprovisioning planes simpler, faster, and cheaper.

- Southwest offered passengers no baggage transfer services to other carriers—passengers with checked baggage who were connecting to other carriers to reach their destination were responsible for picking up their luggage at Southwest's baggage claim and then getting it to the check-in facilities of the connecting carrier. (Southwest only booked tickets involving its own flights; customers connecting to flights on other carriers had to book such tickets either through travel agents or the connecting airline.)

- In mid-2001 Southwest implemented use of new software that significantly decreased the time required to generate optimal crew schedules and help improve on-time performance. With 2,700 daily flights, approximately 3,000 pilots, and 6,000 flight attendants, there were 750,000 crew duties that had to be covered. Over the course of a week, there were nearly 2 million variables and 90,000 constraints that had to be satisfied in coming up with the optimal crew schedule.

- Also in 2001, Southwest was converting from cloth to leather seats; the team of Southwest employees that investigated the economics of the conversion concluded that an all-leather interior would be more durable and easier to maintain, more than justifying the higher initial costs.

Southwest's operating costs as a percentage of its revenues were consistently the lowest in the industry—see Exhibit 6. Exhibit 7 shows a detailed breakdown of Southwest's operating costs for the period 1995–2000.

Southwest's Focus on Customers and Customer Satisfaction

Southwest went all-out to make sure passengers had a positive, fun flying experience. Gate personnel were cheery and witty, sometimes entertaining those in the gate area with trivia questions or contests such as "Who has the biggest hole in his or her sock?" Casually dressed flight attendants greeted passengers coming onto planes, offering friendly encouragement to customers looking for open seats. Flight attendants were encouraged to let their personalities show, to joke with passengers, and even to play gags. On some flights, attendants played harmonicas and sang announcements to passengers on takeoff and landing. On one flight while passengers were boarding, an attendant with bunny ears popped out of an overhead bin, exclaiming "Surprise!" When passengers sometimes asked what kind of meal they were getting, attendants had been known to pick up a magazine and tear out pictures of dishes and take it to them. The repertoires to amuse and entertain passengers varied from flight crew to flight crew.

Over the years, Southwest employees had built up quite a reputation for treating customers with courtesy, going out of their way to present a happy face to passengers,

***exhibit* 7**   Trends in Southwest Airline's Operating Expenses per Average Seat Mile, 1995–2000

Expense Category	2000	1999	1998	1997	1996	1995
Salaries, wages, and benefits	2.41¢	2.39¢	2.35¢	2.26¢	2.22¢	2.17¢
Employee retirement plans	.40	.36	.35	.30	.23	.23
Fuel and oil	1.34	.93	.82	1.11	1.19	1.01
Maintenance materials and repairs	.63	.70	.64	.58	.62	.60
Agency commissions	.27	.30	.33	.35	.35	.34
Aircraft rentals	.33	.38	.43	.45	.47	.47
Landing fees and other rentals	.44	.46	.45	.46	.46	.44
Depreciation	.47	.47	.47	.44	.45	.43
Other expenses	1.44	1.49	1.48	1.45	1.51	1.38
Total	7.73¢	7.48¢	7.32¢	7.40¢	7.50¢	7.07¢

Source: Company annual reports.

and displaying a fun-loving attitude. Even so, the company had, on occasion, encouraged some of its not-so-pleasant customers to patronize other carriers. One woman who flew Southwest frequently became known as "Pen Pal" because she wrote in a complaint after almost every flight—she objected to the seating arrangements, the lack of meals, the color of the planes, the sporty uniforms of flight attendants and gate personnel, the boarding procedure, and the casual atmosphere.[19] While several employees wrote responses trying to explain to her why the company did what it did, the woman's complaints were eventually bumped up to Herb Kelleher; he quickly penned a short note: "Dear Mrs. Crabapple, We will miss you. Love Herb." Kelleher made a point of sending congratulatory notes to employees when the company received letters from customers complimenting particular Southwest employees; complaint letters were seen as learning opportunities for employees and reasons to consider making adjustments.

In 1993, Southwest wrote a book describing what constituted "positively outrageous service" and why delivering it depended on an employee's attitude and personal commitment to serving others in a caring manner, actually enjoying meeting people and being around passengers, and conveying the feeling to passengers that they got a kick out of doing their job, not on religiously following a series of prescribed steps. In 1989, when Colleen Barrett felt the company was being too rigid, she sent a memo to all station managers asking them not to use rules and regulations as a crutch in refusing customer requests:

> No Employee will ever be punished for using good judgment and good old common sense when trying to accommodate a Customer—no matter what our rules are. Let's start leaning towards our Customers again—not away from them. Let's start encouraging our line employees to be a little more flexible and to take that extra minute to accommodate special needs. Let's start encouraging our Supervisors to give our Customers the benefit of the doubt.[20]

Southwest was convinced that conveying the Southwest spirit to customers was the key to competitive advantage; as one Southwest manager put it, "Our fares can be

---

[19]Freiberg and Freiberg, *NUTS!*, pp. 269–70.
[20]As cited in ibid., p. 288.

matched; our airplanes and routes can be copied. But we pride ourselves on our customer service."[21]

Marketing and Promotion

To celebrate its 30th anniversary in 2001, Southwest announced special $30 one-way fares to 30 destinations from 35 cities for travel between June 25 and October 26. The special fares required seven-day advance purchase, and passengers had to make reservations and buy their tickets at the company's website. In addition, the company instituted reduced fares on flights originating from Phoenix, Baltimore/Washington, and Dallas Love Field when purchased through Southwest.com with a seven-day advance purchase. Southwest's car rental and hotel partners participated in the promotion, offering $30-per-day rentals, $30-off discounts, and $30-per-day hotel rooms at some locations. The 30-year celebration also included decorations in gate areas, prize giveaways, and games in the gate areas so that customers could share in the "Southwest Spirit."

Southwest was known for its unconventional, attention-getting ads (see Exhibit 8), using them to create and reinforce the company's maverick, fun-loving, and combative image and to promote the company's performance as "The Low-Fare Airline" or "The All-Time On-Time Airline" or its Triple Crown awards. The company was continually on the lookout for novel ways to tell its story, make its distinctive persona come alive, and strike a chord in the minds of air travelers. The messages in ads were tightly matched to the company's strategy and were usually worded in a manner calculated to intrigue and entertain the audience and to persuade air travelers that what Southwest offered was of value. One Southwest ad offered all passengers who were embarrassed to fly an airline with the most convenient schedules and fewest customer complaints a paper bag to put over their heads; the ad went on to say that "if, on the other hand, Southwest is your kind of airline, we'll still give you this paper bag for all the money you'll save flying with us." Another of Southwest's TV ads showed a picture of an open bag of peanuts on a tray table, with the announcer saying "Because most of our flights are short, this is what our meals look like on Southwest Airlines . . . It's also what our fares look like." Some of the company's billboards touted the frequency of the company's flights with such phrases as "Austin Auften," "Phoenix Phrequently," and "L.A. A.S.A.P." Another billboard was headlined "Let's Padre."

Management believed that the company's ads helped promote the company's culture and were beneficial in marketing the company's values to employees as well as to customers. Each holiday season since 1985, Southwest has run a "Christmas card" ad on TV featuring children and their families from the Ronald McDonald Houses and Southwest employees.

Other Strategy Elements

Southwest's strategy included several other components:

- *A fare structure that was consistently the simplest and most straightforward of any of the major U.S. airlines*—All of Southwest's different fare options could easily be perused at the company's website, and the company's restrictions on tickets were more lenient than those of its rivals. Most other airlines had complex fare structures with ticket prices varying widely according to how far in advance the

---

[21]Brenda Paik Sunoo, "How Fun Flies at Southwest Airlines," *Personnel Journal* 74, no. 6 (June 1995), p. 70.

exhibit 8   Three Samples of Southwest's Ads

WE CAME. WE SAW. WE KICKED TAIL.

Make that, tails.
Head-to-head against all the major airlines in America, Southwest Airlines just won the first annual Triple Crown ever. Number One in On-time Performance, Number One in Baggage Handling, and

Number One in Customer Satisfaction for all of 1992. How can an airline that specializes in low fares deliver such a consistently high level of Customer Service? Simple. We care! Southwest Airlines. Number One and still climbing.

SOUTHWEST AIRLINES
Just Plane Smart.

Based on on-time arrival, baggage handling and complaint data for all major airlines for January through December 1992, as published in DOT consumer reports. ©1993 Southwest Airlines

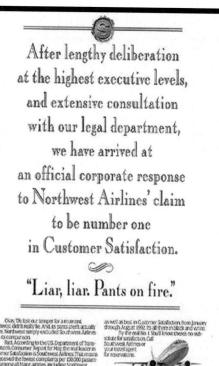

After lengthy deliberation at the highest executive levels, and extensive consultation with our legal department, we have arrived at an official corporate response to Northwest Airlines' claim to be number one in Customer Satisfaction.

"Liar, liar. Pants on fire."

Okay. We lost our temper for a moment. Northwest didn't really lie. And, its pants aren't actually on fire. Northwest simply excluded Southwest Airlines from its comparison.

Fact. According to the U.S. Department of Transportation's Consumer Report for May, the real leader in Customer Satisfaction is Southwest Airlines. That means we received the fewest complaints per 100,000 passengers among all Major airlines, including Northwest.

More facts. The Department of Transportation's Consumer Report also shows Southwest Airlines best in On-time Performance (highest percentage of system-wide domestic flights arriving within 15 minutes of schedule, excluding mechanical delays), best in Baggage Handling (fewest mishandled bags per 1000 passengers),

as well as best in Customer Satisfaction from January through August 1992. Its all there in black and white.

Fly the real No. 1. You'll know there's no substitute for satisfaction. Call Southwest Airlines or your travel agent for reservations.

SOUTHWEST AIRLINES
Just Plane Smart.
1-800-I-FLY-SWA (1-800-435-9792)

©Southwest Airlines 1992

WE'D LIKE TO MATCH THEIR NEW FARES, BUT WE'D HAVE TO RAISE OURS.

No matter what the competition may come up with, Southwest Airlines' everyday low unrestricted fares are still lower than the Big Three. That's a fact that can save you a lot of money every day.

And unlike our competitors, with our low unrestricted fares, we don't charge you a penalty when your plans change. Which makes our fares the smart choice for you and your company. Always have been. Always will be.

SOUTHWEST AIRLINES
Just Plane Smart.
1-800-I-FLY-SWA
(1-800-435-9792)

ticket was purchased, whether the travel dates included a Saturday-night stay (a means of helping distinguish between business and leisure travel), whether it was refundable or transferable, and assorted other factors.

- *Gradual expansion into new geographic markets*—Before adding additional cities/airports to its route system, Southwest endeavored to make sure that it had pretty much saturated the market for daily flights to the cities/airports it currently served. The company tended to add only one or two new cities to each route system in any one year. In selecting new cities, Southwest tried to identify city pairs that could generate substantial amounts of business and leisure traffic, given Southwest's low fares and frequent flight schedule. Management believed that lots of flights met business travelers' needs for schedule convenience and flexibility—if business travelers unexpectedly ran late and missed their flight, then leaving shortly on the next flight was often a good possibility.

- *Additional flights in areas where rivals were cutting back service*—When US Airways acquired California-based Pacific Southwest Airlines in 1990 and began reducing the number of flights on north–south routes in California, Southwest cut some of its fares in California by as much as two-thirds and added more flights from Burbank and Ontario airports (both located just outside Los Angeles) to Oakland—these moves helped Southwest become the second-largest carrier in California behind United. When American Airlines closed its hubs in Nashville and San Jose, Southwest immediately increased the number of its flights into and out of both locations. When Midway Airlines ceased operations in November 1990, Southwest moved in overnight and quickly instituted flights to Chicago's Midway Airport—in 2001 Midway was one of Southwest's biggest destinations with 123 flights daily (see Exhibit 2).

- *An attractive frequent flyer program*—Southwest's Rapid Rewards members received a free round-trip ticket, good for travel anywhere on Southwest's system for up to one year, after purchasing and flying eight round-trips. There were no restrictions on the number of free Rapid Rewards seats on a particular flight and very few blackout dates around holidays. Southwest was considered to have the most generous frequent flyer program in the industry, winning awards for best award redemption, best bonus promotion, and best customer service among all frequent flyer programs.

- *Additional long nonstop flights*—Although over 85 percent of Southwest's flights involved actual in-air flight times of less than 90 minutes, the company was judiciously adding nonstop flights to more distant destinations at those airports where its classic low fares could generate sufficient passenger traffic to achieve high enough load factors and revenues to be profitable. In 2000, about 420 of Southwest's flights were longer than 750 miles—versus fewer than 140 percent in 1995; its longest flight (Providence to Phoenix) was 2,300 miles.

- *Strong emphasis on safety, high-quality maintenance, and reliable operations*—In the 30 years it had been flying, Southwest had never had a plane crash. Southwest had one of the most extensive and thorough maintenance programs in the commercial airline industry. The company's state-of-the-art flight dispatch system helped minimize weather and operational delays.

- *Improved on-time performance, which had slipped significantly in 2000*—The company was adding 5 and 10 minutes to the flight schedules of frequently delayed flights with poor on-time performance.

According to Southwest management, the company's strategy of low-cost, no-frills, reliable, friendly service delivered "more value for less money" to customers rather than "less value for less money." Kelleher said, "Everybody values a very good service provided at a very reasonable price."[22]

SOUTHWEST'S PERFORMANCE UNDER KELLEHER

Southwest had ranked number one in customer satisfaction among U.S. major airlines for 10 consecutive years—1991 though 2000. The company had won numerous awards. In recent *Fortune* magazine surveys, Southwest had been consistently ranked as the most admired airline in America and one of the most admired companies in the world—in 1997, 1998, 1999, and 2000, it was ranked as the most admired airline in the world. For several years running, Southwest had ranked third or higher among the 10 U.S. commercial airlines in the national Airline Quality Rating (AQR) studies conducted by Wichita State University's School of Business and the University of Nebraska at Omaha's Aviation Institute; the AQR system used weighted averages and monthly performance data in the areas of on-time performance, baggage handling, involuntary denied boardings, and a combination of 11 customer complaint categories. Southwest's website had won top awards from both *Business Week* and *PC Magazine*. In 2001, *Business Ethics* included Southwest Airlines on its "100 Best Corporate Citizens" list.

Exhibits 9 and 10 provide comparative statistics on Southwest's performance versus other major commercial airlines.

SOUTHWEST'S PEOPLE MANAGEMENT PRACTICES AND CULTURE

Whereas the litany at many companies was that customers come first, at Southwest the operative principle was that employees come first and customers come second. The importance placed on employees reflected management's belief that delivering superior service required employees who not only were passionate about their jobs but also knew the company was genuinely concerned for their well-being and committed to providing them with job security. Southwest's thesis was simple: Keep employees happy—then they will keep customers happy.

What Southwest management thought about the importance of Southwest's people and their role is reflected in the following excerpt from the company's 2000 annual report:

> Our people are warm, caring and compassionate and willing to do whatever it takes to bring the Freedom to Fly to their fellow Americans. They take pride in doing well for themselves by doing good for others. They have built a unique and powerful culture that demonstrates that the only way to accomplish our mission to make air travel affordable for others, while ensuring ample profitability, job security, and plentiful Profitsharing for ourselves, is to keep our costs low and Customer Service quality high.
>
> At Southwest, our People are our greatest assets, which is why we devote so much time and energy to hiring great People with winning attitudes. Because we are well known as an excellent place to work with great career opportunities and a secure future, lots of People want to work for Southwest . . . Once hired, we provide a nurturing and supportive work environment that gives our Employees the freedom to be creative, have fun, and make a positive difference. Although we offer competitive compensation packages, it's our Employees'

---

[22]Statement made in a 1993 Harvard Business School video and quoted in Roger Hallowell, "Southwest Airlines: A Case Study Linking Employee Needs Satisfaction and Organizational Capabilities to Competitive Advantage," *Human Resource Management* 35, no. 4 (Winter 1996), p. 517.

exhibit 9   Operating Revenues of the Top 10 U.S. Commercial Airlines, 1995–2000 (revenues in millions)

2000 Rank	Airline	2000	1999	1998	1997	1996	1995
1	United	$19,331.3	$17,966.7	$17,517.5	$17,335.2	$16,316.7	$14,894.8
2	American	18,117.1	16,085.5	16,298.8	15,855.8	15,125.7	15,610.2
3	Delta	15,320.9	14,901.4	14,629.8	14,203.9	13,317.7	12,557.3
4	Northwest	10,956.6	9,868.1	8,706.7	9,983.7	9,751.4	8,908.9
5	Continental	9,449.2	8,381.5	7,907.7	7,089.9	6,264.4	5,704.6
6	US Airways	9,181.2	8,460.4	8,555.7	8,501.5	7,704.1	6,984.9
7	Southwest	5,649.6	4,735.6	4,164.0	3,817.0	3,407.4	2,873.5
8	TWA	3,584.6	3,308.7	3,259.1	3,330.3	3,554.4	3,280.9
9	America West	2,309.3	2,164.0	1,983.0	1,887.1	1,751.8	1,561.8
10	Alaska	1,762.6	1,695.6	1,581.3	1,457.4	1,306.6	1,162.9

Note: Federal Express and United Parcel Service are excluded because their business does not consist of carrying passengers.

Source: Department of Transportation, Office of Aviation Analysis, Airline Quarterly Financial Review, Majors, Fourth Quarters 1995–2000.

sense of ownership, pride in team accomplishments, and enhanced job satisfaction that keep our Culture and Southwest Spirit alive and why we continue to produce winning seasons.

The company changed the personnel department's name to the People Department in 1989; the head of the department had the title of vice president of people.

Recruiting, Screening, and Hiring

Southwest hired employees for attitude and trained for skills. Kelleher explained:

> We can train people to do things where skills are concerned. But there is one capability we do not have and that is to change a person's attitude. So we prefer an unskilled person with a good attitude . . . [to] a highly skilled person with a bad attitude.[23]

Management believed that delivering superior service came from having employees who genuinely believed that customers were important and that treating them warmly and courteously was the right thing to do, not from training employees to *act* like customers are important. The belief at Southwest was that superior, hospitable service and a fun-loving spirit flowed from the heart and soul of employees who themselves were fun-loving and spirited, who liked their jobs and the company they worked for, and who were also confident and empowered to do their jobs as they saw fit.

Southwest recruited employees by means of newspaper ads, career fairs, and Internet job listings; a number of candidates applied because of Southwest's *Fortune* listings as one of the best companies to work for in America and because they were impressed by their experiences as a customer on Southwest flights. Recruitment ads were designed to capture the attention of people thought to possess Southwest's "personality profile." For instance, one ad showed Herb Kelleher impersonating Elvis Presley and had the message:

> Work In A Place Where Elvis Has Been Spotted. The qualifications? It helps to be outgoing. Maybe even a bit off center. And be prepared to stay for a while. After all, we have the

---

[23]James Campbell Quick, "Crafting an Organizational Structure: Herb's Hand at Southwest Airlines," *Organizational Dynamics* 21, no. 2 (Autumn 1992), p. 51.

exhibit 10   On-Time Flights, Delays, Mishandled Baggage, Oversales, and Consumer Complaints for Major U.S. Airlines, 1996–2000

Carrier	2000	1999	1998	1997	1996	Rank for Cumulative Period 1996–2000
Percentage of scheduled flights arriving within 15 minutes of the scheduled time						
Alaska	68.1	71.0	72.0	74.7	68.6	9
America West	65.5	69.5	68.5	78.0	70.8	4
American	72.9	73.5	80.1	80.0	72.2	3
Continental	78.1	76.6	77.3	78.2	76.6	5
Delta	75.3	78.0	79.6	74.8	71.2	8
Northwest	77.4	79.9	70.6	75.4	76.6	2
Southwest	75.2	80.0	80.8	82.6	81.8	1
TWA	76.9	80.9	78.3	80.8	68.5	7
United	61.4	74.4	73.8	76.5	73.8	10
US Airways	72.3	71.4	78.9	80.5	75.7	6
Mishandled baggage reports per 1,000 passengers						
Alaska	3.48	5.75	7.27	7.19	7.00	9
America West	6.62	4.52	3.88	3.39	4.38	3
American	5.50	5.21	4.40	4.87	5.47	6
Continental	5.35	4.42	4.06	3.78	4.05	1 (tie)
Delta	4.49	4.39	4.27	4.54	5.19	4
Northwest	5.24	4.81	6.63	6.05	5.34	7
Southwest	5.00	4.22	4.53	3.92	3.96	1 (tie)
TWA	6.06	5.38	5.39	5.44	6.12	8
United	6.57	7.01	7.79	6.70	6.73	10
US Airways	4.76	5.08	4.09	4.24	5.14	5
Involuntary denied boardings per 10,000 passengers due to oversold flights						
Alaska	1.53	0.99	1.49	2.78	2.25	8
America West	1.27	1.38	1.12	1.98	4.36	10
American	0.44	0.42	0.42	0.63	0.79	3
Continental	1.44	0.28	0.13	0.10	0.19	2
Delta	0.34	1.98	1.24	1.53	1.30	6
Northwest	0.43	0.20	0.33	0.53	0.56	1
Southwest	1.84	1.40	1.84	2.16	2.39	9
TWA	2.76	0.88	1.69	1.30	0.87	7
United	1.64	0.69	0.59	0.49	0.54	5
US Airways	0.67	0.57	0.23	0.81	1.34	4
Complaints per 100,000 passengers boarded						
Alaska	2.04	1.64	0.54	0.63	0.51	2
America West	7.51	3.72	2.11	1.51	1.22	10
American	3.54	3.49	1.14	1.06	0.93	7
Continental	2.84	2.62	1.02	0.77	0.58	4
Delta	2.01	1.81	0.79	0.64	0.72	3
Northwest	2.61	2.92	2.21	1.39	0.85	6
Southwest	0.47	0.4	0.25	0.28	0.21	1
TWA	3.47	3.44	1.29	0.83	1.25	8
United	5.3	2.65	1.28	0.95	0.74	9
US Airways	2.59	3.13	0.84	0.78	0.68	5

Source: Office of Aviation Enforcement and Proceedings, *Air Travel Consumer Report,* multiple years.

lowest employee turnover rate in the industry. If this sounds good to you, just phone our jobline or send your resume. Attention Elvis.[24]

All job applications were processed through the People Department.

Screening Candidates   In hiring for jobs that involved personal contact with passengers, the company looked for people-oriented extroverts with a good sense of humor. It tried to identify those with a knack for reading people's emotions and responding in a genuinely caring, empathetic manner. Southwest wanted employees to deliver the kind of service that showed they truly enjoyed meeting people, being around passengers, and doing their job, as opposed to delivering the kind of service that came across as being forced or taught. According to Kelleher, "We are interested in people who externalize, who focus on other people, who are motivated to help other people. We are not interested in navel gazers."[25] In addition to a "whistle while you work" attitude, Southwest was drawn to candidates who it thought would be likely to exercise initiative, work harmoniously with fellow employees, and be community spirited.

Southwest did not use personality tests to screen candidates, nor did it ask candidates what they would or should do in certain hypothetical situations. Instead, it relied on Targeted Selection—an interviewing approach, developed by a Pittsburgh firm, that aimed at matching people's traits to the traits (or target dimensions) for performing a specific job successfully. The hiring staff at Southwest analyzed each job category to determine the specific behaviors, knowledge, and motivations that job holders needed. One trait or target dimension deemed critical for pilots and flight attendants was judgment. Another trait important to all job categories at Southwest was teamwork. Interviewers often asked applicants to tell them about a time in a prior job when they went out of their way to help a coworker or to explain how they had handled conflict with a coworker. Another frequent question was "What was your most embarrassing moment?" Southwest believed that having applicants talk about their past behaviors provided good clues about their future behaviors.

To test for unselfishness, Southwest interviewing teams typically gave a group of potential employees ample time to prepare five-minute presentations about themselves; during the presentations in an informal conversational setting, interviewers watched the audience to see who was absorbed in polishing their presentations and who was listening attentively, enjoying the stories being told, and applauding the efforts of the presenters. Those who were emotionally engaged in hearing the presenters and giving encouragement were deemed more apt to be team players than those who were focused on looking good themselves.

All applicants for flight attendant positions were put through such a presentation exercise before an interview panel consisting of customers, experienced flight attendants, and members of the People Department. Flight attendant candidates that got through the group presentation interviews then had to complete a three-on-one interview conducted by a recruiter, a supervisor from the hiring section of the People Department, and a Southwest flight attendant; following this interview, the three-person panel tried to reach a consensus on whether to recommend or drop the candidate.

In 2000, the company reviewed 216,000 résumés and hired 5,134 new employees.

Training

Apart from the FAA-mandated training for certain employees, training activities at Southwest were designed and conducted by Southwest's University for People, a part

---

[24]Southwest Airlines, and Sunoo, "How Fun Flies at Southwest Airlines," pp. 64–65.

[25]Quick, "Crafting an Organizational Structure," p. 52.

of the company's People Department. Located at Dallas's Love Field, the University for People's curriculum included courses for new recruits, employees, and leadership training programs for both new and experienced managers. The leadership courses emphasized a management style based on coaching and encouraging rather than supervising or enforcing rules and regulations. All employees who came into contact with customers, including pilots, received customer care training. There were also courses on safety, communications, stress management, career development, performance appraisal, decision making, and employee relations. From time to time supervisors and executives attended courses on corporate culture, intended to help instill, ingrain, and nurture such cultural themes as teamwork, trust, harmony, and diversity.

New recruits attended orientation programs held in Dallas, Phoenix, or Chicago. Depending on the influx of new employees, orientation courses were conducted two to five times per week for between 20 and 100 new recruits. The program included videos on Southwest's history, an overview of the airline industry and the competitive challenges that Southwest faced, and an introduction to Southwest's culture and management practices. This introduction, called "The Southwest Shuffle," featured hundreds of Southwest employees rapping about the fun they had on their jobs. Orientation programs at the Dallas headquarters typically included a scavenger hunt where new hires were given a time line with specific dates in Southwest's history and were asked to fill in the missing details by viewing the memorabilia decorating the corridors and getting information from people working in various offices. Another exercise designed to demonstrate the role of creativity and teamwork involved forming teams of eight people and giving them 12 straws, four strips of masking tape, and a raw egg. The objective was to construct a device that would keep the egg intact when it was dropped from a height of 10 feet. After the teams tested their device in front of the whole group, they then shared how they came up with their invention—whose ideas were used, whose expertise came into play, and so on. Usually, at least one team's device worked, but the lesson of the exercise was the value of cooperatively teaming with others to achieve a mutual goal with limited time constraints.

One of Southwest's supervisory training programs involved three teams; one member of each team was blindfolded and asked to throw a ball into a bucket. Unknown to the throwers, the other members on one team could say nothing about where the bucket was, members of the second team were instructed to say only "Good job" or "Keep trying," and the third group was allowed to give its thrower detailed information about where the bucket was. Not surprisingly, the third group's thrower had the most success—an outcome that was intended to demonstrate the value of good coaching on the part of supervisors and good listening on the part of supervisees.

Much of the indoctrination into the company's culture was done informally. However, Southwest made active use of a one-year probationary employment period to help ensure that new employees fit in with its culture and adequately embraced the company's cultural values.

Promotion

Approximately 80 to 90 percent of Southwest's supervisory positions were filled internally, reflecting management belief that people who had "been there and done that" would be more likely to appreciate and understand the demands that people under them were experiencing and also more likely to enjoy the respect of their peers and higher-level managers. Employees could either apply for supervisory positions or be recommended by their present supervisor. All applicants for new positions were subject to a

Targeted Selection process (similar to that used to screen new recruits) so as to improve the chances of matching the right people to the right jobs.

New appointees for low-level management positions attended a three-day "Leading with Integrity" class aimed at developing leadership and communication skills. Employees being considered for managerial positions of large operations (Up and Coming Leaders) received training in every department of the company over a six-month period in which they continued to perform their current job. At the end of the six-month period, candidates were provided with 360-degree feedback from department heads, peers, and subordinates; representatives of the People Department analyzed the feedback in deciding on the specific assignment of each candidate.[26]

Compensation

Southwest's pay scales were at levels close to the industry average, and benefit packages were good relative to other airlines. According to a 1997–98 survey, the average monthly pay of Southwest's pilots was about 10 percent above the industry average; however, they flew an average of 85 hours per month versus an industry average of 80.2 hours.

Southwest introduced a profit-sharing plan for senior employees in 1973, the first such plan in the airline industry. By the mid-1990s the plan had been extended to cover most Southwest employees. As of 2001, Southwest had 12 different stock option programs for various employee groups, a 401(K) employee savings plan that included company-matching contributions, and a profit-sharing plan covering virtually all employees that consisted of a money purchase defined contribution plan and an employee stock purchase plan. Company employees held options on 5.5 million shares at year-end 1998, 5.0 million shares at year-end 1999, and 4.1 million shares at year-end 2000, with a big majority of the options exercisable at prices under $8 (the company's stock price traded in the $15–$20 range during the first nine months of 2001). Company contributions to employee 401(K) and profit-sharing plans totaled $167.1 million in 1998, $192 million in 1999, and $241.5 million in 2000; in recent years, these payments had represented 8 to 12 percent of base pay. Employees participating in stock purchases via payroll deduction bought 677,000 shares in 1998, 649,000 shares in 1999, and 686,000 shares in 2000, at prices equal to 90 percent of the market value at each payroll period. Southwest employees owned an estimated 12 percent of Southwest's outstanding shares. An estimated 200 Southwest employees were millionaires at year-end 2000 by virtue of their investments in their profit-sharing accounts.

Employee Relations

Almost 85 percent of Southwest's employees belonged to a union, making the airline one of the most highly unionized in the United States. The Teamsters Union represented Southwest's airline mechanics, stock clerks, and aircraft cleaners; the Transport Workers Union represented flight attendants; Local 555 of the Transport Workers Union represented baggage handlers, ground crews, and provisioning employees; and the International Association of Machinists represented the customer service and reservation employees. There was one in-house union—the Southwest Airline Pilots Association. Despite having sometimes spirited disagreements over particular issues, Southwest's

---

[26]Sunoo, "How Fun Flies at Southwest Airlines," p. 72.

relationships with the unions representing its employee groups were quite harmonious and nonadversarial for the most part—the company had experienced only one brief strike by machinists in the early 1980s. On one of Southwest's videos, the president of one of the unions said, "Our members enjoy coming to work in the morning."

Management encouraged union members and negotiators to research their pressing issues and to conduct employee surveys before each contract negotiation. One such research effort resulted in the pilots union proposing an unprecedented 10-year contract calling for stock options in lieu of pay increases over the first five years—for years, Southwest's growth had pushed its stock price steadily upward, making stock options very lucrative. Southwest was receptive to the union proposal partly because it tied pilot compensation to the company's financial performance, partly because a long-term agreement with pilots was attractive, and partly because a 10-year contract period was long enough to allow the options granted in the first 5 years to hold significant financial value when they could be exercised. After seven months of back-and-forth negotiations, an agreement was signed in 1995 that froze pilots' salaries for five years, provided for 3 percent annual increases each of the following five years, and linked the size of stock option awards to Southwest's bottom-line performance.

Southwest's contracts with the unions representing its employees were relatively free of restrictive work rules and narrow job classifications that might impede worker productivity. All of the contracts allowed any qualified employee to perform any function—thus, pilots, ticket agents, and gate personnel could help load and unload baggage when needed and flight attendants could pick up trash and make flight cabins more presentable for passengers boarding the next flight.

However, in 2000–2001 the company was locked in contentious negotiations with Local 555 of the Transport Workers Union (TWU), which represented about 5,300 Southwest employees, over a new wage and benefits package; the previous contract had become open for renegotiation in December 1999 and a tentative agreement reached at the end of 2000 was rejected by 64 percent of the union members who voted. A memo from Kelleher to TWU representatives said, "The cost and structure of the TWU 555 negotiating committee's proposal would seriously undermine the competitive strength of Southwest Airlines; endanger our ability to grow; threaten the value of our employees' profit-sharing; require us to contract out work in order to remain competitive; and threaten our 29-year history of job security for our employees." In a union newsletter in early 2001, the president of the TWU said, "We asked for a decent living wage and benefits to support our families, and were told of how unworthy and how greedy we were." The ongoing dispute resulted in informational picket lines in March 2001 at several Southwest locations, the first picketing since 1980. Later in 2001, with the help of the National Mediation Board, Southwest and the TWU reached an agreement covering Southwest's ramp, operations, and provisioning employees.

In August 2001, Southwest's pilots were somewhat restive about their base pay relative to pilots at other U.S. airlines. For example, the maximum pay for Southwest's 3,700-plus pilots (before profit-sharing bonuses) was $148,000, versus maximums of $290,000 for United's pilots, $262,000 for Delta's pilots, $206,000 for American's pilots, and $199,000 for Continental's pilots.[27] Moreover, some veteran Southwest employees were grumbling about staff shortages in certain locations (to hold down labor costs) and cracks in the company's close-knit family culture due to the influx of so many new employees over the past several years. A number of employees who had accepted lower pay

---

[27]Shawn Tully, "From Bad to Worse," *Fortune,* October 15, 2001, p. 124.

because of Southwest's underdog status were said to feel entitled to "big airline" pay now that Southwest had emerged as a major U.S. carrier.[28]

The No-Layoff Policy

Southwest Airlines had never laid off or furloughed any of its employees. The company's no-layoff policy was seen as integral to management efforts to sustain and nurture the corporate culture. According to Kelleher,

> Nothing kills your company's culture like layoffs. No body has ever been furloughed here, and that is unprecedented in the airline industry. It's been a huge strength of ours. It's certainly helped negotiate our union contracts . . . We could have furloughed at various times and been more profitable, but I always thought that was shortsighted. You want to show your people you value them and you're not going to hurt them just to get a little more money in the short term. Not furloughing people breeds loyalty. It breeds a sense of security. It breeds a sense of trust.[29]

Southwest had built up considerable goodwill with its unions over the years by avoiding layoffs.

Management Style

At Southwest, managers were expected to spend at least one-third of their time out of the office, walking around the facilities under their supervision, observing firsthand what was going on, listening to employees and being responsive to their concerns. A former director of people development at Southwest told of a conversation he had with one of Southwest's terminal managers:

> While I was out in the field visiting one of our stations, one of our managers mentioned to me that he wanted to put up a suggestion box. I responded by saying . . . , "Sure—why don't you put up a suggestion box right here on this wall and then admit you are a failure as a manager?" Our theory is, if you have to put up a box so people can write down their ideas and toss them in, it means you are not doing what you are supposed to be doing. You are supposed to be setting your people up to be winners. To do that, you should be there listening to them and available to them in person, not via a suggestion box. For the most part, I think we have a very good sense of this at Southwest. I think that most people employed here know that they can call any one of our vice presidents on the telephone and get heard, almost immediately.
>
> The suggestion box gives managers an out; it relinquishes their responsibility to be accessible to their people, and that's when we have gotten in trouble at Southwest—when we can no longer be responsive to our flight attendants or customer service agents, when they can't gain access to somebody who can give them resources and answers.[30]

Company executives were very approachable, insisting on being called by their first names. At employee orientations, people were told, "We do not call the company chairman Mr. Kelleher, we call him Herb." Managers and executives had an open-door policy, actively listening to employee concerns, opinions, and suggestions for reducing costs and improving efficiency.

---

[28]Melanie Trottman, "Amid Crippled Rivals, Southwest Tries to Spread Its Wings," *The Wall Street Journal,* October 11, 2001, p. A10.

[29]Brooker, "The Chairman of the Board Looks Back," p. 72.

[30]Freiberg and Freiberg, *NUTS!,* p. 273.

Employee-led initiatives were common. Southwest's pilots had been instrumental in developing new protocols for takeoffs and landings that conserved fuel. Another frontline employee had suggested not putting the company logos on trash bags, saving an estimated $250,000 annually. Rather than buy 800 computers for a new reservations center in Albuquerque, company employees determined that they could buy the parts and assemble the PCs themselves for half the price, saving the company $1 million and it was Southwest clerks who came up with the idea of doing away with paper tickets and shifting to e-tickets.

There were only four layers of management between a frontline supervisor and the CEO. Southwest's employees enjoyed substantial authority and decision-making power. According to Kelleher:

> We've tried to create an environment where people are able to, in effect, bypass even the fairly lean structures that we have so that they don't have to convene a meeting of the sages in order to get something done. In many cases, they can just go ahead and do it on their own. They can take individual responsibility for it and know they will not be crucified if it doesn't work out. Our leanness requires people to be comfortable in making their own decisions and undertaking their own efforts.[31]

From time to time, there were heart-to-heart meetings at which frontline employees and managers openly discussed and resolved operating problems and issues.[32] Informal problem avoidance and rapid problem resolution were seen as managerial virtues.

Management wanted Southwest employees to be proud of the company they worked for and its work force practices. In 1998, *Fortune* named Southwest first in its listing of the 100 best companies to work for in America; Southwest was ranked second in 1999, second in 2000, and fourth in 2001.

Core Values

Two core values—LUV and fun—permeated the work environment at Southwest. Much more than the company's ticker symbol, LUV was a recurring theme in Southwest's advertising campaigns. Over the years, LUV grew into Southwest's code word for treating individuals—fellow employees and customers—with dignity and respect and demonstrating a caring, loving attitude. "LUV" and red hearts commonly appeared on banners and posters at company facilities, as reminders of the compassion that was expected toward customers and other employees. Practicing the Golden Rule, internally and externally, was expected of all employees. Employees who struggled to live up to these expectations were subjected to considerable peer pressure and usually were asked to seek employment elsewhere if they did not soon leave on their own volition. To celebrate the company's 30th anniversary in 2001, company flight attendants in serving beverages to passengers were using cocktail napkins with the slogan "30 years of LUV" emblazoned around Southwest's trademark heart.

Fun occurred throughout the company in the form of the generally entertaining behavior of employees in performing their jobs, the ongoing pranks and jokes, and frequent company-sponsored parties and celebrations. On holidays, employees were encouraged to dress in costumes—on one occasion Herb Kelleher, dressed in a bunny costume, passed out Easter eggs to passengers. There were charity benefit games, chili

---

[31]Ibid., p. 76.
[32]Hallowell, "Southwest Airlines: A Case Study," p. 524.

cook-offs, Halloween parties, new Ronald McDonald House dedications, and other special events of one kind or another at one location or another almost every week. Employees were encouraged to come out—even if doing so meant traveling— and have a good time at company events. According to one manager, "We're kind of a big family here, and family members have fun together." Herb Kelleher said, " We demonstrate by example that you don't have to be uptight to be successful." The video showing Kelleher and a group of employees doing "The Southwest Shuffle" contained the following excerpt:

> We're the Southwest team, that's what we are.
> No MVP, we're each a big star.
> It's fun to fly and it's fun to serve,
> And fun is what our customers deserve.

The Culture Committee

Southwest formed a Culture Committee in 1990 to promote "Positively Outrageous Service" and devise tributes, contests, and celebrations intended to nurture and perpetuate the Southwest Spirit. The committee, chaired by Colleen Barrett, was composed of up to 100 employees representing a cross-section of departments and locations; members served a two-year term. Chosen for their zeal in exhibiting the Southwest Spirit and their commitment to Southwest's mission and values, Culture Committee members functioned as cultural ambassadors, missionaries, and storytellers. The committee had four all-day meetings annually; ad hoc subcommittees formed throughout the year met more frequently. Kelleher indicated, "We're not big on committees at Southwest, but of the committees we do have, the Culture Committee is the most important."[33]

Over the years, the Culture Committee had been instrumental in sponsoring and supporting hundreds of ways to promote and ingrain the Southwest spirit. On occasions, members would simply show up at a facility to serve pizza or ice cream to employees. Committee members had been known to show up with paint and equipment to remodel and decorate an employee break room at a terminal facility.

Efforts to Nurture the Southwest Culture   Over the years, Southwest had come up with a wide variety of ways to nurture its core values and perpetuate its unique culture. There was a CoHearts mentoring program, a Day in the Field program where employees spent time working in another area of the company's operations, a Helping Hands program where volunteers from around the system traveled to Southwest facilities that were temporarily shorthanded, and periodic Culture Exchange meetings to celebrate the Southwest spirit and company milestones. Almost every event at Southwest was videotaped, which provided footage for creating such multipurpose videos as *Keepin' the Spirit Alive* that could be shown at company events all over the system and used in training courses. Many of the Culture Committee's activities revolved around promoting the use of red hearts and LUV to embody the spirit of Southwest employees caring about each other and Southwest's customers. The concepts of LUV and fun were spotlighted in all of the company's training manuals and videos. There was an annual "Heros of the Heart Award."

Southwest's monthly newsletter, *LUV Lines,* often described the experiences and deeds of particular employees, reprinted letters of praise from customers, and reported company celebrations of milestones. A quarterly news video, *As the Plane Turns,* was

---

[33]Freiberg and Freiberg, *NUTS!,* p. 165.

sent to all facilities to keep employees up-to-date on company happenings, provide clips of special events, and share messages from customers, employees, and executives. The company had published a book for employees describing "outrageous" acts of service. Sometimes important information was circulated to employees in "fun" packages such as Cracker Jack boxes. Herb Kelleher gave an annual "Message to the Field" that nearly always focused on the accomplishments of Southwest's people and reinforced cultural values; in presenting his 1996 message, he appeared on the podium in a straitjacket to do his part in supporting the company's 25th anniversary theme, "Still Nuts after All These Years."

The Link between Culture and Company Growth   Southwest executives believed that the company's growth was primarily a function of the rate at which it could hire and train people to fit into its culture and mirror the Southwest spirit. With over 100 cities petitioning Southwest to initiate service to their airports, management believed that the company's growth was not constrained by a lack of market opportunities to expand into other geographic locations. Over 10,000 of Southwest's 30,000 employees had been hired since 1995.

Employee Productivity

Management was convinced the company's strategy, culture, esprit de corps, and people management practices fostered high labor productivity and contributed to Southwest's very low labor costs compared to other airlines (see Exhibit 6). When a Southwest flight pulled up to the gate, ground crews, gate personnel and flight attendants hustled to perform all the tasks requisite to turn the plane quickly—employees took pride in doing their part to achieve good on-time performance. Southwest's turnaround times were on average about two-thirds the industry average. One study found that Southwest had an average of 2.2 station personnel per 1,000 passengers in 1994 versus an industry average of about 4.2.[34] According to figures from the Air Transport Association, Southwest had 2,079 passengers per employee in 1999; Alaska Airlines had an passenger/employee ratio of 1,514 to 1, followed by Delta Airlines with 1,493 to 1. United had the lowest 1999 passenger-to-employee ratio, at 938 to 1. In 2000, Southwest's labor productivity compared favorably with the average of its eight biggest U.S. rivals:

Productivity Measure	Southwest	Average of Southwest's Eight Largest U.S. Rivals
Passengers enplaned per employee	2,145	1,119
Employees per plane	83.4	121.7

SOUTHWEST'S NEW LEADERSHIP TEAM

James Parker

Southwest's newly appointed CEO, James Parker, had an association with Herb Kelleher going back 22 years, to the time when they were colleagues at Kelleher's old law

[34]J. H. Gittell, "Cross-Functional Coordination and Human Resource Systems: Evidence from the Airline Industry," doctoral dissertation, Massachusetts Institute of Technology, cited in Hallowell, "Southwest Airlines: A Case Study," p. 527.

firm. Parker moved over to Southwest from the law firm in February 1986. He had maintained a relatively low profile inside the company as Southwest's vice president and general counsel, but he was Southwest's chief labor negotiator—much of the credit for Southwest's good relations with employee unions belonged to Parker. Prior to his appointment as CEO, Parker had been a member of the company's executive planning committee, and his experiences ranged from properties and facilities to technical services to the company's alliances with vendors and partners. Parker and Kelleher were said to think much alike, and Parker was regarded as having a good sense of humor, although he did not have as colorful and flamboyant a personality as Kelleher. Parker was seen as an honest, straight-arrow kind of person who had a strong grasp of Southwest's culture and market niche and who could be nice or tough, depending on the situation. When his appointment was announced, Parker said:

> There is going to be no change of course insofar as Southwest is concerned. We have a very experienced leadership team. We've all worked together for a long time. There will be evolutionary changes in Southwest, just as there have always been in our history. We're going to stay true to our business model of being a low-cost, low-fare airline.[35]

Colleen Barrett

Colleen Barrett began working with Herb Kelleher as his legal secretary in 1967 and had been with Southwest since 1978. As executive vice president—customers, Barrett had a high profile among Southwest employees and spent most of her time on culture building, morale building, and customer service. She and Kelleher were regarded as Southwest's guiding lights, and some analysts said she was essentially functioning as the company's COO prior to her formal appointment. Much of the credit for the company's strong record of customer service and its strong cultural underpinnings belonged to Barrett.

Barrett had been the driving force behind lining the hallways at Southwest's headquarters with photos of company events and trying to create a family atmosphere at the company. Believing it was important to make employees feel cared about and important, Barrett had put together a network of contacts across the company to help her stay in touch with what was happening with employees and their families. When network members learned about events that were worthy of acknowledgment, the word quickly got to Barrett—the information went into a database, and an appropriate greeting card or gift was sent. Barrett had a remarkable ability to give individualized gifts that connected her to the recipient.[36]

Barrett was the first woman appointed as president and COO of a major U.S. airline. In October 2001, *Fortune* included Colleen Barrett on its list of the 50 most powerful women in American business (she was ranked number 20).

CRISIS CONDITIONS STRIKE THE AIRLINE INDUSTRY: THE SEPTEMBER 2001 TERRORIST ATTACKS ON AMERICA

In the days and weeks following the terrorist attacks on the World Trade Center and the Pentagon on September 11, 2001, the commercial air travel system in the United States

---

[35]As quoted in the *Seattle Times,* March 20, 2001, p. C3.
[36]Freiberg and Freiberg, *NUTS!,* p. 163.

was suddenly and unexpectedly in shambles. The unprecedented three-day shutdown of flights, the sudden erosion of passenger traffic, and strict new security measures threw major airlines into a financial crunch of huge proportions and triggered a struggle to revamp flight schedules and respond to sharply lower passenger travel.

Already estimating preattack industry losses in 2001 of close to $1.5 billion due to a slowdown in the economy, airline industry analysts speculated that losses for U.S. airlines in the wake of the terrorist attacks could reach $7 billion in 2001 and that slack demand for air travel could last well into 2002. America West, a low-fare carrier, reported on September 17 that bookings for future flights had dropped 50 percent below usual levels. Many airline executives expressed concerns about an impending liquidity crunch, rapid burns of cash on hand, and the potential for a number of carriers to end up in bankruptcy without some kind of relief from the federal government.

During the three days that flights were suspended by the FAA, airlines burned through an estimated $220 million per day in cash to cover ongoing expenses. On the first day of trading after the terrorist attacks, investor worries about almost-empty flights, higher costs from added security measures, and a clouded financial future for the whole airline industry caused airline stock prices to plunge—see Exhibit 11. With about $26.1 billion in debt as of 2001, billions more in capital lease obligations for planes that had been leased rather than purchased, and ongoing costs for labor, terminal facilities, and maintenance, U.S. commercial airlines typically had to fill close to 65 percent of the available seats in order to break even. For the four weeks immediately following the attacks, load factors at most airlines were in the 40–60 percent range.

Analysts estimated that the nine major U.S. commercial airlines had a combined total of about $9.4 billion in cash and short-term investments as of June 30, 2001. A number of airlines drew on established lines of credit in the week following the attacks to bolster their cash position and help cover expected revenue shortfalls in the weeks and months ahead. Gordon Bethune, CEO of Continental Airlines, indicated that the company expected to take in only half of its normal revenues for several weeks following the attacks; even if Continental cut costs 20 percent, Bethune said, the company would have losses of more than $200 million per month at those revenue levels.[37] On Monday, September 17, 2001, Continental announced that it would not make $70 million in debt payments due that day but it was able to make the payments within the 10-day grace period to prevent defaulting. Continental officials also indicated that a bankruptcy filing was one of the options being considered to cope with its anticipated cash crunch.

Adjustments to flight schedules and crew assignments at some airlines were further complicated by the fact that some nervous airline attendants were no longer willing to fly and by union contracts that contained no-furlough clauses.[38] The union representing flight attendants at Northwest Airlines got unpaid leaves lasting from one trip to several weeks for 300 fearful attendants it represented; both the pilots union and the flight attendants union at US Airways had no-furlough clauses in their contracts (although there was speculation that such clauses might be unenforceable if the airlines could establish that the terrorist attacks were an act of war). At American Airlines, a deal with the pilots union as part of American's recent acquisition of Trans World

[37]"U.S. Airline Industry Faces Cash Crunch, Pleads for a Bailout," *The Wall Street Journal,* September 17, 2001, pp. A1, A6.

[38]"Frightened Workers and Investors Buffet Airlines," *The Wall Street Journal,* September 18, 2001, p. A3, A6

exhibit 11   Selected Operating Statistics of Major U.S. Airlines and Initial Responses to Aftermath of Terrorist Attacks on America

Company	Passengers Carried, 2000	Airplanes	Employees Year-End 2000			Cash on Hand (billions)	Debt to Total Capital, Year-End 2000	First-Day Decline in Stock Price	Announced Cutbacks
			Full-Time	Part-Time	Total				
American	86,200,000	904	86,663	14,536	101,199	$1.49	59.2%	39.4%	20 percent of capacity; layoffs of 20,000+ employees
United	84,461,000	616	90,398	11,416	101,814	1.28	68.5	43.2	20 percent of capacity; layoffs of 20,000 employees
Delta	119,929,500	600	66,758	13,632	80,390	1.51	59.3	44.6	20 percent of capacity; layoffs of 13,000 employees
Northwest	58,721,700	438	50,341	3,548	53,889	1.30	96.4	36.7	20 percent of capacity; 10,000 layoffs
Continental	46,896,000	377	36,156	9,788	45,944	1.01	87.6	49.4	20 percent of capacity; 12,000 layoffs
US Airways	60,636,300	423	41,708	4,125	45,833	1.25	91.6	52.1	23 percent of capacity; 11,000 layoffs; pay cuts
Southwest	63,678,300	356	28,860	828	29,688	1.50	33.3	24.1	None
America West	19,954,000	142	10,992	2,809	13,801	0.17	73.9	65.1	Cut flight schedule by 20 percent; 2,000 layoffs; elimination of food service on all flights while adjusting to new security requirements
Alaska	13,524,700	100	9,112	1,221	10,333	0.47	61.9	28.6	None

Sources: The Wall Street Journal, September 17, 2001, pp. A1, A6; *The Wall Street Journal*, September 18, 2001, pp. A3, A6; U.S. Department of Transportation statistics (for numbers of employees) and various company annual reports for 2000.

Airlines specified that early retirement packages had to be offered to hundreds of American pilots before pilots could be laid off.

Even if air travel rebounded, there were concerns that airlines would be unable to fly the same number of flights that were in place prior to September 11. New security measures were expected to slow passengers moving through terminals and to increase gate turnaround times significantly above the 45-minute norm. Procedures mandated by the Federal Aviation Administration required greater attention to baggage; check-in of passengers at ticket counters rather than at curbside or at departure gates; and careful security screening of caterers, cleaners, and flight crews. These procedures meant lengthening ground times and altering the duties and workloads of various terminal personnel. Adding 30 minutes to each stop would mean that a plane that used to fly six 2-hour trips a day could fly only four or five. Such reduced flight frequencies would mean an increase of several percentage points in breakeven load factors.

In the weeks following the terrorist attacks, Congress passed a $15 billion aid package to assist airlines in coping with their financial crunch—the program involved $5 billion in cash grants to help airlines cover losses and negative cash flows stemming from traffic declines and $10 billion in loan guarantees.

In order to contain costs and detour the need for more planes to accommodate prior flight schedules, many airlines responded with immediate announcements of schedule cutbacks—see Exhibit 11. Before the attacks, major airlines and their commuter partners were making about 29,000 flights a day. Analysts expected that flight schedule cutbacks might have the biggest revenue impact on short-haul point-to-point carriers, which had smaller planes and emphasized quick gate turns and high flight frequencies (to achieve high asset utilization and spread out fixed costs over more passengers). They predicted that hub-and-spoke carriers might be able to recover some of the revenue loss associated with fewer flights by concentrating on high-traffic routes where they could keep their biggest planes filled close to capacity and making most of their flight cutbacks on routes involving lower-traffic spoke locations. All of the airlines were very worried about how long it might take for public confidence in the safety of air travel to be restored and for passenger traffic to rebound to levels above the now-higher breakeven load factors. Some airline executives did not foresee a return to "normal traffic levels" until summer 2002, and there were predictions that (in addition to combined losses of $7–$8 billion industrywide in 2001) losses in the first half of 2002 could total another $15 billion unless traffic levels snapped back quicker than anticipated.

In the last half of September, most major airlines announced cutbacks on international flights—Delta, American, and TWA cut 40 percent of their international flights out of New York's Kennedy International, suspending all service to a number of destinations until March 2002. Domestic flights were also cut, with late-night flights and flights on weak performing routes bearing the brunt. Some routes served by full-size jets were being converted to commuter jet service. Shuttle flights on the Washington–New York–Boston routes were hobbled. United Airlines had announced that it would cease operating its Shuttle by United service on the West Coast, which overlapped with Southwest in such markets as Las Vegas, Oakland, and Los Angeles. US Airways announced it would close down its low-fare MetroJet subsidiary that operated on the East Coast and overlapped with Southwest's service in Providence and Baltimore (one of Southwest's fastest-growing locations). US Airways also announced that it would eliminate 51 of its 75 mainline jet flights from Baltimore, including all nonstop flights to Florida. Delta airlines announced that it would cut the operations of its low-fare operation, Delta Express, by 50 percent; Delta Express served three locations also served by Southwest—Orlando, Tampa, and Hartford. In Orlando, Delta Express said it would cut back from 49 daily flights to 21 (Southwest operated 52 daily nonstop flights out of Orlando to 24 cities).

Southwest was forced to cancel some 9,000 flights during the September 11–14 period, but as of Monday, September 17, 2001, the company was flying its full schedule of 2,772 flights. The company initiated new service to Norfolk, Virginia, on October 7, as planned. Southwest's load factors for the four weeks ending October 14, were 38.5 percent, 52.4 percent, 62.5 percent and 67.0 percent—for the period July 1, 2001, until the attacks, Southwest's load factor was 74.6 percent. The company had decided to tap a $475 million line of credit to provide it with $1.5 billion in cash and cash equivalents as of October 1. In early October, Southwest's chief financial officer indicated that Southwest had incurred losses of $3 to $4 million a day during the shutdown period that extended from September 11 through 13 and that the company's losses had narrowed since then. So far, Southwest Airlines had elected to make no cutbacks of any kind, although it put a temporary freeze on hiring until January 2002, initiated efforts to defer nonessential capital spending and nonessential operating costs, and negotiated a revised delivery schedule for the 132 Boeing 737 jets it had on order (the new schedule called for deferring the delivery of 7 jets scheduled for delivery in September–October 2001 until November 2001 and deferring delivery of 19 Boeing 737s due in 2002 until 2003 and 2004).

In late October 2001, Southwest reported net earnings of $151 million for the third quarter ending September 30, including a special pretax gain of $169 million from a federal grant (stemming from the $5 billion bailout program) and a special $58 million pretax charge associated with the terrorist attacks that included the deferral fees paid to Boeing. Excluding the special gain and charges, Southwest's third-quarter net income was $82.8 million. Southwest indicated that the company incurred operating losses of $95 million between September 11 and September 30 due to depressed traffic and depressed revenues. Management indicated that if "direct and incremental losses" resulting from the attacks continued, as currently expected, Southwest would receive additional federal grants totaling $120 million in the fourth quarter. Jim Parker said that weak air travel conditions had spawned aggressive fare discounting and that Southwest expected lower average fares for the foreseeable future.

Gordon Bethune and the Turnaround of Continental Airlines

Arthur A. Thompson
The University of Alabama

John E. Gamble
University of South Alabama

When Gordon Bethune left his job at Boeing in February 1994 to accept the position of president and chief operating officer of Continental Airlines, Continental was struggling for survival. Even though Continental was the fifth-largest commercial airline, with revenues of close to $6 billion, it had reported a net loss every year since 1985 and it ranked last among the 10 major U.S. commercial airlines in operating performance and customer satisfaction. Bethune was well aware that Continental Airlines had serious operating problems, and, like most operations executives, he looked forward to the challenge of solving the problems and getting Continental on track. But during his first six months on the job, Bethune discovered he lacked the authority and organizational clout to implement the sweeping changes he believed were necessary.

THE CRISIS AT CONTINENTAL AIRLINES IN 1994

Continental Airlines had gone into Chapter 11 bankruptcy protection in 1983 and again in 1990; it emerged from the second bankruptcy proceedings in April 1993. When Bethune came on board in 1994, Continental's finances were still shaky, and the company was struggling to reduce its costs and turn the corner toward profitability. According to statistics compiled by the U.S. Department of Transportation (DOT) and reported in the *Air Travel Consumer Report,* Continental ranked last among the 10 largest U.S. commercial airlines in on-time arrivals (the percentage of flights that arrived within 15 minutes of the scheduled time) in 1993 and early 1994. It also had the highest number of mishandled baggage reports per 1,000 passengers and by far the highest number of complaints per 100,000 passengers. Complaints filed with the DOT by Continental passengers about various aspects of their experiences on Continental flights were 30 percent higher than the ninth-ranking airline and three times the industry average. Continental ranked among the worst (but not last) in the percentage of passengers who were involuntarily denied boarding because of overbooking and other problems.

Over the past 10 years, Continental had had 10 different CEOs. Employees had gone through numerous internal reorganizations, revitalization and turnaround efforts, and strategy shifts—with all the attendant buzzwords and promises of change. Many employees were disillusioned, and morale was low—most workers tried to do their jobs as best as they could; the goal was just to survive. Prior management had tried to rid the company of unions, and during the bankruptcy proceedings of 1993, wages and salaries had been cut. Turnover and use of sick time were quite high; on-the-job injuries were far above the industry average. There was considerable infighting among employee groups and departments. When problems occurred, finger pointing often overwhelmed efforts at constructive problem solving and employees ran for cover, insisting they had followed procedures. Continental's ticket agents and gate personnel spent many stressful hours dealing with dissatisfied and angry passengers—some of Continental's airport personnel, when they were off duty or on break, removed the Continental insignia from their uniforms to avoid having to answer uncomfortable questions from coworkers or customers.[1] According to Gordon Bethune:

> To put it bluntly, the *Good Ship Lollipop* we weren't. That's what I joined in 1994: a company with a lousy product, angry employees, low wages, [and] a history of ineffective management . . .
>
> This was a crummy place to work. The culture at Continental, after years of layoffs and wage freezes and wage cuts and broken promises, was one of backbiting, mistrust, fear, and loathing. People, to put it mildly, were not happy to come to work. They were surly to customers, surly to each other, and ashamed of their company . . .
>
> In a company where cost-cutting was revered, departments fought one another to the death over scarce resources. In a company where management strategies—and management teams—changed overnight, employees schemed above all else to protect themselves, at the cost of their co-workers if necessary. Interdepartmental communication was almost nonexistent.
>
> Everybody was screwing over everybody—no wonder the planes were late and the baggage was lost. The product was crummy. The fundamental reasons for that had nothing to do with flying planes correctly or being able to clean and fix them. It had to do with an environment where nobody could get their jobs done.
>
> The atmosphere was poisonous . . . [and] the organization itself was so dysfunctional that it couldn't have implemented the best idea in the world.[2]

Bethune himself soon became disenchanted because Continental's CEO stymied most of Bethune's efforts to improve Continental's operations unless they also reduced costs. In June 1994, four months after joining Continental, Bethune got an attractive job offer from United Airlines. Continental countered with a handsome financial offer for Bethune to remain; he agreed to stay if the CEO and the board of directors would give him full authority over marketing, scheduling, and ticket pricing—areas of control he thought would help him push through the kind of organizational changes that

---

[1]Gordon Bethune with Scott Huler, *From Worst to First: Behind the Scenes of Continental's Remarkable Comeback* (New York: John Wiley & Sons, 1998), p. 6.

[2]Ibid., pp. 6, 14–15.

were needed to improve Continental's operations and make the company's service more attractive to passengers. The CEO and board agreed to his conditions. But by the end of August, Bethune concluded that his authority was still too limited and that he was not getting adequate support for the sweeping changes he wanted to institute.

In late October 1994, Continental's board, concerned about the potential of further losses and another financial crisis, determined that a change had to be made at the top. Initially, the board decided that it would give the present CEO a six-month leave of absence in the hope that he would decide not to return; Bethune would run the company from his present position as president and COO. However, the CEO decided that he would simply step down immediately. Although it was still not ready to promote Gordon Bethune to the position of CEO, the board told Bethune on October 24 that he could run the company for the next 10 days and would then be given an opportunity to present his plans for Continental's future.

GORDON BETHUNE'S GO FORWARD PLAN FOR CONTINENTAL

Gordon Bethune's first act when he temporarily took over on October 24 was to prop open the doors to Continental's executive suite, which previously had been locked and monitored by security cameras. He wanted people to enter freely at any time, rather than having to show an ID to gain admission, and he wanted to begin to change the atmosphere in the executive suite. Next, he began working on the plan he would present to the board. He asked Greg Brenneman, a Bain & Company vice president with expertise in turning companies around, to help him. Brenneman had been working with Continental for several months on turning around Continental's maintenance operations, which had the highest cost but the lowest dispatch reliability in the industry, and his efforts had produced some good results. Brenneman agreed with Bethune that Continental needed a new direction and a comprehensive plan that would change the entire company.

Meeting at Bethune's house, Brenneman and Bethune came up with what they called the Go Forward Plan. It had four parts—a market plan to fly more profitable routes, a financial plan to put the company into the black in 1995, a product plan to improve Continental's offering to customers, and a people plan to transform the company's culture. All four parts were to be pursued simultaneously and in concert.

The Market Plan: Fly to Win

The guiding principle behind the market plan, which Bethune called Fly to Win, was for Continental to stop doing those things that were losing money or causing the company to lose money and to concentrate on Continental's market strengths. The company was losing money on 18 percent of its routes, many of which were low-fare point-to-point routes where it had a relatively small market share. In taking a hard look at where Continental flew and the number of flights on each route, Bethune and Brenneman determined that Continental Lite, the company's low-fare/no-frills operation that was modeled after Southwest Airlines, was a major money loser. Continental Lite had been created by replacing the first-class seats with coach seats in 100 of Continental's smaller Boeing jets, painting the planes with Continental Lite to identify the product, setting up point-to-point routes that management thought were underserved, offering a number of flights on each route, not serving meals on flights of less than

2½ hours, and flying planes from early morning to late at night to generate as much revenue per plane as feasible.

But Continental Lite had failed to catch on with Continental's customer base. Bethune's diagnosis was that Continental customers preferred to pay full fares for full-service flights—especially on longer flights and flights spanning normal meal hours. Moreover, Continental Lite's costs were too high relative to the revenues being generated by its low-fare approach—Bethune did not believe that Continental Lite's costs could be cut far enough to make its operation profitable and, at the same time, make the Continental Lite product attractive to air travelers. His argument was that just as a pizza restaurant could make a pizza so cheap that no one would want to buy it, you could make an airline so cheap that no one wanted to fly it.[3] Analysis indicated that about one-third of Continental Lite's routes were responsible for about 70 percent of Continental's losses. Fly to Win entailed making drastic cutbacks in Continental Lite flights and substantially revising Continental's route schedule to focus on hub-and-spoke operations rather than point-to-point routes. More flights were scheduled for new spoke locations that held promise of generating enough passenger traffic to generate a profit.

Another part of Fly to Win involved closing the company's money-losing Greensboro, North Carolina, hub and focusing full attention on the Continental's hubs in Newark, Cleveland, and Houston—hub operations in Denver had been abandoned several years earlier. The relatively new Greensboro hub was not generating enough traffic from the various spoke locations to justify trying to continue to win additional market share in the Southeast, where Delta and US Airways had a strong presence. A number of routes were identified where Continental had too many flights with too few passengers and fares too low to make a profit, including the company's intra-Florida routes (where it had ultralow fares to try to compete against Southwest Airlines) and Kansas City to Omaha. These, too, were targeted for cutting; however, the plan called for continuing to serve both Kansas City and Omaha with flights direct from the Houston hub. Bethune and Brenneman discovered that air travel patterns justified adding more flights from Newark to the Houston and Cleveland hubs. And they spotted opportunities to raise fares on some of Continental's routes.

The flight frequency and destination cuts envisioned in Fly to Win meant that Continental would have too many available seats on planes and that there would need to be cutbacks on the size of the aircraft fleet. At the time, Continental had 10 different types of aircraft in its large jet fleet, including a number of the large Airbus 300 (A300) aircraft. The A300 planes were expensive to operate, required special maintenance procedures, and entailed lease payments of up to $200,000 a month. Bethune and Brenneman proposed disposing of all A300 planes in Continental's fleet, thereby removing the necessity of a special parts inventory, special facilities and people, and special procedures. Approaching the companies that had leased the planes to Continental and finding a way to get out of the lease obligations became part of the company's financial plan. Taking the biggest planes in Continental's fleet out of circulation (many of which were only 50–60 percent full on many flights) eliminated most of Continental's excess seat capacity—and with the next-biggest planes flying these same routes at close to capacity, the revenues generated by the A300 flights were retained and profit margins were much better.

Bethune believed all these schedule-fleet revisions would better position Continental in higher traffic markets, allow maintenance to be performed more sensibly and economically, make it possible to reallocate resources into efforts to strengthening Continental's hub operations, and improve the company's overall load factor.

---

[3]Ibid., p. 50.

Efforts to Attract Passengers   Bethune and Brenneman determined that Continental needed to launch a concerted marketing campaign to win back customers that it had lost, especially business travelers. Continental's cost-cutting efforts in prior years had entailed reducing the commissions paid to travel agents (who, at the time, handled 80 percent of all flight reservations), stripping popular features from its OnePass frequent flyer program, and eliminating perks (first-class seats, upgrades, coupons for free drinks) that travel agents could offer corporate customers as inducements to choose Continental flights. Bethune believed such actions had alienated Continental customers, prompting many business travelers to switch to rival carriers. And he believed Continental's poor on-time performance and customer satisfaction ratings, along with lower commissions, had alienated travel agents, causing them to steer customers to other carriers.

To try to win back the confidence and business of travel agents, Bethune proposed going hat in hand to all the major travel agents, apologizing for prior mistakes, promising that Continental's on-time performance and passenger satisfaction levels were going to improve dramatically, reestablishing higher commissions, and giving them a package of incentives they could use to induce their Fortune 500 clients to book more flights on Continental. To try to win back business travelers, Bethune planned to restore the features of the award-winning OnePass frequent flyer program that prior management had dismantled.

The Financial Plan: Fund the Future

In October 1994, Continental was strapped for cash and burdened by debt—it owed considerable money on its aircraft fleet and it had a $2 billion debt hangover from the Chapter 11 proceedings in 1993. Bethune and Brenneman concluded that it was critical for the company to have a credible financial plan for making a profit in 1995. They put together a package of proposed changes involving renegotiation of aircraft lease payments, refinancing some of Continental's debt at lower interest rates, postponing some debt repayments, and raising fares on certain routes. These moves, they projected, held a realistic chance of generating a profit of $45 million in 1995 (a substantial improvement over the $200 million in losses that Continental would likely show for 1994) and would produce sufficient cash flows for Continental to avoid another financial crisis.

The Product Plan: Make Reliability a Reality

The product plan part of Bethune's multifaceted Go Forward Plan—Make Reliability a Reality—aimed at quantum improvements in Continental's on-time performance, baggage handling, and overall flying experience—doing the very things that would please customers and make them inclined to fly Continental again. The centerpiece of Bethune's product plan was to focus employees' attention on on-time performance by rewarding them with a $65 bonus each month that Continental was in the top five U.S. airlines in percentage of flights arriving on-time—as measured and reported monthly by the U.S. Department of Transportation.

The People Plan: Working Together

Bethune believed that the most important component of the Go Forward Plan was to radically change Continental's corporate culture. He was convinced that a successful turnaround at Continental hinged on getting Continental's employees working together and creating a positive work environment. Bethune explained his thinking:

The environment was so bad that regardless of marketing strategies, financial plans, and reliability incentives, there weren't going to be any improvements in Continental's operations until we stopped treating people the way we had been treating them and got them to start working together. You just can't be successful in any kind of business without teamwork.

So part of our plan—and it was vague at this point, even though over the long term it was by far the most important part of the plan—was to make it a corporate goal to change how people treated each other: to find ways to measure and reward cooperation rather than infighting, to encourage and reward trust and confidence.

In preparing for the board meeting, Bethune and Brenneman ran their ideas about changing the corporate culture by Continental's chairman, coworkers they trusted, and by friends and family. At this juncture, the culture-changing effort was general and conceptual rather than a list of specific action proposals.

Bethune's Meeting with the Board

Bethune presented the Go Forward Plan to Continental's board in early November, indicating that it represented a joint effort with Greg Brenneman.[4] After the presentation, which was generally well received, the chairman asked Bethune to excuse himself from the meeting so the board could discuss the exit of the CEO. An hour later, the chairman came to get Bethune, indicating that the board had decided not to name anyone CEO but would have an "office of the chairman" and Bethune would remain as president and COO. Bethune thought that was a mistake and asked to speak with board members. He believed the turnaround effort he proposed required the clear and unequivocal authority of a leader who was designated CEO and enjoyed the full support of the board of directors. Many board members were unconvinced by Bethune's plea that a strong CEO was essential to implement a turnaround plan, and they were not entirely sure that the company's situation was as dire as Bethune indicated. The board asked Bethune to excuse himself again. After an hour and a half, the chairman returned, indicating that a majority of the board had decided to appoint Bethune as CEO. Although he was disappointed that the board had not enthusiastically embraced his Go Forward Plan and then immediately and unanimously elected him CEO, he was nonetheless gratified that he had the chance to see if he could get Continental on track.

THE IMPLEMENTATION AND EVOLUTION OF BETHUNE'S GO FORWARD PLAN, 1995–2000

At the outset, Bethune recognized that Continental's employees would view his actions with suspicion and that he would need to build credibility with them. He judged that employees weren't going to rally around the Go Forward Plan without some good reason to trust that he was different and that his administration was going to do a far better job of really fixing what was wrong with the company than the nine prior executive regimes. Bethune also realized that as CEO at Continental, he would need to draw on many of his prior experiences. He was a licensed airline pilot, qualified to fly Boeing 757 and 767 jets. He had an airframe and power plant mechanic's license. He had been a maintenance facility manager at both Braniff and Western Airlines, and a senior vice president for operations at Piedmont Airlines in the 1980s (before Piedmont was acquired and became a part of US Airways). His operations background at Boeing had

---

[4]Ibid., pp. 26–28.

made him familiar with the aircraft side of commercial airline business and somewhat knowledgeable about the strategies of various airlines and the executives who ran them.

Bethune's First Steps as CEO

The same day he took over as CEO, Gordon Bethune announced the closing of Continental's maintenance operations in Los Angeles. There was not much maintenance to be done in Los Angeles because Continental was shifting its focus to its hubs in Newark, Houston, and Cleveland. Approximately 1,800 people worked at the Los Angeles facility.

Bethune asked Greg Brenneman to remain as a consultant to the company and a close adviser. In May 1995, Bethune named Brenneman Continental's chief operating officer. As COO, Brenneman played a key role in helping implement and execute the Go Forward Plan. In September 1996, Brenneman took on the additional title of president, with Bethune functioning as chairman and CEO.

After dispensing with all the security previously surrounding the executive suite, Bethune instituted open houses for employees on the last working day of each month. Employees were invited to tour the executive offices on the 20th floor of corporate headquarters, visit with Bethune and other executives, and help themselves to food and drinks. Casual-dress Fridays were instituted for all employees except those dealing directly with customers, partly to make Continental managers and executives more approachable. Bethune mandated a no-smoking rule in all company facilities—and he extended the ban on smoking to include all North American and South American flights (over the objections of Continental's marketing people, who contended that such a ban would irritate smoking passengers). The ban was later extended to include all of Continental's European flights and then worldwide, with little apparent effect on ticket sales. At executive meetings, Bethune began sitting at the middle of the long table in the executive conference room rather than at the head of the table. He insisted that meetings begin and end on schedule.

One of his most dramatic actions was to gather a few Continental employees, along with some of the manuals containing the company's regulations and procedures, go out to the parking lot outside the Houston headquarters, and have the employees set fire to the manuals. Word was sent to employees in the field that they were expected to use their best judgment to solve problems and deal with issues, rather than following the rigid procedures described in the manual. A task force was created to go over the entire manual and come up with guidelines that would help employees make good decisions and take appropriate actions—the idea was that Houston headquarters was there to help but not to dictate to the nth degree. Bethune wanted the message to employees to be to "use these guidelines, think things through, and unless you do something completely out of bounds, you don't have to worry about hearing from Houston. Houston wants you to do your job. Houston wants to leave you alone unless you need help. And believe it or not, if you need help, Houston wants to help you."[5]

As of late 1994, Continental's planes were not painted uniformly. Continental was one of the airlines that had been acquired by Frank Lorenzo's Texas International Airlines, which also acquired People Express, New York Air, and Frontier Airlines, merging them all under the name Continental Airlines. Although in earlier years Continental had tried to create a new image with a completely new paint scheme for all its aircraft, only about half the fleet had been repainted because of executive pressures to cut costs.

---

[5]Ibid., pp. 37–38.

At the company's hubs, one could see differently painted Continental planes lined up at the gates. Believing that professional-looking identical planes would send a message to employees and customers that Continental was running a better operation, Bethune ordered that every one of Continental's planes was to receive a fresh paint job by July 1, 1995—there were to be no exceptions. People in Continental's fleet operations said this was too short a time frame in which to get 200 planes repainted; Bethune refused to relent:

> I did something I rarely do: I made a threat. I said, "Yes you can, and you know why? Because I have a Beretta at home with a 15-round magazine, and if you don't get those planes painted by July 1, I'm going to come in here and empty the clip. You're wonderful people and I love you, but you're going to get those airplanes painted or I'm going to shoot every last one of you."[6]

The last one of Continental's planes was painted on June 30, just in time to meet Bethune's deadline.

Meanwhile, Bethune and other Continental executives spread the word among employees that the Go Forward Plan was management's blueprint—there were meetings with employees at virtually every site in the company to introduce the plan and explain how it addressed all of Continental's problems. Many employees had already heard about the open houses and open-door policy, the burning of the manual, the $65 bonus, and some of the other facets, but management wanted to present the plan personally and answer whatever questions employees had. The meetings did not always go smoothly; a number of employees voiced doubt and skepticism, openly expressing their mistrust of what management was telling them. One pilot told Bethune, "You're the tenth guy I've seen, and you sound good, but let me tell you, this goddamn place is broken. There ain't nobody going to fix it, including you. So it doesn't matter what you say, this place is going to fail."[7] Bethune took issue with the pilot, saying in part:

> I don't know about you, but I don't know of any self-respecting pilot, regardless of what predicament the airplane is in—it's on fire, it's upside down, it's spinning around, whatever—who stops trying to fly the airplane before it hits the ground. You don't ever give up and say, screw it, it's over, I can't do anything . . . Listen, I'm the captain of this company now. This is what we are going to do. I'm flying, it's my leg. If you don't like the way I'm working, the jetway is still attached. You can step off if you want to. But I am going to fly this company where it's going.[8]

Bethune's response to the pilot mirrored his concept of what a leader did and what a leader's role was. According to Bethune,

> My definition of a leader is pretty simple. The leader is the person who looks at the big picture and says, "Okay, everybody, go west."
>
> Now west is precisely a compass heading of 270 degrees, but anywhere from about 240 to 300 degrees is heading generally west. So if I say go west, and one person is heading out at about 295 degrees, that's okay with me . . . I don't want to precisely determine how you interpret it when I say, hey, let's go west. You see things a certain way, and what's happening in your department and what's happening to you today may affect what has to happen when I say go west.
>
> On the other hand, the guy who's going 090 degrees, which is due east, is a problem. You have to catch him and readjust his thinking so he's going the right way. If he won't be

[6]Ibid., p. 39.

[7]Ibid., p. 41.

[8]Ibid., pp. 41–42.

readjusted, I say no way buster: You either head west or get out of here. Maybe he needs to go to a company headed east . . .

I'm not saying that everybody has to be marching in lockstep—in fact, that's exactly what we *don't* want. We want people doing their jobs with a minimum of interference from their bosses. That's why we burned the manual . . .

Your real job as boss—my real job as chief executive—is to let people do their jobs. It's to assemble the right team, set the big-picture direction, communicate that, and then get out of the way . . . You have to trust people to do their jobs. That's the strongest leadership there is.[9]

At a meeting with employees in Denver in late 1995, Bethune encountered another vocal employee who reacted to his presentation of the Go Forward Plan and the turn-around actions that were under way by saying, "It sounds fine, but I still don't believe it. We've had too many new programs here and I don't believe it."[10] Bethune tried to reason with the employee, explaining why and how things were on the mend at Continental and the role of the Working Together initiatives. The employee still did not buy what Bethune was saying, at which time Bethune told him what he told the pilot in Newark—that the jetway was still attached and that if he didn't like the direction the company was headed, maybe he should get off the plane. The employee turned and walked out the door; the audience of employees applauded his exit.

Executing the Fly to Win Market Plan

Early on, Continental began treating travel agencies as partners and worked with them closely, creating programs whereby agencies that sold a certain volume of tickets or hit other sales targets specified by Continental would be paid an incentive above the normal commission rate. Programs involving upgrades to first class and discounts for certain travel volumes were created for travel agents to use in marketing Continental to large corporations. In some cases, new destinations were added when feedback from travel agencies indicated that such destinations would be attractive to their corporate clients. Continental wanted to move its business from what Greg Brenneman called the backpack-and-flip-flop crowd to the coat-and-tie crowd (or at least the Patagonia back-pack crowd), believing that such travelers were usually willing to pay higher fares in order not to take chances with their comfort and convenience. To assist travel agencies in marketing Continental to business travelers, Continental sent letters to corporate CEOs, middle managers, and sales representatives who flew frequently, apologizing for the company's poor performance in past years, laying out the customer-related features of the Go Forward Plan, and asking them to give Continental a try. Continental executives made personal calls on the executives of companies that already were doing a lot of business with Continental to thank them for their business, and they made calls on corporate executives of companies where they thought Continental might be able to win a bigger share of the air travel budget.

To help lure Houston-area business travelers back to Continental, Gordon Bethune held a party at his house; invitations were sent to 100 of the company's high-mileage frequent flyers—spouses were invited, too. At the party, Bethune announced that the company had made mistakes in the past and wanted another chance at proving it could be relied on to provide good service. Attendees were presented a leather ticket case.

---

[9]Ibid., pp. 42–43.
[10]Ibid., p. 142.

Continental executives circulated through the crowd, thanking people for coming, asking forgiveness for past sins, and explaining what the company was doing to earn their business.

To grow the business during the 1995–2000 period, Continental gradually added more destinations from its hubs and added more flights to existing destinations. Expansion was particularly aggressive in international markets, with service being added to Rome, Milan, several other European cities, Hong Kong, Tokyo, Tel Aviv, the Caribbean, Guam, South America, Central America, and Mexico. In 2000, Continental had over 2,000 flights going to nearly 90 international and 130 domestic destinations; it served more international destinations than any other carrier. Guam evolved into a fourth, albeit much smaller, hub for a number of Continental flights operating in the Asia-Pacific region; Newark was the primary gateway for flights to Europe (16 cities) and the Middle East; and the Houston hub was the primary gateway for flights to Mexico (20 cities), Central America (every country), and South America (6 cities). The Cleveland hub had international flights to Montreal, Toronto, London, San Juan, and Cancun. In 2000, Continental announced plans to expand its service to 30 European cities within the next three to five years, and it was exploring adding more destinations in the Middle East. Management believed that it could benefit from TWA's decision to cease all transatlantic services from New York—TWA had long been a force in Europe and the Middle East.

The company's website (www.continental.com) was used as an increasingly important distribution channel for marketing tickets to individuals and businesses; in 2000, Continental expanded e-ticketing to about 95 percent of its destinations. Continental had over $5.8 billion in e-ticket sales in 2000, representing 54 percent of total sales. In 2000, Continental partnered with United, Delta, American, and Northwest to create a comprehensive travel planning website called Orbitz (www.orbitz.com) that offered airline tickets, hotel reservations, car rentals, and other services.

Continental Express   Soon after the company decided in 1996 to phase out Continental Lite entirely, management decided to create a feeder operation for its hubs called Continental Express. Continental Express operated as a separate subsidiary with its own president. By 2000, Continental Express had expanded its operations to include about 1,000 daily flights to 70 cities in the United States, 10 cities in Mexico, and 5 cities in Canada; its aircraft fleet consisted mostly of regional jets with some turboprop aircraft. Continental management believed that Continental Express flights allowed more frequent service to small cities than could be provided economically with larger conventional jets and contributed to higher load factors on Continental's regular jet service by feeding passengers into Continental's three major hubs to connect to regular Continental flights. Because regional jets enjoyed better customer acceptance than turboprop aircraft and provided greater passenger comfort, Continental Express was in the process of phasing out the use of turboprop aircraft and using regional jets exclusively by 2004.

Bethune's Row 5 Test   One of the challenges Bethune faced was in deciding what constituted "better" service and "better" performance. In his view, Fly to Win meant that Continental had to fly where people wanted to go, it had to stop doing things that lost money, it had to find out what things customers wanted and provide them, and it had to compete effectively against rivals. He was willing for Continental to do things that added cost, provided they added enough value that passengers were willing to pay for them and the costs could therefore be incorporated in fare prices. When Continental people came up with proposals to spend money to increase the technological sophistication of Continental planes or make other operating changes that had cost-increasing implications, Bethune insisted on applying what he called the "row 5 test"—asking whether a hypothetical passenger sitting in row 5 on a Continental plane would be willing to pay a higher fare in order to have the proposed benefit.[11] Bethune argued, for example, that if the floors on Continental's aircraft maintenance facilities were so clean you could eat off them, Continental was probably paying too much attention to keeping the floors clean. He wanted Continental to add costs only when the expenditure added customer value. In Bethune's view, defining success and good performance in customers' terms did not mean cheap fares or the biggest planes with the most advanced technology or flying to the most exotic locations. Rather, it meant clean, safe, reliable service from well-managed hubs; convenient flight schedules to places customers wanted to go; amenities that made the travel experience more pleasant; and desirable frequent flyer benefits.

Executing the Fund the Future Financial Plan

Despite Continental's having recently emerged from Chapter 11 bankruptcy proceedings, Gordon Bethune and Greg Brenneman believed that there was substantial risk of a third bankruptcy unless the company moved decisively in late 1994 and early 1995 to get its finances in order. Aggressive implementation of Continental's initial financial plan, Fund the Future, to renegotiate aircraft lease payments, refinance some of Continental's debt at lower interest rates (saving about $25 million in annual interest payments), stretch out debt repayments on loans from three years to seven or eight years, and raise fares on selected routes relieved much of the near-term potential for a financial crisis. Whereas in 1994 Continental incurred $202 million in interest costs, by 1996 interest expenses had been reduced to $117 million and were expected to go lower.

But an additional move proved critical. Continental had previously paid Boeing a $70 million deposit for new airplanes on order. As it turned out, Continental determined that it could not afford the new planes and decided to cancel its order—the problem was that Continental's $70 million deposit was nonrefundable (aircraft manufacturers use deposits to help finance initial manufacturing of the planes on order). Boeing had already agreed to refinance Continental's leases at lower rates than called for in the original lease contract. Nonetheless, Continental's financial predicament was such that Bethune felt compelled to telephone his close friend Ron Woodard, the president of Boeing, asking him to return Continental's $70 million deposit for the canceled orders because Continental needed the cash in the worst way. Woodard suspected that Continental was in dire straits and recognized that Bethune was probably pushing Continental in the right direction; despite his reluctance to go against company policy and refund a deposit, Woodard agreed to send Continental a partial $29 million refund. Bethune accepted the offer, indicating that, if possible, Boeing should wire the funds immediately; Woodard laughed but agreed to Bethune's plea.[12]

Cash flows were further improved by the efforts of the company's vice president of purchasing and materials services to sell excess parts inventories and renegotiate maintenance contracts. Another move Continental made to attack the cash shortage in 1994–95 was to enter into code-sharing agreements with other airlines whereby forces were combined to achieve joint operating economies. Code-sharing typically involved two airline partners operating a single flight to a particular destination but having that flight listed in the separate flight schedules of each partner; one of the partner's planes

---

[11]Ibid., pp. 64–69.
[12]Ibid., pp. 84–85.

and crews would be used to operate flight, but both partners could book passengers on the flight to that location, share in the revenues generated, and achieve a better load factor on that flight than they might achieve operating two independent flights. Often, code-sharing partners cooperated in other mutually beneficial ways. For instance, in Phoenix and Las Vegas, where Continental had only two or three flights coming in daily, it partnered with America West to handle the ground work on Continental's flights; in Orlando and Tampa, where Continental had a greater presence than America West, Continental personnel handled the ground work for America West's flights. Each airline thus gained the savings of not having to staff gates that were used for only a few flights a day. During the 1996–2000 period, Continental expanded its code-sharing efforts, entering into agreements with such domestic carriers as Northwest Airlines, Air Canada, American Eagle, and Horizon Airlines and such international carriers as Alitalia, Air France, Virgin Airways, and Air China. A code-sharing agreement with KLM Royal Dutch Airlines involving certain Continental and KLM flights between the United States and Europe was reached in late 2001.

Upset by what he considered untrustworthy information coming from the finance department, Bethune moved to install much stronger financial systems. A new chief financial officer, Larry Kellner, was brought in to overhaul the company's financial systems and generate better information for decision making. Under Kellner's guidance, Continental developed systems that allowed management to have dependable and regularly updated estimates of revenues, costs, profits, and cash flows; every morning by 10:00, executives had a report of the previous day's credit card receipts. Not long thereafter, the system was upgraded to include the capability to produce a 40-item daily forecast that included credit card receipts, fuel costs, maintenance costs, revenue per available seat mile, cost per available seat mile, profit per available seat mile per type of aircraft, profit at each hub, and profit on each route from each hub. According to Bethune, "The measurements became more and more accurate, which meant we could make better and better decisions with increasingly current numbers."[13] For instance, the new financial systems revealed that Continental's European flights were unusually profitable; management used this information to add more European flights and to increase the fares on some of its international routes. It also learned which routes and flights were losing money, thus providing a basis for revising Continental's flight schedules—employees in locations where service was discontinued (or where code-sharing was implemented) were offered jobs in other parts of the company whenever possible. Kellner also came up with a proposal to hedge Continental's jet-fuel purchases and give the company an insurance policy against unexpected increases in fuel costs—in 1995, fuel hedges saved Continental an estimated $3 million as fuel prices rose.

During the 1996–98 period, Continental made inroads on reducing training and maintenance costs by reducing the number of different types of aircraft making up its fleet. The goal was to have only five different types of aircraft by the end of 1999, as compared with nine in 1995. Further maintenance savings were realized as the company took delivery on new Boeing aircraft in 1997 and 1998, reducing the average age of its fleet. Bethune believed that by 1999–2000 Continental would have the youngest, and thus the lowest-maintenance, fleet in the U.S. commercial airline industry.

In July 1997, Continental launched a three-year program to bring employee wages and salaries up to industry standards; the program was completed on schedule in July 2000. At this point, Continental launched another three-year program to bring em-

---

[13]Ibid., p. 88.

exhibit 1   Financial and Operating Summary, Continental Airlines, 1993–2000

	2000	1999	1998	1997	1996	1995	1994	1993
Financial data (in billions, except for per share data)								
Operating revenues	$9,899	$8,639	$7,927	$7,194	$6,347	$5,825	$5,670	$5,767
Total operating expenses	9,215	8,039	7,226	6,478	5,822	5,440	5,681	5,786
Operating income	684	600	701	716	525	385	(11)	(19)
Net income	342	455	383	385	319	224	(613)	(39)[1]
Basic earnings per share	$5.62	$6.54	$6.34	$6.65	$5.75	$4.07	$(11.88)	$(1.17)[1]
Diluted earnings per share	$5.45	$6.20	$5.02	$4.99	$4.17	$3.37	$(11.88)	$(1.17)[1]
Operating data								
Revenue passengers (000s)	46,896	45,540	43,625	41,210	38,332	37,575	42,202	38,628
Revenue passenger miles (millions)[2]	64,161	60,022	53,910	47,906	41,914	40,023	41,588	42,324
Available seat miles (millions)[3]	86,100	81,946	74,727	67,576	61,515	61,006	65,861	67,011
Passenger load factor[4]	74.5%	73.2%	72.1%	70.9%	68.1%	65.6%	63.1%	63.2%
Breakeven passenger load factor[5]	66.3%	64.7%	61.6%	60.1%	60.7%	60.8%	62.9%	63.3%
Passenger revenue per available seat mile (cents)	9.84¢	9.12¢	9.23¢	9.29¢	9.01¢	8.20¢	7.22¢	7.17¢
Operating cost per available seat mile	9.76¢	8.99¢	8.89¢	9.04¢	8.75¢	8.36¢	8.76¢	7.90¢
Average price per gallon of fuel	86.69¢	47.31¢	46.83¢	62.91¢	60.92¢	55.02¢	53.52¢	59.26¢
Actual aircraft in fleet at end of period	371	363	363	337	317	309	330	316
Average age of aircraft fleet (years)	8.0	8.4	11.6	14.3	14.3	n.a.	n.a.	n.a.

[1]Covers only the period April 28, 1993, through December 31, 1993, after Continental emerged from Chapter 11 bankruptcy proceedings that began in 1990; results prior to April 28 are not meaningful due to recapitalization of company and other matters pertaining to the bankruptcy proceedings.

[2]The number of scheduled miles flown by revenue passengers.

[3]The number of seats available for passengers multiplied by the number of scheduled miles those seats are flown.

[4]Revenue passenger miles divided by available seat miles.

[5]The percentage of seats that must be occupied by revenue passengers in order for the airline to break even on an income before income tax basis, excluding nonrecurring charges, nonoperating items, and other special items.

ployee benefits to industry standards by 2003; the program to improve benefits involved increases in vacations, paid holidays, increases in matching contributions to 401(K) programs, and past-service retirement credits for most senior employees.

Exhibit 1 provides a summary of Continental's financial and operating performance for the 1993–2000 period. Continental had paid no dividends on its common stock and had no current intention to do so. Starting in 1998, Continental began a stock repurchase program under which it purchased a total of 28.1 million shares at a cost of approximately $1.2 billion through December 2000.

The Alliance with Northwest Airlines   In 1998, Northwest Airlines purchased an 8.7-million-share block of Continental's common stock, sufficient to give it voting control of Continental. This formed the basis for a long-term global alliance between Continental and Northwest that provided for each carrier to place its flight code on a large number of flights of the other and for sharing of executive lounges in certain airports as well as reciprocal frequent flyer benefits. The alliance also provided for joint marketing activities, while preserving the separate identities of the two carriers.

However, the alliance soon came under fire from the U.S. Department of Justice, which filed an antitrust suit charging that Northwest's controlling ownership in Continental violated Section 7 of the Clayton Act and Section 1 of the Sherman Act. The suit contended that despite various provisions restricting Northwest's ability to exercise voting control over Continental and assure Continental's competitive independence, Northwest's stock ownership had the effect of reducing actual and potential competition in various ways and in a number of geographic markets. Both Northwest and Continental decided to contest the lawsuit. During the 1998–2000 period, while the litigation was pending and working itself through the court process, Continental and Northwest proceeded to implement the terms of their alliance agreement.

Executing the Make Reliability a Reality Product Plan

Boosting On-Time Performance   Because surveys of air travelers consistently showed that on-time arrival was the single most important determinant of customer satisfaction, Bethune opted to use on-time percentage as the chief indicator of how well Continental was performing. The decision to pay employees a $65 bonus for achieving good on-time performance was the result of a company analysis that showed Continental was spending about $5 million monthly taking care of passengers who had missed connecting flights because of late incoming flights—some passengers had to be provided meals and/or housed overnight, and some had to be reticketed to the flights of other carriers. Plus, it took time on the part of ticket agents to handle all these arrangements, adding to staffing costs. Bethune determined that Continental would come out ahead if the company took half of the $5 million and gave it to employees in the form of an incentive to achieve good on-time performance ($2.5 million divided by just under 40,000 Continental employees was roughly $65); Continental managers were not eligible for the $65 bonus because the company already had a performance-based bonus plan for managers.

The $65 bonus plan was announced in January 1995; that month, Continental's on-time percentage was 71 percent, which earned it only 7th place among the top 10 airlines—not good enough for the bonus (which required a ranking in the top 5) but better than the 61 percent on-time arrivals the prior January. In February, 80 percent of Continental's flights arrived on time, good for a fourth-place ranking; Continental cut a special $65 check and sent it to all employees (withholding taxes on the $65 bonus were taken out of the regular paychecks). In March 1995, Continental ranked first in on-time performance, with 83 percent on-time arrivals. In April, Continental was first again. Continental's on-time performance suffered in May, June, and July because pilots initiated a work slowdown as leverage in their contract negotiations then under way with the company. But following the contractual agreement with the pilots' union, Continental's on-time percentage improved to second-best in the industry in August and September, third-best in October, and fourth-best in November.

Given these results, Bethune decided to raise the bar for paying bonuses for on-time performance. The new standard, scheduled to start in January 1996, was that Continental had to finish third or higher for employees to receive a bonus, but the bonus payment was upped to $100. When Continental came in first in on-time performance in December 1995, the month before the new $100 bonus was to go into effect, Bethune decided that all employees should be paid $100 anyway. In 1997, Continental management began noticing that although Continental's monthly on-time percentages were at respectably high levels (sometimes at record levels) there were a number of months when the company did not rank third or higher—partly because other airlines had launched campaigns to improve their own on-time percentages. Continental adjusted the bonus requirements so that the airline had either to rank in the top three nationwide in on-time arrivals *or* to have an on-time arrival percentage above 80 percent—Bethune figured that an on-time arrival percentage above 80 percent represented good performance and merited paying employees a $100 bonus even if Continental was only fourth-best in a given month. The bonus standards were altered again in 2000; a $100 bonus was paid when Continental finished first in on-time performance among the major U.S. carriers, and a $65 bonus was paid when it finished second or third or had an on-time percentage above 80 percent. In 11 out of the 12 months in 2000, Continental gave employees on-time bonus checks, for a total that year of $39 million. During the 1995–2000 period, Continental paid employees a total of $157 million in on-time bonuses.

To further promote better on-time performance, Continental made route revisions for flights that were often delayed. For example, at the congested Newark hub (where at certain times of the day it was not unusual for planes to sit on the runway for 15 to 30 minutes waiting for clearance to take off even if the weather was good) it scheduled most departing planes at peak times to fly out-and-back routes between Newark and particular spoke destinations rather than, say, routing them to Washington and then on to Houston or Denver. Thus, the congestion-related delay of a Continental flight out of Newark would affect passengers on that flight only, thus reducing the number of flights with poor on-time performance.

Improving Baggage-Handling   When the on-time bonus was instituted in 1995, the numbers of lost bags went up at first—partly because flight crews elected not to wait on slow-arriving baggage in order to get planes away from the gates on time. Continental executives chose not to institute a bonus payment for getting passengers' baggage on the planes, believing it was simply the employees' job to ensure that this was done. Bethune explained:

> We had to get the word out that if the number of baggage complaints was increasing, that wasn't going to make it. We didn't want on-time flights without bags, or without people, or with dirty aisles. On-time meant the whole system was working on time, not just part of it. So we explained this to our employees, and baggage started making it onto the planes.[14]

In the following months, Continental's baggage handling improved—during one period, Continental ranked among the top three airlines in fewest number of baggage complaints for 30 out of 31 months. Moreover, management stressed that the on-time arrival percentage was being used as a metric for measuring the reliability of the company's whole operation. They emphasized that "making reliability a reality" meant that a Continental plane should depart on time with a full supply of meals, all its passengers, and all their bags—and then should arrive on time.

Other Product Enhancements   To reduce the time it took Continental reservation agents to answer phone calls and handle the task of making a reservation, Continental increased its call capacity by adding more agents and upgrading its reservation systems software. Calls involving flight status and other standard questions that did not require speaking directly to a reservations agent were automated.

In-flight services were improved on the basis of surveys of customer preferences. Continental began serving Coca-Cola instead of Pepsi and increased the variety of beers available. First-class passengers were given priority baggage handling. New and tastier meals were developed, with Bethune and Brenneman personally testing and approving

---

[14]Ibid., p. 107.

each of the new offerings. In-flight phones were installed in most of Continental's planes by the end of 1997. Music was played as passengers boarded planes.

In 2000, Continental spent $12 million on bigger overhead bins to accommodate larger carry-on bags and provide more storage space for carry-ons—Continental did not use the luggage-sizing templates that some competitors had installed to limit the size of carry-ons. To protect its competitive advantage in accommodating larger carry-on luggage, Continental sued United Airlines, alleging that at Washington, D.C.'s Dulles Airport (where United had 30 gates to Continental's 1), United and two other airlines had set up luggage-sizing templates at security checkpoints that prevented Continental passengers with larger bags from passing through. A federal judge ruled that luggage templates at security checkpoints represented an unreasonable restraint of trade that caused Continental injury; the judge said, "If there is any proof of failure in the market to be gleaned from the record, it is of United's failure to provide what its customers desire."

Executing the Working Together Plan

When Continental's rigid procedures manual was burned and replaced with general guidelines, many company executives feared that employees would "give away the store" in spending money to satisfy stranded or disgruntled passengers or to buy new airplane parts when existing ones could be repaired. But Gordon Bethune wanted employees to be able to use their best judgment, believing that management actions to give employees more free rein to do their jobs would build bridges of trust between management and employees. He further believed that once the company began making money and the profit-sharing plan with employees kicked in, the vast majority of Continental employees would think twice about giving away the store. He was willing to take the risk that some employees would probably be too generous. During the 1995–2000 period, Continental paid employees $545 million in profit-sharing bonuses—the amount for 2000 (paid in February 2001) was $98 million.

To help employees better understand what was expected, checklists were created for pilots in takeoffs and landings, for maintenance technicians in doing engine maintenance, for flight crews in seeing that planes were properly provisioned, for crews in cleaning planes, and so on. The idea was that if certain jobs were broken down into a series of steps, then it would be easier for people to do the jobs they had signed on for.

Open Communications and Teamwork   An 800 voice-mail number directly to Bethune's office was set up for employees to use when they got particularly frustrated or felt a need to talk directly to the CEO—on a normal day, Bethune might get a couple of calls; on days when something unusual happened or when major policy changes were announced, he might get 20 to 25 calls.[15] In addition, another 800 line was set up solely for technical operations problems—an operational response team was on duty seven days a week to provide assistance. There was a hotline employees could call for information about pay, benefits, and their 401(K) program. To keep employees up-to-date on company developments, corporate headquarters distributed a daily update via the company intranet and e-mail, a weekly three-minute voice-mail message from Gordon Bethune giving his take on any new developments at the company, a monthly employee newsletter called *Continental Times,* and a company publication called the *Continental Quarterly* that was mailed to employees' homes. Bethune and the company's head of corporate communications decided in 1995 to install some 600

---

[15]Ibid., p. 115.

bulletin boards in employee break rooms, high-traffic hallways, and common rooms and to post a daily newsletter on the same area of each bulletin board by late afternoon; in 1997, streaming LED display message boards were installed in crew break rooms and office hallways to provide employees with breaking news, the latest daily on-time flight percentages, Continental's stock price, and airport weather reports. Bethune made a point of leveling with employees, keeping them fully informed, and giving straight answers to questions—in contrast to prior management's practice of telling employees as little as possible. The four elements of the Go Forward Plan—Fly to Win, Fund the Future, Make Reliability a Reality, and Working Together—were always discussed in the same order at employee meetings, in company publications, and bulletin board postings; the agenda at the biweekly management committee meetings was also structured according to the four elements of the Go Forward Plan.

The monthly open houses at Houston headquarters were expanded to include employee meetings twice a year at the three hub locations and other Continental facilities with sizable workforces. Bethune wanted all Continental employees to feel like they could get to top-level executives and ask whatever questions were on their minds. An employee at the Newark hub asked Bethune why Continental gave all employees a $65 bonus for good on-time performance when the jobs of many employees did not directly affect such performance. Bethune, holding up his watch, responded, "Which part of this watch don't you think we need?"[16] The employee had no answer and sat down. Bethune believed his question about the watch made a point about the importance of teamwork, the value that each employee contributed, and why it made sense for all Continental employees to win or lose together. Bethune pushed the theme that each Continental employee was a part of what was happening at Continental, that Continental's people *were* the company, and that Working Together was about making Continental a place where people were happy to come to work. Bethune was fond of saying that he had never heard of a successful company that didn't have a good product and where people didn't enjoy coming to work. And he liked to say that running an airline was the biggest team sport in the world.

The Culture-Changing Effort   In Bethune's view, the keys to changing Continental's corporate culture were for management to act differently, for the company to treat its people differently, and for management to look closely at what it was like for Continental employees to come to work every day and deliberately set out to change the things that made the work environment unpleasant or that made employees unhappy. Burning the old manuals; writing new, more open guidelines; and emphasizing teamwork were all deliberate steps that management took to signal employees that the Working Together initiative truly represented a new day at Continental. The final part of the plan was to insist that Continental people treat each other with dignity and respect—the goal was for every worker to treat coworkers like customers or family members. Bethune believed prior management had created a lot of scar tissue and mistrust that needed to be eradicated. "Dignity and Respect" became the company's slogan for 1996.

In early 1995, high-level executives ranked all managerial and supervisory employees on a scale of 1 to 4 with regard to the quality of their work and whether they were team players, with 1 being good and 4 indicating deficient work quality and/or shortcomings in people management skills. During the first nine months of 1995, executives talked to supervisors about their performance, giving them a chance to measure up to expectations. The ratings were fluid, changing as supervisors changed their

---

[16]Ibid., p. 126.

behavior. In October 1995, when it became clear that Continental had too many managers, especially middle managers, Continental decided to dismiss all managers and supervisors with a 4 rating.

Within the executive ranks, there was gradual but big turnover. Of the 61 vice presidents at Continental when Bethune took over, about half either left on their own or were let go for reasons of ineffective management or failing to be team players. Some of those who departed were not happy with the direction Bethune wanted to take the company, and some were not pleased with certain aspects of the programs of change that he instituted. Bethune recruited a number of outsiders for top positions at Continental, hiring several people with whom he had worked at Piedmont Airlines and identifying others by asking trusted acquaintances. In 1998, several Delta Airlines executives told Bethune that Continental had the best management team of any airline. To retain its key executives, Continental adopted a very attractive salary and bonus package. Just as employees got monthly bonuses for on-time performance and had a performance-based profit-sharing plan that paid them up to 15 percent of pretax profits, Continental executives got bonuses based partly on Continental's overall performance and partly on the achievement of individual goals. Bethune preached teamwork among senior executives, warning them that he took a very dim view of people who engaged in power plays, backstabbing, or jockeying for position, and of departments that failed to work cooperatively with other departments.

To build trust, Bethune liked to reward people early and unexpectedly. In mid-1996, Continental was doing so well that it was clear to Bethune the company would hit its performance targets for the whole year; he decided to give Continental's managers 50 percent of the full 1996 bonus at the company's midyear managers' meeting. When he came in to give his luncheon address, Bethune asked the 350 executives there to stand and turn over their chairs—taped to the bottom of each was the manager's bonus check. He told the group, "This is because you've done such an outstanding job—because Continental is going to make its plan this year. Here's the money the company owes you for that success."[17] He got a standing ovation. According to Bethune, "The managers left that meeting like it was halftime of a championship game. They had come in expecting the usual corporate rah-rah and they left with a check for half of their bonus, which they weren't expecting for another six months."[18]

Another visible action was Bethune's mandate for departments to work cooperatively, specifically in the areas of scheduling, flight operations, and aircraft maintenance. Prior to Bethune's joining Continental, marketing and scheduling personnel would work out a flight and route schedule that they thought would attract the most passengers and yield the biggest load factors; then they handed the schedule off to operations to figure out which planes to assign to fly which routes and when and where maintenance on each plane would be done. Often the schedule that was drawn up created all kinds of problems and inefficiencies in flight operations and maintenance—and neither department was inclined to work with the other to resolve the difficulties. Bethune required that people in marketing, scheduling, flight operations, and aircraft maintenance form a team to arrive at a schedule that was workable from all perspectives.

Starting in 1996, Continental began a program to reward employees for perfect attendance. Employees with perfect attendance for a six-month period (either January–June or July–December) were awarded a $50 gift certificate and became eligible for drawings for fully equipped Eddie Bauer Ford Explorers, with the company paying all

---

[17]Ibid., p. 241.
[18]Ibid., pp. 241–42.

sales and gift taxes, title fees, and license fees. Since the program had been initiated, the company had given away 83 vehicles, including 8 for perfect attendance in 2000, at a combined cost of $3.3 million. From July 1 to December 31, 2000, there were 14,980 eligible employees with perfect attendance records. Management officials in Continental's human resources department estimated that the program had saved the company about $20 million through reductions in the absenteeism rate.

Management believed that employee morale at Continental was the highest in the airline industry. Continental's calendar was dotted each year with company picnics, ice cream parties, barbeques, and fried chicken dinners. According to one top executive, "Three to four celebrations a year cost us $20 per employee. Compare that to our payroll and you can't find it. But those are the things people remember."[19] Voluntary turnover rates for Continental's employees were 6.7 percent in 1998, 6.1 percent in 1999, and 5.3 percent in 2000.

At every Continental facility he visited, Bethune preached the importance of teamwork, repeating his analogy of the watch in which every piece was important. In 1998, Bethune wrote in his book *From Worst to First:*

> If you want to make the most sweeping statement you can about the change at Continental since I came on board, it's that now everybody's on the same team and everyone knows it. Everyone knows what the goal is and what his or her part is and how it relates to the goal. Everyone knows what the reward is for making the goal and what happens if we fail.
>
> We're all working from the same plays, the same playbook—plays everyone's had a chance to buy into, plays the people who will be running them had a chance to help design, plays everyone believes in, plays everyone believes can win.[20]

Bethune was a firm advocate of the management principle that what gets measured is what gets managed. It was his philosophy that a company could not just run on autopilot and stay good—it had to keep getting better and better at what it did. He was well regarded by employees. One employee attending a recent ceremony at which the Ford Explorer winners were presented their keys by Gordon Bethune and Greg Brenneman commented, "I started the week we went into bankruptcy 10 years ago. It is now 300 times better. What helps a lot is Gordon and Greg. Their personalities enthuse everybody. They're funny. I love listening to them speak."[21] Bethune talked with every class of flight attendants at the end of their training and he had come up with the idea of putting photographs of employees on ticket jacket covers. He urged Continental employees to thrash the competition; in a *Boston Globe* interview, Bethune said:

> If United Airlines needed help in crossing the street, I'd say sure, "Sure go ahead," and watch them get hit by a truck. I'd say "Sorry, I thought the light was red not green." And then I wouldn't even call 911.[22]

Exhibit 2 shows how Continental's costs compared with those of other major U.S. airlines during the 1995–2000 period.

---

[19]As quoted in "Happy Skies of Continental,": *Continental* (July 2001,), p. 53.

[20]Bethune, *From Worst to First,* p. 181.

[21]As quoted in "Happy Skies of Continental," p. 52.

[22]As quoted in Matthew Brelis, "The Key to Continental's Turnaround is an Empowered Workforce, Not Slash-and-Burn," *Boston Globe,* June 3, 2001, p. E1.

exhibit 2 Comparative Operating Cost Statistics, Major U.S. Airlines, 1995–2000 (in cents per average seat mile)

Carrier	Year	Food	Salaries and Benefits	Aircraft Fuel and Oil	Commissions	Landing Fees	Advertising	Other Operating and Maintenance Expenses	Total Operating Expenses	Rent and Leasing Fees	Interest
American	1995	0.41¢	3.70¢	1.01¢	0.80¢	0.15¢	0.15¢	3.23¢	9.45¢	0.73¢	0.36¢
	1996	0.41	3.38	1.23	0.77	0.16	0.13	2.97	9.05	0.71	0.24
	1997	0.41	3.51	1.21	0.79	0.16	0.11	3.18	9.37	0.69	0.11
	1998	0.40	3.72	1.00	0.75	0.15	0.12	3.24	9.38	0.68	0.00
	1999	0.43	3.81	1.01	0.68	0.16	0.12	3.33	9.54	0.71	(0.02)
	2000	0.44	4.18	1.48	0.60	0.17	0.13	3.49	10.49	0.74	(0.00)
Alaska	1995	0.31¢	2.60¢	1.07¢	0.55¢	0.15¢	0.12¢	3.10¢	7.89¢	1.17¢	0.29¢
	1996	0.30	2.74	1.31	0.60	0.15	0.12	3.03	8.26	1.17	0.20
	1997	0.30	2.99	1.25	0.65	0.16	0.11	3.13	8.60	1.15	0.14
	1998	0.29	3.06	0.94	0.56	0.15	0.13	3.13	8.27	1.15	0.08
	1999	0.28	3.22	1.14	0.53	0.16	0.15	3.29	8.77	1.13	0.06
	2000	0.29	3.53	1.76	0.38	0.18	0.38	3.72	10.25	1.08	0.14
Continental	1995	0.22¢	2.45¢	1.11¢	0.74¢	0.18¢	0.16¢	3.82¢	8.67¢	1.20¢	0.33¢
	1996	0.23	2.65	1.29	0.76	0.20	0.13	4.05	9.31	1.18	0.23
	1997	0.25	2.80	1.34	0.76	0.20	0.15	3.77	9.27	1.12	0.18
	1998	0.26	3.05	1.02	0.69	0.18	0.14	4.08	9.41	1.16	0.16
	1999	0.28	3.10	0.97	0.63	0.18	0.14	4.21	9.51	1.22	0.23
	2000	0.28	3.30	1.62	0.54	0.18	0.07	4.21	10.20	1.23	0.23
Delta	1995	0.26¢	3.25¢	1.11¢	0.85¢	0.20¢	0.13¢	3.06¢	8.86¢	0.81¢	0.19¢
	1996	0.25	3.43	1.35	0.78	0.19	0.09	3.45	9.54	0.69	0.15
	1997	0.26	3.35	1.31	0.73	0.18	0.10	3.15	9.07	0.68	0.12
	1998	0.31	3.36	1.08	0.66	0.16	0.09	3.37	9.04	0.71	0.10
	1999	0.30	3.44	1.07	0.53	0.16	0.10	3.50	9.11	0.73	0.15
	2000	0.27	3.73	1.27	0.42	0.16	0.08	3.51	9.43	0.72	0.28
America West	1995	0.19¢	2.08¢	0.96¢	0.64¢	0.16¢	0.19¢	3.07¢	7.29¢	1.30¢	0.32¢
	1996	0.11	1.91	1.20	0.62	0.16	0.15	3.69	7.84	1.31	0.22
	1997	0.10	1.90	1.13	0.64	0.15	0.13	3.29	7.35	1.32	0.17
	1998	0.10	1.99	0.85	0.48	0.14	0.08	3.72	7.36	1.37	0.14
	1999	0.11	2.07	1.00	0.44	0.13	0.05	3.80	7.60	1.41	0.11
	2000	0.12	2.21	1.54	0.32	0.13	0.09	4.17	8.57	1.58	0.08

exhibit 2 (continued)

Carrier	Year	Food	Salaries and Benefits	Aircraft Fuel and Oil	Commissions	Landing Fees	Advertising	Other Operating and Maintenance Expenses	Total Operating Expenses	Rent and Leasing Fees	Interest
Northwest	1995	0.28¢	3.47¢	1.24¢	0.93¢	0.27¢	0.16¢	2.80¢	9.15¢	0.70¢	0.27¢
	1996	0.26	3.30	1.49	0.90	0.24	0.17	2.84	9.21	0.64	0.21
	1997	0.26	3.25	1.43	0.86	0.23	0.14	2.89	9.06	0.62	0.21
	1998	0.26	3.72	1.19	0.73	0.23	0.20	3.34	9.68	0.64	0.32
	1999	0.27	3.57	1.19	0.71	0.24	0.14	3.03	9.15	0.61	0.35
	2000	0.29	3.65	1.80	0.61	0.24	0.13	3.24	9.96	0.67	0.31
TWA*	1995	0.27¢	3.16¢	1.20¢	0.69¢	0.19¢	0.16¢	2.88¢	8.56¢	0.71¢	0.40¢
	1996	0.27	3.19	1.44	0.66	0.18	0.17	3.34	9.25	0.74	0.31
	1997	0.23	3.45	1.32	0.66	0.18	0.14	3.21	9.20	1.02	0.31
	1998	0.26	3.71	1.00	0.57	0.19	0.17	3.74	9.65	1.33	0.34
	1999	0.25	3.80	1.11	0.51	0.21	0.15	4.23	10.26	1.54	0.27
	2000	0.23	3.72	1.65	0.34	0.20	0.11	3.89	10.14	1.79	0.24
United	1995	0.37¢	3.34¢	1.06¢	0.93¢	0.21¢	0.13¢	2.84¢	8.89¢	0.94¢	0.21¢
	1996	0.37	3.50	1.28	0.90	0.21	0.13	2.95	9.34	0.90	0.13
	1997	0.37	3.74	1.22	0.89	0.21	0.14	2.97	9.53	0.87	0.11
	1998	0.36	3.75	1.03	0.76	0.20	0.15	2.99	9.25	0.83	0.15
	1999	0.37	3.86	1.01	0.65	0.21	0.16	3.15	9.41	0.84	0.17
	2000	0.38	4.16	1.43	0.59	0.20	0.20	3.64	10.60	0.88	0.19
US Airways	1995	0.25¢	4.93¢	1.04¢	0.90¢	0.19¢	0.11¢	4.18¢	11.61¢	1.16¢	0.51¢
	1996	0.24	5.53	1.25	0.93	0.22	0.09	4.64	12.90	1.16	0.49
	1997	0.27	5.39	1.19	0.90	0.20	0.08	5.56	13.58	1.20	0.43
	1998	0.29	5.34	0.90	0.84	0.19	0.06	5.72	13.34	1.15	0.42
	1999	0.29	5.57	1.01	0.74	0.20	0.07	6.09	13.97	1.15	0.30
	2000	0.28	5.35	1.72	0.51	0.20	0.08	5.73	13.88	1.11	0.36
Southwest	1995	0.02¢	2.56¢	1.01¢	0.39¢	0.23¢	0.27¢	2.61¢	7.09¢	0.71¢	0.16¢
	1996	0.03	2.63	1.19	0.40	0.24	0.29	2.73	7.51	0.70	0.09
	1997	0.03	2.72	1.11	0.40	0.25	0.27	2.63	7.40	0.67	0.10
	1998	0.02	2.89	0.82	0.37	0.24	0.27	2.72	7.32	0.64	0.06
	1999	0.03	2.94	0.93	0.33	0.23	0.28	2.73	7.47	0.60	0.04
	2000	0.03	2.99	1.38	0.30	0.22	0.26	2.55	7.72	0.55	0.07

*Acquired by American Airlines in late 2000.

Source: U.S. Department of Transportation, Bureau of Transportation Statistics, Office of Airline Information, Form 41B, Form 41P, Form T100.

CONTINENTAL AIRLINES IN 2001

Recognition and Awards

In January 2001, Continental Airlines was named Airline of the Year by *Air Transport World,* a leading aviation industry trade magazine. As recipient of the same award in 1996, Continental was the first airline to be designated Airline of the Year twice within a five-year period. The magazine cited Continental's employee-friendly culture and said that Continental had the best labor relations of any major U.S. hub-and-spoke carrier. It also noted that Continental had "superior passenger service," especially where business travelers were concerned: "Other airlines infuriate business travelers by limiting carry-on luggage; Continental invests in bigger bins." In 2001, OAG, a division of Reed Business Information and publisher of *OAG Pocket Flight Guides,* named Continental as Best Trans-Atlantic Airline and Best Airline Based in North America; Continental was also honored by OAG as having the best frequent flyer program. OAG awards were based on votes by subscribers to the *OAG Pocket Flight Guide,* most of whom were frequent flyers. The marketing information firm J. D. Power and Associates had named Continental as tops in customer satisfaction for four of the past five years. In 2000 and 2001, Continental was named as the second-most-admired U.S. airline by *Fortune* magazine, trailing Southwest Airlines in both years. However, in the Air Quality Rating 2001 study, conducted jointly by Wichita State University and the Aviation Institute at the University of Nebraska at Omaha and released in April 2001, Continental was ranked 7th among the top 10 U.S. airlines, down from a 2nd-place ranking the prior year; despite leading the industry with 78.1 percent on-time arrivals, Continental was ranked 7th due largely to having involuntarily bumped an average of 18 passengers per 100,000 passengers flown in 2000 (compared with just 3.4 passengers per 100,000 the prior year) and it mishandled an average of 535 bags per 100,000 passengers, up from 442 the prior year. *Worth* magazine, in its April 2001 issue, named Gordon Bethune one of the 50 best CEOs for the third consecutive year. In June 2001, *Aviation Week & Space Technology* gave Continental its highest rating for "outstanding management."

Continental was included for the fourth consecutive year by *Hispanic* magazine on its February 2001 list of the "Corporate 100 Providing the Most Opportunities for Latinos." Since 1998, Continental had recruited more than 3,100 Hispanics to its workforce of 53,000 employees. Approximately 15 percent of Continental's workforce was Hispanic, and 21 percent of Continental's newly hired employees in 2000 were Hispanic.

Gordon Bethune and Greg Brenneman concluded their joint letter to Continental shareholders in the 2000 annual report issued in early 2001 with the following statement:

> We will continue to build on the trust and confidence we have in each other. We remain committed to ensuring that when we win, we all win—employees, customers, and shareholders alike.
>
> "Work Hard. Fly Right" is more than a catchy slogan. It exemplifies who we are and what we do.
>
> As we have often said before—stick with us, we're going no place but up.

The Alliance with Northwest Airlines: A New Arrangement

In January 2001, Continental repurchased 6.7 million of the 8.7 million shares of common stock that Northwest had bought in late 1997 to trigger their global alliance;

Continental paid Northwest $450 million in cash for the 6.7 million shares. However, as part of the deal, Continental and Northwest agreed to extend until 2025 their master alliance agreement that called for code-sharing, reciprocal frequent flyer programs, shared executive lounge access, and various joint marketing agreements. The share repurchase effectively made Continental independent of any outside entity's control for the first time since the company had been formed and thus freed Continental to pursue its own destiny. In addition, it brought an end to the antitrust litigation initiated by the U.S. Department of Justice in 1998. Gordon Bethune declared January 22, 2001, as "Independence Day" at Continental and marked the occasion by paying a $100 cash bonus to Continental's 54,300 employees around the world and holding celebrations at company facilities featuring apple pie and Coca-Cola.

At the time Continental began implementing its global alliance with Northwest Airlines in November 1998, management anticipated that the alliance would be fully implemented by the end of 2001 and would produce an increase of approximately $265 million in operating income for Continental. In mid-2001 it became apparent that the implementation process was going slower than originally expected as a result of delays in establishing common technical platforms and jointly implementing alliances with other carriers. Continental estimated that the shortfall in financial benefits during 2001 would amount to $65 million, but management believed the full benefits would be realized as all of the planned features of the alliance were implemented over the next two to three years.

Executive Changes at the Top

In May 2001, Greg Brenneman, age 39, resigned as Continental's president, COO, and director, electing to devote full time to his own firm, TurnWorks, Inc., which specialized in helping start-up companies and firms going through major transitions. In announcing his resignation, Brenneman indicated he would donate $500,000 to endow two charities that helped Continental employees. Larry Kellner, formerly Continental's chief financial officer and one of Gordon Bethune's first executive hires in early 1995, was elevated to the position of president; Kellner had the distinction in 2000 of having become the first three-time winner of the CFO Excellence Awards named annually by *CFO* magazine. C. D. McLean, former executive vice president of operations, was named Continental's COO and executive vice president.

The Planned Spinoff of Continental Express

In July 2001, Continental announced plans to sell a minority stake in Continental Express through an initial public offering (IPO) of stock. Management indicated that such a move was aimed at raising capital and putting some spark into Continental's stock price, which (like the stock prices of other airlines) had been trending downward in the face of a sluggish economy and weak air traffic. Following the IPO, Continental said it would eventually divest the rest of Continental Express by distributing the remaining shares to Continental stockholders. Having explored the sale of Continental Express off and on for several years, the company decided that the time was now right because the stock market was putting a high value on the shares of fast-growing regional carriers like Continental Express. Over the past 10 years, regional carriers had enjoyed widespread success flying small jets with about 50 seats to lesser-sized destination airports; in many cases, regional carriers faced weaker competition and enjoyed more consistent profitability than the major carriers to which they funneled connecting passengers. Regional carriers had kept costs down by not serving any meals and by negotiating labor contracts calling for substantially lower compensation for pilots, flight attendants, and ground crews than the major carriers. As a result, Wall Street had rewarded regional carriers with substantially higher price–earnings multiples than most major airlines. Since Continental Express had been growing at about 30 percent annually for the past several years, Continental expected that its shareholders would benefit from the higher price–earnings premium being accorded to regional carriers.

Continental's Financial and Operating Performance in 2001

During the first six months of 2001, Continental reported revenues of $5.0 billion, up 3.3 percent over the $4.85 billion in revenues for the first six months of 2000; net earnings for the period were $51 million, down sharply from the $149 million in the first two quarters of 2000. Continental reported earnings of $9 million in the first quarter of 2001 (versus $14 million in 2000) and earnings of $42 million in the second quarter (versus $149 million in 2000). Management attributed the lower earnings in 2001 to the sluggish U.S. and global economies. The company's liquidity was in question, however, with current assets of $2.2 billion and current liabilities of $3.2 billion. Moreover, the company continued to be highly leveraged, with long-term debt of $3.7 billion and stockholders' equity of $1.2 billion. Continental and Southwest Airlines were the only two major U.S. airlines to report a profit for the first six months of 2001.

Exhibit 3 shows selected operating statistics for Continental for the first six months of 2001. Exhibit 4 shows the size and makeup of Continental's aircraft fleet as of June 30, 2001.

Continental's Situation in August 2001   For the first eight months of 2001, Continental reported 80.9 percent on-time performance (versus 77.7 percent for the comparable period in 2000) and passenger traffic increases of 2.7 percent for Continental and 22.9 percent for Continental Express. In August 2001, Continental reported a load factor of 78.1 percent (versus 76.8 percent in August 2000). Passenger traffic in August was up 4.8 percent over year earlier levels. Continental Express, the company's feeder airline to regional hubs, reported a record August load factor of 66 percent, 2.8 percent above August 2000 levels. August 2001 passenger traffic on Continental Express was 26.3 percent above year-earlier levels.

Going into September 2001, Continental and Continental Express were flying over 2,500 flights daily. Continental had reported 25 consecutive profitable quarters and had been designated by *Fortune* as one of the 100 Best Companies to Work For in America in 1999, 2000, and 2001—in the latest *Fortune* listings, Continental was ranked 18.

THE IMPACT OF THE SEPTEMBER 2001 TERRORIST ATTACKS ON AMERICA

Four days after the terrorist hijackings and attacks on the World Trade Center and the Pentagon, Gordon Bethune announced that Continental Airlines would immediately reduce its long-term flight schedule by approximately 20 percent on a systemwide available-seat-mile basis and would furlough approximately 12,000 of its current 56,000 employees in connection with its flight cutbacks. In a press release, he said:

> The U.S. airline industry is in an unprecedented financial crisis . . . Our nation needs immediate congressional action if the nation's air transportation system is to survive.

exhibit 3   Selected Operating Statistics, Continental Airlines,
First Six Months of 2001 versus First Six Months of 2000

| | Six Months Ended June 30 | | Net Increase |
	2001	2000	(Decrease)
Revenue passengers (000s)	23,476	23,285	0.8%
Revenue passenger miles (millions)[1]	32,167	31,496	2.1%
Available seat miles (millions)[2]	44,271	42,334	4.6%
Passenger load factor[3]	72.7%	74.4%	(1.7) points
Breakeven passenger load factor[4]	66.1%	66.0%	0.1 points
Passenger revenue per available seat mile	9.63¢	9.83¢	(2.0)%
Total revenue per available seat mile	10.44¢	10.64¢	(1.9)%
Operating cost per available seat mile	9.65¢	9.71¢	(0.6)%
Average price per gallon of fuel	88.09¢	83.49¢	5.5%
Average fare per revenue passenger	$181.68	$178.72	1.7%
Average daily utilization of each aircraft[5]	10:49	10:37	1.9%
Actual aircraft in fleet at end of period	377	363	3.9%
Average length of aircraft flight (miles)	1,179	1,143	3.1%

[1]The number of scheduled miles flown by revenue passengers.

[2]The number of seats available for passengers multiplied by the number of scheduled miles those seats are flown.

[3]Revenue passenger miles divided by available seat miles.

[4]The percentage of seats that must be occupied by revenue passengers in order for the airline to break even on an income before income tax basis, excluding nonrecurring charges, nonoperating items, and other special items.

[5]The average number of hours per day that an aircraft flown in revenue service is operated (from gate departure to gate arrival).

Source: Continental Airlines 10-Q report, July 2001.

     While we regret the necessity for this massive furlough and substantial schedule reduction, and the adverse impact on our dedicated employees, customers, and communities we serve, we have no choice.

     We are truly sad that this airline has been forced to furlough our hardworking co-workers, but we are fighting to save this industry so that they may return to us one day.

Continental expected that about 3,500 of the announced 12,000 furloughs would be achieved through early retirements and its voluntary leave of absence program. Severance packages to furloughed employees and various other severance and furlough pay provisions were estimated to cost the company slightly more than $60 million. Outplacement job fairs were scheduled for Continental's hub locations in Houston, Cleveland, and Newark.

On Monday, September 17, 2001, Continental announced that it would not make $70 million in debt payments due that day but that it would be able to make the payments within the 10-day grace period to prevent defaulting. Continental officials also indicated that a bankruptcy filing was one of the options being considered to cope with its anticipated cash crunch. Bethune indicated that Continental expected to take in only half its normal revenues during the next several weeks and that even if it cut costs by 20 percent, Continental would incur losses of $200 million per month at those revenue

exhibit 4   Continental's Aircraft Fleet, June 30, 2001

Aircraft Type	Total Seats	Aircraft Owned	Aircraft Leased	Total Aircraft	Average Age*	Aircraft on Order
Continental						
Boeing 777-200	283	4	12	16	1.7	2
Boeing 767-400ER	235	3	2	5	0.2	19
Boeing 767-200ER	174	7	1	8	0.1	2
Boeing 757-300	210	—	—	—	—	15
Boeing 757-200	172	13	28	41	3.9	—
Boeing 737-900	167	—	1	1	0.1	14
Boeing 737-800	155	17	43	60	1.3	33
Boeing 737-700	124	12	24	36	2.0	5
Boeing 737-500	104	15	51	66	4.7	—
Boeing 737-300	124	14	51	65	13.4	—
DC10-30	242	3	11	14	25.5	—
MD-80	141	17	48	65	15.9	—
		105	272	377		90
Continental Express						
Jets						
Embraer ERJ-145XR	50	—	—	—	—	75
Embraer ERJ-145	50	18	72	90	1.9	59
Embraer ERJ-135	37	—	27	27	0.7	23
Total jets		18	99	117		157
Turboprops						
ATR-42-320	46	9	22	31	10.8	—
EMB-120	30	9	10	19	11.0	—
Beech 1900-D	19	—	13	13	4.8	—
Total turboprops		18	45	63		—
Total		141	416	557		247

*In years, as of Year-end 2000.

Note: Continental anticipated taking delivery of 36 Boeing aircraft in 2001 (of which 9 were placed in service in the first half of 2001. Continental Express anticipated taking delivery of 41 Embraer regional jets in 2001 (of which 21 were placed in service in the first half of 2001). Continental planned to retire 14 of its turboprop aircraft during the second half of 2001. As of June 30, 2001, Continental's estimated costs for the Boeing aircraft it had on order totaled $4.2 billion; its commitment for Embraer regional jet aircraft was approximately $2.5 billion. As of June 30, 2001, Continental had approximately $1.3 billion in financing arranged for future deliveries of Boeing aircraft.

Source: Continental Airlines, 2000 10-K report and 10-Q report, July 2001.

levels. If revenue did not snap back quickly, Continental might have to seek bankruptcy protection by as early as November. Bethune further called upon the federal government to enact a major assistance package to help the airline industry cope with the sudden downturn in passenger traffic and the added costs of FAA-mandated airport security regulations regarding baggage handling, passenger screening at security checkpoints, and tighter security screening of caterers, cleaning crews, and flight crews. New security measures were expected to slow passengers moving through terminals, increase the time to process baggage and turn planes at the gates, and otherwise slow down hub operations.

Most of the flight reductions implemented by Continental during the second half of September 2001 involved simply cutting the number of flights between particular locations. However, the flight schedule reduction resulted in Continental's discontinuing service to 10 cities/airports: Atlantic City, New Jersey; Houston/Hobby, Abilene, Tyler, Waco, and San Angelo, Texas; Daytona Beach and Melbourne, Florida; Dusseldorf, Germany; and London/Stansted. The company also announced that it would not implement service to Montego Bay and Kingston, Jamaica, as planned in late 2001. The Denver reservations center was closed, along with the flight attendant base in Los Angeles and several line maintenance facilities. Included in the cutbacks were suspension of flights by all the company's DC-10s to save on maintenance costs and temporary grounding of 14 Continental Express turboprops and 31 other aircraft. Continental also began adjusting its staffing levels at airports on the basis of reruns of its sophisticated simulation models about how passengers would now be moving through airports, given the new screening procedures and the earlier times that passengers would be arriving at airports.

Layoffs at Other Airlines

Meanwhile, other airlines in the United States and around the world were also hastily rearranging their flight schedules to protect their financial positions and respond to air travel reductions, figuring out how best to implement tighter security regulations, and canceling orders or delaying deliveries of new aircraft. Many airlines announced workforce reductions:

- American Airlines—a workforce reduction of 20,000 employees.
- United Airlines—a workforce reduction of 20,000 employees.
- US Airways—a workforce reduction of 11,000 employees and anticipated pay cuts.
- British Airways—a workforce reduction of 7,000 employees.
- America West Airlines—a workforce reduction of 2,000 employees.
- Virgin Atlantic—a workforce reduction of 1,200 employees.
- American Trans Air—a workforce reduction of 1,500 employees.
- Midwest Express—a workforce reduction of 450 employees.
- Frontier Airlines—a workforce reduction of 440 employees.
- Mesaba—undetermined furloughs and significant pay cuts.
- KLM—a workforce reduction of 10 percent.

With layoffs of 30,000 employees at Boeing and another 12,000 at Honeywell (all related to cutbacks in the production of commercial aircraft), close to 120,000 employees were affected by the flight cutbacks and cost-saving measures being initiated across the airline industry.

The Federal Government's Rescue Package

In the days following the September 11 attacks, at the urging of the Bush administration, Congress passed the Air Transportation Safety and System Stabilization Act (ATSSSA), a bailout designed to keep the U.S. airline industry solvent until travel rebounded. The act gave airlines $5 billion in direct payments and provided as much as $10 billion in loan guarantees in an effort to assist airlines in finding funding to finance negative cash flows and cover debt payments even if they had weak balance sheets. Continental received $212.6 million in cash as a result of the $5 billion emergency relief package passed by Congress; the company expected to receive an additional $212 million cash infusion before the end of 2001. The amount of loans that Continental might apply for and receive from the government's emergency $10 billion loan program was still being determined. However, if the federal government required the airlines to put up unencumbered assets to collateralize any loans they might apply for, heavily leveraged airlines like Continental might be put in a bind because they had few unencumbered assets to pledge. It was not yet clear what conditions the government would attach to its loan guarantees, but the requirements were not expected to be so stringent as to disqualify financially weak airlines.

Despite the cash grants made to airlines pursuant to the ATSSSA, a number of prominent U.S. airlines reported heavy losses for the third quarter of 2001. American Airlines posted the largest quarterly operating loss in its history for the three months ending September 30. Northwest reported a third-quarter operating loss of $155 million and indicated that it incurred $250 million in operating losses during the September 11–30 period. Northwest had a load factor of 53.5 percent in the third week of September, but a traffic rebound had pushed the company's load factor back up to 67.9 percent by the third week of October—even so, Northwest indicated that it was still burning through $6 to $8 million a day due to fare discounts aimed at attracting traffic, higher costs per mile, and fewer passengers carried as a consequence of cutting its flight schedule by 20 percent. US Airways reported a third-quarter net loss of $766 million, which took into account special charges and a $331 million grant the airline received as part of the ATSSSA; without the federal grant, US Airways would have lost $1.1 billion in the third quarter. United Airlines reported a third-quarter loss of $542 million before special charges of $865 million for aircraft groundings and impairment, severance costs and early retirements, and early termination fees—a portion of the special charges were offset by a $248 million ATSSSA grant. A few days prior to the announcement, United's CEO sent a letter to company employees indicating that the company would likely go bankrupt in 2002 unless deep cost cuts were made immediately; company officials indicated that United could lose as much as $3 billion in 2001—United's losses from operations through the first nine months of 2001 were $2.8 billion.[23]

Other Developments at Continental Airlines

On September 26, 2001, Gordon Bethune announced that he and Larry Kellner, Continental's president, would not accept any salary or bonus for the remainder of 2001. Bethune's 2000 salary was $966,879, and Kellner's was $581,000—the sacrifice amounted to approximately 25 percent, or $242,000 for Bethune and $145,000 for Kellner (and perhaps more, since their 2001 salaries very likely were greater than for 2000).

In September 2001, Continental incurred a traffic decrease worldwide of 31.0 percent compared to September 2000, with domestic traffic being down 32.3 percent versus 29.0 percent for international flights. Continental's September 2001 load factor was 61.4 percent, 11.0 points below the 72.4 percent load factor reported for September 2000. Continental Express had a traffic decrease of 21.7 percent versus September 2000 and a monthly load factor of 52.0 percent, 6.9 points below the prior September. Continental and Continental Express carried a combined total of 2,915,615 passengers during September 2001, a 32.2 percent drop from the 4,298,885 passengers carried in

---

[23]Company news release, November 1, 2001, p. 11.

exhibit 5 Continental's Passenger Load Factors, September 2001

	Sept. 1–10	Sept. 11–16*	Sept. 17–23	Sept. 23–30
Continental				
Domestic	70.0%	58.0%	46.6%	58.5%
International	76.2	66.6	55.8	47.7
Total	72.4	62.2	50.4	54.1
Continental Express	61.9	41.1	39.0	53.4

*Only 32 percent of planned capacity was operated during this period.
Source: Company records

September 2000. Exhibit 5 shows the company's traffic patterns for various periods in September before and after the terrorist attacks. Traffic on Continental's flights improved even further during the first two weeks of October 2001, with the domestic load factor rising to 71.3 percent and the systemwide load factor increasing to 65.6 percent.

On October 1, 2001, Continental began a program to award double miles to its frequent flyers for travel between October 2 and November 15; it also reduced fares for business travel on most domestic routes for the remainder of 2001. To encourage both business and leisure travel, the company began a reduced fare promotion to select destinations in Mexico, Central and South America, and Europe—passengers could save an additional 10 percent on the sale fares (and frequent flyers got an additional 1,000 bonus miles) by booking their travel at the company's website (www.continental.com).

Continental had installed crossbar or deadbolt cockpit door restraints in all of its aircraft by October 23, ahead of the FAA's targeted November deadline. Management expected to install even stronger doors in all its aircraft over the upcoming months, as manufacturers completed the production of newly designed doors with much-enhanced cockpit security features.

Continental's Third-Quarter Financial and Operating Performance

Continental reported third-quarter net income of $3 million, including a federal grant of $243 million ($154 million after tax) pursuant to the Air Transportation Safety and System Stabilization Act and $85 million in severance costs and other special charges. Excluding the special charges and the federal grant, Continental would have reported a loss of $97 million. Third-quarter revenue was $2.1 billion, down 14.9 percent from the same period last year. The company indicated that cash flow from operations remained negative at $4 to $5 million per day, down from a high of approximately $30 million a day during the three-day air traffic shutdown following the attacks. Management indicated the company expected to receive additional grants under the ATSSSA of approximately $215 million. Continental had unencumbered assets with a book value slightly in excess of $1 billion on September 30, 2001, which could be pledged to collateralize future borrowing.

In the third quarter of 2001, the company took delivery of 14 new Boeing jets and took 49 aircraft out of service; it was in discussions with Boeing concerning deferral of some aircraft on firm order and scheduled for delivery between 2002 and 2005. Exhibit 6 shows Continental's balance sheet as of September 30, 2001. Exhibit 7 provides selected operating statistics for the third quarter of 2001. According to Continental management, recent fare discounting to spur passenger traffic had depressed revenue per available seat mile, helping push the company's break-even load factor in the third quarter of 2001 up sharply, to 78.3 percent.

exhibit 6   Continental's Balance Sheet, September 30, 2001, versus
             December 31, 2000 (in millions of dollars)

	September 30, 2001	December 31, 2000
Assets		
Current assets		
Cash and cash equivalents	$1,201	$1,371
Short-term investments	—	24
Accounts receivable, net	455	495
Spare parts and supplies, net	290	280
Other	306	289
Total current assets	2,252	2,459
Total property and equipment	6,063	5,163
Routes, gates and slots, net	1,048	1,081
Other assets, net	453	498
Total assets	$9,816	$9,201
Liabilities and stockholders' equity		
Current liabilities		
Current maturities of long-term debt and capital leases	$ 349	$ 304
Accounts payable	988	1,016
Air traffic liability	1,124	1,125
Accrued other liabilities	623	535
Total current liabilities	3,084	2,980
Long-term debt and capital leases	4,092	3,374
Other long-term liabilities	1,145	995
Commitments and contingencies		
Continental-obligated mandatorily redeemable preferred securities of subsidiary trust holding solely convertible subordinated debentures	243	242
Redeemable common stock	—	450
Stockholders' equity		
Preferred stock	—	—
Class A common stock	—	—
Class B common stock	1	1
Additional paid-in capital	885	379
Retained earnings	1,510	1,456
Accumulated other comprehensive income (loss)	(4)	13
Treasury stock	(1,140)	(689)
Total stockholders' equity	1,252	1,160
Total liabilities and stockholders' equity	$9,816	$9,201

Source: Company news release, October 31, 2001.

exhibit 7   Selected Operating Statistics for Continental Airlines,
Three Months Ending September 30, 2001, versus 2000
(figures do not include Continental Express operations)

	Three Months Ended September 30		Net Increase (Decrease)
	2001	2000	
Revenue passengers (000s)	11,254	12,155	(7.4)%
Revenue passenger miles (millions)[1]	16,206	17,325	(6.5)%
Available seat miles (millions)[2]	21,994	22,356	(1.6)%
Passenger load factor[3]	73.7%	77.5%	(3.8) points
Break-even passenger load factor[4]	78.3%	67.4%	10.9 points
Passenger revenue per available seat mile	8.59¢	10.06¢	(14.6)%
Total revenue per available seat mile	9.33¢	10.89¢	(14.3)%
Operating cost per available seat mile	9.34¢	9.58¢	(2.0)%
Average price per gallon of fuel	82.37¢	86.52¢	(4.8)%
Actual aircraft in fleet at end of period	342	367	(6.8)%
Average length of aircraft flight (miles)	1,208	1,187	1.8%

[1]The number of scheduled miles flown by revenue passengers.

[2]The number of seats available for passengers multiplied by the number of scheduled miles those seats are flown.

[3]Revenue passenger miles divided by available seat miles.

[4]The percentage of seats that must be occupied by revenue passengers in order for the airline to break even on an income before income tax basis, excluding nonrecurring charges, nonoperating items, and other special items.

Source: Company news release, October 31, 2001.

case | 30

Conseco's Implementation Strategy for a Web-Based Cash Management System

William H. Moates
Indiana State University

Jeffrey S. Harper
Indiana State University

Joseph P. Clarke
Conseco Services, LLC

It seemed as though each of the treasury department's three fax machines would never stop printing wire transfer forms. It was July 31, the last business day of the month for Conseco's cash management department, and the typical deluge of wire activity had already started by 7:30 AM. Conseco's wire volume was averaging 200 to 300 transfers per day, a fairly heavy level in relation to the number of staff within the department—and volume at the end of the month was exceptionally heavy due to the high number of mortgage loan closings. On these particular days, there would be no vacations or floating holidays for the staff. Lunch was brought in to ensure that a full complement of cash management associates would be available throughout the day to process the wire transfer requests.

Robert McNutt, vice president of cash management at Conseco, reflected on how quickly things had changed in his department. He had just completed his 10th year at Conseco, all within the treasury function, and thought he had experienced almost everything from a cash management standpoint. But Conseco's acquisition of one of the nation's leading finance companies, Green Tree Financial Corporation,[1] had changed

[1]Green Tree was subsequently renamed Conseco Finance as part of Conseco's branding campaign.

everything. Following the acquisition, Conseco's average daily wire volume had nearly tripled, and the higher month-end activity could add an additional 100 to 200 wires to the daily total. What complicated the process further was that finance-related wires were originated from a variety of remote sites[2] and were authorized by an array of unfamiliar associates inherited in the Green Tree acquisition. As a result, the Conseco staff in Carmel, Indiana, relied heavily on a multipage authorization sheet (listing approximately 200 associates authorized to approve wires, including each approver's corresponding limit of authority) to determine the validity of a wire approval. To make matters worse, the list changed almost daily.

Thus far, the cash management department was able to keep pace with the volume. Three new open positions, including one at a senior manager level, were filled to accommodate the increased workload. The existing staff was comprised principally of experienced and well-trained associates. Cohesiveness within the unit, particularly on the busiest days, could be considered exemplary. Despite the significant volume of wire transactions, a high level of quality was maintained, as evidenced by the minimal number of errors detected since the department assumed its new responsibilities.

However, McNutt and his cash management associates also knew that the current process would not be effective indefinitely. He thought about the potential problems that would arise if changes were not implemented. This was a labor-intensive process that monopolized much of his staff's time. He was also worried that his best staff might eventually seek out opportunities elsewhere. If he had to limit vacations and floating holidays just to meet the current workload, what would he do if any of his better, more seasoned associates left?

The problems were not going to go away, but the wire transfer forms were beginning to pile up in his in-box. If McNutt did not review and authorize these wires soon, he would delay his staff in executing the transfers. Needless to say, the department could not afford to fall behind. Identifying a possible solution would have to wait for another day.

COMPANY BACKGROUND AND HISTORY

Headquartered in Carmel, a suburb of Indianapolis, Indiana, Conseco, Inc., was one of the leading sources of insurance, investment, and lending products in the United States. In 2001, Conseco had approximately $95 billion in managed assets, 13 million customers, and 14,500 employees. The firm was ranked 231 on the Fortune 500 list, with revenues of $8.3 billion in 2000. The parent company was comprised of subsidiaries serving the insurance/risk management market (13 companies), the investment market (3 companies), and consumer finance/lending services market (6 companies). As such, the company was positioned to offer a vast array of financial services to commercial enterprises as well as to individuals and families.

Conseco was incorporated in 1979 as a life insurance holding company, with the sole business activity of raising capital. In 1982, the company commenced insurance operations after completing its acquisition of Executive Income Life Insurance Company. From 1982 through 1997, the company grew its insurance operations principally through the acquisition of 18 other insurance groups (42 separate insurance companies altogether). At the end of that year, Conseco reported assets of $36 billion and shareholders' equity of just under $4 billion. Conseco common stock had provided its

---

[2]This refers to Green Tree's various divisions (e.g., Manufactured Housing Division, Mortgage Services Division) and, in some cases, branch offices located throughout the United States.

investors a compounded average annual return of 61 percent over the 10-year period ending December 31, 1997.[3] By most accounts, the company was considered one of the great entrepreneurial success stories of the 1980s and 1990s.

Insurance Operations

Conseco's insurance operations consisted of four primary lines of business: life insurance, annuity products, supplemental health insurance, and major medical insurance. In addition to insurance operations, Conseco also owned a full-service investment manager (Conseco Capital Management); a risk management brokerage agency (Conseco Risk Management); and a variety of other small, nontraditional businesses that were either acquired or established to enhance the company's distribution system. Conseco even had a small operation in India named Codelinks that provided programming support to Conseco and other unaffiliated customers.

The company's success could be attributed in part to management's ability (1) to identify good acquisition candidates and (2) to access the capital markets to secure financing. Following each acquisition, redundant expenses were identified and quickly eliminated. With few exceptions, operations of acquired entities were collapsed into centralized processing at the home office in Carmel. Operations were not consolidated for the acquisitions of Bankers Life and Casualty, Colonial Penn, and Pioneer, principally due to either logistical difficulties in moving the operations or a desire to retain some type of unique franchise value implicit in the current location.

One function that was never permitted to remain autonomous was cash management. Conseco's management considered it essential to maintain control of all cash accounts and the movement of all funds. So, early in the process of every acquisition, a Conseco cash management team would gather information on the number of accounts, volume of activity, and authorized personnel on each account. Cash management coordinated the transfer of funds from existing bank accounts of the acquired entity to corresponding bank accounts maintained by Conseco. Control of cash changed concurrently with the change of ownership.

Green Tree Acquisition

In June 1998, Conseco announced the purchase of Green Tree, a finance company that primarily provided financing for manufactured housing, home equity and home improvement loans, and private-label credit cards. Green Tree was also involved in other financing lines (e.g., truck leasing, airplane leasing), although it was principally the manufactured housing and mortgage services that attracted Conseco. Green Tree was acquired to facilitate Conseco's strategic objective of becoming a full-service financial institution. Both companies marketed to Americans whose personal income ranged from $25,000 to $75,000 annually, and Conseco's top management believed that extensive cross-selling opportunities existed between the two entities. If Conseco could tap into Green Tree's extensive customer database with a full line of insurance products, new business sales would surely benefit. Conversely, Green Tree's finance products would also be compatible with the nearly 13 million existing insurance customers of Conseco.[4]

---

[3]Conseco, Inc., investor briefing, December 19, 2000, slide 3.

[4]Conseco, Inc., investor briefing, December 19, 2000, slide 33. Because of its size and certain other logistical difficulties, Green Tree's treasury unit was not consolidated in Carmel for about a year, a deviation from the usual corporate practice.

With a purchase price of nearly $6 billion, some analysts believed that Conseco overpaid for the franchise value of Green Tree. Furthermore, analysts insisted that Conseco might experience difficulty executing its cross-selling initiative. Perhaps more important, certain analysts expressed concern that funding a fast-growing finance company such as Green Tree might place considerable strain on the company's capital resources. Pessimism in the market was one of several factors that had adversely affected Conseco's stock. Additionally, turmoil caused by Russia's economic crisis had caused a flight to quality among analysts, strategists, and fund managers. This in turn triggered a significant decline in the domestic debt and equity markets. A decrease in the company's market capitalization of more than 90 percent over the 21-month period following the acquisition of Green Tree resulted in key management changes during the second quarter of 2000.

On June 28, 2000, Conseco's board of directors announced the hiring of Gary Wendt, former CEO of General Electric Capital Corporation (GECC).[5] Wendt brought with him instant credibility because of his record of success. More important, the board felt that Wendt brought a vision that, based on his prior experience at GECC, would guide Conseco through a very troubled period in the company's history. Three of Wendt's initial objectives were (1) to clearly define strategic business units, (2) to push decision-making authority down to these units, and (3) to implement a practice of process excellence. By defining strategic business units and providing them with the authority to achieve predetermined targets, Wendt began to decentralize the organizational structure. He introduced the concept of process excellence in order to refocus the organization on operational efficiency.

COMPANY CULTURE AND MANAGEMENT STYLE

Prior to the acquisition of Green Tree, Conseco's strategic business plan was principally driven by growth of managed assets and earnings, mostly through acquisitions. Even after two decades, the organization was still characterized by an entrepreneurial orientation and a highly centralized structure. This did not present a problem since corporatewide strategic initiatives could be effectively communicated to all levels of the organization. After all, associates numbered only about 600 in 1992, and the entire organization was centered in Carmel. However, the organization subsequently expanded through a series of acquisitions. As a result, the employee base had expanded to over 6,000 associates by 1997. Furthermore, one-third of these associates were located in Chicago or Rockford, Illinois, and Philadelphia, Pennsylvania. Consequently, the organizational structure as it existed in 1997 did not easily permit information to filter to all levels of employees within the organization. In addition, managers at all levels faced the inevitable problems of integrating the acquired companies into Conseco's organizational structure and culture.

Gary Wendt was deeply committed to process excellence. One of Wendt's first moves as Conseco's new CEO was to flatten the organization and push decision making, and thus accountability, down to specifically defined strategic business units. He also clearly articulated the objectives (both financial and operational) that were expected from these business units. In order to ensure that everyone was on board, Wendt tied officers' compensation to specifically defined goals, many of which corresponded directly to the overall goals of the respective business units.

---

[5]Conseco 10K, December 31, 2000, p. 97.

The impact of this strategy was immediate. Employees at all levels were educated on the goals of their business unit. This in turn enabled each associate, regardless of the level, to see a correlation between his or her work and the goals of the business unit and overall organization. For example, if a particular business unit was required to increase its contribution to earnings per share by 1 percent ($4.5 million of pretax operating income), saving $5,000 annually on unnecessary overnight shipments provided a quantifiable contribution to the unit's goal. A business unit with 900 employees would require average savings of only $5,000 per employee to boost operating income by $4.5 million. When the figures were broken down in this manner, Conseco's associates were better able to measure their contribution to the organization's success. This in turn had a very positive effect on morale throughout the company.

THE CURRENT CONSECO ORGANIZATION

In May 2001, Conseco, Inc.'s corporate headquarters remained in Carmel, Indiana. About 3,300 employees worked on the Carmel campus. Insurance operations were also conducted in Chicago, Rockford, and Philadelphia. Green Tree's corporate headquarters remained in St. Paul, Minnesota. Reporting directly to St. Paul were the manufactured home division (MHD), mortgage services division (MSD), credit card division, floor plan division, Conseco Bank, and Retail Services Bank.

In one of his first directives, Gary Wendt had realigned the various lines of business (e.g., life insurance, annuities, finance products) into distinct strategic business units (SBUs). At the same time, he pushed most of the corporate functions into the SBUs, therefore enabling the business units to better control overhead costs. Cash management, capital management, legal, and corporate finance were about the only remaining corporate functions, with their costs allocated to the SBUs on a quarterly basis.

CASH MANAGEMENT AT CONSECO

The cash management department was primarily responsible for managing daily cash activity, including concentration of cash, funding of accounts, settlement of trade activity and investment of excess funds. Specifically, McNutt's area was responsible for overseeing 67 individual portfolios (19 mutual funds, 19 insurance companies, 26 non-life entities, and 3 finance companies); settling an average of 177 investment trades daily; monitoring 596 operating accounts daily; administering 1,707 bank accounts; and processing between 200 and 500 wire transfers each day.

The team was divided into two groups: daily operations and administrative. Joan Pierson oversaw daily operations. She had three direct reports and a management trainee. Her area was mainly responsible for concentrating cash, reviewing custodial operations, monitoring cash efficiency, handling trade issues and problems, and reviewing and approving wire transfers. James Waters oversaw the administrative group. He had four direct reports and three indirect reports. His area was responsible for technology, account analysis, bank relationships, and bank services. Due to the significant volume of wire transfers, this area shared responsibility with Pierson's group for wire review and approval.

The cash management group was not only well educated but also experienced in cash management operations. In particular, McNutt, Pierson, and Waters had over 50 combined years of cash management experience. Pierson and Waters both came to Conseco from Bank One, one of the nation's largest financial institutions. Of the 13

exhibit 1   Conseco, Inc., Cash Management Organization Chart, April 13, 2001

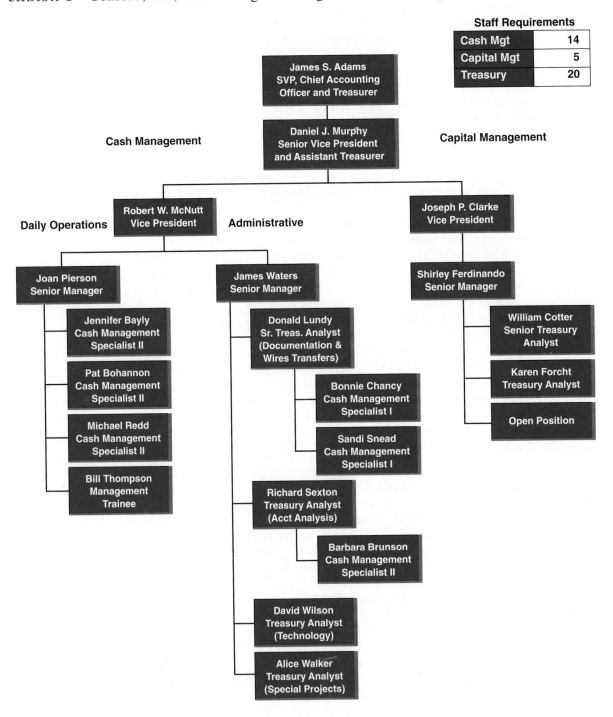

Staff Requirements	
Cash Mgt	14
Capital Mgt	5
Treasury	20

associates who worked in cash management operations under McNutt, 10 had obtained undergraduate degrees and 4 had achieved the designation of certified cash manager. See Exhibit 1 for an organization chart of the cash management group.

THE WIRE TRANSFER PROCESS—BEFORE

Prior to transferring Green Tree's cash management operations to Carmel, Robert McNutt and his group had discussed issues in several areas:

- Logistics (how many remote sites would be transmitting wire information to Carmel).
- Process flow (how information from the faxed wire transfer forms would be entered on the Bank of New York wire system).
- Controls (what controls were necessary to ensure that all wires were processed quickly for the correct amount).
- Staffing (what would be the desirable increase to staff).

The process layout that they developed had proved to be quite effective, if not offering the most efficient use possible of staff resources. In order to incorporate adequate accounting controls, the process flow involved numerous manual processes and hand-offs. Specifically, as faxes from remote locations were received, they were numbered and batched. Certain information from the wire forms was then entered into the Resource IQ system to determine if cash balances were sufficient to fund the wire transfers. If adequate cash was on hand, the wires would be forwarded for further processing. If adequate cash was not available, James Waters's area would investigate the matter.

The batched wire transfer forms were then rekeyed into the Bank of New York wire system for transmission. A member of the cash management group was then responsible for verifying the accuracy of each wire entered into the wire system.[6] Additionally, the individual responsible for verifying the accuracy of the data input was also responsible for verifying that each wire transfer was properly authorized. This procedure involved reviewing the signature on the faxed wire form and comparing it with an authorization listing that consisted of over 200 names of company personnel. Assuming that the wire transfer was properly entered on the wire system and also contained the appropriate authorization, the individual performing the review would sign off on the wire form. Wires over a specific dollar threshold required the signature of at least one officer in the treasury department. Only then could the wires be transmitted to Bank of New York for processing.

Reports generated by the Bank of New York wire system were then used to cross-check all numerically sequenced wire transfer forms. This final check was primarily intended to verify that all wire transfer forms received were actually processed and initiated. The final step involved photocopying all of the wire transfer forms processed that day and forwarding them to St. Paul via overnight delivery. St. Paul required the photocopies so that workers there could rekey the information into Green Tree's general ledger. A process flow diagram for the original wire transfer process is included as Exhibit 2.

Despite the numerous checks and balances incorporated in the process, there remained a problem with the wire transfer forms. Since they were transmitted by fax, the forms were periodically illegible. This resulted in additional calls to the originating locations to clarify information. Although incorrect information was rarely processed completely through the system, the additional follow-up steps created further inefficiencies.

---

[6]Originally, verification and approval of the wires entered onto the Bank of New York system was to be performed by a senior manager or above. However, the high volume necessitated a change. Accordingly, McNutt established a hierarchy for authorizations (e.g., wires under $5,000 could be reviewed and approved by a supervisor) that took some of the burden from his senior managers.

exhibit 2 Conseco, Inc., Cash Management Wire Transfer Process (Before Web-Based Wire Transfer System)

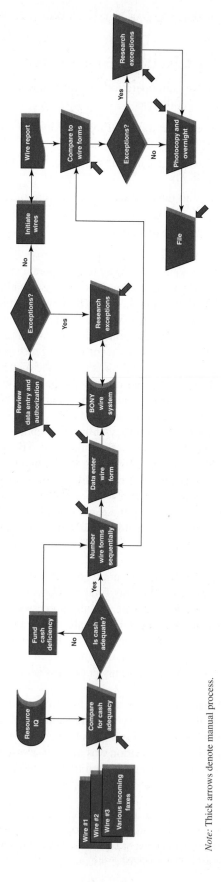

Note: Thick arrows denote manual process.

Internal auditors also expressed concern with the authenticity of faxed approvals. They noted that the signatures contained on faxed wire transfer forms could be copies from previous wires. There was simply no way to tell without calling each location to confirm the wire transfer request—an unrealistic alternative.

McNutt was well aware of the inefficiencies in the workflow. The cash management group had a number of important and unrelated value-added projects that needed to be completed. However, processing of Green Tree's wire transfers monopolized staff, leaving little spare time to dedicate to these open projects. Although McNutt and his group were pleased with their successful integration of Green Tree's substantial wire operations, they were nonetheless viewing these repetitive workflows as tedious and less than challenging. Everyone associated with wire transfers knew that the process would have to be streamlined or simplified, but no one was yet sure how to make it happen.

CREATION AND DEVELOPMENT OF THE NEW SYSTEM

Cash management had historically been quite aggressive at identifying and implementing process improvements. In fact, the treasury function, under the leadership of McNutt and of Daniel Murphy, senior vice president and assistant treasurer, had implemented many of the attributes of process excellence long before the arrival of Gary Wendt. Their previous initiatives had resulted in several million dollars of savings over several years.

The idea of utilizing the Internet to facilitate Conseco's wire transfers stemmed from an industry seminar focused on technology. McNutt and some of his staff periodically attended seminars and product demonstrations sponsored by banks or professional organizations for the purpose of networking as well as staying apprised of current technology trends. It was after one of these sessions that McNutt and others in the cash management group became particularly interested in using the Internet to transfer critical information at much greater speed. In their view, if the Internet allowed information to be transmitted so easily between two remote locations, there should be a way to automate the wire transfer process and eliminate the need to fax wire transfer forms.

Gaining Management Support

The concept of a Web-based wire system met with general approval in Carmel. Specifically, McNutt discussed the scope and purpose of the project with his immediate manager, Dan Murphy, who stated his support for the project. Conseco's internal audit department was also told about the proposed system. From Internal Audit's perspective, this new system would specifically address some of the primary control issues inherent in the current system of faxes and data entry. Murphy's approval and the subsequent sign-off from the internal audit department were encouraging. But Conseco Finance would have to support this plan as well. After all, Finance would ultimately be responsible for financing the project, primarily because its remote branch offices would stand to benefit the most from such an automated wire transfer system. Therefore, it was essential to secure the approval and support of the treasury and accounting departments at Conseco Finance to ensure that the project would proceed.

As it turned out, justifying the project to Conseco Finance did not present much of an obstacle for McNutt and his group. The benefits of implementing a Web-based wire system were compelling for Conseco Finance, cost considerations notwithstanding. Along with improving the wire transfer process at remote locations, one other appealing capability of the new system was the potential for an automatic interface to the Conseco Finance general ledger. The current process required time-consuming manual data entry that was subject to periodic human error. An automatic interface would eliminate unnecessary data entry while improving the quality of recorded wire information. Thus, Conseco Finance's accounting department shared the enthusiasm of the treasury function. With this support from his immediate boss as well as the treasury unit at Conseco Finance, McNutt discussed the concept of a Web-based wire system with Marjie Breisch, assistant vice president of internal auditing in the accounting department of Conseco Finance. Following his initial discussion with Breisch, McNutt was encouraged enough to proceed with the project. Assuming the project could be completed at a reasonable cost, Conseco Finance was supportive.

Programmer Selection and Costs

The next step for the project team was to discuss the feasibility and projected costs of designing a Web-based wire system with a programming vendor. For this stage in the development process, the team opened discussions with Codelinks, a small subsidiary of Conseco with highly educated systems programmers, most of whom were located in India.[7] Codelinks provided technical programming support to different Conseco subsidiaries as needed. It also provided programming support for unaffiliated entities.[8] McNutt had worked with representatives from Codelinks in the past, and he was well aware of the valuable resources they could provide.

The Codelinks subsidiary reacted very enthusiastically to the initial system specifications. Not only could it develop the programming for such a system, but it also believed that there was potential to copyright and sell this software in the business-to-business marketplace on behalf of Conseco, Inc. Codelinks projected a cost of $40,000 for development, which McNutt felt was a bargain given the historical costs of prior purchased technologies (e.g., the treasury workstation). From the corporation's standpoint it was even better, since the Web-based wire system was developed internally by fully utilizing Conseco's own resources (i.e., in this case, a wholly owned subsidiary), thereby avoiding significant charges from third-party vendors.

System Development

The development stage of the Web-based wire system took about eight months. This was due in part to the complexity of the system but also to difficulties in dedicating staff solely to the project. Three people besides McNutt were assigned to the project from the treasury side. Due to staffing limitations, each of these individuals had to continue to complete his normal daily Treasury responsibilities. Consequently, it was rather difficult for McNutt and his team to maintain an uninterrupted focus on the project.

Following some initial high-level discussions with Codelinks representatives in Carmel, the design stage formally began. McNutt's project team first collaborated internally on the design of wire transfer screens along with other preferred requirements of the new system (e.g., control features). Based on these discussions, samples of various wire transfer screens were created in Carmel for the purpose of providing the

---

[7]Codelinks maintained a small office on the Carmel campus. The staff in this office had most of the interaction with McNutt's group, and generally served as an intermediary between Carmel and the Indian programmers.

[8]Codelinks operated as a separate profit center, generating fee income or services provided to unaffiliated entities.

Indian programmers with initial program specifications to get the project started. Codelinks used the initial specifications to design a comprehensive flowchart of transactions, from initial log-in to the final reports generated at the conclusion of a wire transfer.

Much like the screen prints forwarded by treasury to Codelinks, the flowchart provided McNutt's team with a picture of the entire wire transfer process from start to finish. The flowchart also highlighted critical steps that were not originally contemplated by the Carmel treasury group. Creating a picture of the flow of information also served to improve the dialogue between McNutt's group and the programmers, since both parties were now using a common layout of the proposed process.

McNutt's team monitored project status through weekly discussions with the Codelinks representatives in Carmel. They in turn coordinated modifications and other system enhancements to their counterparts in India. Codelinks also established a change log on a secured Web page that allowed the Carmel team to request changes via the Internet. The log served as a useful tool to monitor the status of changes as well since a status code accompanied each change request. Completed changes were archived on the log for informational purposes.

Program changes incorporated by the Codelinks programmers were delivered to Carmel via the Internet. Sample screen prints provided from India incorporated the latest group of changes. Like the earlier flowchart provided by Codelinks, these sample screen prints served as a useful tool to evaluate system development. McNutt's group would generally review the screen prints and discuss them internally before scheduling the next call with Codelinks. Suggested modifications within the Carmel team were agreed on by the group and subsequently entered on the change log. The follow-up conference call with Codelinks served to confirm a general understanding of the status of the project as well as to clarify any outstanding issues.

At this point in the development stage, McNutt sensed that discussions between the two groups were becoming more dynamic, with suggestions coming from both sides. Recommendations were becoming more refined as the system began to take shape. The development was a collaborative process, with frequent exchanges of ideas between Codelinks and McNutt's cash management group. Since this was a homegrown system, specifications were frequently challenged and modified. For instance, at one point a question was raised as to whether there should be only one primary system administrator who was authorized to change passwords. After discussing this as a group, it was determined that no one individual should be able to unilaterally change passwords. Consequently, two approvals were eventually deemed necessary. This was one of the numerous modifications made throughout the development stage as the system began to take form. Through collaboration, an idea was becoming a reality. Furthermore, it was evident to McNutt's group that the collaboration between the treasury function and Codelinks, with its information technology expertise, was creating a more valuable end product.

Throughout the development stage, McNutt did not feel that there was much reason to actively involve associates from Conseco Finance. After all, the actual movement of cash was the responsibility of Carmel's treasury department. Therefore, it was most critical that system specifications met the Carmel-based treasury department's requirements. The Carmel cash management group had always been receptive to suggestions from Conseco Finance's personnel and had periodically revised the wire transfer forms to accommodate their requests (e.g., adding a field for a loan number). All of those changes made previously to the manual forms would be included in the new electronic wire transfer template of the Web-based system, as would informal suggestions made by the treasury unit in St. Paul. Periodically, McNutt apprised the Conseco Finance accounting department on progress, although such communications were infrequent and usually only at the request of the accounting department in St. Paul. On the other hand, the treasury function and business units of Conseco Finance never requested any type of status update during the development stage of the Web-based wire system.

THE WIRE TRANSFER PROCESS—AFTER

The new wire transfer process would almost completely eliminate manual steps that were pervasive within the previous workflow (see Exhibit 3). No longer would cash management rely on fax machines and illegible faxes. Wire information would be transmitted daily from the same remote locations that previously faxed the wires. The forms would be transmitted on electronic templates that could be saved and reused for repetitive wire transfers. Therefore, information arriving in Carmel would already be in an electronic format, eliminating the need for any further data entry. Sending photocopies of wire transfer forms overnight to St. Paul would also be rendered unnecessary with the new system.

The review and approval process in Carmel would also be simplified. The preventive controls incorporated into the system reduced the need to review every wire. Instead, wire information could be spot-checked prior to transmitting the file to Bank of New York.

The remote locations would also benefit from the new system. The remote divisions would be responsible for constructing a hierarchy for authorizing wire transfers. Once these preapproved authorizations were incorporated in the new wire system, subsequent manual verification would no longer be necessary. Perhaps the most significant feature that the new system provided these remote locations was real-time access to wire information. Summary reports could be generated at any remote site. Wires could be tracked on a real-time basis, without the need to call Carmel and await a response.

The system itself was a user-friendly, menu-driven system that would significantly enhance the efficiency and speed of the wire transfer process. A sample screen print is included as Exhibit 4. From an efficiency standpoint, the new system provided the following features:

1. Transmission of wire information was faster and more reliable.
2. The menu-driven system ensured that all required information was included on wire form before transmission could take place.
3. Follow-up phone calls for illegible information were no longer necessary.
4. The automatic download to the Bank of New York wire system eliminated manual input.
5. Spot reviews by cash management personnel replaced detail review of each wire form.
6. Divisions and branches could research the status of their own wires, eliminating the need to telephone Carmel.
7. Photocopies of all faxed wire transfer forms were no longer necessary.
8. Overnight shipments of photocopied wire transfer forms were eliminated.
9. St. Paul could access information for general ledger input one to two days earlier, thus contributing to a quicker financial close.

The efficiencies provided by this system would allow the cash management function to eliminate one and a half positions in McNutt's group. That alone would create at least $60,000 of savings on an annual basis. Eliminating photocopying and overnight

exhibit 3   Conseco, Inc., Cash Management Wire Transfer Process (Steps Eliminated After Web-Based Wire Transfer System)

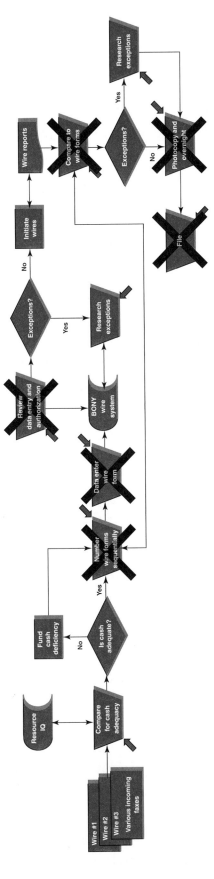

Note: Thick arrows denote manual process.

Note: Research of exceptions is indicative of system support provided to the divisions and branches. The nature of this support will be different from the legacy practices. Still, Carmel's Cash Management group will still be required to follow up special requests.

exhibit 4   Cash Transfer Web Page

Conseco Cash Management – Funds Transfer Page

Submitter - Insurance Wire

|Home |Logout|

Conseco Insurance Beneficiary Bank Only

Current Date   4/19/2001

Future Date

Amount Of Wire $

Purpose Of Wire

Funds From

Company Name   --Select a Company--

Bank Name

City

State

ABA Number

Bank Account Number

Account Description

Funds To

Bene Bank ABA Number

Beneficiary Bank Name

City

State

City and State may differ, please confirm Bank Name and Bank ABA Number.

Beneficiary Name

Beneficiary Name (continued)

Beneficiary Account Number

Reference/Additional Details

(continued)

exhibit 4   Cash Transfer Web Page *(continued)*

Account Number	Account Description	Budget Center/ LOB	Policy/ Agent Number	Amount ($)	Transaction Type
					---Select Type---
					---Select Type---
					---Select Type---
					---Select Type---
					---Select Type---
					---Select Type---
					---Select Type---

G/L entries (Not applicable for transfers to non-Conseco companies)

Account Number	Account Description	Detail Code / Budget Center/ LOB	Policy/ Agent Number	Amount ($)	Transaction Type
					---Select Type---
					---Select Type---
					---Select Type---
					---Select Type---
					---Select Type---
					---Select Type---
					---Select Type---
					---Select Type---

Save as Template   Post Wire   Cancel

mail charges would add another $5,000 in annual savings. More important, management would be able to direct resources toward more value-added projects. Therefore, the explicit cost savings of about $65,000 would be supplemented by implicit cost savings or revenue generation created by other projects.

Efficiency and speed would not be achieved at the expense of management's control over the process. On the contrary, the control environment would be substantially improved as a result of controls incorporated in the system. Some enhancements to the control environment were as follows:

1. Approval of wire transfers would be performed at the remote locations, eliminating the need to rely on faxed approvals.

2. Predetermined authorization limits would be built into the system, eliminating the possibility of someone exceeding their authority.

3. Status of wires could be tracked in real time.

4. Interface with the Bank of New York wire system would eliminate chance of data entry errors.

5. All required approvals would have to be secured before a wire could be initiated.

The primary management controls provided by the new system were as follows:

• *Input controls*	Only authorized personnel would have access to the system.
	Wires would not be initiated if authorization limits have been exceeded.
	Wires would not be initiated if all required information was not input on template.
• *Process controls*	Associates would have real-time access to wire information (i.e., the status of an outstanding wire could be verified instantly).
	Wires could be coded for additional review (e.g., two sign-offs from officers) by an originator at a remote location.
• *Output controls*	Daily wire reports could be used by management to review wire activity.
• *Feedback*	Provides shorter feedback cycles.
	Snared data base of information improves interactive communication between remote locations.

THE MOMENT OF TRUTH—CUTTING OVER TO THE NEW SYSTEM

Cash management met its objective to have error-free beta testing for one month before rolling the software out to remote locations. The rollout itself would occur in stages, with the smaller locations targeted first for obvious reasons (the first location would be the treasury department in St. Paul). Codelinks had prepared a user manual that would be provided to locations as they prepared to transition to the new system. Formal training was not planned, as the menu-driven system was generally self-explanatory. Still, cash management intended to support the transition by making resources available to address specific questions as necessary.

McNutt reflected back on the project, from idea to implementation, with much satisfaction. For the modest cost of $40,000, he had freed up significant staff time (while decreasing his staff by one and a half persons), improved his processing controls, and provided value-added information to his customers. Furthermore, the implementation of this system for wire transfers was only the beginning. He anticipated that in time, an interface with the general ledger was feasible. There would be other possible applications as well, not to mention the possibility that the software could be successfully marketed in the future.

For now, however, it was one step at a time. It was May 31, 2001, and the official cutover date was at hand. He had every reason to be confident. Training was finished, beta testing completed. There were no more delays. A new era for his cash management team was ready to begin.

case 31

West Indies Yacht Club Resort: When Cultures Collide

University of Montana

In early December, Patrick Dowd, a 30-year-old management consultant, stared out his office window at the snowy Ithaca, New York, landscape. Dowd reflected on his recent phone conversation with Jim Johnson, general manager of the 95-room West Indies Yacht Club Resort (WIYCR), located in the British Virgin Islands. Johnson sounded desperate to pull the resort out of its apparent tailspin and noted three primary areas of concern. First, expatriate manager turnover was beginning to become problematic. In the past two years, the resort had hired and then failed to retain three expatriate water-front directors and three expatriate food and beverage directors. Second, although the resort had not initiated a formal guest feedback program, Johnson estimated that guest complaints had increased from 10 per week to more than 30 per week over the past two years. The complaints were usually given by guests to staff at the front desk, written down, and passed on to Johnson: usually, they were centered on the deteriorating level of service provided by local British Virgin Islands employees. Many repeat guests claimed, "The staff just doesn't seem as motivated as it used to be." Third, there appeared to be an increasing level of tension between expatriate and local staff members. In the past, expatriates and locals seemingly found it natural to work side by side; now a noticeable gap between these groups appeared to be growing.

Johnson had come to know Dowd and his reputation for being one of the few expatriate management consultants in the region who seemed to have a real grasp on what it took to manage effectively in the Caribbean. The two had become better acquainted a year or so earlier when the world-renowned sailing school that Dowd was working for, Tradewind Ventures, was contracted to develop new family-focused programs to be offered by the resort. Through this experience, Dowd gained in-depth knowledge of the resort. Dowd's reputation and knowledge of the resort prompted Johnson's call to see if Dowd would be interested in working as a participant observer at the resort to determine the underlying reasons behind his three major concerns. Johnson requested that Dowd work at the resort during three Christmas holiday weeks to observe resort staff during the peak season. Dowd would then present an analysis of his observations and make recommendations regarding what actions could be taken to improve the situation.

All individuals and events are real but the name of the company and its managers and staff have been disguised at the request of the organization. The author also wishes to acknowledge the company's management for their assistance in gathering data for the case.

Copyright © 2001 by the *Case Research Journal* and Jeffrey P. Shay

Although Dowd had never provided consulting in this specific area (i.e., an analysis of the cultural influences on the behavior of workers in the Caribbean), he gladly accepted the challenge: It coincided with this personal experience in the region and recent courses on cross-cultural management that he had taken at Cornell University. Dowd moved over to his bookcase and pulled books, brochures, and other information off the shelf and began reading. He was departing for the British Virgin Islands in one week and wanted to get a head start on his background research.

BRITISH VIRGIN ISLANDS' TOURISM MARKET

Thirty-six islands, 16 of which are inhabited, make up the 59-square-mile chain of British Virgin Islands (BVIs) (Exhibit 1). Unlike the neighboring islands of St. Thomas and St. Croix, which underwent extensive tourism development during the 1970s and 1980s, the BVI government carefully planned and restricted growth. The result was a carefully carved niche in the Caribbean market—positioning the island chain in the exclusive/ecotourism market segment.

From 1950 to 1970, the BVIs hosted the traveling elite. During the early 1970s, the introduction and rapid growth of bareboat chartering (boats ranging from 28 feet to 50 feet, which chartered [rented] to tourists qualified to take the boats out without the assistance of a licensed captain) made the small island chain affordable for tourists with moderate budgets as well. Bareboat charters offered a unique vacation opportunity—one that connected tourists with the islands' rich natural beauty and intriguing history by allowing tourists to visit quiet harbors and villages that were void of larger cruise ships and large hotels. The BVIs' calm waters and steady trade winds were soon filled with charter boats as the chain of islands quickly became known as the premier chartering location in the world. By the early 1990s, there were more than 500 charter boats available in the Virgin Islands, with the largest company, The Moorings, managing more than 190 charter boats in the BVIs alone. Although charter industry growth in the BVIs drew the attention of major developers, the combination of strict government regulations constraining the size of new hotels and resorts and the limited access provided by the small Beef Island Airport kept these developers and mass tourism out. As a result, smaller midscale to upscale hotels and resorts were developed in the BVIs.

UPSCALE HOTELS IN THE BRITISH VIRGIN ISLANDS

Although several midscale hotels were developed and operating in the BVIs by the mid-1980s, there were only four truly upscale hotels in the island chain in addition to WIYCR (Exhibit 1). Each of these hotels provided three meals per day (not including alcoholic drinks) and access to activities (e.g., water sports equipment) as part of the price for the room. Biras Creek was an independent resort located adjacent to WIYCR's property and overlooked the North Sound of Virgin Gorda (Exhibit 2). This resort featured 34 rooms, one restaurant, three tennis courts, a private beach with a bar, a small marina, and several miles of nature trails. Peak season double occupancy rates for Biras Creek ranged from $395 to $695 per night and, similar to WIYCR, this resort was only accessible by sea. After facing high turnover of expatriate resort managers and expatriate assistant managers for the past five years, Biras Creek implemented a policy of hiring individuals for these positions for three-year contracts. After the contract was completed, managers were required to seek employment elsewhere. The

exhibit 1 Map of the British Virgin Islands and Location of Luxury Hotels and Resorts

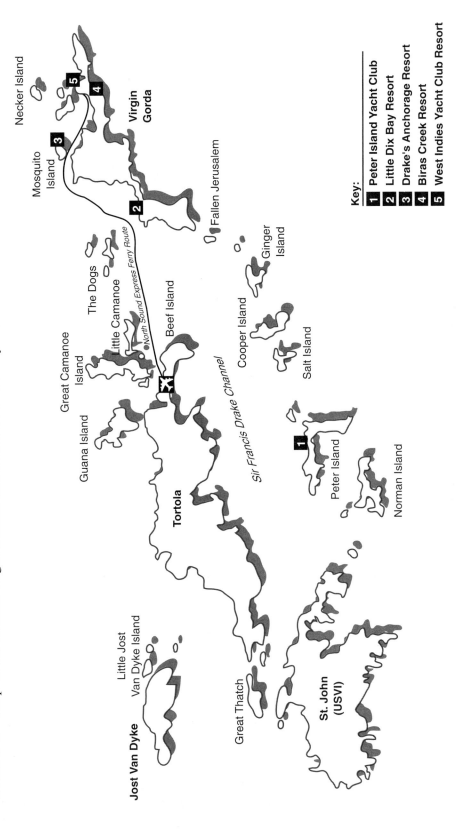

Key:
1 Peter Island Yacht Club
2 Little Dix Bay Resort
3 Drake's Anchorage Resort
4 Biras Creek Resort
5 West Indies Yacht Club Resort

exhibit 2   Virgin Gorda and Its Luxury Hotels

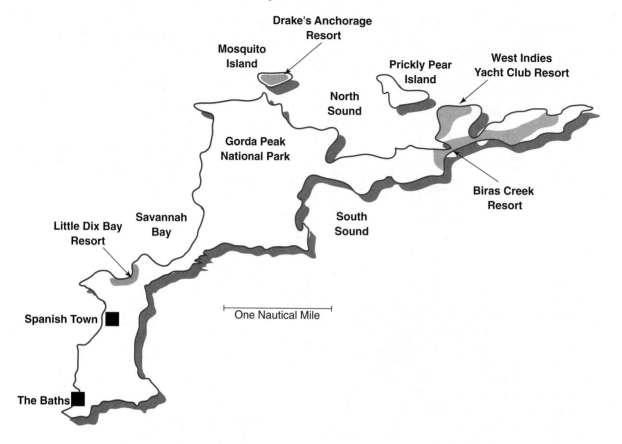

owners felt that most managers became less effective after three years because they suffered from burnout.

Drake's Anchorage was an independent resort located on the 125-acre Mosquito Island, an island situated at the northern entrance to North Sound (Exhibit 2). This small resort offered 12 rooms, a beachfront restaurant, a protected anchorage for charter boats, a picturesque hiking trail, and four secluded sandy beaches. Peak season double occupancy rates ranged from $400 to $600 per night. Expatriate managers oversaw operations at this resort as well. Guests staying at this resort were primarily interested in a relaxing, secluded vacation with limited activities.

Little Dix Bay Resort opened in 1964 as part of the Rockefeller Resort chain. In 1993, after a multimillion-dollar renovation project, Rosewood Hotels and Resorts, a Dallas-based company, acquired the management contract for the resort. This resort offered 98 rooms ranging in price from $480 to $1,000 per night during peak season for a double occupancy room. This resort was located on the northwestern shore of Virgin Gorda and overlooked the Sir Francis Drake Channel, a channel cutting through the heart of the BVI chain (Exhibit 2). In addition to a fine-dining restaurant, the resort offered small boats (i.e., Sunfish, Lasers, and Whalers), waterskiing, and day excursions to snorkeling and diving sites for guests. These amenities made Little Dix the WIYCR's strongest local competitor. Under the management of Rosewood Hotels and Resorts, expatriate managers often rotated every two to three years from one Rosewood property to another. Its prices and impeccable service attracted some of the most affluent tourists visiting the region.

Located on Peter Island, the Peter Island Yacht Club was operated by JVA Enterprises, a Michigan-based firm that acquired the resort in the early 1970s (see Exhibit 1). The resort had 50 rooms, a fine-dining restaurant, a marina, and a beautiful secluded beach. Peak season double occupancy rates ranged from $395 to $525 per night. This resort was also managed by expatriates and had been recently remodeled after being struck by two hurricanes in the early 1990s. Similar to Drake's Anchorage, the Peter Island Yacht Club primarily attracted guests looking for a secluded island vacation with limited activity.

BVI LABOR MARKET LAWS AND REGULATIONS

All hotels operating in the BVIs faced a number of challenges beyond the strict regulations on development. Perhaps the most significant challenge was dealing with local labor market laws and regulations. Despite the restricted growth in tourism, the supply of qualified service employees severely lagged demand. Four general government restrictions and policies exacerbated the challenge of hiring and managing staff. First, organizations were granted only a limited number of work permits to attract more experienced service employees from foreign countries. Expatriate work permits were granted on the basis of the total number of employees working at a resort (i.e., the more employees a resort had, the more expatriates it could hire) and the availability of locals who possessed these skills requisite for the position. The latter meant that resorts had to post positions in local newspapers for at least one month before requesting a permit for an expatriate.

Second, organizations were not permitted to lay off staff during slow seasons. This created significant challenges for resorts like WIYCR that ran at nearly 100 percent occupancy during the peak season (December through May) and as low as 40 percent during the off season (June through November). Especially hurt by this were luxury resorts that required high staffing levels to provide the services that guests expected during the peak months but were then left overstaffed during the off-season periods.

Third, policies restricting the conditions under which an employee could be fired severely limited an organization's ability to retain only the best workers. For example, one hotel manager claimed, "It is hard to fire a local employee even if he steals from us. We are often required to file documents with the government and then attend a formal hearing on why we dismissed an employee. Because it is so difficult to fire someone who steals, imagine how difficult it is to fire someone who doesn't work hard, is always late, or forgets to come to work! Our hands are really tied by these regulations."

Finally, organizations were under extreme pressure to promote BVI locals into management positions whenever possible. As noted earlier, before hiring an expatriate manager a resort had to advertise the position for at least a month. In addition, if a local approached the resort with minimal requisite skills for the job but was enthusiastic and willing to learn, the resort found it difficult in the current environment to overlook the local and hire the expatriate. As a result of these restrictions and policies, managers often found themselves overstaffed with underqualified workers.

Managers overcame these dilemmas in a number of ways. To combat regulations on foreign employees, organizations often paid foreign staff through their offshore corporate headquarters and limited the amount of time they actually spent at the resort, hotel, or other service site. In response to restrictions on laying off staff, organizations offered attractive vacation components to their employment contracts. This allowed the organization to pay lower wages and to decrease excess labor during off seasons. Managers, forced to retain staff regardless of their productivity levels, rationalized that excess labor costs were offset by lower wages in the region, avoidance of costs associated with training a new employee, and the need for extra staff during peak season.

Hotels and resorts also realized that although many entry-level employees could continue to be trained on the job, locals seeking managerial positions would require more formalized training. Unfortunately, neither the BVI nor the U.S. Virgin Islands had developed hospitality management training programs because there was no critical mass of local managers required to start such programs. Instead, hotels and resorts sent promising young staff to service training programs in the Bahamas and Bermuda in an effort to prepare them for management positions.

THE WEST INDIES YACHT CLUB RESORT

In 1964, the Kimball family sailed into the North Sound of Virgin Gorda (Exhibits 2 and 3). The sound's natural beauty captivated the family, and they knew it was a place to which the family would soon return. Nestled on the mountainside of the innermost point, the Kimballs found a shorefront pub and five cottages known as The West Indies Resort. The cottages were rustic, with only cold water running in the bathrooms. It was at the resort's pub that Joe Kimball met Armin Dubois, the property's eccentric owner. Dubois had been a pioneer Virgin Islands yachtsman who had found paradise on these shores and never left.

Under Dubois's management, an old diesel generator supplied lighting, and water was collected on the roofs and stored in cisterns that doubled as cottage foundations. The pub and restaurant served mariners when Dubois felt like it. Dubois established his own protocol. Mariners blew foghorns just off the main dock, and Dubois responded as to whether or not he was open for business. Even after being invited ashore, guests were unsure as to how long the hospitality would last. Dubois was notorious for turning off the generator to let guests know they had outstayed their welcome.

By early 1973, after several visits to North Sound, Kimball asked Dubois if he would sell or lease property so that he could build a family cottage. Dubois replied several months later that he wasn't interested in selling or leasing a small piece of property but would entertain an offer to buy out the whole property. In late 1973, Kimball did just that.

Kimball's painstaking attention to detail fostered development of the property's unique character. His vision was to provide a truly ecology-conscious and comfortable place for travelers to enjoy an environment perfect for sailing, fishing, snorkeling, diving, and combing beaches. To accomplish this, Kimball maintained many of Dubois's earlier practices. For example, the resort continued to generate its own electricity and collect and distill its own water. In addition, the resort used gray water (partially treated water) to irrigate the hillsides and used solar power wherever possible. In sharp contrast to the multistory designs used by other Caribbean developers, Kimball constructed 55 individual bungalows that were scattered along the hillside and preserved the natural beauty for which the resort was known. Kimball differentiated the resort from others in the region by acquiring the world's largest resort fleet of sailboats (e.g., J24s, JY15s, Cal 27s, Freedom 30s, Lasers, Sunfish, Rhodes 19s, Mistral sailboards) and powerboats (e.g., Boston Whalers and sport fishing boats). These carefully selected boats were easy for even inexperienced guests to handle. These acquisitions in conjunction with the resort's sailing instruction program established the resort's reputation as one of the premier water sports resorts in the world. Subsequently, Kimball changed the resort's name to the West Indies Yacht Club Resort to leverage the distinct aquatic recreational activities that the resort offered.

In 1987, with the resort's reputation growing and business booming, Kimball acquired a 15-year renewable management contract for the Sandy Point Resort, located adjacent to his property. The additional facilities, including 40 more rooms, a second restaurant, a swimming pool, a fuel dock, and beach, gave the property the critical mass necessary to compete with local and international competitors. The resort also outsourced the provision of scuba services from the Virgin Islands Dive Company. By 1990, the property had become a fully operational, water sports–oriented, ecology-conscious resort that encompassed more than 75 acres and a mile of beachfront.

The resort faced two major challenges: an occupancy cycle with high peaks and low valleys and changing market demographics. Resort managers estimated that occupancy rates from 1985 to 1990 had ranged from 80 to 100 percent during the peak season from mid-December until the end of May and 40 to 60 percent from June until early December. These fluctuations were thought to occur because people in WIYCR's customer markets sought Caribbean vacations during the colder winter months but found it hard to justify a trip to the tropics when the weather at home was more acceptable. It wasn't until the resort was forced to carry Sandy Point's additional overhead that management realized the need to address occupancy rate fluctuations. One of the most difficult costs to manage was labor. To provide the high-end service for which the resort was known, the number of staff employed by the resort had increased substantially. According to Jim Johnson, the resort was barely able to meet its guests' needs during peak season; during the slow season, the resort was overstaffed.

Changing market demographics also posed a challenge. In the past, the resort predominantly attracted couples of all ages. However, changing market demographics severely hampered its ability to attract both new and repeat guests. Former guests who had begun to raise families of their own recalled the intimate moonlit dinners and walks on the beach but could not recall ever seeing any children and, therefore, did not identify the resort as "family friendly." The resort had never turned away families but had focused marketing efforts primarily on affluent couples without children. Changing demographics forced the resort to reexamine the message conveyed by its advertising.

As a result, the resort launched a new marketing campaign in 1990. Advertising targeted families, and the staff prepared to cater to family-specific needs. The resort created sailing instruction programs for children and a host of activities designed to keep children busy while their parents enjoyed quiet times together. Family excursions onboard some of the resort's larger yachts provided the opportunity for families to sail together and explore some of the less inhabited islands. In addition, the resort added special Christmas, Easter, and Thanksgiving family programs that offered an entertaining atmosphere for the whole family. The resort changed, and the market was responding favorably as occupancy rates began to climb, even during the difficult slow season. Tom Fitch, the director of marketing and special promotions, also implemented several additional marketing initiatives in an attempt to increase occupancy during slower periods (Exhibit 3).

After several years, the resort began to see indications that its family-oriented and other marketing initiatives were working. Although the resort still had some difficulty in attracting guests during the period between June and August, the resort increased its occupancy rates during the period between September and December to 70 to 80 percent. The resort was rated as one of the best tropical resorts in the world by *Conde Nast Traveler* and maintained a strong position in the upscale segment of the BVIs. Peak season rates for double occupancy rooms ranged from to $390 to $595 per day, with meals and access to all water sports equipment included.

exhibit 3   Recent Marketing Initiatives at West Indies Yacht Club Resort

Fast Tacks Weeks. Initial efforts to fill slow-season periods centered on leveraging the resort's competitive advantage. Fitch developed the Fast Tacks Program, which targeted specific sailing groups and utilized the resort's vast sailing resources. These groups ranged from racing to cruising, from families to couples, from senior citizens to young adults. During certain weeks in the historically slow fall season, sailing celebrities were invited and gave specialized seminars to guests. Perhaps the most widely noted week is the ProAm week, in which guests are assigned to teams with some of the top match racing skippers in the world. In addition to becoming a major source of income to the resort, the weeks have become a key free advertising vehicle. Articles in sailing magazines have served not only to promote the weeks themselves but also to increase reader awareness of the sailing experience that the resort can offer.

Family Weeks. To change the resort's image, Fitch marketed special programs during traditional school-break periods to families. These weeks provided special services, including instructional and recreational programs, for children and young adults. By providing a fun yet safe environment for children, the resort left parents free to spend time alone enjoying activities designed for their tastes (e.g., harbor sunset cruises). In addition, there were several family excursions planned throughout the week that offered families an opportunity to enjoy exploring reefs and other islands together.

Capturing the Market Earlier. In addition to the family weeks and Fast Tacks weeks, marketers realized that there was another market that they had been ignoring that could significantly reduce some of its occupancy cycle troubles. Instead of waiting until a couple had established themselves or started a family, why not get them when they were tying the knot? After all, the resort provided one of the most romantic atmospheres in the Caribbean. Moreover, the majority of weddings in North America, the primary market for the resort, occurred during the slow periods of summer and fall. In response to this revelation, the resort began to actively market wedding and honeymoon packages. The resort hoped that these guests would return for second, third, and fourth honeymoons and bring their children when they started their families.

Despite the resort's prime location for water sports activities and strong reputation as the premier water sports resort in the Caribbean, management remained concerned about being able to match the service levels provided by competitors. Increased availability of water sports at competing resorts threatened WIYCR's differentiated market position. WIYCR managers knew that some former guests were vacationing at nearby Little Dix Bay because that resort now offered similar water sports activities and had rates that overlapped those offered at WIYCR. Guests had been dissatisfied with the declining level of service they had experienced during their last visit to WIYCR. WIYCR managers feared that this trend might continue if changes were not implemented soon.

The WIYCR Organization

Company Headquarters   Kimball insisted on managing strategic planning, finance, and reservations activities from an office in Chicago, Illinois (see Exhibit 4). He wanted to live in the United States and attend to other investments (none of which were in hospitality) and argued that these activities were easily separated from the day-to-day operations that took place at the resort. As the resort expanded and Kimball grew older (he was now in his 70s), he visited WIYCR less frequently and never during peak weeks. Moreover, Kimball, who once prided himself on knowing the name of each employee at the resort, knew fewer and fewer of his employees by name. As a

exhibit 4 West Indies Yacht Club Resort Organizational Chart

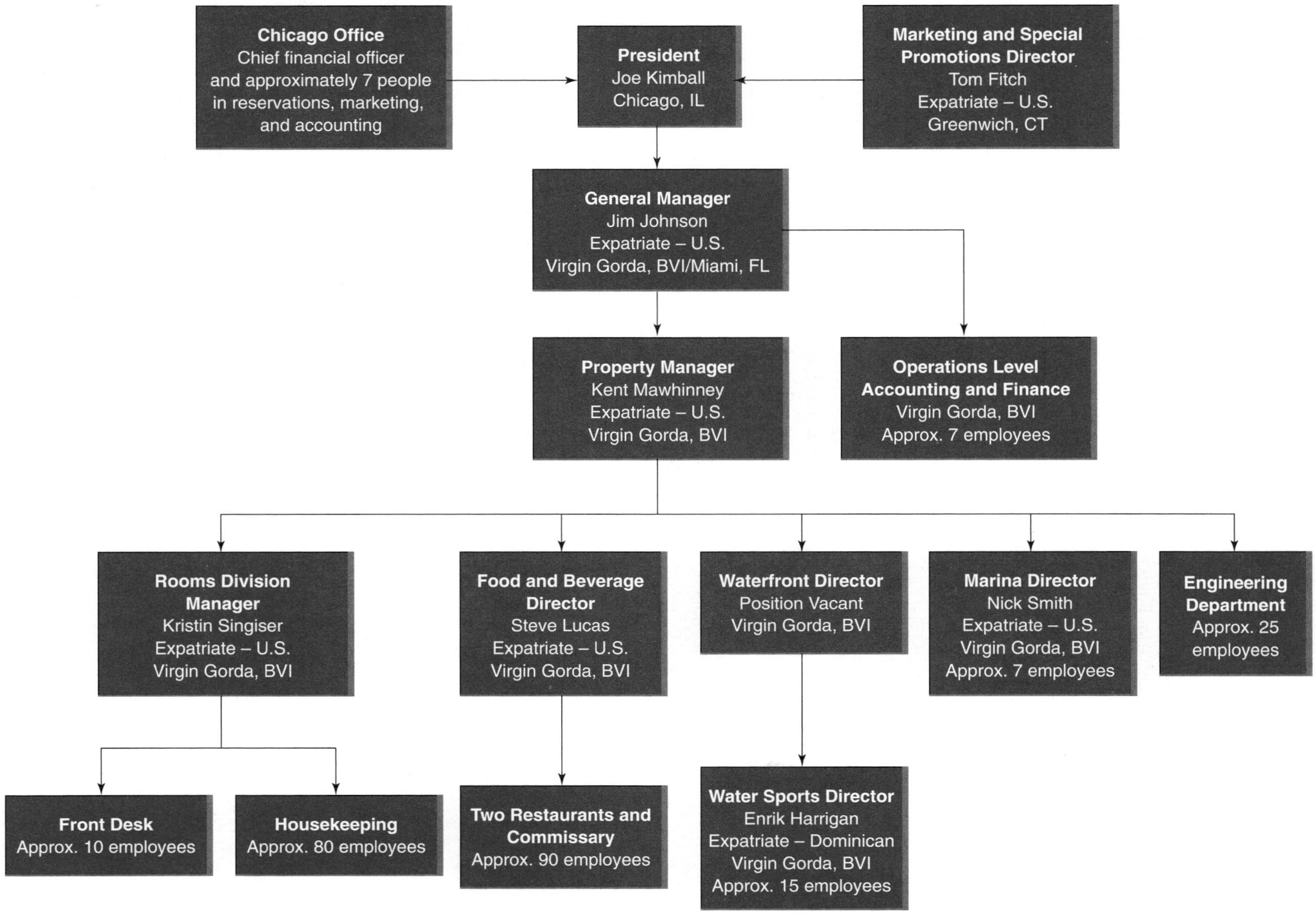

Chicago Office
Chief financial officer and approximately 7 people in reservations, marketing, and accounting

Marketing and Special Promotions Director
Tom Fitch
Expatriate – U.S.
Greenwich, CT

President
Joe Kimball
Chicago, IL

General Manager
Jim Johnson
Expatriate – U.S.
Virgin Gorda, BVI/Miami, FL

Operations Level Accounting and Finance
Virgin Gorda, BVI
Approx. 7 employees

Property Manager
Kent Mawhinney
Expatriate – U.S.
Virgin Gorda, BVI

Engineering Department
Approx. 25 employees

Marina Director
Nick Smith
Expatriate – U.S.
Virgin Gorda, BVI
Approx. 7 employees

Waterfront Director
Position Vacant
Virgin Gorda, BVI

Water Sports Director
Enrik Harrigan
Expatriate – Dominican
Virgin Gorda, BVI
Approx. 15 employees

Food and Beverage Director
Steve Lucas
Expatriate – U.S.
Virgin Gorda, BVI

Two Restaurants and Commissary
Approx. 90 employees

Rooms Division Manager
Kristin Singiser
Expatriate – U.S.
Virgin Gorda, BVI

Housekeeping
Approx. 80 employees

Front Desk
Approx. 10 employees

result, when he did visit the resort the local employees thought that Kimball seemed increasingly removed and distant.

Marketing and Special Promotions   Kimball firmly believed that marketing activities should take place close to WIYCR's target geographic markets. As a result, Tom Fitch, the 32-year-old marketing and special promotions director, managed from a small office in the southwestern corner of Connecticut. Fitch grew up as an active sailing competitor on Long Island Sound (an area that stretches from New York City to the southeastern tip of Connecticut) sailing circuit and was well connected within the sailing industry. Fitch's strong sailing background coupled with being centrally located within the largest sailing community in the United States afforded great opportunities for promoting the resort with its target market. Unlike Kimball, Fitch was always on property during the high season and special promotions weeks. Fitch believed that it was important during these weeks for him to tend to the special needs of guests he had attracted to the resort. Local employees often underestimated the work required to plan and market these programs. Seeing him socialize with guests while on property, local employees questioned whether his job was really full-time once he left the resort and returned to the states. After all, they saw him only periodically when he came in for a few weeks, threw large parties, and frantically tried to assure that the guests' needs were met.

Jim Johnson, General Manager   In the WIYCR organization, the general manager traditionally oversaw all functional areas of the hotel and played an important role in strategic planning. Jim Johnson, the 48-year-old expatriate general manager originally from the United States, was hired in 1990 on the basis of his extensive hospitality experience and academic training. His experience included several years as assistant manager of Little Dix Bay Resort and a master's degree in hospitality management from Cornell University. Johnson worked from his home in Miami, Florida, most of the time in order to spend more time with his family, provide his children with stronger educational opportunities than those offered in the BVIs, and reduce the number of expatriate permits that the resort required. Johnson averaged approximately two weeks at the resort per month, staying for longer periods of time during the high season and shorter periods of time during the low season. Johnson spent most of the time while at the resort in his office and in meetings with the heads of the various departments. Local employees often referred to him as a "behind the scenes" manager; he provided detailed goals, objectives, and actions for his staff but was not present for the execution of plans. Johnson generally felt confident in his management team, especially his property manager, whom he personally recruited and hired.

Kent Mawhinney, Property Manager   The property manager was generally the second in command at the WIYCR and was responsible for implementing the general manager's plans and monitoring the results. Kent Mawhinney, the 40-year-old property manager from the United States, had been hired by Johnson almost three years ago and had an impressive background that included working on the management staff for six years at Caneel Bay, a Rockefeller Resort located on nearby St. John (in the U.S. Virgin Islands). Mawhinney was a hands-on manager who believed that "management by walking around" was needed in the Caribbean. Resort employees knew Mawhinney as a manager who was willing to get his hands dirty, and they greatly appreciated this attitude.

Kristin Singiser, Rooms Division Manager   The rooms division manager was responsible for two departments at the WIYCR: housekeeping and the front desk. To many guests, it seemed like Kristin Singiser had been at the resort forever. In fact,

Singiser had been hired 11 years ago as part of the front desk staff and was now 35 years old. She was born and raised in the midwestern United States. She came to the resort with little hotel industry experience, had only been to the Caribbean as a tourist prior to taking the job, and proceeded to work her way up in the WIYCR organization to her current position. She was well respected by the guests and local staff because of her never-ending energy and constant smile. However, after 11 years at the property Singiser was beginning to get more frustrated with problems she faced over and over again. Her staff knew how Singiser felt but also knew that the issues were mainly between her and the Chicago office.

Steve Lucas, Food and Beverage Director

The food and beverage director was responsible for two restaurants, a commissary, an employee dining facility, and three bars that were located on the WIYCR property. The resort had experienced high turnover in this position, with three food and beverage directors resigning to return to the United States within the past two years alone. Steve Lucas, 28 years old, with recent experience working as the food and beverage director for an exclusive California resort, was currently filling this position. Lucas was from the United States and had an impressive restaurant industry track record. He had been hired by the resort a month earlier and arrived at the property during the first week of December. Lucas had no previous experience working outside the United States.

Nick Smith, Marina Director

The marina director was responsible for the resort's growing marina operations, run largely out of the Davey Jones Marina. This marina included dock space for up to 35 boats, a fuel and water dock, and yacht maintenance services. The marina attracted yachting enthusiasts who were seeking a short stay in a resort environment. Nick Smith was promoted eight years ago to his current position as marina director. Smith, now 45 years old, was originally from the United States and had been working at the resort for nearly 15 years. He lived on the property along with his wife and their six-year-old daughter.

Waterfront Director

The waterfront director's position was created to assign responsibility to oversee the growing water front activities at the resort. The director's responsibilities included overseeing the water sports department and its director (as well as the resort's fleet of day excursion boats), planning and promoting day excursions, and developing and maintaining relationships with the sites that day excursions visited. The resort had hired several expatriates for the waterfront director position. For a variety of reasons, these expatriates had not worked out. Two had become alcoholics, and one had mysteriously packed his belongings and departed in the middle of the night. This position was currently vacant, with most responsibilities assumed by Nick Smith and Enrik Harrigan.

Enrik Harrigan, Water Sports Director

The water sports director was primarily responsible for the resort's fleet of small- to medium-sized boats and its windsurfing program. From 1986 until 1992, the water sports department had been under the leadership of Bill Jones, a Canadian who fell in love with the resort while staying there as a guest. His easygoing management style was well respected by a staff that would seemingly do anything for him. Unfortunately for the resort, Bill returned to Canada in 1992. The next-most-senior member of the water sports staff was 27-year-old Enrik Harrigan, a windsurfing guru from Dominica (part of the Windward Island chain located in the southern Caribbean Sea) who had been working at the resort for about five years. Harrigan assumed the responsibilities as water sports director and was well respected by the staff but found he had difficulty assigning tasks and managing the operation.

DOWD ARRIVES IN THE BRITISH VIRGIN ISLANDS

On December 15, Patrick Dowd arrived at WIYCR. He found it hard to imagine the imminent transformation of the serene British Virgin Islands into an environment overwhelmed by a frenzy of holiday tourist activity. Within a few days, thousands of tourists would invade the BVIs, stretching its natural, human, and capital resources to their limits. The natural beauty that the islands offered was a familiar sight for Dowd, who had spent 10 years working as a management consultant for small- to medium-sized hotels in the Caribbean. Tradewind Ventures, a world-renowned sailing school, introduced him to the British Virgin Islands through summer employment as a skipper and operations director in 1986. For the next six years, Dowd worked year-round for Tradewind Ventures as a management consultant during the winter months and operations director during the summer. During his tenure with Tradewind Ventures, Dowd added the Cabarete Beach Hotel (Cabarete, Dominican Republic) and the West Indies Yacht Club Resort (Virgin Gorda, British Virgin Islands) to his client base. In addition, Dowd had completed his bachelor of science and masters in business administration at Babson College. The primary point of differentiation between Dowd's consulting services and those offered by the larger consulting companies rested in his understanding of the Caribbean market and, most important, its people. His understanding had evolved through interactions both professionally and socially with local nationals from the region. Mike McClane, manager of a nearby charter boat company, respected Dowd's ability to understand the local nationals, saying, "You really must understand my employees. Heck, Small Craft [employee's nickname] considers you a friend, and I'm the only other outsider I know of to accomplish that. It took me five years; you've done it in two summers!"

Driven largely by his desire to study the challenges associated with expatriate management assignments, Dowd had entered the doctoral program in hotel administration at Cornell University the previous September. Dowd hoped that his understanding of the local culture would be enhanced by what he had learned over the past semester in the classroom at Cornell. His first semester introduced him to theoretical explanations for differences in behaviors across cultures. He wondered whether these tools would be helpful for interpreting behaviors and then communicating what they meant to Johnson and his managers.

DOWD'S OBSERVATIONS OF OPERATIONS

Night had fallen on the Caribbean, and as the North Sound Express (a ferry that took passengers from the Beef Island Airport on Tortola to various resort locations on Virgin Gorda—see Exhibit 1) approached the main dock at WIYCR, Dowd noticed the familiar stride of a former colleague from Tradewind Ventures. Dave Pickering, a 22-year-old Cleveland native, had been working in the water sports department for nearly a month and was looking forward to Dowd's arrival. Pickering had worked with Dowd for the past three summers as a skipper and program director at Tradewind Ventures. Although Pickering had worked in the Caribbean for these three summers, his interactions had been primarily with the expatriate staff that Tradewind Ventures brought down each summer. Working side by side with the locals was a much different experience. Pickering had been hired by WIYCR two weeks earlier as part of the water sports staff. He was primarily responsible for teaching sailing lessons, taking guests out on the larger boats, and signing out water sports equipment to guests.

Pickering extended an enthusiastic and firm handshake as Dowd got off the ferry. "Welcome to The Rock," he said. "The Rock" was the term coined by expatriates to describe living at the secluded resort. The two walked up the dock, and Pickering paused for a minute. "Looks like someone forgot to come out and greet the guests again. It will take me a few minutes to give the briefing, so go along to the front desk if you want. I'm sure you're familiar with the routine. We're going out to Saba Rock (a small island about 300 feet off the resort's north beach) in about a half-hour, so why don't you drop your stuff in your room and meet me at the dinghy dock." Dowd nodded headed for the front desk.

Kristin Singiser met Dowd at the front desk, and they exchanged greetings. Suddenly, Singiser looked confused. "Who met you down on the docks?" she asked.

"Dave was down there and is giving the guest briefing," he replied.

"That's odd. Dave is supposed to be off tonight. I wonder who was supposed to meet you down there?" Singiser said with a disturbed look on her face. She assigned Dowd to his room, picked up the radio microphone, and called one of the golf cart chauffeurs to come for him. As Dowd walked out of the lobby, he thought, "What would have happened if nobody showed up to greet us? Sure, I'm working here, but those people who were on the boat with me are paying thousands of dollars to be here. What would they think?"

Although Dowd knew that he had an 8 AM meeting with Johnson, he could not help but enjoy the company of his island friends. Saba Rock was the only real hideout for expatriates and local national employees from WIYCR. A few tourists managed to find a dinghy ride out to the small pub on the half-acre island, but they were usually the more adventurous types and were always welcome.

Pickering always had such a positive disposition; however, tonight a hint of irritability seemed to come across in his voice. You know why I am here . . . right?" Dowd asked.

"Yes, I think so. Kent Mawhinney told me something about you coming down here to observe operations and make some suggestions for improvements. Boy, do I have some suggestions. How about firing everyone and bringing down our old staff from Tradewind Ventures?" he candidly replied. Dowd couldn't help but inquire further. Pickering said that when he arrived a few weeks earlier, the employees really welcomed him aboard. This seemed normal; Pickering had always been considered one of the more affable members of the Tradewind Ventures staff. Pickering said that each day coworkers in the water sports department distanced themselves more and more. Pickering said, "The harder I work, the greater the distance between us becomes."

"I don't understand," Pickering continued. "I've even tried to do some of their work to get back in good favor with them, but nothing seems to work. It's gotten to the point where I think some of these guys don't like me at all."

As Pickering continued, he questioned whether the resort's compensation system could ever work. Employees were paid an hourly rate based on their tenure at the resort. As Pickering understood the resort's compensation system, each year resort employees were given a raise without any performance review. Dowd asked Pickering for some concrete examples why the system wasn't working. Pickering explained, "Even some of the most senior guys in the water sports department hide from work. These senior employees know that they will get raises even if they don't do a good job . . . excuse me, these guys get raises even if they don't do their job at all."

Pickering did not understand why the locals weren't taking advantage of the opportunity to get tips. Pickering was making $50 to $100 extra per day on tips alone; when he told his fellow employees this, they laughed and said it wasn't worth that much to them to have to work so hard. Dowd asked if Pickering had discussed his concerns with any of the managers. Pickering replied that he'd had a few conversations with Mawhinney about it but hadn't been able to find an opportunity to speak with

Johnson. The discussion continued until Dowd's eyes began to grow heavy. He climbed in a dinghy and headed back to the resort.

Johnson arrived at the Clubhouse Restaurant just a few minutes past 8 AM. Dowd had already found his way to the breakfast buffet and sat with a plate full of local fruits and pastries. Johnson seemed rushed and told Dowd that he would have to keep the meeting short. Johnson told Dowd that he did not want to influence Dowd's observations by explaining what he thought were the problem areas at the resort. Instead, Johnson would point out departments generating complaints and let Dowd observe without any biases. Dowd realized that this would be difficult because he knew so many of the employees, but it was a role in which Dowd had been successful in the past. Dowd found that getting to the bottom of problems in organizations in the Caribbean often required gaining acceptance by the group, a status that was achieved only through gaining local employees' trust and establishing friendships. It was only then that employees would open up. Johnson wanted Dowd to focus on front desk, food and beverage, and water sports services and indicate that the resort's staff was at Dowd's service in terms of discussing operations. Johnson finished his coffee, wished Dowd luck, and left. As he watched Johnson walk out the door, Dowd thought, "It's always so easy to pick out the expatriate down here . . . we always seem in such a hurry."

Dowd finished his breakfast and made his way down the shoreline to meet with Mawhinney, the property manager. He was greeted by Mawhinney at the top of the spiral staircase leading to the administrative offices. Mawhinney told Dowd that he was leaving on his daily rounds and asked Dowd to join him. Mawhinney had extensive experience working in the Caribbean, and Dowd knew he would be a rich resource. As they walked off to their first stop, Dowd bluntly asked Mawhinney what he thought the main problems were at the resort. Mawhinney replied that the most basic problem was getting plans implemented. When Mawhinney managed in the United States, his employees had been concerned with the opportunity for advancement and really worked hard to prove themselves. In the Caribbean, things were different. Local employment laws almost guaranteed jobs, and employees knew this. As a result, employees were more concerned with fitting in with their coworkers than with making a good impression. The resort had provided opportunities for some of the locals to be promoted, but few seemed interested. In his opinion, locals did not want the added responsibility, even if it meant more money. In some cases, the resort thought that rewarding the best employees with a title and some authority would help management gain more control over their employees. The result was an employee with a title who was unwilling to take on any of the job's responsibilities. "If the employees only realized what they could have if they worked a little harder and took these positions seriously, they could move up in the organization," Mawhinney commented.

The property tour took about an hour. Mawhinney visited each department head, a mix of local nationals and expatriates (see Exhibit 4). His conversations instilled a sense of urgency to get the resort in shape for the coming week. In each case, he offered assistance in any way necessary to ensure reaching the resort's desired goals and objectives. Dowd was particularly impressed by the amount of detail that Mawhinney recalled regarding each manager's immediate challenges. Mawhinney pointed out to Dowd that one of the main differences between managing in the United States and managing in the Caribbean is how managers have to communicate with employees. Because there is a 70 percent functional illiteracy rate on the property, he could not rely on memos as he had in the States. Instead, he managed by physically demonstrating to his staff what had to be done. For example, Mawhinney's maintenance staff had been told several times that garbage was to be placed in a specific storage area. The staff continued storing the trash in the wrong place until Mawhinney physically showed them where and how it was to be stored.

By 10:30 AM, Mawhinney and Dowd had completed the tour of the resort with the exception of the restaurants. As the two approached the clubhouse dining area, Dowd noticed a man in his early 30s arguing with a local cook who looked to be in his 50s. (Later, Dowd would find out that this was the head chef, who had worked at the resort for more than 20 years.)

"Why didn't you tell me that you couldn't get the ingredients for cheesecake? The menus have already been printed, and now we're going to look like fools! What is wrong with you people?" the man asked the cook.

Mawhinney interrupted, "Steve, what seems to be the problem?"

"Well, once again they failed to tell me that something was wrong," Steve Lucas replied.

Mawhinney looked at the cook and asked if he could have a moment alone with Lucas. The cook welcomed the opportunity to leave the tense situation. Mawhinney calmed Lucas down and said that it was just part of the challenge of working in paradise. Mawhinney guided Lucas back over to Dowd, introduced the two, and informed Dowd that he had to get back to his office for a conference call with the resort's head office in Chicago.

Lucas and Dowd exchanged stories about their backgrounds. Lucas had been hired two weeks ago because the former food and beverage director had quit. When Dowd asked him whether he liked his new job, Lucas replied:

> It's a bit early to tell. One thing is for sure . . . it's a lot more challenging than I ever imagined! I know the staff has been here for a while, but I don't know how they ever managed. They seem to work as a "seat of your pants" type operation. No planning, no commitment, no enthusiasm. It's surprising, because I have heard that this resort is one of the best places for people down here to work. I guess the biggest challenge is the fact that I know the people in Chicago expect big things from me, and I plan to deliver . . . no matter what it takes. I just wish I had more time to train these people properly before we are hit with the big rush next week. Did you know that The Clubhouse and The Carvery are expected to serve 1,000 dinners on New Year's Eve? After dinner, we expect that another 500 to 800 charter boat tourists will be coming ashore for the entertainment at the bar. Meanwhile, my staff is accustomed to our average nightly seating of about 100 for the rest of the year. This will be a big test for them . . . and, I guess for me, as well.

Dowd asked Lucas how he was adjusting to the local culture. "I am having a great time so far. It's so much fun hanging out with a different group of guests every week. I am not looking forward to the slow season around here though. Then, who will I have to hang around with? I haven't made very many local friends and that's mostly because I want to keep business and pleasure separate anyway."

Their conversation went on for another 20 minutes. Finally, Lucas looked eager to get back to overseeing the preparations for tonight's meal, so Dowd closed the conversation and moved on. As Dowd walked away, he stopped to glance back at Lucas. Lucas was hovering over one of his staff, checking to make sure that each ingredient was properly measured before being added to the pot. "What a way to have to manage," Dowd thought.

Singiser entered the restaurant with an apologetic look on her face. "Sorry I am so late. Glad you found yourself a piña colada to keep you occupied," she said.

"So, what took you so long?" Dowd asked jokingly.

Singiser explained that it had been a long day. The Chicago office had overbooked the resort by 20 percent for the coming week without telling the guests that there might be some inconveniences. Therefore, it was her job to greet guests on the dock and tell some of them that they would have to stay on board one of the resort's larger charter boats for a few nights until rooms became available. Meanwhile, other families were told that the children and parents would be staying at opposite ends of the resort. As if dealing with understandably irate guests was not enough, her staff had made several disturbing remarks:

> They asked me, "Why is everyone always coming down on us about providing good service when Chicago pulls a stunt like this?" I just don't know how to reply. My staff faces angry guests all day as a result of this fiasco. How can I expect them to be courteous when the guests are so mad and the staff had no influence on the situation? The worst part is that Chicago has done this to us to for the past three years. Each time, I tell my staff to just manage this time and I'll try to make sure it doesn't happen again. I go to bat for them but seem to strike out every time.

Over a lobster dinner, the two discussed many other challenges that Singiser had faced over the years. Much of the locals' behavior she had become accustomed to, but some things were still frustrating. "Sometimes you feel like the only way you can manage these people is to bash them over the head with it," she commented. Apparently, her style was to demonstrate exactly what she expected of her front desk staff, knowing that some of them would get it right and others would continue to do it their own way. When they continued to do it their own way, it was time for "bashing them over the head with it." Despite all of her frustrations, Singiser was probably the most respected expatriate on the WIYCR staff. Over her long tenure, she had adapted to the local culture, made close friends with locals, and recognized what it took to get things done. However, she still felt challenged when trying to motivate her staff. "Money, opportunity for advancement, all of the normal incentives—they all don't seem to make any impact," she said.

In previous conversations with Singiser's staff, Dowd had solicited their opinions. Most staff said that Singiser was different. She had a sincere interest in them and was involved with the local culture. She frequently took trips with her staff to the neighboring islands and invited employees to her bungalow for dinner on occasion. Sure, she was tough, but her staff felt that managers had to be that way sometimes.

As they finished their meals and enjoyed an after-dinner drink, Singiser suggested that Dowd spend at least a day working alongside the staff at water sports. That would give him an inside look at the department critical to the resort's success. After all, water sports were the main reason that guests chose the resort for their vacation.

Walking down the path to the water sports shack, Dowd knew that he had an interesting day ahead of him. He had extensive water sports experience but had only observed WIYCR's operations from a guest's perspective. Throughout the day, Dowd took mental notes on how the department operated and how the locals worked (or didn't work). Harrigan was behind the desk at the shack most of the day; his assistant Mitchell (a 25-year-old Virgin Gordan) raced about the harbor on a 15-foot Whaler (a small powerboat) taking guests out to boats. It was surprising that Harrigan allowed some of his senior staff to avoid work. Fergus and Muhammad (both in their late 20s and from Virgin Gorda), for example, conveniently wandered off during the peak morning rush. Guests were left standing in line for 15 minutes because the desk was short-staffed. With Fergus's and Muhammad's help at the desk, Dowd thought that the wait could be reduced to five minutes. The daylight sun was waning, and guests wanted to get out on the water. When some of the senior staff did interact with guests, they were reserved and not overly courteous. Guests asked questions, and the staff mumbled incoherent responses. However, one group of guests did have an advantage:

guests who had bought several rounds of drinks for the staff the previous evening. When these guests arrived at the desk, the senior staff would jump to their feet and greet them like these guests were part of the local family. Dowd jokingly referred to this as "pre-service tipping."

Working at the water sports department, Dowd found himself hustling the whole day, thinking that maybe some of it would rub off on his fellow workers. He had a slight advantage over Pickering's socialization into the group because Dowd had worked alongside the local staff during the three previous Thanksgiving vacations as part of a joint project between WIYCR and Tradewind Ventures. The group had accepted him long ago. He thought, "Maybe if they see me working hard, they will think it's OK." By the end of his first day, Dowd had earned $100 in tips. He told the local staff, and they didn't believe him until he laid the money on the counter. He explained how they could easily do the same thing and make a killing this week. They reluctantly replied, "Yeah, right, like we could do that."

At the end of the day, Dowd, Fergus, and Muhammad stopped for a beer at the commissary (a small snack bar). Dowd asked them how they thought things were going in the water sports department. Fergus replied, "Things went more smoothly when Bill [Jones] was around. He gave us clear directions regarding what we had to do for the day, and we did it. Things are different with Enrik [Harrigan]. He's really laid back, and we often don't know what we're supposed to be doing." Dowd also inquired about how they felt about the expatriates that worked at the resort, and Muhammad's comments summarized the discussion: "We have so many managers from the States, and they don't stay here very long. Many of them think they can just come in here, and we'll instantly be their friends. I'm tired of making friends just to have them leave a year later. The worst part is that they think we want to become managers like them. Managing people takes too much effort. I'm just not interested in leaving my friends behind just to make a little more money."

When Dowd was not speaking with the resort's management or its employees, he spent his time with the guests. The following quotes summarized the comments made by guests regarding guest interactions with the resort's staff:

> There is nothing for us to do at night from December 23 until December 26. I know that the staff has to celebrate Christmas, but it would have been nice for us to have something to do.

> I was waiting in line for almost 10 minutes at the bar. They only had two bartenders on, and they moved so slowly. Plus, all the guests are getting their own drinks. Why do they have five waitresses? They just stood there. Can't they work behind the bar, too?

> We were out on the Almond Walk (a terrace area attached to the resort's main restaurant) and thought that a waiter would come by. When we asked one of the waitresses, she said that she was assigned to the dining room. The dining room had served its last guest an hour before and was located about 25 feet from the Almond Walk. Someone should tell them that it's OK to go out onto the walk and serve other guests.

> I asked the restaurant manager to call a waiter over for me, but I'll never do that again. He went over to his wait staff and told them that they were incompetent. I felt so bad. I think that the staff purposely avoided our table for the rest of the night because they were afraid of getting into trouble again.

> I was looking forward to being greeted at the docks by someone who would help me with my bags. After all, I'd just finished a 10-hour trip and am paying a lot of money to be here. When I asked the front desk staff, they apologized and said that someone must have forgotten. It's surprising that I am paying this much money for people to forget. What's that about first impressions being the most important?

Reading the brochure, I really thought that the programs for the kids sounded great. However, the first few days my kids said that the staff weren't very interested in making them have a good time. They seemed like they were more interested in when they got off work than with making my kids have a good time. Then they had Dave. What a difference! The kids came back excited about everything they did that day. He was so energetic and interested in my kids.

I told the front desk that they should really spray for bugs out on the terrace or get one of those bug lamps. There are so many mosquitoes out there in the evening. The staff doesn't seem to be too interested in responding though.

We called maintenance the other day to tell them that our rooms are not fully operational in terms of things like showers, screens and faucets working. It's kind of surprising to be at a resort like this without at least the basics. They said they would send someone by today, but that was three days ago. I think I will go to one of the other managers next.

Today I went to the beach at around 10 AM, and they were already out of towels again. The beach attendant said that he would bring some back as soon as he found them. I guess he didn't find any because it's been three hours, although I did see him standing around at the other end of the resort talking with some friends. Do you think he even looked for them?

Listening to these comments, Dowd wondered which problems related to poor management relations with local staff, which related to simply poor work by the local staff, and which related to poor managing by the expatriates. One thing was sure— issues in all of these areas were beginning to affect the guests.

MAKING SENSE OF IT ALL

Dowd had been at the resort for just one week, and the information from interviews with managers, local employees, and resort guests along with personal observations filled his head as he began to prepare for his meeting with Johnson the following morning. It was clear that there needed to be some changes at the resort if Johnson was going to resolve the issues concerning expatriate turnover, increasing guest complaints, and the level of tension between some of the expatriate managers and the local employees. The first wave of peak season guests, those coming for the Christmas holiday, would arrive tomorrow and stretch the resort's resources to their limits. Dowd wondered how he could best use the information gathered to analyze the current situation and provide some course of action for Johnson that would address his concerns. Dowd sat at his table and began to organize his thoughts.

case 32

AES Corporation: Values, Culture, and Operating Practices at a Global Power Company

Arthur A. Thompson
The University of Alabama

In the spring of 2001, AES Corporation seemed on track for a record-setting year. Since its founding in 1981, the company, headquartered in Arlington, Virginia, had evolved into the world's largest global power company. AES owned or had a part interest in 166 power plants totaling nearly 56,700 megawatts (mW)[1] of generating capability in 24 countries. AES also had 22 separate electric distribution businesses (consisting of substations, poles, wires, transformers, and other equipment associated with delivering electricity); several local natural gas distribution companies; and two steam heat distribution businesses that served a combined total of 17.6 million customers in nine countries around the world. And AES had recently acquired operations engaged in supplying electricity and natural gas to wholesale and retail users in several countries where customers, heretofore captive to local monopoly electricity and natural gas providers, were being given the freedom to choose their energy suppliers. AES's smallest area of operations, begun in 2000, involved providing retail telecommunication services in selected locales in Brazil and the United States. Altogether, as of early 2001, AES's operations included 139 businesses in 32 countries. To further spur the company's growth and expand its geographic operating scope in these market arenas, AES was pursuing some 165 new business opportunities in more than 45 countries.

Since early 1999, AES had more than doubled its electric generating capacity in Latin America, making it the second largest player in the region after Endesa, an

---

[1] A megawatt (mW) equals 1,000 kilowatts (kW); 1 kW of generating capability provides the electricity output sufficient to power ten 100-watt lightbulbs. It takes about 10–15 kW of generating capability to provide electric service to a typical modern home; hence, a 500 mW power plant can supply the electricity needs of approximately 40,000 homes. Modern power plants can range in size from as small as 100 mW to as large as 4,000 mW.

aggressive Spain-based company that was focusing much of its international growth efforts in Latin America. AES's recent acquisition of Chile's Gener SA had made it the leading electricity supplier in Argentina, and it was already the leading electricity supplier in Venezuela and Brazil. Furthermore, AES had major investments in Kazakhstan, the Republic of Georgia (a part of the Soviet bloc), Pakistan, India, the United Kingdom, China, Hungary, Panama, Colombia, and Australia, among others. English was the first language of less than 25 percent of AES's 26,600 employees.

	2000	1999	1998	1997	1996
Assets (millions)	$31,033	$20,880	$10,781	$8,909	$3,622
Revenues (millions)	$ 6,691	$ 3,253	$ 2,398	$1,411	$ 835
Net income (millions)	$ 665	$ 377	$ 311	$ 188	$ 125
Earnings per share ($/share)	$ 1.46	$ 0.96	$ 0.83	$ 0.55	$ 0.41
Shareholders' equity (millions)	$ 4,811	$ 2,637	$ 1,794	$1,481	$ 721

AES's growth during the past five years had been quite impressive: The company's strong performance had rewarded investors handsomely—the company's common stock had split 3-for-2 in 1994, 2-for-1 in 1997, and 2-for-1 in 2000. Even in a severely depressed stock market, the company's shares were trading in early 2001 in the $45–$55 range (equal to a hefty 30 to 40 times the $1.46 per share earned in 2000). The all-time-high stock price was $70, reached in October 2000. AES management expected the company to earn $1.75–$1.90 per share in 2001.

COMPANY BACKGROUND

AES Corporation was cofounded by Roger Sant and Dennis Bakke, a pair of energy conservation enthusiasts who had first learned the energy business working with the U.S. Federal Energy Administration (now the Department of Energy). About the time that Sant decided to give up his post teaching finance at Stanford University's graduate School of Business Administration to become assistant administrator for energy conservation and the environment at the FEA, the Organization of Petroleum Exporting Countries (OPEC) launched its oil embargo and threw the world's energy market into a turmoil trying to cope with short supplies, skyrocketing energy prices, and long lines at gas stations. Dennis Bakke, who had an MBA from Harvard and was an assistant to the head of the FEA, became Sant's chief deputy over energy conservation. Sant quickly determined that innovative energy conservation measures ought to be viewed as a new and reliable "source" of energy, and he was instrumental in helping the FEA marshal convincing evidence that implementing an assortment of conservation measures could mean saving 25 to 50 percent of the oil then used in the United States, the equivalent of $3 to $6 per barrel. His arguments got the attention of President Gerald Ford and led to a meeting with the president's cabinet to discuss an array of energy conservation opportunities.

The Cofounders' Experiences at the Mellon Institute

In 1977, Roger Sant was recruited by Carnegie Mellon University to organize and run the Mellon Institute Energy Productivity Center, a think tank whose mission was to continue to press the theme that energy conservation makes good economic sense. Dennis Bakke joined Sant at the Mellon Center, whose team of experts studied all aspects of energy use—from energy's role in powering machinery and industrial processes to the purposes it served in homes, businesses, and transportation. The research findings led Sant and Bakke to regard energy as a commodity used as a means to other ends, their reasoning being that what energy users were really buying was comfort, convenience, productivity, or mobility and that they would ultimately gravitate toward whatever energy source proved economical, clean, and safe.

They also came to realize that energy conservation was not the sole answer to the "energy crisis" of the late 1970s and early 1980s. Modern industrial societies required energy to grow and function effectively, and large increases in global electricity production were needed if people in developing nations were to avoid perpetual poverty and low living standards. Sant and Bakke concluded that wise energy use was necessary but not sufficient—what also needed to occur was to produce heat, light, and power in the most efficient manner and at the lowest possible cost. They believed that "independent" companies operating in a competitive market arena could do a much better job of boosting efficiency and minimizing costs than could regulated utility monopolies and government-owned electricity providers—though to this point across much of the world the latter had far outnumbered the former.

The Early Years at AES

Sant and Bakke had always viewed their research and consulting jobs at the Mellon Center as temporary, intending all along to start their own business, one that would promote the cause of low-cost, efficient energy use. After four years of honing their ideas about energy and their knowledge about how the energy market functioned, in early 1981 they left Mellon and formed Applied Energy Services, Inc. (which quickly was shortened to just AES). Operations began with eight employees in October 1981; the company initially thought of itself as a consulting and project development company. From the outset, the new company's mission was to build an organization that valued people; that was fair and honest in its dealings with suppliers, customers, employees, and the communities where it operated; that acted in a socially responsible manner; and that made a contribution to society at large. Roger Sant and Dennis Bakke expected the company to be profitable, but maximizing shareholder wealth was not the motivating force for forming the company. Sant and Bakke cared more about the kind of company they could build than the bottom line—their vision and strategic intent was for AES to provide reliable, low-cost electricity to people in a socially responsible way.

Sant and Bakke raised $1.2 million in equity capital in 1982, and AES began in earnest to scout for power plant development opportunities. One of the company's first projects involved using waste coke at Atlantic Richfield's Houston refinery to make electricity.[2] The business model for the project entailed using the heat from burning the waste coke twice—once to turn turbines that would generate electricity that could be sold to Houston Lighting & Power, and again as the hot gas left the turbines, to produce industrial steam that Atlantic Richfield could use in refining crude oil. The technique, known as "cogeneration," was quite cost-efficient—Atlantic Richfield was able to offset some of the costs of its refinery with revenues derived from selling the waste

[2]The following discussion is based on information in Robert Waterman, *What America Does Right: Learning from Companies That Put People First* (New York: W. W. Norton, 1994), and posted on AES's website (www.aesc.com), February 22, 2001. Waterman is a longtime member of AES's board of directors.

coke to AES at a modest price, and AES, with access to very low-cost fuel, could afford to make the heavy capital investment in scrubbers needed to operate the cogeneration facility cleanly. (Scrubbers mixed the sulfur emissions coming from burning coke, which contained 6 to 8 percent sulfur, with limestone to take out the sulfur dioxide that causes acid rain.) However, the project quickly proved a test of AES's commitment to operating in a socially responsible manner—the scrubbing operation produced a steady stream of wet, dirty calcium sulfate, not a hazardous substance or a by-product that violated Environmental Protection Agency standards but still something that had to be dealt with. One AES employee had heard of a process developed by Hitachi that would dry, clean, and turn the dirty calcium sulfate into very pure gypsum. The gypsum could be sold to a nearby plant operated by U.S. Gypsum, a company that made gypsum-based sheetrock commonly used for the walls of homes and buildings. Selling the gypsum would make the AES cogeneration facility an ecosystem that would utilize the waste coke to turn out electricity, steam, clean water, clean air, and gypsum. But further investigation showed that it would cost more to turn the dirty calcium sulfate into gypsum than AES could get by selling the gypsum to U.S. Gypsum. Nonetheless, Sant and Bakke, with the support of other AES employees, made the decision to go forward using the Hitachi process, opting to operate in the most environmentally responsible way despite the bottom-line penalty it entailed. The decision quickly became ingrained in the culture and folklore at AES, symbolizing the company's commitment to generating electricity in a manner consistent with the best environmental practices, even if it meant sacrificing a portion of profits.

AES'S GROWTH IN A RAPIDLY CHANGING INDUSTRY ENVIRONMENT

During the remainder of the 1980s, AES gradually expanded the number of electricity-generation facilities it operated and was constructing—see Exhibit 1 for a summary of company milestones. The company's workforce included 376 people at year-end 1989. By 1991, the company's expansion efforts were hampered by small internal cash flows and a lack of equity capital—investments in new power plants could run as much as $1 million per megawatt of capacity. To raise the equity capital necessary to pursue the rapidly growing number of power-generating opportunities that AES saw, the cofounders elected to take the company public with an initial public offering of common stock in 1991.

The Rapidly Changing Industry Environment

Increasingly during the 1990s, AES began to focus its expansion efforts on the rapidly growing number of opportunities to invest in power plant and electric distribution facilities in foreign countries. These opportunities resulted from a combination of events:

- Beginning in 1989, the British government launched a series of pioneering initiatives to transform its monopolistic and relatively inefficient electric industry into one that embraced an element of competition and would be more market-driven and responsive to the needs and preferences of individual customers. The British approach involved shifting from a vertically integrated electricity monopoly (where the functions of electricity generation, transmission, distribution, marketing, and

exhibit 1 Milestones in AES's Climb to Prominence as a Global Power Company, 1981–2001

Year	Event
1981	AES begins operation in October as Applied Energy Systems, Inc., with eight employees; initial business focuses on energy conservation consulting and developing cogeneration projects at manufacturing plants where steam was an integral part of the industrial process.
1983	AES closes the deal to finance the company's first cogeneration project.
1984	This is the last year the company reports a net loss; AES workforce is up to 89 employees.
1985	AES signs contracts to supply electricity at new plants in Connecticut and Oklahoma; company management begins to see AES's core business as operating power plants.
1986	The first cogeneration plant (at Atlantic Richfield's refining plant in Houston, Texas) begins operations.
1987	The first discussion of shared values appears in annual letter to the shareholders; the first list of names of AES employees (232 people) appears in annual report, a practice that still continues; Dennis Bakke is named president and chief operating officer, while Roger Sant assumes the role of chairman and CEO.
1988	AES becomes the largest independent (nonutility) producer of electric power in the United States, with four plants; the company receives an environmental award from *Power* magazine.
1989	The company receives an award for planting trees in Guatemala to offset the carbon dioxide emissions at one of its new plants; safety becomes a top priority goal at each AES plant; the company moves to new headquarters in Arlington, Virginia, and begins to focus its sights on expanding into international markets; the workforce is up to 376 people.
1991	AES goes public and its stock begins trading on the Nasdaq.
1992	Most AES plants set records for plant reliability; the company's first international acquisition comes with the purchase of two power plants in Ireland.
1993	AES becomes a global company with operations and projects under development in 17 countries; the company makes an acquisition in Argentina and begins business activities in China.
1994	AES initiates dividend payments to shareholders and organizes the company around six mostly geographic divisions; Roger Sant, age 62, turns over the role of CEO to Dennis Bakke, age 48, but retains the title of chairman of the board of directors.
1995	AES is touted as "The Global Power Company" and operates 19 plants in 6 countries.
1996	AES has a banner years in winning new projects and now operates 34 plants totaling over 11,000 mW of generating capacity; its stock is listed on the New York Stock Exchange; its annual report lists the names of 6,000 people comprising the AES workforce.
1997	The company acquires electric distribution businesses in several locations that serve a total of 8 million customers—its first important business investments outside power plant operations; English is the first language of only 8 percent of the 10,000 people who work at AES facilities around the world.
1998	AES is selected as one of the companies to be included in the Standard & Poor's (S&P) 500; an agreement is reached to acquire Cilcorp—a traditional electric and gas utility company operating in Illinois.
1999	AES acquires the 4,000 mW Drax Power Station in North Yorkshire, England, one of the largest coal-fired power plants in the world, for $3 billion; the company enters the competitive market for retail electricity sales in several states in the U.S. that had enacted legislation initiating competition and granting customers the freedom to chose their electricity supplier; the company is organized around 14 business groups, one of which was a telecom operation that could be piggybacked on the assets of its electric distribution businesses.
2000	AES makes a series of acquisitions to greatly expand the company's position in Latin America; it also acquires IPALCO Enterprises, a traditional regulated electric utility with operations in and around Indianapolis, Indiana, and moves to acquire or construct power plants at several other locations in the United States and other foreign countries; it completes a 2-for-1 stock split and is selected for inclusion in the S&P 100 Index.
2001	AES stock is selected for inclusion in the 15-company Dow-Jones Utility Average.

Source: Information posted at AES's website (www.aesc.com), February 22, 2001, and information contained in the company's annual report, 2000.

customer service were all performed by a single, government-owned enterprise) to an deintegrated industry structured around (*a*) investor-owned generating companies competing to serve the daily electric loads of British customers at competitively determined prices that varied across the hours of each day according to hourly demand–supply conditions; (*b*) a separate investor-owned provider of transmission services whose prices for transmission services were regulated; (*c*) a number of investor-owned electric distribution companies, each serving its own defined geographic territory and each providing local distribution services at regulated prices; and (*d*) energy marketers who competed for the patronage of industrial, commercial, and residential customers (all electricity users in Britain could freely switch from marketer to marketer). The total price that British customers paid energy marketers included a competitively determined charge for electricity generation, a regulated charge for transmission services from the power plant to the nearest distribution substation, a regulated charge for delivering the electricity via the local area distribution system to the customer's meter, and whatever markup the energy marketer imposed to cover sales, marketing, and customer service costs and earn a profit. The process of privatizing and deintegrating the electric industry and then giving all electric customers the freedom to choose their electricity supplier took place over a nine-year period in Britain, reaching completion in 1998.

- The British approach was successful enough and attractive enough to capture the attention of governments and policymakers across much of the world. In the mid-1990s, governments in a number of foreign countries began initiating electricity industry restructuring efforts of their own, in many cases adapting certain aspects of the British model to fit local circumstances and political considerations. Laws and regulations were rewritten to allow foreign investment and to permit investor-owned companies, including those based in foreign countries, to own electricity generation, transmission, and distribution businesses. Several countries began the process of privatizing their electricity industries by selling all or part of their government-owned and -operated electric generation, transmission, and distribution facilities to investor-owned companies and, in conjunction with such sales, adopting new policies and regulations that introduced elements of competition into the generation of electricity and into the retail marketing of both electricity and natural gas.[3]

- Some foreign-based electricity providers, facing the specter of a more competitive market in generating electricity, chose to divest some or all of their power generating assets—thus allowing new entrants a way to gain an immediate market foothold by acquiring the facilities that were divested.

- In a number of less-developed or emerging countries, government officials had recently become receptive to having foreign-investor-owned companies like AES come in and participate in the long-term process of constructing and operating efficient, modern power plants that would enable local manufacturers, commercial businesses, and households to gain access to much-needed supplies of electricity at affordable prices.

---

[3]Substantially all of the electric transmission and distribution services continued to be regulated in one way or another in most countries, because of their status as natural monopolies. (Having duplicate sets of transmission and distribution facilities to serve the same customers involved substantially higher costs.) Thus, "deregulation" and restructuring under way in most foreign countries (and in the United States as well) involved introducing elements of competition mainly to the generation and marketing parts of the electricity business.

AES saw the various privatization initiatives of foreign governments, the accelerating global shift away from heavily regulated electricity markets toward more competitive market structures (as had been created in Great Britain), and the fast-rising demand for electricity in emerging countries as an unprecedented growth opportunity—though one with considerable business risk and earnings volatility.

Since the mid- to late 1990s in the United States, the federal government (most particularly, the Federal Energy Regulatory Commission), about 25 state governments, and numerous state regulatory agencies had embraced the global trend of encouraging more open and competitive electricity markets—influenced in large part by the British experience. Federal regulations were adopted that required owners of interstate electric transmission facilities to provide transmission services to all power generating companies and energy marketers on the same terms and conditions that they served their own power plants and end-use customers, thereby opening up the wholesale electricity market to competitively priced generation. Opening up use of interstate transmission systems to all market participants was a key step in paving the way for states to give customers the freedom to obtain their electricity supplies from sources other than their local power company. By early 2001, over 37 million electric customers in the United States (over 30 percent of the total of 120 million electric customers) had freedom of choice, with more scheduled to gain freedom of choice in the 2001–2004 time frame. In 2001, nearly all of the electric utilities in the United States were revamping their operations in one way or another, expecting that industry restructuring somewhat akin to the British model would soon characterize much of the overall U.S. market for electricity. Some regulated electric utilities had elected to sell or auction their power generation plants and retreat to the position of operating their transmission and distribution facilities under a combined state and federal regulatory framework. Others had relied on mergers and acquisitions to enhance their competitiveness and build stronger, more geographically diverse market positions. However, the restructuring outlook in the United States was heavily clouded by recent events in California, where ill-chosen state policies and approaches to industry restructuring had produced rolling blackouts, sharp price increases for electricity, and crisis actions by the California state government to head off bankruptcy of two of the state's major electric utilities.

AES's Transformation into a Global Power Company

Throughout the 1991–2001 period, AES was aggressive in capitalizing on the opportunities afforded by the rapid changes under way in the global electricity industry environment. By 2001, through both acquisitions and new construction—often in places where electricity industry restructuring was actively under way—AES operated more power plants and electric distribution facilities in more locations around the world than any other investor-owned company in either the United States or elsewhere, making its tag line "The Global Power Company" more than just a future intention. Exhibit 2 shows the sizes and locations of AES's operations.

AES's Growth Strategy According to Dennis Bakke, "We don't have a grand central plan at AES. We're pretty much opportunists."[4] Corporate executives at AES

---

[4]Quoted in Pamela Druckerman, "How to Project Power Around the World—U.S. Energy Firm AES Plugs into Seary Turf; Colombia Anyone?" *The Wall Street Journal*, November 13, 2000.

exhibit 2   Locations and Sizes of AES's Businesses, March 2001

Countries Where AES Had Power Plants in Operation or Under Construction	Number of Plants	Total Generating Capacity
United States	25	12,204 mW
Puerto Rico	1	454
United Kingdom, Northern Ireland, and Wales	7	6,123
Argentina	9	2,853
Brazil	52	9,706
Chile	14	1,732
China	9	2,854
Hungary	3	1,281
Kazakhstan	8	8,414
Dominican Republic	9	1,107
Republic of Georgia	3	823
Canada	1	110
Pakistan	2	695
Netherlands	1	405
Australia	3	1,247
Panama	5	397
India	1	420
Venezuela	7	2,265
Mexico	1	484
Colombia	3	1,404
Nigeria	1	290
Bangladesh	2	810
Sri Lanka	1	165
Oman	1	427
Total: 24 countries	169	56,670 mW

Countries Where AES Had Distribution Businesses for Electricity, Gas, or Heat	Number of Distribution Businesses	Number of Customers Served
Brazil	4	12,699,000
Argentina	3	703,000
El Salvador	4	811,000
Republic of Georgia	1	370,000
Dominican Republic	1	400,000
Kazakhstan	6	612,000
United States (Illinois)	1	202,000
India	1	600,000
Venezuela	1	1,159,000
Total: 9 countries	22	17,556,000

continued

exhibit 2 (concluded)

Countries Where AES Had Retail Energy Marketing Businesses	Number of Energy Marketing Businesses	Number of Customers Served
United States	3	154,000
Kazakhstan	1	25
Total: 2 countries	4	154,025

Note: AES did not own 100 percent of all these businesses; it was the majority owner in 102 businesses and a minority owner of 76 businesses, plus it had only the managerial and/or concession rights on 4 other projects. In addition to the listings above, AES owned and operated a coal mine in Hungary that had an annual output of approximately 1 million tons of brown coal; this mine supplied fuel to one of the AES power plants in Hungary.

Source: Compiled by the case researcher from the *AES Summary Fact Sheet* posted on (www.aesc.com), March 22, 2001, and the AES annual report, 2000.

had established no formal growth goals and had crafted no formal strategy or strategic guidelines for the company. Indeed, top management—Roger Sant and Dennis Bakke, in particular—did not dictate where the company should be headed, how fast it ought to try to grow, or what the company's overall strategic themes should be in operating its different businesses and trying to meet budgeted earnings.

For the most part, AES's growth evolved from the efforts of many AES "intrapreneurs" acting opportunistically—AES people at locations around the world were expected to be on the lookout for new acquisition and construction opportunities in their areas and were delegated the freedom and authority to pursue them. The projects that AES won, the acquisitions that it made, and the resulting increases in company revenues and profits flowed from the initiatives and decisions of dozens of geographically scattered AES intrapreneurial teams, each acting more or less independently from the others and each developing its own local area strategies and business plans.

Company intrapreneurs were expected to act responsibly, however, in nailing down an opportunity. This meant doing a thorough job of analyzing the opportunities they elected to pursue, consulting with others in the company to tap their knowledge and experience and to consider their advice, being prudent in how much they bid to win a project or make an acquisition, and taking care to uphold the company's values regarding social responsibility and protecting the environment. And everyone at AES was held accountable for the decisions he or she made. All AES people were expected to pursue projects that would yield an overall after-tax return of 16 to 20 percent on shareholder investment and that would contribute appropriately to meeting the company's budgeted earnings for the year. But this 16–20 percent companywide ROI target was adjusted upward for projects in countries where the economic or political risks were seen as relatively high.

AES's Willingness to Enter Risky Markets One of AES's distinguishing strategy elements was the frequency with which it entered the sometimes topsy-turvy markets of developing countries. AES was not averse to owning and operating facilities in countries that competitors were prone to avoid because of perceived political volatility or unpredictable business conditions. For example, when Venezuelan stocks fell precipitously in the summer of 2000 on fears that populist president Hugo Chavez, a former army paratrooper, would pursue antibusiness policies (based on his frequent tirades against large corporations and the country's wealthy elite—which scared other foreign investors), Dennis Bakke and other AES people in Venezuela met with Chavez, shared with him their vision for AES in supplying Venezuela's needs for electric power, got what they considered a fair hearing with regulators, and won approval to buy 87 percent ownership of the leading Venezuelan electric company. Chavez took an immediate liking to Dennis Bakke, repeatedly asking Bakke to join him in a game of baseball.

AES was proceeding with making new investments in Colombia, even though leftist guerrillas controlled about a third of the country and drug lords posed a continuing political and social problem. The leader of AES's expansion into Colombia was Esteban Walsh, a former U.S. Marine Corps operative who in 1991 had been shot in the leg by Colombian guerrillas in a U.S. operation to deliver drug interdiction boats to the Colombian government. In conducting AES business in Colombia, Walsh made use of his Marine experiences in Colombia, sometimes taking helicopters to avoid getting stopped by rebel roadblocks and deciding against projects that were uncomfortably close to guerrilla-controlled territory. In a *Wall Street Journal* article, Walsh was quoted as saying, "It's not that I'm not scared. A healthy bit of fear is good."[5]

When Brazil, in a surprise move, sharply devalued its currency in 1999, AES incurred $203 million in foreign currency translation losses on its Brazilian projects and, as a result, did not meet its budgeted income and cash flow projections. Nonetheless, this bad experience in 1999 did not stop AES from taking the long-term view and investing over $7 billion in acquiring new Brazilian assets in 2000. Although Argentina had been mired in an economic slump and a political scandal that forced its vice president to resign, in 2000 AES acquired several Argentina-based power plants from U.S. companies that had struggled unsuccessfully to make their plants profitable and were unwilling to ride out the storm in hopes of better days ahead.

AES had also established operations in such "risky" countries as the Republic of Georgia, Kazakhstan, China, India, Sri Lanka, and Bangladesh. In 2000, the company's many ongoing projects in various emerging countries across the world resulted in Dennis Bakke being recognized as "Emerging Markets CEO of the Year" by Europe-based ING Barings. In general, the company was willing to consider establishing facilities "wherever people want us, wherever they need us, and wherever we can live the AES principles consistently."

Risk Management Strategies

Risk Management Strategies   AES managed the risks of its growing portfolio of projects in several ways. First, the company deliberately pursued many relatively small projects so as to minimize the spillover of problems and difficulties at any one project on companywide finances and bottom-line performance. Second, the company generally attempted to hedge certain aspects of each project's financial performance against the effects of inflation; changing interest rates; the prices of fuel used to operate its plants; and, in some instances, exchange rate fluctuations. With only a few exceptions (where AES had opted to participate in competitive energy markets—such as Britain, the United States, Argentina, and Kazakhstan), AES's projects had long-term contracts specifying the prices that AES would be paid for the power output of its plants or the electric distribution services it provided; these prices were typically indexed to inflation, fuel prices, currency exchange rates, and other specified factors to mitigate the risks to AES of selling at contract prices. In several instances, AES had been able to negotiate contractual terms whereby project prices and revenue streams were adjusted for fluctuations in a host country's currency exchange rates.

---

[5]Quoted in ibid.

Third, AES incorporated each project as a separate subsidiary and endeavored to use a project's economics (the long-term contractual revenues and the projected costs and profit margins) to secure loans from lending institutions (including local banks, host-country government agencies, and the World Bank) sufficient to finance a large fraction of that project's acquisition and capital investment costs. Often AES's equity investment in a project/subsidiary was the minimum amount needed to secure as much debt financing as lenders would agree to. Typically, the loans on each project were secured wholly by the equity investment made by AES in the project, the physical assets of the project, and the revenue and cash flow stream associated with the contract. Hence, in the event a particular project was nationalized or fell into deep financial difficulty, creditors' claims had to be satisfied by the assets of that project without any recourse to the assets of other AES projects or to AES as the parent company. On occasion, AES would agree to have the parent company take on some of the debt burden for a particular project if the project was particularly attractive or if there were other compelling reasons for such arrangements. The following table shows how much of AES's long-term debt for the past five years was nonrecourse (project-specific) and how much was guaranteed by the parent company:

	2000	1999	1998	1997	1996
Nonrecourse long-term debt (in billions)	$12.2	$ 8.7	$3.6	$3.5	$1.6
Recourse long-term debt (in billions)	3.5	2.1	1.6	1.1	.5
Total	$15.7	$10.8	$5.2	$4.6	$2.1

Source: AES 10-K report, 2000, p. 22.

Environmental Risks Associated with AES's Power Plant Operations

AES's power plants utilized a variety of fuel sources. Of the company's total installed generating capacity at year-end 2000, 38 percent was fueled by coal or petroleum coke, 18 percent by natural gas, 4 percent by fuel oil, and 33 percent by water. The remaining 7 percent had the capability of using multiple fossil fuels. All of the company's power plants were subject to environmental and land-use regulations of one sort or another. Environmental laws and regulations were typically complex; varied significantly from country to country (and sometimes from location to location within a country, particularly in the United States); were subject to frequent change; and had tended to become more stringent over time. Power plant projects in emerging countries funded partly by the World Bank (a fairly common occurrence) were further subject to World Bank environmental standards.

Sometimes when new or tighter environmental restrictions were imposed, existing facilities were "grandfathered" (exempted from the new regulations because the facility pre-existed the regulation), and sometimes the new regulations applied to both new and existing facilities. Tighter standards for the emission of pollutants (most notably for sulfur dioxides and nitrogen oxides) at existing facilities could require extensive modifications to a facility's technology and operations, entailing sizable capital investments and increases in operating costs. As a general rule, plants fueled by natural gas were much cleaner than plants fueled by coal or petroleum coke and could meet air quality standards with less capital investment and lower operating costs for pollution control activities.

Global warming was a mounting concern in many countries, and there was growing scientific evidence to support the conclusion that the emission of "greenhouse gases"—specifically carbon dioxide (CO_2)—at power plants using fossil fuels (natural gas, coal, and fuel oil) was a significant cause of global warming. While AES took the likelihood of increased capital and operating costs for environmental compliance into account in making acquisitions and in entering into contractual agreements to supply electricity, the company's financial performance was subject to adverse impact by the likely tightening of environmental laws and regulations regarding the power plant operations.

OPERATIONS

AES took pride in operating its facilities with a high level of proficiency. In the company's 1999 annual report Dennis Bakke said, "We think we are the best in the world in plant operations." Reliability, cost reduction, safety, and low environmental emissions were the primary targets of the company's commitment to operating excellence. In 1999, AES power plants worldwide operated at an average of 60 percent of permitted U.S. emission levels; new AES plants had emission levels 5 to 10 times lower than average U.S. plants. The company's average emission levels had been declining annually for a number of years. Nonetheless, the company had several dirty plants in Hungary that were scheduled for shutdown, and some of the company's U.S. plants needed significant cleanup to continue operating.

Average operating costs at the company's facilities had declined for 15 consecutive years—costs per kilowatt-hour of electricity generated, for example, fell by about 7 percent in 1999 and by about 4.5 percent in 2000. The percentage of time that the company's power plants were available to produce electricity (as opposed to being offline for maintenance and repairs) had increased in three of the past four years:

Year	Average Availability
1996	88%
1997	91
1998	92
1999	93
2000	89

The availability problems in 2000 resulted in large part from a fire in the Drax plant in England and to maintenance and repair problems at the company's California plants, which experienced difficulties trying to generate additional electricity aimed at helping alleviate California's electric power shortages. In fact, California environmental officials fined AES $17 million for running its California plants in 2000 so many hours that they exceeded their allowed nitrogen oxide emissions; as a consequence of the fine, AES announced that it would cease running its California plants overtime to help avert blackout and power crises in California. However, the company was proceeding with investments in additional pollution control facilities to reduce nitrogen oxide emissions at its California plants.

AES's distribution businesses were striving hard to reduce the number of minutes that customers experienced electricity outages, thus improving the reliability of its service. The average number of outage minutes was a key performance target, and outage

exhibit 3 Consolidated Income Statement, AES Corporation, 1998–2000
(in millions, except per share amounts)

For the Years Ended December 31	2000	1999	1998
Revenues	$6,691	$3,253	$2,398
Cost of sales	(4,991)	(2,257)	(1,609)
Selling, general, and administrative expenses	(85)	(71)	(56)
Interest expense	(1,299)	(641)	(485)
Interest and other income	245	86	66
Gain on contract buyout	—	91	—
Impairment loss	—	(62)	—
Environmental fine	(17)	—	—
Equity in pretax earnings of affiliates	475	21	232
Income before income taxes, minority interest, and extraordinary items	1,019	420	546
Income taxes	252	111	145
Minority interest	119	64	94
Income before extraordinary items	648	245	307
Extraordinary items—(loss) gain on early extinguishment of debt—net of applicable income taxes	(7)	(17)	4
Net income	$641	$228	$311
Basic earnings per share			
Before extraordinary items	$1.47	$0.64	$0.87
Extraordinary items	(0.02)	(0.04)	0.01
Basic earnings per share	$1.45	$0.60	$0.88
Diluted earnings per share			
Before extraordinary items	$1.42	$0.62	$0.84
Extraordinary items	(0.02)	(0.04)	0.01
Diluted earnings per share	$1.40	$0.58	$0.85

Source: AES annual report, 2000.

rates across the company's distribution businesses worldwide had declined for four straight years.

AES'S FINANCIAL PERFORMANCE

Exhibits 3, 4, and 5 present AES's recent financial statements. While the majority of AES's long-term debt was indeed concentrated in each project, there was about $1 billion in parent-company debt scheduled to come due after 2006. The cash flow to retire this debt was expected to come from the positive cash flows of its individual projects. Exhibit 6 shows a financial breakdown of AES's operations by business segment and geographic segment.

AES'S CORPORATE VALUES

From day one, Roger Sant and Dennis Bakke were committed to the task of building a company that made a real contribution to society. Further, they wanted to create an organization that employees would be enthusiastic about and proud to work for. Four

exhibit 4 Consolidated Balance Sheets, AES Corporation, 1998–2000
(amounts in millions, except shares and par value)

December 31	2000	1999
Assets		
Current assets:		
Cash and cash equivalents	$ 881	$ 669
Short-term investments	1,297	164
Accounts receivable—net of reserves of $201—2000; $104—1999	1,498	934
Inventory	499	307
Receivables from affiliates	27	2
Deferred income taxes	165	184
Prepaid expenses and other current assets	1,206	327
Total current assets	5,573	2,587
Property, plant, and equipment:		
Land	617	216
Electric generation and distribution assets	15,743	12,552
Accumulated depreciation and amortization	(1,304)	(763)
Construction in progress	2,790	1,442
Property, plant and equipment—net	17,846	13,447
Other assets:		
Deferred financing costs—net	375	236
Project development costs	114	53
Investments in and advances to affiliates	3,122	1,575
Debt service reserves and other deposits	517	328
Excess of cost over net assets acquired—net	2,307	1,851
Other assets	1,179	803
Total other assets	7,614	4,846
Total assets	$31,033	$20,880

continued

principles, or values, formed the core of the company's culture and shaped the manner in which AES conducted its business: to act with *integrity,* to be *fair* in conducting its business, to have *fun,* and to be *socially responsible.* AES documents summarized what these values meant:[6]

- *Integrity*—We try to act with integrity, or "wholeness." This means that we honor our commitments. Our goal is that the things AES people say and do in all parts of the Company should fit together with truth and consistency. AES people seek to keep the same moral code at work as at home.

- *Fairness*—It is our desire to treat fairly our people, customers, suppliers, stakeholders, governments and the communities in which we operate. Defining what is fair is often difficult, but we believe it is helpful to routinely question the relative fairness of alternative courses of action. It does not mean that everyone gets treated equally, but instead treated fairly or with justice given the appropriate situation.

---

[6]AES statements posted on the company's website (www.aesc.com), February 28, 2001, and statements included in the company's 10-K report, 2000, pp. 5–6.

exhibit 4   *(concluded)*

December 31	2000	1999
Liabilities and Stockholders' Equity		
Current liabilities:		
Accounts payable	$ 708	$ 381
Accrued interest	404	218
Accrued and other liabilities	1,305	755
Recourse debt—current portion	—	335
Nonrecourse debt—current portion	2,465	881
Total current liabilities	4,882	2,570
Long-term liabilities:		
Nonrecourse debt	12,241	8,651
Recourse debt	3,458	2,167
Deferred income taxes	1,632	1,787
Other long-term liabilities	1,399	602
Total long-term liabilities	18,730	13,207
Minority interest	1,382	1,148
Commitments and contingencies	—	—
Company-obligated convertible mandatorily redeemable preferred securities of subsidiary trusts holding solely junior subordinated debentures of AES	1,228	1,318
Stockholders' equity:		
Preferred stock, no par value—50 million shares authorized; none issued	—	—
Common stock, $.01 par value—1,200 million and 1,000 million shares authorized for 2000 and 1999, respectively; shares issued and outstanding, 2000—481 million; 1999—414 million	5	4
Additional paid-in capital	4,722	2,615
Retained earnings	1,761	1,120
Accumulated other comprehensive loss	(1,677)	(1,102)
Total stockholders' equity	4,811	2,637
Total liabilities and stockholders' equity	$31,033	$20,880

Source: AES annual report, 2000.

- *Fun*—We want all AES people and those people with whom we interact to have fun in their work. AES's goal is to create the most fun workplace since the industrial revolution. The company believes that making decisions and being accountable is fun, and has adopted decentralized organizational principles and practices in order to maximize the opportunity for fun for as many people as possible.

- *Social responsibility*—We believe that AES has a responsibility to be involved in projects that provide social benefits, such as lower costs to customers, a high degree of safety and reliability, increased employment and a cleaner environment. This value has led us to try innovative approaches to environmental cleanup, including helping to fund the planting of trees to seek to offset the global effects of CO_2 emissions and finding ways to maintain plant emissions significantly below permitted levels. The commitment to this value has also led us to pursue projects in countries, which we believe may contribute to economic development in that region of the world.

exhibit 5   Consolidated Statement of Cash Flows, AES Corporation, 1998–2000 (in millions)

For the Years Ended December 31	2000	1999	1998
Operating activities			
Net income	$ 641	$ 228	$ 311
Adjustments to net income:			
Depreciation and amortization	582	278	196
Provision for deferred taxes	45	(1)	69
Minority interest earnings	119	64	94
Undistributed earnings of affiliates	(320)	30	(58)
Other	(38)	40	(73)
Changes in operating asses and liabilities:			
Increase in accounts receivable	(255)	(142)	(10)
Increase in inventory	(84)	(32)	(8)
(Increase) decrease in other current assets	(155)	(95)	14
Increase in other assets	(144)	(45)	(9)
Increase (decrease) in accounts payable	229	(49)	(11)
Increase in accrued interest	127	86	45
Decrease in other current liabilities	(288)	(165)	(32)
Net cash provided by operating activities	459	197	528
Investing activities			
Property additions	(2,150)	(834)	(517)
Acquisitions—net of cash acquired	(1,818)	(5,713)	(1,623)
Proceeds from the sale of assets	72	650	301
Sale of short-term investments	81	49	98
Purchase of short-term investments	(96)	(98)	(2)
Affiliate advances and equity investments	(515)	(193)	(69)
Increase in short-term investments	(1,110)	(80)	(4)
Project development costs	(96)	(84)	(57)
Debt service reserves and other assets	(106)	(85)	31
Net cash used in investing activities	(5,738)	(6,388)	(1,842)
Financing activities			
(Repayments) borrowings under the revolver—net	(195)	102	206
Issuance of nonrecourse debt and other coupon bearing securities	7,051	6,254	1,843
Repayments of nonrecourse debt and other coupon bearing securities	(2,450)	(1,161)	(668)
Payments for deferred financing costs	(136)	(119)	(47)
Repayments of other long-term liabilities	(174)	(44)	(71)
(Distributions to) contributions by minority interests, net	(54)	32	40
Proceeds from sale of common stock—net	1,449	1,305	200
Net cash provided by financing activities	5,491	6,369	1,503
Increase in cash and cash equivalents	212	178	189
Cash and cash equivalents, beginning of year	669	491	302
Cash and cash equivalents, end of year	$ 881	$ 669	$ 491
Supplemental disclosures			
Cash payments for interest—net of amounts capitalized	$1,137	$ 548	$ 415
Cash payments for income taxes—net of refunds	72	45	24
Schedule of noncash investing and financing activities			
Common stock issued for acquisitions	67	48	—
Liabilities assumed in purchase transactions	2,098	3,570	139

Source: AES annual report, 2000.

exhibit 6 AES's Financial Performance, by Business Segment and Geographic Area, 1998–2000 (in millions)

	Revenues	Depreciation and Amortization	Gross Margin	Pretax Equity In Earnings	Total Assets	Investment in and Advances to Affiliates	Property Additions
Year ended December 31, 2000							
Generation	$3,546	$329	$1,350	$ 49	$17,627	$ 584	$1,909
Distribution	3,145	252	350	426	12,195	2,508	241
Corporate	—	1	—	—	1,211	30	—
Total	$6,691	$582	$1,700	$475	$31,033	$3,122	$2,150
Year ended December 31, 1999							
Generation	$1,970	$180	$793	$ 52	$14,250	$ 524	$ 688
Distribution	1,283	97	203	(31)	6,351	1,051	146
Corporate	—	1	—	—	279	—	—
Total	$3,253	$278	$ 996	$ 21	$20,880	$1,575	$ 834
Year ended December 31, 1998							
Generation	$1,413	$126	$ 566	$ 33	$ 5,682	$ 495	$ 369
Distribution	985	70	223	199	4,687	1,438	148
Corporate	—	—	—	—	412	—	—
Total	$2,398	$196	$ 789	$232	$10,781	$1,933	$ 517

	U.S.	Argentina	Brazil	Hungary	Pakistan	United Kingdom	Other*	Total Non-U.S.	Total
Revenues									
2000	$2,506	$ 482	$ 699	$177	$232	$1,110	$1,485	$ 4,185	$ 6,691
1999	1,192	452	376	212	206	207	608	2,061	3,253
1998	655	423	478	227	213	40	362	1,743	2,398
Long-lived assets									
2000	$5,346	$1,624	$2,359	$ 91	$428	$4,483	$4,674	$13,659	$19,005
1999	4,221	1,061	2,588	121	492	4,600	1,375	10,237	14,458
1998	2,329	1,017	848	154	505	224	756	3,504	5,833

*AES has operations in 18 countries which are included in the other category above.
Source: AES annual report, 2000.

Integrity and Fairness

AES's cofounders saw integrity and fairness as basic moral principles that not only were right but that also, when ingrained into AES's ways of operating and practiced daily, would promote trust among company stakeholders and help check unfettered pursuit of profit and self-interest. What Sant and Bakke wanted as much as anything was for AES to conduct its business in a manner that would make AES people proud of the company they worked for. They believed that if AES management garnered a reputation for operating with fairness and integrity it would encourage AES personnel to demonstrate fairness and integrity in their dealings with one another, plus it would help attract job candidates who preached these same values at home.

Early on, AES managers were encouraged to demonstrate fairness and integrity and to expect the same from all company personnel. One AES plant manager, facing a potentially tense contract negotiation session with the local union, decided to do something radically different. When the negotiations began, union leaders, as was the custom, led off by presenting their list of demands. But the plant manager, when asked by the union for the company's initial offer and list of demands and expectations, responded that management had no agenda items for discussion and negotiation. Instead, the plant manager asked the union leaders to figure out what items on their list were truly important to them, which of their demands were in the mutual interest of both the union and the company, and which were fair. He then asked the union to get back to him, indicating that he was prepared to go along with what the union came up with. Shocked by the plant manager's position, the union leaders caucused and began to work on their list. As it turned out, they came up with a reasonable list of demands—all of which AES agreed to. According to a company observer, news of this event spread like wildfire throughout the company and has since become part of the folklore symbolizing what fairness, trust, and open communications really mean at AES.[7]

As part of acting with integrity, it was AES policy to live with prior agreements even though they might be uneconomical for the company. Management honored commitments, and AES people, AES customers, and the communities in which AES operated could rely on management's word. Acting fairly was also interpreted to mean that AES did not engage in one-upmanship to squeeze all it could get out of its negotiations with others—indeed, an earlier version of the company's values statement about fairness explicitly said, "We do not try to get the most out of a negotiation or transaction at the expense of others." Management wanted the company to have a reputation for fairness among outsiders with whom it dealt because deal-making was such a big part of the company's activities.

Fun

Having fun was central to how AES operated. In the AES scheme of things, having fun was not about company get-togethers, toasting company successes, or socializing with coworkers at the office. Roger Sant explained:

> I am pretty skeptical when I see things like beer busts on Friday afternoon. It's certainly appropriate to have parties and celebrate achievements together, but it gets pretty superficial sometimes. That's not my definition of fun; that's something else. Fun is when you are intellectually excited and you are interacting with each other—with one idea leading to

---

[7]Waterman, *What America Does Right.*

another—and you're getting frustrated because there isn't an answer; you work and you struggle and it's great when a plan comes together. It's the struggle, and even the failure that goes with it, that makes it fun.[8]

The emphasis on having fun at AES was intended to foster a culture and work atmosphere where people could flourish, use their talents in very constructive and positive ways, and enjoy the time they spent at work because they were caught up in what they were doing. AES did indeed have company get-togethers to celebrate achievements, but the fun that the two cofounders wanted AES people to have was, as Roger Sant indicated, in the actions and events leading up to the celebrations and parties—the entrepreneurship and business creativity required to make a deal work and win out over competitors, the freedom to run with new ideas and improve how things were done, and the opportunity to take on assignments that broadened one's knowledge and skills. The whole intent, from the cofounders' perspective, was for the fun part to come from the engaging of each person's heart, mind, and soul on a daily basis and the passion surrounding the pursuit of AES's mission of meeting the world's needs for safe, clean, reliable supplies of electricity.

Social Responsibility

Social responsibility was taken very seriously at AES and was a value deeply ingrained in the company's culture and actions. Roger Sant and Dennis Bakke believed that companies exist primarily in order to contribute to society, to help meet societal needs, and to help people live better lives; they thought companies should operate in ways that help communities prosper and thrive.[9] This is why AES's mission was conceived as meeting the need for safe, clean, reliable electricity worldwide and why Sant and Bakke saw social responsibility as a high priority for AES. Bakke and Sant took issue with the conventional notion that companies existed chiefly to make a profit and reward shareholders for their investment; in their view profits at AES, while essential, took a backseat to passionate pursuit of the company's mission, living up to a code of social values, and demonstrating socially responsible behavior. According to Roger Sant,

> You have to make money because the enterprise can't be sustained unless you do. And profits often measure how effectively you are carrying out your mission.[10]

Dennis Bakke, whose father and brother were ministers and who himself was a person of strong religious faith, elaborated several times on the somewhat secondary role of pursuing higher profits at AES:

> Economics, including profits, are important, but service is still our primary purpose and goal. Profits are the just and reasonable payment to the shareholders for believing in us and investing in us. As such, profits are like the salaries and other compensation we pay to AES people for their contribution to the company, the interest and principal we pay to lenders, the taxes we owe to governments for their role in our success, and a host of other forms of remuneration to stakeholders who help us serve effectively. Profits are crucial, but no more so than any of the payments we make to others. None of these groups is more important than the other.[11]

---

[8]Ibid., and (www.aesc.com), February 22, 2001.

[9]Suzy Wetlaufer, "Organizing for Empowerment: An Interview with Roger Sant and Dennis Bakke," *Harvard Business Review*, January–February 1999, p. 120.

[10]Ibid., p. 121.

[11]Dennis Bakke, "Letter to the Shareholders," AES annual report, 1999, p. 16.

> For example, we try not to put profits before environmental concerns, but neither do we renege on our commitment to shareholders or our promise to meet customer needs for reasonably priced electricity in favor of a cleaner environment. Balance among the needs and desires of all players is the key.[12]

AES executives spoke publicly and often about what it meant for AES to behave in a socially responsible manner, with Bakke functioning as the company's chief evangelist for living up to a code of social values. In a 1998 speech to an audience of AES people, Dennis Bakke spelled out his definition of social responsibility and explained how it fit into the scheme of things at AES:

> For much of the last 30 years and even during the early development of AES, my understanding of the prevalent world view of business social responsibility was that business was business and social responsibility was something separate and different from business. We did the best we could with the business and then debated what, if anything, we might do to redeem the bad stuff about the business we had undertaken. I think many of us at AES had that interpretation, and some here may still have it. The logic is that business is bad, or neutral, at best. So if we want to do good for society, we should look outside of business to governments, non-profit organizations, churches, and schools to do good things (socially responsible things). I have come to believe this is not the best way to view social responsibility.
>
> Let's start with a definition. What does the term "social responsibility" mean? I choose "love your neighbor" as a definition. It means putting others' welfare at least equal to yourself, your company and your family, and includes those neighbors who are not yet born—future generations. It also includes the physical environment that helps sustain and enrich your own and your neighbor's life now and in the future.
>
> . . . I have come to believe that the most important thing we can do as a company to love our neighbor is to do a great job achieving our corporate purpose or mission. That is, the most socially responsible thing we can do is to supply safe, clean, reliable, and cost-effective power to tens of millions of people around the world. There are few things more socially responsible. That is our calling, our reason for existing as a corporation. That is how we carry out our love for our neighbor and his/her environment. Do not think of this calling as being other than socially responsible, something that we need to feel guilty about. It is not something that we must make amends for by undertaking extra projects.
>
> Underlying this view is my strong belief in the ability of markets and market prices to force the best decisions for society. That is, to make socially responsible decisions. You see, I do not think that markets are blind, black holes that operate in some kind of amoral, purely economic, non-humane vacuum. What the market really is, is just what AES (multiplied by a few million) is as an organization. It is mostly smart, creative people making billions of decisions about what's best for themselves, their groups, their communities and their world. While far from perfect, no other approach ever tried comes close to results that are as socially responsible as depending on economic market pricing to maximize benefits to society.
>
> Many would argue, in fact, that nothing need be or can be added to market economics that enhances social responsibility. That is not my view despite my general confidence in market decisions. While we have come to believe that most of our social responsibility is rightly carried out through our mission to supply the world with clean, safe, reliable electricity, we are convinced that we can do some legitimate and appropriate extra things that can enhance the positive impact we can have on our neighbors. Over the years my own rationale for holding this view is that markets and market prices have certain weaknesses. Marketplace decisions by individuals have a difficult time in areas related to some aspects of beauty, faith, compassion, character, virtues, truth and human fallibility. Ignorance can also cause problems. This means that market pricing signals and the decisions that result may not always be the most socially responsible. There may be gaps or distortions.

---

[12]Dennis Bakke, "Letter to the Shareholders," AES annual report, 2000, p. 8.

> At AES, we have committed to attack this problem as a small part of our attempt to be socially responsible. We call it our extra social responsibility projects.[13]

AES's guideline for how much it should spend on "extra social responsibility projects" was about 3 percent of pretax income, but the number was always open to discussion and the actual amount spent in any given year could vary above or below the 3 percent figure. A big fraction of the extra spending on social responsibility at AES consisted of matching the charitable giving of AES employees. Roger Sant and Dennis Bakke saw an emphasis on matching the charitable gifts of AES individuals as having several benefits:[14]

- Matching solved the problem of deciding what projects should be the focus of the extra spending and who should make the decision of how much to spend on each project.
- The company's matching of individual charitable contributions encouraged giving to charities by AES people.
- The matching program reduced the company's temptation to do good things for the societal credit or strategic payoff it might receive.
- Matching doubled the impact on the problem being attacked.
- Matching led to better research, better decisions on where to spend, and more commitment—it was too easy to spend other people's money on "do-good" projects.
- Matching better diversified the company's overall attack on societal issues and problems, plus it implied some humility that AES management, acting on its accord, could not be sure which social problems merited the highest priority in every part of the world where the company had a community presence or what actions constituted the best way to attack the problem/issue.

In 1999, AES spent $4 million worldwide on matching employees' charitable contributions and it gave another $6 million for schools, feeding programs, global warming mitigation, tree planting, and other projects—a total amount of dollars close to 2 percent of pretax income. The company's extra social responsibility projects included 173 projects initiated and completed in earlier periods; 9 projects initiated in 1999; and 143 projects from earlier periods that were still ongoing, done annually, and/or in progress. A sampling of these projects is shown in Exhibit 7.

The extent of AES's commitment to bettering society and providing electric services where they were truly needed was reflected in the company's 1999 annual report; Bakke's letter to the shareholders began as follows:

Dear Friends,

Less than 150 feet below us on the banks of a railroad grade from which the floodwaters had recently receded, I saw bloated human bodies being cremated on hastily built fires. Everywhere, gray cattle carcasses littered fields and clogged roads. The stench was powerful, even from the helicopter. Death, destruction and despair that followed in the wake of the massive "super cyclone" that hit Orissa, India, in November [1999] encompassed thousands of square miles. In the face of such enormous damage or loss of 80–90% of the poles and wires within the AES distribution company that serves that area seemed inconsequential. At that moment no one had to remind me why AES was in Orissa. This disaster in a poor, remote Indian state might be the ultimate test of AES's purpose to serve the world's need for electricity, for light and maybe even a little hope. We remain committed to this mission.

---

[13]Dennis Bakke, "A Case for Social Responsibility," speech, June 1998; posted at (www.aesc.com).
[14]Adapted from Ibid.

exhibit 7   Examples of Extra Social Responsibility Projects Undertaken at AES Corporation

Location	Project Description	Year Initiated	Expected Benefits	Status
Brazil	Give discounts on electric bill to hospitals, churches, and schools	1986	Give special assistance to local community	Ongoing
Brazil	Partner with government and other companies in a program to teach young people a profession	1998	Help participants gain the skill needed to give them a better future	Completed
Argentina	Support local university program to operate a fish breeding center	1998	Breeding fingerlingsto be taken to area reservoirs	In progress
Argentina	Help a local organization fund the purchase of mammography equipment	1998	Improve the care capability for cancer patients	Completed
Puerto Rico	Donate toys to elementary school and to low-income children; donations to over 20 sports teams; donations to help hurricane victims	1994–98	Improve local community conditions	Completed
Texas	Sponsor Drug Abuse Resistance Education (DARE) program at local elementary school in Houston area	1990	Furnish T-shirts for all fifth-graders	Annual
Hungary	Conduct energy conservation programs and help stimulate local business development	1997–98	Educate laypeople about energy conservation and efficiency issues, especially for large buildings; donate use of unused AES facilities as site for new industrial park; help recruit entrepreneurs to the area	In progress
Netherlands	Support junior league soccer team; help boy scout troop refurbish a boat	1998	Help youth of local communities where AES has facilities	Ongoing and in progress
Britain	Help fund local road improvements to the appearance of roundabouts on local area roads	1998	Improve the aesthetics of the local environment	Completed
Several locations	Donate time and money to local Habitat for Humanity projects	Various	Help build low-income housing	Some completed and some in progress
Pakistan	Plant an average of 200 acres of trees annually for 30 years with help of local people	1997	Help offset CO_2 effects; help cultivate semi-desert area; provide jobs for local residents	Ongoing
Pakistan	Construct schools in two locations	1997 and 1999	Provide buildings for 800 students formerly being taught outdoors	Completed and in progress
China	Make donations to local schools; provide irrigation to land neighboring AES facility;donate AES land for roads to 5 villages; building an earth-packed road (3 kilometers) from 10 community villages to railway station; donate money to help equip a new firehouse	1997–99	Help 200 students and people of 15 villages; bring 20 acres under new cultivation; improve community facilities	Ongoing and in progress

continued

exhibit 7   *(concluded)*

Location	Project Description	Year Initiated	Expected Benefits	Status
Kazakhstan	Maintain and pay repairs for 3 kindergartens; provide financial aid to local police, local culture center, local paramedics; pay for education of 156 students at various colleges and universities	1996–97	Help support area schools, improve local community organizations and facilities, and help local students	Completed and ongoing
Oklahoma	Support local Boy Scouts and county livestock show; build tower to help county fire departments and EMS units communicate during emergencies; wire and light barn for county fair	1997–98	Improve opportunities for local youth groups; help meet needs in local community	Ongoing and completed

Source: Compiled by the case researcher from documents posted on the AES website (www.aesc.com) as of March 2, 2001.

A week before I left for India, Eduard Shevardnadze, the President of Georgia, met with Roger and me in Washington to thank us profusely for bringing lights to the capital city, Tbilisi, for the whole winter for the first time in years.

And, two months later in Poteau, Oklahoma, 150 community leaders celebrated AES Shady Point and its "first couple" David and Beverly McMillen (who are transferring to lead our newly acquired 4,000 megawatt facility in England). LeFlore County's unemployment has gone from over 13% to about 4% in the 10 years since AES arrived there. Both the economy and life in the community are robust. People there give AES much of the credit.

Another example of AES's desire to serve the often critical needs of emerging countries for low-cost electricity was the August 2000 acquisition of TransCanada Pipeline's 49 percent interest in the Songo Songo Gas-to-Electricity Project in Tanzania (financed in part with loans from the Tanzanian government, the World Bank, and the European Investment Bank). The project, for which AES had operating responsibility, involved the refurbishment and operation of five coastal natural gas wells, the construction of a processing plant and pipeline to Dar es Salaam, and the conversion of a power plant that used fuel oil to one that utilized natural gas as the major fuel source. Goals of the project included developing Tanzania's natural gas reserves and reducing the country's dependence on imported oil.

When environmental groups challenged the merits of a $500 million dam and hydroelectric plant that AES planned to build on the Nile River in Uganda because only 5 percent of Ugandans would benefit from the project (most of the population in Uganda lived in rural areas lacking access to electricity), Bakke stepped forward to defend the socially responsible aspects of the project:

We define environment differently than most people. We include people. The assumption is that it is very good for the world to have more electricity to refrigerate medicines, lights to study by, power to ease housekeeping responsibilities. If they could stop the dam—and they can't—they'd condemn the people of Uganda to having to pay three times more for electricity [as compared to the wind and solar power projects favored by the environment group]. We think we're doing the Lord's work. We're making a big, positive contribution in these places.[15]

---

[15]Quoted in Peter Behr, "Power Surge: Global Market to Test AES's Risk-Based Style," *Washington Post*, December 17, 2000.

Global Application of the Four Values

AES management was committed to ingraining its four values at company projects all across the world, the thesis being that its four values transcended national boundaries and were appropriate for the people and cultures of every country. Company executives claimed the company's experiences to date indicated that its four values were as natural and acceptable to people outside the United States as they were to most Americans. Further, management believed that AES could not be a truly global company if its core values and culture fit only the people of a particular nation or people of a particular religious faith or people of a particular income level or social class. Whereas some global companies had adopted values and business philosophies that were flexible (using the operative approach of "When in Rome, do as the Romans do"), AES strived to operate with the same interpretation of and commitment to the values of fairness, integrity, social responsibility, and fun in every country where it did business. Dennis Bakke explained:

> We hold tightly to a central purpose as to why the company exists and to four SHARED values. We try to define these principles and live the same way in Beijing, Belfast, Boston, and Buenos Aires. That is radical because it is in opposition to some modern ideas about the differences among cultures. We should, of course, do our best to be sensitive to—even celebrate—the differences that do exist among various people groups of the world. But our assumption is that the core values that hold us together and guide our approach to business and life can appropriately transcend the diverse groups of people from many lands where AES attempts to serve.[16]

In the company's 2000 annual report, Roger Sant wrote:

> I remain convinced that AES's values are alive and well and that our culture is as meaningful in Kazakhstan as it is in Arlington. Each new country we enter provides reinforcement of the notion that people are more similar than they are different.

Monitoring How Well the Company Lived Up to Its Four Values

AES conducted annual surveys at each facility location that was at least 50 percent owned by AES to measure how well the company and its personnel were living up to the core values of fairness, integrity, fun, and social responsibility. Management believed the surveys were particularly useful in identifying specific instances where the company had failed and what it could do about those failures. Over 28,000 written responses were received in 1999, and 11,000 AES people responded to the survey in 2000. A response from an AES person in Hungary in 2000 said:

> Keep living the principles and values even if no one else goes along with them or acknowledges your good work. We are trying to live this way, not because it will make us popular or successful or get others to go along with us or even like us. We are trying to live this way because it is the way we think life in business ought to be lived.

Senior executives, including Dennis Bakke, personally reviewed survey responses. (It took Bakke from early August until October to review all 28,000 responses in 1999.) How well AES people adhered to the four values was a significant factor

---

[16]Dennis Bakke, "Potholes in the Road: Part 1," posted in the Founders Corner at (www.aesc.com) as of March 20, 2001.

in evaluating individual and group performance and in determining an individual's compensation.

In addition, senior AES executives spend considerable time visiting different AES facilities, talking to cross-sections of AES people at these facilities, and evaluating the extent to which AES people were embracing and living the four core values.

AES'S RELIANCE ON DECENTRALIZED DECISION MAKING AND EMPOWERMENT

AES management relied extensively on decentralized decision making and empowerment. The cofounders had a strong aversion to management layers and hierarchy, written policies and procedures, job descriptions, organization charts, and anything else that smacked of bureaucracy—partly because Roger Sant and Dennis Bakke, during their time working in government, had seen the negative effects of such practices. Sant and Bakke felt that relying on formal procedures and written documents to set boundaries on people's behavior implied that the company did not trust its people to do the right thing. The organizational system at AES revolved around AES people taking ownership of problems and issues and being willing to accept responsibility for their decisions and actions. AES endeavored to hire and attract people who, on seeing a problem or running across an opportunity, would relish the chance to take it on and see it through to resolution. Roger Sant explained the company's organizational approach:

> Our system starts with a lack of hierarchy. We abhor layers. We avoid them like the plague. The more authority figures you have above you, the more likely it is that you won't make decisions yourself. So we organize around small teams.[17]

The Team-Based Organizational Structure

As of 2001, AES's business operations (power plants, electric distribution businesses, and new business development groups) were grouped into 16 geographic regions, each led by a group manager. Each geographic regional group was responsible for all business activity in its region, including operations, construction, and new business development. Every power plant had a manager, as did every distribution business and every business development group. Each power plant and electric distribution business was organized around 5 to 20 teams (depending on overall business unit size), with each team containing 5 to 20 people, including a team leader. Teams were expected to take full responsibility for their work and be accountable for their actions and decisions—they had the final say on all matters related to their assigned area, but were expected to collaborate and cooperate with other teams as needed to operate as a whole. People were sometimes members of more than one team. Most teams were multidisciplinary, and efforts were made to avoid having internal staff support groups or corporate-level departments for such functions as human resources, engineering, maintenance, marketing, environmental compliance, or finance. The only corporate staff function was accounting—a group of about 30 people at the corporate office gathered financial information from the various projects and business units so that company

---

[17]Wetlaufer, "Organizing for Empowerment," p. 112.

financial statements could be prepared and presented to the public and regulatory authorities.

While AES had organized the whole company around small groups of people who worked closely together in tackling a significant piece of AES business and who, in the process, would hopefully prove to be good advisers and good teachers to their colleagues, most decisions were made by individual team members. Very few decisions were the result of group discussions that led to team consensus, and team leaders seldom made the calls on what to do. Rather, decision-making responsibility was parceled out among team members. The role of the team was to serve as "the community" in which people worked; team members were expected to advise, help educate, and be supportive of the decisions individuals made. The team leader's role was to choose which individuals were to make which decisions and to help coordinate the group effort. Once an individual made a decision, the team (and the company) adopted it as their own. The team member charged with making a decision could seek advice from people outside the team, depending on the scope and consequences of the decision and the time available before a decision had to be made.

Using Job Rotation to Help Build Decision-Making Skills

Since, in a sense, every AES person functioned as a "mini-CEO," there was a strong emphasis on job rotation to help people become well-rounded generalists with first-hand knowledge of many aspects of the company's operations. People were moved from team to team and from facility to facility to better develop their business skills and help prepare them for higher levels of responsibility. Dennis Bakke indicated how this practice resulted in upward mobility for individuals, citing the career path of Pete Norgeot:

> Before joining our Thames plant in Connecticut, he was a heavy-machine operator. His first assignment with us was as a member of the fuel-handling team. He stayed with that team for six months, then shifted to the water treatment team, and then to the boiler team. For three years, he basically went from group to group. He studied all the technical books he could—we have manuals on every aspect of our operation, and you can use them to help prepare for the qualification exams you must pass before you can work in an area. After spending three years at Thames, he learned of an opportunity in our Medway plant in England, and he took it. After a few years, he was selected to be the plant manager at our new Barry facility in Wales.
>
> That kind of movement is typical. For instance, of the original 24 people hired at the Thames plant when it opened in 1988, today two are vice presidents and group managers, eight are plant managers, and seven are team leaders. And they're all generalists. They know most aspects of our operations inside and out.[18]

Although the practice of job rotation to create generalists might admittedly hurt efficiency (because it could dampen individual efforts to gain in-depth, specialized knowledge of one particular area of operations), AES believed that the process of learning and doing new things was what fostered engagement—and led to having fun. In management's view, the trade-off between the efficiency gains of specialization and the advantages of having well-rounded generalists who understood many aspects of company operations, knew something about the business environment, and were in a

---

[18]Ibid., p. 114.

better position to have the good of the company in mind when making decisions was, on balance, a good trade-off.

The Organizational Hierarchy at AES

Team leaders reported directly to the business unit or project manager in most instances, creating an organizational system with essentially four management layers—team leader to business unit manger to geographic regional manager to corporate executive at headquarters.

Most plants operated without shift supervisors. Project subsidiaries were responsible for all major facility-specific business functions, including financing, hiring, and capital expenditures. Every AES person was encouraged to participate in the future planning process for his or her respective facility. The result was a highly decentralized organizational structure where AES individuals had an exceptionally high degree of decision-making authority in their assigned areas; according to Bakke, "Everything about how we organize gives people the power and the responsibility to make important decisions, to engage with their work as businesspeople, not as cogs in a machine."[19]

People in positions of managerial leadership at AES were expected to play four roles in the organization: adviser, encourager, guardian/advocate of the four values, and accountability officer. Giving advice and supporting and encouraging the efforts of teams and individuals were particularly important roles. The culture at AES was one where individual decision makers sought out the advice and opinions of people in leadership positions. AES leaders were typically highly visible and active at company functions (plant openings, company celebrations, and the like), using these times to provide positive reinforcement for ongoing efforts and new initiatives. Serving as chief guardian of the values was a function done mainly in the course of advising others and, on occasion, providing examples and stories about how the values applied in specific instances. The guardian aspect came up infrequently because the four company values were so well known, deeply ingrained, and widely shared. Bakke indicated that most of the time AES people guarded the values without any input from senior managers, citing an instance where AES people pursuing a project in Indonesia decided not to give 15 percent ownership of the project to a member of the governing Suharto family because paying such a "tax" (while not illegal) basically amounted to bribery and did not fit with company's principles of fairness and integrity—AES has no projects in Indonesia, partly because of its unwillingness to engage in often corrupt practices that occur there. Serving as chief accountability officers came into play only if on some rare occasion that teams or business units didn't hold themselves accountable; Sant and Bakke, however, answered for the company to the outside world when things did not go well.

The Assumptions AES Made about People and the Linkages to Decentralization

The company's organizational system and reliance on decentralized decision making stemmed from the "fun" value and the assumptions about people behind that value. The company's cofounders strongly believed that it was not possible to maximize fun for the maximum number of AES people without letting individuals closest to the

---

[19]Ibid., p. 112.

action make decisions for the company. Their belief in and commitment to decentralized decision making flowed directly from several fundamental assumptions they made about people and that undergirded the corporate culture at AES:[20]

- People are creative and trustworthy beings, capable of thinking, reasoning, learning, and making good decisions.
- People are unique, both in gifts and needs.
- People are fallible and will make mistakes.
- People desire to be part of a group or community with a cause and to make a positive contribution to the world.
- People are responsible and accountable for their ideas and actions.

Believing firmly that people could be trusted and were capable of making responsible decisions, both Sant and Bakke had elected to operate AES as a something of a grand experiment in employee governance where decision-making authority and power were widely distributed throughout the organization. To do their part in fostering decentralization, Sant, Bakke, and other top AES executives prided themselves in not calling the shots; they basically refused to approve decisions made by employees at any level or to let anyone else do so. As Bakke put it, "If you have to come to me or anyone else for approval, it's not really your decision, is it?"[21] Thus, an unusually high percentage of all the decisions to pursue new projects and to operate existing projects were made by AES people who were on the ground at the scene of the action and who didn't occupy managerial positions. The acknowledgment by AES top executives that people were fallible translated into a policy of not punishing AES people when the risks of a project went the wrong way and things did not turn out well for the company. (However, underperforming projects did have adverse bonus and compensation consequences for the teams and decision makers that were involved.)

Just how fully AES practiced the principle of decentralized decision making and the high degree of trust that it placed in its people was illustrated by the company's $3 billion acquisition of the 4,000 mW Drax power plant in England. In his letter to the shareholders in the company's 1999 annual report, Dennis Bakke told how the decision came to be made and the rationale for delegating major decisions to people deep in the AES organizational structure:

> The decision was not made by the Board of Directors, not by me (the CEO), not by any of our 20 corporate officers and world group leaders, not by a leader of one of our 79 operating businesses, and not even by the head of one of our business development departments. John Turner made this decision when he had been with the company less than two years. I had not even met him in person before he made the final call. John did follow the requirement of every person who is making a decision at AES. He got advice from every corner of the company, including Board members. But in the end, the decision was his. The advice process, with subsequent decision-making and accountability of the decision maker, has five important functions in our work community:
>
> - *Information sharing:* informs the rest of the organization and connects them to the issue under consideration.
> - *Linkage:* links the decision maker to others in the company and discourages the "Lone Ranger" mentality. The individual is connected to the community.

---

[20]Roger Sant, speech, March 1996; posted in the Founders Corner at (www.aesc.com) as of March 12, 2001.

[21]Carol Bowers, "The Amazing Rise of AES," *Utility Business*, April 2000.

- *Education:* through the AES intranet system, the decision maker is afforded the best education possible from colleagues prior to pulling the trigger.
- *Growth:* stimulates enormous personal growth among frontline decision makers.
- *Fun:* for the people involved, the experience is just plain fun.

John Turner, 41, who was the leader of one of AES's business development teams in London at the time, sent e-mails to numerous AES people across the world, seeking the benefit of their own experiences and their counsel. In arriving at his decision to go forward with the Drax acquisition, Turner contacted board members, officers, and senior managers, seeking information and advice, as well as keeping them informed of where things stood as investigation of the project and negotiations went forward. Turner indicated that plenty of advice was given and many opinions were expressed, but he said, "I don't feel that I was being pushed in any one direction."[22] Sant and Bakke believed that John Turner's actions confirmed their belief that people, almost invariably, would rise to the level of trust and decision-making confidence that the company placed in them.

An AES person in the Netherlands, commenting on the company's reliance on empowerment and decentralized decision making, said:

> I enjoy the freedom and responsibility that I have in my position with AES. I'm grateful that I am trusted to do what is necessary to ensure that my responsibilities are handled and that I will seek advice as needed. In short, no one is looking over my shoulder.[23]

Sant, when he was CEO, and Bakke, during his tenure as CEO, both took pride in making very few decisions over the course of a year. Bakke tried to restrict himself to only one decision annually, stating:

> We group all of our properties into 14 regions, but we keep growing. So every year, I get to re-allocate the world. I pick the groups and the group leaders.[24]

The Role and Makeup of AES's Business Development Teams

Some of AES's biggest and best new business activities came from the entrepreneurial efforts of business development teams composed of personnel whose primary jobs were in the company's power plants or distribution operations. AES made a concerted effort to have operations people on each business development team—partly because of their expertise in sizing up the ins and outs of operating the facilities being considered for new investment, and partly to help develop the company's base of entrepreneurial talent. Including so many members from operations on business development teams resulted in AES having an unusually large number of its people active in exploring such new business opportunities as plant expansions, cogeneration projects to convert waste to energy, project refinancing, investments to extend the life of older AES plants, acquiring an existing plant or distribution business, or constructing a new plant.

---

[22]Quoted in Behr, "Power Surge."

[23]Quoted in the company's annual report, 2000, p. 17.

[24]Bowers, "The Amazing Rise of AES," p. 2.

Controlling the Decisions of Empowered AES Workers

In 1991, a doctoral student doing a study of AES spent several weeks at two of the company's plants and came away somewhat amazed at what he had observed:

> I can't believe what I've been seeing! First, they all tell me that they really look forward to coming to work in the morning. Second, they tell me they have the freedom to do anything they want. I say: Really? There must be some controls. They tell me: "No. We really can do anything we want."[25]

The freedom of AES people to do anything they wanted wasn't literally true because there were boundaries and controls in the form of performance measures, information flows and reports, peer pressure, and compensation incentives. For example, AES had the following set of performance targets in place at its power plants and actual performance on each measure was reported daily to all plant personnel:[26]

- *Safety*: Work-related injuries reportable to the U.S. Occupational Safety and Health Administration (OSHA), with comparisons to the industry average. The objective was an incidence rate of zero.
- *Environment*: The amount of sulfur dioxide emissions (which was typically regulated because this compound was a cause of acid rain); the amount of nitrogen oxide (NO_x) emissions—a cause of smog, and an assortment of other pollutants that varied by plant type.
- *Plant availability*: The percentage of hours the plant was available to produce electricity, as opposed to being offline for maintenance and repairs.
- *Heat rate*: The efficiency with which the plant converted fuel into electricity (the heat rate represents the number of British thermal units [BTUs] of fuel consumed per kilowatt-hour of electricity generated).
- *Cost per kilowatt-hour of electricity generated*: Plant costs divided by kilowatt-hour production.
- *Plant profitability*: The plant's profit (or loss) and return on investment.

AES distribution businesses utilized such performance measures as safety and work-related injuries, outage minutes per customer (the average number of minutes that electric service to homes and businesses was interrupted due to storms or equipment failures), customer complaint frequencies, costs per mile of distribution wire, and profitability.

All facility personnel were expected to do their jobs in a manner that contributed to good performance on the specified measures. Frontline workers were as aware as managers were of a facility's current performance against the target. Because worker compensation incentives were tied to performance of their team and business unit, there was considerable peer pressure among coworkers for each individual to do his or her best to achieve or beat the targeted performance standards.

For the most part, however, there were minimal controls on the expenditures that individual team members could authorize. Dennis Bakke, for example, expressed his displeasure at discovering that AES leaders in a Northern Ireland facility had put the equivalent of a $3,200 limit on purchases by individual team members:

---

[25]Quoted in Waterman, *What America Does Right,* and posted on (www.aesc.com), February 22, 2001.

[26]Based in part on information in Waterman, *What America Does Right.*

Approval processes are inconsistent with our principles. They take the fun—the responsibility and therefore the mental and emotional engagement—out of work. In fact, I think I would like to see approval limits abolished at every level of the company—not just for $2,000, but for $2 million or $200 million.[27]

Information Systems and Information Sharing

Information flowed freely and frequently at AES. There were very few restrictions on the data and information made readily available to AES personnel at all levels, and the company culture encouraged AES people to volunteer their knowledge and advice when asked. All financial and market information was widely circulated, and so were the details of actual and potential acquisitions. For regulatory purposes, all AES people were treated as insiders for stock trading because of the detailed information that was available to organization members. While there were some worries about sensitive information getting leaked to competitors, AES executives felt the benefits of extensive information sharing outweighed the risks—mainly because frontline people could not make wise decisions without accurate and timely information at their fingertips and because it helped AES people become better businesspeople.

COMPENSATION, INCENTIVES, AND PERFORMANCE EVALUATION

Roughly 50 percent of a person's compensation at AES was based on such quantitative factors as financial performance, safety, achievement of a particular facility's operating targets (plant availability, heat rate, cost per kilowatt-hour generated, outage minutes, and the like) and environmental impact measures. The other 50 percent was based on how well people, individually and as a group, understood and adhered to the company's four shared values.

AES's two cofounders believed strongly that it was better for people to be paid a base salary than to be paid an hourly wage. Indeed, for the past five years, AES senior management had been campaigning against what Bakke referred to as "the demeaning practice" of paying people hourly wages plus overtime; company leaders were actively encouraging those who received hourly wages to switch to a compensation system where they received a salary and had incentive opportunities to earn bonuses and stock options, as well as the other freedoms that accompanied salaried employee status. Bakke explained that paying people for time spent on the job ran counter to the expectation that all AES people should use their brainpower and creativity in the course of performing their tasks and making decisions:

> Paying people for the physical time they spend at the workplace (including the curious concept of "overtime") is incompatible with the knowledge and thinking required at all times by all people to excel in a modern business. It also makes it difficult for people to feel and act like fully responsible business people. We have been surprised by how quickly people are switching voluntarily from hourly pay to annual salaries. This year 90% of the AES miners in Hungary have opted for a fixed salary with opportunity for bonus and no overtime pay. At our unionized plant in Pittsburgh, 71% have switched. In businesses owned by AES for at least three years, 89% are now paid like business people rather than hourly workers, up from less than 10% just four years ago. This is not a symbolic change; we believe it helps us reach our goal of making every AES person a businessperson.

---

[27]Quoted in Wetlaufer, "Organizing for Empowerment," p. 117.

As of 2001, about 80 percent of all 26,600 company employees were salaried and the company was continuing its efforts to persuade the remaining 20 percent to voluntarily abandon the hourly-wage-plus-overtime approach. Just over 1,700 AES people switched from hourly to salaried compensation in 2000, including people in the California plants, the Argentine distribution business, Northern Ireland, and several newly acquired facilities. The long-term goal was to have no hourly workers at any AES location in the world.

At most all AES facilities, there were incentive plans for salaried AES people to earn bonuses and qualify for stock options based on the performance of their project/business unit and on the company's overall performance. Hourly workers were generally not eligible for bonuses. For example, AES's Shady Point power plant in Poteau, Oklahoma, had performance targets for safety, plant availability, cost per kilowatt-hour generated, and several other measures. Achievement of each target was worth a specified amount of dollars for the bonus pool; at the end of the year, the total dollar size of the bonus pool was determined based on the plant's performance. The size of each person's bonus was determined by dividing the total dollar amount in the bonus pool by the number of salaried workers at the plant—thus, each salaried person's bonus was the same dollar amount, irrespective of salary and job title. Many of AES's plants used this "equal-dollar" method to allocating bonuses.

All salaried AES employees were eligible for incentive stock option awards. The company's stock option plan was administered by the compensation committee of the board of directors. In determining which employees were entitled to stock options, this committee took into account the nature and length of service rendered by the employee; the employee's past, present, and potential contributions to the success of the company; and other relevant factors. All stock options were granted at an exercise price equal to the market price of the company's common stock on the date of the option grant. Options for 2.4 million shares were granted in 1999, and options for 3.1 million shares were granted in 2000. A total of 8.3 million previously awarded shares was exercised during the 1998–2000 period. Going into 2001, company personnel held unexercised options for just over 15 million shares; 10.9 million of these shared were eligible to be exercised by year-end 2001. Approximately 29 percent of AES personnel owned shares of the company's stock.

There were occasions when failure to achieve certain performance targets cut sharply into bonus compensation. For example, at some AES facilities, if there was one accident, bonuses for everyone at the facility were cut 25 percent, two accidents resulted in a 50 percent cut, and three accidents resulted in no bonuses. In 1998, all employees companywide suffered a 10 percent bonus reduction because there were four fatal accidents at AES plants in China, Kazakhstan, and Pakistan. Dennis Bakke's justification for reducing bonuses companywide was "Our company is a community, and we are accountable to the world as one."[28] All serious mistakes, and mistakes made a second or third time, resulted in financial penalties for the decision makers involved. However, mistakes without significant consequences, made as people were learning, were not penalized.

HIRING AND SELECTION

AES strived to attract and hire the kind of person who, on discovering a problem or new business opportunity, would willingly and readily step up to the plate and take a

---

[28]Ibid., p. 119.

lead role in making things happen and getting something done. The idea was that if you saw a problem, then it was yours and you accepted responsibility for taking the initiative to find a solution. In addition to a person's willingness to take on responsibility, other key hiring criteria included acceptance of AES's values and a candidate's experience and expertise.

Each AES facility had responsibility for recruiting, interviewing, screening, and hiring its own people. There was no AES corporate staff that assisted AES field units with the screening and selection function. The company rarely used headhunters to locate candidates for job openings and did not spend much time recruiting. Very few outsiders were hired into senior positions. Instead, the company preferred to promote from within its ranks and new people typically were hired at the local level to fill openings in the company's plants and electric distribution businesses.

As a rule, the company had a large pool of job applicants to choose from. Many applications were the result of current AES people telling their friends and acquaintances about job openings and about the work environment at AES. In most of the communities where AES operated, grapevine information about AES produced a general consensus that AES was a good company to work for—there was considerable local folklore about the company's operating practices, and many people knew about the company's reputation and the successes it had enjoyed. In Kazakhstan, for example, where AES purchased six plants over an 18-month period and supplied about 30 percent of the market, AES employees who had been with the company scarcely six months did what management considered as "an incredible job" explaining to local government officials that capitalism did not have to be "gangsterism" (which was the perception of many); moreover, they communicated to the local people how AES did business and how it represented a different approach to capitalism—all of which helped AES gain a favorable image locally and attract a better caliber of job applicants for the six plants.

Given the sizable applicant pool at most AES facilities, AES was able to pick and choose among those most likely to fit into the AES scheme of things and to understand what it meant to be an AES person (the company did not refer to its people as workers or employees). People at AES believed there was quite a bit of self-selection on the part of job applicants—that is, job seekers who thought they would like working at AES based on what they knew about the company were strongly inclined to apply for job openings, whereas people who didn't feel comfortable with the emphasis the company placed on its four values or with being held accountable for their actions and decisions looked elsewhere for employment.

Applicants were hired primarily because of their cultural fit and secondarily for their technical skills and experience. Teams interviewed candidates for openings on their teams, having multiple meetings with the candidate and among themselves to try to get a strong sense of whether the candidate would be comfortable in the AES work environment. The interview process aimed at determining whether the candidate would eagerly accept decision-making responsibility and be willing to be held completely accountable for results. Candidates were queried about whether they believed it was the responsibility of companies to try to improve the lives of people and the well-being of society in general and what they defined as having fun on the job; other representative interview questions included:[29]

---

[29]Based on information in ibid., p. 116.

- What does "fair" mean to you? Does it mean treating everyone equally? How important is it for a company to demonstrate fairness in its business dealings?
- What would you do if something needs to be done and no procedure exists?
- What kinds of rewards are most satisfying to you?
- What self-improvement efforts are you pursuing?
- What is the most difficult situation you have confronted at work? How did you handle it?
- Have you ever encountered a situation when people around you weren't being totally honest? What did you do?

The company was especially attracted to candidates who were more evangelical about the company's four values than simply being accepting of these values.

JOB SECURITY

One of the more vexing concerns at AES was the issue of job security. In a number of countries where AES had acquired new power plants and operated distribution businesses, the workforce was larger than AES believed was necessary. In nearly every case, AES had moved aggressively and quickly to eliminate overstaffing and to "right-size" the personnel count at each facility. The fear of job loss created anxiety at some AES locations, prompting examination of whether AES should take pains to keep people employed because it was not "fair" to fire people given the stress and economic hardship that it created. Some people at AES even argued that it was not socially responsible for AES to put people out of their jobs. AES management, however, took a strong position against perpetuating overstaffing, relying on the following arguments:[30]

- The dynamics of the real world are such that every job is subject to constant change. While some jobs change faster than others, all people have to keep changing how they do their work to keep up with the changes swirling about them.
- In the course of doing their jobs, individuals gain new knowledge and new skills, often take on new or different responsibilities, and experience changes in which interests and challenges them. Thus, over time, no one really has the job he or she used to have, even if it is still with the same organization.
- At AES, we expect people to make decisions and be held accountable for them, to broaden their responsibilities, to be part of one or more multidisciplinary teams whose assignments and duties may change from time to time, and to cross-train so as to be able to perform a variety of team tasks. Even for those who stay at AES, the current jobs of team members will look different from the jobs they had in times past and their future jobs will differ from the ones they have now.
- It is irresponsible to keep one more person in an organization than is necessary to meet the organization's performance targets. Even one extra person will reduce the ability of other organizational members to use their gifts and talents to the maximum because some of the responsibility and tasks will have to be shared with the extra person.
- Keeping an unneeded person in an organization is further socially irresponsible because it robs society of the chance to benefit from the unneeded person's gifts

---

[30]Based on information in Dennis Bakke, "Potholes in the Road: Am I Going to Lose My Job?" posted in the Founders Corner at (www.aesc.com) as of March 19, 2001.

and skills in another venue. By freeing a person from an unproductive, overstaffed job, society gains another problem-solving citizen.

- Keeping an unneeded person in a position that cannot fully use that person's skills is not kind or generous to that person because it denies the person the opportunity to grow and develop and, ultimately, contribute as much as he or she is capable of contributing. (In his letter to the shareholders in the company's 1999 annual report, Dennis Bakke related the following in support of this point: "Recently, I heard that if a newborn shark, six or seven inches long, is placed in a home-sized aquarium, it can survive as it grows older but its growth is severely stunted and its body deformed. It becomes extremely aggressive and can be kept from escaping its restrictive environment only with a heavily weighted cover. At AES we do not want people's growth and passion confined like a shark restricted to a small aquarium.")

- Overstaffing further raises operating costs above what they should be, thus making it necessary to raise prices to customers; higher costs further have the effect of risking the viability of the whole business and leave less monies to compensate other employees and reward shareholders.

Application of these principles has kept overstaffing at AES to a bare minimum and, on occasion, resulted in significant workforce reductions at newly acquired facilities. For example, in 1998 AES acquired a power plant in Panama that had a workforce of 300 people, only 100 of whom were really needed. The AES team in Panama implemented a generous voluntary severance program and 200 people chose to leave. As part of the process, AES established a venture loan fund to assist those leaving to start new businesses. A total of 67 new businesses were initiated, ranging from restaurants to retail stores to small manufacturing operations. In Venezuela, when AES acquired Electricidad de Caracas SA in 2000, half of the employees opted for voluntary severance packages, reducing the number of management layers from 14 to 4.

ISSUES AND FUTURE OUTLOOK

AES management was quick to publicly admit the company's shortcomings and mistakes. In the company's 1999 annual report Bakke confessed:

> Our businesses in Brazil were a short-term economic disaster for us in 1999, and for that we are responsible. Someday, in one of these letters, I hope to write you without having to admit mistakes and failures. But, again this year we had lots of them, including our poor performance in Brazil, for which we ask your forgiveness. I guess my minister was correct when he said, "Forgiveness is like taking out the garbage. Once is not enough."
>
> Again, safety was our lowest grade for the year. Eleven of our own people and 8 contactors died at work in 1999. We will continue to give ourselves low marks until there are no deaths. Every leader in the company will have safety high on his or her priority list in the coming year.

In his 2000 annual letter to the shareholders, Bakke said:

> As usual, we made more mistakes than we ought. Plant reliability was down. We probably paid too much for our Drax business in the U.K. In several of our distribution companies, too many people still manage to get electricity without paying. And our safety record, though greatly improved, still falls far short of what we aspire to. We didn't do as much as we would have liked to anticipate the California electricity meltdown. And a couple of our startup businesses didn't do well either.

Exhibit 8 shows the report card that Dennis Bakke gave the company for its performance in 1999 and 2000.

exhibit 8   The Grades Dennis Bakke Gave AES for Its Performance, 1999 and 2000

1999		2000	
Performance Target	**Grade**	**Performance Target**	**Grade**
Finance or refinance 18 previously announced businesses	A−	Gain operating control of AES businesses where AES has a minority ownership position (so as to better install AES values and operating philosophy	A−
Experience no deaths of AES people in the workplace	D	Experience no deaths of AES people in the workplace and reduce public deaths associated with AES distribution operations	C−
Operate businesses cleanly, safely, reliably, and at lower costs	B+	Operate businesses cleaner, safer, more reliably, and at lower cost than in 1999	B
Live AES principles and make everyone an AES businessperson	B+	Live AES principles and make everyone an AES businessperson	A−
Maintain a backlog of over 100 new business opportunities	A+	Nurture fledgling new retail supply and telecom businesses into thriving enterprises	C
Create 12–18 new businesses	A+	Develop 15–20 new businesses (Result: Added 39 businesses with $11 billion in assets)	A+
Make budgeted income and cash flow	C	Make budgeted income and cash flow	B+

Source: Company annual reports, 1999 and 2000.

The construction and operation of power plants and electric distribution facilities had many hazardous aspects, prompting most top-tier companies to place considerable emphasis on workplace safety. AES, despite the priority placed on safety, was experiencing difficulty in reducing work-related deaths at its operations—in 1999, the company had 11 AES people and 8 contractor personnel die in the workplace versus 8 AES people and 12 contractor personnel in 2000. (All of the deaths in 2000 were at facilities owned or controlled by AES three years or less.) There were over 54,000 people at various AES facilities worldwide, although only around 26,600 of these were at facilities under AES's direct operating control. Work-related death and accident rates were highest at facilities under AES control for less than three years. In businesses controlled by AES for three years or more, the company's severe accident rate worldwide was 55 percent lower than for similar U.S. businesses. One of the company's biggest safety-related successes in 2000 was in the Dominican Republic where in 1999, the year before AES acquired its Dominican Republic distribution company, 385 public citizens died in electricity-related accidents; in 2000, under AES operations and control, that number of public deaths was reduced to 29.

While operating costs continued to fall in most of AES's businesses (dropping about 4.5 percent on average in 2000), the company believed that costs were not being driven down fast enough at several locations—the Telasi plant in Georgia, the Hefei and Chengdu plants in China, and the distribution business in India. The company's California plants were not profitable in 2000, partly because of the $17 million fine for excessive pollution; the company's retail energy and telecom businesses were expected to lose money for several years before achieving the scale of operation needed for profitability. In general, the company's foreign distribution businesses were doing a better job of reducing workforce sizes and reducing the frequency and duration of customer outages than they were in doing accurate metering, reducing electricity losses from theft, and collecting past due accounts. The recently acquired Drax plant in England was not meeting bottom-line expectations because of lower-than-expected competitive prices for generation. Also, the company's traditional electric and gas utility business in Illinois, CILCORP (whose acquisition was completed in 1999), did not perform up to expectations in 2000. AES was able to meet its budgeted earnings target and nearly meet its cash flow target in 2000 because of unexpectedly strong performances by the company's power plants in New York and the newly acquired Venezuelan utility.

The gross margins on AES's distribution businesses were sharply lower than for its power generating business (see Exhibit 6) and the company had substantial and rising annual interest expenses (see Exhibit 3) as a consequence of its use of debt to finance new acquisitions and construction. A number of Wall Street securities analysts had commented on the risks inherent in AES's strategy and the potential for shortfalls or volatility in the company's short-term financial performance.

Another ongoing issue revolved around sometimes strained working relationships between AES and a number of its business partners. AES management attributed the company's problems in working well with its partners and strategic allies to clashes between AES's culture and the cultures, values, and operating philosophies of partner companies. Some of AES's partners were highly resistant to the elimination of hourly wages and were less than enthusiastic about AES's views about how to pursue having fun in the workplace. In several cases where culture clashes with partners were making it hard for AES to achieve the hoped-for performance and results on its investments, AES was endeavoring to resolve the conflicts by either seeking majority ownership and operating control over the projects or disposing of its interests in minority-owned facilities.

Near-Term Performance Targets

AES's performance targets for 2001 included the following:

- No work-related deaths of AES people.
- Start 20–25 new businesses.
- Operate company businesses cleaner, safer, more reliably, and at lower cost than in 2000.
- Achieve 2001 budgeted earnings and cash flow.
- Live AES principles and make everyone an AES businessperson.
- Celebrate our 20th year (in part by becoming the sixth American business and the first nontechnology company to earn $1 billion in profits in a single year by its 20th birthday).

Dennis Bakke indicated that AES was looking to become more involved in several African sub-Saharan countries and further invest in the Middle East. Insofar as the impact of the mounting electricity crisis in California was concerned, Bakke said:

> I do not believe the California situation will slow the world's march to privatization and deregulation. The mistakes that California officials made may encourage others to do a better job of restructuring their own electricity sectors. If so, AES and others will likely continue to find numerous opportunities to serve these new markets. Almost certainly the California crisis enhances AES's opportunities for new business in California and the surrounding states.[31]

---

[31]AES annual report, 2000, p. 11.

case | 33 Optivus Technology

Lee Hanson
California State University at San Bernardino

"If we want things to stay as they are, things will have to change. Do you know?"
—Giuseppe di Lampedusa, *The Leopard*

Halloween afternoon, 1999. Jon W. Slater, president and chief executive officer of Optivus Technology, Inc., relaxed in his chair with his brown hair concealed beneath a thick wig of dreadlocks—his costume for the company party carrying on in the big high-ceilinged room outside his office door.

Before him sat Kip Edwards, a man Slater was sizing up for the job of Optivus Technology's very first chief operating officer (COO). Owing to busy calendars, the only time available for the interview had been in the middle of the party. But that hardly bothered the boyish-looking 42-year-old Slater, who was enjoying Edwards's bemused reaction to the holiday attire of his prospective new boss. For if Optivus's new COO needed anything in the days ahead, it would be humor. His job was to help pilot the $9 million high-tech firm and its 80 employees through an expected tripling of staff and a 20-fold growth in revenues as they commenced manufacturing of their unique medical technology.

Making the transition into manufacturing would mean big change for this team-based, highly participatory engineering firm, which had begun in 1987 as a small group of computer engineers at a medical research university, inspired by a heady mission of pioneering new lifesaving technology. In creating the more structured organization needed for production, Jon Slater hoped to be able to preserve the team system around which he had built Optivus after he spun it off from the university in 1993 to commercialize the technology, at least in part. That was his personal preference, and in addition, he sensed that it could prove crucial to the quality of health care Optivus would provide. Nevertheless, as he looked ahead, it was unclear just how much of the original team system and collegial culture Optivus Technology could hope to keep as it undertook its 20-year strategy for battle against the great killer disease, cancer.

PROTON THERAPY: A NEW TREATMENT

Optivus was in the business of marketing, manufacturing, and operating an $85 million cancer treatment system known as proton beam therapy. A form of radiation technology, proton treatment used a "conformal" beam of radiation, created with a device called a proton accelerator, which could be shaped in three dimensions to irradiate the precise site of a tumor at any depth within the body up to 38 centimeters while inflicting minimal damage on surrounding tissue. By contrast, conventional X-ray treatment bombarded the general area of a cancer with rapidly diminishing effectiveness the deeper in the body the tumor lay, and often at great harm to surrounding organs. The capacity to control the proton beam's shape and depth to achieve a near glovelike fit around a tumor made it possible to apply high doses of radiation while inflicting minimal damage to surrounding healthy tissues, thereby averting the pain and disfigurement so often incurred as side effects of X-rays. The curative power of protons lay in the underlying physical processes by which they destroyed cancerous cells. As with any radioactive material, as protons passed the electrons orbiting the atoms of cells, their positive charge attracted the atoms' negatively charged electrons, pulling them from their orbits and ionizing (tearing apart) the atoms. This destruction altered the characteristics of the molecule housing the atom, and consequently of the larger cell. Particularly affected was the DNA or genetic material of the cell, because ionization destroyed its ability to divide or propagate (if sufficiently damaged, the cell lost its ability to repair itself).

In conventional radiation therapy, ionization commenced as soon as the X rays entered the body. As they passed through it, they steadily lost strength, with the result that the targeted tumor often got less than a full dose of radiation. At the same time, organs and tissue in front of and behind the tumor were injured. While healthy cells might be able to regenerate themselves, the patient usually suffered side effects of cell damage. These side effects varied depending on the organs surrounding the tumor, but they often were long lasting, and frequently permanent.

Things were very different with protons. The faster the protons traveled, the less chance they had of interacting with and ionizing other atoms; ionization began to occur as the protons slowed. Since the protons entered the body at the enormous rate of nearly half the speed of light, no appreciable ionization occurred. As the protons began to slow under control of the accelerator, the distance in which they started to ionize was about half an inch, the rate of ionization rising rapidly until it reached its maximum level, called the Bragg Peak, at which the protons were most destructive to cancer cells. The proton beam could be controlled to reach its Bragg Peak at whatever the location and depth of the tumor in a patient's body, and within its three-dimensional confines. As a result, highly concentrated doses of protons, administered over a treatment period of several weeks, could destroy an isolated tumor with minimal damage to cells of surrounding tissue.[1] The "dead" tumor wss gradually absorbed by the body and carried away in the bloodstream as waste material.

The World's First Hospital-Based Proton Treatment Center

The proton beam that targeted cancerous cell growth with such precision was propagated and delivered via an imposing system of ultra-high-tech machinery housed in a concrete-encased, earthquake-resistant facility with foundations over 50 feet in the earth. Staffed by about 60 clinical, technical, and operational personnel, a proton treatment center consisted of several main elements (see Exhibit 1).

A synchrotron—a ring of magnets about 20 feet across—employed an electrified "injector" device to strip protons, the positively charged nucleus of the hydrogen atom, from hydrogen gas. The protons then were accelerated around the synchrotron's ring

---

[1]The average for all types of proton treatment "protocols" was about 20 treatment sessions, with each session averaging about two minutes of patient exposure to the proton beam.

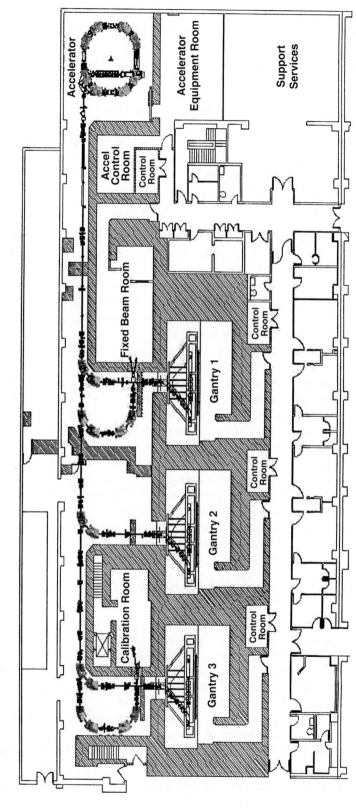

exhibit 1 Proton Treatment Center

Accelerator

Accelerator Equipment Room

Support Services

Accel Control Room

Control Room

Fixed Beam Room

Gantry 1

Control Room

Gantry 2

Control Room

Calibration Room

Gantry 3

Control Room

to a speed of over 75,000 miles per second (hence the name *proton accelerator*), forming a proton beam about three-eighths of an inch in diameter. From the synchrotron, the beam was pulled into a beam transport system, a vacuum tube composed of bending and focusing magnets, which then carried the stream of protons to one of four treatment stations.

The first of these, situated nearest to the synchrotron, was a fixed-beam treatment room in which the proton beam was projected through a stationary orifice for treatment of brain and eye tumors. Next in line were three nearly identical treatment rooms, each served by a beam positioned for aiming via gantries—30-foot-high, 95-ton circular mechanisms resembling Ferris wheels that revolved around each station to permit the proton beam to be directed wherever needed on the patient's recumbent body. A nozzle projecting from the gantry held a device called a bolus—a wax form, varying in size from a human fist to a volleyball, that was precision-machined using computerized milling equipment to the exact shape and contours of the patient's tumor. The bolus permitted the proton beam to be directed onto the tumor with minimal damage to surrounding tissue. In the cylindrical, delivery-van-sized treatment rooms with their futuristic curved walls of molded plastic, patients lay comfortably on a gurney in a plastic pod, or body mold, shaped to their exact form to hold them in the same position for each of their treatment sessions. Looking up or to the side, depending on positioning, all the patients could see of the concealed gantry above them was what appeared to be a big camera eye gazing at them.

Flow of the beam to the treatment rooms (including speed and number of protons, which determined depth of penetration of the beam) was controlled by technicians in computer-packed control rooms situated just to the side of each of the treatment rooms. Another branch of the beam transport system fed into a carbon-filled underground "dump" that absorbed excess proton energy. In six preparation rooms immediately across the hall, patients were readied for movement into the treatment rooms, each patient taking around 10 minutes to be prepped, wheeled in, treated, then brought out once finished. In theory, with all four treatment stations in operation, as many as 320 patients potentially could be treated in a day. In actual practice, owing to patients missing treatments or showing up late, average sustained throughput was less than this, presently 130 patients per day at peak. However, it was anticipated that rates would increase in future years as further enhancements of the technology accelerated patient throughput.

Thus far, the dominant application of proton treatment was for prostate cancer, with less extensive use in tumors of the brain, eye, and other sites where a localized tumor surrounded by normal tissue has not spread (metastasized) to other parts of the body. However, the range of "protocols," or applications, was broadening as increases in clinical experience, diagnostic equipment, and computer-based control capabilities made it possible to apply protons to other forms of cancer and noncancerous growths, such as age-related macular degeneration of the eye. Nearly 50 proton treatment protocols had been approved. Slater and some other experts believed that protons eventually would supplant traditional X-ray radiotherapy—which was used in 50 percent of cancer cases—as well as many types of cancer surgery, such as prostate cancer.[2]

The first high-energy proton accelerator designed specifically for patient use, rather than physics research, began to be constructed in mid-1988 at Loma Linda University Medical Center (LLUMC) in Loma Linda, California, 60 miles east of

---

[2]Proton treatment was not envisioned to replace chemotherapy or hormone therapy used for metastasized, or nonlocal, cancers.

Los Angeles.[3] The facility's fixed beam room, completed in Phase 1 of the project, became operational late in 1990, treating 53 patients in its first full year of operation. The construction of the first gantry and treatment room (Phase 2a), followed by the other two (Phase 2b), was completed in 1994, increasing patient volume dramatically. As of late 1999, over 5,000 patients with cancers and nonmalignant tumors isolated in some 20 different body sites had been treated at LLUMC. Its five-year success rate, documented in a growing volume of clinical studies, had resulted (in 1997) in proton treatment no longer being classified by the Food and Drug Administration as an investigational therapy. It was now endorsed and fully reimbursed by Medicare and many private health insurance carriers.

Optivus' Mission: Present and Future

Optivus Technology, spun off from LLUMC in 1993 to commercialize proton treatment, had a dual corporate mission. Under contract with the university, it was responsible for maintaining and upgrading the operating systems being used by medical staff. This contract was presently the company's main source of revenue. In fulfilling it, Optivus engineers and technicians had pushed the technology steadily to enhance both its capability and capacity. Improvements included complete redesign in 1994 of the treatment computer control system, and in 1996 of the patient digital alignment control system. In 1997, the Phase 1 and Phase 2a beam steering control systems had been upgraded. Certification for ISO 9001 was attained in 1999, which had produced much helpful documentation of systems and procedures. Currently, work was under way to supplant the original "passive" proton beam with an "active" beam transport system that could attack large, irregularly shaped tumors, an innovation that would expand further the range of disease forms treatable with protons. With an active beam system, the proton beam could be scanned, or "rastored," vertically and horizontally over the cancer site in a manner similar to a scalpel paring tissue. This would make it possible to irradiate large sites, such as the chest, without having to realign the patient and incurring the resultant time delays. The active beam system, which was expected to be in operation sometime in 2003, would become a standard feature of all new proton facilities.

The second role of Optivus—and the most exciting for its future—was to market and sell proton beam centers through a technology licensing agreement with Loma Linda University. Jon Slater's ambition was to create as many as 100 proton facilities over 20 years. Although naysayers claimed the huge price tag of a proton treatment center would limit the number that would ever be built, Slater believed the potential market existed simply because proton treatment's actual costs were ultimately lower than alternative treatment modalities once all costs, including treatment of side effects, were taken into account. Furthermore, Optivus's financial projections (corroborated by experience at LLUMC) promised that proton centers could be hugely profitable for a hospital, producing an average annual return on investment of 25 percent, once fully operational.[4] See Exhibit 2 for Optivus's income statements.

Although cost comparisons were limited so far, it was already clear that proton treatment could be less expensive ultimately than cancer surgery. For example, proton treatment for prostate cancer—usually performed on an outpatient basis—averaged $17,000, about the same as the cost of prostatectomy surgery. However, as many as

---

[3]Mike Schwartz, "Tiny Protons Deal a Mighty, Precise Blow: Loma Linda University Medical Center Has the Only High-Energy Proton Laboratory in the World Designed Specifically for Patient Care," *Press-Enterprise*, May 11, 1997.

[4]Internal company projections based on confidential data.

exhibit 2 Optivus Technology's Income Statements, 1994–2001

	Projected 2001	2000	1999	1998	1997	1996	1995	1994
Revenue, net	$8,370,864	$7,690,389	$6,884,940	$5,477,314	$4,967,391	$5,026,957	$4,608,284	$5,407,047
Cost of products and service	6,157,335	5,580,926	4,140,891	3,265,258	1,829,481	2,392,084	2,386,207	2,010,230
Gross profit	2,213,529	2,109,463	2,744,049	2,212,056	3,137,910	2,634,873	2,222,077	3,396,817
General and administrative	2,092,716	1,922,597	1,947,136	2,143,246	2,495,779	1,734,550	1,536,054	1,431,223
Income from operations	120,813	186,866	796,913	68,810	642,131	900,323	686,023	1,965,594
Other income (expense):								
Interest income	60,000	59,074	81,053	85,514	19,238	14,678	26,370	27,461
Interest expense	(20,000)	(24,000)	(4,364)	(13,335)	(9,292)	(18,786)	(20,227)	(22,440)
Other, net	105,148	342	205,494	59,982	(251,497)	(33,396)	2,807	1,462
Total other income	145,148	35,416	282,183	132,161	(241,551)	(37,504)	8,950	6,483
Income before provision for income taxes	265,961	222,282	1,079,096	200,971	400,580	862,819	694,973	1,972,077
Provision (benefit) for income taxes	173,865	55,270	409,500	76,800	233,700	382,300	232,700	854,813
Net income	$ 92,096	$ 167,012	$ 669,596	$ 124,171	$ 166,880	$ 480,519	$ 462,273	$1,117,264

8 percent of prostatectomy patients suffered subsequent problems with incontinence, compared to less than 1 percent with proton treatment. Up to 60 percent of prostate surgery patients were faced with varying degrees of impotence, and while comparative rates with proton treatment were under study, LLUMC researchers believed the level would be less than 30 percent. Whether paid by patients or their insurers, treatment of side effects of prostatectomy could cost as much as two times the surgery itself, leading in some cases to total expenditures of as much as $50,000. These additional costs were largely avoided with proton treatment.[5]

As for conventional radiation, while it was hard to make precise cost comparisons because of the complicated billing and reimbursement practices used in the American health care system, clinical experience and research suggested that proton therapy was ultimately as much as a third less costly. Again considering prostate treatment, up to 5 percent of patients receiving conventional radiation suffered from incontinence problems. As many as 10 percent required treatment for toxic effects of radiation on healthy tissue, compared to less than 1 percent with proton treatment. Again, whether borne by insurers or patients, these costs were reduced if not avoided altogether with proton treatment.

Meanwhile, alternatives to proton treatment seemed unlikely to match its capabilities. One promising radiation technique, Intensity Modulated Radiation Therapy (IMRT), was an extension of conventional treatment that created a conformal beam by using multiple portals to project photons from different angles, rather than the conventional fixed X ray. While much less expensive than proton treatment, IMRT was still subject to the limitations of conventional photon radiation, particularly a dose that was at its maximum power at entry to the body. Because IMRT was a relatively new treatment method, developed in the mid-1990s, outcome studies were likely to be several years in the offing.

A second potential rival to protons was heavy ion therapy, which worked similarly to proton treatment and in fact attacked cancer cells with greater force. Unfortunately, heavy-ion systems were likely to cost over $250 million, three times that of proton facilities. Hence, they were likely to remain beyond affordable cost for most hospitals.[6]

As to gene and drug therapies—the principal nonradiation cancer treatments in which great hopes were being placed—here again the prospects appeared dubious. New research indicated that some 80 percent of cancers were environmental in origin, not genetic,[7] which implied that the potential application of gene therapy to cancer would be limited for years to come, if not always. Nor did the alternative of drug treatment seem likely to be a magic bullet for cancer. The most recent research indicated that while drugs might become part of cancer therapies, they were unlikely to be effective enough to actually eliminate the need for radiation treatment.[8]

Against the future possibilities of alternative cancer regimens, proton therapy was here now. Its costs could be amortized over the estimated 40-year lifetime of a proton facility. The human need was acute, while the market opportunity was huge. In America alone, 100,000 people died every year from relatively localized but uncontrolled cancers that might be treated with proton therapy were it available, and 300,000 people were diagnosed annually with some form of localized cancer. Detection might be

[5]Information on treatment outcomes and costs taken from Optivus internal documents.

[6]David Holley, "Targeting Cancer: Early Clinical Trials of the Use of Heavy-Ion Radiation As a Cancer Treatment Have Shown Promise," *Los Angeles Times*, September 15, 1997.

[7]Paul Liechtenstein, "Environmental and Heritable Factors in the Causation of Cancer," *New England Journal of Medicine* 343 (2000), pp. 78–85.

[8]Shannon Brownlee, "Smart Bombs for Targeting Deadly Tumors," *Time*, January 15, 2001.

made earlier, survival rates increased, and treatment costs reduced if proton treatment could be made more widely accessible. Greater public knowledge of the curative power of proton therapy could also help allay general fear of cancer treatment, which was known to cause many people to delay diagnosis, often with tragic (and costly) consequences.

Moreover, additional proton treatment protocols anticipated to be approved by 2003—treating not just cancer, but neurological diseases like Parkinson's and epilepsy—could increase the potential U.S. patient pool to 1,225,000. Just how large, then, was the potential business market? Given a yearly patient load for an individual proton treatment facility of around 3,000 patients, in the United States alone there was, in theory, a market for as many as 100 proton centers. Worldwide, the potential obviously was vastly greater. And for the time being, at least, Optivus Technology was the only serious competitor in the proton system market.

THE CREATION OF THE LOMA LINDA PROTON TREATMENT CENTER

The potential of proton treatment to provide a superior form of cancer therapy was recognized decades before the imaging and computer technology existed to develop a workable treatment modality that could handle large numbers of patients. In 1946, in a landmark paper entitled "Radiological Use of Fast Protons," Dr. Robert Wilson at the Lawrence Berkeley Laboratory at the University of California first proposed its use, and in 1954 limited medical treatment began at Berkeley, using the lab's synchrotron.[9] Subsequently, some 20 other physics labs and research hospitals in the United States and overseas began taking cancer patients on a limited basis, with 30,000 people having been treated worldwide by the late 1990s (including the 5,000 at Loma Linda).

In the early 1970s, under the leadership of Dr. James Slater, father of Jon Slater, physicians at Loma Linda University Medical Center began to investigate the possibilities of proton therapy for hospital-based treatment. After a series of exploratory studies and discussions, it was concluded that computer and scanning technologies required to locate and make accurate images of tumors were not advanced or cost-effective enough at the time to proceed with creating a hospital-based system. Recognizing, however, that advancing technology would eventually solve these problems, the institution focused on developing other facets of radiation science, including treatment planning, to pave the way for a proton accelerator. In the following years, LLUMC researchers participated with other universities in cancer-related research, while the medical center slowly built up a team of specialists whose skills would be needed to create a proton treatment facility.

In 1984, LLUMC joined with several other universities and institutions, including the Lawrence Berkeley Laboratory and the Fermi National Accelerator Laboratory (or "Fermilab") outside Chicago, to form a national Proton Therapy Cooperative Group (PTCOG). Its purpose was to develop conceptual plans for a proton treatment therapy that would make it possible to design and construct a small number of proton systems to be placed in university hospitals. At the instigation of Dr. Slater, LLUMC entered into a contract with Fermilab in 1985 to develop detailed plans and specifications for creating the first hospital-based proton treatment center, to lead to the creation of an actual facility at the university. Thus was born the proton beam project at Loma Linda.

---

[9]Robert R. Wilson, "Radiological Use of Fast Protons," *Radiology* 47 (1946), pp. 487–91.

LLUMC faced two main challenges in bringing a proton center to life. First was obtaining the capital to fund it, estimated at the time to be nearly $34 million, although in fact that estimate proved to be some $11 million short. Financing ultimately came from several sources. Due to the efforts of a local congressman who championed the proton project from its inception, $20 million was appropriated by the federal government, partly from national defense funds. The remainder was obtained through a national fund-raising campaign, from private donations, and from LLUMC resources. (After the proton center became operational, investments in upgrades and improvements brought its total cost to $130 million—a figure that does not count an estimated $50 million in research and development costs invested by LLUMC over more than 20 years. During the 1990s, the proton facility drew to the medical center some $60 million in additional federal investment, a portion of which was used in upgrading the proton treatment system.)

The other main aspect of the proton center project—contracting to build its housing and components—involved three key elements. First was design and construction of the synchrotron. This was done by Fermilab, which completed and shipped the device to Loma Linda in 1990. Second was design of the proton beam system and of the physical facility to house it. The system design was carried out by Science Applications International Corporation (SAIC), a firm that also was the original commercial licensee for new proton treatment centers but later dropped out, opening up a licensing opportunity that came to be filled by Optivus. Design of the physical facility was done by a Seattle-based architectural firm, NBBJ, while the actual structure was built by McCarthy Construction, a hospital construction company.

The third and final aspect of creating the proton center was to design and engineer the technical interface between the proton accelerator and the sophisticated computer system required to control the beam—a hugely complex challenge of marrying the science of the proton facility with state-of-the-art computer technology. For this task, LLUMC chose to create and hire an internal group of engineers to be given the name of the Radiation Research Laboratory. This team needed a leader. Through a series of logical, if not accidental, events, that role fell ultimately to Dr. James Slater's son, Jon Slater.

JON SLATER'S ROAD TO THE PROTON PROJECT

The computer engineer who came to lead the team that turned Loma Linda's proton treatment center into a reality, and in turn created a company to commercialize it, was in many ways an archetypal entrepreneur.

Jon Slater, born in 1957 in Salt Lake City, spent his teen years in Redlands, California, near Optivus's present location in neighboring San Bernardino, and next door to Loma Linda. He had a typical upbringing for his background, though in school he was not quite the scholar that might have been expected given his father's education, career, and status. As Slater himself would concede, by his teens he was rebellious enough to take seriously just the parts of schooling he liked (mainly science and particularly chemistry, at which he excelled), though never so much as to make trouble that might derail his life.

While in high school, he had worked at the radiation oncology lab at LLUMC, where he assisted physicists and got his first exposure to radiation therapy—hardly imagining that it, and the knowledge he gained there, would figure largely in his life some 15 years later. Out of high school, already interested in computers half a decade before the advent of the personal computer, he attended local community college, majoring in computer science. He became a husband at the early age of 20 when he married his high school sweetheart. (Four years later they had a daughter, the first of four children.) While his wife studied to become a nurse, Slater held down a series of jobs, including used-car salesman, tract-home construction worker (he hung doors and installed dishwashers), and machine operator for a year and a half in a machine shop that made forged pistons for race cars. In the last months of that job, he was involved in the painstaking precision labor of designing high-performance pistons—an experience in exacting engineering and metal fabrication that also would figure in his later life.

In Slater's junior year of college, he and his wife left California to go to the University of Utah for completion of his undergraduate work, after which he continued on in a master's program in computer science. While there, in addition to job stints as a janitor at a public utility, and later in a technical position with a major defense contractor with a branch in Salt Lake City, he worked as a research assistant in the university's radiation oncology department. There he first became truly conversant in the physics of radiation therapy. He also had a hand in developing several computer patents—his first taste of academic research commercialization. His latent rebelliousness (or, as he thought of it, demanding standards of personal responsibility) also showed itself on an occasion when, after a term with a professor he viewed as arrogantly indifferent to both his students and quality of his instruction, Slater orchestrated a protest that led to the professor's being removed from teaching the course. And, one weekend in 1985, during a visit to Salt Lake City, his father first talked with him about the proton project starting to take shape at Loma Linda University Medical Center, showing him sketches of the planned treatment stations.

A Season in Silicon Valley

Jon Slater had completed all of his work on his master's degree, save writing the thesis, when events brought his higher education to a close. On the recommendation of a faculty member who was going there, a high-tech company in northern California's Silicon Valley made Slater a job offer as a computer science engineer. The opportunity seemed too good to pass up, mainly because by this point Slater knew what he wanted to do with his life: found a company of his own to make supercomputers. What the new job provided was a first step down that road.

Slater stayed just a year, giving his notice on the last day of his 12-month contract. It had been time enough for three things to happen to him. First, he saw how Silicon Valley's semiconductor and computer industry companies depended for their success on the talent of people and ideas they could attract—something made possible by the array of higher education institutions in the area that provided a steady flow of collegiate research and graduates into local companies.

Second, he came to the conclusion that, for all the talk about "empowerment" and liberated management practices in Silicon Valley, plenty of the companies there—like all of the conventional ones he'd worked in previously—continued to be run in ways that were anything but empowered. The much-vaunted team systems of high-tech companies often seemed to be a matter of management telling employees, "We're a team—now act like it." Apart from niceties like flextime, from what Slater could tell, even in the world's hottest high-tech zone there was rampant failure to provide the kind of fear-free, creative workplace that fit with his own emerging sense of what makes for real empowerment and corporate performance. This was, in essence, a company that encourages, indeed requires, people to take responsibility for managing themselves. In exchange, employees are permitted and encouraged to challenge the organization whenever and wherever they think it's needed to make things better. Jon Slater didn't see all that much tolerance for such "insubordination" in Silicon Valley in the late 1980s.

The third thing that happened to Slater during that pivotal year was most important for what occurred next. Early in 1987, after he had returned to California, he was
contacted by a friend of his father's and former LLUMC employee who had gone to
the Berkeley radiation lab where he now was consulting with the medical center on the
proton project. Slater was invited to tour the Berkeley facility to assess the challenge
of marrying proton accelerator with computer technology and to convey what he had
seen to his father. The experience was an eye-opener. Slater's imagination was fired by
the technical challenge, which he understood particularly well because of his background in radiation treatment, while at the same time he saw in a new way the human-
itarian implications of creating a successful proton treatment system. And, while it
would be some months yet before it crystallized, the idea was planted in him for a new
entrepreneurial path—one that had the incalculable appeal of saving human life.

Onward to Fermilab

Meantime, Slater had met and befriended a young coworker, an electrical engineer
named David Lesyna. Slater quickly came to feel that Lesyna was something approaching a genius at his work—one who, as it happened, was little more enchanted
with his Silicon Valley life than was Slater, nor any more rooted in the area. By this
point Slater had now begun to talk in depth with his father about the proton project.
James Slater in turn began to suggest that his son come onto the engineering team soon
to be formed. Making up his mind to go, Slater began to court Lesyna to come along.

One thing led to another. That year, LLUMC's governing board had given the
green light to build the world's first proton beam medical center at the university. The
next step was to send an engineering team to the Chicago suburb of Batavia to work
with Fermilab in designing the computer interface and control system needed to enable
large-scale patient treatment. It was a high-stakes, big-pressure task, because construction of the shell of the proton center was scheduled to break ground the following
April, with the computer system still being conceived by Fermilab. Undaunted, that
summer Slater and Lesyna both quit their jobs, then caravaned to Chicago via a long,
leisurely side trip north of the border that let Slater and his wife and two daughters visit
in-laws in Canada.

Slater now envisioned a company to bring proton treatment to market once the
technology was created. The details necessarily were vague, particularly given that
SAIC already had the license to the technology and its intellectual property. But he was
unfazed by that or by the odds he would appear to be facing. His thought was "I'm going to create this thing. Berkeley's going to help me. Fermilab's going to help me." As
things worked out, he and Lesyna, who arrived at Fermilab late in 1987, didn't seek its
help for very long.

FROM RADIATION RESEARCH LAB TO OPTIVUS
TECHNOLOGY

The two men, along with a third colleague recruited by Slater, a University of Utah
computer science classmate named Jim Nusbaum, had no sooner arrived in Batavia
than they discovered that Fermilab staff had a particular concept of how the LLUMC
center's control system would work. In this vision, Slater and his team were to be technicians assisting Fermilab rather than colleagues engaged in a joint creative effort—at
least that was how the three young men saw things. They also observed that an intense
rivalry was at work among the institutions involved in the project, one that actually had

international dimensions, as proton research facilities around the world strove to be first to create a viable hospital-based proton treatment system.

However galling, serving in what amounted to a functionary technical role would have been tolerable if the Fermilab plan for the computer system—which was being designed by physicists, not computer scientists—was demonstrably the best approach to take. But in the opinions of Slater, Lesyna, and Nusbaum it was not, neither on conceptual nor technical grounds. As they saw it, Fermilab was taking a plan-less, "bottom-up" approach to creating the computer control system in which individual components were being developed separately (often using different operating systems and software favored by a particular physicist) in the assumption that all would ultimately coalesce in a functioning control system. They, in contrast, were convinced that a planned, "top-down" design approach was essential to ensure that a properly integrated computer control system would ensue. That they could come up with such a design was a conclusion the three men also reached within a short time, and they set out immediately to develop it. Within about four months, they had conceived and written a 103-page, single-spaced document entitled "Conceptual Design Report for the LLUMC Proton Beam Therapy Treatment Room System." The flavor of this blueprint for a top-down control system design comes through in the following key passage:

> This conceptual design document is concerned with the treatment room system. The scope of this system is from amplification of signals from detectors, to high level user interfaces, to control of the beam bending system, to digital alignment of the patient . . . Specifically, this document describes the treatment room host and all of its associated software modules, all computer control functions in the treatment room; both hardware and software . . . system security, system safety, and a preliminary database definition. (p. 2)

Released on December 7, 1987, the effect of the report at Fermilab was akin to a bombshell; affronted by the defacto slap-in-the-face it presented to their design scheme, the physicists at Fermilab quit the LLUMC design project en masse, though Fermilab did go on to build LLUMC's proton accelerator. By mid-January 1988, Slater's engineering team had removed itself to Loma Linda to go to work carrying out its "Conceptual Design Report."

Spin Off the Technology?

Over the next two years, under Slater's direction, the Radiation Research Lab was staffed to carry out the detailed design and construction of the proton facility's computer system, simultaneously with the phased installation of the synchrotron, gantries, and other components. At the height of the effort, there were some 70 employees writing software programs and, in a warehouse assembly line, making circuit boards, wiring cables, and creating gantry racks to route the cable, although staffing began to be pared back once the proton center had been built and had first begun treating patients. But the conflict with Fermilab had reverberations that affected subsequent events.

A Fermilab official had gone on record at one point to say, "The worst thing that happened on this project was hiring Dr. Slater's son." Such attitudes in turn fueled accusations of nepotism from various quarters within and outside LLUMC. These charges sounded with new force when Jon Slater's older brother, Dr. Jerry Slater, who had just completed his internship in radiation medicine at Massachusetts General Hospital in preparation for joining the proton project, came to Loma Linda in 1988.[10] The

---

[10]Mass General is a major center for training physicians in cancer treatment, and the site of the second hospital-based proton treatment center being built in the United States, by Optivus's rival Ion Beam Applications (IBA).

insinuations of nepotism never came to anything substantive, for several reasons. The reputation of Dr. James Slater, whose arrival at the medical center in 1969 had helped lead to its achieving international recognition in cancer treatment, was unimpeachable. As it also happened, within the university there was a handful of other departments in which several family members had similarly paved the way in giving the medical center unique research specialties and prestige. Finally, once operational, the proton center proved to be a big success for LLUMC on both clinical and financial grounds.

Nevertheless, the dispute did complicate matters as Jon Slater sought to proceed, early in 1991, to found a new company that would license LLUMC's proton beam system to sell to other hospitals. The medical center had intended virtually from the beginning to commercialize its new technology, and in 1987 had licensed it to Science Applications International Corporation. But four years later, SAIC and LLUMC, out of mutual dissatisfaction with their working relationship, agreed to terminate the license. While Slater's original entrepreneurial idea had been to start a company that would subcontract construction of proton center computer control systems to SAIC (which had no such expertise), now the door was opened for a new licensee for the entire facility.

To Slater's thinking, the best approach was to create a new start-up company from among the engineers who had designed the proton center's computer control systems and who knew best how they worked. No outside contractor firm could hope to possess such intimate operating knowledge, which could only be learned by doing despite the best of system documentation (which in any case only partially existed in the early 1990s). At the same time, the medical center itself was unlikely to be effective in attempting to market, sell, and build multiple proton centers in disparate locations in the United States and abroad. As a nonprofit medical institution, it lacked the fundamental market orientation to play such an entrepreneurial role.

What made far more sense was to follow other research universities and spin off a private company to commercialize the technology. The sticking point here was whether to let Jon Slater do it, a debate that was shaped by several factors. Most obvious was the fact that while Slater had business experience and knew the proton beam system inside out, he had never founded a business, let alone a high-tech firm with the financial stakes involved in this venture. Additionally, the university itself had little experience with technology commercialization and so was entering unfamiliar waters. As a religious institution (Seventh Day Adventist), it was hesitant to be party to any commercial relationship that might potentially jeopardize its reputation for compassionate care and commitment to human betterment. Finally, the nepotism issue lingered in the background, there to be raised if someone objected to "giving" the business to Slater.

Ultimately, the matter was resolved in Slater's favor by two things. As it turned out, no major medical device maker, among them General Electric and Siemens, was interested in taking up the LLUMC license, viewing the proton project as too risky. (Indeed, the CEO of Siemens, who visited the university, recommended that the proton center's engineers form a company.) Simultaneously, Slater pursued his vision for a spin-off business tenaciously, gradually building up the expertise he needed to actually found it. He served on an Intellectual Property Committee that LLUMC created to address general issues of technology transfer, in addition to the specific issues surrounding commercialization of the proton beam facility. He also joined a group called Southwest Officers of Technology Transfer (SWOTT), which consisted of collegiate representatives from the western United States whose institutions sought to pursue technology commercialization. There he learned the ins and outs of sponsored research, marketing intellectual property, royalty rates, due diligence, and related matters. At the same time he boned up on the mechanics of cash flow and profit–loss statements, creating wage and benefits packages, designing performance appraisal and profit-sharing systems, and leasing buildings.

Finally, in June 1992 the university governing board voted to approve a licensing agreement with a company, to be named Electus Technology, to market, sell, build, and operate proton beam treatment centers, with a one-time royalty for newly constructed systems to be paid the university. The company would also maintain and upgrade and provide ancillary devices (boluses, pods) to LLUMC's facility under contract. The new business was incorporated in Delaware, with Jon Slater as sole owner. On June 1, 1993, it began life as a private company consisting of 34 employees—a fact that made it somewhat different from the typical start-up, in that Slater had to have functioning payroll and accounting systems and legal contracts in place in order to open his doors. In typical entrepreneur fashion, he hocked himself to the hilt to cover his start-up costs.

One sacrifice Slater and employees did not have to make was to give up plush quarters, since they'd never had any. When formed in 1988, the Radiation Research Lab had leased offices in an old industrial building in San Bernardino near the medical center that one veteran of the site called a "hell hole." There they would stay until 1997, when Optivus finally moved into leased facilities more becoming of a sexy high-tech company.

SELF-DIRECTED TEAMS AT OPTIVUS

Electus Technology became Optivus three-odd years after it was founded, when a company with a name similar to Electus's threatened to sue unless the name was changed.[11] By that time, the team-based structure and management system that was Slater's pride and joy was well-thought-out on both practical and philosophical grounds, albeit a perpetual challenge to make work.

With the small size of the original Radiation Research Lab and the complex tasks its members had to carry out together, a collegial, teamlike operating style, with no real hierarchy or superior–subordinate relations, had been natural if not inevitable. Slater had pursued the team route right from the beginning, for while that was his predilection, another consideration played a role. Given the reality of a grueling timetable for accomplishing many new, untried things (similar to the computer designers portrayed in Tracy Kidder's classic 1980 book, *The Soul of a New Machine*, a lot of the Radiation Research Lab's activity involved learning-as-you-go), Slater believed that success of the venture hinged on knowledge sharing among personnel. He was certain this was most likely to occur if working relations were open and egalitarian, a climate that would work against potential tendencies in some people to hoard knowledge as a means of building power, or to protect themselves out of some murky fear of being fired. Deliberately and overtly then, he sought to create a profoundly different workplace from the others he had known, where he had seen "bureaucracy" (as he called it for lack of a better term) stunt people's capabilities along with the effectiveness and potential of the organization—something that he believed happens routinely.

Whether or not everyone recruited to the Radiation Research Lab felt the same, that was generally how things operated. For most personnel, the majority of whom were engineers of one kind or another, there were no set working hours—much like graduate students, they could come and go more or less as they pleased (though virtually everyone put in grueling, relentless weeks). To a considerable extent, they defined

---

[11]According to company documents, the word *optivus* is Latin for "continuous improvement to reach an optimum."

their own tasks and scheduled their own work, coordinating with colleagues. Slater had an open-door policy and anyone could talk to him at any time (and did). In keeping with the spirit of the venture, hours worked were and continued years later to be self-reported. (By 1994, all this was done via personal computer, though privately Slater regretted that such activity-monitoring ever became necessary. If people were going to cheat on hours, he believed, time clocks wouldn't stop them; meantime, management saddled itself with surveillance costs.) In general, a palpable sense of high purpose and lifesaving mission characterized the experience of the members of the Radiation Research Lab.

In no small part, however, the lab's informal practices—and the continuation of these practices even as personnel count pushed 70—were made possible by the fact that the lab was nested within the medical center organization structure, which handled administrative and support needs. Being a temporary unit of LLUMC also meant that there were few, if any, career ladders in the lab for people to compete for, and so little, if any, internal organization politics tied to such jockeying. While teams had been created earlier on, there were no formal leader positions. Team members coordinated their activities informally.

The "Team to Define Teams" and the Optivus Constitution

Things began to change once the little Radiation Research Lab had been spun off as Electus (later Optivus). Well before the company started up, it was apparent to Slater and to others that greater formalization of structure would be required, and in the preceding year he had begun to think about how he wanted to do it. The need became ever more apparent as, removed from the shelter of the medical center with all its resources and relative security, many employees became anxious about their personal roles and the survival prospects of a business in which so much seemed loose and undefined.

After about a year of attempting to firm things up, Slater decided to form what he called the "Team to Define Teams." It consisted of a diverse set of employees whose task was to come up with a "constitution" to lay out how the company would be structured, and the rules that would govern the team system on which its structure would be based. Given the collaborative organization culture inherited from the Radiation Research Lab, it was a natural way to approach the job. But in hindsight it was, Slater reflected, "a huge mistake," because the "Team to Define Teams was close to dysfunctional." Months went by in which its deliberations could neither converge on one goal nor diverge from any vague, general ones.

Finally, exerting his authority for nearly the first time as CEO, Slater started to write the constitution. The document that eventuated was based on several key elements, "absolutes" for the organization, as he viewed them:

- Structure would be organized around "Specialization Teams" in key areas corresponding to traditional departments (computer sciences, mechanical engineering, electrical engineering, etc.) and "Project Teams," created as necessary to undertake specific projects, for example, upgrading the beam transport system. Both types of teams would carry out the job of defining their operating policies, standards, and practices. Participation on Project Teams was voluntary, and open to all employees.

- Individuals would be fully responsible for their own task allocation. Members of Project Teams could not be forced to do something they hadn't agreed to in joining. They could quit the team without penalty if they chose to.

- Specialization or Project Teams had the right to "fire" the team leader (from the team, not the company). A member or members seeking to fire a team leader had to make their case, and team leaders had the right to defend themselves.
- Documentation of standards and specifications for the proton treatment system was to be developed in all areas that were required for Federal Drug Administration approval to sell it as a medical device. It was the responsibility of team leaders to see that the necessary documentation was produced, and of team members to support them. (This was vital now that the proton system was intended for sale in the market—no sale of new systems would ever be possible without FDA approval.)

The draft constitution encompassing these absolutes was readied and sent out for companywide review in late summer 1994. While it did not have strong buy-in from the Team to Define Teams—some of whose members, nostalgic for the anything-goes Radiation Research Lab days, complained that it imposed too much structure—it generated considerable feedback from employees, if mainly minor clarifications. Once revised, the constitution was adopted in a companywide meeting, leading to the first organization chart for the company, which consisted of just two levels: CEO and teams. Slater's open-door-anytime policy remained in effect.

Slater's overarching goal in creating the constitution and the organizational system it codified was to vest in individual employees the power to determine their actions, the right and responsibility to do so, and freedom from fear of retribution or persecution when they did. Slater believed that when allocation of tasks, and therefore responsibility, is vested in managers, you lose the possibility that individuals can and will do it better because they have and feel the responsibility. "Imagine this is a mirror," he would say to employees, to get them to look to themselves as the source of the problems they encountered—and in turn (and more important) as the source of the solutions.

He had a similar rule of thumb for hiring people. His impression, later corroborated by some research he read, was that people who had not taken personal responsibility by age 13 for some significant thing—say doing a paper route—were unlikely in adulthood to be reliable employees. So in interviews he would ask people to tell him what they had done by that age. His original goal was to hire only people who had a good answer.

Team Training, Employee Performance Evaluation, Stock Options

Such was the theory, or perhaps better put, the working philosophy of Optivus's self-directing team system. By late 1994 it was in place and seemed to have reasonably good commitment from employees. Over the next several years, Slater devoted perhaps 25 percent of his time to shepherding the team effort and trying to work out bugs.

Once into things, two particular needs became apparent. First was training in teams and "empowerment." Second was development of an employee evaluation system that worked to reward—or to bring to bear the necessary sanctions to ensure that people exhibited—personal responsibility of the kind called for in Optivus Technology's team setup. Slater also intended from early on to institute profit sharing as soon as finances would permit.

For purposes of the team training, Slater got in touch with a former professor from his University of Utah days, Bill Guillory, whom he had found a hugely inspiring teacher. Guillory had left the university to create a consultancy that specialized in team building. In 1995, he worked with Optivus to develop a special training video and interactive program that continued to be used into the new century.

A twice-yearly performance evaluation system had been inherited from Radiation Research Lab days, but late in 1995 a new quarterly evaluation system built on the foundation of Guillory's training was instituted that consisted of four modules, completed one per quarter, and included two unique elements of which Slater was especially proud: Everyone evaluated everyone else (including Slater) using a matrix; and each individual did an intensive self-analysis related to job functions that required validation from other employees. This system was used for a two and a half years and then revamped because, essentially, it demanded too much of people; Optivus employees were reluctant to evaluate each other (thus the accuracy became questionable), and they recoiled from the intensive self-analysis required. Ultimately it was voted out, to be replaced by the current evaluation system in which team objectives were developed by the teams to support annual fiscal objectives of the company. Individual employees created annual personal performance objectives (PPOs), which they had to relate clearly, substantively, and with timelines to team goals.

It wasn't clear to Slater whether the new evaluation system was better or worse than the old one; he was fairly certain it lacked the educative value of the original concerning personal responsibility. In general, he viewed conventional performance evaluation systems as a kind of "grand illusion" whose main purpose was to provide a documentation package that made it possible to either fire employees managers wanted to fire or reward the ones they wanted to reward, whatever the reasons.

However, Slater had no doubts about the value of the stock option program that was instituted in 1998, followed by a bonus system that made its initial payout in mid-2000. To establish the stock option plan, which initially covered technical staff but subsequently was extended to all personnel, 20 percent of the company's shares were set aside for employees, with a five-year vesting period (20 percent a year). Formal valuation of the company was made every year, and the value of the stock was set at that time. For the bonus program, an annual bonus rate was established for all employees tied to their salaries, the rate increasing progressively based on position and salary, with the bonus being paid in two outlays at midyear and year-end. At the beginning of the year, employees were notified of the maximum bonus they could earn. An employee's immediate supervisor decided the actual bonus received during each period, based on how well they judged employees had met PPOs. The first payment under the new bonus system was disbursed in July 2000.

Living with Teams Today—and Tomorrow?

In practice, self-directed teams at Optivus appeared to be a case of either liking them or not, with little in between.

For employees who liked the environment—which seemed to be a majority (no survey of attitudes had ever been done)—the lack of emphasis on titles, the opportunity to contribute ideas on anything, or to participate in project teams if you felt able to, could make it the workplace of your dreams. This was especially the case for administrative and nontechnical staff who otherwise could expect to work in a traditional directive, bureaucratic environment. Among the latter, particularly, a visitor was likely to hear praise for the feeling of opportunity, autonomy, and lack of micromanagement ("They watch for results, but they're not breathing down my neck"). There appeared to be none of the feeling of surveillance of other workplaces, where, for instance, supervisors would monitor e-mail. In the case of one employee who had come from a local university, her former manager had asked her to read other employees' e-mail while the manager asked other people to read hers—the manager knew about the Optivus job before the employee could tell her! Alesa Watson, Slater's longtime assistant, liked to talk about a training seminar she went to. Her autonomy in a nonmanagement role was so diametrically at odds with the trainer's assumptions about what Watson's prerogatives "should be" that Watson drove the trainer to distraction talking about what her actual rights and responsibilities were. To end the mutual torment, Watson skipped the second half of the training. "I couldn't go back to a regularly structured company," she said. "I'd get fired in one day!"

Among engineering and professional staff who had the greatest freedom to set their own hours (support staff were more constrained in that regard, as were Manufacturing Team personnel whose responsibility entailed ongoing production of new boluses for patient treatment), again you seemed to either love it or not. For those who did, the working environment was creative, satisfying, and full of possibilities for learning and growth. For those who didn't, the discontent seemed to lie mainly in feelings that roles and responsibilities, both of team leaders and team members, were too ill-defined, while it was difficult to ensure accountability because there seemed to be no real consequences for failing to perform on a team. If team leadership was weak, these problems were heightened accordingly. Some people felt there was little leadership across the board (or from the top down), that indeed, the company was "floundering." Along with that, there was (some felt) a resistance to change that made Optivus slow-moving and belied the flexibility and responsiveness its team environment and empowerment were supposed to help produce. Some also believed that empowerment was often more apparent than real, that sometimes you had it and other times you didn't. Here again, this inconsistency tended to be a reflection of the nature of the team leaders and how they did or didn't lead. Others felt that the vaunted team training was more surface than substance.

One middle-ground critical view was that teams competed with each other too much for resources. Combining this with their constitutional right to self-definition of task and approach, situations could arise where teams worked against each other without realizing it. This dilemma could be compounded by the problem of people over-committing themselves in joining a project team, then subsequently falling down on their responsibilities to both their specialization team and to the project team.

Slater knew that the way Optivus worked was unconventional. On occasion, he'd had the opportunity to tell groups of local executives how his company operated; they would listen intently, nod in agreement as he laid out the benefits of self-management, but then say they'd never dream of trying it themselves. He felt, though, that many of the problems of teams in Optivus could probably be worked out by continuing to experiment and learn. To himself, he dismissed complaints by some managers about the problems supposedly stemming from lack of "control." In reality, a team leader could fire any nonperforming employee from a specialization or project team, if he could—that is, if he was willing and able to—make the case to the rest of the team that firing was in order. In reality, what team leaders called a lack of authority was, he believed, a reluctance to use the power they had, essentially because they had to do it with logic and evidence in a democratic context; they couldn't rely on naked authority, as in a conventional business.

As to the persisting "looseness" of things, Slater thought much of that simply reflected the trade-off that comes from a business choosing to forgo some of the neat orderliness of bureaucratic systems—an "order" that in his view was a kind of self-delusion—and accepting a degree of chaos in pursuit of creativity. Confident of all this, he didn't feel that Optivus was floundering.

Of course, it was always possible that he was wrong or that a perception among employees that they were floundering might become a self-fulfilling prophecy. But there was no doubting that the impending expansion of the organization that would be required to go into production of one, then two, and then still more proton centers would, if Optivus was to succeed, mandate greater structure and standardization. Quite possibly, it would mean less freedom and autonomy for teams in the future, with all that that might imply for the future of Slater's founding vision as well as the daily experience of being in the company.

HIGH-TECH ECONOMIC DEVELOPMENT EFFORTS IN THE ISLAND EMPIRE

Part and parcel with the moving-target chore of making a team-based organization really work for the company, one of Slater's major challenges as Optivus slowly expanded was finding employees with the necessary high-tech skills and education (if not necessarily the industry background) to fill its jobs.

These were problems owing in large part to Optivus's location in the San Bernardino–Riverside region east of Los Angeles—a region known as the Inland Empire (IE). As an economic hinterland along the edge of the greater Los Angeles metropolitan area, the IE long had had a less advanced and dynamic economy than the Pacific Coast areas, with lower average education and income levels among its population. It had little high-tech industry and hence none of the worker pools and job-seeker networks typical of high-tech zones like Silicon Valley or Boston's Route 128. There were few team-based businesses in the region to socialize prospective employees in the norms and methods of team organization, particularly the self-directed Optivus style. To an extent, the region was a huge bedroom community for the coastal zone, several hundred thousand of its million-odd workers daily commuting west to better-paying jobs, spending several hours each day on the freeways. Although the region had been evolving for some years as a continental hub for distribution and transportation, those blue-collar industries didn't offer the kind of incomes provided by sophisticated services, manufacturing, or high tech. Because of these factors, along with the IE's semidesert climate and a physical environment hotter, smoggier, and "grubbier" than Southern California's coastal counties, it was an ongoing problem to induce highly skilled, economically valuable technology workers to move (or to commute) to Optivus's location.

Slater was personally committed to keeping his company in the region that had spawned it, because of his family ties and the fact that, for the time being at least, Optivus was dependent on its clinical and financial ties with Loma Linda University. As a practical matter as well, it was less expensive to live and to run a high-tech business in the IE than in the coastal zone or the San Francisco Bay Area. But Slater recognized that recruiting qualified employees from outside the region would be difficult for as long as Optivus remained a small, unknown technology company. Remembering what he had seen in Silicon Valley, he felt that the main solution was to try to find new people in the various colleges and universities in the area—most importantly by establishing one-on-one relations with faculty and department chairs in campus computer science and engineering departments.

From his earliest days on the proton accelerator project, Slater had sought to develop such ties, both with Loma Linda University and with the nearby Claremont Colleges, where he served on two advisory councils at the Harvey Mudd College of Engineering. This relationship had led to Optivus hosting a number of engineering interns over the years. Then, in the fall of 1996, Slater made important new academic connections as a result of his decision to put some of his time and energies into a budding effort to develop a high-tech strategy for the Inland Empire region.

Public and private leaders in the IE had come to see that if its economic conditions and quality of life were to be improved, the region had to incubate and attract more advanced, high-wage-paying industries. Discussions about how to do this were just beginning when Slater—whose little high-tech company was seen by many in the know as a model for the kind of enterprise the region sought—was drawn into the coterie of businesspeople, university types, and local government economic development officials spearheading the effort to fashion a regional high-tech plan. Slater's own view, shaped by his experience in launching Optivus and his awareness of the lack of local experience with technology commercialization, was rather unconventional. He believed that a regional technology transfer office was needed to pool resources of the area's different campuses to identify and assist with commercializing research that had market potential. Basically, he argued for setting up a regional clearinghouse to spread the costs of running a collegiate technology transfer office while seeking to create new companies and jobs out of local academia, in a kind of miniversion of the Silicon Valley pattern.[12]

For the next several years, while still running his company, Slater participated actively in networking efforts, committee meetings, advocacy group gatherings, conferences, political lobbying, and media shindigs all spawned in one way or another by the high-tech campaign. Although by 2000, no regional technology transfer office had come to pass, a consortium of a dozen or so of the local research and teaching universities and community colleges had been created that sought to be a catalyst for faculty entrepreneurship and technology transfer. If thus far there was little to show for it all in the way of new high-tech businesses, at least there now was a consciousness that local campuses had a potential to actively advance the regional economy and its living standards. Slowly, an infrastructure to make that possible seemed to be taking shape.

Meanwhile, there had been definite payoffs for Optivus. Through involvement with campus presidents, deans, department chairs, and faculty, and by speaking to classes about his company, Slater had raised Optivus's public visibility while developing the direct academic connections he had hoped for. A trickle of talented student interns and graduates (and in a few cases, faculty and well-qualified campus employees) had been channeled into Optivus as positions opened up. Thereby, the looming threat of lack of qualified personnel had been relieved sufficiently to enable the company to continue down its slow path of growth. It remained to be seen whether this local academic spigot would continue to meet Optivus's needs as growth accelerated.

THE SPINOFF OF PERMEDICS

In the midst of these ventures in civic entrepreneurship, Slater also had been focused on still more business entrepreneuring: spinning off a new high-tech company out of Optivus. The new software firm, PerMedics (launched mid-1997), was the outgrowth of an Optivus contract with LLUMC, unrelated to the proton center, for development of a medical activities planning software, eventually called MedPlanner. It quickly became clear that the software could be sold to other hospitals. Planning for a new company to market the software had begun in 1996. In mid-1998, Rob Anglea, who had

---

[12]Andy McCue, "Plugged In: Ideas Began Flowing Like Economic Clusters," *Press-Enterprise*, March 3, 1998.

consulted with Optivus in the preceding two years, joined PerMedics as its president after several other in-house "leaders," as they were called, failed to pan out.

In the months following, the company developed a suite of medical software products. In addition to MedPlanner, these included OptiRad, conceived by a LLUMC physician for radiation treatment simulation and planning (both proton and conventional), and Surveyor, a clinical studies management tool developed by Optivus for the Loma Linda University Cancer Institute. By mid-2000, PerMedics staff was up to 14 people, including a small sales force. For the time being the company shared facilities and human resources support with Optivus, just as the Radiation Research Lab had once been sponsored by LLUMC. Thus far, finance for product development also came from Optivus, but PerMedics was expected eventually to raise its own capital.

Anglea anticipated that PerMedics could grow to $30 million in sales within five years. It had its own informal advisory board separate from Optivus's advisory board, though in the future Anglea thought it might be desirable to tap into the other board as needed. Where Slater's original vision for the company had been built around Med-Planner, under Anglea it had broadened. PerMedics differed also in not being explicitly team-based; presently it was small and informal enough that there was not a lot of structure, but Anglea anticipated that as the company grew he would organize it in a more conventional mode. He also expected that PerMedics would develop its own business identity; conceivably, it could move to another part of Southern California if doing so would help in recruiting software developers. Already the company was fairly autonomous from Optivus and "did" very little with it, apart from supplying Med-Planner and OptiRad. Anglea coordinated with Slater casually and informally.

A newspaper profile of PerMedics had said: "The company's emergence is a typical story in the high-technology industry: Technology is created at a university and found to have commercial use. The company develops it by building its own products to support it. And some of these products have commercial uses of their own."[13] The author might have added that the fact that local business reporters now were sensitized to see such connections was partly a result of Slater's participation in efforts to promote high tech in the region.

OPTIVUS TECHNOLOGY ON THE BRINK OF GROWTH

By mid-2000, Optivus was a more structured company than it had ever been, with levels of management it had lacked in earlier years (see Exhibit 3). Ironically, the buildup was in preparation for growth that was yet prospective: it hinged on sale of a first proton treatment center, followed in turn by subsequent sales—none of which had yet occurred, despite some seven years of marketing and sales efforts by the company.

Since 1993, Slater and his executives had talked with dozens of hospitals. They had been engaged in 10 separate negotiation efforts with potential proton center buyers (virtually all research hospitals) in the United States, Europe, and Asia, getting as far as three signed letters of intent before the deals had fallen through or petered out. The reasons varied. Naturally, all negotiations were influenced to some degree by the seemingly eye-popping $85 million cost of a proton facility, though less by the amount itself than by the challenge posed in building the interest, consensus, and commitment of a hospital or university governing board to buy a system, then securing financing.

---

[13]Michael Diamond, "Helping Better Health Care Compute," *San Bernardino County Sun*, December 29, 1998.

exhibit 3 Optivus Technology's Organization Chart, October 2000

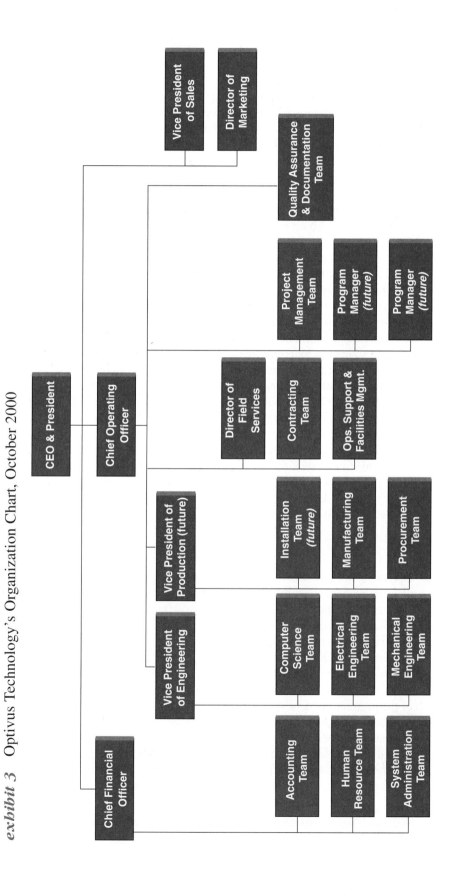

(It was hardly as if $85 million was an inordinate price tag for high technology in the go-go capitalism of the end of the 20th century.) In some cases, talks died because a new hospital administration inheriting negotiations and still feeling its way into its role lacked the self-confidence to continue with a proton center project. Other times, the other party wanted price or other concessions Slater was unwilling to make.

But in no case had negotiations failed because prospective customers questioned the value of proton treatment. To the contrary, the data on proton treatment success rates, its cost savings, and the revenue potential of a proton treatment facility virtually made Slater's case. Consequently, he was not disheartened by the failure so far to land the first contract. He recognized that negotiating failures early in the decade had stemmed in part from worldwide recession combined with health care budget cutbacks, which had both eased with the prosperity accompanying the dawn of the new century. Meanwhile, in each negotiation, he and his bargaining team had learned something new and valuable about how to do things better next time. He believed with complete conviction that the numbers all were on the side of his company and its mission.

He recognized, though, that after a couple of premature public announcements of "impending Optivus contracts" that later fell through—one announcement produced a front-page banner headline in the local paper[14]—there were people in the region who had concluded he was either a scam artist or an incompetent businessman. Where many local leaders had once thought his company was the model of the way ahead for the region, even its great economic hope, some now doubted much would come of it.

Much as he might regret them, such impressions didn't bother Slater. What did cause him some worry was the prospect of Optivus employees losing faith, in him, themselves, and the promise of their work. Some already had, and had departed in consequence. Others, he knew, watched, wondered, and worried. Ultimately, there was nothing he could do about that, for eventually explanations or pep talks from him would just fall on deaf ears. The only thing he could do was keep pushing—and, following the "structure-follows-strategy" maxim of corporate strategy, begin creating the structure needed to implement the growth strategy he and his management team had charted for Optivus.

Optivus's Corporate Strategy and Business Plan

Optivus's strategy was to build at least 100 proton systems in America and overseas over the next 20 years through a process and structure not unlike franchising. All proton facilities would be nearly identical in terms of operating standards and practices and the experience of patients, although the "technology package" could vary depending on the focus of a hospital. For example, one might wish to specialize in breast cancers, another in brain tumors.

A subsidiary of Optivus Technology to be named American Proton Treatment Systems (APTS) would be the parent of subsidiary companies established to operate each of the proton treatment systems Optivus sold to hospitals. Each subsidiary would take a name such as ACME Proton Treatment Associates (see Exhibit 4). Optivus, as parent company, would carry on the planning, marketing, and sales operations of the envisioned national and global organization, as well as product research and development and the accompanying responsibility for advancing the technology, upgrading component systems, and diffusing enhancements to existing and future facilities.

---

[14]Michael Diamond, "Optivus to Build Cancer Center: Inland Empire Company Signs On for a $70 Million Project for a Taiwan Hospital," *San Bernardino County Sun*, January 26, 1998.

exhibit 4   American Proton Treatment Systems Organization Chart

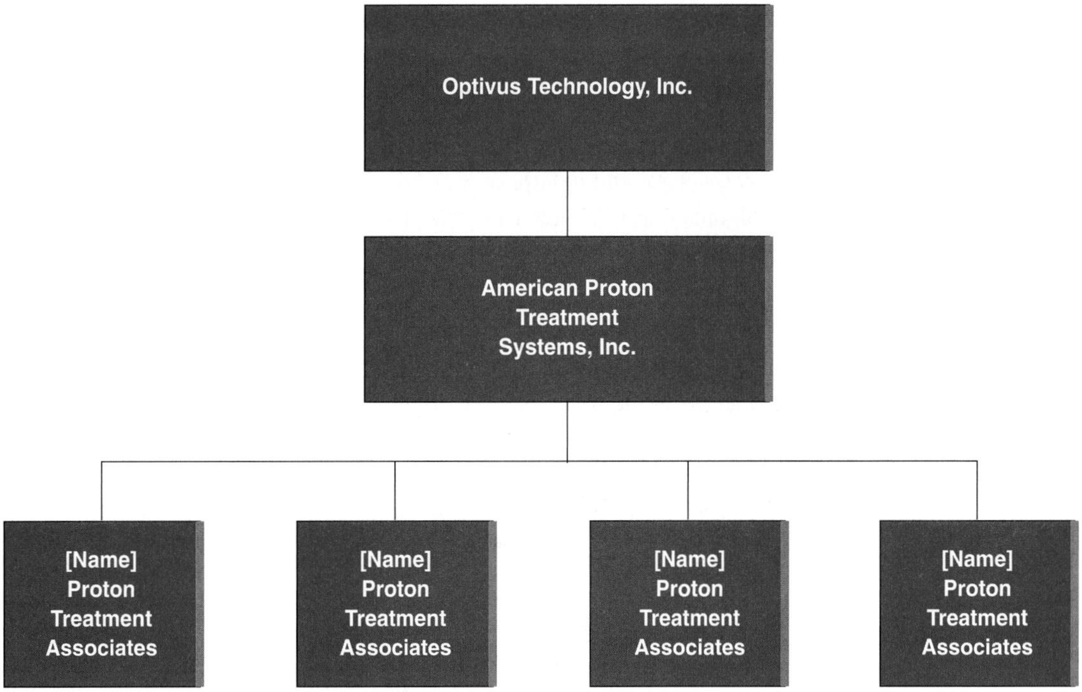

The financial plan to support this business strategy envisioned variation in financing of individual treatment centers, although each was to be an individually incorporated business that raised its own capital and offered its own stock. In general, the intent was for Optivus to hold a partial ownership stake in APTS while APTS would hold partial stakes in each facility and operate the proton center under contract to the site co-owners, working with clinical staff of the affiliated hospitals. In the basic model Slater envisioned, buyers—usually hospitals or their parent organizations—would put up the land for the facility and would build the physical structure to Optivus specifications, which the company would lease back. Depending on the financial resources or preferences of a customer, APTS would supply less or more of the capital, which it would raise in markets and/or secure through corporate strategic alliances. (As of summer 2000, discussions were under way with a European hospital construction firm interested in investing $200 million in APTS in exchange for a 30 percent share of its stock.) Proton technology packages varying between $45 and $60 million would determine the final cost of an individual facility.

A typical facility would take three years to build, varying with soil conditions, weather, and government approval requirements that might affect the schedule. Construction would be carried out by an "Optivus Strategic Partner Team" consisting of a selected group of subcontractor businesses responsible for supplying different services (e.g., architectural design) or components (such as physical shell). It was anticipated that the set of partners would evolve over time.

Marketing of proton treatment was to be carried out on a scale commensurate with Optivus's corporate vision. Up to this time, marketing of what Optivus called its

Conforma 3000™ proton system (the name evoked the conformal characteristics of the proton beam while pointing to the annual patient capability of a facility) had been quite limited, mainly focusing on industry trade shows. But Slater envisioned a marketing strategy that ultimately would target hospitals, insurance companies, doctors, and finally consumers. One marketing theme he toyed with went "If you don't know about proton therapy, it's time you did." Eventually, he hoped to make proton treatment as familiar to the ordinary consumer as Lasik laser eye surgery had become.

Optivus faced one potentially serious competitor. This was Ion Beam Applications (IBA), a Belgian company with 1999 revenues of some $185 million, which was constructing a second U.S. proton facility, called the Northeast Proton Center, at Massachusetts General Hospital in Boston. However, the Mass General facility, begun in 1993, was still under construction in 2000, had yet to treat its first patients, and might be two years yet in doing so. In practice, the $180 million, 30-year investment embodied in Optivus's technology and its commercial experience, coupled with a variety of patents related to its proton beam technology, created large barriers to entry for rivals like IBA. Nonetheless, Optivus's success would hinge on achieving a first-mover advantage in the market as quickly as possible, so that its reputation for clinical success in initial facilities would establish it as the provider of choice. Subsequently, experience and learning effects would give it increasing cost-efficiencies that competitors would have difficulty matching. But to achieve that first-mover position, time was of the essence.

Needless to say, by the time its first proton center contract was signed, Optivus either would have to be at a staffing level (approximately 200 highly skilled people, initially) to proceed with the contract or would have to staff up quickly. Consequently, the company was balanced on a kind of knife-edge. To begin adding new staff prematurely risked bankrupting the business; but to not be able to add them quickly enough risked defaulting on a contract or on multiple contracts if those were to come, which was a distinct possibility—and would be no less of a disaster. It was this uncertainty that permeated the company and made everyone wonder whether they could really pull it off.

The role of new COO Kip Edwards was to provide Optivus with the organizational and operating systems needed to make the leap from its present scale and style of operation to that implied by the company's growth. In other words, his job was to design the structure needed to follow the company's growth strategy.

With his arrival in late February 2000, Edwards had set to work to create the road map for growth. This included a detailed production plan, lacking heretofore, which fully specified costs and identified opportunities for achieving scale efficiencies, so that volume production might reap economies that would make future facilities less costly. A technology plan for three to five years out also had to be developed, to include a financial plan for investing in product development. Additionally, all critical documentation for proton treatment systems had to be properly cataloged, indexed, and packaged for presentation. Finally, there were the management systems to create, or to evolve, to make all of this possible. This last element included recruiting as many as 120 qualified personnel and engineers when the jump-off for growth began.

Edwards had some 20 years' experience in health care administration, including building new hospitals. He saw that Optivus personnel were stressed by understaffing and ongoing uncertainty. Morale had sagged in consequence, though Edwards also felt that that was relative: Compared with many other workplaces Optivus had maintained good morale—indeed, other businesses should have it so good. Edwards hoped that within the next year, greater size would let the company add resources and people that would help relieve strain and make work more enjoyable.

"As Stupid and Ignorant As It Is Possible for a Human Creature to Become ..."

For his part, Jon Slater was now focusing his attention almost entirely on strategic issues of marketing the business and negotiating for contracts. He was, in his words, "letting go of my own intrinsic interest in teams" to concentrate on that strategic role. The ongoing challenge of making a team-based business work had altered Slater's view of something he had long wanted to believe was a basic truth of human nature. Originally, he had thought that he could build the exceptional company he envisioned by recruiting exceptional people who shared his vision and would need no more structure or direction than was absolutely necessary. But about two years before, he had come to the conclusion that his premise was flawed. As he had learned, by definition the exceptional is rare, however attractive a company might become. To sustain exceptional results with growth, a company needed a governing philosophy supported by a structure for implementation which ensured that if a majority of people could not be inspired to share the vision, they could be either influenced, incentivized, or commanded to act in accordance with it—or else leave. Slater's preference in structure was some form of self-directing teams. But the ultimate purpose of Optivus Technology was not employee fulfillment; it was to save people from death by cancer. That would take growth, so that proton treatment centers could be built worldwide. Growth, and whatever internal changes it required, would be the governing consideration in determining the company's structure.

This did not mean, however, that Slater was willing to let whatever happened happen. He recognized that he had to accept some level of bureaucratic structure in order to position the company for growth. His job, if need be, would be to intervene to say, "We're going too far," if he felt that was about to happen. The team system had always had an integral connection in his mind with the nature of the health care Optivus would provide. In working with Bill Guillory in 1995, Slater had clarified and bolstered his ideas about the link between workplace environment and the character of a company. Then, a few years later, he came across a statement from Adam Smith's 1776 bible of capitalism, *The Wealth of Nations,* which solidified his view. The passage in question was from a part of the book that addressed the effect on people of extreme division of labor and simplified work. But Slater felt that it applied little less to the regime of rule-bound, directed work that typifies bureaucracies—which is to say most modern workplaces. A person in such an environment, wrote Adam Smith with brutal eloquence, "generally becomes as stupid and ignorant as it is possible for a human creature to become."

What Smith might have added about the modern workplace, Slater thought, was the element of fear woven through it: fear of offending bosses, fear of control and surveillance, fear of letting go of key information that made you vulnerable—ultimately, fear of being fired. What Slater feared was that such an organization climate, especially in health care, and most especially in a for-profit health provider like Optivus, could lead to fearful and alienated staff treating patients with an equivalent alienation—the wounded abusing the wounded as it were, the maimed tending the crippled. He was convinced this was the experience of too many patients in too many hospitals and other bureaucratically conceived and managed health care organizations.

In his mind, then, the purpose behind Optivus's team system was not to empower employees through self-direction, but rather to empower them through freedom from fear in order to serve best their ultimate clients: cancer sufferers and their families coming into facilities of Optivus Technology and its American Proton Treatment Systems subsidiaries. These would be people riven with fear of death and loss, weakened by suffering and vulnerability. Slater was determined that they should not simply be cured of cancer if they could be, but that in so far as possible, their experience with Optivus's lifesaving technology and the people who applied it were of a piece: that no less than proton therapy, the behavior of Optivus's people was fully and indisputably life-affirming.

In expanding Optivus, his hope was that the value system embedded in its self-directed team structure and its original constitution could be the template for the APTS cancer treatment centers to be created in the years ahead. Thus, as Slater watched the debate unfold about the future of teams, he would be seeking to answer the question of how conventional an organization he was willing to let Optivus become.

case 34

Nike's Dispute with the University of Oregon

Rebecca J. Morris
University of Nebraska at Omaha

Anne T. Lawrence
San Jose State University

On April 24, 2000, Philip H. Knight, CEO of athletic shoe and apparel maker Nike, Inc., publicly announced that he would no longer donate money to the University of Oregon (UO). It was a dramatic and unexpected move for the high-profile executive. A former UO track and field star, Knight had founded Nike's predecessor in 1963 with his former UO coach and mentor, Bill Bowerman. Over the years, Knight had maintained close ties with his alma mater, giving more than $50 million of his personal fortune to the school over a quarter century. In 2000, he was in active discussion with school officials about his biggest donation yet—millions for renovating the football stadium. But suddenly it was all called off. Said Knight in his statement: "[F]or me personally, there will be no further donations of any kind to the University of Oregon. At this time, this is not a situation that can be resolved. The bonds of trust, which allowed me to give at a high level, have been shredded."[1]

At issue was the University of Oregon's intention, announced April 14, 2000, to join the Worker Rights Consortium (WRC). Like many universities, UO was engaged in an internal debate over the ethical responsibilities associated with its role as a purchaser of goods manufactured overseas. Over a period of several months, UO administrators, faculty, and students had been discussing what steps they could take to ensure that products sold in the campus store, especially university-logo apparel, were not manufactured under sweatshop conditions. The university had considered joining two organizations, both of which purported to certify goods as "no sweat." The first, the Fair Labor Association (FLA), had grown out of President Clinton's Apparel Industry Partnership (AIP) initiative and was vigorously backed by Nike, as well as several other leading apparel makers. The second, the Worker Rights Consortium, was supported by student activists and several U.S.-based labor unions that had broken from the AIP after charging it did not go far enough to protect workers. Knight clearly felt

---

Copyright © 2001 by the *Case Research Journal* and Rebecca J. Morris and Anne T. Lawrence.

[1]Philip H. Knight, "Knight's Statement," via press release, www.oregonlive.com.

that his alma mater had made the wrong choice. "[The] University [has] inserted itself into the new global economy where I make my living," he charged. "And inserted itself on the wrong side, fumbling a teachable moment."

The dispute between Phil Knight and the University of Oregon captured much of the furor swirling about the issue of the role of multinational corporations in the global economy and the effects of their far-flung operations on their many thousands of workers, communities, and other stakeholders. In part because of its high-profile brand name, Nike had become a lightning rod for activists concerned about worker rights abroad. Like many U.S.-based shoe and apparel makers, Nike had located its manufacturing operations overseas, mainly in southeast Asia, in search of low wages. Almost all production was carried out by subcontractors rather than by Nike directly. Nike's employees in the United States, by contrast, directed their efforts to the high-end work of research and development, marketing, and retailing. In the context of this global division of labor, what responsibility, if any, did Nike have to ensure adequate working conditions and living standards for the hundreds of thousands of workers, mostly young Asian women, who made its shoes and apparel? If this was not Nike's responsibility, then whose was it? Did organizations like the University of Oregon have any business pressuring companies through their purchasing practices? If so, how should they best do so? In short, what were the lessons of this "teachable moment"?

NIKE, INC.

In 2000, Nike, Inc., was the leading designer and marketer of athletic footwear, apparel, and equipment in the world. Based in Beaverton, Oregon, the company's "swoosh" logo, its "Just Do It!" slogan, and its spokespersons Michael Jordan, Mia Hamm, and Tiger Woods were universally recognized. Nike employed around 20,000 people directly, and *half a million* indirectly in 565 contract factories in 46 countries around the world.[2] Wholly owned subsidiaries included Bauer Nike Hockey Inc. (hockey equipment), Cole Haan (dress and casual shoes), and Nike Team Sports (licensed team products). Revenues for the 12 months ending November 1999 were almost $9 billion.[3] With a 45 percent global market share, Nike was in a league of its own.[4] Knight owned 34 percent of the company's stock and was believed to be the sixth-richest individual in the United States.[5]

Knight had launched this far-flung global empire shortly after completing his MBA degree at Stanford University in the early 1960s. Drawing on his firsthand knowledge of track and field, he decided to import low-priced track shoes from Japan in partnership with his former college coach. Bowerman would provide design ideas, test the shoes in competition, and endorse the shoes with other coaches; Knight would handle all financial and day-to-day operations of the business. Neither man had much money to offer, so for $500 each and a handshake, the company (then called Blue Ribbon Sports) was officially founded in 1963. The company took the name Nike in 1978;

[2]S. Greenhouse, "Anti-Sweatshop Movement Is Achieving Gains Overseas," *New York Times,* January 26, 2000, Section A, p. 10.

[3]L. Lee, "Can Nike Still Do It," *Business Week,* February 21, 2000, p. 120.

[4]J. Martinson, "Brand Values: Nike: The Sweet Swoosh of Success," *The Guardian* (London), Guardian City Pages, July 8, 2000, p. 26.

[5]"The Forbes 400: America's Richest People," *Forbes,* October 11, 1999, p. 296.

two years later, with revenues topping $269 million and 2,700 employees, Nike became a publicly traded company.[6]

From the beginning, marketing had been a critical part of Knight's vision. The founder defined Nike as a "marketing-oriented company." During the 1980s and early 1990s, Nike aggressively sought endorsements by celebrity athletes to increase brand awareness and foster consumer loyalty. Early Nike endorsers included marathoners Alberto Salazar and Joan Benoit, Olympic gold medalist Carl Lewis, Wimbledon champion Andre Agassi, and six members of the 1992 Olympic basketball "Dream Team." Later Nike endorsers included tennis aces Pete Sampras and Monica Seles, basketball great Michael Jordan, and golf superstar Tiger Woods.

Nike became the world's largest athletic shoe company in 1991 when revenues soared to $3 billion, but that was only the beginning.[7] Continued development of "cool shoes," aggressive geographic expansion, and the world dominance of Nike-endorsing athletes resulted in record-breaking performance year after year. By 1998, Nike's total revenues exceeded $9.5 billion.[8] Although the Asian economic crisis and sluggish U.S. sales caused revenues to dip slightly in 1999, Nike easily led the athletic footwear industry, outpacing the number two firm (Adidas) by 1.5 times.[9] Key events in Nike's history are summarized in Exhibit 1.

CUTTING-EDGE PRODUCTS

An important element in Nike's success was its ability to develop cutting-edge products that met the needs of serious athletes, as well as set fashion trends. Research specialists in Nike's Sports Research Labs conducted extensive research and testing to develop new technologies to improve the performance of Nike shoes in a variety of sports. Tom McQuirk, head of the company's Sports Research Labs, stated, "Our job here in sports research is to define human movement in terms of biomechanics and physiology. Our job is to translate activities into a set of performance-enhancing and injury-reducing needs."[10] For example, research specialists studied the causes of ankle injuries in basketball players to develop shoes that would physically prevent injuries as well as signal information to the user to help him or her resist turning the ankle while in the air. Other specialists developed new polymer materials that would make the shoes lighter, more aerodynamic, or more resistant to the abrasions incurred during normal athletic use.

Findings from the Sports Research Labs were then passed on to design teams that developed the look and styling of the shoes. Drawing heavily from trends in popular culture, shoe designers in the Jordan Building of Nike's Beaverton, Oregon, corporate campus blended the technological with the "romance and imagery and all those subliminal characteristics that make an object important to people in less utilitarian ways."[11] Put more simply, the Nike designers took a technologically sophisticated piece of sporting equipment and gave it attitude.

---

[6]"Our History: BRS Becomes Nike," Nike website (www.nikebiz.com/story/before.shtml), accessed February 3, 2000.

[7]Ibid.

[8]Nike, Inc., Form 10-K, 1999.

[9]D. Gellene, "Ad Reviews: Adidas," *The Los Angeles Times,* April 8, 1999, p. C6.

[10]D. R. Katz, *Just Do It: The Nike Spirit in the Corporate World* (Holbrook, MA: Adams Media Corporation, 1995), p. 132.

[11]Ibid., p. 130.

exhibit 1   Key Events in Nike's History

1957	Phil Knight and Coach Bill Bowerman met for the first time at the University of Oregon.
1959	Phil Knight graduated from the University of Oregon with a BBA degree in accounting.
1962	Knight wrote the marketing research paper outlining the concept that became Blue Ribbon Sports (BRS).
1963	The first shipment of 200 Tiger shoes arrived from Japan.
1966	The first retail store was opened.
1969	Knight left the accounting field to devote his full-time efforts to building the company.
1970	Nike's legal dispute with the Japanese supplier resulted in the exploration of manufacturing in Mexico, Puerto Rico, and Canada.
1971	Nike contracted for the production of shoes in Mexico; however, the shoes were a disaster—cracking when used in cold weather.
1972	The first shoes bearing the Nike brand were sold.
1977	Nike contracted with factories in Taiwan and Korea, ending the manufacturing relationship with the Japanese firm.
1978	The split between Blue Ribbon Sports and its Japanese supplier became final. BRS changed to the Nike name for all operations.
1980	Nike sold the first shares of common stock to the public.
1981	Revenues were $457.7 million, and Nike had 3,000 employees.
1982	Phil Knight received the Pioneer Award. The Pioneer Award was given annually by the University of Oregon to a person "whose character places him/her in a position of leadership." The award recognized individuals who led in business, philanthropy, communications, government, or the arts.
1986	For the first time, Nike revenues surpassed the billion-dollar mark.
1990	Growth in international sales helped Nike reach $2 billion in revenues. Nike employed 5,300 people in the United States. The Nike World Campus opened in Beaverton, Oregon.
1991	Revenues reached $3 billion with $869 million in international revenues. Michael Jordan wears Nike shoes while leading the Chicago Bulls to their first NBA championship.
1995	Nike's revenues were $4.8 billion. Nike shoes using the patented Nike Air system were introduced, radically changing shoe design.
1996	Nike's revenues were $6.5 billion. In the Atlanta Olympics, Michael Johnson became the fastest man in the world while wearing a pair of specially designed gold metallic Nike's. Phil Knight donated $25 million to the Oregon Campaign. His gift designated $15 million to the creation of endowed chairs. The remaining $10 million helped finance the construction of a new law school building that was named the William W. Knight Law Center after Phil Knight's father. The $25 million gift was the largest single gift to a university in the Pacific Northwest. Knight's earlier gifts to UO totaled $25 million. Knight funds supported athletics, and the university library was named for his family in the 1980s.
1998	Nike's revenues were $9.5 billion. Basketball shoes slumped as Michael Jordan retired and the NBA played a shortened season due to a labor dispute. Nike's international trading partner, Nissho Iwai of Japan, donated an undisclosed "generous" amount to the UO Knight Library to "honor Mr. Knight's great commitment to supporting the University of Oregon." Nissho Iwai had made a donation to the renovation of the library in 1990. One floor of the library was named for the Japanese company.*
1999	Nike's revenues dipped to $8.8 billion. Revenue decline was attributed to the "brown shoes" movement in the United States and the Asian economic slump.
2000	Phil Knight withdrew his pledge for a $30 million contribution for the University of Oregon's football stadium.

*"Trading Firm Makes Gift to UO Knight Library Endowment," University of Oregon press release, June 11, 1998 (comm.uoregon.edu/newsreleases/official/jun98/G061198_1.html), accessed March 27, 2000.

Sources: "Our History," Nike website (www.nikebiz.com/story/chrono.shtml), accessed February 3, 2000; D. R. Katz, *Just Do It: The Nike Spirit in the Corporate World* (Holbrook, MA: Adams Media Corporation, 1995), Nike, Inc., Form 10-K, 1999.

The Making of Athletic Shoes

Although it was the leading athletic footwear company in the world, Nike never manufactured shoes in any significant number. Rather, from its inception, the company had outsourced production to subcontractors in southeast Asia, with the company shifting production locations within the region when prevailing wage rates became too high. In the early years, it had imported shoes from Japan. It later shifted production to South Korea and Taiwan, then to Indonesia and Thailand, and later yet to Vietnam and China, as shown in Exhibit 2.[12]

The reasons for locating show production mainly in southeast Asia were several, but the most important was the cost of labor. The availability of component materials and trade policies were also factors. Modern athletic shoes were composed of mesh, leather, and nylon uppers that were hand-assembled, sewn, and glued to composite soles.[13] Mechanization had not been considered effective for shoe manufacturing due to the fragile materials used and the short life spans of styles of athletic shoes.[14] Therefore, shoe production was highly labor-intensive. Developing countries, primarily in southeast Asia, offered the distinct advantage of considerably lower wage rates. For example, in the early 19909s, when Nike shifted much of its shoe production to Indonesia, daily wages there hovered around $1 a day (compared with wages in the U.S. shoe industry at that time of around $8 an hour).[15]

Along with lower labor costs, Asia provided the additional advantage of access to raw materials suppliers.[16] Very few rubber firms in the United States, for example, produced the sophisticated composite soles demanded in modern athletic shoe designs. Satellite industries necessary for modern shoe production, plentiful in Asia, included tanneries, textiles, and plastic and ironwork moldings.[17]

A third factor in determining where to locate production was differential tariffs that applied to athletic shoes. The tariffs were determined by the manner in which the upper was attached to the sole of the shoe. The three types—nonmolded, molded, and fox-banded (where a strip of material was applied over the joint of the sole and upper, as in canvas sneakers)—were assessed different tariffs for importation. Variations in the materials used for the uppers also determined the tariff rate. In general, canvas sneakers were assessed higher tariffs than leather molded footwear, such as basketball or running shoes. As a result, differential tariffs prompted shoe companies to outsource higher-margin high-tech athletic shoes while sometimes producing low-margin canvas shoes domestically.[18]

The economic reality for many firms in the athletic footwear industry involved balancing consumer demand for new and innovative styles with pressures to improve the profit picture. Manufacturing new high-technology styles in southeast Asia permitted the firms to take advantage of lower labor costs, lower tariffs, and a better-developed supplier network. Many of Nike's factories in Asia were operated by a small

[12]Although Nike operated shoe factories in New England in the 1970s and 1980s, Nike's annual U.S. production never accounted for more than one week of demand annually. Later, these plants were closed, and Nike stopped producing shoes in the United States, other than prototypes.

[13]Nike, Inc. Form 10-K, 1997.

[14]T. Vanderbilt, *The Sneaker Book* (New York: The New Press, 1998), p. 77.

[15]Katz, *Just Do It*, p. 162.

[16]Vanderbilt, *The Sneaker Book*, p. 81.

[17]Ibid., p. 90.

[18]J. Austen and R. Barff, "It's Gotta Be Da Shoes," *Environment and Planning* 25 (1993), pp. 48–52.

exhibit 2   Location of Shoe Production in Nike Subcontractor
               Factories, 1995–99 Percent of Athletic Shoe Production
               by Country.

	1995	1996	1997	1998	1999
China	31%	34%	37%	37%	40%
Indonesia	31	38	37	34	30
South Korea	16	11	5	2	1
Thailand	14	10	10	10	11
Taiwan	8	5	3	2	2
Vietnam	—	2	8	11	12
Philippines	—	—	4	4	2
Italy	—	—	—	—	2
	100%	100%	100%	100%	100%

Source: Nike 10-K statements, 1995–99.

number of Taiwanese and Korean firms that specialized in shoe manufacturing, many owned by some of the wealthiest families in the region. When Nike moved from one location to another, often these companies followed, bringing their managerial expertise with them.

Nike's Subcontractor Factories

In 2000, Nike contracted with over 500 different footwear and apparel factories around the world to produce its shoes and apparel.[19] Although there was no such thing as a typical Nike plant, a factory operated by the Korean subcontractor Tae Kwang Vina (TKV) in the Bien Hoa City industrial zone near Ho Chi Minh City in Vietnam provided a glimpse into the setting in which many Nike shoes were made.[20]

TKV employed approximately 10,000 workers in the Bien Hoa City factory. The workforce consisted of 200 clerical workers, 355 supervisors, and 9,465 production workers, all making athletic shoes for Nike. Ninety percent of the workers were women between the ages of 18 to 24. Production workers were employed in one of three major areas within the factory: the chemical, stitching, and assembly sections. Production levels at the Bien Hoa City factory reached 400,000 pairs of shoes per month; Nike shoes made at this and other factories made up fully 5 percent of Vietnam's total exports.[21]

A second-generation South Korean shoe worker employed by Nike described the challenges of work in the typical shoe factory as the "three D's." "It's dirty, dangerous,

---

[19]S. Greenhouse, "Antisweatshop Movement Is Achieving Gains Overseas," *New York Times,* January 26, 2000, p. A10.

[20]Descriptions of the Tae Kwang Vina factory in Bien Hoa City were derived from the following: J. Manning, "Nike: Tracks across the Globe,: three-part series in *The Oregonian,* November 9–11, 1997 (available online at www.oregonlive.com/series/nike11091.html); Katz, *Just Do It;* Vanderbilt, *The Sneaker Book;* and *Ernst & Young Environmental and Labor Practice Audit of the Tae Kwang Vina Industrial Ltd. Co., Vietnam,* January 13, 1997 (copy of the audit available at www.corpwatch.org/trac/nike/audit.html).

[21]S. Greenhouse, "Nike Shoe Plant in Vietnam Is Called Unsafe for Workers," *New York Times,* November 8, 1997, p. A1.

and difficult," explained T. H. Lee. "Making shoes on a production line is something people only do because they see it as an important and lucrative job. Nobody who could do something else for the same wage would be here. It's less dirty, dangerous, and difficult than it was in the past—but it's not an easy way to spend a day."[22]

The Chemical Section[23]   Over 1,000 natural and man-made materials were used in the factory to product shoes from scratch. Workers in the chemical or polyurethane (PU) plant were responsible for producing the high-technology outsoles. Production steps in the chemical division involved stretching and flattening huge blobs of raw rubber on heavy-duty rollers and baking chemical compounds in steel molds to form the innovative three-divisional outsoles. The chemical composition of the soles changed constantly in response to the cutting-edge formulations developed by the Beaverton, Oregon, design teams, requiring frequent changes in the production process.

The smell of complex polymers, the hot ovens, and the clanging of the steel molds resulted in a working environment that was louder, was hotter, and had higher concentrations of chemical fumes than allowed by Vietnamese law.[24] Chemicals used in the section were known to cause eye, skin, and throat irritations; damage to liver and kidneys; nausea; anorexia; and reproductive health hazards through inhalation or in some cases through absorption through the skin.[25] Workers in the chemical section were thought to have high rates of respiratory illnesses, although records kept at the TKV operations did not permit the tracking of illnesses by factory section.

Workers in the chemical section were issued gloves and surgical-style masks. However, they often discarded the protective gear, complaining that it was too hot and humid to wear them in the plant. Cotton masks and gloves also were ineffective in protecting workers from solvent fumes and exposure to skin-damaging chemicals.[26]

The Stitching Section[27]   In a space the size of three football fields, row after row of sewing machines operated by young women hummed and clattered. One thousand stitchers worked on a single floor of the TKV factory, sewing together nylon, leather, and other fabrics to make the uppers. Other floors of the factory were filled with thousands of additional sewing machines producing different shoe models.

The stitching job required precision and speed. Workers who did not meet the aggressive production goals did not receive a bonus. Failing to meet production goals three times resulted in the worker's dismissal. Workers were sometimes required to work additional hours without pay to meet production quotas.[28] Supervisors were strict, chastising workers for excessive talking or spending too much time in the restrooms. Korean supervisors, often hampered by language and cultural barriers, sometimes resorted to hard-nosed management tactics, hitting or slapping slower workers. Other workers in need of discipline were forced to stand outside the factory for long periods in the tropical sun. The Vietnamese term for this practice was "phoi nang," or sun-drying.[29]

---

[22]Katz, *Just Do It*, p. 161.

[23]Manning, "Nike: Tracks across the Globe."

[24]Manning, "Nike: Tracks across the Globe, Part II: Poverty's Legions Flock to Nike."

[25]*Ernst & Young Audit.*

[26]Ibid.

[27]Manning, "Nike: Tracks across the Globe."

[28]Manning, "Nike: Tracks across the Globe, Part I: Nike's Asian Machine Goes on Trial."

[29]Manning, "Nike: Tracks across the Globe, Part II: Poverty's Legions Flock to Nike."

The Assembly Section[30]   Women worked side by side along an assembly line to join the uppers to the outsoles through the rapid manipulation of sharp knives, skivers,[31] routers, and glue-coated brushes. Women were thought to be better suited for the assembly jobs because their hands were smaller and more capable of the manual dexterity needed to fit the shoe components together precisely. During the assembly process, some 120 pairs of hands touched a single shoe.

A strong, sweet solvent smell was prominent in the assembly area. Ceiling-mounted ventilation fans were ineffective because the heavy fumes settled to the floor. Assembly workers wore cotton surgical masks to protect themselves from the fumes; however, many workers pulled the masks below their noses, saying they were more comfortable that way.[32]

Rows and rows of shoes passed along a conveyor before the sharp eyes of the quality control inspectors. The inspectors examined each of the thousands of shoes produced daily for poor stitching or crooked connections between soles. Defective shoes were discarded. Approved shoes continued on the conveyor to stations where they were laced by assembly workers and finally put into Nike shoe boxes for shipment to the United States.[33]

Despite the dirty, dangerous, and difficult nature of the work inside the Bien Hoa factory, there was no shortage of applicants for positions. Although entry-level wages averaged only $1.50 per day (the lowest of all countries where Nike manufactured), many workers viewed factory jobs as being better than their other options, such as working in the rice paddies or pedaling a pedicab along the streets of Ho Chi Minh City.[34] With overtime pay at one and a half times the regular rate, workers could double their salaries—generating enough income to purchase a motorscooter or to send money home to impoverished rural relatives. These wages were well above national norms. An independent study by researchers from Dartmouth University showed that the average annual income for workers at two Nike subcontractor factories in Vietnam was between $545 and $566, compared with the national average of between $250 and $300.[35] Additionally, workers were provided free room and board and access to on-site health care facilities.

Many Vietnamese workers viewed positions in the shoe factory as transitional jobs—a way to earn money for a dowry or to experience living in a larger city. Many returned to their homes after working for Nike for two or three years to marry and begin the next phase of their lives.[36]

THE CAMPAIGNS AGAINST NIKE

In the early 1990s, criticism of Nike's global labor practices began to gather steam. *Harper's* magazine, for example, published the pay stub of an Indonesian worker,

---

[30]Vanderbilt, *The Sneaker Book,* p. 84.

[31]Skivers are cutting tools that are used to split leather. In athletic shoe manufacturing, skivers are used to cut away the excess leather when bonding the upper to the sole.

[32]*Ernst & Young Audit.*

[33]Katz, *Just Do It,* p. 160.

[34]D. Lamb, "Job Opportunity or Exploitation?" *Los Angeles Times,* April 18, 1999, p. C1.

[35]B. Baum, "Study Concludes That Nike Workers Can More Than Make Ends Meet," *Athenaeum,* August 27, 1999, (online version available at www.athensnewspapers.com/1997/101797/1017.a3nike.html.

[36]Manning, "Nike: Tracks across the Globe, Part II: Poverty's Legions Flock to Nike."

showing that the Nike subcontractor had paid the woman just under 14 cents per hour, and contrasted this with the high retail price of the shoes—and the high salaries paid to the company's celebrity endorsers.[37] The Made in the U.S.A. Foundation, a group backed by American unions, used a million-dollar ad budget to urge consumers to send their "old, dirty, smelly, worn-out Nikes" to Phil Knight in protest of Nike's Asian manufacturing practices.[38] Human rights groups and Christian organizations joined the labor unions in targeting the labor practices of the athletic shoes firm. Many felt that Nike's antiauthority corporate image ("Just Do It") and message of social betterment through fitness were incompatible with press photos of slight Asian women hunched over sewing machines 70 hours a week, earning just pennies an hour.

By mid-1993, Nike was being regularly pilloried in the press as an imperialist profiteer. A CBS news segment airing on July 2, 1993, opened with images of Michael Jordan and Andre Agassi, two athletes who had multimillion-dollar promotion contracts with Nike. Viewers were told to contrast the athletes' paychecks with those of the Chinese and Indonesian workers who made "pennies" so that Nike could "Just Do It."[39]

In 1995, the *Washington Post* reported that a pair of Nike Air Pegasus shoes that retailed for $70 cost Nike only $2.75 in labor costs, or 4 percent of the price paid by consumers. Nike's operating profit on the same pair of shoes was $6.25; the retailer pocketed $9.00 in operating profits, as shown in Exhibit 3. Also that year, shareholder activists organized by the Interfaith Center on Corporate Responsibility submitted a shareholder proposal at Nike's annual meeting, calling on the company to review labor practices by its subcontractors; the proposal garnered 3 percent of the shareholder vote.

Things were to get worse. A story in *Life* magazine documented the use of child labor in Pakistan to produce soccer balls for Nike, Adidas, and other companies.[40] The publicity fallout was intense. The public could not ignore the photographs of small children sitting in the dirt, carefully stitching together the panels of a soccer ball that would become the plaything of some American child the same age.[41] Nike moved quickly to work with its Pakistani subcontractor to eliminate the use of child labor, but damage to Nike's image had been done.

In October 1996, the CBS News program *48 Hours* broadcast a scathing report on Nike's factories in Vietnam. CBS reporter Roberta Baskin focused on low wage rates, extensive overtime, and physical abuse of workers. Several young workers told Baskin how a Korean supervisor had beaten them with a part of a shoe because of problems with production.[42] A journalist in Vietnam told the reporter that the phrase "to Nike someone" was part of the Vietnamese vernacular. It meant to "take out one's frustration on a fellow worker." Vietnamese plant managers refused to be interviewed, covering their faces as they ran inside the factory. CBS news anchor Dan Rather concluded the damaging report by saying, "Nike now says it plans to hire outside observers to talk to employees and examine working conditions in its Vietnam factories, but the company just won't say when that might happen."[43]

---

[37]J. Ballinger, "Nike: The New Free Trade Heel," *Harper's,* August 1992, p. 119.

[38]Katz, *Just Do It,* p. 166.

[39]Ibid., p. 187.

[40]S. Schanberg, "Six Cents an Hour," *Life,* June 1996, pp. 38–47.

[41]W. J. Holstein, B. Palmer, S. Ur-Rehman, and T. Ito, "Santa's Sweatshops," *U.S. News and World Report,* December 23, 1996, p. 50.

[42]The *48 Hours* report, however, neglected to mention that the supervisor had subsequently been fired and was later criminally convicted in Vietnamese court (Katz, *Just Do It,* p. 188).

[43]CBS News transcript, *48 Hours,* October 17, 1996.

exhibit 3   The Cost of a Pair of Nike Air Pegasus Shoes

| Subcontractor | →A | Nike | →B | Retailer | →C | Consumer |

A. Cost to Nike		B. Cost to Retailer		C. Cost to Consumer	
Materials	$9.00	Nike's operating profit	$6.25	Retail sales personnel	$9.50
Tariffs	3.00	Sales, distribution, and administration	5.00	Rent of retail space	9.00
Rent and equipment	3.00	Promotion/advertising	4.00	Retailer's operating profit	9.00
Production labor	2.75	Research and development	0.25	Other expenses	7.00
Subcontractor's operating profit	1.75				
Shipping	0.50				
Cost to Nike	$20.00	Cost to retailer	$35.50	Cost to consumer	$70.00

Source: Adapted from "Why It Costs $70 for a Pair of Athletic Shoes," *Washington Post,* May 3, 1995.

The negative publicity was having an effect. In 1996, a marketing research study authorized by Nike reported the perceptions of young people age 13 to 25 of Nike as a company. The top three perceptions, in the order of their response frequency, were athletics, cool, and bad labor practices.[44] Although Nike maintained that its sales were never affected, company executives were clearly concerned about the effect of criticism of its global labor practices on the reputation of the brand they had worked so hard to build.

THE EVOLUTION OF NIKE'S GLOBAL LABOR PRACTICES

In its early years, Nike had maintained that the labor practices of its foreign subcontractors—like TKV—were simply not its responsibility. "When we started Nike," Knight later commented, "it never occurred to us that we should dictate what their factor[ies] should look like, which really didn't matter because we had no idea what a shoe factory should look like anyway."[45] The subcontractors, not Nike, were responsible for wages and working conditions. Dave Taylor, Nike's vice president of production, explained the company's position: "We don't pay anybody at the factories, and we don't set policy within the factories; it is their business to run."[46]

When negative articles first began appearing in the early 1990s, however, Nike managers realized that they needed to take some action to avoid further bad publicity. In 1992, the company drafted its first code of conduct (Exhibit 4), which required every subcontractor and supplier in the Nike network to honor all applicable local government labor and environmental regulations, or Nike would terminate the relationship.[47]

[44]Manning, "Nike: Tracks across the Globe, Part II: Poverty's Legions Flock to Nike."
[45]Philip Knight, speech to the National Press Club, May 12, 1998.
[46]Katz, *Just Do It,* p. 191.
[47]Ibid.

exhibit 4   Nike's 1992 Code of Conduct

Nike Inc. was founded on a handshake.

Implicit in that act was the determination that we would build our business with all our partners upon trust, teamwork, honesty, and mutual respect. We expect all of our business partners to operate on the same principles.

At the core of the Nike corporate ethic is the belief that we are a company comprised of many different kinds of people, appreciating individual diversity, and dedicated to equal opportunity for each individual.

Nike designs, manufactures, and markets sports and fitness products. At each step in that process we are dedicated to minimizing our impact on the environment. We seek to implement to the maximum extent possible the three "R's" of environmental action— reduce, reuse, and recycle.

There is No Finish Line.

Memorandum of Understanding

Wherever Nike operates around the globe, we are guided by our Code of Conduct and bind our business partners to those principles with a signed Memorandum of Understanding.

Government Regulation of Business (subcontractor/supplier) certifies compliance with all applicable local government regulations regarding minimum wage; overtime; child labor laws; provisions of pregnancy, menstrual leave; provisions for vacation and holidays; and mandatory retirement benefits.

Safety and Health (subcontractor/supplier) certifies compliance with all applicable local government regulations regarding occupational health and safety.

Worker Insurance (subcontractor/supplier) certifies compliance with all applicable local laws providing health insurance, life insurance and worker's compensation.

Forced Labor (subcontractor/supplier) certifies that it and its suppliers and contractors do not use any form of forced labor—prison or otherwise.

Environment (subcontractor/supplier) certifies compliance with all applicable local environmental regulations and adheres to Nike's own broader environmental practices, including the prohibition on the use of chloro-fluoro-carbons (CFCs), the release of which could contribute to the depletion of the earth's ozone layer.

Equal Opportunity (subcontractor/supplier) certifies that it does not discriminate in hiring, salary, benefits, advancement, termination, or retirement on the basis of gender, race, religion, age, sexual orientation, or ethnic origin.

Documentation and Inspection (subcontractor/supplier) agrees to maintain on file such documentation as may be needed to demonstrate compliance with the certifications in this Memorandum of Understanding and further agrees to make these documents available for Nike's inspection upon request.

Source: Code of Conduct. (n.d.), Nike Inc., at www.nikebiz.com/labor/code.shtml, accessed November 18, 2000.

The subcontractors were also required to allow plant inspections and complete all necessary paperwork. Despite the compliance reports the factories filed every six months, Nike insiders acknowledged that the code of conduct system might not catch all violations. Tony Nava, Nike's country coordinator for Indonesia, told a *Chicago Tribune* reporter, "We can't know if they're actually complying with what they put down on paper."[48] In short, Nike required its subcontractors to comply with existing labor laws, but did not feel it was the firm's duty to challenge local policies that suppressed worker rights or kept wages low in order to attract manufacturing.

In 1994, Nike tried to address this problem by hiring Ernst & Young, the accounting firm, to independently monitor worker abuse allegations in Nike's Indonesian factories. Later, Ernst & Young also audited Nike's factories in Thailand and Vietnam.

---

[48]M. Goozner, "Nike Manager Knows Abuses Do Happen," *Chicago Tribune*, November 7, 1994, p. 6.

Although these audits were not made public, a copy of the Vietnam audit leaked to the press showed that workers were often unaware of the toxicity of the compounds they were using and ignorant of the need for safety precautions.[49] In 1998, Nike implemented important changes in its Vietnamese plants to reduce exposure to toxins—substituting less harmful chemicals, installing ventilation systems, and training personnel in occupational health and safety issues.

In 1996, Nike established a new Labor Practices Department, headed by Dusty Kidd, formerly a public relations executive for the company. Later that year, Nike hired GoodWorks International, headed by former U.S. ambassador to the United Nations Andrew Young, to investigate conditions in its overseas factories. In January 1997, GoodWorks issued a glossy report, stating that "Nike is doing a good job in the application of its Code of Conduct. But Nike can and should do better." The report was criticized by activists for its failure to look at the issue of wages. Young demurred, saying he did not have expertise in conducting wage surveys. Said one critic, "This was a public relations problem, and the world's largest sneaker company did what it does best: It purchased a celebrity endorsement."[50]

Over the next few years, Nike continued to work to improve labor practices in its overseas subcontractor factories, as well as the public perception of them. In January 1998, Nike formed a Corporate Responsibility Division, combining the Labor Practices, Global Community Affairs, and Environmental Action Teams under the leadership of former Microsoft executive Maria S. Eitel, hired to be Nike's new vice president for Corporate and Social Responsibility. Nike subsequently doubled the staff of this division. In May of that year, Knight gave a speech at the National Press Club, at which he announced several new initiatives. At that time, he committed Nike to raise the minimum age for employment in its shoe factories to 18 and in its apparel factories to 16. He also promised to achieve OSHA standards for indoor air quality in all its factories by the end of the year, mainly by eliminating the use of the solvent toluene; to expand educational programs for workers and its microenterprise loan program; and to fund university research on responsible business practices. Nike also continued its use of external monitors, hiring Pricewaterhouse-Coopers to join Ernst & Young in a comprehensive program of factory audits, checking them against Nike's code. At the conclusion of his speech Knight said,

> At the end of the day, we don't have all the answers. Nobody has all the answers. We want to be the best corporate citizens we can be. If we continue to improve, and our industry colleagues and people interested in these issues join in our efforts, the workers are the ultimate beneficiaries.[51]

APPAREL INDUSTRY PARTNERSHIP

One of Nike's most ambitious social responsibility initiatives was its participation in the Apparel Industry Partnership. It was this involvement that would lead, eventually, to Knight's break with the University of Oregon.

---

[49]K. Hammond, "Leaked Audit: Nike Factory Violated Worker Laws," *Mother Jones,* November 7, 1997 (www.motherjones.com/news_wire/nike.html).

[50]S. Glass, "The Young and the Feckless," *The New Republic,* August 25, 1997 (online source at www.corpwatch.org/trac/feature/sweatshops/newprogressive.html). Glass was later fired by *The New Republic,* which charged that Glass had fabricated some of his sources for this and other articles.

[51]Philip Knight, National Press Club luncheon address, May 12, 1998. LEXIS-NEXIS Academic Universe, Category: News (web.lexis-nexisw.com/universe), accessed August 27, 2000.

In August 1996, President Clinton launched the White House Apparel Industry Partnership on Workplace Standards (AIP). The initial group was comprised of 18 organizations. Participants included several leading manufacturers, such as Nike, Reebok, and Liz Claiborne. Also in the group were several labor unions, including the Union of Needletrades, Industrial, and Textile Employees (UNITE) and the Retail, Wholesale and Department Store Union; and several human rights, consumer, and shareholder organizations, including Business for Social Responsibility, the Interfaith Center on Corporate Responsibility, and the National Consumers League. The goal of the AIP was to develop a set of standards to ensure that apparel and footwear were not made under sweatshop conditions. For companies, it held out the promise of certifying to their customers that their products were "no sweat." For labor and human rights groups, it held out the promise of improving working conditions in overseas factories.[52]

In April 1997, after months of often-fractious meetings, the AIP announced that it had agreed on a workplace code of conduct that sought to define decent and humane working conditions.[53] Companies agreeing to the code would have to pledge not to use forced labor—that is, prisoners or bonded or indentured workers. They could not require more than 60 hours of work a week, including overtime. They could not employ children younger than 15 years old, or the age for completing compulsory schooling, whichever was older—except they could hire 14-year-olds if local law allowed. The code also called on signatory companies to treat all workers with respect and dignity; to refrain from discrimination on the basis of gender, race, religion, age, disability, sexual orientation, nationality, political opinion, or social or ethnic origin; and to provide a safe and healthy workplace. Employees' rights to organize and bargain collectively would be respected. In a key provision, the code also required companies to pay at least the local legal minimum wage or the prevailing industry wage, whichever was higher. All standards would apply not only to a company's own facilities but also to their subcontractors or suppliers.

Knight, who prominently joined President Clinton and others at a White House ceremony announcing the code, issued the following statement:

> Nike agreed to participate in this Partnership because it was the first credible attempt, by a diverse group of interests, to address the important issue of improving factories worldwide. It was worth the effort and hard work. The agreement will prove important for several reasons. Not only is our industry stepping up to the plate and taking a giant swing at improving factory conditions, but equally important, we are finally providing consumers some guidance to counter all of the misinformation that has surrounded this issue for far too long.[54]

THE FAIR LABOR ASSOCIATION

But this was not the end of the AIP's work; it also had to agree on a process for monitoring compliance with the code. Although the group hoped to complete its work in 6 months, over a year later it was still deeply divided on several key matters. Internal documents leaked to the *New York Times* in July 1998 showed that industry representatives had opposed proposals, circulated by labor and human rights members, calling for the monitoring of 30 percent of plants annually by independent auditors. The companies

---

[52]"Companies Agree to Meet on Sweatshops," *Washington Post,* August 3, 1996.

[53]For the full text of the Fair Labor Association Workplace Code of Conduct, see www.fairlabor.org/html/amendctr.html#workplace.

[54]Philip H. Knight, statement released to the press, April 14, 1997.

also opposed proposals that would require them to support workers' rights to organize independent unions and to bargain collectively, even in countries—like China—where workers did not have such rights by law. Said one nonindustry member, "We're teetering on the edge of collapse."[55]

Finally, a subgroup of nine centrist participants, including Nike, began meeting separately in an attempt to move forward. In November 1998, this subgroup announced that it had come to agreement on a monitoring system for overseas factories of U.S.-based companies. The AIP would establish a new organization, the Fair Labor Association (FLA), to oversee compliance with its workplace code of conduct. Companies would be required to monitor their own factories, and those of their subcontractors, for compliance; all would have to be checked within the first two years. In addition, the FLA would select and certify independent external monitors, who would inspect 10 percent of each firm's factories each year. Most of these monitors were expected to be accounting firms, which had expertise in conducting audits. The monitors' reports would be kept private. If a company was found to be out of compliance, it would be given a chance to correct the problem. Eventually, if it did not, the company would be dropped from the FLA, and its termination would be announced to the public. Companies would pay for most of their own monitoring.[56]

The Clinton administration quickly endorsed the plan. Secretary of Labor Alexis Herman said, "[We are] convinced this agreement lays the foundation to eliminate sweatshop labor, here and abroad. It is workable for business and creates a credible system that will let consumers know the garments they buy are not produced by exploited workers."[57]

Both manufacturers and institutional buyers stood to benefit from participation in the Fair Labor Association. Companies, once certified for three years, could place an FLA service mark on their brands, signaling to both individual consumers and institutional buyers that their products were "sweatshop-free." It was expected that the FLA would also serve the needs of institutional buyers, particularly universities. By joining the FLA and agreeing to contract only with certified companies, universities could warrant to their students and others that their logo apparel and athletic gear were manufactured under conditions conforming to an established code of fair labor standards.[58] Both parties would pay for these benefits. The FLA was to be funded by dues from participating companies ($5,000 to $100,000 annually, depending on revenue) and by payments from affiliated colleges and universities (based on 1 percent of their licensing income from logo products, up to a $50,000 annual cap).

Criticism of the Fair Labor Association

Although many welcomed the agreement —and some new companies signed on with the FLA soon after it was announced—others did not. Warnaco, a leading apparel maker that had participated in the AIP, quit, saying that the monitoring process would require it to turn over competitive information to outsiders. The American Apparel

---

[55]Steven Greenhouse, "Antisweatshop Coalition Finds Itself at Odds on Garment Factory Code," *New York Times,* July 3, 1998.

[56]For a description of the monitoring process, see www.fairlabor.org/html/ amendctr.html#monitoringprocess.

[57]"Plan to Curtain Sweatshops Rejected by Union," *New York Times,* November 5, 1998.

[58]For a list of signatory companies, universities, and other organizations, see www.fairlabor.org/html/ affiliat.html.

Manufacturing Association (AAMA), an industry group representing 350 companies, scoffed at the whole idea of monitoring. "Who is going to do the monitoring?" asked a spokesperson for the AAMA, apparently sarcastically. "Accountants or Jesuit priests?" The FLA monitoring scheme was also attacked as insufficient by some partnership participants that had not been part of the subgroup. In their view, companies simply could not be relied upon to monitor themselves objectively. Said Jay Mazur, president of UNITE, "The fox cannot watch the chickens. If they want the monitoring to be independent, it can't be controlled by the companies."[59] FLA critics believed that a visit from an external monitor once every 10 years would not prevent abuses. In any case, as a practical matter, they stated that most monitors would be drawn from the major accounting firms that did business with the companies they were monitoring and were, therefore, unlikely to seek out lapses. Companies would not be required to publish a list of their factories, and any problems uncovered by the monitoring process could be kept from the public under the rules governing nondisclosure of proprietary information.

One of the issues most troubling to critics was the code's position on wages. The code called on companies to pay the minimum wage or prevailing wage, whichever was higher. In many of the countries of southeast Asia, though, these wages fell well below the minimum considered necessary for a decent standard of living for an individual or family. For example, *The Economist* reported that Indonesia's average minimum wage—paid by Nike subcontractors—was only two-thirds of what a person needed for basic subsistence.[60] An alternative view was that a code of conduct should require that companies pay a *living wage,* that is, compensation for a normal workweek adequate to provide for the basic needs of an average family, adjusted for the average number of adult wage earners per family. One problem with this approach, however, was that many countries did not systematically study the cost of living, relative to wages, so defining a living wage was difficult. The partnership asked the U.S. Department of Labor to conduct a preliminary study of these issues; the results were published in 2000 (see Exhibit 5).

The code also called on companies to respect workers' rights to organize and bargain collectively. Yet a number of FLA companies outsourced production to nondemocratic countries, such as China and Vietnam, where workers had no such rights. Finally, some criticized the agreement on the grounds that it provided companies, as one put it, "a piece of paper to use as a fig leaf." Commented a representative of the needle trades union, "The problem with the partnership plan is that it tinkers at the margins of the sweatshop system but creates the impression that it is doing much more. This is potentially helpful to companies stung by public condemnation of their labor practices, but it hurts millions of workers and undermines the growing antisweatshop movement."[61]

THE WORKER RIGHTS CONSORTIUM

Some activists in the antisweatshop movement decided to chart their own course, independent of the FLA. On October 20, 1999, students from more than 100 colleges held a press conference to announce formation of the Workers Rights Consortium

---

[59]*New York Times,* November 21, 1997.
[60]"Indonesia: Staying Alive," *The Economist,* June 15, 1991, p. 38.
[61]Alan Howard, "Partners in Sweat," *The Nation,* December 29, 1998.

exhibit 5   Wages, Minimum Wages, and Poverty Lines for Selected Countries
in U.S. Dollars

Country	Year (latest available)	National Poverty Line	Minimum Wage	Prevailing Wage in Apparel and Footwear Industries
China	1997	$21–$27/cap/mo*	$12–$39/mo	$115–$191/mo
Indonesia	1999	$5–$6/cap/mo	$15–$34/mo	$15–$42/mo
South Korea	1999	$182/mo	$265/mo	$727–$932/mo
Thailand	1999	$22/cap/mo	$93–$109/mo	$106/mo
Taiwan	1998	$214–$344/mo	$476/mo	$690–$742/mo
Vietnam[†]	1997	$27–$29/mo	$35–$45/mo	$47–$56/mo
Philippines	1999	$26/cap/mo	$150/mo	$150/mo
Italy	1998	$390/cap/mo	$949–$1,445/mo	$1,280–$1,285/mo
United States	1998	$693/cap/mo	$858–$1,083/mo	$1,420–$1,488/mo

National Poverty Line: Poverty measures reflect an estimate of absolute poverty thresholds based on some specified set of basic needs. Opinions differ as to whether the poverty line should reflect mere physical subsistence levels or sufficient income to provide for a nutritious diet, safe drinking water, suitable housing, energy, transportation, health care, child care, education, savings, and discretionary income. Comparability between countries is difficult because the basis for establishing the poverty level usually differs across countries.

Minimum Wage: The minimum wage-fixing system differs according to the country's objectives and criteria. It is usually set by striking a balance between the needs of the worker and what employers can afford or what economic conditions will permit. A range for minimum wage indicates that the country has differential minimums based on the region, often differing for urban and rural regions.

Prevailing Wage: The prevailing wage reflects the "going rate" or average level of wages paid by employers for workers in the apparel or footwear industries. Positions requiring greater skills, supervisory responsibilities, or workers with longer years of employment typically earn more than the wage reported. Nonwage benefits such as access to health care, paid vacations, supplementary pay, or training are not included in the prevailing wage.

*Per capita per month.

[†]Canada NewsWire, "Nike Factory Workers in SE Asia Help Support Their Families and Have Discretionary Income, According to Preliminary Findings of Study by MBA Team from Dartmouth's Tuck School," October 16, 1997.

Source: U.S. Department of Labor; "Wages, Benefits, Poverty Line and Meeting Workers' Needs in the Apparel and Footwear Industries of Selected Countries," www.dol.gov.ilab/public/media/reports/oiea/main.htm, February 2000.

(WRC) and called on their schools to withdraw from, or not to join, the FLA. The organization would be formally launched at a founding convention in April 2000.[62]

The Workers Rights Consortium differed radically in its approach to eliminating sweatshops. First, the WRC did not permit corporations to join; it was comprised exclusively of universities and colleges, with unions and human rights organizations playing an advisory role. In joining the WRC, universities would agree to "require decent working conditions in factories producing their licensed products." Unlike the FLA, the WRC did not endorse a single, comprehensive set of fair labor standards. Rather, it called on its affiliated universities to develop their own codes. However, it did establish minimum standards that such codes should meet—ones that were, in some respects, stricter than the

---

[62]The website for the WRC is www.workersrights.org. Further material on disagreements within the FLA that led to the WRC's founding may be found at www.sweatshopwatch.org.

FLA's. Perhaps most significantly, companies would have to pay a living wage. Companies were also required to publish the names and addresses of all of their manufacturing facilities, in contrast to FLA rules. Universities could refuse to license goods made in countries where compliance with fair labor standards was "deemed impossible," whatever efforts companies had made to enforce their own codes in factories there.

By contrast with the FLA, monitoring would be carried out by "a network of local organizations in regions where licensed goods are produced," generally nongovernmental organizations, independent human rights groups, and unions. These organizations would conduct unannounced "spot investigations," usually in response to worker complaints; WRC organizers called this the "fire alarm" method of uncovering code violations. Systematic monitoring would not be attempted.

The consortium's governance structure reflected its mission of being an organization by and for colleges and universities. Its 12-person board was composed of three representatives of United Students Against Sweatshops, three university administrators from participating schools, and six members drawn from an advisory board of persons with "expertise in the issues surrounding worker abuses in the apparel industry and independent verification of labor standards in apparel factories." No seats at the table were reserved for industry representatives. The group would be financed by 1 percent of licensing revenue from participating universities, as well as foundation grants.

THE UNIVERSITIES TAKE SIDES

Over the course of the spring semester 2000, student protests were held on a number of campuses, including the University of Oregon, to demand that their schools join the WRC. By April, around 45 schools had done so. At UO, the administration encouraged an open debate on the issue so that all sides could be heard on how to ensure that UO products were made under humane conditions. Over a period of several months, the Academic Senate passed a resolution in support of the WRC. In a referendum sponsored by the student government, three-quarters of voters supported a proposal to join the WRC. A committee of faculty, students, administrators, and alumni appointed by the president voted unanimously to join the consortium.[63] Finally, after concluding that all constituents had had an opportunity to be heard, on April 12, 2000, University of Oregon president David Frohnmayer announced that UO would join the WRC for one year. Its membership would be conditional, he said, on the consortium's agreement to give companies a voice in its operations and universities more power in governance. Shortly after the university's decision was announced in the press, Phil Knight withdrew his philanthropic contribution. In his public announcement, he stated his main disagreements with the Worker Rights Consortium:

> Frankly, we are frustrated that factory monitoring is badly misconstrued. For us, one of the great hurdles and real handicaps in the dialogue has been the complexity of the issue. For real progress to be made, all key participants have to be at the table. That's why the FLA has taken so long to get going. The WRC is supported by the AFL-CIO and its affiliated apparel workers' union, UNITE. Their main aim, logically and understandably, however misguided, is to bring apparel jobs back to the United States. Among WRC rules, no company can participate in setting standards, or monitoring. It has an unrealistic living wage provision. And its "gotcha" approach to monitoring doesn't do what monitoring should—measure conditions and make improvements.[64]

---

[63]Sarah Edith Jacobson, "Nike's Power Game," editorial page letter, *New York Times,* May 16, 2000.

[64]Philip H. Knight, press release, www.oregonlive.com.

DoubleClick Inc.: Gathering Customer Intelligence[1]

Ken Mark
University of Western Ontario

Scott Schneberger
University of Western Ontario

INTRODUCTION

"This Monday, we revealed that the Federal Trade Commission (FTC) began a voluntary inquiry into our ad serving and data collection practices," explained Kevin Ryan, president of DoubleClick Inc. It was Thursday, February 17, 2000, in New York City, and Ryan was preparing to answer media and investor questions.

"We are confident that our business policies are consistent with our privacy policy and beneficial to consumers and advertisers," he continued. "The FTC has begun a series of inquiries into some of the most well-known Web companies, including DoubleClick, and we support their efforts to keep the Internet safe for consumers."

Several Internet privacy activists had filed a formal complaint with the FTC after being informed by media sources that DoubleClick had the ability to determine a person's identity through the use of "cookies" and other databases. Here was an except of an article in an early January 2000 edition of *USA Today:*

[1]This case has been written on the basis of published sources only. Consequently, the interpretation and perspectives presented in this case are not necessarily those of DoubleClick Inc. or any of its employees.

Activists Charge DoubleClick Double-Cross

Web users have lost privacy with the drop of a cookie, they say
By Will Rodger, USATODAY.com

Say goodbye to anonymity on the Web.

DoubleClick, Inc., the Internet's largest advertising company, has begun tracking Web users by name and address as they move from one Web site to the next, USATODAY.com has learned.

The practice, known as profiling, gives marketers the ability to know the household, and in many cases the precise identity, of the person visiting any one of the 11,500 sites that use DoubleClick's ad-tracking "cookies." What made such profiling possible was Double-Click's purchase in June of Abacus Direct Corp., a direct-marketing services company that maintains a database of names, addresses and retail purchasing habits of 90 percent of American households. With the help of its online partners, DoubleClick can now correlate the Abacus database of names with people's Internet activities.

DOUBLECLICK INC.

With global headquarters in New York City and over 30 offices around the world, DoubleClick was a leading provider of comprehensive Internet advertising solutions for marketers and Web publishers. It combined technology, media, and data expertise to centralize planning, execution, control, tracking, and reporting for online media companies. Along with its proprietary DART targeting technology, DoubleClick managed Abacus Direct, a database of consumer buying behavior used for marketing purposes over the Internet and through direct mail.

The privacy controversy over DoubleClick began in the summer of 1999, when DoubleClick announced it was merging with Abacus Direct in a deal valued at more than $1 billion. Privacy experts had feared that DoubleClick would begin merging the two databases at some point. But they said they were unaware that DoubleClick had begun its profiling practice in late 1999. Before its Abacus purchase, DoubleClick had made its money by targeting banner advertisements in less direct ways. DoubleClick ad-serving computers, for instance, checked the Internet addresses of people who visited participating sites. Thus, people in their homes may see ads different from those seen by workers at General Motors, or a machine-tool company in Ohio.

Every time viewers saw or clicked on those banners, DoubleClick added that fact to individual dossiers it built on them with the help of the cookies it stored on users' hard drives. Those dossiers, in turn, helped DoubleClick target ads more precisely still, increasing their relevance to consumers and reducing unnecessary repetition.

The "owner" of those cookies remained anonymous to DoubleClick until it bought Abacus.[2]

Being tracked as they move around the Web "doesn't measure up to people's expectation on the Net," says Robert Smith, publisher of the newsletter *Privacy Journal*. "They don't think that their physical locations, their names will be combined with what

---

[2]These cookies were anonymous because although DoubleClick tracked the cookie (and subsequently, the user), it did not possess any means to identify the owner of the cookie. In effect, DoubleClick was cognizant of the user's surfing habits but not of the surfer's identity. With the additional database containing personally identifiable information, there existed a possibility that the information in the cookie could be matched with a surfer's profile, thus identifying the user.

they do on the Internet. If they [DoubleClick] want to do that they have to expose that plan to the public and have it discussed."[3]

A publicly listed company, DoubleClick traded under the symbol DLCK on the NASDAQ exchange.[4]

DOUBLECLICK'S DART

Developed by DoubleClick and awarded U.S. Patent 5,948,061, Dynamic Advertising, Reporting, and Targeting (DART) was a Web-based, enterprise-class advertising management software package. It performed targeting, reporting, and inventory management, allowing sites (or networks of sites) to manage all or some of their ad serving and reporting functions through DoubleClick's central servers. The benefit to advertising clients was the opportunity to build lifelong relationships with their customers (users) through personalization of advertising messages (see Exhibit 1). A client would begin by placing an advertising campaign with DoubleClick. With the use of DoubleClick's DART technology, advertising messages would be placed on sites most visited by the client's customers, and advertising results tracked. Double-Click would then compile data gathered and present the results of the campaign to the client (see Exhibit 1).

Websites intending to sell banner advertisements could outsource the delivery of the site's online advertisement to DoubleClick. While serving the ads, DoubleClick would then utilize DART to collect, analyze, and optimize online ads and their delivery.

BENEFITS OF DART[5]

Streamlined campaign management, pinpoint targeting, and real-time, actionable reports all add up to one important metric—increased return on investment (ROI). DART for Advertisers gives you the process and tracking refinement that empowers you to continuously optimize your campaigns and tie your marketing programs to real dollars generated. Here are a few of the benefits of using DART for Advertisers:

- **A Web-Based Service Offering**—DART for Advertisers is available from anywhere based on permissions you control. And because it's a service, you get instant upgrades without application deployment or maintenance costs.

- **An Integrated Solution**—DART provides the industry's strongest ad management technology, built-in targeting, and sophisticated reporting that, together, form the cornerstone of closed-loop marketing and enhanced ROI. Its constantly evolving feature set is based on the aggressive demands of leading-edge installed base.

- **Centralized Planning and Control**—No matter how extensive your media plan, DART for Advertisers provides a sophisticated media planning tool and enables you to buy and traffic ads across as many sites as you wish. So you can track requests for proposals (RFPs) and insertion orders, control creative changes and view standardized reports within and across campaigns like never before.

---

[3]As reported in *USA Today,* January 15, 2000.

[4]DoubleClick information and press releases were accessed from www.doubleclick.com.

[5]From www.doubleclick.com, February 29, 2000.

exhibit 1   Central Campaign Management

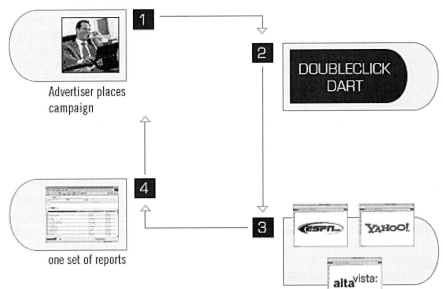

- **High-Level Targeting**—With built-in targeting capabilities, DART offers an unlimited array of targeting criteria to ensure you get the right message to the right person at the right time. DART's targeting capabilities are the best in the industry.
- **Consistent Reporting**—DART provides you a single set of real-time reports that span your entire campaign. Armed with detailed post-click, transaction and reach and frequency information, you can test different executions of selling messages, rich media and ad sizes—and then swap creative instantaneously to maximize campaign effectiveness.
- **Private Labeling**—With DART, agencies gain a competitive advantage by offering the leading online campaign management capabilities within their own suite of products and services.

DELIVERING DART

With an expansive team of engineers supporting DART's complex system, Double-Click served up to 53 billion ads[6] to DART-enabled sites per month to companies in over 13 countries around the world. It accomplished this through the use of 23 global data centers, world-class hosting facilities like Frontier Global Center and Exodus Communications. It also possessed a network of nearly 800 media and ad servers (Microsoft NT Quad Processors) positioned around the world to assure reliability. The architecture it used was 100 percent scalable, running Oracle databases hosted on Sun Solaris equipment. DART's front end (user interface) was hypertext markup language (HTML) compliant and could be accessed from any browser and any platform.

DoubleClick had the ability to segregate ad serving from the site's back-end transaction processing, matching ads in under 15 milliseconds and serving ads at an average rate of one every 24 milliseconds.

---

[6]DoubleClick expected to serve over 53 billion ads per month by June 2000.

exhibit 2   DoubleClick DART in Action

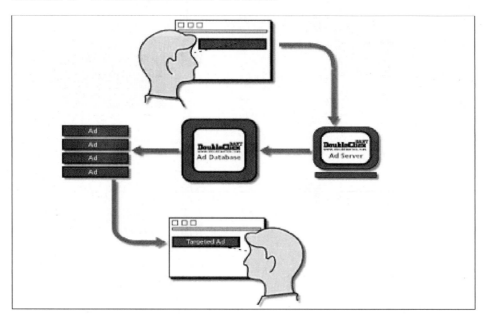

DART IN OPERATION

DART's user profile database recognized unique users by their cookies and delivered a precisely targeted ad every time the user accessed Web pages that were using DART. First, by accessing the Web page, the user would trigger an ad "request" from Double-Click. Next, if that user had previously visited DoubleClick sites, DoubleClick would recognize the user's cookie file and unique number, retrieving the IP address, country domain, company, browser, and operating system. (If not, a cookie would be placed on the new user's computer at this time.) DART would match up a targeted ad to the user-profile, then deliver a targeted ad to the user (see Exhibit 2).

USING COOKIES AT DOUBLECLICK

Cookies were small text files stored on a user's hard drive and were employed by thousands of sites. Cookies enabled sites to "remember" users across site pages and across multiple visits to a site. Using cookies did not damage user files, nor could they read information from a user's hard drive.

This feature enhanced e-commerce and Internet advertising in numerous ways, including allowing personalization features such as stock portfolio tracking and targeted news stories, and enabling shopping sessions and quick navigation across multiple zones of e-commerce sites. Cookies could remember user names and passwords for future visits, control ad frequency or the number of times a user saw a given ad, and could allow advertisers to target ads to a user's interest.

Ryan explained that DoubleClick did not employ cookies to exploit sensitive data.

> DoubleClick has never and will never use sensitive online data in our profiling. It is DoubleClick's policy to only merge personally identifiable information with personally identifiable information for profiling, after providing clear notice of a choice.

exhibit 3

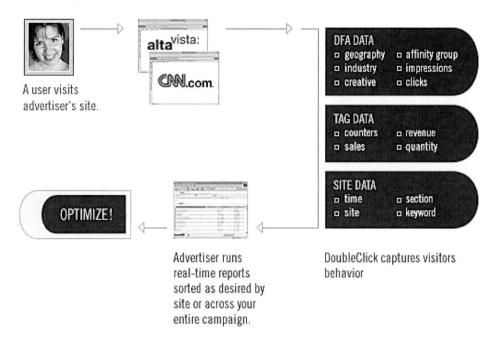

A user visits advertiser's site.

DFA DATA
□ geography   □ affinity group
□ industry   □ impressions
□ creative   □ clicks

TAG DATA
□ counters   □ revenue
□ sales   □ quantity

SITE DATA
□ time   □ section
□ site   □ keyword

DoubleClick captures visitors behavior

Advertiser runs real-time reports sorted as desired by site or across your entire campaign.

OPTIMIZE!

SELLING RESEARCH ON COLLECTED DATA

One of DoubleClick's business units collected traffic and usage data, and analyzed the effectiveness of campaigns. From this research, the document produced for advertising clients was called Spotlight.

Spotlight allowed an advertiser to determine which media placement generated a specific type of post-click activity important to its media plan. Spotlight provided customizable metrics such as the number of registrations, number of sales, number of units purchased, types of services purchased, and actual sales revenue generated as a result of an advertiser's campaign.

Reports offered three levels of reporting including banner level, campaign level, and aggregate activity data at the advertiser level. Another feature offered conversion-to-activity rates by clicks, impressions, and media costs. A third offered a counting methodology that credited activities to the last ad the user clicked on prior to performing the activity, for up to 90 days after the ad had stopped running (see Exhibit 3).

Abacus, the previously mentioned division of DoubleClick, would, on behalf of Internet retailers and advertisers, use additional statistical modeling techniques to identify those online consumers in the Abacus Online database who would most likely be interested in a particular product or service.

A COMPLAINT FILED WITH THE FTC

Jason Catlett of Junkbusters Inc. (an Internet privacy consultancy), David Banisar, deputy director of Privacy International, and the U.S. Electronic Privacy Information Center filed a complaint with the Federal Trade Commission charging that Double-Click had deceived consumers by suggesting the company's technology let them remain anonymous. They expected to enlist a wide array of consumer groups to back their position.

More troubling to privacy advocates was DoubleClick's refusal to state which Internet sites were furnishing them the registration rolls that DoubleClick needed to link once-anonymous cookies to names, addresses, phone numbers, and catalog purchases. Catlett stated,

> The fact that DoubleClick is not disclosing the names of the companies who are feeding them consumers' names is a shameful hypocrisy. They are trying to protect the confidentiality of the violators of privacy.

Jonathan Shapiro, senior vice president and Abacus unit chief bristled at Catlett's characterization, saying, "Any company that uses data from the Abacus database to target Internet ads must disclose it online." Moreover, he added, DoubleClick itself would hand over to privacy advocates the list of participating companies if it could. But as in many lines of business, partners frown when their relationships were disclosed without their permission. Shapiro concluded, "If they all bought a billboard and said they work with us, that would be great."

THE NEW PRIVACY POLICY

Following up on the recently instituted privacy policy, Ryan made this announcement:

> Earlier in February, DoubleClick announced what we believe is the most aggressive Internet privacy policy ever and committed ourselves to a national campaign to educate consumers about online privacy. We also announced that we will only do business with online U.S. publishers that have privacy policies. We have engaged PriceWaterhouseCoopers to perform periodic privacy audits so that consumers remain confident that we are living up to our commitment to protect users' privacy. In addition, we have announced the creation of the DoubleClick Privacy Ad Board, and we are adding a new executive level position of Chief Privacy Officer.

DoubleClick explained in its privacy policy (see Exhibit 4) that it did not collect any "personally-identifiable" information about its users such as name, address, phone number, or e-mail address. It did, however, collect "non-personally-identifiable" information such as the server the user's computer was logged on to, his or her browser type, and whether the user responded to the ad delivered.

Non-personally-identifiable information collected by DoubleClick was used for the purpose of targeting ads and measuring ad effectiveness on behalf of DoubleClick's advertisers and Web publishers who specifically requested it. However, non-personally-identifiable information collected by DoubleClick could be associated with a user's personally-identifiable information if that user had agreed to receive personally-tailored ads.

In addition, with the delivery of ads via DART technology to one particular Web publisher's website, DoubleClick combined the non-personally-identifiable data collected by DoubleClick from a user's computer with the log-in name and demographic data about users collected by the Web publisher and furnished to DoubleClick for the purpose of ad targeting on the Web publisher's website. DoubleClick had requested that this information be disclosed on the website's privacy statement.

There were also other cases when a user voluntarily provided personal information in response to an ad (a survey or purchase form, for example). "That person will receive notice that their personal information is being gathered," stated Shapiro. In those

exhibit 4 DoubleClick Privacy Policy

Privacy Policy

DoubleClick Privacy Statement

Internet user privacy is of paramount importance to DoubleClick, our advertisers and our Web publishers. The success of our business depends upon our ability to maintain the trust of our users. Below is information regarding DoubleClick's commitment to protect the privacy of users and to ensure the integrity of the Internet.

Information Collected in Ad Delivery

In the course of delivering an ad to you, DoubleClick does not collect any personally-identifiable information about you, such as your name, address, phone number or email address. DoubleClick does, however, collect non-personally-identifiable information about you, such as the server your computer is logged onto, your browser type (for example, Netscape or Internet Explorer), and whether you responded to the ad delivered.

The non-personally-identifiable information collected by DoubleClick is used for the purpose of targeting ads and measuring ad effectiveness on behalf of DoubleClick's advertisers and Web publishers who specifically request it. For additional information on the information that is collected by DoubleClick in the process of delivering an ad to you, please click here.

However, as described in "Abacus Alliance" and "Information Collected by DoubleClick's Web Sites" below, non-personally identifiable information collected by DoubleClick in the course of ad delivery *can be associated with a user's personally-identifiable information* if that user has agreed to receive personally-tailored ads.

In addition, in connection solely with the delivery of ads via DoubleClick's DART technology to one particular Web publisher's Web site, DoubleClick combines the non-personally-identifiable data collected by DoubleClick from a user's computer with the log-in name and demographic data about users collected by the Web publisher and furnished to DoubleClick for the purpose of ad targeting on the Web publisher's Web site. DoubleClick has requested that this information be disclosed on the Web site's privacy statement.

There are also other cases when a user voluntarily provides personal information in response to an ad (a survey or purchase form, for example). In these situations, DoubleClick (or a third party engaged by DoubleClick) collects the information on behalf of the advertiser and/or Web site. This information is used by the advertiser and/or Web site so that you can receive the goods, services or information that you requested. Where indicated, DoubleClick may use this information in aggregate form to get a better general understanding of the type of individuals viewing ads or visiting the Web sites. Unless specifically disclosed, the personally-identifiable information collected by DoubleClick in these cases is not used to deliver personally-tailored ads to a user and is not linked by DoubleClick to any other information.

Abacus Alliance

On November 23, 1999, DoubleClick Inc. completed its merger with Abacus Direct Corporation. Abacus, now a division of DoubleClick, will continue to operate Abacus Direct, the direct mail element of the Abacus Alliance. In addition, Abacus has begun building Abacus Online, the Internet element of the Abacus Alliance.

The Abacus Online portion of the Abacus Alliance will enable U.S. consumers on the Internet to receive advertising messages tailored to their individual interests. As with all DoubleClick products and services, Abacus Online is fully committed to offering online consumers *notice* about the collection and use of personal information about them, and the *choice* not to participate. Abacus Online will maintain a database consisting of personally-identifiable information about those Internet users who have received notice that their personal information will be used for online marketing purposes and associated with

exhibit 4 *(continued)*

information about them available from other sources, and who have been offered the choice not to receive these tailored messages. The notice and opportunity to choose will appear on those Web sites that contribute user information to the Abacus Alliance, usually when the user is given the opportunity to provide personally identifiable information (e.g., on a user registration page, or on an order form).

Abacus, on behalf of Internet retailers and advertisers, will use statistical modeling techniques to identify those online consumers in the Abacus Online database who would most likely be interested in a particular product or service. All advertising messages delivered to online consumers identified by Abacus Online will be delivered by DoubleClick's patented DART technology.

Strict efforts will be made to ensure that all information in the Abacus Online database is collected in a manner that gives users clear notice and choice. *Personally-identifiable information in the Abacus Online database will not be sold or disclosed to any merchant, advertiser or Web publisher.*

Name and address information volunteered by a user on an Abacus Alliance Web site is associated by Abacus through the use of a match code and the DoubleClick cookie with other information about that individual. Information in the Abacus Online database includes the user's name, address, retail, catalog and online purchase history, and demographic data. The database also includes the user's non-personally-identifiable information collected by Web sites and other businesses with which DoubleClick does business. Unless specifically disclosed to the contrary in a Web site's privacy policy, most non-personally-identifiable information collected by DoubleClick from Web sites on the DoubleClick Network is included in the Abacus Online database. However, the Abacus Online database will not associate any personally-identifiable medical, financial, or sexual preference information with an individual. Neither will it associate information from children.

Sweepstakes
DoubleClick's Flashbase, Inc., subsidiary provides automation tools that allow our clients to provide online contests and sweepstakes ("DoubleClick sweepstakes").

All DoubleClick sweepstakes entry forms must provide a way for you to opt-out of any communication from the sweepstakes manager that is not related to awarding prizes for the sweepstakes. Entry forms must further provide consumers with a choice whether to receive e-mail marketing materials from third parties. When you enter a DoubleClick sweepstakes, the information you provide is not to be shared with DoubleClick or any third party, unless you agree by checking the opt-in box on the sweepstakes entry form. If you enter a sweepstakes, you agree that the sweepstakes sponsor may use your name in relation to announcing and promoting the winners of the sweepstakes. See the official rules of the sweepstakes you are entering for additional information.

DoubleClick does collect aggregate, anonymous information about the sweepstakes. That information is primarily used to help sweepstakes managers choose prizes and make other decisions regarding the organization of the sweepstakes. DoubleClick does not associate information provided through the sweepstakes with your other web browsing activities or clickstream data.

DoubleClick Research
DoubleClick Research is a subsidiary of DoubleClick, Inc. To review DoubleClick's privacy policy from the beginning, including information on opting out of the DoubleClick cookie, click here. DoubleClick Research provides surveys to users. All research survey responses are voluntary, and the information collected will only be used for research and reporting purposes, to help DoubleClick and our clients determine the effectiveness of our businesses, Web sites, or advertising campaigns.

If you participate in a survey, the information you provide will be used along with that of other study participants (for example, DoubleClick Research might report that 50% of a

(continued)

exhibit 4   *(continued)*

survey's respondents are women). DoubleClick may share anonymous individual and aggregate data with the company that requested the survey for research and analysis purposes.

The only individually identifiable information DoubleClick Research may use is the e-mail address you provide, in order to contact sweepstakes prize winners. DoubleClick Research may also contact you through your e-mail address for other purposes if you tell DoubleClick Research that it may do so; for example, if you indicate in the survey that you wish to join a DoubleClick Research online research panel. When you submit your survey, your e-mail address and your response to the "future contact" question described above are automatically stored in a database that is intentionally separated from your survey responses. Therefore, your e-mail address is not tied back to your survey responses. DoubleClick Research will not share the personally identifiable individual data you enter in response to survey questions with third parties.

For all other purposes, only aggregate data that has been stripped of all personally identifiable information will be used.

DoubleClick Research uses DART ad server technology to transmit the survey. In the course of providing this survey to you, a DoubleClick cookie may be placed on your browser. DoubleClick utilizes cookie technology for many purposes, including targeting ads to you on other web sites. In connection with DoubleClick Research Surveys, the cookie is used to control the research process, primarily to stop people from being asked to take the same survey twice. In addition, the types of advertising you have viewed on web sites during the course of your normal web surfing, such as whether you have viewed a particular ad or how many times you have viewed a particular ad, may be connected to your anonymous survey responses. This information is strictly for research purposes and is totally anonymous.

If your cookies are turned off or you have opted out, DoubleClick Research will be unable to recognize whether or not you have been offered a survey, and may inadvertently offer you the same survey in the future. To read more about DoubleClick's cookies, including information on how to opt-out of a DoubleClick cookie, click here.

Please contact DoubleClick Research at surveyhelp@doubleclick.net if you have questions or comments about DoubleClick Research or your participation in the survey or if you wish to later choose not to receive future email.

E-mail
DoubleClilck uses DARTmail, a version of DART technology, to bring you e-mails that may include ads. E-mail is sent only to people who have consented to receive a particular e-mail publication or mailing from a company. If at any time you would like to end your subscription to an e-mail publication or mailing, follow either the directions posted at the end of the e-mail publication or mailing, or the directions at the e-mail newsletter company's Web site.

In order to bring you more relevant advertising, your e-mail address may be joined with the information you provided at our client's Web site and may be augmented with other data sources. However, DoubleClick does not link your e-mail address to your other Web browsing activities or clickstream data.

Information Collected by DoubleClick's Web Sites
The Web sites owned or controlled by DoubleClick, such as http://www.plazadirect.com/ and http://www.iaf.net/ may ask for and collect personally-identifiable information. DoubleClick is committed to providing meaningful notice and choice to users before any personally-identifiable information is submitted to us. Specifically, users will be informed about how DoubleClick may use such information, including whether it will be shared with marketing partners or combined with other information available to us. In most cases, the information provided by a user will be contributed to the Abacus Online database to enable personally-tailored ad delivery online. Users will always be offered the choice not to provide personally-identifiable information or to have it shared with others.

exhibit 4   *(continued)*

Access

DoubleClick offers users who have voluntarily provided personally-identifiable information to DoubleClick the opportunity to review the information provided and to correct any errors.

Cookies and Opt Out

DoubleClick, along with thousands of other Web sites, uses cookies to enhance your Web viewing experience. DoubleClick's cookies do not damage your system or files in any way.

Here's how it works. When you are first served an ad by DoubleClick, DoubleClick assigns you a unique number and records that number in the cookie file of your computer. Then, when you visit a Web site on which DoubleClick serves ads. DoubleClick reads this number to help target ads to you. The cookie can help ensure that you do not see the same ad over and over again. Cookies can also help advertisers measure how you utilize an advertiser's site. This information helps our advertisers cater their ads to your needs.

If you have chosen on any of the Web sites with which Abacus does business to receive ads tailored to you personally as part of Abacus Online's services, the cookie will allow DoubleClick and Abacus Online to recognize you online in order to deliver you a relevant message.

However, if you have not chosen to receive personally-targeted ads, then the DoubleClick cookie will *not* be associated with any personal information about you, and DoubleClick (including Abacus) will not be able to identify you personally online.

While we believe that cookies enhance your Web experience by limiting the repetitiveness of advertising and increasing the level of relevant content on the Web, they are not essential for us to continue our leadership position in Web advertising.

While some third parties offer programs to manually delete your cookies, DoubleClick goes one step further by offering you a "blank" or "opt-out cookie" to prevent any data from being associated with your browser or you individually. If you do not want the benefits of cookies, there is a simple procedure that allows you to deny or accept this feature. By denying DoubleClick's cookies, ads delivered to you by DoubleClick can only be targeted based on the non-personally-identifiable information that is available from the Internet environment, including information about your browser type and Internet service provider. By denying the DoubleClick cookie, we are unable to recognize your browser from one visit to the next, and you may therefore notice that you receive the same ad multiple times.

If you have previously chosen to receive personally-tailored ads by being included in the Abacus Online database, you can later elect to stop receiving personally-tailored ads by denying DoubleClick cookies.

Your opt-out will be effective for the entire life of your browser or until you delete the cookie file on your hard drive. In each of these instances, you will appear as a new user to DoubleClick. Unless you deny the DoubleClick cookie again, DoubleClick's ad server will deliver a new cookie to your browser.

If you would like more information on how to opt-out, please click here.

Disclosure

DoubleClick makes available all of our information practices at www.doubleclick.net, including in-depth descriptions of our targeting capabilities, our privacy policy, and full disclosure on the use of cookies. In addition, we provide all users with the option to contact us at info@doubleclick.net with any further questions or concerns.

Security

DoubleClick will maintain the confidentiality of the information that it collects during the process of delivering an ad. DoubleClick maintains internal practices that help to protect the security and confidentiality of this information by limiting employee access to and use of this information.

(continued)

exhibit 4 (*continued*)

Industry Efforts to Protect Consumer Privacy

DoubleClick is committed to protecting consumer privacy online. We are active members of the Network Advertising Initiative, NetCoalition.com, Online Privacy Alliance, Internet Advertising Bureau, New York New Media Association, and the American Advertising Federation.

For more information about protecting your privacy online, we recommend that you visit http://networkadvertising.org/, http://www.netgcoalition.com/, and http://privacyalliance.org/. If you have any additional questions, please contact us at info@doubleclick.net.

We also recommend that you review this Privacy Statement periodically, as DoubleClick may update it from time to time.

URL: corporate/privacy/default.asp

Copyright © 1996–2001 DoubleClick Inc.
DoubleClick's DART technology is protected by U.S. Pat. 5,948,061.

Source: www.doubleclick.com, February 2000.

situations, DoubleClick (or a third party engaged by DoubleClick) collected the information on behalf of the advertiser and/or website. This information was used by the advertiser, and/or website, to ensure that users received goods, services, or information requested. Jennifer Blum, Media Relations, stated that only about a dozen of its affiliated sites had started to collect and use personal information. She acknowledged, however, that DoubleClick's goal was to gain agreement from all its partner sites to participate. Where indicated, DoubleClick could use the information in aggregate form to get a better general understanding of the type of individuals viewing ads or visiting the websites. Unless specifically disclosed, the personally-identifiable information collected by DoubleClick in these cases was not used to deliver personally-tailored ads to a user and was not linked by DoubleClick to any other information.

OPTING OUT OF BEING IDENTIFIED

DoubleClick did allow users the option of "opting out" of being identified by DART. By logging on to DoubleClick's site, the user could enter information to allow DoubleClick to recognize the particular user and assign him or her an "opt-out" cookie.

On subsequent visits by the user to DART-enabled sites, the opt-out cookie would disallow DART from assigning other cookies or from identifying the user's computer uniquely. DoubleClick discouraged this approach by stating in its privacy statement:

> DoubleClick believes that all users should have a positive Web experience. Because of this belief, we allow advertisers to control the frequency (the number of times) a Web user sees an ad banner. We also deliver advertising based on a user's interests if that user has chosen to receive targeted advertising. We believe that frequency control, and relevant content makes advertising on the Web less intrusive by ensuring that users are not bombarded with repeat and irrelevant ad messages. Opting-out removes our ability both to control frequency of exposure to individual users and to increase the level of relevant content.

The opt-out would be effective for the entire life of the user's browser or until the user deleted the cookie file on his or her hard drive. In each of these instances, the user would then appear as a new user to DoubleClick—unless the user denied the Double-Click cookie again, a new cookie would be delivered to the user's browser.

DISCLOSURE AND SECURITY

DoubleClick made available all its information practices on its website, www. doubleclick.net, including in-depth descriptions of its targeting capabilities, privacy policy, and full disclosure on the use of cookies. DoubleClick was an active member of the Network Advertising Initiative, NetCoalition.com, Online Privacy Alliance, Internet Advertising Bureau, New York New Media Association, and the American Advertising Federation.

DOUBLECLICK CONFIDENT IN FACE OF INQUIRY

Ryan concluded:

> We renew our challenge to other Internet players to adopt similarly strong privacy policies. We are taking these steps because we believe they are good for consumers, good for our customers, and sound business practices.

In spite of the FTC's inquiries, DoubleClick was confident that its internal practices were sound.

DoubleClick shares, trading at a high of $131 during the beginning of January 2000, had dropped to the $90 range since the charge was announced. Would the move to establish the new privacy policy aid in placating the fears of advertising clients afraid of a consumer backlash? Would the new privacy policy hold up to scrutiny? Was DoubleClick doing enough to satisfy the privacy concerns of Internet surfers? Last, were investors satisfied?

INDEXES

NAME

Abell, Derek F., 16*n, 17, 29, 34n*
Abercrombie, Emily, C–50
Abrams, Sid, C–265
Adami, Norman, C–462
Adamson, D., C–442*n*
Addison, John, C–184 to C–185, C–186, C–198 to C–202
Afuah, Allan, 289
Agassi, André, C–507, C–761, C–767
Agedorn, Aimee, C–153
Ahlstrand, Bruce, 11*n,* 13*n,* 29, 71
Albee, Mrs. P. F. E., C–19, C–37
Alexander, John, 422*n,* 443
Alexander, Marcus, 290, 327, 344*n, 353*
Aleyne, Adrian, 135*t*
Alkema, Robert, C–175
Allaire, Paul, 388
Allshouse, Jane E., C–117*n*
Amara, Roy, 100*n*
Amsden, Davida M., 397*n*
Amsden, Robert T., 397*n*
Anderson, Barbara, 381
Anderson, Martin, C–314, C–315
Anderson, Philip, 401*n, 407n*
Anderson, Sherri, C–552
Andrews, Kenneth R., 63*n,* 72
Anglea, Rob, C–751 to C–752
Ankeny, Jan, C–548
Anslinger, Patricia L., 307*n*
Appel, T., C–260
Argyris, Chris, 386
Armstrong, C. Michael, 354
Armstrong, Douglas, 256
Arnold, David J., 217*n,* 218*n,* 223
Artherton, Andrew, C–323
Ash, Mary Kay, C–35 to C–36
Athos, Anthony, 421
Atkinson, Alan, C–245
Austen, J., C–763*n*
Austin, Nancy, 413*n,* C–566
Austin, Steve "Stone Cold," C–71 to C–72, C–73
Aycock, David, C–394, C–395, C–408 to C–409, C–418 to C–419, C–422, C–423

Baack, Sally, C–225
Badaracco, Joseph, Jr., 68*n,* 70, 450
Bailey, William J., C–263*n,* C–265*t*
Bakke, Dennis, C–696, C–701, C–703, C–704, C–706, C–707, C–712 to C–715, C–713*n* to C–715*n,* C–717 to C–725, C–718*n,* C–728*n,* C–729, C–731
Bales, Carter F., 307*n*
Baliga, B. R., 283*n*
Ballinger, J., C–767*n*
Band, David C., 404*n*
Banisar, David, C–781
Barff, R., C–763*n*
Barnes, Donna, C–315
Barnes, Frank C., C–392
Barnes, James N., C–117*n*
Barney, Jay B., 119*n,* 184*n,* 197, 327
Barrett, Colleen, C–597, C–610, C–623, C–625
Barringer, Bruce, 13*n*
Barringer, Felicity, C–353*n,* C–354*n*

Bartlett, Christopher A., 207*n,* 381, 440*n,* 450
Bartlett, Thomas, C–81*n*
Barton, David, C–116, C–129*n*
Baskin, Roberta, C–767
Batua, Anitish, 255
Baty, Christopher, C–61
Bauerschmidt, Alan, C–536
Baum, B., C–766*n*
Bazdarich, C., C–446*n*
Beckard, Richard, 377, 378*n,* 422*n*
Behr, Peter, C–717*n,* C–723*n*
Beinhocker, Eric D., 273*n,* 274*n, 275,* 289
Bendeich, Mark, C–484*n*
Benjamin, Ed, C–111*t,* C–112*t,* C–114
Benning, Jim, C–354*n*
Benoit, Joan, C–761
Bentz, Leo, C–154
Beringer, Frederick, C–242
Beringer, Jacob, C–242
Bethune, Gordon, C–627, C–630 to C–660, C–631*n,* C–633*n,* C–635*n* to C–638*n,* C–640*n,* C–641*n,* C–644*n,* C–646*n* to C–648*n*
Bhide, Amar, 148, 418
Bickford, Deborah J., 264*n*
Biesada, Alexandra, 134*n*
Birchall, David W., 122*n,* 147
Biren, Beatrix, C–321
Birinyi, Laszlo, 72
Bischoff, Eric, C–68 to C–69, C–70, C–71, C–72, C–73
Blackmon, D. A., C–442*n*
Blazer, Rand, 365
Bleeke, Joel A., 289
Blossman, Jay, C–153, C–179
Bluedorn, Allen C., 13*n*
Blum, Jennifer, C–787
Bodenstab, Jeffrey, 194
Bodett, Tom, 170
Bogner, William C., 118*n*
Boland, Michael A., C–116, C–128*n,* C–129*n*
Bolt, James F., 223
Bontis, Nick, 118*n,* 147
Boone, Jeannie, C–245
Borden, Jeff, C–345*n,* C–349*n,* C–355*n*
Bossidy, Lawrence A., 354, 388
Bourgeois, L. J., 23*n*
Bowerman, Bill, C–759, C–760
Bowers, Carol, C–722*n,* C–723*n*
Bradham, Caleb, C–503
Bradley, Stephen, C–336
Brandenburger, Adam M., 148
Brelis, Matthew, C–648
Brenneman, Greg, 289, C–632 to C–636, C–638, C–640, C–644, C–648, C–651, C–652
Briamonte, Frank, 284
Brodwin, David R., 23*n*
Bromiley, Philip, 17*n,* 29, 71
Brooker, Katrina, C–592*n,* C–596*n,* C–601*n,* C–621*n*
Brown, Byron "Ken," C–253
Brown, John Young, Jr., C–204
Brown, Lew G., C–50
Brown, Robert, 17*n,* 29, 71
Brown, Shona L., 49*n,* 70, 263*n, 264, 265n,* 353

Browning, Peter, C–419, C–423
Brownlee, Shannon, C–738*n*
Brumback, Charles, C–343 to C–344
Bruner, R. F., C–431*n*
Bulkley, D., C–431*n*
Burgelman, Robert A., 29, 39*n*
Burgers, Willem P., 325*n*
Burgess, Ray, 126
Burgmans, Antony, C–470, C–472, C–493
Bush, Laura, C–36
Busse, Keith, C–396, C–419
Byrne, John A., 341, 354, 362*n, 363*

Calantrone, Roger J., 289
Calderon, Claire, C–556, C–557
Caligiuri, Paula M., 408*n*
Calloway, Wayne, 148, C–507, C–509, C–510
Camp, Robert C., 134*n*
Campbell, Andrew, 71, 290, 327, 344*n,* 353
Canetta, Rachel Deane, C–138
Caney, Derek, C–336*n*
Carlzon, Jan, 443
Carroll, Archie B., 446*n, 450*
Carroll, Glenn, 64*n*
Carroll, Lewis, 2
Carson, L. Pierce, C–245
Carter, John C., 24*n,* 354, 440*n*
Case, Steve, 23
Castaldi, Richard M., C–225
Castrogiovanni, Gary J., 283*n*
Catlett, Jason, C–781
Chadwick, Eduardo, C–255
Chaillou, Frederic, C–104, C–114
Chakrabarti, Alek, C–321
Chakravarthy, Bala, 263*n*
Chambers, John, 136, 364
Champy, James, 71, 374*n,* 375*n,* 386, 388
Chandler, Alfred, 373*n*
Chaples, Sherry S., 113
Charan, Ram, 440*n*
Charles, Ray, C–507
Chase, Sanborn, C–394
Chatterjee, Sayan, 304*n,* 307*n*
Chavez, Hugo, C–703 to C–704
Chen, Ming-Jer, 189*n*
Christensen, H. Kurt, 147
Chu, Jessica, 224
Chua, Jean, C–337*n*
Clark, Don, 278
Clarke, Joseph P., C–661
Clawson, James B., C–245
Clement, Ronald W., 450
Clinton, Bill, C–759, C–771
Coblin, Jim, C–410, C–421 to C–422
Coffman, Vance, 447
Cohen, Ben, 63, C–484, C–488, C–489, C–490
Collingwood, H., C–442*n,* C–446*n*
Collins, James C., 29, 39*n,* 45*n,* 71, C–87
Collins, Jim, 393
Collins, John, 258
Collis, David J., 114, 123*n,* 125*n,* 147, 315*n,* 316*n,* 327, 328, 345*n,* 346*n,* 347*n,* 353
Coltrain, David, C–129*n*
Colvin, Geoffrey, 361*n*

Note: Page numbers preceded by C- indicate material in Cases; page numbers in *italics* indicate illustrations; page numbers followed by *n* indicate footnotes; page numbers followed by *t* indicate tables.

Colvin, Jeffrey G., 13n, 39n, 193n
Cone, E., C–438n
Conley, William, C–430, C–438
Cook, Scott, C–366
Cooper, Arnold C., 289
Cooper, Robin, 129n, 133n
Copeland, Thomas E., 307n
Correnti, John, C–396 to C–397, C–419
Coty, Francois, C–33
Couette, Yves, C–490
Courtney, Kevin, C–245
Cousins, John, C–245
Covey, Steven, C–75, C–87
Craig, Kyle, C–206
Cranor, John, C–207
Crockett, Jim, C–68
Cronk, Scott, C–103, C–114
Crosby, Philip, 396
Crutchfield, Scott, C–171
Crystal, Billy, C–507
Cucuzza, Thomas G., 133n
Cunningham, Jim, C–419
Cusumano, Michael A., 188n, 197, 258

Dabels, John, C–102
Daley, William, C–415
Dalton, Mark, C–264
Darr, Eric D., 400n, 402n
Darwin, Charles, 72
Das, T. K., 223
D'Aveni, Richard A., 113, 197, 263n, 289
Dawar, Niraj, 198, 219, 219n, 220n, 221n, 223
Day, George S., 289
Deal, Terrence E., 424n
Deck, Stewart, 377
Defee, Cliff, C–303
Dell, Michael, 23
Deluca, John, C–269
Denton, Keith D., 415
Dess, Gregory G., 197
Diamond, Michael, C–752n, C–754n
Diamond, Neil, C–274
Di Benedetto, C. Anthony, 289
Dickens, Mark, C–438
Dickson, Glen, C–549
DiMicco, Daniel R., C–423, C–424
Dingler, Doretha, C–36
Ditizio, Robert, C–95
Dodd, Tim, C–116, C–129, C–130, C–134,
    C–136 to C–137
Donaldson, Gordon, 27n
Doolin, Elmer, C–503
Dorton, John, C–171
Downs, Harry, 64n, 68n
Doz, Yves L., 148, 172n, 177n, 210n, 214n,
    215n, 216, 223, 311n, 312n, 318n, 323n,
    324, 327
Dragonetti, Nicola C., 118n, 147
Dretler, Thomas D., 223
Driscoll, Dawn-Marie, 450
Drucker, Peter F., 2, 71, 308n, 315n, 371n
Druckerman, Pamela, C–701n
Duncan, W. Jack, 127n, 147
Dunn, Adam, C–104
Durkan, Andrew, C–245
Dutta, Soumitra, C–321
Duvall, M., C–438n

Edmonds, David, C–432
Edwards, Kip, C–732, C–756
Eisenhardt, Kathleen M., 49n, 70, 263n, 264,
    265n, 302n, 327, 353
Eitel, Maria S., C–770
Elliott-Fisk, Deborah, C–245

Enrico, Roger, C–502, C–507, C–510 to C–513,
    C–515, C–517, C–518, C–520, C–531,
    C–532
Erwin, B., C–442n
Estes, Ben, C–349
Evans, Mark, C–260
Evans, Philip, 147, 165n, 256, 387
Evers, William D., C–103
Exelby, J., C–443n

Fahey, Liam, 147, 189n
Falbe, Cecilia M., 39n
Fanning, Shawn, C–336
Farhoomand, Dr. Ali F., C–428
Farkas, Charles M., 29, 450
Farmer, Melanie Austria, 438
Favret, Ben, C–153, C–179
Feder, Barnaby J., 126
Feldman, Lawrence P., 289
Ferratt, Thomas S., 397n
Ferrier, Walter J., 276n
Fiegenbaum, Avi, 103n
Fields, Joe, C–300
Finkelstein, Sydney, 401n, 407n
Finkin, Eugene F., 289
Fiorina, Carly, 2
Fisher, Marshall L., 147
Fishman, Charles, 381
Fishman, Chris, 438
Fitzgerald, Mark, C–343n, C–345n
FitzGerald, Niall, C–470, C–472, C–482, C–493
Flagg, Fannie, C–36
Flaherty, William, C–546
Floyd, Steven W., 23n, 355n, 450
Foreman, George, C–507
Formeski, Tom, C–336n
Foster, Ron, C–79
Fox, Michael J., C–507
Fox, Vicente, C–223
Franklin, Bill, C–593
Franson, Paul, C–229n, C–245
Freberg, Christian, C–116
Freedman, Alix, C–264n
Freeman, Edward, C–278
Freiberg, Jackie, C–591n, C–592n, C–594n,
    C–597n, C–600n, C–610n, C–612n,
    C–613n, C–623n, C–625n
Freiberg, Kevin, C–591n, C–592n, C–594n,
    C–597n, C–600n, C–610n, C–612n,
    C–613n, C–623n, C–625n
Friedman, Lawrence, 223, 289, 387
Frohnmayer, David, C–775
Frost, Tony, 198, 219, 219n, 220n, 221n, 223
Fuller, Jack, C–343, C–347, C–351, C–352,
    C–352n

Gadiesh, Orit, 147
Gallo, Ernest, C–240, C–266, C–267 to C–268,
    C–269
Gallo, Gina, C–268
Gallo, Joe, C–266
Gallo, Joseph, C–266
Gallo, Julio, C–240, C–266
Gallo, Matt, C–268
Galunic, D. Charles, 302n, 327
Gamble, James Norris, C–30, C–31
Gamble, John E., C–17, C–184, C–502, C–590,
    C–630
Gantt, Harvey, C–419
Gates, Bill, 8, 23
Gates, J. Russell, 256
Gellenc, D., C–761n
Gelsi, S., C–441n
Gentry, C., C–437n
George, S., 396
Ger, Guliz, 219n, 223

Gerber, Michael, C–150
Gerety, Mason S., C–302
Gerstner, Louis V., Jr., 30
Ghemawat, Pankaj, 79n, 108n, 113
Ghoshal, Sumantra, 207n, 381, 440n, 450
Gibson, Stan, 136
Gigoux, Mimi, 364
Gilbert, James L., 147
Gilinsky, Armand, Jr., C–95, C–246, C–552
Gillette, Paul, C–264
Ginter, Peter M., 127n, 147
Girard, Kim, 365
Gittell, J. H., C–624n
Giulino, Mike, C–350
Glass, S., C–770n
Gnatt, Brian A., C–276, C–277n
Goffee, Robert, 450
Goizueta, Roberto, C–531
Goldsmith, Marshall, 377, 378n, 422n
Goleman, Daniel, 450
Gomez, Alain, 198
Goodman, Paul S., 400n, 402n
Goodnight, Jim, 438
Goold, Michael, 290, 327, 344n, 353
Goozner, M., C–769n
Gordon, Geoffrey L., 289
Gordon, Mary Ellen, 100n, 101n, 102n
"Gorgeous George," C–62
Gorman, Philip, 113, 223
Goss, Tracy, 421
Gotch, Frank, C–62
Goulet, Philip K., C–536
Govindarajan, Vijay, 129n, 133n, 137n, 147
Graham, Steve, C–302, C–318, C–319, C–320
Grant, L., C–446n
Grant, Robert M., 415
Green, Taylor, C–263
Greenfield, Jerry, 63, C–484, C–489, C–490
Greenhouse, Steven, C–760n, C–764n, C–772n
Griffith, Bill, C–549
Griffith, David A., 256
Grimm, Curtis M., 276n
Grove, Andrew S., 39, 39n, 40, 198
Guillory, Bill, C–747, C–757
Gunnarson, Sarah K., 438n, 450
Guth, William D., 63n
Gutsch, Jeff, C–552, C–557, C–560, C–562,
    C–564
Guy, Michael, C–246

Haberman, Rita, C–108t, C–114
Haeberle, Bo, C–50, C–53, C–54, C–55, C–56,
    C–59
Haeckel, Stephan H., 401n
Hall, Gene, 377, 386, 398n
Hall, William K., 283n
Hallowell, Roger, C–614n, C–622n, C–624n
Halperin, Robert, C–546
Hambrick, Donald C., 189n, 361n, 386
Hamel, Gary, 11n, 18n, 27n, 29, 45n, 49n, 71,
    122n, 147, 148, 170n, 172n, 177n, 197,
    214n, 215n, 216, 223, 235n, 239n, 242n,
    256, 274n, 311n, 312n, 327, 387, 450
Hamermesh, R. G., 269n, 270n, 277n
Hamm, Mia, C–518, C–760
Hammer, Michael, 71, 374n, 375n, 386, 388
Hammett, Jim, C–245
Hammond, K., C–770n
Hanson, Lee, C–732
Hardee, Camilla, 45n, 173n
Hardie, Mark, C–338
Harding, Mike, C–280
Hardy, Quentin, C–363n, C–366n
Harling, Andrew Thomas, C–140, C–146, C–148,
    C–151
Harper, Christopher, C–351n

Harper, Jeffrey S., C–661
Harrigan, Kathryn R., 180n, 189n
Harrop, Peter, C–104 to C–105, C–105t, C–107, C–114
Hart, Bret "The Hitman," C–61, C–70 to C–73, C–72n
Hartman, Jim, C–185 to C–186
Haspeslagh, Phillippe C., 353
Hawkes, Ellen, C–266
Hax, Arnoldo C., 100n, 327
Hayes, Robert H., 114, 183n, 197, 368n
Haynes, Victoria, C–419
Heath, John, C–76
Hedley, Barry, 348n
Heeley, Michael B., 193n
Hegert, M., 129n, 132n, 133n
Heifetz, Ronald A., 450
Henderson, Bruce D., 290
Henshall, Donald, C–296
Herman, Alexis, C–772
Hernly, K., C–442n
Herzberg, Frederick, 388, 415
Heskett, James L., 64n, 409n, 420n, 422n, 423n, 426, 426n, 427n, 428n, 429n, 442n, 450
Hesselbein, Frances, 377, 378n, 422n
Hewlett, Bill, 42
Hilmer, Frederick G., 371n
Hitt, Michael A., 45n, 71, 173n
Hlavacek, Jim, C–419
Hodgetts, Richard M., 398n
Hof, Robert D., 224
Hofer, Charles W., 261n, 262n, 347n, 348n
Hoffman, Richard C., 327
Hoffman, W. Michael, 450
Hoffman, William, 136
Hogan, "Hulk," C–66, C–68
Holland, Robert, C–489
Holley, David, C–738n
Holoman, Chris, C–74
Holson, Laura M., C–353n
Holstein, W. J., C–767n
Hopper, D. Ian, 278
Horton, Tim, C–299
House, Charles H., 42n
House, David, C–299
Hout, Thomas M., 24n, 354, 440n
Howard, Alan, C–773n
Howe, Peter J., 284
Huey, John, 64n
Huler, Scott, C–631n, C–633n, C–635n to C–638n, C–640n, C–641n, C–644n, C–646n, C–647n
Humble, John, 432n
Hustwit, Gary, C–142t
Hutchins, Andrew, C–103, C–104, C–114
Hwang, Peter, 325n

Iacocca, Lee, C–102
Immelt, Jeff, 341
Inkpen, Andrew C., 223
Ireland, R. Duane, 71
Ito, T., C–766n
Iverson, F. Kenneth, C–392 to C–398, C–401, C–406, C–408, C–411 to C–413, C–419, C–422
Iwatani, Yukari, 126

Jackson, David, 432n
Jackson, Michael, C–507, C–511
Jackson, Thomas Penfield, 278
Jacobs, Neil W., C–302
Jacobsen, Kristine, 118n, 147
Jacobson, Sara Edith, C–774n
James, Mike, C–437
Jamison, David B., 353
Janah, M., C–428n, C–438n

Jarvenpaa, Sirkka L., 376n
Jenks, Clifford, C–546
Jeter, Derek, C–518
Johnson, Hugh, C–245
Johnson, Robert Wood, C–34
Jones, Dennis, C–438
Jones, Gareth, 450
Jordan, Lloyd, C–81
Jordan, Michael, C–518, C–760, C–761, C–767
Jung, Andrea, C–17, C–18 to C–19, C–23, C–24, C–36 to C–47
Juran, J., 396

Kahaner, Larry, 71, 104n, 113
Kahn, Meyer, C–455, C–455n
Kami, Michael, 2
Kanter, Rosabeth Moss, 214n, 223, 381n, 386
Kan Yue-Sai, C–33
Kaplan, Robert S., 42n, 71, 116n, 129n, 133n, 147
Kashif, C–141, C–141n
Katz, D. R., C–761n to C–768n
Katz, Jeff, C–116
Katzenbach, Jon R., 386, 415
Kavanagh, Larry, C–418
Kelleher, Denis, C–322n
Kelleher, Herb, C–590 to C–591, C–592, C–595, C–597 to C–604, C–610, C–617, C–620, C–621, C–623, C–624, C–625
Kellner, Larry, C–640, C–652
Kelsey, Dick, C–325n
Kemp, Jeff, C–422
Kendall, Donald M., C–205, C–503
Kennedy, Allen A., 424n
Kennedy, John F., C–85
Kerr, Steven, 407n, 411, 411n, 413, 413n, 415
Kessler, Alan, 126
Khurana, Rakesh, 28n
Kidd, Dusty, C–770
Kidder, Tracy, C–745
Kidwell, Roland E., 283n
Kim, W. Chan, 325n
King, Art, C–557, C–559, C–562 to C–564
King, Rollin, C–590 to C–591, C–592, C–594, C–597, C–598
King, Warren, C–265n, C–278n
Kirkpatrick, Shelley A., 450
Kirsner, Scott, C–348n
Klein, Harold E., 100n, 113
Klein, Saul, C–447
Knight, Philip H., C–759n, C–759 to C–761, C–767, C–768n, C–770, C–770n, C–771, C–771n, C–775, C–775n
Koerber, Kristine, C–245
Kohn, Alfie, 410n, 413n, 415
Konana, Prabhudev, 255
Korte, Barbara, C–557
Kotler, Philip, 186n, 187n, 190n, 261n, 275n, 285n
Kotter, John P., 64n, 409n, 420n, 422n, 423n, 426, 426n, 427n, 429n, 440n, 442n, 450
Kozlowski, Dennis, 298
Kozuh, Alissa, 421
Kraatz, Harry, C–103
Krall, David, C–536, C–546, C–547, C–548
Krause, K., C–432n
Kreiser, Patrick, C–356
Kress, Donald, 114
Kriger, Mark, 39n
Krishnan, R., 415
Kroll, Karen M., 381
Kropf, Susan, C–23, C–41, C–42, C–43, C–44
Krug, Jeffrey A., C–203
Kulkarni, Shashank, 138n
Kutaragi, Ken, 26

Laabs, Jennifer Koch, 381
Lachman, Charles, C–34
La Franco, Robert, 26
Lagerman, John, C–316
LaMar, Ray, C–300
Lamb, D., C–766n
Lampedusa, Giuseppe di, C–732
Lampel, Joseph, 11n, 13n, 29, 71, C–550
Lang, David, C–474n
Langley, Ann, 113
La Point, Kris, C–176, C–178
Lappin, T., C–442n
Larwood, Laurie, 39n
Lauder, Estée, C–31
Lauder, Joseph, C–31
Lauer, Matt, C–102
Lauper, Cyndi, C–66 to C–67
Lauren, Ralph, C–27
Laurie, Donald L., 450
Lawrence, Anne T., C–759
Lawson, Stephen, C–381n
Lay, Herman W., C–503
Layton, Mark, C–302, C–303, C–304 to C–305, C–307, C–308, C–312, C–316, C–317, C–319, C–320
LeBeau, Joe, C–279, C–286
Lee, J., C–760n
Lee, T. H., C–765
Lei, David, 223
Leibovitz, Mitchell, 9
Lemak, David J., 398n
Leonard, Wayne, 418
Lesyna, David, C–742, C–743
Leuchter, Miriam, 363
Leuning, Erich, 176
Lever, William Hesketh, C–471
Levering, Robert, 393
Lewis, Carl, C–761
Li, Chalene, C–346n
Lieberthal, Kenneth, 201n, 217n, 218n
Liechtenstein, Paul, C–738n
Liedtka, Jeanne M., 298n, 327, 379n
Lincoln, Abraham, 328
Linneman, Robert U., 100n, 113
Linsmayer, Anne, C–549
Lipinski, Andrew J., 100n
Lipton, Mark, 29, 71
Lisenby, Terry, C–419
Lister, Sir Joseph, C–34
Little, Darnell, C–351
Littlejohn, Michael, 376n
Livengood, Scott, C–279, C–281, C–286, C–295
Locke, Edwin A., 450
Lodds, Pat, C–185
Lombardi, Vince, 354
Lorek, Laura, 251
Lorenzo, Frank, C–636
Lorsch, Jay W., 28n
Lott, Hamilton, C–401
Love, John M., C–260
Lowy, Alex, 256
Lubatkin, Michael, 304n, 307n
Lublin, Joann S., 383
Lucas, George, C–543
Luchs, Kathleen, 327
Luger, Lex, C–69
Luthans, Fred, 415

McAleer, Joseph, C–280
McCombs, Billy Joe, 179
McConnell, David H., C–19, C–37
McConnell, David H., Jr., C–19
McCormick, Col. Robert, C–343
McCoy, John B., 50, 51
McCue, Andy, C–751n
McGill, A. R., 71

McGreen, James, C–96
Mackay, Graham, C–447, C–450, C–455 to
      C–456, C–458, C–462, C–462n, C–463,
      C–469
McKenna, Jason, C–74, C–75, C–76, C–93 to
      C–94
Mackintosh, Gary, C–116
McMahon, Vince, C–62, C–63 to C–67, C–70
McMahon, Vince, Sr., C–63, C–64, C–65
MacMillan, Ian C., 185n, 186n, 189n, 190n, 275n
McQuirk, Tom, C–761
McTavish, Ron, 39n, 71
Madigan, John W., C–343, C–345, C–346, C–349
Madonna, C–511
Mahler, Gary, C–176 to C–177
Main, Jeremy, 135n, 215n
Majchrzak, Ann, 377, 386
Majluf, Nicolas S., 100n, 327
Malone, Hermione, C–297n, C–298n
Mandela, Nelson, C–460
Mannarelli, Thomas, C–61
Manning, J., C–764n, C–765n, C–766n, C–768n
Mapple, Andy, C–175
Marino, Louis, C–74, C–356
Mark, Ken, C–776
Markides, Constantinos C., 29, 114, 296n, 302n,
      315n, 317n, 386
Marsh, Peter, 298
Martin, Adam, C–274, C–276n
Martinson, J., C–760n
Masaki, Ted, C–328
Massey, Jack, C–204
May, Cliff, C–250
Mayer, Robert J., 289
Mays, Lowry, 179
Mazur, Jay, C–772
Mead, Cheryl, C–556
Mehta, Stephanie N., 365
Michaels, Shawn "The Heartbreak Kid," C–61,
      C–72 to C–73
Middlehoff, Thomas, 224
Miesing, Paul, 39n
Miles, Morgan P., 13n, 39n
Miles, Robert H., 450
Miller, Bill, C–544 to C–546
Miller, James P., C–346n
Miller, Kent D., C–219, C–224
Mills, Mike, C–489n
Milne, A. A., 354
Milne, George R., 100n, 101n, 102n
Mintzberg, Henry, 11n, 29, 49n, 71
Moates, William H., C–661
Mokwa, Michael P., 103n
Moncrieff, James, 29
Mondavi, Michael, C–246, C–251, C–255, C–260
Mondavi, Robert, C–240, C–246 to C–247,
      C–251, C–253, C–256, C–257, C–260
Mondavi, Timothy, C–255
Monroe, Clay, C–376
Montgomery, Cynthia A., 114, 123n, 125n,
      147, 315n, 316n, 327, 328, 345n, 346n,
      347n, 353
Montgomery, Joseph C., 398n
Mooradian, Mark, C–338
Moore, Gordon, 40
Moore, James F., 372n
Moore, Rex, C–361n
Moran, Susan, C–364n
Morgan, Jeff, C–268n
Morris, D., 129n, 132n, 133n
Morris, Rebecca J., C–759
Morrison, Robert, C–502, C–518, C–525
Moscowitz, Milton, 393
Mroz, John Edward, 377, 378n
Mulady, Kathy, 421
Murphy, D., C–442n
Murphy, Patrick E., 432n, 450

Muse, Lamar, C–592, C–593, C–594, C–596,
      C–597, C–598

Nairn, Fiona, C–153
Nakache, Patricia, 365
Nalebuff, Barry J., 148
Nash, Laura, 71
Nash, Sarah, 264n
Nava, Tony, C–769
Ness, Joseph A., 133n
Newman, George, 30
Ng, Pauline, C–428
Nicholson, Robert M., C–230n, C–245
Nielsen, Anders P., 118n
Niles-Jolly, Kathryn, 438n, 450
Noble, Charles H., 103n
Noguchi, Yuki, 284
Nolan, Richard L., 401n
Nooyi, Indra, C–524 to C–525
Norgeot, Pete, C–720
Norton, David P., 42n, 71, 116n, 147
Novak, David, C–207
Novello, Antonio, C–278
Nusbaum, Jim, C–742, C–743

Odak, Perry, C–489, C–490
Ohinata, Yoshinobu, 393n, 415
Ohmae, Kenichi, 72, 223, 296n, 349n
Okawara, Merle, C–380
Olds, Ransom E., C–393
Oleszczuk, Andy, C–346
Olian, Judy D., 396n, 397n, 400n, 416, 430n, 443n
Olusoga, S. Ade, 103n
Omidyar, Pierre, C–356, C–357, C–362 to C–364,
      C–365, C–371, C–375, C–387, C–389
O'Neal, Shaquille, C–507
O'Neill, Darren, C–323
O'Neill, Hugh M., 223
Osgood, Charles, C–269
Oster, Sharon M., 30

Page, Albert L., 289
Paine, Lynn Sharp, 450
Palmer, B., C–767n
Palmer, Jonathan W., 256
Paré, Terence P., 134t
Park, Daewoo, 45n, 173n
Parkening, Christopher, C–141
Parker, James, C–624 to C–625
Parkhe, Arvinde, 223
Pascale, Richard T., 64n, 421
Passarella, Kathy, 437–438
Payne, Kelly, C–264n
Payton, Walter, C–349
Pearson, Andrall, C–503, C–506 to C–507, C–509
Pearson, Ann, C–378n
Pelosky, Robert, 198
Perdue, Arthur W., C–565 to C–566, C–567,
      C–568, C–569
Perdue, Franklin Parsons (Frank), C–565, C–567,
      C–568, C–569, C–569, C–572, C–573 to
      C–574, C–574
Perdue, James A. (Jim), C–565, C–567, C–568,
      C–569, C–572, C–583
Perot, H. Ross, 418
Perrin, Charles, C–17, C–23, C–24, C–36, C–39,
      C–41
Peteraf, Margaret A., 119n
Peters, Eric, C–537
Peters, Tom, 413n, C–395, C–566
Pfeffer, Jeffrey, 386, 387, 404n, 406n, 407n,
      408n, 416, 421, 440n
Picken, Joseph C., 197
Pisano, Gary P., 114, 183n, 197, 368n
Pita, Julie, C–379n
Platt, Lew, C–227

Pollock, Timothy, 113, 223
Porras, Jerry I., 29, 39n, 45n, 71, C–87
Porter, Michael E., 29, 45n, 71, 77n, 79–80, 80n,
      81, 82n, 84n, 87n, 88n, 90n, 93n, 94n,
      100n, 113, 129n, 130, 130n, 131n, 132,
      132n, 133n, 138n, 139n, 148, 149n, 150n,
      151, 153n, 159n, 164n, 165, 166n, 167n,
      174n, 191n, 192n, 193n, 197, 203n, 204n,
      209n, 211n, 214n, 224, 225, 238n, 240n,
      241n, 256, 258, 260n, 266n, 267n, 271n,
      275n, 279n, 295n, 296n, 310n, 311n, 328,
      347n, 350n, 353
Powell, Thomas C., 396, 397, 398n
Prahalad, C. K., 11n, 45n, 71, 122n, 147, 148,
      201n, 210n, 217n, 218n, 318n, 323n,
      324, 387
Preston, James, C–23
Prial, Frank, C–245
Price, Raymond L., 42n
Pritchard, Chris, C–552, C–560, C–562, C–563
Procter, William, C–30
Putnam, Howard, C–598
Putnam, Judith Jones, C–117n

Quelch, John A., 217n, 218n, 223
Quick, James Campbell, C–615n, C–617n
Quinn, Dara, C–332
Quinn, James Brian, 114, 139n, 140n, 184n, 366n,
      367, 371n, 372n, 377, 401n, 407n, 448n

Rackham, Neil, 223, 289, 387
Ramsey, Scott, C–302
Rather, Dan, C–767
Rathle, Mike, C–184 to C–185, C–186, C–198 to
      C–202
Rawley, Curt, C–537, C–544
Reed, Richard, 398n
Reese, Dave, C–317, C–318
Reese, Shelley, C–582n
Reinemund, Steve, C–502, C–522, C–524
Reisberg, Leo, C–80n, C–82n, C–83n
Revson, Charles, C–34
Revson, Joseph, C–34
Rigby, Darrell K., 396n
Robertson, Mike, C–334
Robinson, Edward, 136
Rocklewitz, Rick, C–104, C–114
Rogers, Buddy "Nature Boy," C–62
Rogers, Richard, C–35
Rogers, Sara, C–560 to C–562
Romero, Simon, 284
Roos, Goran, 118n, 147
Roosevelt, Theodore, C–62
Rose, Axl, C–274
Rosen, Hilary, C–322, C–329 to C–330
Rosenoer, Johnathan, 256
Rosenthal, Jim, 377, 386, 398n
Ross, Joel, 2
Rothschild, Baron Philippe de, C–242, C–254
Rothschild, William E., 188n
Royal, Cindy, 381
Rubenson, George C., C–565
Rudolph, Vernon, C–279
Ruff, Richard, 223, 289, 387
Runett, Rob, C–348n, C–354n
Russo, David, 437
Rutkowski, Joe, C–401
Ryan, Ken, 399
Ryan, Kevin, C–775, C–782
Rynes, Sara L., 396n, 397n, 400n, 416, 430n, 443n

St. Clair, L., 71
Salazar, Alberto, C–761
Sampras, Pete, C–761
Samuelson, Ralph, C–153

Sanders, Harland, C–203 to C–204, C–206, C–216 to C–217
Sands, Marvin, C–269
Sands, Richard, C–269
Sannella, Dr. Lee, C–103
Sant, Roger, C–696 to C–697, C–703, C–707, C–712 to C–713, C–715, C–718, C–719, C–722, C–722n, C–723
Santamaria, Jason A., 415
Sathe, Vijay, 425n
Savage, Kathryn S., C–302
Savage, Randy "Macho Man," C–68
Sawyer, Abby, C–245
Saxby, Miles, C–456
Scanlan, Gerald, 404n
Schacht, Henry, 284
Schanberg, S., C–767n
Schendel, Dan, 261n, 262n, 347n, 348n
Scherb, Jeff, C–340, C–353
Schnarrs, Steven P., 197
Schneberger, Scott, C–776
Schneider, Benjamin, 438n, 450
Scholz, Christian, 450
Schotze, Volker, C–104, C–114
Schueller, Eugene, C–28 to C–29
Schuller, Rev. Robert, C–36
Schulman, Lawrence E., 165n
Schulmeyer, Gerhard, 444
Schultz, Howard, 23, 63, C–366
Schwartz, Mike, C–736n
Selby, Richard W., 258
Seles, Monica, C–761
Sells, Robin, C–161
Shadid, Anthony, C–549
Shalaway, Scott, C–57
Shani, Rami, 415
Shank, John K., 129n, 133n, 137n, 147
Shanken, Marvin, C–269
Shapiro, Jonathan, C–782
Sharkey, Andrew III, C–415
Shaw, Gordon, 17n, 29, 71
Shields, Dennis A., C–117n
Shipper, Frank, C–565
Shirley, Mike, C–176
Shirley, Rob, C–154, C–171, C–176, C–177
Shlapak, Fred, 126
Shulman, Lawrence E., 147, 387
Sibley, Bill, C–186, C–187
Siegel, Samuel, C–393, C–394, C–419
Silas, C. J., 418
Silk, S. B., 269n, 270n
Silver, Sara, 284
Silverman, Murray, C–225, C–246
Simms, Mike, C–449n, C–450n, C–461, C–461n
Simons, Robert, 379n, 403n, 404n, 416
Singh, Ravi, 186n
Sinise, Gary, C–537
Sinton, Peter, C–245, C–261
Sionnea, Lucien, C–255
Skanson, Darren Curtis, C–138 to C–139, C–144 to C–146, C–148 to C–151
Skoll, Jeffrey, C–363, C–364, C–366
Slater, Dr. James, C–739, C–740, C–744
Slater, Dr. Jerry, C–743
Slater, Jon W., C–732, C–736, C–739, C–740, C–743 to C–747, C–749, C–751, C–753, C–756, C–757
Slevin, Dennis P., 193n
Sloan, Neysa, C–552
Smith, Adam, 375n, C–757
Smith, Clayton G., 289
Smith, Douglas K., 386
Smith, Fred, C–430, C–442, C–446
Smith, Ken G., 276n
Smith, Robert, C–777 to C–778
Smucker, J. M., 436

Solomon, Digby, C–354
Somerville, Iain, 377, 378n
Sorenson, Ralph Z., C–567
Sorkin, Drew Ross, 341
Sorlien, Gregg, C–225
Sosland, M. I., C–124n
Spacey, Kevin, C–95
Spangler, Todd, 26
Spears, Britney, C–507
Sprague, Courtenay, C–447
Stajkovic, Alexander D., 415
Stalk, George, 147, 165n, 387
Stanley, Morgan, 198
Starr, Gary, C–95, C–96, C–102, C–103, C–114
Stepanek, Marcia, 391n, 428
Sterling, Bill, C–565
Stoddard, Donna B., 376n
Stone, Brad, C–336n
Stone, Martha L., C–340n, C–348n, C–349n, C–354n
Strickland, J., C–74, C–263
Stroh, Linda K., 408n
Strong, Tom, C–79
Stuart, T., 377
Stuckey, John, 180n, 197
Sugiura, Hideo, 223
Sukiennik, Greg, C–288n
Sunoo, Brenda Paik, C–611n, C–617n, C–619n
Sun Zi, 418
Swanson, Robert E., C–103
Swayne, Linda E., 127n, 147
Symonds, William C., 298
Szarka, George, C–351n

Tagiuri, Renato, 63n
Takahashi, Dean, 26
Talley, Scott, C–316, C–317, C–318
Tapscott, Don, 256
Taylor, Dave, C–768
Teece, David J., 122n, 147
Teets, John W., 30
Temple, Terry, C–178
Teng, Bing-Sheng, 223
Terry, Robert J., 290
Thomas, Glen, C–50
Thomas, Howard, 103n, 113, 223
Thompson, Arthur A., C–279, C–470, C–590, C–630, C–695, C–697
Thomson, Alan, 432n
Tichy, Noel M., 71, 418, 440n
Ticoll, David, 256
Tiejten, Nancy, C–36
Timmes, Mark, C–74, C–75, C–76, C–91
Torvalds, Linus, 5
Tovstiga, George, 122n, 147
Tristram, Claire, C–362n, C–376n
Trottman, Melanie, C–621n
Tucker, Laurie, C–438
Tully, Shawn, 209, 215n, C–620n
Turner, John, C–723
Turner, Ted, C–61, C–62, C–67 to C–70, C–71
Twer, Doran, 411n
Tyler, Beverly B., 45n, 173n, C–392

Underhill, Roland, C–401
Upton, David M., 114, 183n, 197, 368n
Ur-Rehman, S., C–767n

Vancil, Richard F., 63n
Vanderbilt, T., C–763n, C–764n, C–766n
Van Wassenhove, Luk, C–321
Veiga, John F., 387, 404n, 406n, 408n, 416
Venkatesan, Ravi, 197
Very, Philippe, 328
Vidal, Jack, C–594

Vogel, David, 64n

Wacholtz, L. E., C–141n
Wade, Judy, 377, 386, 398n
Waitt, Ted, 361
Wallace, Bob, 136
Walsh, Esteban, C–704
Walton, M., 396
Walton, Sam, 64, 64n, 420, 441
Wang, Qianwei, 377, 386
Warner, William, C–537, C–544
Waterman, Robert, C–697n, C–712n, C–713n, C–724n
Waters, J. A., 11n, 13n, 49n
Waters, Richard, 341
Watson, Alesa, C–748 to C–749
Watson, Gregory H., 134n, 147
Watson, Malcolm, C–139
Webb, Allen P., 450
Webb, Maynard, C–378
Welch, Jack, 47, 328, 339, 340, 341, 363, 441–442
Welsh, Ed, C–50 to C–51, C–52, C–56 to C–57
Welsh, Richard, C–50 to C–51, C–52
Wendt, Lloyd, C–344n
Wernerfelt, Birger, 119n
Wesley, Pamela, C–363
Wetlaufer, Suzy, 29, 387, 444n, 450, C–713n, C–719n, C–720n, C–721n, C–725n, C–726n, C–727n
Whinston, Andrew B., 255
White, David, 180n, 197
Whitman, Margaret, C–357, C–361, C–364 to C–366, C–371, C–373, C–375, C–389, C–390, C–391
Wilder, C., C–428n, C–438n
Wilke, John R., 278
Williams, Jason, C–353n
Williams, John, C–141
Williams, Serena, C–40, C–44
Williams, Venus, C–40, C–44
Williamson, Peter J., 114, 296n, 302n, 386
Wilson, Douglas R., C–103
Wilson, Ian, 71
Wilson, Meena S., 422n, 443
Wilson, Robert R., C–739, C–739n
Wilson, Scott, C–52, C–53, C–57, C–59
Winchell, Verne, C–298
Winfrey, Oprah, C–387
Winn, Joan, C–138
Witt, Howard, C–354
Wolverton, Troy, C–356n, C–385
Woodard, Ron, C–640
Woods, Tiger, 190, 367, C–760, C–761
Wooldridge, Bill, 23n, 355n, 450
Wright, Jim, C–597
Wurster, Thomas S., 256
Wyman, Malcolm, C–460, C–462, C–462n, C–468

Yates, Chris, C–302, C–310, C–313, C–314, C–315, C–319, C–320
Yin, Fang, 255
Yip, George S., 86n
Yoffie, David B., 188n, 197
Young, Andrew, C–770
Youngman, Owen, C–339, C–339n, C–343, C–346, C–347 to C–348, C–350, C–351, C–352, C–354, C–355

Zack, Michael H., 118n, 147
Zahra, Shaker A., 113, 118n, 223, 264n
Zajc, Lydia, C–337n
Zedillo, Ernesto, C–222 to C–223
Zimmerman, Frederick M., 283n, 289
Ziv, Nina, C–339

ORGANIZATION

Aaeon Technology, 224
AAMA (American Apparel Manufacturing Association), C–773
Abacus Direct, C–777
Abacus Online, C–781
ABB (Asea Brown Boveri), 380, C–524
ABC, 179, 190, 305
ABC Outdoor, 179
Abitibi-Price, C–305 to C–306, C–319
ABN-AMRO, C–468
Abovenet, C–378
Accenture, C–560
Accompany, 428
Aceralia Corporation, C–424
Acer Computer Group, 265, 312
ACLU (American Civil Liberties Union), 293
ACNielsen/Adams Business Research, C–252
Acura, 169
Adidas, 46, C–767
Adolph Coors Co., *C–465*
Advanced Manufacturing Online, 161
Advanced Micro Devices (AMD), 89, 186–187, 407
A&E (Arts & Entertainment network), 305, 339
Aerospatiale, 216, 372
AES Corporation, 443–444, C–695 to C–731
Agere Systems, 284
AgriRecycle Inc., C–583
AIP (Apparel Industry Partnership), C–759, C–770, C–771, C–772
AIPC (American Italian Pasta Company), C–126 to C–128, C–127*t*
Airborne Express, 87, 159, 401
Airbus Industrie, 176, 216
Air Canada, C–641
Air China, C–641
Air France, C–641
Air Transport Association, C–625
AISI (American Iron and Steel Institute), C–414, C–415
AK Steel Holding Corporation, C–424
Alando.de AG, C–380
Alaska Airlines, C–624
Albani Brewery, C–463
Alberto-Culver, C–29*t*, C–32 to C–33
Albertson's, C–188
Alcan Aluminum, 11
Alcon, 320
Aligent Technologies, 314
Alitalia, C–641
Allied Domecq PLC, C–297
Allied-Signal, 354, 388
AltaVista, C–383
Amalgamated Sugar Company, 394–395
Amazon Auctions, C–382
Amazon.com, 33, 46, 53, 83, 124, 136, 139, 156, 163, 193, 227, 231, 234, 242, 247–248, 251, 275, 362, 445, C–330 to C–334, C–374, C–390
Amazon.com Auctions, C–385 to C–387, *C–386 to C–388*
AmBev (American Beverage Company), *C–464,* C–468

AMD (Advanced Micro Devices), 89, 186–187, 407
American Advertising Federation, C–788
American Airlines, 124, 163, 176, 400, C–613, C–626, C–639, C–656
American Apparel Manufacturing Association (AAMA), C–773
American Beverage Company (AmBev), *C–464,* C–468
American Civil Liberties Union (ACLU), 293
American Eagle, C–641
American Express, 216, C–560
American Greetings, 171
American Iron and Steel Institute (AISI), C–414, C–415
American Italian Pasta Company (AIPC), C–126 to C–128, C–127*t*
American Performance Marine, C–153
American Proton Treatment Systems (APTS), C–754, C–758
American Red Cross, 8
American Standard, 306
American Tobacco, 280
American Trans Air, C–656
American Water Ski Association (AWSA), C–154, C–168, C–169
America Online (AOL), 16, 23, 32, 46, 49, *102,* 173, 176, 178, 192, 193, 227, 242, 245, 248, 278, 362, C–331, C–345, C–348, C–354, C–372
America West Airlines, C–641, C–656
Ameritrade, 161
AMFM, Inc., 179
Amgen, 406
Amora-Maille, C–471, C–482, C–483
Anaheim Angels, 305
Anaheim Mighty Ducks, 305
Andersen Consulting, 136, 176
Anderson Worldwide, C–557
Anheuser-Busch, 44, 67, 91, 275, 293, 373, C–463, *C–464,* C–468
AOL. *See* America Online
Apollo Computer, Inc., C–537
Apparel Industry Partnership (AIP), C–759, C–770, C–771, C–772
Applebee's, C–210
Apple Computer, 37, 280, 293, C–363, C–543
Applied Energy Services, Inc., C–697
APTS (American Proton Treatment Systems), C–754, C–758
Aquatic Propulsion Technology, Inc., C–96
Arbed SA, C–424
Ariba, Inc., 229, 240, 402, C–360
Armco Steel, C–413
Armour, 159
Arrowhead, 320
Arthur Andersen, 66, 394, 395, 401, C–560
Arthur D. Little, 397
Arts & Entertainment network (A&E), 305, 339
Asea Brown Boveri (ABB), 380, C–524
Ashford.com, C–386
AtHome/Excite, 178
A. T. Kearney, 136
Atlantic Richfield, C–697

Atlantic Southeast, 169
Atlas Corporation, 11
AT&T, 9*n*, 28, 36, 43, 100, 137, 173, 176, 178, 215, 226, 284, 298, 316–317, 354, 372, 407
AtYourOffice.com, 251
AuctionWatch, C–383
AutoTrader.com, C–373
Avid Technology, Inc., C–536 to C–548
Avis Rent-A-Car, 8, 190
Avon Products, Inc., 104, 426, C–17 to C–49, C–29*t*
Avstar, C–544
A. W. Perdue and Son, Inc., C–566
AWSA (American Water Ski Association), C–154, C–168, C–169
Azalea Seafood Gumbo Shoppe, C–184 to C–202
Azerty Division (Abitibi-Price), C–305 to C–306, C–319

Baccarat, 280
Bahama Breeze, 301
Bailey's, 305
Bain & Company, C–632
Bajaj Auto (India), 220
Bally (shoes), 280
Banc One Corporation, 11
Bandag, 169
BankAmerica, 250, 426
Bankers Life and Casualty, C–663
Banker's Trust, 178
Bank of America, 50
Bank of New York, C–667, C–667*n,* C–672
Bank One Corporation, 49, 50–51, 250, 410
Barnesandnoble.com, 83
Barnes & Noble, 124, 231, C–143, C–214
BASF, C–312 to C–320
Baskin-Robbins, C–297
Basys Automation Systems, C–542*t*
Bauer Nike Hockey Inc., C–760
Beaird-Poulan, 161, 299
Beatrice Foods, C–280
Beaulieu Vineyards, 305
Bell, 173, 305
Bell Atlantic Corporation, 216, 375
Ben & Jerry's Foundation, C–487 to C–488
Ben & Jerry's Homemade, Inc., 63, 270, C–470, C–484 to C–490
Benson & Hedges, 320
Beringer Wine Estates, Inc., C–242 to C–243, C–260
Bertelsmann AG, 224, C–323
Bestfoods, C–470 to C–471, C–490 to C–491, C–492*t* to C–496*t,* C–493 to C–494
Bestfoods Baking Company, C–471, C–493 to C–494, C–497
Best Practices Benchmarking & Consulting, 136
Bethlehem Steel Corporation, 410, C–395, C–396, C–397, C–407, C–424
BF Goodrich, C–419
Bic, 161
Billpoint, C–379
Biras Creek, C–678
Birmingham Steel, C–419

Note: Page numbers preceded by C- indicate material in Cases; ** indicates disguised company name. Page numbers in *italics* indicate illustrations; page numbers followed by *n* indicate footnotes; page numbers followed by *t* indicate tables.

Black & Decker Corporation, 161, 299, 300
Blimpie's Subs and Salads, C–298
Blockbuster, 133, 178, 314, C–382
Bloom Agency, C–595
BLS (Business Logistics Services), C–439
Blue Diamond, 280
Bluefly.com, 18, 390–391
Blue Mountain Arts, 171
Blue Ribbon Sports, C–760
B&M, 305
BMG Entertainment, C–324, C–335
BMG Music, C–141
BMW, 124, 163, 169, 178, 189, 312, 372
Boats.com, C–374
Bodegas de Santo Tomas, C–244
Boeing, 216, 372, 391, C–635, C–640, C–656
Bombardier, 299
Bombay, 280
Boone's Farm, C–263
Borden Food Holdings Corporation, C–116, C–128, C–133
Borden Foods, C–507, C–513
Borders Books and Music, C–143
Borders Bookstores, 124, 314
Boston Beer Company, C–457
Boston Consulting Group, C–524
Boston Market, C–210, C–212
Botts, C–463
BP Amoco, 34, 204
Brahma, C–464
Braniff, C–591, C–592, C–595, C–596, C–635
Bridgestone, 131
Briggs & Stratton, 9n, 43, 161
Bristol-Myers Squibb, 8, 11
British Aerospace, 216
British Airways, 25, C–656
British Steel, C–413, C–427
British Telecom, 215, 226
Broadcast.com, 193
Broadcom, 226
Brown Forman, C–260
Bruno's, C–190, C–198
Buick, 169
Burger King, 175, 305, C–203, C–209, C–210, C–214, C–219, C–224, C–477t
Business for Social Responsibility, C–771
Business Logistics Services (BLS), C–439
Buy.com, 83, 227, 234, 244
Byron Winery, C–253

Cabarete Beach Hotel, C–688
Cadbury Schweppes, C–477t
Cadillac, 124, 169
Caliber Logistics, C–439, C–440, C–444
Caliber Systems, Inc., C–428, C–439
California Perfume Company, C–19
California Pizza Kitchen, 314, C–507, C–509
Calistoga, 320
Campbell's Soup Company, 163, 280, 293, C–481t, C–497
Camstar Systems, 231
Canada Dry, 280
Canandaigua Wine Company, C–260, C–263, C–269, C–277
Caneel Bay, C–686
Cannondale Corporation, 168–169, 280
Canon, 46, 300
Capital Cities/ABC, 178
Capricorn Records, C–143
Cardinal Health, 34–35
Caribbean Transportation Services, C–441
Carlsberg, C–463, C–464 to C–465
Carl's Jr., C–208, C–210, C–213

Carnation, 320
Carorder.com, 161
Carrier, 305
Carroll's Foods, C–567
CarsDirect.com, C–386
Castrol, 204
Caterpillar Tractor, 45, 46, 163, 392, C–472
CBS, 179, 190, 313, 314
CBS Cable, 314
CBS Marketwatch.com, 314
CBS Television Network, 314
CDW Computer Centers, 440
Centralcer, C–463
Century Business Services, C–560
Century Resorters, C–154
Cessna Aircraft, 305
CFM International, 216
Cha, C–471
Chanel, 163, 170
Chaparral Steel, C–416
Charles Schwab & Co., 49, 163, 227, 247, 249, 406
Chase Manhattan, 161
Château Mouton-Rothschild, C–254 to C–245
Checkers, C–208
Check Point Software Technologies, 227
The Cheesecake Factory, C–210
Chemdex, 161
Cherokee Vineyard Winery, C–252
Chevron, 268–269, 372
Chevys Mexican Restaurants, C–507, C–509, C–510
Chicago Cutlery, 280
Chicago Tribune, C–343, C–344
Chicagotribune.com, C–339 to C–355
Chick-fil-A, 446, C–210, C–212
Chipotle Mexican Grill, C–212
Chris-Craft, C–154
Christian Children's Fund, 293
Christie's, C–359, C–382
Chromatis Networks, 284
Chrysler Corporation, 178, 372
Chuck E. Cheese, C–210
CILCORP, C–731
Cinzano, 305
Circuit City, 90
Cisco Systems, 136, 178, 180, 183, 185, 200, 226, 227, 284, 361, 362, 363, 364–365, 406, C–433, C–435
Citibank, 250
Citicorp, 35, 426
Citigroup, 35, 44
CKE Enterprises, C–210
Claris, C–363
Classic Sports Network, 305
Clear Channel Communications, 178, 179
Cloud 9 Shuttle, 394
CMGI, 313, C–383
CNBC, 339
CNBC Asia, 339
CNBC Europe, 339
CNET, C–350, C–360
CNN, 166
Coca-Cola Consolidated, C–514, C–515
Coca-Cola Corporation, 9n, 32, 43, 100, 109, 124, 133, 217–218, 268, 293, 314, 346, 373, C–260, C–448, C–455, C–458, C–514 to C–515, C–519, C–533
Coca-Cola Enterprises, C–514 to C–515
Codelinks, C–670, C–670n, C–676
Coffee Time, C–300
Cole Haan, C–760
Colgate-Palmolive, C–479t
Collector's Universe, C–377

CollegeBytes.com, C–361
Colonial Penn, C–663
Colorado Creative Music, C–138 to C–152
Columbia, 320, C–141
Comair, 169
Comedy Central, 314
Commerce One, 229, 240
Community Pride Food Stores, 446
Companhia Siderurgica National, C–397
Compaq Computer, 28, 91, 160, 220, 233, 265, 278, C–362, C–372, C–537, C–546
CompuServe, 178, 192
Computer Associates, 402
Computer Identics, C–317
ConAgra, C–477t, C–487
Conseco Capital Management, C–663
Conseco Finance, C–669 to C–672
Conseco, Inc., C–661 to C–676
Conseco Risk Management, C–663
Consumer Reports Online, 248
Contadina, 320
The Container Store, 377
Continental Airlines, 176, C–591, C–592, C–627, C–630 to C–660
Continental Express, C–652 to C–653, C–657
Continental Lite, C–632 to C–633
Cooper Industries, 305
Cooper Tire, 155
Coors, 91, 426
Corel, 178
Corning Glass Corporation, 173, 226
Corporacion Jaboneria Nacional, C–471
Correct Craft, C–154, C–155, C–169, C–170, C–174 to C–175, C–175, C–179
Coty, C–29t, C–33
Country Music Television, 314
Country Style, C–300
Covey Leadership Center, C–87
CPC International, C–491
Cracker Barrel, C–210
Cracker Jack, C–502, C–513
Cray, 367
Cross, 163
Crowell, Weedon and Co., C–401
CVS, 240
CyberCenters, 176

Da Gama Textiles, C–448
Daily News, C–343
Daimler-Benz Aerospace, 216
Daimler-Benz AG, 178, 372
DaimlerChrysler AG, 92, 216, 231
Daisytek, C–302 to C–320
Dakota Growers Pasta (DGP), C–116 to C–137
D'Angelo's Sandwich Shops, C–507, C–509
Danone Group. See Group Danone
Dantroh Japan, C–96
Darden Restaurants, 301
Dazbog Coffee Company, C–300
DeBeers, 190
Deere & Company, 33
Degussa-Huls, 306
Delchamps, Inc., C–189 to C–190
Dell Computer Corporation, 23, 90, 92, 136, 139, 160, 176, 183, 194, 207, 227, 233, 239, 241, 265, 278, 298, 299, 362, 363, 372, 377, 445, C–382, C–435
Deloitte & Touche, C–557
Delta Airlines, 124, 163, 176, 400, C–633, C–639
Deutsche Bank, 178, C–458, C–463
Deutsche Post, C–443
Deutsche Telekom, 173, 226
DGP (Dakota Growers Pasta), C–116 to C–137

DHL, C–442, C–443
Diageo PLC, 68, 175, 305, C–210, C–477t, C–484, C–487
Diamond, 305
DiaSorin, 306
Digidesign, Inc., C–542t
Digital City, C–345
Digital Equipment Corporation, C–537
DigitalFocus, C–540
Digital Java, Inc., C–289
Digital Video Applications Corporation, C–542t
Direct TV, 176
Disney Channel, 305
Disney Radio, 305
The Disney Store, 305
Domino's Pizza, 11, 133, 293, 401
Dom Perignon, 305
Donatos Pizza, C–212
DoubleClick Inc., 46, 193, 227, 362–363, C–776
Drake's Anchorage, C–680, C–681
Drax power plant, C–722
DreamWorks, C–387
Dreyer's Grand Ice Cream, C–484, C–486, C–487, C–490
Droll Yankee, C–56, C–57
Dr Pepper, 163, 280
Drugstore.com, C–386
Dunkin' Donuts, C–296, C–297 to C–298, C–300
Du Pont, 100

E!, 305
Eastman Kodak, 8, 124, 275, 372, 426
East Side Mario's, C–507, C–509
eBay, 156, 168, 193, 227, 237, 242, 247, 275, C–356 to C–391, C–518
Edgars, C–448
Edmunds.com, 227
EDS (Electronic Data Systems), 24, 361
Edward Jones, 440
Egghead.com, C–382, C–387
E. & J. Gallo Winery, 372, C–233, C–240 to C–241, C–259, C–260, C–263 to C–278
Élan Boats, C–153, C–179 to C–183
Elastic Reality, C–542t
Electric Motorbike Inc., C–97
Electronic Arts, 227
Electronic Data Systems (EDS), 24, 361
Eli Lilly, 43
Elizabeth Arden, C–471
Eller Media Company, 179
E-Loan, 46
EMC Corporation, 227
Emerson Electric, 299
Emery Worldwide, 159
EMI-Capitol Recorded Music, C–323, C–324
EMI Recorded Music, C–141, C–335
emPower, C–96
EMusic.com, 234
Engage, 102
Enron, 65–66, 445
Entergy, 418
Enterprise Rent-A-Car, 169
Environmental Defense Fund, C–418
Epic, 320
Equifax, Inc., C–377
Ericsson, 84, 173, 227
Ernst & Young, C–384, C–557, C–769 to C–770, C–770
eShop, C–363
ESPN, 305
The Estée Lauder Company(ies), C–29t, C–31 to C–32
e-Steel.com, 95
Etherian, C–142
eToys, 46, 124, 139, 248, 249

E*Trade Group, 46, 249
EV Global, C–110
Evinrude, C–154
Evoke Communications, C–376
EV Systems, C–96
Excite@Home, C–345
Executive Income Life Insurance Company, C–662
Exodus Communications, 44, 227, C–378, C–779
Expedia, 176
Exxon Company International, 34, 372
Exxon/Mobil, 204
E-Z-Go, 305

Fair Labor Association (FLA), C–759, C–772, C–773
FairMarket, C–360 to C–361
Famous Players, 314
FDX Corporation, 36
FDX Global Logistics, 36
FDX Logistics, C–439, C–441
Federal Express Corporation (FedEx), 36, 87, 95, 140, 159, 163, 166, 250, 293, 401, 406, 407, 421, C–307, C–311, C–318, C–428
Federal Trade Commission (FTC), C–776, C–781, C–788
FedEx Corporate Services Corporation, C–444
FedEx Corporation, C–428 to C–446
FedEx Logistics, C–444, C–445
FedEx Logistics and Electronic Commerce (FLEC), C–439, C–444
Femsa, C–465
Fermilab, C–739, C–740, C–742, C–743
F5 Networks, 226
Fisher-Price, 236
FLA (Fair Labor Association), C–759, C–772, C–773
FLEC (FedEx Logistics and Electronic Commerce), C–439, C–444
Florida Steel, C–416
Footlocker, C–382
Ford Motor Company, 11, 86, 92, 100, 136, 157, 163–164, 178, 216, 218, 231, 293, 372, 426, C–110
Forever Bicycle Company, C–96
Formby's, 280
Forrester Research, 284, C–338, C–358, C–360
Foster's Brewing Group Limited, C–243, C–465 to C–466, C–468
Foundry Networks, 226
Fox network, 179, 190
FreeMarkets, 236
Frescarina, 305
Friendly's, C–210
Frito-Lay Inc., 314, C–205, C–483, C–503, C–509, C–514, C–524, C–525
Frito-Lay International, C–528, C–531
Frito-Lay North America, C–527, C–528
Frontier Airlines, C–593, C–636, C–656
Frontier Global Center, C–779
FTC (Federal Trade Commission), C–776, C–781, C–788
FTD, C–364
FTD.com, 227
Fujitsu, 227
Fuji-Xerox, 135

Galderma, 320
Gamesa, C–507
Gannett, C–353
Gardner-Denver, 305
Gartner Group, C–336, C–358

Gateway Computer, 139, 176, 194, 207, 265, 278, 361, C–378
Gatorade/Tropicana, C–533 to C–534
GE. See General Electric Company
GE Americom, 341
GE Capital, 339
GE Capital Investment Advisors, 340
GE Equity, 339
GE Medical Systems, 407
General Electric Company (GE), 44, 47, 100, 161, 173, 176, 216, 299, 300, 328, 338, 338n, 339–341, 361, 362, 376, 391, 408, 420, 423, 440, 441, C–744
General Foods, 300
General Magic, C–363
General Mills, 406, C–475, C–477t, C–481t, C–487
General Motors, 34, 49, 100, 178, 216, 221, 231, 426, 427, C–777
Gener SA, C–696
George Dickel, 305
Georgetown Steel, C–416
George Weston group, C–493
Gerber, 293
GE Real Estate, 340
Giant, C–110
Giant Records, C–143
Gilbey's, 305
The Gillette Company, 37–38, 275, 301
Girl Scouts, 293
Glass Craft Boat Company, C–154
Glaxo, 139–140
Glen Ellen Wines, 305
Global Crossings, 226
Gnutella, C–326, C–336 to C–337
Godiva Chocolatier, 170
Golden State Vintners, C–253
Goldman Sachs, C–256
Gol-Pak Corporation, C–575
GoodHome.com, 428
GoodWorks International, C–770
Goodyear Tire & Rubber, 131, 165
Gordon's, 305
Granite Rock Company, 392, 393, 440
Great Plains Software, 394, 395
Green Giant, 305
Green Tree Financial Corporation, C–661n, C–661 to C–662, C–662n, C–663n, C–663 to C–664
Greer's, C–198
Greyhound Corporation, 30
Greylock Management Corporation, C–544
Group Danone, C–463, C–481t, C–482, C–519
Grupo Cressida, C–471
Grupo Modelo, C–466, C–468
GTE, 216
Gucci, 165
Guinness Anchor Brewery, 305, C–455, C–466

Häagen-Dazs, 170, 175, 270, 305, C–484, C–486, C–487
Habib's, C–224
Hain, 280
Half.com, C–362, C–374, C–390
Hallmark, 171
Hamilton Substrand, 305
Handspring, C–374
Hanson, PLC, 317
Hardee's, C–208, C–210
Hard Rock Café, C–374
Harley-Davidson, 406
Harris Corporation, 390
Hasbro Inc., C–364, C–366
Health and Hygiene Inc., C–582
HealthSouth, 280

Health Valley, 280
HEAT, *102*
Heftel Broadcasting Co., 179
Heineken, C–455, C–463, *C–466 to C–467,* C–468
Helados Holanda, C–490
Henessey, 305
Hewlett-Packard Co., 2, 42, 64, 91, 160, 176, 183, 220, 227, 233, 278, 314, 361, 392, C–546
Hi-C, 32
Higher Octave, C–141
Hilton Hotels, 204, 206
History Channel, 339
H. J. Heinz Company, 91, 280, C–478
Hollywood.com, 314
The Home Depot, 14, 34, 90, 155, 163, 272, C–382
Homesdirect, C–374
Home Team Sports, 314
Honda, 46, 92, 123, 163, 212, 220, 300, 323, 324, 366, 367
Honeywell, C–656
Horizon, 169
Horizon Airlines, C–641
Hot 'N' Now, C–507, C–509, C–510
Hotwire, 176
Houston Lighting & Power, C–696
H&R Block, C–560
Hueblein, Inc., C–204 to C–205
Hughes Electronics, 176
Hughes Satellite, 173
H. W. Lay Company, C–503

IBA (Ion Beam Applications), C–756
IBM Corporation, 30, 173, 176, 183, 220, 227, 278, 425, 426, 428, C–356, C–362, C–374, C–379, C–390, C–442, C–546
Ice Cream Partners, C–486
Idealab, C–334
Ideal Standard, 306
I-Escrow, C–379
IFPI (International Federation of the Phonographic Industry), C–322
Ikegami Tsushinki Company, C–543
Imperial Chemical, 317
Indmar, C–163
Infinity boats, C–169, C–170, C–176 to C–179, *C–178*
Infinity Broadcasting, 314
ING Barings, C–704
Ingram Micro, 18, 233, *233,* C–305
Inkbusters Inc., C–781
Ink Development, C–363
Inktomi, 193, 227
Intel Corporation, 8, 39, 40, 62, 89, 173, 180, 186, 187, 198, 200, 202, 227, 237, 274, 278, 366, 425, C–543, C–548
Interbrew, *C–467*
Interfaith Center on Corporate Responsibility, C–771
International Federation of the Phonographic Industry (IFPI), C–322
International Home Foods, C–477t
International Olympic Committee (IOC), C–159
International Red Cross, 41
International Water Ski Federation (IWSF), C–159
Internet Advertising Bureau, C–788
Internet Auction Co. Ltd., C–380
Internet Capital Group, 313
Intimate Brands, C–29t, C–32
Intuit, C–366
IOC (International Olympic Committee), C–159
Iomega, 237–238, 285
Ion Beam Applications (IBA), C–756

Iowa Beef Packers, 159
iShip.com, C–379
i2 Technologies, 402
ITT, 317
iVillage, 227, C–345
IWSF (International Water Ski Federation), C–159

Jack in the Box, C–208
Jacobsen, 305
Jaguar, 169, 178
J&B, 305
JCPenney, C–40, C–46, C–381
J. D. Edwards, 231
J. D. Power and Associates, 169, C–160, C–161, C–651
JDS Uniphase, 35, 226
Jeep, 169
Jiang Nan Feng (JNF), C–577
Jiffy Lube International, 169
Jitney-Jungle, C–189 to C–190, C–192
The J. M. Smucker Company, 24, 433, 435–436
JNF (Jiang Nan Feng), C–577
John Deere, C–360
John Hancock, 61
Johnny Walker, 305
Johnson, C–154
Johnson & Johnson, 163, 176, 301, 432, 433, C–29t, C–34
Jollibee Foods (Philippines), 220
Jose Cuervo, 305
JuniperNetworks, 226
Jupiter Communications Inc., C–336, C–338
JVA Enterprises, C–681

Karastan, 163
Kawasaki Steel Corporation, C–424
KB Toys, C–382
Keebler, C–477t
Kellogg's, 218, C–475, C–477t, C–478
Kendall-Jackson Winery, C–227, C–240, C–260
Kentucky Fried Chicken Corporation (KFC), 206, 272, 314, C–203 to C–224, C–502, C–507, C–509, C–510, C–513
King World Productions, 314
Kinko's, 440
Kirin, C–468
KLA-Tencor, 227
KLM Royal Dutch Airlines, 215, C–641, C–656
Kmart, 28, 92, 299, 300, 314, 426, 427, C–381
Knight Ridder, C–353
Komatsu, 45, 46
KPMG Consulting, 365, C–557
Kraft Foods, 178, 300, 320, C–477t, C–480t, C–520
Kraft General Foods, 280
Krispy Kreme Doughnuts, Inc., C–279 to C–301
Kroger Company, 69, 426, C–188
Krug Winery, C–247, C–250
Krupp, C–413

LaMar's Donuts, C–300, C–301t
Lands' End, 34, 406
Lawrence Berkeley Laboratory, C–739
Lee Memorial Hospital, 377
Lee Way Motor Freight, C–205
Lenscrafters, 440
Lever Brothers, C–471
Levi Strauss & Company, 275
Lexmark, 231
Lexus (Toyota Motor Corporation), 124, 178, 189
Libby's, 320
Lifetime network, 305
Lightspan Partnership, C–345
The Limited, 34

Lincoln, 103, 124, 169
Lincoln Electric, 161, 407, 410
Linux, 82
Lion Match Company, C–448
Lion Nathan, C–468
Listerine, 163
Little Caesars, C–210
Little Dix Bay Resort, C–680 to C–681, C–684, C–686
Liz Claiborne, C–771
L. L. Bean, 165
Lloyd's of London, C–377
LLUMC. *See* Loma Linda University Medical Center (LLUMC)
Lockheed Martin Corporation, 433, 434, 446, 447
Loma Linda University Cancer Institute, C–752
Loma Linda University Medical Center (LLUMC), C–735 to C–736, C–738, C–739, C–740, C–741, C–742, C–743 to C–745, C–746, C–751, C–752
Long John Silver's, 8
L'Oréal, C–28 to C–30, C–29t
Lotus, 367, C–442
Lowe's, C–353
LTV Corporation, C–396, C–424, C–427
Lucas Digital, C–543
Lucas Film, C–543
Lucent Technologies Inc., 226, 283, 284, 316
Lucy's LaundryMat, C–298
Lufkin, 305
Lufthansa Airlines, C–443
LVMH (Moët Hennessy Louis Vuitton), 305, C–29t, C–33 to C–34
Lycos, C–372

McCarthy Construction, C–740
McCormick & Company, 44
McDonald's, 14–15, 44, 140, 163, 164, 166, 206, 209, 218, 220, 275, 293, 373, 392, 420, 440, C–203, C–208, C–210, C–212, C–213, C–214, C–216, C–218, C–219
McGraw-Hill Companies, 36
McKinsey & Company, 274, 361, 383, 408, C–454, C–455, C–463, C–489
Macromedia, 227
Macy's, 92
Made in the U.S.A. Foundation, C–767
Mailboxes, Etc., C–379
Malden Mills Industries, 446
Malibu Boats, C–163, C–169, C–170, C–175 to C–176, *C–177*
Margarine Unie, C–471
Margarita, C–531
Marigold Foods, C–487
Marine Design Resource Alliance (MDRA), C–173 to C–174
Marks & Spencer, 346
Marlboro, 320
Marriott Corporation, 204
Marriott Hotels, 437
Marriott International, 440
Mars, Inc., C–487
Martha White, 305
Maruti-Suzuki (India), 218
Mary Kay Cosmetics (MKC), 104, 280, 410, 430, 440, C–29t, C–35 to C–36
Massachusetts General Hospital, C–743, C–743n, C–756
MasterCraft, C–154, C–155, C–159, C–163, C–166, C–169, C–170 to C–174, *C–172, C–173, C–179*
Matsushita, 161
Matsushita/Panasonic, 227
Mattel, 236

Mazda, 405–406, 406
MCI WorldCom, 173, 178
MDRA (Marine Design Resource Alliance),
    C–173 to C–174
Meadowbrook Lane Capital, C–490
MediaOne, 36, 298, 316
Medscape, 314
Medtronic, 408
Mellon Institute Energy Productivity Center,
    C–696 to C–697
MEMC Electronic Materials, 306
MercadoLibre.com, C–380
Mercedes-Benz, 103, 124, 163, 169, 178, C–110
Merck & Co., 35, 139–140, 176, 177, 406, 408,
    437
MerCruiser, C–163
Mercury Marine, C–154
Merrill Lynch, 49, 169, 249, 372
Mesaba, C–656
Metal Blade Records, C–141 to C–142
Metalsite.com, 95
Michelin, 131, 163, 200
Microsoft, C–348, C–351, C–390, C–543, C–548
Microsoft Corporation, 4, 5, 8, 23, 82, 92, 163,
    166, 173, 176, 178, 188, 209, 220, 227,
    237, 268, 275, 277, 278, 339, 361, 390,
    406, 407, 420, 425
Microsoft Network, 188, 245, 248
Micro United, C–305
MicroWarehouse, C–361
Midway Airlines, C–614
Midwest Express, C–656
Mildara Blass Limited, C–243
Miller Brewing Company, 300, 320, 373
Minute Maid, 32
Mitsubishi, 311
Mitsuoishi Shoji Kaisha, Ltd., C–204
MKC (Mary Kay Cosmetics), 104, 280, 410,
    430, 440, C–29t, C–35 to C–36
Moai Technologies, C–360
Mobil, 34
Moët Hennessy Louis Vuitton (LVMH), 305,
    C–29t, C–33 to C–34
Mogen David, C–263
Monarch Company, C–519
Monsanto, 407, 428
Monster.com, 365
Moores Rowland International, C–558
The More Group, 179
Mortgage.com, 46, 49, 139
Moss Adams LLP, C–552 to C–564
Motel 6, 169, 170
The Motion Factory, C–542t, C–548
The Motley Fool, 227
Motorola, 44, 84, 123, 126, 161, 173, 176, 218,
    227, 398, C–524
The Movie Channel, 314
MP3.com, C–334 to C–335
Mr. Coffee, 299
Mrs. Fields Cookies, 392, 402
MSNBC, 188, 339
MSN Gaming Zone, 102
MTV, 67, 314
MTV2, 314
mtv.com, 314
Murray, C–110
Mutual Wholesale Company, C–191
Myhome, C–471

NAA (Newspaper Association of America), 95,
    C–339
Nabisco Corporation, 280, C–205, C–477t,
    C–483
Napster, C–335 to C–336
The Nashville Network, 314

National Consumers League, C–771
National Geographic Channels International, 339
National Marine Manufacturers Association
    (NMMA), C–155, C–156
National Renewable Energy Laboratory, C–110
National Semiconductor Corporation, C–435,
    C–437
National Sporting Goods Association (NSGA),
    C–155
NBBJ, C–740
NBC, 179, 188, 190
NBCi, 339
NBC Television Network, 339
NCA (Nuclear Corporation of America), C–393
NCR, 316
NEC, 227, C–380
Nestlé, 175, 178, 200, 209, 320, C–260, C–475,
    C–479t, C–484, C–486, C–519
Nestlé USA, Inc., C–242
NetCoalition.com, C–788
Netscape, 188, 278
Network Advertising Initiative, C–788
Network Appliance, 227
Newspaper Association of America (NAA), 95,
    C–339
New York Air, C–636
New York New Media Association, C–788
New York Times, C–353, C–354
Nicholson, 305
nick.com, 314
Nickelodeon, 314
Nike.com, 236
Nike, Inc., 46, 190, 252, 361, 372, C–458,
    C–759 to C–775
Nike Team Sports, C–760
Nikki, 204
Nintendo, 102, 227, 319, 323
Nippon Steel, C–413
Nissan, 164, 169, 216
NKK Corporation, C–424
NMMA (National Marine Manufacturers
    Association), C–155, C–156
Nokia Group, 24, 84, 173, 200, 227, 445
Nongbo Topp Industrial Company Ltd., C–96
Nordstrom, 393, 406, 420, 421
Nortel Networks, 226, 284
North American Van Lines, C–205, C–506,
    C–507
North Carolina Coastal Federation, C–418
North Star Steel, C–416
Northwest Airlines, 176, 215, C–627, C–639,
    C–641, C–642 to C–643, C–651 to C–652
Northwest Water, 377
Novell, 178, 227
NSGA (National Sporting Goods Association),
    C–155
Nua, 226n
Nuclear Corporation of America (NCA), C–393
Nucor Corporation, C–392 to C–427
Nucor Steel Corporation, 153, 154, 155, 161,
    270, 410, 430
Nucor-Yamato Steel, C–397, C–423

Oceanline, 102
Ocean Spray, C–507
O'Charley's, C–210
office.com, 314
Office Depot, 250, 251, C–304, C–381
OfficeMax, 314, C–304
Ohlsson's, C–448
OK Bazaars, C–448
Old El Paso, 305
Oldsmobile, 169, C–393
Olive Garden, 301
Omaha Steaks, C–435

Online Privacy Alliance, C–788
On The Border, C–210
OPEC (Organization of Petroleum Exporting
    Countries), C–696
Open Market, Inc., C–442
OpenSite Technologies, C–360
Optivus Technology, Inc., C–732 to C–758
Opus One, C–242
Opus One Winery, C–255
Oracle, 173, 227, 229, 240, 402, C–390, C–546
Orbitz, 176, C–639
Oregon Steel Mills, C–396
Organization for Economic Cooperation and
    Development, C–425
Organization of Petroleum Exporting Countries
    (OPEC), C–696
Otis Elevator, 8, 305, 311, 401
Oxygen SpA, C–97

Pacific Corp., 28
Pacific Southwest Airlines, C–591, C–613
Palm, 126, 176
PalmPilot, 227, 316
Pamlico-Tar River Foundation, C–418
Panasonic, 300, C–546
Papa John's, C–210
Parallax Software, C–542t
Paramount Home Video, 314
Paramount Pictures, 314
Paramount Television, 314
Parcel Plus, C–379
Parkway Food Service, C–191
Patagonia, 280
Paxton Communications, 179
PBG (Pepsi Bottling Group), C–515
PCM, C–163
Peapod, C–345
Pennzoil, 204
People Express, C–635
The Pep Boys—Manny, Moe, & Jack, 9
PepCom Industries, Inc., C–515
PepsiAmericas, Inc., C–515
Pepsi Bottling Group (PBG), C–515
PepsiCo Beverages International, C–532 to
    C–533
PepsiCo, Inc., 109, 124, 148, 301, 314, 346, 361,
    373, C–205, C–205 to C–207, C–217,
    C–260, C–448, C–477t, C–483, C–502 to
    C–535
Pepsi-Cola North America, C–531 to C–532
Perdue Farms Inc., C–565 to C–589
PerMedics, C–751 to C–752
Perrier, 320
Peter Island Yacht Club, C–681
Peugeot, 175
Pfizer, Inc., 37, 176, 433, 434–435
PFS (Priority Fulfillment Services), C–302 to
    C–320
Phi Beta Kappa, 293
Philip Morris Companies, 109, 178, 300, 320,
    346, C–477t, C–480t
Philip Morris/Kraft, C–483
Philips Electronics, 227
Piedmont Airlines, C–634
Pi Kappa Phi fraternity, C–74 to C–94
Pillsbury, 175, 280, 305, C–260, C–477t,
    C–482t, C–486
Pilsner Urquell, C–450, C–463, C–468
Pioneer, C–663
Pizza Hut, 206, 272, 314, C–205, C–207, C–210,
    C–214, C–216, C–502, C–506 to C–507,
    C–509, C–510, C–513
Plate Glass, C–449
PlayNow.com, 248–249
PlayStation, 320

Pluto Technologies International, C–542*t*, C–548
PMC Sierra, 226
Pogo.com, *102*
Polaroid Corporation, 285, 372
El Pollo Loco, C–224
Polygram, C–323
Popeyes, C–212
Popov, 305
Porcher, 306
Porsche, 168
Portera Systems, 428
Pratt & Whitney, 176, 305
PreussenElektra, 306
Priceline.com, 193, 227, 242, 249
PriceWaterhouseCoopers, C–557, C–770
Primo Piatto, C–133 to C–134
Priority Fulfillment Services (PFS), C–302 to
    C–320
Privacy International, C–781
Procter & Gamble, 91, 92, 178, 300, 361, 366,
    406, C–29*t*, C–30 to C–31, C–364, C–449,
    C–475, C–479*t*
Progresso, 305
Prudential Insurance, 190
Publix Supermarkets, 440, C–192, C–198
PurchasingCenter.com, 235
Purvis Farms, C–567
PYA/Monarch, C–198

Quaker Foods North America, C–534
Quaker Oats Company, C–477*t*, C–502 to
    C–503, C–507, C–517 to C–519, C–520,
    C–525, C–528
Quaker State, 204
Quantum Computers, C–544
Qwest Communications, 173, 176, 226

Racal Design Services, C–537
Radegast, C–450
Railway Express, C–565
Rainbow Media Holdings, 339
Ralph Lauren, 163
Randall's, C–198
Ransomes, 305
Recording Industry Association of America
    (RIAA), C–322, C–328, C–336
Red Cross, 293
Redhat Linux, 4, 5
Red Lobster, 301, C–210
Red Rocket, 314
Reebok, C–771
Reed Business Information, C–651
Rembrandt Group, C–448
Remington Products, 410
Renault, 175, 216
Reo Motor Cars, C–393
Republic Steel, C–423
Research Triangle Institute, C–419
Revlon, C–29*t*, C–34 to C–35
Rhino Records, C–142
RIAA (Recording Industry Association of
    America), C–322, C–328, C–336
Richfield Holdings, C–190
Rite Aid, 28
Ritz-Carlton Hotels, 8, 37, 64, 163, 169, 170,
    399
R. J. Reynolds Industries, Inc. (RJR), C–204 to
    C–205, C–206
Robert Mondavi Corporation (RMC), C–241 to
    C–242, C–246 to C–261
Roberts Express®, 36, C–439, *C–440,* C–441
Robin's Donuts, C–300
Roche Holding, Ltd., C–44 to C–45
Rockefeller Resorts, C–680, C–686
Rolex, 103, 163, C–390

Rolling Rock, C–450
Rolls-Royce, 165, 170, 176
Romano's Macaroni Grill, C–210
Roncadin, C–484
Rosewood Hotels and Resorts, C–680 to C–681
Royal Ahold, C–188, C–191, C–589
Royal Dutch/Shell, 34, 274
RPS®, 36, C–439, *C–440,* C–441
Rubbermaid, 123
Russell Corporation, 35
Rutherford Estates, 305
Rx.com, 314

SAB (South African Breweries), C–447 to
    C–469
Safeway, C–188
SAIC (Science Applications International
    Corporation), C–740, C–744
St. Albans Cooperative Creamery, C–488
St. Vincent's Hospital, 377
Salvation Army, 293
Sam Goody, C–143
Sam's Clubs, C–191, C–198, C–199
Samsung, 211, 320, 321
Sandy Point Resort, C–683
SAP, 227, 229, 402
Sara Lee, C–478
SAS Airlines, 443
SAS Institute, 436, 437–438
SBC Communications, 226
Scali, McCabe, Sloves, C–573, C–574
Schindler, 311
Schwinn, C–110
Science Applications International Corporation
    (SAIC), C–740, C–744
Scottish and Newcastle, C462 to C–463, *C–467
    to C–468*
Scotts Stores Group, C–448
ScreamingMedia.com, C–354
SDMI (Secure Digital Music Initiative), C–328
Seagate Technology, 227
Seagram Company, Ltd., C–507, C–514
Sears Roebuck, 46, 92, 379*n*, 426, 427, C–40,
    C–46, C–374, C–381
Sebastian Vineyards, C–260
Secure Digital Music Initiative (SDMI), C–328
Sega, *102,* 319, 323
Seibel Systems, 227
Sempra Energy, 61
Sequoia Capital, C–334
7-Eleven, 272
7UP, 346
SGI (Silicon Graphics), 183
Sharp Corporation, 123
The Sharper Image, C–360
Shato Holdings Ltd., C–298
Shell Oil, 49, 100, 204
Shenandoah Farms, C–567
Shenandoah Valley Poultry Company, C–567
Sheraton, 204
Sherwin-Williams, 179
Shoney's, C–210
Showtime, 314
Siebel Systems, 402
Siemens, 320, C–744
Siemens-Nixdorf Information Systems, 444
Sikorsky, 305
Silicon Graphics (SGI), 183
Simon & Schuster, 314
Singapore Airlines, 124
SlimFast, C–470, C–483 to C–484
Smart & Associates, 361
SMEI (Sony Music Entertainment Inc.), C–326
SMEJ (Sony Music Entertainment [Japan] Inc.),
    C–326

Smirnoff, 305
Smith's Snackfoods Company, C–483, C–507
SMS Schloemann-Siemag AG, C–395
Snapple Beverage Group, C–477*t*
SNECMA, 216
Softbank Corporation, 313
Softech Systems, C–542*t*
Softimage, C–542*t,* C–543, C–545 to C–546,
    C–547
Solaria Estate Vineyard, C–256
Solectron Corporation, 233
Solutia, 428
SonicNet.com, 314
Sonoco Products Company, C–419
Sony Classical, 320
Sony Corporation, 26, *102,* 160, 200, 227, 236,
    270, 319, 320, 322, 323, 366, 445, C–540,
    C–546
Sony Music Entertainment (Japan) Inc. (SMEJ),
    C–326
Sony Music Entertainment Inc. (SMEI), C–326
Sony Music Group, C–141, C–323, *C–324,*
    C–326 to C–330, C–335
Sotheby's, C–359, C–386
Soundings of the Planet, C–142
South African Breweries (SAB), C–447 to
    C–469
South Beach Beverage Company, C–507, C–519
Southwest Airlines, 34, 124, 136, 157, 159–160,
    293, 361, 363, 400, 406, 410, C–632,
    C–633, C–651, C–653
Sports Authority, 314
Sportsline USA, 314
Sprint, 178
Squirrel Defense, Inc., C–50 to C–60
Standard, 306
Standard & Poors, C–424
Staples, 251, C–304
Starbucks Coffee, 23, 63, 123, 183, 275, 378,
    440, C–214, C–292, C–298, C–366, C–487
Steak n Shake, C–210
Stellenbosch Farmers' Winery, C–448
Stinnes, 306
Stokely—Van Camp, C–518
Stouffer's, 320
Stride Rite Corporation, 161, C–364
Subaru, 103
Subway, C–298
Sumitomo Metal Industries, C–425, C–427
Sunbeam, 299
SunChips, C–507
Sundaram Fasteners (India), 221
Sundoor, C–449
Sun Microsystems, 92, 227, 428, C–348, C–378
Suntory, C–260
Supermarkets Online, C–346
SUPERVALU, C–190
Sut's Premium Ice Cream, C–486
Swift and Company, 159, C–566
Sybase, C–546
Symba Ltd., C–531
SYSCO Corporation, C–190, C–191

Taco Bell, 206, 272, 314, 373, C–205, C–207,
    C–208, C–214, C–216, C–502, C–507,
    C–509, C–510, C–513
Taco Bueno, C–210
Tae Kwang Vina (TKV), C–764, C–768
Taiwan Semiconductor Manufacturing, 161, 227
Tanqueray, 280, 305
Target Corporation, C–292, C–381
Tasali Snack Foods, C–507, C–519
Taster's Choice, 320
Tata Finance, 216
TCI (Tele-Communications Inc.), 36, 298, 316
TDI Outdoor Advertising, 314

TD Waterhouse, 249
Technomic, C–296
Tektronix, C–544
Tele-Communications Inc. (TCI), 36, 298, 316
Televisa (Mexico), 220
Tellabs, 406
TEN, *102*
Texaco, 426
Texas Instruments (TI), 312, 372
Texas International Airlines (TI), C–591, C–592, C–595, C–596, C–636
Textron Automotive, 305
Textron Fastening Systems, 305
Textron Financial Services, 305
Textron, Inc., 305
TheStreet.com, 227
Think Mobility, C–110
Thomson, S.A., 198
3Com, 8, 124, 226, 316
3M Corporation, 11, 163, 265–266, 380, 381, 391, 440, 445
Thunderbird Hotel, C–266
TI (Texas Instruments), 312, 372
TI (Texas International Airlines), C–591, C–592, C–595, C–596, C–636
TI (Tribune Interactive), C–340, *C–342*
Ticketmaster, C–382
Tiffany & Co., 103, 165, 280
Times Mirror Company, C–343, C–353
Time Warner, 16, 179, C–72
Timex, 103, 293, 372
Tim Hortons, C–299 to C–300
TKV (Tae Kwang Vina), C–764, C–768
TNT, C–442, C–443
ToGo's Eateries, C–297
To-Kalon Vineyard, C–250, C–251, C–255
Toon Disney, 305
Toshiba Corporation, 22, 124–125, 160, 227
TotalOfficeSupply.com, 251
Totino's, 305
Tower Records, C–143
Towers Perrin, 136
Toyota Motor Corporation, 33, 123, 136, 169, 173, 178, 193, 194, 200, 207, 216, 407
Toyota Motor Corporation (Lexus division), 124, 178, 189
Toys "R" Us, 34, 124, 234, 236, 249, 446
Toysrus.com, C–386
Trader Joe's, 8, 170–171
Tradesafe, C–379
Tradewind Ventures, C–677, C–688
Trane, 306
TransCanada Pipeline, C–717
Trans Texas, C–591, C–592, C–593
Trans World Airlines (TWA), C–626, C–628, C–639
Travelocity, 176
Tree of Life, 280
Trek, C–110
Triarc, Inc., C–477*t*
Tribune Broadcasting Company, *C–341*
Tribune Company, C–340, C–343 to C–347
Tribune Education Company, *C–342*
Tribune Interactive (TI), C–340, *C–342*
Tribune Publishing Company, *C–341 to C–342*
Tricon Global Restaurants, Inc., 206, 272, C–207, C–211*t*, C–214, C–216, C–217, C–507, C–513
Trico Steel, C–427
Trinitron, 320
Tropicana Products, C–207, C–483, C–502, C–514, C–525
Tupperware, 440
TurnWorks, Inc., C–652
TWA (Trans World Airlines), C–626, C–628, C–639

Tyco International, 298

uBid.com, C–383 to C–384, *C–384*
UDV NA Wines, C–260
Uncle Chipps, C–531
Unilever Bestfoods, C–478
Unilever PLC, 178, 218, C–470 to C–501
UNITE, C–773
United Airlines, 124, 176, 400, C–598, C–624, C–631, C–639, C–656
United Biscuits Holdings, C–507
United Breweries, C–448
United Cinemas, 314
United Parcel Service (UPS), 95, 176, 250, 401, C–429, C–442 to C–443
United Stationers, C–305
United Students Against Sweatshops, C–775
United Technologies, Inc., 305
Universal, C–323
Universal Outdoor, 179
University of Oregon, C–759 to C–775
UPN TV, 179, 314
UPS. *See* United Parcel Service
US Airways, C–613, C–626, C–633, C–635, C–656
USA Waste, 178
USA Water Ski, C–167 to C–168, C–169
U.S. Electronic Privacy Center, C–781
U.S. Foodservice, C–190 to C–191, C–200
U.S. Gypsum, C–698
Usinor SA, C–413, C–424
U.S. Postal Service, 36, 87, 97, 401, C–356, C–362, C–369
U.S. Steel, 410, C–393, C–395, C–396, C–413, C–414, C–415
U.S. Steel Group, C–424, C–425
USX Corporation, C–414, C–424, C–425
Utz Quality Foods, 232

Vari-Crafts, C–56, *C–57*
VEBA Electronics, 306
Veba Group, 306
VEBA Oel, 306
VEBA Telecom, 306
VereinsBank, C–457
VeriSign, 227
Verizon, 226
VH1, 314
vh1.com, 314
Viacom, 178, 313, 314, 341
Viacom/CBS, 179
Vignette, C–350
Viking Freight, 36, C–439, *C–440,* C–441
Viña Caliterra, C–255 to C–256
Viña Errazuriz Winery, C–255
Virgin Atlantic, C–641, C–656
Virginia Slims, 320
Virgin Islands Dive Company, C–683
Vist (Russia), 220–221
Viterra, 306
Vodaphone AirTouch PLC, 216
Volkswagen, 164
Volvo, 175
Vulcraft, C–393, C–401, C–402, *C–403,* C–404, C–423, C–427

Walgreen's, 250
The Wall Street Journal, 248
The Wall Street Journal Interactive, C–354
Wal-Mart Stores, 14, 34, 45–46, 50, 64, 90, 91, 92, 103, 124, 155, 160–161, 163, 212, 234, 236, 249, 275, 293, 299, 401, 410, 420, 430, 440, 441, C–188, C–189, C–198, C–199, C–381, C–411, C–476, C–584, C–589

Walt Disney Company, 178, 179, 227, 305, 440, C–365
Warner Brothers, C–143, C–372
Warner-Lambert, 176
Warner Music Group, C–323, *C–324,* C–335
Washington Times-Herald, C–343
Waste Management, 178
Water Sports Industry Association (WSIA), C–160
WB Network, C–345
WCW (World Championship Wrestling), C–61, C–62, C–67 to C–70, C–71
WDAP, C–343
Wells Fargo, 50, 161, 250, C–379
Wendy's, C–203, C–208, C–219, C–224
Wendy's International, C–299
Wente Bros. Vineyards, C–243 to C–244, C–259
Western Airlines, C–635
West Indies Yacht Club Resort **,** C–677 to C–694
Westinghouse, 317
Weyerhaeuser Company, 95
Whirlpool, 161
Whitbread, *C–468*
White Castle, C–208
Whitman Corporation, C–515
Whole Foods Markets, 377, 408
Wilson, 159
Wilson Sporting Goods, C–205, C–506, C–507
Winchell's Donut House, C–298 to C–299
The Wine Group, C–260
Wine Institute, C–256
Wine World Estates, C–242
WingspanBank.com, 50–51
Winn-Dixie, C–190, C–198
Wit Capital, 8
W. L. Gore & Associates, 25, 170, 407, 410, 440, 445
Wolverhampton & Dudley, C–463
Wood Fruitticher, C–198
WordPerfect, 178
Workers Rights Consortium (WRC), C–759, C–773 to C–775
World Bank, C–705
World Championship Wrestling (WCW), C–61, C–62, C–67 to C–70, C–71
WorldCom, 178, 226
World Wrestling Federation (WWF), C–61 to C–73
Wrangler, 401
WRC (Workers Rights Consortium), C–759, C–773 to C–775
WSIA (Water Sports Industry Association), C–160
WWF (World Wrestling Federation), C–61 to C–73
www.avon.com, C–38, C–43

Xerox Corporation, 46, 135, 293, 388, 427
XtraMOBIL, C–96

Yahoo!, 46, 156, 190, 193, 227, 242, 245, 247, 248, C–331, C–334, C–354, C–372
Yahoo! Auctions, C–382, C–384 to C–385
Yamaha, 46, 270, 271
Yamato Kogyo, Ltd., C–396

ZAP Corporation, C–95 to C–114
ZAP Europa, C–96
Zapworld.com, C–96
ZDNet, C–361
ZEV Technologies, C–96

SUBJECT

Access-based positioning, 39n
Accounting:
    activity-based vs. traditional, 133, 134t
    market niche strategies in, C–552 to C–564
    in strategic cost analysis, 133
    unethical behavior in, 65–66
Acquisitions. See Mergers and acquisitions
Activities:
    dispersing, 211
    internal, costs of, 139
    international. See Cross-border activities
    key activities, costs of, 134–137
    linked, 155
    managerial, in strategy execution, 355–356
    in mission statement, 34
    noncritical, outsourcing, 371–372
    operations-driven, 355
    strategic fits in. See Cross-business
        strategic fits
    See also Strategy-critical activities; Value
        chain activities
Activity-based accounting, 133, 134t
Adaptive cultures, 427–429
Ad hoc organizational forms, 445
Administration, 130
Administrative support, 301
Administrative tasks, 370
Advertising:
    on Web sites, 244–245, 247
    See also Marketing; Sales
Agents, C–238 to C–239
Anticipation, in high-velocity markets, 263, 264
Antitrust action, 276
Asset-reduction strategies, 282
Assets:
    competitive assets. See Strengths
    human assets, 118, 118n, 122
    intangible, 118
    organizational, 118
    physical, identifying, 117–118
    undervalued, 303
Attractiveness-strength matrix, 337–338, 338
Auctions, online, C–356 to C–391
Authority:
    for decision-making process, 377, 378
    delegation of, 378
    employee empowerment and, C–721 to C–723
    of employees and departments, 376–380

Backward integration, 180
    buyer bargaining power and, 91
    disadvantages of, 181–182
    suppliers and, 89
Balanced Man project, C–82
Bargaining power:
    of buyers, 90–92, 235–236, 244
    impact of Internet on, 235–236

Bargaining power—Cont.
    leverage with customers, 335
    suppliers and, 88–90
        bargaining leverage with, 155, 335
        impact of Internet technology on, 236
Barriers to entry:
    artificially low, ignoring, 243
    in emerging industries, 260
    example of, C–591 to C–592
    in fragmented industries, 272
    Internet and, 234–235
    manufacturing costs and, C–170
    new competition and, 84, 86, 87
    See also Entry of new competitors
Benchmarking:
    consulting organizations for, 136–137
    continuous improvement and, 393–395, 414
    costs of key activities and, 134–137
    ethics and, 137
    example of, 136
    See also Performance measures
Benefit period, 185, 186
Best-cost provider strategies, 150, 151, 151,
        167–168, 195
    for dot-com companies, 246
    global, 205
    producer strategies, 169
Best practices, 394
    continuous improvement programs and,
        393–400
        capturing benefits of, 398–400
        examples of, 394–395, 399
        total quality management, 395–398,
            396t, 397t
    in strategy implementation, 357, 358
Better-off test, diversification and, 295
BHAG ("big, hairy, audacious goal"), 45, 393
Blocking strategies, 192
Board of directors, 27–28
Bonuses, 406
Boundaryless organization, 340, 341
Brand awareness, C–259 to C–260
Brand diversification, C–251 to C–254, C–478,
        C–479t to C–482t, C–481 to C–483
Brand preferences, 85
Brand reputation:
    brand-name leverage, 322
    building, C–349 to C–352
    business structure, C–438 to C–441
    buyer preferences and, C–286, C–288
    competitive strength and, 336
    cross-border activities and, 212
    dominating, 241–242
    ethics and, C–263 to C–278
    image enhancement, C–43 to C–44, C–44t
    in multinational diversification, 322
    related diversification and, 297, 300

"Brick-and-click" strategies, 249–250, 255
    for direct selling, 252–253
    distribution channels and, 252
    example of, 251
Brick-and-mortar retailers:
    brick-and-click strategies for, 250
    e-commerce and, 231, 232, 234
    Internet strategies for, 230t, 250–253
Broadband technology, 238
Broad differentiation strategy, 151
Brokers, C–238 to C–239
Budget reallocation, market conditions and,
        390–391
Budgets, 357, 358, 390–391, 414
Buildout opportunities, 227
Build-to-order strategy, 160
Buildup period, 185, 186
Bureaucracy, example of, C–472 to C–475
Business definition:
    examples of, 34–35
    specificity of, 35–37
Business environment:
    country-to-country variations in, 202
    customer loyalty and, C–296 to C–297
    environmental scanning, 99–100
    evaluating industry environment, 287
    macroenvironment, 73, 74
    societal considerations and, C–451 to C–452
Businesses. See Companies
Business model(s), 3–4, 48
    case study of, C–279 to C–301
    for e-commerce. See E-commerce
    effects of Internet on, C–324 to C–326
    examples of, 5, 95
    Internet technology and, 239–240
    for local companies, 220–221
    rapid change in, 17
    traditional, C–323
Business philosophy, 63, C–568 to C–569, C–570
Business portfolios. See Diversified firms
Business process reengineering, 159
    case study of, C–661 to C–676
    examples of, 376–377, C–41C–42t
    as strategy-critical activity, 375–376, 386, 414
    TQM contrasted, 398
Business strategy, 208t
    crafting, 54, 54–56
    for Internet. See E-commerce
    performance measures and, C–306 to C–307
    strategy-making pyramid, 49–50, 52
    See also Strategy(ies)
Business-to-business relationships, 90, 92
Business-to-business (B2B) selling, C–310,
        C–358
Business-to-consumer (B2C) selling, C–310
Business units:
    adding as performance test, 349

Note: Page numbers preceded by C- indicate material in Cases; page numbers in *italics* indicate illustrations; page numbers followed by *n* indicate footnotes; page numbers followed by *t* indicate tables.

Business units—*Cont.*
  cross-unit coordination, 380, 381
  example of, C–289 to C–292
  in franchising, C–292
  incompatible, divestiture of, 317
  managers of, C–401 to C–402
  in manufacturing, C–402 to C–406
  organization of, C–402 to C–405, C–665 to
    C–666, C–666
  performance of, 346–347, 346*n*, 352, C–294
Buyer preferences:
  brand reputation and, C–286, C–288
  cross-country, 319
  as driving force, 97–98
  globalization of industry and, C–456
  selection factors, *C–160,* C–160 to C–161,
    C–162*t,* C–163
  understanding, C–148 to C–149
Buyers:
  bargain hunters, 244
  bargaining power of, 90–92, 235–236, 244
  demographics of. *See* Consumer
    demographics
  differentiation strategies and, 163
  equality of, 92
  low-cost provider strategies and, 162
  online buying groups, 235
  perception of value, 149
  product differentiation and, 165
  sellers and, C–366 to C–370
  sophisticated, 266
  See also Customer(s)

Capabilities. *See* Competitive capabilities
Capacity utilization, 156
Capital requirements:
  equity capital, C–390
  Internet technology and, 239–240, 243
  new competition and, 85
  venture capital, 239–240, 243
Cash cows, 343–344
Cash flows, 343
Cash hogs, 343–344
CEO. *See* Chief executive officer
Challenge(s):
  in culture change, 442
  defensive strategies and, 192
  end-run offensives to avoid, 188–189
  market challengers, 277
  strategic, 143–144, 146–147
  stretch objectives and, 46–47
  of sustained growth, C–356 to C–391
Change:
  anticipating, 445
  in business models, 17
  capacity for, 384
  communicating need for, 356–357
  in corporate culture. *See* Culture-changing
    actions
  in costs, 97, 238
  as driving force, 97
  in emerging-country markets, 220–221
  in industries. *See* Industry(ies)
  in management. *See* Management
  organizational, growth and, C–751, *C–753,*
    C–754 to C–755

Change—*Cont.*
  organization building and, 368–369
  in strategy. *See* Strategy(ies)
  technological. *See* Technology(ies)
Chief architect approach, 23, 25
Chief executive officer (CEO):
  corporate culture and, 425, 431
  ethical standards of, 445
  personal involvement of, 431
  responsibilities of, 21, 22
  turnaround strategies of, C–636 to C–638
Clustering, 77, 77*n,* 132, 132*n*
Codes of ethics:
  for conduct of labor relations, *C–769*
  in corporate culture building, 431–432, 432*t*
  examples of, 433–438
  implementing, 433
Collaboration:
  in capability-building, 368, 372–373
  dependence in partnerships, 215
  in organization of future, 384
  responsibility for, 380–381
  between sellers and suppliers, 90, 236–237
  in strategy crafting, 24–26
  See also Management teams; Strategic
    alliances; Strategic partnerships
Collective learning, 11, *12*
Combination diversification strategies, 309
Combination turnaround strategies, 283
Command-and-control paradigm, 377, 382
Communication:
  of incentive programs, 413
  between levels of management, C–691 to
    C–692
  of need for change, 356–357
  problems in, C–689, C–690 to C–691
  public announcements, 192–193
  of strategic vision, 32, 40–41, 41*n*
  teamwork and, C–644 to C–645
Communications, electronic:
  decentralization and, 379
  for Internet. *See* Internet technology
  strategic alliances in, 173
Community:
  company's duty to, 67–68
  economic development in, C–749 to C–780
  stakeholders in, C–352
Companies:
  campaigns against, C–766 to C–768, C–768*t*
  categories of, 338, 338*n*
  comparisons in benchmarking, 134–135
  competencies of, 120, 122
  as coordinated whole, 4
  in crisis:
    bankruptcy, C–630 to C–632
    effects of terrorism, C–625 to C–626,
      C–627*t,* C–628, C–653 to C–660
    end-game strategies for, 281, 283–285
    liquidation of, 283
    turnaround strategies for, 281–283
  cultures of. *See* Corporate culture
  diversified. *See* Diversification; Diversified
    firms
  domineering, 277, 278
  in e-commerce. *See* Dot-com companies;
    E-commerce

Companies—*Cont.*
  established, acquiring, 303
  ethical duties of, 64–68
  financially distressed, 303
  foreign:
    strategic alliances with, 175, 215–217
    subcontractor factories, C–763 to C–766
  global. *See* Multinational corporations
    (MNCs)
  image of, C–489 to C–490
  local. *See* Local companies
  new. *See* New businesses
  present scope of, 6–7
  resource-based view of, 119, 119n
  risk-averse, 16, 63
  risk-takers, 63, C–703 to C–706
  rivalry between. *See* Cross-company rivalry
  sale of, 315, 316
  small. *See* Single-business enterprises
  sustaining rapid growth, 273–275, *275*
  written constitution for, C–746 to C–747
Company stock:
  employee stock ownership, 41*n*
  IPOs. *See* Initial public offerings
  stock options, 406, C–747 to C–748
  value of, C–279, C–282
Company subcultures, 422–423
Compensation systems:
  ethical behavior and, C–759 to C–775
  examples of, C–409 to C–413, C–619
  executive compensation, profitability and, 412
  guidelines for, 412–413
  importance of attractive packages, 362
  living wage, C–763, C–773
  performance evaluation and, C–725 to C–726,
    C–747 to C–748
  recruitment of employees and, 364–365
  See also Incentives; Reward systems
Competencies, 120, 122
  building, 55–56
  cross-border transfer of, 211–212
  distinctive, 122–123
  in mission statement, 34
  in organization building. *See* Organization
    building
  reshaping, 368–369
  as strategy-shaping factor, 62
  SWOT analysis of, 120, 122–125
  See also Core competencies
Competition:
  barriers to entry and, 84, 86, 87
  case studies of, C–61 to C–73, C–126 to
    C–128, C–127*t*
  character of, 76, 111
  emphasis on cost and service, 266
  evolution of strategy and, 16–17
  foreign:
    example of, C–299 to C–300
    strategic inflection points and, 40
  global. *See* Global competition
  impact of Internet on, 232, 234
  industry attractiveness and, 332
  industry conditions and, C–257 to C–260
  international. *See* International competition
  multicountry (multidomestic), 203–204,
    221–222

Competition—*Cont.*
  multinational. *See* Multinational competition
  near-monopoly, C–452 to C–453
  new businesses and, C–55 to C–56, *C–56,
    C–57,* C–68t
  in price, 161
  quality and, 89–90
  regulatory policies and, C–596 to C–597
  strategy and, 12
  strategy crafting and, 55–56
  unfair practices, C–596 to C–597
  See also Cross-company rivalry
Competitive advantage, 148–197
  competitive strategies and. *See* Competitive
    strategies
  competitive strength assessments and, 143
  cooperative strategies and, 172–177
  cross-business potential for, 340–342, *342*
  cross-business strategic fits and, 53
  cross-company rivalry and, 81–82
  defensive strategies and, 62, 191–193, 197
  differentiation-based, 165–166
  of diversified firms, 291–292
  dominating depth and, 367
  economies of scope and, 301–302
  for fast-followers, 242
  in global markets, 204, 222
  key success factors and, 106, 107t, 108, 108n
  mergers and acquisitions and, 177–178,
    177n, 196
  in multinational competition. *See*
    Multinational competition
  multinational diversification and, 318–325
  offensive strategies and, 185–191, *186,* 197
  organizational imperative for, 383
  price-cost comparisons and, 139–140
  related diversification strategy and, 350
  resources and, 123–125
  strategic alliances and, 172–173, 196
  sustainable, 55
    creating, C–146 to C–148
    Internet technology and, 240–242
    investing in, 286
  timing and, 193–194, 197
  unbundling strategies and, 182–185
  vertical integration and, 178–182, 196
Competitive advantage test, 69
Competitive assets. *See* Strengths
Competitive capabilities:
  boundary decisions and, 184
  collaboration in building, 368, 372–373
  competitive advantage and, 165–166
  corporate level management and, 382
  creating or improving, 268–269
  cross-border transfer of, 211–212
  cross-company rivalry in, 345
  identifying, 118
  leading development of, 445
  low-cost leadership and, 160–161
  in multinational competition, 211–212
  organizational. *See* Organizational capabilities
  in organization building. *See* Organization
    building
  related diversification and, 297
  reshaping, 368–369
  strategic partnerships and, 372–373

Competitive capabilities—*Cont.*
  as strategy-shaping factor, 62
  SWOT analysis of, 120, 121t, 122–125
  in technology. *See* Technological capabilities
  unbundling strategies and, 184
  vertical integration and, 181
Competitive conditions, 61
Competitive deficiencies, 121t
Competitive environment, 232–237, C–546,
  C–547t
Competitive forces, 73
  case study of, C–110, C–111t, C–112t, C–113
  five-forces model of, 79–92, *81*
    buyer bargaining power, 90–92, 244
    cross-company rivalry, 81–84
    entry of new competitors, 84–87
    role of suppliers, 88–90
    substitute products, 87–88
  strategic implications of, 92–93
Competitive intelligence:
  customer information:
    gathering via Internet, C–776 to C–788
    sale of, C–781, *C–780*
  evaluating future position, 104–105, 112
  financial information, 346–347, 346n
  monitoring strategies, 103–104, 105t
  predicting competitors' moves, 105–106
Competitive liabilities. *See* Weaknesses
Competitiveness, time horizon of objectives
  and, 45
Competitive position:
  bases for, 39, 39n
  brand awareness and, C–259 to C–260
  broadening diversification base, 312–314
  enhancing, 286
  evaluating future positioning, 104–105, 112
  fortify-and-defend strategies, 273
  industry attractiveness and, 108, 109
  key success factors and, 141, 144
  market advantage and, 118
  narrowing diversification base, 314–316
  overhaul-and-reposition strategy, 347
  in situation analysis, 140–143, 141t, 146
  strategic alliances and, 174–175
  strategic group mapping and, 100–103, 112
  strategic positioning, 39, 39n, C–462 to
    C–468
  strengthening, 55
  See also Market position
Competitive pressures, 84, 323
Competitive strategies, 150–151, *151,* 152t
  best-cost provider strategies, 150, 151, *151,*
    167–168, 195, 206, 246
  differentiation strategies, 163–167, 195
  focused strategies. *See* Focused strategies
  low-cost provider. *See* Low-cost provider
    strategies
Competitive strength assessment, 140–143, 146
  nine-cell matrix for, 337–338, *338*
  rating scales used in, 141–142, 142t
  tests of, 329, 334–338, 335n, 337n, 351
  weighted ratings in, 336–337, 336t, 337n
Competitive superiority, of resources, 124
Competitors:
  choosing whom to attack, 190–191
  comparison to rivals, C–381 to C–387

Competitors—*Cont.*
  diversity of, 83–84
  entry into markets. *See* Entry of new
    competitors
  equality of, 82–83
  international, 200
  predicting moves of, 105–106
  strengths of, offensive strategies against,
    186–187
  study of. *See* Competitive intelligence
  weaknesses of, 187–188, 286
Components, cost of, 159
Compromise strategies, avoiding, 286
Consulting organizations, for benchmarking,
  136–137
Consumer demographics, C–27 to C–28
  as driving force, 96
  in e-commerce, C–361 to C–362
  examples of, C–156, C–158t, C–158 to C–159
Content follower strategy, for runner-up
  firms, 280
Continuous improvement programs:
  aspects of, 397t, 414–415
  See also Best practices
"Cookies," C–777, C–780, C–787 to C–788
Cooperatives, example of, C–128 to C–133
Cooperative strategies, 172–173, 174–177
Cooperative ventures, 118
Copyright, Internet technology and, C–321 to
  C–338
Core competencies, 122
  characteristics of, 366
  developing and strengthening, 366–367, 385
  in foreign markets, 200
  See also Competencies
Corporate citizenship, 446
Corporate culture, 420–440
  adaptive cultures, 427–429
  as ally or obstacle, 423–424
  case study of, C–614 to C–615, C–617 to
    C–624
  change in. *See* Culture-changing actions
  creating strategy-culture fit, 425,
    429–431, 449
  "culture committee," C–623 to C–624
  diversification and cultural fit, 315
  ethics in, 431–433, 432t, 436–437, 449
    enforcement of, 437, 445–446, 447
    ethics test, 439
    examples of, 433–438, C–487 to C–490
  examples of, 421, C–206 to C–207
  fun in, C–708, C–712 to C–713, C–721 to
    C–722
  innovative, 445
  management style and, C–664 to C–665
  in multinational and global companies,
    443–444
  origin of, 420–423
  performance-oriented spirit in, 438, 440
  problems in, C–347 to C–349
  reward systems and, 406, 421–422, 423,
    425, 445
  as situational factor, 63–64
  social responsibility and, C–487 to C–490
  strategy-supportive, 442–444, 448
  strong vs. weak, 449

Corporate culture—*Cont.*
  strong-culture companies, 424–425
  weak-culture companies, 425–426
  total quality culture, 398, 400
  turnaround strategies for, C–634 to C–635,
    C–645 to C–648
  unhealthy cultures, 426–427
Corporate intrapreneur approach, 25, 26, C–703
Corporate-level management:
  access to, C–632
  in adaptive cultures, 428–429
  changes in, C–652
  demands of unrelated diversification on,
    306–307, 309
  divestiture strategies, 308
  incentives for, C–412
  management teams and, C–520, C–524 to
    C–525
  organizing capability-building by, 382
  role in strategy implementation and
    execution, 359
  strategy crafting in diversified firms,
    291–292, 326
Corporate strategy:
  crafting, 50–51, 53, 53–54
  evaluating, 330, 331
  social responsibility and, 59–61
  strategic mistakes in, 315
  in strategy-making pyramid, 49–50, *52*
Corrective adjustments, 447–448
Cost(s), 138, 154–155, 159, 266
  changes in, 97, 238
  competitive strength and, 335
  of differentiation, 166
  duplication costs, 163–164
  fixed costs, 238
  geographic location and, 155, 159
  of internal activities, 139
  lowering, 200, 268
  of manufacturing, 202, 210, C–170
  market share and, 335n
  variations in, 128
  See also Best-cost provider strategies; Low-
    cost provider strategies; Price-cost
    comparisons
Cost advantage:
  controlling cost drivers, 153–157
  dominating advantage, 277–278
  exchange rates and, 202–203
  offensive strategies and, 187
  value chain and, 157–160
Cost competitiveness, 129, 130, 137–139
Cost-cutting strategies, 282–283, 284, 286
  example of, C–605 to C–606, C–607t to
    C–608t, C–609, C–610t
  related diversification and, 297, 299
Cost drivers, 153–157
Cost-of-entry test, 295, 306, 308, 310
Cost segregation, C–556, C–556n
Councils and associations, 136–137
Countercyclical diversification, 307
Creativity, 364, 392, 444
Crosby's 14 quality steps, 396t
Cross-border activities:
  alliances, local companies in, 311–312
  competitive capabilities and, 211–212

Cross-border activities—*Cont.*
  coordination of, 212, 322–323
  diffusion of technical knowledge, 97, 126
  human resources problems and, C–677 to
    C–694
  organizational structure and, C–684, *C–685,*
    C–686 to C–687
  rivalry, 84
  strategy for, 208t
Cross-business strategic fits, 53, 297–301, 302
  along value chains, 297–301
  decentralization and, 379
  distribution activities, 299
  in diversified firms, 291–292
  managerial and administrative activities,
    300–301
  manufacturing activities, 299
  R&D and technology activities, 298
  related diversification strategies, 297–301, 302
  sales and marketing activities, 299–300
  supply chain activities, 298–299
  See also Strategic fit(s)
Cross-company comparisons, 134–135
Cross-company rivalry:
  alliances and, 175
  case study of, C–28 to C–35, C–29t
  common factors in, 82–83
  comparison of competitors, C–381 to C–387
  as competitive force, 81–84
  differences in value chains, 129–131
  example of, C–170, C–171t
  in fragmented industries, 272
  impact of Internet on, 232, 234
  offensive strategies and, 190–191
  in resources or capabilities, 345
  strategic group mapping and, 103
  See also Competition
Cross-country subsidization, 323, 325
Cross-market subsidization, 213
Cross-unit coordination, 380, 381
Culture (diversity):
  company subcultures and, 422–423
  foreign markets and, 201, 216, C–677 to
    C–694
  human resources problems and, C–677 to
    C–694
  incentive systems and, 413–414
Culture-changing actions, 424, 430, 431
  hostility to, 426
  kinds of, 429
  leader's role in, 442–444
  stakeholders as impetus for, 442
  substantive, 430–431
  symbolic, 430
Customer(s):
  access to, C–457
  attracting, C–634
  bargaining leverage with, 335
  company's duty to, 67
  feedback from:
    complaints, C–781 to C–782
    in e-commerce, C–369 to C–370, C–388 to
      C–389
    listening to angry customers, 443
  in foreign markets, 200, 205
  loyalty of, C–296 to C–297

Customer(s), loyalty of—*Cont.*
  in e-commerce, C–375 to C–377
  new competition and, 85
  major, 89
  needs of, 34
  specializing by type, 273
  See also Buyers
Customer information:
  gathering via Internet, C–776 to C–788
  sale of, C–781, *C–781*
Customer service:
  best practices in, 395
  corporate culture and, 421
  differentiation in, 164
  as differentiation strategy, C–588 to C–589
  focus on, C–609 to C–611
  Internet technology and, 230t, 239
  performance-based incentives for, 410
  as strategy-critical activity, 375
Customization of products. *See* Differentiated
    products; Differentiation strategies
Cyclical factors, 332

Decision making:
  authority for, 377, 378, C–721 to C–723
  boundary decisions, 184
  building skills for, C–720 to C–721
  speed of, 215, 217
Declining industries, strategies for, 269–270, 271
Defensive strategies, 62, 191–193, 197
Delegation approach, to strategy crafting, 23–26
Delegation of authority, 378
Delphi method, 100
Demand:
  in fragmented industries, 271–272
  for Internet services, 226
  for products, 83, 94, 266
Deming's 14 points, 396t
Demographics. *See* Consumer demographics;
    Market demographics
Dependence, 180, 215
Developed markets, C–459 to C–460
Differentiated products:
  buyers and, 165
  for foreign markets, 201–202, 218
  in fragmented industries, 272
  vs. standardized products, 98, 162
Differentiation strategies, 105t, 150, 151, 195
  advantages of, 166–167
  backward integration as, 180
  competitive advantage and, 165–166
  costs of, 166
  customer service as, C–588 to C–589
  for declining industries, 270
  disadvantages of, 167
  for dot-com companies, 246
  in emerging industries, 261
  example of, 165
  focused strategies, 170–171
  global, 205
  performance-based incentives and, 410
  for runner-up companies, 279
  stay-on-the-offensive strategy and, 276
  types of, 163–164
  value and, 166
  in value chain, 164

Digital subscriber line (DSL) technology, 238
Direction-setting, 7, C–36 to C–46
Direction-setting tasks, 30–70
  developing strategic vision, 32–41
  establishing objectives, 41–48
  strategy crafting, 48–58
Disinvestment, 61
Distinctive competencies, 122–123
Distinctive image strategy, 280
Distribution:
  "brick-and-click" strategies and, 250
  case study of, C–188 to C–191
  differentiation in, 164
  entrepreneurship and, *C–143,* C–143 to
    C–144, C–151 to C–152
  example of, C–235 to C–236
  joint ventures in, 214
  key success factors in, 107*t*
  multinational diversification and, 319
  order fulfillment issue, 248
  outsourcing distribution services, C–302 to
    C–320
  related diversification and, 299
  strategic alliances in, C–307
  in value chain, *130*
Distribution channels:
  example of, *C–143,* C–143 to C–144
  Internet as, 252, 253, 255
  Internet technology and, 231–232
  new competition and, 86
Distribution strategy, 208*t*
Diversification, 50–51
  brand diversification, C–251 to C–254,
    C–478, C–479*t* to C–482*t,* C–481 to
    C–483
  combination strategies, 309
  countercyclical, 307
  diversification base, 312–316
  failure of, 307, 345–346
  financial resources and, 308, 309
  growth opportunities and, 292–294
  in products and location, C–472
  profitability and, 340–341
  related diversification strategy. *See* Diversified
    firms
  shareholder value as justification, 294–295,
    306, 325
  tests of, 295, 306, 308
  through joint ventures, 311–312
  through mergers and acquisitions, 298
  through strategic partnerships, 311–312
Diversified firms, 290–327
  business definitions of, 36
  business portfolios of:
    assessment of, C–515 to C–516
    example of, 305–306, 339–341
    industry environment and, C–507 to C–510
    managing, 307, 339–341
    organization of, C–478, C–479*t* to C–482*t,*
      C–481 to C–483
    restructuring, C–510 to C–519
    unrelated groups of related businesses, 309
  combination diversification strategies, 309
  corporate strategy for, 50–51, 53, 53–54
  cross-unit coordination in, 380
  evaluating strategies of, 328–352

Diversified firms—*Cont.*
  business-unit performance, 346–347,
    346*n,* 352
  competitive strength, 334–338, 335*n,* 337*n*
  identifying present strategy, 330, *331,* 351
  industry attractiveness tests. *See* Industry
    attractiveness tests
  procedure for, 329–330
  resource allocation priorities, 330,
    347–348, 352
  resource fit analysis, 342–346
  strategic fit analysis, 340–342, *342*
  strategy crafting, 348–351
  examples of portfolio of, 305–306, 339–341
  levels of strategy managers in, 22
  managing business portfolio of, 307, 339–341
  narrow or broad diversification, 309, 326
  organizational structure of, C–472 to C–475
  post-diversification strategies, 312–325, *313*
    to broaden business base, 312–314, 326
    divestiture strategies, 314–316
    multinational strategies, 318–325, 327
    restructuring and turnaround strategies,
      316–318, 327
  related diversification strategies, 296–303,
    297, 325–326
    capturing strategic-fit benefits, 302–303
    competitive advantage and, 350
    economies of scope, 301–302
    example of, 298, 301
    shareholder value and, 308
  related vs. unrelated businesses,
    295–296, *296*
  shareholder value and, 294–295
  strategies for entering new businesses,
    309–312
  strategy crafting for, 330, 348–351
    by corporate-level management,
      291–292, 326
    diversification opportunities, 350
    managing process of, 350–351
    strategy-making pyramid, 52
    tasks in, 291–292, 326
    using performance test, 348–349, 352
  tests for diversification, 294–295
  unrelated diversification strategies, 303–309,
    304, 326
    example of, 305–306
    pros and cons of, 304, 306–308
    shareholder value and, 308–309
  when to diversify, 292–294
    signaling factors, 294
    single-business advantages, 293
    single-business risks, 293–294
Diversified multinational company (DMNC),
  318, 323, 325
Divestiture:
  of cash hogs, 344
  by diversified firms, 314–316
  harvest-divest strategy, 347
  as performance test, 349
  spin-offs, 315–316, C–207, C–513,
    C–652–653
Division managers, C–401 to C–402
Division-of-labor principle, 375*n*
Dominant-business enterprises, 309

Dominating advantage:
  becoming dominating leader, 275
  brand reputation, 241–242
  cost advantage, 277–278
  domineering companies, 277, 278
  in e-commerce, C–371 to C–381
Dominating depth, 212, 367
Dot-com companies:
  adaptive cultures of, 427–428
  business models and strategies for, 246–249
  as entrepreneurship examples, 16
  future of, 254–255
  intellectual capital and, 361–362
  mistakes of, 238, 242, 254
  rivalry and, 234
Driving forces, 93–94
  categories of, 94, 96–99
  examples of, 95
  link with strategy, 99
"Dumping," 128, 213
Duplication costs, 163–164
Duty, ethical, 64–68

E-commerce:
  business models and strategies, 245–253
    "brick-and-click" strategies, 249–250
    for dot-com enterprises, 246–249
    example of, C–372
    innovation in, 248–249
    order fulfillment issue, 248, 253
    product offerings, 247–248
    for traditional businesses, 230*t,* 250–253
    unconventional, 248–249
  business-to-business (B2B), C–310, C–358
  business-to-consumer (B2C), C–310
  consumer demographics in, C–361 to C–362
  customers and:
    customer loyalty, C–375 to C–377
    feedback, C–369 to C–370, C–388 to C–389
    gathering information, C–776 to C–788
  decentralization and, 378
  diversification into, 313–314
  dominating advantage in, C–371 to C–381
  as driving force, 94, 95
  e-business technologies, 157, 161
  electronic value chains, 161
  global e-sourcing, 236
  initial public offerings in, C–371 to C–372
  Internet technology and, 227, C–321 to
    C–338, C–339 to C–355
  mergers and acquisitions in, C–353 to C–355
  in organization of future, 384
  sales strategy, C–43
  support systems for, 401, 402
  sustained growth in, C–356 to C–391
  traditional businesses and, 231, 232, 234
    business models and strategies, 230t,
      250–253
    innovation, C–343, C–345 to C–347
  transformation of organizational structure by,
    C–428 to C–446
  transportation needs and, C–441 to C–442
Economic features of industry. *See* Industry(ies)
Economic value added (EVA), 9, 9*n,* 43
Economies of scale, 301–302
  alternate suppliers and, 89

Economies of scale—*Cont.*
  as cost driver, 153
  dominating cost advantage and, 277–278
  entry of new competitors and, 84–85
  in fragmented industries, 272
  globalization and, 94
  intangible, C–457 to C–458
  in multinational competition, 210, 214
  in multinational diversification, 319
Economies of scope:
  competitive advantage and, 301–302
  in multinational diversification, 319
Efficiency, 97, 229–232
Electronic value chains, 161
Emerging-country markets:
  competition in, 217–218, 222–223
  opportunities in, C–698, C–700 to C–701
  strategies for local companies, *219,* 219–221
    change and, 220–221
    company expertise, 220
    global competition and, 221
    home-field advantages, 219–220
Emerging industries, strategies for, 260–262
Emerging markets:
  developed markets and, C–459 to C–460
  global competition in, 217–218
Employee(s):
  assumptions about, C–721 to C–723
  authority and independence of, 376–380
  commitment of, rewards and, 409–410
  company's duty to, 66–67
  cooperation of, 356, 359
  "employees first" organizational structure,
    C–569, *C–571,* C–572
  empowerment of, 378–379, 400
    decision-making authority, C–721 to C–723
    empowering champions, 444–445
    example of, C–410 to C–411
    management control and, 379, 379*n,* 403,
      404–405, C–724 to C–725
    mistakes in, C–741
    systems to monitor, 403
  encouraging creativity and innovation, 364, 392
  in high-performance cultures, 438, 440
  hiring and selection, C–726 to C–728
  job rotation and, C–720 to C–721
  maltreatment of, C–765 to C–766
  managing, problems in, C–677 to C–694
  nonunion, C–395
  peer evaluation of, 404–405
  productivity of, C–624, C–624*t*
  recruiting and retaining, 361–365, C–615,
    C–617
  response to self-direction, C–748 to C–750
  role of employee training, 369
  strategic role of training, 369
  suggestions of, 408
  TQM and, 397–398, 397*t*
  unionized, C–619 to C–621
  working conditions and, C–759 to C–775
Employee relations:
  principles of, C–409 to C–410
  problems in, C–688
  See also Labor relations
Employee stock ownership, 41*n*
Empowerment. *See* Employee(s)

End-game strategies, 281, 283–285
End-run offensives, 188–189
Entrepreneurship:
  in adaptive cultures, 427
  business spin-offs, C–751 to C–752
  case study of, C–138 to C–152
  distribution and, *C–143,* C–143 to C–144,
    C–151 to C–152
  in emerging industries, 261
  on Internet:
    business models and strategies for, 245–253
    mistakes in, 242–245
  strategic vision and, 39, 39*n*
  strategy crafting and, 13–16
Entry of new competitors:
  barriers to. *See* Barriers to entry
  as competitive force, 84–87
  cost-of-entry test, 295, 306, 308, 310
  as driving force, 97
  in emerging industries, 262
  See also New businesses
Environmental issues:
  in manufacturing, C–418
  in poultry industry, C–581 to C–583, *C–584*
  in power plant operations, C–705 to C–706
  subcontractor factories, C–765
  See also Societal considerations
Environmental scanning, 99–100
Erosion period, 185–186, *186*
Ethical behavior:
  employee working conditions, C–759 to C–775
  social responsibility and, 61, 68, 432
Ethics:
  in administering reward systems, 412, 413
  benchmarking and, 137
  company's ethical duties, 64–68
  competitive intelligence and, 104
  in corporate culture. *See* Corporate culture
  enforcement of, 437, 445–446, 447
  ethical issues in foreign markets, 436
  in fraternal organizations, C–74 to C–94
  of gathering customer information, C–776 to
    C–788
  in marketing, C–263 to C–278
  standards of CEO, 445
  strategy and, 63, 64–68, 445–446
  test of, 439
  unethical behavior:
    example of, 65–66
    strategy and, 64–68
  See also Codes of ethics
European Union, 214
EVA (economic value added), 9, 9*n,* 43
Evaluation:
  as managerial task, 19–20
  by peers, 404–405
  performance evaluation, 116–117, C–725 to
    C–726, C–747 to C–748
  skills required for, 28
  of strategy, 116–117, 146
Exit of firms, 83, 97
Expansion:
  example of, C–566 to C–568
  global, reasons for, 200
  from market niches, C–387 to C–390
  new products or segments, C–397 to C–398

Experience curve effects:
  competitive strength and, 335*n*
  as cost driver, 153–155
  in emerging industries, 260
  locational advantage in, 210
  in manufacturing, 78–79, 79, 79*n*
  in multinational diversification, 319
  new competition and, 85
Expertise:
  cross-border transfer of, 212
  emerging-country markets and, 220
  identifying, 117
  related diversification and, 297, 324
Exporting:
  example of, C–236 to C–240
  export markets, C–258 to C–260
  strategies for, 205–206, C–575 to C–577
External factors (conditions):
  industry attractiveness and, 332
  reshaping competencies and capabilities and,
    368–369
  threats, 121*t,* 127

Fast-followers, 242
Financial objectives, 9–10
  cash management systems and, C–661 to
    C–676
  examples of, 11
  strategic objectives and, 43, 45
  strategy implementation for, C–661 to C–676
  turnaround strategies, C–634, C–640 to
    C–643, C–653, C–658, C–659*t,* C–660*t*
Financial performance, of MNCs, C–707, *C–707*
  to *C–711*
Financial records:
  financial statements, C–48, C–49, C–59, C–60
  information found in, 346–347, 346*n*
  proprietary information, C–580 to C–581
Financial resources:
  capital requirements, 85, 239–240, 243,
    C–390
  diversification and, 308, 309
  government bailouts, C–656 to C–657
  venture capital, 239–240, 243
Financial VP, 21
First-mover advantages, 45, 193–194
  in emerging industries, 262
  myth of, 194, 241–242
  stay-on-the-offensive strategy and, 276
  switching costs and, 241, 254
Five-forces model, 79–92, *81*
  cross-company rivalry, 81–84
  entry of new competitors, 84–87
  role of suppliers, 88–90
  seller-buyer relationships, 90–92, 244
  substitute products, 87–88
Fixed costs, 238
Focused strategies, 105*t,* 150, 151, 168–172,
    195–196
  advantages of, 171
  business definition and, 36
  for declining industries, 269–270
  differentiation-based, 170–171
  disadvantages of, 171–172
  for e-commerce, 248
  example of, 170

Focused strategies—*Cont.*
  global, 205
  low-cost strategies, 169–170
  for market segments, 269–270
  for regional niches, C–552 to C–564
  vacant-niche strategy, 280
Focusers, 277
Folktales, 421
Foreign companies:
  strategic alliances with, 175, 215–217
  subcontractor factories, C–763 to C–766
Foreign competition:
  example of, C–299 to C–300
  strategic inflection points and, 40
Foreign exchange, 202–203, C–222 to C–223
Foreign markets:
  cross-market subsidization and, 213
  culture (diversity) and, 201, 216, C–677 to
    C–694
  customers in, 200, 205
  demographics of, 201
  emerging markets, 217–218
  ethical issues, 436
  joint ventures and, 311–312
  opportunities in, C–698, C–700 to C–701
  products made for, 201–202, 218
  risks in. *See* Risk(s)
  self-contained, 203–204
  situational factors in, 201–203, 204, 221
  strategy options for, 204–209
    example of, C–217 to C–219
    export strategies, 205–206
    franchising strategies, 206
    licensing strategies, 206
    multicountry vs. global, 205, 206–207,
      208*t*, 209
    situation-driven, 201–203, 221
  See also Multinational diversification
    strategies
"Formula facilities," 272
Fortify-and-defend strategies, 273, 276–277, 281,
  347
Forward channel value chains, 131–132, 138,
  155
Forward integration, 180–181
Fragmented industries, 271–273
Franchising:
  business units, C–292
  case study of, C–203 to C–224
  international competition and, C–214 to
    C–215
  strategy for, 14, 205, 206
Fraternal organizations, C–74 to C–94
Full integration, 179
Fully integrated firms, 34
Functional area managers, 22, 56–57
Functional departments:
  authority and independence of, 376–380
  mission statements for, 37–38
  as organizational building block, 374
Functional strategy, 49–50, 52, 56–57

Global companies. *See* Multinational
  corporations
Global competition, 198–223
  acquisitions and, 178

Global competition—*Cont.*
  case study of, C–225 to C–244
  cooperative strategies and, 172
  cross-market subsidization and, 213
  defined, 204
  as driving force, 94, 96
  in emerging markets, 217–218
  exchange rates and, 202–203
  international competition compared, 200
  Internet and, 237
  local companies in, 219, 219–221
  market conditions and, 201–203
    exchange rates, 202–203
    government requirements, 203
    locational advantages, 202
  multicountry competition compared, 203–204
  profit sanctuaries and, 213, 222
  reasons for expansion, 200
  strategic alliances in, 174, 213–217, 222
    examples of, 216
    optimizing, 215–217
    risks of, 177, 214–215
  strategy options for, 204–209
    example of, C–460 to C–468
    export strategies, 205–206
    franchising strategies, 206
    licensing strategies, 206
    options compared, 206–207, 208*t*
  success in, C–458 to C–459
  See also Competition; International
    competition; Multinational competition
Global competitors, 200
Globalization, 199
Globalization of industry:
  as driving force, 94, 96
  example of, C–463 to C–460
  indicators of, C–456 to C–458
Global markets:
  achieving growth in, C–447 to C–469, C–701,
    C–702, C–703 to C–706
  competition in. *See* Global competition
  competitive advantage in, 204, 222
  in fragmented industries, 272
  organization building for, 383
Global strategies, 205, 207, 208*t*
Goals, 42*n*
Goodness of fit test, 69
Government(s):
  financial bailout by, C–656 to C–657
  foreign, 202, 203, 213–214
  political issues, C–418
  See also Regulatory policies
Group gatherings, 430
Growth:
  achieving in global markets, C–447 to C–469,
    C–701, *C–702,* C–703 to C–706
  opportunities for:
    diversification and, 292–294
    in new markets, C–295 to C–296
    product line strategy and, C–201 to C–202
  organizational change and, C–752, *C–753,*
    C–754 to C–755
  rapid, sustaining, 273–275, 275
  sustained, challenges of, C–356 to C–391
Growth rates:
  industry growth rate, 96

Growth rates—*Cont.*
  market growth rate, 332, C–155, C–157*t,*
    C–158*t*
Growth strategy(ies), 14, 279–280
  for global markets, C–447 to C–469, C–701,
    C–702, C–703 to C–706
  growth-via-acquisition, 279–280, C–470 to
    C–501
  organizational structure and, 373–374, 373*n*
  product lines and, C–184 to C–202, C–267 to
    C–268
  for rapid company growth, 273–275, 275
  through outsourcing, C–302 to C–320
Growth-via-acquisition strategy, 279–280, C–470
  to C–501
Guerilla offensives, 189

Harvest-divest strategy, 347
Harvesting, 283–285
Hourly wages, 406
Human assets, 118, 118*n,* 122
Human resources:
  economies of downsizing, 299–300
  flexibility and, 408
  in high-performance cultures, 438, 440
  hiring and selection, C–726 to C–728
  Internet technology and, 230*t*
  job security, C–728 to C–729
  low-cost provider strategies in, 154
  in low-wage countries, 202
  recruitment and retention, 361–365
  sales representatives, C–41 to C–43, C–43*t*
  staffing, 360–365
  staff management problems, C–677 to C–694
  strategies for, 15
  transfer of knowledge and, 345–346
  turnaround strategies for, C–645 to C–648
  union vs. nonunion labor, 155
  use of, C–348
  in value chain, *130*
  See also Employee(s); Managers

Image:
  brand reputation, C–43 to C–44, C–44*t*
  of company, C–489 to C–490
  distinctive image strategy, 280
Immediate abandonment strategies, 281
Inbound logistics. *See* Logistics
Incentives, 357, *358,* 415
  cultural differences and, 413–414
  nonmonetary, 405, 408, 413
  performance-based, 409–410, 412
  performance evaluation and, C–725 to C–726
  production incentives, C–408, C–411
  programs in manufacturing, C–411 to C–412
  results-based, 411–412
  See also Compensation systems; Reward
    systems
Industry(ies):
  change in, 93–100, 111–112
    changing conditions, C–413 to C–416,
      C–423 to C–427
    driving forces and, 93–99
    environmental scanning and, 99–100
    in high-velocity markets, 263, *264*

Industry(ies), change in—*Cont.*
   rapid environmental change, C–698,
     C–699, C–700 to C–706
  competitive structure of:
   case study of, C–104 to C–110, C–105*t,*
     C–108*t,* C–109*t*
   Internet technology and, 237
  conditions in, 83
   changes in, C–413 to C–416, C–423 to
     C–427
   competition and, C–257 to C–260
   entrepreneurship and, C–140 to C–144
   focused strategy and, 171
   new businesses and, C–153 to C–183
   strategy changes and, C–550 to C–551
  definition of term, 77
  economic features of, 76, 111
   experience curve effects and, 78–79,
     79, 79*n*
   in industry and competitive analysis, 76,
     77–79, 78*t,* 79, 80*t,* 110*t*
   sample profile of, 77, 78*t*
   strategic importance of, 80*t*
  effects of Internet technology on, C–321 to
    C–338
  emerging, 260–262
  entering, 291
  establishing industry standards, C–542 to
    C–543
  fragmented, 271–273
  key success factors in, 106, 107*t,* 108, 108*n*
  maturing, 266–269
  service industries, markets in, C–559 to
    C–560
  stagnant or declining, 269–270, 271
  strategies for leaders, 275–277
  terrorist crisis and, C–625 to C–626, C–627*t,*
    C–628, C–653 to C–660
Industry and competitive analysis, 72–112,
  75, 110*t*
  analytical sequence, 73–74, 75
  competitive forces in, 79–93
  competitive intelligence, 103–106
  economic features of industry in, 76, 77–79,
    78*t,* 79, 80*t,* 110*t*
  industry attractiveness, 108–109, 112
  key success factors, 106, 107*t,* 108, 108*n*
  methods of, 76
  process of, 109–111, 110*t*
  role of industry change, 93–100
  strategic group mapping, 100–103
Industry attractiveness:
  competitive forces and, 92–93
  in industry and competitive analysis,
    108–109, 112
  new competition and, 87
  as strategy-determining factor, 61
  vigorous price competition and, 244
Industry attractiveness tests, 329, 331–334, 351
  attractiveness of mix, 332, 334
  diversification and, 295, 306, 308
  individual industries, 331, 332–333
  weighted ratings, 331–332, 333–334, 333*t*
Industry environment:
  diversified firms and, C–507 to C–510
  evaluating, 287

Industry environment—*Cont.*
  example of, C–476, C–477*t,* C–478
  rapid change in, C–698, *C–699,* C–700 to
    C–706
Industry growth rate, 96
Industry trends:
  consolidation trends, C–560, *C–561*
  example of, C–586 to C–588
  product innovation, C–154 to C–155
Industry value chains, *130,* 131–133, 132
  cross-industry chains, 334
  impact of Internet on, 233, *233*
  of maturing industries, 267–268
Information:
  access to, 136, 408
  buyer bargaining power and, 91
  customer information:
   gathering via Internet, C–776 to C–788
   sale of, C–781, *C–781*
  in financial records, 346–347, 346*n*
  importance to strategic leadership, 441
  proprietary, C–580 to C–581
Information systems, 403–405
  customer information, C–776 to C–788
  developing proposals for, C–318 to C–319
  information sharing and, C–725
  logistics and, C–583 to C–586
  online, 400
Initial public offerings (IPOs), 239
  in e-commerce, C–371 to C–372
  examples of, C–256 to C–257, C–514 to
    C–515, C–652 to C–653
Innovation:
  in corporate environment, 442–445
  in designing policies and procedures, 392
  in e-commerce:
   business models and strategies, 248–249
   by traditional businesses, C–343, C–345 to
     C–347
  in employee recruitment, 364–365
  encouraging, in employees, 364, 392
  in marketing, 97, 247
  in product development. *See* Product
    innovation
  in value chains, 267–268
Insular thinking, 426–427
Intangible assets, 118
Intellectual capital, 361–362
Intellectual property rights, C–322 to C–323
Intellectual resources, 118, 118*n,* 122
Internal development, 310–311, 368
International Benchmarking Clearinghouse,
  136, 137
International competition:
  in emerging-country markets, 217–218,
    222–223
  entering new markets, 268, C–45 to C–46,
    C–46t
  franchising, C–214 to C–215
  global competition compared, 200, 221
  in maturing industries, 267
  See also Competition; Global competition;
    Multinational competition
International competitors, 200
International markets, 383, C–379 to C–381
International trade restrictions, 86

Internet, 224–255
  competitive environment and, 232–237
   barriers to entry, 234–235
   buyer bargaining power, 235–236
   competitive rivalry, 232, 234
   industry's competitive structure, 237
   seller-supplier collaboration, 90, 236–237
   supplier bargaining power, 236
  demand for services, 226
  as driving force, 94, 95, 96
  e-commerce models and strategies. *See*
    E-commerce
  effects on business models, C–324 to C–326
  electronic value chains and, 161
  gathering customer information by, C–776 to
    C–788
  online auctions, C–356 to C–391
  online information systems, 400, 403–405
  online training courses, 369
  privacy policies for, C–782 to C–787
  profitability and, 341
  strategic mistakes by early entrepreneurs,
    242–245
   competing on price only, 243–244
   ignoring low barriers to entry, 243
   selling below cost, 244–245
  strategy crafting for, 50–51
  technology for. *See* Internet technology
  as threat to industry, C–322 to C–323
  transfer of expertise by, 212
  use for employee recruitment, 364
  value chain and, 157, 158
Internet-related businesses. *See* E-commerce
Internet speed, 428
Internet technology:
  building, as strategy-critical activity, 375
  capabilities of, 247
  cash management systems, C–661 to C–676
  competing technologies, 228–229, 228*t*
  demand for services, 226
  direct selling to end-users and, 235–236,
    252–253
  effects on industries, C–321 to C–338
  for gathering customer information, C–776 to
    C–788
  impact on value chains, 229–232, 230*t*
   benefits, 232
   distribution channel efficiency, 231–232
   illustration of, 233, *233*
   internal operating efficiency, 229–231
   supply chain efficiency, 229
  inbound logistics and, 230*t,* C–428 to C–446
  for online auctions, C–360
  opportunity and, 254
  outbound logistics and, C–667, C–668, *C–668*
  participants and, 226–229
  proprietary, 241
  strategy-shaping features of, 237–240, 255
  suppliers and. *See* Suppliers
  suppliers of services, 226–227
  support systems, 400–402
  sustainable competitive advantage and,
    240–242
  See also E-commerce
Intranet, 95
Invest-and-grow strategy, 347

Investments:
  of diversified companies, 53–54, 292
  profitability and, C–346
  in research and development, 264–265
  in sustainable competitive advantage, 286
Job seekers, 364–365
Joint ventures:
  in distribution, 214
  diversification by, 311–312
  example of, C–239 to C–240
The Journey project, C–85 to C–91, *C–87, C–90*
Juran Trilogy, 396*t*

Kaizen, 398
Key resource imports, 155
Key success factors (KSFs):
  competitive advantage and, 106, 107*t*, 108,
    108*n*
  competitive position and, 141, 144
  competitive strength and, 335*n*
  determining, 106, 108, 108*n*, 112
  large size, 277–278
  in online retailing, C–358
  resource fits and, 344–345
  types of, 107*t*

Labor relations:
  anti-company campaigns, C–766 to C–768,
    C–768*t*
  code of conduct for, *C–769*
  evolution of labor practices, C–768 to C–770
  foreign subcontractors, C–764 to C–766
  nonunion employees, C–395
  unionized employees, C–619 to C–621
  union vs. nonunion labor, 155
  See also Employee(s); Employee relations
Late-mover advantages, 193
Layered management hierarchies, 382
Leadership, 357, *358*
  in corporate citizenship, 446
  by example, 443
  leadership development academies, 362–363
  leadership styles:
    example of, C–621 to C–622
    strategy implementation and, *358,*
      358–359, 384
  origin of corporate culture and, 420–421, 448
  in strong-culture companies, 425
  See also Strategic leadership
Learning:
  collective learning, 11, *12*
  cost savings and, 154–155
  managing learning process, 217
  profitability and, 340
  support systems and, 402, 402*n*
  See also Experience curve effects
Leveraged buyout, 316
Life-cycle hypothesis, 93, 93*n*
Lifestyles, foreign markets and, 201
Linked activities, 155
Liquidation, 283
Local companies:
  attacking, 191
  cross-market subsidization and, 213
  in global competition, *219,* 219–221

Local companies—*Cont.*
  business models or market niches, 220–221
  expertise and, 220
  home-field advantages, 219–220
  successful initiatives, 221
  as partners in cross-border alliances, 311–312
  Strategies for emerging-country markets, *219,*
    219–221
Location, geographic:
  costs and, 155, 159
  diversification in, C–472
  end-run offensives for, 188–189
  focusing on limited area, 272
  operating procedures and, 391–392
  protection of, Internet and, 234
  regions, niche strategy for, C–552 to C–564
Locational advantages, 202, 210–211, 219–220
Location and construction strategy, 14
Logistics:
  inbound, *130,* 230*t,* C–428 to C–446
  information systems and, C–583 to C–586
  infrastructure for, C–431 to C–432
  Internet technology and, 230*t,* C–428 to
    C–446, C–667, C–668, *C–668*
  outbound, 130, 230*t,* C–428 to C–446
Long-jump strategies, 274, *275*
Long-lasting resources, 124
Long-range objectives, 10, 32, 42*n,* 45–46
"Look-to-buy" ratio, 247
Low-cost leadership, 160–161, 270, 276
Low-cost producer status, 210
Low-cost provider strategies, 150, 151, 194–195
  advantages of, 161–162
  case study of, C–590 to C–614
  cost advantage and, 153–160
  disadvantages of, 162–163
  for dot-com companies, 246
  in emerging industries, 261
  in fragmented industries, 272–273
  global, 205
  illustration of, 154
  performance-based incentives and, 410
  for runner-up companies, 279
  success in achieving, 160–161
  Lower-echelon managers, 24, 359

Macroenvironment, 73, 74
Major suppliers, 89
Malcolm Baldrige National Quality Award, 393,
    396*t,* 397, 399
Management:
  assembling management team, C–102, *C–103,*
    C–104, *C–104*
  change in:
  communicating need for, 356–357
  at corporate level, C–651
  team changes, C–418 to C–419, *C–420*
  as turnaround strategy, C–544 to C–545
  communication between levels of, C–691 to
    C–692
  control by, 379, 379*n,* 403, 404–405, C–724
    to C–725
  decisions as cost driver, 156–157
  examples of management style, C–621 to
    C–622, C–664 to C–665

Management—*Cont.*
  layered hierarchies, 382
  philosophy of, C–408 to C–409, C–563 to
    C–564
  professional, transition to, C–364 to C–366
  signs of good management, 4–6
  staff management problems, C–677 to
    C–694
  strategic role of, C–757 to C–758
  of value chains, 149, 375
Management teams:
  achieving dominance and, 367
  assembling, C–102, *C–103,* C–104, *C–104*
  business-development teams, C–723
  changes in, C–418 to C–419, *C–420*
  peer-based control of, 404–405
  roadblocks to building, C–564
  self-directed, C–745 to C–750
  self-managed, 407
  strength of, 360–361
  top-level management, C–520, C–524 to
    C–525
Managerial tasks:
  evaluation as, 19–20
  in implementing and executing strategy,
    18–19, 355–356, 357, *358,* 388–415
    best practices and continuous improvement,
      393–400
    business strategy, 56
    linking budgets to strategy, 390–391
    policies and procedures, 391–392, 393
    reward systems, 405–414
    strategy implementers, 429
    support systems, 400–405
  in organizational units, 21–22
  related diversification and, 300
Managers:
  budgetary responsibilities of, 390–391
  of business units, C–401 to C–402
  circulation of strategic plans to, 18
  cooperation of, 359
  culture change and, 431
  demands on time of, 20–21
  in diversified firms, 341
  entrepreneurial, 13–16
  evaluating, 363
  functional strategy crafting by, 56–57
  future-oriented concepts and, 32
  industry and competitive analysis by, 111
  leadership roles of, 440–441
  levels of, 22
  lower-echelon, 24, 359
  middle managers, 21–23
  need for strategic vision, 7
  objective setting required for, 9
  personal views as situational factor, 62–63
  pressure to achieve short-range objectives,
    43, 45
  proactive, 4
  "relationship managers," 380–381
  responsibilities for strategy, 21–23
Managing by walking around (MBWA), 441–442
Manufacturing:
  best-cost provider strategy in, 169
  build-to-order, 160, 231–232, 253
  business units in, C–402 to C–406

Manufacturing—*Cont.*
  case study of, C–392 to C–427
  competitive strategies in, 152*t*, 153
  cross-business strategic fits in, 299
  differentiation in, 164
  environmental issues in, C–418
  experience curve effects and, 78–79, 79*n*
  impact of Internet on, 233, *233*
  incentive programs in, C–411 to C–412
  information systems for, 404
  key success factors in, 107*t*
  low-cost provider strategies in, 154
  performance-based incentives in, 412
  production processes, C–407 to C–408
  strategic alliances in, 175
  subcontractor factories, C–764 to C–766
  vertical integration and, 181, 182
Manufacturing costs, 202, 210, C–170
Market(s):
  developed, C–459 to C–460
  developed vs. emerging, C–459 to C–460
  domestic and international, 383, C–379 to
    C–381
  export markets, C–258 to C–260
  opportunities for growth in, C–295 to C–296
  in service industries, C–559 to C–560
  turbulent, 262–266, 264
  See also Emerging-country markets; Foreign
    markets; Global markets
Market challengers, 277
Market conditions:
  adaptation to, 15–16
  best-cost provider strategies and, 168
  budget reallocation and, 390–391
  differentiation strategy and, 166–167
  examples of:
    food industries, *C–117,* C–117 to C–126,
      C–118
    leisure industries, C–163 to C–166
    future conditions, 16–17, 17
    global competition and. *See* Global
      competition
    high-velocity markets, 262–266, *264*
    size and growth rate, 332, C–155, C–157*t*,
      C–158*t*
Market demographics, 201, C–212 to C–214
Marketing:
  approaches to, C–198 to C–201
  celebrity endorsements, C–511, C–518
  competitive strategies in, 152*t*, 153
  differentiation in, 164
  in emerging industries, 260
  entrepreneurship and, C–142 to C–143
  ethics in, C–263 to C–278
  innovation in, 97, 247
  Internet technology and, 230*t*
  introduction of new products, C–216
  key success factors in, 107*t*
  owner as spokesman, C–573 to C–574, *C–574*
  related diversification and, 299–300
  results-based incentives in, 412
  revamping value chain and, 157, *158*
  strategies in, 15, 208*t*
    case studies of, C–38 to C–41, C–39*t*,
      C–97, C–101 to C–102
    for regional niche, C–562

Marketing, strategies in—*Cont.*
    turnaround strategies, C–632 to C–634,
      C–638 to C–640
    unconventional advertising, C–611, C–612
Marketing VP, 21
Market leaders, 190–191, 271
Market niches, 220–221, C–387 to C–390,
  C–552 to C–564
Market niche strategies. *See* Focused strategies
Market opportunities. *See* Opportunity(ies)
Market position:
  competitive approaches and, 150–151
  fortifying and extending, 273
  Internet and, 251–252
  rivalry and, 83
  See also Competitive position
Market segments:
  creating, 189
  domestic, C–574 to C–575
  ethics and, C–272 to C–274
  example of, C–538, C–540 to C–541
  expansion into, C–397 to C–398
  in fast-food industry, C–208 to C–212
  focused strategies for, 269–270
  international, C–575 to C–577
Market share, 279, 335, 335*n*
Market value added (MVA), 10, 10*n*, 43
Maturing industries, 266–269
Medium-jump strategies, 274, *275*
Mentoring, C–563
Merchandising strategy, 15
Mergers and acquisitions:
  acquisition of existing business, 309–310
  building shareholder value by, C–520 to C–535
  business structure and, C–438 to C–441
  case study of, C–116 to C–137, C–470 to
    C–501, C–502 to C–535
  company subcultures and, 422–423
  competing technologies and, 228
  competitive advantage and, 177–178,
    177*n*, 196
  cross-selling opportunities and, C–663 to
    C–664
  diversification by, 298
  in e-commerce, C–353 to C–355
  in emerging industries, 261
  example of, 179
  in maturing industries, 267, 268
  megamergers, C–476, C–477*t*
  in multinational corporations, 422–423,
    C–470 to C–501
  organizational structure and, C–525, C–527 to
    C–528
  rivalry and, 84
  by runner-up firms, 279–280
  in unrelated diversification, 303–304
Middle managers, roles of, 21–23, 359
Mission statement, 32–38
  business definition in, 35–37
  elements of, 34–35
  examples of, 8, 37–38
  for functional departments, 37–38
  profit and, 33
  social causes in, C–487 to C–488
  social responsibility and, 61
  strategic vision contrasted, 6–7

Monetary awards, 407
Motivation (motivational practices):
  by corporate culture, 423–424
  examples of, 405–406
  positive and negative considerations, 409, 440
  problems in, C–689 to C–690, C–692
  in reward systems, 405–409, 415
  value of strategic vision, 41*n*
Multicountry (multidomestic) competition,
  203–204, 221–222
Multicountry strategies, 205, 206–207, 208*t*, 209
Multinational competition:
  competitive advantage in, 209–212
    competencies and capabilities, 211–212
    competitors, 200
    coordinating activities, 212
    examples of strategies, 209
    locational advantages and, 210–211
  economies of scale in, 210, 214
  See also Competition; Global competition;
    International competition
Multinational corporations (MNCs):
  case study of, C–695 to C–731
    company background, C–696 to C–698,
      C–699
    company report card, C–729 to C–731,
      C–730
    compensation and evaluation, C–725 to
      C–726
    corporate values, C–707 to C–709, C–712
      to C–719
    decentralization, C–719 to C–725
    financial performance, C–707, *C–707* to
      C–711
    hiring and selection, C–726 to C–728
    industry environment and, C–698, *C–699,*
      C–700 to C–706
    job security, C–728 to C–729
    operations, C–706 to C–707
  company subcultures in, 422–423
  culture change efforts in, 443–444
  global economy and, C–760
  mergers and acquisitions in, 422–423, C–470
    to C–501
  reward systems in, 413–414
Multinational diversification strategies:
  characteristics of, 318
  opportunities in, 318–325, 327
    brand-name leverage, 322
    combined effects of, 323, 325
    coordination of activities, 322–323
    cross-business or cross-country
      subsidization, 323
    economies of scale and, 319
    economies of scope and, 319
    example of, 320–321, 324
    experience curve effects and, 319
    resource transfer and, 321–322
Multiple strategy horizons, 274–274
Muscle-flexing strategy, 277, 278
Mutual benefit, in strategic alliances, 216
MVA (market value added), 10, 10*n*, 43

"Name-your-own-price," 249
Needs-based positioning, 39*n*
"Network effects," 241, 242

New businesses:
  case study of, C–50 to C–60
  competition and, C–55 to C–56, C–56, *C–57,*
    C–68t
  in emerging industries, 260
  with growth potential, 273–274
  industry conditions and, C–153 to C–183
  internal start-ups, 310–311
  strategies for, C–592 to C–595
  strategies for entering, 309–312
Nine-cell matrix, 337–338, 338
No-layoff policies, 405–406, C–621, C–681 to
    C–682
Nonmonetary incentives, 405, 408, 413
Not-for-profit organizations, 22

Objectives. *See* Financial objectives; Strategic
    objectives
Objective setting, 9–10
  as direction-setting task, 41–48
  top-down, 47–48, 58
  types of objectives, 42–43, 42n, 45
Offensive strategies, 62, 185–191, *186,* 197
  to build market share, 279
  for businesses in crisis, 281
  choice of rival and, 190–191
  competitor strengths and, 186–187
  competitor weaknesses and, 187–188, 286
  end-run offensives, 188–189
  guerilla offensives, 189
  in high-velocity markets, 263, *264*
  preemptive strikes, 189–190
  simultaneous initiatives, 188
  stay-on-the-offensive strategy, 276
Operating strategy:
  crafting, 57
  evolution of, C–421 to C–422
  in strategy-making pyramid, 49–50, 52
Operating unit managers, 22, 57
Operations:
  activities driven by, 355
  call center operations, C–314 to C–315
  corporate intrapreneur approach in, C–703
  environmental issues in, C–705 to C–706
  evaluating, C–688 to C–694
  Internet technology for, 229–231, 240–241
  in multinational corporations, C–706 to C–707
  in value chain, *130*
  vertically integrated, C–577 to C–578, *C–579*
Operations strategy, 15
Opportunity(ies):
  buildout opportunities, 227
  cross-selling opportunities, C–663 to C–664
  for growth:
    diversification and, 292–294, 350
    in new markets, C–295 to C–296
    product line strategy and, C–201 to C–202,
      C–267 to C–268
  identifying, 126
  industry attractiveness and, 332
  Internet technology and, 254
  market opportunities, 227
    emerging-country markets, C–698, C–700
      to C–701
    growth in new markets, C–295 to C–296

Opportunity(ies), market opportunities—*Cont.*
  in SWOT analysis, 121*t,* 125–127
  in multinational diversification strategies,
    318–325
  for product innovation, *C–736,* C–737, C–738
    to C–739
  resource allocation and, 347–348, 352
  as situational factor, 62
Order fulfillment:
  in e-commerce, 248, 253
  growth strategy and, C–307 to C–310
  as strategy-critical activity, 374
Organizational assets, 118
Organizational capabilities, 107*t,* 265,
    367–368, 385
Organizational models, hybrid, C–348
Organizational strategy, 208*t*
Organizational structure(s):
  of business units, C–402 to C–405, C–665 to
    C–666, *C–666*
  centralized, 376–377
  cross-border activities and, C–684, C–685,
    C–686 to C–687
  decentralized, 378–380, C–719 to C–725
  of diversified firms, C–472 to C–475
  "employees first," C–569, *C–571,* C–572
  example of, C–398, C–401
  functional, 375
  future directions, 382–384, 386
  matching structure and strategy, 369–382,
    370, 385
  mergers and acquisitions and, C–525, C–527
    to C–528
  reorganization of, C–441 to C–443
  strategic objectives and, 47–48
  team-based, C–719 to C–720
  tendency to follow growth strategy, 373–374,
    373*n*
  transformation through e-business, C–428 to
    C–446
Organizational units:
  budget reallocations in, 391
  managerial tasks in, 21–22
  mission statements for, 37–38
  as organizational building block, 374
Organization building, 357, *358,* 359–382,
    360, 385
  competencies and capabilities, 360, 365–369
    change in conditions or strategy, 368–369
    core competencies, 366–367
    organizational capabilities, 367–368
    role of employee training, 369
  for international and global markets, 383
  matching structure and strategy, 360,
    369–382, *370*
    building blocks of, 373–376, 373*n*
    cross-unit coordination of, 380, 381
    organizational structure and, 376–380
    organizing effort of, 382
    outsourcing and, 371–372
    partnering and, 372–373
    responsibility for collaboration, 380–381
    strategy-critical activities, 369–371
  staffing:
    examples of, 362–365
    management team, 360–361

Organization building—*Cont.*
  recruitment and retention, 361–365
Outbound logistics. *See* Logistics
Outsourcing, 182–183, 196
  advantages of, 184
  capability-building and, 368
  of credit and collections, C–315 to C–316
  developing proposals for, C–302 to C–320
  disadvantages of, 185
  of distribution services, C–302 to C–320
  in high-velocity markets, 265
  Internet technology and, 234
  of noncritical activities, 371–372
  vertical integration and, 156
Overhaul-and-reposition strategy, 347
Owners/shareholders, duty to, 65

Partial integration, 179
Partially integrated firms, 34
Payoffs, 41, 83
Pay-per-use fees, 248–249
Peers, 404–405, 423
Perceived value, 166, 166*n*
Performance:
  boosting, 291
  business-unit performance, 346–347, 346*n,*
    352
  differentiation and, 165
  financial performance, C–707, *C–707* to
    C–711
  high-performance cultures, 438, 440
  improving, 51
  outcomes linked to reward systems, 409–414
  stimulating, C–475 to C–476
Performance-based incentives, 409–410, 412
Performance evaluation:
  compensation systems and, C–725 to C–726,
    C–747 to C–748
  strategy evaluation and, 116–117
Performance measures, 116, 116*n*
  business strategy and, C–306 to C–307
  compensation systems and, C–725 to C–726,
    C–747 to C–748
  objective setting and, 42
  for successful strategy execution, 399–400
  See also Benchmarking
Performance targets:
  best practices and, 394
  for empowered employees, C–724 to C–725
  lowering, 349
  near-term, C–731
  in objective setting, 9
  reward systems and, 412–413
Performance test, 69
Personal satisfaction, 405, 406–407
Physical assets, 117–118
Piecework pay scheme, 407
Planned strategy, 10–12, *12*
Policies and procedures, 357, *358*
  privacy policies, C–782 to C–787
  strategy-supportive, 391–392, 414
Post-diversification strategies. *See* Diversified
    firms
Preemptive strikes, 189–190
Price(s):
  approaches to, C–406 to C–407

Price(s)—*Cont.*
  competing on base of, 161, 243–244
  cross-company rivalry in, 81–82
  introductory, 162
  "name-your-own-price," 249
  price wars, C–595 to C–596
  volatility of, C–124 to C–126, *C–125, C–126*
Price-cost comparisons, 128–140
  benchmarking costs, 134–137
  competitive advantage and, 139–140
  cost competitiveness and, *130,* 137–139
  strategic cost analysis, 129, 133–134, 134*t*
  value chains, 129–133
Privacy policies, C–782 to C–787
Proactivity:
  benefits of proactive strategy, 28–29
  in developing core competencies, 366–367
  ethical responsibilities and, 68
  in high-velocity markets, 265–266
  low-cost leadership and, 160–161
  proactive managers, 4
Problem cultures, changing, 429–430
Process-complete departments, 374
Process organization, 374, 374n
Process reengineering. *See* Business process
      reengineering
Product(s):
  attributes of, 335
  broad vs. narrow offerings, 247–248
  competitive strategies in, 152*t*
  demand for. *See* Demand
  diversification in, C–472
  first-generation, 261, 262
  getting to market, 374
  limited or simplified, 159
  made for foreign markets, 201–202, 218
  marginal, pruning, 267
  new:
      expansion into, C–397 to C–398
      introduction of, 188, C–216
  new categories of, C–389 to C–390
  quality of:
      consumer preferences and, C–286 to C–289
      improving, 247–248, 375, C–250 to C–251,
          C–267 to C–268
      product innovation and, C–634, C–643 to
          C–645
      superior product strategy, 280
  reviews of, C–274 to C–277
  safety testing, C–169 to C–170
  sales through trade shows, C–159 to C–160
  simplifying design of, 157
  specializing by type, 273
  standardized, 98, 162, 201–202
  standardized vs. differentiated, 98, 162
  substitute, 87–88
  "trailing edge," C–306 to C–307
  value-added, C–574
Product development, C–44 to C–45, C–45*t,*
      C–97, *C–98 to C–101,* C–113 to C–114
Product innovation:
  case studies of, C–26 to C–27, C–50 to C–60,
      C–166 to C–167, *C–168*
  commercial opportunities for, C–736, C–737,
      C–738 to C–739
  as driving force, 96

Product innovation—*Cont.*
  high-velocity markets and, 266
  industry trends, C–154 to C–155
  in maturing industries, 267
  new technology, C–732 to C–758
  production and, C–761, C–763 to C–766
  quality improvement, C–634, C–643 to C–645
  role of suppliers in, C–163
  technological, C–541 to C–542
Production. *See* Manufacturing
Production strategy, 208*t*
Production VP, 21
Product-line strategy, 14–15, 208*t*
  case study of, C–184 to C–202
  growth and, C–201 to C–202, C–267 to
      C–268
Profit(s):
  mission statement and, 33
  new competition and, 86, 86*n*
  unrelated diversification and, 306
Profitability:
  competitive strength and, 336
  conflict with purpose, C–354
  diversification and, 340–341
  executive compensation and, 412
  industry attractiveness and, 108–109, 332
  investments and, C–346
  in maturing industries, 267
  shareholder profitability, C–134 to C–135
  unrelated diversification and, 306
Profit-and-loss responsibility, 22
Profit centers, 374
Profit sanctuaries, 213, 222
Promotion from within, 408, 426
Promotions strategy, 15, C–618 to C–619
Proposals, development of, C–302 to C–320
Purchased supplies, *130,* 138
Purchasing, differentiation in, 164

Quality:
  best-cost provider strategies and, 167
  competition and, 89–90
  Crosby's 14 steps, 396t
  drive for, C–566 to C–567, C–573
  of products:
      consumer preferences and, C–286 to C–289
      improving, 247–248, 375, C–250 to C–251,
          C–267 to C–268
      product innovation and, C–634, C–643 to
          C–645
  recognition and awards for, 393, 396*t,* 397,
      399, C–650
  six sigma program, 340–341
  written quality policy, *C–570*

Rapid followers, 193
Rating scales:
  in competitive strength assessment, 141–142,
      142*t*
  industry attractiveness tests, 331–332,
      333–334, 333*t*
R&D. *See* Research and development
Reactive strategy, 10–12, *12*
  in high-velocity markets, 263, *264*
  strategy crafting and, 48–49

Recruitment and retention, 361–365, C–615,
      C–617
Regulatory policies:
  antitrust action, 276
  business environment and, C–451 to C–452
  customer complaints and, C–781 to C–782
  as driving force, 98
  in foreign countries, C–681 to C–682, C–700,
      C–700*n*
  global competition and, 203
  local, C–277 to C–278
  new competition and, 86
  public safety, C–169
  strong competition and, C–596 to C–597
  See also Government(s)
Related businesses, 295–296, *296*
Related diversification strategies. *See* Diversified
      firms
Research and development (R&D):
  differentiation in, 164
  example of, C–578, C–580, *C–581*
  in Internet technology, 228
  investing aggressively in, 264–265
  locational advantage in, 210–211
  related diversification and, 298
  splintered, 322–323
  in value chain, *130*
Resistance to strategic vision, 41
Resource(s):
  adapting resource base, 126–127
  core competencies, 122
  cross-company rivalry in, 345
  determining value of, 123–125
  distinctive competencies, 122–123
  industry attractiveness and, 332
  intellectual, 118, 118*n,* 122
  low-cost leadership and, 160–161
  sharing, 155–156
  transferring, 321–322
  See also Resource fit analysis
Resource allocation, 330, 333, 347–348, 352
Resource-based view of firm, 119, 119*n*
Resource fit analysis, 330, 342–346, 352
  cash hogs and cash cows, 343–344
  competitive and managerial resource fits,
      344–346
Resource fits, 332, 342, 344–345
Resource strengths:
  developing as performance test, 349
  global strategy and, 207, C–461
  identifying, 117–119, *119*
  matching strategy to, 125
  misjudging, 346
  related diversification and, 297
  as situational factor, 62
  in SWOT analysis, 121*t*
Resource weaknesses:
  global strategy and, C–462
  identifying, 119–120, 121*t*
  matching strategy to, 125
  in SWOT analysis, 121*t*
Response times:
  for corrective action, 448
  Internet technology and, 239
  prompt, 286
  in reward systems, 413

Response times—*Cont.*
shortening, 379
speed of, 265, 427–428
Restructuring strategies, 316–317, 327
Results-based incentives, 411–412
Retail channels, C–46, C–47*t*
Retaliation, 192–193, 286–287
Retrenchment, 314–316
Revenue-increasing strategies, 282
Revenues, ancillary, 242–245, 247
Reward systems, 405–414
compensation system guidelines, 412–413
corporate culture and, 406, 421–422, 423, 425, 445
examples of, 408
honors at group gatherings, 430
in innovative cultures, 445
linking to performance outcomes, 409–414
mistakes in designing, 411
motivational practices, 405–409
in multinational companies, 413–414
negative features of, 407–408, 440
results-based, 411–412
types of incentives in, 405
See also Compensation systems; Incentives
Risk(s):
avoiding, 429
in foreign markets, 200
assessing, C–219 to C–223
risk-taking companies, C–703 to C–706
of strategic alliances, 177, 214–215
industry attractiveness and, 332
reductions in, 98–99
single-business risks, 293–294
unrelated diversification and, 304
Risk-averse companies, 16, 63
Risk management strategies, C–704 to C–705
Risk-takers, 63, C–703 to C–706
Rule-breaking, 49, 84
Rule makers, 49
Runner-up firms:
attacking, 191
customizing strategies for, 277–281
to build market share, 279
content follower strategy, 280
distinctive image strategy, 280
growth-via-acquisition, 279–280
specialist strategy, 280
superior product strategy, 280
vacant-niche strategy, 280

Sales:
business-to-business, C–310
of companies, 315, 316
cross-selling opportunities, C–663 to C–664
of customer information, C–781, *C–781*
direct selling to end-users:
entrepreneurship and, C–149 to C–151
Internet technology and, 235–236, 252–253
increasing, 268
related diversification and, 299–300
results-based incentives in, 412
sales representatives, C–41 to C–43, C–43*t*
sales-tracking systems, 232

Sales—*Cont.*
through product trade shows, C–159 to C–160
See also Marketing
Seasonal factors, 332
Self-managed teams, 407
Seller-buyer relationships, 90–92, 244, C–366 to C–370
Seller-supplier collaboration, 90, 236–237
Selling:
business-to-business (B2B), C–310, C–358
business-to-consumer (B2C), C–310
online sales:
direct to end-users, 235–236, 252–253
as minor distribution channel, 252
mistake of selling below cost, 244–245
Service(s):
Internet services, 226–227, C–360 to C–361
outsourcing, 371–372, C–302 to C–320
value-added, C–379
in value chain, *130*
Service industries, C–559 to C–560
Shareholder profitability, C–134 to C–135
Shareholder value:
building:
as justification for diversifying, 294–295, 306, 325
by mergers and acquisitions, C–520 to C–535
diversification and, 308–309
strategic vision and, 40–41, 41*n*
Short-jump strategies, 274, *275*
"Short-pay" policy, 393
Short-range objectives, 10, 42*n*, 43, 45, 46
Signaling value, 166, 166*n*
Simultaneous offensive initiatives, 188
Single-business enterprises:
advantages of, 293
identifying strategy for, 52
risks of, 293–294
strategy-making pyramid for, *52*
strategy managers in, 22
Situational factors, 58–64, *60*
competitive conditions, 61
corporate culture as, 63–64
in foreign markets, 201–203, 204, 221
personal factors, 62–63
resource strengths, 62
societal concerns, 59–61
in strategy customizing, 287
threats and opportunities, 62
Situation analysis, 114–147
competitive position and, 140–143, 141*t*, 146
format for, 144, 145*t*
price-cost comparisons, 128–140
strategic challenges, 143–144
strategy evaluation, 116–117, 146
SWOT analysis, 117–127
Situation-driven strategies, 201–203, 221
Six sigma quality program, 340–341
Skills, 28, 107*t*, 117, C–720 to C–721
Smart-mover advantages, 242
Social responsibility:
business philosophy and, 63
charitable gifts, C–715
as company value, C–709, C–713 to C–715, *C–716 to C–717*, C–717

Social responsibility—*Cont.*
corporate citizenship and, 446
corporate culture and, C–487 to C–490
corporate strategy and, 59–61
definition of, C–714
environmental issues. *See* Environmental issues
ethical behavior and, 61, 68, 432
strategies for, 15
treatment of employees, C–759 to C–775
workplace standards, C–770 to C–775
Societal considerations:
business environment, C–451 to C–452
as driving force, 98
living wage, C–763, C–773
as situational factor, 59–61
working conditions, C–759 to C–775
See also Environmental issues
Sources of supply, strategy for, 208*t*
Specialist strategy, 280, C–457
Specialized firms, 34
Spin-off businesses:
divestitures, 315–316, C–207, C–513, C–652 to C–653
technology spin-offs, C–743 to C–745, C–751 to C–752
Stagnant (declining) industries, 269–270, 271
Stakeholders:
commitment to, 69
as impetus for culture change, 442
strategy and, C–352 to C–353
Standardized products, 98, 162, 201–202
Star businesses, 343, 343*n*
Start-up companies. *See* New businesses
Stay-on-the-offensive strategy, 276
Stock options, 406
Strategic action plans. *See* Strategic plans
Strategic alliances, 172–173, 196
advantages of, 174–177
competing technologies and, 228
competitive strength and, 335
in distribution, C–307
in emerging industries, 261
examples of, 176
in foreign countries, 126
foreign governments and, 213–214
local companies in, 175, 215–217, 311–312
in global competition. *See* Global competition
increasing use of, 172–173, 196
instability of, 176–177
as performance test, 349
risks of, 177, 214–215
role of "relationship managers" in, 381
in turnaround strategies, C–642 to C–643, C–651 to C–652
as turnaround strategy, C–543 to C–544
Strategic balance sheet, 120, 121*t*
Strategic cost analysis:
developing data for, 133–134, 134*t*
price-cost comparisons, 129, 133–134, 134*t*
value chains and, 129–134, 146
Strategic fit(s), 296
capturing benefits of, 302–303
competitive advantage and, 302
competitive strength and, 335

Strategic fit(s)—*Cont.*
cross-business. *See* Cross-business strategic fits
financial, 344
goodness of fit test, 69
industry attractiveness and, 332
strategy-culture fit, 425
in strategy implementation, 19
Strategic fit analysis, 329, 340–342, *342,* 351–352
Strategic group mapping, 112
constructing map, 100–101
evaluating maps, 101, 103
sample of, 102
Strategic groups, 100, 101, 103
Strategic inflection points, 39, 40
Strategic initiatives, 273–274, *275*
Strategic intent, 45–46
Strategic leadership, 4
benefits of proactive strategy, 28–29
evaluation skills in, 28
in implementation and execution, *358,* 358–359, 384
industry leadership, 276–277
strategy execution and, 449
corrective adjustments, 447–448, 449–450
establishing strategy-supportive culture, 442–444
ethics and corporate citizenship, 445–446
innovation and responsiveness, 444–445
leadership roles of managers, 440–441
monitoring progress, 441–442
See also Leadership
Strategic management process, 2–29
benefits of, 28–29
developing strategic vision, 6–7, 32–41
evaluation, monitoring, and correction, 19–20
five tasks of, 21–28
fundamental nature of, 448
implementation and execution, 18–19
ongoing nature of, 20–21
role of board of directors, 27–28
setting objectives, 9–10, 41–48
signs of good management and, 4–6
strategy and business model in, 3–4
strategy crafting, 10–18, *12,* 48–58
Strategic mistakes:
in declining industries, 270
in designing reward systems, 411
in diversification strategy, 315
of dot-com companies, 238, 242, 254
in employee empowerment, C–741
in entrepreneurship on Internet, 242–245
in maturing industries, 269
selling below cost, 244–245
toleration of, 445
Strategic objectives, 9, 10, 42*n*
establishing, as direction-setting task, 41–48
examples of, 11, 44
financial objectives and, 43, 45
long-range, 10, 32, 42*n,* 45–46
organizational level and, 47–48
short-range, 10, 42*n,* 43, 46
strategic intent and, 45–46
stretch and, 46–47
time horizon of, 45

Strategic objectives—*Cont.*
timing of, 9
See also Objective setting
Strategic partnerships:
business-to-business, 90, 92
in capability-building, 372–373
dependence in, 215
diversification by, 311–312
in emerging industries, 262
global, C–246 to C–261
for high-velocity markets, 265
between sellers and buyers, 92
between sellers and suppliers, 90
value chain activities and, 183
Strategic Planning Institute's Council on Benchmarking, 136, 137
Strategic plans:
action plans, 56
for diversified firms, 291–292
matching to situation, 287–288, 288*t*
creating and modifying, 17–18
examples of, C–553 to C–556, C–754 to C–756, C–755
performance test of, 348–349
revitalizing, C–17 to C–49
Strategic positioning. *See* Competitive position
Strategic vision, 6–7, 32–41
communicating, 32, 40–41, 41*n*
entrepreneurship and, 39, 39*n*
ethics and, 65–66
evolution of, C–421 to C–422
examples of, 8, 33
mission statement and, 6–7, 32–38
revitalizing, C–37 to C–38
strategic inflection points in, 39, 40
time horizon for, 38–39
vision statement, C–89
Strategy(ies), 3–4
budgets linked to, 390–391
changing:
for businesses in crisis, 282
industry conditions and, C–550 to C–551
reshaping competencies and capabilities, 368–369
signaling commitment to, 390–391
components of, 12–13, *13*
customizing, 258–288
for crisis-ridden businesses, 281–285
for declining industries, 269–270, 271
for emerging industries, 260–262
for fragmented industries, 271–273
for industry leaders, 275–277
for maturing industries, 266–269
for runner-up firms, 277–281
to sustain rapid growth, 273–275, 275
for turbulent markets, 262–266, 264
driving forces and, 99
for e-commerce. *See* E-commerce
for emerging markets. *See* Emerging-country markets
ethical issues and, 63, 64–68, 445–446
evaluation of, 116–117, 146
evolution of, 16–17, *17*
financial aspects of, 343–344, 343*n*
flawed, example of, 65–66

Strategy(ies)—*Cont.*
for global competition. *See* Global competition
key action initiatives, C–372 to C–381
managerial tasks in. *See* Managerial tasks
matching organizational structure to, 369–382, *370*
matching to any industry or situation, 287–288, 288*t*
policies supportive of, 391–392
present strategy, identifying, 329, 330, *331,* 351
reactive, 10–12, *12*
in high-velocity markets, 263, *264*
strategy crafting and, 48–49
shaped by Internet technology, 237–240, 255
as sign of good management, 4–6
situation-driven, 201–203, 221
social responsibility and, 64–68
winning, tests of, 68–70
workable, 286
Strategy crafting, 10–18, *12,* 48–58
business strategy, *54,* 54–56
chief architect approach to, 23, 25
collaborative approach to, 24–27
comparison of approaches to, 25–27
components of strategy, 12–13, *13*
corporate intrapreneur approach to, 25, 26
corporate strategy, 50–51, *53,* 53–54
delegation approach to, 23–26
distinctive competencies and, 123
in diversified firms. *See* Diversified firms
entrepreneurship and, 13–16
evolution of strategy, 16–17, *17*
example of, 14–15
functional strategy, 56–57
illustration of, 50–51
operating strategy, 57
performance test in, 348–349, 352
situational considerations in, 58–64, *60*
strategic challenges and, 144, 146–147
strategic plans and, 17–18
strategic vision and, 7
strategy-making pyramid and, 49–50, *52*
ten commandments for, 285–287
uniting efforts in, 57–58, *59*
See also Corporate strategy
Strategy-critical activities:
business process reengineering, 375–376, 386, 414
fragmented and, 380
order fulfillment as, 374
organization building, 369–371
value chain activities, 370, 373–376
Strategy-culture fit, 449
changing problem cultures, 429–430
substantive actions, 430–431
symbolic actions and, 430
Strategy execution, 19–20
case study of, C–41 to C–46
corporate culture and. *See* Corporate culture
ethics and, 445–446
framework for, 356–357
managerial activities in. *See* Managerial tasks
organization building for. *See* Organization building

Strategy execution—*Cont.*
  as sign of good management, 4–6
  strategic leadership and. *See* Strategic
    leadership
  successful, indicators of, 399–400
  turnaround strategies, C–638 to C–640
Strategy implementation, 19–20, 429
  for financial objectives, C–661 to C–676
  leadership styles and, *358,* 358–359, 384
  as operations-driven activity, 355
  organization building for. *See* Organization
    building
  principal tasks in. *See* Managerial tasks
  turnaround strategies, C–635 to C–650
Strategy life cycles, 18
Strategy makers, 429
Strategy-making pyramid, 49–50, *52,* 58, 59
Strengths:
  attractiveness-strength matrix, 337–338, *338*
  competitive:
    of diversified firms, 334–338, 335n, 337n
    evaluating. *See* Competitive strength
      assessment
  identifying, 117–119, *119*
  offensive strategies against, 186–187
  in resources. *See* Resource strengths
  See also Competitive capabilities
Stretch, 46–47
Strong-culture companies, 424–425
Subscription fees, on Internet, 248
Substitute products, 87–88
Superior product strategy, 280
Suppliers:
  bargaining leverage with, 155, 335, C–187
  bargaining power of, 88–90
  company's duty to, 67
  costs of items purchased, 138
  dependence on, 180
  Internet technology and:
    seller-supplier collaboration, 90, 236–237
    supplier bargaining power, 236
    suppliers of technology and services,
      226–227
  roles of, 88–90, C–163
  supply-chain strategy, 138, 138n
  value chain and, 131
Supplies, purchased, *130,* 138
Supply chain:
  cross-business strategic fits in, 298–299
  Internet technology and, 229
  management of, 375
  strategy for, 138, 138n
  supply-chain strategy, 138, 138n
Support functions, 301, 370
Support systems:
  for e-commerce, 401, 402
  installing, 400–405, 415
Sustainable competitive advantage. *See*
  Competitive advantage
Switching costs:
  alternate suppliers and, 89
  buyer bargaining power and, 91
  first-mover advantages and, 241, 254
  low-cost provider strategies and, 162
  rivalry and, 83, 85
  substitute products and, 87, 88

SWOT analysis, 117–127, 146
  competencies and capabilities, 120,
    122–125
  external threats in, 121t, 127
  identifying strengths, 117–119, *119*
  identifying threats, 121t, 127
  identifying weaknesses, 119–120, 121t
  market opportunities, 121t, 125–127
  value of, 127
Symbolic actions, 430
Symbolic egalitarianism, 407
Systems:
  systems development, 357, *358*
  in value chain, *130*

Team approach. *See* Collaboration; Management
    teams
Technical standards, 214
Technological capabilities:
  competitive strength and, 335
  in emerging industries, 260
  Internet technology, 247
  new competition and, 85
  related diversification and, 298
Technology(ies):
  advances in:
    cooperative strategies and, 172, 173, 175
    differentiation and, 167
    as driving force, 96
    improvements in production and, C–416 to
      C–418
    innovation, C–732 to C–758
    multinational diversification and, 322
    offensive strategies and, 187, 189
    best-practices uses of, 394–395
    competing technologies, 228–229, 228t, 260
    cross-border transfer of, 97, 126
    differentiation in, 164, 167
    fast diffusion of, 239, 272
    flexible, 159
    Internet-related. *See* Internet technology
    key success factors in, 107t
    in mission statement, 34
    new:
      product innovation, C–541 to C–542,
        C–732 to C–758
      as threat, C–327 to C–330
      Web site creation, 95
    spin-off companies and, C–743 to C–745,
      C–751 to C–752
    strategic fits in, 298
    in value chain, *130*
Threats:
  as external factors, 121t, 127
  global strategy and, C–462
  identifying, 126
  industry attractiveness and, 332
  new technology as, C–327 to C–330
  as situational factor, 62
Time horizon:
  of objectives, 45
  for strategic intent, 45–46
  for strategic vision, 38–39
Time-paced moves, 265–266
Timing, 156, 193–194, 197

Top-down objective setting, 47–48, 58
Top-level management. *See* Corporate-level
    management
"Topping-out" problem, 267
Total quality culture, 398, 400
Total quality management (TQM), 395–398,
    396t, 397t, 414
  business process reengineering contrasted, 398
  example of, C–577 to C–578
  organizational programs for, 400
Trading platform, C–373 to C–375
Traditional accounting, 133, 134t
Training:
  examples of, C–295, C–617 to C–618
  leadership development academies, 362–363
  strategic role of, 369
Transaction fees, on Internet, 248
Turnaround strategies:
  for businesses in crisis, 281–283
  case study of, C–630 to C–660
  competitive environment and, C–546,
    C–547t
  for diversified firms, 316–318, 327
  examples of, 284, C–536 to C–548

Unbundling strategies, 182–185
Uncertainty:
  in emerging industries, 260, 261
  industry attractiveness and, 332
  Internet technology and, 237–238
  reductions in, 98–99
Unfair competitive practices, C–596 to C–597
Unhealthy corporate cultures, 426–427
Unique resources, 123–124
Unrelated businesses, 295, 296, *296*
Unrelated diversification strategies. *See*
  Diversified firms
Unweighted rating scale, 141, 142t
"Up-or-out" policy, 408–409

Vacant-niche strategy, 280
Value:
  differentiation strategies and, 166
  perceived vs. signaling, 166, 166n
  perception of, by buyers, 149
  of resources, determining, 123–125
  shareholder value, 40–41, 41n
  unique, appeal of, 246
Value chain(s), 129, *130,* 146
  alignment of, C–535
  cost advantage and, 157–160
  cost competitiveness and, *130,* 137–138
  cross-business, 291–292, 297–301
  cross-industry, 334
  electronic, 161
  engineering, for dot-com companies, 246
  example of, 135, *C–324*
  forward channel value chains, 131–132,
    138, 155
  impact of Internet technology on. *See* Internet
    technology
  industry value chains. *See* Industry value
    chains
  innovation in, 267–268
  management of, 149

Value chain(s)—*Cont.*
    for related businesses, 296, *297*
    relatedness in, 324
    revamping, 157–160, *158*
    of rivals, differences in, 129–131
    strategic cost analysis and, 129–134, 146
    in strategic fit analysis, 340, *342,* 351–352
    strategic fits in, 297–301
    for unrelated businesses, 303, *304*
    See also Supply chain
Value chain activities, 153
    cooperative partnerships and, 183
    managing, 139–140
    noncritical, outsourcing, 371–372
    strategy-critical, 370, 373–376
Value chain analysis, 133–134
Values:
    in adaptive cultures, 427, 427*n*
    articulation of, 64, C–708 to C–709
    case studies of:
        in MNCs, C–707 to C–709, C–712 to
            C–719
        refocusing, C–74 to C–94
    core values, C–622 to C–623

Values—*Cont.*
    global application of, C–718
    integrity and fairness, C–708, C–712
    statements of, *C–453*
    unethical behavior and, 65–66
Value statements, 431, 432*t, C–453*
Variable costs, 238
Variety-based positioning, 39*n*
Venture capital, 239–240, 243
Vertical deintegration. *See* Unbundling strategies
Vertical integration:
    benefits of, 156
    competitive advantage and, 178–182, 196
    as cost driver, 156
    disadvantages of, 181–182
    evaluating, 182
    example of, C–294 to C–295, C–566, C–577
    strategic advantages of, 180–181
    value chain and, 130–131
Vice presidents, responsibilities of, 21
"Virtual business model," 249
Vision statement, C–89

Weak-culture companies, 425–426

Weaknesses:
    of competitors, 187–188, 286
    identifying, 119–120, 121*t*
    in resources. *See* Resource weaknesses
Web sites:
    advertising on, 244–245, 247
    of diversified companies, 299
    features and functionality, C–377 to C–379
    site hosting services, C–360 to C–361
    technology for creating, 95
Weighted rating scales:
    in competitive strength assessment,
        141–142, 142*t*
    industry attractiveness tests, 331–332,
        333–334, 333*t*
Winning, commitment to, 68–70
Work environment, 357, *358*
    atmosphere, 408
    corporate culture and, 423
    innovation and responsiveness, 444–445
    politicized, 426
    turnaround strategies for, C–645 to C–648
    working conditions, C–759 to C–775